# THE CAMBRIDGE GUIDE TO
# LITERATURE IN ENGLISH

# THE
# CAMBRIDGE
## GUIDE TO
# LITERATURE
## IN ENGLISH

Edited by Ian Ousby

Foreword by Margaret Atwood

**CAMBRIDGE**
UNIVERSITY PRESS

Published by the Press Syndicate of the University of Cambridge
The Pitt Building, Trumpington Street, Cambridge CB2 1RP
40 West 20th Street, New York, NY 10011–4211, USA
10 Stamford Road, Oakleigh, Victoria 3166, Australia

First published 1988
Reprinted 1989, 1991
Revised paperback edition first published 1992

Printed in the United States of America

*British Library Cataloguing in Publication data*

A catalogue record for this book is available from the British Library

*Library of Congress Cataloging in Publication data*

The Cambridge guide to literature in English/
edited by Ian Ousby; foreword by Margaret Atwood.
    p.      cm.
1. English literature – Dictionaries.
2. English literature – Bio-bibliography.
3. American literature – Dictionaries.
4. American literature – Bio-bibliography.
5. English literature – Commonwealth of Nations authors – Dictionaries.
6. English literature – Commonwealth of Nations authors – Bio-bibliography.
7. Authors, English – Biography – Dictionaries.
8. Authors, American – Biography – Dictionaries.
9. Authors, Commonwealth of Nations – Biography – Dictionaries.
1. Ousby, Ian. 1947–
PR85.C29    1988
820′.9–dc19    87–33129    CIP

ISBN 0 521 26751 x hardback
ISBN 0 521 42904 8 paperback

# Foreword

The new Cambridge Guide to Literature in English, although a comprehensive, authoritative, and up-to-date reference book, is more than that. It is also a testament to the amazing range and vitality of the English language itself.

After its early Anglo-Saxon beginnings, English was profoundly altered by the Norman Conquest of the eleventh century, developed the strength of hybrids and blossomed accordingly. As any translator can tell you, it now contains more words than any other language. As any translator can also tell you, it is grammatically unruly, bafflingly idiomatic, and frustrating to learn. Nevertheless, in dozens of countries and as many cultures, it has flourished.

Possibly because of its mixed ancestry, English, unlike some languages, has never insisted on its own purity. It has grown by assimilation, of words from foreign languages, from dialects, and from its own ever-active slang. It has never been afraid of neologisms, puns, wordplay and slogans. From Chaucer and Shakespeare to the present, it has been in love with the vernacular, and its best writers have not strayed far from the rhythms and vocabularies of speech. A language that ceases to be spoken, and therefore to grow and change, becomes a dead language; but even the briefest glance at any page of this Cambridge guide will indicate that the English language is far from dead.

Perhaps we should say "the English languages", since, being a viral organism, English has mutated, producing many variants which share its main characteristics but which have diverged to become species recognizable in their own right. Thus novels by, for instance, William Faulkner, Chinua Achebe or Anita Desai may contain words and even grammatical constructions which are foreign to readers from the British Isles; American English may sound strange to an Australian, West Indian English to a Canadian; yet each of these "Englishes" can be read by any English speaker, who, by virtue of common ground, is in a position to make at least an educated guess at understanding.

In the past, English followed in the wake of Empire: part of the richness of its written culture has been due to the successes of its navies and armies. Now, however, a good deal of its colour and variety is being generated from those who have taken the language of the former colonizers and moulded it to their own uses. Similarly, women, who for many centuries functioned merely as objects in the grammatical scheme of things – and, if they wrote, were considered remarkable, not for doing it well, but for doing it at all – have begun to reclaim their mothertongue and to describe and explore their own realities with it.

*The Cambridge Guide to Literature in English* reflects these historical shifts and changes, and many others, through its coverage of literary movements, critical schools, journals and genres – but above all through its recording of the lives and achievements of hundreds of individual writers, without whom there would be no movements, schools or journals. For every writer, language is both the power to name the nameless angel which stands between the writer and the wordless reality confronting her. This book bears witness to the writer's ongoing struggle with the language, a struggle that asks from it merely what Jacob asked of his angel: a meaning, and a blessing.

*Margaret Atwood 1988*

# Editor's Note

This volume aims to provide a handy reference guide to the literature in English produced by all the various English-speaking cultures. Its scope thus extends beyond the United Kingdom and Ireland to represent also the USA, Canada, Australia, New Zealand, Africa, India and the Caribbean. The entries fall into three major categories: those dealing with authors; those dealing with major individual works; and those dealing with genres, movements, groups, schools, rhetorical terms, critical concepts, etc. Many of the authors who appear in the guide are still living and publishing. Because of this very broad range, it has been necessary to restrict the consideration of non-English literature which sometimes creeps into such guides. Non-English writers and works are, of course, frequently considered in the context of the genres or movements which they originated or to which they contributed. They are not given separate consideration except in the case of Anglo-Saxon (Old English) literature, which is here treated as part of the 'English tradition', and major examples of medieval literature in Latin, Anglo-Norman and the Gaelic languages, which influenced or flourished beside literature in English. The Bible in English translation receives a separate entry, for reasons too obvious to need stating, but translations of other foreign works are not separately treated.

---

Entries are listed in alphabetical word-by-word order. Headings for authors, movements, literary terms, etc. appear in bold face and headings for titles of books in bold face italics. The appearance of bold face in the course of an entry indicates that the subject receives its own separate entry elsewhere in the guide.

In the case of writers who published under an abbreviated version of their full name, the heading supplies the unused parts in brackets; thus T. S. Eliot appears as 'Eliot, T[homas] S[tearns]'. Writers, like George Eliot and Mark Twain, who are remembered by the pseudonym under which they commonly wrote, are listed under that pseudonym rather than their real name. People who published under their real name as well, or used more than one pseudonym, or adopted an obviously fanciful pseudonym (like 'Q' or 'Phiz'), appear under their real name. Names beginning 'Mc' have been put with those beginning 'Mac'. Medieval writers who take their last name from a place have been listed under their first name: thus Geoffrey of Monmouth is found like that, rather than as 'Monmouth, Geoffrey of'.

Books are listed under their full title (e.g. *The Adventures of Huckleberry Finn*), though this rule has been relaxed in the case of works, like *Comus* and *Gulliver's Travels,* which have become universally known by a title other than the one under which they were originally published. For titles of English books which embody a foreign phrase no attempt has been made to alter the position of the article: Milton's poem will be found under '*Il Penseroso*' not '*Penseroso, Il*'. Sub-titles or alternative titles are supplied immediately after the main heading of book entries.

Archaic spelling has in general been modernized, but phrases which are still universally known and recognized in their original form – like the title of *The Faerie Queene* – have not been tampered with.

Abbreviations have on the whole been avoided and those that do appear are of the commonest sort. The abbreviation '*fl.*', for '*floruit*' ('flourished'), appears in entries for those writers whose exact dates are not known.

*Ian Ousby 1991*

Many people have helped in the making of this book, some of them more than they had bargained. Andrew Brown, Elinor Cole, Geoffrey Day, Paul Hartle, Mark Hendy, Ann Hill, Ann Mason, Sarah Stanton, Ann Stonehouse and Robert Wyke have been particularly long-suffering, and the editor is glad of this opportunity to thank them.

# Contributors

Michael Abbott
Robert Ackerman
James Aikens
Christopher Baldick
Cameron Bardrick
Gillian Beer
Alan Bell
Jeremy Black
MH Black
Paul Bongiorno
John Bradley
Andrew Brown
Jo-Anne Carty
Paul Chipchase
Jean Chothia
David Christie
Alan Clark
Michael Collie
Graham Coster
David Daniell
Geoffrey Day
Seamus Deane
Nicholas Drake
Colin Edwards
John Elsom
Geraint Evans
Mark Fisher
Michael Freeman
Helen Fulton
Robin Gilmour
Jon Glover
Michael Grosvenor Myer
Valerie Grosvenor Myer
Andrew Gurr
Paul Hartle
Laura Henigman

Ann Hill
Meridel Holland
Richard Hollick
Coral Ann Howells
Robin Howells
Jane Hughes
Russell Jackson
Elizabeth Jay
David Johnston-Jones
Grevel Lindop
Tony Lopez
Eric Lott
James Lynn
James Malpas
Robyn Marsack
Desmond Maxwell
David McKitterick
Paul McNeil
Isobel Murray
Alastair Niven
Christopher Norris
Nancy Nystul
Ian Ousby
WR Owens
Graham Parry
Neil Powell
David Profumo
Richard Proudfoot
Arthur Ravenscroft
Bronwen Rees
Jane Remus
Peggy Reynolds
Alison Rimmer
Lucy Rinehart
Gareth Roberts
Jane Roberts

Allan Rodway
Anne Rooney
Clare Rossini
George Rowell
Frank Salmon
Jack Salzman
Andrew Sanders
Christopher Scarles
Raman Selden
Robert Sheppard
Mark Sherman
CH Sisson
Iain Crichton Smith
Brian Stableford
David Staines
Sarah Stanton
Simon Stevens
Margarita Stocker
Ann Stonehouse
Bernard Stonehouse
Sally Stonehouse
Barbara Strang
Jordan Sullivan
John Thieme
Peter Thomson
Nicholas Tredell
Nicholas Tucker
Ann Turner
Norman Vance
Lindeth Vasey
Judy Weiss
Barry Wood
Robert Wyke
Alan Young

# A

**À Beckett, Gilbert (Abbott)** 1811–56 Humorist. Born in London of an old Wiltshire family claiming descent from the father of St Thomas à Becket, he attended Westminster School and was called to the Bar at Gray's Inn. He combined a distinguished legal career with comic writing, particularly for *Punch*, of which he was a founding member. *The Comic History of England* (1847) and *The Comic History of Rome* (1852), published by but not in *Punch*, were his most successful works; both were illustrated by **John Leech**. À Beckett also wrote over 50 plays.

**À Wood, Anthony** See **Wood, Anthony**.

*Aaron's Rod* A novel by **D. H. Lawrence**, first published in 1922.

Aaron Sisson, an amateur flautist, works as check-weighman and secretary to the Miners' Union in a Midlands colliery. He abandons this position, also his wife and his children, in order to join the orchestra of a London opera house. His life thereafter is spent searching for emotional freedom and a fuller sense of 'being'. His quest takes him to Italy and to the Marchesa del Torre, whose lover he becomes, but he is unable to liberate himself from the emotional bondage of conventional relationships. He meets Rawdon Lilly, a Lawrence figure, again in Florence, who tries to persuade Sisson to be his follower. A portrait of **Norman Douglas**, as James Argyle, and his friends is included; this portion of the novel was censored by Lawrence's English and American publishers. At the end of the novel his flute ('Aaron's rod') is symbolically destroyed as a result of an anarchist bomb explosion in Florence.

The biblical Aaron, brother of Moses, was the founder of the priesthood and the first high priest. His rod, the rod of Levi, was made to blossom by God as a sign of his spiritual authority over the children of Israel. He was not permitted to enter Canaan, however, because he doubted God's ability to bring the water of Meribah out of a rock.

**Abbey Theatre** Named after the Dublin street in which it stood, the Abbey opened in 1904 and rapidly established itself as the headquarters of

The Abbey Theatre, Dublin.

the new Irish theatre. The avowed aim of its directors, **W. B. Yeats**, **Lady Gregory** and **J. M. Synge**, was 'to create an Irish National Theatre'. The first phase of the Irish National Theatre Society at the Abbey was notable for the plays of its three directors. A second phase, dominated by the work of **Sean O'Casey**, began with a production of *The Shadow of a Gunman* in 1923 and ended with the decision of the directors to reject O'Casey's *The Silver Tassie* in 1928. Between then and the destruction by fire of the Abbey in 1951, it was the work of lesser dramatists, like **Lennox Robinson** and **George Shiels**, that sustained the theatre. It was not until 1966 that a second Abbey was opened.

*Abbot, The* A novel by **Sir Walter Scott**, published in 1820 and intended as a sequel to *The Monastery*. It is set in the reign of Mary, Queen of Scots, who appears as a character in the story.

**Abercrombie, Lascelles** 1881–1938 Poet and critic. Abercrombie was the son of a stockbroker from Ashton upon Mersey, Cheshire. He was educated at Malvern College and Victoria University, Manchester. After some years as a journalist he became a lecturer in poetry at the University of Liverpool (1919), Professor of English Literature at Leeds University (1922) and Goldsmith's Reader in English at Oxford (1935).

As poet and critic Abercrombie belongs to the Georgian period, before the revolution brought about by **Pound** and **Eliot**. A collected volume, *The Poems of Lascelles Abercrombie* (1930), was supplemented by the posthumous *Lyrics and Unfinished Poems* (1940). Among his critical works were a study of **Thomas Hardy** (1912), *The Idea of Great Poetry* (1925) and *Principles of Literary Criticism* (1932).

**Abinger Harvest** A collection of essays, reviews, poems, etc. by **E. M. Forster**, published in 1936.

The book takes its title from the village of Abinger Hammer in Surrey with which Forster's family had been connected 'for nearly 60 years' and in which he himself lived at the time. About 80 items are reprinted, all of which had appeared in various periodicals between 1903 and 1935. They are arranged not in their order of composition but according to subjects, in five sections:
(1) *The Present*, 'a commentary on passing events', which includes 'Notes on the English Character' (1920), 'Our Diversions' (1917–34) and 'Liberty in England', an address delivered at the Congrès International des Ecrivains at Paris in June 1935.
(2) *Books*, which includes essays and reviews on Ibsen, **T. S. Eliot**, Proust, **Conrad**, **T. E. Lawrence** and **Jane Austen**.
(3) *The Past*, including a delightful note on 'The Consolations of History' (1920), and early essays on Gemistus Pletho, Girolamo Cardan (the 16th-century Italian scientist), Voltaire and Gibbon.
(4) *The East*, a salute to the Orient and Asia, with essays on 'Marco Polo' (1931) and 'The Mind of the Indian Native State' (1922).
(5) *The Abinger Pageant*, a romantic pastoral celebration of local history, and a nostalgic evocation of 'another England, green and eternal'.

**Abrahams, Peter** 1919– South African novelist, born in Vrededorp township. A ship's stoker in 1939–41 and a London journalist in 1941–57, he has since lived in Jamaica. Usually featuring isolated individuals hungering for fellowship, his fiction is often marred by sentimentality, especially the earliest, *Dark Testament* (1942; stories), *Song of the City* (1945) and *The Path of Thunder* (1948). The novel *Mine Boy* (1946), *Return to Goli* (1953), about his 1952 South African visit, and the autobiography *Tell Freedom* (1954) vividly detail black deprivations under apartheid. *Wild Conquest* (1950), a historical novel about 19th-century white–black confrontation, and the novels of remarkable political prescience, *A Wreath for Udomo* (1956), *A Night of Their Own* (1965) and *This Island Now* (1966), respectively about problems of post-independence Africa, anti-apartheid resistance, and neo-colonialism, reveal an acute comprehension of Third-World political issues. His best-written novel, *The View from Coyaba* (1985), persuasively presents the black struggle, world-wide, for freedom and dignity.

**Absalom, Absalom!** A novel by **William Faulkner**, published in 1936. The story is told by several narrators, but in the main represents the attempt of Quentin Compson to understand at once the history of a family and of the American South. Parts of the story are told to Quentin by his father and by Rosa Coldfield, parts by Quentin himself to his college room-mate at Harvard, Shreve McCannon. Pieced together, the story that emerges is as follows:

Thomas Sutpen is born poor in the West Virginia mountains. He runs away at an early age and settles in Haiti, where he marries a planter's daughter, Eulalia Bon. They have a son, Charles, but when Sutpen discovers his wife's partly black ancestry he abandons her and the child. He eventually turns up in Jefferson, Mississippi, with a group of Haitian slaves. By dubious means he acquires a large estate in Mississippi and, unrelenting in his drive for social position, builds a mansion there. He marries the daughter of a respectable family, fathers Judith and Henry, and emerges as the biggest cotton planter in Yoknapatawpha County.

Years later, when Henry comes home from the University of Mississippi, he brings with him his friend – and Sutpen's son by his first marriage – Charles Bon, who becomes engaged to Judith. Sutpen orders Charles from the house. Refusing to believe that Charles is his half-brother, Henry renounces his birthright and follows Charles to New Orleans. They join the Confederate Army (as does their father) at the outbreak of the Civil War. After the war, still angered by Sutpen's refusal to recognize him as his son, Charles determines to marry Judith and returns to the family estate. When Henry learns that Charles is indeed of mixed ancestry, to prevent the miscegenation that would result from his marriage he murders him and then disappears.

Sutpen, meanwhile, wants an heir. With the war over, his plantation in ruins, his son gone, his wife dead and his slaves dispersed, he suggests to his sister-in-law Rosa Coldfield that they try to produce a son; if they are successful he will marry her. Rosa understandably refuses, so he seduces Milly Jones, the granddaughter of a squatter on his land. She bears him not the son he needs to continue the line, but a daughter. When Sutpen repudiates mother and child, Milly's grandfather murders him. Judith Sutpen dies of yellow fever, leaving the mansion to Clytie, Sutpen's mulatto daughter by one of his slaves. Many years later Henry comes home to die. Rosa Coldfield and Quentin Compson (whose grandfather had once befriended Sutpen) find Henry, ill and wasted, hiding in the house. When Rosa sends for an ambulance, Clytie thinks it is a police car come to arrest Henry for Charles's murder. She sets fire to the house, killing herself and Henry, and thus bringing the Sutpen dynasty to an end.

*Absalom and Achitophel* A poem by **John Dryden**, written in heroic couplets and published in 1681. It adapts characters and story from the Old Testament (2 Kings) to create an allegory satirizing contemporary politics. Dryden's main target is the efforts of Lord Shaftesbury and his party to exclude the future James II, a Catholic, from the succession in favour of Charles II's bastard son, the Duke of Monmouth. The poem is famous for its verse portraits. Absalom is Monmouth; Achitophel, his evil counsellor, is Shaftesbury; Zimri (2 Kings 9:31) is the Duke of Buckingham; and David is Charles II. Other figures satirized by Dryden include: Edward Seymour, Speaker of the House of Commons (Amiel, Chief of the Sanhedrin); Titus Oates, fabricator of the Popish Plot (Corah); and Bethel, Sheriff of London (Shimei). A second part (1682) was written chiefly by **Nahum Tate** and revised by Dryden, who contributed 200 lines of savage satire against two of his rivals, **Thomas Shadwell** (Og) and **Elkanah Settle** (Doeg).

**Abse, Dannie (Daniel)** 1923– Poet and doctor. Born into a Welsh-Jewish family in Cardiff (his father part-owned and operated several cinemas in the Welsh valleys), he was educated locally and at the University of Wales before going on to medical training at King's College, London, and Westminster Hospital.

With Howard Sergeant he was joint editor of *Mavericks* (1957), an anthology designed to show the **Movement** as limited and unrepresentative of the time and to stress the importance of 'the image and Dionysian excitement' rather than irony and understatement. Abse's own

work began with *After Every Green Thing* (1949) and continued with many other volumes, notably *Funland and Other Poems* (1973) and *Collected Poems 1948–76* (1977). Without loss of discipline, it attempts to include a wider range of experience – including that of a doctor and a Jewish cultural outsider – in a poetry that remains rooted in the English tradition of intimate address to the reader. *A Poet in the Family* (1974) is autobiographical.

*Absentee, The* A novel by **Maria Edgeworth**, published in 1812. As in *Castle Rackrent*, Maria Edgeworth sets her story on a large landholding in Ireland, and deals here with an absentee landlord (Lord Clonbrony) who is finally persuaded to return to his responsibilities by his son.

**Absurd, Theatre of the** Literally meaning 'out of harmony', absurd was Albert Camus's designation for the situation of modern man, a stranger in an inhuman universe. Recognizing such strangers in stage characters in the 1950s, critic Martin Esslin in 1961 published his influential *Theatre of the Absurd*. He defined plays of the absurd as those that shared a presentation of man's metaphysical absurdity in aberrant dramatic style that mirrored the situation. Never a formal movement, the playwrights of the absurd were centred in post-war Paris, but they soared to international acclaim with the unexpected success of **Beckett's** *Waiting for Godot*. Journalists soon seized upon Esslin's phrase, confusing it with the everyday meaning of absurd as outrageously comic. Esslin's main absurdists are Beckett, Adamov, Ionesco and Genet, with less attention to **Albee** and **Pinter**. Almost every non-realistic modern dramatist has had this label affixed thereafter.

A shared recognition of the incongruity of human life is insufficient to create a distinct or distinguishable group of writers, which is to say that the theatre of the absurd remains, however it is employed, a critical invention. Certain of the techniques used by absurdist writers have nevertheless established themselves in the contemporary theatre, and it is in this formal sense, rather than in any philosophical one, that the idea of a 'theatre of the absurd' has maintained a critical currency-value. The carrying of logic *ad absurdum*, the dissolution of language, the bizarre relationship of stage properties to dramatic situation, the diminution of sense by repetition or unexplained intensification, the rejection of narrative continuity and the refusal to allow characters or even scenery to be self-defining have become acceptable stage conventions. Beckett's question, 'What has one thing to do with another?', is quite as much a formal matter as a philosophical one. The techniques are of the disruptive kind associated with **farce**, but there is no presiding context of harmony to give reassurance to an audience. Instead there are stage images of extraordinary concreteness, dissociated from the milieu that normally defines them.

**Abt Vogler** A poem by **Robert Browning**, published in *Dramatis Personae* (1864). The narrator of this dramatic monologue is the Abbé Georg Josef Vogler (1749–1814), advocate of a new system of harmony based on mathematics and precursor of the musical theories of Liszt and Wagner.

**Academy, The** A periodical founded by Charles Edward Cutts Birch Appleton in 1869. Covering a wide range of topics in art, literature and the sciences, it included **Mark Pattison, Matthew Arnold** and **Thomas Huxley** among its contributors.

**accentual metre** See **metre**.

**Achebe, Chinua** 1930– Nigerian novelist, born at Ogidi, Eastern Nigeria. After secondary schooling at Government College, Umuahia, he graduated from University College, Ibadan, in 1953. He worked in Nigerian broadcasting from 1954, and was Director of External Broadcasting 1951–67. During the Nigerian Civil War (1967–70) he was in Biafran government service. After the war he taught in United States and Nigerian universities. Achebe's indignation at European representations of Africans in fiction prompted him to write his first novel, now an African classic, *Things Fall Apart* (1958), an evocation of the civilized values of pre-colonial African society and of a proud clansman's tragic downfall when British colonialism fractured that society. *Arrow of God* (1964) deals more extensively with similar themes, but *No Longer at Ease* (1960) and *A Man of the People* (1966) treat modern Nigerian urban and political problems satirically. He has also published *The Sacrificial Egg and Other Stories* (1962) and *Girls at War and Other Stories* (1972), and some fiction for children: *Chike and the River* (1966), *How the Leopard Got His Claws* (1972), *The Flute* and *The Drum* (1977). Achebe's war experience is astringently expressed in *Beware, Soul Brother* (1971; as *Christmas in Biafra and Other Poems*, New York, 1972). *Morning Yet on Creation Day: Essays* appeared in 1975. Achebe edits *Okike: Nigerian Journal of New Writing*, and was co-editor of *The Insider: Stories of War and Peace from Nigeria* (1971), *Don't Let Him Die* (1978) and *African Short Stories* (1985). His most recent novel is *Anthills of the Savannah* (1987).

**Ackerley, J[oseph] R[andolph]** 1896–1967 Literary editor. Ackerley was born in London and educated at Rossall School and (after serving in World War I) at Cambridge, where he studied law. During the 1920s he wrote a play, *Prisoners of War* (1925), and visited India as private secretary and tutor in a maharaja's household. His experiences in India were recorded in *Hindoo Holiday* published in 1932.

From 1935 to 1959 Ackerley was literary editor of **The Listener**. During that time he managed to elicit many contributions from distinguished writers, including **E. M. Forster** and **Christopher Isherwood**. *Escapers All*, an anthology, was published in 1932, and two later books, *My Dog Tulip* (1956) and the novel *We Think the World of You* (1960), were about his relationship with a pet Alsatian. *My Father and Myself*, published posthumously in 1968, is a fascinating account of Ackerley's father, who managed to live a secret life behind all the trappings of conventional respectability.

**Ackroyd, Peter** 1949– Novelist and critic. Ackroyd's prolific writing has included poetry and television criticism but it is as a biographer and novelist that he is best known. While his lives of **Ezra Pound** and **T. S. Eliot** have found separate acclaim, a principle of literary and biographical criticism also informs his fiction. *The Great Fire of London* (1982) attempts to apply a Dickensian narrative idiom to a story of a modern attempt to film *Little Dorrit* around the City of London (the capital is a resonant location in all Ackroyd's fiction). *The Last Days of Oscar Wilde* (1983) is an eloquent pastiche of **Wilde**'s final diary. *Hawksmoor* (1985) explores the life of the architect in convincingly 18th-century prose and *Chatterton* (1987) the life of the poet **Thomas Chatterton**.

**acrostic** A poem in which letters in successive lines make a word or pattern. In a true acrostic, like the 'Argument' at the beginning of **Ben Jonson**'s *Volpone*, the word is formed by the first letter of each line. Variants are the mesostich, which uses the middle letters to form a word, and the telestich, using the final letters. See also **palindrome**.

**Acton, Sir Harold (Mario Mitchell)** 1904– Poet, novelist and self-styled 'aesthete'. Acton was born at 'La Pietra', the 14th-century villa in the hills above Florence which is still his home. He was educated at Eton and Christ Church, Oxford. During his second term at Oxford he published a volume of poetry, *Aquarium* (1923); another volume, *This Chaos*, appeared in 1930.

From 1932 to 1939 Acton travelled extensively, visiting Europe, the United States and China – a country with which he felt a special affinity. He translated several works of Chinese poetry and wrote on Oriental art and culture. A novel, *Peonies and Ponies* (1941), was also set in China 'to illustrate the effect of Peking on a typical group of foreigners and the effect of these foreigners on a few Chinese'.

During World War II he served in the Royal Air Force, and afterwards began work on the first part of his autobiography, *Memoirs of an Aesthete* (1948), covering the years 1904–39. The label 'aesthete' had been applied to him since leaving school, but he was careful to associate it with its 'original' meaning. He considered himself a 'citizen of the world' with a duty to 'remind . . . fellow creatures of what they are fast forgetting, that true culture is universal'. A second volume of autobiography, *More Memoirs of an Aesthete*, appeared in 1970.

Acton's historical studies included *The Last Medici* (1932) and *The Bourbons of Naples* (1957). He also published volumes of short stories (*The Soul's Gymnasium and Other Stories* and *Tit for Tat and Other Tales*) and a 'memoir' of **Nancy Mitford**. He was awarded the CBE in 1965.

**Acton, Sir John (Emerich Edward Dalberg), 1st Baron Acton** 1834–1902 Historian. The son of Sir Ferdinand Acton and his German wife, Acton was born in Naples and brought up a Roman Catholic. He received an international education, at Paris, the new Roman Catholic College in Oscott, Edinburgh and Munich, where he studied under the liberal theologian and historian von Döllinger. Elected Whig MP for Carlow in 1859, he was created Baron Acton on Gladstone's recommendation in 1869. From the 1860s he acquired a reputation as a writer and teacher of liberal Catholic ideas, many of which brought him into conflict with the ecclesiastical authorities, notably his rejection of Papal infallibility in *Letters from Rome on the Council* (1870). In 1886 he was instrumental in founding the *English Historical Review*, to which he contributed the article 'German Schools of History'. He was appointed Regius Professor of Modern History at Cambridge in 1895, and became first editor of the *Cambridge Modern History* (1899–1900). Acton's influential series of lectures on modern history and the French Revolution were published posthumously in 1906 and 1910.

**Acts and Monuments** A work of Protestant history and propaganda by **John Foxe**, already known as 'Foxe's Book of Martyrs' in the 16th century. He had written part of the work when he fled to the Continent on Mary's accession. *Commentarii Rerum in Ecclesia Gestarum*, published at Strasbourg in 1554, takes Foxe's history down to the time of **Wyclif** and John Hus. *Rerum in Ecclesia Gestarum*, published in two parts at Basle (1559–63), enlarged the previous version and continued the story almost to the end of Mary's reign. *Acts and Monuments of these Latter and Perilous Days* appeared in 1563, after Foxe's return to England, and was again expanded in 1570. It proved enormously popular, especially in Puritan households, running to two further editions in its author's lifetime and more after his death. With its graphic woodcuts and its vivid portrayal of Roman Catholic persecution, the Inquisition and heroic Protestant martyrdom, *Acts and Monuments* did much to shape anti-Catholic – particularly anti-Spanish – sentiment in the 16th century and afterwards.

***Adam Bede*** **George Eliot**'s first full-length novel, published in 1859. The idea for the story came from the account her aunt Elizabeth Evans, a Methodist preacher, gave of the night she had spent in the condemned cell at Nottingham gaol with a girl awaiting execution for the murder of her child.

Adam Bede, a carpenter in the Midland village of Hayslope, is in love with Hetty Sorrel, niece of the farmer Martin Poyser. The squire, Arthur Donnithorne, is attracted to Hetty and she is vain enough to dream of becoming the squire's wife. Adam watches Arthur's flirtation with growing anxiety and tries unsuccessfully to intervene. Arthur abandons Hetty after seducing her. Adam earns the reward of his loyalty to Hetty when, heartbroken at Arthur's desertion, she agrees to marry him. But she finds herself pregnant and flies from home in a desperate search for her lover. Adam is supported in his grief by Dinah Morris, a young Methodist

Hetty Sorrel and Arthur Donnithorne in the dairy. An incident from *Adam Bede* depicted by the Victorian artist, Edward Henry Corbould. The Royal Library, Windsor Castle.

preacher, with whom his brother Seth is hopelessly in love. Unable to find Arthur Donnithorne, the unfortunate Hetty is arrested, charged with the murder of her child and convicted. Dinah becomes her comforter and the close of the novel describes how Hetty, with Dinah's help, faces her final ordeal. But she is reprieved and her sentence commuted to transportation. Adam later marries Dinah.

The novel was exceptionally well received by contemporary reviewers, who praised its evocation of English rural life and its character studies, particularly Martin's wife, Mrs Poyser.

**Adams, Andy** 1859–1935 American novelist. Adams was born in Indiana but spent much of his life in the Texas cattle country and the mining centres of Colorado. He is best known for his authentic, unsentimental depictions of cowboy life in the days of the open range and of the westward expansion of the railroad. His most notable book is *The Log of a Cowboy* (1903). His other works include *The Outlet* (1905), *Cattle Brands* (1906), *Reed Anthony, Cowman* (1907), *Wells Brothers* (1911) and *The Ranch on the Beaver* (1927).

**Adams, Arthur Henry** 1872–1936 Novelist and poet. Born at Laurence, New Zealand, he worked as a journalist in Australia and New Zealand and visited China in 1900 during the Boxer rebellion. He published several volumes of fiction with an Australasian background including *Tussock Land* (1904), *The New Chum and Other Stories* (1909), *Galahad Jones* (1910), *The Australians* (1920) and *A Man's Life* (1929). His poetry included *My Friend, Remember* (1914), a war poem. He wrote *Three Plays for the Australian Stage* (1914) with a view to helping the establishment of Australian commercial theatre. He also produced light fiction under the pseudonyms of Henry James James and James James.

**Adams, Francis William Lauderdale** 1862–93 Australian poet. Born in Malta and educated at Shrewsbury School, he went to Australia in 1884. His poetry, represented by three volumes, *Henry and Other Tales* (1884), *Poetical Works* (1887) and *Songs of the Army of the Night* (1888), was admired by **W. M. Rossetti** for its 'intensity and fierceness of tone'. Adams also wrote several novels, among them *John Webb's End: Australian Bush Life* (1891), and two volumes of essays on contemporary Australian society and culture, *Australian Essays* (1886) and *The Australians* (1893). A play, *Tiberius*, was published posthumously with an introduction by W. M. Rossetti.

**Adams, Henry (Brooks)** 1838–1918 American historian and man of letters, born in Boston,

the grandson of John Quincy Adams, the sixth President of the United States, and the great-grandson of John Adams, the second President. He wrote numerous histories and political essays, but his two most important works are *Mont-Saint-Michel and Chartres* (privately printed 1904, published 1913), a study of 12th-century culture, and *The Education of Henry Adams* (privately printed 1907, published 1918), an autobiographical exploration of his heritage and a critical examination of the age in which he lived.

His first publication, an essay on Captain John Smith, appeared in 1867. From 1870 to 1877 he taught history at Harvard, where he had himself been educated, and edited *The North American Review*. During this period he produced *Chapters of Erie and Other Essays* (1871, with his brother Charles Francis Adams) and edited *Essays on Anglo-Saxon Law* (1876) and *Documents Relating to new England Federalism 1800–15* (1877). Discouraged by his experiences as a teacher, he left Harvard and went to Washington to observe the political scene at first hand. In 1879 he wrote *The Life of Albert Gallatin* and *The Writings of Albert Gallatin*, both of which examine the career of the *émigré* Swiss who became a controversial politician, Jefferson's Secretary of Treasury, and the author of a pioneering study of the North American Indian. In the following year he anonymously published *Democracy*, a novel about political life in Washington. In 1884 he published the novel *Esther* under the pseudonym of Frances Snow Compton. The heroine was modelled on his wife, Marian, whose subsequent suicide in 1885 apparently brought to a head the discontent that he had been feeling for some time with life in America. He began to travel, first in the Orient with the artist John La Farge and then in the Sierras with the geologist Clarence King.

He returned to Washington to complete his largest-scale historical study, the nine-volume *History of the United States of America during the Administrations of Thomas Jefferson and James Madison* (1889–91). Further travels in the Pacific and in Europe led to *Memoirs of Marau Taaroa, Last Queen of Tahiti* (1893) and *Mont-Saint-Michel and Chartres* (1904). In 1910 he published *A Letter to American Teachers of History*, which was later reprinted in *The Degradation of the Democratic Dogma* (1919) by his brother Brooks Adams. In *The Education of Henry Adams* he self-consciously presents himself as being representative of the American mind at a particular historical moment; he has taken his place as such in the literary and critical tradition.

**Adams, Richard (George)** 1920– Children's author and novelist. Born in Berkshire, the son of a doctor, Adams served in World War II before graduating from Oxford to become a successful civil servant. *Watership Down* (1972) –

his first and most famous book, about the wanderings of a group of rabbits – was rejected by several publishers before appearing to acclaim from both children and adults. *Shardik* (1974) is an ambitious novel about a humanized bear; its horrific accounts of man's cruelty to beasts reflect a major preoccupation in Adams's work. Since then he has written some long, humorous ballads for children but otherwise moved towards adult fiction, with *The Plague Dogs* (1977) and *The Girl in a Swing* (1980), his first exclusively adult book.

**Adcock, Fleur** 1934– New Zealand/English poet. Born in Papakura on New Zealand's North Island, Adcock was educated in Wellington, where she obtained an MA in Classics from Victoria University. After briefly working as an Assistant Lecturer in Classics at the University of Otago, she held various library posts in New Zealand and Britain. She has lived in England since 1963 and has built up a considerable reputation as a sensitive and penetrating observer of contemporary mores. Her poetry is notable for its unsentimental treatment of personal and family relationships, its psychological insights and its interest in classical themes. In her work an ostensibly low-key, ironic manner often takes on a chilling quality as she comments on subjects such as love and the death of relationships. Her volumes of verse include *The Eye of the Hurricane* (1964), *Tigers* (1967), *High Tide in the Garden* (1971), *The Scenic Route* (1974), *The Inner Harbour* (1979), *Selected Poems* (1983) and *The Incident Book* (1986). She has translated a good deal of Latin verse and edited *The Oxford Book of Contemporary New Zealand Verse* (1982).

**Adding Machine, The** A play by **Elmer Rice**, first presented by the Theatre Guild in 1923 at the Garrick Theatre in New York City. It was among the earliest and most successful Expressionist experiments in the American theatre. The central character, Mr Zero, is a slave to routine. When his boss in the department store where he works tells him he has been fired and replaced by an adding machine, he murders the boss with a bill file. Condemned to death and executed, he goes to a pastoral heaven, but is unable to adjust until he is set to work on a giant adding machine. Finally the authorities decide to send him back to earth, where he will operate an even better and more efficient machine.

The point of the play lies not in its plot but in Rice's portrayal of Zero's over-mechanized, joyless existence through carefully chosen, symbolic detail. Even though Zero is not an entirely sympathetic character, the play is a clear indictment of the systematic application of commercial values to crush the soul of the individual.

**Addison, Joseph** 1672–1719 English essayist.

Son of the Dean of Lichfield, he was educated at Charterhouse (where one of his schoolfellows was **Richard Steele**) and at Magdalen College, Oxford, where he became a fellow. Addison was a notable classical scholar, and his Latin verse was commended by **Dryden**. From 1699 to 1703 he travelled on the Continent, with a mind to entering the diplomatic service. In 1704 he published 'The Campaign', a poem in heroic couplets celebrating the English victory at Blenheim.

His Whig supporters in London secured for him an appointment as Commissioner of Excise in 1705; he entered Parliament in 1708 and remained an MP until his death. In 1709 he went to Ireland as chief secretary to Lord Wharton, the Lord Lieutenant, though he lost office with the collapse of the Whig government in 1710, when he returned to London. He became a member of the **Kit-Cat Club**, where his close acquaintances included **Swift** and Steele; the latter was then editor of *The Tatler*, to which Addison contributed papers between 1709 and 1711, in which year the two friends founded *The Spectator*, which ran until 1712, and was revived

An early 18th-century coffee-house. Coffee-houses were the preferred meeting-places of this period for those who sought conversation and an exchange of views, and who provided a public for the writings of Joseph Addison, Richard Steele, and their contemporaries. Frontispiece to *Vulgus Britannicus*, Part IV, 1710.

in 1714. He also contributed to Steele's periodical *The Guardian* during 1713.

*Cato*, his blank-verse tragedy, appeared with great success at **Drury Lane** in 1713, but his later prose-comedy *The Drummer* (1715) was a failure. When the Whigs returned to power in 1715, Addison was returned to office as Chief Secretary for Ireland, becoming a Lord Commissioner of Trade in 1716, the year in which he married the Countess of Warwick. He started a political newspaper *The Freeholder* (1715–16), his last journalistic venture being *The Old Whig*, his contributions to which indicate an estrangement from his old friend Steele. One of the leading editorial journalists of his age, Addison wrote urbane and familiar prose, a model of the 'middle style' so admired in that period. He is buried in Westminster Abbey.

**Ade, George** 1866–1944 American humorist, short-story writer and playwright. Born in Kentland, Indiana, Ade began his career by writing for the Chicago *Record*. Interested in stories of everyday characters, he achieved success with his extensive use of colloquialism in *Fables in Slang* (1899). This form of fable became his trademark and the substance of several more books, including *Forty Modern Fables* (1901), *People You Know* (1903), and *Hand-Made Fables* (1920). Ade was also a popular writer of both musical and dramatic comedies, of which the best known are probably *The Sultan of Sulu* (1903) and *The College Widow* (1904).

**Adelphi, The** A journal founded by **John Middleton Murry** in 1923, appearing monthly at first and then from 1927 as a quarterly (under the title *The New Adelphi* until 1930). Its purpose was chiefly to air the literary and philosophical views of Murry himself and of his friend **D. H. Lawrence**. Murry handed over the editorship in 1930 to Max Plowman and Richard Rees. Before it ceased publication in 1955 it had counted **W. H. Auden**, **T. S. Eliot**, **George Orwell** and **W. B. Yeats** among its contributors.

**Admirable Crichton, The** A comedy by **J. M. Barrie**, first performed at the Duke of York's Theatre, London, in 1902. Crichton, a model butler in the household of Lord Loam, becomes, by a social reversal based on his adaptability and ingenuity, lord of the island when the family is shipwrecked. In the last act, after supervising the rescue, Crichton reverts to his subservient role, with the compliance of the aristocratic Loams.

*Adonais: An Elegy on the Death of John Keats* **Shelley**'s lament for his fellow poet was published in 1821. Written in **Spenserian stanzas**, the **elegy** moves from an account of the mourning at **Keats**'s bier to a triumphant declaration of the immortality of the poet.

**Advancement of Learning, The** A treatise by **Francis Bacon**, properly titled *The Two Books of Francis Bacon: Of the Proficiency and Advancement of Learning, Divine and Humane*, published in 1605. It constitutes the preliminary section of Bacon's great scheme, the *Instauratio Magna* (or 'Great Instauration'), continued in **Novum Organum** (1620). *The Advancement of Learning* itself was extended in the latin version, *De Augmentis Scientiarum* (1623).

It begins by disposing of objections to the idea of learning and championing its advantages. Bacon goes on to attack the various methods of education currently in practice, based on the Aristotelian structures of knowledge, and to suggest they would be improved if the student worked from experiment and observation rather than theory. The principal subdivisions of knowledge (history, poetry and philosophy) are then considered.

**Adventures of Augie March, The** A novel by **Saul Bellow**, published in 1953. Augie March is one of three sons born to a feeble-minded Jewish woman on Chicago's West Side. The father has abandoned the family. Augie's older brother – ambitious for himself and for Augie – marries Charlotte Magnus and tries to arrange a match between Augie and Charlotte's sister Lucy. Georgie, Augie's younger brother, is an idiot whom the family put in a home when they can no longer care for him. Augie attends but does not finish college; becomes involved briefly in union organizing; travels to Mexico; returns to the USA and joins the navy; marries; and, after leaving the service, goes to Europe to write his 'memoir'.

In it he records his encounters with the people who have shaped (or tried to shape) his life. The first, and perhaps most important, is his Grandma Lausch, a Machiavellian *grande dame* who lives with the Marches. There are also William Einhorn, the brilliant and wealthy cripple for whom the teenaged Augie works; the wealthy Renlings from Evanston, who want to adopt him; Mini Villar, the tough waitress who becomes pregnant by another man and whom he helps to obtain an abortion; Thea Fenchel, the rich married woman who takes him with her to Mexico, where she plans to divorce her husband; the millionaire Robey, who hires Augie to help him write a masterwork defining the nature of man; Stella Chesney, the showgirl he marries; and the lunatic scientist Bateshaw, with whom he shares a lifeboat after their ship has been torpedoed.

**Adventures of Hajji Baba of Ispahan, The** An oriental romance by **James Morier**, published in

1824, which recounts the adventures of Hajji Baba, barber, doctor and executioner's assistant, who rises to the position of adviser to the Shah. Morier's uncomplimentary account of Persian society drew a protest from the Persian minister in London which was later printed in a sequel, *The Adventures of Hajji Baba of Ispahan in England* (1828).

### Adventures of Harry Richmond, The A novel by **George Meredith**, published in 1871.

Richmond Roy is the son of a member of the royal family and an actress. Extravagant and charming, he teaches singing in the household of Beltham, a wealthy squire, and charms both his daughters. He elopes with one of them and she bears him a son but his unreliable character drives her to an early grave. Beltham, hating Roy, is determined to gain custody of his daughter's child, Harry Richmond. Roy, however, is obsessed with the idea of obtaining some exalted position for the boy.

Harry loves his charming irresponsible fool of a father, who eventually gets himself accepted at the courts of petty German princes. At one of these Harry and Princess Ottilia fall in love and Roy is determined to overcome all obstacles to the impossible marriage. Beltham, for his part, sees Harry's future in England, married to Janet Ilchester. Harry, through his father, is exposed to embarrassment and humiliation, but he eventually marries Janet and the squire's plans are realized.

### Adventures of Huckleberry Finn, The A novel by **Mark Twain**, published in 1884. Conceived as a sequel to *The Adventures of Tom Sawyer*, it was begun in 1876, the year the earlier book was published, and has far exceeded its predecessor in critical acclaim (if not always in popular attention). Its often harsh satire of life on the banks of the Mississippi, especially concerning the issue of slavery, gives to *Huckleberry Finn* a moral dimension which *Tom Sawyer* generally lacks.

Huck narrates the entire work in his native Missouri dialect, the duplication of which is itself one of Twain's major achievements. The story begins with a summary of *Tom Sawyer* and explains how Huck has fared since being adopted into the home of Widow Douglas and her sister Miss Watson. His blackguard father threatens his relative security by trying to claim the money that Huck and Tom had recovered from the cave of Injun Joe. Eventually Huck is kidnapped by his father and imprisoned in an isolated cabin. He frees himself by making it appear as if he has been murdered, and then flees to Jackson's Island.

While hiding out on the island Huck meets Jim, Miss Watson's goodhearted slave, who has decided to run away because he has overheard a plan to sell him. When Huck discovers that his own 'death' has been blamed on Jim and that a search party may be on its way to Jackson's Island, the two runaways resolve to travel down the Mississippi on a raft. Jim plans to leave the Mississippi at Cairo (the mouth of the Ohio River) and travel up the Ohio to freedom, but they miss Cairo in a dense fog, continue floating downstream, and undergo a series of encounters with feuding clans, murderers, lawless 'aristocrats' and numerous mobs, all of which they survive by luck, wit and determination. The casual cruelty of the river people is often presented, in all its grotesqueness, in an almost offhand manner for satirical effect. Finally, in Arkansas, the two scoundrels who have joined Huck and Jim on their raft, thinking that Jim belongs to Huck and not knowing that there really is a reward on him, tell a local farmer that he is a runaway and offer him to the farmer for a portion of a fictitious reward. By coincidence, this farmer and his wife are Tom Sawyer's Uncle Silas and Aunt Sally Phelps. Huck discovers Jim's whereabouts and tries to free him by posing as Tom. Tom himself happens to arrive and, catching on to Huck's game, poses as his own brother Sid. Tom and Huck free Jim, but only after making him suffer through an absurdly romantic rescue devised by the unsympathetic Tom. All the time Tom knows that Jim is actually a free man, having been freed by Miss Watson (who is now dead) in her will. The rescue goes awry and Tom is shot in the leg. Huck, after fetching a doctor for the injured Tom, becomes separated from him and Jim. Jim gives up his hard-won freedom, or so he thinks, to make sure that Tom receives the attention he needs. Shortly after Jim, Tom and the doctor return to Silas and Sally's farm, Tom's Aunt Polly arrives and sets matters straight. At the novel's end Huck decides to 'light out' for the territories rather than face life with Aunt Sally, who, Huck tells the reader, plans to 'sivilize' him.

### Adventures of Philip, The A novel by **W. M. Thackeray**, with illustrations by him and Frederick Walker, serialized in *The Cornhill Magazine* from January 1861 to August 1862, and published in three volumes in 1862.

Philip Firmin is the son of Dr Brand Firmin, the Brandon of *A Shabby Genteel Story*, who has since made a runaway match with a wealthy woman, Lord Ringwood's niece, and become a fashionable London physician. Philip's mother, now dead, has left him a fortune, and his independent spirit wins him the approval of Lord Ringwood, to the chagrin of his aunt's family, the toadying Twysdens. He suspects his father's shady past, and discovers that he is being blackmailed by Tufton Hunt, the dissolute clergyman who had performed the sham marriage ceremony between Brandon and Caroline Gann in the earlier story. Hunt tries to persuade Caroline, now a nurse, to claim her legal rights, but she refuses to disinherit Philip, to whom she has become devoted after nursing him through a childhood illness.

Meanwhile Dr Firmin has speculated with Philip's fortune and lost it, fleeing to America; and the now penniless Philip is rejected by his cousin Agnes Twysden for a wealthy suitor. The rest of the novel deals with Philip's struggles against his misfortunes, his engagement to Charlotte Baynes, whom he marries despite her mother's opposition, and his early career as a journalist. His father's debts continue to plague him, and his hot temper gets him into trouble, but through the kindness of Arthur and Laura Pendennis, and the unselfish devotion of Caroline Brandon, he and his family survive until the discovery of a lost will of Lord Ringwood's restores him to prosperity.

*Philip* is narrated by Arthur Pendennis, and completes the trio of interconnected and semi-autobiographical novels begun in *The History of Pendennis* and *The Newcomes*. It shows Thackeray's narrative method at its most expansive and self-reflexive.

**Adventures of Sherlock Holmes, The**  See **Sherlock Holmes stories**.

**Adventures of Tom Sawyer, The** A novel by **Mark Twain**, published in 1876. Tom is an intelligent and imaginative boy, who is nevertheless careless and mischievous. In one of the book's most famous episodes he is forced to whitewash the front-yard fence as a punishment for playing truant. He evades the task by pretending it is a great privilege, and then allowing other boys to take over from him – for a considerable price.

Tom lives in the respectable home of his Aunt Polly in the Mississippi River town of St Petersburg, Missouri. His preferred world, however, is the outdoor and parentless life of his friend Huck Finn. When Tom is rebuffed by his sweetheart, Becky Thatcher, he and Huck take to the diversion of playing pirates. By coincidence, they are in the graveyard on the night that Injun Joe murders the town doctor and frames the drunkard, Muff Potter, by placing the knife in his hands. Tom, Huck, and a third boy hide out on a river island in fear of the mestizo murderer, and are believed dead. They finally return to witness their own passionate eulogies, and with much uproar they are discovered in the funeral audience. Later Tom becomes a hero, when at the trial of Muff Potter he stands up and accuses the true murderer. Injun Joe rushes from the room and thus proves his own guilt. Subsequently Tom and Becky abandon a school picnic and get themselves lost

for several days in the very cave where Injun Joe is hiding. They make good their escape, and Tom then returns to the cave with Huck. They find Injun Joe dead, and also find his buried treasure. The two boys return to town as heroic as ever, and the riches are divided between them. Their story is continued in *The Adventures of Huckleberry Finn* (1884).

**AE** (or **A. E.**)  See **Russell, George William**.

**Aelfric** *fl. c.* 955– *c.* 1010 Aelfric *Grammaticus*, 'the grammarian', studied with the Benedictine order at Winchester under Aethelwold, who promoted the monastic reforms of the 10th century. Aelfric moved to teach at Cerne Abbey, where he completed his major works. He composed two sets of homilies in English, largely based on the works of **Bede**, Augustine, Jerome and Gregory, and followed this by a translation of Bede's *De Temporibus*. At Cerne he also wrote his Latin *Grammar* and *Glossary*, and his *Colloquy*, his best-known works. The *Colloquy* was intended as a Latin primer, and has a parallel Old English/Latin text. It consists of dialogues between the teacher and his pupils

God's Covenant with Abraham. An illustration from Aelfric's English paraphrase of the first seven books of the Bible, 1025–50. God descends a ladder from Heaven to address Abraham. *MS Cott. Claudius B. IV, f.29r.* British Library.

who adopt the characters of working people and describe their lives. It gives a vivid picture of the everyday life of the period. Aelfric also wrote a collection of **saints' lives** and translated parts of the Old and New Testaments (see **The Bible in English**) before moving to be abbot of Eynsham, where he wrote a life of St Aethelwold and several minor treatises.

Aelfric's authority was recognized during his own lifetime and he played an important part in spreading the teachings of the 10th-century monastic reform. The lucidity of his style and the variety of religious topics on which he wrote ensured his lasting popularity; his works were copied throughout the Middle Ages and his writings were the first in Old English to be printed.

**Aesthetic Movement** Arising in the 1880s, this movement of mind, or shift in sensibility, had its roots in earlier decades and was also shaped and influenced by contemporary activities in France. Its credo of 'Art for Art's sake' and its aspirations in verse and prose, and on canvas, ran counter to powerful high-Victorian optimism, **Utilitarianism** and belief in morality in art. Touched with melancholy and pessimism, and stirred by exotic art forms, novel precepts and remote cultures, the movement achieved its measure of prominence largely through the writing of the self-effacing Oxford don **Walter Pater**. Anti-bourgeois, escapist, dandiacal, flamboyant, placing form before content and ever seeking aesthetic originality, the movement progressively stressed pure sensation and deified the intensity of the moment. Talents as varied as **Oscar Wilde**, **Lionel Johnson** and **Ernest Dowson** were attracted to various phases of the movement; also associated with it were the young **Yeats**, **Max Beerbohm**, **Arthur Symons**, **Aubrey Beardsley** and **Richard le Gallienne**. *The Yellow Book* and *The Savoy*, both short-lived publications, are revealing of the movement, as is membership of the **Rhymers' Club**.

**Agate, James (Evershed)** 1877–1947 Drama critic. Born in Manchester, he began his career as reviewer for *The Manchester Guardian*. It was as drama critic of *The Sunday Times* from 1923 until his death that Agate established himself as the most feared and most courted of theatrical judges. His exemplary determination to write well did not prevent an occasional waywardness in deciding what to say nor a preparedness to resist radical change in the London theatre. He became too conscious of his own personality, as is disarmingly confessed in the very title of his selection, in nine volumes, from his diary, *Ego* (1938–47). Among his volumes of selected criticism are *Brief Chronicles* (1943), *Red-Letter Nights* (1944) and *Immoment Toys* (1945).

**Age of Innocence, The** A novel by **Edith Wharton**, published in 1920 and set in New York during the 1870s. It tells the story of Newland Archer, a lawyer, and his involvement with two women: May Welland, who becomes his wife, and her cousin, Ellen Olenska, the wife of a Polish count. Ellen, having left her husband, appears in New York, where her unconventional behaviour displeases society. Newland, on behalf of the Welland family, is called upon to dissuade her from divorcing the count. Attracted by her foreign exoticism, Newland falls in love with her, but the constraints of society and his impending marriage to May keep them apart. His interest in Ellen, however, continues after his marriage and prompts May to disclose to her cousin that she is pregnant, whereupon Ellen quickly leaves New York to live in Paris. Thirty years later, Newland, now a widower, visits Paris with his son. As they are about to call on Ellen, Newland decides not to go; he forgoes real contact with her in order to preserve his ideal memories.

**Age of Reason, The** The most famous work by **Thomas Paine**, written during his imprisonment in Paris and published in 1794–6. Showing Paine's inclination towards **Deism**, it makes a stark critique of accepted religious belief and practices. The first part argues that a rational knowledge of God does not accord with traditional conceptions of the Deity; the second illuminates various inconsistencies in the Bible in order to invalidate both literal and figurative readings of the text. The book estranged the author from many of his more orthodox American friends.

**Agee, James** 1909–55 American journalist, social critic, poet and novelist. Born in Knoxville, Tennessee, Agee was educated at Harvard and then moved to New York City, where he worked as a staff writer and eventually as a film critic for *Fortune* and *Time* (1932–48), as well as for *The Nation* (1943–8). He also wrote several filmscripts, including *The African Queen* (1951, with John Huston), *The Bride Comes to Yellow Sky* (1953, based on **Stephen Crane**'s short story) and *The Night of the Hunter* (1955).

He is perhaps best known for *Let Us Now Praise Famous Men* (1941). The product of an eight-week collaboration with the photographer Walker Evans, the work sympathetically depicts the plight of three rural Alabama families during the Depression. Agee's poems and short stories were collected and edited by Robert Fitzgerald in 1968. His two novels, *The Morning Watch* (1951) and *A Death in the Family*, which was published posthumously in 1957 and won the Pulitzer Prize the following year, are partly autobiographical, the first dealing with religious piety and the second with the effects on a family of a father's early death.

**Agnes Grey**  A novel by **Anne Brontë**, published in 1847 and based on the author's experiences as a governess. Agnes Grey, a rector's daughter, is employed by the Murray family. She is badly treated and her loneliness is relieved only by the kindness of the curate, Weston, whom she eventually marries.

**Aidoo, Ama Ata** 1942–  Ghanaian playwright, novelist and poet. Born in the Central Region of Ghana, and originally known as Christina Ama Aidoo, she is a graduate of the University of Ghana, where she was later made a fellow of the Institute of African Studies. She has held other academic posts in West and East Africa and in the USA. She was briefly Minister of Education in the government of Jerry Rawlings, but fell out with him and settled in Zimbabwe. Aidoo is not a prolific writer, but she has proved versatile. Her first play, *The Dilemma of a Ghost* (performed in 1964, published 1965), is still her best-known work – a serious comedy about the pitfalls faced by a black American girl who marries into a Ghanaian family. Marriage is also the subject of *Anowa* (1969), a play based on a traditional legend. Aidoo's other works include *No Sweetness Here* (1970), short stories; *Our Sister Killjoy* (1977), a novel; and *Someone Talking to Sometime* (1985), poems. She is one of the leading writers to be concerned about the position of women in modern Africa, but has also castigated all forms of corruption and chauvinism.

**Aiken, Conrad (Potter)** 1889–1973  American poet, short-story writer and novelist. Born in Savannah, Georgia, Aiken was educated at Harvard, where his contemporaries included **T. S. Eliot** and **Walter Lippmann**. Both his fiction and his poetry reflect his interest in psychology, and his reading of Freud, **William James**, and the French Symbolists, as well as of **Edgar Allan Poe**, his most obvious American antecedent.

His first collection of verse, *Earth Triumphant, and Other Tales in Verse*, was published in 1914, and was followed by *Turns and Movies* and *The Jig of Forslin; A Symphony* (both 1916). His 16 subsequent volumes include *Selected Poems* (1929), for which he won the Pulitzer Prize; *And in the Human Heart* (1940), a sonnet sequence; *Collected Poems* (1952); and *Thee* (1967), a book-length poem. He also published several collections of short stories, including *Bring! Bring!* (1925), *Costumes by Eros* (1928) and *Among the Lost People* (1934); five novels, which appeared together in *The Collected Novels* (1964); and numerous critical essays, collected in *Scepticisms, Notes on Contemporary Poetry* (1919), and *A*

*Reviewer's ABC* (1958). *Ushant*, an autobiographical piece, appeared in 1952.

**Aiken, Joan (Delano)** 1924–  Novelist and children's author. Born in Sussex, the daughter of **Conrad Aiken**, she was educated at home by her mother until finally going to school at the age of 12. Her first collection of short stories for children, *All You've Ever Wanted*, was published in 1953. In a series of vividly imaginative children's novels, beginning with *The Wolves of Willoughby Chase* (1962) and including *Black Hearts in Battersea* (1964) and *The Cuckoo Tree* (1981), she invented not just convincing characters but whole new periods of history where 19th-century England is ruled by a line of Stuart–Tudor monarchs and train journeys are regularly threatened by hordes of marauding wolves. In the foreground, meanwhile, strong melodramas are enacted mixed with unpredictable, quirky humour. Other novels for children include *Midnight is a Place* (1974), an impressive evocation of Victorian industrial brutality, and the supernatural tale of *The Shadow Guests* (1980). Joan Aiken's writing for younger children includes *A Necklace of Raindrops* (1968); she has also written many novels for adults.

**Aikin, John** 1747–1822  Essayist and physician. An MD of the University of Leiden, Aikin early engaged in polemical pamphleteering which offended his patients. A stroke led him to abandon medicine for letters and he produced a number of ephemeral volumes. He wrote several reports on prisons for John Howard and became his literary executor. He is perhaps best known as the brother of **Anna Laetitia Barbauld**, with whom he collaborated on *Miscellaneous Pieces* (1773) and the six-volume *Evenings at Home* (1792–6).

**Ailred of Rievaulx** 1110–67  Abbot of Rievaulx. He was born of a long line of married Benedictine priests in Northumbria, spending his boyhood at Hexham and going to school in Durham. He was received into the household of David I of Scotland, and became steward at his court. In 1134, while returning from a journey to York on the King's behalf, Ailred visited the new Cistercian foundation at Rievaulx, and decided to stay on as a novice monk. He became the confidential adviser of Abbot William, and, in 1142, novice master. He wrote *Speculum Caritatis* at this time, a book inspired by two friends, the prior and another monk; the introductory letter was written by Bernard of Clairvaux. In 1143 he was appointed abbot of St Laurence, a daughter house of Rievaulx, returning to Rievaulx as its abbot in 1147. In 1152–3 he wrote *Genealogia Regum Anglorum*, containing a eulogy of King David. In 1155 he wrote on the Saints of Hexham, to celebrate their translation. Between 1158 and 1163 he composed Sermons on Isaiah and *De Spirituali Amicitia*, in which he wrote of monastic friendships. He also wrote *De Institutione Inclusarum* for his sister. In 1163 he wrote a life of Edward the Confessor at the request of Laurence, Abbot of Westminster. He began *De Anima*, apparently unfinished at his death. His biography was written by Walter Daniel, who entered Rievaulx in 1150.

**Ainger, Alfred** 1837–1904 Essayist. Born in London, the son of a Unitarian family, and educated at University College School and privately. As a boy Ainger was much influenced by **Dickens**, with whose sons he was educated and for whom he acted in the Tavistock House amateur theatricals. Having abandoned his family's Unitarianism, he studied at King's College, London, under **F. D. Maurice**. In 1856 he matriculated at Trinity Hall, Cambridge, and was ordained on graduation in 1860 as an Anglican. He was appointed a canon of Bristol in 1887 and became Master of the Temple in 1894. Ainger was an early contributor to *Macmillan's Magazine*. As an editor and critic he was particularly drawn to the work of **Charles Lamb**, contributing a *Life* to the English Men of Letters series (1882) and editions of the *Essays* (1883), the *Poems and Plays* (1884) and the *Letters* (1888, 1904). He also wrote a life of **Crabbe** for the English Men of Letters series (1903). Ainger's collected *Lectures and Essays* were published in two volumes in 1905.

**Ainsworth, William Harrison** 1805–82 Novelist. The son of a solicitor, Ainsworth was

The rescue of Lady Rookwood. An illustration by George Cruikshank for the 1836 edition of Ainsworth's *Rookwood*.

born in Manchester and educated at the grammar school there. His first novel, *Rookwood* (1834), which gave a romanticized account of the highwayman Dick Turpin, was a great commercial and popular success. He became editor of **Bentley's Miscellany** in 1840 and, at different periods, also edited *Ainsworth's Magazine* and *The New Monthly Magazine*. But he continued to exploit the vein of historical romance he had first tapped with *Rookwood* and wrote 39 novels in all. They include: *Jack Sheppard* (1839), which features another notorious criminal and so helped to fuel the controversy about **Newgate fiction**; *The Tower of London* (1840), about the short reign of Lady Jane Grey; *Old St Paul's* (1841), which uses the Plague and Great Fire of London; *Windsor Castle* (1843), set in the reign of Henry VIII; and *The Lancashire Witches* (1849), set in Pendle Forest. **George Cruikshank** and Phiz (**Hablot Browne**) were notable illustrators of his work. Ainsworth's reputation, which made him the friend of **Dickens** and other notable contemporaries, began to sink even in his own lifetime and has not risen since.

**Akenside, Mark** 1721–70 Poet. The son of a butcher, he himself turned to medicine and conducted a successful practice as a physician in London. Most of his poetry is minor, but *The Pleasures of Imagination* (1744) – revised as *The Pleasures of the Imagination* in 1757 – is remembered for anticipating the concerns of later Romantic poets.

**Alabaster, William** 1567–1640 Divine, scholar, mystical exegete and poet. Alabaster was educated at Westminster School and Trinity College, Cambridge, which he entered as a scholar in 1584. In 1596 he accompanied the Earl of Essex on his Cadiz expedition as chaplain. The rest of his life saw extraordinary religious vacillations, conversions, reconversions and recantations, beginning with his conversion to Roman Catholicism in 1597 and ending with his appointment as Anglican chaplain to King James in 1618. In between he was deprived of Anglican orders, was imprisoned for some time in the Tower of London and visited Rome, where one of his works was denounced by the Inquisition and put on the Index. This latter incident caused a typical recantation, this time of his Roman Catholicism.

Alabaster's Senecan Latin tragedy *Roxana* was performed at Trinity, Cambridge, *c.* 1592 and printed in 1632. **Dr Johnson** praised it as the only Latin work by an Englishman worthy of note before **Milton**'s elegies. *Elisaeis*, his unfinished Latin epic glorifying Elizabeth I, was praised by **Spenser** in *Colin Clout's Come Home Again*, although Spenser's comment that Alabaster was then 'known yet to few' is still true. Alabaster was interested in mystical theology and particularly in eschatology and the Apocalypse. His *Apparatus in Revelationem Jesu Christi* (Antwerp, 1607) was the work put on the Index; *Ecce Sponsus Venit* (1633) is concerned with the end of the world and *De Bestia Apocalypsis* was printed at Delft in 1621. His devotional poems were not printed in his lifetime. They are **metaphysical** in their tone and their use of paradox and typology; many resemble the religious poems of **John Donne**.

*Alastor, or, The Spirit of Solitude* A poem by **Percy Bysshe Shelley**, published in 1816. It reflects Shelley's interest in the figure of the contemplative idealist, condemning his attitude as self-centred while at the same time lamenting the condition of the real world.

**Albee, Edward (Franklin)** 1928– American playwright. Born in Washington, DC, Albee was adopted by the owner of a chain of vaudeville theatres. He rose to prominence in the early 1960s with a series of one-act plays: *The Zoo Story* (Berlin, 1959; New York, 1960), *The Death of Bessie Smith* (Berlin, 1960; New York, 1961), *The Sandbox* (1960) and *The American Dream* (1961). All four plays were impressive formal achievements that expressed disenchantment with American middle-class values in a manner reminiscent of the British theatre's **Angry Young Men** of a few years earlier. In 1962 Albee had his first major success on Broadway with *Who's Afraid of Virginia Woolf?*, a three-act play about a night of drunken verbal conflict between a middle-aged professor and his wife, in which a state of compassion is finally achieved after the 'death' of their imaginary son.

Albee next dramatized **Carson McCullers**'s novel, *The Ballad of the Sad Café* (1963). This was followed by *Tiny Alice* (1964), the story of a rich woman who seduces a Roman Catholic lay brother into marriage and then murders him. He dramatized **James Purdy**'s *Malcolm* in 1966, and in the same year he won the Pulitzer Prize for *A Delicate Balance*, which depicts a family's vain search for happiness and purpose. *Box* and *Quotations from Chairman Mao* were staged in 1968, both works focusing on the banality of human relationships in America. *All Over* appeared in 1971; *Seascape* (1975) won Albee a second Pulitzer Prize. His most recent work has been *Counting the Ways* (1976) and *Listening* (1977), which were both staged in New York in 1979, *The Lady from Dubuque* (1980) and a dramatization of **Vladimir Nabokov**'s *Lolita* (1981).

**Alchemist, The** A comedy by **Ben Jonson**, first produced in 1610 and published in 1612. During an outbreak of the plague in London, Lovewit leaves the city and the care of his house to his servant, Face. Face is a confidence trickster and with his henchman, Subtle, uses Lovewit's house as a centre for his frauds. Subtle poses as an alchemist with possession of the philosopher's stone and therefore the ability to confer knowledge of secret processes for increasing wealth, restoring youth, and generally realizing the dreams of the gullible. Taking part in their operations is Subtle's woman, Doll Common. Their victims represent the foolish and greedy from different walks of life: Sir Epicure Mammon, a knight, is a greedy voluptuary; Abel Drugger a tobacconist; Dapper a lawyer's clerk; Ananias and Tribulation Wholesome are two hypocritical Puritans; young Kastril is newly rich and quarrelsome, looking for a suitable match for Dame Pliant, his sister. The villains come close to exposure when Surly, a gambler, sees through their imposture; and they are finally confounded when Lovewit returns to his house without notice. Subtle and Doll take to their heels and Face is left to explain to his master. Lovewit finds the booty from the frauds in his house and decides to keep it. Face cleverly puts Dame Pliant, who is comely as well as rich, in Lovewit's way. Lovewit marries her and Face is at peace with his master.

Edward Albee, in New York, 1961.

**Alcott, (Amos) Bronson** 1799–1888 American educationalist. Born in Connecticut, and perhaps best known as the father of **Louisa May Alcott**, Bronson Alcott was a pioneer of new educational methods in America. Although he himself had little formal schooling, he became a teacher in 1823, and in 1834 founded his own Temple School. At a time when American education consisted mostly of strict discipline, codified moral instruction, and memorization of texts, Alcott was devoted above all to instilling the joy of learning in his students. Adhering to **Transcendentalist** principles that upheld the unlimited potential of every human being, he encouraged his students to look into themselves to realize their individual intellects. After 11 years at the Temple School he became school superintendent of Concord, Massachusetts, in 1859. There his work initiated the Concord School of Philosophy (1879–88), which was run by his disciple William T. Harris. His books are no longer widely read, but his ideas have had a lasting influence on American education. His major works include *Observations on the Principles and Methods of Infant Instruction* (1830), *Record of a School* (with **Elizabeth Peabody**, 1835), *The Doctrine and Discipline of Human Culture* (1836) and *Tablets* (1868). *Sonnets and Canzonets* (1882) was written in memory of his wife, Abigail May.

**Alcott, Louisa May** 1832–88 American novelist. Daughter of **Bronson Alcott** and author of *Little Women*, she was born in Germantown, Pennsylvania, and grew up in Boston and Concord, Massachusetts. She completed her first book, *Flower Fables*, when she was 16, though it was not published until 1855. During the Civil War she worked as an army nurse in a Union hospital (1861–3), an experience she documented in *Hospital Sketches* (1863). From 1867 she edited a children's magazine, *Merry's Museum*.

Although she produced nearly 300 titles in a variety of genres, Alcott generally is remembered as a writer of domestic novels, of which the best known is *Little Women, or, Meg, Jo, Beth, and Amy*. (The novel originally was published in two parts: the first part, *Little Women*, appeared in 1868; the second part, *Good Wives*, came out the following year. In 1871, the two appeared as a single volume entitled *Little Women and Good Wives*.) She drew upon her own life and family experiences in writing this and her other wholesome domestic tales: *Little Men: Life at Plumfield with Jo's Boys* (1871), *Jo's Boys and How They Turned Out* (1886), *Eight Cousins, or, The Aunt-Hill* (1875), *Rose in Bloom* (1876) and others. Under various pseudonyms, she also wrote melodramatic adventure stories. *Work: A Study of Experience* (1873) is a feminist and autobiographical novel. When, as she noted in her journal, she became 'tired of providing moral pap for the young', she wrote *A Modern Mephistopheles* (1877), in which an innocent young woman resists seduction by the diabolic genius with whom her poet-husband has made a Faustian pact. This novel was republished posthumously with another, *A Whisper in the Dark* (1889), which has a similar theme. She died on 6 March 1888, the day of her father's funeral.

**Alcuin (or Albinus)** *c.* 735–804 Theologian and educationalist. His Anglo-Saxon name was Ealhwine. He studied at the episcopal school in York, was later involved in running it and became its head in 778. In 781 he met Charlemagne at Parma in Italy, and went as head to the palace school at Aachen. He remained there until his death, except for a diplomatic visit to England in 790–2 to renegotiate peace between Charlemagne and Offa, King of Mercia. With a group of scholars under him, he reformed the educational system in France and the reform quickly spread throughout Europe. Under his scheme, education centred on religious texts, Latin and profane subjects which could be of use in religious studies, but not secular topics in their own right. He was responsible for developing the *quadrivium* and *trivium* which shaped the pattern of education throughout the Middle Ages. The matter taught consisted of remnants of classical culture preserved by Boethius, St Augustine, Isidore, Capella and Cassiodorus, and the grammar of Priscian and Donatus. He was active in denouncing the Adoptian heresy, and in its condemnation at the Council of Frankfurt. He was influential in the development of Roman Catholicism and contributed by revising the liturgy, introducing the sung Creed, re-editing the Vulgate Bible and arranging votive masses for days of the week. He retired to be abbot of Tours in 796 and built up the reputation of the school at Tours. A few years before his death he surrendered his abbacies of Tours and Ferrières, but remained head of the school at Tours. Alcuin wrote handbooks to aid the teaching of Latin, religion, arithmetic and computation, and dialogues on rhetoric and dialectic. He also wrote several **saints' lives**, some mediocre verses in Latin, biblical commentaries and studies in theology and philosophy. Over 300 of his letters survive, a valuable historical source.

**Aldhelm, St** d. 709 or 710 Writer of Latin prose and verse. Little is known of Aldhelm's life. He acquired a very good education, apparently spending some time at the School of Canterbury, and became abbot of Malmesbury monastery in 675. An enthusiastic and sympathetic churchman, he is said to have stood on bridges and sung vernacular popular songs to attract a crowd, then switched to religious subjects once he had their attention. He instigated and supervised the building of several churches and monasteries. In 705 he was instrumental in drawing in the Welsh to the orthodox Roman Catholic faith. After this he accepted an extensive bishopric covering Somerset and parts of Devon and Dorset, half of Wessex, with his see at Sherborne. A brilliant and famous scholar, he was partly responsible for the resurgence of learning in England. He wrote treatises, letters and verse in Latin, and probably some verses in English which no longer survive. His works include a treatise on virginity, *De Laude Virginitate*, a version of it in verse, a treatise on writing verse which includes a collection of riddles in Latin verse, and a treatise on the Pentateuch as well as poems and letters. His writing is repetitious, monotonous, bombastic and difficult, showing frequent evidence of his Celtic knowledge and training, but it set the style for the Anglo-Latin poets who came after him.

**Aldington, Richard** 1892–1962 Novelist, poet and biographer. Aldington was born in Hampshire and educated at Dover College and London University. He married the American poet **Hilda Doolittle** (H. D.) in 1913 (divorced 1937) and was a member of the group which introduced **imagism**. His first collection of poems, *Images 1910–1915*, was published in 1915, and his *Collected Poems* appeared in 1928.

During World War I Aldington suffered the effects of gas and shell-shock, and his powerful anti-war novel, *Death of a Hero* (1929), constitutes a savage indictment of the social and intellectual climate of the pre-war era. The 'hero' is so disgusted by his corrupt and wasteful society that he invites his own death by exposing himself to enemy fire. Other novels include *The Colonel's Daughter* (1931), which satirized English village life, and *All Men are Enemies* (1933).

Aldington also translated Julien Benda's *La Trahison des Clercs* as *The Great Betrayal* (1928). He compiled an anthology of **D. H. Lawrence**'s prose, *The Spirit of Place* (1935); his biography of Lawrence, *Portrait of a Genius, But . . .* (1950) caused considerable controversy. His scathing opinion of **T. E. Lawrence** found expression in *Lawrence of Arabia: A Biographical Enquiry* (1955), which savaged commonly accepted interpretations of Lawrence's character and achievements. An autobiography, *Life for Life's Sake*, appeared in 1941, and his correspondence with **Lawrence Durrell**, *Literary Lifelines*, was published posthumously in 1981.

**Aldiss, Brian W[ilson]** 1925– Writer of **science fiction**. Novels like *Non-Stop* (1958) and *Greybeard* (1964) develop stock themes of science fiction in a thoughtful and stylish manner, but in other work Aldiss has pushed the conventions of the genre to new limits. *Hothouse* (1962) is a fantasia of the far future; *The Primal Urge* (1961) and *The Dark Light-Years* (1964) are boisterous satires; *Report on Probability A* (1968) is an exercise in the anti-novel; and *Barefoot in the Head* (1969) is an extravaganza influenced by **Joyce**, set in the aftermath of a psychochemical war. His most sustained exercise in invention is the trilogy *Helliconia Spring* (1982), *Helliconia Summer* (1983) and *Helliconia Winter* (1985), and his versatility is amply displayed in several short-story collections. His non-fantastic fiction, including *The Hand-Reared Boy* (1970), *A Soldier Erect* (1971) and *Life in the West* (1980), draws on his own experiences and displays a sour scepticism.

**Aldrich, Thomas Bailey** 1836–1907 American novelist. Born in Portsmouth, New Hampshire, Aldrich was a successful journalist who edited the *Illustrated News* during the Civil War. In 1866 he became editor of *Every Saturday* and from 1881 to 1890 edited *The Atlantic Monthly*. His first book, a collection of poems entitled *The Bells*, was published in 1855. His best-known work is *The Story of a Bad Boy* (1870), a novel based on his childhood. Other notable works are *Marjorie Daw and Other People* (1873), a collection of short stories, and *The Stillwater Tragedy* (1880), a detective novel.

**Alexander, Sir William, Earl of Stirling** *c.* 1567–1640 Poet and playwright. Courtier to James I and later to Charles I, he became Secretary of State in 1626 and was created Earl of Stirling in 1633, but died in poverty. His best-known work is *Aurora* (1604), a book of songs and sonnets. Other works include *The Monarchick Tragedies* (1603–7), four plays on the theme of destructive ambition, and a long poem, *Doomsday* (1614); these have been described by Maurice Lindsay as 'unactable plays' and 'an unreadable poem'.

**Alexander of Hales** *c.* 1170 or 1180–1245 Philosopher and theologian. Born at Hales in Gloucestershire, he probably trained for the church and held various offices; he became archdeacon of Canterbury in 1235. He studied and taught in Paris, becoming a Master of Arts before 1210 and Master of Theology in 1229. In 1236 he joined the Franciscan order and founded the Schola Fratrum Minorum in Paris. He held the first Franciscan chair in the university, and was largely responsible for establishing the Franciscan order as a teaching body. Basically an Augustinian, he absorbed some Aristotelian doctrines and brought knowledge of this to bear on his theological studies. The contemporary attempt to combine Christian philosophy with classical metaphysics and the Arabic commentaries caused an enduring controversy and debate largely centred on Paris. Although Alexander's name was traditionally attached to the *Summa Theologica*, **Roger Bacon** denies his authorship; it is a composite work of which Alexander wrote some sections. His works include a commentary on the *Sententiae*, part of an *Expositio Regulae*, and sermons. His work influenced St Bonaventure among others, and earned him the title *doctor irrefragibilis*.

**alexandrine** See **metre**.

**Alfred, King** *c.* 848–99 King of Wessex (871–99), largely responsible for the restoration of learning in England after the decay in scholarship which the Norse raids had accelerated.

Alfred's own written works were translations, though he often added new material to his sources. Their order is uncertain, but those that survive are: (1) his translation of Gregory the Great's *Cura Pastoralis*, a manual of instruction for the clergy to which Alfred added a preface describing the contemporary decline in learning and outlining his intention to make education more readily available; (2) a translation of the *Historia Adversus Paganos* of Paulus Orosius, a textbook of universal history to which Alfred added accounts of the experiences of contemporary travellers; (3) a version of Boethius' *De Consolatione Philosophiae*, originally written entirely in prose but with verse renderings of Boethius' metrical passages added later; (4) a translation of Augustine's *Soliloquia*, which was probably Alfred's final work. The last two include much additional material, and his authorship of the last has been questioned, though it now seems likely that he did write it. Alfred probably had a hand in translating a shortened version of **Bede**'s *Historia Ecclesiastica Gentis Anglorum*, at one time attributed wholly to him but written largely in a dialect not his own. He may have been instrumental in planning the **Anglo-Saxon Chronicle**, begun during his reign, but there is nothing to suggest he was involved in writing it.

A great deal of information about the king is given in *De Rebus Gestis Aelfredi Magni* by **Asser**, a Welsh monk who became his friend and teacher. Written in Latin, it chronicles Alfred's life from his birth to 887. The account of national events is largely the same as in the *Anglo-Saxon Chronicle*, but Asser added a great deal about Alfred's character and actions. This is at times naïve, subjective and fulsome in its praise of the king, but nevertheless remains an invaluable source.

**Alger, Horatio** 1832–99 A popular American novelist of boys' books, Alger was born in Massachusetts into a strict Puritan family. He graduated from The Harvard Divinity School, and in 1864 eventually became a Unitarian minister after spending some years as a Bohemian in Paris. He left the ministry in 1866, following alleged liaisons with choirboys, and moved to New York, where he became chaplain of the Newsboys Lodging House, a position to which he devoted most of his remaining years.

Although he wrote several novels for adults (almost all of which were unsuccessful), he is especially known as the author of well over 100 novels for boys, most of them based on a rags-to-riches theme and the moral that a boy can rise from poverty to wealth if he has a good character. The most popular of these were *Ragged Dick* (1867), *Luck and Pluck* (1869) and *Tattered Tom* (1871), all of which appeared initially in serial form. In addition to fiction, but in the same vein, he wrote several biographies of famous self-made men, under such titles as *From Canal Boy to President* (1881, about Abraham Lincoln) and *From Farm Boy to Senator* (1882, about James Garfield).

***Algerine Captive, The*** A novel by **Royall Tyler**, published in 1797 and providing a satiric commentary on contemporary American life. In the first part, Underhill, the narrator, tells of his inappropriately classical education in New England, his own attempts to teach school, and his study and practice of medicine, exposing along the way various instances of American pretension and quackery. He then travels south, serves as a doctor on a slave ship, and sharply condemns American slavery. Abandoned by the ship in Africa, he is himself taken into slavery by the Algerians. The second part of the novel, interspersed with observations about Muslim life, comments obliquely on American culture, as Underhill recounts his first-hand experience of slavery, his resistance of attempts to convert him to Islam, and his various plans to escape. He finally gains his freedom and returns to America.

**Algren, Nelson** 1909–81 American novelist. Algren was born in Detroit, but his work is associated with Chicago, the city where he lived and worked. He graduated from the University of Illinois School of Journalism in 1931 and spent much of the Depression as a migratory worker in the Southwest, an experience which contributed to his earliest fiction. In 1935 he returned to Chicago and published his first novel, *Somebody in Boots*. He became co-editor of *The New Anvil Magazine* in 1939, and his second novel, *Never Come Morning*, appeared in 1942. He is best known for his novel of narcotic addiction, *The Man With the Golden Arm* (1949), which won the National Book Award. Other books are *The Neon Wilderness* (1947), *Chicago: City on the Make* (1951), *A Walk on the Wild Side* (1956), *Who Lost an American?* (1963), *Notes from a Sea Diary: Hemingway All The Way* (1965) and *The Last Carousel* (1973). His last novel, *The Devil's Stocking*, was published posthumously in 1983.

**Ali, Ahmed** 1912– Novelist. He was born in India and educated at Aligarh and Lucknow. While still a student he became centrally involved in Urdu cultural affairs and during his career he has written many short stories in Urdu as well as translated much Urdu poetry into English. After Partition Ali moved to Pakistan and must now be considered a Pakistani writer. His most important novel, however, is *Twilight in Delhi* (1940), written while he was still an Indian. This magnificent historical novel about Muslim life in Delhi is one of the centre-pieces of Indian writing in English. Ali's other novel, *Ocean of Night* (1964), is set in Lucknow and depicts the decline of an aristocratic way of life. It did not achieve the same critical success as *Twilight in Delhi*. Ali is a lyrical writer, with strong undercurrents of melancholy, who at his best has presented the characteristics of Muslim life in India with consummate skill.

*Alice's Adventures in Wonderland* A fantasy by **Lewis Carroll**, originally published as *Alice's Adventures Under Ground* (1865).

Beginning famously as a story told to children on a boating picnic in 1862, it is half dream, half nightmare and always highly diverting. Plunging down a rabbit hole the seven-year-old Alice grows first too large and then too small. When turning for help or enlightenment from the strange characters around her she usually becomes caught up in logic-chopping, parody or pun whether this be with the Cheshire Cat,

Alice and the Queen of Hearts. One of Sir John Tenniel's illustrations for *Alice's Adventures in Wonderland*.

the Mad Hatter, the March Hare or the King and Queen of Hearts. Finally she loses her temper, bringing down this dream world and so waking up. Illustrated by **Sir John Tenniel**, this unique book was an immediate best-seller – much to the surprise of its shy, reclusive author. Its effect upon **children's literature**, in particular the way it favoured good-humoured iconoclasm at the expense of the conventional didacticism of the time, can hardly be exaggerated. Favourite moments include the parodies 'You are old, Father William' and 'Twinkle Twinkle Little Bat', the Lobster Quadrille, the Hatter's Tea Party and Alice's own, understandable comment, 'Curiouser and curiouser'. See also *Through the Looking-Glass and What Alice Found There*.

**alienation** The use of the word 'alienation' (or 'alienation effect') to describe a particular theatrical intention (or technique) derives from the critical writing of the German playwright, Bertolt Brecht. His alienation effects were dramatic or theatrical devices, deployed in order to bring home to audiences the strangeness of social and economic conditions they took for granted. The basic aim is to draw attention to social structures, ideas, principles, motives or conflicts that would normally be ignored, and to draw attention in such a way as to prove them alterable.

Some confusion has inevitably arisen through translation. Brecht coined the word *Verfremdung* to carry his meaning. A kindred word, *Entfremdung*, was already in familiar use. Brecht would certainly have known its application by Marx to the condition of the proletariat in a capitalist economy. Many of Brecht's plays concern themselves with alienation in this sense, and that has confounded the problem. For Brecht, *Entfremdung* was a condition and *Verfremdung* a method of making that condition clear to audiences. He argued that the alienation of the proletariat was not perceived because it was taken for granted, just as an industrialist might honestly believe that a woman's place is in the home despite the fact that he employed women in his factory. Already believing that the alienation of the proletariat was strange, he wished to have people recognize it as strange. That is to say that he wished to alienate alienation – to make strange the condition of proletarian estrangement.

Brecht's use of alienation effects influenced all the major political writers of the post-war English theatre from **John Arden** and **John McGrath** to **David Edgar** and **Howard Brenton**.

*All Fools* A comedy by **George Chapman**, published in 1605 but possibly first performed as early as 1599 and known to have been in the repertoire of the Children of the Revels at the **Blackfriars Theatre** in 1604. Chapman's source was the *Heautontimorumenos* of Terence, though he imported characters from the same author's *Adelphi*. Gostanzo, a dictatorial father, is gulled into collaborating in the love-affairs of his son and daughter.

***All for Love, or The World Well Lost*** A tragedy in blank verse by **John Dryden**, first performed in December 1677 and published in 1678. Dryden's chief source is **Shakespeare**'s *Antony and Cleopatra*, from which he borrows freely; but the two plays are very different. Under the influence of French neoclassical theory, Dryden has regularized Shakespeare, confining the action of the play to the period following the battle of Actium. In *All for Love*, Cleopatra struggles for possession of Antony with his general Ventidius, his friend Dolabella and his wife Octavia. The latter nearly succeeds; Caesar (Octavian) is prepared to come to terms with Antony but requires him to separate from Cleopatra and return to his wife, Octavian's sister. The plan founders when Antony grows jealous of Dolabella, thinking the younger man may supplant him in Cleopatra's affections. His suspicions are skilfully fed by Octavia but, with the desertion of the Egyptian fleet and the report that Cleopatra is dead, the play returns to historical fact and the tragedy runs its course.

***All the Year Round*** A weekly magazine edited by **Charles Dickens** from 1859, when it took over from *Household Words*, until his death in 1870. Like its predecessor, it offered a blend of serialized fiction (including some of Dickens's own later novels) and journalism.

***All's Well that Ends Well*** A comedy by **William Shakespeare**, probably written or revised in 1602–4. Claims for an earlier date are based on the proposal that this is the *Love's Labour's Won*, referred to by **Francis Meres** in *Palladis Tamia* (1598). It was not published until the First Folio of 1623. The source is a story from Boccaccio's *Decameron*, probably read in the English version in **William Painter**'s *The Palace of Pleasure*.

Helena, the orphaned daughter of a famous physician, is a ward of the Countess of Rousillon, whose son Bertram she loves. Bertram is summoned to the court of the incurably ill King of France. His companions are the cowardly braggart Parolles and the loyal old lord Lafeu. Helena follows, hoping to win favour by curing the King. She does so, and is rewarded by the invitation to choose a husband from among the courtiers. She chooses Bertram, whose objections to so mean a match are overrridden by the King. With the help of Parolles, he escapes to the Tuscan wars immediately after the marriage, leaving Helena wedded but unbedded.

The deserted Helena returns to Rousillon, where she receives a cruel letter from Bertram, promising to accept her fully as his wife only if she can get from his finger a treasured ring and bear him a child. Disguised as a pilgrim, Helena traces Bertram to Florence, where he is courting Diana, a widow's daughter. Helena persuades Diana to agree to go to bed with Bertram, asking for his ring as a token. Having ensured that Bertram believes her dead, Helena takes Diana's place in Bertram's bed under the deceptive cover of darkness. Obtaining his ring, she gives him another as a keepsake, and he returns to Rousillon.

Believing, like Bertram, that Helena is dead, Lafeu arranges for him to marry his daughter; but the ring he gives her (Helena's) is recognized by the King, who suspects Bertram of foul play and has him arrested. Diana, who has arrived at court to accuse Bertram of seducing her, is also imprisoned, and it is Diana's mother who produces the necessary bail – a pregnant Helena, bearing Bertram's ring. Confronted by the evidence of his wife's persistence, Bertram accepts the permanence of the marriage with good grace.

*All's Well that Ends Well* has never been a favourite among Shakespeare's plays. Often grouped with *Measure for Measure* and *Troilus and Cressida*, it shares with these other 'problem plays' an implied challenge to ideas of romantic love as a basis for marriage. Some of the plotting is perfunctory and the verse uneven, while neither Helena nor Bertram wins ready sympathy from an audience, particularly an audience that has lost confidence in the 'change-of-heart' convention. It is more fairly viewed as a satirical comedy than as a romantic comedy that has lost its way.

***Allan Quatermain*** A novel by Sir **Henry Rider Haggard**, published in 1887. A sequel to *King Solomon's Mines*, it is more sombre in tone and more scholarly in its delineation of a 'primitive' people.

Curtis and Good return to Africa because of a deep disillusion with 'civilized' living which anticipates the primitivism of **D. H. Lawrence**; Quatermain joins the expedition because his life has become meaningless since the death of his only son. After various preliminary adventures, they reach the lost land of Zu-Vendis by a journey along an underground river. The land of Zu-Vendis is ruled by two queens, one dark, the other fair. Both fall in love with Curtis, who chooses the fair queen, Nyleptha. Her dark sister, Sorais, declares civil war but Curtis and Nyleptha are victorious, and Sorais kills herself. Curtis assumes the kingship, but the price to be paid is the death of both Quatermain and the heroic 'primitive', Umslopogaas. When Umslopogaas smashes to fragments on the sacred stone of the palace his battle-axe, 'Inkosi-Kaas' ('Chieftainess'), he fulfils an ancient prophecy, and a new dynasty rules in Zu-Vendis.

In its disillusionment with Western civilization, its glorification of the 'primitive' in the figure of Umslopogaas and its theme of rebirth through sacrifice, the novel presents a fantasy of an uncorrupted new kingdom, free from the gathering storm of modern degenerate trends.

**allegory** Narrative or description in which the literal events contain sustained reference to a simultaneous structure of other ideas or events. The subject of the secondary level(s) may be philosophical, historical, theological or moral. Allegory does not consist in the simple substitution of one object or action for another, but relies upon a correspondence between the literal and metaphorical levels to help elucidate the meaning. The importance and appropriateness of the juxtaposition of literal and allegorical events, and the degree to which the relationship between the two levels of action is sustained, distinguish skilful from unskilful uses of allegory.

Allegory may be figural or narrative. In the first the form and structure of what is described correspond to the features and structure of what is intended; thus the goddess Fortune is blind to indicate the arbitrary nature of luck. In narrative allegory the sequence of events on the literal level corresponds to a psychological, spiritual, moral or historic progression.

Allegory has its origins in myths, fictional narratives which attempt to explain and contain universal facts of human nature and the material world. All religions therefore have a large allegorical content. In the Middle Ages a fourfold scheme of allegory was seen to operate in the Bible and was emulated in some literary texts. The levels of meaning are (1) the literal, (2) the allegorical, (3) the tropological or moral and (4) the anagogical. These correspond to (1) the historical account, (2) the life of Christ and the Church Militant, (3) the individual soul and moral virtue, (4) the divine schema and the Church Triumphant. The fourfold reading was formulated by John Cassian (AD 360–435), although a similar scheme was proposed by Sallastius (4th century AD). It is a development from exegesis, the explication of biblical passages to develop theological and spiritual significances contained within the literal account of the events of biblical history. Another common method of reading the Bible allegorically is typology, in which the stories of the Old Testament are seen both as historical fact and simultaneously as foreshadowing events of the New Testament.

Although sometimes difficult to penetrate, allegory is generally intended to elucidate rather than obscure, its original purpose being to make universal or divine mysteries accessible to human understanding. The qualities and characteristics of a familiar object or event are used to hint at the nature of the unknown. In literary texts allegory appears in a wide variety of forms. At its simplest and most explicit it is found in **exempla** and **fables**, in which the relationship between the (usually fictional) literal narrative and a spiritual or moral lesson is deliberately indicated or explained by the author with didactic intent. In other cases (e.g. *Piers Plowman*), the relation of literal to other levels is complex and shifting as the author explores difficult concepts and searches for appropriate modes of expression. At other times the intellectual conceit offers a new insight into an idea or event while its actual interpretation is not challenging. Despite the original explanatory intentions of allegory, some 16th-century poets wrote deliberately unfathomable allegories, and sometimes a poet's individual mythological system may render his work almost unintelligible to the reader not supplied with the necessary personal information (e.g. **William Blake**).

Allegory may be religious or secular; it can be presented in verse, prose or drama, and may have political, humorous or didactic intentions. Although it is predominantly associated with the Middle Ages, many later writers have used it in both conventional and original ways (e.g. *The Faerie Queene*, *Pilgrim's Progress*, *Moby-Dick*, *Animal Farm*). The definitive feature of an allegory is its consistent reference to its secondary scheme(s). The two (or more) levels must follow the same structure of progression. Works which intermittently refer to such a secondary level are not strictly allegories, although they are at times allegorical.

### Allen, (Charles) Grant (Blairfindie) 1848–99 Novelist and popularizer of science. Born in Kingston, Ontario, the son of a clergyman of Irish descent, Allen was educated in America, France and England, at King Edward's School, Birmingham, and Merton College, Oxford. He was for many years a teacher, part of the time in Jamaica. He returned to England in the 1870s, and started publishing scientific and evolutionary works, as a follower of **Herbert Spencer**. Among them were *Physiological Aesthetics* (1877), *The Colour Sense* (1879), which won him high praise from the scientific community, *The Evolutionist at Large* (1881) and *The Evolution of the Idea of God* (1897).

Allen was author of numerous short stories and nearly 30 novels. He is remembered now only for his novel, *The Woman Who Did* (1895), which had a *succès de scandale*. Its heroine disapproves of the marriage tie, and chooses to live with her lover and bear his child. However, she suffers the miseries of the outcast when he dies. Feminists considered the book sensational rather than progressive.

**Allen, James Lane** 1849–1925 American novelist and short-story writer. Allen was born in Kentucky and taught there until he moved to New York City in 1893. His first attempts at writing, mostly for *Harper's New Monthly Magazine*, were the short stories, descriptive articles, and critical essays collected in the volume *Flute and Violin* (1891).

In an 1886 article, 'Realism and Romance', which appeared in the New York *Evening Post*, Allen attacked claims for the primacy in American letters of the realist school of **William Dean Howells**, defending the merits of an older romance tradition associated with **Nathaniel Hawthorne** and carried on to some extent by the non-urban, regional writers of his own time. He himself is best known for his romances set in the South, especially *A Kentucky Cardinal* (1894) and its sequel, *Aftermath* (1895). His other works include *Summer in Arcady* (1896), *The Choir Invisible* (1897), *The Mettle of the Pasture* (1903), *The Bride of the Mistletoe* (1909) and *The Kentucky Warbler* (1918). His last collection of short stories, *The Landmark*, was published in the year of his death.

**Allen, Paula Gunn** 1939– American poet. Allen was born in Cubero, New Mexico, of Laguna Pueblo, Sioux and Chicano parentage. She has published five collections of poems: *The Blind Lion* (1974), *Coyote's Daylight Trip* (1978), *Starchild* (1981), *A Cannon between My Knees* (1981) and *Shadow Country* (1982). Many of her poems attempt a modern transformation of the mythic heritage of her people. She explores the nature of the Native American past, the alienation of the mestizo and the trauma of biculturation, and the influence of contemporary white consumer culture on the Native American. In particular, she focuses on the dual role of Native American women as victims and reformers of their culture. Her novel, *The Woman Who Owned the Shadows: The Autobiography of Ephanie Atencio* (1983), tells the story of one woman's psychological journey towards spiritual rebirth and her attempt to adapt to a biculturated world.

**Allen, Walter (Ernest)** 1911– Critic and novelist. Born in Birmingham and educated at King Edward's Grammar School, Aston, and Birmingham University, he worked as a teacher and university lecturer in England, and spent some time in the USA as a visiting lecturer and Professor of English at American universities. He published his first novel, *Innocence is Drowned*, in 1938. This and the two which followed, *Blind Man's Ditch* (1939) and *Living Space* (1940), are pictures of working-class life in England on the eve of World War II. His later fiction includes *The Black Country* (1946), *Rogue Elephant* (1946), *Dead Man Over All* (1950, as

*The Square Peg* in USA) and *All in a Lifetime* (1959, as *Threescore and Ten* in USA).

Allen's critical work was well known through his contributions to *The Times Literary Supplement*, *The New Statesman*, and *New Writing* before he published his study of **Arnold Bennett** in 1948. In the same year came *Writers on Writing* (as *The Writer on His Art* in USA). This was followed by *Reading a Novel* (1949), a study of **Joyce Cary** (1953), *The English Novel: A Short Critical History* (1954), *The Novel Today* (1955), *Six Great Novelists* (biographical studies of **Defoe**, **Fielding**, **Scott**, **Dickens**, **Stevenson** and **Conrad**, 1955), a study of **George Eliot** (1964), and *Tradition and Dream* (1964, as *The Modern Novel in Britain and the United States* in USA).

**Alleyn, Edward** 1566–1626 Actor, known to have been with Worcester's Men in 1583 and with the Admiral's Men at the **Rose** by, at the latest, 1592. It was above all as the creator, for the latter company, of **Marlowe**'s towering heroes that Alleyn was celebrated. Friendship with the Rose's manager, **Philip Henslowe**, was strengthened by marriage to Henslowe's stepdaughter and by a business partnership that eventually made Alleyn a rich man. He retired from the stage in 1597, probably to concentrate on some of Henslowe's business enterprises. Together they ran the Bear Garden, possibly from as early as 1594, and built the Fortune as a new home for the Admiral's Men. Alleyn returned to the stage when the Fortune opened in 1600, but his highly rhetorical style may by then have seemed old-fashioned, particularly by comparison with his rival, **Richard Burbage**. He had probably retired finally from acting by 1604, when he and Henslowe received a joint patent as Masters of the Royal Game of Bears, Bulls and Mastiff Dogs. In 1605 Alleyn was involved in negotiations to purchase the Manor of Dulwich, where, in 1613, he began the building of the College of God's Gift. The papers he deposited there, including Henslowe's *Diary*, provide unique evidence of business practices in the contemporary theatre. Alleyn's social status, confirmed by his second marriage to **John Donne**'s daughter, demonstrates the upward social mobility of actors during the reigns of Elizabeth I and James I.

**Allingham, Margery (Louise)** 1904–66 Writer of **detective fiction**. Born in London, she was educated at the Perse School for Girls in Cambridge and married the artist and editor Philip Youngman Carter in 1927. She made her reputation during the so-called Golden Age of detective fiction with *The Crime at Black Dudley* (1929), *Mystery Mile* (1930), *Look to the Lady* (1931), *Police at the Funeral* (1931), *Sweet Danger* (1933), *Death of a Ghost* (1934), *Flowers for the Judge* (1936), *Dancers in Mourning* (1937), *The*

*Case of the Late Pig* (1937) and *The Fashion in Shrouds* (1938). Her hero, Albert Campion, is a light-hearted aristocrat modelled on **Dorothy L. Sayers**'s Lord Peter Wimsey, but from the start Margery Allingham showed an unusually strong grasp of characterization and a Dickensian eye for the idiosyncrasies of London life. Her post-war novels, particularly *The Tiger in the Smoke* (1952), greatly modify Campion and shed many of her earlier mannerisms. Her last novel, *Cargo of Eagles* (1968), was completed by her husband.

**Allingham, William** 1824–89 Poet. Born in County Donegal, Ireland, Allingham worked in the customs service until 1870, when he retired to become sub-editor of *Fraser's Magazine*; he was editor in 1874–9. By then he had published *Poems* (1850), *Day and Night Songs* (1854), several other volumes of poetry and the rhymed novel of Irish life, *Laurence Bloomfield: or Rich and Poor* (1864). His six volumes of *Collected Poems* (1888–93) are culled from these various earlier works. Allingham's poetry, some of it illustrated by **Dante Gabriel Rossetti** (a close friend), Arthur Hughes and Millais, is graceful and charged with lyric simplicity; it can also become national in spirit and touched by local colour. Through **Leigh Hunt**, Allingham came to know **Carlyle**, **Tennyson** and other Victorian literary lions so that, not surprisingly, his *Diary* (first published in 1907) is a mine of information about Victorian aesthetic life. In 1874 Allingham married the talented watercolourist Helen Paterson.

**alliteration** The repetition of a sound in two or more words. In its commonest form, initial consonants are repeated: 'If Peter Piper picked a peck of pickled peppers'. The repetition of initial vowels tends to make less impact and is therefore less frequent; it is no less alliterative. In the example 'An Austrian army awfully arrayed', it is to be noted that though 'army' begins with the same letter as the other words it does not alliterate with any of them, while 'Austrian/awfully' and 'An/arrayed' alliterate only with each other. Such repetition of initial sounds is sometimes styled initial-rhyme (or head-rhyme). The repetition of internal sounds (like the second 'p' in 'Piper' and 'pepper') is sometimes styled hidden alliteration. Often, though not always, this latter kind of alliteration is also an example of consonance or assonance.

Consonance (apart from its unspecialized sense of agreement or harmony) consists in the repetition of similar consonants along with different vowels ('pipe/pep' or 'rife/reef'), assonance being the reverse ('grope/throne'). Since both by definition avoid rhyme, consonance and assonance are the main forms of that near-rhyme (or para-rhyme or half-rhyme) which

features so prominently in modernist poetry and old-fashioned nursery rhymes alike.

Initial, internal, and final repetitions are often inextricably intertwined (as in 'life's fitful fever') or the effect of one is almost identical with that of another (as with the internal alliteration of the 'Peter Piper' example). It seems sensible, where it is critically convenient, to speak of alliteration for all cases, including those that are also examples of consonance, assonance, or para-rhyme – using those terms for cases where the intertwining, if it exists, is not inextricable or the effects are significantly different. Such does, in fact, seem to be normal critical usage.

**alliterative verse** Originally Old English, alliterative verse continued to be composed until the end of the 15th century in England and into the early 16th century in Scotland. Between the Old English works and those of the late 13th century no examples of alliterative verse survive, but it is usually thought that it continued to be composed orally before enjoying a revival in the later Middle Ages.

Initially the unrhymed alliterative line had four major stresses, two in each half-line. Any number of minor stresses could be included. Usually the two major stresses of the first half-line and the first of the second half-line alliterate, but this was subject to variation for effect. Consonants alliterate with the same consonant, but all vowels (and some words beginning with 'h') were deemed to alliterate with each other. Towards the end of the period in which alliterative verse was being written, variations in the line form and the use of rhyme began to appear. A special poetic vocabulary, marked by a wide range of synonyms for common nouns, with different initial letters, developed to allow the poet greater flexibility; many of these words are not found outside alliterative poetry.

The best-known examples in Middle English are *Sir Gawain and the Green Knight* and *Piers Plowman*; all Old English verse is alliterative.

*Alton Locke: Tailor and Poet* A novel by **Charles Kingsley**, published in 1850. It reflects the social and political turbulence of the 1840s, expressing Kingsley's **Christian Socialism** and making a significant contribution to the debate about the 'Condition of England' (see **Condition of England novel**).

Alton Locke, the son of a small shopkeeper, is apprenticed to a tailor and experiences the squalid conditions of sweated labour. A talent for poetry develops with his consciousness of the need for social reform and he takes readily to Chartism. His poetry brings him into contact with Eleanor Staunton, her cousin Lillian, and Saunders Mackaye, a Scottish bookseller loosely modelled on **Thomas Carlyle**. At the urging of

Lillian and her well-to-do father, Alton allows his revolutionary verse to be made innocuous before publication; this earns him the contempt of his Chartist comrades. Their taunts lead him to undertake a mission that provokes a riot, and he is sentenced to three years in prison. Lillian, with whom he has fallen in love, marries someone else during his imprisonment, and it is Eleanor who stands by him when he falls ill with typhus. She nurses him back to health and explains to him her own views on reform and the role of Christianity. Disillusioned by demagogy and violence, Alton becomes a Christian Socialist, and at the close of the story dies on his way to the USA.

**Aluko, T[imothy] M[ofolorunso]** 1918– Nigerian novelist. A Yoruba, he was born in Ilesha, Nigeria, and educated at Government College, Ibadan, and Higher College, Yaba, Lagos, before undertaking training in civil engineering and town planning at the University of London. He has held many senior positions in Nigeria, including that of Director of Public Works in Western Nigeria. He has written many satirical novels, among them *One Man, One Wife* (1959), the first full-length novel in English to be published by a Nigerian publisher, *One Man, One Matchet* (1964), *Kinsman and Foreman* (1966), *Chief the Honourable Minister* (1970), *His Worshipful Majesty* (1973) and *Wrong Ones in the Park* (1982). Aluko's is a contemporary world, one in which the clash between old and new values gives rise to comedy. Perhaps because his tone is hardly ever judgemental, Aluko has not been regarded as one of the most important African novelists, but he has been consistently popular.

**Alvarez, A[lfred]** 1929– Critic, anthologist and poet. Born in London, he was educated at Oundle and Corpus Christi College, Oxford. He was poetry editor of *The Observer*, 1956–66, and drama critic of *The New Statesman*, 1958–60. His most famous book is *The New Poetry* (1962), an anthology whose combative introduction rejects the gentility of the **Movement** and most current English verse, preferring the work of **Robert Lowell**, **John Berryman** and **Sylvia Plath**. Plath's suicide is a major element in *The Savage God: A Study of Suicide* (1971), which, with *Beyond All This Fiddle: Essays 1955–1967* (1968), defines his taste for poetry and art which expresses extreme states of psychic disorder. His own poetry reveals an acute understanding of **Frost**, **T. S. Eliot** and **Donne**, of whom Alvarez has written a study, *The School of Donne* (1961). In the volumes *Fantasy Poets 15* (1952), *Apparition* (1971) and *Autumn to Autumn, and Selected Poems 1953–76* (1978) dark irony and mordant wit are used to treat the ebb and flow of human relationships, often simple enough in themselves but made monumental by the economies of his language. Alvarez has also published two novels, *Hers* (1974) and *Hunt* (1978).

**Amadi, Elechi** 1934– Nigerian novelist, autobiographer and playwright. Of the Ekwerri people, Amadi was born in Aluu near Port Harcourt in Eastern Nigeria. He was educated at Government College, Umuahia, and later graduated in mathematics and physics from the University of Ibadan. He spent his early career as a land surveyor and then as a teacher in the Military Academy in Zaria. Although he left the army in 1965 to teach at the Anglican Grammar School in Igrito, Port Harcourt, he later rejoined it, on the Federal side, during the Civil War – though only after having been twice detained in 'Biafra'. He wrote about his experiences of this period in *Sunset in Biafra* (1973), an unusual account of the war because few people from Eastern Nigeria shared Amadi's political perspective. Amadi is the author of a trilogy of novels entitled *The Concubine* (1966), *The Great Ponds* (1969) and *The Slave* (1978), which are rural in setting and which draw much from the traditional spiritual and mythic life of his area. His fourth novel, *Estrangement* (1986), portrays the desolation and confusion in society and personal relationships which followed the Nigerian Civil War. His plays, including *Isiburu* (1973), *The Road to Ibadan* (1977) and *Dancer of Johannesburg* (1978), are slight in scale and not well known. Amadi is regarded as one of the leading African novelists, but perhaps because there is a deliberate lack of historical specificity in much of his work he has tended to languish in the shade of **Chinua Achebe**.

***Amazing Marriage, The*** A novel by **George Meredith**, published in 1895. Carinthia Jane Kirby is the daughter of a sea captain and a runaway countess. She is the charge of her uncle, the miserly Lord Levellier. Lord Fleetwood, immensely rich and spoiled, meets Carinthia at a ball and is so charmed that he proposes to her during a quadrille and is accepted.

Fleetwood, realizing his own irresponsibility, hopes Carinthia will realize it too. But she doesn't, and Lord Levellier is determined to hold Fleetwood to the engagement so he can be rid of her. Fleetwood goes through with the marriage – and treats her abominably, eventually abandoning her and their child.

Carinthia makes her way to Whitechapel to the house of Gower Woodseer, whom she met in Europe. Woodseer's father is a minister among the poor and Carinthia is given shelter there. Gower, also a friend of Fleetwood, tries to effect a reconciliation, but when he succeeds with Fleetwood it is already too late – Carinthia has determined to go as an army nurse to Spain with her brother Chillon. Fleetwood ends his days as a Roman Catholic monk.

**Ambassadors, The** A novel by **Henry James**, first published in serial form in *The North American Review* in 1903. It was published in volume form later that year, containing two chapters which had not appeared in the magazine version. James himself considered the novel his most 'perfect' work of art.

Lambert Strether is sent to Paris by Mrs Newsome, a wealthy widow, to persuade her son Chad to return to Massachusetts and his responsibilities as head of the family business. Strether's success as an ambassador will ensure his marriage to Mrs Newsome when he returns. *En route* to Paris, he meets Maria Gostrey, an expatriate American whose witty and sympathetic observations introduce him to the pleasure of European life. In Paris, he finds Chad an assured and sophisticated young man who is not eager to return to America. Strether is introduced to Madame de Vionnet, a charming French woman who has clearly been the refining influence on Chad's life.

Strether's letters to Mrs Newsome reveal his declining enthusiasm for his embassy, and she sends further ambassadors – her daughter Sarah and Sarah's husband and sister-in-law – to appeal to Chad. They receive little help from Strether, and their lack of success with Chad estranges Strether from Mrs Newsome. In the ensuing action Strether makes two discoveries: that Chad's liaison with Madame de Vionnet is an intimate one, and that his own sympathies rest with Chad. He remains detached, however, content to observe life rather than participate in it, and ultimately returns to his life as a widower in Massachusetts.

**Ambler, Eric** 1909– Novelist. Born and educated in London, he became an apprentice engineer and advertising copywriter before devoting himself to writing after the success of his first novel, *The Dark Frontier* (1936). His many popular thrillers are all sustained by a successful formula, usually involving an ordinary Englishman who becomes caught up in a web of international espionage and intrigue. With their fast-moving plots and carefully controlled suspense, the novels were early models for subsequent writers in the genre. His many titles include *Epitaph For a Spy* (1938), *The Mask of Dimitrios* (1939; published in the USA as *A Coffin for Dimitrios*), *Journey into Fear* (1940), *Judgment on Deltchev* (1951), *The Night-Comers* (1956), *Passage of Arms* (1959), *Dirty Story* (1967) and many more. He has also written many screenplays, beginning with *The Way Ahead* (with Peter Ustinov, 1944).

**Amelia** The last novel by **Henry Fielding**, published in 1751.

William Booth, an attractive but impetuous young army officer, has married the virtuous and beautiful Amelia against her mother's wishes. The couple run away and fall foul of the predatory world of London, which is the focus of the book's intense social scrutiny. Imprisoned unjustly in Newgate, William is there seduced by Miss Matthews, an unscrupulous adventuress, but his weakness is contrasted to the resolute behaviour of Amelia herself, who meanwhile resists the amorous attention of several ardent males. She forgives William for his infidelity, but their situation grows still more miserable as his folly then leads him to gambling in an attempt to release them from poverty, and he is imprisoned for debt. Their desperate suffering is alleviated by the happy discovery that her mother's will was a forgery and that Amelia, not her sister, is the rightful heiress to her property. William is released, and the couple retire to the country.

Unlike Fielding's other fiction, *Amelia* is a domestic novel set in one place. It is less sprightly than his previous works, and its depiction of social evil and legal injustice is generally gloomy, although certain minor characters (Dr Harrison the honest clergyman, the brave Colonel Bath) do enliven the representation of human behaviour.

**American, The** A novel by **Henry James**, published in *The Atlantic Monthly* between June 1876 and May 1877, and as a volume in 1877. Christopher Newman, a bachelor who has become wealthy through shrewd business dealings in America, travels to Paris to find a wife. Though an accomplished businessman, he is naïve about European ways. Mrs Tristram, an expatriate American, serves as a sort of guide and confidante to him, much as Maria Gostrey serves Lambert Strether in *The Ambassadors*.

Newman becomes engaged to Claire de Cintré, a widow and the daughter of an aristocratic French family, the Bellegardes. But the Bellegardes decide they cannot sacrifice the family pride, even to Newman's wealth, and they terminate the engagement. Meanwhile Newman has introduced Valentin Bellegarde, Claire's brother and his own friend and ally, to Noémie Nioche, a young woman who copies great paintings for a living. Because of his involvement with Noémie, Valentin fights and dies in a duel. Just before dying, however, he provides Newman with the means of compelling the Bellegarde family to allow him to marry Claire: he sends Newman to Mrs Bread, the Dowager Marquise's maid, who reveals that the Marquise had caused her husband's death by withholding his medicine. In the end, however, Newman decides not to use this information to force the marriage, and the novel closes with Claire's becoming a Carmelite nun.

**American Crisis, The** A series of 16 pamphlets by **Thomas Paine**, published between 1776 and 1783, the first of which begins 'These are the times that try men's souls.' They made an important contribution to the American Revolutionary cause and influenced the direction of the early nation's political and philosophical ideology. They discuss human nature and the individual's proper relationship to the state, tyranny, the spirit of liberty and the future of colonialism.

**American Mercury, The** An American magazine of literary criticism and social commentary founded in 1924 by **H. L. Mencken** and **George Jean Nathan**. When Nathan left the journal in 1925 Mencken assumed sole editorship, a position he retained until his own departure in 1933. The journal, which ceased publication in 1975, featured fiction, essays, and social and political commentary by such authors as **Vachel Lindsay, Theodore Dreiser, W. E. B. DuBois, Ben Hecht, James T. Farrell, Edgar Lee Masters, William Faulkner, William Saroyan, Lionel Trilling, Mark Van Doren, Thomas Wolfe, Pearl S. Buck, Conrad Aiken, Eugene O'Neill, Dorothy Parker** and **Sherwood Anderson**.

**American Notes** **Charles Dickens**'s account of his first visit to America in 1842, published later the same year. It is based on notebooks and letters home, and so mainly takes the form of a casual travel journal, but also includes serious consideration of the treatment of the blind at the Perkins Institute in Boston, the prison system in Philadelphia and slavery in the southern states. Although Dickens had originally travelled to America in hope and had planned to correct the hostile accounts given by earlier visitors from England, his own book becomes savagely critical as it proceeds. Its views are supplemented by the satirical American episodes in his next novel, *Martin Chuzzlewit*.

**American Senator, The** A novel by **Anthony Trollope**, published in *Temple Bar* (May 1876 to July 1877).

Senator Gotobed comes to England at the invitation of John Morton, whom he has met in Washington, in order to study English institutions. He stays in the town of Dillborough and visits Bragton Hall. His comments are outspoken and diverting, but some contemporary reviewers thought the novel spoiled by the addition of two love-affairs.

**American Tragedy, An** A novel by **Theodore Dreiser**, published in 1925, and based on an actual New York murder case of 1906.

Clyde Griffiths, anxious to escape his family's dreary life, goes to work as a bellboy in a luxury hotel. He enjoys the lively society of his more sophisticated co-workers until he is involved in a car accident and found to be legally culpable. Fleeing the scene, he meets his uncle Samuel Griffiths, a successful manufacturer in New York State, who gives him a job in his Eastern factory. Clyde falls in love with Sondra Finchley, a rich girl from a nearby town, who represents the elegance and culture to which he has always aspired. Meanwhile, however, he has seduced a young factory worker, Roberta, who becomes pregnant and demands that he marry her. Seeing marriage to Sondra within his grasp, Clyde decides to dispose of the unfortunate Roberta. He takes her to a lake resort, deserted at that time of year, where he plans to murder her. He lacks the resolution to carry out his plan, but when the boat accidentally overturns he swims away and leaves Roberta to drown. He is accused of her murder, and the rest of the novel traces, in relentless detail, the investigation of the case, and Clyde's indictment, trial, conviction and execution.

**Amis, Sir Kingsley** 1922–    Novelist and poet. Born in Clapham, he was educated at the City of London School and St John's College, Oxford. He became a lecturer in English at Swansea, then at Cambridge, and during the 1940s and 1950s became associated with writers of the **Angry Young Men** generation and poets of the **Movement**.

His own poetry was represented in **Robert Conquest**'s influential anthology, *New Lines* (1956). Volumes include *Bright November* (1947), *A Frame of Mind* (1953), and *A Case of Samples* (1956). *Collected Poems 1944–1979* was published in 1979. *The New Oxford Book of Light Verse* (1978) is one of several anthologies of poetry he has edited.

Sir Kingsley Amis.

It was with his first novel, **Lucky Jim** (1954), that Amis achieved wider popular recognition. *That Uncertain Feeling* (1955), *I Like it Here* (1958), set in Portugal, and *Take a Girl Like You* (1960) displayed his talent for comic and mildly satiric writing, continued with increasing vehemence in *One Fat Englishman* (1963), *Ending Up* (1974) and *Jake's Thing* (1978). *Colonel Sun* (1968), published under the pseudonym of Robert Markham, is a James Bond thriller in imitation of **Ian Fleming**, whose work he had praised in *The James Bond Dossier* (1965). *The Riverside Villas Murder* (1973) is a pastiche of **detective fiction**, set in the author's childhood in the 1930s. More sober novels were *The Anti-Death League* (1966), an atheistic protest cast in the form of a spy story; *The Green Man* (1969), about the supernatural; and *The Alteration* (1976), set in a parallel contemporary world in which there has been no Reformation and the Papacy still wields supreme power. Recent novels include *Stanley and the Women* (1984) and *The Old Devils* (1986), awarded the Booker Prize.

Amis's non-fiction covers a variety of topics, including **science fiction** (*New Maps of Hell*, 1960, and *The Golden Age of Science Fiction*, 1981) and wine. His critical study, *Rudyard Kipling and His World* (1975), was followed by a biography of **Kipling** in 1986. He was knighted in 1990.

**Amis, Martin** 1949– Novelist and journalist. The son of **Kingsley Amis**, he went to Exeter College, Oxford, and wrote his first novel, *The Rachel Papers* (1973), when he was only 21. He turned to writing full-time following a period of editorial work with **The Times Literary Supplement** and *The New Statesman*. His first three novels, of which *Dead Babies* (1975) and *Success* (1978) are the second and third, are ferociously witty, scabrously scatological, and balefully satirical of modern-day metropolitan torpor and cultural trendiness. Amis's fourth, *Other People* (1981), is a fragmented, nightmarish psychological thriller, while *Money* (1984) is a longer work set in high-life America, which revives his penchant for gross, excessive comedy. *Einstein's Monsters* (1986) is a collection of short stories on the theme of nuclear destruction. Amis also writes astringent literary journalism, and his non-fictional pieces on contemporary America have been collected in *The Moronic Inferno* (1986).

**Amis and Amiloun** A Middle English **verse romance** of the late 13th century, adapted from *Amis et Amile*, a 12th-century French romance. Amis and Amiloun are foster-brothers of noble birth, separated after the death of Amiloun's parents. Amis is subjected to trial by combat after succumbing to advances from the daughter of his overlord and foster-father, but is unable to defend himself because of his guilt. Despite a divine warning that he will be stricken with leprosy and reduced to beggary, Amiloun impersonates him in the combat and kills his accuser. Years later, the leprous Amiloun eventually finds his foster-brother who obeys the bidding of an archangel to cure him with the blood of his own children, but as Amiloun is cured Amis's children are restored.

**Ammons, A[rchie] R[andolph]** 1926– American poet. Born in North Carolina, Ammons was educated at the University of California at Berkeley. His first book of poetry, *Ommateum with Doxology*, appeared in 1955 (the title refers to the compound eye of an insect). *Expressions of Sea Level*, the volume which established him as a major poet, was published in 1964; in the same year he accepted a post at Cornell University, where he continues to teach creative writing.

Ammons's work, characterized in particular by its precise descriptions of the natural world, also includes *Corsons Inlet* (1965), *Northfield Poems* (1966), *Uplands* (1970), *Briefings* (1971), *Collected Poems: 1951–1971* (1972), *Diversifications* (1975), *The Snow Poems* (1977), *Highgate Road* (1977), *A Coast of Trees* (1981), *Worldly Hopes: Poems* (1982) and *Lake Effect Country: Poems* (1983). He has published two long poems as books, *Tape for the Turn of the Year* (1965) and *Sphere: The Form of a Motion* (1974). *The Selected Poems 1951–1977* appeared in 1977 and *Selected Longer Poems* in 1980.

*Amoretti* **Spenser**'s contribution to the English **sonnet** vogue of the late 16th century was published together with *Epithalamion* in 1595. It consists of 89 sonnets (83 repeating 35) followed by four short lyrics.

*Amoretti* ('little loves') is a record of a courtship which reflects Spenser's wooing of Elizabeth Boyle: Spenser's three Elizabeths, his mother, queen and love, are mentioned in 74. Earlier sonnets follow **Petrarchan** conventions: love's warfare (11), with its ambush (12), siege (14) and archers (16), and the cruel tyrannical mistress (10). The sequence covers a period of just over two years, beginning in a New Year (4) and punctuated by another New Year (62) and two Easters (22 and 68). It is remarkable among English Renaissance sonnet cycles for this chronological narrative, its comparatively unconventional and characterized mistress and its innovative rhyme scheme of linked quatrains (abab bcbc cdcd ee). The courtship and the time scheme may well be intended to culminate in the marriage-day celebrated in *Epithalamion*.

**Amory, Thomas** *c.* 1691–1788 Irish writer. Educated at Trinity College, Dublin, Amory studied medicine for a time but was able to afford a life of leisure, which he spent in Dublin and London. He was acquainted with **Swift** and is known as the author of *Memoirs of Several Ladies of Great Britain* (1755) and *The Life and Opinions of John Buncle, Esquire* (1756 and 1766). In the *Memoirs of Several Ladies of Great Britain* Mrs Marinda Benlow is a **bluestocking** and the story wanders off into a curious tour of the Hebrides, where Amory places a Green Island of exotic flora, on which stands a ladies' academy. *The Life and Opinions of John Buncle, Esquire*, practically a sequel, purports to be an autobiography. The narrator, like the author, is a Unitarian, amorous but virtuous – seven wives of beauty and intelligence die within a few years of marriage to him. His matrimonial ventures take him to remote and beautiful places, and give rise to many entertaining digressions.

***Amours de Voyage*** A verse novel in five cantos by **Arthur Hugh Clough**, first published in 1858.

Narrated chiefly by Claude, a doubting intellectual, and cast in epistolary form, *Amours de Voyage* is more a series of reflections on contemporary problems than a tale of incident and event. Such story as there is concerns the tenuous relationship between Claude and Mary Trevellyn, a tepid affair that comes to nothing at the end of the book. The various letters are written from Rome, Florence, Bagni di Lucca and other towns visited by the middle-class English in the last century. Claude is a condescending, self-mocking, critical young man who loftily contemplates art, ancient and modern Rome, patriotism, love, politics, Christian belief, and those subjects that absorbed the attention of Clough himself during his short life. The work bears distinctly autobiographical overtones.

**amphibrach** See **metre**.

**amphimacer** See **metre**.

**anacreontic** In English verse, the term loosely denotes poems celebrating wine, love and song, after the example of the Greek lyric writer Anacreon of Teos (6th century BC) and his subsequent classical imitators. **Cowley** first used the English term in his *Anacreontiques* (1656) and the Irish poet **Thomas Moore** published a celebrated verse translation in 1800, the *Odes of Anacreon*, for which **Byron** dubbed him 'Anacreon Moore'.

**anagnorisis** The term used by Aristotle in the *Poetics* for the moment in tragedy when a character moves from ignorance to knowledge, particularly knowledge of his or her tragic fault. More loosely, it refers to the **denouement** of a drama.

***Analogy of Religion, The*** See **Butler, Joseph**.

**Anand, Mulk Raj** 1905– Indian novelist, born in Peshawar. From 1930 to 1945 he divided his time between literary London and Gandhi's India, until undertaking his long editorship of the Bombay arts magazine *Marg*. Sophisticated and cosmopolitan, impatient of transcendentalism, sceptical of religion, Anand looks Indian life fully in the face. His realistic novels, angry at injustice, satirical yet warm, reveal generosity of heart and great sympathy with the unfortunate: a hereditary latrine-cleaner in *Untouchable* (1935), an itinerant labourer in *Coolie* (1936) and a simple villager in the trilogy *The Village* (1939). *Across the Black Waters* (1940) is involved in Europe's mud in Flanders. In *The Sword and the Sickle* (1942) profit and loss have replaced traditional moral imperatives. *The Big Heart* (1945) shows traditional coppersmiths under pressure from factory owners. Anand's sympathies embrace even the privileged in *Private Life of an Indian Prince* (1953), though *Lament on the Death of a Master of Arts* (1967) is a mawkish novella. His art engages fully, however, with the physical and emotional destitution of a peasant woman in *The Woman and the Cow* (1960; reissued as *Gauri*, 1976). Of his projected series of seven markedly autobiographical novels, *The Seven Ages of Man*, four have appeared: *Seven Summers* (1951), *Morning Face* (1968), *Confessions of a Lover* (1976) and *The Bubble* (1984). Anand has published over half-a-dozen volumes of short stories. His fiction consistently upholds the value of living and awareness.

**anapaest** See **metre**.

**anaphora** The rhetorical device of repeating the first word or words of successive sentences or clauses. Famous examples are John of Gaunt's eulogy on England in **Shakespeare**'s *Richard II* ('This royal throne of kings, this scept'red isle,/ This earth of majesty . . .') and the opening paragraphs of **Dickens**'s *Bleak House* ('Fog everywhere. Fog up the river . . .').

***Anastasius, or, Memoirs of a Modern Greek*.** A **picaresque** novel published in 1819, once believed to be the work of **Byron** but in fact by **Thomas Hope**. A rich and much-travelled man, he made extensive use of his knowledge of the Near East, writing his novel in the form of an autobiography by an unscrupulous Greek of Chios in the 18th century.

***Anatomy of Abuses, The*** See **Stubbes, Philip**.

***Anatomy of Melancholy, The*** A colourfully written paramedical treatise by **Robert Burton**, published in 1621. This curious work is elaborately subdivided but comprises three main parts: the first deals with the causes and symptoms of melancholy, the second with its cures and the third with specific melancholies attaching to love and religion. Physical and mental health are only the starting point of Burton's study, which digresses continually to encompass topics such as politics and religion, its pages abounding in quotations from wide-ranging sources including the Bible, the classics and learned works by contemporaries. The style is both comic and serious in flavour, lively as well as informed.

**Ancients and Moderns, The** A literary and cultural debate of the Augustan period. See **Sir William Temple**, **Richard Bentley** and *The Battle of the Books*.

**Ancrene Riwle** (or *Ancrene Wisse*) A devotional manual in Middle English prose (*c.* 1200), also extant in French and Latin versions. It was written for a small group of anchoresses – women who, after a period of instruction, took vows of chastity and obedience and were confined to an eremitical cell to spend the rest of their lives in devotion. The anchoress was considered dead: she received the last rites before entering her cell and the burial service was used at her inclusion. The cell was sometimes sealed.

The work deals with the 'inner' and 'outer' rules of the anchorite life, i.e. both the psychological and physical aspects of devotion and conduct. Its approach reflects the change which took place in the 12th century, subordinating the rules of formal prayer to the private meditations of the individual. Despite its austere subject matter, the work is enlivened with many graphic details of everyday life and with brief **allegories** and **exempla**. Its highly accomplished style has sophistication and charm.

**Anderson, Jessica** Contemporary Australian novelist. Born in Brisbane of English and Irish ancestry, Jessica Anderson has lived most of her adult life in Sydney, apart from a period of three years in London. Before turning to writing novels around the age of 40 she had worked at a variety of occupations, including that of drama scriptwriter for the Australian Broadcasting Commission, for whom she adapted several classic novels. Her first novel, *An Ordinary Lunacy*, was published in 1963. It has been followed by *The Last Man's Head* (1970), *The Commandant* (1975) and the two novels for which she is best known, *Tirra Lirra by the River* (1978) and *The Impersonators* (1980). *Tirra Lirra by the River* takes the form of an elderly woman's account of her life in Queensland, Sydney and London. Her life appears to have been a series of escapes from one constricting environment to another, but gradually, as her narrative unfolds, she comes to terms with herself in her present situation, which is the most confined of all: she is bedridden in Queensland after a serious illness. *The Impersonators* is about an Australian woman who has lived abroad rediscovering her native Sydney, but also offers a vivid portrait of a divided Australian family in the 1970s. Like *Tirra Lirra*, it embodies a strong, albeit delicately realized, feminist vision in its portrayal of the constrictions to which women are subject. Anderson's prose style is characterized by a flair for the poetic and a laconic irony, which has been seen as reflecting her admiration for such English writers as **Henry Green**, **Evelyn Waugh** and **Muriel Spark**. The most significant Australian influence on her work is that of **Christina Stead**.

**Anderson, Maxwell** 1888–1959 American playwright. Born in Atlantic, Pennsylvania, Anderson spent much of his childhood travelling through Pennsylvania, Ohio, Iowa and North Dakota, following the 'call' of his father, a Baptist preacher. He attended the University of North Dakota, and then taught school in North Dakota and California. Newspaper work in San Francisco led to the offer of an editorship on *The New Republic*. He moved to New York City, where he soon began writing for the theatre.

His first play, *White Desert* (1923), about struggling North Dakota miners, was a failure, but a second, *What Price Glory?* (1924), written in collaboration with Lawrence Stallings, won acclaim for its realistic portrayal of soldiers during wartime. The 1930s were successful years for Anderson; during that decade he wrote and saw produced *Elizabeth the Queen* (1930), a blank-verse tragedy; *Night Over Taos* (1932); *Both Your Houses* (1932); *Mary of Scotland* (1933); *Valley Forge* (1934); *Winterset* (1935), a verse tragedy based on the Sacco and Vanzetti case; *Wingless Victory* (1937); *High Tor* (1937), a comedy about a struggle over land rights; *The Masque of Kings* (1937); *The Star Wagon* (1937); *Knickerbocker Holiday*, a musical comedy written in collaboration with his close friend Kurt Weill; *Key Largo* (1939), another tragedy; and *Journey to Jerusalem* (1940), a retelling of the story of Christ's childhood.

During World War II he produced two anti-Nazi plays, *The Miracle of the Danube* (1941) and *Candle in the Wind* (1941), and two more plays about the lives of soldiers, *The Eve of St Mark* (1942) and *Storm Operation* (1944). 1946 saw the appearance of *Truckline Cafe* and *Joan of Lorraine*; in 1948 he completed his Elizabethan trilogy with *Anne of the Thousand Days*. *Lost in the Stars* (1950), another collaboration with Weill, was an adaptation of **Alan Paton**'s novel, *Cry the Beloved Country*. Among his last plays were

*Barefoot in Athens* (1951), about Socrates, and *The Bad Seed* (1954).

**Anderson, Sherwood** 1876–1941 American novelist and short-story writer. Anderson was born in Camden, Ohio, and completed his education at the age of 14. He drifted from job to job, served in the Spanish–American War (1898–9), married, and managed a paint factory in Elyria, Ohio. Then, apparently, he left family and job and went to pursue a literary career in Chicago, where he met **Carl Sandburg**, **Ben Hecht**, **Floyd Dell** and others.

Anderson's first book, *Windy McPherson's Son*, was published in 1916. Other early works include *Marching Men* (1917), a novel about coal miners in Pennsylvania, and *Mid-American Chants* (1918), a volume of unrhymed verse. He received his greatest recognition following the publication of **Winesburg, Ohio** (1919), a collection of inter-related stories of small-town life, and the novel **Poor White** (1920), which explores the effects of technological change on American culture. His later work includes collections of short stories – *The Triumph of the Egg* (1921), *Horses and Men* (1923) and *Death in the Woods* (1933) – and the novels *Many Marriages* (1923), *Dark Laughter* (1925), *Tar: A Midwest Childhood* (1926) and *Beyond Desire* (1932). His autobiography, *A Story Teller's Story*, was published in 1924. A volume of *Letters* was issued in 1953, and a critical edition of his *Memoirs* in 1973. The influence of his flat, minimalist prose style, evocative of a bleaker vision of life than had previously been characteristic of American writing, can be seen in such writers as **Ernest Hemingway** and **William Faulkner**.

**Andrea del Sarto** A dramatic monologue by **Robert Browning**, published in *Men and Women* (1855). Andrea del Sarto (1486–1531) was a contemporary of Michaelangelo and Raphael; Browning's sub-title, *The Faultless Painter*, echoes the description he earned during his lifetime. In *The Lives of the Painters* Vasari wrote that Andrea del Sarto was less devoted to his art than to his wife Lucrezia. Browning's poem makes him aware of his deficiencies, talking to Lucrezia with sad resignation about his enslavement.

**Andreas** Old English poem preserved in the **Vercelli Book**. It relates the deeds of Sts Andrew and Matthew, its ultimate source being the Greek *Acts of Andrew and Matthias*. Matthew, persecuted, blinded, imprisoned and condemned by the cannibal Mermedonians, prays for help and God instructs Andrew to go to him. At first he protests that he cannot travel fast enough, but Christ steers his ship and with divine aid he reaches Matthew, restores his sight and releases him and other prisoners. Andrew is betrayed to the angry cannibals by a demon and tortured, but he has divine protection and cannot be killed. He is miraculously healed, flowers spring from the trace of his blood and the city is destroyed by a flood which only recedes when Andrew, at the bidding of some of the citizens, requires it. The dead are resurrected and the whole race converted. The poet takes every opportunity to expand the narrative with description and dialogue and pays great attention to the creation of atmosphere, setting and sentiment. The style shows the influence of **Cynewulf** and the poem has sometimes been attributed to him.

**Andrew of Wyntoun** *c.* 1355–1422 Scots chronicler. Little is known of his life but he was a canon regular at St Andrews and prior of St Serf's Inch, Lochleven, in 1395–1413. His single surviving work, his *Orygynale Cronykil*, was written in the late 14th century and is probably the earliest surviving example of Scots verse. It relates in octosyllabic couplets the history of Scotland from the Creation to the reign of Robert I. It is in nine books, the first five dealing with events from the Creation and mythical genealogies of the Britons and the last four tracing the history of Scotland from the time of Malcolm III. There is some inaccuracy in the relation of historical fact, but the *Cronykil* is nevertheless interesting as a record of early events in the history of Scotland. (See also **chronicle**.)

**Andrewes, Lancelot** 1555–1626 Churchman and translator of the Bible. Educated at the Merchant Taylors' School, he went to Pembroke Hall, Cambridge, where he became a fellow in 1576. In 1589 he became both master of his college and vicar of St Giles, Cripplegate. The living was attached to a prebend of St Paul's Cathedral and it was there that his preaching brought him to the attention of Queen Elizabeth. She offered him two bishoprics, which Andrewes declined, though he did become Dean of Westminster in 1601.

A distinguished scholar and master of 15 languages, Andrewes was foremost among the 54 translators selected to work on the Authorized Version of the Bible in 1604 (see **The Bible in English**). King James made him Bishop of Chichester (1605), then of Ely (1609) and of Winchester (1619).

Andrewes recoiled from the extremism of the Puritans, and was one of the shaping influences in Anglican theology. His sermons are classics of Anglican homiletic, though their appeal has been limited by Andrewes's classical scholarship and his taste for exhaustive textual analysis. *Ninety-Six Sermons* was published in 1629, *A Pattern of Catechistical Doctrine* in 1630, and *Preces Privatae* (Private Devotions) in 1648. **T. S.**

Eliot's essay (1928) is an important modern reappraisal of Andrewes's work.

**Angel in the House, The** A loosely constructed sequence of poems in praise of married love by **Coventry Patmore**, published at intervals between 1854 and 1863. Its first two parts, *The Betrothal* (1854) and *The Espousals* (1856), follow the courtship and marriage of Felix Vaughan and Honoria, a dean's daughter. This deliberately everyday narrative is interspersed with preludes and epigrams setting forth Patmore's philosophy of love and proclaiming the beneficent power of women to make 'brutes men, and men divine'. *Faithful for Ever* (1860) and *The Victories of Love* (1863) continue the story but in a markedly different manner, being written in octosyllabic couplets and taking the form of letters by Felix, Honoria, her unsuccessful former suitor Frederick Graham, and his wife Jane. Although many readers found the two later books weaker than their predecessors, *The Angel in the House* was among the most popular and highly praised poems of its day.

**Angelou, Maya** 1928– Noted for her varied and international involvement in the arts, Angelou was born Marguerita Johnson in St Louis, Missouri. She attended schools in Arkansas and California and then studied music, dance, and drama.

Her theatrical career began when she appeared in *Porgy and Bess* on an international tour sponsored by the US State Department (1954–5). Off Broadway, she performed in *Calypso Heatwave* and *The Blacks*, and in *Cabaret for Freedom*, which she wrote and produced in 1960 in collaboration with Godfrey Cambridge. She has since written for both stage and screen: *The Least of These*, a two-act drama first produced in Los Angeles in 1966; *The Clawing Within* (1966, unproduced); *Adjoa Amissah* (1967, unproduced); *Georgia, Georgia*, filmed by Independent Cinerama in 1972; an adaptation of Sophocles' *Ajax*, first produced in 1974 at the Mark Taper Forum; *And Still I Rise*, a one-act musical first produced in 1976 under her direction at the Ensemble Theatre, Oakland, California; *All Day Long*, filmed by the American Film Institute in 1974 and directed by herself.

Angelou's more recent work has confirmed her reputation as a telling commentator on black American culture. In her five autobiographical volumes she examines the challenges confronting and the potential awaiting black American women: *I Know Why The Caged Bird Sings* (1969), *Gather Together in My Name* (1974), *Singin' and Swingin' and Gettin' Merry Like Christmas* (1976), *The Heart of a Woman* (1981) and *All God's Children Need Travelling Shoes* (1986). Two collections of poetry – *Just Give Me a Cool Drink of Water 'Fore I Diiie* (1971) and *Oh Pray My Wings Are Gonna Fit Me Well* (1975) – and four television documentaries – *Blacks, Blues, Black* (1968), *Assignment America* (1975), *The Legacy* (1976), and *The Inheritors* (1976) – explore the presence of African traditions in American culture.

**Anglo-Norman** The variety of French spoken in England from the time of the Norman Conquest until the end of the Middle Ages. The Norman officials appointed by the conquerors to positions of power naturally spoke Norman. During the ensuing centuries, this insular version of French became increasingly corrupt as it absorbed features of English and developed separately from European French. At first, Norman (and then Anglo-Norman) was the sole language of the aristocracy and, with Latin, the language of official business and of all but the most popular of literature. The growth of English as a literary language during the 13th and particularly the 14th centuries was accompanied by a decline in Anglo-Norman. English was finally re-established as the language of the court, and courtly literature was again written in English. The earliest major writer to favour English as a literary language was **Geoffrey Chaucer**.

The Anglo-Norman language developed from pure Norman as it was infiltrated by English forms and words. There is no point of stasis at which the language can be identified as Anglo-Norman in a 'final' form; corruption continued until the language died out. Anglo-Norman is characterized by a proliferation of variant spellings, and a mixture of English and French constructions. Many types of work were written in it, the *Lais* of **Marie de France** being perhaps the most famous.

See also **English language**.

**Anglo-Saxon Chronicle** The main literary source of Anglo-Saxon history, beginning in the reign of **King Alfred** (871–99) and continuing, in the Peterborough version, until 1134. It is written in Old English prose. The earliest compiler(s) had access to various sources including some universal histories and a set of Frankish annals from the late 9th century. Manuscripts of the first section were in circulation in the early 890s, and some were continued in various religious houses throughout the country. There are seven versions and a fragment extant, some containing common material and others preserving matter of local interest. The quantity and quality of the material recorded varies at different times; the early 9th and mid 10th centuries are least well represented, while the reign of Aethelred and the years from Edward Confessor's reign onwards are treated most fully. Copies of the chronicle were apparently available to **Asser**, William of Malmesbury, Henry of

Huntingdon and Florence of Worcester, writers of histories or chronicles in Latin. (See also **chronicle**.)

**Angry Young Men** A group of writers of the late 1950s, characterized by what Kenneth Allsop defined in *The Angry Decade* (1958) as 'irreverence, stridency, impatience with tradition, vigour, vulgarity, sulky resentment against the cultivated'. These feelings were founded in the sense of betrayal and futility which succeeded the exalted aspirations generated by post-war reforms. **Colin Wilson's** study of alienation, *The Outsider* (1956), was judged by many an important manifesto for the movement. The classic dramatic embodiment is in **John Osborne's** *Look Back in Anger* (1956), whose anti-hero Jimmy Porter has come to represent the definitive 'angry young man'. In fiction the seminal novels are **John Wain's** *Hurry On Down* (1953), **Kingsley Amis's** *Lucky Jim* (1954), **John Braine's** *Room at the Top* (1957) and **Alan Sillitoe's** *Saturday Night and Sunday Morning* (1958).

The prototypical action occurs in a provincial, lower-middle- or working-class setting, around a solitary, rootless male protagonist whose persistent conflicts with and contempt for authority are rendered with a sardonic humour frequently verging on luxuriant scorn. Posterity's critical judgements, however, have tended to see the anger of such works as no more than dissent, less the product of a coherent or constructive social critique than the virtuoso indulgence of sensibility.

**Animal Farm** A novel by **George Orwell**, published in 1945.

The novel is cast in the form of a satirical **allegory** or fable directed primarily against Stalin's Russia. The animals on Mr Jones's farm revolt against their human masters and violently expel them. Led by the pigs, they decide to run the farm themselves on egalitarian principles. However, in time the pigs themselves become corrupted by power and, under their leader, Napoleon (Stalin), a new tyranny is established. Revolutionary idealism is undermined and the slogans which had embodied the new revolutionary order are cynically rewritten ('All animals are equal, but some animals are more equal than others'). Snowball (Trotsky), an idealist, is driven out, and Boxer, the noble carthorse whose courage and strength had helped to make the revolution possible, is sent to the knacker's yard. The final betrayal occurs when the pigs engineer a *rapprochement* with Mr Jones.

The book was originally rejected for publication by **T. S. Eliot** in 1944, though many hailed it as a classic during the cold war era. It represented Orwell's rejection of all revolutionary change, and has remained very popular, especially with younger readers.

**Anna of the Five Towns** A novel by **Arnold Bennett**, published in 1902.

The cultural and economic realities of Bursley, a Potteries town, weigh heavily on the heroine. The harsh codes of Anna's father, Ephraim Tellwright, and of evangelical Methodism, are relieved when she is told of her large inheritance. This prospect of £50,000 makes her the more attractive, however, in the eyes of the successful businessman Henry Mynors. Anna is impressed by Mynors, so that she excludes thoughts of her other wooer, Willie Price, an industrial tenant of her father. But her eventual engagement to Mynors is primarily a means of escape for herself and her sister Agnes; even Mynors's religious fervour wins her respect rather than her love.

Anna's awakening to her true feelings for the helpless Willie Price is cut across by the constraints of class and money. Ephraim sends her to demand payment from Willie and his devious father, Titus; to some extent, she shares her father's distaste for the debtors' predicament. Her love for Price is real, but ineffectual; yet she acts to save him from public disgrace by destroying the forged bill of credit which the Prices have sent to her father. Ephraim disinherits her for this.

While Anna's marriage to Mynors goes ahead, Willie Price learns that his father has embezzled £50 from the chapel building fund before committing suicide. When Willie disappears, the Bursley community believes he has emigrated to Australia. But he has followed his father's example of self-destruction, throwing himself into a disused pitshaft.

**Annals of the Parish, The** A novel by **John Galt**, published in 1821. The Revd Micah Balwhidder records life in his Lowland parish of Dalmailing, often in an unintentionally humorous way, over a period of 50 years (1760–1810).

**Anne of Geierstein** A novel by **Sir Walter Scott**, published in 1829. Set during the reign of Edward IV, the story follows the intrigues of the Lancastrian exiles, Arthur de Vere and his father, the Earl of Oxford, in Switzerland and at the court of Charles the Bold, Duke of Burgundy.

**Anne of Green Gables** A novel by **L. M. Montgomery**, published in 1908.

Matthew and Marilla Cuthbert, an elderly Canadian bachelor and his sister farming on Prince Edward Island, decide to take in an orphan boy to help with the daily chores. By mistake they are sent Anne Shirley instead, an 11-year-old redhead who quickly charms the shy Matthew by her vivacious prattle. His sister is not so easily won over but eventually Anne's vulnerable but deeply affectionate character wins her heart too, with the rest of the novel detailing the mini-adventures of an adolescent girl and her peer group from attempts at amateur dramatics to first courtship. Anne's long-winded, romantic soliloquies are regularly brought down to earth by Marilla's dry interjections, only to soar to new imaginative heights the next moment. Subsequent novels follow Anne's career from teaching college to marriage and domesticity, but without recapturing the charm of the original book.

**Annual Register, The** An annual review of the year's events, in its early years also containing literary essays and poetry, founded by **Robert Dodsley** and **Edmund Burke** in 1758 and still in publication. From a literary point of view *The Annual Register*'s importance derives from the fact that for the first eight years of publication it was edited by Burke, though anonymously, and he continued as a reviewer probably till at least 1773.

**Annus Mirabilis**: *The Year of Wonders, 1666* A poem in **quatrains** by **John Dryden**, published in 1667. It deals with the war at sea against the Dutch, concluding with the victory at the North Foreland in July 1666, and with the Fire of London (September 1666).

**Anson, George, Baron** 1697–1762 Sailor and travel-writer. Born at Colwich in Staffordshire, Anson served in the Navy and finally became First Lord of the Admiralty. His journal of an eventful and hazardous expedition made in 1740–4 was edited as *Voyage Round the World* (1748) by his chaplain, Richard Walter. It includes accounts of the storms at Cape Horn which wrecked four of the seven ships in the squadron, and of the capture in the Pacific of a Spanish galleon with a million and a half dollars.

**Anstey, Christopher** 1724–1805 Born at Brinkley in Cambridgeshire and educated at Eton and King's College, Cambridge, Anstey made his reputation with *The New Bath Guide* (1766). It describes the comic adventures of the Blunderhead family at the fashionable spa town in a series of verse letters.

**Anstey, F.** Pseudonym of the humorist Thomas Anstey Guthrie (1856–1934). Educated at King's College School and Trinity Hall, Cambridge, Anstey was called to the Bar but diverted from the law by the success of *Vice Versa: or A Lesson to Fathers* (1882), the story of a father and son who exchange ages and personalities. He contributed regularly to *Punch* and joined the staff of the magazine in 1887. His large output included *The Brass Bottle* (1900), a comedy about an inefficient jinnee.

**Anthony, Michael** 1932– Trinidadian novelist. He was born in Mayero and had his secondary education until the age of 15 at the Junior Technical School in San Fernando. These two places feature centrally in his fiction. Four of his five novels are concerned with childhood or adolescence. Probably the best known is *The Year in San Fernando* (1965), one of the acknowledged classics of Caribbean literature and a brilliant study of the maturing process whereby a young boy acquires insight into adult and urban life. His other novels of growing up are *The Games Were Coming* (1963), *Green Days By the River* (1967) and *All That Glitters* (1981). After living in Brazil for some time Anthony wrote *Streets of Conflict* (1976), which is set in Rio de Janeiro in the late 1960s. He is also the author of many short stories; some appeared early in his career in such publications as *The Trinidad Guardian* and *BIM* and others are collected in *Cricket in the Road and Other Stories* (1973). Anthony's is a gentle but shrewdly observant talent, perhaps more recognized outside the Caribbean than within it.

**Anti-Jacobin, The** A political journal founded by **George Canning**, published weekly from 20 November 1797 to 7 July 1798. Its platform is described by its title, and it was successful in combating the radical politics and philosophy which the revolution in France encouraged. Among its contributors were Canning, George Ellis (a former Whig) and **John Hookham Frere**, and the editor was **William Gifford**. *The Anti-Jacobin* published news and notable satirical verse including George Canning's anti-French 'The New Morality'.

**The Antiquary** A novel by **Sir Walter Scott**, published in 1816.

Major Neville, calling himself William Lovel, follows Isabella Wardour to Scotland. She has rejected him in deference to her father, Sir Arthur, who believes Neville to be illegitimate. On the way to Scotland, Neville falls in with the Wardours' neighbour, Jonathan Oldbuck, the antiquary of the title, and with him meets the king's bedesman, Edie Ochiltree. Sir Arthur has fallen under the influence of Dousterswivel, a plausible German scoundrel. Lovel saves Sir Arthur and Isabella from drowning, quarrels with Oldbuck's nephew, Hector M'Intyre, and with Ochiltree's help exposes Dousterswivel. Lovel proves to be the Heir of Glenallan and all ends happily.

The success of *The Antiquary*, the author's own chief favourite among all his novels, owes much to the character of the talkative and eccentric Oldbuck.

**antithesis** A rhetorical device which uses opposites balanced and contrasted to create sharpness of effect. Antithetical expression is a particularly marked feature of style in neo-classical poetry, and is an important element in the structure of the 'closed couplet' (see **heroic couplet**): ''Tis the first Virtue, Vices to abhor/ And the first Wisdom, to be Fool no more.' (**Pope**, *Imitations of Horace*.) See also **chiasmus**.

***Antonio and Mellida*** and ***Antonio's Revenge*** A play in two distinct but related parts by **John Marston**, written for performance by the Boys of St Paul's, first performed in 1599/1600 and published in 1602.

*Antonio and Mellida*, despite darker qualities, is essentially a love-story. Antonio, son of Andrugio, Duke of Genoa, loves Mellida, daughter of Piero, Duke of Venice. Genoa and Venice are at war, and Piero puts a price on the heads of Andrugio and Antonio. Disguised as an Amazon, Antonio goes to Venice and persuades Mellida to run away with him. They are captured, and Andrugio offers himself to the enemy in order to save his son's life. To general surprise, Piero relents and consents to the marriage of Antonio and Mellida. This comedic conclusion is overthrown in *Antonio's Revenge*, which is formally a revenge tragedy. Piero kills Andrugio and wins the hand of his widow. He also thwarts Antonio's happiness by contriving to dishonour his own daughter, Mellida, who dies of grief. Antonio is visited by the ghost of his murdered father, whom he revenges by killing Piero. The relationship of *Antonio's Revenge* to **Kyd**'s earlier **The Spanish Tragedy** and to **Shakespeare**'s *Hamlet* has been often noted.

***Antony and Cleopatra*** A tragedy by **William Shakespeare**, first performed *c.* 1607 and published in the First Folio of 1623. The sole source is **Sir Thomas North**'s translation of Plutarch, on which it relies for much of the language as well as for the story.

Infatuated with Cleopatra, Antony neglects his duties as a Roman triumvir and lingers in Alexandria. Only when news of Pompey's rebellion is added to news of the death of Antony's own wife, Fulvia, does he decide, despite Cleopatra's pleas, to leave for Rome with his loyal general, Enobarbus. The uneasy triumvirate of the scheming Octavius Caesar, the foolish Lepidus and the hedonistic Antony is patched up, and Antony agrees to marry Octavius's sister, Octavia. Even Pompey accepts peace terms. Abandoned in Alexandria, Cleopatra beats the messenger who brings news of Antony's marriage.

In Athens with Octavia, Antony hears that Octavius has ridiculed him and sent an army against Pompey. Octavia returns to Rome on a peace mission, and Antony goes back to Egypt and Cleopatra. There he promises the eastern provinces of the Roman empire to her and her

children. Given such a pretext for open hostility, Octavius embarks his army. Against advice from Enobarbus, Antony combines with the Egyptian fleet to engage Octavius at sea. The battle at Actium is turned into a fiasco when Cleopatra's ships flee and Antony follows her back to Egypt.

In despair, Enobarbus deserts Antony. More at home in a land battle, Antony recovers his firmness of purpose, but, after an initial victory, he is again drawn into defeat by the Egyptian army's defection. The fearful Cleopatra hides in her monument and sends Antony a message that she is dead. Defeated and despairing, he falls on his sword, and is carried to the monument, where he dies in Cleopatra's arms. Octavius visits Cleopatra and leaves confident that she will return as his prisoner to Rome. But Cleopatra achieves a new dignity at last, robbing Octavius of his triumph (over Antony as well as her) by arranging for her own death. She has deadly asps smuggled into the monument, dresses herself in her finest robes, and holds the asps to her body. The outwitted Octavius concedes that she be buried with Antony.

Shakespeare's imagination was excited by the contrast between Egyptian opulence and Roman regulation, and he portrays Antony as a man torn between love and duty. The triumph of love is complete only when Cleopatra finds the resolution to kill herself. Richer in language and imagery than the Roman tragedies, **Julius Caesar** and **Coriolanus**, with which it is inevitably associated, *Antony and Cleopatra* is more appropriately viewed as one of the group of great tragedies Shakespeare wrote *c.* 1603–7 than as part of a scattered group of Roman plays.

***Apologia pro Vita Sua*** The spiritual autobiography of **John Henry Newman**, published in seven parts with an appendix between 21 April and 2 June 1864. The full title, *Apologia pro Vita Sua: Being a Reply to a Pamphlet Entitled: 'What, Then, Does Dr Newman Mean?'*, reflected its origin in Newman's public quarrel with the militantly Protestant **Charles Kingsley**. In a review of **J. A. Froude**'s *History of England* (vols. 7 and 8), contributed to *Macmillan's Magazine* in January 1864, Kingsley had written: 'Truth for its own sake has never been a virtue of the Roman clergy. Father Newman informs us that it need not and on the whole ought not to be.' The next month Newman published *Mr Kingsley and Dr Newman*, the record of his unsatisfactory correspondence with Kingsley and his publishers over the offending passage. Kingsley issued his pamphlet and so provoked Newman to write the *Apologia*.

The volume edition (1865) detached the book from the original controversy by omitting the first two parts and the appendix, where he had not spared his opponent, and by using a new sub-title: *Being a History of his Religious Opinions.* Yet the underlying purpose remained the same. Newman had found in Kingsley's jibe a clear statement of the distrust with which the English public had long regarded his career as an Anglican clergyman, his conversion to Roman Catholicism and his subsequent career as a Catholic priest. The response it demanded went beyond theology and polemic, and involved personal justification. Newman's account of himself is designed to assert the sincerity and consistency of his spiritual development. In addition to its value as a record of personal faith, the *Apologia* is also a primary historical source for the **Oxford Movement**.

*Apology for Poetry, An* A critical treatise by **Sir Philip Sidney**, published in 1595 in two separate editions, one bearing the title *The Defence of Poesy*. Few of the ideas it presents are original, being Renaissance critical commonplaces. However, the work is a masterpiece of elegant persuasion, and its easy and engaging style conceals a careful rhetorical structure. Sidney claims that imaginative literature is a better teacher than philosophy or history. He defends it against the charges of time-wasting, lying and allurement to vice, and deals also with Plato's famous decision to ban poets from the state in his *Republic*. In Sidney's view, literature has the power to reproduce an ideal golden world, not just the brazen one we know, and so to offer 'a speaking picture – with this end, to teach and delight'. A digression looks at the state of English literature and finds it sadly wanting, but makes honourable exceptions of **Chaucer**'s *Troilus and Criseyde*, **Surrey**'s poems, *The Mirror for Magistrates*, **Spenser**'s *Shepheardes Calender* and the play *Gorboduc*.

**Apostles, The** Officially 'The Cambridge Conversazione Society', The Apostles was formed in 1820 for the purpose of formal discussion between friends. Early members included **Tennyson** and **Arthur Henry Hallam**. The turn of the century was a period of particular brilliance for the society, largely through the influence of **G. E. Moore**. Among the **Bloomsbury Group**, members included Roger Fry, **Desmond MacCarthy**, **E. M. Forster**, **Leonard Woolf**, Saxon Sydney-Turner, **Lytton Strachey** and **John Maynard Keynes**.

**Apperley, C[harles] J[ames]** 1779–1843 Writer on sport and rural life, under the pseudonym Nimrod. Educated at Rugby, Apperley turned from his life as a Shropshire squire to journalism when the income from his land declined. He contributed to *The Quarterly Review* and *The Sporting Magazine*, and became a staff editor on *The Sporting Review*. His first book, *Memoirs of the Life of John Mytton* (1837), was about a Shropshire neighbour. *The Life of a Sportsman* (1842) contains a vivid picture of country life. His books was illustrated by Henry Alkne. His friend and rival **R. S. Surtees** lampooned Apperley in *Jorrocks's Jaunts and Jollities* and *Handley Cross*.

**Arbuthnot, John** 1667–1735 Physician and originator of 'John Bull', the archetypal Englishman. Born in Kincardineshire, he studied medicine at Oxford and then took his MD at St Andrews University, after which he pursued a distinguished medical career. He was elected a Fellow of the Royal Society in 1704, and was appointed physician to Queen Anne in the following year. A humane man with diverse talents, he was not only progressive in the field of science, but known as a wit and writer of considerable ability. He became a valued friend of **Swift** and **Pope**, a convivial member of the **Scriblerus Club**, and subsequently a leading contributor to the *Memoirs of Martinus Scriblerus* (published in Pope's *Works* in 1741) and to their collaborative comedy *Three Hours After Marriage* (1717). But he is best known for *The History of John Bull* (1712), a popular collection of five satirical pamphlets designed to terminate Marlborough's European campaign, and advocating a return to peace and common sense. His 'A Sermon Preached to the People at Mercat Cross, Edinburgh' (1706) supported the union of Scotland with England. His scientific works include *An Essay Concerning the Nature of Ailments* (1731), which stressed the value of proper diet in the treatment of patients, *An Essay Concerning the Effects of Air on Human Bodies* (1733), and *An Essay on the Usefulness of Mathematical Learning* (1701). He published a single poem, 'Know Thyself', in 1734.

*Arcadia, The* A prose romance, interspersed with poems, by **Sir Philip Sidney**. Enormously popular in its age, it appealed to the Renaissance love of **pastoral** but was also read as a **courtesy book**, a moral treatise, a discussion of love and philosophy, and even a rhetorical handbook. Sidney wrote the bulk of it in 1580 while staying at Wilton House with his sister, the Countess of Pembroke, to whom it is dedicated; he subsequently began but never finished a careful revision. As a result, the work exists in three different forms.

The first, unrevised version, the *Old Arcadia*, was never printed in the 16th century, though copies circulated in manuscript. It was devised as a tragicomedy in five acts, with **eclogues** scattered in the text and groups of eclogues as dividing entr'actes. The story has a serious double plot and a comic underplot. Duke Basilius is warned by an oracle of enigmatic disasters and retires to Arcadia with his wife Gynecia and his two daughters, Philoclea and

Pamela. Two princes, Pyrocles and Musidorus, first cousins and devoted friends, arrive and fall in love respectively with Philoclea and and Pamela. Pyrocles disguises himself as an Amazon, Cleophila, to be near Philoclea. Basilius falls in love with his disguise: Gynecia and Philoclea, seeing through the disguise, fall in love with Pyrocles. Musidorus decides to elope with Pamela and his attempt to rape her is interrupted by rebels. Pyrocles attempts to solve his amatory entanglements by arranging to meet both Basilius and Gynecia in a cave. There, as the oracle predicted, the Duke commits adultery with his own wife. Pyrocles seduces Philoclea, Basilius apparently dies from a love philtre, and Pamela and Musidorus are carried off by rebels. At the end of the work all the major characters are arraigned before Euarchus. Gynecia confesses to killing her husband and is to be buried alive. Pyrocles and Musidorus are condemned to death; Philoclea is to go to a nunnery. Euarchus, the upholder of strict justice, will not alter his verdict even when he realizes that he has condemned his son Pyrocles and his nephew Musidorus. Tragedy is averted and turns to comedy when Basilius revives and asserts the strange workings of providence. A general pardon is extended.

Like *Astrophil and Stella*, the *Old Arcadia* examines the various workings of love on the human character. It can be an ennobling and educative passion, but it can also bring shame, overthrow reason and undermine the life of heroic action. The trial scene at the end raises acute problems of justice and equity.

The second version, known as the *New Arcadia*, was published posthumously in 1590, perhaps under the supervision of Sidney's friend **Fulke Greville**. It presented the revised text of the first three books, all that the author had lived to complete. Sidney's changes, often done painstakingly sentence by sentence, make the unfinished *New Arcadia* longer by 50,000 words than the finished *Old Arcadia* and introduce major differences. There is no attempted rape of Pamela or successful seduction of Philoclea. The opening of the work is different and new subsidiary stories are interlaced, including that of the blind Paphlagonian king which **Shakespeare** borrowed for the Gloucester sub-plot in *King Lear*. The revised *Arcadia* is a more serious work than the first; moral earnestness is constantly deepened, especially in the depiction of Pamela.

In 1593 *The Countess of Pembroke's Arcadia* was published, perhaps under the supervision of the Countess herself. It brought together the first three revised books of the *New Arcadia* and the last two books of the unrevised *Old Arcadia*, thus making a third hybrid version of the text.

Sidney's sources were recognized as early as the 1590s. From Sannazaro's *Arcadia* he took his title and the pastoral setting; from *Amadis of Gaule* chivalric romance and Pyrocles' disguise as an Amazon. Heliodorus' *Aethiopica* influenced the work in many ways, especially in its revised version.

**Archer, William** 1856–1924 Scottish journalist and dramatic critic, whose alliance with **George Bernard Shaw** in the championship of Ibsen was influential in the move to raise the literary standards of British drama at the end of the 19th century. The first of his translations from Ibsen, *Quicksands, or, The Pillars of Society*, was performed in London in 1880, and a collected edition in 11 volumes was published in 1906–8. Archer was a fierce defender of the best of contemporary drama against what he considered a dangerous and indiscriminate preference for the old. *The Old Drama and the New* (1923) is a vigorously argued and unashamedly partisan statement of his critical view that the English drama since **Tom Robertson** has a greater claim for stage performance than all but a tiny minority of earlier plays.

**Arden, John** 1930– Playwright and essayist. Born in Barnsley and educated at Sedbergh School, Cambridge University and Edinburgh College of Art, where he trained as an architect. His first play, *All Fall Down* (1955), was performed by Edinburgh students. It was followed by a radio play, *The Life of Man* (1956), and his first professionally staged work, *The Waters of Babylon* (1957), which brought him into membership of the Writers' Group at the **Royal Court Theatre**. *Live Like Pigs* (1958) and the powerful *Serjeant Musgrave's Dance* (1959) established him as the most allusive and original new playwright of the socially conscious renaissance of English drama. *The Happy Haven* (1960), the first of his collaborations with his wife Margaretta D'Arcy, makes adventurous use of half-masks in order to allow young actors to impersonate old people. *The Workhouse Donkey* (1963) explores a by-now familiar concern of Arden's, the conflict between the upholders of rigid values and anarchic subverters of rigidity, in the context of local government. As in *Armstrong's Last Goodnight* (1964) and his play about King John and the barons, *Left-Handed Liberty* (1965), Arden allows his preference for 'curvilinear' Celtic disorder to emerge without his having totally to discredit 'rectilinear' Roman order. In *The Hero Rises Up* (1968) and, unmistakably, in the overtly political plays about Ireland, like *The Ballygombeen Bequest* (1972), the six-part *The Non-Stop Connolly Show* (1975) and *Vandaleur's Folly* (1980), the Roman rigidity of the rulers of British society receives short shrift. Arden has consciously progressed from a liberal socialism to the politics of revolution, particularly with regard to the British 'occupation' of Northern

Ireland. The essays in *To Present the Pretence* (1978) record some of that progress.

**Arden of Feversham, The Tragedy of Mr** An anonymous play, published in 1592 and probably performed the same year; at one time it was attributed to Shakespeare (see **Shakespeare apocrypha**). It is an early example of domestic tragedy and, in so far as it is based on an actual murder which took place at Faversham in Kent, a forerunner of the popular criminal drama of the 18th and 19th centuries. The play shows the initially frustrated but eventually successful attempts of Mistress Arden to rid herself of an unloved husband. The murder is discovered and she is executed for the crime, together with her lover and fellow conspirator.

**Ardizzone, Edward** 1900–79 Children's author and illustrator. Born in China of an Italian father and Scots mother, Ardizzone settled in England at the age of five, first in Ipswich and later in London. After an unsuccessful period of office work he became an artist, specializing in scenes of low life around London pubs and street corners. His first children's book, *Little Tim and the Brave Sea Captain* (1936), was devised for the amusement of his own small son and daughter. Its success established him as a leading author–illustrator with a good eye for adventure and a brilliant, elusive drawing style concentrating on the essentials of line and form, leaving readers to provide the rest from their own imaginations. More books about Little Tim followed after a period as official war artist, when Ardizzone travelled (often under hazardous conditions) in France, Italy, Libya and Germany. He went on to illustrate over 100 books by other writers, but remained best loved for his children's work.

**Areopagitica**: *A Speech of Mr John Milton for the Liberty of Unlicensed Printing to the Parliament of England* **John Milton**'s celebrated plea for a free press and free discussion (1644) takes its title from the Greek *Areopagus*, the hill of Ares in Athens where the highest judicial tribunal of the

The frontispiece to the third edition of *Arden of Feversham*, 1633. The murderers attack Arden as he plays backgammon with Mosbie, his wife's lover.

city used to meet. Having abolished the Star Chamber in 1641, the Parliamentarians effectively reimposed censorship in 1643, and Milton opens his objection by demonstrating that the government was using the methods of those they most decried, namely the Papal regimes. He argues that freedom to pursue learning is essential to the Christian 'ethos', that to read freely is necessary to the development of virtue, and that licensing will in any case prove ineffectual. He appeals rousingly to the 'Lords and Commons of England' not to act repressively upon 'a nation not slow and dull, but of a quick, ingenious and piercing spirit'.

**Areopagus** Letters exchanged between **Edmund Spenser** and **Gabriel Harvey** in 1579–80 refer allusively to an 'Areopagus', an association of aristocratic courtiers and poets which took its name from the hill in Athens where the earliest aristocratic council met. Spenser himself seems to have been on the fringes of the group, but the best-known members were **Edward Dyer**, **Fulke Greville** and **Sir Philip Sidney**. The group's exact nature and constitution is not clear, though it was certainly concerned with prosody and classical metres, perhaps in imitation of the French 16th-century academies. Its members may also have discussed political and religious matters as well as exclusively literary ones.

**Argument Against Abolishing Christianity, An** A satirical pamphlet by **Jonathan Swift** published in 1711. Pretending to be a mild objection to an imaginary campaign to remove Christianity altogether, this ironical performance points out that such a move might be 'attended with some Inconveniences'. Swift was concerned at the extremes of religious thinking then current, and the pamphlet attacks both the 'low' churchmen (freethinkers and Deists) and the high Tories (non-jurors and Jacobites) who together threaten in different ways the strength of the established Anglican church. This echoes the argument in his other pamphlets, *The Sentiments of a Church of England Man* (written 1708, published 1711) and *A Letter Concerning the Sacramental Test* (1708), which express dissatisfaction at the idea of nominal piety, or 'occasional conformity', while his *Project for the Advancement of Religion* (1709) urges the practical solution that the court might take the initiative in moral matters.

**Arlen, Michael** The pseudonym of the novelist and short-story writer Dikran Kouyoumdjian (1895–1956). Arlen was born in Bulgaria of Armenian parents, and educated at Malvern College and Edinburgh. He was naturalized as a British subject in 1922, but chose to live in the South of France from the time of his marriage in 1928 until World War II. In the aftermath of

World War I Arlen embarked on a career as a writer of acerbic but stylish short stories of London life. These included *The Romantic Lady* (1921) and *These Charming People* (1923). He then began writing novels, and *The Green Hat* (1924) became a best-seller. His last novel, *The Flying Dutchman*, was published in 1939. Arlen settled in New York after World War II and lived there until his death.

**Armah, Ayi Kwei** 1939– Ghanaian novelist, born in Takoradi. Educated in Ghana, at Harvard and in New York, he worked as scriptwriter, schoolmaster, translator, journalist and lecturer in Ghana, Algeria, France and the USA before settling in Tanzania (1970). His vivid, eloquent novels lament centuries of African suffering and cultural obliteration. In *The Beautyful Ones Are Not Yet Born* (1968), from a slogan on a Ghanaian bus, and *Fragments* (1970) recurrent imagery of excrement, decay, disease, and society's condemnation of individual integrity as insanity, suggest Armah's total disillusion with independent Africa. *Why Are We So Blest?* (1972) seems utterly nihilistic. In *Two Thousand Seasons* (1973), however, he rewrites the history of both Islamic and Christian assaults upon Africa and, by representing traditional *griots* as inspired seers, stresses the true African way as selfless, mutual caring. *The Healers* (1975), about the crumbling 19th-century Ashanti empire, implies the need today for a truly African cultural integrity.

**Armin, Robert** *c.* 1580–1612 One of the actors in **Shakespeare**'s company, the Lord Chamberlain's Men, Armin became the principal comedian after **Will Kemp**'s departure. He contributed a considerable portion to a play that gave him a fine part, *The History of the Two Maids of More-Clacke* (published 1609). He was also the author of the satirical prose tract *Fool upon Fool, or, Six Sortes of Sots* (1605), which he later enlarged as *A Nest of Ninnies* (1608), and a verse translation of an Italian tale, *The Italian Taylor and his Boy* (1609).

*Arms and the Man* See **Shaw, George Bernard.**

**Armstrong, John** *c.* 1709–79 Poet and physician. The son of a minister from Roxburghshire, Armstrong studied medicine at Edinburgh and practised in London. He wrote *The Oeconomy of Love* (1736), a blank-verse sex manual for the newly married, and *The Art of Preserving Health* (1744), a didactic work pleasantly done in the manner of his friend **James Thomson**, who included a portrait of Armstrong in *The Castle of Indolence*.

**Arnold, Sir Edwin** 1823–1904 Poet and translator. Born at Gravesend in Kent and educated at King's College, London, and University College, Oxford, Arnold won the Newdigate Prize in 1852 with his poem 'Belshazzar's Feast'. In 1856 he became Principal of Deccan College, Poona, and in 1861 joined the staff of *The Daily Telegraph.* Arnold studied Eastern languages and published his first translation, from Sanskrit, in 1861: *Hitopadésa*, 'The Book of Good Counsels'. His blank-verse epic on the life and teachings of the Buddha, *The Light of Asia* (1879), was enormously popular. He did not repeat his success with *The Light of the World* (1891).

**Arnold, Matthew** 1822–88 Poet, critic and educational administrator. The son of Dr **Thomas Arnold** of Rugby, Matthew Arnold was born at Laleham in Middlesex and educated at Winchester, Rugby and Balliol College, Oxford, where in 1843 he won the Newdigate Prize for poetry with 'Cromwell'. He became a fellow of Oriel College in 1845 but left the university shortly afterwards to be private secretary to Lord Lansdowne. He travelled abroad in the late 1840s, and met the Swiss girl Marguerite who haunts much of his earlier lyric poetry. By 1851 he was an inspector of schools, a post which brought him the financial security to marry Frances Lucy Wightman in 1851.

Arnold's poetic career began in 1849 with the publication of *The Strayed Reveller, and Other Poems* by 'A', but by *New Poems* (1867) it was over. Between these dates, however, he published *Empedocles on Etna, and Other Poems* (1852), *Poems* (1853), *Poems Second Series* (1855) and *Merope* (1858). The variety of poetic expression in these volumes is apparent: lyrics (the 'Marguerite' poems, **Dover Beach**, 'Philomela'); poetic drama (**Empedocles on Etna** and *Merope*); narrative poems (**Tristram and Iseult** and **Sohrab and Rustum**); elegies (**Thyrsis, The Scholar-Gipsy** and 'Memorial Verses'). Often deriving from classical subjects, Arnold's poetry is frequently informed by alienation, stoicism, despair, and spiritual emptiness.

In 1858 Arnold became professor of poetry at Oxford, and he perhaps appreciated the mild irony that, save for the 1867 volume, he wrote prose for the rest of his life. Like other Victorian polymaths sensitive to the stresses of the age, Arnold sought to deal with these problems through a series of literary, political, religious and educational writings. Holding an inspectorate in education until his retirement in 1886 and possessed of European rather than insular vision, Arnold contemplated the British and Continental pedagogical scenes through a series of reports on differing educational problems – reports marked by clear writing, advocacy of the humane disciplines, and emphasis on the Bible as a moral and a literary strength. He was also a trenchant critic of elementary and secondary education, of teacher training, and an advocate of state instruction at home and abroad. Above all, his educational writings put the case for a national instruction rising above local and political interests.

In 1865 Arnold produced the first series of his *Essays in Criticism* (the second appearing posthumously in 1888). Here, particularly in 'The Function of Criticism at the Present Time' in the first volume, he develops his view of criticism as a disinterested and flexible mode of thought of application far beyond literature. Such a view leads naturally to the broad consideration of the dilemmas of English society in his great prose work, *Culture and Anarchy* (1869), where culture is recommended as 'the great help out of our present difficulties' and defined as 'the pursuit of total perfection by means of getting to know, on all the matters which most concern us, the best which has been thought and said in the world'. By the 1870s Arnold had joined the long list of Victorian thinkers who turned their attention to the theological controversies of the age, with *Saint Paul and Protestantism* (1870), *Literature and Dogma* (1873), *God and the Bible* (1875) and *Last Essays on Church and Religion* (1877).

Of the major Victorian poets Arnold is perhaps the least generous, but what he lacks in abundance he compensates for in subtlety and variety. His melancholy, delicately moving stanzas are an exquisite register of the feelings of those intellectuals 'wandering between two worlds,/One dead, the other powerless to be born'. The despairing gentleness of Arnold's poetry renders it unique in the Victorian canon. And as a prose writer tackling insuperable problems – in language often sardonic and invariably articulate – Arnold is forthright, courageous and impervious to hostility. In their advocacy of culture, his appeals are as applicable in our own day as a century ago.

**Arnold, Thomas** 1795–1842 Educator and historian. Born in the Isle of Wight and educated at Winchester College and Corpus Christi College, Oxford, Arnold became a fellow of Oriel College in 1815. In 1828 he was appointed headmaster of Rugby School, and set about raising its standards and reputation with characteristic energy. Arnold's regime stressed the importance of classical education and, particularly, religious training; its purpose was to develop the boys' sense of duty and their character. Its success made Rugby the first choice of middle-class parents seeking a public school for their sons; in a larger sense, Rugby became the model for the English public-school system in the 19th century. Arnold returned to Oxford as Regius Professor of Modern History in 1841. His edition of Thucydides was published in 1830–5 and his *History of Rome* (1838–42) left

unfinished. Admiringly described by his former pupil **Thomas Hughes** in *Tom Brown's Schooldays* and made the subject of a respectful biography by **Arthur Stanley**, Arnold was caricatured for a later generation by **Lytton Strachey** in *Eminent Victorians* (1918).

**Arraignment of Paris, The**: A Pastoral A pastoral play in verse by **George Peele**, written to be played before Elizabeth I in her honour and first published in 1584.

Paris is to be found in the company of his wife Oenone, tending his flocks on Mount Ida. The three goddesses Juno, Venus and Pallas bring the golden apple and ask him to decide to which of them it shall be awarded. Paris decides for Venus, who promptly carries him off, leaving poor Oenone deserted. Juno and Pallas accuse Paris of partiality in his judgement and arraign him before the assembled gods. The judgement of who is most deserving of the golden apple is referred to Diana, who evades the tricky choice by awarding it to the nymph Eliza, 'our Zabeta fair'. The play has no worth as a stage piece but is notable for its lyrics, particularly the song of Paris and Oenone, 'Fair and fair, and twice so fair'.

**Arthur Mervyn** A gothic novel by **Charles Brockden Brown**, published in two volumes between 1799 and 1800, and set in Philadelphia during the plague year of 1793.

The novel opens when Dr Stevens, the narrator, finds the 18-year-old Arthur Mervyn, a farmboy who has come to the city, sick with yellow fever in the streets. He takes him home and cares for him. Soon, however, a friend voices the suspicion that Mervyn is not the country innocent he seems, but has been involved in criminal dealings with an embezzler named Thomas Welbeck. Mervyn then tells Stevens his story.

Upon his arrival in Philadelphia Mervyn was employed by Welbeck, but soon began to suspect him of criminal activities. These suspicions were confirmed one night when Welbeck shot a man in his study. At this point Welbeck had told Mervyn *his* story – of how, despite his ideals, he had been guilty of seduction, the theft of $20,000, forgery, and now murder. Welbeck then tried to escape by boat but was apparently drowned. Mervyn returned to the country, taking with him a manuscript of Welbeck's; he found a new home on the farm of a Mr Hadwin, and fell in love with his daughter Eliza. Later he discovered the stolen $20,000 in the manuscript. Back in Philadelphia on an errand, he found Welbeck still alive and searching frantically for the missing manuscript. As a result of their confrontation Mervyn burned the money. By now ill with yellow fever, he wandered into the streets and was found by Dr Stevens.

Mervyn's account dispels suspicion and with Stevens's sponsorship, his future looks promising. He returns to the Hadwin farm and finds that only Eliza has escaped the epidemic, thereby becoming the sole inheritor of the farm. When he arrives back in Philadelphia he has a final confrontation with the now dying and repentant Welbeck. Meanwhile, fresh suspicions about Mervyn's character and activities have arisen, and this time his explanations prove somewhat less satisfactory. Indeed, the second part of the book in general casts some doubt on the validity of the version of his life he had given originally. The novel ends when Mervyn, having re-evaluated his love for Eliza (she turns out not to have inherited the farm at all), falls in love with Mrs Fielding, a widow of means whom he finally marries.

**Arthurian literature** Our fairly unified picture of Arthurian legend derives from **Sir Thomas Malory**'s 15th-century *Le Morte Darthur*. Before Malory this unity does not exist; there is only a great mass of fable, legend and pseudo-history. Arthur's first 'biography' is in Latin, in the *Historia Regum Britanniae* (*c.* 1135) by **Geoffrey of Monmouth**. Before Geoffrey, Arthur makes only scattered appearances in chronicle, folk-tale and art.

1) The Pseudo-Historical Arthur

The earliest portrait of Arthur is of a British commander of Roman descent repelling the Saxon invaders at the siege of Mons Badonicus, probably *c.* 500. *De Excidio et Conquestu Britanniae* (*c.* 540) by Gildas depicts such an unnamed leader, probably Ambrosius Aurelianus whom he elsewhere praises and who is made Arthur's uncle in later chronicles. The early 9th-century *Historia Brittonum* by Nennius, perhaps using Welsh tradition, has the first direct mention of Arthur, depicted as a Christian *dux bellorum* winning 12 battles against the Saxons; the last of these is at Mons Badonis. Nennius also tells the story of the British king Vortigern and a marvellous boy, Ambrosius, the original of Merlin. The mid 10th-century *Annales Cambriae* refers to two battles: Badon in 516, with Arthur victorious, and Camlann in 537, where Arthur and Medraut fell. The Welsh triads, which preserve early, pre-Norman traditions about Arthur, depict him, accompanied by his principal warriors Cei and Bedwyr, as a defender of his country; and it is to this tradition that William of Malmesbury's *Gesta Regum Anglorum* also refers, in 1125.

The 12th century sees the flowering of the 'historical' Arthur through the work of Geoffrey of Monmouth, who presents him as king and leader of a group of mounted knights, a very Norman image. Geoffrey used Gildas, **Bede**, Nennius and insular tradition to create a picture of a great medieval monarch, conqueror

Sir Bedivere, after the last battle, returns Excalibur to the lake at King Arthur's bidding. Arthur, mortally wounded, waits to hear of the sword's reception. From a medieval French manuscript, *MS 10294, f.94*, now in the British Library.

of many peoples including the French and the Romans, a descendant of Constantine and a hub of civilization. He retained the story of the Saxon wars, identifying Badon with Bath. Arthur is the son of Uter Pendragon and Ygraine, with a capital at Caerleon; he possesses the sword Caliburn (Excalibur), the shield Pridwen and the lance Ron; he is married to Guanhumara and his principal warriors are the Normanized Kai and Bedivere, while Gualguanus (Gawain) and Mordred are his sister Morgan's sons by King Lot. Merlin Ambrosius appears as a prophet aiding Uter but never meets Arthur. After a battle with Mordred, who has attempted to usurp his kingdom and marry his queen, Arthur is wounded and translated to Avalon; he is succeeded by Constantine of Cornwall.

The Jersey writer Wace in his *Roman de Brut* (1155) translated Geoffrey's *History* into French, greatly enlarging it. Drawing on other sources, he added more marvels to the story, especially the round table, and under the influence of the new and fashionable romance genre made Arthur's court a centre of *courtoisie*. His Arthur is still in Avalon, his return awaited by the Bretons: references to this belief appear from 1113 onwards. In 1191 fraudulent 'discoveries' of Arthur and Guinevere's tombs at Glastonbury sought both to identify it with Avalon and to quash the idea of Arthur's survival. **Layamon**, a priest in the Severn valley, is the first to put the legend of Arthur into English in his late 12th-century *Brut*, a free and expanded adaptation of Wace.

The pseudo-historical Arthur of chronicle is now swamped by the popularity of the Arthur of romance, and surfaces only briefly in the Saxon wars of *Arthour and Merlin* (English, 13th–14th century) before re-emerging in splendour in the epic alliterative **Morte Arthure** (beginning of the 15th century). Here Arthur's conquests increase to include Italy, but his aggressive wars and reckless pride are depicted as causing Gawain's death and his own downfall.

2) The Arthur of Romance

12th-century romance presents Arthur as the head of a brilliant chivalric court from which individual knights leave on adventures. Much of the material for these romances derives ultimately from Celtic tradition. Welsh poetry before Geoffrey of Monmouth mostly depicts Arthur as the leader of a group of monster-killing heroes. The earliest fleeting reference is in the 7th-century *Gododdin*. Nennius, besides recounting Arthur's battles, alludes to his dog Cabal and the tomb of his son Anir/Amr. Cai and Bedwyr, early associated with Arthur, reappear in the pre-Norman *Spoils of Annwyn*, where Arthur leads an expedition to the Otherworld, and in the Welsh triads, where Gwalchmei (Gawain) and Drystan, lover of Essylt, also occur; here would seem to be the first loose association of the Tristan story with the Arthurian legend. *Culhwch and Olwen* (*c.* 1100), a story contained in the Red Book of Hergest and the White Book of Rhydderch, depicts Arthur as a ruler of Britain able to summon armies from France, who helps Culhwch to overcome supernatural obstacles to win his bride. Beside Cai, Bedwyr and Gwalchmei, Gwenhwyfar makes her appearance here. The figure of Merlin derives in part from the Welsh prophet Myrddin, originally unconnected to the Arthurian

legend and the subject of various prophetic poems, contained in the Black Book of Carmarthen and the Red Book of Hergest, which refer back to 9th-century sources. A story of the abduction of Guinevere, recurrent in the romances, first appears in written form in the *Vita Gildae* (*c.* 1130), by Caradoc of Lancarvan, though, surprisingly, preceded in sculptural form on an archivolt of Modena Cathedral. Welsh Arthurian literature written after Geoffrey of Monmouth, like *Rhonabwy's Dream* (early 13th century), is influenced by him.

The earliest writer of Arthurian romance, and one of the greatest, was the Northern French Chrétien de Troyes, writing in the last quarter of the 12th century. Before him, though the poetry of Southern France has many allusions to the Matter of Britain from 1137 onwards, the troubadours left no romance except the 13th-century *Jaufré*. There is only *Lanval* among the *lais* of **Marie de France** (*c.* 1155–89) – interestingly depicting Arthur's queen as unfaithful, which indicates the vogue of the legend among the Anglo-Normans. Chrétien's five verse romances – *Erec et Enide*, *Yvain*, *Lancelot*, *Le Conte du Graal* and *Cligés* – introduce many of the permanent features of the legend: Lancelot and his love for Guinevere; Gawain as a model of prowess and courtesy, often however surpassed by the eponymous heroes; Kay as a churlish boaster; Perceval and the quest for the mysterious *graal*; and a king subordinated to his knights, inactive and increasingly ignoble. The degradation of Arthur, and of some of his best warriors, has begun. Guinevere has already appeared in an ambiguous light through her forcible annexation by Mordred in Geoffrey's *History*, which Layamon interprets as willing

Perceval at the castle of the Grail. He receives a sword from the Maimed King (left). On the right the Grail is carried to a table. Illustration from a medieval French manuscript. *MS. Fr 12577, f.18v*. Bibliothèque Nationale.

treachery to Arthur; the *Lai du Cor* (1150–75) shows her failing a chastity test.

Chrétien's influence is huge, not least perhaps on a group of Welsh stories, *c.* 1200, about Owain, Peredur and Geraint, part of the so-called **Mabinogion**, which may however derive from his sources, not him. There are many continuations of his unfinished Grail story and several romances inspired by the theme, notably Wolfram von Eschenbach's *Parzival* (1200–12), *Perlesvaus* (1225–50), the *Didot Perceval* (*c.* 1202), and Robert de Boron's *Joseph d'Arimathie* (*c.* 1200). This last interprets the *graal* as the vessel used at the Last Supper and also to catch Christ's last drops of blood at the Crucifixion, and which is brought to England by Bron, the Rich Fisher, Joseph's brother-in-law. Boron's *Merlin* introduced yet more elements to the legend, such as Arthur's fostering by Antor (Ector) and the sword in the stone which designates his kingship.

A version of it forms part of the so-called Vulgate Cycle, a huge 13th-century collection of prose romances by various authors, in five parts: *Estoire del Saint Graal*, prose *Merlin*, *Lancelot*, *Queste del Saint Graal* and *Mort Artu*. These portray Arthur and his court as embodying a worldly chivalry doomed to be surpassed by the spiritual chivalry of the Grail knights, and flawed from the start: Arthur unwittingly and incestuously begets Mordred on his sister Morgause. The quest for the Grail by most of Arthur's hitherto praiseworthy knights, above all Gawain, is barren; Lancelot is displaced as the greatest knight by his son Galaad, and his adulterous love for Guinevere leads to the collapse of the Round Table. Only Galaad, Perceval and Bors achieve the Grail, and only Bors returns to the secular life of Camaalot.

The Vulgate and its successors, such as the *Roman du Graal*, are attempts to combine some of the branches of the Arthurian legend, but there are also vast numbers of miscellaneous romances. In French these range from *Le Bel Inconnu* (1185–90) to Froissart's *Meliador* (1388); there are four in Latin, from the 12th to the 14th century, and many in other languages such as Spanish, Portuguese, Dutch, Norwegian and Icelandic. Though Italy provides us with evidence of early diffusion of the legend in the form of the baptismal names of Artusius and Walwanus, from 1100 on, and the Modena archivolt (1099–1120), there is no accompanying literary record until the 13th-century prose romances. Arthur's popularity is then plain in literature and art (witness the Pisanello frescoes in Mantua) and leads to his later celebration by Boiardo. German versions of the legend appear from the end of the 12th century, at first influenced by Chrétien, and include, in addition to the *Parzival*, Hartmann von Aue's *Erek* and *Iwein* (*c.* 1190, *c.* 1202); Ulrik von Zatzikhoven's *Lanzelet* (from 1194); *Wigalois* and *Diu Krône* (13th century). English romances, in verse and prose, featuring Arthur and his knights range from the second half of the 13th century (*Arthur and Merlin*) to the 16th century. Most notable of these are **Thomas Chestre**'s *Sir Launfal* (*c.* 1350), *Ywain and Gawain* (*c.* 1350), the stanzaic *Morte Arthur* (*c.* 1400), *Sir Gawain and the Green Knight* (late 14th century), and *The Awntyrs of Arthure* (late 14th century) with its reproach of the 'covetous' Arthur and its hint of an adulterous Guinevere. Many of the English romances use French originals but compress and adjust their material to give a clear and action-packed story-line.

Sir Thomas Malory's *Le Morte Darthur*, completed in 1469 or 1470, distils these sources, drawing on both French texts (the Vulgate Cycle, the *Roman du Graal* and the prose *Tristan*) and English ones (the alliterative *Morte Arthure* and the stanzaic *Morte Arthur*). It is the culmination of the tradition, the last and greatest attempt to consolidate all the Arthurian material into a unified cycle. In **Caxton**'s printed text of 1485 it achieves a wider circulation than any of its predecessors, and later reworkings of the legend – such as **Tennyson**'s *Idylls of the King* and **T. H. White**'s *The Once and Future King* – take it as their model.

**As I Lay Dying** A novel by **William Faulkner**, published in 1930. Experimental in both subject and narrative structure, it treats the events surrounding the illness, death and burial of Addie Bundren, wife of Anse and mother of Cash, Darl, Jewel, Dewey Dell, and Vardaman. It is divided into 59 short interior monologues, predominantly in the present tense, spoken both by the seven members of the family and by various other characters, including the Reverend Whitfield, Dr Peabody, and the Bundrens' neighbours, Vernon and Cora Tull.

As the novel opens, Addie lies silently in her bed, watching Cash construct her coffin outside the window. Dewey Dell stands beside her, fanning her and musing about a sexual encounter with Lafe. Jewel, Addie's illegitimate son by the Reverend Whitfield, and Darl, the most devoted son, who is considered 'queer' by the townspeople, are hauling a load of lumber to a Northern town. While they are away, Addie dies. Vardaman, the youngest son, is severely traumatized; he confuses his mother with the large trout he has just caught and bores holes in her coffin to allow her to breathe. Addie's dying wish was to be buried in her home town of Jefferson, Mississippi, and Anse is stubbornly insistent that this wish be fulfilled, despite the series of accidents and setbacks which the family encounters during its 10-day journey to Jefferson with the coffin.

They set out for Jefferson in the wagon, with Jewel astride his own horse, and immediately have problems trying to cross a flooded river. They lose control of the team and Cash's leg is badly broken. While resting at the Armstid farm Anse trades Jewel's horse for a new team, and the volatile-tempered Jewel runs away. They set Cash's leg in concrete, which leaves him crippled for life. The corpse has begun to rot and buzzards are circling in the sky above the wagon, but the family continues toward Jefferson, with the crippled but stoic Cash lying on top of the coffin. Jewel rejoins the group and they stop to rest at the Gillespie farm, placing the coffin in the shade inside the barn. Darl, realizing the absurdity of their venture, attempts to cremate his mother's body by setting fire to the barn; Anse decides to turn him over to the authorities once they have buried Addie.

Once in Jefferson, Dewey Dell, who has discovered that she is pregnant, goes into a pharmacy to get a 'cure'. Skeet MacGowan, one of the assistants, gives her some bogus medicine and then rapes her in the cellar, claiming that she must have a 'hair of the dog' that bit her in order to get rid of her trouble. They bury Addie in the family plot. Darl is taken away to an asylum. Anse confiscates the money which Lafe had given to Dewey Dell to get an abortion and buys himself the set of false teeth he has always wanted. As the family prepares to leave for home, Anse appears with a strange woman and introduces her as the new 'Mrs Bundren'.

*As You Like It* A comedy by **William Shakespeare**, first performed *c.* 1599 and published in the First Folio of 1623. The source is **Thomas Lodge**'s *Rosalynde*.

Oliver de Boys has deprived his younger brother, Orlando, of his birthright, and plans to have him killed by tempting him into a match with the champion wrestler of the ducal court. At the court Orlando meets Rosalind, daughter of the deposed duke, and her cousin and friend Celia, daughter of the usurping duke. Orlando wins his bout and Rosalind falls in love with him; but their love is hopeless in Duke Frederick's unjust court. Orlando flies to the Forest of Arden. Rosalind is banished by the duke. She decides to disguise herself as a boy (Ganymede) and Celia leaves with her, in the role of Ganymede's sister, Aliena. Together with the court fool, Touchstone, they, like Orlando, reach the Forest of Arden.

The forest is also the refuge of the banished duke, whose court in exile includes the solitary and wryly speculative Jaques. Orlando is welcomed by the duke and the unexpected comfort gives him leisure to write love poems for his lost Rosalind and post them on trees. Rosalind and Celia find them, and Rosalind uses her male disguise as a pretext for gently testing Orlando's love. She is disturbed to find herself as Ganymede loved by the pastoral Phebe.

The forest idyll is threatened when Duke Frederick sends Oliver to track down his brother; but Oliver undergoes a change of heart, is saved from death by Orlando and falls in love with Celia. In a joyful scene, Rosalind oversees the matching of Celia and Oliver, Phebe and her equally pastoral lover Silvius, Touchstone and his wench Audrey, and Orlando and herself. Duke Frederick, suddenly repentant, restores his banished brother to the dukedom and himself takes refuge from the world, accompanied by Jaques.

*As You Like It*, despite the subtlety of its construction, acknowledges the more primitive pull of fertility rituals and folk festivities. The release from the pressures and constraints of the court brings to all its leading characters a new understanding of their true priorities. However improbable its incidents may seem on a purely narrative level, the harmony of their outcome is profoundly satisfying. *As You Like It* is the most charitable of Shakespeare's mature comedies.

**Ascension, The** See **Christ**.

**Ascham, Roger** 1515–68 Scholar and teacher. Ascham was educated at St John's College, Cambridge, and was associated with both the college and the university for many years. He graduated as a BA in 1534 (MA 1537). He taught Greek there, even as an undergraduate, to the younger students and became instrumental in establishing the importance of Greek at St John's, becoming Greek reader at the college in 1538. He became a fellow of the college and later public orator to the university, resigning both posts only on his marriage in 1554. As well as being an authority on Greek, Ascham was thoroughly versed in Latin literature, an accomplished musician and a fine calligrapher.

In 1548 he became tutor to Princess Elizabeth, a position to which he was reappointed on her accession. With her he read Cicero, Livy and the Greek New Testament. He was also Latin secretary to Queen Mary, with the extraordinary dispensation that he was permitted to continue in the reformed religion.

Ascham wrote two important works in English. *Toxophilus* (1545), a dialogue on archery, stresses the importance of physical exercise in education and pleads for the use of English. *The Schoolmaster*, printed in 1570 after Ascham's death, was apparently provoked by tales of boys running away from Eton for fear of flogging. It argues against excessive discipline in education, warns against idleness and Italian travel, and recommends a method of teaching

Latin grammar. Although Ascham's English prose style was praised by **Gabriel Harvey** for its elegance and polish, the modern reader is likely to find it pleasingly plain and clear. Among his writings in Latin are translations of commentaries on the epistles to Titus and Philemon (1542), a treatise against the Mass (1577) and volumes of letters.

**Ash, John** 1948– Poet. Born in Manchester, he was educated at Birmingham University, and lived in Cyprus before returning to Manchester and then moving to New York. *Casino* (1978) was an attempt to assimilate, and exorcize, the ghosts of French **Symbolism**. *The Bed* (1981) displays an uncertainty of style as Ash works through various modes of European **modernism** and approximates the work of the few British poets he feels to have acknowledged this tradition, including **Roy Fisher** and **Lee Harwood**.

The poems in *The Goodbyes* (1982) stress their own artifice and social detail is aestheticized into an often humorous mode Ash has called 'urban pastoral'.

In *The Branching Stairs* (1984) the new poems resemble those of his most recent mentor, **John Ashbery**. Throughout Ash's work there is a commitment to innovation that avoids the autobiographical and anecdotal.

**Ashbery, John (Lawrence)** 1927– American poet, born in Rochester, New York, and educated at Harvard, Columbia and New York universities. He worked in publishing until 1955, when a Fulbright Scholarship enabled him to study in France. He became an art critic for the European edition of the *New York Herald Tribune*, and returned to the USA in 1965. The best-known poet of the New York School, he published his first volume, *Turandot and Other Poems*, in 1953. His work is characterized by an essentially sceptical world view, and his poems are generally self-referential and self-enclosed. His other volumes are *Some Trees* (1956), *The Poems* (1960), *The Tennis Court Oath* (1962, Harriet Monroe Memorial Prize), *Rivers and Mountains* (1966), *Sunrise in Suburbia* and *Three Madrigals* (1968), *Fragment* (1969), *The Double Dream of Spring* and *The New Spirit* (1970), *Three Poems* (1972, Shelley Memorial Award), *The Vermont Notebook* (1975, with Joe Brainard), *Self-Portrait in a Convex Mirror* (1975), *Houseboat Days* (1977), *As We Know* (1979), *Shadow Train* (1981), *A Wave* (1984) and *Selected Poems* (1985). He is also the joint author of a novel, *Nest of Ninnies* (1969, with James Schuyler).

**Ashford, Daisy** 1881–1972 Juvenile novelist. Born in Surrey, the daughter of a War Office employee, she spent her childhood in Lewes, Sussex. She dictated her first story at the age of four and thereafter constantly wrote or told stories for her own pleasure. At the age of 13 she finally went off to boarding-school, putting aside writing for the rest of her life. But in 1919, shortly before she married, she came across *The Young Visiters*, a long-forgotten, imperfectly spelled manuscript written when she was nine. It was published the same year with an introduction by **J. M. Barrie**. Within its pages Ethel Monticue, an attractive 17-year-old, is courted both by Bernard Clark, her favourite, and Mr Salteena, crushingly described as 'not quite a gentleman'. In search of self-improvement Mr Salteena visits London to stay with the Earl of Clincham as a paying pupil, leaving the field clear for Bernard to propose to Ethel during a romantic riverside picnic. The young author's lively eye for detail and occasional understandable confusions combine to make this book a classic of unconscious humour, never out of print since its first appearance. Other manuscripts written when she was a child and since published are *Love and Marriage* (1965) and *The Hangman's Daughter* (1982).

**Ashmole, Elias** 1617–92 Antiquary and virtuoso. He was born at Lichfield, Staffordshire, and educated at the grammar school there. While in the service of the king's excise at Oxford in 1645 he entered himself as a student of natural philosophy, mathematics, astronomy and astrology at Brasenose College. He knew the astrologer **William Lilly**. It was with this background of judicial astrology that Ashmole became, in 1646, one of the earliest English Freemasons. Scientific interests (including alchemy) brought him into the company of Rosicrucians and led him to publish his *Theatrum Chemicum Britannicum* in 1652. Alchemy and astrology later gave way to Hebrew, engraving and heraldry: Ashmole was appointed Windsor Herald in 1660, by which time he was already amassing material for *The Institution, Laws and Ceremonies of the Order of the Garter* (1672). In 1650 Ashmole met the naturalist John Tradescant whose collections he later inherited. In 1677 Ashmole decided to give the Tradescant collection and his own additions to it to the University of Oxford, provided a suitable building was made available. The twelve carts bearing Ashmole's collections arrived at the Museum in March 1683 and the Ashmolean was opened, with Dr Robert Plot as curator, in May of that year.

**Ashton-Warner, Sylvia** 1908–84 New Zealand novelist. Born in Stratford on North Island, she was educated at small country schools and subsequently, after training at the Teachers' College Auckland, worked in such schools herself. For 17 years she taught Maori infant classes in the same school as her husband, Keith Henderson. After retiring she was a Visiting Professor of Education at Aspen Community School Teaching Center in Colorado. Her first novel, *Spinster* (1958), did not appear until she was nearly 50, but immediately made an impact in New Zealand as a *roman à clef* and internationally for its **stream-of-consciousness** presentation of the teacher-protagonist's turbulent inner life and its relationship to her professional life. Her next novels, *Incense to Idols* (1960) and *Bell Call* (1965), employ Romantic narrative modes which complement the challenge offered to conventional society and its notions of communication and education. *Teacher* (1963) and *Myself* (1967), supposedly the author's diary from the early 1940s, employ a documentary mode but give the impression of being at least partly fictive. Both focus on the narrator's intensely emotional response to the various aspects of her life. *Greenstone* (1966) is a romance that draws heavily on Maori myth and also, in the title theme which refers to an Old English rune, on Germanic cultures. Through a technique which moves between fantasy and realism, it makes a plea for racial and cultural harmony. Ashton-Warner's other works include *Three* (1970) and *I Passed This Way* (1979).

**Asimov, Isaac** 1920– American writer of science fiction. Born in Russia, Asimov was taken to the USA in infancy. He was something of a child prodigy, graduating from Columbia University in 1939. His academic career was interrupted by the war, but he obtained his doctorate in 1948 and became an associate professor of biochemistry at Boston. He had been selling science fiction stories to the pulp magazines since his teens, though, and became a full-time writer in the late 1950s. He has become one of the leading exponents of the popularization of science, prolifically producing essays and books in which explanation of scientific matters is enlivened by his remarkable relish for the excitement of enlightenment. Some of his pulp science fiction stories are among the most popular ever produced, especially those collected in the three-volume *Foundation* series (1942–50; in book form 1951–3) and the classic collection *I, Robot* (1950), which made famous the 'three laws of robotics'. This programmed ethical system has been further elaborated in the science fiction detective stories *The Caves of Steel* (1954) and *The Naked Sun* (1956) and in the more philosophically inclined robot stories in *The Bicentennial Man and Other Stories* (1976). His other science fiction novels include *The Currents of Space* (1952), *The End of Eternity* (1955) and *The Gods Themselves* (1972), and in recent years he has begun to bind his two most famous series together into a single pattern of future history, in rather more prolix novels:

*Foundation's Edge* (1982), *The Robots of Dawn* (1983) and *Robots and Empire* (1985).

**Aspern Papers, The** A story by **Henry James**, published in *The Atlantic Monthly* from March to May 1888, and as the title piece of a volume of stories in the same year. The narrator, an American editor, travels to Venice to recover the letters written by Jeffrey Aspern, a Romantic poet of the early 19th century, to his mistress, 'Juliana'. He rents rooms from Juliana, now the aged Miss Bordereau, who lives with her niece, Tina, an unattractive spinster. After Miss Bordereau dies, Tina says that she could give the letters only to 'a relative' of the family. The veiled proposal is plain and the editor balks at it. When they next meet, Tina reveals that she has burned the letters.

**Assembly of Ladies, The** A poem of unknown authorship once attributed to **Chaucer** and probably written in the third quarter of the 15th century in the London area. It is a **dream-vision** presented as the work of a woman. A lady tells a knight about her dream of an assembly held by Lady Loyalty in the palace of Pleasaunt Regard at which women air their grievances. Nothing is resolved, and another meeting is planned for finding suitable remedies.

See also **Chaucerian apocrypha**.

**Asser** d. 908 or 910 Reputed author of a Latin biography of **King Alfred**, *De Rebus Gestis Aelfredi Magni*. A monk of St David's and a renowned scholar, he was invited to join the king's household in 885 and took up the offer (after a year of sickness) in 887, dividing his time between home and the royal household. Asser became Alfred's teacher, friend and adviser. He was appointed abbot of monasteries in Congresbury and Banwell, and later Bishop of Devon and Cornwall. At his death he held the bishopric of Sherborne in Dorset.

Although Asser's authorship of *De Rebus Gestis Aelfredi Magni* has been contested, the work is generally accepted as his. It comprises a chronicle of events in England between 849 and 887, and an account of Alfred's life to 887. The historical material comes largely from the *Anglo-Saxon Chronicle* but the account of Alfred presents the observations of a man who knew him well. The work is thus an important historical source, as well as being the earliest biography of a secular figure written in England.

The only known manuscript was destroyed in the Cotton library fire of 1731. Of the two editions based on it, that of 1574 is full of arbitrary alterations while that of 1722, though more reliable, preserves many errors from the earlier edition. The work survives in various corrupt versions with extra passages interpolated by other writers. It was, for example, incorporated virtually in its entirety into the chronicles of Florence of Worcester and extensively copied by Simeon of Durham and in the *Annals* of St Neots.

**assonance** See **alliteration**.

**Astley, Thea** 1925– Australian novelist and short-story writer. Born in Brisbane, Astley was brought up as a Roman Catholic, an important shaping influence on her fiction. She studied arts at the University of Queensland and taught English in Queensland (1944–8) and in New South Wales (1948–67). She was subsequently fellow in Australian literature at Macquarie University (1968–80), when she moved to Kurando, near Cairns, Queensland. Astley has won the prestigious Miles Franklin Award for fiction three times. Her novels frequently focus on outsiders and misfits, and attack the philistinism and hypocrisy of middle-class, small-town Australia. *A Kindness Cup* (1974) exposes the criminal past of some of the leading citizens of a small Queensland town. Her more recent fiction extends the range of targets for satire. *An Item from the Late News* (1982) attacks several sacred cows of Australian society, including the 'mateship' ethos which has played an important part in the national myth. Her other novels include *Girl With a Monkey* (1958), *A Descant for Gossips* (1960), *The Slow Natives* (1965), *A Boat Load of Home Folk* (1968), *The Acolyte* (1972) and *Beachmasters* (1985). She has also published *Hunting the Wild Pineapple* (1979), a collection of related short stories, and *Three Australian Writers: Essays on Bruce Dawe, Barbara Baynton and Patrick White* (1979).

**Astrophil and Stella** A **sonnet** sequence by **Sir Philip Sidney**, the first in English, probably composed in 1582 but not printed until 1591. A preface by **Thomas Nashe** introduced it as 'the tragicomedy of love . . . performed by starlight . . . The argument cruel chastity, the prologue hope, the epilogue despair'. The sequence of 108 sonnets and 11 songs has as its heroine Stella ('star'). Punning use of the word 'rich' in sonnets 24, 35 and 37 invites the reader to identify her with Penelope Devereux, who became Lady Rich on her marriage in 1581. She is courted by Astrophil ('star-lover'), self-consciously preoccupied not only with Stella but also with poetry. He makes a concise list of 16th-century poetic conventions and styles in sonnet 6. He debates the claims of will and wit, reason and passion (4 and 52). He professes originality: the first sonnet has lines of 14 syllables, the second denies that he fell in love at first sight, and he proclaims independence of **Petrarchan** predecessors (15). The sequence presents an unsuccessful courtship in a series of scenes and emotional attitudes. It is also, im-

plicitly, a critical account of conventional attitudes to love and love poetry in the late 16th century.

**Atalanta in Calydon** A verse drama by **Algernon Charles Swinburne,** published in 1865. His intention was 'to do something original in English which might in some degree reproduce for English readers the likeness of a Greek tragedy with something of the true poetic life and charm'. The subject is the myth of Meleager and the hunt for the Calydonian boar, a monster sent by the goddess Artemis to punish King Oeneus for neglecting to honour her. His queen, Althaea, is the mother of Meleager; at his birth the Fates promised him strength and good fortune but warned that his life would last no longer than the stick burning in the hearth fire. When they had left Althaea snatched the stick from the fire, put out the flames, and hid it. When a great hunt was organized to kill the boar, one of the participants was the virgin huntress Atalanta, daughter of Iasius of Arcadia and a favourite of Artemis; Meleager fell in love with her. The boar was killed but a quarrel arose over the distribution of the spoils. When the besotted Meleager gave everything to Atalanta his uncles, Toxeus and Phlexippus (Althaea's brothers), objected. Meleager killed them, and in revenge Althaea burned the stick that measured her son's life and so destroyed him.

Several lyrics from *Atalanta in Calydon* achieved a fame beyond their original context: the chief huntsman's address to Artemis and Apollo ('Maiden, and mistress of the months and stars'); the choric hymn to the goddess that follows ('When the hounds of spring are on winter's traces'); and the chorus's comment when Althaea goes to prepare her son for the hunt ('Before the beginning of years/There came to the making of man').

**Atheist's Tragedy, The** or, *The Honest Man's Fortune* A **revenge tragedy** ascribed to **Cyril Tourneur** on the title page of the edition published in 1611. Scholars have found it difficult to accept that the author of the sombrely splendid *Revenger's Tragedy* also wrote this uneven and often lifeless play.

The atheist of the title is D'Amville, whose determination to provide for his family leads him to kill his brother and to arrange for his own sickly son to marry the wealthy Castabella in place of his nephew, Charlemont, to whom Castabella is betrothed. D'Amville's plans are thwarted by his son's impotence, and there follows an extraordinary graveyard scene in which D'Amville's attempt on the honour of his daughter-in-law is prevented by Charlemont. Charlemont is condemned to death for killing D'Amville's servant, D'Amville himself offers to serve as executioner and 'As he raises up the axe strikes out his own brains'. This (presumably authorial) stage direction is followed by a moralizing speech from the unusually ineffective hero, Charlemont, which concludes that 'patience is the honest man's revenge'.

**Athelston** A short **verse romance** of the mid 14th century based on an Old English story. Four men meet and swear brotherhood, and when one of them, Athelston, becomes King of England he makes the others Archbishop of Canterbury, Earl of Dover and Earl of Stane. Stane marries Athelston's sister and Dover, out of jealousy, tells Athelston that the couple are plotting against him. The King imprisons them and when his queen intercedes for them he assaults her, killing her unborn child. Canterbury now intercedes; Athelston orders him to resign his office and is excommunicated. The threat of a popular rising makes Athelston give way. A trial by ordeal proves Stane innocent, but in the same test Dover is proved guilty and is executed. Stane's son is made Athelston's heir; the poem makes a romantic connection with history by identifying him with St Edmund.

**Athenaeum, The** A weekly literary review founded by James Silk Buckingham in 1828. Its distinguished character was moulded by **Charles Wentworth Dilke**, the editor from 1830 to 1846. **Robert Browning**, **Thomas Carlyle**, **Charles Lamb** and **Walter Pater** were among its contributors in the 19th century. Probably its finest hour came with the brief editorship of **John Middleton Murry** (1919–21), when *The Athenaeum* published work by **Bertrand Russell, T. S. Eliot**, **Aldous Huxley** and **Katherine Mansfield**. In 1921 it merged with *Nation*, appearing as the *Nation and Athenaeum* until it was finally absorbed by *The New Statesman* in 1931.

**Atlantic Monthly, The** A magazine devoted to literature and current affairs, founded in Boston in 1857 by **Oliver Wendell Holmes** and **James Russell Lowell**. Its editors have included **William Dean Howells** and **Thomas Bailey Aldrich**. It regularly features the work of America's most prominent writers, and since 1938 has included articles and essays on international as well as national affairs.

**Atterbury, Francis** 1662–1732 Churchman and theologian. Born at Milton Keynes, Buckinghamshire, he was educated at Westminster School and Christ Church, Oxford. After ordination his progress in the church was rapid, and he became Bishop of Rochester and Dean of Westminster in 1713. In 1720 he was imprisoned for alleged complicity in a plot to restore the Stuarts; he was deprived of his offices and banished in 1723, to die in exile. He was a notable contributor to the Phalaris controversy

(see **Sir William Temple**) and a preacher of renown. His chief published works were concerned with church dogma and include *Sermons* (1740) and *Miscellaneous Works* (1789–98).

**Atwood, Margaret (Eleanor)** 1939– Canadian poet and writer of fiction. Born in Ottawa, educated at the University of Toronto and Radcliffe College, she has been writer-in-residence at several universities in Canada and the United States. Her reputation as an original and accomplished poet was established with *The Circle Game* (1966), *The Animals in that Country* (1968), *The Journals of Susanna Moodie* (1970), *Power Politics* (1973), *You are Happy* (1974), *Selected Poems* (1976), *Two-Headed Poems* (1978), *True Stories* (1981), and *Interlunar* (1983). Atwood's fiction includes *The Edible Woman* (1969), *Surfacing* (1972), *Lady Oracle* (1976), *Life before Man* (1979), *Bodily Harm* (1981), *The Handmaid's Tale* (1985), and two collections of short stories. *Murder in the Dark* (1983) is a volume of prose poems and short fictions. She is also author of *Survival: A Thematic Guide to Canadian Literature* (1972), editor of *The New Oxford Book of Canadian Verse in English* (1982) and co-editor of *The Oxford Book of Canadian Short Stories in English* (1987).

Atwood's work displays a tense formal control accurately matched to her sharp and witty idiom, where the prosaic and the surreal frequently interact. Working within a variety of genres, she combines her exposure of the power politics of nationality and gender with her sense of the imaginative possibilities within fictional and poetic language.

**Aubrey, John** 1626–97 Biographer and antiquary. He was born at Easton Pierse, Wiltshire, and received his early education mainly at home, with brief periods at the 'latin schoole' at Yatton Keynell (1633) and under **Thomas Hobbes**'s old teacher, Robert Latimer, at Leigh Delamere (1634). In 1638 he went to William Sutton's school at Blandford. He entered Trinity College, Oxford, in May 1642 and, though he stayed for only four months, formed a lifelong attachment to the place. He died in Oxford in 1697 and is buried in the church of St Mary Magdalen.

He was admitted as a student of the Middle Temple in 1646. In the late 1640s Aubrey found himself developing a special association with the intellectual *avant-garde* of his day. Although fundamentally royalist, he managed to move easily, in London and Oxford, between groups of various political shadings. He was on terms with such men as Hobbes, Samuel Hartlib, William Petty and John Wilkins. It is no surprise that he was elected a Fellow of the Royal Society in 1663 and presented many papers before it in the years to come.

John Aubrey. A drawing by Faithorne in black-lead and India ink in the Ashmolean Museum, Oxford.

Aubrey was strongly drawn both by the Society's empirical approach (with its basis in the work of **Francis Bacon**) and by his own profound sense of history. He never felt any contradiction between these two major aspects of his highly original imagination. Aubrey's scientific impulse to record led him to prepare works of natural history and comparative religion. He made topographical and archaeological collections in the tradition of **William Camden**: his discovery and survey of Avebury (the most reliable before those of this century) give him some claim to be among the first field archaeologists in Britain. But he is best known for the so-called *Brief Lives*. What began in 1667 as compilations of notes for **Anthony à Wood**'s *Historia et Antiquitates Universitatis Oxoniensis* (1674) and *Athenae Oxonienses* (1691–2) survived to occupy a far more interesting place in the history of biography. Although he took account of certain figures of the previous age (**Shakespeare** and **Raleigh** for example), Aubrey's principal aim was to set down accurate records of the foremost men of his own day. The *Lives* are a serious exercise in biographical truth-telling (perhaps the first in English), packed with detail, mostly observed at first hand and conveyed in an inimitable style. Aubrey's sense of the force of individual personality to which the *Lives* are a monument also informs another of his pioneering works, *An Idea of Education of Young Gentlemen* (manuscript completed 1684), which anticipates much that was thought novel in the educational writings of **John Locke**.

It is to be regretted that Aubrey published only one book in his lifetime: *Miscellanies* (1696). His *Lives, Idea of Education* and other work remained in manuscript for a variety of later editors, not all of them equal to the task, to prepare for publication; some remain unedited to this day. The standard, though somewhat bowdlerized, edition of the *Brief Lives* is that by Andrew Clark (2 vols., Oxford, 1898). *A Perambulation of the County of Surrey*, edited and enlarged by Richard Rawlinson, appeared in 1719 (reprinted 1975). The work on Wiltshire has appeared as *The Natural History of Wiltshire* (1847; reprinted 1969) and *Wiltshire: the Topographical Collections* (1862). *Aubrey on Education* appeared, poorly edited, in 1972. **John Fowles** has supervised an edition of *Monumenta Britannica*. *Miscellanies, Remaines of Gentilisme and Judaisme* and *Observations* are printed as *Three Prose Works*, edited by John Buchanan-Brown (1972). Aubrey is the subject of a biography, *John Aubrey and his Friends* (1948; revised 1963), by **Anthony Powell**, who has also edited the best selection from the *Lives* and other works (1949).

**Audelay, John** Nothing is known of Audelay's life beyond the information afforded by the unique manuscript of his poems. He was blind and deaf and, at least towards the end of his poetic career, ill. He apparently lived at Haughmond Abbey near Shrewsbury. The collection of his poems bears a colophon dated 1426, and he was at some time first priest to Lord Strange (who held the title 1397–1449).

The collection of Audelay's poems comprises 55 religious pieces on various themes, though it is possible that the last two poems are the work of a different writer. The majority of the poems are penitential; while one tells of the joys of the true religious life, most are inspired by a fear of damnation. Their treatment of religious matters is completely orthodox and generally symptomatic of a popular interpretation. The poems fall into three broad categories, the didactic, the narrative and descriptive, and a group of 25 poems labelled as carols for Christmas. The poems show little originality of thought and borrow extensively from each other and from other writers. They exhibit a fondness for metrical experimentation and use a wide variety of verse forms. Audelay's skill in metre was not, however, matched by his use of rhyme, which was often careless and uninspired.

**Auden, W[ystan] H[ugh]** 1907–73 Poet. He was born in York, the youngest son of a doctor and a devoutly Anglo-Catholic mother. His father moved the family to Birmingham a year later to take up a post as schools medical officer for the district. Auden was educated at St Edmund's preparatory school in Surrey (1915–20), where **Christopher Isherwood** was a fellow pupil, at Gresham's School, Holt, Norfolk (1920–5), and at Christ Church, Oxford (1925–8), where Auden changed from science to English and gained a third class honours degree in 1928. Contemporaries at Oxford included **Rex Warner**, **John Betjeman**, **Stephen Spender**, **Cecil Day-Lewis** and **Louis MacNeice**. Auden began to make a name for himself as a poet while still a student: he twice edited *Oxford Poetry* and his first book of poems was printed by Spender in 1928. After Oxford he spent some time in Berlin, where Isherwood was living. On his return to England in 1929 he worked as a tutor and then as a schoolmaster until he obtained work with the GPO film unit who produced *Night Mail*, a documentary film with Auden's text.

His early collections of verse, *Poems* (1930), *The Orators* (1932), *The Dance of Death* (1933) and *Look Stranger!* (1936), established him as the leading figure of his generation. In collaboration with Isherwood he wrote three plays, *The Dog Beneath the Skin* (1935), *The Ascent of F6* (1936) and *On the Frontier* (1939). His brief service as an ambulance driver for the Republicans in the Spanish Civil War resulted in *Spain* (1937). Other travels produced *Letters from Iceland* (with Louis MacNeice, 1937) and *Journey to a War* (with Isherwood, 1939), about China. He emigrated to the United States with Isherwood in 1939 and became an American citizen in 1946.

Left to right: W. H. Auden, Christopher Isherwood, and Stephen Spender. Detail from a photograph by Howard Coster, 1936.

Auden's early work is socially committed left-wing writing with a purpose and direction that is uncommon in its uniformity and power. *The Orators* shows that, apart from his early interest in Old English vocabulary and metrical forms, he was working through and applying the model of **T. S. Eliot**'s *The Waste Land* to his own preoccupation with science and psychology. There is a deliberate materialism derived from his reading of Marx and Freud, but also a complicating wealth of latent thematic material that has to do with the concealment (necessary in that time) of a homosexual writing about his own and his friends' emotional lives.

Auden married Erika Mann in 1935 to provide her with a British passport and thus help her escape from Nazi Germany. His lifelong companion, however, was Chester Kallman, whom he met in America. Once settled in New York, he left behind the conflict between his relatively privileged background and his early political sympathies, though his interest in Freud continued. He became increasingly attracted to his mother's faith, and his Anglicanism left its mark on his poetry. While he could successfully adopt American verse forms, he remained unmistakably a British poet. *New Year Letter* (1941, US title *The Double Man*) was the first of his American books, followed by *For the Time Being: A Christmas Oratorio* (1944), *The Age of Anxiety: A Baroque Eclogue* (1947), *Nones* (1951), *The Shield of Achilles* (1955), *The Old Man's Road* (1956) and *Homage to Clio* (1960).

He was Professor of Poetry at Oxford in 1956–60, becoming a Student (i.e. fellow) of Christ Church in 1962 and returning to live in his old college in 1972. Part of his later life was spent in Kirchstetten, Austria, and his life with Chester Kallman there is celebrated in *About the House* (1967). Final volumes were *City Walls and Other Poems* (1969), *Academic Graffiti* (1971) and *Epistle to a Godson* (1972). He also extensively revised his early work from his later viewpoint as a Christian, presenting his personal canon in *Collected Shorter Poems* (1966), *Collected Longer Poems* (1968) and *Collected Poems* (1976). A useful collection is thus *The English Auden* (1977), which reissued his early poetry and some prose in the versions in which it was first read.

Auden edited *The Oxford Book of Light Verse* (1938) and many other collections and anthologies. His critical writing includes *The Enchafèd Flood* (1951), *The Dyer's Hand* (1963) and *Secondary Worlds* (1968). He also collaborated with Chester Kallman on the libretto for Stravinsky's *The Rake's Progress* (1951).

**Audubon, John James** 1785–1851 American naturalist and artist. Born in Haiti, he was educated in the USA and later in France, where he studied with Jacques-Louis David. Audubon spent much of his life travelling throughout the

USA and Canada to find materials for his wildlife drawings, which became celebrated for their accurate detail and delicate use of watercolour. Many were included in his most famous book, *The Birds of America*, which was published in England between 1827 and 1838. Sections of his journals also have been published, including *Delineations of American Scenery and Character* (1926), *Journal of John James Audubon, Made during his Trip to New Orleans in 1820–21* (1929) and *Audubon's America* (1940).

**Augustan Age, The** A descriptive term applied loosely to the literature and art of the Restoration and early 18th century, though some scholars object sharply to its vagueness. It denotes a period of literary excellence, and refers back to the heyday of classical writing during the reign of the Roman emperor Augustus (27 BC–AD 14) and the stylistic achievements of the Latin poets of the golden age, Virgil, Horace and Ovid, whose writings were much admired and imitated by the authors of this later, **neoclassical** period.

Although the term is imprecise, it is none the less convenient for bracketing together the writings and styles of many authors from **Dryden** and **Butler** to **Dr Johnson**, and is most frequently applied to the work of **Pope** and **Swift**. There were several common literary concerns, especially in verse: the development of an elegant, well-turned style, the pursuit of fluency, precision of expression and a dislike of cant or slang, the observation of decorum, and the cultivation of good taste and the refinement of manner.

The period is characterized by a general desire for common sense and compromise in the face of the wilder extremes of contemporary fashion and thought, and this moderation is sometimes referred to as the 'via media' or golden mean, its artistic manifestation being a delight in proportion, poise and wit. Pope's poem 'The First Epistle of the Second Book of Horace Imitated' (1737) is dedicated 'To Augustus' as a specific reference to the monarch George II, whose other name was Augustus, but this was an ironic inversion of the otherwise complimentary implications of the Latin original since the Hanoverian king ignored rather than patronized the arts, and scarcely even spoke English. **Goldsmith**'s essay on the 'Augustan Age in England' is a *locus classicus* for contemporary discussion on this matter.

*Auld Lang Syne* See **Ayton, Sir Robert** and **Burns, Robert**.

*Aureng-Zebe* A heroic tragedy by **John Dryden**, first produced in London in 1675 and published the following year. It was the last and best of Dryden's plays in **heroic couplets**.

Set in Mogul India, it concerns the love of Aureng-Zebe for Indamora, a captive queen. Their love becomes entangled with a struggle for power in the court of Aureng-Zebe's father, the Mogul emperor, Shah Jehan. Both the emperor and Morat, his son by his second wife Nourmahal, pursue Indamora. Despite this, Aureng-Zebe remains loyal to his father, and after the struggle for the throne has led to the deaths of both Morat and Nourmahal, Shah Jehan rewards Aureng-Zebe by abandoning his pursuit of Indamora.

*Aurora Leigh* A novel in verse by **Elizabeth Barrett Browning**, published in 1856 (postdated 1857).

The poem was conceived at least 10 years before publication and was the author's most sustained piece of work, embodying her 'highest convictions upon Life and Art'. Confronting many contemporary social issues – the role of women, the plight of the poor, and the efficacy of 19th-century Utopian socialism – *Aurora Leigh* received a mixed critical reception but remained widely popular until the end of the century, running to some 20 editions.

The heroine, though a poet, is not an autobiographical portrait. The story traces Aurora's development as an artist in opposition to the active philanthropy of her cousin Romney. The resolution of the work lies in the recognition by both cousins that each has placed too great an emphasis upon limited aspects of man's character; Romney in considering and supplying only the physical needs of the under-privileged, and Aurora in relinquishing all love and companionship in order to pursue her ambitious intellectual ideal of the poet's vocation.

**Austen, Jane** 1775–1817 Novelist. Jane Austen was born at Steventon in Hampshire where her father, who was also her tutor, was rector. On his retirement in 1801 the family moved to Bath, a city that frequently appears in her fiction, but returned to Hampshire after his death in 1805. With her mother and sister, Jane Austen lived first in Southampton and then in Chawton, near Alton, remaining there until she died. Her life was conspicuous for its lack of event – allowing biographers to make it a study in quiet contemplation or quiet frustration – and for the strength of her family ties, most importantly with her sister Cassandra. She died in Winchester at the age of 41 and is buried in the cathedral.

She began her literary career at the age of 15 with *Love and Friendship*, a **burlesque** of **Richardson**; other pieces belonging to the 1790s caricature the sentimentality or excessive 'sensibility' of much late 18th-century literature. Her eye for the ridiculous in contemporary taste also inspired *Northanger Abbey* (published posthu-

Jane Austen. A detail from an unfinished sketch by her sister Cassandra, 1810. This is the only authentic likeness of the author. National Portrait Gallery, London.

favourably by **Sir Walter Scott** and was dedicated to another admirer of her work, the Prince Regent. *Lady Susan*, an **epistolary novel**, and *The Watsons* were not published until they appeared in the second edition of J. E. Austen-Leigh's *Memoir of Jane Austen* (1871). The fragment of *Sanditon* on which she was working in the last months of her life was first published in 1925.

**Austin, Alfred** 1835–1913 Poet. Educated at Stonyhurst and Oscott College, though he abandoned his Roman Catholic faith, he became a barrister. An inheritance gave him sufficient income to turn instead to being a man of letters. An Imperialist and supporter of **Disraeli**, he was joint editor of *The National Review* from 1883 and sole editor from 1887 to 1895. He published 20 volumes of poetry between 1871 and 1908, and, to general mockery, was appointed **Poet Laureate** in 1896. He was especially parodied for his ode on the Jameson Raid. His autobiography appeared in 1911.

**Authorized Version, The**    See **Bible in English, The**.

***Autobiography of a Super-Tramp*** See **Davies, W[illiam] H[enry]**.

***Autobiography of Alice B. Toklas, The*** A fictionalized account by **Gertrude Stein**, published in 1933, of her life with Alice B. Toklas, the ostensible author–narrator of the book. Stein adopts the persona and even the manner of her secretary and long-time companion, but the story she tells is essentially about her own life, as seen from Toklas's point of view.

Stein and Toklas were, as the narrator claims, 'in the heart of an art movement', and *The Autobiography* catalogues the many famous artists and intellectuals with whom they came into contact. The narrator notes how many wives of geniuses she has had to sit with while Stein – also a genius – has been with their husbands; among them the wives of Picasso, Matisse, Braque, Gris, **Ernest Hemingway**, **Sherwood Anderson** and **Ford Madox Ford**. The book also tells of the visit Stein and Toklas made to Alfred North Whitehead's home in England, where they met **Lytton Strachey** and **Bertrand Russell**; and of their wartime involvement with the American Fund for the French Wounded, when they visited French hospitals and were decorated by the French government. It also provides an account of their busy life from 1919 to 1932 – the years of 'constantly seeing people' such as **Ezra Pound**, Tristan Tzara, **T. S. Eliot**, **Djuna Barnes**, Jacques Lipschitz, Jean Cocteau, Marcel Duchamp and **Edith Sitwell**.

***Autobiography of Mark Rutherford, The*** See **White, William Hale**.

mously in 1818 but probably her earliest extended work of fiction), which satirizes her heroine's penchant for **Gothic fiction**, and *Sense and Sensibility* (begun in 1797 but not published until 1811).

Begun in 1796 or 1797 and published after revision in 1813, *Pride and Prejudice* has the same high spirits as its predecessors but, more clearly than they, marks out the territory, the subject and the mode of her mature work. It looks forward to her later novels: *Mansfield Park* (begun 1811, published 1814), *Emma* (begun 1814, published 1816) and *Persuasion* (begun 1815, published posthumously in 1818). In these works Jane Austen chose deliberately to portray small groups of people in a limited, perhaps confining, environment and to mould the apparently trivial incidents of their lives into a poised comedy of manners. Her characters are middle-class and provincial; their most urgent preoccupation is with courtship and their largest ambition is marriage. The task she set herself required careful shaping of her material, delicate economy and precise deployment of irony to point the underlying moral commentary. She developed not by obvious enlargement of her powers but by the deepening subtlety and seriousness with which she worked inside the formal boundaries she had established.

Although her novels did not prove especially popular in her own day, *Emma* was reviewed

*Autocrat of the Breakfast Table, The* First published (1857–8) in *The Atlantic Monthly*, and in volume form in 1858, this book is an expanded version of two earlier papers written by **Oliver Wendell Holmes** while studying medicine at Harvard and published in *The New England Magazine* (1831–2). The book consists of essays, poems, and occasional pieces in the form of table talk in a Boston boarding house. Among those present at the breakfast table, besides the 'autocrat' himself, are the landlady, her daughter, and a poor relation, a schoolmistress, a divinity student and an old gentleman. The autocrat is generally seen as a vehicle for Holmes's own wit and social commentary.

*Ave Atque Vale* An **elegy** by **Algernon Charles Swinburne** to Baudelaire, based on a false report of the French poet's death. It was published in *The Fortnightly Review* for January 1868 and reprinted in the second series of *Poems and Ballads* (1878).

**Avison, Margaret (Kirkland)** 1918– Canadian poet. Born in Galt, Ontario, and educated at the University of Toronto, she has held a variety of posts as secretary, librarian, lecturer, research and social worker. Her literary output has been small, consisting of contributions to magazines and three books of verse, *Winter Sun* (1960), *The Dumbfounding* (1966) and *Sunblue* (1978). Nevertheless, Avison is recognized as one of Canada's finest poets, concentrating with delicate precision upon the nature of imaginative perception in the bleak landscapes of the 20th century.

*Avowynge of King Arthur, Sir Gawan, Sir Kaye, and Sir Bawdewyn of Bretan, The* An anonymous poem in **tail-rhyme** stanzas, probably written around 1425 in the North of England. Arthur and his three knights are hunting near Carlisle when they hear of a great boar. Arthur vows to kill it single-handed before morning, Gawain to watch at the Tarn Wadling and Kay to ride the forest all night, while Bawdewyn, who becomes the central figure, extravagantly vows never to be jealous of his wife, never to deny his food to any man and not to fear death. The poem tells of their adventures, and culminates in three anecdotes by Bawdewyn explaining why he made and honoured such vows. The work has no known single source.

See also **Arthurian literature**.

*Awake and Sing!* A play by **Clifford Odets**, first performed by the Group Theatre in New York in 1935. It was one of the major pieces in the repertoire of that short-lived but important company.

The play describes a crisis in the lives of a Jewish family living in the Bronx during the Depression. Bessie Berger determines to sustain her impoverished family by the force of her own belief in a tolerable present and a better future. Her communist father sees hope only in changing society and makes his grandson Ralph his ally. It is only after his grandfather has committed suicide that Ralph finds the energy to fight.

*Awakening, The* A novel by **Kate Chopin**, published in 1899. It is a study of the inner life and rebellion of Edna Pontellier, the wife of a successful Creole speculator in Louisiana, and the mother of two small boys. While spending the summer at Grand Isle, she flirts with Robert Lebrun, the son of the resort owner, who awakens her to a new sense of spiritual and physical self-awareness. She begins to question the importance of the traditional roles of wife and mother that she has always fulfilled and that she sees embodied in her friend Adele Ratignolle. On her return to New Orleans, she begins to assert her new sense of identity. She develops her artistic nature by painting and attains some financial independence by selling her work. She moves out of the family house, and has sexual relations with another man. Lebrun returns and their intimacy is renewed, but the consummation of their love is prevented when Edna is called to help Adele through the birth of her child. Profoundly distressed by the birth scene, she returns home to find Lebrun gone. She realizes that a succession of lovers will not lead to fulfilment, and that, though she feels neither loyalty nor guilt towards her husband, she cannot escape from her responsibilities to her sons. In a final desperate assertion of her independence, she returns to Grand Isle, and the novel closes as she swims far out to sea to her death.

*Awkward Age, The* A novel by **Henry James**, published serially in *Harper's Weekly* from October 1898 to January 1899 (as a volume, revised, 1899). It is written almost entirely in the form of dialogue. Its heroine, Nanda Brookenham, is a 'knowing' young woman brought up in the permissive and worldly atmosphere of her mother's salon. Aggie, a 'pure' young lady who has been raised strictly, in the Continental manner, by her aunt the Duchess, serves as her foil. The action of the novel revolves around the relations between Nanda and Aggie and two men, Mr Vanderbank and Mr Mitchett.

Nanda loves Mr Vanderbank, but he does not return her feeling. Mr Longdon, an elderly gentleman who once cared for Nanda's grandmother, encourages Vanderbank to marry Nanda, even offering to provide her with a dowry. But Nanda, out of the worldly wisdom that has perhaps made her less marriageable than Aggie, realizes Vanderbank does not love her and, in a typically Jamesian renunciation scene, graciously gives him up. Meanwhile, Mr Mitchett, who had hoped to marry Nanda himself, has been sought by the Duchess as a match for Aggie. Accepting that he cannot have Nanda, Mitchett marries Aggie. Nanda leaves the marriage market and retires to Longdon's country house.

**Awnytyrs of Arthure at the Terne Wathelyne, The** An alliterative poem of the late 14th century written in Northern England or Scotland. There are two *awntyrs* (adventures), but Arthur only features in the second and Gawain is the central figure in each. The Terne Wathelyne is Wadling Tarn near Hesket in Cumberland. Arthur and his court are at Carlisle and are hunting when a storm separates Dame Gaynoure (Guinevere) and Gawain from the remainder of the hunting party. They are confronted by a fearsome figure which emerges from the waters of the tarn, the tormented spirit of Gaynoure's mother. Before vanishing, she warns Gaynoure that she is paying the price for her life of pride and lechery and prophesies the end of the Round Table, Arthur's last battle and Gawain's death. The second adventure tells of the combat between Galleron of Galway and Gawain. Arthur had taken Galleron's lands and given them to Gawain, but peace is restored when Arthur returns Galleron's lands and makes Gawain lord of Wales in recompense. The work has been the subject of controversy, the disparate nature of the two adventures causing some critics to see it as two works brought together. However, the two illuminate each other and share a moral criticism of Arthur's court. See also **Arthurian literature**.

**Awoonor, Kofi** (formerly George Awoonor-Williams) 1935–  Ghanaian poet in English and Ewe. Born in Wheta, he was educated in Ghana, London and New York. His teaching and research in the USA (1967–75) resulted in *The Breast of the Earth: A Survey of the History, Culture, and Literature of Africa* (1975). Under different Ghanaian regimes he has been political detainee and ambassador abroad. His lucid, lyrical English verse in *Rediscovery* (1964), *Night of My Blood* (1971) and *Ride Me Memory* (1973) celebrates African communality as 'the feast of oneness' and tries to bridge modern and precolonial African culture by writing, in his own words, 'traditional oral poetry of the Ewes, with emphasis on lyricism, the chant, repetition of lines, symbolism, and imagery transfused into English through the secondary influence of Pound, Dylan Thomas'. Joint editor of *Poems from Ghana* (1970), he has also written a novel about experiencing shifting cultural values, *This Earth, My Brother . . .* (1972).

**Ayala's Angel** A novel by **Anthony Trollope**, published in three volumes in 1881.

The romantic Ayala and her more practical sister Lucy are the pretty but penniless orphan daughters of Egbert Dormer, an improvident artist. Ayala is taken into the home of her wealthy City uncle, Sir Thomas Tringle, and Lucy goes to stay in the penny-pinching household of another uncle, Reginald Dosett. Ayala's attitude to her rich relations is disrespectful, and when her vulgar but good-natured cousin Tom falls in love with her, and she rejects his persistent proposals of marriage, the two sisters change places. The novel concerns the romantic idealism which leads Ayala to reject her available suitors for an 'Angel of Light' of her imagination, and the comic reversal which comes when she discovers this angel in the ugly, fiery-complexioned but devoted soldier Jonathan Stubbs. Her sister, although living in luxury, remains true to the young sculptor she loves, and is enabled to marry him through the generosity of her uncle Sir Thomas. His own children fare less happily and are the subject of the novel's secondary action.

A playful and self-mocking novel, *Ayala's Angel* shows Trollope lightly experimenting with many of the characteristic themes and situations of his earlier novels.

**Ayckbourn, Alan** 1939–  English playwright, who began his career as an actor, became a producer of radio drama and then, in 1970, artistic director of the Stephen Joseph Theatre in Scarborough. Ayckbourn's sour farces about middle-class anxiety and neurosis have enjoyed an extraordinary vogue in the English theatre since *Relatively Speaking* transferred from Scarborough to London in 1967. Outstanding among them are *How the Other Half Loves* (1969), *Absurd Person Singular* (1972), the trilogy of plays grouped under the title *The Norman Conquests* (1973), *Bedroom Farce* (1975) and *Joking Apart* (1978).

**Ayenbite of Inwyt** A religious tract in prose, written by Dan Michel of Northgate, Kent, and completed in 1340. It is a translation and adaptation of *Le Somme des Vices et des Vertues*, written by Frère Lorens for Philip II of France in 1279. The title means the 'again-biting' (remorse) of the 'inner wit' (conscience). The tract aims to teach the basis of good Christian living and the nature of sin. It is divided into discourses on each of the Ten Commandments, the twelve articles of the Creed and the seven deadly sins, and on learning to die, the knowledge of good and evil, and the virtues. Each discourse is further subdivided. **Allegory** is sometimes used but, unlike many similar works, *Ayenbite* prefers to explain the vices and virtues by analysis of their structure and character rather than by anecdote and **exemplum**.

**Ayer, Sir A[lfred] J[ules]** 1910–89 Philosopher. He was educated at Eton and Christ Church, Oxford, with further study in Vienna; his professorial career has been spent mainly at London (1946–59) and Oxford (1959–78). His first book, *Language, Truth and Logic* (1936, revised 1946), forcefully argued but notably elegant and lucid, provided a link between the logical positivism of the Vienna Circle and nascent English linguistic analysis. *The Problem of Knowledge* (1956) deals with questions of scepticism in philosophy. His autobiographies (1977, 1984) cover his varied social life as well as his intellectual career. A prominent atheist, he was knighted in 1951.

*Aylwin* See **Watts-Dunton, Walter Theodore**.

*Ayrshire Legatees, The* A novel by **John Galt**, published in 1820. It takes the form of letters from Dr Zachariah Pringle and his family in London to their friends in Scotland, describing their impressions of the capital and the events of 1820, when George IV succeeded George III.

**Ayton (or Aytoun), Sir Robert** 1570–1638 Scottish poet. Educated at St Andrews University, Ayton served as secretary to Anne of Denmark, James I's queen, and then to Henrietta Maria, and was a friend of **Ben Jonson** and **Thomas Hobbes**. Fluent in several languages, he was probably the first Scot to write in the English of the south as opposed to the Scottish of his contemporaries. His verses are popular with anthologists; best known is the song 'Should Old Acquaintance Be Forgot', which was credited to Ayton by James Watson in 1711. 'Auld Lang Syne', the melody to which **Burns**'s more famous version is sung, is an old Scots air and would have been known to Ayton.

**Aytoun, William Edmonstoune** 1818–65 Scottish poet and critic. He taught at Edinburgh University as Professor of rhetoric and belles lettres and contributed to *Blackwood's Magazine*. Aytoun coined the term **'Spasmodic'** in unflattering description of the febrile Romantic verse of **Sydney Dobell**, **Philip James Bailey** and **Alexander Smith**, whom he satirized in *Firmilian, or, The Student of Badajoz: A Spasmodic Tragedy* (1854). With Theodore Martin, he was author of the *Bon Gaultier Ballads* (1855), which contain parodies of **Tennyson** and **Elizabeth Barrett Browning**. Aytoun's *Lays of the Scottish Cavaliers* (1849) and *The Ballads of Scotland* (1858) were extremely popular in the 19th century.

# B

**Bab Ballads, The** A series of humorous verses by **W. S. Gilbert**, originally contributed to *Fun* and other periodicals between 1862 and 1871, many with illustrations by the author signed 'Bab' (the version of 'Baby' by which he had been known as a child). A first collected edition was published in 1868, *More Bab Ballads* in 1872, and a comprehensive edition in 1882. The ironic tone and many of the themes of the ballads helped to form the characteristic style and content of Gilbert's work for the theatre, and in 1898 he published the Ballads and a number of lyrics from his operas as *The Bab Ballads with which Are Included the Songs of a Savoyard*. For this edition he redrew many of the original illustrations which he claimed 'erred gravely in the direction of unnecessary extravagance'. The ballads have retained their popularity and have been regularly reissued.

**Babbitt** A novel by **Sinclair Lewis**, published in 1922. It depicts the complacency and materialism of George F. Babbitt, a real-estate agent and representative middle-class family man from the city of Zenith in the American Midwest. After his only real friend, the artist-turned-businessman Paul Riesling, shoots his wife and is sent to prison, Babbitt rebels against commonplace values: he begins a love affair with the widow Tanis Judique, refuses to join the Good Citizens' League, and becomes influenced by the socialist lawyer Seneca Doane. But he soon finds the price of nonconformity too great and once again resigns himself to the superficial values of his business culture. His reconciliation with society is completed by his acceptance back into the Booster Club. At the end of the novel, his son (ironically named Theodore Roosevelt Babbitt) himself rebels against the wishes of his family and the town by leaving college and marrying hastily. Babbitt supports him in this rebellion, hoping that, unlike himself, his son will be able to do as he wants and lead a more independent and fulfilled life.

**Babbitt, Irving** 1865–1933 American scholar and critic. Born in Ohio, Babbitt graduated from Harvard in 1889 and then taught at Williams College (1893–4) and Harvard (1894–

1933). With Paul Elmer More he was a leading figure among the New Humanists. His criticism emphasized the ethical component of art, rejecting more romantic ideals which, in his view, tended too much to establish art or science as objects of veneration. His ideas influenced **T. S. Eliot**, who was his student at Harvard. His major works are *Literature and the American College* (1908), *The New Laokoön* (1910), *Masters of Modern French Criticism* (1912), *Rousseau and Romanticism* (1919), *Democracy and Leadership* (1924), *On Being Creative* (1932) and *The Spanish Character and Other Essays, With a Bibliography of His Publications and an Index to His Collected Works* (1940).

**Back to Methuselah** A play in five parts by **George Bernard Shaw**, sub-titled 'A Metabiological Pentateuch'. Published in 1921 and first produced at the Garrick Theatre, New York, in 1922, it was given its first English production at the Birmingham Repertory Theatre under Barry Jackson in 1923. The five parts, each separately titled, stretch from the Garden of Eden to the year 21,920, allowing Shaw ample space to dramatize the essential opposition, in the development of human society, between stagnation and creative evolution. He defined the modern world's dilemma in a 1944 postscript to *Back to Methuselah*: 'Civilization means stabilization; and creative evolution means change. As the two must operate together we must carefully define their spheres, and co-ordinate them instead of quarrelling and persecuting as we do at present.' Shaw's aim was to demonstrate the capacity of humankind to will its own betterment.

**Bacon, Francis** 1561–1626 Philosopher and essayist. The youngest son of Nicholas Bacon, Lord Keeper of the Seal to Elizabeth I, he was born at York House in the Strand, London, and educated at Trinity College, Cambridge. He entered Gray's Inn in 1576 and, failing to secure any official position in public service, turned to practising the law. He was an ambitious man, and though he enjoyed the patronage of the Earl of Essex, and became an MP in 1584, his career saw no dramatic advances until the death of

Francis Bacon. A detail from the portrait by J. Vanderbank in the National Portrait Gallery, London.

Elizabeth – partly because he had opposed her tax programme in Parliament. Appointed to prepare the case against his own patron following the Essex revolt, in 1601, he dispassionately brought his formidable legal skills to bear upon his friend and secured a conviction. In 1606 he married Alice Barnham.

Under James I Bacon's talents were rewarded. He became Solicitor-General in 1607, Attorney-General in 1613, Lord Keeper of the Seal in 1617, and, finally, Lord Chancellor in 1618. In the same year he was created Baron Verulam, and in 1621 Viscount St Albans. But Bacon was not popular among many of his peers. His most jealous rival was Edward Coke, formerly Chief Justice of the King's Bench, who in 1621 successfully instigated a charge of corruption against him. Bacon admitted accepting bribes, but denied he had ever perverted the course of justice. He was dismissed from office, debarred from Parliament, fined, and sent briefly to the Tower, thence retiring into private life, disgraced.

Bacon devoted much of his subsequent life to writing. His first writing had been political: the *Temporis Pastus Masculus* (1584) outlined a policy of tolerance and moderation, but a *Letter of Advice to Queen Elizabeth* later advocated tough anti-Catholic measures. His *Essays*, published in 1597 in a book of 10, were reprinted in a 1625 edition which contained 58. After *The Advancement of Learning* (1605) he turned to Latin for *De Sapientia Veterum* (1609), later translated as *The Wisdom of the Ancients* (1619). Latin was also chosen for his celebrated *Novum Organum* (1620). He returned to English in *The History of the Reign of King Henry the Seventh* (1622), *Apophthegms New and Old* (1624), and *The New Atlantis* (1626). As well as several works concerning the law, Bacon left assorted unpublished writings on a variety of topics including *Sylva Sylvarum, or, A Natural History*, published in 1627, the year after he died on his estate at Gorhambury, from a chill contracted while studying the properties of snow.

His works are suffused with the curiosity of a scientific mind and are written in an accomplished, even beautiful, style that is concise and frequently epigrammatic. Bacon's greatest achievement is the programme of intellectual and scientific reform proposed under the title of *Instauratio Magna* ('The Great Instauration'), begun in *The Advancement of Learning* and continued in *Novum Organum* and *Sylva Sylvarum*. These works reject the older, Aristotelian structures of knowledge and seek to discover a new system of philosophic instruction based upon a clearer, empirical perception of nature. Ironically, it was Bacon's reputation for polymathic intelligence that gave rise to the so-called **Baconian Heresy**.

**Bacon, Roger** *c.* 1220–*c.* 1292    Philosopher and scientist. Born at either Ilchester in Somerset or Bisley in Gloucestershire, Bacon studied the *quadrivium* at Oxford before going to Paris where he lectured on Aristotle and pseudo-Aristotelian works. After 1247, under the influence of **Robert Grosseteste**, Adam de Marisco and Thomas the Welshman, he was in Oxford engaged in experimental work, studying mathematics, optics, alchemy and astronomy as well as languages. In 1257 he became a Franciscan friar and suffered a long period of illness and his literary and university careers virtually ended. In 1266 he sought the patronage of Pope Clement IV for a projected encyclopaedia of all known science and for reforming the teaching of science. Over the next two years he sent the *Opus Majus*, *Opus Minus* and *Opus Tertium* to the Pope, but the death of Clement IV in 1268 frustrated Bacon's desire to see the sciences fully recognized as part of the university curriculum. Other projected encyclopaedias proved abortive. He was condemned to prison at some time between 1277 and 1279 on account of his unorthodox teaching – probably his attacks on theologians and scholars and his interest in alchemy and astrology. Exaggerated accounts of his experiments made him a figure in popular literature (like *Friar Bacon and Friar Bungay*), and he acquired the title *doctor admirabilis* after his death. His influence was principally as a promoter of science and the teaching of science.

**Baconian Heresy** The theory that **Francis Bacon** wrote the works of **Shakespeare** was first publicly advanced by the suitably named Delia Bacon, an American living in England, in her *Philosophy of the Plays of Shakespeare Unfolded* (1857). **Nathaniel Hawthorne** contributed a cautious preface to the book, more in his capacity as American consul at Liverpool than as literary critic. Miss Bacon died insane after haunting Shakespeare's grave in the belief its opening would settle the question of authorship, but her theory flourished and enjoyed a considerable vogue among amateur scholars, particularly in the closing years of the 19th and the early years of the 20th century. In the hands of supporters like Sir Edwin Durning-Lawrence (*Bacon is Shakespeare*, 1910; *The Shakespeare Myth*, 1912) it rests on a variety of arguments. As a rustic from Stratford, Shakespeare is seen as too boorishly illiterate to make a poet; Francis Bacon, on the other hand, was a man of admittedly wide learning who would have had political reasons for concealing any involvement in the contemporary theatre. The connection between the two is made by pointing out linguistic similarities between Bacon and Shakespeare's work, and by discovering cryptogrammatic references to Bacon's name in the text of the plays. The first stage of this argument, the attack on Shakespeare the man, has also been used to serve rival theories attributing authorship to the Earls of Derby and Oxford, a committee including either or both of these peers, and – in Calvin Hoffman's *The Man Who Was Shakespeare* (1955) – **Christopher Marlowe**.

**Bage, Robert** 1728–1801 Paper-maker and novelist. Son of a paper-maker at Darley, near Derby, Bage was educated at a common school. Married at 23, he set up a paper-mill at Elford, near Tamworth, with his wife's money and continued in this business throughout his life. For a period of 14 years from 1765 he was also engaged in the manufacture of iron, an exercise which was not profitable. He produced six novels: *Mount Henneth* (1781), *Barham Downs* (1784), *The Fair Syrian* (1787), *James Wallace* (1788), *Man As He Is* (1792) and *Hermsprong, or, Man As He Is Not* (1796).

Of these works only the last has been edited this century. An idiosyncratic work, its overt narrator, Glen, disappears shortly after the book opens, and reappears without explanation towards the end. Like all Bage's works, *Hermsprong* is radical if simplistic in its political and social messages. Hermsprong claims to be an American Indian and has fixed views on the importance of physical fitness, the corruption endemic among the rich, and the necessity of female education and equality. At the conclusion Hermsprong, who throughout has been shown as an ideal, is revealed as of a social

acceptability which provides a double barb to the book's sub-title, and Bage also used this to mock the convention within which he was writing. Characterization is not a strong point, but Bage successfully combined polemic and humour, the latter very much in the vein of **Sterne. Scott**, in his preface for Ballantyne's Novelists' Library, while deploring Bage's political and atheist tendencies, argued that his humour and command of dialogue fully warranted his inclusion in the series. Though politically close to **William Godwin** and **Thomas Holcroft**, Bage is by comparison far less ponderous in the presentation of his arguments. In his private life he was, according to Scott, an impeccable exemplar of his beliefs.

**Bagehot, Walter** 1826–77 Political thinker, economist and literary critic. Born at Langport in Somerset, Bagehot went to school in Bristol, attended University College, London, and was called to the Bar in 1852 but chose instead to enter his father's bank. In 1855 he became joint editor of *The National Review* with **R. H. Hutton**, a friend from University College, and in 1860–77 he edited *The Economist*. His most famous work, *The English Constitution* (1867), is a classic appraisal of the workings of government. *Physics or Politics* (1872) attempts to relate contemporary theories of natural selection and inheritance to the workings of the state; *Lombard Street* (1873) and *Economic Studies* (edited by Hutton, 1880) examine the money market and commerce. Bagehot's literary criticism, represented by *Estimates of Some Englishmen and Scotchmen* (1858) and *Literary Studies* (edited by Hutton, 1879), adopts the same stance of the worldly, moderate man which marks his approach to economic and political affairs.

**Bagnold, Enid** 1889–1981 Playwright and novelist. At the outbreak of World War I she turned from art studies to nursing. Her *Diary Without Dates* (1917), based on her nursing experience, offended some of the hospital authorities by its frankness. Her first literary success was with a novel, *Serena Blandish* (1925), later dramatized for the New York stage by **S. N. Behrman** (1929). A more famous novel, *National Velvet* (1935), was seen on the stage in Bagnold's own version (1946), and *Lottie Dundas* (1941) was successful both as a novel and as a play (1943). The social comedy, *The Chalk Garden* (1955), was the last of her plays to achieve theatrical success.

**Bail, Murray** 1941– Australian short-story writer and novelist. Born in Adelaide, he lived abroad in Bombay from 1968 to 1970 and in London from 1970 to 1974. Widely regarded as one of the most cosmopolitan of contemporary Australian writers, he had been publishing fiction in magazines for several years when his short-story collection *Contemporary Portraits* (republished as *The Drover's Wife and Other Stories* in 1986) appeared in 1975. Bail's *avant-garde* fiction frequently takes issue with the realist tradition in the Australian short story, as can be seen in one of his best-known stories, 'The Drover's Wife', which, while it is ostensibly a response to Russell Drysdale's painting of this name, may also be seen as an ironic rebuttal of the narrative manner and values of the classic **Henry Lawson** story with the same title. Much of his work offers a playful, Borgesian treatment of definitions, encyclopaedism and literary tradition. His novel *Homesickness* (1980) takes a group of 13 assorted Australians on a package tour of the world's museums. While this situation affords opportunities for satire, the novel is mainly concerned with the way experience is perceived, specifically the perspectives engendered by tourism, and gradually the motley travellers begin to react to the often absurdist stimuli with which they are confronted in an increasingly uniform way. His most recent novel, *Holden's Performance* (1987), is a comic epic about the passage of an innocent through Australian society. Bail has a strong interest in the visual arts which is frequently reflected in his fiction.

**Bailey, H. C.** See **detective fiction**.

**Bailey, Philip James** 1816–1902 Poet. 'Festus' Bailey was born in Nottingham, educated at Glasgow University and called to the Bar in 1840. In 1839 he published *Festus*, a blank-verse epic based on the Faust legend. Progressively enlarged editions appeared throughout his lifetime, and by the last (1889) *Festus* had swollen to 52 scenes and 40,000 lines, incorporating much of the verse earlier published in *The Angel World* (1850), *The Mystic* (1855) and *The Universal Hymn* (1867). Originally praised by the reviewers, *Festus* was effectively ridiculed by **William Aytoun**, who identified Bailey as father of the **Spasmodic School of Poetry**.

**Baillie, Joanna** 1762–1851 Poet and dramatist, born at Hamilton, Lanarkshire. The first volume of her *Plays on the Passions*, published in 1798, included *De Montfort*, which was produced by **Kemble** in 1800 and in which Mrs Siddons enjoyed considerable success. A second volume of plays appeared in 1802 and a third in 1812. Her drama *The Family Legend* was produced in 1810 and her *Miscellaneous Plays* was published in 1836. Her most notable collections of verse appeared as *Fugitive Verses* (1790) and *Metrical Legends* (1821). She was a close friend of **Sir Walter Scott**.

**Bain, Alexander** 1818–1903 Philosopher. Born in Aberdeen and educated at Marischal College, he was appointed Professor of Logic in the University of Aberdeen in 1860. A friend of **John Stuart Mill** and biographer of **James Mill** (1882), he developed the ideas of **Utilitarianism** in his own writings, which include *The Senses and the Intellect* (1855), *The Emotions and the Will* (1859), *Mental and Moral Science* (1868) and *Logic* (1870).

**Bainbridge, Beryl** 1934– Novelist. Bainbridge grew up in Liverpool in a conflict-ridden but united family whose oddity she has evoked memorably both in non-fictional essays and in her claustrophobic novel, *A Quiet Life* (1976). Her novels, the most highly regarded of which have been *The Dressmaker* (1973), *The Bottle Factory Outing* (1974) and *Injury Time* (1977), are short, terse black comedies in immaculately measured prose: they confront innocent, inadequate characters with situations of incipient menace that frequently break out into grotesque violence. Two novels, *Young Adolf* (1978) and *Watson's Apology* (1984), both adopt historical subjects – the former speculating about the possible youthful sojourn of Hitler in Liverpool, and the latter recreating a notorious Victorian murder case.

**Baker, Father Augustine** 1571–1641 Catholic mystic and author of more than 40 treatises, or 'Directions for the Prayer of Contemplation'. His work was published posthumously as the *Sancta Sophia* (1657), a kind of Catholic parallel to **Traherne**'s *Centuries of Meditations*.

**Baldwin, James (Arthur)** 1924–87 American novelist. The son of a preacher, Baldwin was born in Harlem, New York City. He left home at 17 and eventually made his way to Paris, where he lived for some years and began to write.

His first novel, *Go Tell It On The Mountain* (1953), recounts a young boy's coming to terms with the religious beliefs of his father, a store-front preacher incapable of controlling his desires. His father's lusts and inability to communicate with his children have kept the Lord away from him, for before kneeling to the Lord he must kneel to his father, something he cannot bring himself to do. After a long series of conflicts, he is finally able to reject his father and turn to the Lord at one stroke, and he feels something die in him as well as come alive. He has achieved faith through struggle.

The promise of this first book was borne out in further novels, plays, short stories and essays, which have shown Baldwin to be a powerful and articulate enemy of racial discrimination. After *Giovanni's Room* (1956), which is set in Paris, he returned to black America as a setting for his fiction. *Another Country* (1962) is set in

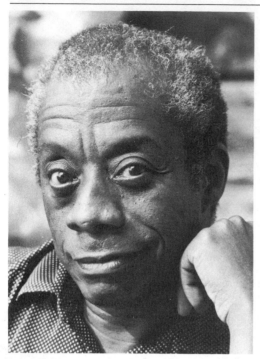

James Baldwin.

New York City and focuses mainly on Harlem society. The death – perhaps suicide – of the main character, Rufus Scott, is representative of the treatment individuals receive in an environment which is essentially hostile and which erects barriers to their desire for love. Other works of fiction by Baldwin include *Going to Meet the Man* (1965), *Tell Me How Long the Train's Been Gone* (1968), *If Beale Street Could Talk* (1974) and *Just Above My Head* (1979). His essays were published in *Notes of a Native Son* (1955), *Nobody Knows My Name: More Notes of a Native Son* (1961, published in England as *No Name in the Streets*, 1972), *The Fire Next Time* (1963), *The Devil Finds Work* (1976), *The Evidence of Things Not Seen: An Essay* (1985) and *The Price of the Ticket: Collected Nonfiction, 1948–1985* (1986). He also wrote four plays: *Blues for Mr Charlie* (produced and published 1964), *The Amen Corner* (produced 1965, published 1968), *One Day, When I Was Lost* (produced 1972, published 1973) and *A Deed from the King of Spain* (produced 1974). *Jimmy's Blues* (1986) is a volume of poetry.

**Baldwin, Joseph G.** 1815–64 American jurist, remembered for his sketches describing his legal career in the Southern backwoods. Born in Virginia, he educated himself in both literature and law, and in 1836 decided to seek work in the comparatively uncivilized region of Mississippi. In 1853 he published *The Flush Times of Alabama*

*and Mississippi*, a collection of sketches and anecdotes about frontier law, which combines serious and moralistic portraits of great men Baldwin admired with comic tales of infamous rascals. The latter pieces remain better known, and include 'Ovid Bolus, Esq.', about a chronic liar, and 'Simon Suggs, Jr, Esq.: A Legal Biography', about a lawyer who cleverly cheats his way to success. Encouraged by the volume's favourable reception, he published *Party Leaders* (1855), a more sober work containing studies of **Thomas Jefferson**, Alexander Hamilton and Andrew Jackson.

**Bale, John** 1495–1563 Playwright. The son of poor parents from Suffolk, he trained for the church but became a vigorous supporter of the English Reformation. His Protestant polemics earned him the patronage of Thomas Cromwell, for whose troupe of itinerant players Bale wrote several anti-Catholic plays between 1537 and Cromwell's fall in 1540. Five of these works survive. *The Three Laws* and the trilogy comprising *God's Promises*, *John the Baptist* and *The Temptation of Our Lord* are **morality plays** in an already well-established style. It is the fifth, *King John*, which earns Bale an important place in the history of English drama, for although such abstract characters as Dissimulation, Private Wealth and Sedition look back to the morality tradition, the portraits of the King, Stephen Langton and Cardinal Pandulphus look forward to the English history plays of **Marlowe** and **Shakespeare**. Unlike Shakespeare's, Bale's King John is an idealized Christian hero battling with the Pope and the whole 'heap of adders of Antichrist's generation'.

**Balfour, Arthur James, 1st Earl of Balfour** 1848–1930 Statesman and philosopher. Born at Whittingehame in East Lothian, he was educated at Eton and Trinity College, Cambridge. He was leader of the Conservative Party (1902–11), Prime Minister (1902–5) and Foreign Secretary (1916–19). His works included *A Defence of Philosophic Doubt* (1879) which expressed his belief that the ultimate convictions of mankind rest on religious faith and are not susceptible to the probing of logic and science. In 1893 he became President of the Society for Psychical Research. He developed his religious position in *The Foundation of Belief* (1895) and in two series of Gifford Lectures, *Theism and Humanism* (1915) and *Theism and Thought* (1923). His other works included *Decadence* (1908), *Criticism and Beauty* (1910) and *Essays Speculative and Political* (1920). His incomplete *Chapters of Autobiography* (edited by Mrs Dugdale) was published posthumously in 1930.

**ballad** Two main types are to be distinguished, the least unsatisfactory names for them, perhaps, being 'traditional' and 'street'. There is no proof that the first type is earlier than the second, though internal evidence points that way. Both have been transmitted mainly through printed **broadsides** (the earliest known example dating from 1513), both have influenced major poets and been imitated by them, but as a popular creative form the traditional ballad seems unlikely to have been composed after the 16th century, while street ballads are still being composed today. The difference may be briefly summed up as follows: the former, deriving from a pre-literate rural community, tended to be tragic, romantic and heroic, telling its story in arbitrary narrative fragments, whereas the latter, developing with the growth of towns and the printing press, tended to be comic, realistic and unheroic, its narrative more leisurely and circumstantial. But frequent and contemporaneous reprinting by publishers unconcerned with authenticity ensures blurring and overlapping – as indeed occurs with the distinction between ballad and folk-song.

All ballads, of whatever type, must not only tell a story in verse but also lend themselves to being sung (if not actually accompanied by a tune). These two defining conditions imply a third: the narrative and style must be simple enough to be followed at a hearing. So most ballads – but by no means all – are written in simple ballad metre: that is to say: in **quatrains** of alternating lines of iambic tetrameter and iambic trimeter (see **metre**). Musical evidence, the fact that most such quatrains rhyme only the second and fourth lines (especially in earlier periods), and the prevalence of 'fourteeners' in the early Elizabethan period, suggest that the normal ballad form, to begin with, was that of long 14-syllable couplets, whose lines were later split into the 8- and 6-syllable lines of the familiar quatrain form. The split led to an increasing tendency to rhyme the first and third lines as well as the second and fourth. Though ballad metre is basically iambic, much syllabic irregularity is common – presumably owing to the demands of music, the early origins of the ballad and the popular audience it mainly catered for.

**ballad metre** See **ballad**.

***Ballad of Reading Gaol, The*** A poem by **Oscar Wilde**, published in 1898, about the hanging of the murderer, Charles Thomas Wooldridge, while Wilde was himself a convict. Its harsh eloquence is in contrast to the aestheticism of Wilde's earlier poems, but shows the same technical control. It concludes with a plea for Christ's forgiveness and a complaint against prison conditions.

**ballad opera** A dramatic form pioneered by **John Gay**, whose *Beggar's Opera* was the most popular play of the 18th century. A combination of **farce**, **pantomime**, street literature, delightful lyrics and musical comedy, the ballad opera enjoyed an intense vogue, and was designed to counteract the modishness of imported Italian opera by offering an entertainment that was British, topical, anti-heroic and satirical of contemporary politics.

**ballade** An Old French verse form, consisting of three eight-line **stanzas**, rhyming ababbcbC, and a four-line envoy, rhyming bcbC (the capital letter indicating that the line is used as a refrain). It is not common in English, and even the best – probably those by **Chaucer** and **Swinburne** – fall far short of the power and mastery of the greatest French exemplar, François Villon.

**Ballantyne, R[obert] M[ichael]** 1825–94 Scottish adventure-story writer. Born and educated in Edinburgh, the son of a newspaper editor, he travelled to Canada at the age of 16 in the service of the Hudson's Bay Company, trading with local Indians in remote areas. Returning to Britain, he produced his first children's book, *The Young Fur-Traders* (1856), based on these memories. This best-seller was followed two years later by his most famous title, *The Coral Island* (1858). Afterwards, he often returned to writing from first-hand knowledge, whether this involved three weeks on Bell Rock (*The Lighthouse*, 1865) or a short spell as a London fireman (*Fighting the Flames*, 1867).

With over 80 books to his credit, written in less than 40 years, Ballantyne was one of the most popular adventure-story writers of all time. Today his books seem over-concerned with details of local flora and fauna, as well as obtrusively pious. *The Gorilla Hunters* (1861), sequel to *The Coral Island*, is disturbing in its callous enthusiasm for every sort of wild-animal slaughter. But in his day Ballantyne provided entertainment popular with both child and adult, the fruits of his own hard work, adventurous life and strong conviction of his importance as a mentor to the young.

**Ballard, J[ames] G[raham]** 1930– Novelist. Ballard began his career as a writer of *avant-garde* **science fiction**, but diversified in the mid-1960s into surreal contemporary fiction. He was born in Shanghai and his internment by the Japanese during World War II provided material for his most successful novel, *Empire of the Sun* (1984), shortlisted for the Booker Prize. His early science fiction novels focus on the psychological adaptations made by his central characters to natural catastrophes, the most famous being *The Drowned World* (1962), *The Drought* (1965) and *The Crystal World* (1966). Some of his science fiction short stories, especially those in *The Four-Dimensional Nightmare* (1963) and *The Terminal Beach* (1964), are among the finest products of the genre. His collection of 'fragmented novels', *The Atrocity Exhibition* (1970), and his novel *Crash* (1973) are the most striking examples of his experimental writings, but subsequent novels, like *The Unlimited Dream Company* (1979), revert to more orthodox narrative technique. His most recent novel is *The Day of Creation* (1987).

**Bancroft, George** 1800–91 American historian. Born in Massachusetts, Bancroft graduated from Harvard at the age of 17, and the following year went to Germany, to study history in Berlin under Hegel and in Göttingen under Heeren and Eichhorn. Though trained for the ministry, he held a variety of government positions: Secretary of the Navy (1845–6); Minister to England (1846–9); and Minister to Germany (1867–74). A Jacksonian Democrat, he supported the Manifest Destiny policy in the 1840s.

His life work, the 10-volume *History of the United States* (1834–75), tells the story of the progressive tendency toward liberty exemplified by American history, culminating in the American Revolution. Bancroft's progressivist notions of history, imbibed in Germany, his extensive use of manuscript sources, and his interest in the human characters underlying historical events place him in a class with his major American contemporaries, **William Hickling Prescott**, **John Lathrop Motley**, and **Francis Parkman Jr**, whose historiographical ideas and practices were similar. The *History*, highly nationalistic and characterized by a resounding rhetoric, was a popular work in its own day.

**Banim, John** 1798–1842 Irish dramatist and novelist who collaborated with his elder brother **Michael Banim** on *Tales by the O'Hara Family* (1825–7). His tragedy *Damon and Pythias* was produced at **Covent Garden** in 1821, and his satirical essays *Revelations of the Dead Alive* appeared in 1824.

**Banim, Michael** 1796–1874 Irish novelist and elder brother of **John Banim**, with whom he collaborated in *Tales by the O'Hara Family* (1825–7). *The Croppy* (1828) is a novel set in the Irish rebellion of 1798. His other fiction includes *Father Connell* (1842) and *The Town of the Cascades* (1864).

**Bannatyne, George** 1545–?1608 Anthologist. Bannatyne was born in Newtyle, Angus, and became a prosperous merchant in Edinburgh. While isolated by the plague in 1568 he compiled a manuscript anthology of Scottish poetry

of the 15th and 16th centuries. The 'Bannatyne Manuscript' of some 800 pages is now in the Advocates' Library, Edinburgh. It contains works by major poets such as **Dunbar**, **Henryson** and **Sir David Lindsay**, works by minor poets who would be otherwise unknown, and much anonymous verse. This collection influenced the revival of interest in Scottish poetry in the 18th century. In Edinburgh in 1823 the Bannatyne Club was founded, under the presidency of **Sir Walter Scott**, to encourage the study of Scottish history and literature.

**Baraka, (Imamu) Amiri** 1934– American poet, playwright and editor. Born LeRoi Jones in Newark, New Jersey, he has been a prominent voice in the black movement since the mid 1950s. He studied at Howard University and then served in the airforce as a gunner; on his discharge in 1956 he began his career as a writer and activist. He established his reputation under his given name of LeRoi Jones; in 1965 he converted to Islam, changed his name to Imamu Amiri Baraka, and moved to a black ghetto in Newark, where he founded the Spirit House Theatre. His other activities have included the founding of Totem Press (1958), which prints the work of contemporary poets, directing of the Black Arts Repertory Theatre in Harlem, and teaching contemporary poetry and creative writing at Columbia, the New School for Social Research, and the State University of New York at Buffalo.

His first published work was a play, *A Good Girl Is Hard To Find* (1958). In 1961 he published *Preface to a Twenty Volume Suicide Note*, a collection of personal and often domestic poems typical of his early period. This was followed by two plays, *The Baptism* (1964) and *The Toilet* (1964), particularly concerned with issues of personal identity. His work then became progressively more radical and more involved with issues of racial and national identity; *Dutchman* (1964), *The Slave* (1964) and *Slave Ship: A Historical Pageant* (1967) all deal with black–white relations and, as works of 'revolutionary theatre', demonstrate Baraka's self-awareness as a leader of a black arts movement which seeks to use dramatic presentation as a weapon against American racism. After 1974 his political ideology underwent a change; his separatist fervour gave way to a revolutionary commitment to the overthrow, by blacks and whites alike, of an oppressive capitalist system. Plays like *S-1* (1976) and *The Motion of History* (1977) exemplify this third stage of his literary career. In addition to other volumes of verse, he has also published *Blues People: Negro Music in White America* (1963); *Tales* (1967), a book of short stories; *Raise, Race, Rays, Raze: Essays Since 1965* (1971); *The Autobiography of LeRoi Jones* (1984); and *Daggers and Javelins: Essays* (1984).

**Barbauld, Anna Laetitia** 1743–1825 Editor, poet and anthologist. Born Anna Aikin at Kibworth, Leicestershire, she was educated by her father and learned, unusually for a girl in her times, French, Italian, Latin and Greek. In 1773 she published a collection of her poems and in the same year collaborated with her brother, **John Aikin**, on *Miscellaneous Pieces*, essays mainly on literary topics. The following year she married a dissenting minister of French birth and they moved to Palgrave, Suffolk, where they ran a boys' school until 1785. During this period her writings were didactic and her *Hymns in Prose for Children* (1781) proved highly successful both in England and, in translation, in Europe. In 1808 her husband died, having been insane for some time, and she then entered her most prolific literary period. Soon after being widowed she undertook a 50-volume anthology *The British Novelists* (1810). This was prefaced by a lengthy and intelligently argued essay 'On the Origin and Progress of Novel-writing' in which she attempted to define the genre, and which revealed her wide reading of fiction in other languages. The works of the selected authors, with the exception of **Francis Coventry**, were each prefixed by a biographical and critical notice, in a number of cases this being the first critical discussion of the writer in question. The set was sufficiently successful as to be reprinted in 1821. Possibly her most important contribution to literature was as the editor of **Samuel Richardson**'s correspondence (6 vols., 1804), and edition which has never been superseded and which is central to intelligent discussion of Richardson's fiction. Her own slightly less voluminous correspondence with, among others, **Hester Chapone**, **Maria Edgeworth**, **Priestley**, **Crabb Robinson**, **Scott** and **Wordsworth**, throws interesting light upon contemporary literary and moral concerns.

**Barbellion, W. N. P.** Pseudonym of Bruce Frederick Cummings (1889–1919), diarist. Born at Barnstaple, Devon, Cummings was a self-educated biologist who eventually became an official of the British Museum (Natural History), South Kensington. Disseminated sclerosis impaired his scientific work and he turned an increasingly self-critical eye on himself. *The Journal of a Disappointed Man*, covering the years 1903–17, was published a few months before his death in 1919 as extracts from the diaries of Wilhelm Nero Pilate Barbellion. It reveals a brave, intelligent personality whose ambitions and aspirations are bedevilled by lack of opportunity and poor health. It is vivid, humorous and objective: 'a self-portrait in the nude' was the author's phrase for it. *A Last Diary* (1920) gives additional information.

**Barbour, John** *c.* 1320–95 Scottish poet. Probably born in Aberdeen, he spent most of his life there and was appointed archdeacon of Aberdeen in or before 1357. In 1364, 1365 and 1368 he studied in Oxford and Paris; in 1372 he was appointed Clerk of Audit and Auditor of the Exchequer to Robert II. His surviving poem, *The Bruce*, gives a patriotic account of the life of Robert the Bruce (Robert I) and his liberation of Scotland from English domination. Two other works, *The Brut* and *The Stewartis Original*, are lost, a record of them surviving only in **Andrew of Wyntoun**'s *Orygynale Cronykil*. The first related mythical history of Britain from its foundation by Brutus and the second traced the pedigree of the Stewarts from Banquo.

*Barchester Towers* A novel by **Anthony Trollope**, the second of the **Barsetshire** sequence, published in three volumes in 1857.

A sequel to *The Warden*, the novel opens with the death of the Bishop of Barchester and the fall of the Conservative ministry which would appoint his son Archdeacon Grantly to succeed him. The incoming Whigs appoint the time-serving Dr Proudie, who comes to Barchester with his Low Church wife and evangelical chaplain Obadiah Slope, an unctuous hypocrite. Mrs Proudie and Mr Slope set about reforming the easygoing diocese, and battle is joined between them and the traditionalists led by Dr Grantly. Mrs Proudie wants to appoint the hard-pressed Mr Quiverful to the vacant wardenship of Hiram's Hospital, but the ambitious Slope, discovering that the newly widowed Eleanor Bold has £1200 a year, manoeuvres to reappoint her father Mr Harding to his old post. When the absentee cleric Dr Vesey Stanhope returns to Barchester, however, Slope becomes infatuated by his *femme fatale* daughter, the crippled Signora Neroni. In the ensuing complications Slope and Mrs Proudie fall out, Quiverful is appointed to the wardenship, and Slope fails in his schemes and is dismissed by the Bishop. Pursued by Slope and Bertie Stanhope, a charming wastrel, Eleanor chooses instead Francis Arabin, the shy cleric brought from Oxford to Barchester to be Dr Grantly's High-Church champion. They marry and Arabin becomes Dean of Barchester.

A classic comic novel, dealing with the clash between old and new ways, *Barchester Towers* made Trollope's reputation with the Victorian reading public.

**Barclay, Alexander** ?1475–1552 Poet and translator. Barclay was a monk and priest at the college of Ottery St Mary, Devon, and later a Benedictine at Ely. He survived the Reformation and in 1546 was presented with a vicarage at Great Baddow in Kent, and with another vicarage in Somerset in the same year. He was a

The frontispiece to Alexander Barclay's translation of Sebastian Brant's *Narrenschiff* (1494) was first published in 1509.

prolific translator: Pierre Gringore's allegorical **dream-vision** *The Castle of Labour* (?1505), Sallust's *Jugurthine War* and Mancinus's *The Mirror of Good Manners* (?1523). His two most important works are his translation of Sebastian Brant's *Das Narrenschiff* as *The Ship of Fools* (1509) and his *Egloges*, which are partly a translation of the work of Aeneas Piccolomini (later Pope Pius II) on the miseries of courtiers and partly an imitation of the pastorals of Mantuan. *The Ship of Fools*, illustrated with woodcuts, is **estates satire** and contains some personal attacks on local Devon clergy and **John Skelton**. The *Egloges* are important as early English attempts at the **pastoral** form later to be used by **Spenser** in *The Shepheardes Calender*.

**Barclay, John** 1582–1621 Miscellaneous writer in Latin. The son of a Scottish jurist, he was born in France at Pont-à-Mousson and was connected with the court of James I. His *Euphormionis Satyricon* (1603–7) is an episodic collection of satire, adventures and discourses modelled on Petronius. *Icon Animorum* (1614), translated by **Thomas May** as *The Mirror of Minds* (1631), is a book of essays on national and temperamental types. *Argenis* (1621) is an allegorical romance with a contemporary setting. It was printed over 40 times in the original Latin, but none of the many English translations secured a lasting place; the last, by **Clara Reeve**, was a revision of Kingsmill Long's translation of 1625 and was published as *The Phoenix* (1772).

**Barclay, Robert** 1648–90 Quaker apologist. He was born at Gordonstown in Elginshire and educated at the Scottish Catholic College in Paris. In 1667 he followed his father in joining the Quaker movement and, because of his wide learning, became its leading theologian. His first published work was his *Catechism and Confession of Faith* (1673). In 1676 he published a Latin apologia supporting the Quaker theses he had circulated and defended at Aberdeen; the English version was called *Apology for the True Christian Religion, as the Same is Set Forth and Preached by the People Called in Scorn 'Quakers'* (1678). It is the main exposition of Quaker principles and also contains a strong attack on Calvinism. Barclay was held in favour by James II, and assisted **William Penn** in the founding of Pennsylvania; he was himself appointed governor of East New Jersey in 1683.

**Barfoot, Joan** 1946– Canadian novelist. Born and brought up in rural Ontario, she now lives in London, Ontario, where she works as a journalist. She has published three novels: *Abra* (1978), reissued in Britain as *Gaining Ground* (1980); *Dancing in the Dark* (1982); and *Duet for Three* (1985). These are all women-centred fictions which present female protagonists isolated by choice, insanity or old age from defining social contexts. In her explorations of women's search for separate identity, Barfoot offers an interesting variant of feminist writing.

**Barham, Revd R[ichard] H[arris]** 1788–1845 Author of *The Ingoldsby Legends*. Born in Canterbury, he inherited the 'moderate estate, somewhat encumbered' of Tappington Everard at the age of seven. After attending St Paul's School and Brasenose College, Oxford, he became a clergyman in Kent and later, in 1821, a minor canon of St Paul's. While recovering from a carriage accident he wrote and published an unsuccessful novel, *Baldwin: or A Miser's Heir* (1820). He contributed to *Blackwood's Magazine* and edited *The London Chronicle* – work he described in his diary as 'rubbish' – but achieved fame only with *The Ingoldsby Legends*, appearing in *Bentley's Miscellany* and *The New Monthly Magazine* from 1837 onwards and in various collections from 1840. Barham was a friend of **Thackeray**, **Dickens**, **Samuel Rogers** and **Sydney Smith**. His son published his life and letters in 1870.

**Baring, Maurice** 1874–1945 Novelist, essayist and playwright. Born in London, he was educated at Eton and Trinity College, Cambridge. From 1898 to 1904 he served in the Foreign Office, mainly in Moscow, and then became foreign correspondent for *The Morning Post* and *The Times* (1904–12). While in Moscow he discovered the works of Chekhov and helped to introduce these and other works of Russian literature to the West. *Landmarks in Russian Literature* (1910) was followed by *An Outline of Russian Literature* (1914) and *The Oxford Book of Russian Verse* (1924).

Baring was closely associated with two better remembered contemporaries, **Hilaire Belloc** and

G. K. Chesterton, whose social and religious preoccupations he shared. His own creative output included the novels *Passing By* (1921), *C* (1924) and *Cat's Cradle* (1925), and a novella, *The Lonely Lady of Dulwich* (1934), often cited as his best work. His plays – like the novels, reflecting the liberal humanism of his social milieu – include *The Black Prince* (1902) and *Diminutive Dramas* (1911). Two historical tales, *Robert Peckham* (1930) and *In My End is My Beginning* (1931), show the influence of Roman Catholicism, to which he became a convert. Baring's autobiography, *The Puppet Show of Memory*, was published in 1922.

**Baring-Gould, Sabine** 1834–1924 Novelist, amateur antiquary and hymnist. He was born in Exeter and educated at Clare College, Cambridge. Ordained in 1864, he was rector of Lewtrenchard in Devon for the last 40 years of his life. His first novel, *Through Fire and Flame* (1868), described his marriage to a mill girl in 1867, and this was followed by over 30 others, of which *Mehalah* (1880) is often considered most noteworthy. Among his non-fictional works were several volumes of *The Lives of the Saints* (1872–7), a biography of **R. S. Hawker**, *The Vicar of Morwenstow* (1876), and numerous works of travel, folklore and local legend (see **folk revival**). His many hymns included 'Onward Christian Soldiers'.

**Barker, George (Granville)** 1913– Poet. Born in Loughton, Essex, Barker was educated at Regent Street Polytechnic. Although he has held university posts in Japan and the USA, he has lived mainly by his writing. His initial volumes were *Thirty Preliminary Poems* (1933), *Poems* (1935) and *Calamiterror* (1937). This early work is marked by a superficial, misunderstood surrealism, garbled rhetoric and a facile fluency with evocative, musical words. He is sometimes associated with the **New Apocalypse** movement and compared to **Dylan Thomas** – mistakes which have dogged Barker throughout his career. *Lament and Triumph* (1940) and *Eros in Dogma* (1944) are better books, and *News of the World* (1950) shows a new limpidity of language. His first masterpiece, though, was the notorious *True Confession of George Barker* (1950), disgracefully omitted by his publishers from the *Collected Poems 1930–1955* (1957). Collections in the 1960s include *The View from a Blind I* (1962) and *Dreams of a Summer Night* (1966). As well as autobiography, Barker's main form has been the elegy, which dominates *The Golden Chains* (1968), 'At Thurgarton Church' and *In Memory of David Archer* (1973). Perhaps his best work has come in the 1970s and 1980s: after *Dialogues, Etc.* (1976), he published *Villa Stellar* (1978), in which a quiet, elegiac mode dominates. *Anno Domini* (1983) is one of the major poems of the post-war period. A 'definitive' *Collected Poems* (1987) brings most of his work back into print. He has also published *Essays* (1970), and novels including *The Dead Seagull* (1950).

**Barker, Harley Granville** See **Granville-Barker, Harley**.

**Barker, Howard** 1946– Dramatist. Born in Dulwich, he was educated at Battersea Grammar School and the University of Sussex, where he read history. His first plays, produced at the **Royal Court Theatre** and the Open Space, looked at British society from the stance of the underworld as well as the underdog – twin gangsters in *Alpha Alpha* (1972), pimps in *Claw* (1975) and the criminal who invades the house of the judge who condemned him in *Stripwell* (1975). Barker is adept at choosing telling dramatic situations in which many different incidents can take place, but he reverses what might be regarded as the moral expectations. The prison governor in *The Hang of the Gaol* (1978) becomes an arsonist, while the entrepreneur who capitalizes on graveyard mementoes in *The Love of a Good Man* is the hero of a black comedy set in 1920, after the carnage of the World War I. In *No End of Blame* (1980) he debates the issue of the different censorships, East and West.

**Barker, James Nelson** 1784–1858 American dramatist. Born in Philadelphia, Barker followed his father's example by becoming mayor of that city in 1819 after a distinguished military career. He later served as Comptroller of the United States Treasury. Only 5 of his 10 plays have survived. *Tears and Smiles* (1807), a comedy of manners, was first produced in Philadelphia. His operatic play, *The Indian Princess, or, La Belle Sauvage*, was produced in 1808; the first extant play to deal with American-Indian life, it was mounted in London in 1820 as *Pocahontas, or, The Indian Princess*. Barker's biggest success, *Marmion, or, The Battle of Flodden Field* (1812), was based on **Walter Scott**'s poem. Although he originally advertised the play under the pen name of Thomas Morton, Barker acknowledged his authorship after its implicit criticism of the British stance toward the United States during the war of 1812 was enthusiastically received by the public. His second romantic comedy, adapted from a French novel about medieval Spain, was published as *How to Try a Lover* in 1817, and produced as *The Court of Love* in 1836. *Superstition, or, The Fanatic Father* (1824), a tragedy in verse, is about a Puritan refugee who leads attacks against the Indians, and deals with religious intolerance and witch-hunting.

***Barlaam and Josaphat*** A **saint's life** written in

Middle English in the 14th century. When it is prophesied that Josaphat, son of a heathen king, will become a Christian his father keeps him in seclusion. He eventually releases him, however, and Josaphat is converted by a holy man, Barlaam. Josaphat converts his dying father, gives up his kingdom and ends his life as a hermit.

The origin of the story is Greek but this English version is translated from the *Legenda Aurea*, later translated again by **Caxton** as *The Golden Legend*. The text appears in the Vernon Golden Legend of *c.* 1385, which translates selected stories, and in one manuscript of each of **The South English Legendary** and *The Northern Verse Homily*.

**Barlow, Joel** 1754–1812 American poet, best remembered as one of the **Connecticut Wits**, though he eventually became politically estranged from the group. Born in Redding, Connecticut, he attended Dartmouth College and in 1774 transferred to Yale, where he met others of the Wits, with whose orthodox Calvinism and aristocratic politics he sympathized. After the Revolutionary War, in which he served as Chaplain for the Third Massachusetts Brigade, he founded *The American Mercury* with Elisha Backock, studied law, and was admitted to the Bar in 1786. Throughout this period he maintained contact with the Wits and contributed to their most notable production, *The Anarchiad*, a satire in mock-heroic verse which

Joel Barlow, the Connecticut poet. Detail from A. B. Durand's engraving of the painting by Robert Fulton.

attacked democratic liberalism in favour of federalist conservatism and was published between 1786 and 1787 in *The New Haven Gazette* and *The Connecticut Magazine*. In 1787 Barlow published *The Vision of Columbus*, an epic poem in which he envisions America's glorious future.

In 1788 he went to France, where he lived periodically for 17 years, an experience which changed his political perspective. Contact with prominent European liberals – **Horne Tooke**, **Mary Wollstonecraft**, **William Godwin** – and a re-evaluation of the writings of **Thomas Jefferson** and of his friend **Thomas Paine** transformed him into a champion of democracy, a change evident in three pamphlets in the 1790s: *Advice to the Privileged Orders*; *The Conspiracy of Kings*; and *A Letter to the National Convention of France*, for which he was awarded French citizenship. In 1796 he published his renowned *Hasty Pudding*, a mock epic in three cantos which celebrates a native American dish as well as 'simplicity of diet'. He returned to the USA in 1805 and in 1807 published **The Columbiad**, a revision of *The Vision of Columbus*. Accepting an appointment as US minister to France in 1811, he went back to Europe and died in Poland on his way to negotiate a treaty with Napoleon.

**Barnaby Rudge** A novel by **Charles Dickens**, first published serially in **Master Humphrey's Clock**, February–November 1841.

Set at the time of the 'No Popery' riots of 1780 provoked by Lord George Gordon, the narrative of *Barnaby Rudge* derives from the unsolved murder of Reuben Haredale, a crime committed 20 years before the start of the novel. Reuben's brother Geoffrey is a rough, fundamentally upright Roman Catholic gentleman hostile toward the hypocritical, unprincipled Mr (later Sir John) Chester whose honourable son, Edward, loves Geoffrey's niece, Emma. Although markedly at odds, the two older men conspire to frustrate this match. Approximately halfway through the novel the Gordon riots erupt and Geoffrey Haredale's house, The Warren, is razed to the ground by an anti-Catholic mob. Emma and her confidante, the beguiling Dolly Varden, daughter of the hale and hearty locksmith Gabriel Varden, are kidnapped. Ultimately both are rescued by Edward Chester and Joe Willet, Dolly's one-armed soldier-suitor. When the riots are quelled it is revealed that Mr Rudge, Reuben Haredale's former steward and a shadowy figure throughout the novel, had murdered his master. He is hanged and his son Barnaby, a poor half-crazed youth who has been unwittingly drawn into the anti-Papist camp, only narrowly escapes the gallows. Sir John Chester dies in a duel with Haredale.

A rich cast of characters includes the snivelling Miss Miggs (servant to the Vardens), Simon Tappertit ('captain of the "Prentice

Knights"'), John Willet (Joe's father and a stupid, obstinate old publican), Mrs Varden (the locksmith's tiresome wife), Gashford (the treacherous secretary to Lord George Gordon), Dennis (the despicable and cowardly hangman), Hugh (the intelligent but undisciplined, irresponsible apprentice) and John Grueby (loyal servant to Lord George).

**Barnes, Barnabe** ?1569–1609 Poet and dramatist. Barnabe was the son of Richard Barnes, Bishop of Durham. He had an eventful life, travelling with Essex to Normandy (1591) and being arraigned before the Star Chamber for poisoning (1598). His poetic works are his **sonnet** sequence *Parthenophil and Parthenope* (?1594), which exists in a unique copy, and *A Divine Century of Spiritual Sonnets* (1595). He wrote one prose work, *Four Books of Offices* (1606). One play, *The Battle of Hexham*, is lost but *The Devil's Charter* survives. An anti-Catholic portrayal of the magician and poisoner Pope Alexander VI, it was performed only once, before King James at Whitehall in 1607.

**Barnes, Djuna** 1892–1982 American novelist, playwright and poet. Born in Cornwall-on-Hudson, New York, Barnes began her career in New York City as a journalist and graphic artist, but spent much of her later life among the post-war Paris expatriates. In her early years in New York she was associated with the experimental Provincetown Players, who produced three of her one-act plays in 1919 and 1920. Her first publication was a collection of poems, *The Book of Repulsive Women* (1915). Her stories and short plays were collected in *A Book* (1923); the stories were revised and reissued subsequently as *A Night Among the Horses* (1929) and later still as *Spillway* (1972). In 1929 she published her first novel, *Ryder*, a satiric chronicle of family history; and *Ladies' Almanack*, a celebration of lesbian life and loves in the form of a quasi-medieval calendar or miscellany. Her best-known work is the novel *Nightwood* (1936), which concerns the relationships of a group of expatriates in Paris and Berlin. *The Antiphon* (1958) is a full-length revenge tragedy in blank verse, which again takes up issues of family history.

**Barnes, Julian** 1946– Novelist. Barnes began his literary career as one of the group of urbane, precociously witty young writers on **Ian Hamilton**'s *New Review*, for which he wrote the infamous 'Edward Pygge' gossip column. His first two novels, *Metroland* (1981) and *Before She Met Me* (1982), combine flamboyant wit and scatological comedy with a psychological sensitivity that recalls Flaubert, Barnes's acknowledged master. Flaubert is obliquely the subject of his third novel, *Flaubert's Parrot* (1984), which mixes biographical investigation, historical speculation and whimsical fantasy in a work of great originality. His latest book, *Staring at the Sun* (1986), is comparably heterogeneous, moving from the inter-war years to the near future and from social realism to satirical fantasy.

**Barnes, Juliana** See **Berners, Juliana**.

**Barnes, Peter** 1931– Dramatist. He was educated at Stroud Grammar School. His plays combine trenchant satire with a delight in shock effects. Although his first play, *Sclerosis*, an attack on British colonialism, was seen in Edinburgh and London in 1965, Barnes achieved success with his second play, *The Ruling Class* (1968), which contained many distinguishing features of his style – fierce parody of the English upper classes, rapid changes of mood and atmosphere from the farcical to the macabre, an unusual delight in rhetoric and several *coups de théâtre*. In subsequent plays, he has chosen major moral and historical themes as subjects for black comedy – the Spanish Succession in *The Bewitched* (1974), the holocaust in *Laughter!* (1978) and the *Black Death in Red Noses* (1985). Barnes consciously looks back to the Jacobeans and to the German dramatist Frank Wedekind for his technical style, despising naturalism. He has adapted plays by **Ben Jonson** (whom he admires more than **Shakespeare**) and Wedekind's *Lulu* plays (1971).

**Barnes, William** 1801–86 Dialect poet and philologist. Born into a family of farmers near Sturminster Newton in the Blackmoor Vale, Dorset, Barnes became a schoolteacher, was ordained in 1838 and graduated as a 'ten-year man' from St John's College, Cambridge, in 1850. From 1862 until his death he served as rector of Winterbourne Came, near Dorchester. His writings on philology – most notably *Tiw: or A View of the Roots and Stems of English as a Teutonic Tongue* (1861) – reject the importation of foreign words and advocate a return to the purity of Anglo-Saxon English. To Barnes, the speech of his native county was the truest survival of Anglo-Saxon, and so he turned to it in his three collections of *Poems in the Dorset Dialect* (1844, 1859, 1862). His command of folk idiom and lyric form gave his poetry more than a philological value, and helped attract a distinguished, if small, circle of admirers. His neighbour **Thomas Hardy** contributed an obituary to *The Athenaeum*, a poem about his funeral ('The Last Signal') and a selection of his poetry (1908).

**Barnfield, Richard** 1574–1627 Poet. Barnfield graduated from Brasenose College, Oxford, in 1592. He was the author of *The Affectionate Shepherd* (1594), a series of homoerotic eclogues telling of the love of Daphnis for Ganymede; *Cynthia*, published together with 20 sonnets in 1595; and a satire, *The Encomion of Lady Pecunia* (1598), in mock-praise of money. Two of Barnfield's poems appeared in **The Passionate Pilgrim** (1599). He was a friend of **Thomas Watson** and later of **Michael Drayton**, and is mentioned as a pastoral poet by **Francis Meres** in *Palladis Tamia*.

**Barrack-Room Ballads and Other Verses** A collection of poems by **Rudyard Kipling**, first published in 1892. Along with subsequent verse collections, *The Seven Seas* (1896), *The Five Nations* (1903) and *The Years Between* (1919), whose underlying preoccupation is with the life of the British soldier overseas, these are among the most popular of Kipling's large output of verse.

Recent criticism has begun to acknowledge the satirical force and originality of Kipling's depiction of the harsh life of the ill-paid common soldier. The patriotic concerns of a poem like 'The Widow at Windsor' are consciously undercut by the language of the proletarian soldier; his soliloquy, addressed in colloquial speech to a silent listener, characteristically shows the influence of **Browning**. Frequently, a comic cockney dialect is used to give one person's reaction to a situation. Kipling draws upon popular traditions of ballad and street-song in giving his speaker a representative rather than an individualized voice. Indeed, the music-hall songs are often felt (as in 'Mandalay') along with hymn tunes, behind his syllabic lines. The border ballads can also be discerned as an influence, more particularly in the poems written in Scottish dialect. More generally, it is the voice of the Irishman and the cockney which can be heard – the same that he represented in his stories of the same period, **Soldiers Three** (1893).

*The Complete Barrack-Room Ballads of Rudyard Kipling*, collected by Charles Carrington, was published in 1973.

**Barren Ground** A novel by **Ellen Glasgow**, published in 1925. It tells the story of Dorinda Oakley, a lower-middle-class country woman who goes to work in Nathan Pedlar's store, hoping the money she earns will restore her father's farm – the barren ground. She falls in love with Jason Greylock, but he is committed to another woman. Dorinda travels from her native rural Virginia to New York City, where, after a street accident, she supports herself by caring for her doctor's children. Another doctor proposes to her, but she refuses him. In her spare time she studies new techniques in agriculture. When her father dies, she returns to Virginia and single-handedly establishes a prosperous dairy farm. After her mother's death, she marries Nathan Pedlar, the man for whom she once worked and a widower with

children. After his death, Dorinda, out of kindness, shelters the degenerate Jason Greylock. But she no longer loves him, and in fact plans never to marry again, being thankful 'to have finished with all that'. The title takes on further significance when one considers that Dorinda, although she nurtures other people's children and restores fertility to her family's farm, has no offspring of her own.

**Barrett, Elizabeth** See **Browning, Elizabeth Barrett**.

**Barrie, Sir J[ames] M[atthew]** 1860–1937 Scottish playwright and novelist, ninth of the 10 children of a Scottish handloom weaver. His mother's early encouragement is commemorated in his biography of her, *Margaret Ogilvy* (1896), and Barrie's often-observed tendency to shrink from the realities of adult life may owe more to his relationship with her than to the painful failure of his marriage.

Barrie began to publish journalistic criticism while he was at Edinburgh University and worked as a journalist in Nottingham and London from 1883 to 1890. Sketches of Scottish life, published in various papers, brought him his first success when they were collected as *Auld Licht Idylls* (1888). Theatrical recognition came later. The farce *Walker, London*, produced as *The Houseboat* in 1892, was a vehicle for the popular comedian J. L. Toole. *The Little Minister* (1897), a dramatization of his own sentimental novel published six years earlier, was a more substantial success, and a profitable association with the American impresario Charles Frohman determined him to devote his talent to the theatre. Two of his best plays, **Quality Street** and **The Admirable Crichton**, were produced in London in 1902, to be followed two years later by the overwhelming triumph of **Peter Pan**. It is unfortunate that Barrie has become so identified with *Peter Pan*. He was too ready to resort to cloying fantasy, as he did again in *Dear Brutus* (1917) and *Mary Rose* (1920), but although his solutions were characteristically sentimental, the problems he investigated were real enough. There is a shrewd feeling for the theatre in **What Every Woman Knows** (1908), the single completed act of *Shall We Join the Ladies?* (1921) and the excellent one-act comedy *The Twelve-Pound Look* (1910). Barrie was knighted in 1913.

**Barrow, Isaac** 1630–77 Divine. The son of a linen merchant, Barrow entered Trinity College, Cambridge, in 1647, during the Civil War; despite his Royalist sympathies he became a fellow of the college in 1649, and was ordained in 1659. A notable scholar, he became Professor of Greek at Cambridge in 1660 and Professor of Geometry at Gresham College, London, in the same year, and was appointed the first Lucasian

Professor of Mathematics at Cambridge in 1663. He resigned the last post in 1669 to his pupil, **Sir Isaac Newton**, preferring to concentrate on theological studies. Charles II made him a royal chaplain, a DD by royal mandate (1670) and Master of Trinity (1673). His sermons were famous for their reasonable views in an age of pious recrimination. Apart from two works on geometry, *Exposition of the Creed, Decalogue and Sacraments* (1669) was published during his lifetime; theological works edited after his death include *A Treatise on the Pope's Supremacy* (1680). Barrow's prose style was praised by **Coleridge** in his *Anima Poetae*.

**Barry, Philip** 1896–1949 American playwright, born in Rochester, New York. He attended both Harvard and Yale, and his first play was produced at Yale in 1919. *You and I* (1923) was his first professional production. A number of his other plays – such as *Holiday* (1929), *Tomorrow and Tomorrow* (1931), and *The Animal Kingdom* (1932) – are comedies that puncture the snobbish pretensions of wealthy society. His other works include *Here Come the Clowns* (1938), *The Philadelphia Story* (1939), *Liberty Jones* (1941) and *The Foolish Notion* (1945). *Second Threshold*, another comedy, unfinished at his death, was completed in 1951 by **Robert Sherwood**.

*Barry Lyndon* A novel by **W. M. Thackeray**, serialized as *The Luck of Barry Lyndon* in *Fraser's Magazine* in 1844, subsequently revised and reprinted as *The Memoirs of Barry Lyndon* (2 vols., 1852).

Set in the 18th century, this is the autobiography of an Irish adventurer whose boastful accounts of his exploits serve only to reveal the extent of his villainy. Redmond Barry of Brady's Town fights a duel and escapes to Dublin, where he changes his name to Barry Redmond, lives a fast life and falls into debt. He enlists as a soldier and fights on both sides in the Seven Years War, eventually meeting up with his lost uncle, Cornelius Barry, who as the Chevalier de Balibari joins with Barry in a career of card-sharping. After various adventures abroad, he lays siege to, and by subterfuge succeeds in marrying, a wealthy widow, the Countess of Lyndon. He changes his name again to Barry Lyndon and embarks on a career of extravagance, ill-treating his wife, bullying his stepson, and wasting their fortune. With the death of his son Bryan in a riding accident, Barry's luck starts to run out. The family regains control of the estate, and Barry is forced to live abroad on a pension. With the death of Lady Lyndon he becomes penniless, and ends his life in the Fleet prison, tended by his faithful old mother.

The novel is a notable contribution to rogue literature, after the manner of *Jonathan Wild* by Thackeray's admired master, **Fielding**, and is interesting as a sustained exercise in the use of the unreliable narrator.

**Barsetshire Novels, The** A sequence of novels by **Anthony Trollope**, consisting of *The Warden* (1855), *Barchester Towers* (1857), *Doctor Thorne* (1858), *Framley Parsonage* (1860–1), *The Small House at Allington* (1862–4) and *The Last Chronicle of Barset* (1866–7).

**Barstow, Stan[ley]** 1928– Novelist. Born into a Yorkshire mining family and educated in Ossett, Barstow has produced many novels about Yorkshire life, but remains best known for his first book, *A Kind of Loving* (1960), which is a later example of the provincial working-class realist fiction developed by **John Braine** and **Alan Sillitoe** in the late 1950s. Barstow's novel follows the fortunes of office-worker Vic Brown, who is forced to marry his pregnant girlfriend, and also traces the changes in popular culture as the influence of television and pop music, immigration and new money, begin to reach Brown's conservative, conventional Northern town. Barstow's most recent novel is *Just You Wait and See* (1986).

**Barth, John (Simmons)** 1930– American novelist, born in Cambridge, Maryland, and educated at the Johns Hopkins University, where he now teaches. After publishing short stories in various periodicals, he attracted considerable critical attention with a novel, *The Floating Opera* (1956). This book, about a nihilist who, contemplating suicide, decides not to kill himself after all, is informed by a sense of the absurd that has coloured all Barth's work. His other novels are *The End of the Road* (1958), *The Sot-Weed Factor* (1960), *Giles Goat-Boy, or, The Revised New Syllabus* (1966), *Chimera* (1972), which won the National Book Award, *Letters* (1979) and *Sabbatical* (1982). *Lost in The Funhouse* (1968) is a volume of short stories. *The Friday Book*, a collection of non-fiction pieces, was published in 1984.

**Barthelme, Donald** 1931–89 An American short-story writer and novelist, Barthelme was born in Philadelphia and grew up in Texas. His first book, *Come Back, Dr Caligari*, a collection of stories, appeared in 1964. *Snow White* (1967), a novel set in Greenwich Village, is a contemporary reworking of the popular fairy-tale. The fragmented narrative is made up of word games and random allusions to both literature and popular culture, taking the disintegration of language as a central metaphor for the breakdown of personal relationships. His later collections of stories – *Unspeakable Practices, Unnatural Acts* (1968), *City Life* (1970), *Guilty Pleasures*

(1974) and *Amateurs* (1976) – continue his satiric commentary on contemporary American life and language. His second novel, *The Dead Father* (1975), is a humorous story about paternity and the fragmentation of the self. His other publications include *Great Days* (1979), *Sixty Stories* (1981), *Over Night To Many Distant Cities* (1983) and *Paradise* (1986).

**Barthes, Roland** See **post-structuralism**, **semiotics** and **structuralism**.

*Bartholomew Fair* A comedy by **Ben Jonson**, performed in 1614 but not published until 1631. The fair of the title was held annually at Smithfield on St Bartholomew's Day, 24 August. Jonson takes it as the setting for one of his most adventurous and original plays. The play contains a number of stories, but spreads them so loosely that it seems scarcely dependent upon plot at all. Jonson gives us a gallery of vivid characters. Adam Overdo, a justice, comes to the fair to spy out its iniquities and is engulfed by them. The country squire, Bartholomew Cokes, brings his lively betrothed, Grace Wellborn, but, simpleton that he is, is easily outwitted by her rival suitors, Winwife and Quarlus, and robbed of everything including his future wife. His servant Waspe has a biting tongue, but in the topsy-turvy world of the fair the biter is bitten, and Waspe ends up in the stocks, as does

The frontispiece for an 18th-century edition of Ben Jonson's *Bartholomew Fair*.

the hypocritical Puritan Zeal-of-the-Land Busy, his mind more fixed on food than on fastidious faith. Like all the other characters, but more greedily, Busy is drawn to the stall of the foul-mouthed pig-woman, Ursula, whose roast pork and small beer attract the crowds. Almost as if beguiled by the earthy liveliness of the fair, Jonson in this play is more intent on observing than correcting the behaviour of his contemporaries.

*Bartleby the Scrivener* See *Piazza Tales, The*.

**Barton, Bernard** 1784–1849 Poet. Born in Carlisle and educated at a Quaker school in Ipswich, Barton worked for most of his life as a bank clerk in Woodbridge, Suffolk. Although collections such as *Metrical Effusions* (1812), *Poems* (1820) and *Devotional Verses* (1826) secured him a steady following as a writer of homely and unaffected religious verse, he is now hardly read and is chiefly remembered for his friendship and correspondence with **Southey** and **Charles Lamb**, who was intrigued by his staunch Quakerism and whose advice, 'Keep to your bank, and the bank will keep you,' was undoubtedly sound. **Edward FitzGerald** wrote Barton's biography (1849) and, at the elder poet's earnest wish, made an unhappy marriage with Barton's daughter.

**Bartram, John** (1699–1777) and **Bartram, William** (1729–1823) American naturalists and travellers. A Philadelphia Quaker, John Bartram went on various expeditions in his official capacity as botanist for the American colonies, keeping records in his journals and publishing *Observations on the Inhabitants, Climate, Soil . . . Made by John Bartram in his Travels from Pensilvania to Lake Ontario* (1751). On his later trips he was accompanied by his son William, who made ornithological and anthropological as well as botanical contributions, and painted some of the flora and fauna he observed. William is most remembered, though, for his descriptions of the American landscape and imaginative, romantic reflections on the wilderness and natural man in his *Travels through North and South Carolina, Georgia, East and West Florida, the Cherokee Country, the Extensive Territories of the Muscogulges, or Creek Confederacy, and the Country of the Chactaws* (1791).

**Bates, H[erbert] E[rnest]** 1906–74 Novelist and short-story writer. Born in Northamptonshire, Bates published his first novel, *The Two Sisters*, in 1926. His many popular novels and collections of short stories include several with rural themes, such as *The Poacher* (1931), and a substantial body of fiction derived from his wartime service as an RAF Squadron Leader. Such collections of short stories as *The Greatest*

*People in the World* (1942) and *How Sleep the Brave* (1943) were originally published under the pseudonym of 'Flying Officer X'. His most famous novel (which, like many of his books, was made into a successful television drama), *Fair Stood the Wind for France* (1944), is about the fortunes of a British bomber crew shot down in occupied France. A striking short novel, *The Jacaranda Tree* (1949), derives from Bates's later war experience in the Burma campaign. Later novels include *The Darling Buds of May* (1958) and *Oh, To Be in England* (1963).

**Bateson, F[rederick] (Noel) W[ilse]** 1901–78 Critic. Born in Styal, Cheshire, and educated at Charterhouse and at Trinity College, Oxford, Bateson undertook during the 1930s the huge task of editing *The Cambridge Bibliography of English Literature* (1940). He spent the war as an agricultural administrator, also writing articles on agricultural policy. In 1946 he took up a fellowship at Corpus Christi College, Oxford, which he held until his death in 1978. In 1951 he founded the periodical **Essays in Criticism**, which assumed the leading position in academic criticism soon vacated by the demise of **Scrutiny** (in which Bateson had debated the principles of literary criticism with **F. R. Leavis**). As the title of his book *The Scholar-Critic* (1972) suggests, Bateson aimed to inform literary-critical judgements with higher standards of historical and linguistic scholarship. His other major works, *English Poetry and the English Language* (1934), *English Poetry: A Critical Introduction* (1950) and *Essays in Critical Dissent* (1972), all stress the importance of the context, historical and linguistic, in which literary works were written.

**bathos** An unwitting drop from elevation into triteness or triviality, or pathos so overdone that it tumbles into the ludicrous. Many enjoyable excruciating examples are to be found in *The Stuffed Owl* (1930), an anthology of bad verse, edited by D. B. Wyndham Lewis and C. Lee.

**Battle Hymn of the Republic, The** An American patriotic song, written by **Julia Ward Howe** in 1861, after visiting a Union army camp near Washington. The melody was provided by *John Brown's Body*, a song popular with the soldiers. The hymn was given its title by James T. Fields, who published it in *The Atlantic Monthly* in 1862.

**Battle of Brunanburh, The** An Old English poem of 73 lines giving an account of a battle which took place in 937 between an army of Norsemen and Scots and another of West Saxons and Mercians. The location of Brunanburh is unknown, but it was apparently near the sea. The poem relates the course of events, employing some conventional motifs and rhetoric but

without singling out specific individuals or feats. It is a vivid account, perhaps by an eyewitness of the battle. **Tennyson** wrote a version of *The Battle of Brunanburh* in modern verse.

**Battle of Life, The** A Christmas story by **Charles Dickens**, published in 1846 and collected in *Christmas Books* (1852).

The story follows the fortunes of Dr Anthony Jeddler, who regards the world as 'a gigantic practical joke', and his two daughters Grace and Marion. Into the girls' lives come the honest young medical student Alfred Heathfield and Michael Warden, a wastrel who later reforms. The narrative depicts the two interrelated love-affairs, the absences and returns of the suitors, the hazards of developing love, the nobility of sacrifice and, in Dr Jeddler's case, a modification of his reading of life. Lesser figures – the lawyer Snitchey, the sour servant Benjamin Britain (known as 'Little Britain') and the worthy servant Clemency Newcombe – round off a brisk, expressive tale.

**Battle of Maldon, The** A fragment of a poem in Old English, probably composed at the end of the 10th century; the manuscript was lost in a fire in 1731, but a transcript had been made. The beginning and end of the poem are lost; the surviving section occupies 325 lines. The battle, which took place in 991, is also described in the **Anglo-Saxon Chronicle**.

The poem tells how the Vikings landed near Maldon in Essex and demanded tribute; this was contemptuously rejected by the Saxon leader Byrhtnoth. The ensuing battle was delayed by the tide, but the over-confident Byrhtnoth allowed the Danes to cross the causeway before joining battle. He was killed and the Saxons fled, led by Godric. Aelfwin drew them together again to rejoin the fight but the Saxon leaders continued to fall. The fragment breaks off at this point.

Despite its late date, the work is heroic and archaic in character. Its presentation of values and the type of the warrior recalls **Beowulf** and the Germanic epics, though here the traditional values are seen to be in decline. In contrast to *The Battle of Brunanburh*, the poem relates the actions of individuals and presents a short series of speeches of explanation, encouragement and boasting.

**Battle of the Books, The** A prose satire by **Jonathan Swift**, written in 1697 and published in 1704. It remains the classic, humorous treatment of the debate between Ancients and Moderns, then treated as a serious cultural issue. His patron, **Sir William Temple**, had published in 1690 his *Essay upon the Ancient and Modern Learning* in which the majority of contemporary writers and philosophers were unfavourably and condescendingly compared with their ancient classical counterparts. Temple's stance was utterly opposed to the New Learning and all it represented, the attitude initiated by **Francis Bacon**'s challenging of the Aristotelian system and subsequently developed by Descartes, and the work of the Royal Society. In extolling the virtues of the ancient authors, Temple unfortunately singled out the epistles of Phalaris, which were later proved to be spurious; **Richard Bentley** and William Wotton, leading scholars of the 'modern' camp, launched an attack upon him, and Swift replied in kind on his patron's behalf.

This mock-heroic drama is set in the Royal Library, where the books championing the ancient and modern causes are preparing to fight over which party should rightfully occupy the higher peak of Parnassus. A dispute meanwhile arises between a resident spider and a bee entangled in his web, and the matter is summarized by the intervention of Aesop who identifies the spider with the Moderns (who spin out empty pedantry) while the bee, going directly to Nature, like the Ancients, succeeds in producing honey and wax, which are 'sweetness and light'. The verdict goads the Moderns into attack, and battle commences. Under the protection of Pallas, Homer leads the Ancients against the Moderns (patronized by the Goddess 'Criticism') under the leadership of **Milton**. Individual duels are nicely matched, as when Virgil takes on his translator **Dryden** (whose helmet is nine times too large for him) and Aristotle shoots Descartes while aiming at Bacon. It ends in mid-battle, supposedly because of a defective manuscript.

Though similarly sceptical about ideas of progress, Swift's spirited defence of Temple's position was largely dictated by personal loyalty, and the *Battle* is closely modelled on the latter's *Essay*. The Preface opens with Swift's memorable contention that, 'Satire is a sort of glass, wherein beholders do generally discover everybody's face but their own.'

***Battle-Pieces And Aspects of the War*** A book of poems by **Herman Melville**, published in 1866. The 72 poems commemorate the tragedy of the American Civil War and its impact on the nation. The sense of Northern victory and celebration is muted; many poems dwell upon the tragic loss of young men cut down in battle. Among the more notable pieces are 'The Portent', on the hanging of John Brown; 'Misgivings', on slavery; and 'Shiloh: A Requiem'. The volume also contains a prose appendix appealing to Northern readers for a humane rather than vengeful attitude toward the South during Reconstruction.

**Baughan, Blanche** 1870–1958 New Zealand poet. Born in Putney, London, she was educated at Brighton High School and Royal Holloway College, University of London. She emigrated to New Zealand in 1900 and her best work belongs to the first decade of her life there. After an illness in 1910 she felt that her gift for poetry had deserted her. In subsequent years she mainly devoted herself to social work and became an important figure in the movement for prison reform. She also wrote numerous works on New Zealand rural life and topography, of which *Brown Bread from a Colonial Oven* (1912) is the best known. Her finest poetry is contained in the volumes *Reuben and Other Poems* (1903) and *Shingle-Short and Other Verses* (1908). The latter contains many dramatic monologues written in a colloquial style and penetrating studies of society's pariahs and misfits. Its success in rendering aspects of the New Zealand experience represents a remarkable achievement for a comparatively recent immigrant.

**Baum, L[yman] Frank** 1856–1919 American children's writer. Born in New York, the son of a wealthy businessman, Baum worked as a journalist and playwright before setting off across America doing a variety of jobs including selling crockery and general shop-keeping. His first children's book, *Mother Goose in Prose* (1897), was based on stories told to his own children. Its last chapter introduced Dorothy, the farm-girl who reappeared in *The Wonderful Wizard of Oz* (1900). This was immediately successful, leading to 14 more titles in the same vein. In 1902 Baum wrote the lyrics for a musical based on his famous book, and later three different film versions followed, the last starring Judy Garland in 1939. After Baum's death 26 more adventures of Oz appeared written by diverse authors including Baum's own son. The series finished in 1951 having sold over seven million copies. Never particularly well written, Baum's stories succeeded through their racy good humour and their straightforward moral framework in which virtue and loyalty are always finally rewarded.

**Bawden, Nina** 1925– Novelist for adults and children. Born in London, she completed her education at Oxford. Her novels for adults provide a consistently incisive analysis of life among the upper middle classes, concentrating on the way that emotional disturbances can threaten or destroy an otherwise comfortable existence. *The Birds in the Trees* (1969) describes how a tormented adolescent puts intolerable pressure on himself and his family, while *Anna Apparent* (1972) explores the way illegitimacy and subsequent adoption can present lifelong problems – a point also taken up in *Familiar Passions* (1979). Her most recent novel for adults is *Circles of Deceit* (1987). The principal characteristic of her novels for children is a good-humoured understanding of the child's point of view. Adventure stories such as *The Witch's Daughter* (1966) that start with obvious heroes and villains soon introduce greater complexity. Her most successful novel, *Carrie's War* (1973), drew on autobiographical memories of wartime evacuation to Wales. Mr Evans, the penny-pinching grocer with whom the book's young characters are billeted, comes to appear a rather sad person, finally inspiring sympathy rather than active dislike.

**Baxter, James K[eir]** 1926–72 New Zealand poet, dramatist and critic. Born in Dunedin, he was educated in Quaker schools in New Zealand and England and at Otago University, Dunedin, and Victoria University, Wellington, where he obtained his BA in 1952. He worked as a labourer, journalist and teacher and edited the Wellington magazine *Numbers* from 1954 to 1960. Much of his career represented a crusade against what he saw as his country's lack of spirituality. Early bohemianism and Christian concern found a focus when he was converted to Roman Catholicism in 1958. He subsequently founded a religious commune on the Wanganui River and was active in various social-welfare schemes, including projects to house the homeless in Wellington and Auckland. One of New Zealand's finest poets, Baxter achieved early recognition with the appearance of his volume of verse, *Beyond the Palisade* (1944), when he was just 18. This was the first of more than 30 books of poetry which he published before his death at the age of 46. His early verse is notable for its lyrical rendition of the New Zealand rural world and the effect of this landscape on its inhabitants. It was followed by a period in which Baxter concentrated on narrative verse and ballads and other poems about local figures like the mill girl, the hotel licensee and the hermit. The poetry he wrote before his conversion is collected in *In Fires of No Return* (1958). After 1958 he went through what by his own standards was a comparatively unproductive period, but his career was reinvigorated when he took up a Burns Fellowship at the University of Otago in 1966. *Pig Island Letters* (1966) and *Jerusalem Sonnets* (1970) are outstanding works from his later period. In the latter volume he evolved a fluid sonnet form to express his highly personal sense of religious conviction. *Howrah Bridge* (1961) and *Autumn Testament* (1972) are among his other notable volumes of verse. Baxter began to write plays in the late 1950s, but it was during his time at the University of Otago, when seven of his plays were performed in Dunedin, that his talent as a dramatist first received recognition. These plays included *The Band Rotunda* (1967), *The Sore-Footed Man*

(1967), *The Devil and Mr Mulcahy* (1967) and *The Temptations of Oedipus* (1970). His criticism includes *Recent Trends in New Zealand Poetry* (1951) and *Aspects of Poetry in New Zealand* (1967).

**Baxter, Richard** 1615–91 Presbyterian divine. A military chaplain during the Civil War, Baxter disliked the growth of sectarianism in the Commonwealth and contributed to the change of feeling that led to the Restoration. He accepted the position of royal chaplain, but refused a bishopric and suffered persecution under James II for his uncompromising conscience. He was sentenced to imprisonment in 1685 and vilified by Judge Jeffreys for libelling the established church. A prolific writer of devotional literature, Baxter is best known for *The Saint's Everlasting Rest* (1651), *A Call to the Unconverted* (1658) and his moving, intimate tribute to his beloved wife who died in 1681, *A Breviate of the Life of Margaret Baxter* (1681). His own account of his turbulent life, *Reliquiae Baxterianae*, was published in 1696.

***Bay Psalm Book, The***: or, *The Whole Book of Psalmes Faithfully Translated into English Meter* The authoritative hymnal of the Massachusetts Bay Colony and the first book published in America (Cambridge, Massachusetts, 1640). The translation, by **Richard Mather**, **John Eliot** and Thomas Weld, replaced the Sternhold and Hopkins version, which the Bay Puritans rejected because it sacrificed the literal rendering of the Hebrew text to poetic effect. *The Bay Psalm Book*'s motto, 'God's Altar needs not our Polishings', makes clear the Puritan translators' insistence on a direct confrontation with the Word of God, unmediated by added ornaments. Following a second printing in 1647, it was revised by Henry Dunster (the president of Harvard) and Richard Lyon, and reprinted in 1651 with the title *The Psalms, Hymns and Scriptural Songs of the Old and New Testament*, an edition which was reissued several times over a period of almost a century.

**Bayly, (Nathaniel) Thomas Haynes** 1797–1839 Poet, dramatist and novelist. Born at Bath and educated at Winchester and St Mary Hall, Oxford, Bayly was celebrated in his time as the author of sentimental songs and ballads, most notably 'I'd be a butterfly', 'She wore a wreath of roses', and 'Oh no, we never mention her'. Among his 36 plays the farce *Perfection, or, the Lady of Munster* enjoyed considerable commercial success. His novels include *The Aylmers* (1827). A collected edition of his *Songs, Ballads and Other Poems* was published in 1844.

**Baynton, Barbara** 1857–1929 Australian short-story writer. Born in Scone, New South

Wales, the daughter of a staunch Presbyterian mother, she was brought up in the Hunter River area. She married a selector who, after they had had three children, later left her. She moved to Sydney and married again, this time to a retired surgeon, Thomas Baynton, in 1890. In the decade that followed, she first began to write fiction and her stories appeared in the *Bulletin*, along with the work of such important shapers of the Australian myth of the bush as **Henry Lawson** and **A. B. Paterson**. In the first years of the 20th century she visited London where her volume of short stories, *Bush Studies*, the work on which her reputation rests, was published in 1902. After the death of her husband in 1904, she moved between London and Australia and in 1921 entered into a third, short-lived marriage to Lord Headley. Baynton's picture of the bush, while not without humour, presents it as a harsh, inimical environment. It represents a contrast to the robust nationalism of Paterson and even to the equivocal treatment of the bush which characterizes many of Lawson's short stories. In classic stories such as 'Squeaker's Mate' and 'The Chosen Vessel' she vividly dramatizes the plight of bush women, frequently regarding them as victims of both malevolent nature and male brutality. Baynton also published a novel, *Human Toll* (1907). Despite the slender nature of her output, she occupies an important place in Australian literature as an early critic of the romantic view of the bush.

***Be Domes Daege (Of Doomsday)*** An Old English poem of 300 lines based on the Latin *De Die Judicii* attributed formerly to both **Alcuin** and **Bede**; the translation is eloquent and capable. The poem exhorts men to confess, urging them to contemplate doomsday, the torments of hell and the bliss of Heaven, and to shun luxury and tolerate hardship in expectation of salvation.

**Beardsley, Aubrey (Vincent)** 1872–98 Illustrator and writer. In a career that began virtually in childhood but was cut short by his early death from tuberculosis, Beardsley created a visual style for the 1890s with his sensuous black-and-white drawings. He illustrated **Wilde**'s *Salome* and became art editor of *The Yellow Book* in 1894, but lost the job when Wilde's public disgrace began the following year. He also illustrated **Pope**'s *The Rape of the Lock* (1896) and **Jonson**'s *Volpone* (1898). A censored version of Beardsley's erotic novel *The Story of Venus and Tannhauser* originally appeared in *The Yellow Book* as *Under the Hill*; it was privately printed without expurgation in 1907.

**Beats, The** A group of writers centred in San Francisco and New York City in the latter half of the 1950s. The term 'beat' was first used by

**John Clellon Holmes** in his 1952 novel, *Go*, the first literary description of the people of the Beat movement and their milieu. The name 'beat' has been variously interpreted as meaning 'beaten down' and 'beatific'; members of the group shared an antagonism toward middle-class values, commercialism and conformity, as well as an enthusiasm for the visionary states produced by religious meditation, sexual experience, jazz, or drugs. The poet **Allen Ginsberg** and the novelist **Jack Kerouac** were perhaps the most prominent spokesmen for the movement, which also included **William S. Burroughs**, **Gregory Corso**, **Gary Snyder**, and **Lawrence Ferlinghetti**, whose City Lights Bookstore, founded in San Francisco in 1953, was a gathering-place for Beat writers.

**Beattie, James** 1735–1803 Philosopher and poet. Born a farmer's son in Kincardineshire, he rose steadily in the academic world to become Professor of Moral Philosophy at Marischal College, Aberdeen, in 1760. His *Essay on the Nature and Immutability of Truth* (1770) was a celebrated attack on the philosophy of **David Hume**. In 1771 Beattie published the first book of *The Minstrel*, a poem in **Spenserian stanzas** on the development of an imaginary poet in past times. The second book appeared in 1774 and Beattie became an honoured poet in his lifetime, praised by **Samuel Johnson**. Like the rest of his verse, *The Minstrel* is largely forgotten, though it shows what one critic has called 'a thin-coloured talent for nature-painting'.

***Beauchamp's Career*** **George Meredith**'s novel published serially in *The Fortnightly Review* (August 1874–December 1875) and in volume form in 1876. Nevil Beauchamp's career is traced from an early commission in the navy through his attempt to stand for Parliament after the Crimean War. Nevil is also torn between two loves, for a married Frenchwoman, Renée de Croisnel, and for Cecilia Halkett. He resists the temptation to join Renée in her flight from her husband, but loses Cecilia to a cousin. After recovering from a severe illness, during which he manages to reconcile his aristocratic uncle to his Radical friend Dr Shrapnel, Nevil marries Shrapnel's ward but is drowned while attempting to rescue a child from the sea. The novel offers a powerful picture of the workings of contemporary political life.

**Beaumont, Francis** 1584–1616 Playwright. Beaumont was born into the rural gentry of Elizabethan England, left Oxford without a degree in 1598 and entered the Inner Temple to study law in 1600. He probably studied very little, and there is no evidence that he ever practised law. His fashionable interest in suberotic Ovidian verse was expressed in *Salmacis and Hermaphroditus* (published in 1602). His first play, a prose comedy called *The Woman Hater* (1605) written for the boys of St Paul's, may reflect the onslaught of a need for money on a writer who would have preferred to be a poet. It is a servile imitation of the work of **Ben Jonson**, in whose company Beaumont was often seen. *The Knight of the Burning Pestle* (1607), the other piece of which Beaumont is now believed to have been sole author, is altogether finer. It is a witty outcome of avid theatre-going in which the dramatic taste of unsophisticated audiences is mocked without much malice.

Beaumont's collaboration with **John Fletcher** marks a separate and substantial stage in his dramatic career. They seem to have replaced **Shakespeare** in about 1609 as chief dramatists of the **King's Men**, for whom they probably wrote *Philaster* (*c.* 1609), *The Maid's Tragedy* (*c.* 1610) and *A King and No King* (1611). The collaborators were sufficiently sensitive to the shifts in public taste to become leaders of it. Their plays exploited the scenic scope of the indoor theatre at the **Blackfriars**, sacrificing Shakespearean profundity to the less durable appeal of the decorated stage, ambiguity to intrigue and the complexity of metaphor to the easy flow of language. Their influence carried over into post-Restoration drama. It is dangerously easy to detect in their plays the transition from Elizabethan popular drama to the élitist drama of Jacobean and Caroline England. By any but the highest standards, the collaborative work of Beaumont and Fletcher is impressive.

The popularity of the Beaumont and Fletcher plays tempted contemporary publicists and publishers to ascribe to the partnership more work than belonged to it. Beaumont probably abandoned the theatre soon after his marriage to an heiress in 1613, while Fletcher continued to write, either singly or with other collaborators, for over 10 years. Of the 50 or more 'Beaumont and Fletcher plays', only seven or eight can be confidently attributed, in any significant part, to Beaumont. These include *Cupid's Revenge* (*c.* 1611), *The Coxcomb* (1612), *The Scornful Lady* (*c.* 1613) and *The Captain* (1613), in addition to the three finer works already mentioned. Despite this, a folio containing 34 plays and a masque was published under the joint names of Beaumont and Fletcher in 1647 and *Fifty Comedies and Tragedies*, again ascribed to Beaumont and Fletcher and containing eighteen additional pieces, was published in 1679. Through such a casual approach to authorship, Beaumont's reputation was increased and, in particular, that of **Massinger** diminished.

***Beaux' Stratagem, The*** A comedy by **George Farquhar**, first performed at **Drury Lane** in 1707, two months before its author's death.

The frontispiece of a 19th-century edition of Farquhar's *The Beaux' Stratagem*. The second scene of Act V: the servant, Scrub, raises the alarm and interrupts Archer and Mrs Sullen at their dalliance. Victoria & Albert Theatre Museum, London.

Durable and good-humoured, the play is often revived in the modern theatre.

Two improvident friends, Archer and Aimwell, arrive at an inn in Lichfield in quest of a change of fortune. They decide that Aimwell shall pose as his titled brother and Archer as 'Lord' Aimwell's servant. The pretence does not fend off speculation as to who they are, and they are taken for Jesuits and, by the landlord, for highwaymen. Dorinda, daughter of the local Lady Bountiful, falls in love with Aimwell when she sees him in church, and the wife of her oafish brother Sullen is attracted to Archer. When Lady Bountiful's house is attacked by highwaymen, Archer and Aimwell rescue the ladies. Struck by love and remorse, Aimwell confesses the deception to Dorinda, whose love survives the revelation. However, it requires the arrival of a **deus ex machina** in the person of Mrs Sullen's brother, Sir Charles Freeman, to resolve the difficulties. Not only does he bring news that Aimwell's brother is dead and Aimwell's title therefore real, but he also persuades the drunken Sullen to consent to the dissolution of his marriage, thus leaving the way clear for Archer to ask for Mrs Sullen's hand.

**Beaver, Bruce** 1928– Australian poet. Born and educated in Sydney, he worked at various occupations as a young man, before going to New Zealand in 1958. After his return to Australia four years later, he published three volumes of verse before achieving major recognition with *Letters to Live Poets* (1969). He has worked as a freelance journalist. Beaver's rough-hewn early verse is essentially personal and documents a struggle to reconcile the conflicting pressures of modern urban life in a morally responsible vision. *Letters to Live Poets* extended his range to a broader consideration of the conflicts involved in artistic perception itself.

*Lauds and Plaints* (1974) shows an indebtedness to modern American poets, particularly **William Carlos Williams**, and is characterized by its formal innovation. Beaver has been an important influence on the younger generation of Australian poets. His other books include *Under the Bridge* (1961), *Seawall and Shoreline* (1964), *Odes and Days* (1975) and the novel *You Can't Come Back* (1966).

**Beckett, Samuel (Barclay)** 1906–89 Irish-born playwright and novelist, one of the most individual voices of the post-war European theatre. Beckett was born and educated in Dublin. After graduating from Trinity College in 1927 he spent most of his life in Paris, usually writing in French and translating his own work into English. As a young man, he was an associate and assistant of **James Joyce**, with whom he shared a relentless urge to test and extend the scope of words. His first published works were a volume of verse, *Whoroscope* (1930), and a critical study of Proust (1931). *More Pricks than Kicks* (1934) was a volume of short stories, and Beckett's first novel, *Murphy* (1938), made little impact on its first publication. It is almost entirely on his work after 1950 that his fame rests. It earned him the Nobel Prize for Literature in 1969.

Beckett's major novels, the French 'trilogy' *Molloy* (1951), *Malone Meurt* (1951) and *L'Innommable* (1953) – translated into English in, respectively, 1955, 1956 and 1958 – and the English *Watt* (1953), exist in and through their narrators, social misfits, old and ill, embarked on a quest for the explanation of 'I'. Although distinct from the plays, they are not cut off from them. *The Unnameable*, for example, searches for an escape from writing in the spoken word, and the difficult *Comment C'Est* (*How It Is*, 1961) is insistently aural. The short prose fictions that followed *How It Is* replace the puzzled subjectivity of the novels with a bleak objectivity.

Beckett is probably more widely known for his plays, above all for **Waiting for Godot** (first produced in French in 1953 and in English in 1955), than for his novels. They introduced to the post-war theatre a philosophical dimension that bemused and intrigued audiences. Martin Esslin saw Beckett as a leading exponent of the **Theatre of the Absurd**, arguing that his depiction of characters struggling doggedly with beginnings and, especially, with endings, represented a perception of meaninglessness and incoherence. The three full-length plays, *Waiting for Godot*, *Endgame* (first produced in French in 1957 and in English in 1958) and **Happy Days** (1961), if not exactly a trilogy, are all concerned with human suffering, survival – and immobility. The shorter, but still substantial, *Krapp's Last Tape* (1958) and *Play* (1963) seek to identify

moments in the characters' past when something actually happened, as does the uncharacteristically rich radio play *All That Fall* (1957). All of Beckett's stage plays replace conventional decor with stark images. In the fragmentary *Breath* (1970) the image is all we have. The mysterious *Come and Go* (1966), which Beckett calls a 'dramaticule', shows three women behaving according to a regular pattern but not allowing the audience to hear the whispers that might (or might not) motivate their behaviour. In *Not I* (1972) and *Footfalls* (1976), it is the detailed direction of stage lighting that dictates what the audience sees (a mouth and feet respectively) as the spoken words reverberate.

**Beckford, William** 1759–1844 Connoisseur and man of letters. Beckford was born at Fonthill, Wiltshire, the son of an immensely wealthy alderman from whom he inherited a vast fortune. A compulsive builder and collector, he reconstructed his Wiltshire mansion as an elaborate Gothic fantasy, Fonthill Abbey – substantially completed in 1809 but abandoned after the fall of its immense tower in 1825. His travel book *Dreams, Waking Thoughts and Incidents* (1783) was reissued in amended form as the first volume of *Italy, with Sketches of Spain and Portugal* (1834). Beckford's fantastic story **Vathek: An Arabian Tale** was written in French and published in 1787 (an English translation by Samuel Henley appeared in 1786). The two pseudonymous burlesques *Modern Novel Writing, or, the Elegant Enthusiast* (1796) and *Azemia* (1797) were followed by another travel book *Recollections of an Excursion to the Monasteries of Alcobaça and Batalha*, published in 1835.

**Beddoes, Thomas Lovell** 1803–49 Poet. A nephew of the novelist **Maria Edgeworth**, Beddoes was born at Clifton near Bristol and educated at Charterhouse and Pembroke College, Oxford. He studied medicine in several European cities and practised in Zurich but because of revolutionary ideas was denied a university post there. As early as 1821 he published *The Improvisatore* (later suppressed) and, in 1822, *The Bride's Tragedy* which enjoyed a modest success. His most famous work is **Death's Jest-Book** (posthumously published in 1850), a revenge tragedy in the Jacobean manner and demonstrative of his talent for blank verse. Beddoes also wrote several dramatic fragments. As an admirer of **Shelley**, although no slavish imitator, Beddoes shows lyric gifts in the memorable 'Dream-Pedlary' and a few shorter poems. He also produced a handful of macabre lyrics touched by grotesque humour. An anomalous, solitary figure of unique, even bizarre, qualities, Beddoes seemed incapable of carrying through his literary plans and designs. He died by his own hand.

**Bede (or Baeda)** *c.* 673–735 Historian. The Venerable Bede, probably born at Monkton, Durham, went at the age of seven to the monastery at Wearmouth and in 682 to the monastery at Jarrow. He remained there until his death, leaving the area only infrequently for short visits. He became a deacon at 19 and a priest at 30. Bede's interests were wide-ranging, although his predominant concerns were theological. His writings, in Latin, fall mainly into three groups: (1) grammatical and scientific; (2) exegetical; (3) hagiographic and historical. His earliest work was perhaps *De Orthographia*, on spelling, but his most famous was a history of the conversion of the British, *Historia Ecclesiastica Gentis Anglorum*, which remains an important record of the early history of Britain. The work traces the development of Christianity in Britain from the barbarous, disparate Christian and heathen groups left in Britain after the withdrawal of the Roman Empire through the conversion of the British, the unification and consolidation of their Christian faith under the influence of such figures as Sts Patrick, David, Augustine, Ninian, Aidan and Columba. With Christianity came the enriching civilization and culture of Rome, and the decay of Celtic tribalism. During the period covered by Bede church administration changed from the strictly spiritual and hierarchical monastic structure of the Celtic saints to the cohesive and stable administrative diocesan form of the Roman church, which fused spiritual and temporal power in one body. The work was finished in 731, and Bede died in 735. As a historian, Bede was thorough, collating evidence and accounts and verifying his facts wherever possible. He treats his material sympathetically and produces a lively account giving many insights into daily life in the 7th century. His was the first attempt to record the ecclesiastical history of Britain and earned him the title 'The Father of English History'.

**Bede, Cuthbert** Pseudonym of the humorist Edward Bradley (1827–89). Born at Kidderminster and educated at University College, Durham, he was ordained in 1850 and served from 1871 as rector of Stretton in Rutland. Under the pseudonym of Cuthbert Bede he published *The Adventures of Mr Verdant Green, An Oxford Freshman* (1853–6), a comic account of undergraduate life that enjoyed great popularity in its day.

**Beecher, Henry Ward** 1813–87 One of the most prominent preachers in Victorian America, and the brother of **Harriet Beecher Stowe**, the author of *Uncle Tom's Cabin*. After serving as minister to several Indiana churches, in 1847 he was called to the Plymouth Church in Brooklyn, New York, where he remained for the rest of his life. There he preached a theology of love rather than fear, exploiting the emotional Protestant revival tradition while addressing social issues such as education, temperance and slavery. His fame grew as he spoke on lecture tours as well as from the pulpit, and wrote weekly columns for *The Independent*, a widely read sectarian newspaper. In the 1850s he emerged as a major moral spokesman on secular issues of national concern, especially slavery; and though a moderate, he became associated in the popular mind with the radical Abolitionists.

His sermons were published periodically in *The Plymouth Pulpit* throughout the 1860s, and in 1870 he began editing a new journal, *Christian Union*. He was a prominent proponent of votes for women, and became active in the American Woman Suffrage Association. His novel, *Norwood, or, Village Life in New England* (1867), whose characters have long conversations about religious values, sold well. In the 1870s he incorporated many of the new Darwinian ideas to support his old teachings of evangelical liberalism, the community benefits of virtuous self-improvement, and the moral value of material success.

**Beer, Patricia** 1924– Poet. Born in Exmouth, she was educated at Exmouth Grammar School, Exeter University and St Hugh's College, Oxford. She has worked as a lecturer in English in Italy and at Goldsmiths' College, London. An autobiography, *Mrs Beer's House* (1969), describes her childhood. Her verse, in *Loss of the Magyar* (1959), *The Survivors* (1963), *Just Like the Resurrection* (1967), *The Estuary* (1971), *Driving West* (1975), *Selected Poems* (1979) and *The Lie of the Land* (1983), is marked by a development away from traditional forms. Precise and economical, her poems observe everyday matters and West Country scenes. She has also published the influential *Reader, I Married Him: A Study of the Women Characters of Jane Austen, Charlotte Brontë, Elizabeth Gaskell and George Eliot* (1974).

**Beerbohm, Sir Max** 1872–1956 Humorist, essayist and cartoonist. Henry Maximilian Beerbohm was born in London and educated at Charterhouse and Merton College, Oxford. His earliest caricatures appeared in *The Strand Magazine* in 1892 and his first essays in *The Yellow Book* in 1894. The essays were reprinted as *The Works of Max Beerbohm* in 1896. *The Happy Hypocrite* was published in 1897 and in 1898 Beerbohm succeeded **Bernard Shaw** as the dramatic critic of *The Saturday Review*. Beerbohm's famous satire on undergraduate passions and manners, *Zuleika Dobson*, appeared in 1911 and his parodies of, among others, **James**, **Conrad**, **Wells** and **Bennett** in *A Christmas Garland* in 1912. *Seven Men*, which includes the celebrated 'Enoch Soames' and the spoof of portentous historical drama in 'Savonarola Brown', was published in 1919. Notable among the collections of cartoons is *The Poet's Corner* (1904), which wryly comments on major figures in the English literary tradition. In his later years Beerbohm became a noted broadcaster. A selection of his broadcast talks appeared as *Mainly on the Air* in 1946. He was knighted in 1939.

**Beeton, Mrs Isabella Mary** 1836–65 Born Isabella Mayson, she became the author of a famous book on *Household Management*, first published 1859–61 in *The Englishwoman's Domestic Magazine* and as a separate volume in 1861. Usually remembered for its sections on cookery, which have been reprinted many times, the book in its original form gives a full picture of the duties of the Victorian middle-class housewife.

**Beggar's Bush, The** A romantic drama by **John Fletcher** and, probably, **Philip Massinger**, first produced about 1622. It was published in 1661 as the work of **Beaumont** and Fletcher, and is an early example of the use of thieves' and vagabonds' cant in dramatic dialogue.

**Beggar's Opera, The** A **ballad opera** by **John Gay**, with songs arranged by John Christopher Pepusch, who also composed an overture. **Swift** suggested the idea of a 'Newgate pastoral' to

Gay, and the original and astonishingly successful *Beggar's Opera* was apparently his response. Intended partly as an attack on the fashionable excesses of Italian opera, this ballad opera, the first of a genre that achieved rapid popularity, was staged at Lincoln's Inn Fields in 1728 by the theatre's manager, John Rich. Its success, according to a contemporary tag, made Rich gay and Gay rich. Its satire of corrupt government caused sufficient concern to Walpole and his colleagues to lead to the refusal of a performing licence for its sequel, *Polly*, in 1729. *The Beggar's Opera* has been frequently revived, and its musical score set by Benjamin Britten and, for a disappointing film version, by Arthur Bliss. It provided the formal inspiration for Bertolt Brecht's *The Threepenny Opera* (1928), a satire on corrupt capitalism, with original music by Kurt Weill.

Peachum, a receiver of stolen goods, whose creation owed much to the historical character of Jonathan Wild, is mortified when his daughter Polly marries the highwayman Macheath, with whom Peachum has a profitable business arrangement. True to the style of Jonathan Wild, he informs against Macheath. Sentenced to death and imprisoned in Newgate, Macheath is rescued by the warder's pretty daughter, Lucy Lockit. The rivalry between Polly Peachum and Lucy maintains the piece's characteristic balance of romance and cynicism. Recaptured in a brothel, Macheath is saved a second time from the

A scene from Act II of *The Beggar's Opera*. Macheath in prison; Polly and Lucy plead with the Turnkey for his release. The painting by William Hogarth (1729) was commissioned by Sir Archibald Grant and is now in the Tate Gallery, London.

gallows by the improbable intervention of a compulsory happy ending, demanded on behalf of the audience by one of the Players.

**Behan, Brendan** 1923–64 Irish playwright. He was born in Dublin, a child of the tenements. Behan credited his education to his prison terms, though he owed much to his family, well-read, and of strong Republican sympathies. At 14 he joined the IRA, and spent two years in an English Borstal, convicted in 1939 of carrying explosives. Released and deported, in 1942 he got 14 years for shooting at a policeman during an IRA ceremony.

Amnestied in 1947, Behan continued the writing begun in prison, mainly short stories in an inventive stylization of Dublin vernacular. His plays brought him celebrity. In 1954 the Pike Theatre presented *The Quare Fellow*, a grimly comic drama of the hours preceding a prison hanging. Much more than propaganda against judicial execution, it captures, with remarkable economy of form and neutrality of tone, the condition of the outcast and the emotions excited by barbaric revenge. Joan Littlewood's 1956 Theatre Workshop production in London made Behan famous.

Success was unmanageable. Behan's irresolute discipline collapsed into prolonged drinking bouts. *The Hostage* (1958), his next play, derived from his one-act Gaelic play *An Giall*, was acclaimed in London, Paris and New York. Much influenced by Joan Littlewood's improvisational theatre, it travesties with song and dance – and Behan's easy connivance – the tragic simplicity of its original. His last serious work, *Borstal Boy* (1958), is an imaginatively controlled account of his Borstal years, itself the testimony to a sophisticated creative power and great generosity of feeling.

A clamorous Dublin presence, belligerent or convivial, Behan illuminated the theatrical drabness of the 1950s. He subdued his vivid personality to an objective form, and his work, however brief, is continuous with a tradition, that of **O'Casey**'s urban drama.

**Behn, Aphra** 1640–89 Playwright, novelist and translator, probably the first Englishwoman to see herself as a professional writer. Aphra Behn's life was adventurous, although our knowledge of its details is not reliable. She seems to have spent some of her childhood in the West Indies, which she used as the setting for her best prose romance, **Oroonoko** (1688). The date of her marriage to a merchant of Dutch extraction is uncertain, as is the exact nature of her spying mission in Antwerp in 1666. Imprisoned for debt in the late 1660s, she turned to writing plays soon after her release.

Anne Bracegirdle, a celebrated actress of the Restoration, as the Indian Queen in Aphra Behn's *The Widow Ranter* (1689). Mrs Behn was the author of no less than eighteen plays, successful in their day; most of them are forgotten now. From a mezzotint in the Victoria & Albert Museum, London.

Her early work was in what Restoration England took to be the style of **Beaumont** and **Fletcher**. Even the more distinguished comedics, like *The Town Fop* (1676), *The Rover* (1677), *Sir Patient Fancy* (1678), *The Second Part of The Rover* (1681) and *The Lucky Chance* (1686), are variously derivative from the work of earlier writers. The political piece *The City Heiress* (1682) borrows from **Middleton**'s *A Mad World, My Masters*. The farce *The Emperor of the Moon* (1687), based on a scenario from Italian *commedia dell' arte*, helped make popular the Harlequinade, forerunner of the English style of **pantomime**. Behn's plays were successful in their time and several of them merit revival, not least because her advocacy of mature relationships between the sexes is a reminder of the social seriousness that underlies the licentiousness of Restoration drama. Her translations from French and Latin were money-making ventures and have no special claims. Of her fiction, only *The Fair Jilt* (1688), a lively account of a *femme fatale*, and *Oroonoko* rival the plays.

**Behrman, S[amuel] N[athaniel]** 1893–1973 American playwright, born in Worcester, Massachusetts, and educated at Harvard and Columbia. He began his theatrical career as an actor but was forced to give up the stage because of ill health, and took to writing – mostly sophisticated social comedies dealing with success, wealth, love and marriage. His first play, *Bedside Manners*, written with J. Kenyon Nicholson, was produced in New York in 1923; in the following year the two of them collaborated on *A Night's Work*. Behrman's third play, *The Man Who Forgot*, written with Owen Davis, appeared in 1926. Others of his plays include *Serena Blandish, or, The Difficulty of Getting Married* (1929, adapted from **Enid Bagnold**'s novel), *Meteor* (1929), *Love Story* (1933), *End of Summer* (1936), *Wine of Choice* (1938), *No Time For Comedy* (1939), *Jacobowsky and the Colonel* (1944; New York Drama Critics Circle Award), *Jane* (1952, adapted from a **Somerset Maugham** short story), *Fanny* (1954, with Joshua Logan) and his last play, *But For Whom Charlie* (1964). Behrman also wrote more than 25 screenplays between 1930 and 1962. He published several collections of essays which had first appeared in **The New Yorker**, as well as volumes of short stories. *People in a Diary: A Memoir* appeared in 1972.

**Bekederemo, J. P. Clark** (formerly John Pepper Clark) 1936– Nigerian poet and playwright, born in Kiagbodo, Niger Delta. Despite wide reading in European literatures, Bekederemo's imagination, idiom and even his themes are nurtured by traditional Ijaw culture. *Poems* (1962), *A Reed in the Tide* (1965), and *Casualties: Poems 1966/68* (1970) contain some well-wrought, crisp, economical poems. *A Decade of Tongues* (1981) is a selection. The collection *State of the Union* was published in 1985. *Song of a Goat* (1961; reissued with *The Masquerade* and *The Raft* in *Three Plays*, 1964) is the finest of his verse tragedies, in which supra-human fate overwhelms human endeavour. *Ozidi* (1966), a verse play about revenge that dehumanizes, is adapted from the seven-day Ijaw epic drama he translated as *The Ozidi Saga* (1975). In image-laden prose, *The Boat*, *The Return Home* and *Full Circle* constitute *The Bikoroa Plays* (1985), about fratricide and family strife across three generations in a traditional riverine community. *America, Their America* (1964) angrily describes a Princeton year. *The Example of Shakespeare* (1970) consists of critical essays, including a seminal piece, 'The Legacy of Caliban'.

**Belasco, David** 1853–1931 American dramatist, theatrical impresario and director, born and educated in San Francisco. He began his long career as an actor in California, and then in 1882 moved to New York City, where he was to make a major contribution to Broadway theatre, both as author or co-author of over 50 plays and as a deviser of sensational stage effects in the plays he directed at his own Belasco Theatre between 1906 and his death. In 1879 he collaborated with **James A. Herne** on *Hearts of Oak*. The domestic drama *Lord Chumley* (1888) was written with Henry C. DeMille, and *The Girl I Left Behind Me* (1893) with Franklin Fyles. A play set during the Civil War, *The Heart of Maryland*, appeared in 1895. He co-wrote a number of plays with John L. Long, including the one-act tragedy, *Madame Butterfly* (1900), *The Darling of the Gods* (1902) and *Adrea* (1904), which tells of a princess of an Adriatic island in the 5th century. Both *Madame Butterfly* and *The Girl of the Golden West* (1905) were turned into operas by Puccini, first performed as such in 1906 and 1910 respectively. *The Return of Peter Grimm*, based on an idea by Cecil B. DeMille, was produced in 1911.

**Bell, (Arthur) Clive (Howard)** 1881–1964 Critic of art and literature. Clive Bell was born at East Shefford, Bedfordshire, and educated at Marlborough College and Cambridge, where he was influenced by the philosopher **G. E. Moore**'s advocacy of 'the pleasures of human intercourse and the enjoyment of beautiful objects' (*Principia Ethica*, 1903). He became one of the central figures of the **Bloomsbury Group**, and married Vanessa Stephen (sister of **Virginia Woolf**) in 1907. His first book, *Art* (1914), was based on articles originally published in periodicals and introduced his concept of 'Significant Form', which separated and elevated the element of form above content in works of art. With Roger Fry, Bell was one of the first critics to herald the achievements of the Post-Impressionists. His other major works of criticism include *Since Cézanne* (1922), *Civilization* (1928), *Proust* (1929), and *Account of French Painting* (1931). A later work, *Old Friends: Personal Recollections* (1956), includes reminiscences of his friends among the Bloomsbury Group, though it also rejects the label as an invention by journalists.

**Bell, Currer, Ellis and Acton** The pseudonyms of **Charlotte**, **Emily** and **Anne Brontë**.

**Bell, Gertrude (Margaret Lowthian)** 1868–1926 Travel-writer. The daughter of a rich ironmaster, she was born in Washington, County Durham, and educated in London and at Lady Margaret Hall, Oxford. Having learned Persian and Arabic on early travels, she undertook archaeological work in Syria, describing some of her journeys in *The Desert and the Sown* (1907). *Amurath to Amurath* (1911) deals with a later journey. Further travels in Central Arabia followed, and during World War I she was an influential liaison officer between British and Arab interests. In addition to her various archaeological and geographical publications, her vivid personality is well conveyed in her posthumously published letters (2 vols., 1927).

**Bell, Martin** 1918–78 Poet. Born in Southampton, he was educated at Taunton School and University College, Southampton. A member of the Communist Party 1935–9, he worked as a teacher and lecturer, and became Gregory Fellow in Poetry at Leeds University in 1967. He was a leading member of the **Group**, and it was under his influence that it developed into the Poets' Workshop. After appearing in *Penguin Modern Poets 3* (1963), and other anthologies, including *A Group Anthology* (1963), his first hardback publication was his *Collected Poems 1938–67* (1967), his only major book. Deliberately populist, he wrote many poems about his peers, including a satire on the Group's meetings called 'Mr Hobsbaum's Monday Evening Meeting'. His most famous poem, though, is the corruscating attack, 'Headmaster: Modern Style'.

**Bellamy, Edward** 1850–98 American novelist. Born in Massachusetts, Bellamy was working as a journalist when in 1888 he wrote *Looking Backward: 2000–1887*, an immensely popular Utopian romance. For the rest of his life he developed and disseminated the political principles set forth in this book. Above all, these involved a government programme of strict state capitalism, resulting in non–revolutionary socialist reform. A Nationalist party was established to advocate his ideas; in support Bellamy founded the journal *The New Nation* (1891), and later wrote *Equality* (1897), a more theoretical sequel to *Looking Backward*. His earlier, less political writings include *The Duke of Stockbridge* (1879), about Shay's Rebellion, and *Dr Heidenhoff's Process* (1880) and *Miss Ludington's Sister* (1884), novels dealing with psychic phenomena in the tradition of **Nathaniel Hawthorne**. *The Blind Man's World And Other Stories* (1898) was published just before his death from tuberculosis.

**Belle Dame sans Merci, La** A poem of 100 eight-line stanzas translated from the French of Alain Chartier (*c.* 1424) by Richard Ros of Leicestershire about 1450. It consists of a debate about **courtly love** between a lover and his cruel lady. She consistently refuses him, and he eventually dies. Except for changing the metre from tetrameter to pentameter and adding a brief introduction and conclusion, the translator follows the French source closely. The translation was at one time attributed to **Chaucer**, being first printed as his in 1526. See **Chaucerian apocrypha**.

**Bellman of London, The** A pamphlet by **Thomas Dekker**, published anonymously in 1608 and belonging to the popular literature of roguery. The bellman exposes the criminal underworld and finds that there is nothing to choose between the town and the country for villainy.

**Belloc, (Joseph) Hilaire (Pierre René)** 1870–1953 Poet, novelist, biographer, historian and travel-writer. Born of half-French parentage in St Cloud, France, Belloc was educated at Cardinal Newman's Oratory School near Birmingham and Balliol College, Oxford. He became a British citizen in 1902, and from 1906 to 1910 he was Liberal MP for Salford. He abandoned politics after becoming disillusioned with the party system; see *The Party System* (1911, with Cecil Chesterton) and *The Servile State* (1912). During the same period he was literary editor of *The Morning Post*, and he founded *The Eye Witness* in 1911.

Belloc's literary career began with *Verses and Sonnets* and *The Bad Child's Book of Beasts* (both 1896). His other verse included *Cautionary Tales* (1907) and *Sonnets and Verses* (1923). His many biographies, often lively and partisan, included *Danton* (1899), *Robespierre* (1901), *Marie Antoinette* (1909) and *Cromwell* (1927) and he wrote several histories, notably *The French Revolution* (1911) and a *History of England* (1915).

In 1900 he met **G. K. Chesterton** and the two collaborated on a number of works which reflected their common beliefs and interests. Their contributions to *The Speaker*, which adopted an anti-Imperial, pro-Boer line on the Boer war, earned them the nickname 'Chesterbelloc' from **G. B. Shaw**.

Belloc also wrote many books of travel, beginning with *Paris* in 1900; others included *The Path to Rome* (1902), *The Pyrenees* (1909), *The Cruise of the Nona* (1925, containing many personal reflections) and *Return to the Baltic* (1938). Among his essays, memorable collections included *Hills and the Sea* (1906), *First and Last* (1911), *Short Talks With the Dead* (1926) and *The Silence of the Sea* (1940).

His novels, many of which were illustrated by Chesterton, included *Mr Clutterbuck's Election* (1908), *The Girondin* (1911), *The Green Overcoat* (1912) and *Belinda* (1928).

**Bellow, Saul** 1915– American novelist. The son of immigrant Russian parents, Bellow was born in Quebec. The family moved to Chicago in 1924, and Bellow was educated at the University of Chicago, Northwestern University, and the University of Wisconsin. He has followed an academic career since 1938. His first novels were *Dangling Man* (1944) and *The Victim* (1947). *The Adventures of Augie March* (1953) won him his first National Book Award. *Seize The Day* (1956), *Henderson The Rain King* (1959), *Herzog* (1964), *Mosby's Memoirs And Other Stor-*

Saul Bellow.

ies (1968), *Mr Sammler's Planet* (1970; National Book Award), *Humboldt's Gift* (1975) and *The Dean's December* (1982) further contributed to his reputation as an interpreter of the struggles of urban dwellers to define their roles and responsibilities in the modern world. He was awarded the Nobel Prize for Literature in 1976. Among his other books are *Recent American Fiction: A Lecture* (1963), *The Future of the Moon* (1970), *Technology and The Frontiers Of Knowledge* (1975) and *To Jerusalem and Back: A Personal Account* (1976). He edited *Great Jewish Short Stories* (1963) and has written several plays, including *The Wrecker* (1954), *The Last Analysis* (1965) and *A Wen* (1965). A collection of short stories, *Him With His Foot In His Mouth And Other Short Stories*, was published in 1984.

**Bells, The** A melodrama, adapted by **Leopold Lewis** from a French play, *Le Juif Polonais*, by Erckmann and Chatrian. It was first staged at the Lyceum Theatre, London, in 1871. Its success established Sir Henry Irving as a leading actor, and the role of Mathias remained in his repertoire until his death in 1905.

The bells are the sleigh-bells of the Polish Jew, whom Mathias, now a respected burgomaster of the small German town where he was once a poor servant, murdered many winters ago. They ring in his mind, tormenting him with the memory of his crime, eventually driving him to a remorseful death.

**Belton Estate, The** A novel by **Anthony Trollope**, serialized in *The Fortnightly Review* from May 1865 to January 1866, and published in three volumes in 1866.

Clara Amedroz is the daughter of the squire of Belton Castle, Bernard Amedroz, whose spendthrift son and heir has committed suicide. Her cousin Will Belton, a hearty Norfolk farmer, becomes heir to the entailed estate, and on a visit to her father falls in love with Clara and proposes marriage. Clara, however, is in love with Captain Aylmer, an MP and nephew of her wealthy adopted aunt Mrs Winterfield, and she refuses Will. When Mrs Winterfield dies, it transpires that she has left her money to Captain Aylmer, and has committed him by a deathbed promise to propose marriage to Clara. This he does and is accepted, but Clara comes to question his conventional attitudes and lukewarm courtship; when she goes to stay at Aylmer Park after her father's death, and encounters his mother's insolent condescension, she breaks off the engagement. Will Belton has meanwhile proved his devotion and generosity by his determination to surrender the Belton estate to her, and Clara finds that she truly loves him. The novel ends with their marriage.

Although not rated highly by Trollope himself, *The Belton Estate* is of some interest for its characteristically sympathetic exploration of the plight of the single, dependent woman.

**Ben-Hur**: *A Tale of The Christ* A novel by **Lew Wallace**, published in 1880. Judah Ben-Hur and Messala the Roman are apparently devoted friends, but Messala, in search of advancement, accuses Ben-Hur of an attempt on the life of the Roman governor. Ben-Hur is sent to the galleys for life, and his mother and sister are also imprisoned. In the slave train to the coast he is given water by a stranger outside a carpenter's workshop. Years later he returns to Judaea a free man and a Roman officer; soon after, he challenges Messala in the chariot races in Caesarea. His mother and sister, meanwhile, have contracted leprosy. Ben-Hur wins the chariot race; Messala, who has staked everything on the victory, is crippled and ruined. Ben-Hur rescues his mother and sister and they return to Jerusalem – on the day of the Crucifixion. The condemned man is the same one who once aided Ben-Hur as a slave; he dies on the cross, but his passing cures the lepers. Ben-Hur and his family embrace the new faith of Christianity.

**Benchley, Robert (Charles)** 1889–1945 American humorist, drama critic and actor. After graduating from Harvard in 1912 he began his career as a journalist, working on several New York newspapers and magazines. He was theatre critic for *Life* (1920–9) and then for *The New Yorker* (1929–40). During these years he also wrote and published humorous sketches, based on the daily lives of ordinary people and marked by an ironic appreciation of life in an era of rapid and often confusing change. They were collected in *Of All Things* (1921), *Love Conquers All* (1922), *Pluck and Luck* (1925), *The Early Worm* (1927), *20,000 Leagues Under The Sea, or, David Copperfield* (1928), *The Treasurer's Report* (1930), *My Ten Years in a Quandary* (1936), *After 1903 – What?* (1938), *Inside Benchley* (1942) and *Benchley Beside Himself* (1943). In addition to his writing, Benchley made frequent appearances in motion pictures and on the radio.

**Benét, Stephen Vincent** 1898–1943  An American poet, short-story writer and novelist born in Bethlehem, Pennsylvania, Benét is well known for his Pulitzer Prize-winning collection of verse about the Civil War, *John Brown's Body* (1928). Another book of poetry, *Western Star* (1943), deals with American roots in 17th-century European migrations; although it was unfinished at his death it was awarded a posthumous Pulitzer Prize. A collection of short stories, *Thirteen O'Clock* (1937), includes the popular 'The Devil And Daniel Webster', which has been made into an opera and a film. Other volumes of his stories are *Tales Before Midnight* (1939) and *The Last Cycle* (1946). He also wrote five novels, and a number of radio scripts which appeared in a posthumous collection, *We Stand United, And Other Radio Scripts* (1945).

**Benét, William Rose** 1886–1950 American poet, the elder brother of **Stephen Vincent Benét**, and founder of the *Saturday Review* (1924). He published several books of poetry, including *Merchants from Cathay* (1913), *Moons of Grandeur* (1920), *Days of Deliverance* (1944) and *The Stairway of Surprise* (1947). An experimental verse novel, *Rip Tide*, appeared in 1932. He was awarded a Pulitzer Prize for his autobiography, *The Dust Which Is God* (1941).

*Benito Cereno* See *Piazza Tales, The*.

**Benlowes, Edward** 1602–76 Religious poet. The heir of a rich Roman Catholic family, he changed his faith at the age of 25. His staunch support of the Royalist cause in the Civil War reduced him to poverty. His long religious poem, *Theophila, or, Love's Sacrifice* (1652), is a rambling theological romance containing many curious expressions and the occasional fine line.

**Bennett, Alan** 1934–  Actor and playwright, born and educated in Yorkshire. Bennett was a student at Oxford when he contributed to the successful revue *Beyond the Fringe* (1960) and since then, despite his own self-effacing qualities, he has remained in the public eye. His first

two plays, *Forty Years On* (1968) and *Getting On* (1971), are intelligent political comedies. *Habeas Corpus* (1973) is a farce. *The Old Country* (1977) describes, with recognizable reference to the life of Guy Burgess, the experience of an English traitor living out his days in the Soviet Union. *Enjoy* (1980), the least successful of Bennett's stage plays, treats the later years of a working-class couple. Like many English playwrights, he has become increasingly drawn to the wider audience of television.

**Bennett, (Enoch) Arnold** 1867–1931 Novelist, short-story writer, playwright and journalist. He was born at Hanley in the Staffordshire Potteries, where his father Enoch had trained himself as a solicitor. Bennett's decision, made when he was 21, to leave his father's firm was crucial for his future, but he still worked as a solicitor's clerk on moving to London. Although literary success came slowly, he was able to exchange careers in 1893, becoming assistant editor of *Woman* magazine. A short story, 'A Letter Home', was accepted by *The Yellow Book* and a first, highly autobiographical novel, *A Man from the North* (1898), was accepted by John Lane.

Bennett's literary mentors were mostly French, notably Maupassant, Zola and Flaubert. His three-volume *Journal* (1932–3), inspired by the example of the Goncourt brothers, was begun in 1896. His first major achievement,

Arnold Bennett, 1911. Photograph by E. O. Hoppé.

## Benson, A[rthur] C[hristopher]

*Anna of the Five Towns* (1902), was set in the Potteries of his boyhood, the scene for much of his best work. It was joined by novels of a different sort: *The Grand Babylon Hotel* (1902), a comedy thriller about the problems of a millionaire, and *The Gates of Wrath* (1903). Two collections of short stories followed: *Tales of the Five Towns* (1905) and *The Grim Smile of the Five Towns* (1907). The novels which are widely accepted as his greatest achievement came with *The Old Wives' Tale* (1908) and *Clayhanger* (1910). The fortunes of the Clayhanger family are followed further in *Hilda Lessways* (1911), *These Twain* (1916) and *The Roll Call* (1918).

Following the death of his dominating father, Bennett had moved to Paris in 1903. His marriage to Marguerite Soulie in 1907 lasted until their separation in 1921. Bennett had a daughter by the companion of his later years, Dorothy Cheston.

Bennett's interest in the theatre began as a critic, but he was to see many of his own plays produced and took an active part in the management of the Lyric Theatre, Hammersmith, in the 1920s. His greatest success came with *Milestones* (1912), written in collaboration with Edward Knoblock. With his lesser novels, *The Card* (1911), *Mr Prohack* (1922) and *Imperial Palace* (1930), he returned to the subject of the rich and the worldly; the more highly regarded political novel *Lord Raingo* (1926) reflects his knowledge of powerful men like Lord Beaverbrook, who became a close friend. In 1918 Bennett served as Director of Propaganda in the Ministry of Information. It was owing to Beaverbrook that he undertook the influential 'Books and Persons' series for *The Evening Standard* from 1926 until his death. His reputation as a novelist was enhanced by *Riceyman Steps* (1923), in which he again considered the lives of ordinary and undistinguished people, the subject for which he is chiefly remembered.

**Benson, A[rthur] C[hristopher]** 1862–1925 Essayist. Born at Wellington College, Berkshire, and educated at Eton and King's College, Cambridge, he was Master of Magdalene College, Cambridge, in 1915–25. Benson's *Memoirs of Arthur Hamilton* (written under the pseudonym Christopher Carr) appeared in 1886. In *The Schoolmaster* (1902), written while he was a housemaster at Eton, he outlined his educational principles. The studies of **Rossetti**, **FitzGerald** and **Pater** in the English Men of Letters series were published 1904–6. As a poet and hymn-writer Benson is perhaps best remembered for his words to Elgar's first 'Pomp and Circumstance' March, 'Land of Hope and Glory' (1902), originally forming part of the Coronation Ode for Edward VII.

**Benson, E[dward] F[rederic]** 1867–1940 Novelist and younger brother of **A. C. Benson**. He was born at Wellington College, Berkshire, and educated at Marlborough and King's College, Cambridge. Benson wrote some 93 books, the most popular being his comic novels about Dodo (*Dodo, Dodo the Second* and *Dodo Wonder*, 1914–21) and Lucia, starting with *Queen Lucia* (1920) and *Lucia in London* (1927). Between 1911 and 1940 he also published five volumes of personal and family reminiscences.

**Bentham, Jeremy** 1748–1832 Philosopher. Born in London and educated at Westminster and Queen's College, Oxford, he studied law at Lincoln's Inn but never practised as a barrister. In 1776 his legal studies bore fruit in the anonymously published *A Fragment on Government: Being an Examination of what is delivered in William Blackstone's Commentaries* in which he outlined his theory of Enlightenment government and a programme of future reform. The arguments were substantially expanded in the *Introduction to the Principles of Morals and Legislation* (1789), much of the editorial work being done by the Swiss scholar Étienne Dumont. After a period of travel in Russia and eastern Europe (1785–8) Bentham published his plan for prison reform as *The Panopticon, or, Inspection House* (1791). The lack of official interest in his scheme gradually dislodged the early faith in enlightened monarchic reform and stimulated the

Jeremy Bentham. A detail from the portrait by H. W. Pickersgill, 1829. National Portrait Gallery, London.

development of Bentham's most influential philosophical system, the 'philosophical radicalism' known as **Utilitarianism**. This system was formed around the dual ideas that all reform should be dictated by the greatest happiness of the greatest number as a measure of right and wrong, and that human motivation was founded on self-interest. The coincidence of interest and duty became an ideal of social and moral reform. Bentham's *Poor Laws and Pauper Management* (1797, in *Annals of Agriculture*) was to provide the guiding principles for the New Poor Law of 1834 (which was so bitterly attacked by **Dickens** in *Oliver Twist*). Among Bentham's other influential tracts are *Chrestomathia* (1816), which discussed education, *A Catechism of Parliamentary Reform* (1817), *A Radical Reform Bill, with Explanations* (1819) and *A Constitutional Code for the Use of All Nations* (1830). His *Rationale of Evidence* (1825) was edited by **John Stuart Mill**, the son of Bentham's closest Utilitarian colleague, **James Mill**. Bentham founded *The Westminster Review* in 1824 with Mill's assistance as the organ of the Philosophical Radicals and was a guiding force behind the establishment of the University of London. His skeleton is preserved in University College, London.

**Bentley, E[dmund] C[lerihew]** 1875–1956 Journalist, novelist and author of light verse. Born in London, he was educated at St Paul's School and Merton College, Oxford, becoming President of the Oxford Union in 1898. He was called to the Bar in 1902 but spent most of his working life as a journalist, first with *The Daily News* (1902–12) and then as leader writer for *The Daily Telegraph* (1912–34), returning to the paper as its chief literary critic in 1940–7. Bentley earned a minor place in literary history by his invention of the light-verse form known as the **clerihew**, after the middle name he used as pseudonym for his first collection, *Biography for Beginners* (1905), and by his contribution to **detective fiction**. Dedicated to his friend **G. K. Chesterton** and recommended for publication by **John Buchan**, *Trent's Last Case* (1903) was intended as 'an exposure of detective stories' but quickly hailed as a classic of the genre. Bentley revived his artist–detective, with much less success, in *Trent's Own Case* (with H. Warner Allen, 1936) and a collection of short stories, *Trent Intervenes* (1938). *Elephant's Work: An Enigma* (1950) is a thriller. More enduring than these works is 'Greedy Night' (1939), his wickedly accurate parody of **Dorothy L. Sayers**.

**Bentley, Phyllis** 1894–1977 Novelist. The daughter of a textile manufacturer, she was born in Halifax and brought up in Huddersfield in the West Riding of Yorkshire. She completed her education at Cheltenham Ladies' College, where she passed a University of London external examination which granted her a BA. She began her largely autobiographical first novel, *Environment* (1915), while teaching in north London. She subsequently worked as a librarian and a writer for *John O'London's Weekly*. *The World's Bane* (1918), a volume of four allegorical stories influenced by **Olive Schreiner**, was followed by more novels, including *Cat-in-The-Manger* (1918), *The Spinner of the Years* (1928) and *The Partnership* (1928). Her love for the West Riding was encouraged by her friendship with **Winifred Holtby** and her career was helped by **Vera Brittain**. 1932 saw the publication of her best-known novel, *Inheritance*, which chronicles the lives of Yorkshire families involved in the textile industry and draws on her mother's family recollections. Phyllis Bentley also wrote several studies of the **Brontës**.

**Bentley, Richard** 1662–1742 Scholar and antiquarian. Born at Oulton in Yorkshire, he entered St John's College, Cambridge, at the age of 14, and became tutor to the son of Edward Stillingfleet, Dean of St Paul's and Bishop of Worcester.

Bentley's scholarly reputation dates from 1691, when his *Epistola ad Millium* – a learned appendix on the Greek dramatists – was contributed to John Mill's edition of John Malalas, the Byzantine chronicler. In 1692 he became the first Boyle lecturer, taking as his subject 'A Confutation of Atheism', which established him as a skilful defender of orthodox Christianity. He became keeper of the Royal Library in 1694. During the years 1697–9 he was embroiled in the dispute provoked by **Sir William Temple**'s *Essay upon the Ancient and Modern Learning*, his own contribution being to show that the epistles of Phalaris which Sir William had praised as examples of classical excellence were spurious. (See also *The Battle of the Books*.)

He was appointed Master of Trinity College, Cambridge, in 1700, a post he despotically enjoyed for some 40 years despite repeated controversy. As an editor Bentley was renowned for his diligent work on Horace and Manilius, but his arbitrary edition of **Milton**'s *Paradise Lost* (1732) discredited him. He was caricatured by **Pope** in *The Dunciad* as a 'mighty scholiast, whose unwearied pains/Made Horace dull, and humbled Milton's strains' (Book 4, lines 211–12).

***Bentley's Miscellany*** A monthly magazine issued by the publisher Richard Bentley from January 1837. It had originally been proposed that it should be called 'The Wits' Miscellany'. **Charles Dickens**, its first editor, was succeeded in January 1839 by another novelist, **William Harrison Ainsworth**. Contributors included **Francis Mahony** (Father Prout) and **R. H.**

**Barham**, many of whose *Ingoldsby Legends* first appeared in its pages.

**Beowulf** The most famous and the longest surviving poem in Old English, written *c.* 1000 in the West Saxon dialect. It probably developed orally and achieved its present form during the 8th century in Mercia or Northumberland. The setting is southern Scandinavia in the Age of Migration of the 5th and 6th centuries, and the poem makes no reference to Britain. It is an **epic** recording the great deeds of the heroic warrior Beowulf in his youth and maturity.

It tells how the monster Grendel terrorizes the Scyldings of Hrothgar's Danish kingdom until the young Geatish warrior Beowulf eventually defeats him. When Grendel's mother comes to wreak revenge on Hrothgar's men Beowulf is summoned again and in her underwater dwelling kills both her and the wounded Grendel. After receiving his rewards Beowulf returns to his native Geat-land and relates his story. His king, Hygelac, gives him lands which he rules for 50 years. A dragon, which had guarded its hoard in peace for 300 years, is stirred by the theft of a goblet to attack the Geats. Beowulf, now Lord of the Geats, battles with the dragon and, with the help of Wiglaf, kills it. Beowulf is fatally wounded in the fight, but Wiglaf recovers the dragon's hoard before his lord's death. The poem ends with Beowulf's funeral pyre and barrow and a prophesy of disaster for the Geats.

The central story is linked by the names of characters in peripheral episodes to a network of other European legends and epics. Some of the names are historical (as Hygelac, d. 521) and the action is firmly attached at many points to the history of Germanic Europe. The poet sets it in the wider context of the founding of the Scylding dynasty and the Danish race and the imminent destruction of the Geats. As the genealogies of men and monsters root the poem in human and supernatural history, the sustained spatial and temporal precision creates a sense of immediacy and physical reality.

The poem's central preoccupations are with the prowess and glory of the hero Beowulf, his well-deserved fame, and with the feasting and fighting which characterize masculine feudal society, yet the many peripheral episodes introduce conflicts inside the feudal code and with outside forces. The poem incorporates the larger considerations of life and death, war and peace, society and the individual, good and evil. These, and Beowulf's supernatural acts (such as fighting underwater for days), have encouraged Christian, mythic and allegorical interpretations. The progress of the action is slow, with elaboration of other episodes, inset stories and the rhetorical development of laments and speeches reducing the pace. The second half,

after Beowulf's return to the Geats, is often considered inferior, but it is generally accepted that originally *Beowulf* was the work of a single poet.

**Beppo:** *A Venetian Story* A poem by **Byron** in **ottava rima**, published in 1818. It satirizes both English and Italian life, telling of the return during a carnival of a long-lost soldier, Beppo (Giuseppe). Disguised as a Turkish merchant, he finds that his wife has consoled herself with a *cavaliere servente*. The scene is set for a violent confrontation, but the dilemma is resolved over a cup of coffee. **Mock-heroic** in manner and pervaded by gentle irony, the poem marks an important change from Byron's early work and introduces the style (and verse form) he developed and refined in **Don Juan** and **The Vision of Judgement**.

**Berenson, Bernard** 1865–1959 American art historian. Born Bernhard Valvrojenski in Lithuania, he came to Boston with his parents at the age of 10. With the help of **Charles Eliot Norton** he transferred from Boston University to Harvard. After graduating in 1888 he visited Paris, London and Oxford before settling in Italy, where he quickly established a reputation as a connoisseur, particularly of Italian Renaissance painting. His expertise in attributing and authenticating paintings brought wealthy buyers and dealers as clients. His scholarly works include *Venetian Painters of the Renaissance* (1894), *Florentine Painters of the Renaissance* (1896), *Central Italian Painters of the Renaissance* (1897), *The Study and Criticism of Italian Art* (1902) and *Drawings of the Florentine Painters* (1903). *Sketch for a Self-Portrait* (1949) is autobiographical. Berenson entertained **Edith Wharton**, **Henry Adams** and **Kenneth Clark** at his Florentina villa, I Tatti, which he bequeathed with its library and collections to Harvard.

**Berger, John** 1926– Novelist and art critic. Born in London, Berger was a student at the Central and the Chelsea Schools of Art, and afterwards a painter and teacher of drawing. His art criticism is collected in *Permanent Red* (1960) and *The White Bird* (1985), while his combative essay *Ways of Seeing* (1972) – which originally accompanied an influential television series – propounds a Marxist theory of artistic appreciation and argues for a reappraisal of existing canons of taste. Berger's interest in the photographic image is exemplified in two collaborations with the United Nations photographer, Jean Mohr: *A Fortunate Man* (1967), a study of the life of a country doctor in Berger's words and Mohr's pictures, and *Another Way of Telling* (1982).

A major preoccupation of Berger's fiction is the nature and possibilities of individual freedom, whether social, political or sexual. *A Painter of Our Time* (1958) charts the crises and breakthroughs in the progress of a single artist's career; *Corker's Freedom* (1964) portrays the struggles of the eponymous protagonist to break out of a stultifying suburban existence. Berger's most substantial novel is *G*, awarded the Booker Prize in 1972, a quixotic, strenuously thoughtful work that melds fictional narrative, personal reflection, political treatise and historical reconstruction in pursuing the fortunes of the ambiguous central figure – variously the political hero Garibaldi, the pioneering aviator Geo Chavez and the sexual adventurer Don Giovanni.

In recent years Berger has been living in a peasant farming community in the French Jura. So far his sojourn has produced the first book of a projected trilogy, *Into Their Labours*, recording the simple vicissitudes of modern peasant life. *Pig Earth* (1979) mixes poetry, fiction and reportage and introduces a spare, unadorned, often sad and elegiac style to Berger's fiction which subsequent short stories have continued.

**Berkeley, George** 1685–1753 Philosopher. The son of an English family settled in Ireland, George Berkeley was born at Dysert Castle, near Kilkenny, and attended the same school as **Congreve** and **Swift**. Like them he went on to Trinity College, Dublin, where he was ordained and where he became a junior fellow in 1707. His first published works dealt with mathematics, a subject in which he maintained an interest throughout his life; *The Analyst* (1734), written late in his career, asserted that the assumptions of mathematicians were harder to understand than Christian dogma.

But Berkeley's fame was earned as a philosopher. His first book, *An Essay Towards a New Theory of Vision* (1709), advanced a psychological theory of perception based on two propositions: the objects and ideas of sight have nothing in common with the objects and ideas of touch; the connection between them comes only from experience and there is no abstract element common to both. Like **Locke**, Berkeley hated abstractions; he wrote his treatise in English prose that has commanded admiration ever since for its lucidity.

The first part of *The Treatise Concerning the Principles of Human Knowledge* followed in 1710. The second part, concerning morals, existed in a first draft but this was lost while Berkeley was travelling in Italy and he never found the inclination to 'do so disagreeable a thing as writing twice on the same subject'. In essence, the treatise insists that mind is the creative force: rather than being representations of reality, ideas are reality.

This theory of immaterialism is based on the principle *esse est percipi* (to be is to be perceived)

which holds that there is no external reality independent of man's mental perception of things. As a distinguished member of the church (he was later Dean of Derry in 1724, and then Bishop of Cloyne) Berkeley was concerned to oppose any philosophical theories that might nurture atheism or scepticism, and he therefore ranged himself against **Hobbes** and Locke, especially the latter's concept of the dualism of spirit and matter. His argument for belief in the existence of God is an idealistic one, resting upon the notion that Nature is a regular series of material objects that exist continuously in God's own perception, which lends them uniformity. This theory was further defended in his *Three Dialogues between Hylas and Philonus* (1713). **Boswell** records that, in reply to Berkeley's 'ingenious sophistry to prove the non-existence of matter' **Dr Johnson** forcefully kicked a large stone and pronounced, 'I refute it thus.'

In 1713 Berkeley was in England and soon became the friend of **Addison**, **Pope**, **Swift** and **Steele**, and contributed to the latter's *Guardian*. On appointment as Dean of Derry in 1724 Berkeley launched a scheme to found a missionary college in Bermuda, described in his *Proposal for the Better Supplying of Churches in our Foreign Plantations* (1725); he sailed for America in 1728 with the promise of an essential grant from Robert Walpole. Three years went by, which Berkeley spent in Newport, Rhode Island, but the grant never materialized. He formed a Literary and Philosophical Society and wrote the popular *Alciphron, or the Minute Philosopher* (1832), Platonic dialogues on his philosophical principles in the defence of religion. His model for a college was put to excellent use in founding King's College in New York City; it later became Columbia University. After returning to England Berkeley published his *Theory of Vision, or Visual Language Vindicated and Explained* (1733).

In 1734 Berkeley was given the bishopric of Cloyne, a remote diocese in the county of Cork in Ireland, where he remained until 1752, his mind occupied with questions of social reform and religious speculation. *The Querist* (1735) shows the reformer asking penetrating questions about the matter of Ireland. *Siris: A Chain of Philosophical Reflexions* (1744) examines both physical and metaphysical questions chiefly concerning the virtues of tar-water. Berkeley retired to Oxford, where he died. His notes, *The Commonplace Book*, were first published in 1871.

**Berners, John Bourchier, 2nd Baron** See **Bourchier, John**.

**Berners (or Barnes), Juliana** Her name appears at the end of the miscellanea following the hunting treatise in the 1486 edition of *The*

*Book of St Albans*, and she was at one time thought to be the author of all four treatises in the collection. But it is unlikely that she contributed more than the appended lists of 'company terms' and other miscellaneous terminology, and she certainly did not write the entire work. The biographical details usually offered – that she was the daughter of Sir John Berners of Roding-Berners in Essex and later prioress of Sopwell convent – are fabrications by the *Book's* early editors.

**Berry, James** 1924– Poet. Born in Jamaica, James Berry was among the first settlers from the Caribbean to arrive in Britain after World War II. He has lived in England since 1948 and has become a cultural leader in the black community. His collections of poetry include *Fractured Circles* (1979), *Lucy's Letters and Loving* (1982, an enlarged version of *Lucy's Letter*, 1975) and *Chain of Days* (1985). He is also a prolific editor of poetry, his anthologies including *News For Babylon* (1984), a selection of West Indian–British poetry. Berry's poem 'Fantasy of an African Boy' won the National Poetry Competition in Britain in 1981. Berry is often humorous, particularly in his ability to capture Caribbean speech, but he also has a plangent aspect in some of his poems. He is regarded as the doyen, and possibly as the best, of the black poets who, in the 1980s, have made a significant mark on British culture.

**Berryman, John** 1914–72 American poet. Born in McAlester, Oklahoma, Berryman was educated at Columbia University and at Clare College, Cambridge. He taught at Princeton, Harvard, the University of Cincinnati, and, from 1955 until his death, at the University of Minnesota. His poems appeared in small magazines and reviews during the 1930s, and then in 1940 his work was published in *Five American Poets*. His first collected volume was *Poems* (1942), followed in 1948 by *The Dispossessed*. Widespread recognition came with *Homage to Mistress Bradstreet* (1956), and in 1965 he was awarded the Pulitzer Prize for *77 Dream Songs* (1964). The poems in this latter volume became the first section of the lengthy collection called *The Dream Songs*, which was published in its entirety in 1969. He committed suicide in 1972. A posthumous volume of poems, *Delusions* (1972), shows him looking toward the end of his life, also the subject of his novel, *Recovery* (1973). *The Freedom of the Poet*, a collection of his essays on poets and poetry, appeared in 1976. He also wrote a notable biography, *Stephen Crane* (1950), which was revised and reissued in 1962.

**Bertrams, The** A novel by **Anthony Trollope**, published in three volumes in 1859.

After a brilliant undergraduate career, George Bertram visits the Holy Land before settling to a career. There he meets and falls in love with Caroline Waddington, the granddaughter of his wealthy City uncle, also called George Bertram. They plan to marry but she insists that he establish himself financially first, encouraging him in a legal career despite his own inclination to the church. Their engagement drags on for three years until it is broken by mutual consent, and soon after Caroline marries Sir Henry Harcourt, the Solicitor-General and an ambitious politician. Harcourt is disappointed when he fails to gain access to Caroline's grandfather's fortune to support his extravagant way of life, and he becomes jealous of George Bertram, eventually committing suicide after Caroline leaves him and he loses his political position. In due course Caroline and George are reconciled and marry. Secondary plots deal with George's father Sir Lionel, a plausible but irresponsible diplomat, and his attempts to marry a wealthy spinster, and with the love-affair between George's friend Arthur Wilkinson and Adela Gauntlet.

Although Trollope considered the plot of *The Bertrams* 'more than ordinarily bad', the novel is redeemed by his unconventional handling of the hero and heroine as disenchantment overtakes their initial high hopes.

**Besant, Sir Walter** 1836–1901 Novelist and historian. He was born at Portsmouth and educated at Christ's College, Cambridge. His early novels, of which *Ready Money Mortiboy* (1872) and *The Golden Butterfly* (1876) were the most popular, were collaborations with James Rice. His own later historical fiction was less widely read than two realistic works, *All Sorts and Conditions of Men* (1882) and *Children of Gibeon* (1886), which exposed conditions in the East End of London. Sincere and tireless in his philanthropic interests, he helped found the 'People's Palace' in the Mile End Road and was knighted in 1895. A founder in 1884 of the Society of Authors, he campaigned to secure better legal protection for literary works, exposed the fraudulent practices of disreputable publishers and wrote and argued constantly for an agreed system of international copyright. Besant's Royal Institution lecture of 1884 on the status of the novel provoked **Henry James**'s famous reply, 'The Art of Fiction'. An authority on Rabelais and Montaigne and on the exploration of Palestine, Besant planned and inaugurated a great 10-volume topographical survey of London, which appeared after his death under other editors (1902–12).

**Best, George** d. ?1584 Best was a navigator who accompanied Martin Frobisher in his three attempts to find the Northwest Passage in 1576,

1577 and 1578. His account, *A True Discourse of the Late Voyages of Discovery* (1578), was dedicated to Sir Christopher Hatton and was later included in the collection of **Richard Hakluyt**.

***Bestiary, The*** A Middle English poem of the late 12th or early 13th century presenting allegorical and descriptive pieces about real and mythical animals. Although the form was widespread in medieval Europe and many examples in French and Latin survive, only one bestiary in English is extant. All the bestiaries have their source in the *Physiologus* of Thetbaldus, a Latin work of the 11th century, although the origins of the bestiary in Western Europe probably date from the 4th century. Its basic premise is the characteristic medieval view that God may be understood by studying the symbolism of the material world. Using a variety of verse forms, the work gives an account of various animals, describing real and imagined features of them and then explaining their significance. For example, it was believed that the elephant had no knees and had to sleep leaning against a tree; to kill or capture an elephant, the hunter had only to fell the tree and the animal would fall over. The fictitious beasts included the familiar unicorn, phoenix and cockatrice, but also the bizarre manticora with its scorpion's tail, lion's

A drawing from a 12th-century Latin bestiary. A huge legendary fish, the Aspidochelone, deceives mariners into believing that its back is an island; then it submerges and drowns them all. *MS Ii.4.26, f 54v.* Cambridge University Library.

body, man's head, gleaming red eyes, triple row of teeth and liking for human flesh. Often the name of an animal was the source of misunderstanding; barnacle geese were supposed to hatch from barnacles, and the crocodile was thought to be so called because it was saffron (crocus) coloured. The belief that the nature of the beast could be derived etymologically from its name is due to the influence of the 7th-century *Etymologiae* of Isidore of Seville.

Although much of the work seems to be pure invention, many of the fantastic characteristics attributed to real animals can be traced to misinterpretation of accurate observations of animal behaviour. Many of the non-existent animals bear some similarity to real animals and represent the repeated distortion or misrepresentation of the truth rather than total invention.

**Bethell, Ursula** 1874–1945 New Zealand poet. Born in England, she spent most of her life in a family of farmers in the South Island. In the 1930s she established a 'house of Christian learning', a community of women of the Church of England, in Christchurch. In some degree it reflected her own search for a community of like-minded spirits; it was not a success, at least in that regard. Known as the poet of the Cashmere Hills, near Christchurch, she produced domestic, unassertive, openly meditative verse. Her first book of New Zealand poetry, published in London in 1929 under the pseudonym 'Evelyn Hayes', was *From a Garden in the Antipodes*. The recipient of these poems was an English friend, and the shape this epistolary format gave the poems in the volume, as well as the acknowledgement of foreignness and distance, created a delicate balance of inward- and outward-looking meditation. This book and two later volumes, published by the Caxton Press in Christchurch, contain her best work. Her *Collected Poems* appeared posthumously in New Zealand in 1950, also from Caxton.

**Betjeman, Sir John** 1906–84 Poet. He was born in Highgate and educated at Marlborough and Magdalen College, Oxford, where he came into contact with the group of young poets led by **W. H. Auden** without being influenced by their political and artistic stance. He became a schoolmaster and, during World War II, United Kingdom press attaché in Dublin before earning his living as a writer, journalist and broadcaster.

Betjeman's first volume of verse, *Mount Zion* (1931), was followed by *Continual Dew* (1937), *Old Lights for New Chancels* (1940), *New Bats in Old Belfries* (1945), *A Few Late Chrysanthemums* (1954), *Poems in the Porch* (1954), the autobiographical *Summoned by Bells* (1960), *High and Low* (1966), *A Nip in the Air* (1974) and *Church Poems* (1981) among others. His immensely popular *Collected Poems* (1958, revised 1962), edited by the Earl of Birkenhead, was reprinted many times and sold close to a million copies. He succeeded **Cecil Day-Lewis** as Poet Laureate in 1972.

Particularly after his success as a broadcasting personality, Betjeman's very popularity often stood in the way of serious recognition, though this came from fellow poets like Auden and **Philip Larkin**. Technically conservative and deceptively simple in its reliance on regular rhythms and well-worn rhymes, his poetry creates a wry comedy of middle-class life and aspirations that is shot through with sadness. His sense of the smallness and superficiality of contemporary life, his melancholy Christianity and, above all, the abiding sustenance he took from English landscape and English architecture found a voice, too, in his large output of prose from *Ghastly Good Taste* (1933) onwards. His architectural writings were notable for their unfashionable advocacy of Victorian buildings, often in danger of obliteration, and their discerning eye for churches, perhaps best displayed in the introduction to *Collins Guide to English Parish Churches* (1958).

**Betrothed, The** A novel by **Sir Walter Scott**, published with *The Talisman* in 1825 under the general title *Tales of the Crusaders*. In fact, the story is set in the Welsh Marches during the reign of Henry II.

**Between the Acts** A novel by **Virginia Woolf**, published posthumously in 1941.

Virginia Woolf's last novel is set in an English country house, Pointz Hall, owned by the ageing Bartholomew Oliver and his widowed sister, Lucy Swithin. The house is also occupied by their nephew, Giles Oliver, a stockbroker, and his wife, Isa, whose poetic inner thoughts are rendered in **stream of consciousness** and correspond to the metaphorical impulse which underlies the main action.

The novel centres upon the performance of a village pageant during a June afternoon in 1939. This takes place in the grounds of Pointz Hall, and is directed by Miss La Trobe, a lesbian artist whose creative aspirations are continually thwarted by reality. The pageant itself occupies the bulk of the novel, a fragmentary re-enactment of English history by means of songs and tableaux. Naïvely comic aspects are offset by an underlying nostalgia as a communal image of rural England is interwoven with the spectators' varying interpretations.

The author's intention seems to be to celebrate the lasting values in English country life ('We act different parts; but are the same') and to indict the contemporary age for its shallow pretensions. The imminent threat of annihilation in World War II is a recurrent background theme.

When the pageant reaches its climax in the present day (June 1939) the audience is confronted by mirrors and asked how 'orts, scraps and fragments like ourselves' can build the great wall of civilization. A gramophone runs down ambiguously ('*Unity – Dispersity*. It gurgled *Un . . . dis . . .* And ceased') but the novel closes on a note of qualified optimism: 'Before they slept, they must fight; after they had fought, they would embrace. From that embrace another life might be born.'

**Bevis of Hampton (or Beves of Hamtoun)** A **verse romance** in **tail-rhyme** stanzas and octosyllabic couplets, probably written in Southampton *c.* 1300. The story exists in several European languages; the source of the Middle English romance is an Anglo-Norman version. Bevis's father is murdered by his mother's lover and he is taken by pirates and sold as a slave to the Saracen King of Armenia. He gains favour at court and the King's daughter Josian falls in love with him and renounces her faith. Her father objects and contrives to have Bevis imprisoned; Josian is forcibly married but manages to preserve her virginity. After seven years Bevis escapes from prison, rescues her and subdues a giant, Ascopart, who becomes their ally. Bevis goes to England to aid the faithful steward against his father's murderer, now the new Earl of Southampton, but has to return when Josian is condemned to burn for murdering a knight who forced her to marry him. Bevis succeeds in defeating his stepfather and mother, marries Josian and becomes Earl of Southampton but he is forced to flee again when his horse kills King Edgar's son. In his absence Josian gives birth to twins and is abducted by Ascopart. After many years the family is reunited. Despite being needlessly long and packed with spurious incident, the romance is enlivened by touches of humour and the characters of its hero and heroine are sympathetically drawn.

**Bewick, Thomas** 1753–1828 Wood engraver. The son of a small farmer, Bewick was born and educated at Ovingham, Northumberland, and was apprenticed to Thomas Beilby (1744–1817), a Newcastle engraver whose partner he later became. He is credited with having revived wood engraving, a neglected art when he began his career. His first cuts for **Gay**'s *Fables* were completed before the end of his apprenticeship and gained a prize from the Society of Arts. They were published in 1779, and followed by the *Select Fables* of 1784. Although his early work is based on previous illustrators, he invariably improved on their technique, and swiftly developed into an artist of remarkable facility as an interpreter of animal life, and a humorist in the tradition of **Hogarth**. His most original and characteristic work is to be found in the lovingly executed wild-life illustrations and vignettes of country life in *A General History of Quadrupeds* (1790), and *A History of British Birds* (2 vols., 1797, 1804). He also cut blocks for *Poems by Goldsmith and Parnell* (1795); **Thomson**'s *The Seasons* (1805) and *Fables of Aesop* (1818). His admirers included **Wordsworth**, **Carlyle**, **Ruskin** and the ornithologist **Audubon**, who visited him in his workshop in 1827. Apart from a brief period in London in his youth, Bewick spent his life in Newcastle. His *Memoir* (1862) contains absorbing descriptions of his Northumberland childhood and the development of the techniques of his craft.

**Bhattacharya, Bhabani** 1906– Indian novelist, born in Bhagalpur. He studied in Patna and London before travelling widely as journalist and lecturer. The Bengal famine of 1942–3 shocked him into writing his first, uncompromisingly realistic novel, *So Many Hungers* (1947), about 3 million deaths making 'thirty new millionaires'. His fiction confronts many Indian social problems, always with compassion for the victims of injustice: the young wife in an arranged marriage in *Music for Mohini* (1952), villagers resisting greedy businessmen in *A Goddess Named Gold* (1960). This compassion blends particularly felicitously with social satire in *He Who Rides a Tiger* (1954), about caste and wealth, and, less convincingly, within a broadly political dimension, in *Shadow from Ladakh* (1967). In *A Dream in Hawaii* (1978) a holy man paradoxically retains his integrity within American-style commercialized religion. *Steel Hawk* (1968) is a volume of short stories. Bhattacharya has also published non-fiction and translated Rabindranath Tagore.

**Bible in English, The** The task of translating the Bible into English has been in hand in almost every decade since the 1520s. Then, it was a dangerous thing to do. Now, many modern English versions compete for a publishing market.

Before the Reformation, for over 1000 years, the Bible existed primarily in Latin, descended from Jerome's 4th-century versions, known as the Vulgate. Parts were paraphrased or translated, sometimes with some brilliance, into Anglo-Saxon (by **Aelfric**, for example) and Middle English; in the late 14th century the followers of **John Wyclif** translated the entire Vulgate into English for the first time. That Lollard Bible was in two versions, hand-written and prohibitive in cost, yet with a pastoral aim not far from the spirit of the Protestant Reformation, and, in particular, the work of **William Tyndale**. His urgent need to enable 'the boy that driveth the plough' to know Scripture impelled him to give his life to the work, in two senses. His translations of the New Testament, between

1525 and 1534, were from the original Greek (of which a good text had just been established by **Erasmus**), and his translations of the Old Testament books of the Pentateuch (1530 and 1534), Jonah (1531) and Judges to 2 Chronicles were from the Hebrew. This work set a norm.

It is remarkable that the very first printed translations into English remain in many ways the best, even though the language was then considered hardly worthy enough and scholarship has since provided better original texts. Tyndale was a good scholar of Greek and Hebrew at a time when to be so was rare. His sense of how those languages might go into English produced phrases often so clear and arresting that all but the most bizarre of later attempts, even down to our own day, stand in some relation to his work. This is often imperceptibly familiar, because later translations took it over. Yet there have been enough later changes to make his translations still have extraordinary freshness. His serpent says to Eve not 'Ye shall not surely die' as in the Authorized Version (Genesis 3:4) but 'Tush ye shall not die'; of Joseph in Egypt Tyndale says not, as in the Authorized Version, 'and the Lord was with Joseph and he was a prosperous man' (Genesis 39:2) but 'the Lord was with Joseph and he was a luckie felawe'. The sixth chapter of Matthew, part of the Sermon on the Mount, does not end with the Authorized Version's remote and Latinate 'Sufficient unto the day is the evil thereof', but with 'For each day hath enough of his owne trouble.'

Only one copy of Tyndale's first complete New Testament of 1526 survives, so ruthless were the authorities; readers in England were persecuted, and there was a public burning of books at St Paul's Cross. Tyndale worked in permanent exile, often in hiding and even on the run. His enemies caught him in May 1535 and blocked attempts to release him: he was strangled and burned at the stake at Vilvorde, near Brussels, in October 1536. His dying words were, 'Lord, open the King of England's eyes.'

His fellow worker **Miles Coverdale**, whose Englishing of the Psalms is cherished to this day in the **Book of Common Prayer**, used Tyndale's work, some then unpublished, to produce a complete Bible – the first to be printed in English – at Cologne in 1535. A year later Henry VIII gave royal licence for an English Bible. Known as Matthew's Bible, it was said to have been edited by John Rogers, but these names were devices to conceal the work of Tyndale – the elaborate initials 'W. T.' at the end of Malachi, and thus between the Testaments, perhaps covertly indicate this. A revised version by Richard Taverner followed in 1539. Later in the same year the first Great Bible, the only 'official' Bible in English, was ordered to be set up in churches. It was prepared by

Coverdale as another revision of Matthew's Bible (and thus again of Tyndale) and carried a prologue by the Archbishop of Canterbury, **Thomas Cranmer**.

Two decades later the most international of all English Bibles appeared, a remarkable result of humanist and Reformation scholarship. English Protestants escaping from Mary had arrived in Geneva, which was then a powerhouse of textual research and translation into European vernaculars, of secular classics as well as Scripture. The English exiles, including Coverdale, worked on a new translation into English which they were able to present to Queen Elizabeth soon after her accession, in 1560. This, the Geneva Bible, had indexes, copious explanatory notes on every page, maps and elucidatory pictures, in a tradition going back to Tyndale – illumination, as a preface frankly said, 'of all the hard places'. It was a Bible for readers at all levels, and for nearly a century it was the Bible of the English people, influencing **Shakespeare**, **Milton** and many others. It set a new standard in Greek and Hebrew scholarship. In 1576 the New Testament was revised, with only slight changes to the text but complete reworking of the notes, now full and often surprisingly engaging, by Laurence Tomson of Magdalen College, Oxford. In 1599 the Book of Revelation was given vast new notes by the European theologian 'Junius'. In the hundred years of its life, the Geneva Bible came in many forms, large and small, black-letter and Roman, but – especially when it had Tomson's New Testament – it was encyclopaedic. A whole world of learning, often including concordances, the Book of Common Prayer, Sternhold and Hopkins's metrical psalms (see **Psalters**) and changing but usually impressive preliminary matter, it made a *locus* of Reformation and Renaissance scholarship. Even the two Roman Catholic, Vulgate-based retorts to Geneva – a New Testament from Rheims in 1582 and an Old Testament from Douai in 1609 – make use of it, for all their huffing against Protestants. Yet the Geneva Bible has been quite forgotten. Worse, it was replaced for political reasons, being dismissed as bitterly Calvinistic, which it is not. Worst of all, it has been shrivelled to a vulgar nickname and called the Breeches Bible because in Genesis 2:7 it says (as did the Lollard Bibles, incidentally) that Adam and Eve 'made themselves breeches'.

The Bishops' Bible, an attempt led by Archbishop **Matthew Parker** to rival Geneva with a more Latinate, Vulgate-based translation, with few notes, appeared in 1568 but did not establish itself. James I, however, decided that he found the Geneva Bible objectionable and at the Hampton Court Conference of 1604 he initiated a new translation. A panel of 54 scholars was appointed, divided into six groups. **Lancelot**

**Andrewes** was head of one of the groups at Westminster. The Authorized Version (so called, although it was never authorized) or King James Bible appeared in 1611, incidentally to broadside attacks on its accuracy. It carried an obsequious dedication to James which contrasts unhealthily with the urgent religious concern of the dedication of the Geneva Bible to Elizabeth. This translation was in fact largely a revision heavily dependent on the scholarship of the Geneva Bible and the phrasing of Tyndale but taking from the Bishops' Bible and Rheims New Testament a more lofty, Latinate orotundity. The translators' declared aim, 'to make a good one better', was often doubtfully achieved. The Authorized Version certainly contains many famous beauties, such as 'And the glory of the Lord shall be revealed, and all flesh shall see it together: for the mouth of the Lord hath spoken it' (Isaiah 40:5), or Jesus's 'Father, forgive them, for they know not what they do' (Luke 23:34) or 'In my Father's house are many mansions' (John 14:2). But that phrase from Isaiah comes from the Geneva Bible, and the two New Testament phrases come from Tyndale. The much-loved Christmas stories in Matthew 2 and Luke 3 are virtually unchanged from Tyndale and Geneva. Where the Authorized Version differs, whether or not from the Bishops' Bible, it can in fact be very unlovely: 'Nevertheless the dimness shall not be such as was in her vexation' (Isaiah 9:1); 'The treacherous dealers have dealt treacherously; yea, the treacherous dealers have dealt very treacherously' (Isaiah 24:16); 'We do you to wit' (2 Corinthians 8:1); 'I long after you all in the bowels of Jesus Christ' (Philippians 1:8). Though King James had set his translators specifically to avoid marginal notes, the Authorized Version was later printed eight times with Geneva's notes.

The Authorized Version gradually ousted the Geneva Bible. Its overwhelming impact on English literature since its first appearance, though commonly asserted, is in fact quite hard to substantiate. Certainly a reader who does not know an earlier Bible in English will miss much of the meaning of religious writing like the poems of **George Herbert** or the poetry and much of the prose of **Henry Vaughan**, or of a satire like **Dryden**'s *Absalom and Achitophel*. In spite of what is sometimes said, **John Bunyan**'s English comes from common speech rather than the Authorized Version. **Jonathan Swift**, however, in *A Proposal for Correcting the English Tongue* (1712), wrote that 'the translators of the Bible were masters of an English stile much fitter for the work, than we see in any of our present writings' and praised 'the simplicity of the whole'; **Coleridge** believed that 'without this holdfast, our vitiated imaginations would refine away language to mere abstractions'. By the time of its first official revision in the Revised Version of 1881–5, the Authorized Version had become a hallowed classic of English literature, and the revisers could state, wrongly, that it had been revered from its first appearance.

Between the Authorized Version of 1611 and the Revised Version of 1881–5 there were some 150 published translations of all or part of the Bible, some admirable and some odd. Some, like Dr Challoner's revisions of Douai and Rheims, were influential in their time. Between the 1880s and 1939 at least seven 'one-man' translations of the whole Bible into English were printed. Two dozen 'one-man' New Testaments have appeared in the last hundred years, not to mention a host of parts of the Bible. In the last 25 years, for example, over 150 translations of sections of the Bible into English have been published. Modern printing techniques can conceal the sheer size of the undertaking, to say nothing of the necessity of professional expertise in textual scholarship and so many different kinds of Hebrew and Greek. In this century, the modern translations by Moffatt, by Weymouth, by Ferrar Fenton, by Goodspeed, by Knox and by Barclay have been influential and are still well regarded. Just after World War II, the English editions of the (American) Revised Standard Version were widely used; the translations of Paul's letters by J. B. Phillips alerted a generation to the fact that Paul did not write in an archaic code, but made vivid modern sense (as did his original Greek). As the Bible in local vernaculars spreads now across the world – the Bible, or part of it, is to date in over 1700 languages – so more is learned about how the special revelations of the Old and New Testaments might best come across to late 20th-century English-reading people. There are now many different versions of the Bible in English in print, including several attempts to modernize the Authorized Version. Those with greatest impact have been: The New English Bible (1970), which is lucid but sometimes disliked; The Living Bible (1971), a paraphrase; Today's English Version (1976), popularly known by its American title, Good News Bible, which combines accuracy with a relaxed readability that is a long way from the Authorized Version; The Jerusalem Bible (1966), an often ponderous antidote to raciness; and the rather patchwork New International Version (1979). New Testament scholars often use the excellent Translator's New Testament (1973), which hits the theological nail on the head every time; it is designed to help those who translate the New Testament into remoter languages.

More Bibles in English are now sold than ever before. The number of English readers has risen from six million under Elizabeth I to 600 million now. Whether the proportion of Bible students has changed is arguable. It is debatable whether it matters that now so many people do not know that 'the scales fell from his eyes', for example, comes from Acts 9:18 (Tyndale, via the Authorized Version). It is an emotive question whether men and women who lack Greek should have the clear access to the doctrines of the Epistle to the Romans that they can find in very modern translations, rather than a reverential knowledge of the Authorized Version. Tyndale did not die for antiquarianism. He thought of the ploughboy in the field. Certainly the Bible in English has had an effect on our literature that is beyond fathoming. Many hundreds of fine phrases have passed into the language, to form a body of allusions of lapidary beauty unmatched by anything from any other source. In the study of English literature, not to know them is to be deprived of a rich store, as a student is deprived who does not know Virgil. But the greatest impact of the Bible in English has always been from the message and its accessibility. Shakespeare used Bible cadences, of course – from the Geneva and Bishops' Bibles. Deep in him, however, were the roots of the Bible doctrines. This is something of far greater significance than a sentimental regret for the passing of the Authorized Version – with which Shakespeare, in any case, had no connection. If the Bible in English,. even despised modern English, is today being read and understood, Tyndale did not die in vain.

**Bible in Spain, The** **George Borrow**'s colourful narrative of his travels through Portugal and Spain, published in 1843. Ostensibly an account of his five years' service (1835–40) as an agent of the British and Foreign Bible Society, committed to distributing a Protestant New Testament in a Catholic country where it was not wanted, the book describes adventures in remote regions, encounters with gypsies and bandits and frequent confrontations with authority. The inherent absurdity, indeed illegality, of the enterprise added spice to stories often told with great vivacity and directness, the reader having no means of distinguishing between fact and fiction. Based partly on his Spanish notebooks, and partly on the set of remarkable reports he had sent his employers from Spain, it was accepted as authentic both by **John Murray**, a publisher ill-disposed to fiction, and by an Evangelical reading public that most enjoyed sensational adventures when they could be thought to have happened in reality. The book was a best-seller on both sides of the Atlantic and was never out of print during the 19th century.

**Bickerstaff, Isaac** A character invented by **Swift**, supposed to be the author of the *Predictions for the Ensuing Year* (1708), a collection of spoof prophesies at the expense of John Partridge, a cobbler turned astrologer, currently fashionable for his almanac. In Swift's version, Partridge's death is foretold for 29 March and, despite the hapless quack's protestations to the contrary, 'Bickerstaff' successfully 'proved' that his prediction had been fulfilled. This idea caught the imagination of **Steele**, who adopted the nickname of Bickerstaff when he started *The Tatler* in 1709.

**Bickerstaffe, Isaac** 1733–*c*. 1808 Irish-born dramatist who, between 1760 and 1771, was largely responsible for the emergence and fashionable acceptance of English comic opera. His early successes, *Thomas and Sally* (1760) and the excellent *Love in a Village* (1762), had accompanying music by Thomas Arne. *The Maid of the Mill* (1765) and *The Royal Garland* (1768) were provided with music, in part and in whole respectively, by Samuel Arnold. Bickerstaffe's other music dramas were written chiefly in collaboration with **Charles Dibdin**. The best of these is *Lionel and Clarissa* (1768). Two serenatas, written by Bickerstaffe and Dibdin for performance at Ranelagh House, *The Ephesian Matron* (1769) and *The Recruiting Serjeant* (1770), promised new developments in the collaboration, but Bickerstaffe's career was brought to a sudden end in 1772, when he was threatened with arrest as a homosexual. He fled to the Continent, where he lived in obscurity for a further 40 years.

**Bierce, Ambrose (Gwinnett)** 1842–*c*. 1914 American short-story writer, born in Horse Cave Creek, Ohio. He fought in the Civil War, and reached the rank of major, but saw his part as a soldier as little more than that of a paid assassin. This bitterness (his nickname was 'Bitter Bierce') later informed his Civil War stories – stories of defeat and disillusionment. When the war ended Bierce went to California and eventually became a journalist, contributing to the celebrated *Overland Monthly*, which **Bret Harte** had helped to establish. Later he published his own newsletter, and with Harte, **Mark Twain** and **Joaquin Miller** constituted a Western literary circle. With the departure of Twain and Harte for the East, his position as chief arbiter of the Western literary establishment (and later, chief short-story writer) was unchallenged.

He went to England in 1872, where he lived and wrote until 1876. Although he was a busy contributor to periodicals, his success did not match that of his San Francisco period, and he returned there to write for William Randolph Hearst's *Examiner*. In 1891 he published *Tales of Soldiers and Civilians* (entitled *In The Midst of Life* in England and in the 1898 US edition), and *Can Such Things Be?* in 1893. He moved to Washington in 1897 as the capital correspondent for the Hearst papers. He contributed to *Cosmopolitan*

and in 1906 published *The Cynic's Word Book*, a volume of ironic definitions. He also published verse and essays. In 1913, estranged from all family connections, Bierce went to Mexico, where civil war was raging, and disappeared. It is not known exactly when or how he died.

***Big Money, The*** See **USA**.

**Bigg, John Stanyon** 1828–65 Journalist and poet of the **Spasmodic School**. Born at Ulverston in Lancashire, Bigg became editor of its local paper in 1848. In the same year he published his first work, *The Sea King*, a metrical romance in six cantos. He later worked as a journalist in Ulster but returned to his home town in 1860. His other writings include *Night and Soul* (1854), the novel *Alfred Staunton* (1860) and a final volume of poetry, *Shifting Scenes and Other Poems* (1862).

***Biglow Papers, The*** Two series of popular satirical verses by **James Russell Lowell**, written in Yankee dialect. The first series (1848) opposes the Mexican War, and the second (1867) attacks the policy of the Confederate states in the Civil War.

**Bildungsroman** A 'novel of development', tracing the protagonist's growth, usually from birth or early childhood, into adulthood and maturity. The prototype is Goethe's *Wilhelm Meister's Apprenticeship* (1795–6), translated into English by **Carlyle** in 1824. Even an incomplete list of major examples suggests how important a part the form has played in English fiction since then: **Dickens**'s *David Copperfield* and *Great Expectations*, **Samuel Butler**'s *The Way of All Flesh*, **D. H. Lawrence**'s *Sons and Lovers*, **Joyce**'s *Portrait of the Artist as a Young Man* and **E. M. Forster**'s *The Longest Journey*.

**Billings, Josh** Pseudonym of the American comic writer Henry Wheeler Shaw (1818–85), born in Lanesboro, Massachusetts. Like **Artemus Ward**, **Petroleum V. Nasby** and **Mark Twain**, Shaw began his career as a humorist with contributions to local newspapers. These early pieces attracted the attention of Artemus Ward, who helped him publish his first collection, *Josh Billings: Hiz Sayings*, in 1865. Thereafter he became a favourite exponent of agrarian folk wisdom and reached an immense public with his comments on government, fashionable pretension and political corruption. His publications include *Josh Billings on Ice, and Other Things* (1868), *Everybody's Friend* (1874), *Josh Billings' Trump Kards* (1877) and *Josh Billings' Spice Box* (1881). From 1869 to 1880 he published a parody annual called *Farmer's Allminax*. In the tradition of the vernacular humorists of his day, he lectured widely in his Josh Billings persona and commanded a large popular audience.

*Billy Budd, Sailor* A short novel by **Herman Melville**, begun in 1886 but left in semi-final draft form at the time of his death in 1891.

The story is set aboard HMS *Bellipotent* in 1797, a tense period following mutinies in the navy during the war between England and France. Billy Budd, the 'Handsome Sailor' of sailors' folklore, is impressed from a merchant-man, the *Rights-of-Man*. He quickly adjusts to life aboard a man-of-war and is a favourite of the crew, but he becomes the target of the envious and brutal master-at-arms, John Claggart. Claggart concocts a plot of a supposed mutiny and accuses Billy of being involved in it before the ship's commander, Captain Vere. The innocent Billy, unable to answer the charge because of a chronic stammer, strikes Claggart on the forehead and kills him. Vere, though recognizing the falsity of Claggart's story and sympathizing with the agonized Billy, fears reaction among the crew if Billy is not punished for assaulting a superior. He calls a drumhead court and in effect instructs it to find Billy guilty of a capital crime. The court, though troubled by the ambiguities of the case and by Vere's precipitate action, condemns Billy, who is hanged from the yardarm after crying out, 'God bless Captain Vere!' Some time later Vere is killed during an engagement with the French; his last murmured words are Billy's name.

**Bingham, Joseph** 1668–1723 Religious historian. Born at Wakefield in Yorkshire, he attended Wakefield Grammar School, and completed his education at University College, Oxford, where he became a fellow in 1689. In literature he is remembered for his exhaustive *Origines Ecclesiasticae, or, The Antiquities of the Christian Church*, a 20-year labour (10 vols., 1708–22).

*Bingo* A play by **Edward Bond**, first performed at the Northcott Theatre, Exeter, in 1973.

Seeking quiet in retirement at Stratford, **Shakespeare** is trapped between the home pressures of a sick wife and embittered daughter and the external pressures of the local factions for and against enclosures. He is drawn by his friend Combe into collusion in the oppressive Welcombe enclosures. In the second half of the play, Shakespeare talks with the visiting **Ben Jonson** and is further convinced of his own complicity in social oppression. Preferring death to perpetual self-disgust, he kills himself, leaving his daughter Judith to search for his will.

**Binyon, (Robert) Laurence** 1869–1943 Poet and art historian. He was born in Lancaster and educated at Trinity College, Oxford, where his

poem 'Persephone' won the Newdigate Prize. He worked at the British Museum in 1893–1933, first in the Department of Printed Books and later as Keeper of the Department of Oriental Prints and Books. He published *Etchers of the Seventeenth Century* (1895), *Paintings in the Far East* (1908) and *Landscape in British Art and Poetry* (1931). Eight volumes of poetry include *Lyric Poems* (1894), *Winnowing Fan: Poems of the Great War* (1914), *The New World* (1918) and *The Burning of the Leaves and Other Poems* (1944). 'For the Fallen' (1914) and 'The Burning of the Leaves' are standard anthology poems, reflecting his main themes of mutability and decay. He also wrote several odes, including *The Sirens* (1924) and *The Fools* (1928); several verse dramas, including *Arthur* (1923) with music by Edward Elgar, *Brief Candles* (1938) and *The Madness of Merlin* (unfinished, 1947). His translation of Dante's *Divine Comedy* appeared in 1933–43.

*Biographia Literaria* A philosophical and autobiographical work by **S. T. Coleridge**, published in 1817. Originally conceived in 1814 as a brief critical preface to *Sibylline Leaves*, it rapidly grew into a two-volume *causerie* on his 'literary life and opinions'. Unsystematic, inexhaustibly communicative, and untied to a single literary register, it is entirely lacking in the aesthetic and recapitulatory 'finish' of conventional autobiography. Whether his subject matter is his youthful admiration for the sonnets of **William Bowles**, his early friendship with and domestic proximity to **Wordsworth**, or the 'associationist' tradition in philosophy from Aristotle to **Hartley** and the challenge to it issuing from Kant and his German Romantic successors, Coleridge invariably begins, and not infrequently ends, *in medias res*. Important theoretical matters are forced to queue behind passages of advice to would-be writers and the detailed enumeration of the practical difficulties of publishing and editing journals. As in the lectures and *Table Talk*, his method is excitingly oblique and inspirational, the moment of insight sudden and often wonderfully incandescent.

The underlying philosophical concern of the *Biographia* is the process, as opposed to the fact, of human creativity. The predominantly empirical English tradition of literary and philosophical thought bequeathed by the 18th to the early 19th century had tended, for Coleridge, to view culture and creativity as simple givens rather than as the products of a specifically constituted intelligence. His famous definition of the creative intelligence, or the 'Imagination', issues from an exploration (which takes him through pioneering readings of Kant, Fichte, Schelling and the brothers Schlegel) of the structure of the relations between subjectivity and objectivity, self and world, speculative reason and rational understanding (Chapters IX, XII, XIII). As the universal human faculty through which these antinomies are reconciled, or rendered merely apparent, the Imagination is by no means the monopoly of a particular group or a specific practice, though Coleridge is in no doubt that it finds its greatest adepts among poets, and its highest form of expression in poetry and aesthetic culture. Like Friedrich Schiller before him, in the celebrated *Letters on the Aesthetic Education of Man* (1794), though in a more fragmentary form, he envisages the substitution – spearheaded by the greatest among the poetic *avant-garde* of the time – of a dynamic and progressive aesthetic culture for the grievously divided political cultures of the revolutionary and post-revolutionary era.

Having come to the central point of his theoretical meditations, Coleridge abruptly drops it, and Volume II of the book consists largely of a critique of his erstwhile collaborator Wordsworth, interspersed with essays on **Shakespeare**, and the 'origin and elements of metre' and the differences between poetry and prose. Here he turns from the theory to the psychology of the creative process, and the question of the inner preconditions and workings of authentic Imagination. Before **Shelley**'s unpublished *Philosophical View of Reform* of 1820, Coleridge's theory of the imagination and the commitments it enjoined was English Romanticism's most carefully articulated response to the multiple contradictions of early industrial society. Its influence upon later 19th- and 20th-century cultural theory has been, to say the least, pervasive, and its model of the creative process is the one with which students of poetry and literature are still most readily familiar.

**Bird, Robert (Montgomery)** 1806–54 American novelist and playwright. Bird was born in Delaware and attended the University of Pennsylvania, where he received an MD in 1827. He taught for a short period at Pennsylvania Medical College (1841–3) but left to take up a career as a writer. He began with romantic plays about Philadelphia life, including *The City Looking Glass* (1828, first published 1933), and historical dramas: *Pelopidas*, *The Gladiator* and *Oralloosa* (1830, 1831 and 1832, respectively; all published in 1919), and *The Broker of Bogota* (1834, first published 1917). His first novel, *Calavar, or, the Knight of the Conquest*, was published anonymously in 1834 and its favourable reception prompted him to write a sequel, *The Infidel, or, The Fall of Mexico* (1835). He then turned to stories of Pennsylvania society: *The Hawks of Hawk-Hollow* (1835), about a well-to-do family's fatal lack of patriotism; and *Sheppard Lee* (1836), a satire on contemporary society, informed by Bird's Whig politics.

*Nick of the Woods, or, The Jibbenainosay* (1837) is generally considered to be his best novel. Set at the end of the American Revolution, it concerns the abduction of a white woman by Indians who, unlike those of **James Fenimore Cooper**, are not in the least noble. Its leading character is a Quaker known as Bloody Nathan or Nick of the Woods, who kills Indians mercilessly to avenge the murder of his family. Bird published two other books: *Peter Pilgrim, or, A Rambler's Recollections* (1838, travel sketches); and *The Adventures of Robin Day* (1839, a novel).

**Birdsell, Sandra** 1942– Canadian short-story writer. Born and brought up in rural Manitoba, she now lives in Winnipeg. Her two collections of short stories, *Night Travellers* (1982) and *Ladies of the House* (1984), tell of girls' and women's lives in a small prairie community where domestic ordinariness is supplemented by an imaginative sense of family and local history. As a western writer who publishes with a regional press in Manitoba, Birdsell is an important new voice in the long tradition of prairie women's fiction.

**Birmingham, George A.** Pseudonym of James Owen Hannay (1865–1950), novelist and playwright. Born in Belfast into a clerical family, he was educated at Haileybury and Trinity College, Dublin. Ordained as a Church of Ireland clergyman in 1889, he was rector of Westport, County Mayo, from 1892 to 1913, where he became interested in agricultural reform and **Douglas Hyde**'s Gaelic League. He travelled and held various appointments, including army chaplain in France 1916–17 and chaplain to the British legation in Budapest 1922–4, before settling in England in 1924. His early literary work included a clerical biography of his father-in-law and two scholarly volumes on early Christian monasticism, but he turned to novel-writing in 1905. The important early novels such as *Hyacinth* (1906) and *The Bad Times* (1908) are serious, compassionate explorations of the tangle of recent Irish history and contemporary politics from a moderate nationalist standpoint. With the success of the more light-hearted *Spanish Gold* (1908) he won a large popular audience but he unintentionally offended Roman Catholic and extreme nationalist sensibilities with the social criticism of *The Seething Pot* (1905) and the gentle satire of *General John Regan*, a comedy which had been successful in the West End but caused a riot when performed in Westport in 1914. His *Red Hand of Ulster* (1912) poked fun at unionist militancy at the height of the anti-Home-Rule crisis and fantasized about a unionist gun-running expedition which actually took place shortly afterwards. His later books are chiefly well-observed light comedies of Irish (and

English) life. In all he wrote more than 80 books and countless articles and pamphlets on many subjects. His autobiography *Pleasant Places* appeared in 1934.

**Birney, (Alfred) Earle** 1904– Canadian poet and novelist. Born in Calgary, he lived as a boy on farms in Northern Alberta and in British Columbia. After working at a range of jobs, including those of bank clerk and farm labourer, he attended the University of British Columbia and went on to do postgraduate work at the University of Toronto and the University of California, Berkeley. He became a prominent Trotskyist in the 1930s and, while teaching at the University of Utah, was embroiled in controversy because of his political affiliations. During a year at the University of London as a Royal Society of Canada Fellow he travelled to Norway to interview Trotsky. During World War II he served as a personnel selection officer with the Canadian army and afterwards supervised broadcasts to Europe for the Canadian Broadcasting Corporation. From 1946 to 1965 he was Professor of English at the University of British Columbia, where he introduced Canada's first creative writing department.

Birney did not begin writing verse until the late 1930s, but he has come to be regarded as one of Canada's most important poets. His verse deals with an encyclopaedic range of Canadian subjects, but he has also travelled extensively and written poems about virtually every area of the globe. His early writing is characterized by a belief that art can change the course of experience and frequently supposes knowledge of myth and early English cultural traditions. More recently these attitudes have been replaced by an absurdist view of the human experience and from *Ice Cod Bell and Stone* (1962) onwards he has written in a more colloquial North American voice. Birney has written in a wide variety of styles, demonstrating considerable technical virtuosity in all of them. His best work includes the verse drama *Trial of a City* (1952; later republished as *The Damnation of Vancouver*), in which the 'trial' debates whether Vancouver, representing modern urban civilization, ought to be destroyed, and the comic 'military picaresque' *Turvey* (1977). His other volumes of poetry include *David and Other Poems* (1942), *Near False Mouth* (1964) and his *Collected Poems* (1975).

**Birrell, Augustine** 1850–1933 Politician and essayist. The son of a Baptist minister in Liverpool, Birrell became a barrister in 1875 and entered Parliament as MP for West Fife in 1889. He became President of the Board of Education (1905) and Chief Secretary for Ireland (1907), a post he resigned after the Parliamentary storm following the Easter Rising of 1916. Birrell's collections of literary essays, *Obiter Dicta* (1884, 1887 and 1924), were popular; his other writings include a biography of **Charlotte Brontë** (1887) and studies of **William Hazlitt** (1902) and **Andrew Marvell** (1905) for the English Men of Letters series.

***Birth of Merlin, The*** See **Rowley, William** and **Shakespeare apocrypha**.

***Birthday Party, The*** The first of **Harold Pinter**'s plays to attract attention (and abuse), it opened at the Arts Theatre, Cambridge, in 1957.

In a seaside boarding-house belonging to a deck-chair attendant and his eccentric wife, Meg, the only boarder is Stanley, who claims to have been a concert pianist and who suffers from the persecution mania of a neurotic refugee. When two new boarders, a Jew called Goldberg and an Irishman called McCann, come to lodge at the house, Stanley is terrified. At a birthday party, given in his honour, he is driven to hysteria during a game of blind man's buff. The next day, Goldberg and McCann remove him to an unknown destination.

**Bishop, Elizabeth** 1911–79 American poet. Following the early death of her father and her mother's mental illness, she was raised by grandparents in Nova Scotia and in her birthplace of Worcester, Massachusetts. *Questions of Travel* (1965) contains a number of poems about her experiences in Brazil, where she spent 16 years. *Poems: North and South A Cold Spring* (1955) won her the Pulitzer Prize. Another product of her time in Brazil is a translation from the Portuguese of *The Diary of 'Helena Morley'* (1957), the diary of a young Brazilian girl at the end of the 19th century, whom Bishop met when she was an old woman. *The Complete Poems* (1969) won the National Book Award; *Geography III* appeared in 1976. *The Collected Prose* was published in 1984 and includes autobiographical sketches, travel accounts, a memoir of **Marianne Moore**, and several short stories.

***Bishop Blougram's Apology*** A **dramatic monologue** by **Robert Browning**, published in *Men and Women* (1855). The worldly, comfort-loving but highly intelligent Bishop treats his listener, the journalist Gigadibs, to a virtuoso performance that leaves him and the reader still uncertain of the extent or nature of his religious faith. In the process, the poem offers a minute and skilful examination of the various grounds for faith and doubt in the 19th century. Contemporaries widely assumed, and Browning did not deny, that the model for Blougram was Nicholas Wiseman, who in 1850 had become Archbishop of Westminster and Primate of the Roman Catholic Church in England.

**Bishop Orders His Tomb at Saint Praxed's Church, The** A dramatic monologue by **Robert Browning**, published by *Hood's Magazine* in 1845 and again the same year in *Dramatic Romances and Lyrics*. In a well-known passage from *Modern Painters* **John Ruskin** said of this poem, 'I know of no other piece of modern English, prose or poetry, in which there is so much told, as in these lines, of the Renaissance spirit – its worldliness, inconsistency, pride, hypocrisy, ignorance of itself, love of art, of luxury and of good Latin. It is nearly all that I have said of the central Renaissance in thirty pages of *The Stones of Venice*, put into as many lines.'

**Bishops' Bible, The** See **Bible in English, The**.

**Black, William** 1841–98 Scottish novelist, born in Glasgow and educated at Glasgow School of Art. His first novel, *James Merle: An Autobiography*, appeared in 1864 and was followed in 1867 by *Love or Marriage*. Black is best remembered for his novels with a Scottish setting, most notably *A Daughter of Heth* (1871), *A Princess of Thule* (1874) and *Macleod of Dare* (1878). The miscellaneous *The Strange Adventures of a Phaeton* (1872) combines elements of fiction, romance, guidebook and natural description. He contributed a study of **Goldsmith** to the English Men of Letters series in 1878. See also **Celtic revival**.

**Black Arrow, The** A novel by **Robert Louis Stevenson**, serialized in *Young Folks* between June and October 1883 and issued in book form in 1888. It is set in late 15th-century England, during the final stages of the Wars of the Roses. Stevenson himself ridiculed it as a potboiler, an example of what he called pseudo-historic 'tushery'.

Brutally reduced, the diffuse plot has three main strands. The first concerns the conflict between Yorkists and Lancastrians, and the second a group of outlaws, the Brotherhood of the Black Arrow, led by 'John Amend-All' (Ellis Duckworth). The third strand concerns the hero, Richard Shelton, and heroine, Joanna Sedley, and their relations with his treacherous uncle and guardian, Sir Daniel Brackley. Dick rescues Joanna from Sir Daniel, at first believing that she is a boy called 'John Matcham'. The activities of Duckworth and his band eventually lead Dick to suspect that his father was murdered by Sir Daniel. The three stories are eventually resolved after the Battle of Shoreby, where the Yorkists are victorious and Dick is knighted by Richard of Gloucester. He spares his uncle's life but Sir Daniel is killed by Duckworth and the last Black Arrow. The book ends with the marriage of Dick and Joanna and his retreat into private life, as he abandons the 'heroism' which the whole novel has shown to be self-seeking and treacherous.

**Black Beauty** A novel by **Anna Sewell**, published in 1877.

One of the best animal stories ever written, *Black Beauty* charts the decline and fall of a well-bred horse brought low by neglectful grooms and overwork in the cab trade. He also suffers sadly throughout from the hated 'bearing rein', a harness designed to keep a horse's head up however hard the effect upon their breathing. Although the story's gentle Quaker author died a few months after her book was published, with the horses at her own funeral still forced to suffer from the same hated bearing rein, this practice ended soon after partly as a result of her book. Black Beauty himself is finally saved from the knacker's yard to enjoy an honourable retirement. Less fortunate is his high-spirited friend in harness Ginger, whose ignoble death in the streets of London makes for one of the most powerful passages in all **children's literature**.

**Black Dwarf, The** The first of **Sir Walter Scott**'s *Tales of My Landlord*, published in 1816. It tells the story of Elshie of the Mucklestanes, the dwarf of the title.

**Black Elk** 1863–1950 A Sioux warrior and priest born into the Oglala division of the Teton Dakota. His youth coincided with the last years of territorial freedom for the Plains Indians. Black Elk had been instructed as a child in the ancient tribal religions, and his mission to defend the embattled Indian cultures involved both active resistance of US encroachments – he fought at Little Big Horn and Wounded Knee – and the perpetuation of the spiritual vision and commitment of his forefathers. His oral autobiography, *Black Elk Speaks* (1932, recorded and edited by John Neihardt), is a moving account of his life and mission. He also delivered an account of the religious rites of the Oglala Sioux, *The Sacred Pipe* (1953, recorded and edited by John Epes Brown).

**Black Mask, The** A detective magazine, founded in 1920 by **H. L. Mencken** and **George Jean Nathan**. It began by publishing traditional stories with heroes modelled after English characters, but with the introduction of Carroll John Daly's Race Williams, the first of the hardbitten detectives, it began to reflect the realities of post-war America. **Dashiell Hammett**'s Continental Op stories, which began to appear in 1923, and Sam Spade, the hero of *The Maltese Falcon*, mirrored the cynical, detached and disillusioned times of Prohibition. **Raymond Chandler** also published extensively in *The Black Mask*, and by the time Philip Marlowe made his appearance in

1939 the magazine had fathered a unique American hero – the private eye. Other contributors included Erle Stanley Gardner, George Harmon Coxe, Frederick Nebel, Lester Dent and Horace McCoy.

**Black Mountain school** A group of American poets based at Black Mountain College near Asheville, North Carolina, in the early 1950s. A number of poets attended the experimental liberal arts college to study with **Charles Olson**, who was for a time both an instructor and rector of the college. Olson's 'projective verse', which described poems as 'open fields' conducting energy from the poet to the reader, influenced many of his students, among whom were **Robert Creeley**, **Robert Duncan** and **Denise Levertov**. The work of these poets appeared in the influential *Black Mountain Review*, published from 1954 to 1957.

**Blackburn, Paul** 1926–71 American poet. Born in St Albans, Vermont, the son of the poet Frances Frost, Blackburn was educated at the University of Wisconsin and then attended the University of Toulouse from 1954 to 1955 on a Fulbright fellowship. A prolific poet, Blackburn's early work appeared in *The Dissolving Fabric* (1955), *Brooklyn–Manhattan Transit* (1960) and *The Nets* (1961). His middle-period poems were collected in *The Cities* (1967) and *In. On. Or About the Premises* (1968). A substantial number of late poems appeared in *Halfway Down the Coast* and *The Journals*, both published in 1975. *The Collected Poems of Paul Blackburn* appeared in 1985. Before his death of cancer at the age of 44, Blackburn had also established a reputation as a translator of the Provençal troubadours and of the works of Julio Cortázar and Antonio Jiménez-Landi.

**Blackfriars Theatre** The first Blackfriars theatre opened in 1576 to house performances by the Children of the Chapel Royal. The converted room was probably the old refectory of the dissolved Blackfriars monastery inside London's city walls. There are no surviving plans or drawings on which to base reconstructions of this indoor theatre, the first of its kind known to have been open to a paying public. It closed in 1584. 12 years later James Burbage, who had built the outdoor **Theatre** in 1576, leased several rooms in the Blackfriars with the intention of converting them to an indoor theatre for an adult company. The work was halted after a protest by the Blackfriars residents, and it was not completed until 1600, when his son **Richard Burbage** (famous as the creator of many of **Shakespeare**'s greatest roles) transferred the lease to the Children of the Chapel Royal. For several years, the boy actors at the Blackfriars rivalled and sometimes outstripped the adult companies in popularity, but their tenure of the theatre (probably in the converted Parliament Chamber) ended in disarray in 1608. It was then that Richard Burbage led the **King's Men** into occupation of the Blackfriars, which they continued to run in tandem with the outdoor **Globe** until the closure of the theatres in 1642, after which it fell into disrepair.

**Blackmore, Sir Richard** *c.* 1655–1729 Minor poet and physician to Queen Anne. A well-meaning but long-winded writer, he published a *Satyr against Wit* in 1700, which was admired by his friend, Samuel Wesley. Blackmore's uncontrolled epic verses, pious and patriotic, include *The Creation* (1712) and *Redemption* (1722), which attempt to promote adherence to religion on the basis of natural reason.

**Blackmore, R[ichard] D[oddridge]** 1825–1900 Novelist. He was born at Longworth in Oxfordshire and spent most of his childhood on Exmoor in the West Country; after attending Blundell's School in Tiverton he went to Exeter College, Oxford. Called to the Bar in 1852, Blackmore preferred instead to divide his time between writing and market gardening. His earliest published works were poems and translations but he gained his first real success, and lasting fame, as a novelist with *Lorna Doone* (1869), a historical novel set on Exmoor. His other books, all overshadowed by the popularity of *Lorna Doone*, include *Clara Vaughan* (1864), *Alice Lorraine* (1875), *Cripps the Carrier* (1877), *Christowell: A Dartmoor Tale* (1881) and *Springhaven: A Tale of the Great War* (1887), set in southern England during the Napoleonic era.

**Blackstone, Sir William** 1723–80 Jurist. Born in London, and educated at Charterhouse and Pembroke College, Oxford, he became a fellow of All Souls College and the first Vinerian Professor of English Law at Oxford in 1758–66. Appointed a judge in 1770, he had the misfortune to have the loudly sociable **Goldsmith** as a neighbour in the Middle Temple. He is buried at Wallingford.

Blackstone's four-volume *Commentaries on the Laws of England* (1765–9), derived from his annual lectures at Oxford, was admired for its lucid, eloquent exposition, and regarded for many years as a definitive historical account. In it, he advances from the law of nature (being either the revealed or the inferred will of God) to municipal law, which he defines as a rule of civil conduct prescribed by the supreme power in the state, commanding what is right and what is wrong. Yet Blackstone was by no means a scientific jurist. His attempt to find a basis in history and reason for all the most characteristic English institutions was attacked by **Jeremy**

**Bentham** in his *A Fragment on Government* (1776).

**Blackwood's Edinburgh Magazine** The monthly periodical started in July 1817 by the Edinburgh publisher William Blackwood in response to the success of Constable's *Edinburgh Review* and **Murray**'s *Quarterly Review*. Originally Tory in its political outlook, it took violent objection to the so-called **Cockney School** of writers: **Lamb**, **Hazlitt**, **Leigh Hunt** and **Keats**. **J. G. Lockhart**'s attack on Keats (more notorious even than **John Wilson Croker**'s review of *Endymion* in the *Quarterly*) was published in the issue for August 1818. Other notable early contributors were **John Wilson** ('Christopher North'), whose *Noctes Ambrosianae* began publication in 1822, **James Hogg**, **William Maginn** and **Thomas De Quincey**. The *Chaldee MS*, a satire on Whig intellectuals by Lockhart, Hogg and Wilson, appeared in October 1817. In 1857 **George Eliot**'s *Scenes of Clerical Life* was published as separate tales in its pages. Known familiarly to its adherents as the 'Maga', *Blackwood's* survived until 1980.

**Blair, Robert** 1699–1746 Poet. Born the son of a clergyman in Edinburgh, Blair became a clergyman himself. While minister at Athelstaneford in East Lothian he wrote *The Grave* (1743), a blank-verse poem which owed much to **Edward Young**'s *Night Thoughts* and identified him with the **graveyard poets**. Its morbid meditation was popular with middle-class Dissenters for many years, and one edition of the poem (1808) was illustrated by **William Blake**.

**Blaise, Clark** 1940– Canadian novelist and short-story writer. Born in Fargo, North Dakota, to Canadian parents, he grew up in the southern United States with summers spent in Winnipeg, Manitoba. He studied at Denison University, Ohio, and the University of Iowa, and taught English for one year at the University of Wisconsin before going to Canada. He took out Canadian citizenship in 1966 and has taught at Concordia University, Montreal, and York University, Toronto. Blaise now lives in Iowa City, with his wife, the Indian novelist Bharati Mukherjee. His short-story collections, *A North American Education* (1973) and *Tribal Justice* (1974), and his novels, *Lunar Attractions* (1979) and *Lusts* (1983), focus on the often victimized outsider, the isolated individual struggling to find a place in an increasingly bizarre contemporary society. *Resident Alien* (1986) combines autobiographical essays and autobiographical fiction in a further exploration of geographical and personal identity. With Bharati Mukherjee, he wrote *Days and Nights in Calcutta* (1977), a fascinating account of a stay in India where their different approaches and atti-

tudes provide intriguing and complementary analyses.

**Blake, Nicholas** See **Day-Lewis, C.**

**Blake, William** 1757–1827 Poet and painter. Blake's father, James, was a successful London hosier and a Dissenter attracted by the doctrines of Emmanuel Swedenborg; nevertheless his son William was baptized at St James's Church in Piccadilly. Blake never went to school but was educated at home, chiefly by his mother. He read widely in **Shakespeare**, **Milton**, **Ben Jonson** and the Bible, and somehow picked up a knowledge of French, Italian, Latin, Greek and Hebrew. This learning, randomly acquired and independently held, underlay his later writing.

At the age of 14 Blake was apprenticed to James Basire, an engraver specializing in antiquarian and topographical work. Basire sent his pupil to make drawings of Westminster Abbey and other old churches, thus exposing him to the influence of Gothic art. At this time also Blake's fascination with the nude began, through a study of Henry Fuseli's *Reflections on the Painting and Sculpture of the Greeks*. He stayed with Basire until he was 21, but aimed higher than being a journeyman engraver; he was accepted at the recently founded Royal Academy at Somerset House, though he would soon become restless with its traditional approach.

William Blake. A detail from the portrait by T. Phillips, 1807. National Portrait Gallery, London.

In 1782 he married Catherine Boucher, and the Blakes had their first home in Leicester Fields. Among their neighbours were Jane Hogarth, widow of the artist, the pioneer surgeon and anatomist John Hunter, and **Joshua Reynolds**, the painter whose *Discourses on Art* epitomized the **neoclassicism** Blake rejected.

In 1783 two of Blake's friends, the artist John Flaxman and a **bluestocking** named Mrs Mathew, decided to print a collection of his poems. *Poetical Sketches* contained such poems as 'To the Muses' and 'My Silks and Fine Array'. In 1789 he published *Songs of Innocence*, the gentlest of all his volumes of lyrics, and *The Book of Thel*, which illustrates his early mysticism and use of emblems. *Tiriel*, written in 1788–9, is the first of his elaborately symbolic writings. Blake added *Songs of Experience* to an edition of *Songs of Innocence* in 1794; the full title of the volume was **Songs of Innocence and of Experience** *Shewing the Two Contrary States of the Human Soul*. The poems set the world of pastoral innocence and childhood against the world of adult corruption and repression; they contrast the meek virtue of 'The Lamb' with the darker forces of energy in 'The Tyger'.

Blake's dislike of human authority and his radical sympathies found natural expression in friendships with **William Godwin** and **Thomas Paine**, and increasingly in his writing. He published two sets of prose aphorisms under the title *There is No Natural Religion* and a third called *All Religions Are One* (all *c.* 1788), as well as *The French Revolution: A Poem in Seven Books* (*c.* 1791), only one book of which survived. 1790 was the year in which he engraved **The Marriage of Heaven and Hell**, his principal prose work.

The Blakes moved south of the Thames to Lambeth in 1793, the period when he began to work on his 'prophetic books'. In his new home Blake executed some of his most famous engravings, including those for *The Book of Job* and for **Edward Young**'s *Night Thoughts* – though his early admiration for 'graveyard' poetry waned and he came to regard it as insipid. He wrote *The Visions of the Daughters of Albion* (1793), introducing the figures of his personal mythology: Urizen, the grim symbol of restrictive morality, and Orc, the arch-rebel. Urizen appears with all his depressing characteristics in *America: A Prophecy* (1793).

The ideas of *The Marriage of Heaven and Hell* and the personified symbols encountered in *The Visions of the Daughters of Albion* are developed in *Europe* and *The Book of Urizen* (1794), *The Book of Ahania*, *The Book of Los* and *The Song of Los* (1795), in which Blake pursued his exposure of the errors of the moral code. Urizen has been expelled from the abode of the immortals and has taken possession of man; his agent, or archangel, is Enitharmon. Los is apparently the champion of light and the lord of time, but is held in bondage. Orc is the symbol of anarchy, opposed to Urizen. The whole sequence is an inversion of Milton's *Paradise Lost*, which Blake denounced for trying to justify the evil committed by God. His criticism of Christianity is strongest in *Europe* and *The Song of Los*. *Vala* was probably begun in 1795; its rewritten version, *The Four Zoas, The Torments of Love and Jealousy in the Death and Judgement of Albion the Ancient Man*, appeared in 1797. The four Zoas of the title – Urizen (reason), Urthonah (spirit), Luvah (passion) and Tharmas (body) – are traced in a great cloud of symbols. Urizen and Orc oppose each other: the oppressive moral code is condemned; Orc and liberty triumph, and the figure of Jesus as Redeemer is introduced.

In 1800 Blake was taken up by the wealthy **William Hayley**, a bad poet but a patron of good ones, and the Blakes went to live in Hayley's house at Felpham in Sussex. They stayed three years but the association was not a success, and Blake's time at Felpham was soured by his arrest on trumped-up charges of sedition; they returned again to London in 1803. Blake remained there for the rest of his life. At Felpham he had worked on *Milton: A Poem in Two Books, To Justify the Ways of God to Men*; it was finished and engraved between 1803 and 1808. The most famous part of this poem, when Milton returns to earth and in the person of the living poet corrects the spiritual error glorified in *Paradise Lost*, is the conclusion of the preface – the lines beginning 'And did those Feet in ancient time'. *Jerusalem: The Emanation of the Giant Albion*, written between 1804 and 1820, is a complex account of Albion (Man), continually torn between the forces of imagination and the forces of natural religion. *The Ghost of Abel* (1822) came the year after **Byron**'s *Cain* and challenges the younger poet's views in a minute poetic drama of 70 lines. The shadow of Cain is seen as Satan's work, not Jehovah's, and the atonement is made on Calvary.

Other notable poems by Blake are difficult to place in the chronology of his career. *Auguries of Innocence* probably dates from 1802, for example, and *The Everlasting Gospel* perhaps from 1810. Some works were unknown until his papers were examined after his death, while many were not issued in the conventional way. Defying the usual methods of publication, Blake became a one-man industry, designing, engraving and producing his own works like the medieval craftsmen who so intrigued him. Now famous, his engraved books then did not reach more than a small circle of readers. To fellow writers he remained an eccentric and a curiosity, known more through rumour and report than directly through his writings.

The years after Blake's return to London were

trying, if only because he never shook off the poverty which had accompanied him through life. The publisher Robert Hartley Cromek cheated him over the commission of 'The Canterbury Pilgrims'; an exhibition of his work in 1809 was a commercial fiasco, though the *Descriptive Catalogue* is a prized addition to his output. But in spite of these discouragements, he remained tenaciously independent. At his death he left no debts, though he was buried in an unmarked grave at the public cemetery of Bunhill Fields.

One of the most difficult of artists to assess, Blake was a mixture of extremes in both thought and work, by turns profound and naïve. Though the mythology he evolved was highly complex, its allusive sources only now being unravelled by scholars, it was never meant to be private and impenetrable, and the image of Blake as a totally isolated figure is no longer acceptable. His vision of the contradictory forces beneath the appearance of human civilization mirrors the intense political turmoil of Europe (and the New World) during his lifetime. His interest in legend and antiquity was revived with the Romantics' rediscovery of the past, especially the Gothic and the medieval. His insistence on the need to remake those legends in the poet's own terms, and the need to find a new language for expressing them, has pointed the way to the poetry of later generations. But it was left to later generations to recognize his importance.

**blank verse** Verse in unrhymed iambic pentameters (see **metre**). A flexible form able to accommodate a variety of English speech rhythms, it is used in most Elizabethan drama (including the plays of **Shakespeare**) and many long narrative poems (**Milton**'s *Paradise Lost*, **Wordsworth**'s *The Prelude* and **Tennyson**'s *Idylls of the King*).

*Blast: The Review of the Great English Vortex* Intended as a periodical of art and literature, it lasted for only two issues, in July 1914 and July 1915. Its advocacy of **vorticism** signalled an important stage in the development of **modernism** in Britain. The first issue attacked Victorianism and the **Bloomsbury Group**, promoting in their place mechanical, geometric and non-representational elements derived from such art movements as expressionism, cubism and futurism. It carried a manifesto signed by **Ezra Pound** and **Richard Aldington**, both adherents of **imagism**, as well as **Wyndham Lewis**, Henri Gaudier-Brzeska, Edward Wadsworth and several other artists. Lewis and Pound were largely responsible for the dynamically and radically authoritarian tone of the issue, and for its

futurist typography and layout. It contained poems by Pound, Lewis's 'vorticist drama' *The Enemy of the Stars*, and contributions from **Ford Madox Ford** and **Rebecca West**. There were also illustrations of vorticist art, including sculpture by Gaudier-Brzeska and Jacob Epstein and works by Wadsworth, Lewis and William Roberts. The second issue, published as a 'War Number', was mostly written by Lewis, though it contained some poems by **T. S. Eliot**.

*Bleak House* A novel by **Charles Dickens**, published in monthly parts from March 1852 to September 1853.

Although the fortunes of three pedestrian characters – Esther Summerson (who relates much of the story), Ada Clare and Richard Carstone – are central to the plot of *Bleak House*, it is Dickens's merciless indictment of the Court of Chancery and its bungling, morally corrupt handling of the endless case of *Jarndyce* v. *Jarndyce* that gives the novel its scope and meaning. Starting with Esther's account of her lonely, unhappy childhood, her role as protégée of the worthy John Jarndyce (the guardian of Richard and Ada), the tale develops the relations between the three young people, all inhabitants of the Jarndyce household. Ada and Richard marry but he, always vacillating in his choice of career, becomes enmeshed in the Jarndyce lawsuit and dies worn out by its frustrations. The story is enlarged by the introduction of the pompous Sir Leicester Dedlock and his proud wife. Her guilty past – an affair with the now dead Captain Hawdon that produced Esther – is slowly unravelled by the coldly calculating lawyer Tulkinghorn. Before Tulkinghorn can expose Lady Dedlock, he is murdered by Mademoiselle Hortense, waiting woman to her ladyship, who is brought to book by Inspector Bucket. Although Sir Leicester in fact behaves with compassion and understanding when he learns his wife's secret, she flees from home and is found dead by Bucket and Esther, not far from where the Captain lies. In due course Esther, released from an understanding with John Jarndyce, marries the surgeon Allan Woodcourt.

Numerous other characters contribute to the complex portrait of society which emerges from the novel. They include the selfish leech on others, Harold Skimpole (based on **Leigh Hunt**), and the boisterous Boythorn (based on **Walter Savage Landor**); Krook, the rag-and-bottle shopkeeper who dies a hideous death by 'Spontaneous Combustion'; Gridley and the crazed Miss Flite, both ruined by Chancery; Mrs Jellyby, neglectful of domestic responsibilities in favour of 'Telescopic Philanthropy'; the greasy Mr Chadband, a parson 'of no particular denomination'; the grasping Smallweed family; Conversation Kenge and Mr Vholes, lawyers

'Mr Chadband "Improving" a tough subject.' An illustration by Phiz for *Bleak House*. The tough subject is poor Jo, the crossing-sweeper, subjected to the preaching of the smug, greasy Reverend Mr Chadband.

both; and the two sons of Sir Leicester Dedlock's stately old housekeeper, Mrs Rouncewell. Of particular importance to the moral design of the novel is Jo, the crossing-sweeper whose brutish life and death are the instrument for one of Dickens's most savage judgements on an indifferent society.

**Blessed Damozel, The** A poem by **Dante Gabriel Rossetti**, first published in 1850 in the shortlived literary magazine **The Germ**. The Damozel leans out 'from the gold bar of Heaven' yearning for her earthly lover, whose reflections are expressed parenthetically throughout. This highly symbolic work is the embodiment of **Pre-Raphaelite** verse, and it is complemented by a Rossetti painting of the same name.

**Blessington, Marguerite, Countess of** 1789–1849 Authoress. One of the most colourful female figures of the Regency, she was born at Knockbrit near Clonmel, Co. Tipperary. Her father, a dissolute small landowner, forced her to marry the equally dissolute Captain Maurice St Leger Farmer when she was only 14. She left him after three months, and shortly after his death in 1817 married Charles John Gardiner, the 1st Earl of Blessington; their town mansion in St James's Square became a centre of social attraction. Her first work, *The Magic Lantern,*

*or, Sketches of Scenes in the Metropolis*, was published anonymously in 1822. In August of the same year she and Blessington embarked on a tour of the Continent, accompanied by the young Count d'Orsay, with whom she was intimately associated until the end of her life. At Genoa in 1823 the Blessingtons struck up a brief though extremely cordial friendship with **Byron**, the details of which were recorded by the Countess in her *Journal of Conversations with Lord Byron* (1832), the work for which she is now chiefly remembered. Towards the end of 1828, the Blessington ménage shifted its centre of operations to Paris, where the Earl died of apoplexy in 1829. Returning with d'Orsay to London in 1831, she eventually established court at Gore House, Kensington, where for 13 years she was hostess to literary, political and artistic London. Restricted by her husband's death to a jointure that left her merely well-off, she began to write in order to maintain her position. Her prolific output over the next 15 years included countless pieces for periodicals, annuals and magazines; the editorship of *The Book of Beauty* and *The Keepsake*; highly successful travel books such as *The Idler in Italy* (1839) and *The Idler in France* (1841); and numerous novels in three volumes. Although considerable, her earnings failed to keep pace with her needs, and when the inevitable crash came in April 1849 she fled with d'Orsay to Paris, where she died in June.

**Blickling Homilies, The** A series of 19 Old

English homilies (or sermons) found in a manuscript of 971. Their date of composition is not known; since it is not unusual to find archaisms in Old English prose, the fact that their language belongs to the 9th century is far from decisive. The homilies deal largely with stories from the Bible and religious festivals, but one takes as its theme the imminent end of the world, another the futility of worldly pleasures and the importance of the life of the soul, and a third treats the life and incarnation of Christ.

**Blind Harry** *c.* 1440–*c.* 1492 The author of *Wallace* (*c.* 1477), an epic poem in 12 books describing the life of the Scottish hero William Wallace and his struggle against the English. Little is known of Blind Harry's life but the vividness of some descriptive passages in the poem suggests that he had not been blind from birth. His work shows familiarity with the geography of Central Scotland and with contemporary scholarship, and a strong anti-English sentiment.

**Blithedale Romance, The** A novel by **Nathaniel Hawthorne** published in 1852, and based on the author's experience at the **Transcendentalist** Utopian community at **Brook Farm**.

The narrator, Miles Coverdale, goes to the Utopian community of Blithedale, where he meets the famous Zenobia, an exotic feminist, Hollingsworth, a blacksmith turned philanthropist, and Priscilla, a mysterious and fragile seamstress. Zenobia passionately loves the egotistic Hollingsworth, who wishes to turn Blithedale into an institution for criminal reform. Priscilla has escaped to Blithedale from the control of the evil Westervelt, who forced her to pose as the mysterious 'Veiled Lady', through whom he demonstrated his mesmeric powers to Boston audiences. Westervelt also has a mysterious past connection with Zenobia. Sensing competition for Hollingsworth from Priscilla, Zenobia delivers her back to Westervelt. Hollingsworth, however, intervenes to save Priscilla, and pledges himself to her. Meanwhile, it is revealed to all that Priscilla is Zenobia's half-sister, and that apparently she has been chosen to receive the inheritance that Zenobia thought was hers. Hollingsworth has chosen her over Zenobia because he needs the inheritance money to realize his reform scheme. The spurned and impoverished Zenobia drowns herself. Hollingsworth and Priscilla marry, but the egotistical reformer, overcome by guilt for Zenobia's suicide, is a broken man. Coverdale lapses back into a lonely bachelor's life, offering as explanation for his obsession with his three friends that he has all along been in love with Priscilla.

**Blitzstein, Marc** 1905–64 American composer, librettist and lyricist, best remembered for his contributions to the theatre of social protest in the 1930s. His first major work was the oratorio *The Condemned* (1932), based on the martyrdom of Sacco and Vanzetti. This was followed by *I've Got the Tune* (1937), a radio play. His best-known work is the musical play *The Cradle Will Rock* (1937), which fused elements of opera and popular music to portray the tyranny of a wealthy businessman over all aspects of life in a small city. Another play, *No For an Answer*, was produced in 1941 but was soon censored and shut down by the authorities because of its political content. After World War II, during which he served in the US Air Force, he completed a ballet, *The Guests* (produced by The New York City Ballet in 1949), and an adaptation of the text of Brecht's *The Threepenny Opera*, produced off Broadway in 1954 with Lotte Lenya as Jenny. His musical *Regina*, based on **Lillian Hellman**'s play *The Little Foxes*, was first produced in 1949 and later became part of the repertory at The New York City Opera. Hellman's plot and characterizations allowed Blitzstein to continue his criticism of capitalism in America by focusing on the way greed can lead members of a family to destroy one another.

**Blixen, Karen** See **Dinesen, Isak**.

**Bloomfield, Robert** 1766–1832 Poet. Born in the village of Honington, Suffolk, Bloomfield was the son of a tailor, and was taught to read and write by his mother, who ran the village school. After a period as a farm labourer, he ran away to join his older brothers in London, where he became a cobbler, and improved himself by attending meetings of Dissenters, and by reading 'the long and beautiful speeches of Burke, Fox, or North'. He is now chiefly remembered as the author of *The Farmer's Boy* (1800), in imitation of **Thomson**'s *The Seasons*, which had come to the attention of Capel Lofft, who arranged for its publication in a fine quarto edition with wood engravings by **Thomas Bewick**. No fewer than 26,000 copies were sold in three years, and translations appeared in French, Italian, and even Latin. Despite the prevailing demand for authentic rustic poetry, Bloomfield was unable to repeat the success of his life of the orphan ploughboy, Giles, and did not develop significantly as a writer during the two decades after its appearance. Later works include *Rural Tales* (1802), *Good Tidings or News from the Farm* (1804) and *The Banks of the Wye* (1811). His last years were dogged by illness and partial blindness, and he died in extreme poverty.

**Bloomsbury Group, The** The name given to a group of friends – writers, artists and intellectuals – who began meeting in about 1905 at the Bloomsbury house of the Stephen sisters, Vanessa Bell and **Virginia Woolf**. Accurate dating of the group's existence is difficult – the broadest estimate being 1905–41. In 1899 Thoby Stephen, **Clive Bell**, **Lytton Strachey**, Saxon Sydney-Turner and **Leonard Woolf** had all entered Trinity College, Cambridge. By 1905 Thoby had initiated his 'Thursday evenings' when he brought his Cambridge friends to meet his sisters at Gordon Square. After Vanessa's marriage to Clive Bell, Virginia moved to Fitzroy Square and then to Brunswick Square, where she lived with her younger brother Adrian and where **Maynard Keynes** had a *pied à terre* which Duncan Grant also used as a studio. Leonard Woolf rented rooms on the top floor. **E. M. Forster** was a frequent visitor. This was 'Old Bloomsbury'. Thoby's friends, Strachey, Sydney-Turner and Woolf, serious-minded and heavily influenced by **G. E. Moore**'s *Principia Ethica*, formed one element, enlivened by the more worldly and sophisticated Clive Bell and **Desmond MacCarthy**. By 1910 Clive Bell had met Roger Fry, through whom the group's interest broadened to encompass a greater involvement in the visual arts – the first post-impressionist exhibition also took place in that year. During World War I a second generation began to make its appearance, in particular, **David Garnett**, and after the war the circle grew larger and became geographically more dispersed. The Bells, Woolfs and Lytton Strachey all took country houses which members of the group visited, and they also met at the Garsington home of **Lady Ottoline Morrell**. Lytton Strachey's death in 1932 and Virginia Woolf's suicide in 1941 can both be seen as ends of an era.

Although its members denied being a group in any formal sense, they were united in an abiding belief in the importance of the arts. Their philosophy can perhaps best be summarized in Moore's statement that 'one's prime objects in life were love, the creation and enjoyment of aesthetic experience and the pursuit of knowledge'. They were sceptical and tolerant, reacting against the artistic and social restraints of Victorian society. Through writing (biography, novels, art criticism, economics, political theory), painting (in the works of Vanessa Bell and Duncan Grant), publishing (the Hogarth Press started in 1917 and in 1923 published **Eliot**'s *The Waste Land*) and support of new developments in the arts they exercised a considerable influence on the *avant-garde* of the early 20th century. Accused by some of intellectual élitism, the group's reputation faltered in the 1940s and 1950s, but from the 1960s critical interest in their achievements began to revive.

***Bloudy Tenent of Persecution, The*** The first in a series of American Puritan tracts which debate the questions of freedom of conscience and the separation of church and state, *The Bloudy Tenent* was written and published by **Roger Williams** in London in 1644. Provoked by **John Cotton**'s defence of persecution to preserve orthodoxy, Williams presents a two-part dialogue between Truth and Peace. The first part constitutes both a point-by-point rebuttal of Cotton's argument, and a defence of freedom of conscience as an inalienable right. On the grounds that civil power derives from the people and not from God, the second part denounces the ministerial intervention in secular affairs sanctioned by the Puritan theocracy of Massachusetts Bay. Thus, *The Bloudy Tenent* subverts the idea of a national church, the basis of New England's theocratic practices.

**bluestocking** This term for a woman of pronounced literary or intellectual interests gained currency in the 1750s, when **Elizabeth Montagu** held assemblies at her home to which 'literary and ingenious' figures were invited. Conversation on intellectual matters prevailed, instead of cards or entertainments. Among the members of Mrs Montagu's circle were **Hannah More**, **Fanny Burney**, **Hester Chapone** and **Horace Walpole**. The group was nicknamed 'The Blue Stocking Society' probably because of the costume of one of its male members. The term has also come to mean a female pedant.

**Blume, Judy** 1938– American children's author. She was born in New Jersey and educated at New York University. Her first successful book, *Are You There, God? It's Me, Margaret* (1970), is about an 11-year-old girl who longs to reach puberty so that she can wear a bra. Such comparative outspokenness on personal problems or worries became a feature of later novels, and *Forever* (1975) provoked controversy by describing an adolescent girl's first sexual experience in explicit detail.

**Blunden, Edmund (Charles)** 1896–1974 Poet and critic. Born in London, he moved to Kent, which later became the inspiration for much of his poetry. After serving in the Royal Sussex Regiment, he became assistant editor of *The Athenaeum* until 1922. He left England to teach in Tokyo, and became Professor of English Literature in Hong Kong in 1953, and Professor of Poetry at Oxford in 1966.

His early verse appeared in *Georgian Poetry*. Volumes include *The Waggoner and Other Poems* (1920), *The Shepherd and Other Poems of Peace and War* (1922), *English Poems* (1929), *Collected Poems* (1930), *After the Bombing and Other Short Poems* (1950) and *A Hong Kong House Poem* (1962). His autobiographical account of the Great War, *Undertones of War*, appeared in 1928, and *Votive*

*Tablets*, a collection of essays on English poetry, in 1931. He published biographies of **Shelley** (1943) and **Leigh Hunt** (1930), a study of **Thomas Hardy** (1941), pioneering editions of the poetry of **John Clare** (1920), **Wilfred Owen** (1931) and **Ivor Gurney** (1954), autobiographical writings (1931), and *Cricket Country* (1944) and *English Villages* (1947) for the Britain in Pictures series.

**Blunt, Wilfrid Scawen** 1840–1922 Poet, diplomat and Arabist. Born into a landed Roman Catholic family in Sussex, he joined the diplomatic service at 18 and married Annabella King-Noel, **Byron**'s granddaughter, in 1869. His first verse collection, *Sonnets and Songs by Proteus* (1875), contained addresses to women, poems on the Sussex countryside, and adaptations from the Arabic. He wrote and worked in support of Egyptian, Indian and Irish independence, publishing *The Future of Islam* (1882), *Ideas about India* (1885) and *The Secret History of the English Occupation of Egypt* (1907). During a spell in an Irish prison he wrote the sonnet sequence *In Vinculis* (1899). *My Diaries*, published in two volumes in 1919–20, referred to his friendships with Lord Lytton (**Edward Robert Lytton**), Curzon, **William Morris**, **Lady Gregory**, **Alice Meynell** and **Oscar Wilde**. His *Poetical Works* appeared in 1914, and in the same year a birthday celebration, at which roasted peacocks in full plumage were served, was attended by **Ezra Pound**, **W. B. Yeats**, **Richard Aldington**, **T. Sturge Moore** and F. S. Flint.

**Bly, Robert** 1926– American poet, born in Madison, Minnesota, and educated at Harvard and the University of Iowa. His verse is filled with images of rural Minnesota, where he continues to live and write. The natural world, however, often becomes a figure for the poet's unconscious, and Bly's exploration of interior 'landscapes' frequently gives his work a mystical or surreal quality. His first book, *Silence in the Snowy Fields*, appeared in 1962. Since then he has published numerous other volumes of verse and translations; these include *The Light Around the Body* (1967), *Sleepers Joining Hands* (1973), *Point Reyes Poems* (1974), *Old Man Rubbing His Eyes* (1975), *The Morning Glory* (1975), *This Body Is Made of Camphor and Gopherwood* (1977), *This Tree Will be Here for a Thousand Years* (1979), *The Man in the Black Coat Turns* (1981), *The Eight Stages of Translation* (1983) and *Four Ramages* (1983).

**Blythe, Ronald (George)** 1922– Miscellaneous writer. Born in Acton, Suffolk, he has written a novel (*A Treasonable Growth*, 1960), short stories (collected in 1985) and essays on literature, but is principally known for *Akenfield: Portrait of an English Village* (1969). Blythe

used its technique of transcribed interviews with linking commentary again in *The View in Winter: Reflections on Old Age* (1979). *The Age of Illusion* (1963) is a social history of England between the two world wars.

**Blyton, Enid (Mary)** 1897–1968 Children's writer. Born in London, she was educated at a girls' school in Beckenham, anticipating the heroines of her later stories by becoming both head girl and captain of games. She then trained as an infant teacher but soon became known as a writer of stories and poems for children, often of a strongly sentimental character. Quickly becoming commercially successful, contributing a special page for children in *Teachers' World* each week, she not only wrote fiction but also organized competitions and various appeals for charities, some of which she set up herself. Full-length books soon followed, written at such a rate that many believed the quite unfounded rumour that her work was ghosted by a team of writers. In 1942 she published the first of her 'Famous Five' adventures, in which a gang of well-born, privately educated children solve various mysteries in the course of their largely unsupervised vacations. These too were immensely popular, with her various publishers assigning so much of their strictly rationed paper supply to her books that other wartime children's writers found it hard getting into print at all. After the war she created the character of Little Noddy, a humanized toy enjoying mild adventures in a bland, domestic setting. He too was an instant success, although by now critics began questioning both Enid Blyton's limited literary style and the way that many young readers repeatedly turned to her books to the exclusion of more demanding fare. Other objectors drew attention to her racist and snobbish attitudes but have still done little to dent her popularity with children, which continues even today.

**bob and wheel** A wheel is a group of short lines at the end of a longer stanza of longer lines. If its first line is even shorter than the others, it is known as a bob and the whole group is then styled a 'bob and wheel'. The medieval romance **Sir Gawain and the Green Knight** provides the best-known example.

**Bodkin, (Amy) Maud** 1875–1967 Critic. Maud Bodkin was born in Chelmsford, Essex, and educated at the University College of Wales, Aberystwyth. Of the later life of this amateur psychologist little is known: she held no public position or academic post. Her book *Archetypal Patterns in Poetry* (1934) was the first and most important English work on literature to emerge from the psychological school of C. G. Jung. Applying Jung's concept of the collective unconscious to the reading of **Coler-idge**'s *The Rime of the Ancient Mariner*, Bodkin discerned underlying patterns and cycles of death and rebirth also to be found in ancient literatures and religions. Surveying the endurance of these and other 'archetypes' in poetry and drama from Sophocles to **T. S. Eliot**, she argued that poetry, as the objectification of 'universal forces of our nature', allows special access to the collective unconscious of the race. In a sequel, *Studies of Type-Images in Poetry, Religion, and Philosophy* (1951), she developed these Jungian theories in the direction of a synthesis between poetry and religion.

**Bodley, Sir Thomas** 1545–1613 Scholar and diplomat. Born at Exeter, Bodley was brought up on the Continent, chiefly at Geneva, where his parents had taken their family to avoid the persecutions of Mary. In Geneva Bodley was taught divinity by Calvin and Beza. He entered Magdalen College, Oxford, and became a fellow in 1565. A fine Hebrew scholar, he was also instrumental in encouraging the study of Greek at Oxford. In the 1570s he travelled abroad and subsequently became a diplomat. He was Elizabeth I's permanent resident at The Hague in 1589–96, though he found his later years there tiresome and pressed to be recalled. Bodley withdrew from active political service after 1596 and channelled his energies into the establishment at Oxford of the great library which was opened in 1603 and given his name in 1604. Bodley later extended the library building and endowed it with other property, as well as making the University chief beneficiary of his will. (See also **libraries**.)

*Boece* Translation by **Geoffrey Chaucer** of the *Consolatione Philosophiae* of the 6th-century Roman philosopher Boethius undertaken *c.* 1380. While not following the original closely, Chaucer's prose version testifies to his deep sympathy for and engagement with Boethius' work. Its discussion of the 'true good' and the apparent paradox of man's free will and God's foreknowledge influenced his own writing, most notably *Troilus and Criseyde* and *The Knight's Tale* (see *Canterbury Tales*).

**Boece (or Boethius), Hector** ?1465–1536 Scottish historian. Boece's family came from Dundee. He was educated at the University of Paris and later helped Bishop Elphinstone in his plans to set up a university at Aberdeen. His major work was the compilation of a history of Scotland, *Historia Scotorum* (1527), which shows a humanist concern with narrative and rhetoric rather than historical accuracy. **Leland** commented that Boece wrote as many lies as there are waves or stars. **Holinshed** found the story of

Macbeth in the *Historia* and it was thus transmitted to **Shakespeare**.

**Bogan, Louise** 1897–1970 American poet. Born in Maine, Bogan was educated at Boston University and spent most of her life in New York City. She was the regular poetry reviewer for *The New Yorker* from 1931 to 1968, and in 1951 published the highly regarded *Achievement in American Poetry 1900–1950*. Her own poetry was strongly influenced by her study of 16th- and 17th-century English verse, and is characterized by its dramatic structure and highly refined metrical forms. She published six volumes of poems: *Body of This Death* (1923), *Dark Summer* (1929), *The Sleeping Fury* (1937), *Poems and New Poems* (1941), *Collected Poems 1923–1953* (1954) and *The Blue Estuaries: Poems 1923–1968* (1968). A prose collection, *A Poet's Alphabet*, appeared in 1970.

**Boker, George Henry** 1823–90 American playwright and poet. Born into a wealthy Pennsylvania family, Boker was educated at the College of New Jersey (later Princeton University) and went on to study law, but he aspired to the life of a poet. He published his first collection of verse, *The Lesson of Life*, in 1848. *Calaynos*, the first of his 11 plays, only six of which were produced professionally, was staged without authorization in London in 1849. He wrote two comedies in verse, *The Betrothal* (1850), set in Renaissance Italy, and *The Widow's Marriage* (1852, unproduced), and one in prose about contemporary London, *The World a Mask* (1851). His two most successful plays were the historical verse tragedies *Leonor de Guzman* (1853), about the rivalry between the mistress of Alfonso XII and his wife Maria, and *Francesca da Rimini* (1855), based on Dante's story of the lovers Paolo and Francesca. The latter play was unsuccessful at first, but its revival in 1882 won great critical acclaim. Boker's last two plays, *Nydia* (1885) and *Glaucus* (1886), were both based on **Edward Bulwer Lytton**'s novel *The Last Days of Pompeii* (1834); both were unproduced. His patriotism during the Civil War was rewarded by his appointment as United States Ambassador to Turkey (1871–5) and to Russia (1875–8).

**Boland, Eavan (Aisling)** 1944– Irish poet. Born in Dublin, the daughter of a diplomat, she was schooled in London, New York and Killiney, County Dublin, before reading English at Trinity College, Dublin. She has worked as a freelance lecturer, and reviews regularly for *The Irish Times* and *PN Review*. After her 'truly frightful' pamphlet, *23 Poems* (1962), her first full-length book was *New Territory* (1967). Her range of themes is wide: Irish myth and legend, suburbia, the intimacies of love and motherhood. The distinctive development from volume to volume – *The War Horse* (1975), *In Her Own Image* (1980), and *Night Feed* (1982) – is a deepening internal response to external phenomena. She is already one of Ireland's leading poets, and the appearance of *The Journey and Other Poems* (1987), her first book to be published in Britain and a Poetry Book Society Choice, should widen her readership.

**Boldrewood, Rolf** Pseudonym of Thomas Alexander Browne (1826–1915), Australian novelist. He was born in London but his family emigrated in 1830 and he was educated in Sydney. From 1843 to 1871 Browne speculated as a squatter on property in Victoria and the Riverina, New South Wales. Drought ended this career and he became a police magistrate and goldfields commissioner. He was 40 before he began to write. Browne's best-known novel, *Robbery Under Arms*, was published as a serial in the *Sydney Mail* (1881) and in volume form in 1888. This racy tale about an infamous bushranger, Captain Starlight, with its authentic scenes and dialogue, soon established itself as a classic adventure story. Of some 17 other novels the most popular were *The Miner's Right* (1890), *A Colonial Reformer* (1890) and *The Squatter's Dream* (1890), first published in 1878 as *Ups and Downs of Australian Life*.

**Bolingbroke, Henry St John, 1st Viscount** 1678–1751 Statesman and historian. Born at Battersea, he was educated at Eton and (probably) Christ Church, Oxford, and then made the fashionable tour of Europe. He entered Parliament in 1701, supporting **Robert Harley** and the Tories. St John was a fine speaker and became Secretary of State in 1710; in 1712 he was created 1st Viscount Bolingbroke. An opponent of the Hanoverian succession, who wanted the crown to remain with the Stuarts, Bolingbroke was impeached when George I came to the throne in 1714. He fled to France, where he became Secretary of State to Prince James Stuart (the Old Pretender), though the Prince dismissed him in 1716 and Bolingbroke wisely severed his connection with the Stuarts. His friends managed to secure his pardon, and he returned to England in 1725; his property was restored but he was banned from holding office.

Most of his writing dates from his return to England but during his political ascendancy he was the friend and patron of writers. In 1711 he founded the Brothers Club, which included **Swift**, **Arbuthnot** and **Matthew Prior**, as well as adherents of the Tory Party, among its members.

In exile Bolingbroke wrote *A Letter to Sir William Wyndham* (1717, published in 1753), about the Jacobite question. While not entirely honest in its handling of fact, it is persuasively written and of interest for Bolingbroke's comments on his former colleagues – particularly Harley – and for the description of the Old Pretender's court. *Reflections in Exile* was written the year before, in 1716. After he returned to England Bolingbroke was soon in active opposition to the Whigs, now securely in power under Robert Walpole. Nicholas Amherst founded a periodical called *The Craftsman* in 1726 and Bolingbroke was an anonymous and regular contributor. These pieces are printed in *Remarks upon the History of England* (1743) and *A Dissertation upon Parties* (1735). The latter reprints an attack upon Walpole written in 1733; the article did not harm Walpole, however, and Bolingbroke retreated to France once more, to live in his French wife's home at Chanteloup, in Touraine.

*Letters on the Study and Use of History* (published in 1752) were written in 1735: in them Bolingbroke argued that, since history teaches philosophy by example, England should follow the example of her European neighbours and produce written histories. The book was widely read, and not only in England, for Voltaire acknowledged its influence. *A Letter on the True Use of Retirement and Study* and *A Letter on the Spirit of Patriotism* were both written in 1736. The latter (published in 1749), which looks hopefully to a future Tory Party inspired by patriotism, influenced **Disraeli**. *The Idea of a Patriot King* (written in 1738, published in 1749) develops the same idea, while *Some Reflections on the Present State of the Nation* (1749) examines the question of the public debt.

Bolingbroke's writings were collected and published by **David Mallet** in 1754. Included in the edition were *Philosophical Works*, the occasional writings that influenced **Pope** in his **Essay on Man**.

**Bolt, Robert (Oxton)** 1924– Playwright. He studied history at Manchester University before becoming a schoolteacher. The success of *Flowering Cherry* (1957) encouraged him to become a professional writer. His best work includes the large-scale historical plays *A Man for All Seasons* (1960) about Sir Thomas More, *Vivat! Vivat! Regina* (1970) about Elizabeth I and Mary, Queen of Scots and *State of Revolution* (1977) about Lenin, Trotsky and the Russian Revolution.

**Bond, Edward** 1934– Playwright and poet who left school at the age of 14. His farm-working parents had been drawn to London in search of work and Bond's plays are powerfully aware of both rural and urban deprivation. Many of them have caused controversy.

Bond received his first encouragement as a member of the Writers Group at the **Royal**

**Court Theatre**, London, where *The Pope's Wedding* (1962) was given a Sunday night performance. *Saved* (1965) is a bleak presentation of the effects of cultural deprivation. Banned by the Lord Chamberlain because of the scene in which a group of bored youths stone a baby, it brought Bond's name into theatrical prominence. *Early Morning* (1968), a surreal historical fantasy, was the last play to be banned in its entirety by the Lord Chamberlain, whose legal control of theatrical performance was discontinued in the year of its first performance. *Narrow Road to the Deep North* (1968), radically revised as *The Bundle* (1978), impartially compares fascism and imperialism as modes of government. As in *Early Morning*, Bond is here attacking the legacy of Victorian prejudice and pride. *Lear* (1971) is a startlingly cruel reappraisal of **Shakespeare**'s play and *Bingo* (1973) takes Shakespeare himself as its central character, speculating on his complicity in the agricultural enclosures that disinherited the rural population. A concern with the relationship between artist and society is also central to *The Fool* (1975), a disturbing dramatization of scenes in the life of **John Clare**. Other plays in which Bond uses historical settings to expose modern injustices include *The Woman* (1978) and *Restoration* (1981).

**Bond, (Thomas) Michael** 1926– Children's writer. Born and educated in Berkshire, he was a television cameraman before becoming an author. His success began with *A Bear Called Paddington* (1958), which created a favourite character later to appear in numerous sequels popular both in Britain and abroad. Other successful characters Bond has invented include an orphan mouse, first appearing in *Here Comes Thursday* (1966), and a guinea-pig named Olga da Polga.

***Bone Florence of Rome, Le*** An anonymous **verse romance** of the late 14th century written in the North Midlands. Florence, wooed by an aged emperor, is eventually married to Esmere, whom she sends to destroy him. In his absence she is wooed by her brother-in-law and imprisoned for adultery when she refuses him. She flees, and in the ensuing years is falsely accused of murder, sold into slavery and shipwrecked. She eventually becomes a famous healer and all her wrong-doers come to her for aid. They confess, she cures them and is reunited with her husband. The romance is notable for its vivid descriptions and attention to detail, and for its portrayal of the heroine. Florence's endurance, patience and kindness recall the popular story of the 'constant' Constance (see **Emare**); her goodness and the moralizing tone of the end of the poem recall the character of the **saint's life**.

***Bonifacius*** A pamphlet by **Cotton Mather**, sub-titled *An Essay Upon the Good*, published anonymously in Boston in 1710 and discussing the meaning of true Christian conduct. Invoking the traditional Puritan idea that every person has a social as well as a spiritual calling, Mather suggests ways in which people of diverse callings – ministers, lawyers, doctors, magistrates, merchants – may translate Christian principles into their daily lives and activities. He stresses that true Christians fulfil their callings for the good of the whole community, and should direct their energies in responsible and co-operative rather than competitive ways. He pays particular attention to the nurture of pious principles in the family and to the value of organized church prayers.

Although Mather retains his Puritan orthodoxy in *Bonifacius*, his concern with worldly activity is an attempt to apply traditional Puritan teachings to the immediate concerns of his changing society, with its increasingly complex and diversified secular activities. The book went through many printings both during and after Mather's lifetime, and provided something of a programmatic statement of the social vision of the American Protestant sensibility.

**Bontemps, Arna (Wendell)** 1902–73 American novelist, born in Louisiana and raised in California. He received an MA from the University of Chicago in 1943, and spent much of his professional life working at Fisk University, first as a librarian, then as public relations director. His writing is dedicated to portraying the life of black people in America. *Black Thunder* (1936) and *Drums at Dusk* (1939) are novels about slave revolts in Virginia and in Haiti. *God Sends Sunday* (1931) was dramatized by **Countee Cullen** as *St Louis Woman* (1946). *Sam Patch* (1951) is one of many children's books written with **Jack Conroy**. His non-fiction includes *They Seek a City* (1945, with Conroy), *The Story of the Negro* (1948) and *100 Years of Negro Freedom* (1961).

***Book Named the Governor, The*** See **Elyot, Sir Thomas**.

**Book of Common Prayer, The** The name for the service-book used by the Church of England from 1549 until the mid 1970s, when it was largely replaced by Alternative Services, and in particular one called Series 3.

Christian service-books can be traced from the earliest times. The first chapters of Luke's gospel contain four great hymns, later called the Magnificat (1:46–55), the Benedictus (1:66–79), the Gloria (2:14) and the Nunc Dimittis (2:29–32), and there are many evidences of Christian worship in the New Testament – fragments of hymns throughout Revelation, corporate prayer in Acts 4:23–30. Examination of the service-books of the Fathers, for example in 6th-century Rome, reveals eight daily services, mostly of Scripture reading. Complication, accretion and local variation followed over the centuries. Scripture was often replaced by legends – 'some be untrue, some uncertain, some vain and superstitious' as **Thomas Cranmer** wrote. Additional services, for the Virgin Mary, or for the dead, or of other kinds, multiplied so much in number and length as to become impossible, and demanded at least four different service-books; all were in Latin.

At the English Reformation, there was great need for simplification and for standardization over the country – for an agreed order in one book in English. The large number of daily Latin 'uses' was clarified into Matins and Evensong (Morning and Evening Prayer after 1552), Holy Communion and Baptism (two, not seven, sacraments) and five other services, all in English. The first Book of Common Prayer of 1549, under the young Edward VI, was the work, as always, of committees, based on the best 'use', that of Sarum (Salisbury), and influenced by several service-books from the Continent. The special gifts, however, of the Archbishop of Canterbury, Thomas Cranmer, especially in the making in English of the brief, beautiful daily prayers known as 'collects', link his name for ever with the Prayer Book. Though many sentences translate earlier Latin forms, it is wrong to think of the Book of Common Prayer as the-Latin-in-English: it is a Reformed book, with much that is simple, fresh and 'new' only in the sense that it restored earlier forms. This first Edwardian Book of Common Prayer, and all Prayer Books that follow, put daily Bible reading in the House of God first in importance, as the Fathers had done: all the Psalms to be read through once a month, the whole New Testament three times a year, and most of the Old Testament once a year. The Bible was to be read from the Great Bible of 1540, which was **Miles Coverdale**'s printing and continuation of the work of **William Tyndale** (see **The Bible in English**). The Psalms, though based on Coverdale, made use of earlier Middle English Psalters and carried forward a more ancient tradition (see **Psalters**).

Innumerable phrases have come into the language from the Book of Common Prayer, many of them now taken to be proverbial: 'through fire and water', 'the iron entered into his soul', 'like a giant refreshed', 'all sorts and conditions', 'peace in our time'. Cranmer's genius can be felt in the beauty of one collect for Evensong: 'Lighten our darkness, we beseech thee, O Lord, and by thy great mercy defend us from all perils and dangers of this night, for the love of thy only son, our saviour Jesus Christ. Amen.' Such timeless simplicity is found everywhere: 'we have done those things which we

ought not to have done', or 'pour into our hearts such love toward thee' or 'that peace which the world cannot give', or 'serve thee with a quiet mind'.

In 1550 John Merbecke's music for the Prayer Book was printed. Composed on the sound principle of 'one syllable, one note', it was used whenever the services were sung for over 400 years. The First, 1549, Prayer Book was revised in 1552 and, though hardly used, this Second Prayer Book influenced later revisions. After the savagery of Queen Mary's five years, during which Cranmer, among hundreds of others, was martyred, the Third Prayer Book of 1559 was instituted on the accession of Elizabeth. Under her, there was some revision, and additional services and other matter were bound in – the 39 Articles (setting out Anglican belief), some hymns, and sometimes metrical psalms. The compulsory Sunday attendance of almost everyone at Church meant that the ideas and phrases of Cranmer's English liturgy bit deep into the nation's consciousness. The same Hampton Court Conference of 1604 which initiated the Authorized Version under King James produced also the Fourth Prayer Book, with some fresh variations. In 1637 the Scottish Prayer Book was printed in Edinburgh to local hostility; it later influenced Scottish, English and American liturgies. From 1645 to 1660 the use of the Book of Common Prayer was forbidden by law. Its place was taken by the Directory for Public Worship, which gave only general directions to the minister.

At the Restoration the old Book of Common Prayer was instantly in demand, and quickly revised and lavishly reissued. The Fifth Prayer Book was completed in 1661, but as it became attached to the Act of Uniformity of 1662, it has been known ever since as '1662'. This Prayer Book – and Parliament – went a little way to incorporate the professions of opponents, but then threw tolerance away and hardened the divisions in the nation, making non-adherence to the Prayer Book a most serious handicap for several following centuries. **John Bunyan** and thousands of others suffered harshly, and it was a long time before being a Dissenter, a Roman Catholic, a Jew, or what became known as an agnostic, and thus unable to subscribe to the Prayer Book through conscience, did not bring penalties.

The 1662 Prayer Book introduced several hundred alterations, changing obsolete phrases, transferring the source for all the Bible except the Psalms to the Authorized Version, and giving new directions to the minister. The tendency of the revision can be seen in the change from 'Bishops, pastors and ministers' to 'Bishops, priests and deacons'. State services, particularly those for remembering 'King Charles the Martyr' and the Restoration, joined the revised older service commemorating the Gunpowder Treason of 1605. New collects were introduced. Some revision, usually towards elaboration of ritual, was the work of Bishop John Cosin. It was '1662' which represented Anglicanism for three centuries, and transmitted Cranmer's prose and the Prayer Book Psalms across the world; it was the basis of the service-books of what became nearly 20 independent Anglican churches around the globe.

'1662' was richly and frequently issued. In the 100 years from 1660, some 350 fresh editions were published, about 25 of them with full-page engravings, sometimes very lavish. These illustrate Bible events throughout the Church Calendar – the angels appearing to the shepherds, Christ riding into Jerusalem, and so on – followed by pictures of saints. About half the illustrated editions have also, against the appropriate services, an engraving of Guy Fawkes under the eye of God and pictures of the martyrdom of Charles I and the Restoration of Charles II.

Proposals for the further revision of the Book of Common Prayer continued. An attempt under William and Mary in 1689 did not succeed. Movements for Prayer Book reform were strong in the 18th century. A new Scottish liturgy was accepted in 1764, an American Prayer Book in 1789, an Irish Prayer Book in 1877, and the Scottish Prayer Book in 1912. Reform of the Book of Common Prayer was discussed urgently in the 19th century. In 1859 the Gunpowder Treason and Stuart services were dropped. Later proposals were in the direction of more universally Protestant evangelicalism, and more powerfully in the opposite direction, by those who wished that the Reformation had never happened. The wholesale revision proposed in the 1920s was twice rejected by the House of Commons in 1928. The arguments continued, notwithstanding, and some of the 1928 proposals resurfaced in the 1960s, when moves towards alternative services produced three sets. One from the Bishops was called the First Series, and another from the Liturgical Commission was called the Second Series. International religious commissions, dominated by the United States, made proposals which the Church of England largely incorporated in what it called Series 3. This has become standard in many Anglican churches, which now use '1662' for perhaps one early Holy Communion a month. Cranmer and the Reformers (and Merbecke) have been replaced. So, often, have Morning and Evening Prayer. The emphasis is frequently on one weekly 'Parish' or 'Family Eucharist'. The supposed 'popularizing' of the words and order of the services has been in line with the Englishing of the Roman Catholic Mass, but the Church of England must be held responsible for the ugliness of Series 3. Words for people to use together repeatedly in enacting worship have to be specially crafted. The sense of mystery, essential in worship, has in Series 3 been replaced by baffling blocks of language, like the unpunctuated 'You are God we praise you' in the Te Deum. Cranmer's 'The Lord be with you: and with thy spirit' has become in Series 3 'The Lord be with you: and also with you', which is ungrammatical ('and also' is tautological), vacuous, and the result, apparently, of an international commission's insistence that 'spirit' would be misunderstood in English (it remains in European revisions).

Cranmer wrote his Book of Common Prayer in the tradition of several hundred years of excellent English devotional writing, starting from the 12th century: a supple, lively, often beautiful, prose, quiet in manner and simple in effect. This remained a living English inheritance until the mid 1960s. Cranmer wrote – they are the first words of the First Prayer Book – 'There was never anything by the wit of man so well devised, or so surely established, which (in continuance of time) hath not been corrupted.' It has not been time, but the Church of England itself, which has corrupted, since 1965, a Prayer Book once 'so surely established'.

**Book of Martyrs, Foxe's** See *Acts and Monuments.*

**Book of St Albans, The** A collection of four treatises in verse, which had existed separately since *c.* 1400, published at the St Albans press in 1486. They deal with hawking, hunting, coat-armour and blazoning of arms; a further treatise, on fishing, was added for **Wynkyn de Worde**'s edition of 1496. The colophon attributes the hunting book to Dam Julyans Barnes (or **Juliana Berners**) but it is unlikely that she was its author, and the belief of later editors that she wrote the whole collection cannot be supported. *The Book of St Albans* proved enduringly popular and appeared with only slight alterations under different titles in the 16th and 17th centuries.

**Book of Snobs, The** Satirical sketches by **W. M. Thackeray**, published weekly in *Punch* as *The Snobs of England* from 28 February 1846 to 27 February 1847, with illustrations by him, and in book form, revised, in 1848.

Sub-titled 'By One of Themselves' in *Punch*, this portrait gallery of early Victorian snobbery ranges from 'The Snob Royal', 'Military Snobs' and 'Clerical Snobs' to 'Country Snobs' and 'Club Snobs'. Although crude and repetitive in places, these sketches have a keen satirical edge, and prefigure both the social concerns of *Vanity Fair* and Thackeray's mature narrative stance of involved spectator, implicated in the vices he satirizes.

**Book of the Duchess, The** A poem by **Geoffrey Chaucer** on the death of Blanche, Duchess of Lancaster, the first wife of John of Gaunt, in 1368. It was composed within a few years of the duchess's death and is one of the poet's earliest works.

The poem is a **dream-vision** with a long prologue. Unable to sleep because of some sickness or depression, the narrator reads a truncated version of Ovid's story of Ceyx and Alcyone. He tells the story, which ends before the metamorphosis, and prays to Morpheus. He falls asleep and narrates a dream in which he first watches and then wanders away from the hunt of the Emperor Octavian and comes upon a knight in black lamenting. The latter (probably intended to represent John of Gaunt) describes his love for the lady White and his life with her, and tells the dreamer, at first in a metaphor but finally explicitly, of her death. At this point the dream ends and the narrator awakes and determines to write the poem.

**Boorde, Andrew** ?1490–1549 Writer on medicine and travel. Boorde was a Carthusian who was released from his vows in 1529. He was practising medicine in Glasgow in 1536, but much of his time was spent in extensive travel in Europe. His medical works are *A Dietary of Health* (1542), which ran through many editions, and *The Breviary of Health* (1547). His travels equipped him to write the first Continental guidebook in English, *The First Book of the Introduction of Knowledge* (?1548), which is in prose with verse portraits of national types. His other works include a book on astronomy.

**Booth, Charles** 1840–1916 Social critic and reformer. Born in Liverpool to a prosperous Unitarian family, he made his fortune in the shipping business. His interest in public issues developed into active concern about poverty after he opened a London branch of his business in the 1880s. The result was a monumental survey in the tradition of **Henry Mayhew**, taking 17 years and growing to 17 volumes, published in its final form as *Life and Labour of the People in London* (1902–3). **Beatrice Webb**, his wife's cousin, was one of his researchers for the early volumes. Enough of a Manchester liberal to dislike state intervention in business and trade, Booth nevertheless welcomed measures to regulate incomes (he coined the term 'poverty line') and his advocacy of old-age pensions eased the way for their introduction in 1908.

**Borough, The** A poem by **George Crabbe**, published in 1810, in the form of 24 letters from 'a residing burgess in a large sea-port', describing various aspects of life in a town which is clearly based on Crabbe's native Aldeburgh. Much of the poem is rather shapeless and meandering, but it suddenly comes to life towards the end with the introduction of seven letters dealing exclusively with the life history of a single person – either one of the 'Inhabitants of the Alms-House' or one of 'The Poor of the Borough'. Particularly powerful are *Clelia*, which depicts the moral and social decline of an irredeemably trivial flirt, and *Peter Grimes* and *Ellen Orford*, which were combined in Britten's opera *Peter Grimes* (1945).

**Borrow, George (Henry)** 1803–81 Author, translator, linguist and traveller. Born in East Dereham, Norfolk, son of a recruiting officer in the militia, Borrow experienced little childhood stability because of the frequent movements of the regiment around Britain. He had only three or four years of formal schooling, after which he was articled to a firm of solicitors in Norwich, though apparently without any intention of practising law. By 1824, when his father died and the articling period ended, he had a working knowledge of at least 12 languages, including Latin, Greek, French, Welsh, Irish, Italian, German, Danish and Dutch; he later added Portuguese, Russian, Arabic and Spanish. Borrow habitually called himself a philologist or 'Lavengro', throughout his life dabbling in comparative linguistics and verse translation. At least by the time of the family's return to Norwich in 1816, he had begun to associate with gypsies, soon having a good knowledge of their ways.

The years 1824–32 were divided between Norwich and London, where he made a number of attempts to establish himself as a writer. He compiled and edited the six-volume *Celebrated Trials and Remarkable Cases of Criminal Jurisprudence, from the Earliest Records to the Year 1825*; published a translation of *Faustus: His Life, Death, and Descent into Hell* (1825), banned by some libraries because of antisocial interpolations; engaged in hackwork for London booksellers, producing the *Life and Adventures of the Famous Colonel Blood* (1825) and probably other such pamphlets; and put out, by subscription, his *Romantic Ballads, Translated from the Danish* (1826). Not a great deal is known about his personal life: he continued to read widely, he may have travelled, he was certainly from time to time ill, for he was throughout his life the victim of a severe nervous disorder which he and his mother called 'the horrors'.

It was his linguistic proficiency that, in 1832, resulted in an introduction to the British and Foreign Bible Society. Financially supported by an extensive network of local Bible groups, this interdenominational, but predominantly Evangelical organization was committed to the world-wide distribution of the Bible, and particularly the New Testament, usually in specially prepared editions in the appropriate language. Borrow worked for the Society for seven years, first in St Petersburg (1833–5), where he issued a translation of the New Testament into Manchu and produced two volumes of his own verse translations, *Targum* and *The Talisman* (both 1835), and then in Portugal and Spain (1835–40), where he supervised the printing and distribution of the New Testament in Spanish and Basque. For these activities he was arrested on several occasions, and at least once spent some time in gaol. By travelling extensively through dangerous, little-known areas of Portugal and western Spain, Borrow also had those adventures that were soon to give imaginative substance to the two books which made him famous: *The Zincali* (1841) and **The Bible in Spain** (1843).

Borrow married Mrs Mary Clarke in 1840 and for the rest of his life resided on her estate at Oulton, Norfolk, albeit with long periods in Yarmouth (1853–60) and London (1860–?1870). During this period, he wrote the three works on which his literary reputation chiefly depends: **Lavengro** (1851), **The Romany Rye** (1857) and **Wild Wales** (1857). Though he declined to provide the literal autobiography he at one time promised, these works, especially the first two, for many years enjoyed the status of established classics, simultaneously delighting and puzzling the reader with a racy, convincing, but impenetrable amalgam of fact and fiction. He spent his later years in further forays into translation (a second edition of his *Gypsy Luke*) and philology (*Romano Lavo-Lil*), at the same time consolidating his reputation as a traveller by means of walking tours through Norfolk, Wales, Ireland and Scotland.

**Bosman, Herman Charles** 1905–51 South African writer, born at Kuils River, Cape Province. With Afrikaner background but English-medium education, he worked as a schoolmaster in a remote Afrikaner district near Groot Marico, Transvaal. After four and a half years in gaol for fatally shooting his stepbrother in a quarrel, he spent nine years in Europe, then practised journalism in South Africa. His literary reputation rose steadily after his death. It rests especially upon *Mafeking Road* (1947), *Unto Dust* (1963), *Jurie Steyn's Post Office* (1971) and *A Bekkersdal Marathon* (1971) – collections of spirited stories about rural Afrikaner life, original, versatile treatments that include sardonic detachment, shrewd observation, social satire, irony and folk comedy. With humour and pathos *Cold Stone Jug* (1949) recounts his prison experience; *A Cask of Jerepigo* (1957) gathers essays and sketches together; *Jacaranda in the Night* (1947) and *Willemsdorp* (1977) are novels. *Collected Works* (2 vols.) appeared in 1981.

**Boston, Lucy (Maria)** 1892–1990 Children's author. Born in Southport, and educated at a Quaker school and Oxford, she trained as a nurse before turning to poetry and painting. In 1939 she took up residence at the 12th-century manor house near Cambridge which later featured in her children's books. The first of these, *The Children of Green Knowe* (1954), was published when she was over 60. Its successors include *The River at Green Knowe* (1959), *A Stranger at Green Knowe* (1961), *An Enemy at Green Knowe* (1964) and *The Stones of Green Knowe* (1976), which brings the series to an end by describing how the house was originally built. *The Sea Egg* (1967), more strikingly original, tells the story of a greenish stone that hatches a small triton under the gaze of two children holidaying in Cornwall.

**Bostonians, The** A novel by **Henry James**, serialized in *The Century Magazine* (1885–6; volume form 1886). It is a satirical study of the movement for female emancipation in New England. In searching for a tale which would be characteristic of social conditions in the USA, James concluded that the most striking aspect of American life at the time was 'the situation of women, the decline of the sentiment of sex, and the agitation in their behalf'.

The novel recounts the story of a young lawyer from the South, Basil Ransom, who comes to Boston on business. He becomes acquainted with his two cousins, the feminist Olive Chancellor and her sister, the widow Mrs Luna, who soon falls in love with him. Olive takes Basil to a suffragette meeting, where he meets the altruistic philanthropist, Miss Birdseye. At the meeting a beautiful young woman, Verena Tarrant, delivers an eloquent address, and both Olive and Basil are immediately interested in her. Verena is easily persuaded to share Olive's luxurious home, and Olive sets out to make her a leader of the feminist cause, pleading with her to forswear the thought of marriage. Basil, however, increasingly irritated by the attentions of Mrs Luna, falls in love with Verena and attempts to counter Olive's sway over her. As a result, hostility develops between Olive and Basil. Verena is preparing to deliver a course of lectures, but when Miss Birdseye dies she loses confidence in her purpose. She is about to begin her first lecture when Basil's appearance in the hall unnerves her. She finds herself having to choose between Olive and Basil, and to Olive's bitter disappointment she decides to accept Basil's proposal of marriage.

**Boswell, Sir Alexander** 1775–1822 The eldest son of **James Boswell**, born at Auchinleck. Alexander Boswell inherited his father's interest in literature, with a particular interest in his fellow Ayrshireman **Robert Burns**, and initiated the movement for a monument to Burns on the banks of the River Doon. Like many of his contemporaries in Scottish literature he was a collector of songs; he also wrote occasional verse and political squibs. One of his political verses, 'The New Whig Song', was published in *The Glasgow Sentinel* and offended James Stuart of Dunearn. Stuart and Boswell fought a duel on 26 March 1822 and Boswell died of his wounds.

**Boswell, James** 1740–95 Journal writer and biographer of **Samuel Johnson**. Born in Edinburgh, the son of Alexander Boswell (later Lord Auchinleck), judge of the Court of Session, he was educated at Edinburgh High School and studied law, with little enthusiasm, at the Universities of Edinburgh and Glasgow. His father intended a legal career for him, but Boswell had set his mind on other things and left for London in 1760. By turns libertine and puritanical, his colourful life there involved him in a protracted battle of wills with his formidable father, without whose help he was unable to purchase the commission in the Footguards he so desired. He was also ambitious for literary and political reputation, and began to mix in the appropriate social circles.

Already a friend of Thomas Sheridan and **Garrick**, Boswell made the most important literary acquaintance of his life on 16 May 1763,

James Boswell. Portrait by G. Dance, 1793. National Portrait Gallery, London.

when he met Samuel Johnson. Although Boswell started recording closely the activities and conversation of Johnson almost at once, the impression that he had little literary or even social life independent of his friend is wrong. It was largely with the latter's encouragement, though, that he maintained his elaborate view of contemporary London life, published in 1950 as *Boswell's London Journal 1762–3*.

Boswell travelled the Continent from 1763–6, completing his legal studies in Utrecht, meeting Rousseau and **Wilkes**, and visiting Corsica in October 1765. There he gained an introduction to the redoubtable General Paoli, whose independent spirit greatly impressed him, and as a direct result of which he championed the Corsican cause in *An Account of Corsica* (published 1768) and *Essays in Favour of the Brave Corsicans* (1769). Returning to England in 1766 on the death of his mother, Boswell was admitted to the Scottish Bar where, to his father's relief, he began to practise as an advocate in Edinburgh. In 1767 he published *Dorando*, an allegorical romance, set in Spain, concerning the Douglas inheritance case, and in 1769, after numerous well-documented philanderings, he married his cousin, Margaret Montgomerie.

He remained closely in touch with Johnson, however, paying frequent visits to London, and continuing to move in literary circles. Boswell made the acquaintance of **Goldsmith** and **Burke**, and in 1773 became a member of the celebrated literary coterie 'the Club'. He wrote essays under the name 'Hypochondriack' from 1777–83, and continued to pursue a legal career in Scotland, where he succeeded to his father's estate in 1782.

Samuel Johnson died in December 1784, and in the following year Boswell published *The Journal of a Tour to the Hebrides*, a record of his travels through Scotland in 1773. He was called to the English Bar in 1786, and unsuccessfully entertained hopes of a political career in London. During this time, though, with the encouragement of the scholar **Edmond Malone**, he completed the magnificent work for which he is best remembered, *The Life of Samuel Johnson LL.D.*, published in 1791. Boswell spent his remaining years in London where he died on 19 May 1795, after a short illness. He was renowned as good company, with his lively mind and formidable memory, a man exuberant and melancholy by turns. His several journals and private papers, many discovered at Malahide Castle, have been collected and edited by Frederick A. Pottle; they confirm Boswell as a talented writer and a man worth remembering in his own right.

**Bothie of Tober-na-Vuolich, The** A poem in hexameters by **Arthur Hugh Clough**, first published as *The Bothie of Toper-na-Fuosich* in 1848.

It describes the romance of Philip Hewson, an Oxford undergraduate, and Elspie, the daughter of a Highland farmer, during a student reading party in Scotland.

**Bottomley, Gordon** 1874–1948 Dramatist and poet. Born and educated in Keighley, Yorkshire, Bottomley was prevented by ill health from pursuing a career in banking. In enforced leisure, he wrote poetry and plays, and became a contributor to *Georgian Poetry*. Bottomley's interest in Celtic folklore is already evident in his first published collection of poetry, *The Mickle Drede and Other Verses* (1896). His plays are always historically and geographically distanced. The first three to be performed are certainly among his best. *The Crier by Night* (published in 1902; first performed 1916) resolves the cruelty of conflict between the sadistic wife of a farmer and an Irish servant-girl with the aid of a water-spirit. *King Lear's Wife* (published in 1920; first performed 1915), also much concerned with brutality, invents an adulterous affair for King Lear while his wife is dying. *Gruach* (published 1921; first performed 1923) describes the courtship of Macbeth and Lady Macbeth. Bottomley's later dramatic work was written for and confined to amateur performance. It showed the influence of **W. B. Yeats**, in particular his *Plays for Dancers*. Some of the best of it is collected in *Lyric Plays* (1932).

**Boucicault, Dion[ysius] (Lardner)** 1820–90 Irish playwright, actor and theatre manager whose first success came early when *London Assurance* (1841) was staged at the Theatre Royal, **Covent Garden**. Another five-act comedy, *Old Heads and Young Hearts* (1844), offers further evidence of his proficiency. A series of hastily written but clever versions of French plays, including *The Corsican Brothers* (1852) and *The Vampire* (1852), had established him as a leading English dramatist before his emigration to the United States in 1853. There he began a separate and equally successful career, particularly with the melodramas *The Poor of New York* (1857), *Jessie Brown, or, The Relief of Lucknow* (1858) and *The Octoroon* (1859). Three outstanding Irish melodramas, *The Colleen Bawn* (1860), *Arrah-na-Pogue* (1864) and *The Shaughraun* (1874), confirmed his position at the head of the dramatic profession. It was a position that did not survive him. Boucicault wrote too much – nearly 200 plays have been ascribed to him – and too opportunistically, but he had the facility to disguise imitation as innovation and was, at his best, a superb theatrical storyteller.

**Bourchier, John, 2nd Baron Berners** ?1469–1533 Writer and statesman. When young he was involved in a premature attempt to make

Henry Tudor king, and in 1497 he helped in the suppression of the Cornish rebellion against the then Henry VII in support of the pretender Perkin Warbeck. He served the next Tudor monarch, Henry VIII, in various military and diplomatic capacities, including the post of deputy at Calais, and was present at the Field of the Cloth of Gold. In 1516 he became Chancellor of the Exchequer and Holbein painted him in the robes of that office.

As a translator he favoured the works of medieval chivalry and romance, courtesy books and chronicles. His vigorous translation of Froissart's *Chronicles*, faithful in spirit to its original, appeared in two parts in 1523 and 1525. The later chronicles of **Edward Hall** and **Raphael Holinshed** are indebted to it. The chivalric romance **Huon of Bordeaux**, which introduced the fairy prince Oberon to English readers, was not printed until after Berners's death, probably by **Wynkyn de Worde** in 1534. From the French Berners translated *The History of the Most Noble and Valiant Knight Arthur of Little Brittain* (i.e. of Brittany). *The Castle of Love*, of which the first edition was *c.* 1540, was a translation of a courtesy book by Diego de San Pedro. Berners's most popular work was *The Golden Book of Marcus Aurelius*, a translation from the French version of Antonio de Guevara's original Spanish. This appeared in 1535 and went through many editions in the 16th century.

**Bourne, George** See **Sturt, George**.

**Bourne, Randolph** 1886–1918 American essayist and social critic, born in Bloomfield, New Jersey, and educated at Columbia. His first articles, on the revolutionary character of youth, were published in *The Atlantic Monthly* and collected in *Youth and Life* (1913). As his reputation as an essayist rose, he found audiences through *The New Republic*, *The Dial*, and the *Seven Arts*. He was an eclectic reader, and his writings reflected broad interests, notably education (*The Gary Schools*, 1916, and *Education and Living*, 1917), the development of socially responsible fiction, and the depreciation of an ethnically diverse American culture ('Trans-National America', 1916). He was also a fervent pacifist, and after Woodrow Wilson's abandonment of neutrality in 1917 he became an eloquent and increasingly isolated advocate of American non-intervention in World War I (for example in *Untimely Papers*, 1919). His prowess as a conversationalist impressed a generation of writers and critics, including Van Wyck Brooks, Lewis Mumford, and **John Dos Passos**. Among these figures Bourne developed an almost mythic stature. Disfigured – he was a hunchback who had been deformed at birth by an incompetent doctor – but brilliant, he seemed to represent to them the spirit of 1910 which could not outlive the war.

**Bowdler, Thomas** 1754–1825 Editor. Bowdler's edition of **Shakespeare**, *The Family Shakespeare* (1818), made drastic cuts in the text of the plays by omitting 'whatever is unfit to be read aloud by a gentleman to a company of ladies' and so gave rise to the term 'to bowdlerize'. He also prepared an edition of **Gibbon**'s *Decline and Fall of the Roman Empire* on the same principles.

**Bowen, Elizabeth (Dorothea Cole)** 1899–1973 Novelist and short-story writer. She was born in Dublin at Bowen's Court, an 18th-century manor where she spent much of her early childhood and which she eventually inherited in 1930. She was educated at Downe House School in Kent, and lived in Ireland, London, France and Italy until her marriage in 1923. For the next 10 years she was based in London, the setting for many of her novels and short stories. Early volumes of stories, which already displayed her subtle use of language, were *Encounters* (1923), *Ann Lee's* (1926), *Joining Charles* (1929) and *The Cat Jumps* (1934). Later collections included *Look at All Those Roses* (1941) and *The Demon Lover* (1945). Her *Collected Stories*, introduced by **Angus Wilson**, appeared in 1980.

Early novels included *The Hotel* (1927), *The Last September* (1929), *Friends and Relations* (1931) and *The House in Paris* (1935). Best known, however, are *The Death of the Heart* (1938) and *The Heat of the Day* (1949), the latter being a tragic love-story set in war-time London. Later novels were *A World of Love* (1955) and *Eva Trout* (1969).

Elizabeth Bowen's writing follows **Henry James** in its attention to style and its subtle delineation of character (especially female character) and setting. Her impressionistic descriptions of the landscape, both urban and rural, and its seasonal changes add a highly effective dimension to her work.

She also wrote *Seven Winters* (1942), a partial autobiography, and *Bowen's Court* (1942), a history of the family seat.

**Bowering, George** 1935– Canadian poet and novelist. Born and brought up in the Okanagan Valley of British Columbia, he was a Royal Canadian Air Force aerial photographer before attending the University of British Columbia. His early volumes of poetry, strongly influenced by the **Black Mountain school**, include *Points on the Grid* (1964), *Baseball* (1967), *Rocky Mountain Foot* (1968) and *The Gangs of Kosmos* (1969). He has been involved in the publication of a number of influential little magazines and was founding editor of *TISH*, an iconoclastic poetry journal of the 1960s. He has worked in various Canadian universities and now teaches at Simon Fraser University, Vancouver. Around 1970 Bowering turned to longer, book-length poems; these include *George Vancouver* (1970) and *Autobiology* (1972), collected in *The Catch* (1976) and *West Window* (1982). The navigator and explorer Vancouver fascinates him and his most acclaimed novel, *Burning Water* (1980), is a deconstructionist account of Vancouver's search for the Northwest Passage. His fiction, which includes *A Short Sad Book* (1977) and *A Place to Die* (1983), adopts a playful stance towards narrative conventions and shows the influence of **Gertrude Stein**. *In the Flesh* (1974) and *Another Mount* (1979) are among his other volumes of verse.

**Bowles, Paul** 1910– American poet, novelist and short-story writer. Bowles was born in New York City and attended the University of Virginia before going to Paris, where his first poetry was published in the magazine *transitions* during the 1920s. After some years as a composer and music critic, he published his first novel, *The Sheltering Sky*, in 1949. In subsequent works, notably *The Delicate Prey* (1950, in England as *A Little Stone*), *Let it Come Down* (1952), and *The Spider's House* (1955), he continued to explore the theme of spiritually weary Westerners attempting to escape the ennui of their lives only to find themselves displaced in an Orient they find unsatisfying and even frightening.

Resident in Tangier since 1952, Bowles has tape-recorded, transcribed, and translated original accounts of indigenous life, including *A Life Full of Holes* by Driss ben Hamad Charhadi (1964), *For Bread Alone* by Mohammad Choukil (1973) and several by Mohammad Mrabet: *M'Hashish* (1969), *The Boy Who Set The Fire* (1974), *Harmless Poisons, Blameless Sins* (1976) and *The Beach Café and The Voice* (1980). Among Bowles's other books are *Pages From Cold Point and Other Stories* (1968), *Their Heads Are Green and Their Hands Are Blue* (1963, travel sketches), *Scenes* (1968, poems) and *Collected Stories* (1979). *Without Stopping*, an autobiography, was issued in 1972.

**Bowles, William Lisle** 1762–1850 Poet. Educated at Winchester School and at Trinity College, Oxford, in 1804 Bowles was appointed vicar of Bremhill in Wiltshire and prebendary of Salisbury Cathedral; he later became a canon and was made chaplain to the Prince Regent in 1818. He published *Fourteen Sonnets, Elegiac and Descriptive, Written During a Tour* anonymously in 1789. They were the first poems of distinction in the sonnet form for a great many years and were to have considerable influence on the work of **Coleridge** and **Southey**. His edition of **Alexander Pope** (1806) brought him into conflict with **Campbell**, to whom he replied in *The Invariable Principles of Poetry* (1819). **Byron** joined Campbell, but Bowles effectively defended his views.

**Bowra, Sir (Cecil) Maurice** 1898–1971 Scholar and critic. The son of a customs official, Bowra was born in China and educated at Cheltenham and at New College, Oxford. He saw military service in France from 1917 to 1918, and became a fellow of Wadham College, Oxford, in 1922. As warden of this college from 1938 to 1970, Bowra was a celebrated host and raconteur. Among his many works on classical literature are *Tradition and Design in the Iliad* (1930), *Ancient Greek Literature* (1933), *The Greek Experience* (1957) and *Landmarks in Greek Literature* (1966); his more modern interests appear in *The Heritage of Symbolism* (1943) and *The Romantic Imagination* (1949). Bowra also published translations of Greek and Russian poetry, and edited *The Oxford Book of Greek Verse in Translation* (1938).

**Boyd, John** 1912– Irish playwright. Born in Belfast, and educated at Queen's University, Belfast, and Trinity College, Dublin, he became director of the Lyric Theatre, Belfast. His major theme is the North's divided heritage, mainly in an urban setting and expressed in the local idiom paradoxically common to the antagonistic faiths. *The Assassin* (1969) explores the psychology of a clerical demagogue, *The Flats* (1971) places domestic tragedy in the collective violence of the Belfast streets. These naturalistic plays, with *The Farm* (1972) and *The Street* (1977), are acutely discerning of the brutalities behind factional slogans and their travesty of political action.

**Boyd, Martin (A'Beckett)** 1893–1969 Australian novelist. Born in Lucerne and brought up in Melbourne, Boyd divided his time between Australia and Europe. He was studying architecture when World War I broke out; he enlisted in the British army and later transferred to the RFC. In a period of post-war indecision he tried life as a journalist and spent some time in a Franciscan community before becoming a novelist. His first novels were published under the name of Martin Mills, notably *The Montforts* (1928), a dense but elegant and ironic family chronicle of Anglo-Australian life. This remained the theme of his best novels: *Lucinda Brayford* (1946), *The Cardboard Crown* (1952), *A Difficult Young Man* (1955), *Outbreak of Love* (1957) and *When Blackbirds Sing* (1962). Of his other novels the most notable is *Such Pleasure* (1949). He published two volumes of autobiography, *A Single Flame* (1939) and *Day of My Delight* (1965).

**Boyer, Abel** 1667–1729 Historian. A Huguenot, Boyer was educated in the Netherlands and came to England in 1689. In 1703 he began to publish an annual calendar of events and continued this until 1713. He made his mark as a historian with *The History of King William III* (1702) and *The History of the Life and Reign of Queen Anne* (1722). His translation of the *Mémoires de la Vie du Comte de Gramont* (1714) was revised and annotated by **Sir Walter Scott** (1811).

**Boyle, Kay** 1903– American novelist and short-story writer. Born in St Paul, Minnesota, Boyle lived in Europe for 30 years before and after World War II. From 1946 to 1954 she was a foreign correspondent for **The New Yorker**. Among the 24 volumes of fiction she published between 1929 and 1975 were several collections of short stories: *Short Stories* (1929), *Wedding Day and Other Stories* (1930), *The First Lover and Other Stories* (1936), *The White Horse of Vienna and Other Stories* (1936) and *Thirty Stories* (1946). In 1935 and 1941 she was the recipient of the O. Henry Award. Among her novels are *Year Before Last* (1932), *My Next Bride* (1934), *Monday Night* (1938), *The Crazy Hunter: Three Short Novels* (1940), *Avalanche* (1944) and *A Frenchman Must Die* (1946). She often takes as her subject a young and unworldly American who travels to Europe. A vivid depiction of extraordinary instances of brutality or absurdity in life is a particular characteristic of her work. In addition to novels and short stories she has published five books of verse, various works of non-fiction, and books for young people.

**Boyle, Robert** 1627–91 Chemist and philosopher. The 14th child of the Earl of Cork, he was educated at Eton and by private tutors. Around 1655 he moved to Oxford to join the group of proto-scientists centred on John Wilkins, Warden of Wadham, which included Christopher Wren, Seth Ward, William Petty and later Robert Hooke. His early interests were in alchemy. However, following the lead given by Descartes and Gassendi, he became convinced that the structure of matter was corpuscular, and its operations open to rational investigation. His work would be instrumental in turning chemistry from an occult science to a recognizably modern discipline in which theory and practical experiment supported and advanced each other. His method of experiment, observation and hypothesis owed much to **Bacon**'s proposals for a regulated scientific programme. Assisted by Hooke, his most rewarding research was into the behaviour of air and gases. Boyle's law, which stemmed from his work on atmospheric pressure and the vacuum in the 1650s, established the relationship between the pressure and the volume of a gas at a constant temperature. As a founder-member of the Royal Society in 1660, he was associated with all the leaders of the early scientific movement in England.

Boyle was a prolific writer, his most enduring works being *The Sceptical Chymist* (1661), a dialogue in which he attacked the theories of matter based on elements and qualities that derived from Aristotle and Paracelsus, and approached the question of how change occurred in the material world. The book contains a somewhat florid recommendation of the experimental method. *The Origin of Forms and Qualities* (1666) offered a defence of the corpuscular theory of matter, falling back on to Greek atomic theory for support. Boyle's concern with the bases of scientific classification expressed in this book had some influence over **Locke**'s *Essay Concerning Human Understanding*. Later in his life his religious concerns began to merge with his scientific interests, and he was anxious to refute the suspicion that atomism led to atheism. He was a declared opponent of **Hobbes**. His desire to demonstrate the intellectual compatibility between scientific enquiry and revealed Christianity led him to endow the Boyle Lectures, which became a vehicle for those who strove to maintain a consensus between science and religion in the early 18th century. His *Occasional Reflections on Several Subjects* (1665) provided material for Book Three of *Gulliver's Travels*, and was also satirized by **Swift** in *Meditations on a Broomstick*. His sentimental religious romance, *The Martyrdom of Theodora and Didymus* (1687), was later adapted to provide a libretto for Handel's opera *Theodora*.

**boys' companies** Surviving records show that the choristers of the Chapel Royal were performing occasional plays by 1516 and those of St Paul's by about 1525, but the significant decision to present plays in public was taken in 1576, when Richard Farrant, Master of the Children of the Chapel at Windsor, purchased a lease on rooms in the Blackfriars with the aim of converting them for indoor performance. The **Blackfriars** theatre was closed in about 1585, perhaps overshadowed by the greater success of the St Paul's Boys in the plays of **John Lyly**. Increasingly involved in controversy during the 1580s, the boys' companies fell seriously out of favour over their part in the **Marprelate** debate (1588–9) and for nearly 10 years (*c.* 1590–8) they ceased to act in public. But the popularity of boy actors reached a new peak during the first decade of the 17th century. **Marston**, **Dekker**, **Middleton**, **Chapman**, **Webster**, **Jonson**, **Beaumont** and **Fletcher** were among the playwrights who wrote for them. By 1613, fashionable interest had so diminished that the once-great Children of the Chapel Royal were absorbed by an adult company.

**Boz** The early pseudonym of **Charles Dickens**.

*Bracebridge Hall, or, The Humorists: A Medley* A book of 49 tales and sketches by **Washington Irving**, published in 1822 under Irving's pseudonym, Geoffrey Crayon, Gent. It is a sequel to Irving's popular *The Sketch Book*. English, French and Spanish settings are intermingled with American; the best-remembered tales, 'Dolph Heylinger' and 'The Storm-Ship', are set in America.

**Brackenbury, Alison** 1953– Poet. Born in Gainsborough, Lincolnshire, she was educated at St Hugh's College, Oxford. She worked as a librarian until the birth of her daughter in 1983. After two pamphlets, *Journey to a Cornish Wedding* (1977) and *Two Poems* (1979), her first major collection was *Dreams of Power and Other Poems* (1981), which was a Poetry Book Society Recommendation. The title poem is a dramatic monologue, featuring one of history's victims, Arabella Stuart, granddaughter of Bess of Hardwick. Sceptical of autobiographical discourse, she usually employs the technique of presenting objects in which the past is embodied. She is interested in myth and dream, and the poems are located in a known landscape. Brackenbury writes both short lyrics – 'Medicine in Turkey' and 'Summer Fruit' – and long poems, like the title poem from *Breaking Ground and Other Poems* (1984), which evokes episodes from the life of **John Clare**. The winner of a Gregory award, she is a leading female poet of her generation, and the unusual and ambitious directions she pursues are winning her a widening readership.

**Brackenridge, Hugh Henry** 1748–1816 American novelist and poet. Brackenridge was born in Scotland; his family emigrated to Pennsylvania when he was five. He educated himself in the classics while growing up on the frontier, and in 1768 entered Princeton University where he collaborated with **Philip Freneau** on *Father Bembo's Pilgrimage to Mecca* (1770), a fictional prose satire on American manners, and on a patriotic poem, *The Rising Glory of America*. During the Revolutionary War he wrote several patriotic works, including *A Poem On Divine Revelation* (1774) and two plays, *The Battle of Bunkers-Hill* (1776) and *The Death of General Montgomery* (1777). In 1779 he went to Philadelphia and founded the *United States Magazine*, which published patriotic speeches and state constitutions, as well as his own series of fictional essays on Revolutionary themes, 'The Cave of Vanhest'.

He soon moved to Pittsburgh to practise law. There he became involved in politics, but was a true partisan of neither political party. Having founded *The Pittsburgh Gazette* (1786), the first Western newspaper, he frequently contributed

'Children of the Chappell' followed by 'Gentlemen of the Chappell'. The Children of the Chapel Royal Choir and the Children of St Paul's attended the choir schools and were often called upon to entertain at court. In the early years of the 17th century they appeared in works by Jonson, Marston, and Chapman in the theatre at Blackfriars. The boys' companies came to an end when the parents objected to their children's exploitation. *Add.MS 35324, f.31v.* British Library.

satires of both Eastern and Western manners, both Federalist and Republican politics. He acted as mediator during the Whiskey Rebellion (1794), provoked by Alexander Hamilton's excise tax on liquor, and his account of the rebellion was published as *Incidents of the Insurrection in the Western Parts of Pennsylvania, in the Year 1794* (1795). He served on the Pennsylvania Supreme Court from 1799 to 1814, during which time he continued to publish volumes of **Modern Chivalry** (1792–1815), the novel on which his literary reputation chiefly rests.

**Bradbrook, M[uriel] C[lara]** 1909– Critic. Born in Wallasey, near Liverpool, where her father was a coastguard officer, M. C. Bradbrook attended schools in Wallasey and Glasgow before going to study at Cambridge University. She began her long association with Girton College as an undergraduate, becoming a fellow in 1932 and eventually Mistress from 1968 to 1976. She was Professor of English at Cambridge from 1965 to 1976.

Bradbrook's many critical studies range from *Ibsen the Norwegian* (1946) and *T. S. Eliot* (1950) to *Sir Thomas Malory* (1957) and *John Webster: Citizen and Dramatist* (1980). She has written a history of Girton College, and a study of **Malcolm Lowry** (1974). However, she is best known as an authority on **Shakespeare** and the Elizabethan theatre. In this field her works include *Themes and Conventions of Elizabethan*

*Tragedy* (1934), *The Growth and Structure of Elizabethan Comedy* (1955) and *The Rise of the Common Player* (1962). These books, together with *Shakespeare the Craftsman* (1969) and two other works on Shakespeare, have been reprinted as *A History of Elizabethan Drama* (6 vols., 1979).

**Bradbury, Malcolm (Stanley)** 1932– Novelist and critic. Bradbury's first novel, *Eating People is Wrong* (1959), draws on his time at the University of Leicester (the city where he was born and grew up) and is a picaresque, satirical university novel in the manner of **Kingsley Amis**'s *Lucky Jim*. *Stepping Westward* (1965) follows, in similar vein, the fortunes of an English academic in America. *The History Man* (1975), with its bitter portrait of a manically trendy sociology lecturer, was hailed as the definitive fictional response to the culture of the 1960s. *Rates of Exchange* (1982), set in Eastern Europe, continues Bradbury's preoccupation with the academic life but displays greater technical self-consciousness. Its fictional Eastern European country, Slaka, is further explored in a pastiche tourist guide, *Why Come to Slaka?* (1986), while its play with the metaphoric consonances between monetarism and **structuralism** is developed in a recent novella, *Cuts* (1987).

Since 1970 Bradbury has been Professor of American Studies at the University of East Anglia, where with **Angus Wilson**, he has presided over Britain's only notable university course in creative writing. Its students have included **Ian McEwan**, Kazuo Ishiguro, Adam Mars-Jones, Clive Sinclair and Maggie Gee. Bradbury's academic publications include monographs on **Evelyn Waugh** (1962) and **Saul Bellow** (1982), a collection of essays on contemporary fiction, *Possibilities* (1973), and *The Modern American Novel* (1983). *No, Not Bloomsbury* (1987) is a collection of literary journalism.

**Bradbury, Ray (Douglas)** 1920– American novelist and short-story writer. Born in Waukegan, Illinois, Bradbury became a full-time writer in 1943 and contributed numerous short stories to periodicals before publishing a collection of them as *Dark Carnival* (1947). His reputation as a leading writer of **science fiction** was established with the publication of *The Martian Chronicles* (1950; in England as *The Silver Locusts*), which describes the first attempts of Earth people to conquer and colonize Mars during the years 1999–2026; the constant thwarting of their efforts by the gentle, telepathic Martians; the eventual colonization; and finally the effect on the Martian settlers of a massive nuclear war on Earth. As much a work of social criticism as of science fiction, *The Martian Chronicles* reflects some of the prevailing anxieties of America in the early 1950s: the fear of nuclear war, the longing for a simpler life, and reactions against racism and censorship. Another of Bradbury's best-known works, the novel *Fahrenheit 451* (1953), is set in a future when the written word is forbidden; resisting a totalitarian state which burns all the books, a group of rebels memorize entire works of literature and philosophy. Among his other works are the novel *Something Wicked This Way Comes* (1962) and numerous collections of short stories: *The Illustrated Man* (1951), *The Golden Apples of the Sun* (1953), *The October Sky* (1955), *A Medicine for Melancholy* (1959; in England as *The Day It Rained Forever*), *The Machineries of Joy* (1964), *I Sing The Body Electric!* (1969), *The Last Circus and the Electrocution* (1980) and *A Memory of Murder* (1984).

**Braddon, Mary Elizabeth** 1835–1915 Novelist. She was born in London (two years earlier than she later liked to admit), the daughter of an unsuccessful solicitor who eventually deserted his family. In youth she took to the stage, but without abandoning her interest in writing: she began her first novel, not published until several years afterwards, when she was 19. In 1860 she met John Maxwell, a publisher of journals, and lived with him for 14 years before the death of his wife allowed them to marry. *Lady Audley's Secret* (1862), her first published novel, was started in an attempt to rescue one of Maxwell's journals; the journal failed but the novel became the most popular example of Victorian **sensation fiction**. Its success overshadowed the rest of a long and hard-working career in which she produced some 80 novels. Some were in the same vein as *Lady Audley's Secret*: *Aurora Floyd* (1863), *John Marchmont's Legacy* (1863), *Henry Dunbar: The Story of an Outcast* (1864), *Sir Jasper's Tenant* (1865), *Birds of Prey* (1867) and *Charlotte's Inheritance* (1868). Others demonstrate a greater range and seriousness than public or reviewers fully recognized: *The Doctor's Wife* (1864) adapts Flaubert's *Madame Bovary*; *The Lady's Mile* (1866) and *The Lovels of Arden* (1871) are novels of society; *Vixen* (1871) is a satire, *Ishmael* (1884) a historical romance and *Dead Love Has Chains* (1907) a tragedy. Miss Braddon also contributed to many journals, and edited *Belgravia* and *Temple Bar*.

**Bradford, William** 1590–1657 A governor and historian of Plymouth Colony, Bradford was born in Yorkshire. He travelled to America aboard the *Mayflower* in 1620. At Plymouth, on the death of John Carver, Bradford was elected governor, an office which he held from 1621 to 1656 except for five years when he voluntarily stepped down to serve as assistant governor. In 1627, together with seven fellow emigrants and four London merchants, he assumed the colony's debt of £1800 from the original investors. In his various writings Bradford tells of other transactions that provide insight into the colonial government and economy. His *History of Plimmoth Plantation*, written between 1630 and 1651, chronicles the settlement of the Plymouth colony. His incomplete *Letter Book* (1624–30) and his letters to **John Winthrop** show a leader working out the colony's internal problems as well as negotiating with England, the neighbouring Massachusetts Bay Colony, and the Indians.

**Bradley, A[ndrew] C[ecil]** 1851–1935 Critic. Bradley was born in Cheltenham, the son of a clergyman, and the younger brother of the philosopher **F. H. Bradley**. He was educated at Cheltenham College and at Balliol College, Oxford, where he became a fellow in 1874, lecturing in philosophy and English. In 1882 Bradley became the first Professor of Literature and History at Liverpool, and he was later Professor of English Language and Literature at Glasgow from 1890, and Professor of Poetry at Oxford from 1901 until 1906, when he retired from academic life.

Bradley is best known for his *Oxford Lectures on Poetry* (1909) and especially for *Shakespearean Tragedy* (1904), a series of lectures in which he approached the major tragedies of **Shakespeare** through an extended study of the characters, who were presented as personalities independent of their place in the plays. The value of this approach has often been questioned since the 1930s, but Bradley's book is still read.

**Bradley, F[rancis] H[erbert]** 1846–1924 Philosopher. Born at Clapham in London and educated at Marlborough and University College, Oxford, he was elected a fellow of Merton College in 1870. His essay, *The Presuppositions of Critical History*, which contributed to the debate about the **Higher Criticism** (the study of the Gospels as historical records), appeared in 1874. Bradley's most important philosophical works are *Ethical Studies* (1876), *The Principles of Logic* (1883), *Appearance and Reality* (1893) and *Essays on Truth and Reality* (1914), these last two being a discussion of the state of contemporary metaphysical speculation. Bradley's thought was the subject of **T. S. Eliot**'s Harvard PhD thesis, later published as *Knowledge and Experience in the Philosophy of F. H. Bradley* (1964).

**Bradshaigh, Lady** *c.* 1706–85 Letter-writer. Born Dorothy Bellingham, she married Sir Roger Bradshaigh of Haigh, near Wigan, in 1731. On the publication of the first two volumes of *Clarissa* in December 1747 she wrote to **Richardson**, under the pseudonym 'Mrs Belfour', to suggest that Lovelace be reformed by Clarissa's excellence and that the conclusion of the work be their happy marriage. This started an extensive correspondence centring mainly on *Clarissa* and *The History of Sir Charles Grandison*, during the course of which Richardson attempted to explain his intentions in the two works. It is believed that the development of *Sir Charles Grandison* was much influenced by her constant adjurations that Richardson write a book about a good man. Although she considered intelligence to be a defect in a woman, Lady Bradshaigh nevertheless managed to evoke from Richardson some remarkable pieces of self-analysis. Recognizing the commercial and literary value of the correspondence, he persuaded her to edit it for publication. The letters were eventually incorporated into **Anna Laetitia Barbauld**'s edition of Richardson's letters (6 vols., 1804).

**Bradstreet, Anne** 1612–72 America's first published poet, Bradstreet was born and grew up in aristocratic surroundings in England as the daughter of Thomas Dudley, who had been steward to the Earl of Lincoln. She married Simon Bradstreet at 16, and two years later sailed for America with her husband and father on the *Arbella*. Living in Ipswich and then in Andover, she became the mother of eight children. Both her father and her husband eventually became governors of Massachusetts.

Bradstreet's collection of poems, *The Tenth Muse Lately Sprung Up in America*, was published without her knowledge by her brother-in-law in London in 1650. A second edition, with corrections and additional poems, entitled *Several Poems Compiled With a Great Variety of Wit*, appeared in Boston six years after her death. The poems generally follow Elizabethan models, and show the influence of **Spenser**, **Sidney**, Du Bartas and **Raleigh**. There are, for example, quaternions such as 'The Four Elements', 'The Four Humours', 'The Four Ages of Man' and 'The Four Seasons'; a series of emblematic stanzas on the themes of time and mutability; and elegies on Sidney, Du Bartas and Queen Elizabeth. Many of the later poems are more personal in subject and less conventional in form, often meditating on domestic topics from a religious point of view. This group includes poems to her husband and elegies on her dead children.

**Braine, John** 1922–86 Novelist. He was born and educated in Bradford. Before World War II he worked in a shop, a laboratory and a factory; after it he became a librarian in Northumberland and Yorkshire. He is still best known for his first novel, *Room at the Top* (1957), which brought him immediate recognition and was successfully filmed in 1959. One of the classic **Angry Young Men** novels, it features an unscrupulous and opportunistic hero, Joe Lampton, who chooses to marry wealth and success rather than his true love, and offers a sharp picture of Northern life in the 1950s, obsessed with wealth and social status. A sequel, *Life at the Top*, appeared in 1962.

None of Braine's subsequent work attracted comparable attention; later novels include *The Vodi* (1959), set in a tuberculosis sanatorium, *The Crying Game* (1964), *First and Last Love* (1981) and *The Two of Us* (1984).

**Braithwaite, E[dward] R[icardo]** 1912– Guyanese writer, born in Georgetown. His writings, mostly with multi-racial concerns, reflect experience of wartime RAF service, schoolmastering, social welfare and diplomacy. The popular autobiography *To Sir, with Love* (1959), with its film version, describes his years as a black teacher in London, *Paid Servant* (1962) his subsequent social-welfare work. *Reluctant Neighbours* (1972) is further, self-congratulatory autobiography. A travel book, *A Kind of Homecoming* (1962), conveys nostalgic Caribbean sentiments about pre-slavery roots in Africa, while *'Honorary White'* (1975) records a black man's visit to South Africa. His tragic, largely undervalued novel, *A Choice of Straws* (1967), ventures boldly into white working-class racial psychology.

**Braithwaite, William Stanley (Beaumont)** 1879–1962 A black American poet, short-story writer and editor, born in Boston, the son of West Indian parents. He began his literary career with *The Canadian* (1901), a novel which received little attention. His first collection of poetry, *Lyrics of Life and Love*, appeared in 1904; his second, *The House of Falling Leaves*, followed in 1908. He also produced a volume of short stories, *Frost on the Green Tree* (1928), a second novel, *Going over Tindel* (1924), and an autobiography, *The House Under Arcturus* (1941). *Selected Poems* appeared in 1948.

In the first few decades of the century, Braithwaite was influential as an editor and literary critic. For 16 years he published the annual *Anthology of Magazine Verse and Year Book of American Poetry* (1913–29), which served as a major outlet for black writers and poets. He also became a mentor to the younger generation of black writers. In an article entitled 'Some Contemporary Poets of the Negro Race', published in *The Crisis* in 1919, he wrote about the dawning of a 'new movement' in black letters, a flourishing of creative activity which was later termed the **Harlem Renaissance**. He subsequently joined the faculty of the first black graduate school at Atlanta University, where he taught until his retirement.

**Brathwaite, Edward (Kamau)** (formerly L. Edward) 1930– Historian and poet, born in Bridgetown, Barbados. Unlike the more inclusive **Derek Walcott**, Brathwaite tries to establish a Caribbean culture by recording and reorchestrating the surviving echoes of only African culture. His shorter poems appear in *Other Exiles* (1975), *Days and Nights* (1975), *Black and Blues* (1976) and *Third World Poems* (1983), but his excellence as an accomplished and visionary poet was established by three long poems: *Rights of Passage* (1967), *Masks* (1968) and *Islands* (1969), reprinted together as *The Arrivants: A New World Trilogy* (1973). Each of the three parts consists of 'movements' containing varying numbers of shorter poems rhythmically, verbally and thematically interrelated. Brathwaite interweaves popular Caribbean genres like worksongs and calypso with modern 'literary' verse forms. Through the voices of representative personae, *Rights of Passage* meditates upon the slavery-induced rootlessness of West Indians and the dispossession generally of black people.

In *Masks* he finds in West African music, dance and ritual the origins of African cultural fragments, still extant in the Caribbean, which enabled African vitality to transcend the horrors of slavery. In *Islands* Caribbean history is reconsidered, not as pain and despair, but coral growth, as present-day dancing, drumming and masquerade become the means of 'now waking/ making / making / with their / rhythms some- / thing torn / and new'. *Mother Poem* (1977), first in a new cycle about Barbados, is similar in

technique and structure, though the concept of the island as 'mother' is somewhat strained. *Sun Poem* (1982), more persuasive and cohesive, evokes a Barbadian childhood. Brathwaite's historical writings include *The Folk Culture of the Slaves of Jamaica* (1970).

**Brautigan, Richard** 1935–84 American novelist and poet. Born in Tacoma, Washington, Brautigan came to prominence in the mid 1960s as a leading exponent of a new social order. His poetry, of which the best-known collection is *The Pill Versus the Springhill Mine Disaster* (1968), paid homage to an unconstrained sexuality and to the enrichment derived from personal encounters. His novel *Trout Fishing in America* (1967), which sold over two million copies, describes the narrator's nostalgic search for a morning of good fishing in a crystal-clear stream. His quest takes him through a variety of American landscapes – San Francisco city parks, Oregon forests, Idaho campgrounds, a Filipino laundry, and a wrecking yard that sells used trout streams by the foot. The fact that his idiosyncratic quest is never realized becomes a metaphor for the unpromising and unappealing cultural environment that surrounds his journey. *In Watermelon Sugar* (1968) portrays a mode of life in a commune that shuns all standard American values, the residents defining themselves largely in

Richard Brautigan.

opposition to the social structure of the outside world.

Many of his novels display a childlike conception of a world in which one can rearrange, ridicule, or ignore elements that are threatening or irrelevant. His other works of fiction include *A Confederate General from Big Sur* (1964), *Revenge of the Lawn: Stories, 1962–1970* (1971), *The Abortion: An Historical Romance 1966* (1971), *The Hawkline Monster: A Gothic Western* (1974), *Willard and His Bowling Trophies: A Perverse Mystery* (1974), *Sombrero Fallout: A Japanese Novel* (1976), *Dreaming of Babylon: A Private Eye Novel, 1942* (1977), *The Tokyo–Montana Express* (1980) and *So The Wind Won't Blow It All Away* (1982). Among his other collections of poetry are *The Galilee Hitch-Hiker* (1958), *The Return of the Rivers* (1958), *Lay the Marble Tea* (1959), *The Octopus Frontier* (1960), *All Watched Over By Machines of Loving Grace* (1967), *Please Plant This Book* (1968, a combination of poems and seed packets), *Rommel Drives Deep Into Egypt* (1970), *Loading Mercury with a Pitchfork* (1976) and *June 30th, June 30th* (1978). Brautigan was found dead from a self-inflicted gunshot wound in 1984.

**Brave New World** A novel by **Aldous Huxley**, first published in 1932.

In the year 632 After Ford (i.e., the 26th century) the world has attained a kind of Utopia, in which the means of production are in state ownership and the principle 'from each according to his ability, to each according to his need' is rigorously applied. Biological engineering fits different categories of workers – Alphas, Betas, Gammas, etc. – to their stations in life and universal happiness is preserved by psychotropic drugs. As a stranger into this world comes the Savage, raised in a reservation of American Indian primitives. He takes up the threads of arguments introduced by the disaffected intellectuals Bernard Marx and Helmholtz Watson, debating the merits of freedom and passion with World Controller Mustapha Mond. In the end, though, the Savage yields to the temptations of the carefree world, and kills himself in disgust.

*Brave New World* is frequently cited as a horrific work, though it is really a black comedy. It provides a scathing criticism of the values implicit in the myth of social salvation through technological expertise. Modern developments in biological engineering and psychochemistry have preserved, and perhaps increased, its relevance as an exercise in alarmism.

**Brazil, Angela** 1868–1947 Children's author. Born in Lancashire, the daughter of a cotton manufacturer, Angela Brazil was educated at Manchester High School and then at art college.

After her father's early death she became a companion to her mother, with whom she travelled extensively in Europe. She began writing for children at the age of 36, scoring her first success two years later with *The Fortunes of Philippa* (1906), a story about a 10-year-old girl attending boarding-school for the first time. In the more than 50 school novels which followed Angela Brazil created an idealized world, which emphasized the hearty games-playing side of life as well as the strong emotions that often spring up between pupils of the same sex. Her books also contained snippets of general knowledge, and while a few headmistresses banned them for their use of schoolgirl slang, most others accepted them as a wholesome influence. Her last story, *The School on the Loch* (1946), was published a year before her death.

**Breeches Bible, The** See **Bible in English, The**.

**Brennan, Christopher John** 1870–1932 Australian poet. Born in Sydney of Irish parents, Brennan was educated at Sydney University and in Berlin after winning a travelling scholarship. From 1921 to 1925 he was Associate Professor in German and Comparative Literature at Sydney University. His work as a poet was much influenced by the German Romantics and the French symbolist, Mallarmé, with whom he corresponded. Brennan's erudite and crafted verse possesses considerable lyric qualities displayed in his best-known sequence called 'The Wanderer'. He published little in his lifetime; his first publication was *XVIII Poems, Being the First Collection of Verse and Prose* (1897) – of which only eight copies were issued by the author – and his most important collection was *Poems 1913* (1914).

**Brenton, Howard** 1942– English playwright, a leading spokesman for the political drama that flourished during and after the revolutionary year of 1968. Brenton began writing plays while he was a student at Cambridge University, but came to prominence with *Christie in Love* (1969) and *Revenge* (1969). *Magnificence* (1973) is an exploration of urban terrorism and the structures of political power are also the subject of *The Churchill Play* (1974) and *The Weapons of Happiness* (1976), one of the first plays staged in the **National Theatre**'s new premises. The sweep of *Epsom Downs* (1977) is broader, though the focus on class divisions remains. Brenton writes under the influence of Brecht, a fact which is implicitly acknowledged by his translation for the National Theatre of the German playwright's *Galileo* (1980). For *The Romans in Britain* (1980), Brenton provided an elaborate analogy between the Roman invasion and the British 'occupation' of Northern Ireland. The sexual explicitness of one scene gave rise to protest which led to the private prosecution of its director, Michael Bogdanov. After much public controversy, the case was eventually dropped. *The Genius* (1983), though unsuccessful when first staged at the **Royal Court Theatre**, is a provocative confrontation of the political expediency that threatens the tentative balance of nuclear deterrence.

**Breton, Nicholas** ?1555–1626 Poet. Breton's mother was married first to a wealthy tradesman and then to the poet **George Gascoigne**, who influenced Breton's early work. He possibly went to Oxford and then settled in London. His early poetry of the 1570s is laboured with poetic diction and excessive alliteration but improves by the 1590s so that **Francis Meres** in *Palladis Tamia* (1598) can rank him (undeservedly) with **Shakespeare**, **Spenser** and **Drayton** as a lyricist. Some of his best poems appeared in *England's Helicon* (1600). Breton's earliest work is *A Small Handful of Fragrant Flowers* (1575), his latest *Strange News out of Divers Countries* (1622). Between, he produced over 60 works of pastoral and religious poetry, pamphlets, satires, dialogues and letters. His prose works have a moral and pious tone, and the poverty of poets is a constant theme in his poetry.

**Breton lay** The precise form of the original Breton lay is not known; it was apparently a narrative accompanied by music, but in what form is uncertain. The name has become attached to those poems which claim to be adapted from these earlier lyric lays or are Breton in origin. They are exemplified by the collection of **Marie de France**'s *Lais*, written in the late 12th century, simple, relatively short narrative poems, usually treating of love and often involving some elements of magic. Most of the extant English lays were written during the 14th century, and are in couplets or **tail-rhyme stanzas**. They are *Sir Launfal* and *Lai le Freine* (both translated from Marie's *Lais*), *Sir Orfeo*, *Emare*, *Sir Degare*, *Sir Gowther* and *The Earl of Toulous*. **Chaucer**'s *Franklin's Tale* (see *The Canterbury Tales*), while claiming to be a Breton lay, has an Italian source and an uncharacteristically complex narrative structure.

**Brewer's Dictionary of Phrase and Fable** Described as a 'Treasury of Literary bric-à-brac' by its compiler, the educational writer Ebenezer Cobham Brewer (1810–97), the *Dictionary* was published in 1870 and revised by Brewer in 1881 and 1895. It forms a unique compendium of folklore, slang, etymology, mythology and 'words with a tale to tell', as Brewer put it. Since a major revision in 1952, the much-expanded modern editions (notably Ifor H. Evans's Centenary Edition of 1970) have added new curiosities from Australia and America, while some of Brewer's original entries have been omitted.

As a glossary of names from fiction and myth, the *Dictionary* drew heavily on William A. Wheeler's *Noted Names of Fiction* (1866), and has since been superseded by more thorough guides; but its miscellany of adages, superstitions and catchphrases is unrivalled – and delightfully odd. Few other reference books can provide us with a list of German archbishops supposedly devoured by mice (under 'Hatto'), or remind us of the unlucky days of the week for cutting our fingernails (under 'Nail-paring').

**Bridal of Triermain, The** A poem by **Sir Walter Scott**, published in 1813. Framed by the bland courtship of Lucy by Arthur (the poor man and the lady), the central narrative recounts Sir Roland de Vaux of Triermain's quest for Gyneth, daughter of King Arthur and the enchantress Guendolen, who lies sleeping in the Valley of St John as the result of a spell by Merlin.

**Bride of Abydos, The**: *A 'turkish Tale'* Poem by **Byron**, published in 1813. Selim, who is introduced as the son, by one of his female slaves, of the Pasha Giaffir, is in love with his supposed half-sister, the beautiful Zuleika, whom Giaffir has promised in marriage to his fellow tyrant, the elderly Bey of Carasman. The young man is held in contempt by Giaffir, who considers him unmanly enough to be given a key to the harem. Zuleika vows never to part from Selim. He darkly informs her that he is not what he appears and arranges to meet her at night in his secret grotto, where he shows himself in sumptuous pirate costume, and reveals that he is not her brother, but her cousin, the son of the brother whom her father poisoned. He pleads with her to run away with him and share his life of action on the high seas, but Giaffir arrives with his men, and Selim is killed. Zuleika dies of a broken heart, and the Pasha is left with his impotent grief.

**Bride of Lammermoor, The** A novel by **Sir Walter Scott**, published in 1818 in the third series of *Tales of My Landlord*. It tells the story of the Master of Ravenswood's unhappy and eventually tragic love for Lucy Ashton, daughter of a family with whom he has an inherited feud. Lady Ashton, Lucy's mother, opposes the romance and tricks her daughter into marriage with the Laird of Bucklaw by convincing her that Ravenswood has abandoned her. He returns after the wedding to demand vengeance; she becomes insane and murders her husband.

Donizetti used the story as the basis for his opera, *Lucia di Lammermoor* (1835).

***Brideshead Revisited*** A novel by **Evelyn Waugh**, published in 1945.

Sub-titled 'The Sacred and Profane Memories of Captain Charles Ryder', the novel marked a departure from Waugh's earlier satirical works. The hero, Ryder, billeted at Brideshead during the war, recalls his past experiences there as a guest of the Marchmains, a great Roman Catholic family. His acquaintance with them begins at Oxford, where he is dazzled by the good looks and whimsicality of Sebastian Flyte, the younger son of the Marquis of Marchmain. Lord Marchmain has deserted the family to live in Venice with his mistress. Sebastian holds himself aloof from his mother – a fervent Catholic – and sisters Julia and Cordelia, and sinks into alcoholism as the story progresses. He flees to North Africa and, after Lady Marchmain's death, becomes a menial in an African monastery.

Charles Ryder has meanwhile continued to visit Brideshead, where his feelings are centred upon Julia. She, however, marries a non-Catholic, a vulgar politician who fails to qualify as a Catholic convert. With the death of his wife, Lord Marchmain returns to Brideshead and, on his deathbed, is restored to the faith. Julia, who might have married Ryder after her divorce, witnesses her father's reconciliation and she too returns to the faith. Ryder's doubts about his own faith are resolved by her renunciation of him and his agnosticism withers.

The author's preface to the revised edition of 1959 states that the novel is 'an attempt to trace the workings of the divine purpose in a pagan world'. But he also confessed that it was 'infused with a kind of gluttony, for food and wine, for the splendours of the recent past, and for rhetorical and ornamental language' – qualities which have given rise to sharp disagreement about the novel's worth.

***Bridge, The*** A long poem by **Hart Crane**, published in 1930. Begun in 1923, the poem was Crane's attempt to present an affirmative, epic vision of America; New York City's Brooklyn Bridge is its central image. In his prefatory 'Proem' Crane describes the bridge as both 'harp and altar' which will 'lend a myth to God', and he returns to this affirmative vision in 'Atlantis', the final part of the sequence. In the intervening seven sections, however, he explores the negative as well as the positive aspects of the American experience, which are symbolized by literary and historical figures, geographical features and place names, and technological inventions. In the section entitled 'Powhatan's Daughter', for example, the Indian princess Pocahontas becomes a figure representing the beauty of the American landscape; in a subsection entitled 'The River' the Mississippi River is transformed into a natural force fusing history with eternal time; and in 'The Tunnel' the New York City subway becomes a hellish underworld haunted by the ghost of **Edgar Allan Poe**.

**Bridges, Robert (Seymour)** 1844–1930 Poet and critic. Born in Walmer, Kent, he was educated at Eton and Corpus Christi College, Oxford, where he met **Gerard Manley Hopkins**. He practised medicine until 1881. His first volume of *Poems* appeared in 1873, followed by a sonnet sequence, *The Growth of Love* (1876), further collections of short poems and several long poems including *Prometheus the Firegiver* (1883), *Eros and Psyche* (1885) and *Demeter* (1905). During the next decade he wrote eight plays, and his influential criticism included studies of **Milton**'s prosody (1893) and **Keats** (1895). He was interested in the musical setting of poetry, and between 1895 and 1908 wrote four poems set by Parry. He edited the Yattendon Hymnal and wrote *A Practical Discourse on Hymn Singing* (1901).

A one-volume edition of his *Collected Poems* (1912) was very successful, and made his work available to a wider audience. In 1913 he was appointed Poet Laureate, and appropriately produced *The Spirit of Man* (1916), an anthology of prose and verse intended to console and encourage the nation. It included six poems by Gerard Manley Hopkins, whose original and unorthodox work Bridges finally published in 1918. After the war, while living at Boar's Hill, near Oxford, where his neighbours included **Robert Graves**, **John Masefield** and **Robert Nichols**, he published *October and Other Poems* (1920). His experiments in prosody led to the 'loose alexandrines' of *The Testament of Beauty* (1929), a poem in four books on spiritual and artistic wisdom. It was very popular, going through 14 impressions in the first year of publication.

Bridges's poetry is distinguished by its subtle metrics, expert craftsmanship and rationally intelligent subject matter. Much-anthologized poems are 'London Snow', 'Awake my Heart' and 'The Storm is Over'.

**Bridges, Roy[al]** 1885–1952 Australian novelist. Born and educated in Tasmania, Bridges worked as a journalist in Melbourne and Sydney. His first novel, *The Barb of an Arrow* (1909), dealt with the convict days of Tasmania and in many of his novels he returned to themes of the early settlement. He published more than 30 novels, including *By His Excellency's Command* (1909), *Mr Barrington* (1911), *Rat's Castle* (1924) and *The League of the Lord* (1950).

**Bridie, James** The pseudonym of the Scottish playwright Osborne Henry Mavor (1888–1951), who combined an active career as a doctor with his equally active career in the Scottish theatre.

Bridie wrote over 50 plays, many of them first performed in Glasgow despite the fact that he was already well established in London's West End. This regionalism has contributed to the neglect of a writer whose humour has more often a Shavian sharpness than is allowed by critics who compare him to his compatriot **J. M. Barrie**.

Bridie's first major success was *The Anatomist* (1930), a witty scrutiny of medical ethics in the light of Dr Knox and the body-snatchers Burke and Hare. *A Sleeping Clergyman* (1933) also directs its iconoclasm against the medical profession. In *Tobias and the Angel* (1930) and *Jonah and the Whale* (1932), Bridie's target is the humourless fundamentalism that makes of the Bible a book for threatening sinners, and he calls on the Devil to do some of his work for him in *Mr Bolfry* (1943). There are many other effective plays, including *Colonel Wotherspoon* (1934), *Susannah and the Elders* (1937), *Daphne Laureola* (1949) and *Mr Gillie* (1950). Bridie's genial humour is an easily penetrable disguise for his irony.

**Briggs, Raymond (Redvers)** 1934– Children's author and illustrator. Born in London, the son of a milkman, Briggs studied at art college before becoming a successful illustrator, particularly of nursery rhymes. He was first noticed as a writer in *Jim and the Beanstalk* (1970), which introduces one of his many proletarian heroes in the shape of a genial cockney giant. There followed *Father Christmas* (1973), detailing in comic strip a day in the life of an equally working-class Santa Claus who, despite grumbling, has a good heart and is devoted to his pets. He reappeared in *Father Christmas Goes on Holiday* (1975) but was eclipsed by *Fungus the Bogeyman* (1977), which brought Briggs fame amongst adults as well as children, breaking several taboos of **children's literature**. *The Snowman* (1979) was another popular creation; but later books, notably *When the Wind Blows* (1982), a bitter satire on government advice about how to survive a nuclear war, and *The Tin Pot Foreign General and the Old Iron Woman* (1984), an attack on the politics behind the Falklands War, make no pretence of being written for children.

**Brighouse, Harold** 1882–1958 Playwright. Born near and educated in Manchester, Brighouse was working in the cotton trade when Manchester's Gaiety Theatre opened in 1908, providing him with the impetus to write. Of the 70 or so plays he produced between 1909 and 1952, the majority are one-act comedies. The best known of his full-length works is ***Hobson's Choice*** (1915). Its durable popularity has eclipsed the almost equally accomplished *Lonesome-Like*

(1911), *The Odd Man Out* (1912) and *Zack* (1916).

**Brighton Rock** A novel by **Graham Greene**, published in 1938.

The story is set in the criminal underworld of Brighton. Pinkie ('The Boy'), a 17-year-old gang leader hell-bent on establishing himself, plans to murder Fred Hale, a journalist who indirectly caused the death of the gang's former leader. During the attack Hale dies of heart failure, and Pinkie later realizes that he has left a clue in a café which could establish his guilt. He visits the café and, to allay suspicion, dates the innocent young waitress Rose. Later he reluctantly agrees to marry her, thus preventing her from appearing as a future witness against him.

A brief acquaintance of Hale's, the middle-aged Ida Arnold, determines to establish the truth about his death. She attempts (unsuccessfully) to persuade Rose to abandon Pinkie, but he panics and arranges a fake suicide pact with the girl as a means of eliminating her. In the event Rose's conscience will not permit her to go through with the suicide, and Ida Arnold arrives with a policeman to arrest the youth. Pinkie attempts a desperate escape bid by throwing a bottle of vitriol. This is smashed before he does so and the acid blinds Pinkie instead. He falls to his death over the edge of a cliff.

Though Greene originally called the novel 'an entertainment', it is profoundly influenced by his Roman Catholicism. Pinkie's corruption is rendered more complex by the fact that he is a nominal Catholic, and deeply superstitious. His manipulation of the innocent Rose, a practising Catholic, and his detestation of Ida Arnold, a fun-loving hedonist, create an ambiguous moral drama which foreshadows Greene's later novels.

**Brink, André** 1935– South African novelist, born in Vrede. An Afrikaans writer, he has also written in English, especially after his seventh Afrikaans novel, *Kennis van die aand* (1973), became the first Afrikaans book banned in South Africa. He translated it as *Looking on Darkness* (1974) and has since published his novels in both languages: *'n Oomblik in die wind* as *Rumours of Rain* (both 1978), *'n Droë wit seisoen* as *A Dry White Season* (both 1979), *Houd-den-bek* as *A Chain of Voices* (both 1982) and *Die muur van die pes* as *The Wall of the Plague* (both 1984). *The Ambassador* (Johannesburg, 1964; London, 1985; as *File on a Diplomat*, London, 1967) translates his fourth Afrikaans novel. Head of a university department, Brink has with prodigious energy also produced six volumes of short Afrikaans fiction, 12 Afrikaans plays, children's stories, travel books, academic criticism and some 50 translations into Afrikaans of English, French and Spanish books.

Despite his considerable novelistic skills devoted to anatomizing Afrikaner history and morality, his fiction is sometimes ungainly and occasionally, as in the 1984 novel, even gauche.

**Brinkelow, Henry** d. 1546 Satirist. Brinkelow left his order and joined the reform party. His satires include complaints against land enclosures and clerical abuses. Under the pseudonym of Roderigo Mors he wrote *The Lamentation of a Christian* (1542) and *The Complaint of Roderick Mors* (?1542), both first published abroad.

*Britannia* A work of history and topography by the antiquary **William Camden**; its scope is indicated by the sub-title, translated as 'A Chorographical Description of the Most Flourishing Kingdoms of England, Scotland, and Ireland, and the Islands Adjoining, out of the Depth of Antiquity'. It was first published in Latin in 1586 and went through six Latin editions in Camden's lifetime. **Philemon Holland**'s English translation, made under Camden's supervision, appeared in 1610.

Encouraged by **Sir Philip Sidney**, Camden began to gather the materials which were later included in *Britannia* as early as 1571. His holidays from schoolmastering left him free to make the expeditions on which he observed antiquities at first hand. Initially, he had no plans for publication, but he began systematically to compile *Britannia* in 1577 after meeting the geographer Abraham Ortelius. The result was the first practical and historical guide to the British Isles, arranged county by county. Camden treated not only topography and monuments (most famously Stonehenge), but also such subjects as coins and language. He made liberal use of genealogies, maps and illustrative plates. Subsequent copious additions by Camden himself and by succeeding scholars caused later editions to bear less and less resemblance to the first edition of 1586; but the fact that *Britannia* survived so long as the model for antiquarian studies is a tribute to its practicality and usefulness.

**Brittain, Vera (Mary)** 1893–1970 Author of autobiography, poetry and fiction. Vera Brittain was born at Newcastle under Lyme, Staffordshire, the daughter of a wealthy manufacturer. She was educated at Kingswood and Somerville College, Oxford. She married professor George Catlin in 1925.

During World War I she served as a VAD (Voluntary Aid Detachment) nurse, an experience which interrupted her studies at Oxford and which she recounted as part of her autobiographical *Testament of Youth* (1933). The book, which deals with her girlhood (during which she was strongly influenced by **Olive Schreiner**) and recounts her early struggles as a woman to achieve an education, was immediately acclaimed by contemporary writers and has become an important feminist text.

Although she wrote numerous volumes of poetry and fiction, Brittain is more widely known for two later works: *Testament of Friendship* (1940), a memorial to **Winifred Holtby** with whom she developed a close friendship at Oxford; and *Testament of Experience* (1957), a companion to the early autobiography, which covers the years 1925–50.

**broadside** A song or poem printed on one side of a large single sheet of paper, offered for sale on the streets by ballad sellers and hawkers from the Renaissance onwards. Generally doggerel verse or **ballads** to popular airs, broadsides enjoyed a great circulation in particular during the second part of the 17th century when the production of street literature was at a peak.

*Broken Heart, The* A tragedy by **John Ford**. The play was first produced about 1629 and published in 1633.

The setting of the play is Laconia, where Penthea is married to a brutal and jealous nobleman, Bassanes. Penthea was in love with Orgilus; they intended to marry but Penthea's brother Ithocles had forced her to marry Bassanes. She cannot bring herself to return Orgilus' love, feeling herself prostituted in her marriage. Ithocles, meanwhile, has been successful in war; he returns from the conquest of Messene and is greatly favoured by the King, who gives him the Princess Calantha as a bride. Orgilus, whose life has been wrecked, watches Penthea die of self-starvation and is determined to have revenge on Ithocles. At a feast, Calantha hears of the death of Penthea and, soon after, news is brought of the death of her father, the King. A third blow is news of the murder of Ithocles and the apprehension of Orgilus. She continues at the feast, her feelings under control, and waits until the feast is over before ordering the execution of Orgilus. Then she dies of a broken heart.

**Brome, Richard** c. 1590–1652 Playwright. One of the many efficient professional dramatists who continued to provide the Caroline theatre with plays until the closing of the theatres in 1642, Brome is known only by his writing. According to *Biographia Dramatica* (1764) 'his extraction was mean, he having originally been no better than a menial servant to the celebrated **Ben Jonson**', and a Jonsonian influence is certainly detectable in much of his work, though the geniality is Brome's own. Of his surviving plays, the best are *The Northern Lass* (1629), *The City Wit* (c. 1630), *The Antipodes* (1638) and *A Jovial Crew* (1641). That

Brome's talent was recognized in his own time is clear from the earliest extant playwright's contract, drawn up in his name on 20 July 1635.

**Bromfield, Louis** 1896–1956 American novelist and short-story writer. Born in Mansfield, Ohio, Bromfield began studying journalism at Columbia University in 1916 but left shortly thereafter to serve in World War I. Between 1922 and 1925 he worked as foreign editor of *Musical America*. He subsequently wrote columns for *The New Yorker* and *The Bookman* (for which he was also a music and drama critic). His first novel, *The Green Bay Tree*, was published in 1924, and was followed by numerous others, including *Possession* (1925), *Early Autumn* (1926), for which he was awarded the Pulitzer Prize, *The Farm* (1933), *The Rains Came* (1937), *Night in Bombay* (1940), *Wild is the River* (1941), *Mrs Parkinson* (1943) and *Pleasant Valley* (1945). He also published collections of short stories, including *Awake and Rehearse* (1929), *It Takes All Kinds* (1939) and *The World We Live In* (1944); and such plays as *The House of Women* (1927) and *De Luxe* (1935). Bromfield's fiction often reflects a profound distrust of industrialism and materialism, which he saw as dehumanizing factors in 20th-century American life.

**Brontë, Charlotte** 1816–55; **Brontë, Emily** (Jane) 1818–48; **Brontë, Anne** 1820–49 Novelists and poets. They were daughters of the Reverend Patrick Brontë, a Church of England clergyman born in Northern Ireland, and of Maria Branwell, a Cornishwoman. The couple's other children were Maria (1813–25), Elizabeth (1815–25) and Patrick Branwell (1817–48). Maria and Elizabeth were born in Hartshead, near Dewsbury in Yorkshire, where Mr Brontë was curate; the rest were born at Mr Brontë's next curacy in Thornton, near Bradford. In 1820, the year before his wife's death, Mr Brontë took up the living of Haworth, a

Haworth parsonage. The frontispiece illustration for The World's Classics edition of Elizabeth Gaskell's *The Life of Charlotte Brontë*, 1929. By W. J. Linton.

bleak weaving village a few miles north-west of Thornton. The Haworth parsonage and its surrounding moorland became, as it always remained, the centre of his children's lives.

All the girls save Anne attended the Clergy Daughter's School run by the Reverend William Carus Wilson at Cowan Bridge, near Kirkby Lonsdale. Its harsh regime contributed to the early deaths of Maria and Elizabeth, which left Charlotte the oldest child in the motherless family. In 1831–2 she was sent to Miss Wooler's school at Roe Head, near Dewsbury, where she met her lifelong friends Mary Taylor and Ellen Nussey. During Charlotte's subsequent time as governess there (1835–8), Emily also went along as a pupil but was quickly replaced by Anne.

The girls' real education, however, was at the Haworth parsonage, where they had the run of their father's books and were thus nurtured on the Bible, Homer, Virgil, **Shakespeare**, **Milton**, **Byron**, **Scott** and many others. They enthusiastically read articles on current affairs, lengthy reviews and intellectual disputes in *Blackwood's Edinburgh Magazine*, *Fraser's Magazine* and *The Edinburgh Review*. They also ranged freely in Aesop and in the colourfully bizarre world of *The Arabian Nights' Entertainments*; and they pored over lavishly illustrated keepsakes and annuals like *The Gem*, *The Amulet* and *Friendship's Offering* among whose contributors were such artists as the epic painter John Martin, master of the boundless romantic canvas. Over this household presided the forbidding figure of their aunt, Elizabeth Branwell, who had been invited to live with them soon after the death of her sister, and the family servant, Tabitha Aykroyd, who arrived in 1825 and remained until her death 30 years later. Elizabeth Branwell's relentless Calvinistic world – with its threats of eternal punishment, of fiery furnaces and of a vengeful God – had a powerful influence on the young children, while Tabitha's knowledge of folk-tales and superstitions provided another sort of nourishment for their imaginations.

In June 1826 Mr Brontë came back from a visit to Leeds with a box of 12 wooden soldiers he had promised Branwell, and around them his children wove tales and legends associated with remote Africa (where they situated their imaginary Glass Town). Later came other narratives about the kingdom of Angria, whose stories Charlotte and Branwell recorded in minute notebooks two inches by one in size. Yet another 'saga' – the Gondal saga – was created by Emily and Anne. Replete with melodrama and violence, the wondrous and the fantastic, this juvenilia still showed a strong moral strain suggestive of parsonage life and of their aunt's stern Methodism. Much, too, from these youthful writings informs the later fiction and poetry of the Brontë sisters.

Charlotte Brontë. Portrait by George Richmond, 1850. National Portrait Gallery, London.

The strength of the children's attachment to each other and to the Haworth parsonage is shown by the desultory and usually unhappy nature of their forays into the world beyond. Branwell went to London to study painting at the Royal Academy in 1835 but stayed only a few days; thereafter he failed as a portrait painter in Bradford and as a clerk on the local railway. His sisters, meanwhile, worked as governesses. Anne's longest stint (1840–5) was with the Robinson family at Thorp Green Hall, near York, where she was lonely and unhappy in the situation; she left when Branwell, for whom she had secured a tutorial post in the same household, became involved with its mistress. He was dismissed a month later. But the most important sojourn away from home for any of the family was Charlotte's time in Brussels at the pensionnat run by M. Constantin Heger and his wife. Helped by money from her aunt, Charlotte went there with Emily in February 1842 and remained until Elizabeth Branwell's illness demanded her return nine months later. A slightly longer stay to improve her French and German and to develop her teaching of English followed in 1843, though she was back home by January 1844. For much of her stay she was anxious, melancholy and hostile to the atmosphere around her. Her position at the pensionnat was not improved by her growing attachment for M. Heger, who broke off the correspondence she attempted after her return to England.

Charlotte had shown her literary ambition while still at Roe Head by sending her poems to **Southey**, who responded with sage advice. In 1845 her discovery of poems written by Emily further encouraged her to propose a joint volume by all three sisters. In the face of Emily's reluctance, *Poems by Currer, Ellis and Acton Bell* appeared in 1846 but passed unnoticed by the reading public. It was Charlotte who again urged publication of the novels which each of them had by then finished. Her own work, **The Professor**, which drew heavily on her experiences in Brussels, was rejected and did not appear until its posthumous publication in 1857. But the encouragement she received from the publishing house of Smith, Elder and Co. emboldened her to complete and submit **Jane Eyre**. It appeared in October 1847, two months before Emily Brontë's **Wuthering Heights** and Anne Brontë's lesser known **Agnes Grey**, which (unsurprisingly) concerned a governess unhappy in a family she disliked. Anne's second novel, **The Tenant of Wildfell Hall**, appeared in July 1848.

These works, particularly *Jane Eyre*, attracted the public interest that the volume of poems had so signally failed to provoke. It was made the more piquant by the sisters' continued use of their apparently male pseudonyms, Currer, Ellis and Acton Bell, though in July 1848 Charlotte and Anne visited **George Smith** to reveal their identity and to help quell rumours that a single author lay behind the pseudonyms. By this time, however, the family was involved in private sorrow. Branwell's alcoholism, which so clearly cast its shadow over *The Tenant of Wildfell Hall*, contributed to his early death in September 1848. He was followed by Emily, who died of tuberculosis in December, stubbornly resisting the encroachments of the illness until virtually her last hours, and by Anne, who died calmly and resignedly at Scarborough in July 1849.

Charlotte survived to cope with a father now sorely tried and going blind. She published **Shirley** in October 1849 and, in 1853, **Villette**, a novel which, like *The Professor*, drew upon her life in Brussels. Despite her nervous self-consciousness she began to move in literary society, meeting **Thackeray** (to whom she had dedicated *Jane Eyre*) and **G. H. Lewes**, and becoming friendly with **Harriet Martineau** and, particularly, **Elizabeth Gaskell**, her future biographer. In June 1854 she overcame her father's entrenched opposition and married his curate, the Reverend Arthur Bell Nicholls, at Haworth church; the couple lived together with Mr Brontë at the parsonage. She died the following March, apparently from the complications of a chill caught during early pregnancy. Her father survived until 1861 and her husband until 1906.

**Brook Farm** A co-operative reform community, founded in 1841 by **George Ripley** and other **Transcendentalists** on a farm in West Roxbury, Massachusetts, about eight miles from Boston, and set up as a joint-stock company. The Brook Farmers' aim was to simplify and purify economic relations by retreating from an increasingly commercial society and working the farm together to achieve a simplified, near-subsistence existence which would leave time for intellectual and spiritual self-improvement. Many figures prominent in the Transcendentalist movement either lived on the farm or visited it from time to time. These included **Margaret Fuller**, **Ralph Waldo Emerson**, **William Ellery Channing**, **Theodore Parker**, **Orestes Brownson** and **Nathaniel Hawthorne**, who based his novel, *The Blithedale Romance*, on his Brook Farm experience. The Brook Farmers produced two periodical publications: *The Phalanx* (1843–5) and *The Harbinger* (1845–9). The community disbanded in 1847.

**Brooke, Charlotte** 1740–93 Irish translator and poet. The youngest daughter of **Henry Brooke**, and the only one of his 22 children to survive him, she was educated at home by her father. From him she caught an enthusiasm for Irish antiquities further stimulated by the controversies surrounding **James Macpherson**'s alleged *Poems of Ossian* (1765), the Irish antecedents of which were demonstrated by her godfather Sylvester O'Halloran. Her anonymous translation of a poem attributed to the famous Irish bard O'Carolan was included in Joseph Walker's *Historical Memoirs of the Irish Bards* (1786). With her friend **Thomas Percy**'s *Reliques of Ancient English Poetry* (1765) as model she published *Reliques of Ancient Irish Poetry* (1789). This contains not merely some of the earliest verse translations of traditional Irish poems about the Red Branch Knights and the Fenians but also an original composition, *Mäon, an Irish Tale*, coloured by this material. While she has been censured for slack paraphrase and conventionally elegant English metres, her polished translations were often reprinted and did much to stimulate an emerging Irish literature in English. Her other, less noted, works include an unacted tragedy, *Belisarius*, and dialogues for children, *A School for Christians* (1791), as well as an edition of her father's works (1792).

**Brooke, Henry** 1703–83 Irish poet, dramatist and novelist. Brooke came from County Cavan in Ireland and was educated at Trinity College, Dublin. He spent 10 years in London, and began to write when he returned to Dublin. *Design and Beauty: An Epistle* (1734) was followed by a more ambitious poem in six parts, *Universal Beauty* (1734–6), on the perfection of design in the universe. His translation of Tasso's *Gerusalemme Liberata*, Books I and II, followed in 1738 and a tragedy, *Gustavus Vasa*, appeared in 1739. The play was banned, however, because Sir Robert Walpole fancied a likeness to himself in the villain of the piece. It was produced in Dublin as *The Patriot* in 1744. Brooke wrote two novels: *Juliet Grenville* (1774), the second, was soon forgotten but *The Fool of Quality* (1766–72) attracted considerable attention.

**Brooke, Rupert (Chawner)** 1887–1915 Poet. Born in Rugby, he was educated at Rugby School (where his father was a master) and at King's College, Cambridge. He then travelled in Germany and published *Poems* (1911) before taking up a fellowship at King's in 1912. While there he wrote *Lithuania*, a one-act play published posthumously in 1935, and began work on *John Webster and the Elizabethan Drama* (1916). Following a nervous breakdown, he travelled in the United States, Canada and the Pacific during 1913, and joined the RNVR after the outbreak of World War I. His five 'war sonnets', published in *New Numbers* in 1915, included his famous 'The Soldier' ('If I should die, think only this of me'), which drew from his Cambridge contemporary **Charles Hamilton Sorley** the comment that 'he has clothed his attitude in fine words; but he has taken the sentimental attitude'. He died of blood-poisoning *en route* to the Dardanelles in April 1915, and was buried at Scyros.

Brooke's good looks and early death ensured his transformation into a symbol of romantic patriotism – a process encouraged by the posthumous appearance of *1914 and Other Poems* (1915), *Letters from America* (1916), with a preface by **Henry James**, and *Collected Poems* (1918) edited with a memoir by his friend **Edward Marsh**, with whom Brooke had been associated in the anthologies of *Georgian Poetry*. His verse is characteristically Georgian, colloquial and nostalgic; well-known anthology poems include 'The Old Vicarage, Grantchester' (1912), 'Clouds' (1913) and 'The Dead' (1914). A *Complete Poems* edited by Geoffrey Keynes appeared in 1946.

**Brooke-Rose, Christine** 1926– Novelist and critic. Born in Geneva, Switzerland, she was educated at Somerville College, Oxford, and University College, London. In 1956–68 she worked as a freelance journalist in London and since 1975 she has been Professor of American literature at the University of Paris VIII, Vincennes. The scope of her teaching goes beyond American literature to include comparative literature.

Brooke-Rose is a European intellectual, influenced by the French *avant-garde* of the 1950s. Although she rejects the label of 'experimental novelist', the satire of her early work, beginning with *The Languages of Love* (1957), has given way to a concern with the nature of words and the meanings invested in them. *Such* (1966), *Between* (1968), and *Thru* (1975) have been followed, after a nine-year gap, by *Amalgamemnon* (1984). She has also translated Alain Robbe-Grillet's *In the Labyrinth* (1968) and Juan Goytisolo's *Children of Chaos* (1958). Her works of criticism include *A Grammar of Metaphor* (1958), *A ZBC of Ezra Pound* (1971) and *A Rhetoric of the Unreal: Studies in Narrative and Structure, Especially the Fantastic* (1981).

**Brookner, Anita** 1928– Novelist. A lecturer at London's Courtauld Institute of Art, and before that the first woman to be Slade Professor at Cambridge, she began writing fiction only in 1980, but since then has published seven novels in as many years. Her plangent tales of single, solitary women and their failure to secure lasting close relationships, or even reliable friends, have been compared to the novels of **Barbara Pym** and **Elizabeth Taylor**. The first four, *A Start in Life* (1981), *Providence* (1982), *Look at Me* (1983) and *Hotel du Lac* (1984) (which won the Booker Prize), are all unashamedly literary in their allusions, and counterpoint wry, delicate comedy with a remorselessly pessimistic insistence on the disadvantages of opting for timid moral rectitude over worldly self-advancement. Miss Brookner's fifth novel, *Family and Friends* (1985), differs in attempting a concentrated family saga, and draws much on her own East European ancestry, while *A Misalliance* (1986) and *A Friend from England* (1987) return to the single hapless heroine.

**Brooks, Cleanth** 1906– American critic. A Kentuckian by birth, Brooks was educated at Vanderbilt and Tulane Universities before going to Oxford as a Rhodes Scholar in 1929. He taught for 15 years at the Louisiana State University, Baton Rouge, where he edited (with **Robert Penn Warren**) the influential *Southern Review*. From 1947 he taught at Yale University, as Gray Professor of Rhetoric from 1960 to 1975.

A leader of the Southern agrarian group of **New Critics**, Brooks elaborated the critical principles of **T. S. Eliot** in his *Modern Poetry and the Tradition* (1939), examining the poetry of **Yeats** and Eliot as a revival of Metaphysical 'wit'. His other important book, *The Well-Wrought Urn* (1947), comprises a series of close readings of poems from **Donne** to Yeats, concentrating on their ironies and ambiguities in the manner of **William Empson**. With Robert Penn Warren, Brooks wrote *Understanding Poetry* (1938) and *Modern Rhetoric* (1949) – two college textbooks which helped to entrench the New Criticism as an academic orthodoxy. His long (and too modestly titled) *Literary Criticism: A Short History* (with W. K. Wimsatt, 1957) still commands wide respect. Brooks's other works include *The Hidden God* (1963), *A Shaping Joy* (1971) and *The Language of the American South* (1985).

**Brooks, Gwendolyn** 1917– Black American poet, born in Topeka, Kansas, and raised and educated in Chicago. Her first volume of verse, *A Street in Bronzeville*, was published in 1945, and she won the Pulitzer Prize for *Annie Allen* (1949). *Selected Poems* appeared in 1963. She succeeded **Carl Sandburg** as Poet Laureate of Illinois, and in 1968 published the celebratory *For Illinois 1968: A Sesquicentennial Poem*. The first volume of her autobiography, *Report From Part One*, was published in 1972, followed by *The Tiger Who Wore White Gloves, or, What You Are You Are* in 1974.

**Brophy, Brigid (Antonia)** 1929– Novelist and critic. She was born in London and educated at St Paul's Girls' School and St Hugh's College, Oxford, where she was a Jubilee Scholar. She married Sir Michael Levey in 1954. Her nine novels include *Hackenfeller's Ape* (1954), *Flesh* (1963), *The Snowball* (1964), *In Transit* (1970) and *Palace Without Chairs* (1978). Among her non-fiction titles are *Mozart the Dramatist: A New View of Mozart, His Operas, and His Age* (1964), *Black and White: A Portrait of Aubrey Beardsley* (1969) and *Prancing Novelist: A Defence of Fiction in the Form of a Critical Biography in Praise of Ronald Firbank* (1973). She has been Vice-President of the Anti-Vivisection Society of Great Britain and was active in the successful Public Lending Right campaign. Brophy sees all her works as 'baroque' – a device which allows her to present contrastive forces in her novels and create an unexpected view. She has an essentially optimistic outlook, believing in a 'life force' which exists in many complex forms and seeing art as an extension of that force. A lively writer, she embraces many aspects of art with the disciplined mind of a classics scholar.

**Brougham, Henry Peter, Baron Brougham and Vaux** 1778–1868 Lawyer, politician and journalist. Born in Edinburgh and educated at Edinburgh High School and Edinburgh University, he became an advocate in 1800. In 1802 he became, with **Francis Jeffrey**, a founder of *The Edinburgh Review*, contributing three of the 29 articles in the first issue. He published *The Colonial Policy of European Nations* in 1803 and in the same year became a member of Lincoln's Inn. In 1805 he settled in London but continued to contribute regularly to *The Edinburgh Review* including the notorious review of **Byron**'s *Hours of Idleness* which provoked Byron's response in *English Bards and Scotch Reviewers*. Brougham also became active in the movement to abolish slavery. He was called to the English Bar in 1808 and elected MP for Camelford in 1810. In 1810 he successfully defended **Leigh Hunt** in a libel action following the publication of an article on military flogging in *The Examiner*, but in 1812 a second court defence of Hunt failed when the essayist was indicted for a libel on the Prince Regent. Brougham became MP for Winchelsea in 1815 and a prominent member of the Whig opposition. In 1820 he defended Queen Caroline before the House of Lords in the matter of the Queen's degradation and divorce and in the following year he unsuccessfully argued her right to coronation before the Privy Council. Brougham was appointed Lord Chancellor by Lord Grey and was created Baron Brougham and Vaux. A leading advocate of the founding of the University of London and of Parliamentary Reform (his speech on the second reading of the Reform Bill in October 1831 was much praised and was often regarded as a classic of English Parliamentary oratory), he gradually withdrew from politics in the 1850s but was elected Chancellor of the University of Edinburgh in 1859. His published works include: *Practical Observations on the Education of the People* (1825), *Historical Sketches of Statesmen* (1839), *Political Philosophy and other Essays* (1832), *Albert Lunel, or, the Chateau of Languedoc* (novel, 1844), *Lives of Men of Letters and Science* (1845, second series 1846) and *Contributions to the Edinburgh Review* (1856). His memoirs, *Life and Times of Henry, Lord Brougham*, appeared posthumously in 1871.

**Brougham, John** 1810–80 American dramatist, born and educated in Dublin. He wrote or adapted at least 125 plays. His greatest popularity, both as an actor and as a dramatist, was in the years preceding the Civil War, and he is best known for his two-act musical burlesque of 1855, *Po-ca-hon-tas! or, Ye Gentle Savage*. Also notable are his *A Row at the Lyceum, or, Green Room Secrets* (1851), an innovative one-act skit in which a rehearsal is interrupted by an objection from a plant in the audience; and *The Game of Love* (1855), a five-act social satire about marriage between upper and lower classes. His other burlesques include *Metamora, or, The Last of the Pollywoags* (1847), *Columbus* (1857) and *Much Ado About the Merchant of Venice* (1869). He also adapted several contemporary British and American novels for the stage: *Dombey and Son* (1848), *Jane Eyre* (1849), *Vanity Fair* (1849) and *Dred* (1856). His other successes include *Temptation* (1849), *The Irish Immigrant* (1857) and *The Mustard Ball, or, Love at the Academy* (1858).

**Broughton, Rhoda** 1840–1920 Novelist. The daughter of a parson, Rhoda Broughton was born in Wales and wrote copiously from an early age. Two novels, *Not Wisely But Too Well* and *Cometh Up As a Flower* (both published in 1867), were considered audacious in their time and offended Victorian propriety. She said of her own writing that she began as Zola and finished as **Charlotte Yonge**, itself a revealing comment on 19th-century shifts in sensibility. **Trollope** in his *Autobiography* praises the mildly rebellious authoress for her ability 'to make her personages stand upright on the ground. And', he continues, 'she has the gift of making them speak as men and women do speak.'

**Brown, Charles Brockden** 1771–1810 Often considered America's first professional author, Brown was born in Philadelphia into a family of prosperous Quakers. He studied law and during his brief practice in Philadelphia met Elihu Smith, one of the **Connecticut Wits**, with whom in 1790 he formed the Society for the Attainment of Useful Knowledge. Contemptuous of the legal profession, he moved to New York City in 1796 and began writing. His first publication, *Alcuin: A Dialogue* (1798), was a treatise on the rights of women which shows the influence of **William Godwin**. Further stimulated by Godwin's philosophy of rational individualism, and by the novels of **Mrs Radcliffe**, Brown wrote feverishly for the next two years and produced four novels, all of which translate the English Gothic romance into an American idiom: *Wieland* (1798); *Arthur Mervyn* (1799–1800); *Ormond* (1799); and *Edgar Huntly* (1799).

Although widely read in America and England, these novels were not commercial successes. Brown invested in an import business, which collapsed in 1806, and simultaneously engaged himself in more lucrative literary ventures. From 1799 he served as editor of *The Monthly Magazine and American Review*, and at the turn of the century produced two more traditional romances which sold well but lacked the artistic innovation of his previous fiction: *Clara Howard* (1801, in England as *Philip Stanley*) and *Jane Talbot* (1801). *Memoirs of Carwin*, a sequel to *Wieland*, appeared serially (1803–5) in his newly founded and highly successful *The Literary Magazine and American Register* (1803–7), but remained unfinished at his death in 1810.

**Brown, E[dward] K[illoran]** 1905–51 Canadian critic. Born in Toronto, he was educated at the Universities of Toronto and Paris. He subsequently worked in the English departments of the Universities of Toronto and Manitoba, before moving to the United States, where he was chairman of the English department at Cornell and later worked at the University of Chicago. Brown was a wide-ranging critic, but is best remembered for his work on Canadian literature at a time before the discipline had become fashionable. From 1932 to 1942 he was editor of the *University of Toronto Quarterly*. His *On Canadian Poetry* (1943), in addition to helping to construct a canon of what was valuable in Canadian poetry and offering important revaluations of earlier poets' work, did much to establish parameters for Canadian criticism. He particularly stressed the problems that faced the writer in a materialistic society.

**Brown, George Mackay** 1921– Scottish poet and novelist. He was born in Stromness, on the Orkney mainland, where he still lives. He was educated at Stromness Academy, and, from 1951, at Newbattle Abbey, an adult education college near Edinburgh. **Edwin Muir**, the college's warden, encouraged Brown's early work, which includes *The Storm* (1954) and *Loaves and Fishes* (1959). Graduating from Edinburgh University in 1960, he did postgraduate research on **Gerard Manley Hopkins** and published more poetry, *The Year of the Whale* (1965), and his first collection of stories, *A Calendar of Love* (1967). His poems grow out of his life in the Orkney Islands, his sense of their landscapes, and their communities in fishing and farming: the cycle of poems published in 1971 has the title *Fishermen with Ploughs*. Images from work and the seasons, the layers of Orkney history and myth inscribed in literature, rock and the archaeology of the islands are allied to a troubled sense of the impact of the oil industry and the nuclear threat; these form the imaginative and moral location of his work. Much of his writing derives its focus and characteristic shapes from the *Orkneyinga Saga* (the 13th-century Icelandic tales of the Earls of Orkney and of Magnus, the Orkney saint), the poetry of Hopkins and Muir, and the symbolic structures of his own Roman Catholic faith. His novels include *Greenvoe* (1972), an evocation of an imaginary Orkney village; *Magnus* (1973), a lyrical account of the saint's martyrdom; and *Time in a Red Coat* (1984), a richly textured fable about war. Later collections of poetry are *Winterfold* (1976), *Voyages* (1983) and *Andrina* (1983).

**Brown, Dr John** 1810–82 Scottish essayist. Born in Lanarkshire, he attended Edinburgh High School and Edinburgh University and practised medicine in the city. His three-volume collection of essays, *Horae Subsecivae* ('Hours of Leisure', 1858–62), was particularly admired by contemporaries for two items, *Marjorie Fleming* and a story of a dog, *Rab and His Friends*.

**Brown, Rita Mae** 1944– American novelist and poet. Born in Hanover, Pennsylvania, she attended universities in Florida and New York as well as the New York School of Visual Arts. Her first novel, *Rubyfruit Jungle* (1973), estab-

lished her at the forefront of the feminist and gay-rights movements. Other novels include *In Her Day* (1976), *Six of One* (1978), *Southern Discomfort* (1982) and *Sudden Death* (1983). Her poetry has appeared in collections such as *The Hand That Cradles The Rock* (1971) and *Songs to a Handsome Woman* (1973). A collection of essays, *A Plain Brown Rapper*, was published in 1976.

**Brown, Sterling A[llen]** 1901–89 Black American poet and critic, born in Washington DC. He was educated at Williams College and at Harvard. His first volume of poetry, *Southern Road* (1932), with its direct style and use of folk material, shows the influence of **Carl Sandburg**. A leading characteristic of Brown's poetry is the appropriation of folk idioms, such as work-songs and ballads, which he then transforms into contemporary statements of social protest. Most of his work appeared in magazines, with few published volumes. *The Last Ride of Wild Bill, and Eleven Narrative Poems* appeared in 1975 and *Collected Poems* in 1980. An active and prolific critic of black literature in the 1930s, he produced two critical volumes, *The Negro in American Fiction* and *Negro Poetry and Drama*, both in 1937. He was also co-editor of the influential anthology of **Harlem Renaissance** writers, *The Negro Caravan* (1941).

**Brown, Thomas** 1663–1704 Translator and satirist. Born in Shropshire, Brown went to Christ Church, Oxford. Dr John Fell, the Dean, threatened to expel him for some misdemeanour and Brown adapted one of Martial's epigrams to make a famous jingle ('I do not love you, Dr Fell'). He was one of the team who wrote an English version of Paul Scarron's *Le Roman Comique* and, also with others, translated works by Petronius and Lucian. Brown's sketches of London life were published as *Amusements Serious and Comical* (1700). His collected works were published in four volumes (1707–11).

**Brown, William Hill** 1765–93 American novelist, poet and essayist, born in Boston, the great-great-grandson of **Increase Mather**. In 1789 he published his first book, *The Power of Sympathy*, which is generally considered to be the first American novel. He contributed prose and poetry to the *Massachusetts Magazine* and the *New England Palladium*, occasionally using the pseudonym Pollio. As The Yankee he wrote literary and political essays for Boston's *Columbian Sentinel*. He died during an epidemic, probably of malaria, at the age of 28. Several works were published posthumously: a tragedy entitled *West Point Preserved, or the Treason of Arnold* (1797); various poems and prose pieces published in the *Boston Magazine* and the *Emerald* (1805–7); and his second novel, *Ira and Isabella, or, The Natural Children* (1807), whose plot is similar to that of *The Power of Sympathy* except that it has a happy ending.

**Brown, William Wells** *c.* 1816–84 Black American writer, born into slavery in Kentucky, and raised in St Louis. After gaining his freedom he aided fugitive slaves in Ohio. His autobiographical *Narrative of William W. Brown, a Fugitive Slave* was published in 1847 by the Massachusetts Antislavery Society, and he soon became widely known, both in the USA and abroad, as a leading black advocate of Abolition.

Soon after the publication of his *Narrative* Brown turned to other forms of writing. A collection of poems, *The Anti-Slavery Harp*, appeared in 1848, and *Three Years in Europe, or, Places I Have Seen and People I Have Met* in 1852. *Clotel, or, The President's Daughter* was published in London in 1853. Long thought to have been the first novel published by a black American, this story of the mulatta daughter of **Thomas Jefferson**'s black slave was issued in the USA in 1864, without reference to the President, as *Clotel: A Tale of the Southern States*. Brown's other works are a play entitled *The Escape, or, A Leap For Freedom* (1858), and the essay *The Black Man: His Antecedents, His Genius, and His Achievements* (1863), which was later expanded into *The Rising Son* (1873).

**Browne, Hablot K[night]** 1815–80 Illustrator. Under the pen-name of Phiz he took over the illustrations for *Pickwick Papers* after the suicide of the artist Robert Seymour in 1836, and went on to provide the plates for many other novels by **Dickens**: *Nicholas Nickleby*, *Martin Chuzzlewit*, *Dombey and Son*, *David Copperfield*, *Bleak House*, *Little Dorrit* and *A Tale of Two Cities*. He also illustrated works by **William Harrison Ainsworth**, **Charles Lever** and **R. S. Surtees**.

**Browne, Sir Thomas** 1605–82 Scientific and religious writer. Born in London and educated at Winchester and Oxford, he studied medicine at Montpellier, Padua and Leyden, qualified as a doctor and practised first in Oxford, then in Norwich, where he settled in 1637. A fervent Royalist and anti-Puritan, Browne remained in Norwich through the Civil War, and eventually became a celebrated figure there, being knighted by Charles II during the royal visit of 1671.

Browne was the author of several prose tracts distinguished by a widely enquiring intelligence and liveliness of expression, the first of which, *Religio Medici* (an examination of his religious beliefs), was published in 1642 but was written several years earlier. This was followed by *Pseudodoxia Epidemica* (or *Vulgar Errors*) in 1646. *Hydriotaphia* (or *Urn Burial*), a reflection on burial ceremonies, and *The Garden of Cyrus*, a treatise on the application of the quincunx; both

appeared in 1658. The latter was the last of the author's works to be published during his lifetime; posthumous publications included *Certain Miscellany Tracts* (1684) and *Christian Morals* (1716; later edited by **Samuel Johnson** in 1756). He also conducted an extensive and interesting correspondence with such distinguished contemporaries as **Aubrey**, **Evelyn** and Ashmole.

**Browne, Thomas Alexander** See **Boldrewood, Rolf**.

**Browne, William** 1591– *c.*1643 Pastoral poet. Born in Tavistock, Devon, and educated at Exeter College, Oxford, and at the Middle Temple, Browne was a scholarly admirer of the works of **Spenser**, **Sidney** and **Drayton**, and was himself the writer of mature poetry, later to influence **Milton** and **Keats**. His principal work is *Britannia's Pastoral*, a long poem in three books (the first published in 1613, the next in 1616, but the third not until 1852) combining stock motifs of the rural tradition with occasional descriptive freshness. He collaborated with **George Wither** and others on *The Shepherd's Pipe* (1614), a collection of pastorals, and was also the author of several epitaphs, including the famous one on the Countess of Pembroke beginning 'Underneath this sable hearse', formerly attributed to his friend **Ben Jonson**.

**Browning, Elizabeth Barrett** 1806–61 Poet. Born the eldest of the 12 children of Edward Moulton-Barrett and his wife Mary at Coxhoe Hall, near Durham. While she was still quite young her father purchased the estate of Hope End, near Malvern and it was there that most of her childhood and youth were passed. A precocious and ardent student, Elizabeth Barrett studied with a governess and undertook to share her brother's lessons in Latin and Greek. At the age of 15 she suffered a serious illness, but recovered sufficiently to take full part in family life, though her studies and writing always took first place.

She began to write verse at an early age, celebrating family feast days as the 'Poet Laureate' of Hope End. Her first volume, *The Battle of Marathon*, was privately printed in 1820, and her second was published in 1826; both are undeniably juvenile productions, at once imitative and pedantic, but in the latter Elizabeth Barrett's distinctive style begins to emerge. Her translation of Aeschylus' *Prometheus Bound* (1833) she later repudiated as 'cold as Caucasus, and as flat as the nearest plain', and she expiated her sin by making a new version (published in *Poems*, 1850).

In 1832, business difficulties forced Edward Moulton-Barrett to leave Hope End and, after a period at Sidmouth, he finally settled with his family in London at 50 Wimpole Street, in 1838.

There, Elizabeth Barrett enjoyed a moderately full literary life, corresponding with **Mary Russell Mitford** and **R. H. Horne** and her cousin and literary confidant, John Kenyon. *The Seraphim and Other Poems* was favourably received when it appeared in 1838.

In the same year she suffered a lung haemorrhage and removed to Torquay where she remained convalescent for three years. During this period, at her request and against the wishes of their father, her brother Edward spent much time with her. In 1840 she suffered a severe relapse when her brother Samuel died on the family estates in Jamaica and, shortly afterward, Edward also perished in a sailing accident in Torbay. His sister's anguish was augmented by guilt, and the memory of the event remained painful in the extreme. Returning as an invalid to London, Elizabeth Barrett embarked on a productive period, writing a series of notable essays on English literature and the Greek Christian poets for *The Athenaeum* (1842) and collaborating with R. H. Horne on the *New Spirit of the Age* (1843).

The volume of *Poems*, which included 'A Drama of Exile' and 'Lady Geraldine's Courtship', was published in 1844 to considerable critical acclaim. One of her admirers was **Robert Browning** (whose verse she had complimented in 'Lady Geraldine'), and he was prompted to write expressing his appreciation: 'I do, as I say, love these books with all my heart – and I love you too.' A correspondence soon developed,

Elizabeth Barrett Browning. A photograph taken in 1858 by Cyrus Macaire.

growing rapidly into love after Browning's first visit in May 1845. In order to avoid her father's expected prohibition, the poets were married secretly in September 1846, departing for Italy a week later. After a sojourn in Pisa they moved to Florence, settling at Casa Guidi, where their son Robert Wiedemann Barrett Browning was born in 1849.

In 1850 Elizabeth Barrett Browning published a further volume of *Poems*, among them the **Sonnets from the Portuguese**, written during her courtship. This was followed by **Casa Guidi Windows** (1851). On the death of **Wordsworth** in 1850 *The Athenaeum* had proposed Elizabeth Barrett Browning as an appropriate successor to the post of Poet Laureate (on the grounds that the appointment of a woman poet would be a fitting compliment to the Queen, and would assist two poets for the price of one), but it was the publication of **Aurora Leigh** (1856) which secured her recognition as the foremost woman poet in English. Her political *Poems Before Congress* (1860) was, however, received by the critics with dismay, as hysterical and unwomanly.

In June 1861, saddened by the deaths of her sister Henrietta, and the Italian leader, Cavour, she fell ill at Casa Guidi and died there. She is buried in the Protestant Cemetery in Florence. Her *Last Poems* (1861) were prepared for publication by her husband.

**Browning, Oscar** 1837–1923 Historian and educationalist. He was educated at Eton under W. J. Cory (poet of Ionica, and composer of 'The Eton Boating Song') and became an assistant master there from 1860 to 1875. He then became a history lecturer at King's College, Cambridge, gaining notoriety for his snobbery and argumentativeness. Among his works were a biography of **George Eliot** (1890), a childhood acquaintance, and various historical studies. He is frequently mentioned in memoirs by his former students; see, for example, **A. C. Benson**'s *Memories and Friends* (1924) and **E. F. Benson**'s *As We Were* (1930).

**Browning, Robert** 1812–89 Poet. Born at Camberwell in South London, the son of a scholarly man whose estrangement from his own father led to his taking a post as clerk in the Bank of England. Largely educated at home, Browning read widely among the books of his father's extensive library. At 16 he began to study at the newly established London University, but returned home after a brief period.

He wrote verse from an early age, taking as his literary hero **Shelley**, who influenced much of his work and prompted him to adopt vegetarian and atheist principles for a time. In 1833 he published anonymously *Pauline: A Fragment of a Confession*. It was briefly noticed in a few journals, but more important was the reaction

Robert Browning. A detail from the portrait by M. Gordigiani, 1858. National Portrait Gallery, London.

of **J. S. Mill**, who noted in the young poet 'a more intense and morbid self-consciousness than I ever knew in any sane human being'. Mill's remark has often been considered influential in directing Browning toward the dramatic creation of character so typical of his poetry. His next work, *Paracelsus* (1835), dealt with the life of the Swiss alchemist, a subject suggested by the poet's friend Amédée de Ripert-Monclar.

In 1837 Browning wrote a play, *Strafford*, for the actor William Macready. In spite of the efforts of Macready and **John Forster**, who assisted in revising the work for the stage, it was not a popular success. After a visit to Italy (1838), Browning published *Sordello* (1840) which concentrated on 'the incidents in the development of a soul' as evinced in the life of the poet who was Dante's contemporary. From 1841 to 1846 Browning's work was published by Moxon as pamphlets in a series bearing the general title of *Bells and Pomegranates*. These included *Pippa Passes* (1841), *Dramatic Lyrics* (1842), *Dramatic Romances and Lyrics* (1845), *Luria and A Soul's Tragedy* (1846) and the plays *King Victor and King Charles* (1842), *The Return of the Druses* (1843), *A Blot on the 'Scutcheon* (1843) and *Colombe's Birthday* (1844). Many of Browning's best-known poems date from this early 'period; 'Porphyria's Lover' and 'Johannes Agricola' had already appeared in the *Monthly Repository* (1836) and were reprinted in *Dramatic*

*Lyrics* along with **My Last Duchess**, **Soliloquy of the Spanish Cloister** and **The Pied Piper of Hamelin**. *Dramatic Romances and Lyrics* included **How They Brought the Good News from Ghent to Aix**, 'Home Thoughts from Abroad', **The Bishop Orders his Tomb in St Praxed's Church** and 'The Flight of the Duchess'.

Browning paid another visit to Italy in 1844, returning to take part in the chorus of admiration greeting the publication of Elizabeth Barrett's *Poems* that year (see **Elizabeth Barrett Browning**). His enthusiastic first letter to her led to a correspondence, friendship and eventually marriage, which took place in September 1846. Leaving England for Italy, the Brownings settled in Florence where their son was born in 1849, but a few days after the death of Browning's mother.

1850 saw the publication of *Christmas-Eve and Easter-Day* which received little attention but was well reviewed by Joseph Milsand in the *Revue des Deux Mondes*. **Men and Women** (1855) received grudging reviews, though it was read enthusiastically by a small group of adherents, not least the poet and artist **Dante Gabriel Rossetti**. **John Ruskin**, though a friend of the Brownings, made the familiar complaint of obscurity that dogged Browning throughout his career. Among the poems published in *Men and Women* were **Fra Lippo Lippi**, **A Toccata of Galuppi's**, 'Childe Roland to the Dark Tower Came', **Bishop Blougram's Apology**, **Andrea del Sarto** and the eloquent dedication 'One Word More: To E.B.B.'.

After Elizabeth Barrett Browning died in 1861, Browning resolved to leave Italy and settled in England with his son. A year previously he had discovered on a Florentine stall the 'Old yellow book' of documents relating to a 17th-century murder trial and he now began to contemplate his 'Roman murder-story'. Meanwhile *Dramatis Personae* ('James Lee's Wife', **Abt Vogler**, 'Mr Sludge, "The Medium"' and **Caliban Upon Setebos**) appeared in 1864. In 1867 he was elected an honorary fellow of Balliol College, Oxford. **The Ring and the Book** was published in monthly instalments from November 1868 to February 1869. The poem received complimentary reviews and Browning, 'king of the mystics', was at last popular with the reading public.

His vitality continued undiminished as he produced a remarkable series of later works, too frequently undervalued: *Balaustion's Adventure* (1871), *Prince Hohenstiel-Schwangau* (1871), *Fifine at the Fair* (1872), *Red Cotton Night-Cap Country* (1873), *Aristophanes' Apology* (1875), **The Inn Album** (1875), *Pacchiarotto and How he Worked in Distemper* (1876), *La Saisiaz* and *The Two Poets of Croisic* (1878), *Dramatic Idyls* (1879 and 1880), *Jocoseria* (1883), *Ferishtah's Fancies* (1884), *Parleyings with Certain People of Impor-*

tance in their Day (1887) and *Asolando: Fancies and Facts* (1889).

Browning's prolific output during these years nevertheless left him time to produce a translation of Aeschylus' *Agamemnon* (1877), to watch anxiously over the career of his painter son, and to lead a demanding social life. The foundation of the Browning Society (1881) is an indication of the poet's status in old age as sage and celebrity. In 1889, while on a visit to Italy, Browning died at the Palazzo Rezzonico, his son's residence in Venice. Various difficulties made the poet's requested burial in Florence impossible, and his body was returned to England to be interred in Westminster Abbey.

**Brownjohn, Alan** 1931– Poet. Born in Catford, South London, and educated there and at Merton College, Oxford (1950–3), Brownjohn taught at London schools before becoming a lecturer at Battersea College of Education. He has served as a councillor and stood as a Labour candidate for Richmond, Surrey, in the 1964 Parliamentary election.

His first collection was *The Railings* (1961). *Collected Poems 1952–83* appeared in 1983. Associated with the **Group**, Brownjohn has been influenced principally by **Thomas Hardy** and **Philip Larkin**. His verse is scrupulous and controlled in its use of a rather flat language to record and to satirize contemporary British life.

**Brownson, Orestes (Augustus)** 1803–76 American novelist and social critic. Born in Stockbridge, Vermont, into an old Connecticut family, Brownson received no formal education. In the course of his life he underwent several changes of faith. In 1824 he left the Presbyterian church and became a Universalist. By 1832 he had joined the Unitarian church, and finally, in 1844, he became a Roman Catholic. Although he was associated with **Transcendentalism** and the **Brook Farm** experiment, and shared the Transcendentalists' belief that moral reform had to be the basis of political change, his own activities were often more radical than those emanating from that movement. He helped organize The Workingmen's Party in the early 1830s; he agitated for the reform of the penal code and inheritance laws; and in 1836 he founded a church for the working classes in Boston called the Society for Christian Union and Progress.

Brownson provided fora for these ideas in several of the magazines he edited: *Boston Quarterly Review*, *Democratic Review* and *Brownson's Quarterly Review*. Many of his works put forth his religious and social beliefs and describe his changes of faith. In *New Views of Christianity, Society and the Church* (1836), he attacked organized Christianity; *Charles Elwood, or, The Infidel Converted* (1840) is a semi-autobiographical novel about a man's conversion to Unitarianism; *The Meditational Life of Jesus* (1842) outlines his Roman Catholic beliefs; *The Spirit-Rapper: An Autobiography* (1854) is less an autobiography than a novel about the Satanic influences evident in contemporary spiritualism; *The Convert, or, Leaves from My Experiences* (1857) is an account of his personal religious growth.

***Bruce, The*** Poem by **John Barbour** in octosyllabic couplets. It is an epic account of the struggle of Robert the Bruce (Robert I) and Sir James Douglas against the English domination of Scotland. The poem is intensely patriotic, yet avoids elevating the figure of Robert to such mythic status as to undermine his credibility. The descriptions of battles are spirited and vigorous, and the account of Bannockburn is usually judged the poem's finest passage. The tone combines chivalric elements with **verse romance** with touches of humour and a strong historical interest. Apart from some minor errors the poem gives a relatively accurate account of events. It is also notable for Barbour's strong sense of the high value of personal freedom.

**Bruce, James** 1730–94 Traveller. Educated at Harrow, Bruce travelled extensively in Northern Africa and spent two years in Abyssinia, where he succeeded in tracing the source of the Blue Nile. In 1790, he published an account of his journeys, *Travels to Discover the Source of the Nile*, which was considered fanciful until verified by **Burton** and Salt.

**Bruce, Mary Grant** 1878–1958 Australian children's writer. Born in Victoria, the daughter of an Irish surveyor, she began writing as a child and later settled into journalism in Melbourne. As editor of a children's page in *The Leader*, she also contributed her own short stories and serials, the most successful of which finally appeared in book form as *A Little Bush Maid* (1910). This described Billabong, a fictional station in Victoria inhabited by two motherless children, Jim and Norah, with their father, various friends, visiting relatives and servants. Independent, hard-working and adventurous, the Lintons soon became firm favourites with readers, the last of their 15 stories appearing in 1942. Against a physically tough setting, the author creates an idealized rural existence highly acceptable to generations of readers many of whom lived in more urban surroundings. Mary Grant Bruce also wrote *The Stone Age of Burkamukk* (1922), a book of Aborigine legends, and *The Happy Traveller* (1929), about a resourceful young hero escaping from his orphanage.

***Brut*** An alliterative verse chronicle by **Layamon**, written in the late 12th century. The poem is adapted from the French of Wace's *Le Roman de Brut* (1155), itself an adaptation of **Geoffrey of Monmouth**'s *Historia Regum Britanniae* (*c.* 1135). It narrates the history of England from its foundation by the legendary Brutus, great-grandson of Aeneas, who left Italy to seek a new land, destroyed the giants then living in England and built London. King Lear and Cymbeline both appear, but the narrative is memorable for being the first to tell the story of King Arthur in English (see **Arthurian literature**). *Brut* lacks much of Wace's courtliness, resembling more closely the vigorous epic character of Old English poetry.

**Brutus, Dennis** 1924– South African poet. Born in Zimbabwe, but educated in South Africa, he became a schoolmaster and vigorous opponent of apartheid. He was banned in 1961, arrested in 1963, shot in the back while trying to escape, and imprisoned on Robben Island. He went into exile in 1966 and successfully campaigned abroad for South Africa's exclusion from the Olympic Games. Since 1970 he has taught at Northwestern University, Evanston, Illinois.

His first book of poems, *Sirens, Knuckles, Boots* (1962) was published in Nigeria. It vigorously records the strident noises and police violence that accompany black South African life under apartheid, which estranges blacks from a lover-like possession of their land. The central idea of the poet as troubadour, the land as his mistress, integrates his vatic, sometimes bitter utterance on public themes with the great tenderness of his personal love poetry. *Letters to Martha and Other Poems from a South African Prison* (1968) contains some of the most honest and disturbing poetry in English about prison life – sparse, largely non-figurative, relying upon subtle, conversational rhythms and delicate verbal nuances. *Poems from Algiers* (1970) and *Thoughts Abroad* (1970) are poems of exile in which foreign views contain hints of South African landmarks. *A Simple Lust* (1973) collects all the former verse and adds previously unpublished poems. *Stubborn Hope* (1979) and *Strains* (1981) reiterate the exile's concern with his country, but also dramatize a personal, psychological conflict, between apparently irreconcilable urges towards sensual indulgence and spiritual discipline.

**Bryant, William Cullen** 1794–1878 American poet and editor, born in Cummington, Massachusetts. He began writing poetry at the age of 13; his first work, *The Embargo* (1808), satirizes **Thomas Jefferson**'s government. He attended Williams College, then studied law and followed a legal career until he was 31. He was still a young lawyer when the first version of *Thanatopsis*, which he had written when he was 16,

The Prairie Hunter. An illustration for William Cullen Bryant's poem, 'The Prairies'.

appeared in *The North American Review* in 1817. He published a collection, *Poems*, in 1821, and from 1824 to 1825 contributed regularly to the *United States Literary Gazette*. It was during this period that his reputation as a leading American poet was established.

He became an editor of the *New York Review* and *Athenaeum Magazine* in 1825, and chief editor of the *New York Evening Post* in 1829, a position he held for nearly 50 years, during which time he became a vigorous opponent of slavery and an advocate of the new Republican party. His career as a poet continued with the publication of a second collection, *Poems*, in 1832. Late in life he produced blank verse translations of the *Iliad* (1870) and the *Odyssey* (1871–2). Though he was strongly influenced by European Romanticism, and by **Wordsworth** in particular, his verse reveals a concern with distinctively American political and philosophical issues, and reflects a movement, in mid century, from Federalist politics to the New Republicanism.

**Bryce, James, 1st Viscount** 1838–1922 Historian. Educated at the University of Glasgow, Trinity College, Oxford, and the University of Heidelberg, he became a barrister in 1867 and was appointed Regius Professor of Civil Law at Oxford (1870–93). Bryce entered politics in 1880 and was chief secretary for Ireland (1905–6) and ambassador to Washington (1907–13). As a historian, Bryce is remembered for his *The Holy Roman Empire* (1864) and *The American Commonwealth* (1888, revised 1920). Other works include *Studies in History and Jurisprudence* (1901) and *Impressions of South Africa* (1897), a sharply observed picture of the country on the eve of the Boer War.

**Bryden, Bill (Campbell Rough)** 1942–

Dramatist and director. Born in Greenock, he began his career as a documentary writer for Scottish television before being appointed assistant director at the Belgrade Theatre, Coventry (1965–7, and at the **Royal Court Theatre** (1967–9) and an associate director at the Royal Lyceum Theatre in Edinburgh (1971–4). Notable among many Lyceum productions were those of Bryden's own two plays, *Willie Rough* (1972), about the Greenock shop steward who led a shipyard strike during World War I, and *Benny Lynch* (1974). Both plays are distinguished by naturalistic detail, clear handling of complex historical material and socialist fervour which never becomes blindly polemical. In 1975 he joined the **National Theatre**, where his play *Old Movies* (1977) was staged.

**Buchan, John** 1875–1940 Scottish novelist, biographer, historian, essayist, journalist, editor, poet and publisher. Son of a Lowland manse, he received a classical education in Glasgow and Oxford and worked with Milner in South Africa, later becoming a practising London lawyer and virtually editing *The Spectator*. He revitalized Nelson's the publishers, particularly through pocket editions of great literature. In World War I he served in Intelligence, and was then MP for the Scottish Universities. As Lord Tweedsmuir he became Governor-General of Canada.

Buchan is famous for his five Richard Hannay thrillers, particularly the first, *The Thirty-Nine Steps* (1915), his 27th book. His 100 books include nearly 30 novels and seven collections of short stories; many are still widely praised and read, both historical fiction, like *Salute to Adventurers* (1915), *Midwinter* (1923), *Witch Wood* (1927) and *The Blanket of the Dark* (1931), and contemporary tales, like the charming *Huntingtower* (1922) or *Castle Gay* (1930), and the profounder Sir Edward Leithen novels, especially Buchan's last, *Sick Heart River* (1941). His fiction has clarity, atmosphere, good characterization, a grasp of large affairs and an acute sense of landscape. His 24-volume *Nelson's History of the War* (1915–19), partly written from the Front, has a global view free from jingoism. Biographies of Montrose (1913, 1928), Oliver Cromwell (1934), Augustus (1937) and others are admired; that of **Sir Walter Scott** (1932) is definitive. He was a prolific contributor to journals. His fine autobiography, *Memory Hold-the-Door* (1940), may be amplified by the biography by Janet Adam Smith and memoirs by his daughter and sons.

**Buchanan, George** 1506–82 Historian and scholar. Buchanan is the most important of the 16th-century Scottish humanists. He was educated at St Andrews and Paris, where he became an MA in 1528. His career was characteristically humanist: that of teacher, tutor to boys of noble families (including the young James VI), translator, poet and grammarian. He corresponded with the leading scholars of the day, including Languet, **Ascham** and Tycho Brahe. He returned from the Continent to Scotland in 1536 as tutor to the natural son of James V, and with the King's encouragement wrote *Franciscanus et Fratres* attacking the morals of the clergy. Consequently, he had to flee the persecution of Cardinal Beaton to London, Paris and Bordeaux. There in the early 1540s he composed four tragedies: *Baptistes* and *Jephthes* on biblical subjects, and two Latin versions of Euripides, *Alcestis* and *Medea*. While confined in a Portuguese monastery for writing against the Franciscans he produced a Latin paraphrase of the Psalms.

Buchanan returned to Scotland in 1562 and took part in public life. He celebrated the marriage of Mary and Darnley in an epithalamion, but after Darnley's death participated in the commissions against Mary and authenticated her handwriting in the incriminating 'Casket Letters'. He wrote *De Maria Scotorum Regina . . . Conjuratione*, which appeared simultaneously in Scottish as *Ane Detection of the Duinges of Marie Queene of Scottes* in 1571. His later years saw the publication of *De Jure Regni*, a defence of limited monarchy, and his major work, *Rerum Scotiarum Historia*, printed at Edinburgh in the year of his death, 1582.

**Buchanan, Robert (Williams)** 1841–1901 Poet, novelist and playwright. The son of an Ayrshire freethinker, Buchanan was born in Staffordshire and after high-school and university education in Edinburgh sought fame in London. His initial volume of verse, largely derivative, was *Undertones* (1863), followed in quick succession by *Idyls and Legends of Inverburn* (1865), *London Poems* (1866), *Ballad Stories of the Affections* (1866) and *North Coast and Other Poems* (1867). Including verse both lyrical and narrative, much of this work is about the Scottish peasantry and the exacting northern life with which Buchanan felt emotional affiliation, although in *London Poems* he is attracted to those mean streets and squalid city lives that become a literary obsession in the 1890s. With his Celtic poem *The Book of Orm* (1870), followed by *Balder the Beautiful* (1877) and *The City of Dream* (1888), Buchanan shows his north-of-the-border addiction to the mystical in life as well as his affinity with the **Spasmodics** and their penchant for verse on an epic scale. Other poems, more down to earth, were *Saint Abe and His Seven Wives* (1872) and *White Rose and the Red* (1873), which deal with life in the New World.

In the early 1870s Buchanan became embroiled in a vulgar quarrel with the **Pre-Raphaelites** and his criticism of that body, which began as an article in *The Contemporary Review*, developed into the pseudonymous pamphlet 'The Fleshly School of Poetry' (1872), a scurrilous attack that deeply wounded **Dante Gabriel Rossetti** who, however, managed 'The Stealthy School of Criticism' as rebuttal. Rossetti was supported by that ever-eager literary combatant **Algernon Charles Swinburne** with *Under the Microscope* (1872).

Buchanan also wrote plays, with varying success, such as *Lady Clare* (1883), *Sophia* (an adaptation of *Tom Jones*, 1886) and *The Charlatan* (1894). There were, in addition, a good many novels, among them *The Shadow of the Sword* (1876), *God and the Man* (1881), *Foxglove Manor* (1885) and *Effie Hetherington* (1886). Buchanan also wrote some literary essays for the prominent journals of his time.

**Buck, Pearl S[ydenstricker]** 1892–1973 American novelist. Born in Hillsboro, West Virginia, Buck was taken to China as a child by her parents, who went there as missionaries, and spent much of her life there, teaching at various universities. Many of her works of fiction are set in China, including *The Good Earth* (1931), probably her best-known novel, for which she was awarded the Pulitzer Prize in 1932. An epic story about a peasant's relationship with the soil, it is the first in a trilogy called *The House of Earth*, of which the others are *Sons* (1932) and *A House Divided* (1935). Her first novel about Chinese life was *East Wind, West Wind* (1930). Subsequent novels about China include *The Mother* (1934), *This Proud Heart* (1938), *Dragon Seed* (1941) and *Kinfolk* (1949).

A prolific writer, Buck produced over 100 titles: novels, collections of stories, plays, screenplays, one book of verse, books for juveniles, biographies, two autobiographies, a cookbook, and works of non-fiction about the mentally retarded, her philanthropic activities, Russia and missionaries. She also translated and edited works by various Chinese writers. The biographies of her parents, *The Exile* (1936) and *Fighting Angel: Portrait of a Soul* (1936), are considered classics. In 1938 she became the first American woman to win the Nobel Prize for Literature.

**Buckingham, George Villiers, 2nd Duke of** 1628–87 Dramatist. Son of James I's ennobled favourite, he was born in the year of his father's assassination and brought up in the royal household of Charles I. Constantly involved in intrigue, both before and after the Restoration, Buckingham also found time for literary pursuits. Having observed the excesses of heroic tragedy in the Restoration theatre, he wrote, perhaps in collaboration with **Samuel Butler** and others, a burlesque of the style. *The Rehearsal* (1671) long outlived the dramatic taste it satir-

ized, providing a model a century later for **Sheridan**'s *The Critic* (1779). **Dryden**, mocked in the person of Bayes, took his revenge on Buckingham by portraying him as Zimri in *Absalom and Achitophel*. The only other of Buckingham's dramatic work to merit attention is his adaptation of **John Fletcher**'s *The Chances* (1667).

**Buckle, Henry Thomas** 1821–62 Historian. Born at Lee in Kent, he was for most of his life a Londoner. A solitary man, largely without formal education, he used the small fortune inherited from his father to devote himself to studying history from a scientific standpoint influenced by **John Stuart Mill**. The first volume of his ambitious *History of Civilization* appeared in 1857 and the second in 1861, but he died in Damascus with the work unfinished. Buckle's *History* enjoyed a brief popularity before its approach came to appear dated even to those who shared its author's scientific precepts.

**Buckler, Ernest (Redmond)** 1908–84 Canadian novelist. A farmer in Nova Scotia, Buckler was educated at Dalhousie University and the University of Toronto. His best-known novel, *The Mountain and the Valley*, was published in 1952. Other works include *The Cruelest Month* (1963), *Ox Bells and Fireflies: A Memoir* (1968) and *Whirligig: Selected Prose and Verse* (1977). Some of his engaging short stories were collected in *The Rebellion of Young David and Other Stories* (1975).

**Buckley, Vincent** 1925–88 Australian poet and critic. Born of Irish parents in Romsey, Victoria, Buckley was educated by Jesuits in Melbourne and later at the Universities of Melbourne and Cambridge. During World War II he served with the Royal Australian Air Force. He subsequently worked in the public service and then took up an appointment at the University of Melbourne, where he spent all his academic life and where he was Professor of English from 1967. His early work was concerned with the state of contemporary culture, and religion and politics figure prominently. He later rejected much of his poetry and, after the publication of *Golden Builders and Other Poems* (1975), dealt more directly with the process of perception and the way art constructs and enacts meanings. Buckley was also an influential critic. His *Essays in Poetry* (1957) was an important statement on the situation of Australian poetry. He was poetry editor of the *Bulletin* between 1961 and 1963 and published a number of poets who questioned the orthodoxies then prevalent in Australian verse. His other volumes of poetry include *The World's Flesh* (1954), *Masters in Israel* (1961), *Arcady and Other Places* (1966), *Late Winter Child* (1979) and *The Pattern* (1979).

**Buckstone, John Baldwin** 1802–79 English actor, playwright and theatre manager. He was born and brought up in London's East End. After three seasons in the provinces, he made his London debut at the Surrey Theatre in 1823–4, establishing himself in the 'low comedian' line which he sustained for over 50 years. Of the 100 or so dramatic pieces Buckstone wrote between 1825 and 1850, most were short farces, operettas or burlettas, but one of the earliest, *Luke the Labourer* (1826), helped set the fashion for domestic melodrama. *The Wreck Ashore* (1830) is an adventure story larded with low-life comic characters. Here, as in the lively comedy of *The Irish Lion* (1838) and *Single Life* (1839) and in the tear-jerking of *The Green Bushes* (1845), Buckstone upholds manly fortitude and decency, assuring his heroes and heroines the satisfaction of victory or of superior self-sacrifice in defeat. As manager of the **Haymarket Theatre** in 1853–76 he made it the home of comedy, staging the work of **Tom Taylor**, **Westland Marston**, and, after 1870, **W. S. Gilbert**.

**Buke of the Howlat, The** An alliterative poem in Middle Scots, written around 1450 by **Sir Richard Holland**. The poem is a moral **allegory** indicating the dangers of pride and ambition. The owl complains of its dull plumage to the peacock and a parliament of birds is called. They decide nothing can be done, but Dame Nature descends and allows each bird to donate a feather to the owl. The owl becomes too proud of its new appearance and Nature revokes the favour, leaving it in its former state. The poem contains a passage praising the Douglas family to whom Holland was allied.

**Bukowski, Charles** 1920– American poet. Born in Germany, he was brought to the USA by his parents in 1922, and raised and educated in Los Angeles.

His first volumes of verse, *Flower, Fist and Bestial Wall* (1959), *Longshot Poems for Broke Players* (1961) and *Run with the Hunted* (1962), were not widely noticed, but in 1962 *Outsider* magazine named him 'Outsider of the Year' and devoted an issue to his work, bringing him more recognition. Since then he has written some 30 volumes of poetry. These include *Crucifix in a Deathhand: New Poems, 1963–65* (1965), *At Terror Street and Agony Way* (1968), *Poems Written Before Jumping Out of an 8-Story Window* (1968), *The Days Run Away Like Wild Horses over the Hills* (1969), *Burning in Water, Drowning in Flame: Selected Poems 1955–1973* (1974), *Love Is a Dog from Hell* (1977), *Dangling in the Tournefortia* (1981) and *Hot Water Music* (1983). He has also written novels, including *Post Office* (1971), *Factotum* (1975), *Women* (1978) and *Ham on Rye* (1982), and other prose pieces, including *Confessions of a Man Insane Enough to*

*Live with Beasts* (1965) and *All the Assholes in the World and Mine* (1966).

Bukowski's work circulates in limited editions and magazines published by small presses, among an underground rather than a commercial readership. His poetic ancestors are the **Beats**, and he emphasizes immediate, unprettified experience, writing as an alienated outcast, irreverent, angry, and especially critical of the pretentiousness of the academic and commercial mainstream of contemporary American poetry.

**Bullins, Ed** 1935– One of the most prolific playwrights of the black American theatre, Bullins was born in Philadelphia and educated there and in California. His first play, *Clara's Ole Man* (1965), immediately showed his sensitivity to the nature of life in the ghetto; *The Gentleman Caller* (1968), *The Electronic Nigger* (1968), *A Son, Come Home* (1968) and *Goin A Buffalo* (1969) are typical examples of his work's mixture of improvisatory energy and formal discipline. He has planned a cycle of 20 plays to cover the 20th-century life of Afro-American communities, loosely united around the Dawson family. The cycle includes *In New England Winter* (1967), *In the Wine Time* (1968), *The Duplex* (1970), *The Fabulous Miss Marie* (1970), *Street Sounds* (1970), *Daddy* (1977) and *Leavings* (1980). A collection of works written during a militant phase was published in 1971 as *Four Dynamite Plays*. *The House Party* (1973) and *The Taking of Miss Janie* (1975) look back at the politics of the 1960s. After collaborating on the musicals *Sepia Star* (1977) and *Storyville* (1977), Bullins directed the 1978 New York production of his play *Michael. The Hungered One: Early Writings*, a collection of short stories, was published in 1971, and his novel, *The Reluctant Rapist*, in 1973. Since 1967 he has been associated with the New Lafayette Theatre in Harlem, New York, as both playwright and director; he has served as producing director of The Surviving Theatre in New York since 1974.

**Bulwer Lytton, Edward (George Earle Lytton), 1st Baron Lytton** 1803–73 Novelist, playwright, poet. Few English writers are known by such a variety of names. He began as plain Edward Bulwer, though he often called himself Edward Lytton Bulwer (Lytton being his mother's maiden name and one of his several Christian names). He was knighted in 1837, and on his mother's death in 1843 expanded his surname to Bulwer Lytton: hence Sir Edward (Lytton) Bulwer Lytton. Raised to the peerage in 1866, he was known thereafter as Lord Lytton. His son, **Edward Robert Bulwer Lytton**, with whom he is sometimes confused, was created the 1st Earl of Lytton in 1880.

One of the most accomplished authors of his day, he is marked above all by the versatility of his talents. His two dozen novels, written over an active career of 45 years, tackle almost every genre popular with his contemporaries. They include: historical romances, notably *The Last Days of Pompeii* (1834), *Rienzi* (1835), *The Last of the Barons* (1843) and *Harold* (1848); tales of magic, spiritualism and **science fiction** like *Zanoni* (1842), *A Strange Story* (1862) and *The Coming Race* (1871); **silver-fork** novels of high society like *Pelham* (1828); light novels of middle-class domestic life like *The Caxtons* (1849), *My Novel* (1853) and *What Will He Do With It?* (1858); **Newgate novels** like *Paul Clifford* (1830) and *Eugene Aram* (1832); and philosophical novels about gifted young men seeking the meaning of life, like *Godolphin* (1833), *Ernest Maltravers* (1837) and *Alice* (1838). In almost every instance he was immensely successful. 'Everything he wrote' remarked **Edmund Gosse**, 'sold as though it were bread displayed to a hungry crowd.'

He also published 10 plays, of which *The Lady of Lyons* (1838), *Richelieu* (1839) and *Money* (1840) were regularly performed throughout the 19th century, 11 volumes of poetry, two collections of essays, numerous short stories, a history of Athens, translations of Horace and Schiller, and a pioneering sociological study, *England and the English* (1833). From 1831 to 1833 he edited *The New Monthly Magazine*. He entered Parliament in 1831 as a Liberal, resigned 10 years later, returned in 1852 as a Tory, and in 1858 became Secretary for the Colonies. He was a lifelong friend of **Dickens**, and is often remembered for persuading him to change the ending of *Great Expectations*. That he is not much remembered in his own right would have surprised his contemporaries, for during the mid-19th century he was widely regarded as England's leading man of letters.

**Bulwer Lytton, Edward Robert (1st Earl of Lytton)** 1831–91 Diplomat and poet. The son of **Edward Bulwer Lytton**, he pursued a successful career in the diplomatic service, eventually becoming Viceroy of India (1876–80). In his youth he served in Italy where he met **Robert** and **Elizabeth Browning** whose work influenced his poetry. His volumes include *Wanderer* (1857), *Lucile* (1860), *Glenaveril* (1885) and *King Poppy* (1892). His early work was published under the pseudonym of Owen Meredith.

**Bunting, Basil** 1900–85 Poet. Born in Northumberland and educated at Quaker schools and at the London School of Economics, Bunting went to prison as a conscientious objector during World War I. He worked in London as a music critic and in Paris as an editor on *The Transatlantic Review* before seeking out **Ezra Pound** in Rapallo, Italy, where he lived for some time. He published his first poems in the 1930s and during World War II went to Persia to serve first with the British forces and later with the diplomatic service as an interpreter. After being expelled from Persia, he worked as a journalist in Newcastle until his retirement.

Bunting's reputation abroad was established before he was well known in Britain, and his work was first published by small presses, becoming widely known only after the publication of his long autobiographical poem *Briggflatts* (1966), a modern masterpiece that celebrates and seeks to define a distinct Northumbrian community with its own language and history. *Collected Poems* appeared in 1968. A disciple of Pound, whose trace can be found in his brilliant compression and deft use of specific vocabularies, he has in turn had a considerable influence among English and American poets, principally for his command of musical structure.

**Bunting, Edward** 1773–1843 Irish musicologist and collector of folk music. Born in Armagh, he was commissioned at the age of 18 to take down the music at the Belfast Harp Festival. This experience determined him to collect the rich treasures of the Irish folk-music tradition. His three volumes, *A General Collection of the Ancient Irish Music* (1796), *A General Collection of the Ancient Music of Ireland* (1809) and *The Ancient Music of Ireland, Arranged for the Piano Forte* (1840), form the basis for the attempt to preserve Irish traditional music. Bunting's work, continued by **George Petrie**, is an integral part of the **Celtic revival** which is a marked feature of 19th- and 20th-century Irish literature. Bunting settled in Dublin in 1819, where he was organist at St George's Church.

**Bunyan, John** 1628–88 Nonconformist preacher and writer. Bunyan was born at Elstow, near Bedford, the eldest of three children of Thomas Bunyan, a brasier or tinker, and his second wife Margaret Bentley. He was sent to a local school where he learned to read and write before taking up his father's trade. His favourite reading matter as a youth was popular ballads and chapbook versions of chivalric romances. In 1644 Bunyan was enrolled into the Parliamentary army to serve in the Civil War; he spent the next two-and-a-half years as a soldier in the garrison town of Newport Pagnell. Little is known of Bunyan's military career: his only reference to it is to record a providential escape from death when a fellow soldier who had taken his place at a siege was killed. It is likely, however, that he was influenced by radical sectarian preachers who were active in the army.

In 1647, following his discharge from the army, Bunyan returned to Elstow to resume his trade as a tinker. During the next few years he underwent a severe psychological crisis, the

John Bunyan. Portrait by T. Sadler, 1684. National Portrait Gallery, London.

progress of which he later recorded in his spiritual autobiography, **Grace Abounding** (1666). His first wife, whom he married in 1648, possessed a couple of popular religious books, Arthur Dent's *The Plain Man's Path-Way to Heaven* and Lewis Bayley's *The Practice of Piety*, and reading these Bunyan became convinced that he was a sinful creature destined for hell. He tried repeatedly to reform his life, giving up dancing and bell-ringing which were his favourite pastimes, and devoted himself to an intensive study of the Bible. Searching for spiritual enlightenment and fellowship, he came into contact with members of some of the religious sects which had emerged in the 1650s, such as Ranters and Quakers, and read their books, though later coming to reject their doctrines. He was much influenced by reading Luther's *Commentary on Galations*, finding there his own spiritual condition 'so largely and profoundly handled, as if his book had been written out of my heart'. About 1653 he joined an Independent (or Congregational) church in Bedford, but it took several more years of struggle, alternately swinging from moods of blackest despondency to moments of ecstatic vision, before he felt assured that his sins were forgiven and that he was an elect child of God.

The Bedford congregation of which he became a member had been formed in 1650. It developed a comparatively tolerant attitude towards matters which were deemed to be inessential, not insisting, for example, on adult baptism as a requirement for fellowship. Two or three years after joining, Bunyan began to preach in public. His early sermons evidently drew upon his own experience of spiritual conflict. The right of unlearned and unordained men to preach was a fiercely controversial matter in the 17th century, and Bunyan, like other 'mechanick preachers', repeatedly came into conflict with the regular clergy. He also engaged in doctrinal disputes with other sectarian preachers, and his earliest published works, *Some Gospel-Truths Opened* (1656) and *A Vindication of Some Gospel-Truths* (1657), were written against the Quakers. These provoked replies from Edward Burrough, a young Quaker polemicist, and from **George Fox**. Bunyan's first non-controversial work, *A Few Sighs from Hell, or, The Groans of a Damned Soul* (1658), took as its text the parable of Dives and Lazarus, and in it he vigorously castigated the rich for their pride and covetousness, and for their oppression of the poor. This was followed a year later by his most important theological statement, *The Doctrine of the Law and Grace Unfolded* (1659), a lengthy exposition of the Calvinist doctrine of the two covenants of works and grace. He married his second wife, Elizabeth, in 1659, following the death the previous year of his first wife who had borne four children.

With the restoration of Charles II in 1660 the comparative freedom which religious sects had enjoyed under Cromwell came to an end. Bunyan was one of the first Nonconformist preachers to suffer. He was arrested at a meeting at Lower Samsell in Bedfordshire in November 1660 and brought before the local magistrate, who remanded him in custody to appear at the quarter sessions in Bedford in January 1661. The charge was that he did not attend the established church and that he preached without licence to unlawful assemblies, or 'conventicles'. Bunyan's own account of his arrest and trial is to be found in the penultimate section of *Grace Abounding*, and in *A Relation of My Imprisonment*, taking the form of a series of verbatim reports of his trial and subsequent interviews with officials of the court, written for his friends in the Bedford congregation and not published until the middle of the 18th century. Bunyan stubbornly refused to give an undertaking to cease preaching, and spent most of the next 12 years in Bedford gaol in consequence. He occupied himself making shoe laces to help support his family, preaching to his fellow prisoners, and writing. His first prison book, *Profitable Meditations* (1661), presented theological doctrine in verse form in an attempt to reach a wider audience, since, as Bunyan remarked, 'Man's heart is apt in metre to delight.' This was followed by *I Will Pray with the Spirit* (c. 1662), a defence of extempore prayer, and *Christian Behaviour* (1663), a conduct manual. In 1665 he published two more volumes of poetry, as well as *The Holy City*, a millenarian vision of the approaching establishment of the true church on earth, when the saints would no longer suffer persecution. The last and most important prison work to be published before his release in 1672 was his spiritual autobiography, *Grace Abounding to the Chief of Sinners* (1666). It is likely that he also began writing **The Pilgrim's Progress** during this first imprisonment.

Shortly before his release, which came about as a result of a royal pardon following Charles's first Declaration of Indulgence, Bunyan had been appointed pastor of the Bedford congregation. He obtained a licence to preach and for the remainder of his life he was to be an active Nonconformist organizer, travelling throughout Cambridgeshire, Hertfordshire and Bedfordshire, and earning for himself the nickname 'Bishop Bunyan'. His reputation brought him invitations to preach in London, where, however, he became embroiled in doctrinal disputes with a number of Strict Baptists. He also engaged in controversy with the latitudinarian Anglican divine, Edward Fowler, publishing *A Defence of the Doctrine of Justification by Faith* (1672) in response to Fowler's *Design of Christianity* (1670).

The threat of further imprisonment was always present during this period, and a warrant was issued for Bunyan's arrest in 1675, though it seems not to have been put into effect. He was gaoled again for six months in 1677, and it was during this second imprisonment that he put the finishing touches to his masterpiece, *The Pilgrim's Progress* (1678). Such was its success that its publisher, Nathaniel Ponder, became known in the trade as 'Bunyan Ponder'. In the 10 years before Bunyan's death more than 11 authorized editions had appeared, the book had been published in New England, and it had been translated into French, Dutch and Welsh. Following the success of his allegory of the Christian life, Bunyan turned his attention to the ungodly, publishing in 1680 a realistic tale of *The Life and Death of Mr Badman*. Though lacking the imaginative fervour of the earlier work, it presents an unsparing condemnation of the vices of Restoration society. *The Holy War*, published two years later, is in many ways Bunyan's most ambitious work. In 1684, following the appearance of spurious 'continuations' to his *Pilgrim's Progress*, Bunyan published his own Second Part.

As well as these works for which he is remembered, Bunyan continued to publish theological treatises, sermons, verse and controversial works. His bibliography runs to nearly 60 titles, 14 of which were published posthumously. In addition to writing and preaching, Bunyan devoted much energy to the pastoral care of his group of congregations. The *Church Book of Bunyan Meeting* contains entries in his handwriting admonishing wayward professors and recording congregational visits. The latter years of Charles II's reign saw renewed persecution of Nonconformists, and Bunyan's fears for his own security are indicated by the deed of gift which he had drawn up in December 1685, making over all his worldly possessions to his wife. In 1687 the situation was reversed again, when James II offered toleration to both Protestant and Catholic Dissenters. In an attempt to ensure the return of a Parliament which would accept this, he instituted a reorganization of the corporations. Bunyan himself, it is said, was approached by James's agent, Lord Aylesbury, and offered 'a place of public trust', but he evidently refused, no doubt believing that James's real ambition was to enhance the political power of Catholicism in England. He did not live to see the overthrow of James II and the achievement of toleration for Protestant Dissenters under William III. His death in August 1688 was brought about by a fever contracted while riding from Reading to London in heavy rain. He was buried in the famous Dissenting burial ground at Bunhill Fields, Finsbury.

**Burbage, Richard** *c.* 1569–1619 The leading member of the company to which **Shakespeare** belonged. Burbage's father was the builder of the first English playhouse, the **Theatre**, and his son seems to have inherited business sense as well as acting talent. As a founder member of the Lord Chamberlain's Men, later the **King's Men**, and a shareholder in both the **Globe** and the **Blackfriars**, he guided the company to unparalleled fame and remarkable financial equilibrium. Considered by contemporaries a more lifelike actor than his chief rival, **Edward Alleyn**, Burbage is known to have played the title roles in **Hamlet**, **Othello**, **King Lear** and **Richard III**, Ferdinand in **Webster**'s *The Duchess of Malfi* and Malevole in **Marston**'s *The Malcontent*, and it is reasonable to suppose that he created many other major Shakespearean roles. He was also a painter of reputation and it is probably a self-portrait which can now be seen in the Dulwich library.

**Burgess, Anthony** 1917– Novelist. Born John Anthony Burgess Wilson in Manchester, he was educated at the Xaverian College and Manchester University, graduating in philology and literature. After service in World War II he worked as an instructor for the Central Advisory Council for Forces Education and as a grammar-school teacher. From 1954 to 1960 he was an educational officer in the Colonial Service, stationed in Borneo and Malaya. During these years he completed his first three novels,

*Time for a Tiger* (1956), *The Enemy in the Blanket* (1958) and *Beds in the East* (1959), republished together as *The Malayan Trilogy* in 1972 and *The Long Day Wanes* in 1982.

His bleak dystopian novel *A Clockwork Orange* (1962) marked a new development in the Joycean tradition. Its popularity reached the level of a cult after the film version by Stanley Kubrick in 1972. Burgess's prolific output during the 1960s and 1970s also included *The Wanting Seed* (1962), *Nothing Like the Sun* (about **Shakespeare**, 1964), *Napoleon Symphony* (1974) and *ABBA ABBA* (1977). The verbal inventiveness and pointed social satire which characterize his fiction are displayed in the comic sequence about the poet Enderby, whose carnal and cultural career spans England, Rome, Tangiers and New York: *Inside Mr Enderby* (published under the pseudonym Joseph Kell in 1963), *Enderby Outside* (1968) and *The Clockwork Testament* (1974). *Enderby's Dark Lady* (1984) resurrected its hero after he had been dispatched by the author. *Earthly Powers* (1980), narrated by an 81-year-old successful, homosexual writer, Kenneth Toomey, is an ambitious novel about 20th-century life which includes many jokes about major literary figures. *The Kingdom of the Wicked* (1985), shorter but equally ambitious, takes the first years of Christianity as its subject. Major figures, including the apostles and successive Roman emperors, are recreated in a style which has been modestly described as 'rumbustious'.

Burgess has written many critical works, notably on **James Joyce** in *Here Comes Everybody* (1965) and *Joysprick* (1973), on contemporary fiction in *The Novel Today* (1963) and *The Novel Now* (1967), and, as John Burgess Wilson, on the English language. He has also composed several orchestral works, written screenplays and contributed countless reviews and articles to journals and newspapers.

**Burgoyne, John** 1722–92 Soldier and playwright. In command of the British forces at Saratoga in 1777 General Burgoyne lost both an army and a well-earned reputation as a soldier. He had had one play, *The Maid of the Oaks* (1774), staged before the American débâcle. Soon after his return to England, he provided what is virtually a libretto for the music of William Jackson of Exeter, *The Lord of the Manor* (1780). It is a slight piece, with a redeeming trio of soldiers among its characters. A second and more serious musical piece, *Richard Coeur de Lion* (1786), is quite undistinguished. Burgoyne's dramatic reputation rests on his witty comedy, *The Heiress* (1786), whose trivial plot does not obstruct pertinent social comment. **Shaw** made Burgoyne a character in his play *The Devil's Disciple*.

**Burke, Edmund** 1729–97 Political philosopher. Born in Dublin, the second son of a Roman Catholic mother and an Irish Protestant lawyer, Burke was educated as a Protestant, attending Trinity College, Dublin, and then studying law at the Middle Temple in 1750. He was never called to the Bar. His first published works were *A Vindication of Natural Society*, an ironical treatise examining the divisions in society (1756), and *A Philosophical Enquiry into the Origin of our Ideas of the Sublime and the Beautiful* (1757). He married Jane Nugent in 1756, and was a founding editor of *The Annual Register* in 1758. He associated freely in the literary circles of London, befriended **Johnson** and **Reynolds**, and was an early member of 'the Club'.

Burke was a Whig, and became secretary to the Marquis of Rockingham, then Prime Minister, in 1765, entering Parliament as MP for Wendover in the same year. In the Commons he was an outspoken opponent of Lord North's Tory administration, especially over its attempts to repress the American colonies. His published views on the American question, supporting the colonists' cause, include: *Observations on 'The Present State of the Nation'* (1769), *On American Taxation* (1774) and *On Conciliation with the Colonies* (1775). He was strongly opposed to the control exercised over the House by the friends of George III, and forcibly expressed concern in his *Thoughts on the Cause of the Present Discontents* (1770).

At the invitation of the people of Bristol he became their MP in 1774, during which time he made himself famous as an orator, especially for his speech on economic reform in February 1780. But he espoused the cause of free trade with Ireland, became unpopular in his constituency, and lost his seat in the Commons in that year, a defence of his views appearing in *Two Letters . . . to Gentlemen in the City of Bristol* (1778) and the *Speech at the Guildhall* (1780). He

Gillray's cartoon showing Warren Hastings assaulted by Edmund Burke (left), and Lord North and Charles James Fox (right).

also championed the cause of the Irish Catholics, another controversial alignment, of which his letters *To a Peer of Ireland on the Penal Laws* (1782) and *To Sir Hercules Langrishe* (1792) are evidence.

Re-entering the Commons in 1781 as member for Malton, Burke rose to become Paymaster of the Forces (his highest public office) in 1782. Thereafter, two of his chief interests were to be the emancipation of British India and the abolition of the slave trade. In the former matter he became an expert authority, supporting Fox's Bill for reforming the administration, and delivering a celebrated speech in 1785 'On the Nabob of Arcot's Private Debts'. He was a formidable critic of Warren Hastings, the first Governor-General of India, who was impeached for corruption in 1788; Burke led the prosecution, but Hastings was acquitted after a trial lasting 145 days. Always an eloquent defender of the oppressed, Burke then supported William Wilberforce from 1788 to 1789 in his campaign against the slave trade.

In opposition to the principles behind the French Revolution of 1789, Burke published his most famous treatise, **Reflections on the Revolution in France** (1790), a forceful attack on the drastic action of the revolutionaries. He argued against the charge that his attitudes towards the French and the American Revolutions were inconsistent, publishing in 1791 *A Letter . . . to a Member of the National Assembly* and *An Appeal from the New to the Old Whigs*, further discussion of French revolutionary politics appearing in his *Thoughts on French Affairs* (1791), *Remarks on the Policy of the Allies* (1793) and *Letters on a Regicide Peace* (1795–7).

Dogged throughout his career by financial difficulties, Burke was even criticized when, on retiring from Parliament in 1794, he was awarded a pension. He defended himself against the Duke of Bedford and the Earl of Lauderdale with characteristic vigour in *A Letter to a Noble Lord*, in 1796. His published speeches and writings were collected in eight volumes between 1792 and 1827. Burke is remembered for the spirited manner in which he consistently defended the cause of civil justice, for his intellectual integrity and for the magnificent power of his rhetoric; he was a master of persuasive prose.

**Burke, Kenneth** 1897–1986 American critic. Born in Pittsburgh, Pennsylvania, Burke was educated at Columbia University. He wrote essays, short fiction and poetry before becoming the music critic of the *Dial* magazine and, later, **The Nation**. He is best known as a theorist of literary forms, whose studies also encompass history, rhetoric and philosophy. His most famous books, *A Grammar of Motives* (1945) and *A Rhetoric of Motives* (1950), are enquiries into

the ways all human activity is ordered in language.

Apart from his early fiction and poetry, Burke's first works were *Counter-Statement* (1931), *Permanence and Change* (1935), *Attitudes Toward History* (1937) and *The Philosophy of Literary Form* (1941). His fiction and poetry are collected in *The Complete White Oxen* (1968) and *Collected Poems, 1915–1967* (1968). *Towards a Better Life* (1932) is his only novel. His other books include *The Rhetoric of Religion* (1961), *Perspective by Incongruity* (1964), *Terms for Order* (1964) and *Language as Symbolic Action* (1966).

**burlesque** A kind of mockery found in all the arts, and in life too. In literature, a mocking, but not a bitter or contemptuous, imitation of some literary species or specific work or author. In its widest sense, then, it covers **mock-heroic**, travesty, and **parody**. But as the demands of critical precision often require a distinction within this usage, between high-burlesque (otherwise mock-heroic) and low-burlesque (otherwise travesty or burlesque), there seems good reason for following **Dryden** and Boileau, in restricting burlesque to cases where a high theme or subject is travestied by a low style (as in the 'Pyramus and Thisbe' episode in *A Midsummer Night's Dream*). Mock-heroic does the reverse, treating a low theme in a high style (as in **Pope**'s *Rape of the Lock*). Parody, then, is distinguished as the mockery of specific works or authors.

**Burnet, Gilbert** 1643–1715 Historian and divine. Of an Aberdeenshire family, Burnet was born in Edinburgh, but returned to Aberdeen for his education at Marischal College. He became Professor of Divinity at Glasgow University in 1669, and came to England in 1675 as chaplain to the Rolls Chapel, a position he held until 1684. Burnet was on familiar terms with Charles II and James, Duke of York, and was a well-known preacher. However, he offended Charles by remonstrating with him about his conduct and was dismissed in 1684. He went abroad in the following year, where he enjoyed the confidence of William of Orange and Mary, and sailed for England in 1688. He was rewarded with the bishopric of Salisbury (1689).

Burnet's chief works are his *The History of the Reformation of the Church of England*, published in three parts (1679, 1681 and 1714) and his *The History of My Own Times* (published posthumously, 1724–34). His *Reformation* was begun during the years of the 'Popish Plot', when English Catholics endured a reign of terror. *The History of My Own Times* is the work of a good storyteller; his style is conversational, anecdotal, and often prejudiced, but it makes valuable reading. Burnet's contributions to English literature began in history and biography with *The Memoires of the Lives and Actions of James and*

*William Dukes of Hamilton and Castleherald* (1677), constructed from documents and, in the French manner, held together by Burnet's narrative links.

The results of his conversations with the dying **Earl of Rochester**, *Some Passages in the Life and Death of the Right Honourable John Earl of Rochester*, appeared in 1680. *The Life and Death of Sir Matthew Hale* (1682) is a highly regarded short biography of the distinguished jurist. His admired translation of **More**'s *Utopia* was published in 1684. Burnet was a notable moderate and his *Exposition of the Thirty-Nine Articles* (1699) became a standard work in English divinity studies.

**Burnett, Frances (Eliza) Hodgson** 1849–1924 A novelist and children's writer, Burnett was born in Manchester, and moved to Tennessee in 1865. She established a popular reputation with her first publication, a sentimental novel entitled *That Lass o'Lowrie's* (1877), but she is most famous for her children's books: *Little Lord Fauntleroy* (1886), *The Little Princess* (1905) and *The Secret Garden* (1911). Her other works include *Editha's Burglar* (1888), *The White People* (1917), a novel about the supernatural, and *The One I Knew Best of All* (1893), an autobiography. She was also instrumental in establishing the legal precedent which gave American authors control over the English publication of their works.

**Burney, Fanny [Frances]** 1752–1840 Novelist and woman of letters. Daughter of the musician Dr Charles Burney, she was born in King's Lynn and seems to have largely educated herself. Her father was part of **Samuel Johnson**'s circle and she assumed a place in it by right. Her first novel, *Evelina, or, The History of a Young Lady's Entrance into the World* (1778), made her famous and her second, *Cecilia, or, Memoirs of an Heiress* (1782), confirmed her reputation. In 1786 she became Second Keeper of the Robes to Queen Charlotte. Her *Diary* vividly records how uncongenial she found the position; it was only with some difficulty that she obtained permission to retire in 1791.

She married a French refugee officer, General Alexandre Gabriel Jean-Baptiste d'Arblay, in 1793, and in 1796 published her third novel, *Camilla, or, A Picture of Youth*. D'Arblay, who had been adjutant general to Lafayette, returned to France with his English wife in 1802 and Fanny Burney lived there for 10 years, returning to England in 1812, where she published her last novel, *The Wanderer*, in 1814. She spent her time in Bath and, after her husband's death, in London, devoting much of her later career to editing *The Memoirs of Dr Burney*. Of the eight plays she wrote during her life only one, *Edwy and Elgiva*, was produced.

Fanny Burney. Portrait by E. F. Burney, c.1785. National Portrait Gallery, London.

Fanny Burney's diaries are not the least of her literary productions; the *Early Diary 1768–78* (1889) gives firsthand accounts of Johnson and **Garrick**, and her *Diary and Letters 1778–1840* (1842–6) includes the years at court. As a novelist, she inherited the form from **Richardson** and **Fielding** and handled it in a way that would prove useful to **Jane Austen**. Her strength lay in comedy and the comedy of domestic life, developed around innocent heroines like Evelina as they enter a sophisticated social world. 'To read Miss Burney', wrote **Walter Allen**, 'is rather like having a mouse's view of the world of cats: the cats are very terrifying, but the mouse's sense of the ridiculous could not be keener.'

**Burning Babe, The** **Robert Southwell**'s best-known poem was first printed in 1602. In it, the poet feels an unexpected warmth in winter and looks up to see a burning babe who explains to him the significance of his burning. The terms of the explanation spiritualize Petrarchan commonplaces of burning hearts and the sufferings of love with details of Christ's Passion. At the end of the poem the poet realizes that it is Christmas Day. This lyric was much admired by **Ben Jonson** who told **William Drummond** of Hawthornden that if he, Jonson, had written it, he would have been content to destroy many of his own.

**Burns, Robert** 1759–96 Scottish poet. Born the son of a small farmer, William Burnes (the poet was the first to adopt the more familiar spelling), he was brought up in circumstances of agricultural poverty and strict Calvinism. Educated by his father, Burns started work as a farm labourer but became a flax-dresser at the age of 22. On his father's death in 1784, he went into farming with his brother Gilbert at Mossgiel for four years, a period which saw the composition of some of his first verse, such as 'The Tun Dogs' and his unusual cantata *The Jolly Beggars*. It was a time, too, of apparent promiscuity, and Burns formed an attachment to Jean Armour, who became pregnant.

It was not until 1786 that Burns's poetry began to appear in print; this early, 'Kilmarnock' edition of *Poems Chiefly in the Scottish Dialect* contained many of the varied and entertaining pieces of his Mossgiel period, such as 'The Cotter's Saturday Night' and 'Halloween'. The volume brought him fame, and he went to Edinburgh, where the success of his poems led to a new edition being published by William Creech in 1787. Burns was lionized by the literati as an untutored rustic genius, but he disliked hypocrisy and never trusted in that brief fame. During this time he immortalized himself as a songwriter by contributing some hundreds of songs, new and reworked, to James Johnson's *The Scots Musical Museum* (1787–1803), including *Auld Lang Syne* and 'A Red, Red Rose'.

Robert Burns. A detail from the portrait by Alexander Nasmyth, 1787. National Portrait Gallery, London.

Having earned sufficient money to buy a small farm at Ellisland, Burns settled there with his erstwhile consort Jean, now his wife (in the intervening years a number of liaisons had given rise to some passionate verse, addressed to Alison Begbie and Mary Campbell). They led a hard life, had four children, and Burns became an excise man to supplement their meagre income. He developed a pronounced sympathy with the French revolutionary movement, which caused him to be regarded with some suspicion. At length, penury forced them to abandon the farm in 1792, and move to Dumfries where, apart from the 100 or so lyrics he contributed for George Thomson's *A Select Collection of Original Scottish Airs* (published 1793–1811), Burns wrote little of importance except his *Tam O'Shanter* and 'Captain Matthew Henderson'. He died in 1796, at the age of 37, his health undermined by rheumatic fever and a penchant for good living.

Although his origins were genuinely rustic, and he has become a cult figure as a ploughman poet, Burns was proud of his background and had taught himself to read widely among the English and French poets. In the tradition of **Allan Ramsay** and **Robert Fergusson**, whom he admired, he was also skilful in the Scots vernacular, many of his most celebrated lyrics working from the strong native material of Scottish folklore and daily life. His poems about animals are famous, and often anthropomorphic ('To a Mouse'); he also penned some vigorous satires on religion ('The Ordination' and *Holy Willie's Prayer*) and at least one narrative masterpiece, the late *Tam O'Shanter*. His rural poems dating from the late 1780s are consistently the best, with a unique blend of humour and sadness that have made him accepted as the Scottish national poet.

**Burroughs, Edgar Rice** 1875–1950 American popular novelist. Burroughs was educated at a military academy and served briefly in the US cavalry, but failed to find a successful career until he began to write for the pulp magazines in 1912, during which year he published the first of his many interplanetary fantasies (reprinted in 1917 as *A Princess of Mars*) and the first of many novels starring Tarzan, an English aristocrat raised in the African jungle by apes. He wrote extravagant and exotic adventure stories, which might be considered the ultimate daydreams. Tarzan remains his most enduring success, having some significance as a modern hero-myth despite the injury done to the character by many poor films. Burroughs's work deteriorated after 1925, thereafter consisting mainly of lack-lustre sequels, but his early books have an appealing escapist verve which overrides their essential silliness.

**Burroughs, William S[eward]** 1914– American novelist. Born in St Louis and educated at Harvard, Burroughs has spent much of his life in Paris and Tangier. Before leaving the USA he was friendly with **Jack Kerouac**, **Allen Ginsberg**, and the circle of writers later known as **The Beats**.

He wrote of his experience of heroin addiction in *Junkie* (1953), under the pseudonym of William Lee) and *Naked Lunch* (1959). The latter became notorious for its frank treatment of the life of the addict, and was banned on grounds of obscenity. Its bitter rendering not only of the horrors of addiction, but of the far-reaching cultural illusions for which addiction is a metaphor, has made it his most famous book. His subsequent work includes *The Exterminator* (1960, with Brion Gysin), *The Soft Machine* (1961), *The Ticket That Exploded* (1962), *The Yage Letters* (1963, a collection of letters with Allen Ginsberg), *Dead Fingers Talk* (1963), *Nova Express* (1964), *The Job* (1970, an interview), *The Wild Boys* (1971), *Exterminator!* (1973), *Port of Saints* (1973), *The Last Words of Dutch Schultz* (1975), *The Third Mind* (1978), *Ah Pook Is Here and Other Texts* (1979), *Blade Runner: A Movie* (1979), *With William Burroughs: A Report from the Bunker* (1981, interviews), *Cities of the Red Night* (1981), *Letters to Allen Ginsberg 1953–1957* (1982), *The Place of Dead Roads* (1983) and *Queer* (1984).

**Burton, Sir Richard (Francis)** 1821–90 Orientalist, traveller, diplomat and eccentric. He was born at Torquay and baptized at Elstree. His childhood was spent wandering France and Italy, where he became a collector of patois. Largely self-educated, he was wayward, original and brilliant. In 1840, he went up to Trinity College, Oxford, but was rusticated for his unconventional behaviour (which included challenging a fellow student who criticized his moustache to a duel). While at Oxford, Burton had started to study Arabic, without a tutor. A remarkable linguist, he is variously estimated to have mastered 35 languages, or 25 with their various dialects. In October 1842 he joined the Bombay Native Infantry as a subaltern, having worked in London at Hindustani. In India he mastered Gujarati and Marathi, as well as Persian. Appointed assistant in the Sind survey, he frequently mixed in disguise with the people, passing as a native. He contributed to government reports and on his return published four books on India. In 1853 he made the pilgrimage to Mecca, disguised as an Indian Pathan to account for any eccentricities of speech, and relying throughout on his intimate acquaintance with Eastern customs and etiquette. Although he was not the first Englishman to achieve this feat, Burton became famous as a result. The following year he explored the Somali desert,

encountering considerable dangers. The Foreign Office commissioned him to search for the sources of the Nile and in February 1858, along with Speke, he discovered Lake Tanganyika. Burton was the first Englishman to explore Somaliland, the first to discover the central African great lakes, and among the first to reach Mecca. Three years later he explored West Africa. In 1861 he entered the Foreign Office as consul, service which produced numerous further books. His most famous literary work, however, is his translation of *The Arabian Nights* (1885–8) which demonstrates his knowledge of high and low styles in Arabic, and the characteristic speech of all classes. For the last 14 years of his life he worked on a translation of *The Perfumed Garden*, but his widow, who had suffered from his drunkenness and frequent absences, chose to burn it after his death. As a memorial, she built an Arab tent in stone and marble at Mortlake, and set up the 'Burton Memorial Lecture Fund', inaugurated in 1921.

**Burton, Robert** 1577–1640 Author of *The Anatomy of Melancholy* (1621). Born at Lindley in Leicestershire, he was educated at Nuneaton and Sutton Coldfield, then at Brasenose College, Oxford. He was elected a student (i.e. a fellow) of Christ Church in 1599 and remained there for the rest of his life, becoming vicar of St Thomas's, Oxford, and later rector of Seagrave in his home county. *The Anatomy of Melancholy*, much admired by subsequent writers for its curious and colourful mixture of psychological speculation and allusive learning, was his only book. Little more is known of Burton beyond the occasional facts he let drop in the splendidly digressive course of his *Anatomy* and these brief (and perhaps unreliable) remarks by Bishop Kennett in his *Register and Chronicle* (1728): 'The Author is said to have labour'd long in the Writing of this Book to suppress his own Melancholy, and yet did but improve it . . . In an interval of Vapours he would be extremely pleasant, and raise Laughter in any Company. Yet I have heard that nothing at last could make him laugh, but going down to the Bridge-foot in *Oxford*, and hearing the Barge-men scold and storm and swear at one another, at which he would set his Hands to his Sides, and laugh most profusely: Yet in his College and Chamber so mute and mopish that he was suspected to be *Felo de se.*'

***Bussy D'Ambois*** A tragedy by **George Chapman**, written for performance by a **boys' company** in 1604 and published in 1607. Its hero has earned comparison with **Marlowe**'s Tamburlaine. He is based on the historical figure of Louis de Clermont Bussy-d'Amboise, favourite of the Duc d'Alençon, brother of the French king Henry III.

Bussy D'Ambois is introduced to the court as

the protégé of Monsieur (Alençon) and proves himself courageous but insolent. In a quarrel he is forced to defend himself against three courtiers, and kills them; he also quarrels with the Duc de Guise. Monsieur is in love with the Countess of Montsurry (Monsoreau) but she favours Bussy D'Ambois. Giving way to jealousy, Monsieur tells Montsurry that his wife has dishonoured him, and the Count tortures his wife into sending a letter of summons to her lover. He is overpowered and murdered on his arrival.

**Butler, Joseph** 1692–1752 Divine. Born at Wantage in Berkshire, the son of Presbyterian parents, he attended the Dissenting Academy at Tewkesbury. He abandoned Presbyterianism and entered Oriel College, Oxford, in 1714; he was ordained at Salisbury in 1718 and appointed Clerk of the Closet to Queen Caroline in 1736. He became Bishop of Bristol in 1738 and of Durham in 1750.

Butler published *Fifteen Sermons* in 1726. These were delivered while he was preacher at the Rolls Chapel (1718–26) and gained him a reputation as an exponent of natural theology and ethics. Butler's most famous work, *The Analogy of Religion, Natural and Revealed, to the Constitution and Course of Nature* (1736), is a defence of Christianity against the 'natural' religion of **Deism**.

**Butler, Samuel** 1612–80 Satirist. Born the son of a farmer at Strensham in Worcestershire, he was educated at King's School, Worcester, and served in the household of Elizabeth, Countess of Kent, where he met **John Selden**. Butler seems subsequently to have served as secretary to various gentlemen, becoming steward to the Earl of Carbery by 1661. His fame rests on the long burlesque poem **Hudibras**, the first part of which appeared in 1663, the second in 1664 and the third in 1678. Charles II liked it and granted him a pension; Butler also became secretary to the Duke of Buckingham in 1670, accompanied him to France, and may have assisted in the composition of his topical satirical play, *The Rehearsal*. He is reputed, however, to have died penniless, and is buried in Westminster Abbey.

Butler's other works include numerous prose 'characters', epigrammatic 'thoughts' and various verses, the most accomplished of which is his poem *The Elephant in the Moon*, a satire on Sir Paul Neale (of the Royal Society) that concerns a mouse which gets into a telescope. It was printed, along with much of the writing unpublished during his life, in Robert Thyer's collected edition of 1759, *The Genuine Remains in Verse and Prose of Mr Samuel Butler*.

**Butler, Samuel** 1835–1902 Novelist, satirical poet, painter, art critic, amateur scientist and philosopher. Butler, a clergyman's son, was born at Langar Rectory, Nottinghamshire, and educated at Shrewsbury where his grandfather, later a bishop, had been headmaster. The misery of his childhood can be gauged by a *Notebook* jotting on Melchizidech: 'He was a really happy man. He was without father, without mother, and without descent. He was an incarnate bachelor. He was a born orphan.' After attending St John's College, Cambridge, Butler rejected his father's wish that he take holy orders, alleging doubts as to the efficacy of baptism. Instead he emigrated to New Zealand and became a successful sheep-farmer. This period also saw his first publication, *A First Year in Canterbury Settlement* (1863), and the composition of an anonymous pamphlet, *The Evidence for the Resurrection of Jesus Christ as Given by the Four Evangelists Critically Examined* (1865), which was to become the core of *Fair Haven* (1873), a mock defence of miracles, whose satire was so veiled that some orthodox readers missed the joke entirely.

Returning home in 1865, Butler could now afford to embark on the painting career his family had so strongly disapproved. At Heatherley's Art School Butler won for himself the nickname of 'the incarnate bachelor'. Although he struggled to find other emotionally satisfying friendships he remained sharply critical of family ties. For seven years he continued to paint, exhibiting at the Royal Academy, and later turned art critic in *Alps and Sanctuaries* (1881) and *Ex Voto* (1888), written during prolonged visits to Italy.

Unsuccessful investments necessitated a journey to Canada in 1874–5, where Butler found the material for the satirical poem 'A Psalm of Montreal' (1878) and started *Life and Habit* (1877), the first of a series of works, which included *Evolution Old and New* (1879), *Unconscious Memory* (1880), *Luck or Cunning* (1886), to pursue his critical debate with **Darwin**'s theory of evolution. Butler's contention, later applauded by **G. B. Shaw** in his preface to **Back to Methuselah** (1921), was that where variation occurred in the reproductive chain this was not a matter of random chance but a product of the 'Life Force' working through heredity and memory, conscious and unconscious, toward the breeding of the highest form of 'Continuous Personality'.

Butler's eclectic interests and unfocused talent, best displayed in the *Notebooks* (1912), next surfaced in the field of music. In collaboration with his closest friend H. Festing Jones, he composed Handelian pieces and a comic oratorio, *Narcissus* (1888). Two further areas of study produced *The Authoress of the 'Odyssey'* (1897), in which Butler argued that internal evidence proclaimed a female author, and *Shakespeare's Sonnets Reconsidered* (1899), in which Butler represented the recipient of the sonnets as a plebeian lover.

Butler's habits of obsessively revisiting his past life and reworking his literary material emerge most clearly in *Erewhon Revisited* (1899), a sequel to *Erewhon* (1872), and his most influential work, the posthumously published, semi-autobiographical novel, *The Way of All Flesh* (1903).

**Byars, Betsy (Cromer)** 1928– American children's author. Born in Charlotte, North Carolina, and educated at Queen's College, Betsy Byars began writing as her own family was growing up. Following the success of *The Summer of the Swans* (1970) she established herself as a prolific novelist with a strong line in racy humour allied to realistic dialogue. Each novel is seen from a child's point of view and takes up some of children's typically urgent concerns, such as fear of bullying, feelings of rejection or worries about parents' marriages. In her most famous novel, *The Summer of the Eighteenth Emergency* (1973), a bright pupil named Benjie deals with the repercussions of making one joke too many at the expense of a slow, thuggish classmate.

**Byatt, A[ntonia] S[usan]** 1936– Novelist and critic. Like her sister, **Margaret Drabble**, she was educated in York and at Newnham College, Cambridge. She lectured at the Central School of Art and Design and then became lecturer in English and American Literature at University College, London. Besides a critical study of **Wordsworth** and **Coleridge** and a monograph on **Iris Murdoch**, Byatt is the author of four novels, the best known of which, *The Virgin in the Garden* (1978) and *Still-Life* (1985), are the first two parts of a projected sequence tracing English life from the mid-1950s to the present day. Both novels are densely peopled, intricately detailed, unafraid of literary allusion or lengthy dissertation on ideas of art and perception, and anticipate a complete series offering an accurate, pensive account of contemporary middle-class English society. *Sugar* (1987), a collection of short stories on the theme of repetition, shows the weight of family history, tradition and literature recurring over several generations.

**Byrd, William** 1674–1744 American diarist and travel-writer. Throughout his life he lived for long periods in England as well as in Virginia, where he served in various public offices, including, from 1709 to his death, on the Royal Council of Virginia.

Byrd's writings, though not published during his lifetime, provide a vivid picture of his milieu, as well as a satiric commentary on some of his experiences. His journal was discovered in the 20th century, and two portions were published as *The Secret Diary of William Byrd of Westover 1709–1712* (1941) and *Another Secret Diary 1739–1741* (1942). He also wrote important narratives of American travel and exploration. The most famous of these, *The History of the Dividing Line*, is his reworking of the journal he kept while serving on a surveying commission in 1728 to determine the boundary between Virginia and North Carolina. It includes a history of Virginia, satiric digs at North Carolinians, observations on the countryside and Indians, and humorous anecdotes from the surveying expedition. *The Secret History of the Dividing Line*, probably an earlier version, is shorter, and its humour more racy. *A Progress to the Mines in the Year 1732* and *A Journey to the Land of Eden in the Year 1733* are also travel accounts, probably reworked from his journals of the late 1730s.

**Byrom, John** 1692–1763 Poet. A native of Cheshire, he received his early education at Chester and later went to Merchant Taylors' School. At Cambridge he became a fellow of Trinity College, though he lived chiefly in Manchester. He is remembered best for the hymn 'Christians Awake', and for the epigram on King and Pretender showing his Jacobite sympathies: 'But who Pretender is, or who is King,/God bless us all – that's quite another thing.' Byrom studied medicine in Montpellier but never practised. He taught shorthand in Manchester and wrote a quantity of religious verse that is now forgotten, and a pastoral in anapaests (1714). *The Private Journal and Literary Remains of John Byrom* (first published 1854–7) is an important source of information on **William Law**, whom he admired.

**Byron, George Gordon, Lord (6th Baron)** 1788–1824 Poet. He was born in London, the son of Catherine Gordon, a Scottish heiress descended from James I of Scotland, and Captain 'Mad Jack' Byron, a profligate who squandered his wife's money as well as his own. Soon after his son's birth Captain Byron fled from his creditors to France, and Catherine took her son to her home in Aberdeenshire, where they lived in straitened circumstances. Byron's father died when he was three, and the boy was educated at home and later at Aberdeen Grammar School. Scottish scenery and Scottish Calvinism both left their mark on his character.

In 1798 Byron's great-uncle William, the 5th Baron Byron, died, leaving the 10-year-old boy the barony and the family home at Newstead Abbey in Nottinghamshire but very little fortune. He went to Harrow in 1810 and his first poems were written while a pupil there. In 1805 Byron proceeded to Trinity College, Cambridge, where he cultivated a reputation for

Byron in Albanian costume. A detail from the portrait by T. Phillips, 1813. National Portrait Gallery, London.

high-spirited and profligate behaviour that belied the real achievements of his undergraduate years. In January 1807 he published a small volume of verse, *Fugitive Pieces*. A friend advised him that some of the contents were too sensual and Byron destroyed most of the printing; only four copies have survived. The revised volume was published the same year; 'miraculously chaste' was how he described his *Poems on Various Occasions* (1807), which contained 12 new pieces. With remarkable speed Byron published *Hours of Idleness* the same March, a collection of lyrics more distinguished than any of his previous work.

In January 1808 a notice of *Hours of Idleness* appeared in **The Edinburgh Review**, savaging his work and scorning his pretensions. On the title-page Byron had mentioned his minority and the reviewer, **Henry Brougham**, was at pains to point out that this was no excuse for bad verse. Byron responded by revising and extending *British Bards*, a satirical poem he had written, as *English Bards and Scotch Reviewers* (1809). It attacked **Southey**, **Coleridge**, **Wordsworth** and **Scott**, though he was later generous in admitting the hastiness of his judgements. Soon after the publication of *English Bards* Byron came of age and took his seat in the House of Lords; then he left on a tour of the Mediterranean in June 1809 with his friend from Cambridge, John Cam Hobhouse, whose expenses he paid.

Byron's letters from Spain, Portugal and the eastern Mediterranean are remarkably vivid. His *Hints from Horace* was published in 1811, and after visiting the tyrant of Ioannina, Ali Pasha, he began work on another poem; at the same time he encouraged Hobhouse, who was writing his *Journey through Albania*.

After returning to England Byron completed the first two cantos of the poem begun in Albania. *Childe Harold's Pilgrimage* (1812) made him not just a celebrity but the most sought-after figure in English society. Between then and the uproar of 1816 he published *The Curse of Minerva* (1812), *The Giaour* and **The Bride of Abydos** (1813), **The Corsair**, *Lara* and *Jacqueline* (1814), *Hebrew Melodies* (1815), and *The Siege of Corinth* and *Parisina* (1816).

In 1815 Byron married Annabella (Anne Isabella) Milbanke. The unimaginative Annabella was scarcely an ideal wife for the poet, nor he an ideal husband, and their marriage lasted little more than a year. After the birth of their daughter in December 1815 she left him and obtained a separation. The English public was seized with 'one of its periodical fits of morality', as **Macaulay** put it, and, without knowledge of the facts, supported Lady Byron. He left England on 25 April 1816 and never returned.

After sailing up the Rhine to Switzerland Byron joined **Mary Shelley** and **Percy Shelley**. The third canto of *Childe Harold* and *The Prisoner of Chillon* were written in 1816. In January 1817 Mary Shelley's stepsister, Claire Clairmont, bore Byron a daughter who was named Allegra. The liaison continued throughout the year, and Byron agreed to be responsible for supporting Claire and Allegra, but he did not pretend any real attachment. When the Shelley household returned to England in 1817, Byron continued to Venice.

To this period belong *The Lament of Tasso* (1817), **Manfred** (1817), the fourth canto of *Childe Harold* (1818), **Beppo** (1818), **Mazeppa** (1819) and the first cantos of **Don Juan**. His connection with Teresa, Countess Guiccioli, whose home was in Ravenna, began in Venice in April 1819 and proved a lasting one. Byron moved to Ravenna in December of the same year. He remained, meanwhile, in close touch with England despite his exile. Letters to and from friends – his publisher **John Murray**, Hobhouse, Scott, **Thomas Moore** and others – were important to him and he was an avid reader of the English literary reviews. Of the friends who visited him in Venice, Moore wrote a vivid account of Byron's domestic life at this time. Teresa inspired *The Prophecy of Dante* (1821), chiefly by interesting him in the cause of Italian nationalism. At Ravenna Byron wrote another dramatic poem, this time on a Venetian subject, **Marino Faliero** (1821). Two more dramatic poems appeared the same year, *Sardanapalus* and *The Two Foscari*, in a single volume which also included *Cain*; he also wrote more of *Don Juan* and *Heaven and Earth* (1821). His reputation had by now spread beyond England and Byron was famous throughout Europe. After reading *Manfred*, Goethe started a correspondence with the younger poet; *Sardanapalus* is dedicated to Goethe and Byron was honoured in the second part of *Faust*, where he appears as Euphorion, the child of Faust and Helen.

Teresa Guiccioli obtained a separation from her husband and moved to the house of her brother Pietro, Count Gamba. She and Byron, now 15 miles from Ravenna, became more closely involved with the Carbonari, a militant nationalist movement of which Count Gamba was a leader. Byron was a ready adherent and supported it with his money and influence. However, the Carbonari foundered and the Gamba property was confiscated; they fled to Pisa and set up house in the Palazzo Lanfranchi in autumn 1821. Byron found Shelley living in the same city and also made the acquaintance of **Edward Trelawny**, who later wrote a memoir of both poets.

In 1822 the literary quarrel with Southey, begun by a hostile article the older poet contributed to *Blackwood's Magazine* in August 1819, reached a head. Byron had replied in *Some Observations* (1820), accusing the Poet Laureate of slander and apostasy. The next year Southey published *A Vision of Judgement*, and prefaced it with an ill-considered, almost hysterical attack on *Don Juan* and its author as the founder of 'the Satanic school'. Byron's answer was to satirize, with devastating ease, Southey's encomium on the passing of George III in *The Vision of Judgement*, published in **Leigh Hunt's** magazine *The Liberal* in 1822. Charges were brought against the publisher for 'calumniating the late King and wounding the feelings of his present Majesty'. The same year brought Byron news of the death of his daughter Allegra, and saw the departure of the Shelleys and Trelawny for Spezia in May. Byron and the Gambas went to Leghorn, and two months later Shelley was drowned in the Bay of Spezia. After moving on to Genoa, Byron resumed work on *Don Juan*, a new part of which was completed in March 1823. The domestic tragedy *Werner*, the verse tale *The Island* and the satirical poem *The Age of Bronze* were also published in 1823. *The Deformed Transformed*, Byron's unfinished drama, followed in 1824.

The end of the Carbonari and of Italian aspirations to independence from their Austrian overlords in 1821 saw Byron embracing another cause – one perhaps closer to his heart and dating back to his travels in the eastern Mediterranean (1810–11). His interest was apparent in *Childe Harold* and *Don Juan*, and the new cause took on reality in 1821. Greek liberation from centuries of Turkish oppression found a sympathetic response in England and a committee was formed to organize aid. The committee asked Byron, probably the most famous Englishman in Europe, to help; without hesitation he turned all his energies to aiding the Greeks. He armed a brig, the *Hercules*, and set sail from Leghorn with Trelawny and Gamba on 24 July 1823. He reached Cephalonia 10 days later. The factional quarrels which had plagued the Greek rebels dissolved, and some even hinted that he could become king of a free Greece. Byron worked ceaselessly and in January 1824 joined Alexander Mavrocordato (to whom Shelley dedicated his *Hellas*) at Missolonghi on the north shore of the Gulf of Patras. The Greek leader had brought a fleet of ships, and Byron's plan was to attack the Turkish stronghold at Lepanto. But in April he caught a severe chill after being soaked to the skin in an open boat. Rheumatic fever set in and Byron died on 19 April 1824. The Greeks wished to bury him in Athens, but only his heart stayed in Greece. His body was returned to England but refused burial in Westminster Abbey. He was buried in the family vault in the church of Hucknall Torkard, near Newstead Abbey in Nottinghamshire.

**Tennyson**, a boy of 14 when he heard the news of Byron's death, said 'the whole world darkened to me'; on a rock near his home in Somersby he inscribed the words 'Byron is dead'. He spoke for his generation, and indeed for several generations who would labour admiringly or uneasily in the shadow of the legend Byron had left. It was Byron's achievement, as much by his life as his poetry, to organize the new feelings of Romanticism into a stance, a style that the wider public could easily recognize and secretly admire even while publicly condemning it. He bequeathed to posterity the image of the Byronic hero, a Childe Harold or Cain or Manfred, an outcast from his own kind and a wanderer in foreign lands, gloomily absorbed in the memory of his past sins and the injustices done him by society. Like all satisfying legends, it was no less powerful for bearing only a partial resemblance to the man and the poet who inspired it. In personal life, Byron was practical and resilient, fully engaged in the social and political affairs of the world about him. In poetry, he found his characteristic voice not in *Childe Harold* but in mature works like *The Vision of Judgement* and *Don Juan*, where he presents himself as the poised and urbane satirist – heir to the Augustan tradition of **Dryden** and **Pope**.

**Byron, Henry James** 1834–84 English dramatist who made a notable contribution to the development of the peculiarly British style of **pantomime** (Buttons and Widow Twankey are his inventions). Byron's contemporary reputation rested on his prodigiously punning burlesques, written for the Strand and Adelphi Theatres in London between 1857 and 1865. Among the most popular of these were *The Maid and the Magpie* (1858), *Blue Beard from a New Point of Hue* (1860) and *Ali Baba, or, The Thirty-Nine Thieves* (1863). *The Lancashire Lass* (1867) is an unabashed melodrama of the kind Byron delighted to burlesque and *Our Boys* (1875), an accomplished comedy, broke all records with its four-year run at the Vaudeville Theatre.

**Byron, Robert** 1905–41 Travel-writer and journalist. Born at Wembley, he was educated at Eton and Merton College, Oxford. He travelled extensively in Greece, India, Tibet, Afghanistan, Persia, Russia, China and Egypt, and his books, largely the result of these travels, are enthusiastic appreciations of the ancient world. They include *The Byzantine Achievement* (1929), *An Essay on India* (1931) and *The Road to Oxiana* (1937). The last, widely considered his best work, pursues the origins of Islamic architecture and culture from Venice to India. Byron was killed during World War II when his ship was torpedoed.

# C

**Cabell, James Branch** 1879–1958 American novelist. Born in Richmond, Virginia, Cabell is best known for his creation of the mythical French province Poictesme, whose 'history' from 1234 to 1750 he chronicled in a series of allegorical novels which comment obliquely on American life. He went into great detail about the life, customs and liberal morality of the people of Poictesme, and one novel in the series, *Jurgen* (1919), was suppressed as being immoral. The case stirred public curiosity, and Cabell enjoyed a large popular following in the 1920s. He published his first novel, *The Eagle's Shadow*, in 1904. *The Soul of Melicent*, the first in the Poictesme series, appeared in 1913; the last, *Straws and Prayer-Books*, in 1924. He also wrote poetry and non-fiction throughout his career.

**Cable, George Washington** 1844–1925 American novelist and short-story writer. Born in New Orleans, Cable served in the Mississippi Cavalry during the Civil War, and then worked as a surveyor, as a reporter and columnist for the New Orleans *Picayune* (using the pseudonym 'Drop Shot'), and as an accountant and clerk. Though he contributed stories of Louisiana life to *Scribner's Monthly* and *Appleton's Journal* between 1873 and 1879, he did not take up writing as a career until the later date. From 1885 he made annual reading tours of the USA.

One of the leading local-colour writers of the 'New South', Cable produced 18 volumes of fiction between 1879 and 1918. The best of these are generally thought to be the collection of short stories entitled *Old Creole Days* (1879) and the novels *The Grandissimes* (1880) and *Madame Delphine* (1881). He moved to Northampton, Massachusetts, in 1885 and several of his novels – *Dr Sevier* (1884), *Bonaventure* (1888), *John March, Southerner* (1894) and *Bylow Hill* (1902) – treat the collision between Northern and Southern manners and morals. He also wrote a history, *The Creoles of Louisiana* (1884), and a treatise advocating reforms for the improvement of the lives of blacks, *The Silent South* (1885). It was because of the offence these books caused to some of his Southern neighbours that Cable moved to the North.

*Cadenus and Vanessa* A poem by **Jonathan Swift**, written in 1713. Vanessa was Esther Vanhomrigh and Cadenus (an anagram of *decanus* or dean) was Dean Swift. Vanessa fell in love with Swift but he did not return her passion, though he treated her with respect and honoured her with his esteem. The poem gives an equivocal account of their relationship in mock-classical form. Esther Vanhomrigh preserved the poem and it was published in 1726.

**Caedmon** *fl.* 670–80 All that is known of Caedmon is what **Bede** relates in Book 4 of his *Historia Ecclesiastica*: that he was a herdsman ignorant of poetry and unable to sing until one night he was inspired in a dream. On waking he retained his new talent and was advised by Abbess Hild to become a monk. He joined the abbey at Whitby during her rule (657–80), and

The Creation of Light, from the so-called Caedmon Manuscript in the Bodleian Library, Oxford (*MS Junius XI, f.81*). The manuscript, *c.* AD1000, consists of verse paraphrases from Old Testament stories, once believed to be the work of Caedmon.

wrote more hymns. Only the first hymn, nine lines in praise of God the Creator, can be attributed to him with any certainty, though in the past other works have been ascribed to him. Bede seems to imply that Caedmon was the first to write hymns in Old English, but this is not universally accepted.

**caesura** In Greek or Latin prosody, the division of a metrical foot between two words, usually toward the middle of the line. In English, it denotes the natural pause or breathing-space occurring almost anywhere in the line, though most often near the middle, as in these lines from **Shakespeare**'s Sonnet 73:

> This thou perceiv'st, ‖ which makes thy love
>    more strong,
> To love that well ‖ which thou must leave ere
>    long.

**Cahan, Abraham** 1860–1951 American novelist. Having emigrated to the USA from Russia, in 1897 Cahan founded the *Jewish Daily Forward*, a pioneering Jewish newspaper in New York. He had just published his first novel, *Yekl: A Tale of the New York Ghetto* (1896), which had won the enthusiastic support of **William Dean Howells**. Its realistic treatment of the experience of Jewish immigrants became the hallmark of Cahan's work. *The Imported Bridegroom and Other Stories of the New York Ghetto* (1898) further established him as a leader in Jewish American fiction, a position exemplified by his best-known work, *The Rise of David Levinsky* (1917), which portrays a rich but dissatisfied garment manufacturer looking back at his rise from poverty in Russia and in the New York ghetto.

**Cain** A play in three acts, called by its author, **Lord Byron**, 'A Mystery', 'according to the former Christian custom, and in honour of what it probably will remain to the reader'. As with most of his plays, Byron insisted that *Cain* was not for the stage. Its publication (1821) produced a storm of abuse. It was widely considered blasphemous, partly because of Byron's readiness to deploy Cuvier's arguments on the creation of the earth and partly because he so obviously preferred Cain to Abel.

*Cain* follows its hero's rebellion against the post-lapsarian life of toil, his turning to Lucifer to find out more than God will reveal, his journey through the Universe under the guidance of Lucifer, his killing of Abel and the remorse and exile that is the murder's consequence.

**Cain, James M[allahan]** 1892–1977 An American journalist and screenwriter, Cain was also a popular novelist and a prominent member of the 'tough-guy' school – a later manifestation of the uncompromising naturalism of such writers as **Frank Norris** and **Theodore Dreiser**. Born in Annapolis, Maryland, Cain worked as a coal miner, as a teacher, and as a reporter before serving in France as a private in World War I. In 1924 he began to write editorials for the New York *World* under the supervision of **Walter Lippmann**. In 1931 he became managing editor of *The New Yorker*, a position he held for 10 months, and then moved to Hollywood, where he remained for 17 years writing scripts for motion pictures, as well as articles, syndicated columns and several novels.

*The Postman Always Rings Twice* (1934) was adapted for the stage in 1936 and became a movie in 1946. It is the story of Frank Chambers and Cora Papadakis, lovers who murder Cora's wealthy husband for money, making his death look like an accident. Cora then dies in a car crash, and ironically Frank is convicted of murder for her truly accidental death. In *Double Indemnity* (serialized in *Liberty* in 1936, and made into a movie in 1943), an unmarried man and a married woman again plan and execute the husband's 'accidental' death, in this case for insurance money. Cain's other novels include *Serenade* (1937), *Career in C Major* (1938), *The Embezzler* (1940), *Mildred Pierce* (1941), *Love's Lovely Counterfeit* (1942), *The Butterfly* (1947) and *The Root of His Evil* (1951). *Past All Dishonor* (1946) and *Mignon* (1962) are historical novels set during the period following the Civil War.

**Caine, (Sir Thomas Henry) Hall** 1853–1931 Novelist. He was born at Runcorn in Cheshire, the son of a Manx blacksmith. He became a trusted friend of **Dante Gabriel Rossetti** in the last years of the older man's life, and was with him at his death in 1882. His *Recollections of Rossetti* was published the same year. Caine's melodramatic novels, very popular in their day but soon forgotten, include *The Shadow of a Crime* (1885), *The Deemster* (1887), *The Bondman* (1890), *The Scapegoat* (1891), *The Manxman* (1894), *The Prodigal Son* (1904) and *The Woman Thou Gavest Me* (1913). *My Story* (1908) gives an account of his early literary career.

**Caird, Edward** 1835–1908 Scottish philosopher. Born at Greenock, he was educated at Greenock Academy, the Universities of Glasgow and St Andrews, and Balliol College, Oxford, where his tutor was **Benjamin Jowett**. He became fellow and tutor of Merton College and, in 1866, Professor of Moral Philosophy at Glasgow. He succeeded Jowett as Master of Balliol in 1893. He published *The Philosophy of Kant* (1878), *The Critical Philosophy of Kant* (1899), a monograph on Hegel (1883) and *The Religious and Social Philosophy of Comte* (1885).

*The Evolution of Religion* (1893) is based on his Gifford lectures.

**Caird, John** 1820–98 Scottish divine and theologian, elder brother of **Edward Caird**. He became a minister of the Church of Scotland in 1845, Professor of Divinity at Glasgow University in 1862 and Principal in 1873. *An Introduction to the Philosophy of Religion* (1880) seeks to demonstrate the rationality of religion.

**Caldecott, Randolph** 1846–86 Children's illustrator. The son of an accountant, he first worked in a bank before resigning to become an artist. His success in illustrating **Washington Irving**'s *Old Christmas* (1876) prompted Edmund Evans, the eminent printer and engraver who had previously engaged **Walter Crane**, to invite him to illustrate a series of picture-books. Caldecott's illustrations for **William Cowper**'s *John Gilpin* (1876) and *The House that Jack Built* (1878), combining lively action with infectious good humour, soon made his reputation. Other famous commissions to follow included **Oliver Goldsmith**'s *Elegy on a Mad Dog* (1879), *Sing a Song of Sixpence* (1880), *The Fox Jumps Over the Parson's Gate* (1883) and **Samuel Foote**'s *The Great Panjandrum* (1885). Following this last work Caldecott travelled to America for health reasons, only to die soon afterwards of rheumatic fever. Many of his works are still in print, popular not just because of his nostalgic evocation of former rural life but also because of his ingenious ways of commenting on and generally expanding a text, with one line of verse sometimes made to stretch out over a number of pages. It was entirely fitting that the Caldecott Medal, awarded annually to the artist of the most distinguished American picture-book, should take its name from so brilliant and lively an illustrator.

**Caldwell, Erskine** 1903–87 American novelist and short-story writer, born in Georgia, and best known for his portrayal of the experiences of poor whites and blacks in the rural deep South. *Tobacco Road* (1932), the novel which first brought him to prominence, is about a family of white sharecroppers driven to desperate and degenerate acts by the oppression of a changing economic system. It was successfully dramatized by Jack Kirkland in 1933 and ran for over 3000 consecutive Broadway performances. In the same year Caldwell published his second novel, *God's Little Acre*, which consolidated his reputation. *Journeyman* (1935), *Trouble in July* (1940), *A House in the Uplands* (1946), and *Jenny by Nature* (1961) are among his many other novels with Southern settings. He also wrote numerous short stories; collections include *American Earth* (1930), *Jackpot* (1940), and *The Courting of Susie Brown* (1952). Among his works of non-fiction is the documentary study of Southern sharecroppers, *You Have Seen Their Faces* (1937). *All Out On the Road to Smolensk* (1942) is Caldwell's personal account of his work as a war correspondent in Russia. *Call It Experience* (1951) is his literary autobiography. The essays collected in *Around About America* (1964) and *Afternoons in Mid-America* (1976) tell of his travels throughout the USA.

*Caleb Williams, Things as They Are, or, The Adventures of* A novel by **William Godwin**, first published in 1794. As the alternative title indicates, Godwin intended the book as a radical critique of an unjust social system, but he went beyond his merely polemical purpose by his effective use of the conventions associated with **Gothic fiction**.

The story is told by Caleb Williams, the self-educated son of humble parents who has risen to become secretary to the polished and accomplished local squire, Falkland. Out of admiration for his master, and concern for the man's recurrent fits of melancholy, he begins to enquire into Falkland's past. He learns of the violent behaviour of a neighbouring squire, Tyrrel, who humiliated Falkland publicly and was later found murdered. Hawkins and his son, tenants whom Tyrrel had ruined, were tried and hanged for the crime. But Caleb discovers that Falkland is the murderer. Falkland becomes aware of Caleb's knowledge, falsely accuses him of theft and uses his influence to have him imprisoned. Caleb escapes and goes into hiding. Hunted from place to place, he at last confronts Falkland and accuses him of his crimes. Though he has no proof, the strength of Caleb's manner makes Falkland confess. He collapses and dies, leaving Caleb to feel not triumphant but guilty at what he has done to his master.

*Calendar of Modern Letters, The* A monthly literary journal published from 1925 to 1927. The *Calendar* was edited by **Edgell Rickword**, Douglas Garman and Bertram Higgins, and published poems, fiction and essays by **E. M. Forster**, **Robert Graves**, **D. H. Lawrence**, **Wyndham Lewis** and **Edwin Muir**. It questioned the reputations of several established writers – **J. M. Barrie**, **John Galsworthy** and **Rudyard Kipling**, among others – in its celebrated 'Scrutinies' (some of them published after the *Calendar*'s closure in *Scrutinies by Various Writers*, 2 vols., 1928 and 1931) and inspired the founders of *Scrutiny*, including **F. R. Leavis**, who edited *Towards Standards of Criticism: Selections from the Calendar of Modern Letters* (1933).

*Caliban Upon Setebos, or, Natural Theology in the Island* A **dramatic monologue** by **Robert Browning**, published in *Dramatis Personae*

(1864). Browning borrowed the character of Caliban from **Shakespeare**'s *The Tempest*. The 'natural theology' is Caliban's primitive speculation about the character of his God, Setebos, and allows the poet to glance obliquely at several strands of religious thought: stern Calvinism, the then fashionable **Higher Criticism** of the Bible and the contemporary debate about evolution.

**Calisher, Hortense** 1911– American novelist and short-story writer. Calisher was born in New York City and graduated from Barnard College in 1932. Her work is wide-ranging in subject and includes notable studies of family relationships and racial conflict. She began her career with short stories; her early collections include *In the Absence of Angels: Stories* (1952), *Tale for the Mirror: A Novella and Other Stories* (1963) and *Extreme Magic: A Novella and Other Stories* (1964). Her first novel, *False Entry*, was published in 1962, and was followed by *Textures of Life* (1963), *Journal from Ellipsia* (1965), *The Railway Police and The Last Trolley Ride* (1966), *The New Yorkers* (1969) and *Queenie* (1971). Her more recent work includes *Herself* (1972), *Standard Dreaming* (1972), *Eagle Eye* (1973), *The Collected Stories of Hortense Calisher* (1975), *On Keeping Women* (1977), *Mysteries of Motion* (1983) and *Saratoga Hot* (1985).

*Calisto and Melibea: A New Comedy in English in Manner of an Interlude* This early play was adapted from the Spanish by an unknown author and printed by John Rastell in 1530. The original was the *Celestina* of Fernando de Rojas, a novel written entirely in dialogue and obviously suitable for dramatization. It was translated again, with great success, by **James Mabbe** in 1631.

Calisto is a high-born young man who loves Melibea from the moment of first meeting her. She is deterred by the violence of his passion, and Calisto enlists the aid of Celestina, a bawd, to bring Melibea to his arms. Melibea is soon as violently in love as Calisto and Celestina is rewarded, only to be murdered by Calisto's servants, who steal the reward and are executed for their crime. Meanwhile Calisto and Melibea continue with their guilty love until Calisto, keeping a tryst in a tower, falls off a ladder and is killed. The broken-hearted Melibea leaps to her death. The play version is softened by the introduction of a moralizing ending, in which Melibea is persuaded by her father Danio to step no further into vice. He brings her to a timely repentance by telling her the details of a vision, in which the horrors of her avoidable damnation have been revealed to him.

*Call of the Wild, The* A novel by **Jack London**, published in 1903. Buck, the 'hero', is a dog who is kidnapped from his comfortable existence on a California estate, and sold into service as a sledge dog in the Klondike. He proves himself among the other dogs, but is brutally mistreated by a series of cruel masters before being rescued by John Thornton, a gold prospector who treats him with kindness. Fiercely loyal to Thornton, Buck performs several heroic exploits for him, most notably saving him from drowning and winning a wager by drawing a 1000-lb sledge. Later, he fends off an Indian attack during which Thornton is nevertheless killed. Masterless, but now at home in the Alaskan wilds, Buck abandons human civilization to become the leader of a wolf pack.

**Callaghan, Morley (Edward)** 1903–90 Canadian novelist and writer of short stories. Born in Toronto and educated at St Michael's College, University of Toronto, he studied law, but began to write seriously in 1923. As a reporter on the Toronto *Star* he met **Ernest Hemingway** who influenced his early work and encouraged him to publish his first novel, *Strange Fugitive* (1928). Other titles include *They Shall Inherit the Earth* (1935), *More Joy in Heaven* (1937), *The Loved and the Lost* (1951), *The Many-Coloured Coat* (1960) and *Close to the Sun Again* (1975). His distinctively spare prose is displayed to greatest advantage in the collections of short stories, *A Native Argosy* (1929), *No Man's Meat* (1931), *Now That April's Here* (1936) and *Morley Callaghan's Stories* (1959).

**Calverley, Charles Stuart** 1831–84 Poet and parodist. Born at Martley, Worcestershire, he went to school at Marlborough and Harrow. Calverley's practical jokes resulted in his being sent down from Balliol College, Oxford, and he finished his education at Christ's College, Cambridge, where he later became a fellow. He was called to the Bar in 1865 but a severe accident, sustained while skating, disabled him for the rest of his life. He made a reputation as a translator from Greek and Latin, publishing, among other volumes, *Theocritus Translated into English Verse* (1869). But he was best known for the parodies of poets such as **Tennyson**, **Browning** and **Jean Ingelow** which appeared in *Fly Leaves* (1872).

*Cambises, King of Persia* The long title page of the 1569 edition of this play by **Thomas Preston** describes it as a 'lamentable tragedy mixed full of mirth'. It also contains a table showing how eight actors can play all the 38 parts. For the main plot, Preston has drawn on the racy account of Cambises' reign in Book Three of Herodotus' *Histories*. The Cambises of Herodotus is as erratic as he is vengeful, drawn Tamburlaine-like to conquest, sinking into madness and dying exactly as had been predicted by a deceitful oracle. But Preston has added to the characters of his Persian chronicle play abstract figures – Murder, Cruelty, Commons Cry – familiar from **morality plays**, a vice called Ambidexter and the vice's companions in fooling, Huf, Ruf and Snuff. *Cambises* was sufficiently familiar to Elizabethan audiences to draw from Falstaff the warning that 'I must speak in passion, and I will do it in king Cambyses' vein.' The reference is less to the story than to the already stilted and archaic verse form in which Preston wrote it: rhyming couplets composed of seven iambic feet per line, familiarly known as 'fourteeners' (see **metre**).

**Cambridge Platonists** At the University of Cambridge, between 1633 and 1688, there evolved from a group of divines a philosophical approach to religion that marked a path between High Anglicanism and Puritanism. The chief contemporary influence was the philosophy of René Descartes, though they could not accept his materialist view of the inanimate world. The Cambridge Platonists advocated tolerance and insisted on the need for comprehension, seeing reason as the arbiter of both natural and revealed religion: morality itself is based on reason, and reason and religion are essentially in harmony. The chief members of the group were **Henry More**, **Ralph Cudworth** and John Smith.

**Camden, William** 1551–1623 Historian and antiquary, justly praised by **Spenser** as 'the nurse of antiquity/And lantern unto late succeeding age'. Camden attended both Christ's Hospital and St Paul's School and, at Oxford, both Magdalen College and Christ Church. He was second master at Westminster School in 1575 and headmaster in 1593.

Camden travelled the country noting its antiquities, and acquired a knowledge of both Welsh and Anglo-Saxon so that he might read ancient accounts of Britain. The two major results of his erudite and persistent researches were his Latin works, *Britannia* and *Annales*. *Britannia*, a description of England, Scotland and Ireland, first appeared in 1586 and was translated into English under Camden's supervision in 1610. The *Annales* describe and eulogize the reign of Elizabeth I. The first part was printed in 1615, the second at Leyden in 1625 and at London in 1627; the two parts were translated into English in 1625 and 1629 respectively, and the whole work appeared in English in 1635. Camden's minor works include editions of chronicles and other histories, an account of the trial of the conspirators in the Gunpowder Plot, a list of epitaphs in Westminster Abbey, a poem on the marriage of the Thames and the Isis, and his *Remains* (1605), which he described as the 'rubble' of a greater work. In 1621 he endowed a chair of history at Oxford. He is buried in Westminster Abbey.

*Camilla, or, A Picture of Youth* **Fanny Burney**'s third novel, published in 1796. The tale involves a large cast of diverse characters, but concentrates upon the fortunes of Camilla Tyrold, daughter of the respectable but modestly placed rector of Etherington in Hampshire, her sisters Eugenia and Lavinia, her brother Lionel, cousins Indiana and Clermont Lynmere, and her eligible suitor Edgar Mandlebert. With an eye upon the potential market for her novel, Burney calculatedly introduced tender sentiment, dramatic incident and Gothic colour into this work. Nevertheless, as the preface makes clear, the primary interest and skill of the story lies with its delicate and perceptive rendering of 'the human heart in its feelings and changes'.

*Campaspe* A prose comedy by **John Lyly**, first performed under the title *Alexander and Campaspe* by a **boys' company** in *c*. 1584. It was probably Lyly's first play, an elegant dramatization of the story told in Pliny's *Natural History*.

Attracted by his Theban prisoner Campaspe, Alexander the Great commissions Apelles to paint her portrait. Apelles and Campaspe fall in love and Apelles spoils the completed portrait so that Campaspe will have to go on sitting for him. Having tricked Apelles into revealing what he has done, Alexander releases Campaspe to him and returns to war on the famous grounds that 'It were a shame Alexander should desire to command the world, if he cannot command himself.'

**Campbell, Alistair** 1925– New Zealand poet. Born in Rarotonga in the Cook Islands, he moved to New Zealand in 1933 and was educated in Dunedin and at the Victoria University of Wellington. He worked as an editor for the Schools Publication Branch of the Department of Education in Wellington from 1955 to 1972 and as a senior editor for the New Zealand Council for Educational Research from 1972. His first marriage was to the poet **Fleur Adcock**. Originally seen as a member of the 'Wellington group' of poets, Campbell has gone on to carve out a more distinctive reputation for himself, though he has been a far from prolific writer. One of New Zealand's finest writers of lyric verse, he has been deeply influenced by Maori oral culture, as can be seen in his sequence *Sanctuary of Spirits* (1963), which deals with the history of the Maori chief Te Raupahara. A latter-day Romantic, Campbell has demonstrated a strong empathy for nature since the publication of his first volume of poetry, *Mine Eyes Dazzle* (1950). His other volumes include *Wild Honey* (1964), *Kapiti* (1972), *Dreams, Yel-*

*low Lions* (1975) and *Collected Poems* (1982). He has also written plays, television documentaries and children's books.

**Campbell, David** 1915–79 Australian poet. Of pioneer stock, he was born and raised on an isolated sheep-farm near Adelong, New South Wales. He was educated at the King's School, Sydney, and Cambridge University, where his interest in poetry first developed. He was a distinguished athlete and played rugby for England. During World War II he was a pilot in the Royal Australian Air Force and was awarded the DFC and bar. In later life he farmed property near Canberra. Campbell's poetry draws heavily on his formative years. His early verse is mainly nature poetry which conveys a strong sense of equipoise and serenity and is influenced by the Elizabethan lyric. In the 1960s his distinctive poetic manner changed and began to show more involvement with contemporary social issues. His work attempts to bring together the Elizabethan tradition and the Australian ballad tradition of **A. B. Paterson**. His treatment of the bush is notable for its incorporation of Aboriginal elements. His volumes of poetry include *Speak with the Sun* (1949), *The Miracle of Mullion Hill* (1956), *The Branch of Dodonna* (1970), *Selected Poems* (1973) and *Devil's Rock* (1974).

**Campbell, (Ignatius) Roy (Dunnachie)** 1902–57 South African poet, born in Durban. After private study in Oxford and travel in

Roy Campbell. A photograph taken in 1946.

France, he married in 1921 and during two penurious years wrote *The Flaming Terrapin* (1924), a 1400-line rhymed poem about a mythic terrapin which draws Noah's Ark into a revitalized world, symbolizing the released energy of created nature, writ large in images of volcanic flames, lightning and electric current. Back in Durban in 1924–7, he briefly collaborated with **William Plomer** on a radical magazine, *Voorslag* ('Whiplash') and wrote pungent verse about South African provincialism, collected as *The Wayzgoose* (1928). Literary London never forgave him *The Georgiad* (1931), which flays Georgian literature as emasculated, its practitioners as treacherous. *Adamastor* (1931) had revealed Campbell's muse under greater control, capable of savouring calmer experience and defter satire, of expressing a pained sense of exile from sub-tropical climes, yet recognizing 'spirits of power and beauty and delight' in southern Europe. This affinity leads to more contemplative poetry and tauter versification in *Flowering Reeds* (1933) and *Mithraic Emblems* (1936). Although he cuts an uneasy figure as a Franco-apologist in *Flowering Rifle* (1939), he served the anti-Fascist cause in 1939–45. *Talking Bronco* (1946) includes war themes and, in 'Luis de Camões', some of his best poetry. He handsomely repays his debts to Spanish and French literature in translations of *Poems of St John of the Cross* (1951) and Baudelaire's *Les Fleurs du Mal* (1952). The swaggering autobiography, *Light on a Dark Horse* (1951), has contributed to Campbell's undervaluation as a poet.

**Campbell, Thomas** 1777–1814 Poet. Born in Glasgow and educated at Glasgow University, he was the author of a number of poems written before he was 30, some of which have remained popular. His first success was *The Pleasures of Hope* (1799), which has ensured his inclusion in dictionaries of quotations (''Tis distance lends enchantment to the view'). He was skilful and might have achieved more had his inclination to poetry been stronger. He is remembered best for such poems as 'The Battle of Hohenlinden', 'Lord Ullin's Daughter', and 'Ye Mariners of England'.

**Campbell, Wilfred** 1858–1918 Canadian poet. The son of an Anglican clergyman, Campbell was born in Berlin, Canada West (now Kitchener, Ontario). He attended the University of Toronto and the Episcopal Theological School in Cambridge, Massachusetts, and was ordained in 1886. After five years working in various parishes in the United States and Canada, he left the ministry and became a civil servant in Ontario for the remainder of his life. Campbell was influenced by the **Higher Criticism** of the Bible and his poetry reflects the religious doubt of the late Victorian period. His style is often rough and uneven, but he justified such a mode on the grounds that it made for a more spontaneous expression of human emotions than was possible in formally correct poetry. **Longfellow** and the English Romantic poets were significant influences on his work, and during his time in New England he became familiar with **Transcendentalism**. His volumes of poetry include *Snowflakes and Sunbeams* (1888), *Lake Lyrics and Other Poems* (1889) and *The Dread Voice* (1893), in which he paints a very unromantic picture of a non-pantheistic Canadian Nature, which represents a marked shift from the view taken in his earlier verse. In his later years Campbell became a staunch advocate of imperialist values, a stance which can be seen particularly in his last volume of verse, *Sagas of Vaster Britain: Poems of the Race, the Empire and the Divinity of Man* (1914). He also wrote in many other genres, including verse drama, the novel and the travel book. Campbell wrote the Eastern Canada volume of *The Scotsman in Canada* (1911) and edited *The Oxford Book of Canadian Verse* (1913). A writer whose imperialist values caused him to fall out of favour with the generation that succeeded him, he is best remembered today for his poems about the Canadian landscape.

**Campion, Thomas** 1567–1620 Poet and musician. Campion was educated at Cambridge in 1581–4 but left apparently without taking a degree. In 1586 he was admitted to Gray's Inn to study law, participated in its revels of 1588 and contributed some songs to the *Gesta Grayorum* revels of 1594. He studied medicine in France and was practising as a doctor in London in 1606. He became innocently implicated in the scandal surrounding the murder of Sir Thomas Overbury, but was cleared of suspicion in 1615.

Campion was a literary and musical theorist, and a writer of Latin poetry and masques, but he is best known for his lute songs. *Poemata* (1595) was a collection of Latin poems, mainly elegies and epigrams. *Observations in the Art of English Poesy* (1602) was answered by **Samuel Daniel**. In it Campion argued against rhyme and was fighting the cause, already lost, for the application of classical quantitative metres and forms to English verse. *The Lord Hay's Masque* was performed at court 1607. *The Lords' Masque* for the wedding of Princess Elizabeth and *The Somerset Masque* for the marriage of the Earl of Somerset to the Countess of Essex were both performed in 1613.

Campion's lute songs, which make him a worthy rival to John Dowland, were published as *A Book of Airs* (1601), in collaboration with Philip Rossiter, *Two Books of Airs* (?1613) and *The Third and Fourth Books of Airs* (?1617). These books contain great variety: ballads, courtly airs, English versions of Horace, Virgil and Catullus, and spiritual and moral songs. Among the justly famous airs are 'Follow Your Saint', 'Break Now My Heart and Die' and 'There is a Garden in Her Face'.

*Can You Forgive Her?* A novel by **Anthony Trollope**, the first of the **Palliser** sequence, serialized in monthly parts from January 1864 to August 1865.

The novel deals with three related love-triangles, in each of which a woman hesitates between a 'wild' and a 'worthy' lover. In the main plot, Alice Vavasor breaks off her engagement to an honourable country gentleman, John Grey, and is pursued by her reckless cousin George, to whom she was once engaged, and who now seeks her fortune to pay off his debts and enter Parliament. She is attracted to the political life and offers to lend him money, agreeing to marry him after the lapse of a year, but he is disinherited by his grandfather, wins and then loses an expensively contested seat, and escapes to America a ruined man. Grey, who survives George Vavasor's attempts to shoot him, proposes again to Alice and is accepted. The second plot concerns Alice's cousin and friend, Lady Glencora, who has made a prudent marriage with Plantagenet Palliser, the rising Liberal politician, despite her continuing attraction to the charming wastrel Burgo Fitzgerald. She is about to elope with him at Lady Monk's ball when her husband, warned of her danger, arrives to take her home. Realizing that his devotion to politics has made married life dull for her, Palliser refuses the coveted post of Chancellor of the Exchequer to take Lady Glencora on an extended European holiday. The novel ends with the birth of their son, Lord Silverbridge, thus ensuring a succession to the Omnium title, and with Mr Grey's election to the Palliser pocket borough of Silverbridge, thereby satisfying Alice's political interests. A third, comic plot reverses the pattern of the other two, when Alice's aunt, a wealthy widow, chooses a dashing suitor in preference to a solid one.

The novel, which reworks material from Trollope's blank-verse comedy *The Noble Jilt*, shows his subtle understanding of the discontents engendered by conventional Victorian courtship and marriage.

**Canning, George** 1770–1827 Statesman and writer. Educated at Eton and Christ Church, Oxford, he entered Parliament in 1793 and rose to the offices of Foreign Secretary (1882) and Prime Minister (1827). A founder of *The Anti-Jacobin*, Canning also published his *Collected Poems* in 1823.

*Canon's Yeoman's Tale, The* See *Canterbury Tales, The*.

**Canterbury Tales, The** Geoffrey Chaucer's most famous work is an unfinished collection of tales told in the course of a pilgrimage to Becket's shrine at Canterbury. A General Prologue briefly describes the 30 pilgrims and introduces the framework: each pilgrim is to tell two tales on the way to Canterbury and two more on the way back, the teller of the best tale winning a free supper. There follow 24 tales, including two told by Chaucer himself. They are of various types – romance, **exemplum**, **fabliau**, sermon – and from widely differing sources, though usually written in rhyming couplets. The use of a single framework to link a series of stories in this way was not uncommon in the Middle Ages and there is no reason to suppose Chaucer had a specific model for it. His work is remarkable, however, for its integration of framework and tales; the characters established in the General Prologue are developed through linking passages and through the tales they tell, making the collection a sustained piece of social drama.

The structure of *The Canterbury Tales* probably began to emerge *c.* 1387, but the individual stories cannot be dated. The final order Chaucer intended for them has not been definitely established; they are usually given in the order in which they appear in the Ellesmere manuscript. Similarly, some tales were apparently intended for narrators other than the ones who tell them in the text we have.

*The General Prologue* gives an account of the pilgrims as they meet at the Tabard in Southwark and begin their journey under the guidance of the Host, Harry Bailly. They come from all sections of society. Some are described in vivid and realistic detail, combining elements

A woodcut from Caxton's second edition of *The Canterbury Tales, c.*1484. The scene is from the Prologue, and shows the Pilgrims at supper at the Tabard Inn. The same woodcuts were used in the 1498 edition of Wynkyn de Worde.

from the traditional representation of social types with individual characterization.

*The Knight's Tale* is a romance based on Boccaccio's *Teseida*. Not originally intended for the collection, it was adapted to suit the character of the Knight. It tells how sworn brothers, Palamon and Arcite, become rivals for the love of Emelye, the niece of Theseus, whom they first see from their prison window. Out of prison, they are discovered fighting by Theseus, who arranges a tournament to decide their quarrel. Arcite prays to Mars for victory, while Palamon prays to Venus for Emelye. Both requests are granted, as Arcite falls from his horse and dies after his victory and Palamon is later married to Emelye.

*The Miller's Tale* is a bawdy story told by a drunken and quarrelsome character. Like *The Reeve's Tale* which follows, it has several analogues but no known individual source. It describes the cuckolding of an Oxford carpenter by a clerk, Nicholas. Nicholas tricks him into believing that Noah's flood is about to recur, and the carpenter sleeps in a tub suspended under the rafters, leaving Alisoun, his wife, free to sleep with Nicholas. The amorous Absolon also tries to win her love, and Alisoun and Nicholas humiliate him. When Absolon stands under the window craving a kiss, Alisoun thrusts out her backside. But when he returns and Nicholas does the same, Absolon brands him with a red-hot iron. The noise of his screaming wakes the carpenter, who cuts the cord suspending him and plunges from the attic.

*The Reeve's Tale* continues in the same vein and answers the Miller's abuse of carpenters, for the Reeve is himself a carpenter. It tells how a miller is tricked by two clerks whom he has cheated of some of their flour. One sleeps with the miller's daughter and the other rearranges the furniture so that the miller's wife gets into his bed instead of her husband's. The first clerk goes to the miller's bed thinking his companion is in it and boasts of his conquest. The furious miller finds his wife with the other clerk and she accidentally beats him. The clerks further beat him and escape with their retrieved flour, baked into a cake.

*The Cook's Tale* is only a fragment of 57 lines and it is not possible to tell how it was to develop. It opens with an account of an apprentice who loses his position on account of his riotous living and moves in with a prostitute and her husband.

*The Man of Law's Tale* begins the second fragment of *The Canterbury Tales*. After a prologue in which he complains that Chaucer has spoiled all the good stories and announces that he will speak in prose, the Man of Law tells the tale of the unfortunate Constance. She is married to a sultan, converted to Christianity, whose evil mother destroys all the Christians in

The Wife of Bath. One of the illustrations in the Ellesmere MS of *The Canterbury Tales*, now in the Henry E. Huntington Library and Art Gallery, San Marino, California.

the court and sets the widowed Constance adrift in a boat. She lands in Northumberland, where she miraculously cures a blind man and converts her heathen host. A knight in love with Constance, but spurned by her, murders her host's wife and puts the blame on Constance. A mysterious voice condemns him when he swears falsely to her guilt. He is killed, and Constance marries the king and bears a child while the king is away. The king's evil mother interferes with his messages, so that Constance and her child are set adrift again. The king returns and kills his mother. Constance and her son finally come to Rome, where they live with a senator and his wife. They are eventually reunited with Constance's husband and father when these two come to Rome in later years. The story is also told by **John Gower** in *Confessio Amantis* and is the basis of the **verse romance** *Emare*, but Chaucer's immediate source was the Anglo-Norman **chronicle** by Nicholas Trivet.

*The Wife of Bath's Tale*, the first tale of the third fragment, is preceded by a prologue in which the Wife's character – domineering, licentious and pleasure-seeking – is fully developed as she gives an account of her eventful life with five husbands. Her tale continues the theme of women's mastery over men. As a punishment for rape the hero has to discover, within a year, what women most desire. Even-

tually he promises to grant a wish to an old hag in return for the right answer. When he has given the answer in court, 'maistrie' or sovereignty, she demands that he marry her. As they lie in bed together she asks him if he would prefer her ugly and faithful or beautiful and faithless; he allows her the choice and is rewarded by having her beautiful and faithful all the time. The story is a version of the romance, ***The Wedding of Sir Gawen and Dame Ragnell***.

*The Friar's Tale*, an animated and original version of a fabliau from an unknown source, is an attack on the Summoner. A corrupt summoner enters into fellowship with a fiend disguised as a bailiff and agrees to work with him even after learning his true identity. They see a carter cursing his horses but the fiend refuses to take them because the curse is not sincere. The summoner tries to cheat an old woman and when she sincerely wishes him damned the fiend carries him off to hell.

*The Summoner's Tale* answers the Friar with another fabliau from an unknown source about a corrupt mendicant friar. The friar asks a dissatisfied benefactor for more donations and angers him. After preaching against anger he promises to divide whatever he is given among all 12 members of his chapter, and the man tricks him into accepting a fart. A squire, Jankin, wins a new coat by explaining how it may be divided – by seating 12 friars around a cartwheel, each with his nose at the end of a spoke, and letting off the fart from the centre.

*The Clerk's Tale* begins the fourth fragment and gives a version of the folk-tale of Patient Griselda, derived from Petrarch's Latin translation of Boccaccio's telling of it in the *Decameron*. Griselda's husband subjects her to various cruelties, including the feigned murder of her children and his intended divorce and remarriage, in order to test her love and patience. Griselda bears his cruelty to the end, when her children are finally restored to her and her husband again accepts her as his wife. The character of Griselda is stylized to the point of implausibility, a fault recognized in the six stanzas called *Lenvoy de Chaucer* which follow the tale and plead that wives show more independent spirit in the face of stupid, cruel or stubborn husbands.

*The Merchant's Tale* also has its source in folk-tale, though it is richly elaborated and expanded. It tells how the ancient January is cuckolded by Damyan. January is struck blind and becomes jealous but does not know of Damyan's affair with his young wife May, until one day January and May are in the garden and May asks him to help her up into a pear tree to pick pears. Damyan waits in the tree and they make love, at which point January's sight is miraculously restored by Pluto. Proserpina gives May the ability to convince January that she was only struggling with Damyan and had been told that to do so would restore January's sight.

*The Squire's Tale* begins the fifth fragment. It is an unfinished verse romance of no known source, though there are similarities with the story of Cleomades. The King of Arabia and India sends to King Cambyuskan a magic horse, sword, mirror and ring. The brass horse will carry a man anywhere he wishes to go at incredible speed, the sword can cut through all armour and heal wounds, the mirror reveals future misfortunes and the ring gives its wearer the power to understand the speech of birds. The King's daughter wears the ring and hears a falcon complaining of her betrayal by a fickle and dissimulating lover. She takes the bird to court and nurses its self-inflicted wounds. The tale breaks off at this point.

*The Franklin's Tale* is introduced as a **Breton lay** but its source is in Boccaccio's *Filocolo*. It tells the story of Dorigen, wooed by a clerk, Aurelius, in her husband's absence. She refuses the clerk but promises him her love if he can remove all the rocks from the coast of Brittany, so making her husband's return safe. Secure in her belief that the preposterous condition cannot be met, she is horrified when, by enlisting a magician's help, Aurelius makes the rocks disappear. On Arveragus's return he tells his distraught wife she must keep her promise; Aurelius, touched by her love and fidelity to her husband, releases her from her obligation. The tale ends with an appeal to the audience to say which character is most 'fre'.

*The Physician's Tale* is the first in the sixth fragment. It gives a version of the story of Virginia adapted from *Le Roman de la Rose*. The corrupt judge Apius falls in love with the chaste Virginia and invents a charge of abduction to force her father to give the girl to the judge's servant Claudius. However, her father kills Virginia to protect her honour and sends the head to Apius. The corruption uncovered, Apius is imprisoned and kills himself, and Claudius is exiled.

*The Pardoner's Tale* is preceded by a prologue in which he explains how he preaches against all types of sin but himself indulges in various vices and begs from the poor. His tale takes the form of an exemplum inserted in a rhetorically flamboyant sermon. It tells how three drunken men set out to find and destroy Death after one of their friends has died of the plague. An old man directs them to an oak tree, where they find a hoard of gold and kill each other through trickery and treachery born of their greed. The Pardoner ends his sermon by displaying his false relics and appealing to the other pilgrims to part with their money.

*The Shipman's Tale*, which begins the seventh fragment, gives a version of a fabliau telling how a merchant was cheated and cuckolded by a monk. The merchant's wife borrows 100 francs from the monk, who in turn borrows it from her husband. In the merchant's absence his wife and the monk sleep together. On his return the monk tells him he gave the money to his wife; she tells her husband that she thought it a gift and spent it on clothes.

*The Prioress's Tale* follows a polite request by the Host and describes a miracle of the Virgin. It begins with an invocation to the Virgin and continues to tell the story of a Christian child murdered by Jews who is given the power of speech by the Virgin and so is able to reveal his whereabouts by singing, and to explain how he came to his death.

*Sir Thopas* is the first tale told by Chaucer in the collection. It is interrupted after 246 lines by the Host on account of its exceptionally poor quality. It is a pastiche of a verse romance, in six-line stanzas divided into fits of uneven length. The hero, Sir Thopas, rides in search of an elf-queen and is challenged by a giant. He retreats, promising to return. After a conventional arming scene he leaves court again, but the tale is interrupted before anything happens. The parody mimics the dull rhymes, doggerel rhythm, uninspired catalogues and trite superlatives of the worst romances.

*The Tale of Melibee* is Chaucer's second tale. It is a prose **allegory**, a close translation of the

The Franklin. One of the illustrations in the Ellesmere MS of *The Canterbury Tales*, now in the Henry E. Huntington Library and Art Gallery, San Marino, California.

*Livre de Melibé et de Dame Prudence* ascribed to Renaud de Louens, which is itself based on Albertanius of Brescia's *Liber Consolationis et Consilii*. It is long and, to the modern reader, unremittingly dull, but receives an enthusiastic response from the Host. The plot is simple: the house of Melibeus is attacked and his daughter injured, but his wife, Prudence, persuades him to abandon thoughts of revenge and be reconciled with his enemies. The advice of Prudence is delivered largely in proverbs. The allegorical meaning is apparently absurd – the sinner is attacked by the world, the flesh and the Devil and his wisdom injured; he must become reconciled with his spiritual enemies – but the reconciliation perhaps signifies resignation and trust in God's grace.

*The Monk's Tale* follows a prologue in which the Host asks him to tell a story in keeping with his character, perhaps about hunting. Instead the Monk relates a series of tragedies and is interrupted by the Knight after 775 lines because he cannot bear the dismal stories. The sources of the biblical, classical and contemporary figures are Boccaccio's *De Casibus Virorum et Feminarum Illustrium*, *De Mulieribus Claris*, *Le Roman de la Rose*, the Bible, Boethius and Dante.

*The Nun's Priest's Tale* is a **mock-heroic** account of a cock, Chauntecleer. After a premonitory dream which Chauntecleer repeats to his favourite hen, Pertelote, he is approached by a fox who appeals to his vanity to make him close his eyes and crow. The fox seizes Chauntecleer and carries him off, but the cock tricks him into speaking and so escapes from his mouth. The fable is set against a background of world history and philosophy, and is enlivened with humour and vivid characterization. The story is related to the French *Roman de Renart*.

*The Second Nun's Tale* is the first of two in the eighth fragment. It is a **saint's life**, relating the story of St Cecilia from the *Legenda Aurea* (later translated by **William Caxton** as *The Golden Legend*) and following its source closely. The prologue has an invocation to the Virgin based in part on lines from Dante's *Paradiso*. The tale, of 429 lines, tells how the virgin Cecilia converted her husband and his brother to Christianity and then some of their persecutors, and was eventually martyred for refusing to honour the pagan gods. After this tale the Canon and his Yeoman join the party, though the Canon soon leaves again.

*The Canon's Yeoman's Tale* tells of his own experiences with his master practising alchemy. The tale gives details of alchemical processes at length and relates how the canon cheated a priest, tricking him into believing he could transmute mercury into silver and selling him the method for £40.

*The Maniciple's Tale* is the only one in the ninth fragment. It tells the story of the tell-tale bird found in *The Seven Sages of Rome* but adapted by Chaucer from Ovid's *Metamorphoses*. Phebus has a white crow which sings sweetly and talks. Phebus's wife sleeps with a churl in her husband's absence and is betrayed by the crow. Phebus kills his wife. Overcome by anger and remorse, he plucks and curses the bird so that all its descendants are black with a coarse voice.

*The Parson's Tale*, comprising the tenth fragment, is the final tale. It is a prose sermon of great length on the Seven Deadly Sins, treating them in a manner common in manuals of penance. The sources are the *De Poenitentia* of Raymond de Pennaforte and Guilielmus Peraldus's *Summa de Vitiis*. *The Parson's Tale* is followed by *Chaucer's Retracciouns*, a much-debated passage in which the poet renounces all his secular works except **The Legend of Good Women** and asks that they may be excused on account of the many moral works he has written. The sincerity and reliability of the *Retracciouns* must be considered in view of contemporary convention and in their relation to Chaucer's projected character in *The Canterbury Tales*, as well as their position immediately after the overtly moral and didactic *Parson's Tale*.

**canto** A sub-division of a long poem, used by Dante in Italian and in English by, among others, **Spenser** (*The Faerie Queene*) and **Byron** (*Childe Harold's Pilgrimage* and *Don Juan*).

***Cantos, The*** The major work of **Ezra Pound**, widely regarded as one of the most influential poetic works of the 20th century. The first cantos were published in *Quia Pauper Amavi* (1919). A total of 117, some of them fragmentary, appeared over the next 50 years. Thematically and stylistically varied, the cantos deal with people and events in ancient, Renaissance, and modern history, employ diverse languages, and comment on various political and moral problems. The effect is often that of a series of evocative fragments; at other times, such as in the *Pisan Cantos* (1948), the focus is on one subject – in this case, Pound's incarceration in an Italian prisoner-of-war camp during World War II. Other volumes include *A Draft of XVI Cantos . . . for the Beginning of a Poem of Some Length* (1925), *A Draft of Cantos XVII to XXVII* (1928), *A Draft of XXX Cantos* (1933), *Eleven New Cantos, XXXI–XLI* (1934), *The Fifth Decad of Cantos* (1937), *Cantos LII–LXXI* (1940), *Section: Rock-Drill: 85–95 de los Cantares* (1956) and *Thrones: 96–109 de los Cantares* (1959). A collection, *The Cantos of Ezra Pound*, appeared in 1970.

**Cantwell, Robert** 1908–78 American novelist. Born in Little Falls (now Vader), Washington, Cantwell attended the University of Washington. He then served in the coastguard for two years before going to work in a lumber mill. In 1931 he became literary editor of *New Outlook*, and in 1935 literary editor of *Time*. He also worked on the staffs of *Fortune*, *Newsweek*, and *Sports Illustrated*. He is best known as a proletarian writer. His first novel, *Laugh and Lie Down* (1931), describes life in a lumber mill. His second, *The Land of Plenty* (1934), about factory life, is widely considered one of the finest novels to come out of the left-wing movement in the USA. In addition to a few uncollected short stories, he also wrote biography and criticism.

**Canute, The Song of (or Canute Song)** Four lines of Middle English verse said to have been composed by King Cnut as he rowed past Ely and heard the monks sing. The poem describes this experience. It was recorded by a monk of Ely *c.* 1167 although the actual date of its composition is not known.

**Capell, Edward** 1713–81 Shakespearean scholar. He was born at Troston, near Bury St Edmunds in Suffolk, and educated at Bury Grammar School and St Catharine's College, Cambridge. With the passing of Walpole's Licensing Act in 1737 he became Deputy Inspector of Plays, but it was with the age of **Shakespeare** that his real theatrical interests lay. *Prolusions: or Select Pieces of Ancient Poetry* (1760) reprinted the anonymous **Edward III** and considered the case for Shakespeare's authorship (see also **Shakespeare apocrypha**). 20 years' work was brought to a triumphant conclusion with Capell's 10-volume edition of Shakespeare's plays in 1767–8. The preface is important for attempting a contextual study of Shakespeare and challenging 'some good writer' to undertake a biography, a challenge accepted by **Edmond Malone**.

Capell could hardly have expected to survive unscathed in the vicious world of 18th-century Shakespeareans. He prepared an acting edition of **Antony and Cleopatra** with **Garrick** in 1758, but their friendship turned sour. **Steevens** and Malone, it was later alleged, used his notes with unwarrantable freedom. Ironically, Capell had produced *Reflections on Originality in Authors* in 1766. He never published his edition of Shakespeare's poems, and a lack of subscribers delayed full publication of his three-volume commentary on the plays until 1783, after his death. He bequeathed the finer parts of his library to Trinity College, Cambridge, and would no doubt have been pleased that a modern society of Cambridge bibliophiles should bear his name.

See also **Shakespeare: performance and criticism**.

**Capgrave, John** 1393–1464 Historian and religious writer. Born in King's Lynn, Norfolk, he entered the Augustinian order at an early age and was ordained a priest in 1417 or 1418. He became Provincial of the Augustinian friars in England some time before 1456. His works are largely in Latin and comprise theological, historical, hagiographical writings and biblical commentaries. In English he wrote a verse life of St Catharine, a prose life of St Gilbert of Sempringham and a guide for pilgrims to Rome, but his most important contribution to English literature is his prose *Chronicle of England*. It is written in a plain, clear style and is a valuable historical authority on the reign of Henry IV.

**Capote, Truman** 1924–84 American novelist and short-story writer. Born in New Orleans, Capote moved to New York City in 1942. He got a job at *The New Yorker* and also submitted stories to the magazine, but none was accepted. He did publish elsewhere, however, and his short story 'Miriam' won the O. Henry Award in 1946. This distinction led to a book contract, and in 1948 *Other Voices, Other Rooms*, his first novel, was published. This study of youthful innocence in a decadent world was followed by *A Tree of Night and Other Stories* (1949) and *The Grass Harp* (1951), both set in the South. In 1956 he published *The Muses Are Heard*, an account of an officially sponsored tour of Russia by an American company performing *Porgy and Bess*. He turned away from Southern settings with his next novel, *Breakfast at Tiffany's* (1958), a comedy of life in New York City. His next collection of short stories was *A Christmas Memory* (1966). His major publication of that year, however, was *In Cold Blood*, an investigation of the apparently motiveless murder of a Kansas family by two youths. Capote also worked as a journalist and published collections of his pieces in *Local Color* (1950), *Selected Writings* (1963), *The Dogs Bark* (1973) and *Music for Chameleons* (1981).

**Captain Singleton, The Life, Adventures and Piracies of the Famous** A novel by **Daniel Defoe**, published in 1720, it is a narrative of romantic adventure, told in the first person.

Singleton is kidnapped as a child and sent to sea. Off Madagascar he and some of the other sailors mutiny, but their venture fails and they are put ashore. From there he reaches Africa, which he manages to cross, obtaining a fortune in gold on the way. He squanders it recklessly in England and turns to piracy. He sails the high seas as far as China and once more puts together a large fortune. At the end of the novel he is back in England, his adventures over, and married to his shipmate's sister.

Defoe's hero is a man without 'sense of virtue

or religion' because of his upbringing. Virtue is represented by his shipmate and friend William Walters, who is nevertheless a character of considerable charm. In the end, it is William who is Singleton's saviour, both morally and physically. The adventures, many culled from Defoe's wide reading, are compellingly recounted and include escapes, rescues and bizarre encounters in the heart of Africa.

**Cardinal, The** A tragedy by **James Shirley**, first performed in London in 1641, one of the last plays to be staged before the closing of the theatres in 1642. Often considered Shirley's best tragedy, it has an unremarkable plot and a title part strong enough to fill the play with a brooding evil.

The Cardinal, ambitious for his family, enlists the support of the King of Navarre in arranging the marriage of Columbo (the Cardinal's nephew) to Rosaura. During Columbo's absence, Rosaura persuades the King to permit her to marry Alvarez, whom she loves, but Columbo kills Alvarez on the wedding night. Rosaura takes her revenge by having the disaffected Hernando kill Columbo in a duel and the Cardinal becomes the new avenger. His attempt to rape and kill Rosaura is prevented by Hernando, but he succeeds in poisoning her by a trick. Hernando kills the Cardinal before taking his own life.

**Caretaker, The** A play by **Harold Pinter**, first performed at the Arts Theatre, London, in 1960.

Set in a shabby room which belongs to either or both of two brothers, Aston and Mick, the play describes the futile attempts of a derelict, who may be called Davies, to secure for himself a role in and a hold on the room.

**Carew, Thomas** ?1595–?1639 **Cavalier poet**. Son of a Master in Chancery, Carew (pronounced 'Carey') was educated at Oxford, and entered the Inner Temple in 1612 to study law. About a year later he was attached as secretary to Sir Dudley Carleton, the ambassador to Venice and, later, to the Netherlands, but he returned to London in 1616. He was subsequently employed by the British ambassador to France, **Sir Edward Herbert** (later Lord Herbert of Cherbury) and after five years he was accepted at court where his reputation as a lyric poet and stylish personality won him the friendship of Charles I. Best remembered as a love poet (for 'The Rapture', in particular) on a par with the other court poets **Suckling** and **Lovelace**, Carew was a disciple of **Jonson** and **Donne**. He was the author of a masque, *Coelum Britannicum*, performed before the monarch in 1634.

**Carey, Henry** *c.* 1687–1743 Carey is remembered for his song 'Sally in Our Alley'. He was a Yorkshireman, and earned his living as a music teacher. He published *Poems on Several Occasions* (1713) but acknowledged that for him poetry was a pastime, not a profession. He was also author of a burlesque tragedy, *Chrononhotonthologos* ('the Most Tragical Tragedy that ever was tragediz'd'), produced in 1734. He invented the nickname 'Namby-Pamby' for **Ambrose Philips**, and may have been the author of 'God Save the King'.

**Carey, Peter** 1943– Australian novelist and short-story writer. Born in Bacchus Marsh, near Melbourne, Carey was educated at Geelong Grammar School and Monash University, where he studied science. He subsequently worked in advertising in Sydney, and has also lived in the mountainous rain forest country of Queensland and in London. With the appearance of his first short-story collection *The Fat Man in History* (1974), he immediately achieved recognition as one of the finest exponents of the new Australian short fiction. This was followed by a second collection, *War Crimes* (1979), and the novel *Bliss* (1981), a sardonic black comedy. *Illywhacker* (1985), the story of a 139-year-old confidence trickster looking back over his life, is a comic novel of epic scope. Carey writes fables that attempt to extend reality to the limit and his fantasies are characterized by a concrete particularity rare in post-modernist writing. *Exotic Pleasures* (1980) brings together stories from *The Fat Man in History* and *War Crimes*.

**Carleton, William** 1794–1869 Irish novelist. Born of a poor family in Tyrone, he was an acute observer of peasant life. He contributed a number of sketches of the Irish scene to the *Christian Examiner* which were collected and published in 1832 as *Traits and Stories of the Irish Peasantry*. There followed a second series in 1833 and *Tales of Ireland* in 1834. He also wrote a number of novels, of which *Fardorougha the Miser* (1839) is best known. His other novels include *The Misfortunes of Barry Branagan* (1841), *Valentine McClutchy* (1845) and *The Evil Eye* (1860).

**Carlyle, Jane Welsh** 1801–66 Letter-writer and wife of **Thomas Carlyle**. Born at Haddington, East Lothian, she showed herself a precocious scholar in childhood. She inherited her father's estate in Dumfriesshire in 1819 and married Carlyle in 1826. Her shrewdness and astringent wit made her an excellent letter-writer, and her circle of correspondents included many eminent Victorians. *The Letters and Memorials of Jane Welsh Carlyle*, edited by her husband, appeared in 1883.

**Carlyle, Thomas** 1795–1881 Historian, philosopher, essayist and critic. Born at Ecclefechan, Dumfriesshire, the son of a stonemason, he attended the village school and Annan Grammar School before entering Edinburgh University at the age of 15. After completing an arts course he began to study for the ministry but abandoned this course and taught, first at Annan and later at Kircaldy, where he became friends with **Edward Irving**. Returning to the university he studied law for a while, but began to concentrate upon literary work. He wrote contributions for Brewster's *Edinburgh Encyclopaedia* and undertook a thorough study of German literature. His first considerable essay, on Goethe's *Faust*, was published in *The New Edinburgh Review* (April 1822). From 1822 to 1824 Carlyle held a post as a private tutor; during this time he worked at his *Life of Schiller*, published by *The London Magazine* in 1823–4 (and in volume form in 1825), and a translation of Goethe's *Wilhelm Meister's Apprenticeship*, published in Edinburgh in 1824. This was followed by *German Romance* (1827) which included his translation of *Wilhelm Meister's Travels*.

In 1826 he married Jane Welsh, whom he had met through Irving in 1821 (see **Jane Welsh Carlyle**). For two years they lived in Edinburgh, during which time Carlyle wrote for **The Edinburgh Review**, producing, among others, two well-known essays on Jean Paul and on German literature (published June and October 1827).

In 1828 the Carlyles, oppressed by financial difficulties, returned to Jane's farm at Craigenputtock where Carlyle began to write **Sartor Resartus**, published in **Fraser's Magazine** (November 1833–August 1834), while continuing to contribute to *The Edinburgh Review* and other literary journals; *Signs of the Times* (1829) and *Characteristics* (1831) were published during this period. While staying in London in 1831 Carlyle became acquainted with **J. S. Mill**, who later introduced him to **Emerson**, the American philosopher and essayist. Correspondence with Mill interested Carlyle in the French Revolution and, after 1834 when the Carlyles moved to Cheyne Row in Chelsea, he began work in earnest on his history of **The French Revolution**. The manuscript of the first volume was accidentally destroyed while on loan to Mill in 1835, but Carlyle rewrote it and the work was published in 1837.

From 1837 to 1840 Carlyle undertook several series of lectures of which the most significant and successful was that **On Heroes, Hero-Worship and the Heroic in History**, published in 1841. *Chartism* (1839) dealt with contemporary agitation and outlined Carlyle's views on the political and social problems of the day. In **Past and Present** (1843) he drew on the recently published chronicle of Jocelin of Brakelond to argue that the proper regulation of society depended upon the leadership of a strong man of genius. In *Latter-Day Pamphlets* (1850) these views were repeated in more vehement form. With the publication of *Oliver Cromwell's Letters and Speeches* (1845) Carlyle's literary reputation was firmly established. The biography *The Life of John Sterling*, the friend of **Tennyson** and Mill, followed in 1851. Fourteen years and an immense amount of labour were spent on Carlyle's most ambitious work, *The History of Frederick the Great* (1858–65).

In 1865 Carlyle was invited by the students of Edinburgh University to become their Lord Rector and he delivered his inaugural speech on 2 April 1866. He published one more book, *The Early Kings of Norway* (1875), but it is not a notable one. For the most part his writing was confined to letters to *The Times*; one of these, on behalf of Germany in her war against France, impressed Bismarck so much that the Order of Merit of Prussia was conferred on the author. Carlyle refused **Disraeli**'s offer to secure him an honour in England. During his last few years Carlyle completely ceased writing, having lost the use of his right hand; he died on 4 February 1881. His friends wanted a burial at Westminster Abbey but his wishes were honoured and his grave is in Ecclefechan.

In his lifetime, and indeed until the end of the 19th century, Carlyle enjoyed a reputation in striking contrast to his present largely neglected status. To contemporaries he was the leading thinker of his day, a challenging, commanding, if at times exasperating figure to reckon with. There are few Victorians whose work does not reflect his ideas – if only in the process of rejecting them – or echo the colourful, quirky turns of phrase in which he wrote. The social writings of **Ruskin** and the mature novels of **Dickens** are perhaps the strongest examples of his influence. The secret of Carlyle's appeal lay in his affirmation of moral certainties in an age of profound change. Victorian England saw the social upheavals of industrialism, the political turbulence of the demand for wider democracy and the challenge to established religion from the natural sciences. Carlyle responded, not with a philosophical system or with a political programme, but with a list of values to which people could adhere: work, duty and self-abnegation. Above all, in an age of mass movements and mass democracy, he refused to see society in these terms but insisted on the importance of the individual, the private life of service by the ordinary man and the public life of heroism by the leader. From his early lectures on heroism until his last great work, the biography of Frederick the Great, he searched for a satisfactory model of the hero to put before the eyes of contemporaries. The search at first inspired them but, by removing Carlyle from the liberal and democratic tendencies of his age, finally isolated him and paved the way for later neglect.

**Carman, Bliss** 1861–1929 Canadian poet. Born at Fredericton, he was a cousin of **Charles G. D. Roberts**. He studied at the University of New Brunswick, and as an external student at London University. He left Canada to study at Harvard, and worked for a time as a journalist in New York. He published a number of poems in college magazines before the appearance of his first volume *Low Tide on Grand Pré* (1893). This was followed by three works in collaboration with **Richard Hovey** – *Songs from Vagabondia* (1894), *More Songs from Vagabondia* (1896) and *Last Songs from Vagabondia* (1901) – and a series of ballads and myths, *The Pipes of Pan* (1898–1905). Other works include *Behind the Arras* (1895), *A Book of the Sea* (1897), *April Airs* (1916), *Later Poems* (1921), *Far Horizons* (1925) and *Sanctuary* (1929). He also translated the lyrics of Sappho (1904), collaborated on the masques *Daughter of the Dawn* (1913) and *Earth's Deities and Other Masques* (1914), and wrote several books of essays. A prolific and popular poet, Carman was highly regarded during his lifetime.

**carpe diem** Literally, a Latin imperative meaning 'seize the day', an exhortation to make the best use of time before it is too late. The motif derives from Horace, but was frequently imitated by the erotic and devotional poetry of the Renaissance and 17th century; classic expressions of it include **Marvell**'s 'To his Coy Mistress' and **Herrick**'s 'Gather ye Rose-Buds while ye may', both of which cite the urgency of passing time to dissuade a lady from chastity.

**Carpenter, Edward** 1844–1929 Poet, author and socialist reformer. Born at Brighton, he was educated at Trinity Hall, Cambridge, where he became a fellow and was curate to **F. D. Maurice**. In 1874 he abandoned the church to pursue his own brand of primitive communism, much influenced by the writings of **Whitman** and **Thoreau**. Among English writers, he was indebted to **Ruskin** and **William Morris**. He eventually settled at Millthorpe, near Chesterfield, where he earned his living as a lecturer, farmer and controversial author in support of numerous progressive causes (sexual reform, women's rights, vegetarianism) aimed at subverting middle-class convention. He attracted a considerable number of admirers, notably **E. M. Forster**, for his overt homosexuality; and he was an early influence on **D. H. Lawrence**.

Carpenter's best-known prose works were *England's Ideal* (1887), *Civilization: Its Cause and Cure* (1889) and *Love's Coming of Age* (1896). Collections of his poetry included *Narcissus* (1873), *Towards Democracy* (1883–1902), a long poem, published in four parts, which reflected his Whitmanic sense of 'cosmic consciousness' and 'spiritual democracy', and *Sketches from Life in Town and Country* (1908). His autobiography, *My Days and Dreams*, was published in 1916.

**Carr, Emily** 1871–1945 Canadian prose writer and painter. The daughter of a stern Victorian father, she was born and brought up in Victoria, British Columbia, and gives a vivid account of her early years in the first part of her posthumously published 'autobiography', *Growing Pains* (1946). She studied art in San Francisco, London and Paris, where she was influenced by the work of the impressionists, and went on to become Canada's best-known woman painter. However, recognition did not come easily to her. Both her early subjects, which are drawn mainly from the culture of the Indians of Western Canada, and her style, which is characterized by a vivid use of colour and sweeping brush-strokes, made her a controversial figure and her work was generally rejected until a number of her paintings were exhibited at the National Gallery of Ottawa in 1927. There she met artists from the influential 'Group of Seven' and, after having produced far less work during the previous decade, once again began to paint extensively, now mainly turning her attention to the British Columbian landscape. In the intervening years she had supported herself by a variety of means, including running a boarding house in Victoria, an experience which forms the subject of her book, *The House of All Sorts* (1944). It was in her later years, when she was bedridden after a series of strokes and heart attacks, that she turned to writing. Her first book, *Klee Wyck* (1941), is a volume of short stories about the Indians of British Columbia, whose culture is celebrated with a great deal of warmth and empathy. 'Klee Wyck' or 'Laughing One' was the name given to Carr by her Indian friends. It was followed by *The Book of Small* (1942), in which she gives a fictionalized account of her experiences as a child in Victoria. This book is typical of Carr's writing in that it is heavily autobiographical, but in all her work (including *Growing Pains*) details are treated with a certain amount of artistic licence. Carr occupies a particular place in Canadian writing as a fond chronicler of late 19th-century and early 20th-century life, as well as for the close affinity she demonstrates for Indian peoples.

**Carr, John Dickson** See **detective fiction**.

**Carroll, Lewis** The pseudonym of Charles Lutwidge Dodgson (1832–98), humorist and writer of **children's literature**. The child of a scholarly country parson, he was born at Daresbury in Cheshire and attended a Yorkshire grammar school and Rugby. At home during his holidays he took a leading part in family amusements, producing a home-made magazine largely consisting of his own comic verse. At

Christ Church, Oxford, he studied mathematics, obtaining a university post but lecturing and teaching with difficulty because of his habitual shyness and bad stammer. For the same reasons, he preached only occasionally after his ordination in 1861. He produced mathematical textbooks and some occasional comic writing. The instant success of his masterpiece, *Alice's Adventures Under Ground* (now usually known as **Alice's Adventures in Wonderland**, 1865), still came as a surprise both to his friends and to Dodgson himself, who had no idea he had written a book that would revolutionize children's literature, putting all previous literary pieties at risk and opening the door to entertainment in literature for its own sake. At this stage in his life he also took great interest in photography and in the company of young children, particularly girls. Later successes were equally original, notably **Through the Looking-Glass and What Alice Found There** (1871) and a long nonsense poem, **The Hunting of the Snark** (1876). After these Dodgson's genius faded, although his fame continued to grow. Today, while his life has become a quarry for psychological speculation, his best works remain as fresh, original and ultimately elusive as they have always been.

**Carroll, Paul Vincent** 1900–68 Irish playwright. Born in Dundalk, he emigrated when he was 21 and taught in Glasgow until 1937, when his plays gave him financial independence. He was a co-founder of the Glasgow Citizens' Theatre. His early plays – *Things That Are Caesar's* (1932), *Shadow and Substance* (1937) and *The White Seed* (1939) – satirize the clerical authoritarianism of his Irish childhood. Apart from two lightly satiric comedies, *The Devil Came from Dublin* and *The Wayward Saint* (1955), his later work is heavily didactic. The acrid scenes from provincial life in his first three plays put him worthily in the line of **Colum** and **Murray**.

**Carter, Angela** 1940– Novelist and essayist. Born in Sussex, Angela Carter read English at the University of Bristol. She has taught and been writer-in-residence at universities in America and Australia; she wrote extensively about her two years' residence in Japan in essays for *New Society* later included in her collection of journalism, *Nothing Sacred* (1982). Her seven novels and three collections of short stories, often cited as examples of **magic realism**, are influenced more by French literature than English, and mount a witty, resourceful attack on received notions of 'reality' in fiction. They are characterized by extravagant Gothic fantasy, a variety of pastiches – from **science fiction** in early works to 18th-century **picaresque** in her latest novel, *Nights at the Circus* (1984) – and a baroque multiplicity of characters who, in

Angela Carter.

novels like *Heroes and Villains* (1969), change role, status and even sex during the course of the narrative. *Bloody Chamber* (1979), a collection of stories retelling classic fairy-tales in full awareness of their modern symbolism of the unconscious, exemplifies her predilection for myth-making, the unforced feminist imperative that underlies her fiction, and her measured, sensual prose style. Her essay *The Sadeian Woman* (1979) is a consideration of the Marquis de Sade's ideas of repression in the light of what Carter describes as 'the culturally determined nature of women and the relations between men and women that result from it'.

**Carter, Elizabeth** 1717–1806 Translator, linguist and poet. Educated by her father, the perpetual curate of Deal chapel, she learned Latin, Greek, Hebrew, French, German, Italian and Spanish, and subsequently taught herself Portuguese and Arabic. At the age of 17 she started to contribute poems to *The Gentleman's Magazine*, which was edited by her father's friend Edward Cave. A small collection of her verse was published in 1738 as *Poems upon Particular Occasions*; it was followed in 1762 by *Poems on Several Occasions*. Cave introduced her to **Johnson**, and she wrote articles for **The Rambler**, nos. 44 and 100. Johnson thought very highly of her and their friendship lasted nearly 50 years. Similar longstanding friendships with Catherine Talbot and **Elizabeth Montagu** resulted in *A Series of Letters between Mrs Elizabeth Carter and Miss Catherine Talbot from the Year 1741 to 1770* (4 vols., 1809), and of *Letters from Mrs Elizabeth Carter to Mrs Montagu, between the Years 1755 and 1800* (3 vols., 1817), collections valuable for their detailed comments upon contemporary literature and social conventions. In 1739 she published anonymously her translation of Jean Pierre de Crousaz's discussion of **Pope**'s *Essay on Man*, which led to Warburton's defensive response, *A Vindication of Mr Pope's Essay on Man, from the Misrepresentations of Mr de Crousaz*. In the same year she produced, also anonymously, *Sir Isaac Newton's Philosophy Explained for the Use of Ladies*, a translation of Algarotti's *Newtonianismo per le Dame*. Her most important work is a translation of the works of Epictetus (1758). It is a reflection upon 18th-century attitudes that the reviewers seemed more concerned to express surprise that a woman knew any Greek than to comment on the excellence of the work. Johnson considered her knowledge of the language superior to that of anybody he had met.

**Carter, Martin** 1927– Guyanese poet. He was born in Georgetown, and educated there at Queen's College. After a career in the civil service he turned to radical political activity and was detained in 1953. After independence he became for a while Minister of Information and Culture in Prime Minister Burnham's government. It was during his period as a detainee that he wrote *Poems of Resistance* (1954), which first made him a poet of more than local reputation, though this he had in abundance on the basis of *Hills of Fire Glow Red* (1951), *The Kind Eagle* (1952) and *Returning* (1953). Later collections include *Poems of Shape and Motion* (1955), *Conversations* (1961), *Jail Me Quickly* (1963) and *Poems of Succession* (1977). There are many influences upon Carter's writing from both American and European sources, but he is identifiably a Caribbean poet, and it has been accurately said that he combines a tradition of public poetry and an uncomfortable private anguish.

**Cartwright, William** 1611–43 Poet, playwright and preacher, Cartwright was much admired by 17th-century Royalists. Educated at Westminster School and Oxford, where he lived from 1628 until his death, he was claimed as a poetic 'son' by **Ben Jonson**. His comedy, *The Ordinary* (c. 1634), is Jonsonian in style. Two tragicomedies, *The Siege* (c. 1636) and *The Lady-Errant* (c. 1636), are not without ingenuity. *The Royal Slave* (1636) was acted before Charles I and Henrietta Maria in the hall of Christ Church, Oxford. The occasion was a splendid one, with Henry Lawes providing music for the play and Inigo Jones designing it.

Cartwright took holy orders in 1638 and wrote no more plays. He became a noted preacher whose fiery loyalty to the King survives in a Passion Sermon preached at Oxford. The 1651 edition of his works contains 51 commendatory verses by writers of the day.

**Carver, Raymond** 1938–88 American short-story writer and poet, born in Clatskanie, Oregon. His poetry, usually focused on a particular object or aspect of daily life, has appeared in five collections: *Near Klamath* (1968), *Winter Insomnia* (1970), *At Night the Salmon Move* (1976), *Where Water Comes Together with Other Water* (1985) and *Ultramarine* (1986). His short stories have been collected in *Will You Please Be Quiet, Please?* (1976), *What We Talk About When We Talk About Love* (1981), *Cathedral* (1983) and *Fires: Essays, Stories, Poems* (1983). Often appearing in revised form under different titles, his stories have a beguiling surface simplicity. The development of their narratives, however, is accompanied by an intense and dark vision of the contemporary world.

**Cary, (Arthur) Joyce (Lunel)** 1888–1957 Novelist. Born in Londonderry, educated at Clifton and Trinity College, Oxford, he studied art in Edinburgh and Paris (1904–9). He served with a British Red Cross unit in Montenegro during the Balkan war of 1912–13 and later joined the Nigerian political service as a district magistrate and administrative officer. Resigning from the colonial service in 1920, he settled in Oxford with the intention of serving an apprenticeship as a novelist.

His first four novels – *Aissa Saved* (1932), *An American Visitor* (1933), *The African Witch* (1936) and *Mister Johnson* (1939) – were set in West Africa and dealt with the confrontation of tribal culture and British administration. Then followed *Castle Corner* (1938), the only completed novel of a planned trilogy on the decline of the British Empire, and two novels about childhood, *Charley Is My Darling* (1940) and *House of Children* (1941). But his best-known works are the trilogies which explore the worlds of art – *Herself Surprised* (1941), *To Be a Pilgrim* (1942) and *The Horse's Mouth* (1944) – and politics – *Prisoner of Grace* (1952), *Except the Lord* (1953), *Not Honour More* (1955). In both trilogies the story is told through first-person narratives by each of the three main characters. Cary's disciplined presentation of the subjective viewpoint is much admired.

Cary also published two volumes of poetry, *Marching Soldier* (1945) and *The Drunken Sailor* (1947), and several political works including *Power in Men* (1939), *The Case for African Freedom* (1941) and *Britain and West Africa* (1946). His last works, published posthumously, were a book on aesthetics, *Art and Reality* (1958), and an incomplete novel, *The Captive and the Free* (1959).

**Cary, Henry Francis** 1772–1844 Translator of Dante. Born in Gibraltar, he was educated at Christ Church, Oxford, and ordained in 1796. He served as assistant librarian at the British Museum in 1826–37. Although he published a slight volume of verse at the age of 16 (*Sonnets and Odes,* 1788), Cary is best known for his blank-verse translation of Dante's *Divina Commedia* (*Inferno,* 1805–6; *Purgatorio* and *Paradiso,* 1814).

**Cary, Patrick** ?1623–57 Poet. Son of Henry, Viscount Falkland and younger brother to the famous **Lucius Falkland**, Patrick Cary was born in Dublin. His early years were tempestuous, largely owing to his mother's conversion to Roman Catholicism and subsequent estrangement from her husband. When the latter died in 1633, Patrick went to live at Great Tew with Lucius, a staunch Anglican. In 1636, he and his younger brother were abducted by their mother and sent to St Edmund's Priory in Paris. Patrick travelled to Rome, where he remained until 1650; while in residence, he met **Milton, Crashaw** and **John Evelyn.** He entered monastic life briefly, but returned to the world, and England, married and took employment in government service in Ireland, where he died from causes unknown. His poems, written in 1650 and 1651, were unpublished in his lifetime, and first printed in 1771. His secular work, the *Trivial Ballads,* embraces satire, pastoral and love-lyric, and exhibits skilful metrical variety and gentlemanly wit. His devotional meditations are deeply felt, if of uneven quality, echoing both **Donne**'s vigour and **Jonson**'s elegance; the manuscript is embellished with interesting emblematic illustrations in Cary's hand.

**Case-Book of Sherlock Holmes, The** See **Sherlock Holmes stories**.

**Caste** A comedy by **Thomas William Robertson**, first performed at the Prince of Wales's Theatre, London, in 1867. It is the outstanding example of Robertson's innovative realism in the presentation of domestic detail, the 'cup-and-saucer drama'.

Esther Eccles and her lively sister, Polly, are impoverished by their idle, drunken father. Polly may flirt with George's snooty friend,

Captain Hawtrey, but she loves her gas-fitter, Sam Gerridge. Esther, on the other hand, is persuaded almost against her will to marry the genteel George d'Alroy. Transported from Lambeth to Mayfair, she is ill at ease, and her plight is worsened when George is reported missing, believed dead in battle. But George returns, and the problems are resolved.

**Castle Dangerous** A novel by **Walter Scott**, in the fourth and last series of *Tales of My Landlord,* published in 1832. Set in 1306, the story tells how Sir John de Walton and Aymer de Valence defend Douglas Castle for the English king against marauding Scottish troops led by Robert the Bruce and Sir James Douglas.

**Castle of Indolence, The** A poem in **Spenserian stanzas** by **James Thomson**, published in 1748, though he had begun it 15 years before. The first **canto** tells of the wizard, Indolence, and the castle into which he lures world-weary pilgrims. There they surrender to idleness in an atmosphere of delicious ease, until they degenerate and are thrown into the dungeons. The second tells of the Knight of Arts and Industry and his destruction of the castle. Thomson introduces himself ('A bard here dwelt, more fat than bard beseems') and several of his friends into the action of the first canto.

**Castle of Otranto, The**: *A Gothic Story* A novel by **Horace Walpole**, published in 1764. In the first edition it was offered as a translation from an imaginary Italian original, but Walpole acknowledged his authorship in the second edition. These circumstances suggest that *The Castle of Otranto* was playfully conceived, at least in part, but it proved influential in establishing the fashion for **Gothic fiction**.

The story is set in the 13th century. Manfred, Prince of Otranto, is the grandson of a usurper and has no lawful claim to the realm; his grandfather had poisoned the rightful prince, Alfonso. A prophecy foretold that the usurpers would remain in power as long as they had male issue to continue their line and while the castle remained large enough to hold the lawful ruler. Manfred has arranged the marriage of his sole son, Conrad, to the beautiful Isabella, daughter of the Marquis of Vicenzo, but on the night before the wedding Conrad is mysteriously killed. Manfred knows that a gigantic figure haunts the castle and, now suddenly bereft of an heir, he determines to marry Isabella himself and beget another. But Isabella, terrified of Manfred, escapes from the castle with the help of a young peasant, Theodore, who is under suspicion of being connected with Conrad's death. Manfred's daughter, Matilda, loves the handsome peasant, and when he is arrested she releases him. Manfred is convinced that Isabella and Theodore are in love; he learns that Theodore is keeping a tryst by Alfonso's tomb. He goes there, stabs the lady – and discovers that he has murdered his daughter Matilda. The ghost of Alfonso, now grown too enormous to be contained by the castle, overthrows it and rises from the ruins. Manfred confesses the usurpation by his family, and the ghost proclaims Theodore the lawful prince. The tale ends with Theodore and Isabella's marriage.

**Castle of Perseverance, The** A **morality play**, dating from *c*. 1405–25. The surviving manuscript, some 3500 lines of rhyming stanzas, includes a crude drawing of the appropriate stage setting, from which we learn that the play was performed in the round, with the castle in the centre and various scaffolds on the circumference, housing respectively Flesh, World, Belial, Covetousness and God. Beneath the castle there is a bench-bed for the protagonist, Humanum Genus. The play describes the competition between forces of Good and Evil for the soul of humankind. Saved from the scaffold of the World by the Good Angel, Humanum Genus takes refuge in the castle, which offers the protection of Perseverance, a kind of Christian patience in the face of temptation. The castle is assaulted by Satan and his cohorts, who are driven away by the Virtues hurling emblematic roses, but Humanum Genus is drawn towards worldly riches by Covetousness. Death proves the transitoriness of worldly wealth. Defended at the throne of God by Mercy and Justice, Humanum Genus is admitted to Heaven and the play ends with a Te Deum.

**Castle Rackrent** A novel by **Maria Edgeworth**, published in 1801. Thady Quirk, steward to the Rackrent family, relates the history of the family's path to ruin beginning three generations back with the hard-drinking Sir Patrick. Like *The Absentee* the novel criticizes the Irish landlord of the 18th century, vividly depicting the evil results of profligacy and corruption.

**Castle Richmond** A novel by **Anthony Trollope**, published in three volumes in 1860.

Sir Thomas Fitzgerald of Castle Richmond in Ireland is a wealthy landowner whose wife had once been briefly married to a scoundrel long presumed dead. His son and heir Herbert, and his relative Owen Fitzgerald, heir to the estate after Herbert, are rivals for the hand of Lady Clara Desmond, the young daughter of the widowed Countess of Desmond. Owen and Clara plight their troth when she is only 16, but her mother opposes their engagement because of Owen's supposedly reckless bachelor way of life, all the while secretly loving him herself. When Herbert courts Clara, and she accepts him, Lady Desmond is delighted. But a shadow falls on the Castle Richmond family with the appearance of Matthew Mollett, a man claiming to be Lady Fitzgerald's first husband, who has been blackmailing Sir Thomas with the threat of exposing the presumed bigamy and thereby rendering his children illegitimate. The family lawyer advises open acknowledgement of the situation, and Sir Thomas dies from the strain. They prepare to leave Castle Richmond, although the new heir Owen chivalrously offers to surrender his claim, and are on the point of doing so when news comes that Mollett was already married when he married Lady Fitzgerald, and that her marriage to Sir Thomas was legal after all. Herbert's trials have strengthened Lady Clara's love for him, and they marry. Lady Desmond tells Owen of her love for him, but he leaves Ireland, seemingly for good.

*Castle Richmond* is set in 1846–7 and is of interest for its portrayal of the Irish Famine, and for the character of Lady Desmond and her hopeless love for a younger man.

**Cat On A Hot Tin Roof** A play by **Tennessee Williams**, first performed in New York in 1955 and awarded a Pulitzer Prize in the same year. It was revised for a revival in 1974.

The action centres on the wealthy and chaotic Pollitt family in Mississippi, and on the question of the inheritance of Big Daddy Pollitt's 28,000-acre estate. Big Daddy has stipulated that to inherit a share of the estate each of his sons must have children. Brick, the younger son, and his wife Maggie, the 'cat' of the title, are childless – in sharp contrast to Gooper Pollitt and his wife Mae, who already have five children and are expecting another. The discovery that Big Daddy is terminally ill forces the family to confront the tensions and hostilities which have developed as a result of his rigid control of their lives. Obsessed with guilt over his homosexuality, Brick has turned to alcohol. This in turn worsens his relationship with the passionate Maggie, which has already been damaged by the vindictiveness of Gooper and Mae. At the end of the play there is a suggestion that Maggie will be able to seduce Brick and conceive a child.

**catachresis** The misapplication of a word, sometimes ineptly, as in mixed metaphors (see **metaphor**), but often with striking rhetorical effect (as in **Milton**'s 'Blind mouths!' in *Lycidas*).

**catalexis** (or truncation) The omission of the last syllable or syllables from a line in a passage of generally regular verse. Such a line is said to be catalectic when it is one syllable short, brachycatalectic when it is two short. The regular lines of the passage are acatalectic. A line with one or two syllables in excess of the regular number would be hypercatalectic.

**Catch-22** An anti-war novel by **Joseph Heller**, published in 1961. Its non-chronological plotting technique, intended to emphasize the displacements that war produces, makes for a disjointed, fragmented narrative. The story is set in a US army air force base hospital on the fictional island of Pinosa during World War II. Captain John Yossarian is determined to survive the war and will use any means at his disposal to do so. He hopes to get a medical discharge by pretending to be insane, but the 'catch-22' ruling – that anyone rational enough to want to be grounded could not possibly be insane, and is therefore capable of returning to flight duty – keeps him in the war. Finally, after all his friends are killed or missing, he decides to desert to Sweden.

**Catcher in the Rye, The** A novel by **J. D. Salinger**, published in 1951. The 16-year-old Holden Caulfield narrates his own story of rebellion against the banality and 'phoniness' of middle-class values. Expelled from his private school in Pennsylvania, the caustic but quixotic teenager goes to New York City and checks into a cheap hotel. He spends the evening going to nightclubs, but he misses his young sister Phoebe (the only person he feels really close to) and becomes increasingly depressed. On returning to his hotel he has an unsuccessful encounter with a prostitute, and ends up in a skirmish with her pimp. The next day he meets an old girlfriend, Sally Hayes, and takes her skating. His spirits lifted, he suggests that the two of them escape to the New England countryside. Sally rejects this impractical offer and Holden, completely discouraged, gets drunk and then sneaks home to see his sister, telling her that he plans to 'go West'. Later that night he has an unsettling reunion with his former schoolteacher, Mr Antolini, who makes homosexual advances to him. The next morning he goes to Phoebe's school to say goodbye, but he is overwhelmed by his love for her and decides to stay. He then has a nervous breakdown, and tells his story as he is recovering.

**catharsis** From the Greek, a purging or cleansing. In Aristotle's theory of **tragedy**, it refers specifically to the release of emotion caused in the audience by the fate of the tragic hero.

**Cather, Willa (Siebert)** 1873–1947 American novelist. Born in rural Virginia, Cather moved with her family to Red Cloud, Nebraska, in 1883. In an attempt to escape the conservatism of the small town, she moved to Lincoln in 1890 and the following year entered the University of Nebraska. After graduating, she moved to Pittsburgh to pursue a career in journalism. She spent 10 years there, first as a newspaper woman and then as a high-school teacher of English and Latin. *April Twilights*, her only volume of poetry, appeared in 1903. Two years later she published *The Troll Garden*, a collection of short stories which showed the influence of **Henry James**. She later reissued four of these stories and added four more in a collection entitled *Youth and the Bright Medusa* (1920).

When she was 32, Cather moved to New York City and joined the staff of *McClure's Magazine*. Over the next seven years she published stories in *The Century Magazine* and *Harper's Monthly Magazine*, as well as in *McClure's*. In 1912 her first novel, *Alexander's Bridge*, was published. She resigned from *McClure's* and travelled to the Southwest. Her second novel, *O Pioneers!*, appeared in 1913. She returned to the Southwest in the summer of 1915, and her novel of that year, *The Song of the Lark*, is partly set in the ancient cliff-dwellings of Walnut Canyon, Arizona. In her next novel, *My Ántonia* (1918), she returns to the Nebraska of her childhood.

Her first popular success was the Pulitzer Prize-winning *One of Ours* (1922), the story of a boy from the Western plains who joins the army and is killed in France in World War I. Her next novel, *A Lost Lady* (1923), deals with stages of the moral decline of a woman from a small Nebraska town. *The Professor's House* (1925) is set in a small Midwestern college and in New Mexico in the post-war years. *My Mortal Enemy* (1926) is set in New York and on the West Coast in the early 1900s. The New Mexico landscapes in *Death Comes for the Archbishop* (1927) reflect Cather's continuing love for the Southwest. Composed after several visits to Quebec, and set in French Canada at the end of the 17th century, *Shadows on the Rock* (1931) won her the first Prix Femina Américaine in 1933. The three tales that make up *Obscure Destinies* (1932) take place in the Midwest. *Lucy Gayheart* (1935) tells the story of the daughter of a German-born watchmaker who leaves a small Nebraska town to study music in Chicago. *Not Under Forty* (1936) – later renamed *Literary Encounters* – is a volume of critical essays. Cather's last novel, *Sapphira and the Slave* (1940), is the only one of her novels to be set in the Virginia of her grandmothers.

**Catherine**: *A Story, by Ikey Solomons, Esq., junior* A novel by **W. M. Thackeray**, first published in *Fraser's Magazine* (May 1839–February 1840). It is a deliberately sordid tale of criminal life, based on the career of Catherine Hayes, executed in 1726 for the murder of her husband. Thackeray wrote it in reaction against the sentimental views of criminals offered by the **Newgate fiction** popular in the 1930s.

**Cathleen Ni Houlihan** A play by **W. B. Yeats**, first produced in 1902 with Maud Gonne in the title role. It concerns the sacrifice of the private

Maud Gonne in Yeats's *Cathleen Ni Houlihan*, 1902. 'Many songs have been made about me. I heard one in the wind this morning.'

hopes and dreams of Michael Gillane, who leaves his bride to fight for Ireland at the request of the Old Woman, representing Eire. A patriotic and popular play, revived many times and translated into Irish, it inspired the leaders of the 1916 Easter Rising and so raised in Yeats's mind the question posed in 'The Man and the Echo': 'Did that play of mine send out/Certain men the English shot?'.

*Catiline His Conspiracy* A tragedy by **Ben Jonson**, first produced in 1611 and published the same year. The play, rarely revived, follows the events of Roman history in the days of the republic, specifically the conspiracy of 63 BC. Catiline (Lucius Sergius Catilina) was a patrician who had been praetor and governor of Africa but whose dissolute life ruined him financially. He was defeated when he stood for the consulship in 64 BC, the votes going to Cicero and Antonius. Catiline renewed his candidature in the following year but was again rejected. Jonson's play begins at this point. The impoverished and desperate Catiline, with the secret encouragement of Caesar and Crassus, is preparing to overthrow the government. But Cicero is warned by Fulvia of the intention to assassinate him as the first part of the conspiracy; he summons the Senate and accuses Catiline, who immediately leaves the city for Faesulae, where his supporters have raised an army. Proof is delivered to Cicero by the ambassadors of the Allobroges (a Gallic tribe), who had been approached by Catiline for aid. The evidence is submitted to the Senate; Catiline and the other conspirators are sentenced to death. However, Catiline is defeated and killed in battle by the government general Petreius.

**Catnach, James** 1792–1841 Printer and publisher. He was born at Alnwick, Northumberland, the son of John Catnach (1769–1813), a printer there, and, later, at Newcastle upon Tyne. In 1813 James set up business in Seven Dials, London, and prospered with innumerable cheap publications, including ABCs and children's tracts. Some of his output was in the old ballad-publishing tradition, and he helped to preserve the texts of nursery rhymes and carols. He was notorious, however, for his output of topical and sensational material – on crimes, scandals, villainies, prize-fights and political events – which with its crude woodcut illustrations was very widely distributed by itinerant hawkers. Some of his work derives from his own historical collections and he stands late in a long line of succession in the trade; but his emphasis on the sensational did much to kill off the long-established ballad market. He retired from his lucrative business in 1838.

*Cato* A tragedy in blank verse by **Joseph Addison**, first produced in 1713 and published the same year. It enjoyed considerable success in the climate of the time; Queen Anne was dying and the succession was a question that divided the country into two opposing parties. The play has not been revived and is now better known for quotations such as "'Tis not in mortals to command success,/But we'll do more, Sempronius; we'll deserve it.' It is based on the last weeks of the life of Cato (Marcus Porcius Cato, the republican), besieged in Utica by Caesar. Set in 46 BC, Cato has been betrayed by Sempronius, a senator, and the Numidian general Syphax. Faithful to him is Juba, Prince of Numidia. Addison introduces romantic interest in the character of Marcia, Cato's daughter, who is loved by Juba, and in the rivalry of Cato's two sons for the hand of Lucia.

*Catriona* See *Kidnapped*.

**Caudwell, Christopher** Pseudonym of the critic, journalist, poet and detective novelist Christopher St John Sprigg (1901–37), who was born in Putney, the son of a journalist. After leaving school at the age of 15, he worked as a reporter on *The Yorkshire Observer*, and then in London as a writer on aeronautics, launching his own journal, *Aircraft Engineering*. He wrote **detective fiction** under his real name, and textbooks on aircraft. In 1934 he discovered the writings of Marx, Engels and Lenin, and joined the Communist Party the following year. He drove an ambulance to Spain and joined the International Brigade in 1936, and was killed manning a machine gun in the battle of the Jamara river in 1937. His literary reputation rests on his posthumous book *Illusion and Reality* (1937), which attempted to develop a Marxist theory of poetry as a product of the human struggle with nature. *Studies in a Dying Culture* (1938) includes his analyses of Freud, **Shaw** and

**D. H. Lawrence**, and was followed by the philosophical essays in *Further Studies in a Dying Culture* (1949). His other works include *The Crisis in Physics* (1939). *Poems* (1939), edited by his friend Paul Beard, has been superseded by *Collected Poems* (1986). Lacking literary sophistication and sometimes falling into stilted earnestness, Caudwell's plain language and simple forms have an unsentimental realism and urgency. The only directly political poem, 'Heil Baldwin', is often merely propaganda.

**Causley, Charles** 1917– Poet. Born and educated in Launceston, Cornwall, Causley worked briefly as a builder and played piano in a dance-band before spending six years in the Royal Navy. He then returned to Launceston and spent the rest of his working life as a teacher. He began to write poetry in the Navy in 1940.

His first collection was *Hands to Dance* (1951), followed by *Farewell, Aggie Weston* (1951), *Survivor's Leave* (1953), *Union Street* (1957), *Johnny Alleluia* (1961), *Underneath the Water* (1968) and *Figgie Hobbin* (1970). His *Collected Poems* was published in 1975. A writer who uses simple diction, firm rhythms and traditional forms (especially the ballad) with great facility, Causley is well known as a poet of the sea. Religious questioning and the survival of innocence are recurrent themes.

**Cavalier poets** A term loosely describing a group of lyric poets who flourished during the reign of Charles I (1625–49). These courtiers wrote about love and loyalty to the monarch, usually in complimentary poems or lighthearted lyrics. **Lovelace**, **Suckling** and **Carew** were the most prominent, while **Herrick** and **Waller**, though not of their social coterie, often resemble them in literary style and attitude. All owe a debt to **Donne** and **Jonson**.

**Cave, Edward** See *Gentleman's Magazine, The*.

**Cavendish, George** 1500–?61 The biographer of Wolsey, Cavendish was a gentleman usher in the Cardinal's household, which he joined in 1527. He accompanied Wolsey on an embassy to France and was with him when he died at Leicester. *The Life of Cardinal Wolsey* was not printed until 1641 but manuscript copies circulated in the 16th century, making it known to writers like **John Stowe**, who drew on it for his *Annales*. Cavendish's biography is in the medieval tradition of historical writing describing the fall of a great man. Wolsey's sometime glory and magnificence are contrasted with his later disgrace. The work portrays the fickleness of fortune and the transience of honour.

**Caxton, William** *c.* 1415/24–*c.* 1491/2

Printer and translator. Caxton was born in the Weald of Kent and apprenticed to Robert Large, a London cloth merchant, in or before 1438. Large died in 1441 and Caxton seems to have gone to Bruges where he followed a prosperous career. He probably learned to print in Cologne in 1471–2, but he acquired his experience and bought type in Bruges before returning to England to set up his own press near Westminster Abbey in 1476–7, the first printing press in England. When he died it passed to **Wynkyn de Worde**.

Caxton's early printing ventures included an involvement in the production of *Bartholomaeus Anglicus* and perhaps *De Vera Nobilitate* in Cologne, and, in Bruges, the first part of his own translation *Recuyell of the Histories of Troy* (1471–6) from the *Recuiel des Histoires de Troyes* by Raoul Lefevre (1464) and a 15th-century version of Guido delle Colonne's *Historia Troiana*. In England he printed a few works in Latin, but these were religious works, a book of grammar and one of rhetoric, and not the Greek or Latin classics, which appeared only in translation (Ovid, Virgil and Cato). In English he printed works by **Chaucer**, **Gower** and **Lydgate** (but not **Langland**), books on history and geography, **saints' lives** and didactic works, including the **fables** of Aesop (1483/4), prose romances (most notably *The Knight of the Tower*, 1483) and several miscellaneous treatises. He did not print the original work of any living English writer. He was a prolific translator and all the prose romances he printed, except **Malory**'s **Morte Darthur**, were his own work. Best known are his translations of part of the French Renard cycle as **Reynard the Fox** (1481), of the *Legenda Aurea* as *The Golden Legend* (1483), his *Recuyell* and *Esop*, and his *The Game and Play of the Chess* (1474/5). He included some critical comment in the prologues and epilogues he attached to some

The earliest representation of a printing press appears in this illustration from *La Grat Danse Macabre*, Lyons 1499.

of the works he printed, and though his criticism is unoriginal and uninspired, his prose style is vigorous and fluent.

**Cecil, Lord (Edward Christian) David (Gascoyne)** 1902–86 Critic and biographer. The son of the Marquess of Salisbury, Cecil was educated at Eton and Christ Church, Oxford. He taught at Wadham College and New College, Oxford, where he occupied the Goldsmiths Chair of English Literature from 1948 to 1969. In addition to biographical studies of Lord Melbourne, **Max Beerbohm** and **William Cowper**, he wrote *Hardy the Novelist* (1943) and *A Portrait of Jane Austen* (1978), and is best remembered for his *Early Victorian Novelists* (1934). His approach to literature was that of an amateur enthusiast emulating the refined impressionism of **Walter Pater**, a gentlemanly style which earned him the scorn of the Cambridge School led by **F. R. Leavis**. Several of his Oxford lectures were collected in his *The Fine Art of Reading* (1957).

*Cecilia, or, Memoirs of an Heiress* A novel in five volumes by **Fanny Burney**, published in 1782.

Fanny Burney's second novel was written over two years in very trying circumstances – though one misguided (male) friend described the £300 earned for the work as 'A pretty Spill for a young girl in a few months to get by sitting still in her Chamber by a good Fire'. The story concerns the fortunes of Cecilia Beverley, who is victimized by her three unscrupulous guardians, Harrel, Briggs and the Hon. Compton Delvile. Driven by ill usage to insanity and the point of death, Cecilia eventually finds a modicum of happiness with her lover Mortimer Delvile. In spite of its scenes of frantic excitement, hysteria and farce, Burney intended that the work and its characters should be realistic: 'I meant . . . to blend upon paper, as I have frequently seen blended in life, noble and rare qualities with striking and incurable defects.'

The novel was highly successful: its admirers included **Dr Johnson**, **Edmund Burke**, **Hester Chapone**, Mrs Delany and **Edward Gibbon**.

*Celebrated Jumping Frog of Calaveras County, The* This collection of stories was **Mark Twain**'s first published book (1867). The title sketch, which first appeared in the New York *Saturday Press* in 1865, was based on an old California folk-tale. Dan'l Webster, the champion jumping frog, is owned by Jim Smiley. A stranger claims that any frog could beat him, and sends Smiley off to catch another one to have a contest. Dan'l is defeated, but only because, as Smiley discovers after the race, the stranger had managed to fill his gullet with quail shot to weigh him down.

**Celtic revival, the** The revival of interest in the literature and culture of the Celtic people had its origins in **Romanticism** and the 18th-century antiquarianism which preceded it. A number of works in English exploiting what was perceived as the Gothic element in early Celtic literature appeared in the mid 18th century. **Thomas Gray**'s Pindaric ode 'The Bard' (1757) and 'The Triumphs of Owen' (1768) are typical. The latter drew on the first substantial selection of Welsh poetry to be published: *Some Specimens of the Poetry of the Ancient Welsh Bards. Translated into English . . .* (1764), by Ieuan Brydydd Hir (Evan Evans, 1731–88). The growing interest was fuelled by the literary forgeries of the Welsh antiquarian and poet Iolo Morganwg (Edward Williams, 1747–1826) and in particular of the Scotsman **James Macpherson**, whose 'Ossian' poems were the subject of enormous enthusiasm and then fierce controversy. Reliable translations began to appear in the 19th century: Lady Charlotte Guest's *The Mabinogion* was published between 1838 and 1849, Hersart de la Villemarqué's *Barzaz Breiz* and *Les Bardes Bretons du Sixième Siècle* in 1839 and 1850 and **Eugene O'Curry**'s *Lectures on the Manuscript Materials of Ancient Irish History* in 1861.

Translations provided the basis for **Matthew Arnold**'s important 'Lectures on Celtic Literature' at Oxford in 1865–6. His linking together of all the Celtic literatures – Irish, Welsh, Scottish, Cornish, Breton and Manx – was one of the founding steps of modern Celtic scholarship, though many of his other ideas were anticipated by Ernest Renan (1823–92) in *La Poésie des Races Celtiques* (1854). However eccentric some of Arnold's assumptions and conclusions may have been, his lectures led directly to the founding of the Chair of Celtic at Jesus College, Oxford, in 1877, which in turn helped in the establishment of further chairs in the University of Wales and elsewhere. The popular view of Celtic literature and people as mysteriously romantic also owes much to Arnold's description of their gift for style, 'natural magic' and 'Celtic melancholy'.

Throughout the 19th century English authors made use of Celtic material, real or imaginary, in works as various as **Thomas Love Peacock**'s *The Misfortunes of Elphin* (1829), **Tennyson**'s *Idylls of the King* (1942–85) and **Gerard Manley Hopkins**'s 'St Winifred's Well' (written 1879–85). At the same time Irish, Scottish and Welsh writers were exploiting the same material in their English writing. **Yeats**'s collection of stories and folklore, *The Celtic Twilight* (1893), provided a descriptive term for Irish literary activity in the 1890s and early 1900s, although it was made to seem anachronistic by the new generation of writers such as **Joyce** and **Sean O'Casey**. In Scotland this kind of writing, with its implicit belief in ancient heroes and spirits, was produced by **William Black** and **William Sharp**. In the 20th century English writers have continued to make use of Celtic material, and there have been literary revivals in many of the Celtic countries, both in Celtic languages and in English.

**Cenci, The** A five-act tragedy by **Percy Bysshe Shelley**, published in 1819. The single most impressive stage play to have been written by any of the Romantic poets, its subject made performance unlikely in the theatre of the time, though it was considered by **Covent Garden**. It was first produced privately by the Shelley Society in 1886 and has been occasionally revived since then. It provided the French visionary Antonin Artaud (1896–1948) with the basis for a scenario which can be seen as the central text in his 'theatre of cruelty'.

The play is based on the savage history of a 16th-century Roman family. Count Francesco Cenci, a vicious husband and father with a sadistic taste for punishment, combines hatred for his daughter Beatrice with incestuous lust. The family conspires to have him killed. Suspected and tortured, they are brought to trial, and, despite the compassion aroused by their pitiful story and by Beatrice's self-conduct, they are executed. The executions took place on 11 September 1599. Shelley makes Beatrice, whose portrait by Guido Reni he had seen in the Colonna palace in Rome, the central figure of his tragedy.

**Centlivre, Susannah** 1669–1723 Playwright. Susannah Freeman was probably born at Holbeach, Lincolnshire. She was first married at the age of 16 and twice widowed before her marriage to Joseph Centlivre, Queen Anne's cook at Windsor, in 1706. She became an actress but achieved no great distinction, and began writing for the stage under her second married name, Susannah Carroll. 18 of her plays were produced during her lifetime.

Her work was popular in her time and provided useful vehicles for actors. Among her plays may be mentioned *The Gamester* (January 1705, at Lincoln's Inn Fields), adapted from *Le Joueur* by Jean-François Regnard; *The Wonder: A Woman Keeps a Secret* (April 1714, Drury Lane); and *A Bold Stroke for a Wife* (February 1718, Lincoln's Inn Fields). The last two provided successful parts for **David Garrick** and Anne Oldfield.

**Century Magazine, The** An American journal, first published in November 1870 as *Scribner's Monthly, an Illustrated Magazine for the People*, founded by Roswell Smith, Charles Scribner, and Dr Josiah Gilbert Holland, who served as its editor until his death in 1881. Under Holland's control *Scribner's Monthly* featured essays on politics, religion, and current affairs; serial fiction; and numerous high-quality illustrations. Contributors included **George Macdonald**, **Margaret Oliphant** and Jules Verne. It also published most of the 'Nights with Uncle Remus' by **Joel Chandler Harris**.

In 1881 the name was changed to *The Century Illustrated Monthly Magazine*, under the editorship of Richard Watson Gilder. Under Gilder *The Century* displayed an increased concern with public events, but continued to serialize novels, among them **William Dean Howells**'s *A Modern Instance*, *The Rise of Silas Lapham* and *The Minister's Charge*; **Henry James**'s *The Bostonians*; **Jack London**'s *The Sea Wolf*; and **George Washington Cable**'s *Dr Sevier*. In 1925 the title became *The Century Monthly Magazine*, and from May through August 1929 *The Century Magazine*. In the fall of 1929 it became a quarterly publication called *The Century Quarterly*; it was merged with *Forum* in 1930.

**Chamberlayne, William** 1619–89 A minor Caroline poet, Chamberlayne was a physician in Shaftesbury, Dorset. He was the author of *Pharonnida* (1659), a heroic romance in couplets – the poetic fashion of his day – which runs to 14,000 lines. His play *Love's Victory* was published in 1658.

**Chambers, Sir E[dmund] K[erchever]** 1866–1956 Literary scholar. Born in Berkshire, the son of a clergyman, Chambers was educated at Marlborough and at Corpus Christi College, Oxford, where he began his work on **Shakespeare** with an edition of *Richard II* (1891). His working life from 1892 to 1926 was spent as a civil servant in the Education Department (later reconstituted as the Board of Education), and although his researches into the history of English drama were conducted in his spare time, they were outstanding contributions to scholarship. He was the first president (1906–39) of the Malone Society founded by **W. W. Greg** for the reprinting of early English plays, and to this field of learning he brought a civil servant's deliberate care in sifting the evidence of authorship and chronology, as shown in his major works *The Medieval Stage* (2 vols., 1903), *The Elizabethan Stage* (4 vols., 1923) and *William Shakespeare: A Study of the Facts and Problems* (2 vols., 1930). He wrote a survey of Arthurian legend, *Arthur of Britain* (1927), and biographies of **S. T. Coleridge** and **Matthew Arnold**, produced editions of Shakespeare, **Donne** and **Milton**, and also edited *The Oxford Book of Sixteenth-Century Verse* (1932).

**Chance** A novel by **Joseph Conrad**, first published in 1913. The story of the heroine, Flora de Barral, is told by a number of narrators; chief among them is Marlow. Flora is a victim of emotional isolation. On the death of her mother, she is placed by her father, a financier, with an uncaring governess who undermines her childhood self-confidence. After her father's financial ruin and imprisonment, she believes – as her governess wishes – that she is both insipid and unlovable.

Flora's friendship with Mr and Mrs Fyne has mixed consequences. She is rescued from her depression by Captain Roderick Anthony, but their subsequent elopement and marriage is blighted by doubts about her own worth. Anthony, moreover, is told by the Fynes that Flora's motives are self-interested and prudential.

Flora's marriage does indeed provide a refuge for her father on his release from prison; all three live on board Anthony's ship Ferndale. However, Flora's father is unbalanced by his experiences and regards her marriage (which remains unhappy and unconsummated) as a betrayal. It is only his death which enables them to communicate. Flora remains unaware that her father had attempted to poison Anthony and that he had taken his own life when discovered by Powell, the second mate.

Anthony dies after an accident several years later when his ship collides with another. There is some prospect of a romance between Powell and Flora. However, it is the forces which control and over-determine conduct which mostly engage Conrad in the novel, and there is a strongly ironic element in its title.

**Chances, The** A comedy by **John Fletcher**. The date of the first production is unknown; the first published version of 1647 contains a prologue and an epilogue written by another hand. The play is based on a novel by Cervantes. The 'chances' are the coincidences and complications that beset Constantia and the Duke of Ferrara when they decide to elope. Others concerned are Vecchio, a wizard, Dame Gillian, the hostess, and two Spanish gallants, Don John and Don Frederick. The play contains some of Fletcher's best writing.

**Chandler, Raymond (Thornton)** 1888– 1959 American novelist and short-story writer. Chandler was born in Chicago and worked as a journalist and businessman before starting to write **detective fiction** at the age of 45. His stories were published regularly in *The Black Mask* magazine until 1939. In *The Big Sleep* (1939) he introduced his most famous character, the detective Philip Marlowe, who reappeared in many subsequent novels. Chandler's other novels include *Farewell, My Lovely* (1940), *The High Window* (1942), *The Lady In The Lake* (1943), *The Little Sister* (1949), *The Long Goodbye* (1953) and *Playback* (1958). His stories are collected in *Trouble Is My Business* (1950), *Killer In The Rain* (1964) and *The Smell of Fear* (1965). He discusses his work in *The Simple Art of Murder* (1950) and the posthumous *Raymond Chandler Speaking* (1962).

**Changeling, The** A tragedy by **Thomas Middleton** with an uncertainly related tragicomic sub-plot, possibly the work of **William Rowley**, who is known to have been Middleton's collaborator in the play. *The Changeling* was first performed in 1622–3 and published in 1653.

Beatrice Joanna, daughter of the Governor of Alicant, loves Alsemero. In order to avoid her arranged marriage to Alonzo de Piracquo she enlists the dangerous support of her father's physically repulsive servant, De Flores. It is the first in a train of events that draws her, with a terrible logic, into the clutches of De Flores, by whom she is both revolted and fascinated. With Alonzo dead, killed by De Flores, Beatrice Joanna can marry Alsemero, but the marriage is followed by a grotesque scene of feigned virginity, which requires the complicity of her maid Diaphanta. As a dangerous witness to the truth, Diaphanta is also killed by De Flores; but Alsemero has been growing suspicious and it is he who unmasks the 'lovers'. Bound together to the end, Beatrice Joanna and De Flores kill themselves.

The sub-plot concerns the efforts of Antonio to seduce Isabella, the wife of an old and jealous doctor who runs a lunatic asylum. In pursuit of his prey, Antonio (he is the 'changeling' of the sub-plot as Beatrice Joanna, in a subtler sense, is of the main plot) pretends to be an idiot. But Isabella frustrates the attempts to corrupt her, retaining the control of her life that is utterly surrendered by Beatrice Joanna.

**Channing, William Ellery** 1780–1842 American minister and social reformer, born in Newport, Rhode Island. Channing graduated from The Harvard Divinity School, and was ordained in 1803 as a Congregational minister. His 'Baltimore Sermon' (*A Sermon Delivered at the Ordination of the Rev Jared Sparks*, 1819) and *The Moral Argument Against Calvinism* (1820) state plainly his opposition to the dogma and coercion of strict Calvinist theology, and his rejection of the tenet that man is essentially depraved. These revisionist ideas were common among many of Channing's circle, which included such important New England writers as **Ralph Waldo Emerson**, **Henry David Thoreau**, **Margaret Fuller** and **Bronson Alcott**. He put forth his ideas on pacifism, prison reform, child labour, education and slavery – which he opposed fiercely – in many pamphlets and sermons. In his time his views were widely discussed, and his influence was considerable.

**chapbooks** Popular literature, especially profuse during the 18th century, sold by wandering dealers ('chapmen') and comprising ballads, folk-tales, assorted tracts, fairy-tales, contemporary legends and short biographical pieces. Generally illustrated with woodcuts, they numbered 16 or 24 pages depending on format, and were priced at a few pennies.

**Chapman, George** *c.*1560–1634 English poet and playwright whose considerable learning, combined with a belief that the true meaning of poetry need reveal itself only to the few, made his work notoriously difficult and often obscure. Very little is known of his life, but his creative output is clearly divisible.

Of his poetry, as distinct from his translations, the two poetical hymns combined in *The Shadow of Night* (1594) are the earliest to have survived. The three-level **allegory**, philosophical, political and poetic, of the second is particularly complex. *Ovids Banquet of Sence* (1595) obliquely advocates true Platonism as a counter to Ovidian eroticism. The correction and completion of **Marlowe**'s *Hero and Leander* (1598) was undertaken in order to confirm and strengthen the poem's moral seriousness. *Euthymiae Raptus* (1609), better known by its alternative title *The Teares of Peace*, is a carefully constructed defence of learning in which the poetic form of the medieval **dream-vision** is the vehicle for Platonic, Stoic and Christian speculation. *An Epicede or Funerall Song on the Death of Henry Prince of Wales* (1612) laments the loss of a valuable patron.

Of Chapman's translations, the most famous, not least because of a much-quoted sonnet by **John Keats**, are Homeric. *Seven Books of the Iliad* (1598) and *Achilles' Shield* (1598) announced the beginning of what Chapman called 'The Worke that I was borne to doe'. The complete *Iliads* (1611) and *Homer's Odyssey* (1614–15) are translations not only from one language to another, but also from one age and culture to another. Chapman interprets the ethical and philosophical views which he believed to be inherent in the Homeric original. Such monumental labour inevitably eclipses the shorter translations from Petrarch (1612), Musaeus (1616), Hesiod (1618) and Juvenal (1629).

The date of Chapman's first involvement with the theatre is uncertain. He was certainly associated with **Philip Henslowe** and the Admiral's Men in 1595–6, when *The Blind Beggar of Alexandria* was produced, and was considered among the best poets for both tragedy and comedy in **Francis Meres**'s *Palladis Tamia* (1598). Some early plays have obviously been lost. *An Humorous Day's Mirth* (1597) strongly supports claims that Chapman's friendship with **Ben Jonson** was mutually influential. Other surviving comedies, probably written for the **boys' com**panies with which Chapman was associated in the first decade of the 17th century, are *The Gentleman Usher* (*c.* 1602), *All Fools* (1599 or 1604), *Monsieur D'Olive* (1604), *Sir Giles Goosecap, Knight* (*c.* 1604), *The Widow's Tears* (*c.* 1605) and *May Day* (1609). For his part-authorship, with Jonson and **John Marston**, of *Eastward Ho* (1605), a splendid city comedy, Chapman was imprisoned in the Tower of London. In his tragedies he writes repeatedly of deeply flawed Titanic heroes, philosophically removed from the recent French history in which they figured. It is these overreachers who give their names to *Bussy D'Ambois* (1604), *The Conspiracy and Tragedy of Charles, Duke of Byron, Marshal of France* (1608), *The Revenge of Bussy D'Ambois* (*c.* 1610) and *Chabot, Admiral of France* (*c.* 1613). To earn Jonson's commendation, Chapman probably wrote more masques than the single surviving *Memorable Masque of the Middle Temple and Lyncolnes Inn* (1613).

**Chapone, Hester** 1727–1801 Moralist and **bluestocking**. Daughter of Thomas Mulso, a country gentleman, she was taught Latin, French and Italian, and wrote her first fiction at nine. She met Mrs **Elizabeth Carter**, the linguist, and became a friend of **Samuel Richardson**. In Susannah Highmore's sketch of Richardson reading *The History of Sir Charles Grandison* aloud to female friends, she is in the centre. She married John Chapone, an attorney and friend of Richardson, but he died soon afterwards.

Author of tales in verse and essays, she is remembered chiefly for her *Letters on the Improvement of the Mind* (1773), a seminal work in the moral education of generations of girls (see **conduct books**). Lydia Languish, in **Sheridan**'s *The Rivals*, pushes **Smollett**'s and **Fielding**'s novels out of sight, and pretends to be reading Mrs Chapone. Among Mrs Chapone's exhortations are the necessity for humility, sincerity and uprightness of heart; pride and vanity are to be subdued by reason and grace. The affections must be 'regulated' and the temper 'governed'. She also published *A Letter to a New Married Lady* (1777). Her correspondence and a memoir were published posthumously (1807, 1808).

***Charley's Aunt*** An immensely successful farce, the only play by which its author, **Brandon Thomas**, is remembered. It ran for four years after its opening in London in 1892. The play is an elaboration on a simple theme. Lord Fancourt Babberly, an amiable Oxford aristocrat, is prevailed upon to aid the amorous designs of two friends by impersonating his rich aunt. The troubles begin when the real aunt arrives in Oxford.

*Charlotte Temple, A Tale of Truth* A novel by **Susanna Rowson**, published in England in 1791 and in America in 1794. Modelled on **Samuel Richardson**'s *Clarissa*, it sold poorly in England but was a great success in the USA. Rowson's stated intention was to warn against the dangers of seduction, and the book is full of authorial admonitions.

The story recounts the wooing of Charlotte, a 15-year-old pupil at Mme Du Pont's school for young ladies, by Montraville, an army officer. They elope to New York, where Montraville, despite qualms of conscience, soon deserts Charlotte for an heiress, Julia Franklin. Charlotte is now stranded, and pregnant. She looks in vain for help, and is even rebuffed by her former schoolteacher, Mlle La Rue, the woman of moral laxity who had introduced her to Montraville in the first place. Charlotte dies in poverty after giving birth to Montraville's illegitimate child, Lucy. Montraville is conscience-stricken, but returns to Julia. Mlle La Rue dies in ignominy. Charlotte's father adopts Lucy.

*Chaste Maid in Cheapside, A* A comedy by **Thomas Middleton**, first performed in 1611 and published in 1630. One of the richest of London's city comedies, it parades mercantile double-dealing as if it were the norm, exposing its characters' obsessive concern with sex, procreation and genteel inheritance. As so often in the work of Middleton, there is not so much a plot as a variety of plots, unified (if at all) by the shared involvement and eventual discomforting of Sir Walter Whorehound.

Whorehound hopes to marry Moll Yellowhammer, daughter of an avaricious goldsmith. He encourages a strategic marriage between his own discarded mistress (the 'chaste' maid of the title) and Moll's bird-brained brother Tim. But Moll loves Touchwood Junior, and a major strand in the play details their eventually successful struggles to be united. Another follows the adventures of the childless Sir Oliver and Lady Kix, whose fortune Whorehound will inherit. Once again, however, the dissolute Whorehound is worsted when, after some hilarious trickery, Lady Kix is impregnated by Touchwood Senior while the impotent Sir Oliver takes medicine and exercise. Having lost his inheritance and his hopes of marriage, Whorehound turns for help to the Allwits – Mistress Allwit's affair with him has been happily condoned by Allwit because Whorehound has 'maintained my house this ten years' – and is roundly rejected. Now that Whorehound is impecunious, the Allwits plan to set up a bawdy-house in the Strand. Whorehound is arrested for debt. The play's realistic vision is nicely conveyed by the fact that the complacent Allwit comes nearer than any other character to being its 'hero'.

**Chatterton, Thomas** 1752–70 The poet commemorated by **Wordsworth** as 'the marvellous boy . . . that perished in his pride' and to whose memory **Keats** dedicated *Endymion* was born in Bristol, the son of a schoolmaster. His first poem was published when he was 11. He was educated at a charity school, Colston's Hospital, and apprenticed to an attorney when he was 14. His family was associated with the church of St Mary Redcliffe and Chatterton, who could fabricate pedigrees and coats of arms from supposed originals, became interested in the archives of the parish. He made 15th-century Bristol the setting for the supposed poems of 'Thomas Rowley, a Secular Priest of St John's'. His principal source was the documents relating to a 15th-century merchant and mayor of Bristol, William Canynges; he became the imaginary patron of the imaginary Rowley.

In April 1770 he went to London. A practised writer – he had been contributing to London journals since the year before – he might have succeeded in earning a living but the poems which he offered to **Dodsley** and the document he offered to **Horace Walpole** were refused, and only one of the Rowley poems, 'Elinoure and Juga', was published in Chatterton's lifetime (in *The Town and Country Magazine* in 1769). In a fit of depression Chatterton took arsenic and died in a room in Holborn, London, on 24 August 1770. He was not yet 18.

A pen and wash drawing by John Flaxman entitled 'Despair offering a bowl of poison to Chatterton.' The drawing, now in the British Museum Print Room, was executed a few years after Thomas Chatterton's death in 1770.

A single poem, 'Bristowe Tragedie: or The Dethe of Syr Charles Bawdin', was published in 1772; the remainder of the Rowley poems were collected and edited by the **Chaucer** scholar **Thomas Tyrwhitt** in 1777. Tyrwhitt and many others were persuaded that the poems were genuine, but **Gray**, **Percy** and **Thomas Warton the younger** doubted their authenticity. Tyrwhitt himself was induced to reconsider, and the 1778 edition of *Poems, Supposed to Have Been Written at Bristol, by Thomas Rowley, and Others, in the Fifteenth Century* contained 'An Appendix Tending to Prove that They Were Written by Chatterton'.

With their archaic vocabulary and Spenserian style, the poems nonetheless reveal a genuine talent. Chatterton became an object of admiration to the Romantics, who recognized his youthful genius and were impressed by the histrionic circumstances of his death.

**Chaucer, Geoffrey**  *c.* 1343/4–1400   Born before 1346, the son of a wealthy vintner in London, he was perhaps educated at St Paul's Cathedral School and later studied at the Inner Temple. He became a page to Elizabeth, Countess of Ulster, and Prince Lionel, but it is not known how long he remained in this service. It was at least until he was involved in military campaigns in France in 1359–60; he was ransomed in March 1360 and returned to England but was again in France later that year. Nothing is known of his life between 1360 and 1367 except that he entered the king's service; he received a pension from Edward III in 1367. He married Philippa, probably in 1366, and apparently had two sons, Lewis (to whom he dedicated *A Treatise on the Astrolabe*) and Thomas.

Between *c.* 1368 and 1378 he conducted diplomatic missions to Europe, including Italy which he first visited *c.* 1373; Italian culture was to become a strong influence on his poetry. During this period he was also connected with John of Gaunt, either receiving his patronage or being in his service, or both. In 1374 he received a house in Aldgate where he lived until 1386 or 1385. Also in 1374 he undertook a series of professional and official appointments including a post as a customs official. His appointments increased in importance and he became prosperous, but in 1385 he left the Custom House and retired to Kent where he was a justice of the peace and, in 1386, knight of the shire. Whether his retirement was voluntary is unrecorded, but he was not re-elected to Parliament after his only session in 1386. Only after Richard II reached the age of majority and took over from Gloucester in 1389 did Chaucer receive any new preferments. In that year he was appointed Clerk of the King's Works and supervised construction, maintenance and renovation work, travelling constantly for two years. He left the

post in 1391 and became deputy forester of the royal forest of North Petherton, Somerset. This was his last regular office; his appointment was renewed in 1398 but it is not known for how long he maintained it. Late in 1399 he moved to Westminster and he died the following year; his tomb is in Westminster Abbey.

Generally considered to be the greatest English poet of the Middle Ages, Chaucer was recognized during his lifetime and remained extremely influential throughout the 15th century. The canon of his writings has now been established, with only a few short pieces and the translation *The Romaunt of the Rose* remaining uncertain, but from the 15th to the 19th centuries much spurious material was attributed to him (see **Chaucerian apocrypha**). The chronology of his poetry is less certain, and of the longer pieces only *The Book of the Duchess* can be attached to a definite event, the death of Blanche, Duchess of Lancaster in 1368. The other works can be put into an approximate order by their relation to each other, the dates of known sources and the influence of French and Italian literary traditions. *The Book of the Duchess*, some of the short poems and *The ABC* were written before 1372 and show the influence of French poets. Italian influence begins to appear in the works ascribed to the period 1372–80: *The House of Fame, Anelida and Arcite*, early versions

Geoffrey Chaucer. This is the earliest-known portrait, painted for Thomas Occleve's *De Regimine Principum*, in which the later poet pays tribute to Chaucer. The unknown artist worked from memory; Chaucer died in 1400 and Occleve's work was published in 1412. *MS Harley 4866, f.88.* British Library.

of *The Second Nun's Tale* and *The Monk's Tale*, and some of the lyrics form this group. Between 1380 and 1386 *The Parlement of Foules*, *Boece*, *Troilus and Criseyde*, an early version of *The Knight's Tale*, *The Legend of Good Women* and some short poems were written, in all of which the Italian influence appears fully assimilated. *The General Prologue* and the early stories of *The Canterbury Tales* were written between 1387 and 1392, and *A Treatise on the Astrolabe* in 1391–2. The later *Canterbury Tales* and final short poems date from 1393–1400. The doubtful translation of *Le Roman de la Rose* cannot be placed with certainty; it may belong with *The Book of the Duchess* in the period of French influence, but the Prologue to *The Legend of Good Women* links it with *Troilus and Criseyde* (c. 1385).

Although frequently imitated, Chaucer's blend of humour, realism, philosophical depth, poetic virtuosity, and masterful control of dialogue and character was never matched. The pervasive humour (sometimes vulgar) is directed at various targets, and the poet appears as the butt of his own jokes throughout the canon; in *The Canterbury Tales* it is Chaucer who cannot tell a tale competently and in the **dream-visions** he appears as naïve, ignorant and foolish. His translations are highly workmanlike and his use of philosophical ideas, though sometimes derived from intermediate texts, consistently demonstrates his understanding of them. As a story-teller he is supreme, and it is for this that he is known best. In the framework of *The Canterbury Tales* he develops both character and dialogue, and the extended characterization in *Troilus and Criseyde* has made critics liken the poem to a novel. His favourite verse forms are the decasyllabic couplet and **rhyme royal**, but *The Romaunt of the Rose* is in octosyllabic couplets; he also wrote in prose, though less well, in *Boece* and *A Treatise on the Astrolabe*, as well as *The Tale of Melibee* and *The Parson's Tale*.

Chaucer made a crucial contribution to English literature in using English at a time when much court poetry was still written in **Anglo-Norman** or Latin. His confidence in the language encouraged his followers and imitators also to write in English and speeded the transition from French as the language of literature.

**Chaucerian apocrypha** Body of material once attributed to **Geoffrey Chaucer**, much of it included in early editions of his works. It includes over 100 pieces of verse. The 15th-century manuscript distributor John Shirley instigated many of the early erroneous attributions and remains the only authority for some poems still accepted as the work of Chaucer. Early editions such as those of Pynson (1526), Thynne (1532) and Stow (1561) contain several apocryphal works and the canon was not revised until the 19th century. The apocrypha include works by other known poets such as **John Lydgate** (*The Siege of Thebes*, *The Fall of Princes* and others), **Robert Henryson** (*The Testament of Cresseid*), **Thomas Usk** (*The Testament of Love*) and **John Gower**. There are also additions to **The Canterbury Tales** – *The Plowman's Tale*, *The Tale of Beryn* and **The Tale of Gamelyn** – and anonymous pieces on various themes, including **The Assembly of Ladies**, **The Cuckoo and the Nightingale**, **The Flower and the Leaf** and *Jack Upland*. The degree to which these poems are Chaucerian in style and content varies, and some resemble the presently established canon hardly at all.

**Chaudhuri, Nirad C[handra]** 1897– Indian writer, born in Kishorganj, Bengal. His eccentric literary career began late, with *The Autobiography of An Unknown Indian* (1951), which, egotistical yet measured, records the development of his own quirky personality. The travel book, *A Passage to England* (1960), and two biographies, *Clive of India* (1975) and his account of F. M. Muller, *Scholar Extraordinary* (1975), unravel many strands in British–Indian relations. *The Continent of Circe* (1965) argues that Indians are displaced Europeans at odds with their Indian geography. His energy found further exercise in *Culture in the Vanity Bag* (1976) and *Hinduism: A Religion to Live By* (1979).

**Cheever, John** 1912–82 American short-story writer and novelist, born in Quincy, Massachusetts, and educated at Thayer Academy. Much of his fiction deals humorously and compassionately with the spiritually and emotionally impoverished life in materially affluent communities. His first novel, *The Wapshot Chronicle* (1957), won the 1958 National Book Award. In 1965 he received the Howells Medal for Fiction from the National Academy of Arts and Letters. His other novels include *The Wapshot Scandal* (1964), *Bullet Park* (1969), *Falconer* (1977) and *Oh, What a Paradise It Seems* (1982). His short stories, many of which appeared originally in **The New Yorker** and **The New Republic**, were collected in *The Way Some People Live: A Book of Short Stories* (1943), *The Enormous Radio and Other Stories* (1953), *Stories* (1956), *The Housebreaker of Shady Hill and Other Stories* (1958), *Some People, Places, and Things That Will Not Appear in My Next Novel* (1961), *The Brigadier and the Golf Widow* (1964), *Homage to Shakespeare* (1965), *The World of Apples* (1973) and *The Day the Pig Fell into the Well* (1978). *The Stories of John Cheever* was published in 1978 and received a Pulitzer Prize and a National Book Critics Circle Award.

***Cherrie and the Slaye, The*** See **Montgomerie, Alexander**.

**Chesney, Sir George Tomkyns** 1830–95

Novelist. Born in Devon, he pursued a distin-guished military career in India. His first novel, *The Battle of Dorking*, a fictional account of an enemy attack on England, was published by **Blackwood's Magazine** in 1871 and was frequently reprinted. Other novels were *The Dilemma* (1876), set at the time of the Indian mutiny, *The New Ordeal* (1879), *The Private Secretary* (1881) and *The Lesters* (1893).

**Chesnutt, Charles W[addell]** 1858–1932 Black American short-story writer and novelist, born in Cleveland, Ohio, to parents who recently had left Fayetteville, North Carolina, to escape the repression of free blacks in the South at the time. After the Civil War, the family returned to Fayetteville, where Chesnutt's edu-cation included instruction in German, French and Greek. After some years as a schoolteacher in the Carolinas, in 1883 he went to New York City to work as a reporter, and then moved to Cleveland, where he began his career as a writer.

His work came to the attention of a national audience when his story 'The Goophered Grapevine' was published in **The Atlantic Monthly** in 1887. He rapidly mastered the con-ventions of the short narrative aimed at readers of the popular literary magazines of his day, and this urbane, fluent style is seen in his first two collections of stories, *The Conjure Woman* and *The Wife of His Youth and Other Stories of the Color Line*, both published in 1899. Despite his adoption of prevailing literary forms, Chesnutt is considered a pioneer of black fiction, with his probing exploration of racial themes and his realistic view of slavery and the Reconstruction era. In his later works he focused on the prob-lems of racial and class identity in a changing society. He wrote three novels, *The House Behind the Cedars* (1900), *The Marrow of Tradition* (1901) and *The Colonel's Dream* (1906), and regularly published essays and reviews in vari-ous journals.

**Chester cycle of mystery plays** See **miracle plays**.

**Chesterfield, Philip Dormer Stanhope, 4th Earl of** 1694–1773 Statesman and writer. Born in St James's Square, Westminster, he was edu-cated at home and at Trinity College, Cam-bridge. After the customary Grand Tour for the sons of gentlemen he entered Parliament (1716) and became England's ambassador at The Hague from 1728 to 1732. After Walpole's government fell Lord Chesterfield (he succeeded to the title in 1726) entered Newcastle's cabinet as Secretary of State (1744), and became Lord Lieutenant of Ireland from 1745 to 1746. In that difficult post he acquitted himself with honour,

earning the gratitude of the people for his tolerance.

However, Chesterfield found Newcastle a difficult colleague, though he was Secretary of State again from 1746 until 1748, when he retired. He declined the offer of a dukedom. Chesterfield had a number of valued friends whom he kept until death separated them, rang-ing from the Earl of Scarborough to a Dublin bookseller, and from Lady Suffolk to his protégé Chenevix, who later became Bishop of Killaloe in Clare. The letters to his friends are among the most pleasant in the language – spontaneous, witty and full of natural kindness.

But his most famous letters were written to his son and to another godson who was a member of his family and was to become the 5th earl. The son was illegitimate, born in 1732; Chesterfield gave him his name (Philip Stan-hope) and, when the boy was five, began the letters of advice that were intended for no one else's eyes. The godson, also Philip Stanhope, was born when the son was 25; he began to receive letters when he was four, and these were also intended for the recipient only. The letters to both were written in English, French and Latin and all of them contain the affection and shrewdness of a man whose own life had not always been smooth. His son married in secret and had two sons and Chesterfield only became aware of the fact when his son died at the age of 36. He wrote to the widow, Eugenia Stanhope, in the kindest terms and assumed responsibility for his grandsons' upbringing. When he died, Chesterfield's legacy to them did not please Eugenia Stanhope and she realized that his let-ters to her late husband were a valuable prop-erty. The first public appearance of the famous letters was in 1774: *Letters to his Son, Philip Stanhope, Together With Several Other Pieces on Various Subjects*. Some of those to his heir and godson appeared in *The Art of Pleasing: in a Series of Letters to Master Stanhope* and were published in two numbers of *The Edinburgh Magazine* in the same year, and after that more and more of the Chesterfield letters were pub-lished.

Chesterfield has also assumed an undeserved literary notoriety as the epitome of churlish patrons since **Samuel Johnson**, in a celebrated letter of 7 February 1755, rebuked him for not having offered support to the plans for his **Dictionary**, 'till I am known, and do not want it'.

**Chesterton, G[ilbert] K[eith]** 1874–1936 Poet, novelist, journalist and essayist. Born on Camden Hill, London, he was educated at St Paul's School and the Slade. His talent as an illustrator can be seen in his contributions to the novels of his friend, **Hilaire Belloc**, but he made a more definite mark by his own prolific writ-ings. He first published articles in *The Bookman* and *The Illustrated London News* and, like Belloc, contributed to *The Speaker*, in which he made known his anti-Imperial sentiments during the Boer War. His first book was a collection of verse and sketches, *Greybeards at Play – Literature and Art for Old Gentlemen* (1900). This was followed by *The Wild Knight and Other Poems* (1900). Most of his verse, which tends to celebrate the 'Englishness' of England, can be found in *Collected Poems*, published in 1933.

Chesterton's first novel, *The Napoleon of Notting Hill* (1904), was a political fantasy which, like much of his work, reflected his distaste for the modern world of business and centralized power and celebrated the romance of an earlier pre-industrial world. Similar sentiments informed *The Man Who Was Thursday: A Nightmare* (1908). But Chesterton is perhaps best remembered for his detective stories about Father Brown (beginning with *The Innocence of Father Brown*, 1911), an unassuming Catholic priest with a gift for solving complex mysteries. Chesterton himself became a Roman Catholic in 1922.

Among his non-fiction, there are studies of **Robert Browning** (1903), **Charles Dickens** (1906), **George Bernard Shaw** and **William Blake** (both 1910), and **Chaucer** (1932). Works on social, political and religious subjects include *Heretics* (1905), *Orthodoxy* (1909), *St Francis of Assisi* (1923) and *St Thomas Aquinas* (1933). Collections of his essays appeared as *All Things Considered* (1908), *A Miscellany of Men* (1912), *The Uses of Diversity* (1920), and *As I Was Saying* (1936). His *Autobiography* appeared in 1936.

**Chestre, Thomas** 14th-century poet who wrote *Sir Launfal* and possibly also *Libeaus Desconus*. Nothing else is known about him.

**Chettle, Henry** *c.* 1560–*c.* 1607 Particularly active as a dramatist – he had a hand in about 50 plays – Chettle made his first significant contribution to Elizabethan literature as a printer, when he prepared *Greene's Groatsworth of Wit* for publication in 1592. When the printing house in which he was a partner failed, Chettle turned to writing. His satirical dream-fable *Kind Harts Dreame* (1593) is best remembered for its preface, in which he expresses regret for **Greene's** abuse of **Shakespeare**. *Piers Plainnes Seaven Yeres Prentiship* (1595) is a picaresque romance better than many of its voguish kind.

By 1598 Chettle was providing plays for **Philip Henslowe** and the Admiral's Men. That he was living hand-to-mouth is clear from his imprisonment for debt in the Marshalsea that year. Most of his plays are lost. Of those that survive only *Hoffman, or, A Revenge for a Father* (*c.* 1603) is believed to be his alone. It is a **revenge tragedy**. Two pieces written in collaboration with **Anthony Munday** are generally

regarded as his most interesting work, not only because they deal with the **Robin Hood** legend. Both performed in 1598, *The Downfall of Robert, Earl of Huntingdon* and *The Death of Robert, Earl of Huntingdon* illustrate the Elizabethan theatre's avidity to capitalize on success. Chettle collaborated with William Haughton and **Thomas Dekker** on *Patient Grissel* (1600) and with **John Day** on *The Blind Beggar of Bednal-Green* (1600). His elegy on the death of Elizabeth I, *England's Mourning Garment* (1603), is charming but slight.

**chiasmus** A type of **antithesis**. Where the contrasting parts of the normal antithesis stand in the relation ab/ab, those of a chiasmus form a mirror-image, ab/ba: 'A Fop(a) their Passion(b)/ but their Prize(b) a Sot(a)' (**Pope, *Moral Essays***).

**Child, F[rancis] J[ames]** 1825–96 American scholar. He was born in Boston and educated at Harvard University, where he became Boylston Professor of Rhetoric in 1851 and Professor of English in 1876. His friends and colleagues included **Charles Eliot Norton**, **James Russell Lowell** and **Longfellow**. The editor of **Spenser** and the author of philological studies of **Chaucer** and **Gower**, he is remembered for his collections of **ballads**, particularly the five-volume *English and Scottish Popular Ballads*, originally issued in 10 parts between 1883 and 1898. See also **folk revival**.

**Child, Lydia M[aria]** 1802–80 American social reformer and novelist. Born in Medford, Massachusetts, Child is best remembered as a leading Abolitionist. She achieved her greatest success with her 'Appeal in Favor of that Class of Americans Called Africans' (1833). Her persuasive letters to the governor of Virginia were later published as *Correspondence* (1860), and won many adherents to the anti-slavery cause. She also wrote several novels, including *Hobomok* (1824), a didactic story about the Indians of colonial Massachusetts, *The Rebels, or, Boston Before the Revolution* (1825), about the Stamp Tax agitation, and *Philothea* (1836), a romance set in classical Greece.

***Child of the Jago, A*** A novel by **Arthur Morrison**, published in 1896.

'The Jago', Morrison's name for 'The Nichol' in London's Bethnal Green, is the setting for this story about the childhood of Dick ('Dicky') Perrott. A boy with good intentions, he is constantly frustrated by his environment – a violent 'jungle' in which his father is hanged for murder and Dicky himself is killed in a street fight at the age of 17. Morrison's terse, straightforward style owes something to **George Moore** and looks ahead to the social realism of a later generation of writers. His refusal to impose his own moral judgements on the various criminals in the book distinguished him from most of his late-Victorian contemporaries.

**Child's History of England, A** A work by **Charles Dickens**, published at irregular intervals in *Household Words* between January 1851 and December 1853.

As early as 1843, when his son Charley was six, Dickens contemplated writing for him a history of his native country to counter the High Church or Conservative ideas he might otherwise absorb. The result, some years later, was a chronological account of the individual reigns of English monarchs from Alfred to James II; two opening chapters look at the Romans and early Saxons, and an exceedingly brief final one summarizes the period 1688–1837. Written in the broadest outline, the book is a withering condemnation of the humbug attaching to the glorification of past times and people, particularly royalty. King John, for instance, is a 'miserable brute' and Henry VIII 'one of the most detestable villains that ever drew breath'. *A Child's History* has good words only for Alfred and Cromwell.

**Childe Harold's Pilgrimage** A poem by **Byron** in Spenserian stanzas. The first two **cantos** were published in 1812, the third in 1816, and the fourth in 1818. The poem was begun in Albania in 1809 during Byron's visit to the eastern Mediterranean with John Cam Hobhouse.

It describes the wanderings of a young man, disillusioned with his empty pleasure-seeking existence, who looks for distraction in foreign scenes, travelling through Spain, Portugal, Albania and Greece whose 'haunted, holy ground' had made an indelible impression on the poet's mind. The third canto follows the pilgrim to Belgium on the eve of Waterloo, along the Rhine and to the Alps and Jura. Finally, speaking in his own voice, Byron

An illustration for an edition of Byron's *Childe Harold's Pilgrimage* published in 1841. The scene is from Canto III (1816); Brussels on the eve of Waterloo.

describes a literary and historical tour of Italy invoking the associations of Venice, Arqua, Florence and Rome.

*Childe Harold's Pilgrimage* was immediately popular – after the publication of the first two cantos Byron 'woke one morning and found myself famous' – and made the melancholy 'Byronic hero' one of the most recognizable Romantic figures of the age.

**Childe Roland to the Dark Tower Came** A poem by **Robert Browning** published in *Men and Women* (1855). The title is taken from **Shakespeare**'s *King Lear* (III, iv, 173). This masterful and enigmatic nightmare poem was apparently one result of a resolution made by Browning in 1852 to write a poem a day.

**Childers, (Robert) Erskine** 1870–1922 Novelist and political pamphleteer. Born in London, and educated at Haileybury College and Trinity College, Cambridge, Childers served in the Boer War and World War I and worked as a clerk in the House of Commons (1895–1910). He settled in Dublin in 1919, devoted himself to the cause of Irish Home Rule and, after the establishment of the Irish Free State, joined the Irish Republican Army. He was arrested and executed in 1922. Although his political pamphlets on miltary affairs and the Irish question are forgotten, his one novel, *The Riddle of the Sands* (1903), is not. A slow-paced thriller, packed with yachting lore and polemical warnings of Germany's military ambitions, it remains notable for its portrait of the two well-contrasted heroes, the dandified civil servant Carruthers and the homespun amateur sailor Davies.

**Children of the New Forest, The** See **Marryat, Frederick**.

**children's companies of actors** see **boys' companies**.

**children's literature** Stories and poems aimed at children have an exceedingly long history: lullabies, for example, were sung in Roman times, and a few nursery games and rhymes are almost as ancient. Yet so far as written-down literature is concerned, while there were stories in print before 1800 that children often seized on when they had the chance, such as translations of Aesop's fables, fairy-stories and popular ballads and romances, these were not aimed at young people in particular. Since the only genuinely child-oriented literature at this time would have been a few instructional works to help with reading and general knowledge, plus the odd Puritanical tract as an aid to morality, the only course for keen child readers was to raid adult literature. This still occurs today, especially with adult thrillers or romances that include more exciting, graphic detail than is normally found in literature for younger readers. For the boy or girl in the early 18th century the equivalent could have been **Bunyan**'s *The Pilgrim's Progress* (1678), **Defoe**'s *The Adventures of Robinson Crusoe* (1719) or **Swift**'s *Gulliver's Travels* (1726). The fact that all these classics soon appeared in simplified form suggests that such popularity among young readers had not been overlooked.

By the middle of the 18th century there were enough eager child readers, and enough parents glad to cater to this interest, for publishers to specialize in children's books whose first aim was pleasure rather than education or morality. In Britain, a London merchant named Thomas Boreham produced *Cajanus, The Swedish Giant* in 1742, while the more famous **John Newbery** published *A Little Pretty Pocket Book* in 1744. Its contents – rhymes, stories, children's games plus a free gift ('A ball and a pincushion') – in many ways anticipated the similar lucky-dip contents of children's annuals this century. It is a tribute to Newbery's flare that he hit upon a winning formula quite so quickly, to be pirated almost immediately in America.

Such pleasing levity was not to last. Influenced by Rousseau, whose *Émile* (1762) decreed that all books for children save *Robinson Crusoe* were a dangerous diversion, contemporary critics saw to it that children's literature should be instructive and uplifting. Prominent among such voices was Mrs Sarah Trimmer, whose magazine *The Guardian of Education* (1802) carried the first regular reviews of children's books. It was she who condemned fairy-tales for their violence and general absurdity; her own stories, *Fabulous Histories* (1786), described talking animals who were always models of sense and decorum. In less fanciful vein, **Mary Sherwood**'s *The History of the Fairchild Family* (1818–47) contained dark moral warnings together with regular reference to biblical verses. That her book stayed in print so long is a tribute to her powers as a writer; the famous passage, where the Fairchild father takes his children to see a corpse on a gibbet as a final Awful Warning, had actually to be softened in later editions. Not for the first time, children may have thrilled to this part of the text with its horrific, Gothic overtones rather more whole-heartedly than its author intended. The stories of **Captain Frederick Marryat** too, such as *Masterman Ready* (1841) or *Children of the New Forest* (1847), were popular for more reasons than their lengthy digressions on flora, fauna and British history. They also included passages of exciting action where both reader and writer could temporarily forget about self-improvement.

In this way the moral story for children was always threatened from within, given the way children have of drawing out entertainment from the sternest moralist. But the greatest blow to the improving children's book was to come from an unlikely source indeed: early 19th-century interest in folklore. Both nursery rhymes, selected by **James Orchard Halliwell** for a folklore society in 1842, and collections of fairy-stories by the scholarly Grimm brothers, swiftly translated into English in 1823, soon rocketed to popularity with the young, quickly leading to new editions, each one more child-centred than the last. But another folklorist, Sir George Dasent, insisted on keeping his translation of Norse fairy-tales intact, merely suggesting – no doubt unrealistically – that all good children should ignore the two slightly racy examples at the end of the book. Later on, American children also had the chance of enjoying the legends of **Robin Hood** (1883) and King Arthur (1903) skilfully reworked by **Howard Pyle** – another revivalist who provided rich fare for children, however occasionally worrying for the puritan conscience.

Those latter-day followers of Rousseau who still battled for 'sensible' stories continued to have a certain success despite the wrath of **Charles Dickens** in his memorable essay of 1853, 'Frauds on the Fairies'. But by now history was against them: 1846, for example, saw the publication of **Edward Lear**'s *Book of Nonsense*, as anarchic as any rebellious child could wish, while **Thackeray**'s *The Rose and the Ring* (1855) and **Charles Kingsley**'s *The Water Babies* (1863) continued to make an unanswerable case for fantasy and the imagination first, moral lessons second. All it needed was a masterpiece that not only avoided didacticism but actually made fun of it, and two years later this duly arrived with the appearance of **Lewis Carroll**'s *Alice's Adventures in Wonderland* (1865).

From now on younger children could expect stories written for their particular interest and with the needs of their own limited experience of life kept well to the fore. In Britain, **Mrs Juliana Ewing**, **Mrs Mary Molesworth** and **Charlotte M. Yonge** produced excellent stories aimed at young girl readers in this way, something repeated in America by **Susan Coolidge** in *What Katy Did* (1872), **Kate Douglas Wiggin** in *Rebecca of Sunnybrook Farm* (1903), Eleanor H. Porter in *Pollyanna* (1913), and by the Canadian writer **L. M. Montgomery** in *Anne of Green Gables* (1908). For boys, **Thomas Hughes**'s classic *Tom Brown's Schooldays* (1857) spawned a new generation of school-stories.

But while such books for younger children stood out on their own as the next stage after the large picture-books now available for fortunate infants from homes wealthy enough to afford such fare, older child readers and adults still tended to share each other's principal fare. **R. M. Ballantyne**'s adventure stories were popular with all ages, for example, while Gladstone was an enthusiastic fan of **Robert Louis Stevenson**'s *Treasure Island* (1883), although on hearing this news the ungrateful author merely remarked, 'He would do better to attend to the Imperial affairs of England.' Elsewhere, **George MacDonald**'s strange, mystical stories such as *At the Back of the North Wind* (1871) also intrigued a wide audience, while **Anna Sewell**'s *Black Beauty* (1877) was once set as compulsory reading material in prison by way of reform for an adult guilty of animal cruelty.

What eventually determined the reading of older children during this time was often not the availability of special, children's literature as such but their access or otherwise to books that contained within them characters, such as young people or animals, with whom they could more easily identify, or action, such as exploring or fighting, that made fewest demands on adult maturity or understanding. Such a list encompassed **G. A. Henty**'s imperialistic adventures or **Fenimore Cooper**'s *The Last of the Mohicans* (1826; see **Leatherstocking Tales**), **Harriet Beecher Stowe**'s *Uncle Tom's Cabin* (1852), **Louisa M. Alcott**'s *Little Women* (1868), **Mark Twain**'s *The Adventures of Huckleberry Finn* (1884) and **Frances Hodgson Burnett**'s *Little Lord Fauntleroy* (1885), also greatly admired by Gladstone. Mention must also be made of Dickens's novels, with a poll as late as 1888 still revealing him to be the most popular author with older children by a generous margin.

In time, however, adults themselves moved on to a narrower spectrum of imaginative literature, leaving genres they had once freely enjoyed – such as animal or fairy-stories – increasingly to a younger audience. In this way, masterpieces such as **Kipling**'s *The Jungle Book* (1894), **Kenneth Grahame**'s *The Wind in the Willows* (1908) or **Andrew Lang**'s collection of folk-stories would more often be found on children's than on adults' bookshelves. At the same time, magazines sprang up specifically directed at children both in Britain and America, while a new generation of writers such as **E. Nesbit** took the children's story further out of the adult world and more into the details of family life, imaginative games and domestic adventures that adults found less relevant to their current interests. In America, **Frank L. Baum**'s *The Wonderful Wizard of Oz* (1900) was another determinedly child-centred success, despite passages of doctrinaire morality, while Australian children could enjoy their own comic masterpiece with no adult pretensions, **Norman Lindsay**'s *The Magic Pudding* (1918). With poetry, Robert Louis Stevenson's *A Child's Garden of Verses* (1885) set a high standard not equalled until the publication of **Walter de la Mare**'s *Peacock Pie* (1913). More knockabout fare

was provided by **Hilaire Belloc**'s *The Bad Child's Book of Beasts* (1896) only rivalled in popularity years later with the publication of **T. S. Eliot**'s *Old Possum's Book of Practical Cats* (1939). At the same time sentimental verses for and about children, also very popular since the 19th century, finally touched bottom with the saccharine cadences of Rose Fyleman's *Fairies and Chimneys* (1918).

The inter-war period saw a further consolidation of children's literature as an exclusive empire, a process helped by the growing popularity of children's annuals, children's picture-books and the children's comic, now moving well away from its rougher, penny dreadful origins towards something far gentler in taste. With books, plots became considerably softened, with the dangers of Kenneth Grahame's Wild Wood or Kipling's jungle giving way to the gentler concerns of **A. A. Milne**'s Ashdown Forest in *Winnie-the-Pooh* (1926) and **Hugh Lofting**'s amiably eccentric collection of humans and animals in *The Story of Doctor Dolittle* (1922). In **Arthur Ransome**'s adventure stories young people wrestled with sailing boats rather than with hostile enemies, while in **Noel Streatfeild**'s *Ballet Shoes* (1936) the chief fear was failing an audition rather than encountering adult ostracism or family ruin as in tales from earlier writers such as Frances Hodgson Burnett. In America, though, **Laura Ingalls Wilder**'s *The Little House* series (1932–43) continued to describe a past world that could be tough as well as warm and loving. Picture-books also lost some of the matter-of-fact treatment of danger and death found earlier in **Beatrix Potter**'s stories for small children. Instead, **Edward Ardizzone** and William Nicholson in Britain or Munro Leaf and later **Dr Seuss** in America painted a world both safe and ultimately welcoming to all.

The final apotheosis of literary childhood as something to be protected from all unpleasant reality came with the arrival in the late 1930s of child-centred best-sellers intent on entertainment at its most escapist. In Britain, novelists such as **Enid Blyton** and **Richmal Crompton** described children who were always free to have the most unlikely adventures, secure in the knowledge that nothing bad could ever happen to them in the end. The fact that war broke out again during her books' greatest popularity fails to register at all in the self-enclosed world inhabited by Enid Blyton's young characters, and for Richmal Crompton's mischievous creation William a country in arms only provides him with further opportunities for becoming a nuisance. Reaction against such dream-worlds was inevitable, coinciding after World War II with the growth of paperback sales, children's libraries and a new spirit of moral and social concern. Urged on by committed publishers and progressive librarians, writers slowly began to explore new areas of interest while also shifting the settings of their plots from the middle-class world to which their chiefly adult patrons had always previously belonged. In the realms of fantasy a similar spirit of moral toughness is evident in the stories of **C. S. Lewis** and **J. R. R. Tolkien** and later in the stories of **Alan Garner** and **Ursula LeGuin**. Picture-books also began to experiment with offbeat stories and characters, with artist-illustrators like **Maurice Sendak** and **Raymond Briggs** exploring a small child's timeless concern with death and aggression alongside lighter preoccupations.

Critical emphasis, during this development, has been divided. For some, the most important task was to rid children's books of the social prejudice and exclusiveness no longer found acceptable. Others concentrated more on the positive achievements of contemporary children's literature, in particular those of British novelists like **William Mayne**, **Leon Garfield**, **Philippa Pearce**, **Joan Aiken** and **Nina Bawden**; American novelists like **Virginia Hamilton**, **Paula Fox** and **Betsy Byars**; and Australian novelists like **Patricia Wrightson**, **Ivan Southall** and Nan Chauncy. That such writers are now often recommended to the attentions of adult as well as child readers echoes the 19th-century belief that children's literature can often be shared between the generations, rather than act as defensive barrier between childhood and the necessary growth towards adult understanding.

**Chillingworth, William** 1602–44 Divine. A godson of Archbishop **Laud**, Chillingworth became a Roman Catholic in 1630 but returned to the Protestant fold and accepted preferment at Salisbury in 1638. In 1637 he published *The Religion of Protestants a Safe Way to Salvation*, which argued that disagreements among Protestants were not a spiritual hazard and caused heated controversy. A Royalist, he fought at the siege of Gloucester; he was captured at Arundel Castle, where he lay ill, and died the same year. **Nathaniel Hawthorne** may have been remembering his reputation for Protestant polemic when he called one of his characters in *The Scarlet Letter* Chillingworth.

*Chimes, The* A Christmas story by **Charles Dickens**, published in 1844 and collected in *Christmas Books* (1852).

*The Chimes* is an uneasy amalgam of realism and fantasy built around the adventures of the simple, good-hearted Toby ('Trotty') Veck who, mesmerized by chiming bells and influenced by spirits, 'dwarf phantoms' and elfin creatures, witnesses the hardships of his daughter Meg, the falsely accused Will Fern and the orphaned Lilian. These good characters are maltreated or condescended to by Sir Joseph Bowley, Alderman Cute, Mr Filer and others. But the plight of the poor, as well as an appeal for deeper human feeling to be directed towards social improvement, is eloquently voiced by Will Fern. A final burst of goodwill resolves the various problems and effects a happy ending.

**Chopin, Kate** 1851–1904 American novelist and short-story writer. Born Kate O'Flaherty in St Louis, Missouri, to an Irish father and French mother, she moved to New Orleans following her marriage to Oscar Chopin. After the death of her mother and husband, she began to devote herself to writing. Her first novel, *At Fault* (1890), showed the influence of Guy de Maupassant. This was followed by two collections of short stories set among Creoles and Acadians in Louisiana, *Bayou Folk* (1894) and *A Night in Acadie* (1897), which helped establish her as a leading exponent of the 'local colour' school. She also contributed regularly to popular and literary magazines. Her best-known work, *The Awakening*, was published in 1899. Its sympathetic portrayal of a woman who rejects the constraints of marriage and motherhood provoked hostile criticism. The book was banned from the library shelves in Chopin's home town of St Louis, and following a reprint in 1906 went out of print for over 50 years.

**Chrétien de Troyes** See **Arthurian literature** and **courtly love**.

*Christ* An Old English poem in three parts, dealing with the Nativity, the Ascension and Doomsday. It is preserved in the **Exeter Book**. **Cynewulf**'s runic signature appears in the first section; it is not certain whether he also wrote the other two parts. The *Nativity* is freely adapted from the Church antiphon for Advent, the *Ascension* is based principally on a **homily** of Pope Gregory the Great, and the third part, a powerful description of the Day of Judgement with Christ's address to the sinners, has various sources. The dialogue between Mary and Joseph in the first part is the earliest extant dramatic scene in English.

*Christ and Satan* An Old English poem in three parts, or perhaps three separate pieces, found in the Junius manuscript (see **Junius, Francis**). They deal with the Fall of the Angels, the Harrowing of Hell and the Temptation of Christ. The first and third have biblical sources, while the second draws upon the apocryphal *Gospel of Nicodemus*.

*Christabel* An unfinished poem by **Coleridge**, begun during the period of his collaboration with **Wordsworth** on the *Lyrical Ballads* (1798) but first published in *Christabel and Other Poems* (1816). Making evocative use of Gothic and supernatural themes, it tells how the enchantress

Geraldine deceives all but the virtuous Christabel. It uses a new metre, the rhyming four-stressed line.

**Christian Socialism** A response to the Chartist agitation of 1848, Christian Socialism set out to help the working man to help himself and to avert revolution by improving social conditions. Its practical outcome was the founding of the Working Men's College in 1854, the establishment of small self-governing workshops and a revival of the Co-operative Movement. The leader was **Frederick Denison Maurice**; his associates were **Charles Kingsley**, who wrote under the pseudonym Parson Lot, **Thomas Hughes**, author of *Tom Brown's Schooldays*, and 'John Townsend', whose real name was John Malcolm Ludlow (1821–1911). Although Maurice was the figurehead, Ludlow was the mainspring. A barrister, educated in Paris, he was largely responsible for promoting the Industrial and Provident Societies Act of 1852. Kingsley's socialism, as evinced in his novels *Yeast* (1848) and *Alton Locke* (1850), was paternalistic and ultimately impermanent, though his enthusiasm for sanitary reform was passionate. Christian Socialism did not imply radical social change, though Marx's famous phrase about religion being 'the opium of the people' (1844) is echoed by Kingsley: in *Letters to the Chartists* (1848) he wrote that the Bible had been used as 'an opium dose for keeping beasts of burden patient'. The Christian Socialists produced several short-lived journals: *Politics for the People* (1848), *The Christian Socialist* (1850), *Tracts for Christian Socialists* (1850) and *The Journal of Association* (1852).

*Christian Year, The* See **Keble, John**

**Christie, Dame Agatha (Mary Clarissa)** 1890–1976 Writer of **detective fiction**. Born in Torquay, Devon, of an American father and English mother, she enjoyed a quiet, middle-class childhood that set the keynote for her adult life and personality. Only the much-publicized episode of her temporary disappearance in 1926 offers any encouragement to those wishing to connect the author and her work. The more than 80 books she produced made her beyond doubt the most famous detective novelist of the century. Her first novel, *The Mysterious Affair at Styles* (1920), introduced the Belgian private detective Hercule Poirot, whose fictional career extended through many books to *Curtain* (1975). *The Murder at the Vicarage* (1930) introduced the shrewd, gentle Miss Marple, whose fictional career rivalled Poirot's in length and popularity, ending with *Sleeping Murder* (1976). Other detective heroes (Superintendent Battle, Tommy and Tuppence Beresford) proved less durable. Agatha Christie's classic books – *The Murder of Roger Ackroyd* (1926), *Peril at End House* (1932), *Lord Edgeware Dies* (1933), *Murder on the Orient Express* (1934), *Why Didn't They Ask Evans?* (1934), *The ABC Murders* (1936) and *Ten Little Niggers* (1939) – epitomize the so-called Golden Age of detective fiction in the 1920s and 1930s. Perfunctory in setting and characterization, they concentrate almost exclusively on tantalizing ingenuity of plot. Of the several short stories Agatha Christie adapted for the stage, *The Mousetrap* (first produced 1952) and *Witness for the Prosecution* (first produced 1953) were prodigiously successful. She also wrote light romantic novels as Mary Westmacott.

*Christmas Books* A collection of Christmas stories by **Charles Dickens**, published together for the first time in 1852: *A Christmas Carol* (1843), *The Chimes* (1844), *The Cricket on the Hearth* (1845), *The Battle of Life* (1846) and *The Haunted Man* (1848).

*Christmas Carol, A* A novella by **Charles Dickens**, published in 1843. The first and most famous of his popular Christmas stories, it was gathered together with its successors in *Christmas Books* (1852).

The 'ghostly little book', as Dickens called *A Christmas Carol*, starts on Christmas Eve when the grasping miserly Scrooge is visited by the shade of his former partner, Jacob Marley, now dead seven years. This uninvited guest warns Scrooge he is to be haunted by three spirits without whose visits he cannot avoid the endless wanderings now inflicted upon Marley himself. The trio consists of The Ghost of Christmas Past, The Ghost of Christmas Present, and The Ghost of Christmas Yet to Come. Escorted by each in turn Scrooge goes back, invisibly, to the scenes of his youth and, later, to the family life of his loyal clerk, Bob Cratchit, whose household includes the sadly crippled Tiny Tim. With the third Ghost the old miser surveys the ominous shape of things to come should he not change his ways. Chastened by his experiences, and now taught how others suffer in adversity, Scrooge resolves to live in a better way, a decision he celebrates by sending a turkey to the Cratchits, visiting his honest nephew, donating to charity and raising Bob's salary. The tale ends in a glow of warmth and *bonhomie*.

**chronicle** Historical writing of the Middle Ages, in either verse or prose, varying in scope from the universal history to the local record. Written in English, Latin and **Anglo-Norman**, the British chronicles borrowed from each other and adapted each other freely. Despite their large mythic and fictional content, they can be valuable historical sources for contemporary and near-contemporary events.

*The Anglo-Saxon Chronicle* is the earliest vernacular English example and records events from the 9th century to, in one version, 1134. The first important Latin chronicle was the *Historia Regum Britanniae* (*c.* 1135) by William of Malmesbury. William's sceptical reference to King Arthur was developed by **Geoffrey of Monmouth** into a full 'history' of the king and his court imitating the form of the ostensibly accurate historical chronicle (see **Arthurian literature**). Arthur's place in history was consolidated by Wace's Anglo-Norman *Roman de Brut* (1155) and its Middle English version, **Layamon**'s *Brut* (*c.* 1190). Although the chronicles begin with a mythic past, they end in recent history and here they are more trustworthy. **Andrew of Wyntoun**'s *Orygynale Cronykil*, for example, begins with biblical history but culminates in a relatively accurate account of Scottish political history.

Many chronicles are by several hands. Thus the Latin chronicle of Florence of Worcester (d. 1148) was continued by John of Worcester until 1141, then by Henry of Huntingdon until 1152 and thereafter by the monks of Bury St Edmunds. Similarly, in the Middle English chronicle of **Robert of Gloucester** the work of at least two other compilers can be detected.

***Chronicles of the Canongate*** The inclusive title given by **Sir Walter Scott** to stories presented as the recollections of Mrs Bethune, Baliol of the Canongate in Edinburgh. They are written down by her friend Mr Chrystal Croftangry, whose own remarkable story serves as an introduction. The first series, consisting of three stories, was published in 1827 and the second, *The Fair Maid of Perth*, in 1828.

*The Highland Widow.* The story of a widow's struggle to make her son adhere to the traditions of his dead father, one of the Highland rebels in 1745. When the son enlists in an English regiment, her attempts to stop him succeed only in provoking him to kill his sergeant. He is shot for desertion and murder, and she dies alone in her grief.

*The Two Drovers.* Two drovers – a Highlander, Robin Oig M'Combich, and a Yorkshireman, Harry Wakefield – quarrel on their way to England. Robin finally kills his companion and surrenders himself to justice.

*The Surgeon's Daughter.* Richard Middlemass, adopted son of a surgeon, goes to India and falls under the influence of a procuress, Madame Montreville. He attempts to lure Janet Gray, the surgeon's daughter, out to India and into the clutches of Tippoo Sahib, but she is saved by Adam Hartley, Richard's fellow pupil who is in love with Janet. Richard is put to death for his crime.

*St Valentine's Day, or, The Fair Maid of Perth.* A story of Scotland in the 14th century, in the reign of Robert III. The fair maid of Perth is Catharine Glover. The worthless Duke of Rothsay, the king's son, and his evil friend, Sir John Ramorny, try to kidnap Catharine but are driven off by Henry Smith, the armourer, who loves her; Henry strikes off Ramorny's hand during the fight. Ramorny is determined on vengeance: first on Henry, and also on Rothsay whom he blames as the author of his misfortune. He lures Rothsay to Falkland Tower, with the promise of Catharine, and has him murdered. The gentle Catharine, meanwhile, in spite of her father's urging, refuses Henry; his great strength and love of combat are not for her. Henry's rival, Conachar, is also his enemy since their two clans are at feud, and in an arranged battle Conachar is finally confronted by Henry. Conachar's courage deserts him and Henry wins the day when Conachar runs from the field. But Henry is sickened by the carnage and, when he learns that Conachar has killed himself in shame, he resolves to hang up his broadsword for ever. Catharine accepts him in the light of this vow.

***Chrysal, or, The Adventures of a Guinea*** See **Johnstone, Charles**.

**Church, Richard (Thomas)** 1893–1972 Poet and novelist. Born in London, Church attended Dulwich Hamlet School. He was a civil servant for 24 years before becoming a publisher's reader; he was also the Examiner for Voice Production and Verse Speaking for London University. His novels include *The Porch* (1937) and *The Nightingale* (1952). His essentially Georgian poetry is characterized by sturdy craftsmanship and limited ambition; now neglected, he is doomed to oblivion. His many collections include *The Flood of Life* (1917), *The Lamp* (1946), *Collected Poems* (1948) and *The Burning Bush* (1967).

**Churchill, Caryl** 1938– Playwright who began writing while a student at Oxford University. Her best work has been written for, and often in collaboration with, lively and socially alert small-scale theatre companies. *Vinegar Tom* (1976), performed by the feminist group Monstrous Regiment, is a play with songs, based on the trials of the Lancashire witches in 1612. *Light Shining in Buckinghamshire* (1976), about the Levellers in 1647, was the first of several outstanding collaborations with Joint Stock Theatre Company. It was followed by *Cloud Nine* (1978), in which an attack on sexual stereotyping is given a background in imperialism, *Top Girls* (1982), a scrutiny of the hazards encountered by women on the road to competitive success, and *Fen* (1982), a bleak portrait of the lives of working women in East Anglia. *Serious Money* (1987) is about the financial world of the City of London.

**Churchill, Charles** 1731–64 Satirist. The son of a curate of St John's, Westminster, he attended Westminster School and went on to St John's College, Cambridge, but blighted his academic prospects by a secret marriage at the age of 17 to Martha Scott. Though hardly better suited to the Church, he succeeded his father in 1758 as incumbent of St John's. To help support his family Churchill soon turned to writing. Two poems, 'The Bard' and 'The Conclave', failed to find publishers but he published *The Rosciad* with his own money in 1761. This verse satire praising **David Garrick** at the expense of other contemporary actors was an overnight success.

It led to his friendship with **John Wilkes**, whose rakish example Churchill (now estranged from his wife) lost no time in following. *The North Briton*, Wilkes's political weekly, owed a great deal of its success to Churchill, who wrote at least half of it. *The Prophecy of Famine* (1763) was a satirical blast at Bute; but Wilkes made sure that his friend escaped prosecution in the uproar which followed the publication of No. 45 of *The North Briton*, asserting that Churchill had not written it. After Wilkes's departure for exile, Churchill continued his social and political satires: *The Apology* and *Night* (1761) and *Ghosts* (1762) preceded the suppression of *The North Briton*, while *The Conference, The Author, An Epistle to William Hogarth* (1763), *The Duellist, The Candidate, Gotham, Independence, The Times* and *The Farewell* (1764) followed it. In 1764 Churchill sailed for France to visit Wilkes, but died soon after landing at Boulogne. *The Journey*, a fragment, and some satirical verses directed at Bishop Warburton appeared in 1765.

**Churchill, Sir Winston (Leonard Spencer)** 1874–1965 Politician and historian. Born at Blenheim Palace, the eldest son of Lord Randolph Churchill, he was educated at Harrow and Sandhurst. He served with the British forces in India and the Sudan, and was captured by the Boers while acting as a war correspondent in South Africa. He entered Parliament in 1900 and thereafter held the offices of, among others, Home Secretary (1910–11), First Lord of the Admiralty (1911–15), Secretary of State for War (1918–21), Chancellor of the Exchequer (1924–9) and Prime Minister (1940–5 and 1951–5). He published several historical studies including *The World Crisis 1916–18* (6 vols., 1923–31), *The Second World War* (6 vols., 1948–54) and *A History of the English-Speaking Peoples* (4 vols., 1956–8). His biographies include *Lord Randolph Churchill* (1906) and *Marlborough: His Life and Times* (4 vols., 1933–8). He also wrote a novel, *Savrola* (1900), and several books dealing with his early career, among them *My African Journey* (1908) and *My Early Life* (1930). He was awarded the Nobel Prize for Literature in 1953.

**Churchyard, Thomas** ?1520–1604 Poet. Churchyard started writing poetry in the reign of Edward VI and his career lasted long enough for him to celebrate James VI's public entry to Westminster in 'A Paean Triumphal' (1603). His last two works were printed in the year of his death. **Spenser** disguises him as Palaemon in 'Colin Clout' and commented he 'sung so long until quite hoarse he grew'. Churchyard was trained as a soldier and campaigned in Scotland, Ireland, the Low Countries and France. Some of his military experiences appear in his works, e.g. *General Rehearsal of Wars* (1579). He wrote pageant verses, epitaphs, tracts and broadsides. His best works are the 'Legend of Shore's Wife' which appeared in *The Mirror for Magistrates*, the voluminous collection *The First Part of Churchyard's Chips* (1575) and *The Worthiness of Wales* (1587), which has some historical interest.

**Cibber, Colley** 1671–1757 Actor, dramatist and poet. The son of an immigrant Danish sculptor, Cibber joined the company of actors at **Drury Lane** in 1691 and made a major success in the role of Lord Foppington in **Vanbrugh**'s *The Relapse*. There is some irony in that, since Vanbrugh's play was a riposte to Cibber's own *Love's Last Shift* (1696), but it accurately illustrates Cibber's ability to deflect hostility by his provocative and sometimes outrageous good humour. It was an ability that stood him in good stead during his controversial years as co-manager of Drury Lane, 1708–32, and as Poet Laureate, 1730–57. It was the latter appointment that earned him the dubious immortality of **Pope**'s scorn in *The Dunciad*.

Few people, even among his contemporaries, believed that Cibber's verse merited the laureateship, but his services to the theatre have been often underrated. *Love's Last Shift*, his first play, heralded the long reign of sentimental comedy on the English stage. Together with *The Careless Husband* (1704), *The Lady's Last Stake* (1707) and, a riposte to Vanbrugh's *The Provoked Wife*, *The Provoked Husband* (1728), it is among the best of its now-unfashionable kind. Cibber's understanding of contemporary theatrical taste is further exemplified in his cleverly compiled version of **Shakespeare**'s *Richard III* (1700), which replaced the original on the English stage for 150 years, and in his much-loved version of Molière's *Tartuffe, The Non-Juror* (1717). His discursive autobiography *An Apology for the Life of Mr Colley Cibber, Comedian* (1740, revised 1750 and 1756) gives an unrivalled account of the English theatre over four decades.

**citizen comedy** The term is used to describe a group of Elizabethan and Jacobean plays whose setting is London and whose characters are predominantly the day-to-day tradesmen of the city. The satire of mercantile values and financial opportunism is, for the most part, good-humoured, but no quarter is given to social overreaching or the pursuit of commercial success by fraud. Citizen (or 'city') comedy is characteristically moral and determined to castigate whatever or whoever discredits the good name of London. Outstanding examples include **Dekker**'s *The Shoemaker's Holiday* (1599), *Eastward Ho* (1605), on which **Chapman**, **Jonson** and **Marston** collaborated and which outdoes the two joint works of Dekker and **Webster**, *Westward Ho* (1604) and *Northward Ho* (1605), and **Middleton**'s *A Chaste Maid in Cheapside* (1611). The combination of a romantic plot and plain characters was sufficiently familiar by 1607 to provoke the lively mockery of **Beaumont**'s *The Knight of the Burning Pestle*, but citizen comedy was both durable and adaptable. It reflected the secure London base of many of the public stage's greatest dramatists. Jonson, too various and too original to be confined within a category, evoked the teeming life of the city in *Epicoene* (1609), *The Alchemist* (1610) and *Bartholomew Fair* (1614). The increasing tensions of London under the Stuarts, which contributed to the hardening tone and eventual decline of citizen comedy, are well represented by the distance between *Eastward Ho* and **Massinger**'s altogether darker version of the same plot in *The City Madam* (c. 1632).

**Citizen of the World, The** A collection of letters by **Oliver Goldsmith**, purporting to be the correspondence of a philosophic Chinese gentleman, Lien Chi Altangi, living in London. They were written for **John Newbery**'s *The Public Ledger* (1760–1) and published under the present title in 1762. The letters offer a satirical comment on contemporary English life and manners, mental and moral characteristics, and literary matters. Two notable characters appear, Beau Tibbs and The Man in Black.

**City Madam, The** A comedy by **Philip Massinger**, first performed c. 1632 and published in 1659.

Sir John Frugal is a successful merchant; his wife and daughters have grown in affectation and vanity as his wealth has increased. Living in his household is his younger brother, Luke, a ruined prodigal Sir John has helped and whose manner is one of humble gratitude. Exasperated by his family, Sir John pretends to retire to a monastery and hands the management of the household over to his brother. Luke shows his true colours at once, appropriating his brother's fortune and displaying a remarkable rapacity in calling in debts. He ridicules Lady Frugal and her daughters, and is prepared to sell them to three 'Indians' who want three women for human sacrifice. The Indians, however, are in fact Sir John and two young men who unsuccessfully wooed his daughters, so Luke is unmasked. He is driven unrepentant from the house, and the relieved and repentant ladies promise to behave better in future.

The play gives a realistic picture of London society at various levels in the Caroline period, ranging from the integrity of Sir John, the honest merchant, and his family to the stews where the prostitutes Shavem and Secret are ready to fight with knives against fashionable ruffians who would make victims of them. The pretensions of aristocracy are given utterance by one suitor, Sir Maurice Lacy, and vigorously challenged by the other, Master Plenty, a yeoman farmer's son whose wealth and station came from hard work.

**City of Dreadful Night, The** A poem by **James Thomson**, first published in Charles Bradlaugh's secularist magazine, *The National Reformer*, in 1874. It takes its motto from Leopardi: 'In thee, O Death, our naked nature finds repose; not joyful, but safe from the old sadness.' *The City of Dreadful Night* is a work of profound desolation, a requiem to disillusionment and negation. Written in contrasting sections of episodic and ruminative verse, the poem envisions London both topographically and as a terrifying City of Dis, dark, tenebrous and forbidding. It reflects on the meaninglessness of the human condition, on the death-in-life Thomson believed man must endure. Sinister imagery, dramatic scenes, and brooding despair (as in Thomson's arresting description of Dürer's 'Melancholia') render the poem unique in the literature of despondency as well as a landmark in late-Victorian pessimism.

**Civil Disobedience, On the Duty of** An essay by **Henry David Thoreau** which was originally printed in 1849 as *Resistance to Civil Government*, it first appeared under its familiar title in a posthumous collection of essays called *A Yankee in Canada, with Anti-Slavery and Reform Papers* (1866). Citing the controversial Mexican War, slavery and the treatment of Indians, and referring to the night he himself spent in gaol for refusing to pay his poll tax, Thoreau argues that an individual may refuse to participate in a government that does not uphold his or her moral standards.

**Clandestine Marriage, The** A comedy by **George Colman the Elder** and **David Garrick**, first performed at **Drury Lane** in 1766. While it is generally agreed that the original idea of basing a play on the first plate of Hogarth's *Marriage à la Mode* was Colman's and that the brilliant fifth act was written by Garrick, there is no certainty about the sharing out of the rest of the play. Its best part, that of Lord Ogleby, was intended for Garrick, and may have been invented by him, though illness prevented him playing it.

The wealthy merchant, Sterling, plans to increase his social standing by marrying his elder daughter to Sir John Melvil, nephew of the impecunious Lord Ogleby. At the last moment, Melvil expresses a preference for the younger daughter, Fanny, and Sterling complies, to the indignation of his rich sister, Mrs Heidelberg. What no one knows is that Fanny is secretly married to her father's clerk, Lovewell. A series of misfortunes culminate in Lovewell's being found in Fanny's bedroom, and it is Lord Ogleby who unexpectedly saves the situation.

**Clanvowe, Sir John** *c.* 1341–91 Poet and religious writer. Of Welsh ancestry, he inherited an estate on the southern Welsh border. He fought in military campaigns in France, including the battle of Lussac Bridge in 1369. He was knight bachelor to the Earl of Hereford and entered the service of Edward III on Hereford's death in 1373. He was later in the service of Richard II and held political offices in England and abroad. He died near Constantinople in 1391; it is reported that his lover, Sir William Neville, refused food and died a few days later. His two known works are quite disparate in character. *The Cuckoo and the Nightingale*, or *The Book of Cupid*, is a secular poem on the nature of love modelled on **Chaucer**'s *Parlement of Foules* and a part of the **Chaucerian apocrypha**. His other work is a religious tract in prose condemning luxury and worldliness and exhorting his readers to obey the commandments and to love God. Although Clanvowe is counted with Neville, Sir Thomas Latimer, Sir Lewis Clifford, Sir John Montagu and Sir Richard Sturry as one of the 'Lollard knights', the tract does not express **Lollard** sympathies.

**Clare, John** 1793–1864 Poet. The son of an agricultural labourer in receipt of poor relief, Clare was born at Helpston, Northamptonshire, where he worked as a thresher, farm labourer and gardener. His life and work are marked by an intimate sense of place: in his *Autobiography* he describes how, as a child, he once strayed beyond the parish boundary, until he found himself 'out of his knowledge', the sun seeming to shine from a 'different quarter of the sky'. The formative years of his youth were contemporary with the passing of an Act for the enclosure of Helpston and several neighbouring villages, and by the time he began to write a new landscape had been created. His *Poems Descriptive of Rural Life* appeared in 1820, and in the following year he produced *The Village Minstrel*, a long poem in **Spenserian stanzas**. Both works contain moving descriptions of the conditions of the rural poor, together with poignant evocations of the old village landscape of open fields. Although Clare was producing verse that shows him as already the equal of his models, **Goldsmith** and **Thomson**, he was at length dissatisfied with this mode, feeling that their poetic diction was at odds with his own sensibility. In *The Shepherd's Calendar* (1827), *The Rural Muse* (1835) and the posthumous collection *The Midsummer Cushion* he attempted to blend the physical with the linguistic textures of Helpston, employing grammar, vocabulary and syntax that are pronouncedly, though by no means naïvely, athwart the dominant conventions of pastoral.

In 1820 Clare married Martha Turner, and, though he never adjusted to the breakdown of an earlier relationship with Mary Joyce, he seems to have been a dutiful husband and a good father. In 1832 he was offered a cottage in Northborough, a village just three miles northeast of Helpston, but in a landscape so different that he felt wholly estranged there. The poems written at Northborough communicate a deep melancholy and a sense of irretrievable loss. In 1837 he became mentally ill, and was admitted to an asylum in High Beach, Epping. He escaped in 1841 and walked to Northamptonshire, having convinced himself that he would there be reunited with Mary Joyce, to whom he believed himself married. He was committed to the county asylum at Northampton, where he remained for the rest of his life, enjoying considerable freedom and continuing to write poetry. He seems to have recognized his illness as a loss of 'self-identity', in which the enclosures, the move from Helpston and the decline in the sales of his work, with the passing of the vogue for 'peasant' poetry at the end of the 1820s, all played a part. His poetry, much of which was distorted by his publisher's editorial interventions, remained virtually unread until this century, when its reception as a prefiguration of modern, or 'alienated', aesthetic consciousness did much to stimulate the production of new editions based on the original manuscripts.

*Clarel: A Poem and Pilgrimage in the Holy Land* A 7000-line poem by **Herman Melville** in octosyllabic couplets, published in two volumes in 1876. Inspired by Melville's reflections on his visit to the Holy Land 20 years earlier, the poem is an enquiry into and search for faith. Its various characters represent a range of attitudes: some express religious doubts arising from their personal experience or philosophy; others are comfortably certain of their faith. None, however, is able to assist Clarel, an American theology student visiting Jerusalem, to resolve his own uncertainties.

**Clarendon, Edward Hyde, 1st Earl of** 1609–

74 Historian and statesman. The son of a Wiltshire country gentleman, Clarendon attended Magdalen Hall, Oxford, and then practised law. He entered Parliament in 1640 and sat in the Commons throughout the Short and Long Parliaments, first for Wootton Bassett and then for Saltash. He began by being opposed to the King's policies, but soon fell out of sympathy with the tenor of the opposition and with the Presbyterians. By 1641 he had become one of the King's chief advisers.

When Charles I gave the Prince of Wales a council and court of his own in the West Country during the Civil War (1645), Hyde was appointed to it. He followed the Prince into exile and, while in the Scilly Isles, began in 1646 to write his *True Historical Narrative of the Rebellion and Civil Wars in England* – the **History of the Rebellion**, as it is usually known.

At the Restoration he became Lord Chancellor, and at Charles II's coronation was created Earl of Clarendon; he was Charles's chief minister until 1667. The mismanagement of the war with the Dutch (which Clarendon had opposed) gave political enemies a chance to bring about his downfall. Because they feared his possible return to power – his daughter, Anne, was married to James, Duke of York and later James II – Lord Arlington and others moved his impeachment. Charles did not intervene and Clarendon again went into exile, living at

Edward Hyde, 1st Earl of Clarendon. Detail from the portrait, after A. Hanneman, *c.*1650. National Portrait Gallery, London.

Montpellier and then Rouen, where he died. During these years he finished his *History*, though it was not published until 1702–4. His autobiography and *The History of the Irish Rebellion and Civil Wars in Ireland*, which also belong to this period, were both later incorporated into his chief work. His speeches, political tracts and essays were published as *A Collection of Several Tracts* (1727), while his criticism of **Hobbes**, in *Leviathan: A Brief View and Survey*, appeared two years after his death. From the Restoration until his flight from England Clarendon was Chancellor of the University of Oxford, which inherited his manuscripts. The profits from publication of his work provided the funds for the building of the Clarendon Press.

**Clarendon, The Life of Edward, Earl of** The autobiography of the **Earl of Clarendon** was written during his exile in France after his fall from power in Charles II's government. Some of the material in his memoirs paralleled events in his great *History of the Rebellion and Civil Wars in England*, into which he fitted his personal story with great skill. The manuscript was among the papers presented to the University of Oxford by his heirs, and was published separately in 1759.

**Clarissa**, *or, The History of a Young Lady* A novel by **Samuel Richardson**, the first two volumes published in 1747, the last five in 1748. Like his first novel, *Pamela*, it is epistolary in form, the text comprising a four-way correspondence between the principal characters: Clarissa Harlowe's to her friend Miss Howe, and Robert Lovelace's letters to his friend John Belford being the predominant ones.

Clarissa is a well-bred young lady who is attracted to the dashing Lovelace, an unscrupulous man of whom her parents strongly disapprove. In deference to her parents' wishes, Clarissa resists his advances, but also refuses to marry the man they have selected instead, the detestable Mr Solmes. Confined to her room (for the first 500 pages of the plot) she secretly corresponds with Lovelace, and runs away with him, only to discover his real nature is dishonourable.

Installed under the watchful eye of Mrs Sinclair, a bawd, Clarissa is wooed ardently by Lovelace, but his subtlety gives way to impatience and eventually he drugs and then rapes her. Denounced by her family and abused by her seducer, she rejects him totally, ignores the pleas of his family and friends to accept his proposal of marriage, and retires into solitude. She dies of shame and grief, and Lovelace is killed in a duel with her cousin. Belford, the libertine correspondent, turns over a new leaf, becomes Clarissa's executor, and edits her letters.

An illustration for an edition of Richardson's *Clarissa* published in 1768. This is the frontispiece to Vol. III and shows Clarissa and Lovelace at breakfast with Mrs Sinclair and her nieces.

Though the action of the novel encompasses less than one year, the intense degree of characterization is extraordinarily sustained, buoyed up by Richardson's careful unification of the narrative elements. It is widely regarded as Richardson's masterpiece, and, running to over a million words, is the longest novel in the English language.

**Clark, John Pepper** See **Bekederemo, J. P. Clark**.

**Clark, Kenneth Mackenzie, Baron** 1903–83 Art historian and critic. Born in Oxford, educated at Winchester and Trinity College, Oxford, he held various distinguished appointments in the course of a long career, being Director of the National Gallery (1934–45), Surveyor of the King's Pictures (1934–44) and Chairman of the Arts Council of Great Britain (1953–60). As a writer he first attracted attention with *The Gothic Revival* (1928); the many works that followed include *Florentine Painting* (1945), *Landscape into Art* (1949), *The Nude: A Study of Ideal Art* (1953), *Moments of Vision* (1954) and

*Civilisation* (1969), based on a successful television series. His interest in **Ruskin**, which lay behind his first book, was again expressed in the introduction he provided for an edition of *Praeterita* (1949) and in the selection *Ruskin Today* (1964). *Another Part of the Wood* (1974) and *The Other Half* (1977) are volumes of autobiography.

**Clarke, Arthur C[harles]** 1917– Writer of **science fiction**. Clarke was born in Minehead, Somerset, and served in the RAF during the war. He graduated from King's College, London, in physics and mathematics in 1948 and since 1956 has lived in Sri Lanka. As a writer and popularizer of science he has been an ardent champion of the cause of technological progress; a strong interest in space exploration dates from the 1940s, when he first published plans for a hypothetical communications satellite. His early works, *Childhood's End* (1953) and *The City and the Stars* (1956), show the influence of **Olaf Stapledon**, but most of his novels aim at technological realism. They include *Rendezvous with Rama* (1973), *Imperial Earth* (1975) and *The Fountains of Paradise* (1979). Clarke worked closely with Stanley Kubrick on the spectacular film *2001: A Space Odyssey* (1968), and in the sequel *2010: Odyssey Two* (1982) has begun again to re-emphasize the visionary element in his work.

**Clarke, Austin** 1896–1974 Irish playwright, poet and novelist, born and educated in Dublin. He worked first as a university lecturer in Dublin, then as a journalist in England, before returning to Dublin in 1937 to found the Dublin Verse-Speaking Society and, later, the Lyric Theatre Company. Clarke's aim was to revive poetic drama in the **Abbey Theatre**, where he had seen some of **Yeats**'s plays while he was a student. *The Vengeance of Fionn* (1917), first of several volumes of verse before and after *Collected Poems* (1936), is typically a product of his enthusiasm for Irish legend and folk-tales. The first of his verse plays, *The Son of Learning* (1927), is based on a medieval Irish story, as are most of those that followed. Two exceptions are the delicate Pierrot plays, written in free-flowing heroic couplets, *The Kiss* (1942) and *The Second Kiss* (1946). These are one-act pieces. For the three-act *The Moment Next to Nothing* (1958), Clarke returned to a Gaelic story that had already furnished him with the plot for a novel, *The Sun Dances at Easter* (1952), which was banned in Ireland. *The Plot Succeeds* (1950), particularly interesting for its experiments with rhyme, is one of a small number of plays by Clarke that might sustain revival. An autobiography, *Twice Around the Black Church* (1960), and a volume of memoirs, *A Penny in the Clouds*

(1968), show the range and intensity of his Irish studies.

**Clarke, Charles Cowden** 1787–1877 Scholar and critic. Born in Enfield, Middlesex, he became a friend of **Keats**, who attended his father's school. Later he became acquainted with **Leigh Hunt**, **Shelley**, **Hazlitt** and **Dickens**. He was a London bookseller and publisher who wrote and lectured on **Shakespeare**. With his wife **Mary Cowden Clarke** he wrote *Recollections of Writers* (1878).

**Clarke, Gillian** 1937– Poet. Born in Cardiff, she read English literature at University College, Cardiff, and has lived in South Wales all her life, apart from two years with the BBC in London. Until 1984 she combined work as a part-time teacher with editing *The Anglo-Welsh Review*. Two early books of poems, *Snow on the Mountain* (1971) and *The Sundial* (1978), established a strong following in Wales but it was her third collection, *Letter From A Far Country* (1982), that brought a wider audience. *Selected Poems* (1985) established her as a leading woman poet of her generation. Although strongly rooted in both the urban and rural experience of her native Wales, her work transcends regional concerns and approaches archetypal themes of love, death and family life from intimate, almost casual angles. She combines the traditional skills of versification with a sharply accurate, at times visionary use of imagery and language.

**Clarke, Marcus** 1846–81 Australian novelist. Born in London, he was educated at Highgate School, where he was a schoolfellow of **Gerard Manley Hopkins**. He emigrated to Victoria in 1863 and, after four years on a station in the Wimmera, joined *The Melbourne Argus*. He contributed a weekly column as 'the Peripatetic Philosopher' to *The Australian* and, in 1868, became owner and editor of *The Colonial Monthly*, where his first novel, *Long Odds* (1869), was serialized. His best-known work, *His Natural Life* (serialized 1870–2), was the result of a commission from *The Australian Journal* and presented a vivid picture of the penal settlement in Tasmania. His other works included collections of short stories – *Old Tales of a Young Country* (1871) and *The Man with the Oblong Box* (1878) – and a pantomime, *Twinkle, Twinkle Little Star* (1873).

**Clarke, Mary Victoria Cowden** 1809–98 Born Mary Novello, she married the scholar and critic **Charles Cowden Clarke** in 1828. Her *Concordance to Shakespeare's Plays* was published in monthly parts in 1844–5; *Recollections of Writers* (1878) was written in collaboration with her husband.

**Clarke, Samuel** 1675–1729 Divine. Clarke was born in Norwich and educated at Gonville and Caius College, Cambridge. He was appointed chaplain to the Bishop of Norwich in 1698. In 1704 and 1705 he delivered the Boyle lectures known in their published form (1716) as *A Discourse Concerning the Being and Attributes of God*, a carefully reasoned defence of rational theology against the empiricism of **John Locke**.

*Claverings, The* A novel by **Anthony Trollope**, serialized in *The Cornhill Magazine* from February 1866 to May 1867.

Harry Clavering, a schoolmaster resolved to become an engineer, is jilted by the beautiful Julia Brabazon in favour of Lord Ongar, a wealthy debauchee. After a year abroad Ongar dies and Julia returns to London. In the meantime Harry has fallen in love with Florence Burton, the homely daughter of a partner in his engineering firm. He is drawn into contact with Julia again through his concern to protect her from the sinister Count Pateroff and his scheming sister Sophie Gordeloup, who are after her money, and the old feeling between them revives. Julia now wants to marry him and Harry is drawn into a second proposal, but conscience and domesticity win when he realizes that Florence will be a better wife for him. Julia surrenders her claim and fortune smiles on Harry when his two cousins drown in a boating accident, and he finds himself heir to the Clavering estate.

Despite its conventional ending, *The Claverings* offers what was for its time an unconventional and penetrating exploration of the mind of a man in love with two women.

*Clayhanger* A novel by **Arnold Bennett**, published in 1910. The first of a trilogy of novels, it was followed by *Hilda Lessways* (1911) and *These Twain* (1916). A fourth novel, *The Roll Call* (1918), is loosely connected with the series.

Edwin Clayhanger's life over 20 years is traced, from the day he leaves school in 1872 aged 16. The central relationship of Edwin and his father, Darius, was inspired by Bennett's own struggles with a dominating parent. Crucially for their relationship, Edwin is unaware of Darius's cruel upbringing in the workhouse during the 1840s and of the chance in life that came to him from Mr Shushions, the Sunday school teacher, now poor and decrepit himself.

Edwin's dreams of escaping the Potteries town of Bursley, the family printing business, the narrow company of his downtrodden sisters Mary and Clara, and the pious hypocrisies of Auntie Hamps, are held in contempt by Darius. Edwin's association with the cultivated Orgreaves family has introduced him to ideas and unattainable prospects: one of these, at first, is Hilda Lessways. When marriage seems possible, Edwin's request for a rise in salary brings a climactic, unsuccessful encounter with Darius. But Hilda departs mysteriously and he hears of her subsequent marriage.

Years later, Edwin traces Hilda and her son to a Brighton boarding house, and hears of her ruin at the hands of the bigamous George Cannon. The novel ends with their plan to marry. The earlier account of Darius's slow and painful decline into death is more characteristic of the novel than is the note of romance.

**Cleanness** (or **Purity**) An alliterative poem written in the late 14th century in the dialect of the West Midlands. It is usually supposed to have been written by the same poet as **Sir Gawain and the Green Knight**, **Patience** and **Pearl**, and is preserved in the same manuscript. Its theme is the supreme value of spiritual purity and God's rejection of the impure. The 'cleanness' of the title is not simply chastity, but freedom from all kinds of vices which defile the soul in the eyes of God. The poet draws on biblical narratives to illustrate his theme, using the parable of the Guest without a Wedding Garment, the Flood, the destruction of Sodom and Gomorrah, and finally Belshazzar's Feast. These narratives are enlivened by vivid description and given a medieval English setting. The result is powerful and dynamic, the austere subject matter enriched by gentle humour, sincere faith and tenderness. Alone among the four poems attributed to the **Gawain-poet**, **Cleanness** draws on the Apocrypha for some of its material and is clearly dependent on known secular works, citing Jean de Meun's part of the *Roman de la*

A detail from one of the illustrations to *Cleanness* in the *Cotton Nero Ax. MS, f.60*. The little craft is Noah's Ark. British Library.

*Rose* and borrowing from an early French version of *Mandeville's Travels* for the description of the Dead Sea.

**Cleary, Jon (Stephen)** 1917– Australian novelist. Born in Sydney, he joined the army in 1940 and served in the Middle East and New Guinea. His first published volume was a collection of short stories entitled *These Small Glories* (1945). A number of novels followed, including *You Can't See Round Corners* (1947), *The Sundowners* (1952), *Forests of the Night* (1963), *The High Commissioner* (1966), *Season of Doubt* (1968), *Remember Jack Hoxie* (1969), *The Safe House* (1975), *A Very Private War* (1980) and *Spearfield's Daughter* (1982). Cleary's novels are popular tales of adventure and action, generally set in exotic locations and frequently distinguished by their subtle interest in personal dilemmas of indecision and fear of responsibility.

**Cleland, John** 1709–89 Novelist. Educated at Westminster School, he held minor government posts in Smyrna and Bombay before becoming a professional writer in London. He is best known for *Memoirs of a Woman of Pleasure* (1748–9), usually called *Fanny Hill*, for long suppressed as obscene, though it was one of the most popular novels of the 18th century. *Memoirs of a Coxcomb, or, The History of Sir William Delamere* (1751) and *The Surprises of Love* (1764) are his other novels. Cleland also wrote dramatic pieces and philological studies.

**Clemo, Jack (Reginald John)** 1916– Poet. A native of St Austell, he still lives in the cottage in which he was born. Unhelpfully, his poetic career has sometimes been seen merely as a triumph over adversity: deaf from the age of five, and blind since 1955, he has also suffered from heart trouble and cerebral paralysis. His early family life impinges on his work: his father's death and the subsequent religious indoctrination by his mother have significantly shaped his verse, which is concerned with the conflict between grace and nature, and the assimilation of sexuality into Christianity, which surfaces as an erotic mysticism. After his only novel, *Wilding Craft* (1948), came his first volume of autobiography, *Confession of a Rebel* (1949). His first two volumes of verse, *The Clay Verse* (1951) and *The Wintry Priesthood* (1951), feature a tortured Christian existentialism and devastated, metaphysical Cornish landscapes. Clemo's late discovery of **modernism** is evident in *Cactus on Carmel* (1967); other volumes include *Broad Autumn* (1975) and *The Bouncing Hills* (1983). Although Clemo has been praised by **Donald Davie** and **Charles Causley**, the unusual and individual directions in which he has proceeded account in part for the lack of a proper assessment of his work.

*Cleopatra* A tragedy in blank verse by **Samuel Daniel**, published in 1594. It deals with events following the death of Antony. Octavius tries to persuade Cleopatra to leave the monument in which she has taken refuge; he wants to parade her in triumph in Rome. But after a last celebration of great magnificence she takes her life by the application of a venomous serpent. At the same time her son by Julius Caesar, Caesarion, is murdered by Octavius and the line of Ptolemy is extinguished.

**clerihew** A comic verse form invented by **Edmund Clerihew Bentley**, consisting of two rhyming couplets designed to sum up a subject or character:

> The art of Biography
> Is different from Geography.
> Geography is about maps,
> But Biography is about chaps.

**Clerk of Pennecuik, Sir John** 1676–1755 Clerk was one of the circle of friends who grouped around **Allan Ramsay** in the reviving literary life of Edinburgh in the early 18th century. A pupil of Corelli, he composed a set of five cantatas for solo voice in 1698; he also wrote a number of songs. His *Memoirs* give an illuminating picture of his times; they were published by The Roxburghe Club in 1895. Clerk was also the author of *Observations on the Present State of Scotland* (1730).

*Clerk's Tale, The* See *Canterbury Tales, The*.

**Cleveland, John** 1613–58 Poet. The son of a Yorkshire clergyman, he was educated at Christ's College, Cambridge (where he was a contemporary of **Milton**), and became a fellow of St John's in 1634, though he was later deprived of this post for his opposition to Cromwell. He went to Oxford and later joined the Royalist garrison at Newark. Robustly loyal to the cause of the Crown, he was imprisoned by the Parliamentarians in 1655–6, but released after a personal appeal to Cromwell.

As a political satirist and poet he was both formidable and popular. His verse portraits were often anti-Presbyterian and his best poems are 'The Rebel Scot' and 'The King's Disguise'. Though collections of his work continued to appear after the Restoration of the monarchy, he was ridiculed by **Dryden** for the roughness of his effects, and his conceits are often extreme and 'far-fetch't', giving rise to the term 'Clevelandism' to denote implausible comparison, or **catachresis**. Sometimes dubbed 'the last metaphysical poet', he is not widely read today, though some of his verse is memorably vigorous.

**cliché** From the French, 'a stereotype plate'. A trite expression which has lost its cutting edge.

*Cliff-Dwellers, The* A novel by **Henry Blake Fuller**, published in 1893, and one of the earliest American novels to have as its setting the monstrous and impersonal city. A satire on greed and social striving set in Chicago, it depicts the lives of the 'cliff-dwellers' – those inhabiting a skyscraper called the Clifton Building. The characters include Arthur Ingles, the rich owner of the Clifton; Erasmus Brainard, an antisocial banker; Eugene H. McDowell, a crooked real-estate agent; George Ogden, an ambitious clerk who works in Brainard's bank; and the various women who contribute to their fortunes and misfortunes.

**Clive, Caroline** 1801–73 Born Caroline Meysey-Wigley, she married Archer Clive in 1840. Using the pseudonym 'V', she published *IX Poems* (1840), which was well received and followed by several other volumes. Her most popular work was a sensational novel, *Paul Ferroll* (1885).

**Cloete, Stuart** 1897–1976 South African novelist. Born in Paris, he was educated in England. British army service (1914–25) was followed by farming in South Africa. A prolific author of non-fictional works, novels of adventure, and collections of stories, he was at his best in a sequence of realistic, unsentimental novels covering 19th-century Afrikaner history. His first novel, *Turning Wheels*, published in 1937, just before the Voortrekker centenary, was banned for depicting sacrosanct pioneer heroes as human and fallible. Other fictional themes include elephant-hunting (*The Curve and The Tusk*, 1953) and white-slave trafficking (*The Abductors*, 1970). *A Victorian Son* (1971) and *The Gambler* (1973) are autobiographies.

*Cloister and the Hearth, The: A Tale of the Middle Ages* A historical romance by **Charles Reade**, published in 1861 but expanded from a story, 'The Good Fight', which had appeared in *Once a Week* in 1859. The tale is set in the 15th century in Tergou, Holland, and concerns Gerard, a mercer's son, who loves Margaret, the daughter of a poor scholar, Peter Brandt. Both the burgomaster and Gerard's family oppose the marriage and contrive to have Gerard imprisoned. He escapes to join Margaret, but is later forced to flee the country. Gerard wanders through Europe, the incidents of his exile enlivened by atmospheric scenes in taverns, stews, castles and monasteries. In Italy, he hears a false report of Margaret's death and surrenders to debauchery before repenting and becoming a Dominican monk. Gerard returns to Holland, where he discovers Margaret. She has borne him a son who will grow up to be Erasmus. No longer able to marry, Gerard spends the rest of his life at Gouda near his family.

Reade based his novel upon his studies of **Erasmus**'s *Life* and *Colloquies*, and the works of Froissart and Luther.

**closet drama** Plays written to be read rather than performed. There is scholarly dispute over the question of whether Seneca's work provides a classical precedent. Examples in English include, perhaps, **Milton**'s *Samson Agonistes*, **Walter Savage Landor**'s *Count Julian*, **Shelley**'s *Prometheus Unbound*, **Matthew Arnold**'s *Empedocles on Etna* and *Merope*, **Swinburne's** *Locrine*, and **Hardy**'s *The Dynasts*.

*Cloud of Unknowing, The* A mystical treatise of unknown authorship written in the second half of the 14th century, probably in the East Midlands. It is concerned with the preparation of the mind and soul for mystical experience, requiring the obliteration of the Christian's sense of self. The 'cloud' of the title is the gulf between man and God which can be crossed only by love and not by reason. The treatise aims to correct misleading notions drawn from the work of **Richard Rolle** (d. 1349) and is itself later criticized by **Walter Hilton** (d. 1395). Six other works are attributed to the author: *The Epistle of Privy Counsel*, *The Epistle of Prayer*, *Deonise Hid Divinite*, *Benjamin*, *The Epistle of Discretion in the Stirrings of the Soul* and *The Treatise of the Discerning of Spirits*. See also **mystical writing**.

**Clough, Arthur Hugh** 1819–61 Poet. Born in Liverpool, the son of a cotton merchant who emigrated to South Carolina, Clough spent his early years in the USA. During a family visit to England in 1828 he attended school in Chester and the following year was sent to Rugby – then under the headship of **Thomas Arnold** whose son, **Matthew Arnold**, became one of his friends. In 1837 Clough went up to Balliol College, Oxford, and, after taking an undistinguished degree, he became in 1842 a fellow and tutor of Oriel College. But his orthodox faith was challenged, and in 1848 his perplexities over the interpretation of the 39 Articles relative to his university position compelled Clough to resign both his posts at Oriel. In 1849–51 he was principal of a student hostel at University College, London. Shortly thereafter he went as a tutor to Cambridge, Massachusetts, where he was friendly with such New England intellectuals as **Ralph Waldo Emerson** and **Charles Eliot Norton**. Ever restless, Clough returned to England in 1853 to become Examiner in the Education Office, an office he held until his early death in Florence from a cerebral attack complicated by fever. Clough is commemorated in Matthew Arnold's elegiac poem, **Thyrsis**.

Clough wrote almost as much poetry as Matthew Arnold, but only two volumes appeared during his lifetime: **The Bothie of Toberna-Vuolich** (1848), a verse-novel in hexameters, and *Ambarvalia* (1849), 29 shorter poems printed together with some verses by Thomas Burbidge. His *Amours de Voyage* first appeared in *The Atlantic Monthly* in 1858 and his unfinished *Dipsychus*, although mostly written in Venice in 1850, did not come out until 1865. Two other longer poems, both unfinished, *Mari Magno* and *Adam and Eve*, and some lesser prose round off his writings. Long neglected, Clough's poetry has recently received recognition for its lyric quality and for its interpretation of the Victorian spiritual malaise.

**Cobbe, Frances Power** 1822–1904 Religious writer and philanthropist. Her first work, published anonymously, was *The Theory of Intuitive Morals* (1855–7). She travelled widely, producing, among other titles, *Italics* (1864), based on her observation of Italian life. Turning to philanthropic work, she supported female suffrage and opposed vivisection. Most of her numerous published works deal with these topics. Her autobiography appeared in 1894.

**Cobbett, William** 1763–1835 Civil rights activist, journalist, farmer and MP. The son of an innkeeper in Farnham, Surrey, who taught him shorthand and arithmetic, as well as to read and write, Cobbett, otherwise self-educated, acquired at an early age that vigorous, plain style on which his whole career was based. It was 'vehement and brisk . . . free from affectation, loose, irregular and bold'. It was also witty, in the sense that Cobbett perceived connections of which others were unaware. Through the use of his pen he came to be acknowledged as one of the most powerful political influences of his day, writing some 20 million words in all. He ran away from home at the age of 10 or 11 to work in the Royal Gardens at Kew (where he said he first read **Swift**'s *Tale of a Tub*) and then for a second time to London, where he worked as a clerk. Cobbett was posted to America soon after enlisting in the 54th Regiment of Foot in 1784. Though only a sergeant, he soon had effective responsibility for the garrison at Fredericton in New Brunswick because he could read, write and think more clearly than his officers. Back in England in 1792, and married to Anne (Nancy) Reid whom he had met in New Brunswick, Cobbett brought charges of corruption and peculation against his former officers, but had to flee, first to France and then to America, when counter-charges were brought against him by the military establishment. This confrontation with authority set the pattern of his life: 'It is the system, the vermin-breeding system, that I for my part am at war with.' Always a loyalist and a patriot, and never a revolutionary, he became nevertheless what someone called 'a fiercely independent radical reformer', openly and energetically opposed to government corruption, to the vote-buying and patronage that was then normal, to the manipulation of the press by those in power, and to all types of social injustice, irrespective of the actual political system prevailing at the time. In 1792–1800, first in Wilmington and then in Philadelphia, though he earned his living by teaching English to French émigrés, he became as 'Peter Porcupine' (his pseudonym) the outstanding journalist in support of the Washington administration. But in his newspaper, *Porcupine's Gazette* (1797–9), and in pamphlets such as the outspoken *Observations on the Emigration of Dr Joseph Priestley* (1794) he so frequently tracked corruption and hypocrisy to its source in the personal abuse of power that his entertaining scurrility and outspokenness was bound to result, sooner or later, in court action. Libel actions brought against him in 1800 by Judge McKean and Benjamin Rush forced him to leave Philadelphia, ending the first phase of his career as an influential political journalist. Whereas in Philadelphia Cobbett had attacked the American adulation of Napoleon, urging the case for the continuing interdependence of Britain and America, back in England he changed his tune and through his newspaper, *The Political Register*, regularly savaged the British government for corruption and incompetence. Although Cobbett consequently enjoyed immense popularity in the country as a whole, the fact that the government controlled both the press and the courts meant he was soon in trouble. 'Laws grind the poor, and rich men rule the law,' said Cobbett. Tried by one of the infamous special juries in the action brought against him by Spencer Perceval, a cabinet minister, Cobbett was found guilty of seditious libel, fined heavily and sent to Newgate Prison for two years, after which, Habeas Corpus having been suspended, he fled again to America. On Long Island he rented a small farm and lived almost at subsistence level, though continuing to write. When Cobbett returned to England (with, amazingly, the disinterred mortal remains of **Tom Paine** in his baggage) it was to re-engage fearlessly with British political life once again. His target now was to a much greater extent what he took to be the misman-agement of an economy characterized by alarm-ing fluctuations in the price of wheat and the overproduction of paper money. During the turbulent period leading to the Reform Bill of

1832, this political involvement never abated. Nevertheless, he lived more prudently. The farm at Botley he had acquired in 1805 proving impractical because distant from London, he took possession of a smallholding in Kensington, selling seeds and saplings of trees at that time unfamiliar in England – the ability, indeed the right, of a man to live off the soil by means of his own labour being one of the principal tenets of his belief. At the same time he continued to write and publish practical primers, treatises and handbooks for the use of the literate poor. He had earlier published *A Grammar of the English Language* (1818) and *Cottage Economy* (1822). To these he now added *A French Grammar* (1824), *Cobbett's Poor Man's Friend* (1826–7), *The Woodlands* (1828), *The English Gardener* (1828), *Advice to Young Men and (Incidentally) Young Women* (1830) and *A Spelling Book* (1831), to give these only their short titles. The poor would always be poor, he thought, but by their own efforts they could improve the quality of their existence. Late in life, he achieved one of his principal ambitions by being elected MP for Oldham in the Reformed Parliament of 1832. By that time he had already engaged in the travels that resulted in his best-known work, **Rural Rides** (1830). The social indignation of his earlier work is expressed here in more mellow terms. Indeed, for any reader who believes Cobbett's political battles to have been won, this must stand as his literary masterpiece.

**Cockburn, Henry** 1779–1854 Scottish judge and autobiographical writer. Born in Edinburgh of Scots legal stock with Tory connections, he was educated at the High School and University of Edinburgh, and admitted advocate in 1800. Cockburn early attached himself to the Whig opposition but prospered at the Bar in spite of his political opinions. In 1830 he became Solicitor-General for Scotland, assisting his friend **Francis Jeffrey**, then Lord Advocate (whose *Life* he wrote in 1852), with details of parliamentary reform legislation. He was appointed to the bench in 1834 (with the judicial title of Lord Cockburn) and enjoyed modest success as a judge. A lively correspondent in his social circle, Cockburn did not make his literary gifts widely known in his lifetime, but a posthu-mously published volume of reminiscences, *Memorials of his Time* (1856), continued by two volumes of his *Journal* (1874) and one of *Circuit Journeys* (1888), established his reputation. He was the recorder of a rapidly vanishing Scotland whose characters, especially among Edinburgh legal dignitaries, he captured in anecdotal vignettes of memorable quality. His nostalgia for the 18th century and respect for Scottish rural peculiarities were tempered by a commonsensi-cal view of the 19th century and a strong feeling for the metropolitan elegance of Edinburgh, where the civic society, the Cockburn Association, was founded in his memory in 1875.

**Cockney School, The** The term appears to have first been used by *Blackwood's Magazine*, which in October 1817 published an article 'On the Cockney School of Poetry', signed by Z (the editors **Lockhart** and **Wilson**), and headed by some clumsily chiming verses in praise of, among others, **Leigh Hunt** and **Keats**, written by Cornelius Webb, a minor poet and member of Leigh Hunt's Hampstead circle. It was the first of a regular series of extraordinarily venomous, and often personally abusive, attacks over the next few years on Hunt and his friends and collaborators, particularly Keats and **Hazlitt**. Hunt was singled out as the debauched ringleader of a group of literary upstarts, whose humble (i.e. lower middle-class) origins ill fitted them for the poetic calling, which was the preserve of 'men of some rank'. Hazlitt was so angered by Z's unsavoury remarks on his appearance, morals and character that he sued the editors, who settled out of court. In a famous review in the same number (autumn 1818) Keats's *Poems* (1817) and the recently published *Endymion* were cruelly combed for immature verses and 'Cockney' rhymes, and their author derided as an apprentice apothecary 'of pretty abilities, which he has done everything in his power to spoil' – a sneer which was tastelessly repeated after his death.

*Cocktail Party, The* A verse drama by **T. S. Eliot**, loosely based on the *Alcestis* of Euripides and first performed at the Edinburgh Festival in 1949. The outer shell of the play, with its quartet of lovers temporarily adrift from the fashionable society to which they belong, is familiar from drawing-room comedies, but Eliot's deeper concern is with modes of spiritual reconciliation for individual Christians. The central action restores the unsatisfactory marriage of Lavinia and Edward Chamberlayne, with the restoration engineered by the knowing psychoanalyst, Sir Henry Harcourt-Reilly. Its achievement requires, in a way uneasily assimilated by the accomplished triviality of the poetic dialogue, the Christian martyrdom of Edward's lover, Celia, a sacrifice that permits the predominantly secular life of the community to continue.

**Cockton, Henry** 1807–53 Novelist. Nothing is known of Cockton's early life except that he was born in London. He achieved temporary success with broadly comic novels in the manner of the early **Dickens** – notably *The Life and Adventures of Valentine Vox the Ventriloquist* (1840) – but lost the money they earned him by an unsuccessful venture into the malting business at Bury St Edmunds, Suffolk, where he died.

**Coetzee, J[ohn] M[ichael]** 1940– South African novelist, born in Cape Town. His deliberately disorienting, linguistically explosive writing is as much about the nature of language and the techniques of fiction as about the victims of imperialism, neo-colonialism, and apartheid. *Dusklands* (1974) consists of two closely related novellas, one about America and Vietnam, the other about an 18th-century Boer pioneer, both protagonists exercising power brutally over people considered inferior. *In the Heart of the Country* (1977; as *From the Heart of the Country*, New York, 1977) presents the patricidal fantasies of a rebellious Afrikaner spinster, trying vainly to reorder her life imaginatively; it is an overwritten book. The Crusoe-like fear of unidentifiable footprints dominates *Waiting for the Barbarians* (1980), with neither humane imperial-frontier magistrate nor brutal security chief able to discover the external 'enemy' they mistake for their corrosive power-sickness. *Life and Times of Michael K* (1983) displays Coetzee's creativity splendidly in the despised hero's almost epic survival, but also his limitation in the intellectuality of a solipsistic art.

**Cogswell, Fred** 1917– Canadian poet and editor. Born in East Centreville, New Brunswick, he served in the Canadian army in World War II and subsequently attended the Universities of New Brunswick and Edinburgh, from which he received his doctorate in 1952. He then returned to the University of New Brunswick to teach English and spent his entire career there. He was editor of the magazine *Fiddlehead*

J. M. Coetzee.

from 1952 to 1967 and founded Fiddlehead Books, a publishing house which provided an outlet for many young Maritime writers. He was made a member of the Order of Canada in 1981. Cogswell has published numerous volumes of poetry since his first book, *The Stunted Strong*, appeared in 1954. They include *Descent from Eden* (1959), *Lost Dimension* (1960), *Star-People* (1968) and *A Long Apprenticeship: Collected Poetry* (1980). His best work describes the lives of Maritime villagers in a witty, laconic style. Other poems are more personal, recording a subjective response to a variety of everyday experiences. His translations, which include *One Hundred Poems of Modern Quebec* (1970) and *Confrontations* (1976), have helped stimulate interest in Quebec poetry in anglophone Canada.

**Cohen, Leonard** 1934– Canadian poet, novelist and popular composer-singer. The son of a prominent Jewish clothier, he was born and brought up in an affluent district of Montreal and attended McGill University, graduating in 1955. His first volume of verse, *Let Us Compare Mythologies*, appeared the following year. He embarked on graduate study at Columbia University but dropped out to write and perform music. Internationally known as an entertainer, Cohen has also published important works of poetry and fiction. His poetry includes *The Spice-Box of Earth* (1961), *Flowers for Hitler* (1964), *The Energy of Slaves* (1972) and *Death of a Lady's Man* (1978). Like his songs, it explores contemporary mythologies but frequently uses traditional forms. Cohen's novel *The Favourite Game* (1963) was followed by *Beautiful Losers* (1968), a visionary counter-culture religious epic. He declined a Canadian Governor-General's Award for his *Selected Poems* (1968). In 1983 he completed an opera with the Montreal composer Louis Furey. His record albums include *Songs of Leonard Cohen* (1967), *Songs of Love and Hate* (1971), *New Skins for the Old Ceremony* (1974), *The Best of Leonard Cohen* (1975) and *Death of a Lady's Man* (1977).

**Cohen, Matt** 1942– Canadian novelist and short-story writer. Born in Kingston, Ontario, he grew up in Ottawa, attended the University of Toronto and spent a year teaching the sociology of religion at McMaster University, Hamilton. He has mainly lived in Toronto and on a farm in Verona, Ontario, but has also spent periods in France, Italy and the Queen Charlotte Islands, the setting for his fourth novel *Wooden Hunters* (1975). His first two novels, *Korsoniloff* (1969) and *Johnny Crackle Sings* (1971), use experimental forms to explore the dehumanizing pressures of contemporary society. His four 'Salem' novels – *The Disinherited* (1974), *The Colours of War* (1977), *The Sweet Second Summer*

of *Kitty Malone* (1979) and *Flowers of Darkness* (1981) – are written in a realistic mode, which he believes is the dominant tradition in Canadian fiction, and deal with family relationships in a community in rural Ontario. Dispossession and self-exploration are major themes of these and other works. *The Spanish Doctor* (1984) is an epic novel about the Jewish diaspora in medieval Europe. His most recent collection of short stories, *Café le Dog* (1983), also includes pieces which explore the Jewish experience. Other books include the short-story collections *Columbus and the Fat Lady* (1972) and *Night Flights* (1978).

**Coke (or Cook), Sir Edward** 1552–1634 Legal writer. Born in Norfolk, he completed his education at Trinity College, Cambridge, and became a barrister of the Inner Temple. His future was assured when he attracted the attention of Lord Burghley, who made him Attorney-General. His rival for the office was **Francis Bacon**, whose opponent in law he remained. Coke became Chief Justice of the Court of Common Pleas in 1606, and waged a steady war against the courts of privilege; one of his triumphs was the acceptance of the principle that the King could not change the common law by proclamation. King James, and all the adherents of the idea of government by *rex*, were determined to overcome the champion of *lex* and James 'promoted' him to Chief Justice of the King's Bench in 1613. Coke and the other judges were involved in a direct challenge to the King in 1616, when they decided that he could not command the common-law courts to desist from hearing cases pending, even if the royal interest was involved. When summoned before the King's council Coke was the only judge who stood his ground, and the King dismissed him.

Coke's place as a writer on English law is a proud one. His collected *Reports* (13 vols., 1600–15) and *Institutes* (4 vols., 1628–44) contain a superb exposition of the rules of English common law.

***Cold Comfort Farm*** The first and most famous novel by Stella Gibbons (1902–89), *Cold Comfort Farm*, appeared in 1932 and won the Femina Vie Heureuse Prize. An acute and witty parody of the rural fiction made popular by writers like **Mary Webb**, it both mocks and exploits the hysterical intrigue, emotional turmoil and lugubriousness of the genre.

**Colenso, John William** 1814–83 Theologian. Born into a poor family at St Austell he entered St John's College, Cambridge, as a sizar and was elected a fellow in 1837. After some years as a mathematics teacher at Harrow and a tutor in his own college, Colenso became vicar of Forncett St Mary in Norfolk. In 1853 he was appointed bishop of the new diocese of Natal, where his attitude to race relations and his broadminded approach to tribal customs in marriage caused controversy. Colenso provoked a larger storm by his contribution to the **Higher Criticism** in *A Commentary on the Epistle to the Romans* (1861) and *The Pentateuch and Book of Joshua Critically Examined* (1862–79), which challenged the historical accuracy of those books and concluded that they were written during the post-Exile period. In 1863 Bishop Gray of Cape Town deposed Colenso, who in turn challenged Gray's jurisdiction. Colenso was confirmed as holder of the see by the law courts in 1866 and he continued in the affection of his diocese until he died.

**Coleridge, Derwent** 1800–83 Editor, biographer and poet. Son of **S. T. Coleridge**, he was educated at St John's College, Cambridge, and ordained in 1825. As master of the grammar school at Helston in Cornwall, he taught **Charles Kingsley**. He contributed poetry to *Knight's Quarterly Magazine* from 1822. He also published *The Scriptural Character of the English Church* (1839) and a biography of his brother **Hartley Coleridge** (1849), whose works he edited (1851).

**Coleridge, Hartley** 1796–1849 Poet. The eldest son of **S. T. Coleridge**. Born at Clevedon, Somerset, he attended Ambleside school where his education was supervised by **Robert Southey**. He went on to Merton College, Oxford, and later became a probationer fellow of Oriel, but was dismissed for 'intemperance'. He eked out a living by contributing to *Blackwood's Magazine* and *The London Magazine*. He attempted to run a school at Ambleside 1823–8, but finally retired as a recluse to Grasmere. He published *Biographia Borealis* (1833), republished in 1852 as *Lives of Northern Worthies* with marginal observations by S. T. Coleridge. Other works included a slight volume of *Poems* (1833) and a biography of **Andrew Marvell** (1835). Two volumes of *Poems* were published in 1851, accompanied by a memoir by his brother **Derwent Coleridge**.

**Coleridge, Mary Elizabeth** 1861–1907 Novelist and poet. She was born in London, the great-granddaughter of **S. T. Coleridge**'s brother. Educated at home, partly by **W. J. Cory**, she began to write verse as a child, publishing her first volumes *Fancy's Following* (1896) and *Fancy's Guerdon* (1897) under the pseudonym Anodos. Her first novel, *The Seven Sleepers of Ephesus* (1893), was praised by **R. L. Stevenson**; other titles include *The King with Two Faces* (1897), *The Fiery Dawn* (1901) and *The Lady on the Drawing-Room Floor* (1906). Her *Poems Old and New* (1907) and *Gathered Leaves* (1910) were published posthumously.

**Coleridge, Samuel Taylor** 1772–1834 Poet, critic and philosopher. He was born at Ottery St Mary, Devon, where his father was vicar. After his father's death in 1781 he was sent to preparatory school in London and then to Christ's Hospital, where his schoolfellows included **Charles Lamb** and **Leigh Hunt**. Intended for the church, he entered Jesus College, Cambridge, in 1791, joining in the reformist fervour stimulated by the French Revolution. He abandoned his studies in December 1793, enlisting in the Light Dragoons under the name of Silas Tomkyn Comberbache. He was bought out after two wretched months but did not return to Cambridge to take his degree, despite reinstatement in autumn 1794.

In June 1794 Coleridge met **Robert Southey** in Oxford. They decided to establish a commune in New England based on the ideas of **William Godwin**. The scheme – which Coleridge called 'Pantisocracy' – came to nothing, though at Bristol Coleridge allowed Southey to talk him into pledging himself to Sara Fricker, sister of Southey's fiancée Edith. Coleridge's first poems appeared in *The Morning Chronicle* in December 1794. On leaving Cambridge for good that winter, he went to London and then Bristol, lodging with Southey and lecturing on politics, religion and education. His lectures won him the respect of local democrats, including the publisher Joseph Cottle and Thomas and Josiah Wedgwood of the pottery dynasty. After his

Samuel Taylor Coleridge. The portrait by R. Hancock, 1796. National Portrait Gallery, London.

marriage to Sara Fricker in October 1795 he settled at nearby Clevedon. His first volume, *Poems on Various Subjects*, was published by Cottle in April 1796 and his first son, Hartley David, was born in September. Coleridge preached throughout the region, produced 10 issues of a radical Christian weekly, *The Watchman*, wrote philosophical and religious 'conversation poems' and began to read German literature and philosophy. He also took opium during bouts of illness and depression.

In December 1796 the Coleridges moved to Nether Stowey on the edge of the Quantock Hills. **William Wordsworth** and his sister **Dorothy Wordsworth**, whom he first visited in June 1797, were living nearby. The literary partnership that began laid the foundations of English Romanticism. The two poets planned a joint volume of 'experimental' poems, the *Lyrical Ballads*, eventually published in 1798, to which Coleridge's most important contribution was *The Rime of the Ancient Mariner*. He also began, though never completed, three other ballads in the same idiom, the finest of which is *Christabel*. Visitors included Charles and Mary Lamb, the radical John Thelwall and the young **Hazlitt**. The year 1797–8 was a happy, creative period. His second son was born in May 1798 and an annuity from the Wedgwoods allowed him to write full-time. He produced another sequence of conversation poems, addressed to friends: 'This Lime-Tree Bower My Prison', 'Frost at Midnight', 'Fears in Solitude' and 'The Nightingale'. The enigmatic fragment *Kubla Khan* was written in 1797. Other work included the verse tragedy *Osirio*, leading articles for *The Morning Post* on foreign policy, the political ode 'France' and the anti-war poem 'Fire, Famine, Slaughter: A War Eclogue'.

In September 1798 Coleridge visited Germany with the Wordsworths, proceeding alone to Göttingen to attend lectures and read deeply in Kant, Schiller, Schelling and A. W. Schlegel. These studies made him the most influential English interpreter of German Romanticism and the foremost exponent of its organicist doctrines. Back in England the next year, he translated part of Schiller's *Wallenstein* trilogy, contracted for a biography of Lessing and planned an ambitious work of Romantic metaphysics. He also wrote some 50 articles for *The Morning Post* between December 1799 and October 1800. He moved his family to London and then to Keswick in the Lake District to be near Wordsworth. By this time Coleridge's marriage had begun to fail and he fell in love with Sara Hutchinson, whose sister Mary married Wordsworth in 1802. The guilt and stress of this love profoundly affected him over the next decade, forming the background to such poems as 'The Keepsake' (1800), 'On Revisiting the Seashore' (1801), 'To Asra' (1801), 'The Picture,

or, The Lovers' Resolution' (1802) and 'A Day-Dream' (1801–2). A more authentic voice breaks through in 'Dejection: An Ode' (1802), answered by Wordsworth in his 'Intimations of Immortality' ode. Coleridge now became more or less addicted to opium. His energies flowed away from systematic work and into the meditative, confessional *Notebooks*.

In spring 1804 Coleridge left his family in Southey's care and spent two years in the wartime Civil Service at Malta. Little was heard of him in England during this exile. He increased his intake of opium, visited Sicily and Italy, wrote nothing but his notebooks and vainly tried to forget Sara Hutchinson. On his return to England in August 1806 he formalized his separation from his wife. From December 1806 to June 1807 he stayed with the Wordsworths and Sara Hutchinson, then living at Coleorton, Leicestershire, and was present at Wordsworth's reading of the 'Poem to Coleridge' which became *The Prelude*; he replied with the conversation poem 'To William Wordsworth'. In 1808 he delivered 18 lectures 'On Poetry and the Principles of Taste' at the Royal Institute, the first of many series in the next decade. The form was particularly congenial to him, and he drew large, distinguished audiences. Especially significant were the lectures on **Shakespeare** (first published as a two-volume collection of *Shakespearean Criticism* in 1907), developing the idea of a poet's work as epiphenomena, or particular emanations, of a single creative mind and the concept, then completely new, of 'organic' form. In autumn 1808 Coleridge joined the Wordsworths for the last time, spending 18 months at Grasmere. Here he produced *The Friend*, a 'literary, moral and political paper' running for 28 issues in 1809–10 and appearing in book form in 1812, perhaps the closest he came to fulfilling his dream of a synthesis. Politically and intellectually, its project of educating the English mind in post-Kantian idealism showed his development towards a new conservatism.

The final break with Wordsworth, and the last crisis of his relationship with Sara Hutchinson, came in 1810. Coleridge lodged in London, lecturing and writing despite periods of near-suicidal despair and his ever-increasing opium addiction. The few poems of the next years include 'The Visionary Hope' (1810), 'The Suicide's Argument' (1811) and 'Time, Real and Imaginary' (1812). His pro-Government articles in *The Courier* and his attacks on the English Jacobins caused Hazlitt to denounce him as a political turncoat. His play *Remorse*, a reworking of *Osirio*, was produced at **Drury Lane** in 1813. After a physical and mental breakdown in December 1813 Coleridge underwent treatment at Bristol and spent the summer of 1814 with friends near Bath. To this period belong the marginal commentaries added to *The Rime of the Ancient Mariner*, three short essays 'On the Principles of Genial Criticism Concerning the Fine Arts' and *Biographia Literaria*, a kaleidoscope of philosophy, criticism and autobiography, and one of the key texts of English Romanticism.

In the spring of 1816 Coleridge settled at the Highgate home of Dr James Gillman, remaining there for the rest of his life. A chastened but also clarified figure, he became something of a living legend to younger Romantic poets. At **Byron**'s initiative, *Christabel and Other Poems* appeared in 1816, printing 'Kubla Khan' and 'The Pains of Sleep' for the first time. *Sibylline Leaves*, his collected poems, was published in 1817 (and expanded in 1828 and 1834), along with the *Biographia* and *Zapolyta*, a 'dramatic poem . . . in humble imitation of "The Winter's Tale" of Shakespeare'. Yet Coleridge's poetic career was largely over. The philosopher, preacher-lecturer and critic, on the other hand, flourished. He became the centre of a circle of friends and disciples that included Godwin, **Crabb Robinson** and the faithful Charles Lamb.

Coleridge's view of society, culture and religion became more concrete and programmatic. His two *Lay Sermons* (1816–17) develop ideas on morality, national education and the 'organic' structure of society. His 'Treatise on Method', written as introduction to the *Encyclopaedia Metropolitana* and included in the final three-volume edition of *The Friend* (1818), ranges through every conceivable branch of knowledge in dizzying pursuit of the 'self-organizing purpose' of nature, man and science. In 1818–19 he lectured on 'The History of Philosophy' and gave a 'General Course on Literature', described in the *Literary Remains* (1836). *Aids to Reflection* (1824), emphasizing the importance of Christianity as 'personal revelation', influenced the development of the Broad Church movement and the **Christian Socialism** of John Sterling, **F. D. Maurice** and **Charles Kingsley**. In his last years Coleridge renewed his friendship with Wordsworth, with whom he went on a short tour of Germany in 1828, made memorable by a meeting with Friedrich Schlegel. 'Work without Hope', 'Constancy to an Ideal Object', 'Coeli Enarrant' and 'Love's Apparition' are among the most representative of his few late poems. His last major publication, *On the Constitution of the Church and State* (1830), proposed the removal of education and learning from both ecclesiastical and state control and the establishment of teachers, scholars, scientists, artists and priests as an independent 'estate of the Realm' called the 'clerisy' or 'National Church'. Some idea of Coleridge's conversation is given in *Table Talk* (1836), edited by his nephew Henry Coleridge.

Coleridge's reputation as a poet is secured by a small, though radiant, corpus of major works.

The distinctively Continental cast of his thought was excitingly new to British contemporaries. His theory of the poetic imagination as a unifying and mediating power within divided modern cultures provided one of the central ideas of Romantic aesthetics, and his dialectical juxtapositions of reason and understanding, culture and civilization, and mechanical and organic form shaped the vocabulary of its recoil from **Utilitarianism**. Yet much of Coleridge's work is shot through with self-doubt and fears for his Christian belief, a metaphysical anxiety that seems to anticipate modern existentialism.

**Coleridge, Sara** 1802–52 Translator, editor and writer of fairy-tales. Born at Keswick, the only daughter of **S. T. Coleridge**, she married Henry Nelson Coleridge in 1829. She translated Dobrizhoffer's *Account of the Abipones* (1822) and the history of the *Chevalier Bayard* (1825). Her most important work was a romantic fairy-tale in prose and verse, *Phantasmion* (1837). She also published *Pretty Lessons for Good Children* (1845) and edited her father's *Poems* (1852) with her brother **Derwent Coleridge**.

**Colet, John** ?1467–1519 Colet was one of the most important English Christian humanists. He was educated at Oxford and travelled abroad for three years in France and Italy. He lectured in 1496–1504 at Oxford, first on the Epistle to the Romans, and later on 1 Corinthians. Erasmus attended the latter lectures. These expositions abandoned the minute exegesis and allegorical interpretation of the schoolmen. In 1504 Colet became Dean of St Paul's, and *c.* 1509 he founded St Paul's School with William Lily as its first headmaster. With Lily he prepared a Latin grammar and the collaboration was later revised by **Erasmus**. As a humanist he extolled the virtues of pure classical Latin and was influenced by Platonic and neo-Platonic thought. Colet was a close friend and correspondent of Erasmus and **Thomas More**.

***Colin Clout's Come Home Again*** The title of **Spenser**'s pastoral poem is evidently designed to recall the major character in ***The Shepheardes Calender***. Published in 1595 and dedicated to **Raleigh**, it has Colin giving a first-hand account of his adventures to his fellow shepherds, some of whose names, Hobbinol and Cuddy, also recall Spenser's earlier **pastoral**. It offers compliments to Queen Elizabeth (Cynthia) and Raleigh (the Shepherd of the Ocean), laments the death of **Sidney** (Astrophel), and alludes to notable personages of the poet's time, such as the Countess of Pembroke (Urania). It is ambivalent in its feeling about the court which it alternately compliments and criticizes, and is one of Spenser's most autobiographically allusive poems.

*Colleen Bawn, The* A melodrama by **Dion Boucicault**, based on **Gerald Griffin**'s 'true-life' crime novel, *The Collegians* (1829). The play was first performed at Laura Keene's Theatre, New York, in 1860. It is a successfully softened version of a historical murder.

Hardress Cregan, secretly married to Eily O'Connor, the poor-but-honest colleen bawn (Anglo-Irish for 'fair girl'), needs to marry the heiress, Anne Chute, in order to redeem the family's fortunes. He instructs his devoted hunchbacked servant to kill Eily, but the attempt is frustrated by the comic vagabond Myles-na-Coppaleen. Although Myles loves Eily, it is enough for him to see her happily restored to her repentant husband. The creation of Myles gave new life to the figure of the stage Irishman.

**Collier, Arthur** 1680–1732 Churchman and philosopher. A native of Wiltshire, Collier was educated at Pembroke and Balliol colleges, Oxford, and held the living of Langford Magna until his death. His *Clavis Universalis – or a Demonstration of the Non-Existence and Impossibility of the External World* (1713) is interesting because it demonstrated that Collier had arrived independently at the same conclusions as **George Berkeley** had in *The Principles of Human Knowledge*.

**Collier, Jeremy** 1650–1726 Moralist and divine. Educated at Ipswich school and Gonville and Caius College, Cambridge, Collier became rector of Ampton in Suffolk (1679) and lecturer at Gray's Inn (1685). He remained loyal to James II, refusing to take the oath of loyalty to William and Mary, and was imprisoned in 1689 and 1692; in 1696 he incurred further wrath by giving absolution, on the scaffold, to two men charged with attempting to assassinate King William. Collier was outlawed and fled the country; but he returned in 1697 and became a bishop in 1713, though still without taking the oath of loyalty.

A man of unwavering courage, Collier was author of *Essays upon Several Moral Subjects* (3 parts, 1698–1705), *The Great Historical, Geographical, Genealogical and Poetical Dictionary* (1701) and *The Ecclesiastical History of Great Britain* (2 vols., 1708 and 1714). He is best known for his controversial *Short View of the Immorality and Profaneness of the English Stage* (1698), an attack on the leading playwrights of the day, including **Dryden**, **Congreve**, **Vanbrugh**, **John Dennis** and **Thomas D'Urfey**. Both Congreve and Vanbrugh replied to Collier.

**Collier, John Payne** 1789–1883 Shakespearean scholar. Born in London, he qualified as a barrister despite receiving little formal education. He chose instead to work as a journalist, for *The Times* and later *The Morning Chronicle*. His scholarly writings on **Shakespeare** and Renaissance drama were supported by his researches in noblemen's private libraries and his vigorous work for various literary and historical publishing societies. A Second Folio Shakespeare (1632) with supposedly contemporary annotations was the basis for his later work and reputation. The annotations were exposed as forgeries only after embittered controversy. Collier was taken to be the perpetrator rather than the victim of the fraud and, as well as blighting the end of his life, the revelation rendered his previous work permanently suspect.

**Collins, Anthony** 1676–1729 Philosopher. Collins was born in Heston, Middlesex, and educated at Eton and King's College, Cambridge. He became Deputy-Lieutenant of Essex in 1715.

A close friend and admirer of **John Locke**, Collins became a freethinker and deist of considerable influence in his own right. His *Essay Concerning the Use of Reason* (1707) denied the accepted separation between those things that are beyond human reason and those that are not. *A Discourse of Freethinking, occasioned by the Rise and Growth of a Sect call'd Freethinkers* (1713) is a sharp attack on ministers of all denominations and was in its turn attacked by many churchmen, including **Richard Bentley** and **Jonathan Swift**. Collins's *A Philosophical Inquiry concerning Human Liberty and Necessity* (1715) is regarded as an able and clearly written statement of determinism.

**Collins, John Churton** 1848–1908 Critic. The son of a doctor, Collins was born in Gloucestershire and attended King Edward's School, Birmingham, before studying at Balliol College, Oxford. Until his appointment as Professor of English at Birmingham in 1904, he made his living as a private tutor and extension lecturer in London, contributing articles to *The Cornhill Magazine*, *The Quarterly Review* and, later, to *The Saturday Review*. A ruthless critic, he wrote damaging attacks on **Edmund Gosse** and even on his friend **Swinburne**, and offended Oxford University with his agitation for the establishment of an English school there, in his book *The Study of English Literature* (1891) and in earlier articles for *The Pall Mall Gazette*.

Collins edited works by **Robert Greene**, **Tourneur**, **Lord Herbert of Cherbury** and **Milton**, and published *Ephemera Critica* (1901), *Studies in Shakespeare* (1904) and other critical works. Morbidly interested in murder, spiritualism and graveyards, and depressive in temperament, he drowned himself near Lowestoft.

**Collins, Tom** See **Furphy, Joseph**.

**Collins, William** 1721–59 Poet. The son of a hatter, Collins was born in Chichester and was educated at Winchester College and then at Magdalen College, Oxford. He went to London in 1744 with almost no money, determined on a literary career.

Collins began to write poetry as a schoolboy and completed the *Persian Eclogues* (published in 1742) when he was 17. In London he published *Odes on Several Descriptive and Allegoric Subjects* (1746) but did not gain recognition immediately; he accepted an advance from a London bookseller for a translation of Aristotle's *Poetics* and retired to Chichester. Then in 1749 he inherited £2000 and promptly repaid the advance; he also abandoned the translation of Aristotle, but his plans for future work halted when his mental and physical health began to fail. He broke down completely after a journey in France (1750) and died insane at the age of 38, at his sister's house in Chichester.

Collins's temperament was unstable and, for most of his life, his circumstances uncertain: he was always 'doubtful of his dinner and trembling at a creditor', anxieties that his inheritance came too late to allay. Even before his career as a poet broke off, he had never been prolific and he left less than 1500 lines of verse. Yet they show he had the makings of an original artist, struggling to escape the conventions of his time and often succeeding. 'Ode to Simplicity', 'Dirge in Cymbeline', 'Ode to Evening', 'How Sleep the Brave' ('Ode, Written in the Beginning of the Year 1746') and especially the posthumous 'Ode on the Popular Superstitions of the Highlands' (1788) have an honoured place in English poetry.

**Collins, (William) Wilkie** 1824–89 Novelist. Born in London, son of the landscape painter William Collins, he was named after his father's friend Sir David Wilkie. Educated privately, with generous interruptions for travel abroad, he entered Lincoln's Inn in 1846 but quickly showed the real direction of his interest by publishing three books: a memoir of his father (1848); *Antonina, or, The Fall of Rome* (1850), a historical novel in the manner of **Bulwer Lytton**; and the charming *Rambles Beyond Railways* (1851), about a walking tour of Cornwall. He first met **Dickens** in 1851, joining the older novelist in amateur theatricals and becoming a regular contributor to *Household Words*; the two men also collaborated in writing, among other pieces, *The Lazy Tour of Two Idle Apprentices* (1857) and two melodramas, *The Lighthouse* (1855) and *The Frozen Deep* (1857). By himself, Collins produced a succession of short stories and several novels: *Basil: A Story of Modern Life* (1852), *Hide and Seek* (1854) and *The Dead Secret* (1857). They were the prelude to his work of the 1860s, when he emerged as the most skilful

writer of **sensation fiction**, with *The Woman in White* (1860), *No Name* (1862), *Armadale* (1866) and *The Moonstone* (1868). Vigorously observing his own advice to the novelist – 'Make 'em laugh, make 'em cry, make 'em wait' – these books made him one of the most popular writers of the day.

His triumph ended with the decade. Various reasons have been suggested for Collins's subsequent decline in power and the near-eclipse of his former popularity: the death of Dickens in 1870 robbed him of a powerful mentor; his recurrent ill health was aggravated by addiction to laudanum; and his unconventional private life became further entangled, with two mistresses, Caroline Graves and Martha Rudd, apparently sharing his house. Above all, his determination to tackle social issues disconcerted his audience and, at times, dispersed his narrative powers. **Swinburne** commented in a famous doggerel: 'What brought good Wilkie's genius nigh perdition?/Some devil whispered – "Wilkie, have a mission."' Collins attacked athleticism in *Man and Wife* (1870), attitudes to fallen women in *The New Magdalen* (1873), the Jesuits in *The Black Robe* (1881) and vivisection in *Heart and Science* (1883). *The Evil Genius* (1886) dealt with adultery and divorce, *The Legacy of Cain* (1889) with heredity and environment. Not all his later works were failures – though Swinburne thought *The Fallen Leaves* (1879) 'something too absurdly repulsive for comment and endurance' – and Collins periodically returned to mystery and suspense, with varying success, in *Poor Miss Finch* (1872), *The Law and the Lady* (1875), *My Lady's Money* (1878) and *I Say No* (1884). His last novel, *Blind Love* (1890), was completed by **Walter Besant**.

**Colman, George, the Elder** 1732–94 Playwright, journalist and theatre manager. Colman trained, rather casually, as a lawyer in the expectation that he would inherit riches from his uncle, William Pulteney, Earl of Bath. His early involvement with the theatre, a product of his friendship with the equally clubbable **David Garrick**, was amateur. The one-act *Polly Honeycombe* (1760) is light and charming. *The Jealous Wife* (1761), inspired by rather than based on **Fielding**'s *Tom Jones*, is more ambitious. Its extraordinary success, in a style more acerbic than that of sentimental comedy, may have tempted Colman towards the theatre and away from his legal practice. If the Earl of Bath was displeased, we have a ready explanation of his leaving Colman, in 1764, a much smaller inheritance than he had hoped for. Colman's disappointment silenced the carefree tone of his life and work. He was sufficiently provided to abandon the law, but he had now to rely on the patronage of the public. His translation of *The Comedies of Terence* (1765) enhanced his reputation, as did the successful collaboration with Garrick in *The Clandestine Marriage* (1766), but Colman was temperamentally inclined to spend more than he had. It was the need to make money that persuaded him to put his friendship with Garrick at risk by buying a share in the management of the **Covent Garden Theatre**, chief rival to Garrick's **Drury Lane**.

Colman was the active and effective manager of Covent Garden for seven years, 1767–74. His own plays during this period were mostly adaptations, though *The Man of Business* (1774) was a notable exception. Two years after leaving Covent Garden, he was tempted back into management when the death of **Samuel Foote** left vacant the Little Theatre in the **Haymarket**. His last two considerable plays, *The Suicide* (1778) and *The Separate Maintenance* (1779), were first performed there. Increasingly subject to bouts of insanity from 1785, Colman eventually surrendered the management of the Haymarket to his son, **George Colman the Younger**, in 1790.

**Colman, George, the Younger** 1762–1836 Playwright and theatre manager. The son of **George Colman the Elder**, from whom he inherited the Little Theatre in the **Haymarket** in 1794, having already assumed the responsibilities of management five years earlier, he was gregarious, hard-drinking and improvident, but nevertheless defended and improved the status of the Little Theatre, with which he remained associated until 1817. His fourth play, *Inkle and Yarico* (1787), was a deserved success there. Described as an opera, it is a comedy with songs, humanely if uninsistently critical of the slave trade. Colman's undoubted facility as a writer of comic verse (the collection of 'tales in verse', *My Nightgown and Slippers* (1797) has genuine merit) enlivens, with some strain on plausibility, the historical romances, *The Battle of Hexham* (1789) and *The Surrender of Calais* (1791), as well as colouring the otherwise sombre adaptation of **Godwin's** *Caleb Williams*, *The Iron Chest* (1796). Colman's more traditional five-act comedies, *The Heir at Law* (1797), *The Poor Gentleman* (1801) and particularly *John Bull* (1803), are not without incidental merits, but he was at his best as a popular entertainer. It is ironic that his appointment as Examiner of Plays in 1824, and his conduct in the office between then and his death, should have left him with the reputation of a spoiler of other people's entertainment.

***Colonel Jack*** (*The History and Remarkable Life of the Truly Honourable Colonel Jacque, Commonly Call'd Colonel Jack*) A novel by **Daniel Defoe**, published in 1722. Like the earlier *Captain Singleton*, it is a romantic adventure told in the first person.

Abandoned by his parents while a small child, the narrator falls into bad company, becomes a pickpocket, and reaches early manhood living on his wits. 'Colonel Jack' is the nickname given to the hero when he is homeless and in the London underworld. To escape this way of life, he enlists as a soldier but promptly deserts when faced with the prospect of fighting in Flanders. Next he is abducted and shipped to Virginia, where he is sold as a slave to a planter and begins at last to make his way in the world: he is promoted to overseer and eventually freed. He becomes a planter and is so successful that he is able to return to England a rich man. He experiences some vicissitudes in his married life but by the end of the tale he is prosperous and mellow. The early chapters are among the finest in Defoe's fiction.

**Colton, Charles Caleb** ?1780–1832 Author of the immensely popular *Lacon, or, Many Things in Few Words* (1820), a collection of aphorisms, epigrams and essays. Educated at Eton and Cambridge, Colton was a clergyman who felt little inclination for the calling.

**Colum, Padraic** 1881–1972 Irish poet, dramatist, folklorist and children's writer. Born the eldest son of a workhouse master in Longford and educated at a National School, Colum worked in Dublin as a clerk in the Irish Railway Clearing House until 1903, when a wealthy American financed a period of private study. He had already published poems in *The Irish Independent* and *The United Irishman*, edited by Arthur Griffith, the nationalist politician whose biography he eventually wrote (1959). Griffith encouraged his first play, an anti-British propaganda piece called *The Saxon Shillin'*; this led to involvement in the new National Theatre Society and, eventually, work with **Yeats** and **Lady Gregory** in the **Abbey Theatre**, of which he was a founder member. The plays of this period, *Broken Soil* (1903), *The Land* (1905) and *Thomas Muskerry* (1910), are marked by a sombre realism. He left Ireland in 1914 and lived thereafter chiefly in the USA though temporary residence in Paris brought him the friendship of **James Joyce**, commemorated in *Our Friend James Joyce* (1958). His commissioned study of Polynesian folklore in Hawaii resulted in three volumes of stories in the 1920s. He lectured on comparative literature and published many volumes for children retelling Irish, Welsh, classical and Scandinavian myths and legends, while also continuing to write poems and plays. While his later work encompasses Noh plays, experimental drama and explorations of near-Eastern exoticism and fantasy, he is remembered chiefly for the simple rhythmic lyricism of his earlier poetry, celebrating the lives of poor people and animals and the mystery of nature in an already vanishing rural Ireland. An ambitious, neglected novel, *The Flying Swans*, was published in 1957.

**Columbiad, The** An epic poem in heroic couplets by **Joel Barlow** published in 1807, 20 years after it first appeared as *The Vision of Columbus*. The two versions, however, have little in common. In nine books, *The Vision* presents a dialogue between an angel and Christopher Columbus, both of whom ascend the Mount of Vision and survey human history. The angel argues that all historical events, particularly Columbus's discovery, lead to the future glory of America. The poem thus reaffirms America's manifest destiny; it offers an essentially conservative vision congenial to Federalists of the new republic.

By 1807 Barlow had changed his political orientation and had revised the poem accordingly into *The Columbiad*. Now a liberal democrat, he replaced the simple dialogue with a colloquy of different voices, each intended to represent a different political or social interest. He also included further classical allusions, often explained in lengthy scholarly footnotes, and developed the prefaces to each of the nine books into extensive political and philosophical arguments. Ironically, these revisions, which aimed at widening the poem's audience, in fact limited it, and made *The Columbiad* read more like a political treatise than a poem.

**Colvin, Sir Sidney** 1845–1927 Critic of art and literature. Born in Norwood, he attended Trinity College, Cambridge. He served as Slade Professor of Fine Art at Cambridge (1873–85), Director of the Fitzwilliam Museum (1876–84) and Keeper of Prints and Drawings at the British Museum (1884–1912). In addition to his art criticism, chiefly on engravers and engraving, he published volumes on **Landor** (1881) and **Keats** (1887) for the English Men of Letters series, a biography of Keats (1917), and memorials to his friend **Robert Louis Stevenson** in editions of the *Vailima Letters* (1895) he had received from Stevenson and of Stevenson's works (1894–7) and correspondence (1899–1911).

**Combe, William** 1741–1823 Verse satirist and writer of miscellaneous prose. Combe was born in Bristol and educated at Eton, and then Oxford, which he left without taking a degree. He travelled in France and Italy, where he met **Sterne**, and then proceeded to squander his substantial inheritance in London; after which he seems to have been successively a common soldier, a waiter, a teacher of elocution, a cook and a private in the French army. He turned to writing around 1772, and scored his first success as a satirist with *The Diaboliad* (1776), dedicated to Lord Irnham, 'the worst man in His Majesty's dominion', in settlement of a private score. He followed it up with *Diabo-lady* (1777), *Anti-diabolady* (1778), and numerous other works in verse and prose, including *The Devil upon Two Sticks* (1790) and the topographical *Microcosm of London* (1808). His most famous work, ***The Tour of Dr Syntax in Search of the Picturesque***, on which he collaborated with Thomas Rowlandson, appeared in Ackermann's *Poetical Magazine* in 1809, and was followed in 1820 by *The Second Tour of Dr Syntax in Search of Consolation*, and in 1821 by *The Third Tour of Dr Syntax in Search of a Wife*. Combe again combined his talents with Rowlandson's in *The English Dance of Death* (1815–16), which contains some of his best verse; *The Dance of Life* (1816); and *Johnny Quae Genius* (1822), the last, and feeblest, of the Syntax series.

**comedy** The Greeks originally used the word from which 'comedy' derives to describe a choric song of celebration or revel. The transition of the word, from describing a song and dance within a play to describing a kind of play distinct from **tragedy**, was complete by the second half of the 5th century BC. The earliest surviving examples are the satiric comedies of Aristophanes (*c.* 488–*c.* 380 BC). The form of 'old comedy', of which the plays of Aristophanes are the unique evidence, was elaborate, but the content has an air of improvisatory freedom. There was licence for parody, personal abuse and invective and a direct treatment of contemporary social and political issues as well as for the traditional obscenity of fertility rituals. In 'new comedy', as exemplified by the surviving work of Menander (*c.* 342–293 BC) and his Roman successors, Plautus (*c.* 254–184 BC) and Terence (*c.* 190–159 BC), plot is altogether more central, and stock characters of fiction replace the portraits of living people.

It is the much more easily imitable 'new comedy' that lies behind British and Continental comedy. The word has been applied to a great variety of work, of which the simplest common denominator is a happy ending, and a more complex feature is a greater interest in society and its values than in individuals and their destiny. The earliest substantial example in English, *Ralph Roister Doister*, was written in conscious imitation of Terence, who continued to serve as a model to the writers of intrigue comedy for the Elizabethan stage. By exaggerating Terentian stereotypes, **Ben Jonson** invented the 'humours' comedy that was immensely popular after the 1598 performance of *Every Man in his Humour*. City comedies, like *The Shoemaker's Holiday*, also reflect the influence of Terence and Plautus, whose *Menaechmi* provided **Shakespeare** with the plot of one of his earliest successes, *The Comedy of Errors*. Shakespeare's later comedies, as well as the unclassifiable 'last plays', mark a departure from strict classical form. But English comedy followed Jonsonian rather than Shakespearean lines. The comedy of manners that dominated the English stage for four decades after the restoration of Charles II rests on the foundation of a Jonsonian contrast between the truly witty and those who pretend to wit. Too bawdy and too mordant for many of its critics, the Restoration comedy of manners gave way to 18th-century sentimental comedy, in which the emphasis is shifted from the exposure of fools and villains to the rewarding of virtue and prudence.

It has been the tendency, in criticism at least, to celebrate only those writers who have challenged the dominance of **sentimental comedy** in the 18th and 19th centuries – **Goldsmith**, **Sheridan**, the **Boucicault** who wrote *London Assurance*, **Oscar Wilde** – and to neglect or question the achievements of such 'sentimental' writers as **Steele**, **Cibber**, **Cumberland**, **O'Keeffe**, **T. W. Robertson**, **Pinero** and **Henry Arthur Jones**. It was the more robust work of **Shaw** that carried the reputation of comedy into the 20th century, but a distinctive kind of drama, formally classifiable as comedy, is hard to discern in the modern theatre. It survived longer in Ireland, where the plays of **Synge** and **Fitzmaurice** gave early impetus to a uniquely Irish comic drama.

*Comedy of Errors, The* A comedy by **William Shakespeare**, first performed *c*. 1593 and published in the First Folio of 1623. The main source is the *Menaechmi* of Plautus, presumably in an English translation.

The complications of the plot – and complications are its very essence – arise from the fact that Aegeon, a merchant from Syracuse, had identical twin sons and made distinction even trickier by calling them both Antipholus. What is more, Aegeon bought, as servants for his sons, two slaves, also identical twins and also sharing a name, Dromio. The whole purpose of the play is to devise, and then to handle effectively, scenes of mistaken identity.

This early comedy by Shakespeare was immensely successful in the Elizabethan theatre. It was still popular enough in 1604 to be called for performance at James I's court, and it probably remained in the repertoire of the **King's Men** for many years after that. The complications are handled with dexterity and with a mature sense of comic timing.

*Comical Revenge, The, or, Love in a Tub* A comedy by **George Etherege**, first produced in March 1664 and published the same year. The play shows the influence of Molière's early style and is set in the last months of the Commonwealth.

The very slight comic plot concerns Sir Frederick Frolick's wooing by a rich widow, the impudence of a valet, Dufoy, who is wedged into a tub by his irritated fellow servants, and the cheating of a country knight, Sir Nicholas Cully, by Palmer and Wheadle. Cully is married off to Sir Frederick's former mistress Lucy. Sir Frederick decides to marry the rich widow. The serious plot, in rhymed couplets, is almost a satire on the 'heroick' play: Aurelia loves Colonel Bruce, who loves Aurelia's sister Graciana, who loves Lord Beaufort. Bruce and Beaufort quarrel over Graciana and fight a duel; Beaufort wins, and Bruce tries to kill himself in despair. Beaufort takes Graciana; Bruce recovers from wounds both physical and mental, and is comforted by Aurelia.

*Coming Race, The* A novel by **Edward Bulwer Lytton**, published in 1871. An American mining engineer descends to the centre of the earth and encounters a subterranean people with control over a mysterious kinetic energy, called 'Vril', which gives them unbounded powers. The book is in part a satire on Darwinian evolutionary theory and on contemporary ideas about the emancipation of women. For a time the word 'Vril' became associated with any strength-giving elixir: hence Bo(vine)vril.

*commedia dell' arte* The name given to a style of improvised comedy which flourished in Italy from the mid 16th to the mid 18th century, and whose influence was felt throughout Europe. The performed pieces were based, not on an established text (though certain set speeches were commonly learned by heart), but on a scenario which left room for improvised action and dialogue. *Commedia* companies toured Italy and, later, France. Each member adopted a vivid mask, generally retaining that mask throughout his or her career. It was always possible to add a new mask to such well-established ones as Arlecchino, Pantalone, the pedantic Dottore and the bragging Capitano. Thus, Tiberio Fiorilli (1608–94) virtually invented Scaramuccia, who was adopted in France as Scaramouche, and another (unknown) Neapolitan invented Cetrulo, who was modified into Pulcinella, reaching England as Punchinel in about 1650 and becoming familiar as the fairground Punch. Such modifications of a mask are typical. The English Harlequin, though derived from the quick-witted Italian Arlecchino, was utterly unlike him. John Rich (*c*. 1692–1761), who popularized the harlequinade during his long tenure of **Covent Garden Theatre**, played Harlequin as a dumb acrobat, endowed with sufficient magical powers to win his Columbine. The triumph of love in the English harlequinade was an acting out of 'real' struggles of young lovers in the framing play, and it is in the evolution of the harlequinade and the **pantomime** that the influence of *commedia dell' arte* in

England can be most clearly seen. A divergent tradition is that of Pierrot, derived from the mask of Pedrolino by way of Paris.

**Commentaries on the Laws of England** See **Blackstone, Sir William.**

**Common Sense** Published anonymously in Philadelphia on 10 January 1776, this political pamphlet by **Thomas Paine** was the first public statement to urge America's immediate and unqualified separation from England.

Paine's argument divides into four parts. The first insists that in so far as governments are established only to protect the freedom and security of citizens, England has violated its mandate by its economic and political enslavement of the colonies. The second part rejects hereditary succession in favour of democratic election, a process which respects individual talents rather than family lineage in the designation of a ruler. The third and fourth parts celebrate both America's economic security and its potential to safeguard, by example, the inalienable rights of all people. The carefully argued pamphlet sold widely at the time (over half-a-million copies) and helped galvanize the forces which only seven months after its publication began to fight the American Revolution.

**complaint** Conventional poetic expression of personal complaint common in the Middle Ages and used also by the **Cavalier poets** in the 17th century. A first-person narrator describes his sorrow and its causes, often by telling his story. The theme is frequently unrequited or betrayed love, but may also be some other personal grief or a general dissatisfaction with the state of the world or the vicissitudes of Fortune. A complaint may be part of a longer work, like the knight's complaint in **Chaucer**'s *The Book of the Duchess*, or may be self-contained, as in his *Complaint unto Pity*.

**Complaint of the Black Knight, The** A poem usually accepted as the work of **John Lydgate**, mainly written in **rhyme royal**. The narrator walks through a park and overhears a knight in black complaining of the cruelty of his mistress. The poet prays to Venus to make the knight's beloved have mercy on him. The work shows the influence of **Geoffrey Chaucer** and the French poet Froissart.

**Compleat Angler, The**, *or, The Contemplative Man's Recreation* The classic work on fish and fishing by **Izaak Walton** was first published in 1653, and there were four further editions carefully supervised by the author during his lifetime, the last in 1676. It has become one of the most reprinted books in the history of British letters.

Three sportsmen, a fisherman (Piscator, who is Walton himself), a huntsman (Venator), and a fowler (Auceps), travel north through the countryside from Tottenham to Ware along the river Lea on the first day in May; they discuss the relative merits of their respective pastimes. Venator becomes a pupil of Piscator, and is systematically introduced to the arts of angling for various species of freshwater fish, along with a wealth of advice about watercraft, pisciculture and country lore. In the fifth edition there appeared a continuation of Walton's expanded original, a second part by his younger friend **Charles Cotton**, which largely concerns flyfishing on the river Dove, a subject Walton himself knew little about.

The book is often wrongly assumed to be the first of its kind in the language, but is in fact partly an anthology of previous writers on fishing and the mass of related subjects. As well as numerous borrowings and adaptations from the extensive tradition of piscatorial literature, it includes about 40 songs and verses and contains some fine examples of both **pastoral** and devotional writing. It is a unique combination of manual and meditation, and the way in which the personality of the author, both widely read and practically experienced, pervades the whole shape and flavour of the book is the reason for its lasting appeal to sportsman and general reader alike.

**Compton-Burnett, Dame Ivy** 1892–1969 Novelist. Ivy Compton-Burnett was born in Pinner, Middlesex, and educated privately before attending the Royal Holloway College in 1902. Her family background was difficult. The children (five by her father's first wife, seven by his second) were divided by conflicting emotional allegiances. There were numerous family tragedies: her brother, Noel, was killed on the Western Front during World War I, and two of her sisters committed suicide in 1917. In 1919 she began to live with the writer Margaret Jourdain, a relationship which lasted until the latter's death in 1951.

Her first novel, *Dolores* (1911), which she later rejected, was a pale imitation of **George Eliot**, and it was not until *Pastors and Masters* (1925) that she emerged as a writer with a distinct and highly individual style. From the late 1920s until her death she produced a new novel almost every two years: *Brothers and Sisters* (1929), *Men and Wives* (1931), *More Women than Men* (1933), *A House and Its Head* (1935), *Daughters and Sons* (1941), *A Family and a Fortune* (1939), *Parents and Children* (1941), and so on – a total of over 20 novels. *Mother and Son* (1955) won the James Tait Black Memorial Prize.

As their titles suggest, Ivy Compton-Burnett's novels are preoccupied with domestic scenes and family strife: she confines her characters to an Edwardian setting, and isolates them within a claustrophobic and frequently violent world. Her plots are realized almost exclusively through dialogue, dispensing with conventional authorial comment, yet at their best her novels achieve a brilliantly incisive irony, occasionally broadening into satire. Her central theme is the abuse of power (ranging from the petty to the diabolical), and some have found in her work remarkably acute and universal insights into the psychology of persecution.

**Comus** *(A Masque Presented at Ludlow Castle 1634: On Michaelmas Night, Before the Right Honourable, John Earl of Bridgewater, Viscount Brackley Lord President of Wales . . .)* A **pastoral** entertainment by **John Milton**, written at the request of his friend Henry Lawes to celebrate the Earl of Bridgewater's appointment to Wales and the Marches in 1634. Lawes wrote the music, and at the first performance the parts of the lady and her brothers were taken by the Earl's children. It was published in 1637. The title *A Masque* was used in the first three editions but *Comus* is not a **masque** in the court sense, in which singing and spectacle were more important than words. Its theme, the confrontation between virtue and evil, is both serious and recurrent in the rest of Milton's poetry.

Three travellers, a lady and her two brothers, are stranded in a forest by nightfall. The brothers go in search of a spring and, attracted by sounds of revelry, the lady finds a shepherd who offers her shelter in his cottage. He is Comus, son of Circe and Bacchus, and he has dismissed his rout at sight of the lady, his passion having been aroused by her beauty. When the brothers return they are told of what has happened by the benign Attendant Spirit, who has taken the form of a shepherd, Thyrsis. He warns them that Comus is an evil sorcerer who lies in wait for travellers and, in the guise of hospitality, gives them a potion that changes their faces into those of wild beasts. The Attendant Spirit gives the brothers the root of the Haemony plant, of use against all enchantments, and shows them the way to the palace of Comus.

Comus has placed the lady in a chair that holds her fast by magic. His rout is enjoying a feast and the sorcerer presses a glass, containing the potion, on the lady. She refuses it and struggles to rise but he tells her that only his wand can release her. The brothers burst in with drawn swords; they subdue the rout but Comus escapes, taking the wand with him. However, the Attendant Spirit invokes Sabrina, goddess of the nearby River Severn, who releases the lady with pure drops of water from her own spring. After a song of thanks to Sabrina the lady and her brothers, guided by the Spirit, complete their journey to Ludlow Castle.

*Comus* was adapted for the stage in 1738 by John Dalton (1709–63).

**conceit** An intricate metaphorical figure which makes ingenious comparison between two apparently incongruous things or concepts. Originating from the Italian 'concetto', it featured prominently in Petrarch's love poetry (see **Petrarchan**). In England it became one of the exercises of fancy admired by 16th-century poets and was developed by the **metaphysical poets**, particularly **Donne**, whose conceits are sometimes extended throughout an entire poem in a virtuoso display of similitude (the figure of the compasses, for example, in 'A Valediction: Forbidding Mourning'). In other instances the effect is compressed and paradoxical, requiring

Ludlow Castle, where *The Masque of Comus* was first performed. A detail from an illustration in the edition of 1637.

an imaginative and intellectual act on the part of the reader to unravel the analogies. The latter type of conceit has characterized much recent British poetry.

**concrete poetry** An international movement of experimental writers who reduced the poet's sphere of interest from a concern for continuity and the whole texture of language to isolated and particular aspects of visual, phonetic or kinetic structure, abandoning normal forms of meaning for those disclosed at or below the level of the single word. Pioneers of the movement, which is now seen as a phenomenon of the 1960s, were Eugen Gomringer and the Brazilian Noigandres group, though the *Calligrammes* (1918) of Apollinaire were perhaps equally influential. The leading British practitioner was **Ian Hamilton Finlay**, whose work has notably moved on to other fields.

Different accounts of concrete poetry have either stressed its novel and experimental nature, making links with **structuralism** and **semiotics**, or else have claimed a long tradition stemming from older texts whose visual aspects contributed to their meaning. Now that the moment of concrete poetry is past, it can most usefully be seen as an episode in the continuing assertion of an internationalist *avant-garde* that has sought to break with the past and establish formal structures reflecting the scale of alteration that technology has unleashed on the world.

**Condell, Henry** See **Heminges, John**.

**Condition of England novel** In the 1840s the social conscience of the middle-class public was stirred by the miseries of factory life. Rural squalor had been accepted as a fact of life, but industrial squalor, the product of change, aroused concern. The diseases caused by filth and overcrowding were interpreted as God's punishment for neglect and aroused anxiety for 'sanitary reform' (water supplies and sewerage). The concern was largely stimulated by **Thomas Carlyle** in *Chartism* (1839) and *Past and Present* (1843). Carlyle attacked the 'mechanical age', yet found grandeur in Manchester's machinery. He pleaded for 'baths, air, a wholesome temperature, ceilings twenty feet high' in factories. His message was that *laissez-faire* policies, combined with social neglect of the poor in industrial areas where there were no squires or clergymen to lead, were driving the ranks of society further apart and could easily foment revolution. His metaphors were apocalyptic: abysses, crumbling cliffs, falls through glass on to spiked iron railings, horses galloping out of control. The use of power, mechanical and social, the sense of a breach between man and man and the importance of healing it, the importance of education

and the fear of revolution, are themes running through novels of the period. **Elizabeth Gaskell**'s solution in *Mary Barton* (1848) and *North and South* (1855) was the 'regulating law of Christ'. Mrs Gaskell, and **Dickens** in *Dombey and Son* (1848) and *Hard Times* (1854), demand from their manufacturers a change of heart. **Charlotte Brontë** in *Shirley* (1849) offers paternalism: leadership and welfare. **Disraeli**'s solution in *Coningsby* (1844) and *Sybil* (1845) is social welfare plus a firm hand. Although all the novelists echo Carlyle's thought, phrasing and violent imagery, none of them accepts his recognition that factory legislation was inevitable. **Charles Kingsley**'s *Yeast* (1848) and *Alton Locke* (1850) plead for sanitary reform; *Alton Locke* shows how an intelligent, underprivileged working man can be seduced by the doctrines of Chartism. **George Eliot**'s *Felix Holt* (1866) has an incident drawn from *Alton Locke*: the virtuous hero is swept up by a rioting mob and suffers the penalty. *John Halifax, Gentleman* (1857), by **Dinah Mulock** (Dinah Craik), is a cruder example of the genre, but reflects the way the anxieties of one decade had become the accepted social ethics of the next. John Halifax, a gentleman by birth, like previous heroes, like them raises himself from poverty by his own efforts to become a captain of industry, defeating the hereditary landowners. Like the mill-owners in *Shirley* and in *North and South* he stands up to an attack on his property and quells a mob by force of personality. Although his wife is a 'lady', the book shows the hereditary aristocrats as vengeful and decadent. Only when Lord Luxmore's heir has succeeded in business is he deemed worthy to marry a Halifax daughter. In several of these novels, a marriage between the new 'millocracy' and well-born heiresses is offered as a happy omen for future leadership.

**conduct books** 'Improving reading' urged upon young people, particularly girls of the leisured class, especially in the 18th century. Like the Renaissance **courtesy book**, the conduct book touches on manners and deportment, but in the main deals with religion, morality and self-control. In this they are unlike the Victorian etiquette books, handbooks for social climbers. **Lord Chesterfield**'s letters (1774) were considered shocking because, in the words of **Samuel Johnson**, they 'taught the manners of a dancing master and the morals of a whore'. He blamed them for frustrating expectations that advice to the young should be moral.

Probably the most famous and influential conduct books were the *Letters on the Improvement of the Mind* (1773) by **Hester Chapone**, a friend of **Samuel Richardson**, and Fordyce's *Sermons to Young Women* (1767). (Mr Collins in **Jane Austen**'s *Pride and Prejudice*, forswearing novels, reads Fordyce's *Sermons to Young Women*

(1767) aloud to the Bennett girls, causing Lydia to yawn. The joke, of course, is that Fordyce attacks novels and novel-reading.) Among other examples widely read in the 18th century are: Richard Allestree (?), *The Ladies' Calling* (1673) and *The Whole Duty of Man* (1658); Elizabeth Appleton, *Private Education, or, a Practical Plan for the Studies of Young Ladies. With an Address to Parents, Private Governesses, and Young Ladies* (1815); Mary Astell, *A Serious Proposal to the Ladies for the Advancement of Their True and Great Interest* (1701); Thomas Gisborne, *An Enquiry into the Duties of Men in the Higher and Middling Classes of Society* (1794) and *An Enquiry into the Duties of the Female Sex* (1796); the Revd Dr John Gregory, *Legacy to his Daughters* (1774); Miss Hatfield, *Letters on the Importance of the Female Sex: With Observations on Their Manners, and on Education* (1803); Laetitia Matilda Hawkins, *Letters on the Female Mind, its Power and Pursuits. Addressed to Miss H. M. Williams, with Particular Reference to Her Letters from France* (1793); Georges Edmond Howard, *Apophthegms and Maxims on Various Subjects for the Good Conduct of Life &c.* (1767); *Instructions for a Young Lady, in Every Sphere and Period of Life* (1773); **Henry Home, Lord Kames**, *Loose Hints Upon Education, Chiefly concerning the Culture of the Heart* (1781); *The Ladies' Dictionary* (1694); **Hannah More**, *Coelebs in Search of a Wife* (1809); Lady Sarah Pennington, *An Unfortunate Mother's Advice to her Absent Daughters* (1761); *The Polite Lady, or, A Course of Female Education In a Series of Letters, From a Mother to her Daughter* (1775); **Clara Reeve**, *Plans of Education: With Remarks on the Systems of Other Writers. In a Series of Letters between Mrs Darnford and Her Friends* (1792); **Adam Smith**, *The Theory of Moral Sentiments* (1759); Sarah Trimmer, *The Guardian* (a periodical); Jane West, *Letters to a Young Man* (1802) and *Letters to a Young Woman* (1806); Hannah Woolley, *The Gentlewoman's Companion* (1675). Against this background of discussion of female education and female duties, **Mary Wollstonecraft**'s *A Vindication of the Rights of Woman* (1792) may be seen as both traditional in its concerns and revolutionary in its stance.

***Conduct of the Allies, The*** A political pamphlet by **Jonathan Swift**, published anonymously in 1711 under the full title, *The Conduct of the Allies, and of the Late Ministry, in Beginning and Carrying on the Present War*.

Swift's most famous political pamphlet, it was also the single most polished contribution to the propaganda machine controlled by the Tory ministry of **Robert Harley, Earl of Oxford**, in its determination to end the ruinous war with France. As Tory apologist Swift had already alleged, in essays for *The Examiner* (November 1710–June 1711), a Whig conspiracy by the Duke of Marlborough and others to prolong the

war and aggrandize themselves and other 'monied men' at the expense of Britain's true interests. In the *Conduct*, begun in August 1711, he extends the theory to implicate the Allies (the Dutch, Austrians and Portuguese) as fellow conspirators of the Whig grandees. He builds up the case for peace by artful selection and manipulation of facts, revelation of previously secret information, subtle innuendo and audacious logic. Britain is portrayed as the losing party, and the fact that she would emerge with distinct advantages played down; even the failure to secure Spain for the Habsburgs is justified.

Swift's pamphlet greatly strengthened the Tory case, helping to smooth the way for Marlborough's dismissal at the end of 1711 and the Treaty of Utrecht in 1713. The first edition of 1000 copies, appearing on 27 November 1711 and pre-dated 1712, disappeared in two days and a second edition in five hours. 11,000 copies had been sold by the time the sixth edition sold out in January 1712.

***Confederacy, The*** A comedy by **John Vanbrugh**, adapted from *Les Bourgeoises à la Mode* (1692) by Florent Dancourt. It was first produced in October 1705, and published the same year.

Gripe and Moneytrap are both mean moneylenders, grown rich by charging high interest. Gripe falls in love with Mrs Moneytrap; Moneytrap falls in love with Mrs Gripe. The ladies confide in each other and resolve to exploit their husbands' weaknesses. To pay her debts, Mrs Gripe has pawned her necklace to Mrs Amlet, a seller of cosmetics, whose unprincipled son Dick poses as a colonel and pursues Corinna, Mrs Gripe's daughter.

Dick has enlisted the help of Mrs Gripe's maid, Flippanta; his friend Brass acts as his footman. Mrs Gripe and Mrs Moneytrap use the maid and the footman as go-betweens, and each succeeds in extracting money from the other's spouse. Dick Amlet, meanwhile, has stolen Mrs Gripe's necklace from his mother and sends Brass out to sell it. But the goldsmith recognizes it as the one reported lost and takes it to Gripe. His wife, Moneytrap and Mrs Moneytrap are present when the exposure takes place; the wives close ranks and challenge their husbands about the money, freely given though one wife has been forced to pawn her necklace. Dick Amlet's true character being exposed also, his prospects look bleak; but Corinna loves him and his mother makes him a generous cash settlement.

***Confessio Amantis*** ('The Lover's Confession') **John Gower**'s major English poem, in rhyming octosyllabic couplets, was probably completed in 1390. He later revised it twice, the second version replacing the dedicatory preface

The poet makes confession to Genius, the priest of Venus. A scene from Book I of Gower's *Confessio Amantis. MS Egerton 1991, f.7v.* British Library.

praising Richard II with praise of Henry of Lancaster.

The prologue contains a complaint at the state of the world and times, and in the first book the poet states his intention to write instructively and entertainingly about love. The narrator, Amans (or the Lover), complains that he has served love too long and wishes for death. Venus instructs him to confess to her priest, Genius. The poem progresses through confession and enquiry from the Lover, answered by the priest's instruction and exposition, each point being explained through the use of one or more tales. The work deals with the seven deadly sins and the sins of the five senses, but although they provide a structural framework the material treated often bears little relation to them. The seventh book is on Aristotle's counsel to Alexander and the eighth deals with the laws of marriage and incest. Finally the Lover is won over to reason and abandons his cause, being too old to be a lover.

The poem's central interest lies in the collection of tales, taken from various classical and medieval sources. The use of a framework designed to embrace such various elements was not unusual in the Middle Ages and, indeed, several stories used by Gower also appear in another famous example, **Chaucer**'s *Canterbury Tales*.

**Confessional Poetry** A type of verse whose subject matter reveals intimate details of the poet's life, confessional poetry emerged in America in the 1950s. Its chief practitioners included **W. D. Snodgrass**, **Robert Lowell**, **Theodore Roethke**, **John Berryman**, **Sylvia Plath**, **Anne Sexton** and **Adrienne Rich**. In their confessional verse, these poets focus on particularly painful moments in their lives, which they often relate to more general historical or cultural problems. The intimate and intensely autobiographical approach of the confessional poets remains a major influence on contemporary American verse.

***Confessions of an English Opium Eater*** An autobiographical work by **Thomas De Quincey**, first published in two parts in *The London Magazine* in 1821, and as a single volume (with an appendix) in 1822.

De Quincey's account of his opium addiction is interwoven with a description of his life, from early childhood to the present in which he writes. Inevitably, perhaps, the book is open to interpretation as an apology for opium-taking in view of its pragmatic advocacy of the drug as the most efficient available artificial means of inducing intellectual clarity and, above all, visionary waking dreams. What the latter confirm, according to De Quincey, is that 'there is no such thing as *forgetting* possible to the mind'. The tumultuous symbolic actions facilitated by the opium are a retelling of the manifold, and more often than not terrifying, experiences of childhood that have moulded the mind of the adult.

The work was an overnight success and quickly established De Quincey's reputation as a writer. A slight aura of scandal hangs over it to this day, for he does not offer the story of his addiction as a cautionary tale. Not only are the 'pains of opium' too inextricably bound up with its pleasures for that, but its claims to literary significance rest on the lofty, sonorous, and 'impassioned prose' of its climactic dream descriptions. In 1856 De Quincey considerably extended the *Confessions* for a collected edition of his works, but, on his later admission, succeeded more in damaging than enhancing his original slender text. Among his more famous disciples were Branwell Brontë and **Francis Thompson**, though he had had a deterrent effect on the more cautious **Carlyle**. The *Tales* of **Poe** are profoundly influenced by De Quincey, and a large part of Baudelaire's *Paradis Artificiels* consists of verbatim translations of the *Confessions* and *Suspiria de Profundis*.

***Confidence-Man, The****: His Masquerade* A novel by **Herman Melville**, published in 1857, the last to be published during his lifetime. It is a complex exploration of the dialectic between trust and sincerity on the one hand, and manipulation and violation of trust on the other, a conflict which Melville saw as pervading contemporary American society.

The action takes place on the Mississippi river steamer *Fidèle*, and involves a large number of characters, many of whom are different manifestations of a single figure, the confidence-man. He makes his initial appearance as a deaf-mute on the riverboat landing in St Louis. Holding up a chalkboard sign advertising the virtues of charity, he is derided by the crowd, but in his later appearances he proves to be more persuasive. For example, in the guise of a herb doctor he succeeds in persuading a distrusting miser to buy his worthless tonic; in other disguises he sells phoney stock to passengers, petitions for a loan to alleviate alleged hardship, and solicits contributions to Indian missions. In some of his appearances, however, he merely encourages the more disaffected and cynical passengers to keep faith and to trust in the goodness of others.

Throughout the second half of the novel the confidence-man is in the costume of a friendly 'cosmopolitan', Frank Goodman, who engages in philosophical conversations with other passengers, occasionally digressing to tell long stories related to the central themes of the book, especially to that of trust in personal relationships. The narrative ends with a discussion between him and an old man about the status of the apocryphal scriptures, thus fusing the book's thematic concern with trust with the literary issue of narrative as a bearer of meaning.

**Congreve, William** 1670–1729 Playwright. Born in Yorkshire into a military family, he was educated at Kilkenny School and Trinity College, Dublin, where **Jonathan Swift** was a near-contemporary. He entered the Middle Temple in 1690, but never practised law, preferring a fashionable life (he was the lover of the Duchess of Marlborough, who bore him a daughter) and the pursuit of literature, which he began by publishing a novel, *Incognita* (1692). His first play, *The Old Bachelor* (1693), was shaped for performance with the help of **Dryden**. It made Congreve famous, a status confirmed by the success of two further comedies, *The Double Dealer* (1693) and *Love for Love* (1695), and his single tragedy, *The Mourning Bride* (1697). The tragedy is, after the fashion of the time, inflated and self-consciously poetic, but Congreve's comedies are distinguished by the wit and elegance of their dialogue as well as by their skilful plotting and the crafty deployment of contrasting characters and themes. They are mannered explorations of social values, marital practices and the scope given to intrigue and deceit by prurience in high places. It was on Congreve and **Vanbrugh** that **Jeremy Collier** concentrated his fury in his *Short View of the Immorality and Profaneness of the English Stage* (1698). That Congreve was stung by Collier's attack is evident in his own *Amendments of Mr Collier's False and Imperfect Citations* (1698) and, regrettably, in the diminution of his interest in the theatre. He remained involved in the management of Lincoln's Inn Theatre until 1705, but added only one important comedy to the repertoire. This was *The Way of the World* (1700), a masterpiece of manners comedy, less lucidly plotted than *Love for Love* but lively with brilliantly drawn characters and firmly moral in its corrective satire of high society. Its comparative failure on its first performance combined with Collier's continuing grumbles and Congreve's own financial security (he had been granted three lucrative sinecures through the influence of a patron) to hasten Congreve's abandonment of drama. He lived in comfort, numbered **Pope**, Swift and **Steele** among his friends and the actress Anne Bracegirdle among his lovers, and continued to write at leisure. His 18th-century work includes a masque, *The Judgement of Paris* (1701), an operatic piece, *Semele* (1710), which, with additions by Pope, provided Handel with the libretto of his secular oratorio (1744), a prose tale, *An Impossible Thing* (1720), an edition of *The Dramatic Works of John Dryden* (1717) and several poems. Congreve never fully recovered from a fall suffered when his carriage overturned in Bath in 1728. He is buried in Westminster Abbey.

***Coningsby**, or, The New Generation* A novel by **Benjamin Disraeli**, published in 1844. It addresses the problem of leadership for England under a regenerated, idealistic Conservative Party. The answer, for Disraeli, lies in the symbolic marriage of his hero, the aristocratic Harry Coningsby, with a daughter of the 'millocracy', Edith Millbank. Originally Edith's father opposes the match, but later comes round. The true hero of the book, however, is the aloof Sidonia, fiercely proud of his Jewish race and its purity, who looks down on mere Normans and Saxons as parvenus, and who combines wealth, wisdom and cosmopolitan culture. However, while Coningsby and his brother-in-law, Oswald Millbank, go into Parliament, Sidonia does not enter public service, although shown to be the superior of everybody in the book. He has reverted to the faith of his fathers, thus cutting him off from his place as a natural leader in England, and guards the purity of his race by not marrying.

**Connecticut Wits, The** A group of 18th-century American poets, often referred to as the Hartford Wits (because they were centred in Hartford, Connecticut), and drawn together at Yale by shared academic, literary and political values. They advocated a revision of Yale's curriculum to include the study of American literature, and they sought themselves to produce poetry which would simultaneously proclaim and signify America's literary independence. They also adhered to the orthodox Calvinism and conservative Federalism which had found a home in Connecticut.

The group espoused its causes in numerous publications, three of which stand out in American literary history: *The Anarchiad*, 12 papers in **mock-heroic** verse printed serially between 1786 and 1787 in *The New Haven Gazette* and *The Connecticut Magazine*; *The Echo*, a verse satire against anti-Federalists, as well as against **Thomas Jefferson**, and printed in *The American Mercury* between 1791 and 1805; and *The Practical Greenhouse*, a Federalist satire printed in 1799 in the *Connecticut Courant*. All three represent the collaborative efforts of the group's members: **John Trumbull**, **Timothy Dwight**, **Joel Barlow**, Lemuel Hopkins, David Humphreys, Richard Alsop, Theodore Dwight, E. H. Smith and Dr Mason F. Cogswell.

***Connecticut Yankee in King Arthur's Court, A*** A satirical fantasy by **Mark Twain**, published in 1889. It tells the story of Hank Morgan, a master mechanic and chief superintendent at the Colt arms factory in Hartford, Connecticut, who is knocked unconscious during a fight with one of his workmen and awakes to find himself near Camelot in 6th-century England. The Yankee uses his knowledge of history and 19th-century technology to convince King Arthur and the knights of the Round Table that he has magical powers. Having earned the nickname 'The Boss', he then sets himself, in the author's words, to 'the task of introducing the great and beneficent civilization of the nineteenth century' into the chivalric order of Camelot.

Originally conceived by Twain as a comic experiment in anachronistic contrast, the novel gradually developed into a darker, more violent story. Hank's introduction to Camelot of 19th-century 'enlightenment', with its ideology of progress and its powerful gadgets, leads to civil war in Arthur's England, and to an apocalyptic last battle in which both sides are destroyed by advanced technology.

**Connell, Evan (Shelby) Jr** 1924– American novelist, born in Kansas City, best known for his novels *Mrs Bridge* (1959) and *Mr Bridge* (1969). His other novels include *The Patriot* (1960), *The Diary of a Rapist* (1966) and *The Connoisseur* (1974). His short stories are collected in *The Anatomy Lesson and Other Stories* (1957) and *At The Crossroads* (1965). His verse includes *Notes From a Bottle Found On A Beach At Carmel* (1963) and *Points From a Compass Rose* (1973). His essays are collected in *A Long Desire* (1979) and *The White Lantern* (1980).

**Connelly, Marc[us] (Cook)** 1890–1980 American playwright, born and educated in Pennsylvania. Connelly had his first play produced in 1913, two years before he moved to New York to work as a journalist. His first real success as a dramatist came in a series of 10 collaborations with George S. Kaufman, beginning with *Dulcy* (1921) and including *Merton of the Movies* (1922) and a notable expressionist piece, *Beggar on Horseback* (1924), staged in the year in which the partnership broke up. Connelly continued to write plays and screenplays, but only the Broadway production of *The Green Pastures* (1930) confirmed his place in any history of American drama. Based on Roark Bradford's stories of Louisiana blacks and framed by scenes in a Sunday school, it retells Old Testament stories through the innocent voices of uneducated blacks. Flawed by sentimentality, the play retains humour and dignity.

**Connolly, Cyril (Vernon)** 1903–74 Critic and literary editor. Born in Coventry, he was educated as a scholar both of Eton and of Balliol College, Oxford. His reputation for intellectual precocity set him a target of promise that his actual literary output consistently failed to fulfil. His main books are a novel, *The Rock Pool* (1936), the partly autobiographical *Enemies of Promise* (1938) and the nostalgic-hedonist maxims of *The Unquiet Grave* (by 'Palinurus', 1944). *Horizon* (1939–50), the wartime literary monthly magazine which he founded and edited, was one of the most influential intellectual organs of its period. He became principal book reviewer of *The Sunday Times* and published several collections of his reviews and essays, which showed him a skilled arbiter of taste, even if he made a career of underfulfilment.

**Conquest, (George) Robert (Acworth)** 1917– Poet, historian and critic. Born in Malvern and educated at Winchester and Magdalen College, Oxford, Conquest served in World War II, worked for the Diplomatic Service (1946–56), held academic posts in Britain and the United States, and was for a time literary editor of *The Spectator*. He edited and introduced the influential anthology *New Lines* (1956), which helped to establish the poets of the **Movement**. His own verse, in *Poems* (1955), *Between Mars and Venus* (1962) and *Arias from a Love Opera* (1969), shows him a typical Movement poet in his concern for traditional forms and ordinary language, less so in his variety of subjects, which include **science fiction**. He has written and edited many works on Marxism and the USSR.

***Conquest of Canaan, The*** Identified by its author, **Timothy Dwight**, as the first American epic, this poem was written between 1771 and

1773, but not published until 1785. Its 11 books of heroic verse elaborate upon the biblical account of Joshua's conquest of Canaan and, by allusion to people and events of the 18th century, draw a parallel between the Hebrew invasion of Canaan and the English settlement of New England. The poem thus confirms the Puritan conception of America as the seat of the New Jerusalem and in turn provides theological justification for the American Revolution.

*Conquest of Granada, The*, or, *Almanzor and Almahide* A heroic tragedy in two parts by **John Dryden**, written in rhymed couplets and published in 1672. The first part was produced in December 1670, the second in January 1671. **John Evelyn** attended a performance on 6 February 1671 but the entry in his diary confines praise to 'very glorious scenes & perspectives, the worke of Mr Streeter'. The main plot concerns the last days of Granada, before the city falls to Ferdinand and Isabella. The Moorish ruler Boabdelin is harried by the rivalry of the principal families, the Abencerrages and the Zegrys. Almanzor, a noble stranger, arrives in the city and fights for the Moors. Almahide, betrothed to Boabdelin, falls in love with the stranger but repulses his advances. Boabdelin is jealous of Almanzor but needs his prowess. When the Spaniards capture the city Boabdelin is killed and it transpires that Almanzor is of noble Spanish birth. Almahide and Almanzor are married at the end of the play.

**Conrad, Joseph** (born Jozef Teodor Konrad Korzeniowski) 1857–1924 Novelist. He was born in Podolia, now part of the Soviet Ukraine. His parents, Apollo Korzeniowski and Evelina Bobrowski, came from Polish nobility and were opposed to the Tsarist domination of their country. Apollo's involvement in political conspiracy prior to the nationalist insurrection of 1863 resulted in exile to Volgoda, north-west of Moscow. Here Conrad's mother died when he was seven. Apollo returned to Poland, dying of tuberculosis four years later.

It was Conrad's uncle, Tadeusz Bobrowski, who acted as his guide in major decisions at this time, but the early influence of Apollo (notably in introducing him to the works of **Dickens**, **Fenimore Cooper** and **Marryat** in either Polish or French translation) may have shaped his deeper aspirations. Conrad's wish to go to sea, to serve on French vessels, certainly had the advantage of sparing him service in the Russian army. He went to Marseilles, and began the 20 years of his sea career.

In *A Personal Record* (1912) Conrad disclosed significant parallels between the life of a seaman and his embarking on the career of writer in 1894. He discouraged interpretation of his sea novels through evidence from his life, but he

Joseph Conrad, 1904.

was proud of his qualifications and experiences as a sailor. In 1878 he began service on English ships; in 1880 he passed the second mate's examination, and in 1884 that for first mate. He became a naturalized British subject in 1886, and received his master's certificate from the Board of Trade.

Conrad's early sea career had not promised this steady progress, however. While in Marseilles, he was employed by the shipowning firm of Delestang, a family having strong sympathies with the claimant to the Spanish throne, Don Carlos VII. While making his first voyages to the West Indies in the *Mont Blanc* in 1875, and the *Sainte-Antoine* in 1876, Conrad met the Corsican Dominic Cervoni, who became a model for central figures of romantic daring in his fiction. Conrad and Cervoni were involved in a number of gun-running voyages to Spain, for the Carlists, which ended in disaster. These events were depicted impressionistically in Conrad's reminiscences, *The Mirror of the Sea* (1906) and in *The Arrow of Gold* (1919). These reckless and improvident years for the young Conrad culminated in a suicide attempt in 1878; his uncle's letters have shown that this was the truth behind an injury originally thought to have been received in a duel.

During his service with the British merchant navy, Conrad worked on a variety of ships: first with the *Mavis*, on a journey to Constantinople, and then on more than one wool clipper bound for Sydney. Particularly eventful voyages came in 1881, during service with the *Palestine*, when Conrad had his first experience of the East, and with the *Narcissus* in 1884, when he sailed from Bombay to Dunkirk. These were the experiences which underlay the novels *Youth* (1902) and *The Nigger of the 'Narcissus'* (1897), respectively. His later experience as first mate on the *Vidar*, sailing through the Malay archipelago, and as master of the *Otago* in 1888, was to show a wide influence on his fiction: notably the *Otago*'s voyage from Bangkok to Singapore, which is directly discernible within *The Shadow Line* (1917).

It was before his experiences of 1890 as captain of a river steamer in the Congo – later to form the basis of *Heart of Darkness* (1902; published with *Youth*) – that he began writing his first novel, *Almayer's Folly* (1895). When this had been published, with the help of **Edward Garnett**, he was settled in England; in 1896 he married Jessie George.

The period between *The Nigger of the 'Narcissus'* (1897) and *Under Western Eyes* (1911) is commonly regarded as the major phase in his writing life. Other novels of this period were *Lord Jim* (1900), *Typhoon* (1903), *Nostromo* (1904), and *The Secret Agent* (1907). These years brought Conrad recognition from leading Edwardian novelists, **Arnold Bennett**, **John Galsworthy** and **Ford Madox Ford**, with whom he wrote *The Inheritors* (1901) and *Romance* (1903). Among others who regarded him as a major innovator and literary modernist were the fellow expatriates in Sussex and Kent, **Stephen Crane** and **Henry James**. Wider public recognition came with the publication of *Chance* (1913) and *Victory* (1915); *The Rescue* (1920) and *The Rover* (1923) were among his later works.

With his wife and two sons, Borys and John, Conrad revisited Poland in 1914, an inauspicious moment. But having been adopted, as he said, by the genius of the English language, Conrad's life as an author was sedentary, and he suffered from ill health in his last years. He died in 1924 at his home near Canterbury.

**Conroy, Jack** 1899–1980 American novelist and editor. Conroy was born at Monkey Nest coal camp near Moberly, Missouri, and spent several years as a migrant worker in steel mills, rubber factories and coal mines. When the Depression came, he drew on his experiences to write poems and articles about unemployment, which were published in periodicals such as *Northern Lights*, *Unrest* and *The New Masses*. In 1933 his novel *The Disinherited* appeared. A classic of proletarian literature, it explores working-class life in the Depression with unsentimental directness and is widely considered to be Conroy's greatest achievement. He later

founded *The Anvil* and *The New Anvil*, important left-wing magazines which published work by writers such as **Richard Wright**, **Erskine Caldwell**, **Frank Yerby**, **James T. Farrell**, **Michael Gold**, **Langston Hughes** and **Meridel Le Sueur**. Conroy's other books include *A World to Win* (1935), *Anyplace But Here* (1966, with **Arna Bontemps**) and *Writers in Revolt: The Anvil Anthology* (1973, with Curt Johnson). He also wrote children's books with Arna Bontemps, among them *The Fast Sooner Hound* (1942) and *Sam Patch* (1951).

***Conscious Lovers, The*** A comedy by **Sir Richard Steele**, first performed at **Drury Lane** in 1722 and published the following year. The plot is based on the *Andria* of Terence, but Steele has softened and moralized his original. Soon translated into French, the play influenced the development of the *comédie larmoyante*. In England, its success helped oust the comedy of manners from the stage and to show the 18th-century theatre's determination to cleanse the air of Restoration licentiousness.

In Bevil, the hero, Steele has created an ethical absolute of surpassing dullness. What life the play has is confined to below-stairs interludes. Bevil, affianced to Lucinda, heiress to the wealthy Sealand, loves his own ward, Indiana, a destitute orphan whom he found and has brought up. Bevil's worthy friend Myrtle loves Lucinda, who is pestered by the fortune-hunting Cimberton. When Bevil, with the utmost decency, tells Lucinda of his love for Indiana, Myrtle takes offence on Lucinda's behalf and challenges Bevil to a duel. Bevil's declining of the challenge permits him (and Steele) to ridicule the fashion of the duel, but it requires a timely revelation to resolve the play's problems. Indiana is discovered to be Sealand's lost child, a daughter from his first marriage. With the dowry shared between the half-sisters, each is free to marry the man who loves her, and Cimberton, dissatisfied with half a fortune, is happy to withdraw his suit.

**consonance** see **alliteration**.

***Conspiracy and Tragedy of Charles, Duke of Byron, Marshal of France, The*** A double play by **George Chapman**, first performed by a **boys' company** in 1608, when its references to what was very recent history (the Marshal of France had been executed in 1602) gave grave offence to the French ambassador, who succeeded in getting the play banned. Chapman protested to the Office of the Revels of 'Illiterate Authority' that 'sets up his Bristles against Poverty', adding the interesting claim that 'I see not mine own plays; nor carry the Actors' Tongues in my mouth.'

In the first play, the restlessly ambitious Herculean hero is discovered in his conspiracy against the French king, Henry IV, asks forgiveness and is pardoned. In the second play he again conspires, is again discovered and dwindles into cringing despair before being executed.

**Constable, Henry** 1562–1613 Poet. Constable came from a family distinguished for military and public service. He graduated from St John's College, Cambridge, in 1580 and went to Paris, with Walsingham as his patron, in 1583. In the late 1580s he converted to Catholicism, and having again crossed to France in 1591 did not return to England until James's accession in 1603. He had hopes of the king's conversion to Rome, was well received at court, but was confined briefly to the Tower in 1604 after some of his letters were seized. He left England in 1610 and died at Liège. Constable's collection of sonnets, *Diana*, was printed in 1592 and reissued in 1594 with additional sonnets dubiously ascribed to Constable, and some contributions by other poets. His other poetry consists of sonnets to such noble ladies as the Countess of Pembroke and Penelope Rich, and 16 'Spiritual Sonnets' which were not printed until 1815.

**Constantine, David (John)** 1944– Poet. Born in Salford, he read modern languages at Oxford, and has lectured at Durham and Oxford. After a study of Friedrich Hölderlin (1979), his first collection was *A Brightness to Cast Shadows* (1980). Influenced by **Robert Graves**, the poems are erudite, erotic and culturally wide-ranging; he brings a classical, European sensibility to bear on observed reality. His second collection, *Watching for Dolphins* (1983), is a stronger volume. Constantine has a descriptive accuracy, but at times the erudition is too weighty, the biblical and mythical references too conspicuous ('The Diktaean Cave'). His distinctive voice and assured handling of syntax, though, make him a promising talent, and he has a growing reputation. He has also published *Early Greek Travellers and the Hellenic Ideal* (1984).

*Contarini Fleming: A Psychological Romance* A novel by **Benjamin Disraeli**, published in 1832. It purports to be the autobiography of Contarini Fleming, a romantic and idealistic young man, the son of a Venetian noblewoman and an aristocratic British father active in political circles. After a failed marriage to his cousin, Alceste, and a prolonged tour of Europe and the East, he settles in Rome, devoting himself to art.

*Contrast, The* A five-act play by **Royall Tyler**, generally considered to be the first American comedy, and written after Tyler had attended a performance of **Sheridan**'s *The School for Scandal* in New York in 1787. It was produced in the same year and published in 1790. Clearly influenced by the 18th-century English comedy of manners, it was an immediate success.

The 'contrast' of the title is that between Bill Dimple, the representative of European affectation, and Colonel Manly, the representative of American straightforwardness and honesty. Maria van Rough is to marry Dimple, the match having been arranged by her father. The intensely Anglophilic Dimple is carrying on flirtations with two other women, Letitia and Charlotte. Charlotte's brother, Colonel Manly, is in love with Maria. Dimple gambles away his fortune and decides to marry the wealthy Letitia. Maria's father discovers his baseness and gives his blessing to Manly's suit. Dimple is finally thwarted in his ambition when Letitia learns of his flirtation with Charlotte. The subplot reproduces the contrast between national manners in the amorous rivalry between Dimple's servant, the devious and conceited Jessamy, and Manly's servant Jonathan, the prototype of the naïve, goodhearted Yankee.

**Cook, Eliza** 1818–89 Poet. Born in London of a poor family, she was self-educated and began to write verse as a child. Her first volume, *Lays of a Wild Harp*, was published in 1835. *Melaia* (1838) and *New Echoes* (1864) followed. Her well-known poem 'The Old Arm Chair' appeared in *The Weekly Dispatch* in 1836. She conducted *Eliza Cook's Journal* from 1849 to 1854.

**Cook, Capt. James** 1728–79 Navigator. Cook left records of his three principal voyages and also published his *Sailing Directions* (1766–8). The journal of his first voyage (1768–71) was edited by Captain W. J. L. Wharton and published as *Journal During his First Voyage* (1893). *A Voyage towards the South Pole and Round the World in 1772–1775*, the second voyage, was published in 1777. The last, *A Voyage to the Pacific Ocean in 1776–1780*, was published in three volumes (1784): the first two volumes are by Cook, who was killed in Hawaii, and the third, which includes the voyage home, by Captain T. King.

**Cook, Michael** 1933– English-born Canadian playwright. He spent 12 years in the British Army where he wrote, directed and acted in troop entertainments. After teacher training in drama at Nottingham University he emigrated to Canada and settled in Newfoundland, where he was associated with Memorial University. He became deeply involved in local theatre and started writing radio plays. *Colour the Flesh the Colour of Dust* (1972), his first stage play, is a Brechtian examination of the political turmoil in Newfoundland in 1762 as it went from a British to a French to a British colony. *Head, Bones and Soundbone Dance* (1973) is a powerful folk play which captures both the colourful Newfoundland speech and the fatalistic attitudes engendered by the island's harsh life. *The Gayden Chronicles* (1979), commissioned by Festival Lennoxville, tells the story of a British Navy rebel who was hanged in St John's in 1812. Cook's plays are passionate and unsubtle attacks on the emotions that 'celebrate the elemental and instinctive', particularly as found in indigenous cultures.

**Cook's Tale, The** See **Canterbury Tales, The.**

**Cooke, John (Esten)** 1830–86 American novelist. A Virginian, Cooke wrote historical novels of colonial Virginia in the manner of **James Fenimore Cooper**: *Leather Stocking and Silk* (1854), *The Virginia Comedians* (1854) and *Henry St John, Gentleman* (1859). While fighting on the side of the Confederates in the Civil War, he wrote *The Life of Stonewall Jackson* (1863), and later a biography of Robert E. Lee (1871). A series of novels about the Civil War appeared in the late 1860s, but he then turned again to the colonial history of Virginia: *Her Majesty The Queen* (1872), about the Cavaliers; *Canolles* (1877), about Virginia during the Revolution; *Virginia, A History of the People* (1883); and *My Lady Pokahontas* (1885).

**Coolbrith, Ina Donna** 1842–1928 The first published poet from California, Coolbrith wrote verse in a simple lyrical style which marked an important stage in the regional development of Western literature in the USA. Her verse appeared in three volumes: *A Perfect Day* (1881), *The Singer of the Sea* (1894) and *Songs From The Golden Gate* (1895). She also shared the editorship of the **Overland Monthly** with **Bret Harte**.

**Coolidge, Susan** The pseudonym of the American children's writer Sarah Chauncy Woolsey (1845–1905). Born in Ohio, the oldest daughter of a close family, she was educated at private schools and served as a nurse in the Civil War. She became popular with several generations of young readers for the heroine she introduced in her second book, *What Katy Did* (1872) – the tall, rebellious daughter of a small-town family very much like its creator's own. Katy's adventures in succeeding books cover her schooldays, foreign travel and engagement. Susan Coolidge also published several volumes of poetry and edited the correspondence of **Fanny Burney** and **Jane Austen**.

**Cooper, Giles (Stannus)** 1918–66 Playwright. He was born at Carrickmines, County Dublin, and educated at Lancing College. After service in World War II, he worked first as an actor and then as a television script editor. Although best known in his lifetime as a prolific adapter for television (notably the *Maigret* series, which won him a Writer of the Year award in 1961), he produced 70 original plays for radio, television and the stage. He had some critical success in the theatre with *Everything in the Garden* (1962) and created one of the most spectacular television plays of its time, *The Other Man* (1964), an alternative history of Anglo-Nazi relations. But his best work, like *Unman, Wittering and Zigo* (1958), was in radio, a medium whose extreme flexibility suited his acerbic mixture of the absurd and the naturalistic. Pushing out radio's technical frontiers, Cooper pioneered electronic sound-effects to reinforce the cartoon-like nature of some of his stories; he moved adroitly between his characters' inner and outer lives, between dream and reality. A prestigious award for radio drama bears his name.

**Cooper, James Fenimore** 1789–1851 American novelist, born in Burlington, New Jersey, the son of Judge William Cooper, an enterprising and wealthy land agent who founded Cooperstown in upstate New York, a community where Cooper spent much of his childhood. He attended a school in Albany and studied for a time at Yale until he was expelled in 1805. He spent the next five years at sea, first on a merchant ship and then as a midshipman in the US Navy. He left the sea in 1811 to marry Susan Delancy, who was descended from the early governors of New York colony.

The Coopers settled in Scarsdale, where in 1820 he wrote his first novel – *Precaution*, a study of manners in English society in the tradition of **Jane Austen** – after his wife had challenged him to improve upon an English novel he had criticized. His next novel, *The Spy*, appeared in 1821. They moved to New York City in 1822, and in the following year he published a novel of the sea entitled *The Pilot* and the first of the **Leatherstocking Tales**, *The Pioneers*. Firmly set in his career as a writer, he soon established a popular reputation as one of America's leading authors. He planned a series of novels to celebrate each of the 13 original states, and in 1825 published *Lionel Lincoln*, a story of Boston during the Revolution, but the rest of the series never materialized. His next publications were two more volumes of the Leatherstocking saga, *The Last of the Mohicans* (1826) and *The Prairie* (1827).

In 1826 he took his family to Europe and stayed there for almost seven years. Though he served as US consul at Lyons and travelled a great deal, he continued to write, publishing a sea story, *The Red Rover* (1827); a novel of early American frontier life, *The Wept of Wishton-Wish* (1829); and another naval tale, *The Water Witch* (1830). He became friends with **Sir Walter Scott** and with the Marquis de Lafayette, who partly inspired his essay *Notions of America* (1828). A historical trilogy, *The Bravo* (1831), *The Heidenmauer* (1832) and *The Headsman* (1833), completed one of his most active periods.

In 1832 he returned to the USA, where his conservative political essays made him less popular. Non-fictional works of social commentary such as *The Monikins* (1835) and *The American Democrat* (1838) contain rather sharp criticism of American society and the abuses of democracy. The novels *Homeward Bound* (1838) and *Home as Found* (1838) also dramatize his 'aristocratic' social and political beliefs.

In the last decade of his life Cooper published 21 books. The Leatherstocking series was completed with *The Pathfinder* (1840) and *The Deerslayer* (1841), and in 1844 came two sea novels, *Afloat and Ashore* and *Miles Wallingford*, which drew on his own early experiences. *Satanstoe* (1845), the first novel of his trilogy about a New York family (known as the 'Littlepage Manuscripts'), explores problems of property rights in America, from the Colonial period to the 1840s. *The Chainbearer* (1845) is set during the Revolution, and *The Redskins* (1846) tells how the Littlepage family manages, with the help of Indians, to deal with the exploitations of agents and lawyers in developing American society.

**Cooper, Thomas** 1805–92 Chartist poet. Imprisoned for sedition in 1842, he wrote, while serving his sentence, *The Purgatory of Suicides* (1845), an epic on political themes, and *Wise Saws and Modern Instances* (1845). He also published an *Autobiography* in 1872.

**Cooper, William** 1910– Novelist. Born Harry Summerfield Huff in Crewe, he worked as a schoolmaster in Leicester before entering the civil service in 1945 and becoming Personnel Consultant to the Atomic Energy Research Authority in 1958. His most important novel is his fifth, *Scenes from Provincial Life*, which appeared in 1950. With its cynical and pragmatic hero, Joe Lunn, lower-middle-class provincial milieu and quiet realism, it was a seminal influence on writers like **John Braine** and the genesis of the **Angry Young Men** novel. Three sequels have since been added, continuing Joe Lunn's story through his marriage and later years in London: *Scenes from Married Life* (1961), *Scenes from Metropolitan Life* (actually the second of the sequence, but not published until 1982) and *Scenes from Later Life* (1983).

**Coover, Robert (Lowell)** 1932– American novelist. Born in Iowa, Coover studied at Southern Illinois, Indiana, and Chicago universities, serving in the US Navy from 1953 to 1957, and then taught philosophy at several universities. His novels, with their particular emphasis on cultural patterns and movements, are representative of post-modernist fiction. His first, *The Origin of the Brunists* (1966), which received the William Faulkner Award for best first novel of 1966, concerns the founding of a religious cult by the survivor of a mining disaster. *The Universal Baseball Association, Inc., J. Henry Waugh, Prop.* (1968) is an allegorical novel which uses baseball as its central metaphor to satirize American religious attitudes. His third novel, *The Public Burning* (1977), is set in the 1950s and treats the impulses that lead to dogmatic extremism, an interest that has been integral to most of Coover's fiction. *Spanking the Maid* (1981) is a dark story of the obsessive relationship between a man and his maid which focuses on human enslavement to ritual behaviour. Coover has also published short stories which are collected in *Pricksongs and Descants* (1969).

**Coppard, A[lfred] E[dgar]** 1878–1957 Short-story writer and poet. He received a rudimentary education at Board schools in Folkestone and Brighton before leaving at the age of nine to become apprentice to a tailor in Whitechapel at the time of the Jack the Ripper killings. Subsequently he worked as a paraffin vendor's assistant, auctioneer, cheesemonger and soap agent. In 1907 he moved to Oxford to become a clerk at the Eagle Ironworks, where he stayed until he became a full-time writer in 1919. His friends in Oxford included Harold Laski and **L. P. Hartley**, but his nearest literary kin is perhaps **W. H. Davies**. Warm and friendly, with an immense capacity for enjoying life, Coppard added sophistication to the lyrical power which both men possessed. The first of his volumes of poetry, *Hips and Haws*, appeared in 1922, but he is chiefly remembered for the collections of short stories that began with *Adam and Eve and Pinch Me* (1921) and included *The Black Dog and Other Stories* (1923), *Fishmonger's Fiddle: Tales* (1925) and *The Field of Mustard* (1926). They contain tales as diverse as the rich and mysterious 'Dusky Ruth' and 'The Presser', about a 10-year-old boy apprenticed to a Whitechapel tailor, but above all Coppard's work conveys the flavour of the English countryside.

**copyright** In simple terms, copyright is ownership of, and right of control over, all possible ways of reproducing a work – a work in this context being an object which is the product of an original creative act by one or more people, in a form which makes it subject to one or other means of copying. In particular, but not exclusively, copyright protection is given to literary works, dramatic works, artistic works (paintings, drawings, photographs, and so on), sound recordings, films, television and sound broadcasts, and various productions of the new technology.

Beyond this basic definition matters become less easy, because of the inherent complexity of copyright (at least in its modern manifestations), and because of its tendency to mean different things at different times in different countries and even in different minds. In terms of existing laws, for instance, copyright in the UK and in France differs in important respects, despite many common characteristics; and copyright in both countries differs significantly from copyright as a system of international protection. In historical terms, copyright is an evolving legal concept determined by the peculiarities of each particular nation's history, by the growing ease of international communications and by technological developments (the invention of the gramophone, television, the photocopier and so on). And in more general conceptual terms there is unresolvable debate as to whether copyright is properly seen primarily as a negative right (the right to stop), or as a monopoly, or as property, or as uniquely personal (dealing above all with the control of the creator over his creation). Copyright is fixed and final only in so far as it happens to be frozen, for the time being, within the laws of those countries which grant it recognition, and within certain international conventions. Beyond that, there is continuing debate as to the proper nature of copyright as an abstract entity which in turn affects debate as to the correct legislative balance to be struck between the interests of different parties.

To a large extent, the history of copyright begins when you want it to begin. Those who have been interested in dignifying the concept of authors' rights with as long a genealogy as possible have gone back to classical Greek culture, to around the sixth century BC, when it is said that intellectual works began to be considered as the product of one mind rather than as the anonymous property of a whole society. Others have argued that 'true' copyright began in 1709, with the passing of the first national copyright Act in England. However that may be, copyright has been an important subject since the invention of movable type and continues to grow in importance as the world finds more and better ways in which to multiply images, to record, to transmit and to receive. We are all copiers and receivers now: the large institutions with their photocopiers and visual terminals; and the average individual, with an accessible photocopier at work or in the nearest library, a computer in his spare-room, a video-cassette recorder, a television and a radio in his living-room and a tape-recorder close at hand or even in his pocket. What is being devoured insatiably, what is being copied, often illegally – plays, novels, films, poems, operas, computer programs – is the very lifeblood of our culture. The main, almost the sole, legal safeguard of that lifeblood is the law of copyright.

Under most national copyright laws there are two major qualifications for protection. First, that the work is 'original', which does not mean so much being novel in subject matter as being the product of some skill and labour in composition other than the skill and labour involved in mere copying. In the main, emphasis here is on expression rather than content. For example, the copyright in an article expressing a new philosophical theory lies in its unique sequence of words rather than in the theory as such. It does not infringe copyright to paraphrase this theory and publish the paraphrase (although it may be plagiarism). Indeed, the paraphrase secures its own copyright protection as another sequence of words. A common, but over-simple, catchprase in this context is 'copyright is in words and not ideas'. This is certainly true in the example that has just been given, and in the case of any single 'idea'. But if it were generally true, then to translate an English novel into French, or to turn it into a play, would not be an infringement of copyright. It is a matter of degree, and at one extreme a particularly distinctive sequence of events in a play, or whole collection of philosophical ideas, can be regarded as a substantial part of a work, and to express them, or a significant part of them, in other words, or with other characters, or in another medium, will be to infringe copyright.

The creator of a work is normally the copyright owner, and no special act (e.g. registration) is required in order to establish ownership. The main exceptions are where the creator has already assigned copyright to another party, via a contract entered into before the work was begun, or at least before it was finished, or where the act of creation was a legitimate part of the creator's role under a contract of employment (broadly speaking, what US copyright legislation refers to as a 'work made for hire').

The second qualification for protection concerns time. In the main, copyright is finite: after a given period a work goes out of copyright and falls into 'the public domain'. Different countries define the period very differently – from 20 years after first publication at one extreme to 80 years after the author's death at the other – but all would probably justify it in a similar fashion. It is right for the author to control the use of his work during his lifetime and that his immediate dependants or successors should also have some measure of control over it, or at least some financial reward from it. Yet if it still remains in circulation at some stage after his death, then the work must be assumed to have the makings of some kind of classic: it is a candidate for permanent membership of a nation's culture, and should, in some sense, belong to everybody.

Copyright protection extends to all forms of writing, regardless of quality and of character.

The hurried, banal letter is safeguarded as strongly as the great novel. The practical consequences are dictated by the writer's intent. If he is not writing for the public, then copyright merely acts as a protection against unauthorized publication (an unlikely event, but we would not want a law which attempted to discriminate between our letters and the letters of **D. H. Lawrence**). If he is writing for the public, then copyright not only protects his work from the pirate but also provides him with a means by which he can control and encourage the maximum exploitation of his work. For copyright is not one right but a bundle of different rights. The copyright in a novel, for example, will include the prime right to publish in the novel's original language in volume form. But it will also include the right to publish it in translation; the right to turn it into a stage play, and a television play, and a film; the right to read it on radio; the right to take one or more of its characters and 'merchandize' them (as toys, or on T-shirts, for example); and so on. This potential lies in every just-completed novel. For the majority, alas, it remains merely potential: nobody offers publication. For the rest, the offer of publication leads to a publishing contract, one of whose major objects will be to bring about, by a transfer of rights, a state of affairs where some of the potential can be realized.

One important element in the history of publishing in the UK has been a growing concern for the lot of the author. Until 1694, printing and publishing were carried out only with the direct authority of the Crown through the Star Chamber, by a designated group of printers, publishers and booksellers – the Stationers' Company. The official emphasis, that is to say, was not on the rights of the author but on the control of what could be published and the establishment within the Company of a mutually beneficial system whereby each member respected the other's copyrights. It was the expiration of the Act granting the Company this monopoly which led to the making of the first national copyright law in 1709, and it is not to be wondered at that the main thrust of this Act is the protection of the entrepreneur rather than the creator. Compared with the present day, the contractual relationship between the bookseller/publisher and the author, then and for many generations to come, was very simple: the publisher purchased the copyright from the author for one flat fee, and there was an end of it. A typical arrangement of the early 1800s, for example, would have the publisher commissioning a novel in serial form for so many guineas a sheet (16 pages). The guineas bought the copyright as well as the author's time. No further payment would be made if the serial was eventually published in volume form, nor if that volume was reprinted. The growing concern for

the author found expression towards the end of the 19th century in a collective sense with the founding of the Society of Authors and in an individualistic sense in the new profession of author's agent. This, together with the growth in international publishing and the proliferation of separate exploitable rights (film, television, video-cassette, etc.), means that the modern contract between author and publisher will tend to be complex, and will ensure that the author retains a permanent financial interest in the sales of his book and in the leasing of and proceeds from the various subsidiary rights. There are exceptions, which may be well founded, but in the main the transfer of rights will be piecemeal and reversible. Instead of an outright sale, there will be separate leasings of different rights (usually achieved by the publisher or agent on the author's behalf) or of the same rights in different exclusive markets.

All major countries except the People's Republic of China and most minor countries now possess a copyright law, and there are two international conventions which extend copyright protection to all member nations. The protective structure is in place. The problem for the future is to hold it firm against the power, complexity and rapid development of the new technology, while at the same time allowing that technology its proper development and exploitation. This will be difficult, and all the more so because technical innovations proliferate almost daily, while laws change at snail's pace. New applications of the new technology are introduced, become commonplace, and are as like as not replaced by a second generation while copyright committees are still trying to come to terms with the last innovation but three. The most recent major copyright Act became operative in the USA in 1978 after a gestation period of at least 40 years. At the time of writing, the new UK Act is struggling to be born, after years of discussion and not a little delay. One could wish that it had come sooner, and that the legislatures, or more particularly the governments, of all countries would have the will to devise quicker and more flexible means of adapting and extending the protection which societies must give – incidentally and for good cultural and economic reasons to publishers, theatre companies, record manufacturers and the like, crucially and essentially and for the pleasure and enrichment of us all, to the writers, artists and composers of today and tomorrow.

**Coral Island, The** An adventure story by **R. M. Ballantyne**, published in 1858.

Three youths, Ralph, Jack and Peterkin, are wrecked on a desert island and set about surviving in true **Robinson Crusoe** fashion. They make a fire by rubbing two sticks together and climb palm trees to gather obligingly thin-skinned coconuts (a mistake in detail Ballantyne was bitterly to regret). Later adventures include rescuing natives from cannibals and escaping from a shark when fishing on a log. Finally the three heroes return to civilization, none the worse for their ordeal and as chummy still as the day on which they were marooned. Writers since have acknowledged the book's influence, most memorably **William Golding** in his pessimistic reworking of a similar situation, *Lord of the Flies*.

**corantos** See **newspaper, the rise of the English**.

**Corbett (or Corbet), Richard** 1582–1635 Poet and divine. Son of a Surrey gardener, Corbett was educated at Westminster and Christ Church, Oxford, and through the powerful patronage of the royal favourite the Duke of Buckingham he became chaplain to James I, Dean of Christ Church, Bishop of Oxford and finally Bishop of Norwich. He was a celebrated figure of fun, convivial and witty, and a friend of **Donne**, **Jonson** and **Coryate**. His occasional verse is sprightly and ironical, and was published posthumously in *Certain Elegant Poems* (1647) and *Poëtica Stromata* (1648); he is best remembered for 'Farewell, Rewards and Fairies', a nostalgic and accomplished poem on the theme of England's past.

**Corelli, Marie** 1855–1924 Novelist. Born Mary Mackay, the daughter of **Charles Mackay**, she was originally trained for a musical career, but at the age of 30 published her first novel, *A Romance of Two Worlds* (1886). Although disparaged by the critics, her wildly over-written romantic fiction achieved extraordinary popularity. A habit of creating exotic legends about her own life and an unfailing talent for publicity-seeking helped to keep her in the public eye. She spent her latter years in Stratford-upon-Avon, vying with **Shakespeare** as a tourist attraction. Although Queen Victoria was convinced that Marie Corelli's fame would be lasting, her books are now forgotten. In their day, *Barabbas* (1893) and *The Sorrows of Satan* (1895) were perhaps the most famous; others include *Vendetta* (1886), *Thelma* (1887), *Ardath* (1889), *The Soul of Lilith* (1892), *The Mighty Atom* (1896), *The Master Christian* (1900) and *Temporal Power* (1902).

**Coriolanus** A tragedy by **William Shakespeare**, first performed *c.* 1608 and published in the First Folio of 1623. The main source is **Sir Thomas North**'s translation of Plutarch's *Lives*.

Rome's plebeians are a constant, though inconsistent, force in the play. When it opens, they are on the verge of rebellion against their patrician rulers. Persuaded by the tactful Menenius Agrippa to work for the common good, they are immediately incensed by the arrogant scorn of Caius Martius. But crisis is temporarily averted by the appointment of five Tribunes of the People and by the dispatching of Caius Martius to put down a Volscian uprising. His success in capturing the Volscian city of Corioli wins him glory in Rome and the honourable name of Coriolanus. Election to the Senate seems certain, but Coriolanus is too proud to observe the traditional rites of public humility, and the Tribunes refuse to support him.

The Volscian leader Tullus Aufidius, who is Coriolanus' sworn enemy, prepares another attack on Rome. Hated by the plebeians, Coriolanus is finally persuaded by Volumnia, his mother, to face them and ask for their support, but it is a role he cannot sustain. His outburst in the Forum forces the Tribunes to demand his banishment, and Coriolanus presents himself to Tullus Aufidius in Antium, either as a sacrifice or as an ally. He becomes the leader of the Volscian army against Rome, rejects the desperate pleas of the Senators and is persuaded to spare the city only after an astonishing confrontation with his mother, Volumnia. Aufidius sees the peace treaty as a betrayal, and when Coriolanus taunts him, he and the Volscians kill him as an enemy.

The story of Coriolanus was much less familiar to the Elizabethans than that of Julius Caesar or Antony and Cleopatra. This fact alone would distinguish *Coriolanus* from those other Roman plays. It is a stark political tragedy, in which Shakespeare gives unusual attention to the claims of the people on those who undertake to rule them. It is a consideration that relates the play more obviously to *King Lear* among the great tragedies than to *Antony and Cleopatra*. On the other hand, the making and breaking of the individual Coriolanus is told so barely as to invite comparison with *Timon of Athens*, which was probably the next play Shakespeare wrote.

**Corkery, Daniel** 1878–1964 Irish critic, short-story writer and man of letters. Born in Cork, he was educated there and at St Patrick's College, Dublin (1906–7). From 1931 to 1947 he was Professor of English at University College, Cork.

Corkery's book on **Synge**, *Synge and Anglo-Irish Literature* (1931), and his other scholarly works – *The Hidden Ireland* (1925) and *The Fortunes of the Irish Language* (1954) – constitute the most sustained attempt to formulate a nationalist version of the Irish literary tradition. In effect, he ascribed to the Gaelic tradition an authenticity he denied to the English language or to the Anglo-Irish tradition.

Corkery was mentor to younger writers such as **Frank O'Connor** and **Sean O'Faolain** to whom he introduced some of the French and Russian practitioners of the short story. His own fiction varied in quality. Sometimes, as in his novel *The Threshold of Quiet* (1917) and his volume of short stories *The Hounds of Banba* (1920), it was highly sentimental; at other times it was broodingly impressive. His best stories are to be found in the collections *A Munster Twilight* (1916), *The Stormy Hills* (1929) and, to a lesser extent, in *Earth Out of Earth* (1939). He published a number of plays, of which the three one-acters in *The Yellow Bittern and Other Plays* (1920) are the most notable.

**Corn Law Rhymer, The**    See **Elliott, Ebenezer**.

**Cornford, Frances** 1886–1960 Poet. The granddaughter of **Charles Darwin** and the mother of **John Cornford**, she was born and lived in Cambridge. Her *Collected Poems* (1954) includes the famous triolet 'To a Fat Lady Seen from a Train'.

**Cornford, (Rupert) John** 1915–36 Poet and writer on politics. Born in Cambridge, he was educated at Stowe School, Trinity College, Cambridge, and the London School of Economics. He joined the Communist Party in 1933 and in August 1936 he became the first Englishman to go to Spain to fight against Franco, serving with the POUM and the International Brigade before his death at the Cordoba Front. He began writing poetry at an early age, much influenced by his mother, **Frances Cornford**; his work still kept its clarity and direct simplicity after he rebelled in favour of the **modernism** of **Graves**, **Eliot** and **Auden**. A few love-poems and 'Poems from Spain, 1936' are the best, though even some of the earlier poems indicate much talent unrealized because of his allegiance to Communism and his premature death. Jonathan Galassi has edited *Understand the Weapon, Understand the Wound: Selected Writings of John Cornford* (1976).

**Cornhill Magazine, The** A monthly periodical founded by **George Smith** in 1860, with **Thackeray** as its first editor. He established a distinctive brand of family literature for the journal, and contributed two novels of his own, ***Denis Duval*** and ***The Adventures of Philip***. Other contributors included **Elizabeth Barrett Browning**, **Robert Browning**, **Swinburne**, **Elizabeth Gaskell**, **Ruskin**, **George Eliot**, **Charles Reade**, **Matthew Arnold**, **Trollope** and, under the editorship (1871–82) of **Leslie Stephen**, **Thomas Hardy**.

**Cornwall, Barry** Pseudonym of the poet Bryan Waller Procter (1787–1874). Born in Leeds and educated at Harrow, he enjoyed a successful practice as a London solicitor before changing to the profession of barrister. He was a Commissioner of Lunacy from 1832 to 1861. He began to contribute to *The Literary Gazette* in 1815 and thereafter produced several volumes of poetry, chiefly lyrics and songs, among them *Dramatic Scenes* (1819), *Marcian Colonna* (1820), *The Flood of Thessaly* (1823) and *English Songs* (1832). He also wrote a tragedy, *Mirandola* (1821). His daughter was the poet **Adelaide Anne Procter**.

**Corsair, The** A poem by **Byron**, first published in 1814. The story, narrated in **heroic couplets**, concerns an Aegean pirate, Conrad. Warned that the Turkish pasha Seyd is preparing to attack his stronghold, Conrad plans to outwit him. He takes leave of his beloved, Medora, and goes to the Pasha as a dervish who claims to have escaped from the pirates. Conrad's men launch their attack but it fails and he is taken prisoner. Gulnare, the favourite of Seyd's harem whom he has saved during the fighting, falls in love with him and gives him the opportunity to kill the Pasha. Conrad chivalrously refuses and Gulnare kills the Pasha herself. When Conrad escapes she goes with him. Arriving home, he finds that Medora has died of grief after a mistaken report of his death. Conrad leaves his home and disappears, though he returns in disguise as the title character of Byron's *Lara* (1814).

**Corso, Gregory (Nunzio)** 1930– American poet. The son of poor immigrants, Còrso was born and raised in New York City. His youth was difficult and violent, and by the age of 20 he had served three years in prison for attempted robbery. His poetry, which has affinities with that of **The Beats** in its concern with political and social issues, often adopts the stance of a sophisticated child who looks upon a world gone mad. His first volume, *The Vestal Lady of Brattle*, appeared in 1955. Subsequent volumes include *Gasoline* (1958), *Bomb* (1958), *The Happy Birthday of Death* (1960), *Long Live Man* (1962) and *There is Yet Time to Run Back Through Life and Expiate All That's Been Sadly Done* (1965). The title poem of his *Elegiac Feelings American* (1970) is dedicated to **Jack Kerouac**. His recent volumes, which reflect his interest in Egyptology and Eastern religions, include *Egyptian Cross* (1971), *Ankh* (1971), *The Night Last Night was at its Nightest . . .* (1972), and *Earth Egg* (1974). He has also written a play, *This Hung-Up Age* (1955), and a novel, *The American Express* (1961).

**Corvo, Baron**    See **Rolfe, Frederick William**.

**Cory, William Johnson** 1823–92 Poet. Born William Johnson in Torrington, Devon, he was educated at Eton and King's College, Cambridge. He worked as an assistant master at Eton for over 26 years. On inheriting an estate in 1872 he assumed the name of Cory and settled in Hampstead. *Ionica*, a collection of lyrics, was published anonymously in 1858. His *Letters and Journals* appeared in 1897. His best-known works are the poem 'Heraclitus', paraphrasing Callimachus, and the 'Eton Boating Song', written in 1863.

**Coryate, Thomas** *c.* 1577–1617 Traveller and writer. Son of the rector of Odcombe, Somerset, Coryate was educated at Gloucester Hall, Oxford, and became an inveterate traveller. In 1608 he journeyed through Europe, largely on foot, visiting France, Italy, Switzerland, Germany and Holland. On his return in 1611 he published a vivacious account entitled *Coryats Crudities, Hastily Gobbled up in Five Months Travels*, a mishmash of entertaining curiosities and opinionated reportage still of considerable interest as a period piece. It was prefaced with an extravagant number of commendatory verses including contributions from several of the leading poets of the day; these were reprinted separately as *The Odcombian Banquet* (1611). In the following year he embarked on an overland expedition to India, by way of Greece, Turkey, Egypt, Mesopotamia and Persia. He reached Agra, the court of the Mogul Emperor, in 1616, but died exhausted in Surat on his way home. His notes on this journey were preserved in his correspondence, and in *Thomas Coriate Traveller for the English Wits: Greeting from the Court of the Great Mogul* (1611).

**Cotton, Charles** 1630–87 Poet, translator and angler. Son of a generous landowner and *literatus*, who numbered **Donne**, **Jonson** and **Herrick** among his friends, he was born at the family home, Beresford Hall in Staffordshire. Staunchly Anglican and Royalist, he lived most of his life in retirement, and his few ventures into public life brought him no eminent success. Constantly plagued by financial problems of his father's making, his writing brought modest pecuniary relief, particularly his burlesque of the *Aeneid, Scarronnides*, the first Book of which appeared in 1664, to instant and lasting popular success, only ceasing to command reprints in the 19th century. A burlesque of Lucian, *The Scoffer Scoft*, followed in 1675. His translations from the French include military memoirs, Corneille's *Pompey*, and an excellently racy version of Montaigne's *Essays* (3 vols., 1685), which largely supplanted **John Florio**'s 1603 translation until this century. The bulk of his original poetry appeared posthumously, in *Poems on Several Occasions* (1689); it is a true miscellany, but his particular gifts are best represented in burlesques, conversational epistles and poems of

retirement. These last bear eloquent witness to his love of angling, and his enduring fame has been as **Izaak Walton**'s friend and protégé, and as author of the dialogue between Piscator and Viator which forms the Second Part of the renowned fifth edition of *The Compleat Angler* (1676).

**Cotton, John** 1584–1652 American Puritan minister. Born in Derbyshire, Cotton entered Trinity College, Cambridge, at the age of 13. Subsequently awarded a fellowship at Emmanuel College for his proficiency in Hebrew, he served as a lecturer, dean and catechist (1608–12), and in 1612 was appointed vicar of St Botolph's Church in Boston, Lincolnshire, a post which he resigned 20 years later when the Court of High Commission summoned him for instituting Puritan reforms in his parish. In July 1633 he emigrated to Massachusetts Bay aboard the *Griffin* and was chosen to be minister of the Boston church, where he remained until his death.

A distinguished preacher, he took up the issues most pressing to the Puritan consciousness in edifying and affective sermons. *A Brief Exposition on the Whole Book of Canticles* (1642) reads the history of the Christian church in the biblical *Song of Solomon*, an interpretation which theologically justifies the Puritan enterprise in Massachusetts. The sermons collected in *Christ the Fountaine of Life, or, Sundry Choyce Sermons on part of the fifth chapter of the first Epistle of St John* (1651) describe Cotton's ideas about religious conversion, revealing the emphasis he placed throughout his ministry on the irrelevance of good works to salvation. He also wrote several widely read theological tracts. *The Keyes of the Kingdom of Heaven* (1644) was written to persuade the Westminster Assembly to adopt the New England Way of church governance, and *The Way of Churches of Christ in New England* (1645) in an attempt to define Congregational theology and ecclesiology. In 1646 he published *Milk for Babes, Drawn from the Breasts of Both Testaments*, one of the authoritative catechisms which was used widely throughout the 17th century in America. The following year, he responded to **Roger Williams**'s criticisms of New England church policies in *The Bloudy Tenent Washed and Made White in the Bloud of the Lamb*. Having been attacked for the views expressed in *The Way of Churches of Christ in New England*, by Robert Baille, whose critique was published as *A Dissuasive from the Errours of the Time* (1645), Cotton refuted Baille's charges in *The Way of the Congregational Churches Cleared* (1648). That same year he published his most thorough ecclesiastical statement, *A Survey of the Summe of Church Discipline*.

**Cotton, Sir Robert Bruce** 1571–1631 Author of political tracts, antiquary and collector of manuscripts. Educated at Westminster School and Jesus College, Cambridge, Cotton became a Parliamentarian during the reign of James I. He was less important for his own writings than for his library of manuscripts from the dissolved monasteries; this precious material might otherwise have been destroyed or lost. Cotton gave manuscripts to the newly founded Bodleian Library at Oxford in 1602, and allowed **Bacon**, **Raleigh**, **Camden**, **Selden** and **Ussher** access to his collection. The Cottonian Library was left to the nation by his grandson, Sir John Cotton, and housed first in Essex House and then in Ashburnham House, where some of it was destroyed in a disastrous fire of 1731. The remainder passed to the British Museum in 1753. Among the treasures to survive are the single manuscript of *Beowulf*, the manuscripts of *Sir Gawain and the Green Knight* and *Pearl*, several biblical manuscripts and the Lindisfarne Gospels. See also **libraries**.

**Coulter, John** 1888–1980 Irish-Canadian playwright. Born in Belfast, he taught art and textile design there and in Dublin, where he was influenced by the **Abbey Theatre**. His first stage play was published in 1917. In London he did freelance work for the BBC and edited *The New Adelphi*. His friendship with and eventual marriage to the Canadian writer Olive Clare Primrose was the reason for his settling in Canada, where his play, *The House in the Quiet Glen*, won several awards at the 1937 Dominion Drama Festival. Coulter also wrote for radio, and later television, in Canada, the USA and Britain. The Canadian Broadcasting Corporation commissioned libretti for two operas by Healey Willan, *Transit through Fire* (1942) and *Deirdre* (1946). His best-known work is *Riel* (1950), an epic play about the leader of the 19th-century Métis rebellion in Western Canada. The same episode also yielded *The Crime of Louis Riel* (1966) and *The Trial of Louis Riel* (1968).

*Count Robert of Paris* A novel by **Walter Scott**, in the fourth series of *Tales of My Landlord*, published in 1831, the year before Scott's death. The setting is Constantinople at the time of the first crusade; the story deals with the adventures of the oafish Count Robert, his wife Brenhilda, and an impossibly chivalrous English member of the Emperor's Varangian guard, Hereward. The book contains an interesting portrait of Anna Comnena (b. 1083), the daughter of the Emperor and historian of the period (in the *Alexiad*). Otherwise, the novel reflects Scott's waning powers.

*Countess Kathleen, The* The earliest written of the plays of **W. B. Yeats** (published 1892), this dramatized Irish folk-tale was chosen, despite opposition from those who considered it blasphemous, to inaugurate the Irish Literary Theatre in 1899. Set in ancient Ireland during a time of terrible famine, it describes the efforts of the Countess to relieve the sufferings of her people. Appalled that they should sell their souls to demons for food, she eventually sells her own for a sum large enough to help the poor. The demons are denied her because God forgives her. 'The Light of Lights / Looks always on the motive, not the deed.'

The first version of this play was written for Maud Gonne. Yeats later revised and republished it under the title *The Countess Cathleen* (1912).

*Country of the Pointed Firs, The* A novel by **Sarah Orne Jewett**, published in 1896. It concerns an unnamed female narrator's summer vacation in the imaginary town of Dunnet Landing in rural Maine. The townspeople, at first somewhat distant, gradually include the narrator in their daily lives as though she were family. The novel reveals the dramatic depth and intensity in the life of an apparently placid community. It focuses in particular on the characters and abilities of women, and also addresses the issue of ageing and its impact on one's life and activities.

*Country Wife, The* A comedy by **William Wycherley**, first produced in January 1675 and published in the same year. One of the greatest examples of **Restoration comedy**, the play gave some offence even in its own day, and was toned down by **David Garrick** when he presented it as *The Country Girl* in 1766. Wycherley's original is certainly bawdy and the humour is not without savagery, but the play is constructed by a master of comedy.

Pinchwife and his wife Margery go to London for the marriage of Pinchwife's sister, Alithea, to Sparkish. Pinchwife is paying his sister's dowry, the real reason for Sparkish wanting to marry her. He is a foolish character who bores his acquaintances, among them Horner, a cynical libertine who has put it about that he suffers from impotence; jealous and suspicious husbands are content to trust their wives to Horner's company, believing him harmless. Pinchwife has married a country girl much younger than himself, and Margery is agog with excitement at being in London. Sparkish takes Alithea for granted and eventually loses her to Harcourt (the love of Harcourt and Alithea is the play's still centre). The fashionable ladies soon discover that Horner is far from impotent but keep their apparent secret to themselves. Horner finds Margery irresistible; she is driven into his arms by the jealousy of Pinchwife. In a brilliant closing scene the wives discover to their wrath that they all share the same secret, but they have to close ranks and swear to Horner's impotence in order to protect themselves from their husbands' rage. The curtain comes down to a dance of cuckolds.

**court theatres** The various entertainments at the Tudor and Stuart courts were often elaborate enough to demand the temporary adaptation of indoor spaces. The Great Hall at Hampton Court, the Banqueting House as well as the Great Chamber at Whitehall and the Great Halls at Greenwich, Richmond and Windsor were all put to use, particularly during the Christmas festivities at which professional theatre companies were privileged to perform and rewarded well for doing so. Under Charles I, more permanent structures were adapted or built. Inigo Jones converted the Cockpit-in-Court (1629–30) into an intimate theatre along lines already tested at the Cockpit in Drury Lane, and the Stuart delight in **masques** was gratified by the costly erection of the Masquing House (1637), close to Jones's magnificent Banqueting Hall (1619–22). Under Charles II and his successors, the custom of adaptation declined and the court theatres dwindled into insignificance.

**courtesy book** A type of literature particularly popular in the Middle Ages, defining the rules of polite behaviour and the general demeanour and duties of a courtier. Often written in verse and in dialogue, examples are extant in most European vernaculars and in Latin. Courtesy books were intended for the young gentry and aspiring courtiers, and dealt with personal hygiene and cleanliness as well as matters of etiquette, courtly duties and codes of behaviour. In the Renaissance the form changed slightly, following the influential work of Castiglione, *Il Libro del Cortegiano* (1528, translated 1561; see **The Courtier**). These later works were concerned with the integration of a wide variety of intellectual and practical attributes and skills in the ideal man of the age. The last courtesy book in the traditional mould is **Lord Chesterfield**'s *Letters to His Son* (1774).

**Courtier, The** Baldessare Castiglione's dialogue *Il Libro del Cortegiano* was first printed at Venice in 1528. It describes conversations at the court of Urbino, supervised by the Duchess Elisabetta Gonzaga, aimed at defining the perfect courtier. It had numerous Italian editions and was translated into the major European languages. The English translation made in 1561 by Sir Thomas Hoby (1530–66) ran through several editions and it was enormously popular as a **courtesy book**. Its immediate influence is discernible on such educational treatises as **Elyot**'s *The Book Named the Governor* and

Ascham's *The Schoolmaster*, and **Jonson** bases a scene in *Every Man Out Of His Humour* on it.

**courtly love** The modern name for a literary and social concept, originating in the Middle Ages, of a particular kind of love between men and women, involving service and veneration on the part of the man, and a nominal or actual domination on the part of the woman. This reversal of the usual medieval marital relationship took place between a lady who might or might not be married and a man sometimes but not invariably her social inferior. Descriptions consequently insist on its private, discreet and secret nature, on the frustrations and obstacles intensifying it, and on the dangers of its discovery by spies and slanderers. Its aristocratic system of values envisaged love as an educative and ennobling experience, the source of prowess and refinement, and consequently beneficial to society.

Some critics have denied that such a concept ever existed and point to Gaston Paris's coining of the term *amour courtois* in 1883. More widely held is the view that some such variation of romantic love was discussed, and existed as an ideal, if not as a historical fact, from the 12th century onwards, though usually called *fine* (or *verai*, or *bon*) *amour*. Definitions of it have varied according to literary fashion and have proliferated in the 20th century, when increasingly specialized knowledge of the Middle Ages has also resulted in scepticism and an unwillingness to make grandiose hypotheses.

Theories on the origins of courtly love have also proliferated. Dronke has asserted that it is a timeless human experience that transcends geographical boundaries (thus removing its 'courtly' label), and can be found in the earliest poetry. But **C. S. Lewis** and most critics have seen it as a phenomenon arising at the end of the 11th century in the courts of Southern France. Influences contributing to its formation are multiple, probably including the ironical love treatises of Ovid, and Hispano-Arabic literature. Southern France had many and various connections with Spain, and the Norman kingdom of Sicily also provided a bridge to the Arab world. The idea of love melancholy or *amor hereos* is a Graeco-Arabic one that passed into standard European medical knowledge through Avicenna and thence to literature. Both Troubadour and Arabic poetry express similar ideas about love, as simultaneously beneficial and distressing, in similar oxymorons: delight/torment; sickness/medicine; freedom/slavery; life/death.

Whereas the Arab poets frequently wrote of their love for slave girls, the Christians address themselves to noble ladies and use the terminology of feudalism to make the relationship resemble one between vassal and overlord. Here the growth of the concept of courtly love has perhaps been influenced by certain 12th-century social factors. The households of territorial magnates were often full of young men, landless younger sons, receiving their education and chivalric training there and as yet unable to afford marriage. There was often a shortage of women in such households; and in the absence of the overlord on crusade, his wife or sister frequently acted as suzerain. Such a situation may have nurtured love affairs between people of different social standing. The medieval practice of arranged marriages might also have encouraged the ladies to look elsewhere for love, but it is important to remember too that despite the famous dictum (allegedly by Marie de Champagne in 1174) that love and marriage were incompatible, there is much literary evidence to suggest that they were not. Huizinga has widened the discussion of sociological factors contributing to the growth of courtly love by envisaging it as an aristocratic game, played by members of a class who had the leisure to indulge in it, and containing all the satisfying game elements of contest, chance, make-believe and risk.

The poetry of the Troubadours of Southern France, which flourished for about two hundred and fifty years before being dealt a mortal blow by the onset of the Albigensian Crusade in 1209, is responsible for the earliest formulation of courtly ideas about love and for their subsequent wide dissemination throughout Europe. But their poetry shows right from its beginnings, in the literate and civilized court at Poitiers at the end of the 11th century, a range of amorous attitudes: Guilhem IX of Poitou, Duke of Aquitaine, writes both bawdily and seriously, of sensual and aspiring lovers. Distinctions between *Amors* (carnal, treacherous, sterile) and *Fin'Amors* (spiritual, distant, inspiring) continue to be made in the 12th century by poets like Jaufré Rudel (*fl.* 1140s), with his *amor de lonh* (love from afar), and the moralist Marcabru (*fl.* 1138–50). Bernart de Ventadorn (*fl.* 1145–80), on the other hand, accepts love's service completely and identifies *Fin'Amors* as no quasireligious ideal but true, mutual, fulfilled love, a source of improvement for the submissive and patient lover.

The Troubadour ideal of *cortesia* as a high moral code of behaviour based on profane love spread to the Northern French lyric poets and to England, to the *lais* of **Marie de France** (*fl.* 1160–90) and the story of Tristan, both based on Celtic legends. These stories in their outlines are often uncourtly: they depict mutual passion and women often both attainable and active, even (as in Marie's *Lanval* and *Eliduc*) making the first advances; and the linchpin of aristocratic society, the queen, is removed by Tristan to temporary exile. The uncourtly material of legend has in other respects, however, been modified or used to enhance other powerful constituents of courtly love. Hopeless passion makes young men accomplish all kinds of deeds; their suffering due to separation is intensified by all kinds of obstacles – mountains, jealous husbands, jealous wives. The Tristan story, above all, contributes three details endlessly imitated in courtly literature: the body/heart (*cors/cuers*) pun expressing Iseut's dilemma of body possessed by husband and heart by lover; the words 'En vus e ma mort e ma vie'; and the love potion, expressing the sudden and inexorable force of passion. The romances of Chrétien de Troyes (*fl.* 1170–81) likewise link Celtic material and the terminology of courtly love, but much of his work (*Erec*, *Yvain*, *Cligés*) portrays married lovers. The immoral adulterous love of Tristan and Iseut may have inspired his *Cligés*, where the dilemma of *cors/cuers* is ingeniously solved. Marriage is seen as the proper, socially celebrated expression of romantic love, even if there is a subsequent danger that satisfied desire may lead, not to prowess on the knight's part, but inertia (*Erec*). Chrétien's *Lancelot* is the great exception to the rest of his work, and still arouses controversy, since it is the first romance to depict the adulterous love of Lancelot and Guinevere, with hauteur and scorn on the latter's part when her submissive lover does not at once undergo a humiliating ordeal for her sake.

The subject of the romance may well have been imposed on Chrétien by his patroness Marie de Champagne, depicted as denying the compatibility of love and marriage in a much more controversial work, Andreas Capellanus' *De Arte Honeste Amandi* (1175–80). Two-thirds of this popular and much-translated treatise expounds courtly love, its rules and etiquette, to an unknown young man called Walter; the last third claims it has been expounded only so that it should be rejected, as harmful to the soul. Is it a scholastic joke, a seduction manual, a moralistic work or an early documenting of the game of love? Its structure, and some of its sentiments, undoubtedly owe something to Ovid's cynical *Ars Amatoria* and *Remedia Amoris*, and for this reason alone it is probably not worth attaching too much importance to Andreas; certainly we should not assume that his rules present an inflexible code. By the 1180s and 1190s some of the courtly attitudes to love were being parodied, as the romances of the Anglo-Norman poet Hue de Rotelande bear witness. The hugely influential 13th-century *Roman de la Rose,* the work of Guillaume de Lorris and Jean de Meun, is no romance but allegory used for the first time to convey the courtly experience of love. It presents a garden of love which excludes old age and poverty but is open to the rich and leisured; a Lover who falls in love with a Rose (the lady) and has to find a way of wooing and seducing her; and a gamut of opinions on the emotion, from varying characters, which range from the idealistic to the downright cynical.

In medieval English literature, expressions of the courtly ideal of love, other than in the work of **Chaucer**, are less frequently found than on the Continent. An early and delightful use of the *amor de lonh* motif appears in a little story in the **Ancrene Riwle** (*c.* 1200) about a disdainful lady wooed patiently by a king from a distant land – Christ wooing the soul. Courtly terminology often appears in English lyric only to lead us to the supreme Lady, the Virgin Mary. Secular lyrics refer to some of the courtly attitudes and attributes, but often in a modified form: the lady may still be described in terms of *largesse, prouesse* and *lealte* as if she were a feudal overlord; the necessary secrecy of the love affair may be emphasized; but it is not necessarily extramarital and the lady seems attainable, not aloof. English romances, taking their cue perhaps from the 12th- and 13th-century Anglo-Norman ones, which they often adapted or translated, are not notably courtly. The great exception is the 14th-century **Ipomadon**, which translated Hue de Rotelande's *Ipomédon* and retains its extensive reflection on the problems of courtly love and its emphasis on the thoughts and emotions of its characters. The romance portrays its hero and heroine as learning and maturing through the suffering entailed in love, whose natural fulfilment comes in marriage.

But this courtly theme of education through love is comparatively rare in English romances, which are more commonly homiletic in character or, when they use French originals, are less interested in love problems than adventures. So **Ywain and Gawain** (*c.* 1350), a version of Chrétien's *Yvain*, omits the long self-questioning monologues of the original, and the late 13th-century **Sir Tristrem** is predominantly not a love story. The Lancelot story is not taken up till around 1400, in the stanzaic **Le Morte Arthur**, where although love is the chief source of Lancelot's greatness, it is also firmly established as responsible for the fall of Arthur and the Round Table. **Sir Thomas Malory** too, who used the stanzaic *Morte* in his **Le Morte Darthur**, was not entirely happy with the relationship of Lancelot and Guinevere and at times seems to deny the possibility of any carnal union between them. A group of 14th-century romances – **Sir Eglamour of Artois**, **The Earl of Toulous**, **Sir Degrevant**, **Sir Torrent of Portyngale** and **Guy of Warwick** – all portray the hero in love with his social superior, and **Guy**, like its 13th-century Anglo-Norman original, shows him taking to his bed with all the symptoms of love-melancholy. His lady will not return his love until he has proved worthy of her, and is anxious lest her premature yielding should check his prowess, a concern reminiscent of Chrétien's *Erec*. But these courtly features only occur in the first quarter of the romance; the rest is entirely given up to Guy's martial adventures, eventually performed for the greater glory of God rather than for the lady. The 14th-century **William of Palerne** is a fairly faithful translation of its French original and so retains the description of the symptoms of 'courtly love' evinced by its hero. The courtly elements in these works make them exceptional cases among English romances, where the heroines often take the lead in wooing and the heroes may be initially reluctant.

The work of the greatest 14th-century English writers, however, makes it clear that they were thoroughly familiar with and sympathetic to the aristocratic ideal of love. We may not think of the relationship between Gawain and Bertilak's lady, in **Sir Gawain and the Green Knight**, as one of *fine amour*, especially as she is the one who woos, yet the 'luf-talkyng' expected of Gawain and indulged in by both of them is undoubtedly an essential ingredient of *courtoisie* and reminds us of Huizinga's theory of courtly love as an aristocratic game. In **John Gower**'s **Confessio Amantis** the Lover is questioned about his amorous behaviour. He 'confesses' his sentiments and experiences and demonstrates his refined manners and 'fair speech' in his long and devoted service to his lady. But the Lover has grown old in this service and by the end of the poem Love will have no more of him.

This realistic and clear-sighted attitude that accompanies a sympathetic depiction of courtly love is also shared by Gower's friend Chaucer. His first poem, **The Book of the Duchess**, indebted in part to the French love-visions of Machaut and Froissart, celebrates the relationship between yearning knight and virtuous but aloof lady which leads to a happy marriage but is abruptly terminated by death. The knight's feelings are intensified by loss and threaten to overwhelm him. A more detached and comic view of courtly relationships is expressed in **The Parlement of Foules**. The poet dreams of a garden containing a great gathering of birds of all classes, assembled to witness the formel eagle select a mate from among her three noble suitors, all of whom suitably express their devotion in terms of service, fidelity and obedience. Amid ribald comments from the lower orders of birds, the timid formel cannot bring herself to abandon the chaste life as yet, and the decision is postponed for another year. In such a company idealistic posturing has to take its place next to perhaps equally acceptable and more down-to-earth points of view: each perspective on love qualifies the other.

This sympathetic but critical viewpoint is also characteristic of Chaucer's mature works, **Troilus and Criseyde** and **The Canterbury Tales**. Many of the tales in the latter offer a variety of attitudes to love, from the sensual and bawdy to the idealistic, from secular to religious. The two tales which most exemplify courtly attitudes are *The Knight's Tale*, where Emelye's attitude to her two noble lovers reminds us a little of the formel eagle's, and *The Franklin's Tale*, frequently cited as Chaucer's last word on ideal marriage. The *Roman de la Rose* (which Chaucer translated as **The Romaunt of the Rose**) has influenced *The Franklin's Tale*: Jean de Meun puts into the cynical mouth of Amis a discussion of the reversal of roles endured by a woman when courtship is followed by marriage. The *maistrie*, or sovereignty, passes from her to her husband and as a result love dies. *The Franklin's Tale* envisages a union where the husband refuses to exert *maistrie* over his wife and tries to preserve within marriage the mutual honour and tolerance characteristic of their courtship. Their happy relationship is the source of their adherence to *trouthe*, the highest standard of honourable behaviour, by which they act in times of stress and which inspires similarly honourable behaviour in others. *Troilus and Criseyde* is Chaucer's most extended portrayal of a courtly love affair, ending in grief because one of the partners fails to adhere to *trouthe*. With that ending constantly in mind, Chaucer paints a complex, critical picture of his lovers and the ideals by which they talk and strive to act. Courtly behaviour in love is both high-principled and silly, noble and ineffectual. It cannot survive too much pressure from the violent world of war; seen from the cosmic viewpoint Troilus is granted when he ascends to the eighth sphere after death, it is indistinguishable from fleshly lust; seen from the Christian perspective which closes the poem, it is infinitely surpassed by Divine love. Yet courtly love at its greatest is celebrated, as the lovers consummate their union, in an unforgettable scene where the aspirations and desires of both mind and body have been fully satisfied. The patience, suffering, self-abnegation and self-control imposed by courtly ideals have led directly to this transient but intense joy: by no other road could the lovers arrive at their temporary heaven upon earth.

*Cousin Phillis* A novel by **Elizabeth Gaskell**, published in four parts in **The Cornhill Magazine** (November 1863–February 1864). Paul Manning, young and naïve, introduces his friend and superior in the railroad company, Edward Holdsworth, to his relatives, the minister Ebenezer Holman, his wife and daughter Phillis. Though Paul admires Phillis, he is somewhat intimidated by her learning and self-assurance, and for her part, she is attracted by the sophisticated charm of his friend. When Holdsworth departs to take up a job in Canada, Paul, guessing the reason for Phillis's low spirits, is prompted to confide to her Holdsworth's half-formed idea of making her his wife. With this new secret knowledge Phillis rallies, but when, some months later, the news arrives of Holdsworth's marriage to a French Canadian girl, Phillis is stricken and collapses with a brain fever. She eventually recovers, but not until she has learned the real selfishness of immoderate sensibility, and Paul has faced the burden of his irresponsibility. *Cousin Phillis* is a short but brilliantly conceived novel which displays the author's delicate and tactful observation of adolescent emotion.

**Covent Garden, Theatre Royal** When John Rich moved from his theatre in Lincoln's Inn Fields to the newly built Theatre Royal at Covent Garden in 1732, he took with him the patent that entitled him to share with **Drury Lane** the monopoly of the legitimate drama in London. Sustained with varying intensity, the rivalry with Drury Lane continued until 1843, when the patent monopoly was abolished by Act of Parliament. By then, the first theatre, with its capacity of nearly 2000, had been replaced by a second, with a capacity of 3000. This second theatre, designed by Richard Smirke and opened in 1809, was immediately threatened by the most famous of all popular resistance to increased admission charges, the Old Price Riots. John Philip Kemble, acting manager, had to give in to public demand and even to apologize to his victorious audience.

Even under the management of the actor Macready (1837–9), Covent Garden struggled to overcome the costliness of its ambition as a **patent theatre**, and soon after the 1843 act it became primarily an opera-house. After a fire had destroyed the building in 1856, a third theatre, designed by Sir Edward Barry, was erected on the site, and it is this theatre, considerably altered, that now carries the name of the Royal Opera House.

**Coventry, Francis** d. ?1759 Satirist. Educated at Magdalene College, Cambridge, Coventry became vicar of Edgware near London. He was author of a satirical prose tale *The History of Pompey the Little* (1751), giving a lap-dog's observation of life while he is passed from one owner to another with bewildering speed and treated in different ways.

**Coventry cycle of mystery plays** See **miracle plays**.

**Coverdale, Miles** ?1488–1569 Protestant reformer and translator of the Bible. Coverdale was ordained priest in 1514 and became an Augustinian friar in Cambridge. But he developed enthusiasm for reform and by 1528 was preaching against the Mass and devotion to images. A fellow worker with **William Tyndale** in the translation of the Bible, Coverdale was responsible for the English version of the Psalms preserved in the **Book of Common Prayer**. Using Tyndale's work, he published at Cologne in 1535 the first complete English Bible to be printed, and he was editor of the Great Bible of 1539. He became Bishop of Exeter in 1551, but lost the bishopric in Mary's reign and left England to live in Germany and Switzerland. There he joined the group of exiles who worked on the Geneva Bible, presented to Queen Elizabeth in 1560. He had returned to England in 1559 but his Puritanism prevented his ever regaining a bishopric. He was made a DD of Cambridge in 1563, the same year that he became rector of St Magnus at London Bridge; he held the post until 1566. See also **The Bible in English** and **Psalters**.

**Coward, Sir Noël (Pierce)** 1899–1973 Playwright, actor, lyricist and composer, educated privately and at a stage school. Coward had already written several plays and sketches, including some for *The Co-Optimists* (1922), when his comedy *The Young Idea* (1922) announced a distinctive voice of the 1920s. Much better than the more celebrated but contrived *The Vortex* (1924), *The Young Idea* was the first of a succession of stylish comedies, which include *Fallen Angels* (1925), **Hay Fever**

A scene from Act II of Coward's *Private Lives* at the Phoenix Theatre, London, in 1930. Noël Coward as Elyot, Gertrude Lawrence as Amanda. Victoria & Albert Theatre Museum, London.

(1925), ***Private Lives*** (1930), *Design for Living* (1933), *Blithe Spirit* (1941) and *Present Laughter* (1942).

It was not by his plays alone that Coward earned for himself the admiration, and often the envy, of the theatrical profession. He was also a gifted and notably relaxed actor, a showman who learned how to sell a song without singing it and a master of revue. His lyrics, particularly those that look with wry affection at English eccentricity ('The Stately Homes of England', 'Mad Dogs and Englishmen', 'Let's Not Be Beastly to the Germans'), are among the best of their kind. Except in *Bitter-Sweet* (1929), he found it hard to sustain a whole piece with music of his own composition, but individual tunes linger ('Some Day I'll Find You', 'I'll See You Again').

Of Coward's patriotic plays, the ambitious *Cavalcade* (1931) has more admirers than *This Happy Breed* (1942) and *Peace in Our Time* (1947). The best of his later work includes *Look after Lulu* (1959), an adaptation of a Feydeau farce and the three plays performed under the general title *Suite in Three Keys* (1966).

Coward also published two lively autobiographies, *Present Indicative* (1937) and *Future Indefinite* (1954), several volumes of short stories (*The Collected Short Stories*, 1962) and a novel, *Pomp and Circumstance* (1960). Under the pseudonym of Hernia Whittlebot, he published *Poems* (1923) and *Chelsea Buns* (1925). *The Coward Song-Book* (1953) and *The Lyrics of Coward* (1965) are useful collections. Coward was knighted in 1970.

**Cowley, Abraham** 1618–67 Poet. The posthumous son of a wealthy London stationer, Cowley was educated at Westminster School and Trinity College, Cambridge, where he took his BA in 1639, was made a fellow in 1640 and became MA in 1643. Like **Cleveland** and **Crashaw**, he was deprived of his fellowship by the Parliamentary party during the Civil War but had already left Cambridge when this happened. He joined the King at Oxford, and departed for France as secretary to Queen Henrietta Maria in 1644. Ten years later he came back to England and was immediately imprisoned; upon his release he appears to have submitted to the Cromwellian regime but he may have been a Royalist spy. During this time he studied medicine at Oxford and became an MD in 1657. At the Restoration Cowley's fellowship was restored and he was granted land by Henrietta Maria. Thereafter he lived a retired life at Chertsey, devoting his time to botany and to the writing of essays.

Cowley was writing at the age of 10 and had published two romantic epics by the time he was 15; a pastoral drama appeared when he was 20 and he wrote a Latin comedy in the same year. His first collection of verse was *The Mistress: or Several Copies of Love Verses* (1647). In 1656 a multiple collection was published in which *The Mistress* was included; it contained also *Miscellanies*, *Pindaric Odes* and four books of an epic on an Old Testament subject, *Davideis*. Cowley wrote an 'Ode upon the Blessed Restoration' in 1660 and *A Discourse By Way of Vision Concerning the Government of Oliver Cromwell* in 1661. In the same year he published his *Proposition for the Advancement of Experimental Philosophy*. A folio edition of his works published in 1668, the year after his death, contained *Several Discourses by way of Essays, in Verse and Prose*, the essays that kept his name alive.

The poet's reputation earned him a splendid funeral and burial in Westminster Abbey beside **Chaucer** and **Spenser**, but after his death his fame quickly dwindled, though he was a formative influence on **Swift**, and the first subject of **Samuel Johnson**'s *The Lives of the Poets*. His imitations of the high metaphysical style of **Donne** and the difficult measures of Pindar are energetic, learned and difficult to read.

**Cowley, Hannah** 1743–1809 Playwright and poet. Born in Tiverton, Devon, she began writing for the stage eight years after her marriage to a captain in the East India Company. Her first play, *The Runaway* (1776), is a lively comedy, dedicated to **David Garrick**, who may have 'improved' it. *Who's the Dupe?* (1779), her second performed play, remained popular as a two-act afterpiece until the end of the century. In an age of generally turgid sentimental comedy, Cowley's plays are refreshingly sprightly. The best of them, *The Belle's Stratagem* (1780), held its own on the 19th-century stage and was revived in London in 1913. Her characters are recognizably stereotypes, but their dialogue is deft and the contrast between a witty couple and a sentimental one, repeated in *Which Is the Man?* (1783) and *More Ways Than One* (1783), is effective. Hannah Cowley's career as poet involved her in a sentmental verse correspondence with Robert Merry, leader of the so-called **Della Cruscans**.

**Cowper, William** 1731–1800 Poet. Cowper (pronounced 'Cooper') was born in his father's rectory at Great Berkhampstead, Hertfordshire. As a child he attended a private school – where he suffered from bullying – and then Westminster School. His vehement dislike of public-school education was later the subject of 'Tirocinium' (1785). He studied law at the Inner Temple, was called to the Bar in 1754, but made no attempt to practise. He fell in love with his cousin, Theodora Cowper, but his father forbade them to marry, on the grounds of consanguinity.

Already suffering from fitful periods of depression, Cowper deteriorated into unmistakable mania when, at the age of 32, an uncle tried to help him by nominating him for a sinecure as Clerk of the Journals of the House of Lords: the prospect of a formal examination drove him to attempt suicide. He was cured, and settled in comfortable lodgings at Huntingdon, with a small income. Throughout his life, the poet was fortunate to have a wide circle of friends who cared for his welfare. In Huntingdon he met Morley Unwin, a retired Evangelical clergyman, and his wife Mary, with whom he went to live. After Unwin's death in 1767, Cowper moved to Olney in Buckinghamshire, along with Mary and her children, and here he came under the powerful influence of John Newton, a formidable Evangelical pastor with an inclination to Calvinism. The intellectual pressures of this association were not fortunate for Cowper and he declined again into melancholy, though his poetic talents were channelled into several notable contributions to the hymn-book Newton was producing. *Olney Hymns* (1779) includes several by Cowper, such as 'God Moves in a Mysterious Way'.

Cowper again suffered mental collapse but Mary Unwin, to whom he was engaged, nursed him to recovery, and by 1776 he was again corresponding with his friends. Many of his letters are of exceptional quality, and are of

William Cowper. A detail from the portrait by L. F. Abbott, 1792. National Portrait Gallery, London.

importance in revealing his true personality; Cowper did not cultivate the 'art of letter-writing' like many literary correspondents of that century. His letters talk directly and personally to his friends, and show him, when not unwell, cheerfully intent upon a simple country existence. At this period he began to write verse again. His cousin, Martin Madan, had published a book supporting polygamy, and Cowper replied with *Anti-Thelyphthora: A Tale in Verse* (1781), and, at Mary Unwin's instigation, began a series of eight satires. *Poems* (1782) contained these and some short poems. The satires are weakened by the poet's restricted experience of life, but they illustrate his skill with the couplet, and 'Retirement' is the most accomplished. The shorter poems include 'The Shrubbery', 'Boadicea' and *Verses Supposed to be Written by Alexander Selkirk*. At the suggestion of a new friend, Lady Austen, Cowper composed **The Task**, in six books, published in 1785 in a volume which included **The Diverting History of John Gilpin** (1782), also the result of Lady Austen's initiative.

Cowper and Mary Unwin never married, but they remained together and moved in 1786 to nearby Weston Underwood. There he composed a number of short poems published after his death, including 'The Poplar Field', 'On the Loss of the Royal George' and the fine sonnet 'To Mrs Unwin'. In 1785 he started to translate Homer, beginning with a blank-verse version of the *Iliad*. The project was well-subscribed and was published in 1791, though it is not among his best achievements. He also translated works from Latin, Italian and French.

When Mary Unwin died in 1794, the strain was too much for the poet and he became a physical and mental invalid for the rest of his life. He was awarded a royal pension in 1794, and died at East Dereham, Norfolk, in 1800, his last years yielding the depressingly powerful poem, 'The Castaway'. It is sometimes thought that Cowper did not take seriously enough his vocation as a poet, merely because his quieter and more direct verse is less intellectually ambitious and sublime than his distinguished predecessors'. Unwittingly, his example of poetry that addressed the simpler human and rural themes marked the point at which English verse moved away from neoclassical concerns towards the different poetic of the 19th century.

**Cozzens, James Gould** 1903–78 American novelist. Born in Chicago, Cozzens attended Harvard and began his writing career early, publishing in **The Atlantic Monthly** when he was 16. His novels explore the social order of American life and its potential for stability and hierarchy, by portraying professional men caught in moral and cultural dilemmas: *The Last Adam* (1933) is about the medical profession, *Men and Brethren* (1936) about the ministry and *The Just and the Unjust* (1942) about the law. *Guard of Honor* (1948), an ambitious novel set during World War II, won Cozzens the Pulitzer Prize. In 1957 he published *By Love Possessed*, about a lawyer, his most controversial and widely read book. Cozzens has long been the object of controversy; his enquiries into the possibilities of social stability have been criticized by some as dangerously right-wing. His last publications were *Children and Others* (1964, children's stories) and *Morning, Noon and Night* (1968, a novel).

**Crabbe, George** 1755–1832 Poet. Crabbe was born at Aldeburgh, Suffolk, where his father was a collector of salt duties, and educated at schools in Bungay and Stowmarket, before being apprenticed to surgeons at Bury St Edmunds and Woodbridge. In 1772 he met and became engaged to Sarah Elmy, and published his first verse in *Wheble's Magazine*. His first significant poem, *Inebriety*, a didactic satire in the manner of **Pope** on the perils of drink, was published anonymously in 1775. In the same year he returned to Aldeburgh to set up practice as a surgeon, making little money but continuing to read, write and pursue botanical studies. In 1780 he determined upon a literary career and, with £5 in his pocket, a sheaf of manuscripts and a case of surgical instruments, set off for London, where, but for the timely intervention of **Burke**, to whom he appealed as a complete stranger, he would have been imprisoned for debt. With the help of Burke's recommendation and literary connections, *The Library*, another work showing the influence of Pope, was published in 1781, and Crabbe went to stay with his patron at Beaconsfield, where he began work on his next publication, **The Village**. Burke introduced him to Charles James Fox and **Sir Joshua Reynolds** and encouraged him to enter the church. After a brief period as curate at Aldeburgh, Crabbe took holy orders and was from 1782 to 1785 chaplain to the Duke of Rutland at Belvoir. In 1783 he married Sarah Elmy, and in the same year met **Dr Johnson** who read, praised and slightly 'corrected' *The Village*, a work in heroic couplets, which established his reputation following its publication in May. In 1784 he published a brief memoir of Lord Robert Manners, Rutland's brother, who had been killed in action at sea in 1782; and in 1785 a satire, *The Newspaper*.

There now followed a period of 22 years during which Crabbe published nothing of importance, although he wrote and destroyed three novels and continued to be intellectually active, particularly as a botanist and entomologist. In 1789 he took up the living of Muston, Leicestershire, which he held until 1814, but absented himself to Suffolk between 1792 and

Aldeburgh, in a 19th-century coloured drawing in the Moot Hall. George Crabbe was born in Aldeburgh in 1755 and it is the setting for his best-known poetry.

1805. *The Parish Register* appeared in 1807, and inaugurated the second phase of Crabbe's literary career, in which he emerged as a gifted exponent of verse narrative. The main part of the collection narrates the memories of a country parson as he leafs through the register of births, marriages and deaths, and includes 'Sir Eustace Grey', a remarkable poem in eight-line stanzas portraying the demented hallucinations of a patient in a madhouse. The extraordinary vividness of the dream sequences suggests that they may have been written under the influence of opium, which Crabbe is known to have begun taking in 1790. In 1810 he published *The Borough*, a poem in 24 'letters' describing the scenery and life of a country town based on his native Aldeburgh, which was followed in 1812 by *Tales*. His wife, who had suffered from manic depression for many years, died in 1813, following which he was himself for a while dangerously ill. In 1814 he became vicar of Trowbridge, Wiltshire, and was briefly engaged to Charlotte Ridout. He now began to travel more frequently to London, where he became acquainted with **Thomas Moore**, **Samuel Rogers**, **Southey** and **Wordsworth**. His *London Journal* of 1817 was later printed in the *Life* by his son. *The World of Dreams* was written in 1817, and 1819 saw the publication of *Tales of the Hall*. In 1822 he went to Edinburgh to visit **Scott**, with whom he enjoyed a close friendship. In the same year he wrote *In a Neat Cottage*, and in 1823 a collected edition of his *Works* appeared in five- and eight-volume formats. He died in Trowbridge, leaving much unpublished work, some of which was incorporated into the last volume of *The Poetical Works* (8 vols., 1834).

Although Crabbe first gained his reputation as a poet in the age of Johnson, his best work was contemporary with that of the Romantics. He was not, however, simply a survival from the Augustan age, despite his almost unbroken fidelity to the heroic couplet, and firm commit-ment to that period's values of sense, judgement, moderation and balance. His tales are an original achievement in a new art form through which he probed the psychological, social and moral textures of the post-classical epoch. He was much admired by **Jane Austen** (who thought she could see herself as Mrs Crabbe), Scott and **Byron**, who saw him as 'Nature's sternest painter yet the best'.

**Cradle Will Rock, The** A musical drama of social protest, with lyrics and music by **Marc Blitzstein**, first produced in 1937. Blitzstein brought techniques of classical opera together with elements of popular music to tell the story of a strike in 'Steeltown, USA'. The characters are representative types rather than realistic individuals. Mr Mister, who owns the steel mill and everything else in town, is trying to break the strike with the aid of his 'Liberty Committee' – Reverend Salvation, Editor Daily, Yasha (a musician), Dauber (an artist), Dr Specialist, and Professor Trixie and President Prexy from the local university. Most of the play takes place in a courtroom to which the Liberty Committee has been taken, mistakenly arrested along with 'the man who made the speech' – Larry Foreman, a union organizer and the hero of the piece. Through a series of flashbacks the sympathetic Harry Druggist, a former drugstore owner who has become a bum after the death of his son in an explosion caused by Mr Mister's henchmen, explains to Moll, a poor woman who is being framed for soliciting, how each member of the Liberty Committee came to sell his soul and his profession to Mr Mister and his family. At the end of the play, Mr Mister appears and attempts unsuccessfully to buy off Larry Foreman; we are left with the impression that the union will be successful.

**Craik, Dinah Maria** See **Mulock, Dinah**.

**Crane, (Harold) Hart** 1899–1932 American poet. Crane was born in Ohio but spent most of his life in New York City. His parents' unhappy marriage deeply troubled him; alcoholism and his inability to support himself in New York further undermined his stability. He committed suicide at the age of 33.

Strongly influenced by the French symbolists and by **T. S. Eliot**, Crane produced in his relatively brief career a body of poetry that has received considerable critical attention and acclaim. Characterized by dramatic rhetoric and exotic diction, his work often drew on images of water and the sea, which provided him with material for his symbolic and psychological speculations. He is best known for his long poem *The Bridge* (1930), written partly in response to the negativism of Eliot's *The Waste Land*. Each section of the poem focuses on a particular aspect of American history or culture, which Crane then unifies in the figure of the Brooklyn Bridge, which he called 'a symbol of our constructive future'. His first book of poetry, *White Buildings*, was published in 1926, his *Collected Poems* in 1933.

**Crane, Stephen** 1871–1900 American novelist and short-story writer, born in Newark, New Jersey, the son of a Methodist minister. After leaving high school he moved to New York City and worked as a journalist for the *Tribune* and the *Herald* before starting on his first novel, eventually published as **Maggie: A Girl of the Streets** (1893). Though *Maggie* was not widely noticed, his second novel, **The Red Badge of Courage** (1895), was a critical and popular success. In 1896 he published a collection of short stories, *The Little Regiment*, focusing on the Civil War. In the same year, working-class life in New York City provided material for the novel *George's Mother*. *The Third Violet* (1897) is a short novel about a young artist.

Crane's career as a journalist continued during these years and he travelled to the Southwest, to Mexico, and, in 1896, to Cuba. On this last journey he was shipwrecked, spending nearly three days in an open boat at sea, an experience which formed the basis for one of his most famous stories, the title piece of *The Open Boat and Other Stories* (1898). In 1897 he and his companion Cora Taylor travelled to Greece, where he served as a war correspondent. His poor health forced them to leave and they

Stephen Crane.

moved to England, where he met **Joseph Conrad** and **Henry James**, two of his most distinguished admirers. A novel, *Active Service* (1899), was derived from his experience of the Graeco-Turkish War. In 1899 he returned to Cuba, to cover the Spanish–American War, but was again obliged to return to England due to poor health. He died of tuberculosis at the age of 29. Some of his most highly regarded stories appeared in *The Monster* (1898). His poetry was collected in *The Black Rider* (1895) and *War is Kind* (1900). Posthumous publications include the sketches and stories from his life as a correspondent in *Wounds in the Rain* (1900); and *Whilomville Stories* (1900), about a childhood in a small town in New York state.

**Crane, Walter** 1845–1915 Artist and illustrator of children's books. Born in Liverpool, the son of a portrait painter, Crane first trained as a wood engraver before illustrating a children's book at the age of 18. The pioneer colour printer Edmund Evans asked him to illustrate a series of children's picture-books, which appeared between 1865 and 1873 and included classics like *The Railroad Alphabet*, *The House that Jack Built* and *Sing a Song of Sixpence*. While somewhat static in design, they appealed to children because of their strong line, bold colour and the intricate decorative borders which added an extra commentary to each picture. Most popular of all, and still in print today, was *The Baby's Opera* (1877), a collection of traditional nursery rhymes where text, music and illustration come together in one diminutive but pleasing whole. A friend of **William Morris**, Crane also designed mosaics, friezes and wallpapers and became the first president of the Arts and Crafts Society. Best remembered for his children's work, Crane was an important figure in the movement to bring picture-books to a pitch of excellence never seen before and only rarely equalled since.

*Cranford* A novel by **Elizabeth Gaskell**, first published serially in **Household Words** in 1851–3.

Set in early 19th-century England, *Cranford* is a series of vignettes of life in a community of genteel ladies, a world into which very few gentlemen are admitted. A strict social hierarchy obtains among the well-intentioned, basically kind spinsters and widows whose weaknesses and attributes extend across the pages of this mild and gentle book. At the centre of *Cranford* is Miss Matilda (Miss Matty) Jenkyns whose warm heart and tender ways compel affection and regard from all about her. Her quiet life of 'elegant economy' is seen through the eyes of a sympathetic narrator. Revealed, too, are the foibles and attributes of others in Miss Matty's circle: the pompous Mrs Jamieson and her awesome butler, Mulliner; the genial, straightforward Captain Brown, killed while looking up

An illustration by Hugh Thomson for an edition of *Cranford* published in 1898. Miss Matty is apprehensive about being carried in a sedan chair.

too late from reading; Miss Deborah Jenkyns, Miss Matty's elder sister and an ardent Johnsonian; Martha, the cumbersome but loyal housemaid; and several others. The cast is replete with fundamentally decent people touched by the lesser weaknesses of the human animal. But above all, it is Miss Matty, free from any taint of hypocrisy, affectation or unkindness, who emerges as the true Christian.

Although there is a tenuous narrative in *Cranford* that takes Miss Matty from quiet satisfaction through minor crises rising to serious personal adversity and retreating to calm security through the reappearance of a long lost brother, it is the individual moment of revelation that marks *Cranford* as a minor triumph. The passing of Mr Holbrook (a yeoman-farmer who loved Miss Matty), the permission granted Martha to have a follower, and Miss Matty's conduct toward a farmer deprived by a bank failure: these and other scenes are deftly, quietly, and economically written.

**Cranmer, Thomas** 1489–1556 Divine. Cranmer was educated at Cambridge and became a fellow of Jesus College in 1510 or 1511. He found favour with Henry VIII, who sent him on embassies to the Pope in 1530 and the Emperor Charles V in 1532. In 1533 he became Archbishop of Canterbury and remained in office through the Reformation, thus becoming Canterbury's first archbishop in the reformed church. In co-operation with Thomas Cromwell he promoted publication of the **Bible in English** and wrote a prologue to the Great Bible

of 1540. He composed a litany for the reformed church of 1545, was responsible for the publication of the *Homilies* in 1547 and supervised the first and second Edwardian prayer-books of 1549 and 1552 (see **Book of Common Prayer**). His other works include a controversy with Stephen Gardiner, a catechism and a treatise on the Eucharist. Under Queen Mary he was condemned for treason in 1553, degraded from ecclesiastical office and burned as a heretic in 1556.

**Crashaw, Richard** 1612–49 Devotional poet. The son of William Crashaw, a Puritan preacher, he spent his short adult life in increasing reaction against the austerity of his father's religion. He entered Pembroke College, Cambridge, graduated in 1634, and was awarded a fellowship of Peterhouse in the following year. With the defeat of the Royalists in the Civil War he was deprived of his fellowship (1644) but had already left Cambridge the previous year. After two years, mostly in exile, he became a Roman Catholic, and ended his days in a minor office at the Cathedral of Loreto.

Crashaw is best remembered as a religious poet. He sometimes achieves a memorable sequence of lines but the matter of his poetry is, as **D. J. Enright** says, 'lovingly handled, but sometimes too lovingly fondled'. This is clearly seen in his only original secular lyric (his others are versions from other languages) 'Wishes: To His (Supposed) Mistress'. But there are fine lines to be found, especially when the poet's intensity of feeling imposes its own discipline on his baroque extravagance. His first collection, *Steps to the Temple. Sacred Poems with other Delights of the Muses*, was published in 1646; a revised and enlarged edition followed two years later. In 1652 Crashaw's friend Miles Pinkney published a more complete collection, the posthumous volume *Carmen Deo Nostro*.

**Crawford, Francis Marion** 1854–1909 American novelist. Son of the sculptor Thomas Crawford and nephew, on his mother's side, of **Julia Ward Howe**, Crawford was born in Italy. He was educated in the USA and at Cambridge and Heidelberg universities. An accomplished linguist, he travelled extensively, sometimes gathering material for his novels.

His first novel, *Mr Isaacs: A Tale of Modern India* (1882), was an immediate success, and he went on to write almost 50 more romances, historical novels and tales of cosmopolitan adventure which enjoyed a large following. His aim, as he argued in *The Novel: What It Is* (1893), was not to moralize or to paint life in the realistic mode that was then becoming popular, but simply to entertain. Among his other novels are *A Tale of a Lonely Parish* (1886), *Don Orsini* (1891), *Corleone: A Tale of Sicily* (1896), *Via*

*Crucis* (1898), *In the Palace of the King: A Love Story of Old Madrid* (1900) and *The White Sister* (1909). Many of his novels were adapted for the stage. He wrote *Francesca da Rimini* (1902), a play in four acts, for Sarah Bernhardt. His tales of the supernatural, *Wandering Ghosts*, were published posthumously in 1911.

**Crawford, Isabella Valancy** 1850–87 Canadian poet. She was born in Dublin, but her parents settled in Canada in about 1858. After her father's death in 1875 she was the sole support of her mother and sister and began to write for a living. In Toronto she wrote short stories and contributed poems to *The Globe* and *The Telegram*. In 1884 she published a paperbound collection, *Old Spookses' Pass, Malcolm's Katie and Other Poems*, at her own expense. It was well reviewed in England, but only some 50 copies were sold before the author's death. Her *Collected Poems* appeared in 1905 with an introduction by John Garvin. One of Canada's finest early writers, Crawford combines in her poetry exuberance and vigour with a wide range of mythological material drawn from classical legend, biblical and folk-stories.

**Creasey, John** See **detective fiction**.

**Creeley, Robert** 1926– American poet. Born in Arlington, Massachusetts, Creeley attended Harvard but did not graduate. In 1954 he joined the faculty at Black Mountain College in North Carolina, where he was associated with the **Black Mountain school** of poets. When the college closed in 1956 he moved to San Francisco, where he met **Jack Kerouac**, **Allen Ginsberg**, and other writers of the **Beat** movement. His poems, often syntactically compressed and beginning and ending in mid-thought, are collected in *You* (1956), *For Love: Poems 1950–1960* (1962), *Words: Poems* (1967), *Divisions and Other Early Poems* (1968), *St Martin's* (1971), *The Collected Poems of Robert Creeley, 1945–1975* (1982) and *Mirrors* (1983). His prose works include a novel, *The Island* (1963), and a collection of short stories, *The Gold Diggers* (1954), *Was That a Real Poem and Other Essays* (1979) and *The Collected Prose of Robert Creeley: A Story* (1984).

**Creevey, Thomas** 1768–1838 Politician and man of letters. Born in Liverpool, he was elected MP for Thetford in 1802, and later held the seat for Appleby. He became treasurer for Greenwich Hospital in 1860. *The Creevey Papers: A Selection from the Correspondence and Diaries of The Late Sir Thomas Creevey* was published in 1903. This gossipy and irreverent volume is interesting for the light it sheds on the principal figures of the late Georgian period.

**Creighton, Mandell** 1843–1901 Historian. Creighton, who became Bishop of London in 1897, was born in Carlisle and educated at Merton College, Oxford, of which he later became a fellow. He was appointed Professor of Ecclesiastical History at Cambridge (1884) and made a reputation as a historian with his *A History of the Papacy during the Period of the Reformation* (1882–94), which was praised for its detachment and erudition. He became the first editor of *The English Historical Review* (1886), which he directed until he was made Bishop of Peterborough (1891). Other works by Bishop Creighton include *A History of Rome* (1875), *The Tudors and the Reformation* (1876), *Cardinal Wolsey* (1888), *Queen Elizabeth* (1896), *A History of the Papacy from the Great Schism to the Sack of Rome* (1897) and *The Life of Simon de Montfort* (published posthumously, 1905).

**Crèvecoeur, J. Hector St John de** 1735–1813 Born in Normandy, and educated in France and England, in 1754 he went to Quebec to serve in Montcalm's army. He subsequently travelled around the Great Lakes and the Ohio River Valley, New York and Pennsylvania, describing his experiences in *Voyage dans la Haute Pennsylvanie et dans l'état de New York* (Paris, 1801). He became naturalized as an American colonial citizen in New York in 1764. In 1769 he married and settled on a farm in Orange County, New York.

In 1780 the American Revolution forced Crèvecoeur to leave America for Europe, where he moved in fashionable circles and published, under the name J. Hector St John, a collection of his impressions of America called *Letters from an American Farmer* (London, 1782; not published in America until 1793). Returning to the USA after the war in 1783, he found his farm burned, his wife dead, and his children dispersed. He served as French consul and eventually went back to France in 1790. Further letters and essays written during his American period were published in 1925 as *Sketches of Eighteenth Century America*.

***Cricket on the Hearth, The*** A Christmas story by **Charles Dickens**, published in 1845 and collected in ***Christmas Books*** (1852).

John Peerybingle, a stolid but worthy carrier married to the beautiful but much younger Dot, one day brings home an elderly stranger to lodge with them. A strain is placed upon their idyllic marriage when, through the malicious interference of the odious toy-merchant Tackleton, John sees the stranger, divested of his wig and other accoutrements, transformed into a handsome young man whom he mistakenly assumes to be the object of his wife's affections. John is prevented from wreaking vengeance by the intervention of the 'Cricket on the Hearth in Faery shape'. Meanwhile, Tackleton seeks the hand of Dot's friend, May Fielding, but on the morning of their intended marriage it is revealed that she has just been united with the stranger, who is really Edward Plummer, her fiancé of earlier years now home after a long absence. Another narrative strand concerns Edward's blind sister Bertha and their father, the simple Caleb, who works for Tackleton. *The Cricket* concludes with reconciliation and rejoicing, in which even the previously villainous Tackleton joins.

**Crispin, Edmund** See **detective fiction.**

**Criterion, The** A literary journal founded and edited by **T. S. Eliot.** It appeared quarterly from 1922 to 1939, with a short period in 1926 and 1927 as *The New Criterion*, and from 1927 to 1928 as *The Monthly Criterion*. Financial backing came first from Viscountess Rothermere, and later from Eliot's employer, Faber and Faber. It was launched with the publication of **The Waste Land** in its first issue. Eliot's editorial 'Commentary' in each issue expounded his right-wing, Anglo-Catholic and classicist doctrine of order, and at times expressed admiration for fascism. This did not prevent him from opening *The Criterion* to contributions from younger writers of very different persuasions: **W. H. Auden, Hart Crane, William Empson, D. H. Lawrence** and **Stephen Spender** were represented, along with Eliot's mentor **Ezra Pound**. To many who had hailed Eliot's promise in the early 1920s, *The Criterion* proved to be a disappointment, and by 1939 Eliot himself was too dispirited to carry on with it.

**Critic, The, or, A Tragedy Rehearsed** A comedy-burlesque by **Richard Brinsley Sheridan,** first performed at **Drury Lane** in 1779. The piece is modelled on the **Duke of Buckingham's** *The Rehearsal* (1671), which had set the fashion for topical jokes about pompous playwrights and theatrical stupidity. *The Critic* is given added point by the exasperation Sheridan must often have felt as manager of Drury Lane. 'It was to be regarded', according to the compilers of *Biographia Dramatica* (1811 edn), 'in the light of an advertisement published by the manager of Drury Lane, signifying his wish that no more *modern tragedies* might be offered for representation at his theatre.'

*The Critic* is in three acts. In the first, Dangle, a man obsessed with theatrical affairs, reads the paper and discusses the issues of the day. Various figures of the day, in particular **Richard Cumberland** as Sir Fretful Plagiary, are mocked. In the second and third, Puff introduces and then exhibits a rehearsal of his appalling tragedy, the hilarious *The Spanish Armada.*

**Critical Quarterly, The** Founded in 1959 by its editors C. B. Cox and A. E. Dyson, *The Critical Quarterly* publishes poems, reviews and critical articles with a strong focus of interest on modern literature. Its contributing poets have included **Ted Hughes, Philip Larkin, R. S. Thomas** and **Charles Tomlinson**, and it has published articles by **W. H. Auden, William Empson, Raymond Williams** and **David Lodge,** among many others.

**Crock of Gold, The** A fantasy by **James Stephens,** published in 1912. The tale begins by introducing the Two Philosophers who lived in the centre of the pine wood called Coilla Doraca and who married the Grey Woman of Dun Gortin and the Thin Woman of Inis Magrath. Thereafter other characters arrive and vanish at will, among them the Philosophers' children Seumas Beg and Brigid Beg, the farmer Meehawl MacMurrachu and his daughter Caitlin, who follows Pan and marries the god Angus Og. Blending the faery and folk idioms with ancient legend, Stephens created a meandering tale which depends upon his inventive use of inconsequential asides and false trails for its elusive charm.

**Crockett, S. R.** See **kailyard school.**

**Crofts, Freeman Wills** See **detective fiction.**

**Croker, John Wilson** 1780–1857 Essayist and critic. Born in Galway and educated at Trinity College, Dublin, he became a Tory MP, held various offices, and was Secretary of State for the Navy for 20 years. He was a founder of and regular contributor to *The Quarterly Review*, and the author of the notorious attack on **Keats's** *Endymion*. His book, *Essays on the Early Period of the French Revolution* (1857), was a collection of *Quarterly* papers. He edited *Royal Memoirs of the French Revolution* (1823) and **Boswell's** *Life of Johnson* (1831). Croker is the alleged original of the character of Rigby in **Disraeli's** *Coningsby.*

**Croker, T[homas] Crofton** 1798–1854 Irish folklorist. Born in Cork, he received little formal education and served as an apprentice in a mercantile firm from the age of 15. He moved to London in 1818 and gained a clerkship at the Admiralty, where he worked until 1850. Croker was the first collector of folk-tales (chiefly from Munster) to make his material attractive to a wide range of readers. His *Fairy Legends and Traditions of the South of Ireland* (1825) is a classic of its kind. Although he altered the tales to suit his own taste, his work is valuable both as an act of preservation and as a stimulus to further researches and to writers as various as Wilhelm Grimm, **Sir Walter Scott, Maria Edgeworth** and **W. B. Yeats,** all of whom praised Croker highly.

He was a contributor to *Fraser's Mazazine* and a member of the Camden Society, the Percy Society, the British Archaeological Association and a Fellow of the Society of Antiquaries of London. He died at Brompton.

**Croly, George** 1780–1860 Author of historical romances. Born in Dublin and educated at Trinity College, he became rector of St Stephen's Walbrook in 1810. He wrote a tragedy, *Catiline* (1822), and a number of romantic and narrative poems. In *Salathiel* (1829) he employs the theme of the 'wandering Jew' to describe life in Rome under Nero, and Jersualem at the time of its destruction by Titus. *Marton* (1846) is set during the days of the French Revolution and the Napoleonic wars.

**Crompton, Richmal** Pseudonym of the children's writer Richmal Crompton Lamburn (1890–1969). Born in Lancashire, she was educated first in Cheshire and later at London University. While teaching classics at Bromley High School for Girls she wrote short stories for magazines in her spare time. The mischievous small boy called William whom they introduced proved popular enough to justify a collection, *Just William* (1922). It was an instant success, far outselling the adult fiction which Richmal Crompton also began to produce. At first, the 'William' stories were also aimed at a grown-up audience, allowing his creator to enjoy the mayhem he brings to his family and its suburban environs without adding any admonitory note of the sort still expected in books written exclusively for the young. More 'William' books followed in quick succession after she became a full-time writer, a decision forced on her by a serious attack of polio in 1923. Although she occasionally tired of William, turning instead to her more modestly successful adult fiction, she continued the series until her death. By this time more than 8 million copies had been sold, and William's tussles with his irritable father, long-suffering mother and permanently suspicious older brother and sister had also been featured in radio, film and television.

**Cronin, A[rchibald] J[oseph]** 1896–1981 Novelist. Cronin was born in Cardross, Scotland, and educated at Dumbarton Academy and Glasgow University, where he studied medicine. He graduated as a physician in 1919, after working in the naval medical service during World War I. He practised medicine in South Wales, making a special study of industrial medicine, from 1921 to 1924, when he was appointed Medical Inspector of Mines. In 1928–30 he practised in London.

After the success of his first novel, *Hatter's Castle* (1931), Cronin gave up medicine for writing. In the years that followed he produced a large number of popular novels which drew upon his Scottish childhood and his experiences in the Welsh coal-mining valleys. Many were subsequently made into successful films: *Hatter's Castle* in 1941, *The Stars Look Down* (1935) in 1939, *The Keys of the Kingdom* (1942) in 1944 and *The Green Years* (1944) in 1946. A play, *Jupiter Laughs*, was produced in 1940. His autobiography, *Adventures in Two Worlds*, appeared in 1952. His later works included *The Judas Tree* (1961) and *A Pocketful of Rye* (1969).

***Crossing the Bar*** A poem by **Alfred Tennyson**, written in 1889 while crossing the Solent, and published in the same year. Tennyson said that he completed the poem in 20 minutes, though he had had it in mind for some months. It was his wish that it should appear at the end of all editions of his poems.

***Crotchet Castle*** A novel by **Thomas Love Peacock**, published in 1831, which shows off to advantage Peacock's individual brand of romantic satire. As in ***Nightmare Abbey*** and ***Gryll Grange***, the plot is minimal and subordinate to the conversation. The chief participant is the Revd Dr Folliott, gourmet and classicist, who disputes with other characters, notably Mr Skionar, a transcendental philosopher, and Mr MacQuedy, a Scottish political economist.

**Crothers, Rachel** 1878–1958 American playwright, born in Illinois. Crothers's plays brought her box-office success throughout her long career; their central thematic concern – with their realistic characterization, dialogue and settings – was always the possibility of freedom for the modern woman in a world dominated by men. In her first major drama, *The Three of Us* (1906), she relates the story of a determined spinster's attempt to save her and her brothers' interests in a Nevada mine. In *A Little Journey* (1918), a self-centred young woman's world is changed by the experience of a train wreck. *He and She* (1920) examines the conflicts in a woman's life between her artistic career and her role as wife and mother. *Nice People* (1921) describes the rebellion and reform of three flappers. *Mary the Third* (1923) recounts another flapper's feelings about love and marriage. In one of her more enduring social comedies, *Let Us Be Gay* (1929), she examines a woman's attempt to gain freedom through marital infidelity. Her last successful production, *Susan and God* (1937), is the story of another woman's search for independence through religion. Among her other notable plays are: *A Man's World* (1910), *Young Wisdom* (1914), *Old Lady 31* (1916), *39 East* (1919), *Expressing Willie* (1924), *A Lady's Virtue* (1925), *As Husbands Go* (1931) and *When Ladies Meet* (1932).

**Crowe, Catherine** 1800–76 Novelist and short-story writer. Born Catherine Stevens, at Borough Green in Kent, she published children's books, dramas and novels, including *Susan Hopley* (1841) and *Lilly Dawson* (1847). But her most popular work was a collection of stories on ghostly and supernatural themes, *The Night Side of Nature* (1848).

**Crowne, John** *c.* 1640–1712 English playwright whose family emigrated to Nova Scotia in 1656, but returned in 1660 when the land granted to them by Cromwell was seized by the French. Crowne's dislike of court manners may have resulted from his service as a gentleman usher to a London lady. He was the author, none the less, of an impressive court **masque**, *Calisto* (1675). His comedies, much better than his tragedies, are unusually firm in their moral judgements. They include *The Country Wit* (1676), *City Politiques* (1683), the excellent *Sir Courtly Nice* (1685) and *The Married Beau* (1694).

*Crucible, The* A play by **Arthur Miller**, first performed in New York in 1953, at the height of Senator McCarthy's campaign against communists and their associates. The play draws a clear analogy between McCarthy's activities and the Salem witch-hunts.

The play is set in Salem in 1692, and follows the unfolding horror of the witch-trials there. Abigail, the niece of Reverend Parris and a mischief-maker, has led some of the girls of Salem in a naked frolic. To protect herself, she claims to be the victim of witchcraft, and frightens the other girls into making the same claim. When the witch-finders are brought to Salem, Abigail and the girls denounce any member of the community who resists them. One by one the weak and the virtuous are brought to trial, condemned, and hanged. The strongest resistance comes from John Proctor, a good-hearted man whom Abigail had seduced when she was working for his wife. His confession of adultery promises to end Abigail's reign of terror, but his wife lovingly denies it, and Proctor goes to his death knowing that society has lost its ability and its right to distinguish between good and evil.

**Cruden, Alexander** 1701–70 Compiler of *Cruden's Concordance* to the Bible. A strict Presbyterian, he was born in Aberdeen and educated at the university there before moving to London as a tutor and bookseller. He began compiling his *Concordance* in 1736, presenting the first copy to Queen Caroline in 1737; it long remained the standard word-guide to the Authorized Version (see **Bible in English**). Thorough and accurate, but eccentric and sometimes mad, he elevated his career of proof-reading into

'Alexander the Corrector's' campaign of moral castigation. He died disappointed.

**Cruelty, Theatre of** An idea of the anti-rational scope of theatrical performance was outlined by the French actor and writer, Antonin Artaud, in a *First Manifesto of the Theatre of Cruelty* (1932) and a *Second Manifesto* (1933). Believing that 'the theatre only exists on a level which is not quite human', Artaud sought for ways of uprooting the complacency of audiences by drawing attention to the precariousness of conventional moral values. His theatre is concerned with human behaviour under extreme threat of provocation, and his ideas have been influential, even when only partially comprehended, in the modern theatre. No prominent English playwrights can be properly called disciples of Artaud, though he himself enlisted in the prospective repertoire of his theatre **Shelley**'s *The Cenci*, **Tourneur**'s *The Revenger's Tragedy* and **Ford**'s *'Tis Pity She's a Whore*.

**Cruikshank, George** 1792–1878 Caricaturist and illustrator. He was born in London, son of the artist Isaac Cruikshank. In addition to his long and successful career in political caricature, and the impassioned advocacy of temperance which occupied much of his later years, Cruikshank also illustrated books by many contemporaries. These include: **Pierce Egan**'s *Life in London* (1821), though Cruikshank was so dismayed by Egan's departure from any moral design that he left completion of the plates to his brother Robert (?1790–1856); **Dickens**'s *Sketches by Boz* (1836–7) and *Oliver Twist* (1839), in which he is reputed to have used himself as the model for his depiction of Fagin; *Jack Sheppard* (1839) and other novels by **William Harrison Ainsworth**; the first three series of **R. H. Barham**'s *Ingoldsby Legends*; and **Harriet Beecher Stowe**'s *Uncle Tom's Cabin* (1853).

*Cuckoo and the Nightingale, The* (or *The Boke of Cupide*) A poem once attributed to **Geoffrey Chaucer** but now generally accepted as the work of **Sir John Clanvowe** whose name appears at the end of the poem in one of its manuscripts. It was probably written between 1390 and 1403. The poem is a **dream-vision** and records an overheard debate between a cuckoo who is opposed to love and a nightingale who praises it. The narrator drives away the cuckoo and the nightingale pledges loyalty to him. The poem shows the influence of *The Owl and the Nightingale* and Chaucer's *Parlement of Foules*. See also **Chaucerian apocrypha**.

**Cudworth, Ralph** 1617–88 Philosopher. One of the more prominent of the **Cambridge Platonists**, Cudworth had a distinguished academic career. Elected a fellow of Emmanuel College, Cambridge, in 1639, he was appointed Master of Clare Hall by the parliamentary commission in 1645; he became Regius Professor of Hebrew in the same year and Master of Christ's College in 1654. He rejected the Hobbesian type of atheism and was a steadfast opponent of religious dogmatism. His chief work (left unfinished) was *The True Intellectual System of the Universe* (1678); it argues that the Christian religion is the only real source of knowledge. His *Treatise concerning Eternal and Immutable Morality* was published posthumously (1731).

**Cullen, Countee** 1903–46 American poet. A leading figure of the **Harlem Renaissance**, Cullen was reared by foster parents in Harlem, New York. He was educated at New York University and at Harvard. His first verse collections were *Color* (1925), *Copper Sun* (1927), and *The Ballad of the Brown Girl: An Old Ballad Retold* (1927). While in France on a Guggenheim scholarship he wrote *The Black Christ, and Other Poems* (1929), the title piece of which recounts the lynching of a black youth for a crime he did not commit. Cullen's only novel, *One Way to Heaven* (1932), is a social comedy of lower-class blacks and the bourgeoisie in New York City. *The Medea and Some Poems* (1935) is a collection of sonnets and short lyrics together with a translation of Euripides' tragedy (in prose, with the choruses in verse). Cullen also edited the magazine *Opportunity* and compiled an anthology of black poetry entitled *Caroling Dusk* (1927).

**Culler, Jonathan** See **structuralism**.

***Culture and Anarchy*** A volume of essays by **Matthew Arnold**, originating in Oxford lectures and articles for ***The Cornhill Magazine***, published as a book in 1869.

Its sub-title, *An Essay in Political and Social Criticism*, points to Arnold's intentions, for he saw the England of his time as being in political, social and religious ferment, and sought to show that the remedy lay in culture – the supreme realization of the human spirit under reason. Observing in his first chapter, 'Sweetness and Light', that culture is 'a study of perfection' whose 'motto' should be 'To render an intelligent being more intelligent', Arnold avers that a second view of it ought to be 'To make reason and the will of God prevail'. Then follow chapters showing the imbalances, inequities and confusions of English life that impede the advance of culture. Arnold fears a drift towards anarchy through an excess of liberty, of freedom unrestrained by any centre of authority. No one, he believes, has an idea of the state, 'of the nation in its collective and corporate character of controlling, as government, the free swing of

this or that one of its members in the name of the higher reason of all of them, his own as well as that of others'. None of the various classes – barbarians (aristocracy), philistines (middle class) and populace (lower class) – provides an adequate centre of authority. Similarly, the two great traditions of Hebraism, with its 'strictness of conscience', and Hellenism, with its 'spontaneity of consciousness', have vied with each other in English life down the centuries instead of being mutually complementary. Concluding chapters attempt some pragmatic solutions, but Arnold returns to culture as the true saving grace – culture with its development of the individual self in the interests of the greater whole, with its aspiration to a 'fair chance' for the growth of the moral life and with its constant movement towards perfection.

**Cumberland, Richard** 1732–1811 Playwright, too often identified with **Sheridan**'s cruel portrait of him as Sir Fretful Plagiary in ***The Critic***. He was educated at Westminster School and Trinity College, Cambridge, of which he became a fellow in 1752. His subsequent political career was not sufficiently successful to spare him the toil of writing for a living. His **sentimental comedies,** or 'bastard tragedies' as **Goldsmith** called them, often avert disaster only because of a villain's unlikely change of heart in the fifth act. Plays popular in their own time, like *The Brothers* (1769), *The West Indian* (1771) and *The Jew* (1794), can best be read as transitional pieces, carrying sentimental comedy towards **melodrama.** Cumberland wrote nearly 50 plays as well as three novels, *Arundel* (1789), *Henry* (1795) and *John de Lancaster* (1809), a few volumes of negligible verse, two volumes of *Memoirs* (1806–7), scores of journalistic essays and two books on Spanish painters and painting.

**Cummings, Bruce Frederick** See **Barbellion, W. N. P.**

**cummings, e[dward] e[stlin]** 1894–1962 One of the most technically innovative poets of this century, cummings was born in Cambridge, Massachusetts, and graduated from Harvard in 1916. He drove an ambulance in France during World War I, and stayed on in Paris after the armistice. His first published work was a novel, *The Enormous Room* (1922), based on his mistaken imprisonment in a French detention centre during the war. This was followed by collections of verse, *Tulips and Chimneys* (1923) and *XLI Poems* (1925).

*&* and *is 5* (both 1925) presented cummings's new style, which was influenced by jazz and contemporary slang and characterized by an innovative use of punctuation and typography, as in the use of lower case letters for his own

e e cummings, self-portrait.

ingham was apprenticed at age 11 to his brother as a stonemason. As a boy he walked in **Burns**'s funeral procession and nourished his literary ambitions on the works of **Scott**. He became a friend of the self-taught bard **James Hogg**, who, together with Scott, suspected his authorship of *Remains of Nithsdale and Galloway Songs* (1810), a volume of poems which were innocently published by Cromek as authentic old Scottish ballads. In 1813 he published *Songs, Chiefly in the Rural Dialect of Scotland* and in 1814 he was tempted down to London by Cromek, who introduced him to the sculptor Sir Francis Chantrey. From 1814 to 1841 he was Chantrey's trusted assistant, secretary and occasional artistic adviser, pursuing his literary interests in his spare time. From 1819 to 1821 he contributed a series of stories called 'Recollections of Mark Macrabin' to **Blackwood's Magazine**, and then changed to **The London Magazine**, becoming associated with a circle of writers that included **De Quincey**, **Lamb**, **Hazlitt** and **Thomas Hood**. He collected old ballads and stories, published as *Traditional Tales of The English and Scottish Peasantry* (1822) and *Songs of Scotland, Ancient and Modern* (1825). His *Lives of the Most Eminent British Painters, Sculptors and Architects* appeared in six volumes in 1829–33, and in 1834 he produced his edition of *The Works of Robert Burns*, prefaced with a biography of Burns that contained much important new material. His romances and longer dramatic poems are little read today and he is chiefly remembered by a handful of poems and ballads, which include 'A Wet Sheet and a Flowering Sea' and 'Hame, Hame, Hame'.

**Cunningham, J[ames] V[incent]** 1911–85 American poet, born in Cumberland, Maryland, and educated at Stanford. He taught at the Universities of Hawaii, Chicago, Virginia, and, from 1953 until his retirement, at Brandeis. His first volume of poetry, *The Helmsman*, was published in 1942 and was followed by *The Judge is Fury* (1947) and *Doctor Drink* (1950). The poems in all three volumes are notable for their economy of presentation, and their use of precise metres and traditional verse forms. An accomplished Renaissance scholar, Cunningham was drawn to the form of the epigram, publishing *Trivial, Vulgar, & Exalted: Epigrams* in 1957. His later collections include *The Exclusions of a Rhyme; Poems and Epigrams* (1960), *To What Strangers, What Welcome: A Sequence of Short Poems* (1964) and *Some Salt: Poems and Epigrams* (1967). *The Collected Poems and Epigrams of J. V. Cunningham* and *Selected Poems* were both published in 1971. His *Collected Essays* appeared in 1976.

name. Features of this poetry include the use of capital letters and punctuation in the middle of single words, phrases split by parentheses, and stanzas arranged to create a visual design on the page. Formal devices were often used as visual manifestations of theme or tone; the poem's typographical dimension itself becomes a new level of meaning.

cummings's other works include *ViVa* (1931), *No Thanks* (1935), *1/20* (1936), *Collected Poems* (1938), *50 Poems* (1940), *1 x 1* (1944), *Poems 1923–1954* (1954), *Ninety-Five Poems* (1958), *73 Poems* (1963) and *Complete Poems 1913–1962* (1972). He also published two plays, a book of drawings and paintings, a travel book, and *i, six nonlectures* (1953).

**Cunningham, Alan** 1784–1842 Miscellaneous writer. Born at Keir, Dumfriesshire, Cunn-

**Cunninghame Graham, R[obert] B[ontine]** 1852–1936 Short-story writer, essayist, traveller and social reformer. Born in London, the son of a Scottish laird and a half-Spanish mother, he was educated at Harrow and in Brussels. He visited South America at the age of 17 and became an expert horseman. Later he was Liberal MP for North-West Lanarkshire, but became a socialist and disciple of **William Morris,** receiving a six weeks' prison sentence for assaulting the police during a demonstration.

He is chiefly remembered for *Mogreb-el-Aksa* (1898), an extraordinary account of his dangerous journey to discover the forbidden city of Tarudant in Morocco. The book was much admired by **George Bernard Shaw** and **Joseph Conrad.** His other works include *Thirteen Stories* (1900), *A Vanished Arcadia* (1901; the story of the Jesuit settlements in Paraguay), *Success* (1902) and *Scottish Stories* (1914).

**Curnow, Allen** 1911– New Zealand poet and dramatist. Born in Timaru, South Canterbury, the son of an Anglican vicar and a writer of light verse, he was educated at Christchurch Boys' High School and subsequently worked as a cadet journalist on the Christchurch *Sun*. He was a part-time student at Canterbury University before deciding to follow his father into the ministry. He attended St John's College, Auckland, an Anglican theological college, between 1930 and 1933, subsequently obtaining a BA from the University of Auckland in 1938. It was during this period that his poetry was first published in the university magazine, *Kiwi*, and, with poets like **R. A. K. Mason,** A. R. D. Fairburn and **Robin Hyde,** he became a member of the Phoenix group that played an important part in New Zealand's literary renaissance. In 1934 he gave up his theological studies and from 1935 worked as a full-time journalist on the Christchurch *Press*, first as a reporter, then as a sub-editor on foreign news, and for two years in the 1940s as drama critic. In 1949 he worked on *The News Chronicle* in London. After returning to New Zealand in 1950 he became a member of the Department of English at the University of Auckland, where he worked until his retirement in 1976. All Curnow's poetry is strongly concerned with the quest for cultural identity in his native New Zealand and, believing that poets should not cut themselves off from ordinary people, he has been a fierce champion of the demotic voice. The best of his early volumes, *Island and Time* (1941), explores both the geographical and temporal isolation of the poet. His middle verse, collected in *Poems, 1949–57* (1957) is more personal and meditative and demonstrates considerable variety in its range of verse forms. His more recent poetry, such as *Trees, Effigies, Moving Objects* (1972), shows an increased concern with the self-referentiality of language. Curnow's other volumes of verse include *Not in Narrow Seas* (1939), *Sailing or*

*Drowning* (1943), *At Dead Low Water, and Sonnets* (1949), *A Small Low Room with Large Windows* (1962) and *Collected Poems, 1933–1973* (1974). His plays, *The Axe, The Overseas Expert, The Duke's Miracle* and *Resident of Nowhere*, are collected in *Four Plays* (1972).

**Cursor Mundi** (*The Course of the World*) An anonymous Middle English poem in rhyming couplets, probably written in the early 14th century in the North of England. Dedicated to the Virgin Mary, the work is a spiritual history of the world from the Creation to Doomsday. It deals at length with all the principal episodes of both Testaments as well as including apocryphal material. The historical section ends with an exhortation to all people to repent and live a good Christian life, and with a prayer to the Virgin. There follow various miscellaneous pieces, differing from one manuscript to another.

The work was widely known, and survives in several manuscripts. The poet maintains his sense of purpose and the structure of the work despite its length and succeeds in creating a unified poem from diverse material and sources. The work is characterized by the author's humanity and his plain language skilfully written into fluent and regular verse.

**Curzon, Robert, 14th Baron Zouche** 1810–73 Traveller, writer, manuscript collector. He was born in London, and educated at Charterhouse, then Christ Church, Oxford. He travelled to the Levant in 1833–4 and again in 1837–8. These journeys resulted in *Visits to Monasteries in the Levant* (1849), an entertaining account of travel in the Near East and the joys and problems of manuscript collecting in the decaying libraries of Greek monasteries. He wrote *Armenia* (1854) after going there in 1841 as private secretary to Sir Stratford Canning. The manuscripts he collected were deposited in the British Museum after his death. Curzon's life and interests are well documented by a collection of letters (deserving of publication) to his friend the Revd Walter Sneyd; these are now in Keele University Library. Curzon spent his last years quietly at his family home, Parham in Sussex.

**Cymbeline** A play by **William Shakespeare,** first performed *c.* 1610 and published in the First Folio of 1623. There are various sources, of which **Holinshed**'s *Chronicles* is primary only in the sense that it deals with the reign of the early Christian king, Cymbeline.

The emotional centre of the play is the relationship of Imogen, Cymbeline's daughter, and Posthumus Leonatus, whom the King has raised. Angered by their marriage, Cymbeline banishes Posthumus almost as the play opens. The intrigues and complications that delay their reunion make the matter of the play, which can be seen as a prolonged testing of their love. The many strands are kept separate until the extraordinary (and in some eyes clumsy) final act.

The story of Iachimo is one strand. Taking refuge in Rome, the banished Posthumus finds solace in the company of the cynical Iachimo, but wagers Imogen's virtue against Iachimo's boast that he will seduce her. Imogen does, indeed, resist all Iachimo's wiles, and he is forced to cheat by hiding in a trunk to gain access to her bedroom. There he observes the mole on the breast of the sleeping Imogen, takes note of the room's furnishings and steals a bracelet. Confronted with this evidence of Imogen's infidelity, Posthumus swears vengeance and sails for England intent on killing her.

Iachimo is not the only schemer against the marriage. Cymbeline's second wife, a wicked queen of fairy-tale proportions, wants Posthumus dead so that her oafish son Cloten can marry Imogen. The desperate Imogen learns of her husband's anger from his servant Pisanio while they are travelling to Milford Haven for what she had supposed to be a love-tryst. She disguises herself as a boy (significantly named Fidele). Cloten pursues her, determined to kill Posthumus and rape Imogen; but 'Fidele', lost in Wales, has fallen among friends. Neither she nor they know that the two 'sons' of the exiled general Belarius are, in fact, Cymbeline's own lost sons – that discovery must await the final act – but the love between them protects Imogen from Cloten, who is killed and beheaded by one of the boys.

It can be appreciated that the final act has to work hard to achieve all the necessary reconciliations, as well as to achieve a political peace between Rome and Britain. It is not only credibility which the plot strains, but also compre-hension. *Cymbeline* is a difficult play to categorize. The editors of the First Folio grouped it among the tragedies, but its outcome is comedic and even its deeper tones are dependent more on peril than on actual pain. It stands with the group of last plays, **Pericles**, **The Winter's Tale** and **The Tempest**, all written to satisfy the new fashion, encouraged by the staging facilities of the indoor theatre at the **Blackfriars**, for spectacle and romance.

**Cynewulf** An Old English poet of the late 8th and early 9th centuries, Cynewulf is known through the inscription of his name in runic characters after four poems in the **Exeter Book** and the **Vercelli Book**. All that is known of his life is the information drawn from one of his poems, *Elene*: at the time of writing he was old, and he had experienced some sort of spiritual enlightenment when he was granted grace and his poetic gift, but his earlier life he considered sinful.

The poems firmly identified as the work of Cynewulf are those that bear the inscription, *The Ascension* (the second part of *Christ*), *Juliana*, *Elene* and *The Fates of the Apostles*, which tells of the deeds and deaths of the 12 apostles. Various other poems have been attributed to him at different times, but without evidence.

*Cynthia's Revels, or, The Fountain of Self-Love* A comedy by **Ben Jonson**, first performed by a **boys' company** in 1600 and published in 1601. The play was a contribution to the war of the theatres, and much of the satire has lost its point. Virtually plotless, it is chiefly memorable for its self-portrait of Jonson as Crites, an impartial judge of social and artistic standards, and for the lyric hymn to Diana, 'Queen and huntress, chaste and fair'.

# D

**D'Avenant, Sir William** 1606–68 Playwright, poet and theatre manager. Son of the keeper of the Crown Inn in the Cornmarket at Oxford, D'Avenant took pains to encourage the rumour that his true father was **Shakespeare**. In fact, he was the poet's godson.

D'Avenant was educated at grammar school in Oxford, then became page to the Duchess of Richmond and subsequently to **Fulke Greville**, who was his patron for a time and encouraged his interest in the theatre. His plays include *The Tragedy of Albovine* (1629), *The Cruel Brother* (1630) and *The Wits* (1636). From 1635, follow-

ing the pleasure occasioned at court by the best of his **masques**, *The Temple of Love*, he was given charge, including authorship, of all such entertainments during Charles I's reign. *Madagascar, with Other Poems* was published in 1638 and D'Avenant was made Poet Laureate (**Ben Jonson** having died in 1637). He fought as a Royalist in the Civil War and was knighted at the siege of Gloucester in 1643. With **Cowley**, **Waller** and **Thomas Hobbes** he was one of the group of exiles in Paris with Henrietta Maria from 1646 until his appointment as governor of Maryland in 1649. He was captured at sea by

Strolling players performing at a banquet in a rich man's house. From Moyses Waler's *Album Amicorum, c.1610*. During the Puritan interregnum the closure of the playhouses obliged the actors to live any way they could. But a ban on private 'entertainment' was impossible to enforce and D'Avenant had little trouble assembling a company of skilled players at the Restoration. *Add. MS 18991, f.11*. British Library.

Cromwell's forces and imprisoned in the Tower, where he continued work on his verse epic *Gondibert* (1651). His pardon, which came in 1654, was probably the result of **John Milton**'s intervention on his behalf.

Free once more and with his love for the theatre unimpaired by vicissitude, D'Avenant organized clandestine theatrical performances. Cromwell's personal rule had only two years to run and the Puritan attitude to the theatre seems to have relaxed: at any rate D'Avenant secured authority for the presentation of an entertainment which, though given at a private house, could be attended by anyone who paid for admission. So in 1656, at Rutland House, *The Siege of Rhodes* was performed and drama began to return to life in England after being suppressed for 14 years.

At the Restoration D'Avenant received one of Charles II's patents to form a company of players (the other went to **Thomas Killigrew**); he set about recruiting the best of the younger men and introducing new ideas of presentation such as the proscenium, elaborate scenery, and the use of machinery. He produced adaptations of Shakespeare that infuriated many but did serve to bring Shakespeare back to the stage and to nourish the reawakened English theatre. D'Avenant will, and should, always be remembered for the part he played in that reawakening, though his own contributions to English drama have not held the stage. He is buried in Westminster Abbey.

**d'Israeli, Isaac** 1766–1848 Father of **Benjamin Disraeli**, and a man of letters in his own right. He was born at Enfield, of Jewish descent, but quarrelled with the elders of his synagogue and had his children baptized, thus making his son's political career possible. He spent his teens studying philosophy with a tutor in Amsterdam and wrote a poem against commerce, which offended his father, a merchant. He went to Paris, where he frequented literary circles. He spent his life as a literary gentleman and married Maria Besevi, who gave him five children. He died at his home in Buckinghamshire.

His published works are *Curiosities of Literature* (1791), *Essay on the Literary Character* (1795), *Miscellanies, or Literary Recreations* (1796), *The Calamities of Authors* (1812–13) and *Quarrels of Authors* (1814). He also wrote historical works on King James I (1816) and on King Charles I (1828–31). In 1833 he published *The Genius of Judaism*. Three volumes of his projected history of English literature appeared in 1841 under the title *Amenities of Literature*. He also wrote four unsuccessful novels.

**D'Urfey, Thomas** 1653–1723 Playwright and song-writer, remembered above all as the editor of the influential collection of ballads in six volumes, *Wit and Mirth, or, Pills to Purge Melancholy* (1719–20). Born in Exeter, D'Urfey moved to London and became an intimate of both Charles II and James II. He was a versatile dramatist, always willing to adapt to changing tastes. *Madame Fickle* (1676) and *A Fond Husband* (1677) are intrigue comedies in the style of **Wycherley** and **Etherege**, *Squire Oldsapp* (1678) and *The Virtuous Wife* (1679) are more farcical, *Sir Barnaby Whigg* (1681) and *The Royalist* (1682) are political satires, while D'Urfey's best plays, *Love for Money* (1691) and *The Richmond Heiress* (1693), reflect the move towards a greater respect for moral standards in the drama.

**dactyl** See **metre**.

**Dafydd ap Gwilym** *c*.1320–80 Welsh Poet. In English his name means 'David son of William'. He was born in the parish of Llanbadarn Fawr, just outside Aberystwyth. Few details of his life are known but his family certainly belonged to the influential class of Welsh landed gentry known as *uchelwyr*, who maintained their prestige after the English conquest of Wales in 1284 by serving the crown as highly placed administrators. References in the poems indicate that Dafydd moved in a circle of poets and their noble patrons in Cardiganshire but also travelled widely throughout Wales. He had access to English, French and Latin literary traditions, often in oral rather than written form, and probably through the medium of Welsh in many cases.

He composed entirely in Welsh. His collected works, edited by Thomas Parry, consist of about 150 poems, a relatively large number testifying to his stature and popularity long after his death. Only a handful survive in contemporary manuscripts. Even if there were more early manuscripts now lost, it must be assumed that oral transmission played a crucial part in disseminating and preserving his work. Composed within a bardic tradition which had been absorbing Continental themes at least since the Norman Conquest, his poems therefore have affinities with the Middle English **Harley Lyrics** and with **Chaucer**, his contemporary. His themes cover almost the entire range of medieval genres and topoi: **courtly love**, dialogues between lovers, nature description, **dream-vision**, humorous poems in a **fabliau** style. Most of his lyrics use a traditional Welsh bardic metre called the *cywydd*, widely practised in the 14th and 15th centuries. He often employs *dyfalu*, a series of compressed and striking images describing a particular object, and extended metaphors which develop a witty central image throughout the poem. The obligatory bardic device of *cynghanedd*, a complex and highly specific set of alliterative and rhyming patterns within each line of verse, adds richness to a poetry intended to be spoken or sung aloud. His work suggests the concerns of his *uchelwyr* audiences. The recurrent motifs of bardic patronage, the desirability of possessing women and land, and the unremitting satire of bourgeois values, all point to a context in which a traditional Welsh nobility is guarding its privileges as rulers and landowners while aligning itself with the governing English aristocracy.

The complete works of Dafydd ap Gwilym have been translated by R. M. Loomis (1982). Rachel Bromwich has produced a selection with textual notes (1982).

**Dahl, Roald** 1916–90 Children's author. Born in Wales of Norwegian parentage, Dahl was educated at Repton School before serving as a fighter pilot during World War II. In 1943 a children's book *The Gremlins* was published, followed by many adult short stories. He returned to children's fiction with *James and the Giant Peach* (1961), a good-humoured almost surreal fantasy about a boy travelling around the world in an enormous fruit. This was followed by *Charlie and the Chocolate Factory* (1964), which became an international best-seller as well as a successful film. It deals with one small boy's search for the ultimate prize in fierce competition with other, highly unpleasant children, many of whom come to sticky ends as a result of their greediness. The cruelty involved in such descriptions upset many adult critics, as did some of Dahl's grotesque characterizations in other books. But young readers often relish just those excesses that critics tend to deplore; they also enjoy Dahl's immense verbal facility, much in evidence in *Revolting Rhymes* (1982) and *Dirty Beasts* (1984), which take a typically unsentimental look at favourite animals. *The BFG* (1982) won him his first literary prize, perhaps a sign that the former division between his popularity with children and acceptability to critics had begun to heal.

**Dahlberg, Edward** 1900–77 American novelist and critic, born in Boston, the illegitimate son of a lady barber from Kansas City. At an early age, he was sent to an orphanage in Cleveland, Ohio, but ran away and later enrolled at the University of California and then at Columbia. In 1926 he settled in Europe, where he wrote his first book, *Bottom Dogs* (1929), a semi-autobiographical novel about a childhood in slums and orphanages. This was followed by *From Flushing to Calvary* (1932), about the slums of New York City, and *Those Who Perish* (1934), about the effects of Nazism upon American Jews. Dahlberg's interests were wide-ranging: his literary criticism is collected in *Do These Bones Live?* (1941); studies of 'classical sensuality' and myth comprise *The Sorrows of*

*Priapus* (1957) and *The Carnal Myth* (1968); and essays on modern society and modern writers are collected in *The Flea of Sodom* (1950), *Truth is More Sacred* (1961) and *Alms for Oblivion* (1964). *Because I Was Flesh* (1964) is his autobiography. Other books include *Cipango's Hinder Door* (1965, poems), *Epitaphs of Our Times* (1967, letters), *The Confessions of Edward Dahlberg* (1971) and *The Olive of Minerva* (1976).

**Daily News, The** A radical newspaper founded by **Charles Dickens** and edited by him from January until October 1846. He was succeeded by his friend **John Forster**. The newspaper was absorbed by *The Daily Chronicle* in 1930 and became *The News Chronicle*, continuing publication under this name until 1960.

**Daisy Chain, The** A novel by **Charlotte M. Yonge**, published in 1856. The story concerns the large family (the 'Daisy Chain' of the title) of Dr May, who becomes a widower under tragic circumstances in the early chapters. His ugly but warm-hearted daughter, Ethel, with her untidiness, her clumsiness and her marked capacity for scholarship, is the most memorable and best loved of all the characters.

**Daisy Miller** A short novel by **Henry James**, published in 1879. Daisy Miller is touring Europe with her mother and brother. The expatriate American community interprets her innocence and lack of concern for social convention as immodesty and forwardness, and she is ostracized. One of its number, Frederick Winterbourne, though agreeing with that judgement, is also charmed by her innocence. In Rome Daisy takes up with Giovanelli, a young Italian of no social position. Winterbourne meets them one evening viewing the Coliseum by moonlight without a chaperone, and berates Daisy for her lack of social decorum. Shocked and hurt by his reaction, she returns at once to her hotel, where she contracts malaria and dies after a week.

**Dallas, E[neas] S[weetland]** 1828–79 Journalist and literary critic. Born in Jamaica, he was brought to England at the age of four and educated at Edinburgh University, where he studied philosophy under **Sir William Hamilton**. As a journalist, he worked on *The Times* during the editorship of **J. T. Delane**. His critical writing, represented by *Poetics: An Essay on Poetry* (1852) and *The Gay Science* (1866), took a scientific approach to aesthetics, viewing the aim of art as pleasure and the imagination as a function of the unconscious mind.

**Dalrymple, Sir David, Lord Hailes** 1726–92 Scottish jurist, historian and man of letters.

He was born at Edinburgh and educated at Eton and at Utrecht, where he studied civil law. He enjoyed the financial independence simply to have pursued his literary interests, but he became a judge notable for his humanity and an expert legal historian.

Uncomfortable with the major Scottish literary figures (**David Hume**, **Adam Smith** and **William Robertson**), Dalrymple looked south for more congenial correspondents. Political and religious differences did not deter him from forming friendships with such men as **Johnson**, **Burke**, **Horace Walpole**, and Bishops Hurd, **Percy** and Warburton. It was Dalrymple who fired the young **Boswell** with the desire to know Johnson. Thought by Burke 'a clever man and generally knowing', Dalrymple published many works, chiefly of legal history and anti-sceptical Christian antiquarianism. He contributed to *The World* and *The Gentleman's Magazine*. He edited ballads and other ancient Scottish poetry. His most significant historical work was *Annals of Scotland* (1776–9). The *Annals* were praised for their exactness and lightly revised by Johnson, who found the narrative 'clear, lively, and short'. **Gibbon**, too, thought well of Dalrymple's diligence and accuracy as a historian, though Dalrymple later took issue with him in *An Inquiry into the Secondary Causes which Mr Gibbon has assigned for the Rapid Growth of Christianity* (1786).

**Daly, (John) Augustin** 1838–99 American playwright and theatre manager, born in North Carolina and educated in New York City. Daly was first a drama critic, then a professional playwright. *Leah the Forsaken* (1862) was the first of about 100 plays which he wrote or, more often, adapted, in regular collaboration with his brother Joseph. The best include spectacular melodramas like *Under the Gaslight* (1867), *The Flash of Lightning* (1868) and *The Red Scarf* (1868) and comedies about American high society like *Divorce* (1871), *Pique* (1875) and *Love on Crutches* (1884). *Horizon* (1871) is a frontier drama, impressive in its time.

Daly's major contribution to the American theatre was as a company manager and director. At the Fifth Avenue Theatre from 1869 to 1873, and then, particularly, at Daly's Theatre from 1879 until his death, he established ensemble companies, the finest in America, increasing the prestige of his country's actors during tours to London and Paris.

**Dame Sirith** A Middle English **fabliau** written *c.* 1272–83. It tells how Wilekin unsuccessfully tries to seduce Margery in her husband's absence and then goes to Dame Sirith for assistance. She feeds her dog mustard and pepper then takes it to Margery, saying that it is her daughter transformed by a clerk whose advances she refused and showing her the dog's tears as proof. In horror, Margery tells her to bring Wilekin to her and submits to his desires. The major part of the poem is in the form of dialogue and it may have been intended for performance, either by several actors, or, which is perhaps more likely, by a minstrel using mime to distinguish the different characters.

**Damnation of Theron Ware, The** A novel by **Harold Frederic**, published in 1896. Its British title was *Illumination*. It tells the story of a talented young Methodist minister's growing disillusionment with conservative, small-town life in upstate New York, and his attraction for exotic, sophisticated ideas which in the end prove disastrous for him.

Through his friendships with Dr Ledsmar, a scientist, Father Forbes, a Catholic priest, and Celia Madden, the beautiful Catholic church organist, Theron Ware becomes fascinated with experimental science, biblical criticism, and aesthetics, which, together with the life-styles of his new acquaintances, represent for him a new sort of intellectual and personal freedom outside his narrow Methodist experience. He becomes increasingly detached from his wife and congregation, and increasingly drawn to the beautiful and free-spirited Celia; a series of exciting encounters between the two culminate in a kiss at a church picnic. Elated, Theron follows Celia to New York City and calls on her in her hotel room, but she upbraids him for spying on her and taking a prurient interest in her affairs. Devastated by her rejection and by the realization that he has misunderstood her apparent freedom – it rests on a tradition of spirituality and church institutions that are foreign to him – Theron falls ill. When he eventually recovers, he and his wife go west to Seattle, where he will try to go into business and perhaps into politics.

**Dampier, William** 1652–1715 The voyager, discoverer and privateer was born in the West Country, near Yeovil. His career took him to the West Indies, South America, the Pacific, Australia and the East Indies. During one of Dampier's early voyages (1703–4) a Scottish seaman named Alexander Selkirk asked to be put ashore on the Pacific island of Juan Fernández after a quarrel with his captain. (See also **Rogers**, **Woodes** and *Robinson Crusoe*.) Dampier's accounts of his travels and adventures are vivid, entertaining and of considerable historical interest: *A New Voyage Round the World* (1697), *Voyages and Descriptions* (1699) and *A Voyage to New Holland* (1703–9).

**Dana, Richard Henry, Jr** 1815–82 American novelist and social reformer. The son of a minor poet and journalist of the same name, Dana was born in Cambridge, Massachusetts. He went to

Harvard, but at the end of his second year (1834) withdrew because of eye trouble. For the sake of his health he signed on as a seaman for a voyage to California around Cape Horn. He worked on the Pacific coast for a year, collecting and curing hides, and then returned to Boston by sea. He completed his education at Harvard Law School.

Dana's first work, the article 'Cruelty to Seamen', published in the *American Jurist* in 1839, expressed a deeply felt anger at what he had seen on his voyages. In 1840, the year he was admitted to the Bar, he published *Two Years Before The Mast*, the book that made him famous and that described the life of the ordinary seaman as it was lived day by day. The following year saw the publication of *The Seaman's Friend* (in Britain *The Seaman's Manual*), which among other things explained to sailors exactly what their rights – as well as their duties – were. His account of another voyage, *To Cuba and Back* (1859), was not a success.

A champion of the underprivileged, Dana opposed slavery in word and deed. He freely gave assistance to fugitive slaves and in doing so antagonized the Boston mill-owners, because cheap raw materials from the South boosted their profits. He hoped for a political career, but his edition of Henry Wheaton's *Elements of International Law* (1866) involved him in accusations of plagiarism, and his appointment as ambassador to Great Britain was withdrawn by the Senate. Convinced that his life had been a failure, in 1878 he withdrew to Europe, where he died four years later. *Speeches in Stirring Times* (1910) and *An Autobiographical Sketch* (1953) were published posthumously.

**Dance to the Music of Time, A** A sequence of 12 novels by **Anthony Powell**, published between 1951 and 1975.

The sequence is composed of *A Question of Upbringing* (1951), *A Buyer's Market* (1952), *The Acceptance World* (1955), *At Lady Molly's* (1957), *Casanova's Chinese Restaurant* (1960), *The Kindly Ones* (1962), *The Valley of Bones* (1964), *The Soldier's Art* (1966), *The Military Philosophers* (1968), *Books do Furnish a Room* (1971), *Temporary Kings* (1973) and *Hearing Secret Harmonies* (1975).

The sequence is an example of the **roman fleuve**, or 'river novel', and like Proust's *A la Recherche du Temps Perdu* is intended to be read as a unity. It constitutes a history of 20th-century English life. Nicholas Jenkins, its central figure and narrator, is a member of the post-World War I generation and a member of a set in which the life of the artist overlaps with that of polite and fashionable society. In the first novel, *A Question of Upbringing*, Jenkins thinks of 'Poussin's scene in which the Seasons, hand in hand, facing outward, tread in rhythm to the

notes of the lyre that the winged and naked greybeard plays'. Then he imagines 'Human beings, facing outward like the Seasons, moving hand in hand in intricate measure'. Subsequent novels expand Jenkins's world to include a panoramic and satirical view of the changes in the lives and fortunes of the English upper middle classes over the next 50 years – an epic enterprise.

Jenkins's own life takes place 'off stage', but as narrator he is constantly present as the selective recorder of the temporal flow of events. Characters' movements are formalized into the pattern of a dance, and Jenkins's role is that of a musician.

Among the work's memorable characters are the power-hungry Kenneth Widmerpool, whose beginnings are inauspicious, but who eventually achieves formidable influence through a series of ruthless manoeuvres, and Sir Magnus Donners, at whose mansion World War II is fanfared with a charade of the seven deadly sins.

The sequence is named after Poussin's painting.

**Dane, Clemence** Pseudonym of Winifred Ashton (1888–1965), playwright and novelist. Born at Blackheath, she was educated in England and France; after teaching in Geneva for a year, she studied art at the Slade and in Dresden. She gave up painting for acting, then devoted herself to writing. Her first and second novels, *Regiment of Women* (1917) and *Legend* (1919), were widely acclaimed, but she turned her attention to drama before returning to fiction with *Broome Stages* (1931), *The Moon is Feminine* (1938) and *He Brings Great News* (1944).

Dane's career as a playwright began with *A Bill of Divorcement* (1921), about a woman who divorces her husband on grounds of insanity in order to remarry, but comes up against the moral prejudices of the older generation. It was an outstanding success, never quite repeated by subsequent plays like the blank-verse *Will Shakespeare* (1921), *Granite* (1926) and *Wild Decembers* (1932), about the **Brontës**. She also wrote a study of *Tradition and Hugh Walpole* (1929) and a stage adaptation of **Max Beerbohm**'s story *The Happy Hypocrite* (1936).

**Daniel** An Old English poem preserved in the Junius manuscript (see **Junius, Francis**). It tells the story of Daniel from Exodus, which it usually follows closely. Beginning with the fall of the Israelites into sin and Nebuchadnezzar's plundering of Jerusalem, the poem goes on to give an account of Daniel's interpretation of the king's dreams, a vigorous description of the ordeal of the furnace and an incomplete account of Belshazzar's feast. In general the style is flat and uninspiring, but there are occasional redeeming passages.

**Daniel, Samuel** 1562/3–1619 Poet, translator, literary critic, tragedian and author of **masques**. Tradition has it that Daniel was born near Taunton and that his father was a music master. His brother John was also a musician. Daniel tutored the young William Herbert, later **Shakespeare**'s patron, and also Lady Anne Clifford, daughter of the Countess of Cumberland.

Twenty-eight of his sonnets appeared without his authority at the end of the 1591 edition of **Sidney**'s *Astrophil and Stella*. In 1592 Daniel first issued the work for which he is best remembered, *Delia*, a sequence of sonnets showing the influence of Desportes and Tasso. Revised and expanded over the years, the number of sonnets had grown from its original 50 to 57 by the 1601 edition of his *Works*. In 1592 Daniel also published *The Complaint of Rosamond*, in the manner of poems in **The Mirror for Magistrates**, adding to it in 1594 his Senecan closet tragedy *Cleopatra*. *Civil War* was printed in 1595, being expanded from four to five books the same year; it was never completed, though the narrative of the Wars of the Roses had reached the marriage of Edward IV by 1609. Written partly under the influence of Lucan, it in turn influenced Shakespeare's **Richard II** and the **Henry IV** plays. Daniel's *Poetical Essays* (1599) included two new works: *Musophilus*, a verse colloquium on the literary life, and *Octavia*, a verse epistle in the manner of Ovid's *Heroides*.

*A Defence of Rhyme* (1603) is Daniel's answer to *Observations in the Art of English Poesy* by **Thomas Campion**. In it Daniel answers the objections to the use of rhyme in poetry, sensibly arguing that whatever theorists may say, practice and use testify to its power. *Certain Small Poems* (1605) contains *Philotas*, a tragedy on the story of a rebellion against Alexander the Great. It was probably first acted in 1605 and was printed for the first time in this volume. It got Daniel into trouble, as he was suspected of portraying Essex's rebellion sympathetically.

Daniel also wrote court masques. *The Vision of the Twelve Goddesses* was performed at Hampton Court and printed in 1604. *Tethys's Festival* (1610), for the creation of Prince Henry as Prince of Wales, had scenery by Inigo Jones, and *Hymen's Triumph* was played at Somerset House in 1614 and printed in 1615. His masques gained Daniel the favour of Queen Anne, who danced in the Hampton Court masque, and she gave him the office of licensing all entertainments played by the Children of the Queen's Revels. He probably resigned this post to his brother in 1618. Daniel's historical work is *The Collection of the History of England*. The 1612 edition portrays events as far as the reign of Stephen and the enlarged edition of 1618 as far as that of Edward III.

He was admired by his contemporaries for his poetic skill and choice of language. The range of his literary productions and his choice of subjects and forms invites comparison with his contemporary **Michael Drayton**. Daniel's own assessment of his work is modestly confident, 'I know I shall be read among the rest / So long as men speak English.'

*Daniel Deronda* **George Eliot**'s last novel, published in eight parts between February and September 1876. The story is principally concerned with the destinies of two characters, Daniel Deronda, the adopted child of an English aristocrat, and Gwendolen Harleth, the spoiled and selfish elder daughter of a widow. In order to avoid penury as her family approaches destitution Gwendolen agrees to marry Henleigh Grandcourt, fully aware that he has children by his mistress and that his mistress has a prior claim to his hand. The marriage proves unhappy and Gwendolen finds herself drawn for spiritual guidance to Deronda. Deronda, who has rescued the Jewish girl, Mirah Lepidoth, from suicide, gradually discovers a dense Jewish world through Mirah and through her brother, Mordecai. He eventually learns that he too is a Jew and the novel ends with his determination to seek for his ancient racial and religious roots in Palestine.

Although the novel has seemed awkward and unbalanced to some critics, it has also been acknowledged to be George Eliot's most ambitious work, combining profound scholarship and an original power in describing character and thought. The novelist sought both a challenging shape for her narrative and a contrast between the lax, aristocratic mores of her English characters and the fervour and moral intensity of her Jewish ones. Unlike the novelist's earlier work, *Daniel Deronda* has a contemporary setting and radiates disquiet about the future of English society.

**Dark, Eleanor** 1901– Australian novelist. Born Eleanor O'Reilly, she married Eric Payten Dark in 1922. Her novels, which frequently explore the results of catastrophes which precede the action, include *Slow Dawning* (1932), *Prelude to Christopher* (1933) and *Return to Coolami* (1935). *The Timeless Land* (1941) and *Storm of Time* (1948) are fictionalized portraits of the early days of the Sydney settlement.

*Darkness at Noon* A novel by **Arthur Koestler**, written in German and published in translation (by Daphne Hardy) in 1940.

N. S. Rubashov, one of the old Bolshevik founders of the Soviet Union, is arrested during the night by 'No. 1's' (i.e. Stalin's) secret police. During his imprisonment he is subjected to lengthy interrogations, first by Ivanov (an old college friend and former battalion commander), then by Gletkin (a product of the state machinery). After protracted cross-questioning in which he recalls many of his past beliefs and actions, Rubashov is pronounced guilty. His conviction rests partly on the evidence of a young acquaintance, obtained by torture, and partly through his own self-confessed opposition to the system. At the end of the novel he is summarily executed in the cellar of the prison.

Like the earlier *Brave New World* (1932) by **Aldous Huxley**, and the later *Nineteen Eighty-Four* (1949) by **George Orwell**, the novel is a powerful indictment of political tyranny and inhumanity, and did much to alert the West to the reality of Stalinist Russia.

**Darley, George** 1795–1846 Irish poet and critic. He was born in Dublin and educated at Trinity College. From the 1820s he contributed essays, mainly on drama, to *The London Magazine* and later to *The Athenaeum*. His poetry included *The Errors of Ecstasie: A Dramatic Poem, with Other Pieces* (1822), *Sylvia, or, the May Queen: A Lyrical Drama* (1827) and *Nepenthe* (1835). His tragedy *Thomas à Becket: A Dramatic Chronicle* and his notable edition of the plays of **Beaumont** and **Fletcher** appeared in 1840. Darley was also an accomplished mathematician, publishing four popular guides to the subject.

**Darwin, Charles (Robert)** 1809–82 Natural historian and evolutionary theorist. Grandson of **Erasmus Darwin** and son of a doctor, Robert Darwin, he was born at Shrewsbury, where he later went to school. He attended Christ's College, Cambridge, in 1828–31, after a period as a medical student at Edinburgh. Though not seen by his family or himself as intellectual at this time, he impressed James Henslow, Professor of Botany at Cambridge, who encouraged him to study geology and subsequently recommended him as naturalist for the voyage of the survey-ship *Beagle* (1831–6), the most important formative period of his intellectual life. Darwin's wide interests – in geology, zoology, botany, wild-life especially beetles – prepared him for an extraordinarily wide-ranging career of observation and theorizing. His sea and land voyage of five years round the world produced his *Journal of Researches into the Geology and Natural History of the Various Countries Visited by HMS Beagle* (1839), a highly readable and thoughtful account of his response to the tropics, his encounters with 'primitive' peoples, and his realization of how complex are relations between living forms within an environment. These forms include the human and he writes movingly about enslavement and about the conflicts between indigenous Indians and colonizing Spaniards.

Charles Darwin. A detail from the portrait by J. Collier, 1881. National Portrait Gallery, London.

Darwin declared that his reading of **Malthus**'s *Essay on Population* precipitated the formulation of his theory of natural selection, though there are indications in his journals of the late 1830s that he had more or less reached the concept some months earlier. Darwin long delayed publication of his findings: because of the disturbing cultural and religious implications of his views he wished to render his theories as near as possible impregnable by adducing manifold and various evidences. He recognized from the start that 'descent with modification' removed humankind from its centrality in the natural order and undermined the time-honoured religious myths of Genesis. He wrote *The Origin of Species* (1859) rapidly, under the impetus of knowing that Alfred Russel Wallace had reached conclusions similar to his concerning the mechanism of evolutionary development.

Responses to Darwin's theories immediately recognized their implications for humankind, although he had deliberately excluded discussion of 'man's place in nature' from his argument. In particular, objection was made to the implied kinship with other species. One of the earliest literary responses was **Charles Kingsley**'s *The Water Babies* (1863).

Much of Darwin's later work emphasizes the connection of humankind with other species. In *The Descent of Man and Selection in Relation to Sex* (1871) and in *The Expression of the Emotions in*

*Man and Animals* (1872) he juxtaposes material from anthropology, primate studies, and sociology. All these new disciplines had themselves been partly formed by the ideas in *The Origin of Species*. The emphasis on 'sexual selection' opened up connections between evolutionary theory and aesthetics and cultural studies. It also gave an opening to 'social Darwinism'. This draws on the writing of **Herbert Spencer** as much as on that of Darwin: it shifts the sense of 'fitness' from that of the aptness of the organism to its current environment to a quasi-moral concept of 'fitness' as physical and mental power. This produces a hierarchical order in society, a constant struggle for dominance by strong individuals, and a readiness to jettison the weak. Such views form part of the debate in the work of **Jack London** and **Theodore Dreiser** and coloured many later literary responses to Darwin's work.

Among his own contemporaries and at the turn of the century **George Eliot**, **Samuel Butler**, **Thomas Hardy** and **Joseph Conrad** were writers who energetically responded to – and in Butler's case, contended against – Darwin's work. **George Bernard Shaw**, **H. G. Wells** and **Virginia Woolf** demonstrate how differently Darwin could be read in literary terms. In the 20th century his ideas have become part of the apparatus of assumptions to a degree where it is difficult to track them independently, though their power is still manifest, particularly among writers of **science fiction** such as **Isaac Asimov** and Stanislaw Lem.

**Darwin, Erasmus** 1731–1802 Botanist, poet and grandfather of the celebrated naturalist, Erasmus Darwin was born at Elston in Lincolnshire and educated at St John's College, Cambridge. He became a physician and practised for most of his life at Lichfield, where he established a botanical garden and wrote a poem called *The Botanic Garden*, which embodied Linnaeus's system (Part 2, *The Loves of the Plants*, was published first, in 1789; Part 1, *The Economy of Vegetation*, in 1791). The poem is in heroic couplets, with the goddess of Botany's exposition occupying the first four cantos; it was ridiculed by **John Hookham Frere** and **George Canning** in *The Loves of the Triangles*, published in *The Anti-Jacobin*. Erasmus Darwin published his theory of the laws of organic life on the evolutionary principle in *Zoonomia* (1794–6) and *Phytologia* (1799).

**Daryush, Elizabeth** 1887–1977 Poet. Daughter of **Robert Bridges**, she married in 1923 and lived in Persia until returning to England in 1927. An isolated figure, she staunchly ignored the innovations of **Pound** and **Eliot**, clinging to traditional poetic procedures and archaic diction. But she is important for her pioneering technical experiments with syllabic verse, which predate those of **Marianne Moore**, **Auden** and **Thom Gunn**. Admired by **Yvor Winters** (who called her 'one of the few distinguished poets of our century'), **Roy Fuller** and **Donald Davie**, her poems, in *Charitessi 1911* (1912), seven books of *Verses* (1930–71), *The Last Man* (1936), *Selected Poems* (1972) and *Collected Poems* (1976), are notable for their quiet stoicism and questing for disillusioned truth.

***David Copperfield*** A novel by **Charles Dickens**, published in 19 monthly parts from May 1849 – November 1850 (one volume 1850). The novel's full title, *The Personal History, Experience and Observations of David Copperfield the Younger, of Blunderstone Rookery, Which He Never Meant To Be Published On Any Account*, suggests the degree to which Dickens sought to frame his narrative around the personal memoirs of an observant professional writer. David traces his childhood and youth, marred by his widowed mother's remarriage to Mr Murdstone and death, and by his distressing experience working in a London factory (an incident modelled on Dickens's own boyhood suffering). Escaping from London, David takes refuge at Dover with his aunt, Betsey Trotwood, and, after a period of conventional schooling and a brief legal career, becomes a novelist. His marriage to Dora Spenlow proves unhappy but David is

David Copperfield's future is decided. The illustration by Phiz depicting the momentous interview in which Betsy Trotwood confronts the Murdstones. Also present are David (left) and Mr Dick (centre).

nonetheless devastated by her early death. His friendship for James Steerforth is equally disturbed by Steerforth's elopement with Emily, the niece of the Yarmouth fisherman, Mr Peggotty. The novel gradually reveals David's slow grasp of the meaning of his 'Experience', and the disciplining of his heart. He finally finds happiness with the faithful Agnes Wickfield, whom he has known since childhood and whose own future had seemed to be threatened by the wiles of her father's sometime clerk, Uriah Heep. The verbal extravagance, and the pecuniary improvidence of Wilkins Micawber, with whom David lodges during his unhappy London days, is to some extent modelled on that of the novelist's own father, John Dickens. Dickens himself proclaimed that this novel was his own 'favourite child'.

**David Simple, The Adventures of**: *Containing an Account of His Travels through the Cities of London and Westminster in the Search of a Real Friend*. A moral romance by **Sarah Fielding**, first published in 1744.

David Simple discovers that his younger brother, to whom he is devoted, has used a forged will in an attempt to rob him of his inheritance. Disillusioned, David sets out on a journey to rediscover honest friendship. His encounters with Mr Orgueil and his insolent wife, Mr Spatter, who is the chief critic of Orgueil, and Mr Varnish, the chief critic of Spatter, nearly drive him to despair. Then he meets Cynthia, excluded from her father's will and ill-treated by her employer, and Camilla and Valentine, brother and sister who have become the victims of their stepmother's perfidy.

David helps them, and the four become friends. David and Camilla, and Valentine and Cynthia gently fall in love and become betrothed. Camilla and Valentine are reconciled to their father, and the two couples settle down in a happy community established by David's generosity. The novel gives an excellent picture of the London scene and Sarah Fielding's moralizing is skilfully controlled. The book was very popular in France.

**Davidson, Donald (Grady)** 1893–1968 American poet, critic and historian, born in Tennessee, Davidson helped found (1922) and edit (1922–5) *The Fugitive*, the magazine of a group of Southern writers that included **John Crowe Ransom**, **Allen Tate** and **Robert Penn Warren**. Of those in the group, Davidson remained the most committed to its aims to preserve both a distinctly Southern literature and the traditional agrarian economy of the South. His poems were published in *An Outland Piper* (1924), *The Tall Men* (1927), *Lee in the Mountains, and Other Poems* (1938), *The Long Street* (1961) and *Poems, 1922–1961* (1966). His other writings include *The Attack on Leviathan; Regionalism and Nationalism in the United States* (1938), *Still Rebels, Still Yankees, and Other Essays* (1957), *Southern Writers in The Modern World* (1958) and *The Spyglass: Views and Reviews, 1924–1930* (1963). He also contributed to *I'll Take My Stand: The South And The Agrarian Tradition* (1930).

**Davidson, John** 1857–1909 Poet, playwright, novelist and essayist. Born near Glasgow, the son of a minister in the Evangelical Union, Davidson briefly attended Edinburgh University and subsequently, in 1877, became a schoolmaster, a calling he reluctantly followed until 1889 when he left Scotland to pursue a literary career in London. Writing extensively from an early age, he was first published in 1885 when a farcical novel, *The North Wall*, and a verse drama, *Diabolus Amans*, appeared. A year later came a chronicle play, *Bruce*, and in 1889, *Plays*, one of which was the unique fantasy *Scaramouch in Naxos*.

Settled in London, Davidson was an occasional visitor at the **Rhymers' Club** where he had the company of **Yeats**, **Beerbohm**, **Gosse** and others of that circle; he also contributed to **The Yellow Book**. During the 1890s Davidson wrote more novels and a great deal of poetry: his *Fleet Street Eclogues* (1893) were followed by *Ballads and Songs* (1894), *A Second Series of Fleet Street Eclogues* (1896), *New Ballads* (1897) and *The Last Ballad* (1899).

In the last decade of his life Davidson was exceptionally prolific in the production of his blank-verse *Testaments* and in poetic drama. Among the latter were *Godfrida* (1898), *Self's the Man* (1901), *The Knight of the Maypole* (1903), *The Theatrocrat* (1905), *The Triumph of Mammon* (1907) and *Mammon and his Message* (1908). The last two formed part of an unpublished trilogy. Of greater significance were the *Testaments*, some of which were published as sixpenny pamphlets; they were entitled *The Testament of a Vivisector* (1901), *The Testament of a Man Forbid* (1901), *The Testament of an Empire-Builder* (1902), *The Testament of a Prime Minister* (1904) and *The Testament of John Davidson* (1908). Short stories, adaptations from the French, journalism and prose sketches also flowed from his pen.

Ever at odds with the world, Davidson nevertheless possessed a lyrical sense as well as a feeling for the ballad form. His philosophy of life, fashioned from contemporary scientific lore, revolt against the Christian God and perhaps touched by Nietzschean thought, was perplexing to many and found few followers. A thwarted, disappointed man, John Davidson drowned himself off the Cornish coast.

**Davie, Donald (Alfred)** 1922– Poet and critic. He was born in Barnsley, Yorkshire, and educated there and at St Catharine's College, Cambridge. After military service, he lectured at Trinity College, Dublin (1950–7), and Cambridge (1958–64), and became Professor of English at Essex (1964–8), where he was also Pro-Vice Chancellor (1965–8). He then emigrated to the United States to become Professor at Stanford and later Vanderbilt Universities.

Davie was the major theorist of the **Movement**: his critical books *Purity of Diction in English Verse* (1952) and *Articulate Energy* (1955) were instrumental in establishing an 'Augustinian' discipline of chastened poetic language as the measure for what poetry should be in recent times. His own poetry appeared in *Brides of Reason* (1955), *A Winter Talent* (1957), *The Forests of Lithuania* (1959) and *New and Selected Poems* (1961). Two volumes of *Collected Poems* followed in 1972 and 1983. The later Davie has partially repudiated the enthusiasm and special 'romanticism' of his early 'Augustinian' protest. Travel and close consideration of European and American literatures have made him critical of what he describes as 'Little-Englandism' among his contemporaries. His later poetry is more experimental and less cerebral. He has also written critical studies of **Scott** (1961), **Pound** (1964) and **Hardy** (1974), and a volume of memoirs, *These the Companions* (1982).

**Davies, Idris** 1905–53 Poet. Born in Rhymney, Monmouthshire, he was the son of a miner and went into the pits himself at the age of 14. After the 1926 General Strike he went to teachers' college and Nottingham University, becoming a schoolteacher in London in 1928. One of the few genuinely working-class poets to emerge from the 1930s, he produced two sequences about the valleys, *Gwalia Deserta* (1938) and *Angry Summer* (1943), as well as *Tonypandy* (1945) and *Selected Poems* (1953). His early death was caused by cancer.

**Davies, John** *c.* 1565–1618 Poet. Usually called John Davies of Hereford (his birthplace) to distinguish him from his contemporary **Sir John Davies**. Davies of Hereford wrote a philosophical poem, *Mirum in Modum: A Glimpse of God's Glory and the Soul's Shape* (1602), the physiological and psychological *Microcosmos* (1603) and *Humours Heaven on Earth* (1605), a description of the plague of 1603. *The Scourge of Folly* (*c.* 1610) is a book of complimentary epigrams addressed to distinguished figures of his time, including **John Donne**, **Shakespeare**, **Ben Jonson** and **Samuel Daniel**.

**Davies, Sir John** 1569–1626 Poet. Davies was educated at Winchester and The Queen's College, Oxford, which he entered in 1585. He stayed there only a year and a half and did not take a degree. He studied law at the New Inn and then the Middle Temple, which he entered in 1588, and became a barrister in 1595. Davies was disbarred in 1598 for a fight in which he hit a friend with a cudgel. This friend was Richard Martin, to whom Davies refers as my 'better half, my dearest friend' and to whom he dedicated *Orchestra*. Davies was reinstated in 1601 after apologizing and with the insistent support of Lord Keeper Egerton. During this period he became a founder member of the Society of Antiquaries.

Davies was one of the messengers who carried the news of Elizabeth's death to James VI in 1603. He gained the new King's favour and his legal career flourished. He was knighted and made successively Solicitor General of Ireland, and, at the King's personal insistence, Speaker of the Irish Parliament in 1613. He would have become Lord Chief Justice of England but died the day before he was to have assumed the office.

Davies's most intense period of poetic activity was between 1593 and 1599. *Orchestra, or, A Poem of Dancing* (1596) begins with Antinous persuading the chaste Penelope to dance. It becomes a celebration of ordered movement: Love instructs the created world to dance. Traditionally the poem has been seen as a solemn celebration of the harmonious and hierarchical 'Elizabethan world picture', although Davies's contemporaries saw it as a frivolous poem, and the author himself invokes 'Terpsichore, my light muse'. *Nosce Teipsum* (1599, 'Know Thyself') is an expository poem on natural philosophy and the immortality of the soul, its faculties and its relation to the body and to the senses. There was a family tradition that Davies wrote it after his expulsion from the Middle Temple. *Hymns of Astraea* (1599) is a collection of **acrostic** poems spelling out 'Elisabetha Regina'.

Davies's other poetry includes the usual sonnets produced by poets in the 1590s, and also 'Gulling Sonnets' which revolt against and mock Petrarchanism. He was also a writer of occasional verse, some for entertainments, verse paraphrases of the Psalms, and satirical epigrams which earned for him the description of 'our English Martial'. The *Epigrams and Elegies* (?1590), which also included posthumous works by **Marlowe**, were burned on the instruction of the Archbishop of Canterbury in 1599. Davies also wrote works on Ireland and on the offices of High Steward and Earl Marshal.

**Davies, Robertson** 1913– Canadian novelist, playwright and critic. Born in Thamesville, Ontario, he was educated at Upper Canada College, Queen's University, and Balliol College, Oxford. He spent some time in England as an actor before returning to Canada to become literary editor of *Saturday Review*. He later worked as editor of *The Peterborough Examiner* and as a publisher. He was Professor of English at the University of Toronto, and later Master of Massey College. He created the inhabitants of 'Salterton', the town described with wit and generosity in *Tempest Tost* (1951), *Leaven of Malice* (1952) and *A Mixture of Frailties* (1958). Other works include *Fifth Business* (1970), *World of Wonders* (1975) and *What's Bred in the Bone* (1986), shortlisted for the Booker Prize. He has also written numerous plays and critical works, especially on **Shakespeare**. He is a Senator of the Stratford Shakespeare Festival and has written three books on the festival with Tyrone Guthrie.

**Davies, W[illiam] H[enry]** 1871–1940 Poet and writer of autobiography. He was born at Newport, Monmouthshire, the son of a publican, and was educated at elementary school before drifting through a series of labouring jobs. In his twenties he took to the road, making his way to New York, then to the Klondike. In Canada he was injured while jumping a train and had a leg amputated. He returned to England and lived in dosshouses for sixpence a night. A prolific poet, he published at his own expense, and sent *The Soul's Destroyer* (1905) to well-known people asking them to forward the price of the book. *New Poems* (1907) and *Nature Poems and Others* (1908) followed, attracting praise from **Edward Thomas** among others. 600 poems appeared in his *Collected Poems* of 1943, some of which were brief nature lyrics, and others which reflected the harsher side of his life on the road. His *Complete Poems* appeared in 1963, with an introduction by **Osbert Sitwell**.

The *Autobiography of a Super-Tramp* (1908) appeared with a preface by **Shaw** and has become Davies's best-known book. He was also the author of two novels, *A Weak Woman* (1911) and *Dancing Mad* (1927), and further autobiography in *Beggars* (1909), *The True Traveller* (1912), *A Poet's Pilgrimage* (1918) and *Later Days* (1925). *Young Emma* (posthumously published, 1980) recounted his courtship and marriage to his young wife in 1923.

**Davin, Dan[iel]** 1913– New Zealand novelist and short-story writer. Born in Invercargill of Irish parents, he was educated at Roman Catholic schools and at the University of Otago, before attending Balliol College, Oxford, as a Rhodes Scholar from 1936 to 1939. During World War II he served first with the Royal Warwickshire Regiment and then with the New Zealand Division in Greece, Crete (where he was wounded), North Africa and Italy. He was awarded the MBE and three times mentioned in dispatches. After the war he returned to Oxford and worked for the University Press, rising to become Director of its Academic Division in

1974. Since retiring, he continues to live in Oxford. Davin established his reputation as one of the leading New Zealand writers of his generation in the late 1940s, with the publication of his novels, *Cliffs of Fall* (1945), *For the Rest of Our Lives* (1947) and *Roads from Home* (1949), and his volume of short stories, *The Gorse Blooms Pale* (1947). Much of his work deals with his Irish Catholic New Zealand upbringing, but he has also written fiction based on the war experiences of the New Zealand Division in *For the Rest of Our Lives* and on the experiences of New Zealanders in post-war London in *The Sullen Bell* (1956). Whatever the locale the characteristic mode of Davin's fiction is reflective and his concerns are primarily social and psychological. Sometimes considered to be a writer who has failed to fulfil his early promise, he has also published *Not Here, Not Now* (1970), *Breathing Spaces* (1975), a number of critical works and anthologies and a volume of memoirs, *Closing Times* (1975).

**Daviot, Gordon** See **Mackintosh, Elizabeth**.

**Davis, Dick** 1945– Poet. Born in Portsmouth, he was educated at King's College, Cambridge, where he met **Robert Wells** and Clive Wilmer, sharing the volume *Shade Mariners* (1970) with them. He has travelled widely, teaching in Teheran (1970–8), California and Durham. A practitioner of the 'plain style', he reached maturity early, and it is difficult to date individual poems from his three collections, *In The Distance* (1975), *Seeing The World* (1980) and *The Covenant: Poems 1979–1983* (1984). In a tradition running through **Ben Jonson, Yvor Winters**, **J. V. Cunningham** and **Thom Gunn,** Davis's poems have clarity of diction and syntax, use traditional forms and metre, and are morally evaluative. As yet little recognized, he is an outstanding talent among flashier and overpraised contemporaries. He has also edited a selection of **Thomas Traherne**'s writings (1980), written *Wisdom and Wilderness: The Achievement of Yvor Winters* (1983), and with his wife, Afkham Darbandi, translated *The Conference of the Birds* (1984) from a 12th-century Persian religious allegory by Farid Attar.

**Davis, Jack** 1917– Australian poet and playwright. Born in Perth, Western Australia, he is, with **Colin Johnson** and **Kath Walker**, one of the few prominent Aboriginal writers – that is, authors who express themselves in print rather than in an oral form. He draws much from the traditions of his own people, the Nyoongarah of the south-west of Western Australia, but writes in English. He was director of the Aboriginal centre in Perth from 1967 to 1971 and he has actively supported Aboriginal political and cultural causes. Most of his published work has come fairly late in life. It includes two volumes of poetry, *The Firstborn* (1970) and *Jagardoo (Poems from Aboriginal Australia)* (1978), which express Aboriginal attitudes in a direct and personal manner. Davis is also the author of two widely praised plays: *Kullark (Home)* (1979), which portrays the devastating impact of the European settlers upon traditional Nyoongarah life, and *The Dreamers* (1982), in which the squalor of contemporary Aboriginal life is contrasted with nostalgia for the past. Davis himself performed in the original production of this play. The central motif in Davis's work is his pride in being an Aboriginal and his belief that his people can restore much of their cultural dignity in a contemporary Australia that will itself be enriched by this renewed infusion.

**Davis (or Davys), John** ?1550–1605 Davis was a navigator and explorer, one of the many who made attempts to discover the Northwest Passage. On one such trip in 1587 he established friendly relations with the Eskimos. Seeking a passage through the Straits of Magellan he discovered the Falkland Islands in 1592. Davis commanded one of the ships sent against the Armada and sailed with **Raleigh** to the Azores and Cadiz. He was killed by Japanese pirates on a voyage to the Indies. *The Seaman's Secret* (1595) is a treatise on navigation and *The World's Hydrographical Description* (1595) deals with the Northwest Passage.

**Davis, Rebecca (Blane) Harding** 1831–1910 American novelist and short-story writer. Much of Davis's fiction is set in her native Philadelphia, including her best-known story, 'Life in the Iron Mills' (published in *The Atlantic Monthly* in 1861), which portrays the frustrated and tragic life of Hugh Wolfe, a furnace-tender in an industrial mill, and his cousin Deborah, who brings herself to ruin when she tries to help him. One of the earliest exponents of the American realist school, Davis again portrayed the bleak lives of industrial workers in her novel *Margaret Howth* (1862), and of blacks in *Waiting for the Verdict* (1868). *John Andross* (1874) is a tale about political corruption.

**Davis, Richard Harding** 1864–1916 American journalist, novelist, short-story writer and playwright – one of the most prolific and popular writers of his day. Born in Philadelphia, the son of **Rebecca Harding Davis**, he became at a young age one of the leading journalists in America. In 1890 he was appointed managing editor of *Harper's Weekly*, and his travels in that capacity provided the material for *The West from a Car Window* (1892), *The Rulers of the Mediterranean* (1893), *Our English Cousins* (1894), *About Paris* (1895) and *Three Gringos in Venezuela and Central America* (1896). His subsequent experi-

ences as a war correspondent gave rise to *Cuba in War Time* (1897), *A Year from a Reporter's Note-Book* (1898), *The Cuban and Porto Rican Campaigns* (1898), *With Both Armies in South Africa* (1900), *Notes of a War Correspondent* (1910), *With the Allies* (1914) and *With the French in France and Salonika* (1916).

Davis also published over 80 short stories, 7 novels, and 25 plays. He was successful in all genres, although not much of his work survived his own day. His 11 short-story collections span his career from *Gallegher* (1891), *Van Bibber and Others* (1892) and *Ranson's Folly* (1902) to *The Lost Road* (1913) and *The Boy Scout* (1917). His novels include *Soldiers of Fortune* (1897), *The Bar Sinister* (1903) and *Vera the Medium* (1908). Among his most popular plays are *Ranson's Folly* (1902) and *Miss Civilization* (1905).

**Davis, Thomas (Osborne)** 1814–45 Irish poet and journalist. Posthumous son of an English army doctor and an Irish mother, Davis was born in Mallow and educated at Trinity College, Dublin. He was called to the Bar in 1837 but made his living chiefly by writing. Despite Protestant Tory antecedents and later Benthamite leanings he emerged in the early 1840s as the leading literary exponent of romantic nationalism in verse and prose. Much of his writing first appeared in *The Nation*, the patriotic newspaper he helped to found in 1842. Despite the historically well-informed reasonableness of his essays, stressing English and Scottish as well as Gaelic ingredients in Irish nationality, his verse could be bombastic and even racialist in its endeavours to provide Irishmen with new songs and ballads popularizing the spirit and sentiment of the old Gaelic tradition as he perceived it. His political fervour as much as his poetry deeply influenced later poets such as **Yeats**, who commended his 'moral radiance', and **Patrick Pearse**, who saw him as one of the four evangelists of Irish separatism. His best work, such as his poetic 'Lament for Eoghan Ruadh O'Neill' and *The Patriot Parliament of 1689* (1843), explores the disasters and achievements of the Irish past as stirring commentary on present possibilities.

**Dawe, (Donald) Bruce** 1930– Australian poet. Born at Geelong in Victoria, he left school at an early age and held a variety of jobs including farmhand and copyboy. Later he became a lecturer at Toowomba in Queensland. His inventive and witty poems use the everyday structures of Australian speech with new resourcefulness, and are distinguished by an element of simple nobility. 'Drifters' and 'Homecoming' – an elegy for the dead of the Vietnam War – are well known. His collections include *No Fixed Address* (1962), *A Need of Similar Name* (1965), *An Eye for a Tooth* (1968), *Beyond the Subdivision* (1969), *Heatwave* (1970),

*Condolences of the Season* (1971), *Just a Dugong at Twilight* (1975) and *Sometimes Gladness: Bruce Dawe. Collected Poems 1954–1978* (1978).

**Day, Clarence (Shepard)** 1874–1935 The son of a stockbroker, Day was born in New York City and educated at Yale. He served in the US Navy during the Spanish–American War, then worked as a businessman in New York, and eventually became a regular writer for *The New Yorker*. He is best known for his autobiographical writings, which include *God and My Father* (1932), *Life with Father* (1935), *Life with Mother* (1937) and *Father and I* (1940) – all characterized by their humorous examination of upper-class life in 19th-century New York. *Life with Father* was dramatized in 1939 by Howard Lindsay and Russel Crouse, and became a long-running success. Day's other publications include *This Simian World* (1920), *Thoughts Without Words* (1928), *In the Green Mountain Country* (1934), *Scenes from the Mesozoic and Other Drawings* (1935) and *The Crow's Nest* (1921), which was enlarged in 1936 as *After All*.

**Day, John** 1574–1640 Playwright and poet. Born in Norfolk and educated at school in Ely and at Gonville and Caius College, Cambridge, Day was active in the London theatre for a decade after 1598, initially as one of **Philip Henslowe**'s circle of writers. Of six extant plays in which he is known to have had a hand, four are probably his alone. They are: *Law Tricks* (1604) and *The Isle of Gulls* (1606), satiric comedies written for **boys' companies**; the attractive *Humour Out of Breath* (*c.* 1608); and the pastoral dialogues of *The Parliament of Bees* (published in 1641), which exhibits Day's poetic skills at their most fanciful. With **Henry Chettle**, Day wrote *The Blind Beggar of Bednal-Green* (1600) and with **William Rowley** and George Wilkins the patriotic picaresque piece *The Travails of the Three English Brothers* (1607), based on the adventures of the extraordinary Shirley family. This play contains an interesting scene in which the Shakespearean clown **Will Kemp** exhibits his skills, though it is not known whether Day was the author of it. *The Parnassus Plays* have also been attributed to Day.

**Day, Thomas** 1748–89 Educationalist and children's author. Born in London of wealthy parents and educated at Oxford, Day was an early, eccentric disciple of Rousseau. Attempting to bring up two orphan girls on the lines laid down in *Émile* with a view to marrying the more apt pupil, Day eventually chose a more conventional heiress when neither of his protégées wished to fall in with his scheme. In 1783 he wrote the first part of *The History of Sandford and Merton*, the second part following in 1786 and the final instalment in 1789. Totally didactic in purpose, the story followed the lives of Tommy Merton, the idle son of a rich gentleman, and Harry Sandford, the industrious son of a hardworking farmer. Tommy always does everything wrong, a point in no danger of being lost on the good Harry, ever on hand to set a better example. This unlikely tale became a best-seller during the next century, although it was probably always more popular with parents than with children. Day subsequently wrote *The History of Little Jack* (1788), another moral tale, about a child suckled by goats then raised by a God-fearing old man before returning to civilization to make his fortune.

**Day of Doom, The** A didactic poem by **Michael Wigglesworth**, published in 1662. Subtitled 'A Poetical Description of the Great and Last Judgement', it describes how God rewards the virtuous sheep with eternal life and condemns the sinful goats to eternal damnation. Cast in ballad lines of seven feet, it was easily memorized and was soon selected to supplement the catechism in the education of the young American Puritan: within a year of the first printing all 1800 copies had been sold, which suggests that one out of 35 New Englanders owned the poem by 1663. During the next 100 years it was reprinted frequently, and found its way into virtually all Puritan homes.

**Day-Lewis, C[ecil]** 1904–72 Poet and detective novelist. Born in Ballintubber, now in the Republic of Ireland, he was educated at Sherborne School and Wadham College, Oxford. At Oxford he first came into contact with **W. H. Auden** and the group of young poets around him. He worked reluctantly as a teacher in private schools until 1935, when he became a freelance writer. Of all the left-wing Auden group he was the only one to join and be active in the Communist Party, from 1935 until 1938. His first mature collections, *Transitional Poem* (1929) and *From Feathers to Iron* (1931), are lyric sequences, and in *The Magnetic Mountain* (1933) and *A Time to Dance* (1935), there is a clash between his Marxist politics and his tendency to Romanticism. *Overtures to a Death* (1938) contains his best political poems, 'Newsreel' and 'The Bombers'. Despite *An Italian Visit* (1953), with its chatty, travelogue poems, and *Collected Poems* (1954), his reputation declined after the war, as the intriguing conflicts of his Marxist poems were replaced by the dry formalism of *Pegasus* (1957), *The Gate* (1962) and *The Room* (1965). Increasing respectability brought many honours: he delivered the Clark lectures at Cambridge in 1946 (published as *The Poetic Image* the following year), served as Professor of Poetry at Oxford in 1951–6 and was appointed **Poet Laureate** in 1968 after the death of **John Masefield**. His collection *The Whispering Roots*

(1970), if unexciting, showed that public office had not dimmed his skill. The *Poems of C. Day-Lewis 1925–1972* appeared in 1977. He also made verse translations of Virgil, with *The Georgics* (1941), *The Aeneid* (1952) and *The Eclogues* (1952). Under the pseudonym of Nicholas Blake he made a distinguished contribution to **detective fiction** with some 20 novels, beginning with *A Question of Proof* (1935). Their hero Nigel Strangeways was originally modelled on Day-Lewis's friend Auden. *The Buried Day* (1960) is a volume of autobiography.

**De Boissière, Ralph** 1907– Novelist. A difficult writer to define nationally, he was born and educated in Trinidad but emigrated in 1948 to Australia, where he has written books with both Caribbean and Australian settings. Among his Caribbean works the best is probably *Crown Jewel* (1952), for a long time the neglected masterpiece of West Indian writing but successfully republished in 1981. Set in Trinidad on the eve of World War II, when the colonial presence is concealing injustices on a huge scale, it is a novel about political aspirations and popular culture. His principal later novels are *Rum and Coca-Cola* (1956) and *No Saddles for Kangaroos* (1964). He has been compared to the masters of European fiction, but his historical sensitivity is firmly rooted in the Caribbean.

**De Forest, John W.** 1826–1906 American novelist. Born in Connecticut, De Forest went to live in Syria with his brother when ill health prevented him from attending college. After his return to the USA he began to write. His *History of the Indians of Connecticut* (1851) was marked by a strict objectivity which later became a characteristic of his fiction. He served for three years as a Union army captain in the Civil War and in 1867 published *Miss Ravenel's Conversion from Secession to Loyalty*. A romance set during the Civil War and Reconstruction, it includes some grimly realistic battle scenes which anticipate those of **Stephen Crane**. Among De Forest's later novels are *Kate Beaumont* (1872), about South Carolina plantation society; and *Honest John Vane* (1875), a satire of political corruption. His Civil War memoirs, *A Volunteer's Adventures*, appeared posthumously in 1946; *A Union Officer in the Reconstruction* followed in 1948.

**De Jong, Meindert** 1906– American children's writer. Born in Holland, he emigrated with his family to America at the age of eight. But his best book, *The Wheel on the School* (1954), is set in his native country and describes how a group of Dutch schoolchildren plan to entice a stork back to nest on the roof of their school – a traditional sign of good fortune. By contrast, *The House of Sixty Fathers* (1956) memorably describes the plight of an abandoned Chinese boy during World War II, drawing on the author's experiences as a war historian in the Far East. Subsequent novels have returned to a Dutch setting: *Far Out the Long Canal* (1964) deals with a village frozen up during the winter and *Journey from Peppermint Street* (1968) is a lovingly detailed account of a boy's trip through North Holland on a visit to relatives.

**de la Mare, Walter** 1873–1956 Poet, short-story writer and anthologist. Born at Charlton, Kent, and educated at St Paul's Choir School, he worked for an oil company, and wrote poems for children, and poems about childhood for adults. His first volume, *Songs of Childhood*, was published in 1902 under the pseudonym Walter Ramal. 18 further volumes, including five of collected poems, were published before the definitive *The Complete Poems of Walter de la Mare* (1969). The best-known single volumes are *Peacock Pie: A Book of Rhymes* (1913), *Memory and Other Poems* (1938), *The Burning Glass and Other Poems* (1945) and *Winged Chariot* (1951). His lyrical poems of childhood and fantasy use a great variety of verse forms, and were described by **Edward Thomas** as 'the most original featherweight poetry of our time'. His volumes of short stories include *Broomsticks* (1925), *The Lord Fish* (1933) and *The Scarecrow* (1945). His main anthologies are *Come Hither* (1923), for children; *Behold This Dreamer* (1939); and *Love* (1943). De la Mare also published three novels, *Henry Brocken* (1904), *The Return* (1910) and *Memoirs of a Midget* (1921); critical works on **Rupert Brooke** and **Lewis Carroll**; and an edition of **Christina Rossetti**. He is buried in St Paul's Cathedral.

**de la Roche, Mazo** 1879–1961 Canadian novelist. Born in Toronto, she grew up on a fruit farm in Ontario. This experience gave her the background and setting for her novels, best characterized as regional idyll. Her early works, *Explorers of the Dawn* (1922), *Possession* (1923) and *Delight* (1926), attracted little attention, but *Jalna* (1927), set in an old house of that name, won *The Atlantic Monthly*'s $10,000 prize. Its sequel, *The Whiteoaks of Jalna* (1929), continued her success and another 14 novels were eventually added to the series. She also produced several other novels, including a number for young people, some one-act plays, historical studies and an autobiography, *Ringing the Changes* (1957). The romantic and optimistic character of her works ensured their popularity for some time.

**de Man, Paul** See **deconstructive criticism**.

**de Morgan, William (Frend)** 1839–1917 Artist and novelist. Born in London, he attended University College, London, and studied at the Royal Academy School. A friend and colleague of **William Morris** in the Arts and Crafts Movement, he made stained glass and, after 1870, the decorative tiles for which he is still remembered. Only in retirement did he turn to writing, achieving considerable success with *Joseph Vance* (1906) and eight more novels; the last two were completed by his wife, the artist Evelyn de Morgan. Digressive and reminiscential, they cast a Dickensian eye over the London of de Morgan's youth.

**De Profundis** An extended letter by **Oscar Wilde** to **Lord Alfred Douglas** ('Bosie'), written during the author's imprisonment in Reading Gaol. It complains of Bosie's selfishness, shallowness, parasitism, greed, extravagance, tantrums, pettiness and neglect, while praising the selfless devotion of Robert Ross ('Robbie'). Ross, who became Wilde's literary executor, gave the work its present title (from the opening line of Psalm 130) and published an edited version in 1905. A fuller text appeared in 1949.

**De Quincey, Thomas** 1785–1859 Prose writer. The son of a linen merchant, De Quincey was born in Manchester and received his first education from one of the guardians appointed after his father's death in 1793. From 1796 he lived with his mother at Bath, where he attended the grammar school and quickly acquired a reputation as an outstanding classicist. Following a trivial accident he was moved to an inferior school at Winkfield, Wiltshire, where he lost interest in formal education, and then to Manchester Grammar School from which he ran away in July 1802. Two years earlier he had first read *Lyrical Ballads* and now thought of presenting himself to **Wordsworth** in the Lake District, but decided that he could in the circumstances hardly expect to make a favourable impression on his hero and embarked instead on a tour of Wales. Completely destitute, he reached London in November, suffered extreme deprivations and befriended a young prostitute named Ann. The story of this London venture is told in the first part of the *Confessions of an English Opium Eater*. In March 1803 he was reconciled with his mother and guardians, and in December he entered Worcester College, Oxford. He read voraciously, made few friends at college and frequently absented himself to London, where in 1804 he first took opium to alleviate a prolonged attack of facial neuralgia. He experimented intermittently and secretly with the drug over the next nine years, until he became thoroughly addicted in 1812–13. He had begun a correspondence with Wordsworth in 1803, and in the summers of 1805 and 1806 travelled to the Lakes in order to visit him, but was on each occasion overcome at the last moment by feelings of his own inadequacy

Thomas De Quincey. A detail from the portrait by J. Watson-Gordon, 1845. National Portrait Gallery, London.

which forced him to turn back. A similar diffidence seems to have caused him to absent himself from the second part of his final examinations at Oxford in the spring of 1808, when success seemed certain. In August 1806 he came of age and inherited a modest sum which he soon spent, largely on books. He also made an anonymous loan of £300 to **Coleridge** whom he met in Bridgwater in the summer of 1807, and through whom he finally met Wordsworth at Dove Cottage, Grasmere, the first encounter leaving very favourable impressions on both parties, and on **Dorothy Wordsworth**. He now became totally devoted to his new friends, and when they moved to Allan Bank he took over the lease of Dove Cottage, which he held until 1834. The next few years were devoted to reading, social life and the performance of literary services to Wordsworth and Coleridge. Anticipating the exhaustion of his private means, he made a desultory attempt in 1812–15 to obtain legal qualifications. By 1813 he was a confirmed opium-addict, which estranged him from the Wordsworths, who also looked with disfavour on his affair with Margaret Simpson, a local farmer's daughter, whom he married in 1817, following the birth of a son in November 1816.

But for the need to support a family, De Quincey might never have become a writer. His work was almost entirely composed of contributions to magazines, and was collected only a few years before his death. From 1821 to 1824 he wrote mainly for *The London Magazine*, where *Confessions of an English Opium Eater* appeared in 1821, bringing him immediate notoriety and recognition. His 48 pieces for the periodical are remarkably varied both in quality and character, and include articles on Goethe, Herder, Richter, **Malthus**, Rosicrucians and Freemasons, English and German dictionaries, education, and one of his best critical essays, *On the Knocking at the Gate in Macbeth*. Following the demise of *The London Magazine* in turned to Edinburgh, and with the appearance of the first part of his article on Lessing in **Blackwood's Magazine** in November 1826 began the association which was to produce some of his best work in the next 23 years, including his long historical series entitled *The Caesars*, *The Last Days of Immanuel Kant*, his important article *Rhetoric*, and one of his humorous masterpieces, **On Murder Considered as One of the Fine Arts**. His Gothic novel *Klosterheim* appeared as a separate volume in 1832. Despite his productivity, De Quincey led a hand-to-mouth existence: he was briefly imprisoned for debt in 1832, forced into bankruptcy in 1833 and even harassed by creditors at the funeral of his son Julius in September of the same year. He now switched to *Tait's Edinburgh Magazine* in which he began publishing the 'Sketches . . . from the Autobiography of an English Opium Eater' (later entitled *Autobiographic Sketches*), and **Recollections of the Lakes and the Lake Poets** (1834–9), which effectively set the seal on his alienation from Wordsworth, Coleridge and **Southey**. *The Revolt of the Tartars* (1837), the uncompleted series *Suspiria de Profundis* (1845) with its magnificent dream-visions, and the two remarkable articles on *The Glory of Motion* and *The Vision of Sudden Death*, which make up *The English Mail Coach* (1849), appeared with *Blackwood's*, which also published his book, *The Logic of Political Economy* (1844); for *Tait's* he wrote an account of his gradual estrangement from Wordsworth and a criticism of his poetry, as well as articles on **Godwin**, **Hazlitt**, **Shelley**, **Keats** and **Pope**. In 1852 De Quincey turned to arranging and revising his life's work for Hogg's collected edition, entitled *Selections Grave and Gay from Writings Published and Unpublished*, which began appearing in 1853 and was completed with the 14th volume the year after his death.

***De Sapientia Veterum*** A Latin treatise by **Francis Bacon**, published in 1609 and translated into English by **Sir Arthur Gorges** as *The Wisdom of the Ancients* in 1619. Like many Renaissance philosophers, Bacon believed that the Greek myths formed a repository of ancient wisdom concerning the phenomena of the physical world and the principles of human nature that had been coded into their narrative. Like the parables of the Bible, the fables of the myths relate an engaging story that pleases the common hearer, but communicates also a knowledge of profounder matters to a philosophic audience. The Greeks, Bacon maintained, had known many of the secrets of nature that were coming to light again in his own time; the Egyptians too had possessed much secret wisdom that they had recorded in their hieroglyphic inscriptions. In *De Sapientia Veterum* Bacon attempted to interpret a number of the most notable fables to reveal their esoteric content. The story of Cupid is read as an allegory of the atomistic nature of matter and of the causes of motion in the physical world. Proteus tells of the properties of matter and of the transformations that matter may undergo. Pan describes the state of nature and the unity of the natural world beneath the variety of appearances. The Orpheus myth hints at the civilizing effects of philosophy: 'persuasion and eloquence insinuate the love of virtue, equity and concord in the minds of men' and inspire the achievements of high culture. These achievements are destroyed by the vicissitudes of time, though they may with difficulty be restored. Proserpina explains the perpetual fertility of the earth. Other myths provide evidence of the profound knowledge of political behaviour and of the difficulties of the moral life possessed by the poets of antiquity and preserved in their fictions. The work now serves as a useful key for deciphering the meaning of mythological figures in Renaissance art and poetry.

**De Vere, Aubrey Thomas** 1814–1902 Irish poet and essayist. The son of another poet, Sir Aubrey de Vere, he was born at Curragh Chase in County Limerick and educated at Trinity College, Dublin. In England he became a close friend of **Tennyson** and **Browning**. His conversion to Roman Catholicism in 1851 was followed in 1854 by his appointment as Professor of Social and Political Science at the new Catholic University in Dublin, where **Newman** was Rector. De Vere's works include *The Waldenses and Other Poems* (1842), *English Misrule and Irish Misdeeds* (1848) and three volumes of *Critical Essays* (1887–9). His *Recollections* appeared in 1897.

***Death Comes for the Archbishop*** A novel by **Willa Cather**, published in 1927 and based on the careers of two French missionaries, Jean-Baptiste Lamy and Joseph Machebeuf, who worked in the New Mexico territory in the mid 19th century.

Bishop Jean Latour arrives in the New Mexico territory shortly after it has been annexed by the USA. With his vicar, Father Joseph Vaillant, who is also his long-time friend, he establishes a new diocese. Latour is withdrawn and ascetic; Vaillant is practical, vigorous and cheerful. Together they overcome the persistence with which the native Navajo and Hopi Indians cling to their ancient superstitions, and they confront the antagonism of the corrupt Mexican priests already present in the territory. They establish mission schools in remote areas and, after some years, succeed in building a cathedral at Santa Fe.

The cathedral is the outer symbol of the achievement of these two devoted men – of their success in adapting an Old World religion to the New World. Though Latour brings two architects from France to design the cathedral, it is very much inspired by the landscape of the Southwest, a landscape Cather vividly evokes for her readers. Shortly after gold is discovered at Pike's Peak, Vaillant becomes bishop in Colorado, and the two friends part. Later, Latour is made an archbishop. Vaillant is the first to die, and the novel closes with Latour's own death, mourned by all in his diocese – Mexicans, Indians and Americans alike.

**Death of a Salesman** A play by **Arthur Miller**, first performed and published in 1949. It won instant critical acclaim, running for 742 performances at the Morosco Theatre in New York City and winning both the Pulitzer Prize and the New York Drama Critics Circle Award.

It relates the tragic story of a salesman named Willy Loman, who is not the great success that he claims to be to his family and friends. After 35 years on the road trying to earn money and recognition, and measuring his own worth by the volume of his sales, Willy has begun to lose his way on trips and to run off the side of the road in his car. His devoted wife Linda and his two grown sons, Biff and Happy, who are home for a visit, worry about him. He is eventually fired because he no longer brings in the business that he used to when he was younger. He begins to hallucinate about significant events from his past: he remembers encouraging his sons to lie if it helped them to be successful and well liked; he recalls the pathetic scene of being discovered with a prostitute by his older son, who arrives unexpectedly at his hotel room seeking fatherly advice; he has imaginary conversations with his successful brother Ben. Finally, deciding that he is worth more dead than alive (the insurance money will support his family and help Biff get a new start in life), he kills himself in his car on a last trip. Critics have disagreed whether his suicide is meant to be seen as a last desperate and tragic assertion of the American dream or as an act of cowardice and selfishness.

**Death of the Heart, The** A novel by **Elizabeth Bowen**, published in 1938. A sensitive study of adolescence, it shows the influence of **Henry James**, particularly *What Maisie Knew*, but does not suffer by the comparison.

After her father's death Portia Quayne, an innocent and emotionally vulnerable girl, has spent her childhood in dreary hotels with her mother Irene. When Irene dies Portia, then 16, is sent to London under the care of her half-brother Thomas and his wife Anna. They are a sophisticated couple, unable to cope with the terrifying honesty of Portia's emotional life and ill-equipped to show real warmth or understanding. Her only ally is an elderly female servant, Matchett, inherited along with the furniture after old Quayne's death.

Enrolled at a private academy, Portia befriends Lilian and falls in love with Eddie, an admirer of Anna's, who in his conceited but despairing way encourages her to depend upon him. Unknown to Portia, Anna has already discovered her diary, a naïve but searching account of the shallow lives around her. The girl's misplaced trust in Eddie prompts her to show him her diary, over which he and Anna gain much mirth. During a holiday on the South Coast, she is shaken when Eddie flirts with Daphne Heccomb, the daughter of the house. Portia's blind faith in him is destroyed completely when she later learns how her diary has been used. In desperation she flees to the hotel room of Major Brutt, a sympathetic but equally helpless acquaintance. She refuses to return home unless Thomas and Anna 'do the right thing'. After deliberating what this might be, they decide that the right thing to do is to dispatch Matchett to bring her back.

**Death's Jest-Book**, or, the Fool's Tragedy A play by **Thomas Lovell Beddoes**, begun in 1825 and revised continually during the author's lifetime. It was posthumously published in 1850 and no less than three versions exist in manuscript. It has not been staged but contains some fine blank verse, the song 'Dream Pedlary' and the dirges for Sibilla and Wolfram. The play concerns the brothers Wolfram and Isbrand who enter the service of Duke Melveric, Wolfram as a knight and Isbrand as a court fool. They seek vengeance on the Duke for the death of their father and the dishonour of their sister. Wolfram is obliged to rescue the Duke and Sibilla, another captive, whom he loves, from the Moors. He succeeds in his knightly mission but discovers that the Duke is in love with Sibilla and looks upon Wolfram as his rival. The Duke kills Wolfram before returning to his own country but he is haunted by his victim's ghost. From that point the play's action becomes very confused and a supernatural element is introduced into a Jacobean welter of horrors. The Duke, at least, gets his just deserts in the end.

**debate poem** Medieval poetic tradition in which opposed parties contest one or more issues. The debate form is very old, dating back to Plato and the Old Testament. Boethius' *Consolatione Philosophiae* provided the most popular philosophical debate of the Middle Ages, and the form was also very common in secular Latin poetry. In the vernacular it was used for both serious and humorous ends. Often the opposed characters are animals, birds, inanimate objects or allegorical personifications, and the subject of debate ranges from spiritual problems (see *Vices and Virtues*) to personal relationships (*De Clerico et Puella*) and petty squabbling covering a variety of topics (*The Owl and the Nightingale*). The form was used for political **allegory** and **satire**, as in *Wynnere and Wastoure*, for serious philosophical debate and for humour; *The Owl and the Nightingale* is a brilliant comic use of the genre. The debate may be inconclusive or it may be resolved by a third party. A related form is the parliament involving more than two participants (see *The Parliament of the Three Ages*, *The Parlement of Foules*).

**Decline and Fall** The first novel by **Evelyn Waugh**, published in 1928.

The novel recounts the 'decline and fall' of Paul Pennyfeather, a theology undergraduate at Oxford when the story begins. Debagged by fellow students, Paul is caught running through the quadrangle of 'Scone College' and sent down for indecent behaviour. He becomes a schoolmaster at Llanabba Castle, a small boarding school in Wales hopelessly administered by an outrageous staff which includes Mr Prendergast, a former clergyman, and Captain Grimes, a one-legged drunkard who commits bigamy with the headmaster's daughter, Flossie Fagan. Paul is taken up by the sophisticated and wealthy Margot Beste-Chetwynde, mother of Peter, one of Paul's pupils. He is offered and accepts the position of private tutor to Peter, and is initiated into Margot's high-society life in Mayfair and at King's Thursday, a 'modernized' Tudor mansion. She and Paul become engaged, but he finds himself under arrest for having unwittingly involved himself in her activities in the white-slave trade. Tried and convicted, Paul is sentenced to seven years in prison – a natural enough environment, he feels, for anyone brought up in an English public school. There he finds Captain Grimes, a fellow prisoner, and Prendergast, now the prison chaplain. Shortly after his confinement, however, Margot engineers Paul's escape and he is transported to her villa in Corfu. At the end of the novel he returns as a 'very distant' cousin of Paul Pennyfeather – and bearing his own name – to resume his studies at Oxford.

**Decline and Fall of the Roman Empire, The History of the** Edward Gibbon's great work of classical history was published in three instalments: vol. 1 in 1776, vols. 2 and 3 in 1783, and vols. 4, 5 and 6 in 1788. These correspond to the major divisions in his narrative: from Trajan and the age of the Antonines to the reign of Constantine, from the foundation of Constantinople to the Western Empire of Charlemagne, from the establishment of the Western (Holy Roman) Empire to the long history of the Eastern (Byzantine) Empire and the taking of Constantinople by the Turks in 1413. Gibbon traces the events of more than 13 centuries. The establishment of Christianity is dealt with in detail, though his sceptical attitude provoked much criticism. Gibbon examines the encroachment of the Teutonic tribes who eventually held the Western Empire in fee, the rise of Islam, and the Crusades. He looks backward in history to illuminate the period of his work and forward from it to show what has been its legacy.

*The Decline and Fall* is a model of clarity and completeness, as accurate as the condition of historical research in Gibbon's day could make it. He is scrupulous in acknowledging his sources, and only in respect of available knowledge has he been superseded. The history is finely organized, the narrative power unflagging, the arguments irresistibly persuasive and the viewpoint elegantly detached. Such qualities have guaranteed his work a permanent place of honour in historical literature.

**deconstruction** A school of criticism, or approach to reading literature which owes its development mainly to the writings of Jacques Derrida (1930– ). His paper 'Structure, Sign, and Play' (1966) inaugurated a new critical movement in the United States (especially at Yale University).

Key Derridean concepts include 'presence', 'logocentrism', 'phonocentrism', 'supplement' and 'differance'. Since Plato, Western thought has used various concepts – such as 'substance', 'essence', 'end', 'cause', 'form', 'being' and so on – in order to centre discourses and to permit distinctions between truth and falsehood. Logocentrism is the desire for a centre. This principle involves the privileging of one term over another. For example, speech, in Rousseau and others, is placed hierarchically above writing. This particular 'violent hierarchy' is called 'phonocentrism' (centring on the voice). The deconstructor begins by reversing the hierarchy (writing before speech) and then by displacing the new hierarchy, thus leaving a certain indeterminacy in the particular discursive field. The term 'differance' describes the process which prevents signs from achieving a full 'presence'. 'Differance' in French combines two meanings – to 'differ' and to 'defer'. Signs acquire meanings within a system of differences, and at the same time meaning is deferred by the endless chain of signifiers which is generated as soon as we begin to interpret. The 'supplement' describes the unstable relationship which exists between terms like 'speech' and 'writing'. One term both takes the place of and supplements the other.

The Yale deconstructors include Barbara Johnson, Paul de Man, Geoffrey Hartman and J. Hillis Miller. Johnson has written excellent essays on Barthes, Derrida and Lacan. She deconstructs **Poe**'s 'The Purloined Letter' via a reading of Derrida's deconstruction of Lacan's reading of the story, showing that both readings of Poe unconsciously privilege particular concepts. De Man's work (e.g. *Blindness and Insight* (1971) and *Allegories of Reading* (1979)) explores the way rhetoric (especially figurative language) prevents discourse from unequivocally referring to things or communicating meanings. Criticism itself is caught up in the same figurative dislocation of meaning. Critical commentary is always allegory: it stands in the place of another discourse. De Man also believes that literary texts are 'self-deconstructing', and that therefore the critic has only to collude with the text's own literary processes. Hartman takes to an extreme the post-structuralist view of criticism as an activity within literature. He combines a fondness for verbal play and a reluctance to abandon the humanistic tradition of anglophone criticism. Hillis Miller preserves some of the rigorous textualism of his New Critical phase, which was followed by a period of phenomenological criticism. However, he accepted Derrida's criticism of the former critical methods' faith in the stability and unity of text or consciousness. His recent work explores the unpredictability and heterogeneity of literary language.

**Deeping, (George) Warwick** 1877–1950 Novelist. Born in Southend, he was educated at the Merchant Taylors' School in London and at Trinity College, Cambridge, where he read science and medicine, finishing his medical training at the Middlesex Hospital. A prolific writer, he produced 70 novels and five volumes of short stories, which attempt to keep alive the idea and spirit of Edwardian Britain. Early novels like *Uther and Igraine* (1903), *Bertrand of Brittany* (1908) and *The Red Saint* (1909) were popular historical romances. Deeping's experiences in the Royal Army Medical Corps during World War I were the inspiration for his most famous work, *Sorrell and Son* (1925), the moving story of Captain Sorrell trying to make a life for his young son Kit in severely reduced circumstances. Later novels included *Old Pybus* (1928), *Corn in Egypt* (1941) and *The Laughing House* (1947).

**Deerslayer, The** See **Leatherstocking Tales, The**.

BUT·STOOD·TURN'D·SIDEWAYS; LISTENING;

The end of William Morris's poem 'The Defence of Guenevere'. An illustration by Jessie M. King for the 1900 edition.

**Defence of Guenevere and Other Poems, The** The first collection of verse by **William Morris**, published in 1858. The title poem and the three which follow it represent the beginning of a projected set of poems on **Arthurian** themes. It was probably **Tennyson**'s publication of *Idylls of the King* in 1859, coupled with the harsh critical judgement of *The Defence of Guevenere* as 'Pre-Raphaelite minstrelsy', which dissuaded Morris from continuing his cycle. The larger part of the other poems in the collection are either taken from or based on the chronicles of Jean Froissart. A third group reflects Morris's interest in the worlds of dream and fantasy, deriving from his childhood reveries and reading of the Romantics. Two of these poems, 'The Blue Closet' and 'The Tune of Seven Towers', were written in imaginative juxtaposition with watercolours by **Dante Gabriel Rossetti**.

**Defence of Poetry, The** An essay by **Shelley**, written in Italy in 1821 and posthumously published in *Essays, Letters from Abroad, Translations and Fragments*, edited by **Mary Shelley** (1840). Shelley's most famous prose work is an amplification of arguments first advanced in earlier essays and prefaces, notably the first two chapters of *A Philosophical View of Reform* (1820), and was written as a rejoinder to his friend **Thomas Love Peacock**'s *The Four Ages of Poetry* which had appeared in Charles Ollier's *Literary Miscellany* (1820). Somewhat tongue-in-cheek, Peacock had suggested that since poetry had degenerated into the pursuit of a sort of pseudo-simplicity, the brightest talents of the age would be far more usefully employed in the new sciences of economics and political and social theory, which could help to improve the world.

Shelley's use of 'poetry' is inclusive, referring to literature as a genre *per se*, imaginative writing in general, and poetry considered as a human faculty. The essay is essentially aimed against **Utilitarian** definitions of value and happiness accompanying the growth of industrial culture. Poetry is the 'expression of the Imagination', whose unifying and synthesizing operations are distinguished from Reason's neutral observation of differences and calculation with known quantities. In a rapid review of classical and European literature Shelley discusses the characteristic features of poetic thought and inspiration, the problems of literary translation, the function of erotic writing in periods of social decline and the wider connections between poetry and politics.

The case for the 'Defence' as a whole rests on the role of poetry as a force for social freedom and creative eros. The modern age, as Shelley sees it, possessed more knowledge than it could cope with. The science of economics had not led to the 'just distribution of the produce which it multiplies', while the question of meaning was subordinated to the 'accumulation of facts and calculating processes'. 'We want the creative faculty to imagine that which we know . . . we want the poetry of life.' In burnished passages on **Chaucer**, Dante and **Milton**, he argues that, with their special capacity to sense connections between individual experience and social and intellectual change, poets both anticipated and provided the ideas by which subsequent ages lived. The celebrated (though often misunderstood) peroration hails them as unconscious 'ministers' of a benificent 'Power which is seated on the throne of their own soul', as 'mirrors of the gigantic shadows which futurity casts upon the present' and as 'the unacknowledged legislators of the World'.

**Defoe, Daniel** 1660–1731 Novelist, journalist and entrepreneur. Born in the year of the Restoration, the son of James Foe, a butcher of Stoke Newington, Daniel altered his surname to the more fashionable Defoe in 1703, the year he began depending on writing for his living. The Act of Uniformity was passed when he was two, and Defoe – a lifelong Presbyterian – was educated at Stoke Newington Academy, a

Daniel Defoe. Portrait by M. van der Gucht after J. Taverner, 1706. National Portrait Gallery, London.

school for Dissenters. He had a contemporary there by the name of Timothy Cruso. He went into trade and travelled extensively in Europe until his marriage in 1683 to Mary Tuffley, when he was a hosiery merchant in Cornhill. He took part in Monmouth's rebellion in 1685, but later became a supporter of William III, joining his army in 1688 – the first of several changes of allegiance that subsequently earned him a mercenary reputation.

Throughout his remarkably varied life, Defoe was fascinated by trade and mercantile projects. His first writing was on economics (the *Essay on Projects* of 1697) by which time he had gone bankrupt as a hosier, though in 1700 he started up a tile factory in Tilbury. His first literary success was *The True-Born Englishman* (1701), a satiric poem championing the cause of the foreign-born monarch, but (unusually among the famous writers of his period) he subsequently wrote little satire. His skills in stylistic impersonation and irony, however, were superlative, in 1702 he published a pamphlet entitled *The Shortest Way with the Dissenters* in which Defoe (himself a Dissenter, and therefore in favour of religious toleration) mimicked the extreme attitudes of High Anglican Tories and pretended to argue for the extermination of all Dissenters. In the politically volatile atmosphere of the time the leaders of neither party were amused; the author was fined, imprisoned and pilloried, but it made him a popular hero.

While in prison Defoe wrote a mock ode, *Hymn to the Pillory* (1703).

His spell in prison put paid to his Tilbury project, and Defoe appears subsequently to have been wary of partisan affiliations in his politics. In 1704 Defoe published his first issue of **The Review**, a newspaper that continued to appear until 1713, and to which he contributed, thrice weekly, articles on an impressive variety of topics from the commercial to the moral. The literary essay, which Defoe partly pioneered, was emerging as one of the distinctive genres of the period. He was assisted in this project by the politically moderate **Robert Harley, Earl of Oxford**, who was astute enough to recognize the early propagandist potential of the press. In Defoe he had the most versatile journalist of the age. Harley began to employ him as an under-cover field-agent, in particular monitoring activities in the North accompanying the Union with Scotland (1707), a clandestine occupation that suited Defoe's personality.

Defoe changed his allegiance once more in 1712, when the Tories were ousted by the Whigs, and he entered the service of Godolphin. His own political beliefs remained resolute, irrespective of changes in party policies; a committed anti-Jacobite, Defoe published *Reasons against the Succession of the House of Hanover* (1712) a satirical piece that was again mistaken by the authorities. He was imprisoned for treasonable publication, and *The Review* ceased publication. Defoe went on to edit *Mercator*, a trade journal, and in 1714 supported the notion of free trade in his *A General History of Trade*. In that year, the death of Queen Anne saw the accession of the Hanoverians to the throne; Defoe became agent to Lord Townshend (the Whig Secretary of State) in 1715, thereby escaping punishment for his libel against Lord Annesley. During this period he may have been operating in a double capacity as informer, reporter, and monitor of events.

By 1720 Defoe had ceased to be politically controversial in his writings. *The Family Instructor* (1715–18) was a conduct book, *The History of the Wars of his Present Majesty Charles XII King of Sweden*, *Memoirs of the Church of Scotland* (1717) and *The Life and Death of Count Puktil* (1717) were all works of historical interest. His earliest venture into fiction had been *A True Relation of the Apparition of one Mrs Veal* – an embroidered account of a current ghost story. No rigid barriers between fact, fiction or rumour were then considered important, but in his 60th year Defoe seems to have discovered a new well of talent for writing fictional narrative, and during the next five years he produced a flow of important books. They began with the first part of **Robinson Crusoe** (1719), followed shortly by *The Farther Adventures of Robinson Crusoe*, **Memoirs of a Cavalier** and

**Captain Singleton** (1720), **Moll Flanders, A Journal of the Plague Year**, and **Colonel Jack** (1722) and **Roxana** (1724). These books alone would have rendered their author memorable, but his pen continued to be peculiarly prolific: *The Great Law of Subordination Considered* (1724), an examination of the treatment of servants, *A Tour Thro the Whole Island of Great Britain* (3 vols., 1724–7) an outstandingly evocative guide book, *The Complete English Tradesman* (1726), which identifies the new respectability of the merchant classes, and *Augusta Triumphans* – an optimistic Utopian project – were all to follow.

It has proved difficult to ascertain the extent of Defoe's canon but, with over 500 verified publications to his name, he is the most prolific author in the English language. His enduring reputation rests now upon his novels, the genre in which he was one of the great innovators, but he was also an outstanding journalist, producing over 250 pamphlets alone, in an age where such publications had a crucial and positive power. He brought versatile skills to the essay but he was recognizably unlike most of his important contemporaries in the **Augustan Age**. Street-wise where they tended to be aesthetic, he was a master of the plain style, almost, in fact, a utilitarian clarity, rather than the politely allusive mode cultivated by **Swift** and **Pope**. That he was superbly ignored by Swift – himself a propagandist of Harley – is perhaps a measure of the way he was regarded: 'the Fellow that was Pilloryed, I have forgot his name' was the extent of the Dean's recognition in 1709.

Phenomenally industrious, Defoe seemed capable of turning his hand to any endeavour. As a novelist he was interested in social man rather than individual psychology, and his fiction reveals a swashbuckling love of travel, adventure and piracy that has subsequently become the stock material of many books. As a writer on economics he championed mercantile expansion and the concept of self-sufficiency, and was later (misleadingly) hailed as a prophet of the Industrial Revolution. But in the end little is really known about him as a person, except that he was a phenomenon of literature, a prodigious one-man industry of great variety and skill. He died on 26 April 1731 at his lodgings in Ropemakers' Alley, Moorfields.

**Deighton, Len** 1929– Novelist. Before finding success in 1962 with his first book, Deighton worked variously as a railway clerk, waiter, illustrator in New York and director of an advertising agency. His early spy thrillers, such as *The Ipcress File* (1962) and *Funeral in Berlin* (1964), were praised for their laconic style and unobtrusive authenticity. Subsequently, his many novels have alternated between exhaustively researched and bulky thrillers about World War II air combat, of which *Bomber*

(1970) and *Goodbye Mickey Mouse* (1982) are popular examples, and returns to the theme of espionage, most recently in his *Game, Set and Match* trilogy (1983–5).

**Deirdre of the Sorrows** A tragedy by **J. M. Synge**, first produced at the **Abbey Theatre** in 1910, a year after the author's death. Had he lived, Synge would certainly have revised the text, written during illness and depression.

The story comes from the Saga of Cuchulain. Synge would have known the verse plays on the same subject by **Yeats** and AE (see **Russell, George William**), as well as **Sir Samuel Ferguson**'s poem. Deirdre, destined to be the wife of Conchubor, High King of Ulster, runs away with her lover Naisi. After seven years in Alban, they are enticed back to Conchubor's court. Naisi and his brothers are killed there, and Deirdre kills herself with Naisi's knife.

**Deism** A theological position which accepted the Supreme Being as the source of finite existence but denied the supernatural element in Christianity, as well as rejecting Christian revelation as the only way to salvation. **Edward Herbert** (Lord Herbert of Cherbury) was the first English philosopher to advance these ideas, and **John Locke**'s *The Reasonableness of Christianity* (1695) gave support by its contention that man and his use of reason are evidence enough for the existence of God, who must have given man the capacity. Deism played an important role in 18th-century thought and controversy, influencing Voltaire, Rousseau and Diderot in France and spreading to Germany through a translation of **Matthew Tindal**'s *Christianity as Old as the Creation* (1730). See also **Joseph Butler, Samuel Clarke, Anthony Collins**, and **John Toland**.

**Dekker, Thomas** *c.* 1570–1632 Playwright and pamphleteer whose vivid accounts of London life make plausible the assumption that he

The plague depicted on the title-page of Thomas Dekker's pamphlet *A Rod For Run-awayes* (1625).

was a Londoner by birth and upbringing. Nothing more certain is known of him before references in **Philip Henslowe**'s *Diary* to his plays (and to his debts) in the period 1598–1602. Dekker was prodigiously busy in these early years – Henslowe lists 16 plays in which he had a hand in 1598 – but his industry could not keep pace with his expenditure. He was briefly imprisoned in the Poultry Counter in 1599 (Henslowe arranged his release), and problems with money were probably constant, worst of all in 1613–19, when he was in the King's Bench Prison.

Of the 50 or so plays to which Dekker's name is linked, only 20 have survived, together with various **masques**. The earliest, *Old Fortunatus* (1599), is a rambling moral tale describing the misfortunes that follow the decision of an old beggar and his sons to choose riches from among the benefits offered them by Fortune. The second, *The Shoemaker's Holiday* (1599), is Dekker's masterpiece. Both in its variety and in its boisterous portraits of London's citizens it advanced the development of a distinctive comic form. The other plays of which Dekker was sole author are, in comparison, disappointing. *Satiromastix* (1601) is an unattractive rejoinder to **Jonson**'s wittier abuse of Dekker (in *The Poetaster* as well as the earlier caricature of Orange in *Every Man out of His Humour*), notable only for its contribution to the war of the theatres. The structural weaknesses of this play are shared by *The Whore of Babylon* (*c.* 1606), *If It Be Not Good the Devil Is in It* (*c.* 1610) and *The Wonder of a Kingdom* (published in 1636).

Of Dekker's many collaborations the most effective include: with **Webster**, *Westward Ho* (1604) and *Northward Ho* (1605); with **Middleton**, *The Honest Whore* (1604; a second part, probably by Dekker alone, was produced in 1605) and *The Roaring Girl* (published in 1611); with **Massinger**, *The Virgin Martyr* (1620); with **Ford** and **William Rowley**, *The Witch of Edmonton* (1621); and with **Chettle** and William Haughton *Patient Grissel* (1600).

Dekker's moralizing, occasionally observable in his plays, is explicit in the series of pamphlets, the best of which were written 1603–10. They include *The Wonderful Year* (1603), *The Seven Deadly Sins of London* (1606), *The Bellman of London* (1608), *Lantern and Candlelight* (1608) and *The Gull's Horn-Book* (1609). At his best Dekker writes with exuberance, and always with an affection for and interest in erring humanity.

**Delafield, E. M.** Pseudonym of the novelist Edmée Elizabeth Monica Dashwood, *née* De La Pasture (1890–1943). She was born in Monmouthshire, and worked as a nurse during World War I. After the war she became a civil servant in the Ministry of National Service, then served as a magistrate. Her prolific career as a writer of mildly satiric novels about the day-today upheavals of provincial life began with numerous books which found a small but devoted readership. *Messalina of the Suburbs* (1923) was based upon a famous murder case. *The Diary of a Provincial Lady* (1930) became a popular success and gained her an increasingly large public. It was followed by *The Provincial Lady Goes Further* (1932), *The Provincial Lady in America* (1924) etc., a series which provided the basis for a successful film. Delafield's other works included the novels *Faster! Faster!* (1936), and *Nothing is Safe* (1937); three plays, *To See Ourselves* (1930), *The Glass Wall* (1933) and *The Mulberry Bush* (1935); and a study of the **Brontës** (1938).

**Delane, J[ohn] T[haddeus]** 1817–79 Editor of *The Times*. Born in London, he was educated at King's College, London, and Magdalen Hall, Oxford, and called to the Bar in 1847. The most famous Victorian editor of *The Times* (1841–77), he assembled a distinguished team of journalists around him and took an influential public role, particularly in his attacks on the mishandling of the Crimean War. According to **Alexander Kinglake**, historian of the War, Delane was 'passionately imbued with the spirit of journalism'.

**Delaney, Shelagh** 1939– English playwright. Born in working-class Salford, Delaney left school at 16 and began writing her first and best-known play a year later. *A Taste of Honey* was staged by Joan Littlewood's Theatre Workshop in 1958. It tells the story of a white teenage girl's coming to terms with her loveless home and her pregnancy after a brief encounter with a black sailor. The play's success was the result of its unadorned contemporaneity, centrally expressed in the girl's recognition that 'I really do live at the same time as myself, don't I?'. Neither Delaney's second play, *The Lion in Love* (1960), nor her later work in drama and fiction have achieved equal acclaim.

**Delany, Mary** 1700–88 Letter-writer. She was married first to Alexander Pendarves (d. 1725) and then to Patrick Delany, Dean of Down (d. 1768). Mary Delany was famous for her intricate paper mosaics of flowers, but her lasting reputation rests upon her six-volume *Autobiography and Correspondence* (1861–2), which includes her letters to and anecdotes of **Swift**, and her extensive correspondence on literary and social matters with such other major **bluestockings** as **Elizabeth Carter**, **Elizabeth Montagu** and **Sarah Chapone**.

**Dell, Floyd** 1887–1969 American novelist. Born in Illinois, Dell settled in New York City in 1913. A radical journalist, he edited *The Masses* (1914–17) and *The Liberator* (1918–24).

After the success of his first novel, *Moon-Calf* (1920), about the disillusionment of the post-war generation, he turned most of his energy to fiction. *The Briary-Bush* (1921) is a sequel to *Moon-Calf*, and *Janet March* (1923) and *Runaway* (1925) are also about the confusion and turmoil of life in the jazz age. His other works include *An Old Man's Folly* (1926), *Upton Sinclair* (1927) and *Love in the Machine Age* (1930). Together with Thomas Mitchell, Dell dramatized his novel *An Unmarried Father* (1927) as *Little Accident* (1928). *Homecoming* (1933) is his autobiography.

**Della Cruscans** A short-lived school of sentimental poetry, founded by Robert Merry (1755–98). After an undistinguished career at Harrow and Christ's College, Cambridge, he toyed with the Horse Guards, gambling and travel, before arriving in Florence in 1784. There he edited two miscellanies, the *Arno* (1784) and the *Florence* (1785), containing his own effusions and those of Mrs Piozzi and other dilettanti. He managed to join the Florentine Accademia della Crusca ('of the chaff or bran'), founded in 1583 to guard the purity of the Italian language. Its emblem, a sieve, emphasized its sifting function – to which Merry seems to have been engagingly blind. Having offended the English Florentines, he returned to England in 1787 and published his 'Adieu and Recall to Love' over the signature 'Della Crusca' in *The World* for 29 June of that year. Its depth of sentiment so moved the playwright **Hannah Cowley** that she responded in *The World* a fortnight later with 'The Pen', signing herself 'Anna Matilda'. Pseudonymous imitators rushed to swell the poetical correspondence, and the English Della Cruscans were launched.

A collection by 'Anna Matilda' and 'Della Crusca' was published in 1788. Bell published *The British Album*, containing examples of the school's productions, in 1789. This went quickly through four editions, the last prompted by **William Gifford**'s *The Baviad* (1791). This satire on Della Cruscan excess and nonsense was reinforced by the same author's *Maeviad* of 1795. Merry and Mrs Cowley met, apparently for the first time in 1789. Thereafter 'Della Crusca' produced 'The Interview' and 'Anna Matilda' replied in saddened strain, but their literary affair, their influence on poetry and their school soon ended.

**Deloney, Thomas** ?1543–1600 Author of ballads, pamphlets and prose fiction. Deloney was by trade a silk-weaver: **Thomas Nashe** calls him the 'balletting silk-weaver of Norwich'. Nothing is known of his early life and education, but his works suggest that he knew Latin and some French. Some of the contemporary university-educated writers of prose fiction regarded him as a mere ballad-maker and popular romancer, an opinion which continued in a subsequent low critical regard for Deloney's works as 'popular'.

His early works were ballads and broadsides, including three on the Spanish Armada, and many of them were of the kind that Autolycus has in his pack in *The Winter's Tale*. *The Lamentation of Beckles* and *The Death and Execution of Fourteen Most Wretched Traitors* (both 1586) may have been the kind of ballads which earned **Greene**'s oblique and disdainful dig at 'such trivial trinkets and threadbare trash'. *Canaan's Calamity* is an attempt at a poem of greater length and sustained construction.

His works of prose fiction were produced in 1596–1600. They draw on Tudor jest-books and such popular works as the chronicles of **Edward Hall** and **Holinshed** and **Foxe**'s *Acts and Monuments*. They describe the careers and adventures of artisans, travelling craftsmen and the middle class, with sympathetic dipictions of the experiences of ordinary life, although there are also moments of fashionable **euphuism** and romance. *Thomas of Reading* (licensed 1602) depicts the clothier's craft, *Jack of Newbury* (licensed 1597, first extant edition 1619) that of the weaver, and *The Gentle Craft* (licensed 1597, first extant edition 1637) shoemakers. The latter contains the story of Simon Eyre, a shoemaker who became Lord Mayor of London. It was the source for **Dekker**'s *The Shoemaker's Holiday*. Deloney's works glorify the English artisan. They are patriotic and fiercely anti-Catholic and anti-Spanish. He shows a special gift for reproducing the conversation of naïve women and Long Meg of Westminster in *The Gentle Craft* is his finest creation. He has good claim to have formed the English 'novel'. **Kemp** said that Deloney 'died poorly . . . and was decently buried'.

**Deloria, Vine, Jr** 1933– American Indian writer, a Standing Rock Sioux, born and raised on a South Dakota reservation. His writings consistently advocate a separatist political strategy for American Indians. These include the satiric *Custer Died For Your Sins: An Indian Manifesto* (1969); *We Talk, You Listen: New Tribes, New Turf* (1970); *God is Red* (1973), a critique of the Judaeo-Christian religious tradition; *Behind The Trail of Broken Treaties: An Indian Declaration of Independence* (1974), an examination of the events which led to the 1973 conflict at Wounded Knee; *Indians of The Pacific Northwest: From the Coming of The Whiteman to The Present Day* (1977); and *The Metaphysics of Modern Existence* (1979).

**Democracy in America** (*La Démocratie en Amérique*) A classic interpretation of American civilization by Comte Alexis de Tocqueville (1805–

59), published in two parts in 1835 and 1840. De Tocqueville's predictions about the course democracy would follow in the USA were based not only on what he had read about America but also on his own observations, made while on an official visit to the USA to study its penal system.

In the first part he discusses America's geography, political institutions and processes, and society. He argues that Anglo-Americans have been able to take possession of and settle such a large portion of the continent because they have the habit of democratic self-government that he considers essential to civilization, and he predicts that they will continue successfully to expand their territory. Noting that the tendency toward equality is advancing throughout the western world, he declares that – at the time he writes – equality is most advanced in the USA. In the second part he analyses the effect of democracy on intellectual movements, art, religion, taste and mores. He concludes that democracy and increasing equality will lead to greater mediocrity of individual achievement, even as it makes possible greater general comfort and greater achievements by the state.

**Democratic Vistas** A prose pamphlet by **Walt Whitman**, first published in 1871. It was later included in *Two Rivulets* (1876), the second volume of the sixth edition of *Leaves of Grass*. Whitman was an ardent democrat and a passionate individualist. *Democratic Vistas* asserts his belief in the compatibility of the two positions and sees their union as the basis for a cultural order in the USA that would be independent from that of Britain.

**Demos**: *A Story of English Socialism* A novel by **George Gissing**, published in 1886. It is in fact an attack on the validity of socialism, portraying its leaders as short-sighted, self-deceived, self-serving and ultimately corrupt. Gissing shows individual members of the working class (especially women) as sensitive, high-principled and altogether noble, but his working-class agitators, such as Richard Mutimer and Daniel Dabbs, take to capitalist practices as soon as they have the chance. The story hinges on the establishment by Mutimer of a model community, an Owenite ironworks in an unspoiled valley (see **Owen, Robert**). There is a complex plot involving a will which is lost and found (its acknowledgement by the finder's husband becoming a test of honour). The socialist–capitalist loses his money, which reverts to the rightful, aristocratic owner, and the ironworks is closed, with loss of jobs. The peasantry have become unsettled, but the beauty of the landscape is restored, and Gissing seems to endorse this solution to the problem of industrial relations, expressing in his narrative voice the opinion that it takes three generations to produce a cultured person.

**Denham, Sir John** 1615–69 Poet. Born in Dublin and educated at Trinity College, Oxford, Denham studied law at Lincoln's Inn and was called to the Bar in 1639. He was a staunch Royalist, and his fortunes rose and fell with the King's. The Restoration saw him rewarded with a knighthood and a post as Surveyor of the Royal Works; he also served as MP for Sarum.

Denham was 26 when his blank-verse tragedy, *The Sophy*, was published. In the same year his most famous work, the long poem *Cooper's Hill*, appeared. Set in the country near his home at Egham and concentrating on landscape description, the work influenced the topographical poetry of the 18th century and, in **Samuel Johnson**'s words, conferred on Denham 'the rank and dignity of an original author'. His use of the couplet strengthened the case for its adoption in the interest of discipline and rhythm. Denham also worked on translations of Homer and Virgil.

*Denis Duval* An unfinished novel by **W. M. Thackeray**. The completed parts were published in *The Cornhill Magazine* from April to June 1864. The author had died in December 1863. The setting is Rye in the late 18th century. Denis Duval tells of his involvement with the smugglers of the area, of his love for Agnes de Saverne and the story of her victimized mother, and of the villainous de la Motte. Thackeray left sketches for the remainder of the book, which took him back to the sort of full-scale historical novel he had attempted so successfully in *Henry Esmond*.

**Dennis, Clarence Michael James** 1876–1938 Australian journalist and writer of verse. Educated in Adelaide, Dennis followed a varied career before joining the staff of *The Melbourne Herald* in 1922. His first volume was *Backblock Ballads* (1913), followed by *The Songs of a Sentimental Bloke* (1915) and *The Moods of Ginger Mick* (1916). Their everyday language, teasing humour and use of bush themes made them immensely popular, particularly with soldiers in the trenches. Later volumes were *Digger Smith* (1918) and *Rose of Spadgers* (1924), a sequel to *Ginger Mick*.

**Dennis, John** 1657–1734 Critic. The son of a prosperous saddler, Dennis was born in London and attended Harrow School. At Cambridge, he was expelled from Gonville and Caius College for stabbing a fellow student, but finished his education at Trinity Hall. After university he travelled in France and Italy and became a member of **Dryden**'s circle when he returned to England. An unsuccessful dramatist (he wrote eight plays, including *Appius and Virginia*, 1709, satirized by **Pope**), Dennis had more success as a critic, though he became cantankerous in later life and was ridiculed by Pope in *The Dunciad*. His principal essays are *The Impartial Critick* (1693), an attack on **Thomas Rymer**; *The Advancement and Reformation of Modern Poetry* (1701), *The Grounds of Criticism in Poetry* (1704) and *Three Letters on the Genius and Writings of Shakespeare* (1711). Dennis's *Original Letters, Familiar, Moral and Critical* (1721) remains a valuable source of information on the literary world of his time.

**Dennis, Nigel (Forbes)** 1912–89 Novelist, dramatist, critic and journalist. He was born in Surrey, brought up in Rhodesia and educated partly in Austria. In 1931–49 he worked as a journalist in the USA, publishing his first novel, *Boys and Girls Come out to Play* (1949), shortly after his return to England. The startlingly inventive *Cards of Identity* (1955) established him as a satirical novelist, but he then turned to the theatre, writing plays that deplored the debasement of standards under facile democracies and denounced left-wing totalitarianism. In *Cards of Identity* (1956), which he adapted from his novel, the target is the manipulation of mass opinion. *The Making of Moo* (1957) derides the idolatry of religion, Christianity included. In *August for the People* (1961) an aristocratic landowner who denounces the common man finds himself besieged by common men who agree with him. A brilliant journalist, Dennis also co-edited *Encounter* and contributed reviews and columns to *The Sunday Telegraph* which displayed his acid wit and the clarity of his writing style.

**denouement** The final unravelling of a complex plot, usually involving revelations of such things as mistaken identity, lost children, disguised motives, etc. While the term may be broadly applied to the closing scenes of many plays, it refers most accurately to the formula of the **well-made play**.

*Deor* A short Old English poem found in the **Exeter Book**. It is written in the form of a first-person narrative by a minstrel called Deor. The narrator tells of five well-known miserable situations from history and mythology and then of his own misfortune, probably fictional: his position as official poet and its attendant benefits have been given to another. He comforts himself with the thought that God will soon improve his fortunes and offers solace throughout in a refrain which says that these other sorrows passed and so shall his own. *Deor* is similar in form and function to a longer poem, *Widsith*.

**Derrida, Jacques** See **deconstructive criticism**.

**Desai, Anita** 1937– Indian novelist, born in Mussoorie. A very polished writer, she describes surface realities sharply, but uses them also as markers for her characters' interior lives; indeed, *The Village by the Sea* (1982), though intended for children, achieves social commitment simply through the great clarity of its scenes of poverty. *Cry, the Peacock* (1963) and *Voices in the City* (1965) feature sensitive Hindu women of orthodox background seeking unorthodox means of fulfilment that lead to despair and insanity. In *Bye-Bye, Blackbird* (1971) two Indians in England gradually understand their relationship with India. The claustrophobia of family-bound women is explored in *Where Shall We Go This Summer?* (1975) and *Fire on the Mountain* (1977). Particularly distinguished is *Clear Light of Day* (1980), about an embittered woman discovering her own human shortcomings. *In Custody* (1984), her first novel centred on a male character, is convoluted in style and thematically hazy.

**Desani, G[ovindas] V[ishnoodas]** 1909– Indian novelist. Born in Nairobi, Kenya, he spent World War II in Britain and now lives in the USA. He is ranked among the most important 20th-century Indian writers in English on the strength of one novel, *All About H. Hatterr* (1948). An eccentric and comic book about an Anglo-Indian in search of wisdom, it combines linguistic dexterity and philosophical curiosity. It has been admired enthusiastically by both Indian and Western critics, the latter including **T. S. Eliot** and **Anthony Burgess**, and is said to have influenced **Salman Rushdie**. Desani has written nothing else substantial, though he has been a regular contributor from abroad to *The Illustrated Weekly of India* and is the author of a play, *Hali* (1950).

*Deserted Village, The* A poem by **Oliver Goldsmith**, published in 1770. This pastoral elegy takes the theme of the vanished rural past of England, destroyed by the Enclosure Acts and the depopulation of agrarian communities once the Industrial Revolution was concentrating workers in the cities. Revisiting an idealized village, Auburn, the poet laments that money and progress should have become more important than human destinies, and that such a previously happy place has decayed. **Crabbe's** *The Village* was in part a reaction to the mood of this poem.

*Desperate Remedies* The first published novel by **Thomas Hardy**, appearing in 1871. Having failed to find a publisher for his first attempt at fiction, *The Poor Man and the Lady*, Hardy deliberately adopted the formulae of the popular **sensation novel** in this work.

Set mainly in Dorset, this complicated narrative of intrigue, violence and deception follows the welfare of Cytherea Graye, a young woman forced to become lady's maid and later companion to the imperious Miss Aldclyffe, mistress of Knapwater House, who years earlier had an illegitimate son given the name Aeneas Manston. It is Miss Aldclyffe's hope that Manston, whose post as her land agent she arranges, should marry Cytherea, although the latter is in love with Edward Springrove, a fledgling architect and son of a neighbouring farmer. But Manston is already married to a down-at-heel American woman named Eunice who pursues him to the West Country where she is presumed to have perished in a fire at the Three Tranters Inn; in fact, Manston murdered her and placed her remains in the smouldering ashes of the fire. A combination of circumstances moves Cytherea to accept Manston in marriage at which point it is revealed that Springrove, who had unwisely attached himself to a local girl, has been jilted. After much investigative work Manston is brought to book as the murderer of Eunice and hangs himself in his cell. Miss Aldclyffe dies and Cytherea and Springrove are reunited.

**detective fiction** A sub-genre of fiction which presents a mysterious event or crime, usually but not necessarily murder, at first concealing the solution from the reader but finally revealing it through the successful investigations of the detective. **W. H. Auden** summarizes a typical plot: 'a murder occurs; many are suspected; all but one suspect, who is the murderer, are eliminated; the murderer is arrested or dies'.

Historians of the form have tried to trace its origin to the puzzle tales of the Enlightenment (Voltaire's *Zadig*) or even to the Bible (Daniel, Susanna and the elders), but there is a general agreement that its real history starts in the 19th century. **Edgar Allan Poe** brought all the basic ingredients together in his 'tales of ratiocination' of the 1840s. His detective, the brilliant and eccentric Dupin, is accompanied by an obligingly imperceptive friend who narrates the story; he confronts mystery with a coherent, though not exclusively scientific, methodology of detection; and he produces the solution with a triumphant flourish that both surprises and satisfies the reader. Without providing either a murder or an infallible detective, **Wilkie Collins** showed in *The Moonstone* (1868) how the formula could be expanded to fit the requirements of the full-length novel. In his **Sherlock Holmes stories**, begun in the late 1880s, **Sir Arthur Conan Doyle** masterfully orchestrated the hints Poe had sketched out.

The success of Sherlock Holmes rapidly bred imitation, ranging from distinguished contributions like **G. K. Chesterton**'s Father Brown stories and **E. C. Bentley**'s *Trent's Last Case* (1913) to forgotten works like **Arthur Morrison**'s Martin Hewitt stories and **M. P. Shiel**'s tales of Prince Zaleski. It also bred new awareness of the form, a new attempt to distinguish detective fiction from all the other types of popular fiction which dabble in crime and mystery. According to Monsignor Ronald Knox (1888–1957) and his followers in the Detection Club, detective fiction should be concerned with puzzles rather than crime as such, and it should elaborate its puzzles in strict obedience to the rules of logic and fair play. From such prescriptions arose the so-called Golden Age of the detective novel in the 1920s and 1930s. Writers became known for their expert refinements of the puzzle: R. Austin Freeman (1862–1943) for his scientific expertise; Freeman Wills Crofts (1879–1957) for his juggling with timetables and alibis; John Dickson Carr (1905–77) for his variations on the locked-room mystery; and, most famous of all, **Agatha Christie** for her ingenuity in making the least likely suspect turn out to be the murderer.

Setting and characterization inevitably took second place, but they, too, followed well-worn paths. Detectives tended to be gentleman amateurs rather than policemen or private enquiry agents. H. C. Bailey (1878–1961) was perhaps the first, in his Reggie Fortune stories, to make his gentleman amateur a facetious dandy, but Fortune was soon joined by a lengthening list of detectives who owed as much to **Saki** and **P. G. Wodehouse** as they did to Conan Doyle: Lord Peter Wimsey (**Dorothy L. Sayers**), Albert Campion (**Margery Allingham**) and even Nigel Strangeways (Nicholas Blake, the pseudonym of **Cecil Day-Lewis**). Settings were equally genteel, with country houses and Oxbridge colleges among the favourites, and with the work of Michael Innes (**J. I. M. Stewart**) offering perhaps the best representative selection.

Detective stories in this classic mould were not confined to England, as the popularity of S. S. Van Dine (Willard Huntington Wright, 1880–1939), Ellery Queen (Frederic Dannay, 1905–82, and Manfred B. Lee, 1905–71) and Rex Stout (1886–1975) in America showed. Nor did they entirely disappear after the 1930s. Christie, Allingham, Blake, Innes and **Ngaio Marsh** all continued their careers after the war, with some adjustment to the change in public taste, and were joined by Edmund Crispin (Robert Bruce Montgomery, 1921–78) and Michael Gilbert (1912– ). Contemporaries like P. D. James (Phyllis White, 1920– ) in England and Emma Lathen (Mary J. Latsis and Martha Henissart) in America can still follow the classic formula. But it came increasingly under challenge from writers who, whatever else they may not have shared, were agreed in finding it restrictive and in wishing to break down the barriers that separated detective fiction from other popular forms like the thriller, adventure story, chase novel and spy story, or from the concerns of serious literature.

By far the most significant challenge came from America, where **Dashiell Hammett**, **Raymond Chandler** and other contributors to *The Black Mask* pioneered 'hard-boiled' detective fiction. Its aims were succinctly indicated by Chandler when he praised Hammett for putting murder back in the hands of people who commit it with real weapons for real reasons, not just to provide the reader with a puzzle. With its tough, down-at-heel private eyes and its sleazy urban world of vice and hoodlums, hard-boiled detective fiction now dominates the American approach as thoroughly as Conan Doyle once did the English. In England itself, the form has never taken root, but two other tendencies – both with international ramifications – are worth noting. The first is the 'crime novel', so called because an interest in the criminal and criminal psychology can overshadow or even replace the element of mystery. Pioneered by Anthony Berkeley Cox (1893–1971), writing as Francis Iles in the 1930s, it has since attracted distinguished adherents in the American Patricia Highsmith (1921– ), Julian Symons (1912– ) and, intermittently, Ruth Rendell (1930– ). The second is the 'police novel', in which a determination to make good the genre's earlier neglect of the police can produce works ranging from strictly procedural novels like those of John Creasey (1908–73) or the American Ed McBain (**Evan Hunter**), to the atmospheric fiction of Nicolas Freeling (1927– ). Indeed, Freeling's work, with its policemen–heroes at odds with the bureaucracy that gives them authority, its enquiry into the social and personal origins of crime and its ability to propound a neat puzzle when the occasion requires, comes as close as any to epitomizing the eclectic variety open to the contemporary detective novelist.

***deus ex machina*** The Latin phrase means 'the god from the machine'. It refers to the practice on the classical Greek stage of lowering the gods in a large crane, or 'mechane', as if they were flying down to earth. It was often the task of a god to resolve problems insoluble by human agency, and so the phrase has become more widely applied, to describe any character, or even any device, employed arbitrarily by the playwright in order to bring the plot to its desired end.

***Devil is an Ass, The*** A comedy by **Ben Jonson**, first produced in 1616 and published in 1631. The play exposes the activities of 'projectors' (in modern terms, fixers and confidence tricksters), witchfinders and healers of demoniacs (supposed victims of satanic possession). The plot concerns Meercraft, a projector, who proposes a scheme for reclaiming land. His victim is Fitzdottrel, who parts with his estate on the promise of being made Duke of Drowndland. Fitzdottrel, in turn, deceives the law by pretending to be bewitched. Another character in the plot is Pug, a minor devil allowed out by Satan for one day to practise his wickedness on earth. But the wickedness he encounters on earth is worse than his own; he is completely outwitted by human knaves and ends up in Newgate gaol.

**Dewey, John** 1859–1952 American philosopher and educationalist, born in Burlington, Vermont. He taught at the University of Michigan and then at the University of Chicago, where he founded the Laboratory School for experimental education. He was a professor of philosophy at Columbia University from 1905 until his retirement in 1929.

Many of his works are concerned with reforms in education, politics and religion. His numerous writings greatly influenced the development of educational techniques both in the USA and abroad. His publications in this field include *Psychology* (1887), *Moral Principles in Education* (1909), *Interest and Effort in Education* (1913), *Democracy and Education* (1916), *Experience and Education* (1938), *The Public Schools and Spiritual Values* (1944). Dewey started out as a Hegelian, but his study of **Darwin** led him to a philosophical pragmatism more in the tradition of **William James**. His philosophy, which he termed 'instrumentalism', with its emphasis on the practical problems of social construction, is elaborated in such works as *Outlines of a Critical Theory of Ethics* (1891), *Studies in Logical Theory* (1903), *Reconstruction in Philosophy* (1920), *Human Nature and Conduct* (1922), *Experience and Nature* (1925), *The Quest for Certainty* (1929), *Art as Experience* (1934) and *Freedom and Culture* (1939).

**Dial, The** A New England quarterly magazine started in 1840, and the chief periodical of the **Transcendentalist** movement. It published the literary, philosophical and religious statements of its founders, who included **Margaret Fuller** and **Ralph Waldo Emerson**, as well as the poetry of **Jones Very** and **William Ellery Channing**. Although it was published for only four years, *The Dial* had a major influence on the intellectual life of 19th-century New England. In addition to Fuller and Emerson, its editors included **Henry David Thoreau**.

**Dialogues Concerning Natural Religion** A work by **David Hume**, written in the 1750s but not published until 1779, three years after his death.

The narrator is Pamphilus, and the interlocutors are the philosopher Cleanthes, the sceptic Philo and the orthodox Christian Demea. The subject is the nature of God (the existence of God is not in question) and the dialogues examine further the questions raised in the essay on miracles in *An Enquiry Concerning Human Understanding* and *The Natural History of Religion*. In particular, the issue of divine providence is debated and held in doubt. With their varying pace and rhythm, sharp exchanges and interruptions, the dialogues achieve a remarkable impression of recorded discussion.

**Diana of the Crossways** A novel by **George Meredith** published in 1885. The central character, Diana Warwick, is accused of adultery by her husband, a government official of limited sensibilities. An action for divorce is brought, citing the eminent Lord Dannisburgh, but fails and the couple agree to live apart. Diana forms a close relationship with a rising young politician, Percy Dacier, and their affair ends only when Dacier discovers that Diana has betrayed to the press a political secret confided in her. After the death of her husband she marries an old admirer, Thomas Redworth. The nervous, impulsive, inconsistent character of the heroine has always been admired by critics of the novel.

**Diaper, William** *c.* 1686–1717 Poet. The author of *Nereides, or, Sea-Eclogues* (1712), a whimsical production in verse where the speakers are mermaids and mermen. Diaper is best known for his translation of the first part of Oppian's *Halieuticks*, a Greek poem of epic proportions describing and classifying fish and methods of fishing.

**Diary of a Nobody, The** Comic novel of late-Victorian manners by **George** and **Weedon Grossmith**, published in 1892. 'Why should I not publish my diary . . . because I do not happen to be a "Somebody"?' demands city clerk Charles Pooter, the unreliable narrator. The humour derives from the socially and physically accident-prone Pooter's unconsciousness of how ridiculous he makes himself by his petty snobberies, and from his invariably unsuccessful wrangles with his rebellious son Lupin. Nevertheless, a character of respectability and even integrity emerges, so that the reader rejoices in the eventual rise in the fortunes of Pooter and his faithful, though frequently irritated, wife Carrie.

The current fashion for bicycling is exemplified by Pooter's dignified but dull friend Cummings, and that for imitations of the famous contemporary actor Irving by Lupin's friend Fosselton. Among the host of other characters who cross the Pooters' path are the hearty Mr Gowing, and his vulgar friend Padge, 'who appeared to be all moustache'.

**Dibdin, Charles** 1745–1814 Playwright, actor and composer, Dibdin had his first comic opera, *The Shepherd's Artifice* (1764), produced at **Covent Garden** before he was 20. Much of his early work was done in collaboration with **Isaac Bickerstaffe**, for whose *The Padlock* (1768) he not only wrote the music but also created the role of Mungo. He provided both text and music for *The Wedding Ring* (1773), *The Deserter* (1773), the excellent **ballad opera** *The Waterman* (1774) and upwards of 40 subsequent pieces. A commercial venture into equestrian drama at the Royal Circus in 1782 ended in failure and imprisonment for debt, but the series of one-man shows which Dibdin wrote and performed in 1788–93 helped to restore his uncertain fortunes. Among the many ballads for which he was famous in his time, 'Tom Bowling' has proved the most durable. His prose work included a five-volume *History of the Stage* (1795) and several forgotten novels, of which *Henry Hooka* (1806) was the last.

**Dick, Philip K[endred]** 1928–82 American writer of **science fiction**. Dick spent most of his life in California. His early paperback novels were written quickly to earn a living, but *The World Jones Made* (1956) and *Eye in the Sky* (1957) contain striking material. His mature work often studies the effect on human life and values of the gradual mechanization of the environment. Another theme is the unreliability of perception, and Dick's novels are most impressive when they deal with false realities created by hallucinogenic drugs or schizophrenic delusion. They include *The Man in the High Castle* (1962), *Martian Time-Slip* (1964), *Now Wait for Last Year* (1966), *Do Androids Dream of Electric Sheep?* (1969), *Flow My Tears, the Policeman Said* (1974) and *A Scanner Darkly* (1977). In his last years, having had his own problems with schizophrenia, Dick turned with deepening interest to metaphysics and hypothetical theology in *Valis* (1981) and *The Divine Invasion* (1981). His non-science fiction work, including *Confessions of a Crap Artist* (1975) and *The Transmigration of Timothy Archer* (1982), shows his concern for the plight of meek people confronted by the uncaring hostility of others.

**Dickens, Charles (John Huffam)** 1812–70 Novelist. Born at Portsmouth, the son of John Dickens, a well-intentioned but irresponsible clerk in the Navy Office, and his wife Elizabeth, Charles Dickens had an unsettled childhood in London, Chatham and, ultimately, London again. At Chatham from 1817 until 1821/2 the boy came under the beneficent eye of the schoolmaster William Giles, who recognized his talent and gave him particular attention. Always a voracious reader, the young Dickens fell upon the works of **Smollett**, **Fielding** and Cervantes; his restless imagination also responded to exotic tales like *The Arabian Nights*, public recitations, play-acting, colourful pageantry and magic-lantern displays. But with his father's transfer to London, he was for several years neglected while his feckless parents slid further into financial difficulties that resulted in John Dickens's imprisonment for debt in the Marshalsea. Two days after his 12th birthday Dickens was put to work in Warren's blacking factory, a humiliating experience which he nursed in memory until the end of his life. So profound a mark did his father's imprisonment and his own miserable months at Warren's leave on him that it was not until the publication of the biography by **John Forster**, after Dickens's death, that his family knew of these early experiences.

When he was released from the Marshalsea John Dickens sent his son to Wellington House Academy, an institution of negligible value to the boy but an improvement on his recent mode of living, and there he remained until the spring of 1827. He then became office boy in a firm of attorneys, mastering shorthand and rising swiftly to work as reporter in that 'confusion of different courts', Doctors' Commons. In 1829 he had met and fallen in love with Maria Beadnell. Her family disapproved of her literary suitor and their association ended after four difficult years – although, like so much of Dickens's early experience, it provided material for later fiction.

Charles Dickens. A detail from the portrait by A. Scheffer, 1855. National Portrait Gallery, London.

Characteristically alert to self-advancement, the young Dickens was by 1832 working for his uncle's Hansard-style publication, *The Mirror of Parliament*, and also reporting for *The True Sun*. Shortly afterwards, in 1833, he was Parliamentary journalist for the Liberal *The Morning Chronicle*, often travelling into the country to report political meetings for the paper. During the 1830s he also wrote sketches for a variety of journals, among them *The Monthly Magazine* edited by his friend George Hogarth. From these reportorial experiences and writings came his first book, *Sketches by Boz* (1836–7), in which he for the first time adopted the pseudonym derived from his own infant pronunciation of 'Moses' as 'Boses'. Of note, too, is that Dickens from his earliest years developed a wide knowledge of the squares, highways, courts, alleys, markets and gardens of London. His endless wanderings, literally from one end of the city to the other, not only contributed to *Sketches by Boz* but gave rise to situation after situation and description after description in his later writing.

Welcomed into George Hogarth's family, Dickens courted the eldest daughter of the household, the pretty Catherine, and the couple were married at St Luke's, Chelsea, in April 1836. The same month saw the inauspicious beginning of *The Posthumous Papers of the Pickwick Club*, better known as *The Pickwick Papers*. Its fourth number, introducing Sam Weller, elevated Dickens to a literary and financial position from which he never descended.

With success assured, Dickens worked and lived with even greater intensity and purpose than before. Overlapping with the serialization of *Pickwick Papers* came first *Oliver Twist* (1837–9) and then *Nicholas Nickleby* (1838–9). In the autumn of 1839, as *Nicholas Nickleby* came to its conclusion, Dickens conceived the ill-fated *Master Humphrey's Clock*, a weekly miscellany with its framework of an antiquarian extracting tales, sketches and stories from his 'old quaint queer-cased clock'. Sales very soon fell off and Dickens had to expand a short story originally designed for the miscellany into a full-length serial, *The Old Curiosity Shop* (1840–1); this he quickly followed with *Barnaby Rudge* (1841).

Dickens's business and personal life were equally busy. Ever prickly with publishers, he quarrelled with John Macrone and in 1839 friction with **Richard Bentley** caused him to resign the editorship of *Bentley's Miscellany*. He moved in 1837 to Doughty Street and two years later to something more palatial on Devonshire Terrace. He enlarged his family, was elected to the Athenaeum, met his future biographer John Forster, rescued his parents several times from financial difficulties and widened his circle of friends beyond the humbler spheres of journalism.

In January 1842 Dickens arrived to an enthusiastic welcome in Boston for his first American visit. He travelled to New York, Philadelphia, Baltimore, Washington, DC, and Richmond, Virginia, as well as various smaller cities and towns; he went down the Ohio river to Cincinnati and briefly up to Canada. But his *American Notes* (1842) and the American episodes in his next novel, *Martin Chuzzlewit* (1843–4), caused lasting resentment among his American audience. In 1843, prompted by the sight of the Ragged Schools, he produced his first and most famous Christmas story, *A Christmas Carol*. In the spring of the next year he went to live in Genoa – partly, he claimed, for financial reasons – and, with his usual energetic curiosity, made a round of visits to Vesuvius, Rome, Naples, Florence and Venice before returning to England in 1845. *Pictures from Italy*, published that year, was less controversial than *American Notes*. In the mid 1840s, too, Dickens produced *The Chimes*, *The Cricket on the Hearth*, *The Battle of Life* and *The Haunted Man*, which were republished together with *A Christmas Carol* as *Christmas Books* in 1852. As a journalist, he edited the newly founded *Daily News* for a mere 17 numbers in 1846 before a disagreement with the publishers, Bradbury and Evans, caused him to withdraw. In 1850 he founded his own magazine, *Household Words*, succeeded by *All the Year Round* in 1859.

More important was the publication of *Dombey and Son* (1846–8), the novel which ushered in the mature period of his art and was followed in the next decade by *David Copperfield* (1849–50), *Bleak House* (1852–3), *Hard Times* (1854), *Little Dorrit* (1855–7) and *A Tale of Two Cities* (1859). Where his early work had overflowed with improvisatory energy, the novels of the 1850s and beyond are more tightly controlled. No less wide-ranging in their subjects, they are unified by theme, image and symbol as much as by their complex and ramifying plots.

Outside literature, Dickens's energy continued unabated. He indulged his love for the theatre and delighted in assembling companies, mounting productions at Knebworth House and Rockingham Castle, arranging theatrical benefits for the bankrupt dramatist **Sheridan Knowles** and the penniless widow of **Douglas Jerrold**, and acting in *The Frozen Deep* (a play he wrote in collaboration with his friend **Wilkie Collins**) and other pieces. He also continued his interest in social problems, concerning himself with capital punishment, the reform of prostitutes and model flats in Bethnal Green among other issues. Inevitably, he moved again – to Tavistock House – and then, in the spring of 1857, to Gad's Hill in his beloved Kent. He toured Switzerland and Italy with Wilkie Collins and the painter Augustus Egg, and visited France several times. By the late 1850s, too, he had met and been captivated by the young actress Ellen Ternan, whose shadow hovers over his later fiction. His marriage, which had deteriorated over the years, came to an end with the notorious revelation in *Household Words* (June 1858) of 'Some domestic troubles of mine, of long-standing' and a permanent separation from Catherine.

Ever aware of his inability to rest or settle, even if beset with domestic difficulties, Dickens planned a series of public readings from his work, the first of them given in 1858. Highly successful, they were repeated throughout England and on his second visit to the United States in 1867. Further readings took place on his return to England, but by then the strain had grown too great and they were curtailed. It is ironic that the 1860s should also have produced some of his best work: *Great Expectations* (1860–1), *Our Mutual Friend* (1864–5) and the tantalizingly incomplete *Mystery of Edwin Drood*, halted in its serialization by his death in June 1870.

It is hard to accept that in the space of 58 years Dickens should have written even as much as the foregoing, though his canon also includes *A Child's History of England* (1851–3), many short stories, several comic plays and other writings. A complete edition of his letters has long been in progress and his speeches have already been edited. So prolific is his output and so frenzied his life, it seems miraculous he lived as long as he did.

**Dickey, James (Lafayette)** 1923– American poet and novelist. Born in Atlanta and educated at Vanderbilt University, Dickey has taught at various colleges in addition to working in advertising. Much of his work is concerned with the causes and consequences of guilt arising from the personal cruelties of life in the Southern backwoods, and from the collective cruelties of nations.

He published his first volume of poetry, *Into the Stone and Other Poems*, in 1960. Subsequent collections are *Drowning with Others* (1962), *Helmets* (1964), *Two Poems of the Air* (1964), *Buckdancer's Choice* (1965), *Poems 1957–1967* (1968) and *The Eye-Beaters, Blood, Victory, Madness, Buckhead and Mercy* (1970). *Babel to Byzantium*, a collection of criticism, was published in 1968; *Deliverance*, a best-selling novel about a violent Georgia canoe trip, in 1970. His most recent publications are *The Zodiac* (1976), *The Strength of Fields* (1979), *The Water-Bug's Mittens: Ezra Pound* (1979), *The Central Motion: Poems 1968–79* (1979), *The Early Motion* (1981) and *Puella* (1982).

**Dickinson, Emily** 1830–86 American poet. One of the three children of Edward Dickinson, a respected state legislator, US congressman and judge, she was born and lived all her life in Amherst, Massachusetts. She attended Amherst Academy and the Mount Holyoke Female Seminary. Although her early years were filled with the normal social activities of the daughter of a prominent citizen, she began to withdraw from the world outside her home. By the age of 30 she had become an almost total recluse, never leaving her father's house and garden, dressing completely in white, receiving very few visitors, and carrying on most of her many friendships, like those with the novelist **Helen Hunt Jackson** and the Reverend Charles Wadsworth, through a regular correspondence. At the age of 32, at the end of what seems to have been the most intense and prolific period of her creative life, Dickinson sent some of her poems to Thomas Wentworth Higginson, the minister, author and critic. This marked the beginning of a long and sustained correspondence between the two that only twice (in 1870 and 1873) actually resulted in meetings. Although he encouraged her writing and assumed the role of her mentor, Higginson did not attempt to get her work published. In fact, only seven of her poems were published during her lifetime.

After her death, her sister Lavinia found over a thousand poems in her room, all bound neatly in home-made booklets. Almost all were short lyrics; most were untitled and undated; some appeared in several versions. The first volumes of Dickinson's poetry to be published were edited by Higginson and Mabel L. Todd, an Amherst friend, in 1890 and 1891. Uncertain about public reaction to her work, Higginson and Todd changed metres and rhymes, altered metaphors, and substituted conventional grammar for the original complex syntax. Despite their caution the critical reception was mostly unfavourable. Other volumes, also marred by insensitive and unnecessary editing, were edited by Dickinson's niece, Martha Dickinson Bianchi, and Alfred Leete Hampson, and published in 1914, 1924, 1929, 1930, 1935 and 1937. *Bolts of Melody: New Poems of Emily Dickinson*, edited by Todd and her daughter, Millicent Todd Bingham, was published in 1945; it was more faithful than previous volumes to Dickinson's original texts, and included many poems that had been suppressed by her relatives. In 1955 Thomas H. Johnson prepared a three-volume variorum edition, *The Poems of Emily Dickinson*, containing all 1775 known poems, and this text is now accepted as the authoritative edition. Johnson and Theodora Ward edited her massive correspondence, *The Letters of Emily Dickinson*, which appeared in 1958.

The subjects of Dickinson's poetry are the traditional ones of love, nature, religion and mortality, seen through her Puritan eyes, or, as she described it, 'New Englandly'. Much of the dramatic tension stems from her religious doubt; she was unable to accept the orthodox religious faith of her friends and schoolmates, yet she longed for the comfort and emotional stability that such faith could bring. Many of her lyrics, in their mixture of rebellious and reverent sentiments, illustrate this conflict. Her poetry is also notable for its technical irregularities, which alarmed her early editors and reviewers. Her characteristic stanza is four lines long, and most poems consist of just two stanzas. Other characteristics of her style – the frequent use of dashes; sporadic capitalization of nouns; convoluted and ungrammatical phrasing; off-rhymes; broken metres; bold, unconventional and often startling metaphors; and aphoristic wit – have greatly influenced 20th-century poets and contributed to Dickinson's reputation as one of the greatest and most innovative poets of 19th-century American literature.

**dictionaries** See **English dictionaries**.

*Dictionary of the English Language, A* **Samuel Johnson**'s monumental work was first published in 1755. The project had been announced in a *Plan* of 1747, dedicated at the prompting of the bookseller **Robert Dodsley** to the **Earl of Chesterfield**; Johnson's own uneasiness about patronage was justified by his later quarrel with Chesterfield. The *Dictionary* represented eight years' labour, and the work was done while Johnson had several other projects on hand, driven as he was by the need to earn his living. One of these was *The Rambler*, and he concluded that series of essays with a declaration that he had striven to refine the language to grammatical purity 'and to clear it from colloquial barbarisms, licentious idioms, and irregular combinations' (1752).

The *Dictionary*'s full title reflected the extent of Johnson's purpose: *A Dictionary of the English Language: In Which the Words are Deduced from Their Originals, and Illustrated in Their Different Significations by Examples from the Best Writers. To Which Are Prefixed a History of the Language, and an English Grammar.* His earliest authorities were **Sidney** and **Spenser**, for he held firmly that the golden age of the English language began with the Elizabethans; he also honoured, as fully as the knowledge of his time permitted, provincialisms and dialect. He set himself to reject all the 'Gallick structure and phraseology' which the language had absorbed since the Restoration and which threatened to make the English 'babble a dialect of France'. In the 18th century there was only scant etymological knowledge to help Johnson but he brought to his task massive common sense, just as he brought his extraordinary wealth of reading to bear on the choice of illustrative quotations. The result was not definitive but pioneering, a dictionary which has influenced and inspired all later attempts in the field. See also **English dictionaries**.

**Digby, Sir Kenelm** 1603–65 Writer on science and religion. A Roman Catholic, Digby was educated at Gloucester Hall (now Worcester College), Oxford, and became a successful naval commander. He interested himself in science and became a founder-member of the Royal Society in 1660. His first work, not published until 1827, was his *Private Memoirs*, written in 1628 to refute gossip about his wife, Venetia Stanley. In 1638 he published a reaffirmation of his Catholic faith, *Conference with a Lady about Choice of Religion*, after toying with Protestantism, and a criticism of **Sir Thomas Browne**'s *Religio Medici* (*Observations upon Religio Medici*) in 1643. A Royalist, he pleaded the cause of King Charles in Rome, and was banished in 1649, the year of the King's execution. He lived in Paris, where he became a friend of Descartes, until the Restoration, when he returned to England as Chancellor to Queen Henrietta Maria. Other works were *Of the Immortality of Man's Soul* (1644), *On the Cure of Wounds* (1658) and *A Discourse Concerning the Vegetation of Plants* (1660), an address to the Royal Society on the necessity of oxygen to plant life.

**Digby, Kenelm Henry** ?1797–1880 Enthusiast for medieval culture. A descendant of **Sir Kenelm Digby**, he was born in Ireland and educated at Trinity College, Cambridge. He converted to Roman Catholicism in 1825. Digby combined admiration for medieval religion with a love of chivalry he had already announced during his undergraduate years by holding mock tournaments and keeping an all-night vigil in King's College Chapel. *The Broad Stone of Honour, or, Rules for the Gentlemen of England* (1822) set forth his ideals with copious quotation from classical and medieval sources – and at greater and greater length, swelling to four volumes in 1828–9 and to five in 1877. It had considerable influence on the 19th-century cult of medievalism, particularly among the **Pre-Raphaelites**. The 11-volume *Mores Catholici, or, Ages of Faith* (1831–42) dealt with the Catholic virtues. Digby later turned to verse and religious painting.

**Dilke, Charles Wentworth** 1789–1864 Critic and editor. Following exactly in his father's footsteps, Dilke entered the Navy Pay Office, where he remained until its abolition in 1836. His liberal sympathies and literary interests brought him into contact with **Leigh Hunt** and his circle, and he is particularly remembered for his close friendship with **Keats**, who enjoyed the freedom of his home at Hampstead and often used to go there to write. His continuation and completion of **Dodsley**'s *Old Plays* (1814–16) was, in its time, an important contribution to the rediscovery of forgotten dramatists of the Elizabethan age. Although most of his numerous contributions to periodicals such as *The London Review*, *The London Magazine* and *Colburn's New Monthly* were on literary topics, he wrote, in 1821, a political pamphlet, in the form of a letter to Russell, calling for the repeal of the Corn Laws. From 1830 to 1846 he was editor-in-chief of *The Athenaeum*, introducing the then comparatively new principle of complete editorial independence, and vastly improving the paper's circulation. In 1846 he was called in to manage the affairs of *The Daily News*, following the departure of its founder-editor, **Charles Dickens**. In 1849 he retired from newspaper management and was, for the remainder of his life, chiefly active as a literary historian, publishing mainly in his own *Athenaeum* and Thoms's recently founded *Notes and Queries*. He is best known for his detective work on the *Letters of Junius* (see **Junius**), and researches into the early life and career of **Pope**.

**Dillon, Wentworth, 4th Earl of Roscommon** *c.* 1633–85 Translator. The nephew and godson of Thomas Wentworth, Earl of Strafford, Dillon was born in Ireland and educated at the University of Caen. He was interested in founding a British Academy on the lines of the Académie française to 'refine and fix the standard of our language'. He was the author of an *Essay on Translated Verse* (1684) and a blank-verse translation of Horace's *The Art of Poetry* (1680), and was among the first to recognize the greatness of **John Milton**.

**dimeter** See **metre**.

**Dinesen, Isak** The name used by the Danish-born writer Karen Christentze Blixen, *née* Dinesen (1885–1962). She wrote in English, rewriting her work for Danish publication. Born to well-to-do parents living at Rungsted (on the coast between Copenhagen and Elsinore), she was educated at home, then at Lausanne. She attended the Royal Academy of Fine Arts in Copenhagen, and studied art there and later, spasmodically, in Paris and Rome. At the beginning of 1913 she went to East Africa to marry her cousin, Baron Blor von Blixen-Finecke, and farmed coffee outside Nairobi, in a district subsequently named 'Karen' after her. In 1931 she returned to Denmark, divorced and with the farm bankrupt. Her first book, *Seven Gothic Tales*, appeared in 1934, a collection of sometimes portentous neo-Gothic stories in which reality is distorted, the macabre ever-present, and desire never naturally fulfilled. *Out of Africa* followed in 1937, drawing upon her own experiences, and written in an episodic style remarkable for its clarity of phrase and intellectual breadth. *Shadows on the Grass* (1960) continued the same theme. Other collections, *Winter's Tales* (1942), *Last Tales* (1957) and *Anecdotes of Destiny* (1958), deal with provincial as well as sophisticated situations and the insoluble difficulty of reconciling art and nature, while demonstrating erotic tension and many facets of alienation. Popular in her own time, she was particularly well received in America.

**Dipsychus** A verse drama by **Arthur Hugh Clough**, written in 1850 and first published in 1865.

This near-plotless duologue of 13 scenes between Dipsychus (an individual of two natures) and the Spirit is set in a Venetian palazzo, but there is little or no action. The scenes range across problems of society, religion, the professions and the contemplative life, as the protagonist searches his inner self, for *Dipsychus* is essentially a work of introspection. While the much-debated role of the Spirit fluctuates, that amorphous being often takes the part of tempter, a summoner to the worldly, and asserts itself as a presence conducive to satire. Like other writings of Clough, *Dipsychus* articulates the role of the intellectual adrift in the world; and after much inner strife Dipsychus, in submission, bids farewell to the

> pious sweet simplicities of life,
> Good books, good friends, and holy moods,
> and all
> That lent rough life sweet Sunday-seeming
> rests,
> Making earth heaven-like.

**Disraeli, Benjamin, 1st Earl of Beaconsfield** 1804–81. Novelist and politician. The eldest son of **Isaac d'Israeli**, he was born in London and, despite his Jewish descent, was baptized at the age of 13. Aged 17, he was articled to a firm of solicitors, but by the time he was 20 he had given up the law. He gambled on the Stock Exchange, lost, attempted to found a new daily paper, *The Representative*, and lost money again. In 1826 he published his first novel, *Vivian Grey*, which gave the youthful hero his own wit and arrogance and (like several later works) introduced society figures under transparent disguises. The novel succeeded. Disraeli toured Italy and in 1827 published a satirical work, *The Voyage of Captain Popanilla*. He entered Lincoln's Inn to read for the Bar but, still in debt, succumbed to depression and went back to his father's house. In 1831 he published another society novel, *The Young Duke*. His tour of Spain, Greece, Albania and Egypt proved a formative experience, leaving its mark on much of his later writing, including his next novels, *Contarini Fleming* (1832) and *Alroy* (1833).

In 1832 Disraeli took up politics as his main career, unsuccessfully contesting his first two seats as a Radical and then switching to the

Benjamin Disraeli. A detail from the portrait by C. Bone, 1828. National Portrait Gallery, London.

Tories. He was defeated twice more, but established a political reputation with pamphlets and letters to *The Times* arguing that the Tories were really the champions of national liberty against an oligarchy. He published a satire, *The Infernal Marriage* (1834), and two more novels, *Henrietta Temple* (1837) and *Venetia* (1837), a fictionalized account of events in the lives of **Shelley** and **Byron**. In that year Queen Victoria ascended the throne and Disraeli succeeded in becoming Conservative MP for Maidstone. In 1839 he married Mrs Mary Anne Wyndham Lewis, widow of a previous Conservative member for Maidstone. During his early years in the Commons Disraeli showed his concern for the condition of the working class and associated himself with other reforming Tories in the 'Young England' group. The same attitudes underlie the trilogy of novels for which he is best known: *Coningsby, or, The New Generation* (1844), *Sybil, or, The Two Nations* (1845) and *Tancred, or, The New Crusade* (1847). They are characterized by the strength of their interest in current social problems, their informed historical discussion and their search for a true morality, a true patriotism.

Disraeli first achieved political office in Lord Derby's Conservative administration of 1852. He was twice Prime Minister, in 1868 and in 1874–80. In 1876 he took the title Earl of Beaconsfield, one he had invented for a character in his first novel. His success in politics overshadowed, but did not end, his writing career. *Lothair* (1870) is a novel about religious conflict; *Endymion* was published in 1880, the year before his death. He also left nine chapters of an unfinished novel, *Falconet*.

**dissociation of sensibility** A term coined by **T. S. Eliot** in his influential essay 'The Metaphysical Poets' (1921). Eliot argued that writers of the late 16th and early 17th centuries, particularly **John Donne**, had possessed a unity of thought and feeling, making for 'a direct sensuous apprehension of thought' and 'a mechanism of sensibility which could devour any kind of experience'. After Donne's time, with the influence of **Milton** and **Dryden**, English poetry was impoverished by a dissociation of sensibility. Poets of the 18th and 19th centuries, Eliot concluded, thought but could not feel their thoughts.

**dithyramb** Originally a Greek choric hymn accompanied by music and describing the adventures of Dionysus, the term is now used for verse or prose of a wild, passionate or excited nature, or for any wild chant or song. Perhaps the finest example of dithyrambic verse in English is **Dryden**'s 'Alexander's Feast'.

**Dixon, H[enry] H[all]** 1822–70 Sporting journalist. Educated at Rugby and Cambridge, he flirted with the law but turned to sporting journalism, writing as 'The Druid', and carved himself a niche in the middle ground between the aristocratic world of **C. J. Apperley** ('Nimrod') and the debased, pugilistic arena of **Pierce Egan**. He traversed England and Scotland indefatigably on foot or pony, writing largely of bourgeois sporting personalities, professional hunt-servants and jockeys, sporting dogs, race-horses and the like; he also discoursed on cattle-dealers and farm stock. His best-known books are: *Post and Paddock* (1856), *Silk and Scarlet* (1859), *Scott and Sebright* (1862), *Field and Fern* (1865) and *Saddle and Sirloin* (1870). Some of his allusions are obscure today but his work still provides a vivid picture of mid-century, middle-class sporting and farming life.

**Dixon, Richard Watson** 1833–1900 Poet. He was educated at King Edward VI School, Birmingham, and Pembroke College, Oxford, where he became a member of the **Pre-Raphaelite Brotherhood** and close friends with **William Morris**, Burne-Jones and **Rossetti**. After his ordination, he was assistant master at Highgate School, where he taught **G. M. Hopkins** in 1861. He maintained his friendship with Hopkins, praising his poetry for 'forcibly and delicately giving the essence of things in nature' and trying to get 'The Loss of the Euridyce' printed in a Carlisle newspaper. Dixon's own first collection of verse, *Christ's Company* (1861), was praised by Rossetti and **Swinburne**. He later held various preferments in the North of England and published several more volumes, including *Historical Odes* (1864), *Mano: a Poetical History* (1883), *Odes and Eclogues* (1884) and *Lyrical Poems* (1887). *Mano* was a long narrative poem set in the 10th century, recounting the adventures of a Norman knight. Other anthology poems are 'Dream', 'The Wizard's Funeral' and 'Love's Consolation'. His main prose work was a *History of the Church of England from the Abolition of Roman Jurisdiction* (1878–1902). **Robert Bridges** edited a selection, *The Last Poems* (1905).

**Dobell, Sydney (Thompson)** 1824–74 Poet. He was born at Cranbrook in Kent and privately educated in Cheltenham. *The Roman: A Dramatic Poem* (1850) supported the cause of Italian nationalism. The first part of *Balder* appeared in 1853 but Dobell never completed the poem, so damaging was the ridicule inflicted by **William Aytoun**, who parodied its plot in *Firmilian* (1854) and identified its author as part of the **Spasmodic School of Poetry**. Dobell's other volumes included *Sonnets on the War* (with **Alexander Smith**, 1855) and *England in Time of War* (1856), about the Crimean campaign. His essays, *Thoughts on Art, Philosophy, and Religion*, appeared posthumously in 1876.

**Dobson, Austin (Henry)** 1840–1921 Poet and biographer. Educated at Beaumarchais Grammar School and in Strasburg, he served with **Gosse** at the Board of Trade. His knowledge of the 18th century is apparent in his biographies of **Hogarth** (1879), **Steele** (1886), **Goldsmith** (1888), **Horace Walpole** (1890), **Richardson** (1902) and **Fanny Burney** (1903). His verse often used French forms such as the triolet and rondeau. His volumes include *Vignettes in Rhyme* (1873), *Proverbs in Porcelain* (1877) and *At the Sign of the Lyre* (1885). *Collected Poems* appeared in 1897, and a collection of later essays in 1921.

**Dobson, Rosemary** 1920– Australian poet. Born in Sydney of Australian and English parents, she is the granddaughter of **Austin Dobson**. After studying art at the University of Sydney, she taught art at her former school, was employed on cipher work during World War II and then entered publishing. For several years she lived in London and now lives in Canberra. Dobson's detached, reflective verse has not received a great deal of popular attention, but its craftsmanship and formal elegance have few rivals in Australian literature. Her training in art frequently manifests itself in poems about painters, painting and design. Like much of her verse, the title-poem of one of her finest volumes, *The Ship of Ice* (1948), illustrates the timelessness of art, its power to immortalize a fleeting moment. *Child with a Cockatoo* (1955) includes several meditations on painting. *The Ship of Ice* also contains 'The Devil and the Angel' sequence in which the Devil and the Archangel Michael invite a series of representative figures to choose between Heaven and Hell. Dobson's subsequent poetry is increasingly concerned with her personal experiences, especially that of motherhood, and Greek themes. Her other volumes include *In a Convex Mirror* (1944), *Cock Crow* (1965), *Collected Poems* (1973) and *Greek Coins* (1977).

***Doctor Faustus, The Tragicall History of*** A tragedy in blank verse and prose by **Christopher Marlowe**, first produced *c.* 1589 but not published until 1604. An edition of 1616 is more reliable, but both are faulty. The medieval legend of the bargain with the Devil first found its way into printed form at Frankfurt in 1587, when the chief character was identified with a Doctor Georg Faust, a necromancer of the late 15th and early 16th centuries in Germany. In the Frankfurt *Volksbuch* he is called Johann Faust and Marlowe uses the same name (John) in his (the first) dramatization of the story. The play was acted by the same company who produced ***Tamburlaine***, The Admiral's Men, who were now called the Earl of Nottingham's Men – in recognition of their patron's new eminence. **Edward Alleyn** played Doctor Faustus.

Faustus is weary of scientific study and turns to magic. He invokes the aid of the Devil, who sends his agent Mephistophilis in the form of an ugly beast. Faustus commands him to change his shape to that of a friar, which Mephistophilis meekly does. Faustus makes his bargain: Lucifer will give him 24 years of life, with Mephistophilis to do his bidding, but at the end of that time Faustus will be taken, body and soul, by Lucifer.

The title-page illustration of Christopher Marlowe's *The Tragicall History of the Life and Death of Doctor Faustus*, 1620 edition.

The contract gives Faustus everything he asks for, except for certain questions Mephistophilis will not answer ('Now tell me, who made the world?'). Faustus's guardian angel goes on trying to redeem him, while a Bad Angel goes on persuading him he is damned. Lucifer himself comes to Faustus and shows him the pleasures in the seven deadly sins. After a confrontation with the Pope and cardinals in Rome, Faustus invokes the ghost of Helen of Troy. An Old Man pleads with Faustus to step back from the brink – there is still hope of redemption. Faustus makes his choice: he invokes the spirit of Helen again and embraces her ('Her lips suck forth my soul'). The climax of the play is Faustus's monologue anticipating the terrors that await him in his last hour of mortal life ('See, see, where Christ's blood streams in the firmament! One drop would save my soul, half a drop. Ah, my Christ!'). It is a magnificent poem, a great theme expressed in language that is equal to it.

*Doctor Thorne* A novel by **Anthony Trollope**, the third of the **Barsetshire** sequence, published in three volumes in 1858.

The unmarried Dr Thorne, a country practitioner, lives in Greshamsbury with his niece Mary. He alone knows the secret of her birth, that she is the illegitimate child of his brother Henry by the sister of a local stonemason, Roger Scatcherd. Imprisoned for murdering his sister's seducer, Scatcherd, now Sir Roger, has risen to eminence as a successful railway contractor, although his life is vitiated by the drunkenness he has passed on to his enfeebled only son Louis. Mary has grown up as the friend of the local squire's family, the Greshams, and she and the young heir Frank are in love; but the estate is burdened with debt and Frank is required to 'marry money'. The novel deals with the trials the young couple have to endure, as Frank's relatives first ostracize Mary, then aided by their aristocratic relations, the De Courcys, plot a marriage between him and the much older Miss Dunstable, the shrewd and kindly heiress to a patent medicine fortune. When Sir Roger dies, however, soon followed by his son Louis, Mary falls heir to his fortune, and the obstacles to her marriage with Frank dissolve, his family choosing to ignore the fact of her low birth now that money is in prospect. A subsidiary plot deals with the relations between Frank's sister and a social-climbing lawyer, and his eventual marriage to her treacherous De Courcy cousin.

*Doctor Thorne* was Trollope's best-selling novel in his own lifetime, and represents an extension of the Barsetshire range to take in the life of county society.

**Doctorow, E[dgar] L[awrence]** 1931– American novelist. Doctorow was born in New York City and educated at Kenyon College and Columbia University. His first novel, *Welcome to Hard Times*, was published in the USA in 1960 (in Britain as *Bad Man from Bodie*, 1961). In 1971 he published *The Book of Daniel*, the novel which brought him his first public acclaim, a fictional account of the espionage trial of Julius and Ethel Rosenberg and its aftermath. His fiction is typified by its use of historical figures, most notably in *Ragtime* (1975), in which the lives of three fictional families at the beginning of the 20th century are entwined with figures such as Henry Ford, Emma Goldman, Harry Houdini, **Theodore Dreiser** and Sigmund Freud. His other works are the novels *Big as Life* (1966), *Loon Lake* (1980), and *World's Fair* (1985); the play *Drinks Before Dinner* (1979); and *Lives of the Poet, Six Stories and a Novella* (1984), which addresses the position of the writer as both participant in and observer of society.

**Doddridge, Philip** 1702–51 Nonconformist divine. Born in London the twentieth and final offspring of an oilman, he was always delicate, and only one of his siblings reached adulthood. Educated privately, then at the school at Kingston founded by his grandfather, he finally moved to a school at St Albans. The Duchess of Bedford offered to fund a university course but he felt unable to conform. In 1723 he received his certificate of approbation and was ordained a presbyter in 1730. He was a major influence in the unification of Nonconformist groups. In an attempt to alleviate ill health he voyaged to Lisbon, but died there. His collected works appeared at Leeds in 10 volumes in 1802–5 and the most important are *The Rise and Progress of Religion in the Soul* (1745) and over 350 hymns, which may be compared to those of **Isaac Watts**. In 1747 he produced *Some Remarkable Passages in the Life of Colonel James Gardiner*, an account of a reformed rake.

**Dodgson, Charles Lutwidge** See **Carroll, Lewis**.

**Dodsley, Robert** 1703–64 Publisher and author. Born near Mansfield, Nottinghamshire, educated at the free school where his father was headmaster, and apprenticed to a stockingmaker who ill-treated him, the young Dodsley ran away and found work as a servant, eventually becoming footman to the Hon. Mrs Lowther. He was fortunate in his employer, for she helped him publish his poem *Servitude* (1729) and called attention to her footman's gifts. Literary London became interested in Dodsley, and the friendship of **Pope** and **Swift** eventually brought him to the notice of John Rich.

Dodsley's play *The Toyshop: A Dramatic Satire* (written about 1732) was successfully produced by Rich at **Covent Garden** in 1735 and Dodsley used his modest success to open a bookshop at Tully's Head in Pall Mall. Pope invested £100 and **Horace Walpole**, **Lord Lyttelton** and Joseph Spence helped him select poetry when he became a publisher. In addition to the works of Pope, Dodsley issued those of **Thomas Gray**, **Mark Akenside**, **William Collins**, **Edward Young** and **William Shenstone**; he also published work by **Samuel Johnson** and **Oliver Goldsmith**. His great service to the poets of his time was the publication of their work in permanent volumes called *A Collection of Poems by Various Hands*, the first of which was published in 1748; six volumes appeared in 10 years. They are valuable to students of the period, as his collection of *Old Plays* (12 vols., 1744) is to students of drama.

Dodsley's tragedy *Cleone* was produced in 1758. In the same year he founded, with **Edmund Burke**, *The Annual Register*, which still continues to appear.

**Dodsworth** A novel by **Sinclair Lewis**, published in 1929. Sam Dodsworth, a successful automobile manufacturer in the city of Zenith in the American Midwest, sells out to a larger company and retires. Still vigorous in his middle age, a dreamer and an idealist, he travels with his wife Fran to Europe.

Fran is spoiled, affected, and easily awed by European manners and titles. Wishing to appear a woman of the world – to become European – she flirts with other men and becomes increasingly impatient with Sam's supposed gaucheness. Eventually they separate and she plans to marry Kurt von Obersdorf, a young Austrian aristocrat. But the marriage does not take place: Kurt's mother disapproves of Fran – a soon-to-be-divorced, middle-aged American. She begs Sam's forgiveness, and though in the meantime he has met Edith Cortright, a refined and understanding American living in Italy, he takes Fran back. Soon, however, her shallowness and petulance make him realize how much he cares for Edith. He divorces Fran and returns to Edith in Europe.

**Dombey and Son** A novel by **Charles Dickens**, published in 20 monthly parts from October 1846 until April 1848 (and in volume form, 1848). Its full title, *Dealings with the Firm of Dombey and Son, Retail, Wholesale and for Exportation*, is deliberately ambiguous in its reference to both a family and a family business. The stern, unbending Mr Dombey, preoccupied with his desire for a son and heir to the firm, ignores and resents his eldest child, a daughter, Florence. When a son is born at the beginning of the book, Mrs Dombey dies in childbirth and the boy, Paul, proves to be constitutionally weak. He grows to be more fond of his sister than of his father, and has the habit of disconcerting those who attempt to instruct him by his quick perceptions. Little Paul Dombey dies in

the fifth number (Chapter 16) and the bereavement serves to alienate Florence further from her father, despite her desperate eagerness for his love. Dombey's second marriage, to the widowed Edith Grainger, proves loveless and childless. The passionate Edith finally runs away with the manager of Dombey's business, the predatory Carker, though she soon abandons him and he is killed in a railway accident. Dombey's ensuing mental and physical decline parallels his business difficulties. Only as a ruined man can he at last respond to Florence's enduring love.

*Dombey and Son* is commonly taken to herald the start of Dickens's maturity as a novelist, for its careful planning marks a break from the high-spirited improvisation which often sustains his early fiction. The central idea – that 'Dombey and Son should be a Daughter after all' – controls the book's shape, though Dickens is also deeply concerned with the theme of pride. The novel contrasts the cold unhappiness of the Dombey household with the cheerful homes of the Toodle family and of Sol Gills and his nephew Walter Gay (Florence's future husband). The story of Paul's birth, education and death was edited as 'The Story of Little Dombey' to make a favourite set-piece in Dickens's immensely succesful public readings.

**Domett, Alfred** 1811–77 Politician and poet. Domett was born at Camberwell Grove, Surrey, and became a barrister of the Middle Temple after leaving St John's College, Cambridge. He emigrated to New Zealand, where he became Prime Minister. After his return to England in 1871 he published two books of poetry reflecting his experiences, *Ranolf and Amohia* (1872) and *Flotsam and Jetsam* (1877). 'A Christmas Hymn', which was once a familiar anthology piece, was one of the occasional poems published by **Blackwood's Magazine** before Domett went to New Zealand. A friend of

Don Juan fighting with the Sultan. An illustration from an edition of Byron's *Don Juan* published in 1850. The incident occurs in Canto VIII.

**Robert Browning**, Domett is the 'Waring' of Browning's well-known poem (1842).

*Don Juan* Lord **Byron**'s unfinished 'epic satire' in **ottava rima** published in 16 **cantos** between 1819 and 1824. The first two cantos appeared in 1819, cantos 3–5 in 1821, 6–14 in 1823 and cantos 15 and 16 in 1824.

Byron's central character is not the aggressive libertine of tradition, but a passive, if unprincipled, innocent who learns through the variety of his complex international experience. The poem opens with the 16-year-old Juan being sent away from his native Seville by his mother as a result of an intrigue with Donna Julia. On the way from Cadiz his ship is wrecked in a storm and the crew and passengers are obliged to drift in the ship's longboat; their privations lead to the consumption first of Juan's spaniel then of his tutor, Pedrillo. Byron's description of both the storm and the subsequent cannibalism contains some of his most powerful, as well as his most wry, descriptive verse. Juan is eventually cast up on a Greek island where he meets Haïdée, the daughter of a pirate. The two fall in love, but their passion is disrupted by the return of Haïdée's pirate-father, who sends Juan away in chains to be sold as a slave. Haïdée dies of grief. Juan is sold in Constantinople to a sultana who has fallen in love with him, but their relationship is soured by her perpetual jealousy and Juan is obliged to escape to the Russian army then besieging Ismail. Distinguishing himself in the Russian service, he is sent with dispatches to St Petersburg where he inevitably attracts the attentions of the Empress Catherine. He is sent to England on a diplomatic mission; the last cantos of the unfinished poem recount his amorous adventures and contain much satirical comment on contemporary English society, politics and literature.

*Don Juan* is Byron's most sustained masterpiece. Its tone is varied and its loose structure allows the poet to intermix his gifts as a lyrical, satirical, comic and narrative writer. The poem offers a wide-ranging ironic comment on human passions, whims and shortcomings. It also contains the much-anthologized lyric 'The Isles of Greece' (Canto 3), Byron's powerful song to a nation still occupied by the Ottomans.

**Donleavy, J[ames] P[atrick]** 1926– Novelist and playwright. Born in Brooklyn, New York, he served in the US Navy before going to Trinity College, Dublin. His experiences of Dublin literary life provided the material for his most famous novel, *The Ginger Man*, first published in Paris in 1955, then in a revised edition in New York in 1958 and in a 'complete and unexpurgated' edition in New York in 1965. A dramatized version was withdrawn in Dublin in 1959, but staged in England in the same year and in New York in 1963. Its hero, Sebastian Dangerfield, became a minor cult figure. Donleavy's second novel, *A Singular Man*, appeared in 1961, as well as the play *Fairy Tales of New York*. They were followed by a volume of short stories, *Meet My Maker the Mad Molecule* (USA, 1964), *The Saddest Summer of Samuel S.* (USA, 1966) and two other novels with Irish settings, *The Beastly Beatitudes of Balthazar B.* (1968) and *The Destinies of Darcy Dancer, Gentleman* (1977). Donleavy's parents were Irish; in 1967 he became an Irish citizen and settled in Ireland. His comic gift and his sexual candour were once more appreciated than they are now.

**Donne, John** *c.* 1572–1631 Poet and divine. He was born in Bread Street, London, his father a prosperous ironmonger and his mother the daughter of **John Heywood**, the dramatist. Donne was brought up as a Roman Catholic. He was educated at Hart Hall, Oxford, and left in 1584 without a degree, which would have required him to take the Oath of Supremacy. According to his earliest biographer, **Izaak Walton** (whose *Life* appeared in 1640), Donne then went to Cambridge and travelled abroad. He entered Lincoln's Inn in 1592, and embarked on a period of womanizing and writing verse. The dating of most of his poetry is problematic, but to this period of the 1590s probably belong most of his fine love poetry and the five *Satires*, which were some of the first formal verse-satires in the language.

In 1596 he sailed on the Cadiz expedition when the Spanish fleet was defeated, and in the

John Donne. Collection of the Marquess of Lothian.

following year he joined the inconclusive expedition to the Azores, where he wrote 'The Calme'. On his return he became chief secretary to Sir Thomas Egerton, a former lawyer, Lord Keeper of the Great Seal. Donne now lived next to the Palace of Whitehall, and he met Ann Moore, 14-year-old daughter of Lady Egerton's brother, Sir George Moore. In 1601 Donne became MP for Brackley, one of Egerton's pocket boroughs, but he was not active in the House. At the end of this year he drastically altered the course of his life by marrying Ann (at 17 still a minor) in secret. This amounted to social suicide. The union was discovered, and in 1602 Egerton had the poet briefly imprisoned and permanently dismissed from office. At the age of 30, Donne was married and jobless.

Doubts have been raised about the happiness of this fateful marriage, but they had 12 children, of whom seven survived. Their domestic circumstances were impecunious, and the poet was dogged by intermittent illness. In 1605 he travelled to Europe with Sir Walter Chute, returning in 1606 and settling in Mitcham. Donne preferred the busy life of the metropolis to rural calm; he tried to attract the attention of potential patrons such as the Countesses of Bedford and Huntingdon, but advancement was not forthcoming. In 1607 he wrote *Biathanatos*, an erudite prose-work about Christianity and suicide. He was becoming increasingly involved in religious thought, having drifted from Catholicism; his spiritual commitment was unresolved, though, and he declined the suggestion of his friend Thomas Morton, Dean of Gloucester, that he should be ordained. In 1610 he published his most notable prose-work, *Pseudo-Martyr*, designed to persuade English Roman Catholics to take the Oath of Supremacy. This and *Ignatius His Conclave* (1611), a satire on the Jesuits, met with the approval of James I.

About this time, Donne became frustrated and seriously depressed. His near-despair is reflected in the *Holy Sonnets* which he was then composing. He cultivated a convivial circle of literary acquaintances centring on the Mitre Tavern, and these included **Jonson**, **Drayton** and Inigo Jones. He also made an important new friend in Sir Robert Drury, a vivacious landowning gentleman with whom Donne travelled to Amiens and Paris in 1611, returning the next year via Germany.

He and his wife settled in a small house in Drury Lane, and Donne assiduously presented complimentary verses to individuals in court circles, but failed to find preferment. The Church looked increasingly like the only prospect for professional success, and on 23 January 1615 he took Holy Orders. James I appointed him a royal chaplain, and he began to acquire a reputation as a fine preacher. In 1616 he was made Reader in Divinity at Lincoln's Inn, a post which suited his combination of talents, and he held two livings, one in Kent and the other in Huntingdon.

Just when his fortunes appeared to be improving, Donne's wife died on 15 August 1617, after giving birth to a stillborn child. The poet's grief at her death is powerful proof of his devotion to her; he never quite recovered, and according to Walton he was thereafter 'crucified to the world'. The religious dimension to his life certainly seems to have deepened. In 1619, Donne spent seven months travelling with Viscount Doncaster in an unsuccessful attempt to mediate between the Catholic Emperor of Germany and the troublesome Protestant subjects in Bohemia. He returned to London in 1620, his depression somewhat alleviated, and in the following year was made Dean of St Paul's, a busy administrative and spiritual occupation at which he excelled. His financial position was finally secure. In 1623 his eldest daughter, Constance, married the celebrated actor Ned **Alleyn** (by then 58) who was the founder of Dulwich College.

Late in 1623 Donne became seriously ill during an epidemic, and began work on his *Devotions upon Emergent Occasions* (1624) consisting of meditations, expostulations and prayers, including Meditation 17 which begins 'Perchance he for whom the bell tolls' and is one of the best-known passages of English prose. He also wrote some verse, including the poem 'In Sicknesse'. In 1624 he was made Vicar of St Dunstan's-in-the-West, where Walton was a parishioner. On 27 March 1625, James I died, and Donne preached his first sermon before Charles I. He retired from London to Chelsea to avoid the plague, but later delivered some of his most powerful sermons on the theme of suffering. Donne became unwell again in 1630, but, emaciated and suffering from infections of the mouth, he nevertheless insisted on preaching the sermon on the first Friday in Lent, 1631, before the King at Whitehall. The theme was 'Death's Duel', and it was to be his last. The poet died on 31 March 1631, and is buried in St Paul's; he personally designed his monument, and it survived the Great Fire.

Very little of Donne's verse appeared in print during his lifetime. There was a publication of his *Collected Poems* in 1633, mostly comprising his earlier work. His poetry is generally divided into the secular – often amatory – lyrics, and his later religious verse, although the latter was evidently an organic development from the former. Most of the poems for which he is best known belong to his pre-marriage, London days of the 1590s, contained in *Songs and Sonnets* – this includes 'The Good Morrow', 'The Canonization', 'The Bait', and songs such as 'Go and Catch a Falling Star'. To the same period belong his *Elegies*: characteristically sinuous, colloquial and racy, these poems have nothing of the smoothness subsequently identified with the elegiac mode. Elegies 16 and 19 are celebrated examples of the young poet's energetically passionate verse, in the form of addresses to a real or imaginary mistress, and they represent a new force in English poetry. Donne's verse was frequently erotic and physically urgent; he was the first writer to use 'sex' in its present sense. Between 1593 and 1598, he worked on his verse *Satires*, the trend of which shows early evidence of his rational strength. In 1601 he published an ambitious but unfinished poem, *Metempsychosis*, a complicated explanation of the nature of good and evil as manifested in the progressive metamorphoses of the soul, from its vegetable origins in Eden to its embodiment in mankind.

Much of Donne's poetry confronted the theme of death; in his *Holy Sonnets*, mostly written before he was ordained, there is the memorable poem beginning 'Death, be not proud', and he was also the author of two notable poems commemorating the death of Elizabeth Drury, the daughter of his friend and patron – 'The First Anniversary' (1611) and 'The Progress of the Soul' (1612). His religious poems are more difficult than the secular, since they are sometimes intellectually unresolved, but they are uniformly forthright and sincere. As a devotional poet Donne is less stylistically arresting, less facetious, and less sure of his direction; the poems mirror what was evidently a fierce struggle of the spirit to conquer doubt and achieve faith. As a writer of religious prose he is best known for his *Sermons*, 160 of which were published after his death, in 1640, 1649 and 1660 successively. They are often brilliant and severe.

Generally regarded as the foremost of the **metaphysical poets**, Donne was always an uneven writer. His secular poems were original, energetic and highly rhetorical, full of passionate thought and intellectual juggling. His love poetry often turns on paradox and puns, and was designed to work forcefully against the tired conventions of the **Petrarchan** school of **Sidney** and **Spenser**. His adroitness in argument and his skill at impersonating different states of mind make Donne's poetry intense and often riddling. His roughness of rhythmic effect, though, caused him to fall out of favour with succeeding generations of readers until his rediscovery in the 20th century.

**Doolittle, Hilda** 1886–1961 American poet. Doolittle, who used the pen-name of HD, was born in Bethlehem, Pennsylvania. In 1911 she went to live in Europe, and soon became part of the group known as the **imagists**. A leading member of the group was **Ezra Pound**, to whom she had been briefly engaged, and it was he who arranged for her first publications – in

*Poetry* magazine and then in the anthology *Des Imagistes* (1914). In 1913 she married the English poet and novelist **Richard Aldington**. Her first collection of verse, *Sea Garden* (1916), drew heavily on her passion for the literature of classical Greece. Indeed, all her early collections include translations from – and many poems inspired by – the works of Sappho, Meleager and Euripides among others. All reveal her gift for concise and direct visual description; she often uses a natural object (a plant, a rock, a wave, a bee) to stand for a human mood or emotion, a method consistent both with the principles of imagism and with the practice of the Greek poets she loved.

She stayed in England throughout World War I, which brought many changes to her life, including the dissolution of her marriage, the birth of her daughter, and the beginning of her association with Bryher (Winifred Ellerman), the English novelist and patron of the modernist arts, who became her lifelong companion. More collections of poetry followed: *Hymen* (1921), *Heliodora and Other Poems* (1924), and *Red Roses for Bronze* (1929). In the 1920s she also began to write prose fiction. *Palimpsest* (1926) consists of three sections, one set in classical Rome, one in post-war London, and one in the Egypt of the excavators; each is told through the stream of consciousness of a central female figure (each one an artist), and the three are unified by themes of sexual betrayal and the woman's attempt to find personal fulfilment through love and art. *Hedylus* (1928), set in ancient Alexandria, deals with the relationship between a woman poet and courtesan and her son, also a poet. During this period Doolittle worked on several prose works with explicitly lesbian themes, which she chose not to publish during her lifetime: *Pilate's Wife*, *Asphodel*, and *Her* (published as *Hermione* in 1981).

Her psychoanalysis by Freud (1933–4) and her experience of London during the blitz of World War II provided two of the main sources for her long poem *Trilogy*, which comprised *The Walls Do Not Fall* (1944), *Tribute To The Angels* (1945) and *The Flowering of the Rod* (1946). Her other works include *Hippolytus Temporizes* (1927), a drama in classical form; *By Avon River* (1949), a tribute in verse and prose to **Shakespeare** and the Elizabethans; another novel, *Bid Me To Live* (1960), treating life in London during World War I; *Helen in Egypt* (1961), a long poem about Helen of Troy; three memoirs: *Tribute to Freud* (1956), *End To Torment: A Memoir of Ezra Pound* (1979) and *The Gift* (1982); and a final set of poetic sequences, *Hermetic Definition* (1972).

**Dos Passos, John (Roderigo)** 1896–1970 American novelist. The illegitimate son of a prominent American attorney, Dos Passos was born in Chicago, but spent much of his early life living abroad with his mother. He returned to the USA to attend Harvard, and then served as an ambulance driver in France and Italy during World War I. He drew upon his war experiences for his first two novels, *One Man's Initiation: 1917* (1920) and *Three Soldiers* (1921), both of which portray revolt against mindless discipline. In 1922 he published a collection of essays, *Rosinante to the Road Again*, and a volume of poems, *A Pushcart at the Curb*. *Streets of Night*, a novel he had begun while still a student at Harvard, appeared in 1923.

Dos Passos came to prominence with **Manhattan Transfer** (1925), a novel set in New York City and in which he introduced the stylistic innovations he would develop further in his greatest work, **USA**. During the mid 1920s he also became involved with experimental drama, and in 1926 the New Playwrights Theatre performed his play *The Moon is a Gong* (later renamed *The Garbage Man*). His other plays are *Airways, Inc.* (1928) and *Fortune Heights* (1934). His involvement with the New Playwrights Theatre brought him into contact with political radicals, and he began to publish in **The New Masses**, a left-wing periodical. His reputation as a proletarian writer was enhanced by the publication of his novel *The 42nd Parallel* (1930), which, with *1919* (1932) and *The Big Money* (1936), makes up the trilogy **USA**. The trilogy tells the stories of numerous representative Americans, the narratives intersecting and continuing from one novel to the next. They are interspersed with sections called 'The Camera Eye' (**stream-of-consciousness** passages about the experiences of the unnamed narrator), with 'Newsreels' (impressionistic collections of slogans, popular song lyrics, newspaper headlines, and extracts from political speeches), and with brief biographical vignettes of actual figures, such as **Randolph Bourne**, **Thorstein Veblen**, Theodore Roosevelt, Henry Ford and Rudolph Valentino.

He became disillusioned with communism and broke completely with the left at the time of the Spanish Civil War, as is made clear in his novel *The Adventures of a Young Man* (1939). This work, together with *Number One* (1943), a novel about the dangers of demagogy, and *The Grand Design* (1949), about the threat of bureaucracy, make up another triology – *District of Columbia*. His later novels include *Chosen Country* (1951) and *Midcentury* (1961). He also wrote numerous works of non-fiction: *The Head and Heart of Thomas Jefferson* (1954), a full-length biography of one of his heroes; *The Best of Times: An Informal Memoir* (1966); and several collections of essays and reportage, which reflect his increasingly conservative political stance. *The Fourteenth Chronicle* (1973) contains selections from his letters and diaries.

**Double Dealer, The** A comedy by **William Congreve**, first performed in London in 1693. More satirical and more rigidly classical in form than his first play, *The Old Bachelor* (1693), it was, according to **John Dryden**, who admired it, 'much censured by the greater part of the town'. The malice of Maskwell, the double-dealer, and the rhetorical force of the Touchwoods' passion are certainly more than can be easily resolved by a happy ending.

Lady Touchwood, a woman motivated by passion, desires Mellefont, who is her husband's nephew and heir. Mellefont prefers Cynthia, daughter of Sir Paul Plyant. Determined to obstruct their marriage, Lady Touchwood enlists the aid of Maskwell, a former lover expert in deceit. Playing the part of Mellefont's friend, Maskwell tricks both Sir Paul Plyant and Lord Touchwood into suspecting that Mellefont is having affairs with their wives. The ruse works and Mellefont is disinherited and banned from marrying Cynthia. But Maskwell overreaches when he claims Cynthia for himself. The jealous Lady Touchwood cannot accept being supplanted and their plotting is discovered when Lord Touchwood overhears her furious attack on Maskwell's duplicity. Mellefont and Cynthia are at last free to marry, and Maskwell and Lady Touchwood are consigned to the ignominy of oblivion.

**Double Falsehood, or, The Distressed Lovers** See **Shakespeare apocrypha**.

**Douce, Francis** 1757–1834 Antiquary. A student of Gray's Inn, Douce became keeper of manuscripts at the British Museum where he catalogued the Lansdowne Manuscripts and revised the catalogue of the Harleian Manuscripts, but left after a disagreement. His *Illustrations of Shakespeare* (1807) was a collection of the principal sources and analogues of the plays. In 1823 he was left a considerable sum by the sculptor Nollekens, which enabled him to indulge in his longstanding desire to acquire books and *objets d'art*. He left his outstanding collection of books, manuscripts, prints and coins to the Bodleian Library.

**Doughty, Charles Montagu** 1843–1926 Travel-writer and poet. Born at Theberton Hall, Suffolk, and educated at Gonville and Caius College, Cambridge, he began travelling as a student, visiting North Africa, Syria and Arabia in 1870. After settling in Damascus in 1875 in order to learn Arabic, he made the pilgrimage to Mecca in 1876 by joining a camel caravan. He continued with the caravan to central Asia, finishing his journey at Jedda. The account of his journey is contained in his most famous work, *Travels in Arabia Deserta* (1888), a book written in a self-consciously archaic style and in the manner of the Elizabethan travel-writers. Doughty's poetry includes *The Dawn in Britain* (6 vols., 1906–7), *Adam Cast Forth* (1908), *The Clouds* (1912) and *Mansoul, or, The Riddle of the World* (1920).

**Douglas** A blank-verse tragedy by **John Home**, first performed in Edinburgh in 1756. Its success there was repeated in London the following year and the play retained its hold in the theatre for almost a century. For its author *Douglas* was a turning-point, since the outraged reaction of the Church of Scotland's dignitaries brought his career as a minister to an end.

The plot is based on an old Scottish ballad. Its central characters, Young Norval and Lady Randolph, exhibit the exalted sentiments that satisfied Home's quest for a 'celestial melancholy'. Young Norval is the son of Douglas. His mother, embroiled in the feuds of the Scottish clans, is married to Lord Randolph after the birth of her son, and the infant son exposed to the elements by her father, Sir Malcolm. Presumed dead, the boy has been saved and brought up by Norval, a shepherd. He wins the favour of Lord Randolph by saving his life and is briefly restored to his loving mother. But Lord Randolph's heir, the villainous Glenalvon, is jealous of Young Norval. After his various attempts to calumniate him have failed, Glenalvon tries to kill him, but Young Norval, now boasting the name of Douglas, kills Glenalvon, only to be killed by the deceived Lord Randolph. Lady Randolph commits suicide.

**Douglas, Lord Alfred (Bruce)** 1870–1945 Poet. He was born near Worcester and educated at Winchester and Magdalen College, Oxford. His intimacy with **Oscar Wilde**, to whom he was introduced in 1891 by **Lionel Johnson**, eventually provoked Douglas's father, Lord Queensberry, to intervene; Wilde's unsuccessful suit against Queensberry brought about his own downfall. In prison Wilde addressed the bitter *De Profundis* to Douglas.

Apart from his translation of Wilde's *Salome* into English (1894) and his two books, *Oscar Wilde and Myself* (1914) and *Oscar Wilde: A Summing-Up* (1940), Douglas produced several volumes of verse, notably *The City of the Soul* (1899), *Sonnets* (1909), *Sonnets – In Excelsis* (1924) and *Sonnets and Lyrics* (1935). He was editor of *The Academy* in 1907–10 and published *The Autobiography of Douglas* in 1929.

**Douglas, Gavin** ?1475–1522 Scottish poet. Douglas came of a noble and powerful family: his father was Earl of Angus. He graduated MA from St Andrews (1494) and probably also studied at Paris. Among ecclesiastical offices he held were the deanery of Dunkeld, the provostship of St Giles Cathedral in Edinburgh, and

finally the bishopric of Dunkeld to which he was consecrated in 1515. The last was a post he sought for some time and had difficulty in obtaining. After Flodden Douglas's attention became more and more engaged by politics, as the dowager Queen Margaret, widow of James IV, married Douglas's nephew. He was ambitious but often disappointed or hampered in his hopes for high office by clan and ecclesiastical rivalries. In 1515 he was charged with irregularities in obtaining benefices and imprisoned, despite the protestations of the Pope and Queen Margaret. In 1521 he went to London, apparently to gain Henry VIII's support for his interests, and was accused of high treason by the Scottish Lords of Council in 1522. He died in exile, probably from the plague.

Douglas says that his translation of the *Aeneid* was completed 22 July 1513. His other major work, *The Palace of Honour*, was probably finished by 1501, but was not printed until later (London *c*.1553, Edinburgh 1579). This poem was designed for a courtly audience and dedicated to James IV. It is an allegorical **dream-vision** in which the poet sees first the pageants of Minerva, Diana and Venus. He is tried on a charge of blasphemy before the Court of Venus and only saved by the intervention of the muse Calliope. The poem's quest for Honour is finally achieved in the third part, as the poet reaches Honour's palace on a high mountain.

*King Hart* is only doubtfully ascribed to Douglas. It was first printed in 1786 and is a homiletic **allegory** at times very like **Everyman**. King Hart (the soul) is imprisoned in mid-life by Lady Plesaunce and finally faces mortality. *Conscience*, probably by Douglas, is an attack on the cupidity of churchmen. **Bale**'s *Index Britanniae Scriptorum* mentions other works by Douglas, but these are now lost.

**Douglas, George** Pseudonym of the Scottish novelist George Douglas Brown (1869–1902). Born in Ayrshire, he was educated at Glasgow University and Balliol College, Oxford. In London he earned his living contributing short stories and boys' stories to magazines. His realistic story of Scottish life, *The House with Green Shutters*, appeared in 1901.

**Douglas, (George) Norman** 1868–1952 Novelist and travel-writer. Norman Douglas was born in Austria; his father was a Scot, his mother Scottish-German. He was educated at Uppingham School and Karlsruhe. From 1893–1901 he served in the British Foreign Office, working as a diplomat to St Petersburg, then settled in Italy on the island of Capri.

His career as a writer began with books on zoology, but in 1901 he published *Unprofessional Tales* (under the pseudonym Normy), which was not successful. *Siren Land* (1911), like his subsequent two works (*Fountains in the Sand*, 1912, about Tunisia, and *Old Calabria*, 1915), was essentially a travel book which reflected Douglas's wide-ranging interests as biologist, geologist, art lover, archaeologist and classicist. However, it was with **South Wind** (1917) that he achieved his first, and only popular success. The novel caused considerable debate because of its frank discussion of moral and sexual questions. *They Went* (1920) and *In the Beginning* (1927) are novel-fantasies about early mankind, and *Looking Back* (1933) is a fragmentary autobiography.

**Douglas, Keith (Castellain)** 1920–44 Poet. Born in Tunbridge Wells and educated at Christ's Hospital and Oxford, where **Edmund Blunden** was his tutor, Douglas served during World War II in North Africa and was injured by a land-mine. He soon returned to active service in Normandy, where he died in 1944.

His war poems face the prospect of death without recourse to heightened rhetoric or mournful sentiment. *Selected Poems* appeared in 1943 and *Alamein to Zem Zem*, an account of his experience in the desert campaign, was published posthumously in 1946. **Ted Hughes**'s enthusiastic introduction to a selection of Douglas's verse (1964) brought him a wider audience. A revised *Collected Poems* was issued in 1966 and a *Complete Poems* in 1979.

**Douglass, Frederick** 1817–95 Black American writer, born into slavery on a plantation in Maryland. He received no formal education, but learned to read first by bribing young white schoolchildren to help him, then by studying a copy of the journal *The Columbian Orator*. He worked for a while in a Baltimore shipyard, and then taught school to fellow slaves before escaping in 1838 to Massachusetts, where he was employed as a lecturer by anti-slavery societies.

He became known as one of the most eloquent anti-slavery orators of his day, and in 1845 published the *Narrative of the Life of Frederick Douglass, an American Slave*, which was circulated widely and soon translated into a number of languages. Fearing capture as a fugitive, he spent two years in England and Ireland, returning to the USA in 1847 to purchase his freedom and to establish an anti-slavery journal in Rochester, New York – *The North Star* (1847–64), later called *Frederick Douglass' Paper*. In 1858 he founded a second journal, *Douglass' Monthly*, which continued until 1863. His editorial essays in these publications comprise a substantial portion of his writing. His position as a leading spokesman against slavery was strengthened by the appearance of his enlarged autobiography, *My Bondage and My Freedom* (1855). His influence in American political life at this time was considerable. He was in personal contact with Abraham Lincoln, and during the

Civil War he organized two black regiments for the Union. In 1881 he published his third autobiographical work, *The Life and Times of Frederick Douglass*, a central text of the slave narrative tradition and of American autobiography in general. He continued in public service late in life as recorder of deeds for the District of Columbia (1881–6), and as US minister to Haiti (1889–91).

*Dover Beach* A poem by **Matthew Arnold**, published in *New Poems* (1867), which despite its brevity is probably the best known of all his works. The poet contemplates the sea, finding in it melancholy reminders of the uncertainties of belief brought about by modern life. He turns instead to faith in human relationships: 'Ah, love, let us be true to one another!'

**Dowden, Edward** 1843–1913 Critic and scholar. Born in Cork and educated at Queen's College and at Trinity College, Dublin, he was appointed Professor of English Studies at Trinity College in 1867. The editor of 12 **Shakespeare** plays for the original Arden edition, he also wrote *Shakspere: A Critical Study of His Mind and Art* (1875) and *A Shakspere Primer* (1877). His other critical works include a study of **Southey** (1879) for the English Men of Letters series, a substantial biography of **Shelley** (1886) and a life of **Browning** (1905) for the Temple Biographies. His *Poems* appeared in 1876.

**Dowson, Ernest (Christopher)** 1867–1900 Poet. Born in Kent and educated at The Queen's College, Oxford, he left without taking a degree, and joined the London society of **Beardsley**, **Wilde** and **Richard Le Gallienne**. He was a member of the **Rhymers' Club**, and contributed poems to *The Yellow Book* and *The Savoy*. In 1891 he met the 12-year-old Adelaide Foltinowicz, and she became the symbol of love and innocence in his otherwise world-weary poetry. He became a Roman Catholic in 1891–2, and after the suicides of both his parents within a few months of each other in 1895, he travelled aimlessly between France, Ireland and London. **Yeats** described him as 'timid, silent, a little melancholy'.

His verse first achieved attention with *Poems* (1896). *Decorations* (1899) included some experiments with prose-poems, and *The Pierrot of the Minute* (1897) was a one-act verse play. His *Poetical Works* appeared in 1934, and his *Letters* (1967) were edited by H. Maas and D. Flower. The poems are written in a variety of stanza-forms, and express ennui (as in 'Non Sum Qualis Eram' and 'Vitae Summa Brevis') and a correspondingly idealized love (in 'Poet's Road').

**Doyle, Sir Arthur Conan** 1859–1930 Novelist. Born in Edinburgh, son of an unsuccessful architect and nephew of the artist **Richard Doyle**, he attended the Jesuit Stonyhurst College and studied medicine at Edinburgh University. He practised briefly in Plymouth, an experience reflected in *The Stark Munro Letters* (1894), and then at Southsea (1882–90), where a lack of patients gave him the time to write. The first of his **Sherlock Holmes stories** (see also **detective fiction**) was *A Study in Scarlet*, published in *Beeton's Christmas Annual* for 1887. It was followed by another novel, *The Sign of Four* (1890), but the popularity of his detective really dated from the series of short stories he contributed to *The Strand Magazine* from 1891, collected as *The Adventures of Sherlock Holmes* (1892) and *The Memoirs of Sherlock Holmes* (1894). Doyle's attempt to kill off his creation was unsuccessful and Holmes reappeared in two novels, *The Hound of the Baskervilles* (1902) and *The Valley of Fear* (1915), and several collections of short stories, *The Return of Sherlock Holmes* (1905), *His Last Bow* (1917) and *The Case-Book of Sherlock Holmes* (1927).

Doyle's resentment at being identified solely as the creator of Sherlock Holmes was excessive but understandable. Just as his life reflected the many interests of the Edwardian gentleman – particularly sport and military affairs – so his

Sir Arthur Conan Doyle the slave of his creation, Sherlock Holmes. Cartoon by Bernard Partridge, 1926. National Portrait Gallery, London.

career established him as a versatile and hard-working writer. His historical fiction comprises *Micah Clarke* (1889), *The White Company* (1891), *Rodney Stone* (1896), *The Exploits of Brigadier Gerard* (1896), *Uncle Bernac* (1897), *The Adventures of Gerard* (1903) and *Sir Nigel* (1906). *The Tragedy of the 'Korosko'* (1898) is an adventure story. He also turned his hand to **science fiction** in the Professor Challenger stories, *The Lost World* (1912), *The Poison Belt* (1913) and *The Land of Mist* (1926). The last of these reflects the belief in spiritualism which preoccupied much of his later life; he published a history of the subject in 1926.

**Doyle, Sir Francis Hastings Charles** 1810–88 Poet. Born at Nunappleton in Yorkshire, and educated at Eton and Christ Church, Oxford, he became a fellow of All Souls and succeeded **Matthew Arnold** as Professor of Poetry. He was the author of popular ballads, notably the patriotic 'Private of the Buffs' and 'The Red Thread of Honour', and one about racing, 'The Doncaster St Leger'.

**Doyle, Richard** 1824–83 Cartoonist and illustrator. Born in London, 'Dicky' Doyle was son of the artist John Doyle. At the age of 19 he joined the staff of *Punch* and designed its famous cover, but resigned in 1850 because of the journal's anti-Catholic bias. Thereafter he became a distinguished book illustrator – his light, playful sketches accompanied **Ruskin**'s *King of the Golden River* (1851) and **Thackeray**'s *The Newcomes* (1853–5) among other works – though he did not live long enough to collaborate with his nephew, **Sir Arthur Conan Doyle**.

***Dr Jekyll and Mr Hyde, The Strange Case of*** See ***Strange Case of Dr Jekyll and Mr Hyde, The***.

***Dr Wortle's School*** A novel by **Anthony Trollope**, serialized in ***Blackwood's Magazine*** from May to December 1880, and published in two volumes in 1881.

Dr Jeffrey Wortle, a high-spirited and worldly clergyman, runs a successful private school to which he appoints Mr Peacocke as an assistant master, and Peacocke's beautiful American wife as matron. Although Peacocke proves an excellent master, mystery surrounds the couple's history and it is revealed early in the novel that they are not in fact married. While teaching in Missouri he had met and befriended the ill-treated and deserted wife of one Ferdinand Lefroy, a soldier of fortune, and had married her when news came of his death – an event Peacocke made every effort to verify. But Lefroy reappears, and the scandal of their seeming bigamy follows the couple to England. The novel deals with Dr Wortle's courage in standing by his conviction of the Peacockes' integrity against pressure from his bishop, the press and the malevolent gossip of an ex-parent. His stand is rewarded when Peacocke goes to America and returns with proof of a rumour that Lefroy had subsequently died. The scandal subsides when the couple are married again in London. The conventional love interest is provided by the romance between the doctor's daughter Mary and one of his former pupils, Lord Carstairs.

*Dr Wortle's School* deals impressively with a subject peculiarly congenial to Trollope's art, the clash between social convention and the intricacies of the individual case.

**Drabble, Margaret** 1939– Novelist. Born in Sheffield, she was educated at the Mount School, York, and Newnham College, Cambridge. Her novels frequently present an individual's struggle against a conventional or repressive background. They include *A Summer Birdcage* (1963); *The Garrick Year* (1964); *The Millstone* (1965); *Jerusalem the Golden* (1967), about a young woman's rebellious quest for experience in London; *The Waterfall* (1969); *The Ice Age* (1977), a tragicomedy about the *Angst*-ridden middle age of Anthony Keating, onetime producer of TV 'social conscience' programmes; and *The Radiant Way* (1987).

She has also written studies of **Wordsworth** (1966) and **Arnold Bennett** (1974) and edited *The Oxford Companion to English Literature* (1984). *A Writer's Britain* (1979) is an account of the relationship between the writer and landscape. Other works include a play, *Bird of Paradise* (1969), and a book for children, *For Queen and Country* (1978). A lecturer for the Arts Council and the British Council, and past chairman of the National Book League, she was awarded the CBE in 1980 for her services to English literature.

**Dracula** A novel by **Bram Stoker**, published in 1897.

Presented in diaries, letters and news items, this story of the bloodsucking vampire who preys on the living and can be repelled by garlic and crucifixes, is both absurd and powerful. It opens with the diary of Jonathan Harker, a London solicitor who falls victim to Count Dracula in his Transylvanian castle. The Count then travels to England, arriving at Whitby, where the story is taken up in accounts by Harker's fiancée Mina Murray, her friend Lucy Westenra and Dr John Seward. Van Helsing, a Dutch doctor and expert in vampirism, leads the attempt to frustrate the Count. Lucy falls a victim to Dracula and becomes, in her turn, a vampire, but a merciful stake through the heart brings her peace. He turns his attention to Mina, but is followed back to Transylvania and finally vanquished.

There are effective passages describing Dracula's midnight landing at Whitby and his mastery over the zoophagous lunatic in Seward's private asylum, but in general the English scenes do not compare in power with those set in Transylvania. The episode where Harker sees Dracula crawling face downwards, like a giant bat, along the stone wall of his castle is particularly memorable.

Like *Frankenstein*, *Dracula* has become modern myth – the subject of many film versions, imitations and parodies. Tourists to Romania, a country Stoker himself never visited, are now shown 'Dracula's Castle' as tourists to Verona are shown 'Juliet's balcony'.

**dramatic irony** See **irony**.

**dramatic monologue** A development of the **soliloquy**, but not written for the stage or forming part of a play, the dramatic monologue is a poem consisting of a speech by a single character who reveals his thoughts, character and situation. In the 19th century, when literature became increasingly preoccupied with the individual viewpoint, **Robert Browning** found it an ideal form and **Tennyson** several times used it (in, for example, *Tithonus*). In the 20th century, **T. S. Eliot** and others have turned to the dramatic monologue.

***Dramatis Personae*** A collection of poems by **Robert Browning**, published in 1864, the first he issued after the death of **Elizabeth Barrett Browning** in 1861. It includes *Abt Vogler*, 'Prospice' and 'Rabbi Ben Ezra' as well as significant longer poems: 'A Death in the Desert', 'Mr Sludge, "The Medium"' and *Caliban Upon Setebos*.

***Drapier's Letters, The*** A group of seven pamphlets by **Jonathan Swift**, five published in March–December 1724 and two in 1735, written in the character of a Dublin draper, M. B. Drapier. The original five attack the patent acquired by William Wood for supplying Ireland with copper coinage. George I had given the patent to his ageing mistress, the Duchess of Kendal, and she in turn had sold it to Wood, a mineowner and dealer in iron, for the then enormous sum of £10,000. When the Irish Parliament protested to the King in 1723 he promised an enquiry, which opened in April 1724. By then the first of Swift's pamphlets against the 'obscure Ironmonger' had appeared. The scheme to coin 'Wood's ha'pence' was withdrawn and the satirist became a national hero. Swift's interest in the matter was part of his campaign against the arrogant and thoughtless treatment of Ireland by the English.

**Drayton, Michael** 1563–1631 Poet. Drayton's youth was spent in the service of Sir Henry

Goodeere to whom he was indebted for his education. Goodeere's daughter Anne was partly the inspiration for the figure of 'Idea' who appears in Drayton's work.

Drayton's career covers a wide span of time: his first published work appeared in 1591 and his last in 1630. He wrote in nearly all the kinds of poetry available in his time, was sensitive and responsive to fashions in poetic taste and open to influence from a great diversity of sources. He constantly revised and reissued poems, often giving them different titles. As well as there being several separate editions of various works, there are also two collections of his poems by Drayton himself, printed in 1605 and 1619. These collections often contain yet further versions of poems, and a poem by Drayton can exist in as many as five different forms.

*The Harmony of the Church* (1591) is a dull metrical version, marred by excessive alliteration, of some songs and prayers from the Old Testament and the Apocrypha. Drayton responded to the fondness for **pastoral** in the 1590s with *Idea: The Shepherds' Garland* (1593), whose nine **eclogues** show the strong influence of **Spenser**'s *The Shepheardes Calender*. It was revised and reissued in 1606. *Idea's Mirror* (1594) is the first version of the **sonnet** sequence *Idea*, Drayton's contribution to the sonnet vogue of the 1590s. *Endimion and Phoebe* (1595) is an erotic mythological poem, a fashionable form used by **Marlowe** in *Hero and Leander* and **Shakespeare** in *Venus and Adonis*. It was revised and appeared again as *The Man in the Moon* (1606 and 1619). The 1590s also saw Drayton's first attempts at historical poetry with the 'legends' of *Piers Gaveston* (?1594) and *Matilda* (1594). For his historical poems Drayton thoroughly researched his chronicle sources. **Raphael Holinshed** was a favourite source for him as for Shakespeare. *Robert of Normandy* (1596, revised 1605 and 1619) is his most medieval legend: Robert's story is told, in the presence of his ghost, by Fame and Fortune. *Mortimeriados* (1596), rewritten and much altered as *The Barons' Wars* (1603), describes the troublesome reign of Edward II and is much indebted to Marlowe's play. The first version is a series of scenes and tableaux, the revision is several hundred lines longer, changes its form from **rhyme royal** to **ottava rima** and displays a more serious interest in the subject of civil war. Mortimer and the queen also become more prominent figures. The 1603 text was again revised for the 1619 collection.

*The First Part of Sir John Oldcastle* (published 1600) is Drayton's only extant play, although there are records of others which are now lost. These, like the surviving play, seem to have been collaborations with other dramatists, and many were on historical subjects. As Drayton responded to popular taste in his poetry, so *Sir*

*John Oldcastle* cashed in on the success of Shakespeare's *Henry IV* plays. *England's Heroical Epistles* (1597) earned for Drayton the title of 'our English Ovid'. Its classical model is Ovid's *Heroides* and like Ovid's work it is a collection of letters exchanged by notable lovers. Instead of Ovid's mythological characters Drayton gives us figures from English history: Henry II and Rosamond, Richard II and Isabel, the Earl of Surrey and Geraldine, and so forth. The couplets are full of elaborated conceits and rhetorical balance. These poems are among Drayton's most immediately readable works. Drayton's constant interest in history is displayed in his annotation of these poems. *The Legend of Great Cromwell* (1607) sees Drayton returning to the legend form. Its main source is **Foxe**'s *Acts and Monuments* and it shows the precarious rise to power of a 'new man' of the Tudor age. It is remarkable for its detached view of the reign of Henry VIII, refusing to slip into an easy 'Protestant' bias. It is the only one of Drayton's historical legends to be included in *The Mirror for Magistrates*, appearing in the 1610 edition. *The Owl* (1604 and 1619) is medieval in character as it is a satire in the form of a beast fable. *Poems Lyric and Pastoral* (1606) contains some important poems in the manner of Horace's *Odes*. Drayton was the first English poet of the Renaissance to issue a collection of poems in imitation of the *Odes*. His major work, **Poly-Olbion**, appeared in two parts in 1612 and 1622.

In 1627 a number of new poems appeared together: *The Battle of Agincourt* is an attempt at epic which again drew on chronicle sources, and *The Miseries of Queen Margaret* is indebted to Holinshed and Shakespeare's *Henry VI* plays. Also in this volume is *Nimphidia*, which has won Drayton more popularity than any of his other works. It is a **mock-heroic** series of 'Nimphalls' or fairy poems. The influence of *A Midsummer Night's Dream* is everywhere apparent, especially in the quarrel of Oberon and his queen. *The Muses' Elizium* (1630) sees Drayton, like Shakespeare, returning to pastoral at the end of his career and describing the poet's paradise.

**Dream of Gerontius, The** A poem by **John Henry Newman**, published in two parts in *The Month* (April and May 1865) and in book form in 1866. It is the dramatic monologue of a just soul on the point of death. Edward Elgar's oratorio setting was composed in 1900.

**Dream of John Ball, A** A tale by **William Morris**, serialized in *The Commonweal* between 13 November 1886 and 22 January 1887 (published in book form 1888).

Morris describes a dream transporting him back to Kent during the 1381 Peasants' Revolt. He witnesses a battle in which the Sheriff of Kent's men are repulsed by peasants inspired by the words of John Ball, a dissenting priest. Later Morris and John Ball discuss the peasants' hopes for change and, as Morris describes the Industrial Revolution and 19th-century society, John Ball realizes he is himself dreaming of the future course of history and of still unfulfilled ideals.

In its use of the dream motif for the exploration of both historical and future aspiration *A Dream of John Ball* is the forerunner of Morris's greatest socialist literary effort *News from Nowhere*. However, the implicit alliance of Christian morality and socialist ethics is an unusual retrospective glance at his earlier religious beliefs.

**Dream of the Rood, The** An Old English poem preserved in the **Vercelli Book**, probably dating from 750 or earlier. The narrator describes a dream in which he saw the Holy Cross alternately as a beautifully adorned symbol and as the historical, blood-stained cross. The cross speaks to him, telling him the history of the Crucifixion in terms of its own experience, and its emergence as a glorious symbol of Christ's Passion. After the dream, the poet says, he felt a longing for his own death and salvation, and determined to live a pure life. The poem is the most original, imaginative and moving of Old English religious poems.

**Dream Songs, The** An open-ended sequence of poems by **John Berryman**, first published in its entirety in 1969 and made up of two earlier volumes entitled *77 Dream Songs* (1964) and *His Toy, His Dream, His Rest* (1968). Through the dreams of a character called Henry, Berryman presents a meditation on American literary and cultural history. Several of the 'songs' are dedicated to Berryman's contemporaries, including **John Crowe Ransom**, **Saul Bellow**, **Robert Lowell** and **Adrienne Rich**. Many of the details of Henry's character and life reflect those of Berryman himself, including the profound impact of a father's suicide and the difficulties of overcoming alcoholism.

**dream-vision** A medieval poem about a dream. Its substance is allegorical – though the extent to which **allegory** is sustained depends largely on the skill of the poet – and may be secular or religious, comic or serious. Though differing widely in form and content, medieval dream-visions share a few common features: they are told in the first person, they have a certain supernatural or surreal content and they involve some kind of instruction for the dreamer. In many the dreamer is naïve or ignorant, has a companion or guide and encounters a beautiful dream landscape.

The chief influences on the form were the Latin *Somnium Scipionis* of Cicero with Macrobius's commentary on it, and the French *Roman de la Rose* by Guillaume de Lorris and Jean de Meun, but the classical and biblical traditions of revelations and visions were equally important. The three greatest medieval poets all wrote dream-visions: **Geoffrey Chaucer** (who translated the *Roman de la Rose* as *The Romaunt of the Rose*) in *The Book of the Duchess*, *The Parlement of Foules*, *The House of Fame* and the Prologue to *The Legend of Good Women*; **William Langland** in *Piers Plowman*; and the **Gawain-poet** in *Pearl*. Chaucer's dream poems were widely copied and the form continued into the 16th century, with such writers as **Gavin Douglas** (*The Palace of Honour*), **John Skelton** (*The Garland of Laurel*) and **William Dunbar** (*The Thrissil and the Rois*). It did not then vanish but later dream-visions, like **William Morris**'s *News from Nowhere*, are usually the result of deliberate medievalizing. The preoccupation with dreams in modern literature – **James Joyce**'s *Finnegans Wake*, for example – often acknowledges the medieval tradition but is likely to be influenced by modern psychological theory.

**Dreiser, Theodore (Herman Albert)** 1871–1945 American novelist, known for his naturalistic portrayal of the tragic conditions of early-20th-century life in the USA. Dreiser was born in Terre Haute, Indiana, the ninth child of German-speaking parents. The poverty of his childhood and the harsh bigotry of his father are reflected in his fiction. He briefly attended Indiana University, and then obtained a job on the *Chicago Globe* as a reporter before moving to New York City in 1894.

His first novel, *Sister Carrie* (1900), was accepted by **Frank Norris** for Doubleday Page & Co., but Mrs Doubleday objected to its realistic style and subject matter, and interfered with its publication, with the result that it was not widely distributed. Continuing to work as a journalist, Dreiser managed to earn a fairly comfortable living as an editor for Butterick, a company specializing in women's magazines, and 10 years passed before the publication of his next novel, *Jennie Gerhardt* (1911). Like *Sister Carrie*, which was reissued in 1912, this new novel was attacked for its candid depiction of American life and for its unconventional subject matter. *The Financier* (1912) and *The Titan* (1914) were the first two novels of Dreiser's 'Cowperwood' trilogy based on the life of the business magnate, Charles T. Yerkes. (The trilogy was completed with the posthumous publication of *The Stoic* in 1947.) In 1915 he published *The Genius*, a partly autobiographical novel examining the artistic temperament, but popular acclaim came only with the publication of *An American Tragedy* (1925), which was based on the Chester Gillette–Grace Brown murder case of 1906. Another novel, *The Bulwark*, was published in 1946, the year after he died.

Apart from his novels, Dreiser wrote an

account of a visit to the Soviet Union, *Dreiser Looks at Russia* (1928), and gave further expression to his growing hopes for socialism in *Tragic America* (1931) and *America is Worth Saving* (1941). He also published *Plays of the Natural and Supernatural* (1916), the tragedy *The Hand of the Potter* (1918), and books of verse, short stories, essays and autobiography.

**Drennan, William** 1754–1820 Irish pamphleteer and poet. The son of a prominent Presbyterian minister, he was born in Belfast and educated at Glasgow and Edinburgh universities, where he was a pupil and close friend of **Dugald Stewart** and met **David Hume**. He qualified as a doctor in 1778 and returned to practise in Ireland. Proudly conscious of his radical heritage as a Dissenter, he made his mark as a spirited, libertarian political writer with his *Letters of an Irish Helot* (1784) and was a founder and active member of the society of United Irishmen. One of his best poems, 'The Wake of William Orr' (1797), is an elegy for the first United Irishman to be executed. Drennan himself was tried for sedition in 1794 but acquitted. After the defeat of the United Irishmen's Rising in 1798, in which Drennan played no part, he withdrew from active politics but maintained his leading role in the cultural and intellectual life of Belfast. His verse is lyrical, witty, iconoclastic or fiercely patriotic by turns; for the last quality at least it won the admiration of **Thomas Davis**. His most famous poem, 'Erin to Her Own Tune and Words' (1795), set to a traditional air, is the source of the phrase 'the Emerald Isle'. His *Fugitive Pieces in Verse and Prose* appeared in 1815, a translation of Sophocles' *Electra* in 1817 and *Glendalloch and Other Poems*, incorporating poems by his two sons, posthumously in 1859. A selection of his vividly informative letters was published in 1931.

**Drinkwater, John** 1882–1937 Playwright and poet. Born at Leytonstone, Essex, and educated at Oxford High School, he worked for the Northern Assurance Company in Nottingham and Birmingham before accepting Sir Barry Jackson's offer of the post of manager of what was to become the Birmingham Repertory Company (1909). His early verse plays, like *Cophetua* (1911) and *X = O: A Night of the Trojan War* (1917), are mostly short experimental pieces and his major achievement is a sequence of historical plays written in prose. *Abraham Lincoln*, written for Birmingham in 1918, was produced successfully in London in 1919 and enjoyed an international reputation. His other plays include *Mary Stuart* (1921), *Oliver Cromwell* (1921), *Robert E. Lee* (1923) and the comedy *Bird in Hand* (1927). His volumes of verse include *The Death of Leander and Other Poems* (1906), *Lyrical and Other Poems* (1908),

*Cromwell and Other Poems* (1913) and the wartime volume *Swords and Ploughshares* (1915). Drinkwater's critical work includes a study of **William Morris** (1912) and biographies of **Samuel Pepys** (1930) and **Shakespeare** (Great Lives series, 1933).

**Drummond, William Henry** 1854–1907 Canadian poet. Drummond's family emigrated from Ireland to Canada when he was 11 years old. The boy studied telegraphy and found his first job at Bord-à-Plouffe on the Rivière des Prairies. In this region, not far from the American border, Drummond was fascinated by the stories told by the travellers, backwoodsmen, and French-Canadian dwellers in the small town. He resumed his education by 1876 and graduated in medicine at Bishop's College, Montreal, in 1884. He practised as a doctor for some years and lectured in medical jurisprudence at his old college; in 1905 he became rich through a successful venture, with his brother, in a silver mine at Cobalt in Ontario.

As a poet, Drummond succeeded in capturing the patois of the French-Canadian people. His four volumes of verse were *The Habitant* (1897), *Johnny Courteau* (1901), *The Voyageur* (1905) and *The Great Fight* (1908). A collected volume, *The Poetical Works*, was published in 1912.

**Drummond of Hawthornden, William** 1585–1649 Poet. Born at the manor of Hawthornden near Edinburgh, he was educated at Edinburgh University and studied law in France. He lived at Hawthornden from 1610 and was to have married Mary Cunningham of Barns in 1615. She died on the eve of the wedding and much of Drummond's work reflected his grief.

Drummond was a Royalist and anti-Presbyterian and wrote many pamphlets in support of his views. His first published poem was a lament on the death of Prince Henry in 1613, *Tears on the Death of Moeliades*. The year after the death of Mary Cunningham he published *Poems, Amorous, Funereal, Divine, Pastoral, in Sonnets, Songs, Sextains, Madrigals* (1616), and in 1617 contributed to the verses written to celebrate the visit of James I to Edinburgh ('Forth Feasting', published in *The Muses' Welcome*, 1618). Drummond corresponded with **Michael Drayton**, and **Ben Jonson**'s visit to Hawthornden in 1618 prompted him to keep notes of the occasion, eventually published in 1832.

A collection of religious verse, *Flowers of Sion* (1623), contains the religious sonnets 'Saint John Baptist' and 'For the Magdalene', which are among his best-known works, and the prose essay on death *A Cypress Grove* (written in 1630).

Drummond married Elizabeth Logan in 1632 and wrote the words for the entertainment

The interior of Drury Lane Theatre in 1813, rebuilt after the fire of 1809. Engraving by W. Hopwood. Victoria & Albert Theatre Museum, London.

staged for the Scottish coronation of Charles I in 1633. He died in 1649, the year of the King's execution. His poetry echoes his wide reading, and is in places elegant and musical.

**Drury Lane, Theatre Royal** The first theatre on the site was opened in 1662 to house the **King's Men** under the management of **Thomas Killigrew**. Letters Patent from Charles II awarded to Killigrew and to **William D'Avenant** a monopoly on performances of the legitimate drama within the City of Westminster, and Drury Lane has retained its status as a **patent theatre** ever since, though the monopoly was abolished by Act of Parliament in 1843.

The capacity of the first theatre was 700. The second, possibly designed by Sir Christopher Wren, opened in 1674 and had a capacity of 2000. It prospered, particularly from 1709–33 under the management of **Colley Cibber** and others, and from 1747–76, under **David Garrick**. Garrick was succeeded by **Richard Brinsley Sheridan**, whose tenure began with a production of *The School for Scandal*. Increasingly involved in politics, Sheridan entrusted the active management of the theatre from 1788 to the actor John Philip Kemble, and it was he who supervised the rebuilding in 1791–4.

This third theatre, designed by Henry Holland, with a capacity of 3611, was destroyed by fire in 1809, leaving Sheridan in financial difficulties. The enterprising brewer, Samuel Whitbread, led the fund-raising for the building of a fourth theatre, opened in 1812 and designed by Benjamin Wyatt. Its capacity was 2283. Despite many alterations, this is the theatre that now stands. Considered too big and too uneconomic as a home for legitimate drama after the loss of the monopoly, Drury Lane became famous as the home of spectacle and **pantomime** during

the successive managements of Augustus Harris (1879–96) and Arthur Collins (1896–1923). It is now reliant on musicals.

**Dryden, John** 1631–1700 Poet Laureate and dramatist. Born at the vicarage of Aldwinkle in Northamptonshire, Dryden came from a family of moderate Parliamentary supporters with Puritan inclinations. He was educated at Westminster when the formidable Richard Busby was the headmaster, and there he read voraciously, especially among the classical poets. While still at school, he published his first verses, an elegy 'Upon the Death of Lord Hastings' (1649), but he was not prolific while young. He went to Trinity College, Cambridge, in 1650 and took a BA in 1654. In 1659 he wrote his impressive 'Heroic Stanzas' on the death of the Lord Protector, though he readily adapted to the Royalist climate of the Restoration, and wrote *Astraea Redux* in 1660, to welcome back the monarch. This was later interpreted as a mercenary move, but it was merely the product of common sense and moderation; from the start, Dryden's attitudes were ranged against extremism of any kind, and he became an exponent of the golden mean in art, politics and morality.

Much of Dryden's Restoration verse is professionally tailored to specific public occasions; he was a born Laureate. At the coronation he wrote 'To His Sacred Majesty, A Panegyric . . .' (1661), followed by verses addressed tactfully 'To My Lord Chancellor', **Clarendon**, in 1662. He began assiduously to write plays, a good way of drawing the attention of the public, since the playhouses (under the imported French tastes of the court) were busily fashionable. *The Wild Gallant*, his first, was a prose piece started in 1663 – the year he married his theatrical partner's sister, Lady Elizabeth Howard – but is otherwise unremarkable. *The Rival Ladies* (1664) used the rhymed couplet, and proved more popular. In 1665, the theatres closed owing to the plague, and the court removed to Oxford; Dryden wrote one of his most successful heroic dramas, *The Indian Emperor*, which established his reputation, and the confidence of a distinctive style.

Well-liked as a person, Dryden was rather a modest, private character, though he has been chastised (notably by **Dr Johnson**) as a mere professional opportunist. He was made a Fellow of the Royal Society, and in 1667 he published his poem **Annus Mirabilis**, a work representative of his efficient public mode, and which was instrumental in securing him the position of the Poet Laureate in 1668 on the death of **Sir William D'Avenant**, the first poet officially to hold the title. In 1670 he was appointed Historiographer Royal.

From 1668 onwards, Dryden began a busy

period of dramatic and critical writing. His many plays include *Secret Love* (1667), which was popular in London after the scares of the plague; *The Conquest of Granada* (1668), a controversial study of religious and civil disorder; and *Tyrannic Love* (1669) which treats the martyrdom of St Catherine and the lust of Emperor Maximin, full of histrionic touches, and *Marriage à la Mode* (1672) is the most durable of his earlier comedies, and was produced the next year. Of scant dramatic value was *Amboyna* (1673), a piece of anti-Dutch propaganda, followed in 1674 by the poet's bizarre tribute to **Milton** in the form of a musical adaptation of *Paradise Lost*, entitled *The State of Innocence*; perhaps an apt title for the idealistic spirit in which it was conceived for the new Theatre Royal. It was never performed. With *Aureng-Zebe* (1676) and *All for Love* (1678) – the latter his first in blank verse – Dryden returned to real drama, and wrote some of his most stirring verse, but he was beginning to be disenchanted with the cut-throat competitiveness between the theatrical companies, and the personal criticism his opponents began directing at him. He was lampooned by **Rochester**, and his heroic style was satirized mercilessly as bombast in *The Rehearsal* (1671), a burlesque play partly by **Buckingham**. On 18 December 1679, he was physically ambushed and badly beaten in a mysterious attack in Rose Alley, Covent Garden, an incident generally taken as proof of the seriousness with which his public position was beginning to be regarded. His unfortunate adaptation (1679) of **Shakespeare**'s *Troilus and Cressida* earned him, excusably, additional ridicule.

By the year 1681, Dryden was beginning to direct his interests towards politics and that quickly maturing political adjunct, satire. He effectively discredited Shaftesbury and the supporters of Monmouth during the Exclusion Crisis with his masterfully rational *Absalom and Achitophel* (1681), a miniature epic of ingenious exactitude supporting the legitimacy of James, Duke of York, to succeed his brother to the throne, despite his Catholic sympathies. Dryden found himself once again the target for personal vituperation, but Charles II was pleased at his onslaught against the Whigs, and at his next poem *The Medal* (1682) a dutiful but baldly partisan attack on Shaftesbury's supporters, which in turn provoked a spate of counter-attacks of which **Thomas Shadwell**'s *The Medal of John Bayes* was the sharpest. The 'paper war' was now in full swing, and Dryden replied with *Mac Flecknoe*, his most entertaining poem, written around 1678, pirated in 1682 and officially published in 1684.

With *Religio Laici* in the same year he examined with seriousness the squabbling history of religious factions and, in 1686, after a period of spiritual uncertainty, he embraced Roman Catholicism. This was the year after James II, a crypto-Catholic, ascended the throne, and Dryden was attacked as a turncoat, though in fact it was an act of courage. Apart from several 'official' odes in this period he composed in 1686 a movingly lyrical ode 'To the Pious Memory of . . . Mrs Anne Killigrew', a painter who drowned in the Thames, and he began to translate from the classics. *The Hind and the Panther* (1687) is a lengthy allegorical fable about Protestant and Papist beliefs in which Dryden criticizes the Anglican church. With the (Protestant) Revolution of 1688, Dryden was deprived of the Laureateship because of his religious beliefs and, ironically, replaced by Shadwell. He was now in his fifties and, having published his convictions in verse, he turned himself afresh to the theatre.

He contributed the libretto to Henry Purcell's operatic celebration of the English monarchy, *King Arthur* (1691), and wrote a tragicomedy about sin, *Don Sebastian* (produced in 1690), a comedy of errors, *Amphitryon* (1690), *Cleomenes: The Spartan Hero* (1692), and finally the unsuccessful *Love Triumphant* (1694), announcing in the Prologue that it was to be his last play. Dryden's productions were by then coming into competition with the work of younger playwrights such as **Congreve**. In his later years, Dryden turned to translations: most significant was his commercially profitable edi-

John Dryden. A detail from the portrait after Sir Godfrey Kneller, 1698. National Portrait Gallery, London.

tion of Virgil (1697), but his handsome volume of translations from the satires of Persius and Juvenal (1693) is additionally valuable for its preface, the excellent *Discourse concerning the Original and Progress of Satire*. In 1693 he also published his second ode for St Cecilia's Day, 'Alexander's Feast'. His last major achievement was *Fables, Ancient and Modern* (1700), paraphrases of Ovid, Boccaccio and **Chaucer**, the preface to which is a fine example of his prose. Indeed, much of his prose is distinguished for its critical acuity, taking the form of essays or prefaces to plays; his *Essay of Dramatic Poesy* (1668) and *Essay of Heroic Plays* (1672) are the foremost. He also wrote a life of Plutarch (1683).

The poet died on May Day 1700, and is buried in Westminster Abbey. Dryden was a self-critical and civilized writer who brought to the language a clarity and balance of phrase that influenced many of the 18th-century authors of neoclassical verse. His stringent cultivation of the heroic couplet was perhaps unrivalled in his day. He was in every sense a professional and dedicated writer, and his attitudes were characterized by reasonableness and common sense; he is today admired but not quite enjoyed. In his preface to the play *Evening's Love*, Dryden summarized his aesthetic: 'The employment of a poet is like that of a curious gunsmith, or watchmaker: the iron or silver is not his own; but they are the least part of that which gives the value: the prize lies wholly in the workmanship.'

**Du Bois, W[illiam] E[dward] B[urghardt]** c. 1868–1963 Black American writer, born in Great Barrington, Massachusetts, and educated at Fisk University and at Harvard. He taught economics and history at Atlanta University from 1896 to 1910 and soon became famous for his studies of the status of black people in the USA: *John Brown* (1909), *The Negro* (1915), *The Gift of Black Folk* (1924) and *Black Reconstruction* (1935). Sketches and verses about the life of blacks make up *The Souls of Black Folk* (1903) and *Darkwater* (1920). *Color and Democracy: Colonies and Peace* (1945) argues for the rights of small nations and rejects all aspects of imperialism. He also wrote a novel, *Dark Princess* (1928), about a black man who becomes involved in a struggle to unify the 'dark peoples' of the world. With Guy Benton Johnson he co-edited the *Encyclopedia of the Negro* (1945). The autobiographical *Dusk of Dawn* (1940) was, he declared, 'the autobiography of a concept of race'. For 24 years he edited the magazine *Crisis*.

He left Atlanta University to help found the National Association for the Advancement of Colored People, but later became impatient with the association's moderation. In 1949 he became director of the Peace Information Cen-

ter in New York, and in 1961, at the age of 93, joined the Communist Party. He died in Ghana where, as editor of *Encyclopedia Africana*, he had gone to live in 1961. He became a Ghanaian citizen in the year of his death.

**Du Maurier, Dame Daphne** 1907–89 Novelist. Born in London, daughter of the actor Sir Gerald Du Maurier and granddaughter of the novelist **George Du Maurier**, she was educated privately in Paris. For most of her adult life she has lived in Cornwall, whose wild weather and scenery contribute the setting and atmosphere for her most successful novels. These are tense romances, of which the most famous are *Jamaica Inn* (1936), *Rebecca* (1938) and *My Cousin Rachel* (1951). Her short story 'The Birds' may, however, prove her most lasting monument as a result of its classic film treatment by Alfred Hitchcock in 1963. Her memoirs were published in 1967 as *Vanishing Cornwall*.

**Du Maurier, George (Louis Palmella Busson)** 1834–96 Novelist and artist. He was born in Paris, the grandson of refugees from the French Revolution and the son of a naturalized Englishman. In 1851 he entered University College, London, studying chemistry and becoming an analytical chemist, but returned to Paris in 1856, later living in Belgium and Holland. Although the sight of his left eye was almost gone, he turned to drawing and in 1860 sent his first work to **Punch**, becoming a regular contributor. His most famous novel was **Trilby** (1894); his others were *Peter Ibbetson* (1891) and *The Martian* (1897). He also wrote humorous verse. He was the father of the actor Gerald Du Maurier and grandfather of the writer **Daphne Du Maurier**.

**Dubliners** A volume of short stories by **James Joyce**, published in 1914. Some had originally appeared in the magazine *Irish Homestead*, under the pseudonym Stephen Dedalus, in 1904 and the last, 'The Dead', was finished in 1907. The book's publication was delayed, much to Joyce's exasperation, because a printer objected to passages in the story 'Two Gallants'. Joyce told his publisher, Grant Richards, that it was not his fault if 'the odour of ashpits and old weeds and offal' hung around his attempt to 'write a chapter in the moral history of my country'. He had chosen Dublin 'because that city seemed to me the centre of paralysis'. The stories were arranged by Joyce to present Dublin in four of its aspects – childhood, adolescence, maturity and public life – and he claimed to have written them in a style of 'scrupulous meanness'.

**Duchess of Malfi, The** A tragedy by **John Webster**, published in 1623. The date of the first production is not known but is believed to have been before 1614. The plot is based on a story by Matteo Bandello.

The Duchess of Malfi is a widow. One of her brothers is a cardinal; the other, her twin brother Ferdinand, is Duke of Calabria. Both are inordinately jealous of their noble status and warn their sister that she must not remarry. They also hope to inherit her territory. But the Duchess has fallen in love with her steward, Antonio, and secretly marries him. The suspicious brothers introduce a spy into her household in the person of Bosola, an escaped galley slave.

Suspicious of his mistress's condition, Bosola seeks confirmation by offering her fresh apricots which the Duchess devours greedily. Shortly afterwards she gives birth to a son. Some time later, aware of gathering suspicion, she and Antonio separate and flee. The Duchess is captured and confined to her house, where she and her children are eventually murdered.

After the murder of the Duchess, Ferdinand and the Cardinal decide they must remove Bosola, who has been shaken by his victim's courage and now regards his masters with loathing. When he realizes that they are in a hurry to be rid of him he determines on revenge. He kills the man he believes is the Cardinal, finding to his horror that it is in fact Antonio, whom he had determined to save; despair is added to remorse. The unbalanced Ferdinand now descends into total insanity. Bosola succeeds in murdering the Cardinal but is himself killed by the mad Ferdinand; his single consolation is to see the madman killed by Antonio's friends.

**Duck, Stephen** 1705–56 Poet. An untutored agricultural labourer, Duck taught himself by reading books on arithmetic and *Paradise Lost*, using a dictionary, and began to write doggerel verse based on the ballad form as well as classical models. His patrons included Joseph Spence, Professor of Poetry at Oxford, and Lord Macclesfield, who brought the 'thresher poet' to the attention of Queen Caroline. She settled him at Windsor with a pension. When **Laurence Eusden** died in 1730, Duck and **Colley Cibber** were considered for the vacant post of Poet Laureate, which gave rise to some humorous letters between **Pope** and **Swift** at their expense. Duck became a clergyman after the death of the Queen in 1737, and as a preacher at Kew Chapel he drew considerable crowds, chiefly out of curiosity. Most of his verse is occasional, and much is absurd; his early *The Thresher's Labour* has some pastoral merit, but Duck is notable mainly as a peasant poet, a phenomenon intriguing to the Romantics. In 1756 he drowned himself in a trout stream outside the Black Lion Inn at Reading.

**Dudek, Louis** 1918– Canadian poet. Born in Montreal of Polish parents, he attended McGill University and Columbia University, and taught in New York at City College before returning to Montreal in 1951. He lectured at McGill until his retirement in 1982. Dudek published his first volume of poetry, *East of the City*, in 1946. His early work is realistic and shows strong egalitarian sympathies. In 1952, with **Raymond Souster** and Irving Layton, he founded Contact Press, an outlet for early volumes by many important Canadian poets who came to the fore in the 1960s. *Delta*, the literary magazine he published from 1957 to 1966, advocates the same ideal of an urbane and morally responsible art which appears in his later poetry, a marked departure from his early work. By this time Dudek was also influenced by modernist aesthetics and particularly by **Ezra Pound**, with whom he conducted a lengthy correspondence. His best work is to be found in his long poems, *Europe* (1954), *En Mexico* (1958) and *Atlantis* (1967). Other volumes include *The Transparent Sea* (1956), *Laughing Stalks* (1958), *Collected Poetry* (1971), *Cross-Section* (1980) and *Continuation 1* (1981).

**Duenna, The** A comic opera with text by **Richard Brinsley Sheridan** and music by Thomas Linley. It was first produced at **Covent Garden** in November 1775, and published in the same year. The plot concerns Don Jerome and his desire for a match between his daughter Louisa and Isaac. But Louisa is in love with Antonio and she enlists the help of her duenna as intermediary with him. Don Jerome finds out; he locks up Louisa and dismisses her duenna. Louisa escapes from the house disguised as the duenna, who takes her place. Isaac is deceived into marrying the duenna and into bringing about the marriage of Louisa to her Antonio.

**Duffy, Maureen (Patricia)** 1933– Novelist, dramatist and poet. Born in Worthing, Sussex, she read English at King's College, London, and worked as a schoolteacher from 1956 to 1961. Her first novel, *That's How it Was* (1962), is the story of an illegitimate child's relationship with her mother, recounted with simplicity, directness and great feeling. *The Paradox Players* (1967) displays Duffy's talent for making her characters live, describing the people who inhabit a Thames houseboat during a bitter winter. The novel which attracted most attention was *The Microcosm* (1966), a study of lesbianism centred on the lives of three women and the club where they meet. Duffy's topics have ranged widely over the years. *Gorsaga* (1981), set in the future, follows the life of Gor, a young gorilla created by AID in a laboratory and brought up as a human child. Her most recent novel, *Change* (1987), is set in wartime Britain and deals with young people growing to maturity in extreme and dangerous conditions.

Duffy is an intensely literary author whose work also includes a major study of **Aphra Behn**, *The Passionate Shepherdess* (1977). A leader in the campaign for Public Lending Right, she is a tireless champion of the rights of authors.

**Dugdale, Sir William** 1605–86 Antiquary. Born at Shustoke, near Coleshill in Warwickshire, he became a pursuivant extraordinary in the reign of Charles I. Dugdale's *The Antiquities of Warwickshire* (1656) is regarded as the fullest and most accurate of its kind until that date, setting a new standard for local antiquarianism. His *Monasticon Anglicanum*, an account of English monastic foundations, was published in three volumes in 1655, 1661 and 1673; and the valuable record of old St Paul's before it was destroyed by fire, *The History of St Paul's Cathedral*, appeared in 1658. *The History of Imbanking and Drayning of Divers Fenns and Marshes* (1662) goes far beyond the brief suggested by the title and includes an account of Hereward the Wake. His other works were *Origines Juridicales* (1666), a history of the administration of law in England (1675–6); and *A Short View of the Late Troubles in England* (1681), an expression of his Royalist principles. Dugdale has a high place among English antiquarians for his careful scholarship and clear, attractive style.

**Duggan, Eileen** 1894–1972 New Zealand poet. Born in Tua Marina on South Island into an Irish immigrant family, she was educated at Marlborough High School and Victoria University, where she received a first-class honours degree in history. She subsequently worked as a teacher and as a lecturer in history at Victoria University and wrote a regular page for *The New Zealand Tablet* for many years. One of the first New Zealand poets to establish an international reputation, she was awarded the OBE in 1943. Duggan's work is characterized by its Roman Catholicism, its interest in Maori culture and its attempt to pioneer a sense of a local identity in New Zealand verse, which was an important influence on the following generation of poets. Her work demonstrates a strong feeling for the landscape in which she grew up, as well as an optimistic religious faith. Her volumes of verse include *New Zealand Bird Songs* (1929), *Poems* (1937), *New Zealand Poems* (1940) and her best collection, *More Poems* (1951), which transcends the Georgian simplicities of her early work.

***Duke's Children, The*** A novel by **Anthony Trollope**, the sixth of the **Palliser** sequence, serialized in *All the Year Round* from October 1879 to July 1880 (3 vols., 1880).

Now a widower and no longer Prime Minis-

ter, the Duke of Omnium is left alone to adjust to his children's generation and its freer ways. His eldest son, Lord Silverbridge, has been expelled from Oxford and has fallen in with the disreputable Major Tifto, through whom he loses heavily in gambling on horses. He causes further heartache to his father by standing for Silverbridge as a Conservative rather than as a Liberal. The Duke is tolerant of his son's waywardness, and pays his gambling debts, but advises an early marriage to steady him. He approves of Silverbridge's attraction to the poor but well-connected Lady Mabel Grex, but when he falls in love with the beautiful and wealthy American girl, Isabel Boncassen, the granddaughter of an obscure Dutch immigrant, the Duke's pride of caste is stung. His daughter, Lady Mary Palliser, also disappoints him by falling in love with Frank Tregear, a young man of promise but without wealth or social rank, who had been encouraged by Lady Glencora before her death. The Duke refuses his consent to Silverbridge's marriage to Isabel, and she will not marry without it; but gradually the girl's charm and his son's determination win him over. Recognizing in his two older children something of their mother's stubborn spirit, he surrenders gracefully, and the novel ends with the two marriages. This closing harmony is shadowed by the loneliness of Lady Mabel Grex, who loses both the man she loves, Tregear, and the man who could have given her wealth and social position, Silverbridge.

*The Duke's Children* is concerned more with family relationships than with politics, and shows the Duke of Omnium coming to terms with a generation in many ways less principled and public-spirited than his own. Isabel Boncassen anticipates **Henry James**'s American girl, Isabel Archer, in *The Portrait of a Lady* (1881).

**dumb show** Dumb shows flourished as a feature of tragedies in Tudor England, making a spectacular element in the actionless plays that followed in the wake of *Gorboduc* (1562). Early dumb shows were typically allegorical, employing symbolic figures rather than characters from the play itself, but the professional playwrights of Elizabethan England saw the theatrical advantage to be gained by using dumb shows to focus the audience's attention on significant deeds outside the strict time-sequence of the play. There are famous examples in **Kyd**'s *The Spanish Tragedy* (c. 1589), **Peele**'s *The Old Wives' Tale* (published 1595) and the anonymous *A Warning for Fair Women* (1599). Like other writers of plays on legendary heroes, **Anthony Munday** found the dumb show a valuable means for introducing episodes without spreading his plots too wide. **Shakespeare** was less addicted to them than many of his contemporaries, although the dumb show that introduces the play-within-the-play in *Hamlet* is much the best-known example in Elizabethan drama. It is deployed in a consciously archaic way, since the vogue for introductory dumb shows had long passed. Still more unusual is its pre-enactment of the whole substance of the ensuing play rather than of a single episode. During the Jacobean period, the dumb show became increasingly associated with the **masque**, although **Webster** and **Middleton** are among the dramatists who continued to exploit it to sensational effect.

**Dunbar, Paul (Laurence)** 1872–1906 Black American poet and novelist, born in Dayton, Ohio, the son of former slaves. His first collection of verse, *Oak and Ivy*, was printed privately in 1893, and was followed by *Majors and Minors* in 1895. **William Dean Howells** became interested in his work and wrote the preface to a third volume, *Lyrics of Lowly Life* (1896). Dunbar soon received national recognition and embarked on a number of lecture tours.

Known in his day primarily as a writer of dialect verse, he has been severely criticized for his nostalgic and sentimental depiction of black life in the South. He himself, however, was dissatisfied with the limited basis of his reputation, and in some of his works he reveals a concern with the troubled social climate of his times. His other collections of poetry include *Lyrics of the Hearthside* (1899), *Lyrics of Love and Laughter* (1903) and *Lyrics of Sunshine and Shadow* (1905). He wrote four novels: *The Uncalled* (1898), *The Love of Landry* (1900), *The Fanatics* (1901) and *The Sport of the Gods* (1902).

**Dunbar, William** ?1465–?1530 Very little is known of Dunbar's life: even the dates of his birth and death are uncertain. He graduated MA from St Andrews in 1479, probably became a Franciscan novice and travelled abroad for some period between 1479 and 1500. In 1501 he went to England, probably in connection with the arrangements for the marriage of James IV of Scotland and Margaret, daughter of Henry VII.

Dunbar is usually considered to be one of the most important **Scottish Chaucerians**. He refers to 'noble **Chaucer** of makaris [i.e. poets] all' in *Lament for the Makaris* and Chaucer as 'rose of rethoris [i.e. rhetoricians] all' in *The Goldyn Targe*. His main debt to English poets, as the second apostrophe to Chaucer suggests, is to their rhetoric and diction. This is mainly seen in his court poetry. *The Thrissil and the Rois* is a nuptial song for the marriage of James IV and Margaret Tudor in 1503. It is an allegorical **dream-vision** in Chaucer's **rhyme royal** stanza and is at times reminiscent of *The Parlement of Foules*. Amid heraldic animals and flowers Nature crowns a lion, eagle and thistle pre-eminent among animals, birds and plants. The thistle is

James and the rose Margaret. Similarly courtly is *The Goldyn Targe* with its aureate diction, 'Up sprang the goldyn candill matutyne/With clere depurit bemes cristallyne.' In this allegorical dream the poet finds himself at the court of Venus, only temporarily defended by the golden shield of reason against the arrows of beauty. Nature, Venus and classical deities mingle with personified abstractions.

At the other extreme from the diction and style of these dream-visions is *The Flyting of Dunbar and Kennedie*, although this too was probably intended for a courtly audience. **Sir Walter Scott** thought it the most repellent poem he knew in any language. It is a stylized *tour de force* of mutually exchanged abuse, each contestant striving to outdo the other in brilliantly inventive invective: 'Chittirlilling, ruch rilling, like schilling in the milhous/Baird rehator, theif of nator, fals tratour, feyindis gett.' The flyting is not to be taken as indicating personal animus, for Dunbar's fellow poet Walter Kennedy is referred to fondly in *Lament for the Makaris*. The *Tretis of the Twa Mariit Wemen and the Wedo* seduces its reader into an expectation of the courtly with its opening on midsummer eve and its picture of fair ladies gathering garlands in an arbour. But the poem mixes high and low styles, for there follows a deliberately gross and cynical discussion of marriage and sex by the three speakers. The poet asks his audience at the end to choose one of the speakers as wife.

Among Dunbar's other longer poems is *Dance of the Sevin Deidly Synnes*, a dream, or rather trance, in which the poet sees the devil Mahoun goading unshriven sinners into a *danse macabre*. The seven deadly sins, headed by Pride, the most deadly, appear in turn and dance. Mahoun finally calls for a Highland fling but the Highlanders make such a noise with their Gaelic that they are smothered in smoke in the deepest pit of hell. *Lament for the Makaris* is a familiar medieval meditation on the transitoriness and mutability of life, 'The flesch is brukle [fragile].' The poem is also known by its originally liturgical refrain, '*Timor mortis conturbat me.*' Among those taken by death we find Chaucer, **Henryson** and **Gower**.

Dunbar's poetry includes those kinds well established in the Middle Ages: dream-vision, the court poem and moralizing reflection (especially on 'this warld unstabille'). He also wrote religious poems, some of which are typically medieval macaronic lyrics (poems which mix the vernacular with Latin). These include 'Et Nobis Puer Natus Est' on the Nativity and a poem on the Resurrection with its splendid opening line 'Done is a battell on the dragon blak'.

**Duncan, Robert (Edward)** 1919–88 American poet, born in Oakland, California, and at the University of California at Berkeley. His first volume of poetry, *Heavenly City, Earthly City*, was published in 1947. Following the publication of *Medieval Scenes* (1950), *Poems 1948–49* (1950) and *The Song of the Border-Guard* (1951), he became associated with the **Black Mountain school** of poets in North Carolina. Mysticism and frequent allusion to major literary figures – Dante in particular – which had been hinted at in his earlier work, emerged as the mark of his later writing: *Caesar's Gate: Poems 1949–1950* (1956), *Letters* (1958), *Selected Poems 1942–50* (1959), *The Opening of the Field* (1960), *Roots and Branches* (1964) and *Bending the Bow* (1968). After a self-imposed silence of 15 years, he published *Ground Work: Before the War* in 1984.

**Duncan, Sara Jeanette** 1861–1922 Canadian novelist who grew up in Brantford and was educated there and in Toronto. She taught for some years before becoming a journalist, writing for *The Toronto Globe* and *The Washington Post*. In 1888 she became parliamentary correspondent for *The Montreal Star*. In 1891 she married Everard Charles Cotes, a British journalist in India, which provided the setting for some of her novels. Of more than 20 novels, the most notable are *A Social Departure, or, How Orthodocia and I Went Round the World by Ourselves* (1890), *An American Girl in London* (1891), *The Imperialist* (1904), set in the small Canadian town of 'Elgin', and *Cousin Cinderella, A Canadian Girl in London* (1908).

***Dunciad, The*** A satirical poem by **Alexander Pope**, first published anonymously in 1728; he did not acknowledge his authorship until 1735. The first *Dunciad* consisted of three books; a fourth, *The New Dunciad*, was published in 1742 and the complete work in 1743.

The subject of the satire is dullness, but the object was Pope's desire to hit back at **Lewis Theobald**, who had severely (and accurately) criticized Pope's edition of **Shakespeare**. Pope made him the original 'hero' of *The Dunciad* but moved **Colley Cibber** into that position in the poem's final form. Cibber had alluded to the play, ***Three Hours after Marriage***, to which Pope had contributed, in his production of ***The Rehearsal***. The body of the satire is full of ridicule for those writers who had earned the poet's displeasure or disapproval, but it is also a brilliantly wrought attack on literary vices.

The four books describe the triumph of dullness. In Book I the character Bayes (Colley Cibber) is trying to decide where his talents will best be deployed. The **Poet Laureate**, **Laurence Eusden**, has died and Bayes's decision is made for him; the goddess anoints him king in place of Eusden, who now 'sleeps among the dull of ancient days'. Book II describes the celebrations

following the enthronement of Bayes as King of the Dunces; his domain is the empire of Emptiness and Dullness. The celebrations as described are a burlesque of the funeral games for Anchises in the *Aeneid*, just one of the poem's many mock-heroic features. Everyone falls asleep while poetry is being read. In Book III Bayes, sleeping in the goddess's lap, sees in his dreams the past and future triumphs of the empire of Dullness extended to all arts and sciences, the theatre, and the court. Bayes's guide in his dream is **Elkanah Settle**, who had been one of **Dryden**'s literary opponents. Book IV sees the dream realized: the goddess gives her messengers instructions to discover silly pursuits that will be encouraged. Thought is discouraged and Dullness triumphs. The final vision of cultural chaos is a triumph of Pope's art, part comic and part serious.

**Dunlap, William** 1766–1839 One of the earliest American playwrights, and the first to make the theatre his profession, Dunlap was born in Perth Amboy, New Jersey. He studied painting in New York and then in London under Benjamin West (1784–6), but abandoned art for the theatre soon after his return to the USA. His democratic patriotism is evident in the first of his plays to be produced, *The Father, or, American Shandyism* (1789), and in the military tragedy *André* (1798), which concerns an incident in the Revolutionary War. Dunlap wrote over 65 plays, many of them adaptations from foreign works, particularly the fashionable shocking dramas of the German August von Kotzebue. In 1805 he turned to management but was plagued by financial problems. He left the theatre in 1811, and from 1816 until his death resumed his interrupted career as a painter. His advocacy of native art is voluminously represented in *A History of the American Theatre* (1832) and *A History of the Rise and Progress of the Arts of Design in the United States* (1834).

**Dunn, Douglas (Eaglesham)** 1942– Poet. Born in Inchinnan, Renfrewshire, he was educated locally, becoming a librarian before reading English at Hull University (1966–9). After graduating he worked as a librarian there until 1971, when he became a freelance writer, returning to Scotland in 1984. The poems in his fine first collection, *Terry Street* (1969), influenced by **Philip Larkin**, are detailed observations of underprivileged lives. After *The Happier Life* (1972), his third collection, *Love or Nothing* (1974), shows strong elements of fantasy. *Barbarians* (1979) articulates, like **Tony Harrison**'s work, the resentment of the working class towards 'a culture of contrivance'. *St Kilda's Parliament* (1981) is a surrealistic, if uneven treatment of Scottish obsessions, and *Elegies* (1985) mourns the death of the poet's wife. The winner of many awards, Dunn is one of the most important of younger contemporary poets. He has also published a volume of stories, *Secret Villages* (1985), and has edited *A Rumoured City: New Poets from Hull* (1982).

**Duns Scotus, John** ?1265–1308 Schoolman. He was born in Scotland, possibly at Duns near Berwick. After completing his studies at the universities of Scotland and England between 1291 and 1293, he went to the University of Paris for further studies under Gonsalvus of Spain and James of Quarcheto. He commented on the *Sentences* of Peter Lombard at Cambridge between 1297 and 1300. Between 1300 and 1301 he lectured on the *Sentences* at Oxford (*Opus Oxoniense*), breaking off after Book III to go to Paris where he finally completed the commentary on Book IV (*Reportata Parisiensia*, 1303). He commented, in addition, on Aristotle and Porphyry. He returned to Oxford in 1303, after refusing to subscribe to a petition against ‘Boniface VIII; he then returned to Paris, where he took his *magisterium,* recommended by Gonsalvus. He travelled to Cologne in 1307, dying there on 8 November 1308. In spite of his being much venerated by the Friars Minor, he was accused in 1315 of holding opinions that came dangerously close to Pelagianism, and ten ‘*temerariae opiniones*’ were put forward for condemnation.

It is in his commentaries, particularly on the *Sentences,* that Scotus elucidates his own complex synthesis of Aristotelian, Thomistic and Augustinian ideas. He rejected an Aristotelian emphasis on knowledge and intellect, substituting an emphasis on freedom, love and the will. He is thought of as a philosopher of ‘realism’, positing the close correspondence of our concepts to the real, and seeking to establish a more perfect foundation for our universal concepts. He attempted to construct a valid and complete proof of the existence of God. **Gerard Manley Hopkins**’s understanding of Scotus’s ideas on *haecceitas* (the individuating differences in a thing, as opposed to those features it shares in common with other individuals) contributed to the development of his own ideas about individuation.

**Dunton, John** 1659–1733 Bookseller. A characteristic publisher of his times, Dunton strove to print material that would satisfy the newly expanding readership of the Augustan age. In 1690 he started publishing *The Athenian Gazette* (later renamed *The Athenian Mercury*), a journal initially dealing with intellectual and philosophical curiosities, but deteriorating with popularity into a sometimes preposterous triviality. The *Mercury* was the place where **Swift** first appeared in print, with an inferior encomiastic ode. Dunton was also the author of

many political pamphlets, and *The Life and Errors of John Dunton* (1705).

**Durham** The latest datable poem in Old English, written between 1104 and 1109. It describes Durham’s position in terms of the countryside surrounding the city, and the relics of the famous saints, bishops and scholars kept there.

**Durrell, Gerald (Malcolm)** 1925– Writer on travel and natural history. Durrell was born in Jamshedpur, India, the son of a civil engineer and a younger brother of **Lawrence Durrell**. Brought up in France, Italy, Switzerland, Greece and Britain, he was educated privately and developed a strong interest in natural history, especially animals. In 1945 he became a student keeper at Whipsnade Zoo, and from 1947 travelled widely (Cameroons, Guiana, Argentina, Cyprus, etc.) on expeditions to collect animals for zoos. In 1950 he began writing for journals and radio, mostly about his travels and animal life, and in 1951 completed his first book, *The Overloaded Ark*. A succession of light-hearted but informative books followed, developing themes of travel, natural history and conservation, and including *Three Singles to Adventure* and *The Bafut Beagles* (1953), *The Drunken Forest* (1955), *My Family and Other Animals* and *The New Noah* (1956). In 1958 Durrell settled in Jersey, Channel Islands, founding a zoo and later (1964) the Jersey Wildlife Preservation Trust, which breeds rare and threatened species. Travels and writing continued, later books including *Encounters with Animals* (1959), *A Zoo in my Luggage* (1960), *Island Zoo* (1961), *The Whispering Land* (1962), *Menagerie Manor* (1964), *Birds, Beasts and Relatives* (1969), *Beasts in my Belfry* (1973), *The Stationary Ark* (1976) and *How to Shoot an Amateur Naturalist* (1984). He has also written novels, many articles for journals, and programmes for TV and radio. He was appointed OBE in 1983.

**Durrell, Lawrence (George)** 1912–90 Novelist, poet and travel-writer. The elder brother of **Gerald Durrell**, he was born in India and educated at Darjeeling and at St Edmund’s School, Canterbury. His first volume of poetry, *Quaint Fragment: Poems Written between the Ages of Sixteen and Nineteen*, was published in 1931. His first novel, *Panic Spring*, appeared under the pseudonym Charles Norden in 1935, though a second novel, *Pied Piper of Lovers*, was published the same year under his own name. The Eastern Mediterranean, where he spent a great deal of his life, formed the background to much of his best-known work, notably his books on Greece, *Prospero’s Cell* (1945) and *Bitter Lemons* (1957), and the four novels forming the *Alexan-*

*dria Quartet*: *Justine* (1957), *Balthazar* (1958), *Mountolive* (1958) and *Clea* (1960). Later volumes of poetry include *The Ikons* (1966) and *The Vega and Other Poems* (1973); *Collected Poems* appeared in 1960. Durrell's later fiction includes *Tunc* (1968), *Nunquam* (1970) and *Monsieur* (1974). Lectures delivered while he was teaching for the British Council in Greece and Argentina were published as *A Key to Modern Poetry* (1952).

**Dutch Courtesan, The** A comedy by **John Marston**, first published in 1605. It was first produced at least two years before that, in the reign of Elizabeth I; the title-page states that it was played 'by the children of her Majesties revels'.

The Dutch courtesan of the title is Franceschina. Her protector is Freevill, who falls in love with Beatrice, the daughter of Sir Hubert Subboys, and decides that he must end the liaison with Franceschina. Meanwhile he takes his stiff-necked friend Malheureux with him on a visit to Franceschina; he intends to amuse himself at his friend's uneasiness, but Malheureux conceives a violent passion for her. When Franceschina discovers Freevill's plans to marry she uses Malheureux's passion for her; she will respond if he will kill Freevill and bring her proof by taking from his hand a ring given him by Beatrice.

Malheureux recoils from the proposal and reveals it to Freevill, who arranges a mock fight, gives his friend the ring, and goes into hiding. But when Malheureux takes the ring to Franceschina she denounces him as a murderer to Sir Hubert and Freevill's father. Malheureux finds himself charged with Freevill's death and sentenced to the gallows. Freevill reappears in time to rescue him.

Freevill, who comments on the motives and emotions of the others and manipulates them some of the time, is one of the most unpleasant characters in Jacobean drama. Late in the action he declares himself enchanted with the prospect of marriage to Beatrice, while looking forward to the confounding of Franceschina: 'Providence all wicked art o'er tops.' If that were true he could expect to find himself brought down very hard some time in the future. But there is no such moral framework in *The Dutch Courtesan*: expedience is all in Marston's play.

**Dutchman** A one-act play by **Amiri Baraka** first performed in 1964 when the author was still known as LeRoi Jones, *Dutchman* had a successful first New York run of 366 performances and drew attention to the growth of a black American theatre. It won the Obie Award for the best American play of the 1963–4 season.

Set in the New York subway in summer, the play depicts the fatal encounter of Lula, a provocative white woman, and Clay, a somewhat naïve, middle-class black man. Their initially flirtatious conversation becomes more antagonistic as Lula taunts Clay for playing the role which the dominant white society has handed him. He finally responds to her with all the force of the racial hatred that he has suppressed in order to survive, claiming that for the black man repression and conformity are necessary because murder is the only alternative. Furious at losing control of the situation, Lula fatally stabs him and orders the other subway riders to remove his body. As they are doing so, another young black man enters the subway car and Lula begins her act again. The constant references to Adam and Eve, fairy-tales, and the Flying Dutchman, as well as the physical setting of the play, make it a more mythic than realistic representation.

**Dwight, Timothy** 1752–1817 American poet. One of the founding members of the **Connecticut Wits** and the grandson of **Jonathan Edwards**, Dwight was born in Massachusetts and matriculated at Yale at the age of 13. At 19 he was made tutor, a position he filled with such zeal that he suffered a nervous breakdown at 25. To aid his recuperation he undertook extensive walking and horseback journeys, which provided the material for his *Travels in New England and New York* (4 vols., 1821–2). During the Revolutionary War he served as an army chaplain and in 1783 became pastor of the Congregational church at Greenfield Hill, Connecticut. While serving there, he wrote his most widely read poems, which attempt to inculcate Calvinist and Federalist values: *The Conquest of Canaan* (1785), *Greenfield Hill* (1794) and *The Triumph of Infidelity* (1788). In 1795 he became president of Yale, in which capacity he successfully advocated the enlargement of the curriculum and published a number of statements of his political views, among them *The True Means of Establishing Public Happiness* (1795) and *The Duty of Americans, at the Present Crisis* (1798). *Theology, Explained and Defended* (1818–19), a five-volume collection of 173 sermons, makes a complete statement of his theology.

**Dyce, Alexander** 1798–1869 Scholar. Born in Edinburgh, educated at the High School there and at Exeter College, Oxford, he took Anglican orders and served as a curate until 1825, after which he devoted himself to literary work in London. His editorial work, which had begun as an undergraduate, was mainly concerned with the early dramatists: **Fletcher**, **Webster**, **Greene**, **Shirley**, **Middleton**, **Marlowe** and especially **Shakespeare** (9 vols., 1857). Other publications include an edition of the play *Sir Thomas More* for the Shakespeare Society (1844). His extensive library, strong in classical and European verse as well as Elizabethan authors, was bequeathed to the South Kensington (Victoria and Albert) Museum.

**Dyer, John** *c.* 1700–58 Poet. A native of Dyfed, Dyer was educated at Westminster School. He studied painting with Jonathan Richardson but was an unsuccessful artist. He was ordained in 1741, and was the incumbent of Coningsby and Kirkby in Lincolnshire when he died. Dyer is remembered in English literature for his poem *Grongar Hill* (1727), a poem which celebrates the valley of the River Towy in Dyfed, and is regarded as proto-Romantic. Dyer used the octosyllabic couplet of **Milton**'s *L'Allegro* and brought a remarkable freshness of observation to the countryside. Later but unsuccessful poems were *The Ruins of Rome* (1740) and *The Fleece* (1757), a faintly absurd treatment of the wool trade.

**Dyer, Sir Edward** 1543–1607 Poet, courtier and diplomat. A Somerset gentleman, he was educated at Oxford, and gained access to the court as a protégé of the Earl of Leicester. A man of speculative interests, he was one of the backers of Frobisher's expeditions to the far north of America in the 1570s; later in life he became fascinated by alchemy, and developed a strong friendship with the magus John Dee. In 1575 Dyer participated in the Woodstock entertainment for Queen Elizabeth; concealed in an oak, and accompanying himself on his lute, he sang an exquisite song complaining of his neglect at court. Thereafter he prospered. He was a close friend of **Sir Fulke Greville** and **Sir Philip Sidney**, who composed a song in praise of their three-in-one friendship, 'Join Mates in Mirth to Me'. Sidney also introduced Dyer into his *Arcadia* as the shepherd Coridon, and Dyer wrote a moving elegy on the death of Sidney, 'Silence Augmenteth Grief'.

**Nashe** wrote of Dyer that he was the first 'that repurified Poetrie from Art's pedantism, and instructed it to speak Courtly'. He liked a plain style, but his lyrics have sweetness and good measure. Their prevailing character is introspective and melancholy. Like so much Elizabethan courtier verse, his lines require a musical accompaniment to achieve their full effect. Only a handful of his poems survive, preserved in commonplace-books. The most famous lyric ascribed to him, 'My Mind to Me a Kingdom Is', was set to music by William Byrd and printed in 1588.

**Dylan, Bob** Stage- and pen-name of Robert Allen Zimmerman (1941– ), folk-singer, songwriter, poet and rock-musician. Educated at the University of Minnesota, Dylan made his reputation with his early records, *Bob Dylan* (1962), *Times They Are A-Changin* (1964) and *Another Side of Bob Dylan* (1964). His *Greatest Hits* was issued in 1967 and his *Greatest Hits vol. 2* in 1971.

As a folk- and protest-singer, Dylan's name was closely linked with the Civil Rights Movement and he performed many concerts with fellow singer Joan Baez. He then changed his style of music to modern rock, taking a position in its vanguard with committed songs and work of more substance than is usual in that medium. More lyrical than **Ginsberg**, less self-tortured than **Kerouac**, Dylan's work has many common themes with the **Beats**. After disappearing from public view for some time amid much rumour and speculation (he was the victim of a serious motorcycle accident in 1966), Dylan produced albums closer to Country and Western music than his previous style. A quieter and more introspective figure who has declared himself Christian and who continues to be an important lyricist, he has lately appeared in films and written music for films. His books include *Tarantula* (1966), *Approximately Complete Works* (1970), *Poem to Joanie* (1972), *Words* (1973), *The Songs of Bob Dylan 1966–75* (1976), and *XI Outlined Epitaphs and Off the Top of My Head* (1981).

***Dynasts, The*** **Thomas Hardy**'s 'Epic-Drama of the War with Napoleon', published in three parts in 1904, 1906 and 1908, is a long poem rather than a play intended for the stage. Its 19 acts and 130 scenes trace Napoleon's career from 1805 until his defeat at Waterloo some 10 years later, a period that had fascinated Hardy for many years. The structure of *The Dynasts* embodies what he liked to call his philosophical 'impressions'. The actions of the huge cast of human characters, from Napoleon down to the common soldiers and ordinary people of Wessex, are subject to the Immanent Will, the controlling power of the universe but a blind, unheeding force which bears no resemblance to the Christian God. Events are commented on by 'impersonated abstractions or Intelligences, called Spirits', including the Ancient Spirit of the Years, the Spirit of the Pities, the Spirit of Rumour and the Spirits Sinister and Ironic. *The Dynasts* combines a variety of verse forms with scenes and descriptions in prose.

# E

**Eagleton, Terry** See **Marxist criticism**.

*Earl of Toulous, The* A **verse romance** written around 1400 in the North-east Midlands. It is, by its own account, a **Breton lay**. The Earl promises a prisoner freedom in exchange for a meeting with his beautiful Empress, the wife of the Earl's enemy. He goes disguised as a hermit and she gives him a ring as a love-token. The Emperor later goes away and entrusts his wife to knights who try unsuccessfully to woo her. They hide a naked youth in her chamber then vociferously 'discover' and kill him; the Empress is accused of adultery. Hearing of her need of a champion the Earl disguises himself as a monk, hears her confession and, assured of her innocence, successfully defends her. The Emperor accepts the Earl's friendship and on his death the couple marry.

The story is based loosely on historical fact. In 831 the Empress Judith, second wife of Louis le Debonnaire, was accused of adultery with Bernard I, Count of Barcelona and Toulouse, but acquitted, and later Bernard offered battle with anyone who doubted his innocence.

**Earle, John** *c.* 1601–55 Essayist. A fellow of Merton College, Oxford, at the age of 18, Earle wrote *Microcosmography, or, A Piece of the World Discovered in Essays and Characters* (1628). Although the book appeared anonymously, its author's identity was no secret and Earle became famous. It is a collection of 'characters', or descriptions of behavioural types, a form much in fashion at the time. Easily recognizable from the day-to-day life he knew, Earle's characters are presented with insight and reckoned to be among the best of their kind. *Microcosmography* ran to four editions in 1628 and enlarged editions in 1629 and 1633.

Earle became tutor to Prince Charles, remaining loyal to him throughout the Civil War. He translated *Eikon Basilike* into Latin during his 16 years' exile as a Royalist. At the Restoration he became Dean of Westminster and later Bishop of Salisbury.

*Earthly Paradise, The* A poem by **William Morris**, published in three volumes between 1868 and 1870. It consists of 24 tales in verse, with a prologue and linking narrative.

A group of Norsemen flee the plague by setting sail across the western sea in search of the Earthly Paradise where nobody grows old. After long and fruitless journeying they at last arrive, old and tired, at 'a nameless city in a distant sea' where Greek culture and civilization have been preserved. They are made welcome and spend their remaining years there. Twice a month they meet their hosts at a feast and exchange stories. One of the Norsemen tells a tale of their past and one of their hosts relates a classical legend. Lyric poems connect the months and describe the landscape of the changing year.

Obviously medieval in both its form and content, *The Earthly Paradise* deliberately creates a dreamlike atmosphere. In a famous passage the prologue offers the reader an escape from the industrial society that Morris himself so despised: 'Forget six counties overhung with smoke,/Forget the snorting steam and piston stroke.' The appeal was popular with the Victorian public and *The Earthly Paradise* helped establish Morris as one of the leading poets of the day.

*East Lynne* A novel by **Mrs Henry Wood**, published in 1861. Immensely popular in its day, it was also dramatized with great success. Lady Isobel Vane marries Archibald Carlyle but deserts him to go abroad with Sir Francis Levison. After he abandons her, she is disfigured in a train crash. Returning to England, she works unrecognized as governess to her own children and asks for Carlyle's forgiveness on her deathbed.

**Eastman, Charles (Alexander)** 1858–1939 Born of mixed Santee Sioux and white parentage, Eastman was the best-known Native American writer of the early 20th century. He received his BA from Dartmouth in 1887 and his MD from Boston University Medical School in 1890. He treated the victims of the Wounded Knee Massacre in 1890, and that same year married Elaine Goodale, with whom he collaborated on all his books (though only

*Wigwam Evenings* bears both their names). Between 1890 and 1910 he held a number of positions connected with the Bureau of Indian Affairs; he also lectured in America and England, meeting many of the great literary and political figures of his day.

Through his writings Eastman attempted to bridge the gap between Indian and white culture by describing the life, customs and legends of his people for a primarily white audience. Four of his books were for children: *Indian Boyhood* (1902), *Red Hunters and the Animal People* (1904), *Old Indian Days* (1907) and *Wigwam Evenings: Sioux Folktales Retold* (1909). In *The Soul of the Indian: An Interpretation* (1911) he describes the Indian system of ethics and Indian attitudes toward nature. *The Indian To-day: The Past and Future of the First Americans* (1915) is an overview of Indian history. *From the Deep Woods to Civilization: Chapters in the Autobiography of an Indian* appeared in 1916. *Indian Heroes and Great Chieftains* (1918) is a collection of short biographies of Sioux leaders.

**Eastman, Max** 1883–1969 An American critic, poet and essayist from New York City, Eastman came to prominence as the author of *Enjoyment of Poetry* (1913), a critical study which is still his best-known work. He co-founded and edited the left-wing magazines *The Masses* (1913–17) and *The Liberator* (1918–22), and later published *Marx, Lenin, and The Science of Revolution* (1926). With the rise of Stalin, however, he turned against the left, publishing *Artists in Uniform: A Study of Literature and Bureaucratism* (1934), a collection of literary and political essays; *Marxism, Is It Science?* (1940); and *Reflections on the Failure of Socialism* (1955). From 1941 to his death he was an editor for *Reader's Digest*. His memoirs of famous friends, including Isadora Duncan, Anatole France, Charlie Chaplin and Leon Trotsky, appeared in *Heroes I Have Known* (1942) and *Great Companions* (1959). His collected poems were published as *Poems of Five Decades* (1954), and his autobiography as *Love and Revolution* (1964).

***Eastward Ho*** A comedy by **George Chapman**, **Ben Jonson** and **John Marston**, first performed at **Blackfriars** by the Children of the Revels and published in 1605.

The plot tells of Touchstone, a goldsmith, his two daughters, Mildred and Gertrude, and his two apprentices, Golding and Quicksilver. Gertrude, who wants to be fashionable and ride in her own coach, marries Sir Petronel Flash, who turns out to be a penniless adventurer. The industrious apprentice, Golding, has eyes for the unpretentious Mildred, who is happy to marry him and proud to see him become deputy alderman. Sir Petronel filches Gertrude's dowry and sends her off on a coach to an imaginary castle. As soon as she is gone he sets off for Virginia in company with the idle apprentice, Quicksilver, who has robbed his master. They are arrested when their ship is wrecked on the Isle of Dogs and brought up before Golding, the deputy alderman. A term in prison makes them repent and they are eventually released through Golding's good offices.

The play is interesting for its setting; like **Dekker**'s *The Shoemaker's Holiday* of 1600 it dealt with tradesmen and their lives. A passage in Act III was considered to be insulting to the Scots and gave offence at the Stuart court. The three authors were punished with imprisonment.

**Eberhart, Richard** 1904– American poet, born in Minnesota and educated at Harvard. He has published almost 30 volumes of poetry: the first, *A Bravery of Earth*, appeared in 1930; the most recent, *The Long Reach: New and Uncollected Poems 1948–1984*, in 1984. Among his other volumes are *Reading the Spirit* (1936), *Poems New and Selected* (1944), *Undercliff: Poems 1946–1956* (1956), *The Quarry* (1960), *Selected Poems 1930–1965* (1965; Pulitzer Prize 1966), *Fields of Grace* (1972) and *Collected Poems 1930–1976* (1976; National Book Award 1977). His poetry tends to be contemplative and lyrical. His themes, often expressed in a philosophical idiom, range from confrontations with death to meditations inspired by scenes in nature. Many of his poems, especially those of his later years, are concerned with the nature of the poetic process itself. He is also a playwright; his *Collected Verse Plays* appeared in 1962.

***Ecce Homo*** See **Seeley, J. R.**

**eclogue** From the Greek word for 'selection', it hence originally referred to a short poem or section of a longer poem. The term was later applied to the **pastoral** poems of Virgil and, in the Renaissance, to verse dialogues on pastoral themes (like **Spenser**'s *The Shepheardes Calender*). By the 18th century a distinction was drawn between pastoral, which described a context, and eclogue, which described a verse form. The term can also mean merely a dramatic argument in verse, not necessarily connected with pastoral.

**Eden, Richard** ?1521–76 Collector and translator of accounts of travel. He was educated at Queens' College, Cambridge, and for a while held a position in the Treasury. His translations include part of Munster's *Cosmographiae* as *A Treatise of the New India* (1553), *The Decades of the New World* (1555), which is a collection of travels mainly from Peter Martyr of Angleria, a translation of Martin Cortes's *Arte de Navegar* as *The Art of Navigation* (1561), and *The History of*

*Travel in the West and East Indies*, published posthumously in 1577.

**Edgar, David** 1948– Playwright. He was educated at Oundle and Manchester University, where he studied drama, and wrote his first plays during a period as a journalist in Bradford. They were lively contributions to the radical revolutionary theatre that flourished for a decade after 1968. *Destiny* (1976), an absorbing exploration of British fascism, revealed Edgar's craftsmanship and signalled a greater complexity in his treatment of social forces. *Mary Barnes* (1977) and *The Jail Diary of Albie Sachs* (1978) are sophisticated examples of documentary drama. The resourceful dramatization of **Dickens**'s *Nicholas Nickleby* (1981) for the **Royal Shakespeare Company** and *Maydays* (1983), an ambitious analysis of the labour movement, have confirmed Edgar's status in the modern English theatre.

**Edgeworth, Maria** 1767–1849 Novelist. She was born at Black Bourton in Oxfordshire, the daughter of Richard Edgeworth, MP for the Irish constituency of Edgeworthstown in County Longford. On her father's second marriage in 1773 she went to Ireland, but returned to England to attend school in Derby (1775–80) and London (1780–2). Her first published work, *Letters to Literary Ladies* (1795), was a defence of female education. The first volume of *The Parent's Assistant*, a collection of stories for children, appeared in 1796; its sixth volume was completed in 1800, the *Little Plays* being added later as a seventh volume. She collaborated with her father on the two-volume *Practical Education* in 1798, adapting and modifying the theories embodied in Rousseau's *Émile*. Her first novel for adult readers, *Castle Rackrent*, appeared anonymously in 1800 and was followed by *Belinda* (1801), *Modern Griselda* (1804) and *Leonora* (1806). The first series of *Tales of Fashionable Life* appeared in 1809 and the second, containing *The Absentee*, in 1812. Her later fiction included *Patronage* (1814), *Harrington* (1817), *Ormond* (1817) and *Helen* (1834). She completed the second volume of her father's *Memoirs* in 1820.

In 1823 she visited Scotland, being warmly received by **Sir Walter Scott**, an admirer of her work. He visited her at Edgeworthstown in 1825 and continued a regular correspondent. Although they did not otherwise come into contact, **Jane Austen** sent Maria Edgeworth a copy of *Emma* in 1816 and commended *Belinda* in *Northanger Abbey*.

**Edinburgh Review, The** A quarterly magazine founded in 1802 by **Francis Jeffrey**, **Sydney Smith** and **Henry Brougham**. It was published by Constable in Edinburgh and by Longman in

London, the first issue appearing on 10 October 1802 as *The Edinburgh Review and Critical Journal*. Circulation rose to 13,500 by 1818. **Sir Walter Scott**, a notable early contributor, gradually withdrew his support because of a conflict between his own Tory prejudices and the Whig prejudices of the journal's editors. Apart from Jeffrey and his co-founders, other contributors included **Hazlitt**, **Henry Hallam**, **Francis Horner** and, in later years, **Macaulay**, **Carlyle** and **Thomas Arnold**. The *Edinburgh* was the most influential magazine of its day, setting new standards for outspoken and deliberate criticism; its demand for disciplined literary feeling made it particularly harsh on the work of **Wordsworth**, **Coleridge** and **Southey**, the so-called **Lake Poets**. An unfavourable review of **Byron**'s *Hours of Idleness* by Brougham provoked the poet's *English Bards and Scotch Reviewers*. The *Edinburgh* ceased publication in 1929.

**Education of Henry Adams, The** The autobiography of **Henry Brooks Adams**, privately printed in 1907 and published in 1918. Among other things, Adams describes his experience as both student and teacher at Harvard, his impressions of England during the years of the American Civil War, and the impact on him of **Charles Darwin**'s theories, but he notably omits his marriage and his wife's suicide. Sub-titled *A Study of Twentieth-Century Multiplicity*, the book illustrates Adams's 'dynamic theory of history' by contrasting the dynamo, the symbol of the accelerating forces of modern life, with the Virgin, the symbol of the 12th century and the subject of his earlier book, *Mont-Saint-Michel and Chartres* (1904).

**Edward III, The Reign of** A chronicle play published in 1596. The authorship is unknown, though the suggestion that **Shakespeare** had a hand in it has not been completely rejected (see **Shakespeare apocrypha**). Apart from its historical content, dealing with Edward III and the Hundred Years War, the play is concerned with the King's unwelcome attentions to the Countess of Salisbury, which nearly drive her to suicide.

**Edward the First, The Famous Chronicle of King** A historical play by **George Peele**, which loosely follows the reign of Edward I. It was written for **Philip Henslowe**'s company, The Admiral's Men, and probably played at the **Rose**, Henslowe's theatre in Southwark. It was published in 1593.

**Edward the Second, King of England, The Troublesome Reign and Lamentable Death of** A historical tragedy in blank verse by **Christopher Marlowe**, first produced by the Earl of Pembroke's Men *c.* 1592 and published in 1594.

**Shakespeare**'s success with *Henry VI* in 1592 had helped to make the English history play an attractive medium for dramatists.

The play begins with Edward's recall of his favourite Gaveston upon his accession to the throne (Gaveston had been banished by the King's father, Edward I), and follows the grim events that succeed. These include the growing hatred of the Queen, Isabella of France (the She-Wolf), the revolt of the barons culminating in their capture and murder of Gaveston, the rise of Hugh le Despenser in Edward's affections, the Queen's alliance with her lover Mortimer and the successful rebellion, the execution of Despenser and his father, and the confinement of the King in Berkeley Castle and his degradation and murder.

As drama, *Edward II* is the best constructed of all Marlowe's works, though its detractors complain that it lacks the grandeur and lofty language of the others. It is more personal than historical, though the history is well handled and the march of events perfectly clear: this results in due weight being given to the characters of Isabella and Mortimer.

**Edwards, Jonathan** 1703–58 American Puritan minister and religious philosopher, born in East Windsor, Connecticut, and educated at Yale. In 1727 he was ordained minister of the church in Northampton, Massachusetts, where he served jointly with his grandfather, **Solomon Stoddard**, until Stoddard's death in 1729. His early sermons include *God Glorified in the Work of Redemption* (1731) and *A Divine and Supernatural Light* (1734), the latter notable for its emphasis on the aesthetic dimension of religious experience. His preaching helped precipitate the religious revival that swept through western Massachusetts in 1734–5, and later contributed to the 'Great Awakening' (1740), which spread through the colonies in general (see *Sinners in the Hands of an Angry God*). These awakenings prompted Edwards to reflect on the nature of religious experience. His *Faithful Narrative of Surprising Conversions* (1737) and *The Distinguishing Marks* (1741) describe and defend the 1735 revival and the Great Awakening, respectively. *Some Thoughts Concerning the Present Revival* (1743) speculates on the millennial possibilities raised by the Awakening. *A Treatise Concerning Religious Affections* (1746) is his systematic exposition of his understanding of religious psychology, while his diary and *Personal Narrative* (*c.* 1740, not intended for publication) tell the story of his own conversion.

Dismissed by his Northampton congregation in 1750 for his unorthodox views, he went to Stockbridge, where he ministered to an Indian mission. During this period he wrote *Freedom of the Will* (published 1754), *The Great Christian Doctrine of Original Sin Defended* (published 1758), *The Nature of True Virtue* (published 1765) and *The Great End for Which God Created the World* (published 1765), works of religious philosophy which expand on his conception of religious experience. Fusing an orthodox Calvinism with Lockean psychology and Newtonian physics, he explains religious conversion in 18th-century rationalist terms. In 1757 he was appointed president of the College of New Jersey (later Princeton University), but died from a smallpox inoculation soon after taking office. At the time of his death he was working on his systematic sacred history, *The History of the Work of Redemption*, based on sermons delivered in 1739. The series was published in 1774 and held an important place in American millennial thought.

**Egan, Pierce** 1772–1849 Comic writer and sporting journalist. Born in London, he first established a reputation as a sports reporter for the newspapers. In 1818 he began the serial publication of *Boxiana, or, Sketches of Modern Pugilism*, which continued until 1824. In 1820 he began monthly publication of the book by which he is best remembered, **Life in London,** *or, The Day and Night Scenes of Jerry Hawthorn Esq. and His Elegant Friend Corinthian Tom*. This comic portrait of Regency manners proved enormously popular. Egan's weekly newspaper, *Life in London and Sporting Guide*, later merged into *Bell's Life in London*, first appeared in 1824.

**Egan, Pierce** 1814–80 Novelist and son of the author of **Life in London**. His many historical novels include *Wat Tyler* (1841) and *Paul Jones* (1842). He was editor of *Home Circle* in 1849–51 and from 1857 contributed serial novels to *The London Journal*, among them *Love Me, Leave Me Not* (1859–60), *The Poor Girl* (1862–3) and *Eve, or, The Angel of Innocence* (1867). Egan is recognized as one of the pioneers of cheap literature.

***Eger and Grime*** A **verse romance** of the mid 15th century written in the North of England; it survives only in 17th-century copies. Eger's lady Winglaine wants a supreme warrior as her husband. Going into a strange land, Eger is attacked by a giant knight, Gray-steele, who cuts off his finger; he is cared for by Loosepaine, who gives him shirts and wine as tokens. On Eger's return his sworn brother Grime goes to avenge him and takes the tokens to Loosepaine, but she sees his hands are intact and he tells her his errand. She tells him that Gray-steele grows weaker from noon to night, which enables Grime to slay the giant and return to Eger with the proof. Eger marries Winglaine on the strength of his supposed victory, and Grime marries Loosepaine. The romance is notable for its use of direct discourse, often humorous and realistic, which gives the narrative a dramatic quality.

**Egerton, George** Pen-name of the short-story writer Mary Chavelita Dunne (1859–1945). Born in Australia, daughter of a spendthrift cashiered Irish army officer and a Welsh mother, she had some schooling in Germany before nursing briefly in London, struggling for a living in New York and eloping to Norway with a bigamist. In Norway she encountered the advanced social and sexual views of Ibsen and Strindberg. She also met Knut Hamsen, whose novel *Hunger* she translated in 1899 and to whom she dedicated her first and best collection of short stories, *Keynotes*. This was published by John Lane in 1893, with illustrations by **Aubrey Beardsley**, on the strong recommendation of **Richard Le Gallienne**. The following year Lane published a further collection, *Discords*, and persuaded her to contribute to the first number of *The Yellow Book*. She published two more volumes of short stories, *Symphonies* (1896) and *Fantasies* (1898), and two novels, *The Wheel of God* (1898) and *Rosa Amorosa: the Love-Letters of a Woman* (1901) which, like her stories, drew heavily on her own varied and colourful experiences. Her first marriage to George Egerton Clairmonte broke up in 1895; after her second marriage (1901) to Golding Bright, a drama critic turned theatrical agent, she wrote for the stage, accepting trenchant advice from **G. B. Shaw** and attracting the interest of actresses such as Lillie Langtry but failing to win either commercial success or critical approval. In her stories an impressionist technique identifies moments of significant female – and feminist – consciousness, blending realistic structures and detail with Utopian fantasies of self-realization and freedom for the 'new woman'.

**Eggleston, Edward** 1837–1902 American novelist. Born into a strict Methodist family in rural Indiana, Edward and his brother **George Eggleston** were educated in back-country schools. Edward had a busy career as a Bible agent and then as a Methodist minister on circuit; he also wrote and edited juvenile magazines as an extension of his Sunday-school teaching. He was 37 when he abandoned Methodism and went to New York City, where he founded a Church of Christian Endeavour in Brooklyn. He remained its pastor for five years, before retiring to devote himself entirely to writing.

His first success, and the novel for which he is best known, was *The Hoosier Schoolmaster* (1871), a realistic if somewhat pious presentation of rural life in Indiana which made excellent use of local dialect. His next novels were also set in the Midwest during the period of the country's expansion: *The End of the World* (1872, set in Indiana), *The Mystery of Metropolisville* (1873, set in Minnesota), *The Circuit Rider* (1874, set in Ohio) and *Roxy* (1878, set in Indiana). For a

Edward Eggleston.

brief period he devoted his attention to writing history and biography, an enterprise which produced several works, among which the uncompleted *History of Life in the United States* (1888) is the most memorable. Before his death he wrote three more novels: *The Hoosier Schoolboy* (1883), a boy's view of the life described in *The Hoosier Schoolmaster*; *The Graysons: A Story of Illinois* (1888), based on Abraham Lincoln's days as a lawyer in Springfield, Illinois, when he successfully defended a man accused of murder, and *The Faith Doctor* (1891), a satirical view of the wealthy devotees of the then-new Christian Science movement.

**Eggleston, George Cary** 1839–1911 American novelist and editor. The younger brother of **Edward Eggleston**, George became a teacher in back-country Indiana at the age of 16. His experiences provided his brother with the material for two novels, *The Hoosier Schoolmaster* (1871) and *The Hoosier Schoolboy* (1883). After serving in the Confederate army during the Civil War, he practised law for a time before becoming a journalist. He served as editor of the New York *Evening Post* and worked for Joseph Pulitzer on the New York *World* for 11 years. He also wrote a number of books for boys, and several novels set in the South, including *A Man of Honour* (1873), *Dorothy South* (1902), *The Master of Warlock* (1903) and *Evelyn Byrd* (1904). With Dorothy Marbourg he co-wrote the novel *Juggernaut* (1891), which is set in Indiana. His autobiographical volume, *A Rebel's Recollections*, based on his experiences during the Civil War, appeared in 1874.

**Eglinton, John** Pen-name of the Irish essayist and critic William K. Magee (1868–1961). Born in Dublin, he was for a time a schoolmate of **Yeats** at the High School before going on to a distinguished career at Trinity College. From 1895 to 1921 he was a librarian at the National Library, Dublin, appearing in this role in the 'Scylla and Charybdis' chapter of **Joyce**'s *Ulysses*. He was friendly with many of the leading figures of the Irish revival, particularly **George Russell** (AE), **George Moore** and Stephen MacKenna. As founder–editor of the literary magazine *Dana* (1904–5) he published the work of distinguished contemporaries but refused the chance to serialize Joyce's *Portrait of the Artist as a Young Man*.

Yeats admired Eglinton's criticism and published a selection as *Some Essays and Passages by John Eglinton* (1905), drawing on *Two Essays on the Remnant* (1894) and *Pebbles from a Brook* (1901). Eglinton's best work appeared in *Anglo-Irish Essays* (1917), but he wrote little of importance for many years afterwards. He moved to England after the founding of the new Irish state in 1922 and it was there that he produced his most notable later works, *Irish Literary Portraits* (1935) and *Memoir of AE* (1937).

**Egoist, The** A novel by **George Meredith**, published in 1879.

The central character of Meredith's 'comedy in narrative' is Sir Willoughby Patterne, rich and handsome, selfish, fatuous, and conceited. He is loved by Laetitia Dale and does nothing to discourage her; but he has proposed to Constantia Durham, who has accepted him. Constantia, however, learns in time what sort of man he is and elopes with an officer of Hussars.

Patterne recovers from the humiliation and pursues Clara Middleton, a professor's daughter. Clara is subjected to a whirlwind courtship, and won, but she knows about Constantia and is equivocal about marriage. Her father, an epicurean, is enlisted on his side by Patterne, who can lavish hospitality on him. Others involved are Vernon Whitford, a handsome scholar, and the boy Crossjay, a poor relation of Patterne. Patterne had once been arrogantly rude to Crossjay's father and the boy gleefully avenges the insult when he overhears Patterne proposing to Laetitia Dale – he is becoming worried by Clara's prevarication and wants to hedge his bets.

Crossjay tells Clara, who has in any case fallen in love with Vernon. Patterne turns to Laetitia who, with pride intact, refuses him. In the end, Patterne, stripped of his pretensions, persuades Laetitia to marry him.

The character of Dr Middleton, Clara's father, is modelled on **Thomas Love Peacock**, Meredith's father-in-law.

**Egoist, The** *The New Freewoman*, a feminist journal founded in 1913 by Dora Marsden and **Rebecca West**, changed its name, at the prompting of **Ezra Pound** and **Richard Aldington**, to *The Egoist: An Individualist Review* in 1914. The journal then became, under the editorship of Harriet Shaw Weaver, a vehicle for Pound's **imagism**. **Hilda Doolittle** and Richard Aldington acted as assistant editors, as did (from 1917) **T. S. Eliot**, who contributed a number of critical articles. *The Egoist*'s most notable contribution to literature was its serial publication of **James Joyce**'s *A Portrait of the Artist as a Young Man* in 1914 and 1915. The review closed in 1919, but its name survived in that of Harriet Shaw Weaver's Egoist Press, which published an edition of Joyce's *Ulysses* in October 1922.

**Eikon Basilike**: *The Portraiture of His Sacred Majesty in His Solitudes and Sufferings* A book of which John Gauden, Bishop of Winchester, later claimed authorship. It was presented as the prayers and meditations of Charles I during his imprisonment and was published on the day of the King's burial, 9 February 1649, running to 40 editions before the Restoration in 1660. Gauden probably compiled his book from the notes and memoranda left by Charles, and succeeded remarkably well in presenting the late King as a royal martyr. The title means 'the royal image'. It prompted a reply from **John Milton** and was translated into Latin by **John Earle**.

**Ekwensi, Cyprian** 1921– Nigerian novelist. Born in Minna, he was educated in Nigeria, Ghana and London. He attracted some acclaim with *People of the City* (1954), a novel about rural Nigerians corrupted by city glitterings. Though somewhat artless, he successfully registers and dramatizes the attitudes of ordinary people buffeted by historical change, as in his best novel, *Jagua Nana* (1962), about a Lagos prostitute. *Beautiful Feathers* (1963) satirizes politicians, *Iska* (1966) illustrates the dangers of tribalism, *Survive the Peace* (1976) chronicles Biafran defeat in 1970. He has also written many children's tales, numerous short stories and *Burning Grass* (1962), a novel about wandering Fulani herdsmen.

**Eldershaw, M. Barnard** The pseudonym of two Australian writers working in collaboration, Flora Sydney Patricia Eldershaw (1897–1956) and Marjorie Faith Barnard (1897– ). Educated in Sydney, Flora Eldershaw was senior mistress at the Presbyterian Ladies College, Croydon. Marjorie Barnard was also educated at Sydney University and was librarian at the Commonwealth Scientific and Industrial Research Organization. Their best-known novels, *A House is Built* (1929) and *Green Memory* (1931), were set in 19th-century Australia. They also wrote *The Glass House* (1936), *Plaque with Laurel* (1937), *Tomorrow and Tomorrow* (1947) and *Phillip of Australia: An Account of the Settlement at Sydney Cove 1788–92* (1938).

**elegy** In Greek and Roman literature, any poem using the 'elegiac couplet' (a dactylic hexameter followed by a dactylic pentameter). Since the Renaissance it has come to mean a sustained poetic meditation on a solemn theme, particularly on death (e.g. **Milton**'s *Lycidas* or **Shelley**'s *Adonais*). The 'elegiac stanza' (a quatrain of iambic pentameters, rhyming abab) takes its name from **Thomas Gray**'s famous *Elegy Written in a Country Churchyard*.

*Elegy Written in a Country Churchyard* A poem by **Thomas Gray**, first published in 1751. One of the best-known elegies in the language, this accomplished piece was begun in 1742, and is written in quatrains of iambic pentameters. The churchyard in question is at Stoke Poges, Buckinghamshire, where Gray himself is now buried. The poem is melancholy and reflective, as the poet muses upon the conditions of rural life, human potential, and mortality. At its close, the elegy casts forward to the prospect of the poet's own death, and considers the possibility that Art – in the shape of the poem itself – might offer a more durable memorial against time. The gentle gloominess of this elegy is characteristic of the work of several poets sometimes classified as the **graveyard poets**.

*Elene* An Old English poem by **Cynewulf** preserved in the **Vercelli Book**, it tells of St Helena's discovery of the Cross in the Holy Land.

An illustration from the 1769 edition of Thomas Gray's *Elegy Written in a Country Churchyard*. The poem was first published in 1751.

The story occupies 14 sections of the poem; a 15th provides the only information known about Cynewulf and contains his runic signature. At the time of writing, he says, he was old and dying; his early life was sinful but a spiritual experience brought him enlightenment and the gift of poetry.

**Eliot, George** Pseudonym of Mary Anne (or Marian) Evans (1819–80). Novelist, critic and poet. She was born at South Farm, Arbury, Warwickshire, where her father, Robert Evans, was a land agent. She was educated at several schools, among them Miss Wallington's Boarding School in Nuneaton, where she came under the beneficent influence of a Miss Maria Lewis, her own mother having died when she was 16. She also attended the Misses Franklins' School in Coventry, where she shed her provincial accent and studied the piano and French. During her early years she also read widely in theology, the Romantic poets and German literature. When her father retired in 1841 they went to live at Foleshill near Coventry, and there Mary Anne Evans was drawn to an intellectual circle that included Charles Bray and Charles Hennell, whose influences directed her towards freethinking in religious opinion. Her refusal in January 1842 to attend church with her father suggested a coalescence of her spiritual position. A few years later she completed the translation

George Eliot. Photograph by Mayall, 1858.

The drawing room at The Priory, Regent's Park, which became the home of George Eliot and George Henry Lewes in 1863, and thereafter a meeting place for London's intelligentsia. An illustration for *George Eliot's Life* by J. W. Cross (1885).

of *The Life of Jesus, Critically Examined by Dr David Strauss*, published by John Chapman in 1846 (see **Higher Criticism**). Then followed Continental travel with the Brays, after which she went to London and was closely associated with the amorous Chapman, now proprietor and publisher of the radical *Westminster Review*, of which she was assistant editor from January 1852 until January 1854. For her services she received no salary but board and lodging at 142 Strand, where Chapman conducted a curious *ménage*-cum-boarding-house which was a haven for middle-class intellectuals. George Eliot's next publication of consequence was a translation of Feuerbach's *Essence of Christianity* (1854). By this time she had met **George Henry Lewes**, with whom she went to live in October 1853. Their union, happy despite Lewes's irregular marital situation, lasted until his death in 1878.

George Eliot's interest in writing fiction goes back to her schooldays in the early 1830s, when she wrote a story entitled 'Edward Neville', but her debut as a fully fledged writer of narrative did not come until the serial publication in *Blackwood's Edinburgh Magazine* in 1857 of 'The Sad Fortunes of the Reverend Amos Barton', 'Mr Gilfil's Love-Story' and 'Janet's Repentance'. The next year these tales were collectively published as *Scenes of Clerical Life*. Well received, they were followed by *Adam Bede* (1859), *The Mill on the Floss* (1860) and *Silas Marner* (1861). After a brief Florentine visit George Eliot deserted her native literary landscapes to publish serially in *The Cornhill Magazine* (1862-3) the Renaissance novel *Romola*. Next came *Felix Holt the Radical* (1866) in some respects anticipatory of *Middlemarch: A Study of Provincial Life*, published in independent parts in 1871-2; and in 1874-6 came *Daniel Deronda*, in

format the same as its immediate predecessor. Her last work was *The Impressions of Theophrastus Such* (1879), a series of essays linked by a narrator. George Eliot also wrote some novellas and a surprising amount of poetry, including *The Spanish Gypsy* (1868), the product of a trip to Spain in 1867, and *The Legend of Jubal and other Poems* (1874). In addition, she was one of the finest letter-writers in the language.

After the death of Lewes, she married John Walter Cross, a man many years her junior, in the spring of 1880; she died in December of the same year. Cross's biography was published in 1885. In a century of gifted women writers George Eliot stands pre-eminent.

**Eliot, John** 1604-90 American Puritan minister, born in England, and educated at Cambridge. He emigrated to Massachusetts in 1631 and in the following year became minister at the church in Roxbury. He contributed, along with several other New England ministers, to the English translations in the **Bay Psalm Book** (1640). Over the next decade he learned the language of the Massachusetts Indians and began attempts to Christianize them. His missionary efforts received some support from the Massachusetts General Court, and in 1651 he established the first of a series of 'praying Indian Towns', at Natick. His pamphlet *The Christian Commonwealth*, written in 1649 and published in 1659, set forth his notions for the governance of these Indian communities. He also compiled a primer to teach the Indians to read, and translated the Bible into the Algonquian dialect. Known as the 'Apostle to the Indians', Eliot was a venerable figure in the Massachusetts Bay community. A youthful **Cotton Mather**, who knew him in his old age, memorialized him in a biography included in the *Magnalia Christi Americana*.

**Eliot, T[homas] S[tearns]** 1888-1965 Poet, critic and dramatist. He was born and brought up in St Louis, Missouri, though his Unitarian family had strong ties with Massachusetts. In 1906 he went to Harvard University, where his teachers included **George Santayana** and **Irving Babbitt**. The latter in particular influenced his ideas about the dynamic relationship between past and present, as well as his bias against **Romanticism**. At Harvard he also became interested in Dante, Jules Laforgue and French **Symbolism**. His formal studies were in philosophy, and after gaining his BA and MA he began a doctoral thesis but chose not to take the degree. The thesis was eventually published as *Knowledge and Experience in the Philosophy of F. H. Bradley* (1964).

Eliot left America in 1914, and after studying briefly in Germany, at the Sorbonne and at Merton College, Oxford, settled in London the

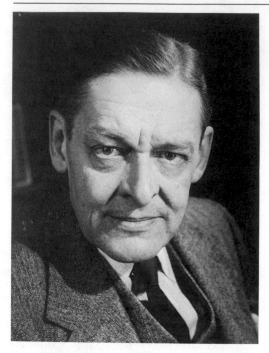

T. S. Eliot, 1960.

following year. His troubled marriage to Vivien Haigh-Wood lasted from June 1915 until their separation in the early 1930s. She died in 1947 and Eliot was married a second time, to Valerie Fletcher, in 1957. During his early years in London he taught at Highgate School, reviewed books for *The Times Literary Supplement*, and, from 1917, worked for Lloyds Bank. After a short term as assistant editor of *The Egoist*, he became editor of a newly founded quarterly review, *The Criterion*, in 1922 and held the post until it ceased publication in 1939. He also worked as a director of its publisher, Faber and Faber, aiding many younger poets in their careers.

He himself had begun to publish poetry with the help and encouragement of **Ezra Pound**. *The Love Song of J. Alfred Prufrock*, written while he was at Harvard, appeared in 1915 in the American magazine *Poetry* and in 1917 was collected in his first volume, *Prufrock and Other Observations*, published by Harriet Shaw Weaver. It was followed by two more collections: *Poems* (1919), which contained 'Gerontion', printed by **Leonard Woolf** and **Virginia Woolf** at their Hogarth Press and published in the USA the following year, and *Ara Vos Prec* (1920). His next major work was *The Waste Land*, published in the first issue of *The Criterion* in 1922 and dedicated to Pound in acknowledgement of his considerable editorial role in crafting the final version. After the initial controversy it provoked by its innovatory technique and its apparently pessimistic

tone, the poem came to be accepted as a central text of **modernism**. Eliot's position as a major force in 20th-century letters was confirmed by the critical essays which, throughout his career, offered a theoretical counterpart to the example of his own poetry. His first collection, *The Sacred Wood* (1920), reprinted the essay on *Hamlet* (with its concept of the **objective correlative**) and the highly influential 'Tradition and the Individual Talent', rejecting Romantic individualism in favour of a belief in the 'impersonality' of poetry. *Homage to John Dryden* (1924) contained his essays on **Marvell** and the **metaphysical poets**, praised for their unified sensibility in contrast to the **dissociation of sensibility** which afflicted later writers.

*For Lancelot Andrewes: Esasys on Style and Order* (1928), in which Eliot described himself as 'classical in literature, royalist in politics, and Anglo-Catholic in religion', emphasized the main direction of his development during the 1920s, a direction neither anticipated nor welcomed by many of his first admirers. He had joined the Church of England in 1927, the same year that he became a British citizen. The increasingly religious tendency of his poetry can be traced in *Poems 1909–25* (1925), which includes 'The Hollow Men', and *Collected Poems 1909–35* (1936), which added 'The Journey of the Magi' (1927) and 'Ash Wednesday' (1930). Its chief fruit – and the major achievement of Eliot's later career – was *Four Quartets*, consisting of 'Burnt Norton' (1935), 'East Coker' (1940), 'The Dry Salvages' (1941) and 'Little Gidding' (1942), first published together in 1943. *Old Possum's Book of Practical Cats*, his collection of humorous verse for children, appeared in 1939. *Collected Poems 1909–62* was published in 1963.

Cultural problems absorbed much of Eliot's energies as critic after he joined the church. The *Use of Poetry and the Use of Criticism* (1933), based on lectures delivered at Harvard, and the incautious *After Strange Gods: A Primer of Modern Heresy* (1934) both show the fascination that authority and control in life and literature had for him during this troubled period of his life. They were followed by *The Idea of a Christian Society* (1939), but his most influential exercise in social criticism is undoubtedly *Notes Towards a Definition of Culture* (1948). Other collections include *On Poetry and Poets* (1957) and *To Criticize the Critic* (1965).

Eliot's attempt to revive verse drama, foreshadowed in *Sweeney Agonistes: An Aristophanic Fragment* (1932) and advanced further by his pageant play *The Rock* (1934), was perhaps most successful in *Murder in the Cathedral* (1935), where Yeatsian spiritual vigour and dramatic crispness helped carry off the historicism. This was not always the case in his later plays, *The Family Reunion* (1939), *The Cocktail Party* (1950),

*The Confidential Clerk* (1954) and *The Elder Statesman* (1959), where the burden of philosophical ideas and the conventions of the contemporary stage sit uneasily together.

In 1948 Eliot received both the Nobel Prize for Literature and the Order of Merit. Such honours acknowledged his vital role in showing poetry how to become modern. 'Tradition and the Individual Talent' spoke of tradition not as inertly inherited but as achieved 'by great labour' and as bringing a perception 'not only of the pastness of the past, but of its presence'. With its dense, even riddling, allusions to earlier literature *The Waste Land* had crucially redefined the traditions of use to the modern poet, abandoning Victorianism and the lingering traces of Romanticism. Eliot's praise of the Elizabethan dramatists and the metaphysical poets in his criticism confirmed a preference for intellectual toughness, energy and wit that left its mark on most of the poets (as well as the critics) who immediately followed him. Yet the rightward tendency of his beliefs in politics and religion, though shared by several poets of his own generation, limited his influence over younger writers from **Auden** onwards. Since his death it has further diminished, with the lyricism of **Yeats** and the stubborn individuality of **Hardy** exerting their rival claims with increasing power.

**elision** In verse, the slurring or omission of an unstressed syllable so that a line may conform to a metrical pattern, or the omission of part of a word for ease of pronunciation. The effect is most frequently accomplished by the omission of a final vowel preceding an initial vowel, as in 'th'Eternal', but it also occurs between syllables in a single word, as in 'ne'er' for 'never'.

**Elkin, Stanley (Lawrence)** 1930– American novelist, born in New York City and educated at the University of Illinois. His novels tend to explore the nature of evil, frequently through a comic examination of both ordinary and extraordinary situations. His first novel, *Boswell* (1964), traces its protagonist's struggle to satisfy the needs of his ego, which culminates in a wrestling match with the Grim Reaper. His second novel, *A Bad Man* (1968), treats a salesman's compulsion to make 'the ultimate sale' regardless of its consequences. Other novels include *The Dick Gibson Show* (1971), *The Franchiser* (1976), *The Living End* (1980) and *The Magic Kingdom* (1985). Elkin has also published short stories in *Criers and Kibitzers, Kibitzers and Criers* (1966) and *The Making of Ashendon* (1972). His collection of novellas, *Searches and Seizures* (1973), has been published in England under two different titles: *Eligible Men* (1974) and *Alex and the Gypsy* (1977). *Stanley Elkin's Greatest Hits*, an omnibus collection, appeared in 1980.

**Elliott, Ebenezer** 1781–1849 The Corn Law Rhymer. Born at Rotherham in Yorkshire and largely self-educated, he ran an iron business in Sheffield for much of his working life. A Chartist, he derived his nickname from his simple, direct verses attacking the Corn Laws and describing rural poverty: *The Village Patriarch* (1829), *Corn-Law Rhymes* (1831) and *The Splendid Village* (1833–5).

**Ellis, (Henry) Havelock** 1859–1939 Writer and sexual scientist. Born at Croydon and educated at private schools in Surrey, he was advised at the age of 16 to make a year's sea voyage for reasons of health. Travelling in a ship under his father's command he reached Australia and settled there for four years, working as a teacher. He returned to England in 1879 to become a medical student, but after qualifying eight years later he rarely practised professionally. During his time as a medical student he became acquainted with many prominent socialists and began writing for magazines. Ellis acted as the first editor of the Mermaid series of unexpurgated reprints of Elizabethan and Jacobean drama. He also edited the Contemporary Science series. His interest in scientific and social progress is evident in his *The New Spirit* (1890) and in an increasing concern with sexual matters. His study *Man and Woman* was published in 1894 and his once notorious *Studies in the Psychology of Sex* appeared in six volumes between 1897 and 1910. *The Erotic Rights of Women* followed in 1918. Three series of essays entitled *Impressions and Comments* appeared in 1914, 1921 and 1924. His autobiography, *My Life*, was published posthumously in 1940.

**Ellison, Ralph (Waldo)** 1914– Black American novelist, essayist and short-story writer. Born in Oklahoma City, Ellison attended Tuskegee Institute in Alabama (1933–6), where he studied music and became an accomplished trumpet player. He then moved to New York City to study sculpture, and soon began writing book reviews, essays and short stories, encouraged by **Richard Wright**. In 1942 he helped to found and edit the short-lived *Negro Quarterly*.

After World War II he worked for seven years on the novel that made him famous, *Invisible Man* (1952). This semi-autobiographical account of a black man's gradual self-discovery remains Ellison's only major work of fiction to date. For over two decades he has reportedly been working on a second novel, parts of which have been published, including one entitled 'And Hickman Arrives'. His short stories have never been collected, though several are widely anthologized, among them 'Flying Home' and 'King of the Bingo Game'. He has, however, collected some of his many essays on black music, literature and American culture in *Shadow and Act* (1964) and *Going to the Territory* (1986).

Ellison's reputation as the most important literary heir to Richard Wright – matched only by that of **James Baldwin** – remains strong. *Invisible Man* was attacked by the radical left in the 1950s and by black nationalists in the 1960s, but it has weathered critical controversy and remains one of the central texts of the 20th-century Afro-American experience.

**Ellwood, Thomas** 1639–1713 Poet and early Quaker. A friend of William Penn, Ellwood was for some years reader to the blind **Milton**, to whom he suggested the theme of *Paradise Regained*. He was himself the author of *Davideis* (1712), a religious poem concerning the Israelite King David, as well as *A Collection of Poems on Various Subjects* (1710) and *The History of the Life of Thomas Ellwood* (1714), an account of his imprisonment for his religious beliefs.

*Elsie Venner: A Romance of Destiny* A novel by **Oliver Wendell Holmes**, published serially in *The Atlantic Monthly* (as *The Professor's Story*, January 1860–April 1861), and as a volume in 1861. In it Holmes sought to 'test the doctrine of "original sin" ' – to question the belief that holds individuals responsible for antenatal influences upon them.

Elsie Venner, whose mother was bitten by a rattlesnake three weeks before Elsie's birth, has been infected with the venom and now exhibits peculiar, snake-like qualities: her eyes glitter; she is wild, seemingly insane; she both fascinates and frightens those around her. The professsor in the story is a professor of medicine who becomes interested in Elsie's abnormal behaviour after he is told about her by Bernard Langdon, one of his students who has temporarily taken a job as a teacher at the school Elsie attends. Elsie falls in love with Bernard; she even saves his life, exerting her snake-like powers to enchant a rattlesnake that is about to strike and kill him. But he does not love her. Rejected by him, Elsie falls ill and, gradually losing her snake-like strangeness, dies. Helen Darley, a schoolteacher whose sympathy is stirred by the strange, motherless girl, attends her to the end. Old Sophy, a faithful servant, dies only days after Elsie, and at *her* death an earthquake buries Rattlesnake Ledge with all its poisonous snakes.

**Elyot, Sir Thomas** ?1499–1546 A lexicographer and administrator, Elyot is best known for *The Book Named the Governor*. He was clerk to the Privy Council in 1523–30 and knighted in 1530. *The Book Named the Governor* (1531) was dedicated to Henry VIII. It draws on many sources, one of the most important being Castiglione's *The Courtier*. It is a plan for bringing up

gentlemen's sons and manifests the usual humanist concern for education. Perhaps as a result of the favourable reception of this book Elyot was made ambassador to Emperor Charles V. As important as *The Book Named the Governor* is Elyot's Latin–English *Dictionary* (1538), which formed the basis for the work of some subsequent English lexicographers. It appeared again in a revised form as the *Bibliotheca Eliotae* (1542). His translations include a work of Isocrates, as *The Doctrinal of Princes* (1534), and *The Image of Governance* (1541) from Eucolpius. Elyot's *Castle of Health* (1539) is a medical treatise written by a layman and adorned with anecdotes. He also wrote Platonic dialogues and produced translations of parts of Plutarch and a sermon on mortality by St Cyprian.

*Emare* A **verse romance** dating from about 1400. Emare's father is a widowed emperor with an incestuous obsession for his child. He gives her a richly embroidered robe which endows her with an unearthly beauty, but when she rejects his advances he sets her adrift in an open boat with her robe. She lands in Galys where she eventually marries the king, against his mother's advice. While he is away at battle Emare gives birth to a son, Segramour. Her mother-in-law contrives to have Emare set adrift again. Emare and Segramour come to Rome and are taken in by a merchant; they are eventually reunited with both the king and emperor when they come to Rome on pilgrimages.

The poet says his source was a **Breton lay**, but no French version analogous to *Emare* is known. The story is substantially the same as that of the 'constant' Constance, well known in the Middle Ages, and told by **Gower** in *Confessio Amantis* and **Chaucer** in *The Man of Law's Tale* (see *The Canterbury Tales*).

**emblem book** A book made up of symbolic pictures or engravings to which mottoes and verbal explanations are attached, of a proverbial or gnomic nature. The earliest European example was *Emblematum Liber* (1531) of Andrea Alciati, but Geoffrey Whitney's *Choice of Emblemes* (1586) was the first to appear in English. The most popular was **Francis Quarles**'s *Emblems* (1635), consisting of pictures, verses and verbal illustrations from previous authorities. Emblem books offered instruction on religious and moral subjects, and they became valuable source-books for poetic imagery.

**Emecheta, Buchi** 1944– Nigerian novelist. Born in Lagos, she moved to Britain in 1962. As a black woman in Britain, she courageously overcame appalling social conditions, which gives power and authenticity to her first two novels, *In the Ditch* (1972) and *Second-Class Citizen* (1974), published together as *Adah's Story* (1983). Her championship of women's rights provides the compassion, and occasionally unrelieved anger, of her other novels, mostly set in West Africa: *The Bride Price* (1976), *The Slave Girl* (1977), *Destination Biafra* (1982), *Naira Power* (1982), *Double Yoke* (1982) and *The Rape of Shavi* (1983). She has also written children's books and television plays.

**Emerson, Ralph Waldo** 1803–82 The American essayist, philosopher and poet was the son of William Emerson, the minister of the First Unitarian Church of his native Boston. After completing his education at Harvard, Emerson himself became a minister in 1829. The orthodoxy of Unitarianism, however, though far removed from the original Calvinism of New England, was something he could not accept. In 1832, shortly after the death of his first wife, he resigned his ministry and sailed to Europe, his mind disturbed by personal grief and religious confusion. During the year he spent in Europe, he met **Samuel Taylor Coleridge** and **William Wordsworth**, and commenced a lifelong friendship with **Thomas Carlyle**.

Contact with European thought stimulated his interest in religion and philosophy, and back in Boston he drifted away from preaching into the broader field of lecturing. With the growth of the lyceum movement in the Northeast and Middle West in the early 1830s, he found that he could command large audiences who came to hear him expound his natural philosophy. He

Ralph Waldo Emerson.

drew much of his lecture material from his personal journals, which he had begun in 1820 and continued throughout his life. In 1835 he married Lydia Jackson and moved to Concord, Massachusetts, where his ancestors had first settled in the New World and where **Transcendentalism** took form. He became part of the circle which included **Nathaniel Hawthorne**, **Bronson Alcott**, **Henry David Thoreau** and **Margaret Fuller**.

Emerson's first book, *Nature*, was published in 1836; *The American Scholar*, an oration in which he applied Transcendentalist views to national and cultural questions, followed in 1837. His assertion that human thought and action proceed from Nature was a radical departure from tradition; **Oliver Wendell Holmes** referred to his philosophical position as an 'intellectual declaration of independence'. In 1838 he delivered the 'Divinity School Address' at Harvard. The statement of his belief that the individual's intuitive spiritual experience was of more importance than any formal church ensured his exclusion from that university for almost 30 years. In 1840 he became involved in the publication of the Transcendentalist quarterly magazine, *The Dial*, and two years later became its editor. His reputation, already considerable in the USA, became firmly established in Europe, too, with the publication of two volumes of essays in 1841 and 1844. He earned further distinction as a poet with his first collection, *Poems* (1847), and later with *May-Day and Other Pieces* (1867).

He went to England in 1847 and lectured in Oxford and London, where he renewed his friendship with Carlyle and met other English intellectuals. The lectures were published under the title *Representative Men* (1850). *English Traits* (1856) contains his observations on the English character. During this period, as his journals show, he became deeply interested in the issue of slavery and saw Abolition as a matter of paramount importance. Two further volumes of his lectures were published as *The Conduct of Life* (1860) and *Society and Solitude* (1870). In 1866 Harvard conferred on him the degree of Doctor of Law. His *Journals* were published in 10 volumes (1909–14).

*Emma* A novel by **Jane Austen**, begun in January 1814, completed in March the following year and published in 1816. The author said she feared that nobody but herself would like the heroine, an indication that she had deliberately subdued the high-spirited comedy of manners practised in earlier novels to offer instead a study in development and education. Emma Woodhouse changes from being vain and self-satisfied, blind to her own feelings and dangerously insensitive to the feelings of others, in a slow, painful progress toward maturity.

Emma is left alone with her hypochondriacal father and feels bereft of companionship when her governess, Miss Taylor, leaves the household to marry a neighbour, Mr Weston. She makes a protégée of Harriet Smith, an illegitimate girl of no social status, and sets about arranging Harriet's life.

George Knightley of Donwell Abbey is a friend of the Woodhouse family and his younger brother John is married to Emma's sister Isabella. He disputes Emma's smug assumption that Anne Taylor's marriage is largely due to her skill as a matchmaker and frowns on her attempts to manipulate Harriet into what she decides is a good marriage. One of his tenants, a young farmer named Robert Martin, proposes to Harriet but Emma sees to it that Harriet turns him down. She tries instead to effect a match for Harriet with Mr Elton, a young clergyman, in spite of Knightley's warning. Elton despises Harriet and has set his sights on Emma herself.

For her part, Emma half fancies herself in love with Mr Weston's son by his first marriage, Frank Churchill, who has now appeared on the scene. Harriet, meanwhile, has become interested in George Knightley's unaffected warmth and intelligence. Emma, reassuring Harriet after the departure of Elton, is now considering Frank Churchill for her. Without giving the thought expression, Emma has always regarded Knightley as hers and the realization that Harriet might supplant her in Knightley's affections, together with the discovery that Frank Churchill is engaged to Jane Fairfax, forces her to examine her own conduct and resolve to behave better. Knightley proposes to her while Harriet, left to decide for herself, marries Robert Martin.

***Empedocles on Etna*** A poem by **Matthew Arnold**, published in 1852. The philosopher Empedocles (*c.* 450 BC) journeys to the volcano, Etna, in Sicily with the physician Pausanias. They are joined by the poet Callicles. The philosopher's despair does not yield to the wisdom of the physician or the strength of poetry and at the end he kills himself in the crater of Etna. The songs of the poet Callicles were published separately by Arnold in 1855 in *Poems: Second Series* before he republished the whole poem in 1867.

***Emperor Jones, The*** A play in eight scenes by **Eugene O'Neill**, produced by the Provincetown Players in 1920 and published in 1921. It is an early example of O'Neill's symbolic expressionism and of his progressively more experimental use of dramatic devices. Brutus Jones, a black man who has escaped from an American prison, becomes the emperor of a West Indian island. When he learns from his cockney major-domo, Henry Smithers, that his subjects have rebelled,

he boasts that he can escape through the forest. He has stored money and food in various places, foreseeing that his reign would be short, and created the legend that he can be killed only by a silver bullet. The reduction of the proud bully to a terrified savage as he is hunted down to the relentless beating of native drums is a theatrical *tour de force*.

**Empson, Sir William** 1906–84 Critic. A Yorkshireman born in Yokefleet, Empson was educated at Winchester College and at Magdalene College, Cambridge, where he studied mathematics and then, under **I. A. Richards**, English. Here he wrote his best-known critical work, *Seven Types of Ambiguity* (1930), a detailed study of multiple shades of meaning in poetry, which encouraged the trend towards close verbal analysis in modern criticism. During the 1930s he taught English at the Universities of Tokyo and Peking, returning to Peking after working for the BBC Far Eastern Section during the war. In 1953 he returned to England as Professor of English Literature at the University of Sheffield, where he remained until his retirement in 1971.

His poetry, especially in *Poems* (1935), is as complex as his critical theories demanded it should be: a modern counterpart of metaphysical poetry in its use of scientific conceits and cerebral puzzles. Empson's second volume of poems, *The Gathering Storm* (1940), draws upon his experiences in the East as the world drifted towards war; he revised these works for *Collected Poems* (1955). In his critical work Empson was something of a maverick: *Some Versions of Pastoral* (1935) extends the definition of its subject to embrace proletarian fiction and **Alice in Wonderland**; *The Structure of Complex Words* (1951) outlines an elaborate system for analysing the different senses of certain versatile words; and *Milton's God* (1961) uses the theological problems of **Paradise Lost** to launch an assault upon the cruelty and 'wickedness' of Christianity. The essays in his posthumous *Using Biography* (1984) defend the use of biographical information in criticism, against the dogmas of **New Criticism**. He was knighted in 1979.

**encomium** Originally a Greek choral song in praise of a hero; now, any composition in verse or prose which praises a person, idea or occasion. Encomiastic poetry enjoyed a minor vogue in the 17th and 18th centuries, **Dryden**'s 'A Song for Saint Cecilia's Day' being perhaps the most famous example.

***Encounter*** Political, cultural and literary journal founded in 1953. Its editors and co-editors have included **Stephen Spender**, **Nigel Dennis**, Frank Kermode, **Anthony Thwaite** and Melvin Lasky. *Encounter*'s stance has always been Anglo-

American, both in its political concerns and its literary interests. A controversy in the 1960s following the revelation of CIA involvement in its funding caused Spender to disassociate himself from it. The magazine is notable for having published **Nancy Mitford**'s 'U and non-U' treatise on acceptable and infra-dig behaviour (1955) and **C. P. Snow**'s defence of his 'Two Cultures' thesis (1959–60), as well as much distinguished modern poetry.

**end-stopped line** A line of verse in which both the sense and grammatical structure are self-contained, without the need for **enjambement**, or running-on. End-stopped couplets occur frequently in 18th-century poetry, as in these lines from the fourth of **Pope**'s *Moral Essays*:

> Who then shall grace, or who improve the soil? –
> Who plants like Bathurst, or who builds like Boyle.
> 'Tis use alone that sanctifiers expense,
> And splendour borrows all her rays from sense.

**Endgame** A play by **Samuel Beckett**, given its first performance in French (as *Fin de Partie*) in London in 1957. Beckett's own English translation was first presented in New York in 1958.

In a room, evidently isolated from all external contact, sits Hamm, immobile and dependent on his servant Clov for everything from painkillers to conversation. He aspires to an end of which the prospect constantly eludes him. Master and servant are locked in resentful symbiosis – if Hamm cannot stand, Clov cannot sit. Towards the end of the play, Clov tells Hamm that he can see a boy in the wasteland outside the room. Before his last exit he asserts to Hamm that he is leaving for ever, but we have not sufficient confidence in an ending to believe him.

**Endymion** **Benjamin Disraeli**'s last novel, published in 1880. Set in the political world of the 1830s, it describes the rise to positions of eminence by Endymion and Myra Pitt Ferrars, twin children of a promising politician who dies penniless. Myra succeeds because she is beautiful and captivating; her husband, the Foreign Secretary Lord Roehampton, is able to help Endymion. Contemporaries could recognize a portrait of Lord Palmerston in Lord Roehampton and a satirical portrait of **Thackeray** as St Barbe.

**Endymion: A Poetic Romance** A poem in four books by **John Keats**, published in 1818, dedicated to the memory of **Thomas Chatterton**.

Its basis is the Greek legend of Endymion, variously a prince of Elis or a beautiful young shepherd, who falls asleep on the slopes of Mount Latmos. The moon goddess Selene (Cynthia in Keats's version) falls in love with him and makes him sleep eternally so that she may always enjoy his beauty. In Keats's poem Cynthia takes him away to eternal life with her, but into this fabric are woven the stories of Venus and Adonis, Glaucus and Scylla, and Arethusa, as well as an ambitious, if not completely successful, allegory of the quest for perfection and the distraction of human beauty. The famous 'Hymn to Pan' is in Book 1; the roundelay 'O Sorrow', leading into the lovely song of the Indian maid, 'Beneath my palm trees, by the river side', is in Book 4.

The poem was made the object of a notoriously savage attack by **John Wilson Croker** in *The Quarterly Review*.

**Endymion: The Man in the Moon** A prose comedy by **John Lyly**, first performed in 1588 by the Boys of St Paul's. An elaboration of the classical myth of the sleeping shepherd, *Endymion* owed its contemporary reputation to its easily read allegory of court intrigue rather than to its slender plot. Lyly cleverly exploited the skills of his chorister–actors by incorporating several songs as well as a dance of fairies, and stage directions reveal the importance of scenic effects and spectacular costume, not least in a **dumb show** depicting a dream. Endymion (the Earl of Leicester) abandons Tellus, the earth (Mary Queen of Scots), for love of Cynthia, the moon (Queen Elizabeth). Tellus employs the witch Dipsas to put Endymion to sleep for 40 years, but Cynthia kisses Endymion to break the spell. There is further allegorical reference to such court notables as **Sir Philip Sidney** (Eumenides) and Lady Rich (Semele).

**Engel, Marian** 1933–85 Canadian novelist. Born in Toronto, Engel grew up in various towns in Ontario. She was educated at McMaster and McGill Universities and subsequently lived abroad for a number of years, studying French literature in Provence and teaching in the United States and Cyprus. After returning to Canada, she took an active part in the Canadian writers' movement and was first Chairperson of the Writers' Union of Canada. Most of her novels focus on the roles of women in contemporary consumer society. Her best-known work, *Bear* (1976), is about a woman who leaves her urban life and her job in a historical institute to do research on the northern shore of Lake Superior and discovers her identity through an erotic relationship with a large pet bear. Sometimes regarded as a parody of female quest novels, such as **Margaret Atwood**'s *Surfacing*, in which a return to animal roots provides a new sense of identity, *Bear* is at the same time a penetrating and witty exploration of this theme itself. Engel's other novels include *The Honeymoon Festival* (1970), a study of motherhood, *Monodromos* (1973; reissued as *One-Way Street*, 1974), a tragicomic account of a Canadian woman's life on a Greek island, and *The Glassy Sea* (1978), in which the protagonist joins an Anglican order of nuns. She also published two short-story collections, *Inside the Easter Egg* (1975) and *The Tattooed Woman* (1985).

***England's Helicon*** This collection of mainly pastoral poems was printed in 1600. It depicts a world of love, music and dance and is generally acknowledged to be the finest of the Elizabethan poetic miscellanies, containing verses by **Peele**, **Greene**, **Sidney**, **Drayton**, **Marlowe** and **Spenser**. Some of the poems are taken from Elizabethan song-books and appear later with musical accompaniment. Titles of a number of the lyrics ('jig', 'roundelay' and 'madrigal') testify to their musical nature. The collection does not seem, however, to have achieved the popularity of predecessors like **The Paradise of Dainty Devices**. A second edition, adding nine new poems, came out in 1614.

***England's Parnassus*** A collection of 'elegant extracts', or selected quotations, from the Elizabethan poets, published in 1600. The compiler is believed to have been Robert Allott.

**English dictionaries** Behind today's dictionaries lies a long tradition that began with the glossing of Latin. From glosses written over Latin texts there grew up separate collections, organized sometimes alphabetically and sometimes by meaning. As Englishmen became eager to learn the languages of the modern world, publishers brought out dictionaries for Italian and Spanish, and even polyglot dictionaries, but the first English dictionary did not appear until as late as 1604: Robert Cawdrey's *A Table Alphabetical, Containing and Teaching the True Writing, and Understanding of Hard Usual English Words*. As the title suggests, its immediate forerunners were teaching manuals and works on grammar and orthography. Cawdrey was indebted to the title-page of Coote's *The English Schoolmaster* (1596) for the phrase 'unskilfull persons', which must designate a part of the readership he aimed at. In their turn Bullokar's *An English Expositor* (1616), Cockeram's *The English Dictionary* (1623), Blount's *Glossographia* (1656) and Phillips's *New World of English Words* (1658) depend on one another for basic materials, growing in bulk and pretension but still concentrating on difficult words. In the next century, recognizing the need for general treatment of the vocabulary, compilers admitted more everyday words into their dictionaries.

**Samuel Johnson**'s *The Plan of a Dictionary of the English Language* (1747) signals a new direction. His introduction reads almost like a programme for an English Academy, and it marks the culmination of a long campaign for just such a body as France and Italy had, a campaign that

numbered many writers among its advocates – **Chapman**, **Cotton**, **Drayton**, **Dryden**, **Evelyn**, **Cowley**, **Waller** and **Swift**, for example. With the publication of Johnson's **Dictionary of the English Language** (1755), the idea of an Academy lost ground, evidence of the immediate recognition commanded by his two folio volumes. The most notable innovation was his systematic use of quotations, taken largely from literature 1560–1660, to illustrate usage and justify definitions. (The next major step forward was taken over half a century later with Charles Richardson's inclusion of quotations from 1250 onwards in his *Encyclopaedia Metropolitana*, published in 1819.) Some contemporaries labelled Johnson 'the man who has conferred stability on the language of his country', but Johnson himself recognized that a dictionary cannot 'embalm' language or 'secure it from corruption and decay'. He acknowledged the usefulness to him of one preceding 18th-century dictionary in particular – Bailey's *Dictionarium Brittanicum: A More Complete Universal Etymological Dictionary than Any Extant* – and he greatly increased the representation of everyday words in his own work. More important, he produced a dictionary in which encyclopaedic entries play little part. With him, the English dictionary has moved on from the 'difficult words' tradition.

Although Johnson's achievement was pioneering, not definitive, his dictionary cast a long shadow. Its status was not challenged until the appearance of the **Oxford English Dictionary** and, to a lesser extent, **Webster's Dictionary**.

***English Humorists of the Eighteenth Century, The*** Lectures by **W. M. Thackeray**, first delivered in 1851 and published in 1853.

Thackeray lectured on **Swift**, **Congreve**, **Addison**, **Steele**, **Prior**, **Gay**, **Pope**, **Hogarth**, **Smollett**, **Fielding**, **Sterne** and **Goldsmith**. Largely biographical and anecdotal in approach, his hearty condescension to his subjects reveals more about Victorian attitudes to the 18th century than about the period itself.

**English language, the** To every human being his mother tongue is of unique importance. Objectively, however, we can claim that English is unique among the languages of the world. It has at present the widest use of any language in history, both in numbers of users (among whom native speakers are probably in a minority) and in range of uses. The corollary of this is that it has an extraordinary diversity of forms. Only mankind's exceptional capacity for abstraction enables us to conceive of such a thing as *the* English language underlying the hugely different realizations we are liable to encounter. But the right-hand man of this capacity for abstraction is the written form of the language. This prevails world-wide, with only trivial divergences, and of course has long been the vehicle of literature. Even where writers attempt to portray dialect their portrayal has for centuries been mediated by the conventions of standard orthography.

What is true of the current range of English is almost matched by the duration and diversity of the historical record. At 1400 years this is by no means the longest in the world, but it is among those of high duration, and it incorporates changes, sometimes obvious, sometimes covert, of immense extent and profundity.

*External history.* The language came to England in the mouths of Germanic settlers who arrived in substantial numbers from the mid 5th century, though some had certainly come earlier. They were of various tribes, including Angles and Saxons, from a long stretch of the northern European littoral. Their dialects, which were closely related but not uniform, belonged to the wider Germanic (Gmc) family, itself a subgroup of Indo-European (IE), whose membership includes the Celtic (the antecedent language family in Britain), the Italic-Romance (including Latin and all its modern descendants), the Hellenic, the Balto-Slavonic, the Indo-Iranian, and many others. As always happens, the new societies in what is now England developed their own linguistic norms; their members converged in usage, and in doing so diverged from that of the Germanic communities they left behind. Extension of settlements throughout the country was a protracted business. Once settlements were made the village would constitute, for most people, their effective circle of communication. Under such conditions distinct dialects develop in two or three generations, and it is natural to suppose that this happened from village to village in pre-Conquest England. Customarily four large dialect areas are recognized, not because speech in these areas can have been internally uniform, but because this is as much as we can detect from the surviving written records: these are the South-eastern, South-western, Mercian (Midland) and Northumbrian. The language from the settlement to the Norman Conquest is called Old English (OE), and in late OE West Saxon had national currency as a standard for written prose.

The first settlers were only minimally literate. A tiny minority of them were masters of the runic method of inscription in angular symbols designed for carving, developed in the Gmc world probably about AD 200. Literacy in the normal sense was a by-product of the conversion to Christianity, beginning in the south with the Roman mission of Augustine in 597, and almost simultaneously with Celtic missions in the north. The alphabet developed for OE was basically Roman, omitting *j*, *q*, *v*, and usually *k* and *x*, and adding one Celtic and two runic symbols. The first written English words in it date from 597, but continuous documents in English are considerably later, though some incorporate 6th-century material which at first had been transmitted orally. Literacy remained rare, the province of two minority groups, the clergy and a handful of well-born laymen. Surviving pre-Conquest manuscripts are a small fraction of what must have existed, but even if all had survived their representation of the language would have been selective. Manuscript production was costly in materials and skilled labour and would have been authorized only for purposes which seemed convincing to ecclesiastical authorities or landowners. The surviving records are also unevenly distributed over a period of five centuries and a wide geographical area.

From the close of the 8th century, Viking raids and eventual settlement over most of northern and eastern England brought into contact two languages closely related in origin and mutually comprehensible. In 1066 came a shock as profound but wholly different in kind. The Normans (themselves originally Vikings – Northmen) were, by comparison with 11th-century Englishmen, barbarians whose strength lay in military and administrative success, the bringer of wealth. Once again the great religious houses were as much a target as the great secular estates – now not for plunder but for takeover. In most parts of the country control of the leading scriptoria soon passed into Norman hands; documents not written in Latin were for the most part written in French, and original English texts are rare from 1066 to *c.* 1200. We have least documentation for the century that seems to have witnessed the deepest and swiftest changes ever to have affected the language. Norman influence was not, like Scandinavian influence, variable by locality, but variable by class, affecting most those who had most to do with centres of wealth and power, where **Anglo-Norman**, or Norman-French, was current. In 1204 new legislation prevented the holding of estates in both England and France. Thenceforth those who stayed were committed to England. Their families grew up English-speaking and English began to extend into public and governmental functions. During the same period English took its first small step overseas, to Ireland, with the settlement of an English landowning cadre in 1210.

In the following centuries two developments proceeded hand in hand – a vast increase in the number and types of English documents and an extension of the use of English for all public purposes. Generally, the forms of writing show marked discontinuities from those current in OE, mainly under French influence; what is more, the national currency of one standard form has been lost. Most scribes clearly wrote within a tradition they had learned, but these traditions were local, and so diverse that a recent survey has identified over 1100 of them in a single century. However, the increased public role of English created a need for standardization. From 1330 to 1430 four successive and competing standards have been identified. Type III is familiar today as **Chaucer**'s English, and Type IV is the ancestor of the modern standard. When printing was introduced in 1476 the existence of identical multiple copies made standardization even more important. Neither 15th-century nor 16th-century printed English is standard in the modern sense of being virtually self-consistent and uniform, but it is broadly true that, punctuation apart, **Caxton** established the range of options within which the modern system would be selected. In large measure the spellings we now use are those favoured by **Johnson** in his *Dictionary of the English Language* (1755), but he correctly claimed that most of his preferences were determined by tradition.

English from about the Norman Conquest to the emergence of Type IV is known as Middle English (ME), and from the mid 15th century to the present as Modern English (ModE), within which Present-day English (PE) is distinguished. There are long periods of overlap and transition, and change takes place at different rates from dialect to dialect; the dates are not meant to be precise.

The 16th century saw the inception of two main developments which were to continue to the present day. Externally these involved the first planting of the language outside Europe, through exploration, trade, settlement and colonization, in Africa, America and the Far East. In most of these distant places the English were preceded by and interacted with other Europeans – Portuguese, Spanish, Italian, French and Dutch. They encountered new flora, fauna, topographical and climatic features, commodities, processes, social organizations, and languages, not only the languages of Africa, Asia and America; there was greater linguistic influence from other Europeans than there had ever been in Europe, except from the French. They developed new institutions and established new kinds of official. Everything had to be named. The linguistic effect was overwhelmingly on the repertoire of nouns.

Among the commodities were human cargo, slaves from many African tribes transported in conditions where inevitably their African linguistic heritage was blended with the language of the owners to create new languages whose Englishness is hotly disputed.

In the late 18th century Australia and New Zealand were settled, and in the 19th century southern and eastern Africa.

Meanwhile, the War of Independence in America was rapidly followed by Webster's declaration that 'our honor requires us to have a system of our own, in language as well as government' (1789). *Webster's Dictionary* encoded this, the source of the differences in written standard English between America and Britain to this day.

English was therefore in an unprecedented position when the 19th–20th-century explosion of scholarship, scientific discovery and technical development took place. So many of the early advances were made by English speakers and published in England that researchers everywhere had to know English, and its scholarly use snowballed. When a language of worldwide currency was required for international air traffic it had to be English. In many countries where English has no native speakers it is the only practicable medium of higher education. Its world-wide role has increased, not shrunk, with the decline of the Empire.

Reverting to the 16th century, we can state that the second main development is preoccupation with the identification and fostering of a spoken standard on a par with the written one. Commentators agree in giving it a socio-geographical basis: it is the speech of courtly (not ordinary) Londoners, but it can also be heard from a thinly scattered population of gentry in every county. Though there were to be many modifications, we recognize for the first time a distinctively modern variety-structure typical of England – not of Britain, and certainly not of English world-wide.

*Internal structure.* A systematic account of a language needs to describe two interdependent systems – systems of transmission and of meaning. The primary means of transmission is speech; secondary, less widely distributed but not necessarily derivative, is writing. The meanings and distinctions which can or must be transmitted are organized in two ways: they may be realized by open-class items, infinitely extensible rapidly changing repertoires, the vocabulary of a language, notably nouns, verbs, adjectives and adverbs; or closed-system items, each set few in number, rarely added to or lost, its members interdependent. These constitute the grammar and may be realized by abstract contrasts, such as tense, or by wordlike items, such as prepositions, conjunctions and personal pronouns.

Only the briefest characterization of the English sound system is possible. Writing in English centres on letters, and it may be for this reason that we tend to think of strings of distinctive segments (phonemes) as the essential constituents of speech. They do indeed have an important function; changing the initial segment enables us to distinguish *bin* from *din*, *kin*, *gin*, etc., the middle one *bin* from *ban*, *bun*, *bean*, etc., and the final one *bin* from *bid*, *big*, etc. Most varieties of English have at all times had rather more than 40 of these distinctive sounds, and though their lexical distribution has changed through time the overall shape of the system has been remarkably constant. But in many ways the suprasegmentals, which writing largely ignores, are more primary in English than the segmental sounds. These involve syllables, what shapes they can take, how stress contrasts are distributed over them, and temporal patterning (rhythm) and pitch movement (intonation). An example of the dominance of suprasegmentals can be seen in the vowel system: stressed syllables are the domain of a system of some 20 different vowels; unstressed syllables of only two. With minor variations this has been true for 1000 years.

In what we do know of OE vocabulary over half the words (normally the commonest) are of IE origin, about one sixth Gmc, one sixth borrowed from Latin (usually the rarest), and the rest from minor or unknown sources. Vocabulary then, as at all times, responded to new demands to a large extent by word formation (WF) (chiefly compounding, as in modern *blackbird*, or derivation, as in *blacking*). In late OE clearly Scandinavian influence must have been great in the north and east, but few loanwords appear in the record till ME; those that have stayed in the language include basic words of every grammatical class, e.g. *law* (replacing OE *ae*), *egg* (replacing OE *aeg*), *ill*, *take*, *till*, *they*, *their*, *them*; hundreds have been lost. The influence of French, mainly after the Norman Conquest, was also slow to appear in the record. However, by the late 14th century Chaucer alone uses some 4000 French loans, which represent almost all semantic fields. In subsequent centuries loans flooded into English from over 100 other languages, but at all times French and classical loans have been most numerous.

Since the Norman Conquest additional methods of formation have come into prominence: zero-derivation, in which a word is established in a new grammatical class without change of form (cf. *look*, *walk*, *love*, sbs. and vs.); back-derivation, as when *peddle*, *burgle* are formed from *pedlar*, *burglar*; various sorts of sound-motivation, such as vowel gradation in *flim-flam*, *shilly-shally*, or of graphic motivation, as in the acronyms *radar*, *NATO*; there are also invented and blended words (e.g. *blatant*, *brunch*). In the present century about 30 words a day, on average, have been added to the repertoire. Naturally there are losses as well as gains – of the recorded OE stock about seven items have been lost for every four preserved. Survivals may not be obvious – they can undergo radical change of shape (OE *nafo-gar*, PE *auger*) or meaning (OE *thing*, 'meeting').

It is in grammatical structure that English has undergone the most sweeping changes. Three are of central importance. First the structure of the noun phrase (NP), which in OE was more like its Latin than its PE counterpart in its range of declensions, genders, cases, and rules of concord. By early ME the present simplified system was complete in essentials. What have remained constant are rules of order (*the duke's large well-built timber-framed hunting-lodge*, for instance).

In the verb phrase (VP) Gmc had diverged sharply from IE. An older system of rich inflectional contrasts gave way to an oversimplified tense system inherited by OE. The past tense was marked either by internal change or, following a Gmc innovation, by adding a suffix; thus OE *he rad* (corresponding to PE *he rode, was riding, has ridden, had ridden*) or *he lufode* (*he loved*, etc.). In contrast with the past was the non-past tense, corresponding to everything else (*he rideþ*, PE *he rides, is riding, will/shall ride*). This drastically reduced system was already being re-expanded in Gmc and the process has continued ever since, using not inflection but preverbal particles, auxiliaries, forming at any one time a closed system. The perfective (forms in *has/have/had* plus past participle) is pre-English, and so is a new passive (in OE with *weorþan*, 'become', later with *be*, plus past participle). Within OE clearly modal uses begin (those now involving *will, would, shall, should, can, could, may, might, must*) but the modals did not emerge as a system till early ModE nor take their full present functions till *c.* 1700. The aspect contrast (*he is riding* carved out of the former territory of *he rides*) did not come into its own till the 17th century (though scattered examples are frequent before that) and is still evolving. The semantico-syntactic categories have been refined; referential distinctions (number and person) have declined. Except in *be* (*was, were*, a pure number contrast) only the non-past is affected, distinguishing third person singular from the rest – singular or plural – by addition of *-s*. However, the largely syntactic contrast of subjunctive with indicative has also been almost completely lost.

Verbs are central to the functioning of negation, and here too change has been profound. OE negated by putting *ne* before the verb, a pattern that goes back to IE. This changed steadily and *c.* 1600 began to take on its present shape, which has two essential features – first the use of *not*, *n't* after the finite verb; second, the requirement that *not*, *n't* be attached only to auxiliaries, so that if no auxiliary is present the dummy *do/does/did* must be inserted (*he isn't riding* but *he doesn't ride*). The interrogative was made in OE by simple inversion of subject and verb; now this too must have an auxiliary as its domain and calls on *do/does/did* in the absence of any other (*he's riding, isn't he?* but *he rides, doesn't he?*).

The third major area of change is clause

structure. In OE, as in Latin for the same reason, the subject did not always need to be expressed. The nucleus of the clause, the prime domain of rules of order, was therefore the verb and whatever nominal structure was needed to complete it. With the reduction of verb inflections expression of the subject became indispensable; it was given initial position, and if it had no semantically required realization a dummy was inserted (*It's raining*; *There isn't enough*). From the 15th century the nucleus of the sentence has been subject–verb, in that order (except for interrogation or special effect). Rules of order were also much affected in OE, as in modern German, by the nature of the clause and its type of onset. All these special patterns were abandoned in favour of the nuclear type.

It is no wonder that a language which has been the vehicle of much of the experience of so much of humanity should also be the vehicle of the world's richest literature, not only English literature but that of English-speaking communities in every continent and of an unparalleled number of great writers whose mother tongue was not English. Yet, as we have seen, 'English' subsumes many Englishes. Each has in its repertoire many 'false friends', words and structures that look familiar but have quite different functions in the text from those the reader expects. Constant vigilance is needed to save the inexhaustible well from turning into a snake-pit.

**English Review, The** This literary periodical was founded in 1908 by **Ford Madox Ford** with the financial backing of Arthur Marwood. Ford's editorship lasted little over a year (to 1910), but it was the most promising period for the journal, which published work by **Thomas Hardy**, **Henry James**, **H. G. Wells** and **Wyndham Lewis**, and introduced the poems of **D. H. Lawrence** to the reading public. Ford's successor, Austin Harrison, continued to publish Lawrence's stories and essays, but Lawrence dismissed the *Review* after Ford's departure as 'piffling'. After Harrison's resignation in 1923 the journal was edited by Ernest Remnant and later by **Douglas Jerrold**, and was finally absorbed into *The National Review* in 1937.

**enjambement** From the French 'in-striding'. In English poetry it refers to the continuation of the sense and grammatical structure from a line of verse into the one that follows, or from one couplet into the next. See also **end-stopped line**.

**Enoch Arden** In its day one of the most popular poems by **Tennyson**, written in 1861 and 1862 and published in 1864. It was based on a prose sketch written for the poet by his friend, the painter Thomas Woolner. A similar theme appears in **Elizabeth Gaskell**'s novel *Sylvia's Lovers* (1863) and in **Adelaide Anne Procter**'s poem 'Homeward Bound' (1858).

Enoch Arden marries Annie Lee but, when he can no longer support his family from his work as a fisherman, is forced to set sail on a merchantman. In his absence Annie falls into financial difficulties and is helped by Philip Ray, once Enoch's rival for her love. Enoch's ship is wrecked and he is believed dead, so Annie finally marries Philip. But Enoch has survived and, after being rescued from a lonely desert island, returns. He sees the happiness of Annie and Philip and the children, and quietly resolves to leave them be. Nobody recognizes him but he confides his secret to Miriam, the local innkeeper, when he knows he is dying. She conveys his last blessing to his wife and children, and to Philip.

**Enquiry Concerning Human Understanding, An** A philosophical work by **David Hume**, originally published as *Philosophical Essays Concerning Human Understanding* in 1748 and retitled in 1758. It recasts the arguments in Book I of *A Treatise of Human Nature* and adds an essay on miracles, once considered notorious for its scepticism, which denies that miracles can be proved with any amount or type of evidence and concludes that they cannot be part of a reasonable foundation for a system of religion.

**Enquiry Concerning Political Justice** A libertarian philosophical treatise by **William Godwin**, completed and published in 1793, with revised second and third editions appearing in 1796 and 1798. It is Godwin's major theoretical work and brought him immediate, though short-lived, fame upon its publication during the critical years of the French Revolution. Impressed by **Paine**'s *Rights of Man* (1791), yet dissatisfied with its lack of conceptual rigour, he embarked upon a work that would philosophically place the principles of politics on an immovable basis and annihilate all oppositions'.

Its methodological springboard is a strongly Rousseauian attack on the 'natural' rights tradition since **Locke**, and on the idea of the origin of human society in a contract founded upon promise. Promises according to Godwin merely postponed into a vague future the exercise of virtue, performance of duty and promotion of the happiness and moral well-being of others, which he saw as the sole purpose of human existence, leaving the individual indefinitely free to pursue his own selfish interests. What he goes on to recommend, however, is in many ways the opposite of Rousseau's advocacy, in the famous *Social Contract*, of popular sovereignty and state sponsorship of economic justice and civic sensibility. *Political Justice* represents the fulfilment of the anarchic potential of classical enlightenment rationalism: itself systematic to the point of pedantry, it is essentially a repudiation of political systems as such. Although its political programme was revolutionary in that it projected the abolition of law, government, marriage and all apparatuses of inequity and coercion, there could be no question of bringing this about by insurrection, political agitation or even group solidarity. Reason's means could not differ from reason's end, which was the universal rejection of institutionalized justice itself rather than the violent or inflammatory confrontation of specific cases of its fallibility. People might, therefore, influence each other to embrace the good solely through informal reasoned persuasion: once a person became a member of a political association, he committed his reason to the care of others, and was thus self-estranged. The ultimate triumph of rationality and correct moral sentiment was inevitable, however, and with it injustices would fall away of themselves.

The book's meteoric fall from grace in the second half of the 1790s is, to some extent, explained by the conservative mobilization of British public opinion against radical and dissenting intellectuals, but it was also soon under attack from liberals and radicals as well, to whom it gave little ideological support in the new era of counter-revolutionary repression. Today the work is seen as a canonical text of anarchism. Its influence on the Romantic generation of writers was profound, and its themes echo in the writings of Tolstoy, Proudhon, Kropotkin and **Thoreau**.

***Enquiry into the Present State of Polite Learning in Europe, An*** Appearing in 1759, this short but ambitious treatise was the first important work by **Oliver Goldsmith**. He traces the course of polite learning from classical times to his own and examines its state in western Europe. He finds it comprehensively in decay in England and lists the reasons: university education is inadequate, poetry is divorced from nature and stifled by pedantry, and drama is bound by the rules of current taste.

**Enright, D[ennis] J[oseph]** 1920–  Poet. Born in Leamington and educated at Leamington College and Downing College, Cambridge, Enright taught English literature at overseas universities, mostly in the East, before returning to Britain to take up posts at the Universities of Leeds and Warwick in the 1970s.

His anthology *Poets of the 1950s* (1955) helped to establish the **Movement** as the representative grouping of poets of that time. His own work, beginning with *The Laughing Hyena* (1953), is gathered in *Collected Poems* (1981). Typically set in the landscape of the East, his poems are often concerned with inequality in human circum-

stances and speak passionately for the poor and oppressed. His treatment of this theme avoids sentimentalism, using understatement and irony to carry the load of pity or indignation.

He has edited a selection of **Milton** (1975), **Johnson**'s *Rasselas* (1976) and *The Oxford Book of Contemporary Verse 1945–80* (1980) and has written novels for children, including *The Joke Shop* (1976), *Wild Ghost Chase* (1978) and *Beyond Land's End* (1979). *Memoirs of a Mendicant Professor* (1969) is autobiographical.

***Entail, The*** A novel by **John Galt**, published in 1823. Claud Walkinshaw, a packman, is obsessed with recovering the estates which formerly belonged to his family and can achieve this only by disinheriting his eldest son in favour of his second, an idiot. The story follows the disastrous recoil on the Walkinshaw children and grandchildren.

***Eothen*** See **Kinglake, Alexander William**.

**epic** One of the earliest literary forms, and the subject of critical discussion from Aristotle to the present day. The following, however, seem to be the generally agreed minimal requirements for a work to qualify for the title. It should be a long narrative, normally in verse, dealing with one important major action or theme – however much it may be amplified or buttressed by subsidiary actions. It should also normally have a certain sublimity of style and grandeur of content. The work of Homer and Virgil provides the main precedent in classical literature, while the most obvious examples in English are *Beowulf*, **Spenser**'s *The Faerie Queene* and **Milton**'s *Paradise Lost*.

'A comic epic in prose' therefore carries an implication of paradox. Yet this claim, made by **Fielding** for *Joseph Andrews* but best exemplified by **Joyce**'s *Ulysses*, is not quite a contradiction in terms, since it does indicate something of the scope and endeavour of these works.

**epic simile** (or Homeric simile) A **simile** of such length and ramification that it seems to operate rather as a separate ornament, or small inserted lyric, than as a narrative function. Unlike the normal brief simile, that is to say, it deliberately suspends the action – giving pause for contemplation – instead of advancing or vivifying it. As the name implies, it is a conspicuous feature of **epic**, and the extended comparison between Satan and Leviathan (the whale) in Book I of **Milton**'s *Paradise Lost* provides a famous example.

***Epicoene, or, The Silent Woman*** A comedy by **Ben Jonson**, first produced in 1609 and published in 1616.

The plot concerns the deception of Morose, a

self-centred bachelor who hates noise. Suspecting that his nephew, Sir Dauphine Eugenie, finds him ridiculous, Morose plans to remove him from his will; he also intends to marry if he can find a woman who is quiet enough. His barber, Cutbeard, tells him of such a woman and brings Epicoene, soft-spoken and of few words. Morose marries her and she immediately becomes talkative and quarrelsome. Then the house is invaded by noisy well-wishers, among them Sir Jack Daw and Sir Amorous LaFoole, who both claim to have enjoyed Epicoene's favours in the past. In the end Morose is forced to accept his nephew's offer of help in getting rid of Epicoene, and to agree to restore his nephew's inheritance. Sir Dauphine then removes Epicoene's wig and reveals that 'she' is a youth trained for the plot. Morose has to abide by his bargain, while Daw and LaFoole cover their embarrassment as best they can.

**Epicurean, The** A romance by **Thomas Moore**, published in 1827. The story tells how Alciphron, a 3rd-century Epicurean philosopher, visits Egypt to search for the secret of eternal life. Assisting a priestess, Alethe, in her duties, he discovers that she is a secret Christian. Through her he too is converted to Christianity, and when she suffers martyrdom he is condemned to the mines, where he dies.

**epigram** 'Her whole life is an epigram, smart, smooth and neatly penn'd, / Platted quite neat to catch applause with a sliding noose at the end.' This example by **Blake** both exploits and defines what the epigram has come to signify: a witty and well-turned saying with a sting in its tail. The word's Greek derivation, however, means simply an 'inscription', terse and lapidary by necessity, suitable for funerary or celebratory monuments, and the collection gathered in *The Greek Anthology* (which consists of 6000 poems from 7th century BC to 10th century AD) includes many non-satirical poems. Greatest and most influential of the classical epigrammatists is the Latin poet Martial (c. AD 38–104), whose epigrams fully reflect the capaciousness of the genre, both in form (many are pithy distichs, others extend to 50 lines or more) and in variety of content. His scurrility has been much exaggerated, and his work embodies **Camden**'s definition of the epigram: 'short and sweet poems, framed to praise or dispraise'. With Catullus, Martial provided the model during the vogue for the epigram in the Renaissance, with **Thomas More** (writing in Latin) as the acknowledged master and **Sir John Harington** a lively practitioner. **Ben Jonson**'s *Epigrams* (1616) brilliantly vivify the spirit of Martial in English; **Robert Herrick**, in *Hesperides* (1648), was perhaps the last English poet to master the epigram's full tonal range. Later epigrammatists emphasized satirical wit at the expense of serious directness. They include **Prior**, **Pope**, **Swift**, **Goldsmith**, **Cowper**, **Burns**, **Byron**, **Landor** and **Coleridge**, with the last offering a famous definition: 'What is an epigram? a dwarfish whole, / Its body brevity, and wit its soul.' **Hilaire Belloc**, **Robert Graves** and **Stevie Smith** have been among the distinguished exponents in this century.

**Epigrams** A collection of poems by **Ben Jonson**, published in the 1616 edition of his works. The epigrams themselves, strongly influenced by Martial, show the poet's sharp and satirical view of contemporary manners. Better known are the sweeter-toned addresses, compliments and epitaphs; in the last category are poems on the poet's son ('On My First Son') and a child actor ('On Salomon Davy, a Child of Queen Elizabeth's Chapel').

**epistolary novel** A novel in which the story is told through an exchange of letters between the characters. The form was made fashionable in the 18th century by **Samuel Richardson**, though he used it loosely enough to allow his characters' letters to grow into private journals; **Smollett**'s *Expedition of Humphry Clinker* shows that it was still popular towards the end of the century. Since then it has been used occasionally – in, for example, **Swinburne**'s *Love's Cross Currents* (1877) and **John Barth**'s *Letters* (1979) – but has not been consistently favoured by major novelists.

**Epithalamion** **Spenser**'s marriage song was published together with *Amoretti* (1595) and may well be intended as the culmination of the sonnet sequence. Spenser himself had married Elizabeth Boyle in June 1594. The poem begins with the invocation of the muses before dawn, describes the awakening of the bride and then progress to church, the wedding ceremony and the onset of night, and ends with a prayer in the bridal chamber for 'fruitful progeny'. Blending classical formulae with Christian sentiment, it is a poem of jubilant festivity, full of music and light, and is considered one of Spenser's finest minor poems.

**epyllion** The word (from the Greek, 'little epic') was first used in the 19th century to describe classical poems that told a story whose subject was love, with mythological allusions and at least one major digression. The tradition dated from the time of Theocritus (d. 250 BC); *Peleus and Thetis* by Catullus (d. c. 54 BC) is a late Roman example. The term became applied to post-classical literature, especially the erotic treatment of mythological narratives in Renaissance poetry. **Shakespeare**'s *Venus and Adonis* and **Marlowe**'s *Hero and Leander* are major English examples, **Thomas Lodge**'s *Scillaes Metamorphosis* (1589) and **Francis Beaumont**'s *Salmacis and Hermaphroditus* (1602) minor ones.

**Erasmus, Desiderius** ?1466–1536 Erasmus was acknowledged in his own time as the greatest humanist and scholar of the northern Renaissance. He was born in Rotterdam and went to school in Deventer 1475–83 with the Brethren of the Common Life, whose *devotio moderna* with its emphasis on personal piety and works of charity influenced his later thinking. He became an Augustinian canon and was ordained priest in 1492, but obtained dispensations throughout his life which enabled him to leave the cloister and live in the world. His experiences at the University of Paris 1495–9, where he studied for the degree of Doctor of Theology, were less than happy. He complained of addled eggs and the stench of the bedrooms. More importantly, he was irritated by the wrangling subtleties of the scholastic theologians there. His career displayed all the facets of the Renaissance humanist. He became Latin secretary to the Bishop of Cambrai in 1494, and was tutor to boys of noble families, including two English boys.

His achievements as an editor, translator and writer were outstanding, and it was with justice that the German humanists hailed him as the light of the world. He edited Jerome (1516), and among the other fathers of the Church whose work he either edited or translated were Cyprian (1520), Hilary (1523), Ambrose (1527), Chrysostom (1530) and Origen (1536). He also edited Pliny and Seneca and translated Lucian. In 1504 Erasmus discovered a manuscript of Lorenzo Valla's *Adnotationes* on the New Testament and his edition of that work appeared in 1505. His *Novum Instrumentum*, an edition of the Greek text of the New Testament with a new parallel Latin version which superseded the Vulgate in its elegance and accuracy, was printed in 1516. It also contained notes by Erasmus, some of which criticized the state of the Roman Catholic church. In his prefatory essay Erasmus wishes that every woman might read the Gospel and that the farmer at his plough might sing snatches of scripture. Erasmus made a vast collection of Greek and Latin proverbs, the *Adagia*, which grew and grew so that the Venetian Aldine edition of 1508 contained over 3000. Towards the end of his life he made a similar collection of classical anecdotes, the *Apophthegmata* (1531). The *Enchiridion Militis Christiani* (dagger of the Christian soldier) (1503) is a manual of simple piety which is intended, in Erasmus's words, to kindle a warm love of the scriptures in generous hearts. *Institutio Principis Christiani* (1516) is a work on the education of the Christian prince. *Colloquia* are dialogues on various subjects.

Erasmus's relations with England were close. On his first stay in 1499–1500 he met the young Henry VIII, and made the acquaintance of English humanists, finding congenial friends in **William Grocyn**, **Thomas Linacre**, William Latimer, **John Colet** and above all **Thomas More**. He was in England again in 1505 and 1509–14. During this last visit he lectured at Cambridge on Greek and theology, and to this third visit belongs the composition of the *Moriae Encomium* ('Praise of Folly') (1511) which in its title puns on the name of his greatest English friend. This paradoxical self-praise by Folly herself satirizes clerical abuses, corruption and ignorance, and ends with the praise of Christian folly, the simple Christian and the ultimate folly of Christ's crucifixion.

Erasmus's other works are too numerous to mention. There were many 16th-century English translations of the *Colloquia* and of his devotional works, and selections from the *Adagia* were also Englished. A translation of the *Enchiridion* as *The Manual of the Christian Knight* (1533) is attributed to **William Tyndale**, and **Miles Coverdale**'s *A Short Recapitulation* of the *Enchiridion* was printed at Antwerp in 1545. **Udall**'s *Apophthegmes* appeared in 1542 and a complete Latin and English *Adagia* in 1621. There were also Chaloner's *Praise of Folly* (1549) and Paynell's *Complaint of Peace* (1559), a translation of *Querimonia Pacis*.

Despite his constant criticism of clerical abuse and folly and theological over-niceties, Erasmus could never bring himself to join Luther and finally opposed him in a treatise on free will, *De Libero Arbitrio* (1524). However, there is much truth in the cliché that the Reformation was an egg laid by Erasmus and hatched by Luther.

**Erewhon** A satirical novel by **Samuel Butler**, published in 1872. Erewhon (an anagram of 'nowhere') is discovered by Higgs, the narrator, on the far side of a chain of unexplored mountains in a remote colony. His description embodies Butler's attack on the mental and moral stagnation and hypocrisy he found in England, and on his society's attitudes to crime, religion and the rearing of children. Higgs escapes from Erewhon in a balloon he constructed himself, accompanied by a girl with whom he has fallen in love.

**Erewhon Revisited** **Samuel Butler**'s sequel to his satirical novel **Erewhon**, published in 1901. Twenty years after escaping from Erewhon, Higgs has a strong desire to revisit the place. When he arrives he discovers that his ascent into the sky by balloon has called into being a religion, Sunchildism, and that a great temple to him is about to be dedicated. Higgs is horrified at the way people's credulity is being exploited by the Professors Hanky and Panky.

**Ervine, St John (Greer)** 1883–1971 Irish playwright, novelist and critic. Born in Belfast, he was a drama critic in Dublin when he began writing plays. *Mixed Marriage* (1911), the first to be produced at the **Abbey Theatre**, is a bold treatment of Catholic–Protestant relationships and their likely cost in human happiness. *Jane Clegg* (1913) and *John Ferguson* (1915) are strong plays, 'well-made' in the theatrical fashion of their time (see **well-made play**), but not afraid to address serious problems seriously.

Ervine became manager of the Abbey Theatre in 1915, but left to serve in the Royal Dublin Fusiliers. After the war, in which he was wounded, he settled in London. He was drama critic for *The Observer* 1919–23 and for the BBC for some years after 1932. He continued to write social dramas, like *The Ship* (1922), *Robert's Wife* (1937) and *The Christies* (1947), but also comedies, like *The First Mrs Fraser* (1929), almost in the style of **Noël Coward**, and *Boyd's Shop* (1936), a gentle study of Irish village life. His novels include *Mrs Martin's Man* (1914) and *Alice and the Family* (1915) and his biographical studies *Parnell* (1925), *God's Soldier: General William Booth* (1934), *Craigavon, Ulsterman* (1949), *Oscar Wilde* (1951) and *Bernard Shaw* (1956).

*Essay Concerning Human Understanding* A philosophical treatise by **John Locke**, published in 1690. Further editions, with important revisions by the author, were published in 1694, 1700 and 1706. *Some Thoughts on the Conduct of the Understanding in the Search of Truth*, originally designed as a chapter of the *Essay*, was published posthumously in 1762.

Locke rejected the doctrine of inborn ideas or knowledge, maintaining that the source of knowledge is experience. His intention in the *Essay* was to enquire into the origin and extent of man's knowledge; he also examined the nature and limits of knowledge, what man can hope to know and what he cannot. In the course of his argument Locke threw new light on the working of the human mind and the association of ideas, and thereby influenced generations of poets and novelists. His philosophy is conveyed in lucid and unadorned prose.

*Essay of Dramatic Poesy* A critical symposium by **John Dryden**, written while he was living at Charlton in Wiltshire to escape the plague in London. It was first published in 1668. Those taking part are **Charles Sackville**, **Earl of Dorset** (Eugenius), **Sir Robert Howard** (Crites), **Sir Charles Sedley** (Lisideius) and Dryden himself (Neander). The four friends are boating on the Thames. After discussing the fighting between the Dutch and English fleets in the Thames estuary (June 1665), they go on to discuss the English drama of earlier days and in their own time, comparing English drama with French. There is lively discussion of the use of rhyme in drama and a fine appreciation of the art of **Shakespeare**. The *Essay* is notable for Dryden's fine and succinct prose.

*Essay on Criticism, An* A poem in heroic couplets written by **Alexander Pope** when he was 21 and first published in 1711. Didactic in purpose, it contains a description of the rules of taste and the principles by which a critic should be guided; a demonstration follows showing departures from these principles by certain critics. The classical inspiration for the poem was Horace's *Ars Poetica* and it is a remarkbly sophisticated performance; the skill with which Pope used the form and the concentration of witty utterance it contained made him famous. Some of the lines have the status of proverbs: 'A little learning is a dangerous thing' and 'Some praise at morning what they blame at night; / But always think the last opinion right.'

*Essay on Man* A poem by **Alexander Pope**, in four epistles, addressed to his friend Henry St John, **Lord Bolingbroke**. The poem was partly inspired by Bolingbroke's occasional philosophical writings. The first three epistles were published anonymously in 1733; the fourth was published in 1734 under Pope's name. The original plan was for a poem upon the nature of man on a more ambitious scale but Pope did not continue. The first epistle is concerned with the nature of man and his place in the universe; the second with man as an individual; the third with man in society; and the fourth with man and the pursuit of happiness. The purpose is to demonstrate the essential rightness of the world as ordered by God; man's inability to realize this is the fault of his limited perception. The result is conventional enough in its thought, but its expression is enlivened by Pope's gift for witty aphorism.

*Essays, The*, or, *Counsels, Civil and Moral* **Francis Bacon**'s essays were first published in a book of 10 in 1597, followed by a book of 38 in 1612, and a third in 1625 containing 58. They are mostly reflections and observations shaped into advice for the conduct of a successful life. Some deal with matters of great importance, such as government (on the 'Greatness of Kingdoms'); others with topics such as architecture ('Of Building') and aspects of human behaviour including ambition and cunning. Incorporating numerous quotations from earlier writers, the essays are full of acute intelligence and wit. The turn of phrase is aphoristic: 'If the hill will not come to Mahomet, Mahomet will go to the hill'; 'Money is like muck, not good except it be spread.' The celebrated essay 'Atheism' was first published in the edition of 1612.

***Essays and Reviews*** A collection of theological essays, published in 1860. The editor was Henry Bristow Wilson and his eminent contributors were: **Benjamin Jowett**, Professor of Greek at Oxford; **Mark Pattison**, Rector of Lincoln College, Oxford; Baden Powell, Professor of Geometry at Oxford; Frederick Temple, Chaplain to the Queen and to the Earl of Denbigh, and headmaster of Rugby; Rowland Williams; and C. W. Goodwin. Influenced by the **Higher Criticism**, the authors argued for a liberal Christianity which took account of modern biblical research and modern science. In the ensuing controversy they were nicknamed the 'Seven Against Christ' and Jowett's essay, 'The Interpretation of Scripture', was discovered to give the greatest offence; he never wrote on theological subjects again. The book was condemned by a meeting of bishops in 1861 and by the Synod of the Church of England in 1864.

***Essays in Criticism*** Two collections of essays by **Matthew Arnold**, the first series published in 1865 and the second posthumously in 1888.

Of the nine essays in the first volume, mainly devoted to Continental and classical subjects, the most important is 'The Function of Criticism at the Present Time', a sustained attempt to broaden and elevate the role of criticism. According to Arnold, criticism 'obeys an instinct prompting it to know the best that is known and thought in the world, irrespective of practice, politics, and everything of the kind'. Disinterested and flexible, it can 'see the object as in itself it really is' and 'make the best ideas prevail'. Criticism can thus not only shape 'the creative epochs of literature' but play its role in other areas of knowledge and in society, whose contemporary problems Arnold eloquently notes.

The second collection likewise begins with a challenging essay, 'The Study of Poetry', notable for its theory of 'touchstones' of poetic excellence: one should 'have always in one's mind lines and expressions of the great masters . . . and apply them as a touchstone to other poetry'. Brief passages from Homer, Dante, Virgil, **Shakespeare** and **Milton** demonstrate the theory and assert the 'penetrative power' of poetry, whose attributes are matter and substance, manner and style, and 'high seriousness' (a quality which Arnold, surprisingly, denies to **Chaucer**). Otherwise, the aim of the volume is more narrowly informative than its predecessor. It includes essays on Tolstoy, Amiel, Milton, **Gray**, **Keats**, **Wordsworth** and **Byron** ('first and pre-eminent in actual performance, a glorious pair, among the English poets of this century') and **Shelley** ('a beautiful and ineffectual angel, beating in the void his luminous wings in vain').

***Essays in Criticism*** Borrowing its title from **Matthew Arnold**, this critical quarterly was founded by the Oxford critic **F. W. Bateson** in 1951, partly in emulation of and partly as a rival to the Cambridge-based *Scrutiny*. T. S. Eliot and J. M. Murry were among the first contributors, and since then *Essays in Criticism* has published articles by **William Empson**, **Donald Davie** and many other leading literary critics. After Bateson's death in 1978 the journal passed into the hands of his co-editors Stephen Wall and Christopher Ricks.

***Essays of Elia, The*** The miscellaneous essays that **Charles Lamb** contributed under the pseudonym of Elia to ***The London Magazine*** between August 1820 and December 1823, beginning with 'Recollections of the South-Sea House'. The essays contain much observant social and literary criticism, and are also prized for the reminiscences of childhood ('Christ's Hospital Five-and-Thirty Years Ago', 'Blakesmoor in H—shire') and for the descriptions of characters from Lamb's wide range of acquaintances. Also included are the purely fanciful or melancholy exercises which have become famous anthology pieces: 'Dream Children', 'A Dissertation upon Roast Pig' and 'A Chapter on Ears'.

The first collection of *The Essays of Elia* was published in 1823; the remainder appeared, with other essays, as *The Last Essays of Elia* (1833).

**Esson, Louis** 1879–1943 Australian playwright, educated in Melbourne. After leaving university without a degree, Esson became a journalist. More significant to his writing was his interest in the Australian outback. A political comedy, *The Time is Not Yet Ripe* (1912), was given an amateur performance, and Esson became one of the founders of a distinct Australian drama. The Pioneer Players, which he helped establish and run in Melbourne from 1922 to 1926, staged his second full-length play, *The Bride of Gospel Place* (1926). This, like the one-act *The Woman Tamer* (1910), is set in Melbourne. Esson's outback plays include the full-length *Mother and Son* (1923) and two one-act tragedies, *Dead Timber* (1911) and *The Drovers* (1920).

**estates satire** A medieval satirical tradition expounding the characteristics, duties and failings of the different social 'estates' or classes. Society is divided by function (often occupation) rather than social rank, typical categories being pope, priest, prince, knight, nun and wife. All the religious classes were placed at the top of the hierarchy, all classes of laymen beneath them, and all classes of women at the bottom. Characteristics were attributed to each social group, and the estates were criticized for failing to fulfil their duties to each other and society as a whole. Works dealing explicitly and solely in estates satire are mostly Latin, but many other works use material from the tradition, for example, *Piers Plowman*, the General Prologue to *The Canterbury Tales*, *Mum and the Sothsegger* and *Wynnere and Wastoure*.

**Esther Waters** A novel by **George Moore**, first published in 1894. The author was strongly influenced by his years in France and had written several novels in a realistic vein before this one but *Esther Waters*, with its sympathetic treatment of the characters and faithful portrayal of all levels of society, departed from Victorian conventions and gave Moore his first great success.

Esther Waters is a religious girl, a member of the Plymouth Brethren, who leaves home to escape from a drunken stepfather. She goes into service at Woodview, the home of the Barfield family whose main interest is their racing stables; the exception is Mrs Barfield, who – like Esther – belongs to the Plymouth sect. Esther, aged only 17, is easily seduced by the footman, William Latch, who then deserts her. Esther is dismissed, and only Mrs Barfield tries to be kind. She bears a son and endures a bitter and humiliating struggle to rear him. Esther is admired by a respectable man, a Salvationist, who wants to marry her; but William Latch comes back into her life and for their son's sake she marries him. William makes a good husband and father; but he is a publican in Dean Street in Soho as well as a bookmaker, and his constant attendance at races ruins his health. Further misfortune comes when he is suspected of using the pub as an unlicensed betting centre and the house is closed. William dies, leaving his family penniless; but Esther's son is soon able to fend for himself and at the close of the novel Esther returns to Woodview. Mrs Barfield, now an impoverished widow, lives alone in a corner of the old house, and there at last Esther finds peace.

**Ethan Frome** A novel by **Edith Wharton**, published in 1911. On a poor farm in western Massachusetts Ethan Frome struggles to wrest a living from the soil. His slatternly wife Zeena (Zenobia) is a whining hypochondriac and spends much of Ethan's hard-earned money on quack remedies. Her cousin, Mattie Silver, is left destitute when her parents die and the farm is the only place she can go. Ethan and Mattie are attracted to each other and Zeena's jealousy is aroused. After a year Zeena drives Mattie off the farm to make way for a hired woman, and Ethan takes her to the railroad station through the snow. Realizing that he cannot bear to part from her, he causes an accident that he hopes will kill them, but the pair survive the crash and spend the remainder of their lives as invalids under the care of Zeena.

**Etherege, Sir George** *c.* 1635–91 Playwright, whose work profoundly influenced the development of drama in Restoration England. Little is known of Etherege's early life. He came from an Oxfordshire family of modest means and may well have spent some time in France. Certainly his knowledge of French manners and literature was sufficient to justify such an assumption.

Etherege's first play, *The Comical Revenge, or, Love in a Tub* (1664), was sufficiently successful to win him a place in society. He entered whole-heartedly into the rakish world of Charles II's London, had a daughter by the actress Elizabeth Barry and included the dissolute **Earl of Rochester** among his intimates. His second play, *She Would If She Could* (1668), is more characteristically a Restoration comedy than his first. It won him further acclaim and may have contributed to his being appointed secretary to the ambassador to Constantinople from 1668–71. The responsibility did nothing to reform him and he resumed his wild life in London on his return to England. His last and greatest play, *The Man of Mode* (1676), is a fully fledged Restoration comedy, more intolerant of dullness and affectation than of libertinism.

On the death of Charles II in 1685, Etherege was appointed ambassador to the Imperial Court at Ratisbon. He may have been knighted in the same year. The letters he wrote to friends in England, first collected in *The Letterbook of Sir George Etherege* (1928), are among the best of the period. A fuller selection of *Letters* (1974) and a volume of slight but elegant *Poems* (1963), together with the three plays, complete the literary output of one of the leaders of Restoration taste.

**Ettrick Shepherd, The** See **Hogg, James**.

**Eugene Aram** A novel by **Edward Bulwer Lytton**, published in 1832, and based on a true story. Aram is a high-minded scholar who, some 14 years earlier, had been driven by extreme poverty to become an accomplice to a murder, and is now racked by guilt. He falls in love but is denounced on his wedding day and sentenced to death. As a sensational example of **Newgate fiction** the book was furiously condemned in some quarters as immoral, but it confirmed Bulwer Lytton's standing, in the year of **Scott**'s death, as England's most popular novelist.

**Euphues** The hero of **John Lyly**'s two prose works, *Euphues, or, The Anatomy of Wit* (probably first published in 1578) and *Euphues and His England* (1580) gave his name to the exaggeratedly elegant style known as **euphuism**. Lyly probably found the name in **Roger Ascham**'s *The Schoolmaster*: 'euphues' is Greek for 'well-endowed'.

The slight plot of *The Anatomy of Wit* is borrowed from Boccaccio, though it is also a variation on the popular Reformation story of the Prodigal Son who wastes his talents. Euphues, a young Athenian, leaves his native city (which may represent Oxford) to visit Naples (which may represent London). There he makes the acquaintance of Philautus and they pledge friendship. Unfortunately, Euphues takes the place of Philautus in the affections of Lucilla. On his return to Naples Philautus discovers this and reproaches Euphues, and there is a mutual exchange of letters. Euphues visits Lucilla only to find that he in turn has been replaced by Curio. Lucilla's father berates her, Euphues and his friend are reconciled, and the book ends with a series of letters. These events are only the skeleton of the book, which is fleshed out with discourses on wit, religion and education, all expressed with the most elaborate rhetorical artifices. Above all, Lyly treats the familiar Renaissance themes of love, friendship and the possible conflicts between them.

The work was enormously popular, running to five editions by 1581 and provoking several imitations. In the sequel, *Euphues and His England*, dedicated to the Earl of Oxford, Euphues and Philautus visit England and the narrative chronicles Philautus's love-affairs. Lyly is fervent in praise of English virtue, and especially the virtue of the English gentlewoman. Euphues ends the story by returning to Greece and entering a monastery, while Philautus gets married.

**euphuism** This elaborate and elegant prose style takes its name from **John Lyly**'s *Euphues*, where it first appears in full flower, though there are hints earlier in *The Dial of Princes* by **Sir Thomas North** and in **George Pettie**'s *Petite Palace of Pettie His Pleasure*. Its characteristic quality is an obvious and exaggerated artifice complete with the figures and 'flowers' of rhetoric, and a fondness for *sententiae* (moral maxims). Lyly has an especial liking for balanced antitheses, often reinforced by alliteration: 'Here may you see, gentlemen, the falsehood in fellowship, the fraud in friendship, the painted sheath with the leaden dagger, the fair words that make fools vain.' He decorates his prose with numerous historical or mythological allusions: 'If incantations or potions or amorous sayings could have prevailed, Circes would never have lost Ulysses, nor Phaedra Hippolytus, nor Phyllis Demophoon.' Another feature is what **Sidney** refers to in *Astrophil and Stella* as the determination to 'with strange similes enrich each line/Of herbs or beasts which Ind or Afric hold'. For these Lyly's source is often Pliny: 'so

that thinking to present me with your heart you have thrust into my hands the serpent Amphisbena, which having at each end a sting, hurteth both ways'.

Although Lyly's imitators display the worst aspects of this style, in Lyly's hands it remained a disciplined medium displaying the possibilities of a 'new English' style.

*Europeans, The* A novel by **Henry James**, published serially in *The Atlantic Monthly* (July–October 1878), and as a volume, in slightly revised form, later that same year.

Felix Young, an artist, and his sister Eugenia, the wife of a German nobleman who is about to renounce her for reasons of state, come from Europe to Massachusetts to visit their relatives, the Wentworths. Though concerned about the 'peculiar influence' these European cousins may exert on his family, the elder Wentworth establishes Felix and Eugenia in a nearby house. Relations between the cousins become friendly. Wentworth's daughter Gertrude falls in love with Felix, and he with her; his son Clifford becomes infatuated with Eugenia, who is looking for a wealthy husband and welcomes his attentions. Gertrude, however, already has an 'understanding' with Mr Brand, the Unitarian minister. Although she does not in fact care for Mr Brand, her sister Charlotte does. Robert and Lizzie Acton further complicate matters: Robert is drawn – but not unreservedly – to Eugenia; Lizzie hopes to win Clifford Wentworth.

At the end of the novel, Mr Wentworth consents to the marriage of Felix and Gertrude; Clifford, having overcome his infatuation for Eugenia, marries Lizzie Acton; Mr Brand discovers that he cares not for Gertrude but for Charlotte, and marries her. Robert Acton and Eugenia do not, however, make a fourth happy couple. Though attracted to her, Acton cannot overcome his scruples about her past and about the calculating way in which she uses her feminine wiles. Eugenia returns to Europe alone.

**Eusden, Laurence** 1688–1730 Poet Laureate from 1718 until he died, Eusden was a writer of minor verse whose work is dwarfed by the greater achievements of his contemporaries like **Pope**, who assigned him a place in the realms of Dullness in his reductive satire on contemporary culture, *The Dunciad*.

*Eustace Diamonds, The* A novel by **Anthony Trollope**, the third in the **Palliser** sequence, serialized in *The Fortnightly Review* from July 1871 to February 1873, and published in three volumes in 1873.

The beautiful but shallow Lizzie Eustace is left a wealthy widow when her husband of a few months, Sir Florian Eustace, dies. The plot centres on the Eustace family diamonds which

Lizzie claims belong to her, a claim denied by the family lawyer, Mr Camperdown. She turns for protection first to Lord Fawn, a dull but ambitious politician in need of money, and they become engaged, Fawn all the while insisting, however, that she return the diamonds. She turns next to her cousin Frank Greystock, another poor man with political ambitions, and he becomes attracted to Lizzie and her fortune while visiting her at her Scottish castle, despite his existing engagement to Lucy Morris, governess to the Fawn family. On the journey south Lizzie's hotel bedroom is robbed at Carlisle, and she claims that the diamonds have been stolen, although in fact she has secreted them under her pillow. But when her London home is robbed, and the diamonds taken in earnest, her dishonesty becomes apparent in the subsequent police investigations. Lord Fawn breaks his engagement and she loses the disillusioned Frank, who finally marries Lucy. Rejected even by the Byronic Lord George Carruthers, to whose 'Corsair' charms she has been attracted, Lizzie ends by marrying the shady Mr Emilius, a converted Jew turned fashionable preacher.

*The Eustace Diamonds* is one of Trollope's darker novels, a study in moral duplicity with a plot that owes something to **Wilkie Collins**'s *The Moonstone*.

**Evan Harrington** A novel by **George Meredith**, first published serially in *Once a Week* in 1860.

Although the death of Melchisedec ('the Great Mel') Harrington – an exquisitely mannered tailor once mistaken for a marquis – occurs on the first page of the book, his elegant ghost hovers over the subsequent narrative. Melchisedec had four children: Caroline (now married to Major Strike), Harriet (wife of the rich brewer Andrew Cogglesby), Louisa (wife of the Portuguese Count de Saldar) and Evan, the only son. The sisters – particularly Louisa – are dedicated to furthering his fortunes by having him marry the eligible Rose Jocelyn of Beckley Court. Although he comes to love Rose, Evan wants to clear his late father's name of debt. Countless sisterly sacrifices are made to conceal their humble background while Evan, who has turned tailor, through a characteristically Meredithian twist of plot falls heir to Beckley Court. Together with misleading letters, renunciation of the estate by Evan (which earns him 'the soul of a gentleman') and other conveniences allowed by the Comic Muse, the novel concludes with the hero gaining both Rose and a diplomatic post in Naples.

*Evan Harrington* is too long to sustain its attenuated narrative, though the story does gain momentum in its later stages. Nevertheless, the book remains notable for its crispness of language, comedy, analysis of snobbery and the lively characterization of lesser figures like Jack Raikes, George Uploft and Mr Parsley, as well as the striking effect of Louisa, the wily Countess.

**Evangeline, A Tale of Acadie** A narrative poem by **Henry Wadsworth Longfellow**, published in 1847, and set in Acadia, a province of Canada roughly corresponding to present-day Nova Scotia. Composed in unrhymed hexameters, the poem recounts the frustrated love story of Evangeline Bellefontaine and Gabriel Lajeunesse, whom the French and Indian Wars have separated. Gabriel and his father, a blacksmith, make their way to Louisiana. Evangeline follows them and eventually finds Gabriel's father, but he has become separated from his son. Together they fruitlessly search for Gabriel. After many years, Evangeline, prematurely aged, becomes a Sister of Mercy in Philadelphia. During a pestilence there she recognizes a dying old man as her lover. She dies of grief, and they are buried together.

**Eve of St Agnes, The** A narrative poem in **Spenserian stanzas** by **Keats**, written in 1819, published in 1820. The tale's setting is a night of dancing and revelry in a medieval mansion on a freezing winter's evening in the distant past. Madeline has learned that on this night, St Agnes's Eve, a virgin may be granted a vision of her lover, and she prepares to leave the ball and retire to bed. Unknown to her, her lover Porphyro, a son of her family's deadliest enemy, has stolen unseen into the castle, where he pours out his heart to Angela, a sympathetic old 'beldame'. He persuades her to hide him in a place in Madeline's apartments from where he can observe her undressing for sleep, and to prepare an exotic supper for two. Enticed by his soft lute-playing, Madeline emerges from her dreams to find him by her bedside. Silently they slip through the sleeping halls and 'away into the storm', leaving old Angela to die 'palsytwitched' and the Baron to his dreams of 'many a woe'.

**Leigh Hunt**'s judgement that it was 'the most delightful and complete specimen' of Keats's genius is shared by many of the poem's modern readers. It is an extraordinarily skilful Romantic montage of popular legend, **Shakespeare**'s *Romeo and Juliet*, motifs from **Chaucer** and Boccaccio, and the atmospherics of Gothic romance. The narrative is fast moving, at times even dramatic; most striking of all, however, is the richness and radiant sensuousness of the imagery, particularly in the central bed-chamber sequence.

**Evelina, or, A Young Lady's Entrance into the World** An epistolary novel by **Fanny Burney**, published anonymously in 1778.

The novelist's first published work, written,

according to herself, for 'private recreation' and printed 'for a frolic, to see how a production of her own would figure in that author-like form'. The germ of *Evelina* was an early story, apparently entitled 'The History of Caroline Evelyn', which retailed the unhappy career of Evelina's mother. Fanny Burney destroyed it along with numerous other juvenile works.

After her mother's death, Evelina was brought up by the Revd Arthur Villars in the rural seclusion of Berry Hill. When she reaches 17 the sensible Lady Howard declares that 'it is time that she should see something of the world. When young people are too rigidly sequestered from it, their lively and romantic imaginations paint it to them as a paradise of which they have been beguiled; but when they are shown it properly, and in due time, they see it such as it really is, equally shared by pain and pleasure, hope and disappointment.' In seven months (and three volumes) Evelina undergoes her education in self-knowledge, prudence and discretion under the tutelage of Villars, Lady Howard and the judicious Lord Orville, whom she eventually marries.

The novel rapidly became a fashionable success, sold many copies, and attracted the admiration of **Edmund Burke**, **Joshua Reynolds** and **Dr Johnson**, who said that it gave the impression of 'long experience and deep and intimate knowledge of the world'. The work still offers sophistication and sensibility, an accomplished and witty style, and vivid portraits of the undesirable relatives, Sir John Belmont, Mme Duval and the Branghtons, who embarrass and disconcert the heroine.

**Evelyn, John** 1620–1706 Diarist and early Fellow of the Royal Society. The son of Richard Evelyn, a Surrey gentleman, he was educated at Balliol College, Oxford, and travelled extensively on the Continent. He was a Royalist supporter, a civilized and elegant-minded man of means, who left England after the execution of Charles I in 1649, to avoid living under the Commonwealth. During his years of exile he conducted a correspondence with Charles II, returning to England in 1652 for the rest of the Interregnum. Following the death of his son at the age of five, Evelyn translated from the Greek *The Golden Book of St John Chrysostom* (1659), a work on the education of children; the 'Epistle Dedicatory' is an early example of the evocative powers of his style, 'My tears mingle so fast with my inke that I am forced to breake off here, and be silent.'

Evelyn was elected one of the first Fellows of the Royal Society, formed shortly after the Restoration, and he interested himself in a wide variety of topics with the enthusiasm of an intelligent amateur. In 1661 he published *Fumifugium, or The Inconvenience of the Air and Smoke of London Dissipated*, proposing certain practical remedies for metropolitan pollution, none of which was implemented by the authorities. The following year he wrote *Sculptura*, a book on engraving. The Royal Society was consulted by the Navy Office (where, coincidentally, Evelyn's friend **Samuel Pepys** was working) over the impending shortage of timber for shipbuilding, and Evelyn was allocated the problem. The result was his influential and informed *Sylva, or, A Discourse of Forest Trees* (1664), a manual of arboriculture. After the Great Fire of 1666, he submitted some constructive proposals for the rebuilding of the capital, and he also wrote a treatise on *Navigation and Commerce* (1674), as well as essays on topics from vineyards to medals.

He is best remembered, though, for his diary. Its inevitable comparison with the diaries secretly kept at the same time by Pepys is not a helpful one, since the two documents are a totally different pair of records. Evelyn's annals are never risqué nor intimate: the record covers the whole span of his life, and started as a series of jottings and memoirs which he began to organize in 1660. The resulting volume, *Kalendarium*, reveals little about the personality of its author – a carefully remote figure – but offers a fascinating account of the principal events of his lifetime, and some penetrating character sketches of public figures. He frequently draws material from contemporary publications to

John Evelyn. Portrait by R. Nanteuil, 1650. National Portrait Gallery, London.

illustrate events, but after 1684 the document becomes more like a diary proper.

It was not published until 1818. The papers had remained unrecognized by generations of Evelyn's family, but were rediscovered by the antiquarian William Upcott and edited by William Bray as *The Memoirs of John Evelyn*. The immediate interest in Evelyn led directly to the rediscovery of Pepys's diaries in Cambridge shortly thereafter. The definitive edition, by E. S. de Beer, was published in 1955 and runs to six volumes.

**Every Man in His Humour** A comedy by **Ben Jonson**, first performed in 1598 by the Lord Chamberlain's Men (see **King's Men**). **Shakespeare** was a member of the company and his name appears on a surviving cast-list of the play. In a revised version published in 1616, Jonson changed the names and the setting from Italy to London. The great popularity of the play created a fashion for 'humours' comedy (see **wit**). Characters whose behaviour is governed by a single dominant emotion or 'humour', grotesquely obsessive, became familiar figures on the contemporary stage, though few writers could match the relish with which Jonson exhibited and exploited the foibles of the foolish.

The merchant, Kitely, has a younger brother who brings his boisterous friends to the house. Dame Kitely is young and pretty and her husband is jealous, thinking that his brother's friends have designs on her. One of the young men, Edward Knowell, suffers from his father's excessive concern for his moral welfare; he woos Kitely's pretty sister, Bridget. An associate of the group of young men is Captain Bobadill, an old soldier who is both vain and cowardly, forever boasting of his valour. Knowell's servant, Brainworm, maliciously plays on Kitely's jealousy and Dame Kitely's credulity to bring about a confrontation between them in a house where each believes the other present for an immoral purpose. Captain Bobadill's pretensions are exposed. Misunderstandings are resolved at the end by Justice Clement, a shrewd observer of human folly, and Knowell wins Bridget's hand.

**Every Man out of His Humour** An almost plotless comedy by **Ben Jonson**, first performed at the **Globe** in 1599. Obviously intended to capitalize on the success of *Every Man in His Humour*, it is a much less attractive piece, though certain foolish 'humours' are nicely hit off in Fungoso, Sogliardo and Sir Fastidious Brisk, and Jonson's adversaries in the war of the theatres, **Marston** and **Dekker**, are waspishly portrayed as Clove and Olive.

**Everyman** This best known of all English **morality plays** dates from around the end of the 15th

A woodcut from an edition of *Everyman* published in 1530.

century. It is closely related to a Flemish play, first printed in 1495. *Everyman* survives in four versions, two of them fragmentary. It combines rhymed couplets and stanzaic forms that may seem rhythmically crude at times but rarely impede the dramatic movement.

The play details the progress of its hero from complacency through fear and despair at the prospect of his death to a Christian resignation that is the prelude to redemption. Seeking for companions on his last journey, he finds only one, Good Deeds, prepared to accompany him all the way to the grave.

**Ewart, Gavin (Buchanan)** 1916– Poet. He was born in London and educated at Wellington College and Christ's College, Cambridge, where he read Classics and English and was taught by **F. R. Leavis** and **I. A. Richards**. After serving in North Africa and Italy during World War II, he worked briefly in publishing and for a longer spell in advertising, becoming a freelance writer in 1971.

Ewart contributed to **Grigson**'s *New Verse* at the age of 17. His first collection was *Poems and Songs* (1939). He has a great facility for light and comic verse, is a skilful parodist and has a reputation for erotic writing (his *Pleasures of the Flesh* was banned by W. H. Smith & Son in 1966). The *Collected Ewart 1933–80* was published in 1980, the same year that his anthology, *The Penguin Book of Light Verse*, also appeared.

**Ewing, Juliana (Horatia)** 1841–85 Writer of **children's literature**. Born Juliana Gatty, the oldest daughter of a Yorkshire vicar, she frequently told stories to her younger siblings before getting into print at the age of 20 in **Charlotte M. Yonge**'s magazine *The Monthly Packet*. In 1866 her mother **Margaret Gatty** launched her own children's journal, *Aunt Judy's Magazine*, for which Juliana contributed a serial story later published as *Mrs Overtheway's Remembrances* (1869). This was a charming family story told with conviction and a rare feeling of accuracy for the normal ups and downs of family life. A succeeding novel, *Jan of the Windmill* (1876), told the story of a foundling later to become a celebrated artist. But perhaps Mrs Ewing is best remembered now by association, in that *The Brownies and Other Tales* (1870) influenced Sir Robert Baden-Powell and gave him the name for the junior section of the (Girl) Guide Movement. Following marriage and a posting with her husband overseas, Mrs Ewing died prematurely after a long period of ill health. Although little read today, she was an important figure in the history of children's literature, helping begin the long process of rejecting didacticism in favour of unsentimental realism.

*Examiner, The* A weekly journal begun in August 1710, as an instrument of Tory propaganda, by **Robert Harley** with the help of **Bolingbroke, Francis Atterbury, Matthew Prior** and other willing Tory pens. **Swift** edited it anonymously from 2 November 1710 to 14 June 1711, contributing 33 essays which provoked its opposing journal, Arthur Mainwaring's *Medley*, to accuse *The Examiner* of working 'a World of Mischief'. Swift went on to write more propaganda, **The Conduct of the Allies**, and **Delarivière Manley** replaced him as editor. *The Examiner* survived until 1716, though issued sporadically toward the end of its life.

*Examiner, The* A radical weekly magazine founded in 1808 by **Leigh Hunt** and his brother, John. It played an important role in bringing the poetry of **Keats** and **Shelley** before the public, thus identifying Hunt and his friends in the eyes of their detractors as the **Cockney School** of poetry. A libel against the Prince Regent was punished with a heavy fine and two years' imprisonment for the brothers; Leigh Hunt continued to edit the journal from his prison cell. *The Examiner* survived until 1881.

*Excursion, The* A poem in nine books by **William Wordsworth**, published in 1814. As early as 1798 Wordsworth had planned what he describes in his preface as a 'philosophical poem, containing views of man, nature, and society, and to be entitled *The Recluse*, as having for its principal subject the sensations and opinions of a poet living in retirement'. *The Excursion* was the only part of the project that Wordsworth completed, but it is still his longest work.

The poet travels with a Wanderer; through him he meets the Solitary, a recent enthusiast for the French Revolution and now dispirited by events in France. The Solitary is reproved for his lack of faith and loss of confidence in man. A Pastor enters the scene, offering the consolations of virtue and faith and illustrating his sermon with accounts of the lives of those buried in his churchyard. At the Pastor's house the Wanderer offers his conclusions, philosophical and political. The last two books present Wordsworth's thoughts on the Industrial Revolution and the havoc it played with the lives of the poor. He makes a strong plea for the education of children.

**exemplum** A short narrative tale illustrating a moral point. Exempla frequently appear in medieval didactic works (such as **Handlynge Synne**) and in homilies or sermons. They are sometimes employed in secular works, like **Gower**'s **Confessio Amantis**.

**Exeter Book, The** An important collection of Old English poems compiled *c.* 975 and donated by Bishop Leofric (d. 1072) to Exeter Cathedral, where it remains. It includes some of the most important surviving poems in Old English – *Christ, Deor, Juliana, The Phoenix, The Seafarer, The Wanderer, Widsith, The Whale, Wulf and Eadwacer, The Husband's Message, The Wife's Complaint* – and a collection of riddles.

*Exodus* An Old English poem preserved in the Junius manuscript (see **Junius, Francis**) which retells the story of the Exodus from Egypt. The biblical narrative is transformed into a vivid and evocative account which does not follow the source in all its details. It was at one time incorrectly attributed to **Caedmon**.

*Expedition of Humphry Clinker, The* A novel by **Tobias Smollett**, published in 1771. In this, his last novel, Smollett used the epistolary form, with five of his characters writing the letters and offering different views on the cavalcade of episodes which make up the book.

Matthew Bramble, a cranky but kind-hearted Welsh squire, travels through England and Scotland with his family: his unpleasant and domineering sister Tabitha, hungry for a husband; his amiable nephew Jerry, just down from Oxford; his teenage niece Lydia; and Tabitha's maid, Winifred Jenkins. Humphry Clinker, an ostler, becomes their postilion and proves a resourceful and devoted servant. The family's travels take them to Bristol, Bath, Harrogate, York, Scarborough and Durham, where they are joined by Lieutenant Obadiah Lismahago, an eccentric and impecunious Scots soldier.

Humphry, a Methodist, converts Tabitha; Tabitha succeeds in marrying Lismahago; Lydia falls in love with a handsome young actor who, fortunately, proves to be of good family; Humphry is falsely arrested and imprisoned; Winifred and Humphry fall in love, and Humphry proves to be Matthew Bramble's long-lost son.

His characters' adventures give Smollett an opportunity to comment on English life and manners in the 1760s, especially in the spa towns and resorts. Matthew Bramble, in particular, savagely criticizes much of what he sees – disliking equally the Palladian architecture of Bath and the Gothic architecture of York Minster, and being disgusted by the fashionable society he encounters. Despite his acerbic tone, and despite Smollett's predilection for violent or coarse descriptive episodes, *Humphry Clinker* is more gentle in its humour than Smollett's earlier work. It has often been considered the finest of his novels.

**expressionism** In 1901 the French painter Julien-Auguste Hervé wanted to distinguish his painting from impressionism and used the word expressionism, a word that found its way into several European languages. The first English dictionary definition was 'a style of painting in which the artist seeks to express emotional experience rather than impressions of the physical world; hence a similar style or movement in literature, drama, music, etc.'. That definition points to one widespread use of expressionism, as the antithesis of **realism**. In painting it usefully distinguished painters such as Van Gogh and Matisse, who forcefully conveyed their private experience, from the early impressionists who tried to paint external reality. Edvard Munch's *The Scream* is perhaps the most readily identifiable expressionist painting.

As a literary term expressionism has most often been applied to the theatre, describing Central European, especially German, productions between 1907 (the date of Oskar Kokoschka's *Murder, the Hope of Women*) and the mid 1920s. These plays, by Reinhard Sorge, Walter Hasenclever, Georg Kaiser, Ernst Toller and others, were marked by their non-realistic form and highly personal, idiosyncratic view of life. The plays often feature an autobiographical protagonist involved in a quest for his essential identity, other characters being reduced to stereotypes or nameless designations, The Man, The Father, etc. Short, often static scenes without causal links and staccato, telegrammatic dialogue interspersed with long rhapsodies characterize the formal structure. In Germany it was a drama of protest, young men rebelling against the proprieties of family life in the pre-war empire, boldly tackling taboo subjects like incest and parricide. Expressionist plays demanded a highly visual production style and a new generation of actors specializing in broad gesture and strident voice. Retrospectively, the term expressionist was applied to the plays of Büchner, Strindberg and Wedekind. In Germany expressionism soon developed a politically radical and Marxist temper and evolved into the 'epic' theatre of Brecht. German expressionist novelists included Franz Werfel, Max Brod and Karl Kraus.

It was mainly through the theatre that expressionism travelled from Germany. Its most successful exponents in America were **Eugene O'Neill**, particularly in *The Emperor Jones* (1920) and *The Hairy Ape* (1922), and **Elmer Rice** in *The Adding Machine* (1932), although the experiments of **Thornton Wilder**, **Tennessee Williams** and **Arthur Miller** also owe something to expressionism. The second act of **Sean O'Casey**'s *The Silver Tassie* (1929), set at the front during World War I, is overtly expressionist in style, while the rest of the play, set in Ireland, is realist. O'Casey's later plays make use of expressionist method.

The term has also been applied to film, music and architecture as well as poetry (such as parts of **T. S. Eliot**'s *The Waste Land*, for example) and some fiction (such as the Nighttown episode of **Joyce**'s *Ulysses*).

**extravaganza** The essence of 19th-century theatrical extravaganzas was their gaiety and spectacle. The finest exponent, **J. R. Planché**, based his extravaganzas on well-known myths or fairy-tales, embellishing them with punning rhyming couplets and frequent songs. They were travesties rather than satires, good-humoured to the point of blandness. Both in subject-matter and reliance on lavish visual effects they shadow the rise of the English **pantomime**.

*Eyeless in Gaza* A novel by **Aldous Huxley**, published in 1936.

The novel is largely autobiographical and charts the career of Anthony Beavis from early childhood in 1902 to his discovery of mysticism in 1935. Through a series of flashbacks, which occupy entire chapters ('August 30th 1933', 'November 6th 1902', 'June 17th 1912', etc.) key moments in Beavis's life are interwoven. Several secondary characters are similarly observed as their relationships with Beavis change over the years, including Brian Foxe (a sensitive and intellectual schoolfriend who later commits suicide), Hugh Ledwidge and his wife Helen (who becomes Beavis's lover), and Mark Staithes (who in adulthood turns to Marxism).

The main burden of the novel is to reveal Beavis's increasing sense of the futility and meaninglessness of his life – and by extension, the meaninglessness of contemporary Western society. Accompanying Staithes to Mexico to join a revolution ('Simply to be shaken out of negativity') Beavis's whole life is changed. Staithes loses a leg after a minor wound becomes infected, and the doctor who treats him, an anthropologist named James Miller, introduces Beavis to mysticism and pacifism: 'Frenzy of evil and separation. In peace there is unity. Unity with other lives. Unity with all being.'

ters who exemplify the 'negative' forces of Western society, and includes a famous shock-passage in which Beavis and Helen, having made love on the flat roof of their Mediterranean villa, are bespattered with the blood of a dog thrown from an overhead aircraft (Chapter 12).

The title and epigraph are from **Milton**'s *Samson Agonistes*: 'Eyeless in Gaza at the Mill with slaves'.

**Ezekiel, Nissim** 1924– Indian poet, born in Bombay. He and **A. K. Ramanujan** are probably the finest Indian poets in English. Both are 'academic' in the senses of quietly explorative, speculative, meditative, yet in both there is a wholly undogmatic religious strain, Ezekiel's Judaic, Ramanujan's Hindu. Reacting deliberately against the oratorical transcendentalism of the verse of Aurobindo Ghose (1872–1950), Ezekiel cultivated a direct, often conversational English to convey his predominant moods of questioning and scepticism. His early verse, in *A Time to Change* (1951), *Sixty Poems* (1953) and *The Third* (1958), is rational and reflective (even when the mode is passionate), much concerned with failures in human relationships and personal living, so that 'time is only meditation,/ Prayer and poetry, poetry and prayer'. Some poems express the desire for simple domestic happiness as background to self-examination, but later verse declares that happiness impossible, even as the need for self-discovery intensifies. Restrained, tautly articulated confession of personal failure, even though aprehended as part of a whole generation's collapse of faiths, makes the poems in *The Unfinished Man* (1960) the most impressive he has written, though he continued to produce finely-turned satirical and confessional poems in *The Exact Name* (1965) and *Hymns in Darkness* (1976). In *Latter-Day Psalms* (1982), which includes poems from earlier volumes, he acknowledges that a vestigial religious precipitate lies suspended within his low-key scepticism; nine Old Testament Psalms are ironically adapted to these times. University teacher, art critic, and literary editor, he has also published *Three Plays* (1969).

# F

**Faber, Frederick William** 1814–63 Poet and hymn-writer. He was born at Calverley in the West Riding of Yorkshire and educated at Shrewsbury and Harrow schools and at Balliol College, Oxford. He became a scholar of University College, Oxford, in 1834 and a fellow in 1837. He was ordained in 1839 and appointed rector of Elton in Huntingdonshire in 1841. Having come under the powerful influence of **J. H. Newman**, he was received into the Roman Catholic church in 1845 and joined the Oratorian order in 1848. Faber established the London Oratory in 1849. His volumes of verse include *The Styrian Lake and Other Poems* (1842), *The Rosary and Other Poems* (1845) and *Hymns* (1848). His 150 *Collected Hymns* was published in 1862.

**fable** A short allegorical narrative relating the actions of anthropomorphized animals and objects and distinguished by a consciously derived moral. Traditionally the form is said to have originated with the work of Aesop, according to Herodotus a deformed Phrygian slave of the mid 6th century BC, but the earliest known fable is that of the hawk and the nightingale in the *Works and Days* of Hesiod (*c.* 8th century BC). The earliest attributable fables are the work of Phaedrus (*c.* AD 40) based on the lost collections of Demetrius Phalereus (4th century BC). The Latin fables of Phaedrus and the Greek collection of Babrius (2nd or 3rd century AD) led to the works of Avianus (4th century) and Romulus (10th century) on which the medieval pseudo-Aesopian collections are based. The oldest of these is the work of Marie de France (12th century). Single fables appear in English in *The Owl and the Nightingale*, *Piers Plowman* and **Chaucer**'s *Nun's Priest's Tale* (see *The Canterbury Tales*). Fables were also used as religious **exempla** and collected as such. The Aesopian collections of **Robert Henryson** (*The Morall Fabillis*) and **William Caxton** appeared at the end of the 15th century. Later writers of fables include **John Dryden**, **John Gay**, **Christopher Smart**, **William Cowper**, **George Orwell** and **James Thurber**.

*Fable for Critics, A* A verse satire by **James Russell Lowell**, first published anonymously in 1848. At a gathering on Olympus a critic is asked by Apollo to give an account of the state of letters in America. Those who come under his review are **Oliver Wendell Holmes**, **Ralph Waldo Emerson**, **Bronson Alcott**, **Henry Wadsworth Longfellow**, **William Cullen Bryant**, **Margaret Fuller**, **Washington Irving**, **John Greenleaf Whittier**, **Edgar Allan Poe**, **Nathaniel Hawthorne** and Lowell himself. Among the most acute of the critical portraits are those of Emerson ('A Greek head on right Yankee shoulders, whose range/Has Olympus for one pole, for t'other the Exchange'), Hawthorne ('There is Hawthorne, with genius so shrinking and rare/That you hardly at first see the strength that is there'), and Poe ('There comes Poe, with his raven, like Barnaby Rudge,/Three fifths of him genius and two fifths sheer fudge').

*Fable of the Bees, The* See **Mandeville, Bernard de**.

**fabliau** A medieval comic tale. The plot is usually about trickery and sex, and the viewpoint is cheerfully amoral, a disreputable character profiting and a respectable one suffering from the adventure. The genre first emerged in France in the late 12th century. English examples, which are all in verse, include **Chaucer**'s *The Miller's Tale* and *The Reeve's Tale* (see *The Canterbury Tales*) and the anonymous *Dame Sirith*.

*Faerie Queene, The* Edmund **Spenser**'s longest, most complex and greatest poem. The first three books appeared in 1590 with the author's epistle to his friend **Sir Walter Raleigh**, offering hints for interpretation of the work and indicating a plan of 12 books in all. The plan was apparently never completed. An edition of 1596 added Books IV–VI, while the first folio edition of the poem, published 10 years after Spenser's death, again added the two Mutability cantos, cautiously stating that they seemed to be part of some subsequent book of *The Faerie Queene*.

The main story is described in the letter to Raleigh as the quest of Arthur, who appears intermittently throughout, for Gloriana, who is one of the projections of Elizabeth in the poem

A woodcut from the first edition of the first three books of Spenser's *The Faerie Queene*, 1590.

as 'a most royal queen or empress'. The Queen also appears as Belphoebe, 'a most virtuous and beautiful lady', and in other guises.

Book I depicts the knight of holiness, Redcross, whose mission is to protect Una and free her besieged parents from a dragon. He is distracted by the magician Archimago and the disguised Duessa, imprisoned in the castle of the giant Orgoglio and freed by Arthur. As a penitent he is healed in the House of Celia, kills the dragon and finally marries Una. The book is concerned with the fate of the individual Christian seduced by false religion and finally triumphant with the assistance of truth. More topically it displays a Protestant bias against the falsehoods of Rome. Its incidents are heavily influenced by the Apocalypse and Protestant commentary on it.

In Book II, Guyon is the patron of temperance. Having established a Christian framework of reference in Book I, Spenser draws some of the ideas in this book from classical sources. Guyon's adventures depict an Aristotelian definition of virtue as the mean between defect and excess, and his voyage to Acrasia's Bower of Bliss is strongly coloured by the story of Odyss-

eus. Guyon's destruction of the Bower, which is a masterpiece of alluring sensuousness, has caused problems for those readers who see Spenser's poetic skill at odds with a moral intention.

In Book III both the narrative technique and the nature of the quest change. Britomart, the female knight of chastity, does not have the primary mission of destroying evil, but of finding Arthegall, her future husband. Interlaced with her story we find the beginnings of the stories of estranged lovers, Amoret and Scudamour, Florimell and Marinell. Centrally placed in this book is the fruitful Garden of Adonis. At the end of the book Britomart frees Amoret from the enchanter Busirane, and in the 1590 edition Amoret and Scudamour were reunited. Spenser changed the ending in 1596, to delay the reunion until the next book.

Book IV is the book of friendship. It continues the stories of the separated lovers from the previous book and reunites most of them. Britomart and Arthegall pledge their love, but their story is not concluded until Book V. Book IV, meanwhile, is taken up with the story of Cambel and Triamond and their respective loves for Cambina and Canacee, a complicated quartet of relationships which suggests the book's theme of concord. Concord and union are embodied in the lovers of Book III finding each other and the magnificent description of the marriage of the Thames and the Medway which completes the book.

Book V is the most topical. It concerns the quest of Arthegall, the knight of justice, to destroy the giant Grantorto and to rescue Irena. Its incidents allude to Elizabeth's dealings with the Netherlands, France, Spain and Ireland. The trial of Duessa by Mercilla in Canto ix provoked a complaint by James VI in 1596 that his mother, Mary Queen of Scots, was slandered in the person of Duessa. No action seems to have been taken, in spite of James's request that Spenser be tried and punished.

Book VI recounts the mission of Calidore, the knight of courtesy, to capture the Blatant Beast. Towards the end of the book, in a pastoral interlude, he stumbles across Colin Clout, the poet–shepherd of *The Shepheardes Calender*, piping to the three Graces dancing on Mount Acidale. Their triple movement of giving, receiving and giving again provides the pattern of courtesy for the book and its incidents. At the end of the book the Blatant Beast escapes from the world of the poem and threatens the poet's own work.

The Mutability cantos apparently contain no knight and no quest, and do not belong to the world of the preceding six books. They describe the threat of the giantess Mutability to claim the created universe as being under her sway. She is arraigned on Arlo Hill before Nature herself who enigmatically pronounces that the giantess is herself evidence of constancy and stability, since change itself is a constant phenomenon. In the last two stanzas the poet finally turns from this 'state of life so tickle' to contemplate eternity. The poem reaches its tremendous climax in a prayer to 'the God of Sabaoth'.

No account of *The Faerie Queene* can do justice to its variety, complexity and richness, and any critical approach must be, in the words of one of Spenser's recent editors, 'only incomplete'. Even Spenser's letter to Raleigh 'expounding his whole intention' is not an infallible guide. In both its poetic style and thought *The Faerie Queene* is syncretic. Spenser blends heroic poetry with **allegory**. The heroic models for the poem are distantly the epics of Homer and Virgil, while Spenser's immediate Italian predecessors are Ariosto and Tasso, especially Ariosto's *Orlando Furioso*. Spenser's stanzaic form varies Ariosto's **ottava rima** and adds a final **alexandrine** to produce the nine-lined Spenserian stanza which he bequeathed to later poets such as **Thomson** and **Byron**. The letter to Raleigh suggests an Aristotelian scheme of virtues, but the idealism of the poem and its assumption that the visible reflects abstractions has Platonic overtones. The poetic techniques include epic formulae, rhetorical devices and emblematic representations, and Spenser's sources for his imagery range from medieval descriptions of the virtues and vices to court pageants and **masques**. Some 19th-century readers admired the visual element in *The Faerie Queene* but found its moralism distasteful. Spenser would not have understood, for the work is a sustained example of the speaking pictures intended to delight and instruct that **Sidney** talks of in his *Apology for Poetry*.

Even so, the various meanings of the various pictures and narratives in *The Faerie Queene* are too dense to be easily unpacked. Thus Duessa may suggest falsehood, false religion, the Roman Catholic church, Mary Queen of Scots and many other meanings at different times, or more than one of those coexisting at one particular moment. As one medieval writer on allegory stated, the whole created world is a book and a picture and a mirror to mankind, offering divine truths. Spenser's imitation of a world offers images that multiply rather than delimit possible meanings.

**Fair Em, the Miller's Daughter of Manchester** See **Shakespeare apocrypha**.

**Fair Maid of Perth, The** See *Chronicles of the Canongate*.

**Fair Maid of the West, The** A romantic comedy in two parts, of which the first may have been performed before 1610 and the second

as late as 1630. The author was **Thomas Heywood**, whose best 'adventure' play it is.

The Earl of Essex's expedition is about to leave Plymouth for the Azores in 1597. Besse Bridges, 'the flower of Plymouth', is saved from molestation by Spencer; but he has the misfortune to kill the man while protecting Besse and has to flee the country. To provide for Besse he makes her the proprietress of the Windmill Tavern in Fowey. Spencer sails for the Azores, where his compulsive gallantry leads him to try and stop a quarrel; he is wounded and, apparently dying, sends a farewell to Besse, leaving all his property to her.

Besse fits out a ship to go to the Azores and bring Spencer's body back to England for burial. She finds him alive but a prisoner of the Spaniards. After many adventures, however, she rescues her gallant Spencer and they sail home to happiness.

**Fair Penitent, The** See *Fatal Dowry, The*.

**Fair Quarrel, A** A comedy by **Thomas Middleton** and **William Rowley**, published in 1617 and probably performed a year or two earlier.

Captain Ager challenges a fellow officer to a duel; he regards a comment made by the other as an insult to his mother's virtue. Before the duel takes place Ager visits his mother and recounts the incident to her, wanting to be certain that his fight will be justified. His mother is indignant at first but when she realizes that a duel will follow she wants to avert the danger to her son; she acknowledges the truth of the accusation.

Ager calls off the duel and his opponent brands him as a coward. He now has grounds for a confrontation and renews his challenge. He fights and wounds his opponent, who withdraws the charge of cowardice; the two are finally reconciled. The main story is supported

An illustration from the title-page of Middleton and Rowley's comedy, *A Fair Quarrel*, 1617.

by a bawdy sub-plot (probably the work of Rowley) but the principal interest of the drama lies in Ager's moral dilemma.

**Fairburn, A[rthur] R[ex] D[ugard]** 1904–57 New Zealand poet and personality. A journalist, radio scriptwriter and university tutor (in art history), he was a restless, ardent publicist for good causes (art galleries, New Zealand wine, good sewage) and a sharp satirist of small-minded prejudices of many kinds. His poetry veered from the satirical and epigrammatic to the lyric. His longer poems, about the identity of New Zealandness, are variable in quality, but develop an intensity of mood and colour of phrase which his shorter poems can only occasionally match. His lyricism easily became sentimental, and his humour could be crude. His best writing, though, is coolly meditative, and offers memorable phrasings of gnomic power. He began writing poems in the 1930s, along with friends such as **Denis Glover** and **R. A. K. Mason**. They shared a concern to establish a distinctively local voice and forms, though each took different routes to find them. Fairburn used some of Glover's ballad forms, and much of Mason's irony, while insisting on his own personal vision and idiom. *Dominion* (1938), which was reprinted in *Three Poems* (1952), and *Strange rendezvous* (1952) contain his best work. His *Collected Poems* appeared posthumously in 1966, and a selection of his letters in 1984.

**Fairfax, Edward** ?1568–1635 Translator and poet. He was born in Leeds, the illegitimate son of Sir Thomas Fairfax of Denton, Yorkshire, and was probably educated at Clare Hall, Cambridge. He was acclaimed for his translation of Tasso's *Gerusalemme Liberata*, retitled *Godfrey of Bulloigne* (1600). His other works, unpublished in his lifetime, include eclogues, epitaphs and *Daemonologia*, an account of witchcraft as sensationally practised upon his own family in 1621–3.

**Faithful Shepherdess, The** A pastoral comedy by **John Fletcher**, first produced about 1608 and published about 1610. The play did not succeed on the stage and is generally regarded as too undramatic for revival, being lengthy and devoted to a formal theme too thin to be called a plot. Nevertheless, it is acknowledged as a poetic masterpiece and Fletcher's finest work in this vein.

The faithful shepherdess of the title is Clorin, who has vowed fidelity to her dead lover and lives by his grave. She is skilled in the use of herbs, which she gathers for the good of others. Thenot is attracted by her exemplary devotion. Amarillis loves Perigot, who loves Amoret. Repulsed by Perigot, Amarillis tries to seduce him by assuming the form of Amoret. Cloe, the

wanton shepherdess, abandons the retiring Daphnis in favour of Alexis. The Sullen Shepherd is always ready to connive at the furtherance of lechery. Misunderstandings abound, while virtue and chastity are sorely tried.

**Falconer, William** 1732–69 Poet. Born in Edinburgh, the son of a barber, the young Falconer went to sea and was shipwrecked off the mainland of Greece. As a result, he wrote a narrative poem in rhyming couplets, *The Shipwreck*, published in 1762, which became popular and was admired by **Burns**. It was reprinted in 1764 and 1769, the year in which Falconer published *An Universal Dictionary of the Marine*, and was also drowned when the frigate *Aurora*, on which he was serving, went down in a gale.

**Falkland, Lucius Cary, 2nd Viscount** 1610–43 Royalist. Falkland had a house at Great Tew, near Oxford, which became the meeting place for a circle of thinkers and writers including **Ben Jonson**, **Thomas Carew** and **Edmund Waller**. He entered Parliament in 1639, where he argued forcibly for the preservation of the reformed Anglican church, for moderation and for the ideal of a constitutional monarchy. He was Secretary of State in 1642 when the Civil War broke out, though his strong desire for peace had already led him into disagreement with Charles I. **Clarendon**, who wrote a 'character' of Falkland, suggests that the outbreak of hostility left him permanently disillusioned. He was killed in the Battle of Newbury at the age of 33.

**William Godwin**, who probably learned of Falkland's career through Clarendon's account, borrowed his name for the flawed but noble character in his novel *Caleb Williams*.

**Falkner, J[ohn] Meade** 1858–1932 Novelist. Born in Wiltshire, the son of a clergyman, he was educated at Oxford before setting out on a successful career with the Armstrong-Whitworth armaments company. He was a book collector as well as an author in his spare time. His first novel, *The Lost Stradivarius* (1895), was soon eclipsed by his extremely popular *Moonfleet* (1898), an adventure story set in the 18th century and obviously indebted to **Stevenson**'s *Treasure Island*. Its young hero, John Trenchard, is an unwilling witness to smuggling in Dorset; kidnapped to Holland, he returns with a price on his head, still determined to clear his name. Nothing Falkner wrote afterwards had the same power. His last novel was lost in manuscript on a train journey.

**Fall of Princes, The** A poem by **John Lydgate** in rhyme royal and divided into nine books. Written between 1431 and 1439, it was the most popular and influential of his works. It tells the tragic stories of all the major historical and mythical figures from Adam to King John of France. The ultimate source is Boccaccio's *De Casibus Virorum Illustrium* (1355–60) but Lydgate relied upon an expanded French prose version by Laurent de Premierfait, *Des Cas des Nobles Hommes et Femmes* (1409). He adapted Premierfait, in particular adding 'envoys' apparently requested by his patron Humphrey, Duke of Gloucester, to offer a remedy to the ill fortune narrated. The philosophical content of the poem is confused, especially in its varying portrayal of Fortune as indiscriminate and as the agent of divine retribution. The work constantly looks back to **Geoffrey Chaucer**, whose *Monk's Tale* (see *The Canterbury Tales*) is its closest English analogue, mimicking the earlier poet's use of humour. The poem's value lies in its immense influence as a store of traditional and moral tales rather than in any intrinsic literary merit. It was also the inspiration for later works of a similar nature, most notably the *Mirror for Magistrates*.

**Fallon, Padraic** 1905–74 Irish poet and playwright. Born in Athenry, Co. Galway, and educated at St Joseph's College, Roscrea, he worked for many years as a customs official in Dublin and in Wexford. He wrote a large number of verse plays which were broadcast on Radio Éireann and published poems in a variety of periodicals. It was only with the collection *Poems*, published in the year of his death, that he was revealed as a writer of considerable stature. The neglect he suffered during his life has not yet been sufficiently repaired. His radio plays, largely treatments of legendary Gaelic material, are widely regarded as among the most successful of their kind; outstanding among them are *Diarmuid and Grainne* (broadcast 1950) and *The Vision of Mac Conglinne* (broadcast 1953). He also wrote plays for the stage, but neither these nor his radio plays have been published.

**Famous History of Sir Thomas Wyatt, The** A historical drama by **Thomas Dekker** and **John Webster**, published in 1607 and probably produced a few years before. The Wyatt of the title is the son of the poet **Sir Thomas Wyatt**. He raised an unsuccessful rebellion in 1554 against the accession and marriage of the Catholic Mary Tudor. Its failure led to his own execution and endangered the lives of those who might have been regarded as the focus for a new revolt.

**Fanny Hill** (*The Memoirs of a Woman of Pleasure*) See **Cleland, John**.

**Fanshawe, Lady Ann** See **Fanshawe, Sir Richard**.

**Fanshawe, Sir Richard** 1608–66 Poet and translator. The fifth son of Sir Henry Fanshawe

of Ware Park, Hertfordshire, the poet was educated at Thomas Farnaby's renowned Cripplegate school and at Jesus College, Cambridge, where he showed promise as both classical scholar and poet. A staunch Royalist, Fanshawe was active in Charles I's service, was Secretary of War to the future Charles II and was taken prisoner at the battle of Worcester in 1651. After the Restoration, he was elected MP for Cambridge University and subsequently sent as ambassador to Portugal and then to Spain. In 1666, shortly after receiving news of his recall, he died of an ague in Madrid. His widow, Lady Ann Fanshawe (1625–80), piously recorded his adventurous life in her *Memoirs*, written in 1676 but not published in full until 1829.

Fanshawe's most important literary work consists of his translations, published in 1647 and 1655 respectively, of Guarini's *Il Pastor Fido*, the most important Renaissance pastoral drama, and of Camoens's *Lusiadas*, the great Portuguese national epic, of which Fanshawe's is the first English version. His versatility and resourcefulness as a translator can also be seen in *Selected Parts of Horace* (1652), Mendoza's *Querer por Solo Querer* and *Fiestas de Aranjuez* (1654, published 1671) and his version, in Spenserian stanzas, of the fourth book of Virgil's *Aeneid*, published in 1648, together with shorter poems and translations, in the second edition of *Il Pastor Fido*. In 1658 he published *La Fida Pastora*, a Latin version of **John Fletcher**'s play *The Faithful Shepherdess*.

**Far from the Madding Crowd** A novel by **Thomas Hardy**, first published serially in *The Cornhill Magazine* between January and December 1874 and in volume form the same year. The first of Hardy's books to achieve popular success, it was also the first to use the name 'Wessex' for the fictional territory he adhered to in his subsequent novels and much of his poetry. The title is taken from **Gray**'s *Elegy Written in a Country Churchyard*.

Rejected by the capricious Bathsheba Everdene and financially ruined by his sheepdog driving his flock over a cliff, Gabriel Oak is forced off his land. Instrumental in quelling a fire at Bathsheba's farm, he is hired by her and soon rises from shepherd to bailiff. Unwisely, Bathsheba sends her neighbour, Farmer Boldwood, an anonymous valentine, which he takes so seriously as to fall in love with her. Meanwhile, the braggart Sergeant Troy has failed to marry the pregnant Fanny Robin because she went to the wrong church for the ceremony. Troy then courts Bathsheba and marries her secretly at Bath. But it is not a happy union and Troy, remorseful at Fanny's death in childbirth in the grim Casterbridge workhouse, leaves his wife and is mistakenly thought to be drowned; later he reappears as a member of a travelling

Troy at the coffin of Fanny Robin and her baby; Bathsheba looking on. An illustration by Helen Allingham for Hardy's *Far from the Madding Crowd*, serialized in *The Cornhill Magazine* in 1874.

circus in the West Country. However, believing him dead, Bathsheba accepts the frenetic attentions of Farmer Boldwood. Troy appears at their engagement party to claim his wife. This enrages Boldwood, who shoots Troy dead and then tries unsuccessfully to turn the gun on himself. Surrendering to the police, Boldwood is tried and condemned to execution, but his sentence is commuted to detention for life. Soon afterwards Oak, who has been overseeing the farms of Bathsheba and Boldwood, proposes for the second time and is accepted by her.

**Farah, Nuruddin** 1945– Somali novelist. Born in Baidoa, formerly part of Italian Somaliland, he has mastered at least five major languages as a consequence of his background and education: Somali, Amharic, Arabic, Italian and English. He went to school in Ethiopia and then attended the Istituto Magistrale di Mogadishu. His university education was in Chandigarh, India, and he then returned to Somalia where he taught in secondary schools and at the National University of Somalia. During this time he wrote in Somali as well as in English, following on the creation of a written form of the Somali language in the early 1970s. He had already had published one novel in English, *From a Crooked Rib* (1970), the study of a girl's resistance to the traditional life she is expected to lead in a nomadic Somali community. It has been hailed as one of the best portrayals of a woman in African fiction. It has been followed by several novels which present modern Somali society as a corrupt and repressive tyranny, including *A Naked Needle* (1976), *Sweet and Sour Milk* (1979), *Sardines* (1981), *Close Sesame* (1983) and *Maps* (1984). The middle three of these form a trilogy entitled *Variations on the Theme of an African Dictatorship*. Farah, who has not lived in Somalia since 1974, is increasingly seen as one of the major writers of Africa, as much for the quality of his characterization as for the acuity of his political and historical judgement.

**farce** Although 'farce' did not enter the English dramatic vocabulary until after the Restoration, its techniques were familiar from folk-drama, from the popular jigs of the Elizabethan theatre and from the more literary interludes of such 16th-century exponents as **John Heywood**. The word derives, by way of the French theatre, from the Latin *farcire*, 'to stuff', and must reflect, in part, the highbrow assumption that, while horseplay might enliven the theatrical event, it could be no more than the seasoning of something more serious in its totality. The broad comic episodes of **Marlowe**'s *Doctor Faustus* would be the model of this kind of farce, but the genre could not be so confined. It established an independent popularity with the audiences of the 18th and 19th century, who relished the scope it provided to outstanding comic actors. But the lowly status of farce in the hierarchy of drama delayed its development in England, where it was conventionally expected to last for a single act and to provide a colourful afterpiece to the long theatrical bill. It was the polish and artfulness of **Pinero**'s farces, of Brandon Thomas's isolated masterpiece *Charley's Aunt* and of **Wilde**'s *The Importance of Being Earnest* that established new possibilities. A mode in which obedience to its own internal logic takes precedence over extra-theatrical plausibility and in which extreme crisis for the characters is a source of hilarity for the audience permits an unusually direct challenge to conventional authority and even to the prevailing morality. A study of farce in the 20th century must take account, not only of **Ben Travers**, **Alan Ayckbourn** and **Noël Coward**, but also of **George Bernard Shaw**, **Tom Stoppard**, **Joe Orton**, **Peter Barnes** and **Beckett**'s *Waiting for Godot*.

***Farewell to Arms, A*** A novel by **Ernest Hemingway**, published in 1929. Set mainly in war-torn Italy of 1917–18, the story focuses on Frederic Henry, an American ambulance driver for the Italian army. He meets a young English nurse, Catherine Barkley, at a military hospital and they begin a relationship which gradually becomes passionate. When Frederic is severely wounded in an enemy mortar attack and is sent to Milan for surgery and therapy, Catherine follows him and obtains a nursing position in the hospital where he is being treated. Shortly before he is to return to active duty Catherine informs him that she is pregnant. The two decide not to marry (as their private commitment is deemed bond enough), but look forward to the birth of their first child.

Frederic returns to active duty but, following

disastrous engagements with Austrian forces, the Italians are compelled to retreat. Eventually, Frederic deserts and flees to neutral Switzerland with Catherine. In Montreux they enjoy an idyllic autumn and winter, remote from the direct impact of the war. In March 1918 Catherine gives birth, after a difficult labour and emergency surgery, to a stillborn son; she dies from complications soon after the birth. The story of the romance is set alongside a powerful portrayal of the horrors of war and its threat of the total destruction of civilization.

**Farjeon, Eleanor** 1881–1965 Children's writer. Born in Hampstead, she led an intensely literary and imaginative existence as a child, memorably recorded in her autobiography, *A Nursery in the Nineties* (1935). Never going to school, she wrote numerous stories and poems, some of which eventually appeared in *Nursery Rhymes of London Town* (1916). Her first novel, *Martin Pippin in the Apple Orchard* (1921), mixed prose with verse, each story steeped in folk-song and traditional country lore. Other successful publications for children included a play, *The Glass Slipper* (1944), written in conjunction with her brother Herbert. A collection of her best children's stories entitled *The Little Bookroom* (1955) won her both the Carnegie and the Hans Christian Andersen International Medal for services to children's literature. She was a close friend of **Edward Thomas**, and her *Edward Thomas: The Last Four Years* (1958) includes selections from their correspondence.

**Farnol, (John) Jeffery** 1878–1952 Novelist. Born in Warwickshire, he was educated privately and at the Westminster School of Art. He married an American and lived in the USA from 1902, working as a scene painter. He had begun to write when he was 19 but his first novel, *The Broad Highway*, did not appear until 1910. Its success enabled him to return to England and make writing his career, producing romantic cloak-and-dagger novels often set in the Georgian or Regency period. He is probably best remembered for *The Amateur Gentleman* (1913); other works include *Our Admirable Betty* (1918), *The Crooked Furrow* (1939), *The Happy Harvest* (1939) and *The Glad Summer* (1951).

**Farquhar, George** *c.* 1677–1707 Irish-born playwright whose work is often seen as the humane culmination of English Restoration comedy. Farquhar was born in Derry, attended Trinity College, Dublin, for a little over a year, worked for a Dublin bookseller and then as an actor at the Smock Alley Theatre, Dublin, and left for London in 1697. The last 10 years of his short life were spent in England, with the brief exception of a military campaign in Holland as a Lieutenant in the Militia (1700). He had been

encouraged to make the move to London by his actor-friend, Robert Wilks, who was instrumental in the staging at **Drury Lane** of Farquhar's first play, the derivative intrigue-comedy *Love and a Bottle* (1698). His second play, *The Constant Couple* (1699), brought the promise of fame. Contemporary audiences warmed particularly to Sir Harry Wildair, a Restoration libertine on the surface but in reality warmhearted and kindly. The part was created by Robert Wilks, but sustained a unique place in the theatrical repertoire for over a century as a breeches role for such outstanding actresses as Peg Woffington and Dorothy Jordan. Anxious to capitalize on the success of *The Constant Couple*, Farquhar wrote an untidy sequel, *Sir Harry Wildair* (1701), following it with an adaptation of **Fletcher**'s *The Wild Goose Chase* as *The Inconstant* (1702). With *The Twin-Rivals* (1702), he turned away from Restoration comedy towards the more demure morality of a theatre in retreat from **Jeremy Collier** and other reformists. The failure of this sentiment-laden comedy was only partially redeemed by the successful afterpiece, *The Stage Coach* (1704). Farquhar, who had married in 1703 only to find his wife not the heiress he had fondly hoped, joined the Grenadiers to support himself, her and the first of their two daughters. Out of his experience as a recruiting officer in the Midlands he wrote the first of his great comedies, **The Recruiting Officer** (1706). The vitality of this play, as of its brilliant successor, **The Beaux' Stratagem** (1707), owes more to its vigorous pursuit of the values of romantic love than to its occasional exercises in epigrammatic cynicism. In both plays Farquhar extends the range of Restoration comedy by removing it from a fashionable London setting to the fresher air of the provinces. It is a context that allows the celebration of the boisterousness of low and middle life in early 18th-century England. Despite the popularity of his last two plays, Farquhar died in poverty.

**Farrar, Frederick William** 1831–1905 Religious writer and author of books for children. Farrar was born in Bombay and educated at London University and Trinity Hall, Cambridge. As headmaster of Marlborough (1871–6) he was influenced by **Thomas Arnold**'s pioneering example at Rugby. He finally became Dean of Canterbury. Farrar published a large number of sermons and theological writings, including *The Life of Christ* (1874), but he was chiefly famous, and is now remembered, for his three heavily moralistic stories for children: *Eric, or, Little by Little* (1858), *Julian Home: A Tale of College Life* (1859) and *St Winifred's, or, The World of School* (1862).

**Farrell, J[ames] G[ordon]** 1935–79 Novelist.

Born in Liverpool and brought up in Ireland, Farrell contracted polio while a student at Oxford – an experience he later recapitulated in his second novel, *The Lung* (1965). His major achievement is his 'Empire trilogy', dramatizing episodes in the history of the British Empire. *Troubles* (1969) is set in Northern Ireland during the civil disturbances of the 1920s; *The Siege of Krishnapur* (1973), for which Farrell won the Booker Prize, covers the Indian Mutiny; and *The Singapore Grip* (1978) presents the fall of Singapore during World War II. Farrell's work combines a scrupulously researched historical verisimilitude with a Dickensian multiplicity of characters and exaggerated, quirky comedy. It is also richly symbolical, representing through the protracted physical decay and destruction of an embattled English-run Grand Hotel in *Troubles*, or the Collector's Residency in *Siege*, or the rubber traders' godowns in *Singapore Grip*, the progressive obsolescence and decline of the Empire. A subsequent novel about British India, *The Hill Station* (1981), was left unfinished at Farrell's untimely and accidental death while fishing.

**Farrell, James T[homas]** 1904–79 American novelist, born and educated in Chicago. He supported the Communist Party from 1932 to 1935, but was one of the first American intellectuals to break with it over the totalitarian character of Stalin's regime. The work for which he is best known, *The Studs Lonigan Trilogy*, began to appear in 1932 with the publication of *Young Lonigan: A Boyhood in Chicago Streets*. Set on the South Side of Chicago, the novel charts the effects of middle-class morality and adult corruption on the young protagonist, the son of an Irish house-painter, who soon learns the way of life of the street corner and the poolroom. *The Young Manhood of Studs Lonigan* (1934) and *Judgment Day* (1935) continue the story of Studs's violent and dissolute life until his death from a heart attack at the age of 29. The trilogy is a powerful indictment of the American Dream – the belief that it requires only individual initiative to achieve wealth, status and, above all, happiness – and it registers this indictment through a series of failures: the failure of urban industrialism to provide an adequate moral vision; the failure of the twin mythologies of Church and Nation to sustain an understanding of a hostile world; and the failure of Studs, inculcated with these broken ideals, to develop his potential.

Farrell's second series of novels was in five volumes: *A World I Never Made* (1936), *No Star is Lost* (1938), *Father and Son* (1940), *My Days of Anger* (1943) and *The Face of Time* (1953). Linked thematically with those of the earlier trilogy, these novels revolve around the contrasted lives of two families, the middle-class

O'Flahertys and the working-class O'Neills. A third series – *Bernard Clare* (1946), *The Road Between* (1949) and *Yet Other Waters* (1952) – chronicles the difficulties faced by radical literary intellectuals after World War II.

Farrell's subsequent work marked a new departure. Though he continued to believe in struggles for freedom, he rejected Marxist–Trotskyite politics. (In the 1950s he became associated with the anti-Communist American Committee for Cultural Freedom, but resigned when he learned that it was funded by the CIA.) A series from this period, known as *A Universe of Time*, offers an account of an aspiring young writer in the 1920s. Books in the series are *The Silence of History* (1963), *What Time Collects* (1964), *When Time Was Born* (1966), *Lonely for the Future* (1966), *A Brand New Life* (1968), *Judith* (1969) and *Invisible Swords* (1970). Among the other books published by Farrell during his prolific career are *A Note on Literary Criticism* (1936), *Ellen Rogers* (1941), *The League of Frightened Philistines and Other Papers* (1945), *This Man and This Woman* (1951), *An Omnibus of Short Stories* (1956), *Boarding House Blues* (1961), *Selected Essays* (1964), *New Year's Eve/1929* (1967) and *The Dunne Family* (1976).

*Fashion* A comedy by **Anna Cora Mowatt**, first performed in New York City in 1845. Mr and Mrs Tiffany, newly rich, have established themselves in an opulent house in New York, but Mrs Tiffany's remorseless pursuit of fashion outruns her husband's resources. He takes to forgery to cover his expenses, but is discovered and blackmailed by his clerk, Snobson, to whom he is forced to promise his daughter Seraphina, even though her fortune has attracted the affections of Count Jolimaitre. At the last minute Tiffany is saved by his honest friend, Adam Trueman, who sees that Snobson is packed off to the remoteness of California and who exposes Jolimaitre as a fraud, the lover of Mrs Tiffany's maid.

**Fast, Howard** 1914– American novelist. Fast was born in New York City; during the 1940s and 1950s he became known for a series of novels which reflected his left-wing politics. Many of them were set during the American Revolution, and all displayed a strong sense of class consciousness: for example, *Conceived in Liberty* (1930), *The Unvanquished* (1942), *Citizen Tom Paine* (1943), *The Proud and the Free* (1950) and *April Morning* (1961). Other works which focus on particular moments in the history of the USA include *The Last Frontier* (1941), about the 1878–9 campaign against the Cheyenne Indians; and *Freedom Road* (1944), dealing with black Southern legislators in the Reconstruction period. *The American* (1946) is about Illinois governor John Peter Altgeld, and *Clarkton*

(1947) details the events of a recent strike in a Massachusetts mill-town. Fast is also the author of numerous historical novels set in ancient times, including *My Glorious Brothers* (1948), set in ancient Israel; *Spartacus* (1951), about a Roman slave revolt; *Moses, Prince of Egypt* (1958); and *Agrippa's Daughter* (1964). *The Naked God* (1957), a work of non-fiction, tells of Fast's disenchantment with the Communist Party during the Stalinist era. His most recent novels include *The Immigrants* (1977), *The Second Generation* (1978), *The Establishment* (1979), *The Outsider* (1984) and *Immigrant's Daughter* (1985). Under the pseudonym E. V. Cunningham he also has written more than a dozen novels of suspense and mystery.

**Fatal Curiosity, The** A tragedy by **George Lillo**, first produced at the **Haymarket Theatre** in May 1736 and published in the same year. Like his other better-known tragedy, *The London Merchant*, it deals with the lives of humble people, but is written in blank verse rather than prose. The play is set in Jacobean England and is based on an old story of murder in Cornwall. The Wilmots are an elderly couple reduced to poverty; at the prompting of his wife, the old man murders a stranger who has deposited a casket with them. The dead man turns out to be their son, whom the couple had believed to be drowned at sea.

Lillo's play was the inspiration for the German dramatist Friedrich Werner in his *Die Vierundswanzigste Februar* (1810), and Albert Camus handled the same theme in *Le Malentendu* (1945).

**Fatal Dowry, The** A tragedy by **Philip Massinger** and **Nathan Field**. It was first published in 1632 and only a corrupt text exists. The exact date of its first performance is not known.

Charalois's father, an old soldier distinguished for his service as marshal to the Duke of Burgundy, fell on hard times and died in a debtor's prison. Charalois cannot claim his father's body for burial until the debts are settled; but the creditors accept his offer to enter prison as succeeding debtor and release the old soldier's body for an honourable funeral. Charalois goes to prison with his friend, the soldier Romont. Charalois's loyalty to his father's memory and Romont's loyalty to his friend move Rochfort, former president of the Parliament, to help them; he procures their release and gives Charalois his daughter's hand in marriage.

The daughter, Beaumelle, is still attracted to a former suitor; one day Romont comes upon her and Novall embracing. Charalois is reluctant to believe his friend; but he surprises the lovers together, kills Novall in a duel, then calls on Rochfort to judge his daughter. Beaumelle is found guilty by her father whereupon Charalois kills her. Rochfort, shocked by Charalois's lack of mercy, hands him over to justice as a double murderer. Charalois is acquitted, but is killed in revenge by a friend of Novall.

**Nicholas Rowe** refashioned the play as *The Fair Penitent*; it was produced in May 1703 and first published in the same year. The characters have different names and the emphasis lies with the dilemma of Calista (Beaumelle), given to Altamont (Charalois) by her father Sciolto (Rochfort); she is unable to end her liaison with Lothario (Novall) and is observed by Horatio (Romont) in her guilt. The character of Lothario is completely different; he is still a libertine but Novall was no more than a meanspirited dandy in the earlier play. Calista is the fair penitent of the title and the end of the play finds her both sorry and reconciled. **David Garrick** played Lothario with great success and Calista was one of Sara Siddons's famous roles. **Samuel Johnson** much admired Rowe's play, which held the stage for over a century.

**Fatal Marriage, The**, or, *The Innocent Adultery* A tragedy by **Thomas Southerne**, first produced in February 1694 and published the same year. It was based on a novel by **Aphra Behn**, *The Nun, or, The Perjur'd Beauty* (1688?). The play was revived, somewhat altered, by **David Garrick** as *Isabella, or, The Fatal Marriage*.

**Father and Son** See **Gosse, Sir Edmund (William)**.

**Faulkner, William (Cuthbert)** 1897–1962 American novelist. Faulkner was born in New Albany, Mississippi, into a family which had played a prominent role in the history of the South. His grandfather had served as a colonel in the Confederate army, and had come home to pursue a career as a lawyer, politician, railroad builder and civic benefactor. The strict family code of honour, its sense of white social status and its often violent exploits would provide a good deal of material for Faulkner's fiction. When he was five the family moved to Oxford, Mississippi, which became his permanent home. He left high school in 1915 and took a clerical job at his grandfather's bank. In 1918, after being rejected by the US military because he was too short, he enlisted in the Royal Canadian Air Force, but the war ended while he was still in training, and he returned to Oxford. He enrolled as a special student at the University of Mississippi, and published poems and drawings in student magazines. His first book, a collection of poems entitled *The Marble Faun*, was published in 1924.

His first novel, *Soldiers' Pay*, was written in New Orleans in 1925 and published in the following year. The story centres on the return of a soldier who has been physically and psychologically disabled in World War I, and

William Faulkner, 1950

early novels in that it does not concentrate on a single family, but it involves similar issues of human need, dissatisfaction, crisis, and redemption through endurance. Also set in Yoknapatawpha county, it broadens the social scope of Faulkner's fiction through the attention it pays to the individual's sense of place in a racist society.

In 1929 Faulkner married Estelle Oldham Franklin, and in the following year purchased the traditional pillared house in Oxford which he named Rowan Oak. His fiction, however, enjoyed no more than mediocre sales, and he was frequently in financial straits. To earn money over the next 20 years he worked periodically as a scriptwriter in Hollywood. Among his more notable credits are versions of **Ernest Hemingway**'s *To Have and Have Not* (1945) and **Raymond Chandler**'s *The Big Sleep* (1946). His next novel, *Pylon* (1935), treats another of his strong interests, aviation, focusing on the lives of four adults and a child who travel nomadically from air show to air show to compete in races. He returned to Yoknapatawpha county with **Absalom, Absalom!** (1936), which concerns the frustrated attempts of Thomas Sutpen to found a Southern dynasty in 19th-century Mississippi. Sutpen's story is reconstructed by Quentin Compson, one of the characters in *The Sound and the Fury*, who is obsessed by the way in which the South's guilt in the matter of interracial relationships is embodied in the misfortunes of the Sutpen family. Following *The Unvanquished* (1938), *The Wild Palms* (1939) and *The Hamlet* (1940) – the first of three novels about the Snopes family – came *Go Down Moses* (1942), a novel composed of several interrelated stories about Southern blacks. One of these, 'The Bear', is among Faulkner's most frequently reprinted pieces. *Intruder in the Dust* (1948) tells the story of Lucas Beauchamp, a black man who is unjustly accused of murder but who is eventually acquitted despite the racial prejudice that permeates society. Faulkner was elected to the American Academy of Arts and Letters in 1949, and was awarded the Nobel Prize for literature in the following year. His *Collected Stories* (1950) received a National Book Award in 1951.

*Requiem for a Nun* (1951), a sequel to *Sanctuary*, offers a less brutal treatment of sexual themes than its horrifying predecessor. As his Nobel Prize address made clear, Faulkner wanted his new work to be more affirmative, more insistent on the power of humankind to endure and to prevail. The change of tone is reflected in *A Fable* (1954), an allegory of the story of Jesus in a World War I setting which won a Pulitzer Prize in 1955. *The Town* (1957) and *The Mansion* (1959) complete the Snopes family trilogy – a penetrating examination of the social fabric of the South. Faulkner's final novel, *The Reivers* (1962), which also won a Pulitzer Prize, is a

whose subsequent illness and death change the lives of his family and friends. Faulkner's second novel, *Mosquitoes* (1927), set in New Orleans, is a satirical tale about a group of Southern artists and intellectuals. His next novel was the first to be set in the fictional Mississippi county of Yoknapatawpha, which was to provide the setting for many of his best-known works. Originally called *Flags in the Dust*, it was rejected for publication but later accepted in an edited version, retitled *Sartoris*, and published in 1929. (The uncut *Flags in the Dust* finally appeared in 1973.)

Faulkner's most productive period began with **The Sound and the Fury** (1929), about another Yoknapatawpha county family, in which he experimented with narrative technique by using multiple points of view. Perhaps due to its fragmented, non-chronological structure, it met with only limited success. **As I Lay Dying** (1930) was still more splintered in form, being composed of 59 monologues by a variety of characters which gradually reveal the intricate ties that bind and frustrate the poor-white Bundren family of Yoknapatawpha county. In an effort to win a popular audience, Faulkner wrote *Sanctuary* (1931), which was in fact an even more controversial work than its predecessors because of its graphic description of a horrific rape. With its more conventional form, however, it sold well amid the scandal it aroused. **Light in August** (1932) differs from his other mildly comic portrait of some of the characters introduced in his earlier books. He died in the year of its publication. His other works include *Knight's Gambit* (1949), a collection of detective stories; *Uncollected Stories of William Faulkner* (1979); and a collection of poems originally written for his wife, *Vision in Spring* (1984). This last is one of several books which Faulkner wrote to present as gifts; another is the allegorical story *Mayday* (written 1926, published 1976), about the adventures of a medieval knight.

**Fauset, Jessie R[edmon]** 1882–1961 Black American novelist and editor, born in New Jersey, and educated at Cornell and the Sorbonne. While editor of **W. E. B. Du Bois**'s magazine *Crisis*, she encouraged and published many of the new writers who constituted the **Harlem Renaissance**. She herself wrote four novels, all depicting the experience of black women, and all asserting the need to accept one's heritage rather than to escape it: *There is Confusion* (1924), *Plum Bun* (1929), *The Chinaberry Tree* (1931) and *Comedy: American Style* (1934).

**Fearing, Kenneth (Flexner)** 1902–61 American poet, born in Oak Park, Illinois, and educated at the University of Wisconsin. His first collection, *Angel Arms*, appeared in 1929 and defined the focus of much of his work: an urban and mechanized society lacking in human compassion. Among his other volumes are *Dead Reckoning: A Book of Poetry* (1938), *Afternoon of a Pawnbroker and Other Poems* (1943), *Stranger at Coney Island and Other Poems* (1948) and *New and Selected Poems* (1956). He also wrote several novels, including *The Hospital* (1939) and *The Big Clock* (1946).

**Federal Theatre Project** Founded in 1935 as a branch of President Franklin Delano Roosevelt's Works Project Administration, the Federal Theatre Project was intended to provide employment for out-of-work actors and theatrical workers, and to create a censorship-free forum for innovative productions. Under the directorship of Hallie Flanagan, the project mounted approximately 1000 shows in 30 states, varying from children's plays to dance productions to classic plays to a jazz version of **Gilbert** and Sullivan's *The Mikado* to a Voodoo *Macbeth*. Altogether it employed over 10,000 people, including E. G. Marshall, Burt Lancaster, Orson Welles, John Houseman, and **Langston Hughes**. Some of the most controversial offerings were the 'Living Newspapers', the documentary-style dramas originated by **Elmer Rice** in New York. Censorship in fact plagued many of the Project's productions, such as Welles and Houseman's version of **Marc Blitzstein**'s leftist musical drama, *The Cradle Will Rock*

(1937). Continuing conservative opposition to the radical nature of such productions brought about the abolition of the entire Project by Congress in 1939.

**Feinstein, Elaine** 1930– Novelist, poet and translator. Born in Bootle and brought up in Leicester, where she attended Wyggeston Grammar School, she read English at Newnham College, Cambridge. From 1960 to 1962 she worked for Cambridge University Press and from 1967 to 1970 she was assistant lecturer at the University of Essex.

Her first novel, *The Circle* (1970), examines a woman's attempt to reconcile her need for independence with her desire for everything that marriage might bring. Its successors include *The Amberstone Exit* (1972), in which dreams, images and memories pass through the mind of a woman about to give birth, and *The Survivors* (1982), an epic by comparison to her usually short fiction, which incorporates part of her own history into the story of two Jewish families who escaped from Russia at the turn of the century. Her latest novel is *The Border* (1984). Volumes of poetry include *The Celebrants and Other Poems* (1973), *Some Unease and Angels* (1977) and *Feast of Eurydice* (1980). Feinstein has also published highly acclaimed translations of the poems of Marina Tsvetayeva (1971) and from the work of Margaret Aliger, Yunna Moritz and Bella Akhmadulina (1978). *A Captive Lion*, her biography of Tsvetayeva, appeared in 1987.

***Felix Holt, the Radical*** A novel by **George Eliot**, first published in 1866.

Relinquishing thoughts of a materially rewarding life, the respectably educated Felix Holt returns to his native village in North Loamshire and pursues the humble trade of watch and clock-keeping in order to maintain his needy mother. He is a forceful young man of honour and integrity, burning to participate in political life so that he may improve the lot of his fellow artisans and encourage them to assert themselves. Contrasted with Felix Holt is the intelligent, economically secure Harold Transome, just returned from the Middle East to assume responsibility for Transome Court, the local manor-house rapidly falling into decay. A good businessman and a widower with a small son, Transome intends to enter Parliament as a Liberal, thus taking up a political position contrary to the family's traditional Toryism. He is opposed to the questionable electioneering practices of the time – the early 1830s – and his growing disdain for his agent, the dishonest lawyer Jermyn, forms an important narrative line in the book. Much action in *Felix Holt* centres upon the hustings and the drunken behaviour of the mob, whose violent activities

Felix Holt tries unsuccessfully to quell. For his efforts he receives a four-year prison sentence for alleged manslaughter. Both Felix Holt and Harold Transome vie for the hand of Esther, supposed daughter of the quixotic Dissenting minister, Rufus Lyon. A young woman of charm and virtue, Esther has a legitimate claim, through a long legal rigmarole, to the Transome estates, but she resigns it shortly before marrying Felix Holt. The narrative is enhanced by character studies of Harold Transome's mother and the corrupt political agent Johnson, as well as by the lesser figures of Mr Christian, Sir Maximus Debarry and the loyal servant Denner.

*Female Quixote, The* See **Lennox, Charlotte**.

**feminist criticism** The past two decades have seen a marked growth of interest in feminist literary studies. It is possible to distinguish four main lines of approach. Firstly, there is the rediscovery of works by forgotten women writers, novels and poems which have often had to wait until now for a modern reprint and a properly informed readership. Several publishers (e.g. Virago, Pandora, The Women's Press) have built up impressive lists of such work and laid the ground for a major reassessment of the place of women writers in literary history. Critics have played their part by interpreting the texts, filling in the background detail and – not least – explaining how it is that a dominant male tradition has effectively written them out of its purview. It is no longer a question of admitting a few women (**Jane Austen**, the **Brontës, George Eliot**) as remarkable exceptions to the rule, and otherwise tracing the 'rise of the novel' through a series of great male writers.

The second approach is through the reinterpretation of women's experience as reflected in various kinds of writing. This means identifying explicitly with female characters, often against the grain of a dominant ideology which tends to distort, repress or simply ignore that experience. Thus feminist critics propose new readings of familiar texts, readings that challenge the established (male) idea of how women are supposed to think, feel or act. This has led to some powerful revisionist accounts of 19th-century fiction, rejecting (for instance) the typecast notion of female 'hysteria' as a weakness peculiar to heroines like Maggie Tulliver in *The Mill on the Floss*.

This raises the obvious question: is there such a thing as 'feminine writing', marked by certain characteristic features of language or style? Some feminists would endorse this idea, arguing that women have access to a realm of experience from which male language is effectively debarred. **Virginia Woolf** spoke of a 'woman's sentence', a mode of writing as yet barely glimpsed in occasional, fragmentary forms but holding out the promise of deliverance from male habits of thought. The distribution of character-roles in her fiction clearly supports this idea, with the men often trapped in a grimly repressive, 'rational' way of thinking while the women enjoy a much greater freedom of intuitive sympathy and grasp. More recently, certain French critics (among them Luce Irigaray and Hélène Cixous) have developed the theme of an *écriture féminine*, a departure from standard language patterns. When women write they are in touch with libidinal energies and drives which can find no place in the regimented discourse of male (patriarchal) reason. Men may perhaps gain access to such writing, and may even themselves *produce* it in certain rare cases. It could be argued that Molly Bloom's soliloquy of unpunctuated **stream-of-consciousness** prose, which ends **James Joyce**'s *Ulysses*, is a more striking example of *écriture féminine* than anything to be found in Virginia Woolf.

Other feminists reject the very notion of some essential difference between male and female writing. They point out that any politics based on this idea will run the risk of simply inverting the old, hierarchical distinction between male and female, leaving its terms still securely in place. For these critics, sexual difference is a matter of biological fact and nothing more. Culture establishes gender-roles which condition men and women to behave differently and accept a dominant patriarchal order. This extends to the politics of writing and reading. Thus women in fiction are typically assigned to a passive or typecast role, reflecting conventional male ideas of female psychology or nature. Such criticism can take various forms. It may focus on the clearly marked sexist assumptions of an author like **Ernest Hemingway**, his habit of casting women characters either as young, desirable and empty-headed, or as archetypal earth-mother figures, no longer posing a seductive threat. In each case the woman serves merely to bolster a sense of security and power in the male protagonist.

Another line of argument is well represented by Judith Fetterly's book *The Resisting Reader*. As the title suggests, Fetterly is most interested in the way women read and – more specifically – the way they read texts (like those of Hemingway or **Henry Miller**) which are drastically reductive of female 'nature' and experience. A feminist approach to such texts would interpret them very consciously against the grain, refusing to be a passive (unresisting) reader. And this feminist approach would extend beyond works of literature to the whole domain of culture where women are often coerced into false or contradictory positions. Thus *The Sun* newspaper in Britain has a large female readership, despite its overtly sexist treatment of woman as a mere commodity or object of mass-produced male fantasy. That such crude examples are not so remote from the high ground of literary culture is one of the main lessons to be learned from present-day feminist criticism.

**Fenton, Sir Geoffrey** ?1539–1608 Translator. He campaigned in Ulster and took an active part in the administration there. He had Elizabeth's confidence and she interceded personally on one occasion to release him from the debtors' prison in Dublin. His *Certain Tragical Discourses* (1567) were translations of stories, originally by Bandello, from Belleforest's French version. Fenton's version is loaded with rhetorical devices, proverbs and maxims. *Golden Epistles* (1575) is a similar work, a translation of pieces gathered from Guevara and other authors. His major work is a translation of the Italian historian Guicciardini's *La Historia d'Italia*, again from a French version, as *The History of Guicciardin Concerning the Wars of Italy* (1597).

**Fenton, James** 1949– Poet and journalist. Born in Lincoln and educated in Durham and at Magdalen College, Oxford, Fenton won the Newdigate Prize for poetry. He worked as a journalist in England, Indo-China and Germany before becoming theatre critic for *The Sunday Times*. His first collection was *Terminal Moraine* (1972), but his reputation so far rests on *The Memory of War* (1982), poems based on his experience as a war reporter, which were well received and compared to the early **Auden**.

**Ferdinand Count Fathom, The Adventures of** A novel by **Tobias Smollett**, published in 1753. His third novel, it is by no means among his stronger works, but it is notable for moving away from the **picaresque** and anticipating features of the **Gothic novel**.

The child of a camp-follower to Marlborough's army, Ferdinand is an amoral, self-seeking villain. He adopts the title of Count Fathom and a benevolent German nobleman, Count de Melville, receives him into his family. Ferdinand hopes to marry the Count's daughter but fails. He turns to plundering the Count's house with the help of the daughter's maid. He cheats Renaldo, the Count's son, and tries to seduce his fiancée, Monimia. She escapes his attentions by feigning death. Eventually Ferdinand's wickedness is revealed and Monimia is restored to Renaldo. Ferdinand is saved from punishment when Renaldo relents towards him, and as a result he reforms.

**Ferguson, Adam** 1723–1816 Philosopher and historian. Born at Logierait in Perthshire and educated for the ministry at the universities of St Andrews and Edinburgh, Ferguson served in the Black Watch regiment before succeeding **David Hume** in the library of the Faculty of Advocates. At Edinburgh University he was successively Professor of Natural Philosophy, of Moral Philosophy and of Mathematics. His *Essay on the History of Civil Society*, which received favourable notice when it was published in 1767, attributed social decline to the failure of citizens to play their due part in public affairs. *The History of the Progress and Termination of the Roman Republic* (1783) provided a carefully designed introduction to **Gibbon**'s great work on the Roman Empire.

**Ferguson, Sir Samuel** 1810–86 Poet and antiquary. The son of a Scots–Irish family, Ferguson was born in Belfast and educated at Trinity College, Dublin. Later he studied law and was called to the Bar in 1838; he became a Queen's Counsel in 1859. A scholar and antiquary, Ferguson became Deputy Keeper of the Irish Records in 1867; he had published his first poems in 1861 and more were to be published by his widow after his death. He was knighted in 1878.

Ferguson was not himself a poet of great distinction. His contribution to literature was his part in the restoration, from the original Irish, of the ancient literature which had been lost to generations brought up and taught in another language. *Lays of the Western Gael* (1864) contained 'The Tain-Quest', his version of the *Táin Bó Cúailgne* (The Cattle Raid of Cooley), and brought back to poetic circulation the myth of Cuchulain and the redoubtable Queen, Maev of Connaught. Other poems concerned Fergus, Conor, Deirdra and Dermid (in Ferguson's spelling). *Congal* (1872) is a poem on the last heroic stand of Celtic paganism against triumphant Christianity. Among other works by Ferguson were *Deirdra* (1880), *The Forging of the Anchor* (1883) and *Ogham Inscriptions in Ireland, Wales and Scotland* (1887). A collection of his prose tales was edited by Lady Ferguson and published as *Hibernian Nights' Entertainment* (1887).

**Fergusson, Robert** 1750–74 Scottish poet. Fergusson was born in Edinburgh, attended the High School for three years and then studied for two years at Dundee University on a bursary. He went to St Andrews University as a divinity student but had to leave after four years because of his father's money troubles. He succeeded in getting work as a copier in the Commissary Clerk's office, where he stayed for the rest of his short life.

Fergusson's first poems were lyrics to Scots airs but they were written in imitation of English styles; he did not find his true voice until he turned to the vernacular. Walter Ruddiman, proprietor of *The Weekly Magazine, or*

*Edinburgh Amusement*, published Fergusson's *The Daft Days* in January 1772 and became the poet's patron. Gifted with wit and the ability to make friends, Fergusson became sought after in Edinburgh literary circles but, early in 1774, he fell victim to religious mania. He died insane in October of that year, at the age of 24.

Fergusson was the poet of Edinburgh, the smoky city to which he gave a nickname in his most famous poem, *Auld Reekie*, which traces the progress of an Edinburgh day. He was the most notable Scots poet of the 18th century before **Burns**, who admired him, learned from his work and sometimes feared his own career might come to the same premature and unhappy end.

**Ferlinghetti, Lawrence** 1919– American poet and publisher. Born in New York City and educated at the University of North Carolina, at Columbia and at the Sorbonne, Ferlinghetti played a major role in the **Beat** movement of the 1950s. With Peter D. Martin he founded City Lights in San Francisco, America's first all-paperback bookstore. As publishers of City Lights Books and the Pocket Book Series, Martin and Ferlinghetti made available the work of such poets as **Gregory Corso**, **Allen Ginsberg** and **Denise Levertov**.

Ferlinghetti's work is experimental in form and often light or satiric in tone; underlying it, however, is a clear interest in social and cultural issues, and it frequently attacks American values and political policies. His first book of poetry was *Pictures from the Gone World* (1955), others include *A Coney Island of the Mind* (1958), *Starting from San Francisco* (1961, revised 1967), *The Secret Meaning of Things* (1969), *Open Eye, Open Heart* (1973) and *Landscapes of Living and Dying* (1979). His recent volumes include *The Populist Manifestos* (1981) and *Endless Life: The Selected Poems* (1981).

**Ferrar, Nicholas** 1592–1637 Scholar and founder of the Little Gidding community. Born in London, Ferrar entered Clare College, Cambridge, in 1605 and became a fellow in 1610. A brilliant scholar, he travelled on the Continent for five years before entering Parliament in 1624. His religious aspirations led him to retire to Little Gidding, an estate near Huntingdon belonging to his mother, where he was joined by his brother and brother-in-law and their families, and they established a community life based on Church of England principles. In 1626 he was ordained a deacon by **Laud**, and the community of some 30 people lived an ordered life of prayer and active good works. The Puritans denounced it as an attempt to reintroduce Catholic practices in England; a Parliamentary raid in 1646 ended Little Gidding.

Ferrar's manuscripts were destroyed, so his only surviving writings are his published translations of Lessius' treatise *On Temperance* and Valdez's *Divine Considerations*, the latter with notes by **George Herbert**, a close friend who entrusted Ferrar with the publication of his poems. For Little Gidding, see also *John Inglesant* and *Four Quartets*.

**Ferrier, Susan (Edmonstone)** 1782–1854 Novelist. The daughter of an Edinburgh official, who was a colleague of **Sir Walter Scott**, Susan Ferrier led a quiet life, managing her father's household after her mother's death. She knew the literary society of Edinburgh through her father's friends and was warmly esteemed by Sir Walter Scott. Her three novels of Scottish life – *Marriage* (1818), *The Inheritance* (1824) and *Destiny* (1831) – mix comedy resembling **Jane Austen**'s with explicit didacticism.

**Field, Nathan** 1587–*c.* 1620 Elizabethan actor and playwright, the son of a Puritan clergyman who must have deplored his theatrical career. Field was educated at St Paul's School, and became a chorister in about 1600. It was as a boy actor in the early years of the 17th century that he made his reputation. Praised by **Ben Jonson**, in many of whose plays he acted, Field graduated to membership of adult companies, ending his acting career as a member of the **King's Men**.

Field's two London comedies, *A Woman Is a Weather-Cock* (*c.* 1609) and *Amends for Ladies* (*c.* 1610), are fashionably bawdy. He is known to have collaborated with **Massinger** in *The Fatal Dowry* (*c.* 1618) and with **Fletcher** in several plays, including *The Honest Man's Fortune* (1613) and *The Knight of Malta* (*c.* 1618). That Field shared some of the soaring ambition of his most famous acting role, the hero of **Chapman**'s *Bussy d'Ambois*, is suggested by his involvement with the Countess of Argyll, by whom he is supposed to have had a child.

**Fielding, Henry** 1707–54 Novelist and dramatist. Born of aristocratic descent, at Sharpham Park, Somerset, Fielding was educated at Eton and went to London to pursue legal studies during the late 1720s. Because of a disputed inheritance he was short of money, and his chief aspiration was to become a playwright. He briefly attended Leyden University but returned to London, where he wrote some 25 plays between 1728 and 1737. These were various and accomplished in nature, not depending upon the prevailing fashion for tired, Restoration-style dramas but embracing several forms, from the **ballad opera** to the conventional five-act comedy.

He had an early success with *Tom Thumb: a Tragedy*, produced at the **Haymarket Theatre** in April 1730 and in a revised version the following

Henry Fielding, by Hogarth, drawn from memory after the novelist's death.

year as *The Tragedy of Tragedies*, where it enjoyed a long run of practically 40 nights. It is a blank-verse burlesque of the traditions of heroic drama set in an absurd court of King Arthur and offering a humorous attack on Sir Robert Walpole. As with Fielding's other satirical plays, it is dense with contemporary allusions and classical echoes, which is why they are nowadays seldom revived; his *Pasquin* (1736), though, is an entertaining 'Rehearsal' piece that offers some modern potential. *The Historical Register for the Year 1736*, another dramatic satire, was produced in 1737, the year in which the authorities determined to stem the flow of political jibes appearing on stage and introduced the Licensing Act to impose censorship on the production of plays.

So in 1737, at the age of 30, Fielding cast around to discover new outlets for his witty inventiveness. He had a wife to support, having married in 1734 Charlotte Cradock, who was later to provide the model for two of his fictional heroines. He resumed his legal studies (eventually being called to the Bar in 1740) and also applied himself to a spell of political journalism. He edited *The Champion* from November 1739 to June 1741, a thrice-weekly publication

in which under the pseudonym of Captain Hercules Vinegar he continued to oppose Walpole's government. After the latter's fall, Fielding edited *The True Patriot* (November 1745 to June 1746) and then the burlesque *Jacobite's Journal* from December 1747 until November 1748, a platform for his strongly Hanoverian views, following the Jacobite Rebellion of 1745.

Fielding was a good stylistic mimic, and adept at literary parody. The popularity of **Samuel Richardson**'s *Pamela, or, Virtue Rewarded* (1740) prompted him in the following year to reply in print with a skilful parodic squib entitled *Shamela* (1741), which makes the innocent virtue of Richardson's original heroine appear scheming. Fielding followed up this idea with his first – and funniest – novel *Joseph Andrews* (1742) in which the central character is Pamela's brother. The shapely narrative follows the mishaps of the innocent Joseph and his companion, the unworldly Parson Adams, as they travel through the predatory world of Georgian England. Though suffering from the perennial problem of how to render virtue colourful, it is a most witty book with numerous comic episodes, and it was a popular success.

In 1743, he published the three volumes of his *Miscellanies*; part three comprised *The Life of Jonathan Wild the Great*, a finely ironical contemporary fable that pretends to equate goodness with greatness and concerns the 'heroic' character of the century's most notorious underworld figure (who had been hanged in 1725). These volumes also contain his *A Journey from this World to the Next*, a spirited satire in the Lucianic mould which describes the progress of the soul. His beloved Charlotte died in 1744 and, to the sneers of his critics, Fielding in 1747 married her former maid, Mary Daniel. It was about this time that he began work on his formidable novel *Tom Jones*.

In 1748 there came an important development in Fielding's life, when he was appointed a Justice of the Peace for Westminster and for Middlesex. His serious concern at the social abuses and judicial corruption of the times is reflected in his essays: *A Charge Delivered to the Grand Jury* (1749), *An Enquiry into the Causes of the Late Increase of Robbers* (1751), *Examples of the Interposition of Providence in the Detection and Punishment of Murder* (1752) and *A Proposal for Making an Effectual Provision for the Poor* (1753). As a magistrate, Fielding was both dedicated and effective: together with his blind half-brother, John, he was responsible for Britain's first organized detective police force, the Bow Street Runners.

There appeared in 1749 *The History of Tom Jones, a Foundling*, the comic novel which is probably his greatest literary achievement; it was published in a revised version later that year. Of scrupulous architectural design, this lengthy work is distinguished by its un-idealized hero and the way in which his fortunes are described by a separate narrator who is virtually a character in his own right. Less exuberant by contrast is his last novel, *Amelia* (1751), which probably mirrors his own grim experience of social hardships in the metropolis and is a gloomy book, somewhat flawed by its own convictions.

In January of the following year, Fielding returned to journalism and edited *The Covent Garden Journal*, under the pseudonym Sir Alexander Drawcansir. Among the essays he contributed were his literary altercations with **Smollett**. But his health was deteriorating – he suffered from asthma and gout – and on 26 June 1754 he set sail for the less inclement climate of Lisbon, with his wife and daughter. It was there that he died, on 8 October, and lies buried in the English cemetery. *The Journal of a Voyage to Lisbon*, published in 1755, is a sharply observed but unavoidably depressing account of his final travels.

Despite certain legends of his rakish life-style, Fielding as a man had a deserved reputation for generosity of spirit, and had a natural sympathy for his fellow man. In religion he was a Broad Anglican (or Latitudinarian) and he believed in the principle of benevolence or 'good nature', which he defined in *The Champion* as 'a delight

William Hogarth's engraving, 'Gin Lane'. Hogarth's friend Henry Fielding was a dedicated and far-seeing magistrate who saw the need for a properly organized force to maintain law and order. His pamphlet, *An Enquiry into the Causes of the Late Increase of Robbers* (1751), is believed to have inspired Hogarth's engraving. Victoria & Albert Museum, London.

in the happiness of mankind'. The example of his later life shows this in practice; as a novelist, too, he is a committed critic of society's corruptions and hypocrisy. (In this, as in other ways, he is frequently compared to his friend William Hogarth.) He brought to the novel a new degree of psychological realism and a linear narrative strength, but the influences upon him were many and various, including the tradition of classical epic prose romances, the European **picaresque**, and the learned fooling of the Scriblerian satirists. His own dramatic experience introduced a new sophistication in both structure and the representation of comic character through dialogue. Though the plays themselves are largely forgotten, **G. B. Shaw** considered him (in 1906) 'the greatest practising dramatist, with the single exception of Shakespeare, produced by England between the Middle Ages and the nineteenth century'.

**Fielding, Sarah** 1710–68 **Henry Fielding**'s younger sister was born in East Stour in Dorset. She went to live in Hammersmith and became the friend of **Samuel Richardson**. She published *The Adventures of David Simple* in 1744 and achieved considerable celebrity. *Familiar Letters between the Principal Characters in David Simple* was published in 1747, and a second edition of *The Adventures* in the same year; Henry Fielding contributed prefaces. *The Governess, or, The Little Female Academy* (1749) preceded a continuation of *David Simple, Volume the Last* (1753). Other works were *The Cry: a New Dramatic Fable* (1754, with Jane Collier), *The Lives of Cleopatra and Octavia* (1757), *The History of the Countess of Dellwyn* (1759) and *The History of Ophelia* (1760). Sarah Fielding published a translation of Xenophon's *Memorabilia* and *Apologia* in 1762.

**Fiennes, Celia** 1662–1741 Travel-writer. Born at the manor of Newton Toney, near Salisbury, she was granddaughter of the 1st Lord Saye and Sele. From 1685 until about 1703 she travelled extensively around England (initially for reasons of health, but also for a broadening of the mind) and began to record in journals what she saw. This account was primarily designed for her own family, but it constituted the most comprehensive impression of the countryside since the work of **Camden**. However, it remained in manuscript form until it was roughly transcribed and published in 1888, by the daughter of the 16th Lord Saye and Sele, as *Through England on a Side Saddle in the Time of William and Mary*. A fine scholarly edition, *The Journeys of Celia Fiennes*, by Christopher Morris, appeared in 1947, and divides the travels geographically into four parts.

As a document of period detail, this account is of interest and importance as social history, but it is also very readable. The style is natural and personal, opinionated and sometimes quirky, but full of enthusiastic observation and recording a wide variety of topics, from gardening to processes of manufacture. Her enquiring attitude decried insularity, observing that too many 'Gentlemen in general service of their country . . . are ignorant of anything but the name of the place for which they serve in Parliament.'

*Fiesta* See *Sun Also Rises, The*.

**Figes, Eva** 1932– Novelist. Born in Berlin, she left Germany with her family in 1939, and was educated at Kingsbury Grammar School and Queen Mary College, London. She worked as an editor at Longmans in 1955–7, Weidenfeld and Nicolson in 1962–3 and Blackie in 1964–7. Her first novel, *Equinox*, appeared in 1966; its successors include *Winter Journey* (winner of the Guardian Fiction Prize, 1968), *Nelly's Version* (1977), *Light* (1983) and *The Seven Ages* (1986). She has also written several radio plays: *Time Regained* (1980), *Days* (1981; adapted from her own novel of the same name published in 1974) and *Between Friends* (1982). A lyrical writer whose prose flows smoothly, Figes has been compared to **Virginia Woolf** in her preoccupation with exploring the inner self. She acknowledges Kafka as a major influence. The darker elements in her work are the shadows cast by the Holocaust, and she remains very much part of a European tradition. She has also translated works by Martin Walser, Bernhard Grzimek and George Sand.

*Fight at Finnsburh, The* A fragment of 48 lines of Old English verse preserved in a corrupt 18th-century copy from a lost manuscript. The story the poem apparently told was well known and forms the subject of the minstrel's song in *Beowulf* after the defeat of Grendel. The fragment describes the defence of the hall in which Hnaef and his men are under attack and the whole poem probably told of a feud between the Danes and Frisians. The relationship between the part of the tale preserved in the fragment and the section told in *Beowulf* has been a topic of controversy and research.

**Findley, Timothy** 1930– Canadian novelist. Born and educated in Toronto, he was an actor in Canada, Britain and the United States between 1950 and 1962. During this time he also worked in Canadian television and wrote dialogue in Hollywood. He had begun to write fiction in the 1950s and from 1962 he turned to writing full-time. With his collaborator William Whitehead he has won several awards for television scripts. His first novel, *The Last of the Crazy People* (1967), is a study of a decaying southern Ontario family, which serves as a social microcosm. *The Butterfly Plague* (1969) offers a similar perspective on a Hollywood family. Findley is best known for his novel *The Wars* (1977), the story of a young Canadian officer in World War I who reacts against the horror of the trenches with a treasonable act of heroism that is deemed 'mad'. Written by a narrator who investigates a variety of written, oral and pictorial sources, Ross's story also affords a vivid picture of the way notions of character and personal history are constructed. *Famous Last Words* (1981) is the fictional story of **Ezra Pound**'s Hugh Selwyn Mauberley. Set at the end of World War II, it blends the conventions of the thriller with an exploration of the darker side of 20th-century history and mythologies, particularly the relationship of artistic élitism and fascism. *Not Wanted on the Voyage* (1984) is a highly imaginative account of the Great Flood. Findley has also published a collection of short stories, *Dinner Along the Amazon* (1984).

**Finlay, George** 1799–1875 Historian. Finlay was one of the enthusiasts for Greek freedom who had been with **Byron** in Missolonghi. He was born at Faversham in Kent and studied law at Glasgow University and at Göttingen. He went to Greece in 1823 and after the struggle for independence had succeeded he decided to settle there. He bought an estate in Attica and eventually died in Athens. His histories of Greece eventually covered the centuries that followed the subjugation by the Romans to its hard-wrested freedom from the Turks. *Greece under the Romans* (1844), *The History of Greece from its Conquest by the Crusaders to its Conquest by the Turks, and of the Empire of Trebizond* (1851), *The History of the Byzantine and Greek Empires 716–1453* (1853), *The History of Greece under Othman and Venetian Domination* (1856) and *A History of the Greek Revolution* (1861) supplemented the histories of Grote and Thirlwall and are pioneer works in their treatment of a continuous theme. They were published collectively as *A History of Greece from its Conquest by the Romans to the Present Time: 146 BC to AD 1864* (1877). Many of Finlay's letters from Greece were published in *The Times* (1864–70). They are historically valuable but so far have not been collected.

**Finlay, Ian Hamilton** 1925– Poet and artist. Born in Nassau and brought up in Scotland, Finlay became widely known as the leading British exponent of **concrete poetry** in the 1960s. In 1969 he moved to Stonypath, Lanarkshire, and began his work with inscriptions and landscape gardening, which uses imagery of the sea, the classical world and modern warfare and continues to cross over the traditional divisions between modes of artistic production. His work is represented in the Tate

Gallery and the Scottish National Gallery of Modern Art, but is still primarily involved with the poetic use of language. *Selected Ponds* (1976) shows the landscape and inscription work to good effect.

*Finnegans Wake* An experimental novel by **James Joyce**, published in 1939. He began the work in 1922, and individual sections had previously been published as *Work in Progress* during the 17 years of its composition.

This was the last and most revolutionary work by Joyce, representing his most extreme experiments with language and making extensive use of **stream of consciousness**. Puns, verbal compounds, and foreign words are combined with allusions from every conceivable source to create an obscure and densely structured text. Its apparent aim is to relate the minimal central story to a much wider historical, psychological, religious and artistic cosmology, a procedure which has been likened to that of scholasticism and medieval **allegory**.

On a literal level, the novel presents the dreams and nightmares of Humphrey Chimpden Earwicker (a Dublin tavern-keeper) and his family (wife Anna, their sons Shem and Shaun, and daughter Isabel) as they lie asleep throughout one night. This, however, provides only a rationale for what is really a novel without narrative or plot, and in which all human experience is ultimately viewed as fragmentary. Major sources of influence have been identified in Vico's ideas of cyclical repetition, Freud's dream psychology, and Bruno's theory of the complementary but conflicting nature of opposites.

The title is itself a compound of Finn MacCool, the Irish folk-hero who is supposed to return to life at some future date to become the saviour of Ireland, and Tim Finnegan, the hero of a music-hall ballad, who sprang to life in the middle of his own wake.

**Firbank, (Arthur Annesley) Ronald** 1886–1926 Novelist. Firbank was the son of a wealthy company director and was born in London. He was educated at Uppingham School and went on to Cambridge, but left in 1909 without graduating and travelled in the Mediterranean. He became a Roman Catholic while at Cambridge. Delicate in health and thoroughly eccentric, Firbank, whose character is described by his friend **Osbert Sitwell** in *Noble Essences*, had wealth enough to indulge his own way of life. His first book of stories, *Odette d'Antrevernes*, and *A Study in Temperament* were published in 1905. The series of novels for which he is best known began with *Vainglory* (1915) and continued with *Inclinations* (1916), *Caprice* (1917), *Valmouth: A Romantic Novel* (1919), the short story *Santal* (1921), *The Flower*

*Beneath the Foot* (1923), *Prancing Nigger* (1924) and *Concerning the Eccentricities of Cardinal Pirelli* (1926). *The Princess Zoubaroff: A Comedy* (1920) was not produced during his lifetime, and several short poems were published posthumously.

Firbank's novels carry what **A. Alvarez** has described as 'a sense of ominous unease'. They are witty, arch and meticulously, even artificially, written.

*Firmilian, or, The Student of Badajoz* A parody by **William Edmonstone Aytoun** of the poets he dubbed the **Spasmodic School: Sydney Dobell, Philip James Bailey** and **Alexander Smith**. It was published in 1854. Firmilian, writing a poetic tragedy about Cain, decides that to do his subject justice he needs personal insight into the 'mental spasms of the tortured Cain'. He starts committing crimes, with ludicrous consequences.

**Fisher, Roy** 1930– Poet. Born in Handsworth, Birmingham, and educated locally and at Birmingham University, Fisher worked as a school and college teacher, becoming head of the English Department at Bordesley College of Education in Birmingham (1963–71) and lecturer in American Literature at the University of Keele (1971–82). Since 1982 he has been a freelance writer and musician, playing piano in a jazz band.

Influenced by the American **Black Mountain school**, Fisher's **modernist** and experimental approach put him out of key with British trends in the era of the **Movement**. His work (and life) has been deliberately provincial, seeking material in the industrialized landscape of the Midlands and making a poetry that is intensely English despite its superficial similarity with American forms. Fisher's early work was published by fugitive small presses. His poem 'City', however, has become well known and **Donald Davie** wrote about it at some length in his study of **Thomas Hardy** (1972). His *Poems 1955–80* was published in 1981 and *Furnace*, a long poem, in 1986.

**Fisher, St John** 1459–1535 Fisher was a humanist and Roman Catholic martyr who resisted Henry VIII's attempts to gain supremacy over the English church. He was ordained priest in 1491 and gained the patronage of Lady Margaret Beaufort whose confessor he became in 1497. He encouraged her patronage of the University of Cambridge where she founded a professorship in divinity in 1503 and Christ's College in 1505. The establishment of St John's, its sister college, was finally supervised by Fisher in 1511. Fisher was president of Queens' College in 1505–8 and became Chancellor of the University and Bishop of Rochester in 1504. He encouraged Hebrew at the University and persuaded **Erasmus** to lecture there on Greek in 1511–14.

A staunch supporter of the Roman Catholic church, Fisher was a controversialist against Lutheranism and preached against its heresies. He defended Catherine of Aragon in 1529 and opposed both the granting to Henry of the title Supreme Head of the Church in England and the Supremacy Act of 1534. He was condemned for not reporting the subversive prophecies of Elizabeth Barton and was imprisoned in the Tower with **Thomas More** for refusing the oath consequent upon the 1534 Act of Succession. His position became even more dangerous when Paul III made him a cardinal in 1535. He was tricked into denying the King's headship of the church, condemned for treason and beheaded on Tower Hill, his head being afterward displayed on London Bridge. Fisher was beatified by Leo XIII in 1886 and canonized by Pius XI in 1935.

Fisher's complete Latin *Opera* were first published at Wurzburg in 1597. His controversialist works against Luther, like *Assertionis Lutheranae Confutatio* (1523), were printed in England, as were some of his vernacular sermons, the sermon on the penitential psalms (1508) and an English sermon against Luther (1521).

**Fitch, William Clyde** 1865–1909 American dramatist. Born in Elmira, New York, Fitch studied journalism at Amherst College before becoming a journalist in New York City. His first play, *Beau Brummel* (1890), was a vehicle for the popular actor Richard Mansfield. Over the next 20 years he wrote nearly 60 plays, earning for himself a fortune and for Broadway a new status as the home of American drama. His best plays are society melodramas which combine surface realism with emotional excess. They include *A Modern Match* (1892), *Barbara Frietchie* (1899), *The Climbers* (1901), *Captain Jinks of the Horse Marines* (1901), *The Girl with the Green Eyes* (1902), *The Truth* (1906) and *The Woman in the Case* (1909).

**Fitzball, Edward** 1793–1873 Playwright. Born plain Edward Ball in Cambridgeshire, he turned to writing when his Norwich printing-house failed, and produced at least 150 plays as well as four novels, six volumes of bouncy verse and an informative autobiography, *Thirty-Five Years of a Dramatic Author's Life* (1859). Most famous for his spectacular melodramas, he wrote nothing better than *Jonathan Bradford* (1833), based on a recent murder. His quest for gallery-gripping effects can be read in his titles: *The Burning Bridge* (1824), *The Earthquake* (1828), *The Negro of Wapping* (1838), *The Wreck and the Reef* (1847). It was the bursts of red and blue fire rather than the skeletal text that brought *The Flying Dutchman* (1827) its phenomenal popularity. His output, in both quantity and quality, is typical of the journeyman dramatist's work in the busy London theatres. Adaptations of popular novels, thefts from the French stage, comic operas, burlesques: whatever was wanted Fitzball provided at the rate of six a year.

**FitzGerald, Edward** 1809–83 Poet and translator. Born Edward Purcell (his father had married a Miss FitzGerald and in 1818 assumed her name) in Bredfield, Suffolk, into a wealthy family, FitzGerald was educated at the King Edward VI Grammar School in Bury St Edmunds and at Trinity College, Cambridge, where he encountered **Thackeray**, **Tennyson** and others soon to become eminent Victorians. FitzGerald pursued no career and passed almost his entire life in his native county. One of his earliest publications was the obituary in *The Ipswich Journal* of his friend, **Bernard Barton**, the Quaker poet who died in 1849 and whose daughter FitzGerald was to marry in 1856; later the same year he wrote a striking *Memoir* for a collection of Barton's writings. But FitzGerald's first volume was *Euphranor* (1851), a Platonic dialogue about the Victorian obsession with the rebirth of chivalry; next came *Polonius: A Collection of Wise Saws and Modern Instances* (1852) and in 1853 his translation of *Six Dramas of Calderon* (he was to translate two more plays by the Spanish dramatist in the next decade). In the early 1850s FitzGerald took up Oriental studies in earnest and in 1856 came his translation *Salámán and Absál, an Allegory Translated from the Persian of Jámi*. This was followed in 1859 by his major literary work, the anonymous pamphlet entitled **The Rubáiyát of Omar Khayyám**. In later years FitzGerald translated the *Agamemnon*, *Oedipus Tyrannus* and *Oedipus Coloneus*, worked on a dictionary of the correspondence of Madame de Sévigné and assembled some readings from **Crabbe**, a poet he admired. His correspondence, marked by wit and sympathy, places him among the masters of epistolary art.

FitzGerald always loved the sea and maintained a yacht which he sailed off the Suffolk coast; he also enjoyed friendships among the local fisher-folk. An eccentric from a family of eccentrics, his marriage was a disaster and lasted less than a year. A shy, unobtrusive man given to melancholy introspection, FitzGerald was an undeniable influence on the late Victorian literature of pessimism mainly through his adaptation of the *Rubáiyát*, a poem whose extraordinary popularity survives even into our own time.

**Fitzgerald, F[rancis] Scott (Key)** 1896–1940 American novelist and short-story writer. Fitzgerald was born in St Paul, Minnesota, and entered Princeton University in 1913. In 1917 he left before graduating to take up a commission in the US Army. While stationed near Montgomery, Alabama, he courted and became engaged to Zelda Sayre, herself an aspiring writer. After his discharge from the army in 1919, he moved to New York City and worked briefly for an advertising agency. That same year he sold his first story, 'Babes in the Wood', which appeared in *The Smart Set*. He returned to St Paul and rewrote a novel he had begun while in the army; originally entitled 'The Romantic Egotist', it appeared in 1920 as *This Side of Paradise* and was an almost immediate success. Its hero, Amory Blaine, like Fitzgerald himself, goes to Princeton, where he becomes a member of the literary coterie. He serves in World War I (unlike Fitzgerald, he is sent to France and sees action) and then works in advertising. He has several romantic affairs, none of them lasting. At the end of the novel, aged 24, he recognizes that his own egotism has prevented his finding happiness.

Fitzgerald and Zelda Sayre were married in 1920, and in the same year his first collection of short stories, *Flappers and Philosophers*, was published. Fitzgerald's second novel, *The Beautiful and Damned*, appeared in 1922, and was less well received. Its main character, Anthony Patch, is an alcoholic whose goal in life is to inherit and spend his grandfather's money. Though he is eventually successful in contesting the will that has disinherited him, by the end of the novel he and his wife Gloria have declined both physically and spiritually because of their dissolute, alcoholic life-style. (For much of his life Fitzger-

Scott Fitzgerald and Zelda Sayre in 1919, at the Sayre home in Montgomery, Alabama. They were married in 1920.

ald was himself an alcoholic.) Another collection of short stories, *Tales of the Jazz Age*, which included 'The Diamond as Big as the Ritz', was published in 1922. 'The Jazz Age' is Fitzgerald's own descriptive phrase for the 1920s, and his early financial success as a writer enabled him and Zelda to lead the kind of decadent, boisterous existence it suggests.

In October 1922 the couple moved to Great Neck, New York. (Living in this affluent Long Island community provided Fitzgerald with material for his next novel, **The Great Gatsby**.) While there he renewed his acquaintance with **John Dos Passos** and became friendly with **Ring Lardner**. He also revised his play *The Vegetable*, which had an unsuccessful one-week run in 1923, and continued to turn out stories for magazines in order to finance his extravagant life-style. Because they could live more cheaply in Europe than in the USA, the Fitzgeralds went to France in April 1924. There Fitzgerald met two other expatriate American writers – **Ernest Hemingway**, who became a close friend, and **Gertrude Stein**. In 1925 he published what many consider his best novel, *The Great Gatsby*, and in 1926 a third collection of short stories, entitled *All the Sad Young Men*.

During the next five years the Fitzgeralds travelled back and forth between Europe and America several times. Zelda had the first of her nervous breakdowns in April 1930; she was hospitalized periodically, both in Europe and the USA, from then until her death in 1948. Fitzgerald published his fourth novel, **Tender is the Night**, in 1934; pressed for money, he was disappointed that it did not sell better, though it was generally well received by the critics. Another collection of stories, *Taps at Reveille*, followed in 1935. That same year he began to write confessional essays about his broken health and exhaustion as a writer. The essays – 'The Crack-Up', 'Pasting It Together' and 'Handle With Care' – were published in *Esquire* magazine in 1936, and were subsequently included in *The Crack-Up* (1945), a collection of Fitzgerald's essays, notes and letters edited by his friend **Edmund Wilson**.

For a few months in 1927, and then again in 1931 and 1932, Fitzgerald worked in Hollywood as a screenwriter. In 1937 he returned to accept a lucrative contract with Metro-Goldwyn-Mayer. He worked on various screenplays, but completed only one (*Three Comrades*, 1938), and was eventually fired because of his drinking. Though he occasionally visited Zelda, who by this time was in a hospital in North Carolina, he became involved with another woman, the columnist Sheilah Graham, whom he met in Hollywood in 1937. (In fact, he died in her apartment, of a heart attack, in December 1940.) During his last months Fitzgerald returned to writing fiction, producing several short stories which were collected and published in 1962 as *The Pat Hobby Stories*. He also began a novel about a Hollywood producer, *The Last Tycoon*, which, though unfinished, was published in 1941.

**Fitzgerald, Robert D[avid]** 1902–87 Australian poet. Born in Hunter's Hill, Sydney, of Irish ancestry, he attended Sydney Grammar School and, briefly, studied science at the University of Sydney. He was articled to a firm of surveyors in 1922 and qualified in 1925. Between 1926 and 1936 he worked as a surveyor in Fiji, an experience which gave his poetry a cultural dimension not to be found in the work of his Australian contemporaries. On returning to Australia, he continued to work as a surveyor and, between 1939 and his retirement in 1965, he was employed by the Department of the Interior. He won numerous awards for his poetry, including an OBE for services to literature in 1951. Fitzgerald's work is particularly concerned with philosophical issues and frequently discusses the problem of free will. His early verse belongs in the tradition of French and German Romanticism, which in Australia had been followed by his precursor, **Christopher Brennan**. Throughout his work there is also a strong humanitarian concern and he made his voice felt over such issues as Australian involvement in Vietnam. His best work included 'The Hidden Bole', an elegy on the death of the dancer Pavlova, which appeared in *Moonlight Acre* (1938) and which explores the nature of time and art, and *Between Two Tides* (1952), an account of a struggle between two Tongan chiefs and a meditation on how choices are made. His finest achievement was *The Wind at Your Door* (1959), a poetic attempt to come to terms with Australian ancestry, which is perceived as having two opposing strains: free settler and convict, victor and victim. Fitzgerald's other poetry included *The Greater Apollo* (1927), *To Meet the Sun* (1929), *This Night's Orbit* (1953), *Forty Years' Poems* (1965) and *Product* (1978).

**Fitzmaurice, George** 1877–1963 Irish playwright, born in County Kerry to a Protestant clergyman and his Roman Catholic wife. His first published work, sketches of peasant life in Kerry, appeared in newspapers, and Irish peasants were the subject of his first play, *The Country Dressmaker* (1907), produced at the **Abbey Theatre**. The same theatre staged Fitzmaurice's idiosyncratic tragicomedies in one act, *The Pie-Dish* (1908) and *The Magic Glasses* (1913). Service in the British Army during World War I brought to an end Fitzmaurice's theatrical career. Increasingly reclusive, he resisted performance of his plays, and it was not until the posthumous publication of his *Collected*

*Plays* (1967–70) that interest in this remarkable writer was revived. A tragedy, *The Moonlighter* and such comic fantasies as *The Enchanted Land, The Ointment Blue* and *The Dandy Dolls*, show Fitzmaurice's range and originality.

**Flatman, Thomas** 1637–88 Poet and painter. A fellow of New College, Oxford, Flatman was much admired as a painter of miniatures. His *Poems and Songs* was published in 1674 and his verse occasionally appeared in anthologies; he also composed some hymns.

**Flecker, James (Herman) Elroy** 1884–1915 Poet and dramatist. Born in Uppingham, he was educated at Trinity College, Oxford, and followed a career in the Consular Service, posted to Constantinople and Beirut. He published volumes of lyric poetry influenced by the last years of the **Aesthetic Movement**: *The Bridge of Fire* (1907), *Forty-Two Poems* (1911) and *The Golden Journey to Samarkand* (1913). He contributed to **Georgian Poetry**; wrote a dialogue on education, *The Grecians* (1910), and an experimental novel, *The King of Alsander* (1914). Two verse plays, **Hassan** (1922) and *Don Juan* (1925), appeared after his early death from tuberculosis. His *Collected Poems*, edited by **J. C. Squire**, appeared in 1947.

**Flecknoe, Richard** c. 1600–c. 1678 Minor poet and playwright. Of his youth little is known beyond what he reveals in a book of letters written to friends while on his travels, *Relation of Ten Years Travels in Europe, Asia, Africa and America* (1654). He was probably Irish and may once have been a priest. He wrote five plays, of which only one, *Love's Dominion* (1654), was ever performed; *Enigmatical Characters*, a collection of prose sketches (1658); and a book of verse, *Epigrams of All Sorts* (1670). His *Short Discourse on the English Stage* (1664) roused **Marvell** to lampoon him (*An English Priest at Rome*) and **Dryden** to satirize him (*Mac Flecknoe*).

**Fleming, Ian (Lancaster)** 1908–64 Novelist. Educated at Eton and Sandhurst, he worked as a journalist for Reuters and *The Times* (for both of which he served in Moscow) before writing the first of his 13 James Bond thrillers, *Casino Royale* (1952). The knowing exotic detail and the worldly wit of these books, and the glamorous, racy adventures of their protagonist, combined to make James Bond one of the most popular secret agents in the history of spy fiction. A parallel series of visually spectacular, and immensely successful, film adaptations starring first Sean Connery and then Roger Moore and Timothy Dalton further increased Fleming's and Bond's reputations. Since Fleming's death attempts have been made by **Kingsley Amis**, in *Colonel Sun* (1968), and recently by

John Gardner to extend the life of James Bond in several pastiche thrillers.

**Fletcher, Giles (Sr)** 1546–1611 The diplomat and poet Giles was the father of the poets **Phineas** and **Giles Fletcher**, and the uncle of the dramatist **John Fletcher**. He was educated at Eton where he contributed Latin epigrams to the collection presented to Queen Elizabeth on her visit of 1563. He went as a scholar to King's College, Cambridge, in 1565 and graduated MA in 1573. He lectured at King's, and to the University on Greek, became deputy Public Orator in 1577, and a senior fellow of King's in 1578. He became chancellor of the diocese of Sussex in 1582, an MP for Winchelsea in 1584 and, on the queen's recommendation, remembrancer (official letter-writer) of the City of London in 1585.

He was successful as a diplomat, negotiating over trade with Hamburg, and in 1588 was sent as an ambassador to the Tsar in Russia where he negotiated a favourable trade treaty for England. His impressions of Russia are recorded in *Of the Russe Commonwealth*. *Licia* (1593) is a collection of sonnets and also contains an ode, a dialogue, some elegies and a monologue by Richard III on his rise to power. Fletcher's attempt to gain Burghley's patronage for a Latin history of the reign of Elizabeth was unsuccessful. He was examined and briefly taken into custody after Essex's Rebellion, Essex having been his patron for some time.

**Fletcher, Giles (Jr)** 1585–1623 Poet. The younger son of the diplomat and poet **Giles Fletcher**, he was educated at Westminster School and Trinity College, Cambridge, where he became reader in Greek. In 1619 he was appointed rector of Alderton in Suffolk, where he died at the age of 38. He is remembered for his long allegorical poem in eight-line stanzas, *Christ's Victory and Triumph in Heaven and Earth, Over and After Death* (1610), a Baroque religious effusion, popular in his day and influenced by **Spenser**.

**Fletcher, John** 1579–1625 This elegant and prolific dramatist, son of a bishop of London, was more exclusively committed to the theatre than most contemporary writers of comparable standing. Little is known of his life after he left Cambridge. It was probably as one of **Ben Jonson**'s circle that he met Francis Beaumont in London. Together the two friends, who had provided the fashionable **boys' companies** with some marketable plays, took over as leading dramatists for the **King's Men** after that company began to perform in the indoor **Blackfriars**. The extraordinary success of the partnership, most notably in *Philaster* (c. 1609), *The Maid's Tragedy* (c. 1610) and *A King and No King* (1611), encouraged their contemporaries and immediate successors to ascribe to them far more work (over 50 plays) than the seven or eight confidently allowed by modern scholars. See **Francis Beaumont** for further details of the collaboration.

If, as is widely accepted, Fletcher was the sole author of *The Faithful Shepherdess* (c. 1609), *Bonduca* (1609–?14), *Valentinian* (1610–?14), *Monsieur Thomas* (1610–?15), *The Mad Lover* (c. 1616), *The Chances* (c. 1617), *The Humorous Lieutenant* (c. 1619), *The Island Princess* (c. 1620), *Women Pleased* (1620–?23), *The Pilgrim* (c. 1621), *The Wild-Goose Chase* (c. 1621), *Rule a Wife and Have a Wife* (1624) and *A Wife for a Month* (1624), then there is substance in the claim that Fletcher, although a subtle contriver of individual scenes, was less adept in the composition of whole plays. He was, however, a willing collaborator, most notably after the retirement and early death of Beaumont, with **Shakespeare** in *Henry VIII* (1613) and *The Two Noble Kinsmen* (1613) and with **Massinger**. Effective products of this latter collaboration include *Sir John van Olden Barnavelt* (1619), *The Custom of the Country* (c. 1619), *The Beggar's Bush* (c. 1622) and *The Spanish Curate* (c. 1622).

Fletcher's influence on the 17th-century development of a comedy of manners and his sophisticated treatment of tragicomedy are signs of his flexible talent and of the alertness with which he perceived the changing tastes of Stuart England.

**Fletcher, John Gould** 1886–1950 American poet, born in Little Rock, Arkansas, and educated at Harvard. In 1909 he went to live in England, and in 1913, at his own expense, he published his verse in five volumes: *The Book of Nature, The Dominant City, Fire and Wine, Fool's Gold* and *Visions of the Evening*. Though critical reception was mixed, he did receive favourable notice from **Amy Lowell**, who became his close friend. In 1914 he became associated with the **imagists** and contributed to Lowell's anthology *Some Imagist Poets*. *Irradiations: Sand and Spray* appeared in 1915, and *Goblins and Pagodas* in the following year. He remained in Europe until 1933, contributing to *The Criterion* (1923–7) and becoming friends with **T. S. Eliot**, **Donald Davidson** and **John Crowe Ransom**. He returned to the USA in 1933, and in 1938 his *Selected Poems* received the Pulitzer Prize. Though he is strongly identified with the imagists, his later works reflect his association with the Southern Agrarians, and his continuing interest in Eastern mysticism (which had been evident in his early verse). His other works include *Japanese Prints* (1918), *The Tree of Life* (1918), *Parables* (1925), *Branches of Adam* (1926), *The Black Rock* (1928), *XXIV Elegies* (1935) and *South Star* (1941). His prose writings include *Paul Gauguin: His Life* *and Art* (1921), *John Smith – Also Pocahontas* (1928) and *The Two Frontiers: A Study in Historical Psychology* (1930). His autobiography, *Life Is My Song*, appeared in 1937.

**Fletcher, Phineas** 1582–1650 Poet. The elder son of **Giles Fletcher (Sr)** and the brother of **Giles Fletcher (Jr)**, Phineas Fletcher was born at Cranbrook in Kent. He was educated at Eton and King's College, Cambridge, where he stayed for 11 years, writing some minor verse. He was ordained in 1615 and became chaplain to Sir Henry Willoghby; he was rector of Hilgay from 1621 until his death. Fletcher was the author of some vehemently anti-Catholic verse, of which *The Locusts or Apollyonists* (1627) is a typical piece. Like his brother, he wrote in imitation of **Spenser**: his erotic narrative, *Britain's Ida* (1628), was ascribed to Spenser in order to safeguard the true author's ecclesiastical position. *The Purple Island* (1633) is a convoluted allegory examining the physical and mental nature of mankind, in which virtue and vice are interminably at war. Fletcher's pastoral play, *Sicelides: A Piscatory* (published in 1631), never received its intended performance before James I.

**Flint, F[rank] S[tuart]** 1885–1960 Poet. Born into appalling poverty in Islington, Flint left school at 13 and joined the civil service at 19. An autodidact, he mastered 10 languages and quickly became the leading authority on contemporary French poetry. His first collection, *In The Net of Stars* (1909), features conventional love poems but *Cadences* (1915), published after he had met **Pound** and **T. E. Hulme** and which appeared in Pound's *Des Imagistes* anthology (1914), made an important contribution to **imagism**. It is written in accordance with Flint's theory of 'unrhymed cadence'. His final volume, *Otherworld: Cadences* (1920), reverts to his initial Romanticism, towards narrative rather than the juxtaposed images of imagism. After giving up writing, he continued to work for the Ministry of Labour until 1951.

*Flores and Blancheflour* A **verse romance** in couplets composed *c.* 1250. One of the earliest English romances, it is based on a lost French version. Blancheflour is a captive maiden brought up with Flores, son of the King of Spain. They fall in love, but the King disapproves and while Flores is absent Blancheflour is sold as a slave. On his return Flores is told she is dead and tries to kill himself. At this his parents reveal the truth and he goes to seek her. He traces her to the harem of the Emir of Babylon and bribes his way into the harem concealed in a basket of flowers, but the reunited couple are discovered and condemned to death. Each is reluctant to use a magic ring which will save only one of them. This, and their story, move the Emir and he allows them to marry.

**Florio, John** ?1553–1625 A lexicographer and translator, Florio was the son of an Italian Protestant refugee. He studied at Oxford and, in 1604–19, was groom of the privy chamber to Queen Anne. His translation of Giovanni Battista Ramusio's account of the voyage of Jacques Cartier was printed in 1580 as *Navigations and Discoveries. Florio his First Fruits* (1578), a grammar and dialogues in English and Italian, was followed by *Florio's Second Fruits* (1591). His Italian–English dictionary, *A World of Words* (1598), was enlarged in a second edition as *Queen Anne's New World of Words* (1611). *Giardino di Ricreazione* (1591) is a collection of Italian proverbs. His greatest work was a translation of the *Essais* of Montaigne (1603, revised 1613). The freedom of this translation is sometimes achieved at the cost of accuracy. **Shakespeare** was one of its readers, as some of Gonzalo's speeches in Act II of *The Tempest* draw on Florio's translation of Montaigne's essay 'Of Cannibals'.

*Flower and the Leaf, The* An anonymous poem written in the third quarter of the 15th century. It was at one time attributed to **Chaucer** (see **Chaucerian apocrypha**) and has more recently, but improbably, been attributed to the author of *The Assembly of Ladies*. The narrator is female, but it is impossible to deduce the sex of the poet.

The lady observes the followers of the Flower and those of the Leaf jousting and singing on a summer day. The Flower's followers faint in the heat and are drenched by a storm, but those of the Leaf shelter and then comfort the others. The allegory is explained to the lady as demonstrating the contrast between those who are faithful and chaste and those who are idle and pleasure-seeking. Asked which side she favours, she opts for the Leaf.

**folk revival, the** The antiquarian researches of **Thomas Percy**, **Allan Ramsay**, **Burns** and **Scott** in the late 18th century and the folkloric researches of the German Grimm brothers in the early 19th century had become influential throughout the English-speaking world in the late 19th century. There was a flurry of activity by middle-class intellectuals anxious to preserve a traditional peasant culture which they saw as threatened by industrialization, urbanization and the spread of mechanical forms of entertainment.

Much of this energy was devoted to Celtic culture and forms part of the **Celtic revival**. The folk revival in England was spearheaded by the work of **Sabine Baring-Gould**, who collected and published folk-songs in and around his

Devon parish, and by Frank Kidson in Yorkshire; and in the USA by **Francis J. Child**'s collection, still regarded to a considerable extent as definitive, of *The English and Scottish Popular Ballads* (1882–98). In the early 20th century, the work of collecting was continued and expanded by such influential young musicians as Ralph Vaughan Williams, Percy Grainger and E. J. Moeran, and by literary amateurs like George Gardiner and the Hammond brothers in Hampshire and the South, and Alfred Williams in the Upper Thames Valley.

The most important and industrious of the collectors of this period was Cecil J. Sharp (1859–1924), who operated widely throughout England and the Eastern USA, and after whom the London headquarters of the English Folk Dance and Song Society is named. His original interest was in folk-dance; his song collecting was started by his having overheard a song in Somerset, sung at work by his clerical host's gardener, the felicitously named John England.

The second phase of the revival, following World War II, differed in that it was brought about largely by left-wing thinkers, often themselves of working-class origin, who saw folksong as a means of politicizing the working class through involvement in its own traditional artefacts. Ewan MacColl and A. L. Lloyd in England, Hamish Henderson in Scotland and Pete Seeger in the USA all come into this category: all were performers as well as writers and collectors. **Arnold Wesker**'s Centre 42 project was also involved in the folk movement. Lloyd's *Folk Song in England* (1967) is an attempt to chart its subject's development in Marxist terms, and with Vaughan Williams he edited the influential *Penguin Book of English Folksongs* (1959).

Aesthetic appreciation of folk-song spread across the social and political spectrum, but the left continued to predominate in the resultant folk-club movement. Performance took equal pride of place with scholarship in this phase. The bowdlerization of love-songs which their *zeitgeist* had forced on to the earlier collectors was despised and the songs were restored and republished. Many singers steeped in traditional song, such as MacColl, Cyril Tawney, Peter Bellamy, Bob Pegg and Peter Coe, were successful in creating new songs convincingly in the traditional idiom which the revival had brought to a wider audience.

The extent to which the working class has actually been involved in *any* phase of the revival, the most recent any more than the earlier manifestations in the 18th, 19th and early 20th centuries, has been cogently questioned by Dave Harker, a Trotskyist, in *Fakesong* (1985).

*Fool of Quality, The* A novel by **Henry Brooke**, published in five volumes (1766–72).

Henry, second son of the Earl of Moreland, is called a 'fool of quality' because he seems dull and unintelligent in comparison with his elder brother. Rejected by his parents, he is reared by his foster-mother and educated by his uncle. He grows into a young man of strength, beauty and virtue who spends his time helping the unfortunate.

On this slender framework Brooke hangs a number of discourses on various aspects of the human condition and, in the latter part, on Christian mysticism in the form of a discussion between the author and a friend. The device is cumbersome, but the book does raise issues that were soon to be taken up by Rousseau, **William Godwin** and **Thomas Paine**. **John Wesley** admired Brooke's ideas and made an edited version of the book for use by Methodists (1781), while **Charles Kingsley** wrote an admiring preface to the 1859 edition. See also **sentimental novel**.

**foot** See **metre**.

**Foote, Samuel** 1720–77 Playwright and actor. He was born into a wealthy Cornish family and educated in Truro and at Oxford, which he left without taking a degree. Foote lived extravagantly, and it was after a brief imprisonment for debt that he decided to try his hand as an actor. His talent for mimicry brought him considerable notoriety, and it was this gift that he decided, opportunistically, to exploit in his own dramatic writing. Almost all his plays include satiric portraits of living individuals, most famously George Whitefield and his Methodist associates in *The Minor* (1760). Many of Foote's victims objected, and it was the Duchess of Kingston's fury at her portrait as Lady Kitty Crocodile in *A Trip to Calais* (1775) that indirectly brought his theatrical career to an end. Tried on a trumped-up charge of homosexual rape, Foote was acquitted but effectively silenced. During an adventurous life, he had been often in trouble. His evasion of the licensing laws – he would charge admission for 'tea' or 'chocolate' and provide satirical entertainment 'free' – offended the Lord Chamberlain in the 1740s and again in 1762–6. A riding accident, the result of a practical joke, led to his having a leg amputated in 1766, and, in compensation, some aristocratic friends procured for him a summer licence to perform plays at the **Haymarket**. Still determined to act, Foote wrote for himself a number of 'cripple' plays, including *The Devil upon Two Sticks* (1768) and *The Lame Lover* (1770). His last considerable play, *Piety in Pattens* (1773), was a vigorous attack on the fashion for sentimentalism. Like all his best work, including *The Author* (1757), *The Mayor of Garret* (1763), *The Patron* (1764), *The Commissary* (1765) and *The Nabob* (1772), it shows a talent for controversy and an ability to stretch the limits of the farcical 18th-century 'after-piece'.

***For the Term of His Natural Life*** See ***His Natural Life***.

**Ford, Ford Madox** 1873–1939 Novelist and editor. He was born Ford Hermann Hueffer. His father, Dr Franz Hueffer, was music critic of *The Times*; his grandfather was the painter Ford Madox Brown, and his uncle was **William Rossetti**, the brother of **Dante Gabriel Rossetti** and **Christina Rossetti**. Brown illustrated Ford's first book, *The Brown Owl* (1892), though Ford was to disclose his mixed feelings about the **Pre-Raphaelites** in his later art criticism.

Ford's writing was varied during the years of his early marriage to Elsie Martindale in 1894. He collaborated with **Conrad** over *The Inheritors* (1901) and *Romance* (1903), and produced historical–topographical works, verse, science fiction and historical romance (*The Fifth Queen* trilogy, 1906–8).

As editor of *The English Review*, founded in 1908, Ford became a notable figure in London. Its high quality owed much to his sponsorship of unknown writers (including **Ezra Pound**, **Wyndham Lewis** and **D. H. Lawrence**) as well as established figures like **James**, **Hardy**, **Bennett**, **Galsworthy** and **Yeats**. He lost control of the *Review* in 1910, a time of crisis associated with his romance with **Violet Hunt**.

Ford published numerous works before World War I, including two novels, *A Call* (1910) and *The Good Soldier* (1915). Two works of propaganda as well as 'Poems Written on Active Service' (in France with the Welsh Regiment) date from the war years. He changed his name to Ford in 1919.

After the war Ford lived in isolation in the country with the painter Stella Bowen. A tetralogy, *Parade's End*, was published between 1924 and 1928, while he was living in France, the country which eventually became his homeland. In Paris, in 1924, he founded *The Transatlantic Review*; **Hemingway** was deputy editor, and they published work by Pound, **Joyce**, **Gertrude Stein**, **e e cummings** and **Jean Rhys**.

Ford wrote about the Paris years in *It Was the Nightingale* (1933), one of many works of personal recollection. During his last years he lived frugally in the South of France with an American, Janice Biala, and expressed his liking for a self-sufficient life-style in *From Minstrels to the Machine* (1938) and other later works. He also gave support to many of the younger American Southern Agrarians such as **Allen Tate**, **Caroline Gordon**, **Katherine Anne Porter** and **Robert Lowell**. He was briefly associated with a college in Michigan, and it was here that he planned his monumental last work, *The March of Literature* (1939), a survey of ancient literature and Mediterranean culture.

**Ford, John** c. 1586–c. 1640 Little is known of the life of this playwright. He was born in Devon, and probably educated at Oxford and the Middle Temple. He had published poems and prose some years before his first known involvement in the theatre, already displaying the interest in moral paradox that characterizes his best plays. The order and precise dating of his dramatic work is the subject of scholarly debate. He began, probably, as a collaborator with **Dekker** and **Rowley** in *The Witch of Edmonton* (1621), and was again associated with Dekker in *The Welsh Ambassador* (1623) and a masque, *The Sun's Darling* (1624). Of the work of which he was sole author, two comedies, *The Fancies, Chaste and Noble* (c. 1636) and *The Lady's Trial* (1638), are slight pieces. Ford's startling interest in morbid psychology and emotional excess belongs more readily to tragedy. *The Lover's Melancholy* (1628) is a comedy that edges towards tragedy. *Love's Sacrifice* (c. 1632) is a tragedy of almost unrelieved gloom, notable for its creation of a magnificent villain in D'Avalos. It is the two tragedies, ***The Broken Heart*** (c. 1629) and ***'Tis Pity She's a Whore*** (c. 1631), together with the chronicle play ***Perkin Warbeck*** (published 1634), that have established for Ford a unique place in the drama of Caroline England.

***Forest, The*** **Ben Jonson** gave this name to the collection of short poems he included in the edition of his works published in 1616. Some of his best-known pieces appear in the collection: 'That Women Are But Men's Shadows', 'To Penshurst', 'Come My Celia, Let Us Prove' and the celebrated 'Song: To Celia' ('Drink to Me Only, with Thine Eyes').

**Forester, C[ecil] S[cott]** 1899–1966 Novelist. Born in Cairo, he was educated at Dulwich College, and studied medicine at Guy's Hospital before turning to writing. His first successful novel, *Payment Deferred* (1926), set during World War I, was made into a play (1931) and later a film. This was followed by *Brown on Resolution* (1929), then a biography of Nelson and two of his best-known novels of the Peninsular War: *Death to the French* (1932) and *The Gun* (1933). More popular historical fiction followed: *The African Queen* (1935; successfully filmed in 1952) and *The General* (1936) – both of which reworked the characteristic Forester theme of individual fortitude in war.

He became a journalist during the Spanish Civil War and his novels continued with the immensely popular 'Hornblower' books, starting with *The Happy Return* (1937). Hero of the Napoleonic Wars, Hornblower was partly modelled on Nelson, and in a further dozen novels published over the next 25 years Forester charted his career from midshipman to admiral.

During World War II Forester devoted himself to writing propaganda for the Allied cause, much of it for American consumption. *The Ship* (1943) resulted from a mission in HMS *Penelope* which he undertook at the invitation of the Admiralty. He suffered from ill health for the latter half of his life, and settled in the United States at the end of the war. *Long Before Forty*, an autobiography up to his 31st year, was published posthumously in 1967.

**formalism** The term is applied on the one hand to a generalized tendency, and on the other to certain specific schools and movements within literary criticism. Aristotle was the greatest precursor of formalist method, with his emphasis on the structure and defining characteristics of **tragedy**. Since then, criticism has tended to fluctuate from age to age between a broadly Aristotelian concern with systematic theory and a more subjective, less methodical style of approach. In the present century formalism has enjoyed a widespread revival of interest among critics determined to rescue their discipline from the vagaries of individual taste.

The Russian Formalists of the 1920s were the first to raise this doctrine into a high point of principle. Their efforts were concentrated on two main topics: the language of poetry and the structure of narrative discourse (folk-tales, novels and short stories). They saw poetry as a special kind of language, set apart from everyday prose by its use of certain devices – **metaphor**, **metonymy**, rhyme, **alliteration**, etc. – which focused attention on its formal or aesthetic attributes. The effect of such devices, so they argued, is to 'defamiliarize' the normal relation between language and reality, word and world, thus forcing us to break (momentarily at least) with our routine, jaded habits of perception. This power of 'making strange' – *ostranenie* in the Russian – is achieved through the 'foregrounding' of various stylistic features that emphasize the difference between poetry and prose, and thus prevent us reading straight 'through' the text to its mere paraphrasable content. In their work on narrative the Formalists again made a virtue of system and method. On the surface, it might seem impossible to achieve any unified general theory that would encompass all the myths, stories and elaborated plots that make up the corpus of world literature. But beneath this surface – so the Formalists argued – there exist certain deep regularities which amount to a 'grammar' of narrative types. Criticism is best, most usefully employed in deducing these deep-laid structures of the text, and not in the mere piling-up of endless new interpretations. It can then be placed on a

truly scientific and co-operative footing, as well as being able to profit from advances in neighbouring disciplines like structural linguistics.

The practitioners of **New Criticism** in the 1930s and 1940s have also been described as formalists, since they read poetry with a keen attentiveness to its formal and rhetorical structure. They were, however, much less concerned with matters of theory and method, preferring to operate with a handful of non-technical terms ('ambiguity', 'irony', 'paradox', etc.) whose looseness of definition was compensated by their flexibility in use. More recently, the proponents of French **structuralism** have played an active role in reviving and developing the legacy of the Russian Formalists.

***Fors Clavigera*** A compendium of some half-million words by **John Ruskin**, published as monthly letters to the workmen and labourers of England between January 1871 and March 1878 (when he became mentally ill) and intermittently thereafter. The enigmatic title suggests more than 'Fortune with the nail', as Ruskin himself informs the reader. 'Fors' he associates with 'Force' (the power of doing good work), with 'Fortitude' (the bearing of pain, if necessary, in the execution of that work) and with 'Fortune' (the 'necessary fate of man'). Similarly, 'Clavigera' is laden with meanings: the 'Club', the 'Key' and the 'Nail' – with Herculean strength, patience and the law, respectively. While *Fors Clavigera* includes many urgent messages on social issues, it moves into other discussions, often highly discursive. The most incongruous subjects jostle each other for attention, and the whole is a dazzling show of linguistic pyrotechnics. As autobiography, often cloaked in symbolism, the book is important in unlocking some of Ruskin's psychological complexities.

***Forsaken Merman, The*** A poem by **Matthew Arnold**, published in *The Strayed Reveller and Other Poems* (1849). A merman laments his wife, a girl from the land; she bore him children and then felt the call of her own world in the sound of church bells at Easter. She leaves her sea king and never returns. In its melancholy and its preoccupation with loss, *The Forsaken Merman* sounds a note that recurs throughout Arnold's poetry and, indeed, the poetry of many mid-Victorian contemporaries.

**Forster, E[dward] M[organ]** 1879–1970 Novelist and essayist. Forster was born in London and educated at Tonbridge School and King's College, Cambridge. His father died in 1880 and Forster's childhood was dominated by his mother and several adoring aunts. Tonbridge left him with an utter dislike of public-school values. Cambridge (1897–1901) proved more congenial, and in 1901 he was elected to the **Apostles**, through which he met members of what was to become the **Bloomsbury Group**. After graduating he travelled to Italy and Greece with his mother, and on his return began to contribute to the Cambridge-based journal, *The Independent Review*. His first short story, 'The Story of a Panic', appeared in 1904.

In 1905 Forster spent several months in Nassenheide, Germany, as tutor to the children of the Countess von Armin. He returned to England (Weybridge) for the publication of his first novel, ***Where Angels Fear to Tread*** (1905). The following year he lectured on Italian art and history for the Cambridge Local Lectures Board and became the tutor and close friend of an Indian Moslem, Syed Ross Masood. ***The Longest Journey*** (1907), his second novel, and ***A Room With a View*** (1908) were widely reviewed, but it was with ***Howards End*** (1910) that he fully established his reputation. However, a relatively minor volume of short stories, *The Celestial Omnibus* (1911), was followed by a period of silence which lasted for over a decade.

In 1912 Forster visited India with R. C. Trevelyan, G. Lowes Dickinson and G. H. Luce. After observing the British in India at close quarters, he developed an intense loathing for imperialism. Upon his return he wrote ***Maurice***, a novel depicting a successful homosexual relationship, which was circulated privately but not published until 1971, after his death.

E. M. Forster, *c.* 1910.

Following the outbreak of World War I, Forster joined the International Red Cross and served in Alexandria until 1919. Copies of his *Alexandria: A History and a Guide* (1922) were destroyed in a fire before circulation, and the book was not revised and reprinted until 1938. During the war he met the Greek poet, C. P. Cavafy, a selection of whose poems he published in translation in his collection of Alexandrian essays, *Pharos and Pharillon* (1923).

In 1921–2 Forster returned to India as secretary and companion to the Maharajah of the native state of Dewas Senior and resumed work on a novel which he had begun, and then put aside, after his first visit. ***A Passage to India*** (1924) was his most acclaimed novel; it was also his last, and for the remaining 46 years of his life he devoted himself to other activities. His Clark lectures were published as *Aspects of the Novel* (1927), and he was offered a three-year fellowship at King's College. *The Eternal Moment*, a volume of pre-war short stories about the supernatural, appeared in 1928, and ***Abinger Harvest*** (1936) was a collection of the shorter essays and criticism.

Forster was an active member of PEN, arguing (in 1928) against the suppression of **Radclyffe Hall**'s *The Well of Loneliness*, and later (in 1960) in defence of **Lady Chatterley's Lover**. In 1934 he became first president of the National Council for Civil Liberties. After his mother's death in 1945 he was elected an honorary fellow of King's and lived there for the remainder of his life. *Billy Budd* (1949), based on **Melville**'s novel, was a libretto written with Eric Crozier for Benjamin Britten's opera; a collection of essays, reviews and broadcasts, *Two Cheers for Democracy* (1951), reflected his concern for individual liberty; and *The Hill of Devi* (1953) recalled his second visit to India and included letters sent from Dewas Senior.

In 1949 Forster refused a knighthood, but 20 years later, the year before his death, he was awarded the Order of Merit. *The Life to Come* (1972), a collection of earlier short stories which like *Maurice* treated the homosexual theme, had also to await posthumous publication.

**Forster, John** 1812–76 Essayist and biographer. Born in Newcastle, he attended the grammar school there before entering University College, London. He studied law and was called to the Bar in 1843, but was increasingly attracted to journalism and the literary life. A close friend of **Dickens**, he succeeded the novelist as editor of ***The Daily News*** in 1846. He also edited *The Foreign Quarterly Review* (1842–3) and *The Examiner* (1847–55). Forster is remembered for his biographies of Dickens (1872–4) and another friend, **Walter Savage Landor** (1869). Among his other works were studies of **Goldsmith** (1848, enlarged 1854) and **Defoe** and **Charles Churchill**

(1855), and *The Arrest of the Five Members by Charles the First* (1860). He completed only the first volume of a life of **Swift** (1876) before his death.

**Forsyte Saga, The** A sequence of novels by **John Galsworthy**, comprising *The Man of Property* (1906), *In Chancery* (1920) and *To Let* (1921, with two interludes, 'Indian Summer of a Forsyte', 1918, and *Awakening*, 1920), published together in 1922.

It traces the fortunes of three generations of the Forsyte family, beginning in the prosperous upper middle class of Victorian London during the 1880s and ending in the early 1920s. Soames Forsyte, a successful solicitor, buys land at Robin Hill on which to build a house for his wife Irene and future family. Irene falls in love with its architect, Bosinney. Soames vindictively sues the latter for exceeding the estimates and Irene deserts him to live with her lover. Bosinney is run over and killed, and the Irene is forced to return to her husband. The second novel, *In Chancery*, follows her love-affair with Soames's cousin, Jolyon. She divorces her husband and they marry. Soames himself marries Annette Lamotte, who gives birth to a daughter, Fleur, Irene and Jolyon produce a son, Jon.

*To Let* describes how Jon and Fleur, now both 19 years old, fall in love. However, when Jolyon informs his son of the past feud the latter finally decides that he cannot marry Fleur. Instead he travels to America. Fleur now throws herself at a long-standing admirer, Michael Mont, a fashionable baronet's son, and the two are married. After Jolyon's death, Irene joins Jon in America. Soames learns that Annette has been unfaithful to him and is left desolately contemplating the sale of Robin Hill. The Forsyte family begins to disintegrate when Timothy Forsyte, the last of the old generation, dies at the age of 100.

**Fortescue, Sir John** *c.* 1394–*c.* 1476 Author of legal treatises. Born in Norris in Somerset, Fortescue was admitted to Lincoln's Inn *c.* 1415 and by 1430 was a serjeant-at-law. He became a Member of Parliament in 1421, was appointed Chief Justice in 1442 and knighted the following year. He supported Henry VI against the Yorkists and fled into exile with the king in 1461. At the battle of Tewkesbury (1471) he was taken prisoner but he submitted to the new king, Edward IV, and was pardoned and admitted to the Council.

Fortescue wrote legal treatises in both English and Latin, his most famous being *De Laudibus Legum Angliae* (1468–70, published in 1546), written for the education of the young Prince Edward. His *De Natura Legis Naturae* (1461–3) was rendered into English as *Monarchia, or The Difference between an Absolute and a Limited Monarchy*. His formal retraction of his pro-Lancastrian arguments was written in English, *A Declaration upon Certain Writings* (1471–3), as was his most important work, *The Governance of England* (*c.* 1473). This is the earliest constitutional treatise in English, and shows an acute insight into the failure of the Lancastrian system of government. Fortescue's clear, straightforward use of the vernacular was an important early influence upon the development of English prose.

**Fortnightly Review, The** A periodical founded by **Anthony Trollope**, Frederic Chapman the publisher and a number of friends and supporters to provide a platform for serious liberal opinion. The first number appeared in May 1865, edited by **G. H. Lewes**, with contributions from **Bagehot**, **George Eliot**, **Frederic Harrison**, Trollope and J. F. W. Herschel the astronomer. Its policy of printing the contributors' names was novel, and was later copied by many rival periodicals. It was not at first financially successful, and after November 1866 it was published once instead of twice a month. Its circulation recovered under its second editor, **John Morley** (1867–82): his contributors included **Meredith**, **Mill**, **Huxley**, **Arnold**, **Swinburne**, **Spencer**, Bagehot and **Leslie Stephen**. Morley's agnostic temper and the doctrinaire Positivism of his assistant, Frederic Harrison, gave the magazine its characteristic tone of opposition to traditional theology and eager support for humanitarian rationalism. **Frank Harris** (editor 1886–94) rescued the *Fortnightly* from a period of decline by publishing much specifically creative literary work and by flouting respectable taste. Under W. L. Courtney (1894–1928) the *Fortnightly* was urbane, academic and distinguished. It ceased publication in 1954.

**Fortune Theatre** Built in 1600, just outside Cripplegate in the Liberty of Finsbury, the Fortune was the home of the Lord Admiral's Men (renamed Prince Henry's Men in 1603) and the main outdoor rival to the **Globe** during the first two decades of the 17th century. From the surviving building contract, we know that **Henslowe** wished it to incorporate many features of the Globe. The first Fortune was destroyed by fire in 1621. The second Fortune, opened in 1623, was the first brickbuilt outdoor theatre, but despite this costly innovation its reputation soon deteriorated. It was partially demolished in 1649.

**Fortunes of Nigel, The** A novel by **Sir Walter Scott**, set in London in the reign of James I. It was published in 1822.

Nigel Oliphaunt, Lord Glenarvon, is in desperate need of a large sum of money which his father advanced to the King during a crisis in his fortunes. Without it Nigel will lose his heavily mortgaged estates. He comes to London and is received by the King, who signs an order on his behalf on the treasury of Scotland. But Prince Charles and the Duke of Buckingham covet the Glenarvon estates, and they send their favourite Lord Dalgarno, apparently to befriend Nigel but in fact to lead him into trouble and earn the King's displeasure. Margaret Ramsay, a London clockmaker's daughter, is uneasy about Nigel's friendship with Dalgarno: that gentleman's wronged wife, Hermione, is Margaret's patroness. Then Nigel discovers Dalgarno's true design and strikes him, an offence which, at the court of King James, could cost him his right hand. Nigel escapes to the underworld of Alsatia, while Margaret enlists the help of Lady Hermione and Richard Moniplies, Nigel's servant, on his behalf.

Nigel is taken, and sent to the Tower. Margaret tries to rescue him and at last disguises herself as a page to gain the King's attention. She succeeds, and at the same time secures reparation for Lady Hermione. Nigel marries Margaret and returns to Scotland. Dalgarno pursues him but is killed by robbers on the way.

***Fortunes of Richard Mahony, The*** A novel by **Henry Handel Richardson**, published in three parts as *Australia Felix* (1917), *The Way Home* (1925) and *Ultima Thule* (1929). The author drew heavily on the facts of her own father's madness for the closing chapters of the book.

Richard Townshend Mahony, a brilliant young doctor, is fascinated by the accounts of Australia and the gold rush which he reads in the English press. He gives up his practice and emigrates, arriving in Melbourne in the 1850s. Six months of prospecting at Ballarat finds him doing very badly and he uses his last resources to buy a barrow-load of sundries. With these he opens a 'Diggers Emporium'. A friend, Purdy Smith, who followed his example and emigrated to Australia, introduces him to the Beamish family in Melbourne; at their hotel he meets Mary Turnbull, a girl from England whom he marries. The emporium at Ballarat prospers until Mahony refuses to support the diggers in a militant action against the authorities. They boycott his store and he is forced to sell up.

Mary persuades Mahony to return to medicine, but in spite of his ability he lacks sympathy for his patients. He also becomes morbidly sensitive to patronage, real or imagined, and alienates patients at all levels of society. He retreats into himself, preoccupied by books, and turns first to religion and then to spiritualism. When things seem at their lowest ebb some shares in a dubious mine soar in value and the

Mahony fortunes are reversed. He and Mary return to Europe and he spends lavishly.

The crash comes when Richard's agent absconds. He returns to Australia and learns that he is ruined, but hides the full truth from Mary, who has joined him with their children. The strain of trying to get his affairs back in order takes severe toll of Richard, who eventually suffers mental and physical collapse. At the end of the tale Mary, resolute and uncomplaining, works as a postmistress in a remote settlement, nursing her husband in the last weeks of his life. The novel is unhurried and covers a broad canvas of events and characters.

***42nd Parallel, The*** See **USA**.

**Foucault, Michel** See **post-structuralism**.

***Four Birds of Noah's Ark, The*** This devotional work by **Thomas Dekker** is a collection of prayers. The four birds are the eagle, dove, phoenix and pelican. It was first printed in 1609.

***Four Georges, The*** Lectures by **W. M. Thackeray**, first delivered in America in 1855, and published there in book form in 1860.

Anecdotal and impressionistic, like his lectures on the **English Humorists**, Thackeray's rather bland account of the Hanoverian kings comes to life in his contemptuous portrait of George IV, a 'fribble dancing in lace and spangles'.

***Four Hymns*** **Spenser**'s *Four Hymns*, dedicated to the Countess of Cumberland and the Countess of Warwick, were printed together with the second edition of *Daphnaida* (1596). Their **rhyme royal** stanzas show the formal influence of **Chaucer**. They are in honour of Love, Beauty, Heavenly Love and Heavenly Beauty. Spenser's dedication, written from Greenwich, claims that the first two belong to 'the greener times of my youth' and that the hymns to Heavenly Love and Heavenly Beauty were written 'by way of retraction to reform' them. They are among Spenser's more difficult poems, part of the difficulty being their relationship to each other. They are at least intermittently influenced by Platonic and neo-Platonic theorizing about love, the notion in the *Symposium* that love is a desire for beauty partly explaining the double pairing of the poems. Platonic influence can also be detected in the parentage of Love in the first hymn and in its account of Love as the agent of creation. The second pair of poems is explicitly Christian in sentiment and tone, describing God's love in the Incarnation and the mysterious figure of Sapience enthroned in heaven. All four poems demonstrate a typically complex Renaissance synthesis of ideas about love, mingling Platonic philosophy and Renaissance commentaries on it, with theological language and Protestant piety and, at least in the first poem, the pains of the suffering poet–lover.

**Four Quartets** A group of four long poems by **T. S. Eliot**, published separately between 1935 and 1942 and collected in 1943.

Together, they make a meditative or devotional sequence, linked by common themes – consciousness and memory, the individual's relation to time and the transcendent experience of timelessness – and by recurrent motifs. This unity contrasts with the deliberately fragmentary method of *The Waste Land*, just as the openly religious character of *Four Quartets* contrasts with the apparently prevailing pessimism of the earlier work. Each of the four poems is firmly anchored in a place. 'Burnt Norton' (1935) meditates on a country house in the Cotswolds with a rose garden pervaded by children, or the memory of children. 'East Coker' (1940) takes its title from the Somerset village of Eliot's ancestors, where he himself chose to be buried, a fitting scene for meditation on transience and eternity. Like other poems in the sequence, it includes a moving consideration of the creative act itself. 'The Dry Salvages' (1941), named after a group of rocks off the Massachusetts coast, evokes memories of America, including Eliot's boyhood in St Louis. 'Little Gidding' (1942) refers to the religious community established near Huntingdon by **Nicholas Ferrar** in the 17th century, destroyed by Cromwell's troops and later rebuilt. It provides the setting for a meditation on war, destruction and reconciliation, and for a restrainedly jubilant ending which gathers together the arrivals and departures which have pervaded the sequence into an endless cycle of spiritual quest.

**fourteeners** See **metre**.

**Fowler, Henry Watson** 1858–1933 Lexicographer and grammarian. Educated at Rugby and Balliol College, Oxford, he taught for a few years, first at Fettes and afterwards at Sedbergh. From 1899 he lived in London, reading, and writing literary essays, apart from brief volunteer service as a private in World War I. In collaboration with his brother Francis George Fowler (1870–1918) he produced a four-volume translation of Lucian (1905) and *The King's English* (1906). His *Concise Oxford Dictionary of Current English* (1911), an abridgement of *The Oxford English Dictionary*, was the first of a series of Oxford dictionaries, the best known being the *Dictionary of Modern English Usage* (1926; re-edited in 1965 by **Sir Ernest Gowers**), long consulted as authoritative for both word usage and grammar.

**Fowler, Katherine** 1632–64 Poet. Also known by her married name, Katherine Philips, she was the daughter of a London merchant and married James Philips, a man of means from Cardigan, in 1647. A member of London's literary society, she organized a salon for the discussion of poetry and religion; **Vaughan, Cowley** and **Jeremy Taylor** were part of the circle. She became known by the admiring title 'Matchless Orinda' and was made the subject of several verses. Her own work includes verses prefixed to Vaughan's *Poems* (1651), a translation of Corneille's *Pompée* (performed in 1663) and a posthumous collection of verses in 1667. Cowley wrote an elegy at her death.

**Fowles, John (Robert)** 1926– Novelist. After reading French at New College, Oxford, and serving in the Royal Marines, Fowles became a teacher and spent some time working on the Greek island of Spetsai before the success of his first novel, *The Collector* (1963), enabled him to write full-time.

His fiction is characterized superficially by an extreme heterogeneity of subject-matter and treatment, and fundamentally by its preoccupation with the possibilities of genuinely free action. *The Collector* is a psychological thriller in which a girl, Miranda, is kidnapped by a psychotically possessive pools winner. *The Magus* (1966; revised 1977) is a long, compulsive masquerade of sexual enticement and historical manipulation set on a Greek island. *The French Lieutenant's Woman* (1969) is a careful pastiche of a Victorian novel undercut by 20th-century literary and social insight. Its heroine, the governess Sarah Woodruff, is one version of the elusive, inscrutable woman who appears throughout Fowles's fiction, notably in the title novella of *The Ebony Tower* (1974), a collection of shorter fictions. *Daniel Martin* (1977) is a dense, realistic **Bildungsroman** rooted in post-war Britain and propounding 'an unfashionable philosophy, humanism'. *Mantissa* (1983) is a sexual *jeu d'esprit* and satire of contemporary structuralist ideology, while his most recent work, *A Maggot* (1985), is a murder mystery set in the 18th century and written as a pastiche transcript of the subsequent interrogations.

*The Aristos* (1964; revised 1980) is a 'self-portrait in ideas' setting forth the personal version of existentialism which underlies the novels. Fowles's concern with the strategies of fictional narrative and the implications of conventional ways of writing fiction is explicated in the valuable 'Notes on an Unfinished Novel' in *The Novel Today*, edited by **Malcolm Bradbury** (1977).

**Fox, George** 1624–91 Founder of the Society of Friends. The son of a Leicestershire weaver, he was born at Fenny Drayton and apprenticed to a shoemaker. He abandoned churchgoing to preach his own belief that God spoke directly to the individual soul. Though he suffered imprisonment, Fox also attracted an increasing number of followers; from these beginnings the Society of Friends (or Quakers) was born. An organizer of genius, he made several missionary journeys to Ireland, Holland, America and the West Indies. He married Margaret Fell in 1669.

Fox is also remembered for his remarkable *Journal*, the story of his spiritual search told with simplicity and illustrated with vivid vignettes. It was prepared for publication by a committee of fellow Quakers in 1694. *A Collection of Epistles* was published in 1698, and *Gospel Truth* in 1706.

**Fox, Paula** 1923– American novelist and children's writer. Born in New York, she worked in publishing and journalism before turning to writing. Her children's novels mark a distinct break with the more secure world described by older authors. Their young heroes and heroines often suffer from prolonged confusion, some of which will be shared by inexperienced readers. In *How Many Miles to Babylon?* (1967) a small black boy is kidnapped by older children who want to use him for thieving; how much he ever understands about his adventures is never made clear. Other novels repeatedly take up the theme of youthful alienation, most memorably in *The Slave Dancer* (1973), about Jessie, a boy kidnapped into slavery in New Orleans in 1840, and his horrific experiences on a slave-ship.

**Fox and the Wolf, The** A Middle English poem in couplets written *c.* 1250–75, probably in the South of England. It narrates an episode from the *Roman de Renart* in which the fox, after an unsuccessful raid on a poultry yard, is driven by thirst to jump into the bucket of a well and gets trapped at the bottom. He dupes the wolf, Sigrim, into believing he has gone to heaven and persuades Sigrim to make his confession and leap into the other bucket to join him. The fox escapes, leaving the wolf trapped, to be soundly beaten by the monks who own the well.

The poem has features of both beast-epic and **fable**; it is the only piece of its kind extant from this period. The plot is handled with vigour and humour, and the anthropomorphism of the two animals is skilfully accomplished. Apart from **Chaucer**'s *The Nun's Priest's Tale* (see **Canterbury Tales**), it represents the only branch of the Renard cycle in Middle English before the appearance of **Caxton**'s translation, *Reynard the Fox*.

**Foxe, John** 1516–87 Martyrologist. Foxe went up to Oxford *c.* 1532 and became a fellow of Magdalen College in 1539. His radically Protestant views caused him to resign his fellowship in

An illustration from the 1610 edition of Foxe's *Acts and Monuments*. Henry VIII tramples on Pope Clement and receives the English Bible from Cranmer. Cardinals Pole and Fisher go to the Pope's assistance.

1545 and move to London. There he became tutor to the children of the Earl of Surrey, who had been executed in 1547. To the years of this tutorship belong his early religious and moral tracts. On the accession of Mary, the Roman Catholic Duke of Norfolk, the children's grandfather, was released and Foxe lost his post. He fled from England to Strasburg, taking with him his manuscript describing the persecution of reformers in Europe which was later to grow into his **Acts and Monuments**.

From Strasburg he moved to Frankfurt and then to Basle, where he earned money correcting proofs for a printer. In 1556 his Latin play *Christus Triumphans* was printed at Basle. It is a rather crude apocalyptic work which was later performed at Trinity College, Cambridge, and printed in an English translation in 1578. From abroad Foxe issued *Ad Inclytos ac Praepotentes Angliae Proceres* (1557), an appeal to the English nobility to restrain Mary in her persecutions of Protestants. He returned to England after Elizabeth's accession and was ordained priest by Grindal in 1560. He never gained high office in the Anglican Church because of his extreme Protestantism (he particularly objected to wearing a surplice). Among his later works are the anti-Catholic *A Sermon of Christ Crucified* (1570), which was preached at Paul's Cross, an edition of Anglo-Saxon texts of the Gospels (1571) and a Latin treatise on the Eucharist (?1580).

**Fra Lippo Lippi** A poem by **Robert Browning**, published in **Men and Women** (1855). Filippo Lippi (*c.* 1406–69) was a painter of the Florentine school and a Carmelite monk. Taking hints from a passage in Vasari's *Lives of the Painters*, Browning gives Lippi a lively dramatic monologue expressing his discontent with the constraints of monasticism and with the purely spiritual art his superiors want him to produce. Instead, the painter prefers a realism that attends to the fleshly details of the world around him.

**Frame, Janet** 1924– New Zealand novelist. Born in Dunedin, she was brought up in Oamaru (the 'Waimaru' of her novels) on the eastern coast of South Island as a member of a poor family in a generally affluent farming area. She attended Dunedin Teachers College and Otago University and subsequently became a teacher, but left the profession within a year and earned a living looking after four elderly women in a boarding house. Her first book, *The Lagoon* (1951), a collection of short stories, was written at the age of 21. She was deeply affected by the drowning of two of her sisters in separate accidents in 1937 and 1947 and had a number of nervous breakdowns. From 1947 to 1955 she spent most of the time in psychiatric hospitals, an experience which is treated in several of her novels, where 'madness' becomes a metaphor for escape from the constrictions of society and schizophrenia is seen to involve breaking down structures which inhibit personal growth. She subsequently went overseas, spending most of 1957 in Ibiza and Andorra and subsequently living in England for seven years, an experience which is described in the third volume of her autobiography, *The Envoy from Mirror City* (1985). Generally regarded as New Zealand's finest living novelist, Frame has won several awards for her fiction in her own country and in 1983 was awarded the CBE. Her first novel, *Owls Do Cry* (1957), is a strongly autobiographical account of growing up in a small New Zealand town. *Faces in the Water* (1961) describes a journey through madness, in which autobiography and fiction intermingle. Novels like *The Edge of the Alphabet* (1962), *Scented Gardens for the Blind* (1963) and *Living in the Maniototo* (1981) are about communication and the problems of realizing experience in language, a major concern of all Frame's fiction. Set in England, *The Adaptable Man* (1965) represents a departure from her earlier work in that it deals with a larger cast of characters and appears to be more concerned with providing a picture of society, but again the novel is about alienation and the problems of conformity. *Intensive Care* (1970) and *Daughter Buffalo* (1972) grew from periods Frame spent at a writers' colony in the United States and both expose humanity's capacity for death and destruction. Frame's other novels include *A State of Siege* (1966) and *The Rainbirds* (1968), reissued as *Yellow Flowers in the Antipodean Room* (1969). She has also published three

other collections of stories and sketches, a children's book and a volume of verse, *The Pocket Mirror* (1967). The first two volumes of her autobiography are *To the Island* (1982) and *Angel at My Table* (1984).

**Framley Parsonage** The fourth of **Anthony Trollope**'s **Barsetshire Novels**. It was published in *The Cornhill Magazine* from January 1860 to April 1861.

The living of Framley is given to Mark Robarts by the widowed Lady Lufton; he is a close friend of her son, Lord Ludovic Lufton. Through Lord Lufton Mark meets Mr Sowerby and the Duke of Omnium, neither of them ideal companions for a young clergyman, since Sowerby is a spendthrift and Omnium is disreputable. After agreeing to support bills for Sowerby, Mark gains a prebendary at Barchester through his influence and the Duke and proceeds to conduct himself in a way that annoys his patroness, Lady Lufton.

Lord Lufton falls in love with Lucy Robarts, Mark's sister, but his mother opposes the match. Lucy will not marry Ludovic without Lady Lufton's complete acceptance of her and eventually her integrity and Ludovic's persistence carry the day. Mark, meanwhile, has been getting into deep water and is rescued by the generous Ludovic; he forswears the idle life which is really beyond his means. Sowerby himself is near ruin – his property is heavily mortgaged to the Duke – and hopes to marry the rich Miss Dunstable; but she refuses him and marries Dr Thorne. The novel features familiar Barsetshire characters: the Grantlys and their daughter Griselda, who marries Lord Dumbello; Bishop and Mrs Proudie; and the Revd Josiah Crawley.

**Francis, Sir Philip** 1740–1818 Civil servant and politician. Born in Dublin and educated at St Paul's School in London, Francis held minor public offices before becoming a councillor to the Governor General of India in 1773. His disagreements with Warren Hastings led to bitter enmity and caused Francis, after his return to England in 1781, to join **Burke** in the unsuccessful prosecution of Hastings on charges of corruption and cruelty. In 1784 Francis entered Parliament, giving up his seat in 1804; he owed his knighthood to his friendship with the Prince Regent.

There is evidence for identifying Francis as the **Junius** of the famous letters which appeared in *The Public Advertiser*, published by his old schoolfellow Henry Sampson Woodfall. However, Woodfall denied Francis's authorship and some of Francis's friends are treated harshly in the letters.

**Frank, Waldo (David)** 1889–1967 American

novelist and critic, born in Long Branch, New Jersey, and educated at Yale. A member of *avant-garde* literary circles, he advocated social and political reform in his novels, which include *City Block* (1922); *Holiday* (1923), an examination of racial problems in the South; *The Death and Birth of David Markand* (1934), about an American businessman's decision to alter his life-style radically; and *The Bridegroom Cometh* (England 1938, America 1939), which tells of a woman's discovery of faith while working for social reform. *Chalk Face* (1924) is a horror novel, *New Year's Eve* (1929) an expressionistic play. He also wrote a good deal of historical and social criticism: *Our America* (1919), *Salvos* (1924), *The Re-Discovery of America* (1929) and *America Hispana* (1931); a study of industrial America, *In the American Jungle* (1937); *Birth of a World* (1951), about Simon Bolivar; a collection of sketches about Israel, *Bridgehead* (1957); and *The Prophetic Island: A Portrait of Cuba* (1961).

*Frankenstein, or, The Modern Prometheus* A **Gothic novel** by **Mary Shelley**, published in 1818. She had begun it in 1816 when she, her husband **Shelley**, and **Byron** wrote ghost stories to pass the time during a summer in Switzerland.

Frankenstein, a student of natural philosophy in Geneva, builds a creature in the semblance of a man and gives it life. Possessed of unnatural strength, the creature inspires horror in those who see it but is miserably eager to be loved. The unhappy Frankenstein deserts the creature but is pursued to Chamonix, where he agrees to make a mate. However, a wave of remorse makes him destroy the female he has been constructing, and the creature swears revenge on his creator. He kills Frankenstein's bride on their wedding night. Frankenstein's father dies of grief, and the scientist's mind gives way. Eventually he recovers and sets out to destroy his creation. After a chase across the world, the two at last confront each other in the Arctic wastes. Frankenstein dies and the creature, mourning the loss of the man who gave him life, disappears into the frozen wilderness, hoping for his own annihilation.

**Franklin, Benjamin** 1706–90 American politician and man of letters. Born in Boston, he received little formal education. At the age of 12 he was apprenticed to his half-brother, the printer James Franklin, to whose *New England Courant* he contributed the essays that were published anonymously in 1722 as *The Letters of Silence Dogood* and which are notable for their humorous commentary on **Cotton Mather**'s *Bonifacius*. He moved to Philadelphia in 1723, and then travelled to England to buy equipment for a press of his own. During a stay of two

years he wrote and published *A Dissertation on Liberty and Necessity, Pleasure and Pain* (1725).

He returned to Philadelphia in 1726 and eventually succeeded in setting up his own press. In 1729 he published the first issue under his own proprietorship of *The Pennsylvania Gazette*, the newspaper which he managed and contributed to until 1766. Three years later he launched the widely read *Poor Richard's Almanac* (1732–58) and *The General Magazine* (1741). He also became actively involved in the public affairs of Philadelphia: he was responsible for drawing up the plans for the lighting and maintenance of the city's streets, for a police force, and for a circulating library; he founded a city hospital, and an Academy for the Education of Youth which later became the University of Pennsylvania. Between 1751 and 1753 he published the results of his celebrated kite experiments in *Experiments and Observations on Electricity*.

He spent most of the 1760s in England, working to advance the cause of colonial representation in Parliament. He returned to Philadelphia in 1769 and founded the American Philosophical Society. He then went back to England, until, convinced that his efforts to promote the colonial cause had failed and that war was inevitable, he returned to America in 1775. He served in the Continental Congress and was part of the committee that ordered the drafting of the *Declaration of Independence*. While serving as Postmaster-General he was sent by the Congress to France, where he remained throughout the war and negotiated an economic and military alliance. When he returned to America in 1785, he was appointed president of the Executive Council of Pennsylvania, a post which he filled for three years, and participated in the Constitutional Convention; he signed the Constitution in 1787 and died three years later in Philadelphia.

Franklin produced numerous tracts on issues such as politics, legal theory, education, language and population control. These, along with a varied and large body of correspondence, constitute a witty and informative history of 18th-century America. His writings of note include *A Scheme for a New Alphabet and Reformed Mode of Spelling* (1768); *Edict of the King of Prussia* (1773) and *Rules By Which a Great Empire may be reduced to a Small One* (1773), both of which oppose the Townshend Acts; *Remarks Concerning the Savages of North America* (1784); 'On The Slave Trade' (1790), a memorandum to Congress which advocates the abolition of slavery; and his *Autobiography* (begun in 1771 and never completed).

**Franklin, (Stella Maria Sarah) Miles** 1879– 1954 Australian novelist. Born near Tumut, New South Wales, Miles Franklin worked as a freelance writer in Sydney and Melbourne until

'Americans throwing the cargoes of the Tea Ships into the River at Boston.' An 18th-century engraving depicting the celebrated act of resentment against the Townshend Acts, which Benjamin Franklin worked so hard to get repealed.

1905, when she travelled to the United States, she remained abroad, living in England and America, until 1927. Her best-known novel, *My Brilliant Career* (1901), was described as 'the very first Australian novel' on account of its original and distinctive Australian character. *My Brilliant Career* and its sequel *My Career Goes Bung* (published in 1946, some 40 years after it was written) describe the adventures and misadventures of Sybylla Melvyn, who aspires to the cultivated life of a writer but is hampered by the backwardness and rigid convention of bush society. The character of Sybylla, with her determined independence, fiery self-confidence and inopportune blundering, is curiously attractive, and was for some time thought to be an autobiographical portrait. In fact, Miles Franklin expressed astonishment at 'the literalness with which *My Brilliant Career* was taken'. Other novels include *Some Everyday Folk – and Dawn* (1909), *Old Blastus of Bandicoot* (1931), *Bring the Monkey* (1933) and *All That Swagger* (1936).

**Franklin's Tale, The** See *Canterbury Tales, The*.

**Fraser, George MacDonald** 1925– Novelist and historian. In 1946–7 he served as a Lieutenant with the Gordon Highlanders, later producing two collections of stories about life in a Highland regiment, *The General Danced at Dawn* (1970) and *McAuslan in the Rough* (1974). *The Steel Bonnets: The Story of the Anglo-Scottish Border Reivers* (1971) is a work of history. Fraser is best known for his novels based on the subsequent military career of the bully from Thomas Hughes's *Tom Brown's Schooldays*, Flashman: a memorable anti-hero, always where the action is, and, despite native cowardice, emerging with glory. From *Flashman* (1969) onward, these cover the Afghan Wars, Crimea, Indian Mutiny, etc., lightly carrying considerable knowledge and research. *Mr American* (1980), a view of Edwardian England through the eyes of a transatlantic visitor, comes most to life when the now aged Flashman briefly appears as a minor character. In *The Pyrates* (1983) the element of burlesque has the upper hand.

**Fraser, G[eorge] S[utherland]** 1915–80 Critic and poet. Born in Glasgow, Fraser was educated at Glasgow Academy, Aberdeen Grammar School and St Andrews University. After serving in the Middle East during the war, he became a critic, and from 1959, worked as a lecturer at Leicester University. His early poetry, in *The Fatal Landscape* (1941) and *Home Town Elegy* (1944), shows a neoclassical strain and lyrical clarity that has little to do with the excesses of the **New Apocalypse** movement, with which he was associated. A minor poet, his other collections include *The Traveller Has Regrets* (1948), *Conditions: Selected Recent Poetry* (1969), and the posthumous collected *Poems of G. S. Fraser* (1981). He is more important as the foremost journalistic critic of his era; his publications include *The Modern Writer and His World* (1953), a study of **Dylan Thomas** (1957), *Vision and Rhetoric: Studies in Modern Poetry* (1959) and *A Stranger and Afraid: Autobiography of an Intellectual* (1983).

*Fraser's Magazine* Founded by **William Maginn** and Hugh Fraser, this monthly magazine commenced publication in February 1830 and ceased in October 1882. Although it remained in the forefront of Victorian periodicals, it enjoyed its heyday under Maginn's editorship. Contributors included **Carlyle** and **Thackeray**, as well as **John Galt, Charles Kingsley, J. A. Froude** and **James Spedding**. Maginn was succeeded in the editorial chair by **Francis Sylvester Mahony** (Father Prout), Froude, **William Allingham** and others.

**Frayn, Michael** 1933– Dramatist, novelist and journalist. Born in London, he was educated at Kingston Grammar School and Emmanuel College, Cambridge. He first established his reputation with witty, gently satirical columns in *The Manchester Guardian* and *The Observer* and a series of novels in the same vein, including *The Russian Interpreter* (1966), *Towards the End of the Morning* (1967) and the fantasy, *A Very Private Life* (1968). At Cambridge he had already written revue sketches. He turned again to the theatre with a quartet of short plays, *The Two of Us* (1970), and *The Sandboy* (1971), showing his instinct for comic dialogue. His true strengths did not emerge until three comedies in the mid 1970s: *Alphabetical Order* (1975), about mayhem in a newspaper cuttings library; *Donkeys' Years* (1976), about university loves; and *Clouds* (1976), perhaps the most original, based on his experiences as a journalist on a visit to Cuba. *Liberty Hall* (1979) satirizes a writers' collective established by the state in Balmoral Castle. His greatest commercial success came with *Noises Off* (1982), a backstage comedy about an appalling touring company. Frayn has also translated and adapted work by Chekhov and Tolstoy for the **National Theatre**.

**Frazer, Sir James (George)** 1854–1941 Historian of 'primitive' religion and classical scholar. Born into a pious (Free Church of Scotland) middle-class family in Glasgow, Frazer was educated at the University of Glasgow and then at Trinity College, Cambridge. He was a fellow of Trinity from 1879 until his death. His best-known work is *The Golden Bough* (2 vols., 1890; 3 vols., 1900; 12 vols., 1911–15; abridged edition, 1922). In it he sifted the burgeoning ethnographic literature from a rationalistic, comparative, and evolutionary point of view in describing the religious behaviour of the entire primitive world. To this encyclopaedic survey he added a discussion of the religions of classical antiquity to produce an attractive, if simplistic, thesis: that everywhere in human mental evolution a belief in magic preceded religion, which in turn was followed in the West by science. Although he employed the attitude and language of objective science,

Frazer's analysis of the religions of the ancient eastern Mediterranean constituted an effective, because well-written, attack on what he regarded as the outworn absurdities and mistakes of religion in general and Christianity in particular. Between the wars he was widely read, and certain images drawn from his work (like that of the Fisher King) attained general intellectual currency: **T. S. Eliot**'s *The Waste Land* (1922) is perhaps the best example of *The Golden Bough*'s literary influence. Frazer produced many other works in the history of religion, but as an 'armchair' anthropologist his standing today among students of religion is low; his more purely classical work, like his commentary on Pausanias (1898) and his edition of Ovid's *Fasti* (1929), has fared better among scholars.

**Frederic, Harold** 1856–98 American novelist, born in Utica, New York. As a young man he worked as a journalist, eventually as the London correspondent for *The New York Times*. He then gave up journalism for fiction, and became a pioneer of the American realist movement. His first novel, *Seth's Brother's Wife* (1886), portrays life on an American farm, and also examines the worlds of politics and journalism. *The Lawton Girl* (1890) and *The Return of the O'Mahoney* (1892) extended his reputation as a local colourist. *In the Valley* (1890) focuses on the American Revolution; *The Copperhead* (1893) and *Marsena and Other Stories* (1894) deal with the Civil War. His best-known novel, **The Damnation of Theron Ware** (1896), depicts the religious and psychological decline of a Methodist minister. His last three novels – *March Hares* (1896), and the posthumously published *Gloria Mundi* (1898) and *The Market Place* (1899) – are historical tales set in England.

**free verse** See **metre**.

**Freeling, Nicolas** See **detective fiction**.

**Freeman, Edward Augustus** 1823–92 Historian. Born at Harborne in Staffordshire, he was privately educated before going to Trinity College, Oxford, where he became a fellow. Freeman was a regular contributor to periodicals, including *The Saturday Review*, and later published his essays in book form as *Historical Essays* (four collections, 1871, 1873, 1879 and 1892). He published his lectures on *The History and Conquests of the Saracens* in 1856, *The History of Federal Government* in 1863, and his best-known work, *The History of the Norman Conquest of England: Its Causes and Its Results*, in 1867–79. Among his other works are *A History of Europe* (1876), *The Turks in Europe* (1877), *The Historical Geography of Europe* (1881), *The Reign of William Rufus and the Accession of Henry I*

(1882), *William the Conqueror* (1888) and *The History of Sicily from the Earliest Times* (1891–4). Freeman was also the author of a number of essays on architecture.

**Freeman, Mary (Eleanor) Wilkins** 1852–1930 American short-story writer and novelist. Born in Randolph, Massachusetts, Freeman began by writing stories for children, but soon devoted her attention to an adult audience. In 1887 she published her first collection, *A Humble Romance and Other Stories*, and followed this in 1891 with *A New England Nun and Other Stories*. Both volumes focus on the lives of women in small New England villages who are placed in situations where they must defend their own values against those of the community. Freeman also wrote novels, plays and poems. *Pembroke* (1894), one of her more successful novels, is a fine study of the New England character and of conventional life there. Her other works include *Giles Corey, Yeoman: A Play* (1893), *Madelon* (1896, a novel), *Silence and Other Stories* (1898), *The Heart's Highway: A Romance of Virginia* (1900), and *The Fair Lavinia and Others* (1907). With **William Dean Howells** and **Henry James** among others, she was one of the contributors to *The Whole Family, A Novel by Twelve Authors* (1908).

**Freeman, R. Austin** See **detective fiction**.

**French, David** 1939– Canadian playwright. Born in Newfoundland and raised in Toronto,

Mary Wilkins Freeman.

he began his career as an actor and writer for television. *Leaving Home* (1972), his successful first stage play, and *Of the Fields Lately* (1973) explore archetypal family conflicts in the specific context of the Mercers, an 'immigrant' Newfoundland family in Toronto. French returned to the Mercers for a third work, *Salt-Walter Moon* (1984). The same autobiographical impulse, but in a very different genre, lies at the base of his most produced and praised play, *Jitters* (1979), a backstage comedy which offers an affectionate view of theatrical life as it is coloured by the specific problems and insecurities of producing theatre in Canada.

**French Lieutenant's Woman, The** A novel by **John Fowles**, published in 1969. It was widely praised for its attempt to combine the scope and solidity of Victorian fiction with experimental narrative devices.

At Lyme Regis on the Dorset coast Charles Smithson, a young Victorian palaeontologist, is struck by a solitary female figure standing at the far end of the Cob staring out to sea. She turns out to be Sarah Woodruff, an enigmatic governess ostracized by the community for her reported liaison with a French sailor who has since deserted her. Although he is already engaged to Ernestina Freeman, Charles is first beguiled and eventually infatuated by the woman, but on the single occasion when the affair is consummated he discovers Sarah to be a virgin. Charles and Ernestina's engagement is broken off, and the novel supplies alternative endings to Charles's story – both a happy and lasting reunion with Sarah and a bleak realization that they are irrevocably separated.

**French Revolution, The** A history by **Thomas Carlyle**, first published in 1837.

Carlyle's formidable warning to the British aristocracy, published half a century after the French Revolution, opens in 1774 with the death of Louis XV and closes a generation later in October 1795 with Bonaparte putting down the Insurrection of Vendémiaire. Thus the reign of the unfortunate Louis XVI occupies a central place in this sweeping prose work. Although Carlyle has been accused of bending history to his visionary philosophy, *The French Revolution* remains an epic work that traces with poetical and historical power the dramatic end of a long-established regime, the consequent Terror and the inevitable decline of insurrection. It is rich in portraits (of Robespierre and Mirabeau, for example) and descriptive set-pieces (of the murder of Marat, the flight to Varennes, the mutiny at Nancy). Carlyle alters his viewpoint effectively throughout the book, writing of some events as a moralist, of some as a detached observer and of some as a near-participant.

**Freneau, Philip (Morin)** 1752–1832 The major American poet of the 18th century. Of Huguenot ancestry, Freneau was born in New York City and grew up in Monmouth, New Jersey. He attended the College of New Jersey (later Princeton University), where he met **Hugh Henry Brackenridge** with whom he collaborated on the poem *The Rising Glory of America*, which was read at their graduation in 1771 and published the following year. A short collection of poems, *The American Village*, appeared in 1772 and was followed by 'Pictures of Columbus' in 1774. When the Revolution began he contributed patriotic poems in support of the American cause to the newspapers, but in 1776 he withdrew from politics and travelled to the West Indies.

The exotic settings of the Caribbean inspired him to write occasional poetry, some of which he published in Brackenridge's *United States Magazine* in 1779, together with poems on more patriotic themes, such as 'George the Third's Soliloquy', 'The Loyalists', and 'America Independent'. In 1780 he was captured by the British and held prisoner on the *Scorpion* in New York harbour. His brief but harsh captivity prompted him to write *The British Prison Ship*, published as a broadside in 1781. In 1781–2 he contributed essays and further Revolutionary War poems to the *Philadelphia Freeman's Journal*, celebrating American heroes and attacking the British. He continued to express a passionate patriotism and hatred for the British in many of his later poems and journalistic writings – most notably in the *National Gazette* (1791–3), a Philadelphia journal that he founded and edited at **Thomas Jefferson**'s urging.

Between 1784 and 1790 he spent a good deal of time at sea, as captain of a trader. His poems during this period include *Journeys from Philadelphia to New York* (1787), which introduced the humorous persona of Robert Slender, weaver, one of the fictional voices which Freneau would use in later political essays. With the folding of the *National Gazette*, he returned to Monmouth, where he published an almanac, and founded and edited the *Jersey Chronicle*. *Letters on Various Interesting and Important Subjects*, a collection of some of the pro-Jefferson 'Robert Slender' letters that had appeared in the Philadelphia journal *Aurora*, was published in 1799. The 'Slender' series ended with Jefferson's election in 1801. *Poems on American Affairs* (1815) contained verses occasioned by the war of 1812, as well as poems exploring deistic ideas, among them 'On the Universality and Other Attributes of the God of Nature'. Freneau spent his last years living in poverty in New Jersey. He died of exposure after being caught in a snowstorm.

**Frere, John Hookham** 1769–1846 Translator and poet. Born in London, he was educated at Eton and at Gonville and Caius College, Cambridge, and enjoyed a distinguished career as a diplomat. In the world of literature, he joined **Canning** (a lifelong friend whom he had first met at Eton) in publishing *The Anti-Jacobin* and played a part in founding *The Quarterly Review*. His translations from the Spanish appended to **Southey**'s *Chronicle of the Cid* (1808) were much admired. He also published translations of several plays by Aristophanes between 1839 and 1842. His witty mock-heroic poem, *Prospectus and Specimen of an Intended National Work by William and Robert Whistlecraft of Stowmarket in Suffolk, Harness and Collar Makers. Intended to Comprise the Most Interesting Particulars Relating to King Arthur and his Round Table* (1817), revived the stanza form used by Pulci and other Italian poets and prompted **Byron** to adopt it in *Beppo* and *Don Juan*. In 1819, however, Frere was one of the 'committee' of Byron's acquaintances who recommended against the publication of the first canto of *Don Juan* because of its indecency.

**Freudian criticism** See **psychoanalytic criticism**.

***Friar Bacon and Friar Bungay, The Honorable History of*** A comedy in prose and verse by **Robert Greene**, first printed in 1594 but probably produced a few years before. Friar Bacon and Friar Bungay are based on the 13th-century Franciscans of Oxford, **Roger Bacon** and Thomas Bungay.

Bacon makes a brass head with the help of Bungay; then, with the help of the Devil, confers the power of speech on it. It will utter in the course of a month but they must be present to hear it speak or all their labours will go for nothing. After a three-week vigil, day and night, Bacon hands the watch over to Miles, his servant, and falls into an exhausted sleep. When the head speaks it utters but two words, 'Time is', which Miles does not think important

The title-page illustration of the 1666 edition of Greene's *Friar Bacon and Friar Bungay*, first published in 1594.

enough to justify waking his master. Next the head says, 'Time was' and then 'Time is past', before it falls on the floor, breaking into pieces. Bacon awakes, and the unfortunate Miles receives the full fury of his wrath. A sub-plot tells of the love of Lord Lacy and the Prince of Wales for the pretty Margaret, a gamekeeper's daughter. A notable scene has Bacon and Bungay and a German rival displaying their powers before the Kings of England and Castile and the Emperor of Germany.

***Friar Daw's Reply*** See ***Jack Upland***.

***Friar's Tale, The*** See ***Canterbury Tales, The***.

**Friel, Brian** 1929– Irish playwright, born in Omagh and educated there and in Derry, where he taught 1950–60. His first play, *This Doubtful Paradise* (1959), was staged in Belfast, but most of his subsequent work has been first performed in Dublin. His first major success was *Philadelphia, Here I Come!* (1964), less a play about emigration than about the anguish of uncommunicated love between a son and his father. Subsequent plays have demonstrated Friel's ability to establish a strong central situation and explore its ramifications. They include: *The Loves of Cass McGuire* (1966); *Lovers* (1967), which consists of two loosely linked plays; *Crystal and Fox* (1968), an evocation of a shoddy touring theatre and its self-destructive leader; *The Freedom of the City* (1973), which highlights the tragic incongruities of events leading to the killing by the authorities of three Londonderry demonstrators; *Volunteers* (1975), whose title refers to a group of Irish prisoners oddly engaged in an archaeological dig; *Faith Healer* (1979), a compilation of monologues describing the life and death of a charlatan; and *Translations* (1980), set in 1833 when the English army was given the task of rationalizing Celtic place-names in order to make the first maps of the region. Friel's short stories have been collected in *The Saucer of Larks* (1962), *The Gold in the Sea* (1966) and *The Diviner* (1983).

**Frost, Robert (Lee)** 1874–1963 American poet, born and raised in San Francisco. His father's death in 1885 forced the family to return to their native New England, where they settled in Lawrence, Massachusetts. Frost went to Dartmouth College but withdrew in his first term to return to Lawrence and support his family by teaching. He married in 1895 and applied to Harvard as a special student; he was accepted into a three-year programme but withdrew after two years. Following the deaths of his son Elliott, his mother and his daughter Elinor, he fell into a deep depression and seriously contemplated suicide. In 1912 he and his family moved to England, where he found a publisher for his first book of verse, *A Boy's Will* (1913). The collection was well received and was soon followed by a second, *North of Boston* (1914). These publications, along with his friendship with poets such as **Ezra Pound** and **Edward Thomas**, increased his exposure in literary magazines. In 1915 he returned to the USA and settled on a farm in New Hampshire.

There Frost the poet was nurtured. Like that of many great national poets, his verse relies heavily on the language of the people. Many of his poems take the form of dramatic monologues or dialogues, using and transforming the New Englander's patterns of speech which he heard each day on his farm. His third collection, *Mountain Interval*, appeared in 1916, and he began to attract national attention. *New Hampshire* (1923) was awarded a Pulitzer Prize. Following the publication of *West-Running Brook* (1928), his *Collected Poems* (1930) won him a second Pulitzer. The distinction was bestowed twice more, for *A Further Range* (1936) – making Frost the first to win the Pulitzer Prize three times – and for *A Witness Tree* (1942).

His work developed further in the 1940s with the production of *A Masque of Reason* (1945) and *A Masque of Mercy* (1947) – dramatic poems in blank verse, portraying biblical characters and exploring the relation of man to God in the modern world. In 1947 he published *A Steeple Bush*, a collection of lyrics. Despite increasingly poor health, he wrote poetry to the end of his life; his last collection, *In the Clearing*, appeared in 1962. His poetry is among the most accessible of modern writers, given the central theme of all his collections: the quest of the solitary person to make sense of the world.

**Froude, James Anthony** 1818–94 Historian. The younger brother of **Richard Hurrell Froude**, James Anthony was born at Totnes in Devon. He was educated at Westminster School and Oriel College, Oxford, where like his brother he came under the influence of **John Henry Newman**. Newman's conversion to Rome weakened Froude's faith in Christianity; he wrote about this period of life in *Shadows in the Clouds* (1847) and *The Nemesis of Faith* (1848), two essays in semifictional autobiography. Two years later he met **Thomas Carlyle** and became his lifelong friend and disciple.

Like other 19th-century historians Froude wrote a great deal for journals, contributing essays, mainly historical, to **The Westminster Review** and to **Fraser's Magazine**, which he edited (1860–74). A notable essay, *England's Forgotten Worthies* (1852), printed in *The Westminster Review* attracted some attention. The first two volumes of *A History of England from the Fall of Wolsey to the Death of Elizabeth* were published in 1858 and the work was completed in 12 volumes in 1870. Froude was severely criticized for his presentation of history: he followed Carlyle in the belief that only extraordinary men initiate and control great events, and his approach was often polemical. In spite of that his history was highly successful, even while **Macaulay**'s work was still in progress. The reasons for its success were Froude's narrative gifts, his scrupulous research (he frequently paraphrases original documents and carefully identifies them), and his excellent prose style. *The English in Ireland in the Eighteenth Century* (1872–4) grew out of a series of lectures which Froude delivered in the USA. This book also became the centre of controversy and **W. E. H. Lecky** dealt with it very firmly in his *The History of England in the Eighteenth Century* (1878–92).

In 1874 Froude went on a government mission to South Africa to investigate the possibilities of federation; he also travelled in Australia (1884) and the West Indies (1886) and published *Oceana, or, England and Her Colonies* (1886) and *The English in the West Indies, or, The Bow of Ulysses* (1888), both readable and interesting for the contemporary view. As Thomas Carlyle's literary executor he was from 1881 engaged in the publication of the biographical remains of his friend and of **Jane Welsh Carlyle**. He performed the task with commendable frankness. Froude's memoirs of Carlyle are published in *Thomas Carlyle: A History of the First Forty Years of His Life* (1882), *Thomas Carlyle: A History of His Life in London* (1884) and *My Relations with Carlyle* (1886).

Froude was appointed Regius Professor of Modern History at Oxford in 1892. Among his other works were the collections of his best essays, *Short Studies on Great Subjects* (four series, 1867, 1871, 1877 and 1883); *Bunyan* (1880), for the English Men of Letters series; *The Knights Templar* (1886); *Lord Beaconsfield* (1890); and *The Divorce of Catherine of Aragon: Being A Supplement to The History of England* (1891).

**Froude, Richard Hurrell** 1803–36 Religious controversialist. The elder brother of the historian **James Anthony Froude**, and one of the early leaders of the **Oxford Movement**, Froude was born near Totnes in Devon. He contributed to *Tracts for the Times* and was the intimate friend of **John Henry Newman**; after his early death Newman wrote a preface to his friend's *Remains*. These were edited by J. B. Mozley (1838 and 1839) and were chiefly extracts from his private diary. They caused a disturbance in the Movement by their hostility to the leaders of the Reformation.

**Fry, Christopher** 1907– English playwright who alternated teaching and acting until service in the Non-Combatant Corps, 1940–4. His early plays attracted little attention, but the Bristol production of *A Phoenix Too Frequent*

(1946), a lively version of the Widow of Ephesus story, proclaimed the arrival of a new contributor to the revival of verse drama. Fry followed it with *The Firstborn* (1948), one of a number of plays in which he uses biblical themes to celebrate life's beauty and mystery. *The Lady's Not for Burning* (1948) shows Fry's delight in language at its best. He later described it as the 'spring' piece in a seasonal cycle, completed by an 'autumn' play, *Venus Observed* (1950), the 'winter' *The Dark Is Light Enough* (1954) and *A Yard of Sun: A Summer Comedy* (1970). Since *The Lady's Not for Burning*, Fry has not found it easy to share with audiences his own belief that poetry is 'the language in which man explores his own amazement'. *A Sleep of Prisoners* (1951) is among the best of his subsequent work, together with several effective adaptations of French plays, *Ring Round the Moon* (1950) and *The Lark* (1955) from Anouilh, *Tiger at the Gates* (1955), *Duel of Angels* (1958) and *Judith* (1962) from Giraudoux and *Cyrano de Bergerac* (1975) from Rostand.

**Frye, (Herman) Northrop** 1912– Critic. Frye was born in Sherbrooke, Quebec, and studied at the University of Toronto, before becoming a minister of the United Church of Canada in 1936. He has lectured on English literature at Toronto since 1939, as Professor at Victoria College from 1947 and as University Professor since 1967. After his first book, *Fearful Symmetry: A Study of William Blake* (1947), Frye elaborated an ambitiously comprehensive theory of literary models and genres in his most important work, *Anatomy of Criticism* (1957). In this book Frye divides literature into four categories which have a mythic or 'archetypal' basis in the seasonal cycle: comedy (spring), romance (summer), tragedy (autumn) and irony (winter). The leading exponent of 'archetypal' criticism, Frye has applied his theories to **Shakespeare**, in *A Natural Perspective* (1965) and *Fools of Time* (1967), and to **Milton**, the English Romantic poets, and **T. S. Eliot**, among others. His other critical works include *Fables of Identity* (1963), *The Stubborn Structure* (1970), *The Critical Path* (1971) and *The Secular Scripture* (1976).

**Fudge Family in Paris, The**, Edited by *Thomas Brown the Younger* Verse letters by **Thomas Moore**, published in 1818, satirizing the manners and behaviour of the English abroad. A sequel, *The Fudges in England*, appeared in 1835.

**Fugard, Athol** 1932– South African actor, director and playwright, born in Middelburg, Cape Province. Despite periodic work in British and American theatre, Fugard's innovative drama has been forged under 'poor theatre' conditions with black-township groups. He deals compassionately with stunted, deprived lives, whether in black ghettos, as in *No-Good Friday* (produced 1958) and *Nogogo* (produced 1959; both published with *Dimetos*, 1977), or amid the tensions of unfulfilled, white lower-middle-class households in *Hello and Goodbye* (produced 1965, published 1966) and *People Are Living There* (produced 1969, published 1970). He directly confronts the inhuman apparatus of the apartheid state in *The Blood Knot* (produced 1961, published 1963), about brother exploiting brother; *Boesman and Lena* (produced 1969, published 1973), about dispossession and non-entity, perhaps his most powerful play; *Statements after an Arrest under the Immorality Act* about miscegenation as an official crime (produced and published 1974); and *'Master Harold' . . . and the Boys* (produced 1982, published 1983), a searing semi-autobiographical revelation of youthful racial arrogance. *Dimetos* (produced 1975, published 1977) and *A Lesson from Aloes* (1981) find gleams of hope even in tragic guilt and self-betrayal. Fugard helped the black actors Kani and Ntshona create *Sizwe Bansi Is Dead* (produced 1972), satirizing the 'pass laws', and *The Island* about political detention (produced 1973; both published in *Statements*, 1974), while *The Road to Mecca* (1985) movingly presents an Afrikaner woman's rejection of conformity and spiritual darkness. Fugard has also written a novel, *Tsotsi* (1981), and film scripts, and directed and acted in films.

*Fulgens and Lucrece* A two-part play (or **interlude**) written by **Henry Medwall** for perform-

The title-page of Henry Medwall's *Fulgens and Lucrece*, which was first performed *c.*1497. The illustration comes from a rare copy of the first published text, between 1512 and 1516; it is believed to have been the first printed English play.

ance as a banquet entertainment. It was probably first performed in 1497 and published *c.* 1515, and is the first secular drama in English to have survived in full. The main plot of the play is predominantly in **rhyme royal** stanzas. It takes the form of an illustrated debate as to whether merit and service to the state better qualifies the title of 'gentleman' than birth. The pretext is the choice before a Roman senator, Fulgens, and his daughter, Lucrece, of the more suitable of two potential husbands for Lucrece. The eventual choice falls on the worthy but low-born Flaminius.

If that were the whole story, *Fulgens and Lucrece* would be nothing more than a curiosity. What gives it interest is the sub-plot, in which two servants involuntarily parody their betters in their rivalry for Lucrece's waiting-maid.

**Fuller, Henry Blake** 1857–1929 American novelist and short-story writer. Fuller was born in Chicago, and except for two years spent touring in Europe (1878–80) lived there all his life. His best-known novel is probably *The Cliff-Dwellers* (1893), which satirizes the social ambitions of people living in a skyscraper apartment building. *With the Procession* (1895) also deals with social climbers, in this case a middle-class family. *Bertram Cope's Year* (1919) takes up the topic of homosexuality. In all three novels Fuller sought to deal in a realistic manner with social issues of his time. His other novels include *The Chatelaine of La Trinité* (1892), *The Last Refuge: A Sicilian Romance* (1900), *On the Stairs* (1918), *Gardens of This World* (1929) and *Not on the Screen* (1930). Among his collections of short stories are *The Chevalier of Pensieri-Vani* (1890), *Waldo Trench and Others: Stories of Americans in Italy* (1908) and *Lines Long and Short: Biographical Sketches in Various Rhythms* (1917). He also wrote plays, among them *O, That Way Madness Lies: A Play for Marionettes* (1895) and *The Red Carpet* (not published until 1939).

**Fuller, John (Leopold)** 1937– Poet. Born in Ashford, Kent, son of **Roy Fuller**, he was educated at St Paul's School and New College, Oxford. He worked at the University of New York, Buffalo, and at Manchester University before becoming a fellow of Magdalen College, Oxford, in 1966.

Fuller's many volumes of poetry include *Fairground Music* (1961), *Lies and Secrets* (1979), *Waiting for the Music* (1982) and *The Beautiful Inventions* (1983). A technically sophisticated writer, he often uses unexpected imagery, riddles and word-games in a poetry diverse in manner and subject. *The Sonnet* (1972) is a valuable guide to the form, and his novel *Flying to Nowhere* (1983) is as intelligent and entertaining as the poems.

**Fuller, (Sarah) Margaret** 1810–50 A leading figure of the **Transcendentalist** circle of Concord, Massachusetts, Fuller was born in Cambridgeport. She became **Bronson Alcott**'s assistant, a friend of **Ralph Waldo Emerson**, and head of a school in Providence. She was an early feminist and, as a member of the foremost group of intellectuals in New England, she enjoyed the stimulus of views and discussions that helped prompt her to write the monumental *Woman in the Nineteenth Century* (1845).

She edited *The Dial* from 1840 to 1842, and in 1843 published *Summer on the Lakes* after a visit to Chicago – her first encounter with the expanding West and the frontier. At about the same time she became literary critic of **Horace Greeley**'s New York *Tribune*, by which in 1846 she was sent to Europe; her distinguished 'letters from abroad' appeared on the *Tribune*'s front page. While in Italy, she married the Marquis Angelo Ossoli and in 1850 they sailed for America with their infant son, but their ship was wrecked in a storm off New York. The whole family perished. In addition to her own work Fuller left another impression of her dynamic personality; she was the inspiration for Zenobia in **Nathaniel Hawthorne**'s *The Blithedale Romance* and for the eponymous heroine in **Oliver Wendell Holmes**'s *Elsie Venner*.

**Fuller, Roy (Broadbent)** 1912–91 Poet and novelist. Born in Failsworth, Lancashire, he was educated at Blackpool High School, before qualifying as a solicitor and working for the Woolwich Building Society, becoming a director in 1969. During the war he served in the Royal Navy. Between 1968 and 1973 he was Professor of Poetry at Oxford; his lectures were published in *Owl and Artificers* (1971) and *Professors and Gods* (1974). His first collection of verse, *Poems* (1939), showed the influence of **Auden**, but he found his own voice in *The Middle of a War* (1942) and *A Lost Season* (1944), which reflect his wartime experience. *Epitaphs and Occasions* (1949) is his last volume in his early style, characterized by left-wing sympathies and an interest in man as a social animal. Later he became interested in outlining individual psychologies, and perhaps his best collections are *Counterparts* (1954), in which Fuller started to experiment with syllabics, *Brutus's Orchard* (1957) and *Buff* (1965), coming after *Collected Poems 1936–1961* (1962). The poems, typically, are logical progressions from particular observation to general reflection. He is a master technician, but his interest in form, his detachment, and his urbane tone and easy use of irony open him to criticisms of unadventurousness. His powers remain undiminished, though, in later collections, which include *New Poems* (1968), *From the Joke Shop* (1971), *Tiny Tears* (1973), *The Reign of Sparrows* (1980) and *Conso-*

*lations* (1987). *New and Collected Poems* appeared in 1985. His novels are more than an interesting sideline: after the melodrama of *Fantasy and Fugue* (1954), *The Ruined Boys* (1959) achieves Fuller's usual subtle characterization and quiet evocation of the real world. Other novels include *Image of a Society* (1956), the ambitious but flawed *The Father's Comedy* (1961), *The Perfect Fool* (1963) and the excellent *My Child My Sister* (1965). His son is the poet **John Fuller**.

**Fuller, Thomas** 1608–61 Royalist divine. Fuller was born at Aldwinkle St Peter's in Northamptonshire. He began his career as the youngest MA to come out of Cambridge University – he was 20 years old. He became a Bachelor of Divinity in 1635, and had by this time established himself as a preacher, and had been prebendary of Salisbury and rector of Broadwindsor. In 1641 he was appointed preacher to the Chapel Royal at the Savoy and during the Civil War was chaplain to the Royalist commander Sir Ralph Hopton. A Royalist and an Anglican, Fuller returned to London after the surrender of Exeter. He was allowed to preach but led an unsettled life until he secured the curacy of Waltham Abbey in 1649. He was reinstated at the Restoration, and became a royal chaplain.

Fuller was a celebrated preacher in his lifetime and also a prolific writer; he wrote poems and histories, and his first book of note was about the Crusades, *The History of the Holy War* (1639–40). His *Good Thoughts in Bad Times* (1645), *Good Thoughts in Worse Times* (1647) and *The Cause and Cure of a Wounded Conscience* (1647) were tracts for his troubled times and were praised by **Coleridge** but these were less popular than the earlier *The Holy State and The Profane State*, a book of 'characters' and essays on diverse subjects. Later works are *A Pisgah-Sight of Palestine* (1650) and *The Church History of Britain: from the Birth of Christ till 1648* (1655).

His most celebrated book *The History of the Worthies of England* was never finished, but was published posthumously in 1662; it is by no means as dull as its title suggests, being a county-by-county survey of England in which Fuller describes the topography, characteristics and famous names associated with the different areas of the realm, including biographical sketches, aspects of local history and lore, and natural curiosities, all memorably treated in a frequently witty style.

**Furnivall, F[rederick] J[ames]** 1825–1910 Philologist and literary scholar. The son of a wealthy doctor, Furnivall was born in Egham, Surrey, and educated at University College, London, and Trinity Hall, Cambridge, after which he practised as a barrister. He joined the Philological Society in 1847, becoming editor of the Society's New English Dictionary in 1861. This project, which he had first proposed and for which he dragooned many volunteers into collecting material, was later to become the *Oxford English Dictionary*. Furnivall was a passionate organizer: he founded the Early English Text Society (1864), the Chaucer Society (1868), the Ballad Society (1868), the New Shakspere Society (1873; one of its novelties being this spelling), and the Wyclif (1881), Browning (1881) and Shelley (1886) Societies. For the Chaucer and Early English Text Societies he edited a great number of editions, and he also edited **Shakespeare**. Furnivall was a fervent vegetarian, socialist, teetotaller, agnostic and oarsman, and taught at the Working Men's College, which he helped to found in 1854.

**Furphy, Joseph** 1843–1912 Australian novelist. The son of Irish immigrant parents, Furphy was born near Melbourne, Victoria. After a sketchy education, and work on farms, roads, and goldfields, he became a teamster in the Riverina area of New South Wales. The failure of his business in 1884 obliged him to sell his bullock teams and find work in a foundry at Shepparton in north Victoria.

Furphy's first stories were published in *The Bulletin* in 1889 under the pseudonym of Tom Collins. In 1897 the literary editor of the paper, A. G. Stephens, was the recipient of a large unwieldy manuscript entitled *Such Is Life: Being Certain Extracts from the Life of Tom Collins*. Revised and shortened, it was published in 1903. From the rich material trimmed from *Such Is Life* two more books were published after Furphy's death: *Rigby's Romance* (1946) and *The Buln-Buln and the Brolga* (1948).

There is no formal plot in *Such Is Life*, a picaresque novel of many digressions and reflections which one American critic, C. Hartley Grattan, described as 'a primary document for any student of Australian attitudes'. Furphy described his work as being of 'Temper democratic; bias offensively Australian'.

# G

**Gaddis, William** 1922– American novelist, born in New York City and educated at Harvard though he left the university in 1945 without taking his degree. His first novel, *The Recognitions* (1955), focuses on a group of artists and poets in Greenwich Village during the late 1940s and early 1950s. Its dominant motifs of ruse and forgery are encountered on many levels – social, aesthetic, theological and sexual. A lengthy and complex work, it was not well received by the critics. His second novel, *JR* (1975), is written entirely in dialogue and takes place mostly at a school on Long Island. It enjoyed a more favourable critical reception, and better sales, than its predecessor, and received the National Book Award in 1976. *Carpenter's Gothic*, published in 1985, examines the impact of the Vietnam war on the lives of those who endured it.

**Gaines, Ernest J.** 1933– Black American novelist and short-story writer, born in Oscar, Louisiana. The son of a plantation worker, Gaines himself began working in the fields at a young age. In 1948 his family moved to Vallejo, California. After spending two years in the army, he attended San Francisco State College and then Stanford University. His fiction mostly treats black life in the bayou region of Louisiana. His first novel, *Catherine Carmier* (1964), tells of the difficulties encountered by a young black college graduate when he returns home to Louisiana. *Of Love and Dust* (1967) is set on a Louisiana plantation in the 1940s. *Bloodline* (1968) is a collection of five stories. His best-known novel, *The Autobiography of Miss Jane Pitman* (1971), consists of the recollections of a 110-year-old black woman, whose experiences range from slavery to the civil rights movement of the 1960s. Gaines's concern with the effects of racism and the possibilities of social change is further revealed in *My Father's House* (1978), a novel which examines the conflict between a black preacher and his more radical son.

**Gale, Zona** 1874–1938 American novelist and short-story writer. Born in Wisconsin, Gale first rose to prominence as a writer in the 'local colour' vein. Among her early works are the novel *Romance Island* (1906) and a collection of short stories entitled *Friendship Village* (1908). After World War I her sentimental tendencies gave way to a sterner realism in novels such as *Birth* (1918), and her best-known book, *Miss Lulu Bett* (1920), a portrayal of bleak Midwestern life and the middle-aged woman who suffers it. *Faint Perfume* (1923) also centres on the stifled hopes and empty existence of a Midwestern spinster. In her later novels, however, Gale departed from the realism of her most highly acclaimed works. *Preface to a Life* (1926) and *Borgia* (1929) are representative of this later phase, during which she became interested in Eastern mysticism as a possible answer to the kind of suffering portrayed in her earlier novels. Her final works, *Papa La Fleur* (1933), *Light Woman* (1937), and the posthumously published *Magna* (1939), share a concern with the gap between the pre-war and post-war generations. Some of her best short stories are collected in *Yellow Gentians and Blue* (1927) and *Bridal Pond* (1930).

**Gallant, Mavis (née Young)** 1922– Canadian short-story writer and novelist. Born in Montreal and brought up bilingually till the age of 10, she then lived in Ontario and the USA, returning to Montreal in 1941 where she worked for the National Film Board and the *Montreal Standard*. Since 1950 she has lived abroad, mainly in Paris, returning to Canada for brief visits and as writer-in-residence at the University of Toronto (1983–4). As a regular contributor to **The New Yorker** since the 1950s she has published over 100 stories, and her collections of short stories and two novels, *Green Water, Green Sky* (1959) and *A Fairly Good Time* (1970), have appeared in the USA and the UK. Her short-story collections include *The Other Paris* (1956), *My Heart Is Broken* (1964; in Britain as *An Unmarried Man's Summer*), *The Pegnitz Junction* (1973). Her first book to be published in Canada was *The End of the World and Other Stories* (1974) but only with *From the Fifteenth District* (1979), *Home Truths* (1981) and *Overhead in a Balloon* (1985) has she been widely read in Canada. She received the Governor

General's Award for *Home Truths* and was awarded the Order of Canada in 1981. She has also written one play, *What Is to be Done?* (1983). An expatriate writing with a mercilessly detached awareness about isolation and displacement in Paris, Montreal or in post-war Germany, Gallant is recognized as one of Canada's best short-story writers.

**Galsworthy, John** 1867–1933 Novelist and dramatist. Born at Coombe, Surrey, and educated at Harrow and New College, Oxford, he studied law and was called to the Bar in 1890. He practised briefly, but could afford to travel and made a voyage to the Far East; on another journey he met and encouraged **Joseph Conrad**, and the two became lifelong friends.

Galsworthy's career as a playwright began with the success of *The Silver Box* (produced 1906) which first employed his favourite device of presenting parallel and contrasted families – one rich, the other poor. In all he wrote over 31 full-length plays and a number of equally successful one-acters. Many commented on social injustices, and one of them, *Justice* (produced 1910), led to reform of the practice of solitary confinement in prisons. *Strife* (produced 1909) remains one of the most successful English plays about the effects of a strike. *The Skin Game* (produced 1920) is a trenchant commentary on jealously guarded privilege and social snobbery. His *Collected Plays* appeared in 1929.

John Galsworthy, 1921. Photograph by E. O. Hoppé.

His first successful novel was *The Man of Property* (1906), which together with *In Chancery* (1920) and *To Let* (1921, with two interludes, 'Indian Summer of a Forsyte', 1918; and *Awakening*, 1920) made up his best-known work **The Forsyte Saga**, published in 1922. A second Forsyte chronicle, *A Modern Comedy* (1929), included *The White Monkey* (1924), *The Silver Spoon* (1926), *Swan Song* (1928) and two interludes, 'A Silent Wooing' and 'Passers By'.

Galsworthy was awarded the OM in 1929, and the Nobel Prize for literature in 1932. Posthumous publications included a trilogy, *End of the Chapter* (1925), on the family history of the Charwells (relatives of the Forsytes) and *Collected Poems* (1934). His works have never received much critical acclaim, but they have remained extremely popular, especially since the advent of television adaptations.

**Galt, John** 1779–1839 Novelist and essayist. The son of a sea captain, Galt was born in Irvine, Ayrshire, and spent his early life in Greenock. He went to London in 1804 and set up as a merchant, writing in his spare time and publishing verse and occasional prose pieces. His business failed in 1808 and he set off on a commercial journey to the Continent, where he made the acquaintance of **Byron**. He continued in the poet's company to Greece and Turkey and subsequently published an account of his journeys in 1812 in *Voyages and Travels in the Years 1809, 1810 and 1811*. He also wrote a biography of the poet, *The Life of Lord Byron*, in 1830, but it was not well received. After 1813 he was back in London for various business posts.

He wrote a great deal, but it was not until his work was published in **Blackwood's Magazine** in 1820 that he achieved distinction. He dealt with his Scottish background in **The Ayrshire Legatees** (1821) and produced a successful novel about contemporary Lowland Scots. **The Annals of the Parish** (1821), **The Provost** (1822), and **The Entail** (1823) are in the same vein and these are the books by which John Galt is best remembered. In 1826 he went to Canada as secretary to a company for development in what is now Ontario. He stayed for three years and then lost his post when the company's affairs went through a bad period. He returned to England but, short of money, was soon in debt and spent some months in prison. His straits were relieved by a gift of £200 from King William IV, but he wrote little of note in his remaining years.

*Game at Chess, A* A political allegory in the form of a comedy by **Thomas Middleton**. On its first performance in 1624 the play was a sensational success. The audience had no difficulty in recognizing that the Black Knight represented the hated Spanish Ambassador, Gondomar, who had given great offence by his attempts to

The title-page illustration of Middleton's comedy, *A Game at Chess*, 1624.

secure an alliance between Protestant England and Catholic Spain through the marriage of the Prince of Wales to a Spanish princess. Diplomacy and confrontation are cleverly presented in terms of chess. The political detail may be obscure for a modern reader, but the lines of the play remain brilliantly clear. After nine successive performances at the **Globe** (an extraordinary number for the period) the play was banned and a warrant issued for Middleton's arrest.

**Gamelyn, The Tale of** See *Tale of Gamelyn, The*.

**Gamester, The** A comedy by **James Shirley**, first performed in London in 1633 (published 1637). Its hero, Wilding, is not only addicted to gambling but also in love with his wife's ward, Penelope. The play details the tricks by which his resourceful wife cures him of his adulterous love and exposes him to the dangers of his addiction.

**Gamester, The** A tragedy by **Edward Moore**, first performed at **Drury Lane** in 1753. It is a mawkish piece in the domestic style recently popularized by **George Lillo**. Beverley, the gamester, is the dupe of the villainous Stukeley. It is a typically heart-wringing trick that he should poison himself just as he is to inherit sufficient wealth to make a fresh start.

**Gammer Gurton's Needle** A comedy that was possibly written in 1553 and vies with *Ralph*

*Roister Doister* for the honour of being the first English comedy if the later date for **Udall**'s work is accepted. Authorship has been attributed to at least three people but the favourite is William Stevenson, identified by Henry Bradley from the 'Mr S. Mr. of Art' on the title-page of the printed edition of 1575, which also refers to the work as 'Played on Stage, not longe ago in Christes Colledge in Cambridge'. An earlier printed edition (c. 1563) has not survived, but Stevenson fulfils the requirements of the evidence: he was styled Master (Mr) of Arts in 1553–4 at Christ's College, where he produced plays from 1550 to 1554. The play is notable for its total Englishness; there is no trace whatever of the influence of Terence or Plautus, hitherto inescapable. It is written in rhymed doggerel.

The action turns on the losing of Gammer Gurton's needle, with which she mends the clothes of Hodge, her servant; the resolution is the finding of the needle in the seat of Hodge's breeches. The play is rich in character and the inventiveness never flags. Among the characters are: Diccon of Bedlam, who enjoys mischief-making; Gammer Gurton's enemy Dame Chat; Doctor Rat the curate; the servants Tib, Doll, and Spendthrift; and Gib the cat.

**Garden of Proserpine, The** A poem by **Algernon Charles Swinburne**, published in *Poems and Ballads* (first series, 1866). One of Swinburne's most anthologized pieces ('Here, where the world is quiet'), it is deliberately pagan in spirit. The poet's note says that it was intended to capture 'that brief total pause of passion and of thought, when the spirit, without fear or hope of good things or evil, hungers and thirsts only after the perfect sleep'.

**Gardiner, Samuel Rawson** 1829–1902 Historian. Born in Hampshire and educated at Christ Church, Oxford, he became a teacher in London and devoted most of his spare time to reading at the British Museum Library and the Public Record Office, preparing the material for his history of England in the early Stuart and Commonwealth periods. He published *Parliamentary Debates in 1610* (1862) and *A History of England from the Accession of James I to the Disgrace of Chief Justice Coke* (1863). The series continued with *Prince Charles and the Spanish Marriage* (1869), *A History of England under the Duke of Buckingham and Charles I* (1875), *The Personal Government of Charles I* (1877) and *The Fall of the Monarchy of Charles I* (1882). The entire work is known as *The History of England from the Accession of James I to the Outbreak of the Civil War*. Gardiner ended his great chronicle with *The History of the Great Civil War* (1886–91) and *The History of the Commonwealth and Protectorate* (1894–1901), which was completed by C. H.

Firth with *The Last Years of the Protectorate* (1909).

He became a lecturer in 1872 and later Professor of Modern History at King's College, London; he was offered but declined the Regius Professorship at Oxford and became Ford Lecturer in 1896. He was elected a fellow of All Souls (1884) and of Merton (1892). Among his other works were *The Thirty Years War* (1874), *A School Atlas of English History* (1892) and his Ford Lectures, *Cromwell's Place in History* (1897).

**Gardner, Dame Helen (Louise)** 1908–86 Scholar and critic. Educated in London at the North London Collegiate School and at St Hilda's College, Oxford, she became Merton Professor of English Literature at Oxford (1966–75) after a distinguished tutorial career. Her two editions of **John Donne**, *Divine Poems* (1952) and *Elegies, and Songs and Sonnets* (1965), are important for both text and commentary; *The Art of T. S. Eliot* (1949) and her textual study of **Eliot**'s *Four Quartets* (1978) are pioneering studies. As a critic she belonged to no 'school' but upheld traditional humane values (see, for example, her *The Business of Criticism*, 1960). She edited the *New Oxford Book of English Verse 1250–1950* (1972), providing a selection to replace **Quiller-Couch**'s anthology. She was created a Dame of the British Empire in 1967.

**Gardner, John** 1933–82 American novelist, short-story writer and scholar, born in Batavia, New York. For most of his life he taught medieval literature and creative writing at various American universities.

*The Wreckage of Agathon* (1970) – published after the critical failure of his first novel, *The Resurrection* (1966) – is set in ancient Sparta and presents a seer, Agathon, and his companion, Demodokos, who have been imprisoned and engage in a dialogue concerning individual freedom and civil restraint. His most highly praised book, *Grendel* (1971), retells the story of Beowulf from the monster's point of view and focuses on the potential meaninglessness of life, a theme also examined in *The Sunlight Dialogues* (1972). In 1973 he published *Nickel Mountain*; set in upstate New York, it records the life of Henry Soames, a middle-aged motel proprietor who searches for a way of living in the face of intense loneliness and fear of a fatal heart attack. Gardner's first collection of short fiction, *The King's Indian Stories and Tales*, was published in 1974. Two years later came the novel *October Light* (1976), an examination of the problems of ageing, which was awarded the National Book Critics Circle award in 1976. His other fiction includes the novels *Freddy's Book* (1980) and *Mickelsson's Ghosts* (1982), and a collection of stories entitled *The Art of Living and Other Stories*

(1981). He also wrote an epic poem, *Jason and Medea* (1973); three libretti, *William Wilson*, *Frankenstein* and *Rumpelstiltskin* (collected in *Three Libretti*, 1979); and a volume of *Poems* (1978). His theories of fiction are developed in *The Forms of Fiction* (1962), *On Moral Fiction* (1978) and the posthumously published *The Art of Fiction: Notes on Craft for Young Writers* (1984).

**Garfield, Leon** 1921– Children's author. Born and educated in Brighton, Garfield went to Art College before serving in the Medical Corps during the war. After that he worked in the hospital service as a biochemical technician before turning to full-time writing in 1966. By then he had already produced *Jack Holborn* (1964), a strongly imaginative, rambling adventure story written in a style owing something to **Fielding** and **Dickens** but perfectly in keeping with the stage-coaches, dark streets and candle-lit rooms of the 18th-century background in which this and most of his later novels are placed. Such dramatic settings are amply reflected in exciting plots that concern pickpockets (*Smith* 1967), highwaymen (*Black Jack* 1968), lost heirs, escape from prison, stolen wills, false accusations and all the other apparatus of traditional melodrama. Even so, the larger-than-life villains who populate Garfield's earlier books give way in later works to more ambiguous characterizations, where the unheroic often turn out to have hearts of gold and the initially plausible prove false friends. *The Strange Affair of Adelaide Harris* (1971) is a comic, fast-moving farce set in Regency Brighton. The constant moral battle that surfaces in all his work is also memorably depicted in *Garfield's Apprentices* (1976–8), short stories about young people making their way in different trades but also having to decide upon important choices in their personal affairs.

**Garioch, (Sutherland) Robert** 1909–81 Scottish poet and translator. Born in Edinburgh, he was educated at the Royal High School and Edinburgh University before training as a teacher at Moray House College of Education. After service in World War II, including several years as a prisoner of war, he taught in and around Edinburgh until his early retirement in the 1960s. He received a Scottish Arts Council award in 1968 and was writer-in-residence (1971–3) at Edinburgh University and with Radio Forth. His *Two Men and a Blanket: Memoirs of Captivity* appeared in 1975 and *Collected Poems* in 1977. Robin Fulton has edited his *Complete Poetical Works* (1983) and *A Garioch Miscellany* (1986).

Most of Garioch's poetry is written in a form of Scots which brings together contemporary colloquial speech and literary diction. He is predominantly an urban poet – taking **Robert**

**Fergusson** rather than **Burns** as his model – and translated into Scots both the sonnets of 19th-century Roman dialect poet Belli and the free verse of Apollinaire. Many of his best-known poems combine a gift for comic impersonation with satirical observations of civic follies, hypocrisy and pretence. In 'At Robert Fergusson's Grave' and such longer meditations as 'The Wire' and 'The Muir', he shows that underlying his sense of the various comedies of urban discontent there is a more sombre vision and a broader ambition for the use of Scots in the modern world.

**Garland, (Hannibal) Hamlin** 1860–1940 American short-story writer and novelist. Garland spent his youth on farms in Iowa, South Dakota and his native Wisconsin. In 1884 he moved to Boston, where he was befriended by **William Dean Howells**, but he returned to the Midwest in 1887 and dedicated himself to depicting the life there and urging reforms to better it. His stories and sketches, written mostly before 1890, won acclaim when collected in *Main-Travelled Roads* (1891). Two other collections – *Prairie Folks* (1892) and *Wayside Courtships* (1897) – were combined in 1910 and published as *Other Main-Travelled Roads*.

His writing often tended toward propaganda, especially in his novels. *Jason Edwards, An Average Man* (1892) is a plea for the Single Tax Theory of **Henry George**; *A Spoil of Office* (1892) campaigns for the Populist Party. Less political novels include two books about life in Dakota farm country, *A Little Norsk* (1892) and *Rose of Dutcher's Coolly* (1895). *The Captain of the Gray-Horse Troop* (1902) and *Cavanagh, Forest Ranger* (1910) are novels about the Far West. *A Son of the Middle Border* (1917) and *A Daughter of the Middle Border* (1921) are autobiographical narratives. His essays on his theory of realistic fiction, which he called 'veritism', appeared as *Crumbling Idols* (1894).

**Garner, Alan** 1934– Children's author. Born in Cheshire, the setting for many of his stories, Garner won a scholarship to Manchester Grammar School before going to Oxford University. Shortly after, he began writing his first children's book *The Weirdstone of Brisingamen* (1960), a powerful mixture of fantasy and everyday reality. *Elidor* (1965) and, most memorably, *The Owl Service* (1967) concentrated on the role myth and legend can still play. Partly inspired by **The Mabinogion**, *The Owl Service* looks at the way ancient hatreds erupt through the modern adolescent inhabitants of a Welsh valley. *Red Shift* (1973), another technically innovatory novel, presents three parallel stories of intolerance that have all occurred at the same place during different periods of history. *The Stone Book Quartet* (1976–8) is made up of four brief stories drawn from the author's own past family of local craftsmen and told in Cheshire dialect.

**Garner, Helen** 1942– Australian novelist and short-story writer. Born in Geelong, Victoria, she was educated at the University of Melbourne. She worked as a secondary schoolteacher in Melbourne until she was dismissed for answering frankly her pupils' questions about sex. She subsequently became a freelance journalist before turning to writing fiction. Garner achieved overnight fame with the publication of her first novel, *Monkey Grip* (1977), made into a film in 1981. Written in the fragmentary postmodernist style which typifies all her work, it relates the narrator–heroine's addiction to romantic love to her lover's addiction to hard drugs. Her subsequent fiction, *Honour and Other People's Children* (1980), two novellas published together, *The Children's Bach* (1984), a novel, and *Postcards from Surfers* (1985), a volume of short stories, has secured her reputation as one of the finest of contemporary prose stylists. Her work chronicles contemporary Australian lifestyles, at home and abroad, in a highly evocative, elliptical style which can be comic and frequently reflects on the processes of art.

**Garner, Hugh** 1913–79 Canadian novelist and short-story writer. Born in England in Batley, Yorkshire, he was taken to Toronto in 1919. After working briefly as a copy boy on *The Toronto Star*, he led an itinerant life in the Canadian West and was gaoled as a vagrant in West Virginia. He subsequently enlisted to fight for the Loyalists in the Spanish Civil War and served in the Canadian navy in World War II. After the war he embarked on his writing career and his first novel, *Storm Below*, which was based on his wartime experience, appeared in 1949. A butchered version of an earlier novel, *Cabbagetown*, followed in 1950, with the complete text not being published until 1968. *Cabbagetown* is a vivid account of the working-class district where Garner grew up in the 1930s and his finest novel. His other novels include *The Silence on the Shore* (1962), *A Nice Place to Visit* (1970), *The Intruders* (1976) and three police novels, *The Sin Sniper* (1970), *Death in Don Mills* (1975) and *Murder Has Your Number* (1978). His short stories are collected in the volumes *The Yellow Sweater* (1952), *Hugh Garner's Best Stories* (1963), *Men and Women* (1966), *Violation of the Virgins* (1971) and *Hugh Garner Omnibus* (1978). *One Damn Thing After Another* (1973) is his autobiography.

**Garnett, David** 1892–1981 Novelist. Garnett was the son of Constance and **Edward Garnett**, and grandson of **Richard Garnett**. He was born in Brighton and educated privately, then at the

Royal College of Science, where he studied botany. He married the illustrator Rachel Alice ('Ray') Marshall (d. 1940) who illustrated his early works, and after her death Angelica Bell, daughter of Vanessa. As a conscientious objector during World War I he worked as a farm labourer. After the war he started a bookshop in Soho with the journalist and drama critic Francis Birrell who, like Garnett, was associated with the **Bloomsbury Group**.

His first novel, *Lady into Fox* (1922), was a prose fantasy about a young wife, Sylvia Tebrick, who while out walking with her husband is suddenly changed into a vixen. This was followed by two more novels in the same genre, *A Man in the Zoo* (1924), about a man who donates himself as a specimen to the zoo, and *The Grasshoppers Come* (1931). Neither achieved the same success as his first. Garnett's subsequent novels relinquished fantasy, and *A Rabbit in the Air* (1932) drew on his early attempts to become an aviator. *Aspects of Love* (1955) was a delicate and bizarre love story. His later works included *A Shot in the Dark* (1958) and *A Net for Venus* (1962).

His non-fiction includes an edition of the letters of **T. E. Lawrence** (1938), a 10-volume edition of the novels of **Peacock** (1924–34) and his own correspondence with **T. H. White** (1968). *The Golden Echo* (1953), *The Flowers of the Forest* (1955) and *The Familiar Faces* (1962) comprise his autobiography.

**Garnett, Edward (William)** 1868–1937 Critic, biographer and essayist. Born in London and educated privately, he was the son of **Richard Garnett** and husband of Constance Garnett, the translator of the Russian classics. He is chiefly remembered as the influential publisher's reader (latterly with Jonathan Cape) who encouraged the talents of many leading contemporary writers, including **Joseph Conrad**, **D. H. Lawrence** and **E. M. Forster**.

His own works, generally considered less important, include critical biographies of Hogarth (1911) and Turgenev (1917), a volume of essays, *Friday Nights* (1922), and *The Trial of Jeanne d'Arc and Other Plays* (1931).

**Garnett, Richard** 1835–1906 Biographer, poet and short-story writer. Born at Lichfield, Garnett worked for the British Museum Library from the age of 16 until he retired in 1899. He was Superintendent of the Reading Room from 1875 to 1884, edited the library's first printed catalogue, and was responsible for the introduction of photography in the library. His knowledge of the classics and of international literature was reputed to be encyclopaedic – the result of a prodigious memory – and he published several short biographies, including works on **Milton**, **Carlyle** and **Emerson**. He

edited *Relics of Shelley* (1862), and wrote a *History of Italian Literature* (1897), but he is chiefly remembered for his collection of short stories, *The Twilight of the Gods* (1888), many of which had originally been published in *The Yellow Book*. Both his son, **Edward Garnett**, and his grandson, **David Garnett**, became writers.

**Garrick, David** 1717–79 English actor who was also an efficient dramatist and a prolific adapter of plays by other dramatists. Born in Hereford and educated in Lichfield, where **Samuel Johnson** was one of his teachers, Garrick accompanied Johnson to London in 1737. For four years he took part in amateur theatricals while working in the wine trade, but the sensation caused by his playing of Richard III (in **Cibber**'s version of **Shakespeare**'s play) in an unlicensed theatre in Goodman's Fields in 1741 decided him to make the stage his career. From then until his retirement in 1776, above all during his 30 years as manager of **Drury Lane** (1747–76), he was the leader of English theatrical taste and an actor whose superiority, though sporadically challenged, was never decisively defied.

Garrick's plays and adaptations have been too readily neglected. Prominent among his lively farces and afterpieces are *The Lying Valet* (1741), *Miss in Her Teens* (1747), *The Irish Widow* (1772) and *Bon Ton, or, High Life above Stairs* (1775). Of a dozen or so adaptations from Shakespeare, none of which say much for the 18th century's understanding of the original, *Florizel and Perdita* (1756) and a musical version of *The Tempest* (1756) are of some interest. Above all his achievements in his own authorial right stands his collaboration with **George Colman the Elder** on *The Clandestine Marriage* (1766). Garrick's letters, collected in three volumes (1963), give some indication of his wit and the uncertainty of his wisdom.

**Garrison, William Lloyd** 1805–79 American Abolitionist leader, editor and lecturer, born in Newburyport, Massachusetts. For five years, he edited *The Genius of Universal Emancipation* with the Quaker Benjamin Lundy. Lundy eventually found his approach too radical, and the two parted company. Garrison then founded the Abolitionist newspaper *The Liberator* in 1831, and in the following year launched a vigorous attack on the American Colonization Society. He continued publishing the influential *Liberator* throughout the Civil War. His own books include *Thoughts on African Colonization* (1832), *Sonnets* (1843), and a collection of essays and speeches entitled *Selections* (1852).

**Garth, Sir Samuel** 1661–1719 Physician and poet. Garth was a member of the **Kit-Cat Club**, a Whig coterie centred on **Jacob Tonson**, the publisher. He wrote a burlesque poem *The Dispensary* (1699) which poked fun at the apothecaries who attempted to resist the supply of medicines to dispensaries beyond their control. The poem enjoyed a certain vogue and was praised by **Pope**.

**Gascoigne, George** ?1525–77 Soldier, Member of Parliament, translator and poet. Gascoigne's significance in Renaissance literature is that he did many things for the first time, or almost the first time, in the period, especially in the domestication of literary kinds and forms. He was educated at Cambridge and studied law at Gray's Inn, for which he translated two plays. He served with English troops in the Low Countries, where he was captured by the Spanish, and sat as an MP for Bedford in the reigns of both Mary and Elizabeth (1557–9).

*A Hundred Sundry Flowers*, a collection of verse, prose and plays, appeared without Gascoigne's authority in 1573. It contained his plays *Supposes* and *Jocasta*, an incomplete work of prose fiction *The Adventures of Master F. I.*, some poetry and an incomplete version of *Dan Bartholomew*. Gascoigne's authorized version of this collection, *The Posies of George Gascoigne* (1575), made a few changes: there are some minor deletions, passages in *The Adventures of Master F. I.* are expurgated, marginal comments added to the plays, and *Dan Bartholomew* is completed. *Posies* also contained *Certain Notes of Instruction in English Verse*, an early treatise on prosody in English. The plays in this collection had both been performed at Gray's Inn (1566) and *Supposes* was put on again at Trinity College, Cambridge (1582). *Supposes*, a prose play of mistaken identity which anticipated **Shakespeare**'s *The Comedy of Errors* and provided the sub-plot of *The Taming of the Shrew*, is the first successful English adaptation of Italian comedy. It is from Ariosto's play *I Suppositi*. *Jocasta* claims to be translated from Euripides' *Phoenissae* but is in fact a translation, with the help of Francis Kinwelmarsh, from Dolce's *Giocasta*. It was the first Greek tragedy played on the English stage. *The Glass of Government*, Gascoigne's other play (printed in 1575), is a closet drama which has the form of a Roman comedy and offers a variation on the popular theme of the Prodigal Son. There is no indication of any early performance. Among the other works in the 1573 collection, *The Adventures of Master F. I.* is a very early example of an original English prose narrative in the Renaissance. *Dan Bartholomew of Bath* is an amatory poem.

*The Steel Glass* (1576) is a very early example of non-dramatic blank verse in English. The honest and satirical steel glass reflects the state of the commonwealth and the work attacks worldliness and ends with praise of an ideal clergy. Another of Gascoigne's poems is *The Grief of Joy*. Until it was printed in 1869 this existed only in an unfinished text which was written by 1576. It is a **rhyme royal** reflection, in imitation of Petrarch's *De Remediis Utriusque Fortunae*, on the vanity of beauty and strength. *The Complaint of Philomene*, an Ovidian narrative, was printed with *The Steel Glass* (1576), although the preface to the latter work says that it was written some 12 years earlier. *The Spoil of Antwerp* (1576) is a piece of war journalism; *The Drum of Doomsday* (1576), treating the frailties and miseries of life, is a translation of part of a treatise by Innocent III. Gascoigne also wrote a **masque** for Viscount Montague (1571), and contributed to the Queen's entertainment on her progresses to Kenilworth and Woodstock in 1575: *Zabeta* (which was probably not presented) for Kenilworth and *The Hermit's Tale* for Woodstock.

**Gascoyne, David (Emery)** 1916– Poet. Born in Harrow, and educated at Salisbury Cathedral Choir School and the Regent Street Polytechnic in London, he is widely known as the most representative English surrealist. At the age of 16 he published his first volume, *Roman Balcony* (1932), and became a *habitué* of London's literary Fitzrovia, also spending time in Paris. *A Short Survey of Surrealism* (1935) established him as the leading English authority on the subject. Its publication was followed by the first international surrealist exhibition in London in 1936, the same year that he issued his surrealist poems in *Man's Life is This Meat*. Gascoyne's early work.is extreme in its break with normal coherence and argument, absolutely resisting the reader's expectations of meaning and control. He later became interested in developing narrative continuities, which he disrupted with insights from Hölderlin and **Lawrence**. *Hölderlin's Madness* (1938), *Poems 1937–42* (1943) and *Night Thoughts* (1956) are his most important works. His *Collected Poems*, first published in 1965, was revised in 1970 and 1978.

**Gaskell, Elizabeth (Cleghorn)** 1810–65 Novelist and biographer. Born in Chelsea, London, the daughter of William Stevenson, civil servant and sometime Unitarian minister, Elizabeth Gaskell was brought up in Knutsford, Cheshire, by an aunt. She was educated at the Avonbank School in Stratford-upon-Avon and subsequently spent two years in the family of a distant cousin, the Revd William Turner, of Newcastle upon Tyne. In fact, her earlier years were peripatetic, a series of temporary sojourns, although at one of them she met her future husband, the Unitarian parson William Gaskell, author of many tracts and pamphlets relating to his calling, who held a chair of English History and Literature at Manchester New College. They were married in August 1832 and henceforth Mrs Gaskell's life was in northern England.

Although she had early tried her hand at short-story writing, it was not until 1848 with the publication of her first novel, *Mary Barton*, that Mrs Gaskell came upon the literary scene. This book, sub-titled *A Tale of Manchester Life*, was commenced shortly after the death of her little son, William, and its writing was suggested to her as a distraction from grief. It is a tale of industrial strife and unrest, touched by the melodramatic, and growing out of the Chartist movement of the 1840s.

*Mary Barton* earned Mrs Gaskell the friendship and respect of **Dickens**, who encouraged her to continue to contribute to his magazine, *Household Words*. *Cranford* appeared at irregular intervals in its pages from December 1851 until May 1853. Set in a thinly disguised Knutsford, it is a gentle understated tale of a retiring spinster and the little circle around her – a book that pronounces, if the word is not too strong, on the fundamental verities and decencies of the human condition. *Ruth* (1853) came next, boldly dealing with the concealment of an unmarried mother's problems. *North and South*, another industrial story of disquiet and confrontation, appeared in 1855. An eight-year interval in novel-writing closed with *Sylvia's Lovers* (1863). *Wives and Daughters*, posthumously published in 1866, stands in striking contrast to her early work and is in the tradition and style of **Jane Austen**.

Elizabeth Gaskell. Portrait by George Richmond, 1851. National Portrait Gallery, London.

Given her close friendship with **Charlotte Brontë** – the two writers first met in August 1850 – it was not surprising that she should have undertaken a biography after Charlotte's early death in 1855. *The Life of Charlotte Brontë* (1857) does not pretend to critical analysis; rather, it is a factual narrative, full in background and analytical of character, a book written out of sympathy and understanding for its subject. But just as Mrs Gaskell raised hackles over her treatment of illegitimacy in *Ruth* and of social strife in *North and South*, so she encountered antagonism over her account of the Brontë children at the Clergy Daughters' School at Cowan Bridge and, in particular, for her indiscreet allusions to Branwell Brontë's relations with a Mrs Edmund Robinson in whose household he was tutor. This last resulted in threats of legal action and, ultimately, withdrawal of questionable passages from the biography after its second edition. Yet, despite the problems surrounding *The Life of Charlotte Brontë*, the biography endures with acclamation.

Throughout her career Mrs Gaskell wrote longer short stories bordering on the novella. Several volumes were collected, among them *Life in Manchester* (1848), *Lizzie Leigh and Other Tales* (1855), *Round the Sofa* (1859) and *Cousin Phillis and Other Tales* (1865). Her control of the form appears in **Cousin Phillis**, 'Lizzie Leigh', 'Lois the Witch' and in more than a handful of others as well.

In a century rich in women writers Mrs Gaskell stands to the forefront in her sympathy for the deprived, her evocations of nature, her gentle humour and her narrative pace. Of note is her exceptionally direct development as novelist from loosely structured melodramatic writing to the urbanity and balanced form of her later work, particularly *Wives and Daughters*.

**Gass, William** 1924– American novelist, short-story writer and scholar, born in Fargo, North Dakota. A professor of philosophy at Washington University in St Louis, he writes fiction that is notable for its experimental use of language. *Omensetter's Luck*, his first novel, was published in 1966. Comprising three sections, each written in a different rhetorical style, it presents the conflict between Omensetter, who represents physicality and mindlessness, and Jethro Furber, who is intellectual and religious. *Willie Masters' Lonesome Wife*, a novella, appeared in 1971 and is still more experimental, containing unusual typography, parodies, footnotes, and authorial interruptions of the narrative. Gass has also published collections of short stories: *In the Heart of the Heart of the Country and Other Stories* (1968) and *The First Winter of My Married Life* (1979). His non-fiction works include *Fiction and the Figures of Life* (1970), *On Being Blue: A Philosophical Inquiry* (1975), *The*

*World Within the Word* (1978) and *Habitations of the Word: Essays* (1985).

**Gatty, Margaret** 1809–73 Children's writer. Born Margaret Scott, she married the Revd Alfred Gatty. Mrs Gatty founded *Aunt Judy's Magazine* in 1866 and edited and contributed to it until she died; it was enormously popular with children. She was best known for her *Parables from Nature*, published in a series of five books (1855–71). Other titles that enjoyed great popularity were *The Fairy Godmothers* (1851), *Aunt Judy's Tales* (1859) and *Aunt Judy's Letters* (1862).

**Gawain-poet, The** Author of *Sir Gawain and the Green Knight*, to whom are attributed also the other poems in manuscript **Cotton Nero A x**, **Cleanness**, **Patience** and **Pearl**. The theory of common authorship is based on similarities of style and diction. The poet's identity is not known; several names have been suggested, but none is conclusively supported by the evidence.

**Gay, John** 1685–1732 Poet and dramatist. Born in Barnstaple, Devon, Gay was brought up by his uncle, educated at Barnstaple Grammar School and then apprenticed to a London silk-merchant in the Strand. Socially at ease

Sir Gawain beheads the Green Knight; Arthur and Guinevere look on. Late 14th or early 15th-century illustration from *MS. Cotton Nero A x, f.90v*. British Library.

from the start of his urban life, Gay befriended **Aaron Hill** and began to move in literary circles. His first publication was *Wine* (1708), an anonymous blank-verse poem written to celebrate the Union of Scotland with England, a convivial piece overburdened by its Miltonic echoes. He met **Pope** and began to frequent the fashionable coffee-houses. His first attempt at drama, *The Mohocks* (1712), a 'Tragical-comical Farce' about a band of aristocratic thugs, was never acted.

Gay had contributed to Lintot's *Miscellany* and *The Examiner*, and his essay *The Present State of Wit* (1711) drew attention to his presence in polite literary circles. In 1712 he was appointed secretary to the Duchess of Monmouth, which alleviated his immediate financial worries. 1713 saw the publication of *The Fan* (a pale imitation of *The Rape of the Lock*) and the more accomplished *Rural Sports*, a **georgic** poem dedicated to Pope, containing some delicate mock-heroic passages and managing a genuine celebration of the English countryside combined with a characteristically comic dimension. Its use of animal parallelism anticipates his later *Fables*. Gay's first substantial success came with *The Shepherd's Week* (1714), his wittiest poem, part parody and partly true to life, a pastoral cycle designed to support Pope's opposition to **Ambrose Philips**. Gay left the Duchess of Monmouth in 1714, and became secretary to Lord Clarendon on a mission to Hanover, but his hopes of advancement in public office collapsed with the death of Queen Anne in 1714, and the fall of Harley's Tory government.

The audience at the first night of his *What d'ye Call it* (1715) were so convinced by Gay's burlesque skills that they mistook the satire for tragedy and were moved to tears. One of his distinctive strengths as a writer was a quick ear for rhythms of speech and tones of voice, and this, combined with his lively interest in ballads and street literature, contributed much to the success of his poem *Trivia, or, The Art of Walking the Streets of London* (1716), an extended Juvenalian survey of the conditions of life in the capital, both realistic in atmosphere and parodic in style. His next work was a dramatic collaboration with his fellow members of the **Scriblerus Club**, Pope and **Arbuthnot**, *Three Hours After Marriage* (1717), which was a flop. **Dr Johnson**, no great admirer of Gay, whom he regarded as an idle dilettante, wrote approvingly 'it had the fate which such outrages deserve', for the first night culminated in fisticuffs behind the scenes between Gay and the leading actor **Colley Cibber**, who had not realized his part was a lampoon of himself.

In 1720, Gay's *Poems on Several Occasions* appeared, containing various eclogues and songs, and made him some money, which he promptly invested in the South Sea Company.

When the 'Bubble' burst, Gay was ruined, and his health had also begun to deteriorate. He stayed with Pope and with Burlington, visited Bath for the 'waters', and, in a final attempt to secure preferment at court, began work in 1726 on his *Fables*, addressed to young Prince William. The first volume of these appeared in 1729 and proved popular, demonstrating the poet's gentle eye for detail and real affinity for natural topics; the second part, more serious, was published posthumously.

Since 1722, Gay had maintained a vigorous correspondence with his older friend **Swift**, and it was the latter who provided the idea for Gay's greatest work, *The Beggar's Opera*. This **ballad opera** pokes fun at the imported fashion for opera, and inverts the heroic values of polite society by translating hypocrisy into the underworld of London's criminals. The Duchess of Queensbury – Gay's new patron – offered to back it, and the play was produced by John Rich at Lincoln's Inn Fields on 29 January 1728. It was prodigiously successful, running for an unprecedented 62 nights, and is reported to have made 'Gay rich, and Rich gay'. In a lean century for good drama, it was by far the most popular play, and contains some 69 songs. The sequel, *Polly* (1729), was suppressed by Walpole, who was tired of being satirized, but this merely made it a *cause célèbre*, and the printed version sold quickly. It was finally produced in 1777. His friends started to worry at Gay's life-style, since he began to indulge freely in gambling and drinking, living a life of leisure at Bath or with the Queensburys. He died in 1732 and is buried in Westminster Abbey. His refusal ever to be solemn about life is epitomized by the epitaph he composed for himself: 'Life is a jest, and all things show it;/I thought so once – and now I know it.'

Gay's literary reputation has proved difficult to determine. As a dramatist, he wrote some 13 pieces, all overshadowed by his runaway success with *The Beggar's Opera*; these include *The Wife of Bath* (1713) ('it received no applause' observed Johnson), *Dione* (1719), an impossible pastoral, and the libretto for Handel's *Acis and Galatea* (1732). As a poet, he was a master of the heroic couplet, and his songs and fables continued to be read after his death, for their sweetness of sound and neatness of phrase. Though his sybaritic life-style and lack of ambition perhaps prevented him from achieving more, Gay should not suffer by comparison to his more serious Scriblerian associates. He was intellectually acute, and a lively personality who made friends easily; Voltaire, for example, is said to have 'loved Gay vastly'.

**Gee, Maurice** 1931– New Zealand novelist. Born in Whakatane on North Island, Gee has lived in many parts of New Zealand and London. He worked as a teacher and librarian before turning to full-time writing in 1975. His novel *Plumb* (1978), the winner of several literary prizes, is a vivid picture of New Zealand life in the first half of the century, centred on the trials of conscience of a domineering Presbyterian minister. It is the first part of a family chronicle, which has been completed by *Meg* (1981), the story of Plumb's youngest child, and *Sole Survivor* (1983), in which the action reaches the present day. All three parts of the Plumb trilogy demonstrate a deft handling of first-person narrative and are carefully crafted explorations of the interaction between past and present. Gee lives in Nelson and, in addition to his adult novels, writes children's fiction and television scripts. His other books include the novels *A Special Flower* (1965), *In My Father's Den* (1972) and *Games of Choice* (1976), and a volume of short stories, *Good Morning, Comrade* (1975).

**Gelber, Jack** 1932– American playwright, born in Chicago, and educated at the University of Illinois. Of the dozen or so of his plays that have been produced in New York, the 1959 Living Theatre production of *The Connection* has received the greatest critical acclaim. About four heroin addicts waiting in an apartment for a 'connection' to bring their drugs, the play uses jazz, poetry and the improvisation techniques of popular theatre deliberately to collapse the traditional sense of distance between audience and actors. His other plays, all of which employ radical dramatic methods to explore the relationship between performer and audience, include *The Apple* (1961), *Square in the Eye* (1965), *The Cuban Thing* (1968), *Sleep* (1972) and *Jack Gelber's New Play: Rehearsal* (1976). He has also written a screenplay of *The Connection* (1961), adapted **Norman Mailer**'s *Barbary Shore* (1974) for the stage, and written a novel, *On Ice* (1964).

**Gems, Pam (Iris Pamela)** 1925– Dramatist. Born in Hampshire, she was educated at Brakenhurst County Grammar School and at Manchester University. Two lunchtime plays, *My Warren* (1973) and *After Birthday* (1973), were followed by a full-length work, *The Amiable Courtship of Ms Venus and Wild Bill* (1975). Her first great success, however, came with *Dusa, Fish, Stas and Vi* (1977), a study of four girls rooming together in a London flat. The accuracy, good humour and specific awareness of feminist (as well as feminine) issues brought her recognition as a leading woman playwright, although her appeal was never confined to female audiences. The **Royal Shakespeare Company** produced *Queen Christina* (1977), her musical biography *Piaf* (1980), *Camille* (1984) and *The Danton Affair* (1986).

*Generides* A late 14th-century **verse romance** composed in the Midlands. It survives in two versions, one of 10,000 lines in couplets and the other 7000 lines in seven-line stanzas.

Knowing his wife is unfaithful with his steward, King Aufreus meets the Princess Sereyne on a hunt; he begets a son, Generides, whom she rears. When he is grown up he goes to Aufreus's court but leaves after the Queen tries to seduce him, travelling to Persia where he falls in love with the Sultan's daughter, Clarionas. He is betrayed and imprisoned but later released to fight as the Sultan's champion. Meanwhile Aufreus loses his kingdom and wife to the treacherous steward and marries Sereyne. Generides eventually marries Clarionas after defeating a rival who kidnaps her and despite the malicious attempts of the Queen, estranged from Aufreus, to separate them. The steward is defeated by Generides and the Queen also dies. The romance, well told and engaging, is a composite of many common themes and motifs. It has no known source; despite its Indian and Middle Eastern setting it is unlikely that it is of Eastern origin.

*Genesis* An Old English poem preserved in the Junius manuscript (see **Junius, Francis**). Once thought to be the work of **Caedmon**, it is now known to be a composite of two works, neither of which can be attributed to Caedmon. The major part of the poem, known as *Genesis A*, was written in the 8th century by a northern monk. It begins with an account of the war in heaven and then proceeds to relate the story of the Book of Genesis up to Chapter 22. Interpolated are over 600 lines of a 9th-century poem, *Genesis B*, translated from a German source and telling the story of Satan. The subject matter is the same as that of **Milton**'s *Paradise Lost*, and there are some striking resemblances between the two works.

**Genette, Gérard** See **structuralism**.

**Geneva Bible, The** See **Bible in English, The**.

**Gent, Thomas** 1693–1778 Printer, poet and writer of topographical works. Born in Ireland, Gent was apprenticed to a Dublin printer who so ill-treated him that he ran away, eventually arriving in London. After various adventures he was admitted to the Stationers' Company in 1717, and shortly after was involved in illicit printing for **Atterbury**. In 1722 he produced an abridgement of *Robinson Crusoe* with 30 rather crude woodcuts of his own design, and in that year or 1723 he set up in business for himself. Hearing that the woman he loved, Alice Guy, had married a former fellow apprentice, he wrote a highly successful poem, *The Forsaken Lover's Letter to His Former Sweetheart*, but on

hearing of her widowhood shortly after he hastened to York and married her, thus acquiring the business of his now dead rival. He became the only master printer in York and, it is thought, in the North of England. He produced a number of topographical works, written and printed by himself, of which the most important are his *History of York* (1730) and *History of Ripon* (1734) which contains a poem in praise of Fountains Abbey by Peter Aram, father of the murderer Eugene Aram. His autobiography (1832) contains a considerable amount of interesting material about the printing trade and literary world in the early 18th century and also shows him to have been extraordinarily cantankerous. His topographical works, which were embellished with at times grotesque woodcuts, are now regarded as valuable both for their idiosyncratic printing practices and their detailed information.

***Gentleman Dancing-Master, The*** A comedy by **William Wycherley**, first produced in March 1672 and published in 1673. The play, which approaches deftly turned farce, had its source in the Spanish *El Maestro de Danzar* by Calderón.

***Gentleman's Magazine, The*** A periodical founded by Edward Cave (1691–1754), the enterprising son of a cobbler in Rugby, who became a printer in London. He launched it in 1731 under the pseudonym of Sylvanus Urban. It began as a review of news, essays and comment from other journals but by January 1739 it was publishing original work and **Samuel Johnson** became a regular contributor. Johnson's suggestions to Cave influenced the character of the paper and it assumed a more serious tone, publishing parliamentary reports, maps, reviews of publications and music. *The Gentleman's Magazine* continued to be published until 1914.

***Geoffrey Hamlyn, The Recollections of*** A novel by **Henry Kingsley**, published in 1859. The setting is Australia, where the author spent some years after leaving Oxford under a cloud. The story leads up to the many reasons why a group of settlers prepare to leave England and then follows their fortunes in the vast undeveloped continent. Kingsley was an excellent reporter and presents a vivid picture of the landscape and the hazards faced by the emigrants.

**Geoffrey of Monmouth** d. ?1155 Chronicler. Probably born in Monmouth and having some connection with Caerleon-on-Usk, he was at Oxford from 1129 to 1151, perhaps a canon of the secular college of St George which was dissolved in 1149. He probably lived in London from 1148 to 1151, though maintaining his

Oxford connections. In 1151 he became Bishop Elect of Asaph and was ordained a priest in 1152. Evidence of doubtful reliability alleges he died in 1155.

Three works of his survive, all written in Latin: *Historia Regum Britanniae* (*c.* 1135), *Propheti Merlini* and *Vita Merlini*. The *Prophecies* and *Life* were conceived separately but finally incorporated into the *History*. The *History* traces events from the legendary founding of Britain by Brutus, grandson of Aeneas, to the death of the last British king, Cadwallader, in 689. Although some of the narrative bears a remote resemblance to actual events, the majority is pure invention. It relates the lives of, among others, Kings Cole, Lear, Cymbeline and Arthur, Julius Caesar, Claudius, Vespasian and Gorboduc, and events such as the founding of London, the moving of Stonehenge to Salisbury Plain by Merlin, and the coming of St Augustine to Britain. But it is for the history of King Arthur that the work is best known. Occupying over a fifth of the work, Arthur's mythical life and deeds are reported for the first time. His marriage to Guinevere, Mordred's treason, his disappearance to Avalon and the exploits of Gawain, Bedevere, Cador and Kay are all related, though Lancelot does not appear.

Geoffrey's intentions were primarily patriotic and artistic; he aims not simply to produce a detailed chronicle but to enliven and enrich history. He orders his potentially rambling and chaotic material into a strict form, and portrays

An illustration from Geoffrey of Monmouth's *Prophetia Merlini* in a 13th-century manuscript. Merlin, standing on a cloud, shows his prophecy to Vortigern. *MS Cotton Claudius B. VII, f.224.* British Library.

his main characters sharply. He alleges that his source was a book, apparently in Welsh, given to him by Walter, Archdeacon of Oxford, but the book (if it ever existed) no longer survives. No single source can be identified, though Geoffrey frequently uses and sometimes refers to many other works, and takes much from **Bede**, the 6th-century *De Excidio et Conquestu Britanniae* of Gildas and the 9th-century *Historia Brittonum* of Nennius. Geoffrey's *History* in turn formed the basis of Wace's *Roman de Brut* and of the vast ensuing body of **Arthurian literature**.

**Geoffrey of Vinsauf** d. *c.* 1210–20 Rhetorician. Little is known of the life of Geoffrey, although hints in his work suggest he was an Englishman, flourishing in the second half of the 12th century. He was a teacher of the future Richard I and it is thought that he studied in Paris, and that he visited Rome on at least one occasion. Three major works survive: the *Documentum de Modo et Arte Dictandi et Versificandi*, the *Summa de Coloribus Rhetoricis*, and the influential handbook, the *Poetria Nova*, which was cited by **Chaucer** in **The Canterbury Tales**. In the *Poetria Nova*, poetry is studied as an aspect of rhetoric, and Geoffrey draws heavily on two main sources, the pseudo-Ciceronian *Ad Herennium* and Horace's *Ars Poetica*. Geoffrey urges poets to improve their skills by acquiring a thorough knowledge of the rules of poetic composition (*ars*), studying and imitating the great poets of the past (*imitatio*) and practising steadily (*usus*). The *Poetria Nova* is a valuable source of information on the rhetorical devices, techniques and methods of ornamentation prescribed by medieval theoreticians as necessary to polished and felicitous poetry.

**George, Henry** 1839–97 American journalist and political reformer, born in Philadelphia. After moving to California in 1857, he worked variously as a ship's storekeeper, a gold-digger and a typesetter, before settling down to a career as a crusading journalist and newspaper editor in San Francisco.

His first major political statement was an editorial in **Overland Monthly** (October 1868) entitled 'What the Railroads Will Bring Us', in which he argued that the present organization of the railroad industry would serve only to make the rich richer and the poor poorer. His first two separate publications, both pamphlets, *The Subsidy Question and the Democratic Party* and *Our Land and Land Policy*, appeared in 1871. The latter contained the first statement of his Single Tax Theory; he developed this in his most important economic treatise, *Progress and Poverty* (published in 1879 at his own expense), arguing that the gap between the rich and the poor could be closed by replacing the various taxes levied on labour and capital with a single tax on the rental value of property. *Progress and Poverty* eventually sold more than two million copies. In four subsequent works he applied his Single Tax Theory to a number of social and economic issues: *Social Problems* (1883), *Protection or Free Trade* (1886), *Perplexed Philosopher* (1892) and *Science of Political Economy* (1897). During the last 16 years of his life he made six lecture tours in Europe, where his theories were even more influential than in the USA.

**George Barnwell** See *London Merchant, The*.

**George Silverman's Explanation** A short story by **Charles Dickens**, published in *The Atlantic Monthly* (1868). The narrator is rescued from a boyhood in the slums of Preston, studies at Cambridge and becomes a clergyman; he attempts to act from the noblest of motives, but remains haunted by guilt and is accused of being selfish.

**Georgian Poetry** An anthology published in five volumes between 1912 and 1922, planned by its publisher **Harold Monro**, **Rupert Brooke** and **Edward Marsh**, the editor. The early, influential volumes included Brooke, **Lascelles Abercrombie**, **Gordon Bottomley**, **W. H. Davies**, **Walter de la Mare**, **John Drinkwater**, Ralph Hodgson, **D. H. Lawrence** and **John Masefield**. Their poetry tended to be colloquial and lightly shocking in its realism, yet they were never a coherent movement. Later volumes included the work of **Blunden**, **Graves**, **Rosenberg** and **Sassoon**. Graves, in particular, rejected the early Georgians as 'principally concerned with Nature and love and leisure and old age and childhood and animals and sleep and similar uncontroversial subjects' and for having no experience of the 'grinding hardships of trench-service'. The group was also criticized by **Pound**, **Eliot** and the **Sitwells**, whose anthology *Wheels* was intended as a **modernist** alternative.

**georgic** A poem designed to offer instruction on some branch of skill or art, the most famous example being the *Georgics* of Virgil, which discussed the conditions of life in the countryside under Augustus Caesar, and various aspects of farming and husbandry. Numerous imitations were written during the 17th and 18th centuries, poems about sheep-shearing, cidermaking, physical health and country sports; the subject was the occasion of an important essay by **Addison**, *Essay on the Georgic* (1697), in which he distinguishes it from the **pastoral**.

**Gerard, John** 1545–1612 Herbalist. Gerard was for some years apprenticed to a barber-surgeon in London before being granted leave to establish his own practice. He developed an interest in plants and in his garden in Holborn cultivated gifts of rare plants and seeds. His catalogue of the plants there was printed in 1596. Gerard also supervised Lord Burleigh's gardens in the Strand. His *Herbal* (1597) was in fact a completion of an unfinished translation by a Dr Priest of Dodoenus, *Stirpium Historiae Pemptades Sex* (1583). The *Herbal* was illustrated with over 1800 woodcuts (including an early depiction of the potato), very few of which were original as they came from Tabernaemontanus, *Eicones Plantarum*. The description of the plants includes their habitat and times of flowering. Gerard gives many of the plants their old English names, includes popular legends (the goose-tree which bears shells that eventually hatch into barnacle geese) and describes the 'virtues' of plants: the lettuce cools heartburn and causes sleep, narcissus root pounded with honey is good for burns. A second edition, revised by Thomas Johnson, was printed in 1633.

**Germ, The** The literary magazine of the **Pre-Raphaelite Brotherhood**, it lasted for only four issues, published between January and April 1850. It contained poetry by **Dante Gabriel Rossetti** (*The Blessed Damozel*), **Christina Rossetti** and **Coventry Patmore**, Rossetti's short story *Hand and Soul* and reviews of contemporary verse by his brother, **William Michael Rossetti**, who was also the editor.

**Gest Hystoriale of the Destruction of Troy** A **verse romance** written in the second half of the 14th century. It is the longest of the Middle English poems in **alliterative verse**, and is divided into a prologue and 36 books. It treats the history of Troy from the story of Jason and the Golden Fleece and the destruction of the Old Troy to the destruction of the New Troy, the adventures of the Greeks after its fall and the

'Cordelia' by Ford Madox Brown. One of the illustrations published in *The Germ*, the short-lived periodical published by the Pre-Raphaelite Brotherhood in 1850 to propagate its views.

death of Ulysses. It includes the story of Troilus and Briseida, invented by Benoît de Sainte-Maure and told in his *Roman de Troie* (*c.* 1160) and later told by **Chaucer** in *Troilus and Criseyde*. While based on Guido's *Historia Destructionis Troiae*, the poem treats the material of its source freely, adding, omitting and adapting episodes. Except for some moralizing digressions the story is vigorously told and the characters are vividly portrayed.

***Gesta Romanorum*** A collection of tales from various sources which took shape in Europe during the 14th century. The title is misleading, since few of the stories are concerned with Rome and some are Eastern in origin. Each tale was designed to point a moral, though this is transparently contrived in many cases. Popular as a storybook, the collection was plundered for subjects by succeeding generations. Originally written in Latin, it appeared in several vernacular translations, including one in Middle English. The first printed version in English was issued by **Wynkyn de Worde** in 1510.

**Ghose, Zulfikar** 1935– Poet and novelist, born in Sialkot, India (now Pakistan). An emigrant to Britain and then the USA, Ghose inhabits the interstices of an Indian–Pakistani–British–American network of allegiances, antipathies and doubts, and skilfully exploits such multivalent experience. *The Loss of India* (1964) contains verse nostalgic for a lost past, tentative in an uncertain present. *Jets of Orange* (1967) again laments loss, and records Indian subjects with a sensitive outsider's detachment – which operates also in the pungent satirical verse of *The Violent West* (1972). His stories in *Statement against Corpses* (1964), with **B. S. Johnson**, and in the novels *Contradictions* (1966) and *The Murder of Aziz Khan* (1969) seek a 'still point' between, respectively, being alive and observing death, Western rationality and Eastern 'nothingness', outside physicality and interior sensibility. Two critical works, *Hamlet, Prufrock, and Language* (1978) and *The Fiction of Reality* (1984), point to the nature of Ghose's impressive output of sophisticated and challenging novels since 1972: a trilogy, *The Incredible Brazilian* (1972), *The Beautiful Empire* (1975), *A Different World* (1979); then *Hulme's Investigations into the Bogart Script* (1981), *A New History of Torments* (1982) and *Don Bueno* (1983). *Confessions of a Native-Alien* (1965) is an autobiography.

**Gibbon, Edward** 1737–94 Historian. The son of a family of comfortable circumstances, Gibbon was born at Putney. He was educated at Westminster School, and entered Magdalen College, Oxford, as a gentleman-commoner just before his 15th birthday. But he was disappointed in Oxford, finding it self-satisfied and

Edward Gibbon. Portrait by H. Walton, *c.* 1773. National Portrait Gallery, London.

outdated. He studied by himself and was received into the Roman Catholic church in June 1753. In alarm, Gibbon's father sent him to Lausanne and a tutor in the form of a Calvinist minister, Pavillar, who managed to reconvert him. At Lausanne, too, Gibbon formed the only romantic attachment of his life, to Suzanne Curchod, who eventually married Jacques Necker; the attachment was broken off because Gibbon's father disapproved.

Gibbon returned home in 1758, and in 1761 published his first work, *Essai sur l'Étude de la Littérature*; an English version appeared in 1764. He served in the Hampshire militia for four years and reached the rank of colonel (1759–63). After his service Gibbon visited Europe, spending some time in Paris and Lausanne, and proceeded to Rome intent on archaeological study. He reached the city in October 1764 and on the 15th of that month he found the historical subject he sought. 'It was at Rome . . . as I sat musing amidst the ruins of the Capitol, while barefoot friars were singing vespers in the Temple of Jupiter, that the idea of writing the decline and fall of the city first started to my mind.' He had, meanwhile, been producing a mass of miscellaneous reviews and exercises, including the *Observations of the Design of the VIth Book of the Aeneid* (1770). His father died in the same year, leaving financial problems for his son to clear up; Gibbon did, however, manage to salvage enough money to establish himself in

London, with its libraries, intellectual stimulus and scholarly society.

Gibbon became an MP in 1774. The House of Commons was 'a school of civil prudence, the first and most essential virtue of an historian', as he wrote in his memoirs. He was a steadfast supporter of Lord North's government and was rewarded with the post of Commissioner of Trade and Plantations in 1779, holding it until its abolition in 1782. His political career amounted to little but his literary career had begun: the first volume of *The History of the Decline and Fall of the Roman Empire* was published on 17 February 1776 and was greeted with general praise, except from orthodox Christians. In England certain theological critics, including **Richard Watson** and Henry Edwards Davis, attacked Gibbon in print, and he replied at last with his *A Vindication of Some Passages in the Fifteenth and Sixteenth Chapters* (1779), in which he refuted completely their charges of plagiarism and misrepresentation. Similar attacks continued throughout his lifetime.

The second and third volumes of the *History* were published in 1781 and at that time Gibbon resolved to extend it to cover the Eastern Empire, Byzantium, as well. He was weary of London and moved to Lausanne in 1783. He completed his *History* there in 1787 and took the three volumes to London in 1788 for the publisher. *The Antiquities of the House of Brunswick* was begun but Gibbon, who had no German, did not complete it. He left Lausanne in 1791 and returned to England, where his closest friend, John Baker Holroyd, now Earl of Sheffield, offered him the hospitality of Sheffield Park in Sussex and his London house. Lord Sheffield was to prepare his friend's *Memoirs of My Life and Writings* for publication (1796), as well as his (admirably edited) collections of *Miscellaneous Works*. Gibbon died in London on 16 January 1794 and lies buried in the Sheffield family tomb in Fletching church in Sussex.

**Gibbon, Lewis Grassic** Pseudonym by which the Scottish writer James Leslie Mitchell (1901–35) is best known. Born into a crofting family at Auchterless, Aberdeenshire, Mitchell was brought up in the Howe of Mearns, south of Stonehaven, the setting of his best-known work, the trilogy of novels collectively called *A Scots Quair*. He was educated at Arbuthnott School and briefly at Mackie Academy, Stonehaven, and became a journalist in Aberdeen and Glasgow. He was early a convert to socialism, his views reinforced by the urban poverty and unrest on Clydeside. Jobless, he served in the Royal Army Service Corps in Persia, India and Egypt, and later in the Royal Air Force until 1929. A packed and remarkable writing career was cut short when he died in Welwyn Garden City in 1935. He was interested in history, archaeology and anthropology, and as James Leslie Mitchell he published *Hanno; or, The Future of Exploration* (1928), *Niger: The Life of Mungo Park* (1934) and *The Conquest of the Maya* (1934), all informed by his version of Diffusionist theory. He believed in a Golden Age for man as a nomadic hunter, which was destroyed by agriculture and consequent civilization. He published seven English novels and many stories under his own name. Lewis Grassic Gibbon was the pen-name he used for his specifically Scottish undertakings, *A Scots Quair* and the collaborative work with **Hugh MacDiarmid**, *Scottish Scene, or, The Intelligent Man's Guide to Albyn* (1934), an important contribution to the **Scottish renaissance**. In the trilogy *Sunset Song* (1932), *Cloud Howe* (1933) and *Grey Granite* (1934) he returned to the Mearns and made a courageous, successful attempt to render the rhythms and cadences of North-East dialect, while using only a handful of local words.

**Gibbons, Stella** See *Cold Comfort Farm*.

**Gibson, Graeme** 1934– Canadian novelist. Born and educated in Ontario, Gibson has travelled widely in Europe, the United States and Latin America. He has published three novels: *Five Legs* (1969), *Communion* (1971) and *Perpetual Motion* (1982). These are experimental but carefully constructed. All are set in southern Ontario, but the first two deal with private contemporary experience, which is conveyed in a **stream-of-consciousness** style, whereas *Perpetual Motion* is a historical novel leaning to **magic realism**. All are concerned with man's relation to nature and spirit, though this is perhaps most evident in the last novel, where a 19th-century farmer's obsession with a mammoth bone and a machine serves to link past and future or earth and industrialism. Gibson has also published a collection of interviews, *Eleven Canadian Novelists* (1973). Prominent in Canadian cultural politics, he was an organizer and founding member of the Writers Union of Canada and its Chairman in 1974–5, Canada's first exchange writer at the University of Edinburgh 1978–9, and President of PEN Canada (Anglophone) in 1987.

**Gibson, Wilfred Wilson** 1878–1962 Poet. Gibson was born at Hexham in Northumberland and educated privately. He published his first collection of poems, *Urlyn the Harper and Other Songs*, in 1902, and thereafter his work appeared regularly in *New Numbers* and in **Edward Marsh**'s *Georgian Poetry*. His output was considerable, his commonest subject being the plight of the unfortunate, particularly the ordinary men and women at the mercy of industrial and political change. Gibson's *Collected Poems* (1926) was followed by another dozen collections before his death. *Within Four Walls* (1950) contains five verse plays.

**Gifford, William** 1756–1826 Satirist and critic. Born at Ashburton in Devon, a glazier's son, Gifford was apprenticed to a shoemaker, but through the kindness of a local surgeon was able to enter Exeter College, Oxford, in 1782. He first came to notice with two satires, *The Baviad* (1791) and *The Maeviad* (1795), directed against the **Della Cruscans**. In 1797 he became editor of *The Anti-Jacobin* and in 1809 editor of *The Quarterly Review*. His criticism is characterized by sourness and conservatism. He was satirically portrayed as Mr Vamp in **Thomas Love Peacock**'s *Melincourt* (1817) and rebuked by **William Hazlitt** in *A Letter to Gifford* (1819).

Gifford also translated the satires of Juvenal (1802) and Persius (1812), and prepared notable editions of several Jacobean dramatists: **Philip Massinger** (1805), **Ben Jonson** (1816), **John Ford** (posthumously published, 1827) and **James Shirley** (completed by Alexander Dyce, 1833).

**Gilbert, Michael** See **detective fiction**.

**Gilbert, Sir Humphrey** ?1539–83 A soldier and navigator, Gilbert was the stepbrother of **Sir Walter Raleigh**. His suggestions for voyages to discover the Northwest Passage, including those in his *A Discourse of a Discovery for a New Passage to Cataia* (written in 1566 and printed in **George Gascoigne**'s edition of 1576), received no or reluctant support from Elizabeth, who eventually granted him a charter in 1578 to settle heathen lands not yet settled by any Christian ruler. In 1583 he claimed Newfoundland for the Queen but on the journey home he was lost at sea in an Atlantic storm. The scene is described in **Hakluyt**'s *Voyages*.

**Gilbert, William** 1544–1603 Gilbert was probably the most distinguished scientist of Elizabeth's reign, although one who still lived in an animistic universe. He began to practise medicine in London in 1573, became physician to Elizabeth in 1601 and then James I in 1603. His work *De Magnete* (1600) was the first to use the term 'electrical force'. He agreed with Copernicus that the earth revolved on its axis. At his death he left manuscripts which were edited by his brother and published as *De Mundo Nostro Sublunari Philosophia Nova* (1651).

**Gilbert, W[illiam] S[chwenck]** 1836–1911 Playwright, librettist and lyricist. Born in London of a naval surgeon with literary leanings and a mother from whom both father and son became estranged, Gilbert was educated at Great Ealing School and University College, London. He had little success in his early career as a barrister and turned to journalism, contributing from 1861 humorous verse to *Fun* and other periodicals, much of it collected and published as *The Bab Ballads*. After considerable apprentice work for the theatre, particularly in the field of burlesque, he achieved popularity with a verse-play, *The Palace of Truth* (1870), and followed this with other successful plays, usually in a vein of fantasy, such as *Pygmalion and Galatea* (1871), *The Wicked World* (1873), *Sweethearts* (1874) and *Engaged* (1877). His career as a librettist was founded on his partnership with the composer Arthur Sullivan, beginning uncertainly with *Thespis* (1871), but flourishing from *Trial by Jury* (1875) onwards, and producing the series known as the **Savoy Operas**, which proved enormously popular up to *The Gondoliers* (1889), though losing favour thereafter. Gilbert's prominence as a librettist led to a diminution in his output as a playwright, though he wrote several ambitious if less appreciated later plays, including *Broken Hearts* (1875) and *Gretchen* (1879).

Unlike his mentor **T. W. Robertson**, Gilbert tended to avoid the contemporary scene and a realistic approach, and (whether writing verse or prose) developed a style marked by formality and paradox. His profoundly pessimistic view of the selfishness of human nature (seen in its purest form in *The Palace of Truth* and *Engaged*) was made more palatable in comic opera, and it is by his collaboration with Sullivan that his work continues to be represented in the theatre. His plays lacked the fashionable settings and social relevance which the Victorian audience hailed in the 'society' drama of **Wilde**, **Pinero** and **Jones**, and his reputation was eclipsed by these authors in the 1890s. He remains nevertheless the most original writer for the Victorian stage. Gilbert was knighted in 1907, the first author to be so honoured specifically for services to the drama.

**Gildas** See **Arthurian literature**.

***Gilded Age, The**: A Tale of Today* A satirical novel by **Mark Twain** and **Charles Dudley Warner**, published in 1873 and dramatized by Twain and G. S. Densmore in the following year. The novel comments on the greed, exploitation and economic speculation during the period of post-Civil War Reconstruction (the era itself has been named after the book). Set in Missouri, New York and Washington, DC, the story tells of various unscrupulous individuals, their personal relationships, and their rather dubious financial enterprises.

**Gillette, William (Hooker)** 1855–1937 American actor and dramatist, born in Connecticut. Gillette's early career was advanced by **Mark Twain**, a family friend. He gained a considerable reputation as an actor, writing parts for himself in which his restrained style and fondness for underplaying could be exploited. His career as a dramatist was launched in 1881 with the production of two plays: *The Private Secretary* and *Esmeralda*, the latter written in collaboration with **Frances Hodgson Burnett**. *All the Comforts of Home* (1890) and *Too Much Johnson* (1894) were adaptations of French farces. His best-known works are two original melodramas about the Civil War, *Held by the Enemy* (1886) and *Secret Service* (1895); and *Sherlock Holmes* (1899), a dramatization of **Arthur Conan Doyle**'s stories in which Gillette himself starred for over 30 years. A short comic sequel, *The Painful Predicament of Sherlock Holmes*, and a melodrama entitled *Clarice* were both produced in 1905.

**Gilman, Charlotte Perkins** 1860–1935 American feminist writer, born in Hartford, Connecticut. *In This Our World* (1893) is a collection of poems about 19th-century womanhood. *Women and Economics* (1898) is a strong indictment of patriarchal culture; other reforming works, including *Concerning Children* (1900) and *The Home: Its Work and Influence* (1903), discuss the detrimental effects that restrictions on women have on the family. *The Yellow Wallpaper*, written in 1890 and published in 1899, is a semi-autobiographical treatment of a woman writer's breakdown and the subsequent 'rest cure' prescribed by her physician husband; the cure forbids her to write and leads to true madness. From 1909 to 1916 Gilman edited *The Forerunner*, a magazine consisting entirely of her own articles and fiction dealing with women's issues. Two of her novels, *What Diana Did* (1910) and *The Crux* (1911), appeared in this periodical, as did *The Man-Made World*, which, with the independently published *His Religion and Hers* (1923), further developed her ideas about sexual relations and oppression in modern society. Her autobiography was published in 1935.

**Gilmore, Dame Mary** 1865–1962 Australian poet. Born Mary Jean Cameron in Goulburn, New South Wales, she worked as a teacher and journalist before joining William Lane's idealistic experimental community in Paraguay. Returning to Australia after the failure of the venture, she wrote for *The Sydney Worker* conducting the woman's page for 23 years. She published 10 books of verse including *Marri'd and Other Verses* (1910), *The Passionate Heart* (1918) and *The Wild Swan* (1930), each typically enthusiastic and radical in tone. She was created a Dame of the Order of the British Empire in 1936. Her poems include 'Old Botany Bay', 'Eve-Song' and 'The Mopoke, Memory'.

**Gilpin, William** 1724–1804 Travel-writer. Educated at The Queen's College, Oxford, Gilpin became a schoolmaster and clergyman in Boldre, Hampshire. He achieved considerable

success with his accounts of tours through Britain and established himself as a leading authority on the **picturesque**. The books, all delicately illustrated by the author and all showing as great a concern for the abstract principles of beauty as for the particular scene, covered the following areas: the Wye Valley and South Wales (1782), the Lake District (1786), the Highlands (1789), the New Forest (1791), the West Country and the Isle of Wight (1789), the coasts of Hampshire, Sussex and Kent (1804), Cambridge, Norfolk, Suffolk, Essex and North Wales (1809). Also notable is the collection *Three Essays: On Picturesque Beauty; On Picturesque Travel; On Sketching Landscape* (1792). The vogue for picturesque travel he helped encourage is satirized in **William Combe**'s *Tour of Dr Syntax in Search of the Picturesque*.

**Ginsberg, Allen** 1926– American poet, born in New Jersey. He attended Columbia University and then held a number of jobs, from dishwashing to book-reviewing for *Newsweek*. His first collection, *Howl and Other Poems* (1956), established him as a major poet and, with **Jack Kerouac** and **William Burroughs**, as a leader of the **Beats**. His other collections include *Kaddish and Other Poems* (1961), *Reality Sandwiches* (1963), *Planet News* (1964), *The Fall of America: Poems of these States, 1965–1971* (1972), *First Blues: Rags, Ballads, and Harmonium Songs, 1971–1974* (1975), *Poems All Over The Place: Mostly Seventies* (1978), *Collected Poems 1947–1980* (1984) and *White Shroud: Poems 1980–1985*

Allen Ginsberg.

(1986). Some of his talks on poetry and politics are included in *Allen Verbatim* (1974). *Journals, Early Fifties Early Sixties* was published in 1977. *Selected Gay Poems and Correspondence*, a collection of poems and letters exchanged between Ginsberg and Peter Orlovsky, appeared in 1978.

**Giovanni, Nikki (Yolande Cornelia)** 1943– Black American poet, born in Knoxville, Tennessee, and educated at Fisk University. Her first two collections of poetry, *Black Feeling, Black Talk* (1968) and *Black Judgment* (1969), are set against the background of the civil rights movement and trace the development of a young black woman into a fiery militant. In *Recreation* (1970) and *Spin a Soft Black Song* (1971) Giovanni's voice has softened somewhat, and the expression of political concerns is balanced with social and political statement. Her examination of the black experience is further developed in *My House* (1972), *Ego-Tripping and Other Poems for Young People* (1974), *The Women and the Men* (1975), *Cotton Candy on a Rainy Day* (1980) and *Those Who Ride the Night Winds* (1983). *Gemini: An Extended Autobiographical Statement on My First Twenty-Five Years of Being a Black Poet* was published in 1971.

**Gissing, George (Robert)** 1857–1903 Novelist. Educated at a Quaker boarding school, Alderley Edge, Cheshire, and Owen's College, Manchester (which later became the University of Manchester). He was expelled for stealing and spent a month in prison. Aged 19, he wandered for a year in America, then settled in London. A classical scholar, he survived by private coaching at just over a shilling (5p) an hour. He married two lower-class girls in succession and was disappointed when they were not grateful. He was an obsessively hard-working and prolific artist, obsessed with his vocation, proud and lonely because conscious of humble origins. His only friend was **H. G. Wells**, from a similar background. Gissing wrote, characteristically, about poverty and failure, but as a writer he was successful and respected as a naturalist novelist in the French manner, though he never became rich. His first novel, **Workers in the Dawn** (1880), was published when he was 23. It was followed by *The Unclassed* (1884), *Eve's Ransom* (1885), *Isabel Clarendon* and **Demos** (both in 1886), *Thyrza* (1887), *A Life's Morning* (1888), *The Nether World* (1889), *The Emancipated* (1890), **New Grub Street** (1891), *Born in Exile* (1892), **The Odd Women** (1893), *Sleeping Fires* (1895), *The Whirlpool* (1897), *Human Odds and Ends* (short stories, 1897), *The Town Traveller* and a critical study of **Dickens** (both in 1898), *The Crown of Life* (1899), *Our Friend the Charlatan* (1901) and *By the Ionian Sea* (impressions of Italy, 1900); **The Private Papers of Henry Ryecroft** (1903) is semi-autobiographical. The narrator has been freed from financial anxiety by a legacy as Gissing had been by his industry. After his death came *Veranilda* (1904), a historical romance of 6th-century Italy, in which he used his knowledge of the late Latin historians and Italian antiquities, *Will Warburton* (1905), *The House of Cobwebs* (short stories, 1906), *The Sins of the Fathers* (1924), *The Immortal Dickens* (1925), *A Victim of Circumstances* (1927), *Brownie* (1931), *Notes on Social Democracy* (1968), *George Gissing's Commonplace Book* (edited by J. Korg, 1962) and *The Diary of George Gissing, Novelist* (edited by P. Coustillas, 1978). Since 1960 he has received increasing critical attention.

**Glanvill, Joseph** 1636–80 The son of a Puritan family in Plymouth, Glanvill became interested in neo-Platonism and science while at Oxford and later became an Anglican clergyman who ended his days with the living of the Abbey Church in Bath. He was 25 when he published *The Vanity of Dogmatizing* (1661), a pioneering work which argued for a scientific approach to learning. He published a new edition as *Scepsis Scientifica* (1665), with some revisions. *The Vanity of Dogmatizing* contains the story of the Scholar Gipsy, which inspired **Matthew Arnold**'s poem. Glanvill's *Plus Ultra* (1668) emphasizes further the value of experimental science. Among his other works is *Saducismus Triumphatus* (1681), an attempt to prove the existence of witchcraft; as a minister of the Church, he believed that to deny the existence of witches was to deny the existence of God.

**Glasgow, Ellen** 1874–1945 American novelist, born in Richmond, Virginia. She published her first novel, *The Descendant*, in 1897, and her only volume of poetry, *The Freeman, and Other Poems*, in 1902. The economic and social conditions of the old agrarian South form the subject of a series of historical novels, beginning with *The Voice of the People* (1900) and including *The Battle-Ground* (1902), *The Deliverance* (1904), *The Wheel of Life* (1906), *The Ancient Law* (1908), *The Romance of a Plain Man* (1909) and *The Miller of Old Church* (1911). Her next two novels, *Virginia* (1913) and *Life and Gabriella* (1916), examine the position of women in the modernization of the Old South. Her other novels include *The Builders* (1919), *One Man in His Time* (1922), **Barren Ground** (1925), *The Romantic Comedians* (1926), *They Stooped to Folly* (1929), *The Sheltered Life* (1932) and **Vein of Iron** (1935). In 1941 she was awarded a Pulitzer Prize for *In This Our Life* (1941), a study of the decay of an aristocratic Virginia family. Two volumes of her stories have been issued: *The Shadowy Third* (1923) and *Collected Stories* (1963). A collection of the prefatory essays to her novels, *A Certain Measure*, was published in 1943, and an autobiographical reminiscence, *The Woman Within*, in 1954.

**Glaspell, Susan** 1882–1948 American playwright and novelist, born and educated in Iowa. With her husband, George Cram Cook, she was a founder of the Provincetown Players, later made famous for the promotion of **Eugene O'Neill**'s early plays. *Suppressed Desires* (1915), written in collaboration with Cook, was the inaugural play of the Provincetown Players. Glaspell followed it with a number of deft one-act pieces, including *Trifles* (1916), *The People* (1917), *The Outside* (1917) and *Woman's Honor* (1918). Her concern that room should be maintained for broad personal and social exploration is also evident in full-length plays like *Inheritors* (1921), in which a Midwestern college struggles to maintain the liberal spirit of its foundation, *The Verge* (1921), in which a woman finds herself simultaneously on the verge of madness and of true discovery, and *Alison's House* (1930), a sensitive account of events and decisions in the quiet life of **Emily Dickinson**.

Glaspell's novels are unimpressive, but her short stories, collected in *Lifted Masks* (1912) and *A Jury of Her Peers* (1927), display the intensity of her quest for a just society. *The Road to the Temple* (1927) is an evocative account of her life with George Cram Cook, written after his death in Greece in 1923.

**Glass Menagerie, The** A play by **Tennessee Williams**, first produced in 1944, and published in the following year. It was the play that established Williams in the American theatre.

Described by Williams as a 'memory play', it is framed by the recollections of Tom Wingfield, whose impressionistic narratives, accompanied by images projected on a screen, introduce a number of the scenes. Tom recalls his life in St Louis with his mother Amanda, a faded Southern belle who clings persistently to glamorous illusions about her past, and with his sister Laura, a crippled and painfully shy young woman whose intensely private world is centred on a treasured collection of small glass animals. Amanda, whose husband has long since deserted the family, has transferred her romantic hopes to Laura, continually asking her about her non-existent gentlemen callers. She persuades Tom, who has become a compulsive movie-goer to escape this intolerable situation at home, to invite his friend Jim O'Connor to dinner. Jim turns out to be the same young man with whom Laura was infatuated at high school; for a moment her sensitivity and reserve are eased by his warmth, but then, suddenly embarrassed, he tells her he is engaged to another girl, and leaves. Amanda is enraged with Tom for what she thinks was a deliberate practical joke. Finally pushed too far, Tom runs out of the house, never to return. The play ends with Amanda comforting Laura, and with Tom's final narration filled with pain for his sister.

**Globe Theatre** The first Globe was constructed early in 1599, partly out of timbers salvaged by the acting company to which **Shakespeare** belonged from their previous home, the **Theatre**. It stood on the south bank of the Thames, a short distance west of what is now Southwark Cathedral. It was in the Globe that most of the great plays of Shakespeare's maturity were first performed. Destroyed by fire in 1613, the Globe was reconstructed and reopened in 1614 and remained in use until the closing of the theatres under Cromwell. It was torn down in 1644.

**Glover, Denis** 1912–80 New Zealand poet. Born in Dunedin, he was educated at Auckland Grammar School and at the University of Canterbury, where he subsequently taught English between 1936 and 1938. He also taught typography at this time, and in 1936 in Christchurch founded Caxton Press, a significant outlet for New Zealand writers during the years of growth which followed. During World War II he was an officer in the Royal Navy and was awarded the DSC. After the war he worked as a journalist and publisher. A prominent figure in New Zealand letters, Glover was a president of New Zealand PEN. He first achieved recognition as a poet in the 1930s when, with his close associate **Allen Curnow**, he was a member of the Phoenix Group. His early poetry earned him a reputation as an *enfant terrible* and works like *Six Easy Ways of Dodging Debt Collectors* (1936) and his contributions to *A Caxton Miscellany* (1937) are wittily impudent reflections on the local cultural situation. Throughout his life he was a staunch champion of directness in verse but, despite their apparently rough-hewn quality, his poems exhibit considerable craftsmanship. Many can be seen as embodying a dialogue between the tough, supposedly unsentimental, male self-sufficiency that characterized the pioneer generation and a need for emotional liberation that is hard to acknowledge. In all, Glover published more than 20 volumes of verse, of which *Recent Poems* (1941), *Sings Harry* (1951), *Arawata Bill* (1953), a highly popular sequence about a wandering prospector, and *Since Then* (1957) are among the best-known. His *Selected Poems* was published in 1981.

**Glover, Richard** 1712–85 Poet and dramatist. Born in London, where his father was a successful merchant, Glover followed the same career and was Member of Parliament for Weymouth (1761–8) in opposition to the ruling party headed by Pitt. He wrote a great deal of poetry in indifferent blank verse, including *Leonidas* (1737) in nine books and *The Athenaid* (posthumously published, 1787) in 30 books. He was the author of two tragedies, *Boadicea* (1753) and *Medea* (1767), both produced at **Drury Lane**, and one, *Jason* (posthumously published, 1799), which was not produced. *Admiral Hosier's Ghost* (1740), a ballad on the misfortunes of Hosier and his fate in the West Indies, was very popular and was included in **Thomas Percy**'s *Reliques of Ancient English Poetry*.

**Glyn, Elinor (née Sutherland)** 1864–1943 Novelist. She was born in Jersey of Canadian parents and educated privately. Her 21 romantic novels were popular and controversial for their treatment of sex, particularly women's sexual feelings. *Three Weeks* (1907), the best known if only because of the erotic scenes played out on the notorious tiger-skin, describes in purple prose the sensual awakening of Paul, a young English nobleman, in his affair with a Slavonic beauty of noble rank. As in Elinor Glyn's other novels, the ending punishes the lovers, thus upholding the moral code and averting the censor's wrath.

**Go-Between, The** A novel by **L. P. Hartley**, published in 1953.

The narrator is an old man, Leo Colston, who in 1952 recalls events during the summer of 1900 while he was holidaying with a schoolfriend, Marcus Maudsley, at Brandham Hall near Norwich.

Besotted with Marcus's sister, Marian, the adolescent Leo confesses that he would do anything for her. Later he meets a local farmer, Ted Burgess, and agrees to deliver a clandestine message to Marian – so becoming their go-between. In his naïvety, Leo imagines numerous innocent explanations for the letters he is asked to carry, but his curiosity to discover the truth leads him to read an unsealed note from Marian and he gradually begins to comprehend the relationship between the lovers. At the same time his own painful awakening into the adult world has begun.

Marian is to become engaged to Lord Hugh Trimingham. Leo, in a fit of conscience, refuses to deliver any more notes. He relents under Marian's scorn, but begins to feel exploited. On Leo's 13th birthday Mrs Maudsley, Marian's mother, intercepts him while he is carrying a message. He refuses to give it up, but later in the day she forces him to accompany her to a distant outhouse where they discover the couple making love.

Leo learns afterwards that Ted Burgess has committed suicide. In an epilogue, Leo visits Marian 50 years later and she implores him to fulfil one last commission: to make contact with her grandson and explain to him the true nature of what happened so long ago – a tragic story of thwarted love.

**Goblin Market** A poem by **Christina Rossetti**, published in 1862. It tells the story of two sisters, Lizzie and Laura, who are tempted by the goblins to eat their delicious but dangerous fruit. Laura succumbs and eats, but afterwards can no longer hear or see the goblins, though she grows ill with longing to taste their fruit again. Lizzie determines to buy fruit for her sister but the goblins, angered by her refusal to eat any herself, deny the request and pelt her with their wares. Thus Laura is saved and her craving satisfied, as she licks the juices with which Lizzie is covered. This cryptic fairy-tale is notable for its use of alliteration and its metrical inventiveness.

**Godden, (Margaret) Rumer** 1907– Novelist. Brought up in Bengal, she came to England at the age of 11 for her education but later returned to India. Beginning as an adult author, she won acclaim with a series of successful novels including *Black Narcissus* (1939), *Breakfast with the Nickolides* (1942) and *The Greengage Summer* (1958), a haunting story of first love set in France and now also considered a children's book. Her first book written expressly for children, *The Dolls' House* (1947), was followed by *The Mousewife* (1951), another typically original story, about the friendship between a mouse and a dove, based on a note found in **Dorothy**

Laura at Goblin Market, buying with her golden hair. Dante Gabriel Rossetti's frontispiece illustration for the 1865 edition of the poem by his sister, Christina. *Goblin Market* was first published in 1862.

Wordsworth's diary. Other successful books include the award-winning story *The Diddakoi* (1972) and *Peacock Spring* (1978), another tale of disappointed love, this time set in India and as before suitable for both old and young readers.

**Godolphin, Sidney** 1610–43 Poet and translator. Son of Sir William Godolphin of Godolphin, Cornwall, and educated at Exeter College, Oxford, Sidney Godolphin was a devoted Royalist, who entered Parliament in 1628, took up arms for the King in 1642 and was shot in a skirmish at Chagford. He is buried at Okehampton. A friend of **Lucius Falkland** and **Clarendon**, he is characterized as 'little Sid' in **Suckling**'s *Sessions of the Poets*. His translation of Book IV of Virgil's *Aeneid* was published in 1658, completed by **Waller**, but his occasional poems, both love lyrics and devotional work, were first collected in 1906.

**Godric, St** d. ?1170 Author of three fragments of verse written before 1170. Before becoming a hermit at Finchdale, near Durham, he was an uneducated pedlar. A contemporary Latin life of the saint alleges that words and music of the first and best-known of his poems, 'Cantus Beati Godrici', were inspired by the Virgin as he knelt in prayer. The Virgin promised to succour him whenever he uttered the eight-line poem, a plea for help in obliterating sin and attaining the bliss of Heaven. A four-line hymn given to him by his dead sister in a vision consoled him in his bereavement. His third poem, 'Cantus Sancto Nicholao', was inspired by an Easter vision in which St Nicholas appeared to Godric. It asks the saint to bring the poet to bliss. The poems are metrically irregular but close to a four-stress line; they do not appear to have been influenced by foreign or Latin verse. Although of little literary merit, they are important as the earliest examples of native popular verse in Middle English.

**Godwin, William** 1756–1836 Philosopher and novelist. He was born into a family that had produced three generations of Dissenting ministers and was educated at the famous Hoxton Dissenting Academy. In 1778 he became minister to a congregation at Ware in Hertfordshire. His Calvinist faith was progressively undermined by his reading of the French philosophers Rousseau, d'Holbach and Helvétius, however, and in 1783 he gave up his ministry and embraced atheism. He moved to London, where he was to spend the rest of his long life, initially contributing essays and reviews to various weekly literary and political journals. With the coming of the French Revolution he grew interested in political philosophy and emancipatory politics, and began to attend meetings of radical political groups and societies. He was

present at the famous pro-revolutionary sermon, given in London on 4 November 1789, by the great Dissenting minister and political radical **Richard Price**. Godwin's own response to the debates and polemics of the revolutionary epoch, the celebrated *Enquiry Concerning Political Justice*, conceived in 1791, was an immediate success upon its publication in 1793. Among its young admirers were **Wordsworth**, **Southey** and **Coleridge**. The inner social and psychological drama masked by its often over-elaborate philosophical punctiliousness is impressively externalized in *Caleb Williams*, the novel which followed it in 1794. Somewhat ironically, in view of his stated antipathy to revolutionary violence, the loyalist reaction orchestrated by Pitt discovered its scapegoat in Godwin, and within two years he had been systematically defamed. It was a blow from which he never recovered intellectually, and which was to sour his personal relations and dealings in the decades ahead.

Godwin was the anarchist of the Age of Reason. Nothing if not consistent in his rationalistic individualism, he opposed both all existing institutions and all organized resistance to them. He never revised his model of reason, and jealously defended his system against the slightest imputation of activism. He insisted that differences and conflicts between men could be resolved only through sober and exhaustive discussion on a person-to-person basis. Such a proceeding presupposed the very rationality that was to be its outcome, and he was frequently accused of facile optimism by his radical opponents in the London Corresponding Society. Although he would continue to be alarmed by the Society's endorsement of agitational methods, his anonymously published *Cursory Strictures on the Charge Delivered by Lord Chief Justice Eyre to the Grand Jury* did much to persuade the jury to return a verdict of innocent in the trial of several of its members for treason in 1794.

In 1797 he wrote *The Enquirer*, another long essay in political philosophy which restates most of the themes of his earlier work. In the same year his wife **Mary Wollstonecraft** died a few days after the birth of their daughter, **Mary Shelley**, future wife of **Shelley**. His life of Wollstonecraft, *Memoirs of the Author of the Vindication of the Rights of Woman*, appeared in 1798. He also edited her *Posthumous Works* and portrayed her in his novel *St Leon* (1799). His subsequent remarriage to a Mrs Clairmont was largely an alliance of convenience.

Few of his many literary and publishing projects succeeded, and he had already become a relatively obscure and forgotten figure at the time of his discovery by the young Shelley in 1812. In 1814, however, Shelley – already married and the father of two small children – eloped abroad with his beloved daughter Mary and step-daughter Claire Clairmont, eventually marrying Mary in 1816 after the suicide of Harriet Shelley. Perhaps the best that can be said in summary of the relations between philosopher and poet is that Godwin managed to extract back in cash what Shelley had borne away in kind, though he responded with such coldness and moralistic insensitivity to the wave of family tragedies that fell upon the couple in Italy, that Shelley was at one stage compelled to intercept his correspondence with Mary.

During the last two decades of his life, Godwin repudiated many of the more radical aspects of *Political Justice* and in the late 1820s spoke out against the increasingly powerful movement for parliamentary and suffrage reform. The only significant work of the period was his study *Of Population* (1820), an answer to **Malthus**'s *Essay on the Principle of Population*, in which he argues that rational man would appreciate the madness of unlimited procreation, and voluntarily restrain his passions in order to curb population growth. His last years brought more financial distress, exacerbated by Shelley's death in 1822. Mary returned to England in 1823 and he saw a good deal of her in his declining years. His *Thoughts on Man*, which retreats from many of the positions taken in 1793, was published in 1831. His substantial literary output includes a life of **Chaucer** (1803–4) and the novels *Fleetwood* (1805), *Mandeville* (1817), *Cloudesly* (1830) and *Deloraine* (1833). In 1833, with the Whigs in power for the first time since the French Revolution, he was awarded the sinecure of Yeoman Usher of the Exchequer at £200 a year. He died at the age of 80 and was buried next to Mary Wollstonecraft.

**Gogarty, Oliver St John** 1878–1957 Irish man of letters and poet. Born in Dublin, he was educated at the local Christian Brothers School, then at Stonyhurst and later at the Jesuit boarding-school, Clongowes. He attended the Royal University in Dublin and transferred to the medical school at Trinity College. At Trinity, Gogarty made a number of important friendships and laid the basis for his reputation as a wit and bon viveur. He is best remembered for his friendship with **James Joyce**, especially for the time he, Joyce and an English friend stayed in the Martello tower at Sandycove in the autumn of 1904. This provided the basis for the opening chapter of *Ulysses*, where Gogarty appears as Buck Mulligan. He published three volumes of poetry: *An Offering of Swans* (1923), *Wild Apples* (1928) and *Selected Poems* (1933). He was much overpraised by **Yeats** in the preface to the *Oxford Book of Modern Verse* (1936) but is still remembered for some poems and, most of all, for his memoir, *As I Was Going Down Sackville Street* (1937), and the libel suit which followed its publication. His second memoir is *Tumbling in the Hay* (1939); this was preceded by the less entertaining *I Follow Saint Patrick* (1938). Gogarty was appointed a Senator of the Irish Free State in 1922. An attempt was made on his life and his country property, Renvyle House in County Galway, was burned. He left Ireland in 1939 and spent the rest of his days in America, dying in New York. In the USA, he published three novels and an autobiography, *It Isn't That Time of Year At All* (1954). His *Collected Poems* appeared in 1950.

**Golagros and Gawain** A Middle Scots romance of the later 15th century in **alliterative verse** written in 13-line stanzas. The story is freely adapted from two episodes from the First Continuation of the *Conte du Graal* of Chrétien de Troyes. The first tells how Kay's request for hospitality for Arthur and his knights is refused because of his churlishness, while Gawain's polite request is granted. In the second episode Arthur demands homage from Golagros who refuses. There follows a siege and many duels, and Gawain finally defeats Golagros. Gawain accedes to Golagros's request that he accompany him as though defeated and Golagros is so pleased with Gawain's generosity and courtesy that he yields to Arthur. The conventional characteristics of Kay and Gawain, respectively rude and courteous, are of central interest.

**Gold, Herbert** 1924– American novelist. Born in Cleveland, Ohio, Gold served in the US army during World War II, and then attended Columbia University. A number of his novels are autobiographical: *Therefore Be Bold* (1960) tells of the experience of a Jewish adolescent growing up in Cleveland; *Fathers: A Novel in the Form of a Memoir* (1967) draws on Gold's experiences as a father to his five children and as a son to his own father; *Family: A Novel in the Form of a Memoir* (1981) is about a Jewish immigrant family. His other novels are *Birth of a Hero* (1951); *The Prospect Before Us* (1954); *The Man Who Was Not With It* (1956), probably his best-known work, the story of a dope-addict carnival barker and his world; *The Optimist* (1959); *Salt* (1963); *The Great American Jackpot* (1971) and *Waiting for Cordelia* (1977), two stories about a sociology student at Berkeley in the 1960s; *Swiftie the Magician* (1974); *He/She* (1980); *True Love* (1982); *Mister White Eyes* (1984), about a journalist's search for love and simple human feelings through, or despite, his profession; and *A Girl of Forty* (1986). Gold's short stories and essays have been collected in *15×3* (1957), *Love and Like* (1960), *The Age of Happy Problems* (1962), *The Magic Will: Stories and Essays of a Decade* (1971) and *A Walk on the West Side: California on the Brink* (1981). His autobiography, *My Last Two Thousand Years*, appeared in 1972.

**Gold, Michael** 1894–1967 American proletarian writer. Born Itzok Isaac Granich to Jewish immigrants, Gold was raised on the Lower East Side of New York City. The major themes of his work are derived from this background. His best-known book, *Jews Without Money* (1930), is a fictionalized autobiography which describes Jewish ghetto life and ends with a political rally in Union Square at which the protagonist is converted to the cause of Communist revolution.

During the years of radical ferment before World War I Gold published articles and stories in *The Masses* and in the Socialist *New York Call*, and had three of his one-act plays produced by the Provincetown Players. In 1920, after returning from Mexico, where he had evaded the draft, he became an editor of *The Liberator*, the successor of *The Masses*. **The New Masses**, which he founded as a successor to *The Liberator*, espoused under his editorship the cause of proletarian literature which sought to represent the working class as the saving grace of America – its last hope for true democracy. His fiery columns for *The New Masses*, notable for their polemical Communist views, have been collected in *The Mike Gold Reader* (1954) and *Mike Gold: A Literary Anthology* (1972), which also reprints articles from *120 Million* (1929) and *Change the World* (1937), his earlier collections of *New Masses* prose.

**Golden Bough, The** *See* **Frazer, Sir James**.

**Golden Bowl, The** A novel by **Henry James**, published in 1904. Adam Verver is an American millionaire living in Europe with his daughter Maggie and amassing an art collection. Maggie is of marriageable age, and her friend Fanny Assingham finds her an Italian prince, Amerigo. The beautiful Charlotte Stant comes to London to stay with Fanny, who knows that Charlotte and Amerigo had once been in love but could not marry since they were both penniless. Charlotte has no trouble persuading Amerigo to accompany her when she goes shopping in search of a wedding present for Maggie. At an antique dealer's she wants to give Amerigo a present also, a gilded crystal bowl. The presence of a flaw in the bowl brings it within the range of her purse; Amerigo, however, is disturbed that the bowl is flawed and declines the gift.

A year later, following the birth of a child to Maggie and Amerigo, Adam Verver, now a grandfather but not yet 50, proposes to and marries Charlotte. But Charlotte and Amerigo have not forgotten their original feelings for each other, and they meet in secret. For her father's birthday Maggie buys a gilded crystal bowl. She has not noticed that it is flawed, but the dealer feels compelled to point it out and calls on her. He recognizes the photographs of Amerigo and Charlotte and tells Maggie that the pair had visited his shop and rejected the bowl during the days of her engagement to Amerigo. Maggie sends for Fanny and makes clear that she knows the whole truth about Charlotte and Amerigo. She smashes the golden bowl just as Amerigo enters the room. Amerigo stops seeing Charlotte; Adam gives no hint to her that he knows of her liaison; Maggie conducts herself with unruffled serenity. Charlotte, wondering at her lover's withdrawal, cannot provoke Maggie to any kind of exchange. Adam finally resolves the situation by deciding to return to America with Charlotte.

**Golden Legend, The** A collection of biblical narratives and saints' lives with some explanation of parts of the Mass and articles of faith. Originally a 13th-century Latin work, the *Legenda Aurea* of Jacobus de Voragine, it was translated into French in the 14th century by Jean de Vignay and into English in the 15th century. The best-known English version is that printed by **Caxton** *c.* 1487.

**Golden Treasury, The** *See* **Palgrave, Francis Turner**.

**Golding, Arthur** ?1536–1605 Translator. Golding produced very few original works: an account of a murder (1577) and the description of an earthquake (1580). His Puritan cast of mind is demonstrated by some of the texts he chose to translate: Calvin's commentary on Daniel (1570) and Calvin's sermons on Job (1574), on Ephesians (1576) and on Deuteronomy (1576). He also completed **Sir Philip Sidney**'s translation of de Mornay's *Trueness of the Christian Religion* (1587). Among classical texts, he produced translations of Caesar's *De Bello Gallico* (1565) and Seneca's *De Beneficiis* (1578).

Golding's most important translation was of Ovid's *Metamorphoses*, the first four books appearing in 1565 and the complete work in 1567. One of the finest and most faithful of Elizabethan classical translations, the work was dedicated to Leicester. The dedicatory verse epistle, which talks of Ovid's 'dark philosophy of turned shapes', allies itself with the tradition of finding **allegory** in *Metamorphoses*: Phaethon signifies ambition, Arachne contest with our betters, and Midas covetousness. **Shakespeare** certainly knew Golding's Ovid, as Prospero's speech 'Ye elves of hills . . .' (**The Tempest**, Act V) draws on Golding's translation as well as Medea's original speech in *Metamorphoses*, Book VII.

**Golding, William (Gerald)** 1911– Novelist. Born at St Columb Minor in Cornwall, Golding was educated at Marlborough and Brasenose College, Oxford. After working in the theatre as writer, actor and producer, he became a schoolteacher and served with the Royal Navy during World War II. He published a volume of *Poems* (1935) but it was in 1954, with the publication of his first novel *Lord of the Flies*, that he achieved success. This was followed by *The Inheritors* (1955), about the ascendancy of brute force in primeval man; *Pincher Martin* (1956), in which a drowning man is tormented by the moral paradoxes of his past life; and *Free Fall* (1959). Subsequent works included *The Spire* (1964), *The Pyramid* (1967), *The Scorpion God* (1971), *Darkness Visible* (1979) and *Rites of Passage* (1980), which won the Booker Prize. *The Paper Men* (1984) is an account of a famous author, Wilfred Barclay, whose life is plagued by the unflagging attention of an American academic called Turner. *Close Quarters* (1987) is a sequel to *Rites of Passage*.

Much of Golding's writing explores moral dilemmas at the centre of human existence, and he frequently places his characters in extreme situations to suggest a 'mythological' dimension to their lives. Profoundly obsessed with the subject of evil and original sin, he treats these subjects in a way that transcends the boundaries of orthodox Christianity.

His other works include a play, *The Brass Butterfly* (1958), and collections of essays, *The Hot Gates* (1965) and *A Moving Target* (1982). He was awarded the Nobel Prize in 1983.

**Goldmann, Lucien** See **Marxist criticism**.

**Goldsmith, Oliver** ?1730–74 Playwright, poet, novelist and essayist. A son of the Irish Protestant clergy on both sides of the family, he was born at either Pallas, County Longford, or Elphin, Roscommon, and passed much of his childhood at Lissoy, Westmeath. After being miserable at various grammar schools, where he was beaten as a dunce and persecuted by his fellows, he went at the age of 16 to Trinity College, Dublin, as a sizar, performing menial jobs and living in a garret. After university he sought ordination, but arrived for interviews dressed in scarlet; applications for other jobs, and a plan to emigrate to America, were similarly unsuccessful, though he did work briefly as private tutor to a rich family. Given £50 to apprentice himself to the law, he gambled it all away. He spent a few months each at Edinburgh and Leiden Universities, but did not apply himself; the authenticity of the medical degree he later claimed has not been established. In 1755–6 he busked his way through France, Switzerland and Italy, playing Irish tunes on his flute and eking out his earnings with food distributed at convent gates. It was at this time that he started his poem *The Traveller*, eventually published in 1764. On his arrival in England in 1756 he scraped a living as messenger, teacher and assistant to apothecaries and physicians.

In 1758 he translated Marteilhe's *Memoirs of a Protestant, Condemned to the Galleys of France for his Religion*, and in 1759 he produced his first important work, **An Enquiry into the Present State of Polite Learning in Europe**. It was still possible in those days for an educated man to make a meagre living as a Grub Street hack, and Goldsmith settled to writing reviews for **Smollett**'s *Critical Review* and contributing essays to *The Busy Body*, *The Weekly Magazine*, *The Royal Magazine* and *The Lady's Magazine*. In 1760–1 he wrote his 'Chinese Letters' for **John Newbery**'s *The Public Ledger*, a satirical view of Britain through the eyes of an imaginary foreigner, republished in 1762 as **The Citizen of the World**.

In 1761 he moved to no. 6 Wine Office Court, off Fleet Street, and met **Samuel Johnson**, later becoming a member of the Club. Goldsmith's talents at this time seemed to be for gathering ideas and information from other people's books and reducing them to clarity. In 1762 he wrote essays for *Lloyd's Evening Post* and his biography of the arbiter of Bath society, *The Life of Richard Nash*. Goldsmith's finances were never stable, and he was about to be arrested for debt when Dr Johnson sold the manuscript of Goldsmith's sole novel, **The Vicar of Wakefield**, for him. It was published in 1766 in Salisbury, a share having been sold by Newbery to a bookseller there.

In 1762 Goldsmith moved to Newbery's house in Islington. During the years that remained to him before his early death from a kidney infection he continued his diverse output with, among other work, *An History of England in a Series of Letters from a Nobleman to His Son* (1764); two anthologies, *Poems for Young Ladies* (1766, dated 1767) and *The Beauties of English Poesy* (1767); *The Roman History* (1769); and biographies of **Thomas Parnell** and **Bolingbroke** (1770). His *Grecian History* and his *History of the Earth and Animated Nature* both appeared posthumously in 1774.

Goldsmith had sold his oratorio libretto *The Captivity* in 1764. His first comedy, **The Good-Natured Man**, was produced at **Covent Garden** in 1768 after being rejected by **Garrick**; its more famous successor, **She Stoops to Conquer**, was staged in 1773. His most famous poem, **The Deserted Village**, which draws in part on his childhood memories of Ireland, appeared in 1770. *The Haunch of Venison*, posthumously published in 1776, is a lively expression in comic verse of gratitude for a gift from his friend Lord Clare.

Goldsmith's coffin was followed by **Burke** and **Reynolds**, his bust in Westminster Abbey executed by Nollekens and his epitaph written by Johnson. The respect and affection which contemporaries felt for him was often mixed with exasperation at his gaucheness, vanity and habit of dwelling on imagined slights. Johnson said of him, 'No man was more foolish when he had not a pen in his hand, or more wise when he had', while Garrick's impromptu epitaph was, 'Here lies Nolly Goldsmith, for shortness called Noll,/Who wrote like an angel, but talked like poor Poll.' Subsequent critics, faced with the journeyman work by which Goldsmith earned his bread, have dismissed him as lightweight, inaccurate and superficial. Yet the diversity of his talent speaks for itself: he left a novel, *The Vicar of Wakefield*, which is still read, a poem, *The Deserted Village*, which has enriched the language with quotations that have become proverbial, and a comedy, *She Stoops to Conquer*, which still holds the stage.

**Gone With The Wind** A novel by Margaret Mitchell (1900–49), published in 1936 and awarded the Pulitzer Prize in the following year. An immediate best-seller, to date it has sold more than 25 million copies and been translated into 27 languages. It was made into a celebrated motion picture in 1939.

The novel opens, just before the outbreak of the Civil War, on a Georgia plantation, Tara, the home of Scarlett O'Hara, a spoilt and wilful 16-year-old Southern belle. Against the backdrop of the war, the defeat of the South, and Reconstruction, the story follows the life and loves of Scarlett. Ashley Wilkes, with whom she is hopelessly infatuated, marries Melanie Hamilton; Scarlett marries Melanie's brother Charles out of spite, but soon becomes a young war widow. Having survived the siege and burning of Atlanta, she saves the lives of Melanie and her newborn child by leading them through the lines to the O'Hara plantation. Back at Tara, she finds her mother dead, her father demented, the slaves freed, and the plantation in ruins. The novel now focuses on Scarlett's determination to restore Tara. In need of money, she marries Frank Kennedy, her sister's fiancé, because he owns a profitable business. After he too is killed she marries Rhett Butler, a profiteer who has made a fortune from the war. Through him she acquires the wealth and power she craves, but throughout their marriage he struggles against her continuing passion for Ashley, and at the end of the novel, when Scarlett has finally come to realize her love for Rhett, he walks out on her with the famous words 'My dear, I don't give a damn.'

**Good Soldier, The** A novel by **Ford Madox Ford**, sub-titled 'A Tale of Passion' and published in 1915.

The narrator, John Dowell, who has recently been made aware of the deception within his marriage, controls our view of this 'the saddest story'. For nine years he and his wife Florence, both American, have joined Edward Ashburnham, the good English soldier, and his Irish-Catholic wife Leonora at the German spa town of Nauheim. Using the pretence of having a bad heart, Florence has kept their marriage unconsummated, while conducting illicit affairs. Ashburnham has been her principal lover, while he has conducted his liaisons under the cold, watchful eye of Leonora. The warm-hearted Edward, beloved of the tenants on his land, is drawn into a tragic infatuation with Nancy Rufford, to whom he and Leonora are guardians.

A sense of fatalism overtakes the characters, indicated by a strange coincidence of dates. Florence, learning of Edward's culminating passion, commits suicide on the date of her birth, and of her marriage. (Ford chose 4 August 1914, the date of the German invasion of Belgium.) The love of Edward for Nancy, of which each is only too aware, is ironically shared by Dowell; equally, he values the friendship of Ashburnham. The denouement is both melodramatic and formally ordered. Nancy is dispatched to her father in India; Ashburnham commits suicide. Dowell buys Ashburnham's estate, where he looks after a real invalid: Nancy, destroyed mentally by the adult world's hypocrisies, has returned to the estate.

**Good-Natured Man, The** A comedy by **Oliver Goldsmith**, first produced at **Covent Garden** in 1768 and published in the same year.

Sir William Honeywood despairs of his nephew, who is both generous and improvident. Young Honeywood is in love with the wealthy Miss Richland, but he is too wanting in self-confidence to propose. Sir William has him arrested for debt, to let him see who his true friends are and to stop him wasting his generosity on importuners. Young Honeywood believes that Lofty, a government official, is responsible for his release; Lofty is pressing his suit with Miss Richland and Honeywood, mistakenly grateful, recommends him to the lady. In fact it was Miss Richland who secured his release. The exasperated heroine and uncle between them expose Lofty's imposture and secure the marriage of Honeywood and Miss Richland.

The sub-plot concerns Croaker, Miss Richland's guardian, who wants his son Leontine to marry the heroine. Sent to Lyons to bring his sister home from school, Leontine returns with Olivia, a girl he has fallen in love with. He passes off Olivia as his sister and, in an effort to strengthen the pretence, proposes to Miss Richland; but the heroine knows the truth and mischievously accepts him. In desperation Leontine and Olivia try to elope but their plan is frustrated by Sir William. However, he persuades Croaker to consent to their marriage. Miss Richland, the heroine, indicates the departure from the **sentimental comedy** fashionable at the time: she is the equal of most of the male characters and superior to some of them.

***Goodbye to All That*** An autobiography by **Robert Graves**, published in 1929 and revised in 1957, covering his childhood, career at Charterhouse, World War I experiences, and post-war life in Wales, Oxford and Egypt. It ends with a farewell to 'godawful' England, its characters and historical time. Highly controversial and successful when first published, it is organized in scenes of anecdote and caricature, and eschews respect for historical fact in favour of deliberately anti-literary black farce and comedy.

**Goodman, Paul** 1911–72 Novelist, critic and writer on contemporary society. Born in New York City, Goodman wrote numerous books on a wide range of topics, including *Utopian Essays and Proposals* (1962), on political theory; *Gestalt Therapy* (1951), on psychology; *Communitas* (1947, with his brother Percival), on city planning; and *Compulsory Mis-Education* (1964), on education. *The Empire City* (1959), a novel set in New York from 1930 to 1950, first appeared as a series of shorter novels. *The Grand Piano* (1942), *The State of Nature* (1946) and *The Dead Spring* (1950). In 1960 he published an influential study of youth and delinquency, *Growing Up Absurd*. *Making Do* (1963), an autobiographical novel, was followed in 1966 by a non-fictional work of autobiography, *Five Years: Thoughts During a Useless Time*. He also wrote several volumes of literary criticism, and served as film editor for **The Partisan Review** and television critic for **The New Republic**. His *Collected Poems* appeared in 1974.

**Googe, Barnabe** 1505–94 Poet and translator. Googe was a long-lived kinsman of William Cecil, Elizabeth I's minister, who employed him in Ireland for 10 years. He was an industrious translator of Latin anti-Catholic pieces, and his Puritan nature is plainly apparent in his *Eclogues, Epitaphs and Sonnets* (1563), his chief claim to notice as a poet. The **eclogues** are among the earliest examples of pastoral poetry in English, though like those of his near-contemporary **Alexander Barclay** they display little of the spirit of their classical originals.

***Gorboduc, or, The Tragedy of Ferrex and Porrex*** A blank-verse tragedy by **Thomas Norton** (Acts 1–3) and **Thomas Sackville** (Acts 4 and 5) first acted in 1561 and printed in 1565. The origin of the story is found in **Geoffrey of Monmouth**'s *Historia Regum Britanniae*.

Gorboduc and Videna are King and Queen in legendary Britain and their sons are Ferrex and Porrex. The sons quarrel over the division of the kingdom and Porrex murders his brother. In revenge Videna kills Porrex and the Duke of Albany tries to seize the kingdom. Civil war ensues, and the people turn on Gorboduc and Videna and kill them. At the end of the play the royal line is extinguished and the country is in chaos.

The play adheres to the Senecan model and there is almost no action; it could be read as effectively as it could be played. But by departing from both the morality tradition (there are no personifications, only characters) and the Aristotelian unities of time and place, it moved towards the flexible action in plays of the great age of English drama.

**Gordimer, Nadine** 1923– South African novelist, born in Springs, Transvaal. Perhaps the most gifted post-1945 South African writer, Gordimer has consistently attacked apartheid, while acknowledging that as a white South African within the system she is, however unwillingly, a privileged beneficiary. Her fiction records the corrosive effects of apartheid with great accuracy and honesty. Precision of observation and style were evident in her first two short-story volumes, *Face to Face* (1949) and *The Soft Voice of the Serpent* (1952), capturing deftly single instants, symptoms and symbols of the South African malaise. This crystalline, detailed style (consolidated in the stories of *Six Feet of the Country*, 1956, and *Friday's Footprint*, 1960) sometimes slips into fuss in her first three novels, *The Lying Days* (1953), basically hopeful about South Africa, *A World of Strangers* (1958), detached and sceptical, and *Occasion for Loving* (1963), disillusioned by racial misunderstanding.

Detail without distraction, hope renewed but on a limited, risky level, characterize the stories in *Not for Publication* (1965) and the economical, tightly structured novel *The Late Bourgeois World* (1966). In the novels *A Guest of Honour* (1971) and *The Conservationist* (1974), Gordimer's art achieves assured maturity, successfully integrating the immediately personal with the panoramically political. The daughter of devout Afrikaner Marxists in *Burger's Daughter* (1979) painfully formulates her own creed before she too is imprisoned. In *July's People* (1981) psychological disintegration is pushed even further than in *The Conservationist*, as civil war bares the mutual falsity of supposedly enlightened personal relationships. In *A Sport of Nature* (1987) an attractive white girl becomes a political activist. Gordimer still regularly publishes short-story collections: *Livingston's Companions* (1972), *Selected Stories* (1975), *Some Monday for Sure* (1976), *A Soldier's Embrace* (1980) and *Something Out There* (1984).

**Gordon, Adam Lindsay** 1833–70 Australian poet. The son of a retired Indian Army officer, Gordon was born in the Azores and educated at Worcester Royal Grammar School. A classical education and the background of a cultured home encouraged an interest in poetry which stayed with him throughout his short but adventurous life. When he was 20 Gordon's father sent him to Australia. He arrived in Adelaide in 1853 and worked as a mounted trooper, horse breaker, livery-stable keeper, and more notably as a steeplechase rider, a field in which he became famous. His first published work, *The Feud*, appeared in 1864 and he contributed regularly to *Bell's Life in Victoria* and *The Australasian*. A collection was published as *Sea Spray and Smoke Drift* (1867). *Ashtaroth, A Dramatic Lyric*, an unsuccessful exercise on the Faust theme, was published in the same year. Further poems were published in **Marcus Clarke**'s paper *The Colonial Monthly*. He retired from steeplechasing in 1870 and his volume of poems *Bush Ballads and Galloping Rhymes* (1870) earned him praise but little else. He returned to steeplechasing and suffered a serious fall from which he never really recovered. He committed suicide at the age of 37.

**Gordon, Caroline** 1895–1981 American novelist and short-story writer, born in Trenton, Kentucky. In her first novel, *Penhally* (1931), she contrasts the grandeur of the ante-bellum South with its diminished condition after the Civil War. *Aleck Maury Sportsman* (1934) has a hero based on her own father. *None Shall Look Back* (1937), modelled on Tolstoy's *War and Peace*, has as its hero an actual figure from the Civil War – General Nathan Bedford Forrest. Her other novels are *The Garden of Adonis* (1937), *Green Centuries* (1941), *The Women on the Porch* (1944), *The Strange Children* (1951), *The Malefactors* (1956) and *The Glory of Hera* (1972). In 1934 she was awarded the O. Henry Prize for her short story 'Old Red', which was later published in the collection *The Forest of the South* (1945), again in *Old Red and Other Stories* (1963) and in *The Collected Stories of Caroline Gordon* (1981).

**Gore, Catherine Grace** 1799–1861 Novelist and dramatist. Born Catherine Moody, Mrs Gore produced 70 assorted works in under 40 years, including plays and occasional pieces. She was known best for her novels of fashionable life and high society, which established her as a leading practitioner of **Silver-fork** fiction. They include *Manners of the Day* (1830), *Mrs Armytage, or, Female Domination* (1836), *Cecil, or, The Adventures of a Coxcomb* (1841) and *The Banker's Wife* (1843). Her fiction was parodied by **Thackeray** in *Punch's Prize Novelists* (1847).

**Gorges, Sir Arthur** 1557–1625 Poet and translator. Son of the vice-admiral Sir William Gorges, he was born probably at Butshed Manor, near Plymouth, and educated at Oxford. He entered royal service in his early twenties. Closely involved with **Sir Walter Raleigh**, he fell from favour under James I and spent the remainder of his life managing his family's property and many lawsuits. **Spenser** praised him in the guise of 'Alcyon' for his amatory songs and sonnets, written in 1580–90, several of which appeared in Elizabethan poetical miscellanies. Gorges prepared a manuscript collection, 'his vanities and toys of youth'; also in manuscript is his chivalric narrative, *The Olympian Catastrophe* (1612), a memorial tribute to Prince Henry modelled on Spenser's *Faerie Queene*. A complete edition of both was published in 1953. Gorges translated Lucan's *Pharsala* in 1614 and, in 1619, **Bacon**'s *De Sapientia Veterum* and *Essays*, the latter into French.

***Gospel of Nicodemus, The*** An account of the events succeeding the accusation of the Jews including the death, resurrection and Ascension of Christ, the acts of Joseph of Arimathea and of Pilate, and the Harrowing of Hell. It first appeared around AD 400, and exists in an Old English translation and a version in Middle English verse and prose. The work greatly influenced medieval art, theology and literature, providing the basis of the Harrowing of Hell episode in **miracle plays**.

**Gosse, Sir Edmund (William)** 1849–1928 Critic and essayist. Edmund Gosse was born in London, the son of Philip H. Gosse, a distinguished zoologist and a devout member of the Plymouth Brethren. He was educated privately, becoming an assistant librarian at the British Museum (1867), a translator at the Board of Trade (1874), lecturer in English literature at Trinity College, Cambridge (1884), and librarian of the House of Lords (1904). He published poems and plays, and was a central figure in London literary life, a friend of **Swinburne**, **Robert Louis Stevenson**, **Thomas Hardy** and **Henry James**. After World War I he became a contributor to *The Sunday Times* with a regular and influential essay on current books. He was knighted in 1925.

As a critic Gosse wrote *Thomas Gray* (1882), *Jeremy Taylor* (1903) and *Sir Thomas Browne* (1905) for the English Men of Letters series, as well as *The Life of Algernon Charles Swinburne* (1917). These works are less important than his interest in Scandinavian culture, expressed in *Studies in the Literature of Northern Europe* (1879), influential translations of two plays by Ibsen, *Hedda Gabler* (1891) and *The Master Builder* (with **William Archer**, 1893), and a book on the dramatist (1907).

Gosse's best remembered work is *Father and Son*, published anonymously in 1907. Sub-titled 'A Study of Two Temperaments', it recalls his isolated, bleak childhood with the widowed Philip Gosse and is remarkable for its blend of sympathy and irony; the atmosphere of the rigidly devout household is finely conveyed.

**Gosson, Stephen** 1554–1624 Anti-theatrical pamphleteer. Born in Canterbury and educated at Oxford, he renounced his youthful interest in drama – he is known to have written some pastoral plays – under Puritan persuasion. Never formally a Puritan, Gosson became an Anglican clergyman. His Paul's Cross sermon of 1598 was published as *The Trumpet of War*. His *The School of Abuse* (1579), attacking poets and actors, was dedicated without permission to **Sir Philip Sidney**, whose *Apology for Poetry* was written partly to confute him. The controversy was still at its height when Gosson wrote *Plays Confuted in Five Actions* (1582).

**Gothic fiction** A type of novel or romance popular in the late 18th and early 19th century. The word 'Gothic' had come to mean 'wild', 'barbarous' and 'crude', qualities which writers found it attractive to cultivate in reaction against the sedate **neoclassicism** of earlier 18th-century culture. Gothic novels were usually set in the past (most often the medieval past) and in foreign countries (particularly the Catholic countries of southern Europe); they took place in monasteries, castles, dungeons and mountainous landscapes. The plots hinged on suspense and mystery, involving the fantastic and the supernatural.

Elements of the form begin to appear as early as **Smollett**'s *Ferdinand Count Fathom* (1753), but the first Gothic novel proper is **Horace Walpole**'s *The Castle of Otranto* (1764). Later novelists associated with the fashion for Gothic were **Clara Reeve**, **Ann Radcliffe**, **William Beckford**, **M. G. ('Monk') Lewis** and **C. R. Maturin**. Their influence can be felt in some Romantic poetry (for example, **Coleridge**'s *Christabel*), **Mary Shelley**'s *Frankenstein*, the stories of **Edgar Allan Poe** in America, and the novels of the **Brontë** sisters.

**Gould, Nathaniel ('Nat')** 1857–1919 Sporting novelist. Gould was born in Manchester and educated privately at Southport. In 1878 he joined the staff of the *Newark Advertiser* and in 1884 travelled to Australia remaining there for 11 years as a journalist in several cities. His first novel, *The Double Event*, linking his interest in racing with his knowledge of Australia, appeared in 1891. He returned to England in 1895 and continued to write and publish prolifically. His later fiction includes *Banker and Broker* (1893), *The Famous Match* (1898) and *Left*

in the Lurch (1903 in *Nat Gould's Annual*). His other work includes *On and Off the Turf in Australia* (1895) and *Town and Bush* (1896).

**Gower, John** *c.* 1330–1408 Poet. Little is known of Gower's life. His family originated in Yorkshire, but he apparently lived in Kent and London, owning estates also in Suffolk and Norfolk. By 1398, and probably from 1377, he lived in the Priory of St Mary Overy in Southwark. He knew **Geoffrey Chaucer**, who dedicated *Troilus and Criseyde* to him.

He wrote in French, Latin and English, one major work in each language. The first of these, *Le Mirour de l'Omme*, or *Speculum Meditantis* (1376–9) is a moral poem in French. Its subject is the effects of sin upon the world, and it is divided into three unequal parts. The first is a schematic analysis of the seven deadly sins and their opposite virtues, the second part examines the effects of sin on different social ranks and the third outlines the way to redemption through repentance and the intercession of the Virgin. *Vox Clamantis* (1379–82) again attacks man's sinfulness, analysing the corruption of Ricardian society. The first book, added after the Peasants' Revolt of 1381, is an apocalyptic vision of political and social chaos. Sometime after the deposing of Richard II in 1399 Gower added a sequel to *Vox Clamantis*, the *Cronica Tripertita*, finally condemning the King. *Confessio Amantis*, written in 1386–90 and revised in 1393, is in a lighter tone. It presents a collection of tales and **exempla** set within the framework of a lover's confession to Venus's priest.

Gower's only other work in English is the poem 'To King Henry IV, in Praise of Peace'; he also wrote some short Latin verses and, in French, the *Cinkante Balades*. During the 15th century he was lauded with Chaucer and **Lydgate** as one of the greatest English poets. He appears in **Shakespeare**'s *Pericles* as the Chorus.

**Gowers, Sir Ernest (Arthur)** 1880–1966 Writer on writing. Educated at Rugby and Clare College, Cambridge, Gowers was a distinguished civil servant. His rigorous insistence on simple clear English from his juniors led to an invitation from the head of the Civil Service to produce a brief paper on writing English: *Plain Words: a Guide to the Use of English* (1948). This was followed by his *ABC of Plain Words* (1951), and both were later published together as *The Complete Plain Words* (1954). He was responsible also for a second edition of **Henry Fowler**'s *A Dictionary of Modern English Usage* (1965). His influential *A Life for a Life? The Problem of Capital Punishment* (1956) grew out of his work as chairman of the Royal Commission of 1949–53.

*Grace Abounding to the Chief of Sinners* John Bunyan's narrative of his spiritual development, published in 1666. He tells of his birth and misspent youth, his service in the Parliamentary army and his scrapes with death. He describes how his religious awakening began with the reading of two devotional books which his wife brought to him among her few possessions at their marriage in 1648, and how he joined a Nonconformist group in Bedford. The book is remarkable for its ruthless self-examination and for Bunyan's agonized awareness that each step forward could lead him into the sin of pride. Like his other works, it is intense and forthright.

**Graham, W[illiam] S[ydney]** 1918–86 Poet. Born in Greenock near Glasgow, educated locally and trained as a draughtsman, he went on to Newbattle Abbey College to study literature and philosophy.

Graham's first book was *Cage Without Grievance* (1942); the best-known single volume is *The Nightfishing* (1955). *Collected Poems 1942–77* was published in 1979. Influenced by Rimbaud and **Hart Crane**, his early work is remarkable for its exotic mix of imagery from industrial and rural scenes. He went on to produce a more developed poetry of considerable power using the extended metaphor of the voyage, inward and outward, to examine language and being. His long residence in and around St Ives in Cornwall brought him in touch with many influential artists of the post-war era; his poems and elegies for them make him the poet of a community which his work helped to define. The hard-won simplicity of his later work combines a single-minded attention to philosophical interests with a rare and Scottish humour.

**Grahame, Kenneth** 1859–1932 Children's author and essayist. Born in Edinburgh, Grahame went to live with his grandmother in Berkshire as a child after the death of his mother. After attending school in Oxford he was forced to join the Bank of England instead of going to university as he wished.

His books of essays *The Golden Age* (1895) and its sequel *Dream Days* (1898) paint a convincingly unsentimental picture of childhood, with the adults in these sketches totally out of touch with the real concerns of the young people around them, including their griefs and rages. After marriage in 1899 Grahame took to telling stories to his young son Alastair, continued in a series of letters. These formed the basis for *The Wind in the Willows* (1908), which after several rejections came out to scant critical acclaim. Its fame quickly grew and the addition of illustrations by **E. H. Shepard** and then **Arthur Rackham** finally led to its present classic status. Grahame produced no further written work of

substance, becoming something of a recluse after the suicide of his son at the age of 19.

*Grammar of Assent, The* A theological essay by **John Henry Newman**, published in 1870. It argues that religious certainty comes not from logic, but from intuition, the conscience and the heart. Newman postulated the 'illative sense', which 'concerns itself with principles, doctrines, facts, memories, experiences, testimonies in order to attain insights too delicate and subtle for logical analysis'. The *Grammar* was an attempt to show that 'common sense' was as much a part of religious faith as it was of 'science and progress'. Newman's statement is Romantic in that it posits a 'religious imagination' and a 'whole man', not just the intellect.

**Grand Guignol** A particularly lurid and violent form of drama, in which the violence threatened but characteristically averted in melodrama is carried through into performance. The name is derived, by ironic transference, from the 19th-century French marionette, Guignol. Immensely popular in Montmartre, Grand Guignol was confined, in 19th-century England, to the penny gaffs of London's East End. There are few notable examples in English. **James Elroy Flecker**'s *Hassan* has elements of the genre, as does Patrick Hamilton's proficient thriller, *Gaslight* (1938), but it is film that most insistently preserves the decadence of Grand Guignol.

*Grandissimes, The: A Story of Creole Life* A novel by **George Washington Cable**, published in 1880, and set in New Orleans in the early 19th century. A feud between the Grandissimes and the De Grapions, aristocratic families of Louisiana, leads to a duel in which Mr Nancanou – related by marriage to the De Grapions – is killed. His widow, Aurora, the last survivor of the De Grapion family, goes to live with her daughter Clotilde in New Orleans. Impoverished, they live in seclusion. Through old Dr Keene, Honoré Grandissime meets Joseph Frowenfield, a young apothecary who is in love with Clotilde De Grapion. Through Joseph, Honoré meets Aurora and falls in love with her. Because Aurora is poor, and serves as a reminder of past hostilities between the two families, the Grandissimes oppose Honoré's marriage to her. However, family objections to the union are cleared away in a deathbed scene: Honoré's uncle Agricola is dying from stab wounds inflicted by Honoré's quadroon half-brother. It was the arrogant Agricola who had killed Aurora's husband, but before he dies he reveals that 20 years earlier he had promised Aurora's father to allow the peace-engendering union between Aurora and Honoré. Obsessed with preserving the 'race', Agricola now finds the union desirable again because it will continue the French Creole 'aristocracy' to which the two families belong.

**Granta** Cambridge University student magazine from 1889 until the mid 1970s, it published early work by **E. M. Forster**, **A. A. Milne**, **Ted Hughes** and **Sylvia Plath**. After a period of moribundity it was resurrected in 1979 under the editorship of Bill Buford as a quarterly literary magazine. It has published work by **Martin Amis**, **Ian McEwan**, **A. N. Wilson**, **James Fenton**, **Salman Rushdie**, **John Berger** and **George Steiner** among others, and American writers such as **Raymond Carver** and other exponents of what it has called 'dirty realism'.

**Granville-Barker, Harley** 1877–1946 Actor, director, playwright and scholar whose career was much affected by his contact with the eccentrically single-minded Shakespearean director, William Poel. Poel chose Barker (he hyphenated his name after his second marriage in 1918) as his Richard II in 1899. Poel's plain staging and pursuit of the original Elizabethan style affected Barker's own immensely influential productions of *The Winter's Tale*, *Twelfth Night* and *A Midsummer Night's Dream* at the Savoy Theatre, London, in 1912–14 as well as his sensitive *Prefaces to Shakespeare* (1927–47). When **George Bernard Shaw** chose Barker to play Marchbanks in the 1900 production of *Candida* by the Stage Society, a second major influence entered Barker's life. The Barker–Vedrenne seasons at the **Royal Court Theatre** (1904–7) established Shaw as a major force in the British theatre, and Barker's own plays, particularly *The Voysey Inheritance* (1905), *Waste* (1907) and *The Madras House* (1910), show a Shavian commitment to intelligent debate.

**Grapes of Wrath, The** A Pulitzer Prize-winning novel by **John Steinbeck**, published in 1939, that tells the story of Oklahoma farmers who are driven off their land by soil erosion. The Joad family drives to California, hoping to take advantage of what they imagine to be a land of plenty. The grandparents die on the way, and the Joads arrive only to be worn down by the impossibly hard life of migrant fruit-pickers. They find a temporary respite in a government labour camp, but when it closes they are forced to take work at a blacklisted orchard. There Tom Joad joins with Jim Casy, a minister turned labour organizer. During ensuing strike violence Casy is killed, and Tom, who had once served time for killing a man in Oklahoma, kills again to avenge Casy's death. In panic, the Joads flee and try to hide Tom, but they are exhausted by struggle and starvation. Finally Ma Joad decides that for the good of all the family Tom must leave. The rest of the family struggles on together, though to what end and in what direction nobody knows. At the controversial end of the novel, the eldest daughter, Rose of Sharon, who has just given birth to a stillborn child, nurses an anonymous starving man with her own milk.

**Graves, A[lfred] P[ercival]** 1846–1931 Irish essayist, songwriter, poet and editor. The son of the Revd Charles Graves, FRS, mathematician and later protestant Bishop of Limerick, he was born in Dublin and educated at Trinity College. He was successively a clerk in the Home Office, a school inspector and an education official in London. Despite these responsibilities he quickly made a name for himself as an Irish writer and published three volumes of Irish songs (1873, 1882, 1892) including the rollicking 'Father O'Flynn', written in 1875 with music by C. V. Stanford. He also wrote the libretto for *The Postbag: A Lesson in Irish* (1902), a one-act opera with music arranged from old Irish airs. He was twice president of the London Irish Literary Society, which encouraged the Irish Literary Revival, and to this end he edited anthologies of Irish poetry and song, wrote *Irish Literary and Musical Studies* (1913) and contributed a valuable chapter on Anglo-Irish literature to the *Cambridge History of English Literature* (1916). Though he knew little Irish and no Welsh he made good use of translations from both languages in popular works such as *A Celtic Psaltery* (1917) and *Songs of the Gael* (1925). His own more serious poetry, lyrical and fluent, engaged increasingly with the heroic world of Irish myth and legend popularized by **Yeats** and **Lady Gregory**, a development commended by **Douglas Hyde** in his introduction to *Irish Poems* (1908). In 1930 Graves published his lively autobiography *To Return to All That*, in part a response to *Goodbye to All That* by his son **Robert Graves**, which had appeared the previous year.

**Graves, Richard** 1715–1804 Novelist. Born at Mickleton in Gloucestershire and educated at Pembroke College, Oxford, Graves became a fellow of All Souls and rector of Claverton, near Bath, in 1749. A popular figure in Bath society, he also enjoyed a correspondence with distinguished people. Among his friends was the poet and landscape gardener **William Shenstone**, whom Graves portrayed in two of his novels and made the subject of a volume of *Recollections* (1788).

Graves is best remembered for his novel, *The Spiritual Quixote* (1773), satirizing the Methodist preacher George Whitefield, whom he had known at Pembroke College. His other novels, interesting for their portrayal of social conditions in the age, are *Columella, or, The Distressed Anchoret* (1779), *Eugenius, or, Anecdotes of the Golden Vale* (1785) and *Plexippus, or, The Aspiring Plebeian* (1790).

**Graves, Robert (von Ranke)** 1895–1985
Poet, novelist and critic. The son of **A. P. Graves**, he was born in Wimbledon and educated at Charterhouse. On the outbreak of World War I he took a commission in the Royal Welsh Fusiliers, meeting **Siegfried Sassoon** in 1915. He was severely injured, and reported dead by *The Times*, in 1916. At the end of the war he married Nancy Nicholson, daughter of the painter William Nicholson, and studied at St John's College, Oxford, where he became a close friend of **T. E. Lawrence**, whose biography he later wrote (1927). In the 1920s he formed an association with **Laura Riding**, living, writing and running the Seizin Press with her. His controversial memoir *Goodbye to All That* (1929) ends with their departure from England following her attempted suicide.

They stayed briefly with **Gertrude Stein** in Paris and then settled in Deya, Mallorca. The outbreak of the Spanish Civil War forced them to leave and, after brief periods in Lugano, Brittany and London, they sailed for America in 1939. Their association ended and Graves returned to England, living in Galmpton, Devon, with Beryl Hodge, who became his second wife. In 1946 he returned with her to Deya. He gave the Clark Lectures at Cambridge in 1954–5 and was Professor of Poetry at Oxford in 1961–6.

Robert Graves. Pastel portrait by Eric Kennington, official war artist from 1916 to 1919.

His early poems, in *Over the Brazier* (1916), *David and Goliath* (1916), *Fairies and Fusiliers* (1917) and **Edward Marsh**'s *Georgian Poetry*, were dominated by World War I. The subsequent volumes which made up his long poetic career show the development of a highly individual style, continually evolving yet always returning to tradition, classical literature and mythology for new inspiration. *Poems 1914–26* (1927) tried to describe and resolve what he called his 'pier-glass haunting' in forms and diction borrowed from nursery rhymes, nonsense verse, ballads and riddles. *Poems 1926–30* (1931) included 'To the Reader over My Shoulder', 'Lost Acres', 'Warning to Children' and 'Welsh Incident' (originally called 'Railway Carriage'). *Collected Poems* (1938) included 'Time', 'To Bring the Dead to Life', 'New Legends', 'The Terraced Valley' and 'No More Ghosts'. *Poems 1938–45* (1946) printed several of his finest poems ('To Sleep', 'Under the Pot' and 'The Thieves'), plain in diction, refusing public themes and concentrating on love. There are also elements of a new mythology in 'To Juan at the Winter Solstice'. The later poems included in *Collected Poems* (1975) show him attempting to be the 'real, perpetually-obsessed Muse poet'.

Graves's poetry went hand in hand with a huge output of critical, scholarly and speculative studies. Influenced by W. H. R. Rivers, the neurologist, anthropologist and early follower of Freud, he elaborated a theory of the equivalence between dream psychology and poetic methods of associative and critical thinking in *On English Poetry* (1922), *The Meaning of Dreams* (1924) and *Poetic Unreason* (1925). His collaboration with Laura Riding resulted in *A Survey of Modernist Poetry* (1928), highly critical both of popular attitudes to poetry and of **modernism** in its more fashionable forms. *The White Goddess* (1948) elaborated his mythology of poetic inspiration. Other prose works included the controversial *The Nazarene Gospel Restored* (1953) and *Jesus in Rome* (1957), both written in collaboration with the Hebrew scholar Joshua Podro, *The Greek Myths* (1955), *The Crowning Privilege* (1955), *Oxford Addresses on Poetry* (1962), *The Hebrew Myths* (1964), *Mammon and the Black Goddess* (1965), *Poetic Craft and Principle* (1967), *The Crane Bag and Other Disputed Subjects* (1969) and *Difficult Questions, Easy Answers* (1972). The later works often assert the value of poetry and mythology over science and technology by challenging academic and popular conventions.

His first novel, *No Decency Left* (1932), was written in collaboration with Laura Riding. A version of **Dickens**'s *David Copperfield*, *The Real David Copperfield* (1933), was followed by *I, Claudius* (1934), narrated by the idiosyncratic Emperor Claudius. Still his most popular work, it was also the first of 13 novels which solved, in a highly commercial way, historical puzzles and conjectures. They include *Claudius the God* (1934), *Count Belisarius* (1938), *The Story of Mary Powell, Wife to Mr Milton* (1943), *The Golden Fleece* (1945), *King Jesus* (1946) and *Homer's Daughter* (1955).

Graves also published work for children in *The Penny Fiddle* (1960) and *Ann at Highwood Hall* (1964), two volumes of selections from his early poems illustrated by **Edward Ardizzone**, and *The Myths of Ancient Greece* (1961) and *The Siege and Fall of Troy* (1962). His popular translations include Apuleius' *The Golden Ass* (1951), Lucan's *Pharsalia* (1956), Suetonius' *The Twelve Caesars* (1957) and *The Anger of Achilles: Homer's Iliad* (1957).

**graveyard poets** The common term for those 18th-century writers, never a formal school, who found inspiration in graveyards and the contemplation of mortality. They were especially fashionable in the 1740s and 1750s, but can be seen to feed the therapeutically melancholic side of **Romanticism**.

A generous collection of graveyard writing might include **Thomas Parnell**'s 'Night-Piece on Death' (published 1721); **Robert Blair**'s *The Grave* (1743); **Edward Young**'s *Night Thoughts* (1742–6); **James Hervey**'s prose *Meditations among the Tombs* (1746–7); **Thomas Gray**'s *Elegy Written in a Country Churchyard* (1751), the *locus classicus* of its poetic kind; Beilby Porteus's 'Death', winner of the Seatonian Prize in 1759; and, as a late flower of the tradition, William Dodd the forger's *Thoughts in Prison* with all its attendant documents (1777).

***Gravity's Rainbow*** A novel by **Thomas Pynchon**, published in 1973. A lengthy and extremely dense text, it involves more than 400 characters, and concerns itself with the historical trends identifiable in American society since World War II. It defies any summary statements, but can generally be said to treat scientific and technological discoveries as historical events and forces, and to explore the modes of consciousness which they generate. One of its central metaphors is the all-pervasive paranoia which has been crucial in other of Pynchon's works. Its allusions range from classical music theory to film and comic-strip characters. The literary figures evoked include **William Faulkner**, **Emily Dickinson**, Rainer Maria Rilke, Jorge Luis Borges, and **James Joyce**, to whose *Ulysses* the novel has been frequently compared.

**Gray, Alasdair** 1934– Novelist. A native of Glasgow, where he still lives, Gray pursued a career as an artist and illustrator before turning to fiction when in his forties. His home city provides the location for his first two novels, *Lanark* (1981) and *1982, Janine* (1984). Both are huge, sprawling picaresque narratives that display a Sternian diffuseness, a Joycean eclecticism and a hallucinatory, fantastic dimension, as well as reminders of Gray's graphic arts skills in their eccentric typology and marginal embellishments. His shorter fictions are collected in *Unlikely Stories, Mostly* (1983). A recent, slighter novel, *The Fall of Kelvin Walker* (1985), follows the fortunes of a typically hapless, itinerant, dissipated protagonist during his sojourn in London. Gray is the most prominent member of a new wave of original Scottish writing, which also includes James Kelman and Agnes Owens, and the stylish publishing programmes of several recently formed Scottish publishing houses.

**Gray, Simon** 1936– Playwright, whose first major success, *Butley* (1971), reflected his wry view of his own career as a university lecturer in English. It had been preceded by three proficient plays, *Wise Child* (1967), *Dutch Uncle* (1968) and *Spoiled* (1971). Butley's sad cynicism is present also in Simon Hench, the leading character of *Otherwise Engaged* (1975). In *Rear Column* (1978), a historically based play about a British expeditionary force in colonial Africa, the emptiness beneath the surface of English cynicism degenerates into open sadism. The comedy thriller *Stage Struck* (1979) is in a lighter vein, but *Quartermaine's Terms* (1981) returns to the familiar Gray territory of overt wit and hidden anguish. His latest work is *Melon* (1987).

**Gray, Thomas** 1716–71 Poet. The only one to survive of the 12 children born to his parents, Gray was educated at Eton (where his two uncles were teaching) and there formed a friendship with **Horace Walpole**, Richard West and Thomas Ashton which was nicknamed the 'Quadruple Alliance'. In 1734 he was admitted to Peterhouse, Cambridge, and considered embarking on a legal career, but was undecided. In 1739–41 he toured France and Italy with Walpole, taking down notes and maintaining a regular correspondence with his friends in England, but they quarrelled at Reggio and Gray returned to England with other friends. At this time he was working on some Latin verses.

The death of his father left Gray financially independent in 1741, and he began writing his tragedy *Agrippina* in 1742. On 1 June of that year West died, just after Gray (in one of the frequent letters they exchanged) had sent him his *Ode on the Spring*. The poet included a lament, *Liber Quartus* (1742), in the Latin poem on which he was working, a translation of **Locke**'s *Essay Concerning Human Understanding* entitled *De Principiis Cogitandi*. In October he returned to Peterhouse and was based in Cambridge for the rest of his life. At his mother's house in Stoke Poges he wrote the *Sonnet on the Death of Richard West*, his ode *On Adversity*, the

*Ode on a Distant Prospect of Eton College* and the unfinished *Hymn to Ignorance*. Graduating as Bachelor of Laws in 1743, he became reconciled with Walpole the following year, and in 1747, on the death of Walpole's cat, Gray sent him the *Ode on the Death of a Favourite Cat, Drowned in a Tub of Gold Fishes*. His other friends at this time included **Christopher Smart**, **William Mason** and **Conyers Middleton**.

On 12 June 1750, Gray sent Walpole the completed manuscript of the poem that was to immortalize him, **Elegy Written in a Country Churchyard**. Published by Dodsley in 1751, it marked Gray's rise to fame as a poet. Apart from a small collection, *Designs by Mr R. Bentley for Six Poems by Mr T. Gray* (1753), which contained *A Long Story* and the *Ode to Adversity*, Gray published little more in the way of poetry. His two Pindaric odes *Progress of Poesy* and *The Bard* were printed by Walpole in 1757 at his Strawberry Hill press. In December of that year he was offered the post of Poet Laureate, on the death of the incumbent, **Colley Cibber**, but declined it.

Pursuing a plan to write the history of English poetry (for which he might have been ideally suited) Gray moved to London in 1759 and spent two years researching in the British Museum. Over the succeeding years he made several tours around England and Scotland, and recorded his impressions in his letters – a medium in which he positively excelled. He returned to Cambridge in 1761, having completed a number of imitations of Celtic and Norse verse, including *The Fatal Sisters* and *The Descent of Odin*. These were included in a collected volume of his *Poems* published in 1768 by Dodsley, and in Glasgow by Foulis. Later that same year he was appointed to the sinecure position of Regius Professor of Modern History at Cambridge, and in 1769 he wrote a masterful *Ode* at the installation of the Duke of Grafton as Chancellor of the University. Gray enjoyed a final expedition to the Lake District in 1769, as recorded in his prose *Journal* (published 1774); he died at Cambridge in 1771, and was buried next to his mother in the graveyard at Stoke Poges that was the subject of his most celebrated achievement in life.

As a poet, Gray managed a relatively slender output, but his verse was polished and exact, and his voice distinctive in its nice balance between introspection and sentiment. His erudition and familiarity with the rhythms and verbal effects of so much other poetry lends his own writing a delicacy that was subsequently admired by the Romantic poets, and is still accessible today.

**Great Expectations** A novel by **Charles Dickens**, published as a serial in **All the Year Round** from December 1860 to August 1861.

Narrated in the first person by Philip Pirrip (Pip) as he reflects on the three stages of his 'great expectations', the novel opens on the Kentish marshes where he lives an orphaned childhood under the harsh hand of his sister and her kindly blacksmith husband, Joe Gargery. One day Pip helps a starving convict, Abel Magwitch, who is soon recaptured and taken back to the nearby prison ship ('The Hulks'). Pip is later summoned to Satis House, home of the wealthy eccentric Miss Havisham, who has lived in seclusion since being jilted by her fiancé. He quickly becomes devoted to Miss Havisham's ward Estella, who treats his developing love only with deliberate cold-heartedness. Pip is aided in his ambition of becoming a gentleman by a generous allowance, paid through the lawyer Jaggers, which he mistakenly assumes to come from Miss Havisham. He relinquishes his humble companions and goes to London to acquire polish, good manners and a smattering of education with the help of his room-mate Herbert Pocket. Urban life leads him into vain and extravagant ways. Magwitch reappears, having illegally returned to England after being transported, and reveals that he is Pip's benefactor, bent on using the fortune he has amassed in Australia to repay the boy's kindness. Pip plans to get Magwitch safely out of the country but the convict is mortally hurt, arrested and brought to trial; he dies before the sentence is carried out. Estella, dramatically revealed as Magwitch's daughter, marries an upper-class lout, Bentley Drummle, who gravely mistreats her before his early death. Pip, learning both loyalty and Christian humility from his experiences, returns to England after a successful career and meets Estella. In the book's original ending the two still remain separate, but at the urging of **Bulwer Lytton** Dickens altered the conclusion to give *Great Expectations* a conventional happy ending.

Despite its neatly melodramatic plotting and its richly stocked gallery of comic minor characters – the histrionic Wopsle, the pompous Pumblechook, the eccentric Wemmick – *Great Expectations* is a book of sober and sustained purpose. The gradual discovery of human values Pip makes as he passes through the various stages of his 'great expectations' enacts a familiar Dickensian fable, enriched here by the presence of Pip's narrative voice to trace the processes of memory.

**Great Gatsby, The** A novel by **F. Scott Fitzgerald**, published in 1925.

The narrator, Nick Carraway, rents a cottage in West Egg, Long Island, next door to the mansion of Jay Gatsby and across the water from the home of Tom Buchanan and his wife Daisy, Carraway's cousin. Gatsby's mansion is the scene of extravagant nightly parties, attended by many people who are uninvited and do not know their host. Carraway, both cynical and curious about Gatsby, soon becomes his confidant. He learns that Gatsby had met Daisy while he was in the army during World War I, and that they had fallen in love and planned to marry. Daisy, however, had grown impatient for him to return and had married Tom, a rich though boring man from Yale. Having risen from his lowly origins as Jimmy Gatz through dubious business deals, Gatsby is obsessed with winning Daisy back. He persuades Carraway to arrange a meeting between them, and Daisy, after initial resistance, succumbs to her former lover's generous attentions, impressed by his newly acquired wealth.

Tom, Daisy, Gatsby, Carraway and Carraway's girlfriend, Jordan Baker, spend a day together in New York City. Tom, who himself has had a longstanding affair with Myrtle Wilson, the wife of a Long Island garage owner, becomes aware of Daisy's attentions to Gatsby. Gatsby tries to convince Daisy to leave Tom. Tom, in turn, tries to discredit Gatsby by revealing that he has made his money from bootlegging. Gatsby and Daisy leave in Tom's automobile, with Daisy driving. Myrtle Wilson, recognizing the car as it passes her husband's garage, runs out into the street and is hit and killed by Daisy, who drives on. Taking revenge on Gatsby, Tom tells Wilson it was Gatsby who killed his wife, and Gatsby, attempting to protect Daisy, lets the blame fall on himself. Wilson murders Gatsby and then commits suicide. Carraway is left to arrange Gatsby's funeral, which hardly anyone attends, and Tom and Daisy retreat 'back into their money, or their vast carelessness, or whatever it was that kept them together'.

***Great Hoggarty Diamond, The***  A story by **W. M. Thackeray**, published in *Fraser's Magazine* (September to December 1841). The Hoggarty Diamond, given to Samuel Titmarsh by his aunt, involves him with swindlers and shady dealings, from which he is rescued by his wife.

**Greeley, Horace** 1811–72 American journalist. Born in New Hampshire, Greeley grew up in Vermont and in 1831 went to New York City, where he worked as a printer before becoming editor of *The New Yorker* in 1834. In 1841 he founded *The Tribune*, the New York daily that he would edit until his death. Greeley was a consistent exponent of American democratic principles, and this was reflected in his editorial support of reform movements, of the new Republican party in the 1850s, of emancipation in the 1860s, and of amnesty and universal suffrage in the period of Reconstruction. An opponent of the more radical Republicans in the 1870s, he was chosen as the Democratic presidential candidate in 1872; he was defeated by Ulysses S. Grant, however, and died within the month. Colourful, eccentric, independent, often controversial, Greeley's editorials were nevertheless influential throughout his career. Among his other writings were travel books: *Glances at Europe* (1851), and *An Overland Journey* (1860); *The American Conflict* (2 vols., 1864–6), an important contemporary history of the Civil War; and *Recollections of a Busy Life* (1868), an autobiography.

**Green, Henry** 1905–73 Novelist. The pseudonym of Henry Vincent Yorke, an engineer and later managing director of his family's engineering company in Birmingham. He was born in Tewkesbury, Gloucestershire, and educated at Eton College and at Magdalen College, Oxford. While still at university he attracted critical attention with his first novel, *Blindness* (1926). He also began but did not complete a second, *Mood*. *Living* (1929) is set in the sort of engineering works he knew very well (he worked as a foundryman) and *Party Going* (1939) among an upper-class group who have wealth but no sense of responsibility. Green's next book was a chapter of autobiography *Pack my Bag: A Self Portrait* (1940). He resumed his career as a novelist with *Caught* (1943), a story of the Auxiliary Fire Service in World War II, and *Loving* (1945), which is of the same wartime period but set in a remote castle in Ireland. *Back* (1946), *Concluding* (1948), *Nothing* (1950) and *Doting* (1952) complete the list of his fiction.

Henry Green is distinguished as a novelist by his elegant impressionistic prose, his indirect and oblique dialogue, and his rapid cutting from scene to scene. His work displays a talent for observation, and a vein of poetry, in evidence most strongly, perhaps, in *Living*.

**Green, John Richard** 1837–83 Historian. Green was born in Oxford and educated at Magdalen College School and Jesus College, Oxford. He was ordained and served as a curate in various parts of London until ill health forced him to give up his duties; he became librarian of Lambeth Palace in 1869. This post gave him an opportunity for historical research; he became a frequent contributor to *The Saturday Review* and achieved a notable success with *A Short History of the English People* (1873), which proved the most popular history since **Macaulay**'s. Green's narrative and descriptive powers are of a high order: they give life to his account of the literary and artistic events, as well as the political and economic ones, which make up the history of a nation. *Stray Studies from England and Italy* (1876) is a collection of essays; in the following year Green began publication of an extended version of his 'short' history as *A History of the English People* (4 vols., 1877–80). With the help of his wife, Alice Stopford Green, he expanded certain themes in *The Making of England* (1881) and *The Conquest of England* (1883).

**Green, Matthew** 1696–1737 Poet. Born in the City of London, Green was a civil servant who wrote a fluent poem in octosyllabics, *The Spleen* (1737), discussing boredom or depression and offering solutions for its prevention and cure.

**Green, Paul (Eliot)** 1894–1981 American playwright. Green was born in Lillington, North Carolina, and educated at the University of North Carolina, where he also taught from 1923 to 1924. His prolific dramatic output began with realistic folk-plays which portrayed the lives of blacks and poor whites in North Carolina. Outstanding among these is the one-act *White Dresses* (1923), one of the six plays for the black theatre published under the title *Lonesome Road* (1926). Another piece in the same collection was later expanded into the full-length *In Abraham's Bosom* (1926), for which Green won the Pulitzer Prize in 1927. Staged in New York by the Provincetown Players, it is an angry story of the persecution and lynching of a black teacher. *The House of Connelly: A Drama of the Old South and the New* (1931), the first production of the **Group Theatre**, deals with the deteriorating fortunes of a white landowning family in the South. *Tread the Green Grass* (1932) is one of a number of 'symphonic dramas', combining dance and music with dialogue. *Johnny Johnson* (1936), written for the Group Theatre, is a fiercely anti-war musical play with music written by Kurt Weill. Green's hatred of violence is again vividly expressed in *Hymn to the Rising Sun* (1936), which exposes the sadistic practices of state penitentiaries. He also dramatized **Richard Wright**'s novel *Native Son* (1941), produced a new revival version of *Peer Gynt* (1951), and wrote 11 screenplays, among them an adaptation of John Howard Griffith's *Black Like Me* (1964).

After 1937, when he wrote *The Lost Colony* for a large-scale outdoor performance on the site of **Sir Walter Raleigh's** landing on Roanoke Island in North Carolina, Green devoted most of his attention to the writing and staging of 'symphonic' pageant-dramas about American history, usually designed for outdoor performance in their appropriate geographical location. Other such productions include *The Common Glory* (1947) in Williamsburg, Virginia; *Faith of Our Fathers* (1950) in Washington, DC; *The Stephen Foster Story* (1959) in Bardstown, Kentucky; and *We the People* (1976) in Columbia, Maryland.

**Green, Thomas Hill** 1836–82 Philosopher. Green was educated at Rugby and Balliol College, Oxford, where he became White's Professor of Moral Philosophy in 1878. He made his first contribution to philosophy in 1874 with two extended introductions to an edition of **David Hume**'s *Treatise of Human Nature*; here he presented detailed criticisms of **John Locke**, **George Berkeley** and Hume, arguing that neither **John Stuart Mill** nor **Herbert Spencer** had advanced beyond the ideas presented by Hume in 1739. He suggested that students of philosophy should study the work of Kant and Hegel rather than that of the English empiricists. Green's principal work was *Prolegomena to Ethics* (1883).

***Green Carnation, The*** A novel by **Robert Hichens**, published in 1894. It is a *roman à clef* about **Oscar Wilde** and **Lord Alfred Douglas**, presented without disguise as Esme Amarinth and Lord Reggie. Written in a brilliant pastiche of the style of Oscar Wilde, the book appears to be loving homage in the flattering form of parody, but the story is ambiguous. Lord Reggie toys with the idea of marriage to Lady Locke, a widow. Though attracted, she decides to refuse him when she overhears Lord Reggie offering a green carnation to her son, Tommy, who is infatuated by Reggie's charm. For Lady Locke, the green carnation is a 'tainted motto' of Lord Reggie's 'unnatural' life. Hichens's own stance is equivocal. In the introduction written in 1948, he describes his own friendship with Douglas, who introduced him to Wilde, and writes of Wilde's kindness to him. The book was published anonymously, though Wilde and Douglas expressed their delight to the author at once. It was withdrawn when Wilde's troubles with the law began.

***Green Mansions***: *A Romance of the Tropical Forest* A novel by **W. H. Hudson**, published in 1904.

Abel Guevez de Argensola (Mr Abel) travels into the Venezuelan jungle (the 'green mansions') as a political refugee and eventually settles with the Indian tribe of his friend Runi. Exploring a forbidden part of the forest he hears and is enchanted by a beautiful voice, which he learns belongs to Rima, the daughter of an evil spirit called Didi. Abel meets Rima, who turns out to be a beautiful girl whose spirit has strong affinities with that of the forest itself. He also meets her grandfather, Nuflo, and he and the old man set out to try to locate Rima's mother. Abel and Rima are by now deeply in love.

After a long and arduous journey the two men return to the forest to discover that Rima's hut has been attacked and destroyed by the Indians. Rima herself has been trapped and burnt on a pyre surrounding a great tree in the forest. Abel is consumed by grief and revenges himself by attacking the Indians' village and slaying Runi. Afterwards he returns to civilization, bearing Rima's ashes in an urn, where he lives apart with his memories.

The Hudson Memorial in Hyde Park presents a sculpture of Rima by Sir Jacob Epstein, commissioned in 1925.

**Greenaway, Kate** 1846–1901 Children's illustrator and writer. Born in London, the daughter of a successful wood-engraver, Kate eventually studied at the Slade School in London. Her first major success as a writer–illustrator was *Under the Window* (1879), printed in colour and selling over 100,000 copies. Her pictures here of demure little girls, accompanied by her own verses, helped popularize a particular fashion for high-waisted, frilly dresses and sun-bonnets. A friend of **John Ruskin**, she produced a large number of best-sellers, many of them in print today. Particularly good are her alphabet book, *A Apple Pie* (1886), and *Mother Goose, or, The Old Nursery Rhymes* (1881), although her essentially decorative, static style of drawing was not equal to the demands of the more vigorous nursery rhymes. But her charming characterizations of the young have always been appreciated by parents and teachers, even if children themselves may sometimes have found them a little too sweet and well mannered.

**Greene, (Henry) Graham** 1904–91 Novelist. Graham Greene was born in Hertfordshire and educated at Berkhamsted School (where his father was headmaster) and Balliol College, Oxford. He joined the staff of *The Times* (1926–30) and married in 1927.

In 1935 Greene made a journey across Liberia (described in *Journey Without Maps*, 1936) and on his return was appointed film critic of *The Spectator*. (He became literary editor in 1940.) In 1937 he was joint editor with John Marks of the short-lived periodical *Night and Day* (July to December), which collapsed after a libel suit over Greene's review of the film *Wee Willie Winkie*. The following year he was commissioned to visit Mexico to report on the religious persecution there, and during World War II he worked for the Foreign Office, mainly in Sierra Leone (1941–3). He was made a Companion of Honour in 1966, and a Chevalier de la Légion d'honneur in 1969.

A key event in Greene's life was his conversion to Roman Catholicism in 1926. His first novel, *The Man Within* (1929), was a historical thriller which reflected many of the themes of pursuit, guilt, treachery and failure which became the hallmark of his fiction. His first popular success came with *Stamboul Train* (1932), another thriller with a more topical and political flavour, and the first of a series of novels which Greene termed 'entertainments'. These continued with *It's a Battlefield* (1934),

Graham Greene, 1964.

*England Made Me* (1935), *A Gun for Sale* (1936), *The Confidential Agent* (1939), *Loser Takes All* (1955) and *Our Man in Havana* (1958).

*Brighton Rock* (1938), which was called 'an entertainment' in the USA and 'a novel' in England, was the first explicitly Catholic novel introducing his central concept of 'the appalling strangeness of the mercy of God'. This theme has also been detected in *The Power and the Glory* (1940), *The Heart of the Matter* (1948), *The End of the Affair* (1951) and *The Quiet American* (1955). Four other novels of this type (*A Burnt-Out Case*, 1961, set in the Belgian Congo; *The Comedians*, 1966, set in Haiti; *The Honorary Consul*, 1973, in Paraguay; and *The Human Factor*, 1978, in the London underworld of spies) dealt with the committed and the uncommitted caught up in places and events in which the 'comedians' were those who would never feel the need for any kind of commitment.

Greene also published a light-hearted novel called *Travels with My Aunt* (1969) and several volumes of short stories: *The Basement Room and Other Stories* (1935), *Nineteen Stories* (1947), *Twenty-One Stories* (1954) and *May We Borrow Your Husband?* (1967). His plays include *The Living Room* (1953), *The Potting Shed* (1957), *The Complaisant Lover* (1959) and *Carving a Statue* (1964), as well as the screenplay *The Third Man*, filmed by Carol Reed in 1949. He wrote a number of stories for children, a chapter of autobiography called *A Sort of Life* (1971) and *Lost Childhood, and Other Essays* (1951).

**Greene, Robert** *c.* 1558–92 Pamphleteer and playwright, born in Norwich and recipient of degrees from both Cambridge and Oxford. Greene married in 1585, but soon deserted his wife to lead a life of pleasure in London. For many of the details of his dissipation we are reliant on his autobiographical pamphlets. These range from superior journalism to self-excoriating penitence. Of the first kind are his descriptions of low life in London in *The Art of Conny-Catching* (1591). 'Conny-catching' is the Elizabethan equivalent of confidence trickery, and Greene's treatment of it is racy, humorous and direct. Of the second kind is *Greene's Groatsworth of Wit, Bought with a Million of Repentance* (1592), famous for its attack on **Shakespeare** as 'an upstart crow, beautified with our feathers'.

In order, perhaps, to buy his pleasures, Greene wrote prolifically. Early pamphlets in the style of **Lyly** culminated in his continuation of *Euphues* in *Euphues, his Censure of Philautus* (1587). A series of prose romances modelled on **Sidney**'s *Arcadia* included *Pandosto* (1588), on which Shakespeare based *The Winter's Tale*, and *Menaphon* (1589), which contains the beautiful lyric, 'Weep not, my wanton'. Of his extant plays, the earliest is *Alphonsus, King of Aragon* (*c.* 1587), a shameless imitation of **Marlowe**'s rhetoric, and the best *Friar Bacon and Friar Bungay* (*c.* 1589). *A Looking-Glass for London and England* (*c.* 1590), written in collaboration with **Thomas Lodge**, is a satirical dramatic treatment of material handled more light-heartedly in Greene's pamphlets. *James the Fourth* (*c.* 1591)

The title-page illustration for Robert Greene's pamphlet, *A Quip for An Upstart Courtier*, 1592.

interestingly combines the techniques of the chronicle play with fairy fantasy.

**Greenwood, Walter** 1903–74 Novelist. Walter Greenwood was born in Salford, Lancashire, of working-class parents. He was educated at a local council school, and for many years after leaving school he held a succession of ill-paid jobs. There were also long periods of unemployment and financial hardship on the 'dole'. *Love on the Dole*, published in 1933, was his first novel and his only commercial success. It is a documentary work which focuses on the misfortunes of the Hardcastle family, particularly the daughter Sally, during the prolonged Depression of the 1930s. The book achieved wide popularity, and a dramatized version (with Ronald Gow) was produced in 1934. Still later, in 1941, it was made into a successful film.

Greenwood wrote several other novels and an autobiography, *There Was a Time* (1967).

**Greg, Sir W[alter] W[ilson]** 1875–1959 Literary scholar. Born in Wimbledon, the son of a political journalist, Greg was educated at Harrow and at Trinity College, Cambridge, where he achieved only a pass degree in medieval and modern languages. His intellect was aroused, however, by the work of the Bibliographical Society, which he joined in 1898. A private income enabled him to devote the rest of his life to bibliography and textual criticism, although he did from 1907 to 1913 hold the post of librarian at Trinity College. In 1906 he founded the Malone Society for the reproduction of early (i.e. pre-1640) English plays, acting as its general editor from 1906 to 1939, when he succeeded **E. K. Chambers** as president. After producing editions of *Sir Thomas More* (1911) and other plays, Greg went on to publish *Dramatic Documents from the Elizabethan Playhouses* (1931) and *English Literary Autographs 1550–1650* (1925–32). The greatest task of his later years was the compiling of *A Bibliography of the English Printed Drama to the Restoration* (1939–59), while his major editorial achievement of this period was the two texts of **Marlowe**'s *Doctor Faustus* (1950). His other important works were *The Editorial Problem in Shakespeare* (1942), *The Shakespeare First Folio* (1955) and *Some Aspects and Problems of London Publishing 1550–1650* (1956). Greg was knighted in 1950 for services to English literature.

**Gregory, Horace (Victor)** 1898–1982 American poet, born in Milwaukee, Wisconsin. His first volume of poetry, *Chelsea Rooming House*, appeared in 1930. His early verse was strongly influenced by Marxist thought, but in 1935 he angered other left-wing writers by asserting that art should be apolitical. Throughout his career, however, he remained concerned with the plight of the poor and dispossessed in America's cities. His other volumes of poetry include *A Wreath for Margery* (1933), *No Retreat* (1933), *Chorus for Survival* (1935), *Poems 1930–1940* (1941), *Selected Poems* (1951), *Medusa in Gramercy Park* (1961), *Alphabet For Joanna: A Poem* (1963), *Collected Poems* (1964) and *Another Look* (1976). With his wife, the poet **Marya Zaturenska**, he edited various poetry anthologies, and wrote *A History of American Poetry 1900–1940* (1946).

**Gregory, Lady (Isabella) Augusta** 1852–1932 Dramatist. Augusta Persse, the daughter of a wealthy family, was born at Roxborough House near Coole in Galway. Her father's lands were adjacent to those of the Gregorys at Coole Park and she married Sir William Gregory in 1880. After her husband's death in 1892, Lady Gregory increasingly devoted her time to the study of Irish folklore and mythology, in which her interest was further stimulated by her meeting **W. B. Yeats** in 1896. Coole Park became his retreat and refuge. It was a friendship that led, in 1899, to the founding of the Irish Literary Theatre and to the renascence of Irish drama in the **Abbey Theatre** after 1904. Lady Gregory's involvement in the running of the Abbey was multi-faceted. She was one of its most prolific playwrights as well as being a director, occasional stage manager and frequent adviser. *Our Irish Theatre* (1913), an autobiographical reminiscence, is an important sourcebook of the Abbey's early history.

Lady Gregory's one-act plays about the Irish peasantry contain much of her best writing.

Lady Gregory. A detail from the portrait by Flora Lion, 1913. National Portrait Gallery, London.

This includes *Spreading the News* (1904), *The Rising of the Moon* (1906), the tragedy *The Gaol Gate* (1906) and *The Workhouse Ward* (1908). Of her Irish folk-history plays, the best are *The White Cockade* (1905), *The Canavans* (1906) and *The Deliverer* (1911). *Hyacinth Halvey* (1906) is a contemporary comedy that shares the affectionate patriotism of Lady Gregory's Irish adaptations of Molière, *The Doctor in Spite of Himself* (1906), *The Rogueries of Scapin* (1908) and *The Would-Be Gentleman* (1926). The first three of these were published in *The Kiltartan Molière* (1910). Lady Gregory's *Journals 1916–30* (1946) are invaluable and impressive.

**Greimas, A. J.** See **semiotics** and **structuralism**.

**Grenfell, Julian (Henry Francis)** 1888–1915 Poet. The eldest son of Lord Desborough, he was educated at Eton and Balliol College, Oxford, and became a professional soldier. His poem 'Into Battle', published in *The Times* on the day he was killed in May 1915, is the one by which he is best known. His output was small and his poems are usually to be found in anthologies, such as **T. Sturge Moore**'s *Some Soldier Poets* (1919).

**Greville, Charles Cavendish Fulke** 1794–1865 Politician. Greville, who was born at Wilbury in Wiltshire, became Clerk to the Council in 1821 and held office until 1859. His brother Algernon Sidney Greville was Wellington's private secretary and Greville became the intimate friend of both Wellington and Palmerston; he knew every statesman of any account in his lifetime. He published anonymously *The Past and Present Policy of England to Ireland* (1845), in which he advocated a more liberal policy for religious endowments. But more interesting are his memoirs, which are probably the most rewarding of their kind; with Greville's portraits of the principal figures of the period they are indispensable to students of English history and politics from the accession of George IV to 1860. *The Greville Memoirs* appeared in three series: the first (1874) covers the reigns of George IV and William IV, the second (1885) the years 1837–52, and the third (1887) the years 1852–60. The second and third series were edited by Henry Reeve, who considered it advisable to suppress some of the contents. The complete text was eventually published in 1938.

**Greville, Sir Fulke, 1st Baron Brooke** 1554–1628 Courtier, poet and dramatist. Greville's family were Warwickshire landowners and he was sent to Shrewsbury School in the same year as **Sir Philip Sidney**, his exact contemporary and later his close friend. After completing his education at Jesus College, Cambridge, he went to court and became a member of the **Areopagus**

club with Sidney, **Spenser** and others. He represented Warwickshire in Parliament and enjoyed a long and distinguished public career under both Elizabeth and James I. He was knighted in 1597, served as Treasurer of the Navy from 1589 to 1604, and was Chancellor of the Exchequer from 1614 to 1622. James I made him first Baron Brooke in 1621, presenting him with Knowle Park and Warwick Castle. Greville was murdered by a servant who believed that his master had left him out of his will. Apart from Sir Philip Sidney, whose pall-bearer he had been in 1586, he numbered among his friends **Samuel Daniel**, **Francis Bacon**, **William Camden** and **Edward Coke**.

Greville's own writings were not published during his lifetime. The most famous is *The Life of the Renowned Sir Philip Sidney*, probably written between 1610 and 1614 and first published in 1652. The sequence of songs and sonnets called *Caelica* contains love poems as well as religious and philosophical verses. It was first published in 1633, together with Greville's two tragedies, *Alaham* and *Mustapha*, both reflecting his strong interest in political ideas. A third, on Antony and Cleopatra, reflected his feelings about the fall of his friend the Earl of Essex; but Greville destroyed it. He also wrote verse treatises on political subjects.

**Grey, (Pearl) Zane** 1872–1939 American novelist. Born in Zanesville, Ohio, Grey graduated from the University of Pennsylvania in 1896 with a degree in dentistry. He practised in New York City from 1898 to 1904, during which time he began to write fiction. His first novel, a romance entitled *Betty Zane*, was privately published by him in 1903 but received little public attention. In 1907 his wife convinced him to make his first trip to Arizona, in the company of C. J. 'Buffalo' Jones, a retired buffalo hunter. The journey proved to be the turning point in his career. He began writing Western novels in the tradition of **Owen Wister**, and developed the conventions of the Western into a formula with enormous popular appeal.

He wrote 60 books, which sold over 15 million copies in his lifetime, making him the single most popular author of the post-World War I era in America. Over 100 Western films were based on his stories. In novels such as *Riders of the Purple Sage* (1912), *To the Last Man* (1922), *Nevada* (1928), *Wild Horse Mesa* (1928) and *Code of the West* (1934) he presents the West as a moral landscape against which his protagonists struggle, and by which they are either destroyed or redeemed, according to their response to its violent code.

**Grierson, Sir Herbert J[ohn] C[lifford]** 1866–1960 Literary scholar and critic. Born into a landowning family in Shetland, Grierson attended the Aberdeen Gymnasium and King's College, Aberdeen, before studying at Oxford University. He was, from 1894 to 1915, the first Professor of English at Aberdeen, where he established the canon of **Donne**'s poetry, producing a two-volume edition of the *Poems of John Donne* (1912); he also edited (with W. M. Dixon) *The English Parnassus: An Anthology of Longer Poems* (1909). In 1919 he moved to the University of Edinburgh, where he occupied the chair of Rhetoric and English Literature until 1935. Here he compiled the work for which he is best known, his anthology of *Metaphysical Lyrics and Poems of the Seventeenth Century* (1921). His introduction to this book inspired **T. S. Eliot** and others to bring about a major critical reassessment of the **metaphysical poets**. Grierson also acted later as co-editor of **Sir Walter Scott**'s *Letters* (12 vols., 1932–7), and wrote a biography, *Walter Scott, Bart.* (1938). He maintained his interest in 17th-century literature, as author of *Cross Currents in English Literature of the XVII Century* (1929), and as editor (with G. Bullough) of *The Oxford Book of Seventeenth-Century Verse* (1934).

**Grieve, Christopher Murray** See **MacDiarmid, Hugh**.

**Griffin, Gerald** 1803–40 Novelist and poet. Born at Limerick, he came to London in 1823 but returned to Limerick in 1838 and joined the Christian brothers. His novel, *The Collegians* (1829), was highly regarded, but Griffin's fame was eclipsed by **Dion Boucicault**, who dramatized it as *The Colleen Bawn* in 1860 and scored one of the great successes of the Victorian theatre. The novel underwent a second transformation as *The Lily of Killarney*, a once popular opera by Julius Benedict, in 1863.

***Griffith Gaunt*** A novel by **Charles Reade**, published in 1866, about a marriage in difficulties because of religious differences. It involves a duel with pistols, a 'gentleman's by-blow', mistaken identity, unjust suspicions aroused by a 'female Iago', a bigamous marriage and a trial for murder. The two wives, improbably, become close friends and a rejected suitor of the legal wife makes an honest woman of the low-born but high-minded victim. The period is the 1740s, though there are few attempts at period style. The book was considered daring.

**Griffiths, Trevor** 1935– Playwright, born and educated in Manchester. Griffiths is one of the most articulate of a generation of socialist dramatists. Much of his finest work has been written for television. His stage plays include: *Occupations* (1970), in which left-wing pragmatism is set against the fervour of the Italian Marxist Gramsci; *The Party* (1973), a political debate-play; and the excellent *Comedians* (1975), in which a training school for comedians provides the context for an angry survey of British social attitudes.

**Grigson, Geoffrey (Edward Harvey)** 1905–85. Poet and man of letters. Born in Pelynt, Cornwall, he was educated at St Edmund Hall, Oxford, and worked as a journalist. His poetry is overshadowed by his achievements as a man of letters; he founded and edited the influential modernist periodical *New Verse* (1933–9), and he was an acerbic, controversial literary journalist, given to attacking inflated reputations – in particular, **Edith Sitwell** – and championing excellent but little-known poets, such as **E. J. Scovell** and **Clere Parsons**. His early poetry, in *Several Observations: Thirty-Five Poems* (1939), *Under the Cliff* (1943) and *The Isles of Scilly* (1946), consists of precise, imagistic observations of the world. Later poems are less austere, more emotional, including the excellent sequence of love-poems *Legenda Suecana* (1953). After *Collected Poems* (1963), other volumes include *A Skull in Salop* (1967), *Ingestion of Ice Cream* (1969), *Discoveries of Bones and Stones* (1971), *Collected Poems 1963–1980* (1982) and *Montaigne's Tree* (1984). He wrote an autobiography, *The Crest on the Silver* (1950), and many books on nature, literature and art, as well as editing several Faber anthologies and selections of **John Clare** and **William Barnes** which helped to restore them to common currency.

**Grimald, Nicholas** 1519–62 Translator and poet. After studying at Christ's College, Cambridge, Grimald became chaplain to Bishop Ridley and consequently fell under suspicion in Mary's reign, a suspicion he dispelled by abandoning Protestantism. The first extant edition of his translation of Cicero's *De Officiis* is dated 1556, but there may have been an earlier one. His Latin paraphrasis of Virgil's *Georgics* was printed in 1591. He wrote two plays, both in Latin and both printed at Cologne. *Christus Redivivus* (1543), on the Resurrection, is subtitled a tragicomedy (*comoedia tragica*) and probably had performances in Germany. *Archipropheta* (1548) is a tragedy on the life and death of St John the Baptist. Grimald's main significance for English literature lies in his contribution of some 40 poems to *Tottel's Miscellany*, which he may have edited.

**Grocyn, William** ?1446–1519 Humanist. Grocyn's significance lies in his introduction of the study of Greek at Oxford, and his connections with the circle surrounding **Erasmus** and **Thomas More**. He was educated at Winchester School and New College, Oxford, which he entered in 1465, and afterwards held various ecclesiastical offices. He studied in Italy under Poliziano and learned Greek with the tutors of the children of Lorenzo de' Medici. In Italy he became acquainted with the Venetian printer Aldus Manutius. On his return to Oxford he taught Greek there, although according to one of Erasmus's letters he had taught Greek at Oxford even before his Italian visit of 1488. When **John Colet** became Dean of St Paul's, Grocyn preached there at his invitation, notably on pseudo-Dionysius. The only known works of Grocyn are a letter of his to Aldus prefaced to **Linacre**'s *Sphaera Procli* (*c.* 1499) and an epigram on a lady who threw a snowball at him.

**Grose, Francis** ?1731–91 Antiquary and draughtsman. Grose was born at Greenford, Middlesex, the son of a Swiss jeweller. He did not attend a university, but studied art and became a member of the Incorporated Society of Artists. He was best known as a maker of 'tinted drawings, chiefly of architectural remains'. Grose was Richmond Herald in 1755–63, and then served in the army until his death. Between 1773 and 1787 he published the four folio volumes of his *Antiquities of England and Wales*; the text was not entirely his own but he was responsible for most of the drawings. In 1789–91 he published *The Antiquities of Scotland*; his *Antiquities of Ireland* appeared posthumously in 1791–5. *Essays on Gothic Architecture* (1800) contained work by, among others, Grose and **Thomas Warton the younger**.

The art of caricature, military antiquarianism (especially armour), local proverbs and superstitions all caught the interest of this 'antiquarian Falstaff'. He was also a pioneer in the lexicography of slang and published *A Classical Dictionary of the Vulgar Tongue* in 1785. This was reissued in 1811 as *Lexicon Balatronicum. A Dictionary of Buckish Slang, University Wit and Pickpocket Eloquence*, and edited by **Pierce Egan** in 1823.

**Grosseteste, Robert** ?1167–1253 Churchman and scholar. Grosseteste was born in Stradbroke, Suffolk. His early years are poorly documented; he would seem to have studied at Oxford, then Paris, returning to Oxford to be Rector Scholorum and perhaps the first chancellor of the university. When the Franciscans arrived in England in 1224, Grosseteste was appointed their lecturer. He maintained warm lifelong relations with them. He held several preferments between 1214 and 1232, all of which he resigned because of illness, except his Lincolnshire prebend. When Hugh de Wells died in 1235, Grosseteste was elected his successor as bishop of Lincoln. He was immediately active in the reform of abuses, beginning a series of 'visits' to monasteries, a much disliked practice. He was involved in disputes with Henry III over various church appointments, with Arch-

Robert Grosseteste depicted in the *Harleian MS. 3860, f.48r*. British Library.

bishop Boniface over the latter's right to 'visit', and with the Pope, again over church appointments. In 1252, shortly before his death, he withstood the King's appeal for money for a new crusade.

Grosseteste was an energetic writer, and regarded by contemporaries as one of 'the greatest clerics in the world'. The range of materials covered is immense. There are letters; sermons; biblical and Aristotelian commentaries; translations from the Greek (including John of Damascus, *The Testament of the Twelve Patriarchs*, Dionysius the Areopagite, and Aristotle); scientific treatises; and a long Anglo-Norman allegorical poem on the history of salvation from the Fall of Adam to the Resurrection of Christ.

Matthew Paris's *Chronicle* contains many fascinating anecdotes of Grosseteste's life.

**Grossmith, George** 1847–1912 and **Grossmith, Weedon** 1854–1919 Joint authors of *The Diary of a Nobody* (1892), which Weedon also illustrated, and for which they are now principally remembered. George started his career as a police court reporter for *The Times*, Weedon as an artist. Both brothers later became actors, George creating many of the most famous bari-tone *buffo* roles in **Gilbert** and Sullivan's **Savoy Operas**, and Weedon eventually becoming manager of Terry's Theatre. Weedon also wrote a novel, *A Woman with a History* (1896), and several plays, of which the most successful was *The Night of the Party* (1901). George published two volumes of memoirs, *Reminiscences of a Clown* (1888) and *Piano and I* (1910).

**Grote, George** 1794–1871 Historian. The son of a banking family, Grote was born at Beckenham in Kent and educated at Charterhouse School. He was a follower of **Bentham** and **James Mill**, publishing pamphlets in support of reform. He entered the family business in 1830, and in 1832 became MP for the City of London. Since 1823 he had worked intermittently on his *A History of Greece*, and after retiring from Parliament (1841) and banking (1843) he devoted himself to its completion. It was published in 12 volumes (1845–6) and surpassed the similar work (1835–44) by his friend from Charterhouse days, **Connop Thirlwall**. Grote wrote two works on Greek philosophy: *Plato and the other Companions of Sokrates* (1865) and *Aristotle* (posthumously published, 1872).

**Group, the** Informal circle of poets which flourished from the mid 1950s until 1965. Although it was initiated by **Philip Hobsbaum** in Cambridge, the Group came to meet in **Edward Lucie-Smith**'s home in London, once a week, to discuss and give unrestrained yet objective criticism of each other's poems. Those attending included **Peter Porter**, **George Mac-Beth**, **Peter Redgrove**, **Alan Brownjohn** and many lesser writers. The Group came to prominence with *A Group Anthology* (1963), edited by Hobsbaum and Lucie-Smith. The participants' critical perspective demanded poems that were immediately and easily understood, and poems were accordingly written to be read aloud, giving attention to the possibilities of the spoken voice. From 1965, under the influence of **Martin Bell**, the Group transmuted into the Poets' Workshop.

**Group of Noble Dames, A** Ten short stories by **Thomas Hardy**, first published in various periodicals in 1889 and 1890, and collectively in 1891.

Set in various Wessex mansions and castles, the tales derive from Dorset history and over half arise from Hardy's close reading of John Hutchins's *History and Antiquities of the County of Dorset* (1861–73), in his library at Max Gate. They deal with such themes as 'the poor man and the lady', confusion (intentional or unintentional) of identity and sexual temptation; characteristic Hardyean devices of secrecy, deception, death from a broken heart, melodrama and irony are used. There were many changes effected from serial to book and much rewriting, bowdlerization, deletion and amplification were deemed necessary.

**Group Theatre, The** A New York theatrical organization, founded in 1931 by a group formally associated with the Theatre Guild, including Lee Strasberg, Harold Clurman and Cheryl Crawford. In rebellion against the apolitical nature of the Guild's productions, the founders were committed to the stage as a forum for the open discussion of political and social issues. **Paul Green**'s *The House of Connelly* (1931) was their first production. The Group helped to launch the careers of the playwrights **Clifford Odets** and **Marc Blitzstein**, and during its nine-year career produced some of the most enduring plays of the decade, including **Sidney Kingsley**'s *Men in White* (1933), Paul Green and Kurt Weill's *Johnny Johnson* (1936), Irwin Shaw's *The Gentle People* (1939), **William Saroyan**'s *My Heart's in the Highlands* (1939) and many plays by Clifford Odets, among them *Awake and Sing!* (1935), *Waiting for Lefty* (1935), *Golden Boy* (1937), *Rocket to the Moon* (1938) and *Night Music* (1940). The Group ceased production in 1940.

**Grove, Frederick Philip** 1871–1948 Canadian novelist and essayist. Born in Russia, the son of a wealthy family, Grove spent his youth travelling Europe with his mother and attempting various careers in a dilettante fashion. While touring Canada he heard of his father's death and bankruptcy and thereafter spent many years working as an itinerant farm hand in the West. At 42 he became a teacher in Manitoba and worked at his writing, but the first book to be accepted, *Over Prairie Trails*, did not appear until 1922. It was followed by *The Turn of the Year* (1923) and *Settlers of the Marsh* (1925), a powerful and penetrating novel, condemned at the time as obscene. Persevering in spite of considerable hardship, Grove published *A Search for America*, a book he had been working at for many years, in 1927. His later works were *Our Daily Bread* (1928), *It Needs to be Said* (1929, a volume of essays), *The Yoke of Life* (1930), *Fruits of the Earth* (1933), *Two Generations* (1939), *The Master of the Mill* (1944) and *Consider Her Ways* (1946). *In Search of Myself* (1946) is an autobiography. Regarded as Canada's first accomplished exponent of realistic fiction, Grove left 'Felix Powell's Career' and 'The Seasons', which he thought his best work, unfinished at his death.

**Grub Street** A term used to denote the category of busy hack writers and impoverished scribblers, journalists and word-peckers on the fringes of the professional literary industry, derived from an actual street in Moorfields which no longer exists. It is particularly applied to certain categories of minor Renaissance and Augustan literature – almanacs, verses, pamphlets, broadsides – of indifferent literary quality. There is a definitive study of this subculture in *Grub Street* (1972) by Pat Rogers. See also **Gissing, George**.

**Grundy, Sydney** 1848–1914 Playwright. He was born and educated in Manchester, where he was working as a barrister when his first play, *A Little Change* (1872), was staged. Grundy's normal practice was to adapt, and if necessary clean up, French plays. The bowdlerized and reshaped versions of Alexandre Dumas, *père* – *A Marriage of Convenience* (1897), *The Silver Key* (1897), *The Musketeers* (1898), *The Black Tulip* (1899) – are typical, as is his best-known work, *A Pair of Spectacles* (1890), an adaptation from *Les Petits Oiseaux* by Labiche and Delacour. An outspoken opponent of the 'demoralizing' Ibsen, Grundy nevertheless provided Lillie Langtry with a *succès de scandale* in *The Degenerates* (1899), and enjoyed playing with fire in *A Fool's Paradise* (1889), a response to the Maybrick trial, and *Slaves of the Ring* (1894), in which he brushed with the adulterous passion of Tristan and Isolde. In the year of his death he published an outrageously reactionary booklet, *The Play of the Future: by a Playwright of the Past*.

***Gryll Grange*** **Thomas Love Peacock**'s last novel, published in 1860–1. The setting is a house party held at the edge of the New Forest. The host, Mr Gryll, personifies the England of the immediate rosy past, as it exists in the minds of those who dislike the present. Taking part in the conversations which make up much of the book are: Dr Opimian, an amiable clergyman, comfortable and erudite; Mr Falconer, a Romantic, though he has no delusions about reforming mankind; and Miss Ilex, an old maid of real charm.

***Guardian, The*** Daily single-folio half-sheet of essays and letters, edited mainly by **Richard Steele**, in March–October 1713.

*The Guardian* was founded by Steele and edited by him throughout its short run, except for the month of July when **Joseph Addison** took over while Steele successfully contested the parliamentary seat at Stockbridge, Hants. The authorship of the 175 numbers has still not been satisfactorily established (see edition by J. C. Stephens, 1982): the major contributors were Addison and Steele; **Tickell** produced a series of papers on pastoral poetry which constitute the most important statement of the rationalist approach to this genre; **Pope** contributed at least eight issues, the most famous (No. 40) being an ironic paean on the pastorals of **Ambrose Philips**. Other contributors include **Berkeley**, Eustace Budgell, **Gay**, Hughes and Philips. Initially

*The Guardian* appears to have been designed to follow the supposed adventures of Nestor Ironside and his acquaintance in a way such as to appeal to the female readership. Like *The Tatler*, but unlike *The Spectator*, *The Guardian* was also intended to include items of news. At first Steele proclaimed the paper's political impartiality, but this, and the Ironside element, soon evaporated, and by April he was openly attacking the Tory *Examiner*; a measure of political neutrality returned during Addison's brief control. *The Guardian* was brought to an unexpectedly sudden conclusion on 1 October 1713, and five days later Steele issued the first number of *The Englishman*.

**Gude and Godlie Ballatis** This was a collection of Protestant hymns compiled and partly composed by the brothers James, John and Robert Wedderburn. The earliest surviving copy is 1567, but there must have been earlier editions. Many of the hymns are sacred versions of popular ballads and some are anti-Catholic in sentiment.

**Guest, Lady Charlotte** See **Celtic revival, the** and *Mabinogion, The*.

**Guest, Edwin** 1800–80 Historian and philologist. Born at King's Norton in Worcestershire and educated at Gonville and Caius College, Cambridge, Guest became a fellow of the college in 1824 and Master in 1852, a position he held until his death. With **Thomas Arnold, A. P. Stanley** and **Connop Thirlwall**, he was a founder of the Philological Society in 1842. Guest wrote *A History of English Rhythms* (1838) and various papers on philology and Romano-British history.

**Guilpin, Everard** *fl.* 1595–1600 Satirist. Little is known of Guilpin, save that he was educated at Emmanuel College, Cambridge, and Gray's Inn. His *Skialetheia* (1598), a collection of epigrams, displays intimate knowledge of contemporary theatre.

**Gull's Hornbook, The** **Thomas Dekker**'s pamphlet was first printed in 1609. In its preface it acknowledges a debt to Dedekind's *Grobianus*, which was translated as *The School of Slovenry* (1605), but Dedekind's work is simply Dekker's starting-point. Dekker's work parodies **courtesy books** and gives satiric instructions to gallants on how to behave in taverns and playhouses.

**Gulliver's Travels** (*Travels into Several Remote Nations of the World, in Four Parts, by Lemuel Gulliver . . .*) A prose satire by **Jonathan Swift** first published, anonymously, in 1726, and subsequently one of the most reprinted books in the English language.

Swift probably began work on this book in 1721, and its original conception seems to have been as part of the *Memoirs of Martinus Scriblerus*. It is divided into four books, but the third was written last of all. Books I and II are the best known, but usually in an abridged form, since there is a degree of physical coarseness in the original, which has become misleadingly notorious.

In Book I, Lemuel Gulliver (the narrator) is a ship's surgeon who is shipwrecked on the island of Lilliput, where he is taken prisoner by the population, who are only six inches tall, the rest of their country being in proportion accordingly. The Emperor and his diminutive court

Gulliver waiting to be hauled up to the flying island of Laputa. An illustration from the edition of 1731. *Gulliver's Travels* was first published in 1726.

offer a physical counterpart to the small-minded attitudes shown as underlying human behaviour, for they are suspicious, deceitful and petty. There are several specific satires on contemporary topics such as religious disputes (which end an egg should be opened) and in-fighting at court (rope-dancing).

In Book II, Gulliver's next voyage sees him stranded in Brobdingnag, a kingdom where the gigantic inhabitants are twelve times taller than himself. The Englishman's own attitudes and pomposity are exposed when, after a series of undignified adventures, he is interviewed by the King about European civilization. The swaggering description by Gulliver of the marvels of gunpowder and the splendours of the judicial system, to his surprise, fill the monarch with horror and he ends the audience with this verdict: 'I cannot but conclude the Bulk of your Natives, to be the most pernicious Race of little odious Vermin that Nature ever suffered to crawl upon the surface of the Earth.'

Book III is less unified, and has always held least appeal. Gulliver visits Laputa, a flying island where the nobles quite literally have their heads in the clouds. So immersed are they in impractical theories of knowledge that nothing works properly. He visits nearby Lagado and in particular the Academy there (a satire on the Royal Society), which is full of 'projectors' working on outlandish scientific schemes (breeding sheep with no wool, extracting sunbeams from cucumbers), several of which projects had real counterparts in Swift's age. Gulliver visits Glubbdubrib, the Island of Sorcerers, where famous historical figures are summoned from the past, to his disillusionment. He also meets the terrifying race of immortals, the Struldbruggs, whose fate is to become increasingly decrepit and despised.

The fourth part is perhaps the most intellectual in concept, describing his visit to the country of the Houyhnhnms, a race of coldly rational horse-like creatures who govern their nature dispassionately, and keep in subservience a race of filthy brutes called Yahoos, to whom Gulliver distastefully finds himself bearing resemblance. This part of the book aims to counterpart the two extremes in human potential, the bestial physicality and the remotely rational; it has been taken as evidence of Swift's supposed misanthropy, but is less pessimistic than that. Gulliver returns home thoroughly imbalanced in outlook, and passes most of his time in the stable, preferring the intellectual company of his horse to that of his human family.

From the earliest days of its popularity, Gulliver's Travels has fooled readers into agreeing with attitudes it satirizes: one contemporary reader declared he didn't believe a word of it. It is a seriously reductive work, a satire on pride and folly; Gulliver himself is a human ambassador, gullible, snobbish and servile, and his opinions are often ridiculous, yet common. The book is also lastingly funny, the hero's antics arising entertainingly from the bizarre proportions of his various surroundings: there is an element of the fantastic, as well as the satirical, and it is this which has maintained its appeal for children in many languages.

There is debate about whether the Travels counts as an early novel, or not. It is safest to label it a philosophical romance, largely because there is little structural unity, and no identification with a central character. Among other things it is also in part a parody of travel literature, then much in fashion with the work of **Dampier** and with **Defoe**'s *Robinson Crusoe*.

**Gunn, Mrs Aeneas** 1870–1961 Australian novelist. Born Jeanie Taylor, she was educated at the University of Melbourne and conducted a private school with her sister until her marriage in 1901. She accompanied her husband to the Northern Territory where he was manager of Elsey cattle station until his death in 1903. Out of her brief exposure to the outback Mrs Gunn created *The Little Black Princess* (1905) and *We of the Never Never* (1908). Presenting an idealized picture of Aboriginal life and of relations between the white farmers and the native population, the two books attained widespread popularity both at home and abroad.

**Gunn, Neil M[iller]** 1891–1973 Scottish novelist. He was born in Dunbeath, Caithness, the setting of some of his best-known novels, *Morning Tide*, *Highland River* and *The Silver Darlings*. He passed by examination into the Civil Service, returned to Scotland in 1909 and entered the Customs and Excise service in 1911, working for various distilleries and publishing *Whisky and Scotland* in 1935. With the critical success of *Highland River* (1937) he became a full-time writer, interspersing his early novels with generally less successful plays. *Morning Tide* (1930) was his first financially successful book, and the first of his sensitive and symbolic accounts of a boy's growing up in the Highlands, the centre of many of the novels. He also attempted historical fiction. *Sun Circle* (1933) deals with the Viking invasion of Scotland, *Butcher's Broom* (1934) with the Highland Clearances in Sutherland, and *The Silver Darlings* (1941), widely considered his best novel, with the aftermath of the Clearances. During World War II, spurred on by the complaint of his friend **Naomi Mitchison** that the pastoral idyll of *Young Art and Old Hector* (1942) was an insufficient response to the dangers of fascism, he wrote *The Green Isle of the Great Deep* (1944), in which Art and Hector find their way to a dystopian world. The case against totalitarian rule and police states was repeated in later books. A friend of **Hugh MacDiarmid**, Gunn was also a socialist and involved in the politics of nationalism: although not himself a Gaelic speaker, he was concerned at the decline of Gaelic speech and culture. His later fiction culminates in the 'wise humour' of a more 'metaphysical' vision of existence in *The Well at the World's End* (1951). He produced essays, short stories, travel writings and *The Atom of Delight* (1956), his autobiography.

**Gunn, Thom[son] (William)** 1929– Poet. Born in Gravesend, he attended University College School, London, and, after national service, read English at Trinity College, Cambridge. The tight verse forms and anti-Romanticism of his first collection, *Fighting Terms* (1954), bracketed Gunn as a **Movement** poet, though he lacked that group's reductive irony. In 1954 Gunn moved to the USA, where he held a creative writing fellowship at Stanford University and came under the influence of **Yvor Winters**. He has lived in the USA ever since. His second collection, *The Sense of Movement* (1957), is dominated by a Sartrean existentialism, and by an intriguing tension between the traditional form and the contemporary subject matter. *My Sad Captains* (1961) marks the start of his experiments with syllabics, and contains a tenderness missing in the earlier work; action is replaced by contemplation. Many critics have seen a falling-off in his more recent volumes: *Touch* (1967), *Moly* (1971), which, with its poems coming out of experiences of LSD, and its imagery of merging and metamorphosis, is a product of late-1960s hope, and *Jack Straw's Castle* (1976). Yet Gunn refuses to stand still and has developed unpredictably, experimenting with free verse. After *Selected Poems 1950-1975* (1979), his most recent volume has been *The Passages of Joy* (1982), in which he is open about his homosexuality; relaxed and anecdotal, it is his best collection for years. He has also published *The Occasions of Poetry: Essays in Criticism and Autobiography* (1982). That his poetic roots are in the 16th and 17th centuries is shown by his editions of the work of **Fulke Greville** (1968) and **Ben Jonson** (1974). Although he is widely taught in schools – because of the joint *Selected Poems* (1962) with **Ted Hughes**, with whom he shares only the most superficial similarities – he is not regarded with the same enthusiasm that greeted his work in the 1950s; he remains, though, one of the finest of post-war poets.

**Gurney, Ivor (Bertie)** 1890–1937 Poet and composer. Born in Gloucester, he attended the Royal College of Music from 1911, and served in the Gloucester Regiment on the western front as a private from 1915. After being gassed and wounded at Passchendaele in September 1917,

he was sent to Bangor War Hospital, Edinburgh. He published two volumes of poetry, *Severn and Somme* (1917) and *War's Embers* (1919). The war damaged an already unstable mental condition, and he was committed in 1922. From December of that year until his death he stayed at the City of London Mental Hospital, Kent, where he continued to write and compose.

All his papers were preserved by Marion Scott. When preparing some texts for an issue of *Music and Letters* devoted to Gurney in 1938, Gerald Finzi wrote that 70 out of every 100 poems showed 'no sign of mental disturbance'. The first edition of the poems was by **Edmund Blunden**, whose selection of the post-war work appeared in 1954. A second by Leonard Clark in 1973 was followed by the *Collected Poems* edited by **P. J. Kavanagh** (1982) – yet this, too, was a selection because Gurney often wrote several poems on one theme or idea, rather than drafts of a developing single poem. The poems in the two early volumes are either reflections on the Gloucestershire countryside (such as the song 'Only the Wanderer') or local incidents in the trenches. His best war poems, such as 'The Silent One', were written later and are modest and unrhetorical. The poems written in mental hospital are uneven, apparently lacking in control but often recovering vision and language to illuminate something anew. Gurney was impressed by the poetry and prose of **Edward Thomas**, and set six of the poems to music in the sequence *Lights Out* (1918–25). He also composed two cycles on poems by **A. E. Housman**, *Ludlow and Teme* and *The Western Playland* (both 1919).

**Gustafson, Ralph** 1909– Canadian poet. Born in Lime Ridge, Quebec, he was educated at Bishop's University, Lennoxville, and Oxford University. After a brief period teaching school in Canada, he lived in England, where his first volumes of verse were published, from 1934 to 1938. He then settled in New York, working for the British Information Services between 1942 and 1946. He returned to Canada in 1960 and was Poet-in-Residence and Professor of English at Bishop's University. For many years he was a music critic for the Canadian Broadcasting Corporation and his poetry is characterized by an attempt to achieve the condition of music. Gustafson is one of the most prolific and accomplished Canadian poets of his generation. His career falls into several distinct phases. The conventional romantic verse of his English years yielded to the new sardonic style he found in New York, apparent in *Flight into Darkness* (1944). With his return to Canada, his poetic style changed again and his more recent work, especially that which deals with his experiences as a traveller, is frequently confessional. It includes *Rivers among Rocks* (1960), *Rocky Mountain Poems* (1960), *Sift in an Hourglass* (1966), *Ixion's Wheel* (1969), *Corners in the Glass* (1977), *Soviet Poems* (1978) and *Conflicts of Spring* (1981). *The Moment is All* (1983) is a selection of his verse from 1944 to 1983. Gustafson has also edited several anthologies including *The Penguin Book of Canadian Verse* (1958).

**Guthlac, St** Two versions of Guthlac's life exist in Old English verse, known as *Guthlac A* and *Guthlac B*. The first was probably written during his lifetime or shortly after his death, while the second is based on the Latin *Vita Guthlaci* by Felix of Crowland. Both describe the life of the saint who became a monk and then a hermit (in 699) living a life of severe asceticism in the Lincolnshire Fens. He died in 714 or 715 and Crowland Abbey was later built on the site of his burial.

**Guy Livingstone** A novel by **George Alfred Lawrence**, published in 1857. Guy is the true patrician hero, with the virtues and failings of his class: pride, courage, sportsmanship and readiness to fight. He starts by protecting a weaker boy (the narrator) at school, rescues him from police custody after an Oxford rag with a well-aimed blow, and defeats a professional boxer. In the hunting field none can match him. Guy becomes engaged to a gentle girl called Constance but his engagement is broken because of the machinations of heartless Flora. Guy and Constance are reconciled only on her deathbed. Eventually a fall on the hunting field cripples Guy and he dies. The author describes

St Guthlac travelling to Crowland in a fishing boat. From the 12th-century *Guthlac Roll*, now in the British Library.

aristocratic violence with bloodthirsty gusto, and his moral stance is ambiguous.

**Guy Mannering** A novel by **Sir Walter Scott**, published in 1815.

The action takes place in the 18th century. The title notwithstanding, it is the story of Harry Bertram, heir to Ellangowan, kidnapped as a child at the instigation of the lawyer Glossin, who hopes to gain the estate himself. Bertram grows up with the name of Brown, serves with the army in India, earns the good opinion of his colonel, Guy Mannering, and falls in love with the colonel's daughter Julia. A misunderstanding leads Mannering to believe that Harry is paying attentions to his wife. A duel follows and Harry is left for dead, but he recovers and returns to England. Finding that Julia is in Dumfries, in the neighbourhood of Ellangowan, he makes his way there.

On his journey he helps the Lowland farmer Dandy Dinmont beat off a gang of thieves, and on arrival at Ellangowan (now in the hands of Glossin) he is recognized by Meg Merrilies, a gypsy woman devoted to the Bertrams. Glossin is determined to have Bertram murdered before he can discover his true parentage. The plot is frustrated by Meg, with the help of Dandy, and Glossin meets his death at the hands of his henchman, Hatteraick. The novel ends happily, with Bertram regaining his inheritance and Guy Mannering's good opinion, thus leaving the way clear for his marriage to Julia.

**Guy of Warwick** An early-14th-century Middle English **verse romance**, ultimately derived from an Anglo-Norman romance composed *c.* 1232–42. There are several versions of the Middle English poem, the majority written in rhyming couplets; the complete romance runs to around 12,000 lines. In plot and style it resembles *Bevis of Hampton*.

The poem tells of Guy, spurned by his beloved Felice because of his low status. He fights in tournaments abroad and then undertakes various adventures for seven years. He returns to England and marries Felice, but after 50 days leaves England and his pregnant wife on a pilgrimage to atone for his earlier life as a warrior. After many adventures he returns incognito to live as a hermit, only revealing himself to Felice shortly before his death; she dies soon afterwards. The story also describes the adventures of Guy's son Reinbrun, stolen by pirates at the age of seven, and the steward who searches for him. The poem is over-long and packed with spurious incident, but it enjoyed popularity for several centuries, first in its original form and later in adaptations.

# H

**H.D.** Pseudonym of **Hilda Doolittle**.

**Habington, William** 1605–54 Poet. Habington was the son of a Roman Catholic gentleman of Worcester who suffered imprisonment for his involvement in the Gunpowder Plot. He published *Castara*, a book of verse celebrating his marriage to Lucy Herbert, anonymously in 1634. An edition of 1635 added elegies on the death of a friend, while a third (1640), in which Habington is identified as the author, included religious verse as well. Habington also wrote, with his father, Thomas, *The History of Edward the Fourth* (1640), *Observations upon History* (1641) and a play, *The Queen of Arragon* (1640).

**Haggard, Sir Henry Rider** 1856–1925 Romance writer, agricultural reformer and servant of the Empire. He was the eighth of the 10 children of William Haggard, a Norfolk squire, and his wife, Ella, herself an amateur author. Haggard was educated, not at a public school like his brothers, but at a London day-school, privately, and at Ipswich Grammar School, since he was seen by his father as the family dunce. Because he failed the army entrance examination, he joined the colonial service as personal aide to Sir Henry Bulwer, the designated Lieutenant-Governor of Natal. His two periods of residence in South Africa (1875–9 and 1880–1) were the formative years of his life. He took part in Theophilus Shepstone's annexation of the Transvaal (1877) and for the rest of his life remained convinced of the British obligation to imperial responsibility – a view he shared with his close friend, **Rudyard Kipling**.

In 1881 he began to read law; he was called to the Bar in 1885. But the runaway success of *King Solomon's Mines* (1885), *Allan Quatermain* (1887) and *She: A History of Adventure* (1887) meant that instead he became an established member of the literary scene of the 1880s, as a co-founder (with **Robert Louis Stevenson**) of a new 'school of romance' which was seen by the literary journals of the period as a healthy antidote to both analytic and naturalist fiction. Haggard's romances develop a private myth of the heroic. His fascination with the Zulu culture can be seen in his portraits of Umbopa in *King Solomon's Mines* and Umslopogaas in *Allan*

*Quatermain* and *Nada the Lily* (1892), as well as in his distinguished Zulu trilogy, *Marie* (1912), *Child of Storm* (1913) and *Finished* (1917). His versions of the 'primitive' are complex, by no means simply paternalist or racist, and his novels draw upon a considerable knowledge of history, tradition and mythographic theory, probably encouraged by his friendship with **Andrew Lang**, with whom he collaborated in the writing of *The World's Desire* (1890). Apart from his African romances, his best works are *Eric Brighteyes* (1891), a re-creation of the spirit of the Icelandic sagas, and *Montezuma's Daughter* (1893), a version of Cortes's conquest of Mexico which, in its sympathy for a martyred culture and its hostility to colonialism, anticipates **Conrad**'s *Heart of Darkness*.

Haggard's marriage in 1880 to Louise Margitson, heiress to the estate of Ditchingham House, Norfolk, led to his expertise in farming – an interest which produced *A Farmer's Year* (1899) and, more importantly, *Rural England* (1902). This vast survey of agricultural decline brought him into professional contact with **Thomas Hardy**. Haggard served on many Royal Commissions, and it was for his public service that he was knighted in 1912. His autobiography, *The Days of My Life*, was published posthumously in 1926.

**Hail and Farewell** An autobiographical trilogy by **George Moore** (*Ave* 1911, *Salve* 1912, *Vale* 1914), which offers a subjective but interesting account of the Irish literary circle whose leading personalities were **W. B. Yeats** and **Lady Gregory**, and whose collective achievement was the establishment of the Irish literary theatre (see **Abbey Theatre**).

**Hakluyt, Richard** ?1552–1616 Historian and travel-writer. He was educated at Westminster School and Christ Church, Oxford. He was ordained some time before 1580 and held various ecclesiastical posts, including the chaplaincy to the English ambassador in Paris and the arch-deaconry of Westminster, to which he was appointed in 1603. His interest in travel was aroused when, as a boy, he visited the Middle Temple and his imagination was stirred by being shown 'certain books of cosmography with an universal map'. He decided to dedicate himself to collecting, publishing and translating accounts of voyages. He was acquainted with sea-captains like **Sir Humphrey Gilbert** and Martin Frobisher, corresponded with the map-makers Ortelius and Mercator, and gave information to the newly founded East India Company. He also gave public lectures on exploration and is regarded as the first professor of modern geography at Oxford. His activities and campaigns for voyages of discovery gained the interest and approval of some of Elizabeth's most influential advisers: Lord Burghley, Sir Francis Walsingham and Sir Robert Cecil. His views on the foundation of a plantation in America are set out in a preface to **John Florio**'s translation of an account of the voyage of Jacques Cartier.

In publishing and collecting voyages Hakluyt deserved **Michael Drayton**'s epithet 'industrious'. *Divers Voyages Touching the Discovery of America* was published in 1582 and a translation from the French, *A Notable History Concerning Four Voyages Made by Certain French Captains into Florida*, in 1587. In support of **Raleigh**'s plan for colonizing Virginia he wrote *A Discourse Concerning the Western Planting* in 1584, although this was not printed until 1831. His major work, *The Principal Navigations, Voyages and Discoveries of the English Nation* (1589), was enlarged and published in three volumes in 1598–1600. After his death **Samuel Purchas** continued his work with the aid of Hakluyt's manuscripts. As well as containing information that was useful to his contemporaries, Hakluyt's *Voyages* are full of adventurous stories: Cabot's discovery of Hudson Bay, Drake's raid on Cadiz and the last fight of the *Revenge* under Sir Richard Grenville.

**Haldane, J[ohn] B[urdon] S[anderson]** 1892–1964 Geneticist and popularizer of science. The nephew of **Richard Burdon Haldane**, he was born in Oxford and educated at Eton and New College, Oxford. During service in World War I he studied the effects of gas warfare and was involved in designing a more effective gas mask. In 1919 he became a fellow of New College and taught physiology. Two years later he was appointed Reader in Biochemistry at Cambridge, and in 1933 he became Professor of Genetics at University College, London (later Professor of Biometry, 1937–57).

During the Spanish Civil War Haldane joined the Communist Party, and became chairman of the editorial board of *The Daily Worker* from 1940 to 1949. In 1957 he emigrated to India, where he established a genetics and biometry laboratory, and became a naturalized citizen in 1960.

Haldane's scientific works include *Enzymes* (1930) and *The Causes of Evolution* (1932), but it was as a popularizer of science that he became more widely known. His imaginative speculations about the future (see *Possible Worlds*, 1927) provided many of the scientific ideas to be found in the works of **Aldous Huxley** (see *Brave New World*). *The Marxist Philosophy and the Sciences* (1938) was one of several works which emphasized the social and political context of science; others include *Science and Everyday Life* (1939) and *Everything has a History* (1951). Haldane was also the author of a collection of children's stories, *My Friend Mr Leakey* (1937).

**Haldane, Richard Burdon, 1st Viscount** 1856–1928 Lawyer, politician and philosopher. Richard Haldane was born in Edinburgh and educated at the universities of Edinburgh and Göttingen. He became a Queen's Counsel in 1890 and was a Liberal MP from 1885 to 1911. An associate of **Sidney** and **Beatrice Webb**, he helped found the London School of Economics in 1895.

In 1905–12 Haldane was Secretary of State for War, during which time he formed what was to become the Territorial Army (1907), and in 1912 he became Lord Chancellor. He was dismissed from office two years later for allegedly pro-German views. By the end of World War I he had joined the Labour Party, and was again appointed Lord Chancellor by Ramsay MacDonald in 1924.

Haldane was also a philosopher. His many works include *The Pathway to Reality* (1903), *The Reign of Relativity* (1921), *The Philosophy of Humanism* (1922) and *Human Experience* (1923). He was also responsible for a translation of Schopenhauer's *The World as Will and Idea* (1883–6).

**Hale, Sir Matthew** 1609–76 Judicial writer. Educated at Magdalen Hall, Oxford, Hale became a judge in the Court of Common Pleas (1654), Baron of the Exchequer (1660) and Chief Justice of the King's Bench (1671). As a writer on law Hale is best known for his *History of the Common Law in England* (1713), published, like most of his work, after his death. He was the subject of a biography by **Gilbert Burnet**.

**Hale, Sarah** 1788–1879 A noted New England humanitarian. Hale edited *The Ladies' Magazine* from 1828 to 1837, and *Godey's Lady's Book* for the next 40 years. Her novel *Northwood: A Tale of New England* (1827) is a didactic condemnation of slavery. Her short stories were collected in *Sketches of American Character* (1829). The later part of her career was dedicated to compiling her massive *Women's Record* (1853; expanded 1855 and 1870), an encyclopaedic work that details the achievements of over 1500 distinguished women. By no means a radical feminist, Hale upheld a traditional view of women as bearers of spiritual and moral virtue. She was, however, a forceful advocate of education for women, as well as for child welfare and the abolition of slavery.

**Hales, John** 1584–1656 Scholar and divine. Fellow of Merton College, Oxford, Regius Professor of Greek, Canon of Windsor and fellow of Eton, Hales was, according to **Clarendon**, 'one of the greatest scholars in Europe'. In religion, he contended that guidance of Scripture was the rightful way for each individual, and he opposed both the coercion of Rome and the extremism of Calvinism. His sermons and tracts were collected by **John Pearson** and published as *Golden Remains* (1659).

**Haliburton, Thomas Chandler** 1796–1865 Canadian satirist and humorist. Born and educated in Windsor, Nova Scotia, he was called to the Bar in 1820 and eventually became a judge of the supreme court of the province. In 1829 he published *A Historical and Statistical Account of Nova Scotia* (the source of **Longfellow**'s *Evangeline*), and was persuaded by the publisher Joseph Howe to contribute to the latter's paper, *The Novascotian*, in 1835. Haliburton's contributions took the form of the 'Sam Slick' papers – observations by a shrewd itinerant clockmaker on life on the Eastern shore of America. The sketches were collected and published as *The Clockmaker, or, the Sayings and Doings of Samuel Slick* (1837) Further series followed, including *The Attaché, or, Sam Slick in England* (1843–4), which was, in effect, a reply to **Dickens**'s *American Notes*. Among other titles by Haliburton are *The Letter Bag of the Great Western, or, Life in a Steamer* (1840) and *The Old Judge, or, Life in a Colony* (1849).

Haliburton retired to England in 1856, where he held the parliamentary seat for Launceston for six years. **Artemus Ward**, the American humorist, declared that the American homespun philosophy and frontier humour practised by Ward himself, **Mark Twain** and **Josh Billings** stemmed directly from Haliburton.

**Hall, Anna Maria** 1800–81 Irish novelist. Born Anna Maria Fielding in Dublin, she lived in England from the age of 15, marrying **Samuel Carter Hall** in 1824. Her most successful works were delicate and humorous portraits of Irish life, among them *Sketches of Irish Character* (1829), *Lights and Shadows of Irish Life* (1838), *Marian* (1839) and *The White Boy* (1845). She also edited magazines and annuals, including *Finden's Tableaux* and *The Juvenile Forget-Me-Not*.

**Hall, Edward** ?1498–1547 A lawyer and historian, Hall went to school at Eton, graduated BA from King's College, Cambridge, in 1518 and then proceeded to Gray's Inn. He was a staunch supporter of Henry VIII and the Tudor dynasty. *The Union of the Two Noble and Illustre Families of Lancaster and York* (the first edition of 1542 is very rare, second edition 1548) traces a providential pattern in English history, beginning with the accession of Henry IV and ending, in Grafton's edition and continuation from Hall's notes (1550), with the death of Henry VIII. The work was prohibited in the reign of Queen Mary. It was a source for later historians, especially **Raphael Holinshed**, and dramatists. Because Holinshed drew on Hall it is at times difficult to be certain which **Shakespeare** is using in his history plays, but Hall seems to have contributed directly at least details to the *Henry VI* and *Henry IV* plays, *Henry V*, *Richard II* and *Richard III*.

**Hall, John** 1627–56 Essayist, poet and translator. A member of the group of friends that included **Thomas Stanley** and William Hammond, John Hall earned praise from **Robert Herrick**, **Henry More** and **Thomas Hobbes** in the course of his short career. His work included a book of lively essays, *Horae Vacivae* (1646), *Poems* (1647) and the first English translation of Longinus. *An Humble Motion to the Parliament of England Concerning the Advancement of Learning: and Reformation of the Universities* was written when he was 22.

**Hall, Joseph** 1574–1656 Satirist and divine. Born at Ashby de la Zouch and educated at Emmanuel College, Cambridge, Hall took holy orders and was appointed chaplain to Prince Henry (1608); as Dean of Worcester he was one of King James's representatives at the Synod of Dort. He became Bishop of Exeter (1627) and of Norwich (1641). A friend of **John Donne** and **Sir Thomas Browne**, he was a versatile writer of verse satires, devotional literature, and 'characters'. His *Episcopacy by Divine Right, Asserted by J. H.* brought him into conflict with **Milton** (1641) and he was one of the 13 bishops imprisoned by Parliament in 1642. In 1647 he was evicted from his palace and retired to a small farm. He was the 'Remonstrant' of Milton's *Animadversions* (1641).

Hall was one of the first English writers to attempt concerted verse satires following classical models; they were published as *Virgidemiarum* (1597 and 1598). He also published a prose satire *Mundus Alter et Idem* (1605), *Characters of Virtues and Vices* (1608) and *Heaven upon Earth* (1606). His best-remembered devotional work is *Meditations and Vows* (1605). The *Mundus Alter et Idem* was translated into English by J. Healey (1609).

**Hall, (Marguerite) Radclyffe** 1886–1943 Novelist and poet. Born in Bournemouth, she was educated at King's College, London, and in Germany. She published four volumes of verse – *'Twixt Earth and Stars* (1906), *Poems of the Past and Present* (1910), *Songs of Three Countries* (1913) and *The Forgotten Island* (1915) – before producing the novels for which she is known. *The Forge* appeared in 1924, followed by *The Unlit Lamp* (1924) and *Adam's Breed* (1926), which won the Femina Vie Heureuse and Tait Black Memorial prizes. *The Well of Loneliness* (1928), a sympathetic study of lesbian experience, was the subject of a notorious obscenity trial and for some years the book was banned in England. It has since been frequently reprinted. Her later works include *The Master of the House* (1932), *The Sixth Beatitude* (1936) and a volume of short stories, *Miss Ogilvie Finds Herself* (1934).

**Hall, Samuel Carter** 1800–89 Journalist and art critic. Founder and editor of *The Art Journal*, author of *A Book of Memoirs of Great Men and Women* (1871) and co-author (with his wife **Anna Maria Hall**) of several volumes, including *Ireland: Its Scenery, Character etc.* (1841–3).

**Hall, Willis** 1929– Dramatist. Born and educated in Leeds, he began by writing plays for radio. His first stage success came with a military drama set in Malaysia, *The Long and the Short and the Tall* (1958). His adaptation of François Billetdoux's *Chin Chin* (1960) also had a long London run. He has collaborated with **Keith Waterhouse** in many works for stage, screen and television. Their plays together include an adaptation of Waterhouse's novel *Billy Liar* (1960), *Celebration* (1961), *All Things Bright and Beautiful* (1963) and a comedy of adulteries, *Say Who You Are* (1965), as well as adaptations of Eduardo de Filippo's *Saturday, Sunday, Monday* (1973) and *Filumena* (1973).

**Hallam, Arthur Henry** 1811–33 Poet and essayist. After Eton, he went to Trinity College, Cambridge, where he was elected to the **Apostles** and became the close friend of **Alfred Tennyson**. Hallam's sudden and untimely death in Vienna prompted Tennyson's *In Memoriam*. His *Remains in Verse and Prose* (1834) was edited by his father, **Henry Hallam**. His essay on Tennyson's early poems (*The Englishman's Magazine*, August 1831) proves him one of the poet's most discerning critics.

**Hallam, Henry** 1777–1859 Historian. Educated at Eton and Christ Church, Oxford, he obtained a sinecure appointment as Commissioner of Stamps and, on inheriting his father's estates in Lincolnshire, was able to devote himself to writing, first as a contributor to *The Edinburgh Review*. *A View of the State of Europe during the Middle Ages* (1818) took 10 years to complete and was notable for its pioneering use

of primary sources. It was followed by *The Constitutional History of England from the Accession of Henry VII to the Death of George II* (1827), and *An Introduction to the Literature of Europe in the 15th, 16th and 17th Centuries* (1837–9). He also edited the *Remains in Verse and Prose* (1834) of his son, **Arthur Henry Hallam**.

**Halleck, Fitz-Greene** 1790–1867 An American poet and member of the **Knickerbocker Group**, Halleck was born in Guilford, Connecticut. He worked first in banking and then as personal secretary to John Jacob Astor. He collaborated with Joseph Rodman Drake on the satirical 'Croaker' poems, published anonymously in 1819 in the New York *Evening Post* and collected as *The Croaker Papers* in 1860. His long poem *Fanny* (1819) satirized New York society in the manner of **Byron**. Travelling in Europe in the following year, he wrote 'Alnwick Castle', influenced again by Byron, and by **Scott**; *Alnwick Castle, with Other Poems* was published in 1827. Other notable poems include 'Red Jacket' (1827), 'The Field of Grounded Arms' (1831), and 'Young America' (1865). His collected *Poetical Works* were published in 1847.

**Halliwell (afterwards Halliwell-Phillipps), James Orchard** 1820–89 Shakespearean scholar. Born in Chelsea and educated at Cambridge, he was elected a Fellow of the Royal Society in 1839. Of his numerous works the most important are the *Life of Shakespeare* (1848), *New Boke about Shakespeare and Stratford-on-Avon* (1850), a *Dictionary of Old English Plays* (1860) and an edition of **Shakespeare** (1853–65).

**Halper, Albert** 1904–84 American novelist, born in Chicago into a poor family of Jewish immigrants. His first books were *Union Square* (1933); *On the Shore* (1934); *The Foundry* (1934), which deals with electrotype workers in Chicago just before the 1929 crash; and *The Chute* (1937), about workers in a mail-order house. *Sons of the Fathers* (1940) is the story of a Jewish immigrant. His subsequent work includes *The Little People* (1942, short stories), and the novels *Only an Inch from Glory* (1943), *The Golden Watch* (1953), and *Atlantic Avenue* (1956). *Goodbye, Union Square*, his memoir of the 1930s, appeared in 1970.

**hamartia** From the Greek, 'error'. In Aristotle's theory of **tragedy**, the mistake or failing which brings about the hero's downfall. 'Tragic flaw', the usual English translation, can mislead by its concentration on moral weakness – encouraging readers to view Hamlet's fate as a condemnation of his uncertainty, or Othello's as a condemnation of his jealousy – since hamartia can also be a matter of ignorance or mistaken judgement.

**Hamburger, Michael (Peter Leopold)** 1924–
Poet and translator. Born in Berlin of a German
family which emigrated to Edinburgh and then
London in 1933, Hamburger was educated at St
Paul's School and at Oxford. His first collection
of poems, *Flowering Cactus* (1950), was followed
by many others, including *Travelling* (1969) and
*Ownerless Earth: New and Selected Poems* (1973),
concerned, as their titles suggest, with a kind of
rootlessness. Hamburger draws on the European tradition as much as the English, and is also
a distinguished translator of Hofmannsthal
(1961), Grass (1966), Hölderlin (1966) and Paul
Celan (1980). His critical book *The Truth of
Poetry* (1969) is a useful introduction to the
themes of modern poetry from Baudelaire to the
1960s. His *Collected Poems* was published in
1984.

**Hamilton, Charles (Harold St John)** 1876–
1961 Author of popular boys' stories. Born in
London, the son of a journalist, he was probably
educated at small private schools rather than the
sort of major public school he later described in
his fiction. He had stories accepted by boys'
magazines and comics while still a schoolboy,
and in 1906 he created a fictional public school
called St Jim's for the boys' weekly *Pluck*.
School stories followed in *The Gem*, *The Magnet*
and other papers, with Hamilton producing
about 70,000 words a week under various
pseudonyms. As Frank Richards he created the
enduring characters Harry Wharton and Billy
Bunter of Greyfriars school for *The Magnet*. He
made a well-argued reply to **George Orwell**'s
criticism of such stories in the essay 'Boys'
Weeklies' (1939). A Billy Bunter revival after
World War II resulted in books about Bunter
and about Tom Merry, and kept him fully
occupied until his death. The more than 50
fictional schools he invented and the more than
72 million words he wrote make Hamilton the
most prolific author in the history of juvenile
fiction.

**Hamilton, Mary Agnes** 1884–1966 Novelist.
Born Mary Agnes Adamson, she was educated
at Newnham College, Cambridge, and in Germany; she later became Labour MP for Blackburn (1929–31) and a governor of the BBC
(1933–7). Her novels include *Less Than the Dust*
(1912), *Dead Yesterdays* (1916), *Special Providence*
(1930) and *Life Sentence* (1935). She also wrote
biographies of **Carlyle** (1926), **John Stuart Mill**
(1933) and **Sidney** and **Beatrice Webb** (1933).
Her autobiography, *Uphill All the Way*,
appeared in 1953.

**Hamilton, (Robert) Ian** 1938– Poet, critic
and editor. Born in King's Lynn, Norfolk, he
was educated at Darlington Grammar School
and Keble College, Oxford. He founded and
edited *The Review* (1962–72), which was succeeded by the glossy and controversial *New
Review* (1974–9). Though distinctive and influential, Hamilton's own poetic achievement is
limited to one major collection, *The Visit*
(1970), containing 33 dense, short poems, none
of them more than a page long, which are
simple in structure but mesmeric in what they
leave unsaid or merely suggested. He is better
known for his criticism, in *A Poetry Chronicle:
Essays and Reviews* (1963), *The Little Magazines:
A Study of Six Editors* (1976) and his sympathetic
and informative biography of **Robert Lowell**
(1982).

**Hamilton, Thomas** 1789–1842 Scottish
novelist and the younger brother of **Sir William
Hamilton**. He was author of a popular novel
*Cyril Thornton* (1827), a lively account of university and military life which went through
three editions in the writer's lifetime.

**Hamilton, Virginia (Esther)** 1936– American children's author. Born in Yellow Springs,
Ohio, the granddaughter of an escaped slave,
she is a leading black author for children, with a
constantly inventive, individual imagination
that defies neat classification. Her most famous
story, *M. C. Higgins the Great* (1974), concerns a
boy who lives on top of a high steel pole set
deep in the mountainside. Other novels include
a **science fiction** trilogy and *The Planet of Junior
Brown* (1971), a moving story of homeless children trying to survive in a big city.

**Hamilton, Sir William** 1788–1856 Scottish
philosopher. Born in Glasgow and educated at
Balliol College, Oxford, he studied law and
became an advocate in 1813. In 1816 he established his claim to the baronetcy of Hamilton of
Preston. His reputation as a philosopher was
secured by a series of contributions to *The
Edinburgh Review* (1829–36) and he was elected
Professor of Logic and Metaphysics at Edinburgh in 1836.
  Hamilton's collected articles were published
in *Discussions on Philosophy and Literature, Education and University Reform* (1852). *Lectures on
Metaphysics and Logic* appeared posthumously
(1859–60). He also prepared an edition of the
works of **Thomas Reid**, completed by H. L.
Mansel and published in 1846. Hamilton is
notable for his contribution to the study of
German philosophy, and for his influential theories concerning the association of ideas, unconscious mental modifications and the inverse
relation of perception and sensation. **J. S. Mill**
attacked him as a representative of the 'intui-
tional' school in his *Examination of Sir W. Hamilton's Philosophy* (1865).

*Hamlet, Prince of Denmark* A tragedy by **William Shakespeare**, first performed *c.* 1601. A bad, perhaps pirated, Quarto (Q1) was published in 1603. A second (Q2), published in 1604, has significant differences from the text of the First Folio of 1623. Both are used by modern editors. Various sources have been proposed, among them a lost play (*Ur-Hamlet*) on the same subject. We do not know whether Elizabethan audiences were familiar with the story before Shakespeare wrote his play.

The recent death of King Hamlet has brought his brother Claudius to the Danish throne. Claudius has also married the King's widow, Gertrude. Prince Hamlet, spectacularly mourning both his father's death and his mother's remarriage, undermines Claudius's attempts to sustain the morale of Denmark in the face of a threatened Norwegian invasion, led by the young and warlike Fortinbras. Told by his friend Horatio of the recent appearances on the battlements of his father's ghost, Hamlet decides to watch with him. The ghost appears and tells Hamlet that Claudius poisoned him. Hamlet swears vengeance. But the act is not a simple one, and the ghost not necessarily trustworthy. Hamlet's urge to verify Claudius's guilt combines with an equally strong need to confirm his mother's innocence.

The arrival of a company of actors at the Danish court provides him with an opportunity. He persuades them to revive an old play whose story offers a persuasive parallel to that of Claudius. Hamlet's eccentric behaviour is, by now, indistinguishable from madness. The court chamberlain, Polonius, is convinced that Hamlet is mad. How else is he to explain his treatment of Ophelia, Polonius's daughter? Claudius gives himself away at the performance of the play, and orders Hamlet to go to England, where he plans to have him killed. But Hamlet escapes his pursuers, confronts Gertrude in her chamber and stabs to death the eavesdropping Polonius, apparently on the assumption that it is Claudius, not Polonius, behind the arras.

Determined to avenge Polonius's death, his son Laertes returns to Denmark, where he finds Ophelia mad. News reaches Claudius that Hamlet is back in Denmark. He plots with Laertes a duel in which Hamlet's death will be assured by a poison-tipped sword. News of Ophelia's death by drowning strengthens Laertes's resolve. The duel takes place and culminates in the death of Gertrude, Laertes, Claudius and Hamlet. The play ends with Fortinbras of Norway, newly proclaimed King of Denmark, ordering a military funeral for Hamlet.

Because the figure of Hamlet has so fascinated successive generations, the play has provoked more discussion, more performances and more scholarship than any other in the whole history of world drama. It stands at the very centre of Shakespeare's dramatic career, on the one hand concluding a decade that had seen the composition of the mature comedies and English history plays, and on the other preceding the sequence of great tragedies. In no other play does Shakespeare subject to such detailed scrutiny the whole art of theatre itself. It is not an accident that the play-within-the-play holds a central position in the pattern of the drama; all the characters are affected by the compulsion to act a part. It is an aspect of the topsy-turvydom of Denmark under Claudius that real feeling should present itself as seeming. The histrionic temperament has never been so fully explored.

**Hammett, (Samuel) Dashiell** 1894–1961 American novelist, born in Maryland. He served in the US army during World War I and then went to work for the Pinkerton Agency in San Francisco as a private detective. His experiences served him well when he turned to writing **detective fiction** and published his first novel, *Red Harvest*, in 1929. He used an unadorned realistic style – later christened the 'hard-boiled style' – that suited his material perfectly. Hammett's heroes are not merely tough; they often confront violence with full knowledge of its inherently corrupting potential.

Hammett's other books include *The Dain Curse* (1929), *The Maltese Falcon* (1930), *The Glass Key* (1931) and *The Thin Man* (1934). He also published a number of short stories in the magazine *The Black Mask*, which were collected in *The Adventures of Sam Spade* (1944), *The Creeping Siamese and Other Stories* (1950) and *The Continental Op* (1974). His longtime companion, the playwright **Lillian Hellman**, contributed a memoir of him to her selection of his short stories called *The Big Knockover* (1966), which also includes his unfinished autobiographical novel, *Tulip*.

**Hammon, Jupiter** 1720–1800 A slave in a Long Island household, Hammon became the first published black poet in America when *An Evening Thought* appeared in 1760. He is also known for his essay *An Address to the Negroes of the State of New York* (1787), in which he insisted that his fellow slaves be patient, and urged owners to free slave children. His work helped generate support for the Abolitionist movement growing in the northern states at the time.

**Hammond, Henry** 1605–60 An Anglican clergyman who is sometimes called the father of English biblical criticism, Hammond published his *Paraphrase and Annotations on the New Testament* in 1653. He also published a number of theological works and sermons, which are highly regarded for their clarity and their quality of Christian tolerance (1649, 1657 and 1660). His *Twenty-Nine Sermons Preached on Several Occasions* was published posthumously (1664).

**Hampton, Christopher (James)** 1946– Dramatist. Born on Fayal in the Azores, he was educated at Lancing College and at New College, Oxford. His first play, *When Did You Last See My Mother?* (1966), was produced while he was still an undergraduate. From 1968 to 1970 he was resident dramatist at the **Royal Court Theatre**, where his finely balanced study of the relationship between Rimbaud and Verlaine, *Total Eclipse* (1968), was staged, together with his comedy of linguistic misunderstanding, *The Philanthropist* (1970). He has also sought to provide modern, actable versions of European Classics, including plays by Chekhov, Ibsen, Molière and the Austrian dramatist Horvath. Horvath's memory also inspired *Tales from Hollywood* (1983), set in the émigré community in California during the war. He can be a technically inventive writer, as he showed in *Savages* (1973), about a British diplomat captured by guerillas in South America. His most distinctive voice, however, comes through the cleverly crafted, amusing but thoughtful comedies, of which *Treats* (1976) is a good, and underrated, example.

**Hand of Ethelberta, The** A novel by **Thomas Hardy**, first published serially in *The Cornhill Magazine* from July 1875 to May 1876 (in volume form 1876). The author's only venture into social comedy, it is among the least read of his works.

Despite being the daughter of a butler, the heroine Ethelberta Chickerel has married the son and heir of Sir Ralph and Lady Petherwin; he, however, has died on his honeymoon and a needless quarrel with her mother-in-law has deprived Ethelberta of a handsome bequest. Determined to make her way, she gives readings and achieves recognition as a 'Professed Story-Teller'. Meanwhile, three suitors pay her court: the painter Eustace Lovell; Alfred Neigh, a rich young man; and the elderly, affluent Lord Mountclere, of dubious reputation. Ethelberta marries Mountclere over her family's protestations, while an earlier, faithful suitor, the organist Christopher Julian, secures the hand of her sister Picotee, who has loved him from the beginning of the story.

**Handful of Dust, A** A novel by **Evelyn Waugh**, published in 1934.

Containing many of the qualities typical of Waugh's satirical novels (mainly written during the 1930s), *A Handful of Dust* recounts the story of Tony Last, proud owner of an English country house, Hetton, 'entirely rebuilt in 1864 in the Gothic style'. Last's wife, Lady Brenda, is infatuated with a young socialite, John Beaver, and frustrated by her husband's old-fashioned ways. She deserts the family after her son, John Andrew, is killed in a hunting accident. Tony refuses to grant her a divorce, fearing the cost of alimony and the consequent loss of his beloved Hetton. He departs for an extended trip to Brazil and accompanies a casual acquaintance, Dr Messinger, up the Amazon. They run into trouble; Tony falls ill and Messinger is drowned. At the point of death Tony is rescued by a mad recluse, Mr Todd, who has lived in the jungle for nearly 60 years. Tony recovers but is forced by circumstances to remain in the jungle. Against his will he becomes Mr Todd's 'companion', and is induced to spend the rest of his life reading Dickens aloud to the old man every afternoon. Meanwhile, at home in England, Tony is reported dead and Brenda has remarried a politician, Jock Grant-Menzies, her relationship with Beaver having faded. Hetton passes into the hands of Tony's cousin, Richard Last.

An 'Alternative Ending' follows in which the author offers a happier version of events. Tony returns from his travels, Hetton having been entirely redecorated in his absence. He is met by a repentant Brenda, whose relationship with Jock has been aborted. Husband and wife retire in marital security to the family seat at Hetton.

**Handley Cross** A novel by **R. S. Surtees**, first published in book form in 1843; an expanded version, illustrated by **John Leech**, followed in 1854. It tells how the sporting grocer Mr John Jorrocks progresses from weekend hunting near London to the mastership of the Handley Cross foxhounds in (it would seem likely) Sussex. He recruits as huntsman the likeable and skilful, albeit drunken, James Pigg of Newcastle and makes a (pretty useless) whipper-in of his cockney servant Binjimin. He is assisted by Charlie Stubbs (Stobbs in the 1854 version) who is paying court to his gorgeous niece Belinda, although the appalling Mrs Jorrocks would rather she married the equally dreadful Captain Doleful. There are many hunting scenes described with Surtees's usual dash and authenticity, coupled with various ridiculous adventures; towards the end of the novel Jorrocks is certified insane but returns triumphant to the discomfiture of his wife and Doleful. A feature of the novel are Mr Jorrocks's public lectures on hunting, delivered in the broadest cockney but replete with technical knowledge and sound common sense.

**Handlynge Synne** A translation by **Robert Mannyng of Brunne** of the *Manuel des Pechiez* of William of Wadington. The work, in 12,000 lines of rhyming couplets, was written in the first decade of the 14th century while Mannyng was attached to the priory of Sempringham. It is a free translation, omitting or modifying much of Wadington's work and adding new material. The poem treats consecutively the Ten Commandments, the seven deadly sins, sacrilege, the seven sacraments, the twelve requisites of penance and the twelve graces of shrift. The account of each item is accompanied by a varying number of skilfully told **exempla** and anecdotes. It is these short tales, drawn from a wide variety of sources, which are the work's main attraction.

***Handy Andy***: *A Tale of Irish Life* A comic novel by **Samuel Lover**, published in 1842. It tells of Andy Rooney, the hopelessly inefficient servant of Squire Egan, and Egan's rivalry with Squire O'Grady. After a succession of humorous incidents, Andy proves to be the heir of Lord Scatterbrain.

**Hanley, James** 1901–85 Novelist, playwright and writer of short stories. Born in Dublin of a working-class family, he received an elementary education before going to sea at the age of 13. After 10 years as a seaman he earned a precarious living as a butcher, clerk, railwayman and postman, finally becoming a journalist. His first novel, *Drift*, appeared in 1930 as did *A Passion Before Death*. *The Last Voyage*, *Men in Darkness: Five Stories* and *Boy* all appeared in 1931 and established him as a novelist with a powerfully direct and painstaking style. *The Furys* (1935), *Secret Journey* (1936) and *Our Time is Gone* (1940) comprise a trilogy portraying the misery of life in the Dublin slums. Other titles include *Captain Bottell* (1933), *Quartermaster Clausen* (1934), *People are Curious* (1938, short stories), *Hollow Sea* (1938), *The Ocean* (1941), *A Walk in the Wilderness* (1950, short stories), *The Closed Harbour* (1952), *Another World* (1972), *A Woman in the Sky* (1973) and *A Kingdom* (1978). *Broken Water* (1937) is a volume of autobiography. Hanley's plays include *Say Nothing* (1962) and *The Inner Journey* (1965).

**Hannay, James** 1827–73 Novelist and journalist. Born at Dumfries, he served in the navy for five years before being dismissed for insubordination. He contributed to **Punch** and edited the Edinburgh *Evening Courant* in 1860–4. He published two novels of naval life, *Singleton Fontenoy* (1850) and *Eustace Conyers* (1855).

**Hannay, James Owen** See **Birmingham, George A.**

**Hanrahan, Barbara** 1939– Australian novelist and artist. Born and brought up in Adelaide, she lived in London for many years before returning to Adelaide. Hanrahan first achieved recognition as an artist and has had numerous solo exhibitions of her work, in Australia and Europe, since 1964. Her paintings are displayed in the National Gallery of Australia. Her first novel, the autobiographical *The Scent of Eucalyptus* (1973), is her best-known work. Set in her native Adelaide, it is a sensitive and evocative account of an adolescent girl's growth. Its sequel, the equally poetic *Kewpie Doll*, appeared in 1984. Since turning to fiction, Hanrahan has published nine novels in 12 years. Her second, *Sea-Green* (1974), is another highly personal work, in which the heroine leaves suburban Australia for London. It was followed by a group of novels set in the historical past of the 19th and early 20th centuries: *The Albatross Muff* (1977), *Where the Queens All Strayed* (1978), *The Peach Groves* (1979) and *The Frangipani Gardens* (1980). These novels frequently use grotesque elements and the perspective of a child with voyeuristic tendencies. Hanrahan's most recent novel, *Annie Magdalene* (1985), represents an attempt to redefine the parameters of biography by promoting a woman who would generally be regarded as having lived an unextraordinary domestic life to the status of heroine and insisting on her uniqueness.

**Hansberry, Lorraine** 1930–65 American playwright. Born in Chicago and educated at the University of Wisconsin, Hansberry was the first black woman to have a play produced on Broadway. Her best-known play, *A Raisin in the Sun* (1959), is a sympathetic examination of the economic, educational and racial concerns of a family of black Chicagoans who plan to move into a white neighbourhood. It was enormously successful, running for 530 consecutive performances, and winning a New York Drama Critics Circle Award. *The Sign in Sidney Brustein's Window* (1964) is the story of a group of Jews, other whites, and blacks in New York's Greenwich Village. In 1964, the year before her death, Hansberry wrote the captions for the photographs in *The Movement*, a documentary of the Civil Rights Movement. After her death her husband assembled *To Be Young, Gifted and Black* (1969) from her letters, diaries and other unpublished material. *Raisin*, a musical adaptation of her best-known work, was produced in 1973.

***Happy Days*** A play by **Samuel Beckett**, first performed in English in New York in 1961, directed by Alan Schneider. The French version (*Oh! les beaux jours*) was distinguished by Madeleine Renaud's performance of the single speaking part.

Buried first to her waist and then to her neck in sand, Winnie joyfully itemizes the trivial details of her existence. Her only on-stage witness is her silent partner, Willie.

*Hard Cash* A novel by **Charles Reade**, published in 1863 as a sequel to *Love Me Little, Love Me Long* (1859).

David Dodd, a sea-captain intent on supporting his family with the 'hard cash' he has earned in India, loses his reason when the money is misappropriated by the dishonest banker Richard Hardie. He is confined to an asylum along with Hardie's son Alfred, committed to prevent him exposing his father's misdeeds. The situation gives Reade scope for vigorous condemnation of the abuses prevalent in private asylums. The story ends with Dodd's escape and return to sea, the rescue of Alfred and the exposure of Richard Hardie.

*Hard Times* A novel by **Charles Dickens**, published as a serial in *Household Words* from April to August 1854.

Dickens's fable traces the life of the warm-hearted Sissy Jupe, a circus child deserted by her ailing father, from her adoption into the household of the fact-ridden retired hardware merchant Thomas Gradgrind, whose children Tom and Louisa are reared in ignorance of love and affection. The consequences of lovelessness are devastating for both. Louisa is driven to a miserable marriage with the boastful and wealthy Josiah Bounderby and then almost to an affair with the dandified James Harthouse. Tom descends to thieving, and is saved only through Sissy and the circus folk. Of comparable significance is the story of Stephen Blackpool, the honest worker in Bounderby's mill, who is burdened with a drunken wife and loved by the factory hand Rachel. Ostracized by his fellow workmen. Stephen is driven out of the community and suspected in his absence of Tom Gradgrind's crime. He is exonerated only after death.

The novel depends on the opposition between Fact, Dickens's name for the cold and loveless attitude to life he associated with **Utilitarianism**, and Fancy, which represents all the warmth of the imagination – a contrast which gives it both tension and unity. Although compact and fast-moving, pressing its message home with persistence and conviction, *Hard Times* also presents several memorable minor characters. They include the fact-crammed Bitzer, ideal product of M'Choakumchild's school; the snobbish Mrs Sparsit, Bounderby's housekeeper; the windy trade union organizer Slackbridge; and the kindly members of Sleary's circus troupe.

**Hardy, Thomas** 1840–1928 Poet and novelist. Hardy was born in Higher Bockhampton, Dorset, the son of Thomas Hardy, a builder and master mason, and his wife Jemima. He attended first a village school provided by Mrs Julia Martin, the local lady of the manor to whom he became closely attached; at the same time his mother encouraged him by giving him **Dryden**'s *Aeneid* and **Johnson**'s *Rasselas* as reading matter. In 1850–6 he went to a school in nearby Dorchester conducted by the British and Foreign School Society, whose headmaster Isaac Last ensured his able pupil was well grounded in mathematics and Latin. During these school-days the young Hardy absorbed much local folklore and became familiar with the grimmer facts of village life, of starvation and cruelty and of transportation for trivial offences. He joined his father as violinist in the village band which played at church services, weddings and other local occasions. Hardy's love of nature and sympathy for animals developed during these introspective and solitary years.

It was in the years 1856–62, when Hardy was apprenticed to a local architect, John Hicks, that he acquired the friendship of the poet, parson and antiquary **William Barnes** and the brilliant but erratic Horace Moule (later to commit suicide), both of whom offered him intellectual stimulation. And although this was the time of **Darwin**'s *Origin of Species* and *Essays and Reviews* Hardy the churchgoer remained unshaken in his faith. A five-year stint in London from 1862 to 1867 at the architectural offices of the celebrated Arthur Blomfield followed the apprenticeship with Hicks. While Hardy's innate morbidity responded to the seamy side of London, he also enjoyed the musical, theatrical and other artistic

Thomas Hardy, 1914. Photograph by E. O. Hoppé.

offerings of the capital. In 1865 he made an early appearance in print with 'How I Built Myself a House' and also won a couple of architectural prizes. By now, too, he was sending (and getting back) poems hopefully dispatched to periodicals. More significantly perhaps, he was failing to meet those challenges to his orthodoxy which resulted in a loss of faith and serious undermining of his health.

By 1867 Hardy was back again with Hicks and soon afterwards, his health restored, was writing the lost and partly cannibalized novel, *The Poor Man and the Lady*, in which **George Meredith**, then a reader for Chapman and Hall, saw merit although he advised against publication. In 1869 when Hicks died G. R. Crickmay, who had taken over the firm, offered Hardy a position in the Weymouth office and it was there he began to write **Desperate Remedies** (1871), his first published novel. That same year his employer sent him to survey the church at St Juliot in Cornwall where he met his first wife, Emma Lavinia Gifford. Prior to this time Hardy appears to have experienced one or two disappointments in love, but shadow and speculation cloud this area of his life.

For a quarter-century following 1871 Hardy produced one novel after another. After *Desperate Remedies* came **Under the Greenwood Tree** (1872) and a year later **A Pair of Blue Eyes**, followed in 1874 by **Far from the Madding Crowd**, whose startling success enabled him to marry Emma Gifford. After a honeymoon at Brighton and on the Continent the couple stayed briefly in London but gravitated toward Hardy's rural roots in the West Country, living first at Swanage where he worked on **The Hand of Ethelberta** (1876); then they came to rest for a couple of years at Sturminster Newton – the time of the 'Sturminster Newton idyl' – where he wrote **The Return of the Native** (1878). In March 1878 they moved to Upper Tooting in London, where they lived for three years while he wrote **The Trumpet-Major** (1880) and **A Laodicean** (1881); although it was a time of illness and marital strain, Hardy met literary people, went to the theatre and dined at various clubs. By June 1881 he and Emma were back in Dorset living at Wimborne, where he wrote **Two on a Tower** (1882). His next major work was **The Mayor of Casterbridge** (1886). In June 1885 the Hardys had moved into Max Gate on the edge of Dorchester, where they were to spend the rest of their lives.

They maintained the habit of going to London for three months or so right after Easter for 'the season'. There are mixed impressions of their accommodation to a more sophisticated milieu but evidence suggests their provinciality rendered them ill at ease during such visits. Also, they travelled on the Continent in 1887 and visited Ireland in 1893. During these years,

too, Hardy seemed to enjoy friendships with attractive, socially prominent women. All in all their lives appear active and full, even if their marital difficulties increased.

Yet the writing went on. And in those years Hardy showed interest in the short story by publishing *Wessex Tales* (1888), **A Group of Noble Dames** (1891), and *Life's Little Ironies* (1894), which, with the later volume *A Changed Man and Other Tales* (1913), round off his significant contributions to the genre. But as if this was not enough, novels of stature also appeared: **The Woodlanders** (1887), **Tess of the d'Urbervilles** (1891) and **The Well-Beloved**, published in 1897 but written several years earlier. Above all, this was the time of **Jude the Obscure** (1895), a novel reflecting the distressing tensions of his married life. Its bizarre reception influenced his decision to give up writing novels.

Hardy had been writing poetry since his youth. He published a vast amount in the last 30 years of his life, after he ceased work as a novelist, beginning with **Wessex Poems and Other Verses** (1898) and **Poems of the Past and Present** (1902). The three parts of the epic verse-drama **The Dynasts** came in 1903, 1905 and 1908; in 1908 he also edited selections from the poetry of his old friend William Barnes. **Time's Laughingstocks and Other Verses** (1909) was followed by **Satires of Circumstance, Lyrics and Reveries** (1914), a collection of particular interest for the elegiac 'Poems of 1912–13' written out of personal remorse and expiatory sadness at the sudden death of Emma Hardy in November 1912. The poetry continued: **Moments of Vision and Miscellaneous Verses** (1917), **Late Lyrics and Earlier** (1922), **Human Shows, Far Phantasies, Songs and Trifles** (1925) and the posthumous **Winter Words in Various Moods and Metres** (1928). *The Famous Tragedy of the Queen of Cornwall* (1923) is a verse-drama about Tristram and Iscult.

Increasingly the mantle of the Grand Old Man of English letters tightened across Hardy's shoulders as distinctions and accolades – the Order of Merit and various honorary degrees – came to him. He continued to live simply in the melancholy twilight of Max Gate, and in 1914 married Florence Emily Dugdale (1879–1937). With her he destroyed many letters, notes and writings of a personal nature, received the inevitable admirers and receded into old age until death came peacefully to him in January 1928. *The Early Life of Thomas Hardy, 1840–1891* (1928) and *The Later Years of Thomas Hardy, 1892–1928* (1930), two often misleading volumes which Hardy himself had compiled in his last years, were published under his wife's name.

**Hare, David** 1947– English playwright whose early work was written while he was a student at Cambridge. The university is the setting for one of his best plays, *Teeth 'n' Smiles* (1975), which follows the sordid progress of a pop group hired to play at a May Ball. The context allows Hare to analyse with some acerbity the operation of privilege in British society. *Fanshen* (1975) is a straightforward presentation of an alternative social system, that of Revolutionary China. Less sceptical and much less critical than his plays about British power politics, it is an unusual example of effective writing for an ensemble company (Hare wrote it with and for the Joint Stock Theatre). *Plenty* (1978), which Hare wrote and directed for the **National Theatre**, is a bleak encounter with the moral bankruptcy of post-war Europe, more successful than the ambitious *Map of the World* (1983), also written and directed for the National Theatre.

**Harington, Sir John** ?1560–1612 Courtier, wit, epigrammatist and translator. The godson of Elizabeth I, he was educated at Eton and King's College, Cambridge. He is chiefly remembered for his epigrams and his translation of Ariosto's *Orlando Furioso* (1591); the phrasing of its dedication to the Queen supports the tradition that she imposed the task on him as a penance after he had translated only the ribald twenty-eighth canto for the amusement of her maids of honour. *A New Discourse of a Stale Subject, Called the Metamorphosis of Ajax* (1596) – in fact three treatises published together – announced the invention of a water closet ('a jakes') with a display of erudition, indecency and satire that identifies Harington as an early English imitator of Rabelais. The satire, rather than the indecency, gave offence and he fell from royal favour.

**Hariot (or Harriot), Thomas** 1560–1621 Mathematician and astronomer. Hariot was one of the circle around **Sir Walter Raleigh**, who sent him as scientific adviser on Sir Richard Grenville's expedition to Roanoake Island, 1585–6. Hariot's account of this journey was published as *A Brief and True Report of the New Found Land of Virginia* (1588). The famous 'Baines Note', reporting the shocking opinions of **Christopher Marlowe**, mentions Hariot's association with Raleigh. Marlowe is reported as saying that 'Moses was but a juggler and that one Heriots, being Sir W. Raleigh's man, can do more than he.' Hariot also contributed to the development of algebra in England, through his posthumously published treatise on equations, *Artis Analyticae Praxis ad Aequationes Algebraicas Novo Methodo Resolvendas* (1631). This work also introduced the signs > (greater than) and < (less than). As an astronomer he observed sunspots and, independently of Galileo, the moons of Jupiter.

**Harland, Henry** 1861–1905 American novelist, born in New York City. After a brief period at the Harvard Divinity School, he embarked on a literary career under the pseudonym of Sidney Luska. Pretending to be Jewish, he wrote several realistic novels about Jewish immigrants in New York: *As It Was Written: A Jewish Musician's Story* (1885), *Mrs Peixada* (1886), *The Yoke of the Thorah* (1887) and *My Uncle Florimund* (1888). In 1889 he went to Paris, and dropped his assumed character with the publication of the collection *A Latin Quarter Courtship and Other Stories* (1889) and the four novels *Grandison Mather* (1889), *Two Women or One* (1890), *Two Voices* (1890) and *Mea Culpa* (1891). He moved to England in 1890, where he became the first editor of *The Yellow Book*, the activity for which he is best remembered. He then wrote a number of stories and romances, including *Mademoiselle Miss and Other Stories* (1893), *Grey Roses* (1895) and *Comedies and Errors* (1898). His most successful novels were *The Cardinal's Snuff Box* (1900) and *My Friend Prospero* (1904).

**Harlem Renaissance** Also called the 'New Negro' or Black Renaissance, the Harlem Renaissance is a term used to designate a period of cultural activity by black American artists from the early 1920s through to the early 1930s. As **Alain Locke** noted in his introduction to the anthology *The New Negro* (1925), there was felt to be a new spirit of achievement and opportunity for collective creative expression by black writers, in contrast to the solitary efforts of earlier literary figures. The movement was also marked by an emphasis on the African heritage of American blacks.

Four major writers who established their reputation during this period were **Claude McKay**, **Jean Toomer**, **Countee Cullen** and **Langston Hughes**. The publication of *Harlem Shadows* (1922) brought McKay recognition as a poet, and his novels *Home to Harlem* (1928) and *Banjo* (1929) were equally well received. Before going south in 1922 Jean Toomer spent time in Harlem, and he remained in contact with New York intellectuals throughout his life. His *Cane* (1923), with its experimental style and form, and its complex examination of black heritage and culture, is a central text of the Renaissance. Cullen's *Color* (1925) is noted for its lyrical exploration of the writer's African heritage, and Hughes's *The Weary Blues* (1926) embodies the spirit of the Renaissance with its celebration of black culture and folk traditions. Other writers who came to prominence at this time were **Zora Neale Hurston**, **Jessie Redmon Fauset**, **Arna Bontemps** and **Sterling A. Brown**. Lesser figures who contributed to the Renaissance include the novelists Walter White, Nella Larsen, George Schulyer, Wallace Thurman, Eric Walrond and Rudolf Fisher. Among the other poets connected with the movement were Waring Cuney, Frank Horne, Gwendolyn B. Bennett and Helene Johnson.

**Harley, Edward, 2nd Earl of Oxford** 1689–1741 Patron of literature and book collector. Only son of **Robert Harley, 1st Earl of Oxford**, he was educated at Westminster School. A close friend of **Pope**, with whom he corresponded in 1721–39, he was also friendly with **Swift**. **Matthew Prior** died at Harley's country seat at Wimpole, Cambridgeshire.

Harley was a manager of the Society for the Encouragement of Learning, and in keeping with this position, having inherited a fine library from his father, which he further improved at immense cost, he generously allowed scholars to publish material, and often also gave financial aid. Among others, Pope published the poems of **Wycherley**, William Oldys received material and money towards his *Life of Sir Walter Raleigh*, and Ames, the historian of printing, was given unlimited access to the library. On Harley's death most of the collection was sold. The printed material, 50,000 books, 41,000 prints and 350,000 pamphlets, was bought by Thomas Osborne, the bookseller, who then employed a number of scholars, including Oldys, to catalogue it as *Catalogus Bibliothecae Harleianae*, published in five volumes (1743–5) with an introduction by **Johnson**. A selection of the material by Oldys appeared in eight volumes (1744–6) also prefaced by Johnson. The manuscripts, in 7639 volumes together with over 14,000 rolls, charters and similar legal material, were sold to the nation and now form the Harleian Collection in the British Library. Among these volumes are the **Harley Lyrics**, the finest extant collection of Middle English lyric poetry.

**Harley, Robert, 1st Earl of Oxford** 1661–1724 Politician. Son of Sir Edward Harley, he was educated at private school near Burford, Oxfordshire. Gradually moving across the political spectrum, he became leader of the Tory Party and effectively Prime Minister under Queen Anne. On the accession of George I (1714) other notable Tories, including **Bolingbroke**, fled the country, but Harley remained and impeachment proceedings were started against him. These ground to a halt in 1717 as a result of procedural disagreement between the two Houses of Parliament, and he was acquitted. When in power he had been an effective manipulator of propaganda and had employed, among others, **Defoe** as a political pamphleteer. Much of the correspondence between the two is still extant in the British Library, and reinforces Earl Cowper's view of Harley: 'If any Man was born under Necessity of being a knave, he was.' In rather more laudable fields he was an as-

sociate member of the **Scriblerus Club** and an avid book collector, founding the excellent library subsequently further enlarged by his son **Edward Harley**.

**Harley Lyrics, The** A collection of early Middle English lyrics, preserved in British Library MS 2253 and first assembled by **Robert Harley, 1st Earl of Oxford** and his son **Edward Harley**. It is the earliest extant collection and contains more than half the secular lyrics surviving from before the 15th century. Apparently the work of several authors, the lyrics are of diverse types and treat both religious and secular topics. They range from the humorous 'Man in the Moon' to the justly famed love song 'Alysoun' and an evocative love song to Christ, 'Suete Iesu, King of Blysse'. (See also **medieval lyric**.)

**Harper, Frances E. (Watkins)** 1825–1911 Black American poet, born in Baltimore, Maryland. Her first volume of verse, *Poems on Miscellaneous Subjects* (most of them expressing antislavery sentiments), was published in 1854. It proved extremely popular and by 1874 had gone through 20 editions. Her other works include *Moses, A Story of the Nile* (1869), *Poems* (1871), *Iola Le Roy, or, Shadows Uplifted* (1892), about the tragic life of a young octoroon woman before and during the Civil War, and *Atlanta Offering, Poems* (1895).

***Harper's New Monthly Magazine*** Founded in 1850 under the title *Harper's Monthly Magazine* by the publishing firm of Harper and Brothers in New York City with Henry J. Raymond as editor, by 1860 its circulation had reached 200,000. It initially concentrated on publishing established British authors, such as **Dickens**, **Thackeray**, **Trollope** and **Hardy**, but under the editorship of Henry M. Alden (1869–1919) it drew regularly on American writers also, among them **John De Forest**, **Hamlin Garland**, **William Dean Howells** and **Sarah Orne Jewett**. Though fiction remained its main offering, after 1900 (and under its new title of *Harper's New Monthly Magazine*) it devoted more space to political and social issues, and featured articles by well-known public figures such as Woodrow Wilson, Calvin Coolidge and Theodore Roosevelt. In 1925 the shortened title of *Harper's Magazine* was adopted and it is now commonly known simply as *Harper's*.

**Harpur, Charles** 1813–68 Australian poet. His first volume, *Thoughts: A Series of Sonnets* (1845), was followed by *The Bushrangers: A Play and Other Poems* (1853). *The Bushrangers* was the first play written by an Australian-born author to be printed in the colony. His later volumes were *A Poet's Home* (1862), *The Tower of the Dream* (1865) and *Poems* (edited by Henry

Maydwell Martin, 1883). Harpur has been described as 'the grey forefather' of Australian poets because of his early distinctive use of Australian subject matter in such poems as 'The Creek of the Four Graves', 'The Bushfire' and 'Ned Connor'.

**Harraden, Beatrice** 1864–1936 Novelist and suffragette. Born in Hampstead, she was educated in Dresden, then at Cheltenham College, Queen's College, and Bedford College, London, where she graduated in 1883. She was an ardent suffragette and became a leader in the Women's Social and Political Union, selling newspapers and making numerous public speeches in support of feminist causes. Her extensive travels on the Continent were followed by a visit to the USA in 1894–5 to help foster international comity.

Her first published book, *Things Will Take a Turn*, appeared in 1891, but she had already contributed many short stories to *Blackwood's Magazine*. Success came with *Ships That Pass in the Night* (1893) which sold over a million copies. Set in a winter resort for consumptive patients in the Kurhaus at Petershof, its heroine, herself a consumptive, dies at the end of the novel in a street accident. It reflects many of her feminist beliefs and has been described as 'rhapsodical, elusive and deliberately parabolic'. *In Varying Moods* (1894) was a collection of short stories written in Sussex, Cannes and Mentone. Other titles included *Hilda Strafford* (1897), *The Fowler* (1899), *Katharine Frensham* (1903), *Interplay* (1908), *Youth Calling* (1924) and *Search Will Find It Out* (1928). She was awarded a Civil List pension in 1930 for her services to literature.

**Harrington (or Harington), James** 1611–77 Political theorist. Educated at Trinity College, Oxford, Harrington was a republican who had travelled extensively in Europe and was for a time in attendance to the Elector Palatine. In 1656 he published *The Commonwealth of Oceana*, a political romance in the manner of **Thomas More**'s *Utopia*, presenting his idea of an ideal state; the features of this commonwealth include liberty, equality, restrictions on property, and a democratically elected 'Archon', or ruling Prince. These political ideas later influenced the early settlers of America, and are in sharp contrast to the scheme set down in **Thomas Hobbes**'s *Leviathan* (1651). Harrington was imprisoned for his views at the Restoration.

**Harris, Frank** 1856–1931 Journalist and literary editor. Born James Thomas Harris in Galway, Ireland, he travelled to New York in his early teens and worked at a series of menial jobs before returning to Europe. As a journalist, he gained a considerable reputation on the London literary scene, editing *The Evening News* (1882–6), *The Fortnightly Review* (1886–94) and *The Saturday Review* (1894–8), which he transformed into the leading weekly with a new bias towards the arts. Regular contributors included **G. B. Shaw**, **H. G. Wells** and **Max Beerbohm**, all of whom later testified to Harris's flair for controversial and often scandalous assaults on Victorian standards.

His notoriety as a braggart and liar was epitomized in *My Life and Loves* (4 vols., 1922–7), highly unreliable memoirs of his early life as a precocious intellectual and sexual buccaneer. His other publications included short stories (*Elder Conklin*, 1894; *Montes the Matador*, 1900), novels (*The Bomb*, 1908; *Great Days*, 1914) and two plays (*Mr and Mrs Daventry*, 1900; *Shakespeare and His Love*, 1910). His literary studies were enthusiastically received in some quarters, but never won scholarly acclaim. *The Man Shakespeare* (1909) was followed by *The Women of Shakespeare* (1911), and biographies of **Wilde** (1916) and Shaw (1931). His *Contemporary Portraits* (1915–23) met with the same kind of reception. A highly individual figure, Harris has continued to attract and frustrate readers, though many of his finer qualities as a writer have been overshadowed by an almost pathological boasting.

**Harris, George Washington** 1814–69 American short-story writer. Born in Pennsylvania, Harris was a Tennessee River steamboat captain before he turned to writing. His best-known work is *Sut Lovingood: Yarns spun by a 'Nat'ral Born Durn'd Fool'* (1867). A collection of tall tales and sketches, full of Southwestern frontier dialect and robust humour, it is a clear forerunner of some of **Mark Twain**'s early writings.

**Harris, Joel Chandler** 1848–1908 American short-story writer, best known as the creator of Uncle Remus. He was born in Georgia, where from an early age he worked on plantations and imbibed the black folklore that was to inform the style and subject matter of his fiction. The first of the Uncle Remus stories, 'The Story of Mr Rabbit and Mr Fox, as Told by Uncle Remus', was published in 1879. *Uncle Remus: His Songs and Sayings* appeared in 1881 and was followed by *Nights With Uncle Remus* (1883), *Uncle Remus and His Friends* (1892), *Mr Rabbit at Home* (1895), *The Tar Baby and Other Short Rhymes of Uncle Remus* (1904) and *Uncle Remus and Br'er Rabbit* (1906). These stories offer traditional black folk-wisdom in what **Mark Twain** considered a flawless duplication of Southern black speech. Harris's special interest in the animal mythology of black folklore has brought to American culture such figures as Br'er Rabbit and Br'er Fox. His other works include *Mingo and Other Sketches in Black and White* (1884), and two novels, *Sister Jane: Her Friends and Acquain-*

*tances* (1896) and *Gabriel Tolliver: A Story of Reconstruction* (1902). *On the Plantation* (1892) recounts the childhood experiences that inspired so much of his work.

**Harris, (Theodore) Wilson** 1921– Guyanese novelist, born in New Amsterdam. While a government surveyor in Guyana he published three volumes of verse, before he moved to London in 1959. He has since become one of the most innovative novelists writing in English. His free-ranging, non-logical, highly metaphoric, associative techniques in prose derive from a poetic imagination fired intellectually by extensive reading (not least by Jung's use of the mythic), and visually by the savannahs, the powerful river currents, and the swirling rock strata of Guyana. In *Palace of the Peacock* (1960), *The Far Journey of Oudin* (1961), *The Whole Armour* (1962) and *The Secret Ladder* (1963), published together as *The Guyana Quartet* (1985), Harris uses physical landscape as metaphor, even allegory, to dramatize the workings of the human psyche and establish its capacity to resist ossification by the categorical and static. The multi-racial Guyanese population also helped inspire his vision of the interpenetrability, rather than the antagonism, of different cultures. So, in his other 'Guyanese' novels, *Heartland* (1964), *The Eye of the Scarecrow* (1965), *The Waiting Room* (1967), *Tumatumari* (1968) and *Ascent to Omai* (1970), character is developed not towards stability, but fluidity, thus inducing new awarenesses and reinterpretations of experience. Since his volumes of salvaged or imagined pre-Columbian legends, *The Sleepers of Roraima* (1970) and *The Age of the Rainmakers* (1971), Harris has written novels set in Scotland, South America, Mexico and London: *Black Marsden* (1972), *Companions of the Day and Night* (1975), *Da Silva da Silva's Cultivated Wilderness* with *Genesis of the Clowns* (1977), *The Tree of Life* (1978), *The Angel at the Gate* (1982) and *Carnival* (1985). In them his profound practical concern for human survival is even more intensely conveyed through the kaleidoscopic interacting of past and present, painting and literature, art and religion. His critical writings include *Tradition, the Writer, and Society* (1967) and *The Womb of Space: The Cross-Cultural Imagination* (1983).

**Harrison, Frederic** 1831–1923 Philosopher and critic. He was educated at King's College, London, and Wadham College, Oxford. Called to the Bar in 1858, he was Professor of Jurisprudence and International Law to the Inns of Court in 1877–89. Originally a member of the Church of England, Harrison became in 1870 a believer in Auguste Comte's creed of **Positivism** and took a leading role in spreading its doctrines. His contemptuous remarks on culture stimulated **Matthew Arnold** to reply in *Culture and Anarchy* (1869). Harrison's own voluminous output included *Order and Progress* (1875), *Victorian Literature* (1895), *Carlyle and the London Library* (1907), *The Philosophy of Common Sense* (1907) and *The Positive Evolution of Religion* (1912). His *Autobiographical Memoirs* appeared in 1911.

**Harrison, Tony** 1937– Poet, translator and dramatist. Born in Leeds and educated at Leeds Grammar School and Leeds University, Harrison spent four years lecturing in West Africa and a year in Prague before returning to Britain to become the first Northern Arts Literary fellow in 1967–8, a post he again held in 1976–7. His poems and translations have won many prizes, and his work for the theatre has been performed by the **National Theatre**, the New York Metropolitan Opera and Channel Four Television.

Apart from his career as Britain's leading theatre poet, Harrison is known for his Meredithian sonnet sequence 'The School of Eloquence' (1978) which takes language as the site of conflict in the class war. Operating within the traditional English forms of poetry, he dramatizes the divisions of modern Britain in *Continuous* (1981) and *V.* (1985). His *Dramatic Verse 1973–85* (1985) includes all his major theatre works to date except *The Mysteries* (1985), and his *Selected Poems* was issued in 1984.

**Harrison, William** 1534–93 Historian and topographer. Harrison was educated at St Paul's School, Cambridge and Oxford, where he graduated MA in 1560. His *Description of England* was incorporated into the *Chronicles* of **Raphael Holinshed**. It gives a vivid picture of social conditions in Elizabethan England with its food, institutions, customs, inns and fairs.

**Harrower, Elizabeth** 1928– Australian novelist. Born in Newcastle, New South Wales, she spent the first 12 years of her life there before moving to Sydney. In 1951 she went to Europe and lived in Scotland before settling in London. Her first two novels, *Down in the City* (1957) and *The Long Prospect* (1958), were published during this period in Britain. In 1959 she returned to Australia and worked briefly for the Australian Broadcasting Commission, and, for a longer period, in publishing. Most of her fiction deals with struggles in personal relationships and with conflicting moral issues. *The Catherine Wheel* (1960) describes the experiences of a young Australian law student in London, focusing on her infatuation for a self-centred and unreliable young man. Like *The Watch Tower* (1966), it sees female passivity as colluding with male egotism to perpetuate the subordinate role of women in relationships. In the latter novel the title refers to an elegant house in a respectable Sydney suburb, which appears to offer a haven for the heroine and her sister, but emerges as an emotional and intellectual prison for the two women. In addition to her four novels, Harrower has also written numerous uncollected stories.

**Harry, Blind** See **Blind Harry**.

**Harte, (Francis) Bret[t]** 1836–1902 American short-story writer, born in Albany, New York. At the age of 18 he went to California, where he worked as a prospector, a teacher, a Wells Fargo expressman, and then as a journalist. In 1860 he settled in San Francisco, and began to contribute to the *Golden Era* and *The Californian*. As editor of the latter he commissioned weekly articles from his friend **Mark Twain**.

He was appointed secretary of the US Mint in San Francisco in 1863. He continued to write, however, and his first book of poems, *The Lost Galleon*, was published in 1867. *Condensed Novels and Other Papers*, parodies of distinguished authors, appeared in the same year. In 1868 he helped to establish **Overland Monthly** as an outlet for Western writers. He edited the journal for two years, and contributed a number of his own stories to it. In 1870 he published a comic ballad, *Plain Language from Truthful James*, as well as the collection of Western stories which made him famous, **The Luck of Roaring Camp and Other Sketches**. He returned to the East, where he lived and wrote until 1878, when he was appointed US consul in Germany. He was consul at Glasgow from 1880 to 1885 and spent the rest of his life in London. His stories are collected in *Mrs Skaggs's Husbands* (1873), *Tales of the Argonauts* (1875), *An Heiress of Red Dog, and Other Sketches* (1878), *A Sappho of Green Springs, and Other Stories* (1891) and *Colonel Starbottle's Client, and Some Other People* (1892). He also published several novels, including *Gabriel Conroy* (1876) and *Jeff Briggs's Love Story* (1880); and two plays, *Two Men of Sandy Bar* (1876) and *Ah Sin* (1877), the latter of which he wrote with Mark Twain.

**Hartley, David** 1705–57 Philosopher. Hartley was born at Luddenden, near Halifax in Yorkshire, and was educated at Bradford Grammar School and Jesus College, Cambridge. He became a physician, was a fellow of Jesus College, and is remembered for one of the earliest attempts at psychological enquiry in English. *Observations on Man: His Frame, His Duty and His Expectations* (1749) relates psychology to physiology, and contributed to the development of the 'association of ideas' theory.

**Hartley, L[eslie] P[oles]** 1895–1972 Novelist and short-story writer. L. P. Hartley was born at Whittlesey in Cambridgeshire and educated at

Harrow and Balliol College, Oxford. During World War I he served in the Norfolk Regiment, and afterwards spent much of his life in Venice.

His first short stories were published in a volume called *Night Fears* (1924). This was followed by numerous other collections, among them *The Killing Bottle* (1932), *The Travelling Grave* (1951), *The White Wand* (1954) and *Two for the River* (1961), which have established his reputation as a leading writer of the genre. His novels began with *Simonetta Perkins* (1925), which was set in Venice, but it was with his trilogy, *The Shrimp and the Anemone* (1944), *The Sixth Heaven* (1946) and the title volume, *Eustace and Hilda* (1947), that Hartley won his greatest critical accolade. The trilogy charts the relationship between Eustace and his elder sister Hilda, through childhood to adulthood in Oxford and Venice, and is indebted (without detriment) to the work of **Henry James** and the teachings of Freud about the influence of early childhood on the formation of character.

Hartley's best-known novel, **The Go-Between** (1953), a beautifully observed portrayal of Edwardian England, won the Heinemann Foundation Award. His other novels include *A Perfect Woman* (1955), *The Hireling* (1957), *Facial Justice* (1960), *The Brickfield* (1964) and its sequel *The Betrayal* (1966), *Poor Clare* (1968) and *The Love Adept* (1969). He was also the author of a volume of critical essays, *The Novelist's Responsibility* (1968).

**Hartman, Geoffrey** See **deconstructive criticism**.

**Harvey, Gabriel** ?1550–1631 Scholar. Gabriel Harvey was educated at Christ's College, Cambridge, becoming a fellow of Pembroke Hall in 1570 and of Trinity Hall in 1578. It was at Pembroke Hall that he made the acquaintance of **Spenser**. He pursued learned interests in rhetoric, neo-Aristotelian philosophy and law; his wide learning is also attested by the copious marginalia he left in his books. Harvey's earliest published work was *Smithus* (1578), an elegy on his patron Sir Thomas Smith. An exchange of letters with Spenser, concerned partly with metrics, was printed in 1580. In it *The Faerie Queene* is mentioned for the first time, as are other poems by Spenser no longer extant and presumably since lost. Harvey attacked the dead **Robert Greene** in *Four Letters* (1592), provoking a reply by **Thomas Nashe** in *Strange News*, also known as *Four Letters Confuted* (1593). The pamphlet war was continued when Harvey replied to Nashe in *Pierce's Supererogation* (1593), and, after a temporary truce, broke out again, to be ended by episcopal decree in 1599. The last 30 years of Harvey's life were spent in Saffron Walden.

**Harvey, William** 1578–1657 Physician. Born in Folkestone, Kent, Harvey attended King's School in Canterbury. From Gonville and Caius College, Cambridge, he went on to take his medical degree at the University of Padua where Galileo was a teacher. In London he became a physician at St Bartholomew's Hospital and lecturer at the College of Physicians, where he expounded his theory of the circulation of the blood in 1616. He did not publish his treatise on the subject until 12 years later, in *Exercitatio Anatomica de Motu Cordis et Sanguinis in Animalibus* ('On the Movement of the Heart and Blood in Animals', 1628). Harvey's theories, the result of observation and experiment carried out without the help of a microscope, were substantiated only after 200 years of slow acceptance. Harvey also made considerable contributions to the knowledge of embryology and comparative anatomy. He was physician to Charles I, and was present with him at the Battle of Edgehill.

**Harwood, Gwen[doline] (Nessie)** 1920– One of Australia's foremost lyric poets. Born in Taringa, Queensland, she did not publish her first book of poems until she was 43. *Poems* (1963) was followed by *Poems: Volume Two* (1968) and *New and Selected Poems* (1975). Tense and controlled poems like 'In the Park', 'Prize-Giving' and 'Cocktails at Seven' draw scenes of middle-class despair, vacillating between rage and elegy.

**Harwood, Lee (Travers Rafe)** 1939– Poet. Born in Leicester and educated at Weybridge and Queen Mary College, London, Harwood lives in Brighton, where he works for the Post Office. His first major collection, *The White Room* (1968), won praise from **John Ashbery**. Its successors include *Landscapes* (1969), *The Sinking Colony* (1970) and *Monster Masks* (1985), and translations from Tzara (1975). His work is well represented in anthologies.

**Hassan** A play by **James Elroy Flecker**, written in 1913–14 and first performed in German in Darmstadt in May 1923. For the first English performance, later in the same year, Delius provided music and Fokine a balletic choreography. It ran for eight months at His Majesty's Theatre, a spectacular successor to *Chu-Chin-Chow*. It is written in highly charged prose, with interspersed poems.

Hassan, a middle-aged confectioner in old Baghdad, becomes embroiled in the cruel and corrupt court of the Caliph as a result of his love for the courtesan, Yasmin. The Caliph takes sadistic revenge on Rafi, the King of the Beggars, who has tried to rescue from the Caliph's harem his virginal lover, Pervaneh. Having been forced to watch the perverted execution of Rafi and Pervaneh, Hassan escapes with Ishak, the court poet, on the golden road to Samarkand. There is enough voyeurism and sadism in the play to explain the hesitation of Lord Cromer, the Lord Chamberlain of the time, to grant it a licence in 1923.

**Haunted Man and the Ghost's Bargain, The** A Christmas story by **Charles Dickens**, published in 1848 and collected in *Christmas Books* (1852).

The sadly reflective, learned Mr Redlaw is visited by an evil phantom who makes a compact with him to obliterate the sorrow, wrongs and troubles he has known. In return, Redlaw agrees to transmit this oblivion to others. But his influence is baleful upon everyone he encounters – the student Edmund Denham, the amiable Adolphus Tetterby and the good-natured William Swidger. These and others fall away from their better selves, if only temporarily, when confronted by Redlaw. Ultimately, through the purity, goodness and gentleness embodied in William's wife, Milly, the unhappy man's bargain is terminated.

**Havelok the Dane** Verse romance composed *c.* 1280–1300, probably in the North-east Midlands.

The story, told in couplets, is English in character and while the romance apparently has an Anglo-Norman source – a similar tale features in Gaimar's *Histoire des Engles* – no European romance of Havelok survives. All attempts to link the Havelok of the poem with a historical figure have proved inconclusive, though some of the characters live on in local folklore. The romance tells of Havelok, son of the Danish king, who is handed over by his guardian to the fisherman Grim to be killed. Magic tokens reveal his importance and lead Grim to flee with him to England. Havelok grows very strong and works as a scullion in the service of Godrich, evil guardian of the heir to the English throne, Goldborough. Godrich had promised her father he would marry Goldborough to the strongest man in the land, and hopes to gain the throne himself by marrying her to Havelok. Havelok's identity is revealed by his magic tokens to his wife and again when the couple have returned to Denmark. The two evil guardians are defeated and Havelok becomes king of Denmark and England.

**Hawes, Stephen** d. ?1523 Poet. Very little is known of Hawes's life except that, by his own account, he was groom of the chamber to Henry VII. His poetry belongs in spirit to the Middle Ages and shows the influence of **Chaucer**, **Gower** and especially **Lydgate**. Hawes is medieval in his allegorizing, especially in the allegorical treatment of love, and in his reflections on the instability of fortune. However, his concern with the education of princes shows the influence of the 'New Learning'. The first editions of his works were printed by **Wynkyn de Worde** and are bibliographical rarities. *The Pastime of Pleasure* (the only copy of the first edition of 1509 is incomplete) deals with the education of the knight Graunde Amoure, by way of the seven liberal arts, to make him worthy of the lady La Belle Pucel. *The Example of Virtue* (earliest surviving edition, 1510) and *The Comfort of Lovers* (earliest surviving copy, ?1510) are also love-allegories. *The Conversion of Swearers* (1509) attacks blasphemy and *A Joyful Meditation* (a unique copy of the first edition of 1509 is at Cambridge) celebrates the coronation of Henry VIII.

**Hawker, R[obert] S[tephen]** 1803–75 Poet. The son of a doctor (later in holy orders), Hawker was born in Devon and educated at Cheltenham College and Pembroke College, Oxford, where he won the Newdigate Prize for poetry. Ordained priest in 1831 he became, three years later, vicar of Morwenstowe on the North Cornish coast. He described his parishioners as a 'mixed multitude of smugglers, wreckers and dissenters of various hues'. Twice married, a High Churchman who converted to Rome on his deathbed, 'Passon' Hawker was an eccentric and an antiquarian prone to superstition and addicted to the occult. He was a vigorous, irrepressible personality of ready wit who affected the fisherman's jersey as emblematic of his calling and who is comparable to St Francis in his devotion to animals, many of whom accompanied him into his church.

By Victorian standards Hawker's output was modest, although his first volume, the anonymous *Tendrils by Reuben*, appeared when he was only 18. In 1826 a local newspaper published 'Song of the Western Men', his best-known poem. Other volumes include *Records of the Western Shore* (1832), *Poems* (1836), *Ecclesia* (1841), *Reeds Shaken with the Wind* (1st series, 1843; 2nd series, 1844) and *Cornish Ballads* (1869). *The Quest of the Sangraal* (1864) is generally acknowledged as his most ambitious work and often compared with **Tennyson**'s *Idylls of the King*, another Victorian treatment of Arthurian legend. Hawker's poetry deals with saints' legends, smuggling, village life and other motifs closely associated with Cornwall, often cast in ballad form; there are also verses dedicated to the Christian life. Hawker wrote on antiquarian subjects, dabbled in translation and contributed to a number of prominent journals. His prose work, *Footprints of Former Men in Far Cornwall* (1870), is a rich source of the mysterious, the supernatural and the forbiddingly unusual that attaches to Cornish lore and legend.

**Hawkes, John (Clendennin Burne, Jr)** 1925– American novelist, born in Connecticut and educated at Harvard; he has taught at Brown University since 1958. His first novel, *The Cannibal* (1949), is a bleak and formally complex work about the horrors of World War II. Subsequent novels, such as *The Beetle Leg* (1951), *The Goose on the Grave* (1954), *The Lime Twig* (1961) and *Second Skin* (1964), continued to evoke the extremes of violence he saw as characteristic of the modern world. His more recent work includes a collection of stories called *Lunar Landscapes* (1969), and the novels *Death, Sleep and the Traveller* (1974), *Travesty* (1976), *The Owl* (1977), *The Passion Artist* (1979), *Virginie: Her Two Lives* (1981), *Innocence in Extremis* (1985) and *Adventures in the Alaskan Skin Trade* (1985).

**Hawkins, Sir Anthony Hope** See **Hope, Anthony**.

**Hawkins, Sir John** 1532–95 Sailor. A relative of Drake, Hawkins was a naval commander and, in his reconstruction of the fleet, the architect of the Elizabethan navy. His early career was as a slave-trader, running slaves from Guinea to the West Indies in three voyages during the years 1562–9. The third disastrous voyage is described in his *A True Declaration of the Troublesome Voyage of Mr John Hawkins (1569)*. He was instrumental in discovering the Ridolfi Plot of 1571 to put Mary Queen of Scots on the English throne. He died at sea on an expedition with Drake to raid the Spanish West Indies.

**Hawthorne, Nathaniel** 1804–64 American novelist and short-story writer, born in Salem, Massachusetts, into a prominent family whose ancestors were among the earliest settlers of the colony. Later in life, he was especially preoccupied, and troubled, by his descent from John Hathorne, a judge in the Salem witch trials of 1692. Hawthorne grew up in seclusion with his widowed mother, his father, a sea-captain, having died of yellow fever in 1808. When he was 11 they moved to Maine. There he attended Bowdoin College and made a number of important and lasting friends, including **Henry Wadsworth Longfellow** and the future president Franklin Pierce.

After graduating in 1825 he returned to Salem and, determined to become a writer, worked on short stories and historical sketches. In 1828, anonymously and at his own expense, he published *Fanshawe*, a novel based on his college life. While the book itself received only slight critical attention and an ashamed author burned the unsold copies, it did initiate a long, productive friendship between Hawthorne and the publisher Samuel Goodrich. He returned to writing short fiction, and in historical and allegorical tales began to explore the impact of which includes stories such as 'Ethan Brand' and 'My Kinsman Major Molineux'. The publication of *A Wonder Book* (1852), which retells Greek myths for children, and *Tanglewood Tales* (1853) marked the end of his most prolific period.

In 1853 Franklin Pierce became President and Hawthorne, who had written a campaign biography for him, was appointed US consul at Liverpool. He lived in England for four years and in Italy for two, returning to the USA in 1860 and publishing his final novel, **The Marble Faun**. He tried to regain his former creative energy, but without success. Four unfinished novels were found among his papers after his death in 1864; they were eventually published as *Septimius Felton; or, the Elixir of Life* (1872), *The Dolliver Romance* (1876), *Dr Grimshawe's Secret* (1882) and *The Ancestral Footstep* (1883). His last publications were *Our Old Home* (1863), a book of essays on England, and various pieces in **The Atlantic Monthly**. After his death his wife edited and published his notebooks, which appeared as *Passages from the American Notebooks* (1868), *Passages from the English Notebooks* (1870) and *Passages from the French and Italian Notebooks* (1871). Modern editions of these works include many of the sections which she cut out or altered.

Nathaniel Hawthorne.

harsh Puritanism on the guilty conscience of New England. Many of these stories were published in Goodrich's *The Token*, an annual giftbook, and were later collected in *Twice-Told Tales* (1837, expanded 1842).

Hawthorne then worked for Goodrich as an editor and hack writer from 1836 to 1839, when he accepted a post as surveyor of the Boston Custom House. His involvement with the Boston literary circle led him to quit his post in 1841 and to invest in the communal experiment at **Brook Farm**. That same year he married Sophia Peabody, herself an active participant in the **Transcendentalist** movement. Soon, however, the retiring Hawthorne was disappointed by communal life; in 1842 he and his wife moved to Concord, where they lived in the Old Manse, a former home of **Ralph Waldo Emerson**. He returned to serious writing, and in 1846 published *Mosses from an Old Manse*, which includes the famous story 'Young Goodman Brown'. After serving as customs surveyor at Salem for three years (1846–9), at the age of 45 he finally produced his first significant long work of fiction. *The Scarlet Letter* (1850), still considered the most important of his works, won almost immediate acclaim. It was rapidly followed by **The House of the Seven Gables** (1851) and **The Blithedale Romance** (1852), which was based on his Brook Farm experience. Hawthorne was never again to equal the productivity of this three-year period, during which he also published *The Snow Image and Other Tales* (1851),

**Hay, Ian** Pseudonym of the novelist and dramatist Major-General John Hay Beith (1876–1952). Hay was educated at Fettes and Cambridge. During World War I he served as a member of the British War Mission to the USA. *The First Hundred Thousand* (1915), an account of the enlisted men during the early stages of the war, achieved considerable contemporary popularity. Hay's novels, invariably written in a light-hearted vein, were frequently about life in English boys' boarding-schools. *A Safety Match* (1911) was the most famous; others included *A Man's Made* (1909), *The Middle Watch* (1930) and *The Housemaster* (1936).

As well as adapting many of his own novels for the stage, Hay dramatized stories by **P. G. Wodehouse**, a close friend, with whom he shares many literary qualities.

**Hay Fever** A comedy by **Noël Coward**, first performed at the Ambassadors Theatre, London, in 1925. It is a skilfully composed account of a weekend at the home of the eccentric Bliss family. The wife, a retired actress who continues to act in her private life, the husband and the two children have all invited guests to stay without telling each other. The bewildered guests, subjected to the Bliss version of bickering hospitality, creep away at breakfast on the second day, leaving the unnoticing family arguing about the exact topography of Paris.

**Haydon, Benjamin Robert** 1786–1846 Painter and diarist. The son of a printer and bookseller, Haydon was born in Plymouth, and attended the Royal Academy before beginning a turbulent career as a painter of classical, biblical and historical subjects. After considerable initial success as a purveyor of large canvases in the Renaissance manner to the houses of the rich and great, he alienated his patrons and influential well-wishers with the often intemperate manner of his advocacy of otherwise sound and progressive schemes for the promotion of art education, the decoration of public buildings and the establishment of schools of design. He was among the first to appreciate the extraordinary merit of the Elgin Marbles, and was instrumental in securing their purchase for the British Museum. His friends included **Keats, Wordsworth, Hazlitt** (all of whom were portrayed in the crowd of his painting 'Christ's Entry into Jerusalem'), **Leigh Hunt** (in whose *Examiner* he virulently attacked the Academy), David Wilkie, M. R. Mitford and **Elizabeth Barrett Browning**. Although consumed to the point of madness by the desire for glory with the brush, he was, in the event, a better writer and lecturer than painter, and is now best known for his posthumously published *Autobiography and Journals* (1853), a treasure-trove of anecdote and vivid observation of his famous contemporaries, and his *Lectures on Painting and Design* (1846), first given at the London Mechanics' Institution and subsequently to working-class audiences in the provinces. A courageous and soaringly idealistic figure, he was at length unable to surmount his many professional disappointments and committed suicide, the coroner's jury returning a verdict of insanity. His extravagant personality intrigued **Dickens**, who used him, along with Leigh Hunt, as the model for the infantile egomaniac Harold Skimpole in *Bleak House*.

**Hayley, William** 1745–1820 Poet and biographer. Born at Chichester and educated at Eton and Cambridge, Hayley spent most of his life at Eartham, Sussex. Although now of mainly antiquarian interest, his poetry, of which there is a great deal, was widely read in its day, and the considerable popular success of his two most ambitious works, *The Triumphs of Temper* (1781) and *The Triumphs of Music* (1805), earned him **Byron**'s ridicule ('Forever feeble, forever tame') in *English Bards and Scotch Reviewers*. His *Ballads Founded on Anecdotes of Animals* (1805) were written for and illustrated by **Blake**. Other literary friends included **Cowper**, of whom he wrote a *Life* (1803), and **Southey**, who thought him good in everything 'except his poetry'. The appearance of an article on Hayley by Southey for *The Quarterly Review* was long delayed by the editor on the grounds that he 'could not bear to see Hayley spoken of with decent respect'.

Other biographical works by Hayley include lives of **Milton** and the portrait painter Romney. In 1790 he declined an offer of the Poet Laureateship.

**Haymarket Theatre** A carpenter called John Potter built the Little Theatre in the Haymarket in 1720 as a speculative challenge to the monopoly of the **Patent Theatres**. **Henry Fielding** staged anti-Walpole satires there in 1735–7. During the management of **Samuel Foote**, 1747–76, the theatre was given a licence for summer performance of plays, when the Patent Theatres were closed. This first Theatre Royal, Haymarket was replaced in 1820 by a larger building, designed by John Nash. The portico alone has survived subsequent improvements. Until 1843, when the Patent Theatres' monopoly of legitimate drama in London was terminated, the Haymarket had a unique role as the only testing-ground of new plays other than the vast and costly Patent Theatres.

**Haywood, Eliza** c. 1693–1756 Hack. Little is known of Mrs Haywood's private life. She was an actress in Dublin around 1715 but shortly after moved to London, where she wrote a few unsuccessful plays, and collaborated with William Hatchett on *Tom Thumb the Great* (1733), a comic opera with music by Arne, adapted from **Fielding**'s *Tragedy of Tragedies*. From 1744 to 1746 she edited *The Female Spectator*, a monthly collection of essays. In a career which spanned nearly 40 years she produced many novels, ranging from collaboration with **Defoe** on *The Life of Mr Duncan Campbell* (1720), through the *roman à clef*, *Memoirs of a Certain Island Adjacent to Utopia* (1725), to *The History of Jemmy and Jenny Jessamy* (1753), which was praised by **Scott** for its pathos in *Old Mortality*. She consistently asserted the didactic moral purpose of her work, both in prefaces and in the body of the texts, but was nevertheless condemned by **Pope** in *The Dunciad* as 'the libellous Novelist' and by **Swift** as a 'stupid, infamous, scribbling woman'.

**Hayward, Sir John** ?1564–1627 Historian. Hayward graduated MA from Pembroke College, Cambridge, in 1584. His *The First Part of the Life and Reign of King Henry IV* (1599), which was flatteringly dedicated to Essex, included an account of the deposition of Richard II. This aroused the suspicion of Elizabeth who was sensitive to possible analogies between Richard and herself (in 1601 she commented to William Lambard, 'I am Richard II, know ye not that?'), especially when her relationship with Essex was worsening. Hayward was brought before the Star Chamber and imprisoned, only being released after Essex's execution. **Bacon**'s opinion was that although the work was not treasonable, its extensive borrowings from Tacitus made it felonious. In the reign of James, at the suggestion of his son Prince Henry, Hayward wrote *The Lives of the Three Normans, Kings of England* (i.e. William I, William II and Henry I) which was printed in 1613. *The Life and Reign of King Edward VI* was published posthumously in 1630. Another edition of this work (1636) contains *The Beginning of the Reign of Queen Elizabeth*, part of a larger work which remained in manuscript until it was printed in 1840. *The Sanctuary of a Troubled Soul* (1616) is a collection of prayers and meditations; *David's Tears* (1622) is a commentary on three of the penitential psalms.

*Hazard of New Fortunes, A* A novel by **William Dean Howells**, published in 1890. The early chapters, set in Boston, tell how Fulkerson, who is involved in syndicated journalism, convinces Basil March to move to New York City and serve as the literary editor of a new magazine called *Every Other Week*. Basil and his family make the move – they 'hazard' this new enterprise. They soon encounter Jacob Dryfoos, an old farmer who became rich when natural gas was discovered on his Ohio farm and who increased this wealth through real estate and stock-market speculation. He has moved his family from Ohio to New York in order to launch his children in society, and has financed *Every Other Week* in order to give his son Conrad something to do. Conrad, however, wishes to become a minister and shows little interest in the magazine, spending much of his time in charity work among the poor. He meets and becomes infatuated with Margaret Vance, a young society woman who also spends her spare time doing charitable work.

Basil March hires Lindau, an elderly socialist of German extraction who had taught Basil German when he was young, to translate pieces for the magazine. The idealistic Lindau interests young Conrad, but Jacob Dryfoos is enraged when he learns that Lindau is a socialist, and orders March to dismiss him. March refuses to do so, but Lindau – morally outraged at having received money (even if indirectly) from Dryfoos, a strike-breaking capitalist – resigns and returns all the money he has earned from the magazine. Near the end of the novel, both Conrad and Lindau appear on the scene of a streetcar workers' strike. Conrad is killed by a stray bullet from a policeman's gun, and Lindau dies later from injuries inflicted by the police who are breaking the strike. Disheartened by his son's death, Jacob sells the magazine to Fulkerson and March, and travels to Europe with his wife and daughters to try their 'fortunes' in European society. Margaret Vance becomes an Episcopalian nun.

**Hazlitt, William** 1778–1830 Essayist, journalist and critic. Hazlitt was born at Maidstone, Kent, where his father, a friend of **Joseph Priestley** and **Richard Price**, was a Unitarian minister. After a period in America the family settled at the village of Wem, Shropshire, and here Hazlitt spent most of his youth, receiving his first education from his father. An intellectually precocious boy (his first essay, 'A Project for a New Theory of Criminal and Civil Legislation', appeared in 1792), he was intended for the ministry and attended the Unitarian college at Hackney in 1793–5. But he soon developed an 'extreme distaste' for the religious life and spent the next three years reading and painting. Through his father he became acquainted with **Coleridge**, who introduced him to **Wordsworth**, and although he was later to quarrel bitterly with them on politics and criticism, it was largely under the stimulus of their 'winged words' during the heady period of the *Lyrical Ballads* that his 'understanding' found 'a language to express itself'. He continued to paint, however, producing portraits of his two friends, as well as Hartley and **Lamb**, and it was not until 1804–5 that he decided that his real talents lay in philosophy and literature. In London Lamb introduced him to **Godwin** and other literary figures, and he began a long career as a prolific critic, journalist, essayist and lecturer. Although his sympathies were radical and republican, his temperament precluded precisely defined loyalties, and he was always something of a one-man political party: he was strongly in support of the French Revolution, and deeply concerned about social conditions in England, yet his admiration for Napoleon lacked discrimination, and his attacks on opponents were often manifestly rancorous. In 1805 he published *An Essay on the Principles of Human Action*, a systematic defence of the unity of the mind against prevailing doctrines of sense impressions, which was followed in 1807 by his *Reply* to **Malthus**'s *Essay on Population*, in which he sides with Godwin, and *The Eloquence of the British Senate*, an annotated selection of parliamentary speeches by **Burke**, Chatham, Fox, the younger Pitt and others. In 1808 he was married to Sarah Stoddard, with whom he settled first at Winterslow, near Salisbury, and then in London. In 1810 he lectured *On the Rise and Progress of Modern Philosophy*, and in the same year published his *New and Improved Grammar of the English Language*, based on the linguistic theories of **Horne Tooke**. He now exchanged philosophy for literature and journalism, and until 1814 was a parliamentary reporter for *The Morning Chronicle* when he became the paper's theatrical critic. He was by now also writing essays for *The Champion*, **Leigh Hunt**'s *Examiner* and *The Edinburgh Review*. His *Characters of Shakespeare* appeared in 1817, and established him as a Shakespearean critic second only to Coleridge. The volume was dedicated to Lamb, with whom he enjoyed a long, if sometimes bumpy, friendship. It found an ardent admirer in **Keats**, who was also deeply impressed, and influenced in his own writing, by *The Round Table* (partly by Leigh Hunt; also 1817), and, above all, the *Lectures on the English Poets* (1818), which immediately anticipate his idea of the poet as an individual of **negative capability**. Hazlitt's next important critical work was the *Lectures on the English Comic Writers* (1819), which was followed in the same year by his *Political Essays* addressing the conditions of the poor.

In 1820 Hazlitt, who had been living apart from his wife, became passionately involved with Sarah Walker, his landlord's daughter. It was an attachment that was to bring him close to insanity over a period of three years. After divorcing his wife in Scotland, he returned to London to discover that the young lady had transferred her affections to another, if indeed she had not been deceiving him all along. His *Liber Amoris* (1823) was, to his contemporaries, an embarrassingly transparent description of the whole affair, and was charitably described by **De Quincey** as a kind of necessary exorcism, 'an explosion of frenzy . . . to empty his overburdened spirit'. His *Characteristics*, in imitation of La Rochefoucauld, appeared later in the same year. In 1821 Hazlitt had angered Leigh Hunt with a rather spiteful attack on **Shelley** in his *Table Talk* (1821–2), an action for which he now made at least partial amends by contributing five pieces to *The Liberal* (1823–4), a journal planned, with Hunt as editor, by **Byron** and Shelley in Italy, shortly before the latter's death. In 1824 Hazlitt was married to a Mrs Bridgewater, a union which came to a mysteriously abrupt end in 1825, following his return from a European tour. Over the next two years he published two collections of essays containing some of his best work, *The Spirit of the Age* (1825) and *The Plain Speaker* (1826). One of his most unusual pieces is his account of his conversations with the painter Northcote, which appeared as *Boswell Redivivus* in 1827. The major project of his solitary last years was his *Life of Napoleon* (4 vols., 1828–30); although he considered it his most important work, it is a rather poorly researched and one-sided account and has never commanded a wide readership.

Hazlitt's claim to literary fame is unusual in that it is founded almost exclusively on his work as a descriptive and critical essayist. Although he was often condemned as a hack, his ideas on art and creativity were highly regarded by later 19th-century writers and critics. Taken as a whole, his writing represents an early attempt at a critical history of English literature, and the establishment of the criteria of a canon. Whilst his judgements are based on conspicuously 'Romantic' ideas, he was hostile to Wordsworth's subjectivism and Coleridge's system-building, and fought against their tendency to exempt the artist from social and political responsibilities. On the other hand, however, his own lack of system prevented any bridging of the political and the aesthetic, and his appeal to well-tempered 'feeling' as a barometer of the good in art begs as many questions as it answers.

**Hazzard, Shirley** 1931– Australian novelist and short-story writer. Born and educated in Sydney, she went overseas with her parents in 1947. Her father was a trade commissioner and his postings took the family to Hong Kong and Wellington. In New Zealand Hazzard herself worked in the British High Commission. From 1952 she worked for the United Nations in New York, with a year at Naples, where she was a translator, in 1957. In 1962 she resigned her post to write full-time. She lives in Manhattan, but returns frequently to Italy, the setting for her first two novels, *The Evening of the Holiday* (1966) and *The Bay of Noon* (1970). She first achieved recognition for her short stories, many of which were published in **The New Yorker**, and which were subsequently collected in *Cliffs of Fall* (1963) and *People in Glass Houses* (1967), a series of satirical sketches about the UN. Hazzard's early novels are formally assured works, in the tradition of Flaubert and **Henry James**, which follow the fortunes of female spiritual questers. Her reputation increased considerably with the publication of *The Transit of Venus* (1980). Winner of the US National Book Critics' Award for the best novel of the year, it propelled her into the best-seller lists. It extends the themes of her earlier fiction and encompasses a broad survey of the political and social movements of post-war society. This is subtly realized through an account of the odyssey of two sisters in Australia and England.

*He Knew He Was Right* A novel by **Anthony Trollope**, serialized in weekly numbers from October 1868 to May 1869, and published in two volumes in 1869.

Louis Trevelyan, a gentleman of education and secure private means, marries Emily Rowley, eldest of eight daughters of a colonial administrator. He becomes unreasonably jealous of the frequent visits made to their house by Colonel Osborne, a middle-aged friend of her father with the reputation of being a Lothario, and forbids Emily to receive him. She submits, but when Trevelyan vacillates and Osborne resumes his visits, her husband's jealousy becomes obsessive, hard words are exchanged, and they separate, she taking their young son with her. Sure that he is right in his suspicions, and insisting on a promise never to see Osborne again which Emily feels she cannot give, Trevelyan hires a private detective to watch her and with his help abducts the boy. They go to Italy where Trevelyan declines into a state of complete mental and physical breakdown. Emily follows him there and persuades him to return to England, where he dies. In one of several sub-plots Emily's sister Nora falls in love with Trevelyan's friend Hugh Stanbury, choosing him in preference to a wealthy aristocratic suitor, Mr Glascock. The novel's interest in the question of women's independence is reflected in the hostile portrait of an American feminist, Wallachia Petrie.

**Head, Bessie** 1937–86 South African novelist. Born in Pietermaritzburg, she lived in Botswana from the mid 1960s. In *When Rain Clouds Gather* (1968), *Maru* (1971) and *A Question of Power* (1974), her first three novels, she established connections between personal morality and political integrity; each investigates a lonely character's private problems within a corporate environment, so that the two intermesh. *Maru* and, especially, *A Question of Power* fearlessly confront the nightmares of personal alienation and political tyranny through kaleidoscopic imagery of racism and sexism. *The Collector of Treasures* (1977) contains village tales that she collected and shaped. *Serowe: Village of the Rain Wind* (1981) recreates from oral tradition the history of the Bamangwato capital in Botswana, while *A Bewitched Crossroad* (1984) is a novel about peace and security under the benevolent Bamangwato king, Khama III (1875–1923), after the early 19th-century 'Wars of Calamity' in Central and Southern Africa.

**Head, Richard** ?1637–?1686 Bookseller and hack. Of English parentage, Head was born in Ireland; his father, a domestic chaplain, was murdered in the rebellion of 1641, and the family escaped to England. Head was educated at Bridport Grammar School and was admitted to Oxford, but left before taking a degree, occupying himself initially in the bookselling trade and subsequently as a poorly paid publisher's hack. He was eventually drowned. His most famous work, often reprinted, is the licentious picaresque fiction *The English Rogue: Described in the Life of Meriton Latroon, A Witty Extravagant* (1665), much of which is autobiographical. His many other productions include an eccentric comedy of Irish life, *Hic et Ubique, or, The Humours of Dublin* (1663).

**Headlong Hall** A satire by **Thomas Love Peacock** published in 1816. The first of Peacock's novels, it is a reworking of the themes of his two unpublished farces 'The Dilettanti' and 'The Three Doctors'. Like most of his subsequent works it is cast in the form of a comic Platonic symposium. The disputatious group of guests invited to spend Christmas at Squire Headlong's Welsh country house represents a broad spectrum of contemporary opinion on matters cultural, philosophical and scientific. The principal figures are Mr Foster the perfectibilian, Mr Escot the deteriorationist, Mr Jenkison the status quo-ite, and the Reverend Doctor Gaster, a gourmandizing cleric who has caught the Squire's eye with a learned treatise on the art of stuffing a turkey. They are joined by Dr Cranium, the phrenologist, and his daughter Cephalis; Mr Milestone, the landscape gardener, Mr Panscope the polymath, and assorted musicians, poets, and daughters of marriageable age. The central debate addresses the question of civilization and progress. Foster rehearses the rational optimism of Condorcet and **Godwin**, while the pessimist Escot is a blend of Rousseau, **Malthus** and the notes to **Shelley**'s *Queen Mab*, and, though sometimes cranky, generally emerges ahead of his complacent opponent on points. In a finely worked comic episode Mr Milestone's expert comment on the unimproved appearance of his gardens causes his host to call immediately for explosives to blow away an offending rock, with near-fatal consequences for two of the guests. The Squire again proves true to his name during the denouement, when in a matter of almost as many minutes, he arranges no fewer than four marriages, including his own.

**Heaney, Seamus (Justin)** 1939– Irish poet. Born in Mossbawn, County Derry, Northern Ireland, the son of a Roman Catholic farmer and cattle dealer, Heaney won scholarships to St Columb's College, Londonderry, and Queen's University, Belfast. He worked as an English teacher at St Thomas's secondary school, Belfast, and at St Joseph's College, before being appointed a lecturer at Queen's University. He was guest lecturer at the University of California, Berkeley, in 1970–1, and in 1976 settled in Dublin to work as part-time lecturer in a Catholic college of education.

His early collections, *Death of a Naturalist* (1966) and *Door into the Dark* (1969), were praised as nature poetry of the kind written by **Ted Hughes**. *Wintering Out* (1972) and *North* (1975) established him as a more substantial writer, engaging with serious cultural and political issues of Irish identity in a territory torn by dispute. *Field Work* (1979) is gentler in its approach but contains public and political poems of great achievement such as 'Casualty' and 'The Toome Road'. *Selected Poems 1965–75* was published in 1980, together with *Preoccupations*, selected essays and lectures from 1968 to 1978. *Sweeney Astray* appeared in 1983 and *Station Island* in 1984.

**Hearn, (Patricio) Lafcadio (Tessima Carlos)**
1850–1904 Born in Greece of Irish–Greek
parentage, Hearn was educated in France and
England. In 1869 he emigrated to the USA and
attempted a journalistic career, but his progress
was hampered by poverty and the scandal
caused by his living with a black woman. His
first successful newspaper articles were colourful descriptions of Creole life based on his
experiences in New Orleans in 1877. *Gombo
Zhebes*, published in 1885, was a collection of
proverbs in French from Louisiana and the West
Indies; this was followed in 1890 by *Two Years
in the French West Indies*. Hearn then travelled to
Japan to write a series of articles for *Harper's
New Monthly Magazine*, and in fact remained
there for the rest of his life, becoming a Japanese
citizen and adopting the name Yakimo Koi-
zumi. His works describing the Japanese land,
people and customs include *Gleanings in Buddha-
Fields* (1897), *In Ghostly Japan* (1899), *A Japanese
Miscellany* (1901) and *Japan: An Attempt at Interpretation* (1904). *Chita* (1889) is a novel set on the
Gulf Coast of Louisiana.

**Hearne, John** 1926– Jamaican novelist. Born
in Montreal, Canada, he saw wartime RAF
service, and has taught and been an Arts Centre
director. In his elegantly written novels articulate, middle-class characters respond generously
to calls upon their humanity, but with disastrous personal consquences, as in *Voices under the
Window* (1955), *Stranger at the Gate* (1956) and
*Autumn Equinox* (1959). *The Faces of Love* (1957)
and *Land of the Living* (1961) explore complex
relationships between intellectual lovers. Set on
a slave-ship, *The Sure Salvation* (1981) is an
ingenious treatment of racial conflict. As John
Morris, he co-authored two thrillers with Morris Cargill.

**Hearne, Thomas** 1678–1735 Antiquary. He
was born at Littlefield Green in Berkshire and
educated at St Edmund Hall, Oxford. In 1712 he
became keeper of the Bodleian Library but was
deprived of his office as a **nonjuror** in 1716,
thereafter refusing invitations to political office
of any kind and adhering to his Jacobite convictions.

Hearne was author of *Reliquiae Bodleianae: or
Some Genuine Remains of Sir Thomas Bodley*
(1703) and *Ductor Historicus: or A Short System of
Universal History and an Introduction to the Study of
It* (1704–5); he was the editor of a valuable series
of texts by English chroniclers and published
editions of **John Leland** and **William Camden**.
He appears as Wormius in **Pope's** *The Dunciad*.

**Heart of Darkness** A story by **Joseph Conrad**,
written in 1899 and published in 1902 in *Youth:
A Narrative, with Two Other Stories*. The narrator, Marlow, tells the story to four friends as

they wait for the tide to turn on a ship in the
Thames estuary. Employed by a European trading company, Marlow's earlier destination had
been another ancient river, in Africa: he was to
replace a river-steamer captain killed by natives
in a quarrel over two black hens. Meeting with
the representatives of Western civilization, both
at the trading post and the Central Station (to
which he has to trek) only adds to the ominous
and unreal aspect of his adventure. The atro-
cious suffering of the native workers witnessed
by Marlow goes unnoticed by his colleagues,
who are in Africa solely to extract its ivory.

Marlow becomes curious about a man called
Kurtz, an agent who has surpassed all others: his
reputation for acquiring ivory is apparently
matched by his general cultivation and idealism.
Having found his steam-boat grounded, Marlow's efforts to refloat her are given the added
motive of reaching Kurtz, who is seriously ill.

The discovery of the true motives of the
Company officers (they are impeding the rescue
attempt) is only a rehearsal for Marlow's later
insights into the mind of Kurtz. Expecting to
meet an apostle of Western altruism, Marlow
finds a man who has made himself the natives'
god; their rites have become his, and the diabolical truth about Kurtz's behaviour is signalled
to Marlow when he sees that the posts outside
Kurtz's hut are decorated with human heads.
Marlow, who has spoken of the value of
restraint, retains paradoxical admiration for
Kurtz, whose deathbed cry – 'The horror! The
horror!' – intimates a kind of desperate self-
knowledge.

**Heart of Midlothian, The** A novel by **Sir Walter Scott**, published in 1818 as the second series
of *Tales of My Landlord*.

The heart of Midlothian is the Tolbooth
prison, and the story opens with the Porteous
Riots of 1736. Porteous, commander of the city
guard, had opened fire without reasonable
provocation at the hanging of a robber named
Wilson. Porteous was acquitted at his trial but
the mob, led by Robertson (an associate of
Wilson), stormed the prison. Robertson loves
Effie Deans, imprisoned within on a charge of
child murder, and the attack on the prison thus
has a double motive for him. The mob drags
Porteous from the prison and lynches him; Effie
refuses to escape, preferring to face trial, knowing herself innocent. But at her trial her sister
Jeanie, having taken the oath, cannot bring
herself to lie and thus ensure Effie's acquittal.
Effie is convicted and sentenced to death.

Jeanie sets out to walk to London to gain
audience with Queen Caroline and is fortunate
in having the help of the Duke of Argyle. The
Queen is moved by Jeanie's honesty and a
pardon is secured for Effie. Jeanie is enabled to
marry her suitor, Reuben Butler. Robertson is

now revealed as George Staunton, a rather wild son of good family and the father of Effie's child. He persuades Effie to marry him and, as Lady Staunton, she learns that the son whom she had been accused of murdering is alive. He had been stolen by a crazed girl, Madge Wildfire, and was eventually left with a band of robbers. Staunton is unwittingly killed by his own son when he tries to retrieve him from the robber band.

Modern readers and critics, who have on the whole reversed the judgement of earlier generations and allowed Scott's work to sink into neglect, have usually agreed that *Heart of Midlothian* is the finest of his novels and that Jeanie Deans is his best-realized character. The book is notable, too, for the lyric, 'Proud Maisie', sung by the dying Madge Wildfire.

*Heart of the Matter, The* A novel by **Graham Greene**, published in 1948.

The novel is located in typical Greene territory: a physical and moral wilderness in West Africa where the harsh climate and the still harsher struggle for survival furnish the backdrop to an intense moral drama. The story takes place during World War II. The deputy commissioner of police, Scobie, a Roman Catholic, becomes the victim of his own compassion for others: first for his unstable wife, Louise, then for a young widow, Helen, with whom he has an affair. Finding himself in debt, Scobie borrows money. This initiates a progressive descent into 'hell' which is observed throughout by a young intelligence agent, Wilson.

Increasingly, Scobie's attempts to retrieve his life only compromise him further, and he inadvertently causes the death of his servant Ali. He decides to commit suicide, a mortal sin in terms of his Catholic creed, and endeavours to conceal this from his wife by fabricating his diary. Wilson, who is in love with Louise but acts in his official capacity, uncovers the deceit after Scobie's death, thereby exposing the final tragic paradox in the latter's life.

Though many critics, including **George Orwell** and **Walter Allen**, have rejected the novel as sentimental and contrived, it epitomizes Greene's fiction and has continued to be one of his most-discussed works.

*Heartbreak House* A play in three acts by **George Bernard Shaw**, sub-titled 'A Fantasia in the Russian Manner on English Themes'. The author began the play before World War I but it was not produced until 1920, at the Garrick Theatre, New York. The first London performance was at the **Royal Court** in 1921. The play was published in 1919 and the action takes place, ostensibly, during the war since it closes during an air raid. But the war is not mentioned by any of the characters and the air raid has to be seen as a device to bring about a resolution. Shaw wrote that '*Heartbreak House* . . . is cultured, leisured Europe before the war'; he presents a series of extraordinary encounters and mistaken identities in a crazy house (part of which has been rebuilt as the after-deck of a sailing ship) owned by the eccentric retired Captain Shotover, aged 88, and presided over by one of his daughters, Mrs Hector Hushabye. She invites her friend, Ellie Dunn, to stay. Ellie Dunn is engaged to Boss Mangan, an oaf of a millionaire, for the sake of her father Mazzini Dunn who, though clever and an idealist, has been outmanoeuvred by financiers. Ellie confides to Mrs Hushabye that she has fallen in love with Marcus Darnley, whom she met at a concert; but he turns out to be Hector Hushabye, a pathological liar and philanderer. Captain Shotover wonders if Ellie's father can be the boatswain and ex-pirate he once employed; but that man, Billy Dunn, turns up to burgle the house and be killed in the air raid with Boss Mangan. Another visitor to the house is Lady Utterword, another of the captain's daughters, whose husband has been governor of all the Crown Colonies in succession.

The great virtue of *Heartbreak House* lies in the exploration of motive in a very uncertain world, mostly through the conversations between Captain Shotover and Ellie; she seems able to focus his sympathy and intelligence better than anyone and provokes his comments on the present, which he observes from the eminence of his great age.

**Heath, Roy (Aubrey Kelvin)** 1926– Guyanese novelist, who lives in London. His description of himself as 'a chronicler of Guyanese life in this century' is both accurate and understated. His novels range over slum poverty in *A Man Come Home* (1974), middle-class respectability in the trilogy, *From the Heat of the Day* (1979), *One Generation* (1981) and *Genetha* (1981), country-village destitution in *Kwaku* (1982), and the clash between the values of 'civilization' and the hinterland in *Orealla* (1984). His fiction transcends the regional, however. Despite all the dissonances of Guyanese life that he faithfully records, he has developed a narrative technique that successfully blends social realism with the Amerindian, African and Indian folk legend and myth in Guyanese popular beliefs, in order to analyse modern problems like male–female relationships, personal liberty, and bourgeois ambitions in poverty-stricken communities. His treatment of psychotic behaviour in *The Murderer* (1978) constitutes original, ironical commentary on the 'normal'.

**Heath-Stubbs, John (Francis Alexander)** 1918– Poet. Born in London and educated at

The Queen's College, Oxford, he worked as a teacher and in publishing before taking up fellowships and professorial posts at Leeds, Alexandria and Michigan. His first poems appeared with the work of **Keith Douglas** and **Sidney Keyes** in *Eight Oxford Poets* (1941). Later volumes, including *Wounded Thammuz* (1942), *Beauty and the Beast* (1943), *The Triumph of the Muse* (1958), *Selected Poems* (1965), the epic *Artorius* (1973), *The Watchman's Flute* (1975), *A Parliament of Birds* (1975), *Birds Reconvened* (1980) and *Naming the Beasts* (1982), established him as a traditionalist with an interest in classical subjects and forms. His many translations include the poetry of Leopardi (1946) and Hafiz (1952) and a version of *The Rubáiyát of Omar Khayyám* (1979). He was awarded the Queen's Gold Medal for Poetry in 1973. He has written critical studies of **Beddoes**, **John Clare** and **George Darley**, in *The Darkling Plain* (1950), and of **Charles Williams** (1955).

**Heber, Reginald** 1783–1826 Bishop and hymn-writer. Educated at Brasenose College, Oxford, where he won the Newdigate Prize with his poem 'Palestine', he was elected a fellow of All Souls, and ordained in 1807. In 1822 he was appointed Bishop of Calcutta and he died in Trichinopoly four years later. He was the author of a *Narrative of a Journey through the Upper Provinces of India 1824–1825* and a few volumes of poetry, but he is best known for his hymns, which include: 'Brightest and Best of the Sons of the Morning!', 'From Greenland's Icy Mountains', 'The Son of God Goes Forth to War' and 'Holy, Holy, Holy! Lord God Almighty!'.

**Hecht, Ben** 1894–1964 American playwright, screenwriter and novelist. Hecht was born in New York City but his family later moved to Racine, Wisconsin, where he attended high school. After a brief period at the University of Wisconsin he moved to Chicago. He worked for many years there as a reporter, establishing a reputation as the most creative and energetic newsman in the city. In the early 1920s he began writing novels, the most successful of which was *Erik Dorn* (1921), a work inspired in part by his years in Germany following World War I as foreign correspondent for the Chicago *Daily News*. He did not achieve national prominence, however, until he began writing plays in the mid 1920s. He scored a huge success with *The Front Page* (1928, co-written with **Charles MacArthur**), about Chicago newspapermen. He and MacArthur also co-wrote the popular comedy *Twentieth Century* (1932). From the early 1930s Hecht turned his attention to screenwriting, and he and MacArthur enjoyed further collaborative success. Their screenplays include *Nothing Sacred* (1937), *Wuthering Heights* (1939), *Spellbound* (1945) and *Notorious* (1946).

**Heinlein, Robert A[nson]** 1907–88 American writer of **science fiction**. Heinlein's first intention was to make a career in the US navy, but poor health forced him to retire after four years' service in 1934. His love of military life and ideals, and his regret at missing the action of World War II, are obvious in the glorification of heroism which permeates his fiction. He began publishing science fiction stories in the pulp magazines in 1939, and was the first writer to fit a number of stories together into a coherent future history – all of the relevant stories were assembled into the collection *The Past Through Tomorrow* (1967) and that history features as an 'alternate world' in some of his recent novels. Heinlein's understanding of technology and enthusiasm for the myth of the conquest of space made him an outstanding pulp writer, and he was one of the first science fiction writers to break into more respectable markets. In the 1950s he wrote many novels aimed at teenagers, as well as the political fantasy *Double Star* (1956) and the future war story *Starship Troopers* (1959), but changed direction abruptly with *Stranger in a Strange Land* (1961), a best-selling novel with a messianic hero whose promotion of libertarian politics and morals managed to anticipate both the 1960s counter-culture and the right-wing backlash of the 1970s. In the last phase of his career, his work became increasingly idiosyncratic, extensive elaboration of his personal preoccupations largely displacing plot and invention.

*Heir of Redclyffe, The* A novel by **Charlotte M. Yonge**, published in 1853. Sir Guy Morville, generous and impulsive, secretly pays the debts of his reprobate uncle but is consequently unable to explain his supposed extravagance to his guardian. His delicate and malicious cousin Philip accuses Guy of gambling, which prompts Guy's guardian to banish him from his house and the presence of his daughter Amy, whom he loves. Guy is later rehabilitated and married to Amy. Travelling to Italy, the pair encounter Philip dangerously ill with fever. Forgiving all injury Guy nurses him back to health but subsequently contracts the fever himself and dies. When Amy's child, a girl, is born, Philip becomes the heir of Redclyffe. The novel was immensely successful, passing through 17 editions in 15 years.

*Heiress, The* A comedy by **John Burgoyne**, first produced at **Drury Lane** in 1786, and published in the same year. It was a great success, being quickly translated and played in France and Germany.

The plot concerns the wooing of Lady Emily Gayville by Clifford, her brother's close friend. Lord Gayville himself is expected to marry the vulgar Miss Alscrip, daughter of a newly rich family, because of her wealth. When Miss Alscrip is introduced to Emily, Gayville is made painfully aware of how silly and pretentious his fiancée is. Then he encounters a girl in the street, Miss Alton, and loses his heart to her. He follows her to her modest lodging and is so eager that he embarrasses her; to escape his attentions she goes into service, with Miss Alscrip. All ends well when she is discovered to be Clifford's long-lost sister, and the true heiress to the Alscrip fortune.

**Heller, Joseph** 1923– American novelist, born in Brooklyn, and educated at New York and Columbia Universities. His best-selling anti-war novel *Catch-22* appeared in 1961, since when he has published three more novels: *Something Happened* (1974), *Good as Gold* (1979) and *God Knows* (1984). He has also written a play, *We Bombed in New Haven* (1968). *No Laughing Matter* (1986), written with Speed Vogel, is an account of Heller's experience as a victim of Guillain-Barré syndrome.

**Hellman, Lillian (Florence)** 1907–84 American playwright, born in New Orleans. She started work as a publisher's reader while still a student at New York University and already had several years' experience as a reader of plays and filmscripts when she wrote her first play, *The Children's Hour* (1934), which tells of the havoc caused by a malicious schoolgirl's invention of a lesbian relationship between her two teachers. Though controversial, the play was an immediate success. She followed it with *Days To Come* (1936), which was a failure, and with several filmscripts. In 1937 her anti-fascist convictions led her to visit Spain. Her second successful play, *The Little Foxes* (1939), dealt with the breaking up of a Southern family, the Hubbards, through greed, cruelty and hunger for power; it was followed by two anti-Nazi dramas, *Watch on the Rhine* (1941) and *The Searching Wind* (1944). *Another Part of the Forest* (1946) took a second look at the Hubbard family, some 20 years earlier, revealing the sources of their cruelty and hatred for one another.

Called to testify in 1952 by the House Un-American Activities Committee, she agreed to talk about her own involvement with radical movements but refused to discuss the involvement of others. She was not sent to gaol, but many friends were, including her companion, **Dashiell Hammett**. One of her three autobiographical volumes, *Scoundrel Time* (1976), tells the story of this period of her life. The others, *An Unfinished Woman* (1969) and *Pentimento* (1973), are largely concerned with her childhood experiences and early political and personal involvements. She wrote two other plays, *The Autumn Garden* (1951) and *Toys in The Attic* (1960).

**Helps, Sir Arthur** 1813–75 Essayist, historian and novelist. Educated at Eton and Cambridge, he was appointed Clerk to the Privy Council in 1860, a post which led to his friendship with Queen Victoria. He edited *Speeches and Addresses of the Prince Consort* (1862) and Victoria's own *Leaves from the Journal of Our Life in the Highlands* (1868). He also published: three plays; three novels (including *Realmah*, 1868); aphorisms (*Thoughts in the Cloister and the Crowd*, 1835); essays and dialogues (*Essays Written in the Intervals of Business*, 1841, and *Friends in Council*, four series, 1847–59); biography (*Columbus*, 1869, and *Hernando Cortes*, 1871); and history (*The Conquerers of the New World*, 1848–52, and *The Spanish Conquest in America*, 1855–61).

**Helwig, David** 1938– Canadian poet, novelist and short-story writer. Born in Toronto, he grew up there and in Hamilton and Niagara-on-the-Lake, Ontario. He attended the Universities of Toronto and Liverpool, where he did postgraduate work between 1960 and 1962. Since then, apart from a period as a story editor for Canadian Broadcasting Corporation television, he has taught at Queen's University, Kingston, Ontario. Helwig's earliest poems, first collected in *Figures in a Landscape* (1967), deal mainly with everyday, domestic subjects, but his subsequent work has tended to focus on the sinister and violent. *Atlantic Crossings* (1974) – which describes journeys to the New World by St Brendan, a slave trader, Columbus and a Norse woman – attempts a reassessment of Canadian history. *The Glass Knight* (1976), *Jennifer* (1979), *It is Always Summer* (1982) and *A Sound like Laughter* (1983) form a tetralogy of novels set in Kingston. Helwig's other works include: the volumes of poetry *The Sign of the Gunman* (1969), *The Best Name of Silence* (1972) and *A Book of the Hours* (1979); the novel *The Day Before Tomorrow* (1971); and the short-story collection *The Streets of Summer* (1969). He has also edited *A Book about Billie* (1972), a work that demonstrates his fascination with the darker side of life, from taped interviews with a habitual criminal, and has co-edited several short-story anthologies.

**Hemans, Felicia Dorothea** 1793–1835 Poet. Born in Liverpool, the daughter of George Browne, a merchant, and his first wife, Felicity Wagner, she was educated by her mother. Her parents encouraged her literary aspirations and arranged for the publication of her earliest volumes, *Poems* and *England and Spain, or, Valour and Patriotism*, in 1808. Her first important collection was *The Domestic Affections* (1812). In the same year she married Captain Alfred Hemans, but the marriage ended in separation in 1818. Working to support her five sons, Felicia Hemans produced numerous volumes of poetry, most notably, *The Forest Sanctuary* (1825), *Records of Woman* (1828) and *Songs of the Affections* (1830). Of her two plays, *The Siege of Valencia* and *The Vespers of Palermo* (both published in 1823), only the latter was produced on stage, with little success. An accomplished scholar and an acknowledged beauty, she was the friend of **Scott** and **Wordsworth**. Her best-known poems are 'The Better Land', 'The Landing of the Pilgrim Fathers in New England' and 'Casabianca' ('The boy stood on the burning deck').

**Heminges, John** d. 1630 Actor and theatre administrator, one of the original shareholders in the Lord Chamberlain's Men, later the **King's Men**, when it was formed in 1594. Heminges acted little after 1611, devoting his time instead to the increasingly complex financial affairs of the company. With his friend, fellow actor and fellow administrator Henry Condell (d. 1627), he undertook editorial responsibility for the **Shakespeare** folio of 1623, saving for posterity 20 plays which might otherwise have been lost. The two men were both churchwardens of St Mary's, Aldermanbury, and their careers illustrate the ready acceptance of professional actors in the busy commercial world of Elizabethan and Jacobean London.

**Hemingway, Ernest (Miller)** 1898–1961 American novelist and short-story writer. Born in Oak Park, Illinois, Hemingway spent much of his early life in the Great Lakes region, which provided the settings for his early stories. After graduating from high school he worked as a reporter for *The Kansas City Star*, and then volunteered for service in World War I. He served with an ambulance unit and was wounded in 1918. After the war he worked as a journalist in Chicago and Toronto, and in 1921 married Hadley Richardson, seven years his senior. The couple moved to Paris, and made frequent excursions to Spain and to the Austrian Alps. Hemingway made friends easily; among those who encouraged him in his literary career were **Ezra Pound**, **Gertrude Stein** and **Ford Madox Ford**. His first collection of stories, *In Our Time* (1925), consists of 15 tales – some of them relating the experiences of the young Nick Adams in the Great Lakes region and in Europe. His first novel, *The Torrents of Spring*, appeared in 1926. His second, and the one which first made him famous, was *The Sun Also Rises* (1926), about the disillusionment of the 'lost generation' – young British and American expatriates in France and Spain – in the aftermath of World War I.

In 1927 Hemingway and Hadley Richardson were divorced and he married Pauline Pfeiffer. Later that year he published the collection *Men Without Women*, which contains some of his

Ernest Hemingway, 1944.

most popular stories. 'The Killers' tells of Ole Andreson, whom two thugs have been hired to kill, and of his surrender to the fact that his death is inescapable. 'The Undefeated' depicts the pointless heroism of Garcia, an ageing bull-fighter facing his last fight. 'Fifty Grand' is a brutal and cynical tale of prizefighters, in which Jack Brennan bets money on his own defeat. Hemingway's next novel, *A Farewell to Arms* (1929), is the poignant story of Frederic Henry, an American lieutenant in the Italian ambulance corps during World War I, and Catherine Barkley, an English nurse on duty in Italy. *Death in the Afternoon* (1932), a study of bullfighting, was followed by *Winner Take Nothing* (1933), a collection of short stories including 'A Clean Well-Lighted Place', 'The Sea Change', and 'A Natural History of the Dead'. *Green Hills of Africa* (1935) is about big-game hunting. *To Have and Have Not* (1937) is a short novel about smuggling in the Key West–Havana region. The collection *The Fifth Column and the First Forty-Nine Stories* (1938) includes the story 'The Snows of Kilimanjaro'. *The Fifth Column*, a play about espionage in the Spanish Civil War, was subsequently produced in New York and in wartime England. The conflict in Spain, in which Hemingway was involved as a war reporter, also provided the background for *For Whom the Bell Tolls* (1940), an ambitious novel with the theme (implied in the title, with its quotation from **John Donne**) that the loss of freedom anywhere is a diminution of it everywhere. Hemingway was at the height of his fame and the book sold well: 270,000 copies in the first year.

In 1940 Hemingway was divorced from his second wife and married Martha Gellhorn. This marriage also ended in divorce, in December 1945, and he married his fourth wife, Mary Welsh, in March 1946. He spent World War II as a war correspondent, and in 1950 he published *Across the River and Into the Trees*, his first novel in a decade. It was poorly received, but he came back with *The Old Man and the Sea* (1952), a parable of inner strength and courage about a Cuban fisherman's struggle to bring home a great marlin he has caught. Two years later Hemingway won the Nobel Prize for literature. In the last years of his life he was troubled by failing artistic and physical powers; he committed suicide on 2 July 1961. *A Moveable Feast*, a memoir of his years in Paris after World War I, was left completed but unrevised at his death. It was published in 1964. *Islands in the Stream* (1970) and *The Garden of Eden* (1986) are posthumously published novels; *The Dangerous Summer* (1985) is an account of his trip to Spain in 1959.

**Henderson, Hamish** 1919– Scottish poet, songwriter, folklorist and translator. Born in Blairgowrie, Perthshire, he read modern languages at Downing College, Cambridge, served in military intelligence in North Africa in World War II and became a lecturer in the School of Scottish Studies at Edinburgh University in 1951. His only volume of poetry, *Elegies for the Dead in Cyrenaica* (1948, reissued 1977), is a tribute to 'the dead, the innocent' on both sides of the war in the 'brutish desert'. Henderson edited *Ballads of World War Two* in 1948 and in 1977 made a collection of songs on record, *Freedom Come All Ye*. His best-known songs – 'The John Maclean March' and 'Free Mandela' – show his strong socialist and republican sympathies. He is a distinguished translator of modern Italian poets such as Montale, Quasimodo and Ungaretti and has published an edition of Gramsci's *Letters from Prison* (1974).

**Hendry, J[ames] F[indlay]** 1912–86 Poet and anthologist. Born in Glasgow, Hendry studied French and Russian at Glasgow University, and German in London. After intelligence work during the war, he worked as a translator and interpreter before becoming Professor of Modern Languages at Laurentian University, Ontario. He was a central figure in the **New Apocalypse** movement, introducing the first of its three major anthologies, *The New Apocalypse* (1939), and editing the other two, *The White Horseman* (1941) and *The Crown and the Sickle* (1943), with **Henry Treece**. Hendry's *Myth and*

*Social Integration* (1940) is the major statement of the aims of the movement. Poems in *The Bombed Happiness* (1940) have tortuous, doomladen imagery. *The Orchestral Mountain* (1943) attempts to connect the myth of Orpheus and Euridice with the death of the poet's wife. A minor poet, he also published *Marimarusa* (1979) and *A World Alien* (1980).

**Henley, W[illiam] E[rnest]** 1849–1903 Poet, critic and editor. Born in Gloucester, he was struck down as a child with tuberculosis and consequently had a leg amputated. He was treated in Edinburgh by Joseph Lister and during a long convalescence began his 'In Hospital' poems (first published in 1875), which have been hailed as early examples of free verse. It was also in Edinburgh that he met **Robert Louis Stevenson** (who used him as a model for Long John Silver in *Treasure Island*), and they formed a close friendship which was later to end in a bitter quarrel. He became editor of *The Magazine of Art* in 1882, and brought the work of Whistler and Rodin to a wider public. In 1889 he returned to Edinburgh to edit *The Scots Observer* (later *The National Observer*), an imperial review which aimed to increase Scottish cultural and political influence, and which introduced **Kipling**. In 1894 he returned to England and edited the short-lived *New Review*, before settling to poetry in his last years.

Henley is best known for the poem 'Invictus' (1875), which contains the lines 'I am the master of my fate:/I am the captain of my soul.' His poetry collections include *A Book of Verses* (1888), *The Song of the Sword* (1892), *London Voluntaries* (1893), *For England's Sake* (1900) and *Hawthorn and Lavender* (1901). There are two volumes of art and literary journalism: *Views and Reviews I* and *II* (1890 and 1892). Among many anthologies the best known is *Lyra Heroica* (1891), a selection of verse for boys. There was an influential edition of **Burns** (1896–7) and the *Tudor Translations* (1892–1903). He wrote four plays with Stevenson: *Deacon Brodie* (1882), *Beau Austin* and *Admiral Guinea* (1884) and *Macaire* (1885).

**Henri, Adrian** See **Liverpool poets**.

*Henrietta Temple* A novel by **Benjamin Disraeli**, published in 1837.

Ferdinand Armine, son of poor but noble parents, enters the army and is soon in debt; but he has hopes of a legacy from his grandfather. When this does not materialize, he proposes to his cousin, Katherine Grandison, because she is wealthy. But he falls in love with the penniless Henrietta Temple and becomes engaged to her, too. Ferdinand's treachery is exposed and Henrietta deserts him. In Italy Henrietta meets Lord Montfort, whom she consents to marry at her father's urging. Katherine, meanwhile, has forgiven Ferdinand and released him. She and Count Mirabel undertake to remedy Ferdinand's situation. He meets Henrietta again and her love for him is reawakened, while Lord Montfort is drawn to Katherine. Lord Montfort gives up Henrietta, who inherits a fortune and helps Ferdinand. Katherine marries Lord Montfort.

**Henry, O.** Pseudonym of the American short-story writer William Sidney Porter (1862–1910), born in North Carolina. He founded *The Rolling Stone*, a comic weekly magazine, in 1894. Five years later, while serving a three-year prison sentence for alleged embezzlement in Columbus, Ohio, he began to write short stories published under the pseudonym of O. Henry. After his release from prison in 1902 he went to New York City, where he became a popular and prolific writer of short stories for magazines. His stories are characteristically marked by a twist of plot which turns on an ironic or coincidental circumstance, and he is a master of the surprise ending. His first collection, *Cabbages and Kings* (1904), is set in South America; his second, *The Four Million* (1906), in New York City. His other volumes are *Heart of the West* (1907), *The Trimmed Lamp* (1907), *The Gentle Grafter* (1908), *The Voice of the City* (1908), *Options* (1909), *Roads of Destiny* (1909), *Whirligigs* (1910) and *Strictly Business* (1910). Four more volumes were published posthumously: *Sixes and Sevens* (1911), *Rolling Stones* (1912), *Waifs and Strays* (1917) and *Postscripts* (1923).

**Henry IV, King** A history play in two parts by **William Shakespeare**. The shaping of the plot, drawn largely from **Holinshed**'s *Chronicles*, permits the conclusion that Shakespeare had the second part of this history play in mind when he prepared the first. Even so, the two parts are distinct, and it is quite orthodox to perform them separately.

**Part One**. Probably first performed in 1597 and first published in Quarto (Q1) in 1598. Modern editors collate this text with that in the First Folio of 1623.

The historical events described in the play begin with the uprising of Owen Glendower and the defeat of the invading Scots by Henry Percy (Hotspur) and culminate in the defeat and death of Hotspur at the Battle of Shrewsbury (1403). The decisive usurper, Bolingbroke of *Richard II*, has been transformed into a careworn king, thwarted in his desire to expiate his crime by leading a crusade by the threat of civil war. Henry IV is further troubled by his son's waywardness. Prince Hal beguiles the time in the company of the fat knight, Sir John Falstaff, drinking in taverns and plotting practical jokes. By comparison, Hotspur seems all the more a hero. But when Hotspur, angered by the King's refusal to ransom his brother-in-law Mortimer, joins forces with Glendower, it is Prince Hal who saves the day at Shrewsbury, fighting gallantly in defence of his father and killing Hotspur in single combat – a death for which Falstaff claims the credit.

**Part Two**. Probably first performed in 1598 and first published in a censored Quarto (Q1) in 1600. Modern editors collate this text with that in the First Folio of 1623.

The play covers, in a highly compressed form, the period from the Battle of Shrewsbury to Henry IV's death in 1413. After his triumph at Shrewsbury, Prince Hal has returned to the riotous company of Falstaff and his cronies, but takes up arms when the rebel forces gather again. Falstaff, recruiting in the Cotswolds, finds a welcome with Justice Shallow, with whom, in his youth, he 'heard the chimes at midnight'. Prince John, younger son of Henry IV, persuades the rebels to disperse their army and then arrests the leaders for high treason. The dying King hears of this successful campaign. He falls asleep with the crown beside him, and Prince Hal, thinking him dead, holds the crown that will be his. They are reconciled, and the feeble King advises his son to unite England by undertaking a foreign campaign.

Overjoyed to hear of Hal's succession, Falstaff boasts of his future under the new King, but the transformed Henry V spurns him in public during his coronation procession.

The two parts of *Henry IV* are an extraordinary achievement. The bare bones of the old-fashioned chronicle play are fleshed out with the riches of what is almost social history. Hotspur is a hero whose home-life is that of a benevolent merchant. Falstaff is both knight and vagabond, a vital link for the future king between the court he knows and the submerged life of London's back streets. Falstaff's trip into the Cotswolds introduces yet another layer of English life, that of rural culture. And Shakespeare has found a different language for each of the social strata he exhibits. So popular was the magnificent creation of Falstaff that he had to write **The Merry Wives of Windsor** to satisfy popular demand. This is fair evidence of the great contemporary popularity of *Henry IV*.

**Henry V, The Life of** The last in the series of history plays by **William Shakespeare**, first performed *c*. 1599 and first published in a corrupt (probably pirated) Quarto (Q1) in 1600. The text in the First Folio of 1623 is probably taken from Q2 (1602). Shakespeare's main source was **Holinshed**'s *Chronicles*, though he seems also to have consulted **Edward Hall**'s *The Union of the Two Noble and Illustre Families of Lancastre and York*.

This most obviously patriotic of the English

history plays is the only one that openly celebrates the achievements of a successful king. Mocked by the French, who revive memories of his frivolous youth, Henry displays his political astuteness by quelling a rebellion at home before going on to demonstrate his military prowess in a French campaign of which the Battle of Agincourt is the highlight. Magnanimous in victory, he charmingly woos the French princess, Katharine, and the play ends with their marriage plans sealed with a kiss.

A low-life sub-plot involves, first, the reported death of Falstaff and then the unruly conduct of various of his old associates, Pistol, Bardolph and Nym. Symbolizing the bonds of loyalty that hold Henry's united kingdom, but oddly ill at ease in both main and sub-plot, are four English, Welsh, Irish and Scottish commanders, Gower, Fluellen, Macmorris and Jamie.

*Henry V* is a slightly disappointing sequel to the splendid achievements of **Henry IV**. The formula is similar, but the absence of Falstaff leaves Henry, even on his disguised trip around the Agincourt camp-fires, awkwardly isolated from the people he inspires and rules. Shakespeare seems sometimes overstretched in his attempt to win his audience's admiration for 'the mirror of all Christian kings'.

*Henry VI* A history play in three parts, of which **William Shakespeare** was the main, but almost certainly not the sole, author. The first part may date from as early as 1590, and the second and third can be presumed, from Elizabethan theatre practice, to have followed fairly closely. It may be that this uneven trilogy contains the first surviving stage composition by Shakespeare. The only reliable text is that published in the First Folio of 1623. The main sources are **Holinshed**'s *Chronicles* and **Edward Hall**'s *The Union of the Two Noble and Illustre Families of Lancastre and York*.

*Henry VI* is an episodic account of the reign of Henry V's son, from the years of his infancy to his murder by Richard, Duke of Gloucester. Whereas Part I divides its attention between factional quarrels in England and the war in France, the last two parts confine themselves to the dynastic struggles that have come to be known as the Wars of the Roses. The complex history of plot and counter-plot is uncertainly controlled, and the trilogy is less successful as a whole than it is memorable for a handful of episodes and characters.

*Henry VIII, The Life of King* A historical play, probably written collaboratively by **William Shakespeare** and **John Fletcher**. The likely date of first performance is 1613 and the first publication was in the First Folio of 1623. **Holinshed**'s *Chronicles* is a main source.

The play is at its most impressive in chronicling the guile of Wolsey and his sudden downfall and the anguish of Queen Katharine. Its popularity on the 19th-century stage owed more to the taste for pictorial splendour and to its purple patches of rhetoric than to its intrinsic merit as a play. The history was perhaps too recent and too contentious to allow the authors' well-tried theatrical imaginations sufficient freedom. If this was Shakespeare's last work for the theatre, it is a disappointingly half-hearted end.

*Henry Esmond, The History of* See *History of Henry Esmond, The*.

**Henry the Minstrel** See **Blind Harry**.

**Henryson, Robert** d. *c.* 1508 Scottish poet. All that is known of Henryson's biography is that he lived in Dunfermline and died before the end of 1508, when **William Dunbar** wrote of him as already dead. It has been suggested that Henryson was a schoolmaster and that he studied medicine or law (or both), perhaps at Bologna, but none of this is certain. His poetry shows him well-read in the Church Fathers and the biblical commentaries, and familiar with the work of Aristotle and Boethius.

An important and influential Middle Scots poet, he is one of the group known as the **Scottish Chaucerians**. Despite the obvious influence of **Chaucer**, Henryson's originality and skill are the most striking features of his work. His best-known poems are: *The Testament of Cresseid*, an alternative ending to Chaucer's *Troilus and Criseyde*; *The Morall Fabillis of Esope the Phrygian*; *Orpheus and Eurydice*; and *Robene and Makyne*, a version of pastoral. He also wrote a number of shorter works, several of them meditations on mortality, and two didactic allegories. *The Bludy Serk* is a brief narrative of a knight who rescues a maiden from a giant's castle but is killed in the process, leaving her a bloody shirt by which to remember him; it is interpreted in terms of Christ's sacrifice for the soul betrayed by the devil. *The Garmont of Gud Ladeis* is similar, describing an allegorical garment made up of various virtues.

**Henslowe, Philip** d. 1616 Theatre manager. Henslowe was the son of the master of the game in Ashdown Forest. He was probably born *c.* 1550 and was certainly living in the Liberty of the Clink in London by 1577. Having been apprenticed to a dyer, he made himself rich by marrying his master's widow. The match brought Henslowe a step-daughter and, in 1592, a son-in-law through her marriage to the most famous actor of the day, **Edward Alleyn**.

Henslowe's interest in theatrical property was well established by then. The **Rose**, built in 1587 or 1588, was his, together perhaps with the theatre in Newington Butts. In partnership with Alleyn in 1604, he purchased the patent as

Master of the Royal Game of Bears, Bulls and Mastiff Dogs, thereby crowning a decade of commercial interest in animal-baiting. Henslowe was the most consistently successful of all the Elizabethan speculators in entertainment. In 1600, when the Rose looked like losing out to the **Globe**, he built the **Fortune** north of the river, specifying in the building contract those features of the Globe he was keenest to have copied, and he may well have had some share in the management of the **Swan** as well. Finally, in 1614, he brought together his interests in animal-baiting and drama in the building of the **Hope** on Bankside. This was to be an adaptable arena, with 'a stage to be carried or taken away' when the business of the day was not drama.

That Henslowe took an interest in theatre is irrefutable evidence of its potential profitability in Elizabethan England. He was a businessman, and not an over-scrupulous one. Apart from maintaining some share in his brother's mines in Ashdown Forest, he was involved also in the manufacture of starch, in real estate, in pawnbroking and in money-lending. It was, in some part, by usury that he maintained his hold over actors and playwrights. It is the preservation of his *Diary* among the papers deposited in Dulwich College by Edward Alleyn that gives Henslowe a peculiarly vital place in the study of the Elizabethan theatre. The *Diary* is less the systematic record of a fanatical bookkeeper than fitful evidence of a wealthy man's attempt to keep his affairs in better order. The manuscript includes his brother's mining accounts, records of Henslowe's private affairs, three sets of pawn accounts, a list of unlikely cures for ailments and, crucially, records of theatrical income and expenditure at the Rose. It can be most conveniently read in the single volume edition by R. A. Foakes and R. T. Rickert (1961).

**Henty, G[eorge] A[lfred]** 1832–1902 Popular author for boys. Born near Cambridge, the son of a stockbroker, and educated at Cambridge University, Henty served first in the Crimean War and later covered other important armed conflicts as a war correspondent. Such background was to serve him well when he first started writing for boys in 1868, with around 80 subsequent novels (sometimes three per year) as often as not concentrating on action-packed episodes from British history. Typical titles include *Under Drake's Flag* (1883), *The Lion of the North* (1885) and his last book, *With the Allies in Pekin* (1904). Enjoying huge sales both in Britain and America, his books long remained popular – **George Orwell** making several sardonic references to their unquestioning patriotism in his journalism. Today they are interesting only as period pieces.

**heptameter** See **metre**.

**Heraud, John Abraham** 1799–1887 Poet. Born in London, educated privately. He made a career as a contributor and editor working for *Fraser's Magazine*, *The Athenaeum* and the *Illustrated London News*. His powerful grandiose style is best represented in *The Descent Into Hell* (1830) and *The Judgement of the Flood* (1834). He also wrote a successful play, *Videna, or, the Mother's Tragedy* (1854).

**Herbert, A[lan] P[atrick]** 1890–1971 Novelist. Herbert was born at Ashstead in Surrey and educated at Winchester and New College, Oxford, where he studied law. After war service with the Royal Navy in Gallipoli and France, during which he was wounded, he became private secretary to an MP. His war experiences resulted in two volumes of poetry (1916 and 1918) and the novel *The Secret Battle* (1919), an account of the horrors of warfare. He was a regular contributor to *Punch* and joined the magazine's staff in 1924. His first stage play, a Christmas piece called *King of the Castle*, was written in the same year, as was the first of his mock law reports. These were later collected as *Misleading Cases in the Common Law* (1929) which ridiculed absurdities of court procedure. *Holy Deadlock* (1934) was a novel which exposed the need for reform of the divorce law, a task which Herbert personally undertook as Independent MP for Oxford University (1935–50). The stormy battle over his Marriage Bill was related in *The Ayes Have It* (1937), while *Independent Member* (1950) described his years in Parliament, during which he continued to fight for a variety of legal reforms. His most popular novel, *The Water Gipsies* (1930), reflected his long-standing love for the English waterways.

Herbert also wrote the libretti for a number of successful musicals, including a revue, *Riverside Nights* (1926), and several operas, *Tantivy Towers* (1930) and *Bless the Bride* (1947) among others. Herbert was knighted in 1945. *APH: His Life and Times*, an autobiography, appeared in 1970.

**Herbert, (Alfred Francis) Xavier** 1901–84 Australian novelist. Born at Port Hedland in Western Australia, he trained as a pharmacist at the University of Melbourne, but abandoned a job as a hospital pharmacist at the age of 24 in favour of a career in literature. He served as Protector of Aborigines at Darwin from 1935 to 1936. In 1975 and 1976 he held appointments as writer-in-residence at the Universities of Newcastle, NSW, and Queensland. His best-known work is a sprawling chronicle of Aborigines and white men set in the Northern outback and entitled *Capricornia* (1938). Other novels are *Seven Emus* (1958) and *Soldiers' Women* (1960). In *Poor Fellow My Country* (1975) Herbert returned to the outback with a massive saga, notable for its passages dealing with Aboriginal life. He is also the author of *Larger Than Life* (1963, short stories) and *Disturbing Element* (1963, autobiography).

**Herbert, Edward, 1st Baron of Cherbury** 1583–1648 Philosopher, poet and diplomat. The elder brother of **George Herbert**, the poet, he was educated at University College, Oxford, and in 1606 moved to London to enter court circles. He was ambassador to France (1619–24) and travelled widely. His foremost work was *De Veritate*, a philosophical treatise in Latin, published in London in 1625, a metaphysical work that aligned him with the **Cambridge Platonists**; the principles of natural religion he propounded have earned him the title the 'Father of **Deism**'. He also published some spirited English verse.

In 1632 Charles I created him Baron Herbert of Cherbury, and he was appointed to the Council of War. Herbert was reluctantly active as a Royalist soldier until 1644, when he retired to Montgomery Castle, but submitted to Parliament the following year, and received a pension. His *The Life and Reign of Henry VIII* (1644) is not outstanding, but his *Autobiography* (though stopping at 1624) is an interesting revelation of the times, and was first published in 1764 by **Horace Walpole**. Herbert's career was one of early promise but no ultimate greatness.

**Herbert, George** 1593–1633 Poet and divine. A member of the noble family that included the earldoms of Pembroke and Montgomery among their holdings, Herbert had an elder brother, Edward, later **Baron Herbert of Cherbury**, and another who became Master of Revels, Sir Henry Herbert. Himself an outstanding scholar, he was educated at Westminster, and Trinity College, Cambridge, where he was a fellow at 22, and Public Orator to the University from 1619 to 1627. Before the death of James I, Herbert seems to have entertained aspirations for public advancement, acting as MP for Montgomery in 1624–5, but he became a deacon in the following year, which debarred him from civil office. His mother, who was a patron of **John Donne**, died in 1627, and Herbert married Jane Danvers in 1629.

During this period of professional indecision (he had resigned his oratorship) Herbert was working on the poems which were later published together as *The Temple*. He became a priest in 1630, obtained the living of Bemerton in Wiltshire, and continued there as a conscientious and benevolent rector until his wavering health gave out, and he realized he was dying. Early in 1633, therefore, he sent a consignment of verse to his friend **Nicholas Ferrar**, asking for his opinion. Herbert died on 1 March 1633. Later that year appeared his collection *The*

George Herbert. Engraving by Robert White, 1674, after the poet's death. British Museum Print Room.

*Temple, Sacred Poems and Private Ejaculations*, a body of some 160 poems, which went through 13 editions by 1680. The chief quality of these often exquisite and short poems is the ingenious nature of their images and their carefully wrought shapes. The tenor is generally religious, and in the mode of devotional verse Herbert ranks as one of the foremost writers in this busy literary era, though his conceits may sometimes appear extravagant. His poetry found favour with later poets, **Cowper** and **Coleridge** in particular. He was the author of the short prose work *A Priest to the Temple* (1652), offering guidance to country priests, and **Isaak Walton** wrote a biography of him, which was first published in 1670.

**Herbst, Josephine (Frey)** 1897–1969 American novelist and journalist, born in Sioux City, Iowa, and educated at the University of California at Berkeley. Her first two novels were *Nothing is Sacred* (1928) and *Money for Love* (1929). These were followed by *Pity is not Enough* (1933), *The Executioner Waits* (1934) and *Rope of Gold* (1939), a trilogy dealing with the decay of capitalism and the emergence of a revolutionary movement which falters and fails to bring about the new communist social order it seeks. Like many other writers of her generation, Herbst aligned herself with the political left. In 1935 she went to Germany as a special correspondent for the *New York Post* and subsequently travelled to Spain to cover the Civil

War. Her other publications include two novels, *Satan's Sergeants* (1941) and *Somewhere the Tempest Fell* (1947). At the time of her death she was at work on *The Burning Bush*, a literary and personal history of the 1920s and 1930s, and *Hunter of Doves* a collection of novelettes.

**Herd, David** 1732–1810 Scottish ballad collector and anthologist. Born in Kincardineshire, he spent much of his life as a clerk in Edinburgh, where he moved in convivial literary circles. He accumulated a good deal of older Scottish traditional verse, notably in *Ancient and Modern Scottish Songs . . . Collected from Memory, Tradition, and Ancient Authors* (2 vols., Edinburgh, 1776).

***Hereward the Wake*** **Charles Kingsley**'s last completed novel, published in 1866. It weaves a romantic and adventurous story from the legends about the English outlaw who led a rising against William the Conqueror in 1070 and was defeated at Ely.

***Hermsprong*** See **Bage, Robert**.

**Herne, James A.** 1839–1901 American playwright, born in Cohoes, New York, to an immigrant Irish family. When he was 20 he joined a theatre group, through which he eventually met **David Belasco**, with whom he collaborated on many productions. Their first significant work was *Chums* (1879), later retitled *Hearts of Oak* (1880). This sentimental domestic melodrama about an old sailor who adopts two orphans and falls in love with one of them is notable for its early indication of Herne's tendency toward realism in the subject matter, dialogue, characterization and staging of his plays. Herne later outlined his convictions about dramatic writing and presentation in the article 'Art for Truth's Sake in the Drama' (1896). His next play, *The Minute Men of 1774–75* (1886), was less successful, and in 1888 he wrote and produced the unconventional temperance drama, *Drifting Apart*. The most important of his contributions to American dramatic realism is *Margaret Fleming* (1891), the story of a woman's response to her husband's infidelity. Clearly influenced by Ibsen in both subject and style, the play was acclaimed by **Hamlin Garland** and **William Dean Howells** but relentlessly attacked by the critics. His next play, *Shore Acres* (1892), an equally realistic but happier story of life in New England, was very successful, and broke performance records in Boston. He wrote two more plays: *The Reverend Griffith Davenport* (1899), a Civil War story based on Helen H. Gardner's novel *An Unofficial Patriot* (1894); and *Sag Harbor* (1900), a reworking of the themes of *Hearts of Oak* in which two brothers are rivals for the love of the same woman.

***Hero and Leander*** An erotic poem (or **epyllion**)

left incomplete by **Christopher Marlowe** at his death in 1593 and finished by **George Chapman**. Marlowe's share of the poem, published by itself in 1598, is its first two 'sestiads'. The word was coined by Chapman by analogy with 'Iliad'; it derives from Sestos, where the poem is set, and may also indicate Chapman's six-fold division. All six sestiads appeared later in 1598.

Marlowe's poem derives from the story by Musaeus, an Alexandrian poet of the 5th century. No English version of Musaeus's poem seems to have been available to Marlowe, but there were Latin, Italian and French translations. Marlowe's version is Ovidian in tone and manner: the digressive story of Mercury and the country maid and decorative mythological allusiveness showing the influence of the *Metamorphoses*. The speaking voice of the narrator owes much to another Ovidian work, the *Amores*, which Marlowe translated. Marlowe's poem relates the meeting, wooing and eventual sexual consummation of the love of Hero and Leander. Having wooed Hero, 'Venus' nun', at Sestos, Leander swims to her turret, in the course of his swim naïvely rejecting the amorous advances of Neptune. It ends with the dawn breaking after a night of love.

Chapman's continuation, sestiads III–VI, is twice as long. Marlowe had a wry and detached narrator relating the passage of two lovers from innocence to experience. Chapman continues the story with conceit, **allegory** and personified abstractions, notably the goddess Ceremony. A change of tone is announced at the beginning of sestiad III and Chapman's continuation is more concerned with morality and decorum.

***Heroes, The*** **Charles Kingsley**'s version, intended for children, of the Greek myths of Perseus, Theseus and Jason. It was published in 1854.

***Heroes, Hero-Worship, and the Heroic in History, On*** A group of six lectures by **Thomas Carlyle**, delivered in May 1840 and published the following year. In the first lecture he said: 'The History of the World is but the Biography of great men . . . Could we see *them*, we should get some glimpses into the very marrow of the world's history.' His premise was that heroism could manifest itself in any field of human ability, and he proceeded to describe the different forms taken by the hero in different phases of human history: Divinity (Odin), Prophet (Mahomet), Poet (Dante and **Shakespeare**), Priest (Luther and Knox), Man of Letters (**Johnson**, Rousseau and **Burns**) and King (Cromwell and Napoleon).

**heroic couplet** In English verse, a pair of rhyming iambic pentameters (see **metre**). The form was developed most notably by **Chaucer** and championed by **Dryden** (especially in his *Essay of Dramatic Poesy*) against the **blank verse**

of much English tragic drama. Dryden was also responsible for promoting its use in non-dramatic verse, cultivating the poised, epigrammatic effects which predecessors like **Ben Jonson**, **Donne** and **Waller** had occasionally managed and which 18th-century successors like **Pope** and **Johnson** emulated. The 'closed couplet' uses the **end-stopped line**, but the 'open couplet' uses **enjambement**.

**Herrick, Robert** 1591–1674 Poet and divine. Apprenticed at the age of 16 to his uncle, a goldsmith named Sir William Herrick, he did not go up to Cambridge until 1613. He graduated with an MA in 1620, went to London, and began to mix in the artistic circles of the capital, where he became a friend of **Ben Jonson**, the writer with whom he is now most identified. Although he was beginning to write, none of Herrick's work was yet published in print; in 1623 he took Holy Orders, and acted as chaplain to Buckingham on the expedition to the Ile de Ré. Herrick continued to write verse prolifically – during the course of his life he was responsible for some 2500 compositions, many dating from the 1620s – and in 1629 was appointed by Charles I to the living of Dean Prior in the diocese of Exeter. He enjoyed the calm parish life of Devon, but was ejected under the Commonwealth for refusing the Solemn League and Covenant, and returned to London, though he was reinstated in 1662. He died, a bachelor, at the age of 83, in his parish.

In 1648, the year after he was compelled to leave Dean Prior, Herrick published his major collection, *Hesperides*. This volume consists of 1200 poems, many of them short, and taking an impressive variety of forms including elegies, epitaphs, epigrams, anacreontics (drinking-songs of the Jonsonian type), hymns, songs (many later set to music) and imitations of the Roman poets Horace and Catullus. Some of the epigrams are positively vile, while elsewhere Herrick is capable of beautifully wrought lyrics which have invited analogies with his earlier craft as a goldsmith; 'The Funeral Rites of the Rose', or 'The Lily in a Crystal' demonstrate the intricate style of his more delicate lyrics, and there is a whimsical grace in much of his love poetry, such as 'To the Virgins, to make much of time', a classic exposition of the **carpe diem** theme. 'Oberon's Feast' and 'Oberon's Palace' are two of his fantasy pieces about faeries. Included separately in *Hesperides* was the subsection *Noble Numbers*, a body of devotional verse which is less individual, and unlike his secular verses is not visually brilliant or embroidered with pretty conceits. Although perhaps never a profound poet, Herrick was a distinguished verbal craftsman, and his erotic poems can be highly sensory. **Swinburne** praised him as 'the greatest song-writer ever born of English race'.

**Herrick, Robert** 1868–1938 American novelist, born in Cambridge, Massachusetts, and educated at Harvard. Many of his novels depict professionals or businessmen who struggle to achieve worldly success only to find that it leaves them unhappy and unfulfilled. In his first novel, *The Man Who Wins* (1897), the character who comes to this realization is a doctor who has given up research for a lucrative medical practice. *Web of Life* (1900) also has a doctor as its hero; *The Common Lot* (1904), an architect. *The Real World* (1901, republished as *Jock O'Dreams* in 1908), *A Life for a Life* (1910) and *Waste* (1924) all tell the stories of business executives who come to regret their material success. *Memoirs of an American Citizen* (1905), perhaps his best-known novel, is the story of Van Harrington, who makes a fortune and wins a seat in the Senate but, unlike Herrick's other leading characters, exhibits no regret. *Sometime* (1933) is a satirical Utopian novel. Herrick also published several collections of short stories: *Love's Dilemmas* (1898), *Their Child* (1903), *The Master of the Inn* (1908), *The Conscript Mother* (1916) and *Wanderings* (1925). He died in the Virgin Islands, where he had served for three years as secretary to the governor.

**Herschel, Sir John Frederick William** 1792–1871 Astronomer. The son of Sir William Herschel, born at Slough and educated at Cambridge, he was a founder of the Royal Astronomical Society and Secretary to the Royal Society 1824–7. He discovered many new stars, clusters and nebulae. His writings include *Outlines of Astronomy* (1841) and *Familiar Lectures on Scientific Subjects* (1867).

**Hervey, James** 1714–58 Essayist. A prominent member of early Methodist circles, Hervey was born at Hardingstone in Northamptonshire and completed his education at Lincoln College, Oxford. He became rector of Collingtree and Weston Favell in his native county. *Meditations among the Tombs* (1746–7), *Reflections on a Flower Garden* and *Contemplations on the Night* (both 1747) were popular in their day, appealing to the same tastes as the work of the **graveyard poets**.

**Hervey, John, Baron Hervey of Ickworth** 1694–1743 Politician. Son of the Earl of Bristol, he was educated at Westminster School and Clare College, Cambridge, and went on a tour to Europe in 1716 when, in Hanover, he befriended the Prince Frederick (son of George II). In 1720 he married Molly Lepell, a London beauty who was maid of honour to the Princess of Wales. Hervey was a political supporter of Walpole and in 1730 he was appointed Vice-Chamberlain to George II; from 1733 until Walpole's fall in 1742 he was Lord Privy Seal and enjoyed the confidence of Queen Caroline.

As a friend of the accomplished **Lady Mary**

Wortley Montagu, Hervey became a hated enemy of her admirer, **Alexander Pope**, who penned a most withering verse-portrait of him as Sporus in the *Epistle to Dr Arbuthnot*, one of his keenest satires, and also in ***The Dunciad***. Hervey attempted to respond in kind, but Pope's representation of him as an unnatural, dangerously pernicious fop has had a lasting impression on Hervey's reputation. His own *Memoirs of the Reign of George the Second* (published in 1848) offer a satirical portrait of the times, remarkably frank about the motives and methods of his contemporaries seeking preferment.

***Herzog*** A novel by **Saul Bellow**, published in 1964. It won the National Book Award for fiction in 1965 and became a best-seller. Its leading character is Moses Herzog, a 47-year-old scholar, twice divorced, who undergoes an emotional, intellectual and moral crisis. As the novel opens, he is tucked away in a house in the Berkshire Mountains. It is summer, and since spring he has been composing letters to various persons – dead or alive, obscure or famous – in an effort 'to explain, to have it out, to justify, to put in perspective, to clarify, to make amends'. Among those he addresses in these 'mental letters' (not all of which he commits to paper) are the women in his life, friends, relatives, his psychiatrist, politicians, philosophers (such as Heidegger and Nietzsche), the public (in letters to the editor), even God. Flashback scenes provide the reader with information about Herzog's relations with his family, his two ex-wives (Daisy and Madeleine), his Japanese mistress Sono, and his current lover, Ramona.

Herzog travels to Chicago, intent on avenging himself on Madeleine and her lover, Valentine Gersbach, formerly Herzog's friend. He takes his father's gun and goes to the home that Valentine and Madeleine share. Peering through a window, he watches Valentine tenderly bathe his (Herzog's) daughter Junie; his humanity is touched and his homicidal urges subside. While taking Junie on an outing they are involved in a minor car accident. The police investigating the accident discover the gun, for which Herzog has no permit, and arrest him. His brother posts his bail, and he returns to the Berkshires for a final week of letter-writing. At the end of the novel he rejects his brother's suggestion that he go into a mental hospital; he engages a local couple to help him put his dilapidated summer place to rights again; he makes plans to have his son Marco (his child by Daisy) visit him; and he prepares for a dinner with Ramona. Herzog's excursions – physical and mental – have left him in relative peace, and for the time being he has 'no messages for anyone'.

**Hewett, Dorothy** 1923– Australian playwright, poet and novelist. She was born in Perth and educated at Perth College and the University of Western Australia. In 1948 she moved to Sydney, where her experience of factory work inspired her only novel, *Bobbin' Up* (1959). She returned to Perth in 1960. Her first play was the working-class drama *This Old Man Comes Rolling Home* (1967). Mainly expressionistic works featuring music and poetry, her plays depict complex women characters trapped in ageing, domesticity and the stereotyped images of women, or evoke an idyllic pastoral world. They include *The Chapel Perilous* (1971), *Bon-Bons and Roses for Dolly* (1972), *The Tatty Hollow Story* (1974), *Pandora's Cross* (1978), *The Man from Muckinupin* (1979) and *The Fields of Heaven* (1982). She has also published four volumes of poetry: *Windmill Country* (1968), *Rapunzel in Suburbia* (1975), *Greenhouse* (1979) and *Alice in Wormland* (1985). She was made a Member of the Order of Australia in 1986.

**Hewitt, John (Harold)** 1907–87 Irish poet. Born in Belfast of Nonconformist 'planter' stock, Hewitt was educated at the Methodist College and Queen's University, Belfast. He worked in museums and art galleries in Belfast and Coventry until his retirement in 1972. Hewitt first gained attention as a nature poet and celebrant of local landscapes, particularly the Glens of Antrim, but his inherited Nonconformity and his reading of **Paine**, **Cobbett** and **Morris** made him a political dissenter. In his poetry this activated a stubbornly radical quest for an Ulster identity predicated on neither an increasingly strident Protestant unionism nor the traditions of Catholic and Celtic nationalism, but on the dialect and idiom generated by local history and environment. Since his *Collected Poems* (1968) he has published seven more collections, most recently *Freehold and Other Poems* (1986), which reprints his historical verse play *The Bloody Brae* (1931), a still-timely plea for tolerance and forgiveness of past hatreds. Published in the shadow of sectarian violence, these later volumes have ranged beyond it in unsentimental evocations of localities, childhood, travel and failing sight. Hewitt's verse is characteristically 'mannerly', formally disciplined and understated but precisely observed, thoughtful and humane. His lifelong concern with the art, poetry, speech and traditions of his native province, reflected in numerous essays and articles as well as in his anthology *The Rhyming Weavers and Other Country Poets of Antrim and Down* (1974), has influenced younger poets such as **Seamus Heaney** and **Tom Paulin**.

**Hewlett, Maurice (Henry)** 1861–1923 Novelist and poet. Hewlett studied law and was called to the Bar but never practised. He was Keeper of Land Revenue Records in 1896–1900. His first novel was *The Forest Lovers* (1898), a medieval romance that became an immediate success. Other romances followed with *Richard Yea and Nay* (1900) and *The Queen's Quair* (1904). A trilogy of modern life – *Halfway House* (1908), *Open Country* (1909) and *Rest Harrow* (1910) – centred on John Maxwell Senhouse, a gentle itinerant scholar. In 1916 he published a long narrative poem, *The Song of the Plow*, which considers the lot of the agricultural labourer. His volumes of essays include *In a Green Shade* (1920), *Wiltshire Essays* (1921) and *Extemporary Essays* (1922).

**hexameter** See **metre**.

**Heylyn, Peter** 1600–62 Religious controversialist. Educated at Magdalen College, Oxford, Heylyn was a supporter of Archbishop **Laud**. His principal work was *Ecclesia Restaurata, or, The History of the Reformation of the Church of England* (1661). Two posthumously published works were *Cyprianus Anglicus, or, The History of the Life and Death of Archbishop Laud* (1668), which was a defence of the dead Archbishop against attacks by **William Prynne**, and *Aerius Redivivus, or, The History of Presbyterianism* (1670), which sees Calvinism as the destructive force behind religious strife in England. Heylyn was also the author of a description of the known countries of the world, *Microcosmus: A Little Description of the Great World* (1621), enlarged and republished as *Cosmography* in 1652.

**Heyward, DuBose** 1885–1940 American poet, novelist and playwright, born in Charleston, South Carolina. His first volume of verse, *Carolina Chansons*, appeared in 1922 and was followed by *Skylines and Horizons* (1924) and *Jasbo Brown* (1931). In 1925 he published *Porgy*, a novel about black life in South Carolina, set in a tenement neighbourhood in Charleston called Catfish Row. A dramatic version of the book was written jointly by Heyward and his wife Dorothy in 1927, and was awarded a Pulitzer Prize. The work was adapted by George Gershwin into the opera *Porgy and Bess* in 1935. Characterized by a use of regional materials and Southern folklore, Heyward's other novels include a chronicle of the Civil War entitled *Peter Ashley* (1932) and *Star Spangled Virgin* (1939), which explores the response of the Virgin Islanders to the New Deal. *Mamba's Daughters* (1929), a novel about the life of a black mother, was dramatized in 1939 by Heyward and his wife.

**Heywood, John** c. 1497 – c. 1580 Dramatist. Little is known about the early life of John Heywood beyond **Anthony à Wood**'s statement that he was educated at Broadgates Hall (later Pembroke College), Oxford, but found it 'not suiting with his airy genie'. He married the daughter of John Rastell, the printer, whose wife was **Thomas More**'s sister, Elizabeth. (Heywood's daughter was **John Donne**'s mother.) The connection with More proved very valuable to Heywood, who became a singer and player of the virginals at the court of Henry VIII from 1519 to 1528. He became a court pensioner in 1528 and held office in the City of London, later becoming a freeman. He remained in favour at court until 1544, when as a zealous Roman Catholic he was involved in a conspiracy directed against **Thomas Cranmer**. He was actually convicted of treason but he saved his life by recanting. Later he became a favourite of Queen Mary's, but upon the accession of Elizabeth and the end of Catholic hopes in England he went into exile. He was last heard of in Malines, in the Netherlands, in 1578.

Heywood published several collections of epigrams and proverbs, and contributed to court **masques** during the reigns of Edward VI and Mary. But his importance to English literature lies in his contribution to the development of English drama. His short dramatic interludes marked a complete departure from allegory and instruction, being concerned with the human comedy in terms of his own world. Among them were *The Play of the Weather* (1533), *A Play of Love* (1533) and *A Dialogue Concerning Witty and Witless* (first printed 1846). He moved nearer to true stage comedy with *The Play Called the Four PP* (c. 1544), in which Palmer, Pardoner and 'Pothecary dispute the value of their respective occupations. They are joined by a pedlar, who offers a prize to the one who shows the greatest capacity for lying. The palmer wins by declaring that he had never known 'any woman out of patience'. Heywood is plainly restoring the comedy of which **Chaucer**, in narrative if not in drama, had been a master.

Heywood was perhaps the first true exponent of English stage comedy, though his own particular contribution was not developed and exists in a peculiar isolation – he lived until the time of the Armada but his interludes were written in the reign of Henry VIII.

**Heywood, Thomas** 1573–1641 Playwright, actor, poet and pamphleteer. Much of his work has been lost and much that remains is ephemeral: interest in his mayoral pageants, for example, is likely to be confined to scholars. Of the 220 plays to which he claimed to have contributed, some 30 have survived. They include: an outstanding domestic tragedy, *A Woman Killed with Kindness* (1603); a frolicsome adventure play in two parts, *The Fair Maid of the West* (published 1631); a chronicle history play, *If You Know Not Me, You Know Nobody* (1605); an ambitious but oddly perfunctory dramatization of Greek mythology in five plays, *The Golden Age*, *The Silver Age*, *The Brazen Age* and the two parts of *The Iron Age* (1611–13); and a late collaboration with **Richard Brome**, *The Late Lancashire Witches* (1634). The excesses of his chivalric romance, *The Four Prentices of London* (published 1615) are nicely satirized by **Francis Beaumont** in *The Knight of the Burning Pestle*, but Heywood's feeling for the theatre of his time should not be underrated. It is well represented in *An Apology for Actors* (1612), a spirited and informative defence of the theatre against Puritan attacks.

**Hiawatha, The Song of** A long narrative poem by **Henry Wadsworth Longfellow**, published in 1855. The poem tells how Hiawatha is reared by Nokomis, daughter of the moon, who helps him acquire the wisdom and power necessary for an Indian hero and leader. Upon reaching manhood, Hiawatha seeks to avenge his mother Wenonah, against his father, the West Wind. The combat ends in reconciliation, and Hiawatha becomes the leader of his people. Although his rule is marked by peace and prosperity, hard times come to his tribe; his wife, Minnehaha, dies, and he follows her to the land of the North Wind, having first advised his people to accept the white man, whose coming he has predicted. Longfellow based the metre of his poem on that of the Finnish epic *The Kalevala*; its hypnotic rhythm has often been parodied.

**Hibberd, Jack** 1940– Australian dramatist. Born in Warracknabeal, Victoria, and brought up in Bendigo, he studied medicine at the University of Melbourne, graduating in 1964. He subsequently worked as a doctor until 1973, since when he has devoted himself to the theatre full-time, remaining in Melbourne, while several of his contemporaries have moved elsewhere. During the 1960s he was an important figure in the move to create a new Australian theatre. A Melbourne University group in which he was prominent took shape as the La Mama Theatre Company and later, in 1969, as the Australian Theatre Company. Hibberd was influential both as dramatist and director in this attempt to bring a more populist and experimental theatre into being, and was involved during this period with other innovatory figures in Australian drama, such as Peter Romeril and **David Williamson**. His early plays, like *White with Wire Wheels* (1967), an examination of Australian male values, employ a rough vernacular style. *Dimboola* (1969), one of Australia's most performed plays, is an affectionately satirical treatment of a country wedding. *A Stretch of the Imagination* (1972), a monologue by an old man facing death, blends comedy and pathos and is widely regarded as his finest work to date. Its protagonist is a quintessentially Australian character, a teller of tall tales who brings together positive and negative aspects of the national legend. It is typical of Hibberd's attempt to create a popular theatre dealing with leading figures and events in Australian popular folklore. The same concerns inform his plays *Captain Midnite VC* (1972), *A Toast to Melba* (1974) and *The Les Darcy Show* (1975), in each of which a national figure is presented with a mixture of fondness and satire. Other plays by Hibberd include *Peggy Sue* (1974), *One of Nature's Gentlemen* (1976) and a number of plays published in the left-wing Melbourne quarterly, *Meanjin*.

**Hichens, Robert (Smythe)** 1864–1950 Journalist and novelist. Eldest son of Canon Hichens, Rector of St Stephen's, near Canterbury, Hichens studied piano and organ at Bristol and the Royal College, London, before deciding, aged 24, that his talent was not strong enough. He had been writing lyrics and songs from his teens, and these brought him a steady income. He joined a school of journalism, an experience described in his novel *Felix* (1902), and succeeded **Shaw** as music critic of *The World*. He was author of 66 books, but his most famous work is his first novel, *The Green Carnation* (1895), written when he was 29. In later years Hichens went to live in Sicily, spending three weeks in a Trappist monastery.

**Higgins, Matthew** 1810–68 Jacob Omnium, the journalist. Born at Benown Castle, County Meath, and educated at Eton and at University College, Oxford, he spent some years managing his inherited estates in British Guiana. He showed his skill as a controversialist in his pamphlets and writings on the Irish question in 1847, often using the name or initials of 'Jacob Omnium, the Merchant Prince', the title of a satire on mercantile dishonesty published in *The New Monthly Magazine* in 1845. He moved much in London society, sporting as well as literary, and was a friend of **Thackeray**. His many pseudonymous letters to *The Times* (up to 1863) and his periodical contributions had a high reputation.

**High Wind in Jamaica, A** See **Hughes, Richard**.

**Higher Criticism, The** The study of the Bible as literature, concentrating on literary technique and sources. Pioneered by 18th- and 19th-century German scholars, it grew out of the older textual criticism concerned with the establishment of the best texts. David Friedrich Strauss (1808–74) denied the historicity of all supernatural elements in the Gospels in his *Das Leben Jesu* (1835–6). He argued that they were 'myth', developed between the time of Christ and the writing of the Gospels in the 2nd century. **George Eliot** translated Strauss in 1846, remarking that it made her ill 'dissecting the beautiful story of the Crucifixion'; the long-term effect was loss of her faith. Joseph Ernest Renan's *Vie de Jésus* (1863) also demythologized the life of Christ by portraying Jesus as an amiable rabbi.

The Higher Criticism implied that the Bible was not the directly inspired word of God but a human artefact; it was less a repository of incontrovertible truth than an anthology of literary beauties. This tendency in biblical studies was part symptom, part cause of the 19th-century decline in religious belief. It seemed that scholarship combined with Darwinian science and geological research to undermine the bases of Christian fundamentalism.

See also **John William Colenso** and *Essays and Reviews*.

*Highland Widow, The* See *Chronicles of the Canongate*.

**Highsmith, Patricia** See **detective fiction**.

**Hill, Aaron** 1685–1750 Theatre manager, playwright and versifier. Educated at Barnstaple Grammar School and Westminster, Hill travelled to Constantinople at the age of 15 and toured the area with a tutor for three years, publishing *A Full Account of the Ottoman Empire* in 1709. His first play, *Elfrid*, flopped in 1709 and was rewritten as *Athelwold* with only fractionally greater success in 1731. At the **Haymarket Theatre** in 1710 he staged *Rinaldo*, his own translation of Rossi's libretto to music by Handel. He became friendly with **Richardson** and on the appearance of *Pamela* (1740) wrote him a sycophantic letter which Richardson printed in the preface to the second edition. Hill's astonishing belief in his own importance and ability led him to write letters advising **Garrick** how to act, **Walpole** how to conduct political life, and **Pope** how to write. Pope retaliated by putting him in **The Dunciad**. He died the night before the intended first performance of his translation of Voltaire's *Merope*. Nearly all his writings are quite properly forgotten. His two lasting achievements were in stage scenery: a practicable mountain in *Rinaldo* and the first practicable bridge in his production of *Henry V* at **Drury Lane** in 1723.

**Hill, Geoffrey** 1932– Poet. Born in Bromsgrove, Worcestershire, and educated at the local grammar school and Keble College, Oxford, Hill began graduate work there before being appointed a lecturer at the University of Leeds and then at Cambridge, where he teaches at present.

His books are *For the Unfallen* (1959), *King Log* (1968), *Mercian Hymns* (1971), *Tenebrae* (1978) and *The Mystery of the Charity of Charles Péguy* (1983). His poetry has an integrity of purpose built from sustained attention to particular themes. The tone is elegiac, and the poems often imagine and give a voice to embattled or suffering figures from both distant and more recent history. Hill's precision of language is unequalled among his contemporaries, though his range is restricted and without humour except a kind of grim wit. It is the intensity of his work and his ambivalent attitude to Christianity that accounts for his reputation as a serious poet; rigour and discipline are the virtues attributed to him in critical accounts. *Mercian Hymns* is a sequence of prose-poems using the historical and legendary figure of Offa to connect the idea of kingship with the private responsibilities of the individual and those of the poet to his people and his time.

**Hill, Susan** 1942– Novelist, short-story writer and author of radio plays. Born in Scarborough, she studied at King's College, London. A frequent theme of her fiction is loneliness, which her best work treats with a lucid psychological precision and narrative composure: *In the Springtime of the Year* (1974) explores the aftermath of a woman's bereavement; *A Change for the Better* (1969) depicts a group of damaged, isolated people brought together in a hotel. *I'm the King of the Castle* (1970), probably her best-known book, won praise for its piercing fable of the brutality latent in childhood innocence. Her resolution to give up novel-writing to look after a family (she is married to the Shakespeare scholar Stanley Wells) has been partly retracted after some years' silence with the publication of *The Woman in Black* (1983), a generic ghost story.

*Hillingdon Hall* A novel by **R. S. Surtees**, published in volume form in 1845. It is the third in the Jorrocks trilogy begun with **Jorrocks's Jaunts and Jollities** and **Handley Cross**, and it deals with his life in retirement, when he devotes himself largely to farming. Much of the humour lies in his enthusiastic but inexpert adoption of new 'scientific' ideas: he is brought back to earth by his former huntsman, James Pigg, who rapturously rejoins his establishment. There is little about hunting and more than is usual with Surtees concerning human relationships and social intercourse. Jorrocks becomes a JP, a role which he fills with characteristically outrageous gusto; and we leave him at the point when he has been elected to Parliament. Mrs Jorrocks is as appalling as ever as 'grande dame' of the village.

**Hillyer, Robert (Silliman)** 1895–1961 American poet, novelist and critic, born in East Orange, New Jersey, and educated at Harvard. He served in World War I, then returned to Harvard, where he taught from 1919 to 1945. His first volume, *Sonnets and Other Lyrics*, was published in 1917. *The Hills Give Promise* appeared in 1923. His novel *Riverhead* (1932) was followed in 1933 by *The Collected Verse of Robert Hillyer*, for which he won the Pulitzer Prize. Subsequent publications include *First Principles of Verse* (1938, a critical work), *Pattern of a Day* (1940, poetry), *My Heart for Hostage* (1942, a novel), *Poems for Music, 1917–1947* (1947), *The Death of Captain Nemo, a Narrative Poem* (1949), *In Pursuit of Poetry* (1960, a critical work) and *Collected Poems* (1961). He generally wrote in traditional verse forms, most notably the sonnet and the heroic couplet.

**Hilton, James** 1900–54 Novelist. James Hilton was born at Leigh in Lancashire, and educated at school and university in Cambridge. As a free-lance journalist he contributed to many newspapers and journals. He first made his name with *Goodbye, Mr Chips* (1934; serialized in *The British Weekly* in 1933), a sentimental tale about an English public school master. His other best-selling novel was *Lost Horizon* (1933), which described 'Shangri-La', an imaginary land isolated in the heart of Asia where the inhabitants were liberated from the stresses of normal life. The name has since been used to signify any idyllic retreat from the world.

Hilton's other novels include *Murder at School* (1931; written under the pseudonym Glen Trevor), *Contango* (1932), *Knight Without Armour* (1933), *We are not Alone* (1937) and *Random Harvest* (1941), about a man suffering from amnesia. During the 1940s Hilton became a Hollywood scriptwriter, and he died in California.

**Hilton, Walter** *c*. 1340–96 Author of *The Scale of Perfection* (or *The Ladder of Perfection*) and of several minor treatises and letters in English and Latin. After studying at Cambridge he became a hermit, but later became an Augustinian canon at Thurgarton priory, Nottingham, where he died. *The Scale of Perfection* is a devotional treatise in two parts, one written considerably later than the other. The first book aims to show how the soul must obliterate the image of sin, replace it with the image of Christ and practise virtue in the attempt to attain perfection. The second book explains the distinction between the active and contemplative lives of the religious and describes the beginnings of contemplation. The similarities between the work and *The Cloud of Unknowing* suggest that Hilton was familiar with *The Cloud*, but it is unlikely that he was its author.

**Himes, Chester (Bomar)** 1909–84 Black American novelist, born in Jefferson City, Missouri. In 1928 he was sentenced to 20 years in the Ohio State Penitentiary for armed robbery. There he witnessed the prison fire of 1930 that killed 320 convicts, an event which became the subject of his first well-known story, 'To What

Red Hell?' (1934). His novel *Cast the First Stone* (1952) is also based on his experiences in prison. He was paroled in 1936 and went to Cleveland, Ohio, where he became friends with **Langston Hughes** and **Louis Bromfield** before moving to Los Angeles, where he became involved in the communist movement. He has lived as an expatriate in France and Spain since 1953.

His first novel, *If He Hollers Let Him Go* (1945), is a story about racial conflict in the defence plants of Los Angeles during the war years. *Lonely Crusade* (1947) examines racial discrimination and violence in the wartime labour unions of California. In 1954 he published *The Third Generation*, a study of the middle-class black experience. *The Primitive* (1955) explores interracial sexuality, a topic taken up later in *Pinktoes* (Paris, 1961; New York, 1965). His later work is dominated by a series of books about the experiences of two Harlem detectives. These novels, in which he continues to examine the themes of racism and violence, include *The Real Cool Killers* (1959), *All Shot Up* (1960), *Cotton Comes to Harlem* (1965), *The Heat's On* (1966), *Blind Man with a Pistol* (1969) and *A Case of Rape* (1980). His autobiography, *The Quality of Hurt*, was published in 1972, followed by *My Life of Absurdity* in 1976.

**Hind and the Panther, The** A poem in three parts by **John Dryden**, published in 1687, two years after his conversion to Roman Catholicism. The first part characterizes various religious sects and identifies them with the emblems of specific animals, the chief pair being the 'milk-white Hind' of the Roman church, and the aggressive Panther, representing Anglicanism. In the second part, there is a theological argument between the two churches. The third and most notable part spills over into temporal satire and invokes two celebrated fables: the swallows and the martin (told by the Panther), and the pigeons and the poultry (told by the Hind).

The significant associations of the beast emblems are at times difficult to follow, but the doctrinal centre of this poem is Dryden's insistence on divine mystique, the belief that essential truth in things 'darkly writ' is accessible only through absolute faith. It is the poet's affirmation of his belief in the indefinable, and the infinite. Despite its earnestness of theme, this poem contains some of Dryden's most accessible verse – particularly the Hind's rebuke to her son, in Part 3 – as well as reflecting the practical and social difficulties involved in translating a faith from one affiliation to another.

**Hindle Wakes** A play by **Stanley Houghton**, first performed in London in 1912, when it was greeted with particular favour by supporters of the movement for women's emancipation.

Fanny Hawthorne, a weaver at Jeffcote's Lancashire cotton mill, and Alan Jeffcote, son of the owner, have spent a weekend together in Llandudno. Both sets of parents agree that they must marry, but Fanny ruins the plan by refusing to marry Alan just 'to turn him into an honest man'. She prefers to leave home and live on her earnings as a weaver.

**His Last Bow** See **Sherlock Holmes stories**.

**His Natural Life** A novel by **Marcus Clarke**, serialized in the *Australian Journal* March 1870 – June 1872, and later published in a thoroughly revised and shortened form in 1874. It was not until 1885, some four years after the author's early death, that the revised version was given the longer title of *For the Term of His Natural Life*.

In the original version, the dissolute son of the wealthy Sir Richard Devine is accused, while travelling in London under the pseudonym of Rufus Dawes, of the murder of his accomplice in a proposed fraud, Hans Blinzler. Though circumstantial evidence is strong against him, Dawes refuses to reveal the truth in an effort to protect his wife, Blinzler's daughter. His sentence of death is commuted to transportation. At the notorious Norfolk Island settlement in Australia he finds a cruel and sadistic persecutor in the commandant, his cousin Maurice Frere, who marries and destroys Dora, a girl Dawes had saved while she was a child and has loved faithfully ever since. After 30 years of suffering, all is finally resolved when Dawes reclaims his true identity and is reunited with his wife, while his adopted daughter Dorcas, the child of Dora and Frere, marries his upright nephew Arthur Devine.

In the revised version the lengthy prologue is cut to give a more melodramatic explanation for Dawes's sentence, and the work ends as Dawes dies reunited with Sylvia (Dora in the original) while escaping from Norfolk Island in the doomed *Lady Franklin*.

The authority and gloomy power of the novel stem partly from Clarke's extensive use of public records and recollections of the penal settlements, and partly from his own authentic and intense response to the harsh beauty of the Australian landscape and its contradictory society consisting of the convicted and the free.

**History of Great Britain, The** **David Hume**'s *History* first appeared between 1754 and 1762, the whole first being published together in 1763.

In its final form the book extends from Caesar's invasion to the flight of James II in 1688, but Hume had originally begun with the Stuarts and worked backwards. 17th-century history best embodied his concern with the progress of society, by which he largely meant the development of political liberty. This interest leads him to concentrate less on the public history of wars and treaties than some earlier chroniclers and less on character studies of history's chief actors than some later ones. His analysis of the social and economic conditions which make 'liberty' possible, and of the relations between liberty and necessary authority, is conducted from a broadly Whig standpoint but without conspicuous partisan loyalties. The attempt at philosophical impartiality is matched by a prose style which is, according to **Buckle**, 'polished as marble, but cold as marble too'.

The *History* was the most popular of Hume's works in his lifetime, its success giving him financial independence for much of his later career, and remained standard for long afterwards.

**History of Henry Esmond, The** A novel by **W. M. Thackeray**, published in three volumes in 1852.

Henry Esmond, who tells the story of his life in a predominantly third-person narrative mode, grows up believing he is the illegitimate son of the 3rd Viscount Castlewood, who dies at the Battle of the Boyne. A lonely childhood in Jacobite circles is lightened when his cousin Francis Esmond inherits the title, and comes to live at Castlewood with his young wife Rachel and their two children, Frank and Beatrix. Their kindness to Henry wins his devotion, but when he unwittingly brings smallpox to the house, and Rachel's looks suffer as a result, husband and wife become estranged. She generously pays for him to go to Cambridge, and he returns to find the dissolute Lord Mohun a regular guest, gambling with Lord Castlewood and pursuing his wife. The two lords fight a duel in London and Castlewood is killed. At his death he gives Henry a written confession, which reveals him to be legitimate and the true heir of Castlewood, but Henry burns the document, refusing to disinherit his patron's son. He is imprisoned for his part in the duel, and rejected by Rachel, although the vehemence of her accusation is one of several signs in the novel of her hidden, guilty love for him.

On his release from prison Henry goes abroad to fight in the War of the Spanish Succession. He returns to an emotional reunion with Rachel at Winchester, and finding Beatrix grown into a proud and beautiful woman, falls in love with her. His pursuit of this worldly beauty at home alternates with his military service abroad in Marlborough's campaigns. He fights at Blenheim and Ramillies, and in Brussels learns of his Flemish mother and visits her grave. Beatrix is now established at court and becomes engaged to the Duke of Hamilton. But the Duke and Lord Mohun fight a duel, and both are killed. In a last effort to please Beatrix, Henry joins in a plot to restore James Edward Stuart, the Old

Pretender, to the throne on the death of Queen Anne. The plot fails because of the Prince's reckless pursuit of Beatrix to Castlewood, when he should have been with his followers in London. Disillusioned with power and worldliness, Esmond marries Rachel, the woman he has always called his 'mistress', and retires with her to a life of domestic tranquillity in Virginia.

*Henry Esmond* is generally considered the finest Victorian historical novel, achieving Thackeray's stated aim to make 'history familiar rather than heroic' (Preface). The elegance of its historical pastiche is enriched by psychological undercurrents and a feeling for the secret life of memory.

**History of Mr Polly, The** A novel by **H. G. Wells**, published in 1910.

Alfred Polly, now 37 years old, has always lived half in an impeding world of real misfortunes and half in a joyous imaginative world, often associated with the past. Polly has suffered from an appalling education followed by several years apprenticed, unsuitably, to a low-class draper. A legacy from his father has worsened his lot: his own shop is unprofitable, and marriage to his cousin Miriam has been loathsome, and produced severe indigestion for 15 years.

Polly escapes after a comically abortive attempt at suicide, when he starts a fire and fails to cut his throat. As a result of his actions during this 'great Fishbourne fire', bundling his neighbour's mother-in-law across the rooftops, Polly is proclaimed a hero. In his fat, romantic way, he tends to achieve his weak ambitions by accident.

When Polly abandons his home for a life on the road, the novel endorses his Utopian dreams of escape. The landscapes of rural England, around the Potwell Inn and its plump landlady, are a haven from the pressures of his class and its failed commercial prospects. But Polly is able to settle at the Inn only after proving his manhood in a fight against the criminal Uncle Jim, and after Miriam has been awarded life insurance for the husband that she imagines to be dead.

**History of Pendennis, The** A novel by **W. M. Thackeray**, with illustrations by him, serialized in monthly parts from November 1848 to December 1850.

Arthur Pendennis's father, a medical man turned country squire, dies while his son is at school, and he is brought up by his unworldly widowed mother, who lives at Fairoaks with her adopted daughter Laura Bell. The young Pen falls in love with a travelling actress, Miss Fotheringay, but is saved from an imprudent marriage by his worldly uncle, Major Pendennis, who persuades the girl and her father, the tipsy Captain Costigan, to break off the engagement. Pen then goes to Oxbridge, where he

becomes idle and extravagant, fails his exams and gets into debt; his mother and Laura pay his debts and he takes his degree. Back at Fairoaks he flirts with Blanche Amory, the shallow and coquettish daughter of the second wife of Sir Francis Clavering, the local baronet, and dutifully proposes to Laura, who rejects him. Pen goes to London to study law, but through his friendship with George Warrington, whose chambers he shares, he starts to write for the 'Pall Mall Gazette' and publishes a successful fashionable novel, 'Walter Lorraine'.

Introduced to London society by his uncle, Pen meets Blanche again, and in turn introduces her to his friend Harry Foker, who falls in love with her. Pen becomes attracted to a porter's daughter, Fanny Bolton, but resolves not to seduce her. He falls ill and is nursed by Fanny, but unknown to him she is dismissed by his mother, who wrongly suspects her of being his mistress. When he subsequently challenges Mrs Pendennis with suppressing Fanny's letters, his own innocence becomes apparent, and mother and son are reconciled before her sudden death. Major Pendennis tries to arrange a worldly marriage between Pen and Blanche, using his knowledge of scandal in the Clavering family to persuade Sir Francis to give up his seat in Parliament to Pen, and they become engaged. When Pen discovers the scandal, that Blanche's father is alive and a criminal, he repudiates the arrangement but decides to honour his engagement. Blanche, however, has transferred her affections to Foker, now the wealthy inheritor of the family fortune. Pen is now free to propose to Laura, whom he has come to love, and she accepts him.

This leisurely **Bildungsroman**, often compared to **Dickens**'s contemporaneous *David Copperfield*, was Thackeray's attempt to portray a representative gentleman of the age, 'no better nor worse than most educated men' (Preface). It has autobiographical elements, especially in the portrayal of London literary life and the fashionable novel industry.

**History of Plimmoth [or Plymouth] Plantation** A history of the pilgrim settlement at Plymouth, Massachusetts, by **William Bradford**, probably begun in 1630. He worked on it until 1651, during most of which time he served as the colony's governor. After his death the unpublished manuscript passed to his nephew, **Nathaniel Morton**, who consulted it when writing *New England's Memorial* (1669). It remained unpublished until 1856. The first book, most likely written between 1630 and 1633, tells of the origins of the Separatist movement in England, the settlement in Leyden, the plans to emigrate to New England, and the voyage aboard the *Mayflower*. Book II, written between 1646 and 1650, is a collection of annals recording the sacred and secular affairs of the colony for the years 1620–46. Throughout both books Bradford included primary material – laws, letters, charters, a list of passengers on the *Mayflower* – which has proved an important source for subsequent historians.

***History of Sir Charles Grandison, The*** A novel by **Samuel Richardson**, published in 1753–4.

The story is told through letters. Harriet Byron, an attractive young lady, arrives in London society and excites the desires of Sir Hargrave Pollexfen, a wealthy, dishonourable swaggerer who is unused to being rebuffed. Harriet repeatedly refuses his insolent proposals of marriage until in a rage he has her abducted from a masked ball and, still failing to bully her into a secret marriage, packs her off to his country estate in a carriage. She is fortunate enough to be saved by the intervention of the wealthy and gallant Sir Charles Grandison, and the pair become enamoured of each other.

While in Italy, though, Sir Charles had previously become attached to Clementina della Porretta, daughter of a noble family which was indebted to him for his services; the two had not actually married due to the differences in their religions. Clementina, more distraught than he at the prospect of their being apart, now suffers a mental breakdown and her parents beg Sir Charles to return urgently to Italy, to save her at any price. The lady recovers when he arrives, and the hero's honour is saved from a difficult dilemma by Clementina's decision that their religions constitute too great an impediment after all. So, with a clear conscience, Sir Charles returns to England and happily marries the lovely Harriet.

Throughout this long novel the portrayal of sustained virtue threatens to become incredible, but there are many touches of delicate sensibility and feeling, and a sureness in domestic description that won the book the admiration of **Jane Austen**.

***History of the Fairchild Family, The*** See **Sherwood, Mary Martha**.

***History of the Rebellion and Civil Wars in England, The*** The title usually given to the **Earl of Clarendon**'s history of his times, *The True Historical Narrative of the Rebellion and Civil Wars in England*. It was begun in 1646, when Edward Hyde (as he then was) accompanied Prince Charles into exile in the Scilly Isles, though not completed until the author's second exile, begun in 1667, and not published until 1702–4. The *History* is a landmark in English historical literature, as well as a valuable source of information about the political upheavals of the 17th century. Clarendon wrote as an eyewitness to events, aided by his lawyer's training in the making of considered judgements and, particularly, by a remarkable gift for characterization.

***History of the Reign of King Henry the Seventh, The*** A biography by **Francis Bacon**, published in 1622, his first work after being dismissed from office. As well as careful historical documentation, Bacon brings his own legal and political experience to bear on the subject. The result is not a chronicle but a coherent interpretation, in which the King is viewed as a Machiavellian figure.

***Histrio-Mastix*** See **Prynne, William**.

**Hoadly, Benjamin** 1676–1761 Churchman and theologian. Hoadly was born at Westerham in Kent and educated at St Catharine's College, Cambridge. He became Bishop of Bangor, Hereford, Salisbury and Winchester successively. A serious illness in youth had left him so incapacitated that he usually preached on his knees. A sermon delivered before George I in 1717 argued that the Gospels afford no warrant for any visible church authority and provoked the 'Bangorian controversy', so called because both Hoadly and his main opponent, **Thomas Sherlock**, had at different times held that see. Hoadly was the author of a number of religious works, including *A Plain Account of the Nature and End of the Lord's Supper* (1735), which maintained that the Last Supper was merely commemorative.

**Hoadly, Benjamin** 1706–57 Dramatist. The son of the bishop who bore the same name (q.v.), Hoadly was a physician in the royal household and became the friend of **David Garrick**. Like many others he owed such success as he was to enjoy as a playwright to the great actor, who staged Hoadly's comedy, *The Suspicious Husband*, at **Covent Garden** in February 1747 and found an excellent part as Ranger, an audacious rake. Hoadly was the author of some medical textbooks; no other play of his was produced though he is believed to have written a total of three.

**Hoban, Russell** 1925– Novelist and children's writer. Born in Pennsylvania, Hoban settled in London in 1960. For many years an illustrator, he became a writer for children before turning to adult fiction as well. *The Mouse and his Child* (1969) is now regarded as a modern classic of **children's literature**. His first three novels – of which the third, *Turtle Diary* (1975), is considered the most substantial – are whimsical, wistful fables of loneliness and aspiration, which often break out in zany comedy. Hoban's fourth full-length fiction, *Riddley Walker* (1980), marked a major advance: ostensibly a scenario of a Britain reverted to primitivism after a late 20th-century holocaust, it is also a religious enquiry into the essence of knowledge, achieved through a broken-down phonetic diction that Hoban has formulated for his narrator, which is simultaneously halting and opaque, and capable of poetic precision. A further novel, *Pilgermann* (1983), set in the Holy Land, continues Hoban's metaphysical and mystical fabulation. *The Medusa Frequency* (1987) is a slighter, more anarchic fantasy preoccupied with word processors, Indian music and Greek myths.

**Hobbes, John Oliver** Pseudonym of the novelist and playwright Pearl Mary Teresa Craigie, *née* Richards (1867–1906). Born in Boston, she was educated in America, England and France before finally settling in England. She contributed many articles to various newspapers and periodicals, but is chiefly remembered for her first novel, *Some Emotions and a Moral* (1891), and for her play *The Ambassador* (1898). Her other novels included *The Sinner's Comedy* (1892), *The Serious Wooing* (1901) and *The Flute of Pan* (1905). Another play, *The Wisdom of the Wise* (1900), achieved some contemporary success. She also published essays on **George Eliot** (1901) and George Sand (1902).

**Hobbes, Thomas** 1588–1679 Philosopher. The son of a parson, Hobbes was born in Wiltshire. He graduated from Magdalen College, Oxford, in 1608 and became tutor to William Cavendish (later 1st Earl of Devonshire), remaining as secretary and companion. The connection proved invaluable to Hobbes: he enjoyed opportunities to travel (during which he met Galileo, Descartes and Père Mersenne), had access to fine libraries, and was able to spend five years (1621–6) working with **Francis Bacon**. He also made the acquaintance of **Ben Jonson** and **Lord Herbert**. He left England in 1640 with the first group of Royalist émigrés and lived in Paris for the next 11 years. He was appointed tutor to the Prince of Wales (later Charles II) in 1647.

Hobbes had meanwhile discovered geometry and this, with the influence of Galileo, had helped clarify his ideas of philosophy as something that could be demonstrated in positive terms: 'the rules and infallibility of reason'. He wrote *Elements of Law, Natural and Politic*, which was circulating in 1640, although it was not published until the 19th century. While in France he worked on a plan for an extensive treatise, beginning with matter as the first part, and going on to deal with human nature, society and government.

Events in England, where the Civil War had begun in earnest in 1642, persuaded him to embark at once on the proposed third part, *Elementorum Philosophiae Sectio Tertia De Cive* (1642). The English text appeared in 1651 as *Philosophical Rudiments Concerning Government and Society*.

Thomas Hobbes. A detail from the portrait after J. M. Wright, 1670. National Portrait Gallery, London.

The year 1651 also saw the publication in London of Hobbes's most famous work, *Leviathan: or, The Matter, Form, and Power of a Commonwealth Ecclesiastical and Civil*, mistaken by some Royalists as an argument in favour of Cromwell's kingship. Dismissed by the Prince of Wales, Hobbes returned to England, where he completed the first part of his projected treatise, *De Corpore*, in 1655 and published *Questions Concerning Liberty, Necessity and Chance* (1656). The second part of his treatise, *De Homine*, came in 1658.

Hobbes had returned to the Cavendish family in 1653 and spent the rest of his life with them. Charles II granted his old tutor an annual pension, though he could do nothing to stop the Commons' bill against blasphemous books, among which *Leviathan* was listed. Hobbes was forbidden to publish any political and religious books and those published were publicly burned. In his old age he embarked on a translation of Homer, publishing his *Odyssey* at the age of 85 and his *Iliad* in the following year, having previously translated Thucydides in 1629. He died at the age of 92 and posthumously published works include *Behemoth: the History of the Civil Wars of England* (1679 and 1681) and *A Dialogue between a Philosopher and a Student of the Common Laws of England* (1681).

Hobbes was a materialist who argued from first principles: he refused to assume, because it was the habit of his time to proceed too easily from assumption. His dismissal of Christian terminology in his religious comments not only provoked a storm of abuse but obliged his contemporaries to argue with him in print. In the absolute precision of his language, Hobbes was the most impressive and influential philosopher of his time. *The Complete Works* were edited by Sir William Molesworth (1839–45).

**Hobsbaum, Philip (Dennis)** 1932– Poet. Born in London, he was educated at Belle Vue Grammar School, at Downing College, Cambridge, under **F. R. Leavis** and at Sheffield University under **William Empson**. He currently lectures in English at Glasgow University. He edited the magazine *Delta* (1954–5). The founder of the **Group**, he went on to edit *A Group Anthology* (1963) with **Edward Lucie-Smith**. His own poetry, influenced by **Robert Lowell** and **Philip Larkin**, is characterized by tones of loss and regret. His main collections are *The Place's Fault* (1964), *In Retreat* (1966), *Coming Out Fighting* (1969) and *Women and Animals* (1972).

***Hobson's Choice*** A comedy by **Harold Brighouse**, first performed in 1915 and frequently revived, as, for example, in an excellent National Theatre production at the **Old Vic** in 1965.

Hobson is a hard-headed and dominating cobbler, more dependent on his daughter Maggie than he cares to recognize. The play details the means by which Maggie breaks down her father's resistance to her marrying his downtrodden employee Will Mossop at the same time as she makes Will aware of his own potential.

**Hoby, Sir Thomas** See *Courtier, The*.

**Hoccleve, Thomas (or Occleve)** *c.* 1368/9 – *c.* 1437 Middle English Poet. Born perhaps in Hockliffe, Bedfordshire, he trained at one of the Inns of Court, becoming a clerk in the office of the Privy Seal in 1387 or 1388. In 1395 he was granted a corrody at Hayling but resigned it after four years and remained at the Privy Seal until *c.* 1422–3. Details of his private life given in his poetry indicate that he suffered from eye-strain and backache, and found his work as a copyist unsatisfying. His claims to living in penury and having spent his youth in debauched and extravagant living beyond his means may be a literary pose; the debauched youth is a common topos. An ardent opponent of the **Lollards**, he had hoped to become a priest but was unable to secure a benefice and instead married in 1410–11. He suffered a period of mental illness after 1416, but claims to have recovered by 1421. He was granted a minor benefice at Southwick priory in 1424 and probably remained there until his death.

Hoccleve was active as a poet from 1402 to 1422. Autobiographical or pseudo-autobiographical material is found in many of his best-known poems – in *La Male Regle*, a confessional and begging poem relating the excesses of his youth and asking for payment of his annuity, in *Hoccleve's Complaint* and *Dialogus cum Amico*, and in *De Regemine Principum*, where a description of his life and over 30 exempla are combined with political complaint and advice on good government. He also wrote: a poem in praise of women, *Lepistre de Cupide*, freely adapted from Christine de Pisan's *L'Epistre au Dieu d'Amours*; *Ars Sciendi Mori*, an adaptation from part of Heinrich Suso's *Horologium Sapientiae* on the art of dying; the *Tale of the Emperor Jerelaus*, a version of the story of *Le Bone Florence of Rome*; and many short, mostly religious, pieces.

**Hodgins, Jack** 1938– Canadian novelist and short-story writer. Born and brought up in a logging and farming community on Vancouver Island, he attended the University of British Columbia, where he studied creative writing under **Earle Birney**. He returned to Vancouver Island and worked as a high-school teacher before becoming a full-time writer. During the 1970s Hodgins travelled to Ireland and Japan and his novel *The Invention of the World* (1977), which includes a quest for origins that takes some of the characters back to Ireland, is influenced by the oral storytelling traditions of Irish epic. His other books are the novel *The Resurrection of Joseph Bourne* (1979) and two volumes of short stories, *Spit Delaney's Island* (1976) and *The Barclay Family Theatre* (1981). All his fiction deals with Vancouver Island and the seven daughters of the Barclay family provide points of contact between the different books. This strong regional flavour is combined with a post-modernist approach that has affinities with Latin American **magic realism**. He lived in Ottawa for a number of years, but has now returned to Vancouver Island.

**Hodgson, William Hope** 1877–1918 Novelist. Hodgson escaped from an unhappy home by going to sea in his teens, but abandoned that career after eight years in 1899. He opened a school of physical culture but made more money by writing articles for the popular magazines. He diversified into fiction with short stories of the sea, many of them horror stories featuring monstrous life-forms. Two of his novels, *The Boats of the 'Glen Carrig'* (1907) and *The Ghost Pirates* (1909), are in the same vein, but *The House on the Borderland* (1908) is a visionary allegory extending over vast reaches of time and space and *The Night Land* (1912) is a bizarre far-future fantasy, difficult to read because of its mock-archaic style. Hodgson drew on his experience to bring a dramatic realism to his sea stories, making their fantastic elaborations all the more striking, and his poetry is affectively powerful when it draws on similar resources. The cosmic perspective of his more ambitious work is a remarkable, if eccentric, product of its age, even more humbling in its implications than that displayed by **H. G. Wells** in *The Time Machine*. Hodgson was killed in action in World War I.

**Hoffman, Charles Fenno** 1806–84 American poet, novelist, and travel-writer, born in New York City. In 1833–4 he made a journey on horseback through the scarcely settled regions of Illinois and Michigan, and published an account of his experiences in *A Winter in the West* (1835). *Wild Scenes in the Forest and Prairie* followed in 1839. *Greyslaer*, a novel published in 1840, deals with a notorious Kentucky murder case and was a popular success. Three books of verse appeared between 1842 and 1847; many of the poems evoke the Hudson River setting of his New York home. A collection, *The Poems of Charles Fenno Hoffman*, was published in 1873.

**Hofmann, Michael** 1957– Poet. Son of the distinguished German novelist Gert Hofmann, he was born in Freiburg and was educated at Winchester and Magdalene College, Cambridge, where he read English, before pursuing postgraduate studies at Regensburg and Cambridge, on Rilke and **Lowell**. His first two collections, *Nights in the Iron Hotel* (1983) and *Acrimony* (1986), mark him out as an original, unusual talent. His poems are off-beat, anecdotal meditations on the detritus of contemporary urban society ('Mannequin' or 'From Kensal Rise to Heaven'), lonely, alienated people ('Boys' Own') or personal disappointment and failure ('A Brief Occupation'), told in a flat, laconic voice. 'The Nomad, My Father' and Part II of *Acrimony*, 'My Father's House', are wrested out of the poet's resentment of his unfathomable father, and his itinerant childhood.

**Hogarth, William** 1697–1764 Painter. The son of an unsuccessful schoolteacher, Hogarth was apprenticed to a silver-plate engraver, set up on his own as an engraver and began to design and execute book illustrations of which the most outstanding are his series to *Hudibras*. In 1729 he clandestinely married the daughter of Sir James Thornhill, the Serjeant-Painter, and in 1757 was appointed to the same position, the intervening holder of the post having been his brother-in-law. His works were immensely popular, but disparaged by other artists for that very reason. His major literary work was *The Analysis of Beauty* (1753) in which he attempted to argue that it was possible to explicate beauty in geometric terms: that the best paintings were constructed according to the principle of the pyramid – the major features of the painting being bounded by an isosceles triangle – and that within this triangle the eye was led by a serpentine 'line of beauty'. This attempt at rationality failed principally because of the inadequacy of Hogarth's verbal dexterity when it came to specifying how serpentine the line was to be. The idea was taken up by **Sterne** in *Tristram Shandy* in his description of Trim reading the sermon, and Hogarth provided a plate illustrating the scene, a composition not notable for its beauty. A close friend of **Fielding**, Hogarth was justly praised in the preface to *Joseph Andrews*, and produced a plate in return illustrating the essential differences between character and caricature Fielding had laid down. Many writers of the time complimented Hogarth on his skill in representing realistic images of life. From a literary point of view his main achievement was a legal victory in the matter of **copyright**. The Act 8 Geo. II, c. 13 (1735), laying down the principle of copyright in engravings, went through Parliament mainly at his instigation and is sometimes known as Hogarth's Act.

**Hogg, James** 1770–1835 Poet and prose writer. Hogg was born at Ettrick Forest, Selkirkshire, the second of four sons of an impoverished farmer, and received only a smattering of formal education. In 1790–1800 he was shepherd to a farmer on the Douglas Burn, Yarrow, where he had access to books and began to write verse. His early collection, *Scottish Pastorals, Poems, Songs etc.*, attracted the interest and friendship of **Scott**, for whose collection *Minstrelsy of the Scottish Border* he and his mother supplied ballads from their recollections of oral tradition. His first volume of original ballads, *The Mountain Bard*, appeared in 1807. After various misfortunes as a sheep-farmer he settled in Edinburgh, where he published *The Forest Minstrel* (1810), a miscellany padded with 'every ranting rhyme . . . that I ever made in my youth', and started *The Spy*, a critical weekly which folded after a year. *The Queen's Wake* (1813) established his reputation as a poet, and led to good friendships with **Byron**, **Wordsworth**, **Southey** and John Murray, who published an English edition of the work. He joined the editorial board of *Blackwood's Magazine*, to which he made many contributions and in which he appeared as the 'Ettrick Shepherd' in the regular editorial feature, *Noctes Ambrosianae*. It was he who later claimed credit for the initial conception of the notorious *Chaldee MS* of 1817, a scurrilous literary prank for which Blackwood's were fined in court but which also considerably boosted sales of their 'Maga'. In 1815 he published *Pilgrims of the Sun*, which was followed in 1816 by *The Poetic Mirror, or, the Living Bards of Great Britain*, a series of remarka-

The frontispiece to Vol. II of *The Poetical Works of The Ettrick Shepherd* (1838–40) by James Hogg. The engraving is of the town of Jedburgh.

bly deft parodies of the Romantic poets. The two volumes comprising *The Jacobite Relics of Scotland* (1819) contain not only poems from the period before the fall of the Stuarts but also some of Hogg's own best lyric poetry. His principal prose works are: *The Three Perils of Man* (1822) and its weaker sequel, *The Three Perils of Women* (1823); *The Private Memoirs and Confessions of a Justified Sinner* (1824), for long neglected, but now recognized as his masterpiece; and *The Domestic Manners and Private Life of Sir Walter Scott* (1834). His edition of **Burns** (with **Motherwell** as co-editor) appeared in 1834–5.

In 1816 Hogg's patroness, the Countess of Dalkeith, died, bequeathing him the farm of Eltrive Lake in Yarrow at a nominal rent. Here he lived for most of the rest of his life, combining farming with writing. Wordsworth's poem 'Upon the Death of James Hogg' expresses a respect and an affection which were shared by many contemporaries.

**Hoggart, Richard** 1918– Critic of literature and contemporary culture. A Yorkshireman, Hoggart was educated at Cockburn High School and the University in his native Leeds. He returned from military service in 1946 to a tutorship at the University of Hull, and later lectured in English at the University of Leicester before becoming Professor of English at the University of Birmingham in 1962; here he founded the Centre for Contemporary Cultural Studies in 1964. He was an Assistant Director-General of UNESCO from 1971 to 1975, and then Warden of Goldsmiths' College, University of London, from 1976 to 1984. He has also held influential positions in broadcasting policy and on the Arts Council of Great Britain.

With the work of **Raymond Williams**, Hoggart's writings – especially *The Uses of Literacy* (1957) – have helped to broaden the scope of literary study to include questions of working-class culture, education and the communications media. His other books include *Auden* (1951), *The Critical Moment* (1964), *Speaking to Each Other* (2 vols., 1970), and his Reith Lectures, *Only Connect* (1972).

**Holcroft, Thomas** 1745–1809 Playwright and novelist, born in London, the son of a shoe-maker. His *Memoirs* (posthumously published in 1816, edited by **William Hazlitt**) give an account of his early struggles as pedlar, Newmarket stable-boy, tutor and strolling actor. His acting was unimpressive, but his experiences furnished the material for his first novel, *Alwyn, or the Gentleman Comedian* (1780). The later novels, *Anna St Ives* (1792) and *Hugh Trevor* (1794), reflect his friendship with **Thomas Paine** and **William Godwin**. In the panic that afflicted England in the wake of the French Revolution, Holcroft was indicted for high treason in 1794. Despite his acquittal, he remained under suspicion as a free thinker for the rest of his life.

Holcroft's dramatic writing began with a comedy, *Duplicity* (1781), a solemn warning against gambling. The best of his subsequent plays include his resourceful adaptation of Beaumarchais's *The Marriage of Figaro* as *The Follies of a Day* (1784), *The School for Arrogance* (1791), the outstandingly successful **The Road to Ruin** (1792) and *Love's Frailties* (1794). To Holcroft belongs the credit of writing the first English play to declare itself, in the French style, a **melodrama**. This was *A Tale of Mystery* (1802), an adaptation from Pixérécourt's *Coelina*.

**Holden, Molly (Winifred) (née Gilbert)** 1927–81 Poet. Born in Peckham, South London, but brought up in the Wiltshire countryside, she was educated at Commonweal Grammar School, Swindon, and at King's College, London, where she read English. Writing was late in coming, and after the pamphlets *A Hill Like a Horse* (1963) and *The Bright Cloud* (1964), she was afflicted by multiple sclerosis, of which she eventually died. Her unflamboyant, fragile poems, which capture subtle details and movements in nature, belong to the tradition of **John Clare**, **Thomas Hardy** and **Edward Thomas**. Formally elegant, they show a stoical attitude to life. Her other collections include *To Make Me Grieve* (1968), *Air and Chill Earth* (1974) and *The Country Over* (1975). The posthumous *New and Selected Poems* (1987) includes 36 from more than 400 uncollected poems.

**Hole in the Wall, The** A novel by **Arthur Morrison**, published in 1902.

After his mother's death, Stephen Kemp goes to live with his grandfather, Captain Nat Kemp, at a public house, The Hole in the Wall, in London's East End. The child is gradually drawn into the seedy world his grandfather inhabits. The plot revolves around the struggle for possession of illegal insurance money gained after the sinking of the *Juno*. Stephen quite innocently retrieves the money in a pocket-book, dropped after its unlawful owner is violently murdered; his grandfather wishes to keep it to buy Stephen's future. As pressure mounts on the Captain from other contenders for the money, he decides to surrender it and then bring the whole case before the authorities. However, his plan is frustrated and The Hole in the Wall is burned to the ground. At the end of the novel, Captain Kemp rebuilds his public house, but with another name, and turns to legitimate business. Stephen is sent to school at last.

The novel is remarkable for its unsentimental portrayal of East End life during the 1890s, and, despite its debts to Zola, displays considerable originality.

**Holiday Romance, A** A light-hearted story in four parts by **Charles Dickens**, written in imitation of children's prose. It first appeared in the Boston magazine *Our Young Folks* between January and May 1868.

**Holinshed, Raphael** d. ?1580 Little is known of Holinshed's life before he worked *c.* 1560 as a translator for the London printer Reginald Wolfe. At his death in 1573, Wolfe left unfinished a universal history, which was compiled from various sources, including the historian **John Leland**. Holinshed, who had also been working on the project, continued Wolfe's work in the modified form of a British history. **Richard Stanihurst** was engaged to continue the description of Ireland, **William Harrison** to help with the description of England and Scotland. The description of Scotland draws on **Hector Boece**'s *Scotorum Historiae*, that of England on **Edward Hall**'s *Union of the Two Noble and Illustre Families of Lancaster and York*. In 1577 the two folio volumes of *Chronicles* appeared. The whole work was dedicated to Lord Burghley, the sections on Scotland and Ireland, with their separate title-pages, respectively to Lord Leicester and Sir Henry Sidney. The work deals with British history up to 1575. On Holinshed's death, the printers employed John Hooker, with the help of various assistants, to continue the work, and the 1587 edition, in three volumes, inserted many new passages and continued the chronicles to 1586. The first edition had suffered some censorship of passages concerning Ireland; the second, which included topical events, was more heavily censored.

Holinshed's *Chronicles* was a favourite source-book (probably in the 1587 edition) for **Shakespeare**, and **Marlowe** drew on it for *Edward II*. Not only do most of Shakespeare's histories draw on Holinshed, but so do moments in his tragedies *Macbeth*, *King Lear* and *Cymbeline*.

**Holland, Norman** See **psychoanalytic criticism**.

**Holland, Philemon** 1552–1637 Translator. Holland was educated at Trinity College, Cambridge, took a degree in medicine in 1597, and taught at Coventry for 20 years, becoming an usher at the Free School (1608) and a master there in 1628. In 1632 he was honoured with the freedom of the city. His mastery of Greek and Latin combined scholarship with a true feeling for antiquity, and he translated from Livy (*Roman History*, 1600), Pliny (*Pliny's Natural History of the World*, 1601), Plutarch (*The Philosophy, Commonly Called the Morals*, 1603) and Suetonius (*The History of the Twelve Caesars*, 1606). These were followed by a translation of Ammianus Marcellinus (1609), **William Camden**'s *Britannia* (1610) and Xenophon's *Cyropaedia*, an account of Persia, in 1632. Acknowledged as one of the foremost translators of his age, Holland wrote in a style both lively and immediate, in his words a 'meane and popular stile'.

**Holland, Sir Richard** *fl.* 1450 Scottish poet. Very little is known about his life except that he was a supporter of the Douglases in the court of James II; after their fall he may have retired to Shetland. His only extant work is **The Buke of the Howlat**, an allegorical alliterative poem into which he interpolated the history of the Douglas family's fate.

**Hollander, John** 1929– American poet and critic, born in New York City, and educated at Columbia and Indiana Universities. His verse, poignant and witty, formally strict and sometimes esoteric, has earned him a reputation as one of the foremost contemporary poets. His books include *The Untuning of the Sky* (1961, a critical study), *Movie-Going* (1962), *Visions from the Ramble* (1965), *The Quest of the Gole* (1966, a children's book), *The Night Mirror* (1971), *The Head of the Bed* (1974), *Tales Told of the Fathers* (1975), *Spectral Emanations: New and Selected Poems* (1978), *Rhyme's Reason* (1981, a study of poetic forms), *Powers of Thirteen* (1983) and *In Time and Place* (1986).

**Hollo, Anselm (Paul Alexis)** 1934– Poet and translator. Born in Helsinki, Hollo was educated at the Universities of Helsinki and Tubingen, West Germany. After living in England from 1958, where he worked for the BBC European Radio Services, he moved to America in 1967, where he has taught at many universities. His English poems, including *St Texts and Finnpoems* (1961), *History* (1964) and *The Coherences* (1968), were reprinted in *Maya: Works 1959–1969* (1970) and in *Sojourner Microcosms: new & selected poems 1959–1979* (1979). His poems, influenced by **Ezra Pound** and **William Carlos Williams**, are affirmations of all forms of life, and have strong ecological concerns; he is interested in language as it is spoken. American volumes include *Sensation* (1972), *Finite Continued* (1980) and *no complaints* (1983). He is also a translator to and from English; he has translated Yevtushenko, Vosnesensky and Kirsanov (in *Red Cats*, 1962), Brecht, Genet and Blok into English, **Allen Ginsberg**, **Gregory Corso** and Williams's **Paterson** into German, and Ginsberg into Finnish.

**Holme, Constance** 1881–1955 Novelist. She was born in Milnthorpe, on the shores of Morecambe Bay. A true regional writer, she set many of her novels in her native area. Her most famous book, *The Lonely Plough* (1914), takes a landed estate and the relationship between landlord, agent and tenant as its subject, reflecting her own descent from a line of land agents. Her other books include *The Splendid Faring* (1916), which won the Femina Vie Heureuse Prize, *The Old Road from Spain* (1916), *Beautiful End* (1918),

*The Trumpet in the Dust* (1921), *The Things Which Belong* (1925) and *He-Who-Came* (1930).

**Holmes, John Clellon** 1926–88 American novelist, essayist and poet. Born in Holyoke, Massachusetts, Holmes was educated at Columbia University and the New School for Social Research in New York City. A member of the **Beat** generation of artists and writers, he recorded first-hand the life-style of this circle of friends in his first novel, *Go* (1952; in England as *The Beat Boys*). In *The Horn* (1958) he describes the jazz scene of the day; *Nothing More to Declare* (1967) is a collection of essays chronicling the Beat movement. He published two collections of poems, *The Bowling Green Poems* (1977) and *Death Drag: Selected Poems* (1979). The memoir *Visitor: Jack Kerouac in Old Saybrook* was published in 1980.

**Holmes, Oliver Wendell** 1809–94 American novelist, essayist and poet, born in Cambridge, Massachusetts, and educated at Harvard, where he received his MD in 1836. In the same year he published *Poems*, a collection of occasional and

Oliver Wendell Holmes as seen by the cartoonist, Spy.

witty verses. He published two considerable medical works, *Homeopathy and Its Kindred Delusions* (1842) and *The Contagiousness of Puerperal Fever* (1843). In 1847 he became Parkman Professor of Anatomy and Physiology at Harvard, a chair he held until his retirement in 1882.

Holmes was extremely popular as a teacher, and was famous also for his humorous essays and poems and his entertaining after-dinner speeches. During the late 1850s *The Atlantic Monthly*, which he co-founded with **James Russell Lowell** in 1857, published many of his essays – which were then collected in the successful *The Autocrat of the Breakfast Table* (1858) – as well as poems such as 'The Chambered Nautilus' and 'The Deacon's Masterpiece'. Among later collections of his essays are *The Professor at the Breakfast Table* (1860), *The Poet at the Breakfast Table* (1872) and *Over the Teacups* (1891). Drawing upon his scientific training, he wrote three novels about characters who are psychologically disturbed. All three explore the biological and psychological factors determining human behaviour, and reject any theological version of determinism. The first, *Elsie Venner* (1861), was the most successful; it was followed by *The Guardian Angel* (1867), and *A Mortal Antipathy* (1885).

**Holtby, Winifred** 1898–1935 Novelist. Born in the East Riding of Yorkshire, she was educated at Scarborough and Somerville College, Oxford, but gave up her studies to join the Women's Auxiliary Army Corps in France during World War I. After the war she became an ardent feminist and lecturer on politics, and joined the staff of *Time and Tide*. She was director from 1926 and made many contributions to other papers, including *The Manchester Guardian*.

Her original and pithy style is best savoured in her last novel, *South Riding* (1936), the portrait of a Yorkshire community, whose heroine, Sarah Burton, is a strong-willed headmistress. Most notable among her earlier works are *The Crowded Street* (1924), *The Land of Green Ginger* (1927), *Poor Caroline* (1931; a subtle indictment of moribund charities) and *Mandoa! Mandoa!* (1933; set in Africa and satirizing the unfortunate effects of European civilization).

Her other works include a critical study of **Virginia Woolf** (1932) and two volumes of short stories, *Truth is Not Sober* (1934) and *Pavements at Anderby* (1937). Her life and achievement are commemorated in **Vera Brittain**'s *Testament of Friendship* (1940).

**Holy War, The**, *Made by Shaddai upon Diabolus* The last major work by **John Bunyan**, published in 1682. It is a complex religious **allegory**, operating on an epic scale, which links the conversion of the individual soul to the early history of the world, to events in recent and contemporary English history, and to the forthcoming millennium described in the apocalyptic books of the Bible.

The City of Mansoul (man's soul) has been conquered by the wiles of Diabolus, and King Shaddai, the builder of the city, sends his captains to recover it. His son Emmanuel leads the besieging army. The city is regained and the King returns, but gradually it relapses into evil ways and Diabolus again takes possession. Emmanuel, however, holds the citadel and Diabolus is eventually defeated.

**Holy Willie's Prayer** A satirical poem by **Robert Burns**, published in *Poems Chiefly in the Scottish Dialect* in 1786. It is a dramatic monologue, the reflections of Holy Willie, a bigoted elder of the Kirk. With considerable eloquence and the conceit of the humourless, Willie exposes himself as a canting hypocrite. He is based on William Fisher, an elder of the parish church of Mauchline. Fisher fell from grace in 1790, accused of drunkenness by the Kirk, and froze to death in a snow-filled ditch in 1809. He was also believed to have been guilty of pilfering from the almsbox and Burns refers to the charge in a later poem, 'The Kirk's Alarm' (1790).

**Homage to Catalonia** An autobiographical work by **George Orwell**, published in 1938.

During the Spanish Civil War Orwell fought in the militia of the far-left Workers' Party of Marxist Unity (POUM), and the book is an account of his time in Spain from December 1936 to July 1937. Having volunteered with no definite party allegiance, he had originally believed that he was fighting for 'common decency', 'the defence of civilization against a maniacal outbreak by an army of Colonel Blimps in the pay of Hitler'. However he rapidly discovers that as a militiaman 'one was also a pawn in an enormous struggle . . . between two political theories': that held by the Communist United Socialist Party of Catalonia (PSUC) ('The war first and the revolution afterwards') and that held by the more libertarian POUM and its anarchist allies ('The war and the revolution are inseparable'). Parts of the book record his personal experiences – of boredom and frustration and, occasionally, danger – and there are many general observations about Spain and Spanish life. Other parts of the book analyse the politics of the struggle: the 'racket' of newspaper reports (except those by *The Manchester Guardian*), and the suppression of the POUM by the Soviet-backed forces. After the battle for Barcelona in May 1937, between anarchists and POUMists on one side and Communists and bourgeois loyalists on the other, and witnessed by Orwell and his wife, the author returns to the front line. He is shot through the throat, hospitalized, and nearly arrested as a member of the POUM. He and his wife escape from Spain and return to England: 'probably the sleekest landscape in the world . . . [that will] . . . never wake till . . . jerked out of it by the roar of bombs'.

**Home, Henry, Lord Kames** 1696–1782 Scottish judge and philosophical writer. Born at Kames, Berwickshire, and educated in Edinburgh for the Scots Bar, he was admitted advocate in 1724 and raised to the bench (with judicial title of Lord Kames) in 1752. Apart from his writings on law, ethics, history and agricultural improvement, his works include the three-volume *Elements of Criticism* (1752), an influential analysis of literary style. He was a prominent figure of the Edinburgh enlightenment.

**Home, John** 1722–1808 Scottish playwright, famous in his life as the author of the popular tragedy *Douglas* (1756). Home was born in Leith and educated at Edinburgh University. He fought against the forces of Bonny Prince Charlie in 1745–6 and was briefly imprisoned at Falkirk in 1746. From 1747 to 1757 he was Presbyterian minister at Athelstaneford, but resigned his living in the wake of the scandal over the production of *Douglas*. Moving to London as private secretary to the Earl of Bute, Home embarked on a moderately successful literary career. *Douglas* was followed by five more tragedies, of which the best is probably *The Siege of Aquileia* (1760), but none rivalled the extraordinary success of *Douglas*. Granted a pension by George III, whom he had tutored, Home returned to Scotland in 1770, wrote his last two plays there, *Alonzo* (1773) and *Alfred* (1778), and settled into silence, broken only in 1802 when he published his *History of the Rebellion of the Year 1745*.

**Home, William Douglas** 1912– Dramatist. Born in Edinburgh, he was educated at Eton and Oxford. His comedies of upper middle-class and political life made him a natural successor to **Frederick Lonsdale** in the post-war West End theatre; they include *The Chiltern Hundreds* (1947), *The Manor of Northstead* (1954), *The Reluctant Peer* (1964), *The Jockey Club Stakes* (1970), *Lloyd George Knew My Father* (1972) and *The Dame of Sark* (1974). His skill in calculating what the stars of his generation could achieve was supported by a sound playwriting technique, whose main weakness lay in a facile sentimentality. *Now Barabbas . . .* (1947), however, showed his ability with a serious theme about prison life, while *The Secretary Bird* (1968) remains a thoughtful comedy abut a *ménage à trois*.

**Homecoming, The** A play by **Harold Pinter**, first performed in Cardiff by the **Royal Shakespeare Company** in 1965.

After six years in America, Teddy returns with his wife Ruth to the all-male household presided over by his cantankerous father, Max. Exacerbated by the presence of a woman, the rivalries and competitiveness of the household find alternately veiled and direct expression. At the end, Teddy returns alone to his university job in America, leaving Ruth as mother or whore to his family.

**Homeric simile** See **epic simile**.

**homily** Didactic religious address or sermon, usually one expounding a biblical text. See *Blickling Homilies*.

**Honest Whore, The** A play by **Thomas Dekker** in two parts, the first published in 1604 and the second in 1630. **Philip Henslowe**'s diary gives us the information that **Middleton** contributed to the first part. The setting is apparently Italy but the atmosphere is Dekker's own London.

In the first part Count Hippolito is in love with Infelice, the Duke's daughter. The Duke is not in favour of the marriage and packs his daughter off to a convent, giving out the news that she is dead. His friends take Hippolito to the house of the beautiful Bellafront, but Hippolito discovers that she is a harlot and abuses her. Then he is brought news that Infelice is alive. He rescues and marries her. The angry Duke, arriving too late to prevent the marriage, is reconciled to it. Bellafront, meanwhile, has abandoned her old life, having fallen in love with Hippolito. The Duke arranges the marriage of Bellafront to Matheo, her first seducer.

In the second part Matheo, Bellafront's husband, is in prison. He is vicious and worthless but Bellafront is now a devoted wife; she goes to Hippolito to seek his help. Matheo is released, but Hippolito has now been married for some time and Bellafront's beauty arouses him. Matheo stops at nothing to find the means to support his pleasures and suggests that his wife resume her old way of life to supply him with money. But his servant, Orlando, is in fact Bellafront's father and he keeps a sharp eye on both Matheo and Hippolito. It is Orlando who saves his daughter when she is falsely accused of being a prostitute and ordered to a house of correction and who proves her innocent when Matheo accuses her of betraying him with Hippolito.

**Hood, Hugh** 1928– Canadian novelist and short-story writer. He was born in Toronto, the son of an English-Canadian father and a French-Canadian mother. Educated at Roman Catholic schools and at the University of Toronto, he has taught English at St Joseph's College, Hartford,

473

Connecticut, and, since 1961, at the Université de Montréal. Hood first achieved recognition as a writer of short stories, but has subsequently become better known as a novelist. His fiction describes specific occupations, physical objects and the workings of bureaucratic and other systems in a detailed and knowledgeable manner. Several of his early novels take an artist as their protagonist: *White Figure, White Ground* (1964) is centred on a painter, *The Camera Always Lies* (1967) on an actress, and *A Game of Touch* (1970) on a cartoonist. *You Cant Get There From Here* (1972) is a political novel set in a bilingual African state which evokes Canada. In 1975 Hood published *The Swing in the Garden*, the first in a projected series of 12 novels, entitled The New Age/Le Nouveau Siècle. Three other volumes of the series have followed: *A New Athens* (1977), *Reservoir Ravine* (1979) and *Black and White Keys* (1982). Proustian in conception, this ambitious sequence, which aims to provide a survey of Canadian life from the 1880s to the year 2000, has so far received a mixed response. Hood is essentially a novelist of ideas and his intellectual Catholicism frequently manifests itself in the form of religious allegory. His volumes of short stories include *Flying in a Red Kite* (1962), *Around the Mountain* (1967), *The Fruit Man, the Meat Man and the Manager* (1971), *Dark Glasses* (1976) and *None Genuine Without This Signature* (1980). He has also published *The Governor's Bridge* (1973), a volume of social and personal essays.

**Hood, Thomas** 1799–1845 Poet. Son of a London bookseller and educated privately, he was apprenticed as an engraver, latterly to Le Keux, but ill health led him to abandon that career and turn to writing. He worked for *The London Magazine*, where he met **De Quincey**, **Lamb** and **Hazlitt**, and in 1825 in collaboration with **J. H. Reynolds** produced *Odes and Addresses to Great People*, a popular success. *Whims and Oddities* appeared in two series in 1826–7, the first series containing his two best-known comic poems: 'Faithless Nelly Gray' and 'The Ballad of Sally Brown and Ben the Carpenter', both of which demonstrate a remarkable skill in punning. In 1829 he became editor of *The Gem*, and published works by, among others, **Tennyson**, and the following year started *The Comic Annual*. Among his hack works were various dramatic pieces and a three-decker novel, *Tylney Hall* (1834). After a financial disaster he spent 1835–40 on the Continent, though still producing *The Comic Annual*, returning to England to write for *The New Monthly Magazine*, becoming editor in 1841. In it he printed 'Miss Kilmansegg', a grotesque satire on the Victorian worship of money, in which the heroine is eventually murdered for her artificial gold leg. Praised by **Dickens**, the poem may be compared to *Our Mutual Friend*. Hood's major serious poem, 'The Song of the Shirt', appeared anonymously in *Punch* in 1843. Based upon an account in *Punch* by **Douglas Jerrold** of a woman accused of pawning articles belonging to her employer, the poem is a powerful attack on exploitation. It was immediately reprinted by *The Times* and other newspapers, translated into French, German, Italian and Russian, dramatized by **Mark Lemon** as *The Sempstress*, printed on broadsheets and cotton handkerchiefs, and highly praised by many leading literary figures, including Dickens. Now principally known as a versifier with a penchant for puns, Hood has few rivals in English for his comic verbal dexterity.

**Hook, Theodore Edward** 1788–1841 Novelist, dramatist and wit. Educated at Harrow, Hook moved in fashionable circles and in 1813 was appointed Accountant General in Mauritius. He was recalled after four years because of a deficiency amounting to £12,000 (he described it as 'a disorder in his chest') and was subsequently imprisoned, though his worst crime was neglect of duty. In 1820 he became editor of the Tory *John Bull*, and published his first stories in 1824 in a volume called *Sayings and Doings*, the first of a series of four. Other books were *Maxwell* (1830), *Gilbert Gurney* (1836) and *Jack Brag* (1837). He was the model for **Thackeray**'s Mr Wagg in *The History of Pendennis*.

**Hooker, Richard**, ?1554–1600 The greatest of the Elizabethan Anglican theologians, Hooker was born and went to school in Exeter. With Bishop Jewel as his patron he was sent to Corpus Christi College, Oxford, graduating MA in 1577 and becoming a fellow of the college in the same year. He became Assistant Professor of Hebrew at the University and was Master of the Temple in 1585–91. He died at Bishopsbourne in Kent, where he had become vicar.

Unlike many of his contemporaries, Hooker still respected much of medieval scholastic theology and especially St Thomas Aquinas. His great work, *Of the Laws of Ecclesiastical Polity*, is an apology for the Elizabethan religious and political settlement. Books I–IV were published in 1594 and Book V in 1597. Other books, VI and VIII (1648), and VII (1661), are of doubtful authority. *Ecclesiastical Polity* was partly Hooker's contribution to the controversy started by the Puritan *Admonition to Parliament* (1572). This pamphlet was answered by Whitgift, Cartwright replied to Whitgift, and Hooker to Cartwright. For Hooker the Anglican tradition relied on the Bible, the Church and reason. Reason pronounced on those matters where the voices of the Bible and the Church were silent or unclear, and also interpreted those voices.

Richard Hooker. The portrait by Wenzel Hollar executed in 1657, many years after Hooker's death. British Museum Print Room.

Natural law, which governs the universe, and whose voice is 'the harmony of the world', is an expression of God's reason. *Ecclesiastical Polity* also insists on the unity of Church and state and suggests a contractual theory of political government. Some of Hooker's minor works appeared, printed at Oxford, in 1612 and 1614.

As well as being an exceptional apologist, 'judicious' Hooker, as he is described on his monument in Kent, is a master of a prose style with long Latinate syntactical structures, discreetly adorned with rhetorical devices, which serve his purpose of careful distinction and qualification.

**Hooker, Thomas** 1586–1647 An American Puritan minister, and one of the first generation of emigrants to New England. Born in Leicestershire, and educated at Emmanuel College, Cambridge (a Puritan stronghold), he fled to Massachusetts in 1633 having been summoned by Archbishop **Laud** to answer for his Nonconformism. Called to the church at Newton, he served as pastor there and then in 1636 migrated with his congregation to Hartford, in the Connecticut Valley.

Admired by his contemporaries as one of the most eloquent preachers in New England, Hooker was the most thorough exponent of the theory of preparation, or the set of steps that a Christian goes through during conversion; his *The Soules Preparation for Christ* (1632) and the expanded *Application of Redemption, By the Effec-*

*tual Work of the Word, and the Spirit of Christ, for the bringing home of Lost Sinners to God* (published posthumously in 1656) are expositions of part of that process. His other works include *A Survey of the Summe of Church Discipline* (1648), an exposition of the independent Congregational church polity, and a defence of it against English Presbyterian critics. *The Poore Doubting Christian Drawn Unto Christ* (1629) is a pastoral manual for dealing with religious melancholy or 'cases of conscience'.

**Hope, A[lec] D[erwent]** 1907– Australian poet. Born in Coona, New South Wales, he was educated at Sydney University and Oxford. Returning to Australia, he taught at Sydney Teacher's College and then at Melbourne University. He was Professor of English (1951–68) at the Australian National University in Canberra. Hope's first poems appeared in magazines after World War II; his first collection was *The Wandering Islands* (1955) and he was welcomed as a poet who made skilful use of traditional verse forms for shrewd comment on modern values. *Poems* (1960), *New Poems 1965–1969* (1969), *Dunciad Minor: An Heroick Poem* and *A Midsummer Eve's Dream: Variations on a Theme by William Dunbar* (both 1970), *A Late Picking: Poems 1965–1974* (1975), *A Book of Answers* (1978) and *The Drifting Continent* (1979) have given him a leading place in modern poetry and he has been awarded the Arts Council of Great Britain Poetry Award (1965), the Britannica Australia Award for Literature (1965), the Levinson Prize for Poetry (1968), the Ingram Merrill Award for Literature (1969) and the Robert Frost and Age Book Awards (1976). An influential critic, Hope has published his essays in *Australian Poetry* (1960), *Australian Literature 1950–1962* (1963), *The Cave and the Spring* (1965), *Native Companions* (1974), *The Pack of Autolycus* (1978) and *The New Cratylus* (1979). His *Collected Poems 1930–1970* was published in 1972.

**Hope, Anthony** Novelist. Pseudonym of Sir Anthony Hope Hawkins (1863–1933). Educated at Balliol College, Oxford, he practised at the Bar until 1894. During this time he published a number of short stories and an unnoticed novel, *A Man of Mark* (1890). In 1894 he achieved success with *The Dolly Dialogues* (a series of witty sketches of the London Season, first published in the *Westminster Gazette*) and, in particular, with his famous Ruritanian novel **The Prisoner of Zenda**. The romance was a sensation and earned high praise from **Robert Louis Stevenson** and **Andrew Lang**. An equally popular sequel, *Rupert of Hentzau*, appeared in 1898. Other novels include *Tristram of Blent* (1901), *Sophy of Kravonia* (1906) and *Lucinda* (1920). He was knighted for his services at the Ministry of

Information during World War I. His autobiographical reminiscences were published in *Memories and Notes* (1927).

**Hope, Thomas** ?1770–1831 Novelist and art connoisseur. Using his fortune with discernment, Hope collected art and patronized major contemporary artists. He produced some notable works on ancient costume and an influential book on taste and design, *Household Furniture and Interior Decoration* (1807). His most inventive and brilliant work, however, was the satirical novel *Anastasius, or, Memoirs of a Greek* (1819), published anonymously and once attributed to **Byron**.

**Hope Theatre** Built in 1614 on the south bank of the Thames, the Hope was designed to accommodate animal-baiting as well as drama. Until his death in 1616, **Philip Henslowe** held a half-share in the lease. **Ben Jonson**'s *Bartholomew Fair* was performed there in 1614 but animal-baiting increasingly took precedence over plays. The building was closed in 1642 and demolished in 1656.

**Hopkins, Gerard Manley** 1844–89 Poet. He was born in Stratford, Essex, of well-to-do parents who encouraged him in drawing and music. At Highgate School he was taught by **Richard Watson Dixon** and won the poetry prize in 1860. He read Classics at Balliol College, Oxford, in 1863–7 and became known as the 'Star of Balliol' after he got a First. He was taught by **Jowett** and **Walter Pater**, began a close friendship with **Robert Bridges**, and fell under the influence of the latter days of the **Oxford Movement**. In 1866 he was received into the Roman Catholic Church by **Newman**, at whose

Oratory School in Birmingham he taught briefly during 1867. In 1868 he became a novitiate of the Society of Jesus, passing the years which followed at a succession of its foundations: Manresa House in Roehampton, Stonyhurst College in Lancashire and St Beuno's in North Wales. After his ordination in 1877 he ministered to parishes in Chesterfield, London, Oxford, Liverpool and Glasgow, before returning to Stonyhurst as teacher of Greek and Latin in 1882–4. His last, uncongenial post was as Professor of Classics at University College, Dublin, where he died of typhoid fever.

Doubting his ability to combine poetry with his vocation, Hopkins burned most of his early work when he became a Jesuit and resolved 'to write no more . . . unless by the wish of my superiors'. He remained silent until 1875, when the rector at St Beuno's encouraged him to write 'The Wreck of the *Deutschland*', dedicated to the memory of five Franciscan nuns drowned with the sinking of the *Deutschland* in the Thames estuary that year. An ode of 35 stanzas, it is divided into two parts, which deal with the dramatic episodes of the wreck, Christ's Passion, and the poet's relation to both events and to God. It ends with a prayer for the conversion of England. The editor of *The Month*, a Jesuit periodical, accepted the poem before deciding that he 'dared not print it'. 'The Loss of the *Eurydice*' (1878) met a similar fate. Hopkins continued to write, producing 'God's Grandeur', 'The Windhover' and 'Pied Beauty' before his ordination and ending his poetic career, during the bleak Dublin years, with the 'terrible' sonnets, 'Tom's Garland' and 'That Nature Is a Heraclitean Fire'. He circulated his poems in letters to Dixon and Bridges but made no attempt to publish them, believing that this

An illustration from *The Illustrated London News*, 18 December 1875. The *Deutschland* in the Thames Estuary after the wreck of 7 December.

could bring him only 'private notoriety'. A small selection appeared in anthologies after his death, but he did not gain an audience until Robert Bridges's edition in 1918. This late publication date effectively made the difficulties and idiosyncrasies of his work seem to anticipate modern poetry, and Hopkins's reputation eventually grew to make him a major influence on later writers.

His small body of work dwells chiefly on his spiritual relations with God, manifest not just in the agonized questioning of his later poems but also in the subtle yet ecstatic response to nature which is perhaps his most characteristic note. His view of the created world is controlled by what he called 'instress' and 'inscape', which mean, respectively, the animating energy in art, nature and God, and the distinctive organic form of a thing. His notebooks, journals and letters also clarify the principles behind his innovative use of language. Hopkins distinguished broadly between 'poetry proper, the language of inspiration' and 'Parnassian poetry', which was 'the language of poetry draping prose thought'. His own pursuit of a language of inspiration that would capture experience afresh led him to break with the conventional poetic diction of his time, reviving archaisms, borrowing dialect words and using coinages of his own. The emphatic or 'oratorical' rhythm of his poems (which were meant 'less to be read than heard') he called 'sprung rhythm' – an attempt to reconcile speech rhythms with the greatest possible poetic emphasis, which is scanned by stresses rather than by the number of syllables (see also **metre**).

**Hopkinson, Francis** 1737–91 American essayist, born in Philadelphia. In 1774, under the pseudonym of Peter Grievous, he published the pamphlet *A Pretty Story*, a propagandistic but humorous allegory of a family of sons (the colonies) wronged by their wicked stepmother (Parliament). During the Revolution he wrote satires for the *Pennsylvania Packet*, the *Pennsylvania Gazette* and the *Pennsylvania Magazine*, including, for the latter, essays in the persona of 'The Old Bachelor'. He also served in the Second Continental Congress (he signed the Declaration of Independence) and then in a variety of positions in the revolutionary government. Among his most popular political writings at this time was a ballad, 'The Battle of the Kegs' (1778), which ridiculed the British for overreacting to a colonial military ruse. In December 1781 his *The Temple of Minerva*, a dramatic masque with music celebrating the American cause, was performed for General Washington in Philadelphia. His next notable productions were further satires in support of the Constitution, including 'The New Roof' (an allegory referring to the proposed new govern-

ment), which appeared in the *Pennsylvania Packet* in 1787. He spent his last years as a judge, and also published some volumes of songs. His revised *Miscellaneous Essays* appeared posthumously in 1792.

**Horestes** See **Puckering, Sir John**.

**Horne, Richard Henry [or Hengist]** 1803–84 Poet and essayist. Born in London, he was educated at Sandhurst. He led an adventurous early life, serving in the Mexican navy during the war of independence. His first work was a poem 'Hecatompylos', published in **The Athenaeum** in 1828. He is chiefly known as the author of an epic poem *Orion* (1843) which he priced at one farthing – according to **Elizabeth Barrett Browning** – as a satirical comment upon the contemporary valuation of poetry. He served as commissioner of enquiry into factories and his report on the employment of children in mines and factories provoked Elizabeth Barrett Browning to write 'The Cry of the Children'. His book of critical essays *A New Spirit of the Age* (1844) – **Robert Browning** and Elizabeth Barrett Browning being among the contributors – remains an illuminating account of notable contemporaries. In 1852 he joined the gold rush to Australia and held several official posts there before returning in 1869. His *Australian Autobiography and Australian Facts and Prospects* (1859) give an account of his experiences.

**Horner, Francis** 1778–1817 Lawyer, politician and economist. Of mixed Scottish and English ancestry, Horner was born in Edinburgh where he was educated at the High School and the University. In 1795–7 he resided in England, apparently in order to tone down a strong Scottish accent, returning afterwards to Scotland, where, together with his friend **Brougham**, he became a leading member of the Speculative Society. He was called to the Scottish Bar in 1800, and the English in 1807. A highly capable product and exponent of Scottish **Utilitarianism**, he was thrice elected to Parliament in the liberal Whig interest, and earned a distinguished reputation as a speaker on economic affairs and the slave trade, and as a member of select committees. With **Jeffrey**, Brougham and **Sydney Smith** he founded **The Edinburgh Review**, contributing no fewer than four articles on politics and political economy to its first number in 1802, and numerous reviews and articles up to 1809. He died of consumption at Pisa. His *Memoirs* were edited by his brother, Leonard Horner, in 1843.

**Hornung, E[rnest] W[illiam]** 1866–1921 Novelist and short-story writer. Born in Middlesbrough, Yorkshire, he attended Uppingham School and lived in Australia (1884–6) before returning to England and marrying the sister of **Arthur Conan Doyle**. He is remembered as the creator of A. J. Raffles, the gentleman-burglar whose exploits are related by his faithful friend Bunny in several collections of short stories, *The Amateur Cracksman* (1899), *The Black Mask* (1901), *A Thief in the Night* (1905), and a novel, *Mr Justice Raffles* (1909). Raffles was also popular on the stage and in the cinema, where he was portrayed successively by John Barrymore, Ronald Colman and David Niven. Several of Hornung's other books, notably *Stingaree* (1905), use an Australian background.

**Horovitz, Frances (née Hooker)** 1938–83 Poet. Educated at Bristol University and RADA, she worked as a schoolteacher and broadcaster until her death from cancer in 1983. Her books include *Poems* (1967), *The High Tower* (1970), *Water Over Stone* (1980) and *Snow Light, Water Light* (1983). She is also represented in *Children of Albion* (1969), edited by her husband **Michael Horovitz**.

**Horovitz, Michael** 1935– Poet. Born in Frankfurt, and educated in London and at Brasenose College, Oxford, he edited *Children of Albion: Poetry of the 'Underground' in Britain* (1969) and is editor and publisher of the magazine *New Departures*. His books include *The Wolverhampton Wanderer* (1971) and *Growing Up: Selected Poems and Pictures 1951–79* (1979).

**Horse's Mouth, The** A novel by **Joyce Cary** published in 1944, the culminating volume of a trilogy which includes *Herself Surprised* (1941) and *To Be a Pilgrim* (1942). Perhaps the best known of Cary's works, the novel traces the last stages in the career of Gulley Jimson, an amoral and egocentric artist endowed with a powerful genius and a grandiose conception of the artist's role which coincides uneasily with the values of modern society. An edition with illustrations by the author was published in 1957.

**Horse-Shoe Robinson**: *A Tale of the Tory Ascendancy* A historical novel by **John Pendleton Kennedy**, published in 1835 and set in Virginia and the Carolinas during the last months of the American Revolutionary War. The characters include Mildred Lindsay, whose father is a Tory; Tyrrel, the British spy Mildred's father wants her to marry; Arthur Butler, a Revolutionary patriot whom Mildred loves; and the title character, Horse-Shoe Robinson, a blacksmith. Mildred and Arthur are secretly married. When Arthur is captured by the British, Horse-Shoe Robinson comes to the aid of Mildred, who undergoes several adventures before being reunited with her husband. Tyrrel is eventually hanged as a spy.

**Hospital, Janette Turner** 1942– Canadian novelist. Born and educated in Australia, she travelled in England, America and India and has lived in Canada since 1971. She frequently visits Australia and has been writer-in-residence at MIT in Boston. Her novels, which are variously set in India, Australia and North America, include *The Ivory Swing* (1982), *The Tiger in the Tiger Pit* (1983) and *Borderlines* (1985). Hospital writes about nomads, whom she describes as 'characters who cross borders, who straddle cultures and countries, who live with a constant sense of dislocation'. Her fiction is international rather than distinctively Canadian.

**Hostage, The** A play by **Brendan Behan**, first staged in Gaelic in 1957 and given a famous production by Joan Littlewood at the Theatre Royal, Stratford East in 1959. The plot is tragic in outline, but the treatment is predominantly comic, and the action interspersed with songs.

An English soldier is brought to an Irish brothel as a hostage. The play's interest is centred on the lives and attitudes of the people he encounters there and on the basic humanity that draws them together. The soldier is killed during a raid on the brothel by the forces of law during a clumsy attempt to rescue him, but is resurrected to lead the final chorus.

**Houghton (William) Stanley** 1881–1913 One of the group of Manchester playwrights who contributed to the repertoire of the newly formed Gaiety Theatre, Houghton was a drama critic and book-reviewer for *The Manchester Guardian* when his first play, *The Dear Departed* (1908), was staged. His lively opposition to the cant of respectability was further revealed in the excellent **Hindle Wakes** (1912) and *The Younger Generation* (1910).

**Hound of the Baskervilles, The** See **Sherlock Holmes stories**.

**House at Pooh Corner, The** See **Milne, A. A.**

**House of Fame, The** An unfinished poem in octosyllabic couplets by **Geoffrey Chaucer**, written between 1374 and 1385. The poem is a **dream-vision** in which the narrator is transported to a temple of glass where he sees images of famous warriors and lovers. He emerges into a desert and is carried off by a talking eagle which promises to take him where he may learn about love. He is dropped next to a tower of ice on which the engraved names of the famous are melting and unreadable. He enters a castle of beryl and sees Fame, a woman of indeterminate, varying height who has numerous eyes, ears and tongues. He watches petitioners being indiscriminately awarded or refused fame and notoriety, and learns of the arbitrary nature of fame.

He then sees the house of Rumour built of sticks and is guided into it by the eagle; the poem breaks off as he is approached by an imposing figure. Attempts have been made to read the poem as an **allegory** of incidents in Chaucer's own life or events at court, but not enough parrallels can be drawn to prove any particular interpretation correct.

*House of Life, The* A **sonnet** sequence by **Dante Gabriel Rossetti**, first published in full in *Ballads and Sonnets* (1881).

The 101 **Petrarchan** sonnets constituting the final form of *The House of Life* (the title derives from astrology) are a perplexing mixture of love, mysticism, Dantesque lore, exaltation, natural phenomena, deep despair and, in particular, autobiography. Groups of sonnets adhering to one motif or theme cluster together while others, especially in the second part of the sequence, tend to the miscellaneous and individual. As often with Rossetti, there are eccentric rhymes and arcane diction as well as obscure phraseology; but as an embodiment of a universal passion, often richly embroidered, rarely removed from the realms of mysticism, *The House of Life* is a landmark in Victorian aestheticism.

*House of Mirth, The* A novel by **Edith Wharton** published in 1905. Set in New York society during the first years of the 20th century, it records the disastrous social career of Lily Bart, a penniless orphan who is related to some of the city's prominent families. Supported by her wealthy aunt, she more or less makes a career of being a house guest in the homes of her more fashionable friends. Now that she is 29, she must secure a rich husband to ensure herself a place in society. She nearly captures Percy Gryce, a pious and somewhat stuffy heir to a large fortune, but loses him when she chooses to spend a Sunday with Lawrence Selden rather than go to church with Percy. Although she is attracted to Selden, she does not think of him as a potential husband: he is sufficiently genteel but not sufficiently rich, and has to earn his living as a lawyer. She also rejects Simon Rosedale, who is certainly rich enough but not yet accepted by genteel society. When she is unjustly accused of having an affair with another woman's husband, she is ostracized by society and her chance of finding a husband is ruined. Disinherited by her wealthy aunt, she is forced to take a job as a milliner to support herself. The novel concludes with her death from an overdose of a sedative.

*House of the Seven Gables, The* A novel by **Nathaniel Hawthorne**, published in 1851 and inspired by the author's own family history. (According to legend, Hawthorne's great-grandfather, a judge at the Salem witch trials, was cursed by one of his victims.)

The story is set in the mid 19th century. Generations earlier, 'Wizard' Maule had pronounced a curse on Colonel Pyncheon just prior to being hanged for witchcraft. With Maule dead, Pyncheon was able to take possession of a plot of land, the ownership of which he and Maule had long disputed, and build the House of the Seven Gables on it. The current owner of the house is the hypocritical Judge Pyncheon, who does not occupy the decaying house himself but allows his poor cousin Hepzibah and her debilitated brother Clifford to live there. Clifford has just returned after spending 30 years in prison, a sentence he received from his cousin the Judge, having been wrongfully convicted of murdering their rich uncle. Clifford and Hepzibah are joined by Phoebe, a young cousin from the country, and Holgrave, a daguerreotypist who takes lodgings in the house. Believing that Clifford knows where the deeds to the 'murdered' uncle's property are, Judge Pyncheon threatens to have him put away as a lunatic, but the Judge then dies unexpectedly and Hepzibah and Clifford inherit his considerable wealth. Holgrave reveals that he is the last descendant of 'Wizard' Maule and explains how both the 'murdered' uncle and the Judge were victims, not of any human wrongdoing, but of the Maule 'curse. Holgrave and Phoebe plan to marry, a union which will remove the curse from the house.

*House with the Green Shutters, The* A novel by **George Douglas**, published in 1901.

The story concerns the family of John Gourlay, a wealthy but arrogant and mean-spirited businessman in the small Scottish town of Barbie. His overweening pride leads him to insult and then to combat the humble but increasingly successful grocer, James Wilson. Disaster strikes when Gourlay's son, sensitive and intelligent, alternately ignored and petted, returns to his father's house in a drunken rage and murders him.

**Household, Geoffrey (Edward West)** 1900–88 Writer of thrillers and adventure novels. Born in Bristol, he was educated at Clifton and Magdalen College, Oxford. After working abroad as a businessman, he achieved fame with his second novel, *Rogue Male* (1939), in which the hero attempts to assassinate a foreign dictator (presumably Hitler) and is himself hunted through England by an enemy agent. Most of the 20 novels that followed drew on Household's interest in the psychology of the chase, notably *Watcher in the Shadows* (1960), *Dance of the Dwarfs* (1968) and *Rogue Justice* (1982), a belated sequel to his most famous book. *Against the Wind* (1958) is autobiographical.

*Household Words* A weekly magazine owned and edited by **Charles Dickens** from 1850 until 1859, when it was superseded by *All the Year Round*. The name (from **Shakespeare**'s *Henry V*) announced its intention of providing family entertainment in the form of wholesome fiction and journalism. Dickens published his own novels in the journal and attracted contributions from **Bulwer Lytton**, **Wilkie Collins**, **Elizabeth Gaskell** and **Charles Lever**.

**Housman, A[lfred] E[dward]** 1859–1936 Poet and scholar. Born and brought up in the Bromsgrove area, he attended St John's College, Oxford, where, despite a reputation as a brilliant student, he managed to obtain only a pass degree. For the next 10 years he worked as a clerk at the Patent Office in London, publishing the scholarly work on Propertius, Ovid and Juvenal which earned him the Professorship of Latin at London University in 1892. His definitive edition of the works of Manilius appeared in five volumes between 1902 and 1930. He became Kennedy Professor of Latin at Cambridge, and a fellow of Trinity College, in 1911.

*A Shropshire Lad*, Housman's collection of nature and love poems, was published at his own expense in 1896. Its idealized vision of the English countryside and its lyric pessimism made it extremely popular during World War I, two decades later. Despite this success Housman largely turned away from poetry, though he did publish *Last Poems* (1922). *More Poems* appeared posthumously in 1936 and 18 additional poems were published in the memoir (1937) by **Laurence Housman**, his brother. *Collected Poems* appeared in 1939. Housman is also known for his lecture, *The Name and Nature of Poetry* (1933), less so for *Praefanda* (1931), an anthology of Latin passages on sex which he published, with an ironic preface, in Germany.

**Housman, Laurence** 1865–1959 Artist, art critic, poet and dramatist. Brother of **A. E. Housman**, he was a protean figure, writing on feminism, socialism and pacifism, publishing volumes of light verse, popular novels (including *Thimblerigg*, 1924, a political satire of Lloyd George) and the notorious and much-parodied *An English Woman's Love Letters* (1900). He is best known for his plays, which included *Bethlehem* (1902), *Angels and Ministers* (1921), *The Little Plays of St Francis* (1922) and *Victoria Regina* (1934). These 'royal playlets' remained unperformed until 1937 when the Lord Chamberlain's ban on the impersonation of the royal family was lifted. He also published an autobiography, *The Unexpected Years* (1937), and a memoir of his brother containing poems and letters (1937). His *Collected Poems* appeared in 1937.

**Hovey, Richard** 1864–1900 American poet, born in Illinois, and educated at Dartmouth College. In collaboration with the Canadian poet **Bliss Carman**, he wrote three volumes celebrating life on the open road: *Songs From Vagabondia* (1894), *More Songs From Vagabondia* (1896) and *Last Songs From Vagabondia* (1901). *Along the Trail* (1898) was published in the year of the Spanish–American War. Drawing on the Arthurian legends, Hovey attempted to create a cycle of poetic dramas, but he did not live to complete it; *The Holy Graal* (1907) contains the fragments. A posthumous collection of poems, *To the End of the Trail*, was published in 1908.

*How They Brought the Good News from Ghent to Aix* A poem by **Robert Browning** published in *Dramatic Romances and Lyrics* (1845). Despite appearances, the narrative does not refer to any historical event. Browning admitted that he had simply wanted to evoke the rhythm of horses galloping; his success made the poem a favourite anthology piece.

**Howard, Bronson (Crocker)** 1842–1908 American playwright. Born in Detroit, Howard had his first dramatic success with *Saratoga* (1870), a comedy of upper-class life which was produced by **Augustin Daly** and later adapted for the London stage as *Brighton* (1874). *The Banker's Daughter* (1878), a revised version of his *Lillian's Last Love* (1873), and *Young Mrs Winthrop* (1882) confirmed his reputation as a dramatist. In all his plays he was concerned with the shaping power of American society and convention upon human relationships. His epic Civil War drama, *Shenandoah* (1888), was one of the most successful of its kind. Its first staging in 1888 in Boston was a failure, but when it reopened in New York the following year it was a huge success, with a first run of 250 performances. His last popular work was *The Henrietta* (1887), a satiric comedy of Wall Street life that ran for 68 weeks and established his reputation as a pioneer in realist drama.

**Howard, Sir Robert** 1626–98 Playwright, courtier and politician. Howard was the son of the Earl of Berkshire and as a fervent Royalist was imprisoned during the Commonwealth and honoured after the restoration of Charles II.

Howard's first play, *The Blind Lady* (1660), is a halfway house between Jacobean tragedy and the new heroic tragedy, but *The Indian Queen* (1664) is fully fledged heroic drama, the first of its kind. Of his four comedies, the best is *The Committee* (1662), notable for its creation of the comic Irish servant, Teague, and for the strength of its female characters. After 1668 Howard abandoned the theatre for a career in politics.

**Howard, Sidney (Coe)** 1891–1939 American playwright, born in Oakland, California. After serving in World War I, he became a journalist in New York. He began his career as a playwright in 1923 and had his first success in the following year with *They Knew What They Wanted*, based on the story of Paolo and Francesca. His most experimental play, *Yellow Jack* (1924), written with Paul de Kruif, deals with the research which led to the identification of the cause of yellow fever. Other plays include *Lucky Sam McCarver* (1925), *The Silver Cord* (1926) and *The Late Christopher Bean* (1932).

**Howards End** A novel by **E. M. Forster**, published in 1910. It centres upon the relationship between the cultivated and intellectual Schlegel sisters (Margaret and Helen) and the more practical and business-orientated Wilcox family (Henry, his sons Charles and Paul, and daughter Evie). Helen is briefly enamoured of Paul Wilcox, but immediately regrets her impulsiveness. Margaret meets a poor young married man, Leonard Bast, and establishes a friendship with Mrs Wilcox, the owner of Howards End. The latter, who is dying, bequeaths the house to Margaret in a note, but this is destroyed by the Wilcoxes before its contents are published. Leonard Bast, meanwhile, has become a close friend of the sisters, and they apply to Henry Wilcox for advice when the Basts' circumstances become straitened. Outraged by his indifference, Helen conducts Bast and his wife, Jacky, to the Wilcoxes' second home at Oniton during Evie's wedding celebrations. Wilcox and Jacky recognize each other as ex-lovers, but Margaret, who has by now become engaged to Wilcox, forgives his past adultery and they marry. Helen, carrying Leonard's child, retreats to the Continent, and Charles Wilcox thrashes Leonard to death for what he takes to be callous seduction. Charles goes to prison. Helen's child is born, and the sisters are reunited at Howards End.

'Only connect . . .', the famous epigraph to the novel, expresses Forster's lifelong belief in salvation through fraternal sympathy.

**Howe, E[dgar] W[atson]** 1853–1937 American novelist and editor. Born in Indiana, Howe owned and edited the *Daily Globe* of Atchison, Kansas (1877–1911), and *E. W. Howe's Monthly* (1911–37). He also published novels and collections of editorials and aphorisms. His novel **The Story of a Country Town** (1883), despite its melodramatic plot, is widely regarded as a landmark of American realism, and drew high praise from **Mark Twain** among others when it first appeared.

**Howe, Julia Ward** 1819–1910 American poet and humanitarian, a tireless worker for women's suffrage, prison reform and the abolition of slavery. With her husband, Samuel Gridley Howe, she edited the Abolitionist newspaper *Commonwealth* in Boston. Although she is probably best remembered as the author of **The Battle Hymn of the Republic** (1861), she published several collections of poetry, including *Passion Flowers* (1854) and *Later Lyrics* (1866). She also wrote *Sex and Education* (1874), *Modern Society* (1881), *Margaret Fuller* (1883) and *Reminiscences* (1899).

**Howell, James** *c.* 1594–1666 A minor diplomat in the reign of Charles I, Howell was a much-travelled man and a fine linguist. He became an MP in 1627, and was imprisoned as a Royalist for eight years from 1643. At the Restoration he was appointed Historiographer Royal.

At the time of his arrest Howell was the author of two books, *Dodona's Grove* (1640), a political allegory, and *Instructions for Foreign Travel* (1642). He also wrote political pamphlets, and his years in prison saw the beginning of the book by which he is remembered, *Epistolae Ho-Elianae: Familiar Letters*, written to imaginary correspondents about a multitude of subjects. The four books (1645, 1647, 1650 and 1655) are the most arresting source of detail about many contemporary events. Other books are his satiric *Perfect Description of the Country of Scotland* (1649) and *Londinopolis: An Historical Discourse or Perlustration of the City of London* (1657).

**Howell, Thomas** *fl.* 1560–80 Poet. Little is known of Howell, but he was probably a West Country man, educated at Oxford. His life was spent in service to the noble Herbert family, whom he celebrates in his poetry, *New Sonnets, and Pretty Pamphlets* (undated, licensed 1567–8), *The Arbour of Amity* (1568) and *H. His Devices* (1581); the last contains the first allusion to **Sidney**'s *Arcadia* (printed 1590).

**Howells, William Dean** 1837–1920 American novelist, journalist, editor and critic. Known in his lifetime as the 'dean of American letters', Howells was born in Martin's Ferry, Ohio. His family moved from town to town in Ohio, and he began to work as a typesetter for his father (a printer) when he was only 9 years old, so he received little formal education. Between 1851 and 1861 he worked as a compositor, reporter, news editor of the *Ohio State Journal* (1860), correspondent of the Cincinnati *Gazette*, and contributor to his father's newspaper *The Sentinel*. In 1860, he and John J. Piatt published *Poems of Two Friends*. In the same year he wrote a campaign biography of Abraham Lincoln, for which he was rewarded with an appointment as US consul in Venice (1861–5). Drawing upon his experiences in Italy, he wrote *Venetian Life* (1866) and *Italian Journeys* (1867). On his return to the USA he settled in Boston and became associated briefly with *The Nation*. He then became assistant editor of *The Atlantic Monthly* (1866–71), and from 1871 to 1881 served as its editor-in-chief. From 1886 to 1892 he wrote an editorial column for *Harper's Monthly Magazine*, and in 1892 he served as co-editor of *Cosmopolitan* magazine.

The first of his 40 or so novels, *Their Wedding Journey*, was published in 1872 and was followed by *A Chance Acquaintance* (1873); in both of them he makes use of his travel experiences. *A Foregone Conclusion* (1874) and *The Lady of the Aroostook* (1879) deal with the contrast between Americans and Europeans. With *The Undiscovered Country* (1880), a novel about spiritualism and the Shakers, *Dr Breen's Practice* (1881), and *A Modern Instance* (1882), Howells moved beyond the comedy of manners to novels dealing with larger social issues. *A Modern Instance*, for example, depicts a society in which traditional religious and family values are disintegrating in the face of commercial influences. *A Woman's Reason* (1883) came next and was followed by *The Rise of Silas Lapham* (1885), which, like *A Modern Instance*, examines critically the effect of material success on the human soul. *Indian Summer* and *The Minister's Charge, or, The Apprenticeship of Lemuel Barker* were both published in 1886, and a scholarly work, *Modern Italian Poets: Essays and Versions*, followed in 1887.

In 1888, after completing *April Hopes* (1888) and *Annie Kilburn* (1889), Howells moved from Boston to New York City. Fascinated by the city's contrasts of wealth and poverty, and appalled by the brutal treatment of striking workers, he produced *A Hazard of New Fortunes* in 1890. That same year he published *A Boy's Town*, an autobiographical work. *The Quality of Mercy* (1892), is a novel about embezzlement; *An Imperative Duty* (1892) has a black heroine. *The World of Chance* (1893), like a *Hazard of New Fortunes*, examines the lack of causality in human affairs. His later fiction includes a Utopian novel, *A Traveller from Altruria* (1894), *The Landlord at Lion's Head* (1897), *The Kentons* (1902), *The Son of Royal Langbrith* (1904), *New Leaf Mills* (1913), *The Leatherwood God* (1916) and the posthumous *The Vacation of the Kelwyns: An Idyl of the Middle Eighteen-Seventies* (1920).

Among his notable critical works are *Criticism and Fiction* (1891) and *Life and Literature: Studies* (1902). His reminiscences in *Literary Friends and Acquaintance: A Personal Retrospect of American Authorship* (1900) and *My Mark Twain: Reminiscences and Criticism* (1910) are important documents since his editorial duties brought him into contact with numerous writers. He was a close friend of **Oliver Wendell Holmes**, **James Russell Lowell**, **Henry James** and **Mark Twain**. Young authors such as **Hamlin Garland**, **Paul Dunbar**, **Stephen Crane**, **Frank Norris** and **Robert Herrick** all received encouragement from the older Howells, who from 1908 to 1920 was president of the American Academy of Arts and Letters.

**Hoyt, Charles Hale** 1860–1900 American playwright, born in Concord, New Hampshire. Between 1883 and 1899 he wrote and produced 17 farces and one comic opera. His early plays, like *A Bunch of Keys* (1883), the story of an incompetent hotel manager, are pure farce and slapstick comedy; his later works, like the comical melodrama *A Midnight Bell* (1889) and the political satire *A Texas Steer* (1890), are more socially aware. In 1892 he leased the Madison Square Theatre in New York, which later became known as Hoyt's Theatre. Among the plays he wrote and produced are: *A Trip to Chinatown* (1891), about down-and-out characters in the Bowery; *A Temperance Town* (1893), about the Prohibition movement; *A Milk White Flag* (1894), about home guard companies; *A Runaway Colt* (1895), about corruption in baseball teams; and *A Contented Woman* (1897), about the women's suffrage movement.

**Huchown of the Awle Ryale** Huchown is mentioned in the *Cronykil* of **Andrew of Wyntoun**, *c*. 1420, as the author of some Arthurian poems. Named as his work are the *Geste of Arthure*, *Awntyre of Gawayn* and *Pistel of Swete Susan*. The first two are lost; they have been dubiously identified as the alliterative **Morte Arthure** and the **Awntyrs of Arthure**. The last-named poem is probably the extant *Pistil of Swete Susan*. Various other works have been attributed to him but without evidence; equally unsupported is the identification of him as Hew of Eglinton.

***Huckleberry Finn*** See *Adventures of Huckleberry Finn, The*.

***Hudibras*** A satiric poem in three parts by **Samuel Butler**. Each part consists of three **cantos** and the whole is written in octosyllabic couplets: Part 1 was published in 1663, Part 2 in 1664 and Part 3 in 1678. The character of Hudibras (the name comes from *The Faerie Queene*) was based on Sir Samuel Luke, whom Butler served as secretary for a time. Luke was a colonel in Cromwell's army and a zealous Puritan. The strongest influences on Butler were Cervantes and Rabelais.

In Part 1 Hudibras, a Presbyterian, goes forth 'a-colonelling'. He rides a worn-out horse and bears rusty arms. His squire Ralpho is an Independent, and the two never cease from pedantic religious squabbling. They come upon a crowd preparing for a bear-baiting, a sport

Hudibras and the rich widow, whose sympathy he is trying to arouse. Loud knocking at the door warns him that he is facing exposure as a fraud. An illustration from an edition of 1710 of Butler's *Hudibras*. The incident occurs in Part 3, Canto 1.

condemned by Puritans; they attack the bear-baiters and put their leader Crowdero in the stocks. The bear-baiters rally and counter-attack; they capture Hudibras and Ralpho and release their leader. Hudibras and Ralpho are put in the stocks, where they continue to bicker with each other.

In Part 2 Hudibras is visited in the stocks by a widow whose property he covets. The widow exposes his mercenary motives, and requires him to undergo a whipping in order to regain her favour. Ralpho suggests that the penance could be accepted by proxy. His master is delighted and selects Ralpho as his substitute, to the latter's fury. After a quarrel they consult an astrologer, Sidrophel, to discover Hudibras's prospects with the widow. Hudibras learns that Sidrophel is a fraud; he beats him, robs him, and leaves him for dead, leaving Ralpho to face any charges. (Sidrophel is a satiric representation of Sir Paul Neale of the Royal Society.)

In Part 3 Hudibras visits the widow and gives her a fictitious account of all he has endured for her sake. But Ralpho has forestalled him and he is exposed once more. A loud knocking strikes terror into him; he believes supernatural agents are pursuing him and he hides under a table. The

astrologer's friends, in fiendish disguises, haul him out and thrash him, and make him confess his many sins. On the advice of a lawyer, Hudibras starts to woo the widow by letter.

At this point Hudibras is forgotten and the last two cantos of Part 3 are concerned with the activities of the Republicans just before the Restoration. Butler gives a notable study of Anthony Ashley Cooper, who became the Earl of Shaftesbury – the Achitophel of **Dryden**'s *Absalom and Achitophel*. Part 3 came 14 years after Part 2, and Butler died two years later.

The poem was exceedingly popular (Part 1 went through nine printings in the year of publication) but the targets of its satire are now too remote to preserve its original incisiveness. It is one of the best examples of an often fierce literary backlash to the tyranny of the Commonwealth, and anti-Puritan satire was a virulent strain in verse for several decades. Butler's unequivocal attack on hypocrisy and self-delusion was later directly influential on **Swift**, who also echoes the distinctive octosyllabics and mock-heroic style of this poem, which give rise to the term 'Hudibrastics'.

**Hudson, W[illiam] H[enry]** 1841–1922 Novelist and naturalist. Born in Argentina of American parentage, he worked on his father's farm until he was 15, when his health gave way and he became unfitted for outdoor work. He emigrated to England in 1869 and became an occasional contributor to various periodicals. *The Purple Land that England Lost* (1885), a series of stories set in South America, later became famous; other stories and two novels, *A Crystal Age* (1887) and *Fan* (1892), followed, but most of his writing during the 1890s was the work of a naturalist with an attractive, clear-cut style. He earned literary acclaim with *The Naturalist in La Plata* (1892), *Birds in a Village* and *Idle Days in Patagonia* (both 1893), *British Birds* (1895), *Birds in London* (1898), *Nature in Downland* (1900) and *Birds and Man* (1901).

In 1901 Hudson met **Richard Garnett**, who was to give him much encouragement, and in the same year he was awarded a Civil List pension, which enabled him to travel through England. *El Ombu and Other Tales* (1902) and *Hampshire Days* (1903) were followed by a romance, **Green Mansions** (1904), his first real success. He published 12 more books, of which *A Shepherd's Life* (1910) and the autobiographical *Far Away and Long Ago* (1918) have established his place in literature. Other works included *A Little Boy Lost* (1905), *Afoot in England* (1909) and *The Birds of La Plata* (1920). His letters to Garnett were published in 1923.

**Hueffer, Ford Madox** See **Ford, Ford Madox**.

**Hughes, Langston** 1902–67 Black American novelist, short-story writer, poet and playwright. Born in Joplin, Missouri, he attended Columbia University in 1921, but left to participate in the more lively activity in nearby Harlem. He was celebrated early on as a young poet of the **Harlem Renaissance**; his poetry appeared in *The Crisis* (1923–4) and was included in **Alain Locke**'s important anthology *The New Negro* (1925). With the support of **Carl Van Vechten**, he published his first volume, *The Weary Blues*, in 1926, and in the same year wrote a critical essay for *The Nation*, 'The Negro Artist and the Racial Mountain'. His second volume of poetry, *Fine Clothes to the Jew*, appeared in 1927, and his first novel, *Not Without Laughter*, in 1930.

During the 1930s Hughes embraced radical politics, publishing a collection of satiric short stories, *The Ways of White Folks* (1934). In two later collections, *Laughing to Keep From Crying* (1952) and *Something In Common* (1963), he again highlights the absurdities inherent in racial prejudice. His play *The Mulatto* was produced on Broadway in 1935, and he founded black theatre groups in Harlem, Chicago and Los Angeles. His drama is collected in *Five Plays* (1963). Other volumes of his poetry include *Shakespeare in Harlem* (1942), *Fields of Wonder* (1947), *Montage of a Dream Deferred* (1951), and *Ask Your Mama* (1961). He published two autobiographies: *The Big Sea* (1940) and *I Wonder as I Wander* (1956). He also wrote numerous books, essays and articles on social, historical and musical subjects, and edited collections of black folklore, poetry and stories. In the latter part of of his life he devoted his creative energies to writing the 'Simple Stories', which involve a seemingly slow-witted black character who always out-smarts his antagonists: *Simple Speaks His Mind* (1950), *Simple Takes a Wife* (1953), *Simple Stakes a Claim* (1957) and *Simple's Uncle Sam* (1965). His second novel, *Tambourines To Glory*, was published in 1958.

**Hughes, Richard (Arthur Warren)** 1900–76 Novelist and playwright. Hughes was born in Weybridge, Surrey, and educated at Charterhouse and Oriel College, Oxford. After graduating in 1922 he helped found the Portmadoc (Caernarvonshire) Players and directed the company until 1925; he was Vice President of the Welsh National Theatre from 1924 to 1936.

Hughes's first two works, a volume of poetry, *Gipsy Night*, and a one-act play called *The Sister's Tragedy* (produced at the **Royal Court Theatre**), both appeared in 1922. In 1924 he wrote the first radio drama, *Danger*, for the BBC, and his *A Comedy of Good and Evil* was performed at the Royal Court. *Confessio Juvenis* (1926) was a volume of his collected poems.

In the 1920s Hughes travelled extensively in Europe and North America, though he did not visit Jamaica until after he had made it the setting for his first and most famous novel. *A High Wind In Jamaica* (1929; in the USA as *The Innocent Voyage*) is a stirring tale about seven English schoolchildren who are kidnapped by Captain Jonsen and his crew of pirates during a voyage to England. In the course of their subsequent adventures one of the girls, Emily (aged 10), is panicked into killing another of the pirates' victims, a Dutch captain. When they eventually reach England the children – much to their amazement – are welcomed as heroes and heroines; and it is Emily's hysterical recollection of the murder which is mistakenly used to indict the pirates. The novel was unusual for its unsentimental portrayal of childhood, which broke with Victorian conventions and pioneered a new realism.

Hughes's next novel did not appear until 1938. *In Hazard: A Sea Story* tells of men at sea whose lives are first threatened by a hurricane, powerfully described, and then by fears of a mutiny.

In 1961 Hughes broke a long silence with the first volume of an ambitious multi-volume novel (*The Human Predicament*), which was to include historical as well as fictional characters. Only two titles were published. The first volume, *The Fox in the Attic* (1961), opens in Wales at the end of World War I. However, *The Wooden Shepherdess* (1973), the second in the sequence, met with little critical enthusiasm.

Apart from early short stories (*A Moment of Time*, 1926; and *The Spider's Palace and Other Stories*, 1931) Hughes was the author (with J. D. Scott) of *The Administration of War Production* (1956), an official history of World War II.

**Hughes, Ted (Edward James)** 1930– Poet. Born in Mytholmroyd, Yorkshire, and educated at Mexborough Grammar School and Pembroke College, Cambridge, Hughes began by studying English but later changed to Archaeology and Anthropology. At Cambridge he met **Sylvia Plath**, whom he married in 1956.

His first collection of poems, *Hawk in the Rain*, was published in 1957 – the year that he went with Sylvia Plath to live in America, where they stayed until 1959. *Lupercal* (1960) was followed by two children's books: *Meet My Folks* (1961) and *Earth Owl* (1963). Hughes has written a great deal for the theatre, both for adults and for children. The volumes of poetry that followed *Lupercal* include *Wodwo* (1967), *Crow* (1970), *Season Songs* (1974), *Gaudete* (1977), *Cave Birds* (1978), *Remains of Elmet* (1979) and *Moortown* (1979).

Hughes's mature work is original, skilful and inventive. His forms owe something to **Lawrence** and a little to **Hopkins**, but his version of the animal world is quite his own – isolating cruel and predatory instincts, and projecting

Ted Hughes.

them on creatures of his own invention. He directs us to the distance of civilized society from its vital origins. His portrayal of female character as devouring and fearful apparently connects with his praise of isolation in a kind of lonely masculinity.

Hughes has edited selections from the work of **Keith Douglas** (1964) and **Emily Dickinson** (1968). His own *Selected Poems 1957–81* was published in 1982. He succeeded **Sir John Betjeman** as Poet Laureate in 1984.

**Hughes, Thomas** 1822–96 Novelist and biographer. Born the son of a country gentleman at Uffington in Berkshire, Hughes was educated at Rugby and Oriel College, Oxford. He was called to the Bar in 1848, served as a Liberal MP and ended his long and energetic career as a circuit judge in Chester. While studying for the Bar he became a supporter of **Christian Socialism**, with his friends **F. D. Maurice** and **Charles Kingsley**. He helped to found the Working Men's College in London and acted as its principal in 1872–83.

Hughes's most famous work is *Tom Brown's Schooldays* (1857), a lightly fictionalized account of his old school under the headship of **Thomas Arnold**. Its 'muscular Christianity', a code which stressed ethical behaviour and athleticism but neglected academic values, is tempered by a good humour that prompted Kingsley to call it 'the jolliest book ever written'. Hughes never

repeated the success: *Tom Brown at Oxford* (1861) lacks the interest of its predecessor while an intervening novel, *The Scouring of the White Horse* (1861), is a slight compilation of the legends connected with the countryside of his birth. In later years Hughes produced admiring biographies, *Alfred the Great* (1869) and *David Livingstone* (1889), a book on his religious views (*The Manliness of Christ*, 1879), and the touching *Memoir of a Brother* (1873) in tribute to George Hughes.

**Hulme, Keri** 1947– New Zealand novelist, short-story writer and poet. Born in Christchurch of mixed Maori, Scottish and English parentage, she identifies most strongly with her Kai Tahu Maori origins, though they only represent one-eighth of her ancestry. She has worked in television, a factory and farming, and as a whitebait fisher on New Zealand's West Coast. A painter as well as a writer, Hulme published numerous stories and poems in magazines and a volume of poetry, *The Silences Between (Moeraki Conversations)* (1982), before becoming internationally famous with her novel *The Bone People* (1984). Originally published by a small feminist collective, the novel won the New Zealand Book Award for fiction and the Pegasus Award for Maori Literature and was subsequently published in Britain, where it won the 1985 Booker Prize. *The Bone People* is a heavily autobiographical work, which explores the spiritual legacy of Maori myth in a complex, poetic structure.

**Hulme, T[homas] E[rnest]** 1883–1917 Poet, essayist and 'philosophic amateur'. Born in Staffordshire and educated at Newcastle under Lyme and St John's College, Cambridge, he was killed in action at Nieuport in September 1917. Only six of his poems were published during his lifetime, five of them as 'The Complete Poetical Works of T. E. Hulme' in Orage's *New Age* (February 1912). He also published articles on 'Romanticism and Classicism' and Bergson in the same magazine in 1911, and translated Bergson's *Introduction to Metaphysics* and Georges Sorel's *Reflections on Violence* in 1913. Much of his work survived only in notebooks, which were edited by **Herbert Read** in two volumes, *Speculations* (1924) and *Notes on Language and Style* (1929). Hulme advocated the 'hard, dry image', and his theories of **imagism** influenced both poetry and the visual arts. **T. S. Eliot** described him as 'classical, reactionary and revolutionary'.

*Human Shows, Far Phantasies, Songs and Trifles* The penultimate volume of verse by **Thomas Hardy**, first published in 1925, when he was 85. It is a collection of older, revised, and recently written poems commemorating associations and affections of the past, among them his first wife Emma, his sister Mary, and his long-dead friend Horace Moule. Also gathered here are poems of philosophical reflection, of narrative (often in the ballad tradition), of love (in sundry phases), of the poor man and the lady (even at this late date in the poet's life) and of contemporary event (the hanging of Edith Thompson in 1923). It is a distinctly heterogeneous collection.

**Hume, David** 1711–76 Philosopher and historian. He was born in Edinburgh, the second son of Joseph Hume, laird of Ninewells, near Berwick. Originally intended for the law, he left Edinburgh University without taking a degree to engage in private study at home and then in France (1734–7). At La Flèche he began *A Treatise of Human Nature*, publishing the first two volumes in 1739 and the concluding one in 1740. It was received with indifference, despite Hume's addition of an abstract later in 1740.

His next work, the first of the *Essays, Moral and Political*, appeared in 1741, followed by the second volume in 1742 and three more in 1748. By this time, his application for the chair of moral philosophy at Edinburgh University having failed, Hume had begun to combine the role of man of affairs with man of letters. In 1745 he became tutor to the Marquis of Annandale, in 1747 he accompanied General St Clair as judge advocate on the disastrous expedition to Port

David Hume. A detail from the portrait by Allan Ramsay, 1766. National Gallery of Scotland, Edinburgh.

L'Orient, and in 1748 he went with the general on diplomatic missions to Vienna and Turin. *An Enquiry Concerning Human Understanding* originally appeared as *Philosophical Essays Concerning Human Understanding* in 1748 and *An Enquiry Concerning the Principles of Morals* in 1751.

In 1752 Hume was appointed Advocates' Librarian in Edinburgh, a post he held until 1757. *Political Discourses* (1752) was translated into French and helped a growing reputation in Europe, consolidated by his most popular work, *The History of Great Britain* (1754–62), which in its final form extended from Caesar's invasion to the flight of James II in 1688. *Four Dissertations* (1757) contained *The Natural History of Religion*, *Of the Passions*, *Of Tragedy* and *Of the Standard of Taste*; his dissertations on suicide and immortality were suppressed until after his death, when they appeared anonymously as *Two Essays* (1777).

Hume's sceptical stance, not always appreciated by his fellow countrymen, gave him much in common with French intellectual and literary life. His contact with France was deepened when he served, in 1763–5, as secretary to the Embassy in Paris. He returned to England with Rousseau, but the association led to a public quarrel and Hume published their correspondence in his own defence in 1766. He became Under-Secretary of State in 1767–8, but finally settled in Edinburgh, dying of cancer in 1776. His curiously detached autobiography, *The Life of David Hume, Written by Himself*, was published by his friend **Adam Smith** in 1777. *Dialogues Concerning Natural Religion*, written in the 1750s but reserved for posthumous publication, appeared in 1779.

**Hume, Fergus** 1859–1932 New Zealand writer of **detective fiction**. Ferguson Wright Hume was educated at Otago and admitted to the New Zealand Bar in 1885. His first novel, *The Mystery of a Hansom Cab* (1886), gained immediate popularity, some half a million copies being sold in the author's lifetime. He was one of the first writers to concentrate on detective and mystery novels, producing some 140 books, none of which equalled the success of his first.

***Humorous Lieutenant, The***; or, *Generous Enemies* An eccentric comedy of intrigue by **John Fletcher**, first performed *c.* 1619 (published 1647). The play's title comes from the character of a lieutenant who suffers from a mysterious infirmity that makes him courageous in battle. When cured his courage deserts him; but it returns when he is convinced he is unwell again. The main plot concerns Celia who is held captive at the court of King Antigonus. Both the King and his son Demetrius fall in love with her and while Demetrius is at the wars Antigonus pursues his suit with Celia. She, however, loves Demetrius and resists him. Demetrius, returning victorious from the war, is greeted with the news that Celia is dead. Antigonus, leaving Demetrius to his despair, then tries to obtain a response from Celia with a love philtre. Unfortunately, the humorous lieutenant accidentally drinks the philtre and immediately falls in love with the King. Celia eventually persuades Antigonus, by her loyalty and virtue, to restore her to Demetrius.

**humour** See **wit**.

**Humphrey, William** 1924– American novelist and short-story writer, born in Clarksville, Texas, and educated at Southern Methodist University and the University of Texas. His novels are set primarily in the Red River country of north-east Texas. His first, *Home from the Hill* (1958), is a family tragedy, which emphasizes the continuance of early Southwestern mores and their conflict with modern values. This was followed by *The Ordways* (1965), which stresses the need for a quality of self-reliance tempered by forgiveness and understanding for others. He has published two other novels, *Proud Flesh* (1973) and *Hostages to Fortune* (1984). His two volumes of short stories, *The Last Husband and Other Stories* (1953) and *A Time and a Place: Stories* (1968), were incorporated into *The Collected Stories of William Humphrey* (1985). A volume of criticism, *Ah! Wilderness! The Frontier in American Literature*, appeared in 1977.

*Humphry Clinker, The Expedition of* See *Expedition of Humphry Clinker, The*.

**Hunt, (James Henry) Leigh** 1784–1859 Poet, journalist and critic. Hunt was born at Southgate, Middlesex, and educated at Christ's Hospital. His first book of poems appeared in 1801, when he was only 17. In 1805 Hunt began to write theatre criticism, publishing a collection entitled *Critical Essays on the Performers of the London Theatres* in 1807. From 1808 he edited the radical weekly, *The Examiner*, which he had founded with his brother John. An uncomplimentary article about the Prince Regent led to Hunt and his brother suffering a heavy fine and two years' imprisonment. He continued the editorial work from his cell, where he was visited by **Byron**, **Lamb** and **Cowden Clarke**. Through *The Examiner* he introduced the work of **Keats** and **Shelley** to the public. Meanwhile, he wrote *The Feast of the Poets* (1814), *The Story of Rimini* (1816), *Foliage* (1818) and *Hero and Leander* (1819). In 1819–21 he conducted another journal, *The Indicator*.

In 1822 he travelled to Italy to join Byron and Shelley in setting up a periodical to be called *The Liberal*. However, Shelley's untimely death and Byron's departure for Greece brought the project to an end after only four issues had appeared. Near destitute, Hunt returned with his family to England; his *Lord Byron and Some of His Contemporaries* (1828) offers a jaundiced view of Byron's part in the affair. He went on to conduct – effectively, to write – *The Companion* (1828), the new *Tatler* (1830–2) and *Leigh Hunt's London Journal* (1834–5). His later works include: *Amyntas: A Tale of the Woods* (1820), translated from the Italian of Tasso; *Captain Sword and Captain Pen* (1835); *A Legend of Florence* (1840), a play produced with some success at **Covent Garden**; *Imagination and Fancy* (1844); *A Jar of Honey from Mount Hybla* (1848) and *The Old Court Suburb* (1855). He published an entertaining autobiography in 1850.

Hunt's short poems 'Abou Ben Adhem' and 'Jenny Kissed Me' (about **Jane Welsh Carlyle**) are favourite anthology pieces, but his most significant role was as a discerning and influential critic, recognizing the genius of Keats and Shelley. His personality is known to have given **Dickens** the hint for his portrait of the romantic, effusive and unworldly Skimpole in *Bleak House*, though Dickens insisted that Skimpole's selfish irresponsibility was not in Hunt's character.

**Hunt, Violet** 1866–1942 Novelist. The daughter of the painter Alfred William Hunt, she studied art, but turned to literature and produced her first book, *The Maiden's Progress: A Novel in Dialogue*, in 1894. Other novels include *Unkist, Unkind* (1897) and *The Tiger Skin* (1924). Her reminiscences of the **Pre-Raphaelites**, *Those Flurried Years* (1926) and *The Wife of Rossetti* (1932), are interesting if unreliable.

*Hunted Down* A crime story by **Charles Dickens**, written for and first published in *The New York Ledger* in 1859. The villain, Slinkton, was based on the poisoner and forger Thomas Griffiths Wainewright.

**Hunter, Evan** 1926– American novelist. Born Evan Lombino in New York City, he also writes under the pseudonym of Ed McBain. (During the 1950s he published novels under two other pseudonyms: Hunt Collins and Richard Marsten.) His best-known novel is probably *The Blackboard Jungle* (1954), about an urban high school, for which he drew upon his own teaching experiences. The novels he writes as Evan Hunter generally deal with social problems: *Second Ending* (1956) is concerned with drug addiction; *Mothers and Daughters* (1961) with the emptiness of middle-class life; *Sons* (1969) with the Vietnam War; *Love, Dad* (1981) with the hippie movement. As Evan Hunter he has also written plays and screenplays. As Ed McBain he has written the popular 87th Precinct series of detective novels, among them *Cop Hater* (1956) and *Fuzz* (1968). A prolific writer, since the mid 1950s he has produced approximately one novel per year under each of his two main pseudonyms.

**Hunting of the Snark, The** A poem by **Lewis Carroll**, published in 1876.

This mock-heroic nonsense poem concerns the quest, led by the lugubrious Bellman, for a mysterious Snark who finally turns out to be a dangerous Boojum instead. Further precis is impossible, given the poem's deliberate lack of logic and its specially invented vocabulary ('Jubjub', 'Bandersnatch' and of course the haunting figure of the Snark itself).

**Huon of Bordeaux** The translation by **John Bourchier, 2nd Baron Berners**, of this 13th-century *chanson de geste* introduced a subsequently popular story to English literature. Huon unwittingly kills Charlemagne's son. He is reprieved from sentence of death and set apparently impossible tasks, for example to bring back some hair from the Emir of Babylon's beard and to kiss his daughter. These he accomplishes with the help of Oberon, king of the fairies.

**Hurston, Zora Neale** 1903–60 American novelist. Born in Eatonville, Florida, the first incorporated black town in America, she won a scholarship to Barnard College and studied with the anthropologist Franz Boas, under whose direction she began an accomplished career as a folklorist. *Mules and Men* (1935) and *Tell My Horse* (1938) gather black traditions of the American South and the Caribbean. Her best-known novel, *Their Eyes Were Watching God* (1937), portrays the life of Janie Crawford, an independent black woman and folk heroine. She also published *Moses: Man of the Mountain* (1939), a novel which examines the figure of Moses as he appears both in the Old Testament and in black myth, and an autobiography entitled *Dust Tracks on a Road* (1942). Her popularity and critical reputation have grown since her death; in 1979 the black novelist **Alice Walker** edited a collection of her writings, *I Love Myself When I Am Laughing*. A volume of short stories, *Spunk*, appeared in 1984.

**Husband's Message, The** An Old English poem preserved in **The Exeter Book**. The message, apparently carved on a staff in runic letters, is to a woman of royal rank; her husband has been forced to flee because of a vendetta and he sends her assurances of his love, pleading with her to take ship for the south and join him in the spring. It is not clear whether the *Message* begins with Riddle 60, which immediately precedes it in the manuscript. The poem may be connected with **The Wife's Lament**, also in The Exeter Book.

**Hutchinson, Lucy** b. 1620 The wife of Colonel John Hutchinson, a prominent Puritan soldier in the Civil War, Lucy Hutchinson wrote *The Memoirs of the Life of Colonel Hutchinson* and a fragment of autobiography for the interest of her descendants. The *Memoirs* were not published until 1806 (edited by J. Hutchinson and including the autobiography). The book is valuable both for its picture of the life of a Puritan family of some distinction and for its comments on those around her. The colonel emerges as a quiet man who found himself swept along by the tide of events and did his conscientious best. He was a soldier on the rebel side, an MP, and a signatory of Charles I's death warrant (1649). At the Restoration he was in mortal danger. His wife sent an eloquent letter of penitence to the Speaker of the House of Commons and he was left in peace for two years, but was then arrested for alleged complicity in plots against Charles II and died in prison.

**Hutchinson, R[ay] C[oryton]** 1907–75 Novelist. He was born in Watford and educated at Monkton Combe School and at Oriel College, Oxford. *The Unforgotten Prisoner* (1933) deals with poverty and distress in post-war Germany, and *Testament* (1938) with the Russian Revolution; the latter established his stature as a novelist. Of his later novels, *A Child Possessed* (1964), on the love of a French *routier* for his idiot child, is the best. His finest work grappled with grand themes, often of tragedy in foreign countries he did not know well personally, but he deals skilfully with individual character as well as great historical movements. His writings were much praised and attracted a loyal but small readership.

**Hutton, R[ichard] H[olt]** 1826–97 Journalist, theologian and literary critic. Born in Leeds, he attended University College, London, where he first met **Walter Bagehot**. He abandoned his original purpose of becoming a Unitarian minister, but never his preoccupation with religion and problems of faith. In 1855 he joined Bagehot in editing *The National Review*, and in 1861 he became joint editor and part owner of *The Spectator*, contributing incisive reviews of contemporary literature to its pages. Hutton's books include: *Essays: Theological and Literary* (1871); *Essays on Some of the Modern Guides of English Thought in Matters of Faith* (1877), which considers **Carlyle**, **Matthew Arnold**, **George Eliot**, **F. D. Maurice** and **Newman**, later the subject of a full-length study (1891); *Criticisms on*

*Contemporary Thought and Thinkers* (1894); and *Aspects of Scientific and Religious Thought* (1899).

**Huxley, Aldous (Leonard)** 1894–1963 Novelist and short-story writer. Huxley was born at Godalming, Surrey, of a distinguished family which included **T. H. Huxley**, his grandfather; **Mrs Humphrey Ward**, his aunt; Leonard Huxley, his father, an editor of *The Cornhill Magazine*; and **Sir Julian Huxley**, his elder brother. He was educated at Eton and Balliol College, Oxford.

After graduating in 1915 Huxley became a journalist, briefly joining the staff of *The Athenaeum* and writing drama criticism for *The Westminster Gazette* (1920–1). Several volumes of poetry appeared before 1920 (*The Burning Wheel*, 1916; *Jonah*, 1917; *The Defeat of Youth*, 1918; and *Leda*, 1920) but it was with his fiction that Huxley made his name. A collection of short stories, *Limbo*, was published in 1920, and this was followed by *Crome Yellow* (1921) which launched his reputation as a witty and satirical commentator on contemporary events. Similar qualities were evident in *Antic Hay* (1923), *Those Barren Leaves* (1925) set in Italy, where Huxley and his wife lived during the 1920s, and *Point Counter Point* (1928), which contained thinly disguised portraits of **D. H. Lawrence** and **John Middleton Murry**, both close friends of the author.

With *Brave New World* (1932) Huxley turned his attention to the threat of world domination by scientific totalitarianism. His subsequent novels were equally marked by qualities of Swiftian despair and disgust.

Aldous Huxley, 1931.

*Eyeless in Gaza* (1936) was the last novel to be written in England. In 1937 Huxley moved to California and *After Many a Summer* (1939) is set in Los Angeles. Other novels during this period included *Time Must Have a Stop* (1944), *Ape and Essence* (1948) and *The Genius and the Goddess* (1955).

*Island* (1962) invokes a Utopian community with a new spiritual perspective and reflects Huxley's own search for an extension of awareness. His quest, which had begun with *The Perennial Philosophy* (1946), led him to experiment with altered states of consciousness through the use of mescalin, described in *The Doors of Perception* (1954) and its sequel, *Heaven and Hell* (1956).

Huxley's other works include *The Devils of Loudon* (1952), a study of demonic possession during the reign of Louis XIII (adopted by **John Whiting** as the basis for his play *The Devils*, 1961), and numerous essays (in *Collected Essays*, 1959). He also wrote two travel books (*Jesting Pilate*, 1926; and *Beyond the Mexique Bay*, 1943) and edited *The Letters of D. H. Lawrence* (1932), with an introductory essay which has been widely acclaimed. Huxley's short stories, also considered by many to be among his best work, were reprinted in *Collected Short Stories* (1957).

**Huxley, Sir Julian (Sorell)** 1887–1975 Biologist and writer. The elder brother of **Aldous Huxley**, he was educated at Eton and Oxford, where he won the Newdigate Prize for poetry. He held various academic posts in England and the USA. His books include *Essays of a Biologist* (1923), *Religion Without Revelation* (1927), *The Captive Shrew and Other Poems* (1932), *Man in the Modern World* (1947), *Evolution in Action* (1953) and *New Bottles for New Wine* (1957). He was Director-General of UNESCO in 1946–8 and was knighted in 1958.

**Huxley, Thomas Henry** 1825–95 Scientist. Born at Ealing, he was educated at his father's school and at London University, where he studied medicine. He continued his studies at Charing Cross Hospital and was particularly interested in comparative anatomy. In 1846 Huxley went to sea as assistant surgeon on HMS *Rattlesnake*, and became a Fellow of the Royal Society through his studies on marine organisms (1851). His lectures, essays and books cover natural science, philosophy and religion; his approach to religion is indicated by his invention of the word 'agnostic' to describe himself. He published *On the Educational Value of the Natural History Sciences* (1854), *On Races, Species and their Origin* (1860), *Evidence as to Man's Place in Nature* (1863), *On the Methods and Results of Ethnology* (1865), *The Evidence of the*

*Miracle of Resurrection* (1876), *The Advance of Science in the Last Half-century* (1887), *Social Diseases and Worse Remedies* (1891) and *Evolution and Ethics* (1893). His essays and lectures were published as *Collected Essays* (9 vols., 1893–4). Huxley was a powerful supporter of **Charles Darwin** – arguing the case for evolution against Bishop Wilberforce at the famous Oxford meeting of the British Association in 1860 – and an advocate of free investigation and enquiry.

**Hyde, Douglas** 1860–1949 Irish scholar, poet and translator. Born into a family of Irish Protestant clergymen in County Roscommon, Hyde was educated at home where he was stimulated to learn Irish by contact with the still current oral tradition of songs and stories. When he went to Trinity College, Dublin, in 1880, he had already amassed a considerable collection of Irish manuscripts and books. He began to publish original poems in Irish under the pseudonym 'An Craoibhin Aoibhinn' ('The Pleasant Little Branch'). He translated three stories from the Irish for **Yeats**'s collection of *Fairy and Folk Tales of the Irish Peasantry* (1888) and in the same year contributed some English poems on Irish cultural themes to *Poems and Ballads of Young Ireland*, to which Yeats also contributed. Increasingly convinced that literature in the Irish language was 'a true possession of national importance' and that it was gravely endangered by the dominant English language and culture in Ireland, he associated with Yeats in founding the National Literary Society and in his inaugural address as president in 1892 spoke of 'The Necessity of De-Anglicising Ireland'. He helped found the Gaelic League in 1893 with the hope of preserving and spreading the Irish language, Irish games and Irish dancing. He was president until 1915, resigning when he felt the sense of national identity the League had revived and stimulated was becoming too overtly political. His most influential publication was *Love Songs of Connacht* (1893), printing the Irish originals alongside verse translations and carefully literal prose versions which revealed to Yeats and others the possibilities of an authentically Irish idiom in English. Hyde's important *Literary History of Ireland*, deliberately confined to literature in Irish, appeared in 1899. He wrote *Casadh an tSugain* (1901), later translated by **Lady Gregory** as *The Twisting of the Rope*, and other Irish plays for public performance, collected in 1905, as well as compiling volumes of folk-stories, songs and religious poems translated from the Irish. He was Professor of Modern Irish at University College, Dublin, in 1905–32, and first president of the Irish Republic in 1938–44.

**Hyde, Robin** Pseudonym of Iris Guiver Wilkinson (1906–39), New Zealand novelist and poet. Born in Cape Town in 1906, she was taken to New Zealand as an infant. She was educated in Wellington, where she was regarded as a schoolgirl prodigy and later attended Victoria College. She worked on the Wellington *Dominion* from 1923 to 1926 and subsequently pursued a career as a freelance journalist and writer. From 1931 to 1933 she was editor of the *New Zealand Observer*. In 1938 she left New Zealand and travelled in China during the Sino-Japanese war, an experience she describes in *Dragon Rampant* (1939), before settling in England later in 1938. She committed suicide in 1939. Hyde's fiction includes *Passport to Hell* (1936), an account of the early life of Douglas Stark, a World War I bomber pilot, and its sequel, *Nor the Years Condemn* (1938), which give a vivid picture of New Zealand life in the early years of this century. A similar interaction between private and public history occurs in her best two works, *Check to Your King* (1936), a fictionalized biography of Charles, Baron de Thierry, who attempted to establish a Utopian community for English settlers and Maoris in early 19th-century New Zealand, and the autobiographical *The Godwits Fly* (1938). Her best-known poetry was produced towards the end of her life and did not achieve full recognition until the publication of her posthumous volume, *Houses by the Sea* (1952), a sequence begun in New Zealand and continued after she left, which recreates the natural and social environment in which she grew up in a style that moves between lyrical retrospection and an investigative ironic tone. *Persephone in Winter* (1937) is the most substantial of the volumes of verse she published in her own lifetime.

***Hyde Park*** A comedy by **James Shirley**, first produced in 1632 to celebrate the opening of Hyde Park as a place of recreation for the public. The play, first published in 1637, has the slightest of plots and comments on the fashionable life of Caroline London.

***Hydriotaphia*** (or *Urn Burial*) A treatise by **Sir Thomas Browne**, published with *The Garden of Cyrus* (1658) and taking as its point of departure the discovery of some ancient grave urns at Walsingham in Norfolk. Browne broadens his enquiry to consider the many ways mankind has disposed of its dead, and his zestful, idiosyncratic scholarship ranges over a wide field. His theme is brought to a close with an eloquent chapter expressing the Christian view of mortality.

***Hymn to Proserpine*** A poem by **Swinburne**, first published in *Poems and Ballads* (1st series, 1866).

Addressed to Proserpine, Queen of the Underworld, by a pagan Roman of the 4th century of the Christian era, this dramatic monologue sets forth the Heraclitan doctrine of flux and change as forcefully as it challenges fundamental Christian beliefs. The speaker, possibly Julian the Apostate, denies Christianity while acknowledging its considerable power, mercy and compassion. But he sees it as swept away by forces of change, and hails the power of Proserpine with the conviction that 'Thou art more than the Gods who number the days of our temporal breath;/For these give labour and slumber, but thou, Proserpine, death.' From death comes sleep, which contents the speaker. The poem ends on this note, deliberately at variance with Christian belief.

*Hypatia, or, New Foes with an Old Face* A historical novel by **Charles Kingsley**, published in *Fraser's Magazine* from January 1852 to April 1853 and in volume form in 1853.

The setting is Alexandria in the 5th century AD, a city governed ineffectually by the pagan prefect, Orestes, and threatened by the barbarian tribes advancing from the heart of Europe. The Christian church is the strongest power in Alexandria and, guided by the patriarch Cyril, it opposes the neo-Platonic philosophy expressed in the teachings of Hypatia, daughter of the mathematician Theon. Philammon, a young Christian monk, arrives from the desert and is repelled by the mindless fanaticism of his fellow monks. He is drawn to the beautiful Hypatia and the moderation and humanity of her doctrines. At the same time, he is discouraged by the weary scepticism of the intellectual, Raphael. Violence explodes when the Christians are led to believe that Hypatia has set the prefect against them. Philammon witnesses a mob cut her to pieces outside the academy and returns, disillusioned, to the solitude of the desert.

**hyperbole** In rhetoric, an exaggerated or extravagant statement designed to command attention or invoke reaction. A famous example is the question asked of Helen of Troy by **Marlowe**'s Faustus:

Is this the face that launched a thousand ships
And burned the topless towers of Ilium?

*Hyperion* Two unfinished poems by **John Keats**, written in 1818–19. One version was published in 1820, the 'Advertisement' to the volume stating that it was included at the publisher's wish, not the poet's. 'The poem was intended to have been of equal length with **Endymion**, but the reception given to that work discouraged the author from proceeding.' The second version is called *The Fall of Hyperion: A Dream* and was published by **Monckton Milnes** in 1856. It is also a draft, not a finished poem, and Keats gave it up (he said in a letter of 21 September 1819) because 'there were too many Miltonic inversions in it'.

The first version, called 'A Fragment' by Keats, tells the story of Hyperion from Greek mythology. Saturn and the other Titans, grieving over their fall and considering how they may regain their power, place their hopes in the only Titan who remains undeposed, the sun-god Hyperion. But with the advent of Apollo, god of knowledge, poetry and music, the Titans' rule is ended. The second version is a dream related by the poet. Because of his awareness of misery in the world, he is granted entry to a shrine. Moneta, the Titans' priestess, describes the fall of Hyperion and the coming of Apollo. An old order has gone, yielding place to a new.

# I

**iamb** See **metre**.

**iambic pentameter** See **metre**.

***Iceman Cometh, The*** A play by **Eugene O'Neill**, first performed in New York in 1946. The play was one of O'Neill's personal favourites, in which he attempted to portray man as a 'victim of the ironies of life and of himself'.

The men who gather in Jimmy-the-Priest's saloon, as well as its owner Harry Hope, are good natured and trusting in the value of love and honour. When the salesman Hickey tries to persuade them to abandon their illusions and return to reality, the truths they discover and reveal cause them to despair. Only the cynical philosopher Larry Slade can stand up to Hickey, and it is he who eases the desperate Parritt's route to suicide. When, at the end of the play, it is revealed that Hickey too has been living a lie, the discovery gives Slade no pleasure; it merely confirms his belief in the necessity of pipedreams.

***Idea*** **Michael Drayton**'s sonnet sequence first appeared as *Idea's Mirror* in 1594; it was reissued with substantial changes and additions in 1599, 1600, 1602, 1605 and 1619, and also in collections of Drayton's poems.

The sequence shows the influence particularly of **Sidney**'s *Astrophil and Stella*, and Drayton's claim to originality in the prefatory sonnet to the 1594 version paradoxically quotes Sidney's 'I am no pickpurse of another's wit.' Echoes from **Spenser**'s *Amoretti* and **Marlowe**'s *Edward II* can also be heard. Drayton was sensitive to comments from fellow poets and made revisions to accommodate their criticisms. His changes usually reject the extravagant conceits of earlier versions and increase the clarity of logic and poetic structure, but the later editions also contain sonnets that seem akin to the new metaphysical style in poetry. 'Since there's no help' (added in 1619), which combines colloquial language in the octave with an allegorized deathbed scene in the sestet, is usually considered Drayton's finest.

***Idea of a University, The*** Collected lectures, dating from 1852 onwards and published in 1873, by **John Henry Newman**, arising out of his experience as Rector of the new Roman Catholic university in Dublin. Newman wished to establish a Catholic university with the intellectual breadth of Protestant Oxford. The justification of a 'liberal education' was the 'enlargement of the mind'. Knowledge, despite having absolute value for Newman, was not the highest good. He argued that knowledge and reason were 'sure ministers to Faith' and that 'Right Reason . . . leads the mind to the Catholic Faith.' **Walter Pater** said the book was 'the perfect handling of a theory'.

***Ideal Husband, An*** A play by **Oscar Wilde** (1895). The most strongly plotted of his earlier works for the theatre, it deals with political corruption, public and private honour, blackmail, repentance and forgiveness.

***Idler, The*** A series of papers contributed by **Samuel Johnson** to *The Universal Chronicle or Weekly Gazette* from 15 April 1758 to 5 April 1760. The papers are similar in character to *The Rambler* but are shorter in length and generally lighter in tone. Representative characters are not given Latin names as they are in *The Rambler* but English ones – Tom Restless, Jack Whirler, Mr Sober, the author (Johnson himself) and the critic Dick Minim.

A monthly journal appearing from 1892 to 1911, edited by **Jerome K. Jerome** and Robert Barr, was also called *The Idler*.

**idyll** From the Greek, 'little picture'. It is used of a descriptive piece of poetry or prose, usually with a **pastoral** or rural scene.

***Idylls of the King, The*** A sequence of poems by **Alfred Tennyson**, his own most ambitious work as well as the most ambitious contribution to **Arthurian literature** since **Malory**. The poems were written at different stages in his career. When he was 24 he wanted to compose a 'whole great poem' about Arthur and started with 'Morte d'Arthur', published in 1842. The reviews, however, were discouraging and Tennyson did not return to the subject until 1859,

The dying Arthur. One of Dante Gabriel Rossetti's designs for Tennyson's *The Idylls of the King.* City of Birmingham Museum and Art Gallery.

when he published a volume, *The Idylls of the King*, containing 'Vivien', 'Enid', 'Elaine' and 'Guinevere'. 'The Coming of Arthur', 'The Holy Grail', 'Pelleas and Ettarre' and 'The Passing of Arthur' appeared in 1869, 'The Last Tournament' in 1871 and 'Gareth and Lynette' in 1872. 'Balin and Balan' was published in *Tiresias and Other Poems* (1885). 'Enid' was later divided into 'The Marriage of Geraint' and 'Geraint and Enid'. In its final order the sequence runs as follows:

*The Coming of Arthur.* Arthur, the newly crowned king, sets out to restore order to the kingdom and subdue the unruly barons. He falls in love with Guinevere, daughter of Leodegran, King of Cameliard. Successful in his campaigns, he seeks her hand but Leodegran hesitates because of Arthur's mysterious origins. He is persuaded by Bellicent, wife of King Lot of Orkney, who tells him the truth about Arthur's birth, upbringing and coronation and about Merlin and Excalibur. Arthur and Guinevere are married. The source is Malory's *Le Morte Darthur*.

*Gareth and Lynette.* Arthur's court, not long established, is the goal of all aspiring young men, one of whom is Gareth, son of King Lot of Orkney and his Queen, Bellicent. His mother reluctantly grants him permission to go to the court on condition that he present himself as a knave and serve in the kitchens for a year. Gareth works his allotted term under Kay, the Seneschal. Lynette, a noble lady, comes to Arthur's court to plead that Lancelot may rescue her sister, Lyonors, who is besieged in her castle by four knights. Gareth, the year over but still appearing a kitchen scullion, claims the adventure and Arthur grants his wish. Lynette is disgusted and treats Gareth with elaborate discourtesy, addressing him as 'Sir Kitchen-Knave'. But he defeats the first three knights and then confronts the last, costumed as Death. Lancelot arrives and Lynette wants him to undertake the last combat. But Gareth fights and prevails, and finds the fourth knight is just a boy, brother of the other three, in hideous armour that strikes dread into the hearts of those who try to help Lyonors. The source of the poem is Malory's *Le Morte Darthur* in which Gareth marries Liones, the lady he rescues. Tennyson leaves the name of Gareth's partner undeclared, saying that tales vary as to Lyonors or Lynette.

*The Marriage of Geraint* and *Geraint and Enid.* The sources were the story of *Gereint and Enid* in **The Mabinogion** (1838–49; translated by Lady Charlotte Guest) and the *Erec* of Chrétien de Troyes. Geraint, one of Arthur's knights, is married to Enid, daughter of Yniol. Uneasy about the character of the Queen, Guinevere, he decides to withdraw from the court and remove Enid from her influence. A remark of Enid's is misunderstood by him and he believes her faithless. He keeps her with him during his knightly encounters but forbids her to speak to him. But her devotion to him in all sorts of dangers reassures him of her love and fidelity.

*Balin and Balan.* This was the last poem of *The Idylls* to be written, and was intended to introduce the story of Merlin and Vivien. The source is Malory's *Le Morte Darthur*. Balin (Balin le Savage in Malory) is a violent and irascible but brave knight who is devoted to Queen Guinevere. His brother Balan, leaving to pursue a dangerous half-human forest demon, warns Balin to curb both his temper and his devotion. Disturbed by the Queen's friendship with Lancelot, Balin curses himself for a fool and leaves the court, then kills Sir Garlon, who dishonours the Queen's name. Garlon's father, King Pellam, who is descended from Joseph of Arimathea, orders his knights to pursue Balin, who flees through Pellam's castle looking for a weapon. He finds a spear before an altar and uses it to vault through a casement to make his escape. Later he is found asleep in the forest by Vivien, the Queen's favour hanging on a tree above him. From pure malice, Vivien confirms Balin's unease about the Queen. In a fury he destroys the emblems of his devotion, but his wild cries are heard by Balan, who believes he has found his quarry and rides to the attack. Balan fails to recognize his brother and both die in combat. Vivien rides away, unconcerned.

*Merlin and Vivien.* In Tennyson's version Vivien is the child of a king whom Arthur defeated; she dwells at the court of King Mark of Cornwall where she hears a minstrel sing of the purity of the knights and ladies of Arthur's court. She goes to Camelot with a distressed and pleading countenance and begs, as an orphan, protection from the Queen. She tries to sow suspicion and to seduce the King but finally decides that Merlin, the master of all secret arts, will serve her purpose better. When Merlin leaves the court for Broceliande, Vivien follows him. She succeeds in extracting from him a charm which she uses to seal him up for ever in a giant oak tree. The character of Vivien in Tennyson is his own invention, but the story of Merlin's enchantment is in Malory's *Le Morte Darthur*.

*Lancelot and Elaine*. The story of Elaine, 'the lily maid of Astolat', and her hopeless love for Lancelot follows closely the events related in the French prose *Lancelot* and the English *Le Morte Arthur* (not to be confused with Malory's *Le Morte Darthur*), but does not continue to Agravain's betrayal of Lancelot and Guinevere.

*The Holy Grail*. The quest for the Holy Grail, in Tennyson's poem, is related by Sir Percivale, who has left the court to become a monk. The first vision of the Grail is conveyed to a holy nun, Percivale's sister, who tells her brother that 'all the world be healed' if a quest for the Grail succeeds. She recognizes in Galahad, the youngest of all the knights, the requisite purity of character and makes him a sword-belt of her hair. Galahad occupies the Siege Perilous, the vision of the Grail is seen by the knights of the Round Table, and the quest begins.

*Pelleas and Ettarre*. Pelleas, innocent and idealistic, sets out for Arthur's court to seek knighthood. On the way he encounters, and falls in love with, Ettarre, beautiful but vain. Pelleas is welcomed by Arthur, gains his knighthood, and wins the prize at a tournament, which he offers to Ettarre. But she, having obtained her desire, returns to her own castle and refuses to admit Pelleas. She sends her knights to kill him but he defeats them one by one. Then all three attack and bind him; he is taken before Ettarre, to whom he declares his continued loyalty. He is ejected, to be discovered by Gawain, who undertakes to further Pelleas's suit but betrays him with Ettarre. Pelleas, heartbroken, rides away. His feelings change from grief to bitterness after he encounters Percivale and learns from him that Lancelot and Guinevere, too, are false. When he meets Lancelot he attacks him furiously, telling him 'a scourge am I to lash the treasons of the Table Round'. Lancelot defeats him and the two return to Camelot. Pelleas scorns the Queen's gracious questioning and leaves the court. In gloomy silence Guinevere and Lancelot foresee 'the dolorous day to be', while Modred watches and waits.

*The Last Tournament*. The last tournament is held on a wintry day, when all glory is rapidly fading from Arthur's court. Lancelot rescues a baby girl from an eagle's nest and takes the child to Guinevere; but in spite of her loving care the baby dies. The Queen gives a ruby necklace found on the child to Arthur to use as a prize in a tournament: 'Perchance – who knows? – the purest of thy knights/May win them for the purest of my maids.' The Tournament of Dead Innocence is presided over by Lancelot, Arthur having departed with the younger knights to quell the growing disorder in the kingdom. Before leaving he tells Lancelot of his depressed state of mind. Lancelot knows too well that Arthur's depression is soundly based; he presides over the tournament with a heavy heart. The ruby necklace is won by Tristram, who does not want it for his wife but for his paramour, Isolt, the wife of King Mark. At Tintagel he offers his prize to Isolt but is surprised and executed by King Mark. Arthur's campaign has reinforced his depression. He encounters the hate-filled Pelleas as the Red Knight and returns to his castle to find that Guinevere has departed. He is greeted by his jester, Dagonet, in tears: 'I am thy fool,/And I shall never make thee smile again.' Tennyson himself was pleased with his creation of the 'half-humorous half-pathetic fool Dagonet'.

*Guinevere*. Tennyson's account of the progress of Guinevere's remorse is his own invention. In Arthur's absence Guinevere, overwhelmed by guilt, implores Lancelot to leave the court and arranges a last meeting. The lovers are overheard by Vivien and surprised by Modred, whereupon Guinevere resolves to seek sanctuary in a nunnery at Almesbury while Lancelot returns to his own land. Among the novices she discovers that the names of Guinevere and Lancelot are notorious as faithless wife and false friend. Arthur comes to the nunnery and Guinevere begs his forgiveness. For three years, until her death, Guinevere remains with the nuns in penitent sorrow.

*The Passing of Arthur*. Bedivere tells the story of Arthur's last days. All the knights are slain in the great battle except Bedivere, Modred and Arthur. Arthur overcomes Modred in single combat but himself receives a mortal wound. He bids Bedivere throw Excalibur into the lake and the knight, overcoming his reluctance and fulfilling the command the third time it is given, sees 'an arm clothed in white samite, mystic, wonderful' receive the sword. Bedivere carries Arthur down to the water's edge to await the barge, with its three queens, which will bear the dying king to Avilion. He comforts Bedivere as best he can, in the famous lines beginning: 'The old order changeth, yielding place to new, / And God fulfils himself in many ways . . . .'.

**Ieuan Brydydd Hir** See **Celtic revival, the.**

*Ignoramus* A farcical comedy by George Ruggle, produced at Cambridge University in 1615 during a visit by King James and Prince Charles. The King enjoyed the performance so much that he asked for it to be repeated on a subsequent visit. The play is a satire on lawyers and the title refers to the Recorder of Cambridge, Francis Brackyn, who is burlesqued as the foolish victim of various adventures. (Brackyn was also a target in *The Parnassus Plays*.) Ruggle based his play on an Italian comedy by Giambattista della Porta (1538–1613) called *La Trappolaria*.

George Ruggle (1575–1622) was a fellow of Clare College who is believed to have written other plays, but *Ignoramus* is the only one to survive. It was published in 1630.

**Ihimaera, Witi** 1944– New Zealand novelist and short-story writer. Born in Gisborne on North Island, Ihimaera is the most significant Maori writer to have emerged to date. He went to school in Gisborne, but frequently visited his grandparents in the nearby village of Waituhi, which figures prominently in many of his stories. Later he attended the Universities of Auckland and Wellington and has worked in the New Zealand diplomatic corps. His collection of short stories, *Pounamu, Pounamu* (1972), was the first work of fiction published by a Maori. *Pounamu* is a type of jade the Maoris used for their ornaments and weapons prior to the advent of Europeans and in the novel comes to symbolize pre-Western Maori culture, and particularly its intense relationship with the land. Ihimaera followed this work with two novels, *Tangi* (1973) and *Whanau* (1974). 'Whanau' refers to the Maori extended family, and three generations figure in the novel, with a grandfather and his grandson sharing a common reverence for the traditional culture and the intervening generation seen as having drifted away from the old Maori ways. *The New Net Goes Fishing* (1977), a collection of short stories, mainly deals with the problems of contemporary urban life, but again demonstrates a concern with retrieving the spiritual legacy of the past. Along with D. S. Long, Ihimaera has edited *Into the World of Light: An Anthology of Maori Writing* (1982), which surveys the rapid development of the literature in the previous dozen years. Ihimaera has also written operas.

*Il Penseroso* A poem by **John Milton**, the companion piece to his *L'Allegro*, written in 1632 during vacations from Cambridge at his father's house in Horton. Milton had not then gained his later fluency in Italian and the title is a mistaken form of 'Il Pensieroso', meaning 'the contemplative'. The poem invokes the goddess Melancholy (*L'Allegro* deals with happiness, by contrast) and celebrates the delights of solitude, withdrawal, rumination, music, drama and epic poetry.

**Iles, Francis** See **detective fiction**.

*Imaginary Conversations of Literary Men and Statesmen* A series of dialogues by **Walter Savage Landor**. The first two volumes were published in 1824, the third in 1828 and the fourth in 1829. The dialogues range from classical times to Landor's own day, some containing action and incident. They cover a wide field of topics – dramatic, satirical, idyllic, social, political and literary. Among the best known are: 'Epicurus and Leantion and Ternissa', 'Leofric and Godiva', 'Dante and Beatrice', 'Leonora d'Este and Father Panigarola', 'Princess Mary and Princess Elizabeth', 'Lord Bacon and Richard Hooker', 'Calvin and Melancthon' and 'Aesop and Rhodope'.

*Pericles and Aspasia* (1836) and *Imaginary Conversations of Greeks and Romans* (1853) are in the same style. *Pericles and Aspasia* began as one of the conversations but outgrew the form and became a series of letters, covering the period from their first meeting at the theatre to the death of Pericles during the plague in Athens in 49 BC.

**imagism** A poetic movement in England and the USA from 1909 to 1917. Influenced by the aesthetic theories of **T. E. Hulme**, it found its leading spokesman in **Ezra Pound** who, with F. S. Flint, wrote an imagist 'manifesto' published in *Poetry* magazine in 1913. Among the tenets they put forth were a free choice of subject matter (often focusing on single, concentrated moments of experience), conciseness of expression, concreteness of imagery, and rhythm composed 'in sequence of the musical phrase, not in sequence of a metronome'. *Des Imagistes*, the first imagist anthology, was edited by Pound and published in 1914. Among the contributors were Pound himself, Flint, **Richard Aldington**, **Hilda Doolittle**, **Ford Madox Ford**, **Joyce**, **Amy Lowell** and **William Carlos Williams**. After 1914 Amy Lowell assumed leadership of the movement, helping to publish three further anthologies, all entitled *Some Imagist Poets* (1915, 1916, 1917).

**imitation** As a literary genre, the term signifies the attempt by one writer to rework the structure and theme of an earlier writer's work, recast in a contemporary mood. The form is most prominent in verse, and the most notable examples date from the late Renaissance period, culminating in the work of the Restoration and Augustan poets, who frequently wrote imitations of the famous classical poets, Juvenal and Horace being the most cultivated. By this means satire could be updated, for instance, but the framework of similarities to an age long past could be invoked for special effect. The form is distinct from a translation and allows considerably more poetic licence. The Latin original ('imitatio') and its Greek counterpart ('mimesis') have a stricter intellectual connotation, referring to the whole process of the representation of reality through the written word.

**Imlay, Gilbert** 1754–1828 American novelist and radical, born in New Jersey. Although little is known about his life, he seems to have been forced out of the USA in 1785 or 1786 after having become involved in dubious land speculation in Kentucky. During the 1790s he lived in London where he wrote and published two works. *A Topographical Description of the Western Territory of North America* (1792) portrays the post-Revolutionary West in a series of letters written to a friend in England. *The Emigrants* (1793), epistolary in form, is the first novel about the frontier area of Pennsylvania, which at the time extended from Pittsburgh west to the Mississippi; the novel envisions America as a promised land, and champions social reform, the rights of women and liberal divorce laws. In Europe Imlay frequented the radical circles of his fellow Americans, **Joel Barlow** and **Thomas Paine**, and for a time lived with **Mary Wollstonecraft**, who bore him a daughter.

***Importance of Being Earnest, The**: A Trivial Comedy for Serious People* A comedy by **Oscar Wilde**, first produced in February 1895 at the St James's Theatre, London. It was the author's last play and has proved his most enduringly

A scene from the first production of *The Importance of Being Earnest* at the St James's Theatre, London, on 14 February 1895. In Act II of Wilde's comedy are, left to right, Allan Aynesworth as Algernon, Evelyn Millard as Cecily, and George Alexander as John Worthing. Victoria & Albert Theatre Museum, London.

popular. The slender but deftly worked plot concerns two fashionable young gentlemen, John Worthing (Jack) and Algernon Moncrieff (Algy), and their eventually successful courtship of Gwendolen Fairfax and Cecily Cardew. More important than the plot is the continual flow of witty, uncompromisingly artificial dialogue and the characterization, especially of Gwendolen's mother, Lady Bracknell, and also of Miss Prism and Canon Chasuble.

***In a Glass Darkly*** A book of short stories by **Sheridan Le Fanu**, published in 1872. It is presented as a collection of cases investigated by Dr Martin Hesselius, who explores the supernatural in terms of psychopathology. With such stories as 'Green Tea', 'The Watcher', 'The Room in the Dragon Volant' and 'Carmilla' (about vampirism) the book has become a classic of mystery and occult literature.

***In Memoriam A. H. H.*** A poem by **Alfred Tennyson**, consisting of 132 connected lyrics, published in 1850.

Tennyson had been meditating a long poem for some time before the death of his friend **Arthur Hallam**, which became the occasion for composition. Some verses were written soon after Hallam's death in 1833, and Tennyson went on adding to them at intervals. The poem was privately printed in a trial edition in March 1850 and published anonymously in May of that year. The title was suggested by Emily Sellwood, the poet's future wife. An alternative title was 'Fragments of an Elegy', and Tennyson occasionally referred to the poem as 'The Way of the Soul'.

*In Memoriam* encompasses the fluctuating states of shock, despair, resignation and reconciliation as the poet explores his experience of bereavement. The three Christmas lyrics (XXVIII, LXXVIII and CIV) locate the process in a lengthy three-year cycle. Among the many remarkable passages is lyric CIII, which describes a symbolic voyage ending in a vision of Hallam as Tennyson's muse. The epilogue, in the form of a prothalamion on the marriage of the poet's sister Cecilia, was designed to bring the work to an optimistic close.

In many ways the cornerstone of Tennyson's reputation with his contemporaries, *In Memoriam* remains a highly original and influential work. **T. S. Eliot** noted some part of the reason for this when he drew a parallel with 20th-century reaction to his own poem, ***The Waste Land***: 'It happens now and then that a poet by some strange accident expresses the mood of his generation, at the same time that he is expressing a mood of his own which is quite remote from that of his generation.'

***In Our Time*** A collection of short stories by

**Ernest Hemingway**, published in 1925 and augmented in 1930. The hero of several of the stories is Nick Adams. In 'Indian Camp', the first story in the 1925 edition, he is a young boy who goes with his father, a doctor, to help a pregnant Indian woman through a difficult delivery. The story ends in startling fashion with the discovery that during the delivery the woman's husband has slit his own throat. 'Big Two-Hearted River', the two-part story with which the collection ends, is set several years later. Nick, now an adult, is psychologically shattered by his experiences in World War I. He goes alone on a trout-fishing trip in the woods of Michigan; fishing allows him to concentrate on doing one thing at a time in an almost ritualistic manner and .proves to be a healing experience. Other notable stories in the collection are 'The Three-Day Blow', 'Mr and Mrs Elliot' (apparently a caricature of **T. S. Eliot** and his wife), 'Cross-Country Snow', and 'My Old Man'. Another story, 'On the Quai at Smyrna', was added to the 1930 edition. Between the stories are a series of vignettes about World War I and bullfighting which complement the stories and add to the narrative unity of the volume as a whole.

**In the Midst of Life** A collection of stories by **Ambrose Bierce**, first published in 1891 under the title *Tales of Soldiers and Civilians*. More than half of the stories are concerned with soldiers' lives during the American Civil War, and reflect Bierce's own revulsion for the life he experienced as a Union soldier. Violence – particularly its psychological effect – and the macabre are dominant themes. Among the best-known of the stories are 'The Middle Toe of the Right Foot', about a murderer who is haunted to death by his victim; 'A Horseman in the Sky', in which a young Union soldier is forced by circumstances to shoot and kill a Confederate officer, who happens to be his father; and 'An Occurrence at Owl Creek Bridge', which presents the fantasy that a man who is being hanged experiences in the last seconds of his life.

**Inchbald, Elizabeth** 1753–1821 English playwright and novelist, born near Bury St Edmunds in Suffolk. She ran away from home in 1772, defying a speech impediment to become an actress. Little is known of her marriage to Joseph Inchbald (d. 1779), a minor actor. That she loved the much greater actor, John Philip Kemble, is well known, not least from the reasonable inference that he served as the model for Dorriforth in her novel *A Simple Story* (1791). Inchbald's acting career continued until 1789, after which time she devoted herself to writing. Her first play, *A Mogul Tale* (1784), cleverly exploited the current craze for hot-air balloons. It was followed by a number of come-

dies, of which the most successful were *I'll Tell You What* (1785), *Everyone Has His Fault* (1793), *Wives as They Were, and Maids as They Are* (1797) and *To Marry, or Not to Marry* (1805). *The Child of Nature* (1788) is a more ambitious piece, as was the adaptation of Kotzebue's *Lovers' Vows* (1798) whose rehearsal in the Bertram household causes such consternation in **Jane Austen**'s *Mansfield Park*. Inchbald was also the editor of three collections of plays, *The British Theatre* (25 vols., 1808), *Farces* (7 vols., 1809) and *The Modern Theatre* (10 vols., 1809).

**Indian Summer** A novel by **William Dean Howells**, published in 1886. It tells the story of a middle-aged American newspaper publisher, Theodore Colville, who travels to Florence to take up an interest in architecture he had abandoned years before. He encounters a friend from his childhood, Evalina Bowen, now a widow. Imogene Graham, Evalina's young friend and protégée, is attracted to Colville. Mrs Bowen tells her of an unhappy youthful romance of Colville's which had left him broken-hearted, and Imogene, her sympathy stirred, conceives a romantic attachment to him. The relationship comes to an end, however, when she experiences true love for the young clergyman Morton. This clears the way for the marriage of Colville and Evalina, who have secretly loved one another almost from the beginning of the novel.

**Indicator, The** A periodical published by **Leigh Hunt** in 1819–21.

**Infernal Marriage, The** A light-hearted tale by **Benjamin Disraeli**, published in 1834, which uses the story of Pluto and Proserpine as a vehicle for satire on contemporary politics.

**Inge, William** 1913–73 American playwright and novelist, born in Independence, Kansas. His first play, *Farther Off From Heaven* (1947), was followed by *Come Back, Little Sheba* (1950), about a married couple's fruitless battle with alcoholism. *Picnic* (1950), the story of a sexually attractive stranger's relationships with several lonely women in a small Kansas town, won both the Pulitzer Prize and the New York Drama Critics Circle Award. Continuing his examination of the frustration of Midwestern life, he wrote *Bus Stop* (1955), the story of a love-affair between a nightclub singer and a lonely cowboy; and *The Dark at the Top of the Stairs* (1957), the semi-autobiographical psychological drama of the Flood family. Two studies of modern Oedipal situations, *A Loss of Roses* (1959) and *Natural Affection* (1963), and the domestic comedy *Where's Daddy?* (1966), were less successful. In 1961 he reworked his one-act play *Glory in the Flower* (1959) into the screenplay for *Splendor in the Grass*. His last play was *The Last Pad* (1970), about three men on death row. After 1970 he turned to writing novels. *Good Luck, Miss Wyckoff* (1971) relates the story of a white schoolteacher whose affair with the black janitor costs her her job and changes her life. His second novel, *My Son is a Splendid Driver* (1972), the first-person narrative of a lonely teacher, is clearly autobiographical. He committed suicide shortly after publication.

**Ingelow, Jean** 1820–97 Poet and novelist. A native of Boston in Lincolnshire, Jean Ingelow became a professional writer after moving to London. She enjoyed considerable success with 25 books of verse, children's stories, and novels. Her *Mopsa the Fairy* (1869) was a children's favourite for a number of years and some of her poems became popular anthology pieces. The most notable of these were 'The High Tide on the Coast of Lincolnshire, 1571' and 'Divided' from *Poems* (1863) and 'A Story of Doom' from the collection of that name (1867). Her novels are *Off the Skelligs* (1872), *Fated to be Free* (1875) and *Sarah de Beranger* (1879).

**Ingoldsby Legends, The** Humorous mock-medieval ballads by **R. H. Barham**, published in *Bentley's Miscellany* and *The New Monthly Magazine* from 1837 onwards and in various collections from 1840. Their main interest is as a repository of early 19th-century slang and as precursor of the work of **W. S. Gilbert** in their outrageous rhymes and lively anapaestic rhythms.

**Inheritance, The** A novel by **Susan Ferrier**, published in 1824.

The Earl of Rossville repudiates his son when he marries beneath him, but admits his daughter-in-law and his granddaughter, Gertrude, to his presence after the death of his son. Gertrude thus becomes heiress presumptive to Rossville. She falls in love with the profligate Colonel Delmour, and, after the death of the Earl, becomes engaged to him, to the despair of her cousin, Edward Lyndsay, who loves her. A coarse American stranger now appears on the scene claiming to be Gertrude's father – a claim which is eventually proved true. Gertrude's mother, despairing of children of her own, had adopted the child of a servant. Gertrude's 'inheritance' is therefore nullified. Colonel Delmour shows his true character and abandons her, but Edward Lyndsay remains faithful and eventually wins her.

**Inn Album, The** A dramatic poem of approximately 3000 lines by **Robert Browning**. The story concerns two couples who are never named, and whose fates are unavoidably intertwined. The visitors' book at the inn where the four are staying is used by the characters to convey messages, make assignations and record threats. Published in 1875, the poem is given a contemporary setting, though it draws upon the career of a notorious Regency rake for its plot, and includes numerous specific allusions to events and preoccupations of the 1870s.

**Innes, Michael** See **Stewart, J. I. M.**

**Innocent Voyage, The** See **Hughes, Richard**.

**Innocents Abroad, The**, *or, The New Pilgrim's Progress* A travel book by **Mark Twain**, published in 1869 and based on his visit to Europe and Palestine during the summer and autumn of 1867. It took shape from letters he wrote to the San Francisco *Alta California* and the New York *Herald* and *Tribune* while on his journey. Comprising the often humorous narrative of a shrewd American in the Old World for the first time, the book marked the beginning of the most productive and successful period of Twain's career.

**inscape** and **instress** See **Hopkins, Gerard Manley**.

**Instructions to a Painter** A sub-genre in 17th-century verse. Several poems incorporate the formula in their titles, the most notable examples being by **Marvell**, **Denham**, **Waller**, **Jonson** and **Herrick**. These poems offer a portrait or caricature of a contemporary figure, presented in the form of guidelines to an artist for a picture. The intent is usually satiric, and the subject made grotesque or ridiculous, though the form was sometimes used for Royalist panegyrics during the Restoration.

The tradition is an ancient one, stretching back to the satirical thumbnail sketches of Martial, and was in vogue at Venice in the 17th century. In England, its popularity seems to have died out with the reign of Queen Anne; **Steele** ridiculed such poems in the third number of his *Tatler* (14 April 1709). **Cowper** and **Elizabeth Barrett Browning** produced later examples.

**Intelligencer, The** A weekly paper started in Dublin by **Swift**, the first number appearing on 11 May 1728, and for its short life written by him and Thomas Sheridan. It ran to 19 numbers, the essays ranging from discussion of the state of Ireland (particularly its poverty) to a famous defence of **Gay's** *The Beggar's Opera* (in the third number). Swift's general aim was 'to inform, or divert or correct, or vex the Town'.

*The Intelligencer* was also the name of a newspaper published in the 1660s by **Roger L'Estrange**.

**interlude** The name, from the Latin *interludium*, given to the short dramatic sketches performed during intervals in banquets. The English origins cannot be exactly traced, though professional or semi-professional performers were active for many years before the first recorded reference to Players of the King's Interludes in 1493. The work of **John Heywood**, in particular, illustrates the importance of the 16th-century interlude in the evolution of English drama.

**Invisible Man** A novel by **Ralph Ellison** published in 1952. Widely regarded as one of the major works of recent American fiction, *Invisible Man* combines elements of realism, surrealism, and folklore. Set in the 1930s, the book details the often incoherent experiences of its nameless black narrator – as a bright high-school student in the South, as a disoriented college student who is eventually expelled from the Southern 'negro' college he attends, as a factory worker in New York City, and as a rising figure in left-wing politics. His life is marked by various traumas of racial and individual identity, but it is through these experiences that he eventually achieves self-consciousness. This self-consciousness is inscribed in the title: he realizes that black skin in American society makes one 'invisible' to white eyes. The novel's climax recounts a race riot in Harlem, during which the narrator observes both the destructiveness of black nationalism and the failure of communist attempts to reform society. He retreats, in his invisibility, to an underground sewer, which he furnishes and lives in while writing his book. At the end of the novel he is better off in one respect than when he began: his consciousness of the social phenomenon of 'invisibility' has provided him with the possibility for free personal action. *Invisible Man* is also the title of a novel (1897) by **H. G. Wells**.

**Iolo Morganwg** See **Celtic revival, the.**

**Ipomadon** A late 14th-century **verse romance** translated from Hue de Rotelande's Anglo-Norman *Ipomédon* (*c.* 1190). The English poem is written in 12-line **tail-rhyme** stanzas in the North Midlands dialect. There are two other English versions: *The Lyfe of Ipomydon*, in couplets and *Ipomedon*, in prose.

The romance tells of Ipomadon's quest for the hand of the daughter of the Duke of Calabria, who has vowed to marry the most proficient knight in the world. In her court he devotes himself to hunting and shows no interest in arms. He leaves in disgrace and wins fame in foreign lands, later returning in disguise to win her in a tournament but leaving without claiming his prize. At this time he is attached to the court of Sicily where, again, he is known as a foolish and cowardly hunter. Ipomadon wins more glory abroad and becomes King of Apulia on his father's death. Hearing his beloved is besieged he returns to Sicily from where, disguised as a fool again, he is led to his lady's castle by a rude maiden and a dwarf. He defeats her suitor and the couple are eventually married.

The story is humorous and entertaining; it is packed with elaborate description and detail, the emotions of the lovers are sympathetically and realistically described (often in the form of soliloquies), and the courtly milieu is skilfully evoked. The lack of motivation for the hero's prolonged deception and delay does not detract significantly from the poem.

**Ireland, David** 1927– Australian novelist. Born in Lakemba in the suburbs of Sydney, Ireland worked at a variety of occupations, including those of gamekeeper and oil-refinery worker, an experience on which he based his second novel *The Unknown Industrial Prisoner* (1971), before becoming a full-time writer in the early 1970s. Ireland's fiction employs discontinuous narrative, surrealism and a range of metafictive techniques, and is frequently highly political in its criticism of the status quo. His first novel, *The Chantic Bird* (1968), has been described as an Australian *Catcher in the Rye*. It is the confession of a youthful outsider who blends an anarchistic disregard for contemporary society with a fondness for his small brothers and sisters and the girl who looks after them. *The Unknown Industrial Prisoner* uses a fragmentary narrative mode to attack the dehumanizing pressures of working for a multinational oil-company. *Burn* (1974) is a 'day in the life' of a half-caste Aborigine about to be evicted from his hut, and once again involves an exploration of the plight of the marginalized outsider. *A Woman of the Future* (1979) blends realism and surrealism in its treatment of a protagonist, apparently representative of Australia, who remains innocent whatever degradations she superficially undergoes. Ireland's novels are frequently concerned with gender stereotypes and subcultures: *The Glass Canoe* (1976) is about a group of drinkers in a Sydney pub, who again represent an Australian microcosm; *City of Women* (1981), a novel set in a Sydney without men, follows the fortunes of a lesbian separatist. Before turning to fiction, Ireland wrote plays and verse. His novel *The Flesheaters* (1972) was adapted from his best-known play, *Image in the Clay* (1964).

**Ireland, William Henry** 1777–1835 Shakespearean forger. The possibly illegitimate offspring of the engraver Samuel Ireland (d. 1800), he was educated at private schools in Kensington, Ealing, Soho and France, and then articled to a conveyancer in New Inn. Taking advantage of both his access to old legal documents and his father's astonishing credulity, he began in 1794 to produce a whole series of forgeries, including a mortgage signed by **Shakespeare** and **Heminges**, many books into which he copied Shakespeare's signature, the whole of *King Lear* and excerpts from *Hamlet* in the author's 'own hand'. In 1795 his naïve father announced an exhibition of these items, and it is a reflection on the age that such personages as **Joseph Warton**, **Boswell** (who went on his knees and kissed the relics) and **Henry Pye** all accepted their authenticity. Ireland overreached himself when he offered his father two entirely new Shakespeare plays, *Vortigern and Rowena* and *Henry II*. The former was accepted by **Sheridan** for performance at **Drury Lane**, for which Ireland received an initial payment of £250 and a share of profits. The play was denounced as a forgery by such genuine scholars as **Ritson**, **Steevens** and **Malone**. The major performers, including Mrs Siddons, developed diplomatic illnesses, and at the only performance the audience made it clear that they did not expect to see the piece again. Though his son admitted the deception and published *An Authentic Account of the Shaksperian MSS*, Samuel Ireland refused to believe him and even published the two plays shortly before his death. William Henry, after an initial period of obloquy, set up a circulating library in Kennington from which he sold copies of his famous forgeries, which he seems to have considered worthy of praise.

**Irish Sketch Book, The** A travel book by **W. M. Thackeray**, with his own illustrations, published in two volumes in 1843.

One of the best of Thackeray's travel writings, this account of a journey round Ireland made in 1842 paints a vivid picture of the country on the threshold of the Great Famine.

**Iron, Ralph** See **Schreiner, Olive**.

**Iron Heel, The** A novel by **Jack London**, published in 1908. A socialist vision of the historically inevitable demise of capitalism, though written when London was at the height of his popularity, the book was banned in various parts of America and met with strong objections to its radical political stance. The story is set in the years 1912–32 and is supposedly a transcription of a manuscript written at the time by Avis Cunningham Everhard and edited 700 years later by Anthony Meredith, who lives in the fourth century of the Brotherhood of Man. London, through his fictitious editor Meredith, provides extensive footnotes which enable him to voice his passionate opposition to capitalism and to project the ultimate success of socialist revolution in the USA.

Avis Cunningham tells how she became a revolutionary socialist after meeting the dynamic proletarian philosopher Ernest Everhard and then observing the social conditions of her native city, San Francisco. The two join the revolutionary movement and become leaders in the fight against the Oligarchy, the Iron Heel of the title. The Oligarchy – a defensive, proto-fascist conglomeration of major trusts and their private militias – is formed after socialism has already made a significant impact on capitalist security. Ernest and Avis marry against a background of the Oligarchy's consolidation of power and the dramatic escalation of social and political unrest. Despite the efforts of the Iron Heel, socialism retains some political power and Ernest is elected to Congress. While he is making an inflammatory speech a bomb is thrown from the House balcony. Although innocent, Ernest and 51 other socialist Congressmen are arrested, tried, and convicted of the bombing. By the time they escape, the Oligarchy has cornered world markets and precipitated global violence. In disguise, Ernest and Avis enter its service and plan a massive revolt, which is sabotaged in the novel's climactic scene of city-wide destruction and slaughter in Chicago. The revolution is crushed, but the socialists remain determined. The manuscript ends abruptly on the eve of a second uprising. Ernest has already been executed. Avis's fate is unclear, though the editor assumes that she too is executed. The reader learns that the Iron Heel is finally overthrown 300 years after the events related in the 'Everhard Manuscript'.

**irony** A mode of discourse, whether lyric, narrative or dramatic, that purports to convey a latent meaning different from – indeed, usually opposite to – the ostensible one. The term has been stretched to cover understatement, naïvety, **hyperbole**, pun, paradox and in fact (especially in modern criticism) any contrast or ambiguity – indeed, to cover anything other than plain literal statement. But, on both etymological and practical grounds, these are better regarded as means of irony or, according to the literary circumstances, as overlapping concepts. If irony is thought of as a dissembling, in keeping with its origin in the 'eiron' (a dissembler), then it becomes a term still broad but limited enough to be critically useful. Like Socrates, though, the eiron dissembles not to deceive but to enlighten. So irony, properly speaking, is a dissembling that is meant to be seen through.

The dissembling element, however, is not a husk to be discarded when the real meaning is perceived. The fact of opposition is as central to the ironic experience as the fact that it is overcome. Only then will there be the characteristic effect of inward amusement, smiling enlightenment, through the release of tension. The perception of irony thus involves both discernment and detachment – a fact that renders it the most effective weapon of **satire** and (as tragic irony, a form of dramatic irony) the saving grace of tragedy, distancing us from horror.

All irony is necessarily either textural or structural: inherent either in verbal constructions, making an immediate impression, or in the memory-dependent constructions of plot or story. These two kinds of irony are normally distinguished as verbal and dramatic irony, the one relying on treatment, the other on content. Sarcasm is verbal irony that is crude rather than clever; it is rightly regarded as inferior since it denies the reader the higher pleasures of discernment and detachment. **Jane Austen**'s description in *Sense and Sensibility* of Robert Ferrars as having 'a person and face of strong, natural, sterling insignificance' provides an example of verbal (textural) irony. *Oedipus Rex* provides many examples of dramatic (structural) irony, such as the fact that his pursuit of the criminal leads Oedipus to himself, the fact that his vengeance falls on his own head, or the fact that in the end (like Tiresias whom he castigates at the beginning) he comes to 'see' only when blinded.

All irony can also be divided into two other broad categories: covert and overt. It would be convenient were these synonymous with the verbal and dramatic categories. But, though overt irony can always be brought within 'dramatic' boundaries and covert irony is usually verbal, the match is not exact.

Only covert irony is straightforwardly ironic in the sense given above, since it relies on a difference between ostensible and latent meaning, and thus requires of the reader or hearer some reconstruction. Overt irony, on the other hand, as the name implies, is not a 'dissembling' statement or event – unless one postulates a benevolent deity, an idea of some built-in justice in nature. Colloquial speech provides many examples. The verbal irony, 'Lovely weather again!', said of pouring rain, requires a little reconstruction to find the real sense and is therefore a minimal example of covert irony. 'He went to help in the crash, phoned for an ambulance, and it knocked him down when it came – it was ironic' is an example of overt irony: it is not ironic at all, just a straight account of an absurd accident, unless we implicitly assume a world in which such 'injustice' is, or ought to be, ruled out.

Dramatic irony – a state of affairs very different from what the protagonists think – is normally overt. The audience usually sees this disparity throughout, and is thus more discerning and detached from the action than the protagonists. This state is similar to the experience of real, or covert irony; but it is not identical with it, since no reconstruction is required, no ostensible meaning is to be seen through – save in so far as the audience may partially identify itself with the protagonists. Even then, this form of irony is really near to being overt; at most it is pseudo-covert.

Other varieties of irony are all particular variants of the general categories, and may be briefly itemized. The term 'Socratic irony' refers to discrepancies between ostensible ignorance or simplicity and actual acuteness. It is verbal and covert. Romantic irony is also verbal, but perhaps more often pseudo-covert than strictly so, since it lies in discrepancies of tone and statement that result from an authorial detachment from the created characters and action, which allows unexpected moods or comments to be expressed; this is not necessarily a 'seeing through'. **Byron** provides many examples, such as the following attitude to multiple rape of the elderly (in Canto 8 of *Don Juan*):

Some odd mistakes, too, happen'd in the dark,
    Which show'd a want of lanterns, or of taste –
Indeed the smoke was such they scarce could mark
    Their friends from foes, – besides such things from
      haste
Occur, though rarely, when there is a spark
    Of light to save the venerably chaste:
But six old damsels, each of seventy years,
    Were all deflower'd by different grenadiers.

Tragic (or Sophoclean) irony lies in the distance between what the protagonists expect and the disastrous way things turn out; it is dramatic and usually overt or at most pseudo-covert, as the audience is usually in the know from the beginning. Irony of fate (or cosmic irony) lies in the difference between the just or orderly way the gods or fate or nature might be expected to behave and the cruel or random way it does in fact treat the protagonists; it is dramatic and overt. Witness the treatment meted out to **Hardy**'s heroine in *Tess of the d'Urbervilles*.

Finally, if irony is essentially a form of dissembling discourse, how is it recognizable as such? In literature, some contextual element must make recognition possible (whereas in conversation mere ironic intention and a tone of voice may suffice). In verbal irony, which is normally formal and covert, discrepancies in the immediate linguistic context usually give the clue (witness that 'insignificance' in the Jane Austen quotation above). In dramatic irony, which is normally contentual, and pseudo-covert or overt, it is indicated either by discrepancies between what the character thinks and what the audience is shown to have reason to believe, or between what is shown to be the case and what, in the context of some metaphysical assumption, ought to be the case.

This gives us, so to speak, a basic ironic scale. If irony is taken to be essentially a dissembling mode of discourse whose discrepancies require some restructuring in order to bring about a smiling enlightenment as the ostensible is suffused by the latent, then at the top we have verbal irony, which is typically covert. In the middle is that dramatic irony which depends on the audience's knowing more than the characters – pseudo-covert because the author rarely dissembles the truth from the audience, so that any restructuring depends on a provisional identification with the characters. At the bottom is that kind of overt dramatic irony which, to be irony at all, depends on some extra-textual metaphysical assumption.

**Irving, Edward** 1792–1834 Minister and founder of the 'Catholic Apostolic Church'. Born in Annan and educated at Edinburgh, he formed an early friendship with **Thomas Carlyle**. After ordination as a minister of the Church of Scotland he preached at Hatton Garden and Regent Square in London, where he attracted a congregation of admirers and sightseers. His *Homilies on the Sacraments* (1828) were attacked as heretical and resulted in his expulsion from the church. He therefore founded his new 'Irvingite' sect, espousing the principles of the early Christian church and testifying to the revival of the gift of tongues, of which there was a high incidence among his adherents.

**Irving, Washington** 1783–1859 One of the first American writers to earn an international reputation, Irving was born in New York City, the youngest of 11 children. He studied law, and in 1802–3 contributed letters to the *Morning Chronicle*, a newspaper edited by his brother Peter. These were published in 1803 as *The Letters of Jonathan Oldstyle, Gent*. In 1807 he began to publish *Salmagundi*, a serial that ran through 20 numbers, written in collaboration with his brother William and **James Kirke Paulding**. His *A History of New York* (1809), by the imaginary 'Diedrich Knickerbocker', was an instant success. A burlesque of contemporary historical narratives, it also lampooned **Thomas Jefferson** and his policies. The name Knickerbocker was later used to identify the first American school of writers, the **Knickerbocker Group**, of which Irving was a leading member.

In 1815 he went to England to work in the family business there; he remained in Europe for 17 years. He became friends with **Sir Walter Scott**, visited **Coleridge**, and in 1820 published *The Sketch Books of Geoffrey Crayon, Gent*. A collection of tales and sketches, including 'Rip Van Winkle' and 'The Legend of Sleepy Hollow', the book was a tremendous success both in England and America. His next collection, *Bracebridge Hall* (1822), was also well received, but *Tales of a Traveller* (1824) was not. Travelling in Germany, France and Spain (where he was a diplomatic attaché at the American embassy in Madrid), he met and became friends with John Jacob Astor, **Mary Shelley** and **Henry Wadsworth Longfellow**. While living in Spain he published *Life and Voyages of Columbus* (1828) and *Conquest of Granada* (1829), both based upon careful historical research. He moved to London in 1829 to become secretary to the American Legation under Martin Van Buren. He published *Voyages and Discoveries of the Companions of Columbus* in 1831, and *The Alhambra*, concerning the history and legends of Moorish

Washington Irving's house at Sunnyside, his estate on the Hudson River near Tarrytown. Irving lived there from 1836 to 1842, and from 1846 until his death in 1859.

Spain, in 1832. Returning to America, where he was enthusiastically received, he travelled in the far West. In 1835 he published *The Crayon Miscellany*, which consists of *Abbotsford and Newstead Abbey*, *Legends of the Conquest of Spain* and *A Tour of the Prairies*. *Astoria* (1836), written at the suggestion of John Jacob Astor, is about the Astor fur-trade empire; it was received well in England but not in America. *Adventures of Captain Bonneville, USA* appeared in 1837. His later publications include *Mahomet and his Successors* (1850), *Wolfert's Roost* (1855) and his five-volume *Life of Washington* (1855–9).

***Isabella, or, the Pot of Basil*** A poem in **ottava rima** by **John Keats**, written in 1818–19 and published in 1820. The story is drawn from Boccaccio's *Decameron*. Isabella falls in love with Lorenzo, a young man employed by her family. Her proud brothers murder Lorenzo and conceal his body in a forest. But when Lorenzo appears to Isabella in a vision and relates the story of his fate, she finds the hidden grave, cuts off the head of her lover and, taking it home, places it in a pot which she plants with basil. While the basil flourishes, moistened by Isabella's tears, the girl herself wastes away. Their suspicions aroused, her brothers steal the pot of basil and, horrified at their discovery, flee from Florence. Isabella, bereft of Lorenzo and the pot of basil, loses her reason and dies.

Keats was never satisfied with the poem – 'There is too much inexperience of life, and simplicity of knowledge in it' – and said that if he were a reviewer, he would describe it as a 'weak-sided Poem'.

**Isherwood, Christopher (William Bradshaw)** 1904–86 Novelist. He was born at High Lane, Cheshire, and educated at St Edmund's preparatory school in Surrey (where he first met **W. H. Auden**), Repton (where he first met **Edward Upward**) and Corpus Christi, Cambridge. His first novels were *All the Conspirators* (1928) and *The Memorial* (1932). His life in Berlin, where he supported himself as a teacher of English from 1929 to 1933, led to the books by which he is usually remembered. *Mr Norris Changes Trains* (1935), set against the background of Hitler's rise to power, centres on the protagonist's intermittent encounters with the seedy and unsavoury Mr Norris. *Goodbye to Berlin* (1939) is another episodic and semi-autobiographical work which describes the Bohemian society of Berlin with wit and sympathy. The most famous sketch is 'Sally Bowles', about a cabaret artiste of extraordinary and idiosyncratic charm. It was later dramatized by John van Druten as *I Am a Camera* (1951) and turned into a musical, *Cabaret* (1968). Isherwood collaborated with Auden on three plays, *The Dog Beneath the Skin* (1935), *The Ascent of F6*

Isabella and the pot of basil. An illustration for Keats's poem by George Scharf, 1854.

(1936) and *On the Frontier* (1939) and an account of their visit to China, *Journey to a War* (1938). The semi-autobiographical *Lions and Shadows* (1938) included portraits of his friends, Auden, Upward, **Stephen Spender** and **Vernon Watkins**.

He emigrated to the United States with Auden in 1939, becoming an American citizen in 1946. In California he wrote screenplays and took an increasing interest in Indian philosophy and religion, shown by his translation of the *Bhagavadgita* (with Swami Prabhavananda, 1944) and a study, *Ramakrishna and His Disciples* (1965). Later novels are *Prater Violet* (1945), *The World in the Evening* (1954), *Down There on a Visit* (1962) and *A Single Man* (1964). *The Condor and the Cows* (1949) is a travel book about South America, *Exhumations* (1966) a miscellany of stories, essays and verse, and *Christopher and His Kind* (1972) a frank account of his homosexuality.

***Israel Potter: His Fifty Years of Exile*** A novel by **Herman Melville** serialized in *Putnam's Monthly Magazine* in 1854–5 and published separately in 1855. It is loosely based on an obscure tract, *Life and Remarkable Adventures of Israel R. Potter*, which was published anonymously in 1824.

Israel Potter is a young Yankee from Massachusetts who leaves his home, works as a surveyor, hunter, fur trader and whale harpooner, and then enlists in the Revolutionary army in 1775. He serves at Bunker Hill, is taken prisoner by the British, and taken to England. After escaping, he adopts a series of disguises and meets George III. Falling in with clandestine friends of America, he is sent to Paris with messages for **Benjamin Franklin** and meets John

Paul Jones. Impressed into the British navy on his return to England, Israel contrives his ship's capture by Jones. He serves under Jones aboard the *Bon Homme Richard* in the raids on Scotland and in the capture of the *Serapis*. Later, he makes his way to London, where he marries and has a family. Owing to his poverty he is unable to return to America until 45 years have passed. Well past 80, he makes the voyage to Boston and revisits the scenes of his youth.

**It Is Never Too Late to Mend** A novel by **Charles Reade**, published in 1856. It tells two parallel stories. The first, about a young man who emigrates to Australia to take part in the gold rush, describes the perils of a miner's life. The second, about a thief serving a vicious sentence, deplores the dreadful fate of those sentenced to prison and transportation.

**Ivanhoe** Walter **Scott**'s most popular novel, and the first of his works to be set in England, was published in 1819. The period is the reign of Richard I.

Wilfred of Ivanhoe incurs the displeasure of his father Cedric because of his love for

Rebecca and Sir Brian de Bois-Guilbert. The frontispiece to *Ivanhoe* in the 1830 edition of The Waverley Novels.

Rowena, his father's ward. Cedric, dedicated to the restoration of the Saxon line, plans to marry Rowena, a descendant of King Alfred, to Athelstane of Coningsburgh who is also of the royal Saxon race. Ivanhoe serves with King Richard in the crusades, while in England the King's brother John tries to usurp the throne, depending on the disloyal Norman barons for support. John is unexpectedly assisted in his plans when Richard is captured by Leopold of Austria on his way back from Palestine.

At length, arriving in England in disguise, Richard appears at the tournament at Ashby de la Zouch, where he helps Ivanhoe defeat the knights of John's party, among them the Templar, Sir Brian de Bois-Guilbert. At the tournament Sir Brian falls in love with Rebecca, a beautiful and courageous Jewess, enamoured of Ivanhoe. Rebecca, her father Isaac, Rowena, Cedric and the wounded Ivanhoe are taken captive by the Norman barons and imprisoned in Torquilstone Castle. The King and a Saxon force, with the help of Locksley (**Robin Hood**) and his band of outlaws, take the castle and release the prisoners – with the exception of Rebecca, who is carried off to the Preceptory of Templestowe by Bois-Guilbert.

Bois-Guilbert's designs on Rebecca are frustrated by the arrival of the Grand Master of the Order. But Rebecca is further imperilled by a charge of witchcraft. She demands trial by combat and Ivanhoe appears as her champion, opposing Bois-Guilbert, chosen as her reluctant accuser. In the conflict, Bois-Guilbert falls dead, untouched by Ivanhoe's lance, a victim to his own conflicting emotions. Rebecca, seeing Ivanhoe's love for Rowena, leaves England with her father.

Scott was severely criticized by historians for his inaccurate account of Saxon–Norman enmity persisting into the 12th century. But the success of his novel lies with its skilful blend of fact, myth and romance, combined with a vivid, if fanciful, interpretation of medieval life.

**Iyayi, Festus** 1947– Nigerian novelist. He was educated at Annunciation Catholic College, Irrua, Government College, Ughelli, the Kiev Institute of National Economy and the University of Bradford, where he took a doctorate. He now lectures in business administration at the University of Benin, Nigeria. Although his family background is rural, he has specialized in his fiction in presenting the poverty, corruption and alienation of city life, and can be regarded as being the central writer of a new generation of Nigerian novelists who have turned aside from the anti-colonial and often village-based themes of earlier writers. His three novels are *Violence* (1979), *The Contract* (1982) and *Heroes* (1986), which is one of the best novels on the subject of the Nigerian Civil War.

# J

*Jack Juggler* (*A New Interlude for Children to Play, Named Jack Juggler*) A comedy written in the late 1550s and first printed in 1562. It has been attributed to **Nicholas Udall** without much evidence and the true authorship is unknown. It is based on the *Amphitruo* of Plautus but considerably toned down since it was written to be acted by schoolboys at Christmas. Jupiter and Amphitryon are removed from the plot entirely and Mercury becomes the trickster Jack Juggler, who takes over the identity of Jenkin Careaway. The other characters are as English as the London street in which the action takes place: the maid is Alison Tripandgo, the mistress and master are Dame Coy and Master Bongrace. The play ends with a cautionary epilogue on the times.

*Jack Upland* The first of a sequence of three pieces in a style somewhere between prose and rough alliterative verse; *Jack Upland* is usually classified as prose. It is an attack on the greed and hypocrisy of the friars, in particular the mendicant order of the Franciscans. The second piece, *Friar Daw's Reply*, answers the charges, defending in particular the Dominican order, and attacking the Lollards as heretics. The third piece, *Jack Upland's Rejoinder*, is written in a coarser tone and attacks Friar Daw personally rather than answering his arguments. The three pieces have been most recently dated 1390, 1420 and 1450 respectively. It is unlikely that they are the work of a single poet.

**Jackson, Helen (Maria) Hunt** 1830–85 American novelist and poet, born in Amherst, Massachusetts. Her poetry is collected in *Verses by H. H.* (1870) and *Sonnets and Lyrics* (1886). Her concern with the US government's unjust treatment of the American Indians prompted her to write *A Century of Dishonor* (1881), a historical study, and *Ramona* (1884), a novel. Among her other publications are works for children, a travel book, and numerous magazine articles, some of which were written under the pseudonym Saxe Holm. She is also known as the friend of **Emily Dickinson** who most vehemently urged her to publish. Her novel

*Mercy Philbrick's Choice* (1876) is probably a fictionalized portrait of Dickinson.

**Jackson, Holbrook** See *New Age, The.*

**Jackson, Laura Riding** See **Riding, Laura**.

**Jackson, Shirley** 1919–65 American novelist and short-story writer, born in San Francisco. Her first novel, *The Road Through the Wall*, appeared in 1948, the year in which *The New Yorker* published her best-known short story, 'The Lottery'. Although the novel escaped critical notice, the story – a depiction of a communal rite in which each year a person chosen by lot is stoned to death – established her reputation. Her next novel, *The Hangsaman* (1951), explores the schizophrenia of a young girl named Natalie Waite and typifies that portion of Jackson's oeuvre concerned with the dark side of human nature. She also produced a quantity of humorous stories and articles, some of which were collected in *Life Among the Savages* (1953) and *Raising Demons* (1957). Her other works include *The Bird's Nest* (1954), *Witchcraft of Salem Village* (1956), *The Bad Children* (1959), *The Sundial* (1958), *The Haunting of Hill House* (1959), *Special Delivery* (1960), *We Have Always Lived in the Castle* (1962), *Nine Magic Wishes* (1963) and two collections edited by her husband, *The Magic of Shirley Jackson* (1966) and *Come Along With Me* (1968).

**Jacob, Naomi (Ellington)** 1889–1964 Novelist. Born at Ripon, Yorkshire, she followed her first novel, *Jacob Ussher* (1926), with numerous titles including *The Loaded Stick* (1935), *Straws in Amber* (1938), *Morning Will Come* (1953) and, most notably, *Four Generations* (1934). She also wrote a series of autobiographical volumes and a biography of Marie Lloyd (1936).

*Jacob's Room* A novel by **Virginia Woolf**, published in 1922.

This was the first of Virginia Woolf's novels to be published by the Hogarth Press, founded with her husband, **Leonard Woolf**, in their home at Hogarth House in Richmond in 1917. It is an episodic tale which attempts to evoke the inner life of Jacob Flanders (based upon the character of her brother Thoby), and his social milieu during the first decade and a half of the 20th century.

At the beginning, Jacob is discovered wandering on a Cornish beach away from his recently widowed mother. As the novel proceeds, numerous impressionistic scenes – some involving **stream of consciousness** – capture the thoughts of surrounding characters, and there are many brief descriptions of the external landscape which have been noted for their poetic qualities.

After Cambridge, Jacob is glimpsed at social gatherings in London, with his mistress, and abroad at Versailles and in Athens, including a visit to the Acropolis. The novel ends during World War I. Jacob has been killed and two friends are visiting his room in Bloomsbury to dispose of his possessions, the mundane and arbitrary record of a human life: odd bills, letters of invitation, a pair of old shoes.

The novel was hailed by friends such as **T. S. Eliot**, but attacked by others for its lack of plot. It represents its author's first move towards experimentation, for which she was later recognized.

**Jacobs, W[illiam] W[ymark]** 1863–1943. Author of some 20 volumes of humorous stories about barge crews, night-watchmen and other coastal workers. His first collection was *Many Cargoes* (1896); others are *The Skipper's Wooing* (1897), *Light Freights* (1901) and *Sea Whispers* (1926). He also wrote tales of horror, the best known being the gruesome story of 'The Monkey's Paw'.

**Jacobson, Dan** 1929– South African novelist, born in Johannesburg. After a short spell on a kibbutz, he settled in Britain in 1958. His novels examine uncontrolled states of mind in varying relationships with personal or political power. *The Trap* (1955) and *A Dance in the Sun* (1956), and even the more genial, though satirical, *The Price of Diamonds* (1957), hint at manic depths beneath apparently stable Northern Cape surfaces. After *Evidence of Love* (1960), about interracial love, Jacobson creates a hero of conflicting loyalties in the accomplished, saga-like *The Beginners* (1966), before adapting, in *The Rape of Tamar* (1970), Old Testament material for a modern study in treacherous cynicism. *The Wonder-Worker* (1973) ventures into a schizophrenic mind, while *The Confessions of Joseph Baisz* (1977) moves between egocentricity and tyrannical dictatorship. Of his short-story volumes, *Beggar My Neighbour* (1964) is probably the best. *Time and Time Again* (1985) is an autobiography.

**Jago, Richard** 1715–81 Poet. Jago was born at

Beaudesert near Henley-in-Arden in Warwickshire and was a friend of **William Somerville**. He was admitted to Oxford as a servitor, and was ordained about 1739. He is remembered for his poem in four books called *Edge-hill, or, The Rural Prospect Delineated and Moralised* (1767), which describes the prospect of Warwickshire observed at various times of day from the ridge where the battle took place during the Civil War.

**Jakobson, Roman** See **structuralism**.

**James I of England** 1566–1625 King of England and Scotland. James Stuart, son of Mary, Queen of Scots, and Henry, Lord Darnley, became James VI of Scotland in 1567, when barely a year old. Among his tutors was the renowned Latin poet **George Buchanan**. Upon the death of Elizabeth I in 1603, he succeeded, at the age of 37, to the English crown, and ruled both realms, styling himself (without parliamentary approval) 'King of Great Britain'.

A learned man, if exaggeratedly vain of his learning, he published several important works. *The Essays of a Prentice, in the Divine Art of Poesy* (1584) consists of original poems, translations of Du Bartas and Lucan, and, most significantly, the first Scots contribution to literary criticism in the Renaissance. *His Majesty's Poetical Exercises at Vacant Hours* (1591) includes further translations from Du Bartas. James expressed his philosophy of government in the anonymously published *The True Lawe of Free Monarchies* (1598) and *Basilikon Doron* (1599), both reissued and acknowledged in London in the year of his accession. His fascination with witchcraft bore fruit in *Daemonologie* (1597), which attacks **Reginald Scot**'s sceptical *Discovery of Witchcraft* (1584). Perhaps his most enduring literary production is *A Counterblast to Tobacco*, issued anonymously in 1604, but acknowledged in the folio collection, *The Works of James I* (1616). Both as practitioner and as a patron, particularly of the development of the English **masque** by **Ben Jonson** and Inigo Jones, James exercised a considerable influence on the culture of Stuart England.

**James I of Scotland** 1394–1437 Son of Robert III of Scotland, James was kidnapped by pirates in 1406 while on his way to France, given up to Henry IV of England and imprisoned until 1423. Robert died shortly after his son's capture, leaving James King of Scotland. On his release he married Joan Beaufort. He was assassinated at Perth.

The earliest reference to the King as a poet appeared in the 16th century, when *The Kingis Quair* was attributed to him, the poem being said to record his love for Joan Beaufort. There is little evidence to support the claim beyond the poem's autobiographical content and the manuscript colophon. It remains uncertain whether James was the author, whether indeed he was a poet at all, and which (if any) other surviving poems are his work.

**James, Alice** 1848–92 American diarist, born in New York City, the sister of the novelist **Henry James** and the philosopher **William James**. The family's life, and especially Alice's, was disrupted by the separations imposed by the Civil War, and she began to manifest the classic symptoms of neurasthenia. Like many women in the 19th century, and despite her intellectual acumen and curiosity, she was deprived of the formal education given her brothers. Her family, while respecting her abilities, coddled and protected her throughout her many illnesses. She suffered the first of several breakdowns at the age of 19.

Her letters and diary show that she was an astute critic of the work and careers of both her famous brothers and the issues of her time. The diary, which she seems to have intended for publication, was begun in December 1886, after she and her companion, Katherine Loring Peabody, had settled in England. Written over the next five years, the later portions were dictated to Peabody, as Alice was too ill to write herself. In March 1892 she died of breast cancer following a gradual decline. One of the major themes of her diary is her awareness of her approaching death, and her confrontation of that finality. Because of her brother Henry's belief that it would violate the family's privacy, the diary was not immediately published. In fact, it was not published until 1934, under the title *Alice James: Her Brothers – Her Journal*. It has since been republished as *The Diary of Alice James* (1964). A selection of her letters, *The Death and Letters of Alice James*, appeared in 1983.

**James, C[yril] L[ionel] R[obert]** 1901–89 Essayist and journalist. Born in Tunapuna, near Port of Spain, Trinidad, James came to England in 1933. He was assistant cricket correspondent of *The Manchester Guardian* under Neville Cardus in 1933–5, returning to the paper in 1953. His Marxist sympathies were developed during a prolonged stay in America between 1938 and 1953. His works include a novel, *Minty Alley* (1936), *The Black Jacobins: Toussaint L'Ouverture and the San Domingo Revolution* (1938) and several volumes of political essays, among them *Mariners, Renegades and Castaways* (1953). But he is best known for a unique book on cricket, *Beyond a Boundary* (1963), which combines autobiography, cultural and social history, aesthetic appreciation and political polemics – an approach prompted by James's introductory question, 'What do they know of

cricket, who only cricket know?'. His other writings on cricket were collected in 1986.

**James, George Payne Rainsford** 1799–1860 Author of over 100 historical novels. Born in London, he was a British consul for many years, holding office in the United States and Europe. His first novel was *Richelieu* (1829), followed by *The Huguenot* (1838), *The Man-at-Arms* (1840), *Arabella Stuart* (1844), *The Cavalier* (1859) and *The Man in Black* (1860). He also wrote historical and biographical works, including *Memoirs of Great Commanders* (1832) and a *Life of the Black Prince* (1836). His style was parodied by **Thackeray** in *Punch's Prize Novelists*.

**James, Henry** 1843–1916 American novelist, short-story writer, playwright, critic and essayist, born in New York City, the brother of **William James** and **Alice James**. He was educated by private tutors until the age of 12, and then at schools in Boulogne, Paris, Geneva, Bonn and – when the family returned to the USA – at Newport, Rhode Island. He entered Harvard Law School in 1862 but withdrew after a year and, with the encouragement of **Charles Eliot Norton** and **William Dean Howells**, began to concentrate his energies on writing. In the 1860s his early reviews and critical essays were published in *The North American Review* and *The Atlantic Monthly*.

In 1869 he made his first extended visit to Europe as an adult, and in the same year published a farce, *Pyramus and Thisbe*. His first novel, *Watch and Ward*, appeared serially in *The Atlantic Monthly* in 1871 (and in volume form in 1878). He went to Europe again in 1872 and stayed for two years; his experiences during this trip are reflected in *A Passionate Pilgrim and Other Tales* (1875) and *Transatlantic Sketches* (1875). He spent 1875 in Paris in the company of Turgenev, Daudet, Flaubert, the Goncourts and Zola. The following year he settled in London, where he lived until 1896. *Roderick Hudson* (1876) was the first novel of this period, and was followed by *The American* (1877) and *The Europeans* (1878). The essay *French Poets and Novelists* appeared in 1878, and the novel *Daisy Miller* in 1879. In the same year he produced a study of **Nathaniel Hawthorne** for the English Men of Letters series, a short novel entitled *An International Episode*, and the collection *The Madonna of the Future and Other Tales*. Two more novels, *Confidence* and *Washington Square*, appeared in 1880.

Early in 1880 he visited Florence – one of the cities which serve as the setting for his next novel, *The Portrait of a Lady* (1881). In 1882 he travelled in France, an experience which prompted the travel sketch *A Little Tour in France* (1884). A collection of short stories, *The*

*Siege of London*, and a travel book, *Portraits of Places*, appeared in 1883. In the following year he published *Tales of Three Cities*, and 'The Art of Fiction', his well-known essay about his chosen craft. He wrote prolifically over the next few years, producing the novels ***The Bostonians*** (1886), ***The Princess Casamassima*** (1886), *The Reverberator* (1888), ***The Aspern Papers*** (1888) and *The Tragic Muse* (1890). A collection of essays, *Partial Portraits*, appeared in 1888.

In 1890 he turned his attention to drama, writing several drawing-room comedies and adapting *The American* for the stage. A collection of short stories, *The Lesson of the Master*, which includes 'The Pupil', 'The Solution', and 'Sir Edmund Orme', appeared in 1892 and was followed by another, *The Real Thing and Other Tales*, in 1893. His play *Guy Domville* opened in London in January 1895, but was not a success. He returned to fiction and produced two more volumes of short stories – *Terminations* (1895), which includes 'The Altar of the Dead', and *Embarrassments* (1896), which includes 'The Figure in the Carpet' – as well as three short novels – ***The Spoils of Poynton*** (1897), ***What Maisie Knew*** (1897) and *In the Cage* (1898).

The range of his literary acquaintance was remarkable: between 1896 and 1901 he met **Joseph Conrad**, **Stephen Crane**, H. G. Wells and **George Gissing**, and received visits from **Ford Madox Ford**, **William Dean Howells**, **Oliver Wendell Holmes**, **Sarah Orne Jewett** and others.

Henry James, 1913. Photograph by E. O. Hoppé.

***The Turn of the Screw***, his celebrated tale of the uncanny, first appeared in serial form in 1898, and was followed by the novel ***The Awkward Age*** in the following year. *The Soft Side*, consisting of 12 stories, was published in 1900, and the novel ***The Sacred Fount*** in 1901. Over the next three years he produced his last three major novels: ***The Wings of the Dove*** (1902), ***The Ambassadors*** (1903) and ***The Golden Bowl*** (1904). His famous short story 'The Beast in the Jungle' appeared in the collection *The Better Sort* in 1903, the year in which he began his long friendship with **Edith Wharton**.

After a 21-year absence, James returned to the USA in August 1904. While there he lectured, stayed in the home of **Henry Adams**, and met President Theodore Roosevelt. For the New York Edition of his works, which was published between 1907 and 1909, he made revisions to some of his novels and wrote 18 new prefaces. In 1907 he published an account of a journey in the USA, *The American Scene*. He visited Italy and France again in 1907–8 and published a collection of essays about his travels, *Italian Hours*, in 1909. In the following year he returned to America. *The Finer Grain*, a volume of short stories, appeared in 1910; *The Outcry*, his last completed novel, in 1911. Before going back to England he received an honorary degree from Harvard (1911); in the following year he received one from Oxford. Nearing the end of a long and productive career, he published two volumes of autobiography, *A Small Boy and Others* (1913) and *Notes of a Son and Brother* (1914). A third volume, *The Middle Years*, appeared posthumously in 1917. *Notes on Novelists* was published in 1914. During World War I he became involved in war relief work and served as chairman of the American Volunteer Motor Ambulance Corps. Having lived for years in England, he became a British citizen on 26 July 1915. In December of that year he suffered two strokes. George V awarded him the Order of Merit on New Year's Day 1916. He died on 28 February 1916, leaving two unfinished novels, *The Ivory Tower* and *The Sense of the Past*.

**James, M[ontague] R[hodes]** 1862–1936 Scholar and writer of ghost stories. He was educated at Eton College and King's College, Cambridge, and elected a fellow of King's in 1887. In the course of his distinguished career he became Provost of King's in 1905 and Provost of Eton in 1918, serving also as Director of the Fitzwilliam Museum (1893–1908) and Vice-Chancellor of the University of Cambridge (1913–15). His broad scholarly interests embraced biblical studies, palaeography (he made pioneering descriptive catalogues of Western manuscripts in Cambridge and elsewhere) and the art and literature of the Middle Ages (he gave expert advice on the restoration of the stained glass in King's College chapel and Great Malvern priory church). Beyond the scholarly world James is best remembered for the recreations embodied in *Ghost Stories of an Antiquary* (1904), *More Ghost Stories of an Antiquary* (1911), *A Thin Ghost, and Others* (1919), *The Five Jars* (1922) and *A Warning to the Curious, and Other Ghost Stories* (1925). His *Collected Ghost Stories* appeared in 1931. The first volume contained the famous and much-anthologized 'Oh, Whistle and I'll Come to You, My Lad'. With their effective use of understatement and scholarly detail, his tales of the supernatural strongly influenced later practitioners of the genre.

**James, P. D.** See **detective fiction**.

**James, William** 1842–1910 American philosopher, born in New York City, the elder brother of the novelist **Henry James**. He received his MD from Harvard Medical School in 1869 and became an instructor in physiology at Harvard in 1872. As his interest shifted to psychology, in

William James.

a pioneering venture he opened a laboratory of psychology at Harvard in 1876.

For the next 12 years he spent his spare time working on *The Principles of Psychology*, which was published in 1890. It remains a classic in its field, even if later investigations – many of which it inspired – have superseded it. In 1897 he published a collection of essays, *The Will to Believe*, in which he defined his position as that of a 'radical empiricist'. His international reputation increased when he was appointed Gifford Lecturer on Natural Religion at Edinburgh University from 1901 to 1902. His two sets of lectures there were published as *The Varieties of Religious Experience* (1902). In 1907 he published *Pragmatism*, whose thesis that an idea has meaning only in relation to its consequences in feeling and action won him new followers, but was also attacked in some quarters. *The Meaning of Truth* (1909) was his answer to these critics. Though he retired from Harvard in 1907, where he had been Professor of Psychology (1889–97) and Philosophy (1897–1907), he continued to write and lecture; indeed, during this time he was probably the most honoured philosopher in America. He explained his metaphysical principles in *A Pluralistic Universe* (1909), a series of lectures he had delivered in Oxford in 1908. Posthumous publications were *Some Problems of Philosophy; A Beginning of an Introduction to Philosophy* (1911), *Memoirs and Studies* (1911) and *Essays in Radical Empiricism* (1912).

**Jameson, Anna Brownell** 1794–1860 Art and literary critic. Born Anna Murphy in Dublin, she moved to England and became a governess. Her experiences touring Europe in this capacity gave her the material for her first book, *Diary of an Ennuyée* (1826). After separating from her husband, Robert Jameson, whom she had married in 1825, she began to earn a reputation as a critic, with *Loves of the Poets* (1829) and *Characteristics of Women* (1832; later called *Shakespeare's Heroines*). Her books on art include *Memoir of the Early Italian Painters* (1845) and *Sacred and Legendary Art* (1848). Of her travel books, *Winter Studies and Summer Rambles* (1838) gives an interesting account of the lives and customs of the Canadian Indian tribes.

**Jameson, (Margaret) Storm** 1891–1986 Novelist. Born in Whitby, where her family were shipbuilders, she went to Leeds University. Her many novels include sagas depicting English life between the wars, notably two trilogies about a family of Yorkshire shipbuilders: 'The Triumph of Time', comprising *The Lovely Ship* (1927), *The Voyage Home* (1930) and *A Richer Dust* (1931), and 'The Mirror in Darkness', comprising *Company Parade* (1934), *Love in Winter* (1935) and *None Turn Back* (1936). She also wrote poetry, essays, criticism and biography. Her wartime work as president of PEN, assisting European refugee intellectuals, is related in one of her several substantial volumes of autobiography, *Journey from the North* (1969). She was married to the historian Guy Chapman.

**Jane Eyre** A novel by **Charlotte Brontë**, published in 1847.

Jane Eyre is an orphan living with her unlikeable aunt, Mrs Reed, and her unattractive cousins. Jane does not embody Mrs Reed's conception of a properly childlike personality, John Reed bullies her, and Jane's imagination and independent spirit make her an alien in the household. At length she is sent to Lowood Asylum, a charitable institution where appalling physical conditions are somewhat palliated by the friendship of the gentle, long-suffering Helen Burns and Maria Temple, the mistress. An outbreak of typhus fever leads to public interest and an improvement in conditions. Helen dies of consumption, but not before Jane has learned from her that self-control is the surest means of retaining self-respect in adversity. After some years as pupil and teacher, Jane leaves Lowood to take up the position of governess at Thornfield Hall, where she finds she has one charge, Adele Varens, the ward of the master Edward Rochester. Life at Thornfield is pleasant but stultifying and Jane welcomes the return of Edward Rochester as a lively distraction. Soon she finds herself drawn to him, while he, attracted by her wit and self-possession, after various misunderstandings, asks her to become his wife.

She consents gladly, though she is somewhat disturbed to find the short period of their engagement marred by Rochester's determination to deck her out in fine clothes and jewels quite unsuitable to her own conception of herself as quiet and quakerish. Their wedding is interrupted by the unexpected arrival of Richard Mason, who reveals that Rochester is already married to his sister Bertha, a raving lunatic, even then confined at Thornfield Hall. Jane's strong sense of self-reliance and respect forces her, despite her yearning to comfort her lover, to flee temptation.

Destitute, Jane is finally taken in by a clergyman, St John Rivers, and his compassionate sisters Diana and Mary. With them, she discovers solace in intelligent intercourse and reasserts her independence by taking a post as local schoolmistress. Not wanting to be discovered by Rochester, she has assumed the name of Jane Elliott, but a slip discloses her true name and leads to the revelation that the Riversers are her cousins and she sole heir to a fortune which she joyfully shares with her relatives in recognition of their legitimate claim. St John, powerful and dedicated but narrow-minded in his ideas of duty and sacrifice, proposes that Jane should accompany him as his wife in his mission to India. Her intelligence rejects the proposal but, swayed by emotion, Jane is nearly brought to consent when a voice, recognizably Rochester's, calls to her out of the air. Resolved to discover his fate, she returns to Thornfield to find it a blackened ruin and the master maimed and blind – the result of his vain efforts to save his mad wife from the flames. Jane banishes Rochester's dejection when she returns to him, able at last to contract a marriage which includes spiritual equality, intellectual companionship and sexual passion.

*Jane Eyre* was not Charlotte Brontë's first novel – *The Professor* had been written earlier – but was composed after that work's rejection in response to the publisher's demand for 'thrilling excitement'. It attracted immediate attention, but praise for its narrative force and the vivid way Jane's feelings are rendered was mixed with criticism. The merciless portrait of Lowood and its headmaster, Brocklehurst, offended Evangelicals. Above all, contemporaries were made uneasy by the book's morality: though Jane's actions observe the conventional code of female behaviour they still embody a disturbingly powerful statement of woman's claim to independence.

**Jane Shore, The Tragedy of** A play by **Nicholas Rowe**, first produced in February 1714 and published the same year. It traces the fall from favour of Jane Shore, daughter of a Cheapside mercer and a goldsmith's wife who became mistress to Edward IV. After the king's death she fell victim to Richard III, who charged her with witchcraft and made her endure public penance in 1483. She died in poverty about 1527.

**Janet's Repentance** See *Scenes of Clerical Life*.

**Jarrell, Randall** 1914–65 American poet and critic, born in Nashville, Tennessee, and educated at Vanderbilt University. He served in the US Army Air Corps from 1942 to 1946, and then taught English literature and creative writing at various universities. His volumes of poetry are: *Blood for a Stranger* (1942); *Little Friend, Little Friend* (1945); *Losses* (1948); *The Seven-League Crutches* (1951); *Selected Poems* (1955); *Uncollected Poems* (1958); *The Woman at the Washington Zoo* (1960), which consists of poems and translations, and for which he received the National Book Award in 1961; a second edition of *Selected Poems* (1964); and *The Lost World* (1965). Published posthumously were *Complete Poems* (1969), and *Jerome: The Biography of a Poem* (1971), which uses works by Albrecht Dürer as illustrations. His verse is characterized by a particular colloquial quality – a modern plainness. It emphasizes the grotesqueness of a reality made more – not less – chaotic by modern science; war is an important theme in several of his poems, including one of his best known – 'The Death of the Ball Turret Gunner'.

His critical writings include *Poetry and the Age* (1953), *The Third Book of Criticism* (1969) and *Kipling, Auden, & Co.: Essays and Reviews 1935–1964* (1979). *A Sad Heart at the Supermarket* (1962) includes both fables and essays. He held editorial positions on several periodicals: *The Nation* (1946), *The Partisan Review* (1949–51), the *Yale Review* (1955–7) and the *American Scholar* (1957–65). He translated, among other works, Chekhov's short stories, Grimm's fairy tales, and Part I of Goethe's *Faust*. *Pictures from an Institution*, his only novel, was published in 1954. He also wrote books for children. He was killed in an automobile accident.

**Jebb, Richard Claverhouse** 1841–1905 Greek scholar. Born in Dundee, and educated at Charterhouse and Trinity College, Cambridge, Jebb became Professor of Greek at Glasgow University (1875–89) and then at Cambridge (1889–1905). He also served as MP for Cambridge University in 1891–1900. His works include *The Attic Orators from Antiphon to Isaeus* (1876–80), editions and translations of Theophrastus (1870), Sophocles (1883–96) and Bacchylides (1905), and a biography of **Richard Bentley** for the English Men of Letters series (1882).

**Jefferies, (John) Richard** 1848–87 Journalist and novelist. He was born at Coate Farm, Liddington, near Swindon. Memorialized by a monument in Salisbury Cathedral and a bust in Taunton Shire Hall, he is mostly remembered for a body of novels and essays celebrating the countryside of southern England in a remarkably detailed but unsentimental way. He knew all country matters intimately, having the knack, acquired at an early age, of writing about them in an unpretentious, economical plain prose that was consistent both with his farming background and his early training as a reporter. From 1864 he worked for *The North Wiltshire Herald*, issuing the locally printed *Reporting, Editing and Authorship* in 1873. He established himself in the public view during the early 1870s by means of articles he wrote, as naturalist, for **The Pall Mall Gazette** and also by a long letter to *The Times* on the plight of the agricultural labourer in Wiltshire. After his marriage in 1874 he began to supplement his journalism by fiction, starting with a series of melodramatic and for the most part unsuccessful novels: *The Scarlet Shawl* (1874), *Restless Human Hearts* (1875) and *The World's End* (1877). In these books neither the aristocratic characters nor the sensational plots quite ring true. More convincing are his last novel, *Amaryllis at the Fair* (1887), with

its portrait of his father as Iden, and, among his earlier works, the autobiographical *Bevis, the Story of a Boy* (1882) and the actual autobiography, *The Story of my Heart* (1883), books which still await biographical and critical analysis. Jefferies's reputation chiefly depends, however, not on fiction or autobiography but on books, written in the style of the essayist, reflecting his close engagement with and knowledge of rural England. These include *The Amateur Poacher* (1879), *The Gamekeeper at Home* (1880), *Hodge and his Masters* (1880), *Greene Ferne Farm* (1880), *The Open Air* (1885) and the posthumous *Field and Hedgerow* (1889), in which detailed descriptions of natural scenes and objects are not complicated by irony, rhetoric or the type of authorial comment that goes beyond the author's exact knowledge. Within this narrow range, Jefferies came to be recognized as a master of straightforward descriptive prose. The vaguely poetic nostalgia for rural innocence that, for many urban and suburban readers, was and is part of the pleasure of reading these books was probably not shared by Jefferies, whose cast of mind was more pessimistic, or at least more practical than romantic. Few 'could long remain poetical', he once said, 'upon bread and cheese'. Present but not precisely visible in the opaque documents of the naturalist was the thoroughgoing distaste for 19th-century industrial civilization implicit in *After London* (1885). Presenting, like other novels of the time, a vision of future disaster, it suggests that the individual must trust for his survival in his knowledge of the earth, and the animals and plants from which, without any other human being's help, he can gain sustenance. The vision is not just pre-industrial, but also pre-agricultural. If the attempt of the main character in *After London* to slip secretly away in his canoe from the world of other people is a fantasy expressing a fear of people that is the corollary of Jefferies's love of nature, it is nonetheless a fantasy with disturbing personal and social implications, something underlined by the story's ambivalent ending (or endings). Though his last years, and his last books, were tragically darkened by the long suffering of tuberculosis, *After London* is not just a consequence of that suffering but reaches back imaginatively to his beginnings, spanning much of his career in mood and effect.

**Jeffers, (John) Robinson** 1887–1962 American poet. Born in Pittsburgh, the son of a theologian and classical scholar, Jeffers spent most of his life in Carmel, on the Monterey coast of California. He called for a poetry of 'dangerous images' which would 'reclaim substance and sense, and psychological reality'. Many of his poems are based on biblical stories or Greek and Roman myths, and their language has a classical directness and clarity. His first two volumes, *Flagons and Apples* (1912) and *Californians* (1916), were relatively conventional; it was not until the publication of *Tamar and Other Poems* (1924) that his particular dramatic and rhetorical power became clear. The title poem is based on the Old Testament figure, and exhibits Jeffers's preoccupation with the themes of lust, incest and the corrupt nature of man. His many other volumes include *Roan Stallion* (1924), *The Woman at Point Sur* (1927), *Cawdor and Other Poems* (1928), *Dear Judas and Other Poems* (1929), *Give Your Heart to the Hawks and Other Poems* (1933), *Be Angry at the Sun* (1941), *The Double Axe* (1948) and *Hungerfield, and Other Poems* (1954). His best-known play, *Medea*, was staged in New York in 1947 and 1965.

**Jefferson, Thomas** 1743–1826 The third President of the United States, born in Virginia, and educated at the College of William and Mary. In 1774 he published *A Summary View of the Rights of British America*, which marked him as one of the primary exponents of the colonies' grievances against the King. He went on, as a member of the Second Continental Congress, to draft *The Declaration of Independence* (1776). During the American Revolution he served in the Virginia legislature (1776–9) and then as the state's governor (1779–81). Though a landed and wealthy slaveowner himself, he espoused a vision of an agrarian society based on an independent yeomanry, and defended the principle of individual freedom against entrenched privilege and government encroachments. He also supported the gradual abolition of slavery. During his tenure as governor of Virginia, he produced the first version of his **Notes on the State of Virginia**, an answer to a series of questions from abroad about his native state. It was published in 1785. He then served as American minister to France, and in 1788 published *Observations on the Whale-Fishery*. He returned to America in 1789, and between 1790 and 1793 served as George Washington's Secretary of State. He became Vice President in 1797, and President in 1801. He served two terms as President, during which he approved the 1803 Louisiana Purchase from France, which doubled the size of the USA at the cost of four cents per acre.

Jefferson had lifelong interests in science, architecture and education. He served as president of the American Philosophical Society from 1797 to 1814. After leaving the presidency, he founded and helped to draw up plans for the University of Virginia, chartered in 1819. The Library of Congress was begun when he sold his personal library to the national government in 1815. He was also the author of *A Manual of Parliamentary Practice* (1801), and a *Life of Captain [Meriwether] Lewis* (1814). Among the papers unpublished at his death were his *Autobiography*, the *Anas* (political memoirs), and 'The Morals of Jesus of Nazareth', extracts from the Bible which reflected his deistic beliefs.

**Jeffrey, Francis** 1773–1850 Lawyer, editor and literary critic. Born in Edinburgh, Jeffrey attended Edinburgh High School before studying at Glasgow and Oxford Universities. Called to the Bar in 1794, he was one of a group of Edinburgh lawyers who strongly supported Whig ideas of reform. He became MP for Edinburgh in 1832 and Lord of Session in 1834, as Lord Jeffrey. His contribution to literature was the founding, with **Sydney Smith** and **Henry Brougham**, of *The Edinburgh Review* in 1802. He became its editor in 1803 and held the post for 25 years, establishing himself as an influential critic who (despite his dislike of **Wordsworth**'s poetry) raised the standard of public taste. He published a selection from his papers in 1844.

**Jellicoe, Ann** 1927– Playwright and director who wrote for the **Royal Court Theatre** during the early days of the English Stage Company. *The Sport of My Mad Mother* (1958) may owe some of its improvisational energy to the workshops of the Royal Court Writers' Group, of which Jellicoe was a leader. *The Knack* (1961) is a small-scale comedy, which was made into a successful film. Jellicoe directed both plays for their original performances, as she did the less successful but oddly impressive *Shelley* (1965).

In 1979, having moved from London to Lyme Regis, Ann Jellicoe began a second career, as writer and director of the Colway Theatre Trust. For the Trust she wrote two large-scale community plays, *The Tide* (1979) and *The Reckoning* (1980). Staged in small towns in the south-west of England, and using events and characters from those towns' history, these plays deploy up to 100 actors, musicians, etc.

**Jenkins, (John) Robin** 1912– Scottish novelist. Born in Flemington, Lanarkshire, Jenkins was educated at Hamilton Academy and Glasgow University, and became an English teacher in Glasgow and later Dunoon, with lengthy spells of teaching abroad. A member of the Independent Labour Party, he was a conscientious objector, and spent the war years in forestry, an experience reflected in his best-known novel, *The Cone-Gatherers* (1955), and perhaps his most austere, *A Would-be Saint* (1978). Although a brilliant student, Jenkins did not enjoy his education: some autobiographical material can be detected in *Happy For The Child* (1953). Education also supplies material for *The Changeling* (1958), where a naïve middle-class teacher tries to transform a slum pupil through a holiday idyll. One of his best and funniest books, *Guests of War* (1956), is based on his experience of accompanying Glasgow slum children evacuated to the prosperous town of Moffat in the Scottish Borders. An acute awareness of class prejudices characterizes all his Scottish novels. As a novelist, Jenkins is above all a moralist, and his acute criticism of the baleful effects of Calvinism culminates in his comic masterpiece *Fergus Lamont* (1979), a triumphant return to the notion of the Justified Sinner celebrated by **James Hogg**. *The Awakening of George Darroch* (1985), his only historical novel, is about the Disruption of the Church of Scotland in 1843. Other characteristic subjects include football as a Scottish substitute for religion (*The Thistle and the Grail*, 1954), and the United States nuclear presence at the Holy Loch, near Dunoon (*A Toast to the Lord*, 1972). Each of his spells abroad produced novels. Afghanistan – his 'Nurania' – in particular inspired *Dust on the Paw* (1961), a widely praised study of race prejudice. Time in Spain resulted in *The Sardana Dancers* (1964), and teaching in Borneo – 'Kalimantan' – inspired *The Holy Tree* (1969) and *A Figure of Fun* (1974). His short stories were collected in *A Far Cry From Bowmore* (1973).

***Jennie Gerhardt*** A novel by **Theodore Dreiser**, published in 1911. Jennie, pretty but poor, helps her mother scrub floors in a fine hotel in Columbus, Ohio. There she meets Senator George Brander, and when her brother is arrested for stealing coal and Brander arranges his release, she gives herself to him out of gratitude. She becomes pregnant, and her father – a rigidly moral Lutheran – forces her to leave home. Her situation worsens when Brander dies.

After the birth of her daughter, Vesta, Jennie goes to work as a maid for the Bracebridges, a wealthy Cleveland family. She meets Lester Kane, who is attracted to her and, by being kind to her family, eventually persuades her to live with him. His family, socially prominent in Cincinnati, disapproves of the relationship. His father dies and leaves his inheritance in the trust of his brother Robert, stipulating that Lester can have it only if he abandons Jennie. Though he suffers pangs of conscience, he does indeed leave her, and eventually marries Letty Pace Gerald, a widowed socialite. Vesta dies and Jennie fights against despair by adopting two orphans.

Lester falls ill and summons Jennie to his deathbed, declaring that he was wrong to leave her and that he has not found greater happiness by doing so. Jennie is with him when he dies but withdraws before the arrival of his wife, who has been travelling. She attends his funeral, masked behind a heavy veil, and watches his coffin being loaded on to the train for the trip to Cincinnati.

**Jennings, Elizabeth (Joan)** 1926– Poet. Born in Boston, Lincolnshire, she was educated at Oxford High School and at St Anne's College, Oxford, where she read English. After working as a librarian and a publisher's reader, she became a freelance writer in 1961. The restraint and clarity of diction of her first collection, *Poems* (1955), marked her out as a member of the **Movement**, but her Roman Catholicism gave her work a quiet vulnerability and made faith rather than reductive irony its dominant quality. Her early work, in *A Way of Looking* (1955) and *A Sense of the World* (1958), culminated in *Song for a Birth or a Death and Other Poems* (1961). Showing simplicity and a belief in traditional formal properties, she writes with correctness and good manners. *Recoveries* (1964) and *The Mind Has Mountains* (1966) come from a period of severe mental illness, and although they achieved popularity in the 1960s, are not her best work. Similarly, Jennings has chosen to reprint very little from the subsequent collections, *Lucidities* (1970) and *Relationships* (1972). More recent volumes have returned to more typical subject matter: love, friendship, childhood, places, religion and works of art, where painting, her 'second favourite art', is well represented. Her later work, in *Growing Points* (1975), *Consequently I Rejoice* (1977), *Moments of Grace* (1977), *Celebrations and Elegies* (1982) and *Extending the Territory* (1985), gains power from the sense of triumph over disruptive mental forces and has the quiet authority of someone who has survived. A second *Collected Poems* (1986) won unanimous critical acclaim and the prestigious W. H. Smith Literary Prize of 1987. Jennings has also written studies of religion and poetry, *Every Changing Shape* (1961) and *Christianity and Poetry* (1965).

***Jenny*** A ballad by **Dante Gabriel Rossetti**, begun in 1847 and eventually published in 1870. Jenny is a prostitute. The poet regards her with sympathy as a victim of her time and circumstances, scorned by her virtuous sisters and, more tellingly, by the men who use her. Rossetti's only poem with a contemporary subject, it has a close connection with his only painting on a contemporary theme, the unfinished 'Found'.

**Jerome, Jerome K[lapka]** 1859–1927 Humorist and novelist. The son of an ironmonger, Jerome was born at Walsall in Staffordshire and brought up in east London, where he became an actor and a reporter for various newspapers. *On Stage and Off* (1885) and *Idle Thoughts of an Idle Fellow* (1886) were lighthearted essays which set the tone for his most enduring work, *Three Men in a Boat* (1889), about an accident-prone rowing holiday on the Thames. *Three Men on the Bummel* (1900) took the same characters on a tour of Germany. Jerome founded *The Idler*, a humorous periodical, in 1892, and wrote many plays with some contemporary success. Best known of these was *The Passing of the Third Floor Back* (1907). His own favourite work was *Paul Kelver* (1902), an autobiographical novel. *My Life and Times* (1926) was autobiographical.

**Jerrold, Douglas (William)** 1803–57 Dramatist and journalist. Jerrold was born in London and spent part of his youth as a sailor before starting his successful career in literature. In 1827 his farce *Paul Pry* was staged at the Coburg and he became resident playwright there. A melodrama, *Fifteen Years of a Drunkard's Life* (1828), did equally well and he had a major success in *Black-eyed Susan* (1829). His next play was the melodrama *The Mutiny at the Nore* (1830), and *The Rent Day* (1832) was a drama, but he generally wrote comedy: *The Bride of Ludgate* (1831), *Beau Nash* (1834) and *Time Works Wonders* (1845).

In 1841 Jerrold joined the staff of a new weekly called **Punch** and from that date devoted most of his time to journalism. He was equally successful in his new role, signing his contributions 'Q'. His *Mrs Caudle's Curtain Lectures* (1845) helped to establish the paper's popularity and were published in book form (1846). Mrs Caudle is a nagging wife who always gets into her stride at bedtime when her suffering husband is hoping to sleep. From 1852 until his death Jerrold edited *Lloyd's Weekly Newspaper*.

**Jerrold, (William) Blanchard** 1826–84 Journalist and editor. The son of **Douglas Jerrold**, he was educated in London and France and planned a career as an artist before his sight failed. He wrote four plays, including *Beau Brummel*, and succeeded his father as editor of *Lloyd's Weekly Newspaper*. He wrote a biography of his father (1859) and provided the text for Gustave Doré's famous volume of illustrations, *London: A Pilgrimage* (1872).

*Jew of Malta, The Famous Tragedy of the Rich* A tragedy, with comic elements, by **Christopher Marlowe**. It was first produced in about 1590 but not published until 1633. The published text is believed to contain a number of alterations made during production and these are usually attributed to **Thomas Heywood**. The play was very popular and gave **Edward Alleyn**, the creator of Tamburlaine and Doctor Faustus, another great opportunity as an actor.

Barabas, a successful Jewish merchant of Malta, counts his riches and ponders on the Christians' envy of his success, and their persecution of his people. He knows them for hypocrites who use their religion as their excuse. Barabas longs for the power that would enable him to deal with his enemies.

The Turks demand tribute from Malta and the governor of the island decides to extract the money from the Jews. Barabas resists but his wealth is taken by force and his house confiscated – the governor turns it into a nunnery. He decides to revenge himself on those who have wronged him and embarks on a campaign of destruction. Abigail, his daughter, has a Christian lover and he disposes of both of them. He poisons wells and destroys the entire nunnery, his former house, with poisoned porridge. But his plan to destroy the Turkish commander and his retinue at a banquet by means of a collapsible floor goes awry. He is betrayed and meets his death in a cauldron under the same floor.

**Jewett, Sarah Orne** 1849–1909 American novelist and short-story writer, born and raised in South Berwick, Maine. Her father was a doctor, and she often travelled with him to outlying farms and fishing towns, and observed at first hand the decay and depopulation that afflicted them. (Deephaven, the harbour town of her early stories, was modelled on that of York, near her own home town.) Her observation of this desolation, coupled with her reading of **Harriet Beecher Stowe**'s stories of New England life, provided the stimulus for her own first efforts at fiction; she decided to record the life of her own state and succeeded in getting a story accepted by *The Atlantic Monthly* when she was 19. A collection of such pieces was published as *Deephaven* in 1877 and established her at once as a writer of considerable talent.

Sarah Orne Jewett.

She then published two novels, *A Country Doctor* (1884) and *A Marsh Island* (1885), and further collections of stories – *A White Heron* (1886), *The King of Folly Island* (1888), *A Native of Winby* (1893) and *The Life of Nancy* (1895). In 1896 came the book that gave her a lasting place in American literature, **The Country of the Pointed Firs**. Her later work included two books for children; a historical romance, *The Tory Lover* (1901); and some poems that were posthumously published as *Verses* in 1916.

**Jewsbury, Geraldine Endsor** 1812–80 Novelist. Born in Derbyshire, she became the intimate friend of **Thomas** and **Jane Carlyle**. Her desire to work as a journalist was frustrated by ill health, but she produced several notable and unjustly neglected novels: *Zoe: The History of Two Lives* (1845), *The Half-Sisters* (1848), *Marian Withers* (1851), *Constance Herbert* (1855), *The Sorrows of Gentility* (1856) and *Right or Wrong* (1859).

**Jhabvala, Ruth Prawer** 1927– Indian novelist. Born in Cologne of Polish parents and educated in England, she migrated to India after marriage in 1951 and to the United States 30 years later. Though a satirically minded outsider, she has also experienced Indian joint-family life, and skilfully exploits this duality in her fiction. *To Whom She Will* (1956), *The Nature of Passion* (1957) and, more confidently, *The Householder* (1960) deal with personality clashes and 'Westernized' attitudes within urban families. *Esmond in India* (1958) and, more imaginatively, *Heat and Dust* (1975) are about Westerners trying to understand India and Indians. The technically adventurous *A New Dominion* (1973; in the USA as *The Travelers*) and the

Ruth Prawer Jhabvala.

more authoritative *A Backward Place* (1963) are about the interaction of Indians and expatriate Westerners. Satire flares brightly in *In Search of Love and Beauty* (1983), about European exiles in New York. *Like Birds, Like Fishes* (1963), *A Stronger Climate* (1968), *An Experience of India* (1971) and *How I Became a Holy Mother* (1976) are collections of stories. Part of the Merchant-Ivory film-making team, she has written some half-dozen film scripts.

**Jocelin of Brakelond** *fl.* 1173–1215 Monk and chronicler. Jocelin, whose name derives from the street in his native Bury St Edmunds, Suffolk, entered monastic life in 1173, holding an increasingly important series of posts in the great abbey at Bury until 1215, when his name disappears from the records. The subject of his Latin *Chronicle* is the life of the monastery, particularly under the rule of Abbot Samson, elected in 1182, whom Jocelin served as chaplain and of whom he paints an extraordinarily vivid and telling portrait. For six years Jocelin was 'constantly' with the Abbot 'night and day', and his narrative, striking for its human informality, describes a religious magnate, 'more remarkable for counsel than for piety' perhaps, who ruled the abbey's human and material resources with an iron will. He recounts Samson's vicissitudinous early career, his beautification of the abbey church and his sermons to the local people, delivered in his native Norfolk dialect. The chronicle ends eight years before Samson's death in 1211 at the age of 77. No other work by Jocelin survives, although he records composing an account of the martyrdom of St Robert, a child allegedly murdered in 1181 by the Jews of Bury and buried in the abbey church.

Jocelin's *Chronicle*, first published in 1840, won fame in the pages of **Carlyle**'s *Past and Present* (1843), in which Book Two is wholly devoted to the Abbot and his 'Boswell', the latter sentimentally characterized as 'a learned, grown man, yet with the heart of a child'. As a result of Carlyle's enthusiasm, an English translation appeared in 1844.

***John Bull, The History of*** The collective title of a group of pamphlets by **John Arbuthnot**, first published in 1712 and rearranged for publication in **Pope** and **Swift**'s *Miscellanies* of 1727. A satire directed against the war with France, it marks the first appearance of the typical Englishman, John Bull.

John Bull (England) and Nicholas Frog (Holland) are engaged in a lawsuit with Lewis Baboon (Louis XIV, Bourbon). Their case is fought and won by the attorney Humphrey Hocus (Marlborough). Then John Bull discovers an intrigue between Hocus and Mrs Bull (the Whig Parliament). Mrs Bull dies during the ensuing rumpus and John Bull marries again;

the new Mrs Bull is the Tory Parliament and John Bull has spent a great deal in litigation, thereby losing the 'Plumbs' he had acquired by 'plain and fair dealing'. John Bull is 'an honest plain-dealing Fellow' who honours his mother (the Church of England) but is easily deceived by partners, apprentices and servants.

**John Buncle, Esquire, The Life and Opinions of** See **Amory, Thomas**.

**John Gilpin, The Diverting History of** A comic ballad by **William Cowper**, published anonymously in *The Public Advertiser* in 1782, later published in the same volume as *The Task* in 1785. Cowper heard the story of the linen draper John Gilpin from his friend Lady Austen and wrote his ballad on the subject the following day. The story tells of John Gilpin of Cheapside and his wife, who decided to celebrate their wedding anniversary at The Bell, Edmonton. Mrs Gilpin and the children will travel by chaise and pair, while John Gilpin will proceed on horseback. But he loses control of his borrowed horse, which carries him 10 miles further, to Ware, and back again. The real John Gilpin was a citizen of London who owned land at Olney in Buckinghamshire, where Cowper lived for some years.

**John Halifax, Gentleman** A novel by **Dinah Mulock**, published in 1856. The hero is an orphan who in spite of his poverty and friendless condition is sustained by a proud consciousness of independence and integrity. He is given work by Abel Fletcher, the tanner of Norton Bury, and befriended by his son Phineas, who writes his biography 50 years after their first meeting. Through industry and perseverance John succeeds in the world and marries Ursula March. Thereafter Phineas's part in the action dwindles, somewhat to the detriment of the book. (See also **The Condition of England novel**.)

**John Inglesant** A historical novel by **Joseph Henry Shorthouse**, privately printed in 1880 and published in 1881. It is set in the early 17th century and gives a skilful portrait of the age's religious and political tensions.

John Inglesant comes under the influence of a Jesuit emissary, who sees in the highly wrought, sensuous young man excellent material for service in the religious intrigues of the later years of Charles I. Inglesant is strongly influenced by the community of Little Gidding (see **Nicholas Ferrar**) and the King's approval of it is a factor in his decision to undertake dangerous service in the Royalist cause. When secret negotiations to bring an Irish army into England come to light, the King repudiates him. Inglesant refuses to expose the King, even though his own life is in peril.

After Charles's execution, Inglesant goes to Italy where he hopes to find the Italian who murdered his brother. The author now moves his story of religious tensions to Rome, where Inglesant witnesses the drawn-out intrigues that attend the election of a successor to Innocent X. He meets Molinos, the Spanish mystic who was ultimately condemned for the influence of his doctrine of Quietism, and is temporarily drawn to the idea that human endeavour is futile except in devotion to God. The climax of the story comes with Inglesant's encounter with the murderer, now in his power. He renounces vengeance, believing it God's prerogative.

**John of Salisbury** c. 1115–80 Philosopher. After a failed boyhood apprenticeship to a necromancer, John of Salisbury went on to study under Peter Abelard and to work for the papal curia at Rome. He became Treasurer of Exeter Cathedral and, in 1176, Bishop of Chartres. His writings reveal a broad education not only in the classics, philosophy and the Bible, but also in canon law. His *Policraticus*, a major medieval work, deals, often satirically, with the ethics of politics and the state. The *Metalogicus* combines the studies of logic and metaphysics, while the *Historia Pontificalis* is a delightful account of life in Rome, full of anecdotes and vignettes of the characters whom John had met while at the curia. A close friend of Cardinal Nicholas Brakespear (the future Pope Adrian IV), John was at the centre of medieval church and intellectual life. Two of his biographies of leading churchmen, Anselm and Thomas Becket, survive, as does a collection of his letters, witty, polished and erudite.

**Johns, W[illiam] E[arle]** 1893–1968 Children's author and creator of Biggles. Born in Hertford and educated at the local grammar school, Johns trained as a surveyor before enlisting in World War I, first as a trooper and later in the Royal Flying Corps. After various sorties as a pilot he was shot down and imprisoned, managing to escape despite his wounds before final recapture. After the war he stayed in the RAF as an officer, becoming founder-editor of the monthly *Popular Flying* in 1932. It was in those pages that his legendary hero Captain James Bigglesworth (Biggles for short) first made an appearance in a series of short stories. Along with his inseparable companions Ginger, Algy and Bertie, Biggles provided young readers with an idealized image of toughness, honesty and stoicism. Johns went on to write over 70 Biggles novels, many of which remain in print today. In his undemanding but entertaining style, he also wrote about the adventures of the only slightly less popular commando hero, Gimlet, and created a female Biggles in 'Worrals of the WAAF'.

**Johnson, Barbara** See **deconstructive criticism**.

**Johnson, B[rian] S[tanley]** 1933–73 Novelist. Born in London, Johnson campaigned vigorously through his short writing life (he committed suicide at the age of 39) for a renaissance of technical innovation and experimentation in the English novel. His own fiction demonstrates his admiration for **Joyce**, **Beckett** and **Flann O'Brien** in its deliberate abjuration of realistic homogeneity and for **Sterne** in its playfulness with the physical form of the novel. *Albert Angelo* (1964) contains a hole in page 149 which is later revealed to represent the knife-cut which killed **Christopher Marlowe**, and is also offered as the chance to read the future (on a subsequent page) through the past (a previous page). Johnson himself intrudes into *Christie Malry's Own Double Entry* (1973) to converse with the book's hero, while *The Unfortunates* (1969) is notorious for being published in a box of 27 loose-leaf sections, to be shuffled and read in any order, to embody in literal reading terms the haphazard, unreliable recollections of the narrator. Other novels include *Travelling People* (1963), *Trawl* (1966) and *See the Old Lady Decently* (1975). The extremity of Johnson's technical adventures, which have occasionally earned him the charge of gimmickry, may be seen as acknowledgement of the immense task of reversing the realistic bias of post-war British fiction.

**Johnson, Colin** 1929– Australian Aboriginal novelist. He is still best known for his first novel, *Wild Cat Falling* (1965), a brief but intense book focusing on a 19-year-old half-Aboriginal, half-white 'anti-hero'. The novel shows some of the problems of such a person defining his identity in modern Australia, but it also portrays many of the anguishes of early adulthood. Some of its philosophical elements anticipate Johnson's own conversion to Buddhism, which has taken him to remote parts of Asia. He has, however, been an active supporter of Aboriginal rights in his native country. His other fiction includes *Long Live Sandawara* (1979), which switches between north-west Australia in the 1890s and the slums of modern Perth, and *Doctor Wooreddy's Prescription for Enduring the Ending of the World* (1983), which is set in the Australian states of Tasmania and Victoria at the time of the first contact between the local Aboriginals and white men.

**Johnson, Edward** 1598–1672 American historian and prominent figure in the Massachusetts Bay Colony. Johnson was born in Canterbury. Leaving his wife and seven children, he travelled to New England with **John Winthrop** aboard the *Arbella* in 1630, returning home the following year. In 1636 he and his family emigrated to Massachusetts, where he held numerous and influential civic positions. He is best remembered, however, for his history of New England: *The Wonder-Working Providence of Sion's Saviour in New-England* (1654).

**Johnson, Emily Pauline** 1862–1913 Canadian poet, the daughter of an Indian chief and an Englishwoman. She earned a living as a contributor to periodicals and by reciting her own verse under her Indian name of Tekahionwake. Her best works demonstrate a keen sympathy for, and understanding of, Indian life: *White Wampum* (1895), *Canadian Born* (1903) and *Flint and Feathers* (1913).

**Johnson, James Weldon** 1871–1938 American novelist and poet. Born and educated in Florida, Johnson was one of the most influential black figures of his day. While practising law in Florida (he was the first black admitted to the state Bar after the Civil War), he collaborated with his brother in writing popular songs and spirituals. One of these, 'Lift Every Voice and Sing', became known as the black anthem. In 1912 he anonymously published his first novel, *Autobiography of an Ex-Colored Man*, about a light-skinned black man who poses as a white. It was reissued in his own name in 1927, the year he published *God's Trombones: Seven Negro Sermons in Verse*. *Black Manhattan* (1930) is a black history of New York City. His autobiography, *Along This Way* (1933), tells of his political activities as US consul in Nicaragua and Venezuela (1906–12), and of his role as a major figure in the National Association for the Advancement of Colored People. Other volumes of his poetry are *Fifty Years and Other Poems* (1917), *Saint Peter Relates an Incident at the Resurrection Day* (1930) and *Selected Poems* (1935).

**Johnson, Linton Kwesi** 1952– Poet. Born in a rural part of Jamaica, he came to England at the age of nine. He was educated in London at Tulse Hill Comprehensive School and Goldsmiths' College. His poetry, which has a huge popular following, particularly among young black people, is often urban in theme and filled with street-wise aggression. He can, however, be quietly lyrical and always shows himself in command of sound effects and metre. Almost all his poetry is written in the so-called 'dub' mode and requires performance to be fully appreciated. Johnson's poems are often directed at problems of race and social injustice in Britain. Though his recorded poems give a better idea of his talents, Johnson has, unlike some of his similar contemporaries, allowed his work to be printed. His printed collections include *Voices of the Living and the Dead* (1974), *Dread Beat and*

*Blood* (1975) and *Inglan is a Bitch* (1980). His records include *Poet and the Roots* (1977) and *Bass Culture* (1980). His is one of the major talents in black British literature and almost certainly the best known, with many imitators who share his interest in matching words to music.

**Johnson, Lionel (Pigot)** 1867–1902 Poet and critic. Born in Kent, he grew up in Wales, and had a very successful academic career at Winchester and, from 1886, at New College, Oxford. After graduating, he began to publish reviews and articles in several London newspapers and periodicals. He was received into the Roman Catholic church in 1891. A member of the **Rhymers' Club** and a close friend of **W. B. Yeats**, he began to explore his Irish ancestry in 1893, when he visited Dublin. He jointly edited *The Irish Home Reading Magazine* during 1894, and was an active member of the Irish Literary Society in London. His early full-length study of **Thomas Hardy** (1894) was followed by *Poems* (1895) and *Ireland With Other Poems* (1897) which included 'Ways of War' (dedicated to John O'Leary). *Posliminium*, a posthumous collection of essays, appeared in 1912, and his *Complete Poems* edited by I. Fletcher in 1953. Although his Irish poems are rhetorical, his other work 'conveys an emotion of joy, of intellectual clearness, of hard energy', as W. B. Yeats wrote. Johnson influenced Yeats's early work, especially *The Wind Among the Reeds* (1899), and he appears in 'In Memory of Major Robert Gregory' as a man of learning who 'brooded upon sanctity'. He acknowledged his own alcoholism in 'Mystic and Cavalier': 'Go from me, I am one of those who fall.'

**Johnson, Louis** 1924– New Zealand poet and editor. Schoolmaster, educational journalist and copywriter, he based himself in Wellington, where he was born, from 1944. He founded *The New Zealand Poetry Yearbook* (1951) and became an influential force among poets of the 1950s and 1960s, particularly in directing attention to the values of contemporary American poetry, and the concern of poets such as **Charles Olson** for a sense of locality and cultural identity. Through the 1970s he lived in the USA, but returned to New Zealand in the early 1980s. As an editor he was controversial, dextrously using arguments about poetry to educate his readers. His own poetry is intricate and careful, owing much to **Wallace Stevens** and something to the **Black Mountain school** of poets. It uses the surprising adjective brilliantly in short, composed, allusive poems based on the persona of the meditative observer, but always outwardly directed, a poet speaking to poets. His early poetry was published in *The Sun Among the Ruins* and *Roughshod Among the Lilies*, both published by **Denis Glover**'s Pegasus Press in 1951, and *New Worlds*

*for Old*, 1957. His later work has mostly appeared in Australia and the USA.

**Johnson, Pamela Hansford** 1912–81 Novelist and critic. Born and educated in London, she married **C. P. Snow** in 1950. Her first novel, *This Bed Thy Centre* (1935), was followed by many others including *The Trojan Brothers* (1944), *An Avenue of Stone* (1947) and *Catherine Carter* (1952). Her talent for light satire is best revealed in the 'Dorothy Merlin' trilogy: *The Unspeakable Skipton* (1959), *Night and Silence, Who is Here* (1962), and *Cork Street, Next to the Hatter's* (1965). A gentle satire of literary life, it became her best-known work. Later titles included *The Honours Board* (1970), about the close relationships between the staff at a traditional English public school, *The Good Listener* (1975) and *The Good Husband* (1978).

Her non-fictional works included critical studies of **Ivy Compton-Burnett**, Proust and **Thomas Wolfe**, and a book about contemporary society in the wake of the Moors Murders, *On Iniquity* (1967), based on her experiences as a reporter at the trial. She wrote one play, *Corinth House* (1948).

**Johnson, Samuel** 1709–84 Lexicographer, critic, scholar, poet and man of letters. Born the son of a bookseller in Lichfield, Johnson was throughout his life prone to ill health. At the age of three he was taken to London to be 'touched' for scrofula. He entered Pembroke College, Oxford, in October 1728, and during his time there he translated into Latin *Messiah*, a collection of prayers and hymns by **Alexander Pope**, published in 1731. Johnson was an impoverished commoner and is said to have been hounded for his threadbare appearance; the customary title 'Dr' by which he is often known is the result of an honorary doctorate awarded him by the University in 1775. His father died in 1731, and left the family in penury; Johnson was a teacher at the grammar school in Market Bosworth during 1732, and then moved for three years to Birmingham, his first essays appearing in the *Birmingham Journal*. There he completed his first book, *A Voyage to Abyssinia* (published 1735), a translation from the French version of the travels of Father Jerome Lobo, a Portuguese missionary.

In 1735 he married Mrs Elizabeth Porter ('Tetty'), a widow 20 years his senior, and the couple harboured enduring affection for each other. They started a school at Edial, near Lichfield, but the project was unsuccessful, so they moved down to London in 1737, accompanied by one of their former pupils, **David Garrick**. Johnson began earning a steady living in the employ of Edward Cave, the founder (in 1731) of *The Gentleman's Magazine*. To this he contributed copious and varied writings: essays,

Samuel Johnson. A detail from the unfinished portrait by J. Barry, *c*.1777. National Portrait Gallery, London.

Latin verses, biographies and political commentaries on parliamentary proceedings. In 1738 he published his poem **London**, a Juvenalian imitation approved by Pope.

The death in 1743 of his erstwhile friend, the poet **Richard Savage**, prompted the first of Johnson's biographical pieces, published in 1744. The publisher Robert Dodsley then persuaded him to address to **Lord Chesterfield** his *Plan of a Dictionary of the English Language* in 1747, but little help was forthcoming, and for the next eight years Johnson laboured intermittently with this project, a lexicographical milestone. In 1749 he published *The Vanity of Human Wishes*, his longest and most enduring poem, and in that same year his loyal friend Garrick fulfilled a promise by staging a production of Johnson's indifferent, moralistic tragedy *Irene* (completed 12 years previously); it appeared at **Drury Lane** and altogether earned its author a welcome £300. In 1750, Johnson undertook another enterprise for Cave, a twice-weekly periodical called *The Rambler*, which ran until 1752, all but four of its 208 numbers being written, anonymously, by Johnson himself, and comprising moral essays and commentaries. The project was applauded by **Samuel Richardson**.

In 1752 he contributed to John Hawkesworth's periodical *The Adventurer*, and at Cave's death in 1754 Johnson wrote a life of the bookseller for *The Gentleman's Magazine*. The next year saw the publication of *A Dictionary of the English Language*, and the notorious rebuff with which he greeted the delayed endorsement of this project by Chesterfield. His entry for 'patron' in the *Dictionary* reflects the compiler's feelings: 'Commonly a wretch who supports with insolence, and is paid with flattery.' An abridged form of the *Dictionary* appeared in 1756, but Johnson was hardly earning a living, having to pen numerous political articles, reviews and essays for various periodicals including the *Universal Visitor* and the *Literary Magazine*. He wrote his lives of **Sir Thomas Browne** and **Roger Ascham** (published in 1756 and 1761 respectively), and from 1758 to 1760 contributed *The Idler* series of papers to the *Universal Chronicle*. In 1759 his philosophical romance *The Prince of Abyssinia, A Tale* (later known as **Rasselas**) was published shortly after the death of the author's mother.

At the behest of Lord Bute, the new monarch George III awarded Johnson in 1762 an annual pension of £300, which somewhat relaxed his straitened circumstances. On 16 May the following year he first met the young Scot **James Boswell**, who was later to become his biographer. In 1764 – along with his friend Joshua Reynolds, the painter – Johnson founded 'the Club', an artistic 'coterie' whose meetings at the Turk's Head in Gerrard Street were attended by **Burke**, **Goldsmith**, Garrick, Boswell and Charles James Fox. In this year he made the acquaintance of Henry Thrale, a prosperous and cultured brewer, and his diminutive wife Hester, who offered generous hospitality to Johnson during crucial years when depression hovered over his life. In 1765, after considerable delays, his eight-volume edition of *The Plays of William Shakespeare* appeared, followed by Johnson's own *Preface*; subsequent scholarship may have superseded most of the editorial work, but the prefatory essay remains one of the most sensible introductions to its subject.

By now a deservedly celebrated literary figure whose opinions on a variety of subjects were eagerly noted in metropolitan circles, Johnson finally agreed to Boswell's request that they embark together on a tour of Scotland. His observations were published as *A Journey to the Western Islands of Scotland* (1775). At the suggestion of a number of London booksellers, he began work in the spring of 1777 on a series of 'little prefaces' for a planned edition of the works of certain English poets, and these penetrating biographical essays were published separately in 1781 as *The Lives of the Poets*, 52 compelling studies which show him both informed and opinionated as a literary critic. In 1781 Henry Thrale died, and Hester sold off the brewery, and began to see less of Johnson; in June 1783 she announced her intention to marry Gabriele Piozzi, a music teacher, and Johnson's outraged response caused their sad estrangement. He spent the summer of 1784 touring England, visiting Lichfield, Birmingham and Oxford, and returning to London in mid-November, dropsical and depressed. Samuel Johnson died during the night of 13 December and is buried in Westminster Abbey.

Johnson's massive literary reputation is in part dependent on Boswell's unique biography, which fused the personality of the author with his writings and raised him to legendary status. A pioneering scholar, celebrated conversationalist in an age when this was considered a minor art form, and eloquent sage, Johnson is sometimes wrongly considered a reactionary embodying the High-Tory principles of the dwindling Augustan age, but this view misrepresents him. Though famous in later years, he preserved both his humility and his scepticism, and never forgot the real hardships of his early life as a struggling hack. He was not a philosopher who discovered an original system of thought, but his wisdom shaped a stern and practical critique of both human behaviour and literature. Pathologically lazy himself, he chastised idleness in others; fearful of insanity, he was fascinated by irrationality in others; he applauded originality, clarity, honesty and the perception of general truths, and these values operated in his life as well as in his writings.

As a writer of prose, Johnson changes somewhat with maturity; his early work tends to be sententious and pompous, but he evolved a quite distinctive blend of precision and aphorism, characterized by counterpoint and reasoned argument. He was also the author of an Introduction to the *Harleian Miscellany* (1744, see **Harley Lyrics**), *Miscellaneous Observations on the Tragedy of Macbeth* (1745), some Prologues (the most notable being for Garrick on his management of Drury Lane, and the indignant Prologue to *Comus*) and the political tracts *The False Alarm* (1770), *Thoughts . . . respecting Falkland's Islands* (1771), *The Patriot* (1774) and *Taxation no Tyranny* (1775). In 1776 he wrote a parliamentary speech for General Hamilton, *Considerations on the Corn Laws*. In addition to hymns, prayers and sermons, Johnson wrote a number of poems in English and Latin throughout his life, verses ranging from the stately to the personal, including excellent imitations from the classics, elegies, satires and odes. Though he lacks in verse the verbal agility of Pope (to whom he is frequently compared) he wrote several memorable poems which perhaps reveal more about his charitable, even passionate, nature than the public mode of his more familiar prose; 'Old Age' and 'On the Death of Dr Robert Levet' have a particular place in the line of 18th-century verse. For these many achievements, Johnson is often considered the greatest man of letters England has produced.

Boswell's *Life of Samuel Johnson LL.D.* (1791) is the main, but not the only, source of biographical detail; Mrs Piozzi's *Anecdotes* (1786), for example, also contains informative insights. The *Correspondence* was edited by R. W. Chapman in 1952.

**Johnston, Sir Charles (Hepburn)** 1912–86 Poet and translator. Educated at Winchester and Balliol College, Oxford, Johnston entered the diplomatic service in 1936, serving in Tokyo (where he was interned when Japan entered the war), Cairo, Madrid, Bonn, Amman and Aden, before becoming British High Commissioner in Australia (1965–71). Although he had already published two volumes of verse – *Towards Mozambique* (1947) and *Estuary in Scotland* (1974) – his first major success was his translation of Pushkin's *Eugene Onegin* (1977). This was followed by annual privately printed volumes – *Poems and Journeys* (1979), *Rivers and Fireworks* (1980), *Talk about the Last Poet* (1981), *Choiseul and Talleyrand* (1982) and *The Irish Lights* (1983) – which mixed new and old poems with translations from Latin and Russian, especially Pushkin and Lermontov. His range is wide – epigrams, autobiographical poems, dramatic monologues – and he is an original narrative poet, influenced by **Byron**. His major original poems are 'In Praise of Gusto' and 'Elegy', although there is reputedly an as yet unpublished masterpiece. His admirers include **Vikram Seth**, **Roy Fuller** and **Peter Levi**.

**Johnston, (William) Denis** 1901–84 Irish playwright, born in Dublin and educated at Cambridge and Harvard, where he trained for the law. Associated with both the **Abbey Theatre** and the Gate Theatre in Dublin from 1927 to 1936, Johnston had his first play, an expressionistic satire called *The Old Lady Says 'No!'* (1929), produced at the Gate. *The Moon in the Yellow River* (1931), his most popular play, is a powerful portrait of political and moral divisions in post-Civil War Ireland. Together with *The Scythe and the Sunset* (1958), a play about the Easter Rising written in conscious recollection of **O'Casey**'s *The Plough and the Stars*, it showed Johnston's ability to write realistic drama that is easy of access. Many of his more experimental plays troubled critics and public. *A Bride for the Unicorn* (1933), *Storm Song* (1934) and *The Golden Cuckoo* (1938) are among these. Johnston wrote both a play about **Swift**, *The Dreaming Dust* (1940), and a contentious study in critical biography, *In Search of Swift* (1959). *Nine Rivers from Jordan* (1953) is an impressionistic account of his wartime experiences. *The Brazen Horn* (1977) proposed a personal mystical philosophy.

**Johnston, George (Henry)** 1912–70 Australian novelist. He was born in Melbourne and educated at Caulfield State School, Brighton Technical College and the National Gallery Arts

School in his home city. He was a journalist who in 1942 became a war correspondent in New Guinea, Italy, Burma and China. He drew from this period of his life in many of his writings. He later lived for 10 years on the Greek island of Hydra, where he wrote his most famous work and also achieved success as a thriller writer under the pseudonym 'Shane Martin'. Although he is the author under his own name of several other novels, among them *The Darkness Outside* (1959) and *The Far Face of the Moon* (1964), his fame rests today on a trilogy of self-examining novels: *My Brother Jack* (1964), *Clean Straw for Nothing* (1969) and *A Cartload of Clay* (1971). The first two books in the trilogy both won the Miles Franklin Award; the third was incomplete at the time of Johnston's death. Together they brilliantly present aspects of 20th-century Australian life, depicting as they do so archetypal qualities in the Australian male character.

**Johnston, Jennifer** 1930– Irish novelist. She was born in Dublin, the daughter of the playwright **Denis Johnston** and the actress Shelagh Richards, and educated at Park House School and Trinity College, Dublin. She lives in Northern Ireland, near Derry. Johnston has published six novels to date, most notably *The Captains and the Kings* (1972), *How Many Miles To Babylon?* (1974) and *Shadows on Our Skin* (1977). The best of her work continues the tradition of the Irish 'Big House' novel, centring on the decay of the Protestant gentry and their embattled position in modern Ireland. It is, in essence, a new version of the old clash between 'culture' and philistinism, although it gains new life from Johnston's sympathetic portrayal of the relationships which survive the inherited political and economic as well as religious attitudes of her characters. In the less successful *Shadows on Our Skin* she moves beyond her customary range and attempts to show the pressure of the Northern Irish troubles on a working-class family.

**Johnstone, Charles** *c.* 1719–*c.* 1800 Journalist and satirist. Born in Ireland and educated at Trinity College, Dublin, Johnstone practised as a lawyer before going to Calcutta in 1782, where he became a journalist and newspaper proprietor. He was the author of *Chrysal, or, The Adventures of a Guinea* (1760–5), satirical episodes from the life of the times, told by a guinea as it is passed from hand to hand. Most notable are the scenes at the Hellfire Club and the successful manoeuvres of an ambitious wife on behalf of her clergyman husband.

**Jolley, Elizabeth** 1923– Australian novelist and short-story writer. Born in Birmingham to an English father and a Viennese mother who was the daughter of an Austrian general, she was brought up in a German-speaking household and educated at a Quaker boarding-school. During World War II she worked as a nurse. In 1959 she migrated to Western Australia and regards herself as a writer from this region. In 1974 she began attending classes at Fremantle Arts Centre, whose highly successful small press subsequently published her fiction. She had been writing since childhood, but her first book, *Five Acre Virgin and Other Stories*, did not appear until 1976. Since then she has become regarded as one of the finest of contemporary Australian writers of fiction. Her novel *Miss Peabody's Inheritance* (1983) is an impishly funny book which engages in a playful treatment of the conventions of schoolgirl fiction, received female stereotypes and the relationship between writer and reader, as well as exploring and contrasting Australian and English cultural codes. Along with *Mr Scobie's Riddle* (1982), a post-modernist novel set in a nursing home and another penetrating study of comic eccentricity, it represents her best work. Jolley's other books include the novel *Palomino* (1980) and volumes of short stories, *The Travelling Entertainer* (1979) and *Woman in a Lampshade* (1983). She is also a successful writer of radio plays.

**Jolly Beggars, The** A verse cantata by **Robert Burns**, first published in a Glasgow chapbook in 1799. An assortment of wretched folk are described enjoying themselves singing and drinking an evening away, despite the low quality of their daily lives. Each character sings a song in turn, and these are linked by descriptions of the singer, so evocative and precise that it is thought Burns was directly moved to compose the piece by a visit he paid in person to Poosie Nansie's tavern in Mauchline.

**Jonathan Wild the Great, The Life of** A satirical novel by **Henry Fielding**, published in 1743 as part of his *Miscellanies*. It gives a fictionalized version of the life of an infamous criminal executed earlier in the century, ironically presented as an example of heroism and greatness. Wild's success in the underworld is offered as a parallel to the values at work in polite society and government, where, Fielding implies, greatness and influence are sanctioned irrespective of motive or morals. Sir Robert Walpole is the chief target for this aspect of the satire.

Wild is baptized by Titus Oates, and shows an early propensity for underhand behaviour; he goes to work for Snap, warden of a sponging-house (where arrested debtors were detained before being imprisoned) and is tutored in the arts of extortion and exploitation. He becomes chief of a gang of thieves, taking the lion's share of the profits and safeguarding himself by turning over to the law any subordinates who question his leadership.

He marries Laetitia Snap, his former employer's amusingly hypocritical daughter, and concentrates on ruining his virtuous former schoolfellow, the jeweller Heartfree. Wild robs him and then gets him imprisoned for bankruptcy; he tricks Mrs Heartfree into fleeing the country and accuses her innocent husband of having murdered her. The jeweller is rescued from the scaffold by the exposure of Wild, who is hanged in his stead, a 'hero' and 'great man' to the last.

**Jones, Henry Arthur** 1851–1929 Playwright. Jones was born at Grandborough in Buckinghamshire, the eldest son of a farmer. He began work at the age of 12 in drapers' shops; he then worked in a London warehouse and as a commercial traveller, using his leisure to extend his reading and further his education. He wrote a novel and some one-act plays, none of which were accepted; he eventually achieved a modest success with a domestic drama, *It's Only Round the Corner*, performed at the Theatre Royal, Exeter, in 1878, and later in London as *Harmony* (1884).

Jones made the drama his profession after 1878, and 45 full-length plays by him were staged in London and New York between 1878 and 1917. *A Clerical Error* (1879) was produced by Wilson Barrett, for whom Jones and Henry Herman devised a spectacular melodrama called **The Silver King** (1882). This was one of Barrett's most successful parts and the long run established Jones's reputation. He then turned to more serious theatre; he was interested in the drama of ideas and the drama as a vehicle for social criticism. With Herman he adapted Ibsen's *A Doll's House* as *Breaking a Butterfly* (1884) and in his own work displayed a talent for naturalistic dialogue and portrayal of character. However, it is now generally agreed that his drama lacked the firm philosophical basis that would have given his social and moral criticism a permanent place in the English theatre. His most notable plays were *Saints and Sinners* (1884), *The Dancing Girl* (1891), *The Case of Rebellious Susan* (1894) and *The Triumph of the Philistines* (1895). *Michael and His Lost Angel* (1896) was severely criticized because one of the central scenes contained a public confession of adultery by a priest. The star, Mrs Patrick Campbell, left the cast during rehearsals and the play was taken off after 10 performances. But Jones went on to further success with **The Liars** (1897) and *Mrs Dane's Defence* (1900). The last two plays are occasionally revived.

**Jones, James** 1921–77 American novelist. Born in Robinson, Illinois, Jones served in the US Army in the Pacific from 1939 to 1944. *From Here to Eternity* (1951), his first and best-known novel, is a realistic story of army life in Hawaii on the eve of the attack on Pearl Harbor; it won him the National Book Award and became a best-seller. His career continued with *Some Came Running* (1957), *The Pistol* (1959), *The Thin Red Line* (1962), *Go To The Widow-Maker* (1967) and *A Touch of Danger* (1973). His short stories are collected in *The Ice Cream Headache* (1968) and *The Merry Month of May* (1971). *Viet Journal* (1974) describes his visit to Vietnam.

**Jones, LeRoi** See **Baraka, Amiri**.

**Jones, (Walter) David (Michael)** 1895–1974 Poet and artist. Born of a Welsh father in Brockley, Kent, he studied at Camberwell Art School in 1909–14, joined the Royal Welsh Fusiliers and served as a private on the western front in 1915–18. He was profoundly affected by the war landscape, describing it as 'a place of enchantment'. In 1919 he studied at Westminster Art School, and was received into the Roman Catholic church in 1921. In the same year he began to learn carpentry and engraving under Eric Gill at Ditchling, Sussex, and lived with Gill's family in Capel-y-Ffin, South Wales, during 1925. He joined the Society of Wood Engravers in 1927, producing illustrations for a number of private presses. Following a breakdown in 1933, he visited Jerusalem and Cairo, landscapes which became crucial to his work. *In Parenthesis* (1937) was followed by *The Anathemata* (1952), *The Sleeping Lord and Other Fragments* (1974), *The Kensington Mass* (1975) and *The Roman Quarry and Other Sequences* (1981). *Epoch and Artist* (1959) and *The Dying Gaul* (1978) are collections of essays and articles.

Combining prose, verse, illustration and lettering, Jones's work makes highly allusive and associative use of a variety of sources of ritual and romance. A central theme is the need to connect a consciousness of the remote and recent past with the post-war world, and to re-establish traditional meanings and symbols. *In Parenthesis* relates the war experience of Private John Ball to chivalric antecedents, and the modern Waste Land to **Malory's** *Morte Darthur*. It avoids the 'wholesale slaughter' of the later war years. *The Anathemata*, divided into eight sections, is a much wider chronicle of the 'Western Christian *res*' and was much admired by **W. H. Auden**, **Kathleen Raine** and **Edwin Muir**. It has an important preface which explores succinctly the problems of the 'sign maker' in the modern world. The later works are complete fragments relating to the Crucifixion.

**Jones, Sir William** 1746–94 Jurist and orientalist. Educated at Harrow School and University College, Oxford, Jones was judge of the High Court at Calcutta from 1783 until his death. He published several works on law and oriental languages but is best remembered for his mastery of Sanskrit and his insistence, in his essay in *Asiatic Researches* (1786), on its study as the common source of Greek and Latin. Jones's declaration, together with **John Horne Tooke**'s advocacy of the study of Gothic and Anglo-Saxon (published in the same year), saw the birth of the science of comparative philology.

**Jonson, Ben[jamin]** 1572–1637 Poet and playwright. Probably born in Westminster and educated at Westminster School, Jonson may have worked with his stepfather, a master bricklayer. He is identified as an actor and playwright in 1597 by references in the papers of **Philip Henslowe**. Before that he had probably served as a soldier in Flanders, was certainly married and had fathered the first of several children. If, as seems likely, he was one of the actors imprisoned after the performance of *The Isle of Dogs* in 1597, he had good reason to tread warily. The fact that he never did so is evidence of an unusually combative temperament. The following year he killed a fellow actor, Gabriel Spencer, in a duel but had the wit to escape execution by pleading benefit of clergy. The reputation for fearless speaking of his mind has clung to him ever since.

The presentation of his second known play, *Every Man in His Humour*, in 1598 turned Jonson into a celebrity and created a brief fashion for 'humours' comedy. He followed it, less successfully, with *Every Man out of His Humour* (1599) and *Cynthia's Revels* (1600), satirical comedies which displayed Jonson's classical scholarship and his delight in formal experiment. His quickness to take offence and a stubborn belief in his own superior talent made him a leading participant in the war of the theatres, in which **Marston** and **Dekker** were his chief adversaries and to which *The Poetaster* (1601) was his unattractive major contribution. His decision to portray himself in that play as Horace is indicative of his early admiration for the poet whose *Art of Poetry* he translated. (The translation was published posthumously in the revised *Works* of 1640.)

Jonson's next play, *Sejanus, His Fall* (1603), brought further trouble. He was summoned before the Privy Council to answer charges of 'popery and treason'. He had converted to Roman Catholicism in 1598, and it has to be admitted that a play by a Catholic detailing conspiracy and assassination at court was a supremely tactless contribution to the first winter season of the **King's Men** under their new patron, James I. Like his later Roman tragedy, *Catiline His Conspiracy* (1611), *Sejanus* is too ponderous to stand comparison with **Shakespeare**'s Roman plays. Together with his contributions to *Eastward Ho* (1604), for which he was

once again briefly imprisoned, it put in jeopardy his emerging role as court poet and **masque** writer to James I. *The Masque of Blackness* (1605) was the first of many collaborations with Inigo Jones, a collaboration threatened and finally destroyed by rivalry. Jonson's status as a writer of masques remains almost as secure as his status as a writer of comedies.

The plays on which his enduring reputation rests are all comedies and all written between 1605 and 1614. They are *Volpone* (1605), *Epicoene, or, The Silent Woman* (1609), *The Alchemist* (1610) and *Bartholomew Fair* (1614). It is here that Jonson's stagecraft is at its most ingenious. The incidents and episodes are artfully controlled and yet preserve an air of improvisatory spontaneity. The characters, though strictly defined by their names, seem willing to command the freedom of the stage. The cutting edge of Jonson's comedies is sharp. They are peopled with deceivers and dupes, and the virtuous intelligent have an unusually small part to play. The 'image of the times', promised in the Prologue to the revised *Every Man in His Humour* (1616), is an uncomfortable one. It is an age of usury, in which human folly gives living room to moral outrage. Pug, the junior devil permitted a day of malpractice on earth in *The Devil Is an Ass* (1616), finds himself out of his depth among humans more devious than he.

The comparative failure of *The Devil Is an Ass* may have discouraged Jonson. It was nine years

Ben Jonson. A detail from the portrait after A. Blyenberch. National Portrait Gallery, London.

before his next comedy, *The Staple of News* (1625), was staged and his effective dramatic output is completed by *The New Inn* (1629) and *A Tale of a Tub* (1633). But Jonson was not inactive at any time. His vivid sense of his own stature is represented by the unprecedented publication, in folio, of his dramatic and poetic *Works* (1616) and by his continuing provision of masques at court. He was rewarded with a royal pension and appointment as Poet Laureate. The songs and poems in the masques, together with the collected verse of **Epigrams** and **The Forest** (both 1616) and **Underwoods** (1640), explain his contemporary influence among younger poets, the self-styled 'tribe' or 'sons' of Ben. His prose style, founded like his poems on classical precedent, is memorably sketched in the published notes of **William Drummond of Hawthornden** (1632), which record conversations held during Jonson's visit to Scotland in 1618–19, and in the posthumously published **Timber** (1640).

Jonson's profound knowledge of London life was aptly rewarded by his appointment as City Chronologer in 1628, the year in which he suffered a severe stroke. Many of the friends who remained loyal to him in his last years attended his funeral in Westminster Abbey and contributed to the collection of memorial elegies, *Jonsonus Virbius* (1638). One of them, the forgotten Jack Young, inscribed the words 'O rare Ben Jonson' on his gravestone.

**Jorrocks's Jaunts and Jollities** A collection of 10 stories by **R. S. Surtees**, drawn from the pages of the *New Sporting Magazine* and published in book form, with illustrations by Phiz (**Hablot K. Browne**), in 1838. Other editions, illustrated by Henry Alken, appeared in 1843 and 1869; the latter included three extra episodes. The stories cover the adventures of John Jorrocks, the sporting London grocer, in the hunting field – also racing, shooting, fishing, eating, drinking and driving – and there is a fantastic jaunt to France. Surtees's friend and rival **C. J. Apperley** is lampooned in one story (as he is in the later novel, **Handley Cross**). The stories are full of humour and crude life. Besides Jorrocks, we meet his marvellously vulgar wife, his young Yorkshire friend Charlie Stubbs (modelled on Surtees himself) and his scapegrace servant Binjimin.

**Joseph Andrews** A novel by **Henry Fielding**, first published in 1742 with the full title *The History of the Adventures of Joseph Andrews, and of his Friend Mr Abraham Adams. Written in Imitation of Cervantes, Author of Don Quixote.*

The hero of the book is the brother of Pamela Andrews, the heroine of **Samuel Richardson**'s **Pamela**, and is a footman in the London household of Lady Booby, a lascivious lady who (along with her unprepossessing companion Mrs Slipslop) has designs upon his chastity. Joseph resists these enticements and resolves to take to the road and return to his sweetheart, Fanny. He is accompanied by Parson Adams, a comically absent-minded and gullible curate from the vicinity of Sir Thomas Booby's country seat, who is intent on getting his sermons published; the two central figures meet up in an inn, following the innocent Joseph's drubbing by robbers. Adams is returning to the country, having forgotten to bring the sermons in question.

The adventures and misfortunes of this pair are characterized by near-scrapes, embarrassments and exploitation; life on the road subjects them to a rich cast of hypocritical and dishonest figures, clergy, squirearchy and criminals alike. True to comic convention, the main characters all converge for a final show-down at the Boobys' country seat, through a series of humorous coincidences. Squire Booby has meanwhile married Pamela (Joseph's sister) and the novel ends by revealing that Joseph is in fact the son of a respectable couple, and not Pamela's brother.

*Joseph Andrews* is often considered the author's happiest work. Initially a lampoon on Richardson's over-virtuous characters, it rapidly develops an original shape of its own, and extends the range of the novel form by its refusal to depend on exclusive and extensive identification with the sensibility of any central character. Fielding widens the social forms of the novel, setting his characters at large in the 'theatre of the road', the action of the novel more public and more dramatic than ever before. In his 'Preface to the Reader', the author claims to be 'the founder of a new province of writing', but the achievement is in large part a synthesis, a timely conflation of earlier forms of literary narrative with contemporary realism and a trenchant eye for telling detail. Such influences include the classical epic (and its mock-heroic application in certain episodes), the biblical epic (which echoes through the moralistic themes of the book), the questing features of medieval romances (also reflected in the names of certain characters) and, perhaps most importantly, the influence of the **picaresque** tradition of Cervantes and Lesage. Despite this interweaving, the novel is an early masterpiece of the genre – comic in its characterization, yet seriously enquiring in its vignettes of contemporary behaviour.

**Journal of a Tour to the Hebrides with Samuel Johnson, The** A narrative by **James Boswell**, published in 1785, describing the journey he had undertaken with his friend in 1773. In *A Journey to the Western Islands of Scotland* **Johnson** himself gave a formal account of their itinerary, using its main stages as an opportunity to reflect on life and manners. Boswell, by contrast, writes informally about the discomforts, hazards and passing incidents of the journey, and concentrates in particular on bringing the character of his travelling companion vividly to life.

The original manuscript, which was seen by Johnson and prepared for publication by Boswell with the help of **Edmond Malone**, was edited by Frederick A. Pottle and C. H. Bennett and published in 1936. This edition restored a previously unpublished third of Boswell's original.

*Journal of a Voyage to Lisbon, The* See **Fielding, Henry**.

*Journal of the Plague Year, A* An imaginatively reworked account, part fact and part fiction, of the outbreak of the Great Plague in 1664–5, written by **Daniel Defoe** and published in 1722. The eyewitness who purports to be the author of this document, 'H.F.', is a saddler in Whitechapel, who remains in London throughout this public disaster and provides a graphic commentary on the rise of the epidemic, the reactions of the populace, the precautions taken by the authorities and the drastically changing atmosphere in the capital as it gradually becomes depopulated. The infected are imprisoned in their houses, other terrified citizens flock out to the country, and grass grows in the streets.

For this, his most realistic and evocative work, Defoe probably had to invent relatively little; he skilfully weaves together diverse source material, including Plague Bills of mortality, statistics, written historical accounts, anecdotes and hearsay. He had an uncle, Henry Foe, who was himself a saddler in St Botolph's at the time of the plague. The work was prompted by a recent outbreak of plague in Marseilles, and part of its intention is to provide a warning for the future. Defoe's representation of human behaviour under such pressure is critical, as he notes their various reactions to rumour and panic, the indifference and inefficiency of certain authorities, the attitudes of the court and the church, the self-interest of some citizens and the stupidity of others. The narrative is full of highly concentrated effects, vignettes of lively human activity, and is written with Defoe's finest colloquial energy. It is both a study in human isolation and a life-affirming work that considers the life of a city under threat, its character altered by the cessation of trade and business. To many it is Defoe's most attractive book. **Sir Walter Scott** wrote, in 1834, 'Had he not been the author of *Robinson Crusoe*, De Foe would have deserved immortality for the genius he has displayed in this work.'

*Journal to Stella* A collection of private letters sent by **Jonathan Swift** from London between September 1710 and June 1713 to his close friend Esther Johnson and her companion Rebecca Dingley, back in Dublin. Swift was in London on an official commission to plead a case for the Irish clergy, and these letters provide in the first instance an intriguing inside view of the teeming metropolitan world of political intrigue, party wrangling, gossip and literary chitchat. Already a man of some reputation, Swift had many powerful acquaintances, and the early letters show him eagerly involved in such business, but gradually he becomes anxious and disillusioned, longing for the quieter and more civilized company in Ireland, as his health deteriorates and his affections begin to become complicated. 'Stella' was his later nickname for Esther Johnson (though not at this period), to whom he had acted as tutor while they were both living in the household of **Sir William Temple** at Moor Park. Swift formed a lifelong attachment of an enigmatic nature with her, but was careful never to address himself to her alone. The letters are written partly in a teasing form of baby-talk (the 'little language') which shows the formidable satirist's softer side; though they were never designed for publication, a selection appeared in 1766, and an edition was prepared by his cousin, Deane Swift, in 1768.

*Journey to the Western Islands of Scotland, A* **Samuel Johnson**'s description, published in 1775, of the three-month tour he made in 1773 with **James Boswell**.

After welcoming him at Edinburgh, Boswell took his friend north to St Andrews and Aberdeen, where Johnson was given the freedom of the city. They paid a visit to Lord Monboddo, the eccentric law lord, and then travelled west to Inverness. From here they went on horseback to Glenelg and took a boat to Skye, where they visited Flora MacDonald. They set out for Mull but a storm drove them to the island of Coll, where they were obliged to stay for two weeks. After Mull, their journey took them to Iona and thence to Oban. At Inverary they were guests of the Duke of Argyll, who provided them with good horses and made their journey much easier. At Glasgow University the faculty entertained Johnson, and at the family seat Boswell's father, Lord Auchinleck, clashed with his famous guest. (Boswell later declined to record the details of the quarrel.) Johnson left for London from Edinburgh.

Where Boswell's account of the tour, *The Journal of a Tour to the Hebrides with Samuel Johnson*, is casual and anecdotal, Johnson offers a formal survey. He went to Scotland not to see 'fine places, of which there were enough in England; but wild objects, – mountains, – peculiar manners; in short, things which he had not seen before'. His interest lay in exploring the variety and extent of nature, particularly of human nature. His aim was to record local differences in a scientific spirit and universal truths in a philosophical one. Apart from being more sympathetic to Scotland than the popular legend of Johnson's opinions on the subject would admit, the book is one of the finest achievements of 18th-century travel literature.

**Journey's End** A play by **R. C. Sherriff**, first performed in London in 1928. It is perhaps the best-known play about World War I. Set in a dugout in the British trenches in 1918, it is a powerful study of bravery and cowardice under fire. The part of Stanhope, a brave man broken by battle fatigue and threatened by the hero-worship of Raleigh, a new arrival who had been a junior at the public school of which Stanhope had been a star pupil, was created by the unknown Laurence Olivier.

**Jowett, Benjamin** 1817–93 Scholar and divine. Educated at St Paul's School and Balliol College, Oxford, Jowett became a fellow of his college in 1838, Regius Professor of Greek in 1855 and Master of Balliol in 1870.

The influence of Greek studies and his interest in German philosophy made Jowett a theological liberal, and his *Epistles of Paul to the Thessalonians, Galatians and Romans* (1835, revised 1855 and 1859) was notable for its fresh and original approach. 'The Interpretation of Scripture', Jowett's contribution to *Essays and Reviews* (1860), caused angry debate and cast grave suspicion on his orthodoxy. In the field of classical studies his translation of Plato (1871) became a standard work; his Thucydides followed in 1881 and the *Politics* of Aristotle in 1885.

At Balliol, Jowett taught **Walter Pater** and took a sympathetic interest in the wayward undergraduate career of **Swinburne**. His presence was influential in making **Robert Browning** decide that certain of his manuscripts should be donated to the college.

**Joyce, James (Augustine Aloysius)** 1882–1941 Irish novelist, short-story writer and poet. Joyce was born in Dublin and educated at Jesuit schools (Clongowes Wood College, Kildare; Belvedere College, Dublin) and University College, Dublin, where he studied modern languages. He graduated in 1902.

His first published piece was an essay on Ibsen ('Ibsen's New Drama') written as an undergraduate and published in *The Fortnightly Review* in 1900. He cultivated the acquaintance of (among others) **Yeats**, **Synge**, **Lady Gregory** and **George Russell** ('A.E.') who were fostering the Irish cultural renaissance, but in 1902, dissatisfied with the narrowness of Irish life, he spent a year in Paris. Though he lived in poverty, he read widely – notably Dujardin's experimental

novel *Les Lauriers sont coupés* (1888), upon which he later modelled his own **stream-of-consciousness** technique.

He returned to Dublin on his mother's death in 1903, and during the following year he met Nora Barnacle, whom he lived with for the whole of his life and eventually married in 1931. In the same year he began working on a long autobiographical novel, *Stephen Hero* (later reworked as *A Portrait of the Artist as a Young Man*, 1916), and he and Nora moved to Zurich. However, Joyce failed to obtain work there and they soon moved to Trieste, where he was employed at the Berlitz school in 1905.

*Chamber Music* (1907), a volume of poetry, was published in London but made no money. This was followed by *Dubliners* (1914), a collection of technically conventional but delightfully evocative stories based around his native city. After a dispute with the Irish publishers over

James Joyce, aged 22. Photographed by his friend, Constantine P. Curram, 1904.

several references to the British royal family, Joyce withdrew the book and it was published in London. **Ezra Pound** reviewed it enthusiastically in *The Egoist*; he also read parts of the autobiographical novel and arranged for its publication in serial form: *A Portrait of the Artist as a Young Man* appeared in *The Egoist* in 25 instalments from February 1914 to September 1915. The complete volume was published the following year.

Joyce was obliged to leave Trieste during World War I and he moved back to Zurich. With the support of Yeats and Pound, he received a grant from the Royal Literary Fund and a Civil List grant (1916) while working on his next novel, *Ulysses* (1922). Like his earlier book, it too began publication in serial form (in *The Little Review*, New York), appearing between April 1918 and December 1920, when the periodical was prosecuted for publishing obscene matter. *Exiles* (1918), a play in three acts, was unsuccessfully performed in Munich in 1919, but had to wait until 1926 for its first London performance, by the Stage Society. *Ulysses* was finally published in Paris (2 February 1922) where Joyce, Nora, and their two children had finally settled in 1920. Harriet Shaw Weaver (co-editor of *The Egoist* until its demise in 1919), a lifelong friend and benefactress, arranged for the novel's importation and sale in England. Copies were seized by the Customs and those which reached New York were burned by the United States postal authorities. The first English edition appeared in 1936.

In 1923 Joyce began the composition of *Finnegans Wake* which was published as *Work in Progress* in 12 parts between 1928 and 1937. It was published complete in 1939. *Poems Penyeach*, a small collection of new poems, appeared in 1927.

Joyce suffered from a lifelong eye complaint, provoked by an attack of rheumatic fever during his twenties and complicated by glaucoma in 1917. Despite several operations his sight steadily grew worse. Then in 1932 his daughter Lucia was diagnosed as schizophrenic and his general health began to deteriorate. With the outbreak of World War II the family returned to Switzerland, where Joyce died after an operation on a duodenal ulcer on 13 January 1941.

*Ulysses* and *Finnegans Wake* were viewed by many writers and critics as modern masterpieces (most notably by **T. S. Eliot**, Pound, Yeats, **Hemingway** and **Arnold Bennett**), though others (including **Virginia Woolf**, **Gertrude Stein** and the critic **Walter Allen**) showed far less enthusiasm. Joyce's influence on the development of **modernism** (especially stream of consciousness) is undisputed, however, and his work has attracted an immense amount of critical exegesis.

***Jude the Obscure*** A novel by **Thomas Hardy**, published in its complete form in October 1895. An abridged version appeared in *Harper's New Monthly Magazine* (December 1894 to November 1895).

Jude Fawley, a stonemason with a talent and passion for scholarship, is trapped into marriage by Arabella Donn. Unable to cope with his miserable situation, it is only after he is deserted by Arabella that Jude, resurrecting his old love of learning, makes his way to Christminster (which represents Oxford) where he earns his living as a labourer while aspiring to be a student.

Jude meets and is attracted to his cousin Sue Bridehead who, though intelligent and well read, is emotionally immature. She marries Phillotson, Jude's former schoolmaster, but, finding the sexual aspects of her marriage repellent, she flees her husband and lives with Jude, though their union is not consummated for some time. Although free to do so, Sue refuses to marry Jude, succumbing to a sense of atavistic guilt and fatalism. Two children are born to them, and Jude's son by Arabella, the uncannily adult 'Father Time', also lives with them. But, as social outcasts living in abject poverty, both Jude and Sue are bitterly unhappy and while she retreats into a morbid Christianity, Jude moves toward atheism. When Sue tells 'Father Time' that she is expecting another baby he kills the two children and himself, 'because we are too menny'. In a misguided attempt at expiation Sue returns to Phillotson. Jude declines, resentfully cared for by Arabella, and eventually dies alone, neglected both by her and the city of learning which had once epitomized the scope of his ambition.

Many contemporary readers and reviewers were outraged by what they perceived as the indecency of Hardy's novel of the 'deadly war waged between flesh and spirit', and Hardy wrote no more fiction.

***Judith*** An Old English poem preserved in the same manuscript as ***Beowulf***. It is incomplete, but it is not certain how much has been lost; the remaining fragment is 350 lines long. The poem, based on the biblical narrative, tells the story of Judith's execution of Holofernes and her flight, and the Hebrew defeat of the Assyrians. It does not follow its source closely but adapts it into a compelling narrative, most notably in the description of the battle with its references to the attendant carrion-eaters. It is an accomplished poem, with some dramatic speeches and skilful handling of the action.

***Julian and Maddalo, A Conversation*** A poem by **Percy Bysshe Shelley**, written during his visit to Venice in 1818 but not published until 1824. The conversation, presented as a dialogue in couplets, is between Shelley (Julian) and **Byron** (Maddalo). Wandering through Venice and its environs (a scene which gives Shelley opportunity to introduce some highly effective descriptive passages), the two poets discuss concepts of religion, progress and freedom. They visit an incarcerated maniac whose bitter and profound effusions become in some sense the summary of their debate. Through the intervention of a child, innocence and virtue are proposed as lasting values, but the poem retains its presiding cynicism.

**Julian of Norwich** 1342–after 1429 Mystic. Little is known about her life besides the information she gives in her single work, *A Revelation of Divine Love*. Early in life, she says, she prayed for a serious illness which she felt would benefit her spiritually. In May 1373, at the age of 30 and a half, she lay ill for three days and experienced 16 revelations of various content. She contemplated them for 15 years until it was revealed to her that her experience had been a token and manifestation of Christ's love. They were recorded some time after this final revelation by a scribe, Julian herself being illiterate. By 1394 she had become a recluse, living as an anchorite attached to St Julian's Conesford in Norwich. She was visited there by **Margery Kempe** in about 1413, a record of the visit appearing in *The Book of Margery Kempe*.

*Juliana* A short poem in Old English by **Cynewulf**, preserved (except for a few missing pages) in the **Exeter Book**. Its subject is the martyrdom of Juliana, a Christian virgin persecuted in AD 303. She is tortured and imprisoned after refusing marriage and paganism. A devil disguised as an angel visits her in prison, but she realizes his true identity and forces him to tell her of the devil's evil works. The first attempts to martyr her fail, and her executioners are converted and also martyred. The poem follows its Latin source closely.

*Julius Caesar* A tragedy by **William Shakespeare**, first performed in 1599 and published in the First Folio of 1623. For the story and much of the language, Shakespeare relied on **Sir Thomas North**'s translation of Plutarch.

Having defeated Pompey, Julius Caesar represents, for the majority of the Roman people, the promise of a new prosperity. But he is mistrusted by Pompey's former supporters and by a group of variously motivated patricians, who share a belief that he wishes to be crowned and a fear of the consequences if he is. The leader of the disaffected patricians is Cassius, a shrewd politician who knows how much would be gained if Brutus, the most respected of republicans, can be persuaded to join the conspiracy. There is enough evidence in Caesar's behaviour of an ambition to be crowned to tilt Brutus's judgement in Cassius's favour.

Ignoring the warning of a soothsayer, Caesar decides to go to the Capitol, and is there assassinated by the conspirators. Mark Antony, as clever as Cassius, is allowed by Brutus to address the crowd in the Forum after Brutus has explained to them the reasons for Caesar's murder. His skilful rhetoric turns the people against the conspirators, and civil war is again inevitable. Brutus and Cassius flee the city and gather their forces, while Antony, Lepidus and Caesar's great-nephew Octavius form a triumvirate, organize a brutal proscription and prepare for war.

After quarrelling with Brutus, Cassius learns that Brutus's wife, Portia, has committed suicide. Partly out of remorse, he accepts Brutus's decision to march on Philippi and confront Antony's army, though he does not agree with it. The battle is lost, and Brutus and Cassius kill themselves. The play ends with Octavius's ominously ambiguous proposal that he and Antony should 'part the glories of this happy day'.

The unusual structure of the play has been often observed. To some it has seemed like two tragedies in one, first Caesar's and then Brutus's; but it is equally possible to see it as a sophisticated **revenge tragedy**, in which Antony takes on the role of Caesar's avenger, and the second half of the play completes the true tragedy of Julius Caesar. For Shakespeare, the shift from English history in the recently completed *Henry V* to Roman history released a new confidence.

*Jungle, The* A novel by **Upton Sinclair**, published serially in the socialist weekly *Appeal to Reason* in 1905, and in book form in 1906. It portrays the appalling labour and sanitary conditions in the Chicago stockyards and slums, as seen through the eyes of Jurgis Rudkus, a young Lithuanian immigrant. Sinclair chronicles the exploitation and victimization of Jurgis and his family, who live and work in Packington, the stockyard district. Jurgis experiences successive changes of fortune and employment. He works in the fertilizer plant after being injured in the slaughterhouse, and serves time in gaol for attacking a foreman who has taken advantage of his wife, Ona. The Rudkus family is plagued by ill fortune and sickness, culminating in the deaths of Ona and both the children.

After his incarceration, Jurgis is blacklisted in Packington; finds work in a harvester plant and then in the steelworks; escapes from the city briefly to lead the life of a tramp in the open country; survives as a thief upon his return to Chicago; works as a scab during a meat-packers' strike; serves as the tool of a corrupt politician; then ends up back on the street, outcast and unemployable. Finally, Jurgis is introduced to socialist thought at a political meeting which he attends in order to escape the cold. The novel ends with an affirmation of the need for socialist reform by the workers of Chicago.

**Jungle Book, The** and **Second Jungle Book, The** Collections of short stories and poems by **Rudyard Kipling**, published in 1894 and 1895 respectively. The sequence of stories about the boy Mowgli, accidentally thrust out of the human community into the jungle, forms the core of these collections. His growth from jungle boyhood to dominance over the animals, and his eventual return to human service as a forest ranger, provide the basic framework. The code of conduct in the animal world is severe and requires a high level of responsibility; this is demonstrated in 'Letting in the Jungle', where retribution is brought on the village which sought to destroy Mowgli. In comparison with the jungle law and the stoic social duty of the animals, humanity is unruly and undignified.

Mowgli's discovery of his inner nature takes the *Jungle Books* close to the conventions of the **Bildungsroman**. There are strong elements of myth, too, in the recurring *leitmotif* of a fallen Eden: Mowgli is effectively shut out from his boyhood paradise when the blood-tie with humanity reclaims him. The theme of a divided emotional and cultural allegiance is present in the stories outside the Mowgli group, notably in 'The Miracle of Purun Bhagat', about a man who has to adjust from Western codes of conduct to the life of the Hindu holy man.

**Junius** The pseudonym adopted by the author of a series of letters which appeared in *The Public Advertiser* between 1769 and 1771, making unsparing attacks on public figures from a Whig viewpoint. The letters are shrewd and well judged when the writer turns to political argument. The Duke of Grafton, Lord North, Lord Mansfield and George III were all targets; Junius entered the lists on behalf of **John Wilkes** and later attacked the Earl of Chatham and Barrington, the War Secretary. The identity of Junius has never been discovered, though **Sir Philip Francis** has for long been a favourite candidate. An edition of the letters was published by Henry Sampson Woodfall, editor of *The Public Advertiser*, in 1772.

**Junius, Francis (or François Dujon)** 1589–1677 Philologist. Junius was born in Heidelberg and became librarian to Thomas Howard, 2nd Earl of Arundel. He was also tutor to Howard's son and became a friend of **John Milton**. He collected Anglo-Saxon manuscripts, which he later presented to the Bodleian Library in Oxford. He published *De Pictura Veterum* (1637) and an edition of **Caedmon** (Amsterdam, 1655),

and wrote an *Etymologicum Anglicanum* (first printed in 1743), which was much used by **Samuel Johnson** while preparing his dictionary. Junius also gave his philological collections to the Bodleian and helped the Oxford University Press with the printing of Gothic, Anglo-Saxon and Runic material.

The Junius Manuscript contains scriptural poems in Old English that Junius believed to be the work of Caedmon. See **Genesis**, **Exodus**, **Daniel**, and **Christ and Satan**.

**Juno and the Paycock** A play by **Sean O'Casey**, first performed at the **Abbey Theatre** in 1924, when its topicality – it is set in Dublin at the height of the civil war of 1922 – added to its controversial popularity.

The play centres on the Boyle family, inhabitants of a Dublin tenement. Jack Boyle, known as 'Captain' because he was once at sea, is an idler who leaves the care of home and family to his wife Juno. Their daughter Mary is intelligent, their son Johnny a maimed and neurotic victim of Irish violence. When Jack Boyle learns that he has inherited a large sum of money, he borrows money from friends and neighbours and spends it in loquacious drinking bouts with his equally incorrigible crony, Joxer Daly. But that would be his way of life whatever his circumstances. He remains comically and horrifyingly unaffected by the domestic tragedies that surround him. Mary, courted by the attractive Charles Bentham, rejects Jerry Devine, a leader of the local labour movement. But Bentham is after Mary's money and, having seduced and impregnated her, leaves her when it is discovered that Boyle will, after all, inherit nothing. Even the faithful Jerry abandons her

O'Casey's *Juno and the Paycock* at the Royalty Theatre, London, in 1925 when the Abbey Theatre's production was first seen outside Ireland. Sidney Morgan as Joxer, seated, Arthur Sinclair as Boyle, standing.

when he discovers that she is pregnant. Johnny, having suffered nightmares, is finally revealed as the informer whose betrayal led to the death in an ambush of his neighbour, Robbie Tancred. He is taken off to be executed by the Republican Army. Only now does Juno abandon her feckless husband, who is still talking with Joxer in the empty flat when the play ends.

*Jurgen: A Comedy of Justice* A romance by **James Branch Cabell** published in 1919, part of his 18-volume 'Biography of the Life of Manuel'. It was suppressed on grounds of obscenity from 1920 to 1922. Like others in the cycle, it is set in the mythical kingdom of Poictesme. The pawnbroker Jurgen is married to the voluble Dame Lisa. He says some sympathetic things about the Devil, who overhears him and rewards him by making Lisa disappear into a dark cave. Feeling obliged to seek his wife, Jurgen also enters the cave and has several adventures – some of them amatory – with various mythical figures. He encounters the Centaur Nessus, Guenevere, Thragnar, Merlin, Dame Anaïtis (The Lady of the Lake), Queen Helen and others. He lives for a while in Hell, where he encounters Grand-father Satan. He then goes to Heaven, where he assumes the identity of Pope John XX. Finally he meets Koshchei, a powerful being who tempts him with beautiful women. After Jurgen has rejected them all, Lisa is returned to him and they resume their normal life. His adventures take exactly a year, extending from one Walpurgis Night to the next.

*Just So Stories* A collection of 12 stories and 12 poems by **Rudyard Kipling**, published in 1902.

This is the only book for which Kipling supplied his own illustrations. It was written to be read aloud by adults to children. The interplay between the human and the animal worlds in the first seven stories is a simpler and more playful device than in the earlier *Jungle Book*. The language made 'appropriate' for the animals veers between the childlike and the (usually pompous) diction of a grown-up world. The element of teasing is most obviously apparent in such stories as 'How the Leopard Got Its Spots', where Kipling travesties the Darwinian notion of evolutionary progression; the humour can satisfy both children and adults.

# K

**kailyard school** The name for a group of Scottish writers who flourished during the last decade of the 19th century. 'Kailyard' means 'cabbage patch' and was used by Ian Maclaren (born John Watson, 1850–1907) as the motto for his collection of stories, *Beside the Bonnie Briar Bush* (1894). Apart from Maclaren, the group included **J. M. Barrie** and S. R. Crockett (1860–1914), author of *The Stickit Minister* (1893). Their books about humble, homespun topics, often written in the vernacular, promoted a sentimental image of small-town life in Scotland and were, briefly, extremely popular.

*Kangaroo* A novel by **D. H. Lawrence**, published in 1923.

It is set in Australia, where Lawrence and his wife, Frieda, had spent four months in 1922. The central characters are Richard Lovat Somers, a writer, and his wife, Harriet. Jack Calcott, a neighbour, introduces Somers to Benjamin Cooley (nicknamed 'Kangaroo'), a Jewish barrister and leader of a radical political party. Cooley tries unsuccessfully to enlist Somers's support for his programme, a combination of fascism and Lawrentian 'blood consciousness'. After a political meeting in Canberra Hall has been violently disrupted, the Somerses leave for America. The novel includes a vivid chapter, 'The Nightmare', which details Lawrence's experiences in and reactions to World War I.

The novel is principally a vehicle for Lawrence's own passionate observations about politics and life in the post-World War I years, particularly in Australia, though it also contains several memorable descriptions of the landscape. Like his novelette *St Mawr* (1925), it reflects his view of England as a country which has suffered a 'genuine debasement' and is heading for cultural and political bankruptcy.

**Kavanagh, Julia** 1824–77. Novelist. Born in Thurles, County Tipperary, and educated at home. Much of her early life was spent in France, which provided the setting for many of her novels. She earned her living at literary work by snatching spare hours from the task of caring for an invalid mother. Her works include *Madeleine* (1848), *Nathalie* (1850), *Daisy Burns* (1853), *Adèle* (1858), *Bessie* (1872) and *Woman in France in the Eighteenth Century* (1850).

**Kavanagh, Patrick (Joseph)** 1904–67 Irish poet. The son of a small farmer and village shoemaker, Kavanagh was born at Mucker near Inniskeen, County Monaghan. He had little formal education and followed his father into peasant farming, but an interest in poetry led him to write and study privately and in 1928 his poems began to appear in Dublin newspapers. *Ploughman and Other Poems*, his first book, appeared in 1936. His early life formed the basis for an autobiography (*The Green Fool*, 1938) and is analysed more cynically in his novel *Tarry Flynn* (1948). In 1937 he left his farm, and thereafter worked as a freelance writer in Dublin, where he became a controversial figure, admired for his poetry but often disliked for his scathing criticism of the city's literary society. Kavanagh resented what he saw as **Yeats**'s romanticized view of the Irish peasantry, and his major poem, *The Great Hunger* (1942), is a grimly compassionate account of the cultural and emotional poverty of Irish rural life, written in partially rhymed free verse influenced by the early **Eliot**. A costly and unsuccessful libel action against a Dublin magazine and a period of serious illness damaged Kavanagh's later work but in 1955, after major surgery for lung cancer, he experienced a renewal of poetic power, shown in *Come Dance with Kitty Stobling* (1960). An incomplete *Collected Poems* appeared in 1964 and the *Complete Poems* in 1972. Kavanagh is now generally recognized as the major Irish poet of the mid 20th century. His realistic treatment of rural life and his confidence (expressed in a sonnet entitled, with characteristic irony, 'Epic') that the 'parochial' or local subject need not entail a narrowly 'provincial' treatment, exerted an important influence on the early work of **R. S. Thomas** and on subsequent Irish Poets, notably **Seamus Heaney**, who introduced Kavanagh as a character in his long poem *Station Island*.

**Kavanagh, P[atrick] J[oseph] (Gregory)** 1931– Poet. Born in Worthing, Sussex, he was educated at schools in North Wales and Switzerland, and after drama school in Paris and national service, at Merton College, Oxford. Subsequently he has worked for the BBC and the British Council, as an actor, and since 1970 as a full-time writer. Formally traditional and influenced by **Wordsworth**, **Yeats** and **Edward Thomas**, Kavanagh's poems are preoccupied with the pains and joys of life, the hope given by love, and death – particularly the death of his wife, which is the informing event behind his fascinating autobiography, *The Perfect Stranger* (1966). His collections include *One and One* (1959), *On the Way to the Depot* (1966), *About Time* (1970), *Edward Thomas in Heaven* (1974) and *Life Before Death* (1979), and are well represented in *Selected Poems* (1982) and *Presences: New and Selected Poems* (1987). Abandoning debilitating irony, his poems are vulnerable and restrained, and have not received the attention they deserve. His novels include *A Song and Dance* (1968) and *A Happy Man* (1973).

**Kaye-Smith, Sheila** 1887–1956 Novelist. Born in Sussex and educated privately, she became a Roman Catholic in 1929. Her first novel, *The Tramping Methodist* (1908), started a series of rural novels focusing on a Sussex family, the Alards; the best known are *Sussex Gorse* (1916), *Tamarisk Town* (1919), *Green Apple Harvest* (1920), *Joanna Godden* (1921) and *The End of the House of Alard* (1923). *The History of Susan Spray* (1931), *Ember Lane* (1940) and *Mrs Gailey* (1951) are among her later novels. *Three Ways Home* (1937) is an autobiography.

**Keary, Annie** 1825–79 Novelist. She wrote two notable books for children, *The Heroes of Asgard* (with her sister Eliza Keary, 1857) and *Sidney Grey* (1857). Her novels for adults include *Oldbury* (1869), *Castle Daly* (1875) and *A Doubting Heart* (1879), which was unfinished at her death.

**Keats, John** 1795–1821 Poet. Keats was born at Moorfields, London, where his father was the manager of the large livery stables belonging to his father-in-law. He was the oldest of four children who remained deeply devoted and intensely loyal to each other: George was born in 1797, Tom in 1799, and Frances (Fanny) in 1803. After their father's death in 1804 their mother remarried, but was soon separated from her second husband and went with the children to live with her mother at Edmonton, where she died of tuberculosis in 1810. From the ages of 10 to 14 John divided his time between his grandmother's home and Clarke's School at Enfield. Here he was noted more for his love of cricket and boxing than for any studiousness until his final two years, when he began to read voraciously, particularly books on Greek myth-

John Keats. The charcoal drawing by the poet's friend Joseph Severn, who was with Keats during his last hours. Victoria & Albert Museum, London.

ology, and started a translation of Virgil's *Aeneid*. At the end of 1810 he was taken out of school and apprenticed to a surgeon-apothecary at Enfield, but continued to visit the school to pursue his friendship with **Charles Cowden Clarke**, the headmaster's son, and some years his senior, who encouraged his interest in literature. His ambition to become a poet was fired by his first acquaintance with **Spenser**'s *Faerie Queene* which, according to Clarke, 'he ramped through . . . like a young horse turned into a Spring meadow'. His first poem, *Lines in Imitation of Spenser*, was written in 1814, but was not immediately followed by work of the same high promise. In 1814 he quarrelled with his master, Hammond, and went to live on his own in London, resuming his surgical studies in 1815 as a student at Guy's hospital. To this year belong the odes 'To Hope', 'To Apollo', the 'Sonnet Written on the Day after Mr Leigh Hunt Left Prison', and three sonnets on Woman. In the autumn of the same year he began to read **Wordsworth**, whose new influence is discernible in the sonnet 'O Solitude', and with whom he, in common with other second-generation Romantic poets, developed a literary love–hate relationship. In 1816 he became a Licentiate of the Society of Apothecaries but had, by the end of the year, effectively abandoned all thought of pursuing his profession, despite precarious financial circumstances. 'O Solitude' appeared in the May number of the liberal journal, *The Examiner*, and through Cowden Clarke he met its editor, **Leigh Hunt**, who instantly took him under his wing and helped to broaden his literary acquaintance. New friends included **John Hamilton Reynolds** and the painter **Benjamin Haydon**, to whom he addressed the sonnet 'Great Spirits Now on Earth Are Sojourning'. He also met **Shelley**, from whom he was, however, always careful to preserve a certain distance, sensing in the slightly older poet's dominating personality a potential threat to his own 'unfettered scope'. In the 'Young Poets' issue of *The Examiner* in November 1816 Hunt hailed Keats, Shelley and Reynolds as the most promising writers of their generation, and printed Keats's sonnet 'On First Looking into Chapman's Homer'. To 1816 belong also the important poems 'I Stood Tiptoe upon a Little Hill' and 'Sleep and Poetry' which appeared, together with sonnets, rhymed epistles and miscellaneous poems, in his first volume of poetry, *Poems*, published in March 1817. Sales of the book were poor and, apart from some flattering reviews by friends, its appearance passed unnoticed, though, ominously for Keats, his name was linked with that of Hunt as a member of the '**Cockney School**' in the autumn number of *Blackwood's Magazine*.

Keats was a good deal out of London in 1817, spending the spring at Shanklin, on the Isle of Wight, and Margate, where he was joined by his brother Tom. In the summer he joined his friend Bailey at Oxford. It was at about this time that he first began to use his letters to his brothers, sister and friends as the vehicle of his most considered thoughts on poetry, love, philosophy, his own personality and the people and events surrounding him. Vivid, witty and revealing, they were published in 1848 and 1878, and have come to be almost as highly regarded as his poetry, to which many of them supply valuable commentaries. The year also brought new acquaintances such as **Charles Wentworth Dilke** and Charles Armitage Brown, who were his neighbours at Hampstead, and saw the completion, in November, of *Endymion*, his most ambitious poetic project to date, and supposedly undertaken in friendly rivalry with Shelley, who was writing his *Laon and Cythna* (later called *The Revolt of Islam*) at the same time. During the winter of 1817–18 he was frequently in the society of his friends, and towards Christmas briefly stood in for Reynolds as theatrical critic for *The Champion*, producing a fascinating article on the Shakespearean actor Kean. At some point in December he read passages of *Endymion* to Wordsworth, who frostily complimented him on 'a pretty piece of paganism'. With **Charles Lamb** and Wordsworth he was present at Haydon's 'immortal dinner' on 28 December, and regularly attended **Hazlitt**'s lectures on English poetry, which greatly helped him to shape his own ideas on poetry and on the poet as an individual of

'**negative capability**'. Much of his most interesting thinking is contained in his correspondence with Reynolds, with whom he also planned a volume of verse tales drawn from Boccaccio, to which his *Isabella, or, the Pot of Basil*, a work which marks a great advance in his poetic technique, was written as a contribution. Tom Keats was now seriously ill with tuberculosis, and he was devoting much of his time to nursing him, first at Teignmouth and then in London. *Endymion*, which he dedicated to **Chatterton**, was published in the spring of 1818. In June his brother George, one of his closest confidants, married and emigrated to America. Accompanied by Brown, he spent the summer touring the Lakes, Scotland and Northern Ireland. His impressions of the scenery, which was of a kind entirely new to him, are reflected in passages of *Hyperion*. The fatigue and exposure of West Highland travel, however, brought on a throat infection from which he was never afterwards free. Returning to London, he spent the next three months attending Tom. To the pains of the permanent departure of one brother, and the imminent death of another, were added the withering attacks on *Endymion* and his earlier poems in the autumn numbers of *Blackwood's*, and *The Quarterly Review*. Deeply wounded, he thought of giving up poetry, but rallied himself to write to George that, despite the reviews, 'I think I shall be among the English poets after my death', and began work on *Hyperion*. After Tom's death in December he moved to Brown's house at Hampstead, which was close to the home of Fanny Brawne, with whom he fell deeply and jealously in love. It was a relationship that seems to have brought him little real happiness, and was undoubtedly complicated by his lack of means to support a wife and, above all, by the morbid turn given to his thoughts by the development of his illness.

Keats's astonishing poetic development and productivity during the next year is comparable to Shelley's in Italy over roughly the same time-span. In the winter of 1818–19 he worked mainly on *Hyperion*. *The Eve of St Agnes* and the fragmentary *Eve of St Mark* were composed during a visit to Dilke's parents and relatives in Sussex at the end of January. Returning to Hampstead in early February, he idled for a while and then, between March and May, wrote several of the reflective odes which have done more than anything else to secure him his place among the English poets: the odes 'On Indolence', 'On a Grecian Urn', 'To Psyche', 'To a Nightingale' and 'On Melancholy'. The enigmatic ballad *La Belle Dame Sans Merci* was copied for dispatch to George in April. Other poems of the spring are the sonnets on 'Fame', and 'Why Did I Laugh Tonight'. In the second half of 1819 he wrote (with Charles Brown) the tragedy *Otho the Great*, began another play on the subject of King Stephen, and finished *Lamia*, which was followed by the beautiful 'Ode to Autumn' and the second version of *Hyperion*, called *The Fall of Hyperion*. It was, however, also a year of unhappy love and increasing financial difficulties, his slender private means now exhausted, and the existence of a legacy from his maternal grandfather now having apparently been forgotten by both his family and his former guardian. Returning from America on a flying visit, George found him ill and dejected, 'not the same being'. He began the unfinished 'Cap and Bells', but in February 1820 he became seriously ill with tuberculosis, and, after seeing his second volume of poems through the press, was soon too weak to write. This volume was published under the title *Lamia, Isabella, The Eve of St Agnes and Other Poems* in July 1820, and included most of the great odes, *Hyperion*, *Fancy* and other works. The reviewers were this time generous in their praise, with even *Blackwood's* toning down its criticism of the poet it had so recently attempted to discredit as a mere imitator of Leigh Hunt. But this was now rather beside the point: Keats was nursed by the Hunts and then by Fanny and Mrs Brawne, but his condition gradually worsened and, in a last desperate bid for recovery, he put his affairs in order and sailed for Italy with his friend, the painter Joseph Severn, in September 1820. He declined Shelley's generous, but typically lordly, invitation to join him at Pisa, and went instead to Rome, where he died the following February.

Keats's reputation continued to grow during the 19th century, when his admirers included **Tennyson**, **Matthew Arnold** and the **Pre-Raphaelite** poets. In the 20th century he is, together with Wordsworth, perhaps the most widely read and familiar of the English Romantic poets, and some of his odes ('To Autumn', for example, or 'On a Grecian Urn') are as well-known as anything by **Shakespeare**, to whom he has, indeed, often been compared. Recent biographical studies have, in many respects, deepened the tragedy of his life by showing him to have been, while still in health, in many ways the precise opposite of the overburdened, sensitive soul of the posthumous legends.

**Keble, John** 1792–1866 Poet and clergyman. Born at Fairford in Gloucestershire, the son of a High Church clergyman, he studied at Corpus Christi College, Oxford. A brilliant scholar, Keble was elected a fellow of Oriel College at the age of 19. While acting as his father's curate at Fairford, he published *The Christian Year* (1827), a collection of poems for the Sundays and holy days of the church calendar which became perhaps the most popular religious verse of the 19th century. Its success led to his appointment as Professor of Poetry at Oxford in 1831.

A leading figure in the **Oxford Movement**, Keble contributed nine of the *Tracts for the Times*, which affirmed the principles of the Movement and gave it its early name, Tractarianism. He published an edition of the works of **Richard Hooker** (1836) and contributed a translation of St Irenaeus to the *Library of the Fathers* (posthumously published, 1872). His later sacred poetry included an English *Psalter* (1839) and *Lyra Innocentium* (1846). Keble became parish priest at Hursley, near Winchester, in 1836 and never sought preferment. Keble College, Oxford, was founded in his memory in 1870.

**Kelly, George (Edward)** 1887–1974 American playwright, born into a prominent Philadelphia family. His first successful full-length play was *The Torchbearers* (1922), a satiric account of a stagestruck woman's involvement with a 'little theatre' movement. His second play, *The Show-Off* (1924) a comedy about a braggart, was developed from his earlier one-act play *Poor Aubrey* (1922). *Craig's Wife* (1925), which won the Pulitzer Prize in 1926, is a character study of a grasping and self-centred woman that shows the influence of August Strindberg. *Daisy Mayme* (1926) and *Behold the Bridegroom* (1927) are domestic stories of rich and wilful women. Kelly's next two plays focused on conflict between generations: the unsuccessful *Maggie, the Magnificent* (1929) tells of a daughter's rebellion against her domineering mother; *Philip Goes Forth* (1931), which was better received, describes a son's conflict with his father over the choice between a theatrical career and a career in the family business. *Reflected Glory* (1936) further examines the conflict between the theatre and family responsibilities. His last two plays, *The Deep Mrs Sykes* (1945) and *The Fatal Weakness* (1946), are about suspicion and self-deception in marriage.

**Kelly, Hugh** 1739–77 Dramatist. Born in Killarney and apprenticed to a staymaker in Dublin, Kelly moved to London in 1760 and struggled for a living as a writer. He was, at various times, editor of the *Court Magazine*, *The Lady's Museum* and *The Public Ledger*, winning more enemies than friends by his time-serving support of the government against **John Wilkes**. His *Thespis* (1766), written in emulation of **Charles Churchill**'s *The Rosciad*, is a gossipy account of **Drury Lane**'s leading actors and actresses, the very people who made his reputation by their performance of his mildly satiric **sentimental comedy** *False Delicacy* (1768). *A Word to the Wise* (1770) and *The Man of Reason* (1776) were unsuccessful, and Kelly owes his brief reputation as a leading writer of comedies to *False*

*Delicacy* and his version of Molière's *The School for Wives* (1773). His own finances were not much helped by his theatrical fame and he died in poverty.

**Kemble, Fanny (Frances Anne)** 1809–93 Actress, dramatist, poet and autobiographer. Born into a distinguished theatrical family, the daughter of Charles Kemble and the niece of Sarah Siddons and John Philip Kemble, she was more ambitious to write than to act. She made her stage debut in 1829 in a bid to rescue her father from financial disaster at **Covent Garden** and succeeded in parts from **Shakespeare** and as Lady Teazle in **Sheridan's** *The School for Scandal*. She also acted in her own tragedy, *Francis I* (1832), which required the audience's indulgence as well as her father's. After an American tour (1832–3) she stayed behind in Philadelphia to marry Pierce Butler in 1834. She left him in 1845 after disagreements over slavery – she being an ardent Abolitionist and he a slave-owner – and he divorced her in 1849. After a year in Rome she reluctantly returned to the English stage, at first reduced to provincial tours but then supporting herself for many years (1848–74) by public readings from Shakespeare. Her *Poems* appeared in 1844 and her *Plays* in 1863. In retirement she supplemented her *Journal* (also called *Journal of a Residence in America*, 1835) and *Journal of a Residence on a Georgian Plantation in 1838–39* (1863) with several frank and discerning volumes of reminiscence, *Record of a Girlhood* (1878), *Records of Later Life* (1882) and *Further Records* (1890), and a novel, *Far Away and Long Ago* (1889).

**Kemble, John Mitchell** 1807–57 Philologist and historian. The son of the actor Charles Kemble and the elder brother of **Fanny Kemble**, he was born in London and educated at Trinity College, Cambridge. His interest in philology was developed by further study at Göttingen with Jakob Grimm, who became his friend. He published *The Anglo-Saxon Poems of Beowulf* (1833–7) and a scholarly work on the early history of England, *Codex Diplomaticus Aevi Saxonici* (1839–48). His *The Saxons in England* (1849) argued that England's stability in a Europe racked by disturbance was owing to the principles and institutions inherited from Teutonic invaders.

**Kemp (or Kempe), Will** c. 1560–c. 1603 Famous as a clown in the Elizabethan theatre, Kemp was a member of the Lord Chamberlain's company at the time when the decision was made to build the **Globe** on the south bank of the Thames in 1597–8. He is known to have played Peter in *Romeo and Juliet* and Dogberry in *Much Ado About Nothing*. What is not known is the reason for his decision to leave **Shakespeare** and his colleagues before they began operations at their new theatre. Whether or not it was a result of a dispute over the relative merits of plays and the post-play jigs in which Kemp specialized, the actor took his genius for self-advertisement elsewhere, most notably to Norwich on the famous morris dance of which he wrote an account in *Kemp's Nine Days' Wonder, Performed in a Dance from London to Norwich* (1600).

**Kempe, Margery** Mystic and autobiographer active in the early 15th century. All that is known of Margery Kempe's life is recorded in her single work, *The Book of Margery Kempe*. Although she is thought of as a mystic, the work does not strictly belong with the other **mystical writings** of the Middle Ages, as it is principally autobiographical, recording her spiritual experience but not exploring or describing it in detail.

After an early life devoted, by her own account, to pride and worldliness, Margery was converted to a life of chastity and worship. She abandoned her brewing business in her native King's Lynn and tried, eventually succeeding, to persuade her husband to allow her to live in chastity. She dressed in white and travelled in England, Europe and the Holy Land on pilgrimages, relating her mystical experiences and offering divinely inspired advice. She was not universally popular and attracted criticism from both inside and outside the orthodox Church. Her mystical experiences were accompanied by fits of hysterical weeping which often alienated others. She claimed that all her actions were dictated by God, though often God's will seems happily to have coincided with momentary convenience and she was sometimes accused of being a charlatan and a hypocrite. She records that she visited **Julian of Norwich** in her travels. Her book is a valuable and interesting account of her personality and life as an enthusiast in the community, but as a mystical work it is disappointing.

**Ken, Thomas** 1637–1711 Poet and prelate. Born at Berkhamsted, Hertfordshire, Ken was orphaned while young, and lived with **Izaak Walton**, a relation by marriage. He was educated at Winchester and New College, Oxford, taking holy orders in 1661–2. He was chaplain to Charles II from 1680, and sailed with the English expedition to Tangier (1683–4), when he conversed frequently with **Samuel Pepys**. In 1684, he was appointed Bishop of Bath and Wells, reputedly at the King's wish to have no one but 'the little black fellow that refused his lodging to poor Nelly', an allusion to Ken's having declined to allow Nell Gwynne to lodge at his prebendal house in Winchester. Ken attended Charles's deathbed, and absolved him. During James II's reign, he was one of the famous group of seven bishops confined to the Tower for opposition to the King's pro-Catholic policies, but at the Glorious Revolution of 1688 he became a prominent **nonjuror**, refusing to swear allegiance to William and Mary. In 1691 he was deprived of his see and he spent the remainder of his life in retirement, mostly at Lord Weymouth's seat at Longleat, Wiltshire, where he died in 1711. In his lifetime, Ken was renowned for his piety, charity and asceticism, and it was widely believed that **Dryden** modelled his 'Character of a Good Parson' (1700) on him; he wrote several devotional works, in both prose and verse, most notably his *Hymns on the Christian Festivals* (published 1721) and the famous 'Morning, Evening and Midnight Hymns', composed for the use of Winchester scholars, and first published in 1695.

**Kendall, Henry (Clarence)** 1839–82 Australian poet. Born near Ulladulla in New South Wales, he worked in a solicitor's office and later for the State Survey Department. His first poems were sent to Henry (later Sir Henry) Parkes, who published them in his paper, *The Empire*; Kendall's first collection, *Poems and Songs*, appeared in 1862. Some new poems were published in London, in *The Athenaeum* on 27 September of the same year – the first recognition of an Australian poet by an English journal. At its best Kendall's work is a vivid realization of Australia and of the natural beauty which appealed to his lyric gifts. After 1862 his published volumes were *The Bronze Trumpet: A Satirical Poem* (1866), *Leaves from Australian Forests* (1869), *Songs from the Mountains* (1880), *Orara: A Tale* (1881) and *Poems* (1886).

**Keneally, Thomas (Michael)** 1935– Australian novelist. Educated at St Patrick's College, Strathfield, he studied for the New South Wales Bar and began writing while working as a schoolteacher in Sydney. He was a lecturer in drama at the University of New England in 1968–70. His first novel, *The Place at Whitton* (1964), was followed by *The Fear* (1965), *Bring Larks and Heroes* (1967), *Three Cheers for the Paraclete* (1968), *The Survivor* (1969), *A Dutiful Daughter* (1971, the novel Keneally considers his best), *The Chant of Jimmie Blacksmith* (1972), *Blood Red, Sister Rose* (1974), *Season in Purgatory* (1976), *Ned Kelly and the City of the Bees* (1978, a work for children), *A Victim of the Aurora* (1978), *Passenger* (1979), *Confederates* (1979) and the widely praised *Schindler's Ark* (1982), which won the Booker Prize. His most recent novel is *The Playmaker* (1987).

**Kenelm Chillingly** A novel by **Bulwer Lytton**, published in 1873 and employed as a vehicle for many of the author's criticisms of contemporary society.

Thomas Keneally.

**Kenilworth** A novel set in Elizabethan England, by **Sir Walter Scott**, published in 1821. The story is Scott's interpretation of the events which led to the mysterious death of Amy Robsart in 1560.

Amy has been persuaded to contract a secret marriage with the Earl of Leicester, favourite of the Queen. She is kept at Cumnor Place, near Oxford, by the villainous Richard Varney and she is believed to be Varney's mistress by her rejected suitor Edmund Tressilian. Failing to persuade her to return to her father's house, Tressilian goes to the Queen and charges Varney with seduction. To protect Leicester, Varney declares that Amy is his wife, and Elizabeth orders Amy to appear before her at Kenilworth, where she will stay in the course of a royal progress. Varney and Leicester suggest that Amy should present herself as the wife of the former, but Amy indignantly refuses and, aided by Tressilian, makes her own way to Kenilworth where she is discovered by the Queen who finally extracts a confession of the truth from Leicester. Meanwhile he, suspecting the relation between Tressilian and his wife, orders Varney to carry her back to Cumnor Place and murder her. Tressilian arrives too late to prevent the 'accident' which results in Amy's death.

**Kennedy, John Pendleton** 1795–1870 American novelist and essayist. While practising law in his native Baltimore, Kennedy took to writing and produced *The Red Book* (1818–19), which – like **Washington Irving**'s *Salmagundi* – included sketches, satirical essays and poems. Under the pseudonym of Mark Littleton he then published

*Swallow Barn* (1832), a collection of sketches set in Virginia. His first and best-known novel, **Horse-Shoe Robinson**, appeared in 1835, and was followed by *Rob of the Bowl* in 1838. He was a friend of Irving and **Oliver Wendell Holmes**, and the American host to **William Makepeace Thackeray**. He was also one of the first to recognize **Edgar Allan Poe**, to whom he awarded first prize in a short-story contest he judged.

**Kennedy, Margaret (Moore)** 1896–1967 Novelist. She was educated at Cheltenham and Somerville College, Oxford. Her first book, *A Century of Revolution* (1922), was a work of history. Her first novel, *The Ladies of Lyndon* (1923), was well received but it was *The Constant Nymph* (1924) that made her famous. Margaret Kennedy's poised style, cool wit and skilful characterization made her novels welcome for three decades: *Red Sky at Morning* (1927), *The Fool of the Family* (1930), *Return I Dare Not* (1931), *A Long Time Ago* (1932), *Together and Apart* (1936), *The Midas Touch* (1938), *The Feast* (1950), *Lucy Carmichael* (1951), *Troy Chimneys* (1953, James Tait Black Memorial Prize), *The Oracle* (1955), *The Heroes of Clone* (1957), *A Night in Cold Harbour* (1960), *The Forgotten Smile* (1961) and *Not in the Calendar* (1964). For the theatre she wrote *Come With Me* (1928, with Basil Dean), *Escape Me Never* (1933), *Autumn* (1937, with Gregory Ratoff) and *Happy with Either* (1948). *Jane Austen* (1950) is a critical biography and *The Outlaws on Parnassus* (1958) a study of the art of fiction.

**Kentucky Cardinal, A** A short novel by **James Lane Allen**, published in 1894. Adam Moss is an amiable but reclusive nature lover who prefers his garden and the migrating birds it harbours to human society. The Cobb family moves into the house next door and disturbs his seclusion, but he soon feels himself drawn to the eldest daughter, Georgiana, who also loves birds. He falls in love with her, but she is hesitant. As proof of his love, she asks him to capture and cage a cardinal, a bird that lives in his garden and whose trust he has slowly gained. He does as she asks, thinking that his gesture will show her that he is ready to put aside animal attachments for human. The bird soon dies in captivity, and Adam and Georgiana quarrel about the meaning of the incident. Eventually, however, they forgive each other and plan to marry.

*Aftermath* (1895), the sequel, tells of their marriage. Adam tries to become more involved in town life and pays less attention to nature, but he finds only that human behaviour, especially with pre-Civil War tensions rising, is violent and foolish. Georgiana dies after giving birth to their first child, and Adam consoles himself by returning his attention to his first love, nature.

**Kenyon Review, The** Founded in 1939 by **John Crowe Ransom**, the magazine soon became a leading organ for 'New Criticism'. Contributors of non-fiction have included **Allen Tate**, **Cleanth Brooks**, R. P. Blackmur, **Robert Penn Warren**, **William Empson**, **Paul Goodman**, **Kenneth Burke**, Leslie Fiedler, **Northrop Frye**, Marshall McLuhan, **Lionel Trilling**, Harry Levin and **Stephen Spender**. The emphasis shifted from criticism to poetry and fiction when Robie Macauley became editor in 1958. Contributors during this period included **John Barth**, **Flannery O'Connor** and **Thomas Pynchon**.

**Ker, W[illiam] P[aton]** 1855–1923 Critic and scholar. Ker was born in Glasgow, where he attended the Academy before going on to Glasgow University. Later he went to Balliol College, Oxford, and became a fellow of All Souls College in 1879. He was Professor of English Literature and History at Cardiff from 1883 to 1889, when he accepted the chair of English Language and Literature at University College, London. Later he directed the University of London's school of Scandinavian Studies, and was elected Professor of Poetry at Oxford in 1920. His high reputation as an authority on medieval literature was established by his works *Epic and Romance* (1897), *The Dark Ages* (1904) and *Essays on Medieval Literature* (1905). His *Collected Essays* (edited by C. Whibley) appeared in 1925.

**Kerouac, Jack** 1922–69 American novelist, born Jean-Louis Kerouac in Lowell, Massachusetts, and educated at Columbia University. He spent time as a merchant seaman and in wandering around the USA before publishing the first of his semi-autobiographical novels, *The Town and the City* (1950), about a family in his home town of Lowell. **On the Road** (1957), his best-known book, is concerned with the life-style and the often aimless search for significant experience of what later became known as the Beat Generation (Kerouac was the first to use the term). The book established Kerouac as the novelist of the **Beats** just as *Howl* had identified **Allen Ginsberg** as their poet. *The Subterraneans* and *The Dharma Bums* (both 1958), *Tristessa* (1960), *Big Sur* (1962) and *Desolation Angels* (1965) are all products of the Beat consciousness; *Doctor Sax* and *Maggie Cassidy* (both 1959) and *Visions of Gerard* (1963) are evocations of Kerouac's boyhood. *Satori in Paris* (1966) is an account of his quest for his Breton ancestors. Among his other books are *Lonesome Traveller* (1960, travel sketches), *Mexico City Blues* (1959, verse) and *Book of Dreams* (1961). *Visions of Cody*, written in 1951–2, was published posthumously in 1972.

**Kesey, Ken** 1935– American novelist, born in

Colorado, and educated at the University of Oregon. In the early 1960s he volunteered for government drug experiments, and subsequently became an aide on a psychiatric ward in a Veterans' hospital. He made use of this experience in his first novel, *One Flew Over the Cuckoo's Nest* (1962), which is set in a mental hospital. His second novel, *Sometimes a Great Notion* (1964), focuses on the lives of a logging family in the Northwest. *Kesey's Garage Sale* (1973) is a collection of essays, letters, interviews, stories, and drawings. He has since published instalments of a novel in progress, *Seven Prayers to Grandma Whittier*, in his magazine *Spit in the Ocean*.

**Keyes, Sidney (Arthur Kilworth)** 1922–43 Poet and playwright. Born in Dartford, Kent, he was educated there, at Tonbridge School and at Oxford, where he read history. While an undergraduate he edited *The Cherwell* and introduced *Eight Oxford Poets* (1942), which included work by himself, **John Heath-Stubbs** and **Keith Douglas**. He enlisted in 1942 and was killed in Tunisia the following year. In his first volume, *The Iron Laurel* (1942), his eye for dramatic detail is apparent in the most successful poems, 'The Buzzard' and 'William Wordsworth'; the symbols in the long 'The Foreign Gate' deprive the writing of immediacy and pressure. *The Cruel Solstice* (1943) included poems which brought symbolism more urgently near to the realities of wartime life ('War Poet' and 'To Keep off Fears'). Michael Meyer edited *Collected Poems* (1945); *Minos of Crete: Plays and Stories* appeared in 1948. As the reputations of other poets of World War II like Douglas and **Alun Lewis** continue to grow, it remains to be seen whether Keyes can excite as he did in the 1940s. His most enduring poems ('The Migrant', 'The Kestrels') are those in which landscapes, seascapes and birds appear in their least symbolically forced settings.

**Keynes, J[ohn] M[aynard], 1st Baron Keynes of Tilton** 1883–1946 Economist. J. M. Keynes was born in Cambridge, and educated at Eton and King's College, Cambridge, where he subsequently lectured on economics. In 1906 he entered the Civil Service and was a member of the Royal Commission on Indian Finance and Currency. During the inter-war years Keynes published numerous works, including *A Treatise on Probability* (1921), *A Tract on Monetary Reform* (1923), *The End of Laissez-Faire* (1926) and *A Treatise on Money* (2 vols., 1930). However, *A General Theory of Employment, Interest, and Money* (1936) was by far his greatest and most influential work. It revolutionized the approach to unemployment by arguing for greater government spending on public works,

and became the major framework in the formation of the Welfare State.

While at Cambridge Keynes was influenced by the teaching of **G. E. Moore**, the philosopher whose ideas provided the **Bloomsbury Group** with many of its aesthetic and intellectual theories. Keynes became a central member of the Group, and Keynesian economics was based upon the assumption that prosperity would provide the foundation for cultural progress.

Keynes founded and endowed the Arts Theatre at Cambridge and became first chairman of the Arts Council of Great Britain in 1945. Among his more general contributions to literature were *Essays in Persuasion* (1931), *Essays in Biography* (1933) and *Two Memoirs* (posthumously published 1949), which revealed an original and lively prose style combined with novelistic powers of 'character drawing'.

**Kickham, Charles J[oseph]** 1828–82 Irish novelist. He was born in County Tipperary, the son of a prosperous farmer and shopkeeper, and ended his rather desultory education at the hands of private tutors after an accident with gunpowder left him deaf and disfigured. He was strongly influenced in his youth by the nationalism of the Young Ireland movement, and joined the revolutionary Fenian organization in 1860. One of the editors of the Fenian newspaper *The Irish People*, he was arrested in a police raid on the paper's offices in Dublin in 1865, and sentenced to 14 years' penal servitude but released after four years in English prisons, his health broken. He remained politically involved and was a leading member of the IRB, the Irish Republican Brotherhood. He wrote the novel *Sally Cavanagh* (1869) while in prison but his true fame as a novelist depends upon *Knocknagow, or, the Homes of Tipperary* (1879), one of the most popular novels in Irish literary history. Essentially a tale of the depopulation of the village of the title through the workings of the land-laws and landlord greed, its appeal lies in its reconstruction of the detail of Irish country life. Kickham's achievement as a novelist cannot be separated from his career as an Irish nationalist rebel.

***Kidnapped*** and ***Catriona*** A novel and its sequel by **Robert Louis Stevenson**. *Kidnapped* was published in 1886 and *Catriona* in 1893.

After the death of his father, David Balfour goes for help to his miserly uncle, Ebenezer. But Ebenezer, who has unlawfully seized David's estate, first attempts to kill him and then, when this fails, has him kidnapped and put aboard a ship bound for the Carolinas. During the voyage Alan Breck, a Jacobite rebel homesick for his native country, is rescued from a sinking boat. When the ship is wrecked off the coast of Mull, David and Alan travel together and acci-

An illustration from an edition of *Kidnapped*, published in 1887. Alan Breck survives the collision in the fog. Stevenson's novel was first published in 1886.

dentally witness the murder of Colin Campbell, the king's factor on the forfeited estate of Ardshiel. Suspicion falls on them and they are forced to take flight across the Highlands. The story ends with their safe escape, Ebenezer's exposure and the restoration of David's estate.

In the sequel David is in love with Catriona, daughter of the renegade James More. When James Stewart of the Glens is falsely accused of the murder of Colin Campbell, David comes forward on his behalf and finds his own life threatened. The story is concerned with David's escape from the plot against him and with Alan Breck's escape to safety in France.

**Killigrew, Thomas** 1612–83 Playwright and theatre manager. Born in London, Killigrew became page to King Charles I, and was in the suite of Prince Charles when he went into exile in 1647. At the Restoration the Prince, now Charles II, made him groom of the bedchamber and Killigrew enjoyed the King's friendship all his life. Killigrew's career as a minor playwright was interrupted by the closing of the theatres in 1642, by which time he had written, among other pieces, the coarse and popular *The Parson's Wedding*. This was based on the Spanish of Pedro Calderón de la Barca and probably first produced in 1640. Revived after the Restoration, in 1664, it achieved mention in **Samuel Pepys**'s diary as 'an obscene, loose play'. Restoration comedy took a new turn after the success of *The Parson's Wedding*.

However, like **William D'Avenant**, Killigrew holds a place in the history of English drama as one of those who did most to revive it after the Puritan interregnum. Charles II gave him a patent to open a playhouse, The King's House, in a disused tennis court in Vere Street. Killigrew's theatre burned down in 1672, but was rebuilt by Wren and reopened two years later. One of the first training-schools for actors was founded by Killigrew at the Barbican. He became Master of the Revels to Charles II in 1673. His brother William, and his son Thomas, both wrote plays, while another son, Charles, took over the management of the Theatre Royal in 1671.

**Kilroy, Thomas** 1934– Irish playwright and novelist. Born in Callan, County Kilkenny, and educated at University College, Dublin, he has been Professor of English at University College, Galway, since 1978. His novel *The Big Chapel* (1971) won a number of English and Irish awards, but outside his academic pursuits Kilroy has been primarily a dramatist, with *The Death and Resurrection of Mr Roche* (1968), in which other-worldly anticipations undermine an all-male drinking party; *The O'Neill* (1969); *Tea and Sex and Shakespeare* (1976); *Talbot's Box* (1977), in which kaleidoscopic, stylized scenes enact the life and death of the Dublin 'worker's saint', Matt Talbot; and most recently, *Double Cross* (1986).

**Kilvert, (Robert) Francis** 1840–79 Clergyman and diarist. The son of a country clergyman, Kilvert was born in Hardenuish, Wiltshire. Educated at home and at Wadham College, Oxford, he was ordained and served as a curate at Langley Burrell, Clyro, from 1865 to 1872. He became vicar of Bredwardine in Herefordshire in 1877 and died in office.

On Kilvert's sudden death of peritonitis five weeks after his marriage to Elizabeth Anne Rowland (1846–1911), his wife destroyed two large sections of his extensive diary, probably for personal reasons (they are believed to have held an account of his courtship of her); a further 19 volumes were later destroyed by his niece. The remaining three volumes, covering the period 1870–9, were discovered by **William Plomer** and published separately in 1938–40, and in one abridged volume in 1944. Kilvert's *Diary* is a sensitive document of life in the Welsh border country at that time, depicting in vivid detail the local landscape in which he delighted, and the pains and pleasures of rural parish society. The clear and unaffected style of the diary reflects the author's gentle and attractively unworldly personality.

**Kim** A novel by **Rudyard Kipling**, published in 1901. In it he explored many of his childhood memories of India, and it is generally considered to be his most successful full-length novel. His father, Lockwood Kipling, supplied the illustrations and advised Kipling on the Buddhist elements in the story.

Kim (Kimball O'Hara) is the orphan son of an Irish colour-sergeant and a nursemaid in a colonel's family. In his early life in the streets of Lahore, he shows self-reliance and resourcefulness, running errands for Mahbub Ali, who works for the British Secret Service. Kim meets a Tibetan Lama who is on a quest to be freed from the Wheel of Life. The boy attaches himself to the old man as chela, or disciple; however, Mahbub uses Kim to carry a vital message to Colonel Creighton in Umballa. The journey of Kim and the Lama on the Grand Trunk Road is rich with incident and encounters: elements of the picaresque are reflected in the depiction of the two 'pilgrims' as a kind of Quixote and Sancho Panza.

Kim's education takes a different turn when he is recognized by the chaplain of his father's old regiment. He is dispatched to the school of Anglo-Indian children at Lucknow, but rejoins the Lama during the holidays. Also, Mahbub takes him to Simla, where another agent, Lurgan, acts as a kind of benign Fagin in instructing Kim in the arts of spying and disguise.

The great game of imperial espionage against the Russians plays its most active role through Kim when he rejoins the Lama in an expedition to the hill country of the North. Kim's resourcefulness and worldliness are exercised in capturing documents from the enemy spies. At the same time, Kim is united with the Lama at the end of the latter's quest for the sacred River of the Arrow. Kim's destiny is left undecided, with the antithetical values of contemplation and the life of action both exerting their attractions upon him.

**King, Francis (Henry)** 1923– Novelist and short-story writer. Born and initially brought up in Switzerland, he also spent part of his childhood in India – the setting for his graphic murder mystery, *Acts of Darkness* (1983). He wrote his first three novels while still an undergraduate at Balliol College, Oxford. Subsequently he worked for the British Council in Italy, Greece, Egypt, Finland and Japan, before starting to write full-time in 1964. His fiction displays a careful, sensitive concern with the impulses of human action, a fluent narrative skill and a preoccupation with decadent, sometimes horrific, aberrations of behaviour. Novels

An illustration by John Lockwood Kipling for his son Rudyard's novel, *Kim* (1901). 'On the Road.'

include *To the Dark Tower* (1946), *The Dividing Stream* (1951), *The Widow* (1957), *The Custom House* (1961), *Flights* (1973) and *The Action* (1979). *Voices in an Empty Room* (1984) investigates the world of the paranormal. Collections of short stories include *The Brighton Belle and Other Stories* (1968) and *Hard Feelings and Other Stories* (1976). He has also published an exemplary short biography of **E. M. Forster** (1978) and edited **Lafcadio Hearn**'s *Writings from Japan* and the diaries of **J. R. Ackerley**. He is now President of the British division of the writers' organization, PEN.

**King, Henry** 1592–1669 Poet. Son of the Bishop of London who ordained **John Donne**, King became an acquaintance of that poet and eventually his executor. Educated at Westminster School and Christ Church, Oxford, he took his DD in 1625, and became Bishop of Chichester in 1642; ejected by the forces of Parliament in 1643, he took refuge with friends until regaining his see at the Restoration. A resolute opponent of Puritanism, King was an impressive preacher, and also the author of several occasional verses which include elegies on Donne, **Jonson** and **Raleigh**. His best-remembered poem is the elegy on his first wife, *The Exequy*. His work first appeared in book form in 1657.

**King, William** 1663–1712 Poet and polemicist. A contemporary of **Swift** and **Arbuthnot**, King was educated at Westminster School and Christ Church, Oxford, and became a lawyer. He held various minor posts in Ireland for six years (1702–8) and was appointed gazetteer (1711) after his return to England. Like Swift he was a High-Church Tory and contributed to the 'Battle of the Books' with *Dialogues of the Dead*, an attack on **Richard Bentley** written with Charles Boyle (1699). His first considerable piece was *Dialogue Showing the Way to Modern Preferment* (1690). King is often praised by scholars of the period for his urbane and witty poem *The Art of Cookery, in Imitation of Horace's Art of Poetry* (1708), and for the burlesques and light verse collected in *Miscellanies in Prose and Verse* (1709) and *Useful Miscellanies* (1712).

*King Alisaunder* An anonymous **verse romance** of the early 14th century written in octosyllabic couplets, probably in or near London.

The poem tells the mythical history of Alexander the Great, from the magical circumstances surrounding his conception to his death. The early part of Alisaunder's life to his deafeat of Darius occupies the first half of the romance, while the second half deals with his travels and conquests in the East, with many pseudo-geographical descriptions of the lands visited and the marvels encountered there. The poem was intended for oral delivery. Prose and alliterative treatments of the story also exist, some only as fragments. A Scottish version, *The Alexander Buik*, was once attributed to **John Barbour**.

*King and No King, A* An intrigue-laden tragicomedy by **Beaumont** and **Fletcher**, first performed by the **King's Men** in 1611 and published in 1619.

After a long war between Iberia and Armenia victory goes to Arbaces, King of Iberia, in single combat against Tigranes of Armenia. Arbaces offers Tigranes his liberty and continued peace if he will marry Panthea, his sister. Tigranes declines, for he loves Spaconia. He sends her to Panthea; he hopes that Spaconia will enlighten Panthea and enlist her help in opposing the marriage. Panthea has grown up during Arbaces's absence at the war and when she appears her beauty disturbs not only Tigranes but her brother too. Arbaces tries to smother his incestuous passion; then he discovers that his feelings are reciprocated. The intervention of Gobrias, Lord Protector of the kingdom, reveals that the two are not related – he is Arbaces's father. The Queen Mother had despaired of bearing children and Gobrias had given her his infant son; Panthea was born to the late king and his queen six years later. There is no impediment to their union now; and Tigranes is also free to marry Spaconia.

*King Hart* (or *Heart*) See **Douglas, Gavin**.

*King Horn* A Middle English **verse romance** in couplets. Written around 1225 in the South Midlands, the romance follows an Anglo-Norman source but has its origins in Old English storytelling. The poem recounts the life of Horn, set adrift as a child by pirates who have killed his father, the King of England. He is brought up by King Aylmer of Westnesse, whose daughter Rymenhild falls in love with him. They enjoy a clandestine affair until they are betrayed and slandered and Horn is consequently exiled. He avenges his father's death and lives abroad for seven years before Rymenhild, forcibly betrothed to King Mody, recalls him. He attends the wedding disguised as a beggar, making himself known to Rymenhild by puns and tokens. He kills Mody, denounces and eventually kills the slanderer, regains his kingdom and marries Rymenhild.

The vigorous narrative is compact and economical, being devoid of the spurious incidents which so often mar romances. The treatment of the central couple is sensitive and has a certain degree of psychological realism. Two related poems, *Horn Child* and the *Ballad of Hind Horn*, are not as successful.

**King James Version, The** See **Bible in English, The**.

---

**King John, The Life and Death of** An early history play by **William Shakespeare**. Its relationship to the anonymous *The Troublesome Reign of John, King of England* has given rise to much speculation. That play was first published in 1591, and it may be that Shakespeare's text, first published in the First Folio of 1623, is a playhouse revision of the older text, prepared for a performance in *c.* 1595. It is certainly tempting to explain away the defects of Shakespeare's version by supposing it to be a piece of theatrical cobbling.

The King is determined to keep his throne despite the better claims of his young nephew, Arthur, who has the support of the King of France as well as a legitimate succession from John's older brother, Geoffrey. Harassed not only by the French, but also by Arthur's mother Constance and by Cardinal Pandulph, the papal legate, John bribes Hubert de Burgh to blind Arthur. In a memorable scene, the boy's pleas so move Hubert that he spares him. But Arthur later jumps to his death while trying to escape. The French invade and defeat John, who takes refuge in Swinstead Abbey. There he dies, believed poisoned by a monk. The French troops return home, leaving Cardinal Pandulph to negotiate an honourable peace.

The rantings of Constance attracted many notable 19th-century actresses, but the chief splendour of the play is the loyal but outspoken Bastard, Faulconbridge, under whose guidance the new king, Henry III, must try to restore England after the ravages of King John's reign.

---

**King Lear** A tragedy by **William Shakespeare**, first performed *c.* 1605. The text of the First Folio edition (1623) is more authoritative than that of the 1608 Quarto. In writing the play, Shakespeare turned to various sources, including **Holinshed**'s *Chronicles* and **Sir Philip Sidney**'s *Arcadia*.

The aged British King decides to share his kingdom between his three daughters and spend his remaining years as a regular guest at their courts. The plan goes awry when his youngest (and favourite) daughter refuses to earn her share by joining her sisters in exaggerated public declarations of love for her father. The angry King divides the kingdom between Goneril and Regan, his elder daughters, and Cordelia is accepted, without dowry, as wife to the King of France. She leaves the country.

Lear finds Goneril's grudging hospitality an outrage and leaves for Regan's castle. But Regan puts even greater restrictions on his entertainment. The incredulous King first rants against his cruel daughters and then runs out, accompanied by his Fool and guided by the loyal Duke of Kent, to risk the hardships of the heath rather than accept terms from his daughters. Tried beyond his strength, he goes mad, and, in his madness, encounters his own unprotected humanity.

When Goneril, Regan and Regan's husband the Duke of Cornwall hear that a French army has landed, and that Lear is being taken to Dover to be reunited with Cordelia, they torture and blind the Duke of Gloucester, whose pity for the King has led him to assist his escape to Dover. Lear finds Cordelia at Dover and is restored to sanity; but the French lose the battle and Cordelia and Lear are captured. The Duke of Gloucester's bastard son, Edmund, powerful because he is the lover of both Regan and Goneril, gives orders that they should be put to death. Edmund is defeated in single combat by his legitimate brother, Edgar. His dying confession comes too late to save Cordelia, and Lear brings onstage the corpse of his hanged daughter. He dies asserting that Cordelia is still alive.

The formal achievement of the play is extraordinary. Lear's tragedy is paralleled by that of the Duke of Gloucester, who trusts the wrong son, Edmund, and rejects the right one, Edgar. It is Edgar who guides his blinded father towards the release of death and who avenges him by killing Edmund. The two tragedies touch each other throughout the play, most memorably in the grotesque meeting, near Dover, of the mad Lear and the blind Gloucester. It is Edgar who, with Goneril's husband the Duke of Albany, carries the hopes of a better future at the end of the play.

*King Lear* can be read in various ways – as a theological drama, as a philosophical one, as a supreme example of Shakespeare's intuitive egalitarianism or even as a melodrama lifted towards tragedy only by its superb poetry. It is the most titanic of Shakespeare's great tragedies.

---

**King Solomon's Mines** A novel by **Sir Henry Rider Haggard**, published in 1885, his first successful work, although *Dawn* (1884) and *The Witch's Head* (1884) had already appeared.

The novel was inspired by **Robert Louis Stevenson**'s *Treasure Island* and makes use of Stevenson's framework of a treasure-map and a perilous quest. Three European heroes, Sir Henry Curtis, Captain John Good RN and the narrator, Allan Quatermain, accompanied by their native servant, Umbopa, set off to find Curtis's missing brother, George, who has gone to look for the treasure of King Solomon's mines in the lost land of the Kukuanas. After an archetypally perilous journey over waterless desert and freezing mountains, they encounter the villainous King Twala and the horrific witch-doctor, Gagool. Umbopa turns out to be the rightful king, and civil war breaks out.

Umbopa is victorious in the decisive battle, and Twala is killed in single combat with Curtis. Guided by Gagool, the heroes set off to find Solomon's diamond mine, but are tricked by Gagool and left to die in an underground vault. They escape and return to life and, finally, to civilization; on their return journey the missing brother is found.

Although Haggard's attitude to the 'savage' is ambivalently divided between the evil Twala and the heroic Umbopa, the final abdication of European influence and the sealing-off of the lost land to its own separate development show Haggard's uneasiness about the impact of intrusive European culture on 'primitive' peoples.

**King's Men** The finest of Elizabethan theatre companies, it was formed in 1594 as the Lord Chamberlain's Men, taken into his personal patronage by James I in 1603 and renamed the King's Men. Four of the original shareholders were still with the company at that time, Richard Burbage, Augustine Phillips, **John Heminges** and **William Shakespeare**. They had overseen the move from the **Theatre** to the **Globe** in 1599, losing **Will Kemp**, whom they replaced with Robert Armin, on the way. It was at the Globe that the company confirmed its supremacy, duly rewarded by the new King. As well as Shakespeare's plays, the repertoire of the King's Men included work by **Jonson**, **Webster**, **Tourneur**, **Middleton**, **Marston**, **Beaumont** and **Fletcher**. In 1608 they added the indoor **Blackfriars** to the outdoor Globe, continuing to perform at both until the closure of the theatres in 1642. After Shakespeare's retirement, Fletcher became the 'attached' playwright of the King's Men, to be succeeded in turn by **Massinger**. Evidence of the bonds of loyalty and friendship that united the company survives in wills and in the decision to assemble the plays of their late colleague in the priceless Shakespeare Folio of 1623. Like all of London's professional groups, the King's Men were disbanded during the Interregnum, and it was a quite different and less remarkable company that assembled at **Drury Lane** in 1662, under the nominal leadership of **Thomas Killigrew** and the patronage of Charles II.

**King's Tragedy, The** A poem by **D. G. Rossetti** published in *Ballads and Sonnets* (1881), in which Catherine Douglas (Kate Barlass) tells the story of the murder of **James I of Scotland** and her own vain attempt to save him.

**Kingis Quair, The** A poem in **rhyme-royal** stanzas written in a northern dialect. **James I of Scotland** has been proposed as its author but there is no substantial evidence to support the attribution, which rests largely on the supposed autobiographical content of the poem. It tells how an imprisoned king falls in love with a woman he sees from the window of his tower. The central part of the poem is a **dream-vision** in which the king learns about love and fortune. On waking he receives a message carried by a dove foretelling his fortune in love and he eventually weds the lady. While notable for its description, the poem has a very weak plot serving principally to support the moral allegory of the dream-vision. The verse is strongly influenced by **Chaucer** and its philosophical content derived from Boethius.

**Kinglake, Alexander William** 1809–91 Historian and travel-writer. Born at Taunton in Somerset and educated at Eton and Trinity College, Cambridge, Kinglake was called to the Bar in 1837 and maintained a successful practice until 1856. He is best remembered as the author of *Eothen, or, Traces of Travel Brought Home from the Near East* (1844), a brilliant and evocative account of his adventures. He followed the British Army to the Crimea and at the request of Lady Raglan, widow of the commander-in-chief, wrote his meticulous history, *The Invasion of the Crimea* (1863–87).

**Kingsley, Charles** 1819–75 Novelist and clergyman. Son of the vicar of Holne in Devon, he was educated at King's College, London, and Magdalene College, Cambridge. In 1842 he became curate, and two years later the vicar, of Eversley in Hampshire; he held the living until his death, combining his parochial duties with the many other activities of his restless, combative life. He served as Professor of Modern History at Cambridge in 1860–9, and was appointed Canon of Chester in 1869 and of Westminster in 1873.

*The Saint's Tragedy*, a drama about the life of St Elizabeth of Hungary, appeared in 1848. Kingsley's other writings at this period show the influence of **Thomas Carlyle** and **F. D. Maurice**, leader of the movement for **Christian Socialism**. Kingsley contributed to *Politics for the People* (1848) and *The Christian Socialist* (1850–1) under the pseudonym of Parson Lot. *Yeast*, serialized in *Fraser's Magazine* in 1848 and issued in book form in 1850, was followed by *Alton Locke* (1850). With passionate and emphatic realism they expose the social injustice suffered by agricultural labourers and workers in the clothing trade. *Alton Locke* also deals memorably with the scandal of London's inadequate sanitation, as well as describing the Chartist agitation of the 1840s. *Hypatia* (1843), a historical novel about the conflicts of early Christianity, is regarded by many as his finest work. *Westward Ho!* (1855), another historical novel, turned to the Elizabethan era and the landscape of Kingsley's West Country childhood. *Two Years Ago* (1857) has a contemporary setting.

Charles Kingsley. A detail from the portrait by L. Dickinson, 1862. National Portrait Gallery, London.

Other works include: a volume of natural history, *Glaucus, or, The Wonders of the Shore* (1855); *The Heroes* (1856); *The Water Babies* (1863); a course of lectures given at Cambridge, *The Roman and the Teuton* (1864); *Hereward the Wake* (1865); an account of his journey to the West Indies, *At Last* (1871); and a volume of accomplished essays, *Prose Idylls* (1873).

Kingsley was notable for his application of Christian ethics to the social problems of the age and for a commitment to change that stopped well short of radicalism. His own brand of athletic, hearty Protestantism, popularly dubbed 'muscular Christianity', frequently led him into conflict. In 1864 Kingsley published the review of **Froude**'s *History of England* which angered **John Henry Newman** and prompted the composition of *Apologia Pro Vita Sua*.

**Kingsley, Henry** 1830–76 Novelist and younger brother of **Charles Kingsley**. He was an undergraduate at Worcester College, Oxford, but left under a cloud to spend five years (1853–8) in Australia, serving for a time in the Sydney mounted police. *Geoffrey Hamlyn* (1859), the novel he published on his return to England, took Australia as its setting. It was followed by a romance, *Ravenshoe* (1862), *Austin Elliott* (1863) and *The Hillyars and the Burtons* (1865), another Australian novel. Kingsley became editor of *The Edinburgh Daily Review* in 1869 but left that post to become a reporter with the German armies during the Franco-Prussian War. Among his 16 other novels were *Leighton Court* (1866), *The Boy in Grey* (1871) and *Reginald Hetherege* (1874).

**Kingsley, Mary** 1852–1931 See **Malet, Lucas**.

**Kingsley, Mary (Henrietta)** 1862–1900 Travel-writer. She was born in Islington, the niece of **Charles Kingsley**. In 1893 she travelled to West Africa in order to study primitive religion and published her original and informative account of that journey in *Travels in West Africa* (1897).

**Kingsley, Sidney** 1906– American playwright, born Sidney Kirschner in New York City, and educated at Cornell. His first play, *Men in White* (1933), examines the conflict in a young intern's life between dedication to his medical practice and concern for his personal happiness. Produced by the **Group Theatre**, it was a major critical success, and won a Pulitzer Prize in 1934. His second and longest-running play, *Dead End* (1935), is a realistic examination of how crime breeds among the young of a poor community. His next two plays, *Ten Million Ghosts* (1936) and *The World We Make* (1939), were critical and popular failures. With *The Patriots* (1943) he again received critical acclaim, and won the New York Drama Critics Circle Award. *The Patriots* is a historical drama about the conflict between **Thomas Jefferson** and Alexander Hamilton, and a defence of democracy and call for unity on the eve of World War II. In his next two plays he addressed the problems of the police or totalitarian state: *Detective Story* (1949) is the realistic portrait of a tough New York cop's harsh treatment of two suspects; *Darkness at Noon* (1951) is the award-winning adaptation of **Arthur Koestler**'s novel about conditions in Stalinist Russia. His last two works were *Lunatics and Lovers* (1954), a first attempt at farce; and *Night Life* (1962), a grim portrait of New York nightclub life.

**Kingsmill, Hugh** 1889–1949 Novelist, biographer, literary critic, parodist, anthologist. Kingsmill was educated as a day-boy at Harrow, at Oxford, where he failed to get a degree, and at Dublin, where he succeeded. The second son of Sir Henry Lunn, the travel agent, he worked for his father's firm until he was 38, when divorce made it impossible for him to remain with the Free Church Touring Guild. Thereafter he supported himself precariously on literary earnings.

His first novel, *A Will to Love*, was published in 1919, shortly after his release from prisoner-of-war camp in Germany. This was followed by *The Dawn's Delay* (1924) and *Blondel* (1927). Biographies of **Matthew Arnold** (1928), **Frank Harris** (1932), **Samuel Johnson** (1933), **Dickens** (1934) and **D. H. Lawrence** (1938) gained him a reputation for irreverence. Better received was *The Return of William Shakespeare* (1929), in which **Shakespeare** returns from the dead for six weeks, reads what the critics have said about him and delivers a long oration on the meaning of his works. Among Kingsmill's anthologies are *Invective and Abuse* (1929), *Made on Earth* (on marriage; 1937) and *The High Hill of the Muses* (studies of Johnson 'without Boswell'), published posthumously in 1955. He collaborated with William Gerhardi on *The Casanova Fable* (1934), with Malcolm Muggeridge on two books of parodies, *Brave Old World* (1936) and *Next Year's News* (1938) and with Hesketh Pearson produced a series of 'conversational travel books', *Skye High* (1937), *This Blessed Plot* (1942) and *Talking of Dick Whittington* (1947). Kingsmill wrote articles and book reviews for a number of periodicals and was literary editor of **Punch** and of *The New English Review*. A collection of his essays published in 1949 as *The Progress of a Biographer* contains much of his best work. A critic of deep perception and sensibility, he is scarcely known by the general reading public today.

**Kinnell, Galway** 1927– American poet, born in Providence, Rhode Island, and educated at Princeton and the University of Rochester. His first books were *What a Kingdom It Was* (1960), *Flower Herding on Mount Monadnock* (1964) and *Body Rags* (1968), which established him with many critics as a contemporary master of free verse. *The Book of Nightmares* (1971) confirmed this judgement, and emphasized the sacramental dimension apparent in all his work: poems approximating a personalized chant that accepts death as part of the primal rhythm. His other collections are *First Poems 1946–54* (1970), *The Shoes of Wandering* (1971), *The Avenue Bearing the Initial of Christ into the New World* (1974), *Three Poems* (1976), *Mortal Acts, Mortal Words* (1980), *Selected Poems* (1982, Pulitzer Prize) and *The Past* (1985). He has also published a novel, *Black Light* (1966); a collection of interviews, *Walking Down the Stairs* (1978); and a number of translations of French writers.

**Kinsella, Thomas** 1928– Irish poet and translator. Kinsella was born in Dublin and abandoned a science course at University College, Dublin, for a career in the Irish Civil Service (1946–65). He subsequently taught English at the University of Southern Illinois and, since 1970, at Temple University, Philadelphia, though he continues to spend time in Dublin. One of the most prolific and respected of contemporary Irish poets, his published volumes range from *Poems* (1956) to *Songs of the Psyche* (1985). Some of his collections such as *Fifteen Dead* (1979), elegies for contemporaries, have directly confronted the social and political realities of contemporary Ireland and its heritage of political violence. The characteristic themes of his calmly objective earlier poetry are more

personal: love's difficulty, nightmare and illness, the sometimes ominous unpeopled serenities of the countryside. From about 1968 a new emphasis emerges, registering aspirations to imaginative or mythic structure and order rising above the sharply realized disorder, dislocation and mess of the contemporary European experience. *Nightwalker* (1968), influenced by **Eliot** and (self-consciously) by **Joyce**, signals this departure, recording a sense of personal and cultural disarray. His later poems have largely abandoned formal elegance and accessibility for ambitiously experimental explorations of psychic, historical and cultural origins and evolution. At the same time, Kinsella has emerged as a distinguished translator from the Irish, completing a version of the ancient *Cattle Raid of Cooley* (*The Tain*) and, with Sean O'Tuama, editing and translating *An Duanaire: Poems of the Dispossessed* (1981). His sense of responsibility to Gaelic tradition coexists with a profound sense of discontinuity with that fragmented tradition, finally broken with the triumph of the English language in Ireland in the nineteenth century. He has illustrated this perception in his translations from the Irish and selections from English Irish poetry in *The Oxford Book of Irish Verse* (1986).

**Kipling, Rudyard** 1865–1936 Poet, novelist and short-story writer. He was born in Bombay, where his father taught at a school of art before becoming Director of the Lahore museum. The family connections on his mother's side were distinguished: one of her sisters married the painter Edward Burne-Jones,

Rudyard Kipling, 1923.

An illustration by Rudyard Kipling for one of his *Just So Stories* (1902). 'How the Camel got his Hump.'

a second was the mother of the politician Stanley Baldwin. When Kipling and his sister were sent to Southsea, England, in 1871, the boy's unhappiness – which was to be recalled in the story 'Baa, Baa, Black Sheep' (1888) – was alleviated by visits to the Burne-Jones household. This uncle, along with **William Morris**, inspired the move in 1878 to the United Services College, Westward Ho!, in Devon. Rudyard's five relatively happy years at school underlie the popular *Stalky & Co.* (1899).

Moving back to India in 1882, he began his early career as a journalist in Lahore on *The Civil and Military Gazette*. His familiarity with all ranks of the Anglo-Indian community contributed to the freshness of the poems and tales that he began to write for the *Gazette*. Many of these were subsequently published as *Departmental Ditties* (1886) and *Plain Tales From the Hills* (1888). Other tales which established his reputation in India were published in booklet form by the Indian Railway Library. The stories of *Soldiers Three* (1892) began in this form, along with *The Phantom Rickshaw* and *Wee Willie Winkie* (both 1888).

Travelling more widely as an editor for *The Pioneer* of Allahabad, Kipling moved from India in 1889. In England he rapidly established himself in literary London, winning friendship as well as praise from **Henry James**, **Rider Haggard** and **W. E. Henley**. Henley published Kipling's poems in his *Scots Observer*; these were later collected as *Barrack-Room Ballads and Other Verses* (1892). With the collections of short stories, *Life's Handicap* (1891) and *Many Inventions* (1893) Kipling set a pattern for his major writings. The novels of this period, *The Light that Failed* (1891) and *The Naulahka* (1892, written in collaboration with Wolcott Balestier), were relative failures; both have strongly anti-feminist elements. In 1892 Kipling married Balestier's sister, Caroline, and they spent the years 1892–6 near her family in Vermont, USA. Stories from *The Jungle Book* (1894) and *The Second Jungle Book* (1895) were written here. The elder of Kipling's daughters died in 1899 on a return visit to the USA. By the time his son John was born in 1897, the family had moved back to England, settling in Sussex in 1902. His best-known novel, *Kim*, was published in 1901.

Kipling began to visit South Africa regularly after 1898, including a period during the Boer War. Here he began the *Just So Stories* (1902). This collection, along with *Puck of Pook's Hill* (1906) and *Rewards and Fairies* (1910), shows an unusual sympathy with the children he was partly writing for. In 1907 he became the first English writer to receive the Nobel Prize for literature. He continued to publish collections of short stories for adults throughout the rest of his life, including *Traffics and Discoveries* (1904), *Actions and Reactions* (1909) and *A Diversity of Creatures* (1917), containing the famous 'Mary Postgate'. This story is only one example of his ability to reflect on empire and warfare with an eye to the personal bitterness and the cost of sustaining imperial ideals.

Although his reputation had begun to wane before his death, Kipling is increasingly admired for the variety of his subject matter, and for the mastery of his craft in many of his poems and short stories. To the late collections, *Debits and Credits* (1926) and *Limits and Renewals* (1932), there was added his posthumous work of autobiographical fragments, *Something of Myself* (1937).

**Kipps: The Story of a Simple Soul** A novel by **H. G. Wells**, published in 1905.

Arthur Kipps remembers little of his mother, who left him to be raised by an uncle and aunt, shopkeepers in New Romney. Those, like George Woodrow, schoolmaster at the genteel Cavendish Academy, who pose as social mentors to the inarticulate Kipps, are of little service. Kipps's natural feelings for Ann Pornick, a childhood sweetheart, prove a saving grace in the years of deadening apprenticeship to Mr Shalford the draper, in Folkestone. More particularly, Ann's influence contrasts with that of Helen Walshingham, Kipps's wood-carving teacher, who changes her attitude to him when she hears that he has inherited a fortune from his grandfather. Kipps's legacy leads to a bitterly comic process of social initiation, with Helen taking a leading part in his loss of self-esteem.

Kipps again meets Ann, now a servant at the house where he is a dinner guest. They decide to marry but Kipps soon learns that his money has been embezzled by Helen's brother. Kipps's social misfortunes are discussed by his friends, the impoverished, drunken playwright Chitterlow and the bitter working-class intellectual, Masterman. It is the unexpected success of Chitterlow's play, in which Kipps had invested, which restores the fortunes of Kipps, Ann and their child.

**Kit-Cat Club** A group of 18th-century writers with Whig sympathies, including **Joseph Addison**, **William Congreve**, **Richard Steele**, **Sir John Vanbrugh** and the physician **Sir Samuel Garth**. The club originally met at the London house of a pastry-cook, Christopher Katt (or Catling), whose mutton pies were called kit-cats, but later moved to the home of the secretary, **Jacob Tonson** the publisher. Many of the members were painted by Sir Godfrey Kneller in portraits slightly less than half-length but including the hands, a size of canvas now termed *kit-cat*.

**Kizer, Carolyn (Ashley)** 1925– American poet. Born in Spokane, Washington, Kizer was educated at Sarah Lawrence College and at the University of Washington, where she studied under **Theodore Roethke**. In 1959 she founded the magazine *Poetry Northwest*, which she edited until 1965. Her first volume of verse, entitled simply *Poems*, appeared in 1959. She has continued her exploration of feminist issues in subsequent collections such as *The Ungrateful Garden* (1961), *Knock Upon Silence* (1965) and *Midnight Was My City: New and Selected Poems* (1971). In 1984 she published two more volumes, *Mermaids in the Basement* and *Yin*, the latter of which received the Pulitzer Prize.

**Klein, A[braham] M[oses]** 1909–72 Canadian poet. Born in Montreal of an orthodox Jewish family, he practised as a barrister from 1933–54. As a poet, one of the so-called 'Montreal group', he is highly regarded. Among his books of verse are *Hath Not a Jew* (1940) and his best-known collection, *The Rocking Chair* (1948). *The Second Scroll* (1951) is a short novel accompanied by poems and brief scenes of verse drama.

**Knickerbocker Group** An early-19th-century school of American writers, primarily associated by their common location in New York City. Deriving their name from **Washington Irving**'s pseudonym, Diedrich Knickerbocker, the major figures in the group were Irving himself, **William Cullen Bryant** and **James Kirke Paulding**. **Joseph Rodman Drake** and **Fitz-**

**Greene Halleck** were also prominent in the school, which tended toward sophistication in style and conservatism in politics. Many of the members were published in *The Knickerbocker Magazine*.

***Knickerbocker Magazine, The*** A monthly magazine founded in New York in 1833 by Lewis G. and Willis G. Clark. Although dominated by the local writers of the **Knickerbocker Group**, almost every living American writer of distinction was at some time published in the magazine – **Washington Irving**, **Henry Wadsworth Longfellow**, **Nathaniel Hawthorne**, **John Greenleaf Whittier**, **William Dean Howells**, **Oliver Wendell Holmes** and **William Cullen Bryant** among them. The magazine continued until 1865.

**Knight, G[eorge] (Richard) Wilson** 1897–1985 Critic. Born in Sutton, Surrey, and educated at Dulwich College and at St Edmund Hall, Oxford, Knight served in the Royal Engineers from 1916 to 1920, then worked as a schoolteacher in Kent and Cheltenham before becoming Professor of English at the University of Toronto in 1931, where he also undertook and performed in productions of **Shakespeare**'s plays. After another spell of schoolteaching during the war, he returned to university life at Leeds in 1946, becoming Professor of English literature from 1956 until his retirement to Exeter in 1962.

Although he also wrote critical books on Ibsen, **Byron** and **John Cowper Powys**, Knight's life's work was devoted to Shakespeare, about whom he wrote 13 books. The most important of them, *The Wheel of Fire* (1930), pioneered a major new movement in Shakespearean interpretation, which concentrated on the 'spatial'

The cover design of *The Knickerbocker Magazine*, published from 1833 to 1865.

dimension of the plays: Knight replaced the traditional reading of plot and character with a view of Shakespeare's plays as expanded poetic metaphors. This approach was taken up by **L. C. Knights** and other Shakespearean critics, and applied to prose fiction by **F. R. Leavis** and **Q. D. Leavis**. Knight's other principal works of Shakespearean interpretation are *The Imperial Theme* (1931), *The Shakespearean Tempest* (1932), *The Crown of Life* (1947) and *The Mutual Flame* (1955). He also wrote *Principles of Shakespearean Production* (1936).

**Knight, Richard Payne** See **picturesque**.

**Knight of the Burning Pestle, The** A burlesque comedy, once attributed to the partnership of **Francis Beaumont** and **John Fletcher**, but now believed to be the work of Beaumont alone. It was first produced, without great success, by a **boys' company** in 1607. It affords a precious glimpse of stage practices in the indoor theatres of the time, and a wittily critical view of both contemporary drama and the attitudes of London's merchant class.

At a performance of *The London Merchant* a grocer and his wife in the audience interrupt the play with a demand that their apprentice, Ralph, shall have a part in it. To fit Ralph's aspirations the play is interspersed with scenes written by the grocer himself and renamed *The Knight of the Burning Pestle*. Ralph becomes a 'grocer errant', with a burning pestle as his device, and has wild adventures that include the defeat of Barbaroso, a villainous barber. His scenes are a burlesque of romantic knight errantry. Interspersed with Ralph's histrionic pretensions is the main plot concerning another apprentice, Jasper, who is in love with Luce, daughter of the merchant who is his master. The merchant favours Humphrey, but Jasper carries off Luce when she is about to be married to his rival. Luce is brought back by her furious parents and locked up, so Jasper feigns death and gets himself taken to the house in a coffin. He appears to the merchant as a ghost and succeeds in gaining his consent for the marriage by frightening him.

**Knight's Tale, The** See **Canterbury Tales, The**.

**Knights, L[ionel] C[harles]** 1906– Critic. Born in Grantham and educated at Cambridge University, Knights began lecturing in English at the University of Manchester in 1933 before becoming Professor of English at Sheffield University from 1947 and at Bristol University from 1953, returning to Cambridge as Edward VII Professor of English Literature from 1965 to 1973. He founded *Scrutiny* in 1932, and as co-editor until 1953 he led that journal's work on **Shakespeare** and 17th-century literature. His best-known work is the essay 'How Many

Children Had Lady Macbeth?' (1933), a milestone in Shakespeare criticism, which attacked the literal-mindedness of **A. C. Bradley**'s work on Shakespearean characters, thus clearing the ground for new methods of metaphorical interpretation led by **G. Wilson Knight** and exemplified by Knights himself in *Some Shakespearian Themes* (1959) and *An Approach to Hamlet* (1961). Knights's criticism, particularly in *Drama and Society in the Age of Jonson* (1937), shows a strong sociological interest. His essays were published as *Explorations* (1946), *Further Explorations* (1965) and *Explorations 3* (1976).

**Knolles, Richard** ?1550–1610 Historian. Knolles studied at Oxford, became a fellow there and then master of the grammar school at Sandwich. His *General History of the Turks* (1603) was one of the earliest English examinations of the Ottoman Empire and its influence on his poetry was acknowledged by **Byron**.

**Knowles, James Sheridan** 1784–1862 Dramatist. Knowles was born in Cork, the son of a lexicographer, but moved with his family to London in 1793 and studied medicine at the University of Aberdeen. After early practice as a doctor, he became an actor in 1808, a schoolmaster in 1811, an actor again from 1832 to 1843 and an evangelical preacher after 1844. His decidedly sanctimonious *Lectures on Dramatic Literature* (2 vols., 1873) are pulpit pieces, written with the brief authority of a former playwright, considered in his time a rival to **Shakespeare**. Almost forgotten today, Knowles is a victim of his own inflated reputation. Much of that reputation was owed to the actor, William Macready, whose moving portrayal of suffering fatherhood in Knowles's *Virginius* (1820) brought the playwright into prominence. Later paternal tragedies included *William Tell* (1825) and *John of Procida* (1840). Written, like all his 23 plays, in over-regular blank verse, they are too mawkish to survive 20th-century appraisal. The romances, modelled on **Fletcher** rather than Shakespeare, are more successful. They include *The Beggar's Daughter of Bethnal Green* (1828), revised as *The Beggar of Bethnal Green* (1834), and the understandably popular *The Hunchback* (1832). Best of all, though entirely neglected because of Knowles's claims as a writer of tragedies, are the comedies, *The Love-Chase* (1837) and *Old Maids* (1841).

**Knox, John** ?1514–72 Knox was the most important and the most vehement of the Scottish Reformers. He was born in East Lothian and trained for the priesthood. His conversion to Protestantism was influenced by the religious leader George Wishart, who was subsequently burned as a heretic. Knox was preaching the reformed religion by 1547. During the reign of

John Knox. An engraving made in 1798 from a portrait painted during Knox's lifetime. National Gallery of Scotland, Edinburgh.

the Protestant English king Edward VI, he was licensed as a preacher in England, had an itinerant ministry in the South of England and was even offered the bishopric of Rochester.

On the accession of Mary he fled abroad, becoming pastor of an English congregation in Frankfurt am Main and then minister to Protestant exiles in Geneva, where he met Calvin. He regarded his years in Geneva as his happiest. From abroad he published his *A Faithful Admonition* (1554) to the English Protestants and from Geneva his treatise on predestination and the famous *The First Blast of the Trumpet Against the Monstrous Regiment of Women* (1558). This argued that women in authority are contrary to religion and natural law, and was directed against the three female Catholic rulers of France, Scotland and England (Catherine de' Medici, the regent Mary of Guise and Mary Tudor). Its publication coincided with Mary Tudor's death. The treatise, and Knox's belief that magistrates and the nobility may resist a ruler endangering true religion, did not endear him to Queen Elizabeth and she banned him from England.

He was recalled by the Protestant party to Scotland in 1559, during the troubled times after the death of Mary of Guise. Knox was instrumental in the organization and the liturgy of the Scottish Reformed Church, with its moderately Calvinist faith, elected ministry and prohibition of the mass. Mary Queen of Scots arrived in Scotland in 1561 and Knox was granted a famous series of audiences which culminated in Mary losing her temper and accusing Knox of treason, a charge which her Privy Council refused to uphold. Knox lived to see Mary's abdication in 1567 and died at Edinburgh in 1572, a year in which, although ill, he preached a fiery sermon on the St Bartholomew's Day Massacre in St Giles's Cathedral. His *First Book of Discipline* (1559) advocated a national system of education. His major work *The History of the Reformation of Religion within the Realm of Scotland* (1587) contains in its fourth book accounts of the interviews with Mary Queen of Scots.

**Knox, Monsignor Ronald**  See **detective fiction**.

**Koch, Christopher** 1932– Australian novelist. Born in Hobart, Tasmania, he was partly educated at a Christian Brothers' school, an experience on which sections of his novel *The Doubleman* (1985) are based. While an undergraduate at the University of Tasmania, he began writing his first novel, *The Boys in the Island*, subsequently published in 1958. In 1955 he travelled to Europe, spending time in India, which provided the inspiration for his second novel, *Across the Sea Wall* (1965), on the way. He subsequently lived in London for two years, before returning to Australia in 1957 and joining the Australian Broadcasting Commission where he worked as a radio producer and eventually became Federal Head of Radio for Schools. In the early 1970s he left the ABC to become a full-time writer. His third novel, *The Year of Living Dangerously* (1978), generally regarded as his finest work, is set in Sukarno's Indonesia, where he also lived and worked briefly. Koch now lives in Sydney. He first came to the fore, with **Patrick White** and **Randolph Stow**, as a novelist attempting to provide an alternative to the naturalism which had dominated Australian fiction until the 1950s. He is a meticulous stylist, who has written only four novels in 30 years and has revised two of these for republication. He attempts to write prose which approximates towards poetry in its symbolic density. His themes are an encounter with a romantic 'otherland' and an exploration of the dualities he finds at the heart of the human condition. Brought up as a Roman Catholic, he became interested in Gnosticism after spending time in Asia, and in *Across the Sea Wall* and *The Year of Living Dangerously* he explores the alternative spiritual possibilities which Eastern religions and cultures offer the Australian psyche. *The Boys in the Island* and *The Doubleman* are notable for graphic evocations of Koch's native Tasmania.

**Koch, Kenneth** 1925– American poet. Born in Cincinnati, Ohio, he was educated at Harvard (BA, 1948) and Columbia (PhD, 1959). In the 1950s, with **Frank O'Hara** and **John Ashbery**, he became one of the leading poets of the New York School, which sought to oppose the academic austerity of mid-century American poetry. Much of his early work in particular was influenced by that of the French surrealist Jacques Prévert, whom he discovered during three years spent in Europe. Like others of the New York School he makes frequent use of urban settings and metaphors. His volumes include *Poems* (1953), *Ko, or a Season on Earth* (1959), *Permanently* (1960), *Thank You and Other Poems* (1962), *Sleeping With Women* (1969), *The Art of Love* (1975), *The Duplications* (1977), *Sleeping on the Wing* (1981), *Selected Poems* (1985) and *On the Edge* (1986). As well as teaching poetry at Columbia University, he has taught the writing of poetry to children and the elderly, and published two books on the subject: *Rose, Where Did You Get That Red? Teaching Great Poetry to Children* (1973) and *I Never Told Anybody: Teaching Poetry in a Nursing Home* (1977). He has also written several plays which have been produced off-Broadway. A collection entitled *Bertha and Other Plays* appeared in 1969.

**Koestler, Arthur** 1905–83 Novelist. Born in Budapest and educated in Vienna, he wrote his first books in Hungarian, but later used German and, after 1940, English. In 1926 he left Vienna for Palestine and a Zionist settlement, returning to Europe to become foreign editor of the Berlin *BZ am Mittag* in 1932. Having joined the Communist Party in 1932, he spent some time in the Soviet Union. During the Spanish Civil War he travelled there as a reporter and was arrested and imprisoned by the fascists. He was released in an exchange of prisoners, but was later interned in Paris as a suspect alien. Escaping to England he was there interned again. *The Scum of the Earth* (1941) is his account of these experiences, and his first book written in English. Koestler broke with the Party in 1938, and his novel *Darkness at Noon* (1940) condemns the totalitarian rule of the Stalin era. *Arrival and Departure* (1943) examines the motives of those dealing with resistance groups, and *The Yogi and the Commissar* (1945) is a volume of essays on the contemporary political scene. *Thieves in the Night* (1946) is a novel concerning hopes for a Jewish state, and *Promise and Fulfilment* (1949) is a historical account of the Jews in Palestine from 1917 to 1949. *The Age of Longing* (1951) is a novel set in the immediate future when all societies are threatened by nuclear extermination. *Arrow in the Blue* (1952) and *The Invisible Writing* (1954) are autobiographi-

Arthur Koestler, 1959.

cal. Claiming the right to a dignified death, Koestler and his wife died together by their own hands.

**Kogawa, Joy** 1935– Canadian poet and novelist. Born in Vancouver, a third-generation Japanese-Canadian, she and her family were interned and then sent as workers to the beetfields in Alberta under the Canadian government's dispersal policy for citizens of Japanese origin during World War II. She did not return to British Columbia but attended university in Saskatchewan and Alberta, the Royal Conservatory of Music and the Anglican Women's Training College in Toronto. She has worked as a schoolteacher and now lives in Toronto. She has published three collections of poetry – *The Splintered Moon* (1967), *A Choice of Dreams* (1974) and *Jericho Road* (1977) – though she is known best for her novel *Obasan* (1981). As the first novel about the Japanese-Canadian experience, it is a combination of documentary realism and lyrical protest against the silences of official history. Kogawa speaks out of her own double inheritance as a strongly individual voice within the Canadian multicultural tradition.

**Kolatkar, Arun** 1932– Indian poet. He was born in Kolhapur and works as a graphic artist in Bombay. His reputation as a poet in English is based mainly on his short volume, *Jejuri* (1976), which won the Commonwealth Poetry Prize in 1977. These pithy and sharply observed poems convey a true sense of Indian regional life. Kolatkar also writes in Marathi and translates between his two languages of expression. As well as being the leading poet of Maharashtra, he is regarded as one of the outstanding poets in English in India, though this claim is based upon a comparatively small and limited range of work.

**Kopit, Arthur L.** 1937– American playwright, born in New York City and educated at Harvard. His best-known work parodies the theatre of the absurd: *Oh Dad, Poor Dad, Mama's Hung You in the Closet and I'm Feelin' So Sad*, sub-titled 'a pseudo-classical, tragi-farce in a bastard French tradition', was published in 1960, but not produced professionally until 1962. Six other plays are collected in *The Day the Whores Came Out to Play Tennis* (1965). A satirical drama examining myths of the American West, *Indians*, was produced in London in 1968. *An Incident in the Park, or Pardon Me, Sir, But Is My Eye Hurting Your Elbow?* also appeared in 1968. Other plays include *What's Happened to the Thorne's Place* (1972); *Louisiana Territory, or, Lewis and Clark – Lost and Found* (1975); *Secrets of the Rich* (1976); *Wings* (1978); and *Good Help is Hard to Find* (1982).

**Kroetsch, Robert** 1927– Canadian poet, novelist and critic. Born in Heisler, Alberta, Kroetsch attended the University of Alberta, then worked in the Canadian North and joined the US Air Force before attending graduate schools at McGill University, Montreal, Vermont and Iowa. He taught English at the State University of New York, Binghampton, and since 1978 has been Professor of English at the University of Manitoba. He has travelled extensively on lecture tours to China, Europe and Australia. He has published seven novels: *But We Are Exiles* (1965), *The Words of My Roaring* (1966), *The Studhorse Man* (1969) which received the Governor General's Award, *Gone Indian* (1973), *Badlands* (1975), *What the Crow Said* (1978) and *Alibi* (1983). He is a distinguished poet with seven books to his credit, the best known being *Seed Catalogue* (1977) and *Field Notes* (1981), a continuing poem of which *Advice to My Friends* (1985) is the second volume. It is as a post-modernist novelist and critic in *Labyrinths of Voice* (1982) and *Essays* (1983) that Kroetsch's voice is most distinctively Canadian in his mythologizing of the prairie.

***Kubla Khan, or, A Vision in a Dream*** A 54-line fragment of an unfinished poem by **Samuel Taylor Coleridge**, published in *Christabel and Other Poems* (1816). In the preface Coleridge gave a famous account of how he came to write the poem and why it was never completed: 'In the summer of the year 1797, the author then in ill health, retired to a lonely farmhouse between Porlock and Lynton . . . In consequence of a slight indisposition, an anodyne [probably laudanum] had been prescribed, from the effects of which he fell asleep in his chair at the moment he was reading the following sentence, or words of the same substance in **Purchas**'s Pilgrimage: "Here the Khan Kubla commanded a palace to be built, and a stately garden thereunto. And thus ten miles of fertile ground were enclosed with a wall." The author continued for about three hours in a profound sleep.' Coleridge goes on to say that he composed between 200 and 300 lines in his sleep, and hastened to write them down when he woke. 'At this moment he was unfortunately called out by a person on business from Porlock, and detained by him above an hour.' On returning to his room Coleridge found that the rest of the poem had passed from his memory.

**Kumin, Maxine** 1925– American poet and novelist, born in Philadelphia and educated at Radcliffe College. She has published several volumes of poetry including *Halfway* (1961), *The Privilege* (1965), *The Nightmare Factory* (1970), *Up Country: Poems of New England* (1972, Pulitzer Prize 1973), *House, Bridge, Fountain, Gate* (1975), *The Retrieval System* (1978), *Our Ground Time Here Will Be Brief* (1982) and *The Long Approach* (1985). Among her works of fiction are the novels *Through Dooms of Love* (1965), *The Passions of Uxport* (1968), *The Abduction* (1971) and *The Designated Heir* (1974); and a collection of short stories, *Why Can't We Live Together Like Civilized Human Beings?* (1982). A collection of essays entitled *To Make a Prairie: Essays on Poets, Poetry, and Country Living* appeared in 1979. Her verse focuses in general on themes of loss and survival, and she frequently emphasizes the importance of family bonds. In her most recent works she has stressed the role of the poet and dealt with the threat of Armageddon that seems to hover over contemporary society.

**Kunene, Mazisi** 1930– South African poet. Of Zulu inheritance, he is a graduate of the University of Natal, though he later studied Zulu literature at the School of Oriental and African studies in London. He was in charge of African Studies at the University College of Lesotho from 1958 to 1962 and has subsequently held other university positions outside South Africa. He has been an active representative of the African National Congress in Europe and the USA, as a result of which he can no longer live in South Africa. His collections of poetry include *Zulu Poems* (1970) and *The Ancestors and the Sacred Mountain* (1982), both of which are steeped in the Zulu oral tradition while at the same time sounding a strong note of political dissent. His major achievements have been in two long epic works, *Emperor Shaka the Great* (1979) and *Anthem of the Decades* (1981), both of which help to dignify the modern African by extolling the great Zulu cultural and historical inheritance. *Anthem of the Decades* tells of the origin of life as conceived by an African community, and by taking such a perspective of time spells out great hope for the future. Kunene writes in Zulu and then makes his own English-language version of his work. In scale Kunene is probably the most ambitious poet in modern Africa.

**Kunitz, Stanley** 1905– American poet, born in Worcester, Massachusetts, and educated at Harvard. His first volumes were *Intellectual Things* (1930) and *Passport to the War: A Selection of Poems* (1944). Acclaim, however, did not come until *Selected Poems: 1928–58* appeared in 1958 and won the Pulitzer Prize. Since then he has published *The Testing Tree* (1971), *The Lincoln Relics* (1978), *The Poems of Stanley Kunitz: 1928–1978* (1979) and *The Wellfleet Whale & Companion Poems* (1983). A book of essays and interviews, *A Kind of Order, A Kind of Folly: Essays and Conversations*, appeared in 1975, and *Next-to-Last Things: New Poems and Essays* in 1986.

**Kuppner, Frank** 1951– Poet. Born in Glasgow, Kuppner read English and German at Glasgow University, later qualifying as an engineer. He earns a living by typing theses and theatre reviewing. His first volume, *A Bad Day For the Sung Dynasty* (1984), consists of 511 quatrains, or one long poem of 511 stanzas, based on Chinese paintings. It is remarkable for its variety: the formality of Chinese landscape mixes with a ludic playfulness, bizarre humour alternates with stunning lyricism and satire, tones veer from bathos to obscenity. His second collection, *The Intelligent Observation of Naked Women* (1987), features five sequences, including 'An Old Guide-Book to Prague', which attempts elegiac tones. Kuppner remains an eccentric, unpredictable talent.

**Kyd, Thomas** 1558–94 Dramatist. Born in London and educated at the Merchant Taylors' School, Kyd practised as a scrivener, was for some years in the service of an unknown lord, was arrested for heresy in 1593 because of his association with **Christopher Marlowe**, was probably tortured, and died soon after his release. That is almost all we know about him. Even our belief in his authorship of the brilliantly original *The Spanish Tragedy* (*c.* 1589) rests on a reference in **Thomas Heywood**'s *Apology for Actors* (1612). *The Spanish Tragedy* was the influential adaptation of Senecan tragedy to the English stage. It displays Kyd's inventiveness and his sense of theatre, lending credibility to the view that he wrote a lost *Hamlet* of which **Shakespeare** made use. The only other surviving play of which we can be fairly certain Kyd was the author is *Cornelia* (1594), a version of Robert Garnier's Senecan tragedy, performed in France as *Cornélie*.

**Kynaston, Sir Francis** 1587–1642 Kynaston was the author of a romance in verse, *Leoline and Sydanis*, and the translator into Latin of **Chaucer**'s *Troilus and Criseyde*. He opened an academy for young gentlemen and the sons of noblemen, the Museum Minervae, where they could learn the basics of science, languages and courtly accomplishments.

# L

*L'Allegro* A poem by **John Milton**, written in 1632. Its title means 'the cheerful man' and the work is the young poet's celebration of mirth, in the delights of rustic scenery and also in the busy city. Its companion piece, *Il Penseroso*, celebrates the qualities of meditative retirement.

**L'Estrange, Roger** 1616–1704 Journalist and translator. The son of Norfolk landowners, L'Estrange was an active Royalist during the Civil War, taking part in an abortive Royalist rising in Kent in 1648. He escaped to the Continent, where he first used his talents as a writer with political pamphlets against the army leaders and the Presbyterians. He contributed to the climate of opinion that made the Restoration possible and in 1663 was appointed Surveyor of the Imprimery (of printing presses) and licenser of the press. From 1663 to 1666 L'Estrange published two newspapers, *The Intelligencer* and *The News*, but he had less success than **Henry Muddiman**, whose *London Gazette* ousted all rivals. Another paper published by L'Estrange was the *City Mercury*, founded in 1675. His supposed connection with the Popish Plot forced him to leave England, but he was able to return in 1680, and published *The Observator* (1681–7), attacking Titus Oates particularly and Dissenters and Whigs generally. He earned a knighthood from James II in 1685.

The Revolution and the accession of William and Mary ended L'Estrange's career as a journalist; he was deprived of his office as Surveyor and imprisoned several times. In later life he supported himself by his translations, a field in which he had already enjoyed some success: among them were Erasmus's *Colloquies* (1680 and 1689), *The Fables of Aesop and Other Eminent Mythologies* (1692) and the works of Josephus (1702).

*La Belle Dame Sans Merci* A ballad by **Keats**, written in 1819 and first published in **Leigh Hunt**'s *The Indicator* the following year. The title derives from Alain Chartier's *La Belle Dame Sans Merci* (1424) which Keats probably read in a Middle English translation. A deceptively slight and self-ironizing work, it tells of a knight's fatal enthralment by a beautiful 'lady', who appears partly as a witch and partly as some 'fairy's child'. It contains what must be one of the most succinct poetic rehearsals of the morbid aspect of Romantic love, though its unconscious profundities are, in turn, often emphasized at the expense of the prevailingly playful tone. Keats did not consider it a major piece, but it was later taken very seriously by the **Pre-Raphaelites**, and **William Morris** considered it to be 'the germ from which all the poetry of his group had sprung'.

**La Guma, Alex** 1925–85 South African novelist, born in Cape Town. Clerk, labourer, journalist, one of the 156 successful defendants in the notorious Treason Trial (1956–61), he was detained in 1960, under house arrest in 1962–6, and twice in solitary confinement before the family emigrated to London in 1966. He represented the African National Congress in Havana (1978–85).

*A Walk in the Night* (1962) is his first novel, a short, accomplished story about the Cape Town slum, District Six, which it evokes vividly in terse, sparse descriptions. While La Guma's novels engrave the iniquities of apartheid in the scrupulously detailed language of realism, they also assert a romantic faith in his characters' potential for compassion: *And a Threefold Cord* (1964) counters miserable, deprived, shantytown living with the inhabitants' sense of community; within the prison in *The Stone Country* (1967), a precise metaphor for South Africa itself, some humane responses miraculously survive. While inadequate action in *In the Fog of the Season's End* (1972) makes heroic rhetoric about underground resistance seem pretentious, *Time of the Butcherbird* (1979), set in a tribal area, succeeds in correlating the pursuit and punishment of a private atrocity with communal resistance to the enforced removal of villagers from their ancestral lands. *A Soviet Journey* (1978) is a travel book.

**La Ramée, Louise de** See **Ouida**.

**Lacan, Jacques** See **psychoanalytic criticism**.

*Lady Anna* A novel by **Anthony Trollope**,

published in *The Fortnightly Review* (April 1873 to April 1874). The spirited heiress Lady Anna, daughter of an earl, is successfully wooed by Daniel Thwaite, a hard-working tailor from Cumberland. In spite of opposition and the advice of artistic and aristocratic friends, Anna marries Daniel and they leave for Australia.

*Lady Audley's Secret* A novel by **Mary Elizabeth Braddon**, published in volume form in 1862 after being serialized in *Robin Goodfellow* from September 1861 and then, after the failure of that journal, in *The Sixpenny Magazine* from March 1862.

George Talboys returns from Australia to learn that the wife he had abandoned is now dead. His friend Robert Audley takes him for a holiday near Audley Court, the seat of Robert's uncle, Sir Michael, and his beautiful young wife. When Talboys disappears, Robert investigates the mystery, becoming transformed from an idle dandy into a man of serious purpose. His enquiries show that Talboys's wife is Lady Audley; she had faked her death and married Sir Michael bigamously. Lady Audley tries to kill Robert by burning down the inn where he is staying, but he survives to make her confess that she had pushed Talboys down the well at Audley Court when he confronted her. Her crimes are the result of hereditary insanity and she is permanently committed to a private asylum. In a final twist to the story, George Talboys turns out to be alive, having secretly left the country after surviving the attempted murder.

Written in great haste but with a breathlessly readable plot and a striking central character in Lady Audley, the novel became the most famous example of Victorian **sensation fiction**, reviled by critics and moralists but loved by the public.

*Lady Chatterley's Lover* A novel by **D. H. Lawrence**, written and privately printed in Florence in 1928. The first unexpurgated English edition did not appear until 1960.

Constance (Connie) Chatterley is married to Sir Clifford, a wealthy and cultured mineowner in Derbyshire. A war wound has left him paralysed and impotent, and he increasingly devotes all his energy to the management of his mines and to himself. Constance grows restless within the confines of their marriage. She has a brief and superficial affair with Michaelis, a young playwright, then enters into a passionate relationship with Sir Clifford's gamekeeper, Oliver Mellors. He is an ex-officer who rose from the ranks, a forthright, individualistic man uncontaminated by industrial society.

Connie becomes pregnant and attempts to conceal the father's identity from her husband. She later confesses and asks him for a divorce. Sir Clifford considers Mellors his social inferior,

therefore not worthy, and refuses to release her. The lovers depart and, though separated, wait hopefully for a time when the obstacles between them will have been surmounted and they can be united.

The novel was denied full publication in England for over 30 years because of its sexual explicitness. An expurgated version, released in 1932, contained none of Lawrence's detailed descriptions of the sexual act and eliminated all four-letter words. After Sir Allen Lane's Penguin Books received a favourable High Court judgement in 1960 the unexpurgated text became freely available in England. The prosecution, under the Obscene Publications Act, became a major test-case, and the verdict marked a famous victory in publishing history. Defence witnesses at the trial included **E. M. Forster**, **Helen Gardner** and **Richard Hoggart**, who also wrote a celebrated introduction to the second Penguin edition in 1961. Lawrence's two earlier versions of the novel have been published independently as *The First Lady Chatterley* (1944) and *John Thomas and Lady Jane* (1972).

*Lady of Shalott, The* A poem by **Alfred Tennyson**, published in 1832 and revised for the 1842 edition of his *Poems*. The setting is Arthurian. The lady of the title leads an isolated life on an island, never looking out of her window but instead weaving pictures from a mirror's reflection of the scene. When Sir Lancelot passes by,

Lancelot and the Lady of Shalott. An illustration by Dante Gabriel Rossetti for the Moxon *Tennyson*, published in 1857. Other illustrations were contributed by Millais and Holman Hunt.

she is tempted to gaze directly on reality and dies. Like many of Tennyson's early poems, the work displays a ripe luxury of imagery and language, both manipulated with extraordinary skill. On a figurative level, the main interest of the poem lies in its consideration of the relationship between life and art.

The theme was suggested by an Italian story, *Donna di Scalotta*, in *Cento Novelle Antiche* of the 14th century. Tennyson gave the story a different treatment in 'Lancelot and Elaine', one of the *Idylls of the King*.

**Lady of the Lake, The**  A poem in six **cantos** by **Sir Walter Scott**, published in 1810. The lake is Loch Katrine, the Lady is Ellen, daughter of the outlawed James of Douglas, and the period is the early 16th century.

Roderick Dhu, the Highland chief, gives hospitality to a mysterious knight, James Fitz-James. Roderick loves Ellen, but she has given her heart to Malcolm Graeme. Threatened by the royal armies, Roderick summons his clan, but Douglas, believing himself to be the cause of the royal army's approach, decides to go to Stirling to surrender to the king. Fitz-James returns to offer refuge to Ellen, but withdraws when Ellen declines, confessing her love for Malcolm. Fitz-James gives her a ring which will secure the king's favour in an emergency. On the road to Stirling Fitz-James meets Roderick with whom he quarrels and fights. Roderick is worsted, and taken to Stirling as Fitz-James's prisoner. When Ellen arrives in Stirling to plead for her father, using the ring to gain an audience, Fitz-James proves to be none other than the king himself. Roderick dies of his wounds, but Douglas is pardoned and Ellen marries Malcolm. The poem includes Ellen's memorable song 'Rest, warrior, rest', and the beautiful funeral lament, 'He is gone on the mountain'.

**Lady Windermere's Fan**  A play by **Oscar Wilde** (1892). His first theatrical success, it deals with a blackmailing divorcée driven to self-sacrifice by maternal love. The dialogue has the paradoxical, witty comments on society that made Wilde famous.

**Lady's Not for Burning, The**  A verse comedy by **Christopher Fry**, first performed at the Arts Theatre, London, in 1948 and an outstanding success when it transferred to the Globe with John Gielgud as Thomas Mendip.

The story, conveyed in highly artificial but consistently lively verse dialogue, concerns Jennet Jourdemayne, accused of murder by witchcraft, and Thomas Mendip, impelled by world-weariness to 'confess' to the murder. When the corpse turns up alive, Thomas finds himself surprised into wanting to live by his love for Jennet.

**Lai le Freine**  A fragment of a **verse romance** in couplets, written in the early 14th century in the south-east. One of the better Middle English **Breton lays**, it is derived from one of **Marie de France**'s *Lais*, *Lai le Fresne*, but does not follow its source closely. The poet adds a lengthy prologue, alters the setting, adds, omits and adapts sections, increases dramatic effect and adds concrete detail to the story of his source. The poet was perhaps the author of *Sir Orfeo*.

The wife of a knight slanders her neighbour, who has borne twins, as unfaithful. When she then bears twin girls herself she avoids embarrassment by having one taken away and abandoned, with a robe and a ring, in an ash tree near a convent. The nuns who bring the girl up christen her Freine, 'ash'. When mature, she lives as the mistress of a knight, Guroun, who is eventually persuaded to marry and weds Freine's sister. The fragment ends here, but in the source Freine covers the bridal bed with her robe and it is recognized by her mother who confesses her crime. Guroun's marriage is dissolved and he weds Freine. The story contains several common medieval motifs which are not specifically Breton. Analogues of the story are found in other European languages and were written over several centuries.

**Laing, B[ernard] Kojo**  1946–  Ghanaian novelist. Born in Kumasi, he was educated at schools in both Ghana and Scotland, before taking his degree at the University of Glasgow. He has worked in government administration and as secretary to the Institute of African Studies at the University of Ghana, but now runs a private school in Accra. His reputation is so far based on only one book, a novel called *Search Sweet Country* (1986), but this has been praised as one of the major novels of modern Africa and is likely to be very influential. Set in Accra in the mid 1970s, it is an attempt to define the nature of modern Ghanaian identity, with implications in this for the rest of Africa. It is, however, the technical accomplishment of the book which has been particularly admired since it appears to extend the possibilities of the form of fiction in Africa.

**Lake Poets (or Lake School), The**  A term applied to **Wordsworth**, **Coleridge** and **Southey** because of their close association with the Lake District. It was apparently first used by *The Edinburgh Review* in 1817.

**Lalla Rookh**: *An Oriental Romance*  Four narrative poems, with a connecting tale in prose, by **Thomas Moore**, published in 1817.

Lalla Rookh, the daughter of the Emperor Aurungzebe, journeys from Delhi to Cashmere where she is to be married to the King of Bucharia. The journey is enlivened by the stor-

The Veiled Prophet of Khorassan. Engraving from a drawing by Richard Westall for Thomas Moore's *Lalla Rookh*, 1817.

ies told by Feramorz, a young poet from Cashmere, who joins her retinue. Also present is the self-important chamberlain Fadladeen, who vents his irritation at the mishaps of the journey in criticism of Feramorz's poetry.

*The Veiled Prophet of Khorassan.* The beautiful Zelica, mourning her lover Azim, whom she believes to have died in battle, is lured with promises of admission to Paradise into marrying Mokanna, an imposter posing as a prophet. Returning from the wars, Azim joins a force raised by the Caliph to punish Mokanna. Zelica, seeking death, dons the veil of the false prophet and is killed by Azim who believes her to be Mokanna.

*Paradise and the Peri.* A peri was, according to Persian mythology, a beautiful but malevolent sprite. In later Islamic tradition they are gentle spirits, the children of fallen angels who waft the pure in spirit to the gates of paradise. In Moore's poem the peri laments her exclusion from heaven, and is promised admission if she will bring the gift most dear to the Almighty to heaven's gates. She brings the blood of a young warrior who dies to free India from the tyranny of Mahmoud of Gazna: the gates remain closed. She brings the last sigh of an Egyptian girl who dies of grief when her lover dies of plague: the gates remain closed. She brings the tear of a repentant criminal, wrung from him by the prayers of his child, and heaven's gates are opened to her.

*The Fire-Worshippers.* The Ghebers were the fire-worshippers of the ancient Persian religion, who resisted the advance of Islam. A young Gheber, Hafed, falls in love with Hinda, daughter of the emir Al Hassan of Arabia, who has come to crush the Ghebers. Hafed scales the eminence where Hinda has her bower and she falls in love with him, though she discovers his true identity when the Ghebers capture her. Al Hassan's army defeats the Ghebers and rescues his daughter from them, whereupon Hafed throws himself on a funeral pyre. Hinda drowns herself on the way back to her father's headquarters.

*The Light of the Haram.* Selim is the son of the Emperor Akbar and his beloved wife is Nourmahal; they quarrel during the Feast of Roses in the Vale of Cashmere. Nourmahal is determined to win back her husband's love, and learns a magic song from the enchantress Namouna. At a banquet given by Selim she enters masked, and sings the magic song, thereby regaining her husband's love.

As Lalla Rookh's journey to Cashmere proceeds, she falls in love with the young poet. When she arrives, she is delighted, and the chamberlain discomfited, to discover that the supposed poet is none other than her prospective husband, the King of Bucharia.

**Lamb, Charles** 1775–1834 Essayist and poet. Charles Lamb was the youngest child of Elizabeth and John Lamb, a clerk to Samuel Salt, a lawyer, at whose house in Crown Office Row Lamb was born. He went to school in Fetter Lane and later entered Christ's Hospital, where he formed a lifelong friendship with **Coleridge**. In his youth Lamb spent some time at Blakesware in Hertfordshire where Mary Field, his grandmother, was housekeeper. After 1789 Lamb was employed in the South Sea House and later at the East India House where he worked until his retirement in 1825. In 1796 his

Christ's Hospital in 1784. Charles Lamb and Samuel Taylor Coleridge were schoolfellows there. Christ's Hospital, London.

sister Mary Ann Lamb (1764–1847) murdered their mother in a fit of insanity and was confined to an asylum, at length being released into her brother's care. Lamb himself suffered a period of insanity in 1795–6.

Lamb contributed four sonnets to Coleridge's *Poems on Various Subjects* (1796). In 1798, with Charles Lloyd, he published *Blank Verse* which included 'The Old Familiar Faces'. *A Tale of Rosamund Gray and Old Blind Margaret* also appeared in 1798, followed by *John Woodvil* (1802; initially entitled 'Pride's Cure'), a tragedy, and *Mr H* (1806), a farce. As a contributor to *The Albion*, **The Morning Chronicle** and *The Morning Post* and as the popular host to intellectual gatherings which included Coleridge, **Southey**, **Leigh Hunt**, **Benjamin Haydon**, **Crabb Robinson**, **Thomas Talfourd** and the mathematician Thomas Manning, Lamb established a reputation in literary circles. **William Godwin**, another acquaintance, suggested that Lamb contribute to his 'Juvenile Library' and so, with his sister, he produced the well-known **Tales from Shakespeare** (1807). Other books for children were: *The Adventures of Ulysses* (1808); *Mrs Leicester's School* (1809), written with Mary and containing reminiscences of their childhood; *Poetry for Children* (1809); and *Prince Dorus* (1811), a fairy-tale in verse.

Lamb's contributions to journals included his essay 'On the Character and Genius of Hogarth' (published by Leigh Hunt's *Reflector* in 1811), 'On the Tragedies of Shakespeare', and a review of **Wordsworth**'s **The Excursion** (published with editorial alterations by **The Quarterly Review** in 1814). He is best remembered for the series of essays he contributed under the name of Elia to **The London Magazine** from 1820 to 1823. They were collected in 1823, and a second series, *The Last Essays of Elia*, appeared in 1833. Deliberately good-humoured and ranging in subject from personal reminiscence ('Christ's Hospital Five-and-Thirty Years Ago', 'Blakesmoor in H—shire') to light-hearted speculation ('A Dissertation upon Roast Pig'), they had a lasting influence on the tradition of essay-writing in England.

In 1827 Lamb, his sister and Emma Isola, an orphan whom they had adopted, moved to Enfield and later to Edmonton, where he died and was buried. Talfourd published a volume of his letters with a biographical sketch in 1834 and *Memorials of Charles Lamb* in 1848. Lamb's gentle and engaging personality, his debilitating stammer, his burden of responsibility and his whimsical humour attracted many friends whose memoirs record their lasting admiration.

Charles Lamb. A detail from the portrait by William Hazlitt, 1804. National Portrait Gallery, London.

***Lamia*** A poem by **John Keats**, written in 1819 and published the following year. The serpent Lamia is transformed by Hermes into a beautiful maiden. She loves a young man of Corinth, Lycius, who, though a serious student, is enchanted by her beauty and retires with her to an exquisite but mysterious and secret palace. After some time in blissful union, Lycius overrules Lamia's fears and insists on inviting his friends to a sumptuous feast. Among the guests comes Apollonius, the sage philosopher, who recognizes Lamia's true nature. She vanishes with a 'frightful scream' and Lycius dies.

The subject is borrowed from **Robert Burton**'s **The Anatomy of Melancholy** (III, ii, 1, 1), which quotes Philostratus's *De Vita Apollonii*. The poem's central theme – the tension between appearance and reality – occurs elsewhere in Romantic poetry, most notably in **Coleridge**'s **Christabel** and **Thomas Love Peacock**'s *Rhododaphne*, which both portray dissembling woman. Keats's poem regards Apollonius's coldly scientific attitude with ambivalence.

**Lamming, George** 1927– Caribbean novelist. He was born in Barbados and his first novel, *In the Castle of My Skin* (1953), which draws upon his boyhood there, is a finely wrought account of growing up in poverty in a community undergoing fundamental social change. Its immediate success opened literary London to Lamming. *The Emigrants*, about West Indian disillusion with life in Britain, appeared in 1954. *Of Age and Innocence* (1958) contrasts peasant wisdom and youthful tolerance with violent,

Caribbean, pre-Independence politicking, while in *Season of Adventure* (1960) the heroine painfully achieves Caribbean identity by accepting what she had previously despised. Rather less accessible with their tumbling, swirling issues are the two ambitious novels: *Water with Berries* (1971) and *Natives of My Person* (1972). *The Pleasures of Exile* (1960) consists of Lamming's essays. He edited an anthology of black writing, *Cannon Shots and Glass Beads* (1974).

**Lampman, Archibald** 1861–99 Canadian poet. Born at Morpeth, and educated at Trinity College, Toronto, he graduated in 1882. He worked as a teacher for a time and later joined the Post Office Department in Ottawa. His reputation rests upon two small collections published in his lifetime, *Among the Millet* (1888) and *Lyrics of Earth* (1893). *Alcyone* (1899), which includes 'The City of the End of Things', was in preparation at the time of his death. His emphasis is upon natural themes, and his setting is Canadian; a broadening of interest is seen in *At the Long Sault* (1943), a collection of hitherto unpublished poems edited by Lampman's friend **Duncan Campbell Scott** in collaboration with **E. K. Brown**.

**Lancelot of the Laik** A Middle Scots romance written in the last quarter of the 15th century. The poem is a clumsily managed **dream-vision** in which the poet, inspired by the God of Love to write a work for his lady, decides to translate part of a French Lancelot story. The poem, a paraphrase of part of the Vulgate *Lancelot*, is incomplete, and includes an incongruous digression on the political duties of a king, usually thought to have been intended for James III (1460–88).

**Land of Cockaygne, The** A Middle English poem composed in Ireland during the second half of the 13th century. It presents a lively parody of the Christian Paradise and of the Earthly Paradise of European tradition, describing a land devoid of all unpleasant things where the buildings are edible, the monks and nuns enjoy a guiltless, licentious life and geese fly ready-roasted. The land can be reached only by wading through the filth of swine for seven years.

**Landon, Letitia Elizabeth** 1802–38 Poet and novelist, who generally used the initials L. E. L. She was among the most popular and prolific authors of her time. Her first volume *The Fate of Adelaide* (1821) was followed by *The Improvisatrice* (1824), *The Troubadour* (1825), *The Venetian Bracelet* (1829) and *The Vow of the Peacock* (1835), among others. She also contributed to numerous periodicals and her poems were collected in 1850 and 1873. She married

George Maclean, governor of Cape Coast Castle in West Africa, in 1838, and died there shortly afterwards. Her most successful novel was *Ethel Churchill* (1837); others were *Romance and Reality* (1831), *Francesca Carrara* (1834) and *Duty and Inclination* (1838).

**Landor, Walter Savage** 1775–1864 Poet and essayist. Born at Ipsley Court, the son of a doctor, he was educated at Rugby School and Trinity College, Oxford. He was sent down in 1794 and published his first collection of poems in the following year, but suppressed the work soon after. It was followed by *Gebir* (1798), an exotic poem in seven books, and *Count Julian* (1811), a tragedy. Subject to an inflammable temper which made his residence in Monmouthshire untenable, he left England in 1814 living abroad in Como, Pisa and Florence. He did not return to England until 1835 when he separated from his wife, Julia Thuillier, whom he had married in 1811. From 1824 to 1829 he published *Imaginary Conversations of Literary Men and Statesmen*. Other works included *Citation and Examination of William Shakespeare Touching Deer-Stealing* (1834), *Pericles and Aspasia* (1836) – a work which began as one of his imaginary conversations, *Pentameron* (1837), the trilogy *Andrea of Hungary, Giovanna of Naples* and *Fra Rupert* (1839–40), *The Hellenics* (1847), *Poemata et Inscriptiones* (1847) and *Imaginary Conversations of Greeks and Romans* (1853).

In 1858 Landor again departed for the Continent on account of an action for libel arising out of a lampoon included in *Dry Sticks Fagoted* (1858). He returned to Florence, an extraordinary and irascible old man, where **Robert Browning**, who had long admired his work, attempted to protect and care for him. Landor's boisterous manner and short temper were tolerantly caricatured by **Dickens** in the character of Boythorn in his *Bleak House*.

An accomplished writer of prose, Landor is not remembered for his poetry, but much of it displays a distinguished simplicity: 'Lately Our Poets Loitered in Green Lanes', 'Dying Speech of an Old Philosopher', 'Mother I Cannot Mind My Wheel', 'Rose Aylmer' and 'To Ianthe'.

**Lane, Edward William** 1801–76 Arabic scholar. Born at Hereford and educated at Bath and Hereford Grammar Schools, he published his classic *Account of the Manners and Customs of the Modern Egyptians* in 1836. Other works were a translation of the *Arabian Nights' Entertainments* (1838–40) and *Selections from the Kur-an* (1843). His *Arabic Lexicon* was left unfinished at his death, and was completed by his nephew S. Lane Poole.

**Lang, Andrew** 1844–1912 Poet, scholar and man of letters. Born in Selkirk, he was educated at St Andrews, Glasgow and Balliol College, Oxford. Lang became a fellow of Merton College but settled in London as journalist and man of letters in 1875. There was almost no type of writing that he did not touch: essays, reviews, literary controversy, plays, novels and biographies all form part of his collected works.

His first volume of poetry, *Ballads and Lyrics of Old France*, had appeared in 1872, before he left Oxford; it was followed by *Ballades in Blue China* (1880 and 1881), *Helen of Troy*, a narrative poem in six books (1882), *Rhymes à la Mode* (1885), *Grass of Parnassus* (1888), *Ban and Arrière Ban* (1894) and *New Collected Rhymes* (1905). As a classical scholar he worked mostly on Homer. As a historian he was chiefly concerned with Scotland, though he also wrote a book on Joan of Arc, *The Maid of France* (1908). As a biographer he wrote lives of Sir Stafford Northcote (1890) and **J. G. Lockhart** (1896). As an anthropologist he published *Custom and Myth* (1884), *Myth, Ritual and Religion* (1887) and *The Making of Religion* (1898).

Lang's involvement in scholarly controversy about folk-tales led to his best remembered work. In contrast to Max Müller, Professor of Philology at Oxford, he did not believe that all fairy-tales originated in Central Asia and were spread by travellers over the rest of the world. Instead, he thought such tales to be relics of savage customs and thoughts common to early man – such as the belief that animals can understand and speak in human language. He began his famous collections with *The Blue Fairy Book* in 1889; eleven more volumes, known by the colours in their titles, enjoyed great popularity, the last appearing in 1910. Taken from many different sources, these stories were rewritten by Lang's wife and a committee of ladies in the same spirit that they altered his *Arabian Nights' Entertainments* (1898) to 'omit pieces suitable for Arabs and old gentlemen'. Lang also edited one of the best and most inclusive of nursery rhyme anthologies still in print today, *The Nursery Rhyme Book* (1897).

**Langland, William** *fl.* 1360–87 The author of *Piers Plowman*, a religious allegory in **alliterative verse** dating from the second half of the 14th century and extant in three versions. Nothing is known of Langland's life beyond what can be deduced from the poem and a few details from notes in a 15th-century manuscript of the C-text. Traditionally, he is supposed to have been the son, perhaps illegitimate, of Stacy de Rokayle, an Oxfordshire gentleman, and to have been educated at the priory of Great Malvern until the death of his father curtailed his education. His poem suggests a knowledge of the Malvern Hills. His familiarity with the Scriptures is abundantly clear from the text, although his knowledge of biblical commentaries, the patristic writers and other areas of scholarship was patchy. The three versions of the poem represent substantial revisions, apparently undertaken by the poet himself and spread over a period of around 25 years; the A-text was written during the 1360s and the C-text was probably completed by 1387.

The poem manifests a passionate concern with the corruption of secular society, the regular clergy and the mendicant orders, and its consequences for the spiritual welfare of the populace. His dreamer-narrator's search for 'true' Christianity and the path to salvation involves an introspection and a condemnation of the established Church which also characterize the writings of **Wyclif** and the **Lollards** and inspired the **mystical writers** of the period. Langland's poem was lauded as a herald of Lollardy and the Reformation by his successors, though wrongly so. He sought reformation within the Church in its established form rather than the radical doctrinal and institutional changes demanded by the Lollards and later reformers.

**Lanier, Sidney** 1842–81 American poet and critic. Born in Macon, Georgia, Lanier graduated from Oglethorpe University in 1860. After writing his only novel, *Tiger Lilies* (1867), he turned to poetry, greatly influenced by his work as a professional musician. Two years after the publication of his first book of poetry, *Poems* (1877), he became a lecturer at Johns Hopkins University in Baltimore. His *The Science of English Verse* (1880) remains an important study of English prosody. Most of his other works were published posthumously. His collected *Poems* appeared in 1884 and was reissued with additions in 1891 and 1916. *Poem Outlines* – also verse – was published in 1908. Among his critical works are *The English Novel and the Principles of its Development* (1883), *Music and Poetry: Essays upon Some Aspects and Interrelations of the Two Arts* (1898) and *Shakespeare and his Forerunners: Studies in Elizabethan Poetry and its Development from Early English* (1902).

***Lantern and Candlelight*** This pamphlet by **Thomas Dekker** was his greatest publishing success and was first printed in 1608. It is a description of Jacobean low-life with its rogues and canting terms, and contains an early account of English gypsies. It was written as a continuation of *The Bellman of London*. The third edition of 1612 added a section entitled 'O per se O' and the fourth edition (1616) chapters on prison life, of which Dekker had personal experience. The title refers to the story of Diogenes the Cynic searching with candle and lantern in broad daylight for an honest man.

***Laodicean, A*** A novel by **Thomas Hardy**, first

published serially in the European edition of *Harper's New Monthly Magazine* between December 1880 and December 1881 and in book form in 1881.

Paula Power, the Laodicean or vacillator, is left Stancy Castle in Somerset by her wealthy father. She and George Somerset, a young architect, fall in love but by virtue of her nature she will not agree to an engagement. Then Captain de Stancy, a member of the family who once owned the castle, seeks her hand and, after procrastination, is accepted. He is assisted in his quest for Paula by his illegitimate son, Will Dare, a conniving villain who blackens Somerset's character. Upon discovery of Dare's knavery Paula breaks her engagement and follows Somerset to Normandy, where they are reconciled and married. But their intention of living in the restored castle is thwarted when Dare contrives to burn it to the ground, leaving only the very stout walls.

**Lardner, Ring[gold] (Wilmer)** 1885–1933 American short-story writer, born in Michigan. He worked as a sports reporter for various newspapers and eventually a syndicated columnist. The letters he wrote in the guise of 'Jack Keefe', a newcomer to a professional baseball team, made him famous. They first appeared in *The Chicago Tribune* and were collected as *You Know Me, Al: A Busher's Letters* (1914). Lardner had a sharp-edged sense of humour and a remarkable ear for vernacular speech. Americans of every walk of life appeared in his stories, their utterances establishing their characters. He demonstrated his talent for verse in the *Bib Ballads* (1915). *Gullible's Travels* (1917) is a collection of satirical stories, and was followed by more of the same in *Treat 'em Rough* in 1918. His only novel, *The Big Town*, was published in 1921. By the time he published *How to Write Short Stories (With Samples)* (1924), he already had a large and enthusiastic following. His later works are the collections: *What of It?* (1925), *The Love Nest* (1926), *Round Up* (1929) and *First and Last* (1934).

**Larkin, Philip (Arthur)** 1922–85 Poet, novelist and essayist. He was born in Coventry and educated locally at the King Henry VIII Grammar School before reading English at St John's College, Oxford. After graduating in 1943, he took a post in the library at Wellington in Shropshire and remained a librarian throughout his career, working at universities in Leicester and Belfast before moving to the University of Hull in 1955.

In the 1940s he had published two finely understated novels, *Jill* (1946) and *A Girl in Winter* (1947). Conversely, his early poems, collected in *The North Ship* (1945), give little indication of his future distinction as a poet:

written under the pervasive influence of the early **Yeats**, they are uncharacteristically rhapsodic and rhetorical. A privately printed pamphlet, *XX Poems* (1951), marked the emergence of his true poetic voice, but it was the publication of *The Less Deceived* (1955) which brought Larkin's mature work before the public for the first time, and established his public persona and recurrent themes. Partly because of its title, taken from the poem 'Deceptions', *The Less Deceived* left some readers with a misleading impression of unrelieved scepticism in Larkin's work. While developing many of the themes from the previous book, his next collection, *The Whitsun Weddings* (1964), is guardedly, and therefore all the more convincingly, celebratory in nature. The magnificent title-poem, describing the poet's journey by train from Hull to London, is justly his best-known work. *High Windows*, Larkin's final book of poems, appeared in 1974. At its heart are two substantial poems about ageing, illness and death: 'The Old Fools' and 'The Building'. The stance is one of clear-eyed endurance: as Larkin put it in a later, uncollected poem, 'Aubade', 'Death is no different whined at than withstood.' There are also poems of regret for a vanished or vanishing England, 'Going, Going' and 'Show Saturday', where the formulaic conservatism seems to come a shade too easily, but the tone of affirmation often persists.

From 1961 until 1971 Larkin wrote a regular column on jazz records for *The Daily Telegraph*: most of these reviews appear, with a teasingly polemical anti-modernist introduction, in *All What Jazz?* (1970). Similarly anti-modernist principles informed his editing of *The Oxford Book of Twentieth-Century English Verse* (1973). *Required Writing* (1983) is a witty and engaging selection of his occasional articles and reviews. An edition of his collected poems by **Anthony Thwaite** and a biography, by **Andrew Motion**, are in preparation.

Larkin's reputation rests on what **Peter Levi** has called '85 perfect poems', the contents of his three mature collections. Working with traditional, often ingeniously constructed poetic forms, he simultaneously extended the territory of poetry in his generous, wry and emotionally complex treatment of contemporary English life.

***Last Chronicle of Barset, The*** The final volume in **Anthony Trollope**'s **Barsetshire** series, published in 1867. In his *Autobiography* Trollope named it as his own favourite among the novels.

The story is mainly concerned with Josiah Crawley, the poor but righteous and intractable curate of Hogglestock. When Lord Lufton's agent, Mr Soames, loses his pocket-book in Crawley's house and Crawley later cashes a cheque for £20 it contained, the clergyman falls under suspicion of theft. His explanation that the money was a gift from Dean Arabin is inadequate and he is committed for trial. The bishop's wife, Mrs Proudie, plays a leading part in the persecution which now focuses on Crawley. Archdeacon Grantly's son, Major Henry Grantly, is in love with Crawley's daughter Grace and insists on becoming engaged despite his father's opposition; a serious breach between them is the result. When the whole affair reaches a crisis, it is resolved by Mrs Arabin (the former Eleanor Harding), who reveals that she had slipped the cheque into a letter from her husband to Crawley. His innocence established, Crawley is appointed to the parish of the late Mr Harding. Archdeacon Grantly is won over when he meets Grace Crawley, and welcomes her as his daughter-in-law. The novel also contains the death of the dreadful Mrs Proudie and follows Johnny Eames's ever-hopeful pursuit of Lily Dale.

***Last Days of Pompeii, The*** A novel by **Edward Bulwer Lytton**, published in 1834. The action takes place just before and during the catastrophic eruption of Vesuvius in AD 79. The book has some lively pictures of 1st-century Roman life (including an early Christian sect), and a particularly memorable villain – Arbaces, the Priest of Isis.

***Last of the Barons, The*** A novel by **Edward Bulwer Lytton**, published in 1843, and set during the Wars of the Roses. The hero of the title is the Earl of Warwick, known as 'the kingmaker'. The book was intended as a political allegory: Warwick's defeat at the Battle of Barnet represents the overthrow of the hereditary feudal order by the new commercial classes, and prefigures the Reform Bill's eclipse of the landowning Tory aristocracy by Whig industrialists.

***Last of the Mohicans, The*** See **Leatherstocking Tales, The**.

***Last Puritan, The: A Memoir in the Form of a Novel*** A novel by **George Santayana**, published in 1935. Oliver Alden – the 'Last Puritan' – is the heir of a wealthy, established New England family. He and his mother are abandoned by his drug-addict father, who has rebelled against the puritanical values of New England and sails about the world in his yacht, employing Jim Darnley to accompany him on his travels. Oliver is raised by his mother. At the age of 17 he joins his father for a cruise and becomes Jim Darnley's friend. He then enrolls at Williams College where he is both studious and athletic. His father commits suicide. Oliver becomes friendly with a European cousin, Mario, whom his father has supported, and courts another cousin, Edith. After graduation Oliver visits the

Darnleys in England, where he meets and falls in love with Jim's sister Rose. But Rose falls in love with Mario (who does not love her in return) when he in turn visits Oliver at the Darnleys. World War I having begun, Oliver follows Mario's example and enters the army. Rose refuses Oliver's proposal of marriage. He leaves for France, and is killed there. His estate goes to the Darnleys.

***Late Lyrics and Earlier*** Poems by **Thomas Hardy**, first published in 1922. Music is the main theme of this volume, a number of whose lyrics have been set by various composers. As in other collections of Hardy's verse, there is the characteristic subject matter – mismatings, dramatic moments, misunderstandings, sardonic memories, grotesque happenings – together with technical virtuosity of a singular order. But a lyric presence predominates in this volume, which is replete with impressions of earlier times frequently recalled and evoked through the rhythms of the ballad or the folksong.

**Lathen, Emma** See **detective fiction**.

**Latimer, Hugh** ?1485–1555 Preacher and Protestant martyr. Latimer was ordained c. 1510 and gained a great reputation as a preacher at Cambridge, where he was educated; in 1522 the university licensed him to preach anywhere in the country. He preached before both Henry VIII (the annulment of whose marriage to Catherine he supported) and Edward VI. However, some of his sermons, which attacked purgatory and the veneration of saints, led to a charge of heresy and he was excommunicated until he made his submission in April 1532. In 1535 he became Bishop of Worcester but resigned his see when he refused to subscribe to the Act of Six Articles (1539), which were designed to halt the further spread of reforming ideas. He was confined to the Tower in 1546 but released on the accession of Edward VI. On the accession of Mary he was again committed to the Tower in 1553 and sent to Oxford with Ridley and Cranmer to defend his views before divines from both universities. He was condemned as a heretic, excommunicated and burned with Ridley in 1555.

Latimer's vernacular sermons are vividly graphic, engaging and anecdotal. 'Sermon on the Card' was preached c. 1529 and disparages 'voluntary' works (e.g. pilgrimages) and encourages 'necessary' ones (e.g. mercy). It develops an extended metaphor of card-playing: 'Now turn up your trump, your heart (hearts is trump, as I said before)'. His most famous sermon 'Of the Plough' was preached on New Year's Day 1548 at Paul's Cross. It envisages the preacher as God's ploughman and urges London to repent of its covetousness: 'Charity is waxen cold, none helpeth the scholar nor yet the poor.' Collections of Latimer's sermons were printed in Elizabeth's reign: *Twenty-Seven Sermons* in 1562 and *Fruitful Sermons* in 1571, with many reprintings in the 16th century.

**Laud, William** 1573–1645 Divine. The son of a Reading clothier, he was educated at St John's College, Oxford, and enjoyed a distinguished career as a cleric before becoming Charles I's Archbishop of Canterbury. His defence of order and ceremonial against Puritan demands for change, and his allegiance to the king in his conflict with Parliament, led finally to his impeachment. He was tried in 1644 and executed the following year. Some of his sermons were published in 1651 and a collection of his writings in 1695–1700. Their literary value is slight, but *The History of the Troubles and Trial of William Laud*, written by himself in the Tower and published with his diary in 1695, has some historical interest.

**Lauder, William** d. 1771 Schoolteacher and literary hoaxer. Educated at Edinburgh University, he was an excellent classical scholar who translated Grotius's *Eucharista* and edited a collection of Scots neo-Latin religious poetry. He is principally renowned, however, for his fraudulent attempt to convict **Milton** of plagiarizing from Masenius's poem *Sarcotis* and Grotius's *Adamus Exil* in **Paradise Lost**. He first made the allegations in a series of articles for *The Gentleman's Magazine* beginning in February 1747. Interest being aroused, Lauder issued an extended version of these pieces as *An Essay on Milton's Use and Imitation of the Moderns in his 'Paradise Lost'* (1749). **Samuel Johnson**, who had first introduced Lauder to the editor of *The Gentleman's Magazine*, Edward Cave, contributed a prospectus for the proposed publication of *Adamus Exil*. The works of Masenius and Grotius were not readily available in England, and Lauder had simply inserted extracts from William Hog's Latin translation of *Paradise Lost* into genuine passages from their writing. The scale and brazenness of the forgery was exposed by John Douglas in 1750. An apology, dictated by Johnson and signed by Lauder, appeared as *A Letter to the Reverend Mr Douglas, Occasioned by his Vindication of Milton* (1751), though Lauder subsequently retracted it. His reputation never recovered and he emigrated to Barbados, where he died in poverty. Johnson's opponents attempted, with little success, to implicate him in the fraud.

**Launcelot Greaves, The Life and Adventures of Sir** A novel by **Tobias Smollett**, published in volume form in 1762. His fourth novel, it is generally regarded as one of his weakest. Sir Launcelot Greaves is an 18th-century Don Quixote, riding about England in armour with his ludicrous squire, Timothy Crabshaw. The humour is harsh and the main interest of the book lies in its picture of England before the Industrial Revolution and in a few of its characters: the rogue Ferret, Mrs Gobble, the justice's wife and Captain Crowe, the naval knighterrant.

**Launfalus Miles** See **Sir Launfal**.

**Laurence, (Jean) Margaret** 1928–87 Canadian novelist. She was born in Neepawa, Manitoba and educated at the University of Manitoba. She travelled to England and to Africa, which was the background for her novel, *This Side Jordan* (1960), and the stories in *The Tomorrow-Tamer* (1963). Other novels are *The Stone Angel* (1964), *A Jest of God* (1966), *The Fire-Dwellers* (1969) and *The Diviners* (1974). Regarding herself as a religious writer, Laurence tackled moral and social issues, particularly in the 'Manawaka' novels, set in the fictional Prairie town of that name. *Long Drums and Cannons* (1968) is a study of Nigerian literature.

**Laus Veneris** A poem by **Swinburne**, first published in *Poems and Ballads* (1st series, 1866).

Both a peroration on physical love and a treatment of the Tannhauser legend *Laus Veneris* (Praise of Venus) is a reworking of the medieval tale to stress the tragedy of the knight's return to Venus. He depicts Tannhauser in thrall to the goddess in whose lair, the Horselberg, he is ensnared. Tannhauser's vain remonstrations and struggles, his pilgrimage to Rome, his confession to the Pope and the papal response are related in elaborate and luxuriant language. The poem follows the metrical scheme of *The Rubáiyát of Omar Khayyám*.

**Lavengro: The Scholar – The Gypsy – The Priest** A fictionalized autobiography by **George Borrow**, published in 1851. 'Lavengro' is the gypsy name for a philologist.

The book which for many generations of readers established George Borrow as the master of vigorous but unaffected prose narrative was at first intended to be an autobiography which would build on the success of *The Bible in Spain* through accounts of Borrow's other travels and adventures, notably in Russia. However Borrow discovered while writing the book that he was unwilling to present his life straightforwardly in a coherent, chronological narrative. By a quirk of genius he seemed to perceive that the avoidance of the literal truth, frustrating though that might be to readers who knew part of his actual life story, would create imaginative space for a set of episodes of the open road that expressed his narrative self in a convincing manner. He said nothing of Russia, though he had lived there for two years (1833–5). He concealed his early family life behind irresistibly romantic portraits of his father and mother. He drew a veil over the seven-year period (1825–32) which preceded his employment with the British and Foreign Bible Society. Written episodically and with disregard for chronology, *Lavengro* consists of a series of brilliantly conceived episodes concerning the adventures of an almost penniless young man who, leaving London in 1825, wanders about England for a year or more, consorting with tinkers, innkeepers, Nonconformist ministers, eccentric old gentlemen, chaste young women and gypsies. Though many of Borrow's contemporaries distrusted the book, it was soon recognized as a narrative masterpiece. *The Romany Rye* (1857) is a sequel.

**Lavin, Mary** 1912– Irish short-story writer and novelist. Born in Walpole, Massachusetts, she was brought to Ireland when she was 11 and brought up in Dublin. She studied English at University College, Dublin, and taught for two years before marrying and going to live in Co. Meath at Bective Bridge. Her first collection of stories, *Tales From Bective Bridge* (1942), was followed by a dozen other volumes published over the next 40 years. Mary Lavin's work was especially well received in the USA, although she was also recognized in Ireland as one of the foremost practitioners of the short-story form so popular with Irish writers then and since. Her work provides a sharp view of the small tensions of Irish middle-class life: children, widows and young people of marked sensitivity are observed within a stifling, comfortable environment, and their loneliness is enhanced by the intensity with which they experience love in a society dominated by pragmatic considerations. Among her best-known volumes are *The Long Ago and Other Stories* (1944), *The Becker Wives and Other Stories* (1946), *At Sallygap and Other Stories* (1947) and *In The Middle of the Fields* (1967). Her *Collected Stories* were published in 1971. Although she much prefers the short-story form, Mary Lavin has published two novels, *The House In Clewe Street* (1945) and *Mary O'Grady* (1950).

**Law, William** 1686–1761 Religious writer. Born at King's Cliffe, Northamptonshire, and educated at Emmanuel College, Cambridge, he became a fellow of Emmanuel in 1711, after being ordained. Law was a **Nonjuror**, refusing to take the Oath of Allegiance to George I, and was deprived of his fellowship and forbidden to take up any Church appointment. In 1717 he published the first of *Three Letters to the Bishop of Bangor*, a reply to Bishop **Hoadly**'s defence of

the Church's submission of loyalty to George I (*Preservative against the Principles and Practices of the Non-Jurors*, 1716). *Remarks on a Late Book Entitled The Fable of the Bees* (1723) is a reply to the satire of **Bernard de Mandeville**; and in 1726 he wrote *The Absolute Unlawfulness of the Stage Entertainment*, which attacked the contemporary theatre.

In 1726 Law also published *A Practical Treatise on Christian Perfection* and in 1728 came *A Serious Call to a Devout and Holy Life*, the two books by which he is best known. They constitute a guide to the full practice of Christian ideals in everyday life, are written in vigorous prose, and carried a strong appeal in the simplicity of their teaching. *A Serious Call* had great influence: **Samuel Johnson** admired it and **John Wesley** declared that the beginnings of Methodism were to be found in it. *The Case of Reason* (1731) was Law's answer to the deists; he saw reliance on reason as a fundamental error, since both man and the universe are mysteries that admit of no explanation.

In middle life Law became interested in the writings of the German Lutheran mystic, Jakob Boehme, but as a mystic he lost the loyalty of some of his former disciples and Wesley became estranged from him. Among his mystical writings are *The Spirit of Prayer* (written in two parts, 1749 and 1750), *The Way to Divine Knowledge* (1752), and *The Spirit of Love* (again in two parts, 1752 and 1754).

From 1727 to 1737 Law was tutor to Edward Gibbon (the father of the historian) and remained the family's spiritual guide until 1740.

**Lawler, Ray[mond] (Evenor)** 1921– Australian playwright, born in Footscray, Melbourne. Having left school at 13, Lawler worked in a factory before becoming an actor. His first play, *Cradle of Thunder* (1949), was given an amateur production, but his second, *Summer of the Seventeenth Doll* (1955), was selected as the first native Australian play to be performed by the Australian Elizabethan Theatre Trust in Sydney. It stands unchallenged as the first sign of a new movement in the Australian theatre. The greatness thrust upon Lawler was hard to sustain. *The Piccadilly Bushman* (1959), written during his long residence in Ireland, is still preoccupied with Australian themes, unsatisfactorily embodied in the expatriate actor who is its central character. *The Unshaven Cheek* (1963), an exercise in flashbacks, and the more accomplished *The Man Who Shot the Albatross* (1972), which is an experimental play about Captain Bligh's two years as governor of New South Wales (1806–8), were departures from the realistic style that Australian audiences expected from Lawler, and to which he returned with two plays treating earlier years in the lives of the characters of *Summer of the Seventeenth Doll*, *Kid Stakes* (1975) and *Other Times* (1976).

**Lawless, Emily** 1845–1913 Irish poet and novelist. Born in County Kildare, the daughter of the 3rd Baron Cloncurry, she was educated privately and led a retired life, producing several novels, generally serious and thorough studies of the Irish peasantry. They include *A Millionaire's Cousin* (1885), *Hurrish* (1886), and *Grania* (1892). *With the Wild Geese* (1902), a volume of poetry, was well received by contemporary critics.

**Lawrence, D[avid] H[erbert] (Richards)** 1885–1930 Novelist, short-story writer, poet, critic, playwright and essayist. He was born at Eastwood, Nottinghamshire, and educated at Nottingham High School and University College, Nottingham. His father was a coal-miner, his mother from a family with genteel aspirations; emotional friction between the parents, and Lawrence's close relationship with his mother, left important traces in his later writing. He was subject to illness, including lung infections, from a very early age and ill health dogged him throughout his life, culminating in his death from tuberculosis at the age of 44.

For a brief period after leaving school in 1901 Lawrence became a junior clerk in a surgical appliance factory. From the following year until 1906 he worked as a pupil-teacher, at Eastwood and then at Ilkeston, while saving the money necessary to take a training-course at University College. He matriculated at 22 and joined the staff of Davidson Road School in Croydon, an important move towards emotional and financial independence and the prelude to his literary career.

In 1909 a number of his poems were submitted by his friend from youth, Jessie Chambers, to **Ford Madox Ford** of *The English Review* and

these were published in the November issue. Ford also read his first novel, *The White Peacock* (1911), and successfully recommended it to William Heinemann, who subjected it to some censorship. Lawrence gave up teaching after a serious illness and his second novel, *The Trespasser*, followed in 1912. Early in the same year he met Frieda Weekley (*née* von Richthofen), daughter of a German baron and wife of a professor at Nottingham whom Lawrence knew. They went to Germany together and were married after Frieda's divorce in 1914. *Sons and Lovers* (1913), which draws on Lawrence's childhood and contains a portrayal of Jessie Chambers (the Miriam of the novel), has always been one of his most popular books.

During World War I the Lawrences at first lived in London, then moved to Cornwall; they developed close friendships with many of the leading literary figures of the period. **David Garnett** was already a friend; others included **Aldous Huxley**, **Bertrand Russell**, **Lady Ottoline Morrell**, **Katherine Mansfield**, **John Middleton Murry** and **Richard Aldington**. *The Rainbow* (1915), considered by many critics to be his best novel, was prosecuted by the authorities and banned on grounds of obscenity. Further harassment occurred when the Lawrences were accused of spying for the Germans; they were officially expelled from Cornwall in October 1917. He had completed another novel, *Women in Love*, but was unable to find a publisher. Two volumes of poems appeared, *Look! We Have Come Through!* (1917) and the misnamed *New Poems* (1918), but in 1919 he and Frieda left England for Italy. *Women in Love* was published privately in 1920 in New York, defeating court action there in 1922; an English edition followed in 1921 with changes dictated by censorship and a threatened libel suit. With *The Lost Girl* (1920), which won the James Tait Black Memorial Prize, and *Aaron's Rod* (1922), Lawrence at last had the financial security to

Industrial Nottingham in 1901.

travel. An incomplete novel written in 1920–1, *Mr Noon*, carrying forward his life following *Sons and Lovers*, was published in 1984.

Between 1922 and 1926 he and Frieda left Italy to live intermittently in Ceylon, Australia, New Mexico and Mexico, and these provided the settings for several of his subsequent novels and stories. *Kangaroo* (1923) was written during a four-month stay in Australia, where Lawrence met M. L. Skinner (with whom he collaborated on *The Boy in the Bush*, 1924); *The Plumed Serpent* (1926) was inspired by his stays in Mexico. His last novel, *Lady Chatterley's Lover*, was published in Florence in 1928 and an expurgated edition in England and USA in 1932, but had to await favourable court verdicts in 1959 and 1960 respectively before it became freely available in its original form. The first two versions of the novel were published independently as *The First Lady Chatterley* (1944) and *John Thomas and Lady Jane* (1972).

In 1925, after a severe illness in Mexico, it was discovered that Lawrence was suffering from tuberculosis, and he was given a year or two to live; there is contradictory testimony about whether he was told what he had, but he never called his disease by name. He and Frieda returned to Europe, but his health continued to decline. He finally died at Vence, in France, on 2 March 1930.

Although his literary career spanned only two decades, the body of work is considerable. His short stories, generally considered to be among the best in the genre, first appeared in small collections: *The Prussian Officer* (1914), *England, My England* (1922), *The Woman Who Rode Away* (1928), *Love Among the Haystacks* (1930) and *The Lovely Lady* (1933). They were gathered into three volumes in 1955. He also wrote novelettes, which include some of his best writing: *The Ladybird*, *The Fox*, *The Captain's Doll* (1923); *St Mawr* together with *The Princess* (1925); *Sun* (1926); *The Escaped Cock* (1929; also known as *The Man Who Died*), and *The Virgin and the Gipsy* (1930). His poetry, first collected in a two-volume edition in 1928, includes *Love Poems* (1913), *Amores* (1916), *Look! We Have Come Through!* (1917), *New Poems* (1918), *Bay* (1919), *Birds, Beasts and Flowers* (1923), *Pansies* (1929), *Nettles* (1930) and *Last Poems* (1932).

Among the non-fiction, *Psychoanalysis and the Unconscious* (1921) and *Fantasia of the Unconscious* (1922) provide illuminating insights into his view of life. *Studies in Classic American Literature* (1923), one of the earliest appreciations of (mainly 19th-century) American writers, concludes with highly idiosyncratic but delightfully entertaining essays on **Moby-Dick** and **Whitman**. He also wrote about **Thomas Hardy** in 'Study of Thomas Hardy' first published in *Phoenix*.

In addition Lawrence wrote plays, several about mining families, which were collected in

D. H. Lawrence in 1908, at University College, Nottingham.

*The Complete Plays* (1965); excellent travel books of which three are set in Italy: *Twilight in Italy* (1916), *Sea and Sardinia* (1921) and *Etruscan Places* (1932); and one of essays about Mexico and New Mexico, *Mornings in Mexico* (1927); he also compiled several volumes of general essays, *Reflections on the Death of a Porcupine* (1925) and *Assorted Articles* (1930). During the lean war years Lawrence contracted to write a school history, *Movements in European History* (1921), which had to be published under a pseudonym Lawrence H. Davison; it was bowdlerized for use in Ireland. He also translated several volumes of Verga. 13 of his paintings were seized by the police in the London exhibition in July 1929 and returned to Lawrence only after he promised never to bring them back to England; most of his pictures were reproduced in *The Paintings of D. H. Lawrence* (1929). Many of his uncollected stories, essays and introductions were included in *Phoenix: The Posthumous Papers* (1936) and *Phoenix II: Uncollected, Unpublished and Other Prose Works* (1968). *The Letters of D. H. Lawrence* (to be published in 8 vols., ed. J. T. Boulton, I to IV published) include all of the author's correspondence during a brief but intensive career. His complete works are being published in the new, authoritative Cambridge edition.

**Lawrence, George Alfred** 1827–76 Novelist. Educated at Rugby and Balliol College,

Oxford, he was called to the Bar in 1852. His popular novel *Guy Livingstone* (1857) introduced 'muscular blackguardism' (as opposed to **Charles Kingsley**'s 'muscular Christianity') in the character of the brutally strong and unprincipled hero. Eight other novels followed, including *Sword and Gown* (1859), *Barren Honour* (1862), *Breaking a Butterfly* (1869) and *Hagarene* (1874).

**Lawrence, T[homas] E[dward]** 1888–1935 Soldier and author, commonly known as 'Lawrence of Arabia'. He was born at Tremadoc in Caernarvonshire, the illegitimate son of Sir Robert Chapman. Educated at Oxford High School and Jesus College, Oxford, he travelled to the Middle East in 1911 as an archaeologist. In World War I he worked in the intelligence section of the Arab Bureau, and in 1916 organized the revolt of the Arab tribesmen against the Turks, acquiring a tenacious reputation as a legendary hero, enhanced by his appearance with the Arab delegation at the Versailles conference. Refusing numerous honours, and dissatisfied with British policy towards the Near East, he enlisted in the Royal Air Force under the name of Ross, and later, Shaw, serving until 1935.

*The Seven Pillars of Wisdom: A Triumph* was published in a limited edition, with illustrations by Eric Kennington, in 1926. A shortened version, *Revolt in the Desert*, was published in 1927. Accepted by some contemporary critics as a literary masterpiece, *The Seven Pillars of Wisdom* has also been condemned as an example of monstrous self-aggrandizement. Apart from contributions to early archaeological reports and occasional introductory essays, Lawrence published a translation *The Odyssey of Homer* (1932) and *The Mint* (limited edition, 1936), a curiously uncertain and ambiguous account of Lawrence's experience of life in the ranks, subtitled 'Notes made in the RAF depot between August and December 1922, and at Cadet College in 1925'. *The Letters of T. E. Lawrence* (1938) was edited by **David Garnett**.

**Lawson, Henry** 1867–1922 Australian poet. The son of a Norwegian sailor who became a gold prospector, Lawson was born at Grenfell in New South Wales. He had only a rudimentary education, restricted by deafness from the age of 10, and started to earn his living when he was 13. After his parents separated he went to Sydney with his mother, who launched a socialist periodical, *The Republican*, to which Lawson contributed his first writings. He also wrote for *The Boomerang* (a radical Brisbane weekly) and *The Sydney Worker* but, like his contemporary **A. B. Paterson**, he found his best form and outlet in *The Bulletin*. He went to live in the outback in the north of New South Wales in

1892 and the bush ballads and stories that resulted from his stay there became a popular feature of *The Bulletin* in the 1890s. He married in 1896 and travelled to Europe and New Zealand, returning to Australia in 1902. The best of Lawson's work was written by the turn of the century; after 1901 he seemed unable to recapture his laconic humour and fine balance of style, and his later work is marred by sentimentality. Lawson's first collection was *Stories in Prose and Verse* (1894), followed by *While the Billy Boils* (1896), *On the Track* (1900) and *Joe Wilson and His Mates* (1901). A collection in three volumes, *The Stories of Henry Lawson*, was edited by Cecil Mann (1965).

**Lawson, John Howard** 1894–1977 American playwright. Born in New York City and educated at Williams College, Lawson helped shape the theatre of social consciousness in the 1920s and 1930s. His first play, *Processional* (1925), is a protest against the harshness of life during a coal strike in West Virginia. Lawson was among the first playwrights to move to Hollywood, where he became active as a leader of the Communist faction. *Marching Song* (1937) was another leftist play, which showed the triumph of labour's solidarity against the persecutions of an uncaring management. His career was cut short when he was summoned before the House Un-American Activities Committee. As one of the 'Hollywood Ten', he served a one-year sentence (1950–1) for contempt of the House. *Parlor Magic* (1963) was the only play he produced after the effective blacklisting of his name. His other plays include *Roger Boomer* (1923), *Nirvana* (1926), *Loudspeaker* (1927), *The International* (1928), *Success Story* (1932), *Gentlewoman* (1934) and *The Pure in Heart* (1937).

*Lay of the Last Minstrel, The* A poem in six **cantos** by **Sir Walter Scott**, published in 1805. It was the first of Scott's romances in this form. The story is told by an ancient minstrel, the last of his race, and set in the 16th century.

The widowed lady of Branksome Hall blames her husband's death on Lord Cranstoun, who is in love with her daughter Margaret. Margaret returns his love but the feud between the two families prevents a marriage. Margaret's mother resorts to sorcery to revenge herself on Cranstoun, commissioning the dubious Sir William Deloraine to steal a magic book from the tomb of the alchemist Michael Scott in Melrose Abbey. Deloraine's encounter with Cranstoun after the theft serves to introduce the character of Gilpin Horner, Cranstoun's goblin page. This legendary Border character was the real inspiration of the poem (suggested to Scott by the Countess of Dalkeith); in spite of his wilful pranks, he is the agent for the reconciliation of the two families and the union of Margaret and Lord Cranstoun.

**Layamon** All that is known of Layamon comes from an early version of his sole surviving work, *Brut*, written in the late ·12th century. He was, he says, a priest at Areley Kings in the Severn valley and there decided to write his history of England from its foundation by the legendary Brutus. The poem, based on Wace's *Roman de Brut* (1155), is notable for its contribution to the development of **Arthurian literature**.

**Layard, Sir Austen Henry** 1817–94 Archaeologist and excavator of Nineveh. After working for some years in the office of a London solicitor he became, almost accidentally, interested in the excavations in western Asia which resulted in the publication of his famous works *Nineveh and its Remains* (1848–9) and *The Ruins of Nineveh and Babylon* (1853). From 1861–6 he held the office of Under-Secretary for Foreign Affairs and was later Ambassador to Madrid and Constantinople. He was a close friend of **Charles Dickens**.

*Lays of Ancient Rome, The* A sequence of poems by **Thomas Babington Macaulay**, published in 1842. Macaulay was prompted by Barthold Niebuhr's suggestion, in *The History of Rome*, that Livy's narrative was based on traditional ballads. 'Horatius' tells of the defence of the Sublician Bridge against the Etruscans by Horatius Cocles; 'The Battle of Lake Regillus' describes the Romans' defeat of the Latins (*c.* 496 BC) with the divine aid of Castor and Pollux; 'Virginia' concerns the maiden killed by her father, Virginius, to save her from the lust of Appius Claudius; and 'The Prophecy of Capys' tells of the prophecy of the future greatness of Rome by the blind Capys to Romulus.

**Layton, Irving** 1912– Canadian poet. Layton was born in Romania but his family emigrated to Canada in 1913, settling in Montreal where Layton studied agriculture before entering McGill University. He graduated in 1936 and served with the Royal Canadian Air Force during World War II. Layton was a teacher after the war and editor of *First Statement*, a literary magazine which later merged with *Preview* to become *Northern Review*. He was also lecturer in modern poetry at Sir George William's University and Professor of English at York University. Layton's career as a poet began with *Here and Now* (1945). *In the Midst of My Fever* (1954), *The Bull Calf and Other Poems* (1956), *A Red Carpet for the Sun* (1959), *The Swinging Flesh* (1961), *The Shattered Plinths* (1968) and *Droppings from Heaven* (1979), are among his numerous volumes. Layton's early work was designed to oppose the austerity of the poetry

being published in Canada at the time. His later work discloses his increasing resentment of social inequality and a deepening sensitivity.

**Le Carré, John** Pseudonym of the novelist David John Moore Cornwell (1931– ). After a public school education, he attended the universities of Berne and Oxford, taught briefly at Eton and then spent five years in the British Foreign Service. His novels about the grey, duplicitous underworld of the secret service have increasingly come to be regarded less as thrillers than as original, perceptive documentations of the post-1945 Cold War climate.

Le Carré's third novel, *The Spy Who Came In From The Cold* (1963), made his reputation, and remains his most concentrated and grim portrait of the self-despising ideology and shabby, compromised life of the spy. A previous novel, however, *Call for the Dead* (1961), introduced Le Carré's best-known character, George Smiley, who has subsequently reappeared in two later books, *Tinker, Tailor, Soldier, Spy* (1974) and *Smiley's People* (1980). A highly successful television dramatization of the former confirmed Le Carré's popularity. His other novels have included *The Looking-Glass War* (1965); *A Small Town in Germany* (1968); *The Honourable Schoolboy* (1977); *The Perfect Spy* (1986), drawing on his own relations with his domineering, raffish father; *The Naive and Sentimental Lover* (1971), forsaking espionage; *The Little Drummer Girl* (1983), about the cause of Palestinian liberation; and, in response to the end of the Cold War, *The Russian House* (1989).

**Le Fanu, (Joseph) Sheridan** 1814–73 Novelist. Born in Dublin of a family related to **Richard Brinsley Sheridan**, he was educated at Trinity College and called to the Bar in 1839, though he did not practise. He contributed to the *Dublin University Magazine* and became well known with the publication of his Irish ballads, 'Phaudrig Croohoore' and 'Shamus O'Brien' (1837). His first novel, *The Cock and Anchor*, appeared in 1845. He became proprietor and editor of the *Dublin University Magazine* in 1869. In all, he published some 20 books including novels, stories and verse, the latter including a drama 'Beatrice', 'The Legend of the Glaive' and 'Song of the Bottle'. He is best known, however, for his ingenious and skilfully constructed tales of mystery and terror, notably *The House by the Churchyard* (1863), *Uncle Silas* (1864) and a volume of short stories, *In a Glass Darkly* (1872).

**Le Gallienne, Richard (Thomas)** 1866–1947 Poet and essayist. Born and educated in Liverpool, he worked as a chartered accountant before the publication of *My Lady's Sonnets* in 1887. His best-known book of verse, *The Lonely*

*Dancer*, was published in 1913. His style is characteristic of the 1890s, being uncompromisingly mannered and artificial. *The Romantic Nineties* (1926) gives a valuable account of the circle which included **Wilde**, **Arthur Symons** and **Aubrey Beardsley**. Other volumes of reminiscences are *Quest for the Golden Girl* (1896) and *From a Paris Garret* (1936).

**LeGuin, Ursula** 1929– American writer of science fiction, born in Berkeley, California, and educated at Radcliffe College and Columbia University.

Her first three novels, *Rocannon's World* (1966), *Planet of Exile* (1966) and *City of Illusions* (1967), are characteristic of all her work in their rejection of the technological concerns of more traditional science fiction and in their interest in humanism and anthropology. Her most acclaimed work, *The Earthsea Trilogy*, is composed of *A Wizard of Earthsea* (1968), *The Tombs of Atuan* (1971) and *The Farthest Shore* (1972). While working on the trilogy she also wrote *The Left Hand of Darkness* (1969): set on an imaginary planet populated by 'androgynes', the novel reflects LeGuin's interest in Taoist thought. In some of her later works she has been critical of contemporary American political and social values: *The Word for World is Forest* (1972), about Vietnam, *The Dispossessed* (1974), a fantasy set on an anarchist moon colony and its capitalist mother planet, and *The New Atlantis* (1975), which presents a futuristic vision of totalitarianism in the USA.

Her other works include *The Lathe of Heaven* (1971), *From Elfland to Poughkeepsie* (1973), *Dreams Must Explain Themselves* (1975), *Wild Angels* (1975), *The Wind's Twelve Quarters* (1975), *Orisinian Tales* (1976), *Very Far Away From Anywhere Else* (1976), *The Water is Wide* (1976), *Lesse Webster* (1979), *Malafrena* (1979), *The Language of the Night* (1979), *The Beginning Place* (1980), *The Eye of the Heron and Other Stories* (1980) and *Hard Words and Other Poems* (1981).

**Le Sueur, Meridel** 1900– American radical and feminist writer. Born in Murray, Iowa, Le Sueur spent her childhood in Texas, Oklahoma and Kansas. Her father was a socialist lawyer and participated in various reform movements on behalf of farmers and workers. After a period in New York City, where she studied at the American Academy of Dramatic Art and lived in an anarchist commune with Emma Goldman, among others, she moved to Hollywood and began to write articles and stories for radical publications such as *The Daily Worker* and *The New Masses*. Her first novel, *The Girl* (1939), examines the lives of various women whom she had known and observed in the 1930s. *Salute to Spring* (1940) is a collection of short stories

describing the struggle of ordinary women's lives during the Depression. *North Star Country* (1945) is a history of the Midwest in which she grew up. She continued to write radical journalism throughout the 1950s and 1960s. A volume of her poetry, *Rites of Ancient Ripening*, was published in 1975. Her other books include *Conquistadors* (1973), *The Mound Builders* (1974) and a series of children's books. Her work as a whole helped to establish a tradition of feminist dissent on which the women's movement of today is partly based.

**Leacock, Stephen** 1869–1944 Canadian writer, best known as a humorist. Born in England at Swanmore, Hampshire, Leacock was taken to Canada when he was six. He grew up in the Lake Simcoe region of Ontario and was educated at Toronto's leading secondary school, Upper Canada College, and at the University of Toronto. After graduating in 1891, he taught Modern Languages at Upper Canada College. He subsequently studied political economy at the University of Chicago and was appointed a lecturer at McGill University in 1901. He published his first book, *Elements of Political Science*, which became a standard college textbook, in 1906. In 1907–8 he went on a lecture tour of the British Empire, speaking on Imperial Federation. He was appointed Head of the Department of Political Economy at McGill on his return and continued there until his retirement in 1936. The first of his many humorous works, *Literary Lapses*, appeared in 1910. Leacock subsequently published an average of one humorous book a year for the remainder of his life. These include *Nonsense Novels* (1911), *Sunshine Sketches of a Little Town* (1912), *Arcadian Adventures with the Idle Rich* (1914), *Moonbeams from the Larger Lunacy* (1915), *Further Foolishness* (1916), *Frenzied Fiction* (1918), *Winnowed Wisdom* (1926), *My Remarkable Uncle* (1942) and *Last Leaves* (1945). Like his two great mentors, **Dickens** and **Twain**, Leacock undertook highly successful lecture tours. *My Discovery of England* (1922) and *My Discovery of the West* (1937) grew out of such tours. From 1908 onwards he spent his summers at a home he built on the shores of Lake Couchiching in Orillia, Ontario, the original of the 'little town' of Mariposa of his *Sunshine Sketches*. Leacock's greatest talent was as a master of the short sketch or extended anecdote and his work has a strong oral flavour. It belongs in the tradition of such North American humorists as **Artemus Ward**, Mark Twain and, in Canada, **Thomas Chandler Haliburton**. Most of Leacock's books are miscellanies, but the finest of them, *Sunshine Sketches of a Little Town*, *Arcadian Adventures with the Idle Rich* and *My Discovery of England*, are more unified. *Sunshine Sketches* is a satirical but affectionate portrait of small-town Canada.

*Arcadian Adventures* is a much more trenchant satire of the self-seeking plutocracy of a large American city and is informed by Leacock's work as an economist. *My Discovery of England* parodies the travel journals of Europeans abroad by using the provincial as a yardstick for measuring the metropolitan. Leacock was a staunch advocate of the values of the British Empire and the Victorian ideal of progress, and saw Anglo-Saxon humour as an expression of the growth of a humanitarian society. He demonstrated this belief in a series of books on humour and humorists published in the 1930s. These include *Mark Twain* (1932) and *Humour: Its Theory and Technique* (1935).

**Leader, The** A weekly periodical founded by **G. H. Lewes** and Thornton Leigh Hunt, published from 1850 to 1866.

**Lear** A play by **Edward Bond**, first performed at the **Royal Court Theatre**, London, in 1971.
  *Lear* is a complex reworking of **Shakespeare**'s *King Lear* in which the original is scarcely recognizable. Bond's interest is in 20th-century political forces and in the process of political discovery that leads the old king from an opening scene in which he shoots a worker in order to enforce the speedy building of a wall to a final scene in which he himself is shot for trying to dig up the same wall.

**Lear, Edward** 1812–88 Artist, traveller and nonsense poet. Born in London, the son of a stockbroker and the youngest of 20 children, he was educated at home, chiefly by his sister Anne, but was obliged to start earning his living at the age of 15. He was commissioned to make drawings of the parrots in the Zoological Gardens, and this led to his being engaged as an artist by the Earl of Derby, who kept a menagerie at Knowsley Hall. Lear's task was to produce illustrations for a description of the inhabitants. Successfully establishing himself as an accomplished artist, Lear was eventually engaged to give drawing lessons to Queen Victoria. He travelled extensively in the Mediterranean and visited India and Ceylon, finally settling at San Remo in Italy.
  While working at Knowsley Hall, Lear wrote nonsense poetry for the Earl of Derby's children; later he made nonsense drawings to accompany them. This singular talent produced some of his most enduring work. Lear's verse was published as *A Book of Nonsense* (1845; enlarged 1861, 1863, 1870), *A Book of Nonsense and More Nonsense* (1862), *Nonsense Songs, Stories, Botany and Alphabets* (1871), *More Nonsense, Pictures, Rhymes, Botany, Etc.* (1872) and *Laughable Lyrics, a Fresh Book of Nonsense Poems* (1877). *Queery Leary Nonsense* (1911) contained new material and was compiled by Lady Stra-

One of Edward Lear's illustrations for *A Book of Nonsense*, 1845. 'There was an Old Man in a tree, who was horribly bored by a bee . . .'

chey; *Teapots and Quails* (1953) contained unpublished fragments and was edited by P. Hofer and A. Davidson. *The Complete Nonsense of Edward Lear* (1947) was edited by Holbrook Jackson. His numerous well-known poems include 'The Owl and the Pussycat', 'The Jumblies' and 'The Courtship of the Yongy-Bonghy-Bo'. He was also an accomplished exponent of the limerick form, and did much to popularize such verse jingles.
  Lear's travel books include *Illustrated Excursions in Italy* (1846), *A Tour in Sicily* (1847), *Journal of a Landscape Painter in Albania, Illyria etc.* (1851), *Journal of a Landscape Painter in Southern Calabria* (1852), *Journal of a Landscape Painter in Corsica* (1870) and *Italian Journal* (1873–5). *The Letters of Edward Lear* (1907) and *Later Letters* (1911) were edited by Lady Strachey, and are valued for their discerning pictures of his times. **Tennyson**'s poem 'To E. L. on his Travels' was addressed to Lear.
  Although at the centre of a wide circle of gifted literary and artistic friends, Lear suffered throughout his life from loneliness, depression and melancholy, conditions partly attributable to his subjection to epilepsy. In some sense all the isolated and marked creatures of his fantasy, the Yongy-Bonghy-Bo, the Dong with the Luminous Nose and the Pobble Who Has No Toes, are partial self-portraits.

**Leatherstocking Tales** A series of five novels by **James Fenimore Cooper**, set in the early frontier period of American history. They take their name from their central protagonist, Natty Bumppo, who is variously called Leatherstocking, Deerslayer, Hawkeye and Pathfinder. The chronological sequence differs from the dates of composition. *The Pioneers; or the Sources of the Susquehanna* (1823) was the first volume to be written, followed soon after by *The Last of the*

An illustration for the *Seaside Library* edition (1878) of James Fenimore Cooper's *The Deerslayer*, first published in 1841. Deerslayer (Natty Bumppo) is seen with Judith Hutter.

*Mohicans: A Tale of 1757* (1826) and *The Prairie: A Tale* (1827). Cooper later completed the series with *The Pathfinder; or the Inland Sea* (1840) and *The Deerslayer; or the First War Path* (1841).

The first novel in order of events (though the last to be written), *The Deerslayer*, relates Bumppo's experiences as a young man, and takes place in upstate New York in the early 1740s. The action begins as Deerslayer and his friend Hurry Harry approach Lake Glimmerglass, or Oswego, where the trapper Thomas Hutter lives with his daughters, the beautiful Judith and the feeble-minded Hetty. Hutter's floating log fort is attacked by Iroquois Indians, and the two frontiersmen join in the fight. Harry and Hutter are captured. Deerslayer is joined by his Mohican friend, Chingachgook, whose bride Hist is being held by the Iroquois, and they eventually manage to ransom the two men. They then try to rescue Hist, but Hutter is killed and Deerslayer is captured in the attempt. The frontiersman is released on parole so that he may see his friends for the last time and, keeping his word, he returns to the Indian camp to await his death. Judith, however, manages to delay the proceedings long enough for Chingachgook to arrive with a troop of English soldiers and save Deerslayer's life.

The next novel in the series, *The Last of the Mohicans*, presents Bumppo in his maturity, and is set in 1757 during the Seven Years War between the French and the British. (In this novel he is known as Hawkeye.) Cora and Alice Munro are on their way to Fort William Henry to join their father, the commander. They are accompanied by Major Duncan Heyward and a singing teacher, David Gamut. Their Indian guide, Magua, plans to betray the group to the Iroquois, who are fighting on the side of the French. Magua's plan, however, is frustrated by Hawkeye and his friends Chingachgook and Uncas, who are the last Mohican chieftains. The group arrives at the fort, but Munro is forced to surrender to the French commander Montcalm. Although supposedly given safe conduct, the English are attacked and the girls captured by Delawares and Hurons. The former take Cora; the latter, Alice. Alice and Uncas, also a prisoner, manage to escape. Uncas is then welcomed at the camp of the Delawares and named successor to the old chief. Magua, however, has laid claim to the captive Cora, and he eventually kills both the young woman and Uncas. Hawkeye avenges the death of his friend and kills Magua.

*The Pathfinder* takes place soon after *The Last of the Mohicans*, in the same conflict between French and Indians and the British colonials. Mabel Dunham is making her way to Oswego, the British fort on Lake Ontario, to join her father. She is accompanied by a group consisting of her uncle, Charles Cap, a Tuscarora Indian named Arrowhead and his wife Dew-in-June, the scout Pathfinder (Natty Bumppo), Chingachgook the Mohican chief, and Jasper Western the sailor. The party is harassed by Iroquois, and Arrowhead and his wife disappear. The rest of the company arrives safely at the fort, then proceeds with Mabel's father on Jasper Western's boat to relieve a post in the Thousand Islands. But Jasper is suspected of being disloyal to the English and is sent back to Oswego, while Dunham and his force set out to attack French supply boats. Dew-in-June then arrives, with the warning that Arrowhead, at the head of an Iroquois force, is leading an attack on the post. The Iroquois are eventually routed by Pathfinder and Chingachgook, and Jasper is arrested as a traitor, to the despair of Mabel who, in spite of a promise to Pathfinder, is in love with Jasper. Muir – the lieutenant who had accused Jasper – is unmasked as the real traitor, and Arrowhead kills him. Dunham dies and Pathfinder, realizing the truth, relinquishes Mabel to Jasper.

The next novel in the series, *The Pioneers*, is set in 1793 in Otsego County in the recently settled region of New York state. While hunting deer, Judge Temple, one of the principal landowners in the area, wounds Oliver Edwards, the companion of the ageing Natty Bumppo, now known as Leatherstocking. The judge and his daughter Elizabeth befriend Edwards, who becomes their overseer, meanwhile maintaining his friendship with Bumppo and with old John Mohegan, whom everyone knows to be the Mohican chief Chingachgook. It is suspected that

Edwards is the chief's son and soon Elizabeth and her friends are disdaining his company. Bumppo is arrested for shooting deer out of season and spends a short time in prison. Elizabeth goes to visit him upon his release but is caught in a forest fire on her return, and is saved by Edwards. Chingachgook is also caught in the fire, and dies in spite of Bumppo's efforts to save him. A party searching for Elizabeth comes upon a demented old man. It is discovered that he is Major Effingham, the Loyalist who had once owned Judge Temple's estate, but who was lost in the war and had his lands confiscated. It is revealed that Oliver Edwards is his grandson. Temple relinquishes half of his estate to Oliver, and he and Elizabeth are betrothed at the end.

*The Prairie* is set in 1804 on the frontier of the great plains. Natty Bumppo – now in his 80s and known simply as the trapper – has joined the western movement. He meets a wagon train, gains an unpleasant impression of its leaders, Ishmael Bush and his brother-in-law Abiram White, and is puzzled by the confinement of a woman in a covered wagon. The trapper's wisdom enables the train to evade an Indian raiding party, and he guides it to a safe camp. A young soldier then joins the camp and Bumppo is overjoyed to recognize Duncan Uncas Middleton, a descendant of his friend Duncan Heyward. Duncan is on a mission for the army but is also seeking his betrothed, Inez de Certavallos, who has been kidnapped and is being held for ransom. The trapper remembers the confined woman, who proves to be Inez, and the two proceed to rescue her. The travel-

'Going down the rapids.' An illustration for James Fenimore Cooper's *'Leatherstocking Tales'*.

lers endure a prairie fire, a buffalo stampede, and capture by the Sioux. A Pawnee raid on the Sioux frees them, but Ishmael Bush catches up with them and accuses Bumppo of the murder of one of his men. There has indeed been a murder, but the guilty man proves to be Abiram White. The arrival of Duncan's soldiers finally provides the party with safety, with the trapper's Pawnee friends watching quietly. The end of the tale brings the frontiersman's life to a close. He dies peacefully on the prairie, surrounded by his friends of both races.

*Leaves of Grass* The major work of **Walt Whitman**, the collection consisted of 12 untitled poems when it was first published in 1855. Over the next 37 years it appeared in five revised editions and three reissues. Whitman added, deleted, or revised poems for each edition.

The first edition of *Leaves of Grass* included the poems that Whitman eventually titled 'Song of Myself', 'I Sing the Body Electric', and 'The Sleepers'. He wrote a now famous preface for it but omitted it from subsequent editions. The second edition appeared in 1856 and contained 20 new poems, among them 'Sun Down Poem' (later renamed 'Crossing Brooklyn Ferry') and 'Poem of the Open Road' (renamed 'Song of the Open Road'). In 1860 Whitman published a third edition, adding 'Out of the Cradle Endlessly Rocking', one of his most memorable poems; the 'Calamus' poems, extolling friendship among men; and 'Enfants d'Adam' (later titled 'Children of Adam'), a group of poems about heterosexual, procreative love. The fourth edition of *Leaves of Grass* (1867) was bound with *Drum-Taps* (which had been published separately in 1865) and with *Sequel*. *Drum-Taps* was a series of poems inspired by what Whitman had witnessed while nursing the wounded during the Civil War, and *Sequel* contained his elegy for the assassinated president, Abraham Lincoln, 'When Lilacs Last in the Dooryard Bloom'd'. For the fifth edition (1871) Whitman incorporated the poems from *Drum-Taps* into the body of *Leaves of Grass*, and also added a new 'annex' – 'Passage to India' – which he later incorporated into the body of the work for the sixth edition (1881). In 1876 a reissue of *Leaves of Grass* appeared sometimes referred to as the 'Centennial' edition. For the 1889 reissue of the 1881 edition, Whitman added another annex, which included a group of new poems entitled 'Sands at Seventy' and a prose piece called 'A Backward Glance O'er Travel'd Roads' – both of which had previously appeared in *November Boughs* (1888). The final version of *Leaves of Grass* to appear in Whitman's lifetime, though sometimes called the 'Deathbed' edition (1891–2), is simply a reissue of the 1881 edition supplemented with 'Sands at Seventy' and 'Goodbye My Fancy'.

Both the form and content of the poems in *Leaves of Grass* were revolutionary; Whitman's sprawling lines and cataloguing technique, as well as his belief that poetry should include the lowly, the profane, even the obscene, have had enormous influence. His intention in writing *Leaves of Grass*, he said, was to create a truly American poem, one 'proportionate to our continent, with its powerful races of men, its tremendous historic events, its great oceans, its mountains, and its illimitable prairies'. In fact, the poem goes beyond its specifically American subject to deal with the universal themes of nature, fertility and mortality.

**Leavis, F[rank] R[aymond]** 1895–1978 Critic. Born the son of a music-shop proprietor in Cambridge, Leavis was educated in his home city at the Perse School and Emmanuel College, where he abandoned his study of history in favour of English. After serving as a stretcher-bearer in World War I he returned to his studies and absorbed the critical teachings of **I. A. Richards**, whose Practical Criticism lectures he attended. He lived by part-time teaching, and during a period as a probationary lecturer married his former pupil Q. D. Roth (see **Q. D. Leavis**) in 1929; but he had to wait until 1936 for a fellowship at Downing College, and 1937 for a university lectureship. During these years he wrote a series of cultural manifestos, *Mass Civilization and Minority Culture* (1933), *For Continuity* (1933), and *Culture and Environment* (with Denys Thompson, 1933), which propose the study of English literature as a base from which to rally the discriminating educated minority against the threats to cultural continuity posed by the processes of industrialism, especially by the cinema, advertising and the spread of 'mass' culture. These arguments formed the basis of the critical campaign undertaken by *Scrutiny*, which Leavis guided as co-editor from 1932 to 1953. His *New Bearings in English Poetry* (1932) began a thorough revision of the English literary tradition, championing **Gerard Manley Hopkins**, **T. S. Eliot**, **Pound** and **Yeats** as the creators of a modernist tradition after the post-Swinburne 'arrest'. The implicit recasting of the poetic tradition (based on the theories of Eliot and I. A. Richards) was defined in *Revaluation* (1936), where Leavis opposed a 'line of wit' from **Donne** to Eliot to the line, with its emphasis on melody and special poetic diction, running from **Milton** to **Swinburne**.

In *The Great Tradition* (1948) he brought the same kind of historical and critical discrimination to the English novel. The 'great' novelists (**Jane Austen**, **George Eliot**, **Henry James**, **Joseph Conrad**) were admired for their life-enhancing moral seriousness. The subsequent rehabilitation of **Dickens** in *Dickens the Novelist* (with Q. D. Leavis, 1970) identified a complementary tradition linking **Blake** and **D. H. Lawrence**, whose work he had defended in *D. H. Lawrence: Novelist* (1955). This shift accompanied his increasingly embattled response to 'technologico-Benthamite' trends in British culture.

Leavis refused to define the theoretical basis of his judgements, though it can be inferred from numerous asides. Historically considered, he belongs to the tradition of **Arnold**, **Ruskin** and other writers on 'the condition of England'. The almost religious seriousness which he introduced to criticism inspired a generation of followers ('Leavisites') with a sense of vocation in teaching a subject deemed central to civilization. His revaluation, not just of the canon of English literature, but of the status of criticism, established him as the most important English-speaking critic of his time.

**Leavis, Q[ueenie] D[orothy]** 1906–81 Critic. Born in London, the daughter of a draper, Queenie Roth was educated at Girton College, Cambridge, studying English under **I. A. Richards**. While researching into the history of the English reading public, she married **F. R. Leavis** in 1929. Her only book, *Fiction and the Reading Public* (1932), offered a sociological diagnosis of trends in English popular culture since the 17th century, tracing how the readership of fiction had progressively split into the 'highbrow' minority interested in the art of the novel and a mass audience consuming popular romances, with best-sellers tending to confuse standards. This early attempt at a sociological approach to literature influenced her husband's critical work and the ethos of *Scrutiny*, to which she was a regular contributor while bringing up her family. She wrote important critical reassessments of **Dickens** in *Dickens the Novelist* (with F. R. Leavis, 1970) and of **Jane Austen**, **Charlotte** and **Emily Brontë**, **Nathaniel Hawthorne** and **Edith Wharton** in essays gathered posthumously, with other work, in *Collected Essays* (three volumes, 1983– ). She had a special interest in women writers.

**Lecky, William Edward Hartpole** 1838–1903 Historian. Born near Dublin, he was educated at Cheltenham College and Trinity College, Dublin. Influenced by **Henry Thomas Buckle**'s approach to history, he published *The Religious Tendencies of the Age* (1860) and *The Leaders of Public Opinion in Ireland* (1861) anonymously. *The Declining Sense of the Miraculous* (1863) became the first two chapters of *A History of the Rise and Influence of the Spirit of Rationalism in Europe* (1865), which argued with considerable force that progress is due to the spirit of rationalism and the tolerance demanded by reason, and is always impeded by theological dogmatism and bigotry. The book made Lecky famous and he followed it with *The History of European Morals from Augustus to Charlemagne* (1869). *A History of England in the Eighteenth Century* (1878–90) was published in eight volumes, which were extended to 12 (1892). Lecky also published some historical essays and two later volumes, *Democracy and Liberty* (1896) and *The Map of Life: Conduct and Character* (1899). From 1895 he sat in Parliament as MP for Dublin University; he opposed Home Rule for Ireland though his sympathies lay with the welfare and interests of that country.

**Lee, Laurie** 1914– Writer and poet. Born in Gloucestershire, he was educated locally at Slad Village School and Stroud Central School. After several years as an office clerk, he travelled on the Continent in 1935–9, returning to work with various film units. During World War II he was Publications Editor at the Ministry of Information, and later he worked for the Festival of Britain.

His first collection of poetry, *The Sun My Monument* (1944), was followed by many others showing his love of the countryside, including *The Bloom of Candles* (1947) and *My Many-Coated Man* (1955). He became popular for his readings during the 1960s. However, he is best known for *Cider With Rosie* (1959), his lyrical and nostalgic autobiography of a Gloucestershire childhood before the advent of motor cars and modern farm machinery. It was followed by *As I Walked Out One Midsummer Morning* (1969), which recounts his adventures as a young man, on the road to London and in Spain, during the early 1930s. He is also the author of several screenplays and travel books.

**Lee, Nathaniel** *c.*1653–92 Dramatist and actor. Lee's theatrical career began when he turned actor after graduating from Trinity College, Cambridge. His first plays, *Nero* (1674), *Sophonisba* (1675) and *Gloriana* (1676), were poetic tragedies, written in heroic couplets and showing an appetite for rhetoric and sensation. His masterpiece, *The Rival Queens* (1677), led the return to blank verse as the poetic style for tragedy. It reveals, as does *Lucius Junius Brutus* (1680), an ability to create complex characters and a recognition of political motives sufficiently acute to lead to the banning of the later play.

Lee was drawn into the dissipated circle of friends surrounding the **Earl of Rochester**, whom he portrays without flattery as Nemours in the satiric sex-comedy, *The Princess of Cleve* (1681). Lee's physical and mental health declined so far that he was confined to Bedlam from 1684 to 1689.

**Lee, Sir Sidney** 1859–1926 Shakespearean scholar and biographer. Born in London, the son of a Jewish merchant, he was educated at the City of London School and at Balliol College, Oxford, where the Master, **Benjamin Jowett**, recognized his promise. In 1882 he became assistant to **Leslie Stephen**, then planning the *Dictionary of National Biography*, succeeded Stephen as editor in 1891 and saw the main project to its conclusion in 1900, working later on supplementary volumes. His principal separate work, a biography of **Shakespeare** (1898), grew from his main *DNB* contributions. Several times revised, it was in its time the fullest statement of the sparse biographical facts, set in a wide literary and historical context with full attention to foreign influences. Having written on the Queen for the *DNB* he prepared a prompt and frank *Queen Victoria, a Biography* (1902) and was later commissioned to write a two-volume *Life of King Edward VII* (1925–7). Neither is as successful as his work on the Elizabethan period, on which he wrote many books and articles. He was knighted in 1911.

**Leech, John** 1817–64 Comic artist and illustrator. Born in London, he attended Charterhouse – where he first met **Thackeray** – and studied medicine at St Bartholomew's Hospital. In 1841 he became a founding member of *Punch*, acting as its chief artist until his death. Outstanding among the 50 books Leech illustrated are **Dickens**'s *A Christmas Carol* (1844), the sporting novels of **R. S. Surtees** and **Gilbert à Beckett**'s *The Comic History of England* (1847) and *The Comic History of Rome* (1852).

**Left Book Club** A London-based publishing venture launched early in 1936 by Victor Gollancz, the Labour MP John Strachey and Harold Laski, Professor of Political Science at the London School of Economics. Its editorial director was John Lewis, co-founder and first president of the Welsh Nationalist Party.

The Club's aim was to combat the rise of Fascism by fostering a United Front, providing its members with books with a Socialist bias, most of which were specifically commissioned. Beginning with a membership of 10,000, numbers rapidly rose to 50,000 by 1939, but then suffered an equally rapid decline after the Nazi–Soviet Pact. The Pact was denounced by many of the Club's leaders, including Gollancz (see *The Betrayal of the Left*, 1941, which he edited), whose earlier pro-Soviet stance had precluded criticism of Stalin's Great Purge and of the Moscow trials (1936–8).

The majority of the Club's publications were factual, and few achieved lasting success. Two exceptions were **George Orwell**'s *The Road to Wigan Pier* (1937), ironically enough a title about which Gollancz had misgivings, and **Clifford Odets**'s play *Waiting for Lefty* (1937).

The Club never recovered from its great slump after 1939, and it was dissolved in 1948.

**Legend of Good Women, The** An unfinished poem by **Geoffrey Chaucer**, immediately preceding *The Canterbury Tales* and making the earliest known use of the **heroic couplet** in English.

A prologue, cast in the form of an allegorical **dream-vision**, uses a debate about the supremacy of the flower or the leaf (see also *The Flower and The Leaf*) to proclaim allegiance to the daisy, Alceste, the leader of 'Good Women'. The prologue goes on to explain the main body of the poem by saying that Chaucer, after having defamed women in *Troilus and Criseyde* and his translation from the French, *The Romaunt of the Rose*, has now been required by the God of Love to write in their praise. (It is not known whether *The Legend of Good Women* was written in response to genuine criticism of his earlier works.) The work is a 'Legend', or legendary, narrating the lives of women who suffered or died as a result of their faithful love. The stories are drawn from Virgil and Ovid, and tell of classical heroines: Cleopatra, Thisbe, Dido, Hypsipyle and Medea, Lucrece, Ariadne, Philomela, Phyllis and Hypermnestra. The legends do not share the fresh and lively poetry of the prologue, and the uniformity of their tone and intention makes them less appealing to the modern reader than many other works by Chaucer. The prologue exists in two versions; the second (which could have been written as late as 1394) is apparently an attempt to make the structure more consistent, but omits several of the most beautiful passages in the earlier version.

**Legend of Montrose, The** A novel by **Sir Walter Scott**, in the third series of *Tales of My Landlord*, published in 1819. Its setting is the rising of the Highland clans against the Covenanters and in support of Charles I in 1644.

Interwoven in the plot is the story of Allan M'Aulay, nephew of a man murdered by Highland raiders calling themselves Children of the Mist. Passionate and vengeful, he falls in love with Annot Lyle, whom he has rescued from the raiders, but she loves the young Earl of Menteith. The Earl returns her affection, though they cannot marry because of an unresolved mystery surrounding her birth. She is eventually revealed to be the daughter of Sir Duncan Campbell, but Allan interrupts her wedding to Menteith to stab his rival and disappear.

The novel is more successful in its portrait of history, particularly the opposing characters of Montrose, the Royalist, and Argyle, than its account of the lovers' problems.

**Lehmann, Rosamond (Nina)** 1903–90 Novelist. She was born in London, the sister of **John Lehmann** and the actress Beatrix Lehmann. She was taught at home before going to Girton College, Cambridge, the background for her first novel, *Dusty Answer* (1927). This was well received and its themes, developing womanhood and the subtle shades of emotional relationships, served the author well in a successful career as a novelist. Her other books were *A Note in Music* (1930), *Invitation to the Waltz* (1932) and its sequel *The Weather in the Streets* (1936), *The Ballad and the Source* (1944) and *The Echoing Grove* (1953). She also wrote a play, *No More Music* (1939), a volume of short stories, *The Gypsy's Baby* (1946) and an autobiographical volume, *The Swan in the Evening* (1967).

**Lehmann, (Rudolph) John (Frederick)** 1907–87 Poet, magazine editor, and publisher. Brother of the novelist **Rosamond Lehmann**, he was born at Bourne End in the Thames Valley and educated at Eton and Trinity College, Cambridge. He is one of the century's leading men of letters, editing *New Writing* (1936–9), *New Writing and Daylight* (1942–6), and, most importantly, *Penguin New Writing* (1940–50), which ran for 40 numbers, sometimes selling 100,000 copies per issue, and featured the work of **Roy Fuller**, **Laurie Lee** and **Henry Reed**. He also edited *The London Magazine* (1954–61). His eponymous publishing imprint issued, among more than 200 titles between 1946 and 1951, Sartre's *La Nausée* and **Saul Bellow**'s *Dangling Man*. Lehmann's verse, including *A Garden Revisited and Other Poems* (1931), *The Noise of History* (1934), *The Sphere of Glass* (1944) and *Poems New and Selected* (1986), came only intermittently, between major publishing and editorial ventures. Marked by unostentatious rhythms and direct treatment of experience, it is now neglected.

**Leland (or Leyland), John** ?1506–52 Antiquary and poet. The earliest of the 16th-century antiquarians, Leland was educated at St Paul's School, Christ's College, Cambridge (where he graduated BA in 1522), and Paris. He became Keeper of Libraries to Henry VIII some time before 1530 and the king's antiquary in 1533. He was granted permission by the king to search the libraries of monasteries and colleges for ancient documents and in 1534–43 toured the country in his researches, intending to write a work called 'History and Antiquities of this Nation'. Leland's career as antiquarian was funded by the revenues from various ecclesiastical preferments. He was a friend of **John Bale** who was engaged in similar researches and who mentions Leland in his play *King John*. Leland presented an account of his researches to Henry VIII and an English version was later published by Bale as *The Laborious Journey and Search of John Leland* (1549). In 1547, in Bale's words, 'a most pitiful occasion fell besides his wits' and Leland became insane. He was given into his brother's care in 1551 and died the next year, his great work still in notes.

Leland's notes passed successively into several hands, including those of Lord Burghley. They were of great use to later topographers and historians like **William Harrison**, **Raphael Holinshed** and **William Camden**, while **Michael Drayton** drew on Leland in writing *Poly-Olbion*. Most of Leland's manuscripts are now in the Bodleian Library, Oxford. His notes were finally published as the *Itinerary* (9 vols., Oxford 1710–12). Leland also wrote a defence of the Arthurian legends, *Assertio Inclytissimi Arthuri* (1544), which was translated as *A Learned and True Assertion of the Original Life, Acts and Death of . . . Arthur* (1582). He wrote a few Latin poems: on the death of **Sir Thomas Wyatt** the elder (1542) and the birth of Prince Edward (1543); *Cygnea Cantio* (1545) which has been suggested as a model for **Spenser's** *Prothalamion*; and *Laudatio Pacis* (Praise of Peace) (1546).

**Lemon, Mark** 1809–70 Co-founder, with **Henry Mayhew**, of *Punch* in 1841. The new journal did not at first succeed, and was subsidized by Lemon's earnings as a playwright. Over 60 of his pieces were performed in London. Meanwhile, he contributed to other journals, and was a founder-editor of *The Field*. He wrote over 100 songs, lyrics, novels, Christmas fairy-stories and a joke-book. He collaborated with **Dickens** in 1851 in a one-act farce, *Mr Nightingale's Diary*, in which they both acted. Eventually *Punch*, which had originally belonged to Lemon, Mayhew and the printer and engraver, was sold to a new proprietor, and Lemon stayed on as editor until he died. He nursed it to success and by the time of his death *Punch* had become a national institution.

**Lennox, Charlotte Ramsay** 1720–1804 Charlotte Lennox was born in New York, the daughter of the lieutenant governor, and went to England at the age of 15. She worked as an actress for a short time and then became a professional writer and novelist. *The Life of Harriot Stuart* (1750) was a sentimental novel of manners but she achieved success with her satire *The Female Quixote* (1752). She dramatized the novel as *Angelica: or Quixote in Petticoats* (1758). *The History of Henrietta* (1758) was followed by a play, *The Sister* (1769). Other novels were *Sophia* (1762) and *Euphemia* (1790).

*The Female Quixote, or, The Adventures of Arabella* depicts a heroine whose world is conjured up from French romances of the previous century – a far more satisfying one for her than the real world. But reality keeps intruding and Mrs Lennox makes some successful comedy out of Arabella's conviction that all men are either suitors or ravishers.

**Leonard, Hugh** Pen-name of the Irish playwright John Keyes Byrne (1926– ). He was born in Dalkey, County Dublin. The **Abbey Theatre** produced Leonard's first two long plays, *The Birthday Party* (1956) and *A Leap in the Dark* (1958). Shortly afterwards he joined Granada television, writing original plays, many adaptations and a farcical series, *Me Mammy*. Leonard is knowledgeable in farce. He has adapted Labiche's *Célimare*; his *The Patrick Pearse Motel* (1971) and *Time Was* (1976) use the genre to satirize Dublin's fashionable outer suburbs. *Da* (1973), enormously successful in New York, is a serio-comic treatment of the same location: *revenants*, re-enacting a writer's Dalkey childhood, confuse his flippant self-confidence. *A Life* (1976) retraces Mr Drumm's path to his desiccated marriage, accounting for and perhaps disturbing his defensive reserve.

**Lessing, Doris (May)** 1919– Novelist. Born to British parents in Khermanshah in Persia, Doris Taylor grew up on a farm in Southern Rhodesia. She worked at various jobs and was twice married, the second marriage taking place in 1945. In 1949 Lessing left Africa for England, taking with her the manuscript of a novel. This was *The Grass is Singing* (1950), a powerful study of a white woman's obsession with her black servant, demonstrating the writer's interest in the private action of the mind which was to distinguish many of her later novels. The work was well received by critics, as was her first volume of short stories, *This Was the Old Chief's Country* (1951).

Her second novel, *Martha Quest* (1952), became the first part of a five-novel sequence collectively entitled *The Children of Violence*. *Martha Quest* draws much of its material from the author's experience of life in a society rigidly governed by convention and prejudice. Other novels in the series reflect her enduring commitment to radical politics, and challenge formalistic literary conventions in their exploration of mental processes and breakdown. The four novels which complete the sequence are *A Proper Marriage* (1954), *A Ripple From the Storm* (1958), *Landlocked* (1965) and *The Four-Gated City* (1969), which takes the tale through to the year 2000. While this sequence was still in progress Doris Lessing also published volumes of short stories – including *Five* (1953), *The Habit of Loving* (1957) and *A Man and Two Women* (1963) – *Fourteen Poems* (1959), and some non-fiction including the autobiographical works *Going Home* (1957) and *In Pursuit of the English* (1960).

*The Golden Notebook* (1962), which was hailed

Doris Lessing.

if not conceived as the expression of feminist politics, examines on several levels and with a minute particularity, the experience of a woman writer. The narrative is split into a conventional novel, ironically entitled 'Free Women', and a series of lyrical and exploratory asides represented by the four notebooks kept by the protagonist, Anna Wulf. Though initially maintaining fragmentation and separation, the several strands of the novel, including the two formal narrative processes, are brought triumphantly together in the final 'golden' notebook.

Lessing's later work has concentrated on the 'space within', beginning with the extraordinarily successful experimental novels, *Briefing for a Descent Into Hell* (1971) and *The Memoirs of a Survivor* (1974), and continuing into the 'space fiction' series, *Canopus in Argos: Archives*. This series presently stands at five novels: *Re: Colonised Planet 5, Shikasta* (1979), *The Marriages Between Zones Three, Four and Five* (1980), *The Sirian Experiments* (1981), *The Making of the Representative for Planet 8* (1982) and *Documents Relating to the Sentimental Agents in the Volyen Empire* (1983). The frequent mention of literary forms in the titles of Lessing's works (notebook, memoirs, archives, documents) attests her conscious interest in, and extension of, the structures available to the experimental writer.

Lessing has since returned to realistic narrative with two novels originally published under the pseudonym of Jane Somers, *The Diary of a Good Neighbour* (1983) and *If the Old Could* (1984), the former being an unsparing study of the privations of old age, and more recently a novel about urban terrorism, *The Good Terrorist*

(1985), and *Prisons We Choose to Live Inside* (1987).

**Letter Concerning the Sacramental Test, A** See **Argument Against Abolishing Christianity, An**.

**Letter to Sir William Wyndham, A** See **Bolingbroke, Henry St John, 1st Viscount**.

**Letters Concerning Toleration** The first of **John Locke**'s *Letters* was published in Latin as *Epistola de Tolerantia* in Holland in 1689. The English version and *A Second Letter Concerning Toleration* appeared in 1690. *A Third Letter for Toleration* followed in 1692. A convinced Christian and an empiricist, Locke was a powerful advocate of free enquiry. He favoured religious liberty for all except atheists and Catholics, and a national church that made possible the freedom of individual opinion which was every man's right.

**Letters from an American Farmer** A collection of 12 essays by **J. Hector St Jean de Crèvecoeur** describing rural life in 18th-century America. They were first published in London in 1782, though they were probably written several years earlier. The first American edition appeared in Philadelphia in 1793.

Addressing his letters to a British correspondent, Crèvecoeur, in the person of 'Farmer James', writes glowingly of the conditions of American agrarian life and of the virtue, independence, industry, and prosperity of the American farmer. In the third essay, 'What Is An American?', he speculates on the roles that the experience of immigration and of working the American land play in the 'Americanization' process that produces this singular breed. He also makes observations on the relationship between the geography of different regions and the typical character and activities of the people therein, discussing on the one hand Quaker simplicity and the whale fishery on Nantucket, and on the other the luxuries of Charleston and the slave system Southerners depend upon. Though extolling the virtues of stable, agrarian life throughout, Farmer James's concluding essay, 'Distresses of a Frontier Man', describes his realization that the agrarian idyll is not possible in the midst of frontier raids and Revolutionary violence; reluctantly he resolves to join the Indians on the frontier, leaving his farm and the political conflict that white, European-American society imposes upon him.

**Letters on the Study and Use of History** See **Bolingbroke, Henry St John, 1st Viscount**.

**Lever, Charles (James)** 1806–72 Novelist. Born in Dublin, he studied medicine at Trinity College and made his name with a succession of lively novels about Ireland and the army: *The*

*Confessions of Harry Lorrequer* (1837), *Charles O'Malley* (1840), *Jack Hinton the Guardsman* (1842), *Tom Burke of Ours* (1844), *Arthur O'Leary* (1844) and *The O'Donoghue* (1845). Their tone was well parodied by **Thackeray** in *Punch's Prize Novelists*. In 1845 Lever toured the Continent in extravagant style, settling in Italy, where he held two consulships as sinecures, at Spezzia (1865) and then Trieste (1867). His later novels were more subdued, partly through an attempt at greater realism and partly through fatigue; they include *Roland Cashel* (1850), *Sir Jasper Carew* (1855), *The Fortunes of Glencore* (1857), *Luttrell of Arran* (1865) and *Lord Kilgobbin* (1872). The failure of *A Day's Ride* (1863) on its original serialization in *All the Year Round* prompted **Dickens** to begin *Great Expectations*.

**Leverson, Ada** 1865–1936 Novelist. Born Ada Beddington in London, she was educated privately. She became a member of the circle which included **Wilde**, **George Moore** and **Max Beerbohm**, and contributed to *The Yellow Book*. Her six novels are *The Twelfth Hour* (1907), *Love's Shadow* (1908), *The Limit* (1911), *Tenterhooks* (1912), *Bird of Paradise* (1914) and *Love at Second Sight* (1916).

**Levertov, Denise** 1923– American poet. Levertov was born in England, where she wrote her first volume of poetry, *The Double Image* (1946). Two years later, after marrying the American writer Mitchell Goodman, she moved to New York City. Her poems are full of sensory detail and often concern the nature of the creative process itself. She writes in the rhythms of speech, using metaphor and allusion sparingly. *Here and Now* (1957) and *Overland to the Islands* (1958) were written in Mexico. The poems in *With Eyes at the Back of Our Heads* (1959) reflect her decision to leave Mexico and return to New York. In 1961 she became poetry editor of *The Nation* and published another collection, *The Jacob's Ladder*. Since then she has concentrated increasingly on political and feminist themes, in volumes such as *O Taste and See* (1964), *A Tree Telling of Orpheus* (1968), *To Stay Alive* (1971), *The Freeing of the Dust* (1975) and *Wanderer's Daysong* (1981). Prose analyses of her own creative process are collected in *The Poet in the World* (1973). See also **Black Mountain school**.

**Levi, Peter (Chad Tigar)** 1931– Poet, critic and translator. Born in Ruislip, and educated at Beaumont and Oxford, Levi trained as a Jesuit and taught at Stonyhurst, the Catholic public school, before being ordained as a priest in 1964. Thereafter he taught Classics at Campion Hall, Oxford, and pursued archaeological work in Greece. His translation of Pausanias' *Guide to Greece* appeared in 1971. He left the priesthood,

married and became a fellow of St Catherine's College, Oxford, in 1977. He was elected Professor of Poetry at Oxford in 1984.

Levi's poetry is characterized by tranquillity and indirectness. *The Gravel Ponds* (1960) shows elements of social concern, combined with a decorative use of nature-imagery. The mature poetry in *Water, Rock and Sand* (1962), *The Shearwaters* (1965), *Fresh Water, Sea Water* (1966) and other volumes gathered in his *Collected Poems* (1976) represents a merging of pastoral themes and images with a Symbolist poetic: aspects of landscape and the seasons are presented in a cryptic, subtly disjunctive manner to evoke elusive states of mind or a mood of philosophical questioning. The formal elegance and inconspicuous originality of Levi's work won him a reputation which grew slowly but steadily among critics and fellow poets, and his volume of elegies (*The Echoing Green*, 1983) was widely praised. A volume of criticism, *The Noise Made by Poems*, appeared in 1977 and an autobiography, *The Flutes of Autumn*, in 1983. He has also published detective novels, travel books and translations of several Eastern European poets.

**Lévi-Strauss, Claude** See *semiotics* and *structuralism*.

***Leviathan, or, The Matter, Form, and Power of a Commonwealth Ecclesiastical and Civil*** A treatise on political philosophy by **Thomas Hobbes**, written during the Interregnum while he was in Paris, as tutor to the future Charles II, and published in 1651.

The title of Hobbes's work refers to the principle of sovereign rule, and the fundamental tenet of his philosophy is that the basis of government must be practical consent, since man is not inherently peaceful, nor prone to communal society in any stable fashion. To preserve man from self-destruction resulting from individual competition, a series of 'articles of peace' needs to be assembled. Hobbes depicted society as a necessary contract whereby voluntary adherence to such articles would result in a 'commonwealth' in which each individual acknowledged his obligation to the peaceful liberty of others on an equal basis to his own. Communal security would be vested in a person, or assembly – the sovereign and indivisible power – ruling under a covenant between each individual governed, and subordinating all other potential power (such as the Church) to its absolute influence.

Hobbes attracted the criticism of both Royalist and Parliamentarian camps by his proviso that a failure on the part of the sovereign to honour the covenant and preserve the electors of office might constitute a case for insubordination to authority. Without this cohesive contract, he memorably contended, 'the life of man is solitary, poor, nasty, brutish and short'.

**Levine, Norman** 1923– Canadian short-story writer and novelist. Born in Ottawa of Polish Jewish parents, Levine served in the Canadian Air Force in World War II. He subsequently studied at Cambridge and McGill Universities, before deciding, in 1949, to live in England, where he spent the next 31 years, mainly in St Ives, Cornwall. In 1980 he returned to Canada and settled in Toronto. Much of his fiction is fictionalized autobiography, dealing with central experiences from his own life. Written in a tight, economic prose style, his stories evoke places vividly and frequently focus on social outsiders, the problems of the writer's life and his Jewish-Canadian upbringing. Levine has written two novels, *The Angled Road* (1952), an introspective war novel, and *From a Seaside Town* (1970). His volumes of short stories include *One Way Ticket* (1961), *I Don't Want to Know Anyone Too Well* (1971) and *Thin Ice* (1979). *Champagne Barn* (1984) is a collection of stories mainly drawn from his earlier volumes. Although he is best known as a fiction writer, he has also published collections of his poetry, much of which is about St Ives, and the autobiographical memoir, *Canada Made Me* (1958), a consideration of Canadian life on 'the other side of the tracks', which offers a critique of the complacency of conservative attitudes in Canada.

**Levine, Philip** 1928– American poet, born in Detroit, and educated at Wayne State University and the University of Iowa. Since 1958 he has taught at California State University in Fresno. His first books of poetry, *On the Edge* (1961), *Silent in America: Vivas for Those Who Failed* (1965) and *Not This Pig* (1968), established him as a bitter and ironic chronicler of the working classes of Detroit and southern California. His subsequent volumes of poetry include *5 Detroits* (1970), *Pili's Wall* (1971), *They Feed They Lion* (1972), *The Names of the Lost* (1974), *Ashes: Poems Old & New* (1979) and *One for the Rose* (1981). *Don't Ask*, a collection of essays and interviews, appeared in 1981 and *Selected Poems* in 1983.

**Lewes, George Henry** 1817–78 Journalist, philosopher, scientist and critic. Born in London, Lewes flirted with various activities – business, the law, medicine and the theatre – before becoming a journalist, writing for *The Morning Chronicle* and *The Penny Encyclopedia*. In 1850 he became editor of *The Leader* with Thornton Leigh Hunt, and later helped to found the influential *Fortnightly Review*, of which he was the first editor. In 1851 Lewes met Marian Evans (**George Eliot**) with whom he lived from 1854 until his death. The couple were unable to marry, although Lewes's wife Agnes was involved in a long-standing liaison with Hunt.

Lewes is probably best remembered today as the supporter and encourager of George Eliot's first efforts in fiction, but his own talents also claim attention and exerted an influence on her work. He wrote two novels, *Ranthorpe* (1847) and *Rose, Blanche and Violet* (1848), ten plays, a *Life of Robespierre* (1849) and a number of books on the contemporary theatre, most notably *Actors and the Art of Acting* (1875). His most important work was *The Life and Works of Goethe* (1855). His writings on philosophy include *A Biographical History of Philosophy* (1845), and *Comte's Philosophy of the Sciences* (1853). *Problems of Life and Mind* (1873–9) was completed after his death by George Eliot. Among his scientific writings are *Seaside Studies* (1858) and *Studies of Animal Life* (1862).

**Lewis, Alun** 1915–44 Poet and short-story writer. Born in Cwmaman, South Wales, he was educated at the University College of Wales, Aberystwyth, and at the University of Manchester. After working as a journalist and teacher he joined the army in 1940, despite pacifist leanings. He died during action in Burma from a gunshot wound which may have been self-inflicted. *Raiders' Dawn* (1942) contained important poems concerned with the identity and environment of industrial Wales, with love and with wartime Britain. *The Last Inspection* (1942) contains 23 wry and observant stories. Poems, stories and letters from India were collected in *Ha! Ha! Among the Trumpets* (1945), with a foreword by **Robert Graves**, and *In the Green Tree* (1948). Confronting the people and ideas of the East gave Lewis a context for his views on the war, just as the Western Desert did for **Keith Douglas**; he emerges, not as a minor 'war poet', but as a mature, wide-ranging writer with a coherent pattern of themes.

**Lewis, C[live] S[taples]** 1898–1963 Critic, theologian, writer of **science fiction** and **children's literature**. Born in Belfast, he read voraciously as a child and started writing early. The death of his mother when he was 10 destroyed a happy and secure childhood and plunged him into education at all-male schools. At these Lewis discovered Wagner, and Norse, classical and Celtic mythology with delight, lost his Christianity, and continued to write. His abilities won him a classical scholarship to Malvern College in 1913, but he disliked it so much that he was soon placed with a private tutor in Surrey, who coached him for a scholarship to Oxford (1916). After war service (1917–18), and a published collection of poems, *Spirits in Bondage* (1918), he entered University College to read classics and philosophy, turning to

English for a fourth year, and winning Firsts throughout.

After his first year at Oxford, Lewis set up a joint home with a Mrs Moore, mother of a friend killed in the trenches. His generosity imposed a financial and emotional burden on him which lasted over 30 years. Lewis became a fellow of Magdalen College in 1925, where he soon was noted as an excellent lecturer and incomparable teacher. A group of his friends, including **J. R. R. Tolkien**, Hugo Dyson and **Charles Williams**, began to meet regularly in his rooms to read their own work to each other.

Between 1929 and 1931 Lewis was converted back to Christianity, an experience charted in his spiritual autobiography, *Surprised by Joy* (1955), and the mainspring of all his subsequent writing, starting with *The Pilgrim's Regress* (1933) and then his science fiction trilogy, *Out of The Silent Planet* (1938), *Perelandra* (1939) and *That Hideous Strength* (1945). The first and still the most famous of his scholarly books was *The Allegory of Love* (1936), but others remain influential: *A Preface to Paradise Lost* (1942), the third volume of the Oxford History of English Literature, *English Literature in the Sixteenth Century, Excluding Drama* (1954), *Studies in Words* (1960) and *The Discarded Image* (1963). What brought him wide popularity, however, were his talks on Christianity broadcast during World War II (collected as *Mere Christianity*) and *The Screwtape Letters* (1942). The seven 'Narnia' stories for children, combining strong imagination and lively adventure with artfully concealed Christian parable, secured him another large audience; they began with *The Lion, the Witch and the Wardrobe* (1950) and closed with *The Last Battle* (1956). In 1954 Lewis moved to Cambridge to occupy the first Chair of Medieval and Renaissance English. In 1956 he married Joy Davidman, who brought him much happiness before her death from cancer in 1960, when Lewis was already suffering from the osteoporosis which would cause his own death.

**Lewis, (Harry) Sinclair** 1885–1951 American novelist, born in Sauk Center, Minnesota. In 1903 he entered Yale University, but left in 1906 to join **Upton Sinclair**'s socialist colony in Englewood, New Jersey. He then became a free-lance writer and editor in New York City before returning to Yale and graduating in 1908. Four years later he published his first novel, a boy's book entitled *Hike and the Aeroplane* (1912), under the pseudonym of Tom Graham.

In 1914 he published *Our Mr Wrenn*, which was followed by *The Trail of the Hawk* (1915) and three more novels before the successful *Main Street* (1920), a satirical portrayal of small-town life in the Midwest. He continued his critique of provincial American life in *Babbitt* (1922). In 1926 he was awarded the Pulitzer Prize for *Arrowsmith* (1925), the story of an altruistic doctor who struggles to resist the temptations of a fashionable and profitable practice in order to pursue a scientific career, but Lewis refused to accept the honour. His next novel, *Elmer Gantry* (1927), is the story of a sham revivalist minister. *Dodsworth* (1929), about a retired automobile manufacturer travelling in Europe, appeared a year before Lewis was awarded the Nobel Prize, the first American to be so honoured.

Lewis's commitment to social and political change is evident also in his novels of the 1930s and 1940s. *Ann Vickers* (1933) is about a discontented Midwestern girl who goes east to college and becomes a social worker; she becomes involved in the women's movement and works for prison reform. *Work of Art* (1934) is about the American hotel industry. During the late 1930s and the 1940s Lewis began a career as an actor. His novel, *It Can't Happen Here* (1935), a warning about the possibility of fascism in the USA, was dramatized and produced by the Federal Theatre Project in cities throughout the country with Lewis himself playing the lead.

The revolt of children against their parents is the subject of *The Prodigal Parents* (1938). *Bethel Merriday* (1940) deals with the career of a young actress. *Gideon Planish* (1943) is about a speech professor who marries a student and then finds himself manipulated into the lucrative advertising profession by his wife. Lewis's next three novels return to the Minnesota setting of *Main Street*. *Cass Timberlane* (1945) is another story of a middle-aged man, a judge, who marries a young girl; *Kingsblood Royal* (1947) deals with race relations; *The God-Seeker* (1949) treats the American Indian question. His last novel, *World So Wide*, was published posthumously in 1951.

**Lewis, Leopold** 1828–90 Playwright. His single claim to fame was his adaptation of *Le Juif Polonais* by Erckmann and Chatrian as *The Bells*. The role of the guilt-stricken Mathias was superbly played by Sir Henry Irving in 1871. Lewis was a solicitor, volatile to the point of instability. Of three later plays staged in London, none succeeded.

**Lewis, M[atthew] G[regory]** 1775–1818 Novelist, playwright and poet. Born into a wealthy family, he was educated at Westminster School and Christ Church, Oxford, before entering the diplomatic service. He wrote *The Monk* (1796), his sensationally successful **Gothic novel**, at the age of 19 during a period as attaché at the British Embassy at The Hague. It earned him the nickname of 'Monk' Lewis. Although it is almost the only work by which he is now remembered, he wrote other novels (*The Bravo of Venice*, 1804; *Feudal Tyrants*, 1806) and plays (*The Castle Spectre*, 1796; *The East Indian*, 1799;

*Alphonso, King of Castile*, 1801; *The Wood Demon*, 1807). He also published several volumes of verse, but his best poem, 'Alonzo the Brave and the Fair Imogine', appeared in *The Monk*. **Hazlitt** considered that he was, after **Ann Radcliffe**, 'the greatest master in the art of freezing the blood', and he is credited with introducing English readers to popular German Romantic literature. Passionately addicted to the company of the rich, the titled and the famous, he dined everywhere and spent much time at ducal country residences. He visited Goethe and Wieland in Weimar, and was on friendly terms with **Byron** ('Lewis was a good man, a clever man, but a bore') and **Scott**. He held a seat in the House of Commons in 1796–1802. After his father's death in 1812 he gave up writing to devote himself to the improvement of the West Indian sugar plantations where most of his money came from, incurring the displeasure of his neighbours by his efforts to better the condition of his slaves. He visited Jamaica twice in the last three years of his life, and died of yellow fever on his way back to England in 1818. He left behind his *Journal of a West Indian Proprietor*, published in 1834, a highly respected work and certainly his most important since *The Monk*.

**Lewis, (Percy) Wyndham** 1882–1957 Artist, novelist and critic. Wyndham Lewis was born on his father's yacht off the coast of Maine (his father was American, his mother British). He was educated at Rugby School, then at the Slade School of Art, after which he lived and studied in Paris for several years. He earned a reputation as a painter, mainly among the *avant-garde*, and with the help of **Ezra Pound** edited the experimental publication **Blast**: *The Review of the Great English Vortex* (1914–15). Originally intended as a periodical, it lasted for only two issues, but the excitement of **vorticism** had considerable impact.

Lewis's novels began with *Tarr* (1918), set in pre-war Paris; it is an intellectual comedy of art, life, and Teutonic romanticism embodied in Kreisler, a would-be artist with no talent. *The Childermass* (1928) was the first novel of a trilogy called *The Human Age*; the other two novels, *Monstre Gai* and *Malign Fiesta*, did not appear until 1955. This remarkable fantasy is located in a waste land outside heaven's gate where the remnants of mankind await inquisition by the Bailiff.

*The Apes of God* (1930) is a satire mocking the fashionable racket of art and literature in the London of the 1920s. Many consider it Lewis's best work, but his next, *The Revenge for Love* (1937), also has its admirers. It is a political satire of the 1930s, set against the background of the Spanish Civil War. *Self Condemned* (1954) was Lewis's last major novel and is semi-autobiographical. Professor Harding, a figure with many

Wyndham Lewis, 1932. Self-portrait. National Portrait Gallery, London.

of Lewis's characteristics, finds himself unable to bear the insanity and cowardice engulfing Europe in the immediate pre-World War II period. He resigns his post and retreats to Canada with his wife, eventually emerging, alone, as no more than a shell of a man.

Lewis brought a painter's eye to his writing, but he rejected many of the techniques of **modernism** practised by his contemporaries. As a critic, he made enemies everywhere: **Virginia Woolf**, **James Joyce**, **D. H. Lawrence**, **Ernest Hemingway**, **William Faulkner** and **T. S. Eliot** were all his targets at different times. Eliot, however, wrote a complimentary preface to the 1960 edition of Lewis's verse satire *One-Way Song* (1933). This celebration of individual will and consciousness opposed the surrender to inwardness and subjectivism, so much an element in the art of the 1920s and 1930s.

Lewis's political and critical essays include *The Art of Being Ruled* (1925), *Time and Western Man* (1927), *Men Without Art* (1934), *The Mysterious Mr Bull* (1938) and *The Writer and the Absolute* (1952). His short stories were collected in *The Wild Body* (1927) and *Rotting Hill* (1951). Chapters of his autobiography were published in *Blasting and Bombardiering* (1937) and *Rude Assignment* (1950).

**Leyden, John** 1775–1811 Polymath. He was born at Denholm, Roxburghshire, and educated at Kirktown and Edinburgh University, where he took all knowledge as his province. Leyden was an early champion of **Thomas Campbell** and was himself encouraged by Richard Heber. The breadth of his interests is extraordinary: he moved easily from composing a discourse on the colonization of North Africa to contributing 'The Elf King', a ballad, to **M. G. Lewis**'s *Tales of Wonder* (1801). A passion for ancient Scottish literature enabled him to help **Sir Walter Scott** with *The Minstrelsy of the Scottish Border* (1802). He edited *The Scots Magazine* during part of 1802 and in 1803 prepared his *Scenes of Infancy* for publication.

Meanwhile, this unstoppable figure had qualified as a doctor in order to take up the post of assistant-surgeon in Madras. His hospital was not allowed to monopolize his time. On an official mission into the Mysore provinces in 1804 Leyden concerned himself with the area's agriculture, geology, public health and languages. He succumbed to fever on this exercise: his method of convalescence was to study Sanskrit and translate from Persian and Hindustani. He extended his growing knowledge of Asiatic languages on a trip to Penang in 1805, finding a moment during a brush with a French privateer to eulogize his Malay dagger in verse.

Back in Calcutta Leyden became not only a professor of Hindustani (1807) but also Judge of the Twenty-four Pergunnahs and Commissioner of the Court of Requests. In 1811 he accompanied his patron, Lord Minto, on an expedition to annex Java, but three weeks after the fall of Batavia caught a fever while foraging in an airless library and died aged 35.

Leyden served both Scotland and Asia well. Scott wrote an appreciative memoir of him for *The Edinburgh Annual Register* of 1811; and he further commemorated him in *The Lord of the Isles* (1815). William Erskine, who completed Leyden's *Commentaries of Baber* for publication in 1826, praised the thoroughness of his classification of Asiatic languages and dialects. Leyden's *Poetical Remains* appeared in 1819 and his translation of *Malay Annals* in 1821. A collection, *Poems and Ballads*, was published in 1858.

**Liars, The** A social comedy by **Henry Arthur Jones**, first performed in London in 1897. It elaborates on the need to lie in a hypocritical society, which turns an innocent friendship into a serious threat to the marriage of Lady Jessica Nepean. The play is expertly crafted and the ice it skates on thin enough to demand all its author's dexterity.

**Libeaus Desconus** ('The Fair Unknown') A **verse romance** of the mid-14th century written in the south of England, perhaps by **Thomas Chestre.**

The poem is an uninspired treatment of the story of the Fair Unknown, Gawain's son Gingelein (or Gauinglain), current in several European languages in the Middle Ages. The illegitimate son of Gawain is brought up by his mother in ignorance of his identity and in isolation in the forest. He steals the armour of a dead knight and goes to Arthur's court where he is knighted as Libeaus Desconus. Despite the initially contemptuous attitude of the court, he soon proves his prowess in various adventures. At one point he is bewitched and lives in idleness and luxury for a year, but resumes his career as a knight and undertakes more adventures. Finally he enters a magic hall where a serpent with a woman's face encircles him. Having been bewitched until she should kiss Gawain or one of his line, she is transformed into a beautiful woman; she weds Libeaus Desconus.

**Libel of English Policy, The** A Middle English poem provoked by the attack on Calais in 1436 and written in that year or 1437. Divided into a prologue and 12 chapters, the *Libel* ('little book') stresses the importance of maritime trade and the need to control Dover and Calais in order to maintain it. It advocates a powerful navy to ensure peace and prosperity for England. The poem was important in its time, and appeared in two later versions. It provides detailed information on contemporary political and commercial conditions.

**Liberal, The** A periodical founded by **Shelley** and **Byron** in 1822, when they were both in Pisa; **Leigh Hunt** was brought from England as its editor. Only four issues appeared, between September 1822 and June 1823, before the venture succumbed to a series of problems: the death of Shelley in July 1822, the growing hostility between Byron and Hunt, and the legal problems arising from the journal's publication of Byron's *Vision of Judgement.*

**Liberator, The** An American Abolitionist weekly journal founded by **William Lloyd Garrison** in Boston in 1831 and edited by him for the next 34 years. From its first issue, *The Liberator*'s editorial policy was unequivocally opposed to slavery, calling for immediate emancipation of the slave population. Its circulation was never higher than 3000, but its radical stance aroused vocal and violent antagonism in South and North alike. A law was passed forbidding its distribution among free blacks, and a reward was offered in South Carolina for information leading to the arrest of anyone who circulated it. The Georgia Senate passed a resolution offering another reward for the arrest of Garrison himself. The last issue was published on 29 December 1865, shortly after the Thirteenth Amendment, abolishing slavery, was ratified.

**libraries** Organized collections of books belonging to an individual, a group or an institution have existed since early classical times. They both serve their own times and also, either in their surviving stocks or in their catalogues, provide records of the tastes, preoccupations, achievements and thought of past generations. Thus they have both a current and historic value. Naturally these functions have resulted in a variety of different kinds of libraries, for different people and in different subjects. The following summary concentrates on those perhaps most obviously of interest to users of this *Guide*.

1 *British Isles*
(a) Monastic and collegiate libraries
The earliest libraries known to have existed in England are those connected with religious houses. At Canterbury, an abbey was established within 10 years of the arrival of St Augustine in 596; Winchester Cathedral priory was founded *c.* 604, and Peterborough Abbey *c.* 655. Though each eventually accumulated sizeable libraries, little evidence survives of their earliest collections. At Wearmouth-Jarrow,

A Jacobean bookcase and chained book in Trinity Hall Library, Cambridge, England.

Benedict Biscop (*c.*628–89), one of the most active bibliophiles of pre-Conquest England, accumulated an outstanding library thanks largely to connections with the Continent (chiefly Italy and Gaul), and the collection was used thoroughly by **Bede** for his treatises and for his *Ecclesiastical History*. At York, there was a library attached to the cathedral school by the mid 8th century, and its contents were recalled in verse by **Alcuin** in his 'Carmen de Pontificibus et Sanctis Ecclesiae Eboracensis', composed at the end of the century. The libraries at both Lindisfarne and York were sacked by the Danes, in 793 and 866–7 respectively. Partly no doubt because of the Viking invasions, and despite the literary revival under **King Alfred**, monastic life (and with it the production of books) did not return generally to normal until the 10th century. The major monastic libraries of which substantial portions survive (very often elsewhere) today include Bury St Edmunds, Christ Church and St Augustine's, Canterbury, Durham, Norwich, Reading, Rochester, St Albans and Worcester (all Benedictine houses) and the secular cathedrals of Exeter, Hereford, Lincoln and Salisbury. Yet apart from these, books are recognizable as having survived in smaller quantities from over 400 other libraries, not including those at Oxford and Cambridge.

The establishment of these two universities in the 13th century brought further developments. At Cambridge, Peterhouse (founded 1284) preserves still much of its medieval library, as do Gonville and Caius (founded 1349) and Pembroke (1347) Colleges. Little is known of the university library before the first years of the 15th century: its earliest catalogue dates from 1424. At Oxford, Merton College (founded 1263–4), Balliol (1261–6), New College (1379), Oriel (1324), Lincoln (1429), All Souls (1438) and Magdalen (1448) likewise preserve notable portions of their old libraries; but the old university library, greatly enriched by the humanist influence of Humfrey, Duke of Gloucester (1390–1447), was dispersed completely at the Reformation. Among other educational establishments, manuscripts survive both from Eton College and from Winchester. In Scotland, catalogues survive for Glasgow University Library from 1475 onwards, and Aberdeen University Library possesses three books known to have belonged to King's College, Aberdeen.

These medieval libraries were generally chained, at least in part, and sometimes remained so until years later. The chains were removed at Eton in 1719, at Merton and Magdalen Colleges only in the 1790s. The most celebrated chained library now extant is at Hereford Cathedral, but there are major collections of chained books, dating from the 16th and 17th centuries, in parochial or school libraries at (among other places) Grantham, Wimborne and

All Saints', Hereford, as well as the grammar schools at Guildford and Bolton.

The suppression of the monasteries in the 1530s, and the accompanying upheavals of the Reformation, resulted in the dispersal or destruction of most books from medieval libraries. Many, however, found their way as groups into other libraries: from Exeter Cathedral into the Bodleian, from Norwich Cathedral into Cambridge University Library, from Bury St Edmunds into Pembroke College, Cambridge. The dispersal encouraged a new generation of private collectors: the antiquary **John Leland** (?1506–52) was already prospecting among ecclesiastical libraries in the 1520s, noting their most important holdings for his master Henry VIII; and **Matthew Parker**, Archbishop of Canterbury (1504–75), amassed a collection especially valuable for its Anglo-Saxon manuscripts, now divided by gift and bequest respectively between Cambridge University Library and Corpus Christi College, Cambridge. Parker's collection included the 6th-century Gospels believed to have been brought to England by St Augustine in 596, and the best manuscript of the Anglo-Saxon Chronicle. In the next generations the mathematician John Dee (1527–1608) and the politician **Sir Robert Cotton** (1571–1631) were only the most important among many who took advantage of the relative wealth of medieval manuscripts on the market, and assembled major collections of their own: Dee's is now dispersed, but Cotton's descended in his family until 1702, when it passed to the state, and then, in 1753, became one of the foundation collections of the British Museum.

Cathedral libraries did not really recover until after the Restoration in 1660, when some of the collections were virtually refounded by men such as Michael Honywood (1597–1681) at Lincoln, George Morley (1597–1684) at Winchester, Henry King (1592–1669) at Chichester, and Henry Compton (1632–1713) at St Paul's Cathedral, London.

At Oxford and Cambridge, the libraries seem to have suffered in the mid 16th century more from neglect than deliberate destruction, as the Catholic reaction to the Protestant Reformation was in turn replaced by the reign of Queen Elizabeth. Their post-Reformation recovery came at the end of the century. At Cambridge, Andrew Perne, Master of Peterhouse, engaged the interest of Matthew Parker, Sir Nicholas Bacon (Lord Keeper) and others in the 1570s. At Oxford, **Sir Thomas Bodley** (1545–1613), a London diplomat and businessman, announced his intention of refounding the university library in 1598: his new library was opened in 1602 and grew quickly, fortified by the gifts elicited by Bodley, the income from the estate of Bodley himself, and an agreement with the London Stationers' Company (concluded in 1611) whereby one copy of every new book printed in London was to be given to Oxford. The gifts of collections of manuscripts by the Earl of Pembroke (1629), **William Laud** (1635–40), **Sir Kenelm Digby** (1634), and, among printed books, the bequests of **Robert Burton** (1640) and the arrival of **John Selden**'s books in 1659 meant that by 1700 the library was the greatest in the country.

(b) Copyright libraries
Under the Licensing Acts of 1662 etc., Cambridge University Library, the Bodleian and the Royal Library were each to receive one copy of every new book published in England. This right was embodied in the Copyright Act (1710) and has been repeated in subsequent legislation, the Royal Library being replaced by the British Museum from the mid 18th century. Between 1710 and 1836 the right was shared with Sion College in London, the Faculty of Advocates in Edinburgh, the Universities of Edinburgh, Glasgow, St Andrews and Aberdeen, and from 1801 to 1836 the King's Inns and Trinity College, Dublin. In 1836 these deposit libraries were reduced to five (British Museum, Oxford, Cambridge, Trinity College, Dublin, and the Faculty of Advocates), the last being succeeded by the National Library of Scotland on its foundation in 1925 and the National Library of Wales (founded in 1907) in 1911. Until 1814 deposit depended on entry in the Stationers' Register, and was therefore irregular; but efforts to improve it during the 19th century were increasingly successful, thanks particularly to Sir Anthony Panizzi (1797–1879) at the British Museum. This long history of deposit has been a principal factor in the emergence of the British Museum (since 1973 the British Library), the Bodleian and Cambridge University Library as the three largest in the country.

In 1753 the British Museum was established by Act of Parliament. Its foundation collections included those of Sir Robert Cotton (including the unique manuscripts of *Beowulf* and *Sir Gawain and the Green Knight*), Sir Hans Sloane (1660–1753), and **Robert Harley** and **Edward Harley**, Earls of Oxford. In 1757 these were increased by the gift by George II of the Old Royal Library, dating back to the reign of Edward IV and including the Codex Alexandrinus (a 5th-century Greek manuscript of the Bible). This gift was followed by George III with the collection of Civil War pamphlets known (after the bookseller who collected them) as the Thomason Tracts, and by the bequest (1799) of C. M. Cracherode (notable for its collection of classical texts and fine printing), as well as by smaller collections such as **David Garrick**'s English plays. The great library assembled by George III and the Prince Regent between 1760 and 1820 was given by George

IV. Other collections acquired in the 19th century included the Arundel Manuscripts, assembled by Thomas Howard, Earl of Arundel (1592–1646) and containing the unique manuscript of the *Ayenbite of Inwit*; the library of the naturalist Sir Joseph Banks (1743–1820); Charles Burney's collection, including both classics and a unique collection of early English newspapers; the collection of Thomas Grenville (1755–1846), outstanding for its Italian and Spanish books; the manuscripts of F. H. Egerton, 8th Earl of Bridgewater (d. 1829); and the Stowe manuscripts, collected by the 1st Duke of Buckingham (d. 1839) but bought only in 1883. In the mid 19th century the British Museum was established as the greatest library in the world, buying in all subjects and in most languages under the auspices of an outstanding series of keepers including (in printed books) Thomas Watts (1811–69) and Sir Anthony Panizzi, and (in manuscripts) Sir Frederic Madden (1801–73). Some important collections, however, went elsewhere, such as that of **John Forster**, biographer of **Dickens**, and **Alexander Dyce**, editor of **Shakespeare**, which went to the South Kensington Museum (now the Victoria and Albert Museum), and much of the working library of **George Eliot**, which is now in Dr Williams's Library, Gordon Square.

The gradual publication of authoritative catalogues of the British Museum's printed books – of early English books in 1884, of 15th-century books from 1908 (still in progress), and of successive editions of the general catalogue itself – emphasized the Museum's leading position, and has contributed profoundly to bibliographical studies: the most recent edition of the General Catalogue (known as GK4) began publication in 1979.

Accessions in the last hundred years have generally been less wholesale than previously, but they include the library of the bibliographer and forger **T. J. Wise** (1859–1937), especially rich in 16th- and 17th-century literature and in 19th-century poetry, collections of illuminated manuscripts from Henry Yates Thompson and Eric George Millar, and bookbindings from Henry Davis (d. 1977). The music collection was transformed by the gift in 1957 of the Royal Music Library, by Queen Elizabeth II, and the acquisition of Paul Hirsch's music collection in 1946. In 1973, by Act of Parliament, the British Library was established, composed of the British Museum Library, the National Reference Library of Science and Invention, the National Lending Library for Science and Technology, the National Central Library and the British National Bibliography.

In the 18th and 19th centuries, both the Bodleian Library and Cambridge University Library consolidated their positions as the major national libraries outside the British Museum.

Cambridge University Library was trebled by the gift (by King George I) of the library of John Moore, Bishop of Ely (d. 1714), the finest of its generation and celebrated for its books printed by **Caxton** and as containing the earliest extant manuscript then known of Bede's *Ecclesiastical History*. However, Oxford in particular attracted a long series of benefactions, most notably Richard Rawlinson's manuscripts (1755), Richard Gough's collection (rich especially in topography) in 1809, **Edmond Malone**'s library in 1821, and **Francis Douce**'s in 1834. More recently the Bodleian has acquired the John Johnson collection of printed ephemera and (by bequest) the considerable collection of Walter N. H. Harding (1883–1973), a Chicago popular musician, devoted partly at least to the history of popular song. Following his death in 1982, Cambridge University Library acquired the collection of Sir Geoffrey Keynes, with its renowned series of author collections including **Donne, Evelyn, Sir Thomas Browne, William Blake, Jane Austen, Rupert Brooke** and **Siegfried Sassoon**. Among the college libraries, that at Trinity College, Cambridge (built to the design of Sir Christopher Wren from 1676 onwards), is the richest in either university; its printed books alone include most of the surviving portion of **Sir Isaac Newton**'s library, the Shakespeare collection of **Edward Capell**, and the collection of 18th-century English literature formed by Lord Rothschild. Colleges at both Oxford and Cambridge house private libraries of unusual distinction: that of **Samuel Pepys** is at Magdalene College, Cambridge, many of the books of Robert Burton (other than those in the Bodleian) are in Christ Church, Oxford, and those of the economist **Malthus** are at Jesus College, Cambridge.

### (c) University libraries

Apart from the university libraries at Oxford and Cambridge with quasi-national status, and apart from the libraries of the ancient Scottish universities already mentioned, the libraries attached to the universities founded in the 19th and 20th centuries have usually come in some way to serve research well beyond their own localities. Of these, the most important is the John Rylands University Library of Manchester, founded by the merger in 1972 of the University of Manchester Library with the John Rylands Library. The latter was founded by Mrs John Rylands in 1900 as an independent collection; it includes the library of the 2nd Earl Spencer (d. 1834), one of the greatest bibliophiles of his age, as well as the manuscripts assembled by the Earls of Crawford in the 19th century. Leeds University, founded in 1875, is remarkable in its library not least for the Brotherton collection (presented 1935). The University of London Library, which includes the

Sir Louis Sterling (1879–1958) collection of English literature and the Goldsmiths' Company library of economic literature, has been housed in the Senate House, just to the north of the British Museum, since 1937–8, though the University itself was founded in 1836. All university-connected libraries grew rapidly in the wake of the Robbins Report on higher education (1963), and the 1960s and 1970s also saw considerable changes in their housing, as new buildings were erected. The subsequent revision of university grants has placed increasing pressure on inter-library co-operation, principally in loans of books: as in the public library sector, this is heavily dependent on the British Library Lending Division at Boston Spa, Yorkshire.

(d) Circulating libraries
The 18th century witnessed a widespread development of circulating libraries, commercially run and charging a small subscription for the loan of books. These paid especial attention to fiction, poetry, travel, biography and periodicals, and were satirized by (among others) **Sheridan** and Jane Austen. By the end of the century they had become immensely fashionable and, because of their buying power, became in the 19th century of crucial importance to publishers of novels especially: the lasting popularity of the 'three-decker' novel was due largely to the most successful of all circulating libraries, that of Charles Edward Mudie (1818–90). Vestiges of these libraries survived until the mid 20th century, either on a small scale or in those run by the chain stores Boots the Chemists and W. H. Smith, stationers and booksellers. These libraries are to be distinguished from those founded in the 19th century by Mechanics' Institutes (in which self-improvement and education played a prominent part) and from the major subscription libraries, of which the most notable are the Leeds Library (founded in 1768) and the London Library (founded in 1841 by **Thomas Carlyle** and others), the latter of which is the largest of its kind in the world.

(e) Public libraries
The earliest English public library to be established was at Norwich in 1608; another was opened at Bristol in 1613. In Manchester, a chained library was founded by the will of Humphrey Chetham (1580–1653). But in London, though a library had been established in 1423–5, the modern Guildhall Library dates only from 1824–8 and as a public library from 1872; the most important early public library there was that founded by Thomas Tenison, Archbishop of Canterbury (1636–1715), whose foundation (attached to St Martin's in the Fields) survived from 1684 to 1861.
Modern public library services date from the

Museums Act (1845) and, especially, the Public Libraries Act (1850) and its successor of 1919. Among the first free public libraries to be established after the 1850 legislation were Winchester (1851), Manchester (1852) and Ipswich (1853). Birmingham Public Library (founded in 1861) contains the Shakespeare library founded in 1864, and many other public libraries have special collections relating to well-known local authors. In many towns, public libraries owed their foundation or improvement to the Carnegie United Kingdom Trust, founded in 1913 by Andrew Carnegie (1835–1919), an American steel magnate who was the son of a Scottish handloom weaver. By 1919 Carnegie and his trust had given over 2800 public libraries, not only in Britain but in most of the English-speaking world as well. During the 1930s the trust took a leading part in making possible organized inter-library loans, by the establishment of regional catalogues. Local authority spending, particularly by county authorities, increased notably after World War II, and by the 1960s encouraged a proliferation of activities sometimes only indirectly related to books. Besides this, special attention has been given generally to improvements to provision for children's reading, and in some parts of Britain an increasingly multiracial society has been met with the provision, gradually improving, of foreign-language materials. On the other hand, in both public and university libraries, the information revolution of the early 1980s, and the advent of generally available computerized databases, have further challenged traditional librarianship and have brought often unexpected costs.

2 USA
In America, virtually the earliest known library dates from the bequest in 1638 of John Harvard to what became Harvard College, later Harvard University. Yale University Library was founded in 1701, and New Jersey College Library, Princeton, was founded in 1746. Outside the college and university community, William Bray gave a library to Annapolis in Maryland in 1696, so beginning a campaign for parochial libraries in both the American colonies and England. As in England, the 18th century saw the growth of subscription libraries, among which the Library Company of Philadelphia (founded 1731 by a group headed by **Benjamin Franklin**) soon incorporated the library of James Logan (1674–1751), the finest to be thus far assembled in North America. At Newport, Rhode Island, the Redwood Library was founded in 1747, using money given to a local literary and philosophical society by Abraham Redwood.
National library provision dates from the foundation of the Library of Congress, estab-

lished by Act of Congress in 1800; the infant library was destroyed by British troops in 1814, and the present collections are based on the library of **Thomas Jefferson** (1743–1826), purchased subsequently that year. Thanks to its position as a copyright deposit library, its world-wide collecting policy, and its role as provider of catalogue records to other libraries (for which cards were first made available in 1901), it is now the most influential, as well as the largest, library in the world. Among many special collections, notable acquisitions include the Lessing J. Rosenwald collection of illustrated books since the 15th century, the John Boyd Thacher collection (including incunables, Americana, and materials relevant to the French revolution), and outstanding assemblages, both printed and manuscript, relating to **Walt Whitman**. Here, as in many other libraries in North America especially, the traditional collecting areas of books, manuscripts, maps and music have been extended to include photographs, sound and video recordings, globes and musical instruments.

The establishment of free public libraries in America depended at first in the 19th century on town or state, rather than Federal, legislation. The first state law was passed in New Hampshire in 1849, followed by Massachusetts in 1851. Among the most important are Boston Public Library (founded 1852), Chicago (whose modern history dates from 1872, after the burning of the city in 1871), and, largest of all, New York Public Library. The last was created, in its modern form, in 1895 from a merger of three collections: the Astor Library, a general reference library founded in 1848 under the terms of the will of a fur-trader and capitalist, John Jacob Astor (1763–1848); the Lenox Library, amassed by the wealthy bibliophile James Lenox (1800–80) and especially rich in Americana, early printed books, and Bibles; and the estate of Samuel J. Tilden (d. 1886).

The libraries of the new American universities founded in the latter part of the 19th century developed slowly at first. Among the most important are now Cornell (founded 1868), the University of California (1869), Texas (1883) and Chicago (1891). Their growth this century has been rapid, like those of the older universities. It has been greatly helped by American tax law and the generosity of private benefactors, quite apart from the imagination and determination of successive librarians. These libraries have also often been more able, as well as more ready, than their English counterparts to buy entire collections, such as Sir Michael Sadleir's 19th-century three-decker novels at the University of California, Los Angeles, or the entire stock of the 19th-century Berlin bookseller S. Calvary at Chicago. At Austin, Texas, the Harry Ransom Center bears witness to inspired and aggressive buying in English literature in the late 1950s and early 1960s; the Latin American collections here are however hardly less outstanding. In 1986 the University of Texas announced the acquisition, thanks to a private benefactor, of the Carl H. Pforzheimer collection of early English literature, assembled originally in the 1920s and 1930s.

The major independent research collections in America have likewise often benefited in this manner. In Chicago, the Newberry Library (founded 1887) contains rich collections on (among others) **Melville**, the history of printing and the American Indian. The Huntington Library, San Marino, California (opened 1920) was founded by the railway entrepreneur Henry E. Huntington (1850–1927), and contains one of the richest collections anywhere of Americana, English literature and incunables. The Pierpont Morgan Library, New York, is likewise still housed in the building erected by its founder, the banker John Pierpont Morgan (1837–1913). In 1924 his son established it as a public reference library, and it owes much of its present character to its formidable first librarian, Belle da Costa Greene. A reminder that neither this kind of collection nor this kind of collecting was a thing of the past came in 1983, when the J. Paul Getty Trust of Malibu, California, negotiated the purchase of the princely collection of medieval manuscripts assembled by the West German book-collector Peter Ludwig.

### 3 Canada

In Canada, Toronto University (founded in 1827 as King's College) dominates the retrospective collections with, in the Thomas Fisher Library, outstanding collections in the history of science and a unique collection of the 17th-century illustrator Wenceslaus Hollar. McGill University Library, an older foundation (1821), is celebrated for the Sir William Osler collection, principally but not entirely on the history of medicine. McMaster University Library, Hamilton, Ontario, was established in 1887, and its library houses the **Bertrand Russell** Archives. Public libraries were founded at Toronto in 1883 and at Ottawa in 1906, though both were long preceded by the Bibliothèque de Québec, founded in 1848. The national libraries at Ottawa and (for Quebec) at Montreal were established in 1953 and 1967 respectively.

### 4 Australia and New Zealand

The different services offered by circulating, subscription, public, university and national libraries naturally developed more quickly in Australia and New Zealand, keeping pace with the rapid expansion of the two countries. Sydney had a subscription library by 1826, which has since developed into the State Library of

New South Wales. Each state now has its own state library, which acts also as a copyright deposit collection. The University of Sydney was founded in 1850, its library a year later, and 1853 witnessed the foundation of both Melbourne Public Library and the University of Melbourne. Under the National Library Act (1960) the National Library of Australia was established at Canberra: among its holdings are the D. Nichol Smith collection of English literature, the C. T. Onions collection of English philology, and the Clifford family library from Ugbrooke Park, Devon, England.

In New Zealand, the two most notable libraries are those of the University of Auckland (founded in 1884) and the Alexander Turnbull Library (since 1966 part of the National Library), which had its origins in the bequest of Alexander Horsburgh Turnbull (1868–1918). The latter has outstanding collections relating to **Milton** as well as to the Pacific. The first Public Libraries Act was passed in 1869, and the public library system has always depended, to an extent matched in few other places, on the postal service for the transport of books between library and borrower.

*5 Africa and Asia*
By the end of the 19th century, only a few of what were to prove to be major international libraries had been established elsewhere in the English-speaking world. The South African Library, Cape Town, was founded in 1818 from money raised by a tax on wine. (The Pretoria State Library was founded in 1887 by Paul Kruger.) In Singapore, the present National Library traces its history back to the Singapore Institution founded by Sir Stamford Raffles in 1823. The National Library of India, in Calcutta, is founded on a public library established in 1836, and was given its modern name in 1953 on removing to a former winter residence of the Viceroys.

With the important exception of Makerere University Library in Uganda, founded as Makerere College in 1922, most changes came after World War II. In Ghana, the Balme Library, University of Accra, was originally founded in 1948. In India, Delhi Public Library was founded in 1951, as part of a UNESCO plan for developing countries. In Jamaica, the University of the West Indies Library opened in 1948. In Kenya, the University of Nairobi Library can be traced from 1956 onwards. In Nigeria, Ibadan University Library was founded in 1948. In Pakistan, the University of Karachi Library was founded in 1952 (Panjab University College, later Punjab University, had however been established in 1882). In Zimbabwe, the University of Zimbabwe (formerly Rhodesia) Library was founded in 1956. In many of these countries, both university and public libraries often reflect British practices, thanks partly to the efforts of the British Council.

***Life and Death of Jason, The*** A narrative poem in heroic couplets by **William Morris**, published in 1867. The story follows the classical myths and the *Argonautica* of Apollonius Rhodius. Morris's version begins with the birth of Jason, his education by Chiron the centaur, his confrontation with the usurper Pelias and his embarkation for Colchis in the *Argo*. The poem then describes the familiar adventures of the voyage, the encounter with King Aeëtes and the meeting with Medea, the theft of the Golden Fleece and the flight of Jason and Medea. After numerous disasters, Jason's life ends in melancholy loneliness as he muses in the shadow of the rotten timbers of his once glorious ship, the *Argo*.

***Life and Death of Mr Badman, The*** A religious **allegory** by **John Bunyan**, published in 1680. It consists of a dialogue between Mr Wiseman and Mr Attentive, who relate and comment on the life of Mr Badman, an utterly immoral character who has recently passed over into damnation. Selfish and deceitful, he courts a rich woman and maltreats her after their marriage, is a swindler in business, behaves drunkenly, and degenerates physically, though he pretends to repent. His wife dies in despair, whereupon he remarries – this time a woman of similar disposition to his own – and at last expires peacefully.

The book shows a considerable degree of realism, especially in its vivid representation of a 17th-century market town, and through the lively credibility of Mr Badman's own character, making an unmistakable contribution to the development of the novel.

***Life in London***, or, *The Day and Night Scenes of Jerry Hawthorn Esq. and His Elegant Friend Corinthian Tom, Accompanied by Bob Logic, The Oxonian, in Their Rambles and Sprees through the Metropolis* A boisterously comic description of life in Regency London by **Pierce Egan**. It appeared in 20 shilling parts (1820–1) and in book form (1821), with illustrations by Robert and **George Cruikshank**.

Corinthian Tom, helped by his friend Bob Logic, shows the sights of the capital to his country cousin, Jerry Hawthorn. Tom is a Regency rake, Bob a man of facetious wit and continual good humour, and Jerry Hawthorn an amiable rustic eager for adventure. In a series of cheerfully coarse episodes the book gives a revealing picture of the manners of the age and an interesting record of fashionable slang.

It was enormously popular with young men who aspired to a dashing life. **Thackeray** confessed that when he read it in youth he believed the three principals 'to be types of the most

'Tom and Jerry in trouble after a spree.' An illustration by George and Robert Cruikshank for *Life in London* by Pierce Egan (1821).

elegant, fashionable young fellows the town afforded' and their activities 'those of all high-bred English gentlemen'. Twenty years later he could find nothing to say in its favour. Egan himself seems to have had second thoughts about his characters as time passed. *The Finish to the Adventures of Tom, Jerry and Logic, in Their Pursuits through Life in and out of London* (1828) has Tom breaking his neck while hunting, his mistress Kate dying of drink, Logic succumbing to his excesses, and Jerry settling down to a quiet life in the country.

**Life of Samuel Johnson LL.D., The** James **Boswell**'s biography of his friend **Samuel Johnson** was published in 1791. The seventh life of Johnson to appear, it gave the fullest treatment of its subject and remains by common consent the greatest biography in the language.

The 22-year-old Boswell first met Johnson, then aged 54, in Tom Davies's bookshop on 16 May 1763. In his journal for 31 March 1772, Boswell writes of his 'constant plan to write the life of Mr. Johnson', though he was at first nervous of divulging the plan to Johnson. Six months later he refers to a 'store of materials' for the *Life*. Johnson became certain of the scheme after reading the manuscript of Boswell's *Journal of a Tour to the Hebrides*, and it had his blessing. Boswell's methods and emphases as biographer coincided with Johnson's own as expressed in *The Rambler* (Number 60).

Working always with a master-plan in mind, Boswell was tireless in his search for authenti-

cated truth. His training as a lawyer helped him sift the evidence of friends and to operate forensically on Johnson himself: he was able to draw him out as no one else could. Johnson was actually made more 'Johnsonian' by Boswell's transformation of his conversation and doings into the scenic forms and polished prose of the published *Life*. Boswell certainly kept immediate rough notes of many of his encounters with Johnson, but when writing up the *Life* he relied mainly upon a prodigious memory and what he called 'a mind impregnated with the Johnsonian aether'.

Because of the date of their first meeting, Boswell's treatment of the last 20 years of his subject's life occupies three-quarters of the book; but his skill in reconstructing the early years is quite remarkable. Another important aspect of the *Life*'s greatness is pointed at by part of its full title: 'The whole exhibiting a view of literature and literary men in Great-Britain, for near half a century, during which he flourished'. Johnson's centrality in 18th-century letters is established not only by Boswell's record of his life and conversation, but also by the success of the work in placing him in a literary and cultural context.

**Life on the Mississippi** A book by **Mark Twain** published in 1883, part history, part geography, part memoir and part travelogue. It opens with a brief history of the Mississippi River from its discovery by Hernando de Soto in 1541 to the early 19th century, which is more or less factual except for a famous passage in chapter 3 in which Twain offers as 'historical' an episode experienced by his fictional character Huck Finn (the passage had originally been intended for inclusion in the novel *Adventures of Huckleberry Finn*). Twain then turns to a more personal form of history, and for the next 19 chapters describes his own childhood and youth, and his life as a river pilot during the antebellum era.

Some seven years later, Twain added the second half of *Life on the Mississippi*, which recounts his experiences during a return trip to the scenes of his youth. He travels from St Louis to New Orleans, observing the changes wrought by, among other things, the railways. He reminisces about friends from that earlier period of his life, and ruminates on the detrimental effects of Southern romanticism, which he links to the historical romances of **Sir Walter Scott** that were so popular in the antebellum South. In his opinion it was this self-conscious romanticism that prevented social and economic progress in the South and made the Civil War inevitable.

*Life's Handicap* A collection of 27 stories, 'Being Stories of Mine Own People', by **Rudyard Kipling**, published in 1891. They helped to establish him as a literary figure in London.

Almost all look back to his experiences of India. One group deals with the characters who also appear in *Soldiers Three*, a separate collection written during the same period; these include 'The Courting of Dinah Shadd' and 'On Greenhow Hill', which have been particularly admired. 'On Greenhow Hill' is unusual in that the setting for the soldier's reminiscences, and his passion for a dying woman, are green Yorkshire valleys. The atmosphere of a group of horror stories permeates the collection as a whole, with its air of haunted lives. The mood of 'The End of the Passage', in which Hummil, the victim of terrifying nightmares, is literally 'scared to death', is also felt in 'The Limitations of Pambé Serang'. Here the consequences of an obsession are played out in a story of vengeance. At the story's climax, the Negro Nureed, who has been pursued across the globe by Pambé for no more than a few lightly traded insults, shows compassion for his sick and poverty-stricken pursuer. The pathos of this moment of reconciliation is violently destroyed: Pambé knifes Nureed, and the tale ends with the murderer being restored to health in order that he may go to the gallows.

*Light in August* A novel by **William Faulkner**, published in 1932. Set in the imaginary Yoknapatawpha County, Mississippi, it has three main characters: Lena Grove, pregnant and unwed, who travels to Jefferson, Mississippi, in search of Lucas Burch, her baby's father; Joe Christmas, a man who is unsure of his racial origins, and who has murdered his lover Joanna Burden; and the Reverend Gail Hightower, a disgraced minister whose wife committed suicide years earlier, and who lives as a recluse, frequently having a fantasy in which he identifies himself with his grandfather, a Confederate officer who died in Jefferson during the Civil War.

The novel opens with Lena's arrival in Jefferson. She finds, not Lucas Burch (who now calls himself Joe Brown), but Byron Bunch – a hardworking, dependable bachelor who immediately falls in love with her. As they meet, Joanna Burden's body is discovered in a blazing house. Hoping for the reward offered for the capture of her killer, Lucas Burch, who has been involved in bootlegging with Joe Christmas since his arrival in Jefferson, accuses Joe of the crime. Meanwhile Byron tends Lena, who is near to giving birth.

Flashback scenes provide the reader with an account of Joe Christmas's life. His mother, Milly Hines, died when he was born; his father, a travelling circus hand, was killed by her grandfather, Eupheus Hines, who was convinced that he had Negro blood in him. Eupheus then left Joe on the steps of a white orphanage on Christmas night (hence his name). At the age of five, when his racial background was again called into question, he was sent to the home of an unbendingly strict and puritanical farmer, Simon McEachern. As a teenager Joe finally fled the frequent beatings administered by McEachern, took to the road, and after many years arrived in Jefferson, where he carried on an intensely sexual relationship with Joanna Burden. Her request that he pray with her – something McEachern had often demanded – prompted him to slit her throat and set fire to the house.

After eluding capture for nearly a week, he is finally taken. His grandparents, the Hineses, arrive from nearby Mottstown, his grandmother insisting on seeing the grandson her husband had robbed her of. They go to the cabin which Joe and Burch had shared, and where Byron Bunch has installed Lena. Mrs Hines attends the birth of Lena's baby. Bunch, who serves to bring together the stories of the three main characters, takes the Hineses to see the Reverend Hightower to seek his assistance. They ask Hightower to provide Joe with an alibi, but he refuses. When Joe breaks free from his gaolers the next day he runs – as if by instinct – to Hightower's home. The National Guard, led by Percy Grimm, pursue him; Grimm shoots and kills him, then castrates him, ignoring Hightower's frantic explanation (a lie) that Joe was with him at the time of the murder. Hightower withdraws once more into his reverie about his grandfather. Lena, now accompanied by her baby and the attentive Byron Bunch, continues her search for Burch, who has once again fled town.

**Lilliburlero** An anti-Catholic song popular with the army. In January 1686, the Earl of Tyrconnel was sent to Ireland as Lieutenant to James II, and a song with the catchy refrain 'Lero, lero, lilli-burlero; lilli-burlero bullen-a-la!' became familiar among the troops. Lord Thomas Wharton was probably the author of the words, and was said to have composed the music, though this is doubtful; the tune was also once attributed to Purcell. Because of its popularity, the song is said to have sung the Catholic James II out of his kingdom. It is a favourite of Uncle Toby's in **Laurence Sterne**'s *Tristram Shandy*, and is included in **Percy**'s *Reliques of Ancient English Poetry* (1786).

**Lillo, George** *c.*1693–1739 Playwright. Believed to have been of Flemish and English parentage, Lillo was born in London. He wrote seven plays and an adaptation of the Elizabethan tragedy, *Arden of Feversham* (1759). Six of his plays were produced: *Sylvia, or, The Country Burial* (1730), a **ballad opera**; *The London Merchant, or, The History of George Barnwell* (1731); *The Christian Hero* (1735); *The Fatal Curiosity* (1736); *Marina* (1738); and *Elmerick, or, Justice Triumphant* (1740). *Britannia and Batavia*, a **masque**, was not performed. *Marina* was based on **Shakespeare**'s *Pericles*.

Lillo's most important works, *The London Merchant* and *The Fatal Curiosity*, were pioneering examples of domestic tragedy. They abandoned the world of kings and courtiers and insisted on the seriousness of high emotion in ordinary people lower down the social ladder. In this respect, they express the same trend in art and society during the 18th century which produced the engravings of **Hogarth** and the novels of **Samuel Richardson**.

**Lilly, William** 1602–81 Astrologer. Lilly wrote a number of pamphlets containing 'Prophesies' and published an annual almanac from the year 1644. He was the author of *Monarchy, or No Monarchy, in England* (1651), the second part of which is called *Secret Observations on the Life and Death of Charles King of England*. He claimed to have foretold the execution of the king.

**limerick** A form of nonsense verse with a strict rhyme scheme (aabba). The name is said to derive from parties where each guest contributed a verse followed by the chorus 'Will you come up to Limerick?' The form was first used in the 1820s and achieved popularity in the work of **Edward Lear**. An example is:

There was a young lady of Clyde
'Twas of eating green apples she died
The apples fermented
Inside the lamented
And made cider inside her inside.

**Linacre, Thomas** ?1460–1524 Greek scholar and founder of the Royal College of Physicians. He was educated at the Cathedral School at Canterbury and at Oxford, where he became a fellow of All Souls. In 1485–97 he travelled extensively in Italy, studied under Poliziano and was awarded an MD from Padua in 1496. On his return he became tutor to Prince Arthur in 1500. He was a friend of **Erasmus** and **Thomas More** who, together with Cardinal Wolsey, were also his patients. He was also one of Henry VIII's physicians. In 1518 he was granted letters patent by the king to set up the Royal College of Physicians and in 1520 was ordained priest. Linacre was one of the first English scholars to cultivate the study of Greek. He translated many of Galen's works into Latin, including *De Sanitate Tuenda* (1517), which was dedicated to Wolsey, and *De Morbis et Symptomatibus* (1524). His work on Latin grammar *Rudimenta Grammatices* (?1555) was originally written for Princess Mary to whom he was Latin tutor.

**Lincoln Center for the Performing Arts** Situated in New York's West 65th Street, this ambitious cultural centre was incorporated in 1956. Its first auditorium, the Philharmonic Hall, was opened in 1962 and the Vivian Beaumont Theater, designed by Eero Saarinen and Jo Mielziner, in 1965. The Center also contains a much smaller 300-seat auditorium, originally called the Forum, but renamed the Mitzi E. Newhouse Theater in 1973, when Joseph Papp began his five-year directorship. The original intention to establish a repertory theatre in the heart of New York has been pursued, with mixed fortunes, by successive directors.

**Linda Tressel** A novel by **Anthony Trollope**, published anonymously in *Blackwood's Magazine* from October 1867 to May 1868. The setting is Nuremberg and the story concerns Linda Tressel, a girl who loves her aunt and guardian Madame Stanbach, a woman of strong Calvinist principles and little charity. Aunt Stanbach decides that Linda shall marry the vulgar and middle-aged Peter Steinmarc, who (the aunt's character notwithstanding) has no time for religion. A contemporary critic found the book 'so improbable and melancholy that it cannot be read with pleasure'. *The London Review* was convinced that the author of both *Linda Tressel* and *Nina Balatka* was a woman.

**Lindsay, Lady Anne** 1750–1825 Scottish poet and diarist. The daughter of the Earl of Balcarres, Anne Lindsay became Lady Anne Barnard by marriage and accompanied her husband to South Africa. Her journals were edited by D. Fairbridge in 1924 as *Lady Anne Barnard at the Cape, 1797–1802* and are a valuable source of information on the first English occupation of the Cape. She is also known as the author of the ballad 'Auld Robin Gray' (1771) and the poem 'Why Tarries my Love?' (1805).

**Lindsay, Sir David** See **Lyndsay, Sir David**.

**Lindsay, Jack** 1900–90 Australian writer, editor and publisher. The son of the distinguished Australian artist and writer, **Norman Lindsay**, he was born in Melbourne and spent his early years in Sydney. After his parents separated, he went to Brisbane with his mother, reading Classics at Brisbane University. In 1924 he published his first book, *Fauns and Ladies*, a celebration of Aphrodite and the rites associated with her. He was a founding editor of *Vision*, a seminal Australian literary magazine which aimed to publish the best of the new poetry, but attacked both modernism and Australian nationalism. His internationalism led to his leaving Australia for London in 1926. In England he edited various journals, of which *The London Aphrodite* was the most significant, and founded Fanfrolico Press, which between 1927 and 1930 published fine limited editions of classical works. His journals and editions contain many illustrations by his father. During World War II he served in the British army, first in the Royal Corps of Signals and later in the Education Department of the War Office. He received numerous awards in Australia and elsewhere, but had comparatively little critical recognition. A prolific writer, Lindsay published over 120 books. These include translations of Aristophanes, Petronius and other classical authors and a number of historical novels and verse-plays. *The Roaring Twenties* (1960), which gives a vivid portrait of Sydney literary life in the early 1920s, is among his most interesting works. It has been reissued as the second part of his autobiographical trilogy, *Life Rarely Tells* (1982).

**Lindsay, (Nicholas) Vachel** 1879–1931 American poet, born in Springfield, Illinois. He studied art in Chicago and New York City, then tramped across much of the USA and began to write verse, which he would often barter for food and lodging. His third collection of poetry, and the first to bring him recognition, was *General William Booth Enters Into Heaven and Other Poems* (1913), the title-piece of which had originally been published in **Harriet Monroe**'s *Poetry* magazine. He was welcomed as a new poet whose work was dramatic and full of incisive rhythms, and one whose vivid imagery was drawn from a broad American background. *The Congo and Other Poems* appeared in 1914, and *The Chinese Nightingale and Other Poems* in 1917.

As a reader of his own poetry Lindsay became a popular figure; indeed, he tried to extend the popularity of poetry in general by presenting it in what he liked to call 'the higher vaudeville'. The method enjoyed only limited success but he retained the hope that he might become the great singer of everyman; he wanted above all to 'reconcile culture and manliness'. This idealism is evident in his *Golden Book of Springfield* (1920), in which he depicts a Utopia based on the 'Gospel of Beauty'. As his audience dwindled and he could no longer support himself by his poetry readings, he became depressed and committed suicide in 1931. His last published work was a book of political essays, *The Litany of Washington Street* (1929). His *Collected Poems* appeared in 1923 and a revised edition in 1925. A volume of *Letters* was published in 1979.

**Lindsay, Norman (Alfred William)** 1879–1969 Australian artist and novelist. Born in Victoria, he first became known as an illustrator and cartoonist. His first novel, *A Curate in Bohemia* (1913), was followed by an enduring fantasy for children, *The Magic Pudding* (1918). *Redheap* (1930), *Saturdee* (1933) and *Halfway to Anywhere* (1947) form a trilogy about boyhood and adolescence in the Ballarat district of Victoria. The first volume was banned in Australia for some years. Lindsay also published three volumes of essays which express his philosophy of life: *Creative Effort* (1920), *Hyperborea: Two Fantastic Travel Essays* (1928) and *Madam Life's Lovers* (1929).

**Lindsay of Pittscottie, Robert** ?1500–?65 Lindsay was the author of *The History and Chronicles of Scotland*, or at least of that part from the accession of James II in 1437 until 1565. The continuation of the narrative up to 1604 is by another hand. The work is Protestant in sympathy, and shows considerable inaccuracy and confusion over dates. It exists in several early manuscript copies and was first printed in Robert Freebairn's edition (Edinburgh, 1728). It was one of **Sir Walter Scott**'s favourite sources and he draws on it in *Marmion*.

**Lingard, John** 1771–1851 Historian. Lingard was born in Winchester, the son of a Roman Catholic family, and educated at the English College at Douai, which he entered in 1782. The Revolutionary wars forced him to leave in 1793 and he completed his training for the priesthood at Crook Hall, near Durham, taking holy orders in 1795. He taught natural and moral philosophy there, and published *The Antiquities of the Anglo-Saxon Church* (1806, enlarged 1845). After

1811, he spent most of his life at Hornby, near Lancaster, making a successful journey to Rome in 1817 to negotiate the reopening of the English College. *The History of England from the First Invasion of the Romans to the Accession of William and Mary* (8 vols., 1819–30) enjoyed considerable success; it was praised for its objectivity, its careful use of original documents and its balanced view of the Reformation. Lingard was also the author of *A New Version of the Four Gospels* (1836).

**Linklater, Eric** 1899–1974 Novelist and writer for radio. He was born in Penarth, Wales, of a family from Orkney, where he spent much of his childhood and later life. He studied medicine and then English literature at the University of Aberdeen. After serving in World War I, he became assistant editor of *The Times of India* from 1925 to 1927. From 1928 to 1930 he held a Commonwealth Fellowship in the United States, and published a satirical novel, *Juan in America* (1931). Other novels of this period, *White Maa's Saga* and *Poet's Pub* (both 1929), were set in the Orkney Islands.

During World War II he commanded a fortress in the Orkneys and later worked for the War Office. He wrote various 'conversation' pieces for radio, including *The Great Ship* and *Rabelais Replies*, and a radio play, *Crisis in Heaven* (all in 1944). The following year he became Rector of Aberdeen University (until 1948) and wrote his most successful novel, *Private Angelo* (1946), a comic account of postwar reorganization in Italy. *The Man on My Back* (1941) and *A Year of Space* (1953) were autobiographical, and among his later works, *Husband of Delilah* (1962) is the best known. Other novels included *The Corpse on Clapham Common* (1971) and *The Voyage of the Challenger* (1972).

**Linton, Eliza Lynn** 1822–98 Novelist. Born Eliza Lynn, the daughter of a clergyman in Keswick, she left home in 1845 determined to earn a living by her pen and published her first novel, *Azeth the Egyptian*, in the following year. From 1848 to 1851 she was on the staff of *The Morning Chronicle* and later worked for *The Saturday Review* and *All the Year Round*. *Amymone* (1848) and *Realities* (1851) having failed, she settled for a time in Paris before marrying William James Linton, the engraver and poet, in 1858. They separated shortly afterward. Her best novels are *The True History of Joshua Davidson* (1872), *Patricia Kenball* (1874) and *The Autobiography of Christopher Kirkland* (1885). In spite of her own success in an independent life, she was a vehement anti-feminist, as *The Girl of the Period and Other Essays* (1883) shows.

**Lippard, George** 1822–54 American novelist, born in Pennsylvania, best known for his sensa-

tional books about the immorality of large cities. The most famous is *The Quaker City, or, The Monks of Monk Hall* (1844), which went through 27 printings in five years and enjoyed lively sales abroad. Like *New York: Its Upper Ten and Lower Million* (1854), it is lurid in plot but reformist in intention, portraying the corruption of the ruling classes and their sexual, political and financial exploitation of the poor. Lippard also wrote romantic historical novels, including *Blanche of Brandywine* (1846) and *Legends of Mexico* (1847).

**Lippmann, Walter** 1889–1974 American journalist and political commentator, born in New York City, and educated at Harvard. He taught philosophy there under **George Santayana**, and was later one of the founders of *The New Republic*. He served as an assistant to the Secretary of War from 1917 to 1919. When he returned to *The New Republic*, he found himself an important spokesman for liberalism. He soon became editorial commentator for the New York *World* (1921–31) and then for the *Herald Tribune* (1931–62). It was during these years that his first books began to appear. *A Preface to Politics* (1913), *Drift and Mastery* (1914), *The Stakes of Diplomacy* (1915), *The Political Scene* (1919), *Public Opinion* (1922), *The Phantom Public* (1925), *A Preface to Morals* (1929), *The Method of Freedom* (1934) and *The Good Society* (1937) represent his attempts to promote a mature liberalism that would depend upon public virtue, individual freedom, and *laissez-faire* economics. His later books include *Some Notes on War and Peace* (1940), *US Foreign Policy* (1943), *US War Arms* (1944), *The Cold War* (1947), *Isolation and Alliances* (1952), *The Public Philosophy* (1955), *The Communist World and Ours* (1959) and *The Coming Tests with Russia* (1961). He was awarded Pulitzer Prizes for reporting in 1958 and 1962.

***Listener, The*** A weekly magazine of general interest published since 1929 by the BBC, *The Listener* has had a strong literary bias, printing occasional articles, broadcast talks and poems by almost every established writer of modern times. **J. R. Ackerley**, editor from 1935 to 1959, elicited contributions from **E. M. Forster** and **Christopher Isherwood** among others; in recent years new poems by **Philip Larkin**, **Ted Hughes** and **George MacBeth** have appeared in its pages. Regular reviewers have included **Edwin Muir** and **Raymond Williams**.

**litotes** A figure of speech which uses understatement for rhetorical effect, a positive being expressed by the negative of an opposite, e.g. 'Shakespeare's was no mean achievement'.

***Little Dorrit*** A novel by **Charles Dickens**, published in 20 monthly parts from December 1855 to June 1857.

Amy, universally called 'Little Dorrit', the youngest child of William Dorrit, a debtor and an inmate of the Marshalsea, was actually born in the prison. She and her father are befriended by Arthur Clennam who has recently returned from a long period abroad, and whose mother employs Little Dorrit as a seamstress. William Dorrit escapes the Marshalsea when he inherits a fortune, and the family, assuming a station befitting their wealth, travel to Italy. There Dorrit, once known as 'the father of the Marshalsea', dies, unable at the last to remember anything but his past years in the prison.

In England, Arthur Clennam, fighting his own battles with the bureaucracy of the Circumlocution Office, is himself victim of a gigantic fraud perpetrated by the eminent financier, Merdle, and is sentenced to the Marshalsea. There he is found by Little Dorrit whose resilient optimism, generosity and humility are unaffected by the social aspirations of her sister and brother. Arthur now recognizes Amy's enduring love for him, but only when the Dorrit fortune is once more lost can the couple be united, to go 'quietly down into the roaring streets, inseparable and blessed'.

A sub-plot centres on Arthur Clennam's mother, a gloomy and bigoted paralytic who, symbolically, lives in a crumbling and mysterious house. This part of the plot involves two villains, the Frenchman Rigaud, alias Blandois, and Jeremiah Flintwich. The latter's wife Affery is a memorable character, much put upon by her husband and mistress, Mrs Clennam, and haunted by extraordinary 'dreams' which turn out to be true events.

Other characters include some of Dickens's most memorable comic creations, among them 'Mr F's aunt' ('There's milestones on the Dover road'), Flora Finching (who is apparently a satirical portrait of Dickens's early love, Maria Beadnell, in middle age), John Chivery, a despairing suitor of Amy's, and Mrs General, the highly correct governess-companion who advocates the words 'Papa, potatoes, prunes and prism' as giving 'a pretty form to the lips'.

The novel, originally given the title 'Nobody's Fault' during composition, emphasizes individual responsibility in all aspects of life, whether commercial, political or personal.

***Little Foxes, The*** A play by **Lillian Hellman**, first performed in New York in 1939. It is an angry study of the voracious capitalism that Hellman believed to have swept aside the older values and traditions of the Southern states. Like the later and less impressive *Another Part of the Forest* (1946), it concentrates on the complex of loyalties and rivalries that bind and divide the newly wealthy Hubbard family. Ben is a bachelor, Oscar has entered into an alliance with the old aristocracy by marrying Birdie, whom he has proceeded to destroy as systematically as the new rapacity has destroyed the old nobility, and Regina has married a liberal financier. To complete a lucrative deal, the three Hubbards need each to provide a large sum. The play details the processes by which Regina's portion is provided, and concludes when she has proved herself stronger than the whining Oscar and more merciless even than the bullying Ben. It is a vigorous and disturbing study of corruption, cruelty and blackmail in a family community that expels any humanity that it cannot silence.

***Little Lord Fauntleroy*** A novel for children by **Frances Hodgson Burnett**, published in 1886. The son of the Earl of Dorincourt becomes estranged from his father because he has married an American. The earl refuses to receive his daughter-in-law who, after her husband's death, takes their son to New York. He is called Cedric Errol, has long curls, is generous, affectionate, and loved by all in his modest neighbourhood, particularly by Mr Hobbs the grocer and Dick the bootblack. When his uncles die he becomes heir of Dorincourt and returns to England with his mother. The old earl still refuses to receive Cedric's mother, and she is obliged to live in a house near the Dorincourt seat. But Cedric wins the earl's love and soon influences him to behave benevolently to his tenants and other poor people. Then a strange American woman appears, claiming that she is the earl's real daughter-in-law and that her son is heir to the estate. She is eventually unmasked by Dick and Mr Hobbs, who journey all the way to England to discredit the impostor's claims. The earl receives Cedric's mother and the three generations settle down happily at Dorincourt, which Cedric – Little Lord Fauntleroy – will inherit.

One of the illustrations by Birch for the 1889 edition of *Little Lord Fauntleroy*, by Frances Hodgson Burnett.

**Little Review, The** A literary periodical published from 1914 to 1929, edited by Margaret Anderson and Jane Heap. Begun in Chicago, the enterprise was moved to New York City in 1917 and to Paris in 1924. Numerous writers from both sides of the Atlantic were represented in its pages, among them **Richard Aldington**, **Sherwood Anderson**, Guillaume Apollinaire, **Djuna Barnes**, **Hart Crane**, **T. S. Eliot**, **Ernest Hemingway**, **Wyndham Lewis**, **Vachel Lindsay**, **Amy Lowell**, **Marianne Moore**, **Ezra Pound** (who also served as the periodical's foreign editor), **Gertrude Stein**, **Wallace Stevens**, Tristan Tzara, **William Carlos Williams** and **William Butler Yeats**. The periodical gained notoriety when its editors were tried and found guilty of obscenity for publishing a portion of **James Joyce**'s *Ulysses*.

**Little Women** A novel by **Louisa May Alcott**, originally published in two parts. The first part, *Little Women, or, Meg, Jo, Beth, and Amy*, appeared in 1868; the second, under the title *Good Wives*, in 1869. In 1871 the two appeared as a single volume, *Little Women and Good Wives*. Subsequent editions have generally included both sections and have been entitled simply *Little Women*.

The March sisters, Meg, Jo, Beth and Amy, are the daughters of an army chaplain in the Civil War who live with their mother (Marmee) in a small town in New England. The story follows the girls' lives and their efforts to increase the family's small income. Jo, the independent and unconventional sister, wants to be a writer and is on the verge of success at the end of the first part. The second part relates the girls' emergence into womanhood. Meg and Amy marry; Beth falls ill and dies. Jo becomes a successful novelist and later marries a professor, Dr Bhaer. Together Jo and Dr Bhaer establish a school for boys, the subject of Alcott's later novels *Little Men* (1871) and *Jo's Boys* (1886).

**Lively, Penelope (Margaret, née Greer)** 1933– Novelist and children's author. Born in Cairo, she grew up in Egypt, settled in England after World War II and took a degree in History at St Anne's College, Oxford. A preoccupation with the effect of the past on the present, often manifested in a supernatural manner, is the hallmark of her books. She began her career as a writer for children, and her first novels *Astercote* (1970), *The Wild Hunt of Hagworthy* (1971) and *The Whispering Knights* (1971) are pleasant if unexceptional adventure stories. Her first work of note was *The Ghost of Thomas Kempe* (1973), winner of the Carnegie Medal for that year. It concerns the ghost of a 17th-century sorcerer who returns to haunt a present-day family; a witty vision of the clash between 17th and 20th centuries, it also portrays the awakening of an awareness of history in James, the boy to whom it falls to exorcize Thomas Kempe. The same idea is repeated in *The Revenge of Samuel Stokes* (1981). *The House in Norham Gardens* (1974), *Going Back* (1975), and *A Stitch in Time* (1976) treat the same theme in a subtler, more evocative way. In *A Stitch In Time*, which won the Whitbread Award in 1976, the heroine becomes obsessed with a sampler embroidered by a girl who lived in the house more than 100 years before. In 1977 Lively wrote her first adult novel, *The Road To Lichfield*, shortlisted for the Booker Prize. The same intermingling of past and present still prevails in her adult fiction, in *Judgement Day* (1980), *According To Mark* (1984) and *Moon Tiger* (1987), which won the Booker Prize.

**Liverpool poets** A group of poets, Adrian Henri (1932– ), Roger McGough (1937– ) and Brian Patten (1946– ), committed to reviving poetry as a public, performed art. They flourished particularly during the 1960s in Liverpool, strongly influenced by the pop music and culture for which the city was then known. *The Mersey Sound* (1967), in the Penguin Modern Poets series, is an anthology of their work.

**Lives of the Poets, The** A series of succinct critical biographies by **Samuel Johnson**, published between 1779 and 1781. Already the author of several literary 'profiles' or 'lives', Johnson was asked in 1777 by a number of London booksellers to prepare introductory essays for an edition of selected poetry. He originally proposed to begin with **Chaucer**, though in the event the *Lives* started several centuries later with **Abraham Cowley**. Even so, they ran to 52 in all and amounted to a comprehensive review of the previous century of verse – a major undertaking for a writer then in his seventies. Of differing lengths, they offer a combination of biographical sketch, analysis of character and subjective opinion which make lively reading. Johnson was an unrelenting, though honest, critic of people and writing, and his comments are sometimes lasting, sometimes just of historical interest, but never dull. There is an unmistakable tendency to chastise those failings in others which resemble his own: indolence, for example, or (as in the case of **Swift**) derangement. But many of the pieces, however subjective, have become landmarks of literary criticism: the lives of **Dryden** and **Gay**, for example, and the dissection of **metaphysical poetry** in the life of Cowley. Others, like the life of **Somerville**, are masterly achievements in Johnson's inimitable style of prose.

**Livesay, Dorothy** 1909– Canadian poet. Born in Winnipeg, she moved to Toronto in 1920 and was educated at the University of

Toronto and the Sorbonne, working later as a social worker in Montreal and New Jersey during the Depression. She has also been a newspaper reporter, teacher of English and writer in residence at many Canadian universities. She now lives on Galiano Island in British Columbia. Her first collection of poems, *Green Pitcher* (1928), appeared before she was 19. Works like *Day and Night* (1944) reflected her left-wing activism during the 1930s and 1940s. *Collected Poems: The Two Seasons* (1972) provides the most comprehensive sample of her work. *The Phases of Love* (1983) is a retrospective collection of previously unpublished love poems, while *Feeling the Worlds* (1985) was published for her seventy-fifth birthday. *The Self-completing Tree* (1986) is her selection from almost 60 years of writing. She has also published a volume of autobiographical short stories, *A Winnipeg Childhood* (1973), and a memoir, *Right Hand, Left Hand* (1977), as well as editing several anthologies of women's poetry. A poet of wide stylistic range, she is regarded as the first major feminist poet in Canada, and is particularly admired for her love poems.

**Livings, Henry** 1929– Dramatist. He was born and educated in Lancashire, where he continues to live. A prolific writer, he has television and radio plays to his credit as well as more than 30 works for the stage. These include *Stop It, Whoever You Are* (1961), *Big Soft Nellie* (1961), *Nil Carborundum* (1962), *Kelly's Eye* (1963) and *Eh?* (1964). Anarchically cheerful, they show special sympathy for the underdog and feeling for North-Country life. Behind the farcical plotting and the caricatures, Livings retains a bleak estimate of man's inhumanity to man, clearly seen in *The Little Mrs Foster Show* (1966).

**Liyong, Taban lo** 1939– Ugandan essayist and poet. He was born in northern Uganda and educated at Gulu High School, Sir Samuel Baker School, the National Teachers College, Kampala, and several American colleges including Howard University. His first book, paradoxically entitled *The Last Word* (1969), was the first indigenously published East African literary criticism. The essays are wide-ranging in setting and subject, conveying the notion of what Liyong terms 'cultural synthesism', an attempt to make sense out of the uniquely fragmented age in which he believes we live. Liyong is no respecter of literary form and in *Eating Chiefs: Lwo Culture from Lolwe to Malkal* (1970) he attempts to create a new medium which can call upon African traditional culture and yet be appropriate to the modern world. He has also written a collection of short stories, *Fixions* (1969), and several volumes of poetry, among which the best known are *Frantz Fanon's Uneven Ribs* (1971), *Another Nigger Dead* (1972)

and *Ballads of Underdevelopment* (1976). His 'funeral dirge', *Meditations of Taban lo Liyong* (1978), was composed after working with a writers' workshop at the University of Iowa. Liyong now lives in Sudan, where he teaches at the University of Juba. His is regarded as an individual voice in African literature, verging at times on the bizarre and eccentric, but his ability to yoke together the principles of traditional culture with modern trends in Western intellectual life has made him a force to be reckoned with.

**Llewellyn, Richard** 1907–83 Novelist and playwright. Born Richard Dafydd Vivian Llewellyn Lloyd in St David's, Pembrokeshire, he was educated in Cardiff and London. At the age of 16 he went to Italy to learn hotel management, and while in Venice he began to study painting and sculpture. In 1926 he enlisted in the regular army. Throughout the 1930s he lived in England, working in film studios as a director. During the war he served as a captain in the Welsh Guards, and for much of his life thereafter he lived abroad. A gifted linguist and avid traveller, he described himself as 'an expatriate Welshman who now lives in the world and will stay there'. Based in North America, he spent several years in Argentina tracing the descendants of Welsh colonists who had settled in Patagonia in the 18th century.

Llewellyn achieved early success with his stage plays, some of which were later filmed. *Poison Pen* (1937) and *Noose* (1947) were popular, but it was with his novel *How Green Was My Valley* (1939), set in a Welsh mining community, that he gained more lasting recognition. It became the first and most famous best-seller of the war years, and its blend of lyricism, realism and humour has represented something quintessentially 'Welsh' for many readers. Other novels included *None But the Lonely Heart* (1943), and *A Few Flowers for Shiner* (1950), both concerned with cockney characters in the London slums. A sequence of spy novels, *The End of the Rug* (1968), *But We Didn't Get the Fox* (1969), *White Horse to Banbury Cross* (1971) and *The Night Is a Child* (1972), concerned a British agent-turned-industrialist called Edmund Trothe. *A Night of Bright Stars* (1979), about a Brazilian pioneer aviator, was set in *fin-de-siècle* Paris.

**Locke, Alain (Leroy)** 1886 1954 Black American editor, critic, philosopher, art historian and educator, born in Philadelphia, and educated at Harvard, Oxford (where he was the first black Rhodes Scholar), and the University of Berlin. From 1918 to 1953 he was Professor of Philosophy at Howard.

His influential career as critic and editor began with the March 1925 publication of a special illustrated edition of *The Survey* magazine, entitled 'Harlem, Mecca of the New Negro'. Locke edited the issue and wrote an introductory essay which announced the arrival of the **Harlem Renaissance**. Contributors to the volume included such young writers and poets as **Claude McKay**, **Jean Toomer**, **Countee Cullen** and **Langston Hughes**. Late in the same year Locke published *The New Negro*, the first literary anthology of the Renaissance. The volume consisted of material from *The Survey* with additional essays, stories, poems and extensive bibliographies. Locke's other publications include a volume edited with Montgomery Gregory, *Plays of Negro Life* (1927), as well as *The Negro and His Music* (1936), *Negro Art: Past and Present* (1936) and *The Negro in Art: A Pictorial Record of the Negro Artist and of the Negro Theme in Art* (1940). He also wrote numerous reviews and essays on black literature and culture, many of which were published in the magazines *Opportunity* and *Phylon* from the 1930s to the early 1950s.

**Locke, John** 1632–1704 Philosopher. Born at Wrington in Somerset, and educated at Westminster School and Christ Church, Oxford, Locke remained at the university to teach Greek and rhetoric. He also studied medicine, though he did not take a degree until 1674, and was interested in the new experimental science being developed by **Newton**, Boyle, **Harvey** and others. In 1667 he joined the household of Anthony Ashley Cooper, Lord Ashley, later 1st Earl of Shaftesbury – a position from which he gained a considerable knowledge of trade, politics and the role of the monarchy. Meanwhile, he received several minor government appointments and kept up his connection with Oxford. Between 1675 and 1679 he was in France, and was dismissed by the university for suspected complicity in Shaftesbury's plots. Shaftesbury's fall came in 1682 and Locke fled to Holland the following year, staying there until the accession of William and Mary. From 1691 until 1700 he was adviser on coinage to William's government and a member of the Council of Trade. He resigned when his health failed, and died at his manor house in Kent.

Locke's earliest published work, *Letters Concerning Toleration* (1689–92), argued the case for religious freedom. *Two Treatises on Government* (1690) was followed by a book begun as a proposed reply, on a single sheet of paper, to the question, 'what objects our understandings were, or were not, fitted to deal with'. It was published in 1690 as the *Essay Concerning Human Understanding*. Four essays on money (1692, 1695 and 1699) showed Locke's wide-ranging knowledge of economics; the future of learning was examined in *Some Thoughts Concerning Education* (1693) and the problems of faith in *The*

John Locke, 1685. Portrait by Sylvester Brownover. National Portrait Gallery, London.

*Reasonableness of Christianity As Delivered in the Scriptures* (1695). He published two replies to attacks on his work in *Vindications* (1695 and 1697). His last years found him increasingly preoccupied with religion; two posthumous publications were *A Paraphrase and Notes on the Epistle of St Paul to the Galatians* (1705) and *A Discourse on Miracles* (1716).

Locke's view of society was based on his belief in religious toleration, parliamentary democracy and the *laissez-faire* system of commerce and trade. In religion, he was an analytical but convinced Christian whose contempt for traditional theological argument earned him the wrath of the Church. As befitted a man who had become a Fellow of the Royal Society in 1666, he followed the principles of the new experimental science in his investigation of the mind, rooting his ideas in evidence. Though he stimulated later metaphysics, he was not concerned with metaphysical speculation: he appealed constantly to experience, from which reason and knowledge proceed.

**Locker (later Locker-Lampson), Frederick** 1821–95 Poet. Born in Greenwich, he worked for a time at Somerset House and at the Admiralty. After he left government service he wrote 'society verse' and published *London Lyrics* (1857), an anthology called *Lyra Elegantiarum* (1867) and a miscellany of verse and prose, *Patchwork* (1879). His reminiscences were published as *My Confidences* (1896).

**Lockhart, John Gibson** 1794–1854 Biographer, critic and novelist. Born at Cambusnethan, Lanarkshire, he was educated at Glasgow and Oxford. Called to the Scottish Bar in 1816, he contributed to **Blackwood's Magazine**. He translated Schlegel's *Lectures on the History of Literature* and published sketches of Edinburgh society in 1819 as *Peter's Letters to his Kinsfolk*. He was editor of the **Quarterly Review** from 1824 to 1853; his uncompromising criticism earned him the nickname of 'The Scorpion'. In 1820 he married Sophia, **Walter Scott**'s eldest daughter. His *Life of Scott* (1838) is one of the finest biographies in the language. He also published a *Life of Burns* (1828) and four novels, *Valerius* (1821), *Adam Blair* (1822), *Reginald Dalton* (1824) and *Matthew Wald* (1824).

*Locksley Hall* A poem by **Alfred Tennyson**, first published in *Poems* (1842), written in the unusual form of eight-stress trochaic couplets. According to Tennyson, *Locksley Hall* 'represents young life, its good side, its deficiencies, and its yearnings'. But beyond its narrative of the hero's frustrated love for his cousin Amy, the poem is invested with ideas and concepts contributing to the formation of the Victorian frame of mind. Much that is contemporary – ballooning, the middle-class intellectual's fear of encroaching democracy, material optimism, emigration, a touch of Carlylean thought implicit in the doctrine of active participation – informs *Locksley Hall*. Biographically the poem may refer to Tennyson's own frustrated love for Rosa Baring in the 1830s or to the breaking of his engagement in 1840 to Emily Sellwood.

*Locrine, The Lamentable Tragedy of* A play first published in 1595 and once attributed to Shakespeare (see **Shakespeare apocrypha**). Modern scholarship has named **George Chapman** as a likely author but definite attribution is not possible.

The Locrine of the title is Logrin, King of Britain, mentioned by **Geoffrey of Monmouth** and **Edmund Spenser** (*The Faerie Queene*, Book I). Locrine's queen is Gwendolen, who watches with growing rage the king's infatuation with Estrildis, a German maiden. Estrildis had come to England with the invasion by the Huns under King Humber, defeated at the battle of the river Albus (called the Humber thereafter). Estrildis bears Locrine a daughter, and Gwendolen has mother and daughter drowned in the Severn.

**Lodge, David (John)** 1935– Critic and novelist. Educated at University College, London, Lodge is now Professor of Modern English Literature at the University of Birmingham. His literary criticism is concerned with the nature of and current possibilities for fiction. *The Language of Fiction* (1966) looks at the variety of verbal modes open to the novelist. *The Novelist at the Crossroads* (1971) assesses the state of contemporary British fiction. *Working with Structuralism* (1981) applies current structuralist analysis to 19th- and 20th-century novels.

Lodge's novels themselves frequently test and exploit the assumptions and conventions of fictional narrative. *The British Museum is Falling Down* (1965) contains parodies of modernist writers like **Joyce** and **Virginia Woolf**; the plot of *Small World* (1983) mimics the structure of an Arthurian romance. But Lodge's fiction is also grounded solidly in the experience of his own time: *Ginger, You're Barmy* (1962) is an early, vigorous evocation of post-war National Service; *Changing Places* (1975), to which *Small World* is the sequel, is a satirical 'campus' novel much in the school of **Kingsley Amis**'s *Lucky Jim* or the early work of **Malcolm Bradbury**; *How Far Can You Go?* (1978) looks at the problems of Roman Catholic faith in Britain in the 1970s.

**Lodge, Thomas** ?1557–1625 Poet, dramatist and writer of prose romances. Lodge was the son of Sir Thomas Lodge, who became Lord Mayor of London in 1562 and was imprisoned for debt soon after. He was educated at Merchant Taylors' School and Trinity College, Oxford, where he graduated in 1577, and was admitted to Lincoln's Inn in 1578. In 1581 he was summoned before the Privy Council, but the charge is unknown. He sailed on expeditions to the Canaries (1588) and to South America (1591). Lodge later received a medical degree from Avignon (in 1600 according to **Anthony à Wood**), and an MD from Oxford in 1602, and practised as a doctor. He was converted to Catholicism and as a recusant spent periods on the Continent, especially after the Gunpowder Plot of 1605. He practised medicine in the Netherlands and finally returned to England in 1611.

Lodge's earliest work is a short pamphlet, *A Defence of Poetry, Music and Stage Plays* (1580), in reply to Gosson's *The School of Abuse*. An *Alarm Against Usurers* (1584) is a prose work about a young gentleman who falls into extravagant ways and has to resort to usurers. Bound in with this work were a prose romance, *The Delectable History of Frobonius and Prisceria*, and a satire, *The Lamentable Complaint of Truth over England*. *Catharos* (1591) is a sermon against usury and lechery presented as a colloquy between Diogenes and two Athenian interlocutors, and *The Devil Conjured* (1596) a defence of the ascetic life in the form of a dialogue between the hermit St Anthony and three visitors. *Wit's Misery* (1596) is a sermon on the seven deadly sins. *Prosopopoeia* (1596), doubtfully ascribed to Lodge, dwells on Mary's tears and thus might provide evidence for a date for Lodge's conversion. *Rosalynde* (1590) is the main source for *As*

*You Like It* and was Lodge's most successful prose romance. *Robert Second Duke of Normandy* and *William Longbeard* were printed in 1591 and 1593 respectively, and *A Margarite of America* (the story of which Lodge says he found in a Jesuit library on his South American trip) in 1596.

Lodge's first verse publication was *Scillae's Metamorphosis* (1589), an erotic epyllion later published as *Glaucus and Scilla* (1610). *Phillis* (1593) is a sonnet cycle which includes imitations of Ronsard and Desportes. *A Fig for Momus* (1595) is a collection of satires in the Horatian manner.

Lodge wrote two plays. *The Wounds of Civil War* was printed in 1594 but probably had its first performance *c.*1586. It deals with the civil wars between Marius and Sulla and draws on Appian's *Roman History* and Plutarch. *A Looking Glass for London and England*, a collaboration with **Robert Greene** printed in 1594, is a sort of morality play based on the story of Jonah, in which Londoners are invited to learn from the fate of Nineveh.

Lodge was also a translator of the works of the historian Josephus (1602) and of Seneca (1614). His medical interests inform *A Treatise of the Plague* (1603) and *A Poor Man's Talent*, which was not printed until 1883.

**Lofting, Hugh (John)** 1886–1947 Children's author. Born in Berkshire and educated at a Jesuit boarding-school in Derbyshire, he went on to train first as an architect and later as a civil engineer. His children's stories originated in the illustrated letters he sent to his family from the front in World War I, describing how army horses managed to fare and how much better off they would be if they had the services of a doctor who could speak their language. This idea was incorporated into *The Story of Dr Dolittle* (1920), where the vague, benign hero learns how to address the many animals who share his home and dominate his surgery. They all sail to Africa to cure a deadly monkey disease. Further adventures are described in many other books, all illustrated with simple drawings by the author. Sometimes attacked today for his occasionally patronizing attitudes to race, Lofting nevertheless created, in the endearingly absent-minded Dr Dolittle, one of the most famous characters in children's fiction.

**Logue, Christopher** 1926– Poet, translator and dramatist. Born in Portsmouth, he attended Portsmouth Grammar School. He served from 1943 in the Commandos in the Middle East until imprisoned for illegal possession of pay-books. He has lived in London and Paris, working on *Private Eye* and as a film actor. His immature early poems, *Wand and Quadrant* (1953), are influenced by **Pound**. *Devil, Maggot and Son*

(1958) was followed by *Songs* (1959), which revealed his conversion to radical socialism and his debt to Brecht, also apparent in stage plays like *Jazzetry* (1959) and *Antigone* (1960). Selections from his earlier books appear in *Ode to the Dodo: Poems 1953–78* (1981), confirming Logue as a writer of populist lyric and satirical verse with a strong sense of the possibilities of the voice. He is best known for his free adaptations of Homer's *Iliad*: *Patrocleia* (1962) and *Pax* (1967) are joined by *GBH* to form the outstanding *War Music* (1981), which has been praised by **P. J. Kavanagh** and **George Steiner**.

**Lollards, The** Originally a group of Oxford adherents to the unorthodox doctrines of **John Wyclif** (*c.*1320–84), they were led by Nicholas of Hereford. Despite continual persecution, as well as recantations by several early supporters, the sect gained in strength and numbers. The Lollards suffered a military defeat at the hands of Henry V in 1414, after which Lollardy was driven underground. It resurfaced several times well into the 16th century. The main demands of the Lollards were for freely available vernacular translations of the Bible (see also **The Bible in English**), and a reduction in the materialism and powers of the Catholic Church. They denied the value of pilgrimages and prayers for the dead, the necessity of confession and the validity of the doctrine of transubstantiation.

*London* A poem in imitation of the Third Satire of Juvenal, by **Samuel Johnson**, published in 1738. The Latin original, a popular model for Augustan poets, presents a dialogue with a friend leaving the metropolis for the country. In Johnson's version the poet Thales, about to leave London for Wales, delivers an eloquent tirade against the 'thoughtless age' in which he lives, denouncing courtiers and flatterers as well as fashion and other general characteristics of the time. The poem is robustly constructed and contains some memorably contemptuous lines, a spirited description of the streets of the capital and a rousing defence of the condition of poverty.

**London, Jack** 1876–1916 American novelist, born John Griffith London in San Francisco. He grew up on the waterfront of Oakland and his schooling was intermittent. Much of his youth was spent on the wrong side of the law. At the age of 17 he signed on a sealing ship which took him to the Arctic and Japan. Depression had struck the USA when he returned, and he was unable to find work. In 1894 he joined a march on Washington to petition for relief for the poor. The petition was not successful, but London, who had just won first prize in a newspaper competition, added the event to his rapidly expanding store of experience. The aspiring writer became also an aspiring reformer. He discovered the 'Communist Manifesto', and from then on was an active socialist. He enrolled in the University of California in 1896, but dropped out after one semester. He continued his education on his own, reading sociology and political science intensively. In 1897 he joined the Klondike gold rush, carrying the works of Darwin and Milton in his backpack. He returned to Oakland in 1898 and began to write about his various experiences.

His early stories were accepted by **Overland Monthly** in the West and **The Atlantic Monthly** in the East, and in 1900 were collected in a volume entitled *The Son of the Wolf*. Like his first novel, *A Daughter of the Snows* (1902), they drew on his experiences in the Klondike. Subsequent collections of his short stories include *Love of Life* (1907), *Lost Face* (1910), *South Sea Tales* (1911), and *The Red One* (1918). His second novel, *The Cruise of the Dazzler* (1902), was based on his own teenage experiences as an oyster pirate. His next novel, the hugely successful **The Call of the Wild** (1903), is the story of a sledge dog in the Klondike who eventually becomes the leader of a pack of wolves. *The People of the Abyss*, also published in 1903, draws on his observation of the slums of London made during a visit to England in the previous year. *The Sea-Wolf* (1904) chronicles the voyage of a ship run by a ruthless captain. In 1905 he published a socialist

Jack London, 1905.

treatise called *The War of the Classes* and a novel, *The Game*, about a man's fatal fascination with prizefighting. *Before Adam* (1906) attempts to recreate a prehistoric community, and *White Fang* (1906) deals with the taming of a wild dog in the Klondike. **The Iron Heel** (1908), set in the near future, tells of socialist struggles against the totalitarian consolidation of capitalist power. **Martin Eden** (1909), more directly autobiographical than most of London's work, is concerned with his attempts to become a successful writer, and then to come to terms with that success. *Burning Daylight* (1910) is set in the Klondike, *Smoke Bellew* (1912) in the Yukon. *The Valley of the Moon* (1912), another socialist novel, is about a working-class couple who escape from the harshness of industrial life in Oakland to an idyllic life on the land. *John Barleycorn* (1913), an autobiographical memoir, deals with the debilitating effects of alcohol. *The Star Rover* (1915) is the story of a San Quentin lifer's spiritual struggles.

With the success of his fiction, London was also in demand on the lecture circuit. He visited Korea, Japan and Mexico as a foreign correspondent and travelled for two years in the South Seas. But for one so celebrated and so rich (during his career he earned over a million dollars) he was an unhappy man who could not reconcile his own success with the things he had seen and endured. He died at the age of 40, perhaps a suicide. *The Human Drift*, a socialist treatise, was published posthumously in 1917.

**London Assurance** A five-act comedy by **Dion Boucicault**, first staged at **Covent Garden** in 1841 and effectively revived by the Royal Shakespeare Company at the Aldwych Theatre in 1970.

Sir Harcourt Courtly, a vain widower who believes himself irresistibly attractive, plans to marry Grace Harkaway, a country heiress 45 years his junior. He arrives at Oak Hall to meet her, but is anticipated by his son Charles, driven out of London by debts and taking refuge under a pseudonym at an address conveniently discovered by his confidence-trickster friend Dazzle. Charles has already fallen in love with Grace, who finds him a challenge to her belief that love is an unnecessary passion. With the help of the sporting Lady Gay Spanker, Charles eventually wins both Grace and his father's forgiveness.

**London Lickpenny** A satirical poem from the first half of the 14th century; it exists in two versions, one in eight-line stanzas and the other in **rhyme royal**. It was at one time wrongly attributed to **John Lydgate**. A countryman coming to London in search of justice finds he cannot be heard without bribing the legal officials. Abandoning his case, he leaves for home and the second half of the poem consists of a series of vividly described scenes from London street life.

**London Magazine, The** The earliest periodical to be called *The London Magazine* was published from 1732 to 1785 but the more famous monthly of the same name appeared between January 1820 and June 1829. Edited by John Scott, it appealed to the readership created by the success of *Blackwood's Magazine* and rivalled its circulation. It published **Thomas De Quincey**'s *Confessions of an English Opium-Eater* and **Charles Lamb**'s *Essays of Elia*, as well as poems by **John Keats** and **John Clare**. Apart from Scott, Lamb and De Quincey, the staff of the magazine consisted of **William Hazlitt**, **Thomas Hood** and **Mary Russell Mitford**. Rivalry between *The London Magazine* and *Blackwood's* was fierce, and Scott successfully exposed the careless libels of his competitor. A duel resulted, in which Scott was mortally wounded.

*The London Magazine* is also the name of a monthly literary journal founded in 1954 by **John Lehmann**, who was succeeded as editor in 1961 by Alan Ross, a poet, travel-writer and cricket reporter. The magazine has shown an interest in international rather than narrowly English literature. Two recent examples of writers whose work it has discovered and propagated are **Tony Harrison** and the Nobel Prize-winning Czech poet Jaroslav Seifert.

**London Merchant, The**, *or, The History of George Barnwell* A tragedy by **George Lillo**, first produced at **Drury Lane** in 1731 and published the same year. The play is often called *George Barnwell*, the title of the ballad on which its plot is based. It follows the downward path of an apprentice, seduced into evil ways by a courtesan, Millwood. Barnwell becomes her creature and even robs his employer, the honest merchant Thorowgood, whose moral probity is expressed in his observations to the upright apprentice, Trueman. Eventually Millwood persuades Barnwell to rob and murder his uncle; the two of them are hanged for the crime. Written in prose and dealing with the fortunes of ordinary people, Lillo's work was an important example of domestic tragedy; it enjoyed a long history of popularity on the boards, as the references to it in the opening chapters of **Dickens**'s *Great Expectations* show.

**London Prodigal, The** A play of unknown authorship, published in 1605 and of interest only because it was once attributed to Shakespeare (see **Shakespeare apocrypha**). A comedy, it is concerned with the wayward young Flowerdale, the prodigal of the title, and how his constant and loving wife reclaims him.

**London Review of Books, The** Modelled on the prestigious *New York Review of Books*, this fortnightly paper devoted to literature, the arts and political philosophy was founded by its editor Karl Miller in 1979. It filled a gap left by a prolonged industrial dispute which had closed *The Times Literary Supplement*, and has survived as an important journal, publishing reviews by Frank Kermode, John Bayley and other leading critics, and poems by **Seamus Heaney**, **Tom Paulin**, **Douglas Dunn**, **Craig Raine** and others. Its letters page has become a forum for lively literary controversies.

**Long Day's Journey Into Night** A semi-autobiographical play in four acts by **Eugene O'Neill**, written in 1940 and first performed in the USA in 1956, three years after the author's death. The action takes place during a single day in August 1912 at the summer home of the Tyrone family (which to some extent is a dramatic recreation of O'Neill's own family). The members of the family are the father, James Tyrone, an actor, the drug-addicted mother, Mary, the elder brother, the alcoholic James, Jr, and the younger brother, Edmund (based on O'Neill himself), who is stricken with tuberculosis. The play explores the tragic nature of family relations, and questions the possibility of forgiveness and redemption. It was awarded the Pulitzer Prize in 1957.

**Longest Journey, The** A novel by **E. M. Forster**, published in 1907.

Frederick Elliot, nicknamed 'Rickie', was a lame and delicate child who hated his father and gave all his affection to his cold and reticent

A scene from *Long Day's Journey into Night* at the Helen Hayes Theatre, New York, in 1956. Jason Robards Jun. and Bradford Dillman as the Tyrone sons.

mother. When the novel opens he is an undergraduate at Cambridge where he is visited by his friend Agnes Pembroke and her brother Herbert, who come to tell him of Agnes's engagement to Gerald Dawes an 'athletic marvel'. Shortly afterwards Dawes dies of a sporting injury, and Rickie and Agnes marry. Thwarted in his attempts to become a writer, Rickie accepts a teaching post offered by Herbert, who is housemaster at Sawston, a minor public school. On a visit to his father's sister, Mrs Failing, Rickie discovers that her drunken but amiable scapegrace of a nephew, Stephen Wonham, is in fact his half-brother, and Rickie assumes that Stephen is his father's illegitimate son. Agnes tries, without Rickie's knowledge, to persuade Mrs Failing to send Stephen away as a remittance man, and the discovery of her action coincides with Rickie's growing disillusionment with Herbert.

Stewart Ansell, Rickie's Cambridge friend, condemns the selfish preoccupations of the Pembrokes, and eventually reveals that Stephen is in fact the son of Rickie's mother. Leaving his wife, Rickie resolves to assist his half-brother, who promises to reform. However, becoming helplessly drunk soon afterward, Stephen falls on the railway tracks at a level crossing and, in attempting to save him, Rickie is fatally injured.

The title of the novel is drawn from **Shelley**'s *Epipsychidion*: 'Who travel to their home among the dead . . ./With one chained friend . . ./ The dreariest and the longest journey go.'

## Longfellow, Henry Wadsworth 1807–82

American poet, born in Portland, Maine. Longfellow became one of the most popular writers of his time, his work ranging from sentimental pieces such as 'The Village Blacksmith' to translations of Dante. He was educated at private schools and at Bowdoin College; after graduating in 1825 he travelled in Europe for three years. On his return he became a professor of languages at Bowdoin and married his first wife, Mary Potter. During this period he published a series of travel sketches called *Outre-Mer: A Pilgrimage Beyond the Sea* (1833–5). On a second trip to Europe his wife died; when he returned he took up a teaching position at Harvard.

His first volume of poems, *Voices of the Night*, and a prose romance, *Hyperion*, were both published in 1839. A second collection of verse, *Ballads and Other Poems*, appeared in 1842. In the following year he married Frances Appleton and settled in Cambridge, where he remained for the rest of his life. His later work reflects his reading of European epics and his interest in establishing an American mythology; it includes *Evangeline* (1847), **The Song of Hiawatha** (1855), *The Courtship of Miles Standish* (1858), *Tales of a Wayside Inn* (1863) and *Christus* (1872).

Henry Wadsworth Longfellow.

## Longley, Michael 1939–

Irish poet. Longley was born in Belfast and attended the Royal Belfast Academical Institution before studying classics at Trinity College, Dublin. After schoolteaching in Dublin, London and Belfast he joined the Northern Ireland Arts Council in 1970 and is now Combined Arts Director. His four published collections have been incorporated into *Poems 1963–1983* (1985), which also includes new poems. His *Selected Poems* appeared in 1981. He has edited a symposium on the arts in Ulster (*Causeway*, 1971) and an anthology of children's verse. Since the appearance of his first collection, *No Continuing City* (1969), he has been praised for the sharp clarity of his visual imagery and his immaculate diction. A versatile lyric poet, he explores strange moments of fulfilment or misgiving, describing love, grief, visited landscapes, country lore, birds and animals. In his imaginative recoil from contemporary political violence and celebration of nature's permanencies he seeks identification not only with other Ulster poets such as his friends **Seamus Heaney** and **Derek Mahon** but also with the lyric poets of Greece and Rome and the poets of World War I. Many of his more recent poems have distilled a laconic tenderness from vividly rendered experiences of sexuality and bereavement, isolation and horror, family memories and mythic history.

## Longstreet, Augustus Baldwin 1790–1870

Born in Georgia and educated at Yale,

Longstreet was at various times a college president, newspaper editor, clergyman and jurist. He founded and edited the *States Rights Sentinel* in Augusta in 1834. He is best remembered for his *Georgia Scenes, Characters and Incidents, &c., in the First Half Century of the Republic* (1835), a collection of 18 humorous sketches which record Georgian customs and language. A pioneering regionalist, he also wrote a series of short stories and a novel, *Master William Mitten* (1864).

**Lonsdale, Frederick** 1881–1954 English dramatist, who began his career with a series of libretti for musical comedy, including *The Maid of the Mountains* (1917). After *Madame Pompadour* in 1923 he turned to social comedies dealing ironically with polite manners and modern marriage, which at the time were compared to **Maugham**. Epigrammatic wit and neatly constructed, near-farcical situations made his work highly successful, and the best of his 11 plays, *The Last of Mrs Cheney* (1925), in which the maid in a gang of burglar-servants gives up her criminal career to marry into the aristocracy, still retains its popularity.

*Look Back in Anger* A play by **John Osborne**, first performed at the **Royal Court Theatre** in 1956, when it spearheaded the post-war revival of the British theatre.

Jimmy Porter, graduate of a redbrick university, runs a sweet stall in a Birmingham market and lives in squalor with a middle-class wife, whom he persistently abuses. When she leaves him, he sets up home with her middle-class actress friend, subjecting her to exactly the same treatment. The play ends with Jimmy and his wife reconciled in a scene which many critics have found falsely sentimental. The play's contemporary importance was not dependent on its flimsy plot, but on the articulate anger of Jimmy Porter, whose tirades against the complacency of the English establishment won Osborne a reputation as leader of a group of **Angry Young Men**.

*Look Homeward Angel. A Story of the Buried Life* An autobiographical novel by **Thomas Wolfe**, published in 1929. It tells the story of Eugene Gant, the youngest of six children born to an eccentric stone-cutter from Altamont, Catawba (modelled on Wolfe's home town of Asheville, North Carolina). Eugene grows up surrounded by a tumultuous, colourful family, and has many encounters with the local townspeople. Along the way he acquires a love of literature, and enters the state university at the age of 16. The novel concludes with his decision to break with his family and set out on a life of his own. A sequel, *Of Time and the River*, appeared in 1935.

*Looking Backward: 2000–1887* A Utopian novel by **Edward Bellamy**, published in 1888. It is narrated by Julian West, a Bostonian, who falls asleep in 1887 and wakes in the year 2000. He finds himself in a brilliant new society in which the lot of man has been drastically transformed. Dr Leete, who revives Julian and takes him into his home, explains how American society came – through peaceful means – to adopt a rigorous socialist programme under which labour is performed according to a system similar to military service. With all basic human needs accounted for and happiness ensured, human ills once thought to be inevitable have simply vanished. Great political, technological and sociological achievements are described in vivid detail. At the end of the novel Julian dreams of a nightmarish return to 19th-century Boston but wakes again in the year 2000 to find that Edith Leete, a descendant of his former fiancée, returns his love. The effect of *Looking Backward* was enormous, comparable perhaps only to that of *Uncle Tom's Cabin*. Numerous Bellamy clubs were founded; political journals and even a Nationalist party all advocated the changes represented in the book.

**Lord Chamberlain's Men** See **King's Men**.

*Lord Jim* A novel by **Joseph Conrad**, published in 1900.

Jim is chief mate on the steamship *Patna*. During a voyage towards Mecca, with its cargo of pilgrims, the ship strikes a submerged object. Watching the small crew lowering a lifeboat to save their own skins, Jim appears to be an idealistic onlooker but then, impulsively, he jumps. The significance of this action is the crux of the novel.

The action moves to Aden, where the narrator, Marlow, observes Jim at the Court of Inquiry. Ironically, and contrary to the crew's belief, the *Patna* had not sunk; but only Jim has elected to face the official consequences of his actions. Marlow is interested in Jim's private consciousness of disgrace: being stripped of his Master's certificate proves to be a public, but not a spiritual, atonement. With Marlow's assistance, Jim moves through a variety of jobs ashore, but the promise of real freedom from 'talkers' (those who know of his sullied reputation) is provided only by a position as agent at the remote trading post of Patusan.

Jim's life at Patusan, recalled by Marlow, has an active and practical character: to the people, including the elderly chief Doramin, he is Tuan, or Lord Jim. His relationship with the woman he calls Jewel, stepdaughter of his corrupt predecessor, contributes to his partial serenity. This is violently disrupted by the arrival of Gentleman Brown and his fellow thieves. Jim pledges to Doramin that Brown will leave the island without bloodshed; he is proved horribly wrong. Doramin's son is killed as a result of Jim's misplaced trust. Taking responsibility for his action, Jim allows himself to be shot by an angry and grieving Doramin.

*Lord of the Flies* A novel by **William Golding**, published in 1954. His first published novel, it is an inverted Victorian boys' adventure story, whose regular allusions to **R. M. Ballantyne**'s *Coral Island* stress Golding's choice of savage knowledge rather than blithe innocence as the conclusion of his fable.

Marooned on a desert island after a plane crash, a party of schoolboys quickly degenerates into vindictive barbarism. The roguish Jack emerges as a calculating and ruthless dictator, while the fat and clumsy Piggy is taunted, tortured and eventually killed with the Christ-like Simon. It is only when the boys are rescued by a British destroyer that Piggy's well-meaning friend Ralph realizes the true extent of their depravity.

Golding has said that the genesis of his novel lay in the brutalities he witnessed during his service at sea in World War II and in his experiences teaching small boys for 13 years. His use of an obvious but effective symbolism throughout the story allows it to work as an allegory of humanity's fallen nature as well as a graphically realistic scenario.

*Lord of the Rings, The* See **Tolkien, J. R. R.**

*Lord Ormont and His Aminta* A novel by **George Meredith**, published in 1894.

The elderly and disappointed Lord Ormont meets Aminta Farrell in Madrid. Although she is of lowly birth, Lord Ormont proposes to Aminta, who accepts him in spite of his age. After a period of travel, the couple return to London, where Ormont refuses to present his wife in society.

She becomes involved with a disreputable set, one of whom, the profligate Morsfield, is particularly spiteful and importunate. Meanwhile Ormont acquires a secretary, Matie Weyburn, who proves to be a youthful admirer of Aminta. Matie disposes of Morsfield, and his obvious liking for Aminta persuades her husband that Aminta should be accorded her appropriate status in society. Nevertheless, Aminta leaves Ormont and later acknowledges her love for Matie. The couple depart for Switzerland in defiance of convention and open a school there. Ormont forgives them before he dies.

*Lorna Doone: A Romance of Exmoor* A novel by **R. D. Blackmore**, published in 1869.

The time is the 17th century, in the reigns of Charles II and James II. The young John Ridd, an Exmoor yeoman, has lost his father – killed by the evil clan of Doone who inhabit a nearby valley and pursue a career of murder and theft. John is determined to exact vengeance on the Doones, and the progress of the story has a further impulse in his love for Lorna, daughter of the head of the clan and the murderer of his father. John Ridd and his friends bring the Doones to account and he rescues the girl from them. It is then revealed that Lorna was stolen; she proves to be the daughter of a noble house. John is acutely aware of the difference in their positions but Lorna's love and faith in him do not waver. Later he is able to render valuable service both to the king and to a kinsman of Lorna; his reluctance is overcome and the story ends happily for the young lovers. Monmouth's rebellion, the Battle of Sedgemoor, and Judge Jeffreys are part of the background of the story.

*Lothair* A novel by **Benjamin Disraeli**, published in 1870.

Lothair is an orphaned nobleman of enormous wealth. His guardians are Lord Culloden, and Grandison, a clergyman who embraces Roman Catholicism and rises so rapidly that he becomes a cardinal. Lothair reaches manhood after a Scots Protestant upbringing and joins Garibaldi's campaign in Italy. His wealth and influence make him a target for the Catholics: Cardinal Grandison, Clare Arundel and Monsignor Catesby combine to try and convert him. Lord Culloden, Lady Corisande and Theodora, the Italian girl who supports Garibaldi, resist their influence. In the campaign against the papal forces Theodora is killed. Lothair promises the dying girl that he will never enter the Roman Church. When Lothair himself is wounded at Mentana the cardinal renews his attempts at persuasion. Lothair, however, eventually returns to England, unconverted, and marries Lady Corisande.

The cardinal is probably Disraeli's best-realized character and the author's wit serves him well when he is demonstrating the cardinal's persuasive powers.

*Lotos-Eaters, The* A poem by **Alfred Tennyson**, first published in 1832 and revised for the 1842 *Poems*. Its subject comes from Book IX of *The Odyssey*, where the sailors returning home after the fall of Troy land on a strange island inhabited by people who eat only the fruit of the lotos plant. Some of the sailors sample it and are filled with a languorous content that makes them reluctant to continue their journey. Tennyson uses all his skill with verbal music in evoking the desire, commonly expressed in his early poetry, to withdraw from the world of work and competitive struggle.

**Love, Nicholas** *fl.* 1410 Translator. The scanty records which survive suggest that he came to prominence in 1409–10, when he was made rector, and then prior, of Mount Grace, a Carthusian house recently established in Yorkshire. At about the same time, his translation of the *Meditationes Vitae Christi*, once attributed to Bonaventura, was approved for copying. The translation, known as the *Mirror of the Blessed Life of Jesu Christ*, omits some of the doctrinal material of its source, and is striking for its concentration on the nature of Christ's humanity, dealing with the events of the Gospels with simple realism and emotional intensity. The *Mirror* was one of many texts which the late medieval church used to combat the perceived heresies of the **Lollards** and the general demand for the translation of the Bible. Love concentrated on orthodox views of the sacraments, offering a detailed and sympathetic interpretation of the significance of Christ's life which could be read by members of the clergy and the laity alike. In the years after the publication of the *Mirror*, Love became preoccupied with the difficulties of running the monastery of Mount Grace and it appears that he had no further time for writing.

**Love and Mr Lewisham** A novel by **H. G. Wells**, published in 1900.

The novel's title suggests the symmetry with which its underlying themes are explored. As a young schoolmaster at Whortley Preparatory School, Sussex, Lewisham dreams of his coming greatness as a scholar and man of influence. His ambition is matched, and appears threatened by, his attraction to the more experienced Ethel Henderson, a young visitor from town. Lewisham's idealism is also offset by inadequate figures of authority in the adult world: Bonover, the shallow headmaster who dismisses him, and particularly Ethel's father, Chaffery, an exponent of deviousness and intelligence in the modern world. Chaffery's ambitions are satisfied by the misuse of spiritualism and science; posing as a medium, he draws from the wealth of his victim, the weak-minded Mr Lagune.

Later, Lewisham follows a principled pathway as a gifted student in London, although distracted by the attentions of the bluestocking, Miss Heydinger. When he meets Ethel again after a three-year gap, his strength of purpose is dominant. He perceives that she is a victim of her unscrupulous father. Their courtship, Ethel's pregnancy and their marriage are all traced with sympathy for the pains as well as the pleasures of married life. Lewisham's ambitious individualism and his desires for a settled life and fatherhood are reconciled.

**Love for Love** A comedy by **William Congreve**, first produced in April 1695 and published the same year. Thomas Betterton and Anne Brace-

Valentine feigning madness, to the alarm of the lawyer, Buckram, in Act IV, scene 2 of Congreve's *Love for Love* (1695). An illustration for an edition published in 1791. Victoria & Albert Theatre Museum, London.

girdle played the parts of Valentine and Angelica.

Sir Sampson Legend has two sons, Valentine and Ben. Valentine, the elder, is a fashionable man-about-town whose extravagance has led him into serious debt. Ben is a sailor, and Sir Sampson's wrath with Valentine's behaviour leads him to favour Ben. He will give Valentine enough money to pay his debts, no more, if he will sign a bond making Ben the heir. Valentine is in love with Angelica; she is wealthy but has not so far accepted him. Sir Sampson has arranged a marriage for Ben with Miss Prue, a foolish country girl. Valentine has no choice but to agree and the bond is prepared by Sir Sampson. But Valentine, realizing that he faces ruin, swallows his pride and pleads with his father, to no avail. He feigns madness to avoid signing the bond that will disinherit him. Ben, meanwhile, has met Miss Prue; their dislike is mutual. Angelica decides to intervene. She uses her charms to extract a proposal of marriage from Sir Sampson, and gets possession of the bond. Valentine, believing that she will marry his father, despairs and declares himself willing to sign the bond. Angelica then reveals her plot, declares her love for Valentine and tears up the bond.

The plot involves some diverting characters, one of the best being Jeremy, Valentine's resourceful servant. Ben, the younger brother, is his own man and will marry to please only himself, father and fortune notwithstanding. Mrs Frail, an amorous woman of the town, would be delighted to take Ben to bed; believing she has Valentine, she finds herself married to Tattle, who has just disentangled himself from Miss Prue.

***Love of King David and Fair Bathsheba, The*** A play in verse by **George Peele**, published in 1599. It contains some of Peele's finest poetry; the most famous piece is Bathsheba's song, 'Hot sun, cool fire, tempered with sweet air'.

***Love Song of J. Alfred Prufrock, The*** A poem by **T. S. Eliot**, published in the American magazine *Poetry* in 1915 and reprinted in his first collection, *Prufrock and Other Observations* (1917). The title is ironic, for the middle-aged Prufrock, the speaker of the poem, shows himself too nervously timid to make the significant gesture that might redeem or free him from the empty social rituals of his genteel world. He remains trapped in a state of wan hopelessness as social habit and consideration of his futility overwhelm him. Both the use of the **dramatic monologue** and the setting, with the seamier side of urban life glimpsed at the edges of Prufrock's bourgeois existence, anticipate *The Waste Land*.

***Love's Labour's Lost*** A comedy by **William Shakespeare**, first performed *c.* 1594. The text of the 1623 Folio is based on that of a Quarto edition published in 1598. A precise source has not been determined, and it may be that this is one of the few plays whose story Shakespeare invented.

Having forsworn the company of women for three years, Ferdinand, King of Navarre, and his three lords, Berowne, Dumain and Longaville, are sorely tried and eventually overcome by the embassy of the Princess of France with her three ladies, Rosaline, Katharine and Maria. The complications are wittily prolonged and the language the most ornate that Shakespeare wrote. This is a play that has been understandably called Mozartian, though **Lyly**'s *Euphues* and the fashion it created was the immediate influence and the object of Shakespeare's affectionate satire. The extravagant conceits of the courtly lovers are a feature of the play, but Shakespeare has also created a gallery of minor characters, the fantastical Spaniard Armado, the pedantic schoolteacher Holofernes, Dull the constable

and Costard the clown being the most notable. They are of the kind that **Ben Jonson** would later develop into 'humours'.

***Love's Last Shift*** A comedy by **Colley Cibber**, first performed in London in 1696.

Loveless, having deserted his wife Amanda after a mere six months of marriage, returns from abroad penniless to resume his rakish life in London. Amanda wins him back by disguising herself as a stranger, conducting an intrigue with him and then, by appealing to his better nature, persuading him to mend his ways.

Provoked by the popularity of Cibber's play, **Vanbrugh** provided in *The Relapse* an immediate sequel, in which Loveless reverts to type. The two plays are a fascinating part of the growing argument about the morality of the English theatre of the period.

***Lovel the Widower*** A story by **W. M. Thackeray**, first published in *The Cornhill Magazine* (1860). Lovel lives with his overbearing mother-in-law, Lady Baker, and a charming governess, Miss Prior, who was once a dancer. Lady Baker uncovers the truth of Miss Prior's past and high-handedly orders her out of the house, but Lovel takes Miss Prior's side and asks her to marry him.

**Lovelace, Earl** 1935– Trinidadian novelist. His fluent narrative gift and inwardness with varieties of Trinidadian speech enable his fiction attractively to penetrate serious contemporary issues, especially the unexpected outcome of social change. In *The Schoolmaster* (1968) the new village school brings seduction and catastrophe; in *The Dragon Can't Dance* (1979) and *The Wine of Astonishment* (1984) the status of formerly admired stick-fighters and despised steel-band players is reversed. From the first novel, *While Gods Are Falling* (1966), to the most recent Lovelace's central preoccupation is whether people have something to live by. *Jestina's Calypso and Other Plays* appeared in 1984.

**Lovelace, Richard** 1618–58 Cavalier poet. The handsome and dashing son of a wealthy Kentish knight, Lovelace gained a romantic reputation in the eyes of contemporaries. He was granted an honorary MA from Oxford at the age of 18, and adorned the courtly and artistic life of London until, in 1639–40, he took up arms for his king in the Bishops' Wars. The victory of the Covenanters made Parliament's will in the matter absolute, and Lovelace defiantly presented a petition for the retention of the bishops in 1642, earning himself seven weeks in the Gatehouse Prison at Westminster. Enforcedly idle, Lovelace spent his money on the king's behalf and his time among the poets and wits of the day. He travelled abroad but returned to England in 1648, when he was imprisoned again, for ten months, probably because of his family's efforts on behalf of the king, which he had financed. He was freed after Charles I's execution and spent the rest of his life in relative poverty. During his second imprisonment he had prepared for publication the collection of verses called *Lucasta: Epodes, Odes, Sonnets, Songs, etc.* Another volume, *Lucasta: Posthume Poems*, was published by his brother a year after Lovelace's death. Lucasta was his fiancée, Lucy Sacheverell.

Lovelace was not a prolific poet, and his reputation depends on a handful of elegant lyrics. His work was almost forgotten until 1765, when **Bishop Thomas Percy** included the lovely 'To Althea from Prison' in his *Reliques of Ancient English Poetry*.

**Lover, Samuel** 1796–1868 Novelist and songwriter. A Protestant Irishman, born in Dublin. As a songwriter, he is best remembered for 'Rory O'More'. He developed the ballad into a novel in 1836 and a play the following year. Lover's *Songs and Ballads* appeared in 1839. As a humorous novelist working in the same vein as **Charles Lever**, he scored his greatest success with *Handy Andy* (1842), which remained popular long after his death. Lover also wrote several plays, successful in their time, and a number of stories about Irish life.

*Loves of the Angels, The* A poem by **Thomas Moore**, published in 1823. The source was the *Koran*, and the tradition of the angels Harut and Marut, whose purpose is to tempt men and teach them sorcery. Moore elaborated this into the story of three fallen angels who loved mortal women. One loves Lea, but loses her when he reveals the word which will open the gates of heaven. Lea speaks the word and rises to the skies. Another loves Lilis, but when he comes to her in all the glory at his command she is consumed. The third loves Nama, and for her sake lives among mortals. Their happiness on earth is imperfect but they look forward to immortality.

**Lowell, Amy** 1874–1925 American poet, born in Brookline, Massachusetts, into a prominent New England intellectual family. She was a champion of modern poetry, introducing **imagism** to America in what many of her critics felt was a bastardized form. Her first volume of verse, *A Dome of Many-Colored Glass*, appeared in 1912; *The Complete Poetical Works of Amy Lowell* in 1955. She is best remembered for individual poems such as 'Lilacs' and 'Patterns'. Her idiosyncratic masculine appearance and her vigorous sponsorship of modern poetry have

invested her with almost legendary status within the American poetic tradition.

**Lowell, James Russell** 1819–91 American man of letters, born in Cambridge, Massachusetts, and educated at Harvard. His first publications were two volumes of verse: *A Year's Life* (1841) and *Poems* (1842). A critic, humorist, and political satirist, in a single year (1848) he published *Poems: Second Series*, **A Fable For Critics**, *The Vision of Sir Launfal*, and the first series of **The Biglow Papers**.

In 1855 he succeeded **Henry Wadsworth Longfellow** as Professor of French and Spanish at Harvard, a position he held until 1886, though he taught very little during the last ten years of his tenure. He did, however, publish seven books of essays. During this period he was also editor of **The Atlantic Monthly** (1857–61) – which he co-founded with **Oliver Wendell Holmes** in 1857 – and, jointly with **Charles Eliot Norton**, of **The North American Review** (1864). He also produced the second series of *The Biglow Papers* (1867), which criticized England's part in the American Civil War, and a reflective poem called *The Cathedral* (1869). He was the US minister in Spain (1877–80), and then in England (1880–5), where he was received as a cultured and charming man who did much to interpret American aspirations and ideals to the Old World.

**Lowell, Robert** 1917–77 American poet, born in Boston, and educated at Harvard and Kenyon College. He was drafted during World War II, but declared himself a conscientious objector and served a prison term (1943–4). In 1970 he moved to England, where he spent a good deal of time until his death in 1977.

The great-grandnephew of **James Russell Lowell**, he was considered one of the leading poets of his generation. His early work, which was formal and highly symbolic, often focused on the history of New England and of his own family, subjects which continued to interest him throughout his life. *Land of Unlikeness* (1944), his first book, dealt especially with his temporary conversion to Catholicism; *Lord Weary's Castle* (1946) was awarded the Pulitzer Prize. It was not until *Life Studies* (1959), however, that he began to exhibit the loose form and sharp irony which characterize his mature work. The poems and prose pieces in *Life Studies* are highly autobiographical, and the book is usually identified as one of the major works of the **Confessional** school. He did not confine himself to purely personal subjects, however; *Imitations* (1961), for example, included translations of classical poets. Later volumes, such as *For the Union Dead* (1964) and *Near the Ocean* (1967), linked an understanding of the self to an understanding of politics and history. His other collections are *The Mills of the Kavanaughs* (1951), *The Voyage, and Other Versions of Poems by Baudelaire* (1968), *Notebook 1967–68* (1969), *Notebooks* (1970), *History* (1973), *For Lizzie and Harriet* (1973) and *The Dolphin* (1973). *Selected Poems* was published in 1976 and a final volume, *Day by Day*, in 1977. His other work includes a number of plays: *Phaedra* (1961), a translation, *The Old Glory* (1965), a version of *Prometheus Bound* (1969) and *The Oresteia of Aeschylus* (1978). *Collected Prose* appeared in 1987.

**Lowndes, Marie (Adelaide) Belloc** 1868–1947 Novelist, short-story writer and playwright. The sister of **Hilaire Belloc** and wife of the journalist Frederic Sawrey Lowndes, she published over 40 novels. Most are skilfully plotted and observed stories of crime or mystery, and several derive from real-life criminal cases. Her most famous book, *The Lodger* (1913), describes how landlady Mrs Bunting comes to realize that her genteel lodger is in fact Jack the Ripper; its highly effective ending finds her incapable of summoning the will to denounce him to the police. *The Lodger* inspired several early film versions, including one by Alfred Hitchcock (1926).

**Lowry, (Clarence) Malcolm** 1909–57 Novelist. He was born at Wallasey in Cheshire, the son of a wealthy Liverpool stockbroker against whom he rebelled while still at public school. He left school and sailed to China as a deckhand on a merchant ship, but was persuaded to complete his education at St Catharine's College, Cambridge. *Ultramarine*, his novel of seafaring, was published in 1933. An alcoholic and a wanderer, Lowry lived in Mexico and then British Columbia for some years. His second novel, **Under the Volcano**, widely regarded as his masterpiece, appeared in 1947. He spent his last years with his second wife at Ripe, near Lewes in East Sussex. The volume of short stories *Hear Us, O Lord, from Heaven Thy Dwelling Place* (1961), *Selected Poems* (1962), *Lunar Caustic* (1968), *Dark as the Grave Wherein My Friend is Laid* (1968) and *October Ferry to Gabriola* (1971) have been published from the mass of work he left behind.

**Lubbock, Percy** 1879–1965 Critic. Born in London, the son of a merchant banker, Lubbock was educated at Eton and at King's College, Cambridge. He worked briefly as a journalist and as a librarian before taking up writing full-time: an occupation interrupted by his service with the Red Cross during World War I. He lived in Italy from 1926 until his death. His writings range from autobiography (*Earlham*, 1922) to fictional travelogue (*Roman Pictures*, 1923) and biography (*Samuel Pepys*, 1909, and *Portrait of Edith Wharton*, 1947). A friend and

disciple of **Henry James**, Lubbock edited the novelist's *Letters* (1920) and the 35 volumes of his *Novels and Stories* (1921–3) while working on his own best-known book, which is also his fullest homage to James: *The Craft of Fiction* (1920). This work, which became an essential point of reference in subsequent discussions of the novelist's technique, is a distillation of the lessons of the Master on artistic form and dramatic presentation in fiction, although Lubbock saw more merit than James could in the 'loose, baggy monsters' of Tolstoy and other European writers.

**Lucie-Smith, (John) Edward (McKenzie)** 1933– Poet, art critic, anthologist. Born in Kingston, Jamaica, he came to England in 1946, and was educated at King's School, Canterbury, and Merton College, Oxford, before national service in the RAF. Between 1959 and 1965 he was chairman of the **Group**, who met in his Chelsea home, and he edited *A Group Anthology* (1963) with **Philip Hobsbaum**. His first collection of verse, though, *A Tropical Childhood* (1961), an evocation of childhood memories, demonstrates **Movement** virtues of clarity and tight literary forms. His involvement with the Group led to an interest in the dramatic monologue and **Browning**'s work – he edited *A Choice of Browning's Verse* (1967) – which is evident in *Confessions and Histories* (1964). An interest in syllabics, the **Black Mountain school** and Elizabethan experiments with classical metres – he edited *The Penguin Book of Elizabethan Verse* (1965) – resulted in the complicated prosodic experiments of *Towards Silence* (1968) and *The Well Wishers* (1974). His interest in *avant-garde* poetry is shown not only in this later work but in his *Primer of Experimental Poetry* (1971). His comic poems, *Beasts with Bad Morals*, appeared in 1984. He is a prolific art critic, and his publications include *Movements in Art Since 1945* (1969), *Work and Struggle: The Painter as Witness 1870–1914* (1977) and *Super Realism* (1979). Other anthologies of poetry include *British Poetry Since 1945* (1970, sensibly revised in 1985).

***Luck of Barry Lyndon, The*** See *Barry Lyndon*.

***Luck of Roaring Camp and Other Sketches, The*** A collection of stories and sketches by **Bret Harte** published in 1870. The stories originally appeared between 1868 and 1870 in issues of **Overland Monthly**, a journal which Harte himself helped initiate as a forum for Western writers. Harte's popular reputation was established with the appearance of this volume, which is known for its sharply naturalistic depiction of frontier life in the American West. As well as the famous title piece, the collection includes 'The Outcasts of Poker Flat', 'Tennessee's Partner' and 'Miggles'. Most of the stories explore the nature of the individual in frontier society, focusing on human relationships in difficult or even tragic circumstances.

**Lucky Jim** The first novel by **Kingsley Amis**, published in 1954. It is the story of Jim Dixon, an assistant lecturer in history in his first term of employment at a provincial university. The plot is a catalogue of Jim's hapless misadventures and disasters as he attempts to settle into his new job and make a good impression. Virtuoso sequences of comic catastrophe include Jim setting his bed on fire with his cigarette while staying at the home of the Professor of History, and a crucial lecture to the faculty at the end of term which turns somehow into a blatant parody of the University Principal and Dixon's own professor. As well as being a work of sustained, often farcical comedy, the novel also derives a scornful, satirical humour at the expense of 'phoniness' and pretension – a characteristic which links it to other contemporaneous fiction such as **John Wain**'s *Hurry On Down*.

**Ludlow, Edmund** 1617–92 Author of memoirs. An MP for Wiltshire, and staunch anti-Royalist, Ludlow rose to become a lieutenant general in Cromwell's army, though later an opponent of his Protectorship. One of the signatories of Charles I's death warrant, he fled England at the Restoration and settled in Switzerland, where he wrote his *Memoirs* (published 1698–9). These offer a unique first-hand account of the major events of the Civil Wars and the changes of allegiance during the Interregnum.

**Ludlow, John Malcolm** See **Christian Socialism**.

**Lukács, Georg** See **Marxist criticism**.

**Luska, Sidney** See **Harland, Henry**.

**Luttrell, Narcissus** 1657–1732 Diarist, historian and collector. He was born in London and educated at Sheen, St John's College, Cambridge, and Gray's Inn. He appears to have practised law and held a number of significant public and legal appointments. He served as Member of Parliament for Bossiney (1679–80) and Saltash (1690–5). He was a Whig at heart – **Jacob Tonson** was one of his friends – but he was also on terms with Tories such as **Robert Harley**.

He published nothing during his lifetime, but began early to collect the books and ephemera upon which he based his two *Popish Plot Catalogues* (published 1956) and *A Brief Historical Relation of State Affairs from September 1678 to April 1714* (6 vols., 1857). The latter compilation and what he called *An Abstract . . .* (edited by Henry Horwitz in 1972 as *The Parliamentary Diary of Narcissus Luttrell 1691–1693*) are now appreciated as indispensable source books for the parliamentary and political history of the period. Luttrell also kept a diary of 'private transactions' between November 1722 and January 1725.

His collection, which was much admired by **Thomas Hearne** and to which he devoted himself during his last years, was dispersed, in stages, after 1786.

**Lyall, Sir Alfred Comyn** 1835–1911 Poet. Lyall was born at Coulsdon in Surrey and entered the Indian Civil Service in 1856. He became Lieutenant Governor of the North-West Provinces and a member of the India Council, and founded the University of Allahabad in 1885. He was the author of *Asiatic Studies* (two series, 1882 and 1899, which dealt chiefly with Hinduism), *Warren Hastings: A Biography* (1889), *The Rise of the British Dominion in India* (1893) and *Tennyson* (for the English Men of Letters series, 1902). His *Verses Written in India* (1889), revised, enlarged and reprinted as *Poems* in 1907, enjoyed some success.

**Lyceum Theatre** Of the several theatres on the Lyceum site, just off London's Strand, the first was opened in 1772. A second, built in 1816, was destroyed by fire in 1830. The third Lyceum opened in 1834 and became famous in the last 30 years of the 19th century as the 'temple' of Sir Henry Irving, its manager from 1878 to 1902. Irving's repertoire combined notable revivals of several plays by **Shakespeare** with indifferent melodramas, and he was resistant to the new movement in English drama initiated by **Tom Robertson**. Irving's Lyceum was demolished in 1904.

**Lycidas** A pastoral **elegy** by **John Milton** on the death of Edward King, a Cambridge contemporary who was drowned in the Irish Sea while returning to Dublin in August 1637. It first appeared in a volume of memorial verses to King published in 1638. The poem moves from personal grief at the loss of this promising man to a larger consideration of the meaning of death, eventually achieving Christian consolation.

**Lydgate, John** *c.*1370–1449 Poet. Born in the village of Lidgate, Suffolk, from which he took his name, he entered the nearby Benedictine abbey at Bury St Edmunds in or before 1382, and was ordained a priest in 1397. He remained in the abbey for most of his life, although he is known to have spent some time in London,

Oxford and Paris, and was prior of Hatfield Broad Oak (Essex) from 1421 to 1432.

Lydgate's works vary considerably in content and style, from very long translations to brief occasional poems and one short prose work on Julius Caesar, *The Serpent of Division* (1422). He is best known for his translations, often long and tedious, from French and Latin. *The Troy Book* (1412–21), a version in decasyllabic couplets of Guido delle Colonne's *Historia Troiana*, was followed by *The Siege of Thebes*, largely drawn from a lost French work but also indebted to Boccaccio and **Chaucer**. In it Lydgate presents himself as a Canterbury pilgrim invited by Chaucer's pilgrims to tell his tale (see *The Canterbury Tales*). In 1426 he began a translation of *Le Pèlerinage de la Vie Humaine* by Guillaume de Deguileville, a long and mediocre moral allegory (though with some humorous touches) which describes the Christian's quest for salvation. *The Fall of Princes* (1431–8) is a **rhyme-royal** translation of a French version of Boccaccio's *De Casibus Virorum Illustrium*. An allegory on chastity translated from French, *Reason and Sensuality* (*c.*1408), is a less austere and more pleasing work, as are the love-allegories *The Temple of Glass* and *The Complaint of the Black Knight*. He also wrote lyrics, specially commissioned occasional pieces, saints' lives (including a life of St Edmund) and versions of Aesop's fables. Much of Lydgate's work attracts little critical praise now, although in the century following his death he was considered the equal of Chaucer and **Gower** and his work was extremely influential. His verse is metrically

John Lydgate presenting his *Troy Book* to King Henry V. The book was written between 1412 and 1421. An illustration from *MS Cotton. Aug IV, f.1*. British Library.

uneven, and marred by frequent use of clichés and aureate diction, and by its verbosity.

**Lyly, John** ?1554–1606 Writer of prose and comedies. He was brought up in Canterbury and probably attended the King's School there, at a time when **Marlowe** was also a pupil. He graduated MA from Magdalen College, Oxford, in 1575 and unsuccessfully petitioned Burghley's support for a fellowship at the college. *Euphues, or the Anatomy of Wit* was an instant success, as was its sequel *Euphues and His England*, and Lyly became the fashionable writer of the 1580s, his euphuism becoming the 'new English'.

In 1583 he married the Yorkshire heiress Beatrice Browne and in the same year gained control of the first Blackfriars theatre. It was there in the early 1580s that his earliest plays, *Campaspe* and *Sapho and Phao*, were performed by Oxford's Boys, a **boys' company** that flourished only briefly. All his plays, with the exception of *The Woman in the Moon*, were played by Paul's Boys. *The Woman in the Moon* is also the only one of Lyly's plays in verse, all the others being prose comedies. After Lyly's first two plays came a series of comedies, the dates of whose composition are largely conjectural: *Gallathea* (1584), *Endymion: The Man in the Moon* (1586–7), *Love's Metamorphosis* (1589), *Midas* (1589), *Mother Bombie* (1589) and finally *The Woman in the Moon* (?1594). Some of the plays also had court performances as well as those in the public theatre: *Sapho and Phao*, March 1584 and *Gallathea*, 1588.

Lyly's comedies, with their patterned artifice, combine Italian pastoralism with the intrigue of the Roman dramas of Plautus and Terence. Their flexible and elegant prose was a marked advance and helped establish prose as a medium for comedy. Some of **Shakespeare**'s comedies owe a debt to Lyly. Moth in *Love's Labour's Lost* is a notably witty and precocious Lylian page, and Beatrice and Benedick's prose fencing in *Much Ado About Nothing* is very like some of Lyly's exchanges.

From 1588 onwards, encouraged by a remark of the queen's, Lyly hoped to gain the office of Master of the Revels, but was never given it. In 1589 he was elected MP for Hindon in Wiltshire, the first of three constituencies he was to represent. Most of the years 1592–6 were spent at his wife's home in Mexborough, Yorkshire. *Pap with a Hatchet* (1589) is Lyly's contribution, on the side of the bishops, to the **Marprelate** controversy.

**Lyndsay (or Lindsay), Sir David** 1490–1555 A poet, dramatist, diplomat and herald, Lyndsay was one of the 'makaris' of early 16th-century Scottish poetry. He was companion, playfellow and story-teller to the young

Sir David Lyndsay reading the Prologue to his *A Dialog betuix Experience and ane Courteour* (c.1553). An illustration from an edition of 1566.

prince James (later James V), and continued in the office of usher to the king until 1522. He was dismissed from office when James fell under the influence of Douglas but returned to the king's service in 1528. Not later than 1529 he became Lyon King of Arms. Lyndsay represented the king on diplomatic missions, such as an embassy to Charles V in 1531. After James's death in 1542 Lyndsay continued as a diplomat and was sent to the court of Henry VIII in 1544 and to that of Christian III of Denmark in 1548.

His literary career started late. *The Dreme*, finished in 1528 and printed in Paris (1558), is a **dream-vision** in which Dame Remembrance shows the poet hell, purgatory and heaven from where he sees the kingdoms of the earth, including Scotland. *The Testament and Complaynt of Our Soverane Lordis Papingo* (finished 1530, printed 1538) has advice to the king and satire against ecclesiastics put into the mouth of a dying 'papyngo' (popinjay or parrot). Lyndsay's frequent satire on ecclesiastical corruption manifests his reforming sympathies. *An Answer Quhilk Schir David Lyndsay Maid to the Kingis Flyting* (1536) is an example of 'flyting', or poetic abuse, of which **William Dunbar** is the most famous exponent. *The Complaynt and Publict Confessioun of the Kingis Auld Hound* (c.1536) is another satirical poem put into an animal's mouth. For Epiphany 1540 Lyndsay produced a play, *Satire of the Three Estates*. He had shown an early interest in drama by acting before James and Margaret Tudor at Holyrood in 1511. His other poems are: *The Tragedy of the Cardinal* (1547), in which the lately dead Cardinal Beaton offers his fall as a warning to princes and prelates, *The History and Testament of Squire Meldrum* (?1550, first printed 1582), a romance about the exploits of a Scottish laird, *The Monarchie* (1554), a long work of over 6000 lines, describing four ancient empires which are succeeded by the anti-Christian papacy and attack-

ing veneration of images and pilgrimages, and *Kitteis Confessioun*, satirizing the confessional. Lyndsay's *Works* were printed at Edinburgh in 1574.

**lyric** Originally from the Greek ('for the lyre'), the term is now commonly used to describe any short poem, especially one expressing the poet's personal sentiments. The lyric mode covers a wide range of topics ranging from the experience of love, to pastoral description and praise of God. See also **medieval lyric**.

*Lyrical Ballads with a Few Other Poems* A collection of poems by **Wordsworth** and **Coleridge**, first published by Cottle at Bristol in 1798. A second edition in two volumes, containing a preface by Wordsworth which replaces his original short 'Advertisement', appeared in 1801, and a third in 1802.

The book has become one of the abiding reference points of English Romantic literature. The idea for it was conceived when the two poets were living as close neighbours in Somerset, and was nurtured by their shared sense of the emotional artificiality of 18th-century poetry and the petrifaction of its conventions. Of the original 23 anonymous poems, only four are by Coleridge: *The Rime of the Ancient Mariner*, 'The Nightingale', 'The Foster-Mother's Tale' and 'The Dungeon', the two last taken from his tragedy 'Osirio'. Wordsworth's contribution includes ballads, songs and narratives such as 'Goody Blake and Harry Gill', 'The Idiot Boy', 'The Thorn', 'The Mad Mother', 'Simon Lee', as well as other lyrical and personal poems: 'The Tables Turned', 'Lines Written in Early Spring', and 'Lines Composed a Few Miles above Tintern Abbey'. The 'Advertisement' characterizes these works as 'experiments . . . written chiefly with a view to ascertain how far the language of conversation in the middle and lower classes of society is adapted to the purposes of poetic pleasure', and challenges readers 'accustomed to the gaudiness and inane phraseology of many modern writers' to rethink their criteria of poetic decorum. Some of the early reviews were far from flattering: **Southey** considered that the author of 'The Thorn' 'should recollect that he who personates tiresome loquacity, becomes tiresome himself', and Dr Burney judged the 'Mariner' to be 'the strangest story of a cock and a bull that we ever saw on paper', conceding, however, that 'there are in it poetical touches of an exquisite kind'.

The second edition includes a further poem by Coleridge, 'Love', but omits his name from the title-page. Wordsworth's claim to effective sole authorship receives additional support from the relegation of the 'Mariner' from first to twenty-third position; from the long new preface, in which he expounds his ideas on poetic diction and the origin of poetry in 'emotion recollected in tranquillity'; and from the second volume, which consists entirely of his own new poems, including important works such as the 'Lucy' poems, 'The Old Cumberland Beggar', and 'Michael, a Pastoral Poem'. In the expanded version prepared for the 1802 edition, he managed to accommodate some of his collaborator's reservations concerning aspects of the preface, but Coleridge later became dissatisfied with the Hartleian, or 'associationist', premises of Wordsworth's poetic theory as a whole, and explicitly distanced himself from the ideas in *Biographia Literaria*. *Lyrical Ballads* paved the way for Wordsworth's later fame as a poet. Its preference for subjects drawn from 'low and rustic life', and the self-mythologizing poetic *persona* were often ridiculed and lampooned, yet no poet of the Romantic generation was to escape the underlying force of its call for a poetic reinterpretation of the world.

**Lyttelton, George, 1st Baron** 1709–73 Poet and patron. Born at Hagley, Worcestershire, the country seat of his father, he was educated at Eton and Christ Church, Oxford, made the Grand Tour, and entered political life as Member of Parliament for Okehampton in 1735. In literature he is remembered as a minor poet and as a generous patron, the friend of **Pope**, **Thomson**, **Henry Fielding** and **William Shenstone**. His poetry includes *Monody* (1747) to the memory of his wife, and *Dialogues of the Dead* (1760). He published *The History of the Life of Henry the Second* in four volumes between 1767 and 1771.

**Lytton, Edward Bulwer** See **Bulwer Lytton, Edward**.

# M

**Mabbe, James** 1572–c.1642 Translator. Educated at Magdalen College, Oxford, Mabbe became a fellow there and later a lay prebendary of Wells Cathedral. His first translation from Spanish was Mateo Alemán's *The Rogue, or, The Life of Guzman de Alfarache* in 1622. It was followed by translations of Fernando de Rojas's *Celestina* as *The Spanish Bawd* (1631) and Cervantes's *Novelas Ejemplares* as *Exemplary Novels* (1640), the most famous of which is *The Spanish Lady*.

**Mabinogion, The** The collective name for a group of 11 medieval Welsh prose tales first published in an English translation by Lady Charlotte Guest (1812–95) between 1838 and 1849. The complete *Mabinogion* is found in the Red Book of Hergest (c. 1400), although fragments in the White Book of Rhydderch (c. 1350) suggest this was an earlier complete version. The tales were composed during the late 11th and 12th centuries, and there may have been a written version as early as 1200. The word *mabinogion* occurs once in the manuscripts but is clearly an error for *mabinogi*. In modern scholarship, *Mabinogi* is used to refer to a group of four of the tales known as 'Pedair Cainc y Mabinogi' ('The Four Branches of the Mabinogi'). The word is apparently derived from the Welsh *mab* ('boy' or 'youth'), but in what sense it describes the 'Four Branches' has not been conclusively established.

The 'Four Branches' are the tales of 'Pwyll', 'Branwen', 'Manawydan' and 'Math', loosely connected stories commemorating ancient strata of Celtic myth and history. Located in a remote pre-Norman past where independent Welsh rulers vie for power, the tales create a strong sense of 11th-century Welsh society and early Norman influence on the material life of the nobility. At the same time, the pervasive presence of the Celtic otherworld recalls the mythological significance of the tales. Lacking a coherent narrative structure by modern standards, the tales possess a powerful unity of style and technique.

Of the other stories, 'Culhwch ac Olwen' ('Culhwch and Olwen') is the longest and the oldest, possibly antedating the Norman Conquest. The tale is set at Arthur's court and describes a sequence of feats which the hero, Culhwch, must accomplish in order to win Olwen, daughter of the giant Ysbaddaden. Since the story was composed before **Geoffrey of Monmouth**'s *Historia Regum Britanniae*, it is a crucial text in **Arthurian literature**, preserving early Welsh traditions about Arthur and his men. The most notable feature of the tale is a long list of all the knights present at Arthur's court, indicating a lost wealth of oral legends and folk-tales.

The *Tair Rhamant* ('Three Romances') of 'Owain', 'Peredur' and 'Geraint' also have a native Arthurian context but are strongly influenced by Continental Arthurian literature. The heroes are depicted as chivalric knights and Arthur himself is the passive king of French romance rather than the active war-leader of the native tradition. The Welsh romances correspond to the 12th-century French romances of 'Yvain', 'Perceval' and 'Erec et Enide' by Chrétien de Troyes, and it is likely that both groups derive from French or Breton versions of original Welsh material.

The remaining tales, 'Breuddwyd Rhonabwy' ('The Dream of Rhonabwy'), 'Breuddwyd Macsen' ('The Dream of Maxen') and 'Cyfranc Lludd a Llefelys' ('The Tale of Lludd and Llevelys'), are 12th-century versions of native historical legends. Arthur and Owain appear in 'Breuddwyd Rhonabwy', which has a contemporary setting and clearly belongs to Welsh rather than French Arthurian tradition. The other two tales, using material found in Geoffrey of Monmouth's *Historia* and its Welsh translations, hark back to the achievements of British Celts in the pre-Saxon era.

At a time when literature in England was dominated by French, the Welsh tales testify to a rich and continuing native prose tradition in Britain. Taken together, the tales illuminate centuries of oral story material as well as contemporary social practice in the immediate post-Norman period. Stories from *The Mabinogion* have inspired several modern English texts, including *The Virgin and the Swine* by Evangeline Walton (1936; reprinted in 4 vols., 1970–4) and *The Owl Service* by **Alan Garner** (1967). *The Mabinogion* has been translated by Gwyn Jones and Thomas Jones (1948), Jeffrey Gantz (1976) and Patrick Ford (1977). See also **the Celtic revival**.

*Mac Flecknoe, or, A Satire upon the True-Blue-Protestant Poet T.S.* A satirical poem by **John Dryden**, published in 1682 but written in about 1678. Its target is **Thomas Shadwell**, who had attacked Dryden, the Poet Laureate, in *The Medal of John Bayes*. Dryden's poem describes how Shadwell assumes the mantle of literary dullness from its previous possessor, **Richard Flecknoe**, and makes him into the epitome of the absurdly untalented poet with a pretentious and empty style. The climax is a comic coronation scene which later influenced **Pope** in *The Dunciad*. Characterized by its mock-heroic manner and its wide allusiveness, Dryden's verse compares the anti-hero Shadwell to Arion, Christ, Romulus, Elijah and a piece of excrement.

**MacArthur, Charles** 1895–1956 American playwright, born in Scranton, Pennsylvania, the son of a Unitarian clergyman. He studied for two years in a theological seminary, then joined the Hearst Press in Chicago as a journalist, and eventually became a popular feature writer. His first play, *Lulu Belle* (1926), was written with his uncle, Edward Sheldon. In 1927 he collaborated with **Sidney Howard** on *Salvation*, an exposé of a female revivalist, produced in the following year as *Salvation Nell*. His long collaboration with **Ben Hecht** began with *The Front Page* (1928), a play about popular journalism set in a press room in the Criminal Courts Building in Chicago. Other works written with Hecht include *20th Century* (1932), *Jumbo* (1935), *Ladies and Gentlemen* (1939) and *Swan Song* (1946).

**Macaulay, Dame (Emilie) Rose** 1881–1958 Novelist. Born in Cambridge, where her father was a lecturer in classics, she was educated at Somerville College, Oxford. Her writing career began with *Abbots Verney* (1906) but it was not until *Potterism* (1920), several novels and two books of verse later, that she attracted popular and critical interest. Its satirical view of modern journalism and commercialization was also her view of modern humanity in general. Before World War II she completed 12 further novels, mixing a tart intelligence with compassion and humour; the best known are *Told by an Idiot* (1923), *Orphan Island* (1924), *Crewe Train* (1926), *They Were Defeated* (a historical novel about the poet **Robert Herrick**, 1932), *I Would Be Private* (1937) and *No Man's Wit* (1940). Her two post-war novels were *The World My Wilderness* (1950) and *The Towers of Trebizond* (1956). She was made a DBE in the year of her death.

Rose Macaulay's non-fiction included collec-tions of essays: *A Casual Commentary* (1925), *Catchwords and Claptrap* (1926) and *The Writings of E. M Forster* (1938); and the travel books *They Went to Portugal* (1946), *Fabled Shore: From the Pyrenees to Portugal* (1949) and *The Pleasure of Ruins* (1953). Constance Babington Smith edited her correspondence with her religious adviser as *Letters to a Friend* (two volumes, 1961–2), as well as *Letters to a Sister* (1964), which includes the fragment of a novel, *Venice Besieged*.

**Macaulay, Thomas Babington** 1800–59 Historian and essayist. The son of Zachary Macaulay, the anti-slavery campaigner and leading 'Clapham Sect' Evangelical, Macaulay was educated at private schools and at Trinity College, Cambridge, where he twice won the Chancellor's Medal for poetry. He was elected a fellow of Trinity in 1824 but made a wider reputation with his articles for the Whig *Edinburgh Review*, notably his essays on **Milton** (1825) and the Utilitarians (1829), and his attack on **Southey**'s *Colloquies* (1830), a classic expression of the Whig faith in 'the natural tendency of society to improvement'. These articles attracted the attention of Lord Lansdowne, through whose influence Macaulay was elected to Parliament as member for Calne. There he threw himself enthusiastically into the campaign for reform, and his speeches in support of the 1831–2 Reform Bill made him famous.

Political rewards followed. In 1832 Macaulay became Secretary to the Board of Control for India and gained entry to the Holland House circle of influential Whigs. After further success in the House, now as a member for Leeds, he was appointed to the new Supreme Council for India with responsibility for drafting legislation. During his four years in India Macaulay initiated major reforms in education and the penal code, and also wrote most of the *Lays of Ancient Rome* (1842) and the famous essay on **Bacon** (1837). He returned home in 1838 and next year became MP for Edinburgh, entering the Cabinet as the Secretary-at-War; he continued to write for the *Edinburgh*, producing important essays on Clive (1840), Warren Hastings (1841) and **Addison** (1843). In 1843 the first collected edition of his *Critical and Historical Essays* was published, and in 1848 the first two volumes of his *History of England*. This was an immediate and spectacular success, selling 3000 copies within 10 days of publication and 13,000 in four months. On the strength of it Macaulay decided to devote himself mainly to literature. He had been defeated at Edinburgh in 1847 and did not return to Parliament until 1852. The fourth and fifth volumes of the *History* were published in 1855, and the following year he resigned his parliamentary seat for reasons of ill health. Macaulay died in 1859, and a fifth volume of his *History*, edited from his surviving papers by his sister, appeared in 1861.

Macaulay's reputation today rests largely on the *History of England*, rightly considered a classic of English historical writing. His original plan was to bring the story down from 1688 to the threshold of the First Reform Bill, thus dealing with the development of Britain 'between the revolution, which brought the crown into harmony with the parliament, and the revolution which brought the parliament into harmony with the nation'. This progressive thrust and conviction of the rightness and adaptability of the English constitution survive in the final work, which deals only with the years 1685 to 1702. That, however, is complete in its way, distinguished by the epic sweep of Macaulay's narrative and his eye for pictorial and dramatic effects – qualities which enrich the Whig thesis of the *History* and save it from the callow buoyancy and easy contrasts which often mar the earlier essays.

**McAuley, James Phillip** 1917–76 Australian poet. Born at Lakemba, New South Wales, McAuley was appointed Senior Lecturer in Colonial Administration at the Australian School of Pacific Administration after World War II. Later he held the chair of English Literature at the University of Tasmania. He published two books of verse, *Under Aldebaran* (1946) and *A Vision of Ceremony* (1956), and edited the literary quarterly *Quadrant*. His work exhibited a commitment to control, formality and sophistication. His poetic theories were further shown by the hoax he concocted with Harold Stewart in 1944, publishing the 'posthumous' works of 'Ern Malley' in the modernist journal *Angry Penguins*. The verses were in fact deliberately concocted nonsense, composed as a parody of contemporary verse, particularly that of **Dylan Thomas** and **Henry Treece**.

**McBain, Ed**  See **Hunter, Evan**.

**Macbeth** A tragedy by **William Shakespeare**, first performed *c*.1606 and published, in an imperfect text, in the First Folio of 1623. The main source is **Holinshed**'s *Chronicles*. In turning to Scottish history and particularly in presenting a sympathetic portrait of Banquo, legendary ancestor of the Stuart kings, Shakespeare clearly intended some flattery to James I; the play also appealed to the king's well-known interest in witchcraft.

*Macbeth* begins with Scotland torn by rebellion. King Duncan's threatened army is rescued by the gallantry of his two generals, Macbeth and Banquo. On their way back to the king, they are confronted by three witches, who prophesy that Macbeth will become Thane of Cawdor and King of Scotland and that Banquo's sons will be kings. Almost at once Macbeth learns that his bravery has been rewarded by his proclamation as Thane of Cawdor. His thoughts are conveyed to his wife in a letter, which also reports Duncan's intention to visit Macbeth in his castle at Inverness. Lady Macbeth immediately resolves to have him killed. She overrides Macbeth's hesitation and has the presence of mind to prepare an alibi after Macbeth has killed the king. Suspicion falls immediately on Duncan's sons, Malcolm and Donalbain, and grows stronger when they flee from Scotland.

Having become king, Macbeth feels no safety. Remembering the witches' prophecy, he resolves to kill Banquo and his son, but the murderers botch their task and the son escapes. Weighed down by guilt and sleeplessness, Macbeth seeks out the witches and takes comfort from their assurance that he will not be defeated until Birnam Wood comes to Dunsinane Castle and that no man born of woman can harm him. But Scotland is suffering under his guilty reign and Macduff, the powerful Thane of Fife, seeks out Malcolm in England. The angry Macbeth orders the slaughter of Macduff's family.

The play's last movement begins as Malcolm's army advances on Macbeth's castle. Distraught with guilt, Lady Macbeth walks and talks in her sleep, betraying the secret of Duncan's murder. But Macbeth is now isolated even from her. He has only the assurance of the witches to protect him from despair. When Malcolm instructs his army to cut branches from Birnam Wood to camouflage their attack on Dunsinane, Macbeth learns that the wood is, indeed, coming to the castle. He is killed by Macduff, having discovered that Macduff was not 'born' but 'untimely ripped' from his mother's womb. Macduff establishes Malcolm on the Scottish throne.

Only at the very end of the play does Macbeth's behaviour recall the heroism of his defence of Duncan. Attaining of the throne brings him no joy, nor even contentment. For the original audience, his passage towards damnation would have been clear, and there is contemporary evidence that the appearance of the witches and of Banquo's ghost was theatrically impressive. The play certainly provides scope for spectacular staging, and is outstanding among the great tragedies for the vigour of its story-telling and the splendour of its famous soliloquies.

**MacBeth, George (Mann)** 1932– Poet. Born in Shotts, Lanarkshire, he was educated at King Edward VII School, Sheffield, and New College, Oxford. From 1955 to 1976 he was a BBC producer responsible for poetry programmes. A central figure in the **Group** in the 1950s, and involved in performance poetry in 1960s, he has published many volumes; they include *The Broken Places* (1963), *The Colour of Blood* (1967), *Collected Poems 1958–70* (1971), *Shrapnel* (1973) and *The Long Darkness* (1983). His main themes are suffering, death, war and violence, though some of his later work is quieter, simpler, and more genuinely moving. Although MacBeth has sometimes used experimental modes, much of his writing remains traditional in formal terms.

**MacCaig, Norman (Alexander)** 1910– Scottish poet. Son of an Edinburgh chemist, but proud of a Gaelic-speaking mother from Scalpay and a majority of Gaelic-speaking grandparents, MacCaig was educated at the Royal High School, Edinburgh, and read Classics at Edinburgh University. He was a primary teacher and latterly headmaster in 1934–67, except for the war years, when he was a conscientious objector. He was Creative Writing Fellow at Edinburgh University 1967–9, and lecturer in English and eventually Reader in Poetry at Stirling University until 1977. Widely regarded as Scotland's finest living poet, MacCaig has had a great number of awards and prizes, including FRSL (1965), OBE (1979) and the Queen's Gold Medal for Poetry (1986). In two early volumes MacCaig dabbled with Apocalyptic mannerisms (see the **New Apocalypse**) and started on what he calls 'the long haul towards lucidity' with *Riding Lights* (1955). Since then he has published 12 more slim volumes, from *The Sinai Sort* (1957) to *A World of Difference* (1983), and his prize-winning *Collected Poems* (1985). His close friend **Hugh MacDiarmid** described MacCaig as apolitical by nature, and he declares himself both a born atheist and a born pacifist. His poems tend to centre on Edinburgh, or on north-west Sutherland, where he spends time each summer. His poetry has moved from tight traditional forms to a more open verse, characterized by sharp wit and playfulness; much of it is 'metaphysical', concerned with the nature of perception. The deaths of Hugh MacDiarmid and **Sydney Goodsir Smith** affected him strongly, and in *Equal Skies* (1980) there is a sequence of poems for another dead friend, Angus MacLeod, which achieves a new depth of emotion. *As I Say It* is a fine album of MacCaig reading his own poems, recorded in 1971.

**MacCarthy, Sir (Charles Otto) Desmond** 1877–1952 Literary and dramatic critic. MacCarthy was educated at Eton and Trinity College, Cambridge, where he was a member of the **Apostles**, and became a close friend of the philosopher **G. E. Moore**, the historian **G. M. Trevelyan** and of Thoby Stephen, brother of Vanessa Bell and **Virginia Woolf**. By 1903 he was writing reviews and dramatic criticism for

*The Speaker.* In 1907–10 he edited *The New Quarterly*, and in 1913 joined *The New Statesman* as dramatic critic, later becoming literary editor (1920–7), where he wrote under the pen-name 'Affable Hawk'. In 1928 he succeeded **Sir Edmund Gosse** as senior literary critic of *The Sunday Times*, continuing to write weekly articles for that paper until his death. He was knighted in 1951.

His critical essays were published in some 10 volumes, but although his many friends expected great things of him, he never produced any major works. His criticism always preserved the precise thought and an element of the philosophic interest that he had learned at Cambridge. Portraits of **Samuel Butler, Meredith, Henry James, Shaw, Conrad, Ruskin** and Asquith are among his most admired pieces and he was among the first to recognize the significance of Ibsen and Chekhov. He was a brilliant conversationalist and a close friend of the Bloomsbury circle although he never saw himself as a 'member' of the Group.

**McCarthy, Justin** 1830–1912 Irish journalist, novelist, historian and politician. Born near Cork, the son of a magistrates' clerk, McCarthy was brought up in genteel poverty. As a young journalist on *The Cork Examiner* he imbibed the political and literary enthusiasms of **Thomas Davis** and the Young Ireland movement, reporting the Irish famine and the treason trials of the Young Ireland leaders in 1848. He moved to Liverpool in 1854 and joined *The Morning Star* in London in 1859. In the 1860s he embarked on a successful career in fiction, publishing some 20 now-forgotten novels. The best is probably *Mononia: a Love-Story of 'Forty-Eight'* (1901), reflecting the country life and political enthusiasms of his Munster youth, though *Dear Lady Disdain* (1875) and *Miss Misanthrope* (1878) were also very popular. He entered Parliament in 1879, becoming vice-chairman of the Irish parliamentary party under Parnell and after 1890 chairman of the anti-Parnellite majority of the Irish members. His immensely popular *History of Our Own Times* was eventually completed in seven volumes (1879–1905), covering the whole of Queen Victoria's reign. To this he added *The Reign of Queen Anne* (1905) and *The History of the Four Georges and William IV* (1884–1901) as well as shorter studies of Sir Robert Peel (1891) and Gladstone (1898). Despite the failure of his health and eyesight in 1897 he continued to write, publishing works such as his good-humoured *Reminiscences* (1899), *The Story of an Irishman* (1904) and *Irish Recollections* (1912).

**McCarthy, Mary** 1912–89 American novelist, short-story writer, essayist and critic, born in Seattle, Washington. After completing her education at Vassar in 1933, she moved to New York

City and wrote book reviews for *The New Republic*, *The Nation* and *The Partisan Review*.

At the urging of her second husband, **Edmund Wilson**, whom she married in 1938, she began to write fiction, and her first collection of stories, *The Company She Keeps*, appeared in 1942. After that she transformed much of her life into fiction. Her experiences as a university teacher provided much of the material for her novel *The Groves of Academe* (1952); she described her childhood in *Memories of a Catholic Girlhood* (1957); her best-selling novel *The Group* (1963) follows the lives of eight Vassar women of the class of 1933 for seven years after their graduation. A social critic and moralist, she was active in the American Left during the 1930s. Her political interests were evident in all her writing, including her travel books (*Venice Observed*, 1956, *The Stones of Florence*, 1959). After a visit to Vietnam in the 1960s, she published critical accounts of the war in *Vietnam* (1967) and *Hanoi* (1968). She also produced works of literary criticism (*The Writing on the Wall*, 1970, *Ideas and the Novel*, 1981) and many more novels, short stories, and essays, including *Birds of America* (1971), *The Mask of State: Watergate Portrait* (1974), *Cannibals and Missionaries* (1979), *The Hounds of Summer and Other Stories* (1981) and *Occasional Prose: Essays* (1985). *How I Grew* (1987) is autobiographical.

**McClure's Magazine** An American literary and political magazine founded by Samuel Sydney McClure and John Sanborn Phillips in June 1893; its last issue appeared in March 1929, after which it merged with *New Smart Set*. In its first period it ranked as one of the three great illustrated ten-cent monthlies. In its second period, beginning in 1902, it pioneered reformist non-fiction, which was later called muckraking journalism. After 1919 the magazine declined, and despite efforts by people such as William Randolph Hearst to infuse new life and money into it, it lost its prestige. Contributors of fiction included **Rudyard Kipling**, **O. Henry**, **Willa Cather** and **Jack London**.

**McCrae, Hugh Raymond** 1876–1958 Australian poet. Born in Melbourne of a literary family, McCrae was articled to an architect, but went to Sydney to work as a freelance writer. He also pursued a brief career as an actor in New York and Australia. Seeing the poet's task as 'to live in making others live', McCrae created a vivid mythological world in the volumes *Satyrs and Sunlight* (1909), *Columbine* (1920), *Idyllia* (1922) and *The Mimshi Maiden* (1938). *The Dr Poissey Anecdotes* (1922) are fictional revelations in the 18th-century manner, and *My Father and My Father's Friends* (1935) is a biography of George Gordon McCrae and his friends **Marcus**

**Clarke**, **Henry Kendall** and **Adam Lindsay Gordon**.

**McCullers, Carson (Smith)** 1917–67 American novelist, born in Georgia, and educated at Columbia and the Juilliard School of Music. Her first novel, *The Heart is a Lonely Hunter* (1940), won her immediate recognition. Her work often focuses on the spiritual isolation of the individual, and on the attempt to overcome this through love. She was also one of the first American writers to deal openly with homosexual relationships. Her second novel, *Reflections in a Golden Eye* (1941), was followed by *The Ballad of the Sad Café* in 1951. She herself dramatized her novel *The Member of the Wedding* (1946), which ran successfully on Broadway. Other works include the play *The Square Root of Wonderful* (1958), the novel *Clock Without Hands* (1961) and *The Mortgaged Heart* (1971), a collection of stories.

**MacDiarmid, Hugh** Pseudonym of the Scottish poet and critic Christopher Murray Grieve (1892–1978). Born in Langholm in the Scottish Borders, he attended Langholm Academy and trained as a teacher in Edinburgh before becoming a journalist in 1912. After serving in World War I, he married in 1915 and returned to journalism in 1920. He published his first book, *Annals of the Five Senses*, under his own name in 1923, but in 1922–3 began to publish poems in

Carson McCullers, 1944. Detail from the portrait by H. V. Poor.

Scots and thereafter, as Hugh MacDiarmid, became the central figure of the 20th-century **Scottish renaissance**. A Communist and nationalist, he became a founder-member of the Scottish National Party in 1928 and was involved in political controversy throughout his life. He was expelled from both the SNP and the Communist Party during the 1930s and rejoined the Communist Party in 1956 after the Hungarian uprising. In 1931 he met his second wife Valda Trevlyn (his first marriage ended in divorce) and in 1933–42 they lived through a period of troubled but in many ways productive 'exile' on Whalsay in the Shetlands. In 1950 he received a Civil List pension and in 1951 he finally settled at Brownsbank, near Biggar. From the early 1960s he began to enjoy growing recognition as a major modern poet. In the last two decades of his life he received many literary honours and travelled extensively throughout Europe and to North America and China.

He had already written a good deal in English before he established his reputation with poems like 'The Watergaw' and 'The Eemis Stane', which demonstrated new potentialities for the use of Scots as a modern literary language. MacDiarmid's revived or synthetic Scots drew on dictionaries, dialect glossaries and literary diction as well as contemporary speech. Two collections of lyrics, *Sangschaw* (1925) and *Penny Wheep* (1926), were followed by *A Drunk Man Looks at the Thistle* (1926), a sequence regarded by many as his masterpiece and certainly the most important single poem in 20th-century Scottish literature. He continued to extend the use of Scots throughout the 1920s and 1930s, in such works as *To Circumjack Cencrastus* (1930) and in styles ranging from the political polemic of *First Hymn to Lenin* (1931) to the meditation of 'By Wauchopeside', 'Whuchulls' and 'Depth and the Chthonian Image'. By the mid 1930s, however, his desire to create a modern epic led him to experiment with what he called 'synthetic English', a poetic idiom created from a variety of esoteric vocabularies and scientific terminologies, particularly geology and modern linguistics. 'On a Raised Beach' (in *Stony Limits*, 1934) is his most impressive achievement in this mode, but he continued the experiment in two major works, *In Memoriam James Joyce* (1954) and *The Kind of Poetry I Want* (1961).

MacDiarmid's two-volume *Complete Poems 1920–76*, edited by Michael Grieve and W. R. Aitken, appeared after his death in 1978 and was reissued, with minor amendments and additions, in 1982. He was a notable translator of Scottish Gaelic and modern European poetry, and edited several literary magazines and poetry anthologies. He also wrote short stories, critical and political essays and the prose autobiography *Lucky Poet: A Self-Study in Literature and Political Ideas* (1943, reissued in 1972). *The Letters of Hugh MacDiarmid*, edited by Alan Bold, appeared in 1984.

**MacDonagh, Donagh** 1912–68 Poet. Born in Dublin, the son of **Thomas MacDonagh**, he became a barrister and later a judge. He published *Twenty Poems* (1934), *Veterans and Other Poems* (1941), *The Hungry Grass* (1947) and *A Warning to Conquerors* (1968). In 1947 his play *Happy As Larry* was a considerable success in London and New York, and several others were performed on radio. Donagh MacDonagh edited *The Oxford Book of Irish Verse* (1958) with Lennox Robinson.

**MacDonagh, Thomas** 1878–1916 Poet. Born in Tipperary, he attended University College, Dublin, and was later appointed its Professor of English Literature. In his time he was a successful and well-regarded poet, publishing *Through the Ivory Gate* (1902), *April and May* (1903), *The Golden Toy* (1906), *Songs of Myself* (1910) and *Lyrical Poems* (1913). Other works were a tragedy, *When the Dawn is Come* (1908), *Thomas Campion and the Art of English Poetry* (1913) and *Literature in Ireland* (1916). Another play, *Pagans*, was published posthumously in 1920.

An Irish volunteer, MacDonagh played a leading role in the Easter Rising of 1916 and was executed after its suppression. He was mourned by **W. B. Yeats** in 'Easter 1916' as one who 'might have won fame in the end,/So sensitive his nature seemed,/So daring and sweet his thought'. *Collected Poems* (1917) was published with an introduction by **James Stephens**.

**MacDonald, George** 1824–1905 Scottish children's author and novelist. The son of a Scottish weaver, he was educated at Aberdeen University before training as a Congregational minister. Finding his own individualistic views unacceptable to his parish, he gradually turned to literature, producing original fairy-stories shot through with an unmistakable blend of Christian symbolism and mystical imagination. His most famous story, *At the Back of the North Wind* (1871), describes a little cabdriver's son called Diamond who ventures forth each night from his bedroom in the company of the North Wind, pictured as a beautiful lady, to travel over the world. Subsequent classics include *The Princess and the Goblin* (1872), a powerful allegory of good and evil, and *The Princess and Curdie* (1883), where the miner's son Curdie has once more to brave dangers from goblins and other misshapen figures in order to save the princess to whom he owes allegiance. MacDonald's adult fiction – the allegorical *Phantastes* (1858) and *Lilith* (1895), and novels such as *David Elginbrod* (1863) – is less well remembered, but his powerful imagination has influenced **G. K. Chesterton**, **C. S. Lewis** and **J. R. R. Tolkien**.

**McEwan, Ian** 1948– Novelist and short-story writer. The first and most famous protégé of **Malcolm Bradbury**'s creative writing course at the University of East Anglia, he attracted immediate and effusive critical attention with his two collections of short stories, *First Love, Last Rites* (1975) and *In Between the Sheets* (1977). These are distinguished by a sensational sexual explicitness, a preoccupation with perversion and obsession, and a perfectly modulated prose style. *The Cement Garden* (1978), his first novel, is more exactly a novella along similar lines, while his second, *The Comfort of Strangers* (1981), is an investigation of psychopathology of greater substance, owing its location and claustrophobic concentration to Mann's *Death in Venice*. *The Child in Time* (1987) is an intense and sober study of the bereavement visited on young parents whose infant daughter is stolen and never found. McEwan is also the author of a thoughtful television play, *The Imitation Game* (1981), about the Bletchley Park code-breaking centre in World War II; an oratorio, *Or Shall We Die?* (1983), which is a polemic against nuclear war; and the screenplay of *The Ploughman's Lunch* (1983), an influential film satirizing the political complacency of Britain at the time of the Falklands campaign and the Greenham Common disarmament protests.

**MacEwen, Gwendolyn** 1941– Canadian poet, novelist, short-story writer. Born in Toronto, where she was raised and educated, she travelled in Egypt, Israel and Greece before returning to Canada. Her first work appeared in *Canadian Forum* before she was 15 and her first novel was completed by the age of 19. A prolific writer in a wide range of forms, she has published many volumes of poetry, among which are her first two collections *Selah* and *The Drunken Clock* (1961), *The Shadow-Maker* (1969), which won the Governor General's Award, *The Armies of the Moon* (1972) and *Earthlight: Selected Poems 1963–1982* (1982); two novels, *Julian the Magician* (1963) and *King of Egypt, King of Dreams* (1971); short stories, *Noman* (1972) and *The Honey Drum: Seven Tales from Arab Lands* (1984); *Trojan Woman* (1981), a play, and translations from Y. Ritsos. Preoccupied with myth, magic and a sacrificial view of life, MacEwen is one of Canada's most intense and accomplished contemporary writers.

**McGee, Thomas D'Arcy** 1825–68 Irish journalist and poet. McGee was born in Carlingford, County Louth, and emigrated to America in 1842. He quickly made his mark as a precocious orator and was editing a newspaper in Boston at the age of 19. He returned to Ireland in 1845 and became London correspondent of *The Freeman's Journal* and the Young Ireland organ, *The Nation*. He neglected his official business to explore Irish history and literature in the British Museum and wrote hurried but valuable pioneering studies of *The Irish Writers of the Seventeenth Century* (1846) and *The Life and Conquest of Art McMurrough* (1847). The facile popular poetry he wrote for *The Nation*, chiefly on nationalist or historical themes, was admired by **Yeats** as technically superior to that of his colleague **Thomas Davis**. He was actively involved in the Young Ireland rising of 1848 and escaped to America, where he continued to lecture and write indefatigably if controversially on Irish subjects. He concerned himself with the welfare and education of the growing Irish expatriate community both in the USA and later in Canada, where he represented Irish-Canadian interests in Parliament and held ministerial rank. He was assassinated in Ottawa in 1868, possibly by an Irish political extremist since he had become critical of the Fenian movement of the 1860s. His best-remembered poems are the dreamily nostalgic 'The Celts' and 'Salutation to the Celts' addressed to the 'sea-divided Gael' throughout the world. His several touching elegies for Irishmen include a tribute to **Thomas Moore**, to whose influence his own metrical virtuosity and lyric grace are largely attributable.

**McGonagall, William** 1830–1902 Scottish versifier, self-styled 'Poet and Tragedian'. A Dundee weaver aspiring to act **Shakespeare** and write great poetry, McGonagall became and has remained a butt for audiences, with the unscanned doggerel and painful rhymes of his *Poetic Gems* (1890). This volume also contains a 'Brief Autobiography' and 'Reminiscences'. In his poetry he specialized in shipwrecks, battles and beauty spots, and perhaps his most frequently quoted work is 'The Tay Bridge Disaster'.

**McGough, Roger** See **Liverpool poets**.

**McGrath, John** 1935– Dramatist. McGrath's first play, *Events While Guarding the Bofors Gun* (1966), is a forceful indictment of British cold-war militarism. Since 1971, when he founded 7:84 Theatre Company (so called on the strength of an economic estimate that 7 per cent of Britain's population owned 84 per cent of its wealth), McGrath has written exclusively for the political fringe of the British theatre, in quest of a popular audience. Plays for the Scottish branch of 7:84 include *The Cheviot, the Stag and the Black, Black Oil* (1973), *The Game's a Bogey* (1974) and *Little Red Hen* (1975). McGrath's intelligently provocative essays on popular theatre, based on a series of seminars at Cambridge University in 1979, are collected in *A Good Night Out* (1981).

**McGuane, Thomas (Francis)** 1939– American novelist, born in Michigan and educated at Michigan State University. His fiction, written with a comic energy, concerns the attempts of individuals to find workable sets of values in the modern world. His books include *The Sporting Club* (1969), *The Bushwacked Piano* (1971), *Panama* (1978), *Nobody's Angel* (1979) and *Something to be Desired* (1984). *Ninety-Two in the Shade*, written in 1973, was filmed in 1975. *To Skin a Cat* (1986) is a volume of short stories. McGuane has also written the scripts for the films *Rancho Deluxe* (1973), *The Missouri Breaks* (1976) and *Tom Horn* (1980).

**Machen, Arthur (Llewellyn)** 1863–1947 Novelist. Born in Caerleon, Monmouthshire, he was educated privately before moving to London in 1880. He was deeply influenced by and steeped in Welsh folklore, and worked for a time as a cataloguer of diabolistic and occult books. Later he joined the Order of the Golden Dawn, a group of theosophists involved in Cabbalistic magic, of which **W. B Yeats** and Aleister Crowley also became members. After many years of neglect he joined the London *Evening News* in 1910 and was 'rediscovered', a process which culminated in the publication of the Caerleon Edition of his works in 1923.

He is chiefly remembered for his supernatural tales, of which the most notable are *The Great God Pan* (1894) and *The Hill of Dreams* (1907), about the aura of a terrifying past which surrounds a Roman fort. His other works include: translations of *The Heptameron* (1886) and *The Memoirs of Casanova* (1894); a volume of criticism, *Hieroglyphics* (1902); *Notes and Queries* (1926) and *Dreads and Drolls* (1926). *Far Off Things* (1922) and *Things Near and Far* (1923) were both autobiographical.

**McIlvanney, William** 1936– Scottish novelist. Born into a mining family at Kilmarnock, Ayrshire, he was educated at Kilmarnock Academy and read English at Glasgow University, becoming a teacher in 1960. He left a senior teaching post to be a full-time writer in 1975, and since then has held creative writing fellowships at Strathclyde and Aberdeen Universities, and in Canada, as well as writing for television and presenting series on books and football. The first of his prizewinning novels, *Remedy is None* (1966), tells how a student is confronted with his working-class origins through his father's death, and *A Gift from Nessus* (1968) is a strong tale of life crisis and marital breakdown. McIlvanney's reputation rests particularly on *Docherty* (1975) and *The Big Man* (1985), both of which make tough examination of the Scots tradition of the 'hard man'. *Docherty* is a historical novel set in 1903–25, celebrating an Ayrshire miner, his family and community, even as it diagnoses their helplessness in the grip of forces they cannot understand or control. *The Big Man*, a starkly contemporary novel set in a small Ayrshire town, finds the manipulative violence of bare-knuckle fighting an appropriate metaphor for life in a capitalist society. Seeking a wider, more popular readership, McIlvanney wrote *Laidlaw* (1978) and *The Papers of Tony Veitch* (1983), murder stories with a difference. He has been criticized for excessive violence and for over-indulgence in witty metaphors, accepting the second charge because 'Ayrshire speech is full of metaphor'. He has published two books of poetry, *The Longships in Harbour* (1970) and *These Words: Weddings and After* (1984).

**MacInnes, Colin** 1914–76 Novelist and journalist. Son of the popular novelist Angela Thirkell and a descendant of **Rudyard Kipling**, he grew up in Australia, where his first novel, *June in her Spring* (1952), is set. He is now remembered, and frequently idolized, for his 'London trilogy' of novels, which offer a vivid, jauntily enthusiastic and often prophetic evocation of a London just beginning to become multi-racial and develop, with the onset of popular music, a militant youth culture. The best of the three books, *City of Spades* (1957), explores London's nascent West Indian community and the alternate pleasures and crises of white–black race relations; *Absolute Beginners* (1959), while predominantly a celebration of youth and style, culminates in the Notting Hill race-riots of 1958. The third novel, *Mr Love and Justice* (1960), a morality fable about the relationship between a policeman and a pimp, is overly schematic. MacInnes is also notable for his essays, originally published in journals like *New Society* and subsequently collected in volumes such as *England, Half English* (1961), which apply incisive and iconoclastic cultural criticism to contemporary topics from the *Oz* pornography trial to cricket.

**Mackay, Charles** 1814–89 Scottish songwriter. Born in Perth, educated in London and Brussels, he was sub-editor of the Glasgow *Morning Chronicle*, editor of the Glasgow *Argus* and later of *The Illustrated London News*. He published several volumes of verse, beginning with *Songs and Poems* (1834). Many of his poems were set to music; it was said that 400,000 copies were sold of 'A Good Time Coming'. His daughter was the novelist **Marie Corelli**.

**McKay, Claude** 1890–1948 American poet and novelist, born in Jamaica. He emigrated to the USA in 1912. His first two collections of poetry, *Songs of Jamaica* (1912) and *Spring in New Hampshire and Other Poems* (1920), attracted favourable critical attention, but it was not until the appearance of *Harlem Shadows* in 1922 that his popular reputation was established. His first novel, *Home to Harlem* (1928), tells of a black soldier's return to the USA after serving in France. *Banjo: A Story Without a Plot* (1929) is about a vagabond's life on the Marseilles waterfront. *Banana Bottom* (1933) examines the dilemma of a young black woman who has returned to Jamaica after an education in England, and explores the racial traditions and attitudes which make her readjustment a painful process. McKay's other publications include a collection of stories, *Gingertown* (1932); an autobiography, *A Long Way From Home* (1937); and a study of the black community, *Harlem* (1940). *Trial by Lynching: Stories About Negro Life in North America* was written in English but first appeared in Russian in 1925, and had to be translated back into English by Robert Winter in 1975.

**MacKaye, Percy (Wallace)** 1875–1956 American playwright, born in New York City and educated at Harvard. His first play, *The Canterbury Pilgrims* (1903), was a blank verse drama about the Wife of Bath's amorous pursuit of **Chaucer**. His later work includes *Jeanne d'Arc* (1906) and *Sappho and Phaon* (1907). His most successful play, *The Scarecrow*, was based on **Nathaniel Hawthorne's** story 'Feathertop'. It was published in 1908, produced at the Harvard Dramatist's Club in 1909, and then opened at Garrick's Theatre in New York in 1911.

MacKaye also wrote about the theatre. *The Playhouse and the Play* (1909), *The Civic Theatre* (1912), and *Community Drama* (1917) all emphasize the communal functions of theatrical production. He wrote one community masque called *St Louis* (1914) for 7500 actors, and on the occasion of **Shakespeare's** Tercentenary wrote another, entitled *Caliban, By the Yellow Sands* (1916). His later work included an ambitious tetralogy of verse plays, *The Mystery of Hamlet, King of Denmark – or, What We Will* (1949), which depicts the major characters in *Hamlet* prior to that play's beginning.

**Mackenzie, Sir (Edward Montague) Compton** 1883–1972 Novelist. Educated at St Paul's School, London, and Magdalen College, Oxford, he studied law, but published *Poems* in 1907 and earned considerable praise with his first novels, *The Passionate Elopement* (1911) and *Carnival* (1912). The best of his many works include *Sinister Street* (2 vols., 1913–14), *Guy and Pauline* (1915), *Sylvia Scarlett* (1918), *Extraordinary Women* (1928), *Our Street* (1931), *The Four Winds of Love* (6 vols., 1937–45) and the well-known Scottish novels, *The Monarch of the Glen* (1941) and *Whisky Galore* (1947). He drew on his experience of serving in the Dardanelles during World War I for *Gallipoli Memories* (1929), *Athenian Memories* (1931) and *Greek Memories*

(1932). His autobiography *My Life and Times* was issued in ten volumes 1963–71.

**Mackenzie, Henry** 1745–1831 Novelist, essayist, editor, dramatist, biographer. Mackenzie was an Edinburgh lawyer, born on the day Prince Charles Edward Stuart landed in Scotland, and educated at the High School and University of Edinburgh. In 1765 he went to London to further his law studies, and became Attorney for the Crown in Scotland and later Comptroller of Taxes. While in London he started his novel, **The Man of Feeling**, published anonymously in 1771, about a man whose morality is too delicate for a harsh world. It was followed by *The Man of the World* (1773), about the selfish pursuit of happiness, and an epistolary novel, *Julia de Roubigné* (1777). **Sir Walter Scott** ranked him with **Sterne** as a practitioner of the **sentimental novel**.

Mackenzie's membership of an Edinburgh literary society led to his editing *The Mirror* (1779–80) and later *The Lounger* (1785–7). He also contributed to the Transactions of the Royal Society of Edinburgh and was one of the original members of the Highland Society. In 1792 he published tracts intended to calm the lower orders and prevent revolution. In 1793 he wrote *The Life of Dr Blacklock*. In 1805 a committee chaired by Mackenzie decided that **James Macpherson's** *Ossian* was not the true Gaelic epic it claimed to be. In 1808 Mackenzie published his complete works, in eight volumes, including an unperformed tragedy, *The Spanish Father*, another tragedy, *The Prince of Tunis*, performed in Edinburgh (1763), and a comedy, *The White Hypocrite*, performed once at the Theatre Royal, **Covent Garden**. He was also the author of a political tract, *An Account of the Proceedings of the Parliament of 1784*, which brought him to the notice of Pitt. His *Anecdotes and Egotisms* were edited by his biographer, Harold William Thompson, in 1927. These jottings give a vivid picture of Edinburgh life, with gossip about the lordly and the famous, as observed by a civilized intelligence.

**Mackenzie, Seaforth** Pseudonym of the Australian novelist and poet Kenneth Ivo Mackenzie (1913–54). Born in Perth, Western Australia, he was a journalist and agricultural labourer. He published two novels, *The Young Desire It* (1937) and *Chosen People* (1938), and two volumes of poetry, *Our Earth* (1937) and *The Moonlit Doorway* (1944).

**Mackintosh, Elizabeth** 1897–1952 Author of **detective fiction** under the pseudonym of Josephine Tey and of plays and novels under the pseudonym of Gordon Daviot. Born in Inverness, she studied at the Royal Academy there and at the Anstey Physical Training College in

Birmingham, going on to teach physical education in schools. Her first detective novel, *The Man in the Queue* (1929, first published as being by Gordon Daviot), introduced the genteel police detective Alan Grant who reappeared as the hero of *A Shilling for Candles* (1936), *To Love and Be Wise* (1951), *The Daughter of Time* (1951) and *The Singing Sands* (1952). *Miss Pym Disposes* (1946), which used her background in physical education, *The Franchise Affair* (1948) and *Brat Farrar* (1949) belonged to no identifiable series. All enjoyed a reputation for their well-crafted stories, and the use of historical mysteries – an 18th-century *cause célèbre* in *The Franchise Affair* and the character of Richard III in *The Daughter of Time* – received high praise. Her career as Gordon Daviot showed the same interest in history, with *Richard of Bordeaux* (produced in London in 1932) and *Queen of Scots* (produced in 1934) among her best-known plays. Other work as Gordon Daviot included radio dramas and three novels, *Kif: An Unvarnished History* (1929), *The Expensive Halo* (1931) and *The Privateer* (1952).

**Macklin, Charles** 1699–1797 Irish actor and playwright who was a notable figure in the London theatre from 1733 until his retirement in 1789. Of his ten plays, some are specifically about the stage, like *The New Play Criticiz'd* (1747) and *Covent Garden Theatre* (1752), and all clearly written from the viewpoint of an actor. *Love à-la-Mode* (1759) is a wittily satirical afterpiece, and *The True-Born Irishman* (1762) and *The Man of the World* (1781), a revised version of *The True-Born Scotsman* (1764), are comedies which provided Macklin with fine opportunities to act out and ridicule national characteristics.

**Maclaren, Ian** See **kailyard school**.

**MacLaverty, Bernard** 1945– Irish novelist and short-story writer. Born in Belfast, MacLaverty took a degree in English at Queen's University. He left Ireland in the early 1970s to live on Islay, off the west coast of Scotland. His first book, *Secrets and Other Stories*, won a Scottish Arts Council award in 1977, as did the novel *Lamb* in 1980. *A Time To Dance and Other Stories* appeared in 1982, and the novel *Cal*, which deals directly with the political violence in Northern Ireland, was widely acclaimed on its publication in 1983. *Lamb* and *Cal* have been made into films.

**Maclean, Sorley** 1911– Gaelic poet. Born in Raasay, Maclean graduated from Edinburgh University and became a schoolteacher, first in Edinburgh and later, as headmaster, in Plockton, Ross-shire. *Dain do Eimhir Agus Dain Eile* (1943) revealed a major new talent, combining traditional and modern elements, and had the effect of leading Gaelic poetry into the 20th century. It is chiefly a book of love poems, many written at the time of the Spanish Civil War and showing a clash between private needs and social responsibilities. Many of them reappeared in *Reothairt is Contraigh, Taghadh de Dhain 1932–72* (1977), rearranged in sections according to theme, with new work which included his most admired single poem, 'Hallaig', about a township depopulated at the time of the Highland Clearances. *Ris a' Bhruthaich* (1985) is a collection of critical essays, particularly concerned with the great 16th- and 17th-century Gaelic songs which have had a profound influence on his own poetry. Maclean's own influence on younger poets has been considerable, and his transformation of traditional Gaelic poetry has done for the latter what **T. S. Eliot** did for English poetry and **Hugh MacDiarmid** for poetry in Scots.

**MacLeish, Archibald** 1892–1982 American poet and dramatist, born in Glencoe, Illinois. He graduated from Yale in 1915 and published his first book of poems, *Tower of Ivory*, in 1917. After serving in World War I he enrolled at Harvard and took a law degree. He practised briefly, but from 1923 to 1928 joined the group of Americans who had settled in Paris.

His early poetry was highly subjective and owed much to that of **T. S. Eliot** and **Ezra Pound**: *The Happy Marriage* (1924), *The Pot of Earth* (1925), *Streets in the Moon* (1926) and *The Hamlet of A. MacLeish* (1928). *New Found Land* (1930) was written after his return to the USA. *Conquistador* (1932), an epic about the conquest of Mexico, was awarded the Pulitzer Prize in 1933. *Frescoes for Mr Rockefeller's City* appeared in 1933. He also wrote skilful and fluent verse plays: *Nobodaddy* (1926) and *Panic* (1935), which dealt with the Wall Street crash. *The Fall of the City* (1937), a denunciation of totalitarianism, was written for radio and reached a wide audience in the USA and England. *Air Raid* (1938) was also written for radio. His *Collected Poems* (1952) won him a second Pulitzer in 1953. Among his later works are three more verse plays: *The Trojan Horse* (1952, for radio), reflecting the contemporary fear of Communist infiltration; *J. B.* (1958), about a modern Job, which brought him a third Pulitzer Prize in 1959; and *Herakles* (1967), which explores the conflict between human needs and reason and science.

Parallel with his career in letters, MacLeish led an active public and academic life. After editing *Fortune* from 1929 to 1938 he became Librarian of Congress (1939–44), Assistant Secretary of State (1944–5), and Boylston Professor of Rhetoric and Oratory at Harvard (1949–62). He also represented the USA in UNESCO.

**MacLennan, (John) Hugh** 1907– Canadian novelist and essayist. He was born at Glace Bay, Nova Scotia, and educated at Dalhousie University, Oxford and Princeton. He taught classics for some years, later becoming Professor of English at McGill University (1967–79). His first (and best-known) novels, *Barometer Rising* (1941) and *Two Solitudes* (1945), employed a blend of realism and symbolism to examine perceptions of Canadian identity in the early 20th century. An accomplished essayist, MacLennan frequently includes lengthy asides of didactic exposition and description in his novels. Other works are *The Precipice* (1949), *Each Man's Son* (1951), *The Watch That Ends the Night* (1959), *Return of the Sphinx* (1967) and *Voices in Time* (1981).

**Macleod, Fiona** See **Sharp, William**.

**MacNeice, (Frederick) Louis** 1907–63 Poet. The son of a Church of Ireland rector, he was born in Carrickfergus and schooled in England, first at Sherborne then at Marlborough. This Irish background – Northern by birth, Southern by parentage – was a lasting source of anger and pleasure to MacNeice. He read Greats at Merton College, Oxford, emerging with a first and a collection of poems, *Blind Fireworks* (1929). Teaching classics at Birmingham University, and later at Bedford College, London, did not engage him: he was writing a pseudonymous

Louis MacNeice, 1946.

novel (*Roundabout Way*, 1932), critical essays (notably *Modern Poetry*, 1938), plays for the Group Theatre, and a widely praised translation of *The Agamemnon of Aeschylus* (1936). He published a further collection of *Poems* (1935), and, in collaboration with **W. H. Auden**, *Letters from Iceland* (1937). On the eve of the war his long poem *Autumn Journal* appeared: capturing the mood of the Munich weeks, the flickering hopes for the Spanish Republic; social and political in circumference, the centre of the poem is always personal. It is a brilliant epitome of his own characterization of the poet as 'able-bodied, fond of talking, a reader of the newspapers, capable of pity and laughter, appreciative of women, susceptible to physical impressions' – a description that indicated his affinities with **Yeats** (see his 1941 study of the poet). MacNeice joined the BBC in 1941 and remained until his death from pneumonia in 1963. He wrote dozens of feature programmes and radio dramas; his play *The Dark Tower* (1947) is a classic of the genre. With a few exceptions, the radio work encouraged MacNeice's tendency towards a fluent superficiality, what he called 'bloom or frill or floating image'. His poems of the 1940s and early 1950s are discursive and have their longueurs; he felt he had returned to 'syntax and bony feature' in his shorter lyrics. With *Solstices* (1961) and *The Burning Perch* (1963) MacNeice's poems achieved a taut intensity reaching beyond one man's experience to attain at times the resonance of myth and dreams. He has always been linked with Auden, **Day-Lewis** and **Spender** under the 'Macspaunday' umbrella, which does his work a disservice: his detachment can be defensive but also freed him from their need to recant. His debonair professionalism as a poet often disguises the pervasive sense of loss in the poems: loss of faith, of love, of belonging to one country. As a love poet, a poet of urban rhythms and delights, as a reporter with an educated and sensuous intelligence, his reputation stands very high. His unfinished autobiography, *The Strings Are False*, was published in 1965, his *Collected Poems* in 1966, and a volume of *Selected Literary Criticism* in 1987.

**McNickle, D'Arcy** 1904–77 A half-blood American Indian of the Flathead (or Salish) tribe, McNickle was educated at the University of Montana, and then at Oxford and Grenoble. His first novel, *The Surrounded* (1936), is about a youth facing an identity crisis: half Flathead Indian and half Spanish, he is torn between the two cultures. *Runner in the Sun: A Story of Indian Maize* (1954) is a novel for young people. His last novel, *Wind From an Enemy Sky*, published the year after his death, deals with the conflicts between Indian and non-Indian cultures. He also wrote *Indian Man: A Life of Oliver LaFarge* (1971), as well as several histories: *They Came*

*Here First* (1949), *The Indian Tribes of the United States* (1962), *Native American Tribalism* (1973), and, with Harold E. Fey, *Indians and Other Americans* (1970).

**Macpherson, James** 1736–96 Poet and translator. Born a farmer's son at Ruthven in Inverness, he studied at Marischal College in Aberdeen and at Edinburgh University before becoming a teacher. In 1758 he published *The Highlander*, a poem in heroic couplets. Macpherson's knowledge of Gaelic poetry prompted the dramatist **John Home** to suggest he undertake some translations. *Fragments of Ancient Poetry Collected in the Highlands of Scotland and Translated from the Gaelic or Erse Language* (1760) was warmly received by **James Beattie**, Hugh Blair, **Adam Ferguson**, **William Robertson** and the rest of Edinburgh literary society. Its preface spoke of a Gaelic epic which, given support and encouragement, Macpherson could recover for literature. The necessary money was found and he published the result of his labours as *Fingal: An Ancient Poem* (1762), closely followed by *Temora: An Ancient Epic Poem* (1763). A collection, attributing the originals to a Gaelic poet named Ossian, appeared in 1765.

Some critics were sceptical of the Ossianic poems. **Samuel Johnson** and **David Hume** challenged their authenticity, and doubts were strengthened by Macpherson's failure to produce the originals. After his death a committee of inquiry headed by the novelist **Henry Mackenzie** concluded that he had treated the Gaelic poems in a free and selective fashion, adding much verse of his own invention. But such considerations did not check the enormous success and the wide influence of Macpherson's Ossianic poems. Their popularity spread beyond Britain to include Napoleon, Goethe and Herder among admirers. By turning attention to wild nature, the mythic past and folk culture, the poems played a crucial role in the emergence of **Romanticism** and, in particular, of the **Celtic revival**.

After his Ossianic poems, Macpherson published mainly historical works: *An Introduction to the History of Great Britain and Ireland* (1771); *The History of Great Britain from the Restoration to the Accession of the House of Hanover* (1775); and *Original Papers: Containing the Secret History of Great Britain from the Restoration to the Accession of the House of Hanover* (also 1775), for which he was paid £3000. A prose version of the *Iliad* appeared in 1773. Macpherson entered Parliament in 1780, acquired the estate of Belville in Inverness, where he died, and was buried in Westminster Abbey.

**Macpherson, Jay** 1931– Canadian poet. Born in England, she emigrated to Canada at the age of nine. She was an undergraduate in Ottawa and took her MA and PhD at the University of Toronto during the 1950s and early 1960s. She is a professor of English at Victoria College, Toronto. Her first poems were published in 1949 and as a graduate student she was the publisher of a Canadian poetry series, Emblem Books, which included the work of **Dorothy Livesay**, Alden Nowlan and **Al Purdy**. During the same period her *Nineteen Poems* (1952) and *O Earth Return* (1954) appeared. These were collected in her poetic cycle, *The Boatman* (1957), which won a Governor General's award for poetry. In 1974 her second collection, *Welcoming Disaster*, appeared, and the two books were republished as *Poems Twice Told* (1981). Macpherson's very concentrated allusive lyrics swing confidently within the tradition of English poetry, supplemented by the oral tradition of ballads and nursery rhymes. Her fascination with biblical and classical myth and its continuities as realized through the poetic imagination suggests her double affinities with European modernism and the Canadian mythopoeic tradition as exemplifed by **Northrop Frye** and **James Reaney**. Her idiosyncratic voice with its elusive mixture of the comic and the sinister and its evocation of duplicitous female archetypes has been an important influence on contemporary Canadian poets, especially **Margaret Atwood**. Macpherson's Canadianness is eclectic, and her imaginative response to landscape finds its overt expression not in her poetry but in her scholarly study, *The Spirit of Solitude: Conventions and Continuities in Late Romance* (1982), which in its epilogue explores Canadian pastoral with the same subtle sense of transformations to be found in her poetry.

*McTeague: A Story of San Francisco* A novel by **Frank Norris**, published in 1899. McTeague (Mac) practises dentistry, though he has never attended dental college or obtained a licence. He is a bear-like man who appreciates little beyond the physical pleasures of eating, drinking and smoking. When his friend Marcus Schouler brings Trina Sieppe to have her tooth fixed, Mac experiences another physical desire – the sexual – which he accommodates by courting and marrying Trina.

Shortly before the wedding Trina learns that she has won $5000 in a lottery. Marcus, who had previously entertained notions of marrying Trina himself, now becomes jealous of Mac's good fortune. The newlyweds live happily enough for a while, though Trina becomes miserly. The tension between Mac and Marcus erupts at a picnic; they wrestle like animals, and Mac breaks Marcus's arm. Marcus takes his revenge by informing on Mac that he is practising dentistry without a licence. Forced to give up his trade, Mac works for a while making dental instruments. When he loses that job also, he has to get money for tobacco, beer and food from Trina, who jealously guards her hoard. Theirs is now a sado-masochistic relationship: Mac beats Trina or bites her fingers to get her to give him the money, and she takes a perverse pleasure in this treatment. Eventually, he beats her to death and runs off with her hoard of gold coins.

He flees to the gold mines in the hills where he grew up, but is easily recognizable because he takes his canary and its gold cage with him. Having abandoned his job in a mine, he encounters a prospector and together they discover a rich vein of gold, but he senses that he is being pursued and moves on towards Death Valley. Marcus, who has joined the posse searching for him, tracks him down there. They fight, and Mac kills him, but not before Marcus has handcuffed himself to Mac. The novel ends with Mac (who still has his canary, but no water) handcuffed to the corpse in the middle of Death Valley.

**Madame Delphine** A short novel by **George Washington Cable**, published in 1881, which tells the story of Delphine Carraze, a quadroon, who lives in 19th-century New Orleans with her daughter Olive. Olive's father, who was white, had left his wife and daughter his property when he died, which was against Louisiana law. Olive falls in love with the banker Ursin Lemaitre, a white man who associates with the pirate Jean Lafitte. A marriage is arranged through Père Jerome, but Lemaitre's affairs come under investigation and he goes into hiding. His friends seize the opportunity to break off what they regard as his disastrous commitment to the daughter of the quadroon. Madame Delphine then declares that Olive is not her daughter, but rather a white woman's child she was given to foster. The marriage takes place. The story ends as Madame Delphine confesses to Père Jerome that she lied for her daughter's sake; she dies as the priest grants her absolution.

**Madge, Charles (Henry)** 1912– Poet and sociologist. Born in Johannesburg, he was educated at Winchester and Magdalene College, Cambridge, and worked as a reporter on *The Daily Mirror* in 1935–6. With Humphrey Jennings he founded Mass Observation in 1937. After social and economic research and planning during World War II, he became a social development officer (1947–50) and then Professor of Sociology at Birmingham University (1950–70). A notable poet of the 1930s, Madge was a Marxist influenced by both **Auden** and the surrealist movement; some of his prose-poems, including 'Bourgeois News', and longer lyrics such as 'The Storming of the Brain' are imaginatively original. His two collections of poetry are *The Disappearing Castle* (1937) and

*The Father Found* (1941). He has published a number of sociological studies, including Mass Observation surveys and (with P. Willmott) *Inner City Poverty in Paris and London* (1981).

**Maggie: A Girl of the Streets** A novel by **Stephen Crane**, privately printed in 1893 under the pseudonym Johnston Smith and entitled simply *A Girl of the Streets*. Set in the Bowery area of New York City, it describes the sordid and almost hopeless existence of Maggie Johnson. As children she and her brothers are alternately neglected and abused by their drunkard parents, and her baby brother Tommie dies as a result of this mistreatment. Her other brother, Jimmie, grows up to be a truck driver, but like his parents he is coarse, cynical, and drinks too much. Her father dies and her mother becomes known to the police for her frequent bouts of drunkenness. Maggie, who dreams of a better life, works in a collar-and-cuff factory and falls in love with a bartender friend of her brother's called Pete. After he seduces and abandons her, her mother and brother disown her. She tries to survive by becoming a prostitute, but eventually drowns herself.

**magic realism** The exact provenance of the term is disputed, but it probably originated in the question posed by the Cuban novelist Alejo Carpentier: 'What is the story of Latin America if not a chronicle of the marvellous in the real?' It was first employed as a literary definition by the American critic Alastair Reid, and referred then to the large body of spectacular, fantastic fiction produced in South American countries after World War II. This powerful and fecund outpouring of a nascent literary autonomy paralleled such nations' newly-won political independence, and came to be known as 'el boum'. Major exponents of 'lo real maravilloso' included Miguel Angel Asturias, Alejo Carpentier, Carlos Fuentes, Julio Cortázar, Mario Vargas Llosa and Gabriel García Márquez, whose novel *One Hundred Years of Solitude* (trans. G. Rabassa 1970) is generally regarded as the paradigm of magic realism.

The genre is characterized by the juxtaposition of apparently reliable, realistic reportage and extravagant fantasy: Márquez's novel will at one moment narrate the building of a new banana-processing plant, at another describe a woman visibly ascending to heaven. While there is a certain inscrutable playfulness to magic realism (Márquez is recorded as proposing that 'you can get people to believe anything if you tell it convincingly enough'), its method was first conceived, more importantly, as a response to the nature of South American reality. In countries previously ruled despotically as colonies and subsequently negotiating independence with no long-established institutions or freedoms, the fact that information can easily be manipulated or even commandeered by power groups makes truth a far more provisional, relative entity – relativism which magic realism both mimics and exploits through its own merging of realism and fantasy. Indeed, the genre's further assumption – demonstrated well in Márquez's recent fable about the responsibility for a mysterious crime, *Chronicle of a Death Foretold* (trans. G. Rabassa 1982) – is that truth is best viewed as a communal, collaborative construct, rather than as residing in the integrity of individual perceptions, whose authority tends merely to that of caprice and rumour. Such emphasis, implying the limitation of individual responsibility and the quixotic unpredictability of fate, makes magic realism an essentially comic genre.

Magic realism has since been identified in other literatures, such as in the work of the Czech novelist Milan Kundera, and the Italian Italo Calvino. The principal examples in British fiction are the novels of the Anglo-Indian writer **Salman Rushdie**. In Kundera's *The Book of Laughter and Forgetting* (trans. M. H. Heim 1982) and *The Unbearable Lightness of Being* (trans. M. H. Heim 1984), or Rushdie's *Midnight's Children* (1981) and *Shame* (1983), the authors use magic realism for sharp political satire in protest at the restrictions placed on information and truth after the Prague Spring or during India's 1977 Emergency, but also for wilful tall-story-telling, in a celebration of the imaginative freedom available in writing.

In the European tradition, it is possible to see Rabelais and Kafka as precursors of the magic realist idiom, while Rushdie's work points back through the English novel to **Sterne**'s *Tristram Shandy*, **Kipling**'s *Kim* and the major novels of **Dickens**.

Other examples of magic realism in recent British fiction are **Graham Swift**'s novel *Waterland* (1983), **Angela Carter**'s *Nights at the Circus* (1984) and the Australian writer **Peter Carey**'s *Illywhacker* (1985).

**Maginn, William** 1793–1842 Journalist. Born in Cork, he attended Trinity College, Dublin, and worked as a schoolmaster before joining the staff of *Blackwood's Magazine* to form one of a gifted trio with **John Gibson Lockhart** and **John Wilson**. He is believed to have suggested the idea for the *Noctes Ambrosianae* dialogues which became so popular a feature of *Blackwood's*. His own contributions to the journal were under the pseudonym of Ensign O'Doherty. A lively and witty journalist, Maginn went to London in 1823 and in 1830 helped Hugh Fraser to launch *Fraser's Magazine*, in which his *Homeric Ballads* and *Illustrious Literary Characters* appeared. He was the model for Captain Shandon in **Thackeray**'s *The History of Pendennis*.

*Magnalia Christi Americana* **Cotton Mather**'s ecclesiastical history of New England, *The Great Works of Christ in America*, was published in London in 1702. Mather began planning his history in 1693 and worked on it throughout the 1690s, during which time some chapters were published separately. It is divided into seven parts: a history of New England's settlement; biographies of governors; biographies of ministers; a history of Harvard College, including biographies of eminent graduates; a description of New England church practices; a collection of instances of special providences in New England; and an account of New England's 'Wars of the Lord', or conflicts with heretics, Indians, and other 'subversives'. Mather's General Introduction, with its Virgilian echoes, announces his epic subject: the work is intended to be a comprehensive and (especially for its European audience) celebratory account, a vision of a providentially guided, Christian New England. Mather consulted and cited numerous original documents for he had access to the papers of many of the actors in his history; as such, the *Magnalia* is a doubly valuable historical document.

*Magnyficence* A morality play by **John Skelton**, first published in 1530 but probably performed in *c.*1516. It owes something to Skelton's experience as tutor to the future Henry VIII and more to his perception of himself as *orator regius*. The central character, tempted by such characters as Cloaked Collusion and Crafty Conveyance, must learn from Adversity, Poverty and Despair to trust more in the advice of Sad Circumspection and Perseverance how best to regulate both himself and those who depend on him. The play is very long and too infrequently relieved by lively encounters.

**Mahapatra, Jayanta** 1928– Indian poet. He was born in Cuttack, Orissa, and has lived there all his life. He was educated at the University of Patna and is by profession a teacher of physics. He writes both in English and Oriya, but it is as an outstanding writer in English that he has received international recognition. His best collections of poetry include *A Rain of Rites* (1976), *Waiting* (1979), *The False Start* (1980), *Relationship* (1980), and *Life Signs* (1983). His poems are wide-ranging in style but all have a close response to the landscape and smells of Mahapatra's part of India.

**Mahon, Derek** 1941– Irish poet. Born in Belfast, Mahon was educated at the Royal Belfast Academical Institution and Trinity College, Dublin, graduating in 1965. He has worked as a schoolteacher, a journalist, scriptwriter and reviewer. He was Visiting Writer at the New University of Ulster at Coleraine in

1977 and held the same position in Trinity College, Dublin, in 1985–6. He now lives in County Cork.

Mahon first came to prominence as one of the leading members of the 'Northern Poets', along with **Seamus Heaney** and **Michael Longley**, in Belfast in the 1960s. Urban and urbane, his poetry is deeply influenced by **Louis MacNeice**, although perhaps stricter in its formality and bleaker in its implications than MacNeice's work. The Northern Irish crisis has deepened its native sense of estrangement and doom, goading him to question the relationship between poetry and public troubles.

His chief collections are *Night-Crossing* (1968), *Lives* (1972), *The Snow Party* (1975), *The Hunt By Night* (1982) and *Antarctica* (1985). Some important changes were made for the collection *Poems 1962–1978* (1979). Mahon also edited *The Sphere Book of Modern Irish Poetry* (1979) and translated Molière's *L'École des Maris* as *High Time* (1984).

**Mahony, Francis Sylvester** 1804–62 Poet under the pseudonym of 'Father Prout'. Born in County Cork, Ireland, Father Prout was educated at Jesuit centres in Amiens, Paris and Rome. A scandal at Clongoweswood, Ireland, where he had a teaching position, forced his resignation. However, he eventually acquired priestly orders and briefly exercised spiritual functions in London. In the 1830s a friendship with **William Maginn** led to contributions to *Fraser's Magazine*, the most famous being *The Reliques of Father Prout*, a pot-pourri of writings about the life of a parish priest interspersed with literary dialogues, verse translations, prose and the supposed discovery of original stanzas in French, Latin and Greek of the songs and verses of such popular melodists as **Thomas Moore** – all showing the quirky, capricious nature of Father Prout's gifts. Witty, well-informed classically, a literary jester who once described himself as 'an Irish potato seasoned with Attic salt', Father Prout had a sentimental side as well. His last years were passed in Paris as correspondent for *The Globe*. This eccentric man is perhaps best remembered for his poem 'The Bells of Shandon'.

*Maid Marian* A novel by **Thomas Love Peacock**, published in 1822. In contrast to his earlier novels, it uses the framework of historical romance, introducing the characters of **Robin Hood** and Richard I into a satire on oppression and extreme doctrines of social order. Coming hard on the heels of **Sir Walter Scott's** *Ivanhoe* (1819), which had introduced Robin Hood as Robin of Locksley, Peacock's novel confirmed the Romantics' interest in the legendary outlaw and contributed much to his present image in popular culture.

*Maid's Tragedy, The* A tragedy by **Beaumont** and **Fletcher**, performed by the **King's Men** in *c.* 1610 and published in 1619. It is a sensational piece, bordering in at least one scene on the pornographic.

Amintor, betrothed to the Lord Chamberlain's daughter Aspatia, is ordered by the king to marry Evadne, sister of Amintor's friend Melantius. On the wedding night, Evadne reveals to Amintor that she is the king's mistress. Shattered but loyal, Amintor conceals the fact, but Melantius discovers the truth, compels Evadne to kill the king and takes possession of the citadel. The rejected Aspatia, disguised as her own brother, provokes Amintor into killing her in a duel. With the king dead, Evadne hopes to persuade Amintor to accept her. When he refuses, she kills herself, as does Amintor on discovering that he has killed Aspatia. Melantius, who has himself contemplated suicide, is pardoned by the new king.

**Mailer, Norman** 1923– American novelist and journalist, born in Long Branch, New Jersey, raised in Brooklyn, and educated at Harvard. He served in the Pacific during World War II and drew upon this experience for *The Naked and the Dead* (1948); an uncompromisingly harsh war novel which is also a bitter commentary on American society. The book made Mailer famous on both sides of the Atlantic. His critical view of society also informed *Barbary Shore* (1951) and *The Deer Park* (1955, dramatized in 1967). *Advertisements for Myself*

Norman Mailer.

(1959) is a collection of stories and essays linked by autobiographical sketches. He excels at what has been called 'the new journalism', a form which he helped to create, which takes actual events and submits them to imaginative transformation. In this mode he registered the transformation of American sensibility in *An American Dream* (1965), *Why Are We In Vietnam?* (1967) and *Armies of the Night* (1968). The last of these, sub-titled 'History as a Novel, The Novel as History', has as its subject the 1967 protest march on the Pentagon; it won both a National Book Award and a Pulitzer Prize in 1969. Mailer's subsequent work includes *Miami and the Siege of Chicago* (1969), *The Prisoner of Sex* (1971), *Marilyn: A Biography* (1973), a study of Marilyn Monroe, *The Executioner's Song* (1979, Pulitzer Prize), a recreation of the events surrounding the execution of convicted killer Gary Gilmore, *Ancient Evenings* (1983) and *Tough Guys Don't Dance* (1984).

***Main Street*** A novel by **Sinclair Lewis**, published in 1920, and his first great success. Carol Milford, after working as a librarian in St Paul for three years, marries Dr Will Kennicott and moves to the small town of Gopher Prairie, Minnesota. She attempts to start an experimental theatre and a discussion group on the appreciation of poetry, but meets only resistance and is finally ostracized by the residents. Her growing sense of discontent is exacerbated by her unsophisticated husband. The story ends with her abandonment of her progressive aspirations and her submission to the complacent values of the small Midwestern town.

***Main-Travelled Roads*** A collection of short stories by **Hamlin Garland**, it comprised just six stories when it first appeared in 1891. Three more were added to the 1899 edition, and a further two to the final edition of 1922. All of them depict life in the rural Midwest as something drab and monotonous which crushes the spirit out of many of those who live it. 'Under the Lion's Paw', one of the original six stories, is a naturalistic tale about the economic survival of the fittest, or (as the narrator makes clear) of the most ruthless. In 'Up the Coulee' an actor returns to the Midwestern farm where he grew up, and sees with fresh eyes the brutality of the life his family leads. Contrasted with the harshness and squalid poverty are the 'silent heroism' of some of the characters and the panoramic beauty of the prairies.

**Mais, Roger** 1905–55 Jamaican novelist. Born in the Blue Mountains area and variously employed after leaving school, he was politically awakened by the Kingston riots of 1938. All his writings concentrate on what he called 'the dreadful condition of the working classes'. Social-realist accounts of human despair in the Kingston slums thus characterize his collections, *Face and Other Stories* (1942) and *And Most Of All Man* (1943), and the novels, *The Hills Were Joyful Together* (1953) and *Brother Man* (1954); without ideological compromise, the more fluid, non-realist *Black Lightning* (1955) suggests that poverty and suffering do not totally preclude fulfilment.

**Maitland, Sir Richard** 1496–1586 Lawyer, statesman and poet. Maitland studied at St Andrews and Paris, served under James V and was Keeper of the Great Seal to Mary Queen of Scots (1562–7). He collected examples of Scottish poetry in the Maitland Folio (begun *c.*1570), continued by his daughter in the Maitland Quarto. These collections, second in importance only to those made by **George Bannatyne**, contain Maitland's own poems (mainly satires and reflections on the disturbed state of Scotland) as well as poems by **William Dunbar**, **Gavin Douglas** and **Robert Henryson**. The manuscripts passed into several hands, including those of **Pepys**, and are now in Magdalene College, Cambridge. A selection was printed in 1786.

***Major Barbara*** A play by **George Bernard Shaw**, first performed at the **Royal Court Theatre**, London, in 1905.

Major Barbara, daughter of the armaments manufacturer Andrew Undershaft, has joined the Salvation Army in revolt against her father's profession. Quite as much a rebel against the conventions of society represented by his wife and son as Barbara is, Undershaft weakens her faith, not only by argument, but also by showing her the model conditions in which his workers live. Barbara is forced to realize that her own fight against poverty is less successful than her father's.

**Makculloch manuscript** One of the earliest Scottish manuscripts extant, containing readings of three poems by **Robert Henryson** and one by **William Dunbar**. It was written in 1477 in Louvain by Magnus Makculloch.

**Malamud, Bernard** 1914–86 American novelist, born and educated in New York City, the son of immigrant Russian parents. His first novel, *The Natural* (1952), deals with baseball as a realm of American heroism and myth. *The Assistant* (1957) is about a poor New York Jewish shopkeeper who takes on a delinquent Italian-American youth as a helper; the young man comes to look on his employer as a father, but the powerful emotional bonds between them are complicated by cultural barriers. His next novels, *A New Life* (1961), *The Fixer* (1966) and *Pictures of Fidelman* (1969), all explore aspects of the personal struggle involved in the Jewish experience. *The Fixer*, the story of a Russian Jew falsely accused of murder, won the National Book Award and the Pulitzer Prize. Later novels are *The Tenants* (1971), *Dubin's Lives* (1979) and *God's Grace* (1982). Malamud's short stories are collected in *The Magic Barrel* (1958), *Idiots First* (1963) and *Rembrandt's Hat* (1973).

**Malcontent, The** A play by **John Marston**, performed by both a **boys' company** and, with revisions probably by **John Webster**, an adult company in 1604, though it may have been first produced a few years earlier. It is commonly regarded as Marston's most accomplished play.

Altofronto, Duke of Genoa, has lost his throne to the usurper, Pietro, but has returned to court disguised as Malevole, a philosopher-buffoon licensed to speak his mind. His ally in the deception is Mendoza, Pietro's first minister. But Mendoza is an ambitious rogue, who has seduced Pietro's willing wife Aurelia and now has his eyes on Altofronto/Malevole's wife Maria. Malevole warns Pietro that Mendoza is plotting against him and persuades him to go into hiding. He then announces that Pietro is dead. Mendoza seizes the throne, banishes Aurelia and plans to rid himself of Malevole. The usurped Duke outwits Mendoza by revealing himself to Pietro in his true guise as Altofronto, and Mendoza's duplicity is exposed during a ball at the ducal palace.

**Malet, Lucas** The pseudonym used by Mary Kingsley (1852–1931), daughter of **Charles Kingsley**, for her published work, most of it fiction. Among her novels, *The Wages of Sin* (1891) and *The History of Sir Richard Calmady* (1901) were highly popular.

**Mallet, David** *c.*1705–65    Poet. Originally called Malloch, he was educated at Edinburgh University and went to London as a tutor in 1723. There he anglicized his name and succeeded in gaining entrance to the circle of friends surrounding **Alexander Pope**. With **James Thomson** he collaborated on a masque, *Alfred* (1740), which is now remembered only for 'Rule Britannia', in fact contributed by Thomson but claimed by Mallet. Mallet himself is remembered for *William and Margaret* (1723), a forerunner of Gothic and Romantic verse developed from the fragment of an old ballad. He was also literary executor to **Henry St John, Viscount Bolingbroke**.

**Mallock, W[illiam] H[urrell]** 1849–1923 Conservative thinker. The nephew of **J. A. Froude** and **Richard Hurrell Froude**, he was born at Cheriton Bishop in Devon and educated at Balliol College, Oxford, where he

won the Newdigate Prize for Poetry. His output of essays, political studies, poetry and fiction was united by his defence of traditional values against liberal theology, the progress of science and new political ideologies. He is chiefly remembered for two satirical works which, in a manner reminiscent of **Thomas Love Peacock**, bring together fictional characters based on famous contemporaries to debate the issues of the day. *The New Republic, or, Culture, Faith, and Philosophy in an English Country House* (1877) pits the views of **Ruskin**, with which Mallock sympathized, against those of **T. H. Huxley**, **Benjamin Jowett**, **Matthew Arnold** and **Walter Pater**. *The New Paul and Virginia, or, Positivism on an Island* (1878–9) – its title referring to Bernardin de Saint-Pierre's novel *Paul et Virginie* (1787) – takes Huxley, **John Tyndall**, **Frederic Harrison** and **Harriet Martineau** as its particular targets.

**Malone, Edmond** 1741–1812 Scholar. Born in Dublin and educated at Trinity College, he entered the Middle Temple in 1763. He met **Johnson**, who became a lifelong friend, in 1765. **George Steevens**, who gave him early encouragement, later dropped him. Malone spent some years on the Continent and back in Ireland before inheriting sufficient money to be able to settle in London in 1776. He then moved in high literary circles. He was a friend of **Reynolds**, who had painted him in 1774 and whose writings he was to publish with a biographical memoir in 1797; of **Burke**, who dedicated his *Reflections on the Revolution in France* to him; and of **Horace Walpole**. He published an edition of **Goldsmith** in 1780.

Malone was devoted to the methodical study of **Shakespeare**. His *An Attempt to Ascertain the Order in Which the Plays of Shakespeare Were Written* was published by Steevens in the second volume of his own edition of Shakespeare in 1778. In 1780 Malone published his two-volume *Supplement* to the Johnson–Steevens edition of 1778, with the first critical edition of **Shakespeare's Sonnets** together with editions of the poems and items from the **Shakespeare apocrypha**. He added two appendixes to his *Supplement* (1783) and new annotations to Isaac Reed's third edition of the Johnson–Steevens *Shakespeare* (1785). It was a dispute about these annotations that led to the break with Steevens. Meanwhile, Malone was at work on his great edition of Shakespeare, which appeared in 10 volumes (or 11, since the first volume is in two parts) in 1790. It is important bibliographically and for its abundance of information about Shakespeare's life and the theatre of his time. Its 'Historical Account of the English Stage' laid the foundations of English stage history.

Shakespeare did not monopolize Malone's efforts. He played an important part in exposing the forgeries of **Thomas Chatterton** and, later, **William Henry Ireland**. In 1785 he assisted **Boswell** with *The Journal of a Tour to the Hebrides* and over the following six years he helped with the preparation of *The Life of Samuel Johnson*, later editing it from its third (1799) to its sixth (1811) edition.

Despite the information he had amassed in his earlier work, Malone had still not produced the biography of Shakespeare which **Edward Capell** had longed for. He resumed research in 1793, but found himself diverted by work on the **Aubrey** manuscripts in Oxford, his duties as Reynolds's executor and the preparation of a four-volume edition of **Dryden**'s prose (1800), which included an important life of the poet. His sight failed in the early 1800s and he died without finishing his biography of Shakespeare. Boswell's son made some order out of Malone's completed work, notes and revisions: the 21-volume *Plays and Poems of William Shakespeare* appeared in 1821.

See also **Shakespeare: performance and criticism**.

**Malory, Sir Thomas** d. ?1471 Author of the long prose work usually known as *Le Morte Darthur*, a title taken from the epilogue of **Caxton**'s edition (1485). Malory's identity is uncertain and several possible figures have been suggested, but there is not enough evidence to make a definite identification. The author himself provides the only certain information: that his name was Thomas Malory, that he was a knight, and that he wrote most if not all of his work while imprisoned in Newgate gaol, where he completed it in 1469–70. *Le Morte Darthur* is divided into eight tales in 21 books, but is usually taken as a single work. It is the greatest of the medieval prose romances, distilling both English and French sources. It has inspired many later translations and adaptations, such as **Tennyson**'s *Idylls of the King*. See also **Arthurian literature**.

**Malouf, David** 1934– Australian novelist and poet. Born in Brisbane of Lebanese and English parents, he was educated at Brisbane grammar school and the University of Queensland, where he taught for two years after graduating. He spent the next decade in England and Italy. In 1968 he returned to Australia and lectured in English at the University of Sydney before once again leaving for Europe and settling in Tuscany. His movement between the two continents is reflected in similar oppositions in his writings. From his technically assured early poems onwards, his work has shown a habitual concern with juxtaposing opposed modes of existence and perception. He first achieved recognition as a poet and has published the volumes, *Bicycle and Other Poems* (1970), *Neigh-*

*bours in a Thicket* (1974), *The Year of the Foxes* (1979), *First Things Last* (1980), *Wild Lemons* (1981) and *Selected Poems* (1981). He has since become better known as a novelist. All his fiction is concerned with artistic process and transformations of identity. *Johnno* (1975), the most conventional of his novels, explores the eponymous hero's rebellion against the constrictions of Brisbane society in the 1940s and 1950s through a comparatively straightforward autobiographical structure, but even here there is emphasis on multiple possibilities and on metaphor rather than literalism. *An Imaginary Life* (1978) and *Fly Away Peter* (1982), which opposes the calm of a Queensland bird sanctuary with the horrors of World War I trench warfare, are both fables about the imagination's capacity for transforming experience and perception. The title-novella of *Child's Play* (1982), which deals with an Italian terrorist planning to assassinate a famous writer, is another study of consciousness in transition. *Harland's Half Acre* (1984) is an account of an artist's attempt to regain the land lost by his ancestors, a goal he eventually achieves through his painting rather than actual repossession.

**Malthus, Thomas Robert** 1766–1834 Economist. Born near Guildford in Surrey, he was educated at Jesus College, Cambridge, became a fellow of his college, was ordained and appointed curate of Albury, Surrey, in 1798. In the same year he published his famous essay, *On the Principle of Population As It Affects the Future Improvement of Society*. Its central proposition was that population increases geometrically while food supply increases mathematically; population levels would outgrow the means of subsistence. After a period of research on the Continent, Malthus published a second edition in 1803. His theory provoked a storm of controversy, largely because of his apparent acceptance (in the first edition) of poverty and disease as necessary checks on population growth, but exerted a lasting influence on 19th-century thought. Malthus's later writings were directly concerned with economics, notably *An Investigation of the Cause of the Present High Price of Provisions* (1800), *Observations on the Effect of the Corn Laws* (1814) and *The Principles of Political Economy* (1820).

**Maltz, Albert** 1908–85 American playwright, novelist and short-story writer, born in Brooklyn, New York. After graduating from Columbia in 1930 he attended the Yale School of Drama, where one of his fellow students was George Sklar. They collaborated on two plays, *Merry Go Round*, which was produced in 1932, and *Peace on Earth*, which was the first production of the newly-formed Theatre Union in 1933. Maltz followed this with another play, *Black Pit*

(1935). His prose fiction includes *The Way Things Are* (stories, 1938), *The Cross and the Arrow* (1944), *The Journey of Simon McKeever* (1949), *A Long Day in a Short Life* (1956), *A Tale of One January* (1966), and *Afternoon in the Jungle* (stories, 1971). He has also written numerous screenplays, of which perhaps the best known are *This Gun for Hire* (1942), *Destination Tokyo* (1943), *The House I Live In* (1945) and, with Marvin Wald, *The Naked City* (1948).

**Mamet, David** 1947– US dramatist. Born in Flossmoor, Illinois, he was educated at Goddard College. His first play, *Lakeboat*, produced in 1970, was followed by several others treating the social and sexual mores of the American experience of Vietnam, including *Duck Variations* (1972), *Squirrels* (1974) and *Sexual Perversity in Chicago* (1974). He is best known for *American Buffalo* (1975), a witty but scathing attack on the decline of American values from the perspective of a Vietnam War veteran. His other plays include *The Woods* (1977), *All Men Are Whores* (1977), *Dark Pony* (1977), *Shoeshine* (1979) and *Glengarry Glen Ross* (1983; Pulitzer Prize 1984).

**Man and Superman** A comedy by **George Bernard Shaw**, first performed in London in 1905 and published in 1908. Shaw's ideas about the 'life force' are embodied in the characters of the battling lovers, Ann Whitefield and John Tanner.

Under her father's will, Ann has two guardians, the respectable Roebuck Ramsden and the shockingly progressive John Tanner. She decides to marry Tanner and the decision, however Tanner may struggle to evade it, proves irresistible. Some of the play's liveliest encounters occur in Spain, whither Tanner has fled to escape Ann. It is in the Sierra Nevada that he dreams the scene, sometimes omitted and certainly separable from the play in performance, 'Don Juan in Hell'.

**Man of Feeling, The** A novel by **Henry Mackenzie**, published anonymously in 1771. Despite the label 'sentimental novel', it has a pervasive and gentle irony. The quixotic hero, 'rather eccentric', leaves home to seek his fortune and is educated in the harsh realities of the world. His good heart and ready sympathies are no protection against its cheats. The novel is a critique of acquisitive society and a warning against being taken in by appearances. Harley is an innocent abroad. Like his predecessor Roderick Random, Harley is robbed by a pair of professional card-sharpers and befriends a prostitute who has known happier days. She and the lower-class characters, including a fortune-telling beggar, all speak with the same antithetical orotundity, the diction of 18th-century moral discourse. In Bedlam Harley meets a girl who has run mad

*Man and Superman.* A scene from the first performance of Shaw's comedy in 1905 at the Royal Court Theatre, London. Lillah McCarthy as Ann Whitefield, Granville-Barker as John Tanner. Victoria & Albert Theatre Museum, London.

for love. The narrative is distanced by the use to which poor Harley's papers are put: a clergyman is using them as wadding for his gun. **Sir Walter Scott** admired the book's 'tone of moral pathos' and its representation of those 'finer feelings to which ordinary hearts are callous'.

**Man of Law's Tale, The** See *Canterbury Tales, The.*

**Man of Mode, The**, *or, Sir Fopling Flutter* A comedy by **George Etherege**, his third and last play, produced in 1676 and published the same year. One of the first great Restoration comedies, it reflects society as seen through the brilliant personification of its types, who come together and separate, forming new pictures and dissolving into further pictures. It is not concerned only with the fashionable, for even the

Etherege's comedy, *The Man of Mode*, Act I, scene 1. Dorimant receiving Medley in his dressing room. Frontispiece to an edition of the play published in 1723. The play was first produced in 1676.

shoemaker and the orange-woman are sharply observed.

Among those present are: the poet Young Bellair and his love Emilia; the old-fashioned Lady Woodvill and the fashionable and wise Lady Townley; Dorimant, the finest of fine gentlemen (perhaps the **Earl of Rochester**), and his follower Medley; Harriet, beautiful and intelligent, who has the measure of Dorimant perfectly; Sir Fopling Flutter, a remarkable creation who, in **Dryden**'s words, is a 'Fool so nicely writ,/The Ladies wou'd mistake him for a Wit'. Dorimant's formidable wit makes him the major character in this passing parade, but he by no means has his own way entirely and in one scene the shoemaker makes short work of his attitudes. He has already discarded Loveit and Bellinda; Harriet is next on his list but this delightful heroine (if the play has a heroine at all) is more than a match for Dorimant, who falls in love with her.

**Manciple's Tale, The** See *Canterbury Tales, The*.

**Mandeville, Bernard de** 1670–1733 Satirist. A Dutchman, he was born at Dort and educated at the Erasmus School in Rotterdam and the University of Leyden, but came to England to practise medicine. He is remembered for his satire in doggerel verse, first published as *The Grumbling Hive, or, Knaves Turn'd Honest* in

1705 and reissued with prose commentaries as *The Fable of the Bees, or, Private Vices, Public Benefits* (1714 and 1723). A second part was added in 1728, and both parts appeared together in 1734. Its mordant view of society as a hive in which mankind flourished through mutual greed, written in deliberate contradiction to the optimistic philosophers of the age, provoked replies from **William Law** in *Remarks on a Late Book Entitled The Fable of the Bees* (1723) and **George Berkeley** in *Alciphron* (1732). Mandeville's other writings include *A Modest Defence of Public Stews, or, An Essay upon Whoring, as it is Now Practis'd in These Kingdoms* (1724), *An Enquiry into the Causes of the Frequent Executions at Tyburn* (1725) and *An Enquiry into the Origin of Honour, and the Usefulness of Christianity in War* (1732).

**Mandeville's Travels** (or *The Travels of Sir John Mandeville*) An account in Middle English prose of travels through Europe and the Near East, purporting to be the work of Sir John Mandeville; the identity of the real author is unknown. Originally written in French, possibly at Liège, *c*.1357, it became immensely popular and was translated into many European languages. Its chief source is a series of itineraries translated into French by Jean de Long of St Omer completed in 1351, which included accounts of the

Pilgrims arriving by ship (above); other pilgrims approaching a city gate. A 14th-century illustration for *The Travels of Sir John Mandeville. Add. MS 24189, f.8.* British Library.

Holy Land by William of Boldensele (1336), of the East by Odoric of Pordenone (1330) and Haiton's *Fleurs des Histoires d'Orient* (before 1308). 'Mandeville' also used the encyclopaedia of Vincent de Beauvais (*c.*1250).

The narrator gives to his account a fictitious framework made up from details from the sources, saying he was born in St Albans and left on his travels on 29 September 1322, and that he wrote his account from memory when suffering from arthritic gout. The figure of Mandeville, one of the earliest fictitious narrators in English literature, gives the work some structural cohesion; it is otherwise a delightful and simply told series of unconnected descriptions and pieces of information. Mandeville describes interesting features of the terrain, flora and fauna and the customs of the inhabitants of countries in Europe and the East together with some traditional stories and legends. Descriptions of legendary creatures appear alongside accounts containing a surprising proportion of accurate observation and scientific fact.

**Manfred** A dramatic poem by **Lord Byron**, written and published in 1817, in temporary interruption of work on the third canto of *Childe Harold's Pilgrimage*. Byron later explained that the poem had been inspired by the awesome scenery of the Alps.

Guilty of some mysterious crime which makes him an outcast from society, Manfred lives a solitary life in the Alps, tortured by remorse. He invokes the spirits of the universe but they do not offer him the oblivion he seeks. He makes a vain attempt to kill himself and then summons up the Witch of the Alps, so that he can visit the realm of Arimanes and the spirits of Evil; but he refuses to submit to them. At his bidding they call up the dead and he encounters the shade of Astarte, the sister whom he loved and whose death is the cause of his guilt. She tells him that he will die the next day. When the evil spirits come to claim him, Manfred rejects his compact with them and they disappear. Though he dies at the time Astarte foretold, his resolution to remain master of his fate never falters.

**Mangan, James Clarence** 1803–49 Poet. Born in Dublin of a poor family, Mangan was educated by a priest who instructed him in languages. He worked as a lawyer's clerk and later in the library of Trinity College while he contributed poems and translations to *The Dublin University Magazine*. Later he contributed verse to *The Nation*, the patriotic paper founded by Charles Gavan Duffy and Thomas Osborne Davis, and published *Anthologia Germanica*, translations from German poets (1845). *The Poets and Poetry of Munster* (1849) was called translations but is more correctly versions in English. He contributed to *Romances and Ballads of Ireland* (edited by E. Ellis, 1850) and left a version of the Irish satire *The Tribes of Ireland* by Aenghus O'Daly (1852). His best-known poems, 'Dark Rosaleen' and 'The Nameless One', are often found in collections of Irish verse.

**Manhattan Transfer** A novel by **John Dos Passos**, published in 1925, generally considered to be his first artistically mature work. It was here that he first employed the themes and techniques that came to characterize his fiction. The novel tells the stories of numerous characters who have in common only their status as New Yorkers, and who come together randomly, impersonally. Each chapter begins with passages comprising observations of city life, slogans, snatches of dialogue, phrases from advertisements, and newspaper headlines. These passages further emphasize that *Manhattan Transfer* is a 'collective' novel about the city of New York – about the shallowness, immorality, and mechanization of urban life – not simply the story of a few characters' lives.

The two most prominent figures are Ellen Thatcher and Jimmy Herf. The novel opens with Ellen's birth; it ends with a scene in which Jimmy, having left his job with the *Times* (a job that never fulfilled him) and having left Ellen (whom he married and with whom he has had a child), hitches a ride out of New York and thus makes his escape. At 18 Ellen marries John Oglethorpe, a bisexual whom she eventually divorces. She then falls in love with Stanwood Emery, an alcoholic playboy who marries someone else while drunk (he eventually dies in a fire); pregnant with Emery's child, she has an abortion. She then achieves success on the stage and marries Jimmy Herf. At the end of the novel she agrees to marry the self-serving lawyer George Baldwin, even though she does not love him.

**Manhire, Bill** 1946– New Zealand poet. Educated in Wellington and the UK, he teaches English language studies at the Victoria University of Wellington. Probably the outstanding younger poet in New Zealand today, he is deeply influenced by both contemporary English and American poets but remarkably free from any evidence of direct influence. A master of the nuances of his localized language, with a broad range of subject and reference, he is concerned with the domestic, the routines of ordinary living and quiet observation. His craftsmanship is of a high order, though never demonstrative. Volumes of verse include *The Elaboration* (1972), *How to Take Off Your Clothes at the Picnic* (1977), which contains some of his most characteristic work to date, *Good Looks*

(1982), and the brilliantly adventurous *Zoetropes* (1984).

**Manley, Delarivière (Mary)** 1663–1724 Novelist. Born in the Channel Islands, she was trapped into a bigamous marriage by her cousin, who then deserted her. In 1696 a comedy, *The Lost Lover*, and a tragedy, *The Royal Mischief*, were performed, the latter with rather more success. Her first **roman à clef**, and the earliest example of such a work in English, is *The Secret History of Queen Zarah and the Zarazians* (1705; second part 1711). Her most notorious work is *Secret Memoirs and Manners of Several Persons of Quality, of Both Sexes*, more usually known as *The New Atalantis* (2 vols., 1709). The scurrilous nature of this work was such that Mrs Manley, the publishers and the printer were all arrested, but throughout her examination she steadfastly asserted that the correspondence between real persons and the characters in her writings was entirely fortuitous. She was finally discharged. The following year she brought out two continuation volumes under the title, *Memoirs of Europe towards the Close of the Eighth Century*. In 1711 she took over the editorship of **The Examiner** from **Swift**, with whom she collaborated in a number of polemic pamphlets: *A Learned Comment upon Dr Hare's Excellent Sermon* (1711), *A True Narrative of What Pass'd at the Examination of the Marquis de Guiscard* (1711) and *A Modest Enquiry into the Reasons of the Joy Expressed by a Certain Set of People, upon the Spreading of a Report of Her Majesty's Death* (1714). In 1720 appeared *The Power of Love, in Seven Novels*, a collection of conventional romances.

**Manning, Olivia** 1908–80 Novelist. Born in Portsmouth, she spent much of her childhood in Ireland, making Dublin the setting of her first novel, *The Wind Changes* (1937). She married a British Council lecturer, R. D. Smith, in 1939 and joined him in Bucharest just as World War II broke out. Her wartime experiences there and in Athens, Egypt and Jerusalem form the basis of her major fictional achievement, six novels grouped into *The Balkan Trilogy* (1960–5) and *The Levant Trilogy* (1977–80). They trace the fate of a newly married English couple, Harriet and Guy Pringle. *The Great Fortune* (1960) and *The Spoilt City* (1962) show the gradual subordination of Bucharest to the Nazis, and *Friends and Heroes* (1965) describes the Pringles' flight to Egypt. The second trilogy (*The Danger Tree*, 1977, *The Battle Lost and Won*, 1978, and *The Sum of Things*, 1980) deals with the desert war in Egypt. While they are notable for their compassionate portrayal of Guy and Harriet's developing marriage, their multitudinous cast of often vivid minor characters and their understated tragicomedy, their major significance resides in the scope of historical event and detail which the whole sequence accumulates. Olivia Manning's other novels include *School for Love* (1951) and *The Doves of Venus* (1955); she also published two collections of short stories.

**Mannyng of Brunne, Robert** c.1283–1338 Author of **Handlynge Synne** and a verse **chronicle**, the *Story of England*. Born at Bourne in Lincolnshire in or before 1283, he was at Cambridge University in c.1300 and spent 15 years as a Gilbertine canon at Sempringham Priory, Lincolnshire (c.1302–17). In 1303 he began his translation, *Handlynge Synne*, from the Anglo-Norman *Manuel des Peches* (c.1250–70) usually ascribed to William of Wadington. The work deals with self-examination to identify sin and prepare for confession, and is illustrated by numerous exempla. Mannyng usually follows his source faithfully but sometimes adapts exempla, and he adds 13 new stories. The *Story of England*, compiled in 1338, is a chronicle in two parts covering the periods from the Flood to the death of Caedwalla (689) and from then until the death of Edward I (1307). The first part is based on *Le Roman de Brut* of Wace, but also draws on Wace's source, **Geoffrey of Monmouth**'s *Historia Regum Britanniae*, on **Bede** and on the Anglo-Norman *Chronicle* of Peter Langtoft. The second section relies principally upon Langtoft's *Chronicle*, again with some additions from other sources, including **verse romances**.

**Mansfield, Katherine** Pseudonym of Kathleen Mansfield Beauchamp (1888–1923), writer of short stories. She was born in Wellington, New Zealand, and was sent to London in 1903 to complete her education at Queen's College. Returning to New Zealand in 1906 she became a wide-ranging reader and began to write. Several 'Vignettes' were accepted in the Australian monthly *Native Companion* in 1907, and in 1908 she returned to London determined on a literary career. She married George Bowden in 1909 but left him soon afterwards. At Bowden's suggestion she submitted some of her short pieces to A. R. Orage, editor of **The New Age**. These were accepted and Mansfield's relationship with the periodical continued.

After meeting **John Middleton Murry** in 1911 she began to publish in *Rhythm*, an *avant-garde* quarterly founded by Murry and Michael Sadleir in that year. Mansfield's health was poor, and like **D. H. Lawrence** (near whom she and Murry lived in Cornwall for some weeks in 1915) she discovered that she was suffering from tuberculosis. Despite periods of recuperation in the South of France, her health continued to decline. She and Murry were married in 1918, but in 1923 she died at Fontainebleau.

Katherine Mansfield is generally acknowledged as one of the finest writers of her period.

Critics have praised her penetrating and relentless intelligence, which is balanced by a delicate sense of form – qualities which ideally suited her chosen genre, the short story. Her first collection, *In a German Pension* (1911), was followed by *Prelude*, a story published singly in 1918, which like much of her best work was centred around her childhood in New Zealand and showed the influence of Chekhov. Others appeared in *Bliss and Other Stories* (1919), *The Garden Party and Other Stories* (1920) and *Other Stories* (1922), the last work published during her lifetime. Posthumous works included *Poems* (1923; edited by Murry), *Something Childish and Other Stories* (1924) and *A Fairy Story* (Stanford, 1932). *The Collected Stories of Katherine Mansfield* (1945) was an omnibus volume. Murry also edited *The Letters of Katherine Mansfield* (1928) and *Katherine Mansfield's Letters to John Middleton Murry: 1913–1922* (1951).

**Mansfield Park** A novel by **Jane Austen**, begun in 1811 and published in 1814.

Sir Thomas and Lady Bertram of Mansfield Park have two daughters, Maria and Julia, and two sons, Tom and Edmund. Fanny Price, niece of Lady Bertram and one of a large improvident family, is brought to live at Mansfield Park where she is patronized by three of her cousins, but finds a friend in Edmund.

When Sir Thomas leaves for the West Indies to look after his interests there, his children, on whom he has always impressed the need for manners and social (rather than moral) accomplishments, demonstrate the deficiencies in their upbringing. Fanny, now in her teens, refuses to take part in the self-indulgent flirtations of her cousins. Maria Bertram, engaged to Mr Rushworth, is attracted to Henry Crawford; his sister Mary fascinates Edmund Bertram. But Maria decides after all to marry Rushworth, whereupon Henry turns his attention to Fanny. When she refuses his proposal, Sir Thomas, now back at Mansfield, is highly displeased at her apparent foolishness.

The unhappy Fanny goes to visit her own family in Portsmouth and, distressed by the noise and disorder of her father's house, longs to be back at Mansfield Park. Meanwhile Maria, now Mrs Rushworth, runs off with Henry Crawford; Julia elopes with a Mr Yates. Edmund, who has taken orders, is still in subjection to Mary Crawford, but she makes it plain that she is not anxious to marry a clergyman. Edmund and Fanny eventually find happiness together, and it is clear that the rest of the characters are unlikely ever to do so.

**Many Inventions** A collection of 14 stories by **Rudyard Kipling**, published in 1893.

The locations, as well as the subject matter of the stories, are various. Of the six Indian tales, two concern characters who also appear in the collection **Soldiers Three**; another six are located wholly or partly in England. Different tales share underlying preoccupations which are characteristic of Kipling. In 'The Disturber of Traffic', the delusions and growing obsession of Dowse, the lonely lighthouse keeper in the Java Straits, are echoed in Charlie's uncertain states of mind in 'The Finest Story in the World'. Charlie's obsession, related to a sceptical narrator, is with the fragments of a story in his mind which then begins to recall moments of previous lives as a Roman galley slave and on a Viking ship. 'The Record of Badalia Herodsfoot' is a realistic account of the heroine's struggle for survival in the London slums of the 1890s. The ill-treatment of Badalia by her husband Tom, and her eventual death at his hands, is set against the life-enhancing story of her practical and unsentimental concern for the community she lives in. Badalia's code of conduct, personally learned and entailing responsibility to the social order, is shared with other of Kipling's heroes, notably one of the 'soldiers three', Ortheris. In 'His Private Honour', Ortheris's conduct is dictated by a code which is seen to transcend the limits of the army rule book.

**Marble Faun, The**, or, *The Romance of Monte Beni* A novel by **Nathaniel Hawthorne**, published in 1860 (in England under the title of *Transformation*). Kenyon and Hilda are two Americans studying art in Rome. With their friend Miriam, an artist, they meet an Italian nobleman named Donatello and notice that he resembles the Marble Faun sculpted by Praxiteles. Handsome, innocent and warm-hearted, Donatello falls in love with Miriam, but realizes that she is troubled by some secret from the past. There are several rumours circulating about Miriam, though none is proven: she may be the heiress of a Jewish banker fleeing from an unwanted marriage; she may be a German princess; she may be the mulatta daughter of a South American planter; or she may be the mistress of an English nobleman come to Italy to pursue her interest in art. Whichever, she is tormented by a mysterious Capuchin monk who has some connection with her past. One night the four friends take a walk among the hills of Rome; Donatello is enraged to find the Capuchin following them, and, perhaps encouraged by a gesture from Miriam, pushes him off a precipice. Unknown to Miriam and Donatello, Hilda witnesses the scene.

Donatello, horrified by what he has done, flees to his ancestral estate of Monte Beni. Miriam, sharing his guilt, follows him; they agree that they must both bear the consequences. He returns to Rome, gives himself up, and goes to prison; she embarks on a penitential pilgrimage. Hilda also remains troubled, feeling tainted by what she has witnessed; setting aside her Puritan training, she finds relief in a Catholic confessional and marries Kenyon. The secret of Miriam's past is never revealed. In the 'Postscript' to the novel, the narrator claims that to seek to know whether Donatello really is a faun, and who Miriam really is, would destroy the poetry and beauty of the story.

*Mardi and a Voyage Thither* A novel by **Herman Melville**, published in 1849. The narrator, Taji, and Jarl, an older seaman, desert their ship in a whaleboat. They encounter the brigantine *Parki*, which has been abandoned by all except a Polynesian couple, Samoa and Annatoo. The four live a contented life on board until the ship sinks during a storm and Annatoo is drowned. The three survivors take to the whaleboat and soon sight land on the horizon – the islands of Mardi. At this point the adventure tale gives way to something of an experimental allegory. The islands of Mardi represent a mythical or transcendental realm where Taji lives happily for a while with Yillah, a young woman he and his companions rescue from a priest who had intended to sacrifice her. In saving her Taji killed the priest, whose sons take their revenge by kidnapping her again. Taji sets out to find his lost love, accompanied by a king, a historian, a philosopher, and a poet. Their search takes them to many lands, whose societies are closely observed and discussed. The voyage is now generally seen as an allegorical exploration of the world of 1848, in which Dominora stands for Great Britain, Porpheero for Europe, and Vivenza for the USA. The travellers eventually reach the land of Serenia, which is ruled by Alma (Christ). The philosopher declares that Alma's doctrine of love is the ultimate wisdom, but Taji observes that man ignores the doctrine. Although his companions try to convince him to give it up, Taji continues his voyage – alone, still in search of what he has lost, still pursued by the priest's sons.

**Marechera, Dambudzo** 1955–87 Zimbabwean writer of fiction. Educated in a mission school, Marechera was later expelled from the University of Rhodesia and had an equally chequered career at New College, Oxford. His first book, *The House of Hunger* (1978), aroused great interest as a cry of distress from one of the new generation of African writers brought up against a background of war and injustice. It comprises a novella and several short stories. It won the Guardian Fiction Award in 1979. Marechera's second book, *Black Sunlight* (1980), is written with the same degree of uninhibited language and deals with the violent world of urban guerrillas in a disordered society. It remains to be seen whether Marechera's writing expressed the restlessness of his own mind or whether it will have a lasting place as the mouthpiece of an alienated generation of young Africans.

**Marie de France** d.*c*.1216 French poet who probably lived in England, writing in **Anglo-Norman** in the late 12th century. Her three surviving works, *Lais*, *Fables* and *Espurgatoire Saint Patrice*, are the oldest works which can definitely be attributed to a woman writer in England or France. Nothing certain is known about her besides her name, her nationality and statement of patronage found in her works. Conjectural identifications of her with historical figures are inconclusive, but the most plausible is that she was the illegitimate daughter of Godefroy d'Anjou, was abbess of Shaftesbury by 1181 and died *c*.1216.

The *Lais*, probably her first work and written before 1189, are a collection of 12 **Breton lays** preceded by a prologue defending literary activity. They are written in octosyllabic couplets. The lays, narratives of adventure with a central theme of love, vary in type and length from a mere snippet of the Tristan legend ('Le Chevrefoil') to the long and involved 'Eliduc'. The *Fables* are a collection of 102 Aesopic fables which she claims are based on an English translation by 'Alvrez' of a Latin collection. Neither the English nor Latin source survives, though the fables can be traced to various collections. The fables are introduced by a prologue and are in octosyllabic couplets. The *Espurgatoire Saint Patrice*, written after 1189 and apparently the last of the three, is a retelling of the popular legend of St Patrick's vision of purgatory.

*Marino Faliero* A tragedy by **Lord Byron**, published in 1821, when it was produced against his wishes at **Drury Lane**. It was one of two historical dramas set in Venice; the other, *The Two Foscari*, was published in the same year. Marino Faliero, Doge of Venice in the 14th century, is a haughty old man who has slighted Michele Steno, a gentleman of poor but distinguished family. Steno writes a gross lampoon on the Doge's chair of state; he is tried and punished by the Council of Forty but Faliero is furious at what he regards as a mild sentence. Faliero plots with malcontents to overthrow the constitution of Venice and take his revenge on the council. But the plot is exposed and Marino Faliero is beheaded on the staircase of the Doge's Palace.

*Marino Faliero* is also the title of a tragedy by **Swinburne** (1885) in which the old Doge is seen more uncritically as a symbol of liberty.

*Marius the Epicurean* A philosophical romance by **Walter Pater**, published in 1885. The story is set in ancient Rome during the time of the Antonine emperors, the zenith of the empire's greatness. The life of Marius is followed from his childhood to his education at Pisa and his adult life in Rome. Pater examines Marius's response to the philosophical influences of his time, to the Roman religion, to the brutal spectacles of the amphitheatre, finally to the growing power of Christianity. Although Marius does not become a Christian, he is strongly attracted by the high principles and commitment of his Christian friend Cornelius. He dies to save his friend's life and the Christian church regards him as a martyr.

**Mark, Jan[et] (Marjorie)** 1943– Children's novelist. She was born in Welwyn Garden City after the evacuation of the City of London Maternity Hospital during World War II, and educated in Ashford and at the Canterbury College of Art. The RAF base near her Norfolk home furnished the setting for her first novel, *Thunder and Lightnings* (1976), a finely observed and gently humorous story which won the Penguin–*Guardian* competition and the Carnegie Medal. *Handles* (1983), which won a second Carnegie Medal, also has a Norfolk setting. *Nothing To Be Afraid Of* (1980), and *Feet* (1983) are collections of short stories. Jan Mark's **science fiction** trilogy for older children, *The Ennead* (1978), *Divide and Rule* (1979) and *Aquarius* (1982), provides a bleak and despairing vision of a corrupt society and its victims.

**Markandaya, Kamala** 1924– Novelist. Born and educated in South India; as Mrs Kamala Purnaiya Taylor she has lived in Britain since her marriage. She is an impressive explorer of human consciousness and of the convolutions of intimate relationships, but her settings sometimes lack precision, and the dialogue across her social range from peasant to prince is not always adequately differentiated. *Nectar in a Sieve* (1954) elevates peasant subsistence to tragic stoicism. The heroine in *Some Inner Fury* (1955) renounces her English lover in the 1940s quit-India agitation; the artist in *Possession* (1963) deserts an English patroness to seek his Indian roots; *A Silence of Desire* (1960) probes the tensions between religious wife and agnostic husband, and in *The Coffer Dams* (1969) an English marriage is strained because the engineer husband and his wife hold opposed attitudes to Indians. In *A Handful of Rice* (1966) urban poverty utterly overwhelms individual effort, while a village forms the setting for the unfolding of young female consciousness in *Two Virgins* (1974). *The Golden Honeycomb* (1977), about a minor princely court, is marred by over-ambitious structuring and some prolixity, but *Pleasure City* (1982) admirably presents a sensitive Britisher and ingenious Indian villager coping with some on-the-spot effects of the historical process of neo-colonialism.

**Markham, Edwin** 1852–1940 American poet, born in Oregon City, Oregon. Although he had little formal education he became a schoolteacher and, inspired by the poets he read, began to write verse himself. His first poem, 'The Gulf of Night', appeared in 1880. His most famous piece, the title poem of his 1899 volume, *The Man With The Hoe and Other Poems*, was inspired by a painting by Millet. Both this collection and *Lincoln and Other Poems* (1901) are largely concerned with the degrading conditions of the American working classes. His other collections, which were less popular, include *California the Wonderful* (1915), *Gates of Paradise* (1920), *Ballad of the Gallows Bird* (1926), *New Poems: Eighty Poems at Eighty* (1932) and *Collected Poems* (1940).

**Markham, Gervase** *c.*1568–1637 A soldier and horseman who, after some years of fighting in the Netherlands, returned to England and became a writer on horsemanship, country pursuits, veterinary medicine and the arts of war. Markham was an extremely busy writer, plagiarist and hack whose books were useful and widely read. *A Discourse on Horsemanship* appeared in 1593 and *Cavelarice, or, The English Horseman* in 1610. Markham supplemented them with a work of veterinary information, *Markham's Masterpiece, or, What Doth a Horseman Lack* (1610). Other books were *Cheap and Good Husbandry for the Well-Ordering of All Beasts and Fowls* (1614), *Country Contentments* (1615) and *Markham's Faithful Farrier* (1629). He also wrote a number of plays and published collections of poems. The performing horse mentioned by Markham in the title of *Cavelarice* was Marocco, famous throughout Europe: **Shakespeare** refers to him in the first act of *Love's Labour's Lost* as 'the dancing horse' of Armado's conversation with his page.

**Marlatt, Daphne** 1942– Canadian poet. Born in Melbourne of English parents, Marlatt lived in Malaysia for six years as a child before moving with her family to Vancouver in 1951. She attended the University of British Columbia, where she studied English and was an editor of the *avant-garde* magazine *TISH*. She subsequently obtained her MA in comparative literature at the University of Indiana and has since worked in Vancouver as a writer and researcher in oral history. Marlatt's poetry is concerned with the perceptual process and with attempting to render this in language. She frequently relates mental states to exterior surroundings. Her long poem *Rings* (1971), which describes the situation of a pregnant woman enclosed in a room with her husband during a snowstorm, offers a vivid picture of the isolation of the individual. *Vancouver Poems* (1972) documents a personal response to the external phenomena of the city.

*Steveston* (1974), generally regarded as Marlatt's most important work to date, is a meditation on the history of a Japanese-Canadian fishing town, which intersperses sociological material about the community with personal reflection. Marlatt's other volumes include *Frames* (1968), *Our Lives* (1975), the novel *Zocalo* (1977), *Net Work* (1980) and *Here and There* (1981).

**Marlowe, Christopher** 1564–93 Playwright. Born in Canterbury, the son of a shoemaker, Marlowe was awarded a scholarship at Corpus Christi College, Cambridge. Possibly while still at the university, he became an agent of Francis Walsingham and a favourite of Walsingham's brother, Thomas. The detail of any missions Marlowe undertook in the secret service of Elizabeth I's great schemer is unknown, and it is no more than intelligent speculation that links his activities as an agent with his death by violence in a Deptford tavern. What is known is that Marlowe took his BA in 1584, his MA (after some hesitation by the university authorities) in 1587, and almost at once presented the London theatre with the startling success of the first part of **Tamburlaine the Great** (1587). The play's rhetoric, its self-proclaimed 'high astounding terms', was superbly delivered by the actor **Edward Alleyn**, leading performer of the Lord Admiral's Men. The second part of *Tamburlaine* (1587) rivalled the success of the first. Marlowe may already have written *Dido, Queen of Carthage* – the chronological order of his work cannot be precisely established – but it

This portrait in Corpus Christi College, Cambridge, is believed to be a true likeness of Christopher Marlowe but proof has never been established.

was *Tamburlaine* that established him as a playwright. The notoriety of his private life, which led to accusations of atheism, blasphemy, subversion and homosexuality, added spice to his reputation. Certainly he was free-thinking and indiscreet. But *Dido*, for all its shortcomings, gives evidence of a serious application to the playwright's craft. Like the translation of Lucan's *Pharsalia* (published in 1600, but possibly completed at Cambridge) and of Ovid's *Elegies* into heroic couplets (published in 1595, but probably also student work), it shows a careful apprenticeship in the classics. Whilst the play is drawn mainly from Book Four of Virgil's *Aeneid*, it reveals a confident familiarity with the whole poem.

After *Tamburlaine*, Marlowe continued to dramatize the careers and aspirations of overreaching heroes whose bold defiance of social, political and religious morality invites admiration at the same time as it deserves condemnation. **The Jew of Malta** (*c*.1589), described as a tragedy, is equally well read as a grotesque comedy in which murderous excess and inflated rhetoric parody statesmanship and the posturings of Christian authority. As in *Tamburlaine*, interest – and most of the best lines – belongs to the utterly unscrupulous villain-hero, Barabas. *The Massacre at Paris* (*c*.1589), which has survived in a manifestly corrupt text, is not unlike *The Jew of Malta* in tone. Its central figure, the Duke of Guise, adopts with similar gusto the self-confessed villainy of Barabas. That the horrific St Bartholomew massacre of 1572 should be treated so sardonically is, of course, disturbing still. In Protestant England, so soon after the event, it must have been risky. So, in a different way, was Marlowe's most accomplished play, **Edward the Second** (*c*.1592), in which the defeat and eventual murder of a homosexual king by powerful barons is depicted with a new and unexpected plainness of style. *Edward the Second* carried the crude chronicle play a long step towards its sophistication in the mature history plays of **Shakespeare**. It is a character tragedy, in which the focus shifts subtly from Edward to his lover Gaveston, to his Queen, Isabella, and to her lover, Mortimer.

The Marlovian overreacher comes to what, in retrospect, seems a logical conclusion in **Doctor Faustus**, and it may be that this sense of logic has contributed to the scholarly claims that this is the last of Marlowe's plays. It survives in two unsatisfactory texts (1604 and 1616), each of which shows the marks of playhouse accretion and adaptation, but Faustus himself and his increasingly symbiotic relationship with Mephistopheles are magnificently unaffected. No one can say what plays Marlowe might have gone on to write. In plague-affected London, he spent the last months before his murder writing the narrative poem **Hero and Leander** (published in 1598), which, together with the lyrical *The Passionate Shepherd*, is his poetic monument.

**Marmion**: *A Tale of Flodden Field* A poem by **Sir Walter Scott**, published in 1808. Like its predecessor, *The Lay of the Last Minstrel*, it is divided into six **cantos**.

The Marmion of the title is a fictitious favourite of Henry VIII who wants to marry the rich and beautiful Lady Clare in spite of his entanglement with Constance de Beverley, a nun who has broken her vows and followed him disguised as a page. Clare herself is betrothed to Sir Ralph de Wilton. Conspiring to accuse de Wilton of treason, Marmion forges an incriminating letter and is helped by Constance, who hopes to recover her influence over him. However, she is betrayed, returned to her convent and walled up alive.

When Ralph and Marmion fight in the lists, Ralph is defeated and left for dead. Clare flees to a convent to escape from Marmion. Ralph survives, goes to Scotland disguised as a palmer and consults the Abbess of St Hilda, who is attended by Clare. The Abbess has proof of Marmion's crime, which she received from Constance before her death, and she entrusts it to the palmer, who can now reveal his true identity to Clare. The climax takes place at the battle of Flodden, where Marmion is killed.

The poem includes the songs 'Where Shall the Lover Rest?' and 'Lochinvar'.

**Marmion, Shakerley** 1603–39 Poet, playwright and Royalist, Marmion was born near Brackley, Northamptonshire, and educated at Oxford. He enjoyed the patronage of **Ben Jonson** and the friendship of **Sir John Suckling**. Of his three plays, *Holland's Leaguer* (1631) is notable for its depiction of the famous Southwark brothel run by Elizabeth Holland. *A Fine Companion* (1633) is a Jonsonian 'humours' comedy. *The Antiquary* (*c.*1635), which mocks the foolishness of old age, is Marmion's best play. His long poem, *Cupid and Psyche* (1637), based on Apuleius' *The Golden Ass*, is among the best examples of Caroline narrative poetry.

**Marprelate, Martin** The name assumed by the author of a series of pamphlets issued in 1588–9 and printed on secret presses in various parts of the country (e.g. Kingston, Coventry, Manchester). They were extreme Puritan attacks on the bishops, part of a war originally occasioned by Whitgift's 1586 Star Chamber decree attempting to suppress Puritan pamphlets. Seven Marprelate tracts are extant, as well as pamphlets associated with the controversy. These pamphlets have the following short titles: *The Epistle* (October 1588), *The Epitome* (November 1588), *Certain Mineral and Metaphysical Schoolpoints* (February 1589), *Hay [i.e.*

*have you] Any Work for Cooper* (March 1589), *Martin Junior* (July 1589), *Martin Senior* (July 1589) and *The Protestation of Martin Marprelate* (September 1589). The bishops replied in *An Admonition to the People of England* (1589) by the Thomas Cooper whose name is alluded to in one of the Marprelate tracts. Richard Bancroft preached a sermon against false prophets and the tracts at St Paul's Cross in February 1589; it was printed the next month. At Bancroft's suggestion the bishops also employed professional writers on their side: **John Lyly**, **Thomas Nashe** and Richard Harvey. Lyly wrote *Pap with a Hatchet* (1589), and *A Whip for an Ape* and *Mar-Martin* (both 1589) have also been attributed, although doubtfully, to him. Nashe contributed *An Almond for a Parrot* (1590) and *The First Part of Pasquil's Apology* (1590), Richard Harvey *Plain Percival* (1589) and *A Theological Discourse of the Lamb of God* (1590). But the professional writers could not match the force of Marprelate's scandalous ridicule and railing against 'swinish rabble, . . . petty Antichrists, petty popes, proud prelates, intolerable withstanders of reformation'. The satire in the tracts is some of the best produced in Elizabeth's reign. The identity of Marprelate is in doubt. John Penry and John Udall were arrested. Penry was executed in 1593 and Udall probably died in prison. Their collaborator, Job Throckmorton, denied complicity at Penry's trial and escaped punishment.

**Marriage** A novel by **Susan Ferrier**, published in 1818.

Lady Juliana, daughter of the Earl of Courtland, elopes with Henry Douglas, a penniless young officer. Her romantic illusions are stripped away quickly: Douglas's Highland home is a cheerless place, containing grim-faced aunts and five dull sisters. Then her expected child proves to be twin daughters. The couple move to London where Henry falls into debt and is imprisoned. Upon his release he joins the army and goes to India.

Lady Juliana's daughters, and their future, are now her main preoccupation: she is convinced that all her troubles are the result of an 'imprudent' marriage. One daughter, Mary, has been brought up in Scotland while the other, Adelaide, grows up in the Earl of Courtland's London home. Mary rejects the ambitious marriage Lady Juliana wants her to make; Adelaide allows herself to be pushed into marriage with an elderly duke. Mary gives her heart to the man of her choice and returns to Scotland with him to settle down contentedly. Adelaide, after less than a year of her prudent marriage, deserts the duke and runs off with a worthless man.

**Marriage à la Mode** A comedy by **John Dryden**, first produced in April 1672 and published in

1673. There are two plots, and neither has any bearing on the other. One, written in 'heroic' verse, concerns Leonidas and Palmyra, daughter of the usurping King of Sicily; Leonidas is in fact the rightful heir and all ends satisfactorily for them. The other, in contrasting 'manners' style, concerns Rhodophil and Doralice, married for two years and bored with each other. Rhodophil's friend Palamede has been ordered to marry Melantha but has meanwhile fallen in love with Doralice, not knowing that she is married to Rhodophil. Rhodophil pursues Melantha, not knowing that she is intended for Palamede; she is determined to be fashionable and her conversation is littered with French phrases, an affectation that has irritated Palamede beyond endurance. The quadrille is played out until each character discovers that he objects to the other's encroachments and that he wants his partner after all.

*Marriage of Heaven and Hell, The* A prose work by **William Blake**, usually dated 1790, expressing his revolt against the accepted values of his age. It is prefaced by a poem, 'The Argument', declaring that the paths of truth have been corrupted by false religion. Of the six sections that follow, 'The Voice of the Devil' attacks the conventional religious distinction between body and soul, proclaims that 'Energy is Eternal Delight' and sides with Satan in **Milton**'s *Paradise Lost*. 'Proverbs of Hell' explores this Romantic doctrine in a series of aphorisms, sometimes deliberately shocking.

**Marryat, Captain Frederick** 1792–1848 Novelist. Born in London, the son of a Member of Parliament, he joined the navy at 14 and was a Commander by the age of 23. After an adventurous career, during which he won the Royal Humane Society's Gold Medal for bravery, he resigned in 1830 to concentrate on writing. He had already published his first novel, *The Naval Officer, or, Scenes and Adventures in the Life of Frank Mildmay* (1829). His first great success, *Peter Simple* (1834), was followed by *Jacob Faithful* (1834) and *Mr Midshipman Easy* (1836), all likewise drawing on Marryat's experience of the sea. After *Japhet in Search of a Father* (1836) and *Snarleyyow* (1837) he made his first contribution to **children's literature** with *Masterman Ready* (1841). Written as a form of rebuke to the romanticism of Johann Wyss's *The Swiss Family Robinson*, the book concentrates on the toughness of life for his marooned Seagrave family, not least in the way it has to fight marauding savages. It is in one such final encounter that the faithful family friend and retainer Ready dies, doing his duty to the last. Although this and other moments in the story are heavily weighed down with moral didacticism, Marryat provided children with one of their best adventure stories for years to come. His other great success as children's writer, *The Children of the New Forest* (1847), left the sea in favour of a story set in the Civil War, with heroic Royalist children hiding from their Roundhead oppressors in the shelter of the forest. There they also learn how to live off the land, before finally claiming their inheritance at the Restoration. One of the first historical novels written for a young audience, it was also one of the most exciting, with its particular prejudices about English history frequently repeated in succeeding children's books touching on the period.

**Marsh, Edward (Howard)** 1872–1953 Civil servant and patron of the arts. Educated at Trinity College, Cambridge, he became a clerk in the Colonial Office (1896) and private secretary to **Winston Churchill** (1906), a post he retained in various guises for 23 years, following Churchill to the Board of Trade, the Home Office, the Admiralty, the War Office and the Treasury. He retired and was knighted in 1937. Marsh was a connoisseur and influential collector of English painting; Mark Gertler, John and Paul Nash, Stanley Spencer and many others owed him uncountable friendly acts of help and advice. He assisted with money and intelligent kindness several generations of poets, including **Flecker**, **de la Mare**, **D. H. Lawrence**, **Graves** and **Blunden**; the five volumes of Marsh's anthology *Georgian Poetry* (1912–22) first brought many of them to public notice. As the literary executor of **Rupert Brooke** from 1915 to 1934 he performed an extremely difficult task with tact and great patience. The habit of elaborate scholarly proof-correction which he exercised on behalf of Churchill, **Somerset Maugham**, **Hugh Walpole**, Sir Ronald Storrs and other writers was a precise, valuable form of literary surgery. Much mocked for his treble voice and fussy manner, he was a painstaking translator of Horace and La Fontaine and a fine gossiping letter-writer.

**Marsh, Dame Ngaio** 1899–1982 New Zealand writer of **detective fiction** and dramatist. Born and brought up in Christchurch, she attended Canterbury University College School of Art from 1915 to 1920. After leaving university, she worked in the theatre, first as an actress and subsequently as a producer. A period as an interior designer in London preceded the publication of her first novel, *A Man Lay Dead* (1934), after which she became a full-time writer. During World War II she served in a Red Cross Unit and from 1944 to 1952 she once again worked as a theatrical producer in New Zealand. She was made a DBE in 1966 and was given the Mystery Writers of America Grand Master Award in 1978. One of the best-known detective-story writers of her generation, she was also a prominent figure in New Zealand theatre. *A Man Lay Dead* established the pattern for her many mystery novels. It introduced her equivalent of **Christie**'s Hercule Poirot and **Sayers**'s Lord Peter Wimsey, Superintendent Alleyn of Scotland Yard, and her penchant for presenting murder as a game. Her plots reflect her theatrical training, demonstrating a tight dramatic construction, and she frequently uses the theatre as a backcloth for her stories and artists as characters. Among her more than 30 novels in the detective-story genre are *Artists in Crime* (1938), *Died in the Wool* (1945), *Opening Night* (1951), *Killer Dolphin* (1966) and *Black as He's Painted* (1974). Her plays include *A Surfeit of Lampreys* (1950) and *False Scent* (1961), both adapted from her own novels. She also wrote travel books in New Zealand and two works on play production. Her autobiography, *Black Beech and Honeydew* (1966), is primarily about her life in the theatre.

**Marston, John** 1576–1634 Playwright. Born in Oxfordshire and educated at Brasenose College, Oxford, Marston first studied and then wrote in lodgings in the Middle Temple. His verse satires, collected in *The Metamorphosis of Pygmalion's Image* and *The Scourge of Villainy* (both 1598), earned him a reputation for bitter invective, further reinforced by his disputes with **Ben Jonson** in the 'war of the theatres', to which parts of *Histriomastix* (1599) refer. Marston had already written, for a **boys' company**, the dark comedy ***Antonio and Mellida*** and its revenge-tragedy sequel ***Antonio's Revenge*** (both 1599). The satiric comedies *Jack Drum's Entertainment* (1600) and *What You Will* (c.1601) were followed by Marston's best plays, ***The Dutch Courtesan*** (c.1604), ***The Malcontent*** (1604) and *Parasitaster, or, The Fawn* (c.1605). These are all comedies, though *The Malcontent* in particular touches on tragedy in its exploration of moral complexities. *The Wonder of Women, or, The Tragedy of Sophonisba* (1606) is an austere Roman tragedy, uneasily accommodating spectacle and sensation of the kind expected in the Jacobean theatre. An unfinished tragedy, *The Insatiate Countess*, was completed by William Barksted and published in 1613.

Marston's volatile temperament is well illustrated by his decision to dedicate *The Malcontent* to his former adversary, Ben Jonson, and by his collaboration with Jonson and **Chapman** on ***Eastward Ho*** (1605), a parody of the newly fashionable 'city comedy'. The whole of the first act is Marston's and his hand is detectable elsewhere in the play, whose references to the Scots so offended James I that Chapman and Jonson were briefly imprisoned. Marston seems to have gone unpunished, but he was imprisoned, for unknown reasons, in 1608, abandoned the theatre after his release, and took holy orders in 1609. From 1616 to 1631, he was rector of Christchurch in Hampshire.

**Marston, John Westland** 1819–90 English playwright and dramatic critic whose best-known play, *The Patrician's Daughter* (1842), was one of many verse tragedies promoted and performed by the actor William Macready. Marston's intelligent theatrical reviews for *The Athenaeum* in the 1860s and his retrospective book *Our Recent Actors* (1888) are substantial contributions to theatrical literature.

**Marston, Philip Bourke** 1850–87 Poet. The son of **John Westland Marston**, he was born in London and lost his sight as a child. He published *Song-Tide and Other Poems* (1871), *All in All: Poems and Sonnets* (1875) and *Wind-Voices* (1883). *Garden Secrets* (1887), *For A Song's Sake and Other Stories* (1887) and *A Last Harvest* (1891) appeared posthumously.

**Martian poets, the** A term coined by **James Fenton** to describe the school or group of poets, first coming to prominence in the late 1970s, whose work presents familiar objects in unfamiliar ways. The leading figure is **Craig Raine**. The title poem of his collection, *A Martian Sends a Postcard Home* (1979), which purports to be a Martian's uncomprehending reaction to everyday things, typifies the technique and suggested the label for the group. Disciples include **Christopher Reid** and David Sweetman.

**Martin, Violet Florence** See **Somerville and Ross**.

***Martin Chuzzlewit*** A novel by **Charles Dickens**, published in 20 parts from January 1843 to July 1844. The full title, as given in the monthly parts, was *The Life and Adventures of Martin Chuzzlewit, His relatives, friends and enemies. Comprising all His Wills and His Ways, With an Historical record of what he did and what he didn't; Shewing moreover who inherited the Family Plate; who came in for the Silver Spoons, and who for the Wooden Ladles. The whole forming a complete key To The House of Chuzzlewit.*

Martin Chuzzlewit is a selfish young man, the despair of his grandfather and namesake, the head of the family. When Martin is articled to Pecksniff the architect, a hypocrite of beatific appearance, old Martin, in an excess of misanthropy, has Pecksniff dismiss the boy.

Old Martin's nephew, Jonas Chuzzlewit, engineers the death of his own father and marries Mercy, one of Pecksniff's two daughters. Although warned by the elder Martin Chuzzlewit of the probable consequences of marriage to Jonas, Mercy had gone her own way, and reaps the results of her thoughtlessness as Jonas treats her with brutal cruelty. Jonas becomes involved in the crooked schemes of Montague Tigg, and succeeds in drawing Pecksniff into their dubious enterprise.

Meanwhile, young Martin has sought his fortune in America with his irrepressible servant Mark Tapley. He is defrauded by the Eden Land Corporation and nearly dies of fever. His convalescence is cut short by the serious illness of Mark, and Martin learns some valuable lessons about the nature of true generosity. Returning to England, resolved to make peace with his grandfather, Martin finds him living in Pecksniff's house, apparently entirely subject to him. Eventually old Martin's purpose of testing both Pecksniff and his grandson is revealed, and Martin is able to marry Mary Graham, Chuzzlewit's companion and adopted daughter. Pecksniff is exposed, and Jonas, when arrested for the murder of Montague Tigg, who had blackmailed him over the death of his father, poisons himself. Tom Pinch, at one time Pecksniff's loyal assistant and adherent, being so innocent and open himself that he was unable to believe the warnings of young Martin and a sensible young friend, John Westlock, is suitably employed by old Martin. Although he cherished an unrequited and untold passion for Mary Graham, Tom's unassuming ideals of happiness are fulfilled when his beloved sister Ruth marries John Westlock, and the three settle down together.

Dickens's energetic wit and inventive characterization are displayed to their full effect in *Martin Chuzzlewit*, even though the famous character of Mrs Gamp, the midwife 'dispoged' to the not altogether occasional glass of gin, and the American episodes, had not been part of his original intention. When concluding the work, the novelist thought it 'in a hundred points immeasurably the best of my stories'.

*Martin Eden* A novel by **Jack London**, published in 1909. Martin Eden, a labourer who was once a sailor, has a questioning mind and has undertaken a programme of self-education. He aspires to a higher sort of life, such as that personified by Ruth Morse, a college graduate and the daughter of a wealthy family. He works hard to succeed as a writer, and his work reflects the influence of **Herbert Spencer**'s ethical theories. Although his friend Russ Brissenden, a socialist poet, believes in his work, he has no success. When a newspaper calls him a socialist Ruth deserts him. Then one of his books brings him both fame and money. Ruth seeks him out, but he realizes her true nature and turns away from her. He becomes depressed, and Russ's suicide makes matters worse. He grows to despise the society that has finally honoured him, and he commits suicide on a sea voyage.

**Martineau, Harriet** 1802–76 Writer on re-

ligion and economics, and novelist. She was born in Norwich, the daughter of a manufacturer and the sister of **James Martineau**. A Unitarian, she began her writing career with religious subjects, in *Devotional Exercises for the Use of Young Persons* (1823) and *Addresses with Prayers and Additional Hymns for the Use of Families* (1826). She subsequently became interested in economics and earned a reputation as a lively expositor of **Utilitarian** ideas, using fiction to advance her theories and proposals for social reform: *Illustrations of Political Economy* (1832–4), *Poor Law and Paupers Illustrated* (1833) and *Illustrations of Taxation* (1834). A visit to the USA prompted *Society in America* (1837), which contains her comments on slavery, and *Retrospect of Western Travel* (1838). Later she wrote two novels, *Deerbrook* (1839) and *The Hour and the Man* (1841), which takes Toussaint L'Ouverture as its subject. An active journalist, she contributed regularly to *The Daily News* and *The Edinburgh Review*, and in 1841 published a book of stories for young people, *The Playfellow*. She had moved steadily away from her religious beliefs, and in 1853 produced a condensed version of Auguste Comte's *Cours de Philosophie Positive*. A *History of the Thirty Years' Peace, 1815–45* appeared in 1849. Her *Autobiographical Memoir*, posthumously published in 1877, is valuable for its first-hand comments on her contemporaries in literature.

**Martineau, James** 1805–1900 Theologian, brother of **Harriet Martineau**. He studied as an engineer, but was ordained in the Unitarian ministry in 1828. In 1840 he was appointed Professor of Mental and Moral Philosophy at Manchester New College. His highly influential works of philosophy include *Ideal Substitutes for God* (1879), *Study of Spinoza* (1882), *Types of Ethical Theory* (1885), *A Study of Religion* (1888) and *The Seat of Authority in Religion* (1888). He also composed poems and hymns and contributed regularly to the *National Review*.

**Martinus Scriblerus, Memoirs of** A satirical work published in the second volume of **Pope**'s *Works* of 1741, this was a collaborative effort by several members of the **Scriblerus Club** (which flourished in a brief formal existence in 1713), but is thought to have been chiefly written by **Arbuthnot**. The purpose of the Club, which consisted of writers, politicians and intellectuals such as **Swift** and Lord Oxford, was to ridicule 'all the false tastes in learning, under the character of a man of capacity enough, that had dropped into every art and science, but injudiciously in each'. Their invented character is therefore a typical scribbler, an earnest, pedantic dilettante with a tendency to misconstrue everything to which he turns his hand.

Martinus is the son of Cornelius, an antiquary

of Munster in Germany, and is brought up and educated in the traditions of the ancient world. In adult life he is by turns physician, philosopher and critic, dabbling and cogitating, and when the book closes (it was unfinished) has just outlined a sketch of his proposed travels, which resembles the later shape of *Gulliver's Travels*.

**Martyn, Edward** 1859–1923 Irish dramatist. Martyn was born in Galway and attended schools in Dublin and Windsor before going to Oxford. A prominent figure in the Irish cultural revival, he was one of the founders of the Irish Literary Theatre, and his plays *The Heather Field* (1899) and *Maeve* (1900) were among its earliest productions. After a disagreement with **Yeats**, Martyn left the Irish Literary Theatre, satirizing Yeats and his circle in two later plays, *Romulus and Remus* (1907) and *The Dream Physician* (1914). *Grangecolman* (1912) was written for the Independent Theatre Company, and in 1914 Martyn founded the Irish Theatre to present plays in Gaelic.

**Martyrs, The Book of** (or *Foxe's Book of Martyrs*) See *Acts and Monuments*.

**Marvell, Andrew** 1621–78 Metaphysical poet and satirist. Born the son of a vicar at Winestead-in-Holderness, Yorkshire, Marvell moved with his family to Hull in 1624, where he was educated at the grammar school. He went to Trinity College, Cambridge, in 1633, and received a wide linguistic training, reading intently the Roman poets such as Juvenal and Horace, whose work was to influence the form of his later poems. His father died in 1641, and Marvell left for the Continent the following year, returning in 1647 after visits to Holland, France, Italy and Spain. While in Rome, he visited **Richard Flecknoe**, who became the subject of a poem. Marvell's travels and broad cultural interests contributed much to the civilized, urbane tone of his verse.

In 1648, he wrote some commendatory verses for **Lovelace**'s *Lucasta*. In 1649 his elegy for Lord Hastings appeared, and in 1650 Marvell's sometimes equivocal political affiliations expressed themselves in favour of Cromwell in 'An Horatian Ode upon Cromwell's Return from Ireland', which voices approval but stresses the conditions upon which such a leadership must be maintained. In 1651 he moved to Yorkshire to act as tutor to the daughter of Lord Fairfax, the Parliamentary general, and during the two years of his residence at Nun Appleton House Marvell probably composed his finest poetry, including his magnificently sustained 'Upon Appleton House', which celebrates the civilized retirement of Fairfax from the world of public affairs.

Marvell became a friend of **Milton**, by whom

he was recommended in 1653 for the post of Assistant Latin Secretary to the Council of State, a post he finally secured in 1657. In the interim, he acted as tutor to William Dutton, later a ward of Cromwell's, from 1653–6. He became MP for Hull in 1659, holding the seat for the rest of his life. With the Restoration, Marvell's moderate eulogies of Cromwell's regime were converted into a reasonable acceptance of monarchical stability, but he rapidly became an outspoken opponent of Charles II's government, its failure to promote religious toleration and its inefficiency in military matters. He travelled to Holland for eleven months (1662–3) and later acted as Secretary to the Earl of Carlisle in an embassy to Russia, Sweden and Denmark, returning in 1665. During the naval wars with the Dutch, Marvell was in a strong position to be critical of the political mismanagement of the campaign, therefore, and in 1667 wrote his comprehensively withering satire *The Last Instructions to a Painter* (not published until 1689), a catalogue of verse-portraits criticizing and pillorying those who had influence on affairs of state. He wrote several other political and religious satires, for which at the time of his death he was well known; these include 'Clarindon's House-Warming', 'The Loyal Scot', 'The Statue in Stocks-Market' and a powerful prose satire, *The Rehearsal Transprosed* (published in two parts, 1672–3), a denunciation of the opinions of Samuel Parker, Archdeacon of Canterbury. On 16 August 1678, Marvell died of a tertian ague and his housekeeper, Mary Palmer, later claimed that they had been married.

Andrew Marvell. From a portrait by an unknown artist, *c*.1660. National Portrait Gallery, London.

Before 1681, little of his poetry had been published, but in that year appeared *Miscellaneous Poems by Andrew Marvell, Esq. . . .*, which omitted his 'Horatian Ode'. Known at his death as a formidable satirist, Marvell was 'discovered' in the 19th century (by **Tennyson**, for instance) as the writer of some beautifully accomplished pastoral poetry about gardens and flowers, and was celebrated as 'the green poet'. These poems probably belong to the period before 1653, and include 'The Garden' (a complicated contemplation on sophistication and innocence), 'The Picture of Little T.C. in a Prospect of Flowers', and 'The Nymph Complaining for the Death of Her Fawn'. As a lyric poet, Marvell was both dramatic and visually exact, and his fascination for small natural detail seems peculiarly representative of the age of the microscope, the miniature and intricate floral horticulture. His chief influence was **Donne** whose metaphysical conceits clearly impressed Marvell, though the latter is stylistically less brittle. His most famous poem is 'To His Coy Mistress', a seductive love poem of the **carpe diem** mode, precisely constructed and erotically pitched. In style and finesse, Marvell's best poetry properly belongs to the earlier years of his century, but his political satires are also of contemporary interest, though coarser in their effects, and show the diversity of verse genres available at that time.

**Marxist criticism** During the 19th century Marx and Engels developed explanations of the historical development of the capitalist mode of production, but had little time to elaborate a cultural theory to explain how literature and art were conditioned or determined by the social and economic forces which constitute the 'base' of a particular historical system. Their asides on this problem varied from rather mechanical statements about culture and ideology being the 'reflexes' in men's brains of real life-processes to more subtle statements (Engels) about the 'relative autonomy' of 'superstructures' (which rest on the base).

After a liberal phase the Soviet Union, during the early 1930s, adopted Socialist Realism as its official doctrine. It demanded that artists should be committed to the working-class cause of the Party, that literature should reflect a progressive outlook on society, provide a sense of the ideal possibilities of social development, and should be accessible to the masses. **Modernist** tendencies in Western literature were regarded as decadent, subjective and pessimistic in outlook, while the 19th-century realist novel was praised as a precursor of the 20th-century socialist-realist novel.

From within Socialist Realism Georg Lukács evolved a sophisticated theory of 'reflection', according to which a novel gives us a structural understanding of social development. In marked contrast, Bertolt Brecht favoured the experimental techniques of modernism (reportage, photo-montage, etc.) and other devices from Elizabethan and Chinese acting, which prevented the theatre audience from adopting a passive and empathic attitude to the actors on stage. The 'alienation effect' aims to preserve critical engagement between actor and audience.

The Frankfurt School, which flourished in Germany and the United States, developed a Hegelian strain of cultural theory, in response to the threats from totalitarianism in the 1930s. Adorno, Horkheimer and others believed that *avant-garde* literature and art played a special role in giving us a 'negative' knowledge of a hostile social world, reflecting the alienated existence of humanity in late capitalist societies. The writings of Walter Benjamin, an associate of Adorno, developed a highly personal mixture of fundamentalist Marxism and Cabbalistic lore.

In the 1960s Marxist criticism entered a new phase of sophistication under the influence of **structuralism**. Lucien Goldmann's 'genetic structuralism' revealed the 'homologies' (structural parallels) between literature, ideas and social groups. In contrast, Louis Althusser argued that the different levels within the social formation have no overall unity but possess their own 'specific effectivity', while the economic level is determinant only 'in the last instance' (Engels's phrase). His disciple Pierre Macherey developed the literary implications of these views.

**Raymond Williams** and Terry Eagleton are the best-known English Marxist critics. The former developed late as a Marxist from an early socialist reinterpretation of **Leavis**, while Eagleton was influenced by Althusser's theories of ideology and then by the tradition of Brecht and Benjamin. In the USA Fredric Jameson wrote under the influence of the Frankfurt School and, later, **post-structuralism**.

*Mary Barton: A Tale of Manchester Life* A novel by **Elizabeth Gaskell**, published in 1848. The background to the story is the 'hungry forties' of the 19th century, when a series of bad harvests, beginning in 1837, coupled with taxation on imports of wheat, placed a heavy burden on the lower-paid workers. The Chartist movement and the Anti-Corn Law agitation arose out of these conditions. (See also **The Condition of England novel**.)

One of the sufferers is John Barton, an upright man and a good worker. He is an active trade unionist. His daughter, Mary, has attracted the attention of Henry Carson, her father's employer. Flattered, she discourages the attentions of Jem Wilson, a young engineer. John Barton's fellow workers, in despair at their condition, which the employers will do nothing to ease, decide to kill Henry Carson as a warning to his class and the lot falls to John Barton to commit the murder.

In the meantime Mary Barton, realizing her foolishness, determines to break with Carson. At this point Carson is murdered and suspicion falls on Jem, his rival for Mary. Mary, discovering that it was her father who shot Carson, is faced with a terrible choice. Since she cannot betray her father's guilt, she has to prove Jem's innocence; her father, meanwhile, is enduring acute mental anguish which Jem's acquittal does nothing to allay. At the end of the book John Barton, on the verge of death, confesses his crime to Henry Carson's father and succeeds in obtaining his forgiveness.

In her Preface to *Mary Barton*, Elizabeth Gaskell explained that she knew nothing 'of Political Economy, or the theories of trade', but that her work grew out of her own observation of the poor and uneducated factory-workers of Manchester. Her merciless descriptions of poverty, her sense of outrage and her boundless sympathy remain a powerful combination, and *Mary Barton* is one of the most important works to have been written in a decade which produced many remarkable novels.

**Masefield, John (Edward)** 1878–1967 Poet, novelist, dramatist and journalist. After an idyllic childhood in Ledbury, Herefordshire, he joined the merchant navy at the age of 13. He suffered from seasickness on his first voyage, to Chile. On a second voyage in 1895 he deserted in New York, reading, writing and taking various jobs in America before returning to England and joining the staff of *The Manchester Guardian*.

His career as a poet began with *Salt-Water Ballads* (1902), which included 'Sea Fever' ('I must go down to the sea again'), later set to music by John Ireland. *Ballads and Poems* (1910) was followed by *The Everlasting Mercy* (1911), the long narrative poem for which he is best known. It tells the realistic story of the sin and redemption of Saul Kane in colloquial, sometimes profane, language. *The Widow in the Bye Street* (1912) and *The Daffodil Fields* (1913) were followed by *Dauber* (1913), perhaps the best of his narrative poems, in which an artist is mocked by the crew on a long sea-voyage. *Reynard the Fox* (1919) is a Chaucerian narrative of a fox-hunt told by a man who dislikes hunting. *Collected Poems* (1923) proved a great success, and in 1930 Masefield became Poet Laureate. His critical reputation waned in later years, but recently he has again been admired for his wide range, encompassing ballads, lyrics, nature poetry and mythological narrative, and for his attempt to make poetry a popular art. A close friend and admirer of **Yeats**, whom he first met in London in 1900, he published *Some*

*Memories of W. B. Yeats* (1940) and an elegy, 'Oh what he was'.

In all, Masefield published more than 50 books. His novels include *Sard Harker* (1924), *The Bird of Dawning* (1933), *Dead Ned* (1938) and *Live and Kicking Ned* (1939). His plays include *The Trial of Jesus* (1926) and *The Coming of Christ* (1928). *The Midnight Folk* (1927) and *The Box of Delights* (1933) were written for children. *So Long to Learn* (1952) and a further fragment, *Grace Before Ploughing* (1966), are autobiographical.

**Mason, A[lfred] E[dward] W[oodley]** 1865–1948 Novelist. He was educated at Dulwich College and Oxford, and became an actor before turning to writing. The best known of his many popular historical novels and adventure stories is *The Four Feathers* (1902). He is also remembered for his contribution to **detective fiction** in creating Inspector Hanaud of the Sûreté, who appeared in *At the Villa Rose* (1910), *The House of the Arrow* (1924), *No Other Tiger* (1927) and *The Prisoner in the Opal* (1929).

**Mason, R[onald] A[lison] K[ells]** 1905–71 New Zealand poet and dramatist. Born and educated in Auckland, he attended the university there in the late 1920s and again in the late 1930s, graduating with a BA in Classics in 1939. In the 1920s he worked as a part-time tutor and in the 1930s as a company secretary and public works foreman. About this time he turned to Marxism and for many years he wrote left-wing political journalism for the magazines *People's Voice* and *Challenge*, which he edited from 1943 to 1954. During this period he was an active trade-unionist and also wrote a number of political plays, including *Squire Speaks* (1938), *China* (1943) and *Refugee* (1945). In later life he worked as a landscape gardener and part-time teacher. Mason's poetry is strongly influenced by his classical education, but also contains a strong religious element, characterized by an emphasis on suffering and an ironic treatment of the Passion. **Blake**, Horace and Catullus are major influences on his verse. His best work belongs to his early life; most of the poems in *The Beggar* (1924) were written before he was 18, but already display considerable technical mastery. *No New Thing* (1934), which brought together poems written between 1924 and 1929, introduced a new concern for craftsmanship into New Zealand verse. After 1934 Mason wrote comparatively little poetry. His other volumes include *In the Manner of Men* (1923), sometimes seen as marking the beginnings of modern New Zealand verse, *End of Day* (1936), *This Dark Will Lighten: Selected Poems 1923–1941* (1941) and *Collected Poems* (1962). A modern Romantic, whose best poetry appears to be an urgent expression of spontaneous feeling, Mason is highly regarded, though seldom imitated, in his native New Zealand.

**Mason, William** 1725–97 Poet, gardener and musician. Son of the Revd William Mason, Vicar of Holy Trinity, Hull, he was educated at Hull Grammar School and St John's College, Cambridge, subsequently being elected, with the help of **Gray**, fellow of Pembroke Hall. Ordained in 1754 he rose to be Canon and Precentor of York in 1762. He died from an injury to his shin while stepping out of his carriage. As a poet he produced rather plodding couplets, though the didactic *The English Garden* (1772–82) appeared in blank verse. As a playwright he also adopted old-fashioned forms: *Elfrida* (1752) and *Caractacus* (1759) were both historical tragedies in classical mode. He was an avid gardener and his designs, which emphasized the informal, anticipated many of the later Romantic notions of the form; his garden at Nuneham for the 2nd Earl of Harcourt still exists. An equally avid musician, he invented the celestinette, wrote essays on cathedral music and was a friend of Thomas Arne. He painted, badly, and translated Du Fresnoy's *Art of Painting* (1782). On the death of Gray, Mason became the poet's literary executor and published Gray's *Life and Letters* in 1774. He is principally remarkable for his friendships, which, besides Arne and Gray, included **Reynolds**, **Horace Walpole**, Mrs Delany, Hurd and **Garrick**. Mason was living proof of the fact that in the 18th century the gentleman amateur could always gain access to the genuinely able. His achievements were second-rate: his friends were first-rate.

**masque** At its height in the court of James I and Charles I, the English masque was a spectacular entertainment, involving dance, drama, music, lavish costumes and splendidly inventive scenery devised by Inigo Jones. The uneasy collaboration of **Ben Jonson** with Inigo Jones lasted from 1605 to 1634 and produced many of the finest court masques. It was the Civil War that brought to an end the vogue for this costly form of entertainment.

The precise origins of the masque are uncertain. In primitive folk ritual, disguised guests would present gifts to their wealthy host (king or nobleman) before joining him and his household in a ceremonial dance, and the fashion for 'disguisings' was revived in Tudor England. The entertainments provided for Queen Elizabeth I during her 'progresses', whilst retaining some of the features of the simple disguising, pointed the way to the vastly more elaborate Jacobean masques, through which Inigo Jones introduced Italian perspective scenery to the English audience.

*Massacre at Paris, The* See **Marlowe, Christopher**.

**Massinger, Philip** 1583–1640 Playwright. Massinger was born in Salisbury and educated at Oxford. By 1606 he had settled in London, where he is first identified as a playwright in a 1613 reference in **Philip Henslowe**'s *Diary*. He was one of the busiest of Jacobean and Caroline dramatists. That he was highly esteemed as a professional writer is strongly suggested by his long association (1613–40, almost without a break) with the leading theatre company, the **King's Men**. Much of his work was collaborative, and much has been lost. Of the surviving plays, the most notable collaborations include, with **Nathan Field**, *The Fatal Dowry* (c.1618), with **Thomas Dekker** *The Virgin Martyr* (1620) and with **John Fletcher** upwards of 20 plays of which the best include *Sir John van Olden Barnavelt* (1619), *The Beggar's Bush* (1622) and *The Spanish Curate* (c.1622). Massinger was buried in Fletcher's tomb in Southwark Cathedral.

In the work of which he is generally supposed to have been sole author, Massinger's independent, satirical temperament is unmistakable. *The Maid of Honour* (c.1621) dared to attack the Elector Palatine and *The Bondman* (1623) criticized the powerful Duke of Buckingham. In *The Renegado* (1624), Massinger risked offending anti-Catholic London by presenting a sympathetic portrait of a Jesuit priest, and the anti-Spanish bias of *Believe As You List* (1631) led to its being banned from performance in its original version. Massinger believed his tragedy about the Emperor Domitian, *The Roman Actor* (1626), to be his best work, but it is the bitter comedies *A New Way to Pay Old Debts* (c.1622) and *The City Madam* (c.1632), with their monstrously energetic central characters, Sir Giles Overreach and Luke Frugal, that have lasted best.

**Masson, David** 1822–1907 Biographer. Born in Aberdeen, the son of a stonecutter, he was educated at the universities of Aberdeen and Edinburgh and became Professor of Rhetoric and English Literature at Edinburgh (1865–95).

In 1859 he founded *Macmillan's Magazine*, which he edited until 1867. Masson's principal work is his exhaustive *Life of John Milton* (7 vols., 1859–94). Other works include *Drummond of Hawthornden* (1873), *Chatterton* (1874), and *De Quincey* (1881); *Essays Biographical and Critical, Chiefly on English Poets* was published in 1856. *Edinburgh Sketches and Memories* (1892), *Memories of London in the Forties* (1908) and *Memories of Two Cities, Edinburgh and Aberdeen* (1911) offer interesting pictures of Masson's career and the circles in which he moved. He was made Historiographer Royal for Scotland in 1893.

**Master Humphrey's Clock** A weekly miscellany by **Charles Dickens**, begun in 1840. It reintroduced the characters of Mr Pickwick and the Wellers, and served as a framework for the publication of **The Old Curiosity Shop**, but was never in itself the commercial success Dickens had hoped. He dropped the title when **Barnaby Rudge** began to appear in weekly numbers in 1841.

**Master of Ballantrae, The**: A Winter's Tale A novel by **Robert Louis Stevenson**, published in 1889. Set in Jacobite Scotland in the period immediately following the 1745 Rebellion, it is based on the story of the Marquis of Tullibardine. Stevenson saw it as a chronicle of domestic animosity, 'a drama in a nutshell'.

The story is told by Ephraim Mackellar, one of Stevenson's most successfully characterized first-person narrators. It follows the lifelong feud between two brothers: James Durie, the Master of Ballantrae, violent, charming and unscrupulous, and the younger Henry, quiet, dutiful and dull. The Master goes off to support the Young Pretender and is reported killed at Culloden. Henry succeeds to the title and the estate, and marries his brother's sweetheart, Alison Graeme. The Master returns, embittered by his exclusion, and proceeds to milk the estate of its revenues. The brothers' enmity culminates in a moonlit duel, and the Master is left for dead. When he reappears a second time the family flee to their estates in America. The Master follows them and Henry's reason gives way when he hears the rumour that the Master will be pardoned and reinstated. The Master evades Henry's murderous attack on him by having his servant bury him alive. When he reappears from the dead for a third time, or appears to do so for a few seconds, Henry dies from the shock and the brothers are buried in a common grave. The novel is complex and subtle, and the reader's sympathies are divided between the two brothers.

**Master of Game, The** A hunting treatise by Edward Plantagenet, 2nd Duke of York, written c.1410. Largely a translation of parts of the *Livre de Chasse* of Gaston Phoebus, Comte de Foix, it includes additional chapters on details of the hunts for the hare and hart. The work deals with the natural history of the prey, the types and care of hounds and how to find a hart, as well as details of the hunt itself. It follows its source faithfully in the translated passages and, while not notable for any literary qualities, it was popular and widely copied during the 15th century.

**Masterman Ready** See **Marryat, Captain Frederick**.

**Masters, Edgar Lee** 1868–1950 American poet and novelist, born in Kansas. Masters practised law in Chicago from 1891 to 1920. His first publications were A Book of Verses (1898) and a blank-verse drama entitled Maximilian (1902). He became famous in 1915 with the publication of **Spoon River Anthology**, a book of epitaphs in free verse about the lives of those buried in a cemetery in rural Illinois. He was never to repeat its success, perhaps because he never again found a subject so perfectly suited to his free-verse style and his vein of irony. He did command attention, however, and published several more collections; three dramatic poems, Lee (1926), Jack Kelso (1928) and Godbey (1931); three novels based on his own youth, Mitch Miller (1920), Skeeters Kirby (1923) and Mirage (1924); and a biographical study of Abraham Lincoln, Lincoln the Man (1931), which is hostile and belittling. In 1924 he returned to the scene of his initial success with The New Spoon River, in which he applied the same technique as in the original volume but this time to the urban life that was beginning to prevail in America. Across Spoon River, an autobiography, appeared in 1924.

**Masters, John** 1914–83 Novelist. Born in Calcutta and educated at Wellington and Sandhurst, Masters joined a regiment in India in 1934, subsequently commanded a brigade of the Chindits in Burma, and was a member of the 19th Indian Division at the taking of Mandalay. He turned to writing after retiring from the army in 1948. His novels are works of fast-moving, epic adventure on a wide canvas, and divide into two groups. The first (for which he is best known) is a series of books about British India, of which notable examples are Nightrunners of Bengal (1951), a historical fiction set during the Indian Mutiny, and Bhowani Junction (1954), about the post-war strife immediately preceding Indian independence. The second phase of his work is a trilogy, Loss of Eden, about World War I, comprising Now, God Be Thanked (1979), Heart of War (1980) and By the Green of the Spring (1981).

**Mather, Cotton** 1663–1728 A third-generation New England Puritan minister, the eldest son of **Increase Mather**, and grandson of **John Cotton** and **Richard Mather**. A prodigy, he entered Harvard at the age of 12 and prepared for the ministry. He was ordained in 1685 and soon after became co-minister with his father of the Second Church of Boston. In 1689 he took some 'possessed' Boston girls into his home to observe and treat them, and then wrote about the cases in Memorable Providences, Relating to

*Witchcrafts and Possessions* (1689). He later published an account of the Salem witch trials and other instances of what he believed to be the operation of evil spirits in *The Wonders of the Invisible World* (1693).

During the 1690s he worked on his history of New England, *Magnalia Christi Americana* (published in London in 1702); he also published numerous sermons expounding Puritan doctrine, and was regarded by many as the pre-eminent spokesman for Puritan culture. *Bonifacius*, published anonymously in 1710, was an attempt to give Puritan piety a social component, explaining how a true Christian acts in an increasingly secular world of complex business and family relations. Like his father, Mather was interested in science, and he was elected to the Royal Society in 1714. *The Christian Philosopher* (1721) includes scientific observations of the natural world with suggestions of their spiritual significance. *The Angel of Bethesda* (1722) was a medical work. With his prominent family and his own political activism and intense religious involvement, in many ways Cotton Mather epitomized his culture; his extensive diary is a massive record of the American Puritan experience.

Among his other works were *Parentator* (1724), a biography of his father, 'Paterna', an unpublished autobiography written for his children, *Psalterium Americanum* (1718) and *Manuductio ad Ministerium* (1726), a handbook for ministers. His lifelong project, *Biblia Americana*, a systematic commentary on the Bible, remained unpublished at his death.

**Mather, Increase** 1639–1723 American Puritan minister, the son of **Richard Mather**, born in Dorchester, Massachusetts, and educated at Harvard and later at Trinity College, Dublin. He married the daughter of **John Cotton**, the prominent Puritan minister, and himself became the minister of the Second Church of Boston, which he served for the rest of his life, latterly with his son, **Cotton Mather**. He also became a fellow of Harvard and eventually its president.

A leading figure in the affairs of Massachusetts, Mather frequently wrote on matters of public import. His election sermon, *The Day of Trouble is Near* (1674), was sometimes interpreted as a prophecy of the Indian wars that followed. *A Relation of the Troubles which have happened in New England, by reason of the Indians there* (1677) is a narrative of Indian relations starting with the first Massachusetts settlements, and *A Brief History of the Warr with the Indians* (1676) is about King Philip's War (1674–6). Both histories interpret the Indian wars as contests between the saints and the forces of the devil; the Indian attacks are seen as judgements on the colonists for apostasy, colonial victories as signs of God's providence.

Mather also wrote frequently on scientific subjects, though his curiosity about natural phenomena was motivated less by an empirical scientific spirit than by a desire to see the glory of God's works in the world. His *Kometographia* (1683) and other works on comets, as well as his *Essay for the Recording of Illustrious Providences* (1685), include detailed observations which point to the mysterious ways of God rather than to rational understanding. No stranger to physical explanations (albeit they were of secondary importance), he was an early champion of inoculation against smallpox, writing in defence of the practice during the epidemic of 1721.

In 1688, he headed a mission to England that obtained a new charter for the colony, and a new governor in the person of Sir William Phips. Mather and Phips returned to Massachusetts, just as the Salem witch trials were beginning. Although Mather believed in the possibility of witches and witchcraft, he later censured the court in his *Cases of Conscience Concerning Evil Spirits* (1693) for basing convictions on 'spectral evidence', which he said could be deceptive. His other writings, which exemplify the Puritan mentality of his time, include sermons on conversion and church membership policy, speculations on the millennium, and his 'Autobiography'.

Increase Mather. The frontispiece to his *Cases of Conscience Concerning Evil Spirits*, 1693.

Mather, Richard

**Mather, Richard** 1596–1669 Puritan minister, and one of the founders of the Massachusetts Bay Colony. Born in Lancashire, he spent a year at Oxford before being ordained in 1619. Due to his nonconformity, he was suspended by Archbishop **Laud** in 1633, and emigrated to New England in 1635. There he was called by the Dorchester church, which he served from 1636 to the end of his life. He became one of the leading ministers in the Bay Colony, contributing to the translations of the Psalms in the *Bay Psalm Book* (1640). In the 1630s and 1640s he produced a series of treatises defending the New England congregational system against Presbyterian opponents, the most significant of which is *Church Government and Church Covenant Discussed* (1643). He took part in the two major synods of his time in 1648 and in 1662. He was one of the main architects of the 1648 Cambridge Synod's *Platform of Church Discipline* (1649), which set out the main principles of New England church polity. His *Journal*, which includes an account of the Atlantic crossing, was published for the first time in the 19th century.

**Mathews, John Joseph** *c.*1894–1979 An Osage Indian born in Pawhuska, Oklahoma, and educated at the University of Oklahoma and at Oxford. His first work, *Wah 'Kon-Tah: The Osage and the White Man's Road*, a historical study of the Osage Indians from 1878 to 1931, appeared in 1932. His other books include *Sundown* (1934), a novel, and *The Osages: Children of the Middle Waters* (1961).

**Matura, Mustapha** 1939– Playwright. He was born in Trinidad and settled in England in 1960. *As Time Goes By* (1967), winner of several drama awards and still regarded by many as his best play, presents an incisive, though often very funny, portrayal of Caribbean immigrant society in Britain. Matura has gone on to examine many aspects of black life, the monologue *Nice* (1973) and *Welcome Home Jacko* (1979) dealing with Britain, and *Play Mas* (1974), *Independence* (1979) and *A Dying Business* (1980) with the Caribbean. His sharp characterization and confident grasp of stage technique mark him out as possibly the most effective, as well as the most widely performed, Caribbean playwright today. He is the founding director of the Black Theatre Co-operative, Britain's leading black theatre company.

**Maturin, Charles Robert** 1782–1824 Novelist and playwright. Of Huguenot descent, Maturin was born in Dublin and took holy orders after studying at Trinity College. He is remembered for *Melmoth the Wanderer* (1820), a powerful example of the **Gothic fiction** then popular. His other novels were *The Fatal Revenge* (1807), *The*

*Wild Irish Boy* (1808), *The Milesian Chief* (1811), *Women, or, Pour et Contre* (1818) and *The Albigenses* (1824). His tragedy *Bertram* was produced with great success at **Drury Lane** by Edmund Kean in 1816, but two other tragedies, *Manuel* (1817) and *Fredolfo* (1819), failed.

**Maud** A poem by **Alfred Tennyson**, published in 1855. It grew out of the lyric 'Oh! that 'twere possible', which was written in 1833–4 after the death of **Arthur Hallam**. The original title was *Maud, or, The Madness*, but in 1875 Tennyson retitled it *Maud: A Monodrama*.

The narrator recounts the melancholy history of his life: his father's death and the ruin of his family, his love for Maud and the duel in which he killed her brother, his flight from home, his descent into insanity and his recovery through patriotic commitment to the Crimean War. Tennyson described the work as 'a little *Hamlet*, the history of a morbid, poetic soul, under the blighting influence of a recklessly speculative age . . . The peculiarity of this poem is that different phases of passion in one person take the place of different characters.' It is outstanding for the virtuosity with which Tennyson uses a variety of metres to convey the hero's different moods.

Dante Gabriel Rossetti's sketch of Tennyson reading his poem, *Maud*, in 1855. City of Birmingham Museum and Art Gallery.

**Maugham, (William) Somerset** 1874–1965
Novelist, short-story writer and playwright.
The youngest of six brothers, Somerset
Maugham was the son of a solicitor to the
British Embassy in Paris. He was orphaned at
the age of ten and sent to England under the care
of his uncle, a clergyman, at Whitstable in Kent.
He was educated at King's School, Canterbury,
and Heidelberg where he studied philosophy for
a year. He returned to England to study medicine at St Thomas's Hospital, Lambeth,
qualifying in 1897. A small private income
allowed him to travel in Europe and he settled in
Paris in 1898.

From his experience of London Maugham
wrote his first novel, *Liza of Lambeth* (1897), a
story of the slums and Cockney life. In Paris he
wrote seven novels, a volume of short stories,
and a travel book about Andalusia in Spain.
Two plays were given a short run in London in
1903–4, but it was with *Lady Frederick* (1907)
that he achieved success as a playwright. This
was followed by a farce, *Jack Straw* (1908), and a
number of other plays which gained him wide
popularity; they include *The Tenth Man* (1910),
*Our Betters* (1917), *The Circle* (1921), *The Letter*
(1927) and *For Services Rendered* (1932). After
*Sheppey* (1933) he gave up writing for the
theatre.

Maugham's first really successful novel was
*Of Human Bondage* (1915) which charts the life

Somerset Maugham, 1911. Photograph by E. O.
Hoppé.

and adventures of a young man in 'Blackstable'
(Whitstable) and 'Tercanbury' (Canterbury) and
is based upon personal experience. It was followed by *The Moon and Sixpence* (1919), set in
Tahiti and involving a Gauguinesque artist,
Charles Strickland. Other novels were: *The
Painted Veil* (1925), *Cakes and Ale* (1930), a
light-hearted comedy, *The Razor's Edge* (1945)
and *Catalina* (1948).

Maugham's short stories were published in
various collections (beginning with *Orientations*
in 1899, and ending with *Creatures of Circumstance* in 1947), and include some that have been
considered among the best in the language.
Many have been made into films and scripted
for the stage.

Maugham's extensive travels are the subject
of *The Land of the Blessed Virgin* (1905), *On a
Chinese Screen* (1922), and *Don Fernando* (1935).
His personal views on life and art can be found
in *The Summing Up* (1938), *Strictly Personal*
(1942), *A Writer's Notebook* (1949) and *Points of
View* (1958). By his own judgement Maugham
was one of the leading 'second-raters'. Critics
have praised his narrative skill and his merciless,
anti-romantic powers of observation.

**Maurice** A novel by **E. M. Forster**, written in
1913–14 and circulated privately but not published until 1971, after the writer's death.

Maurice Hall, aged 14, is to attend public
school. The senior prep school master acquaints
the boy with 'the mystery of sex', an evasive
idealization of relations between the sexes. Maturing, Maurice experiences homosexual tendencies but represses them to avoid conflict with the
prevailing sexual ethos. Cambridge too is 'hell',
but Maurice, now entering his twenties, meets
Clive Durham. After an agonizing and protracted flirtation, first Clive and then Maurice
declare their love and a clandestine relationship
ensues. Maurice leaves Cambridge for clerical
work, and Clive qualifies as a barrister.

Whilst convalescing in Greece, Clive decides
to 'become normal' and breaks off their relationship. Maurice is heartbroken when Clive
marries, and suffers acute isolation. However,
during a visit to the newly-weds he meets Alec
Scudder, Clive's gamekeeper. Alec is about to
emigrate, but approaches Maurice in search of
love. The latter responds, then is suspicious of
Alec's motives and inhibited by class prejudice.
They reach an understanding and spend Alec's
last night in England together. Alec leaves for
Southampton. Maurice, watching the boat sail,
learns that Alec has decided to stay and proceeds
triumphantly to join his lover.

In a 'Terminal Note', added after the final
revision in 1960, Forster explains the inspiration
behind the novel – his visit to **Edward Carpenter**, the 'Whitmannic poet' and primitive socialist, in 1913 – and defends its 'happy ending'. He

Maurice, Furnley

concludes with an impassioned indictment of the persecution of homosexuals in England in the absence of legal reform.

**Maurice, Furnley** Pseudonym of the Australian poet Frank Wilmot (1881–1942). Most of his working life was spent as a bookseller and publisher, though he wrote verse from an early age. His first important book, *Unconditioned Songs*, was published anonymously in 1913. His vivacious poetry draws on the Australian vernacular and is fresh, engaging and playful. Other works are *To God: From the Weary Nations* (1917), *The Bay and Padie Book* (1917), *Eyes of Vigilance* (1920), *Ways and Means* (1920), *The Gully and Other Verses* (1929), *Odes for a Curse-Speaking Choir!* (1933) and *Melbourne Odes* (1934). *Poems by Furnley Maurice* was published in 1944.

**Maurice, (John) Frederick Denison** 1805–72 Clergyman and leader of **Christian Socialism**. He was born at Normanstone, near Lowestoft, the son of a Unitarian minister. In 1823 he entered Trinity College, Cambridge; with his friend John Sterling he moved to Trinity Hall in 1825, but was excluded from both a degree and a fellowship because of his refusal to subscribe to the Thirty-Nine Articles. In 1830, however, he joined the Church of England, studied at Oxford and was ordained in 1834. He was appointed chaplain to Guy's Hospital in 1836, and while there he wrote *The Kingdom of Christ* (1838), a plea for religious unity that was generally misunderstood. In 1840 he became Professor of English Literature and History at King's College, London, and six years later Professor of Theology in the college's new Theological School.

Associating Christian practice with the need for social reform, Maurice held that 'a true socialism is the necessary result of a sound Christianity'. The belief led to the formation of the Christian Socialist group and his connection with J. M. F. Ludlow, **Thomas Hughes** and **Charles Kingsley**. *Theological Essays* (1853) brought Maurice into conflict with authority once more by questioning the accepted doctrine of eternal punishment. He was dismissed from King's College, an event which prompted **Tennyson**'s lyric, 'To the Rev. F. D. Maurice' (1855). In 1866 he became Professor of Moral Philosophy at Cambridge. Maurice's lasting memorial is The Working Men's College, London, which arose from the organization of evening classes and was firmly established in 1854.

His views are expressed in *The Religions of the World* (1847), *Social Morality* (1869) and *Moral and Metaphysical Philosophy* (1871–2).

**Mavor, Osborne Henry** See **Bridie, James**.

**Maxwell, Gavin** 1914–69 Writer, conservationist, traveller. Born at the family home of Monreith, Wigtownshire, Maxwell developed an early interest in the wildlife around him, a boyhood described in *The House of Elrig* (1966). Educated at Stowe and Hertford College, Oxford, he later described his degree in land management as 'a useless achievement'. Invalided out of the army with the rank of Major in 1944, he bought the island of Soay, off Skye, with the aim of setting up a shark fishing industry. The ultimate failure of this project gave him the material for his first autobiographical book, *Harpoon at a Venture* (1952). After trying his hand at journalism and portrait painting, Maxwell travelled in Sicily and Iraq, and produced three further books, including *A Reed Shaken By the Wind* (1956), an award-winning study of the Marsh Arabs of Southern Iraq.

Returning to Britain, Maxwell brought with him an otter cub, starting a relationship which was to dominate much of the rest of his life. The idyllic story of life with this and succeeding otters on the west coast of Scotland was related to great popular response and considerable critical acclaim in *Ring of Bright Water* (1960). It struck a note of innocence and joy which Maxwell failed to recover in the bitter sequels *The Rocks Remain* (1963) and *Raven Seek Thy Brother* (1968), as he was increasingly overtaken by personal and financial insecurities. He died in 1969, a year after the world of 'Camusfearna' was finally destroyed by fire.

**May, Thomas** 1595–1650 Translator, playwright and poet. Born in Sussex, May was educated at Sidney Sussex College, Cambridge. He was one of the many admirers of **Ben Jonson** and Jonson himself praised May's translations of Lucan's *Pharsalia* (1627) and Virgil's *Georgics* (1628). Two earlier efforts by May, *The Heir* and *The Old Couple* (both *c.*1621), were undistinguished comedies; he also wrote three undistinguished tragedies, *Antigone, the Theban Princess* (*c.*1626), *Cleopatra* (1626) and *Julia Agrippina* (1628). His translations from the Latin, which are regarded as his best work, continued with *Selected Epigrams of Martial* (1629) and a further instalment of Lucan, *Continuation* (1630). *The Mirror of Minds* (1631) is a translation of *Icon Animorum* (1614) by **John Barclay**. But his next works were very long and practically unread historical narrative poems, *The Reign of King Henry the Second* (1633) and *The Victorious Reign of King Edward the Third* (1635).

May was a Puritan and embraced the Parliamentary cause during the Civil War. He became secretary to the Long Parliament and his *History of the Parliament in England Which Began November the Third, 1640, with a Short and Necessary*

650

*View of Some Precedent Years* (1647) is a valuable historical document.

**Mayhew, Henry** 1812–87 Journalist. Born in London, the son of a solicitor, and educated at Westminster School, Mayhew worked for a while in his father's office before joining his friend **Gilbert à Beckett** on the illustrated comic weekly, *Figaro in London*. His farce, *The Wandering Minstrel*, was produced in 1834. In 1841 he was one of the original founders of ***Punch***, but a change in the financial control of the magazine caused him to leave it in 1846.

In 1849 Mayhew began to publish *London Labour and the London Poor*, the ambitious, detailed and compassionate survey for which he is remembered. Its first instalments appeared as 'Labour and the Poor' in **The Morning Chronicle** and were continued independently in weekly parts. A collection was gathered together in book form in 1851, and the work was at last completed in four volumes in 1861–2. The fourth volume, dealing entirely with those who lived outside the law, was enlarged and re-published in 1864.

In 1856 Mayhew began to issue a concurrent series called *The Great World of London* in monthly instalments, nine of which were brought together in a volume at the end of the year. It was incorporated with *The Criminal Prisons of London*, which Mayhew himself considered his most important work of social criticism, to form *The Criminal Prisons of London and Scenes of Prison Life* (1862).

Apart from these great achievements, Mayhew's busy career produced only ephemeral journalism. Among more than a score of other books, two works of travel are worth mention: *The Rhine and Its Picturesque Scenery* (1856) and *German Life and Manners As Seen in Saxony* (1864).

Women and children at work salvaging material in a London dust yard. From a sketch made on the spot for *London Labour and the London Poor* by Henry Mayhew, published in 1851.

**Mayne, Rutherford** Pseudonym of the Irish actor and playwright Samuel J. Waddell (1878–1967), the brother of **Helen Waddell**. He was a leading force in the **Ulster Literary Theatre** from its foundation in 1902. His earliest performed work, *The Turn of the Road* (1906), written in two scenes and an epilogue, concerns a farmer's son whose determination to play the fiddle causes his father to disinherit him. Without undue solemnity, it opposes the harsh realities of rural hardship and the legitimate dreams of an alternative life. A three-act comedy, *The Drone* (1908), contrasts the dangerous meanness of Irish puritanism with the feckless good humour of an Irish drone. It is the drone who saves his brother from making a disastrous marriage. Mayne's best work may be the two one-act tragedies, *The Troth* (1908) and *Red Turf* (1911), in which the Irish experience of eviction and land-grabbing is tersely recreated. Mayne had served in the Irish Land Commission after 1909, and his last play, *Bridge Head* (1934), is about the efforts of the Land Commission to apportion land more equitably. Like its immediate predecessor, the comedy *Peter* (1930), it was written for the **Abbey Theatre** in Dublin.

**Mayne, William (Cyril)** 1928– Children's writer. Born in Hull, the son of a doctor, he was educated at Canterbury Cathedral Choir School before working intermittently for the BBC. *A Swarm in May* (1955), set in a choir school like his own, is a gentle adventure story telling how the pupils explore past mysteries. His subsequent works favoured understatement and left readers to draw their own inferences, a characteristic which has led to objections that Mayne's work is too difficult for most children. *Earthfasts* (1966), his first break with strict realism, used one of his favourite themes: the appearance of a figure from the past in modern life. The ambitious *A Game of Dark* (1971) parallels a consuming illness in a family with a fantasy dragon that has to be slain. *The Jersey Shore* (1973), perhaps his most difficult book, conveys an overwhelming sense of place, however fragmentary the story. Later works have continued to explore new settings and ideas.

***Mayor of Casterbridge, The*** A novel by **Thomas Hardy**, first published serially in *The Graphic* from January to May 1886 and in book form the same year. Sub-titled 'The Story of a Man of Character', it endows the rise and fall in its hero's fortunes with the inevitability of tragic process.

Michael Henchard, an out-of-work hay trusser, gets drunk at Weydon Priors fair and sells his wife, Susan, and their daughter, Elizabeth-Jane, for five guineas to a sailor named Newson. Sober the next morning, Henchard swears an oath to abstain from alcohol for

21 years. After 18 years Mrs Newson, believing her sailor-husband drowned at sea, comes with her daughter to seek out Henchard, now a prosperous grain merchant and mayor of Casterbridge. He receives them generously and, at a clandestine meeting with Susan, arranges to court and marry her anew so that respectability may be maintained. A complicating factor, however, is his commitment to Lucetta Le Sueur, a woman of means he was supposed to be marrying; but upon hearing the mayor's true explanation of affairs their engagement is terminated, although Lucetta comes to Casterbridge to live. Meanwhile, Henchard has engaged as his manager the newly-arrived Scotsman, Donald Farfrae, an energetic young man of commercial acumen. Henchard marries Susan, who soon dies but leaves a letter telling him Elizabeth-Jane is really Newson's daughter; this alienates him from Elizabeth-Jane and his bitterness rises to such a point that she leaves home to live as housekeeper-companion with Lucetta. And now Farfrae, who has shown an interest in Elizabeth-Jane, marries Lucetta. Because of Henchard's pig-headedness a rift opens between him and the Scotsman who, going into business for himself, thrives as Henchard declines to the point of bankruptcy. The old liaison between Henchard and Lucetta is publicized and she dies of shame. Newson returns, Elizabeth-Jane and Farfrae marry, and the lonely, embittered Henchard, reduced even below itinerant labour, dies on Egdon Heath cared for by the loyal but simple Able Whittle.

**Mazeppa** A poem by **Lord Byron**, published in 1819. It is based on a story told by Voltaire in his *Histoire de Charles XII* (1731). In the poem the Swedish king, Charles XII, and his officers are resting after their defeat at Pultowa in 1719. They listen to Ivan Stepanovitch Mazeppa telling the story of his life. Born of a noble Polish family, he becomes page to the king of Poland, Casimir V. When his affair with the wife of a wealthy merchant is discovered, he is punished by being bound naked across the back of a horse, which is whipped into madness and gallops away with him. The poor animal races across rivers and through forests with its semiconscious burden and eventually falls dead on the plains of the Ukraine. Mazeppa is rescued and restored to health by the local people, and he becomes their leader. He seizes the opportunity presented by the Swedish invasion to desert and make his way west.

Mazeppa is also the subject of Pushkin's *Pultowa*.

**Measure for Measure** A play by **William Shakespeare**, formally a comedy but so dark in tone that it is more often neutrally classed among the 'problem plays'. It was first performed *c*.1604

and published in the First Folio of 1623. The main source is **George Whetstone**'s *Promos and Cassandra*, a translation of a play by Cinthio.

Disturbed by the unruliness of Vienna, Duke Vincentio resolves to absent himself from rule and entrust law-enforcement to his puritanical deputy, Angelo. Disguised as a friar, the duke remains in Vienna to observe the consequences of his decision. Angelo orders the destruction of the brothels and, invoking a law against lechery, imprisons Claudio for impregnating the woman to whom he is betrothed. Knowing that the penalty is death, Claudio asks his sister, Isabella, a novice in a nunnery, to intercede. Confronted by Isabella, the unyielding Angelo experiences his own lust. He offers Claudio's life as an exchange for Isabella's body. Outraged when Claudio begs her to accept the offer, Isabella abandons him, but is persuaded by the disguised duke to play a trick on Angelo. The duke reveals that Angelo had broken a marriage-contract with a certain Mariana when Mariana's dowry was lost. Mourning her lost love, Mariana now lives in isolation. She would willingly take Isabella's place in Angelo's bed. The substitution is arranged, but the duke's scheme is ruined by Angelo's decision to have Claudio killed despite his promise to Isabella. The fortunate death in prison of a pirate with some physical resemblance to Claudio gives the duke another opportunity to thwart Angelo, whose villainy is unmasked when the duke makes his unexpected 'return' to Vienna. Claudio can now marry the pregnant Juliet, Angelo's punishment is to marry Mariana, and the duke declares his love for the chaste Isabella.

*Measure for Measure* raises more enduring issues than can be resolved by its conventional comic ending. After Isabella's two finely written encounters with Angelo, in which issues of justice and mercy, morality and the law, sin and grace are raised, the hurried plotting of the bed-trick and Claudio's escape seem perfunctory. It may be that Shakespeare was forced, through theatrical exigency, to finish in haste what he had begun in comparative leisure. Associated by date with *Troilus and Cressida* and *All's Well that Ends Well*, this play is also associated in moral tone with these other 'problem' comedies.

**medieval lyric** A short poem originally written for musical accompaniment, or written as if to be sung. It is usually characterized by a repeated stanza form, with a forceful metre, refrain and simple rhyme scheme. More religious than secular lyrics survive, largely because they were often recorded in the margins of manuscripts containing other material – legal and historical records, theological works, and so forth – and these were most often executed in religious houses. Penitential lyrics, prayers to the Virgin and meditations upon Christ's Passion predominate, but are expressed in a wide variety of styles and poetic forms. Amongst the secular lyrics, love is the most frequent theme. The poems record lovers' pleas, bitter recriminations, celebrations of the beauty of the beloved and complaints at fickleness. The voice of the poem is usually, but not invariably, masculine. Some humorous and satiric lyrics survive, a particularly common form being the description of an ugly woman, a parody of the lover's description of a beautiful mistress.

Many lyrics survive independently, but the most famous collection is the **Harley Lyrics**. The authors are generally not known.

**Medwall, Henry** *c.*1462–1502 Dramatist. Little is known about Medwall beyond his work – much of which is now lost – and the fact that he was chaplain to Cardinal Morton. He was ordained an acolyte in 1490, and is thought to have been a member or connection of a noble family since various livings were granted to him by the Crown. The last was at Calais after Morton's death in 1500. His surviving works are a morality play, *Nature* (printed in 1530), and *Fulgens and Lucrece*, the first completely secular play in English. It was first performed about 1497 and first printed between 1512 and 1516.

**Mehta, Ved** 1934– Essayist, biographer and autobiographer. Born in Lahore, he was partly educated outside Asia, at schools and universities in the USA and Britain. These included Oxford and Harvard Universities. He began his career as a journalist, and an element of journalism at the level which occasionally proves it can be an art is evident in many of his essays and memoirs. His most distinguished work is highly personal in its observations. Particularly prominent is *Portrait of India* (1970), a classic interpretation of the sub-continent which first appeared as a series of articles in *The New Yorker*. It is matched by his first major book, *Face to Face* (1957), a description of his early life in India and his struggle for education both there and in the USA. This struggle was compounded by the fact that he had become blind at the age of three. *Walking the Indian Streets* (1963) takes the story a stage further, to the time of Mehta's return to India, and other volumes of autobiography have included *Vedi* (1982), about his childhood attending a school for the blind in Bombay, and *The Ledge Between the Streams* (1985), which takes him up to his 15th birthday. In several of these books he manages to combine an absorbing sense of the ordinary experiences of India with a penetrating account of Indian politics and leadership. Other books include *Daddyji* (1972), a life of his father, and *Mamaji* (1979), a life of his mother; *Fly and the Fly-Bottle* (1963), 'Encounters with British Intellectuals'; *John is*

*Easy to Please* (1971), a small collection of pieces originally contributed to *The New Yorker*; and a satirical novel, *Delinquent Chacha* (1967). Mehta writes in English but is much translated. He is probably the most widely read Indian writer outside India, and a respected if occasionally controversial author within his own country.

**Melibeus, The Tale of** See *Canterbury Tales, The*.

**Melincourt, or, Sir Oran Haut-Ton** The second novel by **Thomas Love Peacock**, published in 1817. Generally regarded as more ambitious and less successful than his first, *Headlong Hall*, it satirizes both the enthusiasms and the reactions of the period after Waterloo, including the current belief in progress. Rich Mr Sylvan Forester has educated the orang-outang of the title so that he appears to be a charming gentleman who plays the flute, and has bought a baronetcy and a seat in Parliament for him. The portrait of Forester himself owes something to Peacock's friend, **Shelley**. Among the book's targets are **Wordsworth** (Mr Paperstamp), **Coleridge** (Mr Mystic), **Southey** (Mr Feathernest) and **William Gifford** (Mr Vamp).

**Melmoth the Wanderer** A Gothic novel by **Charles Robert Maturin**, published in 1820. The hero has made a pact with Satan to prolong his life, but the debt can be transferred if he can find someone else willing to assume it. The situation provides a framework for a series of episodes in which Melmoth approaches various desperate people and tries to persuade them to take on his dreadful debt: one possibility is a man in a lunatic's cell, another is a victim of the Inquisition and a third sees his children dying of hunger. Nobody will change places with Melmoth and he is doomed.

**Oscar Wilde**, a descendant of Maturin, adopted the name of Melmoth in Paris after his release from prison; Sebastian, the Christian name he used, was suggested by the arrows of his convict garb.

**melodrama** The first English play to be advertised as a melodrama was **Thomas Holcroft**'s *A Tale of Mystery* (1802), but the style was familiar many years before the name came into currency. Holcroft's play was an adaptation of a French piece, so it is reasonable to look to France for the origins of the term. The problem is that *mélodrame* has travelled two distinct paths. What began, perhaps with Rousseau's *Pygmalion* (1770), as an art form in which words and music were used in counterpoint or parallel, remains in opera as a term to define spoken passages with musical accompaniment. In drama there is no such precision, and 'melodrama' must serve to describe a mass of plays and films from the anonymous *Maria Marten* (1830) to Hitchcock's *Psycho* or from Schiller's *Die Räuber* (1782) to next week's episode of a television detective series.

It is not easy to arrive at a definition which will satisfactorily account for such a diversity of material, but during its theatrical heyday in the Victorian theatre, English melodrama generally exposed the uncommonly virtuous to the threat of defeat by the uncompromisingly vicious, allowing good to win out only after sensational risks had been taken or fearsome adventures undergone. Constant peril sustains the tension, and ultimate disaster for the 'good' characters is almost always averted in the nick of time. Outstanding examples of effective melodrama include **Douglas Jerrold**'s *Black-ey'd Susan* (1829), **Tom Taylor**'s *The Ticket-of-Leave Man* (1863), **Boucicault**'s *The Shaughraun* (1874) and **Henry Arthur Jones**'s *The Silver King* (1882). These and many more are fine examples of uncomplicated theatrical story-telling.

**Melville, Herman** 1819–91 One of American literature's greatest figures, Melville was born in New York City into an established merchant family. His father became bankrupt and then insane, and died when Melville was 12. At the age of 15 he left school and began working to support his family, first as a bank clerk, then as a teacher, and as a farm labourer. At the age of 19 he sailed on a merchant ship to Liverpool. This was followed by several other sea voyages, one of them a whaling trip during which he jumped ship and lived briefly among the Typee cannibals in the Marquesas.

Although he had no early designs as a writer, he was encouraged to set down some of his more exotic experiences, and the result was *Typee* (1846), loosely based on his encounter with the cannibals. *Omoo* (1847), *Mardi* (1849), *Redburn* (1849), and *White-Jacket* (1850) also treat themes involving life on the sea. These early works won Melville a good deal of popular acclaim; they also stirred controversy because of their sympathy with pagan societies, sometimes to the point of contempt for western attitudes and practices. During this time Melville began to read widely, acquainting himself with a broad range of writers and philosophers. In 1850 he and his wife moved to Pittsfield, Massachusetts, where they became neighbours and friends of Sophia and **Nathaniel Hawthorne**. Inspired by Hawthorne and by his reading, Melville entered into his most ambitious phase. In 1851 he published **Moby-Dick**, the whaling adventure dedicated to Hawthorne that is considered by many to be the greatest work of American fiction. To his intense disappointment the novel was not well received, and from relative popularity he began to fade into obscurity. *Pierre* (1852), a psychological and moral study based

Herman Melville.

on his childhood, and thus removed from the ocean setting of most of his other fiction, was hardly read at all in the 19th century. At odds with his public, and deprived of the company of Hawthorne, who had moved to Concord, Melville turned increasingly to shorter fiction. After the short novel *Israel Potter* (1855) he published **The Piazza Tales** (1856), a collection of stories which includes 'Bartleby the Scrivener', 'Benito Cereno' and 'The Encantadas'. His last novel, **The Confidence Man** (1857), a harsh satire of American life set on a Mississippi River steamboat, represented his most radical innovation in narrative form since *Mardi*.

At the age of 40 he turned almost exclusively to poetry. **Battle-Pieces and Aspects of the War** was issued in 1866, *John Marr and Other Sailors* in 1888, and *Timoleon* in 1891. **Clarel** (1876) is a long poem about religious crisis, based on Melville's trip to the Holy Land in 1857. *Clarel* was the last of his published works; the later volumes were privately printed and distributed among a very small circle of acquaintances. Additional material was published from manuscript long after his death, when his reputation was beginning to revive. Most notably, the unfinished tale **Billy Budd** appeared in 1924. *Journal Up the Straits* (1935), *Journal of a Visit to London and the Continent* (1948), and *Journal of a Visit to Europe and the Levant* (1955), all record his travels in the 1850s. *Weeds and Wildings* (1924) is a collection of previously unpublished poetry; his letters were published in 1960.

**Melville, James** 1556–1614 Poet and diarist. A Scottish Presbyterian minister and educator, Melville graduated from St Andrews in 1571 and received additional instruction in Greek and Hebrew from his uncle. In 1575 he became one of the regents of Glasgow University, in 1580 Professor of Hebrew at St Andrews and in 1589 Moderator of the General Assembly of the Church of Scotland. His strongly Presbyterian views and his opposition to episcopacy in Scotland meant that he had a troubled career, especially after the accession of James VI as James I of England. He wrote poems, some on ecclesiastical affairs in Scotland. *The Diary of Mr James Melville, 1556–1601*, of which the manuscript is in the Advocates' Library in Edinburgh, was first published in 1829. It gives a valuable (and staunchly Presbyterian) account of ecclesiastical affairs in Scotland.

**Melville, Sir James** 1535–1617 Author of memoirs. At 14 Melville was a page to Mary Queen of Scots in France. He served on a mission for Henry II of France, was sent by Mary to negotiate with Elizabeth I and was present at the baptism of James VI, but declined to follow his king to England on his accession as James I. His *Memoirs* give a valuable account of his times. The manuscript was discovered in Edinburgh in 1660 and first printed in 1683.

***Memoirs of a Cavalier, or, A Military Journal of the Wars in Germany, and the Wars in England, from the Year 1632 to the Year 1648*** A novel by **Daniel Defoe**, published in 1720.

The cavalier who tells the story is Andrew Newport, an English gentleman who travels to Europe in 1630. His travels take him to Vienna, and he accompanies the imperial army during the Thirty Years War. He is present at the sack of Magdeburg (a remarkable piece of 'reporting' by Defoe) and after it joins the army of the opposing forces led by Gustavus Adolphus, King of Sweden. After the king's death at the Battle of Lützen in 1632 he returns to England and as a Royalist colonel serves King Charles I, taking the narrative to the Battle of Naseby and the end of the Civil War.

***Memoirs of a Woman of Pleasure*** (*Fanny Hill*) See **Cleland, John**.

***Memoirs of Barry Lyndon, The*** See ***Barry Lyndon***.

***Memoirs of Sherlock Holmes, The*** See **Sherlock Holmes stories**.

***Men and Women*** A collection of poems by **Robert Browning**, published in 1855. He himself felt that the contents showed him writing 'lyrics with more music and painting than

before, so as to get people to hear and see', and the volume was the first of his works to achieve some measure of popular success. Apart from 'Love Among the Ruins', the enigmatic ***Childe Roland to the Dark Tower Came*** and the virtuoso ***A Toccata of Galuppi's***, it included several mature examples of the **dramatic monologue** he made his special métier: ***Fra Lippo Lippi***, ***Bishop Blougram's Apology***, ***Andrea del Sarto***, 'Saul' and 'Cleon'.

***Men at Arms*** See ***Sword of Honour***.

**Mencken, H[enry] L[ouis]** 1880–1956 American essayist, editor and critic, born in Baltimore, Maryland. With **George Jean Nathan** he edited the New York periodical *Smart Set* from 1914 to 1923. He and Nathan also founded the detective magazine ***The Black Mask*** in 1920, and in 1924 ***The American Mercury***, which Mencken edited until 1933. He became famous with the publication of *The American Language* (1919), a study of English as developed and used in the USA. It went through three revised editions, and supplementary volumes were also added, the last in 1948. His essays, with their characteristically caustic and often vulgar tone, were collected in six volumes called *Prejudices*, the first published in 1919 and the last in 1927. Though known primarily as entertainments for middle-class America, they were often sharply critical of what Mencken himself termed the 'booboisie'. He also published plays, several critical works, including books on **George Bernard Shaw** and Nietzsche, and three volumes of autobiography, *Happy Days* (1940), *Newspaper Days* (1941) and *Heathen Days* (1943).

***Menologium*** A poetical calendar in Old English prefixed to one of the versions of ***The Anglo-Saxon Chronicle***. It follows the progression of the year, combining sensitive descriptions of nature with an account of the saints' days observed by the Church. Although predominantly Christian, it shows the influence of some pre-Christian elements.

**Mercer, David** 1928–80 Dramatist. Born in Wakefield, Yorkshire, he wrote prolifically for television, the stage and films. He established his reputation with a television trilogy later published as *The Generations* (1964); a later TV play, *A Suitable Case for Treatment*, broadcast in 1962, was filmed as *Morgan* in 1965. His first West End stage play, *Ride a Cock Horse* (1965), was followed by *In Two Minds* (1967), *Flint* (1970), *After Haggerty* (1970) and *Cousin Vladimir* (1978). As a writer from the working-class North, he frequently took class conflicts and loyalties as his theme, showing their pressures in a series of protagonists who are eccentric, rebellious or in retreat from society. Mercer's dialogue is usually witty, handling profound ideas and complicated themes with energy and grace; his more abstract style of writing, as in *Duck Song* (1974), worked less well in the theatre.

**Merchant of Venice, The** A comedy by **William Shakespeare**, first performed *c*.1596, and published in Quarto (Q1) in 1600 as well as in the First Folio of 1623. A main source was a story by Giovanni Fiorentino. The casket episode is from **Gesta Romanorum**, and Shakespeare may also have had in mind **Marlowe**'s *The Jew of Malta* and the scandalous contemporary reputation of Roderigo Lopez, a Jewish physician executed in 1594 on suspicion of attempting to poison Queen Elizabeth I.

The Venetian merchant Antonio, awaiting the return of his ships, is asked for a loan by his young friend Bassanio, who needs the money to pursue his suit of Portia, heiress of Belmont. Without money until his ships return, Antonio borrows from Shylock, the Jewish moneylender. Shylock, who hates Antonio for his open-handedness (such generosity keeps down the rate of usury in Venice), makes the surprisingly generous offer to accept as a bond for the failure to repay the loan within three months a pound of Antonio's flesh rather than a high interest. Confident of his ships' return, Antonio accepts the bond.

Bassanio wins Portia by choosing the right casket in a test stipulated in Portia's father's will, but celebrations of their marriage are interrupted by the news that Antonio's fleet has foundered, that Shylock has demanded his bond and that the case will be tried before the Duke of Venice. Shylock's hatred of all Christians has been sharpened by the elopement of his daughter Jessica with Bassanio's friend, Lorenzo. Represented in court by an unknown advocate and his clerk (Portia and her maid Nerissa in male disguise), Antonio hears Shylock reject Portia's famous plea for mercy and demand his bond. But Portia triumphantly insists that the bond mentions flesh only, no blood, and the Duke upholds the point. The defeated Shylock is pardoned on condition that he gives half his wealth to Antonio and becomes a Christian.

The celebrations in Belmont, after Portia and Nerissa have revealed their part in the trial to their husbands, are completed with news that Antonio's ships have, after all, returned safely.

The qualities of *The Merchant of Venice* have been, in some ways, distorted by the theatrical impact of Shylock. For almost two centuries (1680–1880), it was normal to perform the play without its final act, so that the curtain-calls could follow Shylock's final exit. In fact the play shows Shakespeare's increasing maturity in the handling of comic form, and is often grouped with *A Midsummer Night's Dream* among the 'middle comedies'.

**Merchant's Tale, The** See *Canterbury Tales, The*.

**Meredith, George** 1828–1909 Novelist and poet. The son of a naval outfitter of Portsmouth, Meredith received part of his education in Germany at the Moravian School at Neuwied. He was articled to a London solicitor at the age of 17, but, more interested in writing than in the law, he published poetry in magazines, beginning with a poem on the Battle of Chillianwallah, which appeared in *Chamber's Journal*. In 1849 he married Mary Ellen Nicholls, the widowed daughter of **Thomas Love Peacock**. She deserted him for the painter Henry Wallis in 1857.

In 1860 Meredith settled down to weekly journalism for the *Ipswich Journal* and to reading for Chapman and Hall, the publishers; in the latter capacity he gave encouragement to the young **Thomas Hardy** and **George Gissing**. His wife died in 1861, leaving him free to marry Marie Vulliamy. The Merediths moved to Flint Cottage at Box Hill in Surrey in 1864; it was to be his home for the rest of his life.

His first published book was *Poems* (1851), which contained the first version of 'Love in the Valley'. Next came two fantasies, *The Shaving of Shagpat* (1856) and *Farina* (1857), and in 1859 his first novel, **The Ordeal of Richard Feverel**. *Evan Harrington*, an autobiographical novel, appeared in 1861, and this was followed by his second volume of poetry, the one that gave him a permanent place as a poet, **Modern Love** (1862).

Over the next 20 years Meredith published a steady flow of novels: **Sandra Belloni** (first called *Emilia in England*, 1864), **Rhoda Fleming** (1865), **Vittoria** (1867), **The Adventures of Harry Richmond** (1871), **Beauchamp's Career** (1876), **The Egoist** (1879), and **The Tragic Comedians** (1880). Another volume of poetry, *Poems and Lyrics of the Joy of Earth*, appeared in 1883, and the novel, **Diana of the Crossways**, two years later.

**Oscar Wilde**, with good reason, described Meredith as 'a prose Browning' and his condensed and loaded prose, discovered in all his novels, is particularly notable in later works: **One of Our Conquerors** (1891), **Lord Ormont and His Aminta** (1894) and **The Amazing Marriage** (1895). His critical essay *On Comedy and the Uses of the Comic Spirit* (1897) is a highly regarded study of the function of comedy in literature. Further volumes of poetry included *Poems and Ballads of Tragic Life* (1887), *A Reading of Life* (1909) and *Last Poems* (1909). Meredith also published a number of short stories.

**Meredith, Owen** The literary pseudonym of **Edward Robert Bulwer Lytton**, 1st Earl of Lytton.

**Meres, Francis** 1565–1647 The clergyman Meres published a sermon and two translations of Spanish religious works, but his importance for Renaissance literature lies in his contribution to a series of apophthegms and *sententiae* inaugurated by the publication of *Politeuphuia* (1598). Meres's contribution, *Palladis Tamia: Wit's Treasury* (1598), written mainly in **euphuistic** prose, has a section entitled 'A Comparative Discourse of our English Poets with the Greek, Latin and Italian Poets'. It offers rapid estimations of mainly contemporary English authors and is important for the dating of **Shakespeare**'s earlier plays. **Chaucer**, 'the god of English poets', is compared to Homer; *Piers Plowman* and **Skelton** are also mentioned. **Michael Drayton** comes out particularly well among the Renaissance poets. The soul of Ovid lives in Shakespeare in his *Venus and Adonis, The Rape of Lucrece* and 'sugred sonnets'. As Plautus and Seneca were the best for Roman comedy and tragedy so Shakespeare 'is the most excellent in both kinds', as witnessed by the comedies he had written by 1598 (*The Two Gentlemen of Verona, The Comedy of Errors, Love's Labour's Lost*, the problematic *Love's Labour's Won, A Midsummer Night's Dream* and *The Merchant of Venice*), and his 'tragedies' (*Richard II, Richard III, Henry IV, Titus Andronicus* and *Romeo and Juliet*). Meres also mentions **Marlowe**, who 'for his epicurism and atheism had a tragical death'.

**Merrill, James** 1926– American poet, born in New York City. His poetry has received four *Poetry* Magazine awards, two National Book Awards, a Pulitzer Prize, and a Bollingen Prize. His early work was published in *Jim's Book* (1942), *The Black Swan* (1946), *First Poems* (1951), *Short Stories* (1954), which despite its title consists of poetry, and *The Country of a Thousand Years of Peace* (1959, revised in 1970). *Selected Poems* was published in 1961 and the collection *Water Street* in the following year. In *Nights and Days* (1966) and *The Fire Screen* (1969) he became increasingly concerned with the visionary and esoteric. *The Divine Comedies* (1976) begins his attempt to mythologize the self in relation to a cosmic order, justifying his homosexuality by arguing that by avoiding procreation he is more like the angels. In *Mirabell* (1978) and *The Changing Light at Sandover* (1982) he again creates 'sacred' books, turning to the ouija board as a source of divine intervention. *From the First Nine*, a volume of selected poems, appeared in 1983 and *Late Settings* in 1985. He has also written two novels, *The Seraglio* (1957) and *The (Diblos) Notebook* (1965).

**Merry, Robert** See **Della Cruscans, The**.

**Merry Devil of Edmonton, The** An anonymous comedy, first performed at the **Globe Theatre** in 1602, and published in 1608. It was found in a volume of Shakespeare in the library of Charles II and for a time was assumed to be one of Shakespeare's plays (see **Shakespeare apocrypha**). **Charles Lamb** attributed it to **Michael Drayton** but it is now acknowledged to be of unknown authorship. The play has a rural setting (Edmonton in those days lay some eight miles from the urban centre of London) and is chiefly concerned with Sir Arthur Clare's objections to the marriage of his daughter Millicent to Raymond Mounchensey. The young couple are helped in their elopement by the kind magician of Edmonton, Peter Fabel. The only part magic has in the play actually takes place in the prologue. Peter Fabel has made a compact with the Devil and his time is up; the Devil comes to collect, but Fabel tricks him into a magic chair, which holds him fast until he agrees to a new deal.

**Merry Tales of the Mad Men of Gotham** A collection of jests of the proverbially wise fools of Gotham by 'A. B.', possibly **Andrew Boorde** (d. 1549). The first extant edition is 1630. The foolishness of the men of Gotham was known in the 15th century, when it is mentioned in the Towneley *Shepherds' Play*. The traditional explanation is that it was a trick to outwit King John who was intending to pass through Gotham, in Nottinghamshire, and perhaps claim the land. By such actions as linking hands around a cuckoo on a bush in order to catch it, the men of Gotham persuaded John that the land was not worth having. There were numerous collections of the jests of the men of Gotham in the 17th century and after.

**Merry Wives of Windsor, The** A comedy by **William Shakespeare**, first published in an unreliable Quarto (Q1) in 1602 and later in the First Folio of 1623. **John Dennis** claimed, in 1702, that the play was written at the Queen's command, and **Nicholas Rowe** embellished the claim in his 1709 edition: 'She was so well pleas'd with that admirable Character of *Falstaff*, in the two Parts of *Henry* the Fourth, that she commanded him to continue it for one Play more, and to shew him in Love.' However attractive the story, it is no more certain than the more recent proposal that it was first performed at the Garter feast of 1597. An equally likely date for the first performance is 1600. The source of the play is unknown, and it may be one of the few examples of a story invented by Shakespeare.

The impoverished Falstaff is lodging at the Garter Inn in Windsor. He decides to woo Mistress Ford and Mistress Page, for money not for love, because he knows that they have control of their husbands' purses. But his scheming is revealed to Ford and Page by Falstaff's disgruntled followers, and the exaggeratedly jealous Ford takes revenge by thrashing Falstaff. To add to the humiliation, the two women play a series of practical jokes on Falstaff, culminating in his being pinched and punched by fairies (the Page family in disguise) in Windsor Forest, to which he has gone, disguised as Herne the Hunter, for an assignation with Mistress Ford. A much subdued Falstaff is finally forgiven and taken home to a fireside and a hot posset. A slightly more serious plot involves the Pages' daughter Anne in an ultimately successful attempt to marry Fenton, the impoverished gentleman she loves, rather than the suitors her parents prefer.

*The Merry Wives of Windsor* is a play written to a well-established comic formula. There seems no reason to doubt that Shakespeare was primarily interested in exploiting the theatrical popularity of Falstaff.

**Merwin, W[illiam] S[tanley]** 1927– American poet, born in New York City and educated at Princeton. His poetry reflects his concern with the effects of the contemporary loss of belief in traditional myths, frequently exploring the sense of emptiness which follows that loss. His first volume, *A Mask for Janus*, appeared in 1952. Among his other works are *Green With Beasts* (1956), *The Drunk in the Furnace* (1960), *The Moving Target* (1963), *The Lice* (1967), *The Carrier of Ladders* (1970, Pulitzer Prize), *The Compass Flower* (1977) and *Feathers From the Hill* (1978). He has also published several translations, including *The Poem of the Cid* (1959), *Spanish Ballads* (1960), *The Satires of Persius* (1961) and *Pablo Neruda, Twenty Love Poems and a Song of Despair* (1969).

**metaphor** Where **simile** asserts the likeness of one thing to another, metaphor asserts their identity. Usually, though not always, something relatively abstract is identified with something relatively concrete, making it more vivid or accessible. Since the mind seems better able to understand a new concept through concrete illustration than abstract explanation, the language is full of dead metaphors, in which illustration has been fully absorbed into concept. 'Metaphor' itself (literally 'a carrying over') is one, and so are 'abstract' and 'explanation'. Certain metaphors, like 'head of State' and 'table leg', seem to inhabit the borderline between death and life.

The terms commonly used nowadays for the figurative or concrete element of a metaphor and its literal or conceptual element are those suggested by **I. A. Richards**: 'vehicle' and 'tenor' respectively. In a good metaphor the two should have enough in common to avoid absurdity while being different enough for the vehicle to enrich the tenor as well as illustrating it. Where tenor and vehicle are particularly difficult to distinguish – as in **Blake**'s 'The Sick Rose' – it is customary to speak of **symbol** (or at least symbolic metaphor).

As might be expected, creative literature uses more live metaphors than ordinary language does. These are distinguished from dead metaphors by the fact that the figurative element has not been absorbed into the conceptual, but it should be emphasized that the specific images conveyed (which may differ somewhat from reader to reader anyway) are less important than the vehicle's ability to make the idea in the tenor powerfully connotative. Thus, in order to appreciate **Shakespeare**'s 'Bare ruin'd choirs where late the sweet birds sang', it is not necessary to create a mental picture of choir stalls superimposed on winter trees, and choir boys on blackbirds or thrushes. On the contrary, what is required is an openness to a common idea and an aura of suggestion and implication. Indeed, what normally characterizes the mixed metaphor is not so much an exaggerated unlikeness between tenor and vehicle as excessively vivid but incongruous images: 'Let us not be afraid to dive in at the deep end, now we have them on the run!'

**metaphysical poets** A term used to group together certain 17th-century poets, usually **Donne, Herbert, Marvell, Vaughan** and **Traherne,** though other figures like **Abraham Cowley** are sometimes included in the list. Although in no sense a school or movement proper, they share common characteristics of **wit,** inventiveness and a love of elaborate stylistic manoeuvres.

Metaphysical concerns are the common subject of their poetry, which investigates the world by rational discussion of its phenomena rather than by intuition or mysticism. **Dryden** was the first to apply the term to 17th-century poetry when, in 1693, he criticized Donne: 'He affects the Metaphysics . . . in his amorous verses, where nature only should reign; and perplexes the minds of the fair sex with nice speculations of philosophy, when he should engage their hearts.' He disapproved of Donne's stylistic excesses, particularly his extravagant conceits (or witty comparisons) and his tendency towards hyperbolic abstractions. **Dr Johnson** consolidated the argument in *The Lives of the Poets*, where he noted (with reference to Cowley) that 'about the beginning of the seventeenth century appeared a race of writers that may be termed the metaphysical poets'. He went on to describe the far-fetched nature of their comparisons as 'a kind of *discordia concors*; a combination of dissimilar images, or discovery of occult resemblances in things apparently unlike'. Examples of the practice Johnson condemned would include the extended comparison of love with astrology (by Donne) and of the soul with a drop of dew (by Marvell).

Reacting against the deliberately smooth and sweet tones of much 16th-century verse, the metaphysical poets adopted a style that is energetic, uneven and vigorous. (Johnson decried its roughness and violation of decorum, the deliberate mixture of different styles.) It has also been labelled the 'poetry of strong lines'. In his important essay, 'The Metaphysical Poets' (1921), which helped bring the poetry of Donne and his contemporaries back into favour, **T. S. Eliot** argued that their work fuses reason with passion; it shows a unification of thought and feeling which later became separated into a **'dissociation of sensibility'**.

**Metcalf, John** 1938– Canadian novelist, short-story writer, and critic. Born in Carlisle, England, he graduated from the University of Bristol and, in 1962, emigrated to Canada where he has held a variety of teaching positions and writer-in-residence posts, currently living in Ottawa, Ontario. In his fiction Metcalf brings a disciplined, sometimes spare poetic style to capture the beauty and the absurdity of modern life; traditional in format and technique, his stories are hauntingly evocative in their depiction of the human condition. His collections of stories include *The Lady Who Sold Furniture* (1970), *The Teeth of My Father* (1975), *Selected Stories* (1982), and *Adult Entertainment* (1986). His two novels, *Going Down Slow* (1972) and *General Ludd* (1980), satirize the pretentiousness of academic life with biting irony. Metcalf has edited many anthologies of new fiction and a series of high school and college textbooks. Increasingly outspoken in his irritation at the Canadian literary establishment, he published some of his literary criticism in *Kicking Against the Pricks* (1982).

**metonymy** A figure of speech which replaces the name of an object by the name of an attribute or something closely connected with it. It is common not just in literary language but in everyday speech, when we use 'the Crown' for the monarchy, 'the pen' for writing or 'the Press' for journalism. See also **synecdoche**.

**metre** Language 'measured', usually by the foot, into line-lengths of patterned verse. Such measuring can be of four kinds: quantitative (by long and short sounds); syllabic (by syllable count); accentual (by stress count); and accentual/syllabic (by both stress and syllable count).

Since both sense and implication in English rely considerably on stress, quantitative and syllabic metre have never become naturalized, though the influence of classical poetry and French poetry, respectively, has encouraged a number of attempts. Accentual metre, with feet made up of one stressed syllable and a varying number of unstressed ones, was used in Anglo-Saxon and much pre-Chaucerian poetry and is still common in nursery rhymes, jingles and popular ballads. **Gerard Manley Hopkins**, who revived it, calls it sprung rhythm (and its unstressed syllables 'hangers' or 'outrides'); 'strong rhythm' is another, more recent name.

Accentual/syllabic metre, however, is by far the most common kind in English poetry – with good reason, for it accommodates itself easily to natural speech rhythms, as syllabic metre does not, and is less prone than accentual metre to lapse into jingle or singsong. The most common type of foot (or component unit of metre) is the iamb, consisting of one unstressed syllable followed by a stressed one: 'The cur|few tolls|the knell|of part|ing day'. The trochee is the reverse: 'Bright the|vision . . . .'. The anapaest has two unstressed syllables followed by a stressed one: 'And his co|horts were gleam|ing with purp|le and gold'. The dactyl is the reverse of the anapaest: 'O for the|wings of a . . .'. The feet often used to vary these metres are the spondee (— —), the pyrrhic (‿‿) and two so-called 'rocking feet', the amphimacer (—‿—) and the amphibrach (‿—‿).

The four-foot line (tetrameter) and the five-foot line (pentameter) seem to provide the best setting for poetry's blend of formality and freedom, and are in fact by far the commonest verse lines. The iambic pentameter, in particular, has come close to dominating English poetry, used without rhymes in everything from Elizabethan drama and **Milton**'s *Paradise Lost* to **Wordsworth**'s *The Prelude* and **Tennyson**'s *Idylls of the King*, and rhymed in the Renaissance **sonnet** and the satirical verse of **Dryden** and **Pope**. The dimeter, trimeter and hexameter (two-, three- and six-foot lines) are less common. The iambic hexameter is usually known as an alexandrine, and Pope vividly demonstrated the reasons for its relative unpopularity among English poets: 'A needless Alexandrine ends the song/That like a wounded snake drags its slow length along'. The monometer (one-foot line) is rare, like the heptameter (seven-foot line), also called 'fourteeners' when its feet are iambic.

Perhaps surprisingly, these patterns are not restrictive. Indeed, they may offer the poet possibilities lacking in innovations designed to free him from the shackles of metre – like free verse (prose rhythm moderated only by line-length). Accentual/syllabic metre has both rhythm and arithmetic at its service; free verse, only rhythm. It can play off freedom against order, emphasize by reinforcing sense with metrical stress or undercut by doing the opposite; it can add a musical or a hypnotic element by modulating or by formalizing its basic regularities; and it can structure the unorganized as in life we must structure the raw sense-experience presented to us. In fact, accentual/syllabic metre not only may but must make some accommodation with the rhythms of natural speech; otherwise it lapses into doggerel, in which sense is subordinated to and trivialized by a mechanical metre. In good verse, then, absolutely regular lines are probably rather less common than those where at least one foot departs from the norm. And in those lines that are entirely regular not all the stresses will be equal. What determines whether a syllable counts as stressed is not the actual amount of breath used but the amount used in relation to the adjoining syllables; the emphases of sense might even result in an unstressed syllable at one point of the line requiring more effort than a stressed one elsewhere. This is probably the main way in which metre makes its accommodation with the rhythms of prose.

Rhythm, however, is more than the organization of sense-groups centred on meaningful stresses, though this is its most obvious feature. Just as the rhythm of a good games player involves the smooth co-ordination of many movements and a sense of timing, so dictional rhythm involves the co-ordination of stress with pitch and tone, pause and speed. Thus it will be affected not only by the emphases required but also by consonantal clusters, word-length and purpose (e.g. introducing, climaxing, coming to a conclusion). For such reasons, lines that are metrically identical may be rhythmically diverse. Consider these two lines, for instance, both in perfectly regular iambic pentameter but utterly different in effect:

(lust) Ĭs pēr jŭr̆'d,| mūrd'|rŏus, blōod|y̆, fūll|ŏf blāme
(Shakespeare, Sonnet 129)
(the weary weight) Ŏf āll|thĭs ŭn|īntel|lĭgĭb|lĕ wōrld
(Wordsworth, 'Tintern Abbey Re-Visited')

The rhythm of the first, conditioned by its extreme content, is a series of pounding body blows, each accented syllable (with the partial exception of 'full') being heavily stressed. The rhythm of the second, mediating a philosophical sense and contemplative mood, is murmurous. Aided by the relative rapidity of three feet being encompassed by one word, 'unintelligible', and the fact that only 'world' is heavily stressed, it passes easily and mildly into consciousness. The interplay of rhythm, metre and meaning, then, is infinitely subtle in the accentual/syllabic system.

Just why poetry at all times and in all places should have adopted some form of metre is not a question that lends itself to simple and certain answer. There is probably some truth in all of the following explanations. In conjunction with rhyme, metre contributes to the heightening of language that poetry seeks. It becomes part of meaning (in its widest sense) as an element of tone and mood. Like rhyme, it acts in the same way as a picture frame, creating aesthetic dis-tance by signalling that the work is an art-object to be contemplated rather than a statement to be acted on. Or, rather contradictorily, it is an aid to rhetoric. Its order may add authority, its repetitions hypnotize or, modulated, bring a music into meaning. In its varying tension with rhythm there may be a liberating sense of play. But more importantly, it seems to share something of our basic physical being. Our whole body is a system of rhythms accommodated to such regularities as heartbeat, breathing, walking, running, and to certain work activities like threshing, hauling, passing objects along a human chain. And singing – perhaps the earliest poetry – hovers between instinctive bodily activity and the activities of work and play. One thing is sure: the patterning of language required by metre is not the arbitrary requirement it might at first seem.

**metrical romance** See **verse romance**.

**Mew, Charlotte** 1869–1928 Poet and short-story writer. The daugher of an architect, she was born and lived in London. Championed by **Harold Monro**, she published two volumes of verse, *The Farmer's Bride* (1916) and *The Rambling Boy*, which appeared the year after her suicide. Their colloquial diction and restrained expression of romantic passion (mostly for women) was admired by **Virginia Woolf**, who thought her 'unlike anyone else', and by **Thomas Hardy**, who became a close friend, secured her a Civil List pension and called her 'far and away the best living woman poet'. Her *Collected Poems and Prose*, edited by V. Warner, appeared in 1981.

**Meynell, Alice (Christiana Gertrude, née Thompson)** 1847–1922 Poet, essayist and critic. Born in Barnes, she spent much of her childhood in Italy and became a Roman Catholic in 1868. She married the journalist and poet Wilfrid Meynell (1852–1948) in 1877, helping him with his periodical, *Merry England* (founded in 1883), to which she contributed a number of critical essays, and joining him in the rescue of **Francis Thompson** from destitution. Literary gatherings at her Bayswater home attracted other writers, notably **George Meredith** and **Coventry Patmore**. Her poetry, the best of which takes religious mystery as its theme, appeared in *Preludes* (1875), *Poems* (1893), *Other Poems* (1896), *Later Poems* (1902), *A Father of Women* (1917) and *Last Poems* (1923), together with a *Collected Poems* of 1912. Among several volumes of perceptive and original essays were *The Rhythm of Life* (1893), *The Colour of Life* (1896), *The Spirit of Place* (1899), *Ceres' Runaway* (1909) and *The Second Person Singular* (1921). A centennial volume of *Poetry and Prose* (1947) was introduced by **V. Sackville-West**.

*Michaelmas Term* A comedy by **Thomas Middleton** performed by a **boys' company** *c*.1606 and published in 1607. It satirizes materialism and mercantile affluence by portraying the self-defeating acquisitiveness of a London woollen-draper, Ephestian Quomodo.

Quomodo tricks Easy, an amiable gentleman from Essex, out of his estates. Gloating over his prospects as a gentleman landowner, he feigns death to determine whether his wife and son deserve their new status. But his 'widow' falls in love with Easy and his son is unmoved by his father's 'death'. To complete Quomodo's downfall, he is tricked into signing a document that returns Easy's land to him.

*Middlemarch: A Study of Provincial Life* A novel by **George Eliot**, first published in four volumes in 1871–2.

Initially the narrative concentrates on the blighted marriage of the wealthy young Puritanical idealist, Dorothea Brooke, to the desiccated middle-aged pedant, Dr Edward Casaubon, who labours fruitlessly on his *Key to All Mythologies*. Upon his death, affection develops between Dorothea and her former husband's cousin, Will Ladislaw, who eventually marries her. Another narrative strand traces the career of the equally idealistic Dr Tertius Lydgate, devotee of scientific progress and of the new medicine in particular, who errs disastrously in marrying the local mayor's daughter, Rosamund Vincy, whose foolish social ambitions ruin his life. A third narrative depicts the down-to-earth relationship between Fred Vincy (Rosamund's brother) and Mary Garth, daughter of the honest estate-manager, Caleb Garth. And finally the affairs of Bulstrode, the rich hypocritical banker who harbours a grim secret, are followed to their humiliating end. The incidents in the lives of the characters are skilfully woven together by George Eliot and fused into a compelling narrative portraying English economic, social, and religious life, as well as offering a profound comment upon the futility of human aspiration during the pre-Reform years 1829–32.

But *Middlemarch* is more than a collection of carefully wrought narratives. As it reaches back and looks forward, many assorted individuals come to life: Dorothea's uncle Mr Brooke, a characteristic 18th-century landowner and source of much unintentional humour; Mrs Cadwallader, the witty wife of the Rector, himself hardly a fisher of souls; Sir James Chettam, a stolid local squire who marries Dorothea's sister, Celia; Mrs Bulstrode, a woman of dignity and integrity, and the billiard-playing vicar, Camden Farebrother. Beyond these is a huge gallery of briefer portraits of servants, auctioneers, clergymen, businessmen, housewives, labourers, tenants, medical men, school-

mistresses, children, apothecaries – indeed the list seems limitless. Each may appear fleetingly, but collectively they form a vivid, energetic, and panoramic picture of the England of their times and in many cases they play a role in the development of the narrative as well.

**Middleton, Christopher** 1926– Poet. Born in Truro, he read German and French at Oxford. He has lectured at the Universities of Zurich and London, but since 1965 he has taught at the University of Texas. Middleton is a prodigious translator of European (chiefly German) literature.

*Torse 3* (1962), his first mature collection, marked the beginning of an extensive quest after innovation and experiment. Elliptical, difficult, impersonal, allusive, pan-European, Middleton's writing eschews both the narrowness of the **Movement** and the self-disclosure of **Confessional Poetry**. His most 'American' poems, 'Apocrypha Texana' in *Two Horse Wagon Going By* (1986), are explicitly those of an outsider. During the 1960s and 1970s he was able to experiment and develop in a non-programmatic way in *Nonsequences/Selfpoems* (1965), *Our Flowers & Nice Bones* (1969), *The Lonely Suppers of WV Balloon* (1975) and *Carminalenia* (1980). (There was also a book of prose: *Pataxanadu and Other Prose*, 1977.) The work selected from these volumes for *111 Poems* (1983) displays the range of technical resources he had used, from impacted 'micropoems', collages, **concrete poetry** and formal texts which disrupt syntax, reference, and which vary the visual disposition of line, through to excursions into free translation and adaptation. His thematic range is equally broad. Since the mid 1970s, in a series of impressionistic notes and essays, collected as *The Pursuit of the Kingfisher* (1983), he has outlined his later poetics, and has emphasized the primitive impulses underlying sophisticated poetic utterance.

**Middleton, Conyers** 1683–1750 Theologian. The son of the rector of Hinderwell, near Whitby in Yorkshire, Middleton became a fellow of Trinity College, Cambridge, and head of the University Library in 1721. He published a *Life of Cicero* in 1741 but is best remembered for *A Free Inquiry into the Miraculous Powers Which Are Supposed to Have Existed in the Christian Church through Several Successive Ages* (1748), which examined and rejected the evidence for post-apostolic miracles. The book caused a considerable disturbance and showed that some of the principles of **Deism** could find a sympathetic response in the ranks of the established Church.

**Middleton, Stanley** 1919– Novelist. During a career as a Nottingham schoolmaster, Middleton has produced 24 novels – a new book appearing regularly once a year – all set in his native Potteries region. His work has been aptly praised as 'implacably domestic', each novel scrutinizing the effect on a central individual of crises of marriage, vocation or – as in works like *Entry into Jerusalem* (1982) or *Valley of Decision* (1985) – artistic achievement. His 1974 novel *Holiday* was a joint winner of that year's Booker Prize. Middleton's novels are noteworthy not for depicting any extraordinary experience, nor for any modulating humour or irony (the lack of both sometimes causing earnestness), but for a studious, fastidiously honest pondering of provincial suburban existence.

**Middleton, Thomas** *c.*1580–1627 Playwright. The son of a master bricklayer, Middleton was probably born in London. He may have spent some time at Gray's Inn after leaving Oxford, and is identified as a working playwright in **Philip Henslowe**'s *Diary* in 1602. His literary ambitions were already evident – he had published three volumes of verse by 1600 – and his industry is attested by the plays he wrote for the **boys' company** of St Paul's at the same time as he was providing material for the adult Admiral's Men. The city comedies, written for boy actors from 1602 to 1607, include some of his best plays, *A Mad World, My Masters* (*c.*1605), *A Trick to Catch the Old One* (*c.*1605) and *Michaelmas Term* (*c.*1606). For adult companies, he wrote, with **Dekker**, *The Honest Whore* (1604) and *The Roaring Girl* (published 1611), and his own comic masterpiece, *A Chaste Maid in Cheapside* (1611). Like all Middleton's plays, these comedies combine several plots, sharing themes and, sometimes, characters. They make moral, but strangely uncorrective, observations on mercantile values and manners.

After 1613, Middleton was responsible for many City of London pageants, serving as City Chronologer from 1620 until his death; but he continued to write plays. Three collaborations with **William Rowley**, in which critics have detected a sharp division between the work of the collaborators, are notable, *A Fair Quarrel* (published 1617), *The World Tossed at Tennis* (published 1620) and the outstanding tragicomedy *The Changeling* (1622), in which Middleton's fluency and craftsmanship are unerring. He is an unfussy poet, with a fine ear for dialogue. That he was also tough-minded is suggested by the sombre perceptions of his insistently unsentimental plays, as well as by the vigour of his boldly anti-Spanish satire in *A Game at Chess* (1624) and the almost mischievous conclusion to his tragedy, *Women Beware Women* (*c.*1625), a scene of slaughter verging on comedy which has reinforced the argument of those critics who believe Middleton wrote *The Revenger's Tragedy*.

*Midsummer Night's Dream, A* A comedy by **William Shakespeare**, first performed *c.*1596 and published in Quarto (Q1) in 1600 as well as in the First Folio of 1623. The story is gathered from a number of sources and amplified by Shakespeare's own invention.

Theseus, Duke of Athens, is to wed the Amazon queen, Hippolyta. Egeus asks for his judgement on his daughter Hermia, who has refused his order to marry Demetrius. Theseus upholds Egeus and the law, which requires that Hermia should obey her father or choose between death and a nunnery. Hermia decides to elope with the man she loves, Lysander, and confides her plans to Helena. Helena, who loves Demetrius, in turn tells him, and the four young people arrive at various points of a wood near Athens.

In this fairy wood, Oberon, king of the fairies, quarrels with his queen, Titania, over the care of a changeling boy. He punishes her by dropping in her eyes the juice of a magic flower, which will make her love the first person she sees on waking. Later, having overheard Helena pleading with Demetrius to love her, he instructs his servant Puck to drop the juice into Demetrius's eyes. But Puck confuses Lysander with Demetrius, with the result that Lysander falls in love with Helena, as does Demetrius when Oberon tries to correct Puck's error.

Also in the wood are several Athenian artisans, rehearsing the play of Pyramus and Thisbe, which they hope to present at the wedding of Theseus and Hippolyta. The dominant one, a weaver called Bottom, is mischievously given an ass's head by Puck, and it is the ass-headed Bottom whom Titania first sees (and falls in love with) when she wakes. Oberon's magic eventually unravels all and, at the wed-

Pyramus and Thisbe, from a woodcut in an edition of Ovid's *Metamorphoses* published in 1538. Bottom and his companions act the story of the lovers to celebrate the marriage of Theseus and Hippolyta at the end of Shakespeare's *A Midsummer Night's Dream*.

ding celebrations of Theseus and Hippolyta, Hermia is matched with her Lysander and Helena with her Demetrius, while Bottom and his fellow actors perform their play to the assembled nobles.

The most persistently popular of all Shakespeare's comedies, *A Midsummer Night's Dream* is much more than a piece of gentle fairy-fun. Its concern with illusion and reality has been amply demonstrated by many critics as has its profound exploration of the whole art of theatre.

**Mill, James** 1773–1836 Philosopher, economist and historian. Born the son of a shoemaker in the Scottish village of Forfar, Mill was a boarder at Montrose Academy before being sent by patrons to train for the ministry at Edinburgh University. In 1802, however, Mill left for London and earned his living as a freelance journalist, editing two periodicals and contributing to others, including *The Edinburgh Review*. His marriage in 1805 resulted in a family of nine children, including **John Stuart Mill**. In 1806 Mill began the lengthy project of writing *The History of India*, published in 1817, in which he concentrated not on wars and the lives of the country's successive rulers, but upon social analysis. Despite his reputation as a radical, the work won him a position with the East India Company. In 1808 Mill met **Jeremy Bentham** and became a warm disciple of **Utilitarianism**. Bentham's reclusive nature facilitated Mill's emergence as leader of the 'philosophical radicals'. He encouraged the work of other disciples, notably that of the economist **David Ricardo**, took an active part in founding the Benthamite organ, *The Westminster Review*, and, in his own writings, such as *Elements of Political Economy* (1821), *Analysis of the Human Mind* (1829) and *Fragment on Mackintosh* (1835), applied Benthamite principles to a wide range of subjects. His psychological justification of Utilitarian theory, found in the *Analysis*, was derived from **Hartley**'s theory of association. J. S. Mill's *Autobiography* (1873) provides a lasting testament to the way in which Mill put theory into practice by beginning the rigorous education, intended to fit his son for future leadership of the Benthamite cause, at the tender age of three when the first important associations are formed.

**Mill, John Stuart** 1806–73 Philosopher, economist and administrator. Born in Pentonville, London, Mill was the eldest son of **James Mill** and received from his father a formidably rigorous education designed to equip him as leader of the next generation of the 'philosophical radicals' (see **Utilitarianism**). Mill's *Autobiography* (1873) tells how he started Greek at three, and at eight, Latin, history, geometry, logic, mathematics and political economy as taught by

John Stuart Mill. A detail from the portrait by G. F. Watts, 1873. National Portrait Gallery, London.

**Adam Smith** and **David Ricardo**. The duty of weighing the evidence for himself, combined with the task of teaching his siblings, prevented his education from being merely mechanical. A year spent in France (1820–1) left Mill with a keen interest in French society and politics and enabled him to pursue further studies in chemistry, botany, mathematics, psychology, Roman law and Aristotle.

In 1823 his father's influence obtained for him a clerkship in the East India Company where he worked until 1858. His spare time was spent editing the papers of **Jeremy Bentham**, writing articles for periodicals, notably the Utilitarian *Westminster Review*, and in discussion with like-minded contemporaries at meetings of the Utilitarian Society (1823–6) and the London Debating Society, where he first encountered **Coleridge**'s views. In 1826 Mill suffered an acute attack of depression which led him to re-evaluate the Benthamite doctrines of his upbringing and to judge that they had wholly neglected the cultivation of the emotions in favour of developing the intellect. The poetry of **Wordsworth**, with its emphasis upon the morally educative role of emotional association, played a restorative part in redressing the balance. By 1830 Mill had begun to revise his philosophical and economic thinking in the light of those aspects of St Simonian, Comtean and Coleridgean ideas which seemed to offer truths neglected by Benthamism. The strength of his initial reaction against 'sectarian Benthamism' was tempered by the constructive eclecticism which was to characterize his thought. As the essays on Bentham (1838) and Coleridge (1840) reveal, Mill saw the moral and mental improvement of mankind, to which he was dedicated, emerging, not from one set of assumptions superseding and defeating another, but from toleration of diversity and the achievement of a synthesis of the elements of truth from competing or apparently outmoded philosophies.

In 1830 Mill met Mrs Harriet Taylor, whom he claimed to be the dominant intellectual influence in his life, and continued an intense but Platonic relationship with her until their marriage in 1851, two years after her first husband's death.

In 1858 Mill retired from the East India Company shortly after his promotion to Chief of the Examiner's Office, and declined government service. After hs wife's unexpected death at Avignon in 1858 Mill bought a house there so that he might be near her grave, returning to London only for short visits every year. In 1865–8 he served as independent MP for Westminster, a seat which he won despite his refusal either to campaign or pay any contributions towards the expenses of a campaign. In Parliament Mill made notable contributions to debates upon Irish land reform and women's suffrage. Attended by his step-daughter, Mill spent much of the rest of his life at Avignon, where he died in 1873.

Mill's influence, as the voice of 19th-century liberalism, sprang in part from his deep-seated conviction of the connection between theory and practice. He was able to deploy his immense learning and capacity for logical analysis in such a way that the central thread of argument always emerged clearly. His major works, therefore, often gained a readership far wider than their apparent subject matter would invite. In books such as *The System of Logic* (1843) or *Principles of Political Economy* (1848) Mill was able to use the platform of theoretical discussion to present his unconventional views on contemporary society. Mill published a plethora of essays and reviews from his early twenties, amongst which the most noteworthy are those on Bentham and Coleridge (1838, 1840), *On Liberty* (1859), *Utilitarianism* (1861), 'Auguste Comte and Positivism' (1865), *The Subjection of Women* (1869) and *Three Essays on Religion* (1874).

**Mill on the Floss, The** A novel by **George Eliot**, published in 1860.

The story concerns Maggie Tulliver and her brother Tom, the children of the miller of Dorlcote, an honest but ignorant and unimaginative man. His wife is weak and foolish. Tom himself, in spite of being dearly loved by Maggie, is resourceful but insensitive. In this oppressive environment Maggie's intelligence, scholarly competence and wide-ranging imagination become liabilities, especially in a woman. She responds to Philip Wakem, the deformed son of the leading lawyer in the nearby town of St Ogg's, as the only person who can appreciate her intellectual life and sympathize with her interests. But Tulliver regards the lawyer Wakem as his enemy and Tom, blindly supporting his father's cause, makes Maggie give up Philip's friendship.

After Tulliver's death Maggie goes to St Ogg's to stay with her cousin Lucy, who is to marry Stephen Guest. He is attracted to Maggie and his irresponsible behaviour on a boating expedition compromises her reputation. Tom turns her out of his house and she is ostracized by local society, except for Lucy, Philip and the rector, Dr Kenn. Autumn brings a flood which threatens the mill, and Maggie attempts to rescue Tom. She fails, and brother and sister are drowned together, but not before they have briefly recaptured the affection they felt for each other as children.

Response to *The Mill on the Floss* has, since its first publication, been divided between admiration of the skill with which George Eliot evokes

An illustration by W. J. Allen for George Eliot's *The Mill on the Floss* (1860). Maggie and Tom meet their deaths in the flood.

rural life as a background to Maggie and Tom's childhood and criticism of the novel's rushed and arbitrary ending.

**Millay, Edna St Vincent** 1892–1950 American poet, born in Rockland, Maine. Her first collection, *Renascence and Other Poems* (1917), consisted of pieces she had written as an undergraduate at Vassar. The poems in a second volume, *A Few Figs from Thistles* (1920), established her as a representative voice of her generation in their freshness, gaiety, and implied rebellion against established moral standards. Her popularity continued to grow with the publication of her third volume, *The Harp-Weaver and Other Poems* (1923), which exhibited her mature style and mastery of traditional verse forms; it received the Pulitzer Prize in 1923. She wrote less as time went on, but her later works showed a new political and social consciousness. They include *Distressing Dialogues* (1924), a book of satirical sketches written under the pseudonym of Nancy Boyd, *Three Plays* (1926), *The King's Henchman* (1927), a libretto, *The Buck in the Snow and Other Poems* (1928) and *Fatal Interview* (1931), a sonnet sequence. Subsequent volumes of verse are *Wine from these Grapes* (1934), *Conversation at Midnight* (1937), *Huntsman, What Quarry?* (1939) and *Make Bright the Arrow* (1940).

**Miller, Arthur** 1915– American playwright, born in New York City, the son of a Jewish manufacturer whose business failed during the Depression, Miller studied journalism at the University of Michigan. His first Broadway play, *The Man Who Had All the Luck* (1944), closed after only four performances.

His next four plays, however, were enthusiastically received by the critics. His concern with the disruptive and inevitable conflict between successive generations was first shown in *All My Sons* (1947, New York Drama Critics Circle Award), the story of a veteran who discovers that his father sold faulty airplane parts to the government. His celebrated modern tragedy **Death of a Salesman** (1949), which received both the Pulitzer Prize and the New York Drama Critics Circle Award, examined similar issues in its portrait of the unsuccessful salesman Willy Loman. Like Ibsen, whose *An Enemy of the People* he translated in 1950, Miller often explores the origins and consequences of shameful actions. **The Crucible** (1953) clearly relates the issues of the 1692 Salem witch trials to those of the era of McCarthyism in the USA. (Miller himself was one of the many who refused to give names when summoned before the House Un-American Activities Committee in 1956 because of his left-wing politics.) *A View from the Bridge* (1955, revised 1956), which also won a New York Drama Critics Circle

Award, is an examination of the tragic consequences of Sicilian-American longshoreman Eddie Carbone's forbidden passion for his niece Catherine. Originally produced together with *A View from the Bridge* was the one-act play *A Memory of Two Mondays* (1955), about a young man's resolve to extricate himself from the drudgery of life in a Manhattan automobile parts warehouse and go to college.

After an eight-year absence from the New York stage, Miller returned with *After the Fall* (1964), a semi-autobiographical play with obvious references to his marriage to Marilyn Monroe; and *Incident at Vichy* (1964), which deals directly with the Nazi persecution of the Jews – an undercurrent in much of his other work. *The Price* (1968), his last international success, again examines the issues of family conflict and filial disloyalty. Subsequent plays include *The Creation of the World and Other Business* (1972), *Up from Paradise* (1974), *The Archbishop's Ceiling* (1977) and *The American Clock* (1980). *Theatre Essays* (1973) is a collection of Miller's writings about his own work, and includes the well-known essay 'Tragedy and the Common Man' (1949). He has also written a novel about anti-semitism, *Focus* (1945), and the screenplay for *The Misfits* (1961). *I Don't Need You Anymore* (1967) is a collection of short stories; *In Russia* (1969), written with his wife, the photographer Inge Morath, and *Salesman in Beijing* (1984) are travel journals.

**Miller, Henry (Valentine)** 1891–1980 American writer, born in New York City. After attending college for just two months, he took various jobs and ended up working for Western Union from 1920 to 1924. He left the telegraph company to pursue his writing, selling poems door-to-door and then opening a speakeasy in order to support himself. In 1930 he moved to Paris, where he lived until 1939. There he wrote his most famous work, *Tropic of Cancer* (1934), an autobiographical narrative describing the promiscuous lifestyle he witnessed in Paris. Because of its sexual frankness, the book was considered pornographic and was suppressed in both the USA and England. (It was not in fact published in the USA until 1961.) *Black Spring* (1936), which consists of ten autobiographical stories, and *Tropic of Capricorn* (1939), an account of his years with the telegraph company, were also suppressed.

Following a trip to Greece in 1939, Miller produced what some consider his best work, *The Colossus of Maroussi* (1941), a travel book which is more about people than places. He returned to the USA in 1940 and toured the country by car. Drawing upon this experience, he wrote *The Air-Conditioned Nightmare* (1945), a book of sketches in which he decries the materialism – the spiritual and cultural desolation – of life in his native land. He expresses similar sentiments in *Remember to Remember* (1947). His concern with the role of the artist within society is evident in both these works, and in his earlier *The Plight of the Creative Artist in the United States of America* (1944). Miller was also a painter, and with Hilaire Hiler and **William Saroyan** he wrote *Why Abstract?* (1945), a discussion of modern painting. Among his other notable works are *The World of Sex* (1940), *Books in My Life* (1951), *The Time of the Assassins: A Study of Rimbaud* (1956) and a trilogy – *Sexus* (1949), *Plexus* (1953, first published in French in 1952) and *Nexus* (1960) – collectively titled *The Rosy Crucifixion*. A heavily illustrated volume entitled *My Life and Times* was published in 1971.

**Miller, J. Hillis** See **deconstructive criticism**.

**Miller, Joaquin** 1839–1913 The pen-name of the American poet Cincinnatus Hiner (or Heine) Miller. Born in Liberty, Indiana, as a young man Miller moved to the Oregon frontier and later lived with Digger Indians in northern California. He published his first collection of poems, *Specimens*, in 1868. In the following year came *Joaquin et al.*, a defence of the Mexican bandit, Joaquin Murietta, from whom he derived his nickname. In 1870 he went to London and there published *Pacific Poems* (1871), which won acclaim from the **Pre-Raphaelites**, especially **Dante Gabriel Rossetti**, who took an active interest in this 'Byron of Oregon' and helped him revise his next book of poetry, *Songs of the Sierras* (1871), which made him famous. He produced numerous other volumes of poetry, novels, plays, including the successful *The Danites of the Sierras* (1877) about the Mormons, and an autobiography, *Life amongst the Modocs* (1873).

**Miller's Tale, The** See *Canterbury Tales, The*.

**Millin, Sarah Gertrude** 1889–1968 South African novelist. Born Sarah Liebson, she was educated in Kimberley, and published her first novel, *The Dark River*, in 1920. She was the author of several novels which are generally regarded as a major contribution to South African fiction during the inter-war period. Among them are *Adam's Rest* (1922), *God's Stepchildren* (1924), *Mary Glenn* (1925) and *The Sons of Mrs Aab* (1931). Her novels have been praised for the awareness they display of the realities and complexities of racial conflict, a subject she explored further in a study entitled *The South Africans* (1926, revised 1934). She also published biographies of Rhodes (1933) and Smuts (1936).

**Milman, Henry Hart** 1791–1868 Historian and poet. The son of a fashionable physician, Milman was born in London and educated at Eton College and Brasenose College, Oxford. He won the Newdigate Prize for Poetry and the Chancellor's Essay Prize, and was made a fellow of his college in 1814. His career as a poet began with *Fazio: A Tragedy* (1815) and *Samor: Lord of the Bright City* (1818). Milman was ordained in 1816 and appointed rector of St Mary's, Reading, in 1818. He continued to write dramatic poetry: *The Fall of Jerusalem* (1820), *The Martyr of Antioch* and *Belshazzar* (1822), *Anne Boleyn* (1826) and *Nala and Damayanti and Other Poems* (translations from the Sanskrit, 1835). He became Professor of Poetry at Oxford in 1821.

Milman is better remembered as a historian. His *History of the Jews* (1830), *History of Christianity* (1840) and *History of Latin Christianity* (1854–5) reflect his admiration for the work of **Edward Gibbon**, whose *Decline and Fall* he edited (1838–9) and whose biography he wrote (1839).

He became rector of St Margaret's, Westminster, in 1835 and dean of St Paul's in 1849. His later publications included *The Life of Thomas à Becket* (1860), *The Annals of St Paul's Cathedral* (1868) and versions of *The Agamemnon* of Aeschylus and *The Bacchae* of Euripides (1865).

**Milne, A[lan] A[lexander]** 1882–1956 Children's author, humorist, novelist and playwright. The son of a Scottish schoolmaster, Milne won a scholarship to Westminster School and later read mathematics at Cambridge. His real interest was in light-hearted writing and at the age of 24 he became assistant editor of *Punch*. After serving as a signals officer in World War I he won additional good opinions as a playwright, with *Wurzel-Flummery* (1917), *Mr Pim Passes By* (1919, published 1922), *The Truth about Blayds* (1921, published 1922) and *The Dover Road* (1921, published 1922). His great success, however, came as a writer of **children's literature**. *When We Were Very Young* (1924) and *Now We Are Six* (1927) were verses about his young son Christopher Robin. The books by which he will always be remembered are *Winnie-the-Pooh* (1926) and *The House at Pooh Corner* (1928). Both were based on the imaginary conversations and adventures of Christopher Robin's toys, with the boy making an occasional, masterful appearance to sort out some minor crisis or muddle. While each toy has one distinctive characteristic – Pooh's greediness, Eeyore's misanthropy or Piglet's timidity – they also emerge as individuals in their own right, talking very much in character and occasionally with an underlying humour more meaningful to adults than to children. But the stories in which they feature are perfectly adapted to young readers' interests, concentrating on topics such as birthday presents, the quest for food and mini-adventures involving unexpected bouts of bad weather, mysterious footprints or getting lost. The little verses sung by Pooh and **E. H. Shepard**'s illustrations are also memorable.

After these little books Milne turned away from children's writing, coming to resent his success in this area at the expense of his other, adult work. This includes: a murder mystery, *The Fourth Wall* (1929); two novels, *Two People* (1931) and *Chloe Marr* (1946); a plea against war, *Peace with Honour* (1934); and an autobiography, *It's Too Late Now* (1939). His last triumph was a stage adaptation of **Kenneth Grahame**'s *The Wind in the Willows* as *Toad of Toad Hall* (1929), which apart from introducing a talking horse stays close to the original plot and is still revived every Christmas for young audiences.

**Milnes, Richard Monckton, 1st Baron Houghton** 1809–85 Man of letters and poet. The son of a wealthy Yorkshire family, he was educated at Trinity College, Cambridge, where he was a member of the group called the **Apostles** which also included **Tennyson** and **Arthur Hallam**. He became MP for Pontefract in 1837 and a peer in 1863.

During an active life he published five volumes of verse but was less important as a poet than as a patron of letters and generous host to writers at his home, Fryston Hall, in Yorkshire. In *The Education of Henry Adams* his American secretary left a vivid account of these gatherings and of guests like **Swinburne**, whose poetry Milnes defended against hostile criticism. He was also notable for helping to secure the reputation of **Keats**, by his *Life, Letters and Literary Remains of John Keats* (1848).

**Milton, John** 1608–74 Poet. Born in Bread Street, Cheapside, he lived with few intermissions in London for the rest of his life. His father, a Puritan convert from a Catholic Oxfordshire family, had set up as a scrivener (a kind of stockbroker) but also composed music. His prosperity facilitated his son's education and granted him the financial independence necessary to pursue, in adult life, a private programme of study. Having attended St Paul's School Milton was admitted to Christ's College, Cambridge, in 1625 but found university life disappointing. Not only does he seem to have quarrelled with his tutor (possibly he was rusticated in 1626, if this was the occasion for his *Elegia Prima*), but he was pejoratively known as 'the Lady of Christ's' by his contemporaries. While at Cambridge he began to write poems in Latin, Italian and English, including 'At a Vacation Exercise'. Although he had intended to join the clergy, after taking his BA in 1629 and MA in 1632 he showed no anxiety to commit himself to a career, defending his studious leisure and poetic interests to his perhaps impatient father in

'Ad Patrem' (*c.*1634). His family had moved first to Hammersmith in 1631/2 and then in 1635 to Horton, Buckinghamshire, where he continued his private programme of study in European, classical and patristic literature, publishing a few occasional poems. Already, in 1629, he had written his first great lyric in English, the 'Ode Upon the Morning of Christ's Nativity'. 'On Shakespeare' was published in the Second Folio of **Shakespeare**'s plays (1632), *Lycidas* in a volume of memorial verses (1638) to Edward King, a Cambridge contemporary who had drowned while crossing the Irish Sea. Milton's musical interests, no doubt encouraged by his father, had already found expression in collaboration with the musician Henry Lawes on two masques: 'Arcades' (1633), commissioned by the Dowager Countess of Derby, and that which is now known as *Comus*, performed at Ludlow in 1634 to celebrate the institution of her son-in-law, the Earl of Bridgewater, as Lord Lieutenant of Wales, and published anonymously in 1637. Evidently Milton's poetic career was not yet established in England, but in 1638 he undertook a Continental tour, finding in Italy both intellectual delight and an appreciative audience for his Italian verses. There he met Galileo, and, in France, the distinguished Dutchman Hugo Grotius. Meanwhile his closest friend, Charles Diodati (himself an Italian resident in England), died. Written shortly after Milton's return to England in 1639, *Epitaphium Damonis* memorializes his friend in his most sustained Latin poem.

Milton's return was prompted, he said, by news of the Bishops' War, although he took no part in the accompanying controversy until the second Bishops' War of 1641, when he published the anti-episcopal pamphlets *Of Reformation*, *Of Prelatical Episcopacy* and *Animadversions*. As events moved towards a full-scale Civil War, Milton intensified his polemics against the established church in *The Reason of Church Government* (the first pamphlet published under his own name) and *An Apology for Smectymnuus* (1642). In these he joined with the Presbyterian '**Smectymnuus**' (among them his former tutor, Thomas Young) against bishops **Hall** and **Ussher** – although he would later be revolted by the authoritarianism of Presbyterians in their turn. Probably he had already abandoned the notion of an ecclesiastical career. For the better part of the 1640s he acted as a private tutor, a pursuit which seems to have followed adventitiously from the educational needs of his nephews, Edward and John Phillips (Edward left a brief biography of his uncle, and in 1694 printed some of his unpublished poems). In 1642 Milton married Mary Powell, his junior by 16 years, but within a mere six weeks she returned to her Royalist relatives. Her desertion provoked Milton's four pamphlets arguing for the legitimacy of divorce on the grounds of incompatibility (*The Doctrine and Discipline of Divorce*, *The Judgement of Martin Bucer*, *Tetrachordon* and *Colasterion*; 1643–5). He urged the novel view that a mismatch of mind and spirit was a better ground for separation than sexual incompatibility or adultery. Despite the public storm aroused by these pamphlets (which blackened his reputation for the rest of his life) he also found time for a treatise *Of Education* (1644), addressed to his friend Hartlib. Inspired by the wide humanist curriculum he had studied at St Paul's and his own experience as a teacher, he advocated a remarkably extensive regimen for the religious, intellectual and physical training of boys as responsible citizens. By this date the question of a new form of church organization was being widely debated, and Milton's career as a public controversialist now found its most impassioned expression in *Areopagitica* (1644), a classical oration pleading for freedom of the press. In the following year he published also a volume of his early poems (including *L'Allegro* and *Il Penseroso*), but they caused no great stir. He was reconciled with his wife in 1645, and their first child, Anne, was born in 1646, followed by Mary (1648), John (1651) and Deborah (1652), but 1652 also saw the death of his son and his wife. The family now resided in Petty France, Westminster.

Meanwhile Milton had pursued his defence of individual liberties, in the conviction that 'all men naturally were born free, being the image . . . of God himself'. His public role in

John Milton. A detail from the frontispiece to the 1668 edition of *Paradise Lost*. The poem was first published in 1667.

the forging of the English Republic was confirmed in 1649 by his pamphlets attacking monarchy and justifying the regicide of Charles I, *The Tenure of Kings and Magistrates* and *Eikonoklastes* (or 'Image Breaker'), a riposte to a work attributed to the king, **Eikon Basilike** ('The Royal Image'). In the same year he was appointed Secretary of Foreign Tongues to the Council of State, a post which required him to translate diplomatic documents and correspondence. In 1657 **Marvell** was appointed as one of his assistants; by then assistance was the more necessary because after 1651 Milton was effectively blind. Despite the signs that his sight was deteriorating, he had continued to write political pamphlets in an official capacity, answering the Royalist propagandist Salmasius in *Pro Populo Anglicano Defensio* (1651). When this produced a storm of controversy on the Continent he returned to the fray in *Defensio Secunda* (1654), against Du Moulin's *Clamor* (which he wrongly attributed to Alexander More). Here and in the *Defence of Himself* (1655) the personal vilifications of his opponents evoke autobiographical digressions of great interest. Although he considered *Pro Populo* his most significant work to date, he also believed that it had required the final sacrifice of his sight, a conviction reflected in one of his sonnets to Cyriack Skinner (1654/5). Such sonnets are among the few poems Milton wrote in the intervals of prose controversy during the late 1640s and 1650s, and several of these – to Fairfax, Cromwell and Vane, and 'On the New Forcers of Conscience' – share the same public themes. In 1655 the massacre of Waldensian Protestants aroused all of Milton's apocalyptic fervour, so strong in his pamphlets, in 'On the Late Massacre in Piedmont'; the same event required his drafting Cromwell's letters of protest to European rulers. The sonnets on personal topics include another on his blindness, 'When I consider how my light is spent', and one mourning his wife; possibly his second wife, since in 1656 he had married Katherine Woodcock. She and their daughter Katherine both died in 1658.

To these personal distresses was added bitter political disappointment, as the Protectorate crumbled after Cromwell's death. Defiantly, Milton published his republican protest, *The Ready and Easy Way to Establish a Free Commonwealth*, even as the restoration of the monarchy loomed in 1660. After the Restoration copies of his works were publicly burned. In danger of execution, he was initially a fugitive, then a prisoner, though after payment of a massive fine he was finally released into a life of relative retirement – owing partly, it is said, to the intercession of Marvell (who spoke for him in Parliament) and **D'Avenant**. In 1663 he married Elizabeth Minshull; apart from a retreat to Chalfont St Giles from the plague of 1665, they settled in Bunhill Row. With renewed leisure for poetry, he completed *Paradise Lost*, which he had probably begun before the Restoration. Its publication in .667 was followed in 1671 by the joint publication of *Paradise Regained* and the verse drama *Samson Agonistes*. This, too, it has been suggested, had been written much earlier, although most scholars remain convinced that it is his last major poem. He also published a revised edition of his first poetic collection (1673), and some pamphlets written at an earlier date: on grammar (1669), on Ramist logic (1672), on *The History of Britain* (1670) and *Of True Religion* (1673). Milton died of gout on 8 November 1674, before the second edition of *Paradise Lost* – divided now into 12 books rather than 10 – was published, prefaced with a commendatory poem by Marvell. The *History of Moscovia* was also published posthumously, in 1682.

Milton was a polymath even by Renaissance standards. Although he had asserted, publicly in *Defensio Secunda* and privately in letters, his conviction that his life should be dedicated to a great literary work, his early poems and letters show signs of a self-doubt engendered by what he regarded as his own dilatoriness. Immersed in controversy during the 1640s and 50s, he considered his pamphlets work of his 'left hand' merely. During this time he sketched out plans for an Arthurian epic as well as for biblical dramas (preserved in a manuscript at Trinity College, Cambridge), including 'Adam Unparadized', a dramatization of Genesis probably influenced by Grotius's *Adamus Exil* (1601), and foreshadowing *Paradise Lost*. Ironically, the work turned a full circle back into drama, for **Dryden** obtained Milton's permission to adapt the epic (*The State of Innocence*, 1677).

Only shortly before Milton's death did his poetry begin to acquire a reputation, but his eminence was confirmed by **Addison**'s *Spectator* papers (1712), the first substantial contribution to Milton criticism. Throughout the 18th century his style was considered a model for the 'Sublime' mode in English poetry, though **Johnson**'s complaint that Milton's language was 'harsh and barbarous' anticipated 20th-century attacks by **T. S. Eliot** and **F. R. Leavis**. In the Romantic period Milton's radical politics appealed especially to **Wordsworth**, **Blake** and **Shelley**. For **Keats** he was 'an active friend to Man all his Life, and has been since his death'. Blake and Shelley contended that in *Paradise Lost* Milton 'was of the Devil's party without knowing it', a view which has exerted considerable influence upon critics and readers in this century.

**Minot, Laurence** The author of 11 fervently nationalist poems, all short and most in **alliterative verse**, written during the 14th century, probably in Lincolnshire. Nothing is known of Minot's life. The poems describe battles and political events which took place between 1328 and 1352, and include accounts of Crécy (1346), Halidon Hill (1333), Sluys (1340), Neville's Cross (1346) and the defeat of the Spanish fleet at Winchelsea (1350).

**miracle (or mystery) plays** Dramatized versions of biblical stories from the Creation to the Resurrection, popular in the Middle Ages. Their early history cannot be confidently outlined, though it is widely accepted that the movement towards dramatizing Christian doctrine and biblical history outgrew the Church in which it began. The medieval Church approved the elaboration of the liturgy into dialogue, in order to make its central doctrine of man's redemption plainer. The establishment in 1311 of the Feast of Corpus Christi provided a focus for a form of worship that was moving further from liturgy and further towards performance. By the middle of the 14th century, sequences of biblical plays were being performed all over England. Responsibility for their production was increasingly entrusted to the trade guilds, each working on individual episodes under the overall control of the corporation.

The survival of certain sequences (or, as they are more commonly known, cycles) of miracle plays seems to be largely haphazard. The Chester cycle is probably the earliest. It consists of 25 plays, in rhyming verse. The York cycle contains 48 plays, in verse forms of varying sophistication. A surviving roll lists the guilds responsible for each play. The Wakefield cycle (or Towneley cycle, after the family to whom the manuscript belonged) has 32 plays, five of them in the nine-line stanza associated with the anonymous Wakefield Master, who was the finest exponent of the form. His work, especially in the *Second Shepherds' Play*, exemplifies the secularization of the stories that may have contributed to church hostility during the 15th and 16th centuries. The *Ludus Conventriae*, believed by many scholars to be East Anglian in provenance, relies on the richness of **alliterative verse** for many of its most forceful effects.

Debate about the staging of the miracle cycles continues. Pageant wagons were certainly used in York, Chester and Wakefield, but that does not license the romantic but impractical assumption that the plays were in continuous performance as the wagons bounced and banged along cobbled streets. We must assume that a fixed site, or a few fixed sites, were designated for presentation of the plays to a festive audience as well as to local dignitaries. It was an occasion for the whole community to take stock of itself, to contribute and, no doubt, to compete. During the religious onslaught of the Reformation, and in its aftermath, the miracle plays lost their communal centrality. The fact that some at least survived is further evidence of a growing secularity. By 1550 they were already relics.

**Mirror for Magistrates, A** A 16th-century collection of didactic poetry illustrating the instability of fortune, the fall of the great and the punishment of the vicious. Its complicated publishing history began with the first edition in 1559, commissioned by the printer John Wayland as a continuation of **John Lydgate**'s *Fall of Princes* (itself an English version of Boccaccio's *De Casibus Virorum Illustrium*). An earlier attempt to publish the book during Queen Mary's reign had been prevented by her chancellor Stephen Gardiner. The authors – the title-page named William Baldwin and George Ferrers as chief collaborators – drew on chronicle sources to provide 19 examples of the fall of famous men from the reigns of Richard II to Edward IV. The poems are connected by prose links and many deal with characters later made familiar by **Marlowe** and **Shakespeare**'s history plays: the Mortimers, Richard II, Owen Glendower, Henry VI ('a virtuous prince'), George, Duke of Clarence and Edward IV (who dies through 'surfeiting and untemperate life').

The 1563 edition added eight more stories, including that of Jane Shore by **Thomas Churchyard** and that of Buckingham by **Thomas Sackville**. The volume makes an interesting comparison with Shakespeare's *Richard III*, containing poems on Richard himself, Hastings and Rivers as well as Sackville's poem. The edition of 1578 added the legends of two characters also found in *Henry VI, Part Two*, Humphrey, Duke of Gloucester and Elinor Cobham, Duchess of Gloucester.

In 1574 *The First Part of the Mirror for Magistrates* appeared. This was not the Baldwin–Sackville work but one by John Higgins, the 'first part' of the *Mirror* in the sense that it gives 16 legends from early British history. *The Second Part of the Mirror for Magistrates* (1578) is by yet another hand, Richard Blennerhassett, and gives 12 legends of early British and Saxon characters.

In 1587 another edition appeared. This was the work of Higgins, and contains an enlarged version of his early British histories and a Sackville–Baldwin *Mirror* which is itself enlarged (for example, by the addition of poems about James IV, Flodden and Cardinal Wolsey). The last reshaping was that of Richard Niccols (1610). It includes material from previous versions, shuffles some of it around, omits the prose links and adds **Michael Drayton**'s legend of Thomas Cromwell.

**C. S. Lewis** said that nobody laid down the *Mirror* without a sense of relief, but **Sidney**'s *Apology for Poetry* calls it 'meetly furnished of beautiful parts' and finds it the only poetry, apart from the work of the **Earl of Surrey**, worth mentioning between **Chaucer** and **Spenser**'s *The Shepheardes Calender*.

**Misfortunes of Arthur, The** A tragedy by Thomas Hughes, first performed by the Gentlemen of Gray's Inn for Elizabeth I at Greenwich in 1588. It was published the previous year. The full title, *The Misfortunes of Arthur (Uther Pendragon's Son) Reduced into Tragical Notes*, gives a hint of the begetting of Arthur on Igerna by Uther and traces the story of King Arthur's reign and death in five acts and an epilogue. Thomas Hughes of Gray's Inn had been a fellow of Queens' College, Cambridge.

**Misfortunes of Elphin, The** A romance by **Thomas Love Peacock**, published in 1829. Peacock used the Welsh Arthurian legends to parody the literary affectations of his day and to satirize contemporary political movements. When Elphin succeeds to the kingdom of Ceredigion, much of his territory has been lost through the negligence of Seithenyn, a drunkard who has failed to keep the walls of the kingdom in good repair and allowed the sea to flood the land. Elphin is imprisoned by a neighbouring prince, Maelgon, but the bard Taliesin secures his release by appealing to King Arthur. The book contains many songs and set-piece speeches; some of them adapt or translate Peacock's Welsh sources, while others, like 'The War-Song of Dinas Vawr', are his own.

**Misogonus** A comedy acted at Trinity College, Cambridge, between 1568 and 1574 and printed in 1577. It varies the theme of the prodigal son, popular with playwrights of the time, by making the prodigal the one who stays at home. Misogonus is vicious and debauched, and wastes the fortune of his father Philogonus. The return of the long-lost elder son, the virtuous Eugonus, brings about Misogonus's repentance. The play is notorious for its coarseness and for the elaborate scenes of Misogonus's dissipation.

The author's identity is not known with certainty but evidence points to Anthony Rudd (c.1549–1615), who became Bishop of St David's in 1594.

**Miss Ravenel's Conversion From Secession to Loyalty** A novel by **John De Forest**, published in 1867. Dr Ravenel is a New Orleans physician who is forced to move north because of his Abolitionist beliefs. The sympathies of his daughter Lillie, however, are with the Confederates. Her conversion begins when she and her father settle in New Boston (based on New Haven, where De Forest lived). There she is wooed by two Union officers, Colbourne and Carter. The more dashing and aristocratic Carter better suits Lillie's Southern sensibility. She marries him and for his sake supports the Northern cause. Although his habits of drinking and womanizing seem to have abated, he begins a secret affair with Lillie's young aunt, Mrs Larue. He breaks off the affair after Lillie gives birth to a child, but Dr Ravenel learns of it and informs his daughter. Lillie eventually leaves her husband and later he is killed in battle; she returns to New Boston and finally marries the virtuous Colbourne. Her conversion to Abolitionism is by now complete. In spite of his preference for the Union cause, De Forest – with his customary harshness – satirizes New England society as well as that of New Orleans. The novel is also memorable for its grimly realistic battle scenes, which anticipate those of **Stephen Crane**.

**Mitchel, John** 1815–75 Irish patriotic writer. Mitchel was born near Dungiven, County Londonderry, the third son of a Presbyterian minister. Though he entered Trinity College, Dublin, in 1830 there is no record of his graduation. He worked in a bank and a solicitor's office, qualifying as a solicitor in 1843. In 1842 he met **Thomas Davis**, joined O'Connell's Repeal Association in 1843, and by 1845 was writing for the Young Ireland paper *The Nation*. More republican and anti-British than his associates, he founded his own more extreme paper, *The United Irishman*, in 1848. Soon afterwards he was arrested and convicted of treason. Sentenced to transportation, he was taken to Bermuda, South Africa and, finally, Tasmania, whence he escaped to the USA in 1853. All these experiences were recorded in his most famous work, the *Jail Journal* (1854), which registers his quarrel not merely with British policy but with the economic triumphalism, as he saw it, of British civilization, well represented by **Macaulay**. He became notorious in America for his defence of slavery before and after the Civil War. His other writings include *The Life and Times of Aodh O'Neill* (1846), an edition of pamphlets on the Irish economy by **Swift** and **Berkeley** (1847), a series of *Letters to the Protestant Farmers . . . of the North of Ireland* (1848, republished as a book 1917) and a *History of Ireland* (1868). His savage and sardonic account of the Irish famine and the Young Ireland insurrection of 1848, *The Last Conquest of Ireland (Perhaps)* (1861), assumes a more or less efficient British strategy of systematic extermination and dispersion of the Irish people and shows his familiarity with the polemical techniques of Swift, to whom he has often been compared. **Patrick Pearse** venerated him as one of the four evangelists of Irish Nationality.

**Mitchell, Adrian** 1932– Poet, novelist and dramatist. Born in London, he was educated at private schools and Christ Church, Oxford.

From the start his poetry was populist, rhetorical and overtly political. Accessible forms, popular idioms and immediacy of image and wit are deployed in polemic against bad government and the threat of nuclear war and in celebration of New Jerusalems. He frequently gives public performances of his work, and it has appeared in two widely read anthologies, **Michael Horovitz**'s *Children of Albion* and *The Penguin Book of Socialist Verse*. *For Beauty Douglas* (1982) brings together poems from earlier volumes, including *Out Loud* (1966) and *The Apeman Cometh* (1975). New poems appeared in *On the Beach at Cambridge* (1986). Mitchell's novels include *If You See Me Comin'* (1962) and *The Bodyguard* (1970). Of his work for the stage, the best known is his adaptation of Peter Weiss's *Marat/Sade* (1966).

**Mitchell, James Leslie** See **Gibbon, Lewis Grassic**.

**Mitchell, Julian** 1935– Novelist and playwright. He was educated at Winchester and Wadham College, Oxford. He began his career with a succession of novels in the 1960s: *Imaginary Toys* (1961), *A Disturbing Influence* (1962), *As Far As You Can Go* (1963), *The White Father* (1964), *A Circle of Friends* (1966) and, most notably, *An Undiscovered Country* (1968). Since then he has concentrated on drama, working for the stage and television. As well as adaptations of **Ivy Compton-Burnett**, his stage plays include *Half-Life* (1977), *The Enemy Within* (1980) and *Francis* (1983), but he is perhaps best known for *Another Country* (1981; filmed 1984), about the making of a traitor.

**Mitchell, Langdon (Elwyn)** 1862–1935 American playwright, born in Philadelphia, the son of the novelist S. Weir Mitchell. He began his career as a dramatist with the romantic tragedy *Sylvian* (1885). His best-known production is *The New York Idea*, which examines contemporary attitudes towards love and marriage. He also wrote stage adaptations of novels, including *The Adventures of François* (1900), from his father's novel of 1898, and *Becky Sharp* (1899) and *Major Pendennis* (1916), both based on famous novels by **Thackeray**. A collection of essays, *Understanding America*, was published in 1927.

**Mitchell, Margaret** See *Gone With The Wind*.

**Mitchell, W[illiam] O[rmond]** 1914– Canadian novelist, raconteur and dramatist. He was born in Weyburn, Saskatchewan, and spent part of his youth in Florida. After his return to Canada in 1931 he studied at the University of Manitoba, did various odd jobs, travelled in North America and Europe, completed his BA at the University of Alberta and became a rural schoolteacher. In 1944 he gave up teaching to become a full-time writer. Mitchell's first novel, *Who Has Seen the Wind*, a classic account of a Prairie boyhood, was published in 1947. From 1948 to 1951 he was fiction editor for the news magazine *Maclean's* and lived in Toronto. Since then, apart from periods as writer-in-residence at various Canadian universities, he has mainly lived in Alberta. Between 1950 and 1958 he wrote over 300 scripts for his popular 'Jake and the Kid' series on Canadian Broadcasting Corporation radio. Thirteen of the original stories for these are collected in *Jake and the Kid* (1961). Mitchell is a seminal figure in the development of recent western Canadian writing. He is popular as a raconteur and humorist and much of his work has its origins in oral story-telling. His fiction stresses the value of the organic, natural life. His other works include *The Kite* (1962), *The Vanishing Point* (1973), *How I Spent My Summer Holidays* (1981), and the plays *The Devil's Instrument* (1973) and *Back to Beulah*, published in *Dramatic W. O. Mitchell* (1982).

**Mitchison, Naomi (Mary Margaret)** 1897– Novelist. Daughter of the physiologist J. S. Haldane and sister of the biologist **J. B. S. Haldane**, she published some 70 books during a long career. The best are generally acknowledged to be the novels and stories of the 1920s and 1930s which evoke classical Greece and Rome: *The Conquered* (1923), *When the Bough Breaks* (1924, short stories), *Cloud Cuckoo Land* (1925), *Barbarian Stories* (1929), *Black Sparta* (1928, short stories), *The Corn King and the Spring Queen* (1931) and *The Delicate Fire* (1933, short stories). *The Blood of the Martyrs* (1939) is an original novel of the early Christians in Rome. *Anna Comnena* (1928) is a biography of the Byzantine princess and historian of the 12th century AD.

**Mitford, Mary Russell** 1787–1855 Author of sketches and short stories, novelist and playwright. The daughter of a country doctor in Alresford, Hampshire, who ruined his family through extravagance, she supported her father by her earnings as a writer. The charming *Our Village: Sketches of Rural Life, Character and Scenery* began as a series of contributions to *The Lady's Magazine* in 1819 and appeared in five volumes between 1824 and 1832. The village is Three Mile Cross, near Reading, which itself was made the subject of *Belford Regis: Sketches of a Country Town* (1835). A novel, *Atherton and Other Tales* (1854), was less successful. Miss Mitford's plays include *The Foscari* (1826), *Rienzi* (1828) and *Charles I* (1834). *Recollections of a Literary Life* (1852) offers bright and gossipy comment on her contemporaries.

**Mitford, Nancy (Freeman)** 1904–73 Novelist and biographer. The daughter of the 2nd Baron Redesdale, she was born in London and educated privately. Her younger sister, Jessica, wrote an account of their family life in *Hons and Rebels* (1960). Nancy Mitford's novels generally describe Bohemian life in upper-class society and combine a witty and satiric tone with a sharp ear for dialogue. *Highland Fling* (1931), *Christmas Pudding* (1932), *Wigs on the Green* (1935), and *Pigeon Pie* (1940) were followed by *The Pursuit of Love* (1945), her first real success. Other successful novels included *Love in a Cold Climate* (1949) and *The Blessing* (1951), which follow the same range of characters through numerous affairs of the heart, and are closely observed studies of English class mores. Her biographies include *Madame de Pompadour* (1954), *Voltaire in Love* (1957), *The Sun King* (1966), and *Frederick the Great* (1970).

With A. S. C. Ross she edited and contributed to *Noblesse Oblige: An Enquiry into the Identifiable Characteristics of the English Aristocracy* (1956), a collection of satirical essays on snobbery. She also edited volumes of revealing family correspondence, *The Ladies of Alderley* (1938) and *The Stanleys of Alderley* (1939).

**Mitford, William** 1744–1827 Historian. Educated at The Queen's College, Oxford, he served in the Hampshire militia at the same time as **Edward Gibbon** and published a treatise on England's military strength. His *History of Greece*, published in five volumes between 1784 and 1818, was suggested by Gibbon and praised by **Macaulay**.

**Mittelholzer, Edgar** 1909–65 Guyanese novelist, born in New Amsterdam. Under his mother's rigid puritanism, he grew up passionate for absolute personal freedom. Veerings between order and licence produce many unresolved contradictions in both his moral vision and fictional design, but his 23 novels helped to create a genuine Caribbean consciousness that incorporates Guyanese history and landscape. The first novel, *Corentyne Thunder* (1941), uneasily shackles the authentic realism with which Mittelholzer depicts Indian peasantry in Guyana with overwritten, romantic description, while *A Morning At the Office* (1950), his second novel, is a polished handling of Jamaican race relations, exemplified in personal interactions within a single office on a single day. Much research went into the Kaywana novels, a Guyanese family saga covering the years 1612–1953: *Children of Kaywana* (1952; including *Kaywana Heritage*, separately published from 1976), *The Harrowing of Hubertus* (1954; later published as *Kaywana Stock*) and *Kaywana Blood* (1958). Here vigorous writing and imaginative sweep are weakened by melodrama, sexual frankness by titillation. *Shadows Move Among Them* (1952) and *The Mad MacMullochs* (1959) figure ideally free, sexually liberated communities, yet both are under authoritarian leaders. Mittelholzer's attack on race prejudice in *A Morning At the Office* seems undermined by the hero's inadequately distanced anti-black sentiments in *Latticed Echoes* (1960). In *The Life and Death of Sylvia* (1953), faith in human resilience, and despair over its failure, seem equally weighted. His last novel, *The Pilkington Drama* (1965), ends with a suicide by fire. So did Mittelholzer's own life.

**Mo, Timothy** 1950– Novelist. Born in Hong Kong of English and Cantonese parents, Mo is best known for his second novel, *Sour Sweet* (1982), a densely realistic portrait of London's Chinese community, remarkable for its wealth of detail but also its spry, bizarre comedy. An earlier novel, *The Monkey King* (1978), was set in Hong Kong, a setting Mo has returned to in *An Insular Possession* (1986), an enormous historical novel about the Opium Wars that forsakes Mo's previous gingery wit for a more studied comedy of manners.

***Moby-Dick**, or, The Whale* A novel by **Herman Melville**, published in New York in 1851 and in London, titled simply *The Whale*, in the same year.

The highly complex story begins with the narrator Ishmael's decision to go to sea. On his way to Nantucket he meets and befriends Queequeg, a harpooner from the South Sea Islands who is the image of the noble savage – a 'George Washington cannibalistically developed'. The two friends sign aboard the whaler *Pequod*, named for the first Indian tribe exterminated by white Americans. Before they set sail, a man named Elijah delivers mysterious warnings

about a disastrous voyage and Father Mapple delivers a symbolic sermon about the prophet Jonah who was swallowed by a whale. The *Pequod*'s mysterious Captain Ahab appears after several days at sea. He reveals to the crew the purpose (as he conceives it) of the voyage: to hunt and kill the white sperm whale, known among whalers as Moby-Dick, a whale that on Ahab's previous voyage had cost him his leg. Ahab's eloquence convinces the crew to pledge themselves to his monomaniacal plan for vengeance. Only Starbuck, the first mate, demurs, feeling that Ahab's mission is a sacrilege and a threat to the financial investment the ship's owners have made. Stubb, the second mate, and Flask, the third, are easily drawn into Ahab's plan. The crew, castoffs and refugees of all races and lands, are in their own way a microcosm of humanity. The harpooners are Queequeg, Tashtego (a Gay Head Indian) and Daggoo (an African). On the first encounter with whales, they find that Ahab has kept hidden his own boat's crew, which is led by Fedallah, a Parsee and fortune-teller.

The narrative is sometimes naturalistic, sometimes fantastic and shaped into obscure parables. Large sections dwell upon the science of whales or upon the intricacies of the whaling business and its history. Amid the often turbulent complexity of the narrative form, the dramatic events unfold slowly. As the men of the *Pequod* sail the open sea in search of a single whale, they still occupy themselves with the regular business of whale hunting. Occasional chases after whales, storms, or meetings with other ships punctuate the long voyage. The crew captures and processes a sperm whale; Pip, a young black cabin boy, becomes caught in a harpoon line and is nearly drowned, whereupon he becomes insane; the *Pequod* nearly founders

A detail from 'Pêche du Cachalot', an aquatint after Garneray, 1850. Melville describes the incident in Chapter 56 of *Moby-Dick*. National Maritime Museum.

when Ishmael drowses at the helm; a meeting with the British whaler, the *Samuel Enderby*, provides Ahab with news that Moby-Dick has been sighted recently; and Queequeg has a coffin made when he nearly dies of fever.

When a lightning storm sets the mastheads ablaze with St Elmo's fire, Ahab delivers a speech to his crew that confirms his mad devotion to the quest; the crew is panic-stricken and Starbuck warns Ahab that God is against him. These ominous events lead up to the eventual sighting of Moby-Dick and the three-day chase with which the novel culminates. On the first day the great whale crushes one of the boats and nearly kills Fedallah. On the second day it drags Fedallah down in Ahab's harpoon line, and Ahab's artificial leg is snapped off as the whaleboat is wrecked. Finally, on the third day, a stricken Moby-Dick charges the *Pequod* and smashes her sides. Ahab, in the whaling boat, manages to strike a final blow but is himself caught in the harpoon line and drowned, tied to the whale. The *Pequod* sinks, taking all of the whaling boats and their crews down in the suction. The only survivor is Ishmael, who is shot back up, clinging to the coffin that had been made for Queequeg.

**mock heroic** A term applied to satire which uses for comic effect an epic style elevated out of all proportion to its trivial or dismal subject matter. Major examples include **Dryden**'s *Mac-Flecknoe* and **Pope**'s *The Rape of the Lock* and *The Dunciad*.

**Modern Chivalry** A novel in seven volumes by **Hugh Henry Brackenridge**, published in instalments between 1792 and 1815. Captain John Farrago and his Irish servant, Teague O'Regan, American versions of Don Quixote and Sancho Panza, travel around the Pennsylvania countryside, their adventures providing the occasion for satirical observations about post-Revolutionary American life and manners.

Farrago is a stuffy, aristocratic landowner; Teague, a stereotypical Irishman – irresponsible, untrained, uneducated, one of the men who have been newly placed in positions of power by the Revolution and the institution of democracy. Much of the book consists of a series of incidents in which Teague is given opportunities – as preacher, Indian treaty maker, potential husband for a well-bred young lady, pupil to a French dancing master – for which, according to an earlier set of values, he is socially unqualified. (He is, in fact, unqualified by any standard.) Farrago's unprincipled attempts to discourage and prevent him from exploiting these opportunities derive from his own desire to keep the old aristocratic system in place, thereby retaining Teague as his servant and preserving his own class's exclusive pre-

rogative to fill these roles. The tensions between them thus dramatize the problem of authority and leadership in a democracy.

**Modern Instance, A** A novel by **William Dean Howells**, published serially in the **Century Magazine** in 1881 and in volume form in the following year.

Bartley Hubbard, a young Boston journalist, is married to Marcia Gaylord. The marriage quickly deteriorates, however, because of his unscrupulous business practices and moral decline. Despite her love for her husband, Marcia leaves him. Hubbard sues for divorce but his suit is defeated and the divorce is granted to Marcia. After the divorce he moves to Arizona where he is killed by someone about whom he has published personal details in his newspaper. Marcia, meanwhile, is courted by Ben Halleck, a highly principled man who cannot decide whether or not to leave the ministry for her. The novel ends without giving his final decision. Howells developed the idea of the divorce theme after seeing a performance of the *Medea*. He referred to the novel as his 'New Medea', a 'modern instance' of what would happen to a gradually estranged couple.

**Modern Love** A sequence of 50 poems, each of 16 lines, by **George Meredith**, published in 1862. It traces the decline of passion and the disintegration of a marriage, with the wife dying and the husband taking a mistress after their separation.

**Modern Painters** A five-volume treatise on art by **John Ruskin**, published intermittently between 1843 and 1860.

The full title of the first volume was *Modern Painters: Their Superiority in the Art of Landscape Painting to All the Ancient Masters Proved by Examples of the True, the Beautiful and the Intellectual, from the Works of Modern Artists, Especially from those of J. M. W. Turner, Esq., R.A.* On one level it is a defence of Turner, whose recent contributions to Royal Academy exhibitions had been widely attacked. But it quickly transcends that goal to advocate Truth and Beauty, whose elusive qualities Ruskin finds best exemplified in Turner's work, to consider art as a social force and to praise Nature. All this is expressed in prose both persuasive and grandiloquent. The second volume (1846) is a more formidable treatise on ideas of beauty and the imaginative faculty.

A decade then elapsed while Ruskin developed theories of architecture, morality and society. The third volume (1856) is appropriately sub-titled 'Of Many Things', for it seems, initially, a bewildering mass of diverse topics. The reader is swept through commentary on painting and poetry, on landscape modern, medieval and classical – all enlivened with proliferating references to Homer, Dante, **Wordsworth**, **Byron**, **Scott** and hosts of others. Chapters such as 'Touching the "Grand Style"' and 'Of the Pathetic Fallacy', as well as discussions of the true and the false ideal and of the teachers of Turner, nevertheless give cohesion and unity to this impressive discourse. With the fourth volume (also 1856), whose five opening chapters interpret Turner's art in the light of the theories advanced earlier, came such memorable chapters as 'The Mountain Gloom' and 'The Mountain Glory', relating these natural phenomena to spiritual, social and aesthetic temperaments. The final volume (1860) is marked by its author's conviction that the entire series reveals Turner as the supreme landscape painter. Yet it is also suffused with disappointment and futility, for Ruskin was by now becoming hopeless in the face of the amount of work remaining to be done in art criticism. There is also a growing desire to speak on social questions, clearly shown in 'The Two Boyhoods' with its malediction on industrial England.

*Modern Painters*, then, is large in its ambition and diverse in its accomplishment. The volumes are born of different moods, varying perspectives and shifting purposes. Yet Ruskin's idealism – be it aesthetic or social – does not waver, and the book at last succeeds in embodying (in the words of one critic) 'Ruskin's comprehensive theory of art criticism'.

**modernism** The term for an international tendency in the arts brought about by a creative renaissance during the last decade of the 19th century and lasting into the post-war years. Strictly speaking, modernism cannot be described as a 'movement' or reliably characterized by a uniform style. Indeed it may be said to have embraced a wide range of artistic movements (including **Symbolism**, impressionism, post-impressionism, futurism, constructivism, **imagism**, **vorticism**, **expressionism**, dada, and surrealism) and to have originated in cosmopolitan circles in Berlin, Vienna, Munich, Prague, Moscow, London and Paris. At a slightly later period it spread to New York and Chicago, and became synonymous with a world-wide reaction against positivism and representational art. Its most notable landmarks in English literature are commonly understood to include **Henry James**'s *The Ambassadors* (1903), **Conrad**'s *Nostromo* (1904), **T. S. Eliot**'s *The Waste Land* (1922), and **Joyce**'s *Ulysses* (1922). One might add the work of **Pound**, **Yeats**, **Ford Madox Ford** and **Virginia Woolf** to a list which is by no means exhaustive.

Technically, modernism was distinguished by its opposition to traditional forms and to the aesthetic perceptions associated with those forms. It was persistently experimental. A common quality was the highly self-conscious manipulation of form, together with an awareness of pioneering studies which were contemporaneous in other disciplines. These included, in psychology, **William James**'s *Principles of Psychology* (1890) and Freud's *The Interpretation of Dreams* (1899); in physics, Einstein's *General Principles of Relativity* (1915); and in anthropology, **Sir James Frazer**'s *The Golden Bough* (1890–1915).

**Herbert Read** suggested that modernism 'is not so much a revolution, which implies a turning over, even a turning back, but rather a break-up, a devolution, some would say a dissolution. Its character is catastrophic.' (*Art Now*, 1933.) Much of the difficulty of modernist texts, which has intimidated some readers, stems from this attempt to 'break up' or re-create the experience of reading. **Stream of consciousness**, the use of myth as a structural principle, and the primary status given to the poetic image, all challenged traditional representation.

*Modest Proposal, A, for Preventing the Children of Poor People from Being a Burden to Their Parents, or the Country, and for Making Them Beneficial to the Public* A satirical pamphlet by **Jonathan Swift**, first published in 1729.

Despite his repeated claims to dislike Ireland, Swift was a patriotic defender of the cause of the repressed Irish nation, the conditions of poverty and the carelessness of absentee English landlords moving him to indignant outrage. The central 'proposal' of this satire is that it would make sound economic sense if the offspring of the Irish poor were farmed for the table of the rich English. With the scrupulous reasoning of an economic 'projector', Swift brilliantly imitates the shape and method of such arguments, adopting a dispassionate, even benevolent tone as he sets down the appallingly plausible plan. As with much of his satire, the basic strategy is the literalization of an idea: since the greedy landlords are metaphorically devouring the profits of the country, they might as well literally eat up the inhabitants. The several advantages of this proposal, which it is suggested will benefit everyone, include the reduction of beggars, the year-round availability of tasty meat, profit to the mothers (or 'dams') and the certainty that husbands would look after their women for a change, as a source of their livelihood. Swift by implication suggests that cannibalism on a commercial scale would be no less justifiable than the economic system which allows England to exploit Irish labour and trade. As a rhetorical performance in satiric impersonation the *Modest Proposal* is probably unrivalled in English prose.

**Moir, David Macbeth** 1798–1851 Scots novelist who wrote much in the manner of his friend, **John Galt**. A doctor in Musselburgh, he contributed regularly to *Blackwood's Magazine* and other periodicals, signing his name with the Greek capital delta. *The Life of Mansie Wauch, Tailor in Dalkeith*, his best-remembered book, first appeared in parts in *Blackwood's* and was published in volume form in 1828. Dedicated to Galt, it is the imaginary autobiography of a small-town tailor and contains much wryly humorous observation.

**Molesworth, Mary Louisa** 1839–1921 Author of books for children. Born Mary Louisa Stewart in Rotterdam, she was educated in Switzerland. Her novel *Lover and Husband*, published in 1869, was followed by several other novels written under the pseudonym Ennis Graham. She later turned to **children's literature** with great popular success. Macmillan made a practice of issuing a book by Mrs Molesworth every Christmas, and **Walter Crane** was one of her illustrators. Among the more than 100 books she wrote are *The Cuckoo Clock* (1877), *The Tapestry Room* (1879), *The Adventures of Herr Baby* (1881), *The Children of the Castle* (1890), *The Carved Lions* (1895), *Peterkin* (1902), *The Little Guest* (1907) and *The Story of a Year* (1910).

*Moll Flanders*, *The Fortunes and Misfortunes of the Famous* A novel by **Daniel Defoe**, published in 1722.

Moll Flanders is born in Newgate, where her mother is under sentence of death for theft. The hanging is delayed because 'being found quick with child, she was respited for about seven months' and then her sentence is commuted to transportation to Virginia. The abandoned child is taken in by the mayoress of Colchester, from whom she passes to another gentlewoman who gives her an education; but the son of the house seduces her. She leads an adventurous love life and eventually marries. She visits Virginia with her husband and finds her mother – and discovers that her husband is in fact her brother. She leaves him and her children and goes back to England, where she falls into bad company and finds herself destitute. She becomes a successful thief but is caught and, like her mother before her, transported to Virginia. On the ship is one of her former husbands, who had been a highwayman, and they renew their liaison. Moll inherits her mother's plantation and prospers. When their sentence runs out, she and her husband return to England, where in comfort and serenity Moll looks back from the age of 70 over 'the wicked lives we have lived'.

*Moll Flanders* owes much of its continuing popularity and its importance in the development of English fiction to the fact it is a novel of character, as opposed to an adventurous romance. The book may not be neat or shapely

in structure – indeed, it is riddled with inconsistencies and contradictions – but Moll herself is made an identifiable personality, and her autobiography continually poses questions about the motives for human conduct. The familiar themes of domestic allegiance and self-sufficiency link *Moll Flanders* with Defoe's other fiction, together with his love of portraying urban low life and foreign travel.

**Molloy, Michael (Joseph)** 1917– Irish playwright. Born in Milltown, County Galway, he abandoned training for the priesthood because of illness, then farmed near his birthplace. His foremost works are *The Old Road* (1943), *The Visiting House* (1946), *The King of Friday's Men* (1948), *The Wood of the Whispering* and *The Paddy Pedlar* (1953). Set in Western Ireland in 1817, *The King of Friday's Men* mourns the passing of a feudal way of life. Molloy deals less certainly with the contemporary residue of those folkways, but *The Visiting House* effectively dramatizes the dying institution where country districts were regaled with songs and stories. Molloy's dialect speech at its fluent best carries his often knotty plots. Though more restricted by his region than either **Synge** or **Fitzmaurice**, Molloy is the last remarkable exponent of their folk-drama.

**Momaday, N[atachee or Navarre] Scott** 1934– American Indian writer, born on a Kiowa reservation in Oklahoma, and educated at Stanford. He first became known as an **Emily Dickinson** scholar and as editor of the poems of **Frederick Goddard Tuckerman**. His first novel, *House Made of Dawn* (1968), which was awarded the Pulitzer Prize, is the story of an Indian named Abel who leaves the reservation when he is drafted, and is forced to confront the non-Indian world and its values. Momaday's next publications were a collection of Kiowa folktales, *The Way to Rainy Mountain* (1969), and a volume of poetry, *Angle of Geese and Other Poems* (1974). One of the foremost American Indian writers, his other books include *The Gourd Dancer* (1976) and *The Names: A Memoir* (1976).

*Moments of Vision and Miscellaneous Verses* Poems by **Thomas Hardy**, first published in 1917. A short poem, 'Moments of Vision', gives the volume its title and also evokes its ambience and tenor, for there is much of Wordsworthian introspection, of inner searching, in the collection. Yet whilst the older Hardy (he was 77 at the time of publication) harks back for subject matter, much of the verse is contemporary in composition and one group of poems is given to war and patriotism. But strong human feelings, the pulsations of the heart and the reverberations of folk-song and rural life create a sustained emotional unity unique in collections of Hardy's poetry. The volume includes 'The Last Signal' (about **William Barnes**), 'The Blinded Bird', 'During Wind and Rain', and 'Near Lanivet' (the latter two among those about Emma, his first wife) and 'Afterwards'.

**Monastery, The** A novel by **Sir Walter Scott**, published in 1820. The setting is the monastery of Kennaquhair (based on Melrose Abbey) in the time of Elizabeth I.

An English adherent of the Catholic cause, Sir Percie Shafton, takes refuge in Scotland, where the Abbot of Kennaquhair lodges him with his tenant, Simon Glendinning. The kind and hospitable Simon has given a home to an orphan girl, Mary Avenel, with whom both his sons have fallen in love. Edward is quiet and studious and Mary prefers the spirited and gallant Halbert.

Halbert falls into conflict with the arrogant Sir Percie and leaves him for dead after a duel. The White Lady of Avenel, a beneficent ghost, restores the English knight to life. Halbert enters the service of the Earl of Murray, prospers and marries Mary. Edward enters the monastery.

**Moncrieff, William Thomas** 1794–1857 Playwright and theatre manager. He was born in London, where he worked from boyhood as a solicitor's clerk before risking a theatrical career. Lessee at various times of the Queen's, Astley's Amphitheatre, the Coburg, Vauxhall Gardens and the City Theatre, Moncrieff was a hack writer who turned out plays to suit the time. Adaptations of popular novels were entrusted to him by managers eager to cash in on the latest vogue. *The Lear of Private Life* (1820), from a novel by **Amelia Opie**, has some interest as a 19th-century domestication of **Shakespeare**. *The Shipwreck of the Medusa* (1820) exploited the excitement created by Géricault's picture. *Tom and Jerry* (1821) was a particularly zestful adaptation of **Pierce Egan**'s *Life in London*. *The Cataract of the Ganges* (1823) was the sensation of its season at **Drury Lane**, less for the text than for the use of a horse troupe and the lavish sets of Clarkson Stanfield and David Roberts. Moncrieff, who wrote over 100 plays, was evidently willing to accept the modest standing of contemporary playwrights.

**Money** A comedy by **Edward Bulwer Lytton**, first produced at the Theatre Royal, **Haymarket**, in 1840 by William Charles Macready, who had suggested the plot to the author.

Alfred Evelyn is a nobody until he suddenly, and entirely unexpectedly, inherits a fortune. Determined to sort out which of his friends are true and which of two women he should marry, Evelyn pretends to have lost all his money through gambling (and the collapse of a bank). The reading of the will in Act One and the gambling scene at Crockford's in Act Three are the outstanding sequences in this socially alert play.

**Monk, The** A novel by **M. G. Lewis**, published in 1796, at the height of the craze for **Gothic fiction** stimulated by **Ann Radcliffe**'s *Mysteries of Udolpho* (1794). It is more sensational than her work, and relies on horror rather than terror; it allows the supernatural elements it uses to remain without natural explanation.

The theme of the story is the sexual repression at the heart of asceticism. A young monk, Ambrosio, famous for his religious devotion, is tempted by Matilda, the model for his own much beloved portrait of the Virgin Mary. Initially she comes to him dressed as a boy entering the monastery as a novice. She initiates him into sexual depravity and he proves insatiable. Matilda helps him to pursue a young girl living with her mother; he ends by destroying both women, who are later revealed to be his mother and sister. He is unmasked and sentenced to death, but believes that the Devil, with whom he has made a pact, will save him. Just as he is hurled to damnation he learns that

'Almighty God! – My mother!' Frontispiece engraving to Vol. III of the 1807 edition of *The Monk* by M. G. Lewis. The novel was first published in 1796.

Matilda is the Devil's emissary. Sub-plots compound the horror of the tale which was considered both ridiculous and indecent by many, though it also enjoyed considerable popularity.

**Monk's Tale, The** See *Canterbury Tales, The*.

**monometer** See **metre**.

**Monro, Harold (Edward)** 1879–1932 Publisher and poet. Born in Brussels, he came to England at the age of seven and was educated at Radley and Gonville and Caius College, Cambridge. Monro is best remembered for the Poetry Bookshop which he established in 1913, to publish, sell and organize public readings of work by contemporary poets. He published **Edward Marsh**'s *Georgian Poetry* anthologies, founded *The Poetry Review* and its short-lived successor, *Poetry and Drama*, and issued pamphlets by **W. W. Gibson** and **John Drinkwater** from his Samuria Press. His *Chronicle of a Pilgrimage: Paris to Milan on Foot* appeared in 1909 and his *Collected Poems* in 1933. This was introduced by **T. S. Eliot**, who saw Monro's work as isolated between the Georgians and the Moderns.

**Monroe, Harriet** 1860–1936 American editor and poet, born in Chicago. She first attracted attention with her *Columbian Ode*, a poem written for the dedication ceremony of the World's Columbian Exposition, held in Chicago in 1892. Her other poetry was published in *Valeria and Other Poems* (1891), *You and I* (1914), *The Difference* (1924) and *Chosen Poems* (1935). She also wrote several verse dramas, five of which were published in 1903 as *The Passing Show*.

In 1912 she founded *Poetry: A Magazine of Verse* to encourage and publish the 'new poetry'. The magazine, which she edited until her death, played a prominent role in the Chicago Renaissance in literature. **Ezra Pound**, who served as *Poetry*'s foreign correspondent for the first six years of its existence, brought **T. S. Eliot**'s early work to Monroe's attention, and she published it in the magazine. Other poets she published include Pound himself, **H. D.**, **Carl Sandburg**, **Vachel Lindsay**, **Edgar Lee Masters**, **Hart Crane**, **Robert Frost**, **Edwin Arlington Robinson**, **Wallace Stevens**, **Edna St Vincent Millay** and **Marianne Moore**. Monroe's autobiography, *A Poet's Life: Seventy Years in a Changing World* (1937), provides an informative account of the changes in the American literary scene during the late 19th and early 20th centuries. *Poets and Their Art*, a collection of her critical essays, appeared in 1932.

**Monsarrat, Nicholas (John Turney)** 1910–79 Novelist. Born in Liverpool, he was educated at Winchester and Trinity College, Cambridge. He is chiefly remembered for his novel of World War II, *The Cruel Sea* (1951). It was preceded by *Think of Tomorrow* (1934), *At First Sight* (1935) and *The Whipping Boy* (1936), and followed by *The Story of Esther Costello* (1953), *The White Rajah* (1961), *A Fair Day's Work* (1964), *The Tribe That Lost Its Head* (1965) and *Richer Than All His Tribe* (1968). Monsarrat died before completing what he considered his major work, *The Master Mariner*, a projected three-volume novel of seafaring life from Napoleonic times to the present; the first part appeared in 1978 and the second (unfinished) after his death. The first volume of his autobiography, *Life is a Four-Letter Word*, was published in 1966, the second in 1970.

**Mont-Saint-Michel and Chartres** A historical study of medievalism by **Henry Adams**, subtitled 'A Study of Thirteenth-Century Unity'. Printed privately in 1904 for distribution among family and friends, and then published by the American Institute of Architects in 1913, it is complemented by his later study of modernity, **The Education of Henry Adams**, itself sub-titled 'A Study of Twentieth-Century Multiplicity'. Adams identifies the dominant cultural power of the Middle Ages as the Catholic faith which informed and unified all artistic and intellectual endeavour, as well as religious and moral thought. In particular, he sees the unifying symbolic 'force' of the Virgin as having provided the spiritual impulse for the arts of the time, which he discusses in separate chapters devoted to architecture, sculpture, stained-glass windows, literature and historical and religious figures.

**Montagu, Elizabeth (née Robinson)** 1720–1800 Leading member of the **bluestocking** circle. She spent several childhood years in Cambridge, at the home of her maternal grandmother and her grandmother's second husband, Dr Conyers Middleton. There she was trained to listen to the conversation of divines, scholars, philosophers, travellers and men of the world. Her father also encouraged her conversational powers, and the brothers and sisters used to debate. In 1742 she married Charles Montagu, cousin of Edward Wortley Montagu. She held regular assemblies for intellectual and literary conversation at her house in Hill Street, near Park Lane. Members of her 'Blue Stocking Society' included **Hannah More**, **Fanny Burney**, **Hester Chapone** and **Horace Walpole**. **Samuel Johnson** christened her 'Queen of the Blues' and thought that 'Mrs Montagu is *par pluribus*. With her, you may find *variety in one*.' They quarrelled however, in 1781, when she criticized the manuscript of his 'Life of Lyttelton' for **The Lives of the English Poets**. She was author of the *Essay on the Writings and Genius of Shakespeare* (1769), defending **Shakespeare** against the attacks of Voltaire.

**Montague, John** 1929– Irish poet and short-story writer. Born in New York, he grew up in County Tyrone in Northern Ireland. He was educated at University College, Dublin, and at the University of Iowa. Between 1956 and 1959 he worked for the Irish Tourist Board and was Paris correspondent for *The Irish Times*. He taught widely in the USA and Canada, and lived for the most part in Paris until 1974, when he returned to Ireland to teach at University College, Cork.

Montague's most important work is contained in six volumes of poetry: *Poisoned Lands* (1961; revised edition, 1976), *A Chosen Light* (1967), *Tides* (1970), *The Rough Field* (1972), *A Slow Dance* (1975) and *The Great Cloak* (1978). He also published a volume of short stories, *Death of a Chieftain* (1964), and edited an important anthology, *The Faber Book of Irish Verse* (1974). A contemporary and friend of **Thomas Kinsella**, Montague introduced American and French influences into Irish poetry at a time when it was becoming introverted and provincial. He and Kinsella were the leading poets with the new Dolmen Press, which was founded by Liam Miller and dominated the scene in Irish poetry until the arrival of **Seamus Heaney**, **Derek Mahon** and others in 1966. Montague has been deeply affected by the crisis in Northern Ireland. His poetry has always sought for a reconciliation between the intimacies of the private life and the brutalities of historical and public experience. *The Rough Field* has been the most influential and best known of his works because of its attempt to achieve this accommodation in a new form.

**Montagu, Lady Mary Wortley** 1689–1762 Poet and letter-writer. Born in London the eldest daughter of the 1st Duke of Kingston, Lady Mary Pierrepoint was well educated and an accomplished 'belle lettriste'. In 1712, against her father's wishes, she married Edward Wortley Montagu, an MP who became ambassador to Constantinople in 1716. The couple became well known in literary circles, associating with **Addison** and **Pope**. Lady Mary stayed in Turkey for two years, returning to London in 1718; while abroad she maintained a lively correspondence, the letters giving a sharp account of life in the Ottoman Court. She introduced the practice of inoculation against smallpox.

Pope had an unhappy disagreement of some sort with Lady Mary in 1723, and was thereafter malicious to her in print on several occasions, although there was still a portrait of her in his room when he died. She went to live abroad in 1738, living in France and Italy and returning to England in 1762, when she died while staying with her daughter, Lady Bute. Lady Mary's publications included *Town Eclogues* (1716) and *Court Poems by a Lady of Quality* (1716), spirited 'vers de société' that are witty and perceptive, and a collection of *Letters* published 1763–7. *The Complete Letters* were published in three volumes, 1965–7, edited by Robert Halsband.

**Montgomerie, Alexander** ?1556–?1610 Scottish poet. Montgomerie held office in the Scottish court, first under the regent Morton and then under James VI, who quotes from his verse in *Rewlis and Cautelis of Scottis Poesie* (1584). In 1594 Montgomerie fell from favour after being implicated in a popish plot. His principal work is *The Cherrie and the Slae* (sloe), first printed in 1597, an allegorical work about the choice between the noble and virtuous cherry and the lowly sloe. It contains debates between such personified abstractions as Hope, Experience, Reason and Cupid. *The Flyting betwixt Montgomerie and Polwart* (1621) is an example of the poetry of exchanged invective. Montgomerie also wrote versions of the psalms, lyrics and songs.

**Montgomery, L[ucy] M[aud]** 1874–1942 Canadian novelist. Born on Prince Edward Island where she spent her youth, she became a teacher and enjoyed a modest success with contributions to periodicals. Later she married Ewen Macdonald, a Presbyterian minister, and settled in Toronto. *Anne of Green Gables* (1908), which began as a serial for a Sunday-school paper, was an immediate success. She followed it with *Anne of Avonlea* (1909), and numerous other titles centring on the life of her scapegrace heroine, Anne Shirley. Other novels include *The Blue Castle* (1926), *Kilmeny of the Orchard* (1910) and the melancholy semi-autobiographical novels, *Emily of New Moon* (1923), *Emily Climbs* (1925) and *Emily's Quest* (1927).

**Moodie, Susanna** 1803–85 Writer of verse, fiction and anecdote. Born Susanna Strickland at Reydon Hall in Suffolk, she married John Dunbar Moodie in 1831 and emigrated to Canada in 1832, where they made a precarious living near Cobourg and later at Rice Lake and Belleville. A book of verse, *Enthusiasm and Other Poems*, was published in 1831 and other volumes were written in Canada to contribute to the family finances, including the novels *Mark Hurdlestone and the Gold Worshipper* (1853), *Geoffrey Monckton* (1853) and *Flora Lyndsay* (1854). Her most enduring works are two books based on her experiences in Canada, *Roughing It in the Bush or Life in Canada* (1852) and *Life in the Clearings Versus the Bush* (1853). She was the sister of **Catharine Parr Traill** and **Agnes Strickland**.

**Moody, William Vaughn** 1869–1910 American playwright and poet, born in Indiana, and educated at Harvard. His first published work was *Class Poem* (1894). *The Masque of Judgment* (1900) was the first part of a verse drama trilogy continued by *The Fire Bringer* (1904) and the uncompleted *The Death of Eve* (1912). *Poems* (1901) contains the often-anthologized pieces 'Gloucester Moors' and 'An Ode in Time of Hesitation'.

Although only two of his plays were produced during his lifetime, Moody's brief career as a dramatist was of considerable importance to the development of the American theatre. Unlike many dramatists of his time, he chose distinctively American subjects for his plays. His enormously popular *A Sabine Woman* (1906), which was later produced and published under the title *The Great Divide* (1909), treats the conflict between the values of established Eastern culture and the realities of free-spirited frontier life, describing the abduction of a woman from Massachusetts by a man from Arizona and the events that lead to their eventual marriage. Its realism challenged the melodramatic conventions of the contemporary American stage. Moody's final play, *The Faith Healer*, appeared in 1909.

**Moonstone, The** A novel by **Wilkie Collins**, published serially in ***All the Year Round*** from January to August 1868 and in volume form the same year.

The story is told in Collins's customary manner, through eyewitness accounts by various characters. The prologue describes how Colonel John Herncastle stole the Moonstone diamond from a Hindu holy place at the siege of Seringapatam. He leaves it to his niece, Rachel Verinder, and Franklin Blake brings it to her Yorkshire home for presentation on her eighteenth birthday. By the next morning the stone has disappeared, and the mystery is investigated first by the slow-witted Superintendent Seagrave and then by the shrewd, melancholy Sergeant Cuff from London. Suspicion falls variously on three Hindus who have been seen in the neighbourhood, the servant Rosanna Spearman and Rachel herself. She inexplicably turns against Franklin Blake and becomes engaged to Godfrey Ablewhite, a pious philanthropist also staying in the house.

With Cuff unable to advance the matter further, Franklin Blake takes over the investigation. To his surprise, he discovers that he himself is the thief: Ezra Jennings, the local doctor's assistant, demonstrates that Blake unknowingly removed the diamond while under the influence of opium. The diamond, meanwhile, is traced to a London bank and Sergeant Cuff re-enters the story to expose Ablewhite as the real villain – but not before Ablewhite has been killed and the diamond retrieved by the mysterious Hindus.

Carefully paced and sharply characterized, the novel made a notable contribution to the growth of **detective fiction**. **T. S. Eliot** called it 'the first, the longest, and the best of modern English detective novels'.

**Moorcock, Michael** 1939– Editor, writer and promoter of *avant-garde* **science fiction**. In the 1960s he transformed and revitalized the magazine *New Worlds*. He has produced many hack 'sword and sorcery' novels, but shown growing artistry in his offbeat novels about Jerry Cornelius. The core of the series is a tetralogy: *The Final Programme* (1968), *A Cure for Cancer* (1971), *The English Assassin* (1972) and *The Condition of Muzak* (1977). Jherek Carnelian is featured in a series of self-consciously decadent far-future fantasies begun with *An Alien Heat* (1972). More recently, Moorcock's virtuosity has been displayed in *Angst*-ridden non-fantasy novels, including *The Brothel in Rosenstrasse* (1982), *Byzantium Endures* (1983) and *The Laughter of Carthage* (1984).

**Moore, Brian** 1921– Irish novelist. The son of a surgeon, he was born in Belfast and educated there at St Malachy's College. He served with the ARP in wartime Belfast – an experience ironically reflected in *The Emperor of Ice Cream* (1965) – before working for the Ministry of War Transport and, after the war, UNRRA. He migrated to Canada in 1948 and worked as a journalist in Montreal. In 1959 he moved to the USA, living in New York and California. His first novel, *Judith Hearne* (1955, later reissued as *The Lonely Passion of Judith Hearne*), recounts the descent into delusion of a sexually obsessed Belfast spinster. Its successors include *The Feast of Lupercal* (1957), *The Luck of Ginger Coffey* (1960), *An Answer from Limbo* (1962), *Catholics* (1972), *The Great Victorian Collection* (1975), *The Mangan Inheritance* (1979) and *The Cold Heaven* (1983). *Black Robe* (1985) concerns 17th-century Jesuits and Canadian Indians but represents a paradigm of sectarian intolerance and mutual incomprehension in contemporary Ulster. His most recent novel is *The Colour of Blood* (1987). The unflinchingly realistic surfaces of the novels, usually reflecting contemporary life as Moore has encountered it in Ireland, Canada and the USA, belie an underlying engagement with the phantasmagoric, the atavisms of myth and ritual and the ordeals of disturbed sexual consciousness, both male and female, sensitively conveyed through internal monologue. His own experience of Catholicism and a divided Ireland has issued in themes of guilt, isolation, ancestral memory and religious unease; his treatment of them has won the respect and admiration of other at least residually Catholic writers such as **Graham Greene**. In *I Am Mary Dunne* (1968), perhaps his best novel, all these concerns are subsumed in a powerful study of imperilled personal identity.

**Moore, Edward** 1712–57 Playwright and poet. Moore was born in Abingdon and trained as a linen draper. He turned to literature when his London business failed, and was one of many writers to enjoy the patronage of **Lord Lyttelton**. Of his three plays, *The Foundling* (1748), *Gil Blas* (1751) and *The Gamester* (1753), only the last is of any enduring significance. A middle-class tragedy about the lure of gambling, its heightened prose and eager pursuit of virtue carried the influence of **George Lillo**, profoundly affecting the development of drama in Germany and easing the passage of **melodrama** into the English theatre. In 1753–6 Moore was editor of *The World* magazine.

**Moore, George (Augustus)** 1852–1933 Anglo-Irish novelist and playwright. George Moore was born at Ballyglass in Mayo, the son of an Irish MP who was also the proprietor of a racing stable. He was educated at Oscott College in Birmingham. He spent ten years in Paris, studying painting and publishing two books of verse, *Flowers of Passion* (1878) and *Pagan Poems* (1881). He went to live in London in 1880, where he published poems, plays, essays, his autobiography *Confessions of a Young Man* (1888), and seven realistic novels which clearly displayed the influence of Zola: *A Modern Lover* (1883), *A Mummer's Wife* (1885), *A Drama in Muslin* (1886), *A Mere Accident* (1887), *Spring Days* (1888), *Mike Fletcher* (1889) and *Vain Fortune* (1891). He achieved a major success with *Esther Waters* (1894), generally acknowledged as his finest work.

Moore's knowledge of painting led him to become art critic of *The Speaker* and he published *Modern Painting* in 1893. He opposed the Boer War and returned to Ireland in 1899. He had been brought up as a Catholic and educated as one; he now became a Protestant and was caught up in the Irish cultural revival, particularly in the growing pains of the Irish National Theatre (see **Abbey Theatre**). The years in Ireland are the subject of a trilogy of reminiscence, *Hail and Farewell* (1911–14); it first appeared as *Ave* (1911), *Salve* (1912) and *Vale* (1914). Among other works published in the years between publication of *Esther Waters* and 1911, when Moore returned to London, were two collections of stories, *Celibates* (1895) and *The Untilled Field* (1903); the novel *Evelyn Innes* (1898) and its sequel *Sister Theresa* (1901), and *Reminiscences of the Impressionist Painters* (1906).

In London Moore went to live in Ebury Street, and made it his home for the rest of his life, acquiring a reputation as a literary sage. His later stage as a writer began with the elaborate and painstaking *The Brook Kerith* (1916), a novel

'George Moore au Café' by Edouard Manet, 1879.

about Jesus. Among other works of this period were the short stories *A Story-teller's Holiday* (1918), the essays *Conversations in Ebury Street* (1924), a translation from the Greek, *Daphnis and Chloe* (1924), the novels *Héloise and Abelard* (1921) and *Aphrodite in Aulis* (1930) and the plays *The Making of an Immortal* (1927) and *The Passing of the Essenes* (1930), which was a revised version of the earlier *The Apostle* (1911).

**Moore, G[eorge] E[dward]** 1873–1958 Philosopher. Born in London, Moore was educated at Dulwich College and Trinity College, Cambridge, where he was a contemporary of **Bertrand Russell**. He was Professor of Philosophy at Cambridge in 1925–39.

Moore broke away from the prevailing idealistic philosophy which held the universe to be an all-inclusive mind, and defended the independent reality of material objects, minds and their states, and such abstract items as concepts and propositions. His first major essay, 'The Refutation of Idealism' (1903; reprinted in *Philosophical Studies*, 1922), argued against the idea that we really perceive nothing but our own sensations. His major work, *Principia Ethica* (1903), rejected the view that moral properties such as goodness can be reduced to 'naturalistic properties' such as happiness or evolutionary success. He argued for 'direct moral awareness' and claimed that the contemplation of beauty and affectionate personal relations are the only supremely good states of mind.

His ideas were profoundly influential on the **Bloomsbury Group**, many of whom had studied under him at Cambridge and were also members of the famous **Apostles**. Other works by him include two important essays, 'A Defence of Common Sense' (1923) and 'A Proof of an

External World' (1939). *Some Main Problems of Philosophy* was published in 1953.

**Moore, Marianne (Craig)** 1887–1972 American poet, born near St Louis, Missouri, and educated at Bryn Mawr College. Her first book, *Poems*, was published in 1921 and was followed by *Observations* in 1924. Her poetry is marked by an unconventional but disciplined use of metrics, and a witty, often ironic tone. Known for their eclectic subject matter, her poems contain references to scientific and historical works and to current affairs, and many are written about exotic animals. They also reveal an abiding interest in aesthetic and philosophical issues. Her other volumes of poetry include *Selected Poems* (1935), *The Pangolin and Other Verse* (1936), *What Are Years* (1941), *Nevertheless* (1944), *A Face* (1949), the Pulitzer Prize-winning *Collected Poems* (1951), *Like a Bulwark* (1956), *O, to Be a Dragon* (1959) and *Tell Me, Tell Me: Granite, Steel, and Other Topics* (1966). Other works include a volume of critical essays, *Predilections* (1955), and two volumes of translations, *The Fables of La Fontaine* (1954) and *Selected Fables of La Fontaine* (1955). *The Complete Poems of Marianne Moore* was published in 1967, and *The Complete Prose of Marianne Moore* in 1986.

**Moore, Nicholas** 1918– Poet. The son of **G. E. Moore**, he was born in Cambridge, went to school in Oxford and Reading, and studied at Trinity College, Cambridge. He has worked as a horticulturalist. He was the editor of *Seven* (1938–40) and *New Poetry* (1944–5). A prolific poet in the 1940s, he was a central figure in the **New Apocalypse** movement, appearing in two of its anthologies: *The New Apocalypse* (1939), introduced by **J. F. Hendry**, and *The White Horseman* (1941), edited by Hendry and **Henry Treece**. Indebted to **Auden**, **Wallace Stevens** and **Blake**, his poetry has a visual clarity and lyrical fluency: surrealism mixes with effects from popular songs. The principal volumes of this early period are *A Wish in Season* (1941), *A Book for Priscilla* (1941), *The Cabaret, The Dancer, The Gentleman* (1942), *The Glass Tower* (1944) and *Recollections of the Gala: Selected Poems 1943–48* (1950). After this he stopped writing, starting again in the 1960s with *Identity* (1969) and *Resolution and Identity* (1970). Overrated in the 1940s, he is little read now but has fervent admirers in **John Ashbery** and **John Ash**.

**Moore, Thomas** 1779–1852 Poet. Born in Dublin and educated at Whyte's School, he took advantage of a slight relaxation of the laws against Catholics to attend Trinity College, Dublin, where he first began to write verse. In 1799 Moore went to London to study law at the Middle Temple, publishing his first work, *Odes of Anacreon Translated into English Verse, with*

*Notes*, in the following year and a volume of amorous verses, *The Poetical Works of the Late Thomas Little, Esq.*, in 1801. He was appointed Admiralty Registrar in Bermuda in 1803, but lightheartedly left his deputy in charge and took the opportunity to travel in Canada and the United States, returning to England during 1804. He was later to regret his negligence. *Epistles, Odes and Other Poems* (1806) was severely criticized by **Francis Jeffrey** in *The Edinburgh Review*, more for its moral tone than its literary quality. The attack did no harm to sales, and Moore not only became a contributor to the *Review* but was later offered its editorship.

Moore published *Corruption and Intolerance: Two Poems with Notes, Addressed to an Englishman by an Irishman* in 1808. More successful was the light satire in *Intercepted Letters: or The Twopenny Post Bag, by Thomas Brown the Younger* (1813). Meanwhile, he was preparing the work which secured his reputation during his lifetime and would prove his most enduring. The ten parts of *A Selection of Irish Melodies* were published between 1808 and 1834. Moore had a keen instinct for the taste of a public wealthy enough to afford a piano and scores, and likely to enjoy a reassuringly sentimental view of Ireland. An example of his judgement is 'The Last Rose of Summer'. The air had been used by R. A. Millikin in the late 18th century for his song 'The Groves of Blarney'; but it was old even then, and had originally belonged to a song called 'Castle Hyde'. Moore's version was borrowed by the German composer Flotow for his opera, *Martha* (1847), and it became world famous. The accompaniments to Moore's songs were arranged chiefly by Sir John Stevenson, and the lyrics were published separately in 1821.

In December 1814 the publisher Longman commissioned Moore to write a romantic poem. The result, *Lalla Rookh: An Oriental Romance* (1817), was not only romantic but exotic – a combination for which the poetry of **Byron** had already created a large public. *The Fudge Family in Paris, Edited by Thomas Brown the Younger* (1818) returned to the vein of light satire which Moore had already exploited successfully in earlier years. In 1819 Moore's deputy in Bermuda misappropriated £6000, and the responsibility fell on Moore himself. He left England with Lord John Russell for a visit to Italy and stayed away until the debt to the Admiralty had been paid, returning in 1822. *The Loves of the Angels*, published in 1823, was a second venture into orientalism, financially as successful as *Lalla Rookh*.

Moore had been a friend of Byron since the latter returned to England from the eastern Mediterranean in 1811. On his death Byron left his manuscript 'Memoirs' to Moore, who destroyed the original but used some material from it to compile his controversial *Letters and*

*Journals of Lord Byron, with Notices of His Life* (1830). **Macaulay** declared that 'it deserves to be classed among the best specimens of English prose which our age has produced'. Other works by Moore include his lives of **Sheridan** (1825) and Lord Edward Fitzgerald (1831), his novel *The Epicurean* (1827), *The Fudges in England* (1835) and *The History of Ireland* (1835–46). He remained a famous and popular figure for the rest of his life, and was awarded a Civil List pension in 1850.

**Moore, T[homas] Sturge** 1870–1944 Poet and art historian. Moore, the brother of the Cambridge philosopher **G. E. Moore**, was born at Hastings in Sussex. Indifferent health brought his schooling to an early end but he succeeded as a wood engraver and later as an art historian, publishing studies of painters: *Albrecht Altdorfer* (1900), *Albrecht Dürer* (1905), *Correggio* (1906) and *Charles Ricketts* (1933). He was a close friend of **W. B. Yeats** and designed the covers for several volumes of Yeats's poetry. Moore's own poetry, often classical in theme, was cordially received by the critics but neglected by the public; it includes *The Vinedresser* (1899), *Danae* (1903), *The Gazelles* (1904), *Marianne* (1911), *Medea* (1920) and *Judas* (1923). His collected poems were issued in four volumes in 1931–3.

**Moorhouse, Frank** 1938– Australian short-story writer. Born and educated in Nowra, New South Wales, he attended Wollongong Technical Institute and subsequently worked as a journalist in Sydney and in country areas. He is now a full-time writer and lives in the Sydney suburb of Balmain, an area he has celebrated in his fiction. As co-founder and editor of the influential alternative fiction magazine *Tabloid Story*, he has had an influence on the contemporary Australian short story beyond that of his own writing. Moorhouse describes much of his work as 'discontinuous narrative'. While more traditional than some other Australian writers of post-modernist fiction, he writes in forms which reflect the fragmentation of contemporary urban life and all his work demonstrates a strong interest in social and cultural issues. His style is frequently journalistic and his writing has been compared with the American 'new journalism'. His books include *Futility and Other Animals* (1969), *The Americans, Baby* (1972), *The Electrical Experience* (1974), *Tales of Mystery and Romance* (1977) and *The Everlasting Secret Family and Other Secrets* (1980). He has also edited an important anthology of Australian contemporary fiction, *The State of the Art: The Mood of Contemporary Australia in Short Fiction* (1983). Moorhouse's work shows a strong interest in breaking down the barriers between contemporary media and he has written the scripts for a number of films, including *Between Wars* (1974) and *The Disappearance of Azaria Chamberlain* (1983).

*Moral Essays* Four poems by **Alexander Pope**, each taking the form of a verse epistle addressed directly to one of his acquaintances. Epistle I, *Of the Knowledge and Characters of Men*, is addressed to Viscount Cobham and sets out the poet's belief that each individual has a key to his particular behaviour, a 'Ruling Passion', which dictates his perspective on life. Epistle II, *Of the Characters of Women*, is addressed to Pope's friend Martha Blount and includes some waspish verse-portraits such as the pointed 'Atossa' (the Duchess of Marlborough) and satires of other contemporary females. Epistle III, to Lord Bathurst (*Of the Use of Riches*), takes the form of a dialogue and praises his subject's well-disposed house and country gardens; it contains the celebrated episodes on the benevolent 'Man of Ross' (John Kyrle, the charitable philanthropist) and the death of Buckingham. Epistle IV, to Lord Burlington, the cultivated patron of art, also considers the uses of wealth, and equates good taste with good sense (morality), comparing the architectural 'finesse' of Burlington with the ghastly uselessness of 'Timon's villa', the embodiment of opulent vulgarity.

**morality plays** Where the **miracle plays** of the late Middle Ages derived from the liturgy and celebrated God as manifest in the life and death of Jesus, the morality plays took their inspiration from the sermon and treated the problems and dilemmas confronting Man. Their form was usually allegorical, with abstractions such as Mercy or Justice and Envy or Lust representing the opposed forces which accompany Man in his progress through life.

The earliest morality play of which we have any knowledge from records is the *Pater Noster* play, which may have been the work of **John Wyclif** and was performed at York. The earliest manuscript to survive, of a play called *The Pride of Life*, is imperfect and may date back as far as the end of the 14th century. The most remarkable collection is *The Macro Plays* (named after the former owner of the manuscripts), which may have come from the abbey at Bury St Edmunds. The three plays in this collection are *Mankind* (c.1473), *Wisdom, Who Is Christ* (c.1460) and the earliest and most elaborate, *The Castle of Perseverance* (c.1425). The most famous morality play belongs to the whole of western Europe: *Everyman* (1495) was probably an English version of the Dutch *Elckerlijk*. It enjoyed a new fame in the German verse translation *Jedermann* by Hugo von Hofmannsthal (1911), which became the opening item of the Salzburg Festival each year in Max Reinhardt's celebrated production.

The morality play did not die with the Middle Ages, for examples abound in England up to 1550. But by then the form had become flexible enough to be used for satire and comedy, and for abstraction to give way to character.

**Morall Fabillis of Esope the Phrygian, The** 12 verse **fables**, derived from Aesop and drawing on a long European tradition of Aesopic writing, by the 15th-century Scottish poet **Robert Henryson**. The fables are allegorical, lightheartedly using animal characters to convey observations and criticisms of human society. Henryson makes original use of his material, often describing animal life in sympathetic detail, and sometimes creating a deliberate discrepancy between the moral given at the end of the tale and the moral suggested by the tale itself.

**Mordaunt, Elinor** Pseudonym of the novelist and traveller Evelyn May Mordaunt (1877–1942). Her first published work, *The Garden of Contentment* (1902), was written in Mauritius and drew on English memories. She later travelled to Australia and all over the world, recounting her experiences in *The Venture Book* (1926), *Purely for Pleasure* (1932) and *Traveller's Pack* (1933). Her numerous novels include *The Rose of Youth* (1915) and *Reputation* (1923). Her autobiography appeared in 1937 as *Sinabada*.

**More, Hannah** 1745–1833 Dramatist and religious writer. The youngest of five sisters, she was born at Stapleton in Gloucestershire and educated at her sisters' boarding school in Bristol, where she learned French, Italian, Spanish and Latin. At the age of 22 she became engaged to a Mr Turner, who never married her but eventually settled a small income on her.

Hannah More's first publication was a pastoral play, *The Search After Happiness* (1773), and she went to London the following year. There she was fortunate in making an impression on Joshua Reynolds and his sister and in gaining through them the entrée to London society. She became the friend of **Johnson, Garrick, Horace Walpole** and the circle of **bluestocking** ladies surrounding **Elizabeth Montagu**. Her play, *Inflexible Captive*, was published in 1774 and her tragedies, *Percy* and *The Fatal Falsehood*, were produced by Garrick in 1777 and 1779.

In her later career she moved away from the stage to religious and didactic writing. *Village Politics* was published in 1793 and *Cheap Repository Tracts* in 1795–8. The Religious Tract Society was formed to continue her work, while she herself went on to support William Wilberforce in his campaign against slavery, to play a pioneer role in the Sunday School movement and to write a popular didactic novel, *Coelebs in Search of a Wife* (1809). Her *Letters*, many to distinguished correspondents, were published in 1834.

**More, Henry** 1614–87 A prominent **Cambridge Platonist**, he was born at Grantham, Lincolnshire, and educated at Eton College and Christ's College, Cambridge. He became a fellow of his college in 1639, and stayed there for the rest of his life, refusing the offers of rich preferments. Although his family tended to Calvinism, More himself remained a steadfast supporter of the Church of England and was Royalist in sympathy during the Civil Wars. Like his fellow Platonist **Ralph Cudworth** he was opposed to the materialism of **Thomas Hobbes**, and eventually rejected the philosophy of René Descartes for the same reason. More was an industrious writer, expounding his ideas in both verse and prose. *Psychozoia Platonica* (1642) was enlarged and included in *Philosophical Poems* (1647). His later works include *Enthusiasmus Triumphatus* (1656), an effective denunciation of Puritan 'enthusiasms' (extravagant claims for their faith and inspiration) and *The Immortality of the Soul* (1659).

**More, St Thomas** 1477–1535 England's foremost Christian humanist and sometime Lord Chancellor, More was a martyr to Catholics and a traitor to extreme Protestants in the 16th century who, like **Foxe** in *Acts and Monuments*, saw him as an enemy to the Gospel. The son of the judge Sir John More, Thomas was educated at St Anthony's School in Threadneedle Street. He spent his youth at the house of Cardinal Morton, who predicted that he would be a 'marvellous man', and, with Morton as his patron, went to Oxford, where he was a pupil of **Thomas Linacre** and **William Grocyn**. He was back in London to study common law in *c.* 1494, being admitted to Lincoln's Inn in 1496 and becoming a barrister in 1501. While at Lincoln's Inn he was testing a vocation for the priesthood by living at a nearby Carthusian monastery and sharing some of the monastic life; the habits of prayer, fasting and penance stayed with him for the rest of his life. He married for the first time in 1504 or 1505, and in 1504 entered Parliament.

He met **Erasmus** on the latter's first visit to England in 1499 and their friendship and correspondence began in that year. During Erasmus's second visit they both produced Latin translations of some of Lucian's works which were printed at Paris in 1506. On Erasmus's third visit to England in 1509 he wrote *Encomium Moriae*, whose title quibbles with More's name, at the house of his friend.

From 1510 to 1518 More was one of the two under-sheriffs in London where he gained a reputation for impartiality and patronage of the

Thomas More. The portrait by Holbein. Royal Library, Windsor Castle.

poor (reflected in the play *Sir Thomas More*). In 1511 his first wife died in childbirth and very soon More was married again, this time to the redoubtable Dame Alice. In 1515 he was part of a delegation to Flanders to sort out disputes about the wool trade; it is with a reference to this delegation that *Utopia* opens. In 1517 a London mob rose against foreign residents and More's quelling of this mob is reflected in a scene, possibly by **Shakespeare**, in *Sir Thomas More*. He was present at the Field of the Cloth of Gold in 1520–1, participated in trade talks at Calais and Bruges and was knighted in 1521.

More helped Henry VIII to write his *Defence of the Seven Sacraments* in answer to Luther, and in response to Luther's reply More, under a pseudonym, wrote *Epistola ad Pomeranum* (1568). With Henry's favour More's career prospered as he became Speaker of the Commons in 1523, Chancellor of the Duchy of Lancaster in 1525 and Wolsey's successor as Lord Chancellor in 1529. His fall came rapidly. He refused to attend the coronation of Anne Boleyn and in 1534 was one of those accused of complicity with Elizabeth Barton, the visionary nun of Kent who opposed Henry's break with Rome. The Lords passed the bill for attainting those accused only when More's name had been deleted. In April 1534 he found himself unable to swear to the Act of Succession and on 17 April he was committed to the Tower. Richard Rich, the Solicitor General, acted as prosecutor

at More's trial in July. More was sentenced as a traitor and executed on 6 July 1535 claiming that he was dying for his faith. He was beatified in 1886 and canonized by Pius XI in 1935.

Many lives of More were written in the 16th century. That by his son-in-law William Roper, with its famous exchanges between More and Dame Alice in the Tower, was not printed until 1626. Nicholas Harpsfield's biography was written in the reign of Mary but not printed until 1932 and Thomas Stapleton's Latin work on the three Thomases (the Apostle, Becket and More) was printed in 1588. Others exist in manuscript, while some are lost.

More's first published work was the Lucian translations in collaboration with Erasmus (1506). His English translation of a Latin life of the Italian humanist Giovanni Pico della Mirandola was printed by **Wynkyn de Worde** in 1510. *Utopia* was published at Louvain in 1516 and in an English translation by Ralph Robinson in 1551. The longest and most important of More's controversialist defences of the Catholic faith, which were written in the late 1520s and early 1530s, is *The Confutation of Tyndale's Answer* (1532); he also wrote against Tyndale's view of the Eucharist in 1534. More's *History of Richard III* exists in both Latin and English versions. It was written c.1513–18 but was left unfinished and was imperfectly printed in English in Grafton's *Chronicle* (1543). The Latin text first appears in print in the Louvain *Opera* (1565). Much of the information for this must have come from Cardinal Morton, and More's *History* was used by **Stow** and **Hall** as well as Grafton, and also by **Raphael Holinshed**. More is therefore responsible for transmitting material used by Shakespeare in his play. While in the Tower More wrote *A Dialogue of Comfort Against Tribulation* (printed in 1553), a supposed English translation of a French version of a Latin dialogue between two Hungarians, Anthony and Vincent. More's English *Works* appeared in the edition by William Rastell in 1557. His Latin works – *Utopia*, the Lucianic dialogues, epigrams and controversialist treatises – were printed at Louvain in 1565.

**Morgan, Charles (Langbridge)** 1894–1958 Novelist and playwright. Morgan was born in Kent, and studied at the naval colleges of Osborne and Dartmouth from 1907 to 1913. He then resigned, intending to go up to Oxford, but rejoined the Royal Navy during World War I. He was captured and interned in Holland until 1917, spending some of this time on parole at Rosendaal Castle. In 1919 he went up to Brasenose College, Oxford, and published his first novel, *The Gunroom*, about his unhappy experiences as a young midshipman.

In 1921 he joined *The Times* and became its drama critic from 1926 to 1939. Under the pseudonym 'Menander' he contributed numerous articles to *The Times Literary Supplement*. His 11 novels include: *Portrait in a Mirror* (1929), *The Fountain* (1932), set in Rosendaal Castle and considered by some to be his most successful work, *The Voyage* (1940), *The Judge's Story* (1947), a fable on the struggle between spiritual and material values (echoed in a collection of essays *Liberties of the Mind*, 1951) and *Challenge to Venus* (1957), his last. His plays are: *The Flashing Stream* (1938), *The River Line* (1952), dramatized from his 1949 novel with the same title, and *The Burning Glass* (1954).

Morgan also wrote a publishing history of *The House of Macmillan* (1943), *Epitaph on George Moore* (1935), a close friend, and *Ode to France* (1942), a country where his work was much admired. He was made a member of the Institut de France in 1957.

**Morgan, Edwin (George)** 1920– Scottish poet, translator and literary critic. He was born in Glasgow and has lived all his life in the city, apart from a period of military service during World War II. He studied at Glasgow University, lectured in English there from 1947 and was titular Professor of English from 1975 until his retirement in 1980. His poetic career stretches from *The Vision of Cathkin Braes* (1952) to *Sonnets from Scotland* (1984) and *From the Video Box* (1986). There are two volumes of selections: *Poems of Thirty Years* (1982) and *Selected Poems* (1985). Inevitably, Glasgow figures prominently in his work – notably in *Glasgow Sonnets* (1972) and *Sonnets from Scotland* – but he is by no means limited to his native city. At once Scottish and European, he is committed to a stylistic pluralism which encompasses concrete poetry, sound poetry and playful experiment (such as 'The Computer's First Christmas Card') as well as more traditional modes. A notable literary critic, he has written on Hugh MacDiarmid and a wide range of contemporary Scottish writers. As a translator he is best known for his Scots versions of Mayakovsky, but he has translated into English the work of several European poets – French, German, Spanish and Hungarian – and shows a particular affinity with modern Italian poets such as Montale and Quasimodo. His translation of *Fifty Renascence Love-Poems* appeared in 1975 and *Rites of Passage: Selected Translations* in 1976.

**Morgan, Lady Sydney** ?1783–1859 Novelist. Born Sydney Owenson in Dublin, she married Sir Thomas Morgan in 1812. She was well known as a writer of Irish romances, the best being *The Wild Irish Girl* (1806), *O'Donnel* (1814) and *The O'Briens and the O'Flahertys* (1827). She also wrote two lively books on France and Italy, and a life of Salvator Rosa.

**Morier, James Justinian** c.1780–1849 Traveller and novelist. The son of the Consul General of the Levant Company, Morier was born at Smyrna and returned to Turkey after being educated at Harrow. He entered the diplomatic service in 1807 and went with Sir Hartford Jones's mission to Persia. In 1812 he published his *Journey Through Persia, Armenia and Asia Minor*, and in 1818 the more notable *Second Journey Through Persia*. After his retirement he used his experiences in several oriental romances, of which the most successful is *The Adventures of Hajji Baba of Ispahan* (1824), a picaresque novel which presents real people in a setting both exotic and authentic.

**Morley, Henry** 1822–94 Editor. Morley was born in London, studied medicine at King's College, London, and practised for a time before turning to journalism. He contributed to Dickens's *Household Words* and *All the Year Round*, edited *The Examiner* and published translations, biographies and miscellanies. Morley, who became Professor of English at University College, London, was active in the field of adult education and produced valuable editions of English classics in cheap format: Cassell's Library of English Literature (1875–81) and Cassell's National Library (begun in 1886). In 1887 he started his ambitious history of English literature, *English Writers*: 11 of a projected 20 volumes were completed, taking his subject as far as Shakespeare before he died.

**Morley, John, 1st Viscount** 1838–1923 Statesman and biographer. Born at Blackburn in Lancashire, he was educated at Cheltenham College and Lincoln College, Oxford. he studied law and was called to the Bar, but did not practise. He contributed to *The Saturday Review*, and later became editor of *The Fortnightly Review* (1867) and *The Pall Mall Gazette* (1881). Morley entered politics in 1883, when he was elected Liberal MP for Newcastle. A staunch supporter of Gladstone, he held office as Chief Secretary for Ireland (1886 and 1892), Secretary of State for India (1905) and Lord President of the Council (1910).

His chief contribution to literature was *The Life of William Ewart Gladstone* (1903). He also edited the English Men of Letters series, to which he contributed the volume on Edmund Burke (1879). Among his other works were *Voltaire* (1872), *Rousseau* (1873), *Diderot and the Encyclopaedists* (1878), *Richard Cobden* (1881), *Machiavelli* (1897), and *Oliver Cromwell* (1900). He also published two collections of speeches on Indian affairs (1908 and 1909) and *Critical Miscellanies* (1871–1908), four collections of essays written for *The Fortnightly Review*.

***Morning Chronicle, The*** A Whig journal founded in 1769 by William Woodfall. It became prominent at the turn of the century under the editorship of James Perry and John Black. Famous contributors included **Sheridan, Charles Lamb, Thomas Moore,** David Ricardo, **John Stuart Mill, W. M. Thackeray** and **Henry Mayhew.** As a young man, **Charles Dickens** was employed by the paper as a reporter and part of *Sketches by Boz* first appeared in its pages. *The Morning Chronicle* ceased publication in 1862.

**Morrell, Lady Ottoline** 1873–1938 Literary patron and socialite. Born Ottoline Violet Anne Cavendish-Bentinck, she lived at Welbeck Abbey before her marriage to the Liberal MP Philip Morrell. From 1908 she entertained a wide circle of political and literary celebrities at 44 Bedford Square, London, and then, during the post-World War I decade, at her country house, Garsington Manor, near Oxford. The circle included **Bertrand Russell, Virginia Woolf, T. S. Eliot, W. B. Yeats, D. H. Lawrence** and **Aldous Huxley.** Lawrence (in *Women in Love*) and Huxley (in *Crome Yellow*) both used her as the model for striking but eccentric fictional characters.

In the late 1920s the Morrells returned to London where she remained until her death. Her *Memoirs*, edited by Robert Gathorne-Hardy, appeared in two volumes in 1963 and 1974.

**Morris, Sir Lewis** 1833–1907 Poet. Born in Carmarthen, educated at Sherborne and Oxford, he was called to the Bar and practised until 1880. He assisted in the foundation of the University of Wales and was knighted in 1895. His cheerful and musical collection, *Songs of Two Worlds* (1871), was well received by the reading public. Still more popular was *The Epic of Hades* (1876–7). Other works included *Gwen* (1879), *Songs Unsung* (1883), *Gycia: A Tragedy* (1886) and *A Vision of Saints* (1890). *The New Rambler* (1905) is a volume of essays.

**Morris, Mervyn** 1937– Jamaican poet. He was born in Kingston and educated at Munro College, the University of the West Indies and the University of Oxford. Although he has been both a schoolteacher and a university administrator, his main career has been as a university lecturer in English. He has published several collections of verse, among them *The Pond* (1973), *On Holy Week* (1976) and *Shadowboxing* (1979). His poems tend to be short and precisely wrought moments of feeling or observation. They are sometimes said to lack commitment – 'Another friend arraigns me:/too detached, he says' – but as personal statements they are deeply felt and well crafted, showing that Caribbean poetry can be about private pains as well as about public causes.

**Morris, William** 1834–96 Writer, artisan and socialist. He was born at Walthamstow in Essex. His father made a fortune trading shares from which Morris benefited in his later pursuits. In 1848–51 he attended Marlborough College and in 1853, intent on ordination, he went up to Exeter College, Oxford. The lifelong friends he made there included Edward Burne-Jones and Charles Faulkner. In 1854 Morris's Oxford circle fell under the influence of the **Pre-Raphaelite** school and in 1855, on their second visit to France, Morris and Burne-Jones jointly renounced their ecclesiastical ambitions in favour of artistic careers which Morris described as 'the embodiment of dreams in one form or another'.

After taking his BA Morris was articled to the Oxford architect G. E. Street. In 1856 Street moved to London, where Morris and Burne-Jones shared rooms in Red Lion Square previously occupied by **Dante Gabriel Rossetti,** whom they had met earlier that year. Morris began designing furniture and, influenced by Rossetti, abandoned architecture for painting. In August 1857 he worked with Rossetti and Burne-Jones on frescoes at the Oxford Union Society; the subjects from **Malory** are an early product of Morris's lifelong love of **Arthurian literature.** His only extant oil painting, 'Queen Guenevere', is a portrait of Jane Burden, whom he had met in 1857.

Morris married Jane Burden in 1859. The next year they moved into The Red House and, as a result of furbishing it himself because of the ugliness of contemporary decor, Morris decided in April 1861 to found a firm for the hand manufacture of 'all things necessary for the decoration of a house'. This was Morris, Marshall, Faulkner and Co. (reconstituted as Morris and Co. in 1875) and thus began the revival of decorative arts for which Morris was largely responsible and about which he delivered much polemic in the ensuing years. Morris's own talents lay in pattern designing (for wallpapers, chintzes, damasks, embroideries, tapestries and carpets), and the firm is also famous for its stained glass and stencilled mural decoration (much in demand by Gothic Revival architects), painted tiles and furniture.

Morris's literary career had begun in 1855 when he excited his Oxford friends with his first mature poem 'The Willow and the Red Cliff'. In 1856 he helped found and finance *The Oxford and Cambridge Magazine*, intended as a successor to the Pre-Raphaelite journal **The Germ.** Morris's contributions to the 12 numbers were five poems, nine pieces of creative prose and four critical articles. In 1858 thirty of his poems were published as **The Defence of Guenevere and Other**

*Poems*. He only published one further collection of verse and this was *Poems by the Way* (1891), a selection of 55 poems written in the intervening 33 years.

As early as 1857 Morris had begun to use classical mythology in the fragment *Scenes from the Fall of Troy* (first published 1915). Though the decade of the 1860s was primarily devoted to work for the firm, he continued to write shorter poems and, in 1867, scored a public success with **The Life and Death of Jason**. This was a much enlarged version of a tale originally intended for the epic **The Earthly Paradise** (1868–70) which secured Morris's reputation as a leading poet of his day. Later Morris returned to classical poetry and translated *The Aeneid of Virgil* (1875) and *The Odyssey of Homer* (1887) into English verse. A projected translation of *The Iliad* only reached some two hundred lines before being abandoned.

In *The Earthly Paradise* tales from classical literature alternate with northern European stories, and Morris's meeting with the Icelandic scholar Eiríkr Magnússon (1833–1913) in October 1868 profoundly affected his literary career. Magnússon, with whom he studied Icelandic, gave him direct access to the sagas. He drew on the *Laxdaela Saga* for 'The Lovers of Gudrun' in *The Earthly Paradise* and experimented with other works such as the *Egilssaga*. He and Magnússon then collaborated on the prose translation of the following: 'The Saga of Gunnlaug the Worm Tongue and Rafn the Skald' (*Fortnightly Review* January 1869), *The Story of Grettir the Strong* (May 1869), *The Story of the Volsungs and Niblungs with certain Songs from the Elder Edda* (1870) and *Three Northern Love Stories and Other Tales* (1875). They further collaborated on the six volumes of *The Saga Library* (1891–1905) which included a translation of the *Heimskringla* begun two decades earlier. Morris's personal affinity with the bleak landscape of Iceland, which he visited in the summers of 1871 and 1873, is attested to by the *Journals of Travel in Iceland* (first published 1911) and by poems in *Poems by the Way* such as 'Iceland First Seen'. In 1876 Morris published his great poetic version of the *Volsunga Saga*, **Sigurd the Volsung and the Fall of the Niblungs**. Fragments also survive showing Morris's interest in Norwegian stories. He visited Norway in 1896, the same year that French tales first published separately appeared together as *Old French Romances*. At the end of his life Morris inevitably turned to 'the first epic of our race', **Beowulf**, and his translation (undertaken with A. J. Wyatt) was published in 1895.

From June 1871 Morris rented Kelmscott Manor in Oxfordshire which he thenceforth regarded as his home. The unhappiness of his personal life at this time (due to his wife's ill health, her affair with Rossetti and his own involvement with Georgiana Burne-Jones) is reflected in his non-Icelandic literature such as the 1872 attempt at a novel (*The Novel on Blue Paper*, first published in 1982 and denounced by Morris as 'nothing but landscape and sentiment') and the plaintive 'masque' *Love is Enough or The Freeing of Pharamond: A Morality* (November 1872). In 1876 his life dramatically moved into a political dimension in outraged response to the Bulgarian atrocities of that year and he became treasurer of The Eastern Question Association. In 1879 he became treasurer of The National Liberal League, from which he resigned in 1880 as his socialistic ideas gained pre-eminence. In 1883 he joined The Social Democratic Federation but left the following year to set up The Socialist League. Finally, in 1890, he founded The Hammersmith Socialist Society. Moving away from the traditions of a literary career Morris declined to be considered as **Arnold**'s successor to the Oxford Chair of Poetry in 1877 and as **Tennyson**'s successor as Laureate in 1892. Much of his writing was now devoted to political polemic and his contiguous theories of art (to Morris art was the 'expression of man's delight in his labour'). *Hopes and Fears for Art* appeared in 1882. During 1884 Morris made 28 contributions to the magazine *Justice* and he edited *The Commonweal* between 1885 and 1890, himself making some 100 contributions. His first explicitly political poem, 'Wake London Lads', appeared in 1878 and set the standard for such later efforts as the collected *Chants for Socialists* (1885), *The Pilgrims of Hope* (*Commonweal* 1885–6) and 'Alfred Linnell Killed in Trafalgar Square November 20 1887: A Death Song'. Morris tried his hand at a socialist play, *The Tables Turned; or Nupkins Awakened* (1887), but his greatest socialist literary efforts were the prose pieces **A Dream of John Ball** (1886–7) and **News from Nowhere** (1890). The latter was first published in book form by Messrs Roberts of Boston, who throughout Morris's life disseminated his works in America.

Morris founded The Kelmscott Press, which began printing in 1891, with the aim of producing books characterized by beauty rather than economy (to this end he designed two type faces, 'Golden' and 'Troy') and of publishing his own works. The great folio **Chaucer** with Morris borders and 87 illustrations by Burne-Jones appeared in 1896 and ranks among the finest books ever made. In 1888 Morris embarked on the last phase of his literary career with *A Tale of the House of the Wolfings and All the Kindreds of the Mark Written in Prose and Verse*. This set the tone for his late prose romances, and the peoples of central Europe (here in the pre-Roman conquest period) featured again in *The Roots of the Mountains* (1889) and *The Story of the Glittering Plain* (1890). Throughout the 1890s Morris worked prodigiously on four further romances: *The Wood beyond the World* (1894), **The Well at the**

'A view of the Manor House at Kelmscott, in Oxford-shire, from the garden gate', the frontispiece to William Morris's *News from Nowhere* (1890).

*World's End* (1896) and the posthumously published *The Water of the Wondrous Isles* and *The Sundering Flood* (both 1897).

Despite his great physique he suffered ill health from 1891. The cause of death according to one doctor was 'simply being William Morris and having done more work than most ten men'.

Morris's importance both in the Arts and Crafts movement and in the history of British socialism is not in doubt. However, little of his vast literary corpus is now read, with the exception of the still popular *News from Nowhere*. This is partly due to the variable quality of much of his work (he wrote with great spontaneity when he could find time amidst all his other endeavours, and he seldom revised) and partly due to his unfashionable interest in epic narrative and Teutonic mythology. Morris had a vision of an England 'over which the shadow of Rome had never descended' and which would have blossomed into a 'splendid branch of the Germanic people, its life and thought nobly expressed in its songs and chronicles'. From the time he began translating Icelandic sagas through to the late prose romances he therefore developed a language from which Latinate and Romance words were increasingly eradicated. In the twentieth century the influence of the prose romances has been greatest on **W. B. Yeats**, whilst in recent years they have acquired a new readership amongst the devotees of **J. R. R. Tolkien** and **C. S. Lewis**.

**Morris, Wright** 1910– American novelist, born in Central City, Nebraska, a town which figures prominently in his fiction. His principal concerns have always been with a definition of the American character, with the American Edenic myth, and with the uses and influences of American history. His narratives are often fragmented and his novels many-voiced and subtly ironic. His novels include *My Uncle Dudley* (1942), *The Man Who Was There* (1945), *The World in the Attic* (1949), *The Works of Love* (1952), *A Field of Vision* (1956, National Book Award), *Love Among the Cannibals* (1957), *Ceremony in Lone Tree* (1960), *Cause for Wonder* (1963), *In Orbit* (1967), *Fire Sermon* (1971), *A Life* (1973), *The Fork River Space Project* (1977) and *Plains Song* (1980). *Collected Stories: 1948–1986* appeared in 1986. He has published three volumes of memoirs: *Will's Boy: A Memoir* (1981), *Solo: An American Dreamer in Europe, 1933–34* (1983) and *A Cloak of Light: Writing My Life* (1985). His literary criticism includes *The Territory Ahead* (1958), *About Fiction* (1975) and a study of American writers entitled *Earthly Delights, Unearthly Adornments* (1978).

**Morrison, Arthur** 1863–1945 Novelist and short-story writer. Born in Poplar, he spent most of his life in the East End of London where his best stories are set. He became clerk to the trustees administering the People's Palace in Mile End Road, where he met **Walter Besant**, probably responsible for appointing him sub-editor of *The Palace Journal*. Morrison afterwards became a freelance journalist, and in 1891 an article in *Macmillan's Magazine* brought him to the notice of **W. E. Henley**, who invited him to write a series for *The National Observer*. The series was published as *Tales of Mean Streets* (1894), which – together with *A Child of the Jago* (1894) and *The Hole in the Wall* (1902) – is his best-known work. In these books Morrison described a world he knew at first hand, and presented the working people and criminals of the slums in terms of their own values and attitudes, without imposing his own moral standards.

He also produced detective stories: *Martin Hewitt, Investigator* (1894), *Chronicles of Martin Hewitt* (1895) and *Hewitt: Third Series* (1896). More interesting than these, and equally little known, is a novel of witchcraft and smuggling in Napoleonic times, *Cunning Murrell* (1900), set on the Essex shore of the Thames estuary. Morrison also collected Japanese prints and paintings, bequeathed to the British Museum at his death. *The Painters of Japan* (2 vols., 1911) was an early and influential study.

**Morrison, Blake** 1950– Poet, anthologist and critic. Born in Skipton, Yorkshire, he read English at Nottingham University before pursuing postgraduate studies in Canada and at

University College, London. He has published a scholarly and informative study of the **Movement** (1980) and a monograph on **Seamus Heaney** (1982); with **Andrew Motion** he edited the controversial *Penguin Book of Contemporary British Poetry* (1982). Morrison's work as a critic precedes and outweighs his poetry, which includes *Dark Glasses* (1984), winner of a Somerset Maugham Award, and *The Ballad of the Yorkshire Ripper* (1987).

**Morrison, Toni** 1931– Black American novelist, born in Ohio, and educated at Howard and Cornell Universities. Her first novel, *The Bluest Eye* (1970), is the story of a year in the life of Pecola Breedlove, a young black girl in Ohio who comes to believe that she has blue eyes. In the course of the year Pecola endures a series of degradations, including incest with her father and subsequent pregnancy, until her fixation with the blue eyes of a friend's doll develops into complete insanity. *Sula* (1973), also set in Ohio, focuses on the friendship between two black women, Sula Peace and Nel Wright Greene, as they mature during the 1920s and 1930s. Their friendship is based on a shared sense of alienation from community and family values, and a similar experience of emptiness in their other relationships – especially with men. *Song of Solomon* (1977) is an intricate narrative about Milkman Dead's exploration of his family history, his quest for a place as an individual within a heritage of slavery and violence. *Tar Baby* (1981) is about motherhood and the relationships between black and white cultures in the Caribbean and America.

*Morte Arthur* A Middle English poem written in the North-west Midlands *c*.1400. Derived from a version of the French prose *Mort Artu*, it tells the same story as the last two tales of **Thomas Malory**'s *Morte Darthur*, on which it had an important influence. Guinevere mistakenly believes Lancelot returns the Maid of Astolat's love and causes him to leave court. She is accused of poisoning a knight and when she learns of Lancelot's innocence he returns to defend her successfully. Agravain, Gawain's brother, betrays Lancelot and Guinevere to Arthur and is killed by Lancelot. Arthur and Gawain besiege Lancelot and Guinevere, and pursue him to Brittany even after the queen has been restored. Arthur and Gawain return to England to deal with Mordred's uprising, but both armies and their leaders are destroyed in the ensuing battle, and Arthur's body is borne to Avalon. Lancelot lives as a hermit-priest and Guinevere as a nun until their deaths. The poem is remarkable amongst medieval **Arthurian literature** in that the powerful, yet simple and concise, narrative moves towards the inexorable destruction of the society of the Round Table without digression or spurious incident.

*Morte Arthure* An alliterative poem written *c*.1360 by an unknown author, at one time thought to be **Huchown of the Awle Ryale**. The principal source was probably a version of Wace's *Roman de Brut*, but it was also influenced by other works and follows none of its sources closely. It relates in epic style Arthur's early victories, his defeat of Lucius, and the revolt led by Mordred in Arthur's absence and the battle culminating in Arthur's death. Arthur, vividly portrayed as a warrior-hero, dominates the narrative; the removal of his body to Avalon is replaced by an account of a solemn and grand burial ceremony at Glastonbury. The poem was used by **Thomas Malory** in his *Morte Darthur*, though he did not follow its additions to the story. See also **Arthurian literature**.

*Morte Darthur, Le* A prose version of the Arthurian legends by **Sir Thomas Malory**, completed in 1469 or 1470. The work was written largely or entirely while Malory was in prison in Newgate. It survives in **Caxton**'s printed text of 1485 and in a manuscript discovered at Winchester in 1934.

The work is divided into eight tales and 21 books. The first tale (Books 1–4) relates Arthur's birth, accession and marriage to Guinevere, his begetting of Mordred by his half-sister Morgan and the establishment of the Round Table. The stories of Merlin and of various knights of the Round Table also appear. The second (Book 5) tells of Arthur's defeat of the Roman emperor Lucius and his coronation by the Pope. The third and fourth tales (Books 6 and 7) are concerned with the stories of Lancelot

An illustration from Wynkyn de Worde's 1529 edition of Malory's *Le Morte Darthur*. Frontispiece to the 21st Book: 'How Sir Mordred presumed and took on him to be King of England, and would have married the Queen.'

Igraine and Uther Pendragon. The frontispiece illustration to the first book of Malory's *Le Morte Darthur* in Wynkyn de Worde's edition, 1529.

du Lake and Sir Gareth of Orkney respectively. The fifth tale (Books 8–12), which occupies almost half of the work, relates the life of Sir Tristram de Lyones, not originally an Arthurian story but one which had independent existence throughout Europe. An accident with a love-potion causes Tristram to fall in love with Isode, the wife of his king and uncle, Mark. The history of the love and jealousy of the three characters is adapted and combined with other exploits including Lancelot's begetting of Galahad, but Malory omits the tragic end of the story of Tristram and Isode. In the Tale of the Sankgreall (Books 13–17) Malory deals with the fragmentation of the Round Table and the quests by all the knights for the Holy Grail. They are successful according to their spiritual purity, only Galahad, Perceval and Bors succeeding completely and taking the Grail to Sarras. The seventh tale (Books 18–19) deals with the adulterous affair of Lancelot and Guinevere, while the final tale (Books 20–21) tells of the destruction of the Round Table through Arthur's discovery of Guinevere's adultery with Lancelot, the war between Lancelot and Arthur, and Mordred's revolt against the king. After his death in the final battle with Mordred, Arthur's body is carried to the Isle of Avalon, and Malory mentions the legend that the king still lives, awaiting the time for his return.

Most of the narrative comes from three French texts, the prose *Tristan*, the Vulgate Cycle and the *Roman du Graal*, and two English works, the alliterative **Morte Arthure** and the stanzaic **Morte Arthur**. Malory's masterly handling of his sources unravelled intertwined narratives and made the Arthuriad more compact by cutting out extraneous material and characters. Whether Malory also created a unified narrative

– or had this as his main purpose – has been a matter of debate. His eight tales share common characters and a common interest in the themes of chivalry, love and religion but have a discontinuity that sometimes dissatisfies modern readers.

See also **Arthurian literature**.

**Mortimer, John (Clifford)** 1923– Playwright and barrister. Educated at Harrow and Brasenose College, Oxford, he served with the Crown Film Unit during World War II. He was called to the Bar in 1948 and became a QC in 1966. His writing has several times drawn on his legal career, in his short play *The Dock Brief*, broadcast on radio and television in 1957, and in his creation of Rumpole, the splendidly disreputable barrister introduced in a volume of short stories, *Rumpole of the Bailey* (1978), and since then the hero of several more collections and several successful television series. Mortimer's work for the stage includes *What Shall We Tell Caroline?* (1958), *The Wrong Side of the Park* (1960), *Two Stars for Comfort* (1962) and *A Voyage Round My Father* (1982), a play based on memories of his father which was also adapted for television. Other work for television has included adaptations of **Robert Graves**'s *I, Claudius* (1972) and **Evelyn Waugh**'s *Brideshead Revisited* (1981), and his own *Paradise Postponed* (1986). *Clinging to the Wreckage* (1982) is a volume of autobiography. Mortimer was created a CBE in 1986.

**Morton, H[enry] V[ollam]** 1892–1979 Travel-writer. H. V. Morton was born and educated in Birmingham. He began his career as a journalist working for various London newspapers, but after the success of *The Heart of London* (1925) and *In Search of England* (1927) he devoted himself to his travel writing.

During his career Morton visited and wrote about numerous countries. A volume on Scotland appeared in 1929, on Ireland in 1930, and on Wales in 1932. He then moved further afield, and his other travel books include one about South Africa (1948), where he finally settled, as well as volumes on the Middle East (1941), Spain (1954), Rome (1957) and the Holy Land (1961).

**Morton, Nathaniel** 1612–85 American colonial historian. Born in the pilgrim community in Leiden, Holland, Morton emigrated to Plymouth Colony in 1623, and went to live with his uncle, Governor **William Bradford**. In 1647 he was appointed secretary of Plymouth Colony, a post which he occupied until his death and which gave him responsibility for keeping the colony's official records. His history of the colony, published in 1669, was entitled *New Englands Memoriall: or, A Brief Relation of the*

*Most Memorable and Remarkable Passages of the Providences of God, Manifested to the Planters of New England, in America: With Special Reference to the First Colony Thereof, Called New Plymouth.* The book relied and elaborated upon Bradford's *History of Plimmoth Plantation*, and provided a source for **Cotton Mather**'s *Magnalia Christi Americana*.

**Morton, Thomas** 1764–1838 English playwright, born in County Durham. Morton was sent to study at Lincoln's Inn, but showed no interest in the law, preferring cricket – he was a senior member of the MCC – and the theatre, in which he won his first success with a musical play, *The Children in the Wood* (1793). There followed a succession of comedies, written for **Covent Garden Theatre**, of which the best are *The Way to Get Married* (1796), *A Cure for the Heart Ache* (1797), *Secrets Worth Knowing* (1798), *Speed the Plough* (1800) and *The School of Reform* (1805). The character of Tyke in the last play was as famous in its time as that of Mrs Grundy in *Speed the Plough*.

**Mosley, Nicholas (Lord Ravensdale)** 1923– Novelist. The eldest son of Sir Oswald Mosley, he was born in London and educated at Eton and Balliol College, Oxford. He has not achieved as much public recognition as other novelists of his generation, perhaps because of his experimental approach to writing. His early novels, *Spaces of the Dark* (1951), *The Rainbearers* (1955) and *Corruption* (1958), are essentially realistic, influenced by **Henry James** and **William Faulkner**. They relate directly to World War II. In the next decade Mosley turned to a simpler style, producing *Accident* (1966), later to be one of Joseph Losey's major films, and *Natalie, Natalie* (1971). Coming after an eight-year silence, *Catastrophe Practice: Plays Not for Acting, and Cypher: A Novel* (1979) signalled his move to a more abstract form. Intended as the first of a seven-volume sequence, it has been followed by *Imago Bird* (1980) and *Serpent* (1981). Mosley's other works, mainly biography, include a study of **Julian Grenfell** (1976), *Rules of the Game: Sir Oswald and Lady Cynthia Mosley 1896–1933* (1982) and *Beyond the Pale: Sir Oswald Mosley and Family 1933–1980* (1983).

**Motherwell, William** 1797–1835 Poet. Born in Glasgow and educated at Glasgow University, Motherwell published a collection of Scottish ballads, *Minstrelsy Ancient and Modern* (1827), and a collection of his own work, *Poems Narrative and Lyrical* (1832). His ballad 'Jeanie Morison' was widely popular. He collaborated with **James Hogg** in editing the poetry of **Robert Burns** (5 vols., 1834–6).

**Motion, Andrew (Peter)** 1952– Poet. Born in London, he was educated at Radley and University College, Oxford. He has been a lecturer in English at Hull University (where he became acquainted with **Philip Larkin**, whose official biographer he is), editor of the *Poetry Review*, and poetry editor at Chatto and Windus. Besides the long poem 'Inland', his first book, *The Pleasure Steamers* (1978), contains work which owes a good deal to the benign influence of **Edward Thomas** and personal poems about his invalid mother. In *Independence* (1981) personal utterance is transmuted into fiction; the sequence is a retrospective narrative spoken by a retired colonial businessman and centred on the year of Indian independence, 1947. Other collections include *Secret Narratives* (1983) and *Dangerous Play* (1984). With **Blake Morrison** he edited the controversial *Penguin Book of Contemporary British Poetry* (1982); he has also published critical books on **Edward Thomas** (1980) and Philip Larkin (1982), and a group biography of George, Constant and Kit Lambert (1986).

**Motley, John Lathrop** c.1814–77 American historian, born in Dorchester, Massachusetts, into a prosperous New England family, and educated at Harvard. He published two novels, *Morton's Hope, or, The Memoirs of a Young Provincial* (1839) and *Merry-Mount: A Romance of the Massachusetts Colony* (1849). He also spent time in the diplomatic service in Russia, Austria and England. *The Rise of the Dutch Republic: A History* was published in three volumes in 1856 after ten years' work in the USA, Holland and Germany. The history, which ends with the death of William of Orange, was well received and soon translated into the principal European languages. Motley followed it with *The History of the United Netherlands*, which examines the years up to the truce of 1609; two volumes were published in 1861 and a further two in 1867. Another history, *The Life and Death of John of Barneveld, Advocate of Holland* (2 vols., 1874), spans the period from 1609 to the Thirty Years War. Motley planned another instalment, which would carry the history to the year 1848, but died before the project was realized.

**Motley, Willard** 1912–65 American novelist, born in Chicago. Motley had a diverse career, which included working as a ranch hand, cook, migrant labourer, and photographer. His observation of the slums of Chicago in the 1940s served as material for his first novel, *Knock on any Door* (1947). His next novels, *We Fished all Night* (1951) and *Let No Man Write My Epitaph* (1958), are also critical examinations of the urban environment. He lived in Mexico for the last 12 years of his life; *Let Noon be Fair*, published posthumously in 1966, traces the gradual corruption and cultural decline of a Mexican tourist town.

**Motteux, Peter Anthony** 1663–1718 Journalist, translator and dramatist. This talented Huguenot, brought up in Rouen, fled to England at the Revocation of the Edict of Nantes in 1685. His early years in England are obscure, but in January 1692 he produced the first number of *The Gentleman's Journal, or, The Monthly Miscellany . . . Consisting of News, Philosophy, Poetry, Music, &c.* This sophisticated literary periodical adopted the epistolary form of the French *Mercure Galant* and ran until November 1694. Largely a clever amalgam drawing on the *Mercure* and a host of unusual sources, the *Journal* includes contributions from Henry Purcell, **Sir Charles Sedley**, **John Dennis**, Tom Brown and **Matthew Prior**. Motteux seems to have brought the word 'journalist' into English; and his *Journal*, coming almost twenty years before **Addison** and **Steele**'s *Tatler*, can claim an important place in the history of English literary journalism.

Motteux completed the translation of Rabelais left unfinished by **Sir Thomas Urquhart**; and he published a translation of *Don Quixote* which, in the version revised by John Ozell, was, like the Rabelais, to remain standard for many years.

Motteux's involvement with the theatre began with his *Love's a Jest* in 1696. Thereafter he composed a multitude of entertainments. His more significant pieces include the tragedy *Beauty in Distress* (1698) and the libretto for *Arsinoë, Queen of Cyprus* (1705). *Arsinoë*, though sung in English, gave the London audience its first hint of the Italian opera which was to become so dominant as to be satirized by **John Gay**'s *The Beggar's Opera* (1728).

In his later years, as his letter to *The Spectator* (Number 288) reveals, Motteux ran a China warehouse in Leadenhall Street. He also dealt in pictures and kept up lively contacts with foreign artists working in England: there is a sketch of Motteux and his family by Pellegrini in the British Museum. Motteux died in exquisitely unfortunate circumstances in a City brothel on his birthday in 1718.

**Mottram, R[alph] H[ale]** 1883–1971 Novelist. He was born in Norwich and educated there and in Lausanne. **Galsworthy**, with whom he became friends in 1904, encouraged him to write but he did not achieve recognition until *The Spanish Farm* (1924), the first part of *The Spanish Farm Trilogy* continued in *Sixty-four, Ninety-four* (1925) and *The Crime at Vanderlynden's* (1926). Set on a farm near the front during World War I, it is the story of the owner, Vanderlynden, his youngest child, Madeleine, and the men who pass through in search of peace and serenity. Mottram wrote 60 books altogether, and many of his later novels are set in East Anglia, where he spent most of his life. He was awarded the honorary degree of Doctor of Letters by the University of East Anglia in 1966.

***Mourning Becomes Electra*** A trilogy of plays by **Eugene O'Neill**, based on the *Oresteia* of Aeschylus, and first produced in New York in 1931. The 13-act trilogy is set in a small New England coastal town at the close of the Civil War. During General Mannon's absence in the war his wife Christine takes Captain Adam Brant as her lover. The grim Mannon house, built in the style of a Greek temple, becomes the setting for the first death, that of General Mannon, poisoned by Christine. Their daughter Lavinia hates her mother as fervently as she loved her father, and finding the remains of the poison, she urges her brother Orin to exact revenge. Orin kills Brant and Christine commits suicide. Driven towards madness by the consciousness of his crime, Orin is taken on a voyage by the unrepentant Lavinia. On their return to the Mannon house, he is still ill but she is transformed into a beauty exactly like her mother (the play was originally intended for performance with masks). Orin's passionate attachment to his mother is now incestuously transferred to Lavinia, and remorse leads him to suicide. Lavinia accepts the punishment of shutting herself away in the decaying mansion of the doomed Mannons.

***Mourning Bride, The*** A tragedy by **William Congreve**, his only essay in the form, first produced in February 1697 and published the same year. A considerable success, it provided a fine part for a tragic actress in the character of Zara, created by Elizabeth Barry. The play has not been revived, but two quotations from it are remembered: 'Music has charms to soothe a savage breast' and 'Heav'n has no rage, like love to hatred turn'd,/ Nor Hell a fury, like a woman scorn'd'.

**Movement, the** A loose grouping of poets who made their names during the 1950s. The term derives from an unsigned article by J. D. Scott, 'In the Movement', published in *The Spectator* on 1 October 1954. Although it can be extended to include novelists and playwrights, it has come to identify essentially those poets included in **Robert Conquest**'s anthology *New Lines* (1956): Conquest himself, **Kingsley Amis**, **Donald Davie**, **D. J. Enright**, **Thom Gunn**, John Holloway, **Elizabeth Jennings**, **Philip Larkin** and **John Wain**. Conquest's introduction claimed that they shared a 'negative determination to avoid bad principles'. In practice, this meant a determination to re-establish the values of rational intelligence and skilful craftsmanship in English poetry. Their stance was ironic and anti-romantic, their manner at times literary, and, to some tastes, academic: detractors have not failed to point out how many Movement poets earned their living in universities. Yet no post-war anthology of new writers has included such an impressive proportion of subsequently distinguished poets as *New Lines*.

**Mowat, Farley** 1921– Canadian writer, essayist, and story-teller. Born in Belleville, Ontario, and raised in Saskatoon, Saskatchewan, he interrupted his education at the University of Toronto for military service in World War II. After the war he spent two years in the Arctic before finishing his university degree and embarking on his highly successful career as a freelance writer. Mowat's first book, *People of the Deer* (1952), denounced the treatment of the Inuit by government officials and by missionaries, and its impassioned prose created an immense readership and immense controversy, two factors that have stayed with Mowat throughout his life. More than 30 books document his unending interest in the north, the wilderness, the animal kingdom, and the disadvantaged peoples. *The Desperate People* (1959), *Canada North* (1967), and *Canada North Now: The Great Betrayal* (1976) study the Canadian north. *Never Cry Wolf* (1963) and *A Whale for the Killing* (1972) are his most famous animal books. His fiction for children includes *The Dog Who Wouldn't Be* (1957), *Owls in the Family* (1961), *Lost in the Barrens* (1965), and *The Boat Who Wouldn't Float* (1968). His military service provides the background for his autobiographical *And No Birds Sang* (1979). He has also edited many journals of early Canadian explorers. Translated into 23 languages and published in more than 40 countries, his 'subjective nonfiction', as he himself describes his writings, has raised public awareness, both in Canada and throughout the world, of mankind's inhumanity to man, to animal life, and to the environment.

**Mowatt, Anna Cora** 1819–70 American dramatist, novelist and actress. Anna Ogden was the ninth of 16 children born in a wealthy American family living in Bordeaux, France, where she spent her early years before the family returned to settle in New York City. She was 15 when she married James Mowatt, a respected lawyer much older than herself. He encouraged her to write, and she published a verse romance, *Pelayo* (1836), and a verse satire, *Reviewers Reviewed* (1837), before turning her hand to novels of New York social life, including *The Fortune Hunter* (1844) and *Evelyn, or, A Heart Unmasked* (1845).

As a figure in New York society, she risked ridicule for her literary aspirations. To turn to the theatre was considered even worse, but when her comic social satire, *Fashion*, opened in 1845 and became widely popular, she was encouraged to take to the stage herself. For nine years she toured as an actress, retiring in 1854 to live in Richmond, Virginia, and after 1861 in Florence, Italy. She spent the rest of her life writing romantic narratives of life in the theatre, *Mimic Life* (1856) and *Twin Roses* (1857), her own *Autobiography of an Actress* (1854) and various historical sketches.

**Mphahlele, Es'kia (formerly Ezekiel)** 1919– South African writer, born in a Pretoria township. Notwithstanding tribal village childhood and urban slum adolescence and manhood, prodigious personal effort led, through menial jobs, teaching, and journalism, to Mphahlele's becoming an African writer and critic of distinction. Leaving South Africa in 1957, he worked in Nigeria, France, Kenya, Zambia and the USA before returning to a professorship in Johannesburg in 1978.

His early sketches of black ghetto experience, *Man Must Live* (1947), were followed by stories of increasing political protest collected in *The Living and the Dead* (1961) and *In Corner B* (1967), with a selection from all these in *The Unbroken Song* (1981). But his narrative art excels in *Down Second Avenue* (1959), now a classic autobiography through its vivid, candid, angry, life-affirming account of a humane personality maturing under grinding poverty and racial oppression. *Afrika My Music: An Autobiography 1957–1983* (1984) is less compelling. The earlier parts of the novel *The Wanderers* (1971) have admirable immediacy, but later it falters thematically and structurally. *Chirundu* (1979) is a lesser novel about political power and corruption. *Father Come Home* (1984) is an affecting tale of African families dispossessed and scattered.

Mphahlele has been an important, influential literary critic. *The African Image* (1962) was a pioneering study both of literature in Africa and its politico-cultural context. The second edition (1974) brought it up to date and related African with Afro-American writing and Black Consciousness, which he also discusses in the essays, *Voices in the Whirlwind* (1972).

***Mr Britling Sees It Through*** A novel by **H. G. Wells**, published in 1916.

With its strongly autobiographical elements, the title of this work reflects Wells's belief that the Great War would be over by 1916. The novel also reflects the disillusionment that had set in since Wells had written *The War That Will End War* (1914). It is centred on the household circle of Matching's Easy, undoubtedly based on Wells's Essex household, Easton Glebe. Through Britling, a mature and successful writer, we are given a picture of Wells's public and private worlds during and just before the outbreak of the war. Britling's early enthusiasms, including his patriotic fervour, are generally endorsed by the detached narrator, only to be destroyed by the shock of learning of the death of Hugh, his son by a first marriage.

The depiction of Britling's boredom with his wife and children, and his marital infidelities, are generally considered among the novelist's less discreet reflections on his life. Britling becomes a more obviously sympathetic character when Hugh's death in the war is announced; this brings into his private sphere the larger public grief at the consequences of war. Particularly with the device of Hugh's bitterly intelligent letters from the trenches, and of the letter that Britling tries but fails to write to the bereaved parents of Heinrich, once his children's tutor, Wells captured the national mood of 1916.

*Mr Gilfil's Love Story* See *Scenes of Clerical Life*.

*Mr Scarborough's Family* A novel by **Anthony Trollope**, published in *All the Year Round* (May 1882 to June 1883). It appeared in volume form in 1883.

The plot concerns the disappointment of Mr Scarborough who, after the birth of a son, Mountjoy, marries his wife again before the birth of a second son, Augustus, to ensure that he can declare the latter his heir, should Mountjoy not prove of responsible character. The novel is enlivened by the characters of Mr Grey, Scarborough's gentle, long-suffering attorney, and his daughter, Dolly, who refuses to marry because all the men she meets compare unfavourably with her father.

*Mr Sponge's Sporting Tour* A novel by **R. S. Surtees**, published in 1853 with illustrations by **John Leech**. Probably Surtees's best novel, it has more form and balance than the others and the central character is convincingly developed. Sponge lives up to his name by forcing himself upon rich men and making up to their daughters. He is, however, redeemed by enormous

'Hercules "takes" a Draper's Shop.' An illustration by John Leech for Surtees's *Mr Sponge's Sporting Tour*, 1853.

courage and skill on horseback and a genuine love of hunting. His peregrinations take us into the company of such extraordinary folk as Lord Scamperdale and Sir Harry Scattercash; and there are some marvellous low-life characters from horsedealers' yards and hunting stables. A sequel, *Mr Facey Romford's Hounds*, was published in 1865, the year after Surtees died.

*Mrs Dalloway* A novel by **Virginia Woolf**, published in 1925.

Clarissa Dalloway, the wife of Richard Dalloway MP and a fashionable London hostess, is to give an important party. Her character is gradually revealed through her thoughts on that day and through her memories of the past, rendered by interior monologue and **stream of consciousness**. So are the other people who have touched her life: her one-time suitor Peter Walsh, lately returned from India after five years' absence, her childhood friend Sally Seton, her daughter Elizabeth and spinster tutor Miss Kilman, a political hostess, Lady Bruton.

A complementary character is Septimus Warren Smith, a shell-shock victim who has retreated into a private world and ends the day by committing suicide. He and Clarissa Dalloway never meet, but their lives are connected by external events and news of his death is casually mentioned by a guest at Clarissa's party. It provokes in her thoughts of her own isolation and loneliness: 'Death was defiance. Death was an attempt to communicate, people feeling the impossibility of reaching the centre which, mystically, evaded them; closeness drew apart; rapture faded; one was alone.'

The novel was generally well reviewed and sold well. It reflects Virginia Woolf's many talents, including the astonishingly well-managed flow of her heroine's thoughts through the course of the day.

*Mrs Warren's Profession* A play by **George Bernard Shaw**, written in 1893, but denied performance by the Examiner of Plays, who considered it immoral. It was given a private performance by the Independent Theatre Club in 1902 and its first public performance in 1925.

Mrs Warren's profession is prostitution. She runs a chain of brothels in the capitals of Europe. She cannot be certain who is the father of her brilliant and independent daughter, Vivie. Shaken by the discovery of the truth about her mother, Vivie rejects both her suitors in favour of continuing actuarial work with her friend Honoria. The conflict between mother and daughter is the dramatic centre of the play. Vivie is not prepared to learn what Mrs Warren is prepared to teach – that prostitution is economically determined by a society that only pretends to outlaw it.

**Mtshali, Oswald Mbuyiseni** 1940– South African poet, born in Vryheid. With *Sounds of a Cowhide Drum* (1971) Mtshali led the great creative outburst of black 'township' poetry, after a decade of black post-Sharpeville literary silence; then came **Serote**, **Sepamla** and the other poets in the anthology, *Black Poets in South Africa* (1974). Mtshali's conversational, free-flowing verse often expresses communal ghetto emotions – frustration, anger, bitterness, pathos, pity – though, despite more poems about 'the jaded soul of the forlorn', *Fireflames* (1980) also looks forward to a time 'long/after the fiendish ideology has been reduced to rubble'.

*Mucedorus, The Comedy of* A play of unknown authorship first published in 1598. Discovered in a volume of Shakespeare in the library of Charles II, it was once regarded as an early work of the poet, though this possibility has now been rejected. (See **Shakespeare apocrypha**.) The story concerns the efforts of Mucedorus, Prince of Valencia, to discover the virtues of Amadine, daughter of the King of Aragon. In the process he falls in love with her, saves her life on two occasions, and successfully overcomes the king's objections to him as a husband for his daughter.

*Much Ado About Nothing* A comedy by **William Shakespeare**, first performed *c.*1598 and published in Quarto (Q1) in 1600 as well as in the First Folio of 1623. The Claudio/Hero plot was already a familiar story and could have been taken from any number of sources. More original is the invention and elaboration of the unwilling love of Beatrice and Benedick.

Claudio, in the service of the Prince of Aragon, Don Pedro, falls in love with Hero, daughter of Leonato, Governor of Messina. The match is welcomed by all but Don Pedro's discontented brother, Don John, who determines to destroy it. With the aid of his henchman, Borachio, he convinces Claudio that Hero is unfaithful, and Claudio waits till the marriage service itself to reject his intended bride. Hero faints away, and Leonato is persuaded to challenge assumptions of her guilt by announcing that she is dead. When the garrulous Borachio is overheard boasting of Don John's trick, Claudio's horror is relieved by Leonato's forgiveness and by Hero's return to life.

In what is formally a sub-plot, but one which attracts more attention than the conventional main plot, Claudio's friend Benedick and Leonato's niece Beatrice fight a duel of wit which, through the manoeuvres of their friends, is exposed as a disguise of their real love for each other. That love is tested when Beatrice, outraged by Claudio's treatment of Hero, demands that Benedick kill him. Benedick challenges Claudio to a duel, but the timely discovery of Don John's duplicity spares the two friends that confrontation. It is characteristic of Shakespeare's inventiveness that the real villainy of Don John should be exposed by a fumbling and incompetent constable, Dogberry. A surviving reference makes it almost certain that the part of Dogberry was written for the famous comic actor, Will Kemp, who left Shakespeare's company shortly after the play's first production.

*Much Ado About Nothing* is a mature comedy with a long history of success in the British theatre. The influence of Beatrice and Benedick was felt in the Restoration comedy of manners, whose competitive loving couples similarly disguise their true affection by verbal combat. Millamant and Mirabell in **Congreve**'s *The Way of the World* are the most famous of a number of examples.

**Muddiman, Henry** b.1629 Journalist. Almost nothing is known of his personal life. A pensioner at St John's College, Cambridge, and later a schoolteacher, he was licensed through the influence of General Monk and the patronage of Sir John Williamson to write a news-sheet under the Long Parliament in 1659. He was remarkably successful, and *The Oxford Gazette*, which he began to publish in 1665, was the ancestor of *The London Gazette*.

**Muggleton, Lodowicke** 1609–98 and **Reeve, John** 1608–58 Founders of the sect known as the Muggletonians. They were cousins, both London tailors, who in 1651 claimed to be the 'Two Last Witnesses' foretold in Revelation 11:3–6; they were to prepare the elect for the coming of Judgement Day. They preached complete freedom of conscience in matters of religion, and their beliefs included the special inspiration of the elect, the mortalism of the soul, and the conviction that matter was composed of the substance of God. They were pacifists and quietists. The sect survived obscurely until the present century, and the recent discovery of a large archive of Muggletonian material has provided historians with an exceptional amount of information about the workings of a radical 17th-century sect.

**Muir, Edwin** 1887–1959 Poet, novelist, translator and critic. Born in Orkney, he moved to Glasgow with his family, worked as a clerk, and began to contribute to A. R. Orage's *New Age*. He married in 1919, moved to London and, at Orage's suggestion, began psychoanalysis. This released the 'mythological dreams' which were to become important for his poetry. He travelled to Prague with his wife Willa, and between 1930 and 1949 they published translations of the novels of Franz Kafka. After the war he returned to Prague to work for the British Council, and then became Director of the British Institute in Rome in 1949. He was Professor of Poetry at Harvard University in 1955–6.

His volumes of poetry include *First Poems* (1925), *Chorus of the Newly Dead* (1926), *Journeys and Places* (1937), *The Narrow Place* (1943), *The Voyage* (1946), *The Labyrinth* (1949) and *One Foot in Eden* (1956). *Collected Poems 1921–1958* was published in 1960. His poetry became increasingly allegorical and philosophical, though he is perhaps best represented by the often-anthologized 'The Horses'. His prose work includes three novels, *The Marionette* (1927), *The Three Brothers* (1931) and *Poor Tom* (1932), and several critical studies, *Transition: Essays on Contemporary Literature* (1926), *The Structure of the Novel* (1928), *Scott and Scotland* (1936), *Essays on Literature and Society* (1949) and *The Estate of Poetry* (1962). His autobiography, *The Story and the Fable* (1940), was revised as *An Autobiography* (1954).

**Mulcaster, Richard** ?1530–1611 Writer on education. Mulcaster was educated at Eton and Christ Church, Oxford, where he graduated MA (1556) with a reputation as one of the best Hebrew scholars of his age. In 1561 he became the first headmaster of Merchant Taylors' School where he remained until 1586. **Spenser** may have been one of his pupils. In 1596 he became high master of St Paul's School. His two works on education, *Positions* (1581) and *The First Part of the Elementary* (1582), show that he held advanced views, advocating university education and adequate salaries for teachers, close contact between teachers and parents, and music in schools. He wrote some Latin verse including an elegy on the death of Elizabeth (1603).

**Muldoon, Paul** 1951– Irish poet. He was born in Moy, County Armagh, Northern Ireland and educated at Queen's University, Belfast, where **Seamus Heaney** was among his teachers. He worked as a producer for the BBC for many years before resigning in 1985. His verse is dazzlingly adroit, developing its peculiar rhetoric in stages to a fine point of sophisticated eloquence. After the first volumes, *New Weather* (1973) and *Mules* (1977), Muldoon seemed to intensify his humour and broaden his range so that *Why Brownlee Left* (1980) and *Quoof* (1984) have come to be regarded as highly important moments in modern Irish poetry. He edited a controversial anthology, *Contemporary Irish Poetry* (1986), and has shown himself to be a fine translator of contemporary Gaelic poetry.

**Mulock, Dinah Maria** (afterwards Mrs Craik) 1826–87 Novelist. Born near Stoke-on-Trent, where her father was a minister, she helped her mother in conducting a school. In 1846 she settled in London, starting her writing career with stories for children. Her first novel, *The Ogilvies*, appeared in 1849 and was followed by *Olive* (1850), *The Head of the Family* (dedicated to **Elizabeth Barrett Browning**, 1852) and *Agatha's Husband* (1853). In 1857 she published her most popular work, **John Halifax, Gentleman**. Later novels included her own favourite, *A Life for a Life* (1859), as well as *Christian's Mistake* (1865), *The Woman's Kingdom* (1869) and *Young Mrs Jardine* (1879). She also published volumes of poetry in 1859, 1875, 1880 and 1881. Of a number of sensible and penetrating essays, 'A Woman's Thoughts About Women' (1853) is most interesting.

***Mum and the Sothsegger*** An anonymous Middle English poem in **alliterative verse**, surviving in two fragments and dating from the first decade of the 15th century. It was at one time known as *Richard the Redeless* and believed to have been written by **William Langland**. The first fragment, in four passus and a prologue, deals with the events of 1399 surrounding the deposition of Richard II and criticizes the king for his unwise behaviour. The second fragment refers to events after 1402 and is not divided into passus. It takes the form of a debate between Mum and the soothsayer (or truth-teller), the former advocating discreet silence and the second adamant that criticism should be voiced. In a dream the narrator is told by a gardener that truth-telling is best, and so he writes the poem. Verbal similarities between the second fragment and the A-text of **Piers Plowman** suggest that the author was familiar with the text. It is generally accepted that the two fragments are from a single work, although this has not been proved conclusively.

**mummers' play** The mummers' play, with its central theme of death and resurrection, belongs less to literature than to anthropology. Associated with the death of winter and the new birth of spring, it is presumed to have survived from the folk festivals of agricultural communities. More than 3000 texts have been recovered by 19th- and 20th-century researchers, who have divided them into three main groups: the Hero-Combat Play, the Sword Play (mainly from the North-east of England), and the Wooing Ceremony (mainly from the East Midlands). Adapted over the centuries, the texts can accommodate heroes from St George to Winston Churchill and villains from the Turkish Knight to Adolf Hitler. Whoever dies can be revived by a remedy of the Doctor's, and the play ends with a procession and the taking of a collection.

**Munby, A[rthur] J[oseph]** 1828–1910 Poet and diarist. He was born near York and educated at Trinity College, Cambridge, writing most of his first volume of poetry, *Benoni* (1852), while still an undergraduate. A reluctant lawyer who always preferred the literary life, he entered Lincoln's Inn, was called to the Bar and worked from 1860 onwards as a clerk with the Ecclesiastical Commission. His subsequent volumes included *Verses New and Old* (1865), *Vestigia Retrorsum* (1891), *Vulgar Verses* (published under the pseudonym of Jones Brown, 1891), *Poems: Chiefly Lyric and Elegiac* (1901), *Relicta* (1909) and several verse romances, notably *Susan* (1893). Their recurrent preoccupation with working women and the frequent theme of the gentleman who falls in love with a servant have an autobiographical counterpart in Munby's love for Hannah Cullwick, a maid of all work whom he met in 1854 and secretly married in 1873. This side to his life, first glimpsed by friends and contemporaries on the publication of his will, is recorded in the diaries he kept from 1859 onwards – used by Derek Hudson as the basis for his account in *Munby: Man of Two Worlds* (1972).

**Munday, Anthony** 1560–1633 Dramatist. Born in London, Munday may have been a boy actor before being apprenticed to a stationer. He was engaged in anti-Catholic espionage from early in his adulthood. There are even suspicions that he was a double-agent, though his religious pamphlets are vigorously and unequivocally Protestant. Munday was certainly capable of changing his mind. Within a few years of writing *A Second and Third Blast of Retreat from Plays and Theatres* (1580), an anti-theatrical tract, he was engaged in writing plays for the public theatre. Not many have survived. *Fedele and Fortunio* (c. 1584), a piece for court performance, is now believed to be mostly Munday's work, as is *John a Kent and John a Cumber* (1594). His is one of many hands at work in the revision of *Sir Thomas More* (c. 1596) and in Part One of *Sir John Oldcastle* (1599). By 1598 he was well enough known to be referred to by **Francis Meres** in *Palladis Tamia* as 'the best for comedy' and 'our best plotter'. The latter skill suggests a journeyman's useful talent for dividing a given story into suitable dramatic episodes. It is certainly arguable that the plotting is better than the writing in the two-part play, written in collaboration with **Henry Chettle**, on the **Robin Hood** legends, *The Downfall of Robert, Earl of Huntingdon* and its sequel *The Death of Robert, Earl of Huntingdon* (both 1598), which completes the list of extant plays known to have been Munday's in whole or in part. In addition, there are several pageants for the City of London, dating from the period 1592–1623 when he was keeper of the pageant properties and the city's official poet.

As translator of many French and Spanish prose romances, Munday made a widely acknowledged contribution to the growth of Arthurian and semi-Arthurian stories in England. There, and in his own *Zelauto* (1580) and *A True and Admirable History of a Maiden of Consolens in Poitiers* (1603), he was also advancing the development of the English novel.

*Munera Pulveris* Essays by **John Ruskin**, first published in *Fraser's Magazine* as 'Essays On Political Economy' in 1862–3 and then in book form as *Munera Pulveris* in 1872.

In *Munera Pulveris* Ruskin attempts to analyse the salient aspects of political economy which he sees as 'a system of conduct' that cannot be achieved 'except under certain conditions of moral culture'. He defines the commercial cornerstones of Wealth, Money and Riches and in each case his definitions assume life-giving qualities, assert human principles and demonstrate adherence to a moral standard – an approach very different from that of Victorian *laissez-faire* capitalism. Many familiar Ruskinian motifs – treatment of the worker, relations between rich and poor, between the powerful and the weak, and the 'national store' of wealth – come under consideration. Although lacking the pungency of *Unto this Last*, *Munera Pulveris* is a noble statement of Ruskin's idealism.

**Munro, Alice** 1931– Canadian novelist and writer of short stories. Born Alice Laidlaw, she grew up in Wingham, Ontario, and attended the University of Western Ontario. Her first book of stories, *Dance of the Happy Shades* (1968), was followed by *Something I've Been Meaning to Tell You* (1974), *Who Do You Think You Are?* (1978, as *The Beggar Maid* in England) and *The Moons of Jupiter* (1982). *Lives of Girls and Women* (1971) is a novel. Her refreshing and poignant stories generally centre on the 'pain of human contact' in the lives of women.

**Munro, Hector Hugh** See **Saki**.

*Murder in the Cathedral* A religious verse drama by **T. S. Eliot**, first produced at the Chapter House of Canterbury Cathedral during the Canterbury Festival of 1935 and published in the same year. The play follows the events in Canterbury after Becket's return in 1170.

A Chorus of Women lament the absence of their archbishop and the people's helplessness in the schism between church and state. A herald announces to them, and to the priests, that Becket is returning; the news is welcome, but all, save the second priest, are fearful of King Henry II's reconciliation with Becket and wonder if it is to be trusted. Becket enters, determined to resolve the crisis, though he knows it may cost him his life. In a long scene, the Four Tempters illustrate the conflict his decision provokes within himself; the temptation to seek martyrdom is powerful. Becket realizes that the only course he can follow is to offer his life to 'the Law of God above the Law of Man'. The Christmas morning sermon of 1170 makes his position clear. Four days later the King's Four Knights arrive and charge Becket with rebellion; he is ordered to depart from England. He refuses, and the abusive knights warn him they will come again. The priests try to persuade Becket to barricade himself in the cathedral. He refuses, and orders them to unbar the door and open it. The knights return, half drunk, and murder him; then they address the audience in turn with a justification of their deed. After they withdraw the stage is left to the priests, who offer thanks to God for having given another saint to Canterbury.

**Murdoch, Dame Iris (Jean)** 1919– Novelist and philosopher. Born in Dublin of Anglo-Irish parents, she was educated at Badminton and at Somerville College, Oxford. She lectured in philosophy at Oxford and then at the Royal College of Art in London. Her philosophical works include *Sartre: Romantic Rationalist* (1953), *The Sovereignty of Good* (1970) and *The Fire and the Sun: Why Plato Banned the Artists* (1977).

Her first novel, *Under the Net* (1954), used a first-person male narrator and displayed her gift for humour. It was followed by *The Flight from the Enchanter* (1955), *The Sandcastle* (1957) and *The Bell* (1958), widely considered her most successful novel, about a declining religious community. Her prolific output has continued with *A Severed Head* (1961), *An Unofficial Rose* (1962), *The Unicorn* (1963), *The Italian Girl* (1964), *The Red and the Green* (1965), *The Time*

Iris Murdoch.

of the Angels (1966), *The Nice and the Good* (1968), *Bruno's Dream* (1969), *A Fairly Honourable Defeat* (1970), *An Accidental Man* (1971), *The Black Prince* (1972), *The Sacred and Profane Love Machine* (1974), *A Word Child* (1975), *Henry and Cato* (1977), *The Sea, The Sea* (1978; winner of the Booker Prize), *The Philosopher's Pupil* (1983) and *The Book and the Brotherhood* (1987). With their blend of realism and symbolism, they reflect her interest in psychological patterns and myths in human relationships. Their narrative skill and talent for irony has also helped attract a wide readership.

Iris Murdoch's plays include an adaptation of *A Severed Head* (with **J. B. Priestley**, 1963), *Servants and the Snow* (1970), *The Three Arrows* (1972) and *Art and Eros* (1980).

**Murphy, Arthur** 1727–1805 Dramatist, editor and critic. An Irishman born in Roscommon, Murphy was a man of unusually broad interests. Educated at the English Jesuit College in St Omer, France, he began his adult life as a clerk and book-keeper, but by 1752 was submitting contributions to **Fielding**'s *Covent Garden Journal* and the *New Craftsman*. From 1753–4 he was editor of the *Gray's Inn Journal* and from 1756–7 of the political weekly *The Test*, through which he supported Henry Fox's attacks on the militarism of the elder Pitt. A committed Tory, Murphy alienated progressive Londoners by his defence of Lord Bute's government in articles submitted to *The Auditor* in 1762, protesting against **John Wilkes** and *The North Briton*. His appointment as commissioner of bankruptcies came in recognition of the journalistic support he had lent to an often unpopular administration.

Remembered primarily as a playwright, Murphy was also an actor from 1754–6, during which time he played Othello at **Covent Garden**. *The Apprentice* (1756) was the first of several accomplished farces that were among the most popular 18th-century afterpieces. Others were *The Upholsterer* (1758), *The Citizen* (1761) and the excellent *Three Weeks after Marriage* (1776), a revised version of *What We Must All Come to* (1764), which had been damned by the public during the furore caused by the prosecution of John Wilkes. The unpopularity of Murphy's politics has disguised from many critics the talent as a writer of unsentimental comedies that ought to have earned him comparison with **Goldsmith** and **Sheridan**. *The Way to Keep Him* (three-act version, 1760; five-act version, 1761), *All in the Wrong* (1761) and particularly *Know Your Own Mind* (1777) have been unfairly neglected in the theatre. Murphy's tragedies, even the best of them, *The Grecian Daughter* (1772), are less effective.

When it is remembered that Murphy sustained an active career as a barrister from 1763–

87, his literary output is prodigious. It includes the first edition of Fielding's works, in four volumes with a biographical and critical introduction (1762), *An Essay on the Life and Genius of Samuel Johnson* (1792), *The Life of David Garrick* (2 vols., 1801) and a translation of *The Works of Tacitus* (4 vols., 1793).

**Murphy, Richard** 1927– Irish poet. Born in County Galway, he spent part of his childhood in Ceylon, where his father was posted as a colonial official, before going to Wellington College, followed by Oxford and the Sorbonne. He has taught at various schools and universities. His first small collection, *The Archaeology of Love*, appeared in 1955 and was followed by *Sailing to an Island* (1963), *The Battle of Aughrim* (1968), *High Island* (1974) and *The Price of Stone* (1985). *Selected Poems* appeared in 1979. In a sense he is the last of the Anglo-Irish poets: he dwells on his Anglo-Irish heritage, similar to **Yeats**'s, represented by demesne and rectory, long-planted trees and service in England's wars and colonies, but he ranges beyond it in search of reconciliation and association with the other Ireland of hovels, famine-memories, the islanders of the West of Ireland and historical disaster continuing into the present. This double allegiance is reflected in technique: Murphy has made some use of the alliterative stress-metres and 'kennings' or terse periphrases of the Anglo-Saxon sea-poems as well as experimenting with the assonance and consonance of Gaelic poetic tradition. His most ambitious poem, 'The Battle of Aughrim', commissioned and broadcast by the BBC, coolly explores the antecedents and reverberations of 'the last decisive battle in Irish history' fought between 'planters' and 'mere Irish' in 1691. In this and other poems he meditates on buildings, stones and earth which have witnessed and survived Ireland's difficult history.

**Murphy, Thomas (Bernard)** 1935– Irish playwright. He was born in Tuam, County Galway. His first play, *A Whistle in the Dark* (1961), concerns an Irish immigrant family in Coventry whose despairs find outlet in brutal violence. After writing television and radio scripts in London, he returned to Ireland in 1970. Subsequent plays explore various modifications of the realism of his first work. *Famine* (1968) was followed by *A Crucial Week in the Life of a Grocer's Assistant* (1969), with a tight, surrealistic structure and Joycean wordplay. In *The Morning after Optimism* (1971) a whore and a pimp are the shadows and finally the murderers of two idealized lovers in a debased Forest of Arden. *The Sanctuary Lamp* (1975) peoples its stage with three grotesque derelicts, while *The Blue Macushla* (1980), set in a night club, is a satire of Irish politics. In *The Gigli Concert*

(1983) an Irish businessman who aspires to sing like Gigli 'consults' an English 'philosophical dynamatologist'. Murphy's latest work is *Bailegangaire* (1986).

**Murray, Sir James A[ugustus] H[enry]** 1837–1915 Lexicographer. A tailor's son from Hawick, he left school before he was 15 and worked locally as a casual labourer while continuing to read up many subjects avidly. From the age of 17 he was a highly successful assistant master at Hawick United School, his zest for learning astonishing all who met him. His move to London, where he at first worked as a bank clerk, was to get his wife into a better climate. Through membership of the Philological Society he met **F. J. Furnivall**, who involved him in preparing medieval texts for the Early English Text Society series, and the headmaster of Mill Hill School, who gave him a teaching job (1870). Despite widespread recognition of his scholarship he schooled himself through a University of London external degree (1874). In 1878 he was appointed editor of *The Oxford English Dictionary*, becoming the driving force behind that formidable project and continuing to pour his enthusiasm and compulsively hard work into it even in his seventies. His achievement brought him many honorary doctorates as well as the award of a Civil List pension (1884) and a knighthood (1908).

**Murray, John** 1778–1843 Publisher. Born in London, and educated at private schools in Edinburgh, Margate and London, Murray was the son of John Murray I (born MacMurray, 1745–93), who founded the publishing house that still exists today. Assuming control of the business after his father's death, he built it up into one of the most prestigious and successful houses of the 19th century. Combining considerable commercial talent with cultivated literary taste, he was one of the new breed of highly professionalized patron-entrepreneurs that emerged at the end of the 18th century. His house at Albemarle Street became a meeting-place for many of the leading literary figures of the day, and he held a reputation for liberality towards his authors, occasionally burning his fingers (**Coleridge** appears not to have produced a line of his translation of Goethe's *Faust*), but in general reaping the rewards of finely judged advances. In 1808 he discontinued his part-interest in *The Edinburgh Review* and, with the encouragement and support of **Scott**, founded the Tory *Quarterly Review* in 1809, installing **William Gifford** as editor and securing the services of **Southey** as his star contributor. He took an active interest in its management, and its influence, both literary and political, was for almost a century rivalled only by that of the *Edinburgh* itself. He was also for a time joint publisher of *Blackwood's Magazine* but pulled out in 1818, in protest at the tone of its attacks on **Leigh Hunt** and **Keats** in the famous 'Cockney School' articles. His single most important author was his friend **Byron**, who awoke to find himself among the immortals after the publication of the first two cantos of *Childe Harold's Pilgrimage*. *The Corsair* reputedly sold 10,000 copies on the first day of its publication alone. Their alliance continued for some time after Byron's departure for the Continent, and only broke down under the strains of *Don Juan*. Murray published, but withheld his imprint on, Cantos I to V, but thereafter his Tory instincts rose in rebellion, and the later cantos, as well as the anti-establishment satire *The Vision of Judgement*, were gratefully snapped up by Leigh Hunt for his *Examiner*. In the complicated controversy relating to Byron's *Memoirs*, which he had bought from **Thomas Moore** in 1821, he was compelled to resell them to Moore who then burned them in the grate at Albemarle Street.

Murray's other authors included **Jane Austen** (on whose novels he later sold the copyright), **Crabbe**, Southey, Coleridge, **Borrow** and the historian Napier. Another very profitable undertaking was the series of guidebooks inaugurated by Mariana Starke's *Guide for Travellers on the Continent* (1820), and continued by his son, the third John Murray (1808–92). In the mid-1820s he suffered his only major financial catastrophe with the discontinuation, after only six months, of the daily newspaper *The Representative* which he had been persuaded to launch by the young **Benjamin Disraeli**.

**Murray, Les[lie] A[llan]** 1938– Australian poet. Born in Bunyah, New South Wales, he attended Sydney University. His poetry is adventurous and commanding, qualities exhibited in 'The Powerline Incantation' and 'An Absolutely Ordinary Rainbow'. Works include *The Ilex Tree* (with Geoffrey Lehmann, 1965), *The Weatherboard Cathedral* (1969), *Poems Against Economics* (1972), *Lunch and Counter Lunch* (1974), *Selected Poems: The Vernacular Republic* (1976), *Ethnic Radio* (1977) and a verse novel, *The Boys Who Stole the Funeral* (1979). *The Peasant Mandarin* (1978) is a collection of essays and reviews. He is co-editor of *Poetry Australia*.

**Murray, Thomas Cornelius** 1873–1959 Irish playwright. Born at Macroom, County Cork, he was headmaster of a County Dublin model school from 1915 to 1932. With **Lennox Robinson**, Murray was one of the 'Cork realists' whose work determined the characteristic style of the **Abbey Theatre** in its early years. In *Birthright* (1910), his first play, a father's jealous care for the disposition of his land becomes a mortal issue between his two sons. It is a theme typical of Murray's sombre vision of a small-farming society obsessed by ownership of their harsh land. His most successful later plays are *Aftermath* (1922), *Autumn Fire* (1924), and *Michaelmas Eve* (1932). In none of them does anyone win: the mother of an idealistic young teacher forces him into a 'practical' marriage with a woman who could 'buy and sell them that talk like angels'; an ageing man marries a young girl who falls in love with his son. In a society bound by strict Roman Catholic teaching, which Murray approved, his characters must simply endure within the restrictions.

**Murrell, John** 1945– Canadian playwright. He was born in the USA but raised in Canada, where he became a teacher before turning full time to the theatre. *Waiting for the Parade* (1977) is a sensitive portrayal of the lives of five women waiting for their men to come home from World War II. *Memoir* (1977), depicting the last days of Sarah Bernhardt, has been produced in more than 20 countries in 15 languages. Murrell has also produced notable translations of the classics, including plays by Chekhov.

**Murry, John Middleton** 1889–1957 Critic. Born in Peckham, London, the son of an Internal Revenue clerk, he was educated at Christ's Hospital and at Brasenose College, Oxford, where he edited the magazine *Rhythm*. In 1912 he met the writer **Katherine Mansfield**, with whom he lived (as her husband from 1918) until her death in 1923, and whose letters and stories he later edited. His close but often troubled association with **D. H. Lawrence** began in 1914, when they drew up an abortive plan for a Utopian community called 'Rananim'. Murry worked in the political intelligence department of the War Office from 1916 to 1919, before becoming editor of *The Athenaeum* from 1919 to 1921. In this post, and as editor of *The Adelphi*, which he founded in 1923, Murry was an energetic force behind the new wave of post-war literature, encouraging and publishing the work of **T. S. Eliot**, **Virginia Woolf** and other modernist writers. His influence subsequently waned as his strongly mystical disposition came to the fore in his work, but he is still remembered for *The Problem of Style* (1922) and particularly for *Son of Woman* (1931), an analysis of D. H. Lawrence's struggles with the female element in his nature. He wrote an autobiography, *Between Two Worlds* (1935), as well as studies of Dostoevsky (1916), **Keats** and **Shakespeare** (1925) and **Swift** (1954).

***Muses' Looking-Glass, The*** A play by **Thomas Randolph**, first performed in 1632 and published in 1638. It is a defence of the dramatist's art and is considered Randolph's best work by scholars of the period. Two Puritans, Bird and Flowerdew, sell posies and feathers in the

Blackfriars playhouse; but at the same time proclaim their abhorrence of theatres. Roscius joins them, persuades them to attend the play with him, explains the action of the piece as it proceeds, and eventually converts them to a more tolerant view.

**Mwangi, Meja (David)** 1948– Kenyan novelist. Born in Nanyuki, he is part of the generation of Kenyan writers to be deeply affected by the Mau Mau emergency of the early 1950s and by the struggle for independence. He was educated at Nanyuki Secondary School and at Kenyatta College, Nairobi. The first book he wrote, though not the first to be published, is *Taste of Death* (1975), which presents the Mau Mau in a heroic light. Most of his later fiction has been concerned with the social conditions of life in post-independence Kenya, the most famous of these being *Going Down River Road* (1976), a novel which despite its comic touch gives a graphic portrait of life in the industrial areas and nightspots of Nairobi. His other books include *Kill Me Quick!* (1973), *Carcase for Hounds* (1974), in which he returned to the subject of the Mau Mau, *The Cockroach Dance* (1979) and *The Bushrangers* (1979), which was based on a film script. Mwangi is sometimes felt to have compromised too much with the standards of popular fiction and his novels certainly have a wide readership in East Africa; yet he remains an astute depicter of modern Kenyan life.

*My Ántonia* A novel by **Willa Cather**, published in 1918. It takes the form of a memoir by Jim Burden, recounting the life of his childhood friend Ántonia Shimerda, the eldest daughter of an immigrant Bohemian family of farmers in Black Hawk, Nebraska.

When Ántonia's father commits suicide, she is forced to work in the fields like a man though she is still in her early teens. Later she goes to work as a hired girl for the Harling family. She remains in this position for some years, leaving only when she refuses to accede to Mr Harling's demand that she cease attending the town's Saturday night dances lest she lose her reputation. She takes up a similar position with Wick Cutter and his wife until Wick's amorous attentions drive her away. Jim enters college in Lincoln, Nebraska, and then moves East to attend Harvard. When he returns to Black Hawk two years later, he learns that Ántonia has been duped by Larry Donovan, a flashy railroad man she had sporadically dated years before, and who had pretended he wanted to marry her. Abandoned by him in Denver, Colorado, pregnant and unwed, she returns to her mother's farm outside Black Hawk and resumes her hardworking routine. In due course she gives birth to a daughter. After a reunion with Ánto-

nia Jim goes East again to attend Harvard Law School. While he is away Ántonia marries a fellow Bohemian, Anton Cuzak, and has a large family. When Jim comes home 20 years later he visits Ántonia and her husband on the farm they have built. He finds her worn down but thoroughly satisfied with her lot.

*My Last Duchess* A **dramatic monologue** by **Robert Browning**, published in *Dramatic Lyrics* (1842). Although the poem is apparently based on an incident in the life of Alfonso II, Duke of Ferarra, and set in the 16th century, the historical background takes second place to Browning's interest in the psychology of the speaker. On the point of marrying again, the duke displays a strikingly life-like portrait of his previous wife. It soon becomes obvious that, in his jealous obsession with the duchess, he had resented her vivacity and arranged her murder.

**Myers, F[rederic] W[illiam] H[enry]** 1843–1901 Poet, critic and psychical researcher. He was born at Keswick and educated at Trinity College, Cambridge, where his academic achievements were exceptionally high. A classics lecturer and fellow of Trinity in 1865, he gave up university teaching to become a school inspector in 1869. His most famous poem, *St Paul* (1867), an exclamatory meditation on the life of the saint, was published in an unusual though not original metre, and was widely parodied. He wrote much ardent, emotional verse on a note of unrest and baffled enquiry, in particular *The Renewal of Youth* (1882). His monograph on **Wordsworth** appeared in 1881 and *Essays, Classical and Modern* in 1883. Myers shared with **Henry Sidgwick** a deep practical interest in the education of women, but his dominant passion was the scientific study of paranormal phenomena and the evidence of life after death. A founder in 1882 of the Society for Psychical Research, he contributed to *Phantasms of the Living* (1886) on the nature of apparitions, and his papers on hallucination, mediumship and double personality were the first of their kind. He married Eveleen Tennant in 1880 and was the first Englishman to swim the river below Niagara Falls.

**Myers, L[eopold] H[amilton]** 1881–1944 Novelist. Myers was born in Cambridge, and educated at Eton and Cambridge, which he left upon the death of his father, **F. W. H. Myers**. A legacy in 1906 gave him financial independence and, except for service at the Board of Trade in World War I, Myers devoted his life to writing and travel. For a brief period he lived in Colorado.

His first published work was a verse play, *Arvat* (1908), but it was 13 years before he managed to complete his first novel, *The Oriss-*

*ers*, published in 1921. This was followed by *The Clio* in 1925. *The Near and the Far* (1929) was the title volume of a tetralogy set in 16th-century India at the court of the Mogul emperor Akbar. With profound moral imagination Myers uses the setting of a past and idealized society to explore the poverty of contemporary existence: its failure to reconcile material and spiritual values. The completed sequence was published as one volume in 1943 and included the other three titles: *Prince Jali* (1931), *The Root and the Flower* (1935) and *The Pool of Vishnu* (1940).

Myers committed suicide at the age of 63.

*Mysteries of Udolpho, The* A novel by **Ann Radcliffe**, published in 1794.

The setting is Gascony and the Italian Apennines at the end of the 16th century. Emily de St Aubert is a beautiful girl of Gascon family; after losing her parents, she becomes the ward of her tyrannical aunt, Madame Cheron. Madame Cheron marries Montoni, a sinister character, and disapproves of Emily's attachment to the Chevalier de Valancourt, whose means are too moderate for the aunt's ambitions. Emily is carried off to Montoni's castle, Udolpho, in the Apennines, where frightening and apparently supernatural occurrences are frequent. Montoni's cruelty brings about the aunt's death and he then turns his attentions to Emily. She manages to escape, however, and returns to Gascony, where she is eventually united with her chevalier. The evil Montoni, who has been pillaging the countryside from his sinister castle, is captured and brought to justice.

The combination of terrifying incidents which befall the heroine and lavishly 'picturesque' settings made for a potent and distinctive formula. In its own age *The Mysteries of Udolpho* was one of the most popular examples of **Gothic fiction**, and it has never entirely lost its appeal.

*Mystery of Edwin Drood, The* **Charles Dickens**'s last novel, left unfinished at his death in June 1870. Only six of the projected 12 monthly numbers were written.

Dickens had set out to write a mystery story, set chiefly in the cathedral city of Cloisterham (closely modelled on Rochester). John Jasper leads a double life as cathedral choirmaster and opium addict, travelling secretly to a London opium den to satisfy his craving. Edwin Drood, on whose mysterious disappearance the story was to have centred, is Jasper's nephew; he was betrothed as a child to Rosa Bud, but the couple are not in love and their engagement is dissolved. Jasper nurses a passion for Rosa. Edwin vanishes on Christmas Eve after a ferocious thunderstorm.

There have been many attempts to complete the novel and much speculation as to its denouement. Most commentators have presumed that Drood has been murdered by Jasper, but other matters are less clear – most notably, the role that would have been played by Neville and Helena Landless, the orphaned twins who have come to live with Mr Crisparkle in Cloisterham, and the true identity of Dick Datchery, the obviously disguised detective who arrives in Cloisterham to investigate Drood's disappearance just as Dickens's fragment breaks off.

**mystery plays** See **miracle plays**.

**mystical writing** Religious prose of the Middle Ages dealing with personal spiritual experiences. The 12th-century renaissance precipitated a more introspective and individual approach to religion, in reaction against the absolute authority of the Church and its role as an essential mediator between man and God at a time when it had become corrupt and embroiled in secular politics. The mystical writers describe widely different experiences and attitudes, but in general they were wholly orthodox. They did not seek doctrinal or social change in any form, and although sometimes a tension between the teachings of the Church and the writings of the mystics may be discerned their allegiance to the Church is usually emphasized. Mystical writing is the only genre in which the work of women authors was prominent in the Middle Ages. See also *The Cloud of Unknowing*, **Walter Hilton, Julian of Norwich, Margery Kempe, Richard Rolle**.

# N

**Nabokov, Vladimir** 1899–1977 American novelist, short-story writer and poet, born into a wealthy and prominent family in St Petersburg. His father, a member of the Russian Constituent Assembly, moved the family to Yalta in 1919 at the start of the Bolshevik Revolution, and following the White army's defeat in the Crimea they went into exile in western Europe. Between 1919 and 1922 Nabokov studied modern languages at Trinity College, Cambridge. While living in Berlin and Paris during the 1920s and 1930s, he produced a critically acclaimed canon of poems, short stories and novels written in Russian and published under the pseudonym of V. Sirin: *Mashen'ka* (1926), *Korol', Dama, Valet* (1928), *Zashchita Luzhina* (1930), *Soglyadatay* (1930), *Podvig* (1932), *Kamera Obskura* (1932–3), *Otchayanie* (1936), *Priglashenie na Kazn'* (1938) and *Dar* (1937–8).

Vladimir Nabokov.

The second phase of his career began in 1940 when he emigrated to America and settled in Boston. While teaching Russian literature at Wellesley College, he published his first novel in English, *The Real Life of Sebastian Knight* (1941), and wrote many of his short stories and poems, which appeared in periodicals such as **The New Yorker**. His second novel was *Bend Sinister* (1947). In 1948 he accepted the position of Professor of Russian literature at Cornell and during his tenure there published his first memoir, *Conclusive Evidence* (1951, later retitled *Speak, Memory* and under this title expanded and revised in 1966). It was also at Cornell that he wrote his most famous novel, *Lolita* (1955). Humbert Humbert, the speaker in this first-person narrative, writes from gaol a confession and explanation of his socially unacceptable lust for adolescent girls, whom he calls 'nymphets'. Humbert details the seduction of his step-daughter, Lolita, and their journey westward. The relationship is broken off when Lolita runs off with the actor Quilty, who abandons her and whom Humbert murders. The critical and financial success of *Lolita* enabled Nabokov to resign his post at Cornell and engage exclusively in literary enterprises. While working steadily on his translation of Pushkin's *Eugene Onegin* (published in four volumes in 1964), he wrote three more novels: *Pnin* (1957), *Pale Fire* (1962) and *Ada, or Ardor: A Family Chronicle* (1969); and two collections of short stories: *Nabokov's Dozen* (1958) and *Nabokov's Quartet* (1966). He also supervised the translation of his Russian novels, a project undertaken by his son Dimitri. **The Enchanter**, a novella showing links with *Lolita*, was lost for 30 years and published in 1987.

**Nahal, Chaman** 1927– Indian novelist. *My True Faces* (1973) is an overwritten novel about a loveless marriage, while *Into Another Dawn* (1977), sunnier and more poised, tells of an Indian's love for an American woman. His most considerable novel, *Azadi* (1975), describes Hindus, Muslims and Sikhs living together peacefully in the Punjab until Partition turned neighbours into enemies, citizens into fugitives. *The English Queens* (1979) cleverly satirizes the

English-speaking Indian élite. *The Crown and the Loincloth* (1981) inaugurates a trilogy about Gandhi. Nahal has also produced a volume of stories, *The Weird Dance* (1965), and some critical studies.

**Naipaul, Shiva[dhar] (Srinivasa)** 1945–85 Trinidadian novelist, born in Port of Spain, younger brother of **V. S. Naipaul**. *Fireflies* (1970) and *The Chip-Chip Gatherers* (1973) satirize the wilting of Hindu culture among Trinidadians of Indian origin, though with compassion for the deracinated; chilling despair characterizes *A Hot Country* (1983), about a corrosive colonialist past producing an 'independent' future of nullity. *North of South* (1978) reports sardonically on travel in Africa, *Black and White* (1980) on American subcultures and the People's Temple mass suicides in Guyana in 1978. *Beyond the Dragon's Mouth* (1984) collects pieces of journalism (some sharp, some metropolitically naïve), autobiography and vital, humane, accomplished stories.

**Naipaul, V[idiadhar] S[urajprasad]** 1932– Trinidadian novelist. Born in Chaguanas, he was educated at the Queen's Royal College, Trinidad, and University College, Oxford. He has lived in Britain since 1950 but travelled extensively. Naipaul is a novelist of distinction, whose fastidious, sardonic tone controls a profound concern with 20th-century uncertainties and such damaging effects of imperialism upon

the people of the Third World as cultural alienation and deracination. His first three books are satirical but genial: *The Mystic Masseur* (1957), *The Suffrage of Elvira* (1958) and *Miguel Street* (1959) mock and delight in, respectively, a colonial politician's career, the running of a Trinidadian election and the antics of some neighbourhood characters. In *A House for Mr Biswas* (1961) he brilliantly portrays a nonentity, simultaneously absurd and heroic, establishing, barely, a distinctive personality for himself. *Mr Stone and the Knights Companion* (1963), his only novel with English characters, is a study of human potential blighted by commercial, urban influences. *The Mimic Men* (1967) shows Naipaul's growing interest in larger themes, the political career of 'Ralph' Singh undermining accepted ideas about post-colonial Third-World politics. *In a Free State* (1971) suggests that all modern notions of 'freedom' are illusions, while the main characters of *Guerrillas* (1975) are rootless, with nothing but their pathetic though persistent attempts to find fulfilment. On an extensive, tragic scale, *A Bend in the River* (1979) proclaims the corruptibility of mankind, the fallibility of most 20th-century shibboleths, yet also the wondrous human ability to survive. His non-fiction is closely related to the novels, especially *The Middle Passage* (1962) to his Trinidadian books and *An Area of Darkness* (1964) to the subsequent fiction. *A Flag on the Island* (1967) is a volume of stories, *The Overcrowded Barracoon* (1972) a volume of articles.

**Nairne, Carolina, Baroness** 1766–1845 Scottish poet. Carolina Oliphant was the daughter of a Jacobite family of Perthshire and married Major William Nairne, who became 5th Baron Nairne in 1824. She is remembered as a songwriter and song collector: in the former activity her Jacobite sympathies are plain, in the latter her tendency was to refine the robust lyrical strength of Scotland which remained intact in the hands of **Robert Burns**. Most of her work was contributed anonymously to *The Scottish Minstrel* (1821–4); it was collected after her death and published as *Lays from Strathearn* (1846). Among her songs are 'Will Ye No Come Back Again?', 'The Auld Hoose', 'The Rowan Tree', 'The Land o' the Leal', 'The Laird of Cockpen', 'Caller Herrin' and 'Charlie is My Darling'.

***Naked and the Dead, The*** A novel by **Norman Mailer**, published in 1948 when the author was 25. Set on a Pacific island during World War II, the story reflects in numerous brutally naturalistic combat scenes Mailer's own army experiences; it won quick acclaim as one of the best personal accounts to emerge from the war. But the major concern of the book centres not on the campaign against the Japanese but on the disparate and often desperate political and moral

V. S. Naipaul.

philosophies of the fighting men – on the problems of the pluralistic American society from which they have emerged. Mailer focuses on 13 characters, whose civilian lives are recalled through flashbacks. The men are thus characterized as carrying not only the weapons of war but also the weight of their pasts – of economic, radical and religious tensions. Mailer's cynicism about America's past and his doubts about its post-war future are expressed largely through the clash between the proto-fascist General Cummings, who holds that the enlisted men must be made into automatons, and Lieutenant Hearn, a rich, educated, and confused liberal, who finds that he cannot argue with true conviction his hope for the survival of a democratic spirit. Rough in language, violent in action, and hostile towards mainstream American values, the novel foreshadows much of Mailer's later writings.

**Narayan, R[asipuram] K[rishnaswami]** 1907– Indian novelist, born in Madras. His deceptively simple English and ironic outlook make him particularly accessible to western readers, though the unobtrusive, wry moral thrust of his fiction also aligns it with traditional Indian story-telling. *Swami and Friends* (1935) and *The Bachelor of Arts* (1937) are episodic novels about boyhood and youthful self-exploration. While *The Dark Room* (1938) treats Hindu marriage sombrely, *The English Teacher* (1945; as *Grateful to Life and Death* in USA, 1953) celebrates fulfilled union, psychically extended after the wife's death. Malgudi, Narayan's fictional South Indian town, provides a solid, realistic setting for his tragicomedy of human aberrations and attainments – with locals overreaching themselves, like the printer in *Mr Sampath* (1949; as *The Printer of Malgudi* in USA, 1955) and the pavement moneylender in *The Financial Expert* (1952), or cyclonic outsiders causing havoc, like the demonic taxidermist in *The Man-Eater of Malgudi* (1962) and the family-planning woman official in *The Painter of Signs* (1976). *Waiting for the Mahatma* (1955) tolerantly exposes the mixed motives of some of Gandhi's followers. Narayan's irony is at its best in *The Guide* (1958) as a loquacious trickster is 'tricked' into becoming a holy man, and *The Sweet-Vendor* (1967; as *The Vendor of Sweets* in USA), in which a sweet manufacturer seeks self-control by conquering taste. Transparently clear narrative itself becomes a device for satirizing human follies in a tiger's 'autobiography', *A Tiger for Malgudi* (1983). Narayan has also published numerous volumes of short stories and a genial autobiography, *My Days* (1975).

**Nasby, Petroleum V[esuvius]** The pseudonym of the American humorist and journalist, David Ross Locke (1833–88). He began by publishing letters in the Findlay, Ohio, *Jeffersonian* in March 1861. The letters, which ridicule the South and the Confederate cause by loudly proclaiming their righteousness in the silliest way possible, drew a large audience throughout the Civil War. (They were also popular with Abraham Lincoln.) A collection appeared in 1864 as *The Nasby Papers*. Locke became editor (in 1865), and later owner, of the Toledo *Blade*, where he continued to publish letters under his pseudonym. A humorist in the style of **Artemus Ward** and **Josh Billings**, he was one of the most successful exponents of the genre of the facetious letter to the editor. Locke also wrote a political novel, *The Demagogue* (1881).

**Nash, Ogden** 1902–71 American poet, born in Rye, New York, and educated at Harvard. Best known as a writer of light, humorous verse, his first books were *Cricket of Cavador* (1925), *Free Wheeling* (1931) and *The Bad Parents' Garden of Verse* (1936). A master of irony, he often questions the commonplace in American life, the objects of his humour ranging from the more general assumptions of society to problems of domestic life, to grammar and prosody itself. His later books include *I'm a Stranger Here Myself* (1938), *Good Intentions* (1942), *Versus* (1949), *Family Reunion* (1950), *Everyone But Thee and Me* (1962), *Marriage Lines* (1964), *Merrill Lynch We Roll Along* (1965), *Bed Riddance: A Posy for the Indisposed* (1970) and the posthumous *A Penny Saved Is Impossible* (1981).

**Nashe, Thomas** 1567–1601 Satirist and pamphleteer. Nashe graduated from St John's College, Cambridge, in 1586. After a tour through France and Italy he settled in London in 1588 and joined the circle of writers that included **Robert Greene**. His first published work was a stern review of recent literature prefaced to Greene's *Menaphon* (1589), which attacks plagiarism from classical authors and ranting tragedies, and praises **Spenser** and **Peele** as well as Greene. *The Anatomy of Absurdity* (1589) is another piece of satire on contemporary literature, attacking artificiality in romances. These early works display a fashionable **euphuism** and Nashe confessed in a later work: '*Euphues* I read when I was a little ape in Cambridge.'

Nashe became involved in the **Martin Marprelate** controversy and various pamphlets have been assigned to him, but only *An Almond for a Parrot* (1590) with any certainty.

Nashe was also involved in a personal controversy with **Gabriel Harvey** and Richard Harvey. Richard attacked Nashe for presumption in the preface to *Menaphon* and Nashe replied in *Pierce Penniless his Supplication to the Devil* (1592). Gabriel Harvey gave a bitter account of the last days of Greene in *Four Letters* (1592) and Nashe replied defending his dead friend in *Four Letters Confuted* (1593, also known as *Strange News of the Intercepting of Certain Letters*). An attempt at peace-making is to be found in *Christ's Tears over Jerusalem* (1593), Nashe's most serious prose work, which offers the fall of Jerusalem as a warning to Londoners. Harvey contributed *Pierce's Supererogation* (1593) and Nashe replied in *Have With You to Saffron Walden* (1596), which added Wrinkle de Crinkledum to the splendid list of absurd names he found for his adversary. The pamphlet war was eventually brought to an end by the decree of Archbishop Whitgift and Bishop Bancroft in 1599 ordering confiscation of books by the two men.

*The Terrors of the Night* (1594) is a series of visions and an account of demons, spirits and superstitions. *The Unfortunate Traveller* (1594) has a claim to be the first **picaresque** 'novel' in English. It gives an account of the adventures of Jack Wilton, an English page, and his hair-raising experiences and narrow escapes from death in France and Italy. *Nashe's Lenten Stuff* (1599), a mock panegyric of a red herring, contains a vivid description of Yarmouth and a splendid burlesque of the story of Hero and Leander. Nashe's prose writings manifest a racy and colloquial diction, grotesque characterizations, fantasy and a dislike of foreigners and Puritans. They are often brilliantly inventive linguistically, but there is a general lack of coherence. The loose picaresque structure of *The Unfortunate Traveller* suited Nashe best.

*Summer's Last Will and Testament* was written for private performance at Croydon, perhaps for Whitgift's household, in the late summer of 1592. It has motifs from folk drama. Summer attended by the seasons, classical deities and Harvest makes his will. Among the characters is Will Summers, Henry VIII's fool who died in 1560, who opens the play and comments on its action. The play contains the poignantly beautiful lyrical lament on transience 'Adieu, farewell earth's bliss'. The title-page of *The Tragedy of Dido Queen of Carthage* (1594) makes Nashe co-author with **Christopher Marlowe**, but Nashe's share of the play is disputed. *The Isle of Dogs*, performed in 1597, is lost. The Privy Council suppressed it as lewd and seditious, searched Nashe's lodgings and arrested several of the suspected authors, including **Ben Jonson**.

**Nathan, George Jean** 1882–1958 American editor and critic, born in Fort Wayne, Indiana, and educated at Cornell. In 1908 he began contributing to *Smart Set*, and in 1914 became its editor in partnership with **H. L. Mencken**, with whom in 1920 he founded the detective magazine *The Black Mask*. He founded *The American Mercury* with Mencken in 1924 and contributed to it from 1924 to 1930 and from 1940 to 1951. In 1934 he helped to found the New York Drama Critics Circle, and was president of the group from 1937 to 1939. His works include the plays *The Eternal Mystery* (1913), *Heliogabalus* (1920, with Mencken), *The Avon Flows* (1937) and the annual record of the New York stage, *The Theatre Book of the Year* (1943–51).

**Nation, The** An American weekly magazine, first published in 1865. Those who sponsored it were concerned with securing full rights for the newly freed American Negroes – a concern recorded prominently in the early issues. Indeed, the National Association for the Advancement of Colored People was first housed in *The Nation*'s office in New York. In its early years it consisted almost entirely of political commentary and literary reviews, but by the 1920s it came to include original works of literature. The first editor was E. L. Godkin, an Anglo-Irish journalist. Subsequent editors have included **William Lloyd Garrison**, Paul Elmer More, Oswald Garrison Villard, Freda Kirchway, Carey McWilliams and Victor Navasky.

**National Theatre** Britain's National Theatre was established only after a long struggle. This began with calls from **David Garrick** in the 18th century, gained widespread support from **Matthew Arnold** among others in the 19th century and was given further impetus with the publication of a detailed scheme by **William Archer** and **Harley Granville-Barker** in 1907. Delays resulting from two world wars, a lack of funds and opposition even within the theatre community were followed by the token laying of a foundation-stone in 1951; even then matters did not advance further until Sir Laurence (later Lord) Olivier lent his support to the chase. He served as director of the National Theatre from its opening at the **Old Vic** in 1962 with a production of *Hamlet* until 1973, when he was succeeded by Sir Peter Hall. In 1976–7 the company moved to a new complex, designed by Denys Lasdun, on the South Bank. It consists of three theatres: the open-stage Olivier, the proscenium arch Lyttleton and the experimental Cottesloe. Despite a decline in public subsidy and some loss of its original idealism, the National Theatre has kept its foremost place among British companies, rivalled only by the **Royal Shakespeare Company**.

**Native Son** A novel by **Richard Wright**, published in 1940. It recounts the story of Bigger Thomas, a black ghetto dweller on the south side of Chicago, who is hired by a wealthy family as their chauffeur. The family's spoiled, liberal-leaning daughter, Mary, and her Communist boyfriend, Jan, befriend him. One night, after Mary has had too much to drink, and while Bigger with the best of intentions is getting her back to her room, he accidentally smothers her with a pillow. A black man with a white woman's death on his hands, he knows that it matters little that his act was not intended, and tries to escape. He goes to his girlfriend for help, but realizing that she is too distraught by the murder to trust him, he kills her too and is soon caught. Waiting in gaol for his trial, he feels for the first time a sense of freedom in having successfully carried out an act he was impelled to do by the social conditions from which he arose. In prison he comes to realize what real emotional connection with a white person can be – through his lawyer, Max, also a Communist. Max tries to get him to articulate the harshness of the conditions which have led to his acts, but he cannot: he is not privy to white society's conditions of articulation; he has too much pride to do anything more than affirm that 'what I killed for, I am!'

**Natural History of Religion, The** One of the *Four Dissertations* by **David Hume**, published in 1757.

Hume examines the theoretical argument that leads to theism and the mental processes from which religion arises. In primitive societies, religious beliefs spring not from any specific instinct, but from the fear of death or pain and the desire for security and pleasure: God is simply a particular providence, not the author of nature. By further insisting that polytheism preceded monotheism in the development of religious beliefs, he concludes that the existence of God cannot be proved by reason.

**naturalism** A term generally applied to art which seeks to adhere to nature. More strictly, it refers to the scientifically based extension of **realism** propounded by Émile Zola in the 1870s and 1880s in essays such as 'Naturalism in the Theatre' and 'The Experimental Novel', and exemplified in his hugely popular cycle of *Rougon-Macquart* novels, which chart the social and genetic development of a single family through several generations of legitimate and illegitimate descendants. In naturalist writing, medical and evolutionary theories of 19th-century science inform readings of human character and social interactions, which are seen as being genetically and historically determined. The struggle of the individual to adapt to environment, the fight for the spouse and the Darwinian idea of the survival of the fittest become central concerns of naturalist fiction and drama.

Inspired by Zola's writing, André Antoine founded the Théâtre Libre in Paris in 1887 and staged plays, including Tolstoy's *Powers of Darkness*, Strindberg's *Miss Julie*, Ibsen's *Ghosts* and Hauptmann's *The Weavers*, which were informed by naturalist ideas and which subsequently became standard works in the new European independent theatres. Plays in English in which naturalist ideas about social and genetic inheritance and the struggle for survival recur, include **Synge**'s *Riders to the Sea* (1904) and **Galsworthy**'s *Strife* (1909). Naturalist ideas occur in **Hardy**'s novels and underpin **Gissing**'s *New Grub Street* (1891) and **George Moore**'s *Esther Waters* (1894) but are less evident in England than in America where **Theodore Dreiser**, **Jack London** and **Stephen Crane** in *Maggie* (1893) are the notable naturalist writers.

**Nature** A book by **Ralph Waldo Emerson**, developed from his early lectures, and published in 1836. In it he sets forth the main principles of **Transcendentalism**, postulating the need for 'an original relation to the universe' and rejecting timeworn attitudes to God and Nature. He elaborates on his conception of Nature as the expression of a divine will, asserting the need for man to establish a relationship with Nature that will allow him to take advantage of its spiritual self-governance, and thereby to reunite himself with his own spiritual source. An expanded second edition was published in 1849.

**Neale, John Mason** 1818–66 Clergyman, church historian and hymn writer. Born in London, Neale was educated at Sherborne School and Trinity College, Cambridge. A convinced High Churchman, he was in sympathy with the **Oxford Movement** and opposed to liberal tendencies in the Church of England. With his friend Benjamin Webb he founded the Cambridge Camden Society for the study of ecclesiastical art in 1839. He was the author of *A History of the Holy Eastern Church* (1847–50) and a number of hymns, some translated from Greek and Latin originals, which were eventually edited by M. S. Lawson as *Collected Hymns, Sequences and Carols* (1914). They include 'O Happy Band of Pilgrims', 'Art Thou Weary', 'Good Christian Men, Rejoice', 'Good King Wenceslaus' and 'Jerusalem the Golden'. A novel, *Theodora Pranza*, recounts the fall of Christian Constantinople; it was serialized in 1853–4 and published in volume form in 1857.

**negative capability** A term coined by **John Keats** to describe the quality he thought essential to the poet: 'when man is capable of being in uncertainties, Mysteries, doubts, without any irritable reaching after fact & reason' (letter to George and Tom Keats, 21–27 December 1817). The same letter goes on to cite **Shakespeare** as the supreme example of negative capability and to note its absence in **Coleridge**, who 'would let go by a fine isolated verisimilitude caught from the penetralium of Mystery, from being incapable of remaining content with half-knowledge'. **Milton** and **Wordsworth** are elsewhere classed with Coleridge, while Keats's original discussion concludes: 'with a great poet the sense of Beauty overcomes every other consideration, or rather obliterates all consideration'.

**Neilson, John Shaw** 1872–1942 Australian poet. Born at Penola, South Australia, Neilson received little formal education and worked as a manual labourer. After the publication of his first two volumes, *Old Granny Sullivan* (1916) and *Heart of Spring* (1919), he was awarded a small literary pension (1922). Poor health and bad eyesight dogged him in later life, but his poetry reflected his dreary circumstances only in displaying an enhanced pity and tenderness for suffering. Later volumes were *Ballad and Lyrical Poems* (1923), *New Poems* (1927), *Collected Poems* (1934), *Beauty Imposes* (1938) and the posthumous edition, *Unpublished Poems of Shaw Neilson* (1947).

**Nemerov, Howard** 1920– American poet, novelist and critic, born in New York City and educated at Harvard. His first volumes of poetry were *The Image and the Law* (1947), *Guide to the Ruins* (1950) and *The Salt Garden* (1955). His subject matter varies from broad philosophical questions to more immediate and contemporary issues. Other collections of verse are *New and Selected Poems* (1960), *The Blue Swallows* (1967), *Gnomes and Occasions* (1973) and *The Western Approaches: Poems 1973–1975* (1975). His prose fiction, which often explores moral problems in modern society, includes *Commodity of Dreams and Other Stories* (1959), and three novels: *The Melodramatist* (1949), *Federigo, or The Power of Love* (1954) and *The Homecoming Game* (1957). His criticism is published in *Poetry and Fiction: Essays* (1963), *Reflexions on Poetry and Poetics* (1972), *Figures of Thought: Speculations on the Meaning of Poetry and Other Essays* (1978) and *New and Selected Essays* (1985). He has also written plays, two of which are included in *The Next Room of the Dream: Poems and Two Plays* (1962).

**Nennius** See **Arthurian literature**.

**neoclassicism** A term for the ideas about art and literature which evolved during the 17th and 18th centuries under the influence of the classical (i.e. Graeco-Roman) tradition.

The survival of classical texts and their transmission to the Renaissance was often haphazard and fortuitous. The satirist Horace (65–8 BC) and the Latin theorists of rhetoric arrived fairly intact but the *Poetics* of Aristotle (384–322 BC), with its discussion of **tragedy**, survived only in a fragment. It was not until a gradual revival of interest among Italian scholars in the 15th and 16th centuries that many works were recovered. An interest in oratory and education in rhetoric

progressively led Renaissance critics to the matter of poetry *per se*. By the end of the 16th century, on the Continent at least, Aristotle was established as the presiding genius of classical criticism, while the philosophy of Plato (427–347 BC) was beginning to attract new commentaries.

In England the classical theory of literature made itself felt in **Sir Philip Sidney**'s *Apology for Poetry* (1595), but it was not until the beginning of the 17th century that such harking-back became current. **Ben Jonson** was an early and erudite poet in the classical mode, imitating Martial and Juvenal, and taking an interest in the theories of dramatic action derived from Aristotle. He was followed in this respect by **Dryden**, both in his criticism – notably his *Essay of Dramatic Poesy* (1668) – and in his plays, which show him as one of the first (and very few) major dramatists in English to temper Shakespearean abundance by observing the strict neoclassical unities of time, place and action.

Although there was never any concerted body of neoclassical principles as such, English writers shared a common ground in their response to the writings of the various ancients. They agreed in admiring the concision, elegance, good taste and wit of their classical predecessors. Their poetry emulated the intelligent articulacy of Horace's verse epistles, or the vituperative energy of Juvenal's satires, or the heroic elevation of Homer's epics. Their theory of literature was shaped by a composite classical influence in which the names of Aristotle and Horace stand out. It followed Aristotle's *Poetics* in making the classification of genres a foremost consideration and Horace's *Ars Poetica* in several vital tenets: the need to discipline the creative impulse by practice and self-control, the usefulness of imitating past models of excellence, the desirability of a literary decorum that matches content to style, and the aim of combining pleasure with instruction. **Pope**'s *Essay on Criticism* (1711) is representative of neoclassical concern with artistry and structure; it is followed by **Fielding**'s Preface to *Joseph Andrews* (1742), several of **Johnson**'s *Rambler* papers (1750–2) and his superlative *Preface to Shakespeare* (1765).

Such theoretical enquiry into the methods and rules of composition stimulated wider interests derived to some extent from the Graeco-Roman tradition: in the connection between nature and art and between the various sister arts, for example, and in the various relations of imagination and reason, taste and sense, originality and imitation, beauty and pleasure. These manifested themselves in discussion of several topics: the merit of ancient versus modern literature (typified by **Sir William Temple**'s essay *Upon Ancient and Modern Learning*, 1690); the functions of satire (Dryden's

*Discourse*, 1693); the pleasures of the imagination (**Addison** in *The Spectator*, 1712, and, later, **Mark Akenside**); and the *ut pictura poesis*, as exemplified in Dryden's *Parallel betwixt Poetry and Painting* (1695).

Behind such theorizing there lay an essential fascination with the systematic principles of art, but as the 18th century progressed an interest in the universal aspects of nature itself came to predominate over any notion of artistic rules. **Burke**'s essay on the *Sublime and the Beautiful* (1757) is just one text which shows less concern for artistic systems than for the spirit or quality of an individual work: 'truth', 'wit' or 'beauty' were more important than the technical correlation of stylistic components. In this way, in fits and starts over the course of several decades, European sensibility shifted its attention to the human faculties involved in art: the workings of the mind and the imagination, and the nature of genius. By the middle of the 18th century poetry written by recipe and formulaic regulations had become stale and outworn. The formal stimulus of the classical revival weakened. By concentrating attention on the poet rather than his audience, his mind rather than his medium, and the nature that was his matter rather than the art which manifested his genius, the later decades of the 18th century moved away from the general body of inherited classical principles toward the poetic which is usually labelled **Romanticism**.

See also the **Augustan Age**.

**Nesbit, E[dith]** 1858–1924 Writer of **children's literature**. Born in London, the youngest daughter of an agricultural chemist, Edith had an unsettled childhood, receiving her education in Britain, France and Germany. Turning to hack literary work after marrying young and in poverty, she eventually discovered her true talent for writing lively family stories unburdened with the heavy moralizing of earlier writers. Her first great success, *The Story of the Treasure Seekers* (1899), concerned the Bastable children and their mini-adventures, often in search of extra pocket money. Succeeding books (written at a great rate but always with a sensitive ear for children's dialogue) mix fantasy with reality, most successfully in *The Phoenix and the Carpet* (1904) and *The Story of the Amulet* (1906). Each of these involve the idea of time-travel, later to be a staple ingredient of so much children's literature. But her most famous novel, *The Railway Children* (1906), has a more realistic setting. The title characters are forced to retreat to the countryside after the arrest of their father on a trumped-up charge. There they make friends with the local railway porter Perks, a character whom E. Nesbit, as a Fabian socialist, treated sympathetically rather than as a figure of fun. The story also involves a political

refugee, theft, misplaced charity and fierce family loyalty – powerful ingredients for young readers, though always balanced by romantic adventures, fortunate coincidences and happy endings. Towards the end of her life her writing lost popularity but made a triumphant comeback for later generations, still selling well today and popular in film and television adaptations.

**New Age, The** A journal founded in 1907 by two members of the Fabian Arts Group, Holbrook Jackson (1874–1948) and A. R. Orage (1873–1934), with financial support from **George Bernard Shaw**. *The New Age* appeared under Orage's editorship until 1922, and lived up to its name by welcoming the early ferment of modernist ideas. In its Edwardian phase, regular contributions appeared from Shaw, **Arnold Bennett** and **J. C. Squire**, but Orage was quick to recruit new talents like **Ezra Pound**, **Katherine Mansfield**, **T. E. Hulme** and **Edwin Muir**, and it was *The New Age* which introduced Freud's psychoanalytic theories to the British reading public.

**New Apocalypse, the** A literary movement which flourished in Britain just before and during World War II in reaction against the committed rationalism of **Auden**'s generation. Responding to what they saw as a crisis in European civilization, writers of the New Apocalypse reinterpreted Freud and Marx in the light of **Lawrence**'s *Apocalypse* (1931) and accommodated diverse strands of a European non-rational impulse, principally **expressionism** and surrealism, within British literary culture. Key figures were **J. F. Hendry**, who introduced *The New Apocalypse* (1939), an anthology of verse, prose and criticism, and **Henry Treece**, who joined Hendry as editor of two further anthologies, *The White Horseman* (1941) and *The Crown and the Sickle* (1943). Poems by **G. S. Fraser**, **Nicholas Moore**, **Norman MacCaig** and **Vernon Watkins** appeared in their pages. Hendry published a major statement of the movement's aims in *Myth and Social Integration* (1940), while Treece contributed a collection of essays, *How I See Apocalypse* (1946). **Dylan Thomas** was also associated with the movement.

**New Atlantis** An unfinished Utopian fiction by **Francis Bacon**, written about 1624 and first published in Latin in 1627, in English in 1629. It recounts the discovery by English mariners of an island in the Pacific called Bensalem. Bacon describes a high civilization of great antiquity, coeval with Plato's lost Atlantis, that has long isolated itself from the world in order to preserve its integrity. The island has however received the gospel of Christianity by miraculous means. Bacon's chief intention in devising this fiction is to introduce his ideal design for a college of sciences, here given the name of

Salomon's House or the College of the Six Days' Works, for its purpose is the study of the entire physical creation. The College is publicly financed, and its members engage in co-operative research. The scope of its activities includes physics, chemistry, mechanics, astronomy, agriculture and medicine; the work is experimental, and the results advance the knowledge and enhance the life of the people of Bensalem. 'The end of our foundation is the knowledge of causes, and secret motions of things, and the enlarging of the bounds of human empire, to the effecting of all things possible.' Salomon's House represents the kind of institution that Bacon hoped King James would establish – James liked to be regarded as the British Solomon – in which the programme of experiments that Bacon had suggested in his *Natural History* would be carried out, following the methods of scientific enquiry that he had laid out in *The Advancement of Learning* and in the *Novum Organum*. Nothing came of his proposals in his lifetime, but in the 1650s there were several schemes to realize his design put forward by Samuel Hartlib, **Abraham Cowley** and **John Evelyn**, amongst others. Eventually, Bacon's hopes were in some measure fulfilled by the foundation of the Royal Society in 1660; the Society's programme of research was undoubtedly inspired by the model provided by Salomon's House.

***New Bath Guide, The*** See **Anstey, Christopher**.

**New Criticism** A term first used by the American critic, Joel Spingarn, in an address at Columbia University in 1910 ('The New Criticism') which anticipated the New Criticism of the 1930s and 1940s. Spingarn employed it to describe a modern trend towards scholarship and the application of extra-literary, statistical, stylometric devices. The term was not generally known until **John Crowe Ransom** used it (in *The New Criticism*, 1941) to prescribe a new 'ontological' approach to literary studies, in contradistinction to traditional criticism which had generalized broadly from biographical dates and influences. His qualified recognition of the contributions of **I. A. Richards**, **T. S. Eliot**, **William Empson** and **Yvor Winters** had the (largely unintentional) effect of promoting them as a new 'movement'. Other critics (including **Robert Penn Warren**, **Allen Tate**, R. P. Blackmur and **Cleanth Brooks**) were later conscripted, though the group always differed widely in its individual aims. Winters, for instance, had been concerned with the moral aspects of form and style (*In Defence of Reason*, 1947), Brooks with the ambiguity of poetic statement (*The Well-Wrought Urn*, 1947), Blackmur with the larger meanings of language (*Language as Gesture*, 1952).

I. A. Richards (*Practical Criticism*, 1929) and Eliot (*The Use of Poetry and the Use of Criticism*, 1933) were formative influences on **F. R. Leavis**, who applied many of the principles of New Criticism and made an enormous impact on the development of literary studies in England during the same period.

As a general rule, the New Critics may be said to have initiated a view of the text as an autonomous whole, an object with its own inherent structure, which invited rigorous scrutiny. They encouraged an awareness of verbal nuance and thematic organization. Although widely rejected as too limited by many more recent schools, New Criticism still has influence; close reading of the text remains a dominant principle in most literary criticism.

***New Grub Street*** A novel by **George Gissing**, published in 1891. Its bleak portrait of the literary world, obviously drawn from Gissing's own years of discouraging struggle, concludes that self-advertisement is a better route to success than any amount of artistic endeavour.

Edward Reardon, the author of two fine books, is hampered by poverty and an unsympathetic wife. Jasper Milvain is a facile and self-interested reviewer. Alfred Yule is a sarcastic, embittered scholar whose learning goes unappreciated. Yule's daughter Marian falls in love with Milvain and, on learning that she has expectations of a legacy, he decides to marry her. When the legacy does not materialize, he withdraws from the engagement. Reardon's wife, Amy, deserts him and this, coupled with his failure to make his mark as a writer, sends him to the grave. Jasper marries the widowed Amy and becomes, in worldly terms, a success.

Other representatives of the literary life are Harold Biffen, earnestly polishing a novel of absolute realism called 'Mr Bailey, Grocer' and Whelpdale, a literary failure who becomes an Adviser to Literary Aspirants and achieves success by thinking up the best name for a magazine full of scraps – a reference to *Tit-Bits*, which had begun publication in 1881.

***New Masses, The*** A journal founded in 1926 in New York City. The original editors were Egmont Arens, Joseph Freeman, Hugo Gellert, **Michael Gold**, James Rorty and John Sloan. Gold became its sole editor in 1928. *The New Masses* was one of the main fora for those writers and intellectuals involved with radical left-wing politics and the Communist party in America. Among its contributing editors were **Sherwood Anderson**, Van Wyck Brooks, **Max Eastman**, **Waldo Frank**, Lewis Mumford, **Eugene O'Neill**, Lola Ridge and **Carl Sandburg**. Contributors of fiction, poetry and critical essays included **Robinson Jeffers**, **Horace Gregory** and **Kenneth Fearing**. The journal ceased publication in 1948.

**New Negro, The** An anthology of essays, stories, a play, and extensive bibliographies of black American writers, edited by **Alain Locke** and published in 1925. It served as a manifesto which marked the crystallization of the concept of the 'New Negro' or **Harlem Renaissance**. In his preface to the volume Locke argued that blacks were making progress in combating prejudice, and that they possessed a new spirit of 'group expression and self-determination' which would in turn enrich American culture as a whole.

**New Republic, The** An American literary and political journal, founded by Herbert Croly in 1914. Its literary editors have included **Edmund Wilson**, Malcolm Cowley, Richard Gilman and Reed Whittemore. Though markedly liberal in its politics, it has published literary and critical pieces by writers of various political orientations, including **Robert Frost**, **George Santayana**, **H. L. Mencken**, **John Dos Passos**, **John Crowe Ransom**, **Allen Tate**, **Archibald MacLeish**, **Willa Cather**, **Ernest Hemingway**, **Eudora Welty**, **Michael Gold** and **Walter Lippman**. From the 1950s the magazine began to print more political commentary and less fiction and poetry.

**New Review, The** A monthly literary magazine edited by **Ian Hamilton**, who had founded and edited its predecessor, *The Review*, it was published from 1974 until its demise for financial reasons in 1979. During its short but controversial life, *The New Review* was notable for its consistency of editorial policy and its preference for short, minimalist poems. It published the verse of **James Fenton** and **Craig Raine**, the irreverent prose of **Julian Barnes** and Clive James, and the fiction of **Ian McEwan**. Typical work can be sampled in *The New Review Anthology* (1985).

**New Way to Pay Old Debts, A** A comedy by **Philip Massinger**, based on **Thomas Middleton**'s *A Trick to Catch the Old One*, first performed c.1622 and published in 1633.

Sir Giles Overreach, a monster of greed, has succeeded in gaining possession of the property belonging to his prodigal nephew, Frank Wellborn. The destitute Wellborn is helped by Lady Allworth, who lets it be known that she intends to marry him. On the promise of so good a match, Sir Giles is prepared to advance money to Wellborn. Sir Giles's daughter, Margaret, is less fortunate. Her love for Lady Allworth's stepson, Tom, is frowned on by Sir Giles, because Tom is no more than a page in the service of Lord Lovell. However, Lord Lovell enters into the plot to outwit Sir Giles, who, believing that his daughter is marrying the lord, finds she has married the page. His unbalanced rage is toppled into madness when he learns that his claim on Wellborn's estate cannot be upheld, and he is carried off to Newgate. Lady Allworth marries Lord Lovell, and Wellborn takes a commission in Lovell's regiment.

The character of Overreach was based on that of a contemporary extortioner, Sir Giles Mompesson. It is a famous actor's part (**Byron** experienced a kind of fit as a result of Kean's powerful playing of it in 1815), and in the 18th and 19th centuries was often allowed to dominate the play in performance.

**New York Review of Books, The** An American magazine founded by Robert Silvers and Barbara Epstein, who are still its editors, to provide book reviews during the New York newspaper strike of 1963. It was financed initially only by revenue from publishers' advertisements. Publishing 22 issues a year in newspaper format, the magazine immediately established itself as a viable addition to the range of review media, specializing in extended essay reviews, often by writers of the left. The *Review* also publishes articles on politics and has been active in protesting against the Vietnam war, the Watergate scandal and, more recently, government policy in Central America. Among its contributors have been Hannah Arendt, J. K. Galbraith, Elizabeth Hardwick, **Mary McCarthy**, **Norman Mailer**, **V. S. Pritchett**, **Susan Sontag**, I. F. Stone, H. R. Trevor-Roper, **Gore Vidal** and **Edmund Wilson**. The *Review* has received the compliment of having *The London Review of Books* modelled after it.

**New Yorker, The** An American weekly magazine founded in 1925 by Harold W. Ross. Many of his contributors, who included Alexander Woolcott, **James Thurber**, **Dorothy Parker**, **Robert Benchley**, **E. B. White**, Peter Arno and Charles Addams, were given the security of salaried employment and allowed to develop their gifts at their own pace. The result was a light, witty style which epitomized literary New York in the 1930s. Ross died in 1951 and was succeeded by William Shawn, who published much notable short fiction, poetry, criticism and non-fiction. Recent contributors have included **Truman Capote**, Saul Steinberg, **John Updike**, **Donald Barthelme**, **Alice Munro**, John McPhee and Jeremy Bernstein. Shawn was succeeded as editor by Robert Gottlieb in February 1987.

**Newbery, John** 1713–67 Publisher specializing in children's books. Born in Waltham St Lawrence, Berkshire, Newbery acquired *The Reading Mercury* by marrying the previous owner's widow. In 1744 he moved to London, where he set up shop as a vendor of patent medicines and a publisher. Most of his large output was designed for children, consisting of moral tales with copious woodcut illustrations. His policy of cheap, visually interesting and overtly didactic works was a major influence in educational publishing. He also issued many small works by **Smart**, who had married a daughter of his wife's first marriage. In 1759 he began to publish *The Public Ledger*, a periodical to which **Johnson** and **Goldsmith** contributed.

**Newbolt, Sir Henry (John)** 1862–1938 Poet and barrister. Educated at Clifton and Corpus Christi College, Oxford, he published many volumes of patriotic ballads and lyrics, including *The Island Race* (1899), *Admiral's All and Other Verses* (1907), *Clifton Chapel and Other School Poems* (1908), *Songs of Memory and Hope* (1909) and *Drake's Drum and Other Sea Songs* (1919), the title poem of which was set to music by Charles Stanford in *Songs of the Sea*. His *A Naval History of the War, 1914–18* appeared in 1920, and his memoirs, *My World as in My Time*, in 1932.

**Newcastle, Margaret, Duchess of** 1623–74 Poet, dramatist and biographer. Born Margaret Lucas, she was an indefatigable writer but is remembered only for her biography of William Cavendish, whom she married in 1645 when he was Marquis of Newcastle. One of the wealthiest peers in England, he served the king faithfully as governor of the Prince of Wales but was dismissed and eventually went to Paris with the queen's suite when she left England at the king's insistence. He was made Duke of Newcastle at the Restoration. His wife's biography (1667) was dismissed as ridiculous by **Pepys** but highly praised in later centuries by **Charles Lamb** and **Virginia Woolf**. It remains a notable document of its age.

*Newcomes, The* A novel by **W. M. Thackeray**, published in 24 parts between October 1853 and August 1855. The story is told by Arthur Pendennis and sub-titled 'Memoirs of a Most Respectable Family'.

Colonel Thomas Newcome is a simple gentleman of the highest honour. His son Clive is in love with his cousin Ethel, daughter of the wealthy banker, Sir Brian Newcome. The union of Clive and Ethel is opposed by most of her relatives – chiefly her mean-minded and snobbish brother Barnes and her grandmother, the Countess of Kew. Yielding to the pressure of her family, Ethel becomes engaged to her cousin, Lord Kew, and then to the spineless and callow Lord Farintosh, but her own character asserts itself and she eventually rejects both of them.

Despairing of Ethel, Clive allows himself to be manoeuvred into marrying the daughter of Mrs Mackenzie, a scheming widow. Rosey Mackenzie proves empty-headed and the household is dominated by her mother. When Colonel Newcome loses his fortune he is bullied and reproached by the vindictive Mrs Mackenzie to such a degree that the bewildered old soldier takes refuge in the Greyfriars almshouse, dying at length in a pathetic deathbed scene. Clive's fortunes are restored by the discovery of a will and, with his wife's death, he is presumably free to marry Ethel.

*Newgate Calendar, The* The title, or generic label, of various 18th- and 19th-century collections describing the careers of notorious criminals. Although they usually claimed to have a moral purpose in recording the downfall of lawbreakers, and sometimes alleged a political purpose in advocating reform of the criminal law, their main interest was always salacious and sensational. The first *Newgate Calendar*, running to five volumes and dealing with crimes from 1700 onwards, appeared in 1774. The lawyers Andrew Knapp and William Baldwin published a second *Newgate Calendar* in four volumes in 1824 and the six-volume *New Newgate Calendar* in 1826. **George Borrow** was one of their staff of contributors. The last of the series was C. Pelham's *Chronicles of Crime, or, The New Newgate Calendar* (1886).

**Newgate fiction** A school of crime fiction popular in the 1830s, chiefly associated with the names of **Edward Bulwer Lytton** and **William Harrison Ainsworth**. The Newgate novelists took real-life cases (often from *The Newgate Calendar*) as the source for their plots and pointed to the treatment of crime in the work of **Fielding**, **Gay** and **Hogarth** as a respectable precedent. According to their many detractors, however, they portrayed the criminal in a dangerously sympathetic manner. In Bulwer Lytton's *Paul Clifford* (1830) he is the victim of social circumstances, while in the same author's *Eugene Aram* (1832) he is a conscience-stricken philosopher. In Ainsworth's *Rookwood* (1834) and *Jack Sheppard* (1839) he becomes a glamorous outlaw. **Dickens**'s *Oliver Twist* (1837–8) and **Thackeray**'s *Catherine* (1839–40) rejected Newgate fiction by offering a harshly realistic view of criminal life.

**Newman, John Henry** 1801–90 Theologian. Of Huguenot and Jewish descent, Newman was educated privately at Ealing and went, aged 16, to Trinity College, Oxford. In 1822 he was elected to a fellowship at Oriel College and in 1826 became Tutor there. The following year he became vicar of St Mary's, Oxford, and in 1832 he resigned his tutorship at the college.

With **Keble** and **Pusey** he played a leading part in the **Oxford Movement**, preaching influential sermons at St Mary's in the late 1830s. Afterwards, Newman regretted that his influence had been on undergraduates rather than on his parishioners. During this period, he defended the Anglican church as the *via media* or middle way between Romanism and popular Protestantism. His researches into early church history led to his publishing, in **Tracts for the Times**, the famous Tract 90 (1841), which argued that the 39 Articles of the Anglican church were compatible with Catholicism. It was condemned by the Bishop of Oxford, and Newman ceased publishing tracts and gave up being editor of *The British Critic*. In 1842 he set up a monastic community at Littlemore, where he continued his studies of the early church. In 1845 he became the most celebrated of the 19th-century converts from the Church of England to Rome. Many clergy followed him. His effect on the Anglican church was eventually to bring the study of patristics into the Anglican purview.

In 1854, Newman went to Dublin as Rector of a new Catholic university. After a disappointing four years, he withdrew and published a series of lectures under the title, **The Idea of a University** (1873). **Charles Kingsley**'s attack on his honesty provoked his **Apologia Pro Vita Sua** (1864, revised 1865) describing the changing convictions which had led him to become a Catholic. In 1870 he published **The Grammar of Assent**, an argument for religious belief. In 1879 Newman was made a Cardinal.

Newman's poem, 'The Dream of Gerontius', and the hymn, 'Lead, Kindly Light', were written in 1832. He also wrote two novels, *Loss and Gain* (1848) and *Callista* (1856).

**News from Nowhere**, *or*, *An Epoch of Rest*, *Being Some Chapters from a Utopian Romance* A prose work by **William Morris**, serialized in *The Commonweal* between 11 January and 4 October 1890 and first published in book form later that year in Boston.

The story falls into three sections. Morris dreams of waking in his Hammersmith house amid a communist society of the early 21st century. He travels through a London so changed that the Houses of Parliament are used as a 'dung market'. The central chapters comprise a detailed discussion with an aged historian, in which the course of history from the 19th century through violent socialist revolution and up to the Utopian present is described. In the concluding chapters Morris journeys up the Thames beyond Oxford to Kelmscott for the hay-making season.

As in *A Dream of John Ball* the central dialogue enables Morris to give a critique of his own time, though here his vision of human social potential is more fully developed. The non-industrial society Morris describes draws upon his beloved medieval period in many details. However, the lack of any central government, legal structure and monetary system is part of a classless non-materialist future. The society envisaged is based on 'the religion of humanity', the sanctity of labour and its inseparability from art. *News from Nowhere* proved a seminal work, reappearing nine times (including in Italian translation) before Morris's death in 1896.

**newspaper, the rise of the English** The early growth of the press was episodic. The first news publications printed in English date from 1620 and came from the Netherlands. Known as corantos (or 'currents' of news), these consisted of a single unfolded sheet carrying two columns of print on each side. They concentrated on international events, a feature of the news section of the press that was to remain true for over two centuries. Both James I and Charles I regarded the development of the press as dangerous and sought to restrict it: in 1632 the Star Chamber prohibited all unauthorized news publications. Stuart suspicion was to some extent justified by the massive expansion of the press that accompanied the English Civil War, when radical opinion was widely disseminated. The response after the Restoration was restraint, the Printing Act of 1662 being based on the theory that the freedom to print was hazardous to the community and dangerous to its ruler, a threat to faith, loyalty and morality.

This restrictive legislation, which limited the number of printers and established a licensing system to enable pre-publication censorship, remained in force until 1695. It did not, however, completely prevent the appearance of newspapers. In 1663 **Sir Roger L'Estrange** was appointed Surveyor of the Press, a position he exploited to produce a newsbook entitled *The Intelligencer*. L'Estrange's monopoly was breached two years later by *The Oxford Gazette*, which rapidly became *The London Gazette*, a half-sheet folio that enjoyed a monopoly of printed news until 1678. The Exclusion Crisis, which began in that year, both raised public interest in political news and made government regulation more difficult. By the end of 1679 more papers were being published than at any time since 1649. Many of the features and devices that were to characterize the 18th-century press, such as a paranoid mentality, rigid convictions and a style that exploited humour, offering mock-advertisements, fictional creeds and fake prophecies, were already present. Ministerial papers were founded to challenge the opposition Whig press, but Charles II wished to end a propaganda war rather than to conduct one: the Whig press was stamped out by prosecutions for seditious libel, and the Licensing Act, which had expired in 1679, was revived in 1685. James II continued the policy of regulation, *The Gazette* regaining its monopoly.

The Glorious Revolution of 1688 was not

followed by any immediate freeing of the press. William III, no supporter of press liberty in the Netherlands, maintained the machinery of press control and unlicensed works were seized. However, difficulties in the enforcement of the Licensing Act in the early 1690s led to increased doubts about the existing regulatory system. The Act expired in 1695 without any agreement as to how to replace it, and, despite considerable support for the idea of press censorship, successive attempts to revive it over the next two decades failed.

The lapsing of the Licensing Act spurred considerable growth. There were 12 London newspapers by 1712 and 52 by 1811 – a number swelled by Sunday papers, the first of which, *The British Gazette and Sunday Monitor*, was begun in about 1779, and all of which were illegal due to sabbatarian legislation. Circulation also increased rapidly, reaching about 44,000 copies a week in 1704. By 1801, 16 million newspaper stamps were issued annually, and in 1851 the comparable figure was 85 million. This growth was accompanied by an expansion in the number of types of newspaper, in no way restricted to London. In 1702 the first daily paper, *The Daily Courant*, appeared. However, in the first half of the century most newspapers were weeklies or evening tri-weeklies. Though the earliest extant copy of a provincial newspaper, *The Bristol Post-Boy*, dates from 1704, it is probable that the first provincial paper was *The Norwich Post*, starting in 1701. By 1748 there were 43 provincial papers, a figure that had more than doubled by the end of the century.

The press was of course not the only type of printed material whose sale rose markedly during the 18th century: **chapbooks**, almanacs and ballad sheets were increasingly popular too. It was not until the 19th century that the press significantly sought to expand into the popular literary market catered for by these other products. If a distinction between polite and popular culture is to be adopted, then the press was clearly a facet of the former. An examination of the literary or theatrical news or the bulk of the advertisements in the London and provincial press does not suggest much of an effort to create or cater for a mass readership, and the bulk of the claims made for its existence relate to London, the only place where unstamped and cheap papers were produced in the 18th century. Newspapers were expensive and their readership was limited by comparison with that of the Victorian period. News and opinion were rapidly disseminated among an appreciable portion of the community, but this hardly amounts to the national political culture whose creation has sometimes been alleged.

A striking feature of the 18th-century press was the active participation of most of the leading men of letters. Writers such as **Addison**, **Bolingbroke**, **Defoe**, **Fielding**, **Goldsmith**, **Johnson**, **Smollett**, **Steele** and **Swift** did not simply contribute items: they also played a major role in founding and running newspapers, and often in conducting press campaigns. Though certain journals, such as *The Spectator* of Addison and Steele, were largely concerned with matters of social conduct and can be understood in terms of the literature of social behaviour, many prominent writers were actively involved in the political press. Swift defended the Tory ministry of **Robert Harley**, and his *Examiner* competed with Mainwaring's Whig *Medley*. Steele was a leading Whig critic of the Harley ministry. Defoe followed an ambiguous course in the political press of the early 18th century. Many prominent literary figures used the press as a vehicle in the criticism of the Walpole ministry. Bolingbroke was one of the joint founders of *The Craftsman* and wrote numerous articles for this influential weekly. Fielding wrote *The Champion* for the opposition before producing *The True Patriot* and *The Jacobite's Journal* for the government of the Pelhamite Whigs. Such intervention by writers could result from political patronage (Lord North, for example, persuaded Johnson to write pamphlets against the supporters of **John Wilkes** and in defence of the policy in the Falkland Islands crisis) but it also reflects the heavily politicized nature of English society and literary life. The age made no attempt to separate literature from the social sphere, and the press simply provided another opportunity for writers to advance their arguments.

The didactic function of the press was not restricted to political opinion. Although political news, particularly that of foreign lands, was the dominant element of the British press, both metropolitan and provincial, English and non-English, instruction was also a recurrent theme. It took many forms, ranging from social manners to religious issues. Much of it was contributed by unpaid correspondents, necessarily so in light of the absence of any reporting staff in the newspapers of the period, and thus provided a significant opportunity for literary enterprise. Unfortunately, as the vast bulk of such material was anonymous or pseudonymous, it is rarely possible to establish the authorship of these pieces and thus to assess the literary impact of the press. The characteristic form of such contributions was the essay, itself a significant development of the early 18th-century press, and these were sometimes written by leading literary figures such as **Boswell**, **Burke**, Goldsmith and Johnson. The essay proved ideally suited both to the press and to the magazines. *The Gentleman's Magazine*, founded in 1731 by Edward Cave, was a monthly deliberately designed to be of general interest which achieved a circulation of 10,000 within a decade and acquired a number of rivals, particularly

*The London Magazine* (1732–85). The rise of such magazines influenced the newspapers, particularly the weeklies, whose readers appear to have expected reflective essays or shorter pieces. The increased number of words per paper, achieved by means of smaller print and more columns per page, ensured that instructive material was not sacrificed to the pressure of more advertising or economic, sport and theatrical reports.

In the 19th century technical innovations, such as the spread of the iron press and the introduction of steam printing, facilitated the mass production of newspapers. This, in combination with the ending of newspaper duties, helped to produce a cheap press and titles such as *The Daily Mail* were printed in quantities and at a price that would have been inconceivable in the Georgian period. The provincial press ceased to be a vehicle for the reprinting of material in the London newspapers. However, the 19th-century press conformed in many ways to the patterns laid down in the earlier period, understandably so as many of the problems of reporting were identical. Similarly, the content of the press was often the same. By the 19th century it is possibly more appropriate to argue that the press played a major role in the creation of a mass readership and constituted its principal source of supply. However, in assessing its significance it is necessary to guard against the tendency to treat the press as a fourth estate. It was not an autonomous agency or force. Instead, in the literary field as in so much else, the press reflected and sought to meet social changes. It did so within the context of competition, but also in a fashion that reflected the conservative nature of the newspaper world, in which well-tried methods that produced successful results were maintained by men whose conception of the potentialities of print was based on experience. The press developed, but was arguably less influential and autonomous than is commonly believed.

**Newton, Sir Isaac** 1642–1727 Scientist and philosopher. Born at Woolsthorpe near Grantham in Lincolnshire, and educated at Grantham grammar school and Trinity College, Cambridge, he succeeded his teacher, Isaac Barrow, as Lucasian Professor of Mathematics in 1669. The preceding years (1664–6) had been spent at Woolsthorpe, beginning the scientific enquiries that led to his theories of gravitation and the spectrum, and the development of the calculus – the instrument he used to discover the results published in *Philosophiae Naturalis Principia Mathematica* (The Mathematical Principles of Natural Philosophy) in 1687. A milestone in the history of science, Newton's *Principia* demonstrated the principle of universal gravitation. His first communications to the Royal Society on light and colour were made in 1672; his *Opticks*

(1704) established him as the founder of the modern science of optics. To this book was attached *Method of Fluxions* – the Newtonian calculus which anticipated Gottfried Leibniz in the same field and caused a bitter dispute between them over priority of invention.

Newton has been called the greatest English scientist. He was honoured generously during his lifetime: he was twice the university's representative in Parliament (1689 and 1701), President of the Royal Society (1703 until his death), Warden of the Mint (1696) and Master in 1699. He was knighted by Queen Anne in 1705.

**Ngugi wa Thiong'o (formerly James Ngugi)** 1938– Kenyan teacher, critic, dramatist, novelist, born in Limuru. He helped establish the Kamiriithu Cultural and Community Centre, where the successful performance of *Nhaahika Ndeenda*, which he co-authored with Ngugi wa Mirii, was banned in December 1977 (English version, *I Will Marry When I Want*, 1982). In *Detained* (1981) he describes his own year-long detention in 1978. He has lived in exile since 1982.

Written before *Weep Not, Child* (1964), *The River Between* (1965) covers white settlers' incursions and Christian missionaries' ventures into Kikuyuland; *Weep Not, Child* projects a sensitive Kikuyu youth's perspective of the Mau Mau War. Both are lucid, freshly written novels of youthful idealism and disillusion. Structurally and thematically, *A Grain of Wheat* (1967) is more complex, searching and mature, exploring various characters' painful confrontation of their own acts of betrayal during the Mau Mau struggle, but with early signs of corruption among post-Independence politicians. The plays *The Black Hermit* (1968), *This Time Tomorrow*, with *The Rebels* and *The Wound in the Heart* (1970), and *The Trial of Dedan Kimathi* (1976, co-author Micere Mugo) dramatize the peasant, proletarian and national struggles. The power-

Ngugi wa Thiong'o.

ful, boldly designed novel, *Petals of Blood* (1977), and *Devil on the Cross* (1982), narratively adventurous but reiterative, eloquently and persuasively expose, in Marxist terms, the exploitation of ordinary Africans by international neocolonialism. Essays in *Homecoming* (1972) and *The Writer and Politics* (1981) discuss the social and political functions of literature, those in *Barrel of a Pen* (1983) Kenyan education, culture and politics.

**nichol, b p** 1944– Canadian poet and writer of fiction. Born in Vancouver, he spent his youth there and in Winnipeg and Port Arthur, Ontario. He attended the University of British Columbia, where he was influenced by the *TISH* group of poets, a counter-culture movement that stressed the importance of the spoken idiom. From 1964 until the early 1980s he worked in Toronto as a therapist. nichol first attracted recognition in the mid 1960s with his **concrete poetry**. In the latter years of that decade he published numerous volumes of poetry, all concerned with the visual or, by using exploratory new forms, with foregrounding the way language operates. *The Year of the Frog* (1967) uses comic-strip techniques. *Ballads of the Restless Are* (1968) and *Dada Lama* (1968) are attempts to reach the oral roots of poetry and language. Since 1970 he has worked in a wide variety of modes, including free verse and **stream-of-consciousness** prose. His best known work is *The Martyrology*, a continuing poem in several parts, of which the first two books appeared in 1972. It is an investigation of the nature of the poetic process, in which the artist is presented as a saint or martyr. nichol has also composed a considerable body of experimental sound-poetry, which he has performed widely. Over the years he has demonstrated his skill in a wide range of modes, always challenging commonly held assumptions about language and the creative process. His other works include *Two Novels* (1969), *Still Water* (1970), *ABC: the Aleph Beth book* (1971), *Love: a Book of Remembrances* (1974), *Craft Dinner* (1978), *Journal* (1978) and *extreme positions* (1981).

**Nicholas Nickleby** A novel by **Charles Dickens**, published in 20 monthly parts from April 1838 to October 1839 and in volume form in 1839.

After the death of the improvident Nicholas Nickleby senior, his widow and children Nicholas and Kate turn for help to his brother Ralph, who has made a fortune as an unscrupulous financier. Kate is apprenticed to a dressmaker, Madame Mantalini, and Nicholas is sent to teach at Dotheboys Hall in Yorkshire. He finds the school a miserable place where the master, Wackford Squeers, starves and ill-treats his pupils, secure in the knowledge that their relieved and uncaring parents will not interfere.

'The internal economy of Dotheboys Hall.' Mrs Squeers dosing the boys with brimstone and treacle. An illustration by Phiz for *Nicholas Nickleby*.

Horrified by his discovery, and particularly by the treatment of the half-witted orphan Smike, Nicholas rebels, thrashes Squeers into insensibility and runs away with Smike. They work where they can, travelling in the pleasant company of Vincent Crummles and his band of actors.

Kate, meanwhile, is exposed to the unwelcome attentions of Ralph Nickleby's friends and business associates, among them the vicious Sir Mulberry Hawk. But they are no match for her and she treats Sir Mulberry with contempt. Alerted to her danger by Newman Noggs, Ralph's eccentric clerk, Nicholas returns to London with Smike and obtains a post in the business of the amiable Cheeryble brothers. Overhearing a conversation in which Kate's name is mentioned with disrespectful insinuation, he thrashes Sir Mulberry. Squeers and Ralph Nickleby conspire to injure Nicholas through Smike, but their plan fails when the ill-used and frail Smike dies with Nicholas at his side. Newman Noggs and the Cheeryble brothers help frustrate the villains' designs completely, and when they disclose that Smike is his own son, Ralph Nickleby hangs himself.

Loosely structured, and taking frequent advantage of its looseness for excursions into sentiment and melodrama, *Nicholas Nickleby* is nevertheless informed by the joyful energy that typifies Dickens's early work. The scenes at Dotheboys Hall and on the road with Vincent Crummles's strolling players are particularly memorable, and Dickens himself was sufficiently proud of his portrait of the garrulous Mrs Nickleby to revive her for his public readings in later life.

**Nichols, Grace** 1950– Poet and novelist. Born in Georgetown, Guyana, she worked as a journalist before coming to Britain in 1977. She first established herself as a children's writer, but it was the award of the Commonwealth Poetry Prize in 1983 for *i is a long memoried woman* which brought her to the attention of a wider audience. She is regarded as one of the best poets in Britain who also happens to be black and female. Concern with race and gender are key topics in her poems, but she treats both with a measure of comedy, particularly apparent in her second verse collection, *The Fat Black Woman's Poems* (1984). However, some poems show a strong sense of the historic injustices perpetrated against black people and against women. Her poetry has a vigorously oral quality, as a result of which both she and her fellow Guyanese poet, John Agard, with whom she lives, are in great demand for public recitals. Grace Nichols has written one novel, *Whole of a Morning Sky* (1986), apparently based on her own growing-up in Guyana.

**Nichols, Peter (Richard)** 1927– Dramatist. Born and brought up in Bristol, he worked as an actor and schoolteacher before starting to write television plays in the early 1960s. His first stage success came in 1967 with *A Day in the Death of Joe Egg*, about the parents of a spastic child. Subsequent works fall, perhaps deceptively, into two categories. There are broad, expansive plays about social or historical themes, written in spacious manner; these include *The National Health* (1969), *The Freeway* (1974), *Privates on Parade* (1977) and *Poppy* (1983). The second category consists of domestic plays, tightly written, naturalistic and exact in their details, such as *Chez Nous* (1974), *Born in the Gardens* (1980), *Passion Play* (1981) and *A Piece of My Mind* (1987).

**Nichols, Robert (Malise Bowter)** 1893–1944 Poet and dramatist. Educated at Winchester and Trinity College, Oxford, he enlisted in the Royal Field Artillery, but was sent back to England suffering from neurasthenia after three weeks in the line. Encouraged by **Edward Marsh**, he contributed to *Georgian Poetry* and published two volumes, *Invocations* (1915) and *Ardours and Endurances* (1917). Both were extremely popular for their celebration of the 'loved, living, dying heroic soldier', and he was compared to **Rupert Brooke**. He toured the United States giving lectures and readings, published *Aurelia* (1920), and became Professor of English Literature in Tokyo in 1921–4. His plays include *Guilty Souls* (1922) and *Wings Over Europe* (1930). His only further volumes of poetry were the satirical *Fisbo* (1934) and *Such Was My Singing* (1942), a selection of his work with an introduction outlining his ideas about poetry and extracts from two long works in progress. **Wilfred Owen** described Nichols's poetry as 'deplorably self-concerned and *vaniteux*', and it is not now critically admired. He was a close friend of **Robert Graves** during the war, who wrote 'To Robert Nichols' in reply to his 'Faun's Holiday'.

**Nicholson, Norman** 1914–87 Poet, dramatist and critic. He was born in Millom, Cumberland; the locality, his family and early life here are evoked vividly in *Wednesday Early Closing* (1975). Several books on Northern geography include *The Lakes* (1977). *The Old Man of the Mountains* (1946) and two other verse dramas have a biblical basis; a fourth, *Prophesy to the Wind* (1950), concerns survival after a nuclear holocaust. The drama and the critical writing – principally *Man and Literature* (1943) – owe much to his interest in **T. S. Eliot**'s work and to his own Anglicanism. But it is a continuity from **Wordsworth** and **Cowper** that informs his poetry, where morality, metaphysics and imaginative vision are located in particular places and communities, and people's relationships with the natural world. *Selected Poems, 1940–1982* represents several earlier volumes, most strikingly *The Pot Geranium* (1954). *A Local Habitation* (1972) and *Sea to the West* (1981) develop his recurrent themes in a more direct, often anecdotal and colloquial manner.

**Nicolson, Sir Harold (George)** 1886–1968 Diplomat, politician and man of letters. Born in Teheran, where his father was the English chargé d'affaires, he was educated at Wellington College and Oxford. In 1909 he joined the diplomatic service and was posted to Madrid, Constantinople, Teheran and Berlin. He married **V. Sackville-West** in 1913. After his resignation from the diplomatic service he entered politics in later life, serving as MP for West Leicester (1939–45) and receiving a knighthood in 1953.

Nicolson began his literary career in 1921 with a study of Verlaine and a novel, *Sweet Waters*. There followed biographical and critical studies of **Tennyson** (1923), **Byron** (1924) and **Swinburne** (in the English Men of Letters series, 1926), as well as *The Development of English Biography* (1927) and *Some People* (1927). Later works included another novel, *Public Faces* (1932), *The Congress of Vienna: A Study in Allied Unity 1812–1822* (1946), a highly praised official biography of King George V (1952) and a biography of the French critic Sainte-Beuve (1957). His *Diaries and Letters* (3 vols., 1966–8), edited by his son Nigel Nicolson, give an interesting picture of political life between the two world wars.

**Nigger of the 'Narcissus', The** A novel by

**Joseph Conrad**, published in 1897. Framed around a sea voyage from Bombay to London, and narrated by an anonymous seaman, the action concentrates on the human community of the ship, the *Narcissus*. The tensions within that small number are as perilous as the weather itself, and are produced partly by two different generations of seamen. Captain Alistoun and the veteran Singleton have the reticence of men primarily concerned with their duties as seamen. Conversely, the detachment from the working community of the younger Donkin and the Negro of the book's title, Wait, comes to represent a powerful, if less practical, set of interests.

The illness and confinement of Wait claim the humanitarian sympathies of the remaining crew. Indeed, at the height of a storm, five men risk their lives to save the trapped Wait from his deck cabin. As Singleton and Alistoun are uneasily aware, the safety of the entire ship is meanwhile at risk. Confrontation between the captain and Donkin (who supports Wait's demands to go back on duty) comes to a head. After Donkin has hurled a belaying pin in his direction, the captain calmly reasserts a seaman-like authority, with the remaining crew looking on. More strangely, Singleton's superstition that Wait will die at the first sight of land proves to come true; before the *Narcissus* comes to port, Wait is buried at sea.

Conrad's Preface is frequently cited as a manifesto of literary Impressionism and of its chief aim: 'it is, before all, to make you see'.

**Night Thoughts** The usual abbreviation by which **Edward Young**'s lengthy didactic poem, *The Complaint, or, Night-Thoughts on Life, Death and Immortality* (1742–6), is known. The first of its nine books is devoted to reflections by the poet. The following seven take the form of a soliloquy rebuking the worldly Lorenzo, who is exhorted to turn to faith and the virtuous life. The final book, called 'The Consolation', includes a vision of the Day of Judgement, a contemplation of eternity, a survey of the firmament, a last exhortation to Lorenzo and an invocation to God. The solemn subject and diffuse manner appealed to the taste of the age, and *Night Thoughts* made Young one of the most popular of the so-called **graveyard poets**.

**Nightmare Abbey** A satirical novel by **Thomas Love Peacock**, published in 1818.

Perhaps the most popular of Peacock's topical satires, its principal target is the contemporary literary intelligentsia, with its predilection for morbid subjects and unworldly philosophical systems. The most persistently foregrounded figure of fun is **Coleridge**, whom Peacock is at pains to unmask as a cultural reactionary, but **Byron**'s misanthropy and **Shelley**'s illuminist politics are also mocked. As usual with Peacock,

there is little in the way of plot, and the narrative frequently makes way for fully dramatic exchanges between the figures. Mr Glowry, once a very harassed husband, now 'a very consolate widower', is the master of Nightmare Abbey on the edge of the Lincolnshire fens, where he lives with his philosophical son Scythrop (Shelley). Taking his cue from the opening of **Godwin**'s *Mandeville*, Peacock has Glowry surround himself with domestics chosen for a depressive appearance or a dismal name: his butler is Raven, his steward Crow, and his grooms are called Mattocks and Graves. He keeps open house for his fellow spirits and relatives who include Mr Toobad, a 'Manichean Millenarian' pessimist, Mr Flosky (Coleridge), Mr Cypress (Byron), and Mr Listless, representing the 'common reader' and currently prostrate with the 'blue devils' of Romantic *ennui*. Their modish melancholy is offset by the unquenchable enthusiasm of the scientist Mr Asterias, whose life is committed to the capture of a mermaid and, in a more serious vein, by Mr Hilary, whose protests against the prevailing 'conspiracy against cheerfulness', and advocacy of nature, Mozart and the life-affirming wisdom of the ancient Greeks, would appear to have the author on their side. Scythrop is hopelessly divided in his affections between his conventionally feminine cousin Marionetta and Toobad's philosophical daughter, Celinda. Refusing to relinquish either, he ends by losing both, the former to Listless, the latter to Flosky; he thinks of a suicide in the manner of Goethe's Werther, but calls instead for a bottle of Madeira.

**Nin, Anaïs** 1903–77 American diarist, novelist and critic, born in Neuilly, just outside Paris. Her father was a Spanish composer, her mother half-French and half-Danish. In 1914 she moved with her mother to New York, where she lived until returning to Paris in 1923. In her early life she was a model, dancer, teacher and lecturer, and she later became a practising psychoanalyst under the tutelage of Otto Rank. She began writing her renowned *Diary* (10 vols., 1966–83) in 1931; her first publication was an essay entitled *D. H. Lawrence: An Unprofessional Study* (Paris, 1932). She turned to fiction with the novel *House of Incest* (Paris, 1936; USA, 1947). Prominent in Paris literary circles, she became the friend of **Henry Miller** and **Lawrence Durrell**. At the beginning of World War II she returned to the USA. Her subsequent work includes a collection of three novelettes, *The Winter of Artifice* (Paris, 1939; USA, 1942), a volume of short stories, *Under a Glass Bell* (1944), and the novels *Ladders to Fire* (1946), *Children of the Albatross* (1947), *The Four-Chambered Heart* (1950), *A Spy in the House of Love* (1954), *Solar Baroque* (1958) and *Collages* (1964). Her volumes of erotica include *Delta of*

*Venus: Erotica* (1977) and *Little Birds* (1979). Her critical studies are *Realism and Reality* (1946), *On Writing* (1947) and *The Novel of the Future* (1968).

**Nina Balatka** A novel by **Anthony Trollope**, published in ***Blackwood's Magazine*** from July 1866 to January 1867. Like ***Linda Tressel***, it appeared anonymously, for Trollope wanted to see if 'he could obtain a second identity'. His belief that 'a name once earned carried with it too much favour' was borne out: discerning critics praised the book but few readers paid attention to it.

The setting is Prague and the subject is the love of Nina Balatka for Anton Trendellsohn. He is Jewish and Nina's family set their faces against her marrying him; for their part, Anton's family are just as strongly opposed to his marrying a Christian. A striking character is the beautiful Rebecca Loth, the Jewish girl who had been intended as a wife for Anton. In a powerful scene she represents to Nina, with unsentimental truth, the consequences of a marriage that will alienate both communities.

**Nine Worthies, The** A group of nine great historical and mythical figures frequently mentioned in medieval and early Renaissance literature. It consists of three pagans (Alexander, Hector and Julius Caesar), three Jews (Joshua, David and Judas Maccabeus) and three Christians (Arthur, Charlemagne and Godfrey of Bouillon). There is some variation, with the occasional addition of a tenth or the substitution of a different name for one of the original nine, but the list remains fairly constant. Occasionally an equivalent list of worthy women was also given. The earliest surviving treatment of the group is in Jacques de Longuyon's *Voeux du Paon* (*c*.1312).

**Nineteen Eighty-Four** A novel by **George Orwell**, first published in 1949.

In 1984 Britain has become Airstrip One in the superstate Oceania, which is perpetually at odds with the other superstates Eurasia and Eastasia. It is ruled by the Party, under the aegis of the possibly non-existent Big Brother, whose image is ever present. The Party's agents constantly rewrite history and are redesigning the language, with the aim of controlling men's thoughts absolutely. A minor Party operative, Winston Smith, commits thought-crimes by keeping a secret diary and loving a girl named Julia, but is seduced into self-betrayal by his superior, O'Brien. His interrogation ultimately leads him to Room 101, where resides every man's ultimate horror. There, his spirit is so utterly broken that he surrenders his identity to the state and learns to love Big Brother.

This brilliant and extraordinarily bitter novel may be regarded as the culmination of the loss of faith in mankind which infected British futuristic fiction in the 1930s and was underlined by World War II. It provides a heavily ironic commentary on the state of the world in 1948, exaggerating all its worst traits to a nightmarish extreme. The development of world politics from 1948 to 1984 did nothing to soothe the anxieties with which it plays.

*1919* See *USA*.

**Noah, Mordecai Manuel** 1785–1851 American playwright, born in Philadelphia into a Portuguese-Jewish family. The first of his plays to be produced was *Paul and Alexis, or, The Orphans of the Rhine* (1812), a melodrama later retitled *The Wandering Boys*. This was followed by his best-known work, *She Would Be a Soldier, or, The Plains of Chippewa* (1819), a patriotic comedy about a young woman who disguises herself as a soldier in order to follow her lover who is fighting in the War of 1812. His other plays include *The Siege of Tripoli* (1820), *Marion, or, The Hero of Lake George* (1821), *The Grecian Captive, or, The Fall of Athens* (1822) and *The Siege of Yorktown* (1824). Whether his subject was ancient or contemporary, Noah always wrote what he himself termed 'national plays', plays that self-consciously recalled and represented the course of the nation's history.

*Noctes Ambrosianae* A series of imaginary conversations published in ***Blackwood's Edinburgh Magazine*** from 1822 to 1835. The idea is supposed to have originated with **William Maginn**, who certainly wrote several of the conversations, but the largest number (41 of the 71 published) came from **John Wilson**. Other contributors were **James Hogg** and **John Gibson Lockhart**. The spirited and wide-ranging dialogues take place at Ambrose's Tavern in Gabriel Road, Edinburgh, with the Ettrick Shepherd (Hogg) and 'Christopher North' (Wilson) among the supposed participants. The *Noctes Ambrosianae* were a favourite feature of *Blackwood's* and contributed greatly to the magazine's success.

**Nonjurors** The name given to those Church of England clergymen who refused to take the Oath of Allegiance to William and Mary in 1689 on the grounds that they could not lawfully break the oath they had given to the deposed James II. Among them were the Archbishop of Canterbury, William Bancroft, and seven bishops.

**Norris, Frank** 1870–1902 American novelist. Born Benjamin Franklin Norris in Chicago, at the age of 14 he moved with his family to San Francisco. He studied in Paris and then attended the University of California from 1890 to 1894.

Frank Norris.

In 1895 he visited South Africa, hoping to find material for travel sketches; instead he reported the conflict between the English and the Boers for the San Francisco *Chronicle*. After being captured by the Boer forces he was deported, and returned to San Francisco where he joined the staff of a magazine called *The Wave*. *Moran of the Lady Letty*, a sea story set off the California coast, was serialized in the magazine and published in book form in 1898. *A Man's Woman*, a romantic adventure story, appeared in 1900. Other contributions to *The Wave* were published in later years: *The Joyous Miracle* (1906, a novelette), and the short-story collections *A Deal in Wheat* (1903) and *The Third Circle* (1909).

In 1898 Norris went to Cuba to report on the Spanish–American War for *McClure's Magazine*, and on his return took a job with the publishers Doubleday, who in 1899 published the love story *Blix* and *McTeague: A Story of San Francisco*. Norris next concentrated his energies on a trilogy, *The Epic of the Wheat*. The first book, *The Octopus* (1901), describes the struggle between farming and railroad interests in California. Norris died in the following year after an appendix operation, and the second novel, *The Pit*, was published posthumously in 1903. The third part, to be entitled *The Wolf*, was never written. *The Pit* concerns the manipulation of the wheat market in Chicago, and *The Wolf* was to tell of a wheat famine in Europe. Also published posthumously were *The Responsibilities of the Novelist* (1903), in which he describes the type of naturalistic writing, based on actual experience and observation, which he had derived from Zola; and the novel *Vandover and the Brute* (1914), which he had started in 1895.

**Norris, John** 1657–1711 Philosopher. The last of the **Cambridge Platonists**, Norris was educated at Winchester and Exeter College, Oxford, and became a fellow of All Souls. He was a follower of Nicholas Malebranche, the French philosopher who combined the ideas of René Descartes with a Platonic mysticism. His chief work was the elaborate two-part *Essay towards the Theory of the Ideal or Intelligible World* (1701 and 1704), which criticizes the empiricist **John Locke**'s *Essay Concerning Human Understanding*. Norris also wrote devotional verses.

**North, Christopher** See **Wilson, John**.

**North, Sir Thomas** ?1535–?1601 Translator. North may have been educated at Peterhouse, Cambridge. He entered Lincoln's Inn in 1557 and accompanied his brother on a diplomatic mission to France in 1574. He was knighted c.1591, and was also a Justice of the Peace for Cambridge.

His translation of Guevara's *El Relox de Príncipes* appeared in 1557 as *The Dial of Princes*. *The Moral Philosophy of Doni*, a translation from Italian of beast fables of eastern origin, was printed in 1570. His most important translation was of Plutarch's *Lives* as *The Lives of the Noble Grecians and Romans* (1579), from a French version by Amyot. The second edition appeared in 1595 and the third (1603), which added new lives, was dedicated to Queen Elizabeth. This was an important source for **Shakespeare**'s knowledge of the ancient world and its great men. Shakespeare seems to have read it by the time he wrote *A Midsummer Night's Dream* and his Roman plays all draw heavily on North. Enobarbus's description of Cleopatra on the river Cydnus in *Antony and Cleopatra* is a reworking of North's prose.

**North American Review, The** A New England quarterly first published in Boston in 1815 under the editorship of William Tudor. Later, as a monthly publication, its editors included **Charles Eliot Norton**, **James Russell Lowell**, **Henry Adams** and Henry Cabot Lodge. Although founded as a literary journal, it began to publish articles on political and social matters when it was moved to New York City in 1878. After World War I it reverted to quarterly publication and continued until 1940. Writers published in the *Review* include **Ralph Waldo Emerson**, **Washington Irving**, **Henry Wadsworth Longfellow**, **Francis Parkman**, **Walt Whitman**, **Mark Twain**, **Henry James**, Leo Tolstoy, Gabriele D'Annunzio, **H. G. Wells**, Maurice Maeterlinck and **Alan Seeger**.

**North and South** A novel by **Elizabeth Gaskell**, published serially in *Household Words* from September 1854 to January 1855 and in volume form in 1855. The north and south of the title are the 'satanic mills' of the industrial north and the leisured life of London society and rural Hampshire. Mrs Gaskell began the book early in 1854, when **Dickens**'s *Hard Times* was being serialized, also in *Household Words*. (See also **The Condition of England novel**.)

Mr Hale, prompted by his conscience, leaves his comfortable living in the village of Helstone to go to the grim industrial city of Milton-Northern, where he teaches aspiring millowners. His wife and daughter, Margaret, accompany him. Margaret detests trade of any kind but soon discovers that the reality behind it all arrests and challenges her: her true character begins to emerge. She takes the side of the workers and confronts John Thornton, the mill-owner who is the employers' leader.

Although he has little sympathy with Margaret's argument for a humane approach to his workers' problems, Thornton is nevertheless strongly drawn to her. When he is attacked by a mob of strikers, Margaret's courage in protecting him convinces him that his feelings are returned. He proposes to her but Margaret rejects him so coldly and firmly that he is deeply hurt. He later sees her with another man and is shocked by her apparent lie when she denies that she has a lover. In fact, the man was her brother Frederick, who had sought her out secretly while in danger of arrest.

Thornton's attitude to the workers causes problems in his business and he is made to realize the need for the warmer approach Margaret had advocated. For her part, Margaret has been deeply affected by her fall in Thornton's estimation and begins to appreciate how much his regard matters to her. The two come together at the end of the novel.

Mrs Gaskell originally planned to call *North and South* 'Margaret' or 'Magaret Hale', and her portrait of the heroine – tough, wilful and self-confidently proud – owes much to her admiration of the work of her friend **Charlotte Brontë**.

**North Briton, The** A political weekly founded by **John Wilkes** in 1762 and run with the help of **Charles Churchill**. Its chief opponent was Lord Bute's paper, *The Briton*, edited by **Tobias Smollett**. Wilkes named his paper ironically: *The North Briton* was supposed to be edited by a Scot who rejoiced to see his fellow countrymen in powerful positions. The paper was suppressed after no. 45, in which Wilkes risked prosecution for libel by his attack on the government.

**Northanger Abbey** A novel by **Jane Austen**, published posthumously in 1818, though it had been begun in 1798 and accepted by a publisher in 1803. Her shortest major work, it makes fun

'Tales of Wonder!' by James Gillray, 1802. Catherine Morland, the heroine of *Northanger Abbey*, was an assiduous reader of Gothic novels. British Museum Print Room.

of the prevailing fashion for **Gothic fiction**, particularly the novels of **Ann Radcliffe**.

Catherine Morland goes to Bath for the season as the guest of Mr and Mrs Allen, and there she meets the eccentric General Tilney, his son Henry and his daughter Eleanor. She is invited to the Tilneys' home, the Northanger Abbey of the title, where she imagines numerous gruesome secrets surrounding the General and his house. Henry proves that her suspicions have no substance but, while she is still recovering from the humiliation, she finds herself ordered out of the house by the General. She returns home and is followed by Henry. He explains that the General, mistakenly believing her to be penniless, had been anxious to keep her away from his son. Restored to a sensible humour by the truth, the General finally gives his blessing to Henry's marriage to Catherine.

**Northward Ho** A comedy by **Thomas Dekker** and **John Webster**, produced about 1605 and published in 1607. The plot concerns the efforts of Greenshield to seduce Mistress Maybury, who rejects him. He tries to convince her husband that she is unfaithful by producing a ring he has stolen from her. Maybury, convinced of her innocence, takes his revenge upon Greenshield with the help of the old poet Bellamont. The character of Bellamont is an amiable caricature of the authors' fellow playwright, **George Chapman**.

**Norton, Caroline Elizabeth Sarah** 1808–77 Poet and novelist. Born Caroline Sheridan, the granddaughter of **Richard Brinsley Sheridan**, she married George Chapple Norton in 1827 but the union was unhappy. Needing to earn money, she published a book of poetry, *The Sorrows of Rosalie* (1829), followed by a romance, *The Undying One* (1830), and a novel,

*The Wife and Woman's Reward* (1835), all with considerable success. She also edited *La Belle Assemblée* and *The English Annual*. In 1836 Norton brought a charge of alienating his wife's affections against Lord Melbourne and, though the suit failed, it brought their marriage to an end. Her marital wrongs prompted her to publish many powerful and eventually influential pamphlets on questions of women's rights. She continued to publish poetry – *A Voice from the Factories* (1836) and *The Lady of La Garaye* (1861) – while her novels include *Stuart of Dunleath* (1851), *Lost and Saved* (1863) and *Old Sir Douglas* (1867). *The Martyn* (1849) is a play. In 1877 she married Sir William Stirling-Maxwell. Her beauty, talent and determination earned Caroline Norton much abuse and much admiration. Her character was said to have provided the model for the heroine of **George Meredith**'s novel, *Diana of the Crossways*.

**Norton, Charles Eliot** 1827–1908 American man of letters, and Professor of the History of Fine Art at Harvard from 1874 to 1898. A regular contributor to *The Atlantic Monthly* and co-editor of *The North American Review*, he also helped to found *The Nation* in 1865. He was a frequent visitor to Europe and had a wide range of friends among writers and artists on both sides of the Atlantic. His *Letters*, published in 1913, are a valuable document of intellectual life in Massachusetts in the latter half of the 19th century. His books include a prose translation of Dante's *The Divine Comedy* (1891–2), editions of **John Donne**'s poetry (1895) and the early letters of **Thomas Carlyle** (1886), and *Notes of Travel and Study in Italy* (1859).

**Norton, Mary** 1903– Children's novelist. Educated in a convent school, she spent much of her childhood in the Georgian manor house in Bedfordshire which became Firbank Hall in *The Borrowers*. After a brief career as an actress she married and went to live in Portugal. She first turned to writing as a means of support in the USA during World War II. Her first books, *The Magic Bedknob* (1943) and *Bonfires and Broomsticks* (1947), since reissued together as *Bedknob and Broomstick* (1970), concern the adventures of three children and Miss Price, the village spinster who is also studying to be a witch. *The Borrowers* (1952), awarded the Carnegie Medal, was the first in a series of five books about a family of tiny people who flee when they are discovered by the 'human beans' and embark on an epic journey across the countryside to a new home.

**Norton, Thomas** 1532–84 Poet and playwright. Norton was co-author with **Thomas Sackville** of *Gorboduc* (first acted in 1561 and printed in 1565) which has claim to be the first proper English tragedy. He was probably educated at Cambridge, became amanuensis to Protector Somerset and married Archbishop Cranmer's daughter. He translated Calvin's *Institutes* (1561), wrote Latin verses, contributed a poem to *Tottel's Miscellany* and as a lawyer was active in the examination of Catholics in the reign of Elizabeth.

*Nostromo* A novel by **Joseph Conrad**, published in 1904. A turbulent political history is part of the background of the coastal Province of Sulaco, the wealthiest region of the South American republic of Costaguana. Along with the San Tomé silver mine, the Englishman Charles Gould has inherited the instability of a civil war between the legal government of Ribiera and the populist party of his military chief, Montero. In order to prevent the confiscation of silver by the rebels, Gould is persuaded to entrust it to Martin Decoud, a journalist with ambiguous commitments to the Ribiera government. Decoud is joined by the Italian Nostromo ('our man'), the Capataz de Cargadores, a local hero, in smuggling the silver out into the gulf. In the darkness, their loaded lighter is hit and damaged by a rebel troopship; forced to run aground on nearby islands, the Isabels, they conceal the silver and Nostromo returns to Sulaco.

Shocked into awareness by their near-disaster, Nostromo considers how far he has been exploited by his allies, who are aware of his appetite for adventure and glory. Decoud's dilemma is more extreme: his usual scepticism turns to near-madness, and he drowns himself, weighted with silver. At this point, Nostromo is persuaded to further, desperate heroism by another bearer of disillusionment: Dr Monygham, who was tortured under the previous political regime, and who is in love with Charles Gould's wife, the humane and wise Emilia. Owing to Nostromo's actions in summoning loyal forces, Sulaco and the Goulds are saved from the violence of the rebels.

The ensuing peace proves to be superficial for most characters. Nostromo, who is betrothed to Linda, the daughter of Giorgio Viola, fosters the belief that the silver has been sunk. But he makes clandestine visits to the Isabels, where Giorgio is appointed lighthouse keeper; here, he steals back portions of the silver and finds himself in love with Giselle, the sister of his betrothed. When he is mistaken for an intruder and shot by Giorgio, the secret of the silver is lost for ever.

***Notes of a Journey from Cornhill to Grand Cairo*** A travel book by **W. M. Thackeray**, with his own illustrations, published in 1846.

This account of a steamer journey round the Mediterranean, made in 1844 at the invitation of the Peninsular and Oriental Company, describes Thackeray's honest and often irreverent response to such landmarks of the ancient world as Athens, Constantinople, Jerusalem and Cairo.

**Notes on the State of Virginia** A book by **Thomas Jefferson**, published in 1785, and designed to answer a set of questions about America circulated among American statesmen by François Marbois, a French representative in Philadelphia during the Revolutionary War. Perhaps the best single expression of Jefferson's ideas, the *Notes* goes beyond its rubric of answering questions from a foreign government about American landscape, customs and institutions, and advocates a specifically Jeffersonian programme: religious toleration, emancipation of slaves, an agrarian ideal. Jefferson also describes the legal history of the colonies, especially Virginia, including an account of the events leading up to the Declaration of Independence.

**novel of sensibility** See **sentimental novel**.

**Novels by Eminent Hands** See *Punch's Prize Novelists*.

**Novum Organum** A Latin treatise by **Francis Bacon**, published in 1620, which forms the second part of the great programme of intellectual and scientific reform that he proposed under the title of *Instauratio Magna* ('The Great Instauration'). *The Advancement of Learning* constituted the preliminary section to this scheme, with its attack on the Aristotelian structures of knowledge that were still dominant in the universities of Europe, coupled with an appeal to develop new, systematic and profitable methods of enquiry into all areas of research. The Novum Organum of the title means 'The New Instrument' that will be employed to advance learning, Organon being the name given to Aristotle's logical treatises as instruments of reasoning. In the work, Bacon deplores the limited understanding that men have of the operations of the natural world, their ignorance of the causes of natural phenomena, and their inability to control the forces of nature for the benefit of mankind. The fault lies principally in the sterile methods of intellectual enquiry that scholastic teachers, weakly imitating Aristotle, employ. In addition, there are various kinds of prejudice that prevent men thinking clearly and objectively. These Bacon characterizes as the Idols of the Mind (which he also describes in *The Advancement*, Book V). He identifies four notable 'fallacies of the mind of man': the Idols of the Tribe, the commonly received beliefs and superstitions of one's society; the Idols of the Cave, the particular foibles of an individual's mind; the Idols of the Market Place, by which phrase Bacon describes the loose meanings of words in common usage, and the lack of a precise and defined relationship between words and things; and the Idols of the Theatre, the various false philosophic systems that present an attractive but misleading view to the mind, in the manner of a stage play that pleases but deceives as it conjures up an imaginary world.

The method of enquiry that Bacon recommends in *Novum Organum*, the reliable new instrument of discovery, is induction: the method of inferring a general law or principle from the observation of particular instances. Induction forms the basis of Bacon's experimental technique, and Book II of his treatise is given over to a practical application of the method in an investigation of the nature of heat.

**Nowra, Louis** 1950– Australian playwright. His plays, often with exotic or historical settings, depict the private worlds of illusion, obsession and madness under pressure from external power structures, and are characterized by episodic construction, heightened language and powerful, even lurid, theatrical effects. They include two radio plays *Albert Named Edward* (1975) and *The Song Room* (1980), *Inner Voices* (1977), *Visions* (1978), *Inside the Island* (1980), *The Precious Woman* (1980) and *Sunrise* (1983), and a television drama, *Displaced Persons* (1985).

**Noyes, Alfred** 1880–1958 Poet, novelist, short-story writer and playwright. Born in Wolverhampton and educated in Wales, he attended Exeter College, Oxford, but concentrated on producing his first volume of poetry, *The Loom of Years* (1902), and left without a degree. Noyes's first wife was American and he spent many of the years before her death in 1926 in the USA, lecturing on 'The Sea in English Poetry' (a favourite topic) at Harvard University in 1913 and teaching **F. Scott Fitzgerald** and **Edmund Wilson** among others at Princeton between 1914 and 1923. His own poetry – which included the blank-verse epic *Drake* (1906–8) and famous shorter poems like 'The Barrel Organ' ('Come down to Kew in lilac time') and 'The Highwayman' – was vigorously traditional and increasingly out of tune with his contemporaries. *The Torch-Bearers*, an ambitious trilogy about science and Christianity consisting of *The Watchers of the Sky* (1922), *The Book of Earth* (1925) and *The Last Voyage* (1930), reflected a growing preoccupation with religion; he converted to Roman Catholicism in 1926. Notable among his fiction are the ventures into fantasy in *Walking Shadows* (1918), *The Hidden Player* (1924) and *The Last Man* (1940). *Two Worlds for Memory* (1953) is autobiographical.

**Nun's Priest's Tale, The** See *Canterbury Tales, The*.

# O

**O Pioneers!** A novel by **Willa Cather**, published in 1913, the story of Alexandra Bergson, the eldest daughter of Swedish immigrants who live on the Nebraska Divide. After her father dies, Alexandra, in her early 20s, manages the Bergson farm and homestead. Her innovative farming ideas meet resistance from her conservative brothers Oscar and Lou, but after the division of the land upon their marriages, Alexandra's fields flourish, and she becomes rich enough to send her youngest brother Emil to college. She develops a close relationship with a young Bohemian woman, Marie Tovesky, who lives with her husband on a neighbouring farm, once the home of Alexandra's childhood sweetheart, Carl Linstrum. Carl, who had left the Divide years ago when he moved east with his parents, returns to visit Alexandra and then travels west to California. Emil graduates from the University of Nebraska and decides to visit Mexico. Back from his travels, he becomes romantically involved with Marie Tovesky. One day Marie's husband finds the two lovers together in a field, and shoots them in a rage. Hearing of the tragedy, Carl returns and marries Alexandra.

**Oates, Joyce Carol** 1938– American novelist, poet, short-story writer and critic, born in Lockport, New York, in the 'Eden County' of many of her novels. She was educated at Syracuse University and at the University of Wisconsin.

Her intense, often violent vision is perhaps most powerfully expressed in the novel *Wonderland* (1971), which is structured around **Lewis Carroll**'s Alice stories, and in the loosely arranged trilogy, *A Garden of Earthly Delights* (1967), *Expensive People* (1968) and *them* (1969, National Book Award). Her other novels are *With Shuddering Fall* (1964), *The Assassins: A Book of Hours* (1975), *Bellefleur* (1980), *Angel of Light* (1981), *A Bloodsmoor Romance* (1982), *Mysteries of Winterhurn* (1984), *Solstice* (1985) and *Marya: A Life* (1986). Her short-story collections are *By the North Gate* (1963), *The Wheel of Love* (1970) which includes the often anthologized 'Where are You Going, Where have You Been' and 'The Region of Ice', *The Goddess and*

*Other Women* (1974), *The Seduction and Other Stories* (1975), *Last Days* (1984) and *Raven's Wing* (1987). Her essays and criticism have appeared in several volumes, including *The Edge of Impossibility: Tragic Forms in Literature* (1972), *The Hostile Sun: The Poetry of D. H. Lawrence* (1973), *Contraries: Essays* (1981) and *On Boxing* (1987). Her volumes of poetry include *Women in Love, and Other Poems* (1968) and *Anonymous Sins, and Other Poems* (1969).

**objective correlative** A term coined by **T. S. Eliot** in his essay on **Hamlet** (1919): 'The only way of expressing emotion in the form of art is by finding an "objective correlative"; in other words, a set of objects, a situation, a chain of events which shall be the formula of that *particular* emotion; such that when the external facts, which must terminate in sensory experience, are given, the emotion is immediately evoked.'

**Objectivism** An American poetic movement of the 1930s, in reaction against **imagism**. The poets concerned – **George Oppen**, **Louis Zukofsky**, **Charles Reznikoff** and **William Carlos Williams** – believed that the principles of imagism were too vague, being applicable to almost any conceivable idea. Instead, they emphasized the importance of the poem as a physical object, and this led to an increased attention to typography as well as to the use of more conventional poetic devices. *An 'Objectivists' Anthology* appeared in 1932, but the movement was not popular and it disbanded soon after this publication.

**O'Brien, Edna** 1932– Novelist and short-story writer. Born in Tuamgraney in County Clare, Ireland, she was educated locally at Scarriff, and at Loughrea in Galway. Later she studied pharmacy in Dublin and became a Licentiate of the Pharmaceutical College of Ireland. Her first novel, *The Country Girls* (1960), introduces 'Kate' Brady and 'Baba' Brennan, two Irish girls who leave their restrictive backgrounds for the excitement of Dublin. They appear again in *The Lonely Girl* (1962) and *Girls in Their Married Bliss* (1963), in which their quest for 'life' eventually leads them to London.

Other novels include *August is a Wicked Month* (1965), *Casualties of Peace* (1966) and *A Pagan Place* (1971; about rural Ireland). *Night* (1972) is narrated by a middle-aged woman as she lies alone in bed. It was followed by *Johnny I Hardly Knew You* (1977).

Much of her writing is concerned with the position of women in society: their lack of fulfilment and the repressive nature of their upbringing. The bleakness of tone, especially in the later novels, is lightened by a lyrical quality associated with nostalgia for Ireland, and by odd moments of joy in which O'Brien's heroines achieve temporary happiness. Her collections of short stories, on similar themes, include *The Love Object* (1968), *A Scandalous Woman and Other Stories* (1974), and *Mrs Reinhardt and Other Stories* (1978; titled *A Rose in the Heart* in the USA).

**O'Brien, Fitz-James** *c.*1828–62 Born in Ireland, O'Brien was already an experienced journalist when he emigrated to the USA in 1852. There he established a popular reputation as a writer of short stories in the fantastic vein, of which his most famous, 'The Diamond Lens', was published in **The Atlantic Monthly** in 1858. It tells of an inventor who creates a powerful microscope, becomes obsessed with the vision of a human-like figure in a drop of liquid, and goes mad when the creature dies. O'Brien also published a play, *A Gentleman from Ireland* (1858). He fought in the Civil War and died at the battle of Bloomery Gap. The posthumous collection *Poems and Stories* appeared in 1881.

**O'Brien, Flann** 1911–66 Irish novelist and journalist. Born Brian O'Nolan in Strabane, he studied Irish, German and philosophy at University College, Dublin. From 1940 he contributed a column to *The Irish Times* under the pseudonym 'Myles na Gopaleen' in which he constantly argued against the use of clichés about Ireland. A collection, *The Best of Myles*, was published in 1968.

O'Brien's first and major novel, *At Swim-Two-Birds* (1939), was recognized in some circles as a masterpiece in direct descent from **Joyce**'s *Ulysses*. Described by **John Wain** as 'hilarious, elegiac, sarcastic, relaxed and genial', it is a massively ambitious work which combines naturalistic and fantastic elements. The narrator, a young Dublin student, conveys different versions of reality, from the 'realistic' presentation of his own everyday circumstances to an account of the Irish folk hero Finn Mac Cool in a 'novel-within-a-novel' by one 'Dermot Trellis'. A further layer of farce enters the novel in the representation of Irish folklore. Like *Ulysses*, to which it owes much but by no means all of its narrative energy, the novel may also be

read as a sustained exploration of the fictional process.

O'Brien's other novels include *The Hard Life* (1961), *The Dalkey Archive* (1964), and *The Third Policeman* (1967). A novel in Gaelic, *An Béal Bocht* (1941), was translated by P. C. Power as *The Poor Mouth* in 1973.

**O'Casey, Sean** 1880–1964 Irish playwright. Born in Dublin, the youngest of an impoverished Protestant family, O'Casey suffered from poor health during his boyhood. Trachoma permanently damaged his eyesight and interrupted his education. Unable to read properly until he was 13, he read avidly from then on. During years of physical hardship as a roadbreaker, docker and hod-carrier he fell increasingly under the influence of the Irish labour leader Jim Larkin. Nationalism took him into the Irish Citizen Army, but his greater concern for the welfare of the proletariat made him resign from it in 1914 to protest against its anti-Union attitudes.

O'Casey's first publication was a broadside, *The Story of Thomas Ashe* (1917), about a friend in the Citizen Army who died on hunger strike, but he was already interested in the work of the **Abbey Theatre**. After rejecting at least three of his plays, the Abbey staged **The Shadow of a Gunman** (1923), following it in regular succession with the one-act *Kathleen Listens In* (1923), O'Casey's first experiment with expressionist techniques, and **Juno and the Paycock** (1924). Another one-act piece, *Nannie's Night Out* (1924), brought him his first experience of hissing from the intensely nationalistic Abbey audience, and **The Plough and the Stars** (1926) provoked a full-scale riot led by objectors to its unheroic portrait of participants in the Easter

Sean O'Casey at a rehearsal of *The Plough and the Stars* in 1926. The playwright in conversation with actress Ria Mooney, who played the prostitute Rosie Redmond.

Rising. Feeling rejected by the theatre whose fortunes his plays had sustained, O'Casey left Dublin for London. Against his expectations, and perhaps against his own dramatic interests, he never lived in Ireland again.

The decisive break came when **Yeats** and his fellow directors at the Abbey decided against staging O'Casey's next play, *The Silver Tassie*, in 1928 (it was first staged in London in 1929 and, in an atmosphere of protest, at the Abbey in 1935). The particular stumbling-block for Yeats was the expressionistic second act, embedded in a play that otherwise closely resembled O'Casey's Abbey successes in the tragicomic realism with which it viewed the urban poor of Dublin. O'Casey had never wished to be limited by the tenets of dramatic realism. *Within the Gates* (1943), his next play, is wholly expressionistic. Set in Hyde Park, and reliant on the careful interweaving of music, dance and stylized dialogue, it explores the conflicting claims made on the Young Woman by her urge for joy and her hope for religious salvation.

O'Casey's later plays never rivalled the popularity of his Dublin tragicomedies. They include several overtly Communist pieces, like *The Star Turns Red* (1940) and *Red Roses for Me* (1943), which is set against a background with which O'Casey was personally familiar – the Irish Transport Workers' strike of 1913. The expressionistic third act, in which a vision of Dublin as it might be is poetically presented, is a feature of this ambitious play. That O'Casey's preoccupation with Ireland remained with him in exile is further illustrated by *Purple Dust* (1943), *Cock-a-Doodle Dandy* (1949), O'Casey's favourite among his plays, *The Bishop's Bonfire* (1955), *The Drums of Father Ned* (1959) and *Behind the Green Curtains* (1962). Many of these Irish plays press home the point that the constraints of a joy-denying church obstruct the Irish instinct for happiness. It is a theme often referred to in the six extraordinary volumes of autobiography, beginning with *I Knock on the Door* (1939) and ending with *Sunset and Evening Star* (1954). The detail is unreliable, since O'Casey allowed remembered experience to liberate his imagination, but the mood is always telling.

**O'Connor, Flannery** 1925–64 American short-story writer and novelist, born in Savannah, Georgia, and educated at Georgia State College for Women. She suffered from a terminal illness, lupus, for much of her adult life and was frequently hospitalized and in great pain until her death at the age of 39.

Despite the brevity of her career, however, she made a strong impression on the American literary scene, and exerted considerable influence on the development of the American short story. Her own Southern origins and devout Roman Catholic faith are evident throughout her fiction, in which she often uses poor, disabled, or socially marginal characters involved in absurd and violent situations to convey the spiritual poverty and crippled intellect of the modern world. Her vision of violent spiritual struggle in the rural South is marked by a grotesque humour and unnerving irony. Her first novel, *Wise Blood* (1952), tells the story of Hazel Motes, the lonely prophet of a 'church without Christ, where the blind stay blind, the lame stay lame, and them that's dead stays that way'. Another novel, *The Violent Bear It Away*, was published in 1960. Her short stories are collected in *A Good Man is Hard to Find* (1955, as *The Artificial Nigger and Other Stories* in England, 1959) and the posthumously published *Everything That Rises Must Converge* (1965).

**O'Connor, Frank** Pseudonym of Michael Francis O'Donovan (1903–66), Irish writer of short stories. Born and educated in Cork, he first began to write in Gaelic. His stories in English were first published by AE (**George William Russell**) in *The Irish Statesman* and collected as *Guests of the Nation* (1931). Collections appeared at regular intervals and his reputation increased with each one: *The Saint and Mary Kate* (1932), *Bones of Contention* (1936), *Three Old Brothers* (1937), *The Big Fellow* (1937), *Crab Apple Jelly* (1944), *The Common Chord* (1947), *Traveller's Samples* (1950), *Domestic Relations* (1957), and *My Oedipus Complex* (1963). *The Wild Bird's Nest* (1932), *Lords and Commons* (1938), and *The Little Monasteries* (1963) are translations of Irish verse.

During the 1930s O'Connor went to work in Dublin, where **W. B. Yeats** (who compared him to Chekhov) persuaded him to become a director of the **Abbey Theatre** and encouraged him to write plays. O'Connor resigned from the Abbey during the censorship quarrels of 1958 and spent the rest of his life in the USA. Among his other works are: the plays *In the Train* and *The Invincibles* (1937), *Moses' Rock* (1938), *Time's Rocket* (1939) and *The Statue's Daughter* (1940); a novel, *Dutch Interior* (1940); and two volumes of autobiography, *An Only Child* (1961) and the unfinished *My Father's Son* (1968). He also wrote numerous critical essays.

*Octavian* A **verse romance** written in the mid-14th century and existing in two versions, one from the North and the other from the South-east. Both were derived from a French version, though the story is extant in several other European and Nordic languages. Florence, wife of the Emperor Octavian, bears twin sons, Octavian and Florentyn. Her jealous mother-in-law (in the northern version, her father) contrives to have the mother and children driven out into the forest. The children are stolen by an ape and a tiger; Octavian is brought up by a lioness, and Florentyn by a Parisian butcher. Florence, sailing to the Holy Land, recovers the young Octavian with his lioness step-mother and lives in Jerusalem. Florentyn becomes a local champion, then defeats a Saracen sultan's giant champion and marries the sultan's daughter. In a battle with the sultan he and the Emperor Octavian are captured with others. The young Octavian and his lioness fight the pagans and free the prisoners. The family is reunited and the mother-in-law burned.

**Octopus, The**: *A Story of California* A novel by **Frank Norris**, published in 1901, the first part of his uncompleted trilogy *The Epic of the Wheat*.

The octopus of the title is the Pacific and Southwestern Railroad, which in the course of the story economically strangles the wheat farmers of California, who are led by Magnus Derrick, the owner of a large ranch near the town of Bonneville. The railroad is the most powerful vested interest in the state; it dominates the government, gains total control of Bonneville, and is behind the movement of all prices and interest rates. Many of the farmers hold their land on option from the railroad, and it dispossesses them at will; it also manipulates freight charges to lower the price of wheat and thereby ruin other farmers when it wants their land too. Derrick's direct opponent is the railroad agent Behrman, who is eventually suffocated when he falls into the wheat he has plundered from the ruined and dispossessed farmers, wheat that he was intending to sell at a huge profit. Derrick himself is ruined when the railroad succeeds in bribing his son Lyman, a lawyer on the state commission, to act against the farmers' interests. Other leading characters are Dyke, the railroad engineer who wants to be a farmer, and Shelgrim, the railroad president, who blandly tells the protesting poet, Presley, that what has happened has nothing to do with the people – it is all a matter of economic forces and the law of supply and demand.

**Octoroon, The** A melodrama by **Dion Boucicault**, first performed at the Winter Garden, New York, in 1859, a few days after the execution of the abolitionist John Brown. The play was adapted from *The Quadroon*, a novel by **Captain Mayne Reid**.

The octoroon of the title is Zoe, a freed slave on the impoverished Southern plantation of the late Judge Peyton, whose daughter by a quadroon slave she is. The play deals with the attempts of the Judge's widow, his nephew George and the virtuous Yankee Salem Scudder to save both Zoe and the plantation from the villainous M'Closky. Exposed as a murderer by Scudder's camera, M'Closky is hunted and killed by the Indian chief Wahnotee, but too late to save Zoe, who kills herself rather than give

pain to George Peyton. When English audiences objected to this ending, Boucicault grudgingly provided an alternative in which Zoe survives.

**O'Curry, Eugene** 1796–1862 Irish scholar. Born in County Clare and self-educated, he was employed in the topographical and historical section of the Ordnance Survey Office in Dublin in 1834. Like his colleagues **George Petrie** and **John O'Donovan**, he made pioneering contributions to the scholarly aspect of the **Celtic revival**. He set to work on the collections of Irish folk material, establishing the British Museum catalogue in the field. In 1850 he became Professor of Irish History and Archaeology at the new Catholic University in Dublin. His famous lectures of 1855 were published in 1861 as *Lectures on the Manuscript Materials of Ancient Irish History*.

**Odd Women, The** A novel by **George Gissing**, published in 1893.

The death of the improvident Dr Madden leaves his three daughters stranded with very little money and no training of any kind. Their loneliness and poverty in London lodgings and their desperate maintenance of middle-class respectability – Virginia has found a secret consolation in gin – are conveyed with considerable pathos. In contrast to the Madden sisters is Rhoda Nunn, an active feminist who proposes to prepare women for some fate other than marriage.

**ode** A lyric poem in rhymed stanzas, generally in the form of an address and exalted in feeling and expression. Famous examples include **Keats**'s odes 'To a Nightingale' and 'On a Grecian Urn' and **Wordsworth**'s 'Ode: Intimations of Immortality from Recollections of Early Childhood'. The Pindaric ode takes its name from the Greek poet (522–442 BC) whose work, designed to honour victors in the Greek games, used an elaborate stanzaic pattern of strophe, antistrophe and epode. **Abraham Cowley** introduced the form into English; he and successors like **Dryden** and **Pope** loosen the stanzaic pattern but keep the poem's public function. **Tennyson**'s 'Ode on the Death of the Duke of Wellington' is a fine late example of the Pindaric ode.

**O'Dell, Scott** 1903–89 American author. Born in Los Angeles and educated at Stanford University, California, O'Dell worked in films and journalism before writing successfully for adults and, later, for children. His most celebrated work, *Island of the Blue Dolphin* (1960), tells how Karana, an Indian girl, survives for 18 years alone on a tiny island, gradually coming to terms with the animal life around her. The whole story is also a form of parable stressing mankind's need to coexist peaceably with his environment. O'Dell's next children's novel, *The King's Fifth* (1966), describes how ruthless foreign adventurers looted South America.

**Odets, Clifford** 1906–63 American playwright, born in Philadelphia, the son of middle-class Jewish immigrants. He left school at the age of 17 to become an actor, working in radio and playing small parts in stock companies and then in Theatre Guild productions. In 1931 he helped found the **Group Theatre**, in which he initially participated simply as an actor. One act of his play *Awake and Sing!* was given a trial reading in 1933 but rejected for production. Then in 1935 he wrote *Waiting for Lefty* in response to a New Theatre League contest for one-act plays. He won the contest and was rewarded with a production. It was an instant success; the Group Theatre reconsidered and produced *Awake and Sing!* (1935), followed by a double bill of *Waiting for Lefty* and *Till The Day I Die*, a short anti-Nazi play Odets wrote quickly for the purpose. His career as playwright and champion of the underprivileged was launched.

He joined the Communist party in 1934, but soon resigned; he later told the House Un-American Activities Committee that he had found it impossible to write in line with a party programme, and that his sympathy for the working classes was due to family experience rather than party ideology. His second full-length play, *Paradise Lost* (1935), dealt with the disintegration of a middle-class family as a result of the Depression. He then accepted a lucrative offer to become a Hollywood screenwriter, but returned to New York to see a new play, *Golden Boy* (1937), through production by the Group Theatre. This play, which was to be his greatest commercial success, is the story of Joe Bonaparte, a talented young Italian violinist who chooses to become a prizefighter, thereby destroying his talent, his integrity and finally himself and the woman he loves. Of Odets's later plays, *Rocket to the Moon* (1938) explores a dentist's mid-life crisis; *Night Music* (1940) is a story of distrustful love between alienated people in Hollywood; *Clash By Night* (1941) depicts a love triangle which ends in murder. *The Big Knife* (1949) concerns Charlie Castle, a Hollywood actor who has compromised his ideals; in *The Country Girl* (1950), another love triangle centres on a self-pitying, alcoholic actor struggling to make a comeback. Odets's last play, *The Flowering Peach* (1954), retells the story of Noah's ark.

**O'Donovan, John** 1809–61 Irish scholar and topographer. Born in County Kilkenny, O'Donovan was appointed to the Ordnance Survey Office in 1829, where he worked with **Eugene O'Curry** and **George Petrie**. Like them

he made an important contribution to the **Celtic revival** by his pioneering researches into ancient Irish civilization. He published *A Grammar of the Irish Language* in 1845, but his masterwork was his edition of *Annala Rioghacta Eireann, Annals of the Kingdom of Ireland by the Four Masters* (7 vols., 1848–51).

**O'Dowd, Bernard** 1866–1953 Australian poet. Educated at the University of Melbourne, O'Dowd was assistant librarian at the Supreme Court, Melbourne (1887–1913) and State Parliamentary Draughtsman (1931–5). He corresponded with **Walt Whitman**, whose sense of the poet's duty as an 'answerer', dealing with the most useful and interesting questions of the age, influenced his work. His volumes of verse included *Dawnward?* (1903), *The Silent Land* (1906), *Dominions of the Boundary* (1907), *The Seven Deadly Sins* (1909), *The Bush* (1912) and *Alma Venus!* (1921). His poetic technique is discussed in the address *Poetry Militant: An Australian Plea for the Poetry of Purpose* (1909).

**O'Faolain, Sean** 1900–91 Novelist, short-story writer and biographer. Born in Cork, he was educated at the National University, Dublin, and at Harvard. During the 1920s he was a member of the Irish Republican Army, and from 1929 to 1933 he lectured in English at St Mary's College, Middlesex. In the 1940s he was editor of *The Bell*, and in 1957 became director of the Arts Council of Ireland.

O'Faolain's first book of short stories, *Midsummer Night Madness* (1932), was followed by a novel, *A Nest of Simple Folk* (1933), about the spirit of Irish rebellion. Other short stories followed, and he was encouraged by the support of **Edward Garnett**. *Bird Alone* (1936) and *Come Back To Erin* (1940), like his earlier novel, dealt with the tyranny and pathos of Irish life and politics, particularly the oppression of Irish Catholicism. Other writing included biographies of Constance Markiewicz (1934), Daniel O'Connell (1938), De Valera (1939) and Hugh O'Neill (1942). *The Short Story* (1948) and *The Vanishing Hero* (1956) were works of literary criticism, and *Vive-moi!* (1964) was his autobiography.

***Officers and Gentlemen*** See *Sword of Honour*.

**O'Flaherty, Liam** 1897–1984 Novelist and short-story writer. He was born at Inishmore in the Aran Islands and trained for the priesthood before abandoning this to study at University College, Dublin. During World War I he served with the Irish Guards in France, and was invalided out because of shell-shock in 1917. In 1922 he joined the militant demonstrations against unemployment in Dublin and was forced to leave the country. He finally settled in Aran.

O'Flaherty's first novel, *The Neighbour's Wife* (1923), was published with the support of **Edward Garnett**, and his second, *The Informer* (1925), is generally considered to be his best. It is a psychological melodrama about the last day of Gypo Nolan, a destitute Irish revolutionary who turns in a comrade for £20. *The Martyr* (1927), *The Assassin* (1928), *The Puritan* (1931) and *Famine* (1937) were equally uncompromising and realistic accounts of the Irish condition, but were less enthusiastically received.

He is better known for his short stories, which were gentler and more lyrical than the novels but managed to avoid sentimentality. Many grew from his island background and displayed a keen observation of the natural world. Others showed his appreciation of the peasant's life and were rendered stylistically distinctive through his modification of English by the patterns of Gaelic speech. Volumes included *Spring Sowing* (1926) and *The Fairy Goose* (1929), collected in *The Short Stories of Liam O'Flaherty* (1956).

*Two Years* (1930), *I Went to Russia* (1931) and *Shame the Devil* (1934) were autobiographical works which included accounts of his extensive travels.

**O'Grady, Standish James** 1846–1928 Irish historian. Born at Castletown Berehaven in Cork, and educated at Tipperary Grammar School and Trinity College, Dublin, he was called to the Bar in 1872 but never practised, preferring the world of letters. An interest in his country's epic past led to the two-volume *History of Ireland* (1878–80), which aroused considerable interest and had great influence on the Irish poets. *The Early Bardic Literature of Ireland* (1879) also helped inspire the **Celtic revival** by popularizing ancient legends. *Red Hugh's Captivity* (1889) and its sequel, *The Flight of the Eagle* (1897), are novels about Ireland in the days of Elizabeth I. Irish myth is the matter of *Cuculain: An Epic* (1882), *Finn and His Companions* (1892), *The Coming of Cuculain* (1894) and *The Departure of Dermot, The Triumph of Cuculain* and *The Passing of Cuculain* (all 1917). *The Bog of Stars* (1893) is a collection of stories about Ireland in the 16th century; *Hugh Roe O'Donnell* (1902) is a play set in the same period.

**O'Hara, Frank** 1926–66 American poet and playwright, born in Baltimore, Maryland, and educated at Harvard and the University of Michigan. His first book of verse, *A City Winter and Other Poems*, was published in 1952. His other volumes are *Meditations in an Emergency* (1957), *Odes* (1960), *Lunch Poems* (1964) and *Love Poems* (1965). His plays are *Try, Try!* (produced in 1951), *Changing Your Bedding* (produced in 1952), *Awake in Spain* (1960), *Love's Labor* (produced in 1960, published 1964) and *The General Returns From One Place to Another* (1964). *Collected Poems* (1971), *Poems Retrieved* (1977) and *Selected Plays* (1978) were published posthumously.

**O'Hara, John** 1905–70 American novelist and short-story writer, born in Pottsville, Pennsylvania, a town which later figured as the 'Gibbsville' of his fiction. His first novel, *Appointment in Samarra* (1934), is set in Gibbsville and is a naturalistic account of three days that culminate in the suicide of Julian English, the victim of a stratified society and of his own reckless sexual appetite. The book was well received, and in the same year O'Hara embarked on a career as a screenwriter in Hollywood which lasted until the mid 1940s. *Butterfield 8* (1935) is a novel about the experiences of a Manhattan newspaperman. *Pal Joey*, published in 1940 and adapted as a musical in the same year, consists of a comic series of letters from a nightclub entertainer to a friend. O'Hara's other novels include *A Rage to Live* (1949), *Ten North Frederick* (1955, National Book Award), *From the Terrace* (1959), *Ourselves to Know* (1960), *The Big Laugh* (1962) and *The Lockwood Concern* (1965). *Sermons and Soda Water*, a collection of three novellas, was published in 1960. His short stories, like his novels, often focus on questions of class and social privilege. His collections include *The Doctor's Son* (1935), *Files on Parade* (1939), *Pipe Night* (1945), *Hellbox* (1947), *Assembly* (1961), *The Cape Cod Lighter* (1962), *The Horse Knows the Way* (1964) and *Waiting for Winter* (1967). His dramatic work was published in *Five Plays* (1961).

**Okai, Atukwei** 1941– Ghanaian poet. Formerly known as John Okai, he was born in Accra and was educated at Gambaga Native Authority Primary School, Nalerigu Middle Boys' School, Methodist Middle Boys' School and Accra High School, before studying for degrees at the Gorky Institute in Moscow and the University of London. He has based his academic career at the University of Ghana, where he teaches Russian language and literature, but he was for a brief time a minister in the first Rawlings government in Ghana. His poetry is little known outside Ghana, both because it incorporates many local references and words and because it relies for a full appreciation upon an element of performance, sometimes accompanied by drums. His collections of poetry include *Flowerfall* (1969), which was published in typescript, *Fontonfrom, and other poems* (1971) and *Lorgorligi Logarithms, and other poems* (1974). His *Selected Poems* came out in 1979. He frequently reads publicly from unpublished collections such as 'Calabash Chorus' or from long unpublished sequences such as 'Rhododendrons in Donkeydom'. He is one of the most metrically inventive African poets, always aware of the aural quality of a poem. He has very effectively amalgamated the traditions of African orality with innovatory modern poetic techniques, while at the same time stretching the possibilities of the English language in Africa.

**Okara, Gabriel (Imomotimi Gbaingbain)** 1921– Nigerian poet. The son of an Ijo chief, he was born at Bumoundi in the Niger delta. He was educated at Government College, Umuahia, Yaba Higher College and, as a mature student, at Northwestern University, USA. He has had careers in publishing and in government information services. During the Nigerian Civil War he was Director of the Cultural Affairs Division of the Biafran Ministry of Education and acted with **Chinua Achebe** as a roving ambassador for the Biafran cause. Among Nigerian poets he has a very high reputation, based on a slim quantity of publications. Many of his best-known poems are frequently included in anthologies, among them 'The Snowflakes Sail Gently Down'. Despite his fame as a poet his first collection, *The Fisherman's Invocation*, did not appear until 1978; it won the Commonwealth Poetry Prize the following year. Okara's poems tend to be lyrical but to be based in some way in his own oral tradition. Apart from his poetry, Okara is known for a novel entitled *The Voice* (1964), which has been much quoted as an attempt to produce a form of English that would have within it the structural principles of his own indigenous Ijo language. Few African novels have aroused so much interest, though it is questionable whether it has had much influence on other writers of prose.

**O'Keeffe, John** 1747–1833 Irish playwright, born in Dublin. Of the 60 plays and operas he refers to in his *Recollections* (2 vols., 1826), most were written after he had settled in London in *c*.1780. Only one, *Wild Oats* (1791), has achieved lasting fame. It is an artificial but quick-moving comedy, whose leading character, a strolling player called Rover, has a dramatic quotation to suit every occasion. O'Keeffe had been blind for several years when he wrote it.

**Okigbo, Christopher** 1932–67 Nigerian poet born in Ojoto village. A graduate in Classics (1956), he worked first in business, then as civil servant, teacher, librarian and publisher. A Biafran major in the Nigerian Civil War, he was killed in action near Nsukka. Most of his poetry was posthumously collected in *Labyrinths* (1971), with an introduction he wrote in 1965; *Collected Poems* (1986) is fuller. Among anglophone African writers, Okigbo has possibly the most fertile, and most mythopoeic, poetic imagination; he always rejoiced in unexpected

correspondences among apparently disparate cultural references. In his own life he could reconcile his Catholicism with his being hereditary priest of a traditional Igbo village deity, and this priesthood is subsumed in his function as a modern poet in English open to influences from the Classics, the Bible, Catholic liturgy, and poets like **Hopkins** and **T. S. Eliot**. To Okigbo poetry is offering, ceremony and ritual, with the celebrant (the speaking voice of the persona in the poem) seeking to break through the mufflings of normality, to reach a truer definition of self and a larger reality, of which snatches of music and gleams of light are revealed to him as intimations. Moreover, 'Heavensgate' (1962) and 'Limits' (1964) are structured like musical compositions with *leitmotifs*, rather than through logical progression. Okigbo the individualist seeking elusive other-worldly revelation is never wholly self-centred, and in his last, 'drum' poems, the poet-prophet, 'I, Okigbo, town-crier', warns of the storm about to break over his people, leaving 'barren farmlands', 'homesteads abandoned', 'corn cobs in burning barns'.

**Okri, Ben** 1959– Nigerian novelist. Born in Lagos, he was educated there privately after a period at Urhobo College, Warri. He was also for a while a student at the University of Essex in England. He is one of a small group of Nigerian writers of the new generation who have largely abandoned the historical themes of the **Chinua Achebe** school or expressions of contempt for those who have held power in independent Nigeria in order to write more personal and introspective novels. These are mainly urban-based and do not attempt to 'Africanize' English in the manner of Achebe. Okri showed a prodigious if slightly unwieldy talent at a very young age. He has written two novels, *Flowers and Shadows* (1980) and *The Landscapes Within* (1981), both of which seem to draw a lot from autobiographical experience. His collection of short stories, *Incidents at the Shrine* (1986), shows an extension of his range, including an atmospheric piece entitled 'Laughter Beneath the Bridge' set at the time of the Civil War.

***Old Bachelor, The*** **William Congreve**'s first play, a comedy, was produced in 1693 and published the same year. Its success on the stage was aided considerably by the performances of Anne Bracegirdle and Thomas Betterton.

The old bachelor of the title is Heartwell, who maintains a pose of despising women. But he falls in love with Silvia and is persuaded to marry her, only to discover that she is Vainlove's discarded mistress. He is later intensely relieved to discover that the parson who married them is Vainlove's friend Belmour, in disguise to pursue an intrigue with Laetitia Fondlewife, already married to an uxorious old banker. Heartwell is still a bachelor, and a husband is found for Silvia in the person of Sir Joseph Wittol, a foolish old man deceived into believing he is marrying the wealthy Araminta. His companion, the bully Captain Bluffe, is similarly deceived into marrying Silvia's maid.

**Old Creole Days** A collection of seven stories of life in 19th-century Louisiana by **George Washington Cable**, published in 1879. (A short novel, *Madame Delphine*, was added in later editions.) The chief setting is the old French section of New Orleans populated by Creoles, Cubans, Spaniards and Santo Domingan refugees, as well as by incoming groups of Germans, Irish and Sicilians. Cable was especially adept in transcribing the varied dialects of the region, but his plots often take a sentimental or melodramatic turn. A typical tale, 'Jean-ah Poquelin', set in the first decade of the century, deals with a once wealthy indigo planter, who now lives a secluded life on his decayed estate near the edge of the burgeoning settlement. Because of the uenexplained disappearance of his half-brother and his militant refusal to let anyone trespass on his property, he has gained a reputation as an evil man who has some great wickedness to hide. After his death it is discovered that he has for many years concealed and cared for his half-brother, now an aged and helpless leper. The collection ends with the tale 'Madame Délicieuse'. It concerns a long-standing quarrel between Madame Délicieuse's fiancé, Dr Mossy, a forward-looking young man who champions scientific advances, and his father, General Villivicencio, who is waging a campaign for public office to restore old Bourbon values and to purge New Orleans of Yankee ideals. Madame Délicieuse, a Creole beauty, engineers a reconciliation between father and son, thus making her marriage possible. The other stories in the volume are 'Café des Exiles', 'Belle Demoiselle Plantation', 'Posson Jone', 'Tite Poulette' and 'Sieur George'.

**Old Curiosity Shop, The** A novel by **Charles Dickens**, first published in the weekly miscellany *Master Humphrey's Clock* from April 1840 to February 1841. It appeared in volume form in 1841.

Little Nell (Nell Trent) lives in the shop of the title with her grandfather, the proprietor. A prey to grasping relatives, he is also a gambler. In an attempt to repair his ruined finances and provide for Nell, he borrows money from Daniel Quilp, evil dwarf, moneylender and smuggler, who has designs on Nell and has persuaded himself that her grandfather is a rich miser. The grandfather loses the borrowed money, and he and Nell flee to the country.

Quilp seizes the shop and sets out in pursuit, determined on revenge.

Nell and her grandfather roam the countryside, reduced to beggary. Kit Nubbles, the errand boy at the curiosity shop who is devoted to Little Nell, does his best to find and help them; he becomes a victim of Quilp's hatred, which nearly succeeds in getting him framed and transported. Nell's great-uncle, returned from abroad, is anxious to trace them, too, but only succeeds when it is too late. Exhausted by her troubles, Nell dies; she is followed soon afterwards by her grandfather. Quilp, trying to evade arrest, falls into the Thames near his wharf on the south bank and drowns.

Although it is today among the least regarded of Dickens's novels, *The Old Curiosity Shop* was at the time an immediate success. **Ruskin** might remark that Dickens butchered Little Nell for the market, but her prolonged deathbed scenes appealed powerfully to the 19th-century love of pathos in literature and her death was the occasion for widespread mourning among Dickens's readers.

**Old Fortunatus, The Pleasant Comedy of** An allegorical play by **Thomas Dekker**, first performed before Elizabeth I on Christmas night, probably in 1598. Its source is the story in the German *Volksbuch* (1509), which had been dramatized by Hans Sachs in 1553.

An old beggar, Fortunatus, meets the goddess Fortune and is offered the choice of long life, wisdom, strength, health, beauty or riches. He takes the last and is given a purse that will yield ten pieces of gold at any time. He goes on his travels with his sons and frequently encounters both Vice and Virtue. He gains possession of the miraculous hat of the Soldan of Turkey, which takes the wearer wherever he wants to go. But Death takes Fortunatus. The purse and hat go to his son, Andelocia, who follows the same way of life as his father and comes to grief when Fortune withdraws the purse and hat. He has learned nothing and without Fortune's favour can make nothing of his life.

**Old Mortality** The second of **Sir Walter Scott**'s *Tales of My Landlord*, published in 1816, and for many years one of his most admired novels.

The title is the nickname of Robert Paterson who, at the end of the 18th century, wandered round Scotland caring for the graves of the Cameronians, strict Covenanters. His stories of the Covenanters form the basis of the novel, one of the principal characters being Graham of Claverhouse, who led the king's forces against them.

The hero of the story is Henry Morton, who shelters John Balfour of Burley, an old friend of his father, not knowing him to be guilty of having taken part in the murder of the Archbishop of St Andrews. Morton's narrow escape from execution, and his anger at the suppression of his countrymen, lead him to join the Covenanters, though he does not share their religious extremism.

Against this background are set the vicissitudes of Morton's love for Edith Bellenden of a royalist family. His rival is the honourable Lord Evandale, who helps save Morton's life, at Edith's plea, when Morton is arrested after the murder of the archbishop. Banished for some years after the defeat of the Covenanters at Bothwell Bridge, Morton returns to England on the accession of William III to find that Edith has given him up for dead and is about to marry Evandale. Preparations for the marriage are halted and shortly afterwards Evandale is attacked by a band of religious fanatics and killed in spite of Morton's desperate intervention.

**Old Vic Theatre** This theatre in the Waterloo Road, London, was called the Royal Coburg when it opened in 1818. By the time it was renamed the Royal Victoria in 1833, it was already a popular home of spectacular and often crude melodrama. Soon referred to as the 'Old Vic', the theatre suffered a decline in fortune and was closed in 1880. From 1881 until 1912 it was owned and managed by Emma Cons, who dedicated herself to the provision of cheap but decent entertainment 'on strict temperance lines'. Her niece, Lilian Baylis, took over the management from 1912 until her death in 1937. It was under her idiosyncratic direction that the Old Vic established its reputation as a theatre for **Shakespeare**. Bombed in 1941 and not fully rebuilt until 1950, the Old Vic, under the direction of Michael Benthall, presented all the plays in the Shakespeare First Folio between 1953 and 1958. It was the first home of the National Theatre company in 1962–76.

**Old Wives' Tale, The** A novel by **Arnold Bennett**, published in 1908.

The lives of two sisters, Constance and Sophia, are the focus of a study of the Baines family, prosperous drapers of Bursley in the Potteries. The story starts in 1860 and ends in about 1906 with the sisters' deaths. 'Mrs Baines', the first of four parts, shows the domestic and commercial struggles of a family in which the father is bedridden. Constance's restricted ambitions, her marriage to the Baineses' apprentice, Samuel Povey, and motherhood, are densely elaborated through Parts One and Two. The parallelism between her life and Sophia's, whose ambition to become a teacher is frustrated, is one component of a highly structured novel.

Constance is left in lonely widowhood when her son Cyril departs to a London art college.

Part Three recapitulates the life of Sophia. We are told of her elopement with Gerald Scales, a glamorous commercial traveller; his desertion of her in Paris; her survival of the Siege of Paris in the Franco-Prussian War; and her achievement of independence as proprietor of the Pension Frensham.

After an exchange of letters, an elderly Sophia returns to the same house in Bursley to live with her sister. Sophia's journey to Manchester, where she is too late to speak to the dying Gerald Scales, strikes a grim keynote to this concluding section, 'What Life Is'.

**Old Wives' Tale, The** A play by **George Peele**, published in 1595. It is usually regarded as Peele's best dramatic work.

Delia has been stolen by the wicked magician Sacrapant and her two brothers are searching for her. But the brothers also fall victim and a gallant knight, Sir Eumenides, sets out to rescue them. Sir Eumenides is aided in his quest by Jack's ghost – Jack was a poor man and when he died Sir Eumenides had borne the cost of a dignified funeral for him. The quest is successful, the magician defeated, and Delia and her brothers rescued.

The play is a satire on the romantic drama of the time, parodying all its absurdities and impossible unreal characters. See also *The Knight of the Burning Pestle*. **Milton** used the basis of the plot for his masque *Comus*.

**Oldham, John** 1653–83 Satirical poet. The son of a Nonconformist minister, Oldham was born at Shipton-Moyne in Gloucestershire. He was educated at Tetbury Grammar School and St Edmund Hall, Oxford, earning his living as a teacher after graduating in 1674.

Oldham impressed contemporaries (**Dryden** among them) as a poet of great promise and his early death from smallpox was mourned as a serious loss to literature. His chief works were *A Satire upon a Woman, Who by Her Falsehood and Scorn Was the Death of My Friend* (1678), *A Satire Against Virtue* (1679) and four *Satires upon the Jesuits* (1681), all written in the aftermath of the discovery of the 'Popish Plot' by Titus Oates. The manner is confident, the matter (especially in the attacks on the Jesuits) aggressive in the extreme. Oldham had a propensity for roughness of effect and for the stylistic excesses of his age. Perhaps Dryden's tribute was earned by Oldham's other works: the ode *Upon the Works of Ben Jonson*, the satires in the manner of Horace and the two translations from Juvenal. His *Poems and Translations*, which appeared in the year of his death, was widely read until the early 18th century.

**Oldmixon, John** 1673–1742 Whig historian. Born at Axbridge in Somerset, he was privately educated in the household of Admiral Blake and later succeeded to the manor of Oldmixon near Bridgwater. His career as a historian began with *A Complete History of England, With the Lives of All the Kings and Queens Thereof to the Death of William III*, which he edited; it was published in 1706 and again, with additions, in 1716. More important was *The British Empire in America* (1708), the first history of that subject. *The Secret History of Europe* (4 vols., 1712–15) was unsparing in its criticism of the Tory party for its willingness to reach agreement with the French. To the third edition (1727) of the *Critical History of England* (2 vols., 1724–6) Oldmixon added an 'Essay on Criticism' that revealed his own fiercely anti-Tory bias and made him the target for **Pope** and other hostile wits. *The History of England During the Reigns of the Royal House of Stuart* (1730) is regarded by some scholars as his best work; it states at length the reason for believing that the Oxford editors of **Clarendon**'s *History of the Rebellion and Civil Wars in England* meddled with the text for political reasons.

**Oldtown Folks** A novel by **Harriet Beecher Stowe**, published in 1869, and set in the fictional Oldtown, Massachusetts, during the post-Revolutionary period. The young Horace Holyoke narrates the rather conventional romance plot about two runaway children who find happiness in spite of their oppressive upbringing in a leading Oldtown family. Holyoke's spiritual turn of mind makes him particularly attentive to the town's religious life. Both children are adopted into clerical families. The boy, Henry, becomes an Anglican minister. Tina marries Davenport, a dashing aristocratic officer, but when Davenport is killed in a duel she eventually marries Holyoke. Other memorable citizens are Parson and 'Lady' Lothrop, and Sam Lawson, whose offhanded commentary provides the novel's comic perspective.

**Oliphant, Laurence** 1829–88 Travel-writer and journalist. Born in Cape Town, Laurence Oliphant became a barrister in Ceylon where his father was Chief Justice, but was chiefly interested in travel and adventure. He published *Journey to Khatmandu* (1852) and *The Russian Shores of the Black Sea* (1853); later he was consulted as an authority upon the outbreak of the Crimean War. He was Lord Elgin's secretary in the USA and Canada (1853–4) and published *Minnesota and the Far West* in 1855. As a correspondent for *The Times* he covered certain aspects of the Crimean War, the Indian Mutiny, and the Risorgimento.

Oliphant accompanied Lord Elgin to the Far East, published a *Narrative of the Earl of Elgin's Mission to China and Japan in the Years 1857, 58, 59* (1859), and sent dispatches to *The Times* from the Franco-Prussian War. To all this can be added a pleasantly satirical novel about London life, *Piccadilly*, which was published in **Blackwood's Magazine** in 1865.

In 1867 Oliphant became so besotted with an American 'prophet', Thomas Lake Harris, that he surrendered his property to him. He went to America with Harris, and with his wife produced a strange book, *Sympneumata* (1885), which they believed to have been dictated by a spirit. Disillusioned with Harris, he removed to Palestine where he founded a community of Jewish immigrants at Haifa, eventually returning to die in England. Oliphant was one of the most remarkable travel-writers his age produced. The autobiographical *Episodes of a Life of Adventure* was published in 1887, after appearing in *Blackwood's Magazine*. His *Life* (1892) was written by his cousin **Margaret Oliphant**.

**Oliphant, Margaret** 1828–97 Novelist and biographer. Born near Musselburgh, Margaret Wilson married her cousin, the artist Francis Wilson Oliphant. Her first novel, *Mrs Margaret Maitland* (1849), began a prolific career in literature extending to more than 100 books and some 200 contributions to **Blackwood's Magazine**. From the *Chronicles of Carlingford*, a series of novels dealing with Scottish life, *Salem Chapel* (1863) and *Miss Marjoribanks* (1866) received particular praise. Her other Scottish novels included *The Minister's Wife* (1869), *Effie Ogilvie* (1886) and *Kirsteen* (1890). *A Beleaguered City* (1880) is a story of the occult. She also wrote histories and biographies, notably a *Life* of her cousin **Laurence Oliphant** (1892) and *Annals of a Publishing House: William Blackwood and His Sons* (1897). Her *Autobiography* (1899) records her efforts to support her own and her brother's children through writing.

**Oliver Twist**, *or, The Parish Boy's Progress* A novel by **Charles Dickens**, first issued in monthly instalments in **Bentley's Miscellany** between February 1837 and April 1839. It was published in book form in 1838.

Oliver Twist is born in the workhouse, where his mother has been brought after being found half-dead in the street. She dies giving birth to him and, until he is nine, Oliver is placed in the care of Mrs Mann at a branch workhouse; then he is taken back by Mr Bumble, the parish beadle, to the workhouse proper. After outraging the authorities by daring to 'ask for more', Oliver is apprenticed to an undertaker, where he is no better used than in the workhouse. He runs away and meets the Artful Dodger (Jack Dawkins), who takes him to Fagin's den in the London slums. Fagin has a stable of boys being trained to steal; his associates are the coarse and brutal burglar Bill Sikes and Nancy, a prostitute.

'Oliver introduced to the respectable Old Gentleman.' George Cruikshank's illustration for *Oliver Twist* depicts Fagin, the Artful Dodger and, right, Oliver.

Oliver is rescued by the benevolent Mr Brownlow but the gang of thieves kidnaps him; prompted by the villainous Monks, they have a special interest in keeping him. They send him out with Bill Sikes to break into a house, but the thieves are surprised and Oliver is shot. The lady of the house, Mrs Maylie, is horrified to discover that the wounded burglar is only a child; she and her adopted daughter Rose take care of Oliver, nursing him back to health.

Nancy, meanwhile, has learned that there is something about Oliver's origins that Monks wants to suppress. She visits Rose Maylie and warns her that Fagin is being bribed by Monks to corrupt Oliver and that there is some relationship between Rose herself and Oliver. With the help of Mr Brownlow, enquiries are begun. Nancy's betrayal is discovered by the gang and Bill Sikes murders her. In the hue and cry that follows he hangs himself accidentally and Fagin and the rest are taken. Monks is investigated by Mr Brownlow and his motives at last revealed: he is Oliver's half-brother, greedily seeking the whole inheritance for himself. Rose Maylie is Oliver's aunt. Fagin is hanged at the end of the story and Oliver is adopted by Mr Brownlow.

Although Dickens wrote *Oliver Twist* while he was finishing **The Pickwick Papers** and editing *Bentley's Miscellany*, the novel is remarkable for its clarity of purpose and its sustained intensity. One aim, as the preface made clear, was to correct the glamorous portrayal of criminals in the popular **Newgate fiction** of the day by showing the sordid reality of the London underworld. Another was to attack the harsh inhumanity of the New Poor Law of 1834. In later years Dickens used an edited version of the murder of Nancy and Sikes's flight from justice in his successful public readings.

**Olsen, Tillie** 1913– American short-story writer and novelist. Her first book, a collection of stories entitled *Tell Me A Riddle* (1962), published when she was nearly 50, draws on her experiences as a working-class wife, mother, wage-earner, and labour activist in San Francisco. The title story, an often anthologized feminist classic, portrays a working-class grandmother at the end of her life retrospectively reviewing her early political and personal aspirations and their gradual fragmentation and frustration by the competing claims of her role as wife and mother. In 1974 Olsen published a novel, *Yonnondio: From The Thirties*, reconstructed from a manuscript begun some 40 years earlier but abandoned and then lost. It is the story, seen through the eyes of a young girl, of a poor family's journey from a mining town to a tenant farm to the slums of an industrial city in an unsuccessful search for a way out of poverty and despair, an unrelenting analysis of the economic roots of oppression. Olsen's collection of essays, *Silences* (1978), draws on both personal and literary sources to explain how social and economic pressures prevent members of oppressed groups from becoming writers.

**Olson, Charles** 1910–70 American poet, born in Worcester, Massachusetts, and educated at Harvard, Yale and Wesleyan Universities. In 1948 he took a position at the experimental Black Mountain College in North Carolina, and from 1951 to 1956 was rector there. Early in his tenure he published an essay entitled 'Projective Verse' (1950), in which he advocated the use of 'open forms' and 'composition by field', arguing that the structure of lines should not be determined by metrical feet but by the breath of the poet. The essay was widely influential and attracted a number of poets to the college, including **Robert Creeley**, **Denise Levertov** and **Robert Duncan**; they became known as the **Black Mountain school**.

Olson's major poetic work, the Maximus Poems, began to appear in 1953. Like **William Carlos Williams**'s *Paterson* the Maximus Poems focused on a single town – in this case, Gloucester, Massachusetts – in which the central figure, Maximus, attempts to discover the energies which shape both personal and social history. The various volumes of the project are *The Maximus Poems 1–10* (1953), *The Maximus Poems 11–22* (1956), a single edition containing poems 1–22 simply entitled *The Maximus Poems* (1960), *Maximus, from Dogtown I* (1961), *Maximus Poems IV, V, VI* (1968) and the posthumously published *The Maximus Poems: Volume Three* (1975). The first complete edition of the series was published in 1983.

Olson's other books of verse include *To Corrado Cagli* (1947), *y & x* (1948), *Letter for Melville* (1951), *This* (1952), *In Cold Hell, in Thicket* (1953), *O'Ryan 1 2 3 4 5 6 7 8 9 10*

(1965), *Selected Writings* (1967), *Archaeologist of Morning: The Collected Poems Outside the Maximus Series* (1970). His prose works include *Mayan Letters* (1953), *Human Universe and Other Essays* (1965), *Causal Mythology* (1969) and *The Special View of History* (1970). *Projective Verse* (1959) and *Poetry and Truth: The Beloit Lectures and Poems* (1971) are books of criticism.

**Omnium, Jacob** See **Higgins, Matthew**.

*Omoo*: *a Narrative of Adventures in the South Seas* A novel by **Herman Melville**, published in 1847, and inspired by the author's second whaling voyage, which was beset by a dry whaling season, a sick captain, and an unsuccessful mutiny. A sequel to the controversial *Typee* and accepted only reluctantly by the publisher, it incited new attacks by critics who objected to Melville's depiction of the failure of missionary work in Tahiti.

The nameless narrator is rescued from the sea after his flight from the Marquesas and signs on the crew of the *Julia*, the ship whose boat has picked him up. The *Julia* proves to be unseaworthy and her captain ill and unstable, but the narrator makes friends with the mate, Jermin, and with the worldly and cheerful Dr Long Ghost. In Tahiti the crew members refuse to take the ship to sea again and are imprisoned. The narrator and the doctor are released and manage to find work on a plantation in Imeeo. Finding that fieldwork is not to their liking, they resort to beachcombing, at the same time exploring the island and observing the people. At the end the doctor stays on in Tahiti while the narrator ships out on the whaler *Leviathan*.

**O'Neill, Eugene (Gladstone)** 1888–1953 American playwright, born in New York City, the younger son of James O'Neill, a popular actor. As a child he toured with his father, and attended a Catholic boarding school and a preparatory school in Connecticut. He enrolled at Princeton University for one year (1906–7), then held a series of jobs including prospecting for gold, several months as a seaman on a Norwegian freighter and a brief spell as a journalist in Connecticut. He then spent time in a tuberculosis sanatorium (1912–13), and his early one-act plays date from this period of confinement. His involvement with the Provincetown Players brought him, and the company, to the attention of the New York public, initially with a sequence of plays about the SS *Glencairn* and its crew: *Bound East for Cardiff* (1916), *In the Zone* (1917), *The Long Voyage Home* (1917) and *The Moon of the Caribees* (1918). Two other plays, not in the Glencairn cycle but drawing on his memories of life at sea, won Pulitzer Prizes in 1920 and 1922 – *Beyond the Horizon* (1920) and

Eugene O'Neill.

*Anna Christie* (1921, first produced as *Chris* in 1920).

O'Neill went on to become a major influence on the development of the modern American theatre, exploring difficult subjects and experimenting with a variety of dramatic styles. Black Americans made up the cast of *The Dreamy Kid* (1919); an interracial marriage is the subject of *All God's Chillun Got Wings* (1924); and in *The Emperor Jones* (1920) a black actor dominates the stage in the central role. The expressionism of *The Emperor Jones* is further developed in *The Hairy Ape* (1922), in which a ship's stoker's alienation from his peers causes him to embrace his own animality, and in the mask-drama *The Great God Brown* (1926). *Strange Interlude* (1928), which won O'Neill a third Pulitzer Prize, portrays the life of its central character, Nina Leeds, through the juxtaposition of conventional dialogue with stylized internal monologue. O'Neill's interest in the familial patterns of Greek tragedy and in Nietzsche's opposition of the Apollonian and the Dionysian is evident in the grim New England tragedy *Desire Under the Elms* (1924), and is the motive force behind *Mourning Becomes Electra* (1931), a reworking of Aeschylus' *Oresteia* in the context of the American Civil War.

After the failure of *Days Without End* (1934), O'Neill, suffering from increasing ill-health which was eventually diagnosed as Parkinson's disease, maintained a long theatrical silence, unbroken by the award of the Nobel Prize in 1936. *The Iceman Cometh* (1946), his first new play to be performed for 12 years, is set in a

Bowery bar. *Long Day's Journey Into Night* (first performed 1956, Pulitzer Prize 1957) is a tortured but compassionate portrait of his own family, a subject he had treated more lightly and with nostalgia in the comedy *Ah, Wilderness!* (1933). *A Moon for the Misbegotten* (first performed 1957) continues the story of the alcoholic elder brother of *Long Day's Journey Into Night*, describing the process of his self-destruction on a Connecticut farm following his mother's death. Of a projected 11-play cycle which was to trace the fortunes of an American family from the 18th to the 20th centuries, only *A Touch of the Poet* (first performed 1957) and the incomplete *More Stately Mansions* (first performed 1962) were actually written. *Hughie*, the single play of another projected series, was first performed in 1958.

***On Liberty*** An essay by **John Stuart Mill**, first published in 1859. He regarded it as the most important of his works. One of his earliest articles had been in support of the freedom of speech and publication which was a Benthamite pre-requisite for good government. By 1859 Mill had realized, partly as a result of reading de Tocqueville's ***Democracy in America***, that democracy did not of itself guarantee freedom; public opinion might be as repressive of minority rights as any other form of dictatorship. He therefore sought to devise a principle by which individual liberty might be legitimated and interference with this liberty limited only to those occasions where its exercise might involve harm to others.

***On Murder Considered as One of the Fine Arts*** An essay in black humour by **Thomas De Quincey**, published in ***Blackwood's Magazine*** in 1827, and followed by a *Supplementary Paper* in the same periodical in 1839.

It purports to be the text of a lecture given in London at a meeting of the Society of Connoisseurs in Murder. After surveying the history of murder since Cain, the speaker addresses the 'Augustan Age of Murder' in the 17th and 18th centuries, before subjecting a number of recently committed murders to detailed aesthetic criticism, based absurdly but logically on **Burke**'s conceptions of the 'sublime'. In defending himself against the charge that his remarks could be taken as an incitement to murder, the speaker argues his purpose to oppose it: 'For once a man indulges in murder, very soon he comes to think little of robbing, and from robbing he comes next to drinking and Sabbath-breaking, and from that to incivility and procrastination.' The sustained poker-faced seriousness of the piece invites comparison with **Swift**, though its sequel featuring the Society's celebration dinner degenerates into rather laboured buffoonery.

***On the Road*** A semi-autobiographical novel by **Jack Kerouac**, published in 1957. One of the most fundamental and popular statements of the **Beat** movement, it tells of a group of friends travelling around America in search of new and intense experiences. The chaos, exhilaration and despair of the quest is conveyed by the headlong style of Sal Paradise's narration. Sal accompanies his friends on four separate trips as they travel the country, spending time in Colorado, California, Virginia, New York and Mexico. Several of the characters are modelled on Kerouac's friends: Dean Moriarty, the guiding spirit of the group, is Neal Cassady; Carlo Marx is **Allen Ginsberg**.

**Ondaatje, Michael** 1943– Poet. Born in Sri Lanka, he was educated at Dulwich College in England and at Bishop's University in Quebec, the University of Toronto and Queen's University, Kingston, Ontario, before becoming a university lecturer. His published work, often dealing with the macabre and bizarre, includes the verse collections *The Dainty Monsters* (1967), *The Man with Seven Toes* (1969), *The Left-Handed Poems: Collected Works of Billy the Kid* (1970), *Rat Jelly* (1973) and *There's a Trick With a Knife I'm Learning to Do* (1979). Among his prose works are *Coming Through Slaughter* (1979) and *Running in the Family* (1982). His most recent novel, *In the Skin of a Lion* (1987), is set in Toronto in the 1920s and 1930s.

***One Flew Over the Cuckoo's Nest*** A novel by **Ken Kesey**, published in 1962, about the inmates of a psychiatric ward. The story is told from the viewpoint of an ex-reservation Indian named Bromden, who pretends to be deaf and dumb. The inmates are kept in place by their dread of Big Nurse. Into this scene comes the reckless, ingenious and defiant McMurphy. Under his leadership the inmates rebel against Big Nurse, the climax – and McMurphy's triumph – coming when they sneak out for a trip on a yacht. However, McMurphy has a lobotomy performed on him by the doctors. Bromden cannot bear to see him in this state. He smothers him out of rage and pity and then heaves a panel of medical equipment through a window to make his escape.

***One of Our Conquerors*** A novel by **George Meredith**, published in 1891.

Nesta Victoria is the illegitimate daughter of Victor Radnor and Natalia Dreighton. Victor's wife, a rich elderly woman to whom Natalia was once companion, is still alive and his life with Natalia is haunted by the fear of exposure. Nesta's suitor, the Hon. Dudley Sowerby, is unenthusiastic when he learns the story of her birth and of her determination to continue her friendship with the hapless Mrs Marsett, the mistress of an army officer. Natalia, also unhappy about her daughter's friendship, falls ill during the crisis and dies. Victor receives news of his wife's death within a few hours of Natalia's passing. The cruel irony of this, and the loss of Natalia, unhinge his mind. Victor lives for a few years, while Nesta eventually marries a more worthy suitor, Dartrey Fenellan.

**onomatopoeia** The formation of a word by imitation of a sound associated with the thing described; for example, 'hurlyburly', 'lullabye', and many of our words for animal calls.

**Opie, Amelia (née Alderson)** 1769–1853 Novelist and poet. Born in Norwich, she inherited radical opinions from her father and in youth became a friend and admirer of **William Godwin** and **Mary Wollstonecraft**. She turned to writing in earnest after her marriage to the painter John Opie in 1798, producing much popular fiction and poetry. Her novels included *Father and Daughter* (1801), *Adeline Mowbray* (suggested by Mary Wollstonecraft's life, 1802) and *Simple Tales* (1806). Their subject is usually domestic, their tone moral and sentimental. After her husband's death in 1807 she returned to Norwich, continuing her career with *Valentine's Eve* (1816) and *Madeline* (1822). She stopped writing novels after her conversion to Quakerism in 1825, but continued to find the lure of literary society irresistible and remained a friend of many leading figures of the day. In later life she devoted much of her energy to the Bible Society and the Anti-Slavery Society. Her last book, a volume of poetry, was *Lays for the Dead* (1833).

**Opie, Peter (Mason)** 1918–82 and **Opie, Iona (Margaret Balfour, née Archibald)** 1923– British folklorists and anthologists. Born in Cairo the son of a doctor but educated in England, Peter Opie married Iona, herself the daughter of an expert on tropical diseases, in 1943. After the birth of their first child in 1944 the couple decided to concentrate on the culture of childhood, producing *I Saw Esau* (1947), a collection of children's skipping and singing rhymes. Their next project was *The Oxford Dictionary of Nursery Rhymes* (1951), an annotated collection that singlehandedly demolished the various false historical interpretations that Mother Goose has always managed to attract over the years. Next, for children alone, came *The Oxford Nursery Rhyme Book* (1955) and *The Puffin Book of Nursery Rhymes* (1963). Meanwhile, their *The Lore and Language of Schoolchildren* (1959) recorded the rhymes, chants and teases popular all over Britain, with *Children's Games in Street and Playground* (1969) doing the same for various non-verbal favourites. The

*Oxford Book of Children's Verse* (1973) collected poems written about rather than by children, and *The Classic Fairy Tales* (1974) reissued some of the most famous of these stories as they first appeared, with a discussion of how and why they were often to change so radically over time. *The Singing Game* (1985) is a masterly survey of another aspect of children's oral culture, completed by Mrs Opie after her husband's death.

**Oppen, George** 1908–84 American poet, born in New Rochelle, New York. His first volume of poems, *Discrete Series*, was published in 1934; his second, *The Materials*, not until 1962. He became a member of the Communist party in 1935, and in 1950 he moved to Mexico to escape pressure from the US government to inform on friends in the Party. He was closely associated with the **Objectivist** school, and was instrumental in providing a forum for new poets through the publishing house (called 'To Publishers') which he founded and operated with his wife from 1930 to 1933. During the next 15 years he worked in a factory in Detroit and as a cabinet-maker in Los Angeles.

He was particularly concerned with how poetry should communicate the realization of concrete objects without drawing attention to itself, formally, as poetry – as artefact. His own verse is characterized by its clarity of images and its lean and precise diction. His other volumes include *This in Which* (1965), *Of Being Numerous* (1968, Pulitzer Prize), *Alpine* (1969), *Seascape: Needle's Eye* (1972) and *Primitive* (1978). *The Collected Poems of George Oppen, 1929–1975* was published in 1975. In 1980 he received the American Academy and Institute of Arts and Letters award.

**Orage, A. R.** See *New Age, The*.

**Orczy, Baroness (Emma Magdalena Rosalia Marie Josefa Barbara)** 1865–1947 Novelist, short-story writer and playwright. Born in Hungary, she was educated in Brussels and Paris and arrived in London with her parents at the age of 15. She studied art and married a fellow student, Montagu Barstow, in 1894. Her fame as a writer of historical romance was established with *The Scarlet Pimpernel*, which introduced her hero, Sir Percy Blakeney, and his exploits rescuing victims from the guillotine during the French Revolution. Written in 1902, the novel was rejected by several publishers and Baroness Orczy had already dramatized it successfully in collaboration with her husband before its first publication in 1905. Its many popular sequels included *I Will Repay* (1906) and *The Elusive Pimpernel* (1908). Baroness Orczy also wrote **detective fiction**, notably in her ingenious stories about 'The Old Man in the Corner' (*The Case of*

*Miss Elliott*, 1905; *The Old Man in the Corner*, 1909; *Unravelled Knots*, 1925) and less successfully in *Lady Molly of Scotland Yard* (1910).

**Ordeal of Richard Feverel, The** A novel by **George Meredith**, published in 1859.

Deserted by his wife, Sir Austin Feverel brings up his son Richard in his own way. Believing all schools to be corrupt, he educates the boy at home. But when Richard reaches adolescence he confounds his father by falling in love with Lucy Desborough, niece of a local farmer. Sir Austin acknowledges her quality but opposes the match because of her humble birth, and the two young people marry in secret.

Richard is devoted to his father, who now ruthlessly manipulates the boy's feelings to separate him from Lucy. Sir Austin sends Richard to London, where his friend Lord Mountfalcon, who has designs on Lucy, puts Richard in the path of a 'fallen' woman of considerable allure. Thinking to redeem her, Richard is easily seduced. He prolongs his absence from home and goes abroad, ashamed of his infidelity. He then learns that he is a father; moreover, Sir Austin is at last reconciled to Lucy as his daughter-in-law through the good offices of Richard's uncle, Wentworth. Richard hurries home. But just when happiness seems to be within his grasp, he discovers Lord Mountfalcon's villainy, challenges him to a duel and is seriously wounded. Lucy loses her reason and dies.

**Oregon Trail, The** The record of a journey by **Francis Parkman** and his cousin Quincy Adams Shaw in 1846, published serially in *The Knickerbocker Magazine* from 1847 to 1849. It appeared in volume form as *The California and Oregon Trail* in 1849, but the 1872 edition restored the original title.

Parkman and Shaw set out from St Louis in April 1846 to explore portions of the northern Great Plains and Rocky Mountains. Travelling

An illustration by Frederic Remington for Parkman's *The Oregon Trail*. 'The Hunting Camp'.

along both the Mormon and Oregon trails, as far west as Fort Laramie, Wyoming, they encountered wagon trains of emigrants, Indians, Mormons, hunters, trappers, traders and buffalo. Excited by rumours that a Sioux chief, 'The Whirlwind' (Tunica), was planning to make war against the Snake Indians, Parkman planned to witness the event and was disappointed when the attack was called off. Leaving Shaw behind, he joined a band of 'Ogillallah' (Oglala) Sioux for a hunting excursion and lived among them for several weeks. Early in August he rejoined Shaw at Fort Laramie and they began their return trip. They travelled south through Colorado, heading towards the Arkansas River, then journeyed eastward along the Arkansas to Missouri, arriving in St Louis in late September.

**Origin of Species, The** A work of natural history by **Charles Darwin**, first published in 1859.

*On the Origin of Species By Means of Natural Selection, or the Preservation of Favoured Races in the Struggle for Life* went through six editions between 1859 and 1872. Darwin responded to objections to his theories of evolutionary process by revising extensively between editions. This book is, with Marx's *Capital*, probably the work which has most transformed the explanatory systems of the past hundred years. In *The Origin* Darwin argues for a theory of 'descent with modification', an apparently modest proposal with extraordinarily far-reaching implications. Species, according to his argument, are not fixed and eternal; rather, in the long history of the physical world many forms have passed away and their offspring have diverged more and more widely from the parent-type. Darwin argues for a 'single progenitor' of life on earth, an irrecoverable form far removed from any current type; he argues further that few current types will survive far into the future. Change has been slow, though probably increasing in pace. Several mechanisms of change, including sexual selection, have operated over the immense time-span of the earth's history. Darwin's most radically innovative idea of agency he called 'natural selection'. 'Artificial selection', or husbandry, has demonstrated (he argues) that it is possible within a few generations to breed plants and creatures whose selected characteristics have advantages for the breeder. 'Natural selection', on the contrary, works unconsciously and to the advantage only of the individual and its progeny within a species, never in order to benefit other species. Natural selection relies on the appropriateness of the organism to its current environment – which, being composed of many forces, is itself unstable. So advantage in one environment will be disadvantage in changed circumstances. Natural selection works by means of descent and relies on variation: individual organisms vary in differing degrees and across a spectrum of characteristics from the parent-generation. Those variations most apt to current physical conditions will prosper and produce offspring, which will in turn vary one from another and in some cases will intensify advantageous characteristics. By this slow means the highly specialized skills of current species have evolved: 'from so simple a beginning endless forms most beautiful and most wonderful have been, and are being evolved' concludes the sixth edition.

Darwin's theory has been extrapolated into many fields and along often opposed consequential sequences. We meet its forms in race-theory, naturalism, musical history, literature, politics, though Darwin always insisted on its entirely biological reference. Most commentators have represented it as a theory of competition though it is now clearly recognized also as an ecological theory. Darwin's name, and mutated forms of his theory, are inescapable in late 19th- and 20th-century literature ranging from **Thomas Hardy** to **Doris Lessing**'s *Canopus in Argos* sequence of science-fiction novels.

**Orion** An epic poem by **R. H. Horne**, published in 1843 at the price of one farthing – a sum chosen, according to **Elizabeth Barrett Browning**, as a satirical comment on the value which contemporary society attached to poetry. The author was subsequently nicknamed 'Orion' Horne, or 'the farthing poet'.

**Orlando** A fantasy novel by **Virginia Woolf**, published in 1928.

Sub-titled 'A Biography' and dedicated to **V. Sackville-West**, the novel traces the career of the androgynous Orlando from the late 16th century to the present day, and contains a great many well-observed literary and historical insights into the ages through which it sweeps.

As a handsome boy of 16, Orlando turns to poetry and completes 'Æthelbert: A Tragedy in Five Acts'. He becomes a favourite of Queen Elizabeth I, who confers on him the Order of the Garter, and the lover of a Muscovite princess. Later he retires from society, writes 'forty-seven plays, histories, romances, poems', and enjoys the company of the irreverent English poet, Nicholas Greene.

Under Charles II, Orlando becomes Ambassador Extraordinary to Constantinople and is rewarded with a dukedom. Then, after spending one night with a dancer, Rosina Pepita, he sleeps for a week and wakes to find that his sex has changed. Lady Orlando now pursues a career in high society through Queen Anne's reign, meeting **Pope**, **Addison** and **Swift**, until (as a Victorian) she eventually marries a sailor, Marmaduke Bonthrop Shelmerdine. Nicholas Greene reappears as the most influential critic of

the Victorian age and arranges for the publication of Orlando's centuries-old poem 'The Oak Tree', which subsequently wins her 200 guineas. She gives birth to a baby, and the novel reaches the present day; as at the beginning, Orlando is a young poet, but this time a female one. The novel ends with her driving back from town to her ancestral home in Kent.

**Orley Farm** A novel by **Anthony Trollope**, published in 20 monthly parts, from March 1861 to October 1862.

Orley Farm is part of the estate of Sir Joseph Mason. Late in life Sir Joseph remarries and a son, Lucius, is born. When he dies Sir Joseph's will leaves the bulk of his estate to his son Joseph by his first wife and, in a codicil, Orley Farm to Lucius. Joseph contests the validity of the codicil but the law upholds it, and the widowed Lady Mason and her son Lucius live there in comfortable circumstances for 20 years. Then one of Lady Mason's tenants, Dockwrath, an attorney of dubious character, is given notice to quit. Feeling unjustly used, Dockwrath reopens the matter of the codicil, and tells Joseph Mason that another document exists signed by his father on the same day as the codicil. The witnesses declare that they signed only one

'Guilty.' Lady Mason confesses her forgery to Sir Peregrine Orme in *Orley Farm*. An illustration by John Everett Millais in Vol. II of Trollope's novel, 1862.

document, though the signatures on both that and the codicil are the same. Lady Mason's friends rally round to support her, and her elderly lover, Sir Peregrine Orme, will not swerve from his belief in her probity. Everything points to forgery, however, and Lady Mason is plainly under severe strain.

The case is brought: Mr Chaffanbrass appears for Lady Mason and all goes in her favour. But her apparently unshakeable resolution breaks down after the trial, and she confesses everything to Sir Peregrine Orme. Orley Farm reverts to Joseph Mason.

The characters of Joseph Mason and his stepmother Lady Mason, so sharply contrasted, are consistent and totally believable; so are the former's resentment, smouldering for 20 years, and the strain on the latter, held at bay for the same period until her resolution is exhausted. The commercial travellers, Kantwise and Moulder, are fascinating representations of one level of the commercial life of the period.

*Ormulum* A series of verse **homilies** written in the early 13th century in the North-east Midlands. In a dedication the author identifies himself as Orm, saying that he is an Augustinian canon writing at the request of his brother Walter, also an Augustinian canon. He says that he will give in English the gospels of the mass book for the entire year, each accompanied by its interpretations and applications. The table of contents lists 242 homilies of which only 32 are extant; the series was probably never finished. The work has no literary merit, but is remarkable for its orthography, the most striking feature of which is the consistent doubling of consonants after a short vowel.

*Oroonoko, or, The Royal Slave* A novel by **Aphra Behn**, published *c.*1678 and included in *Three Histories* (1688). It was adapted for the stage by **Thomas Southerne** in 1695 and enjoyed considerable further success.

Oroonoko, the grandson and heir of an African king, loves the beautiful Imoinda, daughter of the king's general. But the old king himself falls in love with Imoinda and commands that she be taken to his harem. When he discovers that she loves his grandson, he instead has her sold as a slave. The grieving Oroonoko is captured by an English slaver and sold in Surinam, where he finds Imoinda, also a slave. Oroonoko rouses the other slaves and inspires them to make an escape. They are hunted, and eventually induced to surrender to Byam, the deputy governor, on promise of a pardon. But Byam, once he has Oroonoko in his hands, has him flogged. Determined to exact retribution from Byam, Oroonoko realizes that he will not escape the consequences of killing him. At the same time he knows what will happen to Imoinda when he is no longer there to protect her. She understands and surrenders her life to Oroonoko, who is discovered near her body; he is prevented from taking his own life and executed with savage cruelty.

In Southerne's dramatized version Byam is motivated by his passion for Imoinda, and there is a comic sub-plot.

Mrs Behn's novel was the first expression in English literature of sympathy for the plight of slaves, and the author is thought to have had some first-hand experience of Surinam.

*Orphan, The, or, The Unhappy Marriage* A tragedy by **Thomas Otway**, first produced in 1680 and published the same year. The principal parts were played by Thomas Betterton and Elizabeth Barry.

Acasto has brought up Monimia, the orphan daughter of a friend, with his own twin sons, Castalio and Polydore. Monimia's brother, Chamont, is a soldier. The twin brothers have both fallen in love with Monimia; she loves Castalio, but from consideration of Polydore's feelings Castalio pretends indifference. Visiting his sister, Chamont believes that her disturbed emotions can be blamed on one of the twins, but his questions annoy her. Castalio declares his love, and he and Monimia are secretly married.

Polydore does not know of the secret marriage; he overhears his brother arranging to meet Monimia during the night and contrives to take his brother's place. Monimia accepts him and Castalio, arriving later, finds himself barred from his wife's room. The deception is eventually revealed by Chamont, and the three unhappy lovers kill themselves.

*Orpheus and Eurydice* A Middle Scots poem by **Robert Henryson**. It adapts the classical story of Orpheus and Eurydice as a moral allegory of the vulnerability of affection and the relationship between reason and affection. The juxtaposition of narrative and moral is in places discordant, as in *The Morall Fabillis*. The poem has some affinities with both classical and medieval renderings of the story of Orpheus, but is not closely dependent on either. Although there are some powerful lyric and descriptive passages, characterization is minimal, the narrative being subordinated to the moral allegory.

**Ortiz, Simon** 1941– American Indian poet and short-story writer, born in Albuquerque, New Mexico, raised in the Acoma Pueblo community, and educated at Ft Lewis College, the University of New Mexico and the University of Iowa. All his work reflects a strong concern for Indian civil rights. His volumes of poetry include *Naked in the Wind* (1970), *Going for the Rain* (1976), *Fight Back: For the Sake of the People, For the Sake of the Land* (1980) and *From Sand*

*Creek* (1981). His volumes of stories include *Howbah Indians* (1977).

**Orton, Joe (Kingsley)** 1933–67 Playwright and actor. Born in Leicester, he trained at the Royal Academy of Dramatic Art. Orton's exuberant tastelessness established him as a pioneer of a style of black farce. His first plays, *The Ruffian on the Stair* (1964) and *Entertaining Mr Sloane* (1964), derived from **Pinter** the idea of showing how the familiar inhabitants of a room can be menaced by a stranger's intrusion, but Orton's language was already distinct from the studied naturalness of Pinter. He admired the combination of elegance and crudity that he found in the work of the French playwright, Jean Genet, and it was this combination that characterized his best work. In *Loot* (1966), a mother's corpse becomes a comic property. In *The Erpingham Camp* (1967), Orton's malice towards professed religion culminates in an orgy of ritual destruction. In *What the Butler Saw* (1969), polished wit and artful mischief carry the farce tradition of threatened adultery into forbidden realms of incest and violence. Two years before this last play's performance, Orton was bloodily murdered by his male lover, who subsequently took his own life.

**Orwell, George** Pseudonym of Eric Arthur Blair (1903–50), novelist, essayist and journalist. Orwell was born in Bengal and educated in England at St Cyprian's and Eton. In 1922 he joined the Imperial Police in Burma, serving for five years before his mounting dislike of imperialism induced him to resign. He returned to a series of ill-paid jobs in Paris, then London, living in a state of 'fairly severe poverty' before becoming a regular contributor to *The Adelphi* from 1930. His first book, *Down and Out in Paris and London* (1933), described these early experiences and was followed by *Burmese Days* (1934), a novel which continued to reflect his indignation over political injustice.

Orwell's second novel, *A Clergyman's Daughter* (1935), about a middle-class woman's brief period of freedom among the tramps and hoppickers, was followed by *Keep the Aspidistra Flying* (1936), the story of a young bookseller's assistant, Gordon Comstock, whose aspirations and humiliations closely paralleled the author's.

In 1936 Orwell was commissioned by the publisher Victor Gollancz to produce a documentary account of unemployment in the north of England for the **Left Book Club**. The result was *The Road to Wigan Pier* (1937), a milestone in modern literary journalism which has become a classic of its kind. It established Orwell's political outlook as an unaligned democratic socialist, a position which he underlined in *Homage to Catalonia* (1938), about his experiences as a volunteer with the Republican army during the Spanish Civil War.

Under the threat of World War II Orwell wrote *Coming Up for Air* (1939), a novel which reflected in the person of George Bowling, an insurance clerk, many of the frustrations and political concerns which preoccupied Orwell throughout his life. From 1943 to 1945 he was literary editor of *Tribune* and contributed many articles to it and other papers, including *The Observer* and *The Manchester Evening News*. His lucid and colloquial style was ideally suited to journalism, and it was as a pamphleteer that his talents were most in evidence. As he himself admitted, he was not really a novelist: 'One has masses of experience which one passionately wants to write about . . . and no way of using them except by disguising them as a novel.' However, **Animal Farm** (1945) and **Nineteen Eighty-Four** (1949), his pessimistic satires about the threat of political tyranny, have remained his most popular works.

His essays (including *Inside the Whale*, 1940; *Critical Essays*, 1946; and *Shooting an Elephant*, 1950) are gathered in the four volumes of *Collected Essays, Journalism and Letters*, edited by Sonia Orwell and Ian Angus (1968) and contain over 200 pieces on literature, politics and English life.

Orwell's first wife, Eileen, died in 1945. He remarried in 1949, a year before he died of tuberculosis.

**Osborne, Dorothy** 1627–95 The wife of **Sir William Temple**. Her letters to him before their marriage were first published in 1888; a new edition, by G. C. Moore Smith, appeared in 1928.

**Osborne, John (James)** 1929– Playwright. Born in London and educated at a public school in Devon, Osborne wrote his first plays while working as an actor in English repertory theatres. **Look Back in Anger** (1956), the first of which he was sole author, was seen as the harbinger of a revolution in English drama and established Osborne as the leader of the **Angry Young Men**. Those who viewed it, on its first staging at the **Royal Court Theatre** in London, as an attack on British complacency have been disappointed by Osborne's subsequent plays, in which he is more often nostalgically disgruntled than angry. *The Entertainer* (1957) reflects the death of Edwardian values in the declining career of a music-hall comedian. *Luther* (1961) is a character study rather than a social thesis-play. *Inadmissible Evidence* (1964) takes its solicitor-hero through a draining process of self-recognition. *A Patriot for Me* (1966) is as much a spy-story as a study of decadence in the Austro-Hungarian Empire at the beginning of the 20th century. Osborne's other plays include *The Hotel in Amsterdam* (1968), *Time Present* (1968),

*West of Suez* (1971), *A Sense of Detachment* (1972), *The End of Me Old Cigar* (1975) and *Watch It Come Down* (1976). He is the author of a vigorous autobiography, *A Better Class of Person* (1981).

**O'Shaughnessy, Arthur William Edgar** 1844–81 Poet. Born in London and educated privately, O'Shaughnessy spent his working life in the British Museum and the Natural History Museum, where his subjects were fish and reptiles. **Rossetti** and other members of the **Pre-Raphaelite Brotherhood** were both friends and influences on his poetry. He published *An Epic of Women* (1870), *Lays of France* (1872), *Music and Moonlight* (1874) and, with his wife, a volume of verse for children, *Toyland* (1875). Today he is usually remembered only for the delicate 'Ode' in *Music and Moonlight* beginning 'We are the music-makers'.

**Ossian** See **Macpherson, James**.

**O'Sullivan, Vincent** 1937– New Zealand poet, story writer and critic. Educated at Auckland University and Oxford, he has taught at the Victoria University of Wellington and the University of the Waikato, and more recently has worked freelance as a writer, editor and teacher. He shares with **C. K. Stead** and others of the more academic New Zealand poets a self-conscious traveller's stance in many of his poems, though he registers the horrible more readily than most. His 'Butcher' persona, based on a device used by **James K. Baxter**, invests the ironic observer stance with the intensity of satire. A notably flamboyant wordsmith, he has published many books of poetry, beginning with *Our Burning Time* (1965), and including *Bearings* (1973), *Butcher & Co* (1976), *From the Indian Funeral* (1976), and *The Butcher Papers* (1982). His stories, which are technically less adventurous than his poems but dwell on similar moments of savagery, include *The Boy, The Bridge, The River* (1978).

***Othello, the Moor of Venice*** A tragedy by **William Shakespeare**, first performed *c.*1604 and published in Quarto (Q1) in 1622 as well as in the First Folio of 1623. The source is a story in the *Hecatommithi* of Giraldo Cinthio (1565).

Othello, a Moor who has become a trusted general of the Venetian army, has secretly married Desdemona, daughter of a senator, Brabantio. It is immediately revealed to the audience that Othello's ensign Iago, whom Othello believes to be utterly loyal and 'honest', is scheming against him, ostensibly but perhaps no more than partially, because Othello chose Michael Cassio as his lieutenant in preference to Iago. It is at Iago's prompting that Roderigo, a foolish suitor for Desdemona's hand, reports the marriage to Brabantio. The outraged father demands Othello's arrest, but has to accept the whole-heartedness of Desdemona's love when she appears before the senate. The news that the Turks are planning an attack on Cyprus requires Othello's immediate departure. He is joined in Cyprus by Desdemona, Iago, Cassio and Roderigo.

The dispersal of the Turkish fleet leaves Iago free to pursue his schemes in Cyprus. He contrives to discredit Cassio, whom Othello dismisses. Iago advises Cassio to appeal to Desdemona, and implants in Othello's mind a suspicion that Desdemona is more than friendly with Cassio. Her support of Cassio, together with Iago's torrent of innuendo, deepens the suspicion. Iago takes full advantage of Desdemona's accidental dropping of a handkerchief, the very one that Othello gave her as the first token of his love. He secretes it among Cassio's possessions, and the luckless Cassio gives it to his mistress, Bianca. When Othello sees the handkerchief in Bianca's possession, he is convinced of Desdemona's infidelity and humiliates her in public, to the dismay not least of Iago's increasingly troubled wife, Emilia.

Iago incites Roderigo to kill Cassio, but Roderigo manages only to wound him. Iago kills Roderigo to ensure his silence, and Othello, overwhelmed by the horror of a tarnished love, kills Desdemona. In the presence of Venetian emissaries, Emilia now tells the details that reveal Iago's guilt. Iago kills her, is wounded by Othello and escapes. The remorseful Othello stabs himself, the recaptured Iago is condemned to torture and prison, and Cassio is appointed to take command in Cyprus.

Whilst affairs of state are prominent in *Othello*, the domestic tragedy of a fine marriage vindictively destroyed is the play's dominant concern. This narrow focus makes the play unique among Shakespeare's great tragedies, but the towering achievement of both craft and imagination is the plotting and portrayal of the relationship between Iago and Othello. No attempt to explain the motives for Iago's malice can adequately account for its impact. An antagonism that masquerades as friendship is embodied even in the language of the two men. The manner in which Othello's rhetoric is mocked by the prosaic Iago has been the basis of many famous stage rivalries. Very few actors of Othello have been able to hold their own against the undermining thrusts of clever Iagos.

**ottava rima** A verse form using stanzas of eight lines, each with 11 syllables, rhyming abababcc. Italian in origin, it was much used by Tasso, Ariosto, Luigi Pulci and other Italian masters. The *ottava rima* entered English poetry in the Renaissance but did not fully come into its own until the Romantic period, when **Byron**

found it ideally suited to his needs. In his adaptation, the verse line is shortened to 10 syllables.

**Otuel and Roland** A Middle English **verse romance** in **tail-rhyme stanzas**, written before *c.*1330-40 in the East Midlands. It is based on the French romance *Otinel* and forms the second part of the compound romance *Charlemagne and Roland*, of which **Roland and Vernagu** is the first fragment. As a Saracen emissary Otuel delivers an insulting ultimatum to Charlemagne and is challenged by Roland. During the duel a dove alights on Otuel's helmet and he submits, becoming a Christian. He fights as a knight of Charlemagne's in the invasion of Lombardy. The last third of the romance continues the story of *Roland and Vernagu*. Charlemagne defeats the Saracens at Cordova and Navarre, and the story ends with the ambush at Roncesvalles and the emperor's subsequent defeat of the Saracens which form the subject matter of the Old French *chanson de geste*, *La Chanson de Roland*.

**Otway, Thomas** 1652–85 Playwright. Born in Sussex and educated at Winchester and Oxford, Otway failed as an actor some years before he succeeded as a playwright. His first two plays, *Alcibiades* (1675) and *Don Carlos* (1676), are tragedies in the then-dominant style of rhymed couplets and elevated rhetoric, but there are signs, particularly in *Don Carlos*, of a more

Thomas Otway. A detail from the portrait attributed to Soest (undated) in the Poet's Parlour at Knole, where hang several paintings of Restoration poets.

delicate and intimate approach to the creation of character under duress. It is Otway's emotional honesty, together with his satiric denial of hope, that distinguishes his finest tragedies, **The Orphan** (1680) and **Venice Preserved** (1682). Written in sensitive response to their Jacobean models, and benefiting from Otway's encounter with the work of Racine (whose *Bérénice* he had adapted as *Titus and Berenice* in 1676), they are among the finest English blank-verse tragedies. Otway's comedies have not lasted as well, though his adaptation of Molière's *The Cheats of Scapin* (1676) was popular in its time. The plots of *The Soldier's Fortune* (1680) and its sequel, *The Atheist* (1683), are too flimsy to carry the burden of Otway's cynicism. Unable to secure a patron, despite the esteem in which he was held, Otway died in poverty. His unrequited love for the actress, Elizabeth Barry, for whom he wrote several of his finest female characters, is recorded among the *Familiar Letters* collected by Tom Brown and Charles Gildon (2 vols., 1697), which also show the independence of Otway's opposition to the ascendant Whigs.

**Ouida** The pen-name of the novelist Marie Louise de la Ramée (1839–1908), taken from a childish corruption of her Christian name 'Louise'. Born at Bury St Edmunds, where her father taught French, she was encouraged by **Harrison Ainsworth** and her first published works were short stories contributed to *Bentley's Miscellany* in 1859–60. Her first novel, *Held in Bondage* (1863), was followed by *Strathmore* (1865) and *Chandos* (1866). *Under Two Flags* (1867), her most famous work, is a story of the Foreign Legion. Among the rest of her 45 novels were *Tricotin* (1869), *Puck* (1870), *Two Little Wooden Shoes* (1874), *Moths* (1880) and *In Maremma* (1882). Her vivid, artificial brand of hot-house romanticism kept her a popular novelist until about 1890. Afterwards, she lived in poverty for some years before she was awarded a Civil List pension.

**Our Mutual Friend** A novel by **Charles Dickens**, published as a monthly serial from May 1864 to November 1865.

The chief of its several plots centres on John Harmon. He returns to England as his father's heir after many years' absence and is thought drowned under suspicious circumstances, a situation convenient to his wish for anonymity until he can evaluate Bella Wilfer who, by a quirk in the paternal will, he must marry to secure his inheritance. Assuming the name Julius Handford and then that of John Rokesmith, he becomes secretary to Mr Boffin (known also as Noddy and the Golden Dustman) to whom Harmon senior, himself a wealthy dust contractor, has left his property if his son does not marry Bella. The worthy

Boffin asks the lawyer Mortimer Lightwood to offer a reward for the discovery of John Harmon's murderer, whilst he and his wife take Bella under their wing. Harmon falls in love with her, proposes and is scornfully rejected. Boffin and his wife concoct a plan to change her flighty attitude. He affects a miserly unpleasantness and calumniates Harmon, finally discharging him from his post. Distressed by Boffin's conduct, Bella returns to her parents' home and is finally reconciled with Harmon. Soon afterwards, his real identity is established.

A second narrative concerns Lizzie Hexam, daughter of the dishonest waterman Gaffer Hexam, who makes a living by recovering bodies from the Thames and is wrongfully accused of murdering Harmon. Lizzie is passionately loved by Bradley Headstone, schoolmaster of her brother Charley, but she loves the indolent barrister Eugene Wrayburn, a friend of Lightwood. So acute is Headstone's jealousy that he tries to kill his rival; Lizzie saves her lover's life, nurses him back to health and, by marriage, redeems him. Headstone is blackmailed by Rogue Riderhood, and in a mortal struggle both men lose their lives.

Dickens's last complete novel, *Our Mutual Friend* gives one of his densest and most comprehensive accounts of contemporary society, as well as perhaps his bleakest. Its vision of a culture almost stifled by materialistic values emerges not just through its central narratives but through its apparently incidental characters and scenes – the faded aristocrats and parvenus gathered at the Veneerings' dinner table, or Betty Higden and her terror of the workhouse, or the greedy plotting of Silas Wegg.

**Our Town** A Pulitzer Prize-winning play by **Thornton Wilder**, first performed in New York in 1938. Its three acts treat Daily Life, Love and Marriage, and Death, respectively, in the small New Hampshire town of Grover's Corners and focus on two families in particular: the Gibbses and the Webbs. Each act is played without curtain or scenery and is introduced by the Stage Manager in a direct address to the audience.

The first act takes place on 7 May 1901; as it begins, the Stage Manager describes the town and introduces the first characters as they appear on stage and go about the business of starting a new day in Grover's Corners. Act Two, set three years later, traces the courtship and marriage of George Gibbs and Emily Webb and the reaction to this of the older generation. By the third act, which is set in the town cemetery, a further nine years have passed, and the Stage Manager begins by describing the changes they have brought to the town. The central event of the act is Emily's funeral, which is followed by the reactions of both the living and the dead. The occupants of the cemetery are present on stage but remain invisible to the living characters. The voices of the dead are the last heard, as they comment on man's foolishness, his inability to understand the events which structure his life and his ignorance of the nature and meaning of death.

**Overland Monthly** An American literary journal, founded in San Francisco in 1868, *Overland Monthly* was intended to give California and the West a serious magazine and review of the quality of those of New England and the Atlantic states. For the first two-and-a-half years it was edited by **Bret Harte**. It continued in its original form until 1875; then, after a hiatus, was revived in 1883, absorbing *The Californian* at the same time. It published the work of writers such as **Jack London**, **Edwin Markham** and **Frank Norris**, and lasted until 1935.

Thornton Wilder's *Our Town*, at the Morosco Theatre, New York, 1938. The photograph shows a moment from Act II, 'Love and Marriage'.

**Owen, Robert** 1771–1858 Socialist and philanthropist. Born at Newtown in Wales, the son of a saddler and ironmonger, he had become by the age of 19 the wealthy owner of cotton-spinning mills in Manchester. In 1799 he purchased the New Lanark mills in Scotland and set up there his model community and village, with a work force of 2000 people, organized on principles of mutual co-operation. New Lanark became a place of pilgrimage for social reformers, statesmen and royal personages, and its example was instrumental in bringing about the Factory Act of 1817. His ideas of philanthropic education and social improvement were embodied in *A New View of Society*, published in 1813.

In 1821, disappointed with the slowness of reform, Owen left Britain for America to set up another model community at New Harmony, Indiana. On his return to Britain after the failure of the New Harmony experiment he headed a vigorous propaganda campaign and became the pioneer of co-operation between workers and consumers, his ideas strengthening the growing co-operative movement. His *The Revolution in Mind and Practice of the Human Race* appeared in 1849.

**Owen, Wilfred (Edward Salter)** 1893–1918 Poet. Born in Plas Wilmot, Oswestry, he studied at the Birkenhead Institute and the Shrewsbury Technical College, matriculating in 1911 but without the honours necessary to enter university. His mother, to whom he was particularly close, was an Evangelical Anglican, and may have influenced his decision to take an unpaid post as lay assistant to the vicar of Dunsden, teaching Bible classes, leading prayer meetings and attending missionary gatherings. His letters of the period anticipate the social and moral insights of his later war poems. He left Dunsden in 1913, soon afterwards falling seriously ill with congestion of the lungs. In the summer he failed to win a scholarship to read English literature at University College, Reading, and went instead to Bordeaux to teach at the Berlitz School of Languages. He became private tutor to a family through whom he met the poet and pacifist Laurent Tailhade. It is likely that Tailhade's definition of poetry in *Pour la Paix* (1909) as a call to generosity and brotherhood influenced his own.

Owen stayed in France after August 1914 and enlisted in the Artists' Rifles in late October 1915. Commissioned into the Manchester Regiment, then stationed at the Somme, he endured the worst winter of the war, suffering trench fever and concussion. He was diagnosed 'shell-shocked' in May 1917 and sent to Craiglockhart Hospital, Edinburgh, where he edited the hospital magazine, *Hydra*, and in August met **Siegfried Sassoon**. Sassoon's account of the meeting appeared in *Siegfried's Journey* (1945). Discharged in late October, Owen was posted to Ripon before rejoining the 5th Manchesters at Scarborough in June 1918. It was during the period from his convalescence at Craiglockhart until his decision to return to the trenches (rather than take the option of an officer-training post) in August that he drafted and revised his best poems. This return was, he felt, necessary if he were to write poetry 'in no sense consolatory'. He was killed on 4 November on the Sambre Canal, one week before the armistice.

Only four of his poems were published during his lifetime – 'Song of Songs', anonymously, in *Hydra* and three others in **The Nation**. A handful more appeared soon after his death (notably seven in **Edith Sitwell**'s *Wheels* in 1919), but the bulk awaited publication in successively enlarged editions by Sassoon (1920), **Edmund Blunden** (1931) and **C. Day-Lewis** (1963). *The Complete Poems and Fragments* (1983) was edited by Jon Stallworthy. In a draft preface Owen wrote: 'My subject is War, and the pity of War. The Poetry is in the pity.' His best poems, such as 'Strange Meeting', 'Anthem for Doomed Youth', 'Dulce et Decorum Est', 'Futility' and 'Mental Cases', achieve a remarkable nightmare vision which becomes, by virtue of its power and detail, also a protest. **Robert Graves** commented that 'the poetry is not, of course, in the propaganda, but in spite of the propaganda'. **Yeats**, on the other hand, excluded Owen's work from his *Oxford Book of Modern Verse* (1936) because 'passive suffering is not a subject for poetry' and described it, still more dismissively, in a letter as 'all blood and dirt and sucked sugar-stick'. While just possibly an appropriate description of the early Owen's derivative poetic diction, it is inadequate to the forceful language and psychic horror of his war poems.

Herbert Owen, the poet's brother, published a three-volume memoir in *Journey from Obscurity* (1960–5). Benjamin Britten combined several of the poems with the Latin mass for the dead in his *War Requiem* (1962).

**Owl and the Nightingale, The** An anonymous Middle English poem in octosyllabic couplets, written between 1189 and 1216, probably in the South-east. It presents a dispute overheard by the narrator between a sombre owl and a light-hearted nightingale. Their contention covers many topics, from theology to their respective avian characteristics. The debate is inconclusive, the birds leaving to consult the mysterious Nicholas of Guildford for an answer to their quarrel. The work belongs to the tradition of debate poems, but the masterly evocation of the two 'characters' gives it an additional dimension and is the main source of its charm. The poem has been interpreted as allegorical, but its tone is comic and it seems primarily gently satiric, the serious topics of discussion serving to illustrate the folly and contentiousness of man rather than any one of them being the central issue of the poem.

*Oxford English Dictionary, The* It has been variously called the NED (the N standing for 'New'), an abbreviation still sometimes retained for the 125-part dictionary published between 1884 and 1928; HED (the H standing for 'Historical'); 'Murray's dictionary'; and the 'Society's dictionary' (the Society being the Philological Society). OED is now the usual abbreviated title, though this was once restricted to the 12-volume edition published together with the first supplements in 1933. The current series of supplements is now almost complete, and will very likely be known as 'Burchfield's dictionary'. Work is already underway on a vast computerization of all these materials into the NOED (*New Oxford English Dictionary*).

The history of the OED begins with the presentation to the Philological Society of an interleaved copy of Richardson's *New Dictionary of the English Language* (1836–7) by an enterprising firm of publishers, who asked that they be allowed to use any notes made in it. A committee was appointed 'to collect unregistered words in English'. **Richard Chenevix Trench** submitted a paper 'On Some Deficiencies in Our English Dictionaries' (1857), which was influential in securing from the Society the acceptance of a larger scheme 'for a completely new English Dictionary', founded on 'the historical principle'. Herbert Coleridge became general editor in 1859, pigeon holes were constructed for 85,000 slips, and work was assigned to eager amateur helpers, with American contributors to supply the 18th-century materials. Coleridge did much of the groundwork for the OED. On his death in 1861 the general editorship passed to **F. J. Furnivall**, a major producer of slips for the dictionary. Work proper on the OED began only in 1878 when the editorship was offered to **James Murray**, who himself edited nearly half of the 1928 OED. Henry Bradley was appointed co-editor in 1885, William Craigie in 1897 and C. T. Onions in 1914.

The OED is a full survey of the English vocabulary from 1150, and looks back also to the earlier history of those words in use at that date. Full dialect coverage is given into the 15th century. Each main word contains identification of spelling, variant forms and pronunciation, and etymological information. Senses are listed according to their emergence historically, and are illustrated by at least one or two quotations per century of usage. Conceived as an aid to reading English literature, the OED's bias has made it a valued quarry for writers and literary scholars. There are many abridgements and adaptations, most notably the two-volume *Shorter Oxford English Dictionary*, an abbreviation that retains the OED's most essential historical information.

See also **English dictionaries**.

**Oxford Movement, The** Also known as the Tractarian Movement and the High Church Movement. In 1833 **John Keble**, Professor of Poetry at Oxford, preached a sermon attacking what he saw as the dangers threatening the Church of England: erastianism, or subordination to the state, and latitudinarianism, or slackness about dogma, ritual and ecclesiastical organization. Keble's concern was soon echoed by others in the university, notably **E. B. Pusey**, Regius Professor of Hebrew, and **John Henry Newman**, then vicar of St Mary's and a celebrated preacher. The movement to restore High Church principles spread, and Anglo-Catholicism was born. Its doctrines were that the Church of England was a divinely-inspired institution, the validity of the Apostolic succession and the importance of the **Book of Common Prayer**. It led to the reintroduction of ritual, vestments and incense. It stirred young men to 'earnestness', which had originated in Methodist 'seriousness' in the 18th century and in Evangelical doctrines which gained ground early in the 19th century. Its interest in the church of the 17th century and earlier stimulated the 19th-century interest in things medieval. In **Charlotte Brontë**'s novel *Shirley* (1849), there are references to Anglo-Catholic practices, such as Friday fish, and to the surplice-riots which occurred when earnest clergymen adopted them. She caricatures her future husband, the Revd Arthur Bell Nicholls, as Mr Malone. The movement was attacked by the bishops and liberal clergy, who suspected covert propaganda for Rome. Pusey was suspended for heresy from the office of university preacher, after his 1843 sermon, 'The Holy Eucharist, a Comfort to the Penitent'. It aroused a furore because he declared his belief in the Real Presence. He hoped for a reunion of the English and Roman churches and did his best to prevent conversions to Rome, of which Newman's in 1845 is the most famous. See also *Tracts for the Times*.

**oxymoron** A rhetorical device which deliberately joins apparently contradictory words. Oxymoron is a particularly notable feature of **Petrarchan** verse – for example, 'sweet enemy' and 'I burn and freeze like ice'.

**Ozick, Cynthia** 1928– American short-story writer and novelist, born in New York City, and educated at New York and Ohio State Universities. Her first novel, *Trust*, was published in 1966. Written in the first person, it is the story of the unnamed daughter of Allegra

Vand, who searches for the father whom her mother has prevented her from knowing; she no sooner finds him than he dies. *The Pagan Rabbi and Other Stories* followed in 1971. Both this volume and *Bloodshed and Three Novellas* (1976) reflect Ozick's interest in mysticism and the supernatural. In 1981 she published another collection of short works, *Levitation: Five Fictions*. She has twice received the O. Henry Award (1975 and 1980). Her most recent publications are *Art and Ardor: Essays* (1983) and two novels, *The Cannibal Galaxy* (1983) and *The Messiah of Stockholm* (1987). Her fiction explores the dilemmas of being Jewish in a Christian world. She often expresses her ambivalence about writing in English (which, as she notes, is a Christian language) and her fear that creating fictions is itself an act of idolatry.

# P

**Page, P[atricia] K[athleen]** 1916– Canadian poet, novelist and artist. Born in Swanage, Dorset, she moved with her family to Alberta in 1919. She worked at a variety of occupations, including those of shop assistant, clerk and historical researcher before coming into contact with writers in Montreal, where her first poems were published in the early 1940s and her first book, *As Ten as Twenty*, in 1946. Her early work demonstrates a strong political commitment and a concern with psychoanalytic themes. Her novel *The Sun and the Moon* (1944), published under the pseudonym Judith Cape and not issued under her own name until 1973, is about a young woman in touch with strange Gothic forces. After the war she worked for the National Film Board of Canada. The poems of *The Metal and the Flower* (1954) deal with the plight of those on the fringes of society. From 1953 to 1964, when her husband served as Canadian Ambassador in Australia, Brazil and Mexico, she lived abroad, writing comparatively little, but developing a talent as an artist. Since returning to Canada she has held numerous solo exhibitions of her paintings. Her more recent volumes of verse include *Cry Ararat!* (1967) and *Evening Dance of the Grey Flies* (1981), in which she turns to a spare economic verse that represents a marked departure from the style of her earlier poetry and an interest in spiritual self-liberation. All her poetry uses metaphor and symbol to suggest possibilities of human transformation.

**Page, Thomas Nelson** 1853–1922 American novelist and short-story writer, born in Virginia. His work is characterized by its preoccupation with the Old South, whose aristocratic ideals he sentimentalized in much of his writing. *In Ole Virginia, or, Marse Chan and Other Stories*, a collection of short stories, was published in 1887. It was followed by two novels, *On Newfound River* (1891) and *Red Rock: A Chronicle of Reconstruction* (1898). The latter focused on the hardship the Reconstruction period caused to southerners, and became a best-seller. Others of his works are *Two Little Confederates* (1888), a children's story, *The Old South: Essays, Social and Political* (1892), *Social Life in Old Virginia Before the War* (1897), essays, *Gordon Keith* (1902) and *John Marvel, Assistant* (1909), two novels, and *Robert E. Lee, Man and Soldier* (1911), a biography. Page became the US ambassador to Italy in 1913. His last works were *The Land of Spirit* (1913), *Life of Thomas Jefferson* (1918) and *Italy and the World War* (1920).

**Paine, Thomas** 1737–1809 Radical politician and writer, born in Thetford to an Anglican mother and a Quaker father who ran a small farm and made corsets, Paine attended school until the age of 13, when he became an apprentice in his father's shop. Following an unsuccessful attempt to run away to sea in 1756, he began work as a staymaker in 1757 and two

Thomas Paine. A detail from the portrait by August Millière after an engraving of 1793. National Portrait Gallery, London.

years later opened his own shop in Sandwich, Kent. He became a customs officer in 1764, but was dismissed in the following year because of his attempts to organize workers. He then moved to London and worked as a schoolteacher until 1768, when he was reappointed to excise service in Lewes. The publication of his first pamphlet, *The Case of the Officers of Excise* (1772), and his continued activity as a labour agitator led to his dismissal from the post in 1774. He returned to London immediately, and there met **Benjamin Franklin**, who in the same year sent him to America with letters of introduction.

Paine arrived in Philadelphia as a confirmed radical. As editor of *The Pennsylvania Magazine* he attacked the institution of slavery and advocated independence. *Common Sense* (1776), his most influential pamphlet, demanded an immediate declaration of independence. During the Revolutionary War he served in Washington's army and continued his political writing; *The American Crisis*, a series of pamphlets in defence of the war, appeared between December 1776 and April 1783. In 1780 he published *Public Good*, a reiteration of the case for federal union made in *Common Sense* and an objection to the Virginia Plan. After successfully executing a diplomatic mission to France in 1781, he withdrew to his farm in New Rochelle (which the State of New York had given him), where he wrote *Dissertations on Government*, an attack on paper money and a warning on the dangers of inflation.

He returned to England in 1787 and replied to **Edmund Burke**'s *Reflections on the Revolution in France* with *The Rights of Man*, a widely circulated tract published in two parts in 1791 and 1792, which attacked hereditary succession. It was labelled seditious; Paine, who had fled to France, was convicted of treason in his absence and sentenced to banishment. In Paris the revolutionary Assembly made him a citizen of France (1792) and a member of the Convention; but he was a moderate republican – a Girondist, not a Jacobin – and when he opposed the King's execution he nearly went to the guillotine himself. Instead, he was deprived of citizenship and arrested. Assuming that he was safer in prison, Gouverneur Morris, the American minister, did not assist him – a decision which Paine viewed as a plot against him and criticized in *A Letter to George Washington* (1796). Following the Reign of Terror, James Monroe secured his release. The years he spent in prison (1793–5) saw the completion of his most famous work, *The Age of Reason* (1794–6). A stark critique of accepted religious beliefs and practices, the work divides into two parts: the first argues that a rational knowledge of God does not accord with traditional conceptions of the Deity; the second illuminates various inconsistencies in the Bible

in order to invalidate both literal and figurative readings of the text.

Paine, the patriot in 1776, returned to the USA an infidel in 1802. Former friends such as John Quincy Adams ostracized him for his 'atheism', and when he died in 1809 he was refused burial in consecrated ground. Interred on his farm at New Rochelle at a funeral which no one of note attended, his body was exhumed 10 years later by **William Cobbett** and transported to England. Cobbett, however, was not allowed to bury the coffin, and after his own death the body disappeared.

**Painter, William** ?1540–94 Translator. Painter was educated at St John's College, Cambridge, ordained in 1560 and became master of Sevenoaks School in Kent. His *Palace of Pleasure* is a collection of tales based on originals from classical writers, such as Herodotus and Livy, and the *novelle* of Italian authors, such as Boccaccio and Bandello. First published in 1566, it contained some 60 tales. A second volume, printed in 1567, contained another 34 stories, and all the tales were printed again in 1575, when another seven new stories were added. It was a source for plots for Renaissance English dramatists: **Webster**, **Beaumont** and **Fletcher** and **Shirley** all found stories in it. It also probably provided the version of the story of Giletta of Narbonne that **Shakespeare** used in *All's Well That Ends Well*.

*Pair of Blue Eyes, A* A novel by **Thomas Hardy**, first published in *Tinsley's Magazine* from September 1872 to July 1873.

Stephen Smith, a young architect, comes to Endelstow on the north Cornish coast to work on the restoration of the church. There he falls in love with Elfride Swancourt, the daughter of the vicar who, learning that Stephen is of humble origin, opposes the marriage. Elfride, at first agreeable to the idea that they run away to marry, later vacillates and their plans come to nothing. Stephen goes to India in the hope of making his fortune. In his absence Elfride saves the life of Henry Knight, formerly Stephen's friend and patron. Henry and Elfride become engaged. But he proves a stern and rigidly idealistic man: on learning of Elfride's earlier involvement with Stephen he abandons Elfride with harsh words, leaving her heartbroken.

Later, Stephen and Knight meet again. Their conversation reveals to Stephen that Elfride is still free and to Knight that he has behaved cruelly. They both hurry down to Cornwall but the train they take also carries the corpse of Elfride, being transported home for burial. She had married Lord Luxellian, a widowed nobleman, but neither his devotion nor his children's affection could prevent her decline.

Hardy's third published novel, *A Pair of Blue*

*Eyes* has often been overshadowed by the popularity of its successor, *Far from the Madding Crowd*. Yet it remains notable, not merely for showing the full emergence of those ironies of plot which characterize his later and better-known work but also for its autobiographical qualities. The setting, Stephen Smith's profession, his reasons for going to Cornwall, and even his embarrassment about his class origins: all these echo the circumstances of Hardy's courtship of Emma Gifford only shortly before he began writing the novel. The portrait of Elfride herself is perhaps the most interesting of Hardy's several attempts to capture the charm he found in Emma at their first meeting.

**Palace of Honour, The** See **Douglas, Gavin**.

**Palace of Pleasure, The** See **Painter, William**.

**Paley, William** 1743–1805 Theologian and philosopher. Born at Peterborough, he completed his education at Christ's College, Cambridge, where he became a lecturer, a senior wrangler at the age of 20, and a fellow in 1766. His lectures on ethics, much indebted to the theories of **Abraham Tucker**, were expanded and published as *The Principles of Moral and Political Philosophy* (1785). *Horae Paulinae* (1790) sought to demonstrate the historical truth of the New Testament by a close examination of the life and epistles of St Paul. Like much of Paley's work, *A View of the Evidences of Christianity* (1794) earned its wide popularity more by clear presentation and lucid style than by originality of argument. *Natural Theology* (1802) made a more intensive examination of the same issues.

Despite his ability, Paley's advance as an 18th-century churchman was hindered by the latitudinarianism of his younger days. He became rector of Musgrave in Westmorland in 1776 and archdeacon of Carlisle in 1782.

**Palgrave, Sir Francis** 1788–1861 Historian. Born in London, the son of a Jewish stockbroker, he converted to Christianity on his marriage in 1823 and changed his name from Cohen to Palgrave. He studied law, was called to the Bar in 1827, and from 1838 to 1861 served as Deputy Keeper of the Records. *A History of the Anglo-Saxons* (1831) was the first of several works of medieval history, followed by *The Rise and Progress of the English Commonwealth* (1832), *An Essay on the Original Authority of the King's Council* (1834), *Truths and Fictions of the Middle Ages* (1837) and *The History of Normandy and England* (1851–64).

**Palgrave, Francis Turner** 1824–97 Poet and anthologist. The son of **Sir Francis Palgrave**, he was born at Great Yarmouth and educated at Charterhouse and Balliol College, Oxford. He was made a fellow of Exeter College and became a civil servant when he left Oxford, serving as vice-principal of Kneller Hall Training College (1850–5) and later as assistant secretary in the Education Department. Palgrave published several books of verse, among them *Idylls and Songs* (1854), *Hymns* (1867), *Lyrical Poems* (1871), *The Visions of England* (1881) and *Amenophis* (1892). But he is chiefly remembered as an anthologist. *The Golden Treasury* (1861), compiled with the help and advice of his friend **Tennyson**, was a classic statement of Victorian taste in poems and lyrics; it was reprinted many times and a second series appeared in 1896. In 1895 Palgrave became Professor of Poetry at Oxford. His other works include: autobiographical reflections, *The Passionate Pilgrim* (1858), *Essays on Art* (1866) and a volume of lectures, *Landscape in Poetry* (1897).

**palindrome** From the Greek, 'running back again'. A word, phrase or verse which reads the same both forwards and backwards. 'Rotor' is such a word, 'Madam I'm Adam' such a phrase. Like the **acrostic**, palindromic verse is occasionally used as an exercise of writer and reader's ingenuity.

An ancient example which combines both the acrostic and the palindrome is the word square. The Roman word square from Cirencester is one of several variants to survive:

ROTAS
OPERA
TENET
AREPO
SATOR

**Pall Mall Gazette, The** The name was invented by **Thackeray** in *The History of Pendennis* (1848–50) as the title of an imaginary conservative journal 'written by gentlemen for gentlemen'. The evening newspaper of the same name was founded by the publisher **George Smith** and Frederick Greenwood, its first editor, in February 1865; its purpose was to digest the news from the morning papers and to publish substantial articles on political and social questions in competition with the weekly magazines. Among its most distinguished editors were **John Morley** (1880–3), **W. T. Stead** (1883–90), Henry Cust (1892–6) and J. L. Garvin (1911–15). Contributors and reviewers included **Ruskin**, **Arnold**, **Patmore**, **Wilde**, **Pater**, **Wells** and **Kipling**. The political complexion of the paper changed sharply under Morley from conservative to radical and under Cust from radical to independent conservative. The phrase 'the New Journalism' was coined by Arnold in 1887 to describe Stead's brash editorship, and the paper achieved its greatest notoriety at that period with a crusade against child prostitution. As a social and literary influence, its most brilliant success was under Cust. After a long decline it was incorporated in *The Evening Standard* in October 1923.

*Palladis Tamia* See **Meres, Francis**.

**Palliser Novels, The** A sequence of novels by **Anthony Trollope**, consisting of *Can You Forgive Her?* (1864–5), *Phineas Finn* (1867–9), *The Eustace Diamonds* (1871–3), *Phineas Redux* (1873–4), *The Prime Minister* (1875–6) and *The Duke's Children* (1879–80).

**Palmer, Nettie** 1885–1964 Australian critic and woman of letters. Born Janet Gertrude Higgins in Bendigo, she attended the Presbyterian Ladies' College in Melbourne and the University of Melbourne, from which she graduated in 1909. Her next few years were divided between Melbourne and Europe, where she studied languages. In London in 1914 she married the writer **Vance Palmer**, whom she had met in Melbourne. They returned to Australia and settled there the following year. She published two volumes of her early poetry, *The South Wind* (1914) and *Shadowy Paths* (1915). As socialists and promulgators of a national Australian culture, the Palmers became two of the most influential figures in Australian intellectual life in the years to come and Nettie's influence was comparable with her husband's, even though her work, which was mainly literary journalism, has not received the same recognition as her husband's more creative output. Nettie's contribution to Australian social and literary life included work for migrants, acting as a spokeswoman for writers and anti-fascist activity in the 1930s. She also did a great deal to establish the reputation of **Henry Handel Richardson**, of whose work she wrote the first major study, *Henry Handel Richardson* (1950), in Australia. Her most significant literary work was *Modern Australian Literature, 1900–1923* (1924), a pioneering essay which, besides providing a survey of the field in a comparatively small compass, emphasized the difficulties faced by Australian writers, while arguing for the development of an organic local literature. Her other books include a volume of essays, *Talking It Over* (1932), and *Fourteen Years: Extracts from a Private Journal, 1925–1939* (1948), but it is impossible to measure her achievement from her full-length works. It lies rather in her prolific journalism, in which she helped establish the reputation of many of Australia's finest writers.

**Palmer, Vance (Edward Vivian)** 1885–1959 Australian novelist and critic. Born in Bundaberg, Queensland, he spent much of his youth in England and travelling in Europe. He married **Nettie Palmer** in London in 1914. Eager to promote and contribute to a national literature, he attempted to establish himself as a popular writer, producing plays for **Louis Esson**'s Pioneer Players and fiction for the NSW Bookstall Company. It was not until *The Man Hamilton* (1928) that he began to shape a career as a serious novelist. It was followed by *Men Are Human* (1930), *The Passage* (1930), *Daybreak* (1932) and *The Swayne Family* (1934). His later work included a trilogy based on the mining community of Mount Isa, *Golconda* (1948), *Seedtime* (1957) and *The Big Fellow* (1959). Palmer also published poetry, essays, criticism and collections of short stories, among them *Let the Birds Fly* (1955) and *The Rainbow-Bird* (1957).

**Paltock, Robert** 1697–1767 Novelist. Paltock was born in London and became a lawyer. He is remembered for his novel of fantasy, *The Life and Adventures of Peter Wilkins* (1751). The hero is shipwrecked in the far south and reaches a country inhabited by people who can fly by means of an outer silk-like skin which spreads out to enable them to become airborne. One of these, the beautiful Youwarkee, falls out of the sky by Wilkins's hut and he falls in love with her. He marries her and rises to importance in the kingdom. The book was much admired by **Robert Southey** and **Leigh Hunt**.

*Pamela, or Virtue Rewarded* The first novel by **Samuel Richardson**, epistolary in form, the first part being published to great acclaim in 1740.

Pamela Andrews, the heroine, is a teenage maidservant in a household where her mistress has just died. The lady's son, Mr B., conceives a lustful passion for Pamela and, abetted by his servants Mrs Jewkes and Monsieur Calbrand, he tries to take advantage of her position. All these developments are related by means of letters. Pamela is partly revolted and partly attracted by the amorous Mr B. but at length his persistence causes her to leave the house. Mr B. has meanwhile discussed part of Pamela's journal, stolen by Mrs Jewkes, which enables him better to understand her mentality; he writes her a letter asking for her return and at length proposes marriage to her, to her delight.

The second part of the book appeared in 1741 and is less inspiring; it depicts Pamela's social acclimatization to her new position, the changing attitudes of Mr B.'s family, her husband's wayward behaviour and the dignified manner with which she conducts their married existence.

The phenomenal success of the novel, which had a huge cult following and was translated into several languages, is largely due to the plight of the heroine herself and the strongly evocative atmosphere of domestic tension which the author creates. It caught the popular imagination (with a strong following among

'Pamela asks Sir Jacob Swinford's blessing.' Richardson's *Pamela* was published in 1740; Joseph Highmore's series of twelve illustrations from the novel was completed in 1745. Tate Gallery, London.

female and clerical readers) and in commercial terms was the 18th-century equivalent of a runaway best-seller-cum-soap opera. Its literary significance is equally strong, since *Pamela* was an early example of the unified novel of character, which lent popularity and respectability to an emerging form. It also provided a springboard for a number of skits on its success and the 'virtue' of the heroine; **Fielding** was the foremost parodist of Richardson's epistolary style, both in *An Apology for the Life of Mrs Shamela Andrews* (1741), a skilful burlesque on the values and mannerisms of the first part of *Pamela*, and in his adaptation of Pamela's brother (Joseph) as the central figure in his first substantial fiction, *Joseph Andrews*.

**pantomime** The English pantomime developed from two sources: delight in spectacular scenery and costume, and popular interest in story-telling dances. By 1723, particularly at the theatre in Lincoln's Inn Fields managed by John Rich, entertainments known as 'pantomimes' were regular features of the London stage. By the end of the 18th century, stories from British folklore and nursery tales were nudging out the previously established mish-mash of Greek and Roman myths, and the dumb Harlequin, whose danced adventures had been the fanciful centre of the spectacle, was being permitted to talk and sing. Under the influence of Joseph Grimaldi (1778–1837), attention was shifted from Harlequin to the figure of the Clown. It was during this period that the transvestite roles of dame and principal 'boy' became established. The fashion for outrageous punning in rhymed couplets, exemplified in the work of **J. R. Planché** and **H. J. Byron**, combined with a continuing love of spectacle. By mid-century, pantomimes were increasingly associated with Christmas and the involvement of music-hall stars in the latter half of the 19th century confirmed their hold on popular culture.

***Paracelsus*** A dramatic poem by **Robert Browning**, published in 1835. Like many of Browning's works, it portrays an imaginary character based on a historical figure – in this case the Swiss doctor, alchemist and philosopher (1493–1541) – and describes the 'incidents in the development of a soul'. In Browning's poem Paracelsus is a man singlemindedly bent on searching out true knowledge. Eventually, when he is discredited and dying, he sees why he ultimately failed. His great learning was inadequate without the secret now known to him: love becomes the means of knowledge and intelligence the instrument of love.

Though not a commercial success, the poem was praised by a number of thoughtful critics and for many years Browning was known primarily as the author of *Paracelsus*.

***Parade's End*** A tetralogy of novels by **Ford Madox Ford**, consisting of *Some Do Not . . .* (1924), *No More Parades* (1925), *A Man Could Stand Up* (1926) and *Last Post* (1928).

These novels tell of a public and personal struggle for survival by Christopher Tietjens, the second son in a family of Yorkshire squires. Most of the action in the first three novels occurs during World War I, but Part One of *Some Do Not . . .* shows that Tietjens's deepest values are at risk in the pre-war world of London. Christopher's domestic peace is undermined by Sylvia Tietjens, a complex figure who takes pleasure in circulating rumours about their marriage: even Christopher is kept unsure about the true paternity of their son.

Tietjens is betrayed on other fronts, notably by Vincent MacMaster, who gains his knighthood on the strength of Christopher's calculations, from the Imperial Department of Statistics. These events enter into Christopher's consciousness impressionistically. The impersonal narrator, using many time-shifts, is faithful to the characters' inner constructions of reality.

Christopher's meeting with a militant suffragette, Valentine Wannop, provides a comically unlikely beginning to their love-affair, an unconsummated but sustaining passion during the war. In *No More Parades* the action moves to an Allied Base Camp in France. Tietjens copes with its alternate bombardments and boredom, but his wife, Sylvia, brings his domestic and public troubles out to France, arriving in person before his superior, General Campion, an old family friend of hers. Tietjens's efforts to stay in command (of his regiment and, more crucially, of his own mind) reach a crisis. After a bedroom brawl with one of Sylvia's former lovers, he is ordered up to the front line. *A Man Could Stand Up* includes a measured and yet shocking account of trench warfare.

The reunion of Tietjens and Valentine on Armistice Day is followed by the depiction of their country household in *Last Post*. Valentine is bearing Christopher's child, and they live with Mark and Marie-Léonie Tietjens, Christopher's brother and sister-in-law. Through the thoughts of Mark Tietjens, on his deathbed, we receive one person's view of the post-war world: both the suffering involved in Christopher's rejection of a society's hypocrisies, and his survival into a redeemable future.

**Paradise Lost** **John Milton**'s epic poem, published in August 1667. The first edition divided the poem into 10 books; a revised edition was published in 1674 with the 10 books rearranged as 12. Milton had expressed his ambition to write an epic nearly 30 years before, and lists survive naming Samson, King Arthur and Macbeth as possible subjects. *Paradise Lost* was begun in 1658 and completed in 1663, its appearance being delayed by both the Great Plague and the Great Fire.

*Book I.* The argument of the poem concerns the Fall of Man, the origins of his disobedience to God's laws being traced to Satan's efforts to exact revenge for his expulsion from Heaven. Satan and the rebel angels are first shown lying in the burning lake. He rouses his followers and tells them there is hope of regaining Heaven. He orders them into legions, naming the leaders and telling them of a new world being created somewhere in the utter darkness of Chaos. Then he summons a council and the palace of Satan, Pandemonium, is built.

*Book II.* Satan and his followers debate whether or not to wage another war at once to regain Heaven. They finally decide to investigate the new world: Satan himself will go. He passes through Hell Gates past the twin sentinels, Death and Sin, and journeys through the realm of Chaos.

*Book III.* God observes Satan's journey to the newly created world and foretells how Satan will succeed in bringing about the Fall of Man and how God will punish Man for yielding to temptation. The Son of God offers himself as a ransom for Man, to answer for the offence and undergo his punishment. To rejoicing in Heaven, God accepts and ordains his incarnation on a future day. Satan meanwhile has reached the outer rim of the universe; he passes the Limbo of Vanity and arrives at the Gate of Heaven, where he changes his form to deceive Uriel, Guardian of the Sun. From him he learns the whereabouts of the new world, and about Man, the creature God has placed there.

*Book IV.* Satan arrives on earth and finds the

Frontispiece illustration by Sir John Baptist Medina for Book I of the fourth edition of Milton's *Paradise Lost*, 1688.

Garden of Eden, where he observes Adam and Eve. They speak of the Tree of Knowledge and Satan decides to concentrate his temptation on this. Meanwhile Uriel has heard that one of the fallen has escaped from Hell, and warns Gabriel, who in Eden finds Satan at Eve's bower, trying to tempt her in a dream. The tempter is ejected.

*Book V.* Eve awakens, troubled by her dream of temptation, and is comforted by Adam. God sends Raphael to Adam: so that Man may know the nature of his enemy and the need for obedience to God, Raphael tells him of Satan's revolt in Heaven. Satan had gathered many to hear him and had proclaimed his resistance to the supreme authority of God.

*Book VI.* Raphael continues his narrative. Michael and Gabriel command the hosts of Heaven but it is the Son of God who decides the outcome. He orders his angels to hold, then from the centre he charges straight into Satan and his legions, driving them to the wall of Heaven, and down from there into the Deep of Hell. The passage where the Son mounts his attack on the rebels is the literal and thematic centre of the poem, Man's future disgrace being the indirect consequence.

*Book VII.* The archangel tells Adam that God, after the defeat of Satan, decided on another world, from which Man may aspire to Heaven. He sends his Son to perform the Creation in six days.

*Book VIII.* Adam asks for knowledge of the celestial bodies and Raphael tells him that his first need is for knowledge of his own world. Adam then talks to him of Eve and of the passion she arouses in him. The archangel warns him to attend also to his higher instincts, lest he subordinate these to his love for Eve. Then Raphael departs.

*Book IX.* Satan meanwhile has returned to Eden as a mist by night and has entered into a sleeping serpent. He finds Eve working alone and speaks flatteringly to her, extolling her beauty. Eve is curious that the creature has the gift of speech. He tells her he gained it by eating the fruit of a certain tree in the Garden which he shows her, the Tree of Knowledge. At length he weakens her resolve and she eats the fruit. Satan slips out of the Garden and Eve, feeling transformed in awareness, takes more of the fruit and goes with it to Adam who sees at once that she is lost. He eats the fruit also in order to share her transgression: they will fall together. Their innocence departs: they look for cover from their nakedness and the seeds of dissension are shown.

*Book X.* After the transgression, the guardian angels return to Heaven. The Son of God goes to Eden to deliver the judgement on Adam and Eve (as known from the Book of Genesis). Before he leaves the Garden he clothes them, out of pity for their shame in their nakedness. Satan has returned triumphant to Hell; henceforth a path is open for Sin and Death to enter the world of Man. Adam and Eve approach the Son of God in repentance and supplication, begging for mitigation of the doom pronounced upon their children.

*Book XI.* The Son of God intercedes with the Father, but God declares that Adam and Eve must be expelled from Paradise. Michael descends to the Garden and tells them they must go out into the world, which he shows Adam from the summit of a hill. Adam is also shown what will happen in the world until the time of the Flood.

*Book XII.* Michael continues his account of the world, telling of Abraham and of the Messiah promised in the Son's intercession. Adam is comforted by these revelations; he wakes the sleeping Eve and Michael leads them from the Garden.

The poem's greatness is partly a function of its sheer sustained length, but also the visual immediacy with which Milton realizes the imagined scenes. Both Adam and Eve are archetypes with whom a reader can identify as humans, and the network of abstract influences surrounding their central transgression rarely threatens to obscure their essential characteristics. As an embodiment of malicious cunning, Satan is a dramatic and almost recognizable character. Milton has been criticized for glossing over certain contemporary developments in scientific and intellectual thought (the astronomical ambiguities in Book VIII, for example) but the poem's realism is that of myth, and its credibility dependent on the shapes of Christian belief rather than any specific historical details. As a long poem it is a monumental achievement, both intellectually as a work of the literary imagination and for the powerful expanses of its verse which, with the strength of classical precedents behind it, proved inimitable.

**Paradise of Dainty Devices, The** One of the most popular of the Elizabethan miscellanies, this collection of the verse of minor 16th-century poets included the work of **Thomas Churchyard**, Jasper Heywood, William Hunnis and **Thomas Vaux**, the Earl of Oxford. It was originally compiled by Richard Edwards, who also contributed some poems, and published in 1576; there were several later editions, with enlargements.

**Paradise Regained** A poem by **John Milton**, published in 1671. The title suggests that it is a sequel to *Paradise Lost*, with which it shares the theme of temptation, but it is a shorter work and does not attempt the epic splendours of its predecessor.

*Book I.* Jesus hears the call of John the Baptist and goes to Bethabara on the Jordan. He is baptized, and the Father's voice from Heaven proclaims his beloved Son. Satan is alarmed, seeing his dominion over Man threatened, and resolves to outwit the Son of God. In the guise of an aged countryman he approaches Jesus, who is fasting in the desert, and asks him why, if he is the Son of God, he does not make bread of the stones in that desert place? But Jesus recognizes the tempter and resists him; Satan disappears as night falls.

*Book II.* Mary awaits her son's return from the Jordan, unaware that he is in the desert. Satan returns to confer with his diabolical colleagues. Jesus wakes, hunger heavy upon him, and is confronted by the tempter, now in the guise of a man of wealth. He entices him, this time with a richly laden table and the finest wine; waiting to serve are comely youths and maidens and 'all the while Harmonious Airs were heard'. All this is rejected, and disappears. Satan then tells him that all the riches of the world will be at his disposal if Jesus will listen to him. Jesus refutes him: the empires of the earth have come and gone 'In height of all their flowing wealth dissolved'.

*Book III.* Satan persists: he tells Jesus he is

born to the kingdom of David – now under the Roman yoke. Will he not perform his duty and free his country? Jesus answers that he is under his Father's rule and knows the tempter seeks his destruction: Satan retorts that Jesus knows nothing but the meanest aspects of life; he takes him to a high mountain to show him the eastern kingdoms of the earth. He will ally any of these, he says, to Jesus and will restore to him the kingdom of David.

*Book IV.* Satan takes Jesus to the other side of the mountain, and looks west towards the seat of Roman imperialism with the evil Tiberius in power. Satan will help Jesus overthrow him. But who, asks Jesus, made him evil? He rejects the argument of Satan, and also turns his back on the brilliant society of Athens. Satan, having failed, returns Jesus to the desert as the second night falls. On the third day Satan makes his last try, tempting Jesus (as in the Gospel narrative) to prove his godhead. He takes him to the Temple, and sets him on the pinnacle, exhorting him 'Cast thyself down.' Jesus tells him he shall not tempt 'the Lord thy God'. Satan, defeated, falls back into the pit and angels come to bear Jesus away.

**Pardoner's Tale, The** See **Canterbury Tales, The**.

**Paris Sketch Book, The** A travel book by **W. M. Thackeray**, with his own illustrations, published in 1840.

This miscellaneous collection of travel essays, stories, art and literary criticism, interspersed with comment on French manners and society, was the first book of Thackeray's to be published in England, and appeared under the pseudonym 'Michael Angelo Titmarsh'.

**Parker, Dorothy** 1893–1967 American poet, short-story writer and critic, born Dorothy Rothschild in West End, New Jersey. She was raised in New York City, where she was educated at a convent, later moving to an exclusive girls' school in Morristown, New Jersey.

Her first poetry appeared in *Vogue* magazine in 1916. That same year she went to work for *Vogue*, and in 1917 moved on to *Vanity Fair*, where she later served as drama critic (1919–20). In an active career she contributed reviews, articles, columns, poems and short stories to magazines such as *Esquire*, **The New Yorker**, **The Nation**, **The New Republic**, *Cosmopolitan*, *The Saturday Evening Post* and **The American Mercury**. Her writings are characterized above all by a sardonic wit and irreverent sophistication. Her first collection of poems, *Enough Rope* (1926), was a best-seller. It was followed by two other books of verse, *Sunset Gun* (1928) and *Death and Taxes* (1931). Her collected poems, *Not So Deep As a Well*, were published in 1936. *Laments for*

*the Living* (1930) and *After Such Pleasure* (1933) are collections of short stories. *Here Lies*, published in 1939, contains all her fiction written up to that time. She collaborated with **Elmer Rice** on the play *Close Harmony* (1929) and with Arnaud d'Usseau on *Ladies of the Corridor* (1953).

**Parker, Matthew** 1504–75 Elizabeth's first Archbishop of Canterbury was educated at Corpus Christi College, Cambridge, of which he was elected a fellow in 1527 (the same year as his ordination as priest) and Master in 1544. He was licensed to preach by **Cranmer** in 1533, became chaplain to Anne Boleyn in 1535 and was appointed Dean of Lincoln in 1552. In the reign of Mary his preferments were removed and he fled to Frankfurt. On Elizabeth's accession he was consecrated Archbishop of Canterbury at Lambeth Palace in 1559. As a churchman he was moderate, and had to face the opposition of more radical reformers. He concerned himself with the issuing of the 39 Articles and the translation of the Bible in 1568 that became known as the Bishops' Bible (see **The Bible in English**). In 1648 his remains were disinterred by revolutionary Puritans and buried in a dunghill.

He was a scholarly man, and produced editions of early chroniclers – Gildas, **Asser** and **Aelfric** – and of Matthew of Westminster (1567–70), Matthew Paris (1571) and Thomas of Walsingham (1574). His most substantial work was a history of the early English church, *De Antiquitate Ecclesiae et Privilegiis Ecclesiae Cantuarensis* (1572). Parker left his collection of books and manuscripts to Corpus Christi (see **libraries**) and founded scholarships there, one of which was held by **Christopher Marlowe**.

**Parker, Theodore** 1810–60 American theologian and social reformer, born in Lexington, Massachusetts, and educated at Harvard, one of the leading figures of the generation prior to the Civil War.

His sermon *The Transient and Permanent in Christianity*, delivered in 1841, denied the authority of the Bible and the supernatural origin of Christ. Christian theological dogma was transient, Christian moral truths permanent. These beliefs were more fully elucidated in *A Discourse of Matters Pertaining to Religion* (1842). In 1845 he became pastor of the new Twenty-Eighth Congregational Society of Boston, and for the next 14 years he sought to apply Christian morality to contemporary problems, championing before large crowds such causes as prison reform, temperance and women's education. His great passion, though, was the abolition of slavery. He delivered strident and moving denunciations of slavery, was part of the secret committee supporting John Brown and sheltered and encouraged fugitive slaves. His views on the matter were detailed in *A Letter to the People of the United States Touching the Matter of Slavery* (1848).

**Parkes, Sir Henry** 1815–96 Australian politician, journalist and poet. Born in Warwickshire, he emigrated to Australia at the age of 24. Success enabled him to found a liberal newspaper, *The Empire*, and he made a successful career in politics also, becoming Premier of New South Wales. He was one of the moving spirits behind the forming of the Australian Federal Commonwealth, which came into being in 1901, five years after his death. Parkes wrote poetry as a recreation and encouraged the art of poetry in Australia. Of his five volumes of verse the most highly regarded is *Murmurs of the Stream* (1857). Other books by him were *Australian Views of England: Eleven Letters, 1861 and 1862* (1869) and *Fifty Years in the Making of Australian History* (1892).

**Parkinson, John** 1567–1650 A botanist and herbalist of the royal gardens, Parkinson published *Paradisi in Sole Paradisus Terrestris, or, A Garden of All Sorts of Pleasant Flowers Which Our English Air Will Permit To Be Nursed up* (1629) and a massive herbal, *Theatrum Botanicum* (1640), which dealt with nearly 4000 plants and contained 2600 illustrations.

**Parkman, Francis, Jr** 1823–93 American historian, born in Boston and educated at Harvard. In spite of a chronic nervous disorder he travelled extensively in the wilds of America, the information gathered during these excursions providing him with material for his historical works. During the summer of 1846 he and his cousin Quincy Adams Shaw undertook a 1700-mile trek over the prairies and into the Rocky Mountains of the American West. He recorded the experiences of this journey in *The Oregon Trail* (1847), which – owing to his extreme ill health at the end of the journey – he had to dictate to Shaw. In 1851, his *History of the Conspiracy of Pontiac* appeared. It was revised and retitled *The Conspiracy of Pontiac and the Indian War After the Conquest of Canada* in 1870. *Vassall Morton* (1856) is Parkman's only novel.

His great histories of the North American continent are now known under the collective title *France and England in North America*. The individual titles in the series are *Pioneers of France in the New World* (1865), *Jesuits in North America in the Seventeenth Century* (1867), *The Discovery of the Great West* (1869, revised and published as *LaSalle and the Discovery of the Great West* in 1878), *The Old Regime in Canada* (1874), *Count Frontenac and New France under Louis XIV* (1877), *Montcalm and Wolfe* (1884) and *A Half-Century of Conflict* (1892). To write these accounts of the

French and English presence in America – of the men and policies involved – Parkman researched his subject scrupulously, travelling to the scenes of the events he described whenever possible. However much he admired the courage and stamina of the French, his works are not entirely free of a bias toward what he perceived as Protestant democracy (represented by the English) and against Catholic despotism (represented by the French).

***Parlement of Foules, The*** A poem in **rhyme royal** by **Geoffrey Chaucer**, probably written between 1374 and 1381. The form is a **dream-vision**. The narrator describes the *Somnium Scipionis*, which he has been reading, and falls asleep. Following the pattern of the work he has read in which Africanus appeared to the younger Scipio in a dream and showed him heaven and the mysteries of the future, the Chaucerian dreamer is led by Africanus to a garden where he first visits the temple of Venus and then witnesses a congregation of birds of all varieties gathered before the goddess Nature. It is St Valentine's Day, and they are there to choose their mates. A tercel eagle claims the formel eagle on Nature's wrist but the claim is contested by two other tercels of lower rank. All the birds debate the issue and finally Nature rules that the formel herself shall choose between her suitors. She asks for a delay of a year before making her choice, and the other

'The Assemble of Foules.' An illustration for *The Parlement of Foules* in R. Pynson's edition of Chaucer's *Works*, 1526.

birds choose their mates and all sing a roundel in praise of St Valentine and the summer.

The debate between the birds, which is both delightful and comic, has elements of social satire, the hierarchy of birds reflecting distinctions of social class and their debate at times mocking the stylized courtly ideals of love. It is not clear whether any more specific allegorical reference is intended. The poem, an occasional piece celebrating St Valentine's Day, may relate to a particular historical episode: the negotiations to arrange a marriage for Richard II with Anne of Bohemia (1381) and Princess Marie of France (1376–7), and even Chaucer's own marriage in 1376, have all been suggested as the occasion.

*Parliament of the Three Ages, The* A poem in **alliterative verse** written in the North Midlands between 1370 and 1390. After a poaching expedition which gives a detailed account of the butchering of the dead deer, the narrator falls asleep and witnesses a debate between Youth, Middle Age and Old Age. It is not a lively exchange: Old Age dominates, asserting the inevitability of death and the transience of worldly bliss, common themes of medieval literature, and giving an account of the **Nine Worthies**. The latter is longer than the argument demands and was clearly thought to have intrinsic interest. The poem is perhaps the work of the author of *Wynnere and Wastoure*.

*Parnassus Plays, The* A group of plays produced at St John's College, Cambridge, in about 1600. It consists of *The Pilgrimage to Parnassus* and *The Return from Parnassus*; the second play is in two parts and its second part is called *The Scourge of Simony*. Their authorship is not known, though they have been attributed to **John Day**.

*The Pilgrimage* traces the allegorical journey of Philomusus and his cousin Studioso to Parnassus by way of the Trivium (logic, grammar and rhetoric) and Philosophy. They encounter Madido, the votary of wine, Amoretto, the voluptuary, and Ingenioso, who has forsaken the struggle and burned his books. The cousins resist temptation and diversion – and reach their goal. *The Return* is satirical and shows the characters on their way back to London, learning how difficult it is to survive. They are obliged to take humble jobs, though they try the accepted forms of attempting to secure a patron or gull the tradesmen. Eventually they are reduced to being shepherds. The satire continues in *The Scourge of Simony*, which surveys the literary and academic scenes. The separation of town and gown is considered and Brackyn, the Recorder of Cambridge, is subjected to a fair amount of abuse (he also suffers in *Ignoramus*). The merits of contemporary poets are satirically

examined, **Shakespeare** and **Ben Jonson** among them; **Will Kemp** and **Richard Burbage** appear as characters.

**Parnell, Thomas** 1679–1718 Poet. Born in Dublin, and educated at Trinity College, Dublin, he became a canon of St Patrick's Cathedral in 1702 and Archdeacon of Clogher in 1706. After moving to London in 1712, he contributed to *The Spectator* and thereby attracted the attention of **Swift** and **Pope**, and became part of the **Scriblerus** coterie. Pope, denied a university education because of his Catholicism, was particularly impressed by Parnell's formal training in the classics and Parnell contributed *An Essay on the Life of Homer* to Pope's translation of the *Iliad*.

During his lifetime, he published relatively little, apart from *An Essay on the Different Styles of Poetry* (1713), and after his return to Ireland in 1716 he descended into a state of melancholia from which he died. Pope was responsible for the publication of a posthumous selection of his friend's verse, which appeared as *Poems on Several Occasions* (1721) and included his only outstanding verse: 'A Night-Piece on Death' (which anticipates the work of the **graveyard poets**) and the 'Hymn to Contentment', another ode in octosyllabics. 'The Hermit', his narrative poem in heroic couplets, was based on a story in the *Gesta Romanorum*. Parnell remains rather an elusive figure, a minor poet with sufficient affinities with his more illustrious contemporaries to suggest he might have gone on to produce verse of a higher order.

**parody** A form of literary mimicry that holds up a glass in which writers may see their own worst potentialities realized, and take heed. For the reader, it is literary criticism of a particularly palatable kind.

Since outright bad literature may itself resemble a parody of better literature, parody usually mimics the mighty rather than the humble, and often mingles admiration with mockery. However, this is not always the case: witness the parodies of advertisements, newspaper styles, novelettes and so forth in **Joyce's** *Ulysses*.

At its best, parody remains close to the original and is fairly goodnatured; it warns rather than demeans. At one end of its spectrum, however, parody may approximate to **burlesque** by exaggerating mimicry into caricature. At the other end, it may approximate to **satire** by permitting moral criticism to usurp its central function of literary criticism.

Since literary structures tend to be generic, and thus common to writings of very varying quality, parody normally mimics the victim's style or content but merely uses his structure. Exceptionally, however, when some generic type of highly conventionalized structure is mimicked (such as **detective fiction** or the heroic romance), structure as well as style and content may be said to be parodied. In general, though, such cases would be thought of rather as travesties or burlesques.

**Parr, Samuel** 1747–1825 Latin scholar. Educated at Harrow and Emmanuel College, Cambridge, he became the perpetual curate of Hatton in Warwickshire and assembled a library of 10,000 volumes. Parr's scholarship gained him considerable distinction and the nickname of the 'Whig Johnson'; he wrote the Latin epitaph on **Johnson** in St Paul's Cathedral. His writings were collected and published in eight volumes in 1828, and he is the subject of **Thomas De Quincey**'s essay, 'Dr Samuel Parr, or Whiggism in Relation to Literature'.

***Parson's Tale, The*** See ***Canterbury Tales, The***.

***Parson's Wedding, The*** A comedy by **Thomas Killigrew**, written before the closing of the playhouses in 1642 and first produced about 1640. It was published in 1664, the year in which it was revived. Based on an original (and presumably quite different) work by the Spanish playwright Calderón, Killigrew's play is a coarse and uninhibited comedy of sex with its extremes of behaviour personified by the parson and Lady Love-all, an old 'stallion-hunting widow'.

**Parsons, Clere (Trevor James Herbert)** 1908–31 Poet. Educated at Oxford, he produced only one slender volume, *Poems*, published posthumously by Faber in 1932. His early death, and the promise shown in his slender *oeuvre*, can only point to what he might have achieved. Despite the occasional archaic phrase, his poems have a graceful elegance and a distinctive, original voice. Such impressive poems as 'Introduction', 'Suburban Nature Piece' and 'Garden Goddess', which show the influence of **W. H. Auden** and **Laura Riding**, do not deserve the obscurity – they are out of print – into which they have fallen. Parsons has been championed by **Geoffrey Grigson**, who believed that his early death 'probably extinguished a talent as considerable as any', and by **C. H. Sisson**, who refers to his 'few remarkable lyrics'.

***Partisan Review*** An American literary and political journal, founded in 1934. Originally published independently in New York City, it was affiliated with Rutgers University from 1963 to 1978, since which time it has been affiliated with Boston University. Although politically radical, the founders of the journal wished to maintain an independent Marxist position, and not to make it a party organ.

Philip Rahv and William Phillips were the original co-editors. Rahv served until 1969; Phillips still edits the journal. Linked to its Marxist tendency has been its encouragement of *avant-garde* art. Among the many distinguished contributors to the journal have been André Gide, Leon Trotsky, **W. H. Auden**, **Wallace Stevens**, **William Carlos Williams**, **Dylan Thomas**, **T. S. Eliot**, **George Orwell**, **Vladimir Nabokov**, Albert Camus, André Malraux, **Stephen Spender**, **Robert Penn Warren**, **Saul Bellow**, **F. R. Leavis** and Jorge Luis Borges.

***Partonope of Blois*** A 15th-century **verse romance** in couplets; a fragment of a stanzaic version also survives. After becoming lost on a hunt Partonope is carried by a magic ship to a city which is apparently uninhabited. He becomes the lover of an invisible empress, Melior, who promises to wed him if he does not attempt to see her for two and a half years. On return visits to his native France he achieves military glory and is persuaded by his mother to break his promise to Melior. She casts him out and he lives in suicidal despair and near-madness until found by Melior's sister and nursed back to health. He defeats rivals for Melior's hand and eventually regains her love. The poem is based on a French romance, but is not a direct translation of any extant version.

**Partridge, Eric (Honeywood)** 1894–1979 Philologist and lexicographer. Born in Gisborne, New Zealand, he was educated at the University of Queensland and at Oxford. He worked for three years as a schoolmaster before service as a private in the Australian infantry during World War I. University teaching at Oxford, Manchester and London was followed by four years in which he ran his own small publishing business. The 1931 slump brought this to an end, and for the rest of his life he depended on his writing. Partridge specialized in slang and bawdy, areas of the English vocabulary not covered by *The Oxford English Dictionary*. His most popular publications include the *Dictionary of Slang and Unconventional English* (1937), *Usage and Abusage* (1942), *Dictionary of the Underworld* (1950), *Origins* (1958) and *Shakespeare's Bawdy* (1947).

***Passage to India, A*** A novel by **E. M. Forster**, published in 1924.

Adela Quested visits Chandrapore with Mrs Moore in order to make up her mind whether to marry the latter's son, Ronny. He is a city magistrate who exemplifies the narrow anti-Indian prejudices of the imperial bureaucrat. Adela's desire to understand the 'real India', an interest shared by Mrs Moore, annoys the whole white community apart from Cyril Fielding, principal of the government college. Fielding's liberal views have set him apart from his compatriots, and he has nurtured a close relationship with Dr Aziz, assistant to the British Civil Surgeon.

Visiting a mosque, Mrs Moore encounters Aziz and a friendship is established. She and Adela accept his invitation to visit the renowned and mysterious Marabar Caves, but Fielding, who was to have escorted them, misses the train and the party proceeds without him.

The expedition proves to be an unmitigated disaster. Mrs Moore undergoes a traumatic and nihilistic psychic experience from which she never recovers, and Adela believes herself to have been the victim of a sexual assault by Aziz. He is arrested and committed to prison to await trial, and the entire community at Chandrapore is sharply divided into opposing racial factions. Only Fielding continues to assert Aziz's innocence, but their friendship is irrevocably compromised.

Mrs Moore dies on the voyage home, and Adela, under extreme psychological pressure, admits that she was mistaken. Some time afterwards, Aziz and Fielding meet for the last time and discuss the future of India. Aziz, who has now adopted an entrenched radical stance, insists that only when the British are driven out of India can he and Fielding be friends.

**Passionate Pilgrim, The** A slim volume of poems, the earliest surviving complete edition of which is the second (1599), whose title-page bears the ascription 'By W. Shakespeare . . . Printed for W. Iaggard'. Of the 20 poems, five are certainly by **Shakespeare** (three pieces from *Love's Labour's Lost* and versions of *Sonnets* 138 and 144), one by **Marlowe**, two by **Richard Barnfield**, and the remainder still unattributed. Jaggard was undoubtedly trading on Shakespeare's popularity in attributing the whole collection to him, and in his *Apologie for Actors* (1612) the playwright **Thomas Heywood** describes Shakespeare as being 'much offended with M. *Jaggard* that (altogether unknowne to him) presumed to make so bold with his name'. No other of Shakespeare's *Sonnets* appeared in print until 1609. There is no reason to think Shakespeare the author of any of the unattributed poems, although claims have been made for the charming lyric 'Crabbed age and youth cannot live together.' By a fine irony, the great Folio edition of Shakespeare, published in 1623, was printed by the piratical William Jaggard's son Isaac.

**Passionate Shepherd to His Love, The** **Christopher Marlowe**'s poem, an invitation to the loved one to share life in an idyllic world, was first published in an anthology, *The Passionate Pilgrim* (1599), but the text that appeared in *England's Helicon* (1600) is the commonly accepted one. **Sir Walter Raleigh**'s witty counter, *The Nymph's Reply to the Shepherd*, is almost as well known. Together they constitute a classic pairing of romantic extravagance and romantic realism.

**Past and Present** A prose work by **Thomas Carlyle**, first published in 1843.

Its first two books contrast medieval and Victorian England. To that end Carlyle made use of the recently published *Chronicle* of **Jocelin of Brakelond**, an account of life in the 12th-century abbey of St Edmund under the shrewd and sagacious Abbot Samson. Setting this beside Victorian England, Carlyle asks if the medieval peasant, secure in his place in the social order, is not happier and better off than his 19th-century counterpart. The third book, 'The Modern Worker', is in the main a satirical attack on Mammonism, Benthamism, politicians and similar forces that Carlyle considers anathema to society. The final book, 'Horoscope', is an urgent, apocalyptic plea for putting things to rights.

*Past and Present* is notable for Carlyle's concept of the Hero. Through Abbot Samson, the firm, efficient, kindly, astute man of God, Carlyle pleads for a renewal of society, a healthier, abler ordering of human life through good leadership. Thus he suggests Victorian England encourage 'Captains of Industry' as well as a more compassionate understanding among members of society. Also, visionary though he may be, Carlyle makes a number of surprisingly practical suggestions for improvements in the last part of *Past and Present*. As a whole, the book is an arresting combination of the idealistic and the pragmatic; it is laced with humour, rife with fantastic metaphors, and populated by grotesquely named characters such as Sir Jabesh Windbag, Plugson of Undershot and Bobus Higgins. An energetic, explosive and provocative book, *Past and Present* exercised considerable influence over contemporaries' view of their society; see **The Condition of England novel**.

**Paston letters, The** The collected correspondence and documents of the Paston family of Norfolk from the period 1425–95. The letters record the daily lives of three generations of the family and reveal the personalities of individuals as well as many domestic details of the life of a wealthy provincial family in the 15th century. They are a valuable record for both social and literary historians.

**pastoral** Literature about a somewhat idealized rural life, concentrating especially on the loves and laments of shepherds and shepherdesses. The kind is established by Theocritus' *Idylls* in the 3rd century BC. Virgil's *Eclogues* provide the major Roman example. A pastoral poem therefore can also be called an **idyll** or an **eclogue** (or a bucolic). The **georgic** also deals with rural life, but more realistically, concerning itself with farming and its labours rather than with the singing, dancing and loving of shepherds.

The chief example of pastoral romance in English is **Sidney**'s *Arcadia*, **Spenser**'s *Shepheardes Calender* being the chief poetic example. As these examples suggest, there is little pastoral of merit after the Elizabethan period (unless, dubiously, some of **Wordsworth** and **Keats** may count as such). However, **William Empson**'s *Some Versions of Pastoral* seizes on the moral implication of pastoral – that rural life provides a model of a simpler, more wholesome way of life than court or city – and extends the definition to include any such moral world, whether set in the country or not. Hence a Western and a gangster movie alike might count as pastoral.

**Patchen, Kenneth** 1911–72 American poet, novelist and social critic, born in Niles, Ohio. Among his volumes of poetry are *Before the Brave* (1936), *First Will and Testament* (1939), *The Teeth of the Lion* (1942), *Cloth of the Tempest* (1943), *Pictures of Life and Death* (1946), *To Say if You Love Someone* (1948), *Hurrah for Anything* (1957) and *Because It Is* (1960). His prose works include the surrealist allegory *The Journal of Albion Moonlight* (1941), the satirical novel *Memoirs of a Shy Pornographer* (1945), and the novels *Sleepers Awake* (1946) and *See You in the Morning* (1948). His prose poems are collected as *Panels for the Walls of Heaven* (1947) and *The Famous Boating Party* (1954). His later works are *Collected Poems* (1968), *Aflame and Afun of Walking Faces: Fables and Drawings* (1970), *There's Love All Day: Poems* (1970), *Wonderings* (1971) and *In Quest of Candlelighters* (1972).

**Patent Theatres** The Letters Patent, issued by Charles II to **Thomas Killigrew** and **William D'Avenant** in 1662, gave them the sole legal right to arrange performances of plays in the City of Westminster. Killigrew established his company of players at **Drury Lane**, which has remained a Patent Theatre ever since. D'Avenant's patent was invested initially in Lincoln's Inn Fields, then in Dorset Garden, and finally, in 1732, in **Covent Garden**. Despite the often dubious dealings in the assignment of shares in the Patent Theatres, the monopoly of Drury Lane and Covent Garden over the performance of legitimate drama in London was constantly defended until 1843, when an Act of Parliament ended it.

**Pater, Walter (Horatio)** 1839–94 Essayist and critic. Born in London, educated at King's School, Canterbury, and The Queen's College, Oxford, Pater lived an uneventful life at the latter place becoming a fellow of Brasenose in 1864. Shy and remote in personality, he occasionally ventured forth on Continental tours with his sisters, but he preferred the bachelor obscurity of Oxford where he was the diffident centre of a small group of aesthetes. In the 1860s and 70s he began publishing articles on literature, philosophy and the fine arts in the burgeoning journals of the time, but it was his *Studies in the History of the Renaissance* (1873) that secured his reputation. This was followed by *Marius the Epicurean* (1885), *Imaginary Portraits* (1887), the unfinished *Gaston de Latour* (1888), *Appreciations with an Essay on Style* (1889), *Plato and Platonism* (1893), *The Child in the House* (1894), *Miscellaneous Studies* and *Greek Studies* (both posthumous publications, 1895) and the next year, *Essays from 'The Guardian'*. An edition of Pater's collected works came out in 1900–1.

'Appreciation' was a byword with Pater, who rarely if ever took an opposing stance. To him an understanding and an apprehension of beauty were paramount, as was a melancholy recognition of the brevity of human life. But it is misguided to claim for him the worship of the moment or total surrender to the ephemeral and fleeting, for that was a position he later abandoned. Disciples often misrepresent Pater as a hedonistic voice of 'Art for Art's sake' but he never wholly relinquished the ethical implications of aestheticism. There is a morbid side to Pater's work that was seized upon by some of his followers in the 1890s and unhealthily exploited. But whatever his weaknesses Pater is at his finest a matchless prose stylist and he remains a salient figure in the **Aesthetic Movement**.

***Paterson*** A long poem in free verse by **William Carlos Williams**, published in five volumes from 1946 to 1958. The name refers both to a city on the Passaic River near Williams's home town of Rutherford, New Jersey, and to a character in the poem who merges the details of the poet's private life with the public history of the region. Williams said that 'all art begins in the local', and in *Paterson* he combines historical documents, newspaper stories, geological surveys, and personal letters in an attempt to localize his material. The dominant image of the poem is that of the Passaic River, which in its fluid, continual movement unites the particulars of human experience with time. Fragments of a sixth book were published posthumously in 1963 as an appendix to the poem.

**Paterson, A[ndrew] B[arton]** 1864–1941 Australian poet, journalist and novelist. Born near Orange in New South Wales, Paterson was educated in Sydney and later trained for the law. He practised as a solicitor in Sydney until 1899, when he became a war correspondent in South Africa. He edited the Sydney *Evening News* in

1904 and the Sydney *Town and Country Journal* in 1907–8.

Apart from his journalism Paterson also wrote novels, including *The Outback Marriage* (1906), but is famous for the ballads he contributed to *The Bulletin*, the widely read Sydney paper founded in 1880 by J. F. Archibald and John Haynes, while still practising as a solicitor. His collection, *The Man from Snowy River* (1895), became a best-seller. He also gathered authentic bush ballads and published an anthology, *Old Bush Songs*, in 1905. Their slangy idiom and infectious rhythms make Paterson's own poems, and the ones he collected, immediately memorable; everyone in the English-speaking world knows 'Waltzing Matilda', which he adapted from a traditional source. Paterson's ballads create a vivid picture of early Australian life, capturing its hardships, recklessness and grim, matter-of-fact humour. His nickname, 'Banjo', comes from the pseudonym he used in *The Bulletin*. Paterson's *Collected Verse* was published in 1921. His *Happy Dispatches* (1934) is a volume of reminiscences.

**pathetic fallacy** A term coined by **John Ruskin**, in the third volume of *Modern Painters* (1856), for the practice of attributing human emotions to the inanimate or unintelligent world. The opening lines of **Robert Browning**'s 'Porphyria's Lover' provide an example:

> The rain set early in tonight,
>   The sullen wind was soon awake,
> It tore the elm-tops down for spite,
>   And did its worst to vex the lake.

*Pathfinder, The*  See **Leatherstocking Tales, The**.

*Patience* A Middle English poem in **alliterative verse**. Probably written in the second half of the 14th century in the West Midlands, it is usually considered the work of the **Gawain-poet**, the presumed author of **Sir Gawain and the Green Knight**, **Pearl** and **Cleanness**. It is homiletic in intention, aiming to teach the virtue of patience and illustrating it with the story of Jonah, taken from the Vulgate Bible. The skilful, humorous characterization of the surly and disobedient Jonah and the vivid realization of the scenes with a particularly medieval aspect are characteristic of the art of the *Gawain*-poet.

*Patient Grissel, The Pleasant Comedy of* A play by **Thomas Dekker**, written in collaboration with **Henry Chettle** and William Haughton and first published in 1603. The story is based on **Chaucer**'s *The Clerk's Tale*, in *The Canterbury Tales*, which comes in turn from Boccaccio. The play is remembered for Dekker's beautiful songs, 'Art Thou Poor Yet Hast Thou Golden Slumbers? O Sweet Content!' and 'Golden Slumbers Kiss Your Eyes'.

**Patmore, Coventry (Kersey Dighton)** 1823–96 Poet and critic. Born at Woodford in Essex, he was educated at home by an eccentric father, apart from a brief interlude in Paris. In 1846, sponsored by **Monckton Milnes**, he secured an assistant librarianship in the British Museum, where he worked nearly 20 years, and in 1847 he married Emily Andrews.

Soon after his *Poems* (1844) appeared Patmore became associated with the **Pre-Raphaelite Brotherhood**, contributing to their short-lived journal, *The Germ*, in 1850 and interceding successfully with **Ruskin** to support the Brotherhood when it was attacked in the early 1850s. Millais took one of his early verses, 'The Woodman's Daughter', as the subject for a painting. *Tamerton Church-Tower and Other Poems* (1853) was followed by his most popular work, *The Angel in the House*, a loosely constructed sequence of poems in praise of married love which originally appeared in four parts: *The Betrothal* (1854), *The Espousals* (1856), *Faithful for Ever* (1860) and *The Victories of Love* (1863).

His wife Emily died in 1862, though Patmore went on to marry twice more, in 1864 and in 1881. He became a Roman Catholic in the year of his second marriage, and the 42 odes of *The Unknown Eros* (1877) show him entering a new – and to contemporaries, less accessible – literary phase. Their theme once again is love, but now the earthly conception is harmonized with the transcendental. These post-conversion verses apotheosize divine love, complementing and contrasting with *The Angel in the House*. Afterwards Patmore turned chiefly to prose, beginning with the study of metre which introduced his next volume of poems (1878) and continuing with such critical, philosophical and aphoristic studies as *Principle in Art* (1879), *Religio Poetae* (1893) and *The Rod, the Root and the Flower* (1895).

Chiefly identified in his own day as the author of *The Angel in the House*, Patmore had passed from the public view before the end of his career and is now largely forgotten. The very exactitude with which his most successful work captured mid-Victorian values, with its glorification of marriage and domesticity, guaranteed its neglect by later generations. Yet his narrative ability – apparent in his own favourite poem, 'Amelia' – as well as his melodic sense and his occasional delicacy of phrase cannot be denied.

**Paton, Alan (Stewart)** 1903–88 South African writer, born in Pietermaritzburg. His principalship of Diepkloof Reformatory, Johannesburg (1935–48), provided those insights into segregated black living conditions that illumine his first novel, *Cry, the Beloved Country* (1948) and *Debbie Go Home: Stories* (1961; as *Tales from a Troubled Land*, USA, 1965). The contrast in the novel between idealized black rural clergyman and realistic ghetto setting tried to prick white South African Christian consciences; it did alert world opinion to South Africa's long-established racial inequalities. Altogether more accomplished, *Too Late the Phalarope* (1953) explores the tragedy of Afrikaner racial and political inflexibility. President of the Liberal Party (1958–68), Paton wrote two substantial biographies, *Hofmeyr* (1964) and *Apartheid and the Archbishop* (1973). Other publications include *Knocking on the Door: Shorter Writings* (1975), the autobiography *Towards the Mountain* (1981) and *Ah, But Your Land Is Beautiful* (1981), an uneasy combination of 'experimental' fiction and 1950s history.

**Patten, Brian** See **Liverpool poets**.

**Pattison, Mark** 1813–84 Scholar. Born at Hornby in Yorkshire, he went to Oriel College, Oxford, where the Evangelical faith of his childhood was altered by contact with **Newman** and the **Oxford Movement**. He became a fellow of Lincoln College in 1839 and its Rector in 1861, having suffered a decade of disappointment after missing election to the post in 1851. He held liberal views on University affairs and, in later years, on theology, as his contribution to *Essays and Reviews* (1860) demonstrated. In literary studies, he edited poems by **Pope** (1869 and 1872) and **Milton**'s sonnets (1883) and wrote the volume on Milton for the English Men of Letters series (1879). But his chief interest was in the Renaissance scholars Isaac Casaubon and Joseph Scaliger; his biography of Casaubon appeared in 1875 but his work on Scaliger was left incomplete at his death. His wife, the art historian Emilia Francis Strong, was many years younger than himself; she later married the politician Sir Charles Dilke. Pattison's marriage, among other circumstances, has prompted the suggestion that he was the model for Mr Casaubon in **George Eliot**'s *Middlemarch*. His memoirs were published by his widow in 1885.

*Paul Ferroll* A novel by **Caroline Clive**, published in 1855. Its treatment of crime anticipated the popular **sensation fiction** of the next decade. The wealthy and cultured Paul Ferroll murders his malignant, domineering wife, who had used a clever trick to prevent him marrying the woman he loved. His guilt is unsuspected, but after 18 years of happiness and success Ferroll confesses when an innocent person is suspected of the crime. A sequel, *Why Paul Ferroll Killed His Wife* (1860), describes the provocation that drove him to murder.

Mrs Clive had used 'Paul Ferroll' as a pseudonym early in her career.

**Paulding, James Kirke** 1778–1860 American man of letters. Paulding grew up in Tarrytown, New York, where his contemporary **Washington Irving** also lived. His sister Julia married William Irving, Washington's brother. He was a co-founder and major contributor to the literary periodical series *Salmagundi* (1807–8), with Washington and William Irving, and went on to write *The Diverting History of John Bull and Brother Jonathan* (1812). An active participant in the Anglo-American literary dispute over the relative merits of the two nations, he staunchly defended the United States. His *The Lay of the Scottish Fiddle* (1813) parodies **Sir Walter Scott**'s narrative poems, *The United States and England* (1815) is a vigorous defence of the younger nation and *The Backwoodsman* (1818), a long poem written in couplets, celebrates the American frontier spirit. He also produced over 70 tales as well as five novels: *Konigsmarke* (1823), *The Dutchman's Fireside* (1831), *Westward Ho!* (1832), *The Old Continental* (1846) and *The Puritan and His Daughter* (1849).

**Paulin, Tom** 1949– Poet and critic. Paulin was born in Leeds but grew up in Belfast. He studied English at the Universities of Hull and Oxford and is currently a lecturer in English at the University of Nottingham. His poems have been collected in *A Sense of Justice* (1977), *The Strange Museum* (1980) and *The Liberty Tree* (1983). He has also published a critical study of **Hardy**'s poetry (1975) and *Ireland and the English Crisis* (1984), a collection of critical essays. His work is bleaker and more urban than that of other contemporary Ulster poets. It is often informed by a brooding political awareness responding to violence and injustice in Northern Ireland but invoking a more cosmopolitan post-imperial frame of reference. His poetry has paid homage to the radical dissenting tradition of late 18th-century Belfast and the resonances of Ulster dialect verse first explored by **John Hewitt**. His version of Sophocles' *Antigone*, *The Riot Act* (1985), incorporates traces of Ulster dialect to draw attention to Ulster parallels to the tangle of power politics, religion and personal responsibility in the original. It was first produced in Derry by the Field Day Theatre Company of which Paulin, like **Seamus Heaney**, is a director. At its best his poetry is distinguished by clear-sighted moments of vision and exact, sometimes brutally colloquial language.

*Pauline: A Fragment of a Confession* The first published work by **Robert Browning**, a poem in blank verse heavily influenced by **Shelley**, issued anonymously in 1833. It was a complete failure with the public, apparently failing to find a single buyer; **John Stuart Mill** annotated a copy presented to him with the famous remark that 'the writer possesses a more intense and morbid self-consciousness than I ever knew in a sane human being'. In later life Browning was somewhat embarrassed by the poem and included it only with great reluctance in a collected edition of 1867.

**Payne, John Howard** 1791–1852 American playwright and actor, born in New York City. His first play, *Julia, or, The Wanderer* (1806), was staged in New York when he was only 14, and was followed by a successful adaptation of August von Kotzebue's *Lover's Vows* in 1809. In 1813 he went to England, where *Trial Without Jury* (1815), an adaptation from the French, better known by its alternative title *The Maid and the Magpie*, was followed by several other adaptations and then by *Brutus, or, The Fall of Tarquin* (1818), a clever compilation from several sources, which provided Edmund Kean with one of his more notable roles. In 1820, having failed as manager of Sadler's Wells Theatre, Payne was imprisoned for debt. The successful production of *Thérèse, the Orphan of Geneva* (1821), which he wrote in prison, bought his release, and he settled in Paris. The success of *Clari, or, The Maid of Milan* (1823), which contained the famous 'Home Sweet Home', set to music by Henry Bishop, encouraged him to return to London, where he collaborated on a number of plays with **Washington Irving**, including *Charles the Second* (1824). He returned to New York in 1832, but wrote little more for the theatre. He collected voluminous notes on the Cherokee Indians, but published none of them during his lifetime. (Grant Foreman edited *Indian Justice: A Cherokee Murder Trial* in 1934.)

**p'Bitek, Okot** 1931–82 Ugandan poet, born in Gulu. His writings were seminal to the East African search for cultural identity in the 1970s. In *Song of Lawino* (1966), his spirited poem in the manner of Acoli oral verse, the persona of Lawino vigorously defends traditional culture, and scathingly attacks her husband's westernized ways. *Song of Ocul* (1970) is his reply. *Two Songs* (1971) ('Song of Prisoner', 'Song of Malaya', i.e. prostitute) lament the post-Independence penury of most Africans, though Okot always argued, as in *African Religions in Western Scholarship* (1971) and *Africa's Cultural Revolution* (1973), that neo-colonialism was cultural rather than economic.

**Peabody, Elizabeth** 1804–94 American educator, born in Massachusetts, one of the leading literary women of her day. At 18 she opened a school in Boston and began to meet many of the influential New England literati, including **Ralph Waldo Emerson** and **William Ellery Channing**. After serving for many years as Channing's close assistant, in 1834 she began to assist **Bronson Alcott** at his experimental Temple School. The following year she anonymously published *Record of a School*. In 1839 she opened the bookshop in Boston that established her as an important member of the **Transcendentalist** movement; the only source of foreign books in the city, her shop became a centre of intellectual life. (The planning of the **Brook Farm** experiment took place there.) From the printing press in the back of her shop, she published three books by **Nathaniel Hawthorne** (her brother-in-law), several of **Margaret Fuller**'s translations of German works, and from 1842 to 1843 the Transcendentalist journal *The Dial*. She contributed several articles to *The Dial*, but devoted most of her writing to textbooks of grammar and history, including her *Chronological History of the United States* (1856). In 1860 she opened the first American kindergarten, and later published the *Kindergarten Messenger* (1873–7). From 1879 to 1894 she was a member and lecturer at Bronson Alcott's Concord School of Philosophy. Her final days were spent in support of Indian education, and in putting together *A Last Evening with Allston* (1886), which combines memoirs with her early articles for *The Dial*. Her impact on the Boston literary community is reflected in **Henry James**'s characterization of her as Miss Birdseye in *The Bostonians*.

**Peacham, Henry** *c.*1576– *c.*1643 A writer of essays and 'characters', Peacham is best remembered for *The Complete Gentleman* (1622), a book of advice to young men about to enter the world, which contained instructions on art, poetry and heraldry as well as manners. The heraldic definitions in the 1661 edition helped **Samuel Johnson** when he came to compile his *Dictionary of the English Language*. Other works by Peacham were *Coach and Sedan* (1636), *The Truth of Our Times* (1638) and *The Art of Living in London* (1642). His treatise on art, *Graphice*, was first published in 1606 and appeared in many subsequent editions as *The Gentleman's Exercise*.

**Peacock, Thomas Love** 1785–1866 Satirist, poet and essayist. The only son of a London glass merchant, Peacock was born at Weymouth and after his father's early death was brought up by his mother at Chertsey, receiving his only formal schooling at a private school in Englefield Green which he left at the age of 13. A modest inheritance from his father allowed him to live as private scholar and man of letters, and he was not obliged to seek regular employment until he was in his thirties, when he obtained a senior post at the East India Company. In

Thomas Love Peacock. From the portrait by H. Wallis, 1858. National Portrait Gallery, London.

important respects Peacock's development as a writer was inseparable from his close friendship with **Shelley**, whom he first met in 1812. Despite differences of temperament, each man discovered in the other a kindred radical spirit, and if Peacock became something of a literary adviser to Shelley, particularly in respect of the classical literatures in which he was exceptionally well read, it was largely through the younger poet that he acquired greater confidence in his own distinctive creative powers, and was for the first time drawn into a wider literary circle. By the time he made his début as a satirical novelist Peacock's authorial *persona* is already that of the informed insider. His prose satires *Headlong Hall* (1816), *Melincourt* (1817) and *Nightmare Abbey* (1818) all presuppose a reader intimately versed in British intellectual controversy during the years following the end of the Napoleonic wars. Although some of their figures are clearly intended to be identified with real-life counterparts, the primary target of Peacock's urbane ridicule is the particular philosophical, social and political attitudes and ideologies they typify. His most characteristic formal device is the suspension of narrative for a kind of wickedly parodied Socratic dialogue or Platonic symposium, in which the representative minds of the nation argue each other under the well-laden tables of their country hosts. The

satiric disputations are leavened by farcical incidents, witty songs and romantic love-plots ending in incongruous marital alliances. In *Maid Marian* (1822) and *The Misfortunes of Elphin* (1829) Peacock combines topical satire with historical romance, but returns to his earlier, and perhaps more congenial, format in *Crotchet Castle* (1831). 30 years were to elapse before the appearance of his last novel *Gryll Grange* (1860–1), a satire on the mid-Victorian age, and regarded by many readers as his masterpiece.

Peacock's most important poetical writings include *Rhododaphne* (1818), a celebration of natural religion based on Apuleius' treatment of the myth of Cupid and Psyche, which anticipates **Keats**'s *Lamia*; lyrical pieces such as 'Long Night Succeeds the Little Day' (1826) and 'Newark Abbey' (1842); and, perhaps most famously, *The Paper Money Lyrics*, a satirical assault on political economy and the banking fraternity, written in the 1820s, but withheld from publication until the death of **James Mill**, Peacock's immediate superior at India House, in 1837. The fragmentary *Essay on Fashionable Literature* (1818) and *The Four Ages of Poetry* (1820) are Peacock's most systematic critical writings, and the scepticism expressed in the latter concerning the social value and utility of art and literature in an age of philosophy and science provoked Shelley, who perhaps overlooked his friend's tongue-in-cheek manner, to write his *A Defence of Poetry*. In 1820 Peacock married Jane Gryffydh, with whom he appears to have lived happily until she suffered a complete breakdown at the death of their third child, a three-year-old daughter, and continued a mental invalid until her death in 1851. He was also to survive his remaining daughters Jane (d. 1851), and his favourite Mary Ellen, who died at Capri in 1861, following her disastrous marriage to **George Meredith**. In 1837 Peacock succeeded Mill as Examiner at India House, where he remained until his retirement in 1856. His two-part *Memoirs of Shelley* appeared in 1858–60.

**Peake, Mervyn (Laurence)** 1911–68 Novelist, artist and poet. Born at Kuling in China, the son of a medical missionary, he was educated at Tiensin until the age of 11, then at Eltham College in Kent. Later he studied at the Royal Academy School and worked as an artist on the island of Sark in 1934–7. On his return to London he held several exhibitions and published illustrated verse and short stories for children. During World War II he suffered a nervous breakdown and was invalided out of the army. However, he became a war artist, notably for *The Leader*, in which capacity he visited Belsen at the close of the war.

He showed himself a master of the grotesque with his first novel, *Titus Groan* (1946), a minutely detailed Gothic fantasy about the Earl of Groan, the incumbent of Gormenghast, an ancient castle peopled by numerous monumental and bizarre figures. *Gormenghast* (1950) and *Titus Alone* (1959) followed; all were reissued as a trilogy in 1967.

Peake's verse includes *Rhymes Without Reason* (1944), *The Glassblowers* (1950) and *The Rime of the Flying Bomb* (1962), a ballad of the blitz. There is one play, *The Wit to Woo* (1957). Most of his work he illustrated himself; he also provided drawings for editions of **Coleridge**'s *The Rime of the Ancient Mariner* in 1943, and **Stevenson**'s *Treasure island* in 1949. In *A World Away* (1970) his wife Maeve Gilmore provides an insight into his life, tragically marred by Parkinson's disease in the later years. *A Book of Nonsense* was published posthumously in 1972.

**Pearce, (Ann) Philippa** 1920– Children's novelist. Born in Cambridgeshire, the daughter of a flour miller, she grew up in the countryside, finishing her education at Cambridge University. She then worked in the BBC and in publishing, meanwhile producing her first book, *Minnow on the Say* (1955). This is a charming, understated adventure story involving the search for a lost will, but it was her next novel, *Tom's Midnight Garden* (1958), that made her reputation and won her the Carnegie Medal for the most outstanding children's book of the year. It describes the visit of a solitary child, Tom, to an old house where each succeeding night he travels into the past, always meeting an equally lonely Edwardian little girl. Only at the end of the story does he realize that the girl is in fact the present owner of the house in which he is staying, but now turned into a crabbed old lady. Since then Philippa Pearce has written some excellent short stories and another minor classic, *A Dog So Small* (1962), about the clash in a child's mind between fantasy and reality.

**Pearl** A Middle English poem in **alliterative verse**, written in the dialect of the North-west Midlands. It is usually attributed to the **Gawain-poet**, presumed author of **Sir Gawain and the Green Knight**, **Patience** and **Cleanness**, and survives in the same manuscript as these poems, Cotton Nero A x. It was written in the second half of the 14th century, the influence of *Mandeville's Travels* setting the earliest limit of *c.*1357.

*Pearl* has a complex and very tight structure. It is divided into 20 sets of five stanzas, each stanza having 12 octosyllabic lines; the last line of each is a variation on the last line of the first stanza in the group and acts as a refrain. The stanzas rhyme ababababbcbc, c remaining the same throughout each group. The first line of each stanza echoes the last line of the previous stanza. Despite the extreme restrictions of the form, the verse flows easily and realistically reproduces direct speech.

An illustration from the late 14th- or early 15th-century manuscript of *Pearl. MS Cotton Nero A. x, f.41*. British Library.

The poem is an allegorical **dream-vision** and an **elegy** on the death of a young child, probably the poet's daughter. The authenticity of the autobiographical situation cannot be determined and is not relevant. The grieving narrator falls asleep and in a vision visits a beautiful and strange land where he sees, across a stream, the Pearl-maiden, the dead child as a young woman dressed in pearl-encrusted clothing. He questions her and she teaches him points of doctrine, answering his ignorant and impudent comments born of outraged grief with arguments from biblical texts delivered with little sympathy. The Dreamer is naïve and obstinate, unable to see that his understanding of human society has no relevance in the Kingdom of God. He is shown the Heavenly City, the procession of the 144,000 virgin brides of Christ and the Lamb of God bleeding. Overcome by longing, he attempts to cross the stream and awakens to his grief with a better understanding of how to cope with it. The poem draws extensively on the Vulgate Bible, most importantly the parable of the vineyard (Matthew 20:1–16), the vision of the Heavenly City (Revelation 21 and 22) and the procession of the 144,000 virgins (Revelation 14). The symbol of the pearl, central to the poem, is introduced as the narrator mourns his loss in the form of a metaphor: he has lost a precious pearl in the grass. The symbol's meaning is cumulative and complex, involving the biblical pearl of great price (Matthew 13:45–6), concepts of spiritual purity and perfection, the state of salvation and divine grace, and the Kingdom of Heaven.

The poem, one of the greatest medieval allegories, is concerned with grief and spiritual crisis; it shows, in the contrast of the emotional dryness of rational argument and doctrine with the overwhelming love and pity the Dreamer feels for the Lamb, how both reason and love are necessary to faith. *Pearl* combines austerity in the maiden's teaching with humour in the sympathetic portrayal of the Dreamer and, in the parable of the vineyard in particular, makes biblical stories contemporary and familiar in the same manner as *Patience* and *Cleanness*.

**Pearse, Patrick [Padraig]** 1879–1916 Irish poet. Born in Dublin, Pearse was educated by the Christian Brothers and at University College. Although he studied for the Bar, his main work was as a publicist for the Gaelic League and for a revival of Gaelic literature and culture in education and society. He wrote plays, chiefly in Irish, on religious or heroic themes drawn from Gaelic tradition, for performance in the school, St Enda's, he founded in 1908. *The Singer* (1915), the best known, was written in English and concerned rebellion and redemptive blood-sacrifice for Ireland, explicitly compared to the Crucifixion. The note of heroic idealism and patriotic dedication is apparent in some of the later poems in English, such as 'The Fool', 'The Rebel' and 'The Mother'. While Pearse remained a devout Roman Catholic, his poetry and reported speeches develop the cult of the Irish nation into an alternative religion with an atavistic irrationalism bolstered by the sacred writings of Irish political literature since the 18th century. His execution for his part in the Easter Rising of 1916 drew greater attention to his poetry of patriotic dedication, which influenced **Yeats** and later generations of politicians and poets. His *Plays, Stories and Poems* were collected posthumously and published (in English) in 1917.

**Pearson, John** 1613–86 Divine. Pearson was born at Great Snoring in Norfolk, educated at Eton and Queens' College, Cambridge, and ordained in 1639. He lived quietly in London during the Commonwealth and after the Restoration became Master of Jesus College, Cambridge (1660), Lady Margaret Professor of Divinity (1661), Master of Trinity College, Cambridge (1662), and Bishop of Chester (1673). Pearson is acknowledged as the most learned and profound divine of an age rich in contenders. His *Exposition of the Creed* (1659), developed from a series of sermons delivered at St Clement's, Eastcheap, was for long a standard work in English divinity studies.

**Pecock, Reginald** c.1395–c.1460 Religious writer. He was born in or near St David's in Wales and educated at Oxford, becoming a fellow of Oriel College in October 1417. He was ordained a sub-deacon in 1420, and deacon and priest in 1421. He became Master of Whittington College, London, in 1431 and Bishop of St Asaph in 1444. An anti-Lollardist, he concentrated on the points at dispute between the **Lollards** and the orthodox Church. After a sermon preached at St Paul's Cross in 1447 offended both radicals and reformers he moderated his teachings a little. He became Bishop of Chichester in 1450 and in 1455 completed his most important work, *Repressor of Over Much Blaming of the Clergy*. In this he proposes to examine 11 Lollard objections to the clergy but only actually considers the first six, referring his reader to other works for the remaining five. He anticipated **Hooker** in arguing in favour of moral law based on natural reason illustrated by the Scriptures rather than defined or declared by them. In 1546 he issued his *Book of Faith* analysing faith and the roles of reason and Scriptural authority.

Throughout his career he provoked all sections of theological opinion by his writings. In 1457 he was expelled from the Privy Council for denying the authority of the patristic writers, having set natural law above that of the Scriptures and for writing on important theological matters in the vernacular. Given the choice of recanting or being burned, he recanted, first privately and then in public. He resigned his bishopric in exchange for a pension at Thorney Abbey in Cambridgeshire; there is further record of him, but he probably died soon after his move. Besides *Repressor* and the *Book of Faith*, his surviving works are *The Book of Christian Religion*, *The Donet* and *The Follower to the Donet*, the last two in the form of dialogues, all written before 1454. His prose style is clear and forceful, his works well-argued and rational. They are particularly notable for being written in English, a point seized upon by his accusers.

**Peele, George** 1558–96 Playwright. The son of a London salter, Peele was educated at Christ's Hospital and Oxford. Little is known of his life, but he seems to have lived in London after 1581, earning what he could by writing plays, poems and pageants. His later years were spent in sickness and poverty.

Peele's first extant play, *The Arraignment of Paris* (c.1584), is a combination of debate and *pastoral* written for performance before Queen Elizabeth I. Both in metrical variety and the beauty of some of its songs, it is typical of the work of this 'university wit', but it is dramatically slight. *The Battle of Alcazar* (*c.*1589), a fanciful account of a recent Moroccan encounter, owes its dominant style to the **Marlowe** of *Tamburlaine*. *King Edward the First* (*c.*1593), despite its historical characters, is more a romance than a history play. *The Love of King David and Fair Bathsheba* (*c.*1594) is better-constructed, but Peele's best play is the highly original *The Old Wives' Tale* (published 1595), in which his readiness to mix rhetoric, spectacle, robust humour and lyricism is entirely appropriate to the story.

The songs from Peele's plays have been much anthologized. Among his poems are *Polyhymnia* (1590), *The Honour of the Garter* (1593), and *Anglorum Feriae* (1595), all of which seem to have been written for ceremonial recitation at court.

**Peg Woffington** A novel by **Charles Reade**, published in 1853 and based on a play, *Masks and Faces*, he had written in collaboration with **Tom Taylor**. The story concerns the 18th-century actress Margaret Woffington and her conquest of Ernest Vane, a wealthy man who has, unknown to her, recently married. Vane's wife, Mabel, fearful of losing him to her rival, prays to a portrait of Peg Woffington. However, the portrait is not what it seems, for the actress has cut out the poorly executed face and put herself in its stead, to fool a party of visiting critics. She hears the plea and relinquishes Vane, effecting the reconciliation of the young couple before retiring to a life of good deeds.

**Peirce, C. B.** See **semiotics**.

**Pelham**, *or, The Adventures of a Gentleman* A novel by **Edward Bulwer Lytton**, published in 1828. Henry Pelham is a fashionable dandy, whose habit of wearing black for dinner started a trend which has persisted to the present day, but who, for all his apparent foppishness, succeeds in clearing a friend from suspicion of a vicious murder (based on the notorious Thurtell case of 1824). Bulwer Lytton's first full-length novel, and a prime example of the **Silver-fork** tale of high society, it was enormously popular in its day and remains one of his most enjoyable productions.

**Pendennis, The History of** See *History of Pendennis, The*.

**Penguin New Writing** See **Lehmann, John**.

**Peninsular War, The History of the** The title commonly given to *The History of the War in the Peninsula and the South of France from the Year 1807 to the Year 1814*, by Sir William Francis Patrick Napier (1785–1860), published in six volumes (1828–40). An abridgement, *English Battles and Sieges in the Peninsula*, was published in 1852. Napier served with Sir John Moore in Spain in 1808 and subsequently during the rest of the war, and much of his book is eye-witness reporting. It is highly regarded as military history and was warmly praised by the Duke of Wellington.

**Penn, William** 1644–1718 Quaker and founder of Pennsylvania. The son of Admiral Sir William Penn, who captured Jamaica from the Dutch, he was born in London, and was sent down from Christ Church, Oxford, in 1661 for refusing to conform to the rules of the restored Anglican Church. He entered Lincoln's Inn (1665), but was soon a convinced Quaker and published a defence of his new faith in *The Sandy Foundation Shaken* (1668). This attacked both orthodox and Calvinistic doctrines and resulted in his imprisonment in the Tower, where he wrote *No Cross, No Crown* (1669), now a recognized classic of Quaker literature. He had meanwhile become interested in the foundation of a colony in America. The death of his father left him financially secure, and a debt to his father by the Crown was settled by a grant of land in the New World. Penn named it Pennsylvania and hoped to establish liberty of conscience for all settlers, whether Quakers or not. After establishing the colony, Penn returned to England in 1684, and wrote a loyal address to James II and a pamphlet (1687) expressing gratitude for the Declaration of Indulgence.

When James II lost his throne Penn continued their lifelong friendship; he was accused of treason and deprived of the governorship of Pennsylvania. He wrote *Some Fruits of Solitude* (1692), a collection of aphorisms of some literary interest. Pennsylvania was annexed to New York, until 1694, and Penn spent his remaining years in England preaching and writing, except for his spell of retirement to the Colonies in 1699–1701. His last years were troubled: Penn was imprisoned for debt (1707–8) after his steward had successfully swindled him, and he became alienated from his eldest son. He suffered a stroke in 1712 and took no further part in public life.

Penn wrote a great deal, being a man of tireless energy. An advocate of tolerance, a courageous and stubborn upholder of human rights, he was noted for his gentleness and was a worthy representative of the movement he espoused.

**pentameter** See **metre**.

**Pepys, Samuel** 1633–1703 Diarist and naval reformer. The son of a London tailor, John Pepys, he was educated at St Paul's School and

Magdalene College, Cambridge, graduating in 1654. He entered the employ of a relation, Sir Edward Montagu (later the 1st Earl of Sandwich), as secretary in his household, and in 1655 married Elizabeth St Michel, the teenage daughter of a Huguenot family. Pepys was from the start fortunate in his connections. Montagu's patronage coincided with the great Royalist opportunity of the Restoration, and he was commander of the fleet that escorted the monarch back to England – a voyage at which the young Pepys assisted, recording a vivid account of Charles II's fortunes after the battle of Worcester.

On 1 January 1660 (the year of the Restoration) Pepys began his now famous *Diary*, when he was living in Axe Yard, Westminster, in conditions of hardship. Enterprising and fastidious, he managed to secure preferment within the Navy Office, becoming Clerk of the King's Ships, Clerk of the Privy Seal, Surveyor-General of the Victualling Service (1665) and finally Secretary to the Admiralty (1672). In an age when the efficient official was still a rarity, Pepys (though initially preferred through nepotism) became a first-rate civil servant and bureaucrat to whose reforms in supply and administration the Navy was subsequently indebted. He was also a JP, an MP, and a Fellow of the Royal Society, as well as being a man about town and a figure in court circles. His sybaritic personality attracted the attention of both the monarch and the Duke of York, his brother (later James II).

In 1679, Pepys was imprisoned in the Tower of London on the charge of involvement in the 'Popish Plot' and deprived of office. In 1683 he went to Tangier with Lord Dartmouth, and made a record of his experiences there in a journal. He was reinstated as Secretary to the Admiralty in 1684, but had to resign in 1688 with the ousting of James II. He was imprisoned by the new government, released, and in 1700 returned to his house in Clapham, which he shared with his faithful confidant and factotum, William Hewer (who features strongly in the *Diary*).

Pepys was a personal friend of **John Evelyn**, like him an early fellow of the newly-established Royal Society, and a man of lively and enquiring intelligence; it was the publication in the 19th century of Evelyn's *Memoirs* (1818) which led to the rediscovery of the manuscript version of the work for which Pepys is now known across the English-speaking world. Along with a sizeable bequest of contemporary pamphlets, broadsides, ballads and manuscripts, Pepys left to the library at Magdalene six volumes of encoded diaries which were approximately deciphered by a Cambridge undergraduate, John Smith, and shortly thereafter published under the auspices of Lord Braybrooke in 1815. The

Samuel Pepys. Portrait by John Hayls, 1666. National Portrait Gallery, London.

*Diary* covered the period of Pepy's life from the beginning of 1660 until 31 May 1669, when he was compelled to abandon his minute record, due to the apparent onset of blindness – John Smith, his earliest transcriber, suffered the same consequence. The text appeared in varying stages of completeness (both the obscurity of the cipher and the explicit nature of the revelations contributing to a certain caution on the part of publishers) until finally reaching the reading public in the full annotated edition by R. Latham and W. Matthews (Bell and Hyman, 11 volumes) completed in 1983, a masterpiece of lively scholarship.

The *Diary* was never designed for publication during the author's lifetime and, despite its length, it covers a short period of his extraordinarily eventful public and private life. It is a phenomenon of literature, practically a household name. As the private, first-hand record of a historical personality it can scarcely be rivalled, and the decade which is so evocatively chronicled could hardly have been a more colourful one into which an ambitious, self-interested, and passionately enthusiastic young man could have launched himself. More neatly perhaps than any other individual contemporary (bar the monarch himself) Pepys seems to embody the more youthful attributes of the Restoration era – indeed, much of the colourful detail which has reached us has filtered through the very medium of his clandestine document. Pepys's record catches exactly that balance of civility and coarseness, *laissez-faire* and rationalism which typified his age.

Apart from its period interest, which is unequalled, the *Diary* is a fine, quirky achievement of literature – the literature of privacy, self-conscious, voyeuristic, intimate and unique. There is the perceptive analysis of the professional, and the biased aside of the rival. In everything, Pepys is outspoken – the Duchess of Albemarle is 'a damned ill-looking woman', and a production of **Shakespeare**'s *A Midsummer Night's Dream* is said to be 'the most insipid ridiculous play that ever I saw in my life'. The whole document is wonderfully enlivened by the comedy of the diarist's own frank descriptions of himself (set upon by a dog, spotted with a mistress, terrified by a pillow) and his constantly shifting attention, a mind which was 'with child to see any strange thing'.

**Percy, Thomas** 1729–1811 Antiquarian. The son of a Shropshire grocer, he was educated at Bridgnorth grammar school and Christ Church, Oxford. He became vicar of Easton Maudit in Northamptonshire, then chaplain to the king and the Duke of Northumberland, and later Dean of Carlisle (1778) and Bishop of Dromore in Ireland (1782). Percy's interest in ancient and foreign poetry was first expressed in works from the Chinese, which he found in European translations: *Hau Kiou Choaan, or The Pleasing History* (1761) was the first English version of a Chinese novel. The great success of **Macpherson**'s Ossianic poetry stimulated him to publish *Five Pieces of Runic Poetry Translated from the Islandic Language* in 1763 and to begin the collection that became famous as *Reliques of Ancient English Poetry* (1765). His enquiring mind pleased **Samuel Johnson**, who declared that Percy was a man 'out of whose company I never go without having learnt something'.

**Percy, Walker** 1916–90 American novelist, born in Alabama. He attended the University of North Carolina and received an MD from Columbia. Most of his novels are about Southerners, usually alienated individuals in search of fulfilment. His first book, *The Moviegoer* (1961), portrays a New Orleans stockbroker who insulates himself from the real world by going to movies until eventually, during Mardi Gras, a complicated involvement with his neurotic cousin Kate restores him to real life. *The Last Gentleman* (1966) is about a transplanted Southerner who returns home for a visit; in the sequel, *Second Coming* (1980), the same character seeks to affirm the value of his own life in a world which he sees as disintegrating. Percy's novels are often comic, even as they deal with fundamental problems of human experience. *Love in the Ruins* (1971) is a satire about a scientist who seeks to redeem America's mechanistic culture.

*Lancelot* (1977) is a darker work, about a man whose quest for self-fulfilment leads him to a murderous arson. His last novel was *The Thanatos Syndrome* (1987). Percy's essays on language are collected in *The Message in the Bottle* (1975).

**Percy Folio, The** A 17th-century manuscript that **Thomas Percy** acquired from Humphrey Pitt of Shifnal in Shropshire; Percy drew most of the ballads for his *Reliques of Ancient English Poetry* from it. It contains material of various kinds, including an allegorical poem of the 14th century, 'Death and Life', but is most important for preserving ballad poetry. The Percy Folio is now in the British Library and was edited for publication by **F. J. Furnivall** and J. W. Hales (1867–8).

*Peregrine Pickle* The second novel by **Tobias Smollett**, published in 1751. The story is farcical and violent, and it pilloried well-known people. Its reception was mixed and in 1758 Smollett published an expurgated version, softening

Frontispiece illustration to Vol. 1 of an edition of *Peregrine Pickle* published in 1769. Commodore Trunnion aims a blow at Jack Hatchway with his stick; Hatchway deflects it with his wooden leg. Smollett's novel was first published in 1751.

some of the attacks and removing some of the 'low' passages.

Peregrine is a picaresque hero, an ungovernable youth who goes from bad to worse before being tamed by disillusion and imprisonment. He is released by the good offices of those to whom he has formerly been generous and is rewarded by the hand of Emilia, whom he has treated badly, despite their mutual love. The story was considered on the whole improving, but not to be put into the hands of young persons. It has two unusual features: one is the interpolated story of the widowed Lady Vane's remarriage and subsequent adulteries, which she is believed to have paid Smollett to publish; the other is Chapter 95, which deals with Peregrine's purchase of a beggar girl. He has her bathed, her old clothes are burned and new ones bought. Peregrine proceeds to turn her into a fine lady, by means of lessons in dancing and French and a smattering of polite literature. The only difficulty is her inveterate habit of swearing, but she learns to be on her guard. Her social success is considerable, until in a quarrel at cards, she opens 'the floodgates of her own natural repartee'. She elopes with Peregrine's valet and Peregrine gives them a wedding present of £500. The parallels with **Shaw**'s *Pygmalion* have been noted.

**Dickens** preferred *Peregrine Pickle* to **Fielding**'s *Tom Jones*.

**Perelman, S[idney] J[oseph]** 1904–79 American humorist, born in Brooklyn, and educated at Brown University. In 1931 he published the first of hundreds of articles for *The New Yorker*. The success of his first book, *Dawn Ginsbergh's Revenge* (1929), a collection of prose and cartoons, introduced him to Hollywood, where he wrote comic material for the Marx brothers. He also wrote screenplays for 11 films, notably *Ambush* (1939) and *The Golden Fleecing* (1940) – both with his wife Laura Weinstein, the sister of his friend **Nathanael West**. A sharp and humorous observer and critic of contemporary American society, Perelman published some 20 books, mostly collections of his journalistic pieces. He also wrote travel books, including *Westward Ha! or Around the World in Eighty Clichés* (1948) and *Eastward Ha!* (1977).

**Pericles, Prince of Tyre** A play of which **William Shakespeare** wrote a substantial proportion; the first two acts have been often ascribed to George Wilkins. It was first performed c. 1608, published in Quarto (Q1) in 1609 but not included in the First Folio of 1623. It is based on a story in **Gower**'s *Confessio Amantis* and Gower himself appears as Chorus.

While in Antioch, Pericles guesses that King Antiochus has an incestuous love for his daughter, for whose hand Pericles is a suitor. Afraid of Antiochus, Pericles leaves Tyre and is shipwrecked in Pentapolis. There he wins the hand of the king's daughter, Thaisa, in a tournament. They are married and set sail for Tyre, where the king and his daughter have died, leaving Pericles as rightful heir to the throne. But the sea intervenes again. Thaisa gives birth to a daughter, is herself believed dead and her body placed in a chest and put to sea. Pericles entrusts his aptly named infant daughter Marina to the care of Cleon, governor of Tarsus, and returns to Tyre.

The Chorus now explains how 16 years have passed, with Pericles in Tyre and Marina in Tarsus, where her grace and beauty arouse the jealousy of Cleon's wife Dionyza. A plan to kill Marina is foiled when she is kidnapped by pirates and sold to a brothel in Mytilene. Cleon and Dionyza publish it abroad that Marina is dead. Protected from contamination by her purity, Marina attracts the love of Lysimachus, governor of Mytilene. When the despairing Pericles arrives there, it is Lysimachus who accidentally brings about the reunion of father and daughter. Impelled by a dream, Pericles sets sail for Ephesus and is there united with his long-lost wife, who has become a priestess of Diana. Pericles decides that Lysimachus and Marina shall rule in Tyre and he and Thaisa in Pentapolis.

*Pericles* followed the contemporary fashion for extravagant adventure and pictorial staging, but the untidy plotting that accompanies these effects has been a leading cause of its comparative unpopularity. It has often been grouped with *Cymbeline*, *The Winter's Tale* and *The Tempest* and, whatever its defects, its mixture of romance, tragedy and comedy has much in common with these remarkably experimental late plays.

**Perkin Warbeck** A tragedy by **John Ford**, it was published in 1634 but there is no record of its first production.

The historical facts of Warbeck's imposture as Richard, Duke of York (the younger son of King Edward IV), are closely followed. Warbeck (de Werbecque) was the son of a burgess of Tournai; he came to notice during the reign of Henry VII and succeeded in gaining support for a time. The play deals with his arrival at the court of James IV of Scotland, his marriage to Lady Katherine Gordon, and the events surrounding the treason and execution of the disaffected Sir William Stanley in London. James IV leads an expedition to England in support of Warbeck, but deserts him when the Tudor king offers forceful resistance. Warbeck's last attempt sees him landing in Cornwall; but the support he had hoped for is not forthcoming and the play follows his capture and eventual execution. In Ford's play he maintains his royal origins to the end. The love and loyalty of Lady Katherine are movingly portrayed.

**Persuasion** A novel by **Jane Austen**, written in 1815–16 and published in 1818.

Sir Walter Elliot of Kellynch Hall – whose favourite reading is his own entry in *The Baronetage* – has three daughters: Elizabeth, who shares his haughty vanity and, at twenty-eight, has found no one quite good enough to marry; Mary, who has, with some condescension, married Charles Musgrove, the son of the local squire; and the admirable but neglected Anne, who 'was nobody with either father or sister: her word had no weight: her convenience was always to give way; – she was only Anne'. Unable to keep up a style of living appropriate to his status, Sir Walter is forced to let Kellynch to Admiral and Mrs Croft. Anne re-encounters Captain Frederick Wentworth, a brother of Mrs Croft's, whom she had known, loved – and refused – eight years previously when she had yielded to the persuasion of her godmother and friend, the excellent but cautious Lady Russell. Anne, who still loves Wentworth, is at once disappointed and relieved when he appears to care for her no longer.

Wentworth soon becomes a favourite with the Musgrove family, particularly Charles's two high-spirited sisters, Louisa and Henrietta, and within a short time Anne begins to suspect that Wentworth is attracted to Louisa. A cheerful jaunt to Lyme Regis is cut disastrously short when Louisa falls on the steps of the Cobb and suffers a severe head injury. Wentworth's concern seems to confirm Anne's suspicions.

On arriving in Bath, where her father and sister have settled, Anne meets William Elliot her cousin and father's heir. Elliot pays her marked attention, but Anne, who has renewed an old acquaintance with Mrs Smith, a schoolfriend, now a widow and an invalid, learns from her of Elliot's past misdeeds and his present schemes. Unexpected news arrives of Louisa Musgrove's engagement to Captain Benwick, and soon afterward Wentworth appears in Bath, by now anxious to renew his addresses to Anne but uncertain of his reception. Hearing Anne, in a conversation on the quality of love, declare that woman's love is more enduring than man's, especially where the object seems lost for ever, Wentworth understands her remark to refer to her own experience. Leaving Anne an ardent declaration, hastily scribbled, he later overtakes her in the town, and all is at last settled between them before they reach the top of Milsom Street.

Although *Persuasion* is Jane Austen's last novel and was written under considerable difficulties when her health was rapidly failing, it shows barely any sign of loss of power; the social comedy is deftly handled and the overriding tone of the whole is one of serious and profound reflection. Austen's sureness of touch is shown particularly by her revision of the ending, which replaced a witty but somewhat contrived chapter where Wentworth is accidentally forced to be the instrument of Anne's acknowledging her love with two chapters (the present Chapters 22 and 23) where Anne herself, true to her ideals, prompts Wentworth's new understanding.

**Peter Grimes** One of the tales in **Crabbe**'s *The Borough* (Letter XXII). Grimes is a fisherman who from birth has been driven by the desire to inflict pain and hurt. He refuses the authority of men, and even strikes down his own father. He buys apprentices from the London workhouses, who perish under his brutal treatment. He lies to the courts, who can prove nothing against him, but he is eventually forbidden to keep apprentices, and forced to live and work in solitude. The ghosts of his father and the tormented boys rise out of the sea before him, and he goes insane with guilt and remorse. He is brought to a 'parish-bed', where he dies in mental agony. The story, one of the most compelling of all Crabbe's tales, was made into an opera of the same name by Benjamin Britten (1945).

**Peter Pan, or, The Boy Who Would Not Grow Up** A play by **J. M. Barrie**, first performed at the Duke of York's Theatre, London, in 1904 and now established as an annual favourite, with a long succession of well-known actresses in the title role. *Peter Pan* occupies blurred ground

Captain Hook and Peter Pan. An illustration for *The Peter Pan Picture Book* (1907) by Alice B. Woodward.

between drama and pantomime, though it began its life quite simply as a play for children, and its subsequent history owes more to its theatrical than its literary qualities.

The play begins in the Bloomsbury flat of the Darlings, which is visited by Peter Pan, a boy who ran away on the day he was born when he heard his parents talking about what might happen to him when he grew up. The Darlings' dog frightened Peter, and he flew away, leaving his shadow behind him. Unreasonably jealous of the dog's hold on his children, Mr Darling chains her in the yard before taking his wife out to dinner, with the result that Peter can return to find his shadow without intervention. He teaches the three Darling children to fly, after Wendy Darling has sewn his shadow on him, and they accompany him to the Never Land, where he lives with all the lost boys, protected by a tribe of Red Indians. The threat to the children comes from a pirate gang, led by Captain Hook. The gang overcomes the Red Indians while Peter is away, and Wendy, who has become mother to the lost boys, is captured along with all her 'family'. Peter arrives just in time to prevent Captain Hook from making them walk the plank, defeats the villainous pirate in a duel and sees him eaten by the crocodile that has stalked him for years. He then takes Wendy and her brothers back home, declines Mrs Darling's offer to adopt him and is partly compensated for the loss of his beloved Wendy when Mrs Darling promises to let her return to the Never Land each year to do the spring cleaning.

**Peter Wilkins, The Life and Adventures of** See **Paltock, Robert**.

**Peters, Lenrie** 1932– Gambian poet and novelist. Born in Bathurst (now Banjul), The Gambia, he received his secondary education at Prince of Wales School in Freetown, Sierra Leone. He qualified as a doctor in Cambridge and for a time was a surgeon at a hospital in Northampton, England. Returning to The Gambia, he has for many years practised privately as a doctor. His collections of poetry include *Satellites* (1967), *Katchikali* (1971) and *Selected Poetry* (1981). His poems are easily accessible to people brought up in the English literary tradition, seldom calling upon the traditional oral techniques of African poetry. The need to be pan-African in one's outlook is a central interest of all Peters's writings and with an unfashionable lack of doctrine he expresses great fear for the future of the continent: 'madness and infirmity/threaten all who hope for better things'. His novel, *The Second Round* (1965), portrays the predicament of a young doctor returning to Sierra Leone from abroad to be faced with the difficulty of fulfilling people's

expectations of him. Peters is the most prominent Gambian writer and one of the calmest voices in contemporary African literature.

**Petrarchan** After Petrarch, the anglicization of the surname of Francesco Petrarca (1304–74), a major humanist scholar and poet of the Italian Renaissance chiefly remembered for his collection of lyric poems and sonnets, *Rime Sparse* (or *Canzoniere*). The term is sometimes used for the style of his poetry, particularly its use of antithesis, paradox, **oxymoron** and the **conceit**. More usually, it distinguishes what might be regarded as the standard form of the **sonnet** from the Shakespearean sonnet.

**Petrie, George** 1790–1866 Irish antiquarian, musicologist and scholar. Born in Dublin and educated at Trinity College, Petrie edited the short-lived but important *Irish Penny Journal* (1840–1) and was a central figure in the Ordnance Survey Office, where **Eugene O'Curry** and **John O'Donovan** were his assistants. Like them he made a pioneering contribution to the scholarly aspect of the **Celtic revival**. His studies of the Round Towers of Ireland and of the Hill of Tara led to his archaeological work, *The Ecclesiastical Architecture of Ireland* (1845). He is best remembered for his continuation of **Edward Bunting**'s work in preserving the traditional music of the country, *The Petrie Collection of the Ancient Music of Ireland* (2 vols., 1855–82).

**Pettie, George** 1548–89 Very little is known of Pettie's life, except that he graduated from Christ Church, Oxford, and subsequently travelled abroad. Influenced by both the popularity and the name of **William Painter**'s collection of stories, *The Palace of Pleasure* (1566), he issued *A Petite Palace of Pettie His Pleasure*, licensed in 1576 and published soon after, although the first edition is not dated. It consists of twelve stories, which the preface says are intended for gentlewomen, including those of Alcestis, Tereus and Pygmalion. Pettie also translated Guazzo from a French version as *Civil Conversation* (1581). In his prose style Pettie is a precursor of **euphuism**.

**Peveril of the Peak** A novel by **Sir Walter Scott**, first published in 1823.

The novel concerns religious strife in the reign of Charles II. Two neighbouring Derbyshire gentlemen, the Royalist Sir Geoffrey Peveril and the Puritan Major Bridgenorth, quarrel after having managed to live through the Civil War as friends. Julian Peveril, son of Sir Geoffrey and a trusted member of the Catholic Countess of Derby's household on the Isle of Man, falls in love with Bridgenorth's daughter Alice. The machinations of Bridgenorth, his brother-in-law Edward Christian and the licentious Duke of Buckingham threaten the lovers. Julian and his father are arrested for complicity in the Popish plot, but are acquitted thanks to the intervention of Charles II.

**Peyton, K. M.** The pseudonym of the children's writer Kathleen Wendy Peyton, *née* Herald (1929– ). Born in Birmingham and brought up in Surbiton, she went to Wimbledon High School and later to Art College. Already writing children's stories while at school, she published her first book, *Sabre, the Horse from the Sea* (1948), when she was still 19. Several subsequent pony or adventure books were followed by *Windfall* (1963), a more original tale of danger at sea written with meticulous accuracy reminiscent of **Arthur Ransome** at his best. Other successes culminated in *Flambards* (1967), the first of a trilogy about a decayed Edwardian landed family and its various intrigues for restoring its fortunes. High drama is much in evidence throughout, together with a strong feeling for history, particularly in regard to changing ideas about social class. Since then she has written another trilogy about a brilliant but disturbed schoolboy musician first encountered in *Pennington's Seventeenth Summer* (1970), and has also produced an excellent ghost story, *A Pattern of Roses* (1973).

**Phalaris controversy** See **Temple, Sir William**.

*Philaster, or, Love Lies A-Bleeding* A tragicomedy by **Beaumont** and **Fletcher**, first performed *c.*1609, probably at the **Blackfriars**, and published in 1620. It was a popular success. *Philaster* has often been compared with **Shakespeare**'s *Cymbeline*, written at much the same time and for the same company of actors.

Philaster is the rightful heir to the throne of Sicily but the kingdom has been taken by the King of Calabria. He is obliged to live in the usurper's court. He and Arethusa, the usurper's daughter, are in love and Philaster places his page, Bellario, in Arethusa's service as his go-between. A marriage is arranged between Arethusa and the Spanish prince, Pharamond; but Arethusa is able to reveal that Pharamond has been amusing himself with Megra, a lady of the court, and the marriage is called off. Pharamond gets his revenge with the accusation that Arethusa has been conducting an affair with Bellario. Philaster believes the story and, distracted, alters his intention to kill himself to an intention to kill the 'guilty' pair. He is arrested and entrusted to the custody of Arethusa, who promptly marries him, thereby saving his life. Her honour is shown to be intact when it is revealed that Bellario is a girl, daughter of a Sicilian nobleman who, infatuated with Philaster, had disguised herself as a boy to be his page.

The title-page illustration for Beaumont and Fletcher's *Philaster*, 1620. The original spelling is no longer used.

The usurper is overthrown and Philaster is restored to his inheritance.

*Philip, The Adventures of* See *Adventures of Philip, The*.

**Philips, Ambrose** *c.*1675–1749 Poet and the original 'Namby-Pamby'. Educated at Shrewsbury School, Philips became a fellow of St John's College, Cambridge, and a friend of **Addison**. He wrote a version of Racine's *Andromaque* under the somewhat understated title of *The Distrest Mother*, published in 1712, and *A Collection of Old Ballads* (1723). But his chief claim to fame is the degree of contempt he earned from distinguished contemporaries after his *Pastorals* appeared in **Jacob Tonson**'s *Miscellany* of 1709 beside the undoubtedly superior examples by **Pope** (written when he was only 16). Pope elegantly demolished Philips's poetic reputation in *The Guardian* and a 'pastoral war' in print ensued, with **John Gay** parodying Philips in his sequence *The Shepherd's Week*. Philips's verses for children were praised by **Samuel Johnson** but earned him the nickname 'Namby-Pamby' from **Henry Carey**.

**Philips, John** 1676–1709 Poet. Educated at Winchester and Christ Church, Oxford, Philips is remembered as a poet who wrote blank verse during a period when the couplet was the fashionable form. *The Splendid Shilling* (1701) is in burlesque Miltonic verse and contrasts the wellbeing of the man who possesses a shilling with the privation of being a poet. A Tory, Philips was persuaded by **Robert Harley, Earl of Oxford** and **Henry St John, Viscount Bolingbroke** to write a blank-verse poem, *Blenheim* (1705), as a counter to **Addison**'s *The Campaign* (1704) on the same subject. The piece was not a success but *Cider: A Poem in Two Books* (1708) is a notable essay in blank verse in the manner of Virgil's *Georgics*.

**Philips, Katherine** See **Fowler, Katherine**.

**Phillips, John** 1631–1706 Poet, journalist, translator. Educated by his uncle, the Puritan poet, **John Milton**, Phillips wrote one of the most extreme anti-Puritan poems of any literary quality, *The Satire against Hypocrites*, in 1655. Characteristic of a certain breed of professional writer surviving on his wits and a shoestring, he was also the translator of *Pharamond* (by La Calprenède) and *Almahide* (by Madeleine de Scudéry). As well as a number of burlesques, he was responsible for editing the periodical *The Present State of Europe* from 1690 until his death.

**Phillips, Stephen** 1864–1915 Playwright and poet. Born near Oxford, Phillips was an actor in his cousin F. R. Benson's company in 1885–92, but was working as a schoolteacher when his *Poems* (1898) earned him the prestige of a literary award. There followed a short-lived vogue for his sonorous poetic dramas, of which Herbert Beerbohm Tree produced four, *Herod* (1900), *Ulysses* (1902), *Nero* (1906) and *Faust* (1908), and George Alexander staged the best, *Paolo and Francesca* (1902). Success and self-doubt affected Phillips's stability. Unprotected by the theatrical flair of Tree and Alexander, *Iole* (1913) and *The Sin of David* (1914) failed, and the man who had been so recently celebrated as the great reviver of poetic drama died destitute.

**Phillpotts, Eden** 1862–1960 Novelist and playwright. Born in India, he was educated in Devon and remained associated with the county for most of his long, secluded life. He was the author of well over 200 books, the best of them being novels about Dartmoor, like *Children in the Mist* (1898), *The Secret Woman* (1905), *The Thief of Virtue* (1910) and *Widecombe Fair* (1913). With his daughter Adelaide, Phillpotts collaborated in two successful comedies, *The Farmer's Wife* (1924), which was a revision of his own earlier version, and *Yellow Sands* (1926), as well as several shorter pieces.

**Philotas, The Tragedy of** A tragedy in blank verse by **Samuel Daniel**, first published in 1605. The subject is the execution of Philotas, the son of Alexander's great general Parmenion.

**Philotus** A play of unknown authorship probably written about 1600. The earliest known text was printed by Robert Charteris (Edinburgh, 1603), and it represents the only complete survival of Scottish drama apart from the *Satire of the Three Estates* by **Sir David Lyndsay**. The theme is the attempt of two old men, Philotus and Alberto, to marry young and pretty girls, and how their plans are frustrated by the girls, Emilie and Brisilla, with the aid of their lovers.

***Phineas Finn: The Irish Member*** A novel by **Anthony Trollope**, the second in the **Palliser** sequence, serialized in *St Paul's Magazine* from October 1867 to May 1869, and published in two volumes in 1869.

Phineas Finn, a young Irish barrister, is elected to Parliament for his local borough of Loughshane. In London his charm and good looks win him the love of Lady Laura Standish, a politically astute and ambitious woman whom he pursues despite his commitment to an Irish sweetheart, Mary Jones. Forced by family debt to make a wealthy match with the gloomy Scots laird Robert Kennedy, she continues to use her influence to help Phineas to the family pocket-borough, after he rescues Kennedy from a street assault. Phineas turns his attention to another eligible girl, Violet Effingham, and clashes with her fiery suitor Lord Chiltern. The two men fight a duel abroad, which leads to their reconciliation, and Violet marries Lord Chiltern. The background to these amorous intrigues is the new reform bill which Phineas's party, the Liberals, are trying to steer through Parliament. Phineas becomes a junior minister but is forced to resign his post when he votes in support of Irish tenant-right. He attracts the attention of Madame Max Goesler, a wealthy widow and

'You don't quite know Mr Kennedy yet.' Phineas Finn and Lady Laura Standish at Lord Brentford's. An illustration by John Everett Millais for Trollope's *Phineas Finn*, 1869.

companion of the elderly Duke of Omnium, who offers him her hand and fortune to pursue his political career. But the now discouraged Phineas refuses and returns to Ireland, where he marries Mary Jones and becomes Inspector of the Cork Poor Houses.

*Phineas Finn* is the first of the Palliser novels to deal with the workings of Parliament itself. Written at the time of the Second Reform Bill debates, it is thought to portray aspects of **Disraeli** in Mr Daubeny and of Gladstone in Mr Gresham.

**Phineas Redux** A novel by **Anthony Trollope**, the fourth in the **Palliser** sequence, serialized in *The Graphic* from July 1873 to January 1874, and published in two volumes in 1873.

Phineas Finn, now a widower, returns to England and contests the borough of Tankerville, successfully. Lady Laura Kennedy, living apart from her increasingly insane husband, still loves Phineas, but his efforts to mediate between husband and wife only inflame Mr Kennedy's jealousy, who attempts to shoot Phineas but misses. The incident is publicized in its worst light by his old enemy Quintus Slide, the radical journalist, and more scandal ensues when Phineas quarrels publicly with a cabinet minister, Mr Bonteen, who is afterwards found murdered. Phineas is arrested and brought to trial, but the skill of the lawyer Chaffanbrass, and the perseverance of Madame Max Goesler in unearthing new evidence, results in his acquittal. Suspicion falls on Mr Emilius, the estranged husband of Lady Eustace, who escapes prosecution through lack of sufficient evidence. Phineas is re-elected for Tankerville and offered a post in the government, but his sufferings have disillusioned him with public life, and he refuses the post. Meanwhile the old Duke of Omnium has died, attended to the end by Madame Max, who shows her disinterestedness by refusing a legacy left her by the duke. This comes to Plantagenet Palliser's cousin Adelaide, enabling her to marry her penniless suitor Gerard Maule. The novel ends with the marriage of Phineas and Madame Max.

The political pessimism of *Phineas Redux* reflects Trollope's disillusioning experience at the Beverley election of 1868, but is balanced in the novel by the rise of Plantagenet Palliser, now Duke of Omnium, as his ideal statesman.

**Phiz** See **Browne, Hablot K**.

**Phoenix, The** An Old English poem preserved in **The Exeter Book**. It tells the myth of the phoenix and develops it as a Christian symbol. The first part of the poem describes the Earthly Paradise, the phoenix, its flight to Syria and its death and rebirth. It is derived from the Latin poem *De Ave Phoenice* attributed to Lactantius,

but adapts this source freely; the version of the myth used is that given in Pliny's *Natural History*. The second part of the poem introduces a Christian significance not found in *De Ave Phoenice* and makes the bird a symbol of Christ and the Christian life.

**Phoenix and the Turtle, The** This 67-line poem by **Shakespeare** appeared, in the company of verse by **Ben Jonson**, **George Chapman** and **John Marston**, as an occasional poem appended to Robert Chester's *Love's Martyr* (1601). Chester's long, poor poem tells ramblingly of the love of the phoenix and the turtle (i.e. turtledove) and digresses on matters from King Arthur to beast lore and the properties of precious stones. Shakespeare's obscure and enigmatic poem is an elegy for the two birds, and ends with Reason's threnody celebrating their married chastity.

**Phoenix Nest, The** A poetic miscellany published in 1593. It was a gentlemanly enterprise, edited by one R. S. of the Inner Temple, and the contributors as well as the editor are usually identified by discreet initials; they include **Thomas Lodge**, **George Peele** and **Nicholas Breton**. The phoenix of the title is clearly **Sidney**, whose death in 1586 is lamented in several elegies.

**Physician's Tale, The** See *Canterbury Tales, The*.

**Piazza Tales, The** A volume of six pieces of short fiction by **Herman Melville**, published in 1856. Except for the title piece, they had all previously been published individually in *Putnam's Monthly* or in *Harper's New Monthly* in the early 1850s. The volume is introduced by 'The Piazza', Melville's descriptive recollection of his Massachusetts farmhouse, to the north side of which he added a piazza. 'The Bell Tower' is about an ambitious artist named Bannadonna, who attempts to rival God by creating a mechanical man, and is destroyed by his own creation. 'The Lightning-Rod Man' is the story of a man who refuses an insistent lightning-rod salesman because he believes that man should not fear the acts of God. 'The Encantadas; or, Enchanted Isles' contains 10 separate sketches, all concerning the Galapagos Islands.

'Benito Cereno' is set in 1799. The narrator, Amasa Delano, is a sea captain who puts in to an uninhabited island off the coast of Chile to take on water, and encounters a Spanish ship commanded by a seriously ill Benito Cereno. He listens to Cereno's story of the ship's recent misfortunes at Cape Horn, but suspects something amiss in the unruly and insubordinate behaviour of the crew, Cereno's strange relationship with his Senegalese valet Babo, and his ingratitude when Delano offers him aid. As Delano prepares to return to his ship, Cereno suddenly follows him. The crew attack them, but the two captains escape. Cereno then confesses that the apparent crew were in fact slaves, who, led by Babo, had mutinied and demanded that Cereno take them to Africa. When Cereno had succumbed to fever, the mutineers had planned to seize Delano's ship instead. Delano later succeeds in capturing the slave ship, and takes it to Lima, where Babo is executed. Cereno enters a monastery and dies soon after.

The last of the *Piazza Tales* is 'Bartleby the Scrivener'. A Wall Street lawyer hires Bartleby as a copyist. Bartleby is pale, quiet and strange, but extremely diligent in his single task of copying legal documents. To the lawyer's consternation, when Bartleby is asked to do anything other than copy, he replies only, 'I would prefer not to.' Soon, he would prefer not to leave, and begins to live in the office. Baffled, the lawyer moves his office to another building. The new tenant has Bartleby arrested as a vagrant. He dies in prison within days, resisting the attempts of his former employer to help him. The lawyer later hears that Bartleby had previously worked in the Dead Letter Office in Washington, and ponders on the relevance of this fact to his strange behaviour.

**picaresque** The Spanish *pícaro* was a character from low life, living on his wits and often a scoundrel, but the term came to be applied to anyone at odds with society. The *pícaro* first appeared in fiction in the anonymous *Lazarillo de Tormes* (1554). *Guzmán de Alfarache* (1559) by Mateo Alemán was widely read and translated, and the *pícaro* was eventually to appear in the literature of all western Europe. The picaresque novel is the episodic narrative describing the progress of the *pícaro*, but the term is rather loosely used: *Don Quixote*, for example, is told in the picaresque form while being a satirical romance. Le Sage's *Gil Blas* (1715–35) and Hans Jacob Christoph von Grimmelshausen's *Der Abentheurliche Simplicissimus Teutsch* (1669) are picaresque novels in a narrower sense. In English literature the tradition begins with **Thomas Nashe**'s *The Unfortunate Traveller* (1594) and continues in the work of **Defoe** (*Moll Flanders*), **Fielding**, **Smollett** and **Dickens**. By the 19th century the English picaresque novel has on the whole forgotten its origin in the literature of roguery and is usually an episodic story involving a journey. In America, the picaresque novel has an obvious influence on **Twain**'s *The Adventures of Huckleberry Finn* and many later works chronicling the adventures of the open road.

**Pickering, John** See **Puckering, Sir John**.

***Pickwick Papers, The*** The first novel by **Charles Dickens**, formally titled *The Posthumous Papers of the Pickwick Club*, published in monthly parts from April 1836 to November 1837.

The novel takes its loose, easy structure from the travels to Ipswich, Rochester, Bath and elsewhere of Samuel Pickwick and his three fellow members of the Pickwick Club, Tracy Tupman, Augustus Snodgrass and Nathaniel Winkle. Mr Pickwick's innocent and trusting nature repeatedly makes him the butt of comic adventures: struggling with a recalcitrant horse on the way to Dingley Dell; over-imbibing in punch; tenuously disporting himself on the ice; making an untoward appearance in the wrong hotel bedroom; and, in the book's most prolonged episode, unintentionally making his landlady Mrs Bardell think he wishes to marry her, and so provoking her into suing him for breach of promise. Interspersed among these and many other similar adventures are moral and melodramatic stories – 'The Bagman's Story', 'The Convict's Return', 'The Stroller's Tale' and others – which counterbalance the prevailing comedy of the book.

The bustling scenes of *Pickwick Papers* introduce a wide variety of characters: Sam Weller, Pickwick's sharp-witted Cockney servant and his coachman father Tony; the glib strolling player Alfred Jingle, who lives by his wits and his cool nerve, and his rascally servant Job Trotter; the medical student Bob Sawyer ('Nothing like dissecting, to give one an appetite'); the good-natured Wardles; the duel-hungry Dr Slammer of the 97th; the poetical

'The Break-Down.' Pickwick and Mr Wardle, in pursuit of Jingle and Rachael Wardle, are wrecked when the chaise loses a wheel. An illustration by Phiz for *The Pickwick Papers*.

Mrs Leo Hunter; and a host of watermen, lawyers, clerks, fashionable women, military men, footmen, and others. Most heighten the sheer humour of the book, but some strike a deeper note and hint at the force of Dickensian satire and anger against social injustice in later novels. The antics of the Parliamentary candidates Slumkey and Fizkin show Dickens's awareness of corrupt electioneering practices, just as the canting hypocrite Mr Stiggins shows his dislike of evangelical religion. Above all, the characters connected with the lawsuit of Bardell versus Pickwick – the rapacious Dodson and Fogg, the pompous Serjeant Buzfuz – and Pickwick's own experiences in prison near the end of the novel hint at that darker vision which Dickens's later work would explore.

***Picture of Dorian Gray, The*** A novel by **Oscar Wilde**, published by *Lippincott's Magazine* in 1890 and, expanded, in book form in 1890. Once regarded as daringly modern in its portrayal of fashionable *fin de siècle* decadence, Wilde draws on traditional patterns to create a powerful new Gothic tale. Dorian sells his soul to keep his youth and beauty, in an updated version of the Faust story. The tempter is Lord Henry Wotton, who lives selfishly for amoral pleasure; Dorian's good angel or conscience is Basil Hallward, the portrait painter, whom Dorian murders. The book highlights the tension between the polished surface of high life and the life of secret vice. Although sin is punished in the end, the book has a strong flavour of the elegantly perverse. Wilde asserted in his preface to the expanded edition: 'There is no such thing as a moral or an immoral book. Books are well written or badly written. That is all.'

***Pictures from Italy*** A travel book by **Charles Dickens**, published in *The Daily News* in 1845.

It is based on travels beginning in Paris in the summer of 1844 and lasting until the next year. Dickens entered Italy at Genoa, renting a house for some months in the nearby suburb of Albaro. The local festas, gambling, bowls, puppetry, shops, food and wine-drinking are described in compelling detail. Restless as ever, he visits Rome, Pisa, Ferrara, Parma, Florence, Bologna and Venice, which he sees as if in a dream, and goes as far south as Pompeii, Paestum and Naples. He vividly depicts a gory execution in Rome but, above all, he animates every person or scene his pen touches, giving individuality to the work of couriers, the life of inns, the stench of byways, the quarrying of marble, the economy of a palazzo and the ways of Neapolitans. Little is remarked about art or religion, although the activities of Holy Week are drily observed. His experience with *American Notes* may have taught Dickens to deal discreetly with national customs and habits, but *Pictures from Italy* also shows a genuine warmth and friendliness toward its subject markedly absent from the earlier travel book.

**picturesque** The term for an ideal of beauty which flourished, to the point of becoming a cult, during the 18th and early 19th centuries, principally in relation to landscape and gardens and the depiction of these scenes in painting and literature. It signified a departure from **neoclassicism** in its admiration for what was irregular, disordered or decayed, but stopped short of **Romanticism** by admiring these effects in a spirit of judicious connoisseurship (or taste) rather than exalted feeling. The beginnings of the cult may be found as early as **Addison**'s *Remarks on Several Parts of Italy* (1705) and **Pope**'s *Eloisa to Abelard* (1717). It was developed, but never precisely or with complete agreement, by a later generation: **William Mason** in his poem *The English Garden* (1771–81); **Thomas Gray** in his travel journal (published 1775); Richard Payne Knight (1750–1824) in *The Landscape: A Didactic Poem* (1794) and his *Analytical Enquiry into the Principles of Taste* (1805); Sir Uvedale Price (1747–1829) in his *Essay on the Picturesque* (1794); and the landscape gardener Humphry Repton (1752–1818) in various essays published between 1795 and 1816. Probably the most influential figure was **William Gilpin**, in his *Three Essays: On Picturesque Beauty; on Picturesque Travel; on Sketching Landscape* (1792) and his various travel books.

The chief manifestations were a tradition of landscape gardening which stretched from William Kent (1685–1748) to Repton and beyond; an increased interest by travellers in the wilder scenery of Wales, the Wye Valley and the Lake District and in Gothic ruins; and the widespread popularity in England of paintings by Nicolas Poussin (1594–1665), Claude (Claude Lorrain, 1600–82) and Salvator Rosa (1615–73). Literary references to the picturesque occur for the most part from the end of the 18th century onwards. **Ann Radcliffe** and **Sir Walter Scott** described scenery in conventional picturesque terms in their novels. Writers such as **Jane Austen**, in *Northanger Abbey* and *Pride and Prejudice*, and **Thomas Love Peacock**, in *Headlong Hall*, adopted a sceptical attitude, and the cult is satirized by **William Combe** in his very popular *Tour of Doctor Syntax in Search of the Picturesque*.

***Pied Piper of Hamelin, The*** A poem for children by **Robert Browning**, published in *Dramatic Lyrics* (1842). The story of the piper whose music lures away first the rats and then the children of Hamelin is based on what was apparently a common legend of the Middle Ages, though Browning encountered it in the prose compilation, *The Wonders of the Little*

*World* (1678), by **Nathaniel Wanley**. It is now generally believed that the story is connected with the Children's Crusade, when 20,000 children left their homes to follow Nicholas of Cologne and, for the most part, perished without ever reaching the Holy Land.

*Pierce Penniless His Supplication to the Devil* Thomas Nashe's prose pamphlet was printed in 1592. Pierce is prevented by society from using his talents, and he asks the devil for a loan. There is a grotesque characterization of the seven deadly sins which demonstrates Nashe's talent for fantasy: Greed has shoes made of 'crabshells . . . toothed at the toes with two sharp sixpenny nails'. Nashe spends some time in satirizing foreigners and defends the theatre against Puritan critics.

*Pierce the Ploughman's Crede* A Middle English poem in **alliterative verse**, written in the South-west Midlands *c.*1394. An early and competent imitation of *Piers Plowman*, it follows the same basic plan as the first part of **Langland**'s poem. The narrator, ignorant of his Creed, questions friars of various orders but hears only abuse of the others' orders and evidence of corruption. Eventually he meets the poor ploughman Pierce and his family; Pierce offers him comfort, reveals the sins of the friars and teaches him his Creed. The poem is remarkable for its detailed descriptions and accounts of contemporary life.

**Piercy, Marge** 1937– American novelist and poet, born in Detroit. She has been active in the women's movement for many years, and most of her work reflects the consciousness of women's assigned place in a male-dominated society, and the form that relationships take as a result. Her novels include *Going Down Fast* (1969), *Dance the Eagle to Sleep* (1970), *Small Changes* (1973), *Woman on the Edge of Time* (1976), *Vida* (1979), *Braided Lives* (1982) and *Fly Away Home* (1984). Among her volumes of poetry are *Breaking Camp* (1968), *Hard Loving* (1969), *4-Telling* (1971), *To Be Of Use* (1973), *Living in the Open* (1976), *The Twelve-Spoked Wheel Flashing* (1978), *The Moon is Always Female* (1980), *Circles on the Water: Selected Poems* (1982) and *Stone, Paper, Knife* (1983).

*Pierre, or, The Ambiguities* A novel by **Herman Melville**, published in 1852. Pierre Glendinning is the 19-year-old son of a wealthy widow in upstate New York. He is engaged to Lucy Tartan, a young woman from a prominent family, but he then meets Isabel, who claims to be his illegitimate half-sister. He knows that his mother will never accept a girl whose very existence exposes her husband's immoral behaviour. To give Isabel some measure of protec-

tion, he takes her to New York, allowing everyone to believe that he has married her. He confides in his cousin, Glen, who rejects his boyhood companion on hearing the truth. Impoverished, Pierre turns to writing to earn a living, but the novel which results from his exhaustive efforts is turned down for publication. Lucy, meanwhile, has followed Pierre to New York. Isabel shows jealousy at her appearance, and Pierre begins to realize his true feelings about his half-sister. During a confrontation with Glen and Lucy's brother, Pierre kills his cousin. He is arrested, and Lucy and his mother die of grief. Tormented by conflicting emotions about their forbidden love, Pierre and Isabel commit suicide in his prison cell.

*Piers Plowman* An allegorical poem in **alliterative verse** by **William Langland** written in the West Midlands during the second half of the 14th century. It survives in three recensions, known as the A-, B- and C-texts, representing different stages of revision almost certainly carried out by Langland himself. The A-text, of 2500 lines, is the product of the 1360s and was probably completed 1369–70. The B-text was written in the following decade and makes repeated reference to the events of 1376–9. It expands and develops the material of the A-text, trebling its length. The C-text was complete by 1387; **Thomas Usk** (d.1388) borrowed from its unique sections in his *Testament of Love*. It is the same length as the B-text and its alterations seem intended to elucidate the earlier text and to incorporate the significance of recent events. It is not always superior to the B-text and in some places reduces its imaginative power and vividness. The B-text is that which is most commonly read and discussed.

The poem is divided into passus of unequal length, 12 in the A-text, 20 in the B-text and 23 in the C-text. It falls into two parts, known as the *Visio* and the *Vita* after the Latin rubric dividing the B- and C-texts into the *Visio Willilmi de Petrus Plowman* and the *Vita de Dowel, Dobet et Dobest*. The basic format of the poem is a **dream-vision** but in its progress it moves in and out of dream and does not employ consistently the characteristic features of the form. Through a series of allegorical narratives the *Visio* reveals the corrupt state of the world, of secular government, society and the established Church, and makes an attempt to remedy it by creating an ideal society in which each individual exercises humility and submits to the common good. Social reform is inadequate and soon the order breaks down as selfishness and disobedience undermine the structure. The *Visio* initiates the search for Truth and the quests for the means to salvation and for Charity which provide the impetus for the remainder of the poem.

'And as I lay and lened and loked in the wateres, I slombred in a slepying.' An illustration from a manuscript of the second version (B) of *Piers Plowman*. *MS 201 f.1*. Corpus Christi College, Oxford.

The *Vita* is more introspective, exploring the reasons for the failure in the *Visio* by intellectual enquiry. Allegorical narrative is largely replaced by a series of interviews with personified abstractions representing facets of the Dreamer's psyche (Wit, Thought, Conscience) and concepts or ways of life (Study, Clergy, Reason). The Dreamer's search for Dowel, Dobet and Dobest, the various stages of good Christian life and understanding, is beset with problems of incomprehension, backsliding and confusion. At one stage he disappears, to be replaced by Rechelesnesse, representing his wallowing in worldliness and temporary abandonment of the quest in favour of easy and superficial answers. The Dreamer returns to continue his search through more interviews and a vision of the history of Christianity, the progress of which must be echoed in the spiritual progress of the individual. The devil's undermining of man's attempts is revealed and the individual's consequent need for divine grace is stressed. After a vision of the Crucifixion and the harrowing of Hell the Dreamer sees the establishment of the Church and returns to its state of decay in the

14th century with an ultimate realization that the search must begin again.

The figure of Piers Plowman is part of the shifting allegorical fabric of the poem. His first appearance is as a humble servant of God who organizes society into an ideal structure in the allegorical episode of the Ploughing of the Half Acre. After the failure of the social experiment he leads his followers in the search for Truth, disappearing after the reading of an enigmatic pardon from Truth which states only that those who live well shall be saved. During the first stages of the Dreamer's search for the meaning of living well Piers is absent, but he reappears towards the end of the *Vita* as the Good Samaritan and as the incarnated form of Christ, demonstrating the ideal progression of the Christian soul to an imitation of Christ (*imitatio Christi*).

The poem's use of **allegory** is complex, often confusing and unconventional. Its various modes include the personification of abstract concepts, fully developed narrative episodes, **exempla** and tableaux; the whole work has a substructure of biblical reference and exegesis. The poem shifts in and out of allegory, mingling it with the literal, varying and developing its symbols. The meaning of an argument or symbol at any one time is dictated and limited by the Dreamer's capacity for understanding and so changes with the poem's progress. The reader follows the Dreamer's path towards understanding, restricted by and sharing his difficulties. The very impenetrability of the poem, its allegory and its meandering path, is a part of its meaning, mirroring the difficult process of apprehending its critical issues.

Apart from its allegorical content, *Piers Plowman* provides a detailed record of late 14th-century life, covering all aspects of political and theological debate and echoing common sentiments in its satire of the corrupt church and especially the friars. It is packed with details of contemporary life, often portrayed with extraordinary vividness and sympathy, as in the confessions of the Seven Deadly Sins, and the poet's portrayal of common humanity is characterized by deep compassion and astute observation. While the aim of the work was not principally poetic, and it is frequently difficult and daunting for the modern reader, *Piers Plowman* remains one of the greatest literary works of the Middle Ages.

**Pilgrim's Progress, The**: *From this World to that which is to come* A religious **allegory** by **John Bunyan**, Part I published in 1678, Part II in 1684. It is presented as a dream by the author, in which he sees a man called Christian with a book in his hand and a burden on his back, in great distress of mind because the book tells him that he lives in the City of Destruction, and is condemned to death and judgement. Advised by Evangelist to flee towards a Wicket Gate, he sets out forthwith, leaving behind his wife and children who refuse to accompany him. The course of his subsequent pilgrimage takes him through the Slough of Despond, past the Burning Mount, thence to the Wicket Gate, the Interpreter's House, the Cross (where his burden rolls away), the Hill Difficulty, the House Beautiful, the Valley of Humiliation, the Valley of the Shadow of Death, Vanity Fair, Lucre Hill, the River of the Water of Life, By-Path Meadow, Doubting Castle, the Delectable Mountains, the Enchanted Ground and the country of Beulah, until at length he passes over the River and into the Celestial City. On the way Christian has been helped by trusty companions, first Faithful, who is put to death in Vanity Fair, and then Hopeful, who accompanies him into the Celestial City. Both separately and together they encounter a great number of allegorical characters. Some are hostile, like the foul fiend Apollyon who is slain by Christian, Lord Hategood who presides over their trial in Vanity Fair, and Giant Despair who

Christian climbing the Hill Difficulty. An illustration from the 1695 edition of *The Pilgrim's Progress*.

imprisons them in Doubting Castle. Others are seemingly friendly but give the pilgrims dangerous advice; these include Mr Worldly Wiseman, Ignorance, Talkative and By-ends.

In Part II Christian's wife Christiana follows him on pilgrimage, together with her children and their neighbour Mercy. At the Interpreter's House the party is joined by Great-heart, who subsequently slays Giant Despair and various other giants and monsters. They meet with many fellow pilgrims on the way, such as Mr Feeble-mind, Mr Ready-to-halt, Mr Honest, Valiant-for-truth, Mr Stand-fast, Mr Despondency and his daughter Much-afraid, and at the end they all pass over the River one by one.

In Part I Bunyan is drawing on his own experience of conversion which, according to his view of it, is no instantaneous event or abrupt redirection of the spiritual life, but a long and arduous progression. But whereas his earlier autobiographical *Grace Abounding* is notable for its inward-turning, isolated and agonized preoccupation with his individual experience, here the process is given flesh in figurative terms: his own temptation to despair is transmuted into a Giant who locks the pilgrims up; the scriptural texts which had threatened him become demons with which Christian must contend. Part II, by contrast, is much more relaxed in tone, and leisurely in pace: the pilgrims enjoy fellowship together, and they have time to get married and entertain one another. The greater number and variety of pilgrims reflects Bunyan's increased responsibilities as a nonconformist pastor, and this part of the book is more like a social novel in consequence.

From the moment of its publication, Bunyan's allegory of the Christian life has appealed to an extraordinarily wide readership. It has been published in innumerable editions, and has been translated into well over 100 languages. The book's popularity in languages other than English undoubtedly owes something to the folk-tale elements in its structure – the story of a man in search of the truth is one which crosses cultural boundaries. But the book is solidly rooted in Bunyan's own time, and owes a great deal to his experiences as an itinerant sectarian preacher, and prisoner of conscience. Much of its attraction lies in the beauty and simplicity of Bunyan's prose, and in the vividness with which he brings his allegorical characters to life, acutely catching the rhythms of colloquial speech. Though allegorical in form, the work is also profoundly realistic, particularly in its memorable portrayal of the psychological states of the pilgrims as they strive to hold on to their beliefs in a hostile and uncomprehending world.

**Pindar, Peter** The pseudonym adopted by the satirist John Wolcot (1738–1819). Born at Dodbrooke, near Kingsbridge in Devon, Wolcot studied medicine in London and at Aberdeen University, where he took his MD in 1767. In the same year he became physician to Sir William Trelawny, Governor of Jamaica. After two years he took holy orders, and returned to Cornwall to practise medicine. He abandoned it in 1778 and went to London with his protégé, the painter John Opie. He began his own career as a satirist, using the name of Peter Pindar, with *Lyric Odes to the Royal Academicians* (1782–5) in *The Weekly Review*. *The Lousiad* (1785–95), a mock-heroic poem, took the Royal Family as its target, *Ode upon Ode* (1787) the yearly official odes to the king. *Bozzy and Piozzi* (1786) satirized **Boswell** and Mrs Thrale, the friends of **Dr Johnson**. Peter Pindar elsewhere turned his attention to James Bruce (the explorer of Abyssinia), William Pitt and **Edmund Burke**. His verse was collected in 1812.

**Pindaric ode** See **ode**.

**Pinero, Sir Arthur Wing** 1855–1934 Dramatist. Born in London and frugally educated there, Pinero left his father's law office to become an actor in 1874. He was the author of 15 plays by 1884, when he abandoned the stage to commit himself to writing, and his best work post-dates his acting career. He was the leading dramatist of his age in two distinct fields, that of farce and that of the social 'problem' play. Of the first kind, are *The Magistrate* (1885), *The Schoolmistress* (1886) and *Dandy Dick* (1887), all among the finest of English farces. *The Cabinet Minister* (1890) is less secure. Pinero had, by the time he wrote it, established a reputation as a writer of comedy with the sentimental *Sweet Lavender* (1888) and risked that reputation with *The Profligate* (1889), controversial in its time simply because its plot hinged on seduction. Without radically criticizing contemporary moral values, Pinero proceeded to write a succession of social dramas highlighting the plight of women in an unforgiving world. They include **The Second Mrs Tanqueray** (1893), *The Notorious Mrs Ebbsmith* (1895), *The Benefit of the Doubt* (1895), *Iris* (1901), *Letty* (1903), *His House in Order* (1906), *The Thunderbolt* (1908) and *Mid-Channel* (1909). A preparedness to examine, if not quite to challenge, convention is evident also in two effective comedies, *The Princess and the Butterfly* (1897) and *The Gay Lord Quex* (1899). Pinero's best comedy, **Trelawny of the 'Wells'** (1898), is a nostalgic celebration of the mid-Victorian theatre, already lost in the era of the long run. Pinero was knighted in 1909. He continued to write plays for the rest of his life, seeking to maintain a hold in a theatre that changed too fast for him.

**Pinter, Harold** 1930– Playwright. Born and educated in Hackney, London, Pinter trained as an actor at the Royal Academy of Dramatic Art and was a working actor when he began writing plays. Although influenced by **Beckett** and associated with him in the **Theatre of the Absurd**, Pinter is better appreciated as the inventor of a new kind of comedy, sometimes called the 'comedy of menace'. The majority of his plays are set in a single room, whose occupants are threatened by forces or people whose precise intentions neither the characters nor the audience can define. *The Room* (1957) and **The Birthday Party** (1957) were the first to be produced. *The Dumb Waiter* (1960), a brilliantly crafted one-act piece, and **The Caretaker** (1960) established him as a major playwright in the suddenly adventurous British theatre. Four more short plays, *A Slight Ache* (1961), *The Collection* (1962), *The Dwarfs* (1963) and *The Lover* (1963), were followed by **The Homecoming** (1965), perhaps the most enigmatic of all his work. For many critics it marked the climax of his dramatic career. Increasingly involved in writing for films, Pinter wrote a series of short memory plays, abstract and poetic, *Landscape* (1968), *Silence* (1969), the two-act *Old Times* (1971) and *Monologue* (1973). *No Man's Land* (1975), *Betrayal* (1978) and *The Hothouse* (1980), however proficient, lacked the theatrical excitement of his earlier work, with the result that the double-bill of *One for the Road* and *Victoria Station* (1983), zestful and humorous, was greeted with something like relief by his admirers.

**Pioneers, The** See **Leatherstocking Tales, The**.

**Pippa Passes** A dramatic poem by **Robert Browning**, the first of the series called *Bells and Pomegranates*, published in 1841. Pippa is a silk winder who spends her holiday wandering through the small Italian town of Asolo, singing songs and thinking of the local people whom she considers the most blessed: Ottima, Phene, Luigi and the Bishop. In reality, the lives and characters of these four are entirely different from Pippa's innocent imaginings.

**Pirate, The** A novel by **Sir Walter Scott**, published in 1822.

The misanthropic Basil Mertoun and his son, the amiable and attractive Mordaunt, live in a remote part of Zetland. Their landlord is the wealthy Magnus Troil, and Mordaunt is a close friend of Troil's two daughters, Minna and Brenda. When a buccaneer, Cleveland, is wrecked on the coast Mordaunt rescues him and Minna falls in love with him. Mordaunt and Cleveland develop a hatred for each other and Mordaunt finds himself unwelcome at his landlord's house. Brenda, however, remains true to their friendship and he grows to love her.

Eventually the pirates and Cleveland attempt to capture Magnus and his daughters but Mordaunt raises the alarm and they are rescued by a frigate. Minna and Cleveland (who proves to be half-brother to Mordaunt) are thus parted for ever. Mordaunt and Brenda find a happy ending.

*Pistil of Swete Susan, The* See *Susanna, or, The Pistil of Swete Susan.*

*Pit, The*: *A Story of Chicago* A novel by **Frank Norris**, published in 1903, the year after the author's death. It is the second part of his uncompleted trilogy *The Epic of the Wheat*. The 'pit' of the title is the Chicago stock exchange, where Curtis Jadwin is a leading speculator in the wheat market. By the time he gains a monopoly of the wheat stocks, Jadwin's obsession with money and the operations of the pit has driven him almost to madness. In the meantime, however, the growth of farming in the West has increased the supply of grain, and this results in a sharp devaluation of his investment. With a glut of wheat on the market, Jadwin, already in poor health, loses all his money. His rise in the wheat market is paralleled by the decline of his marriage to the attractive Laura Dearborn. Neglected by her husband, she begins to return to the flirtations which had characterized her behaviour prior to their marriage, and she resumes her relationship with the aesthete Sheldon Corthell. At the end of the novel, however, Laura returns to Jadwin; they renew their commitment to each other and are able to look toward the future with hope.

**Plaatje, Solomon Tshekisho** 1877–1932 South African politician and writer, born near Boshof. Court interpreter during the Mafeking siege, he wrote a posthumously discovered *Boer War Diary* (1972). Newspaper editor and first Secretary of the African National Congress (1912), he attacked in his *Native Life in South Africa* (1916) the 1913 Natives Land Act for turning blacks into pariahs in their own country. *Mhudi* (1930), written about 1917, was the first novel to present pre-colonial African society as having humane religious, social, and legal institutions. Other works include *Sechuana Proverbs and Their . . . Equivalents* (1916) and, with Daniel Jones, *Sechuana Reader in International Phonetic Orthography (with English Translations)* (1916).

*Plain Dealer, The* A comedy by **William Wycherley**, produced in December 1676 and published in 1677. Its source is Molière's *Le Misanthrope*. The most mordant of Wycherley's four plays, it is regarded by many as his finest. His friend **John Dryden** described it as one of the most bold, most general, and most useful

satires which has ever been presented on the English theatre'.

The plain dealer of the title is the misanthropic Manly, a sea-captain who believes that only his friend Vernish and his betrothed Olivia are sincere. He returns from the Dutch wars to find that Olivia has married another and has no intention of returning the money he left in her care. Manly uses his page as a go-between in his vengeance on Olivia. Part of his plan is to dishonour her, but he does not know that his page is a girl, Fidelia, who has always loved him and has followed him to the war in disguise. Olivia is charmed by the page and makes an assignation with him; Manly accompanies Fidelia thinking his plan successful and intending to expose Olivia. But Olivia's husband, none other than the supposed friend Vernish, arrives on the scene. In the scuffle that follows Fidelia is wounded and her disguise discovered. Manly is touched by her devotion and sees the worthlessness of his obsession with Olivia. Fidelia wins her man.

**Planché, James Robinson** 1796–1880 Born and educated in London, Planché was a prolific playwright, a musician, historian of costume, herald and antiquarian. He wrote well over 150 plays and libretti, the best known being *The Vampyre, or, The Bride of the Isles* (1820). His crucial role in the development of the English **pantomime** is widely recognized, as is the contribution he made to the thoughtful costuming of **Shakespeare** by his designs for the revival of *King John* at **Drury Lane** in 1823. *Recollections and Reflections* (2 vols., 1872) is a lively and informative autobiography.

**Plater, Alan (Frederick)** 1935– Dramatist. Born in County Durham, he began by writing television scripts and plays, several of which he adapted for the stage. *A Smashing Day* (1965) is about a confused young man; *See The Pretty Lights* (1970) is a tender love-story between a middle-aged man and a teenage girl. His true vitality emerged only when he started to work in a style of regional 'epic', combining songs, music-hall sketches and comedy gags into what were often serious social themes. The most successful of these local documentaries was *Close The Coalhouse Door* (1968), which described the history of coal-mining as seen through the eyes of the Milburn family.

**Plath, Sylvia** 1932–63 American poet, born in Boston, and educated at Smith College. After graduation she won a Fulbright to Cambridge, receiving her MA in 1957. In the same year she married the English poet **Ted Hughes**. She studied with **Robert Lowell** and her work has clear affinities with **Confessional poetry**. However, she often distances herself from her per-

Sylvia Plath.

sonal subject matter by assuming a sharply ironic tone. Whether writing about tulips and elm trees, her experiences as a daughter and a wife, or her suicide attempts, there is an undercurrent of terror in her poems. *The Colossus and Other Poems* (England 1960, US publication 1962) was the only one of her books of poetry to be published before her suicide. Posthumous volumes include *Ariel* (1965), *Crossing the Water* (England 1971, US publication 1972), and *Winter Trees* (England 1971, US publication 1972). A partly autobiographical novel, *The Bell Jar*, was published in 1963 (US publication 1971). Her prose is collected in *Johnny Panic and the Bible of Dreams: Short Stories, Prose, and Diary Excerpts* (1979). *The Journals of Sylvia Plath* appeared in 1982.

***Playboy of the Western World, The*** A comedy by **J. M. Synge**, first performed at the **Abbey Theatre**, Dublin, in 1907, when it was the occasion of a riot, sparked off by the mere mention of an undergarment. The play is one of the masterpieces of the Irish theatre.

The action takes place near a village on the coast of County Mayo during two autumn days. On the first, a stranger called Christy Mahon arrives, confessing himself a fugitive because he has killed his tyrannical father. Overwhelmed by the boldness of the deed, the villagers lionize Christy, who flourishes in the atmosphere of adulation. Pegeen Mike, daughter of the owner of the local shebeen, and Widow Quinn give him his first experience of female admiration. No longer a whimpering weakling, Christy wins a mule race and is rewarded with a promise of marriage to Pegeen Mike. But his triumph is cut short by the return of his father, bandaged but not dead, to reclaim his errant son. For the second time, Christy 'kills' his father with a spade, and for the second time old Mahon rises from the dead. Christy goes with him in the end, but no longer into servitude. Mahon respects him now, and

Pegeen grieves over the loss of her playboy from the west.

**Plomer, William (Charles Franklyn)** 1903–73 Poet and novelist. Born in South Africa, he was educated in England at Rugby. After working as a farmer he founded the literary magazine *Voorslag* with **Roy Campbell** in 1926. Plomer's first, angry novel, *Turbott Wolfe* (1926), precociously treats racism. He travelled widely, living in Japan (1926–9) before settling in England. He worked as a publisher's reader and served in Naval Intelligence (1940–6). Plomer's poems, including *Notes for Poems* (1927), *The Family Tree* (1929), *The Fivefold Screen* (1932), *Visiting The Caves* (1936) and *Celebrations* (1972), fall into two categories. His serious verse, exemplified by 'The Taste of the Fruit', is often moving and elegiac; his light verse, including the satirical balladry of *The Dorking Thigh* (1945), is comparable in stature to that of **Betjeman**. After *Collected Poems* (1960), he received wide recognition, including the CBE and the Queen's Gold Medal for Literature. Besides editing the diaries of **Francis Kilvert** (1938–40) and **Melville**'s poems, he collaborated with Benjamin Britten as librettist for *Gloriana* (1953) and his three 'church operas'.

***Plough and the Stars, The*** A play by **Sean O'Casey**, first performed at the **Abbey Theatre**, Dublin, in 1926, where it was the occasion of a famous riot. The action covers one day in November 1915 and the week of the Easter Rising in 1916. It was O'Casey's blunt and often humorous treatment of the behaviour of ordi-

Sara Allgood as Pegeen Mike and Arthur Shields as Christy Mahon in J. M. Synge's *The Playboy of the Western World* at the Abbey Theatre, 1907.

nary people involved in great events that offended many Irish people. The play is set in the Dublin slums and the title refers to the banner of the Irish Citizen Army, to which O'Casey had once belonged.

The occupants of a Dublin tenement are a cross-section of Irish social and political attitudes. Jack Clitheroe is a member of the Irish Citizen Army. His wife Nora is concerned only for Jack's safety. Nora's uncle, Peter Flynn, supports the independence movement from a safe distance. Jack's cousin, Covey, hopes for social revolution but does nothing to further it. Fluther Good does nothing but talks a lot. Mrs Gogan is ghoulishly fascinated by death, not only because her daughter Mollser is dying of consumption. Bessie Burgess, finest of them all, is a fruit-vendor with a son in the British army, a taste for drink and a heart of gold. The first act ends with Jack Clitheroe angrily brushing off his wife's protests and going to a gathering of the Citizen Army. The extraordinary second act brings some of the occupants together in a Dublin pub, where they hear and respond to the inflammatory speeches of Irish patriots addressing a crowd outside. The last two acts take place during Easter Week 1916. Nora's frantic attempts to keep Jack at home fail and he is killed. Fluther, Covey and others take their chances to loot shops. Bessie Burgess, trying to protect the demented Nora, is shot by a sniper.

***Plowman's Tale, The***, or, *The Complaint of the Plowman* A Middle English poem in **alliterative verse**, probably written in the early 15th century. It is likely that the main part of the poem was written by one, or perhaps two, **Lollard** sympathizers, the prologue being added in the 16th century. In the form of a debate between a pelican and a griffin, the poem attacks the Church and supports Lollard ideals; the Griffin, proponent of the established Church, is defeated. The prologue introduces the tale as that of the ploughman mentioned in the General Prologue to *The Canterbury Tales*; as a consequence the poem was included in early editions of **Chaucer**'s works. (See **Chaucerian apocrypha**.)

***Plumed Serpent, The*** A novel by **D. H. Lawrence**, published in 1926.

Kate Leslie, an Irish widow, visits Mexico in search of some quality that will renew her life. She attends a bullfight and is revolted by what she considers the degeneration of modern Mexico. Then she meets General Don Cipriano Viedma, a pure-bred Indian whose primitive sexual energy she finds mysterious but attractive. Cipriano introduces her to Don Ramón Carrasco, scholar and political leader, whose mission is to dispose of Christianity and revive the old gods of Mexico. Quetzalcoatl, the plumed serpent, will preside and Don Ramón will represent him. This cult is characterized by an actual and symbolic reawakening of primeval sexuality marked by the dominance of the male over the female and of the political leader over the masses.

As Don Ramón rises to lead the people Kate witnesses violent blood sacrifices by Cipriano, but is fascinated by the cult's elemental power. She herself is reborn as Malintzi, a fertile goddess and bride of Cipriano, now elevated by Ramón to the status of war god, Huitzilopochtli. Possessed by the man-god, Kate seems about to become wholly subservient to his will, thereby fulfilling the emotional and symbolic sacrifice demanded of the female in the cult and in Lawrence's own quasi-mystical scheme: but the novel ends with her continued expression of doubt.

**Poe, Edgar Allan** 1809–49 American short-story writer and poet. Born in Boston, Poe was raised by the Richmond merchant, John Allan, after the early death of his parents. Later, by choice, he took Allan as his middle name. The Allans moved to England, where Poe was educated at a private school from 1815 to 1820. He completed his schooling in the USA and entered the University of Virginia in 1826, but left soon after in order to pursue a literary career. His first book, *Tamerlane and Other Poems*, was published anonymously and at his own expense in 1827. It went unnoticed. He then enlisted in the army under an assumed name and incorrect age. He was admitted to West Point in 1830, but in the following year was dismissed for neglecting his duty.

During a brief stay in New York City, he published a volume entitled *Poems* (1831), and then went to Baltimore, where he began to publish short fiction in magazines. The story 'MS Found in a Bottle' (1833) was awarded the first prize in a contest judged by **John Pendleton Kennedy**, who later found Poe an editorial position on the *Southern Literary Messenger* (1835). In 1836 Poe married his 13-year-old cousin, and moved to Richmond, Virginia. During this period, the unfinished tragedy *Politian* (1835–6) was serialized in the *Messenger*, which also published Poe's numerous reviews, essays, poems and stories. He moved to New York in 1837, published *The Narrative of Arthur Gordon Pym* in 1838, then went to Philadelphia, where he served as assistant editor of *Burton's Gentleman's Magazine* from 1839 to 1840. He contributed a number of stories to this magazine, including 'The Fall of the House of Usher' (1839). His first collection of short stories, *Tales of the Grotesque and Arabesque*, appeared in 1840. In the same year he left *Burton's* to begin his own journal, *The Penn*, but when the project failed he became literary editor of *Graham's Magazine* (1841–2), to which he contributed the stories, 'Murders in the Rue Morgue', 'The Masque of the Red Death' and 'The Imp of the Perverse', and an essay entitled 'The Philosophy of Composition'.

The year 1843 saw the freelance publication of 'The Tell-Tale Heart', 'The Black Cat', 'The Pit and the Pendulum', and the prize-winning story 'The Gold Bug'. He returned to New York City in 1844 and began working for the *New York Mirror*. He purchased the *Broadway Journal* in 1845, and in the same year published *Tales* and *The Raven and Other Poems*. The *Journal* folded in 1846, and his young wife died in 1847. His later work includes the ambitious philosophical poem, 'Eureka', a poem entitled 'Ulalume', and the story 'The Domain of Arnheim', all published in 1848. He began a three-month lecture tour in 1849 to raise funds for a proposed magazine, but the strain led to a nervous breakdown. He returned to Richmond, where he produced the poem 'Annabel Lee' and delivered a lecture entitled 'The Poetic Principle'. He died in Baltimore later that year.

**Poema Morale**, *or, Moral Ode* A striking and powerful poem of religious warning, dating from *c*.1150. It treats the common theme of the consequences of wrongdoing, and admonishes the reader to work towards salvation through virtuous living.

**Poems of the Past and Present** A volume by **Thomas Hardy**, first published in 1902. Much of it was written in the 1880s and 1890s, although some goes back as far as the 1860s. Some, too, had already appeared in *The Tatler*, *The Academy*, *The Westminster Gazette* and other publications. Divided into several parts – 'War Poems', 'Poems of Pilgrimage', 'Miscellaneous Poems', 'Imitations', and 'Retrospect' – this richly variegated collection includes some of Hardy's most enduring verse. Beginning with a reverie on Queen Victoria, published in *The Times* a week after her death, Hardy next offers poems on the Boer War which include the finely wrought 'Drummer Hodge'. 'Poems of Pilgrimage' evoke literary and historical memories of **Shelley**, of **Gibbon**, of Rome, of Genoa and of Fiesole. 'Miscellaneous Poems' dwells – often sardonically, sometimes lyrically – on the timeless themes of doom and sadness, of nature and female beauty, of marital and emotional complexities, and they include 'To an Unborn Pauper Child', 'Lizbie Brown', 'The Darkling Thrush', 'The Ruined Maid', 'In Tenebris' (I–III) and 'The Lost Pyx'.

**Poet Laureate** Originally a title given generally to poets in recognition of their achievement, it became in later times an official post awarded to a poet who received a stipend as an officer of the Royal Household. The formal duty of writing occasional verses and appropriate odes for public occasions is no longer demanded, and the title is largely honorific. The stipend, similarly, is nominal. **Ben Jonson** first performed the duties of Poet Laureate, though the post was first bestowed officially on **Dryden**, who was followed by: **Shadwell**, **Tate**, **Rowe**, **Eusden**, **Cibber**, **Whitehead**, **Thomas Warton the younger**, **Pye**, **Southey**, **Wordsworth**, **Tennyson**, **Austin**, **Bridges**, **Masefield**, **Day-Lewis**, **Betjeman** and **Ted Hughes**.

**Poetaster, The**, *or, The Arraignment* A satirical comedy by **Ben Jonson**, directed at contemporary writers. It was produced in 1601 and published the following year. The thin storyline, set at the court of the Emperor Augustus, concerns the efforts of Crispinus (**Marston**) and Demetrius (**Dekker**) to defame Horace (Jonson). Dekker, perhaps helped by Marston, replied with *Satiromastix*.

**Poetical Rhapsody** A collection of Elizabethan verse published by Francis Davison and his brother Walter in 1602. It includes 'The Lie', attributed to **Walter Raleigh**, and poems by **Robert Greene**, **Sir Henry Wotton**, **Sidney**, **Spenser** and **Donne**.

**Poetry**: *A Magazine of Verse* An American journal that prints reviews as well as verse, *Poetry* has been published monthly since its founding in 1912. Virtually every major American poet of the 20th century has published in it at some point. It has also published poetry by British, Irish, French, Italian, Greek, Indian, Israeli, Japanese and Soviet dissident poets. **Harriet Monroe**, its founder, served as editor from 1912 to 1936.

**Poetry Bookshop** See **Monro, Harold**.

**Poliakoff, Stephen** 1952– Dramatist. Born in London, he studied at Cambridge but started to write plays as a teenager, contributing to *Lay-By* (1971), a group play about pornography and rape. *The Carnation Gang* (1973), *Hitting Town* (1975) and *City Sugar* (1975), together with *Heroes* (1974), established him as a prolific, original playwright with an instinct for powerful contemporary metaphors. Subsequent work has included *Strawberry Fields* (1977), written while he was writer-in-residence at the **National Theatre**, *Shout Across the River* (1978), *Favourite Nights* (1981) and *Breaking the Silences* (1984), about the early days of the Russian Revolution.

**Pollock, Sharon** 1936– Canadian dramatist. Born in Fredericton, New Brunswick, she grew up in the eastern townships of Quebec, returning to Fredericton where she attended the University of New Brunswick for two years. Subsequently she worked in amateur theatre, first in New Brunswick and later in Alberta as a member of a touring company, Prairie Players. She won a Dominion Drama Best Actress Award in 1966. She began to write for radio and the stage in the early 1970s. She has held various posts in theatrical centres and at the University of Alberta and has lived in Vancouver, Edmonton and Calgary. Her first play, *A Compulsory Option* (1972), a black comedy, was followed by a series of works which focus on political and social issues in both present and past, often using the historical to cast light on the contemporary. *Walsh* (1974), which first attracted national attention to her work, examines the treatment meted out to Sitting Bull and his followers when they fled to Canada after their victory at Little Big Horn. *Out You Go* (1975) satirizes contemporary politics in British Columbia, while *The Komagata Maru Incident* (1978) finds a parallel for contemporary racism in a 1914 episode, when 400 Sikh immigrants were prevented from entering Canada by a gang of Vancouver hooligans. *One Tiger to a Hill* (1980) attacks the complacency of Canadian attitudes to prison reform. Pollock's best-known play, *Blood Relations* (1980), is about Lizzie Borden, the New England spinster charged and acquitted of the axe murder of her parents in 1892. It is a tightly constructed family drama which represents a departure from her previous work. It exploits the possibilities for ambiguity inherent in dramatic production and leaves the central issue of the protagonist's guilt open, but suggests a revisionist feminist perspective. Pollock has also written a number of children's plays.

**Polly** A ballad opera by **John Gay**, written as a sequel to *The Beggar's Opera*. It follows Polly Peachum to the West Indies in search of the transported Macheath, describing her adventures there and their ironic culmination in her unintended delivering of Macheath to justice on the scaffold.

*Polly*'s banning by the Walpole government in 1729 gave it an unmerited celebrity. It was eventually produced, in a version adapted by **George Colman the Elder**, in 1777.

**Poly-Olbion** An enormous poem by **Michael Drayton**, published in 1612 and 1622, running to some 30,000 alexandrines in rhyming couplets. Its 'Chorographical Description' (that is, a description of a country or locality) embraces both England and Wales: their landscapes, notable sights, ancient history and beliefs. Its chief source was the *Britannia* by the antiquary **William Camden**, who also sub-titled his work 'chorographica descriptio'. The result is both a versified map and a vast storehouse of infor-

mation, much of it of great antiquarian interest. Some of the finest verse is to be found in Drayton's descriptions of landscapes and the countryside.

Drayton was planning this 'Herculean labour' (as one of his friends called it) by 1598 but the first part did not appear until 1612. The splendid title-page of this edition shows Britannia on her throne holding a sceptre and a cornucopia – the latter alluding to the meaning of the title, 'many blessings'. On her garments are rivers and hills of the British Isles. This first part has 18 songs and is annotated with great learning and remarkable accuracy by the antiquary **John Selden**. The remaining 12 songs were finished by 1619 but not added to a new edition until 1622, because of Drayton's difficulty in finding a printer willing to undertake so vast (and apparently unprofitable) a project.

**Pomfret, John** 1667–1702 Poet. The son of Thomas Pomfret, vicar of Luton, the poet was educated at Bedford grammar school and Queens' College, Cambridge. He followed his father's calling, becoming rector of two Bedfordshire parishes. In 1699 he published *Poems on Several Occasions*, but it was to *The Choice*, which appeared the following year, that he owed his immense contemporary popularity. A civilized and elegant account of a life at once genteel and epicurean, it was perfectly suited to the taste of the time. Pomfret's other works include moral reflections, Pindaric essays and the disappointingly unexciting *Cruelty and Lust*. His popularity endured for more than a century, and led **Johnson** to suggest to the publishers of *Lives of the Poets* that he be included (one of only four such additions to the original scheme). 'Perhaps no composition in our language has been oftener perused than Pomfret's *Choice*', he wrote, adding in judicious bafflement, 'He pleases many, and he who pleases many must have some species of merit.' **Robert Southey**, in 1807, seems moved by a similar sentiment: 'Why is Pomfret the most popular of the English Poets? The fact is certain, and the solution would be useful.'

**Poole, John** 1786–1872 Playwright. His first dramatic work, the *Hamlet Travestie* (1811), established a fashion for burlesque versions of **Shakespeare**. Only with *Paul Pry* (1825) did Poole again rise above the journeyman level of other hack dramatists.

**Poor Richard's Almanack** Published by **Benjamin Franklin** under the pseudonym of Richard Saunders, *Poor Richard's Almanack* first appeared in 1732. From 1747 to 1758 it was entitled *Poor Richard Improved*. As well as containing a calendar and astronomical data, it included many of Franklin's well-known maxims dictating homely wisdom, virtue, and frugality. Its fictional author, Richard, and his wife Bridget became popular literary characters. Franklin sold the almanac in 1758, but it continued publication until 1796.

**Poor White** A novel by **Sherwood Anderson**, published in 1920. It tells how late-19th-century technology changes the lives of the inhabitants of Bidwell, Ohio, and particularly that of Hugh McVey, a telegraph operator, who at the beginning of the novel is the shy, inhibited 'poor white' of the title.

McVey invents a mechanical planter which he hopes will improve the life of the local farmers. He is exploited by the enterprising speculator Steve Hunter, who convinces the townspeople to invest in a company which, like the invention, is a failure. Hugh's next inventions, however, a corn-cutter and a device to help load coal on to trains, are extremely profitable. Hunter becomes a millionaire and Bidwell gradually changes into a bustling industrial town. McVey too becomes rich and famous, but is lonely and isolated in his prosperity. He then marries Clara Butterworth, the daughter of a wealthy farmer, and though their marriage is unhappy initially they are reconciled at the end of the novel. Anderson traces Bidwell's economic development from a craftsman's town to an industrial centre and the troubles faced by the inhabitants as a result. Social distinctions based on wealth emerge, and the town's former peaceful existence is marred by outbreaks of violence, strikes, and company lock-outs. Disillusioned, McVey finally realizes the negative effects of industrial progress.

**Pope, Alexander** 1688–1744 Poet and satirist. Born the son of a Roman Catholic linen-draper in London in the year of the Protestant Revolution, Pope had an uneven education and was debarred by his religion from attending university. Precociously bright, he was largely self-taught, learning Latin and Greek from a local priest at eight, and later acquiring knowledge of French and Italian. He is said to have been whipped for satirizing a master at Twyford School. In 1700, the year his family moved to Binfield in Windsor Forest, he contracted tuberculosis, which permanently damaged his health. During his life the poet got progressively weaker (he also suffered from asthma), and physically dependent on others; in middle age, no more than 4ft 6in tall, he was unable to dress without assistance and needed to wear a stiffened canvas bodice to support his spine. Half-jokingly he later referred to 'this long disease, my life'.

While still at school, Pope embarked on his poetic apprenticeship, writing paraphrases and imitations of classical poets and of **Cowley**

**Chaucer** and the Psalms. He claimed to have written his first significant work, *The Pastorals*, at 16; these were published in 1709, and display an extraordinary degree of technical control, and a sensitive awareness of that genre, in the manner of Virgil and **Spenser**.

Pope moved to London and began to move in literary circles. His **Essay on Criticism** was published in 1711 and its accomplished tone drew the attention of **Addison**, with whose powerful Whig friends the young poet began to associate. In May 1712 he published his religious eclogue *Messiah* in **The Spectator**, and also the first version of **The Rape of the Lock** (expanded in 1714), the witty feminized epic which established his reputation in London society. He was a friend of **Wycherley** and **Congreve**, but by 1713 had drifted away from Addison's circle (the Whigs were anti-Catholic) towards the Tory coterie presided over by **Swift**. In 1713, Pope became one of the **Scriblerus Club**.

In 1713 he published *Windsor Forest* (begun in 1704), a Royalist pastoral that combines a celebration of rural Albion with a political affirmation of the peace under Queen Anne, and confirmed his allegiance with the Tories. At this time Pope was working on a most ambitious project, a translation of Homer into heroic couplets; the first volume of the *Iliad* appeared in 1715, and was completed in 1720. The result strays considerably from the original, but is

Alexander Pope. A detail from the portrait, *c.*1727, from the studio of M. Dahl. National Portrait Gallery, London.

'An exact Draught and View of Mr Pope's House at Twickenham.' Detail from an 18th-century engraving.
Society of Antiquaries, London.

distinguished by its own merits, chief among which are its visually arresting descriptions. The translation (and its less fortunate successor, *The Odyssey*, which appeared in 1725–6) freed Pope from both booksellers and patrons by giving him financial independence. He became one of the first professional poets to be self-sufficient as a result of his non-dramatic writings.

The publication in 1717 of his collected works, in a handsome volume, established Pope as the leading man of letters of his day. It included an adaptation of **Chaucer**'s *The House of Fame*, the 'Ode for Music on St Cecilia's Day' and two new love poems; *Eloisa to Abelard* is a bleak study in the self-imposed loneliness of the legendary female whose love has been blighted, while Pope's *Elegy to the Memory of an Unfortunate Lady* is another melancholy piece, about a suicide. These expressions of dejection and rejection are haunting, and are perhaps occasioned by the two affectionate relationships that belong to this period of his life. He formed an attachment with **Lady Mary Wortley Montagu**, the sophisticated wife of the ambassador to Turkey, but the friendship soured and led to unpleasantness after 1723. More successful was the lifelong relationship with Martha Blount, to whom Pope addressed some epistles that are among his most attractive works. In this same year, he collaborated with his fellow Scriblerians **Arbuthnot** and **Gay** on the play *Three Hours After Marriage*, his only venture into drama proper.

Despite the rising accolade with which he was greeted, Pope now seems to have entered a period of doubt about his achievements, and became tired of the literary business. The stricter measures taken against Roman Catholics following the Jacobite rebellion of 1715 meant he could no longer reside in central London, and

in 1719 he moved out to Twickenham, to a villa with a garden that was to be his home for the rest of his life. He began to be fascinated by horticulture and landscape gardening – he was later consulted by Bathurst and Burlington on these subjects – and constructed for himself a shell-lined grotto on the far side of the London road which ran through the end of his garden. Pope was happy at Twickenham, where Lady Mary was a neighbour, and entertained numerous visitors including Swift, whom he helped with the publication of **Gulliver's Travels**.

His *Odyssey*, completed in 1726 with the help of Elizabeth Fenton and William Broome, was another financial success, but it followed one of Pope's less distinguished projects, the edition of *Shakespeare's Works* commissioned by the bookseller **Jacob Tonson**, and published in 1725. It prompted a pamphlet by **Lewis Theobald** entitled *Shakespeare Restored* (1726) pointing out Pope's scholarly deficiencies.

In 1727 two volumes of a *Miscellany* of pieces by the Scriblerian group appeared in print, with a further volume the next year. This contained an early version of Pope's masterful *An Epistle to Dr Arbuthnot* (the full version is 1735) and a prose piece called *Martinus Scriblerus peri Bathous, or, the Art of Sinking in Poetry* which ridiculed the literary capabilities of his former collaborator William Broome (there had been a disagreement), Lewis Theobald (who was to come in for further antagonism), **Ambrose Philips** (with whom Pope had disagreed over the *Pastorals*) and **John Dennis**, the opinionated critic. A comic inversion of Longinus' treatise on the sublime (*Peri Hupsous*), Pope's essay illustrates the lowest qualities in contemporary verse, the tendency for 'bathos' and anticlimax, drawing upon his enemies as examples. For some time he had been working on another seriously ambitious poem, and in 1728 there appeared the first version of *The Dunciad*, a satire in three books on Dullness in contemporary culture. It was enlarged in 1729 and a fourth book was added in 1742; these appeared in a revised version in 1743. Initially, it was Theobald who was the anti-hero of the piece, but by the time of the complete version, Pope had transferred his malignant displeasure to **Colley Cibber**, the Poet Laureate.

Pope had conceived an elaborate 'Opus Magnum' which would comprise four books, though the project was never completed. The first book was his *Essay on Man*, four epistles published in 1733–4, mapping out the intellectual plan for the larger work. The second was to be *The Dunciad* and the third an epic (never finished). The fourth book he did finish, and this appeared as his four *Moral Essays* or *Ethics* (1731–5). Their philosophical content is hardly original, but the poems epitomize the highly developed intellectual concerns with which he was preoccupied. In 1733 he began to produce his miscellaneous *Imitations of Horace* (an idea of **Bolingbroke**'s), 11 translations and adaptations of Horace's *Odes*, *Satires* and *Epistles*. These are probably his easiest verses to enjoy, and demonstrate the fundamental affinity between Pope's genius and the foremost poets of the classical age. Effectively a 'Prologue' to these satires was *An Epistle from Mr Pope to Dr Arbuthnot* (1735), the most brilliantly sustained rhetorical performance that the poet ever achieved. Addressed to his dying friend, the erudite physician who had in turn looked after the poet, these verses embody the ideals of civilized friendship, good sense and honesty as well as offering a series of blistering verse-portraits including one of Addison (written before his death) and Lady Mary Wortley Montagu. As an example of ironic autobiography versified, it has no equal. In 1738 appeared *One Thousand Seven Hundred and Thirty Eight*, two satirical dialogues modelled on Horace. Pope also prepared an edition of his correspondence, doctored to his own advantage, and had it published by Edmund Curll in 1735, though he subsequently pretended the edition was piratical.

Pope's reputation did not long outlive him. The drastic changes of taste later in the 18th century which caused so many Augustan writers to fall into disfavour made his sophistication appear merely a lack of 'feeling' and his satire merely malicious. He did not appeal to writers or readers again until this century, when he has come once more to be highly regarded. Pope is perhaps our foremost poet of culture; the audience to whom he addressed his shapely poems is urban, urbane and civilized. He himself was interested in all the arts except music – he was virtually tone-deaf, though his verse is far from tuneless. He studied painting under Charles Jervas, and was for part of his life almost as much preoccupied with architecture and landscape gardening as with poetry. A sense of proportion and an awareness of contrasting effects within the 'correctness' of a design are consequently features of much of his verse. They do not, however, make it impersonal or unemotional. Pope's writing is continually informed by his own personality, especially in the outstanding verse epistles, and by an exciting, even baroque, sense of performance which is both lively and articulate.

**Porson, Richard** 1759–1808 Classical scholar. Humbly born, Porson attended the village school at East Rushton in Norfolk, but found a patron in Sir George Baker, the physician, who sent him to Eton and Trinity College, Cambridge, of which he became a fellow in 1782. 10 years later, he was elected Regius Professor of Greek in the university. He lacked the stability, however, that good health and a moneyed background might have provided. He was married for a few months to a widow, Mrs Lunan, sister of his friend James Perry, editor of *The Morning Chronicle*, to which Porson was a contributor. His wife died, however, and Porson relapsed into heavy drinking and his habit of procrastination grew upon him. Contemporaries considered he frittered his brilliant talents on journalism. He collapsed in the street and died a few days later. He is buried in the chapel of his old college, near the statue of Newton.

His work was on Aristophanes, Euripides, Athenaeus, and the lexicons of Suidas, Hesychius and Photius. He also annotated Pausanias. His work on Aeschylus laid the foundation for all subsequent editions. He was expert on Greek metres and idiomatic usage. Many of his emendations are now accepted. However, in his day, the tendency was to treat all extant Greek texts as of equal value. Brilliant as his emendations were, some could have been corrected if he had compared printed copies with manuscripts. His notebooks were edited by various persons after his death. The Greek typeface called 'Porson' is supposedly based on his hand.

Porson also contributed to *The Gentleman's Magazine*, including three letters on Sir John Hawkins's *Life of Johnson* and *Letters to Archdeacon Travis on the Specious Verse 1 John v. 7*.

**Porter, Anne Maria** 1780–1832 Younger sister of the more successful **Jane Porter** and, like her, a writer of numerous romances. The most popular was her novel of the French Revolutionary war, *The Hungarian Brothers* (1807).

**Porter, Hal** 1911–84 Australian prose writer, poet and dramatist. Born in Melbourne and brought up in Bairnsdale, a country town in western Victoria, he worked briefly as a cub reporter before becoming a teacher of English and modern languages at schools in Victoria, South Australia, Tasmania and New South Wales. In 1949–50 he taught the children of Australian army personnel in Japan. After returning to Australia, he was Director of the National Theatre in Hobart for three years. In 1953 his varied career took another turn, when he became Chief Librarian of Bairnsdale and Shepparton. From 1961 he devoted himself to full-time writing. Porter worked in many genres, producing short stories, novels, poetry, drama and autobiography, but he is best known for his short stories and his three volumes of autobiography: *The Watcher on the Cast-Iron Balcony* (1963), *The Paper Chase* (1966) and *The Extra* (1975). As the title of the first suggests, he adopts a detached, spectatorial stance. He is both one of Australia's finest prose stylists and a chronicler of many uncelebrated aspects of the country's social life. His novels, *A Handful of Pennies* (1958), set in occupied Japan, and *The Tilted Cross* (1961), which deals with Tasmania's convict past and achieved a considerable international reputation, are sympathetic towards loners and eccentrics. Cosmopolitan in range, Porter's stories are precise and carefully crafted works which extended the scope and style of the Australian short story. They are collected in *A Bachelor's Children* (1962), *The Cats of Venice* (1965), *Mr Butterfry and Other Tales of New Japan* (1970) and *Fredo Fuss Love Life* (1974). His other books include the play *The Tower* (1963), the volumes of poetry, *The Hexagon* (1956) and *Elijah's Ravens* (1968), and the non-fictional *Stars of Australian Stage and Screen* (1965) and *The Actors: An Image of the New Japan* (1968).

**Porter, Jane** 1776–1850 Sister of **Anne Maria Porter** and the author of historical romances which enjoyed considerable success in their day. *Thaddeus of Warsaw* (1803) is one of the earliest examples of the historical novel, though the setting itself was more romantic than the date, which was not far removed from the author's time. The hero, Thaddeus, apparently a member of the Sobieski family, accompanies the Polish patriot army against the occupying Russians. The Poles are defeated, the Sobieski castle is destroyed, and Thaddeus, an exile, arrives in England. There he suffers hardship and deprivation, until he proves to be none less than the long lost son of an English gentleman. *The Scottish Chiefs* (1810) is more ambitious. The story opens with the murder of William Wallace's wife by Heselrigge, the English governor of Lanark, when he tries to make her divulge her husband's whereabouts. It continues with the career of the ill-fated Wallace and his barbarous execution by the English, and closes with the triumph of Bruce at Bannockburn.

**Porter, Katherine Anne** 1890–1980 American short-story writer and novelist, born in Indian Creek, Texas. Her first collection of stories, *Flowering Judas, and Other Stories*, was published in 1930. *Hacienda: A Story of Mexico* appeared in 1934. She received widespread critical acclaim for the volume *Pale Horse, Pale Rider* (1939), which consists of three short novels: 'Old Mortality', 'Noon Wine', and the title-piece, which tells of a short-lived love affair between a soldier and a young Southern newspaperwoman during the influenza epidemic of World War I.

Porter published two further collections of stories, *The Leaning Tower, and Other Stories* (1944) and *The Old Order: Stories of the South* (1944), as well as two volumes of essays, *The Days Before* (1952) and *A Defense of Circe* (1954). Her best-known work, *Ship of Fools*, appeared in 1962 after 20 years in the writing. A bitterly ironic novel, it is set on a German passenger ship sailing from Mexico to Germany in 1931, and explores the origin and potential of human evil through the allegorical use of characters as almost one-dimensional representatives of various national and moral types. *The Collected Stories of Katherine Anne Porter* (1965) received both the Pulitzer Prize and the National Book Award. *Collected Essays and Occasional Writings* appeared in 1970. *The Never-Ending Wrong* (1977) is an account of the infamous Sacco–Vanzetti trial and execution. Her other works include *The Itching Parrot* (1942), *Holiday* (1962) and *A Christmas Story* (1967).

**Porter, Peter (Neville Frederick)** 1929– Poet. He was born and educated in Brisbane, Australia, where he worked as a reporter before emigrating to England in 1951. He became an advertising copywriter in 1959, and since 1968 has earned his living as a freelance broadcaster and journalist.

It is possible to distinguish three main poetic identities in Porter's work: the social satirist, the cultural conservationist and the personal elegist. The social satirist dominates his first three collections, *Once Bitten, Twice Bitten* (1961), *Poems Ancient and Modern* (1964) and *A Porter Folio* (1969). Among the most striking and memorable pieces from this period are 'Annotations of Auschwitz' and 'Your Attention Please', both of which deal with appalling events (one historical, one hypothetical) in a disarmingly matter-of-fact tone. The lack of surface warmth persists in the second phase of Porter's career: *The Last of England* (1970), *Preaching to the Converted* (1972) and *Living in a Calm Country* (1975). In 'The Sanitized Sonnets' he wryly identifies as 'Porter's Complaint' 'an inability to feel anything when feeling/is the whole point of the operation'. Feeling, however, does increasingly emerge. Porter's wife died in 1974, and the poems in *The Cost of Seriousness* (1978) are both shadowed and inspired by her death. 'An Angel in Blythburgh Church', 'The Cost of Seriousness' and the marvellous 'An Exequy' have been widely and justly acclaimed as Porter's finest poems to date. *English Subtitles* (1981) and *Fast Forward* (1984) inevitably seem somewhat slight by comparison, but they continue to display Porter's characteristic blend of cultural erudition and dry wit. A volume of translations, *After Martial*, appeared in 1972, and his *Collected Poems* in 1983.

***Portnoy's Complaint*** A novel by **Philip Roth**, published in 1969, which takes the form of an account by Alexander Portnoy to his analyst of his relationship with his suburban Jewish family: his domineering, guilt-inducing mother who dotes on him and yet waves a knife over his head when he won't eat; his perpetually constipated, weak-spirited insurance salesman father; and his pathetic, conformist sister. Portnoy's guilty responses to his family's needs alternate with self-conscious rebellions against them: as an adolescent he performs brilliantly in school, but he seeks relief and revenge through constant masturbation; as an adult he has a respected job as the Assistant Commissioner for the City of New York Commission on Human Opportunity, but he refuses to get married and instead has affairs with gentile women. Toward the end of the novel, having abandoned his latest lover in Greece, he travels to Israel and meets an Israeli girl. For the first time in his life he is impotent. The girl confronts him with the contradictions of his existence, and embodies for him a noble, self-sacrificing model of Jewishness.

***Portrait of a Lady, The*** A novel by **Henry James**, first published serially in *The Atlantic Monthly* (1880–1), and then in volume form in 1881.

Isabel Archer, of Albany, New York, a penniless orphan, becomes the protégée of her wealthy aunt, Lydia Touchett. She goes to England to stay with her aunt and uncle, a retired American banker, and their tubercular son, Ralph, who persuades his father to provide for Isabel in his will. When Mr Touchett dies, Isabel finds herself rich and goes to the Continent with Mrs Touchett and her friend, Madame Merle. In Florence, Madame Merle introduces her to Gilbert Osmond, a middle-aged widower with a young daughter, Pansy. To preserve her freedom, Isabel has previously turned down proposals of marriage from Casper Goodwood, a rich young American, and from Lord Warburton, an English neighbour of the Touchetts. Now, however, impressed with Osmond's taste and intellectual detachment, she accepts his proposal, only to discover him to be a selfish and sterile dilettante who has married

her for her money. When she hears that Ralph is dying she prepares to depart for England to be with him, but Osmond forbids her to go. It is at this point that she discovers that Madame Merle is Pansy's mother, and she at last understands the woman's part in her marriage to Osmond. She goes to England after a final confrontation with Madame Merle and is at Ralph's side when he dies. Casper Goodwood makes a last attempt to gain Isabel, but though she feels an attraction for him she rejects him and returns to Osmond and Pansy in Italy.

***Portrait of the Artist as a Young Man, A*** An autobiographical novel by **James Joyce**, published in one volume in 1916. It was originally published in serial form in *The Egoist*, February 1914 – September 1915.

Stephen Dedalus (representing Joyce), an intelligent but frail child, struggles towards maturity in Ireland at the turn of the century. The novel traces his intellectual, moral, and artistic development from babyhood to the completion of his education at University College, Dublin.

Stephen's individuality is stifled by many levels of convention, dictated by the family, Catholicism and Irish nationalism. As a child he witnesses a fiery political dispute between supporters of Parnell and anti-Parnellites, and suffers unjust punishment at the hands of a stupid and brutal priest, Father Dolan. Adolescent sexuality causes him moral torment, and this is exacerbated at a school 'retreat' where he hears Father Arnall's famous 'hellfire' sermon.

Rejecting the call to the priesthood, Stephen begins to assert his own identity. At University College he embraces the wider and more rewarding world of literature, philosophy and aesthetics, and by the end of the novel he has freed himself from the claims of family, church and state. He resolves to leave Ireland for Paris to encounter 'the reality of experience' and to forge 'the uncreated conscience' of his race.

The novel was developed from an earlier work, *Stephen Hero*, which Joyce had begun *c.*1904. Part of this earlier work survived and was published in 1944, edited by T. Spencer. Stephen Dedalus reappears as one of the principal characters in *Ulysses* (1922).

**Positivism** Creed deriving from Auguste Comte (1798–1857). Comte believed that humanity, both the individual and the race, progressed by three stages: the theological, the metaphysical and the positive. This cultural maturity was evinced by confining intellectual enquiry to observable facts: philosophy and theology were treated as illegitimate. Women's role was to safeguard the emotions. **Frederic Harrison** was a leading English advocate of Positivism, and **George Eliot** embraced its doctrines for a while. The Positivist philosophy has links with the scientific attitude and led to the 20th-century school of 'Logical Positivists' who deny the existence of metaphysics.

**post-structuralism** Modern critical theory which begins by asserting the unstable relationship between signifier and signified (see **structuralism** and **semiotics**). The signifier refuses to be tied to a single signified, as is evident in jokes, dreams and poetry. This theory of signification is expressed in a number of characteristic post-structuralist positions: (1) the author should not be regarded as the origin of his text or the authority for its meaning (see Roland Barthes's 'The Death of the Author'); (2) there are no objective 'scientific' discourses. Our metalanguages (discourses used to explain other discourses) are always capable of being subjected to other metalinguistic operations *ad infinitum*; (3) literature cannot be isolated as a separate discourse but is always contaminated with the entire universe of discourses.

Barthes's *S/Z* (1970) examines a Balzac short story by cutting it into fragments (lexias) and dispersing them in the infinite sea of the 'already written'. He attacks the structuralist attempt to find *the* structure of narrative, arguing that narrative draws upon the 'codes' which form a grid of possible meanings which permit no ultimate 'closure'. Even though 'readerly' texts try to limit the possibilities of meaning, they can always be read, against the grain, for a certain plurality. The 'writerly' text actually celebrates its openness and encourages the reader's productive activity, which resembles the writer's own in its deployment of the codes. Barthes names five codes: 'hermeneutic', 'semic', 'symbolic', 'proairetic' and 'cultural'.

Under the influence of Nietzsche, who believed that all knowledge is the 'will to power', Michel Foucault (1926– ) examined the historical construction of knowledge. What is considered rational and scholarly is determined not by absolute standards of reason but by unspoken rules, institutional constraints and the power of particular discursive practices. Edward Said (1935– ) takes up Foucault's historical kind of post-structuralism and emphasizes the pressures of reality which constrain the possibilities of knowledge. Literary critics, he argues, can grasp a past text only within the discursive 'archive' of the present.

**Potter, Dennis (Christopher George)** 1935– Playwright. He was born into a mining family in the Forest of Dean and educated at Oxford. Although he has also written for the stage and screen, he is chiefly distinguished as a television playwright. One of the first (with **David Mercer**) to explore the potential of the medium, Potter has created a body of work that uses it

with ingenuity and imagination, from *Vote, Vote, Vote for Nigel Barton* and *Stand Up, Nigel Barton* (both 1965) to *The Singing Detective* (1986). *Son of Man* (1969) was a bold portrayal of a 'human' Christ anguished by self-doubt; *Pennies from Heaven* (1978) anticipated *The Singing Detective* by its use of popular songs to form, divert and generate the action. *Blue Remembered Hills* (1979) cast adults as children, giving their games played in the context of World War II a rare fantasy.

**Potter, (Helen) Beatrix** 1866–1943 Writer and illustrator of **children's literature**. Born the only daughter of well-to-do parents in Kensington, she was taught at home by a governess. To enliven her otherwise dull and sheltered life, she kept a journal in code (deciphered and published by Leslie Linder in 1966) and drew and painted, often using specimens from the nearby Natural History Museum. In 1893 she sent a letter to a young friend illustrated with drawings of animals; with much encouragement from several quarters, she turned this into *The Tale of Peter Rabbit*, privately printed in 1901 and followed the next year by *The Tailor of Gloucester*. Subsequent picture-books for the very young, issued during a long and profitable association with the publisher Frederick Warne, include: *The Tale of Squirrel Nutkin* (1903), *The Tale of Benjamin Bunny* (1904), *The Tale of Two Bad Mice* (1904), *The Tale of Mrs Tiggy-Winkle* (1905), *The Tale of Jeremy Fisher* (1906), *The Story of a Fierce Bad Rabbit* (1906), *The Story of Miss Moppet* (1906), *The Tale of Tom Kitten* (1907), *The Tale of Jemima Puddle-Duck* (1908), *The Tale of the Flopsy Bunnies* (1909), *The Tale of Mrs Tittlemouse* (1910), *The Tale of Timmy Tiptoes* (1911) and *The Tale of Pigling Bland* (1913). Her tales range from stories of escape from near-death to charming, eventless catalogues of animal domesticity. Each one, however, was written with a natural ear for what she described as 'fine-sounding words'. Her illustrations usually showed animal characters wearing human clothes but otherwise treated without sentimentality. After her marriage to a solicitor, William Heelis, in 1913 Beatrix Potter went to live in the Lake District, which she had learned to love during childhood holidays and which she made the setting for many of her books. She put most of her energies into sheep farming and conservation, leaving 4000 acres of land to the National Trust. *The Tale of Little Pig Robinson* (1930) was the only story of note to appear in her declining years.

**Pound, Ezra (Weston Loomis)** 1885–1972 American poet, born in Hailey, Idaho, and educated at the University of Pennsylvania and at Hamilton College in New York State. In 1906 he took up a fellowship at the University of

Pennsylvania, and then taught briefly at Wabash College in Crawfordsville, Indiana. His academic career, however, was short-lived; he sailed for Europe in February 1908 and went to live in Venice.

His first volume of poetry, *A Lume Spento* (With Tapers Quenched) was published in Venice in June 1908. In September of that year he travelled to London, where he renewed his acquaintance with **W. B. Yeats,** whom he had first met during Yeats's visit to the USA in 1903. While in London he also became friendly with **Ford Madox Ford**, **T. E. Hulme**, **James Joyce** and **Wyndham Lewis.** Ford published Pound's 'Sestina Altaforte' in *The English Review* in 1909. Two collections of his poems, *Personae* and *Exultations*, appeared in the same year. *The Spirit of Romance* (1910), a volume of critical essays adapted from lectures he gave in London, further demonstrated the literary erudition that had been evident in his early poetry. His next two collections of poems, *Provença* (1910) and *Canzoni* (1911), again showed the influence of medieval and Victorian literature, of Provençal poets, troubadour ballads, and **Robert Browning.**

His translation of *The Sonnets and Ballate of Guido Cavalcanti* and his volume of poems entitled *Riposte* (both 1912) marked the beginning of his association with the movement known as **imagism**, which encouraged experimentation with verse forms, the economic use of language, brevity of treatment, and concreteness of detail. The movement, with Pound as its central figure, was at its peak between 1912 and 1914. During these years he also established his association with **Harriet Monroe**, and through her magazine *Poetry* promoted the work of fellow imagists, as well as that of **T. S. Eliot** and **Robert Frost**. In 1914 he published an anthology of imagist poetry, *Des Imagistes*, which included contributions by **Hilda Doolittle**, **Richard Aldington**, James Joyce, **Amy Lowell**, and **William Carlos Williams**, as well as by Pound himself. Another influence on him at this time was the sculptor Henri Gaudier-Brzeska, and from their association came the short-lived movement called **vorticism**, which opposed representational art in favour of abstract forms and structures. The movement's journal, *Blast*, to which Pound contributed, survived for just two issues (1914–15).

Pound's next volumes of poetry were *Lustra* (1916) and *Quia Pauper Amavi* (1919). During the course of World War I he became increasingly disillusioned with what he saw as a decayed civilization, and this sense of living in a world of false values found its clearest expression in his 1920 volume, *Hugh Selwyn Mauberly*. Late that year he and his wife Dorothy, whom he had married in 1914, went to live in Paris; there he worked through the first draft

Ezra Pound, 1918. Photograph by E. O. Hoppé.

of *The Waste Land* with T. S. Eliot. He moved from Paris to Italy in 1924, and made a home in Rapallo. An epic poem had been one of his ambitions since his student days, but the form had taken 10 years to evolve. He had begun the *Cantos* before the vorticist period and had worked on them intermittently. The first collection, *A Draft of XVI Cantos*, was published in 1925. He continued to work on this, his modern epic, for the rest of his life; eventually it consisted of 117 Cantos.

*Personae: The Collected Poems of Ezra Pound* was published in 1926; *Selected Poems*, edited by T. S. Eliot, appeared in 1928. *A Draft of XXX Cantos* (1930) continued the sequence, which was further extended by *Eleven New Cantos* (1934), *The Fifth Decad of Cantos* (1937), and *Cantos LII–LXXI* (1940). In 1933 Pound had met Mussolini and been impressed by the dictator's imposition of order on Italy. In 1939 he visited the USA, where his new political beliefs and his anti-semitism alienated many of his friends. When he wanted to return in 1941 he was denied permission. In the same year he began to broadcast for the Axis in Rome. In April 1945 he was arrested by partisans and handed over to the American authorities. He was held under harsh conditions in an American disciplinary centre at Pisa and then transferred to the USA; in November 1945, in Washington, he was declared unfit to stand trial for treason on grounds of insanity, and was confined to St Elizabeth's hospital. While incarcerated at Pisa he had begun an additional volume of Cantos; *The Pisan Cantos* were completed at St Elizabeth's in January 1946 and published in 1948. (Their receipt of the Bollingen Prize for poetry in 1948 caused an uproar which led to the Library of Congress's relinquishing the administration of the prize, which thereafter passed to Yale University.) Pound added to the Cantos with the publication of *Section: Rock-Drill: 85–95 de los Cantares* (1956) and *Thrones: 96–109 de los Cantares* (1959). *The Cantos of Ezra Pound* (I–CXVII) appeared in 1970. *Collected Early Poems* was published posthumously in 1976.

Pound's confinement in St Elizabeth's finally came to an end in 1958, and he returned to Italy. He died in Venice at the age of 87. He himself was uncertain of his achievements, but he is widely recognized as one of the makers of modern poetry. Among his volumes of criticism are *Pavannes and Division* (1918), *Instigations* (1920), *Indiscretions* (1923), *How to Read* (1931), *ABC of Reading* (1934), *Polite Essays* (1937), and *A Guide to Kulchur* (1938). *Gaudier-Brzeska: A Memoir* was published in 1916; his adaptation from the Chinese, *The Classic Anthology Defined by Confucius*, in 1954; and his translation of Sophocles' *The Women of Trachis* in 1956.

**Powell, Anthony (Dymoke)** 1905– Novelist. The son of a serving army officer, he was born in London but spent much of his childhood at army bases. He was educated at Eton and Balliol College, Oxford. Before serving in World War II, he worked for a publishing firm and as a book reviewer and film scenario writer.

Powell's first novel was *Afternoon Men* (1931), a precisely judged satire of the Bohemian world and the futile foolishness of those inhabitants of Chelsea and Bloomsbury who felt their existence justified by mere aspiration. Powell's description is done with remarkable economy and a fine ear for speech. *Venusberg* followed in 1932, and *From a View to a Death* (1933), *Caledonia: A Fragment* (1934; a privately printed verse satire), *Agents and Patients* (1936), and *What's Become of Waring?* (1939) complete his first group of works. The last makes use of Powell's publishing background and tells of a travel-writer, Waring, upon whose works his publishers depend. The death of Waring and the search for a suitable biographer provide the basis of the story; the investigations into Waring's life reveal facts which threaten to undermine the publishers, Judkins & Judkins. Powell's characteristically polished style makes for incisive social comedy.

After World War II Powell published a biographical study, *John Aubrey and His Friends* (1948), and edited a selection of **Aubrey**'s *Brief Lives* in the following year. He also began work on an ambitious sequence of 12 novels, *A Dance to the Music of Time*, which began with *A Question of Upbringing* (1951) and ended with *Hearing Secret Harmonies* (1975). *O, How the Wheel Becomes It!* (1983) was followed by his most recent novel, *The Fisher King* (1986).

Powell's memoirs were published in four volumes under the general title *To Keep the Ball Rolling* (1976–82).

**Power and the Glory, The** A novel by **Graham Greene**, published in 1940.

It arose out of Greene's visit to Mexico in 1937, after he had been commissioned to report on religious persecution there. It is set in the violent context of a new revolutionary republic where the Church is outlawed and priests are banned, and traces the 'martyrdom' of a lapsed priest, guilty of drunkenness and lechery. Despite being outlawed (or perhaps because of it) he rediscovers the integrity of his original commitment and determines to perform his duties until physically prevented by the authorities. His life is contrasted to that of several other characters: a fellow priest, Padre José, who has capitulated to the regime, and a 'gringo' thief and murderer, hunted by the police. His opponent, a police lieutenant, represents the non-religious humanist viewpoint. He is described as a good and honourable man, and is acknowledged as such by the priest when, at the end of the novel, the latter is cornered at the bedside of the dying 'gringo'. The priest's execution is imbued with Christlike implications, and the novel closes on a subdued note of triumph about the Church's survival in the face of religious intolerance.

As in so many of Greene's novels, the thriller element is employed to dramatize an ambiguous moral drama.

**Power of Sympathy, The** A novel by **William Hill Brown**, published anonymously in 1789. Written in epistolary form, it relates the tragic tale of an attempted seduction which, if it had been successful, would also have been incestuous. Based in part on an actual scandal in Boston society, it warns young women of the danger posed by would-be seducers.

A young man, Harrington, is determined to win a young woman, Harriot Fawcet. Unbeknownst to either of them, they are half-brother and sister. Harriot is the illegitimate child of the elder Harrington and an unfortunate woman named Maria. Harrington confides his plans – which to start with are simply to seduce Harriot, but change quickly to marrying her without his father's permission – to his friend Mr Worthy, who sensibly counsels against this course. When the truth of Harriot's parentage is revealed, she collapses and soon after dies.

Grief-stricken, Harrington becomes increasingly unstable and eventually commits suicide.

**Powys, John Cowper** 1872–1963 Novelist. Powys was born in Derbyshire, the brother of **Llewelyn Powys** and **T. F. Powys**. He was educated at Sherborne and Corpus Christi College, Cambridge. His boyhood was spent in the West Country, which provided the setting for many of his later novels, but for much of his life he lived and worked as a lecturer in the United States. He returned to Great Britain in his 60s and lived at Blaenau-Festiniog in North Wales for the remainder of his life.

Powys's career began with poetry and essays. *Odes and Other Poems* (1896) was followed by *Poems* (1899) and *Visions and Revisions: A Book of Literary Devotions* (1915). *Suspended Judgements*, a collection of essays, appeared the following year, and there were many other essays on subjects ranging from literature to religion and philosophy. He also published a group of romances – *Wood and Stone* (1915), *Rodmoor* (1916), and *Ducdame* (1925) – but his reputation as the author of highly individual and immensely long novels with an esoteric interest began with *Wolf Solent* (1929). This was a complex work which, like *A Glastonbury Romance* (1932), blended elements of folklore and the supernatural with elements of the epic. *Weymouth Sands* (1934; republished as *Jobber Skald* in 1935 because of a libel suit, but restored to its original form in 1963) was cast in the same mould and centred upon the unfolding of an intense love–hate relationship between its major protagonists: Jobber, his lover Perdita, and enemy Dog Cattistock.

*Maiden Castle* (1936) is set among the excavations of the Dorchester fort and, like much of Powys's work, it celebrates the power of human fortitude in the face of disillusionment. *Morwy: or The Vengeance of God* (1937), about man's inhumanity to man, was followed by two more historical romances: *Owen Glendower* (1940) and *Porius: A Romance of the Dark Ages* (1951). Other novels included *The Inmates* (1952), about madness, *Atlantis* (1954), a fantastic tale about Homer's Odysseus which ends with the discovery of America, and *The Brazen Head* (1956), about the 'Doctor Mirabilis' Roger Bacon.

Powys's literary stature has been the subject of much debate, and his admirers have largely been confined to those readers who share his interest in the esoteric.

**Powys, Llewelyn** 1884–1939 Novelist and essayist. The brother of **John Cowper Powys** and **T. F. Powys**, he was born in Dorchester and educated at Sherborne and Corpus Christi College, Cambridge. Like his brother, John Cowper, he worked in the United States, but on his return in 1909 he discovered that he was suffering from tuberculosis. From 1914–19 he farmed in Kenya with his brother William. He spent another five years in the United States as a journalist, and then travelled in Palestine and the West Indies. His last years were passed in Switzerland.

Powys wrote many essays and sketches, including *Ebony and Ivory* (1923), based on his experiences in Kenya, and *Skin for Skin* (1925), an account of his illness set in Swiss sanitoria, in Israel, the United States and Dorset. Newspaper serialization made *Earth Memories* (1934) and *Dorset Essays* (1935) perhaps his best-known volumes. His novels included *Black Laughter* (1924) and *Apples be Ripe* (1930).

*Confessions of Two Brothers* (1916) was written in collaboration with John Cowper Powys, and *Damnable Opinions* (1935) reflected the highly individual characteristics shared by all of the Powys brothers. His other autobiographical writings included *The Verdict of Bridlegoose* (1926) and, looking forward to his own approaching death, *Love and Death: An Imaginary Autobiography* (1939).

**Powys, T[heodore] F[rancis]** 1875–1953 Novelist and short-story writer. The brother of **John Cowper Powys** and **Llewelyn Powys**, he was born in Dorchester and educated at schools in East Anglia. In 1902 he returned to East Chaldon in Dorset, the setting for most of his novels and short stories.

Powys's first published work was *An Interpretation of Genesis* (1907), and this was followed by *Soliloquies of a Hermit* (1916), a series of meditations; both works indicated his preoccupation with religious themes. His first fiction appeared in two collections of stories, *The Left Leg* and *Black Bryony* (both 1923), which revealed him to be a master of the short form. *Mr Tasker's Gods* appeared the following year, a highly individual work which introduced many strange and grotesque figures who were to reappear in his subsequent books.

Powys is best known for *Mr Weston's Good Wine* (1927), an allegorical fantasy of love and death in which God and the archangel Michael visit the village of Folly Down in the person of Mr Weston, wine merchant, and his junior partner. In *Unclay* (1931), Powys's other major novel, John Death visits the village of Dodder with orders from God to kill various of its inhabitants. Like *Mr Weston's Good Wine* the book defies classification but is imbued with profoundly moral paradoxes about good and evil.

Powys's other works include *Feed My Swine* (1926; short stories), *The House With the Echo* (1928), *Fables* (1929; also published as *No Painted Plumage*, 1934), *The White Paternoster and Other Stories* (1930), *Captain's Patch* (1935) and *Bottle's Path* (1946), one of a very few books to appear after 1940.

**Praed, Mrs Campbell** 1851–1935 Novelist. She was born Rosa-Caroline Murray-Prior at Bromelton in Queensland, Australia. She grew up in Queensland where her father was Postmaster-General and received some education at Brisbane; *My Australian Girlhood* (1902) is the story of those years. Marrying Arthur Campbell Mackworth Praed in 1872, she lived on his station on Curtis Island until 1876 when the couple settled permanently in England. Of some forty novels at least half draw on her experience of Australia and often revolve around a contrast between the refined English gentleman and the crude, spiky Australian whose qualities prove more enduring. Her novels include *An Australian Heroine* (1880), *Policy and Passion* (1881), *Miss Jacobsen's Chance* (1886), *The Romance of a Station* (1889), *Mrs Tregaskiss* (1895), *Nulma* (1897), *The Maid of the River* (1905), *Opal Fire* (1910) and *Sister Sorrow* (1916).

**Praed, William Mackworth** 1802–39 Poet. Praed was born in London and educated at Eton and Trinity College, Cambridge. He was called to the Bar in 1829 but soon turned to politics and in his short life sat for several constituencies. In 1835 he was appointed Secretary to the Board of Control under Peel but such work was more the foundation for the future political career denied him by early death than a realization of any achievement.

Praed's verse takes varied forms but at its best it is humorous, light, unforced, and of a social inclination redolent of the order to which he belonged. He also wrote some romantic poetry, a mode he often touched with mockery. He had a turn for the grotesquely amusing, as well as a taste for political satire that was frequently expressed through 'squibs' directed against prominent figures like **Brougham** and Palmerston. His *Poems* appeared in 1864.

**Praeterita** The unfinished autobiography of **John Ruskin** first appeared intermittently in 28 parts between July 1885 and July 1889. Although written between bouts of madness, it contains some of its author's most lucid and carefully formulated prose. It is selective in detail, and concentrates on the first half of Ruskin's long life. But *Praeterita* is replete with character sketches of painters, teachers, literary folk, servants and friends, and it is rich in descriptions of nature remembered by Ruskin from his ceaseless travels. Above all, perhaps, *Praeterita* engages as an absorbing portrait of the household of a middle-class 19th-century merchant on the way up, for at times Ruskin's parents seem as much to the fore as their son himself.

**Pragmatism**: *A New Name for Some Old Ways of Thinking* An approximate transcript of the Lowell lectures **William James** delivered in Boston (1906) and repeated at Columbia University (1907), *Pragmatism* was first published in 1907 and is considered by some to be the most significant work of American philosophy. As James describes it, pragmatism is not so much a theory as a method of choosing among theories – a means of mediating between rationalist absolutism and empiricist materialism. Although James distrusts the abstract manipulation of words (rationalism), he does not reject abstraction altogether (as perhaps a rigid empiricist would); rather, he accepts abstractions in so far as they redirect one profitably into experience. Ideals are 'real' because they have results. James argues that truth, an abstraction, does not reside innately within any proposition; rather, one can call a proposition truthful if it has practical consequences. For the pragmatist, therefore, truth is relative.

**Prairie, The** See **Leatherstocking Tales, The**.

**Pratt, E[dwin] J[ohn]** 1882–1964 Canadian poet. Born in Western Bay, Newfoundland, the son of an itinerant Methodist minister, he attended St John's Methodist College and, after working as a preacher and schoolteacher in remote island communities, went to Victoria College, University of Toronto, where he took four degrees, culminating in a doctorate in theology. He was a demonstrator-lecturer in psychology at Victoria College from 1913 to 1920, and from 1920 to 1953 worked in the Department of English there. Pratt is generally regarded as Canada's most important narrative poet, though his work, which embodies central Victorian ideological conflicts, has sometimes been regarded as outmoded. His poetry is particularly concerned with conflicts between man and nature and within nature itself. *The Witches' Brew* (1925), in which three sea-witches attempt to discover what effect alcohol has on fish, is a comic allegory about Prohibition. *The Iron Door* (1927) is an ode written to commemorate his mother's death, which reflects on death more generally and concludes with an ambivalent affirmation of faith. *The Titanic* (1935) places the ship and the iceberg which destroyed it in contrast as an ironic commentary on man's belief in technological progress. Pratt's best-known works are two long poems dealing with subjects from Canadian history which assume epic status: *Brébeuf and His Brethren* (1940) is about a group of missionaries massacred by the Iroquois in the 17th century; *Towards the Last Spike* (1952) deals with the building of the transcontinental railroad in Canada, and national unity and communication more generally. Pratt was a meticulous craftsman who worked in a variety of metrical forms. His other volumes include *Newfoundland Verse* (1923), *Titans* (1926), *The Roosevelt and the Antinoe* (1930), *Verses of the Sea* (1930), *Many Moods* (1932), *The Fable of the Goats* (1937), *Still Life* (1943), *Behind the Log* (1947) and *Collected Poems* (1958).

**Prayer Book, The** See **Book of Common Prayer, The**.

**Pre-Raphaelite Brotherhood** The Pre-Raphaelite Brotherhood, or the PRB as it was known, was founded in 1848 by Holman Hunt, John Everett Millais, **Dante Gabriel Rossetti**, **William Michael Rossetti**, F. G. Stephens, James Collinson and Thomas Woolner. These painters were in youthful revolt against prevailing artistic canons in England, especially those of **Sir Joshua Reynolds** ('Sir Sploshua') and other adherents of the 'grand style' in painting. The group also professed to return to artistic standards prevalent before Raphael. Among further aims were their wishes to express genuine ideas, to study nature in the closest detail, to produce (by their standards) good pictures and statues, to oppose what is learned conventionally and by rote, and to revolutionize colour in painting. *The Germ*, the short-lived periodical they published in 1850, expressed these ideals, and their early work was championed by **John Ruskin**. Symbolism and the love of remote, romantic subject matter informed much of the work of the PRB which, by attracting others, developed into what is termed Pre-Raphaelitism. Although the Brotherhood as such lasted only five or six years before its founders went their different ways, it had a distinct influence upon later 19th-century artists and writers, including such figures as **William Morris**, Edward Burne-Jones, Arthur Hughes and **Coventry Patmore**.

**Prelude, The**, or, *Growth of a Poet's Mind* An autobiographical poem in blank verse by **William Wordsworth**, begun at Goslar in Germany in the autumn of 1798. Unpublished during Wordsworth's life, and known to his circle simply as 'the Poem to Coleridge', the work is available to modern readers in three versions: a two-part text completed in 1799, first published in 1973; the earliest full-length *Prelude* of 1805, edited from the manuscripts by Ernest de Selincourt in 1926; and the poet's own definitive version in 14 books, put aside in 1839, and published after his death in 1850, with its present title, suggested by Mary, his widow. The 1850 text irons away some of the infelicities and clarifies the syntax of the 13-book 1805 version, but late 20th-century critics are generally agreed that it also weakens its poetic force. The work was originally intended to be a 'sort of portico' to 'The Recluse', an ambitious philosophical poem on 'Nature, Man and Society' which Wordsworth began but never completed.

*The Prelude* is a poetic reflection on poetry itself, although this does not become fully evident until the final three books. In the course of the poem the Imagination is progressively distanced from, and finally raised above, all other modes of understanding and acting upon man and the world, becoming 'but another name for absolute strength/And clearest insight, amplitude of mind,/And Reason in her most exalted mood'. The authority for this derives less from any generalizable aesthetic philosophy than from the poet's (i.e. Wordsworth's) own personal experiences and the exemplary significance of his intellectual development. The fortunes of Wordsworth and the fate of poetry are thus essentially one. Wordsworth was not insensitive to the 'self-conceit' implicit in his undertaking, and tried to rectify matters by insisting on the 'real humility', and even 'diffidence', with which he had approached it. The chosen confessional form, however, necessarily places the 'I' of the narrator in the position of principal subject of the narrative. Wordsworth's encompassing claims for his craft are grounded in a comprehensive critique of the negativity of modern civilization. The deadening equation of knowledge with book-learning and writing; the debased conception of human community inscribed upon the streets and buildings of the London metropolis (Book VIII); the bloodless abstractions of the rationalistic philosophy of **Godwin**; and, above all else, the catastrophic degeneration of the French Revolution into 'domestic carnage' and wars of foreign conquest (IX, X, XI) are all, in the final analysis, both causes and symptoms of an estrangement of man from his true purpose and being. Only the poetic imagination, the repository of truths anterior to, and immeasurably larger than, the fragile constructions of the rational understanding, is capable of restoring him to wholeness. The poet's privileged purchase upon truth is the reward of his intuitive intimacies with Nature, who teaches him to avoid the enthralments of 'sensible impressions' and to 'hold communion with the invisible world'. Yet Wordsworth is not a nature mystic: enhanced by vision though it may be, the model for his lost totality is a recognizable social order. Significantly, *The Prelude* begins in, revisits and finally returns in spirit to the world of his Cumberland childhood and youth, with its undisturbed beauty and stillness and the timeless patriarchal simplicity of its social and economic relations. The poem is Wordsworth's greatest work, and it is astonishing that his fame in his own lifetime as the architect of Romantic conservatism was actually achieved without it.

**Prescott, William Hickling** 1796–1859 American historian, born in Salem, Massachusetts, and educated at Harvard. His *History* *of the Reign of Ferdinand and Isabella, the Catholic* was published in three volumes in 1838. He was encouraged by its reception and in the following year began to prepare *History of the Conquest of Mexico*, which was published in three volumes in 1843 and brought him widespread acclaim. Prescott was careful to indicate the tragedy inherent in the advance of the conquistadors; his careful examination of sources and his adventurous narrative method provided a model for a younger generation of historians. *History of the Conquest of Peru* followed in 1847, and the cycle was completed with the publication of three volumes of *History of the Reign of Philip the Second* (1855–8).

**Preston, Thomas** *fl.* 1570 Nothing is known of the life of the author of *Cambises, King of Persia* (1569), though he has often been confused with his namesake, the Vice-Chancellor of Cambridge University. Preston may also have been the author of the heroical romance *Sir Clyomon and Sir Clamydes.*

**Price, Richard** 1723–91 Writer on philosophy and politics. Born at Tynton in Glamorgan, he became a Unitarian minister in London. In 1756 he published *A Review of the Principal Questions in Morals*, arguing that the rightness and wrongness of any action belonged to that action intrinsically and opposing the 'moral sense' view of ethics taken by the **Earl of Shaftesbury** and Francis Hutcheson. Price advocated the reduction of the national debt in *An Appeal to the Public on the Subject of the National Debt* (1772) and strongly supported the American independence in *Observations on the Nature of Civil Liberty, the Principles of Government and the Justice and Policy of the War with America* (1776, supplemented in 1777 and 1778). He became a friend of **Benjamin Franklin** and in 1778 was invited by Congress to live in America. The French Revolution was the occasion for a famous sermon and *A Discourse on the Love of our Country* (1789): 'After sharing in the benefits of one Revolution, I have been spared to be a witness to two other Revolutions, both glorious.' Price's *Discourse* provoked **Edmund Burke** to write his *Reflections on the Revolution in France*, published the following year.

**Price, Sir Uvedale** See **picturesque**.

**Prichard, Katherine Susannah** 1883–1969 Novelist. Born in Fiji, she spent her childhood in Tasmania, and was educated in Melbourne. She worked as a journalist in Melbourne and then went to London, where she spent six years as a freelance journalist and published her first novel, *The Pioneers* (1915). In Australia she took pains to familiarize herself with the background of her novels, travelling the continent and observing the life she depicts with such care. The life of teamsters is featured in *Working Bullocks* (1926); the life of a cattle station and a relationship with an Aboriginal girl in *Coonardoo* (1929), her best novel; and circus life in *Haxby's Circus* (1930). Her trilogy of novels about the goldfields, *The Roaring Nineties* (1946), *Golden Miles* (1948), and *Winged Seeds* (1950), are set in Western Australia, where she eventually made her home. She also wrote verse, including *Clovelly Verses* (1913) and *The Earth Lover and Other Verses* (1932).

**Pricke of Conscience, The** Northern Middle English poem of the first half of the 14th century existing in many versions; the best manuscript has 9000 lines in couplets. It is divided into seven parts and a prologue and deals with man's miserable state, the world and worldly life, death, Purgatory, the signs of Doomsday, the torments of Hell and the joys of Heaven. It is drawn from many sources, Latin and English, amongst the most notable being Pope Innocent III's *De Contemptu Mundi*, Bartholomew's *De Proprietatibus Rerum* (see **John de Trevisa**), Honorius d'Autun's *Elucidarium* and Aquinas's *Compendium Theologicae Veritatis*. It concentrates on spiritual experience and is more introspective than works with similar intentions, such as *Handlynge Synne*. Its title expresses the author's hope that reading the poem will stir men to repentance. The work was immensely popular and is preserved in a very large number of manuscripts.

**Pride and Prejudice** A novel by **Jane Austen**. It was begun in 1796 and completed the following year under the title 'First Impressions', but rejected by a publisher in this form. It finally appeared in 1813, after careful revision and with a new title.

Mr and Mrs Bennet of Longbourn are an ill-matched couple, he detached and ironic, she vulgar, gossipy and mainly engaged in seeking husbands for their five daughters. Netherfield, a house near Longbourn, is leased by the wealthy Charles Bingley, who stays there with his sisters and his friend, the still wealthier FitzWilliam Darcy. To Mrs Bennet's delight, Bingley falls in love with her eldest daughter, Jane. But Elizabeth Bennet, next in age of the Bennet children, frankly dislikes Mr Darcy for his cold and superior manner; her prejudice against him is increased by the story she hears from George Wickham, an engaging young militia officer, of the unjust treatment he has received from Darcy. For their part the Bingley sisters and Darcy find Mrs Bennet and the younger Bennet sisters impossibly vulgar, and prevail on Bingley to detach himself from Jane.

The Bennet family is visited by William Collins, a rector under the patronage of Lady Catherine de Bourgh who will inherit Mr Bennet's entailed property on his death. With great pomposity Mr Collins proposes to Elizabeth but she refuses him, despite the financial convenience of such a marriage. Mr Collins transfers his attentions to Elizabeth's friend, Charlotte Lucas, who accepts him out of expediency. Elizabeth goes to visit the newly married couple and finds that Darcy is in the neighbourhood visiting Lady Catherine, his aunt. He falls in love with Elizabeth but phrases his proposal in so condescending a manner that she refuses, taking the opportunity to upbraid him for his treatment of Wickham and for his role in separating Jane and Bingley. In a letter, Darcy exposes Wickham as an adventurer who had once cherished designs on Darcy's fifteen-year-old sister Georgiana, and protests that he had never been convinced of Jane's love for Bingley.

Elizabeth leaves on a tour of Derbyshire with her aunt and uncle, the Gardiners. They visit Pemberley, Darcy's seat, in the belief he is absent but accidentally meet him. He welcomes them, and his charm and grace begin to impress Elizabeth. Then comes the news that her sister Lydia has eloped with Wickham. Darcy helps trace the runaways and makes sure that they marry. Bingley renews his courtship of Jane and, despite insolent attempts at interference from Lady Catherine, Darcy persists in his wooing of Elizabeth. Both couples are finally united.

**Priestley, J[ohn] B[oynton]** 1894–1984 Novelist, playwright, and broadcaster. Priestley was born in Bradford and educated locally and (after infantry service during World War I) at Trinity Hall, Cambridge. His early publications include *The Chapman of Rhymes* (1918) and *Brief Diversions* (1922; occasional pieces for *The Cambridge Review*). *Papers from Lilliput* also appeared in 1922, the year in which he became a journalist in London.

During the 1920s Priestley wrote several volumes of criticism, including studies of **Meredith** (1926) and **Peacock** (1927), and several novels. However, it was with his novel *The Good Companions* (1929) that he achieved his first popular success, a high-spirited account of three people who, at crises in their lives, join a concert party to become 'The Good Companions' troupe. *Angel Pavement* (1930), a more sombre tale about London life, consolidated his reputation but was less popular.

In 1931 Priestley made his début as a playwright, with a dramatization of *The Good Companions* (with Edward Knoblock). It was spectacularly successful, and many other plays followed. *Dangerous Corner* (1932) employed the theories of J. W. Dunne (see *An Experiment with*

A scene from *The Good Companions* at His Majesty's Theatre, 1931. J. B. Priestley's novel was dramatized by the author and Edward Knoblock and enjoyed further success. The players were, left to right, Adèle Dixon, John Gielgud, Deering Wells, and Lawrence Baskcomb. Victoria & Albert Theatre Museum, London.

*Time*, 1927) to explain such phenomena as precognition; this and similar experiments (*I Have Been Here Before*, 1937; and *Time and the Conways*, 1937) became known as his 'Time' plays.

In 1937 Priestley became president of the London PEN Club, and during World War II he was a highly successful broadcaster. *Postscripts* (1940), *Britain Speaks* (1940) and *All England Listened* (1968) are all selections of his wartime broadcasts. Post-war publications include novels (*Festival at Farbridge*, 1951; *Saturn Over the Water*, 1961; *It's an Old Country*, 1967) and numerous volumes of criticism, including *The Art of the Dramatist* (1957) and *Literature and Western Man* (1960), influenced by Jung.

In total Priestley produced over 60 books and more than 40 plays. His wide-ranging interest in England and the English character, and his appeal to 'the man in the street' have made him one of the most popular 'middlebrow' authors of the 20th century.

His autobiography is incorporated in two volumes, *Martin Released* (1962) and *Instead of the Trees* (1977).

**Priestley, Joseph** 1733–1804 Writer on science, religion and politics. A native of Fieldhead in Yorkshire, Priestley was educated at Batley Grammar School and at Heckmondwike. He trained for the Presbyterian ministry at Daventry and became minister at Needham Market, Suffolk, in 1755 and at Nantwich in Cheshire in 1758, where he opened a school. His views became increasingly controversial and he accepted the ministry of Mill Hill Chapel, an unorthodox church in Leeds, in 1767. The same year saw the foundation of *Theological Repository*, a periodical in which he argued for the autonomy of the individual congregation and the proliferation of sects, attacked the principle of an Established Church and demanded complete toleration for Roman Catholics.

Priestley's first published work was *The History and Present State of Electricity* (1767); the next was to reach a wider audience. *An Essay of the First Principles of Government* (1768) first stated the idea, developed later by **Jeremy Bentham** and the **Utilitarians**, that the happiness of the majority is 'the great standard by which everything relating to that state must finally be determined'. His appointment as librarian to Lord Shelburne in 1772 gave him the leisure to pursue his interest in science and theology, and resulted in *The History and Present State of Discoveries Relating to Vision, Light and Colour* (1772), *Institutes of Natural and Revealed Religion* (1772–4), *Experiments and Observations on Different Kinds of Air* (1774–7), *Disquisitions Relating to Matter and Spirit* (1777) and *A Harmony of the Evangelists* (1777).

In 1780 Priestley moved to Birmingham and became a minister of the New Meeting Society. *A History of the Corruptions of Christianity* (1782) was widely read and widely resented, while *A History of Early Opinions Concerning Jesus Christ* (1786) provoked an attack from Samuel Horsley, Bishop of St Asaph. Priestley denied the infallibility of Christ, though he held throughout his life to a belief in Christ as the Messiah. In 1791 he became one of the founders of the Unitarian Society.

Remaining as radical in his politics as his theology, Priestley earned the nickname 'Gunpowder' Priestley by his support of the French Revolution, expressed in his *Letters to Edmund Burke* (1791). In the same year a mob attacked and wrecked his Birmingham house. After an interval in London, Priestley went to America in 1794 and spent his remaining years in Northumberland, Pennsylvania.

**Prime Minister, The** A novel by **Anthony Trollope**, the fifth in the **Palliser** sequence, serialized in monthly parts from November 1875 to June 1876, and published in four volumes in 1876.

Ferdinand Lopez, an adventurer of doubtful ancestry and profession, wants to marry Emily Wharton. Her crusty but honest father objects to their marriage on the grounds that Lopez is not a 'gentleman', preferring instead the well-bred Arthur Fletcher, a hard-working barrister. Emily and Lopez marry, but his true nature emerges when he gets her to extract money from her father to finance his shady speculations. In a parallel plot Plantagenet Palliser, now Duke of Omnium, becomes Prime Minister at the head of a shaking coalition government, which Lady Glencora helps to sustain with lavish entertaining at Gatherum Castle. There she meets Lopez and foolishly encourages him to stand in the Silverbridge by-election. Although the duke will have nothing to do with it, he is embarrassed when Lopez loses and accuses the duchess of treachery. To protect his wife the duke pays the election expenses demanded by Lopez, and this becomes a source of scandal until Phineas Finn silences the gossip with an effective speech in the House of Commons. Meanwhile the financial affairs of Lopez and his partner deteriorate, and he commits suicide by throwing himself in front of a train. In due course Emily marries Arthur Fletcher and the duke's coalition government falls.

In *The Prime Minister* Plantagenet Palliser is revealed as a man too thin-skinned for party politics but remarkable for his honesty and integrity, Trollope's 'perfect gentleman'.

**Prime of Miss Jean Brodie, The** A novel by **Muriel Spark**, published in 1961.

Miss Jean Brodie is a schoolmistress in Edinburgh during the 1930s. Her ideas about the education of her pupils and about her own role at the Marcia Blaines School for Girls are out of place but representative of 'those women who from the age of thirty and upwards . . . crowned their war-bereaved spinsterhood with voyages of discovery into new ideas and energetic practices in art or social welfare, education or religion'. The 'Brodie set', as her five 16-year-old charges are scornfully nicknamed, are tutored in Renaissance painting, the advantages of cleansing cream over 'honest soap', and the love life of **Charlotte Brontë** and of Miss Brodie herself. She becomes the subject of intense fascination for the girls, and they are increasingly drawn into her emotional life and her relationships with the art master, Teddy Lloyd, and the singing master, Gordon Lowther. The girls too are famous for different things: Monica Douglas for mathematics, Rose Stanley for sex, Eunice Gardiner for gymnastics and 'glamorous swimming', Mary Macgregor for being a scapegoat, and Sandy Stranger for her 'vowel sounds' in recitation.

Sandy has an affair with Teddy Lloyd during the summer of 1938 and the effects of Miss Brodie's teaching concern the headmistress, Miss Mackay. Betrayed by Sandy, Miss Brodie is eventually forced to retire at the end of 1939 on the grounds that she has been teaching fascism. The 'Brodie set' leave school to meet very different and in some cases tragic fates but the colourful and morally ambiguous influence of 'Miss Jean Brodie in her prime' endures long after her death.

**Prince, F[rank] T[empleton]** 1912– Poet and scholar. Born in South Africa, he was educated there, at Balliol College, Oxford, and at Princeton University. During World War II he served in the Intelligence Corps. From 1954 to 1974 he was Professor of English at Southampton University; in 1973 he delivered the Clark lectures at Cambridge. His first book, *Poems*, appeared in 1938 but he established his reputation with the widely anthologized 'Soldiers Bathing', which became the title poem of a later collection (1954). Subsequent volumes include *The Doors of Stone* (1963), *Collected Poems* (1979) and *Later On* (1983). Many poems derive from imaginary confrontations with past events and people, including Michelangelo, **Byron**, **Shelley** and **Rupert Brooke**. Prince's scholarly works include the Arden edition of **Shakespeare**'s *Poems* (1960).

**Prince and the Pauper, The**: *A Tale for Young People of All Ages* A novel by **Mark Twain**, published in England in 1881 and in the USA in 1882. It is set during the last years of Henry VIII's reign and tells how Prince Edward and a pauper boy exchange places by mistake.

The Prince encounters the poor Tom Canty, and is fascinated to see that they appear to be exact twins. They exchange clothes, and the Prince is chased from the palace by guards. He is abused by Tom's family, and then wanders through London in rags until a disinherited knight, Miles Hendson, takes pity on the boy, whom he believes – from his repeated claim to royal birth – to be unbalanced. In Miles's company Edward sees at first hand the wretchedness of the poor and the cruelty of the law. Meanwhile, Tom has been treated as a prince, and when the king dies he is prepared for coronation. Edward makes his way to Westminster Abbey and manages to establish his identity by revealing the whereabouts of the Great Seal. The Prince becomes Edward VI, and during his brief reign does his best to keep in mind the lessons of his own days as a pauper.

**Prince's Progress, The** An allegorical poem by **Christina Rossetti**, published in 1866. A prince sets out confidently and happily to claim his bride. In the course of his long and arduous journey he yields to temptation, seeking mere comfort at first but then turning to one pleasing distraction after another. When he arrives he finds that the princess who had been awaiting him has died of despair.

**Princess, The**: *A Medley* A poem by **Alfred Tennyson**, first published in 1847.

Framed by its setting of the typically English estate of Sir Walter Vivian, who 'all in a summer's day/Gave his broad lawns until the set of sun/Up to the people', *The Princess* consists of a Prologue, Conclusion, and seven parts. They tell the story of a Prince, subject to 'weird seizures', whose betrothed, Princess Ida, daughter of King Gama, rejects marriage, preferring 'to live alone/Among her women' and to found a centre of learning devoted to feminists. The Prince, accompanied by two friends Florian and Cyril, gain admittance to this fortress disguised as women but their identities are soon revealed, although not before the Prince has rescued the Princess from drowning. Further complications of an amatory nature involve Cyril and Florian. The kingly fathers of the Prince and Princess almost do battle; Arac, the Princess's brother, appears, and ultimately his forces and those of the Prince engage in combat. Arac is victorious, the Prince, Cyril and Florian are all wounded, the Princess modifies her stringent antimasculinity, her college is transformed into a hospital, and all parties are happily reconciled.

It is perhaps unnecessary to add that the narrative of *The Princess* is not its principal strength. But the poem is a characteristically Tennysonian work in its dichotomy between the pragmatic and the lyrical. On the one hand, the poem manifests the growing Victorian concern for geology, astronomy, mathematics, evolutionary theory, feminism, domesticity, paternalism, and other aspects of the social hierarchy; on the other, *The Princess* is a poem transformed by some of the finest lyrics in the language. At the end of each section – interpolated in the third edition of 1850 – are such enduring songs as 'Sweet and Low, Sweet and Low' and 'The Splendour Falls on Castle Walls', whilst within the body of the work, originating in the first edition, are 'Tears, Idle Tears' and 'Now Sleeps the Crimson Petal'.

**Princess Casamassima, The** A novel by **Henry James**, published serially in *The Atlantic Monthly* from September 1885 to October 1886, and then in volume form in 1886.

Set in London in the 1880s, the novel portrays a range of characters from all social classes. Its hero is an orphan boy, Hyacinth Robinson, who has been brought up by Miss Pynsent, a quiet little spinster who makes a living as a dressmaker and lives in a lower-class district of London. Hyacinth has seen his mother only once, when she was dying in prison, condemned for the murder of his father, 'Lord Frederick'. He becomes apprenticed to the book-binder Eustache Poupin, a French Communist in exile. While learning his trade he meets Paul Muniment, a proletarian revolutionary, joins a secret society, and commits himself to the movement. He also comes into contact with Christina, the Princess Casamassima, who, separated from her Italian husband (see *Roderick Hudson*), finds the revolutionary movement an outlet for her energies. After Miss Pynsent dies,

Hyacinth travels to Europe and returns with a somewhat altered social vision. Though he no longer supports the society, he receives a summons from it to carry out the assassination of a duke. The Princess Casamassima goes to his apartment, planning to offer to substitute for him, but she arrives too late. He has given up in despair and killed himself.

**Principles of Moral and Political Philosophy, The** A theological treatise by **William Paley**, published in 1785. Its argument is heavily indebted to **Abraham Tucker**'s *The Light of Nature Pursued* (1768–78) but presented with greater system and clarity. Paley's version of theological utilitarianism is firmly grounded in Christianity, and his ethical system requires the acknowledgement of rewards and penalties after death. Paley's skill as an expositor kept his book widely read in academic circles for a number of years.

**Principles of Psychology, The** A book by **William James**, published in 1890. The text, 12 years in the making, was based in part on James's observations at the psychological laboratory he established at Harvard in 1876. In this laboratory, the first of its kind in the USA, James developed his functional approach to psychology. His findings indicated that the mind operates as a part of the body, and that an individual's mental adjustments are in fact environmental responses. In *Principles* he defines the mind as an instrument which, by controlling choice, effort, and will, makes adjustments which are modified by deterministic factors such as heredity and biology.

**Pringle, Thomas** 1789–1834 Poet. Born at Kelso in Scotland, he completed his education at the University of Edinburgh. He published *The Institute: A Heroic Poem* (1811) and became editor of *The Edinburgh Monthly Magazine* in 1817. *The Autumnal Excursion* (1819) was published the same year that financial difficulties led him to accept the post of government librarian in Cape Town. He spent six years in South Africa, where he opened a school and founded a periodical, *The South African Journal*. This led to his dismissal by the governor, who objected to Pringle's politics and rejected his hopes of bringing the country's various cultural groups together. Pringle left South Africa in 1826 and settled in London with his family. He devoted his energies to the Anti-Slavery Society, working closely with Wilberforce and Clarkson, and to giving the first authentic breath of South Africa to English literature. His poems were published in *Ephemerides* (1828) and *African Sketches* (1834). *The History of Mary Prince, a West Indian Slave* (1831) and *Narrative of a Residence in South Africa* (1835) reinforce the humanitarian tone of his poems, which were admired by **Coleridge** and **Tennyson**.

**Prior, Matthew** 1664–1721 Poet and diplomat. Of a humble but respectable Dorset family, Prior was born in Stephen's Alley, Westminster, and sent to nearby Westminster School. His father's death forced his withdrawal for financial reasons but he was 'discovered' by **Charles Sackville, Earl of Dorset**, who financed his return, a generosity warmly acknowledged by Prior in the dedication to his first collection of poems in 1709. He went on to St John's College, Cambridge, being elected a fellow in 1688 and retaining the position until his death.

Prior's diplomatic career began in 1690, as secretary to the British ambassador at The Hague, where he remained for seven years, for much of the time as his country's sole representative. In a series of complex negotiations he won William III's confidence, acting as a trusted itinerant diplomat. The accession of Queen Anne initially brought a reversal of fortunes, but the Tory ministry of **Robert Harley, Earl of Oxford**, revived his career, and in 1711 he was secretly dispatched to France to negotiate peace. The officiousness of a British customs official resulted in a public fiasco, as recounted in Prior's friend **Swift**'s *A Journey to Paris* (1711). Prior remained instrumental in Franco-British peace negotiations, both secret and public, being named Minister Plenipotentiary in 1712. His star reached its zenith when, after the signing of the Treaty of Utrecht in 1713 (popularly known as 'Matt's Peace'), he was Louis XIV's personal guest at Fontainebleau in the autumn. The death of Queen Anne in 1714 brought a new administration, hostile to Prior; returning to England the following year, he was arrested, interrogated and imprisoned for more than a year. He retired to private life, occupied in the preparation of the great subscription edition of his works, a massively handsome folio published in 1718, and in the beautification of the country house, Down Hall, which he had bought with Harley's aid. On 18 September 1721, Prior, whose health had always been delicate, died of cholera. At his request, he was buried in Westminster Abbey at the feet of his favourite poet, **Spenser**.

Prior's fame as a poet was inaugurated by early satires attacking **John Dryden**, particularly the burlesque *The Hind and the Panther Transvers'd to the Story of The Country Mouse and the City Mouse* (1687), parodying Dryden's philosophical *The Hind and the Panther* of earlier that year. Written in collaboration with his friend Charles Montague, this lively and good-humoured travesty was a runaway success. The bulk of Prior's work consists of occasional pieces: epistles, lyrics, patriotic odes, ballads, burlesques and imitations of **Chaucer** and Spenser. His comic writing is made particularly vivid by his wry self-characterization (as Matt). Serious works include *Carmen Secolare* (1700), eulogizing his master William III, and the weighty *Solomon on the Vanity of the World* (1718), in three books. *Alma, or, the Progress of the Mind* (1718), written in prison, is a witty mock-scholastic conversation between Matt and a friend, a burlesque counterpart to *Solomon*. These were the two works Prior himself most valued. In his last years he began work on the superlative *Dialogues of the Dead*, a sequence of imaginary conversations; that between Montaigne and **Locke** is the most brilliant. Prior's voice, vivacious and well-mannered, conforms to his own ideal: 'a style close, distinct, and familiar; and in your writing easy and civil'.

***Prioress's Tale, The*** See *Canterbury Tales, The*.

***Prisoner of Zenda, The*** A novel by **Anthony Hope**, published in 1894. It follows the swashbuckling adventures of Rudolf Rassendyll, an Englishman who bears a striking resemblance to the King of Ruritania. When the monarch is kidnapped by his enemies Black Michael and Rupert of Hentzau, Rassendyll impersonates him and helps thwart the plot to usurp the throne. A sequel, *Rupert of Hentzau*, appeared in 1898.

**Pritchett, Sir V[ictor] S[awdon]** 1900– Writer and critic. V. S. Pritchett was born in Ipswich and educated in London at Dulwich College. He became a journalist in 1923, serving as literary critic of *The New Statesman* for 20 years and a director from 1946 to 1978. Although he is best known as a critic and short-story writer, Pritchett's range is wide and he has also published novels, travel books and biographies. His first book was a travel report, *Marching Spain* (1928); his first novel, *Clare Drummer*, followed in 1929 and his first volume of short stories, *The Spanish Virgin and Other Stories*, in 1932. Among his best-known works are *Dead Man Leading* (1937, novel), *You Make Your Own Life* (1938, short stories), *In My Good Books* (1942, reviews), *It May Never Happen* (1945, short stories), *The Living Novel* (1946 and 1964, essays), *Mr Beluncle* (1951, novel), *The Spanish Temper* (1955, travel), *When My Girl Comes Home* (1961, short stories), *The Working Novelist* (1965, reviews), *A Cab at the Door* (1968, memoir), *George Meredith and English Comedy* (1970), *Balzac* (1973), *The Camberwell Beauty* (1974, short stories), and *Turgenev: The Gentle Barbarian* (1977). V. S. Pritchett was knighted in 1975.

***Private Lives*** A comedy by **Noël Coward**, first performed at the Phoenix Theatre, London, in 1930, with the author, Gertrude Lawrence and Laurence Olivier in the cast.

Elyot and Amanda, divorced, meet again on the occasion of their honeymoons at Deauville after marriage to new partners. Still powerfully attracted to each other, they run off to Paris together, only to rediscover the reasons for the original separation. Their deserted spouses catch up with them just as their quarrels edge towards violence; but the following morning they sneak off again, leaving their partners squabbling. Whatever Elyot and Amanda may do to each other, they always prefer each other's company.

***Private Memoirs and Confessions of a Justified Sinner*** A novel by **James Hogg**, published in 1824. Chilling, psychologically challenging and grimly humorous, it is the most ambitious, and now most widely read, of Hogg's prose works. Set against the background of the violent religious and political divisions of late 17th-century Scotland, the story is divided into two main parts, the first of which contains the 'editor's narrative' of the strife-torn marriage of the Lord of Dalcastle and the mysteriously contrived murder of his son and heir, George Colwan, in circumstances pointing to the complicity of his half-brother Robert Wringhim, a Calvinist bigot. The second part consists of Wringhim's own memoir which is discovered in his grave a century after his presumed suicide. In it he reveals how, with the aid of the uncanny skills of a malign *alter ego*, or *doppelgänger*, he murdered first a preacher, then his brother, and then apparently his mother, having been persuaded by his helper's antinomian sophistry that he was thereby doing God's work, and that no act he might commit could affect his predestined salvation. He gradually realizes that the stranger is in fact the Devil, who appears to have claimed him in the end, for the body found beside the memoir is still firmly covered with flesh and the skull appears to have grown a tiny pair of horns.

***Private Papers of Henry Ryecroft, The*** A novel by **George Gissing**, published in 1903. It takes the form of a journal kept by a recluse who has been helped by a legacy from a friend to withdraw from the London literary world where he had failed as a writer.

**private theatres** The indoor playhouses of Elizabethan, Jacobean and Caroline London were, and still are, sometimes called 'private theatres' to distinguish them from the open-air **public theatres**. The title embodies a fiction which was a useful defence against interference from the civic authorities. They were, in fact, open to the public on the payment of an admission charge which was generally higher than that of the public theatres. But the first actors to use private playhouses were choristers, and it was convenient for their managers to claim that what the public witnessed were private rehearsals of plays in preparation for presentation at court. The title stuck long after it had lost all conviction. The main private theatres were the unknown home of the Boys of St Paul's (*c.* 1575), the first **Blackfriars** (1576), the second Blackfriars (1600), the Whitefriars (1605–8), the Cockpit or Phoenix (1616) and the Salisbury Court (1629). More genuinely private were the **court theatres**.

**problem play** A term in common use by the end of the 19th century to describe plays dealing with contemporary social and moral issues. Even in England and the USA, where he was frequently denounced, Ibsen was the major inspiration of a new seriousness, and his influence lies behind the problem plays of **Pinero**, **Henry Arthur Jones**, **Galsworthy** and **Granville-Barker**, as it does behind the more openly subversive early plays of **Shaw**.

It was F. S. Boas who, in 1896, first applied the term to a group of plays by **Shakespeare**, and it has kept some critical currency as a group title for the three tragicomedies, *All's Well That Ends Well*, *Measure for Measure* and *Troilus and Cressida*. Each of these plays addresses with a harshness untypical of Shakespeare's comedies the interrelationship of private and public morality. Some critics have proposed the advantage of associating *Julius Caesar* and *Hamlet* with Shakespeare's problem plays.

**Procter, Adelaide Anne** 1825–64 Poet. The daughter of B. W. Procter (**Barry Cornwall**), she published several volumes of sentimental verse: *Legends and Lyrics* (two series, 1858 and 1861), *A Chaplet of Verses* (1862) and *The Message* (1892). Her work was popular in its day, and admirers included **Charles Dickens**.

**Professor, The** Charlotte Brontë's first completed novel, written in 1846 but not published until 1857, two years after her death. It draws on the same experiences that she was later to use more successfully in *Villette*. An Englishman, William Crimsworth, goes to Brussels as a schoolmaster and falls in love with Frances Henri, a fellow teacher and Anglo-Swiss girl.

**Prometheus Unbound** A lyrical drama in four acts by **Shelley**, written in 1818–19 and published in 1820.

The action is drawn from Aeschylus' *Prometheus Bound* and what is known of its lost sequel *Prometheus Unbound*, though, as he explains in his preface, Shelley felt obliged to depart from the Greek dramatist's 'feeble' idea of 'reconciling the Champion with the Oppressor of mankind'. A second, more positive, source of inspiration was **Milton**'s Satan, whom Shelley considered to be the real hero of *Paradise Lost*, with God occupying the role of tyrant. Com-

bining, rewriting and updating these two myths, he creates a Prometheus of beauty, energy and moral perfection, who suffers the persecution of a jealous, irrational and wholly vindictive God. His liberation by the personified forces of Hope, Love and 'Necessity' brings about the triumph of mankind over tyranny, and the transfiguration of the world in a new golden age. Partly mythical drama, partly political allegory, the work blends Shelley's preoccupations as poet, philosopher and radical into a sequence of powerful symbolic tableaux, cast in a bewildering variety of forms: dreams, visions, epic narrative, rhetorical soliloquies, songs, choruses and dramatic dialogues.

Act I opens with Prometheus chained to a precipice in the Indian Caucasus, where his heart is daily consumed by Jupiter's eagle. Aided by his mother, the Earth, he recalls his curse of Jupiter, and his hatred for his adversary turns to pity. Mercury is sent by Jupiter with a vast chorus of Furies who tempt him to despair with visions of human inadequacy: he is made to relive the failure of the French Revolution, and sees Christ eternally crucified, and 'Wailing for the faith he kindled'. Panthea (Hope) reminds him of her sister Asia (Love), whom he has forgotten. In Act II Panthea tells Asia of her dream of Prometheus rejuvenated by love, and together they follow the mysterious echo of a second dream to the dark underworld realm of Demogorgon, the 'people-monster', an inscrutable ultimate source of revolutionary power, whom Asia rouses into action with her passionate declaration of love for suffering humanity. Jupiter is summarily overthrown by Demogorgon at the beginning of Act III, and the unchained Prometheus is reunited with Asia. The Spirit of the Hour describes the universal liberation consequent upon the fall of kings, and the end of social classes, nations and racial distinctions. Act IV, which Shelley added as an afterthought, is a kind of coda or epithalamion, sung first by a chorus of Spirits of the Hour and another chorus of the Spirits of the Human Mind; then by the Spirit of the Earth (male) and the Spirit of the Moon (female).

The first two acts of the drama must count among Shelley's poetic masterpieces, though there are considerable differences of opinion on Acts III and IV, which some consider anticlimactic. The centrality of the theme of liberation is clear but Shelley's magic-wand approach to revolutionary processes has been variously commented upon, and the figure of Demogorgon remains open to conflicting readings.

***Proposal for the Universal Use of Irish Manufacture*** The first of **Jonathan Swift**'s pamphlets about Ireland, published in 1720, it protests against the exploitation of the Irish economy by England. The pamphlet proposes that the home-produced cloth of Ireland – devalued because the English in Ireland regarded it without justification as inferior – should be promoted as an industry and that imported fabrics from England should be boycotted.

*Prothalamion* The word was invented by **Spenser** to entitle his poem to celebrate the double betrothal of Katherine and Elizabeth, daughters of the Earl of Worcester. They were married in November 1596, the same year in which the poem was published. 'Prothalamion' is glossed in the poem's title as 'a spousal verse' and Spenser formed the word by analogy with 'epithalamion' (marriage-song). His own *Epithalamion* had appeared in 1595. The poem's ten stanzas, modelled on Italian *canzoni*, offer a description by a discontented courtier of sights along the Thames, the most important being 'two swans of goodly hue' (Katherine and Elizabeth Somerset). Stanza nine makes complimentary reference to Essex. The poem has been praised for its graceful movement and music. Its famous refrain 'Sweet Thames run softly, till I end my song' is echoed by **T. S. Eliot** in *The Waste Land*.

**Prout, Father** See **Mahony, Francis Sylvester**.

*Proverbial Philosophy* See **Tupper, Martin**.

*Provok'd Wife, The* A comedy by **John Vanbrugh**, produced in 1697 and published the same year.

Sir John Brute is a coward and a bully whose wife suffers greatly. Lady Brute has a devoted admirer, Constant, but she has remained true to her marriage vows. Constant's friend Heartfree has always declared his indifference to women, but falls in love with Bellinda, Lady Brute's niece. Bellinda pursuades her aunt to join her in a lighthearted frolic, a meeting with Heartfree

Sir John Brute brawling with the watchman in Act IV, scene 1 of Vanbrugh's *The Provok'd Wife*. A 19th-century illustration. Victoria & Albert Theatre Museum, London.

Act IV.—Scene 1.

and Constant in Spring Garden whilst Sir John is out drinking. Lady Brute finds Constant's attentions persuasive and is about to yield when the jealous and spiteful Lady Fancyfull intrudes upon them. The two couples hurry away from the Garden and repair to Lady Brute's house, where they sit down to cards. Sir John Brute, meanwhile, has been indulging in drunken and vulgar behaviour with Lord Rake and Colonel Bully, and has taken a parson's gown from a poor tailor. He is wearing it when he is arrested for brawling; the magistrate dismisses him and he lurches off home unexpectedly early. Constant and Heartfree hide in a closet, where he discovers them. But he is outfaced by Constant and accepts that the two men are present because of Heartfree's forthcoming marriage to Bellinda, though he is sure in his own mind that he has been cuckolded. Lady Fancyfull does her best to make mischief but fails because her fellow conspirator Rasor, Sir John Brute's valet, baulks at the extent of her spite. The play ends with Bellinda's marriage to Heartfree.

*Provost, The* A novel by **John Galt**, published in 1822, in which he displays his rich humour, ready sympathy and fine command of the Scots vernacular in all its shades. An essay in sustained irony, the book is narrated by Mr Pawkie, who has three times reached the office of provost (mayor). He unwittingly reveals his own canny nature as he reflects on his progress through public life and contrasts the sophistication of the wider world of business and politics with the manners and speech of provincial Scotland.

**Prynne, J[eremy] H[alward]** 1936– Poet. Born in Kent and educated at St Dunstan's College and at Jesus College, Cambridge, where he read English, Prynne spent a year in the United States before becoming a fellow of Gonville and Caius College, Cambridge, in 1962. He is the leading British exponent of a postmodernist, experimental poetry which has its origins in the later work of **Ezra Pound** and in the 'projective verse' of **Charles Olson**. His work avoids concentration on an identifiable subject matter and instead uses enigmatic imagery and disorienting twists and fractures of syntax to force the reader into a self-conscious awareness of the processes of reading and writing. *Force of Circumstance and Other Poems* (1962), *The White Stones* (1969), *Brass* (1971) and *Poems* (1982), bringing together much previous work, are among the numerous volumes which have gained him a small but devoted following among British and American readers and critics sympathetic to the *avant-garde*.

**Prynne, William** 1600–69 Puritan pamphleteer. Born in Somerset, he attended Bath Grammar School and Oriel College, Oxford, and then studied law at Lincoln's Inn; he was called to the Bar in 1628. A fanatical Puritan, Prynne published a 'pamphlet' of over a thousand pages, *Histrio-Mastix* (1632), attacking the playhouses. Archbishop **Laud** decided that the work contained veiled attacks on Henrietta Maria and King Charles, and Prynne was sentenced by the Star Chamber in 1634 to life imprisonment, a huge fine, loss of his law and university degrees, and the pillory, where his ears were 'cropped'. He was later branded for sedition.

Prynne was freed by the Long Parliament in 1640 and emerged as a hero. In 1648 he became MP for Newport and, surprisingly, opposed the trial and execution of Charles I. He became therefore a victim of Pride's Purge and suffered imprisonment again. However, he continued as an MP, opposing the Commonwealth Army and the Rump Parliament until in 1660 he brought in the bill dissolving Parliament for the restoration of the monarchy. Charles II made him Keeper of the Tower Records and Prynne continued writing busily until the end of his days. He was the author of no fewer than 200 miscellaneous works.

**Psalters** The book of 150 psalms in the Old Testament, traditionally ascribed to King David, was the basis for the liturgy of the medieval church. There is a long tradition of Old and Middle English Psalters. The version in the **Book of Common Prayer** is largely based on the translation by **Miles Coverdale** in his first complete Bible of 1535 (see **Bible in English**). Coverdale's metrical version of 13 psalms, *Ghostly Psalms and Spiritual Songs*, with words and tunes mainly adapted from Lutheran sources, was printed *c.*1539. Frequently reprinted – even annually after 1549 – was the *Whole Books of Psalms Collected into English Metre*, by T. Sternhold and J. Hopkins, a version with tunes adapted from the Genevan Psalter. This was the Old Version (hence 'Old Hundredth' as the name of the hymn tune for 'All People That on Earth Do Dwell'). Between this and the New Version by Nicholas Brady and **Nahum Tate** (1696) there were many publications of metrical psalms in various arrangements. The whole Psalter was translated into metrical forms by **Matthew Parker**, **Sir Philip Sidney** and **James I**, and parts by **John Milton**, **Francis Bacon**, **George Herbert**, **Richard Crashaw**, **Henry Vaughan** and others. For over a thousand years the Psalter has been one of the greatest influences on English lyric poetry.

*Pseudodoxia Epidemica, or, Enquiries into Very Many Received Tenents and Commonly Presumed Truths* Often known as *Vulgar Errors*, **Thomas Browne**'s lengthy second work was first published in 1646; revised and expanded editions appeared in 1650, 1658 and 1672. It investigates credulity and popular hearsay, analysing the reasons for mistaken beliefs and tracing their origins in the susceptibility of humans to the dictates of others, as well as the ultimate agency of Satan. Browne enquires widely into instances of such mistakes, wittily and vivaciously rummaging through legends and cherished beliefs which result from gullibility, deceit, custom and superstition.

**psychoanalytic criticism** Freud coined the term 'psychoanalysis' in 1896 to describe a therapeutic technique used to uncover unconscious repressions of childhood emotions. The analytic methods were sometimes applied to literary texts on the assumption that the author's repressed emotions were at work in the text's affective patterns – that texts are shaped by unconscious desire. The unconscious often expresses itself in dreams, jokes and ambiguous uses of language, and especially in figurative language. Freud discovered that forbidden thoughts are retold by patients under the influences of certain mental processes, including displacement (of an emotional focus from one object to another) and condensation (of several ideas into one), which correspond (as Roman Jakobson shows) to two figures of speech – **metaphor** and **metonymy** (see also **structuralism**).

The most important challenge to Freudianism was Jung's school of psychology with its notion of a collective unconscious, manifested in certain recurring images, stories and forms, which Jung called 'archetypes'. Jung's sympathy with visionary experiences made his work attractive to many critics, such as **Maud Bodkin**, **Northrop Frye** and Leslie Fiedler, who traced in literary texts the presence of the archetypal patterns which express the most profound and universal experiences of human existence.

Among modern critical uses of psychoanalysis is the development of 'ego-psychology' in the work of Norman Holland, who concentrates on the relations between reader and text. He argues that readers use texts in order to satisfy unconscious wishes. In recent studies he sees reading as the re-creation of the reader's identity: the text's challenging nature requires some adjustment of identity but also is matched by the self-confirming ruses of the reader.

Jacques Lacan (1901–81) has reinterpreted Freud in the light of structuralism and **poststructuralism**. He questions the static concepts of ego-psychology, and produces a new theory of the 'subject' by inserting a structural linguistics into Freud's theory of the unconscious processes. The 'I' is a signifier which takes on meaning (substantial identity etc.) only within a language system. Sexual identity and position within the family system are a product of this entry into the symbolic system of language.

Before this stage there is only the rule of the 'pleasure principle'. Part of the process of identity formation is the repression of desire following the Oedipal phase. However, the desire will not go away, and, remaining in the unconscious, produces a split subject, which never possesses full 'presence'.

Lacan's theories have encouraged a criticism which focuses not on the author but on the linguistic processes of the text. He himself, in his celebrated study of **Poe**'s 'The Purloined Letter', shows that the text reduplicates the processes of the unconscious: the letter represents the unconscious and its (dis)placements in the story determine the positions of the characters. He reads the story as an allegory of psychoanalyis itself: the letter (signifier) lures both the writer and the reader, for it embodies their unconscious drives. This means that meaning is nothing more than the shifting chains of desire in language. Either the writer or the reader can try to impose his or her desire upon the letter. For Lacan art is never representation: even the most realistic novel involves fantasy and wish fulfilment.

***Public Advertiser, The*** A newspaper founded in 1752 as *The London Daily Post and General Advertiser*; it ceased publication under this name in 1798, when it was amalgamated with **John Newbery**'s *The Public Ledger*. The paper carried home and foreign news as well as a great deal of political correspondence, including a dispute between **John Wilkes** and **John Horne Tooke**. The letters of **Junius** were published in its pages by Henry Sampson Woodfall, editor from 1758 to 1793.

**public theatres** The open-air theatres of Elizabethan, Jacobean and Caroline London were, and still are, sometimes called 'public' playhouses to distinguish them from the equally public but more exclusive indoor **private theatres**. They are, in approximate chronological order, the **Theatre** (1576), the Curtain (1577), a theatre of unknown name in Newington Butts (*c.* 1580), the **Rose** (*c.* 1587), the **Swan** (1595), the **Globe** (1599), the Boar's Head (*c.* 1599), the **Fortune** (1600), the Red Bull (1605), the second Globe (1614), the **Hope** (1614) and the second Fortune (1623).

***Puck of Pook's Hill*** A collection of 10 stories and accompanying poems by **Rudyard Kipling**, published in 1906. The stories were intended for both adults and children. Two children, Dan and Una (loosely modelled on Kipling's own children), meet the nature spirit Puck. They provide the framework for a series of stories reaching back in English history, past the Normans and Saxons to the Roman invaders. Most of the stories show particular individuals who

are able to illuminate their historical predicaments, such as the centurion, Parnesius, whose unorthodox handling of his Imperial duties – in co-operating with the Picts – shows an insight which is absent from the higher échelons of the declining Roman Empire.

The stories point to the capacity of civilization to renew itself. The God Weland, in 'Weland's Sword', is freed from an unwanted heathen immortality by a novice monk, Hugh. While Weland adapts to the Christian world, Hugh becomes a warrior. Along with one of the Norman invaders, Sir Richard Dalyngridge, he brings leadership and good management to the land. The figure of Old Hobden, known to Dan and Una as someone who had instinctive understanding of local traditions and the ways of the world, is also a representative of a stoical spirit in the common man which can endure historical change.

A sequel to the collection, *Rewards and Fairies* (1910), followed a similar format. Both volumes contain some of Kipling's best-known verse. In the latter volume particularly, 'A St Helena's Lullaby', 'The Way through the Woods' and 'If' have been much admired.

**Puckering, Sir John** 1544–96 Sir John Puckering is identified as the 'John Pickering' who wrote *Horestes*, a play which is itself identified as the *Orestes* acted at court in 1567 or 1568 and published just before it was produced. Puckering was a lawyer of Lincoln's Inn who later became Lord Keeper of the Seal and who was an implacable enemy of Mary of Scotland.

*Horestes* was a distinct advance on the bombastic clumsiness of contemporary works such as **Cambises** and *Appius and Virginia*. There are still hangovers from the **morality plays** in the characters who personify Vice, Revenge and Nature; but the action develops steadily and the speeches by the principal characters approach the correct mixture of credibility and poetry.

***Pudd'nhead Wilson, The Tragedy of*** A novel by **Mark Twain**, published in 1894. The title character of this story of confused identities is a lawyer, David Wilson, called 'Pudd'nhead' by a community which ridicules his eccentric ideas and practices.

The story takes place in the Missouri town of Dawson's Landing in the 1830s. Tom, the son of the prosperous slave-owner Percy Driscoll, is born on the same day as Chambers, the son of one of Driscoll's slaves, a light-skinned woman named Roxana, and a Virginian gentleman. The children closely resemble each other. Roxy is afraid that Chambers might eventually be sold down the river, so she switches the two babies to protect her son. When Percy Driscoll dies, his brother Judge Driscoll adopts Chambers, thinking him to be Tom. The boy grows up to be a bully, a gambler, and an arrogant coward. To pay his gambling debts he decides to sell Roxy, but she escapes from her new owners and blackmails him with the secret of his true birth. He resorts to stealing to help pay his various debts, and, during a robbery attempt, murders the Judge with a knife he had stolen from Luigi, one of the aristocratic Italian twins who have recently arrived in town. Although the twins were initially well received, the false Tom had caused a series of disturbances which led to enmity between them and Judge Driscoll. It is therefore supposed by all that Luigi committed the murder. The unpractised attorney 'Pudd'n-head' Wilson successfully proves Luigi's innocence by showing that the fingerprints on the knife belong to the false Tom. He also establishes the true identities of Tom and Chambers. Wilson becomes a town celebrity, the disgraced Chambers is sold down the river as a slave and Roxy is supported by her surrogate son, the true Tom.

**Punch**, *or, The London Charivari* A weekly comic magazine founded in 1841, partly through the efforts of **Henry Mayhew**, with **Mark Lemon** and Joseph Stirling Coyne (1803–68) as joint editors, and a circle of contributors which included **Gilbert à Beckett, Thomas Hood, Douglas Jerrold** and **Thackeray. John Leech** was the chief artist and **Richard Doyle** drew the famous cover. Originally noted for its radical abrasiveness, *Punch* soon settled for a more comfortable style of humour that came to be seen as typically English. Shirley Brooks (1816–74) and **Tom Taylor** were among later editors; its artists included Sir John Tenniel (1820–1914), Charles Keene (1823–91), **George Du Maurier** and Linley Sambourne (1845–1910).

**Punch's Prize Novelists** Parodies by **W. M. Thackeray**, with his own illustrations, published in **Punch** from April to October 1847 and reprinted under the title *Novels by Eminent Hands*.

There are seven parodies of contemporary novelists, including **Bulwer Lytton, Fenimore Cooper, G. P. R. James, Charles Lever** and **Disraeli**, whose *Coningsby* is devastatingly mocked in 'Codlingsby'. Thackeray's playful critique of the military, historical and fashionable fiction of the day throws light on his intentions and achievements in *Vanity Fair*, written at the same time.

**Purchas, Samuel** *c.*1575–1626 Historian and travel-writer. Born at Thaxted in Essex and educated at St John's College, Cambridge, Purchas was vicar of a parish on the Thames estuary for ten years and then became rector of St Martin's, Ludgate. He published *Purchas His Pilgrimage, or, Relations of the World and the Religions Observed in All Ages* in 1613 and *Purchas His Pilgrim: Microcosmus, or, the Histories of Man* in 1619. An assistant to **Richard Hakluyt** in his later years, Purchas inherited the maritime historian's manuscripts and compiled the extensive *Hakluyt Posthumous, or Purchas His Pilgrims: Containing a History of the World, in Sea Voyages and Land Travels by Englishmen and Others* (1625). Of the book's two parts, the first deals with the Mediterranean and the East, the second with the Northwest Passage, Russia (Muscovy), the West Indies and Florida. Although generally considered inferior to Hakluyt's work, it contains some notable accounts, particularly William Adams's description of his journey to Japan and his residence there.

**Purdy, Al[fred] (Wellington)** 1918– Canadian poet. Born in Wooller, Ontario, he left school at 16 and embarked on a wandering life before settling at Roblin Lake at Ameliasburgh. His verse presents the people of modern Canada but is enriched by a vivid background of allusion and imagery drawn from mythological and historical sources. His numerous collections include *Poems for All the Annettes* (1962), *The Cariboo Horses* (1965), *North of Summer: Poems from Baffin Island* (1967), *Wild Grape Wine* (1968), *Love in a Burning Building* (1971), *Hiroshima Poems* (1972), *In Search of Owen Roblin* (1974), *To Feed the Sun* (1976), *A Handful of Earth* (1977) and *Moths in the Iron Curtain* (1979).

**Purdy, James** 1923– American novelist, born in Ohio and educated at the universities of Chicago and Puebla, Mexico. His first book, a collection of short stories entitled *Color of Darkness*, appeared in 1957. Much of his fiction focuses on small-town provincial America; sometimes a character from a small town is transplanted to a large urban setting and the values of each are juxtaposed. His first novel, *Malcolm*, was published in 1959. Other books are *The Nephew* (1960); *Cabot Wright Begins* (1964); *Eustace Chisholm and the Works* (1967); *I Am Elijah Thrush* (1972); a trilogy, *Sleepers in Moon-Crowned Valleys*, comprising *Jeremy's Version* (1970), *The House of the Solitary Maggot* (1974) and *Mourners Below* (1981); and *In the Hollow of His Hand* (1986). He has also published collections of poetry, including *The Running Sun* (1971); some plays are included with short stories in the volume *Children is All* (1962).

*Purity* See *Cleanness*.

**Pusey, Edward Bouverie** 1800–82 Theologian and leading member of the **Oxford Movement**. Educated at Eton and Christ Church, Oxford, he became a fellow of Oriel College in 1822. After studying Hebrew and Arabic at Göttingen and Berlin, he returned to

Oxford, where he was ordained in 1828 and became Regius Professor of Hebrew and Canon of Christ Church. A close associate of **John Henry Newman** and **John Keble** in the Oxford Movement, he contributed essays on the holy eucharist and baptism to *Tracts for the Times*. He defended Newman's analysis of the Thirty-Nine Articles in the controversial 'Tract 90' and was suspended from the office of university preacher in 1843, but remained firm in his allegiance to High Church Anglicanism after Newman's conversion to Roman Catholicism. His *Doctrine of the Real Presence* was published in 1856.

**Puttenham, George** 1529–90 It was probably George rather than his brother Richard (?1520–?1601) who was the author of *The Art of English Poesy* (1589), although each has, at various times, seemed the likelier candidate. Both were nephews of **Sir Thomas Elyot**. George was educated at Cambridge and admitted to the Middle Temple in 1556. The apparent claim of the author of *The Art of English Poesy* to have been at Oxford is one of the details that has cast doubt on George Puttenham's authorship.

The work is a critical discussion of poetry, mainly from the formal aspect. Its three books are concerned respectively, as its title-page announces, with 'poets and poesy', 'proportion' and 'ornament'. Book I defines poetry and claims, as does **Sidney**'s *Apology for Poetry*, that in ancient times poets were priests, prophets and lawgivers. It also makes the same claim as the *Apology* for the antiquity and dignity of poetry, and the educative and reprehensive powers of fiction. Book I also gives major divisions of fiction (e.g. epic, tragedy, comedy) and minor divisons of poems (e.g. of praise, lamentation, marriage). Book II is concerned with metrics, with pattern poems appealing to the eye (like those later written by **George Herbert**), anagrams and devices. Book III is largely concerned with figures of speech and Puttenham gives English equivalents for the technical Greek terms of rhetoric: *ironia* is 'the dry mock', *sarcasmus* 'the bitter taunt', *antiphrasis* 'the broad flout' and *charientismus* 'the privy nip'.

**Pye, Henry James** 1745–1813 **Poet Laureate** from the death of **Thomas Warton the younger** in 1790 until his own death, when **Robert Southey** was appointed to the office. Pye's work – which includes plays, translations from the classics and critical essays as well as poetry – was not highly regarded during his lifetime and has not been reprinted since 1822.

*Pygmalion* A romantic comedy by **George Bernard Shaw**, first produced in German at Vienna in 1913. The first English production was staged the following year with Mrs Patrick Campbell,

Mrs Patrick Campbell as Eliza Doolittle in the first London production of *Pygmalion* at His Majesty's Theatre, 1914.

for whom the part was written, as Eliza Doolittle.

The play turns on the claim made by Professor Higgins, a professor of phonetics, to his friend Colonel Pickering that he could pass off a cockney flower girl, Eliza Doolittle, as a duchess by teaching her to speak properly. She asks Higgins for lessons and he takes her as his pupil. In the course of her education she emerges not merely as a presentable lady but as a beautiful woman of increasing sensitivity. To Higgins, however, she is just a successful experiment. The play, as originally written, ends with Eliza asserting herself as a human being and rejecting Higgins. The film adaptation of 1938, which Shaw approved, brought Eliza and Higgins together at the end. This version was made into the musical comedy, *My Fair Lady* (1956).

Shaw based the character of Professor Higgins on the phonetician and scholar of Old English, **Henry Sweet**.

**Pyle, Howard** 1853–1911 American author and illustrator. Born in Delaware, the son of a Quaker businessman, Pyle studied drawing before travelling to New York in the hope of making good as an artist. After some success contributing to children's magazines, he became famous with his version of *The Merry Adventures of Robin Hood of Great Renown in Nottinghamshire* (1883). There followed a succession of historical romances before he turned to writing and illustrating fairy-stories. His outstanding work, *King Arthur and his Knights* (1913), continued into three more volumes, ending with *The Story of the Grail and the Passing of Arthur* (1910). A perfectionist to the last detail, Pyle was always conscious of the total appearance of a page, at times adding his own decorative surrounds and always making sure text and illustration merged harmoniously together. His pictures also abound in good humour and invention, with the busy movements of numerous characters bringing in a new vigour to American picture-books that has lasted to this day.

**Pym, Barbara (Mary Crampton)** 1913–80 Novelist. Brought up in Shropshire in a solicitor's family, Pym attended St Hilda's College, Oxford, and later worked in London at the International Africa Institute. After success with novels such as *Excellent Women* (1952) and *A Glass of Blessings* (1958), she fell out of favour with her publishers and remained in obscurity until, with the publication of *Quartet in Autumn* in 1977, her work was championed and her reputation rescued by **Philip Larkin**. *The Sweet*

*Dove Died* followed in 1979, and four further novels, *A Few Green Leaves* (1980), *An Unsuitable Attachment* (1982), *Crampton Hodnet* (1985) and *An Academic Question* (1986), have appeared since her death. All Pym's books are wistful, delicate comedies with an unsparingly sad undertow; the frustration in love suffered by hapless spinsters is their common theme, and the intrigue-ridden world of middle-class churchgoing a distinctive milieu.

**Pynchon, Thomas** 1937– American novelist, born in Glen Cove, New York, and educated at Cornell. He worked for a time at the Boeing Aircraft Corporation in Seattle, but little else is known about his life – he avoids interviews – beyond his liking for Mexico. His first novel, *V.* (1963), is a long, dark-toned fantasy – his preferred medium for depicting American life in the latter half of the 20th century. In *The Crying of Lot 49* (1966) he explores the attempts of the modern mind to organize an apparently chaotic universe, and juxtaposes various systems and ideologies that exist in contemporary society. His third novel, *Gravity's Rainbow*, appeared in 1973, and received the National Book Award. He has also published a collection of his early short stories, *Slow Learner* (1984), which includes 'Lowlands' and 'Entropy'.

**pyrrhic** See **metre**.

# Q

Q See **Quiller-Couch, Sir Arthur**.

*Quality Street* A comedy by **J. M. Barrie**, first performed at the Vaudeville Theatre, London, in 1902.

The play is set at the beginning of the 19th century in the home of two sisters, Susan and Phoebe Throssel. Considered a little too lively by their respectable lady visitors, the sisters pin their hopes on the likelihood that a young doctor, Valentine Brown, will propose to Phoebe. When he arrives at the house, however, it is to report that he has enlisted and must leave the next day. Forced by poverty to start a school 'for genteel children', the sisters are aged by hardship. When Brown returns ten years later, having lost a hand in battle, he is shocked by Phoebe's drabness. But Phoebe, letting loose her ringlets and masquerading as her own niece, first captivates Brown and finally drives him into preferring 'the schoolmistress in her old-maid's cap'.

**quantitative metre** See **metre**.

**Quarles, Francis** 1592–1644 Poet. Born in Essex, the son of a surveyor-general of victualling for the Navy, he was educated at Christ's College, Cambridge, before entering Lincoln's Inn. Quarles found favour at court, travelling with the Princess Elizabeth's entourage to Germany for her marriage to the Elector Palatine and writing pamphlets in defence of Charles I. He suffered for his Royalist sympathies when the Parliamentary party came to power, having his property sequestered and his manuscripts destroyed. His wife and nine children were left in poverty at his death.

Quarles's poetry can be direct and appealing but, among the mass of work he published, he is remembered only for *Emblems* (1635), the most popular of 17th-century **emblem books** and perhaps the most popular verse of its age. *Enchiridion* (1640–1), a book of aphorisms, was also highly regarded.

*Quarterly Review, The* A Tory rival of the Whig *Edinburgh Review*, founded in 1809 by **John Murray**, the second John Murray of the distinguished publishing house. Its guiding principles were suggested by **Sir Walter Scott**, a keen supporter of the venture, and the first editor was **William Gifford**. He was succeeded by Sir J. T. Coleridge, nephew of the poet, and **J. G. Lockhart**. The contributors included Scott himself, George Canning, **John Hookham Frere**, **Robert Southey**, **Samuel Rogers**, Gladstone, Lord Salisbury and Sir John Barrow. The first praise of **Jane Austen**, in a review of *Emma* by Scott, appeared in its pages; so did Scott's review of his own *Tales of My Landlord*, a notable piece of lighthearted writing. The *Quarterly* also published **John Wilson Croker**'s savage review of **Keats**'s *Endymion* in 1818, which friends would allege had contributed to the poet's early death.

**quatrain** A four-line **stanza** usually but not necessarily in rhyme. The heroic (or elegiac) quatrain is in iambic pentameter (see **metre**). For the ballad quatrain, see **ballad**.

**Queen, Ellery** See **detective fiction**.

*Queen Mab* A visionary philosophical and political poem in nine cantos, with prose notes, by **Shelley**, privately published and circulated in 1813.

Shelley's first major poem is prefaced by Voltaire's 'Écrasez L'Infâme!', and quotations from Lucretius and Archimedes. The mixed heroic and descriptive blank verse form is indebted to **Milton**'s *Samson Agonistes* and **Southey**'s *Thalaba*. The work opens on the sleeping maiden Ianthe, whose spirit is transported by a spectral chariot to the Fairy Queen's 'etherial palace' in deep space. Here Mab rewards her for her personal virtue with a synoptic vision of historical and present humanity, and the new moral, social and economic order which will inevitably arise from the miseries of time. The Queen's speeches, to which most of the poem is devoted, attack conditions in contemporary England. The most impassioned assaults are reserved for the institutions of monarchy (canto III), law (III), warfare (IV), marriage and commerce (V), and established religion (VI and VII). Canto VIII contains a measured and beautiful evocation of the state of perpetual peace that is to follow the work of 'Necessity'.

Of equal if not greater interest are the 17 prose notes, almost as long as the poem itself when taken together, and clearly intended to be read as part of it. Six are fully developed essays, dealing with the labour theory of value (Note 7); the theory and practice of free love (particularly striking here is the influence of **Godwin** and **Mary Wollstonecraft**) (9); necessity in the moral and material universe (12); atheism (13); Christianity (15); and vegetarianism (17).

Despite certain contradictions, the poem reveals the young Shelley as a poet of a considerably more radical turn of mind than other writers of the Romantic epoch, too radical in fact to be properly published. In 1821, however, *Queen Mab* was pirated by radical publishers, and by 1840 it had gone through no fewer than 14 cheap editions. The most widely read of all Shelley's works, it became known as the 'Chartist's Bible'.

**Queen's Wake, The** A poem by **James Hogg**, published in 1813. The 'Introduction' describes Queen Mary's return from France to assume the Scottish throne and the announcement of her Christmas 'wake' at Holyrood Palace, during which 13 bards – including Rizzio, 'The gaudy minstrel from the south' – compete in song for the glory of their clans and the prize of a jewelled harp. The songs are performed before the court over three nights, and take the form of ballad narrative in various styles. Although not among the winning entries, the story of 'Kilmeny', the rasping 'Witch of Fife' and 'The Fate of Macgregor' are particularly effective. The work was admired by **Byron** and established Hogg's reputation.

**Quennell, Peter** 1905– Biographer and editor. He was born in Berkhamsted and educated at Berkhamsted Grammar School and Balliol College, Oxford. His early reputation as a poet (*Poems*, 1926) launched him on a literary career in which biographical writing has predominated. His books include studies of **Byron** (1934–5), **Ruskin** (1949) and **Hogarth** (1955); *Four Portraits* (1945) deals with **Boswell**, **Gibbon**, **Sterne** and **John Wilkes**. *The Marble Foot* (1976) is autobiographical. From 1951 to 1979 he was the founder-editor of the monthly *History Today*.

**Quentin Durward** A novel of 15th-century France by **Sir Walter Scott**, published in 1823.

King Louis XI of France matches his considerable wits against Charles the Bold, Duke of Burgundy, whose devouring ambitions are a continual threat to crown and country. Louis enlists the aid of William de la Marck, the Wild Boar of the Ardennes, to provoke a revolt against the duke in Liège. Quentin Durward, a young Scot in the king's guard, is sent to conduct the Burgundian heiress, Isabelle de Croye, to the protection of the Bishop of Liège to save her from marriage to Count Campo-Basso, an Italian in the service of the duke. Their journey is beset by dangers, many of them provoked by the duke but complicated by de la Marck's villainous nature. The murder of the Bishop of Liège threatens not only Isabelle's safety but also the king's careful plans for controlling the duke's ambitions. The story ends happily: Quentin Durward kills de la Marck and wins the hand of Isabelle, and Louis outwits the duke.

**Quiet American, The** A novel by **Graham Greene**, published in 1955.

The novel is set in Vietnam during the French war against the Vietminh, and revolves around the death of Alden Pyle (the Quiet American), a naïve and high-minded idealist who has arrived in the country as a member of the Economic Aid Mission, 'impregnably armoured by his good intentions and his ignorance'.

The narrator, Thomas Fowler, is a middle-aged English journalist, cynical and detached: 'Not involved . . . It had been an article of my creed.' Estranged from his wife in England, Fowler lives with an Annamite girl, Phuong. The story alternates between the period immediately after Pyle's murder and the events leading up to it. Vigot, the priest-like Sûreté officer, appears after the event to investigate, and it is partly his presence which causes the narrator to reconstruct the past.

Pyle steals Phuong from Fowler, able to offer her the dream of marriage and a home in America. He has also become involved in subversive politics, and begins to direct funds to a small guerrilla army under the nationalist General Thé in the mistaken belief that it will help the struggle against Communism. When Fowler learns that the American has played a part in a bomb explosion in a local café, causing horrific injuries, he informs on Pyle, thereby promoting the latter's murder. His motives are hardly pure, however, for he is partly driven by jealousy over the loss of his mistress.

At the end of the novel Fowler has retrieved Phuong, and now finds himself in a position to marry her, but he is left wishing that 'there existed someone to whom I could say that I was sorry'.

**Quiller-Couch, Sir Arthur** 1863–1944 Critic, novelist and poet, better known by his pen-name, Q. Born at Bodmin in Cornwall, he was educated at Clifton and Trinity College, Oxford. After working as a journalist he returned to Cornwall in 1892, living at Fowey for the next 20 years. Q used his Cornish background in his novels, among them *Dead Man's Rock* (1887), *Troy Town* (1888), *The Splendid Spur* (1889) and *The Ship of Stars* (1899). Volumes of poetry included *Verses and Parodies* (1893), *Poems and Ballads* (1896) and *The Vigil of Venus* (1912). In 1900 he edited the *Oxford Book of English Verse*, the first of several famous anthologies he compiled for Oxford University Press. He was knighted in 1910 for political services (he had been much involved with the Liberal *Leader*) and in 1912 he was appointed the first King Edward VII Professor of English Literature at Cambridge. Two volumes containing his lectures, *On the Art of Writing* (1916) and *On the Art of Reading* (1920), enjoyed great popularity.

# R

**Rackham, Arthur** 1867–1939 Artist and illustrator. Born in London, the son of a successful civil servant, Rackham studied art at the Slade as well as in Paris. He scored an early success with his illustrations for **R. H. Barham**'s *Ingoldsby Legends* (1898), where his talent for the grotesque first found true expression. Subsequent work included illustrations for *Fairy Tales by the Brothers Grimm* (1900), **Barrie**'s *Peter Pan in Kensington Gardens* (1906) and *Mother Goose: The Old Nursery Rhymes* (1913). There is no denying Rackham's brilliant use of light and shade, but his penchant for sinister detail was sometimes thought too frightening for very young audiences, even though much of his work appeared in limited editions to be treasured as gifts rather than used for casual reading. As he aged his style mellowed, most memorably in the illustrations for a new edition of *The Wind in the Willows* (1940), only half of which were completed at his death.

**Radcliffe, Ann** 1764–1823 Novelist. Ann Ward, the daughter of a London tradesman, grew up in an artistic and cultured circle. In 1786 she married William Radcliffe, who later became proprietor and editor of *The English Chronicle*. Her first novel, *The Castles of Athlin and Dunbayne* (1789), was followed by *A Sicilian Romance* (1790), which **Sir Walter Scott** praised for its quality as a poetical novel, *The Romance of the Forest* (1791), *The Mysteries of Udolpho* (1794), *The Italian* (1797) and *Gaston de Blondeville* (1826). She was also a talented writer of romantic verse which was included in her novels and collected in two volumes (1834). *A Journey Made in the Summer of 1794 Through Holland and the Western Frontier of Germany* (1795) displays her mastery of vivid and atmospheric description of landscape, also used to great effect in her novels.

Although she did not originate the form, Mrs Radcliffe became the best-known exponent of the **Gothic novel**. Her persecuted heroines, wild and lonely settings, cliff-hanging chapter endings and apparently supernatural events epitomize its conventions. Her importance is further acknowledged by the fun **Jane Austen** pokes at the delicious terrors of *Udolpho* in *Northanger Abbey*.

*Railway Children, The* See **Nesbit, E.**

*Rainbow, The* A novel by **D. H. Lawrence**, published in 1915.

The novel chronicles the lives of three generations of the Brangwen family in Nottinghamshire. After the death of his father, Tom Brangwen inherits Marsh Farm in the Erewash Valley and marries a Polish widow, Lydia, who already has a daughter, Anna, by her first marriage. Tom becomes devoted to Anna but estranged from his wife, even after the birth of two sons, Tom and Fred.

Anna marries Will Brangwen, Tom's nephew, like his father (Alfred) a lace-designer and gifted craftsman. They move into a cottage nearby, leased them by Tom, where they spend a rapturous and passionate honeymoon. However, over the succeeding years Anna grows apart from her husband and devotes herself to her six children. The oldest of these, Ursula, 'a free, unabateable animal', becomes strongly attached to her father, and overshadows her more reserved and fanciful sister, Gudrun. Increasingly, the novel's focus shifts towards Ursula, following her development through adolescence and early womanhood. Her grandfather is drowned when she is eight years old and she grows close to her Polish grandmother, Lydia, whose foreign origins intrigue her. Later, as a young woman, she meets and is fascinated by Anton Skrebensky, a Polish connection of Lydia's. He and Ursula begin a passionate relationship, but Anton, an army engineer, departs for the Boer War leaving her sexually overwrought and frustrated. She enters into a brief lesbian relationship with her class mistress, Winifred Inger, who subsequently becomes lover and then wife of her uncle, Tom Brangwen, a colliery manager.

Ursula matriculates and struggles for two years as a schoolteacher in Ilkeston. The Brangwen family moves to Beldover and Ursula studies for a BA degree. Anton returns during her final year and they renew their passionate relationship. Largely as a result of this Ursula fails her degree, but Anton, now an officer, begs her to marry him and live in India. She declines, seeking something more lasting than sexual attraction, but when later she believes herself to be pregnant she writes to him changing her decision. Anton, however, has already settled his future and cables from India that he is married to his colonel's daughter. In the meantime, Ursula has fallen deliriously ill, after experiencing a symbolic charge of horses while out walking. She appears to suffer a miscarriage, but recovers finally to contemplate through her window a rainbow: 'the earth's new architecture' symbolically sweeping away 'the old, brittle corruption of houses and factories'.

The novel was seized by the police shortly after its publication on grounds of obscenity and banned. Unsold copies were destroyed. It was reissued in 1926 from American sheets. The English publisher had extracted some changes out of Lawrence prior to publication, and the American publisher had silently censored further passages. Ursula and Gudrun reappear in Lawrence's next novel, *Women in Love*.

**Raine, Craig** 1944–  Poet. He was born in Shildon, County Durham. The autobiographical prose section in his third collection, *Rich* (1984), describes the eccentricity of his upbringing. Raine was educated at Barnard Castle School and at Exeter College, Oxford, where he read English. He lectured at Oxford before becoming poetry editor at Faber and Faber in 1981. With its original, startling metaphors, his first book, *The Onion, Memory* (1978), set out to reawaken the reader's visual awareness. Presenting domestic objects in unfamiliar ways, Raine celebrates the ordinary. The title poem of his second collection, *A Martian Sends a Postcard Home* (1979), which purports to be an alien's uncomprehending reaction to everyday objects, is typical of his technique. **James Fenton** has dubbed him and his followers the **Martian poets**. Raine's libretto for Nigel Osborne's opera, *The Electrification of the Soviet Union* (1986), commissioned by Glyndebourne, is adapted from Pasternak's novella *The Last Summer*.

**Raine, Kathleen (Jessie)** 1908–  Poet and critic. She was born at Ilford, Essex, and educated there, at Bavington, Northumberland, and at Girton College, Cambridge. Her first collection of poems, *Stone and Flower* (1943), was illustrated by Barbara Hepworth. Notable subsequent volumes include *The Year One* (1952), *The Hollow Hill* (1965), *The Lost Country* (1971), *The Oval Portrait* (1977) and *Collected Poems* (1981). Influenced by **Yeats** and **Edwin Muir**, Raine's poetry is contemplative and lyrical, concerned mainly with the relationship between man and nature, with dreams, and with an inner spiritual quest. As well as an autobiography (*Farewell Happy Fields*, 1973; *The Land Unknown*, 1975; *The Lion's Mouth*, 1977), she has published much influential criticism, not-

ably *Defending Ancient Springs* (1967), *Blake and Tradition* (1969) and *Yeats the Initiate* (1986). She founded *Temenos*, 'a review devoted to the arts of the imagination', in 1981.

**Raleigh (or Ralegh), Sir Walter** 1554–1618  Courtier, adventurer, poet and historian. Born the younger son of a gentleman at Hayes Barton in Devon, he studied at Oriel College, Oxford, for about a year and later entered the Middle Temple. Before this time, in 1569, he had fought with a contingent of volunteers from Devon on the side of the Huguenots; later, in 1580, he fought against the Irish rebels in Munster. He came to the attention of Queen Elizabeth and by 1582 was established as her favourite, rewarded with monopolies, vast estates in Ireland and England, a knighthood, the Captaincy of her Guard and the Vice-Admiralship of Devon and Cornwall. His secret marriage to Elizabeth Throckmorton, one of the queen's attendants, became public with the birth of their son in 1592 and Raleigh was briefly committed to the Tower. The couple settled at Sherborne in Dorset. In 1595 Raleigh led an expedition up the Orinoco and in 1596 he took part in Essex's raid on Cadiz, though he quarrelled violently with Essex the following year.

As the queen's favourite Raleigh had not been popular. His pride and extravagance had excited dislike, and he had acquired a reputation for unorthodox thought. A Jesuit pamphlet of 1592 accused him of patronizing a 'school of atheism' and there were suspicions, too, about his connection with the mathematician **Thomas Hariot**. He was certainly interested in sceptical philosophy, chemistry and mathematics.

In 1603 he was again arrested, this time on suspicion of conspiracy to dethrone James I. After an unfair trial (although Raleigh was by no means entirely innocent) he was again commit-

Sir Walter Raleigh and Arrowmaia, King of Guyana, during Raleigh's second expedition to the Orinoco, 1616. From Theodor de Bry's *Americas*, 1590–1623.

ted to the Tower, where he lived with his wife until 1616. He was released to undertake an expedition to the Orinoco in search of gold, but again arrested after its failure. Raleigh was executed at Westminster in 1618, to become a martyred hero to the Parliamentarians of the next generation.

Very little of his verse appeared in print during his lifetime and some of the surviving works are only dubiously attributed to him. Undoubtedly in Raleigh's hand are 'The Eleventh and Twelfth Books of the Ocean to Cynthia', a formalized courtship devoted to Elizabeth, though it is not certain whether this formed part of a longer work. Perhaps some of the poems in *The Phoenix Nest* are also by Raleigh. Even the authenticity of the famous 'Passionate Man's Pilgrimage' (beginning 'Give me my scallop shell of quiet') is in doubt. Other famous anthology pieces attributed to Raleigh are the reply to **Marlowe's** *Passionate Shepherd to His Love* and the poignant 'What is our life?' which appeared in a madrigal setting by Orlando Gibbons in 1612.

Raleigh published accounts of his voyages and expeditions: *A Report of the Truth of the Fight about the Isles of the Azores* (1591) deals with Sir Richard Grenville's encounter with the Spanish fleet, and *A Discovery of the Empire of Guyana* (1596) describes his 1595 expedition. *The History of the World* (1614), written during his imprisonment, was published unfinished. Raleigh started with the creation and got as far as the 2nd century BC, including the history of the Jews and the Egyptians and some account of the myths of the Greeks. The work was designed for Prince Henry, who had shown some sympathy for his predicament and had visited him in the Tower.

**Raleigh, Sir Walter Alexander** 1861–1922 Critic. Born in London and educated at the universities of Edinburgh and Cambridge, he was Professor of English at Aligarh in India, Liverpool and Glasgow. In 1904 he became the first Professor of English Literature at Oxford. A respected critic in his day, he was the author of, among other books, *The English Novel: From the Earliest Times to the Appearance of Waverley* (1891), *Robert Louis Stevenson* (1895), *Milton* (1900), *Wordsworth* (1903), *Shakespeare* (for the English Men of Letters series, 1907), and *Six Essays on Johnson* (1910). He was knighted in 1911. After World War I Raleigh was chosen to write the official history of the RAF, but he died after completing only the first volume (1922).

**Ralph Roister Doister** A comedy by **Nicholas Udall**, who probably intended it for performance by schoolboys. There is disagreement about its date of composition. Some scholars place it before 1541, when Udall was dismissed from Eton, and others as late as 1553. What is certain is that Udall based the contrasting characters of braggart lover (Ralph Roister Doister) and flattering parasite (Matthew Merrygreek) on the plays of Terence, particularly *Eunuchus* and *Miles Gloriosus*, adding to his classical model such homely English figures as the servants, Meg Mumblecrust and Tib Talkapace, and combining them all in lively rhyming doggerel. The action takes place outside the house of Christian Custance, a widow betrothed to the absent merchant, Gawyn Goodluck. Needing little encouragement from Merrygreek, Ralph determines to woo and win Dame Custance. When his suit is unsuccessful, he determines to take the house by storm, but is routed by the widow and her loyal household. Gawyn Goodluck returns in time to deliver the widow from further harassment.

**Ram Alley, or, Merry Tricks** A coarse, popular comedy produced about 1609 and published in 1611. Nothing is known about its author, Lording Barry. The setting, Ram Alley, was a disreputable part of the City of London off Fleet Street, where Mitre Court now stands.

**Ramanujan, A[ttipat] K[rishnaswami]** 1929– Indian poet, who writes in Kannada and English, born in Mysore. He has taught linguistics in the University of Chicago since 1962. A poet of delicate, thoughtful sensibility, he has always aimed at purity and translucence of expression. The title-poem of his first volume, *The Striders* (1966), refers to water-insects that can stand motionless upon 'the ripple skin/of a stream'. It fittingly describes his preoccupation with the precarious moment of fixity upon an under-torrent of change, caught just long enough for a flash of understanding of experience – his preoccupation as poet but also professional analyst of language, as Hindu of orthodox upbringing living in a largely rationalist Western ethos and as a 20th-century man earning his bread 'in exile'. The title of *Relations* (1971) refers both to kin in India and to intimate connections between moments, incongruous yet illuminating, from different periods of his life. Correspondences, contrasts and contradictions successively turn much of Ramanujan's poetry into daring forays into a 20th-century mind that regards its external and interior environment questioningly. *Selected Poems* (1976) is a choice from the earlier volumes.

**Rambler, The** A twice-weekly essay edited by **Samuel Johnson**, for 208 issues published between 20 March 1750 and 14 March 1752.

All but four of the issues were written by Johnson himself. No. 30 was by Catherine Talbot, No. 97 by **Richardson**, and Nos. 44 and 100 by **Elizabeth Carter**; parts of three others, notably the second letter in No. 15 by **Garrick**, were also from outside contributors. It was not initially a great commercial success, fewer than 500 copies being sold of each number, but extracts from *The Rambler* were frequently reprinted by such journals as *The Gentleman's Magazine* and the whole run was reprinted nine times in Johnson's lifetime. Though at first Johnson wished the work to be anonymous, his style was quickly recognized and the bi-weekly essays did more than any other work, except his *Dictionary*, to establish his reputation.

The quality of writing was uneven, as might be expected in a work produced to such a tight schedule, but Johnson's belief that this was more than an ephemeral periodical may be gauged from the fact that he extensively revised the text twice, for the collected edition of 1752, and for the fourth edition of 1756. *The Rambler* is a highly moral work and, with *Rasselas* (1759), has been regarded as a prose companion to and explication of *The Vanity of Human Wishes* (1749). Very different from *The Spectator*, Johnson's work is much more akin to the essays of Montaigne in tone and ethical approach. He is recorded as saying, 'My other works are wine and water; but my *Rambler* is pure wine.'

**Ramsay, Allan** 1686–1758 Scottish poet and anthologist. Born at Leadhills in Dumfriesshire, he went to Edinburgh and worked as a journeyman wigmaker. In 1712 he founded the Easy Club for the promotion of conversation and the exchange of ideas, and in 1718 he became a bookseller. In the same year he published a broadside edition of *Christis Kirk on the Grene*, a poem attributed to **James I of Scotland**, to which he had incautiously added two cantos of his own. *The Tea Table Miscellany* (1724–32) collected Scots songs and ballads; it was to give **Robert Burns** and other later Scottish writers the impetus for their work. *The Ever Green, Being a Collection of Scots Poems, Wrote by the Ingenious before 1600* (1724) presented the work of such poets as **Robert Henryson** and **William Dunbar** from the Bannatyne Manuscript (see **George Bannatyne**) and so made another contribution to the revival of Scots secular poetry. Ramsay's readiness to 'improve' what he reprinted, later the object of criticism, was again apparent in his *Collection of Scots Proverbs* (1736), which modified originally coarse and vital expressions.

Ramsay began to publish occasional poems of his own in broadsides and periodicals in 1713 and collections of his poetry in 1721; his most notable work is to be found in *Poems* (1728). A pastoral drama, *The Gentle Shepherd* (1725), was staged as a **ballad opera** with Scots airs. Ramsay founded the first circulating library in Great Britain in 1728, and succeeded in opening a playhouse in Edinburgh in 1736, though it was closed by Walpole's Licensing Act of the following year.

**Rand, Ayn** 1905–82 American novelist and social critic. Born and educated in Leningrad, Rand emigrated to the USA in 1926. Her first publication was a mystery play, *The Night of January 16th* (1935). The novel *We the Living* appeared in 1936, and was followed by *Anthem* (England 1938, USA 1946), a short novel which depicts the plight of an individual in the face of an oppressive, totalitarian society. With the publication of *The Fountainhead* in 1943, Rand attracted a substantial popular audience. Her credo that humans are rational, self-interested and pledged to individualism was advocated in *The Objectivist*, a journal she founded in 1962, and in *The Ayn Rand Letter* (1971–82). The novel *Atlas Shrugged* (1957) portrays what she considered to be the inevitable results of altruism – socialism or, worse, anarchy. Her critical works include *For the New Intellectual* (1961), *The Virtue of Selfishness* (1965) and *The New Left: The Anti-Industrial Revolution* (1971).

**Randolph, Thomas** 1605–35 Dramatist. Born near Daventry and educated at Westminster School and Trinity College, Cambridge, Randolph owed his contemporary reputation to the work he produced while at university. The facility with which he wrote is well illustrated by 'An Ode to Master Anthony Stafford', which is a charming poem in praise of country life. His pastoral play, *Amyntas* (1630), is enlivened by its comic scenes, but his other full-length piece, *The Jealous Lovers* (1632), is dramatically insipid. Randolph was better suited to the writing of dramatic sketches. *Aristippus, or, The Jovial Philosopher* (c.1626) proposes that study of the philosophy of drinking should be added to the university syllabus, a theme pursued with variations in *The Drinking Academy* (c. 1626). *The Conceited Pedlar* (1627) is an ephemerally witty monologue. *The Muses' Looking-Glass* (1630), in which an actor out-argues Puritan opposition to the theatre, is Randolph's most interesting work. It reflects the influence of **Ben Jonson**, of whom Randolph was a favoured 'son'.

**Ransom, John Crowe** 1888–1974 American poet and critic, born in Tennessee, and educated at Vanderbilt and Oxford universities. He taught at Vanderbilt from 1914 until 1937. His first collections of verse were *Poems About God* (1919), *Chills and Fever* (1924), *Grace After Meat* (1924) and *Two Gentlemen in Bonds* (1927). While at Vanderbilt he became a member of the group known as the 'Fugitives', from their contributions to the poetry magazine *The Fugitive*, published from 1922 to 1925. This group, which also included **Allen Tate**, **Laura Riding**

and **Robert Penn Warren**, was composed of Southern conservative writers who stood for traditional agrarian values in an age of industrialism.

In 1930 Ransom edited *I'll Take My Stand: The South and the Agrarian Tradition*, a collection of essays by 12 Southern writers of the Fugitive group: the poets **Donald Davidson**, Tate, Warren, **John Gould Fletcher** and Ransom himself; the scholars Stark Young, John Donald Wade and Andrew Lytle; the historian Frank Owsley; the political scientist Herman Clarence Nixon; the psychologist Lyle Lanier; and the economist and journalist Henry Blue Kline. This Agrarian manifesto included a 'Statement of Principles' written mainly by Ransom, which maintained that the industrial way of life was causing unhappiness and unemployment among the work force and destroying the very roots of religion, culture and art. Although they differed considerably in their political affiliations and suggested strategies, the essayists advocated a return to the traditional Southern agrarian way of life as the best antidote to the encroachment of Northern industrialist values and problems. After leaving Vanderbilt, Ransom taught at Kenyon College, Ohio, where in 1939 he founded the *Kenyon Review*, which became one of the most influential academic journals in America. Two years later he gave currency to the principles of the **New Criticism** in a book of that title. His other critical writings include *God Without Thunder; an Orthodox Defense of Orthodoxy* (1930), *The World's Body* (1938) and *Poems and Essays* (1955).

**Ransome, Arthur (Michell)** 1884–1967 Journalist and writer of **children's literature**. Born in Leeds and educated at Rugby, he began his career as an office boy in a London publishing house before becoming a journalist for *The Daily News* in 1912, later for *The Manchester Guardian*. He travelled to Russia in 1913 and produced *Old Peter's Russian Tales* (1916) which became very popular. During the revolution he was an 'on-the-spot' reporter and produced an account of *Six Weeks in Russia* (1919). After extensive travel during the 1920s, including a visit to China, he wrote *Swallows and Amazons* (1931), first of a series of adventure stories for younger readers which reflected his enthusiasm for sailing and the outdoor life. Other titles in this vein included *Pigeon Post* (1936), *We Didn't Mean to Go to Sea* (1938), *The Big Six* (1940), and *Great Northern?* (1947). He was also the author of *Racundra's First Cruise* (1923) and *Mainly About Fishing* (1959).

*The Autobiography of Arthur Ransome*, edited by Rupert Hart-Davis, appeared in 1976.

**Rao, Raja** 1908– Indian novelist, born in Hassan. He was Professor of Philosophy at the University of Texas, Austin, from 1965 to 1983. His early stories were in Kannada and English, the latter published as *The Cow of the Barricades* (1947); a second English collection appeared as *The Policeman and the Rose* (1978). His first novel, *Kanthapura* (1938), successfully attempted 'to convey in a language . . . not one's own the spirit that is one's own'. In the ample manner of the *Mahabharata* and *Ramayana*, and using a purana-like episodic structure, a talkative villager tells how a village community obtains from daily life, with its millennia-old worship of the local deity, the strength for non-violent resistance to the British Raj. Whether Hindu myth still has a viable place in modern, urban Indian life, is the major theme of *The Serpent and the Rope* (1960), Raja Rao's most important book, a taxing but immensely rewarding experience for non-Indian readers. About a spiritual quest in Europe and India, it is a modern rendering of the *Mahabharata* legend of Satyavan and Savithri, dramatizing also the relationships between India and the West, the earthly and the spiritual, the physical and the metaphysical, illusion (the serpent) and reality (the rope). *The Cat and Shakespeare* (1965), the story of a loquacious official helping the narrator receive divine grace (symbolized by the cat), is about self-surrender through love, enabling the human will not to surrender to, but unite with, God's will. *Comrade Kirillov* (1976; in French translation, 1965) chiefly satirizes communism, and argues that all foreign creeds gradually become Indianized.

**Rape of Lucrece, The** A narrative poem by **Shakespeare**, entitled simply *Lucrece* on its first appearance in 1594. Like the slightly earlier **Venus and Adonis**, it was dedicated to Henry Wriothesley, Earl of Southampton. The poem is in seven-line stanzas and describes the rape by Tarquinius, son of the King of Rome, of Lucretia, whose husband Collatinus had extolled her chastity. Shakespeare could have read the story in Livy, Ovid's *Fasti* and **Chaucer's** *The Legend of Good Women*.

The first section describes the furious ride of 'lust-breathed Tarquin' to Collatium, his entertainment there by an unsuspecting Lucrece, his restlessness and night journey by torchlight through the house to her chamber, in the course of which he has an internal debate between 'frozen conscience and hot-burning will'. After Lucrece has been described in bed, she awakens to hear Tarquin's threats and pleads unavailingly with him. In the second section, after the rape, Lucrece rails at length against night, opportunity and 'misshapen time', all of which conspired in her violation. When day comes she sends her husband a letter and views a picture of the fall of Troy, which has poignant parallels with her own case. Collatinus returns with attendant lords and Lucrece, having identified Tarquin as her violator, stabs herself.

In *The Rape of Lucrece* Shakespeare turns from the mythic world of *Venus and Adonis* to a grim tragedy from Roman history. The ambiguous ethics of Lucretia's suicide had been debated from the time of St Augustine, but **Sidney** in the *Apology for Poetry* describes a picture of Lucretia as depicting the outward beauty of virtue. Shakespeare's version is full of ornamented language and conceits, and its obviously self-conscious delight in verbal artifice has led to accusations of lack of feeling in the treatment of so tragic a tale. **Hazlitt** described both this poem and *Venus and Adonis* as 'a couple of ice-houses' and **Coleridge** found *Lucrece* lacking in pathos. The story stayed in Shakespeare's imagination: in *Titus Andronicus* it is cited as a parallel to the rape of Lavinia, in *Cymbeline* the villainous Iachimo remembers Tarquin as he approaches Imogen's bed, and before he kills Duncan, Macbeth personifies murder as having 'Tarquin's ravishing strides'.

**Rape of the Lock, The** A poem by **Alexander Pope**, first published in 1712 (two-canto version) and expanded in 1714 (five cantos). The occasion for this elegant comic piece was the forceful cutting by Lord Petre (a 20-year-old Catholic Peer) of a lock of hair from Lady Arabella Fermor's head, this apparently trivial event causing dissension between their two aristocratic families. Pope's avowed intention was 'a jest to laugh them together again', and the early version of his poem became something of a *cause célèbre* in the metropolitan Catholic circles in which they all moved.

One of the poet's most glittering performances, the *Rape* subjects this event to an extended **mock heroic** treatment, playing upon the war between the sexes, feminizing epic conventions and satirizing the superficial concerns of society women while still celebrating their beauty – something to which the poet was especially attracted. The poem traces the course of the fateful day when Belinda the society beauty wakes up, glorifies her appearance at a ritualistic dressing table (the 'Toilette' scene is one of Pope's most celebrated set-pieces), plays cards, flirts, drinks coffee and has her hair ravaged. As in the pastoral tradition, this action is set within the wider cycle of time itself, so that at the close, when the violated lock is transformed into a new constellation, the immortality of the story is seen to be a function of poetic artifice as well as of feminine charms. The enlarged version of the poem includes some elaborate 'machinery', or accompanying details of supernatural elements surrounding the mortal events, partly modelled on *Le Lutrin* of Boileau. Part love poem and part satire, the *Rape* is a virtuoso piece of writing, designed to demon-

An engraving by M. van der Gucht for the second edition of *The Rape of the Lock*, 1714. Belinda, shorn of a lock of hair by her admirer, is comforted by her friends.

strate 'What mighty contests rise from trivial things.'

**Rasselas, Prince of Abyssinia, The History of** A philosophical romance by **Samuel Johnson**, published in 1759, and said to have been written in the evenings of a single week to pay for his mother's funeral. Johnson was already familiar with much of the background material for such a project (he had translated *A Voyage to Abyssinia* by Father Jerome Lobo in 1735) and the exotic setting ensured the book instant success.

The book (which consists of three parts followed by a sort of 'coda') is concerned with Johnson's habitual theme of the 'choice of life' whereby Rasselas, son of the Abyssinian Emperor, determines to seek the world outside the luxurious 'happy valley' in which he has hitherto been living an insulated existence. Full of theoretical hopes and fruitless meditations, Rasselas escapes from his privileged confines along with his sister Nekayah and the elderly philosopher Imlac; they reach Egypt, where the prince's romantic notions about the conditions of human life are contradicted by the actual instances they encounter. The plot itself is slender, but the whole work is invigorated by Johnson's robust common-sense, occasional glints of humour, and avoidance of the over-melancholy. Idealism and innocence, the pastoral values, are gently deflated but with ample opportunities for wide-eyed raillery. *Rasselas* displays some of the author's finest aphoristic writing (partly in imitation of oriental literary style) but its antithetical method is careful to leave unresolved the larger issues it handles. The Prince encounters apparent paradoxes which prevent him from formulating neat opinions – the monks of St Anthony can only be certain of hardship, the Sultan is tormented by suspicions, the philosopher's wisdom is useless in his grief. 'The Conclusion, in which Nothing is concluded' illustrates the book's deliberate structure, and affirms Johnson's conviction that action is superior to introspection.

**Rattigan, Sir Terence** 1911–77 Playwright. Born in London and educated at Harrow and Oxford, Rattigan committed himself to writing plays on leaving university. *French Without Tears* (1936), a light comedy, established him as a West End favourite, and he is best remembered as the writer of carefully crafted plays and screenplays in which character and plot take precedence over social comment. Rattigan wrote several plays based on historical incidents and characters: *The Winslow Boy* (1946), *Ross* (1960, a perceptive study of **T. E. Lawrence**) and *A Bequest to the Nation* (1970) exhibit his compassion for the humiliated and the ashamed. The same concern characterizes his serious plays, like *Flare Path* (1942), *The Browning Version* (1948), *The Deep Blue Sea* (1952) and *Separate Tables* (1954). Rattigan was knighted in 1971.

*Rattlin the Reefer* A novel by Edward Howard, published in 1836. Howard was a shipmate of **Captain Marryat** and his story is in the same vein as Marryat's own more famous novels of the sea. Marryat himself thought enough of his friend's work to prepare it for publication, and the title-page described it as 'Edited by the author of *Peter Simple*'.

*Rauf Coilyear, The Tale of* A late 15th-century Scottish poem in **alliterative verse**. It relates the story of Rauf, a forthright and independent charcoal-burner who entertains Charlemagne in his hut after the emperor has become lost in a storm. Ignorant of his guest's identity, Rauf treats him politely and hospitably but as an equal. Charlemagne (Charles) invites Rauf to court, reveals his true identity and knights his former host. Rauf fights a Saracen, Magog, and is made a Marshal of France.

**Raven, Simon** 1927– Novelist. Having attended Charterhouse, and then read Classics at King's College, Cambridge, Raven joined the King's Shropshire Light Infantry, with which he served in Germany and Kenya. He resigned his commission as the commander of a rifle company in 1957 in order to become a book reviewer, and published his first novel, *The Feathers of Death*, in 1959. A prolific novelist, who also writes with enthusiasm about cricket and with malicious enthusiasm about public school education, Raven has made his reputation for rakish, witty and satirical fiction with a long *roman fleuve*, *Alms for Oblivion*, whose 10 volumes appeared between 1967 and 1976, beginning with *Fielding Gray* and concluding with *The Survivors*. The work is a gossipy, sharp-tongued and racy account of British high society, whose denizens display a predilection for flamboyance and outrageous intrigue. In 1984 he began a second sequence, *The First-born of Egypt*, with the publication of *Morning Star*.

*Ravenshoe* A novel by **Henry Kingsley**, published in 1861. Part of the book is set in the Crimean War, in which Charles Ravenshoe, the son of a wealthy Catholic family, is seeking obscurity after a series of blows connected with the mystery of his birth. The mysteries are complicated by the neglect of a Jesuit confessor to tell the whole truth and by the villainy of Charles's supposed friend Lord Welter. Charles Ravenshoe survives Balaclava and returns to England a broken man. However, he is helped by friends, the mystery of his birth is cleared up, and all ends well for him.

**Raverat, Gwen[dolen] (Mary)** 1885–1957 Wood engraver and autobiographer. Born in Cambridge into the Darwin family (**Charles Darwin** was her grandfather), she was educated privately and at the Slade School of Art. In 1911 she married the French artist Jacques Raverat (d. 1925). An accomplished pioneer in the revival of wood engraving, she also wrote *Period Piece: A Cambridge Childhood* (1952), originally conceived as a short narrative to accompany reminiscent drawings. Instead, though it is charmingly illustrated, this avowedly 'circular book' portrays her extended family of sisters, cousins, aunts and uncles (many of them people of academic or scientific consequence) in their full range of well-observed eccentricity. An important branch of the 'intellectual aristocracy' is shown in an endearingly domestic light.

**Raworth, Tom** 1938– Poet. He grew up in London and has studied and worked, as writer-in-residence, in Britain, Spain, Mexico and the USA. An important figure in the 'underground' poetry of the 1960s, he edited the magazine *Outburst* and ran the Matrix Press in 1961–3, and co-founded an important small press, Goliard, which published **Charles Olson** and **J. H. Prynne**. His early work, in *The Relation Ship* (1966), *The Big Green Day* (1968) and *Lion, Lion* (1970), conformed to Olson's projectivist doctrine that one perception should lead instantly to another, without reflection, qualification or discrimination, though in Raworth's poetry the effect was often comic and surreal. Instants are recorded without editing in a poem such as 'Stag Skull Mounted', in *Moving* (1971). Such experiments, at the edge of what is recognizably poetry, are related to contemporary developments in conceptual art. The text becomes increasingly minimal. Later long poems, such as *Ace* (1977), *Writing* (1982) and 'West Wind' in *Tottering State: Selected and New Poems 1963–83* (1984), have tended to find an American audience more readily than a British one.

**Read, Sir Herbert (Edward)** 1893–1968 Critic and poet. Born in Yorkshire and educated at Leeds University, he served in France during World War I before becoming Assistant Keeper at the Victoria and Albert Museum (1922–31) and Professor of Fine Art at Edinburgh University (1931–3). He edited *The Burlington Magazine* from 1933 to 1939. Read's critical work includes *Reason and Romanticism* (1926), *English Prose Style* (1928), *Form in Modern Poetry* (1932), *Art and Industry* (1934), *The True Voice of Feeling* (1953) and *The Literature of Sincerity* (1968). He also produced editions of **T. E. Hulme**, Kropotkin, Orage and Jung, and several volumes of autobiographical prose, including *In Retreat* (1925), *Ambush* (1930) and *The Contrary Experience* (1963). His novel *The Green Child* (1945) is an allegorical fantasy. His poetry, which was much influenced by **imagism**, included *Songs of Chaos* (1915), *Naked Warriors* (1919), *The End of a War* (1933) and several *Collected Poems*, the last of which appeared in 1966. He was knighted for services to literature in 1953.

**Reade, Charles** 1814–84 Novelist, dramatist, journalist. Born at Ipsden House, Oxfordshire, seventh son and tenth child of a Tory squire, he was educated privately and went up to Magdalen College, Oxford, with a demyship in 1831. He qualified as a barrister, although he never practised, and went for a while to Edinburgh to study medicine, but was too squeamish to persist. His knowledge of the law led to contractual disputes and litigation. The bibliography of his works is problematic, because 'for his own protection' he had most of his writings privately printed and the record is complicated by his constant reworking of plays as novels and novels as plays, his own and other people's.

In 1844 he was elected Bursar at Magdalen and held various college offices, though he appears to have spent little time at Oxford. As a sideline he was dealing in violins at Birkenhead

and roaming the Continent in search of stock. Later he settled in London and speculated in theatre management, which absorbed a great deal of his earnings. In 1851 he published a dramatization of **Smollett**'s *Peregrine Pickle* at his own expense and became Vice-President of his college. That year he wrote his first play to be performed, *The Ladies' Battle*, and started a collaboration with **Tom Taylor**. They worked together on *Masks and Faces*, the play which made Reade's reputation. In 1852 he went into theatrical management at the Strand Theatre. His play *Gold* was performed. In 1853 he began writing and selling short stories. That year he published a narrative version of *Masks and Faces* under the title *Peg Woffington*, and a novel called *Christie Johnstone* about Scottish fisherfolk. In 1854 he was managing the St James's Theatre with the actress Mrs Laura Seymour. Several of his plays were produced: *Two Loves and A Life* (with Tom Taylor); *The King's Rival* (with Tom Taylor); *Honour before Titles (or Nobs and Snobs)*; *The Courier of Lyons* (later reworked as *The Lyons Mail*); and his version of *Peregrine Pickle*.

He became successful as a novelist in 1856 with *It Is Never Too Late to Mend*, intended to reform prisons. Others followed quickly: *The Course of True Love Never Did Run Smooth* (1857), *Jack of All Trades* (1858), *The Autobiography of a Thief* (1858), *Love Me Little, Love Me Long* (1859) and *White Lies* (1860). In 1861, after a year's concentrated delving into historical records, he published his masterpiece, *The Cloister and the Hearth*. In 1863 his novel, *Hard Cash*, attacked abuses in private lunatic asylums. Other 'novels with a purpose' were *Foul Play* (1868), about abuses at sea; *Put Yourself in His Place* (1870), attacking Trade Union closed shops; and *A Woman-Hater* (1877), about the disadvantages of village life.

In 1866 came another novel, *Griffith Gaunt*, which Reade considered his best work. In 1867 he started collaborating with the Irish dramatist, **Dion Boucicault**, and produced his own dramatization of *Griffith Gaunt*. Boucicault dramatized *Foul Play* in 1868. In 1870 Reade dramatized *Put Yourself in His Place* under the title *Free Labour*. That year he was managing the Adelphi Theatre. His novel, *A Terrible Temptation*, was published in 1871. *A Simpleton* was serialized in 1872, the year he published *The Wandering Heir*, suggested by the Tichborne case; Reade dramatized and produced it himself the following year. In 1874 he published *A Hero and a Martyr*. In 1876 his bronchitis confined him to his house, and he began writing short stories. In 1877 he wrote *Hang in Haste, Repent at Leisure*, a series of letters which led to the reprieve of four people condemned to death for murder. His later years were spent in adapting a play by Sardou, and Zola's *L'Assommoir* under the title *Drink*, which was a commercial success. In 1879 Mrs Seymour, with whom he had lived for 24 years, died and he was broken-hearted. His health never recovered. When he died, he left a completed novel, *A Perilous Secret*, and instructions that his research materials should be available for inspection for two years after his death.

In his day he was ranked with **Dickens** and **George Eliot**. His industry and his capacity for research were prodigious, as his notebooks and scrapbooks show. He is now remembered, if at all, for *The Cloister and the Hearth*.

**Reade, (William) Winwood** 1838–75 Historian, novelist and travel-writer. He studied at Magdalen Hall, Oxford, but left without taking a degree to pursue his interest in the natural sciences, exploring Africa to study the habits of the gorilla and then entering St Mary's Hospital as a student. His travel books deal with his African experiences and his novels imitate the work of his uncle, **Charles Reade**. He made his name with *The Martyrdom of Man* (1872), a history of civilization written from a standpoint frankly hostile to religion. The book remained popular for a number of years after his early death, being praised by **H. G. Wells** and **Conan Doyle**'s Sherlock Holmes among others.

**realism** A term first used in France in the 1850s to characterize works concerned with representing the world as it is rather than as it ought to be, with description rather than invention. Champfleury and Duranty were among its earliest exponents but the term was applied retrospectively to Balzac's *La Comédie Humaine*, begun in 1830, because of its authentic detail, its perceptions about the function of environment in shaping character and the setting of its constituent books in the present or the very recent past. Realism observes and documents contemporary life and everyday scenes as objectively as possible in low-key, unrhetorical prose, drawing its characters from all social levels and reproducing the flavour of their colloquial speech in its dialogue. Because they seek to explore areas of life customarily ignored by the arts, realist writers frequently look to the lowest social classes and to cruelty and suffering for their subject matter.

Realism became the dominant mode of the 19th-century European novel and also of the theatre, from the late 1880s, where it initiated a revival of serious drama and led to the development, by Antoine in Paris and Stanislavski in Moscow, of less histrionic, more natural-seeming acting styles.

The great works of European realist fiction include Flaubert's *Sentimental Education*, Tolstoy's *Anna Karenina* and Dostoevsky's *Crime and Punishment*. Accurate observation and attention to the structures of society make **George Eliot**'s *Middlemarch* and **Elizabeth Gaskell**'s *Mary Barton* notable examples of English 19th-century realism. The chief American realists are **William Dean Howells** and **Sinclair Lewis**, while the line of English realist writing continues in the 20th via **H. G. Wells** (*Tono-Bungay*, 1909) and **Arnold Bennett** (*Clayhanger*, 1910) to the post-World War II evocations of English middle-class life of **Angus Wilson** and the Northern working-class fiction of the 1950s, best exemplified by **Alan Sillitoe**'s *The Loneliness of the Long Distance Runner* (1959).

Realism played an important part in the revival of the English theatre in the first decade of this century (**Granville-Barker**, **St John Ervine**, **Galsworthy**, **Stanley Houghton**) and, again, in the 1950s (**Osborne**, **Wesker**, **Shelagh Delaney**). In Ireland **O'Casey** recreated the texture of tenement life in the setting and language of his early Dublin plays, *Juno and the Paycock* (1925) and *The Plough and the Stars* (1926), while in America **O'Neill** and **Arthur Miller** developed native versions of the dramatic realism of Ibsen and Strindberg. See also **naturalism**.

**Reaney, James (Crerar)** 1926– Canadian poet and dramatist. Born near Stratford, Ontario, Reaney grew up on a farm in a Protestant fundamentalist atmosphere. He attended the University of Toronto between 1944 and 1948 and then taught English at the University of Manitoba until 1960, apart from the years 1956 to 1958, during which he completed his doctorate at the University of Toronto under the supervision of **Northrop Frye**. Since 1960 he has lectured at the University of Western Ontario. While still in his early twenties, he achieved recognition as a poet with a powerful Gothic and regional voice. His first volume, *The Red Heart* (1949), which shows the attempts of a lonely southern Ontario boy to reconcile his reading with the environment around him, was seen as introducing a new strain into Canadian poetry. Subsequently he came to be regarded as a 'mythopoeic' poet writing under the influence of Frye, but far from aspiring towards the universalism favoured by the mythic approach, both *The Red Heart* and his finest volume, *Twelve Letters to a Small Town* (1962), are strongly regional. His other poetry includes *A Suit of Nettles* (1958) and *The Dance of Death at London, Ontario* (1963). Having previously written libretti, in the late 1950s Reaney turned from poetry to the theatre and his first play, *The Killdeer*, was performed in 1960. This was published, with *The Sun and the Moon*, *One-Man Masque* and *Night Blooming Cereus*, in 1962. Like his poetry, these early plays show a world of fantasy and the macabre lurking beneath the surface of rural Ontario. All Reaney's plays use the conventions of melodrama, but from the mid 1960s onwards, his work shows a more conscious awareness of theatrical artifice and is characterized by the use of mime. His dramatic

Rechy, John (Francisco)

masterpiece, the *Donnellys* trilogy, combines mime with music, dance, puppets and magic lanterns. Its three parts, *Sticks and Stones* (1975), *The St Nicholas Hotel* (1976) and *Handcuffs* (1977), tell the story of an Irish immigrant family mysteriously murdered in Lucan, Ontario, in 1880. Reaney's other plays include *Colours in the Dark* (1969), *Listen to the Wind* (1972) and *The Dismissal* (1978).

**Rechy, John (Francisco)** 1934– American novelist, born in El Paso, Texas, and educated there at the University of Texas and at the New School for Social Research in New York City. His work usually concerns a search for love and identity in socially marginal settings; his leading characters tend to be homosexual or bisexual and are frequently associated with danger and violence. His first novel, *City of Night*, appeared in 1963 and was followed by *Numbers* (1967), *This Day's Death* (1969), *The Vampires* (1971), *The Fourth Angel* (1973), *Rushes* (1979) and *Bodies and Souls* (1983). His representations of urban life-styles are generally based on the homosexual communities of major cities such as New York and Los Angeles, and are additionally developed to incorporate the crime and violence of the urban underworld. He has also published a study of urban homosexual life-styles, *The Sexual Outlaw* (1977).

**Recollections of the Lakes and the Lake Poets** A series of autobiographical reflections and literary portraits by **Thomas De Quincey**, first published in *Tait's Magazine* 1834–9. Written some 20 years after the period of his association and intimacy with them, De Quincey's reminiscences of his Lakes-dwelling friends and former neighbours, **Wordsworth**, **Coleridge**, **Southey** and **Dorothy Wordsworth**, are a revealing blend of fulsome admiration and praise for their literary and poetic achievements, and mischievous – occasionally malicious – gossip, unflattering personal description, and the carefully placed negative inference. Except in his rather cruel presentation of Mary and Dorothy Wordsworth, however, the wounded vanity which seems to have been the fruit of his relations with the self-consciously great is never allowed to blunt a fineness of moral and psychological perception. Coleridge is shown in all his intellectual grandeur and human weakness: simultaneously the most original English mind of his time and a compulsive plagiarist. Wordsworth's genius is fully honoured, but he is also the proud bibliophobe – sacrilegiously cutting open precious pages with a used butter-knife on the kitchen table – as well as the supremely competent manager of his own interests. (In a splendidly humorous passage De Quincey shows how the deaths of wealthy friends, benefactors and distributors of stamps are miracu-

lously synchronous with the poet's ever-increasing material requirements.) Southey is effectively damned with faint praise for his moral integrity and love of books. All three have little understanding of political economy, the one area in which De Quincey may justly claim to have outshone them.

**Recruiting Officer, The** A comedy by **George Farquhar**, first performed in London in 1706. Farquhar had served as a recruiting officer in Lichfield and Shrewsbury in 1705–6, and the experience inspired not only the play but also the decision to set it in Shrewsbury, against the prevailing theatrical view that comedy required a London setting.

The plot is slight. Captain Plume recruits men by courting their sweethearts. His sergeant, Kite, poses as an astrologer to persuade the gullible. Sylvia, daughter of Justice Ballance, loves Plume. Disguised as a man, she is handed over to the army by her deceived father. A secondary plot concerns the failure of a rival recruiting officer, Captain Brazen, to win the rich wife he had set his sights on.

**Red Badge of Courage, The** A novel by **Stephen Crane**, published in 1895. In preparation for publication, the story was subject to considerable emendations and deletions. An edition of the original manuscript was published in 1982.

*The Red Badge of Courage*, though only his second novel, established Crane's reputation in critical and literary circles. It is set during the American Civil War, and the frightening realities of battle are violently contrasted with the heroic ideals of conventional war narrative. Henry Fleming proudly enrols as a soldier in the Union army. He is anxious to participate in the glory of the fight, but his expectations are disappointed by his first encounter with the enemy. He witnesses a mass retreat of his fellow soldiers, and receives a head wound from the butt of a gun when he grabs a deserter to ask for an explanation of the disjointed sequence of events. He is temporarily proud of his own bravery, but during a second encounter with the enemy he is overcome by fear and flees from the battle into the forest. There he attempts to find solace in Nature, but fails to justify his desertion in his own eyes. After coming across the spectral figure of a dying soldier, he becomes enraged by the injustices of war. He returns to the lines with the wounded, marked by the 'red badge' of a soldier who has fought but does not tell anyone how he received his wound. Back with his regiment, in the heat of battle he automatically picks up the regiment's colours when they fall from another's hands. But he can no longer be proud of his own heroics. He is filled with guilt and haunted by the memory of the 'tattered' soldier, a wounded man who was deserted on the field.

**Red Book of Hergest** See *Mabinogion, The*.

*Redburn: His First Voyage* A novel by **Herman Melville**, published in 1849. He wrote the book in about ten weeks, drawing on the experiences of his first voyage as an apprentice seaman.

The son of an impoverished New York family, Wellingborough Redburn ships out on the *Highlander*, a trader bound for Liverpool. On this his first voyage, he must learn slowly and painfully not only the sailor's strenuous trade but also that he is the lowest in social standing among the crew. Captain Riga seems to treat him kindly at first, but then ignores him contemptuously; his attempts to approach crew members alternate with their rebuffs and his similarly contemptuous withdrawal. Feeling isolated and receiving few kindnesses, he is disturbed by the deaths of some of the seamen and still more by the torments of the evil and tubercular sailor Jackson.

When the ship reaches Liverpool, Redburn finds that a guidebook belonging to his dead father (who had made business trips abroad) is no longer accurate or useful; feeling dislocated and disillusioned, he explores the city and sees the appalling conditions among the poor. He encounters a spendthrift aristocrat, Harry Bolton, and the two go off to London together. London's glitter, however, only thinly disguises its corruption. Harry, who has run up a gambling debt, is obliged to run away and ship out on the *Highlander* with Redburn for the trip home. Emigrants to America accompany them on this return voyage, and the unhealthy conditions lead to an epidemic and more deaths. Jackson's treacheries continue, though he dies as they near New York; Captain Riga cheats Harry and Redburn out of their wages, but Redburn is happy to be home with his family.

*Redeemed Captive, Returning to Zion, The* An account by John Williams, published in 1707, of his two-year captivity among the Mohawk Indians and French Jesuits in Quebec. Williams (1664–1729) was a minister in the frontier town of Deerfield, Massachusetts, and was taken prisoner during a raid (part of the French and Indian Wars) in 1704. He describes how he saw his wife and two of his children killed, and how he himself was constantly threatened with death during the march with the Indians to Canada. He and the party were delivered to the Jesuits in Quebec and their physical hardships lessened, but the Jesuits tried to convert them to Catholicism, an experience which Williams found almost as harrowing as physical deprivation. The latter part of the narrative contains his exchange of letters with his son, also a captive, who had been separated from him and successfully converted by the Jesuits, but who soon reverted to Protestantism and, together with his father, was released from captivity in 1706. Williams's youngest daughter, however, was not released; in fact she later married an Indian, joined the Roman church, and refused to return to New England. Williams stresses that the afflictions of Indian raids and captivities have been visited on the colony for its sins.

*Redgauntlet* **Sir Walter Scott** returned to a historical setting with this novel, published in 1824, the same year as the unsuccessful *St Ronan's Well*. The background to the story is the supposed return of the Young Pretender after the defeat of the 1745 rebellion to make one more attempt on the throne.

Herries of Birrenswork (Sir Edward Redgauntlet) is a fanatical Jacobite. As part of his plan for helping the Pretender he kidnaps Sir Arthur Darsie Redgauntlet, his nephew and the head of the family. Alan Fairford sets out to rescue his friend Darsie, and their adventures form the substance of the novel. In the end Sir Edward is forced to flee abroad (where he becomes a prior) and Prince Charles Edward's hopes are again crushed.

Scott tells his story in the form of letters. A famous feature of the book is 'Wandering Willie's Tale', a classic ghost story.

**Redgrove, Peter (William)** 1932– Poet and novelist. Educated at Taunton School in Somerset and at Queens' College, Cambridge. After a brief period writing scientific journalism he became a resident author at Falmouth School of Art, where he subsequently taught for many years. In 1956 he became a founder member of the **Group** and his first volume of poems, *The Collector and Other Poems*, appeared in 1960. Several collections have followed, including *At the White Monument* (1963), *Sons of My Skin: Selected Poems* (edited by Marie Peel, 1975) and *The Weddings at Nether Powers* (1979). They exhibit a densely packed and vivid visual imagery. The muscular power and rich language of his poems also marks his novels, which include *In the Country of the Skin* (1973) and *The Beekeepers* (1980). He has collaborated on several books with his wife, the novelist and poet Penelope Shuttle, including a documentary on the human fertility cycle, *The Wise Wound* (1978). His work has developed in a strongly mystical vein, repeatedly exploring the enduring religious and sexual mysteries of man.

**Reed, Henry** 1914–86 Poet. He was born in Birmingham and went to the King Edward VI School and Birmingham University. He worked as a teacher and freelance journalist before serving in the British Army (1941–2) and in the Foreign Office (1942–5). After the war, he worked as a broadcaster, journalist and radio dramatist, being known for the verse plays collected in *The Streets of Pompeii* (1971) and for the satirical prose plays in *Hilda Tablet and Others* (1971). His only volume of poetry, *A Map of Verona* (1946), includes 'Lessons of the War', three poems that deal with army training; of these, the precise and poignant 'Naming of Parts' is often anthologized. The exploratory mode of 'The Place and the Person' calls to mind **T. S. Eliot**'s *Four Quartets*, though Reed is better known for his short, acute parody of Eliot in the same volume, 'Chard Whitlow'.

**Reed, Ishmael (Scott)** 1938– Black American novelist and poet, born in Chattanooga, Tennessee, and raised in Buffalo, New York. With their combination of radical surrealism and angry social satire, Reed's novels aspire to break the cycle of oppression of American minorities. The first of these experimental works, *The Free-Lance Pall-Bearers* (1967), represents a parodic departure from the autobiographical style of earlier black American narratives. *Yellow Back Radio Broke-Down* (1969) portrays the remarkable adventures of a black cowboy. *Mumbo-Jumbo* (1972) sets forth a pseudo-history of racial oppression. *The Last Days of Louisiana Red* (1974) is loosely based on the racial violence in Berkeley in the 1960s. *Flight to Canada* (1976) surrealistically merges the Civil War period with modern America. *The Terrible Twos* (1982) is a fantastic satire of corruption in present and future American society. *Reckless Eyeballing* appeared in 1986. Reed's volumes of poetry include *Catechism of D Neo-American HooDoo Church* (1970), *Chattanooga* (1973) and *A Secretary to the Spirits* (1978). *Shrovetide in New Orleans* (1978) and *God Made Alaska for the Indians* (1982) are collections of essays.

**Reed, Talbot Baines** 1852–93 Author of school stories for boys which glamorized the shibboleths and traditions of public-school life. His most popular titles were *The Fifth Form at St Dominic's* (1887), *Cock House at Fellsgarth* (1891) and *The Master of the Shell* (1894).

**Reeve, Clara** 1729–1807 Novelist. She was born at Ipswich in Suffolk. Clara Reeve earned herself an important place in the development of **Gothic fiction** with *The Champion of Virtue: A Gothic Story*, published in 1777 but revised and republished as *The Old English Baron*. Writing some 12 years after **The Castle of Otranto** had appeared, she acknowledged her debt to **Walpole** while criticizing his performance. Her other novels were *The Two Mentors* (1783), *The Exiles* (1788), *The School for Widows* (1791), *Memoirs of Sir Roger de Clarendon* (1793) and *Destination* (1799). She also published a critical

dialogue, *The Progress of Romance through Times, Centuries and Manners* (1785).

**Reeve, John** See **Muggleton, Lodowicke**.

**Reeve's Tale, The** See **Canterbury Tales, The**.

**Reeves, James** 1909–78 Poet. Born in Middlesex, the son of a businessman, Reeves was educated at Cambridge before becoming a schoolteacher as well as a widely regarded poet, producing some 12 volumes of poetry for adults through his lifetime, including his *Collected Poems 1927–74* (1974). His first collection for children, *The Wandering Moon* (1950), was an instant success with more anthologies following, some illustrated by his friend **Edward Ardizzone**. In later life he took to retelling classics to a child audience, notably in *The Exploits of Don Quixote* (1959) and *Fables from Aesop* (1961). In 1973 he published his *Complete Poems for Children*. Virtually blind in old age, Reeves continued to work as author and editor, sensitive as always to the sound as well as the sense of what he was producing. The irreverent humour, lively imagination and occasional melancholy of his poetry helped make him an especial favourite with all ages of reader.

***Reflections on the Revolution in France*** A political treatise by **Edmund Burke**, published in 1790, the year after the outbreak of the French Revolution. Burke attacks revolutionary movements based on noble humanitarian ends because he believed that people are not at liberty to destroy the state and its institutions in the hope of some contingent improvement. He criticizes those who make an abstraction of liberty without real knowledge of what is meant by it. Equality is contrary to nature and therefore impossible to achieve, while fraternity is dismissed as 'cant and gibberish'. A memorable passage laments that with the destruction of the *ancien régime* 'the age of chivalry is gone . . . and the glory of Europe is extinguished forever'.

The seeming inconsistency of supporting the movement for Irish independence and the rebellion of the American colonists against the English government is justified, he argues, because these were actions on behalf of traditional rights and liberties, while the French Revolution was designed to produce a new social order based on the false rationalistic philosophy at the expense of personal property and the traditional class structure of a Christian kingdom.

Prompted by **Richard Price**'s sermon and *Discourse* in praise of the Revolution, Burke's treatise in turn provoked notable replies from **Thomas Paine** in **The Rights of Man**, James Mackintosh in *Vindiciae Gallicae* and **Mary Wollstonecraft** in her two *Vindications*.

*Rehearsal, The* A burlesque play by **George Villiers, 2nd Duke of Buckingham**, first performed in London in 1671. Its mockery of heroic tragedy probably contributed to the decline of that style.

Bayes brings his friends, Smith and Johnson, to watch the rehearsal of his heroic tragedy. Constantly providing ludicrous annotation to his overblown verse and tragic account of the attempted usurpation of the kingdom of Brentford, he emerges as a pompous fool. Buckingham's original target in the creation of Bayes was probably **William D'Avenant**, but the revised version was aimed at **Dryden**, who retaliated in *Absalom and Achitophel.*

**Reid, Christopher (John)** 1949– Poet. Born in Hong Kong, he was educated at Tonbridge School and Exeter College, Oxford. He works as a literary journalist. His first two collections, *Arcadia* (1979) and *Pea Soup* (1982), concentrating on unusual perceptions of everyday reality and using a technique built on the deliberate misrecognition of signs, identified him with the **Martian poets** and made comparisons with **Craig Raine**, his Oxford tutor, inevitable. Reid's taste for impersonality is emphasized by his third collection, *Katerina Brac* (1985), which purports to be the translated work of its imaginary title character. A widely praised writer, he has won the Somerset Maugham, Gregory and Prudence Farmer awards.

**Reid, Forrest** 1875–1947 Irish novelist. He was born and lived for most of his life in Belfast. At Cambridge he struck up a lifelong friendship with **E. M. Forster** who, with other Cambridge friends like **Edwin Muir** and **Walter de la Mare**, was an admirer of his work. Most of his 16 novels are centred on childhood and set their values against those of the decaying commercial society of North-East Ulster in the early 20th century. *Peter Waring* (1937) is widely regarded as his best work, although the Tom Barber trilogy, *Uncle Stephen* (1931), *The Retreat* (1936) and *Young Tom* (1944), is almost as well known. His autobiographies, *Apostate* (1926) and *Private Road* (1940), are steeped in the nostalgia which characterizes the best of his fiction. Reid also wrote critical studies of **Yeats** and Walter de la Mare.

**Reid, J. Graham** 1945– Irish playwright. He was born in Belfast and educated at Queen's University. Reid's first two plays, *The Death of Humpty-Dumpty* (1979) and *The Closed Door* (1980), tell equally harrowing stories of victims on the periphery of terrorist violence and the widening circle of loss. He has since written a successful television trilogy, *Billy* (1982), and two stage plays, *The Hidden Curriculum* (1982) and *Remembrance* (1984).

**Reid, Thomas** 1710–96 Scottish philosopher. Born at Strachan in Kincardineshire, the parish minister's son, he completed his education at Marischal College, Aberdeen. He was Professor of Moral Philosophy at King's College, Aberdeen, from 1752 to 1764, when he succeeded **Adam Smith** in the same chair at Glasgow University. Reid's first publication was *An Essay on Quantity* (1748) but he made his mark with *An Inquiry into the Human Mind on the Principles of Common Sense* (1764). *Essays on the Intellectual Powers of Man* (1785) and *Essays on the Active Powers of Man* (1788), his later works, confirmed him as the founder of the 'common-sense' school of philosophy, in ranging the principles common to the understanding of all rational men against the scepticism generated by philosophers like **Locke**, **Berkeley**, and **Hume** who could not, he insisted, produce any evidence for their assumptions. Reid's rhetorical prose style has confined his readership to students of philosophy.

**Reid, Captain (Thomas) Mayne** 1818–83 Anglo-American author of adventure stories for boys. Born in Ballyroney, County Down, he was intended for the Presbyterian ministry but, at the age of 19, went to America, where he spent several adventurous years and acquired his captaincy in the Mexican–American war. After his return to Europe in 1849 he settled in England, though he returned to America for a further stay in 1867–70. Reid drew on his American experiences in his popular novels for boys, notably *The Rifle Rangers, or, Adventures in Southern Mexico* (1850), *The Scalp Hunters, or, Romantic Adventures in Northern Mexico* (1851), *The Boy Hunters* (1853), *The Maroon* (1862), *The Cliff-Climbers* (1864), *Afloat in the Forest* (1865), *The Headless Horseman* (1866), *The Castaways* (1870) and *Gwen-Wynne* (1877). *The Quadroon, or, A Lover's Adventure in Louisiana* (1856) was adapted for the stage by **Dion Boucicault** as *The Octoroon* (1859). Reid's later work showed signs of strain, for by this time he was in financial difficulties brought about by his extravagance and weakness for unsuccessful business ventures. He also wrote travel books, poetry, plays and a book on croquet (1863).

*Relapse, The, or, Virtue in Danger* **Sir John Vanbrugh**'s first play, performed in 1696, was a hastily written riposte to **Colley Cibber**'s *Love's Last Shift* (1696). Cibber had shown the rakish Loveless resolved on reform and determined to live faithfully with his wife Amanda. Vanbrugh shows his immediate relapse into his old ways when, on a visit to London, he becomes involved with the witty widow, Berinthia, while Amanda resists the advances of Berinthia's former lover, Worthy.

More substantial than the main plot is a

sub-plot involving some of the most memorable characters in Restoration comedy. Having bought himself a title, Lord Foppington, the epitome of empty fashion, wishes to acquire a wife who can afford him. The choice falls on Miss Hoyden, a spirited girl brought up in rustic seclusion by her father, Sir Tunbelly Clumsy. Outwitted by his young brother, Fashion, who has secretly married Hoyden while claiming to be Lord Foppington, his lordship has to concede defeat.

*Religio Laici, or, A Layman's Faith* A religious poem by **John Dryden**, first published, to considerable acclaim, in 1682. The argument of the piece is in favour of the Christian religion over any belief in **Deism** (the inference of a godlike presence from an examination of the created world), and an affirmation of the primary importance of the Bible as a guide to salvation. The second part of the poem strives to express the infinite preferability of the Anglican church over its Catholic counterpart (Dryden was later to become a convert to Rome), but is generally less successful.

*Religio Medici* The first published book by **Sir Thomas Browne**, it was originally written for his 'private exercise and satisfaction'. The widely circulated manuscript was obtained by a printer and published in 1642 but reissued in an authorized edition in the following year.

The work affirms the author's Christian faith but refers to such a wide diversity of topical thought that the book transcends the normal barriers of devotional literature, becoming a fascinating and allusive investigation of the richness of God's creation. Browne is both sceptical and celebratory, erudite and fantastical in his attitudes, and the whole is realized in some of the century's finest prose, firm and yet idiosyncratic. The book includes two fine prayers in verse, and numerous sections on subjects ranging from the occult to the nature of sleep.

*Reliques of Ancient English Poetry* A collection by **Thomas Percy** of songs, ballads, metrical romances and sonnets, first published in 1765 and expanded in editions of 1767, 1775 and 1794. Some pieces are medieval while others are as late as the early 17th century. Most are drawn from **The Percy Folio**, though Percy followed the custom of his age and edited the original texts freely. The *Reliques* was an important step towards the revival of ballad poetry and its influence was acknowledged by the Romantic poets.

*Renaissance, The* See *Studies in the History of the Renaissance*.

**Renault, Mary** Pseudonym of the novelist Mary Challans (1905–83). A doctor's daughter, born in London, she was educated at St Hugh's College, Oxford. Her work as a nurse provided the background for her early novels: *Purposes of Love* (1939, as *Promise of Love* in USA), *Kind Are Her Answers* (1940), *The Friendly Young Ladies* (1944, as *The Middle Mist* in USA), *Return to Night* (1947), *North Face* (1948) and *The Charioteer* (1953), a story of servicemen and homosexuality during the war. Her reputation rests mainly on her historical novels about the ancient world, notable for combining liveliness with scholarly sophistication: *The Last of the Wine* (1956), *The King Must Die* (1958) and *The Bull from the Sea* (1962), about Theseus; *The Lion in the Gateway* (1964), for young people; *The Mask of Apollo* (1966), *Fire from Heaven* (1970), *The Persian Boy* (1972) and *Funeral Games* (1981), about Alexander; and *The Praise Singer* (1978). *The Nature of Alexander* (1975) is a historical study.

**Rendell, Ruth** See **detective fiction**.

*Representative Men* A book by **Ralph Waldo Emerson**, published in 1850 and consisting of seven essays that were originally delivered as lectures in Boston between 11 December 1845 and 22 January 1846. The series was given again shortly afterwards in Concord, Massachusetts, and again, with various revisions, in England between May 1847 and November 1848. In the opening essay Emerson suggests that truly great men are representative of their time and place: the genius is not aloof from his society, but is the earliest and finest manifestation of that society's possibilities. The six representative men he discusses in the other essays are Plato, Swedenborg, Montaigne, **Shakespeare**, Napoleon and Goethe.

*Restoration* A play with songs by **Edward Bond**, first performed at the **Royal Court Theatre**, London, in 1981.

Lord Are, an impoverished Restoration fop, marries for money the daughter of an industrialist whom he proceeds to ignore. A trick she plays in order to make him notice her misfires, in a scene that combines the macabre and the hilarious, when he stabs her to death in her disguise as a ghost. Are shifts the blame on to his loyal servant Bob, promising that he will protect him when the time comes. As a supporter of the social system that oppresses him, Bob rejects the warnings of Ruth, the black servant-girl he has married – and Lord Are rewards his trust by making sure that he is executed.

**Restoration comedy** With the reopening of London's theatres after the Restoration of Charles II, there came a demand for new plays to fill out the national repertoire. Revivals of the comedies of **Ben Jonson** and **Beaumont** and **Fletcher** and translations of Molière were increasingly replaced by colourless imitations of their work. The fashionable audiences of the period, aping the manners and aspiring to the taste of the new king's court, sought out stronger and more salacious material for the new sensations of the stage, actresses. A competitive comedy of wit and repartee, concluding in marriage only after extensive foreplay with adultery, was pioneered by such gentleman-writers as **Etherege** and **Sedley**. The master-pieces of the genre are Etherege's *She Would If She Could* (1668) and *The Man of Mode* (1676), **Wycherley**'s *The Country Wife* (1675) and *The Plain Dealer* (1676), **Congreve**'s *The Double Dealer* (1693), *Love for Love* (1695) and *The Way of the World* (1700) and **Vanbrugh**'s *The Relapse* (1696) and *The Provok'd Wife* (1697). The plots are characteristically based on the deception of the witless and the would-be wits by the truly witty, and the complications can appear tired and mechanical where the language of the writers is not adequate to sustain them. Opposition to the immorality and decadence of Restoration comedy started early, and came to a head with the publication of **Jeremy Collier**'s *Short View* (1698), in the wake of which Congreve abandoned the theatre. A new comedy of conscience and reformation was signalled by the success of **Colley Cibber**'s *Love's Last Shift* (1696) and immediately challenged by Vanbrugh's sparkling sequel, *The Relapse*. The plays of **George Farquhar** are the outstanding works of transition from the Restoration comedy of manners to the 18th-century **sentimental comedy**.

**Return of Sherlock Holmes, The** See **Sherlock Holmes stories**.

**Return of the Native, The** A novel by **Thomas Hardy**, first published in 1878 in book form and as a serial in the magazine *Belgravia*.

Damon Wildeve, an engineer turned publican, is proprietor of 'The Quiet Woman' on Egdon Heath. He is engaged to the gentle Thomasin Yeobright but carrying on an affair with Eustacia Vye, who lives with her grandfather at nearby Mistover Knap and whose desire in life is 'to be loved to madness'. Wildeve, 'to wring the heart' of Eustacia, marries Thomasin. Meanwhile, Clym Yeobright, the latter's cousin, wearying of his meretricious life as a Parisian jeweller, returns to his native heath intending to become a schoolmaster. Greatly to his mother's disapproval he falls in love with and marries Eustacia, who has unwisely accepted him in the hope he will take her away to the more exciting life of a city, preferably Paris. But Clym's sight fails and he is reduced to furze-cutting for a livelihood, a catastrophe that drives his wife to despair. Then, out of her renewed association with Wildeve, Eustacia becomes partially, but unknowingly, responsible for Mrs Yeobright's death; a quarrel with Clym which arises from that tragedy causes her to leave home. In desperation Eustacia drowns herself in Shadwater Weir and Wildeve loses his life trying to save her. Some 18 months later Clym, remorseful over the deaths of Eustacia and his mother, becomes an open-air preacher and Thomasin marries Diggory Venn, the 'isolated and weird' reddleman who moves in and out of the narrative at psychologically suitable times.

**Revelation of Divine Love, A** A mystical prose work dictated by **Julian of Norwich** some time after 1393. In 86 chapters it gives an account of 16 revelations experienced by Julian and offers some interpretation of them. All are concerned with God's love for mankind and how the Christian should love God, though one is a diabolical vision. The first 15 revelations occurred during a period of sickness and hysteria in 1373; the last was several years later and showed that the revelations had been a manifestation of God's love. The work survives in two versions.

**Revenge of Bussy D'Ambois, The** A revenge tragedy by **George Chapman**, written for indoor theatre performance in *c.*1610 and published in 1613. It is a sequel to *Bussy D'Ambois*.

Clermont D'Ambois, close friend of the Duc de Guise, is a gentleman of honour and courage. The ghost of his murdered brother, Bussy, urges him to avenge the crime; Clermont intends to do so, but only by the honourable method of a formal duel. He sends a challenge to his brother's murderer, Montsurry, who proves himself a coward. When the ghost of Bussy renews his plea, Clermont forces Montsurry to fight and kills him. He then learns that his friend, the Duc de Guise, has been assassinated and, despairing of the vicious time in which he lives, he kills himself.

**revenge tragedy** The fashion for revenge tragedy in Elizabethan and Jacobean England was set by the success of **Kyd**'s *The Spanish Tragedy* (*c.*1589). According to the strict classical precedent of Seneca, a revenge tragedy begins with the appearance of the ghost of a wronged and/or murdered man to a still-living descendant or associate. Having heard the ghost's story, the listener assumes the role of avenger and the play pursues the story through to the completion of the revenge. Rarely adherents of strict form, the Elizabethan playwrights incorporated those features that best suited them whilst re-ordering or abandoning others. **Shakespeare**'s two revenge tragedies, *Titus Andronicus* (*c.*1592) and *Hamlet* (*c.*1601), exhibit almost the full range of their kind. Other notable examples are **Tourneur**'s *The Revenger's Tragedy* (*c.*1606), **Webster**'s *The White Devil* (*c.* 1612) and *The Duchess of Malfi* (*c.* 1613), **Middleton**'s *The Changeling* (1622) and *Women Beware Women* (*c.* 1625), **Marston**'s *Antonio's Revenge* (1600) and **Shirley**'s *The Traitor* (1631), but the theme of revenge so dominated the tragedies of the period that the list could be vastly prolonged.

**Revenger's Tragedy, The** Generally, though not confidently, ascribed to **Cyril Tourneur**, this is one of the finest of Jacobean **revenge tragedies**. Its rapid sequence of vigorous scenes exposes courtly corruption with an unremitting savagery that has led many critics to suppose that its composition was motivated by its author's loathing of humanity. But such biographical speculation tends to ignore its obvious debt to the satiric bite of **Marston** as well as its adherence to the dramaturgical conventions of revenge tragedy. There remains, though, a threatening gleefulness in the death-dealing climax of the masque-within-a-play. The ascription to Tourneur is not helped by the manifest inferiority of his other surviving play, *The Atheist's Tragedy*, and this, together with certain stylistic arguments, has strengthened the critical case that **Middleton** is the author. However, *The Revenger's Tragedy* is distinct from any of Middleton's surviving plays and demands assessment in its own right. It was printed in 1608, after it had established its place in the repertoire of the **King's Men**.

The complex plot centres on two families. The first consists of Gratiana, widow of an Italian nobleman impoverished by the chicanery of the reigning duke, and her three children, Castiza, Hippolito and Vindice. The second consists of the conniving duke, his son Lussurioso, his bastard son Spurio, his second wife and her three sons, Ambitioso, Supervacuo and the unnamed Junior Brother. The primary link in the chain of revenge is established at once, when Vindice enters holding the skull of his loved one, poisoned by the lecherous duke because she would not yield to his lust. Sworn to revenge, Vindice finds opportunity in his employment by Lussurioso, for which purpose he assumes disguise as the mercenary Piato. Lussurioso's object is the seduction of Vindice's sister, Castiza. She angrily rejects the suit, but 'Piato' is horrified to find his mother ready to persuade Castiza to surrender her virginity to Lussurioso. Junior Brother is imprisoned for raping the virtuous wife of the noble Antonio. Without much difficulty the duchess persuades Spurio, the duke's bastard son, to become her lover. The duke continues his career of lust. All the brothers and step-brothers conspire against each other to succeed to the dukedom. Methodically, Vindice, with some help from his brother Hippolito, plots their downfall, aided by their own rivalries. He contrives for the duke a startlingly apt death by applying poison to the skull of his dead lady and tricking the duke into kissing it in the belief that it is his procured new mistress. Junior Brother has already been executed as a direct result of confused orders issued by his elder brothers. The climax comes at the festivities to celebrate the inauguration of the new duke, Lussurioso. In the disguise of masquers, Vindice and Hippolito assassinate Lussurioso and his corrupt noblemen. They are followed by the 'real' masquers, Spurio, Ambitioso and Supervacuo, who, finding Lussurioso dead, turn on each other in a paroxysm of mutual murder. The restoration of the shattered dukedom rests with the virtuous Antonio, whose first act is to order the execution of Vindice and Hippolito, self-confessed murderers of the old duke.

**Review, The** A periodical founded by **Daniel Defoe** with the help of **Robert Harley, Earl of Oxford**, on 19 February 1704, upon Defoe's release from prison. It was first called *A Weekly Review of the Affairs of France, Purged from the Errors and Partiality of News-Writers and Petty-Statesmen, of All Sides*. It had become *The Review* by 11 June 1713, the year it closed, when Defoe went to prison for the second time. After the first six weekly issues it came out twice weekly and from 22 March 1705 was appearing thrice weekly. It was written almost entirely by Defoe himself, a remarkable feat since he was often in Scotland as Harley's clandestine agent during the paper's existence. *The Review* offered well-informed comment on the affairs of Europe (England was at war with France), dealt with aspects of the social life of the day, and kept its readers informed on commerce and trade. Nonpartisan, Defoe gave his opinion on political topics and thus became the first leader writer of the English press.

**Revolt of Islam, The** A poem by **Percy Bysshe Shelley**, in **Spenserian stanzas**, published in 1818. Written in 1817, it was originally called 'Laon and Cythna'; the principal characters, who become lovers, are brother and sister. Charles Ollier, who published the revised poem, persuaded Shelley to change the relationship.

The poem is set in Islam where Cythna, a maiden dedicated to the freedom of her sex from harsh laws, joins forces with Laon, another revolutionary. They unite the people in revolt and for a time succeed; but the ruling tyrants, with reinforced armies, crush the revolt and lay waste the land. Famine and pestilence follow, and at the instigation of a priest Laon and Cythna are burned alive as a sacrifice. Its revolutionary significance lay in Shelley's response to contemporary conditions in England.

**Rexroth, Kenneth** 1905–82 American poet, born in South Bend, Indiana. He led a Bohemian life-style in Chicago in the 1920s, and then moved to San Francisco, where he became active in leftist and union movements and eventually established himself as a central figure in the literary community. His work variously consists of elegiac, erotic, and political verse, and is often surreal and experimental in style. His early volumes of poetry are *In What Hour* (1940), *The Phoenix and the Tortoise* (1944), *The Art of Worldly Wisdom* (1949) and *The Signature of All Things* (1949). Although he later distanced himself from the movement, Rexroth was briefly associated with the **Beats**. His other volumes of verse are *Poems* (1955), *Natural Numbers* (1963), *The Collected Shorter Poems* (1967), *The Collected Longer Poems* (1968), *New Poems* (1974), *The Silver Swan* (1976) and *The Morning Star: Poems and Translations* (1979). He also published a collection of four plays in verse entitled *Beyond the Mountains* (1951) and numerous translations, including *100 Poems from the Japanese* (1954), *100 Poems from the Chinese* (1956) and *100 Poems from the Greek and Latin* (1959). His critical essays are collected in *The Bird in the Bush* (1959) and *Assays* (1961). *An Autobiographical Novel* appeared in 1966.

**Reynard the Fox** A prose translation by **William Caxton**, published in 1481, of the Dutch *Hystorie van Reynaert die Vos*, a version of the composite Renard Cycle. The cycle probably originated in Latin but is best known in its French form, the verse *Roman de Renart* largely produced in the 12th and early 13th centuries. This formed the source of the Flemish *Van den Vos Reynaerde* (probably 13th-century); a later version of this text, the 14th-century *Reinaerts Historie*, was the source of the Dutch prose *Hystorie*. The whole cycle is dominated by the deceitful character of the fox, at first sympathetic but later simply evil, and by an increasing tendency to satiric attack on the nobility and the Church.

The part of the cycle given by Caxton relates how the fox is called to court to answer for his misdeeds. By trickery and corruption he escapes death. On his second trial he is challenged to single combat by the wolf, Isegrim, whom he defeats unfairly. He becomes a favourite at court. The story is a parable, showing how the evil are advanced and teaching avoidance of wickedness.

**Reynolds, John Hamilton** 1796–1852 Poet. The son of a schoolmaster, Reynolds was born at Shrewsbury, Shropshire, and educated at Shrewsbury and St Paul's Schools, and worked in a London insurance office before taking up law. In 1814 he published his first work, *Safie*, an oriental novel in the style of **Byron**, and *The Eden of the Imagination*, which recalls the verse of the late 18th century. In 1815 he became a contributor to the periodical *The Champion*, and his collection *The Naiad: A Tale with Other Poems* appeared in 1816. An article in *The Examiner* at the end of 1816 placed him alongside **Keats** and **Shelley** as one of the most promising writers of the day, but Reynolds failed to find his own voice as a poet, and is now chiefly remembered for his friendship and correspondence with Keats. His most craftsmanly serious work is *The Garden of Florence* (1821). A witty and mercurial figure, his real genius lay in imitation and parody, and his skit on **Wordsworth**'s *Peter Bell*, *Peter Bell, a Lyrical Ballad* (1819), is one of the finest parodies in English literature; it inspired Shelley to try his own hand in *Peter Bell the Third*. *The Fancy* appeared in 1820, and in 1825 he collaborated with **Thomas Hood** in *Odes and Addresses to Great People*.

**Reynolds, Sir Joshua** 1723–92 Portraitist. Son of the master of the grammar school at Plympton-Earl's, Devonshire, where he was educated, Reynolds was apprenticed to Thomas Hudson, the portrait painter, in 1740. He had a highly successful career, culminating in the foundation Presidency of the Royal Academy in 1768. As President, Reynolds delivered the lectures (1769–90) published as *Discourses on Art*. The dedication to the King, prefacing the work, was written by **Johnson**, who also improved the text at various points. Philosophically, these pieces were based upon the theories of Aristotle and Plato in that notions of truth and beauty were the result of generalizing from particular examples, and these notions were inextricably linked with moral qualities. Reynolds also strongly advocated that the aspiring artist should build upon the achievements of his predecessors: copying the works of suitable masters was a key element in the education of the student. Creation was presented as an entirely rational process. The *Discourses* were vitriolically assailed by **Blake**: they are more conventionally seen as perceptive discussions of 18th-century attitudes to art. Reynolds had earlier contributed three papers on art matters to *The Idler*, nos. 76, 79 and 82, and provided the annotations to **William Mason**'s verse translation of Du Fresnoy's *Art of Painting*. In 1781 he toured Flanders and Holland and recorded the tour with detailed notes on all the pictures he had seen, advancing the then unfashionable opinion that Dutch paintings, particularly those of Rubens, were not inferior to the Italian School. Some of his notes on **Shakespeare** were printed in the final volume of Johnson's edition and others in **Malone**'s supplement of 1780. He also left short descriptions of **Garrick**, **Goldsmith** and Johnson which were published posthumously. Johnson described Reynolds as 'almost the only man whom I call a friend', and was encouraged by him to found the literary gathering known as the Club in the winter of 1763–4. Initially the Club had nine members: Johnson, Reynolds, Beauclerk, **Burke**, Chamier, Goldsmith, Hawkins, Langton and Nugent. Others, including Garrick, Banks and Malone, were subsequently elected. **Boswell** dedicated *The Life of Johnson* (1791) to him, as had Goldsmith *The Deserted Village* (1770). In his long and highly successful career (he had 156 sitters in 1759) he painted many literary and theatrical figures, including: Mrs Abington, Baretti, Boswell, Burke, Charles Burney, Sir William Chambers, Kitty Fisher, **Foote**, Charles James Fox, Garrick (seven times), Warren Hastings, Johnson (five times), **Sheridan**, Mrs Siddons, **Sterne** and **Horace Walpole**. Some 700 engraved plates were made of his works, and it has been through Reynolds's eyes that the public have come to see many of these figures.

**Reznikoff, Charles** 1894–1976 American poet, born in Brooklyn, and educated at the University of Missouri and New York University. He is generally identified with the **Objectivist** school, and much of his work emphasizes the role of Judaism in his life. His first publication was a volume of poetry, *Rhythms* (1918). Other volumes include *Poems* (1920), *Uriel Acosta: A Play and A Fourth Group of Verse* (1921), *Chatterton, The Black Death, and Meriwether Lewis: Three Plays* (1922), *Coral and Captive Israel: Two Plays* (1923), *Five Groups of Verse* (1927), *Nine Plays* (1927), *Jerusalem the Golden* (1934) and *Inscriptions: 1944–1956* (1959). A poetic meditation on US history, *Testimony: The United States, 1885–1890*, appeared in 1965; its sequel, *Testimony: The United States, 1891–1900*, in 1968. He also wrote a historical novel, *The Lionhearted* (1944).

***Rhoda Fleming*** A novel by **George Meredith**, first published in 1865.

Interested in metropolitan life, Rhoda and Dahlia, the two daughters of the widowed Farmer Fleming, come to London under the protection of their uncle, Anthony Hackbut, where they encounter the cousins Edward and Algernon Blancove. The former seduces and deserts Dahlia, whose shame is deepened by a miserable marriage to the bigamous and contemptible Sedgett, an alliance contracted in the hope of expiating her shame. After various melodramatic adventures, she attempts suicide whilst the hand of the self-willed, determined Rhoda is successfully sought by the ex-soldier and farm-assistant Robert Eccles.

Although *Rhoda Fleming* is a sombre novel,

several down-to-earth characters – among them Master Gammon, Mrs Sumfit and Mrs Boulby – enliven the pages with their local humour and steadfastness.

**rhyme royal** Stanza form of seven decasyllabic lines rhyming ababbcc. It first appeared in **Chaucer**'s 'Complaint unto Pity' and was used by him also in *Troilus and Criseyde*, *The Parlement of Foules* and in some of *The Canterbury Tales*. It was later used by **Sir Thomas Wyatt**, **Edmund Spenser**, **Shakespeare** (in *The Rape of Lucrece*), **Michael Drayton** and **William Morris** amongst others. Its name probably derives from its use in *Kingis Quair*, at one time attributed to **James I of Scotland**; it is sometimes called the Chaucerian stanza.

**Rhymers' Club, The** A group of poets who met at the Cheshire Cheese in Fleet Street between 1891 and 1894. It included its founders, Ernest Rhys and **W. B. Yeats**, **Richard Le Gallienne**, **Ernest Dowson**, **Lionel Johnson**, **Arthur Symons**, **John Davidson**, T. W. Rolleston, Selwyn Image and Edwin Ellis. According to Yeats's memoir *Four Years: 1887–1891*, **William Watson** joined but never came, **Francis Thompson** came once but did not join, and **Oscar Wilde** would only attend meetings in private houses. Yeats described the meetings as 'always decorous and often dull'. The group published two collections of verse, in 1892 and 1894.

**Rhys, Jean** 1894–1979 Novelist, born in Roseau, Dominica. The painful clarity of her understanding of personal, sexual, or social exploitation gives her writings firm coherence. European, Bohemian, modernist, her stories in *The Left Bank* (1927), together with the novels *Postures* (1928; as *Quartet*, in USA, 1929, and subsequently), *After Leaving Mr Mackenzie* (1930), *Voyage in the Dark* (1934) and *Good Morning, Midnight* (1939) all reveal single-minded craftsmanship in presenting female characters of intense vitality, but deracinated

Jean Rhys.

lonely and directionless. Her finest novel, *Wide Sargasso Sea* (1966), invents the tragic story of Rochester's mad wife in **Jane Eyre**, portraying her as a victim of commercial, decadent colonial society, reduced to the very insanity for which her individuality was mistaken. *Tigers Are Better-looking* (1968) and the finely designed collection, *Sleep It Off, Lady* (1976) contain stories that confirm the imaginative unity of Rhys's work. *Smile Please: An Unfinished Autobiography* appeared in 1979, *Letters 1931–1966* in 1984.

**rhythm** See **metre**.

**Ricardo, David** 1772–1823 Political economist. Born in the City of London into a Jewish family with strong Dutch connections, he had a 'common-school' education followed by two years in Amsterdam, probably at the Talmud Tora, where he was taught by rabbis. This developed the 'taste for abstract and general reasoning' which characterized his deductive method of economic enquiry and eventually dominated the field of economics. Introduced early to the family stockbroking business, he established himself as a jobber in the Stock Exchange and quickly prospered. Between 1806 and 1815 he joined partnerships bidding for the government loans which financed the Napoleonic War, and the victory at Waterloo set the seal on his fortune. He restricted his business activities to concentrate on Parliament (which he entered in 1819 for the pocket borough of Portarlington), his estates (which included Gatcomb Park in Gloucestershire) and writing.

**Adam Smith**'s *Wealth of Nations* had first aroused his interest in political economy. Ricardo's earliest work is in the field of monetary economics, concerned with the high price of gold and the depreciation of paper money, the role of the Bank of England and monetary theory. His writing, never brilliant, is at its clearest in *The High Price of Bullion* (1810) and the *Reply to Mr Bosanquet's Practical Observations on the Report of the Bullion Committee* (1811). His *Proposals for an Economical and Secure Currency* (1816) are grounded in the Quantity Theory of Money, which demonstrates that inflation is caused by too much money in circulation. Ricardo's pamphlets brought him into contact with leading economists, including **Malthus** and **James Mill**. Mill encouraged him to develop the ideas in the *Essay on the Low Price of Corn on the Profits of Stock* (1815) into his major work, *On the Principles of Political Economy and Taxation* (1817, twice revised by 1821). It develops a theory of value which is used to explain how the proportions of the wages of labour and the profits of capital are determined, as well as the effects of taxes. Ricardo did not produce another book, although he wrote a critical commentary

on Malthus's *Principles of Political Economy* not published until 1928. His article 'Funding System' appeared in the *Supplement to the Encyclopaedia Britannica* (1820). His interest in free trade led him to publish *On Protection to Agriculture* (1822). The *Plan for the Establishment of a National Bank* appeared posthumously.

**Rice, Elmer** 1892–1967 American playwright. Born Elmer Leopold Reizenstein in New York City to German-Jewish immigrant parents, Rice left school at the age of 14. He worked for a time as a clerk in his cousin's law office, then studied law, and was admitted to the Bar in 1913, but shortly thereafter gave up this career to become a playwright. His first play, *On Trial* (1914), was a financial and critical success and effectively launched his career. He is often credited with inventing the technique later called flashback: in *On Trial*, a court-room drama, the action switches between testimony and flashbacks initiated by the testimony, moving progressively further back in time to exonerate the accused man. Despite its revolutionary construction, it deals with relatively conventional themes of honesty, infidelity and the preying of the immoral rich upon female innocence. In the course of the long and active career that followed, Rice wrote over 50 plays, of which the best known are **The Adding Machine** (1923) and **Street Scene** (1929), which won him the Pulitzer Prize.

Though his drama ranges from expressionism to naturalism to light-hearted comedy, Rice's devotion to social justice and liberal causes is apparent throughout his work. Two early plays, *The Home of the Free* (1917) and *The Iron Cross* (1917), took up pacifist themes at an unpopular time; *The Subway* (1929) told the story of a young working girl victimized by lecherous men; *See Naples and Die* (1929) and *The Left Bank* (1931) were light-hearted critiques of expatriate morality, for which Rice gathered material on trips abroad. Other plays include *We, The People* (1933), a vehement indictment of conditions during the Depression, including an attack on racial prejudice; *Judgement Day* (1934), a thinly fictionalized account of the trial which followed the Reichstag fire; *Between Two Worlds* (1934), in which characters on a transatlantic voyage debate and play out the contradictions between the American system and the Soviet, which Rice had observed on a long visit to Russia; *Dream Girl* (1945); *Love Among the Ruins* (1963); and *Close Harmony* (1929, also produced as *The Lady Next Door*) written in collaboration with **Dorothy Parker**.

Rice wrote several novels, Hollywood screenplays, an autobiography, *Minority Report* (1963), and a history of the theatre. He also worked as a producer and director, and in 1937, three years after a widely publicized 'retirement from the theatre' prompted by a battle with the critics, formed the Playwrights Company with **Maxwell Anderson**, **Robert Sherwood**, **Sidney Howard** and **S. N. Behrman**. He was a founding member of the American Civil Liberties Union and later of the **Federal Theatre Project**, which employed out-of-work actors, playwrights, and other theatre workers during the Depression.

*Riceyman Steps* A novel by **Arnold Bennett**, published in 1923. The story of Henry Earlforward concentrates on his life in and around the antiquarian bookshop he has inherited in Clerkenwell. His courtship, in middle age, of Violet Arb, the widow who has moved into a neighbouring shop, leads to marriage. But Henry's main passion is with his money and possessions: the novel gives keen insight into the self-centred world of the miser, its glimpses of openheartedness and its gradual decline from the state of emotional under-nourishment to physical illness. Henry's grim calculations over the honeymoon outing to Madame Tussaud's, his gift to Violet of a second-hand safe, and his horrified reactions when Violet has the house vacuum-cleaned, are only part of a detailed narrative, generous in its human interest.

Violet's thwarted attempts to bring warmth into the marriage before her death of a wasting illness are echoed in the life of her maidservant Elsie, and with a note of triumph. Detailed attention is given to Elsie's past, including her marriage, the death of her soldier husband, and her life in cramped lodgings. Her romance with the shell-shocked Joe, whom she nurses through malarial illness, and marries, contrasts with the struggle of Henry with his own illness. Only when near to death does he begin to acknowledge that Violet and he have been victims of a life-denying passion and that he has been responsible for this end.

**Rich, Adrienne (Cecile)** 1929– American poet, born in Baltimore, Maryland, and educated at Radcliffe College. Her first book of poems, *A Change of World* (1951), was published in the Yale Series of Younger Poets. A second volume, *The Diamond Cutters*, appeared in 1955. In the 1960s she turned to increasingly innovative forms and a startlingly frank idiom to explore feminist themes. *Snapshots of a Daughter-in-Law* appeared in 1963. Subsequent volumes were *The Necessities of Life* (1966), *Selected Poems* (England 1966, USA 1967), *Leaflets: Poems, 1965–1968* (1969), *The Will to Change: Poems, 1968–70* (1971), *Diving Into the Wreck: Poems, 1971–72* (1973), *Poems: Selected and New, 1950–1974* (1975), *The Dream of a Common Language: Poems 1974–1977* (1978), *A Wild Patience Has Taken Me This Far: Poems, 1978–81* (1981), *Sources* (1983), *The Fact of A Doorframe: Poems Selected and New, 1950–1984* (1984) and *Your*

*Native Land/Your Life* (1986). A prose work, *Of Woman Born: Motherhood as Experience and Institution* (1976), established Rich as an influential radical feminist critic. She has also published *On Lies, Secrets, and Silence: Selected Prose 1966–1978* (1979) and *Blood, Bread, and Poetry: Selected Prose 1979–1985* (1986).

**Rich, Barnabe** 1542–1617 Author of romances and pamphlets. Rich entered military service in 1562, fought in Queen Mary's wars with France, in the Low Countries and in Ireland, where he spent most of the time between 1572 and 1582. During this time he rose to the rank of captain. His literary career consisted of the production of some 25 books: romances in the popular style of **euphuism**, tracts on military affairs, and the state of government in Ireland, some anti-Catholic works (including an account of a girl's false visions) and satires. His earliest publication was a dialogue on military affairs, *A Right Excellent and Pleasant Dialogue between Mercury and an English Soldier* (1574). His most important work is *Rich his Farewell to the Military Profession* (1581), a collection of eight romances, including 'Apolonius and Silla' which is the source of the plot for *Twelfth Night*. This was followed by a series of euphuistic romances in 1581, 1584 and 1592. His later works were mainly satirical.

*Richard II, The Life and Death of* A historical tragedy by **William Shakespeare**, first performed *c.*1595 and published in two good Quartos in 1597 (Q1) and 1608 (Q4) before the First Folio of 1623. The main source is **Holinshed**'s *Chronicles*.

The play opens with the conflict of two powerful noblemen, Thomas Mowbray, Duke of Norfolk and Henry Bolingbroke, Earl of Hereford. Richard II orders them to settle their differences in a duel at Coventry. With all preparations made, the king suddenly intervenes and banishes both men. Bolingbroke's resentment is exacerbated when Richard takes advantage of John of Gaunt's death to confiscate Bolingbroke's inheritance. He needs the money to finance his Irish wars. But the confiscation gives the calculating Bolingbroke a pretext for bringing an invading force to England. He receives sufficient support from English lords, overtaxed to gratify Richard's extravagance, to encourage him to claim the throne. In a famous scene, the histrionic Richard stages his own deposition. He is then confined to Pomfret Castle, where he reflects on the divine right of kings. Threatened by conspiracies, Bolingbroke exercises a diplomacy and discipline that distinguish him from the deposed king. Sir Pierce of Exton, interpreting Bolingbroke's secret wishes, kills Richard II at Pomfret, but is repudiated by Bolingbroke, now firmly enthroned as Henry IV. The play ends with the new king's expressed intention to expiate the regicide by making a pilgrimage to the Holy Land.

*Richard II*, because it deals with the deposition of an anointed king, was a controversial play. Shakespeare's company earned the queen's displeasure by performing it on the eve of the Earl of Essex's rebellion in 1601. Shakespeare, conscious of the notoriety of **Marlowe's** *Edward II*, wrote it as the tragedy of a misguided king. Although it stands as the first of a sequence of English history plays, to be completed by the two parts of *Henry IV* and by *Henry V*, it was written as a single tragedy.

**Richard III, The Life and Death of** A historical tragedy by **William Shakespeare**, first performed *c.* 1594 and published in Quarto (Q1) in 1597 as well as in the First Folio of 1623. The main source is **Holinshed's** *Chronicles*.

Richard, Duke of Gloucester, conscious of his deformity, determines to force his way to the throne. He has first to eliminate a number of rivals, which he does with the connivance of the Duke of Buckingham. He becomes king, making his position secure by ordering the deaths of his young nephews, sons of the dead Edward IV, and insisting on marrying their sister. But opposition hardens, and Richard is troubled by a prophecy that the Earl of Richmond will become king. Alienated by Richard's ingratitude, Buckingham raises an army, and Richard's increasing isolation is emphasized when Richmond invades. Although Buckingham is captured and executed, the forces of Richmond advance inexorably. Disquieted by dreams on the eve of the Battle of Bosworth, Richard rallies his strength in a desperate fight, but is eventually killed in single combat by the Earl of Richmond, who, as Henry VII, establishes the Tudor dynasty on the throne of England.

The acting potential of the title role ensured for *Richard III* a prime place in the English theatre, particularly in the greatly altered version by **Colley Cibber** (1700). Although the play is historically related to the *Henry VI* trilogy, it is entirely self-sufficient. For the Elizabethan audience, it offered confirmation that the young Shakespeare had the popular touch.

**Richard Coeur de Lyon** A verse romance written soon after 1300, probably in South-east England. Combining history with romance, it tells the story of Richard the Lionheart: his parentage, his triumph over a lion sent to devour him and the Crusade during which he dined on Saracens' heads before eventually capturing Babylon and Jaffa. The central episode of the Crusade includes detailed accounts of military campaigns. Richard's exuberant and dominating personality, which the poem celebrates

with patriotic pride, is explained by his having a supernatural mother. **Sir Walter Scott** drew on the poem for *The Talisman*.

**Richard the Redeless** See *Mum and the Sothsegger*.

**Richards, David Adams** 1950– Canadian novelist. Born and raised in New Brunswick, Richards writes exclusively about Maritime Canada and the tightly-knit, often intense lives of its inhabitants. After studying at St Thomas University in Fredericton, he moved back to his native Newcastle. His first novel, *The Coming of Winter* (1974), is a vividly realistic account of the life of a young New Brunswick mill-worker and is notable for its rendition of the local idiom. *Blood Ties* (1976) employs a slow-paced narrative style, almost entirely reliant on dialogue and deadpan accounts of action and remarkable for its ability to evoke intense emotions without explicitly describing inner feelings. *Lives of Short Duration* (1981) is a more wide-ranging novel which examines the history of a deprived Maritime community through a complex interior monologue technique. Richards has also published a volume of short stories, *Dancers at Night* (1978).

**Richards, Frank** See **Hamilton, Charles**.

**Richards (Franklin Thomas) Grant** 1872–1948 Publisher. The son of an Oxford don, he left school at 16 and joined a wholesale publishing firm. On the staff of *The Review of Reviews* between 1890 and 1896 he made literary friendships which proved valuable when he set up his own publishing firm in 1897. Despite habitual irresponsibility in finance (he twice went bankrupt), Richards developed a strong literary list which included **Samuel Butler's** *The Way of All Flesh* and the poetry and scholarly writings of **A. E. Housman**. His light-hearted autobiography, *Author Hunting* (1934), owes much to the correspondence with **Shaw** that animates it. He also wrote well on Housman (1941), the austere poet having unexpectedly been a close friend of his rapscallion publisher.

**Richards, I[vor] A[rmstrong]** 1893–1979 Critic. Born the son of a factory manager in Cheshire, Richards was educated at Clifton College and at Magdalene College, Cambridge, where he studied Moral Sciences before becoming a lecturer in the recently founded school of English in 1919. In his early writings, *The Foundations of Aesthetics* (with C. K. Ogden and J. Wood, 1922) and *The Meaning of Meaning* (with C. K. Ogden, 1923), he began to use methods of Positivist philosophy to clarify problems of language and art. In the much more influential *Principles of Literary Criticism* (1924) and in *Science and Poetry* (1926) he presented an almost clinical view of poetry as a kind of mental hygiene which reconciles conflicting impulses in the mind. He distinguished the scientific or referential use of language from the 'emotive' uses of language found in the 'pseudo-statements' of poetry, attributing a variety of evils – from bad taste to violent patriotism – to the illegitimate mixture of the two.

Richards's best-known work, *Practical Criticism* (1929), was the result of an experiment in which he gave his Cambridge students a series of unsigned poems for comment. Analysing the written responses, he catalogued the various kinds of misreading to which poems can be subjected. This work displaced the uncritical notions of poetry inherited from the late Victorian age, and it prompted a new 'close reading' of poetry for verbal ambiguities, ironies, and other complexities, not just in the work of Richards's pupil **William Empson** and of the *Scrutiny* school, but in the study of literature throughout the English-speaking world: 'practical criticism' became a standard classroom exercise.

After a year spent teaching in China, Richards moved in 1931 to Harvard University, where he taught until 1963. These years were devoted to the promotion of Basic English, which he had formulated with C. K. Ogden as a simplified system for learners of the language, with a vocabulary of only 850 words. His important works of literary interest in this period were *Coleridge on the Imagination* (1934), *The Philosophy of Rhetoric* (1936), and *Interpretation in Teaching* (1938). *Goodbye Earth, and Other Poems* appeared in 1959, to be followed by three more volumes of verse. His life's work was dedicated to clarity of communication, which he felt vital in an age of world wars.

**Richardson, Dorothy M[iller]** 1873–1957 Novelist. She was born in Abingdon and attended local schools before working as a teacher and a clerk. She married a painter, Alan Odle. After publishing *The Quakers Past and Present* and *Gleanings from the Works of George Fox* (both 1914) she embarked on *Pilgrimage*, the sequence of 12 novels for which she is remembered. Making an early use of **stream of consciousness**, it deals with the life of Miriam Henderson. The individual volumes are: *Pointed Roofs* (1915), *Backwater* (1916), *Honeycomb* (1917), *Interim* (1919), *The Tunnel* (1919), *Deadlock* (1921), *Revolving Lights* (1923), *The Trap* (1925), *Oberland* (1927), *Dawn's Left Hand* (1931), *Clear Horizon* (1935) and *Dimple Hill* (1938).

**Richardson, Henry Handel** The pseudonym of the novelist Ethel Florence Richardson (1870–1946). Born in Melbourne, Australia, she was educated at the Melbourne Presbyterian Ladies College, where she showed a talent for music that led to further study at the Leipzig Conservatorium. At Leipzig she met her future husband, John George Robertson, who became lecturer in English at Strasbourg (1896–1903), and Professor of German Language and Literature at the University of London in 1904.

She successfully used music as the theme for her novel *Maurice Guest* (1908). Her own adolescence provided the background for *The Getting of Wisdom* (1910) and music, again, for *The Young Cosima* (1939). She revisited Australia only once, to ensure the authenticity of the background of *Australia Felix* (1917). This was the first part of a trilogy completed in *The Way Home* (1925) and *Ultima Thule* (1929) and published as **The Fortunes of Richard Mahony** (1930). She left an autobiography, *Myself when Young* (1948), which appeared after her death.

**Richardson, Samuel** 1689–1761 Novelist and printer. Although Richardson was born in Derbyshire, his father was a London joiner and the family had returned to the capital by 1700. HIs father could not afford the classical education necessary to make him a clergyman, and he was bound apprentice to a printer in 1706. He proved diligent, and his reward was the hand of his master's daughter, Allington Wilde. He married in 1721, the year he set up in business by himself as master printer. By this first wife he had five sons and one daughter, all of whom died young. After her death he married Elizabeth Leake, daughter of a fellow printer and sister of a bookseller, who survived him. They had five girls and a boy, of whom four girls survived.

As a boy, Richardson – whose nicknames were 'Serious' and 'Gravity' – entertained his schoolfellows with tales remembered from his reading, and all his tales, according to him, 'carried with them . . . an useful moral'. He served an unofficial apprenticeship as a writer of love-letters for servant girls from the age of 13, and before that as author of a reproving letter to a lady who professed religion but practised slander and backbiting, and by providing prefaces and dedications for booksellers. In 1733, he published *The Apprentice's Vade Mecum*, which urged the ambitious youth to diligence, sobriety, self-denial and morality, an ethic of deferred gratification; this was followed by his own didactic version of *Aesop's Fables*. He also edited *The Negotiations of Sir Thomas Roe in his Embassy to the Ottoman Port for the years 1621 to 1628 Inclusive* (1740) and continued **Defoe**'s *A Tour Through The Whole Island of Great Britain*, which was completed anonymously.

Richardson prospered, and as well as his business address off Fleet Street, had second homes, first near Hammersmith, and later near Parsons Green. In 1754 he was elected Master of

Samuel Richardson, c.1747. A detail from the portrait by Joseph Highmore. National Portrait Gallery, London.

should put Richardson first, then Rousseau; after them, but at an immeasurable distance – Charlotte Lennox, Smollett and Fielding.' She thought both Fielding and **Smollett** 'knew the Husk of Life perfectly well', yet 'for the Kernel – you must go to either Richardson or Rousseau'. Johnson, though he admitted that 'if you were to read Richardson for the story your impatience would be so much fretted that you would hang yourself', believed that 'there is more knowledge of the human heart in one letter of Richardson's than in all of *Tom Jones*'.

Yet Richardson's reputation was in decline even by 1797, when Mary Hay, writing in *The Monthly Magazine*, while admitting Richardson was 'a sovereign genius', complained of his 'false and pernicious principles, the violation of truth and nature, . . . absurd superstitions and ludicrous prejudices' and compared him unfavourably with Fielding and Smollett. During the 19th century, Richardson's supposedly effeminate preoccupations were denigrated in comparison with Fielding's manliness. During the second half of the present century, however, his greatness has been once more acknowledged.

**Richler, Mordecai** 1931– Canadian novelist. Born in Montreal, he dropped out of university and travelled to England where he worked for

the Stationers' Company, and in 1760 he purchased a share of the patent of the printer to the king. In later life he suffered from ill health which he considered nervous in origin. His virtues were those of the industrious apprentice; his weakness was agreed to be his vanity. However, he was a self-made man, who started life with few advantages, and his achievement was distinguished. Among his circle of friends and admirers were two sisters, **Lady Bradshaigh** and Lady Echlin, both of whose correspondence with Richardson survives.

He wrote three novels, becoming famous with the publication of *Pamela* in 1740, consolidating his success with his masterpiece, *Clarissa*, in 1747–8, and adding *Sir Charles Grandison* in 1753–4. Taking up a hint from his friend **Samuel Johnson**, he also published *A Collection of the Moral and Instructive Sentiments, Maxims, Cautions and Reflections, Contained in the Histories of Pamela, Clarissa and Sir Charles Grandison, Digested under Proper Heads* (1755). All three novels are epistolary. Though he did not invent this form, Richardson did invent the novel of common life, eschewing 'the improbable and the marvellous'.

**Henry Fielding**'s mockery was expressed in *Shamela* and *Joseph Andrews*, but otherwise Richardson's reputation stood high during his lifetime. Mrs Thrale wrote in her commonplace book: 'Were I to make a scale of novel writers I

Mordecai Richler.

many years as a freelance journalist, eventually returning to Canada in 1972. His works include *The Acrobats* (1954), *Son of a Smaller Hero* (1955), *Choice of Enemies* (1957), *The Apprenticeship of Duddy Kravitz* (1959), *The Incomparable Atuk* (1963), *Cocksure* (1968), *Hunting Tigers Under Glass* (journalistic pieces, 1968), *The Street* (short stories, 1969), and *St Urbain's Horseman* (1971), a novel which occupied him for several years. Recent works include a children's book, *Jacob Two-Two Meets the Hooded Fang* (1975), and a novel, *Joshua Then and Now* (1980). Richler's sympathies lie with minorities, and many of his novels embrace themes of persecution and escape from the ghetto. His ambivalent attitude to his heritage as a Canadian Jew is skilfully presented in *St Urbain's Horseman*, which combines nostalgia and satire.

**Rickword, (John) Edgell** 1898–1982 Critic. The son of a librarian from Colchester, where he attended the grammar school, Rickword fought in World War I before studying at Pembroke College, Oxford. He was a reviewer for *The New Statesman* and **The Times Literary Supplement** (in which he reviewed **T. S. Eliot**'s **The Waste Land**), before acting as editor of the short-lived **Calendar of Modern Letters** (1925–7). This journal was admired for its exacting critical standards and for its uncompromising 'Scrutinies' of established literary reputations, by (among others) **F. R. Leavis**, who edited a selection of *Calendar* articles in 1933, and who saw his own periodical **Scrutiny** as a continuation of Rickword's efforts. After adopting Marxism in the early 1930s, Rickword became associate editor of *Left Review* in 1934–6 and editor until 1938, and later edited **Christopher Caudwell**'s *Further Studies in a Dying Culture* (1949). He published six volumes of poetry and a short study of Rimbaud, but his most important work is collected in *Essays and Opinions 1921–1931* (1974) and *Literature and Society: Essays and Opinions 1931–1978* (1978).

**Riders to the Sea** A one-act tragedy by **J. M. Synge**, first performed at the **Abbey Theatre**, Dublin, in 1904. Within its very limited length, the play achieves extraordinary emotional intensity.

The single scene is the kitchen of a cottage on one of the Aran Islands. The whole life of the community is centred on the sea. When the play opens, Maurya has already lost four sons and a husband to the sea. A fifth son is missing. Only the youngest, Bartley, remains to help his mother and his two sisters. By the end of the play, the missing son's death has been confirmed and Bartley is dead too, drowned on his way to the horse fair in Connemara.

**Ridge, Lola** 1871–1941 American poet, born in Dublin, Ridge spent her childhood in Australia and New Zealand, emigrated to San Francisco in 1907, and moved to New York City in 1908. In 1918 she published *The Ghetto and Other Poems*, a collection which focuses on immigrant life in New York City and shows the influence of **imagism** on her work. Her next publication, *Sun-Up* (1920), contains poems which explore both the nature of artistic vision and the realities of working-class experience. The collection *Red Flag* (1927) includes tributes to those who lost their lives in revolutionary struggles, as does *Firehead* (1929), which was written in response to the executions of Sacco and Vanzetti in 1927. Her last volume of verse, *Dance of Fire* (1935), reflects her lifelong concern with the exploitation and martyrdom of the working class.

**Riding, Laura** 1901– American poet, short-story writer and critic. Born Laura Reichenthal in New York, she was educated at Cornell University. Her work up to 1926, signed Laura Riding Gottschalk, included poems in *The Fugitive* (see **John Crowe Ransom**) which brought her the Fugitive Group's 'Nashville prize' in 1924; she was welcomed into membership of the Fugitives shortly afterwards. At New Year 1926 she went to England, remaining abroad until 1939. During this period she worked in collaboration with **Robert Graves**, spending 1929–36 with him in Mallorca. She legally adopted the surname Riding in 1927.

*The Close Chaplet* (1926) was the first of 10 volumes of poems preceding *Collected Poems* (1938; with new introduction, 1980). She founded and operated the Seizin Press (1928–38) with Graves and was first author of their *A Survey of Modernist Poetry* (1927), containing close analysis which inspired **William Empson** and influenced the **New Criticism.** Riding, however, was 'seeking in varied writing and work with others . . . to outline ground of moral unity for modern sensibility'; she edited the 'critical summary' *Epilogue* (1935–7) and the symposium *The World and Ourselves* (1938; with new preface, 1969). Books of criticism, such as *Contemporaries and Snobs* (1928) and *Anarchism Is Not Enough* (1928), dealt with **Gertrude Stein, Wyndham Lewis** and **T. S. Eliot** among others. She also published stories, in *Progress of Stories* (1935; enlarged 1982) and *Lives of Wives* (1939; with afterword, 1987), and a novel of Homeric Troy, *A Trojan Ending* (1937; with afterword, 1984).

In the early 1940s Riding 'renounced poetry and literary affiliations, seeing language itself as essential moral meeting-ground'. In 1941 she married Schuyler B. Jackson (d. 1968), writing with him 'Rational Meaning: A New Foundation for the Definition of Words' (as yet unpublished). Laura (Riding) Jackson's contributions to American and UK magazines, resumed in 1962, include language studies, literary–personal memoirs and a developing critique of poetry as an institution – pursued in her introduction to *Selected Poems: In Five Sets* (1970). *The Telling* (1972) is her 'personal evangel'.

**Ridler, Anne (Barbara) (née Bradby)** 1912– Poet. Born in Rugby, Ridler went to Downe House School and King's College, London. In 1935–40 she worked in Faber and Faber's editorial department. She married in 1938 and has four children. Her poetic output has been relatively small: among her collections are *The Nine Bright Shiners* (1943), *The Golden Bird and Other Poems* (1951), *A Matter of Life and Death* (1959), *Selected Poems* (1961) and *Some Time After and Other Poems* (1972). She has also written verse dramas such as *Cain* (1943). Ridler is a devotional poet not only in her explicit concern with faith but in her receptivity to transcendental intimations outside formal religious contexts. She brings a quiet, traditional craft to the evocation of religious experience, married love, children, the sense of mortality, and the feelings aroused by places and paintings. Her poems comprise a distinctive minor achievement. She has affinities with **Wyatt** and **Herbert**, and with **Eliot** and **Larkin**.

*Rienzi: The Last of the Tribunes* A novel by **Edward Bulwer Lytton**, published in 1835. The hero is Cola di Rienzo, a visionary idealist who briefly succeeded in subduing the warring baronial factions of 14th-century Rome and in establishing a Republic with himself as Tribune. He was eventually turned on by the ungrateful people and torn to pieces in the streets. The story thus had a message for post-Reform Bill England: that liberty cannot be imposed upon a nation which is not politically or morally ready to accept its responsibilities.

*Rights of Man, The* A political tract by **Thomas Paine**, published in two parts, in 1791 and 1792. It was written in reply to **Edmund Burke**'s *Reflections on the Revolution in France* (1790), and its defence of the Revolution led to a law against seditious publications. Paine fled to France to escape prosecution.

The first part advocates the theory of a social contract. Sovereignty is inherent in the will of the majority and should be reaffirmed by each generation; no generation has any right to bind its successors to its own order. The social contract should be embodied in a formal constitution; where that did not exist, authority – and therefore tyranny – prevailed. The purpose of government should be the freedom and security of the individual; the rights of man include the maximum freedom of thought and action compatible with the rights of others.

In the second part Paine compares the constitutions of the United States and the new France with English institutions, to the latter's disadvantage. But the work is most interesting in the radical constructive policy which it outlines. Paine advocated, among other things, a tax on income above a certain level, pensions for the aged, the promotion of free education for the poor, family allowances, and the limitation of armaments by treaty.

**Riley, James Whitcomb** 1849–1916 American poet. Riley began his career in 1877 as a writer for the Indianapolis *Journal*. The poems he published in the paper established him as a regional writer of light and sentimental verse. He became known especially for his dialect poems, which include 'Little Orphant Annie', 'The Raggedy Man', and 'When the Frost is on the Punkin'. His great popularity as a poet and lecturer made him one of the wealthiest writers of his time. His most famous collection was *The Old Swimmin'-Hole and 'Leven More Poems* (1883). Other volumes include *Afterwhiles* (1888), *Pipes o' Pan at Zekesbury* (1889) and *Poems Here at Home* (1893).

**Riley, John** 1937–78 Poet. Born into a Methodist, working-class family in Leeds, he read English at Cambridge and became a teacher. He was killed by muggers after his return to Leeds. Founder of the Grosseteste Press and *The Grosseteste Review*, he was also a leading experimental poet. His work owed little to any native tradition but was influenced instead by **Pound**, **Olson** and **Oppen**, and by Hölderlin and Mandelstam, whom he translated. Marked by an increasingly religious perspective and an unparochial sense of place, his poems treat moments of illumination and dislocation with, at times, an elegant lyricism and subtly changing rhythms. Volumes include *Ancient and Modern* (1967), *What Reason Was* (1970), *Ways of Approaching* (1973) and *That is Today* (1978), gathered with other poems in the posthumous *Collected Poems* (1981), which contains the important long poem 'Czargrad'. Ignored by the literary establishment, Riley's work – produced during only 15 years – deserves a wider readership.

*Rime of the Ancient Mariner, The* A poem by **Samuel Taylor Coleridge**, published in *Lyrical Ballads* (1798).

The poem tells of the 'ancient mariner' who meets three gallants on the way to a marriage feast and recounts to one of them the story of his ship, driven south by a storm into the ice of the South Pole. An albatross, which appears as a bird of good omen when the ship escapes from the ice, is wilfully shot down by the mariner. His shipmates at first upbraid him but are willing to condone the crime when they seem to

A detail from one of Gustave Doré's engravings for Coleridge's *The Rime of the Ancient Mariner*. The engraving, published in 1876, is for Part I: the ship is driven towards the South Pole by a storm.

have a clear passage, which they attribute to the death of the bird. The ship is carried north into tropic seas where it is becalmed. Water runs out and the crew blame the mariner; they hang the dead albatross around his neck. After a ghost ship passes the crew begin to die. The mariner's redemption starts with a vision of the creatures of God and the beauty of His world, seen by moonlight. When he is at last able to pray, the dead bird falls from his neck into the sea and the Virgin Mary sends life-giving rain. The mariner is eventually rescued and confesses to a hermit, who shrives him; but he knows his penance will continue throughout his life. He must go on relating his story.

Coleridge wrote *The Ancient Mariner* as a ballad, a form the Romantics brought back into poetic currency. The elaborate prose gloss accompanying the poem in most modern editions was added by Coleridge when he included it in his collection *Sybilline Leaves* (1817).

**Ring and the Book, The** A poem by **Robert Browning**, published in four monthly instalments between November 1868 and February 1869. Divided into 12 books and running to 21,000 lines of blank verse, it is his most ambitious and complex work.

The story comes from a *cause célèbre* in Rome towards the end of the 17th century. Count Guido Franceschini, an impoverished nobleman of Arezzo in search of an advantageous marriage, discovered the Comparinis, an elderly Roman couple who had only one daughter, Pompilia, to inherit their property. A match was arranged and the girl delivered to Arezzo. Pompilia led a wretched life, finding her husband cruel and his younger brother frankly lustful. Her appeals to the archbishop and the governor of the province did nothing for her. Her only help came from a young canon, Giuseppe Caponsacchi, whom she persuaded to take her back to her parents in Rome. Franceschini pursued and caught them, accusing them of adultery and confining Pompilia to a convent. When she was taken to her parents' house to await the birth of her child, Pompilia learned that she had in fact been adopted from the slums of Rome. The enraged Franceschini hired four accomplices and, using Caponsacchi's name to gain entrance to the house, murdered the Comparinis. Pompilia died later of her wounds. Franceschini was arrested and brought to trial with his accomplices. Taking advantage of the fact he had been in minor orders earlier in life, he appealed to Pope Innocent XII for special privilege as a cleric. His plea was rejected. Franceschini was beheaded and his accomplices hanged on 22 February 1698.

The title of Browning's poem is founded on a number of allusions. The 'Book' is 'the Old Yellow Book', the collection of documents about the case he had found on a bookstall in Florence in 1860. The 'Ring' represents the 'pure gold' of fact found in the book, shaped and given form by the 'alloy' of the poet's imagination. The poem begins with Browning's account of his sources and his well-known invocation to the Muse, a tribute to his wife, **Elizabeth Barrett Browning**, who had died in 1861. Succeeding books narrate the story from different points of view: gossips in Rome favourable to Count Guido, those favourable to the hapless Pompilia, an impartial observer (Tertium Quid), Guido himself, Giuseppe Caponsacchi, and Pompilia on her deathbed. These are followed by statements for the defence and for the prosecution, and Pope Innocent's soliloquy on the nature of evil and the fallibility of human judgement, and his decision to let the sentence stand. The closing books are occupied by Guido's expression of abject cowardice when he realizes he is doomed, and the Pope's declaration of Pompilia's innocence.

**Ringwood, Gwen Pharis** 1910–84 Canadian playwright, born in the USA. She wrote her first play, *The Dragon of Kent* (produced in 1935), while studying at the University of Alberta. Four more plays – including her classic,

*Still Stands the House* (1938) – belong to the years 1937–9, when she attended the University of North Carolina. From 1939 she taught playwriting at the University of Alberta. Like many of her plays, her prairie tragedy *Dark Harvest* (1945) is based on local history. Her later works became more socially conscious but still dealt with local concerns. However, her move in 1953 to Williams Lake, a remote town in British Columbia, distanced her from the mainstream of Canadian drama, though she continued to write and work in community theatre. The theatre in Williams Lake was named after her in 1968. She also wrote short stories and a novel, *Younger Brother* (1959).

**Ripley, George** 1802–80 American philosopher and man of letters, born in Greenfield, Massachusetts, and educated at Harvard. His sermon, *Jesus Christ, the Same Yesterday, Today, and Forever*, delivered on 14 May 1834 at the ordination of **Orestes Brownson**, is considered an exemplary pronouncement of the **Transcendentalist** doctrine. In 1836 he helped to found the Transcendental Club and also published *Discourses on the Philosophy of Religion Addressed to Doubters Who Wish to Believe*. This was followed by *The Temptations of the Times* (1837) and *Philosophical Miscellanies* (1838). He then edited 14 volumes of translations of European idealistic philosophy, *Specimens of Foreign Standard Literature* (1838–42).

He handled the business affairs of the Transcendentalist magazine *The Dial* (1840–4) and also assisted **Margaret Fuller** in editing it. He left the ministry in 1841 and established **Brook Farm**, a Transcendentalist experiment in communal living which continued until 1847. From 1845 to 1849 he edited *The Harbinger*, a socialist weekly published by the Brook Farm Community. He became literary critic for the *New York Tribune* in 1849, and continued as critic, philosopher, and political commentator for the *Tribune* and other periodicals until his death. In 1850 he helped to found *Harper's New Monthly Magazine*. With Charles A. Dana he edited a 16-volume work entitled *The New American Cyclopedia* (1858–63).

**Rippingale, C[uthbert] E[dward]** 1825–97 Novelist. The son of a wealthy and strongly Nonconformist manufacturing family in Bradford, he studied at Lincoln's Inn before abandoning the law in favour of writing. His first novels rejected both aspects of his background, *Robert Higden: or, The Sweat Shop* (1851) attacking conditions in the clothing trade and *The Lion Yard Meeting* (1852) the hypocrisies of evangelical religion. Several years of silence followed, and Rippingale's only other novel of the 1850s – *Can These Bones Live?* (1859) – would seem to confirm that it was for him a period of spiritual crisis. Later novels combined High Anglican fervour with a love of medieval chivalry. *The Testing of Sir Richard Fortescue* (1865) and *The Trials of Sir Clarence* (1872) are typical of the books which enjoyed a modest success in appropriate circles and won him praise from **Kenelm Henry Digby** and, more reservedly, **Charlotte M. Yonge**. Toward the end of his life Rippingale devoted his energies to a campaign for standards of purity in stained-glass windows, contributing much of his inherited fortune and many of his own designs to this cause.

**Rise of Silas Lapham, The** A novel by **William Dean Howells**, serialized in *Century Magazine* in 1884–5, and published in volume form in 1885.

Colonel Silas Lapham, originally a Vermont farmer, has risen to wealth through his successful paint manufacturing business. He moves his family to Boston, and urges his wife and daughters to enter fashionable society. He looks forward to a new life, but thinks back on his old business practices with increasing moral discomfort. The family does not fit in well with the high-class Boston set, though one of this set's representatives, Tom Corey, falls in love with the older Lapham daughter, Penelope. The younger daughter, Irene, convinces herself and Penelope that Tom is really in love with her; Penelope refuses his proposal and does not attend the Coreys' dinner party. Her father does, however, and gets drunk, revealing himself as a misfit in genteel Boston society. Meanwhile his business speculations have been unsuccessful and he is threatened with bankruptcy. His partner urges him to save himself by selling some mill property to a British firm, even though he knows it to be worthless. After a struggle with himself, he decides not to make the sale. Economically bankrupt, socially disgraced, but morally restored, he returns to Vermont. Penelope and Tom run away to Mexico to escape the rigid social barriers that have created such unhappiness for them in New England.

**Ritchie, Anne (Isabella) Thackeray, Lady** 1837–1919 Novelist and biographer. Elder daughter of the novelist **Thackeray**, she received an unconventional upbringing as a result of her mother's confinement in a mental asylum, spending her formative years with her grandparents in Paris, and subsequently in her father's bachelor home in London. Paris is the setting of her first novel, *The Story of Elizabeth* (1863), which was followed by seven others, of which *Old Kensington* (1873) and *Mrs Dymond* (1885) are still remembered. In 1877 she married her cousin Richmond Ritchie, a civil servant in the India Office, and they had two children. Although **Virginia Woolf** and others have paid tribute to the impressionistic charm of her novels, her enduring literary work was as a memorialist of the great Victorian writers she had known, notably in her *Records of Tennyson, Ruskin and Robert and Elizabeth Browning* (1892) and *Chapters from Some Memoirs* (1894), and in the introductions she wrote to the 13-volume 'Biographical Edition' of her father's works (1894–8). She is portrayed as Mrs Hilbery in Virginia Woolf's novel *Night and Day*.

**Ritson, Joseph** 1753–1803 Antiquary. Trained as a conveyancer, Ritson early adopted a strict vegetarian diet after reading **Mandeville**'s *Fable of the Bees*, and to this diet has been ascribed his remarkable acerbity in literary disputes and his eventual insanity. His own excessively punctilious scholarship is best seen in his two-volume accumulation of allusions to **Robin Hood** in popular literature which appeared in 1795, with woodcuts by **Bewick**. He issued numerous similar anthologies of popular literature. Most of his literary productions were vitriolic attacks on what he saw as the shortcomings of other editors. His principal targets were **Thomas Warton**'s *History of English Poetry*, **Bishop Percy**'s *Reliques of Ancient English Poetry* and the **Shakespeare** edition of **Johnson** and **Steevens**. His aggressive behaviour was such that he appears to have retained the friendship only of **Surtees** and **Scott**.

**Rivals, The** A comedy by **Richard Brinsley Sheridan**, first performed at **Covent Garden Theatre**, London, in 1775. It was a failure on its opening night and Sheridan rewrote parts of it before its successful second performance 11 days later.

Among the fashionable visitors to Bath is Captain Jack Absolute, humbly disguised as Ensign Beverley to suit the romantic yearnings for love and poverty of his beloved Lydia

A 19th-century illustration for *The Rivals*. Sir Anthony Absolute and his son, Captain Absolute; Lydia Languish and her aunt, Mrs Malaprop, in Act IV, scene 2. Victoria & Albert Theatre Museum, London.

Languish. Lydia's friend Julia, much more robust, is loved by the self-tormenting man of feeling, Faulkland. The play brings the lovers to a happy agreement, after many adventures, and despite the obstacles erected by Lydia's aunt, Mrs Malaprop, and the impecunious Irish knight, Sir Lucius O'Trigger.

Mrs Malaprop achieved a fame beyond the play in which she appears, and her uncertain grasp of long words ('No caparisons, miss, if you please') has given the term 'malapropism' to the language.

**Road to Ruin, The** A comedy by **Thomas Holcroft**, first produced at **Covent Garden** in 1792 and published the same year. It was translated and played in Holland, Denmark and Germany.

Harry Dornton's extravagance causes a run on his father's bank and brings it close to ruin. In love with Miss Warren, he resolves to save the house by marrying the girl's wealthy mother, an unpleasant woman who surrounds herself with sycophantic admirers. Among them is Goldfinch, heavily in debt from his idle fashionable way of life, who is determined to marry Mrs Warren himself. In the end the bank is saved by the genius of Old Dornton's chief clerk, the grim old Mr Sulky. Harry, a reformed character, is able to marry Miss Warren, while her odious mother is disinherited by the discovery of a new will.

**Road to Wigan Pier, The** A work by **George Orwell**, commissioned and published by the **Left Book Club** in 1937.

Orwell's account of 'the great industrial wastelands' of Yorkshire and Lancashire began as an attempt to write the urban equivalent of **Cobbett**'s *Rural Rides*. His mission, as he states it at the beginning of Part Two, is twofold: 'partly . . . to see what mass-unemployment is like at its worst, partly in order to see the most typical section of the English working class at close quarters'. The first prompts a damning record of poverty, apathy, malnutrition, and overcrowding; the second leads him to confront his own class prejudices ('When I was fourteen or fifteen I was an odious little snob, but no worse than other boys of my own age and class'). Fashionable 'bourgeois socialism' provokes his scorn, and there are excellent analyses of middle-class prejudices about 'the lower classes'.

The book concludes with an impassioned exhortation to the Socialist movement to unite lower-middle and working classes, whose interests Orwell believes are essentially the same. This line of polemic did not please his sponsors but, despite Victor Gollancz's reservations, the work proved successful and has remained a classic of literary journalism.

***Roaring Girl, The**, or, Moll Cutpurse* A comedy by **Thomas Middleton** and **Thomas Dekker**, first produced in 1610 and published in 1611. The play is a comment on the notoriety of Moll Cutpurse, a thief and forger whose real name was Mary Frith; she was not apprehended until 1612, when she was sentenced to public penance at St Paul's Cross as part of her punishment.

Sebastian Wentgrave and Mary Fitzallard are betrothed but Sebastian's father, the mean and mean-spirited Sir Alexander, forbids the match. To force his hand Sebastian pays court to the notorious Moll Cutpurse. Moll herself is touched by the young lovers' plight; she agrees to follow Sebastian's scheme and also to be his means of contact with Mary. Sebastian announces that he has fallen in love with Moll Cutpurse and must marry her. The distracted old villain, Sir Alexander, sends his unpleasant servant Trapdoor to worm his way into Moll's confidence and then betray her. But Trapdoor is unequal to the task, and Moll and Sebastian extract Sir Alexander's consent by a carefully staged wedding.

***Rob Roy*** A novel by **Sir Walter Scott**, published in 1817. It is set in the north of England and Scotland in the early 18th century.

The story follows the adventures of Francis Osbaldistone, banished from London by his father, a successful merchant. At the house of his uncle, Sir Hildebrand, he meets Rashleigh, the greedy and malicious youngest son, and Diana Vernon, Rashleigh's cousin on whom he has designs. When Francis is favourably received by Diana, Rashleigh determines to destroy him. He is already plotting to ruin Francis's father. At the prompting of Diana, Francis goes to the Highlands, accompanied by Bailie Nicol Jarvie, to seek the help of Rob Roy MacGregor, the outlaw. In the Highlands Francis witnesses a clash between clansmen and the king's troops and Rob Roy's escape. With the help of the spirited Diana and Rob Roy, Francis is able to unmask Rashleigh's villainy and regain the money which the latter has embezzled from Francis's father. Rashleigh betrays them to the government and Rob Roy kills him.

The historical Rob Roy, a drover, became a powerful and dangerous outlaw when he and his clan were proscribed as Jacobite sympathizers. He was a ruthless opponent of the government but famous for disinterested kindness and his partisanship on behalf of the oppressed. In 1716 he came under the protection of the Duke of Argyle and assumed the name of Campbell.

***Robene and Makyne*** A Middle Scots poem by **Robert Henryson**. Owing something to the traditions of both the *pastourelle* and the debate poem, it tells how the shepherd Robene refuses Makyne's love but is scorned in turn when he later falls in love with her.

***Robert Elsmere*** A novel by Mrs Humphry Ward (**Mary Augusta Ward**) published in 1888.

Robert Elsmere is a young Anglican parson whose faith is untroubled during undergraduate days at Oxford despite encountering two characteristic strains of 19th-century unorthodoxy in the morbidly critical spiritual paralysis of Edward Langham and the philosophic idealism of the Hegelian Grey. After his marriage to a girl of the strictest Anglican Evangelical piety, 'the Thirty-nine Articles in the flesh', Elsmere takes a country living where he combines a life of practical parochial work in the style of **Charles Kingsley** with scientific interests and historical studies. The local squire, Roger Wendover, places at his disposal an extensive library which covers all the main movements of modern thought from the **Oxford Movement** and the **Higher Criticism** to works of more general philosophical and historical enquiry. The squire, a dry rationalist, is the notorious author of a book attacking religious orthodoxy and is engaged on a work on the nature and value of historical testimony. Elsmere's studies gradually lead him to abandon his faith in miracles and in Christ as anything more than a symbol of the divine spirit at work in humanity. His conscience demands that he leave the Anglican church and find a new way of expressing a deeply religious, but undogmatic, piety. Eventually he founds the New Brotherhood of Christianity, an educational settlement in the London slums.

The drama of the novel derives from the emotional anguish experienced by Elsmere as he makes a spiritual pilgrimage which inevitably opens a chasm between the honest doubter and his orthodox wife. In this respect the novel undoubtedly draws upon the strain imposed on Mrs Ward's own parents by her father's changing religious allegiances. The tenor of the novel's discussion of 19th-century religious and sceptical thought is in general closer to the mid than the late 19th-century atmosphere, but the portraits the novel was commonly supposed to offer of **T. H. Green**, **Walter Pater** and **Mark Pattison** ensured its topical success. Gladstone's lengthy review in the *Nineteenth Century* boosted its sales yet further.

**Robert of Gloucester** *fl.* 1250–1300 A monk at Gloucester abbey involved in the writing of a Middle English verse **chronicle**, 12,000 lines long in its earliest version. He was probably the principal author, revising the early part of the work and writing the last section; two other writers apparently worked on the chronicle at some stage.

The chronicle covers the history of England

from the beginning of the reign of Stephen to the death of Henry III. It combines historical fact and legend, a large part of it being devoted to King Arthur. The sources are diverse, ranging from the pseudo-historical **Geoffrey of Monmouth** to more reliable records such as the Annals of Winchester. The most valued portion of the chronicle, apparently reliable and probably first-hand, is the account of the last part of the reign of Henry III, including the battle of Evesham (1265), the death of Simon de Montfort and the town and gown riots of Oxford (1263). The work conveys an enthusiasm for accurate representation and a love of England. It is characterized by sincerity and directness of style, and the author's generosity of feeling.

**Robert the Devil** A popular story of the Middle Ages found in a variety of forms – **exemplum**, romance, drama, ballad – throughout western Europe. The story is the basis of the Middle English romance, *Sir Gowther*.

**Roberts, Sir Charles G[eorge] D[ouglas]** 1860–1943 Poet, writer of short stories and novels, called 'the father of Canadian literature'. Born near Fredericton, he was educated at the University of New Brunswick. He taught for some years before becoming editor of *The Week* in Toronto, where he met and encouraged many young writers. He was professor at King's College in Nova Scotia and later lived in New York, Paris and London, returning to Canada in 1925. He was a prolific writer, producing ten books of poetry – the first being *Orion and Other Poems* (1880) – several romances, and 18 collections of short stories, including *Earth's Enigmas* (1896), *The Kindred of the Wild* (1902), *The Watchers of the Trails* (1904) and *Kings in Exile* (1909). His earlier poetry, found in volumes such as *In Divers Tones* (1886) and *Songs of the Common Day* (1893), is generally thought his best. His *Selected Poems* were published in 1936. He was knighted in 1935.

**Roberts, Michael (William Edward)** 1902–48 Anthologist, poet and critic. Born in Bournemouth, he was educated at King's College, London, and Trinity College, Cambridge. He worked as a teacher, as a wartime propagandist and as a college principal. Roberts's first successes were the Marxist anthologies *New Signatures* (1932) and *New Country* (1933), which featured new poets such as **W. H. Auden**, **C. Day-Lewis**, **William Empson**, **John Lehmann** and **Charles Madge**. His reputation as anthologist was confirmed by the influential *Faber Book of Modern Verse* (1936), which introduced **George Barker**, **David Gascoyne** and **Dylan Thomas** and omitted the Georgians (see *Georgian Poetry*). Roberts's poetry, published in *These Our Matins* (1930), *Poems* (1936), *Orion Marches*

(1939) and the posthumous *Collected Poems* (1958), is now neglected, despite the appearance of a *Selected Poems and Prose* (1980). The poems evoke bleak, mountain landscapes, and explore man's need to accept responsibility for his own life. His diverse prose writings include a fine study of **T. E. Hulme** (1938), *The Recovery of the West* (1941), and the unfinished *The Estate of Man* (1951), which can now be seen as a pioneering ecological work.

**Robertson, Thomas William** 1829–71 Dramatist. Born in Newark, the eldest of 22 children in a theatrical family, Robertson worked on and behind the stage from his childhood to his death. Only a few of the 50 or so plays and adaptations for which he was responsible are of lasting value, but those few are of enormous significance in the development of English drama during the 19th century. It is no exaggeration to say that the six comedies by Robertson, presented at the Prince of Wales's Theatre in 1865–70, set a standard for realistic attention to domestic detail that prepared the way for a revival of serious drama. Their effect on acting styles was more immediate and quite as profound. The best are *Society* (1865), *Ours* (1866), *Caste* (1867) and *School* (1869). *Play* (1868) and *M. P.* (1870) were and are less successful. The term 'cup-and-saucer drama' was applied to Robertson and his imitators. **Pinero**'s warm portrait of him as Tom Wrench in *Trelawny of the 'Wells'* invites more serious attention to a writer who was one of the first to combine the vision of the director and the art of the playwright.

**Robertson, William** 1721–93 Historian. Born at Borthwick, Midlothian, and educated at the common school there, Dalkeith grammar school and Edinburgh University, Robertson was licensed as a preacher in the Church of Scotland in 1741. His *History of Scotland* (1759) was described by **Horace Walpole** as 'what all the world now allows to be the best modern history', and was also praised by **Burke**, **Chesterfield**, **Gibbon** and **Mallet**. Its success was such he was elected principal of Edinburgh University in 1762 and the following year Moderator of the General Assembly of the Church of Scotland, in which capacity he established the independence of the Church from government interference. His *History of Charles V* (1769) was praised by Voltaire and said by Catherine the Great to be 'le compagnon constant de tous mes voyages', while the *History of America* (1777), a work of great popular appeal as a result of the almost simultaneous American War of Independence, is believed to have influenced **Keats**'s view of Cortez. Robertson was one of the original members of **Allan Ramsay**'s Select

Society, and was a major force in the Scottish Enlightenment.

**Robin Hood** An outlaw hero of English folk-tale who first emerged over 600 years ago. The stories attached to Robin Hood and his band of outlaws have changed considerably over the centuries, his continuing struggle against the sheriff of Nottingham and his poaching of the king's deer being their only constant features. Robin Hood's most famous characteristic, his practice of robbing from the rich to give to the poor, is a later addition to the legend and does not feature in the medieval stories. His companions Little John and Will Scarlet (or Scarlok) appear in the earliest versions, but Maid Marian was not introduced until the 16th century. According to the legend, Robin always triumphed over the corrupt forces of law and order and was only killed when he had his blood let by a malicious nun. The first reference to him dates from the last quarter of the 14th century and suggests that he was already a famous figure. The extant parts of the medieval legend are preserved in five poems and a fragment of a play. Several historical figures have been identified as the 'real' Robin Hood, but there is little evidence to support any particular claim or, indeed, to suggest that he was ever anything but a legendary character.

**Robinson, Edwin Arlington** 1869–1935 American poet, born in Head Tide, Maine. His childhood in Gardiner, Maine, provided the background for 'Tilbury Town', the fictional location of many of his poems. His first collection of poems, *The Torrent and the Night Before* (1896), was revised, expanded, and reissued as *The Children of the Night* in 1897. His third book, *Captain Craig* (1902), proved to be the turning-point in his career. Theodore Roosevelt became interested in his work, and secured him a job at the Custom House in New York City. *The Town Down the River* (1910) was successful enough to allow him to give up his job and devote his energies to writing. *The Man Against The Sky* appeared in 1916, and was followed in 1917 by the first part of his Arthurian trilogy, *Merlin*. The volumes *Lancelot* (1920) and *Tristram* (1927) completed his reworking of the medieval legend.

Robinson's mature poetry reveals strong counter-romantic tendencies and is concerned with some of the questions raised by the crisis of World War I. His shorter works in particular are characterized by their direct style and often ironic treatment of subject matter, as in the frequently anthologized 'Richard Cory' and 'Miniver Cheevy'. The 1920s and 1930s were the poet's most productive years. He published *The Three Taverns* in 1920 and *Avon's Harvest* in 1921. His *Collected Poems* (1921) and *The Man*

*Who Died Twice* (1924) were both awarded Pulitzer Prizes. His other publications include *Roman Bartholow* (1923), *Dionysus in Doubt* (1925), *Cavender's House* (1929), *The Glory of the Nightingales* (1930), *Matthias at the Door* (1931), *Nicodemus* (1932), *Talifer* (1933), *Amaranth* (1934) and *King Jasper* (1935). The volume *Sonnets 1889–1927* was published in 1928.

**Robinson, (Esmé Stuart) Lennox** 1886–1958 Irish playwright, actor, director and critic. Born in County Cork, Robinson was associated with the **Abbey Theatre**, Dublin, from 1908, when his first play *The Clancy Name* was produced there, until his death. His work includes serious plays about Irish politics like *Patriots* (1912), *The Dreamers* (1913), *The Lost Leader* (1918) and *The Big House* (1926) and comedies, like *The White-Headed Boy* (1916), the one-act *Crabbed Youth and Age* (1922), *The Far-Off Hills* (1928) and the more experimental *Church Street* (1934). His commitment to the Irish theatre is adroitly illustrated in *Drama at Inish* (1933), also known by the title *Is Life Worth Living?* Robinson wrote *A History of the Abbey Theatre* (1951) and an autobiographical memoir, *Curtain Up* (1942), and edited a useful collection of lectures under the title *The Irish Theatre* (1939).

**Robinson, Henry Crabb** 1775–1867 Lawyer, journalist and diarist. Born in Bury St Edmunds, Robinson was a solicitor at Colchester, and from 1813 to 1828 a barrister on the Norfolk circuit. In 1800–5 he lived in Germany, where he matriculated as a student at the University of Jena in 1802. During this period he met many of the leading German poets and thinkers, including Goethe, Schiller and Herder, and on his return to England was influential in making German literature and philosophy more widely known to British readers. In 1807 he was appointed foreign editor of *The Times*, and was its first war correspondent during the Spanish Peninsular War in 1808–9. A Liberal and Dissenter, he was active in the anti-slavery campaign, and was one of the founders of both University College, London, and the Athenaeum Club. He is, however, now chiefly remembered for his voluminous diaries and letters, first published in 1869, which are a valuable source for the early Romantic period. His friends included **Blake** (of whose last years his is the only first-hand account), **Wordsworth**, **Lamb**, **Hazlitt** and **Coleridge**, of whose public lectures he made careful notes. A renowned conversationalist, Robinson was noted for his Sunday breakfast parties which brought together poets and men of affairs.

***Robinson Crusoe*** (*The Life and Strange Surprising Adventures of Robinson Crusoe, of York, Mariner. Written by himself*) A prose romance by **Daniel**

**Defoe**, published in 1719 when the author was practically 60, and the most enduring of his many fictional works. Although it subsequently assumed a near-mythological status, the story is based squarely upon the true account of Alexander Selkirk, a fugitive sailor who went to sea in 1704 under **William Dampier** and was put ashore (at his own request) on an uninhabited island in the Pacific, where he survived until his rescue in 1709 by **Woodes Rogers**. On his return, he published an account of his experiences, this being a period when travel literature was at the height of popular fashion.

Defoe's imaginative reworking of this essential material therefore enjoys a pronounced degree of realism. Crusoe is a mariner who takes to the sea despite parental warnings, and suffers a number of misfortunes at the hands of Barbary pirates and the elements, finally being shipwrecked off South America. A combination of systematic salvaging, resourcefulness and good fortune enables him to exist on his island for some 28 years, two months and nineteen days (according to the painstaking journal in which the adventures are recorded) during which time he needs to adapt to his alien environment, demonstrate the self-sufficiency so admired by Defoe himself, and come to terms with his own spiritual listlessness. If, as a psychological study in isolation, the book now seems inconsistent and even unconvincing, it should be remembered that the novel was then barely in its infancy, and *Robinson Crusoe* owes more to the previous literary pedigree of Puritan spiritual autobiographies and allegories (**Bunyan**'s *Grace Abounding* was a strong influence); it is at any rate a deliberate amalgam of the specific and the general. The narrative interest combines typical characteristics of the adventure story (for instance, Crusoe's horrified discovery of a strange footprint in the sand) and the exotic fascination of travel literature with a fable more widely representative of human behaviour under conditions of difficulty and pressure.

*Robinson Crusoe* enjoyed instant and permanent success, and has become one of those classics of English literature which (like *Gulliver's Travels*, perhaps, or *Pilgrim's Progress*) appeal at various levels to adults and children alike. It has been subjected to a welter of critical attention, much of which is oddly inconclusive. The economic aspects of Defoe's fiction have in particular prompted the interest of recent scholars: Crusoe's survival and his enterprising behaviour are seen as expressions of Defoe's own belief in the mercantilist mentality of the expanding British Empire (though he was in fact quite sceptical about many economic projects), the marooned Crusoe manufacturing his clothes and educating Man Friday being emblematic of the superiority of civilized man and the nature of the Noble Savage. By com-

'Robinson Crusoe saving his goods out of the wreck of the ship.' An illustration from an edition of Defoe's novel published in 1726. *Robinson Crusoe* was first published in 1719.

parison, the story has been scrutinized for religious and numerological significance, Crusoe's sojourn on the island being interpreted as a period of spiritual gestation and rebirth according to the religious sentiments of the book's Dissenting author.

The truth seems to be that *Robinson Crusoe* draws its strength from this very combination of disparate echoes and shapes: Jonah, Job, Everyman, the Prodigal Son, the colonial explorer and the proto-industrialist are all elements which feature in this archetypal tale in various ways. There was an unsubstantiated rumour that Defoe met Selkirk in person, in 1711; the source of some of the actual details of the book is ultimately less important than the way Defoe managed to transform them into a configuration which has appealed to people's imaginations ever since. Both **Scott** and **Coleridge** were great admirers of the book, despite its occasional raggedness, and it has since been translated into numerous languages.

Defoe continued the story in *The Farther Adventures of Robinson Crusoe* (1719) in which he revisits the island and loses Friday in an attack by savages, and *The Serious Reflections . . . of Robinson Crusoe* (1720), neither of which has achieved a wide recognition outside scholarly circles.

**Rochester, John Wilmot, 2nd Earl of** 1647–80 Poet and wit. Born at Ditchley, near Woodstock, and educated briefly at Wadham College, Oxford, Rochester became one of the most dashing and notorious personalities of the Restoration, a peculiar combination of libertine and intellectual, a favourite of Charles II, who continually fell into disrepute. He distinguished himself by gallant action in the second Dutch War (1665) and was involved in a number of subsequent civil 'imbroglios' for which he was duly banished from court. He once claimed not to have been sober for five years at a stretch; he kidnapped Elizabeth Malet (a wealthy heiress) whom he married in 1667 and surprised by becoming a relatively attentive husband according to the standards of his day. It was no coincidence for such an inveterately posturing personality that one of his mistresses should have been Elizabeth Barry, one of the first really celebrated English actresses. He was intermittently the patron of several poets, and was rumoured to have been responsible for the vicious attack on **Dryden** in Covent Garden (1679), when the poet was severely beaten. The subject of rumour and legend, Rochester's exuberant life-style caused his health to collapse in 1679, alcohol and venereal disease having taken their toll, though he died a reformed character, after the religious instruction of **Gilbert Burnet** during his final months persuaded him to renounce **Hobbes** and scepticism and embrace the Christian faith.

Little of Rochester's poetic output was actually published during his lifetime, but much of it was evidently designed for clandestine circulation in manuscript form, being scurrilous or pornographic in nature ('Signior Dildo', 'The Imperfect Enjoyment', 'A Ramble in St James's Park' and 'The Maim'd Debauchee'). As a satirical poet Rochester was more accomplished than his 'minor' status now suggests; he was later an influence on **Pope** ('Upon Nothing' is recognizably in the paradoxical style of Augustan wit) but his best-known poem is 'A Satire Against Reason and Mankind' (1675), which ranges the sensualist against the rationalist attitude towards the capabilities of the human mind. His other two substantial achievements are the 'Letter from Artemisia in the Town to Chloe in the Country', a pungent social satire on dissembling and gullibility, and the superbly contemptuous 'Allusion to Horace: The 10th Satire of the First Book', both of which establish Rochester as an intelligent and skilful versifier. His inclination for physical self-indulgence cut short one of the most vivacious poetic imaginations of the Restoration years.

**rocking feet** See **metre**.

*Roderick Hudson* A novel by **Henry James**, first published as a serial in *The Atlantic Monthly* in 1875, and then in volume form in 1876. The author revised it for publication in England in 1879.

Roderick Hudson, an amateur sculptor, is taken to Europe by Rowland Mallet, a wealthy connoisseur who is impressed by his talent. In Rome he introduces Roderick to his circle, which includes the French sculptor, Gloriani, who is certain that the young American's talent will never develop. Roderick meets Christina Light, the daughter of an expatriate American widow; he is fascinated by her and deserts his work. In order to force him back into reality, Rowland brings his mother and fiancée, Mary Garland, from New England. Their arrival seems to have its desired effect, and Roderick executes a fine bust of his mother. But then Christina, urged on by her ambitious mother, marries Prince Casamassima (see *The Princess Casamassima*), and Roderick's work comes to a complete halt. Once again Rowland attempts to rekindle Roderick's interest by arranging a visit to Switzerland for Mary, Mrs Hudson, Roderick, and himself. Unfortunately Christina is there too and Roderick borrows money from Mary so that he can follow her. This provokes Rowland to a furious outburst and he condemns Roderick as an ungrateful egoist. Roderick walks off into the mountains where he is caught in a thunderstorm. He is found dead, and it is unclear whether or not he committed suicide.

*Roderick Random, The Adventures of* The first novel by **Tobias Smollett**, published in 1748.

Roderick Random's father disappears and the boy is left in the care of his grandfather, who ill-treats him and leaves him penniless when he dies. Roderick is befriended by his uncle, Tom Bowling, a lieutenant in the navy, and decides to go to London to make his fortune; an old schoolfriend, Hugh Strap, accompanies him as valet. The journey bristles with crude adventures. In London, Roderick qualifies as a surgeon's mate but discovers that a bribe is necessary to secure a commission, not qualifications. He becomes assistant to a French apothecary, but is seized by the press gang.

Forced into service as a common sailor on the man o'war *Thunder*, Roderick proves his qualifications and becomes a surgeon's mate, after all. The *Thunder* takes part in the siege of Cartagena (1741) and Roderick suffers many humiliations and misadventures. While returning to England he is shipwrecked and robbed and, lying naked on the shore, is found and

The frontispiece to Vol. II of *Roderick Random*, 1748. Roderick discovers his long-lost uncle, Tom Bowling, in a tavern.

taken care of by a middle-aged woman poet, whose footman he becomes. He falls in love with the poet's niece, Narcissa, but the presence of suitors of considerable means obliges him to leave. He is kidnapped by smugglers and taken to France, where he finds his uncle Tom Bowling and a 'Monsieur d'Estrapes' – his old friend Strap. The two return to London in their original partnership: Strap sets up Roderick, acts as his valet, and is going to aid and abet Roderick's design to marry an heiress.

Melinda Goosetrap is a likely quarry, but her mother is not impressed. At Bath, Roderick meets Narcissa again. He loses all he has at the gaming tables and, returning to London, is thrown into a debtors' prison. Tom Bowling obtains his release, and takes him aboard his own ship as a surgeon for a trading trip. During the voyage they encounter a wealthy trader, Don Roderigo; he proves to be Roderick's father, who had been disinherited by the evil grandfather and had left the country to make his fortune. They return to England and Roderick marries Narcissa. Strap marries her maid, Miss Williams. Roderick repurchases the family estate and has a rewarding time snubbing those

relatives who, formerly, had scorned him as an impecunious dependant.

Modelled on Le Sage's *Gil Blas*, *Roderick Random* has the savage energy of true **picaresque**. Unlike later novelists in the English tradition – including those whom he strongly influenced, like **Dickens** – Smollett saw no need to soften the roguery of his villains or temper the coarseness of their adventures. It is not a book which can engage the reader's sympathy or moral approval, for there is hardly a pleasant episode in the whole narrative; there is, moreover, a marked obsession with filth and violence. What commands attention is the unabashed vitality of the writing and the vivid portrayal of life in London, at sea and, in later chapters, in fashionable society.

**Roethke, Theodore (Huebner)** 1908–63 American poet, born in Saginaw, Michigan, and educated at the University of Michigan and at Harvard. His first volume of poetry, *Open House*, was published in 1941. In it, as in much of his early work, he returns to the landscapes of his childhood as a means of reconstructing transcendent moments of 'waking'. His second volume, *The Lost Son and Other Poems*, appeared in 1948. In 1954 he received the Pulitzer Prize for *The Waking: Poems, 1933–1953* (1953). *Words for the Wind: The Collected Verse of Theodore Roethke* (1957) won him the 1958 Bollingen Prize and the 1959 National Book Award. His later volumes, which include a good deal of love poetry, are *I am! Says the Lamb* (1961), *Sequence, Sometimes Metaphysical, Poems* (1963) and *The Far Field* (1964). Two collections of prose pieces appeared posthumously: *The Contemporary Poet as Artist and Critic* (1964) and *On the Poet and His Craft: Selected Prose* (1965).

**Rogers, Samuel** 1763–1855 Poet. The son of a banker, Rogers was born at Stoke Newington, then just north of London. He succeeded to his father's fortune and took the opportunity to indulge his fancy for writing poetry. A generous patron at whose table the cultured society of London was always welcome, he commissioned Turner as illustrator for an edition of his *Italy* (1822–8), for which he had followed Childe Harold's footsteps as a tribute to **Byron**. The volume enjoyed considerable popular success. He declined the office of **Poet Laureate** on the death of **Wordsworth**. Among his volumes of verse are *Ode to Superstition* (1786), *The Pleasures of Memory* (1792), *Columbus* (1810) and *Jacqueline* (1814). *Recollections of the Table-Talk of Samuel Rogers* (1856; edited by Alexander Dyce) and *Recollections* (1859; edited by William Sharpe) are valuable sources of information on the artistic life of the period.

**Rogers, Will** 1879–1935 American actor and

humorist, born William Penn Adair, of Cherokee ancestry, in Oologh Indian territory, in what is now Oklahoma. As a young man he travelled the world, and during the Boer War worked as a horse-breaker for the British in South Africa. On his return to the USA he worked as a rodeo cowboy in vaudeville shows, and for several years, starting in 1913, performed in the *Ziegfeld Follies*. In 1919 he became an actor, first in silent films and later in the 'talkies'. In 1926 he began writing newspaper articles which commented humorously on American politics and society; eventually his column was syndicated and reached an estimated 40 million readers. His books include *The Cowboy Philosopher on Prohibition* (1919), *The Illiterate Digest* (1924), *Letters of a Self-Made Diplomat to His President* (1927) and *There's Not a Bathing Suit in Russia* (1927). He died in a plane crash in Alaska. *The Autobiography of Will Rogers* appeared in 1949, and a collection of his newspaper pieces, *Sanity is Where You Find It*, in 1955.

**Rogers, Woodes** d. 1732  A captain in command of two privateering ships, the *Duke* and *Duchess*, during an expedition to the Pacific (1708–11), Rogers wrote a vivid account in his journal, published as *A Cruising Voyage Round the World* (1712). His pilot was **William Dampier**, and Rogers tells of the seizure of Guayaquil in Ecuador from the Spaniards, who were forced to ransom the city, and the captain of a galleon from Manila. Also described is Rogers's visit to the island of Juan Fernández, where they found 'a man clothed in goat-skins, who seemed wilder than the original owners of his apparel'; his name was Alexander Selkirk, whose strange adventures gave **Defoe** the idea for *Robinson Crusoe*. Rogers became Governor of the Bahamas (1718–21 and 1729–32), where he was chiefly responsible for the suppression of piracy.

**Roget's Thesaurus**  Peter Mark Roget (1779–1869), an Edinburgh-trained doctor, spent most of his life in medical and scientific research. His most famous work, however, is his *Thesaurus of English Words and Phrases, Classified and Arranged So As to Facilitate the Expression of Ideas and Assist in Literary Composition* (1852). Roget's taxonomic arrangement of the vocabulary of his day was based on a logically ordered system of six major categories, subdivided into 1000 specific topics. Essentially he presented a classification of 'Ideas', and his categories are often so wide as to be unwieldy. Although most topics do contain self-consistent groupings of vocabulary, many concepts are scattered almost capriciously about the *Thesaurus*. Despite, therefore, its elaborate conceptual framework, which lies behind so many of the revisions, abridgements and related collections, 'Roget' is more often than not viewed as a collection of synonyms. Users generally consult the alphabetically arranged index of common words at the back as a way of finding their way to a topic appropriate to their needs. The *Thesaurus* went through 28 editions in Roget's own lifetime, and editorship descended to his son and later his grandson. The most recent edition (1984), which was much publicized because of its 'positive' editorial treatment of 'sexist' language, also differs markedly from its 1962 predecessor in its treatment of particular areas of the vocabulary – technology, the media, drug abuse and medicine, for example – but retains the traditional framework.

**Roland and Vernagu**  A **verse romance** in **tail-rhyme** stanzas written before 1330–40, probably in the East Midlands. It is the first part of the composite romance *Charlemagne and Roland*, the second fragment of which is **Otuel and Roland**. Its source is the Old French prose *Estoire de Charlemagne* (1206), a translation of the Latin prose *Chronicle of the Pseudo-Turpin* (c.1140). *Roland and Vernagu* relates Charlemagne's journey to Constantinople and return with the relics of the Passion, followed by his conquest of Spain and a long episode in which Roland defeats the Saracen giant Vernagu in a duel after showing him charity and explaining the Christian faith to him. The structure is episodic, with lengthy descriptions of the relics and miracles connected with them or independent of them. The romance is incomplete, breaking off as Otuel hears of Vernagu's death.

**Rolfe, Frederick William**  1860–1913  Novelist and short-story writer, who also styled himself Baron Corvo and Fr (i.e. Father) Rolfe. A Londoner, born in Cheapside and educated in Camden Town, he turned to teaching after he failed to get into Oxford. He became a Roman Catholic convert in 1886 and spent the next few years training for the priesthood, first at Oscott and then at Scots College in Rome, before being finally rejected in 1890. He remained in Rome, calling himself Baron Corvo, but returned to England before the end of the decade to begin his career as a writer. *Stories Toto Told Me* (1898), which first appeared in **The Yellow Book**, was followed by the expanded collection, *In His Own Image* (1901). Rolfe's fascination with late medieval and Renaissance Italy was expressed in *Chronicles of the House of Borgia* (1901), a collection of essays defending the Papal family, and informed two romances, *Don Tarquinio* (1905) and *Don Renato* (1909). His paranoid sensibility and ornate prose style were best displayed in *Hadrian the Seventh* (1904), the story of how George Arthur Rose, a failed priest clearly modelled on the author, is elected Pope. His most famous book, it was successfully adapted for the stage by Peter Luke in 1968. Two posthumously published works belong to the same category of extravagantly fictionalized autobiography: *The Desire and Pursuit of the Whole* (1934), which takes a characteristically savage revenge on Rolfe's friends and patrons, and *Nicholas Crabbe* (1958), based on the unhappy years at the start of his career as a writer. A. J. A. Symons's *The Quest for Corvo* (1934) is a classic account of the biographer's difficulty in separating the reality of Rolfe's life from the lies, fantasy and mystery in which he delighted to shroud it.

**Rolle of Hampole, Richard** *c.*1300–49 Born in Thornton, Yorkshire, he was apparently educated at Oxford, though he never graduated. He was not ordained and there is no evidence to suggest he entered orders, but he became a hermit while still young, living in various parts of Yorkshire, finally near a Cistercian convent in Hampole, where he died. He wrote English and Latin didactic and mystic prose and religious lyrics. His best-known and principal mystical work, *De Incendio Amoris*, was a product of his youth and is marred by attacks on his opponents and by preciosity. He taught that the contemplative must renounce the world and the self in total love of God to receive divine inspiration and revelation, and that knowledge would come in Heaven but love must be exercised on earth. His best writing is to be found in his lyrics on God's love and the Crucified Christ, characterized by fervour and sincerity and devoid of the egocentricity of his prose.

**Rolliad, Criticism on The** A series of Whig political satires which appeared in *The Morning Herald* and *The Daily Advertiser* after the victory of William Pitt and his followers in the election of 1784. The satires took the form of reviews of an imaginary epic called *The Rolliad*. John Rolle was a Tory MP and one of Pitt's supporters; the epic narrated the adventures of his heroic ancestor, the Norman Duke Rollo. The authors, members of the Whig club the Esto Perpetua, included General Richard Fitzpatrick, Lord John Townshend, the antiquary George Ellis, and French Laurence, Regius Professor of Civil Law at Oxford. The *Rolliad* satires were followed by *Political Eclogues*, in which Pitt and his followers appeared as Virgilian shepherds. The death of the Poet Laureate, **William Whitehead**, in 1785 prompted further satire against the Tories from the same group in the form of *Probationary Odes* for the vacant laureateship.

**roman à clef** A 'novel with a key', in which real people appear under fictitious names, lightly disguised and still recognizable. The purpose is often satiric, if only mildly so, as the novels of Thomas Love Peacock and Aldous Huxley's *Crome Yellow* demonstrate; but the portrait of **D. H. Lawrence** as Mark Rampion in Huxley's *Point Counter Point* shows that the form can also express admiration.

**roman à thèse** A 'thesis novel', intended to popularize or propagate an idea or cause. The political novels of **Disraeli** and **Kingsley**'s *Alton Locke* are examples.

**Roman Actor, The** A tragedy by **Philip Massinger**, first produced in 1626 and published in 1629. Although it has not been revived in the modern theatre, Massinger considered it his best work and it was highly regarded in its time. The plot comes from Suetonius, whom Massinger could have read in the translation by **Philemon Holland**.

The Emperor Domitian conceives a passion for Domitia Longina, wife of the senator Aelius Lamia; Domitia is taken from her husband and is made empress. Domitian is intensely jealous, but Domitia does not care for the emperor and falls in love with an actor, Paris. Unfortunately she betrays herself at a performance in which Paris plays a character who threatens suicide when his love rejects him. Domitian is brought information by his wife's enemies; he surprises her with Paris and kills the actor with his own hands. Domitia heaps contempt on the emperor and abuses him for his subservience to his passions, but he cannot bring himself to harm her. However, he adds her name to a list of the proscribed – thus ensuring that someone else will attempt her life. Domitia discovers the proscription while he sleeps and hastily summons those named along with her. Domitian is tricked into leaving the protection of his tribunes by one of the conspirators, Parthenius, with the promise of news of a victory in the east. Among the six who strike him down are Domitia, his niece Julia, and his cousin Domitilla.

**roman fleuve** A sequence of novels, in which the individual books are linked by recurrent characters. These may be drawn from a family (as in **Galsworthy**'s *Forsyte Saga*) or a social milieu (as in **Trollope**'s **Barsetshire Novels** and **Anthony Powell**'s *Dance to the Music of Time*).

**romance** See **verse romance**.

**Romans of Partenay, The** (or *Lusignan*) A **verse romance** of 6600 lines of **rhyme royal** translated in the North-east Midlands *c.*1500 from a French version by La Coudrette (*c.* 1400). Raymond meets the fée Melusine by a fountain after becoming lost on a disastrous hunt and agrees to marry her. Melusine demands that Raymond never try to discover what she does on Saturday nights, but he is persuaded by his brother to break the vow and, spying on her, finds that she turns into a serpent from the waist down. When he reveals his knowledge in an argument she turns into a serpent and leaves him. Her metamorphosis is the result of her mother's revenge on her three daughters for imprisoning their father, who had broken a vow never to visit his wife in childbirth. The other two daughters, Melior and Palestine, are respectively exiled in Armenia and forced to guard the mother's treasure on a mountain in Aragon. The second half of the romance is concerned with the stories of these two and of Melior's ten sons, all deformed in some respect, and in particular of Geoffrey of the Great Tooth, who becomes something of a central figure in a tale without a proper focal point.

**Romanticism** A comprehensive term for the large number of tendencies towards change observable in European literature, art and culture in the later 18th and early 19th centuries. Although it manifested itself everywhere in the form of a pronounced shift in sensibility, Romanticism was not a unified movement with a clearly agreed agenda, and its emphases varied widely according to time, place and individual author. Intellectually it pulled away from the philosophical rationalism and **neoclassicism** of the Enlightenment, developing an alternative aesthetic of freedom from the 'dead' letter of formal rules and conventions, and of uninhibited self-expression, of which the German *Sturm und Drang* movement of the 1770s, which included the early writings of Herder, Schiller (*Die Räuber*) and Goethe (*Werther*), was an important precursor. A corresponding sense of strong feeling, but also of original, fresh and, above all, authentic feeling was also important, and the development of natural, unforced poetic diction became an essential qualification for the standing of the poet (as in the **Lyrical Ballads**). The most typical Romantic attitude is individualism. Underlying the Romantic epoch as a whole is a pervasive sense of the collapse within the individual subject of those intricate systems of moral, religious and psychic control, constraint and limitation which were being shaken apart at the public or institutional level by the American and French Revolutions. Whatever the colour of his politics, the Romantic poet assumes the mantle of prophet, seer and legislator. The Romantic hero is either a solitary dreamer, or an egocentric plagued by guilt and remorse but, in either case, a figure who has kicked the world away from beneath his feet. In their explicitly 'reactionary' phase, writers such as **Wordsworth** and **Coleridge** tended to look back on their earlier revolutionary radicalism as a transgression against an unheeded sense of the

proper truth of things, for which they were punished with a kind of existential vertigo. A similar derangement of the official political economy of the emotions seems to have been the effect, if not the conscious intention, of the **Gothic novels** of **Horace Walpole**, **'Monk' Lewis** and **Ann Radcliffe**, which anticipate and to some extent overlap with Romanticism proper. Other important harbingers of Romanticism were introspective 18th-century poets such as **Blair**, **Chatterton**, **Young**, **Gray** and **Cowper**, as well as the cult of the primitive in the Celtic bardic verse of **Macpherson**'s Ossianic poetry, and the folk ballads collected by **Percy**. The Romantic valorization of personal experience was accompanied by a deepening sense of history which found its expression in the novels of **Sir Walter Scott**; another general feature of the period was the fascination for the private lives of individuals reflected in countless 'memoirs', 'recollections', 'lives', and in the adoption by writers such as **De Quincey**, **Lamb** and **Hazlitt** of autobiography as a literary form. The invasion of the inner recesses of the personality was continued in the analysis of dreams and the irrational, and in drug-taking and dabblings in the occult.

'Romanticism' seems to have assumed its present connotations around the mid 19th century, when the phenomenon to which it referred was already regarded as belonging to a completed past. Except in Germany, the principal protagonists of literary Romanticism were not, themselves, self-consciously 'romantic', nor were they perceived by their contemporaries as belonging to a particular school. The English Romantic poets **Blake**, Coleridge, Wordsworth, **Keats**, **Shelley** and **Byron** divided into two distinct generations, came from disparate backgrounds, differed sharply in their theory and practice, held conflicting political views, and in some cases cordially disliked each other. Friedrich Schlegel's characterization of Romantic writing as medieval, Christian and transcendental as opposed to classical, pagan and worldly was part of a specifically German polemic which was taken up by Madame de Staël in her *De L'Allemagne*, published in England in 1813. It may have fitted Coleridge, appropriately the only English poet with an extensive knowledge of the German theorists, but it seems quite wide of the mark in the case of Byron, Keats and Shelley, who were neo-pagan in their inclinations, liberal-to-radical in their politics and a long way from any idealization of medieval social systems. What the English Romantics did share was a belief in the poet's mission. Perhaps the most lasting achievement of Romanticism, in England and Germany, and later on in France (where writers such as Chateaubriand, Hugo, and De Vigny were strongly influenced by the English poets), was what might be called the institutionalization of the Imagination: the emergence of the poet as a person possessing a special kind of faculty which sets him apart from his fellow men.

**Romany Rye, The** George Borrow's sequel to *Lavengro*, published in 1857.

Though intended to provide the facts omitted from the earlier book, while picking up the story of the author's life after 1825, *The Romany Rye* instead sustains the original narrative in the unchronological, episodic, open-ended way that had already puzzled and irritated literal-minded readers. Yet despite its irony and ambivalence, the book contains some of Borrow's best writing, not least the enigmatic conclusion to the Isopel Berners episode, a tale which soon established itself as a classic of prose romance. But instead of giving the book a conventional structure, Borrow abruptly broke off the account of his life in mid-career and added the 'Appendix', one of the most powerfully written pieces of invective in the English language. To some, the violent attacks on identifiable people seemed tasteless and inappropriate, yet Borrow had hit upon a means by which his interior life could be recoded in psychological rather than documentary terms. The notoriously unsettling 'Appendix' is in fact all of a piece with the narrative that preceded it. Thus the savage attacks on 'gentility nonsense' become the exposition of his suppressed radical self, while his vitriolic dismissal of the critics of *Lavengro* permitted the indirect expression of his own unconventional, anti-bourgeois attitude to life.

**Romaunt of the Rose, The** A fragmentary translation of the French *Roman de la Rose* of Guillaume de Lorris and Jean de Meun. Extremely influential in medieval Europe as a source of the tradition of allegorical **dream-visions**, the French poem was begun by Guillaume de Lorris *c.*1327 with an allegorical account of a lover's pursuit of his beloved. In a dream-vision he visits a delightful garden in which he sees a rosebud and is pierced by one of Cupid's arrows. With the aid and hindrance of various allegorical personifications he attempts to win the rosebud. The work was taken up about 40 years later by Jean de Meun, who added theological, scientific, satirical and philosophical material before concluding with the lover's conquest.

The English translation survives in three fragments, a total of 7700 lines, of which the first fragment has been tentatively attributed to **Chaucer**. 'Thou hast translated the Romaunce of the Rose', says the God of Love to Chaucer in *The Legend of Good Women*. The God's claim that the translation was a crime against women is not supported by the extant fragments, which do not include Jean de Meun's anti-feminist satire but give half of Guillaume de Lorris's account,

Jean de Meun's discussion of love and his account of hypocrisy. Chaucer cannot have been translator of the whole of the extant work – the second fragment shows the influence of a northern dialect – but the style is Chaucerian throughout.

**Romeo and Juliet** A tragedy by **William Shakespeare**, first performed *c.*1595 and published in a corrupt Quarto (Q1) in 1597 and an authentic one (Q2) in 1599 as well as in the First Folio of 1623. The source was a poem by Arthur Brooke, *The Tragical History of Romeus and Juliet* (1562), but the story was, in its main outlines, well known.

The enmity of two great families, the Capulets and the Montagues, is a blight on the city of Verona. After a street brawl, the Prince orders the families to keep the peace on pain of death. Capulet, partly to demonstrate his willingness for Count Paris to marry his daughter Juliet, plans a masqued ball. Romeo, the love-sick son of Montague, decides to attend, effectively masked, in pursuit of his beloved Rosalind. At the ball, he and Juliet meet and immediately fall in love, but Tybalt, recognizing Romeo as a Montague, has to be restrained from fighting him. Romeo waits under Juliet's balcony, and they arrange a secret marriage, with the collusion of their mutual confessor, Friar Lawrence, and Juliet's Nurse.

The marriage takes place, and is immediately followed by disaster, when Romeo tries to prevent a duel between his mercurial friend Mercutio and the angry Tybalt. Mercutio is fatally wounded as a result of Romeo's intervention, and Romeo kills Tybalt as a reprisal. Banished from Verona, he leaves for Mantua after a single night with his new wife. Before Friar Lawrence can find a way of making the marriage public, Capulet decides that Juliet must marry Paris immediately. Friar Lawrence advises Juliet to aquiesce, but gives her a potion to take on the eve of the bigamous wedding. He explains that the potion will give her the appearance of death for 42 hours. She will be taken to the family vault, where the friar will arrange for Romeo to greet her when she wakes.

In plague-torn Mantua, Friar Lawrence's message fails to reach Romeo. Desperate at the news of Juliet's death, Romeo buys poison, goes to the Capulet vault for a last sight of Juliet and, encountering Paris there, kills him and drinks the fatal draught. Juliet wakes, finds Romeo dead and stabs herself with his dagger. The sequence of events, related by Friar Lawrence, serves to reconcile the two warring families.

The achievements of *Romeo and Juliet* have been so long recognized as to threaten the play with over-familiarity. Theatrical popularity has been assured by its clear plotting and the lyrical heights of its love poetry, together with the vivid creation of its minor characters, particularly Mercutio and the Nurse. That Shakespeare could write a tragedy of 'star-crossed' love at much the same time as he was parodying one in the Pyramus and Thisbe play of *A Midsummer Night's Dream* is an indication of his extraordinary range as a writer.

**Romola** A novel by **George Eliot**, published in *The Cornhill Magazine* in 1862–3 and in book form in 1863. It is set in Florence during the 1490s, a period of intense political strife and religious upheaval following the death of Lorenzo de'Medici, the invasion of Italy by the French, and the rise and fall of the fundamentalist Dominican friar Girolamo Savonarola.

Tito Melema, a handsome young Greek, ingratiates himself with the blind scholar Bardo de'Bardi and then marries his high-minded daughter Romola. Though superficially charming, Tito turns out to be utterly unscrupulous; he has robbed and abandoned his adoptive

'The Painted Record.' One of Sir Frederick Leighton's illustrations for *Romola*, first published in *The Cornhill Magazine*, July 1862–August 1863. Romola visits the painter Piero di Cosimo to look at the unfinished portrait of her father, and is surprised to see also a sketch of her husband, Tito.

father, Baldassare, and duped a peasant girl, Tessa, into a mock marriage. When his self-seeking leads him to betray Bardo's solemn trust, and to indulge in unprincipled political duplicity, Romola's love for him is replaced by contempt. She turns for spiritual guidance to Savonarola and for a time becomes his disciple, but rejects him too when his vision of establishing God's kingdom on earth degenerates into religious tyranny. As the several strands of the novel are drawn to a climax, Tito is killed by the demented Baldassare who has found his way to Florence; Romola finds fulfilment through self-sacrifice, in caring for the sick during an outbreak of plague and in looking after Tessa and her children by Tito; while Savonarola, undone by his own fanaticism, is tried for heresy and burned at the stake.

Besides Savonarola, the dramatis personae include Machiavelli, the artist Piero di Cosimo, and 50 or more lesser figures of the time. George Eliot spent months researching the historical background to the story, which abounds with details of almost every aspect of life in renaissance Florence. *Romola* always held a special place in George Eliot's own affections; in 1877 she wrote, 'there is no book of mine about which I more thoroughly feel that I could swear by every sentence as having been written with my best blood'.

**rondeau** Sometimes distinguished from and sometimes taken to be synonymous with the rondel; the English 'roundel' is used for either or both. One could say that the rondeau is a poem of 13 lines in iambic pentameter or tetrameter (see **metre**), divided into two unequal **stanzas**, using only two rhymes throughout and repeating the opening phrase as a refrain at the end of each stanza. The rondel may be 14 lines long and occasionally has a third rhyme. However, poetic practice – in England mostly confined to the late 19th century – varies considerably. **Swinburne**'s roundels, for instance, have three stanzas but only 11 lines, including the refrains; **Chaucer**'s three roundels all have 13 lines and, instead of a refrain, repeat the first three lines at the end, as well as including other repetitions. Perhaps, in the light of these variations – in which the idea of 'rounding' seems most prominent – a looser definition might serve: a short poem, using only two rhymes and repeating some part of the beginning at the end and also, normally, at the end of each stanza.

**Room of One's Own, A** An essay by **Virginia Woolf**, based upon two papers read to the Arts Society at Newnham College and the Odtaa at Girton College, Cambridge, in October 1928. It was published in 1929.

The essay has become a feminist classic.

Woolf begins by announcing her basic thesis: that 'a woman must have money and a room of her own if she is to write fiction'. In answer to the rhetorical question about why there were no famous Elizabethan women writers, Woolf employs the conceit that **Shakespeare** had a talented sister called Judith who was driven to suicide by artistic frustration. She then examines the educational, social, and financial disadvantages and prejudices which have thwarted women writers throughout (English) history. Special tribute is paid to **Aphra Behn**, **Dorothy Osborne**, **Jane Austen** and the **Brontë** sisters.

In the last chapter Woolf discusses 'the androgynous mind' ('If one is a man, still the woman part of the brain must have effect; and a woman also must have intercourse with the man in her') and deplores the male-centred perspective of 'some of the finest works of our greatest living writers' which makes them incomprehensible to women. The essay concludes by exhorting women to struggle to help realize a world in which 'the dead poet who was Shakespeare's sister will put on the body which she has so often laid down'.

**Room With a View, A** A novel by **E. M. Forster**, published in 1908.

Lucy Honeychurch and her chaperone, the genteel Miss Bartlett, are frustrated in their hopes of obtaining a room with a view at the Pensione Bertolini in Florence. Offered an exchange by Mr Emerson and his son, George, Miss Bartlett's sense of social propriety is offended. She graciously accepts the proposal, however, after being reassured by a respectable acquaintance, the Revd Mr Beebe. Lucy, innocent and impressionable, is shown around Florence by the lady novelist, Miss Lavish, one of the novel's many English 'characters' about whom Forster is gently satirical.

Venturing out alone, Lucy witnesses a quarrel between two Italians, one of whom is stabbed and dies in front of her. She faints, and recovers to find herself in the arms of George Emerson. Later, a party from the pensione joins an excursion to Fiesole. During the trip Lucy is again rescued, after a fall, by George and impulsively embraced. She and Miss Bartlett are affronted and take themselves off to Rome, then back to Surrey.

Lucy becomes engaged to the cultured, but shallow and over-protective Cecil Vyse. Her independent spirit is aroused and she eventually rebels. The Emersons, meanwhile, arrive to take up residence nearby. Lucy realizes with some perturbation that she loves George, not Cecil. She extricates herself from the relationship with Cecil, aided by Miss Bartlett, and marries George. The close of the novel finds George and Lucy on their honeymoon in the Pensione Bertolini.

**Rosalynde** A prose romance written by **Thomas Lodge** during his voyage to the Canaries and first printed in 1590. A second edition appeared in 1592, and the eight subsequent editions up to 1642 testify to its popularity. It catered to a popular taste for pastoral, **euphuism** (its sub-title is *Euphues Golden Legacy Found after his Death at Selexidra*) and Arcadian romance.

Based on the 14th-century tale of *Gamelyn*, *Rosalynde* tells the story of the usurper Torismond, which is paralleled by that of Saladyne who dispossesses his brother Rosader. Rosader falls in love with Rosalynde at a wrestling match and the subsequently banished Rosalynde and her cousin Alinda meet him in the forest of Arden. *Rosalynde* provided the basic narrative, main characters and some incidents for **Shakespeare**'s *As You Like It*.

**Rosciad, The** See **Churchill, Charles**.

**Rose and the Ring, The** A comic fairy-tale written and illustrated by **W. M. Thackeray**. It was published in 1855 under the pseudonym of Michael Angelo Titmarsh.

**Rose Theatre** Situated on the south bank of the Thames at Southwark, in the Liberty of the Clink, the Rose was leased by **Philip Henslowe** and became the preferred home of the Lord Admiral's Men during the last decade of the 16th century. It was there that the plays of **Marlowe** were probably first performed. Built in about 1587, it was old-fashioned by 1600, when Henslowe largely replaced it with the **Fortune**, and probably demolished *c*.1605.

**Rosenberg, Isaac** 1890–1918 Poet and artist. Born in Bristol of Russian-Jewish émigré parents, he grew up in Whitechapel in the East End of London, where his father earned a living as a market trader. He became an apprentice engraver in 1911, until a wealthy Jewish family supported him to study at the Slade School. Encouraged by **Gordon Bottomley** and **Ezra Pound**, he published at his own expense two collections of poems, *Night and Day* (1912) and *Youth* (1915), and *Moses: A Play* (1916). Despite his family's pacifism, he joined the army in 1915 and went to France early the following year. Many of his best poems, including 'Break of Day in the Trenches' and 'Louse Hunting', were written at the front, where he also began a second play, *The Unicorn*, which survives only in fragments. He was killed in battle near Arras, on the Somme, in April 1918. In 1922 Bottomley edited a selection of his poems and letters, introduced by **Laurence Binyon**. *Collected Works* (1937), edited by Bottomley and D. W. Harding, gained him a wider recognition. A foreword by **Siegfried Sassoon** praised Rosenberg's experimentation and his 'fruitful fusion between

English and Hebrew culture'. A new *Collected Works* (1979), including paintings, drawings and letters and reprinting Sassoon's essay, was edited by Ian Parsons.

**Rosencrantz and Guildenstern Are Dead** A play by **Tom Stoppard**, first performed at the Edinburgh Festival in 1966, and in revised form by the **National Theatre** in London in 1967. It is a wittily resourceful cross-fertilizing of artistic and philosophical themes, in which the eponymous heroes puzzle over their own identities, their relationship to the great events at Elsinore, the possibility of making decisions and the extent to which their roles have already been determined (in *Hamlet*). The dovetailing with **Shakespeare** is attractively neat.

**Ross, (James) Sinclair** 1908– Canadian writer. Born at Shellbrook, Saskatchewan, he left school at 16 and joined the Royal Bank of Canada in Abbey, Saskatchewan, in 1924. After his retirement he travelled to Europe, living in Athens, Barcelona and Malaga. His first story was published in 1934 but it was not until the publication of his first novel, *As for Me and My House* (1941), that Ross achieved wide recognition. It was followed by *The Well* (1957) and *Whir of Gold* (1970). Between 1934 and 1952 he published several short stories, many of them in the *Queen's Quarterly*; some were collected in *The Lamp at Noon and Other Stories* (1968). Other works are *Sawbones Memorial* (1974) and *The Race and Other Stories* (1982).

**Rossetti, Christina (Georgina)** 1830–94 Poet. The sister of **Dante Gabriel Rossetti** and **William Michael Rossetti**, she was born in London and educated at home by her mother. She showed early promise as a poet, and her grandfather had small collections printed when she was 12 and 15. She was a delicate and religious girl, her devotion to High Anglicanism later moulding much of her finest verse. Her religious convictions seem also to have caused the eventual collapse of her prolonged engagement to the **Pre-Raphaelite** painter James Collinson.

Christina Rossetti's lyrics 'An End' and 'Dream Lane' were published in the first number of *The Germ* (1850) under the pseudonym Ellen Alleyne. She contributed further poems to this and other journals. Her first major collection was *Goblin Market and Other Poems* (1862), followed in 1866 by *The Prince's Progress and Other Poems. Sing Song: A Nursery Rhyme Book* (1872) was illustrated by Arthur Hughes. By the 1880s bouts of ill health had made her an invalid, but she continued to write and publish. *A Pageant and Other Poems* (1881) contained the sonnet sequence 'Monna Innominata', celebrating the superiority of divine love over human passion, while *Time Flies: A Reading Diary*

(1885) consisted of 130 poems and thoughts for each day. The last original work published in her lifetime was *The Face of the Deep: A Devotional Commentary on the Apocalypse* (1892). Her brother, William Michael, edited her complete works (1904).

Her verse is remarkable for its love of verbal invention and of metrical experiment. In both her religious and her secular poetry she shows a keen interest in natural, pictorial imagery, while her addresses to an unnamed lover or suitor suggest both a determination and a carefully controlled ambiguity. Her delicate, frank meditations on death and Heaven are balanced by the imaginative vigour of poems like *Goblin Market*.

**Rossetti, Dante Gabriel** (christened Gabriel Charles Dante) 1828–82 Poet, painter and translator. Rossetti was born in London, the son of Gabriele Pasquale Giuseppe Rossetti, a Neapolitan political exile and sometime Professor of Italian at King's College, London, and of Frances Mary Lavinia Polidori Rossetti, daughter of Gaetano Polidori and sister of **Byron**'s physician, Dr John Polidori. Thus Rossetti's background and heritage were essentially Italian and the London household far more Italian than English. Rossetti was educated in 1836–43 at King's College School, London, where he was well prepared in Latin and French; Italian was of course spoken at home. In 1843–6 he attended Cary's Art Academy in Bloomsbury Street, by which time his inclination toward painting and poetry was apparent. Soon after leaving he spent a brief unfruitful period at the Antique School of the Royal Academy and persuaded Ford Madox Brown to take him as a pupil; his mentor demanded the young aspirant paint picklejars, medicine bottles and other still-lifes, so the association was short-lived. Meanwhile, Rossetti had come to know Holman Hunt and John Everett Millais, and these friendships in turn led in the autumn of 1848 to the formation of the **Pre-Raphaelite Brotherhood** whose other members were Thomas Woolner, Frederick George Stephens, **William Michael Rossetti** and James Collinson. Banding together against the prevailing aesthetic conventionality, the PRB (as it came to be known) sought to effect a revolution in English painting and poetry.

A dominant figure in the early stages of the PRB, Rossetti worked with unusual consistency in the late 1840s and throughout the 1850s both as poet and painter. In the latter capacity he produced such works as 'The Girlhood of Mary Virgin', 'How They Met themselves' and 'Ecce Ancilla Domini'. These works, along with various Dantesque subjects, religious drawings from both Testaments, and Arthurian canvases, are highly symbolic, spiritually charged and redolent of time past, of mysticism, and of other, remote, worlds. But of this period, too,

The Rossetti family, 7 October 1863, photographed by Lewis Carroll. Left to right: Dante Gabriel Rossetti, Christina Rossetti, Frances Rossetti (mother), and William Michael Rossetti.

were early studies for 'Found', a painting of many phases that deals – symbolically and realistically – with the evils of modern city life. As a poet Rossetti complemented his artistic work with an early draft of *Jenny* (a dramatic monologue about a London prostitute), a second version of his best-known poem *The Blessed Damozel* (which appeared in the short-lived PRB magazine *The Germ*), as well as early studies of 'Dante at Verona', 'The Bride's Prelude' and *Sister Helen* (an imitation medieval ballad). Thus Rossetti's poetry, like his painting, was detailed, symbolic, concerned with the remote and sometimes erotic; it was often cast in ballad form and sometimes archaic in language.

The 1850s were also notable in Rossetti's life for the drawings he made for *Poems by Alfred Tennyson* (1857) in which Millais and Holman Hunt also participated. He also engaged to undertake some decorations for the Oxford Union with several of his friends, among them Burne-Jones, **William Morris** and Arthur Hughes as assistants. As the walls were unprepared the subject matter, Arthurian legend, soon deteriorated and later restoration did little to evoke the originals. In Oxford he met Jane Burden, who later married Morris but continued to play an important role in Rossetti's private life. She was one of the many 'stunners', to use the PRB term, whom the poets and painters made their subject: beautiful women with red-gold hair, attenuated fingers, faintly sulky mouths and swan-like necks.

Another stunner was Elizabeth Siddal, whom Rossetti had met and fallen in love with in 1850. They were unable to marry until 1860, and Lizzie died from an overdose of laudanum in 1862. Although Rossetti had not been a faithful husband or lover, her loss affected him deeply and an increasing morbidity became apparent in

his work. However, he published *The Early Italian Poets* (1861), later revised as *Dante and His Circle* (1874), translations from some 60 writers which demonstrate another side of his gifts. Passages from Dante, Guido Cavalcanti, Fazio degli Uberti and many others appear with succinct biographical notes, critical introductions and other editorial apparatus. In the 1860s, too, Rossetti's painting yielded to decorative art – for he was a member of William Morris's firm that undertook work in the 'minor arts' of design for stained glass, furniture, and tiles – and then, as eye strain developed, he turned increasingly to poetry. *Poems* (1870) drew on the manuscripts he had first, in a fit of remorse, interred with Lizzie Siddal but later exhumed. Shortly thereafter he was attacked by **Robert Buchanan** in a scurrilous pamphlet, 'The Fleshly School of Poetry', to which he replied with 'The Stealthy School of Criticism'. By now increasing illness, morbidity and paranoia beset him, and in 1872 he attempted suicide. Yet he published *Ballads and Sonnets* (1881), which included the sonnet sequence *The House of Life* and *The King's Tragedy*, but chloral, imagined treacheries and groundless suspicions took their toll and in 1882, a near-recluse, he died shortly before his fifty-fourth birthday.

There is no doubting that Rossetti's poetry and painting, however far they depart from what is commonly termed Victorianism, were of considerable importance, especially in the last half of the 19th century. Over all his major work hovers the Romantic spirit and, save for the incomplete 'Found' and the narrative *Jenny*, his major work leads us constantly to times past, to medieval colour, to Arthurian legend, to Dantesque mysticism, to the violence of the ballad tradition and to a hot-house eroticism that hardly seems consonant with the fastidious finish and careful composition of the bulk of his artistic production.

**Rossetti, William Michael** 1829–1919 Man of letters. Born in London, the brother of **Dante Gabriel Rossetti** and **Christina Rossetti**, he was educated at King's College School and worked for almost half a century in the Internal Revenue as the main support of his family. One of the founders of the **Pre-Raphaelite Brotherhood**, he edited *The Germ* and wrote about the group and subsequent movements in *Ruskin, Rossetti, Praeraphaelitism* [sic] (1899) and *Praeraphaelite Diaries and Letters* (1900). He also contributed countless articles on literature and art to journals, translated Dante's *Inferno*, wrote a life of **Keats** (1887), produced editions of **Shelley**, **Blake** and **Whitman**, edited the collected works of his brother (1911) and the poetry of his sister (1904), and published *Some Reminiscences* (1906). He was married to Lucy Madox Brown, daughter of the painter Ford Madox Brown.

**Roth, Henry** 1906– American novelist, born in Austria-Hungary to Jewish parents who emigrated to the USA when he was an infant. His reputation is based primarily on the novel *Call It Sleep*. Though it went relatively unnoticed at its initial publication in 1934, it was reissued in 1960 and received widespread critical acclaim. Autobiographical in nature, *Call It Sleep* portrays the mind of David Schearl, the only child of Jewish immigrants who settle in New York City, and centres on his relationship with his family and his experiences in the streets of New York between the ages of six and eight. David has a troubled relationship with his stern father, who sees his son as soft and pampered, and the boy's only security lies in his affection for his sympathetic but socially isolated mother. At the climax of the book he slips a milk ladle into a slot in the live rail of a trolley car line and almost electrocutes himself, causing a blinding flash and a blackout in the neighbourhood. He awakens to a new sense of self-knowledge. Roth's use of dialect and ethnic speech patterns in the book, his vivid descriptions of the diverse streets of New York, and his sensitivity to the processes of David's growth, combine into a powerfully illuminating story.

Roth's literary output since *Call It Sleep* has been modest. He destroyed the manuscript of a second novel, and though he started work on a third it has never been released. He has, however, contributed to various magazines, and published his memoirs, *Nature's First Green*, in 1979.

**Roth, Philip** 1933– American novelist, born in Newark, New Jersey, and educated at Bucknell and at the University of Chicago. His first book, *Goodbye, Columbus* (1959), consisted of a novella and five short stories and won him the National Book Award in 1960. Jewish-American life in particular, and modern American society in general, are the subjects of his subsequent comedies of manners, which include *Letting Go* (1962), *When She Was Good* (1967), *Portnoy's Complaint* (1969), *The Breast* (1972), *The Great American Novel* (1973), *My Life as a Man* (1974) and *The Professor of Desire* (1977). *Our Gang* (1971) is a satire on the Nixon administration. *Reading Myself and Others* (1975) is a collection of essays. His most recent work consists of a semi-autobiographical sequence of novels about the education, sudden fame, and subsequent disillusion of a writer: *The Ghost Writer* (1979), *Zuckerman Unbound* (1981), *The Anatomy Lesson* (1983) and *The Counterlife* (1986).

**Roughing It** An early book of autobiographical episodes by **Mark Twain**, published in 1872, telling the story of his journey from St Louis to Nevada, including visits to a Mormon community in Utah and to Virginia City. He also describes his stay in San Francisco and his visit to the Sandwich Islands (Hawaii).

At the outset Twain portrays himself as an Eastern greenhorn, amused and comically befuddled by strange Western ways. As the story progresses, however, the narrator begins to adjust to the life-style he portrays, and begins to speak from a Western perspective. Though not exactly a coherent picture of life in the American West in the 1860s, the book is held together by the vivid personality and wit of its author.

**Rowe, Nicholas** 1674–1718 Playwright, poet and editor. Born in Bedfordshire and educated at Westminster School, he trained for the law but abandoned it on inheriting the family estate in 1692. Rowe held various official appointments during the later years of his life, serving as Secretary of State for Scotland in 1709–11 and Poet Laureate from 1715 until his death. His best plays held a prominent place in the English repertoire well into the 19th century. *Tamerlane* (1701) is an even more vivid example of the domestication of Elizabethan tragedy than **Dryden**'s *All for Love*. **Marlowe**'s hero is transformed to represent the values of William III in contrast to those of a villainous Bajazet (Louis XIV). It was less popular than Rowe's three 'she-tragedies', *The Fair Penitent* (1703), *Jane Shore* (1714) and *Lady Jane Gray* (1715), the first two of which provided Mrs Siddons with famous roles. *The Fair Penitent* is derived from **Massinger** and **Field**'s *The Fatal Dowry*, from which it deviates into pathos. *Jane Shore* makes of its heroine an unlikely image of domestic virtue and provides her jealous friend, Alicia, with a conclusion in eloquent madness after the fashion of **Otway**'s Belvidera. *Lady Jane Gray* portrays its heroine as a Protestant martyr, who rejects a pardon from the Catholic Queen Mary. Rowe's competent handling of blank verse was extravagantly admired by some contemporaries and temperately praised by **Dr Johnson**. His editorial work on **Shakespeare** (1709) is rightly seen as innovatory. He established his text by comparing copies, made generally thoughtful emendations and supplied logical act and scene divisions. Some of these divisions, like certain of his added stage directions and detailed exits and entrances, reflect and are limited by the regularizing spirit of Rowe's age, and such limitations are fully displayed in his scrupulous Preface.

**Rowlands, Samuel** *c.*1570–*c.*1630 Satirist. Nothing is known of Rowlands's life, though he may have been a cooper and churchwarden of east Smithfield in London. Although he is remembered as a writer of verse and prose satires, he also wrote religious poems, notably

*The Betraying of Christ: Judas in Despair* (1598), *A Sacred Memory of the Miracles Wrought by Jesus Christ* (1618), and *Heavens Glory, Seek it; Hearts Vanity, Fly it; Hells Horror, Fear it* (1628). Among his satires are the spirited *The Letting of Humours Blood in the Head-vein* (1600), *Tis Merry when Gossips Meet* (1602), *Look to it, for I'll Stab Ye* (1604), *Hell's Broke Loose* (1605) and *Democritus: Or Doctor Merry-Man His Medicines against Melancholy Humours* (1607). *A Terrible Battle between the Two Consumers of the Whole World; Time and Death* (1606) is a dialogue in verse and *The Famous History of Guy Earl of Warwick* (1608) a comic ballad. *The Melancholy Knight* (1615) is a verse monologue which ridicules nostalgia for a romantic past.

**Rowlandson, Mary White** *c.*1635–*c.*1678 The wife of an American Puritan minister, Rowlandson lived in the frontier town of Lancaster, Massachusetts. During King Philip's War (1674–6), the Narragansett Indians raided the town, killed some of her family, and took her and two children captive; she was ransomed three months later through the efforts of her husband. Her account of her experiences, *The Soveraignty and Goodness of God, Together with the Faithfulness of His Promises Displayed; Being a Narrative of the Captivity and Restauration of Mrs Mary Rowlandson*, was published in 1682 in Cambridge, Massachusetts. Likening her captivity to a spiritual affliction, she tells how she was taken around the countryside by the Indians, and how she gradually learned how to survive with them. The book went through many editions, becoming a classic of the American captivity genre.

**Rowley, Samuel** *c.*1575–1624 Actor and playwright. A leading member of the Admiral's Men and an 'attached playwright' to his company, Rowley probably agreed not to publish his work. The only known survival, *When You See Me, You Know Me* (1603), is a rambling chronicle play about Henry VIII. His name is associated with the lost *The Taming of a Shrew* (*c.*1589), which **Shakespeare** knew, and **Henslowe** records a payment to him in 1602 for 'additions' to **Marlowe's** *Doctor Faustus*.

**Rowley, William** *c.*1585–1626 Actor and dramatist. Nothing is known of Rowley's life beyond the fact that he was an actor noted for his playing of fat clowns. He collaborated with a number of other dramatists, most notably with **Thomas Middleton** on *The Changeling* (1622) and several other plays but also with **Dekker** and **Ford** on *The Witch of Edmonton* (1621), and probably with **Webster** and **Fletcher** as well. *The Birth of Merlin* (published in 1662) was attributed to Rowley and Shakespeare (see **Shakespeare apocrypha**). His unaided plays include a

muddled tragedy, *All's Lost by Lust* (*c.*1620) and two city comedies, *A New Wonder: A Woman Never Vexed* (published in 1632) and *A Match at Midnight* (published in 1633).

**Rowson, Susanna Haswell** *c.*1768–1824 American novelist, poet and playwright. Born in England, Rowson went to America with her family as a child; her father was a naval lieutenant stationed in Massachusetts. She returned to England in 1777 and later began to write, producing several sentimental novels and books of verse, including *Victoria* (1786), *The Inquisitor; or Invisible Rambler* (1788; US publication 1793), *Poems on Various Subjects* (1788), a collection of poems entitled *A Trip to Parnassus* (1788) and *Mary, or, The Test of Honour* (1789). **Charlotte Temple, A Tale of Truth** (1791; US publication 1794) became the first American best-seller. Rowson and her husband returned to the USA in 1793 to pursue careers in the theatre. Following *Mentoria, or, The Young Lady's Friend* (1791), a collection of essays and tales on education, and *Rebecca, or, The Fille de Chambre* (1792; US publication 1794), Rowson wrote social comedies and romances for the stage: *Slaves in Algiers* (1794), *The Female Patriot* (1794), *The Volunteers* (1795), *A Kick for a Bite* (1795), *Trials of the Human Heart* (1795), and *Americans in England* (1796). She founded a girls' boarding school and left the stage in 1797, devoting her time to more didactic works for youth, including *Reuben and Rachel, or, Tales of Old Times* (1798), *Miscellaneous Poems* (1804), *Sarah, or, The Exemplary Wife* (1813) and *Charlotte's Daughter, or, The Three Orphans* (1828), the sequel to *Charlotte Temple*.

**Roxana, or, the Fortunate Mistress** A novel by **Daniel Defoe**, published in 1724, presented as the autobiography of Mlle Beleau, the beautiful heroine.

The daughter of Huguenot refugees in England, she is ambitious for a more exciting life and parts company with her husband, a London brewer, after squandering his fortune and producing five children. She becomes a high-class kept woman, moving between 'protectors' across England, Holland and France and meanwhile is accorded the nickname 'Roxana', after her dancing, in the manner of Alexander the Great's widow. By now she has amassed a considerable fortune and is married to a wealthy Dutch merchant. Her loyal maid, Amy, accompanies her progress throughout, and is involved in a strategy to remove a difficult problem which crops up in the form of Roxana's daughter, a girl who becomes perilously interested in the Dutch merchant's wife and her origins. Roxana becomes caught between belated maternal feelings and a necessary instinct for self-preservation, but is unable to discover the real outcome of Amy's murderously helpful plans before she learns that her husband knows about her deviousness at long last. He dies shortly afterwards, and his widow receives only a pittance from his fortune, leaving her in penury and penitence.

The psychology of the characters does not always convince and the ending is frequently seen as an anticlimax, but the book has unmistakable energy and a narrative strength which is authentically novelistic.

**Royal Court Theatre** This small theatre in London's Sloane Square, opened in 1888, has twice made a major contribution to the development of English drama. In 1904–7, under the joint management of J. E. Vedrenne and **Harley Granville-Barker**, it established **Shaw** as a force in the British theatre, as well as introducing several socially relevant new plays to a sluggish public. After 1956 it spearheaded the revival of serious drama in England, under the aegis of the English Stage Company. **John Osborne**'s *Look Back in Anger* was the first of a remarkable succession of new plays at the Royal Court, and many dramatists, including **Arden**, **Jellicoe**, **Bond**, **Brenton** and **Hare**, were given their first significant opportunities there.

**Royal Shakespeare Company** The title the Shakespeare Theatre Company adopted in 1961 following the revision of its Royal Charter and its acquisition of a London base at the Aldwych Theatre under the leadership of the Chairman of the Council of its Governors, Fordham Flower, and its Director Peter Hall, appointed the previous year. Based in Stratford-upon-Avon, the Company already ran a distinguished seasonal festival of **Shakespeare**'s plays in the Shakespeare Memorial Theatre, built in 1932 as successor to the building opened in 1879 but destroyed by fire in 1926. Under its new name it further acquired an annual public subsidy, and, through its work at the Aldwych Theatre, a reputation for performing modern plays as well as Shakespeare and the classics which placed it beside (and sometimes in rivalry with) the **National Theatre**. Under the Artistic Directorship of Trevor Nunn (1968–86) two further theatres were opened in Stratford: The Other Place (1974), for studio productions, and the Swan (1986), for the production of plays by Shakespeare and his contemporaries in an environment resembling an Elizabethan theatre. In 1982 the RSC moved its London headquarters to the Barbican Arts Centre, where it has a smaller studio theatre, the Pit, as well as a main auditorium. Trevor Nunn was succeeded by Terry Hands, who had served as Joint Artistic Director since 1978.

*Rubáiyát of Omar Khayyám of Naishápúr,*
*The* A free translation by **Edward FitzGerald** from the Persian, first published (anonymously) in 1859. The author of the *Rubáiyát* (plural of the Persian meaning 'a poem of four lines') was the 12th-century astronomer and poet, Omar Khayyám. In the original the quatrains were placed in alphabetical order, a procedure not followed by FitzGerald who, however, arranged the epigrammatic stanzas to follow the course of the day.

A very free translation, or adaptation, FitzGerald's version distils the spirit rather than extracting the specific meaning from its original. The *Rubáiyát* crept on to the market; only 250 copies of the pamphlet were printed, and a mere two journals (one in a review of one sentence) noted its appearance. Seemingly sunk without trace, the poem, thanks to discerning praise from **Dante Gabriel Rossetti**, **Monckton Milnes**, **Swinburne**, **Ruskin** and **Morris** among others, slowly grew to a recognition it has never forfeited.

In its own time its colourful, exotic and remote imagery and language appealed greatly to the Victorian interest in the Oriental. And its hedonistic philosophy offered escape from a world fast surrendering to scientific determinism. In the poem FitzGerald, albeit unwittingly, offers a luxurious sensual warmth to counter the despair so many saw in the heartless doctrine of the survival of the fittest. The poem also suggests withdrawal from 'this sorry scheme of things', from the dreary responsibilities of a mundane middle-class existence. Neither is the tinge of romantic melancholy that informs many lines without its attraction.

Within its own time, too, the romantic melancholy of the *Rubáiyát* anticipates the pessimistic poetry of **Arnold**, **James Thomson**, **Hardy** and others, whereas its Epicurean motifs suggest the growing tide that swells into the fin-de-siècle to inform the writings of **Swinburne**, **Wilde**, **Beardsley** and **Pater**.

**Rudd, Steele** The pseudonym of the Australian comic writer Arthur Hoey Davis (1868–1935). Born near Toowoomba in Queensland, Davis had a rudimentary education, leaving school at the age of 11 and working as an odd-job man before obtaining a post in Brisbane, eventually becoming Under-Sheriff. In 1895 he began to contribute to *The Bulletin* a series of broad comic sketches about the Rudd family, set in the Darling Downs. They were published in 1899 as *On Our Selection,* and Davis followed the fortunes of his extended and hapless family – Mum, Dan, Dave, Nora, Kate and Sarah, all guided by Dad Rudd – in other volumes: *Sandy's Selection* (1904), *Back at Our Selection* (1906), *Dad in Politics* (1908), *On An Australian Farm* (1910), *We Kaytons* (1921) and *Me an' th' Son* (1924).

**Rudkin, (James) David** 1936– Dramatist. He was born in London and educated at King Edward's Grammar School, Birmingham, and St Catherine's College, Oxford. His first play, *Afore Night Come* (1960), revealed an instinct for high tragedy and myth. The story concerned an itinerant Irish tramp who is murdered by a gang of fruit-pickers, but the heightened language evoked themes of ritual slaughter, infertility and the suppression of the imagination (and Ireland) by British imperialism. The relationship between Ireland and England is the subject of *Cries from Casement as his Bones are Brought to Dublin* (1973) and *Ashes* (1974), his best-known play, about a Belfast couple whose infertility is mysteriously linked to the struggle in Northern Ireland. *Sons of Light* (1976) moves away from a specific political situation towards an allegorical assessment of contemporary man. Rudkin has written extensively for radio and television. An accomplished linguist and musician, he has translated the libretto to Schoenberg's *Moses and Aaron* and adapted Euripides' *Hippolytus*.

**Ruggle, George** See *Ignoramus*.

*Ruin, The* A fragment (45 lines) of an Old English poem preserved in **The Exeter Book**. It gives a descriptive and reflective account of a decaying Roman city, probably Bath since much attention is paid to the springs and baths of the city. In its imaginative evocation of the city's past splendour and its description of current decay the poem is powerful and striking. It owes something to the Classical tradition of the poem in praise of a city (*encomium urbis*) exemplified in **Durham**.

**Rukeyser, Muriel** 1913–80 American poet, born in New York City. Her concern with the Spanish Civil War, women's rights, and the Vietnam War is evident in her numerous volumes of verse, the first of which, *Theory of Flight*, was published in 1935. Other volumes include *U.S.1.* (1938), *The Turning Wind* (1939), *The Green Wave* (1948), *Body of Waking* (1958) and *The Gates* (1976). She also produced one work of fiction, *The Orgy* (1965), and wrote two biographies – *One Life* (1957), about Wendell Wilkie, and *Willard Gibbs* (1942).

**Rule, Jane** 1931– Canadian novelist and short-story writer. Born in Plainfield, New Jersey, she was educated mainly in California; she moved to Vancouver in 1956 and now lives on Galiano Island in British Columbia. She has taught English at Concord Academy, Massachusetts, and the University of British Columbia. Canada's best-known lesbian writer, she has written five novels: *Desert of the Heart* (1964), *This Is Not For You* (1970), *Against the Season* (1971), *The Young in One Another's Arms* (1977) and *Contract with the World* (1980). Her books of short stories include *Theme for Divers Instruments* (1975) and *Inland Passage* (1985). She has also written *Lesbian Images* (1975), a psychological study of 12 women writers including **Gertrude Stein**, Colette and **V. Sackville-West**, and *Outlander* (1980), a collection of essays on lesbianism. Her sense of the importance of women's issues is combined with her ideals of human community and art as celebration.

*Rule a Wife and Have a Wife* A comedy by **John Fletcher**, first performed in 1624 and published in 1640. It is one of several works by Fletcher that had an influence on the development of manners comedy after the Restoration.

Margarita, a rich heiress from Seville, wishes to marry only in order to give a cover of respectability to her amorous intrigues. Her companion Altea, knowing that she wants a fool for a husband, persuades her brother Leon to court her in the guise of a simpleton. Once married, Leon turns the tables on Margarita, eventually winning her admiring agreement to remain faithful.

**Rumens, Carol (née Carol-Ann Lumley)** 1944– Poet. Born in Lewisham, South London, she attended convent schools before reading philosophy at Bedford College, London. Married in 1965, she has worked in advertising and publishing, and as poetry editor for *Quarto* and *The Literary Review*. Her early collections, *Strange Girl in Bright Colours* (1973), *A Necklace of Mirrors* (1979) and *Unplayed Music* (1981), are characterized by detailed observation and accurate descriptions of domesticity and female experience. *Star Whisper* (1983), her most ambitious book, is dominated by a sense of loss and exile. In *Direct Dialling* (1985), her concern with suffering and persecution, especially in Eastern Europe, and the Holocaust, has become paramount. *Selected Poems* appeared in 1987. She has also edited *Making for the Open: The Chatto Book of Post-Feminist Poetry 1964–1984* (1985).

**Runyon, (Alfred) Damon** 1884–1946 American short-story writer and humorist. Born in Manhattan, Kansas, Runyon grew up in Pueblo, Colorado. He began contributing pieces to local newspapers while still at school. He enlisted for the Spanish–American War at the age of 14 and then returned to journalism. During World War I he became a war correspondent for the Hearst papers, and stayed on there as a columnist after the war. The New York scene provided the material for his unique vernacular humour: athletes, show people, gamblers, hustlers, crooks and their women are transformed into recognizable types. His volumes of stories include *Guys and Dolls* (1931), *Blue Plate Special* (1934), *Take It Easy* (1938), *Furthermore* (England 1938; USA

1941), *Runyon à la Carte* (1944), *Short Takes* (1946) and *Runyon on Broadway* (1950). In collaboration with Howard Lindsay, he wrote a farce, *A Slight Case of Murder* (1940), which had a successful run on Broadway.

**Rural Rides** An anthology of essays by **William Cobbett**, selected from pieces composed for his newspaper, *The Political Register*, between September 1822 and October 1826, and published together in 1830 under the full title *Rural Rides in the Counties of Surrey, Kent, Sussex, Hampshire, Wiltshire, Gloucestershire, Herefordshire, Worcestershire, Somersetshire, Oxfordshire, Berkshire, Essex, Suffolk, Norfolk, and Hertfordshire: with Economical and Political Observations Relative to Matters Applicable to, and Illustrated by, the State of those Counties Respectively*. In 1853 Cobbett's son James Paul added further material from *The Political Register*, dealing with his father's eastern and northern tours of 1830 and 1832, to make the present version of *Rural Rides*.

When Cobbett travelled about southern England by coach and on horseback in the 1820s, his immediate purpose was to gather material for *The Political Register*. He wished his campaign for Parliamentary reform to be based on up-to-date, first-hand observation of living conditions in rural England, so that his strictures of corrupt and ineffective government would be well-founded. 'My object was, not to see inns and turnpike roads, but to see the country; to see the farmers at home, and to see the labourers in the fields.' The reader sees with Cobbett's eyes, hears Cobbett's voice. Through page after page of keen observation spiced with indignation and acerbity, the social concerns of the convinced democrat are expressed in witty, flowing, energetic prose that soon established *Rural Rides* as the classic it is still recognized to be. Throughout the book, moreover, Cobbett's radical purposes are never in conflict with his unfeigned patriotism.

**Rushdie, (Ahmed) Salman** 1947– Novelist. Born in Bombay, he migrated to Britain in 1965. Fostered by **James Joyce** and Günter Grass among others, Rushdie's interests are in reshaping the history of his time to make it congruent with identities fractured by imperialism, and in questioning how fiction dare undertake so colossal a task. His novels are important examples of **magic realism**. *Grimus* (1975), a richly entertaining story about a truism, is grandly conceived as an extravagant fable about man's need for myths in a demythologized age. Rushdie's volcanic imagination and narrative gifts come together superbly in *Midnight's Children* (1981), where he succeeds in matching a grand subject, the multitudinousness of India itself, with a narrator's microcosmic personal history and in fashioning out of the absurd incongruity

a novel about the creative process in a world under constant threat. In *Shame* (1983) he is again concerned with the creative process, more than with the wretched of Pakistan, rewriting the history of a country founded in the year of his birth and scarifying its élitist class so that a major character is allegorized into Shame itself.

Nothing in his previous critical success prepared Rushdie or his publishers, Viking/Penguin, for the reception which awaited his next novel, *The Satanic Verses* (1988), making it an *affaire* that raised questions of censorship and freedom of expression. From its abrupt opening, when Gibreel Farishta and Saladin Chamcha suffer their 'angelicdevilish fall' to earth as their hijacked aircraft explodes, *The Satanic Verses* announces its purpose of addressing religion – particularly Islam – not directly but with intense, proliferating and often comic energy. Its kaleidoscopic structure seems designed both to mock and confirm faith. Islamic protest against the novel's 'blasphemy' began with demonstrations and book burnings in England, a publication ban in India, and disturbances in Pakistan, Saudi Arabia, Egypt and South Africa. In February 1989 the Ayatollah Khomeini of Iran proclaimed a *fatwa*, or death sentence, against the author. Rushdie was forced into hiding, from which he has given occasional interviews – charting his progress from defiance to the desire for reconciliation with his persecutors – and published two books: a children's story, *Haroun and the Sea of Stories* (1990), and a volume of essays, *Imaginary Homelands* (1991).

**Ruskin, John** 1819–1900 Critic of art, architecture and society. He was born in London, the only child of a prosperous wine merchant, John James Ruskin, and his wife Margaret. These overly protective parents educated him at home and at small private schools, and his mother accompanied him when he went to Christ Church, Oxford, where he won the Newdigate Prize for Poetry but took a bad degree. He was accustomed to travel from early boyhood, for his father took his son and wife with him when touring England in search of orders for his business; Ruskin was barely six when the little family ventured abroad to savour Continental life. Steeped in the classics (in the original), the Bible and the works of **Sir Walter Scott**, he also studied drawing and in 1832, with the gift of **Samuel Rogers**'s *Italy* illustrated by Turner, began his lifelong devotion to that painter.

Although Ruskin wrote poems and articles (on architecture) in various magazines before he was 20, it was with the first volume of **Modern Painters** (1843) that he first gained public attention by his powers as an art critic. The second volume of *Modern Painters* (1846), essentially a treatise on the imagination, was followed by **The Seven Lamps of Architecture** (1849). **The Stones**

John Ruskin, *c*.1875. A detail from a photograph by Lewis Carroll.

*of Venice* (1851–3), which includes his famous essay on 'The Nature of Gothic', was an epic work over which he spent many months drawing, measuring and accumulating notes in Venice. By now Ruskin was without dispute England's most prominent art critic, and however much he might be resented by more orthodox and less gifted practitioners (particularly architects), his forceful prose, keen eye and revolutionary courage in judgement rendered his position unassailable. By now, too, thanks to generous allowances from his father, he had become an eager collector of Turner's drawings. He was also a champion of the **Pre-Raphaelites**, a student of geology and botany and (like almost all the major Victorians) a victim of spiritual problems and religious doubts. Having survived two love affairs, he had in 1848 married Euphemia (Effie) Chalmers Gray; the marriage was annulled in 1854 on the grounds of non-consummation, and the next year Effie married the painter John Everett Millais.

In 1855 Ruskin began his *Academy Notes* – a beacon in Victorian art criticism – and in 1856 he published the third and fourth volumes of *Modern Painters* as well as *The Harbours of England*, a commentary on marine drawings by Turner. He was also busily engaged in writing notes on the artist and cataloguing his drawings, in an attempt to fulfil the troublesome position of executor to which he had been appointed in Turner's will. Furthermore, in the mid and late 1850s he frequently appeared on the lecture platform; like his work for the Working Men's

College in 1854–8, his addresses showed increasing interest in social and economic problems. But his social concerns are most effectively and directly shown by *Unto this Last*, appearing in *The Cornhill Magazine* in 1860 (the same year as the fifth and final volume of *Modern Painters*) and published as a book in 1862. Of similar importance were the 'Essays on Political Economy' that appeared in *Fraser's Magazine* in 1862–3, subsequently revised and republished as *Munera Pulveris* (1872). The lectures continued and were collected under such arresting titles as *Sesame and Lilies* (1865) and *The Crown of Wild Olives* (1866); in the latter year he also published *The Ethics of the Dust*, dialogues deriving from his interest in Miss Bell's school for girls at Winnington. By this time Ruskin was also in love with the young Irish girl Rose La Touche, some 30 years his junior. The sufferings and perplexities of this relationship were not brought to an end by her death in 1875 at the age of 27, for Rose's memory was to Ruskin a source of deep emotion and turbulence.

The death of his father in 1864 left Ruskin a wealthy man, yet his frenetic activity continued. He published *Time and Tide, by Weare and Tyne*, a series of letters on social problems, in 1867 and *The Queen of the Air*, a study of Greek myths, in 1869. Between the two he sandwiched one of his most humane pronouncements, 'The Mystery of Life and Its Arts' (1868). He became the first Slade Professor of Fine Arts at Oxford in 1870, and in January 1871 he began that vast and remarkable miscellany, *Fors Clavigera*, continued monthly until 1878 and irregularly after that. Two further things of significance happened to Ruskin in 1871: he fell dangerously ill at Matlock in Derbyshire, and he bought Brantwood, the Lake District home where he was to spend his later years cared for by his cousin, Joan Severn. In this same year he was instrumental in founding the Guild of St George, a Utopian organization.

Now, too, he published his Oxford lectures: *Aratra Pentelici*, on sculpture, and *The Eagle's Nest*, on science and art, both in 1872; *Love's Meinie*, on ornithology, in 1873–81; *Val d'Arno*, on Tuscan art, and *Ariadne Florentina*, on wood and metal engraving, in 1876. In 1875 (the year of Rose's death) he began publishing *Mornings in Florence*, the botanical series *Proserpina* and the geological lectures entitled *Deucalion*, all in parts. Further writings – on drawing, on Venice and on fiction – cascaded forth. But Ruskin's mind was seriously disturbed, and in the late 1870s and 1880s he suffered severe breakdowns; indeed, his condition in 1878 was so bad that he could not testify at the notorious libel suit brought against him by the artist Whistler. He managed in February 1884 to deliver the prophetic masterpiece 'The Storm Cloud of the Nineteenth Century' and in 1885 to begin his last enduring work, the autobiographical *Praeterita*, which ran intermittently in parts until July 1889. Under ever-increasing pressure, he deteriorated steadily until, in 1888, he collapsed during a Continental trip and was taken home to Brantwood, where he lived a tragically disturbed life until his death on 20 January 1900.

A man of large and restless mind who alternately impressed and exasperated his contemporaries, Ruskin remains one of the most vital of the great Victorians – made formidable to the modern reader by the sheer bulk and diversity of his writings. As an art critic, his importance goes far beyond his decisive impact on the reputations of Turner, the Pre-Raphaelites and the Italian painters, significant though that is in itself. Works like *Modern Painters* are key documents in the development of the aesthetics of **Romanticism**. As a critic of architecture, Ruskin did far more than praise the Gothic style and so confirm the fashion for medievalism. His discovery in the medieval churches and cathedrals of moral and social values – the freedom of the individual craftsman, the superiority of hand over machine – paved the way for the work of **William Morris** and the Arts and Crafts Movement. Made explicit in his writings on political economy and in his later books, Ruskin's vision of society exerted a powerful influence over those later thinkers who have sought to resist the dehumanizing effects of industrial culture.

***Russe Commonwealth, Of the*** **Giles Fletcher**'s description of Russia, where he was sent as ambassador to the Tsar Fyodor I in 1588, appeared in 1591 and again in an abridged form in the second edition of **Hakluyt**'s *Voyages* (1598). It was the most important book on Russia by a 16th-century Englishman, and its readers included **Ben Jonson** and **John Milton**.

**Russell, Bertrand (Arthur William), 3rd Earl** 1872–1970 Philosopher and mathematician. Bertrand Russell was born at Trelleck in Wales and educated privately and at Trinity College, Cambridge, where he became a fellow in 1895. His first book, *German Social Democracy* (1896), was followed by *An Essay on the Foundations of Geometry* (1877), demonstrating his skill as an exponent in his two chosen fields. He was to become famous for his application of mathematical reasoning to the solution of ethical and political problems.

Russell's work in the field of mathematics and logic began with *The Principles of Mathematics* (1903) which led him to the central insight that 'mathematics and logic are identical'. The paradoxes discovered during his research prompted him to embark on a project (with his former tutor A. N. Whitehead) which resulted in *Principia Mathematica* (3 vols., 1910–13).

After the publication of this, his major academic work, Russell turned to more traditional philosophical problems, and he became increasingly involved in political campaigns. His pacifism led to internment during World War I and the temporary deprivation of his fellowship. His other important philosophical works included *The Analysis of Mind* (1921), *An Inquiry into Meaning and Truth* (1940) and *Human Knowledge: Its Scope and Limits* (1948).

Russell was also the author of many controversial works aimed at a wider audience, including *The Practice and Theory of Bolshevism* (1920), *Why I Am Not a Christian* (1927), *Power, A New Social Analysis* (1938) and *Human Society in Ethics and Politics* (1954). He also wrote two collections of short stories, *Satan in the Suburbs* (1953) and *Nightmares of Eminent Persons* (1954).

He was awarded the Order of Merit in 1949, and the Nobel Prize for Literature in 1950. His *The Autobiography of Russell* came out in three volumes in 1967–9.

**Russell, George William** 1867–1935 Poet, dramatist and painter. His pseudonym, AE (or A. E.), started as a printer's error for AEON (an eternal being in gnostic belief) on the title-page of his first book. An Ulsterman who became a fellow student of **Yeats** at the Metropolitan School of Art, he was a poet and painter of mystical landscapes, incidents and figures owing much to his involvement in Theosophy. His first volume, *Homeward: Songs by the Way* (1894), was followed by *The Divine Vision* (1904), *Gods of War* (1915), *The Interpreters* (1922), *Song and its Fountains* (1932), *The Avatars* (1933), *The House of the Titans* (1934) and *Selected Poems* (1935). In 1902 his poetic drama *Deirdre* was presented with Yeats's **Cathleen Ni Houlihan** by the Irish National Theatre (later the Abbey Theatre), which he helped to form. Russell also pursued a successful career in journalism, editing *The Irish Homestead* (1905–23) and *The Irish Statesman* (1923–30), for which he refused Yeats's poem 'Leda and the Swan'. He also worked for the Department of Agriculture, organizing dairy co-operatives around the country. His friend **John Eglinton** published a memoir of him (1937).

***Ruth*** A novel by **Elizabeth Gaskell**, first published in 1853.

Ruth Hilton, a seamstress, attracts the attention of Henry Bellingham, a country gentleman, while attending ladies at a county ball. Innocent, she is attracted to Bellingham and agrees to go away with him to Wales where he becomes ill and his mother is sent for. Ruth, now an encumbrance and pregnant, is dismissed with £50. Hoping for death, she is befriended by Thurstan Benson, a dissenting parson on holiday in Wales, who summons his sister, Miss Faith Benson, to support his assistance to Ruth.

It is resolved that Ruth shall accompany the generous and kindly Bensons to his northern parish, Eccleston, where she allows herself to be known as a widowed relative, Mrs Denbigh, and it is there her son, Leonard, is born. Ruth becomes a respected member of the household, addresses herself to raising her son, and establishes herself in the community at large. In due course she becomes governess to the Bradshaws, one of Eccleston's most materially successful families and parishioners of Mr Benson.

By unfortunate chance Henry Bellingham, under the name of Donne which he had adopted 'for propriety', reappears in Ruth's life as parliamentary candidate for Eccleston. He offers marriage, which is refused. Soon afterwards Bradshaw senior learns Ruth's secret and dismisses her; as a consequence, she and the Bensons are treated as pariahs and suffer social and financial difficulties. Leonard, too, is humiliated to learn of his parentage and falls ill.

After a time Ruth qualifies as matron in a fever-ward and performs brave deeds during a cholera epidemic, thus rehabilitating herself in Eccleston. Meanwhile the kindly family physician, Dr Davis, ensures Leonard's future by offering to bring him up to medicine, so Ruth's life seems satisfactorily settled. But one more responsibility remains: Bellingham falls ill and she nurses him back to health but dies herself deeply mourned by the local people.

Such are the bones of the main narrative. However, the sub-plot of *Ruth* forms an integral part of the novel by adding a variety of characters, filling out the landscape and even contributing a dash of humour. It also buttresses the main narrative by recounting the attachment of Jemima, one of the Bradshaw daughters, to Walter Farquhar, her father's partner. The character of Jemima is a perceptive study of fundamental kindness temporarily clouded by jealousy and resentment (of Ruth) but ultimately restored through purged pride. Lesser figures – Walter Farquhar himself, old Sally the housekeeper, the bad brother of Jemima, and several others – give substance to the book. The use of natural phenomena, always important to Mrs Gaskell, is well handled and even if some characters and scenes seem stereotyped they are treated with a freshness and sympathy that engage and compel.

**Rutherford, Mark** See **White, William Hale**.

**Ryga, George** 1932– Canadian dramatist. Born in Deep Creek, Alberta, of Ukrainian parents, he spent his early years on a marginal homestead farm. He left school at the age of 12 and worked at a variety of casual jobs, while continuing to educate himself. He briefly attended the University of Texas in 1949, after which he worked as a farm labourer, in the construction industry and at a radio station in Edmonton. Since 1962 he has been a full-time writer. As a young man he was a Communist Party member and was heavily involved in the Canadian Peace Movement. Much of his work as a dramatist has pleaded the case of oppressed minorities. *The Ecstasy of Rita Joe* (1967; first published 1970) is the story of an Indian torn between the traditional ways of her people and the contemporary Canadian urban world. *Grass and Wild Strawberries* (1969; first published 1971) dramatizes another conflict between cultures, in this case between the hippie movement of the late 1960s and middle-class society. Ryga's dramatic technique attempts to recapture the quality of the ballad and he frequently incorporates elements from other media into his plays. These include film projection, recorded sound, dance and song. He has written numerous radio and television plays. His other stage plays include *Indian* (1962; first published 1971), *Captives of the Faceless Drummer* (1971), *Sunrise on Sarah* (1973), *Ploughmen of the Glacier* (1977) and *Seven Hours to Sundown* (1977). He has also published novels and poetry.

**Rymer, Thomas** 1641–1713 Critic and historian. The son of a Puritan country gentleman executed for treason in 1664, Rymer was born at Yafforth in Yorkshire. Educated at Sidney Sussex College, Cambridge, he later studied law and was called to the Bar at Gray's Inn. As a dramatist, he was not successful: his tragedy, *Edgar: or The English Monarch* (1678), was never performed. As a critic, he championed extreme neoclassicism. His first essay was a preface to a translation of René Rapin's *Réflexions sur la Poétique d'Aristote* (1674). *The Tragedies of the Last Age Consider'd* (1678) was praised by **Dryden** but *A Short View of Tragedy* (1693), notorious for its attack on **Shakespeare**, has earned him ridicule. Rymer was appointed Historiographer Royal in 1692 and undertook the task of collecting English treaties, covenants and similar documents in the 20-volume *Foedera* (1704–35).

# S

**Sackville, Charles, 6th Earl of Dorset** 1638–1706 Poet and courtier. Like his fellow wits, **Rochester** and **Sedley**, Sackville was a dissolute young roisterer who later led a more mature and responsible life, leaving England during the reign of James II (with whose sober attitudes he was not in keeping) and playing a role in the Revolution which saw the end of the Stuart dynasty. He served as Lord Chamberlain to King William and was the longest-lived of the clique of Restoration literary blades, though his reputation now rests on a handful of lyrics. He was a patron to **Dryden** and **Prior**, who admired his work in return, and **Pope** later regarded him as one of the wittiest poets of the day. Much of his verse was designed to be circulated in manuscript form, but in 1664 he collaborated with Sedley and others in translating Corneille's *Pompey the Great*, and in 1665 he wrote his celebrated 'To All You Ladies Now at Land', a song composed at sea during the naval campaign of the Second Dutch War, which enjoyed great popularity. Rochester rated him highly as a satirist ('The best good man, with the worst-natured muse') and verses such as 'On Mr Howard' are certainly lively, with an imaginative line in simile and invective. His four poems to Katherine Sedley (later James II's mistress) are also remarkable for their expression of contemporary attitudes to women and the city.

**Sackville, Thomas, 1st Earl of Dorset** 1536–1608 Poet and dramatist. Sackville was educated at Oxford, became a barrister at the Inner Temple and was elected an MP in 1558. He was a successful statesman, becoming a member of the Privy Council and being sent on diplomatic missions to France and the Low Countries. He had the task of announcing her death sentence to Mary Queen of Scots. He was rewarded by Elizabeth with a knighthood and with the title Lord Buckhurst, both in 1567. He became Chancellor of the University of Oxford in 1591, and Lord High Treasurer in 1599, an office in which he was confirmed for life by James I in 1603. The king made him Earl of Dorset in 1604. Sackville contributed the 'Induction' and the 'Complaint of Buckingham' to the 1563 edition of *A Mirror for Magistrates*. He collaborated with **Thomas Norton** on *Gorboduc* and the first edition of 1565 claims that the last two acts are solely by Sackville.

**Sackville-West V[ictoria] (Mary)** 1892–1962 Novelist and biographer. V. Sackville-West was born at Knole in Kent which had been the seat of the Sackvilles since the 16th century. She was educated at home and, in 1913, married the diplomat **Harold Nicolson**, travelling with him to Persia and many other countries. Her first published work was a collection of verse, *Poems of West and East* (1917). This was followed by a novel, *Heritage* (1919), then another volume of poetry, *Orchard and Vineyard* (1921). Other novels, short stories and miscellaneous prose

V. Sackville-West, 1916. A detail from a photograph by E. O. Hoppé.

works followed, but it was with her long poem *The Land* (1926) that she achieved recognition. *The Land* is a realistic pastoral set in the Weald of Kent which details the progress of the seasons and acknowledges the struggle of man with nature. It was awarded the Hawthornden Prize.

Sackville-West produced a total of some 50 books. *Knole and the Sackvilles* (1922, revised 1958) is an account of her family and the family home. *The Eagle and the Dove, A Study in Contrasts* (1943) examines two saints, Teresa of Avila (the Spanish mystic) and Thérèse of Lisieux (the 'Little Flower' of France). *Daughter of France* (1959) is a biography of 'La Grande Mademoiselle'. Among her novels, *The Edwardians* (1930) and *Passion Spent* (1931) have been rated most highly.

Victoria Sackville-West was an expert and passionate gardener, an art which she practised at Sissinghurst, her home with Harold Nicolson, and about which she wrote with great success in a weekly column in *The Observer*. Her contributions were published in several collections (1951, 1953, 1955, and 1958). She was a close friend of **Virginia Woolf**, for whom she was the model for the androgynous hero of *Orlando*.

**Sacred Fount, The** A short novel by **Henry James**, published in 1901. The story takes place at a weekend party at Newmarch, an English country house. The nameless narrator develops the theory of the 'sacred fount' when he observes that his hostess, Grace Brissenden, is much older than her husband, Guy, yet after a few years of marriage seems to be the more youthful and energetic of the two. The narrator speculates that Guy is the 'fount' from which his wife draws her new vitality, and that he is correspondingly devitalized. He then applies this theory to another pair of guests, Gilbert Long and May Server. He posits the passage of vital force from May, who appears to be emotionally disturbed, to Gilbert, who once seemed dull but is now a witty man of the world. He further decides that Gilbert and Grace, the dominant partners of their respective marriages, are drawing closer together, and that so are May and Guy, the weaker partners. But Grace, whom the narrator has taken into his confidence, eventually tells him that he has imagined the whole thing. The reader is left uncertain whether Grace is lying or the narrator has merely invented the idea.

**Sad Fortunes of the Reverend Amos Barton, The** See *Scenes of Clerical Life*.

**Sahgal, Nayantara** 1927– Indian journalist and novelist. Born in Allahabad, she graduated from Wellesley College, Massachusetts, in 1947. As Nehru's niece she was very close to Gand-

hian idealism before Independence and political in-fighting thereafter. Respect for Gandhi's principles and concern with political morality among the élite inform her elegantly written novels: *A Time To Be Happy* (1958), *This Time of Morning* (1965), *Storm in Chandigarh* (1969), *The Day in Shadow* (1971), *A Situation in New Delhi* (1977), *Rich Like Us* (1985), and, with a new imaginative sweep, *Plans for Departure* (1986). *Prison and Chocolate Cake* (1954) and *From Fear Set Free* (1962) are autobiographical.

**Said, Edward** See **post-structuralism**.

**Saint Joan** A play by **George Bernard Shaw**, first produced in New York in 1923. The first English production was in London the following year, when *Saint Joan* was also published.

The play follows the fortunes of the girl from Lorraine, from her first encounter with Robert de Baudricourt, to her meeting with the Dauphin at Chinon, and her subsequent fortunes after she leads the assault on the English and raises the siege of Orleans. After her victory her faith in her inspiration raises the suspicion of heresy: the Earl of Warwick seizes on this. The Bishop of Beauvais and John de Stogumber see her as a girl who may be in error but whose soul can be saved; Warwick sees her as a dangerous enemy to be extinguished. When Joan is taken by the Burgundians she is sold to Warwick, who hands her over to the Church. She is tried for heresy and, terrified by the threat of burning, signs a recantation of her belief in the voices that inspired her. But the alternative sentence, perpetual imprisonment, is worse. Joan destroys her recantation and they hurry her out to the stake. The Epilogue deals with the nullification of the Church's verdict of 1431, and the canonization of Joan of Arc.

The play is Shaw's most widely praised work for the theatre; its central part has attracted distinguished actresses ever since Sybil Thorndike's performance in the first London production.

**St Ronan's Well** A novel by **Sir Walter Scott**, published in 1824. It departs from his usual historical settings and takes place at a fashionable Scottish spa in the early 19th century. The story concerns two half-brothers, sons of the late Earl of Etherington, whose enmity is inflamed by their vexed and tragic relationship with Clara Mowbray, daughter of the laird of St Ronan's. The plot is heavily burdened with improbabilities but Scott's portrait of Meg Dods, the down-to-earth landlady, has been praised.

**saint's life** Prose and verse accounts of saints' lives flourished during the Middle Ages. They are preserved both independently and in collections such as *The Golden Legend* and *The South English Legendary*. Usually taken from Latin *Vitae*, the stories often included fanciful as well as miraculous episodes. Their main purpose is didactic, but clearly they were often felt to be entertaining also. Some saints' lives have features of the **verse romance** and, conversely, there are verse romances (*Emare*, for example) which include features of the saint's life.

**Saintsbury, George (Edward Bateman)** 1845–1933 Literary historian, biographer and critic. Born at Southampton, he was educated at King's College School, London, and Merton College, Oxford. He taught for a number of years and wrote reviews for *The Academy*, gaining attention with his notices of the work of French writers, especially Baudelaire, in 1875.

Saintsbury's first book was *A Primer of French Literature* (1880). *A Short History of French Literature* (1882), a standard book for students for decades, and *Specimens of French Literature from Villon to Hugo* (1883) were followed by *Essays on French Novelists* (1891), and *A History of the French Novel to the Close of the Nineteenth Century* (1917–19). His books on English literature and on the history of criticism extend from 1881 to the year of his death. Among them were a study of **Dryden** in the English Men of Letters series (1881), *Essays in English Literature 1780–1860* (two series, 1890 and 1895), *A Short History of English Literature* (1898), *A History of Criticism* (1900–4), *Minor Poets of the Caroline Period* (1905–21), *A History of English Prosody* (1906–10), *The English Novel* (1913), *The Peace of the Augustans* (1915) and the Oxford edition of the *Works of Thackeray* (1907). Saintsbury contributed 21 chapters to *The Cambridge History of English Literature* and was Professor of Rhetoric and English Literature at the University of Edinburgh (1895–1915). He was also a wine connoisseur and his *Notes on a Cellar Book* (1920) is an acknowledged classic of its kind.

**Saki** Pseudonym of Hector Hugh Munro (1870–1916), short-story writer and novelist. He was born in Akyab, the son of an officer in the Burma police, and brought up by two maiden aunts in Devon. After being educated at a school in Exmouth and at Bedford grammar school, he followed his father into the Burma police but was invalided home. In 1896 he settled in London, contributing political satires to *The Westminster Gazette* (collected in *The Westminster Alice*, 1902). Between 1902 and 1908 he acted as correspondent for *The Morning Post* in Poland, Russia and Paris.

His first book, *The Rise of the Russian Empire* (1899), was the only one written in a serious vein. Thereafter he adopted the pseudonym 'Saki' (the name of the cup-bearer in the last stanza of *The Rubáiyát of Omar Khayyám*) for his

collections of short stories: *Reginald* (1904), *Reginald in Russia and Other Sketches* (1910), *The Chronicles of Clovis* (1912) and *Beasts and Superbeasts* (1914). Whimsical in their plots and light-heartedly cynical in their tone, these stories are also given a darker side by Munro's memories of his unhappy childhood with his aunts. He also published two novels, *The Unbearable Bassington* (1912) and *When William Came* (1913), the latter a satirical fantasy subtitled 'A Story of London under the Hohenzollerns'.

Munro served with the Royal Fusiliers in World War I and was killed on the Western Front in 1916. Two collections of stories and sketches appeared posthumously, *The Toys of Peace and Other Papers* (1919) and *The Square Egg and Other Sketches* (1924).

**Sala, G[eorge] A[ugustus]** 1828–96 Journalist and travel-writer. Born in London, and educated there and in Paris, Sala trained as a miniature painter and worked as a scene painter and book illustrator before turning to journalism and becoming a contributor to **Dickens**'s *Household Words*. *A Journey Due North* (1858), about Russia, derived from articles for *All the Year Round*. *My Diary in the Midst of the War* (1865) was based on his work as correspondent for *The Daily Telegraph* during the American Civil War. His most successful book was *Twice Around the Clock, or, The Hours of the Day and Night in London* (1859), a series of social sketches which had originally appeared in *The Welcome Guest*, a journal he himself edited. Sala also wrote a volume of reminiscences, *Things I Have Seen and People I Have Known* (1894).

**Salinger, J[erome] D[avid]** 1919– American novelist and short-story writer, born in New York City and educated at Valley Forge Military Academy, and at New York and Columbia universities. He published short stories in *The Saturday Evening Post* and other magazines during the early 1940s and served in the US infantry during World War II. His only novel has been the highly successful *The Catcher in the Rye* (1951), narrated by a teenage schoolboy in rebellion against the dubious values of the adult world. In 1953 he published the collection *Nine Stories* (as *For Esmé – With Love and Squalor* in England), in which he introduces the Glass family, characters who reappear in his later works. *Franny and Zooey* (1961) contains two stories about a brother and sister in the family. Buddy Glass is the narrator of two additional collections, *Raise High the Roofbeam, Carpenters* and *Seymour: An Introduction*, both published in 1963.

**Salkey, (Felix) Andrew (Alexander)** 1928– Jamaican writer. Born in Colon, Panama, he worked in London from 1952 to 1976 and has lived since then in the USA. Four children's novels, *Hurricane* (1964), *Earthquake* (1965), *Drought* (1966) and *Riot* (1967), brought him the Deutscher Kinderbuchpreis (1967); four more appeared subsequently. His other novels, however, stress the aridity of Caribbean experience: in a drought-stricken Jamaican parish in *A Quality of Violence* (1959), in the colonial futility of politics in *The Late Emancipation of Jerry Stover* (1968). English society proves no less bleak and inhospitable to West Indians in *Escape to an Autumn Pavement* (1960), *The Adventures of Catullus Kelly* (1969) and *Come Home, Michael Heartland* (1976). *Havana Journal* (1971) and *Georgetown Journal* (1972) are travel books. Salkey has published four volumes of verse and edited anthologies of Caribbean writing.

**Salmagundi**, *or, The Whim-Whams of Opinions of Launcelot Langstaff, Esq. and Others* A series of satirical essays and poems by **Washington Irving**, his brother William, and **James Kirke Paulding**, *Salmagundi* was first published in 20 periodical pamphlets between 24 January 1807 and 25 January 1808, and then issued in two volumes in 1807 and 1808. The authors used a variety of pseudonyms in the manner of *The Spectator* in 18th-century London, representing members of an imaginary club. The essays cover aspects of life in contemporary New York, their political stance favouring aristocratic federalism in opposition to Jeffersonian democracy. A further series of *Salmagundi* papers, of which Paulding was the sole author, was published between May 1819 and September 1820.

**Salome** A play by **Oscar Wilde**, written in 1891 in French, with grammatical help from Pierre Loüys. It deals with Salome's destructive love for John the Baptist.

An English translation by **Lord Alfred Douglas**, with illustrations by **Aubrey Beardsley**, appeared in 1894. Although published translations still bear Lord Alfred's name, the one in current use is not believed to be his. The play first went into rehearsal in 1893, but was banned by the Lord Chamberlain for its depiction of biblical characters; the first production, with Sarah Bernhardt, took place in Paris in 1896, when Wilde was in prison. It was not performed in Britain until 1931. *Salome* inspired Richard Strauss's opera, first performed at Dresden in 1905.

**Samson Agonistes**: *A Dramatic Poem* A tragic poem by **John Milton**, published in 1671. Its subject is the last days of Samson's life, blind (like the poet himself) and a prisoner of the Philistines: 'Eyeless in Gaza at the mill with

slaves'. The 'Agonistes' of the title refers to Samson as an athlete or wrestler.

On a festival day Samson is brought into the open air, where he reflects on his fate: 'Dark, dark, dark, amid the blaze of noon'. The men of Dan, his tribe, find him and try to comfort him; his aged father Manoa also comes and tells him he will attempt to ransom him from the Philistines. The news torments Samson, who feels that his fate is deserved. Manoa, nevertheless, goes ahead to treat with the Philistines for his son's freedom. Dalila is the next character to appear. She pleads for forgiveness for her part in Samson's downfall but he treats her with scorn. She replies that she is like all women and feared that he would abandon her. He still rejects her with contempt, not even allowing her to touch him. She leaves declaring that she is now honoured above all women for her part in his defeat and that she will leave him to his lot. The Chorus watches her go and observes that her new pride is assumed. Next comes Harapha the Philistine, a bully who taunts the fallen Samson. He is disposed of by Samson's furious defiance.

The Chorus praises the hero's unquenchable spirit but is disturbed to see a Philistine officer approaching. His news is that the Philistines want a demonstration of Samson's superhuman strength at the festival to their god Dagon. Samson dismisses him and the Chorus voices unease at what may happen. Samson realizes he has regained all his old strength now that his hair has regrown and, when the officer returns, agrees to go with him. The Chorus watches him depart and at once Manoa hurries in seeking his son: the Philistines have relented, he says, and will accept a ransom. His words are interrupted by the great shouting in the streets as the Philistines see their enemy in chains. The poem ends with the Messenger's arrival and his description of the destruction of the temple and Samson's death.

*Samson Agonistes* is cast in the form of a Greek tragedy, using a Chorus, confining the action to one place and compressing its narrative into the last hours of the hero's life. Although Milton never intended it for the stage, it has been successfully performed. Handel composed an oratorio using the poem as the basis for the libretto.

**Sandburg, Carl** 1878–1967 American poet, born to Swedish immigrant parents in Galesburg, Illinois. He left school at the age of 13 and worked as an itinerant labourer then served in the Spanish–American War, and later found work as a journalist and advertising copywriter. His career as a poet began with the privately printed *In Reckless Ecstasy* (1904), which failed to attract critical attention. From 1910–12 he served as secretary to the socialist mayor of Milwaukee, Wisconsin.

Carl Sandburg, 1956.

In 1914 some of his work was published by **Harriet Monroe** in *Poetry* magazine, and his reputation as a major poet of the Midwest was finally established in 1916 with the publication of *Chicago Poems*, a volume of free verse on 20th-century urban themes. Other collections of poetry followed: *Cornhuskers* (1918), *Smoke and Steel* (1920), *Slabs of the Sunburnt West* (1922), *Good Morning, America* (1928) and *The People, Yes* (1936). His *Complete Poems* (1950) was awarded the Pulitzer Prize. His later verse reveals a rather darker poetic vision, tempered by the experience of the Depression, but throughout his career he retained his optimism regarding the enduring qualities of ordinary working people. In addition to his poetry, Sandburg is known for his two-part biography of Abraham Lincoln: *Abraham Lincoln: The Prairie Years* (2 vols., 1926) and *Abraham Lincoln: The War Years* (4 vols., 1939). He also published several books for children, including *Rootabaga Stories* (1922), *Rootabaga Pigeons* (1923) and *Potato Face* (1930), a novel, *Remembrance Rock* (1948), and an autobiography, *Always the Young Strangers* (1952).

**Sanditon** An unfinished novel which **Jane Austen** worked on during the early months of 1817, the year of her death. Charlotte Heywood is a guest of the Parker family at Sanditon, a seaside village rapidly developing into a fashionable resort. There she meets Lady Denham and her nephew and niece, Sir Edward and Miss Denham.

**Sandra Belloni** A novel by **George Meredith**, published in 1864 as *Emilia in England*.

Emilia Sandra Belloni, an Italian girl with a fine singing voice, leaves her disreputable father and is taken up by the Pole family. Pole is a city merchant with three aspiring daughters and a spineless son, Wilfred. Pericles, a wealthy Greek and business ally of Pole, tries to persuade Emilia into taking musical training in Italy under his direction. But she and Wilfred have fallen in love, and she resists Pericles's persuasions. Pole, involved in speculation by Pericles and brought to the verge of ruin, tries to marry Wilfred to the rich Lady Charlotte Chillingworth. The wretched young man is more than willing but Lady Charlotte sees him for what he is, as do Merthyr Powys and his sister, who have taken a liking to Emilia. Charlotte exposes Wilfred to the girl and the Powyses take Emilia under their wing. To save the Poles – to whom, in spite of everything, she owes much – Emilia persuades Pericles to part with a large sum of money by agreeing to go to the conservatory at Milan. She departs, and both she and Merthyr look forward to her return and their probable marriage. The story continues in Meredith's later novel, *Vittoria*.

**Sandys, George** 1578–1644 Translator, poet and travel-writer. Educated at St Mary Hall, Oxford, Sandys travelled in Italy and the Levant, publishing a widely read account in *A Relation of a Journey Begun An. Dom. 1610: Four Books Containing a Description of the Turkish Empire, of Egypt, of the Holy Land, of the Remote Parts of Italy, and Islands Adjoining* (1615). In 1621 he went to America as treasurer of the Virginia Company for five years and began the translations from Latin for which he was best known. His version of Ovid's *Metamorphoses* appeared in 1626, its trim and regular couplets being much admired by younger poets. A later edition of 1632 added the first book of *The Aeneid*, rendered in the same style, and *Christ's Passion: A Tragedy*, from the Latin of Hugo Grotius, was published in 1640. Sandys also undertook verse translations from the Bible: *A Paraphrase upon the Psalms of David, and upon the Hymns Dispersed throughout the Old and New Testaments* (1636) and *A Paraphrase upon the Song of Solomon* (1641).

**Sansom, William** 1912–76 Short-story writer, novelist and travel-writer. Born in London he was educated at Uppingham School and then studied German in Bonn. He travelled widely in Europe, worked in a City bank and an advertising agency, as well as in radio and films. Throughout World War II he served as a full-time fireman. He began writing when he was very young but was unpublished until he was 30. In 1942 his work appeared in *Penguin New Writing* and *Horizon*. His first collection of short stories, *Fireman Flower*, appeared in 1944. *South* (1948), *Something Terrible, Something Lovely* (1948), *The Passionate North* (1950), *A Touch of the Sun* (1952), *Lord Love Us* (1954), *A Contest of Ladies* (1956), and *Among the Dahlias* (1957) followed. Sansom also wrote film scripts, television plays and lyrics. In 1946 and 1947 he was awarded two literary prizes by the Society of Authors; he was elected a Fellow of the Royal Society of Literature in 1951.

**Santayana, George** 1863–1952 American philosopher, born in Madrid and taken to the USA by his family in 1871. The original form of his name was Jorge Ruiz de Santayana y Borras. He was brought up in Boston and educated at Harvard, where he was Professor of Philosophy from 1889 to 1912. He then returned to live in Europe. *The Life of Reason* (1905–6) is a five-volume study of reason in everyday life, science, art, and literature. He offers the conclusion that the only reality is matter itself and that all else arises from man's experience of, and response to, matter. He took this idea further in *The Realms of Being*, which began with the introductory volume *Scepticism and Animal Faith* in 1923, and was eventually published in four volumes (1927–40). His work also includes three studies dealing with American life: *Philosophical Opinion in America* (1918), *Character and Opinion in the United States* (1920), on the conflict of idealism and materialism, and *The Genteel Tradition at Bay* (1931), a criticism of the 'new humanism'. His one novel, *The Last Puritan*, appeared in 1935. His memoirs, *Persons and Places*, were published in three volumes: *The Backgrounds of My Life* (1944), *The Middle Span* (1945) and *My Host the World* (1953).

**Sapphics** A verse form named after Sappho, the Greek poetess of 7th–6th century BC. It consists of four-line **stanzas**, the first three lines being long (—ᵕ/——/—ᵕᵕ/—ᵕ/——), the fourth short (—ᵕᵕ/—ᵛ). Attempts to reproduce classical quantities in English inevitably seem unnatural, since English is a stressed language, yet if stresses are made to substitute for the long syllables some compromise with sense seems almost unavoidable. There are, however, a number of Sapphic imitations to be found, especially in the Victorian period. (See also **metre**.)

**Sardanapalus** A tragedy by **Lord Byron**, written while he was at Ravenna in 1820 and published in 1821. Charles Kean produced it at **Drury Lane** in 1834. The action is set about 640 BC and based on the history of Diodorus Siculus.

Beleses, a Chaldean soothsayer, and Arbaces, a governor of Medea, organize a revolt against the extravagantly spendthrift king of Assyria, Sardanapalus. The revolt rouses him to action and, with the encouragement of the beautiful Myrrha, his Greek slave whom he loves, he leads his army into battle. But in spite of his valour the fighting goes against him and Sardanapalus has to retreat to his palace. He makes provision for the safe withdrawal of Zarina, his queen, prepares a funeral pyre around his throne and dies on it with Myrrha and his supporters.

**Sargeson, Frank** 1903–82 New Zealand short-story writer and novelist. Born at Hamilton in North Island, he qualified as a solicitor but worked at a number of jobs, becoming familiar with all levels of society and reacting sharply against bourgeois values. The Depression sharpened his sympathies with society's victims. His first stories were published in the 1930s in the Auckland periodical *Tomorrow*. His first collection, *Conversations with My Uncle* (1936), showed his skill at using the language of the ill-educated and semi-literate. Sargeson's *Collected Stories* was published in 1965; he is also the author of *I Saw in My Dream* (1949), *I For One* (1956) and *Joy of the Worm* (1969).

**Saroyan, William** 1908–81 American playwright, novelist and short-story writer. Born in Fresno, California, of Armenian parents, Saroyan spent most of his youth in San Francisco. He left school at 15, worked for a telegraph company, and began writing short stories in the late 1920s. His first collection of short stories, *The Daring Young Man on the Flying Trapeze* (1934), which attracted considerable critical and popular attention, typifies the rather genial vision which characterized his work as a whole. Other volumes of short fiction include *Inhale and Exhale* (1936), *Three Times Three* (1936), *The Trouble with Tigers* (1938), *My Name is Aram* (1940) and *Dear Baby* (1944). His first novel, *The Human Comedy*, appeared in 1943, and was followed by *The Adventures of Wesley Jackson* (1946), *Rock Wagram* (1951), *Mama, I Love You* (1956), *Papa, You're Crazy* (1957) and a story about an ageing author, *One Day in the Afternoon of the World* (1964).

Saroyan perhaps achieved his greatest fame as a playwright. The one-act play, *My Heart's in the Highlands*, was produced in 1939 and published in 1941. *The Time of Your Life* (1939), set in a San Francisco waterfront saloon, was awarded the Pulitzer Prize, but Saroyan rejected it. His other plays include *Love's Old Sweet Song* (1941), *The Beautiful People* (1942), *Across the Board on Tomorrow Morning* (1942), *Hello Out There* (1943), *Don't Go Away Mad* (1949) and *The Cave Dwellers* (1957). He published three autobiographical works: *The Bicycle Rider in*

*Beverly Hills* (1952), *Here Comes, There Goes, You Know Who* (1961) and *Obituaries* (1979).

**Sarton, May** 1912– American poet and novelist. Born in Belgium, Sarton emigrated to the USA in 1916 and became a citizen in 1924. Her first publication was a collection of lyrics entitled *Encounter in April* (1937). Other volumes of verse include *Inner Landscape* (1939), *The Lion and the Rose* (1948), *The Land of Silence* (1953), *In Time Like Air* (1957) and *Cloud, Stone, Sun, Vine* (1961). *Collected Poems* appeared in 1974.

Her novels and poetry address moral and political issues in a controlled and crafted manner, using a distinct and localized idiom. Her novels include *The Single Hound* (1938), about a young English poet, *The Birth of Grandfather* (1957), *The Small Room* (1961), about a young female teacher and a student at a New England college, *Mrs Stevens Hears the Mermaids Singing* (1965), *Kinds of Love* (1970), *As We Are Now* (1973) and *Anger* (1982). Her autobiographical writings include *I Knew a Phoenix* (1959), *Plant Dreaming Deep* (1968), *Journal of Solitude* (1973) and *Recovering* (1980).

**Sartor Resartus** A prose work by **Thomas Carlyle**. It was first published in *Fraser's Magazine* from November 1833 to August 1834 and in book form in the United States in 1836. The first English edition appeared in 1838.

Written under the influence of German Romantic thought, *Sartor Resartus* (The Tailor Re-patched) is constructed in three parts, the first of which satirically examines the philosophy of clothes, their importance as symbols and as coverings of an inner reality. The enquiry is made through the papers and memoranda of the idealistic Professor Diogenes Teufelsdröckh (God sent Devil's-dung) as set forth by a down-to-earth editor. The second movement is largely Carlyle's spiritual autobiography in the guise of Teufelsdröckh's romantic wanderings and peregrinations. These come to a spiritual climax, like one experienced by the author himself, in the chapters 'The Everlasting Nay', 'The Centre of Indifference' and 'The Everlasting Yea'. The final part is a poetic hymn to the romantic aspirant toward a nobler universe.

*Sartor Resartus* is a strangely complex book. Rich in symbol and allegory, frequently rough in humour, bizarre in style, it stands outside the accepted movement of prose writing of its own or any other time. The polarization of light and dark, hot and cold, night and day, as well as the employment of countless poetical figures – cut across by Germanic puns, satirical commentary on contemporary literary figures and hosts of linguistic whims and crotchets – combine to render a unique and often perplexing text. Over all hovers the Divine Spirit whose presence supports the convictions of the romantically intuitive man.

**Sassoon, Siegfried (Louvain)** 1886–1967 Poet and autobiographer. Educated at Marlborough and Clare College, Cambridge, he joined the Royal Welsh Fusiliers in World War I and went to France, where he met **Robert Graves**. He was wounded twice and awarded the MC, which he later threw away. Encouraged by **Bertrand Russell**, he protested in 'A Soldier's Declaration' (July 1917) that the war was 'being deliberately prolonged by those who have the power to end it'. Graves persuaded the War Office not to treat the matter as a disciplinary case. A medical board sent Sassoon to W. H. R. Rivers, the neurologist specializing in neurasthenia, at Craiglockhart Hospital, Edinburgh, where he met **Wilfred Owen**, whose poems he edited in 1920. His own realistic, savagely ironic anti-war poems were published with little critical success in *The Old Huntsman* (1917) and *Counter-Attack* (1918).

After the war he was involved in Labour politics, and became literary editor of *The Daily Herald*. He later returned to his pre-war life of a country gentleman, writing *Satirical Poems* (1926) and the semi-autobiographical trilogy *Complete Memoirs of George Sherston* (1937), consisting of *Memoirs of a Fox-Hunting Man* (1928), *Memoirs of an Infantry Officer* (1930) and *Sherston's Progress* (1936), all published anonymously. He then continued with three volumes of childhood autobiography, *The Old Century and Seven More Years* (1938), *The Weald of Youth* (1942) and *Siegfried's Journey* (1945). His later volumes of poetry included *Vigils* (1935) and *Sequences* (1956). Both were predominantly spiritual in content, and Sassoon became a Roman Catholic in 1957. He published an important biography of **Meredith** in 1948 and his *Collected Poems* in 1961.

**Satchell, William** 1860–1942 New Zealand novelist. Satchell was born in London and completed his education at Heidelberg. He emigrated to New Zealand in the 1880s, settling near Auckland, and published his first novel of New Zealand life, *The Land of the Lost*, in 1902. Others were *The Toll of the Bush* (1905), *The Elixir of Life* (1907) and the highly praised *The Greenstone Door* (1914), a novel about Anglo-Maori relations.

**satire** Satire seems to have begun as magical abuse purporting, like a curse, to wreak effective harm on the victim. Such attacking literature, using invective as its main weapon, would now be styled 'lampoon' rather than satire. On the other hand, when methods of stylistic caricature and farcical content so predominate that malice and morality tend to melt away in the mockery, **burlesque** or **mock heroic** would be preferred. **Dr Johnson** defined satire as 'a poem in which wickedness or folly is censured'. Provided we amend 'a poem' to 'literature' this seems adequate, for though the main weapons of European satire are **irony** and **wit**, it is not necessarily a form of comedy. **Orwell**'s *Animal Farm* is certainly a comic satire, but *Nineteen Eighty-Four* is equally certainly a horrific one.

Since the satirist tends to assume some moral or social norms by which degrees of wickedness or folly can be measured, satire is more frequent in classical periods. Where Romantic satire does exist it needs a higher proportion of wit in order to succeed (witness **Byron**'s *Vision of Judgement* and *Don Juan*), since the writer cannot take it for granted that all his readers share his norms; he must jolly them along, slipping in his punches when he can.

Satire is usually designated as either Juvenalian or Horatian, the former indignantly attacking wickedness, the latter suavely attacking folly. Elizabethan satire is almost entirely Juvenalian, partly because it inherits a morality tradition and partly because of a belief that satire should be rough (the result of an etymological mistake deriving the word from the shaggy satyr of mythology). The satire of the 18th century, on the other hand, as befits a 'polite' age, more often follows Horace; its major exemplar is **Pope**.

*Satire of the Three Estates, Ane Pleasant* A **morality play** by **Sir David Lyndsay**, first performed before the Scottish king, James V, in 1540. A surviving manuscript, dated 1568, records the text of a second performance in 1552, and the printed text (1602) of a third in 1554. The play is written in a variety of metres and mingles couplets with eight- and six-line stanzas. It contains nearly 5000 lines. Part I dramatizes the temptations of Rex Humanitas, beset by evil counsellors and falling prey to Sensuality. Good Counsel, returning to Scotland, is refused access to the court, Verity is clapped into the stocks and Chastity ignored. Only when Divine Correction arrives to reform the Three Estates does moral order return to the court of Rex Humanitas. An interlude details the misfortunes of an impoverished farmer and the chicanery of a pardoner. Part II brings the Three Estates before the King, to be denounced by John the Commonweill. Lords and Commons confess their faults and promise reform, but the Lords Spiritual defy the complainants and are forcibly dispossessed. The play ends with a stringent sermon from Folly.

Lyndsay's intention was to attack corruption wherever he saw it, but it was his vivid attack on the Lords Spiritual that made the play a favourite source for the advocates of reform in the Scottish Church. Modern revivals have found the lively language and the scenes of common life a greater strength than the lengthy debates.

*Satires of Circumstance, Lyrics and Reveries* Poems by **Thomas Hardy**, first published in 1914. Consisting of some poems already published and a number never before in print, *Satires of Circumstance* (misleadingly titled by Hardy's publisher) contains an impressive amount of the poet's finest work. Foremost are the deeply felt 'Poems of 1912–13', which are recollections of journeying in March of the latter year to Cornish scenes he had known over 40 years before when courting his first wife, Emma Lavinia Gifford. These are poems of sadness and meditation upon a flawed, complex marriage; they constitute a chapter of emotional autobiography and, to use Hardy's own term, 'an expiation'. The 1912–13 verses are skilfully wrought, impressively unsentimental and marked by profound regret. Hardy idealizes Emma's youthful beauty ('Beeny Cliff'), laments her sudden death ('The Going'), recalls visiting her at Tintagel ('I Found Her Out There') and replies to her dead spirit ('The Voice'). In poem after poem the tragedy of lost or unrealized love is poignantly suggested. The 'Poems of 1912–13' are among the great achievements of English elegiac verse.

The volume also contains philosophic and religious ruminations, as well as poems on contemporary events and spectral imaginings. Among the finest are 'Channel Firing', 'Wessex Heights', 'When I Set Out for Lyonnesse', 'Ah, Are You Digging on My Grave' and 'Under the Waterfall'.

*Satiromastix* A play by **Thomas Dekker**, perhaps with contributions from **John Marston**, first produced by a **boys' company** in 1601 as a rejoinder to **Jonson**'s *Poetaster* and revived by the Lord Chamberlain's Men (see **King's Men**) later in the same year.

The play is an unsatisfactory mixture, its archaic plot (virgin takes poison rather than lose her honour to the lustful king) largely hidden behind its abuse of Ben Jonson in the character of Horace. Dekker and Marston, in the disguise of Demetrius and Crispinus, ridicule Horace's vanity. Like so much of the writing that grew out of the war of the theatres, the satire is unattractively splenetic now that the quarrel is dead.

*Saturday Review, The* A periodical founded in 1855 by A. J. B. Beresford Hope (1820–87) with John Douglas Cook as its first editor. For many years the periodical maintained an exceptional position in London journalism. With *The Spectator*, it became the most influential paper of the period and published contributions from most of the leading figures in public life.

Politically, it was at first Peelite but rapidly moved towards a Conservative view. Under the editorship of **Frank Harris** (1894–8) its literary interests broadened and there were contributions from **Thomas Hardy**, **H. G. Wells**, **Max Beerbohm** and others. **G. B. Shaw** was its drama critic from 1895 to 1898. In 1899 it was sold to Lord Hardwicke, and was edited by Harold Hodge. It survived until 1938 but, despite some bright periods, it never regained its earlier influence.

**Saunders, James** 1925– Dramatist. Born in London, and educated at Wembley County School and the University of Southampton, he began his career as a chemistry teacher. His early plays were influenced both by poetic drama and the **Theatre of the Absurd**. *Next Time I'll Sing to You* (1963), his first stage success, was suggested by the life of an Essex hermit; loneliness is also a theme in *A Scent of Flowers* (1964), about a young girl who dies from lack of love. *Bodies* (1978), the most successful of his later work, is about two middle-aged couples facing various crises. Saunders also collaborated with **Iris Murdoch** in adapting her novel, *The Italian Girl* (1968), for the stage and adapted Heinrich von Kleist's story, *Hans Kohlhaas* (1973).

**Saussure, Ferdinand de** See **semiotics** and **structuralism**.

**Savage, Marmion** 1803–72 Anglo-Irish novelist. He was the author of six novels, among them a satire on the Young Ireland party, *Falcon Family* (1845). Most of his work was written in London, where he was editor of *The Examiner*.

**Savage, Richard** c.1696–1743 Poet and dramatist. Savage claimed to be the illegitimate son of the 4th Earl Rivers and the Countess of Macclesfield. He wrote a poem, *The Bastard* (1728), censuring his supposed mother and convinced his friend **Samuel Johnson**, who wrote a sympathetic biography in his *Lives of the Poets*, but the story is no longer accepted. Savage's first work was a poem, *The Convocation* (1717), followed by a comedy, *Love in a Veil* (produced in 1718), and *The Tragedy of Sir Thomas Overbury* (produced in 1723). Although Queen Anne paid him a pension for celebrating her birthday with an annual ode, his poetry is forgotten except for *The Wanderer* (1729), a rambling contemplation of the nature of existence which Johnson called 'a heap of shining materials thrown together by accident'. In 1727 Savage was found guilty of killing a man in a tavern brawl but pardoned; he eventually died in a debtors' prison in Bristol.

*Saved* A play by **Edward Bond**, first presented in a club performance at the **Royal Court Theatre**, London, in 1965 after public performance had been banned by the Lord Chamberlain's Office.

Len, an outsider among the drifting gangs of urban youth, moves into the house of his girlfriend Pam and stays even when she takes up with the more bullish Fred. The home is utterly loveless – Pam's parents have not spoken to each other for years – and Len's is the only (mildly) questioning voice heard in the play. Fred tires of Pam after making her pregnant, and the child is another unloved element in the house. Even Len, who knows that he may be the father, has nothing to offer it. Trying to force Fred to come back to the house, Pam leaves the baby with him, having drugged it with aspirins to keep it quiet. In a scene of apparently casual violence (it was the main reason for the play's banning), Fred and his friends tease and jostle the baby before stoning it to death. Fred is imprisoned for the crime, while Pam still hopes to reclaim him on his release. The final scenes of the play show the strangely indestructible Len still living in Pam's house, and the last image is of him silently mending a chair.

**Savile, George, Marquess of Halifax** 1633–95 Politician and writer on politics. Savile was the son of a Yorkshire baronet and entered Parliament in 1660. A man of independent politics, he became Viscount Halifax in 1668, Earl in 1679 and Marquess in 1682. He led the opposition to Shaftesbury and the Exclusion Bill in the House of Lords and carried the house with him. (See *Absalom and Achitophel*.) His influence at court waned with the accession of James II, whom he had criticized freely. As chairman of the committee of peers it fell to Halifax to ask William and Mary to accept the throne of England in 1689. The last office he held before retirement was Lord Privy Seal.

In literature Halifax is remembered for his political tracts and essays, most notably *The Character of a Trimmer* (1688), a bold and seminal pamphlet which contains a famous passage in praise of truth. The main body of his work is to be found in *Miscellanies* (1700) and *A Character of King Charles the Second: And Political, Moral and Miscellaneous Thoughts and Reflections* (1750), both published after his death.

**Savile, Sir Henry** 1549–1622 Scholar and translator. Educated at Brasenose College, Oxford, Savile became a fellow of Merton College and eventually its Warden in 1585. He served both as Greek tutor and Latin secretary to Queen Elizabeth, whom he importuned successfully for the provostship of Eton, which he obtained in 1596. Savile was one of the scholars commissioned by King James to produce the Authorized Version of the Bible (see **Bible in English**). James knighted him in 1604. Savile assisted **Sir Thomas Bodley** in founding his great library and also endowed Oxford with two professorships, in geometry and astronomy, in 1619. Savile translated four books of Tacitus' *Histories* (1519), and edited St John Chrysostom (1610–13) and Xenophon's *Cyropaedia* (1613).

**Savoy Operas, The** A group of 13 comic operas, excluding the early *Thespis* (1871) by **W. S. Gilbert** (librettist) and Arthur Sullivan (composer). They are: *Trial by Jury* (1875), *The Sorcerer* (1877), *H.M.S. Pinafore* (1878), *The Pirates of Penzance* (1879), *Patience* (1881), *Iolanthe* (1882), *Princess Ida* (1884), *The Mikado* (1885), *Ruddigore* (1887), *The Yeomen of the Guard* (1888), *The Gondoliers* (1889), *Utopia Limited* (1893), *The Grand Duke* (1896). Although the first five were originally produced elsewhere, the series is always called after the Savoy Theatre, London, built for their performance by the impresario Richard D'Oyly Carte. They established new standards of writing and presentation for the English musical theatre, proved immensely popular throughout the English-speaking world, and have been widely performed ever since. Gilbert's libretti are characterized by a strong satirical streak allied to a personal vein of fantasy. His lyrics are deftly contrived, often shrewdly pointed, and at their strongest in humorous and patter songs; his sentimental songs tend to be commonplace. The dialogue is marked by an elaborate command of paradox and a profound cynicism sometimes verging on the callous, as in his much criticized presentation of the ageing spinster. This flavour is idiosyncratic enough to justify the term 'Gilbertian', subsequently applied in extra-theatrical contexts. Sullivan's scores admirably complement the libretti, providing in their melody and harmony the warmth which Gilbert's work lacked, and heightening his wit and satire by their vivacity. Like Gilbert, Sullivan did not always avoid the sentimental commonplace. The Savoy Operas represent the main legacy of the Victorian stage to the modern repertory.

*Sawles Warde* A homiletic prose **allegory** written in the late 12th century near the Welsh border. It freely adapts chapters 13–15 in Book IV of *De Anima*, attributed to Hugh of St Victor; these chapters represent a separate work, *De Custodia Interioris Hominis*, circulated in the Middle Ages as the work of St Anselm. *Sawles Warde* uses the common allegorical figures of the body as the house of the soul, the senses as the wards of the heart and the Four Daughters of God (Righteousness, Prudence, Temperance and Ghostly or Spiritual Strength). Wit must rule Will and, with the help of the Daughters of God, guard the house of the soul against the assaults of the Devil. Fear, the messenger of Death, enters and delivers a speech on the horrors of Hell, a catalogue of vividly realized physical torments. The Daughters of God protect the household from fear of death after a period of deliberation and another messenger, that of Mirth, arrives and describes Heaven, giving hope and joy to the soul. The meaning of the allegory is clearly explained and the evocative descriptions of Heaven and Hell add power to the work's message.

**Sayers, Dorothy L[eigh]** 1893–1957 Writer of **detective fiction**, playwright and translator. Born in Oxford, she spent much of her childhood in the Fens (where her father was vicar of Bluntisham-cum-Earith) and returned to Oxford in 1912–15 to study at Somerville College. After working variously as a schoolteacher, publisher's reader and copywriter in an advertising agency, she became a full-time writer in 1931. By this time she had begun her series of detective novels about the elegant and apparently light-hearted Lord Peter Wimsey, eventually to make her one of the most popular writers of the day: *Whose Body?* (1923), *Clouds of Witness* (1926), *Unnatural Death* (1927), *The Unpleasantness at the Bellona Club* (1928), *Strong Poison* (1930), which also introduced Harriet Vane, *The Five Red Herrings* (1931), *Have His Carcase* (1932), *Murder Must Advertise* (1932), set in an advertising agency, *The Nine Tailors* (1934), set in the Fens, *Gaudy Night* (1935), with Wimsey and Vane in Oxford and *Busman's Honeymoon* (1937), in which Wimsey and Vane are married. The later novels in the series determinedly introduce a new note of seriousness. Her only detective novel without Wimsey is *The Documents in the Case* (with Robert Eustace, 1930). She also wrote 11 short stories with the commercial traveller Montague Egg as detective, and contributed thoughtful introductions to two collections of *Detection, Mystery and Horror* (1928 and 1931, called *The Omnibus of Crime* in the USA).

Although she served as President of the Detection Club from 1949 until her death, she had by then abandoned detective fiction for a sequence of radio plays about the life of Christ, *The Man Born To Be King* (broadcast 1941–2) and for translations of Dante's *Inferno* (1949), *Purgatorio* (1955) and *Paradiso* (completed by Barbara Reynolds, 1962) and of *The Song of Roland* (1957).

**Scannell, Vernon** 1922– Poet. Born in Spilsby, Lincolnshire, he was educated at Queen's Park School, Aylesbury, and Leeds University. His unconventional career embraced army service, professional boxing and work in a fairground boxing booth, and teaching before he became a freelance writer and broadcaster. Scannell's many volumes of verse include *Graves and Resurrections* (1948), *A Sense of Danger* (1962), *Epithets of War: Poems 1965–1969* (1969), *Selected Poems* (1971), *The Winter Man* (1973), *The Loving Game* (1975), *New and Collected Poems 1950–1980* (1980), *Winterlude* (1982) and *Funeral Games* (1987). His poems are formally traditional and rooted in recognizable human experience; they are acute observations of the 20th century, with its disillusionments, daydreams and underlying violence. His novels include *The Fight* (1953), *The Wound and the Scar* (1953) and *Ring of Truth* (1983). *The Tiger and the Rose* (1971) is autobiographical.

**Scarlet Letter, The** A novel by **Nathaniel Hawthorne**, published in 1850 and developed from an incident described by him in the story 'Endicott and the Red Cross' (1837).

The novel is set in 17th-century Boston, and opens as a young woman named Hester Prynne emerges from prison with her illegitimate baby in her arms. Charged with adultery, she must stand exposed on the public scaffold for three hours, and must thereafter wear a scarlet letter 'A' on her breast as a lifelong sign of her sin. Her husband is an elderly English scholar who two years earlier had sent her to Boston to prepare a home for them, but had failed to follow her at the appointed time. Unknown to Hester, he had been captured by Indians, and in fact arrives just in time to see his wife publicly condemned. Hester will not reveal the identity of her lover, try as the community does to draw out the secret. Ironically, the guilty man is one of that community's most respected figures, the young minister, Arthur Dimmesdale. A highly conscientious man, he escapes outward condemnation, but is inwardly tormented by sin.

Years pass and Hester settles into her new life. She proves to be a strongminded and capable woman and, in spite of her humiliation, finds a place in Boston society by helping other unfortunates and outcasts. Her daughter, Pearl, has developed into a mischievous 'elfin' child who reminds Hester of her guilt by asking rather acute questions about the minister and the letter. Meanwhile, Hester's husband has taken the name Roger Chillingworth and has settled in Boston as a doctor. He makes Hester swear to keep his identity secret, and indulges his private obsession with finding the identity of her lover. Happening upon Hester, Pearl, and Dimmesdale speaking together one midnight, he guesses correctly at Dimmesdale's guilt. Aware that the minister's failing health is related to his unconfessed sin, Chillingworth pretends to help him medically, while torturing him spiritually with veiled allusions to his crime. Hester intercepts Arthur one day on a walk through the forest and begs him to escape with her to Europe. He would like to do so, and Hester even removes the letter from her breast, but he sees flight as yielding to further temptation. He returns to town, his mind filled with evil thoughts, to finish writing his Election Day Sermon. Hester learns that Chillingworth has blocked her plan of escape by booking passage on the same ship. Having delivered a powerful sermon, Dimmesdale leaves the church and bids Hester and Pearl to join him on the pillory, where at last he publicly confesses his sin. As Dimmesdale dies in his lover's arms, Chillingworth cries out in agony at having lost the sole object of his perverse life. Hester and Pearl, now free from the restraints of the mortified community, leave Boston. The book ends with Hester's return to Boston and her voluntary decision to resume wearing the scarlet letter. While Pearl settles in Europe, Hester continues her life of penance, a model of endurance, goodness and victory over sin.

**scène à faire** The scene of crucial confrontation between two adversaries whose meeting or recognition has been delayed. In the **well-made play** it is the prelude to the **denouement**.

**Scenes of Clerical Life** Three tales by **George Eliot**, marking her début as a writer of fiction. They first appeared in *Blackwood's Magazine* in 1857, and were published in volume form under their collective title in 1858.

'The Sad Fortunes of the Reverend Amos Barton' concerns the well-meaning but maladroit curate of Shepperton and his gentle, graceful wife, Milly. George Eliot delineates Amos Barton's daily life, his awkward relationships with his parishioners, his lack of flexibility, and his alienation from those about him. His gullibility and his wife's innate kindness allow the 'Countess' Czerlaski, a parasitical woman, to impose upon the Barton family to the extent that their meagre resources are strained to the utmost. When poor Milly dies, worn out and tired, Amos Barton is deeply remorseful and, chastened through suffering, acquires the sympathy and understanding of his parishioners. Sadly, as he becomes a true part of the community, his curacy is terminated in favour of another parson and he is compelled to take a parish in an ugly manufacturing town.

Like its predecessor, 'Mr Gilfil's Love-Story' is set in Shepperton, but a good many years before the time of the Reverend Amos Barton. The story centres on the tragic life and love of another incumbent, Maynard Gilfil, once the ward and domestic chaplain of Sir Christopher Cheverel of Cheverel Manor. It is there he meets and comes to love Caterina Sarti (Tina), the talented singer whom Sir Christopher and his wife adopted when her Italian father, a musician, died indigent. Tina is brought to England as one of the Cheverel household, and she develops a fatally consuming passion for the feckless Captain Anthony Wybrow, who trifles with her whilst seeking the wealthy and socially prominent Beatrice Assher as his wife. Wybrow dies suddenly of natural causes whilst waiting to meet Tina, who becomes dangerously unbalanced at her discovery of his body; she flees Cheverel Manor and seeks refuge among humble folk, where Maynard Gilfil finds her and slowly, with the help of his married sister and brother-in-law, restores her to health. He marries her, but so broken is her spirit that she dies after a few months at Shepperton and leaves Mr Gilfil to a lonely old age. 'Mr Gilfil's Love-Story' is a melancholy tale, but the narrative is enhanced by some arresting character studies of local people and by the compassion with which George Eliot invests her protagonist.

'Janet's Repentance', the last and longest of *Scenes of Clerical Life*, tells the tragic tale of the hostility of the drunken, braggard lawyer, Robert Dempster, toward the Reverend Edgar Tryan, who seeks to improve the spiritual life of the complacent, apathetic parishioners of Milby. Tryan provokes Dempster's wrath because he is a civilized Christian gentleman whose brand of Evangelicalism is particularly offensive to the blustering lawyer. In his opposition, Dempster is joined by his wife, Janet, also addicted to drink. Tryan, who is of a delicate constitution, is gravely worn down by his efforts to better the community: preaching three sermons on a Sunday, teaching at night school, giving cottage lectures and paying many pastoral calls. Meanwhile, Dempster seriously abuses his wife, who flees the home and is sympathetically helped toward a finer, gentler life by Tryan. Dempster meets with a serious accident which eventually brings about his death. By now Janet resists the temptation of alcohol, regains her place in Milby and is at Tryan's bedside when he dies, exhausted. But she has attained an inner harmony of mind and spirit and devotes her life to the good of others. The sad narrative is marked, like its predecessor, by some effective sketches of minor provincial people and by its slow-moving rhythmic progression toward an inevitable end.

**Scholar-Gipsy, The** A poem by **Matthew Arnold**, published in *Poems: A New Edition* (1853). It derives from the legend of an Oxford student who left the university to live with the gipsies, told by **Joseph Glanvill** in *The Vanity of Dogmatizing* (1661). In Arnold's poem the speaker has Glanvill's book beside him and envies the scholar-gipsy's escape into the pastoral charms of the countryside around Oxford. For himself and his generation, however, he acknowledges that no such escape is possible from 'this strange disease of modern life,/With its sick hurry, its divided aims,/Its heads o'ertaxed, its palsied hearts'.

**School for Scandal, The** A comedy by **Richard Brinsley Sheridan**, first performed at **Drury Lane** in 1777. Sheridan, who was the leading partner in the management of the theatre, wrote the play in a hurry and under pressure, but even so it is the most accomplished comedy of manners to have been written in the 18th century.

The ageing Sir Peter Teazle has married a young and ingenuous wife, fresh to London and dazzled by its social excitements. Among those she meets are the brothers, Charles and Joseph Surface. Charles is dissolute but good-hearted; Joseph is decorous but hypocritical. Each of them would like to marry Sir Peter's ward, Maria, who is also being courted by Sir Benjamin Backbite, one of the malicious circle headed by Lady Sneerwell. The plot is complex and ingeniously handled. It turns on the return of Sir Oliver Surface from Bengal, his discovery of the true characters of his nephews, and the eventual unmasking of Joseph Surface in a justly famous 'screen scene'. The end sees Charles Surface united with Maria and the much-tried Teazles reconciled.

**Schreiner, Olive** 1855–1920 South African moralist and novelist, born at Wittebergen Mission Station, Cape Colony. Largely self-

A mezzotint of 1783 of the famous screen episode in Act IV, scene 3 of *The School for Scandal*. Sheridan's comedy was first produced in 1777. Victoria & Albert Theatre Museum, London.

educated, her unconventional thinking was coloured by **Herbert Spencer**'s *First Principles* and **Emerson**'s *Essays*. She started writing while a governess from 1874 until she first went to England in 1881. The success of *The Story of an African Farm* (1883) made her the first colonial writer to be clasped to the bosom of literary London. The bleak farm is an unromantic metaphor that undermines the imperial, heroical image of the frontier, while the passionate authority that shapes the heroine's role made the novel an important document for feminists. Two novels she often re-worked were posthumously published by her husband S. C. Cronwright: *From Man to Man* (1926) and *Undine* (1929). The allegory and pulpit rhetoric of the novel *Trooper Peter Halket of Mashonaland* (1897) contribute much to the moral impact of its attack upon Cecil Rhodes and his Chartered Company's barbarous treatment of blacks in 'Rhodesia'.

Olive Schreiner saw herself less as a novelist than a writer trying to transform an uncaring society, hence such works as *Dreams* (1891) and *Dream Life and Real Life* (1893). Her polemical writings consistently championed the victims of injustice: the Boer republics soon to be invaded by Britain in *A South African's View of the Situation* (1898), unfranchised black South Africans in the prescient, still relevant *A Letter on the South African Union and the Principles of Government* (1909) and women in *Woman and Labour* (1911).

**Schwartz, Delmore** 1913–66 American poet, short-story writer and critic, born in Brooklyn, and educated at New York University. The principal concern of much of his work is the complex relationship between the private self and the outside world. The intellectual energy of his writing was reflected also in his career as a teacher at Harvard, Princeton, New York and Syracuse universities, and in his influential position in the group of Jewish writers that emerged after World War II – particularly as a member of the editorial board of **The Partisan Review** from 1943 to 1955.

His first book of stories and poems, *In Dreams Begin Responsibilities*, was published in 1938. Other collections which combine prose and poetry are *Genesis, Book One* (1943) and *Vaudeville for a Princess, and Other Poems* (1950). In 1941 he published a verse-play, *Shenandoah*, and a collection of essays, *The Imitation of Life*. His collection of short stories *The World is a Wedding* (1948) deals with the problems of Jewish life in America. *Summer Knowledge: New and Selected Poems 1938–58* appeared in 1959 and *Successful Love, and Other Stories* in 1961.

**science fiction** Stories which are set in the future, or in which the contemporary setting is disrupted by an imaginary device such as a new invention or the introduction of an alien being. They were first labelled 'science fiction' in American magazines of the 1920s; a term previously used in Britain was 'scientific romance', and many contemporary writers and critics prefer the term 'speculative fiction'. Stories of this kind are distinguished from other kinds of fantastic narrative by the claim that they respect the limits of scientific possibility, and that their innovations are plausible extrapolations from modern theory and technology; relatively few examples, however, are genuinely conscientious in this respect.

Although elements of science fiction appear in many stories of imaginary voyages, it was not until the 19th century that the advancement of science began to inspire a good deal of work in this vein. **Mary Shelley**'s *Frankenstein* (1818) is a notable early example, and science-fictional themes play a significant part in the work of **Edgar Allan Poe** and **Nathaniel Hawthorne**. Following George Chesney's account of an imaginary invasion of England, 'The Battle of Dorking' (1871), there was a spate of future war stories in Britain, and the influence of Jules Verne helped to popularize tales of imaginary tourism involving hypothetical flying machines, submarines and spaceships. Speculation about the future was also encouraged by movements for political reform and by ideas drawn from the theory of evolution. These various threads were drawn together when scientific romance came briefly into vogue in the British popular periodicals of the 1890s. By far the most ambitious and successful author of this period was **H. G. Wells**, whose fertile imagination was fired by **Thomas Henry Huxley**'s lectures on biology and by his fervent socialism. He produced a series of classic scientific romances between 1895 and 1904, including *The Time Machine*, *The Island of Dr Moreau*, *The Invisible Man*, *The War of the Worlds*, *When the Sleeper Wakes*, *The First Men in the Moon* and *The Food of the Gods*.

This was a time when the entire world-view of traditional religion seemed to have crumbled away, to be replaced by a scientific perspective in which the earth was a tiny atom in an infinite universe and man's dominion but a brief moment in an earthly history extending over billions of years. Many of Wells's contemporaries in the genre were sons of clergymen converted to free thought, who often used fiction to work out or display details of the revelation associated with their conversion; they included **M. P. Shiel**, **William Hope Hodgson**, J. D. Beresford and **Grant Allen**. Even some of the writers who were attracted to scientific romance by the opportunities which it offered for writing exotic adventure stories were the free-thinking sons of clergymen; examples include George Griffith, Fred T. Jane and C. J. Cutcliffe Hyne.

'The bone crumbled instantly to white powder.' An illustration from *Stories of Other Worlds* by George Griffith, from *Pearson's Magazine*, January 1900.

Outside the work of Wells the most important scientific romances produced before World War I were Shiel's *The Purple Cloud* (1901), Hodgson's *The House on the Borderland* (1908), Beresford's *The Hampdenshire Wonder* (1912) and *The Lost World* (1912) by **Sir Arthur Conan Doyle**. The most important American writer who contributed to the genre in this period was **Jack London**, in such works as *The Iron Heel* (1907) and 'The Scarlet Plague' (1912).

World War I had a profound effect on British futuristic fiction, and in the period between the wars British scientific romance was dominated by the idea that a new war could and probably would obliterate civilization, plunging mankind into a new Dark Age. This idea can be seen in *People of the Ruins* (1920) by Edward Shanks and *Theodore Savage* (1922) by Cicely Hamilton, and in the work of the new writers who were to be the most prolific producers of scientific romance between the wars: **Olaf Stapledon**, S. Fowler Wright, Neil Bell and John Gloag. Wells's *The Shape of Things to Come* (1933) reaches an optimistic conclusion, but only after describing the devastation of the world by war and plague. A frequent corollary of this notion that man was living on the brink of catastrophe was that he must ultimately be replaced by a new species which had transcended his innate brutality. This preoccupation with the supersession of *homo sapiens* is at its most extravagant in Stapledon's *Last and First Men* (1930) and *Odd John* (1935) but can also be seen in *The Clockwork Man* (1923) by E. V. Odle, in Gloag's *Tomorrow's Yesterday* (1930), in Shiel's *The Young Men are Coming!* (1937) and in Beresford's *'What Dreams May Come . . .'* (1941). Utopian speculation in this period was not entirely stifled, but was undermined and opposed by a determined cynicism seen most comprehensively in *The Question Mark* (1923) by Muriel Jaeger and *Brave New World* (1932) by **Aldous Huxley**.

The USA, by contrast, was relatively untouched by World War I, and its futuristic fictions were haunted by no such anxieties. Interplanetary fiction, which played a very minor role in British scientific romance, enjoyed something of a vogue in America, largely due to the example of **Edgar Rice Burroughs**, who used other planets as settings for gaudy adventure stories like *A Princess of Mars* (1912). Such stories became part of the staple diet of the pulp magazines, and helped pave the way for Hugo Gernsback to introduce magazines specializing in futuristic and interplanetary fiction in the late 1920s; it was he who first popularized the term 'science fiction'. Critics of these exuberant but preposterous space adventure stories contemptuously dubbed them 'space operas', but they embodied a mood of buoyant self-confidence that was current in America at the time. Gernsback's writers were not in the least anxious about the possible destruction of civilization and had no need to imagine new species to replace mankind: in their futures the powers of human creativity, deployed in new technologies, would make men equal to all possible challenges if only they were careful enough, and would enable *homo sapiens* to conquer the universe. American science fiction remained naïve in tone until the mid 1930s, but anxieties bred by the Depression combined with the influence of magazine editor John W. Campbell Jr to encourage a more sober and realistic approach. A new generation of writers recruited by Campbell included **Isaac Asimov**, **Robert A. Heinlein**, Clifford D. Simak, Theodore Sturgeon, **A. E. van Vogt** and Fritz Leiber. These writers brought a measure of intellectual sophistication to science fiction while retaining its imaginative fertility and adventurousness. In the 1940s science fiction remained virtually confined to popular magazines, and the most notable American works of the period were often story series subsequently assembled into book form; they include Asimov's robot stories (*I, Robot*, 1950) and *Foundation* trilogy (1951–3), Heinlein's 'Future History' series, and the series collected in Simak's *City* (1952).

After World War II the British tradition of scientific romance petered out, its last notable practitioners being **C. S. Lewis** and Gerald Heard. Its pessimistic tone, further encouraged by Hiroshima, culminated in such bleak works as **George Orwell**'s *Nineteen Eighty-Four* (1949) and Aldous Huxley's *Ape and Essence* (1949). Works owing their allegiance to this tradition have occasionally been produced since, but scientific romance was almost entirely displaced by and absorbed into American science fiction, which became established in Britain in the late 1940s as part of the more general 'coca-colonization' of British culture. The best of the British writers of futuristic fiction who came to prominence after the war, however, combined the serious and anxious concerns of scientific romance with the greater imaginative scope and ideative playfulness of science fiction. They included **John Wyndham**, **Brian Aldiss**, John Brunner and **J. G. Ballard**, all of whom retained a strong interest in the catastrophist tradition and exemplified it in their best works: Wyndham's *The Day of the Triffids* (1951), Ballard's *The Drowned World* (1962), Aldiss's *Greybeard* (1964) and Brunner's *Stand on Zanzibar* (1968). The most successful of the British post-war writers of science fiction, **Arthur C. Clarke**, is more strongly affiliated to the American optimistic tradition, but shows marked Stapledonian influences in some of his most famous work, including *Childhood's End* (1953) and *The City and the Stars* (1956).

In the USA the popularity of science fiction increased dramatically with the advent of paperbacks, and there was a gradual shift from the short-story form toward novels and, eventually, novel series. Most of the best writers of the 1950s, though, made their names as writers of slick and clever short stories, and some of the apologists for the genre who helped it to gain respectability – notably **Kingsley Amis** – argued that science fiction works best in short-story form because its strengths lie with the ingenious development of ideas rather than with the elaborate characterization that longer works require. The most important new writers to emerge in America in the 50s and early 60s were Frederik Pohl, Cyril M. Kornbluth, James Blish, Robert Sheckley, Poul Anderson, Robert Silverberg and **Ray Bradbury**. Significant works include Bradbury's *The Martian Chronicles* (1950) and *Fahrenheit 451* (1953), Pohl and Kornbluth's *The Space Merchants* (1953), Alfred Bester's *The Demolished Man* (1953) and *The Stars My Destination* (1956), Blish's *A Case of Conscience* (1958) and Walter M. Miller's *A Canticle for Leibowitz* (1960). The last two show a preoccupation with religion which has – rather paradoxically and perhaps surprisingly – become noticeable in modern science fiction. Even where religious ideas are not explicitly evoked there is still a fascination with the relationship between moral and metaphysical issues – in Sturgeon's *More than Human* (1953) and Simak's *Time and Again* (1951), for example.

The mid 1960s saw in both Britain and the USA a modish experimental phase in the development of science fiction. In Britain a 'new wave' was promoted by **Michael Moorcock**, who converted the magazine *New Worlds* into an Arts Council-supported *avant-garde* periodical. In America Harlan Ellison promoted a series of 'taboo-breaking' anthologies begun with *Dangerous Visions* (1967). Moorcock's tetralogy of novels featuring Jerry Cornelius (1968–77) exemplified his new approach, while Ellison's graphic short fictions are best displayed in *I Have No Mouth and I Must Scream* (1967). The best of the experimental new writers were Roger Zelazny, Samuel R. Delany, Barry Malzberg, John Sladek and Thomas M. Disch – all American, though the last two were first received more enthusiastically in Britain. Their most impressive works include Delany's *Dhalgren* (1975) and Disch's *Camp Concentration* (1968). Alongside this *avant-garde*, however, great commercial success was achieved by many more conventional science-fiction writers. Writers like Pohl and Silverberg found new success as novelists, having previously been better known as short-story writers. Asimov, Clarke and Heinlein all attained best-seller status, as did Frank Herbert with his massive novel *Dune* (1965) and **Kurt Vonnegut** with *Slaughterhouse-5* (1969). Following Vonnegut's capture of a cult following on American campuses the American academic establishment began to pay serious attention to science fiction, helping to boost the reputations of **Philip K. Dick** and **Ursula LeGuin**. The former attracted attention because of his ingenuity in presenting images of artificial and hallucinatory worlds which dissolve into confusion, the latter because of her moral earnestness and purity of style. Dick's most important works include *The Man in the High Castle* (1962) and *Do Androids Dream of Electric Sheep?* (1968); LeGuin's two classic novels are *The Left Hand of Darkness* (1969) and *The Dispossessed* (1974).

Before 1965 science fiction was read mostly by young men, but the feminist movement in America generated a new interest in the possibilities of reform in the area of sexual politics, and several new female writers became prominent in the genre in the 1970s, including Joanna Russ and the pseudonymous James Tiptree Jr (Alice Sheldon). In recent years science fiction has been partly displaced in the marketplace by fantasies of magic and swordplay, following the extraordinary success of US paperback editions of **J. R. R. Tolkien**'s *The Lord of the Rings*. The two genres have overlapped in the work of recent best-selling writers like Anne McCaffrey and Piers Anthony. The situation has been further complicated by a resurgence of interest in horror fiction, with writers like Stephen King frequently borrowing science-fictional ideas to mingle and blend with traditional supernatural motifs.

The boundaries of the genre are now more difficult to outline than ever before. Some American 'mainstream' novelists have also begun to use science-fictional elements in their work; examples include **Thomas Pynchon**'s *Gravity's Rainbow* (1973), **Gore Vidal**'s *Kalki* (1978) and Jeremy Leven's *Creator* (1980). This reflects a considerable evolution of science fiction from the days when it was virtually an esoteric literary cult; its imagery has now diffused throughout contemporary culture to become familiar in some measure to everyone. This familiarity has not entirely eroded the contempt in which science fiction was held when it was an absurdly gaudy species of pulp fiction (much of it, in fact, remains both absurd and gaudy, especially in its film and TV manifestations) but it has enabled some writers and individual works to escape stigmatization, and has helped make the products of the scientific imagination available to reputable writers. The difficulty of achieving elaborate characterization and density of environmental detail in futuristic and hypothetical settings still prevents even the best science-fiction novels from living up to the expectations of traditionally-minded literary critics, but the excellence of modern fabulists like Vonnegut and Disch is helping to change hidebound expectations of what novels can and ought to be.

*Scoggin His Jests* The first extant edition of this jest-book is entitled *The First and Best Part of Scoggin's Jests* (1626), but there must have been earlier editions in the mid 16th century. The collection is attributed to **Andrew Boorde**. Scoggin, so the book claims, was a fool at the court of Edward IV, although there seems to have been some confusion with Henry Scogan, a poet and acquaintance of **Chaucer**. Numerous references in English Renaissance literature testify to the popularity of these jokes.

**Scot, Alexander** ?1525–?85 Practically nothing is known of the life of this late Scottish 'maker', or poet. His poems, mainly lyrics, survive only in the collection of Scottish verse made by **George Bannatyne**.

**Scot (or Scott), Reginald** ?1538–99 Writer on witchcraft. Scot was educated at Hart Hall, Oxford, and was MP for New Romney in Kent. *A Perfect Platform of a Hop Garden* (1574) was the first practical treatise on the subject in English. *The Discovery of Witchcraft* (1584) was remarkably rational and sceptical for its time. Scot, who was influenced by the sceptical German writer and doctor, Johann Weyer, does not portray witches as malevolent hags armed with terrific powers to kill and maim. Instead, his witches are 'old, lame, blear-eyed, pale, foul and full of wrinkles; poor, sullen superstitious and papists, or such as know no religion'. They are ignorant, credulous and prone to melancholy and victimization. His scepticism about the supposed activities of witches and spirits was so strong that it laid him open to the charge of sadducism (disbelief in the existence of spirits). There is a tradition that the *Discovery* was burned by the public hangman at the order of King James, who attacks Scot's book in the preface to his *Demonology*. **Shakespeare** and **Thomas Middleton** were among its readers.

**Scott, Dennis** 1939– Jamaican poet and playwright. He first came to the attention of readers outside the Caribbean when his American-published collection of poems, *Uncle Time*, won the Commonwealth Poetry Prize in 1974, a year after its publication. He confirmed his technical assurance and his ability to mix Caribbean subject matter with wider concerns in a second collection of poems, *Dreadwalk* (1982). Scott, who was Principal of the Jamaica School of Drama from 1978 to 1982, and who has been Jamaica's leading theatre critic, is the author of several plays. *An Echo in the Bone* (1974), written for the silver jubilee of the University Drama Society in Jamaica, is the best known: ritualistic and violent in parts, it ambitiously links together different phases in the historical development of black people. A later play, *Dog* (1981), is an allegory about human viciousness. Scott's dramatic talent is innovative in terms of stage technique and seeks to make fundamental statements about man's historical behaviour. His poetry is at times more intimate and personal.

**Scott, Duncan Campbell** 1862–1947 Canadian poet and short-story writer. Scott was born in Ottawa. His father was a Methodist minister and his family lived in various places in Ontario and Quebec. He worked for the Department of Indian Affairs in Ottawa from 1879 until his retirement in 1935. Scott's friend **Archibald Lampman** encouraged him to write and his first book of verse, *The Magic House*, appeared in 1893. He published seven more volumes of poetry, including *New World Lyrics and Ballads* (1905), *Beauty and Life* (1921), *The Green Cloister* (1935) and *The Circle of Affection* (1947). *In the Village of Viger* (1896) and *The Witching of Elspie* (1923) are collections of short stories.

**Scott, F[rancis] R[eginald]** 1899–1985 Canadian poet and lawyer. Born in Quebec and educated at Bishop's College, Lennoxville, Magdalen College, Oxford, and McGill University, he was called to the Canadian Bar in 1927. He became a lecturer at McGill University, where he remained until his retirement. His poetry, beginning with *Overture* (1945), demonstrates the same sense of social responsibility that has made Scott a champion of civil rights and a leading authority on constitutional law; recent volumes include *Selected Poems* (1966), *Trouvailles* (1967) and *The Dance is One* (1973). *Essays on the Constitution*, one of many legal works, was published in 1977.

**Scott, Paul (Mark)** 1920–78 Novelist. Born in London, he spent his army service during World War II in India and Malaya, the only time he ever went to the subcontinent. He was subsequently a publisher and then a literary agent before devoting his time to writing.

His principal achievement is the Raj Quartet of novels and its late coda, *Staying On* (1977), which won the Booker Prize. Like the Quartet, his eight earlier novels show a dense, painstaking realism and are all set in either India or Malaya, except for *The Bender* (1963), which has a London setting and opts for a picaresque manner. The best of them is generally taken to be *The Birds of Paradise* (1962), which illustrates Scott's preoccupation with the process of history and the shifting perspectives of the past, seen to greatest effect in the long, slow movement of the Quartet. *The Corrida at San Feliu* (1964) prefigures the Quartet in its complex, fragmentary narrative structure composed of multiple points of view, a technique Scott learned from **Conrad**.

The Raj Quartet is made up of four novels, *The Jewel in the Crown* (1966), *The Day of the Scorpion* (1968), *The Towers of Silence* (1972) and *A Division of the Spoils* (1974), covering the final five years of British India (1942–7). From a variety of standpoints, ranging from the ostracized Anglo-Indian Hari Kumar to the sadistic, punctiliously disciplinarian Ronald Merrick, Scott explores his theme. This is not just the actual loosening of the British hold on India but, more importantly, the gradual retrospective change in the moral climate among the British community in India, as they are progressively shown to be governing (and then bequeathing to a troubled, uncertain future) an alien, often violently antagonistic land. The final novel in the sequence introduces an element of humour absent from its sober, even solemn precursors, a tendency more marked in the spry, sanguine comedy of *Staying On*, which returns to two minor characters from the Quartet, Tusker and Lucy Smalley, living out a bleak and isolated retirement in India long after independence.

**Scott, Sir Walter** 1771–1832 Poet, novelist, editor and critic. Son of a Writer to the Signet, Scott was born in Edinburgh, the ninth of 12 children, and was early lamed by infantile paralysis, a handicap that rarely inhibited his activities throughout life. He was educated at Edinburgh High School and at Edinburgh University, where his major study was law. He was admitted to the Bar in 1792. Possessed of an astonishingly retentive memory, he read voraciously and devoured antiquarian lore, ballads, fairy-tales, chivalric romances and exotic tales of distant places; further education came from architectural observation and from tales and legends told him by the peasantry with whom he talked in his travels on horseback whilst executing legal business. In 1795 Scott, Sir Walter married Margaret Charlotte Carpenter (Charpentier) and briefly, in 1797, he acted as paymaster, quartermaster and secretary to the Edinburgh Light Dragoons. By 1799 he was Deputy-Sheriff of Selkirk and just on the edge of literary life.

Scott entered literature through poetry and, absorbed as he was in folklore and the supernatural, he started his literary career by anonymously publishing in 1796 an adaptation of ballads by G. A. Burger which he followed in 1801 by contributions to **Matthew Gregory Lewis**'s 'hobgoblin repast', better known as *Tales of Wonder*. About this time, too, he translated Goethe's *Goetz von Berlichingen* and, in 1802–3, put out the *Minstrelsy of the Scottish Border*, an edition of authentic ballads and of some written by contemporary contributors. A metrical version of the romance of *Sir Tristrem* appeared in 1804. Scott's poetic writing so far was dominated by a blend of Gothic-Germanic sorcery and antiquarian enthusiasm.

It was in 1805, with the publication of **The Lay of the Last Minstrel**, based on an old border narrative, that his name became more widely known. This was followed by a number of longer poems, among them **Marmion** (1808), **The Lady of the Lake** (1810), *The Vision of Don Roderick* (1811), *Rokeby* and **The Bridal of Triermain** (both 1813), *The Lord of the Isles* and *The Field of Waterloo* (both 1815), and *Harold the Dauntless* (1817). In addition there were, of course, other shorter poems dating from this period but, ironically perhaps, some of Scott's more memorable verses are found in the novels.

During these poetical years Scott was also involved in prose writing and editorial work on a grand scale, much of it relating to criticism, antiquarianism, and history. Among such works were: *Original Memoirs Written during the Great Civil War* (1806), an edition of **Dryden** with biographical material (1808), *Memoirs of Captain George Carleton* (1808), *The State Papers of Sir Ralph Sadler* (1809), *The Secret History of James I* (1811) as well as numerous book reviews for the Whiggish **Edinburgh Review**, then edited by the fierce **Francis Jeffrey**. And in 1809 Scott had also been a prominent force in the establishing of the Tory-oriented **Quarterly Review**. The magnitude of these enterprises is prodigious.

Writing aside, Scott's energy appears in his printing and publishing agreements with the Ballantyne brothers, James and John. These unfortunately led him toward a position verging on bankruptcy in 1811, the year he purchased Abbotsford. But he was rescued by Archibald Constable, 'the grand Napoleon of the realms of print', who was eager to have the prolific author under his wing. During this time of muddled business interests Scott also embarked on his career as a novelist with the highly acclaimed **Waverley**, some of which had been drafted as early as 1805 and which appeared with the Constable imprint in 1814.

Divers legends surround Scott's phenomenal career as a novelist, but it is safe to say he was at the least partially propelled along that path by the astonishing success in 1810 of the first two cantos of **Byron's** *Childe Harold's Pilgrimage*, whose sophistication quite eclipsed the once successful romance narratives in which the older poet excelled. Be that as it may, after *Waverley* the following novels poured torrentially forth: *Guy Mannering* (1815), *The Antiquary* (1816), *The Black Dwarf* and *Old Mortality* (both 1816 and constituting the first series of *Tales of My Landlord*), *Rob Roy* (1817), *The Heart of Midlothian* (1818; second series of *Tales of My Landlord*), *The Bride of Lammermoor* and *The Legend of Montrose* (1819; third series of *Tales of My Landlord*), *Ivanhoe* (1819), *The Monastery* and *The Abbot* (both 1820), *Kenilworth* and *The Pirate* (both 1821), *The Fortunes of Nigel* (1822), *Peveril of the Peak*, *Quentin Durward* and *St Ronan's Well* (all 1823), *Redgauntlet* (1824), *Tales of the Crusaders*, *The Betrothed* and *The Talisman* (all 1825) and *Woodstock* (1826).

Beyond his novel writing Scott was, throughout these years, again busy with editions, antiquarian studies and literary criticism. A significant monument of the time is his edition of **Swift** (1814), complete with biographical data. This was followed by *Memories of the Somervilles* (1815), *The Border Antiquities of England and Scotland* (1814–17), *Lives of the Novelists* contributed to Ballantyne's Novelists' Library (1821–4) as well as other writings of a dramatic and historical character. The output beggars belief. Furthermore, Scott was entertaining on a baronial scale at Abbotsford, enjoying the role of local Laird, and functioning as a man of law as well as of letters, so it is not surprising that his health was considerably undermined. From 1817 on he experienced attacks of jaundice, bowel trouble, vomiting and stomach cramp, which culminated in 1819 in agonizingly painful seizures and a narrow escape from death. Nevertheless, he continued writing in improved but still impaired health and then, in 1825–6, a financial crisis involving Ballantyne and Co. and Archibald Constable left Scott with a debt of £130,000. Honourably disdaining bankruptcy, he set to work at an even more furious pace and in the next five years came *Chronicles of the Canongate*, with *The Two Drovers*, *The Highland Widow* and *The Surgeon's Daughter* in its first series (1827) and *St Valentine's Day, or, The Fair Maid of Perth* in the second (1828), *Anne of Geierstein* (1829), and *Count Robert of Paris* and *Castle Dangerous* (1832) in the fourth series of *Tales of My Landlord*. But the merciless toil overwhelmed him and he was brought home from Italy, where he had been vainly seeking health, to die at his beloved Abbotsford in September 1832.

Few writers have enjoyed a higher reputation than Scott once did. In his lifetime and for nearly a century after his death he was not merely an immensely popular writer – acclaimed as a poet and often regarded as the greatest novelist in the language – but a major cultural force. His Scottish novels, particularly *Waverley* and *Rob Roy*, did much to rescue that country from the low esteem it had acquired after the 1745 rebellion and to make it at once respectable and romantic. The descriptions of landscape and ruins with which his books abound contributed greatly to the shaping of **Romanticism** in England. Above all, of course, his use of history confirmed that taste for medievalism which lasted throughout the 19th century and the conduct of his historical figures served as the model of that chivalric code by which Victorian gentlemen attempted to live. Yet today Scott is forgotten as a poet and neglected as a novelist. The immense bulk of his writing and the sheer length of his individual works intimidate. His characters are dismissed as artificial, and his plots as stilted and melodramatic; his fascination with history can appear a mere love of fancy dress. These charges carry enough force to prevent any revival of his reputation to its former heights, but they overlook his undoubted merits: his humour, his gift for memorably eccentric characters, his erudite

Sir Walter Scott, 1820. A detail from the portrait by Sir Thomas Lawrence, which was not completed until 1826. The Royal Collection.

and down-to-earth mastery of folklore and, most important, the underlying seriousness of his preoccupation with history and the processes of social and political change.

**Scottish Chaucerians, The** The name given to the 15th- and 16th-century Scottish poets influenced by **Geoffrey Chaucer**, principally **Robert Henryson**, **Gavin Douglas**, **William Dunbar** and the author of the *Kingis Quair*. Although all these poets were openly indebted to Chaucer, the label can mislead by obscuring the original and innovative aspects of their style.

**Scottish renaissance, the** A movement in Scottish literature which flourished between 1920 and 1940. It was originally applied to the work of several minor poets (Marion Angus, Violet Jacob, Sir Alexander Gray and Lewis Spence) who were dedicated to the revival of Scots as a literary language either through its regional dialects or through the revival of the language and traditions of Scottish poets of the 15th and 16th centuries. In 1924, however, the term was given a new meaning and force when the French critic Denis Saurat used it to mark the emergence of **Hugh MacDiarmid**, whose poems in revived or synthetic Scots, especially *A Drunk Man Looks at the Thistle* (1926), transformed Scottish poetry. MacDiarmid committed himself to a vigorous revaluation of Scottish literary traditions and his definition of a renaissance broadened to include not only the recreation of Scots as a national language but also the revival of Gaelic and the re-establishment of separate Scottish social and political institutions. The example of Irish writers, particularly **Yeats,** supported his belief in the need to reverse what he called the 'English ascendancy'. A strong antipathy to the English and towards anglicized Scots became – along with a frequent depreciation of **Burns** in favour of **Dunbar** and **Henryson** – a permanent feature of his literary–political polemic. Although MacDiarmid was the major figure in the renaissance, appropriating and expanding its purposes to meet his own ambitions, at least some of his aims were shared by other writers, notably **Lewis Grassic Gibbon**, **William Soutar** and **Sorley Maclean**. In the 1940s and 1950s a number of younger poets writing in Lallans (as they now called Scots) attempted a second phase of the renaissance, even though MacDiarmid himself was by then writing most of his work in English.

**Scovell, E[dith] J[oy]** 1907– Poet. Born in Sheffield, she was educated in Westmorland before reading English at Oxford. She worked as a secretary and a journalist in London before marrying the biologist Charles Elton and working as his field assistant in northern Brazil and Panama. Although she has written since the 1920s, her first collection was *Shadows of Chrysanthemums* (1944). Other collections include *The Midsummer Meadow* (1946), *The River Steamer* (1956) and *The Space Between* (1982). Her quiet, meditative work, with its exact perceptions of nature, childhood and old age, was neglected in the neo-Romantic atmosphere of the post-war period, but she has been championed by **Geoffrey Grigson**, **Carol Rumens** and John Mole, who called her 'a visionary in sensible shoes'. *Collected Poems* (1988) introduced her to a wider readership.

**Scriblerus Club, The** Formed about 1713, this association of Tory intellectuals and writers enjoyed a brief formal existence, meeting in London to discuss topics of contemporary interest and to enjoy the conviviality of witty conversation. The members were **Swift**, **Pope**, **Arbuthnot**, **Gay**, **Parnell**, **Atterbury**, **Congreve** and **Robert Harley**, **1st Earl of Oxford**. Collectively they invented a character named Martinus Scriblerus, a pedantic hack whose intellectual shortcomings they recorded in the imaginary *Memoirs of Martinus Scriblerus*. Satire directed at bad taste, irrational thinking or political exploitation was common to the independent writings by many of the club's distinguished members, giving rise to the term 'Scriblerian' for such literature.

*Scrutiny* The most influential English critical journal of its time, *Scrutiny* was founded in Cambridge in 1932 by **L. C. Knights** and Donald Culver, and mainly edited until its closure in 1953 by **F. R. Leavis** and **Q. D. Leavis**. It focused on the study of literature, starting from the practice of close critical analysis advocated in Cambridge by **I. A. Richards**, and from the sociological and historical account of English cultural history implicit in Q. D. Leavis's *Fiction and the Reading Public* (1932). The main contributor was F. R. Leavis himself: his *Revaluation* (an account of trends in English poetry, 1936), *The Great Tradition* (the English novel, 1948), and *D. H. Lawrence – Novelist* (1955) were among the books based on articles in *Scrutiny*. Other important contributions were D. A. Traversi's and L. C. Knights's work on Elizabethan drama, D. W. Harding's essays on literature written from the point of view of a psychologist, Martin Turnell on French literature, **D. J. Enright** on German literature and Denys Thompson on English in the secondary school. The stance was that in the secular change from a pre-industrial to an industrial society, and with the rise of mass literacy, popular literature had become the manipulative product of entrepreneurs who could be philistine or unscrupulous. The maintenance of critical standards must become the role of an élite, and the university English school was its natural communications centre. Importantly, in the 1930s it offered a middle ground between Marxism and the right-wing literary politics of **T. S. Eliot**. *Scrutiny* questioned current reputations as well as proposing its own view of literary and cultural history: those whom it thought 'middlebrow' retorted that it was 'puritanical'. Many of the contributors were pupils or colleagues of the Leavises: in the 1950s this began to seem like an orthodoxy. The journal was reprinted as a bound set in 1963; F. R. Leavis edited a two-volume *Selection* in 1968.

**Scupham, (John) Peter** 1933– Poet. Born in Liverpool, he was educated at the Perse School, Cambridge, St George's, Harpenden, and, after national service, at Emmanuel College, Cambridge, where he read English. He works as a teacher and runs the Mandeville Press. A latecomer to poetry, he published his first book, *The Snowing Globe*, in 1972. Subsequent volumes have been *The Gift* (1973), *Prehistories* (1975), *The Hinterland* (1977), *Summer Palaces* (1980), *Winter Quarters* (1983) and *Out Late* (1986). Much of his poetry is domestic: places, objects and heirlooms are his subject matter, examined in great detail and filtered through his deepening sense of history, geology and geography. Together with an elegant, spare lucidity of language, he is a formalist, interested in regular metres and strict rhyme-schemes. His major work is the title sequence of *The Hinterland*, 15 interlocking sonnets. Perhaps because of his antiquarian interests Scupham is not a fashionable poet, but his importance is stressed by his inclusion in both of the 1980s' major anthologies of contemporary poetry, **Blake Morrison** and **Andrew Motion**'s *Penguin Book of Contemporary British Poetry* (1982) and Michael Schmidt's *Some Contemporary Poets of Britain and Ireland* (1983).

**Sea Wolf, The** A novel by **Jack London**, published in 1904. In the fog on San Francisco Bay, two ferry boats collide and Humphrey Van Weyden is thrown overboard. He is saved by a sealing schooner, the *Ghost*, whose captain, Wolf Larsen, presses him into service. He is at once fascinated by Larsen's brute power and repelled by his ruthlessness. They reach the sealing grounds off Japan, where Maude Brewster, a castaway from a shipwreck, is rescued by the *Ghost* and almost at once becomes the object of Larsen's attentions. She finds a sympathetic response in Van Weyden, but the struggle between the two men is hopelessly unequal and she and Van Weyden flee from the ship. They reach a deserted island, but the *Ghost* is driven ashore there. Larsen has been deserted by his crew, and, suffering from cerebral cancer, is blind. Van Weyden and Miss Brewster manage

to make the *Ghost* seaworthy again and set out for civilization; Larsen, defiant to the last, dies on the island.

**Seafarer, The** An Old English poem preserved in **The Exeter Book**. It falls into two halves not connected by their subject matter. The first 64 lines present a monologue by a seafarer about the hardships and dangers of his life and about his love for the sea. The second half of the poem is a homiletic discourse, perhaps intended to draw a general moral from the seafarer's description; it considers the transience of worldly bliss and praises humble, honest living.

**Seasons, The** A poem in blank verse by **James Thomson**, consisting of one book for each season and a final Hymn to Nature. The first three books were originally published separately: *Winter* in 1726, *Summer* in 1727 and *Spring* in 1728. *Autumn* appeared in the first collective edition of *The Seasons* in 1730. From 1738 onwards, aided perhaps by **Pope** and **George Lyttelton**, Thomson made extensive revisions and a much enlarged edition appeared in 1744.

The poem presents a vision of the world progressing amid much change through the cycle of the seasons, each book assembling landscape descriptions, anecdotes and vignettes that show the effect of Nature on human beings. *Winter* describes the bitterness of the elements, the death of a wayfarer in a snowdrift, the comfort of life indoors and the Arctic circle. *Summer* presents outdoor scenes of pastoral industry, and the mythical stories of Celadon and Amelia, and Damon and Musidora. *Spring* gives glowing and verdant descriptions of the season's effect on the whole of Nature, including man, who is seen in the charmingly idealized image of the contented angler. In *Autumn* there is a vigorous account of shooting and hunting, a denunciation of the barbarity of these pastimes, and an episode narrating the love affair of Palemon and Lavinia. The poem as a whole is distinguished by fine, evocative descriptions of rural life.

Thomson's most recent editor, James Sambrook, has pointed out that *The Seasons* cannot easily be assigned to any single genre and looks unmethodical. He suggests that it can profitably be considered as devotional, scientific, georgic, geographical, historical, narrative, descriptive and subjective writing, but that it shows above all the power of landscape as a poetic subject. We find in Thomson the influence of Poussin and Claude, just as we find the influence of Thomson in Turner. *The Seasons* has its roots in Virgil's *Georgics* and in **Milton**; at the same time it marks a shift in taste and sensibility, anticipating elements of the **picturesque** and of **Romanticism**. **Wordsworth** and **Cowper**, in particular, owe a debt to Thomson. *The Seasons* was much translated (especially into German) in the 18th and early 19th centuries. There are even versions in Polish and Hebrew.

***Second Jungle Book, The*** See ***Jungle Book, The***.

***Second Mrs Tanqueray, The*** A play by **Arthur Wing Pinero**, first performed at the St James's Theatre, London, in 1893 with Mrs Patrick Campbell in the title role.

Paula Tanqueray has concealed her past from her respectable husband, Aubrey, but it catches up with her when her step-daughter becomes engaged to her seducer. In opposing the marriage, Paula is forced to confess her own history, and she commits suicide to save herself and those she loves from shame.

***Second Nun's Tale, The*** See ***Canterbury Tales, The***.

***Secret Agent, The*** A novel by **Joseph Conrad**, published in 1907. Revolutionary anarchists, senior Police officers, the Home Secretary, and the mind of a half-idiot are a few of the ingredients of this 'simple tale' (as the novel is ironically sub-titled) set in contemporary London.

Mr Verloc's run-down Soho shop and his marriage to Winnie (which entails responsibility for her brother, the simpleton Stevie) provide cover for his secret life as a double agent. He supplies information to the Russian *agent provocateur*, Vladimir, to Inspector Heat of Scotland Yard, and colludes with an underworld of anarchists. Vladimir conspires to upset the tolerant *status quo* between the Liberal Establishment and the revolutionary groups. Acting on his orders, Verloc provides himself with explosives from the sinister American 'Professor' and enlists Stevie as helpless accomplice for an attack on the Greenwich Observatory.

Stevie's horrifying death in Greenwich Park destroys Verloc's dependence upon both extremism and the banal domesticity which Winnie has selflessly provided. In an ironic and mocking manner, the novel depicts contradictory and self-seeking motives within the police force as well as in the anarchist world. At the Verlocs' home, it is Winnie who breaks apart the circle of collusion: when her husband confesses to his role in Stevie's death, she stabs him with a carving knife. Winnie has been drawn into the insane world of violence. She plans to leave the country with the anarchist Ossipon, but he deserts her on learning of Verloc's murder. Driven to madness, Winnie jumps overboard from a Channel ferry.

***Secret Love, or, The Maiden Queen*** A comedy by **John Dryden**, produced in 1667 and pub-

lished the following year. It was a favourite of Charles II and enjoyed considerable success.

***Secret Service*** A melodrama by **William Gillette**, first performed in Philadelphia in 1895. In its New York production the following year, Gillette himself replaced Maurice Barrymore in the leading role. In a series of fast-moving scenes, the play describes the ruses and eventual unmasking of a gallant Union spy, Captain Thorne, in the Confederate city of Richmond, Virginia. At the last moment his death sentence is commuted, and the audience is left with the prospect of a post-war marriage between him and Edith Varney, the daughter of a Confederate general, for love of whom Thorne had failed to carry out a crucial act of espionage.

**Sedgwick, Catharine Maria** 1789–1867 American novelist, born in Stockbridge, Massachusetts, into a wealthy Calvinist family. Her first novel, *A New England Tale* (1822), became one of America's first best-sellers. It tells the story of the orphaned Jane Elton who, after a difficult adolescence of restrictions imposed by poverty, dependence on others, and Calvinist orthodoxy, finally achieves the emotional maturity to assume the responsibilities of marriage and a family. Sedgwick's second novel, *Redwood* (1824), brought its author a popularity equal to that of her contemporaries **James Fenimore Cooper** and **Washington Irving**. It tells the story of Ellen Bruce, another orphan, who competes with Caroline Redwood for the attentions of Charles Westall. Eventually, Caroline reveals her petty nature and Charles marries Ellen. It is then revealed that Ellen is in fact Caroline's half-sister by their father's secret first marriage, and is thus entitled to a share of the family fortune. The novel envisions a society in which women's influence will produce an age of virtue, family harmony and love. Sedgwick's third novel, *Hope Leslie* (1827), concerns relations between whites and Indians. Set in 17th-century New England, it introduces the theme of miscegenation that was common in subsequent American fiction. Her other works include *Clarence* (1830), *The Linwoods* (1835) and a trilogy consisting of *Home* (1835), *The Poor Man and the Rich Man* (1836), and *Live and Let Live* (1837). Her last novel, *Married or Single?* (1857), reflects her awareness of the social difficulties faced by unmarried women.

**Sedley, Sir Charles** *c.*1639–1701 Dramatist and poet. The younger son of a baronet, Sedley inherited the title on the death of his elder brother. He spent some time at Wadham College, Oxford, but left without taking a degree. In London he settled down to a dissolute life like that of his friend the **Earl of Rochester**. Later, as

MP for Romney, he was an active parliamentary speaker and became something of a patron of men of letters. Sedley was the author of some lyrics, two forgotten tragedies and three comedies, of which the best are *The Mulberry Garden* (1668), influenced by both Molière and **Etherege**, and the ribald *Bellamira, or, The Mistress* (1687), based on the *Eunuchus* of Terence.

**Seeger, Alan** 1888–1916 American poet, born in New York City into an old New England family, and educated at Harvard. Two years after completing his education he departed for Paris. France became his home, and at the outbreak of World War I he enlisted in her defence, joining the Foreign Legion. He served with distinction and was killed in 1916 during the Battle of the Somme. He was posthumously awarded the Croix de Guerre and the Médaille Militaire. His volume entitled *Poems* was published in the year of his death; his famous 'I Have a Rendezvous with Death' had originally appeared in *The North American Review* in October 1916. His *Letters and Diary* was published in 1917.

**Seeley, Sir J[ohn] R[obert]** 1803–95 Historian and essayist. He was born in London and educated at the City of London School and Christ's College, Cambridge, where the poet **Calverley** and the novelist **Walter Besant** were his contemporaries. He held a fellowship at his own college and was appointed Professor of Latin at University College, London, before succeeding **Charles Kingsley** as Professor of Modern History at Cambridge in 1869. His most famous book, *Ecce Homo* (published anonymously in 1865), was an account of the life and work of Christ made controversial by its failure to acknowledge Christ's divinity. Seeley's historical works include *The Life and Times of Stein, or, Germany and Prussia in the Napoleonic Age* (1878) and two books justifying British Imperialism, *The Expansion of England in the Eighteenth Century* (1883) and *The Growth of British Policy* (1895).

**Sejanus, His Fall** A tragedy by **Ben Jonson**, produced in 1603 and published in 1605. The first performance was given by the **King's Men** at the **Globe Theatre** with **Richard Burbage** and **Shakespeare** in the cast. The play, which is rarely revived, follows the career of Lucius Aelius Sejanus, favourite of the Roman Emperor Tiberius, who leaves him in charge of Rome while he spends more and more time on his island, Capri. Sejanus aspires to the purple and poisons the emperor's son, Drusus; he has seduced and hopes to marry his widow, Livia. He also succeeds in discrediting Agrippina, widow of the great soldier Germanicus. But Tiberius grows suspicious and Naevius Sertorius Macro, the ambitious commander of the

Praetorian Guard, is more than willing to supplant Sejanus. Eventually Tiberius denounces Sejanus to the Senate; he is killed by the mob.

**Selborne, The Natural History of** See **White, Gilbert**.

**Selby, Hubert Jr** 1928– American novelist and short-story writer. Born and educated in New York City, Selby drew upon personal experiences for his stories of life in the lowest circles of society. His best-known work, the collection of stories entitled *Last Exit to Brooklyn* (1964), was the subject of a much-publicized obscenity trial in England. It deals with homosexuality, prostitution, and brutality, while exploring human isolation in an urban environment. Selby followed it with three novels: *The Room* (1971), the story of a nameless psychopath awaiting trial, *The Demon* (1976), about a man possessed by lust, ambition and violence, and *Requiem for a Dream* (1978), an examination of drug addiction.

**Selden, John** 1584–1654 Lawyer and scholar. The son of a Sussex yeoman, Selden became a lawyer and was keeper of the records at the Inner Temple. He entered Parliament in 1623, having acquired meanwhile a certain fame as the author of a *History of Tithes* (1618), which angered the Church authorities. No lover of the episcopacy, Selden was a sharp opponent of the crown's prerogative. His clear, detached criticism often earned him the ill will of both sides and he had no patience with parliamentarians who fought to displace princes, only to assume princely powers. He withdrew from public affairs before the trial of Charles I.

His most notable work is the posthumous *Table Talk: Being the Discourses of John Selden Esq . . . Relating Especially to Religion and State*, which was collected by his amanuensis Richard Milward and published in 1689. In it Selden pronounces upon matters of law, personal freedom, and the motives of authority in crisp direct English. He contributed notes ('illustrations') to the first 18 cantos of **Drayton's** *Poly-Olbion* and was also the author of books on antiquities and on law. In *Mare Clausum* (1635) he disputed the principle of sovereignty on the high seas with Hugo Grotius. Selden was a friend of **Ben Jonson** and admired by **Milton**.

**Selvon, Samuel (Dickson)** 1923– Trinidadian novelist of Indian descent. After serving in the RNVR (1940–5), he worked on *The Trinidad Guardian* until 1950, when he migrated to London and, some 30 years later, to Canada. His first, briskly written novel, *A Brighter Sun* (1952), is about an Indian couple of tradition-bound, rural background, married at 16, yet growing into love of each other and understanding of their urban creole neighbours. The sequel, *Turn Again, Tiger* (1958), follows the process of their creolization and mature acceptance, also, of their Indian origins. *An Island Is A World* (1955), *I Hear Thunder* (1963), *The Plains of Caroni* (1969) and *Those Who Eat the Cascadura* (1973), also set in Trinidad, involve the central characters' discovery that individuals within different socio-racial communities seldom correspond with group stereotypes of them. Selvon pioneered the use of Caribbean dialect for other than merely comic effects; he makes it a flexible instrument capable of farce, comedy, satire, and even irony and pathos. All these modes operate in his sharp-edged interpretation of West Indian settlement in Britain in *The Lonely Londoners* (1956), with its jaunty dialect-narrator Moses, and *The Housing Lark* (1965), with such comic episodes as a West Indian Bank Holiday picnic at Hampton Court. Widespread British racism and its concomitant Black Power protests are the major satirical targets in the more pungent *Moses Ascending* (1975) and *Moses Migrating* (1983). Selvon has also written short stories, collected in *Ways of Sunlight* (1958), and numerous radio plays from *Lost Property* (1965) to *Zeppi's Machine* (1977).

**semiotics** (or semiology) The science of 'signs'. The two influential early theorists were C. S. Peirce (1839–1914) and Ferdinand de Saussure (1857–1913). The former made two important contributions to semiology. First, he showed that a sign never arrives at a definite meaning; any definition is always subject to a further definition (rather as in a dictionary any definition can itself be looked up for a further definition). Secondly, he distinguished between three types of sign: the 'iconic' (where sign resembles referent, as in a road-sign for falling rocks), the 'indexical' (where the sign is associated with its referent; smoke equals fire), and the 'symbolic' (where the sign and its referent bear an arbitrary relationship, as in language).

Saussure's writings are devoted to linguistics, but he believed that behind and beyond language lay a whole range of sign systems, the study of which he called 'semiology'. His theory of the divided nature of the sign is fundamental to developments not only in semiology but in **structuralism**, **post-structuralism** and Lacanian **psychoanalytic criticism**. Having made the primary distinction between language as a system (*langue*) and language as individual utterance (*parole*) he went on to reject the view of language as a system of symbols corresponding to referents (things in the world). Words are 'signs' which have two sides (like a sheet of paper): a mark, either written or spoken, called a 'signifier', and a concept, called a 'signified'. In this model of language, 'things' have no place;

words acquire meaning only in so far as they enter a system of relations.

In France under the influence of Claude Lévi-Strauss (1908– ), Roland Barthes (1915–80) and A. J. Greimas (1917– ), semiology has examined social forms (kinship systems, myths, fashions, etc.) as if they were languages. In Greimas, narrative discourse itself is studied as if it were language writ large (see under structuralism).

**Sendak, Maurice (Bernard)** 1928– American children's writer and illustrator. Born in New York, the son of poor Jewish immigrants, he went to work as a window-dresser after leaving school at the earliest opportunity. His talents as an artist were soon noticed. After illustrating the books of others he began supplying his own texts, first in *Kenny's Window* (1956) and more memorably in *The Sign on Rosie's Door* (1958), about a small child putting on a show for her friends. His most famous work, *Where the Wild Things Are* (1963), was also highly controversial, dividing critics between those who thought it too frightening and those who championed its imaginative brilliance. The book itself is about Max, a naughty boy sent in disgrace to his room, where he invents a host of monsters; despite their gargoyle faces and menacing claws, they all agree that Max himself is the wildest thing of all. Subsequent books have included the surreal adventures of *In the Night Kitchen* (1970) and *Outside Over There* (1981), both illustrated with Sendak's characteristic blend of pastel colours, stunted, tough children and dream-like imagery.

**sensation fiction** A school of Victorian fiction which took mystery and crime as its subject and suspense as its narrative method. Like the **Gothic fiction** of the late 18th and early 19th centuries, it appealed directly to the reader's sensations by seeking to induce fear, excitement and curiosity. Unlike Gothic fiction, it preferred a modern setting and sometimes included criticism of current social abuses. The sensation novel enjoyed its heyday in the 1860s, with the work of **Wilkie Collins**, particularly his hugely successful *The Woman in White* (1860), and with **Mary Elizabeth Braddon**'s *Lady Audley's Secret* (1862). **Dickens** was influenced by the form, most obviously in his unfinished *The Mystery of Edwin Drood* (1870), and **Hardy** chose it for his first published novel, *Desperate Remedies* (1871).

*Sense and Sensibility* Jane Austen's first published novel (1811). It began as a story, 'Elinor and Marianne', which the novelist read to her family in 1795. She began to rewrite it in 1797, when she was also drafting the first sketches for *Pride and Prejudice* and *Northanger Abbey* and working on a story, 'The Watsons', which was never completed.

The Dashwoods of Norland Park, in Sussex, have a life interest in the estate while Henry Dashwood lives; on his death it passes to John Dashwood, his son by his first marriage. Henry Dashwood recommends his second wife and his daughters to John when he dies. But John and his wife are selfish and, encouraged by Mrs Ferrars, John's mother-in-law, defeat his father's wish. Mrs Henry Dashwood and her daughters retire to a cottage in Devonshire. Elinor Dashwood and Mrs John Dashwood's brother, Edward Ferrars, feel a mutual attraction but Elinor feels an odd constraint in Edward's relations with her.

In Devonshire, Marianne Dashwood falls passionately in love with the charming and penniless John Willoughby and is deeply distressed when he suddenly leaves for London. Elinor and Marianne go to London, too, at the invitation of their friend Mrs Jennings, and Marianne now finds Willoughby indifferent to her. Her importunities finally provoke an insolent letter from him, announcing his forthcoming marriage to an heiress. Elinor, meanwhile, has learned that Edward Ferrars has been secretly engaged to Lucy Steele for four years. Elinor's self-control enables her to conceal her distress. It is Edward's dependence on his mother that made him conceal his engagement and now Mrs Ferrars, learning of it, dismisses him and settles her property on his silly young brother Robert. Edward, who intends taking orders, has a small living offered him by Colonel Brandon, a quiet worthy man who has long been an admirer of Marianne. But now Lucy transfers her attention to Robert and marries him instead. At last free of a commitment he deeply regretted, Edward proposes to Elinor and she accepts him. The staunch and generous Colonel Brandon wins Marianne, who is brought to see that her passionate sensibility would hardly make for happiness.

**sentimental comedy** Often loosely applied to the plays that replaced the Restoration comedy of manners on the English stage, 'sentimental comedy' properly refers to works of a slightly later date, when the **sentimental novel** had come into fashion and when the mere variety of human emotional experience was an object of fascination. The extravagant success of **Hugh Kelly**'s *False Delicacy* (1768) at **Drury Lane** eclipsed the almost simultaneously produced, and less blandly sentimental, play of **Oliver Goldsmith**'s, *The Good-Natured Man* (1768). Kelly never repeated the triumph of *False Delicacy*, and the most consistently successful purveyor of sentimental comedy was **Richard Cumberland**, particularly with *The Brothers* (1769) and *The West Indian* (1771). It was against

sentimental comedy in general and Cumberland in particular that **Sheridan** sought to revive a comedy of manners. There is no doubt that sentimental comedy blunted the edge of English comedy. Its reliance on benevolence and the timely change of heart to bring matters to a happy conclusion belongs more to **melodrama**, for which it prepared the way, than to the true comic tradition.

*Sentimental Journey through France and Italy, by Mr Yorick, A* The second and last novel of **Laurence Sterne**, published in 1768, shortly before his death. The narrator's journey never reaches Italy, taking him from Calais to Rouen and Paris but stopping short of Lyons. Sterne himself had travelled through France and Italy in 1765–6 to help his consumption; when he used his experiences as the basis for the novel he adopted as persona a character from his earlier *Tristram Shandy*. Mr Yorick finds in everything around him experiences to affect his delicate sensibilities, stimulate his ready sentiments and cause comic confusion. He delights in the small responses of human behaviour, which he greets with benevolence and charity. Genuine pathos in some episodes is balanced elsewhere by erotic suggestiveness, and there are several very entertaining set-pieces. **Tobias Smollett**, whom Sterne met in Italy, is caricatured as the learned Smelfungus.

**sentimental novel** By the middle of the 18th century, when the sentimental novel flourished, the term 'sentimental' had lost its connection with the term 'moral' and had come to mean 'concerned with the emotions'. People liked to believe, with Jean-Jacques Rousseau (1712–78), that the natural emotions were good, kindly and innocent. Society, law and civilization were to blame for corrupting man; left alone by social institutions, he would be wise, happy and good. This was a controversial, though popular, view because it contradicted orthodox Christian teaching that man was born in a state of original sin and could only be saved by God's grace. But for a while orthodox religion lost its hold and the cult of sentimentality filled the vacuum.

Although **Samuel Richardson** did not agree with Rousseau, the highly charged emotions of *Pamela* (1740), and *Clarissa* (1747–8) made an important contribution to the sentimental novel. Indeed, he could be said to have initiated the form, for the distresses of his Clarissa Harlowe set a pattern followed by lesser writers. Novels like **Henry Brooke**'s *The Fool of Quality* (1766–72) and **Henry Mackenzie**'s *The Man of Feeling* (1771) set out to show that effusive emotion was evidence of a good heart, though sentimental characters often found themselves too good for this world and the world too much for them. The heroes and heroines were beautiful, brilliant, talented and morally perfect. **Oliver Goldsmith**'s *The Vicar of Wakefield* (1776), a tragicomedy of clerical life, is frequently included among the hundreds of sentimental novels produced in the period, though it is arguably an early parody.

Sentimentalism was associated with 'sensibility', and although **Sterne** wrote of 'dear sensibility' as 'source inexhausted of all that's precious in our joys, or costly in our sorrows', sensibility had become less fashionable than suspect by the end of the century. **Jane Austen** mocked its excesses in *Sense and Sensibility* (1811), and in *Northanger Abbey* (1818) stressed Catherine Morland's ordinariness by contrast to the heroines of the novel of sensibility (as it came to be called). Sensibility was associated with 'sensations' and thus with sexual excitement, which earned it a bad reputation. **Mary Wollstonecraft** spoke of 'senses . . . inflamed . . . and . . . understandings neglected', making women 'the prey of their senses . . . blown about by every momentary gust of feeling'. **Hannah More** saw in 'ungoverned Sensibility' the roots of profligacy, murder and suicide. In *Strictures on the Modern System of Female Education* (1799), she wrote of the sentimental novel: 'Such is the frightful facility of this species of composition, that every raw girl, while she reads, is tempted to fancy that she can also write . . . the glutted imagination soon overflows with the redundance of cheap sentiment and plentiful incident . . .'; such works 'teach, that chastity is only individual attachment; that no duty exists which is not prompted by feeling; that impulse is the main spring of virtuous actions, while laws and religion are only unjust restraints'. The word 'sentimental' came to mean 'false and self-indulgent feeling' after Schiller's division (1795) of poets into two classes, the 'naïve' and the 'sentimental': 'naïve' writers are natural and instinctive; 'sentimental' ones are forced and artificial.

**Sepamla, Sipho** 1932–  South African poet, born in Krugersdorp. *Hurry Up To It* (1975) and *The Blues Is You In Me* (1976) combine the satirical and subtle with the direct and simple, as, like **Mtshali** and **Serote**, he employs poetry for protest and to develop Black Consciousness. In *The Soweto I Love* (1977) and *Children of the Earth* (1983) plain statement articulates the communal experience of oppression. His first novel is *The Root Is One* (1979); the second, *A Ride on the Whirlwind* (1981), celebrates the school-children–heroes of the 1976 Soweto uprising.

***Serjeant Musgrave's Dance: An Unhistorical Parable*** A play by **John Arden**, first performed at the **Royal Court Theatre**, London, in 1959, when its enigmatic treatment of its title charac-ter's peculiarly violent pacifism puzzled and intrigued critics.

To a northern town, strike-bound and snow-covered, come four uniformed soldiers. Are they strike-breakers? Or are they, as they allow to appear, recruiters? Musgrave himself is strong, brooding and dutiful, outraged when an encounter with a local barmaid causes the accidental death of one of his men. He goes ahead, nonetheless, with his planned meeting in the market-place, dancing his macabre dance of vengeance as the gatling-gun is unveiled and pointed at the crowd – and the audience.

**Serote, Mongane Wally** 1944–  South African poet, born in Sophiatown. Imprisoned without trial in 1969, he now lives in Botswana. In the volumes *Yakhal'inkomo* (1972) and *Tsetlo* (1974) he enunciates the sufferings, anger and bitterness of South Africa's urban blacks in flexible, inventive and self-possessed verse. The long poem *No Baby Must Weep* (1975) is often despairing, but the rapid, jazz-like verse of *Behold Mama, Flowers* (1978) and *The Night Keeps Winking* (1983) affirms faith in ultimate release from bondage. His novel, *To Every Birth Its Blood* (1981), expresses pride in the 1976 Soweto schoolchildren as torch-bearers of the freedom struggle.

**Service, Robert W[illiam]** 1876–1958 Canadian poet and novelist. Born in Preston, Lancashire, he grew up in Scotland, where he worked for the Commercial Bank of Scotland in Glasgow, before emigrating to Canada in 1897. He worked on a farm and later on a ranch in Vancouver Island and then, in 1903, resumed his banking career. In 1904 he was transferred to the Yukon, where the Klondike gold rush had recently taken place, and this provided the impetus for his best-known verse. In rapid succession he published *Songs of a Sourdough* (1907), *The Spell of the Yukon* (1907) and *Ballads of a Cheechako* (1909). The success of the popular ballads in these early volumes enabled him to give up banking and write his first novel, *The Trail of '98* (1910). Service subsequently left Canada and worked as a newspaper correspondent and stretcher-bearer with the Canadian army between 1912 and 1916. *Rhymes of a Red-Cross Man* (1916) came out of this experience. He was a reporter for Canadian Army Intelligence during the last two years of World War I. After the war he settled in France. Service's essentially melodramatic verse is considered of comparatively little literary merit, but his witty ballads of Yukon life, such as 'The Shooting of Dan McGrew', 'The Cremation of Sam McGee' and 'The Law of the Yukon', were immensely popular in his own day. His work shows the influence of **Bret Harte** and **Rudyard Kipling**. Other books include *Rhymes of a Roll-*

*ing Stone* (1912), *Ballads of a Bohemian* (1921), *Bar-Room Ballads* (1940), the novels *The Pretender* (1914) and *The Roughneck* (1923), and two volumes of autobiography, *Ploughman of the Moon* (1945) and *Harper of Heaven* (1948).

**Seth, Vikram** 1952– Poet, novelist and travel-writer. Born in Calcutta, he went to Corpus Christi, Oxford, before studying Chinese economic demography at Stanford and Nanjing Universities. In 1983 he won the Thomas Cook Travel Book award for *From Heaven Lake*, an account of his journey through Sinkiang and Tibet. Influenced by **Thomas Hardy**, **Philip Larkin** and Timothy Steele, the poems in *The Humble Administrator's Garden* (1985) are quiet and graceful, reflecting his encounters with his own and alien cultures. *The Golden Gate* (1986) is a tale of Californian life in verse, using the Pushkin sonnet stanza inspired by **Charles Johnston**'s translation of *Eugene Onegin*.

**Seton, Ernest Thompson** 1860–1946 Canadian naturalist. He was born Ernest Evan Seton Thompson in South Shields, County Durham; his family emigrated to Canada and he was educated in Toronto. Later he studied art in London at the Royal Academy and wildlife in Manitoba, where he became Government Naturalist. He founded the Boy Scouts of America and the Woodcraft League, and wrote a great number of books on wildlife (illustrated by himself) which enjoyed considerable success. Best known are *Wild Animals I Have Known* (1898), *Biography of a Grizzly* (1900), *Lives of the Hunted* (1901), *Biography of a Silver Fox* (1909), *The Arctic Prairies* (1911), *Wild Animals at Home* (1913) and *Woodland Tales* (1921). Apart from several books on scouting and woodcraft, he wrote an autobiography, *The Trail of an Artist-Naturalist*, published in 1940.

**Settle, Elkanah** 1648–1724 Dramatist. Born in Dunstable and educated at Westminster School and at Oxford, which he left within a year, Settle lived in London from 1666. His first play, *Cambyses, King of Persia* (1667), was a grandiloquent heroic tragedy. It was successful enough to encourage him to keep on writing in the same style. *The Empress of Morocco* (c.1671), performed at court and sponsored by the **Earl of Rochester**, is Settle's best-known play. *The Female Prelate, Pope Joan* (1680) was considered offensive by some of Settle's former supporters. He had, by then, joined in the pamphlet wars on the side of the Earl of Shaftesbury, and his *Absalom Senior* (1682) was a poem written as a counter to **Dryden**'s *Absalom and Achitophel*. Settle's reward was Dryden's wicked portrait of him as Doeg in the second part of *Absalom and Achitophel*. It is to this portrait, more than to his

own work, that Settle owes his place in literary history.

Settle was appointed Official Poet to the City of London in 1691 and wrote Lord Mayor's pageants from then until 1708. He achieved some theatrical success with musical pieces, particularly with his adaptation of **A Midsummer Night's Dream** as *The Fairy Queen* (1692), for which Henry Purcell wrote the music. When he fell out of theatrical favour, he wrote drolls (short comic pieces often based on scenes from well-known plays) for Bartholomew Fair. The text of one, *The Siege of Troy* (1707), survives. Settle was taken into the Charterhouse as a poor brother in 1718 and died there.

**Seuss, Dr** Pseudonym of the American children's writer and illustrator Theodor Seuss Giesel (1904–91). Born in Massachusetts, he was educated at Dartmouth College and later attended Oxford University before losing patience with the academic life. Returning to America, he worked in films and advertising before producing his first children's book, *And To Think That I Saw It On Mulberry Street* (1937). It established his distinctive style, marrying catchy, doggerel verse to energetic, sometimes outlandish illustrations. Such a combination also lent itself well to books for early readers, with *The Cat In The Hat* (1957) achieving wonders of surreal humour with only a limited vocabulary. There followed more than 50 such 'Beginner' books, many written and designed by Seuss himself and the rest produced by a company of which he was president. Never a favourite with critics, who complain about occasional violence in his drawings and careless rhyming in his verses, Seuss has always been appreciated by children who usually respond positively to his raw energy and hectic good humour.

***Seven Deadly Sins of London, The*** **Thomas Dekker**'s pamphlet (1606) derives from the tradition of the medieval sermon, but also offers a picture of bustling London life. The Seven Deadly Sins (pride, wrath, envy, lust, gluttony, avarice and sloth), with new names and in modern guises, are admitted to London in a seven-day triumph which recalls contemporary ceremonial entries to the city.

***Seven Lamps of Architecture, The*** A treatise on architecture by **John Ruskin**, first published in 1849.

In Ruskin's words, the purpose of *The Seven Lamps* was 'to show that certain right states of temper and moral feeling were the powers by which all good architecture, without exception, had been produced'. To that end Ruskin claims that architecture should be informed by seven lamps (or spirits): Sacrifice, Truth, Power, Memory, Beauty, Obedience and Life. Each lamp illuminates the author's vision of the heights to which all architecture should aspire. Into his discourse Ruskin weaves problems involving the exertion of the worker, the bearing of labour upon architecture, the matter of ornamentation (its truth or falsity), the significance of colour and the contemporary habit of building houses to last but one generation. The book is a plea for the building as a holy place consecrated in love and affection, stability and contentment. There is, Ruskin avers, a moral duty upon man to build in patience, care and diligence, and where historical building is concerned the Gothic style should prevail because it 'admits of a richness of record altogether unlimited'. His idealism moves him to claim that the earth is an entail rather than a possession and that it belongs as much to those who precede us as to those who will follow and therefore when we build 'let us think we build for ever'.

**Seven Sages of Rome, The** A collection of 15 tales set within a narrative framework and surviving in several versions, of which the earliest was written c.1300–25 in Kent. It is based on a French original, *Les Sept Sages de Rome* (before 1150), but its ultimate source is the western collection analogous to *The Book of Sinbad*.

Diocletian, emperor of Rome, sends his son to be educated by seven sages. The emperor marries a wife who is jealous that the son will succeed and sends for him and his tutors, determined that he should die. One of the sages uncovers the plot and tells the boy not to speak for seven days. The queen tries to seduce him to break his silence and then accuses him to the emperor of trying to rape her. The queen tells seven stories, one each night, to convince her husband of the boy's guilt and the sages tell a tale each morning to persuade him of the queen's duplicity. Each day the king condemns and frees his son. On the eighth day the boy tells a tale after which the queen confesses and is burned. The structural device of a series of tales within a framework was common in the Middle Ages; notable examples are **Chaucer**'s *Canterbury Tales* and **Gower**'s *Confessio Amantis*.

**Sewall, Samuel** 1652–1730 American Puritan writer. The son of New England settlers, Sewall was born in England and returned with his family to Boston in 1661. He received his BA from Harvard in 1671. He served as special commissioner at the witchcraft trials in 1692, but soon regretted the proceedings and, in fact, was the only one of the nine judges to make a public confession of error.

Sewall distinguished himself as a humane and liberal jurist, most notably while he was chief justice of the Superior Judicature (1718–28). His writings testify to that reputation. *The Revolu-*

*tion in New-England Justified* (1691), written in conjunction with Edward Rawson, justifies the uprising of 1689 which deposed Royal Governor Andros. Having produced a text which typically conceives of New England as the eventual seat of the New Jerusalem, *Phaenomena Quaedam Apocalyptica* (1697), Sewall went on to write one of the earliest published arguments against slavery, *The Selling of Joseph* (1700). In 1713 he produced another theological treatise, *Proposals Touching the Accomplishment of Prophesies* (1713). Finally came two tracts that most clearly reveal his kind heart and innovative judgement: *A Memorial Relating to the Kennebeck Indians* (1721), an argument for the humane treatment of the Indians; and '*Talitha Cumi*' (Massachusetts Historical Society, 1873), a rebuttal of a theological position which denied the resurrection to women (the work's Arabic title translates as 'maiden arise' and is taken from Mark 5:41). As a historical document, Sewall's *Diary* is his greatest contribution to colonial literature. Published 1878–82 by the Massachusetts Historical Society, it covers the years 1674–7 and 1685–1729, and offers an intimate and detailed account of day-to-day life in Puritan New England.

**Sewanee Review, The** An American literary journal. Affiliated with the University of the South (Sewanee, Tennessee), *The Sewanee Review* has been published continuously since 1892. Although essentially a critical journal (concentrating in particular on modern English and American literature), it also publishes some poetry and fiction. It has exerted great influence as a journal of the **New Criticism**, particularly under the editorship of **Allen Tate** (1944–6).

**Seward, Anna** 1747–1809 Poet. She was born at Eyam in Derbyshire but spent most of her life in Lichfield, Staffordshire, where she was the centre of a literary circle and was known as the Swan of Lichfield. She met **Samuel Johnson** on his visits to his home town and, though not an admirer, supplied **Boswell** with information for his biography. She bequeathed her poems to **Sir Walter Scott**, who published them with a memoir in 1810. Her letters, carefully written with an eye to publication, appeared in six volumes (1811).

**Sewell, Anna** 1820–78 Novelist. She was born into a family of Norfolk Quakers and sometimes assisted her mother, who wrote verses and stories for children. Not until she was 50, when a childhood accident that had long disabled her at last made her a complete invalid, did she begin writing her only novel, *Black Beauty*. This enduringly popular story of a horse was published in 1877, only a few months before the author's death.

**Sexton, Anne** 1928–74 American poet, born in Newton, Massachusetts. Her poetry, like that of **Robert Lowell**, with whom she studied, is **Confessional** in its use of the ordinary events of the poet's daily life to explore the self and its relation to the world. Among her main subjects were her struggles with depression and mental illness, her experiences as a daughter, wife, and mother, and the natural world, specifically that of the Massachusetts coastline and Maine. Her depression and loneliness finally led to her suicide in 1974. Her first volume was *To Bedlam and Part Way Back* (1960). Subsequent books include *All My Pretty Ones* (1962), *Selected Poems* (1964), *Live or Die* (1966), *Love Poems* (1969), *Transformations* (1971), *The Book of Folly* (1972), *The Death Notebooks* (1974) and *The Awful Rowing Towards God* (1975). Two posthumous collections were edited by Linda Gray Sexton: *45 Mercy Street* (1976) and *Words for Dr Y: Uncollected Poems with Three Stories* (1978).

**Seymour, Alan** 1927– Australian dramatist. Born in Perth, where he was educated in state schools, Seymour was orphaned at a young age. He worked for the Australian Broadcasting Corporation and as a film and theatre critic in Sydney in the 1940s and 1950s. In the early 1960s he went to London for the production of his best known play, *The One Day of the Year*, which had first been performed in Adelaide in 1960, and has since mainly lived abroad. Between 1963 and 1965 he was theatre critic for *The London Magazine*. More recently he has lived in Turkey. Seymour first attracted attention as a dramatist with the performance of his play, *Swamp Creatures* (1957), a surrealist allegory set in a Gothic house, in which experiments to create monster-insects serve as a metaphor for expressing fears of a nuclear holocaust. Experimental in its time, it is a play which is far more typical of Seymour's work than the comparatively naturalistic *The One Day of the Year*, which has come to be regarded as a classic of the Australian theatre. The 'one day' referred to in this title is Anzac Day (25 April), which is used as a focal point for the exploration of issues of national identity. The play's main theme is the conflict between generations in a time of rapid social change. Its appeal can be attributed to its vivid use of the Australian vernacular, careful construction and themes such as the conflict between mateship and individualism which, while quintessentially Australian, have broad resonances which cross cultural boundaries. Seymour's numerous other plays include *A Break in the Music* (1966), which draws on his Perth upbringing, *The Shattering* (1973) and *The Float* (1980). He has also published the novel *The Coming Self-Destruction of the United States of America* (1980) and adapted *The One Day of the Year* into a novel.

**Shabby Genteel Story, A** A story by **W. M. Thackeray**, published in *Fraser's Magazine* from June to October 1840, and in book form in 1852.

George Brandon, a fashionable young gentleman fleeing his creditors, comes to lodge at Margate with the shabby-genteel Gann family. Piqued that the two older daughters are unimpressed by his aristocratic airs, he sets out to seduce the youngest, Caroline, who loves him. Jealousy of a rival leads to love, and he plans to marry her, but his fashionable friends persuade him to go through a mock ceremony. This unfinished story is continued and developed in *The Adventures of Philip*, where Brandon reappears under his real name, Firmin.

**Shadbolt, Maurice** 1932– New Zealand novelist and short-story writer. Born in Auckland, he worked as a journalist for two years after attending Auckland University. Between 1954 and 1957 he was a scriptwriter for the New Zealand National Film Unit and then decided to become a full-time writer. He has subsequently lived in London, Spain and Auckland. Ever since the publication of his first volume of short stories, *The New Zealanders* (1959), Shadbolt's work has chronicled the changing nature of New Zealand life and the problems of sustaining personal relationships in what he presents as an essentially secular and complacent materialistic society. His fiction is characterized by complex plot structures which are often ingeniously handled. He is best known for his novels of the 1970s, *Strangers and Journeys* (1972), which examines the consequences of the failed European attempt to create a Utopia in New Zealand, *A Touch of Clay* (1974) and *The Danger Zone* (1976). *The Lovelock Version* (1980) is a large comic novel, spanning a period of more than a century. Shadbolt has won several awards for his writing, including the Katherine Mansfield Award for short fiction twice. His short-story collections include *Summer Fires and Winter Country* (1963) and *Figures in Light* (1978).

**Shadow of a Gunman, The** A two-act play by **Sean O'Casey**, first performed at the **Abbey Theatre**, Dublin, in 1923. It was the first of O'Casey's plays to be produced there.

In a Dublin tenement in 1920, when the Black and Tans are making their reprisal raids, Donal Davoren, a poet who is believed by fellow lodgers to be on the run from the British, shares a room with Seumas Shields, a feckless pedlar. Donal is, in fact, no kind of gunman or hero, and the play's bitter conclusion (much of its conduct is comic) sees the admiring and admirable Minnie Powell, a girl who lives in the same tenement, killed in an ambush as a result of her attempts to shield Donal.

**Shadwell, Thomas** *c.* 1642–92 Playwright

and poet. Born in Norfolk, Shadwell was at Cambridge University from 1654–6 and studied law (he was a lawyer's son) at the Middle Temple from 1658 until he determined on a literary career. His earliest published work was a play, *The Sullen Lovers* (1668), written on the model of **Ben Jonson**'s comedy of humours. It was a mode that suited Shadwell's firm moral orthodoxy, and he never wholly abandoned it. But Shadwell had a professional preparedness to adapt to changing theatrical fashions. After the comparative failure of *The Humorists* (1670), he incorporated into *Epsom Wells* (1672) the new techniques of the witty society comedy pioneered by **Etherege**. His best plays, *Epsom Wells*, *The Virtuoso* (1676), *The Squire of Alsatia* (1688) and *Bury Fair* (1689), helped to assimilate the Jonsonian urge to instruct through satire into the developing style of English comedy. Not all of Shadwell's successful work is so estimable. His adaptation of *The Tempest* (1674) owed more to the fashion for spectacular opera than to **Shakespeare**. A second opera, *Psyche* (1675), was a tame exploitation of the popularity of the first. *The Libertine* (1675) and an adaptation of *Timon of Athens* (1678) are weak examples of the heroic tragedy brought into vogue by **John Dryden**. Even so, the punishment inflicted on Shadwell's subsequent reputation by the magnificent satire of Dryden's *Mac Flecknoe* (1678) is excessive. He was by no means as dull a writer as Dryden encourages us to believe. That he should have succeeded Dryden as Poet Laureate in 1689 is an irony that has done Shadwell no posthumous favours. His best verse is contained either in his plays or in the satirical prologues and epilogues that accompanied them in the theatre. The Juvenalian satire of *The Medal of John Bayes* (1682) and the version of Juvenal's *Tenth Satire* (1687) has lost its bite and the panegyric of his 'Laureate' poems is predictably empty.

**Shaffer, Peter** 1926– Playwright and novelist. Born in Liverpool and educated in London and at Cambridge, Shaffer first published three novels in collaboration with his twin brother Anthony, but it was the play *Five Finger Exercise* (1958) that first brought him acclaim. Later plays have included clever comedies like *The Private Ear* (1962), *The Public Eye* (1962) and *Black Comedy* (1965), the spectacular *The Royal Hunt of the Sun* (1964) and two highly praised and effective psychological studies, *Equus* (1973) and *Amadeus* (1979).

**Shaftesbury, Anthony Ashley Cooper, 3rd Earl of** 1671–1713 Philosopher. He was the grandson of the 1st Earl of Shaftesbury, politician, champion of the Duke of Monmouth's cause and the Achitophel of **Dryden**'s *Absalom and Achitophel*. Born in London, he was edu-

cated at Winchester College under the supervision of **John Locke**, who had been physician and secretary to his grandfather. After travelling in Europe Shaftesbury entered Parliament, inheriting the title in 1700; he retired from public life because of ill health and in 1711 went to live in Naples, where he died.

After withdrawing into private life Shaftesbury devoted himself to moral philosophy. He rejected the bleakness of **Hobbes** and Locke but at the same time questioned religious dogma; the **Cambridge Platonists** were his philosophical ancestors. His works include *An Inquiry Concerning Virtue* (1699), *A Letter Concerning Enthusiasm* (1708), *The Moralist* (1709) and *Soliloquy, or Advice to an Author* (1710). He collected his writings in *Characteristics of Men, Manners, Opinions, Times* (1711), which contained further reflections and essays on new subjects. A carefully revised text was published in 1714; his unfinished *Second Characters, or the Language of Forms* was published in 1914.

Shaftesbury's prose is uncomplicated and his moral philosophy has no need of technicalities. He disliked religious controversy and regarded it as valueless; he used ridicule against superstition, but thought the use of ridicule as the sole weapon for argument detestable. At a time when many people were dismayed by the rival – and sometimes stridently argued – claims of **Deists**, philosophers and religious dogmatists, Shaftesbury's 'moral sense' had strong appeal and his work was widely read.

**Shakespeare apocrypha** **John Heminges** and Henry Condell, in their epistle 'to the great variety of readers' prefaced to the 1623 Folio collection of **Shakespeare**'s plays, claimed to have included all those previously printed together with 'all the rest'. In fact, they nearly left out ***Troilus and Cressida***, which is missing from the list of contents. Since his lifetime, Shakespeare has been named as the author of other plays which they did not include. ***Pericles*** (1609) is now admitted to the canon. ***The Two Noble Kinsmen*** (1634) continues to provoke debate, but is probably his work, in collaboration with **John Fletcher**. *Pericles* together with six plays printed between 1595 and 1619 as his (or at least as the work of 'W.S.') were added in 1664 as a supplement to the Third Folio (1663). None of the others is now accepted as his, but they provide the basis for what modern scholarship has christened the 'Shakespeare apocrypha'. They are: *Locrine* (1595); Part 1 of *Sir John Oldcastle* (1600), by **Anthony Munday** and others; ***Thomas, Lord Cromwell*** (1602); ***The London Prodigal*** (1605); ***The Puritan*** (1607) and ***A Yorkshire Tragedy*** (1608), both possibly by **Thomas Middleton**.

Two further attributions have seemed plausible enough to receive serious attention. Three pages of the late Elizabethan manuscript of *Sir Thomas More* (?1593–5) are widely accepted as Shakespeare's own revision of a rejected scene. Since **Edward Capell** first suggested it in 1760, many have found reason to entertain his view that *Edward III* (1596) may be wholly or in part the work of Shakespeare; at least he would appear to have been very well acquainted with it. The rest of the conventional group is an anthology of popular drama attributed to Shakespeare on various and tenuous grounds. The plays are **Arden of Feversham** (1592); *Fair Em, the Miller's Daughter of Manchester* (1593); **Mucedorus** (1598); **The Merry Devil of Edmonton** (1608); and *The Birth of Merlin*, printed as late as 1662 and attributed to **William Rowley** and Shakespeare.

Attempts are still occasionally made to attach Shakespeare's name to further unassigned plays of the period, but they rarely achieve much conviction and are more often rationalizations of preconceived conclusions than impartial enquiries. *Double Falsehood, or, The Distressed Lovers* (1728) should probably be added to the core of plays whose attribution is more than fanciful. It is either what it claims to be, namely a thorough reworking for the 18th-century theatre, undertaken by **Lewis Theobald**, of a play by Shakespeare and Fletcher known to us only by its title, *Cardenio*, or an entire fabrication by Theobald himself. Sufficient grounds exist for believing that the play is of Jacobean origin.

**Shakespeare, William** 1564–1616 In a flamboyant age and a notoriously flamboyant profession – he was an active member of a theatre company for at least 20 years – Shakespeare was notably reticent. As a result, scholars have had painstakingly to piece together the story of his life from surviving scraps of evidence, and there remains ample room for speculation.

He was born in Stratford-upon-Avon, where his father was a prosperous glover and one of the town's 14 principal burgesses. In 1565, John Shakespeare was promoted to the rank of alderman and in 1571 was appointed Chief Alderman. It is a reasonable assumption that such a man would send his son to the grammar school in Stratford. The evident decline in John Shakespeare's fortunes after 1576 has allowed speculation that his son did not complete his education. He is known to have married Anne Hathaway in 1582. A daughter was born to the couple within six months. She was the Susanna who later married the physician John Hall and lived prosperously in Stratford. The family was completed with the birth of the twins, Judith and Hamnet, in 1585: Judith lived until 1662 and Hamnet died in 1596.

Virtually nothing is known of Shakespeare's life from 1585 to 1592. One of many possibili-

ties is that he left Stratford with a group of London actors. Certainly his name was sufficiently well known in the London theatre by 1592 to invite **Robert Greene**'s jibe at him as an 'upstart Crow'. Greene had in mind Shakespeare's part in the writing of **Henry VI**. This early collaboration suggests that Shakespeare's apprenticeship as a playwright was served alongside the growing number of aspiring writers, seeking to benefit from the demand for plays in the emergent professional theatre. The texts that survive from the 1590s imply that Shakespeare preferred to work alone, though we do not know what may have been lost. Only in **Sir Thomas More** (*c.*1595) has his hand been confidently detected. By 1594, when he found sufficient money and professional commitment to purchase a share in the newly formed Lord Chamberlain's Men, Shakespeare had probably written his three early comedies, **The Comedy of Errors**, **The Two Gentlemen of Verona** and **The Taming of the Shrew**, two corpse-laden tragedies, **Titus Andronicus** and **Richard III**, and a large share of the three *Henry VI* plays, to which *Richard III* provided a brilliantly original conclusion. He had also reached a fashionable audience with the two narrative poems, **Venus and Adonis** (1593) and **The Rape of Lucrece** (1594). It was sufficient to encourage the mature actors who formed the Lord Chamberlain's Men to accept him, not merely as an actor, but also as a potential resident writer for their proposed London home, the **Theatre** in Shoreditch.

Shakespeare, by an unknown artist. Known as the Chandos portrait, the painting is undated and hangs in the National Portrait Gallery, London.

D. Loggan's 'A Prospect of London as before the Fire.' The South Bank is in the foreground and the theatres are clearly seen.

Living in the region of Bishopsgate, not far from the Theatre, Shakespeare continued to write plays at the rate of approximately two per year. The period 1594–8 may have seen the first productions of *King John* (sometimes dated as early as 1589), the middle comedies *Love's Labour's Lost* (scholars continue to argue about *Love's Labour's Won*, ascribed to Shakespeare by **Francis Meres**), *A Midsummer Night's Dream* and *The Merchant of Venice*, the outstandingly popular tragedy *Romeo and Juliet* and the cycle of English history plays, *Richard II*, the two parts of *Henry IV* and *Henry V*. That he also had aspirations as a gentleman, and sufficient means to support them, is apparent in the application, on his father's behalf, for a coat of arms in 1596. The application was successful. The following year, Shakespeare bought one of Stratford's finest houses, New Place. Early in 1598 he made a small investment in malt (malting was Stratford's principal industry). The London theatres were experiencing hardship at this time, and it is possible that Shakespeare was contemplating the life of a country gentleman with his wife and daughters in Stratford. If so, he changed his mind. With other shareholders of the Lord Chamberlain's Men, he met the landlord's threat of eviction from the Theatre by moving its timbers to the south bank of the Thames and re-erecting them as the **Globe**.

Shakespeare wrote his greatest plays during the first decade of his company's occupation of the Globe. They include the mature comedies, *Much Ado About Nothing* (more probably dating from 1598), *As You Like It* and *Twelfth Night*; the darker comedies, sometimes called **problem plays**, *All's Well that Ends Well*, *Measure for Measure* and *Troilus and Cressida*; a pot-boiler, *The Merry Wives of Windsor*, written in response to demands for more about Falstaff; and the succession of great tragedies, *Julius Caesar, Hamlet, Othello, King Lear, Macbeth, Antony and Cleopatra, Coriolanus* and *Timon of Athens*. It was a period that saw the Lord Chamberlain's Men honoured by the new monarch with the title of the **King's Men** and confirmed in their ascendancy at court. Shakespeare had moved his London lodgings to Southwark, but maintained his financial interests in Stratford. A small investment in land in 1602 was followed by a larger one in 1605. But theatrical fashions were changing. The faddish interest in **boys' companies**, playing in indoor theatres, had attracted the interest of some of the best playwrights of the age. As the interest in the boys waned, these playwrights began to write for the adult companies. **Beaumont** and **Fletcher** were particularly adept at suiting the new fashions almost before they declared themselves, and Shakespeare was probably feeling the need to look to his well-established laurels. When the King's Men decided to invest in an indoor playhouse of their own, at the **Blackfriars**, he joined them, perhaps recognizing the greater scenic scope offered by indoor playing. His last plays, *Pericles, Prince of Tyre* (written in collaboration, probably with George Wilkins), *Cymbeline, The Winter's Tale* and *The Tempest*, are romances, which acknowledge even as they transcend the growing interest in spectacle, magic and improbable resolutions. The collaborations with John Fletcher on *Henry VIII, The Two Noble Kinsmen* and the lost *Cardenio* suggest a dulling of his own creativity. It was at a performance of *Henry VIII* in 1613 that the Globe was burned down. Shakespeare had just bought the upper floor of one of the Blackfriars gatehouses and may not have wished to pay out more money for the rebuilding of the Globe. The probability is that he spent his last years in Stratford.

It was as a poet as well as a playwright that Shakespeare was honoured by his contemporaries. *The Phoenix and the Turtle* had appeared in Robert Chester's *Love's Martyr* (1601). The *Sonnets* (1609), written probably many years before they were published with an enigmatic dedication to Mr W. H., confirmed, if confirmation were needed, his genius. To two fellow actors, **John Heminges** and Henry Condell, is owed the posthumous collection of Shakespeare's plays, known as the First Folio (1623). It was a vast undertaking, without which 20 of Shakespeare's plays may have been lost to posterity. Plays were not highly prized as literature. **Sir Thomas Bodley** had classed most of them among the 'idle books, and riff-raffs' he did not wish to have catalogued in his library in 1612, so that the decision to publish so many by one man, and in the exalted folio form, is evidence of the esteem in which Shakespeare was held, not only by his public, but also by his fellow professionals. The Folio was republished in 1632, 1664 and 1685, and the first scholarly edition of Shakespeare's work, edited by the playwright **Nicholas Rowe**, followed in 1709.

**Shakespeare: performance and criticism** After the Restoration in 1660 **Shakespeare**'s plays were altered to suit new tastes and performance methods. Actresses superseded young men and boys in female roles, perspective scenery was used on stage. The interests of a more exclusive clientele were served. Some plays were radically revised: *The Tempest* acquired new characters, including Miranda's sister and a prince who has never seen a woman, together with more music and grander spectacular effects. In some plays, adaptation was less wholesale, achieved by omission rather than alteration. Critical response to Shakespeare valued energy in language and character but censured what were considered breaches of decorum in plots, imagery and characterization. **Dryden**, in *An Essay of Dramatic Poesy* (1668) and other writings, expressed this mingled dispraise and celebration, crediting Shakespeare with the 'largest and most comprehensive soul' among the moderns. Less willing to admit extenuation was **Thomas Rymer**, whose account of *Othello* insisted on standards of ideal, dignified discourse: the 'tragical part' of the play appeared 'plainly none other than a bloody farce without salt or savour'. The theatre still offered compromise. **Nahum Tate**, having found *King Lear* 'a heap of jewels, unstrung and unpolished', restrung the dazzling disorder to provide a happy ending in which Lear and Gloucester are reprieved and Cordelia is united with Edgar. This denouement, and Tate's omission of the Fool, survived in stage practice up to the early 19th century.

The notion of Shakespeare as a natural genius with more or less pardonable faults was developed in the next century. The works were presented to readers in a succession of handsome and scholarly editions by **Pope** (1725), Hanmer (1743–4), Warburton (1747), **Johnson** (1765), **Capell** (1767–8), **Steevens** (1773 etc.), **Malone** (1790, augmented by James Boswell the younger in 1821). These encouraged attention to Shakespeare's own (rather than his adapters') words. Pope, in the preface to his edition of the *Works*, describes him as 'not so much an imitator as an instrument of Nature'. In Johnson's preface he is the 'poet of nature' who 'holds up to his readers a faithful mirror of manners and life' and whose artistic failings should be forgiven if not imitated.

This confidence in Shakespeare's mimetic powers was reflected in a renewed emphasis on his characters. In the 1740s the actors **David**

**Garrick** and Charles Macklin broke with an oppressively 'formal' manner of playing the tragic roles (represented in the Restoration period by Thomas Betterton and in the early 1700s by James Quin). At the same time the language and structure of the plays gradually returned to the stage, although Garrick's acting texts included a *Romeo and Juliet* in which Juliet awakes in the tomb before Romeo expires (allowing a prolonged pathetic death-scene for both lovers) and a truncated *Taming of the Shrew*. Explorations of psychology – the display of the symptoms of the 'passions' – resulted in performances which impressed audiences as startlingly 'real', for example Macklin's new, serious (and villainous) Shylock and the jarred sensibilities of Garrick's Hamlet. The critic Maurice Morgann, defending his subject against charges of cowardice in an *Essay on the Dramatick Character of Falstaff* (1777), established a precedent for elaborate reconstructions of a dramatic character's personality.

Romantic criticism confirmed Shakespeare's pre-eminence in modern literary culture. In various lectures between 1808 and 1819, in *Biographia Literaria* (1817) and elsewhere, **Coleridge** proclaimed his discovery of the characters as vividly individualized examples of human types. The 'organic regularity' of Shakespeare's characters and plots, distinguished from the 'mechanic regularity' of neoclassical drama, corresponded to the order of nature in exhibiting 'a law in which all the parts obey, conforming themselves to the outward symbols and manifestations of the essential principle'. Obscurities and compression in poetic language were beginning to be valued rather than condemned or merely condoned. **William Hazlitt**'s *Characters of Shakespeare's Plays* (1817), informed by experience of stage performances, described forcefully the aesthetic impact of dramatic characters. The *Tales from Shakespeare* (1807) of **Charles Lamb** and his sister Mary and **Thomas Bowdler**'s notorious expurgation, *The Family Shakespeare* (1807 in 4 vols., 1818 in 10 vols.), helped to make the plays current in education and in middle-class family reading.

In the theatre of the early 1800s the actress Sarah Siddons and her brother John Philip Kemble imbued tragic roles with neoclassical grace and dignity, inspiring sensations of awe rather than intimacy. Kemble often achieved dignity at the expense of emotional power, but some of Siddons's performances were remarkable for psychological complexity. Her Lady Macbeth was both alluring and evil. In contrast with the statuesque effect of Kemble and Siddons, Edmund Kean's acting startled by its carefully prepared effects of sudden and intense emotion. Coleridge compared the audience's experience to that of reading Shakespeare 'by flashes of lightning'. Hazlitt described the 'fresh shocks of delight and surprise' afforded by the rapid transitions in his Shylock (1814). The more measured emotionalism of Kean's contemporary and successor William Charles Macready marked a transition to a recognizably Victorian cultivation of private, domestic feelings. Kemble's acting versions were closer than Garrick's to the original texts, although they were still cut to remove indecencies and suit pictorial staging. Public taste now required costumes and settings that rendered the historical milieu of each play as accurately as possible. Satisfying the taste for historical pageantry was an expensive business, and the actor–managers who presented these shows were expected to dominate them with personal performances of great vigour into the bargain. In the 1840s to 1860s Shakespearean production in London was led by Charles Kean's management at the Princess's Theatre in Oxford Street and the more modest but energetic and idealistic enterprise of Samuel Phelps at Sadler's Wells in Islington. In the 1880s and up to World War I the providers of such 'traditional' Shakespeare were Henry Irving and Herbert Beerbohm Tree. Both were famous for their ability to make characters part of a striking stage-picture: one of the best examples of this was the moonlit scene in Irving's *The Merchant of Venice* when Shylock returned alone to the house from which his daughter had just eloped.

In the 19th century editions began to cater for a variety of tastes and pockets: Charles Knight issued a *Pictorial Shakespeare* in parts between 1839 and 1842, providing a wealth of historical material and illustrations at a popular price; one-volume editions of the works were edited by Clark and Wright (the Globe, 1864), **Furnivall** (the Leopold, 1877) and Craig – whose 1891 Oxford edition has remained in print well into the 1980s. More august scholarly enterprises were the edition by **Halliwell**, or Halliwell-Phillipps, (1853–65) and the New Variorum, begun by Furness in 1874. Cheap reprints of the plays proliferated, and the introduction of Shakespeare into the curriculum of the Board Schools created a market for editions annotated (and expurgated) for the use of pupils.

Victorian criticism focused mainly on character and dramatic effect. **Anna Jameson**'s *Shakespeare's Heroines* (1835) and the writings of the actress Helen Faucit offered sentimental accounts of the female characters. **Carlyle**'s *Heroes, Hero-Worship and the Heroic in History* (1841) included a eulogy of Shakespeare as a type of the 'poet as hero', confirming him in the Romantic tradition of poets-as-legislators. Against this sentiment and celebration should be set a growth of interest in matters of chronology and attempts to find the dramatist's life in his art. **Swinburne**'s *A Study of Shakespeare* (1880), which attempts to combine biography with hero-worship, has the distinction of being the worst book on Shakespeare by a major poet. F. J. Furnivall's energetic work as an editor and as founder of the New Shakspere [*sic*] Society was the basis of much scholarly and critical thinking in the later decades of the century. **Edward Dowden**, in *Shakspere: A Critical Study of his Mind and Art* (1875), traced the playwright's career as a struggle for self-mastery. His *Primer* (1877) made this construction of the biography current at all levels of education. The reverential manner that prevailed in Victorian writing on Shakespeare was challenged by **George Bernard Shaw**, whose dramatic criticism for the *Saturday Review* includes several spirited hatchet-jobs on Shakespearean productions.

**A. C. Bradley**'s *Shakespearean Tragedy* (1904), in some respects a culmination of Romantic preoccupations, also marks a change of attitude in its proposal of a secular, intellectually consistent tragic vision: it has been accused of turning the heroes into Victorian idealists. Although it centres the tragic ethos on individual characters, Bradley's work sets out a world-view bleaker and less sentimental than any offered in earlier criticism. The plays are treated as dramas in the manner of later 19th-century naturalism. Theatrical interpretation was moving away from what had come to seem cluttered scenic realism. William Poel's experiments with Elizabethan staging conventions, and the growth of scholarly interest in theatrical history joined the generally felt impulse to discover non-naturalistic modes of theatre. In **Harley Granville-Barker**'s productions of *The Winter's Tale*, *Twelfth Night* and *A Midsummer Night's Dream* (1912–14) open staging, simplified stylized settings and full texts rapidly delivered revealed Shakespeare as a dramatist whose techniques had little in common with the quasi-operatic spectacle of most Victorian and Edwardian productions. Barker's example and the principles enunciated in his subsequent series of *Prefaces to Shakespeare* (1927–47) set standards for a new generation of interpreters working in the brisker schedules, tighter budgets and integrated ensembles of the repertory theatres. The new, non-commercial companies in the provincial cities and at the **Old Vic** in London offered a greater variety of plays in simpler stagings and quicker succession than had been possible in the commercial actor–managers' theatre.

Criticism in the decades after Bradley extended awareness of Elizabethan literary as well as theatrical conventions. L. L. Schücking's *Character Problems in Shakespeare's Plays* (1919; translated, 1922) and E. E. Stoll's *Art and Artifice in Shakespeare* (1933) were influential in displacing Romantic notions of characterization and dramatic method. Bernard Spivack's *Shakespeare and the Allegory of Evil* (1958) reached back into earlier dramatic and literary works to establish a non-naturalistic system of significance underlying such characters as Iago and Richard III. Bradley's mode of speculation on character had been challenged on other grounds by **F. R. Leavis** and by **L. C. Knights**, whose 'How Many Children had Lady Macbeth?' (1933; reprinted in *Explorations*, 1946) provided a catch-phrase for anti-Bradleyans. The discipline of editorial experience informed **John Dover Wilson**'s teasing out of plot and characterization in *What Happens in Hamlet* (1935). The poetic texture of the plays was investigated by Caroline Spurgeon (*Shakespeare's Imagery*, 1935) and, more subtly, Wolfgang Clemen (*The Development of Shakespeare's Imagery*, 1936; revised and translated, 1951). Studies by **G. Wilson Knight** (notably *The Wheel of Fire*, 1930, on the tragedies) focused on verbal imagery and patterning. This important shift of emphasis, together with the example of the **New Criticism** and **William Empson**'s explorations of ambiguity and word-play, helped to establish a way of reading the plays as poems that characterized much post-1945 criticism. A parallel development was the historical study of 'background', exemplified in Hardin Craig's *The Enchanted Glass* (1936) and **E. M. W. Tillyard**'s construction of a 'world picture' which the plays (especially the histories) were held to set forth. Tillyard's *Shakespeare's History Plays* (1944), although rejected by many as proposing a simplified, conservative intention in the works, mapped out a field of study that would relate the plays to other, non-literary discourses of the period. A. P. Rossiter's essays, collected in *Angel With Horns* (1961), challenge the notion that the plays endorse the 'Tudor myth'.

Thinking on the comedies was given a new impetus by **Northrop Frye**'s formulation of an archetypal comic structure in *An Anatomy of Criticism* (1957) and the complementary thesis of C. L. Barber's *Shakespeare's Festive Comedy* (1959). The bleak outlook in Jan Kott's *Shakespeare, our Contemporary* (1967) has influenced theatrical directors as well as readers; less abrasive, reflecting the more optimistic liberalism of the humanities in the 1960s, was Norman Rabkin's *Shakespeare and the Common Understanding* (1967). A dominant feature of criticism in the 1970s – working alongside **Marxist criticism** and **structuralism** – has been a renewed feminist interrogation of the texts, of which the work of Marilyn French, Coppélia Kahn and Irene Dash is representative.

Research into the conditions of Shakespeare's theatre, consolidated by the documentary labours of **E. K. Chambers**, has resulted in work on the theatrical language of the plays (by J. L. Styan, Nevill Coghill, Bernard Beckerman and others). The use of the play metaphor in Shakespeare, set out concisely in Anne Barton's *Shakespeare and the Idea of the Play* (1969), has been pursued by many critics and directors.

Another kind of stage-centred scholarship concentrates on the plays' stage-life in the centuries since Shakespeare: A. C. Sprague's *Shakespeare and the Actors* (1944) described points of interpretation using prompt-books and reports of performances in a manner that set the standard for many later studies. Investigations of the biographical evidence, although no longer widely accepted as a route into the interpretation of the plays, were set in order by E. K. Chambers's magisterial *William Shakespeare: a Study of the Facts and Problems* (1930) and have been brought up to date by Samuel Schoenbaum, in *William Shakespeare; a Documentary Life* (1975). The same author's *Shakespeare's Lives* (1971) provides an amusing and comprehensive account of the history of Shakespeare biography.

Editions of the plays published since the turn of the century have reflected changes in bibliographical theory and the development of English studies in higher education. The Arden edition (1899–1924) was superseded by the New Arden (1951– ) and a Cambridge edition known as the New Shakespeare (1921–62) is being replaced by a New Cambridge (1984– ). Paperback editions have included the original Penguin series (1937–59), a breakthrough in popular publishing followed by the Pelican (1956–67), the American Signet (1963– ) and the New Penguin (1967– ). The Oxford University Press's editions of individual plays (1982– ), the New Cambridge Shakespeare and the New Arden editions have also appeared in paperback. Important one-volume editions of the complete *Works* are Peter Alexander's (1951), and the American Riverside (1974). A new Oxford edition (1986) offers two versions (rather than a conflated text) of *Lear* and includes the newly attributed poem 'Shall I Die . . .?'.

After Granville-Barker, Shakespearean production in Britain has been characterized by diversity of style: it would be hard to identify a 'tradition'. Directorial practice ranged from the scholarly but enterprising Elizabethanism of Robert Atkins to the cheery, trenchant iconoclasm of Tyrone Guthrie. Between the wars a number of leading Shakespearean actors and actresses established themselves, but their personal styles were diverse: John Gielgud, Laurence Olivier, Ralph Richardson and Peggy Ashcroft worked on occasion with each other, with various directors and in a number of different companies. In the 1940s an actor-manager of the old kind emerged in Donald Wolfit. The parallel institutions of the Old Vic in London and the Memorial Theatre in Stratford were developed (with the advent of state subsidy) into the **National Theatre** and the **Royal Shakespeare Company**. Laurence Olivier's management of the National (Old Vic, 1964–74) began with an unexciting *Hamlet*, but went on to achieve critical acclaim with an all-male *As You Like It* and Franco Zeffirelli's *Romeo and Juliet*. Olivier himself appeared in *Othello* and in Jonathan Miller's production of *The Merchant of Venice*. Neither company can be said currently to offer a 'house style' for Shakespeare, although the RSC's cycle *The Wars of the Roses* (1963–4) set new standards in the presentation of the history plays. A marriage of sorts was arranged between Brechtian epic theatre and a renewed awareness of Elizabethan staging conditions. The scale and breadth of main-stage Stratford productions has been challenged lately by more intimate stagings by other companies. The RSC's own studio work has contributed to this movement: a powerful impression was made by Trevor Nunn's *Macbeth* (1974) and Buzz Goodbody's *Hamlet* (1975). Peter Brook, a *Wunderkind* in the late 1940s and 1950s and now more of a guru, achieved world-wide success with his *Titus Andronicus* (with Olivier, 1956) and *A Midsummer Night's Dream* (RSC, 1970). Mention should also be made of the 'offshoots' in which modern dramatists have reworked Shakespearean material, either in direct confrontation with the originals (e.g. Charles Marowitz's *Hamlet* and other plays) or in order to capitalize on received ideas about characters and circumstances (**Arnold Wesker**'s *The Merchant*; **Edward Bond**'s *Lear*). Some stage versions have hovered between interpreting and revising the plays: Brecht's *Coriolanus* is a famous example.

Shakespeare's plays attracted film-makers from the earliest days of commercial cinema. The first 'talkie' based on Shakespeare was *The Taming of the Shrew* with Douglas Fairbanks and Mary Pickford (1929). In 1936 Max Reinhardt, who had staged the play many times in Europe and America, directed a Hollywood film version with a cast including James Cagney and Mickey Rooney (as Bottom and Puck). Olivier, as actor and director, made popular movies of *Henry V* (1944), *Hamlet* (1947) and *Richard III* (1955); Orson Welles filmed idiosyncratic versions of *Macbeth* (1948) and *Othello* (1950) and an epic compilation of Falstaffian episodes, *The Chimes at Midnight* (1965). Franco Zeffirelli's *The Taming of the Shrew* (1966) and *Romeo and Juliet* (1968) and Roman Polanski's *Macbeth* (1971) have enjoyed great popularity. A *Hamlet* (1964) and *King Lear* (1971) by the Russian director Grigori Kozintsev and Akira Kuroswawa's Japanese versions of the *Macbeth* and *Lear* stories have been widely acclaimed. Shakespeare's plays have been a regular feature of British radio broadcasting since the 1920s, although these productions have never enjoyed the attention lavished on such television adaptations as those included in the BBC's series covering the whole canon (1978–84).

A full survey of the transpositions of Shakespeare's work into the other arts would have to include graphic representations (especially the Shakespearean paintings so popular in the 19th century), music and writings inspired by the plays and poems. It seems prudent to restrict the present account to works offering to *perform* the plays in a new medium.

Shakespearean operas may be said to date from the Restoration versions of *The Tempest* and (with Purcell's music) *A Midsummer Night's Dream*, and incidental music has often been provided on such a scale as to turn the plays into semi-operatic entertainments. A number from Mendelssohn's *Dream* music, long inseparable from the play, was even put to ironic purposes in Brook's production. Giuseppe Verdi's *Macbeth* (1847 and 1865) and *Otello* (1887) are vigorous, perceptive readings of the plays, and his last opera, *Falstaff* (1893), has a poetic quality not usually found in Shakespeare's citizen comedy, *The Merry Wives of Windsor*. A popular and likeable adaptation of the same work is Otto Nicolai's *Die Lustigen Weiber von Windsor* (1849). Benjamin Britten's *A Midsummer Night's Dream* (1960) is considered by many to be the best Shakespeare opera since Verdi. Shakespeare has also been put to good account in musical comedy: Rodgers and Hart made *The Comedy of Errors* into *The Boys from Syracuse* (1938); Cole Porter's *Kiss Me, Kate* (1948) is about the tribulations of actors touring with *The Taming of the Shrew*; and in *West Side Story* (1957) Leonard Bernstein and Jerome Robbins transposed the story of *Romeo and Juliet* to New York.

Choreographers as well as composers have found inspiration in the plays, with results that range from the brief psychodramas of Robert Helpmann's *Hamlet* (1948) and José Limon's *The Moor's Pavane* (1949) to the lavish full-length *Romeo and Juliet* ballets using Sergei Prokofiev's score (1938). *The Taming of the Shrew* was made into a ballet by John Cranko (1969).

**Shakespeare's Sonnets** They were first printed in 1609 by George Eld for Thomas Thorpe. At least some were written earlier, for versions of 138 and 144 appeared in *The Passionate Pilgrim* (?1599), and in 1598 **Francis Meres**'s *Palladis Tamia* spoke of Shakespeare's 'sugared sonnets' circulating among his friends. Since the 1590s saw a great English vogue for the sonnet, initiated by **Sidney**'s sequence *Astrophil and Stella*, it is likely that Shakespeare wrote most of his sonnets before 1600. They are dedicated to Mr W. H., the 'only begetter' of the poems. His identity and whether he is to be identified with the youth addressed in the sonnets is still a matter for debate, which is sometimes only tangentially relevant to the sonnets themselves. Henry Wriothesley, Earl of Southampton, and William Herbert, Earl of Pembroke, have long been popular as candidates for Mr W. H. and also for the youth in the sonnets, who is apparently aristocratic. Similar, and even less successful, attempts have been made to identify the so-called 'Dark Lady' who is the troublesome and unfaithful mistress of the later sonnets, and the 'Rival Poet' of such poems as sonnet 86.

It is uncertain whether the order of the 1609 quarto is authorial. Attempts have been made at rearrangement, but Thomas Thorpe's order remains the usual one. As the sequence of sonnets stands, it falls into two sections: 1–126 are concerned mainly with the youth and 127–154 mainly with the mistress. Shakespeare's sonnets do not even have the barely suggested narrative lines of *Astrophil and Stella* and **Spenser**'s *Amoretti*, but it is just possible to glimpse the poet's love for a young man, whom he initially persuades to marry and beget children, and promises to immortalize, and who is then seduced by the poet's mistress. Within the larger divisions of poems to the youth and to the mistress smaller groups of poems can be identified. Sonnets 1–17 urge the youth to marry as a means of immortality. Their theme and poetic imagery may be summed up by a line from **Erasmus**'s *Education of the Christian Prince*: 'He does not die who leaves behind a living image of himself.' This image, even in the later poems of this first section, becomes the image created by poetry, and the theme is fully expressed at the end of sonnet 18, the famous 'Shall I compare thee to a summer's day', in the triumphant assertion 'So long as men can breathe or eyes can see, / So long lives this, and this gives life to thee.' The poet offers his poetry as a means of immortality for both the youth and himself. The sonnets up to 126 record the oscillations in the relationship between poet and youth: 33–42 tell of a temporary estrangement and then reconciliation. The promises of immortality have to contend with the threat of change and time and 65 is one of the many poems dwelling on 'sad mortality'. Others speak of the discrepancy between the poet's age and the friend's youth. In some poems from 97 onwards we hear of the poet's absence from the youth. The poems to the youth dwell on the great Renaissance themes of friendship, love, death, change and immortality and the relationship of the poet's art to all of these. Sonnet 116, 'Let me not to the marriage of true minds', bravely asserts that 'Love's not Time's fool', but it is untypical in its unshaken faith in the permanence of affection. 126, a truncated sonnet of only 12 lines, may be intended as a conclusion to the first group.

The rest of the sonnets are mainly about the poet's relationship with the mistress. Sonnet 130, 'My mistress' eyes are nothing like the sun', parodies the excessive hyperbole of sonneteering conventions. Many of these poems are bitter about the mistress's infidelity and some express disgust at sexual activity with bawdy

quibbles (135 puns relentlessly on 'will' and 129 describes lust as 'Th'expense of spirit in a waste of shame').

**Wordsworth** in a sonnet about sonnets thought that 'with this key / Shakespeare unlocked his heart' and **Lytton Strachey** talked of the mystery of the sonnets, both anticipating the desire of many readers to find a biographical key to the poems. Wordsworth elsewhere found the sonnets to the lady 'abominably harsh, obscure and worthless', but **Coleridge** thought better of the sonnets as a whole and enthusiastically recommended them to his son. This century has been more attentive to the poetry than the supposed biography and few now could agree with **Hazlitt** that if we had only Shakespeare's poems he would be regarded as a cold and artificial writer. Although, as **W. H. Auden** observed, not all the sonnets are of the same excellence, the very finest of them would alone have assured Shakespeare of that immortality which is one of the sonnets' constant themes.

**Shamela Andrews, An Apology for the Life of Mrs** See *Pamela* and **Fielding, Henry**.

**Shapiro, Karl** 1913– American poet, born in Baltimore, Maryland, and educated at the University of Virginia and The Johns Hopkins University. His first volume was *Person, Place, and Thing* (1942), a collection of love poems in blank verse. He served in the US Army from 1941 to 1945; *V-Letter and Other Poems* (1944), which won him the 1945 Pulitzer Prize, contains war poetry. Later volumes, such as *Poems 1940–1953* (1953), *The House* (1957) and *Poems of a Jew* (1958), are often caustic and iconoclastic in tone and are written in tight, disciplined verse. *The Bourgeois Poet* (1964) marked a distinct change in form, the poems being composed in Whitmanesque prose paragraphs. Subsequent collections, which include *White-Haired Lover* (1968) and *Adult Bookstore* (1976), have tended to return to more traditional forms, notably the sonnet. He has written a number of critical works, among them *Beyond Criticism* (1953, reissued in 1965 as *A Primer for Poets*), *In Defense of Ignorance* (1960), *Randall Jarrell* (1967) and *The Poetry Wreck: Selected Essays 1950–1970* (1975). He edited **Poetry** magazine from 1950 to 1956.

**Sharp, Cecil J.** See **folk revival, the**.

**Sharp, William** 1855–1905 Scottish poet, novelist and biographer, and author of works as Fiona Macleod. Born in Paisley, he attended Glasgow University but left without a degree, travelling to Australia instead. After his arrrival in London in 1878 he soon became a member of the circle of artists and writers centred on **Dante Gabriel Rossetti** and a regular contributor to literary journals. He published hack biographies of Rossetti (1882), **Shelley** (1887), Heine (1888) and **Browning** (1890) and introduced popular editions of poetry. His novels included *The Sport of Chance* (1888) and *The Children of Tomorrow* (1889) and his volumes of poetry *The Human Inheritance, The New Hope, Motherhood and Other Poems* (1882), *Earth's Voices* (1884), *Romantic Ballads and Poems of Phantasy* (1888) and *Sospiri di Roma* (1891). In later years he also wrote rhapsodic verse and prose romances on Celtic themes, represented as being by Fiona Macleod (see also **Celtic revival**). They include *Pharais* (1894), *The Mountain Lovers* (1895), *The Sin-Eater and Other Tales* (1895), *The Washer of the Ford* (1895) and a collection of articles, *The Winged Destiny* (1904). More than a pen-name, Fiona Macleod was a second literary personality whose identity with himself he kept a closely guarded secret. A much-travelled man, Sharp died in Sicily.

**Shaughraun, The** A melodrama by **Dion Boucicault**, first performed at Wallack's Theatre, New York, in 1874 with Boucicault in the title-role of Conn the Shaughraun.

Robert Ffolliott, a convicted Fenian, has escaped from Australia with the help of the feckless but charming Conn. He returns to Ireland to visit his sweetheart Arte O'Neal before embarking for America. Betrayed by his villainous 'friend' Kinchela, Robert is regretfully arrested by the English officer, Captain Molyneux, who has fallen in love with Robert's sister Claire. Once again Conn arranges his escape, but is shot during it. Conn's wake, hilariously observed by Conn himself, is a finely conceived scene, which leads to the final exposing of the villains. Robert Ffolliott is freed under a general pardon to Fenians, and the play ends with the promise of three weddings, Robert's to Arte, Molyneux's to Claire and Conn's to his sorely tried sweetheart Moya.

**Shaw, George Bernard** 1856–1950 Playwright, novelist and critic. Born in Dublin, where he worked for an estate agent after leaving school at 15, Shaw went with his mother, a singer, to London in 1876. There he began a programme of voracious reading. An active interest in socialism was added to his love of music. He became a socialist in 1882 and in 1884 joined the Fabian Society, on whose Executive Committee he served for many years. With the generous aid of **William Archer**, whose interest in Ibsen he shared, Shaw obtained work as a journalist, becoming, as 'Corno di Bassetto', an outstanding music critic on *The Star* (1888–90) and then drama critic for *The Saturday Review* (1895–8). His trenchant articles on the contemporary theatre are collected in *Our Theatre in the Nineties* (3 vols., 1932).

Shaw's first publications were novels, *Cashel Byron's Profession* (1886) and *An Unsocial Socialist*

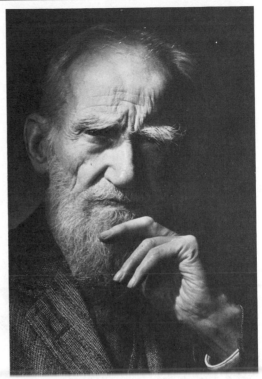

George Bernard Shaw, 1945.

(1887), and he wrote several more, including the socio-political parable, *The Adventures of the Black Girl in Her Search for God* (1932). His social, political and ethical opinions are on display in the wonderfully lively *Prefaces* to his published plays (collected in a single volume in 1934, with revisions and additions in 1938 and 1965), as well as in such studiously and vivaciously controversial works as *Common Sense about the War* (1914), *How to Settle the Irish Question* (1917), *The Intelligent Woman's Guide to Socialism and Capitalism* (1928; revised 1937) and *Everybody's Political What's What* (1944).

From Shaw's friendship with William Archer came the suggestion that they should collaborate on writing a play. They never did, but *The Quintessence of Ibsenism* (1891) is as much a manifesto for Shaw's future work as a playwright as it is an advocacy of Ibsen's genius. **Widowers' Houses** (1892), a vigorous attack on slum landlordism, was produced by J. T. Grein for the Independent Theatre Club. Like **Mrs Warren's Profession** (written 1893, first produced 1902) and *The Philanderer* (written 1893, first produced 1905), it was considered too strong to pass the censor and confined to private performance. *Arms and the Man* (1894), which wittily subverts the conventional view of male gallantry, was the first of Shaw's plays to be presented publicly. It was followed by *Candida* (1897), *The*

Shaw (right) rehearsing *Androcles and the Lion* with Lillah McCarthy and Granville-Barker. St James's Theatre, London, 1913. Victoria & Albert Theatre Museum, London.

*Devil's Disciple* (1897), *The Man of Destiny* (1897), *You Never Can Tell* (1899) and *Captain Brassbound's Conversion* (1900).

Known to the theatrical public as an *enfant terrible*, Shaw owed his emergence into fame to the seasons organized by **Harley Granville-Barker** and J. E. Vedrenne at the **Royal Court Theatre** in 1904–7. They presented the first performances of *John Bull's Other Island* (1904), a provocative thrust at the Irish question, *How He Lied to Her Husband* (1904), **Man and Superman** (1905), **Major Barbara** (1905) and *The Doctor's Dilemma* (1906). It was an unfamiliar experience for the theatre-going public to be drawn into intelligent debate and to encounter unpalatable truths, however beguilingly dressed. *Caesar and Cleopatra* (1907) maintained Shaw's growing reputation for mischief and iconoclasm, as did *Getting Married* (1908), *The Shewing Up of Blanco Posnet* (1909), censured for blasphemy, *Misalliance* (1910), *Fanny's First Play* (1911), *Androcles and the Lion* (1913) and **Pygmalion** (1913).

Shaw contributed four of his most serious plays to the new theatre of the 1920s, **Heartbreak House** (1920), **Back to Methuselah** (1922), **Saint Joan** (1923) and *The Apple Cart* (1929). Of his later plays, the best include *Too True to Be Good* (1932), *The Millionairess* (1936) and *In Good King Charles's Golden Days* (1939). His voluminous correspondence is being edited by Dan H. Laurence (a first volume appeared in 1965), but the fascinating letters to Ellen Terry, Mrs Patrick Campbell and Molly Tompkins have been separately published in *Ellen Terry and Shaw: A Correspondence* (ed. C. St John, 1931), *Correspondence between Shaw and Mrs Patrick Campbell* (ed. A. Dent, 1952) and *To a Young Actress: Letters to Molly Tompkins* (ed. P. Tompkins, 1960), as have the *Letters to Granville Barker* (ed. C. B. Purdom, 1957).

**She: A History of Adventure** A novel by **Sir Henry Rider Haggard**, published in 1887.

The narrator of the story, Horace Holly, an ugly, misogynist Cambridge scholar, becomes the guardian of Leo Vincey, the only son of his only friend. When Leo comes of age, he receives a potsherd and a series of manuscripts which delineate the history of his ancient family. The family name of Vincey is traced back through the Latin 'Vindex' to the Greek 'Tisisthenes', all meaning 'avenger': and Leo's inherited duty is that of revenge. His first ancestor, Kallikrates ('the-beautiful-in-strength'), was murdered by an unknown woman. This revenge-quest takes Leo and Holly to Africa; on their arrival, they narrowly escape death at the hands of the Amahaggar tribe, whose custom is to place red-hot pots upon the heads of strangers. They are then conducted to the underground tombs of Kôr, ruled over by a mysterious queen who has the secret of eternal life: She-Who-Must-Be-Obeyed. This queen, Ayesha, saves Leo's life when he is almost dead of fever and recognizes him as the reincarnation of Kallikrates, whom she murdered because he would not accept her love. She takes Leo and Holly to the Place of Life, an underground cavern where they may step into the Fire of Life and be made immortal. Since Leo fears the ordeal, Ayesha herself enters the Fire and emerges from it immeasurably old and then monkey-like (Darwinistically reliving the biological source of humanity). She dies, asking Leo and Holly to remember her in her eternal youth and beauty. With a superhuman effort, the heroes regain the upper world of ordinary life, but are shattered and transformed by what they have experienced. The novel ends with their setting out for Thibet (*sic*), where they hope to encounter Ayesha again.

Haggard wrote two sequels to *She* – *Ayesha* (1905) and *Wisdom's Daughter* (1923) – though neither has the haunting power of the original. The story has been interpreted mythically many times, notably by Jung, who cites it as the primary example of an 'extraverted' or ignorantly intuitive myth. In fact, *She* is not simply Haggard's naïve plunge into his own subconscious but has close connections with the Cambridge school of mythography summed up in **Sir James Frazer**'s *The Golden Bough*. It also shows Haggard's familiarity with the 19th-century theory that primitive races were the degenerate descendants of people who had been 'civilized' in their own time, as well as expressing his private fears for his own doomed culture and his hopes for redemption through reincarnated love.

**She Stoops to Conquer**, *or, The Mistakes of a Night* A comedy by **Oliver Goldsmith**, first produced at **Covent Garden** in 1773 and published the same year.

Mr and Mrs Hardcastle have a daughter, Kate, and Mrs Hardcastle has a son by a pre-

*She Stoops to Conquer* at Covent Garden, 1773. From a mezzotint after Thomas Parkinson who depicted the incident from the last act in 1779. The characters, left to right, are Mr Hardcastle, Mrs Hardcastle, and Tony Lumpkin. Victoria & Albert Theatre Museum, London.

vious marriage, the oafish and dissolute Tony Lumpkin. Sir Charles Marlow has proposed a match between his son and Kate Hardcastle. Young Marlow and his friend Hastings accordingly make the journey to the Hardcastles' home in the country but, thanks to Tony Lumpkin's misdirections, arrive there believing it to be an inn. The scene is thus expertly laid for the comedy that follows. Young Marlow takes Kate to be a servant and falls in love with her; his mistake frees him of the inhibitions he normally feels in the presence of ladies. Kate's friend Constance Neville falls in love with Hastings; Mrs Hardcastle, who dotes on her son Tony and had intended him to marry Constance, is thoroughly displeased. Sir Charles Marlow's arrival puts everything to rights.

**She Would if She Could** The second of **Sir George Etherege**'s three comedies, first staged in 1668. Unlike his first, *The Comical Revenge* (1664), it has no heroic plot to contrast with the comic plot of sexual misadventures. It is, thus, a better model of what has come to be known as **Restoration comedy**. The characters divide into two groups, with the older trio showing less social and moral perception than the younger quartet. Sir Oliver Cockwood, his wife and Sir Joslin Jolley come to London, bringing with them Sir Joslin's two nieces, Ariana and Gatty, whose charms attract the attention of Courtall and Freeman, two young men-about-town. Determined to taste London's pleasures, the country visitors find their way to the Bear in Drury Lane, where they can both drink and dance. Assignations made there lead to the comic crises of the final act, which are resolved by the pairing up of the young lovers but no

more than partially resolved for their elders, who return, not much wiser, to the country.

**Sheffield, John** 1648–1721 Politician and poet. The 3rd Earl of Mulgrave and (later) 1st Duke of Buckingham and Normanby was born in London and spent most of his flamboyant social and political life at court. His literary works include the *Essay on Satire* (?1680) and *Essay on Poetry* (1682), both published anonymously, a number of love lyrics, and several prose pieces. His reworking of **Shakespeare**'s *Julius Caesar* into two plays, *Julius Caesar* and *Marcus Brutus*, with additional love interest and diminished plebeian presence, was printed in the authorized edition of his *Works* (1723), prepared by his friend **Alexander Pope**. He was a generous patron to **Dryden**, and financed the latter's monument in Westminster Abbey.

**Shelley, Mary (Wollstonecraft)** 1797–1851 Novelist, biographer and editor. The only daughter of **William Godwin** and **Mary Wollstonecraft**, who died a few days after her birth, she was brought up by her father and stepmother. At 16 she ran away to France and Switzerland with **Shelley**, marrying him in 1816 on the death of his wife Harriet. Her most famous work, *Frankenstein, or, The Modern Prometheus* (1818), was begun on Lake Geneva in the summer of 1816 as her contribution to a ghost-story competition devised by **Byron**, Shelley and Byron's friend Polidori. In 1818 the Shelleys left England for Italy, where they remained until Shelley's death in 1822. Of their children only one, Percy Florence, survived infancy, and in 1823 Mary returned with him to England, where she devoted herself to his welfare and education and to her career as a writer. None of her later novels matched the power, originality, and mythical sweep of her legendary first work – both *Lodore* (1835) and *Faulkner* (1837) are little more than romantic pot-boilers – and when public taste began to move away from Byronic heroes and Trelawnyesque adventurers to the new realism of the young **Dickens**, she gave up writing long fictions. Of more abiding interest, however, are: *Mathilde*, an unfinished novel begun in 1819 (published in 1959), which draws strongly on her relations with Godwin and Shelley; *Valperga* (1823), a romance set in 14th-century Italy which portrays the lovelessness and destructiveness of personal political ambition; and *The Last Man* (1826), a politically disillusioned and conservative vision of the end of human civilization, set in the 21st century. The image of Mary Shelley presented by the biographers suggests an intensely private, imaginatively exuberant, yet also emotionally withdrawn figure, whose political melancholy and strong religious faith are intriguingly at odds with the optimistic rationalism of her famous parents, and her poet husband's atheistic radicalism.

In addition to numerous short stories for popular periodicals, particularly *The Keepsake*, she produced several volumes of *Lives* for Lardner's *Cabinet Cyclopedia*, and the first authoritative edition of Shelley's poems, with a preface and valuable notes (4 vols., 1839). Her travelogue, *Rambles in Germany and Italy, in 1840, 1842 and 1843* (1844), was well received.

**Shelley, Percy Bysshe** 1792–1822 Poet. The elder son of Timothy (later Sir Timothy) Shelley, he was born at Field Place, near Horsham in Sussex. He attended Syon House Academy and Eton, where his independence of spirit eventually won him respect and the nickname 'Mad Shelley' was promoted to 'Eton Atheist'. While still at Eton, he privately published a **Gothic novel**, *Zastrozzi* (1810). This was followed by poems written with his sister Elizabeth, published anonymously as *Original Poetry by Victor and Cazire* (1810) and another Gothic tale, *St Irvine, or, The Rosicrucian* (1811). At University College, Oxford, Shelley continued to read radical authors and adopted provocatively eccentric dress and behaviour. With Thomas Jefferson Hogg in spring 1811 he wrote and circulated a pamphlet, *The Necessity of Atheism*, almost the first open profession of atheism to be printed in England. Their refusal to answer questions from the college authorities resulted in their summary expulsion. This affair, and his elopement to Scotland in August 1811 with the 16-year-old Harriet Westbrook, caused a permanent break with his family. Shelley refused his father's demand for a public retraction of the pamphlet, solemnized his 'misalliance' in Edinburgh and renounced his inheritance in favour of a small annuity.

Three years of nomadic living followed. In York Shelley attempted to bring Harriet together with Hogg, and from time to time supplemented the household with other female friends. In the Lakes he found only **Southey** in residence, with whom he argued politics. He corresponded with **William Godwin**, alarming him by the revolutionary rhetoric of *An Address to the Irish People* (1812) and his *Proposals* for new kinds of reform associations. In Dublin he made speeches on the repeal of the Union and Catholic emancipation. *A Letter to Lord Ellenborough* (1812) defended the radical publisher Daniel Eaton. At Lynmouth in Devon, where he tried to set up a small community of free spirits, copies of the democratic broadsheet *A Declaration of Rights* were launched on the sea in bottles and flown across the Bristol Channel in patent Shelley fire balloons. The Shelleys left abruptly on discovering they were being watched by Home Office spies and briefly set up house in Tremadoc, Wales, where he observed the

Shelley. A detail from the portrait by Amelia Curran, 1819. National Portrait Gallery, London.

labourers' living conditions during the harsh winter of 1812. The poetic harvest of this political and philosophical education was **Queen Mab** (1813), a work that brought him no immediate recognition.

In London the Shelleys became frequent visitors of Godwin, who became his philosophical mentor and, before the poet tired of him in 1820, received in return 'the amount of a considerable fortune'. **Thomas Love Peacock** also became a close friend. The birth of a daughter, Ianthe, did not prevent the failure of Shelley's marriage in autumn 1813. The next year he fell in love with Mary (**Mary Shelley**), Godwin's 16-year-old daughter by **Mary Wollstonecraft**, and they eloped, accompanied at Shelley's invitation by Jane 'Claire' Clairmont, who was 15. A triangular relationship developed which endured until Shelley's death. The literary fruit of their Continental journey was an unfinished novella, *The Assassins* (1814), and their combined journal, later reworked by Mary Shelley and published as *History of a Six Weeks' Tour* (1817).

Back in England Shelley fell into financial difficulties, resolved in negotiations following his grandfather's death. Harriet gave birth to their second child, Charles, in November 1814 and the following spring Mary gave birth to a daughter, who died prematurely. Shelley and Mary took a cottage on the edge of Windsor

Great Park where, in a more stable period, he wrote *Alastor* (1816). Its publication coincided with the birth of his favourite son, William. The summer of 1816 was spent with **Byron** at Lake Geneva. Mary began *Frankenstein* and Shelley wrote two philosophical poems, the 'Hymn to Intellectual Beauty' and 'Mont Blanc'.

Shelley married Mary immediately after Harriet drowned herself in autumn 1816. He was taken up by **Leigh Hunt**, who had given him his first favourable notice in *The Examiner* and now introduced him to **Keats**, **Hazlitt** and other members of their circle. At Marlow, where the family settled near Peacock in 1817, he wrote *An Address to the People on the Death of Princess Charlotte*, perhaps his finest political pamphlet, and worked on 'Laon and Cythna', published as *The Revolt of Islam* (1818).

Shelley left England in spring 1818 and spent the rest of his life in Italy, staying first at Lucca, Venice and Este, where he wrote *Julian and Maddalo*, an exploration of his relations with Byron. The 'Stanzas Written in Dejection' belong to the winter at Naples; the 'Roman spring' of 1819 saw completion of the major part of *Prometheus Unbound*. His registration in Naples as father of an illegitimate baby, Elena Adelaide Shelley, still puzzles his biographers. The death in Rome of his adored son 'Willmouse' was a devastating blow. The now childless household settled in Tuscany, first near Livorno, then Florence and finally Pisa, which became more or less their permanent base until 1822.

Despite these difficulties the year from summer 1819 to summer 1820 was Shelley's most creative period. He completed the fourth act of *Prometheus Unbound* and wrote another drama, **The Cenci** (August 1819). News of the Peterloo massacre inspired *The Mask of Anarchy* (September 1819), still perhaps the greatest poem of political protest in the language, though unpublished in his lifetime. The 'Ode to the West Wind' was written at a single sitting on 25 October 1819, shortly followed by the satire *Peter Bell the Third*. The political odes 'To Liberty' and 'To Naples' came in the spring of 1820, the vivid, personal *Letter to Maria Gisborne* in July and *The Witch of Atlas* in August, interspersed with smaller-scale propaganda poems, 'Young Parson Richards', 'Song to the Men of England' and 'Sonnet: England 1819', and such lyric poems as 'To a Skylark' and 'The Cloud'. Percy Florence Shelley was born in November 1819.

During the Pisan period (1820–1) he completed his remarkable political document, *A Philosophical View of Reform* (1820), the entertaining *Essay on the Devil*, **The Defence of Poetry** and a sequence of exquisite short poems: 'To the Moon', 'The Two Spirits', 'The Aziola' and 'Evening: Ponte Al Mare, Pisa'. His satirical

burlesque, *Swellfoot the Tyrant*, was published in 1820. News of Keats's death produced *Adonais* in spring 1821. The absence of Claire left him susceptible to a platonic affair with Teresa Viviani, an heiress immured in a convent by her father. *Epipsychidion* (1821) was the reward of Shelley's self-restraint on this occasion.

At Shelley's encouragement, Byron moved to Pisa in winter 1821. Together they formed the centre of a circle which included Jane and Edward Williams, **Edward Trelawny** and a colourful assortment of exiles, expatriates and adventurers. Shelley translated scenes from Goethe's *Faust* and wrote his last completed verse drama, *Hellas*, to raise money in England for the Greek war of independence. It was published in 1822. March saw the abandonment of *Charles I*, a drama of the Civil War.

After the breakup of the Pisa group the Shelleys moved to the village of Lerici on the Bay of Spezia. Shelley assumed responsibility for Claire, distraught at Byron's news of the death of their daughter, Allegra. He began his last major poem, *The Triumph of Life*, and composed a sequence of short lyrics for Jane Williams: 'The Keen Stars Are Twinkling', 'When the Lamp is Shattered' and the sad 'Lines Written in the Bay of Lerici'. It was also a time of nightmares and premonitory visions. In July 1822 Leigh Hunt reached Livorno to assume editorship of a new journal, **The Liberal**. On the way back from meeting him, Shelley, Edward Williams and their boatboy were drowned in the Bay of Spezia. Shelley's body was cremated on the beach at Viareggio in the presence of Byron, Trelawny and Hunt.

Two collections appeared after his death: *Poetical Pieces* (1823) and *Posthumous Poems* (1824). Mary Shelley's four-volume edition of *The Poetical Works* was published in 1839, an undertaking whose criteria of inclusion were partly influenced by Sir Timothy Shelley, who began the family's attempt to repair his son's tarnished image.

Shelley's colourful life and his achievements as a lyric poet have until recently obscured the central aspects of his art. He drew no essential distinction between poetry and politics. His work continues and revitalizes the radical tendencies of earlier Romantic writing, expanding its critique of social injustice into an attack on specific institutions of oppression. Anticipating the early Marx, Shelley portrayed law and religion as ideological functions of the state, and imaged the growth of capitalist relations of production in terms of its mechanical suppression of the spontaneous growth of human personality. The revolutionary optimism of his great visionary poems is wrung from a painful consciousness of the moral, psychological and historical dimensions of social and political bondage. Taken as a whole, his work represents a decidedly materialist inflection of the Romantic dream of the fusion of poetry and life. He was fascinated by the emancipatory potential of science, and his mythical dramas abound in images of space travel, flight and technologically achieved leisure.

The infelicities of his lesser writing have been carefully rehearsed: excessive rhetoric, abstractionism and the lurking arrogance and emotional chilliness of the poetic voice. Of increasing interest to modern Shelleyans are what might be called the creative contradictions of his work: the tantalizing ambiguity of certain key myths, ideas and images, and the persistence of philosophical idealism in his political thought. Recent criticism has produced a more differentiated view of Shelley, for so long perhaps the least read of English Romantic poets.

**Shenstone, William** 1714–63 Landscape gardener and poet. Born at Halesowen, Worcestershire, Shenstone was educated at a dame school, Halesowen Grammar School and then by a tutor, proceeding to Pembroke College, Oxford, where he was a contemporary of **Johnson**. He did not take a degree. Much of his verse has been properly forgotten; his best-known work, described by **Gray** as 'excellent of its kind and masterly', was *The Schoolmistress* (1742), a revised version of a poem which had appeared in a privately published collection when he had been at Oxford and which he had made every effort to suppress. His major achievement was as a landscape gardener. On the death of his guardian in 1745 he bought the Leasowes and thereafter spent most of his income in efforts to beautify the site. In this he appears to have been relatively successful and an enthusiastic description of the garden by **Dodsley** was printed in the three-volume posthumous collection of Shenstone's works (1764–9). **Horace Walpole** perhaps best summed him up as a man who 'had much more fame than his talents entitled him to'.

**Shepard, E[rnest] H[oward]** 1879–1976 Illustrator. Born in London, the son of an architect, he studied at the Royal Academy, having begun drawing and painting as a small child. He started contributing cartoons to *Punch* in 1907 and maintained the association for the next 50 years. His fame as a children's illustrator was established by his work for **A. A. Milne**'s quartet of Winnie-the-Pooh books (1924–8). Even more successful were his illustrations for a new edition of **Kenneth Grahame**'s *The Wind in the Willows* in 1931, his fine line, liberal use of space and telling eye for detail doing much to make this classic even more accessible to young readers. In later life Shepard was persuaded to add colour to some of these illustrations, but he is best remembered for the original black-and-white drawings.

**Shepard, Sam** 1943– American playwright, born Samuel Shepard Rogers in Sheridan, Illinois, and raised and educated in California. He moved to New York City in 1963 and began writing plays, the first of which, *Cowboys*, was performed in 1964. He has been a leader of the *avant-garde* in contemporary American theatre since his earliest work; to date he has produced more than forty plays as well as several screenplays. His work resists easy categorization but may be said to deal with the vagaries of American mythologies, his plays often focusing on the problems of the individual trying to adjust to historical realities.

His plays include *Icarus's Mother* (1965), *La Turista* (1966), *Melodrama Play* (1967), *Operation Sidewinder* (1970), *Mad Dog Blues* (1971), *The Tooth of Crime* (1972), *Geography of a Horse Dreamer* (1974) and *Angel City* (1976). *Curse of the Starving Class* (1976) was the first play in a trilogy exploring the relationship of Americans to their land, their family and their history. The trilogy continued in 1978 with *Buried Child* (Pulitzer Prize, 1979) and concluded with *True West* (1980). This group of plays, especially, places Shepard in the tradition of **Eugene O'Neill**, with its treatment of a tragic America mired in sin and immorality. Shepard is the only playwright to have received more than two Obie awards (for Off-Broadway productions); he received his tenth in 1979 for *Buried Child*. His plays have appeared in several collections, including *Five Plays* (1967), *Action and The Unseen Hand: Two Plays* (1975), *Four Two-Act Plays* (1980), *Buried Child and Other Plays* (1979), *Seven Plays* (1981) and *Fool For Love and Other Plays* (1984).

**Shepard, Thomas** 1605–49 American Puritan minister, born in Towcester and educated at Emmanuel College, Cambridge. Following his ordination he served as occasional lecturer at Earles-Colne in Essex until 1630, when he was silenced by Archbishop **Laud** for his Puritan leanings and accepted a position as private tutor and chaplain to Sir Richard Darley of Buttercrambe. In 1632 he moved to Hedden, where Bishop Morton of Durham denied him the privilege of public preaching, which drove him to Massachusetts Bay in 1635.

Although Shepard lived only 14 years in New England, he exerted a powerful influence on the Puritan experiment. Between 1636 and 1637 alone, he was appointed pastor of the prestigious church at Newton (Cambridge), convinced his friend John Harvard to locate his college there, married the daughter of **Thomas Hooker**, and played a key role in the Cambridge Synod of 1637 which condemned Antinomianism. His exploration of the stages leading to conversion, *The Sincere Convert* (1641), soon became the most widely read formulation of the theory of preparation. Two of his other tracts, *Theses Sabbaticae* (1649) and *Church Membership of Children and Their Right to Baptism* (1663), demonstrate his contribution to the central ecclesiastical debates of American Congregationalism. Although known as a rigorous theologian and ardent pastor, Shepard tempered his religious conviction with empathy for the common Puritan's struggle with spiritual truths, as is testified to by his sermons, most notably those collected in *The Parable of the Ten Virgins Opened and Applied* (1660) and by his autobiography (first published in 1747 as *Three Valuable Pieces, Viz., Select Cases Resolved; First Principles of the Oracles of God; . . .; And a Private Diary; Containing Meditations and Experiences Never Before Published*).

**Shepheardes Calender, The** Edmund **Spenser**'s first important work was published pseudonymously as by Immerito (unworthy) in 1579. Subsequent editions in 1581, 1586, 1591 and 1597 testify to its great popularity. Its importance was hailed by E. K. (perhaps Edward Kirke), the author of a commentary accompanying the poems. It is one of the few significant works of 16th-century English poetry that **Sidney** can point to in his *Apology for Poetry*, written at about the same time as the publication of *The Shepheardes Calender*. The classic models for Spenser were the *Idylls* of Theocritus and Virgil's *Eclogues*: more recent Continental models were provided by the French poet Marot and the Italian Mantuan. *The Shepheardes Calender* expresses a typically pastoral constant regret for lost golden ages – of purity in love, poetry, morality and religion – and a consequent 'satirical bitterness' about contemporary failings. It consists of twelve poems, one for each month of the year, beginning and ending in winter, with

'Januarye.' A woodcut from the first edition of Spenser's *The Shepheardes Calender*, 1579. Colin Clout, the shepherd boy, compares the bleak season with the bleak progress of his love for Rosalinde. Each month of the poem is illustrated by a woodcut.

Colin Clout's complaints in January and December. The other months contain dialogues of shepherds concerning love, poetry and religious affairs; April contains a panegyric of Eliza, queen of shepherds (Elizabeth I), November is an elegy on Dido ('some maiden of great blood'), and October contemplates the profession and responsibilities of the poet. In October Piers encourages Cuddie to turn from pastoral poetry to sing of wars, jousts and knights. As E. K. points out in his introduction, pastoral was regarded as a literary genre where, following the example of Virgil, poets might test their 'tender wings' before the higher flights of epic: thus, in some sense, *The Shepheardes Calender* is a prologue to Spenser's **The Faerie Queene**.

**Shepherd's Calendar, The** A cycle of poems by **John Clare**, completed in 1823, first published in 1827, and republished from the original manuscripts in 1964 (ed. E. Robinson and G. Summerfield). Perhaps the most widely read of his longer poems, it is the work in which Clare first succeeded in developing his own distinctive pastoral idiom, ignoring the well-meaning, but misplaced, advice of **Lamb** to aim for the 'true rustic style' of **Thomson** and **Goldsmith**. Clare's rural 'realism' – his use of dialect words and the peasant vernacular of his native parish of Helpston, the proliferating detail and extraordinary concreteness of his observation of seasonal changes in nature, his insider's eye for the unromantic harshness of agricultural labour, and his criticism of enclosing farmers and 'tyrant justice' on the land – failed to win the approval of his London publisher, who pruned the text as a whole to half its original length, corrected Clare's idiosyncratic grammar, and introduced punctuation.

**Shepherd's Life, A**: *Impressions of the South Wiltshire Downs* **W. H. Hudson**'s account of life around Salisbury Plain before the automobile age, published in 1910.

Hudson's observations of the wildlife of the country, both flora and fauna, together with his arresting stories about dogs, in themselves make the book worth reading; but the recollections of a shepherd in addition make it a classic of country life from about 1840 to the first years of the 20th century. The shepherd, Caleb Bawcombe, is in his eighties and from early boyhood has tended his master's flocks on the downs; he would not wish for a different life if one were offered him. He trained his sheepdogs, his only company, to the level of almost human response. It is chiefly from Caleb's memories that the vivid parade of human characters is drawn – the villagers and gypsies, employers of every quality from good to tyrannical and greedy, and deer stealers, poachers, and machine wreckers. The author's wrath is aroused most by gamekeepers, to whom everything is subordinate to the care of pheasants and game birds, which are reared with extravagant care so that they may be destroyed.

**Shepherd's Week, The** A series of six pastoral eclogues by **John Gay**, published in 1714. Partly designed to parody the work of **Ambrose Philips**, these witty pieces are at once mock-classical and realistic. In Gay's version, rustic conditions are grubby, superstitious, fractious and exhausting as well as endearing and amorous; the myth of the Golden Age of past innocence is replaced instead by real, sunburnt, lustful, sweating peasants.

**Sheridan, Frances** 1724–66 Novelist and dramatist. The mother of **Richard Brinsley Sheridan**, she was born Frances Chamberlaine in Dublin and married the actor-manager Thomas Sheridan in 1747. They went to London in 1754 when his enterprises failed and she met **Samuel Richardson**, at the height of his success; he read her unpublished novel *Eugenia Adelaide* (it finally appeared posthumously in 1791) and encouraged her to continue writing. She launched her career as a novelist with the popular *Memoirs of Miss Sidney Biddulph: Extracted from Her Own Journal* (1761), heavily influenced by Richardson's *Pamela*. The narrator endures such agonies of love and jealousy that **Samuel Johnson** questioned the author's right to make her readers suffer so much. A sequel recounting Miss Biddulph's further tribulations, *Continuation of the Memoirs*, appeared in 1767, the same year that another novel, *The History of Nourjahad*, was published. Three plays, *The Discovery* (1763), *The Dupe* (1764) and *A Trip to Bath* (1765), were produced at **Drury Lane** (*The Discovery* by **David Garrick**) but not published until 1902.

**Sheridan, Richard Brinsley** 1751–1816 Dramatist. Sheridan was born in Dublin, where his father, Thomas, was manager of the Smock Alley Theatre. His mother, **Frances Sheridan**, achieved fame as a novelist and playwright, and Thomas himself was the author of one of the age's most influential books on rhetoric and acting, *Lectures on Elocution* (1762). They sent their son to Harrow, intending him for the law, but Sheridan became romantically and gallantly involved with the young singer Elizabeth Linley, on whose behalf he fought two duels. The couple married, to the accompaniment of scandalous interest, in 1773, and set up home in London. They had met in Bath, the setting for Sheridan's first play, *The Rivals* (1775). After its stumbling opening night at **Covent Garden**, Sheridan rewrote sections of the play, and it became a favourite with contemporary audiences. Its success loosened Sheridan's pen, and

Richard Brinsley Sheridan. From the portrait by J. Russell, 1788. National Portrait Gallery, London.

two other pieces were produced in 1775, a farce called *St Patrick's Day, or, The Scheming Lieutenant* and a comic opera, with music by his father-in-law Thomas Linley, *The Duenna*.

Impulsively committed to the theatre, Sheridan bought a share in **Drury Lane** in 1776, and wrote all his remaining work for performance there. The best of it was written before the end of 1779: *A Trip to Scarborough* (1777), a softening of **Vanbrugh**'s *The Relapse*, *The School for Scandal* (1777), perhaps the finest of all 18th-century comedies, and *The Critic* (1779). Of his later work only *Pizarro* (1799), a bombastic version of the German play by the modish Kotzebue, matched the success of the work Sheridan produced in his twenties. The second half of his life, after his election to Parliament in 1780 and until his failure to secure a seat in 1812, was more notable politically than theatrically, although he maintained a major share in the management of Drury Lane until its burning in 1809. As a parliamentary speaker, he rivalled **Edmund Burke** and took a famous part in the impeachment of Warren Hastings in 1788–94.

**Sherlock Holmes** A melodrama by **William Gillette**, written with full agreement and some assistance from **Sir Arthur Conan Doyle**. Its first performance was at Buffalo in 1899. The plot is loosely based on three stories by Doyle, 'A Scandal in Bohemia', 'The Final Problem' and *A Study in Scarlet*. Its resolution is far-fetched, depending almost as much on the incompetence of Professor Moriarty and his criminal associates as it does on the resourcefulness of Sherlock Holmes. The play's immense popularity was largely owed to the author's carefully studied playing of the title role. Frederic Dorr Steele, who illustrated the Conan Doyle stories, based his portraits of Holmes on Gillette, so that actor and character became subtly identified in the public mind, both in England and the USA, during the 30 or more years that Gillette toured in the play.

**Sherlock Holmes stories** A total of four novels and 56 short stories by **Sir Arthur Conan Doyle**. They are not just the most famous and enduring contribution to **detective fiction** by any single writer, but also probably the most imitated, parodied and adapted literary works in the language. Already a favourite figure on the stage during Doyle's lifetime (see *Sherlock Holmes*), the detective has since become a staple of the film and television industries.

Holmes and his colleague Dr Watson first appeared in a novel, *A Study in Scarlet*, published in *Beeton's Christmas Annual* for 1887. This was followed by another novel, *The Sign of Four* (1890), but Holmes did not reach a wide readership until Doyle began his short stories for *The Strand Magazine* in July 1891, with illustrations by Sidney Paget, collected as *The Adventures of Sherlock Holmes* (1892) and *The Memoirs of Sherlock Holmes* (1894). In an attempt to free himself from his creation Doyle killed Holmes off in the last of these stories, 'The Final Problem', but the resulting public clamour forced him to return to a subject which he increasingly saw as a distraction from his serious work. *The Hound of the Baskervilles* (1902) narrates an early case of the dead detective, but 'The Adventure of the Empty House', at the beginning of *The Return of Sherlock Holmes* (1905), reveals how Holmes had in fact survived his apparent death at the hands of Moriarty. Gratitude made readers willing to swallow the implausibility, and Holmes appeared in a further novel, *The Valley of Fear* (1915), and two more collections, *His Last Bow* (1917) and *The Case-Book of Sherlock Holmes* (1927).

Some of Holmes's idiosyncrasies were borrowed from Dr Joseph Bell, one of Doyle's teachers at Edinburgh University, but the literary model was **Edgar Allan Poe**'s stories of Dupin. The brilliant but eccentric detective, the admiring friend who narrates the story, the cases which are puzzling and fantastic as much as sensationally criminal, the dramatically revealed solution at the end: all these are elaborated from the earlier writer. To them, Doyle added distinctive touches of his own: a strong feeling for the atmosphere of late Victorian and Edwardian London, an interest in the methods of Victorian science, witty, comic dialogue between the leading figures, a subtle sense of the macabre, and a chivalric concern for justice and the unjustly oppressed. Such qualities are perhaps best displayed in the early short stories, particularly in 'A Scandal in Bohemia', 'The Red-Headed League' and 'The Adventure of the Speckled Band'. Of the novels, *The Hound of the Baskervilles*, mainly set on Dartmoor, is perhaps the most firmly constructed.

**Sherlock, Thomas** 1678–1761 Churchman and theologian. Son of **William Sherlock**, he was born in London and became Bishop of London in 1748 after having previously held the sees of Bangor and Salisbury. He made a reputation as a preacher and, while Master of the Temple (1704–53), opposed **Benjamin Hoadly** in the 'Bangorian controversy' (so called because both men had at different times occupied that bishopric). His exercise in Christian apologetics, *The Trial of the Witnesses of the Resurrection of Jesus* (1729), is his most notable published work. Sherlock was known for being athletic as well as studious, and his prowess at swimming made him the 'plunging prelate' of **Pope**'s *The Dunciad*.

**Sherlock, William** 1641–1707 Churchman and theologian. Born in Southwark and educated at Eton and Peterhouse, Cambridge, he became Master of the Temple, a post in which he was succeeded by his son, **Thomas Sherlock**. He published *A Practical Discourse Concerning Death* in 1689. During the Revolution which forced the abdication of James II he was a **Nonjuror**, but he took the oath to William and Mary in 1690. This change of mind and the book he published the same year, *A Vindication of the Doctrine of the Trinity and of the Incarnation*, made him a target of criticism and his appointment as Dean of St Paul's in 1691 exposed him further. Sherlock suffered most from the witty attacks of **Robert South**, rector of Islip. **Macaulay** admired his published sermons (1719).

**Sherriff, R[obert] C[harles]** 1896–1975 Playwright and screenwriter. Sherriff was born and educated at Kingston upon Thames and at New College, Oxford. His war service in the East Surrey Regiment provided some of the background for his most famous play, *Journey's End* (1928). Of Sherriff's other plays, only *Badger's Green* (1930) and the radio drama *The Long Sunset* (1955) have earned critical attention. His film credits include *The Invisible Man* (1933), *Goodbye Mr Chips* (1939), *Odd Man Out* (1947) and *The Dam Busters* (1955).

**Sherwood, Mary Martha** 1775–1851 Children's writer. The daughter of a country clergyman, she taught religion to the poor before writing various devotional stories for children. In 1803 she went out to India, where she began her celebrated novel *The History of the Fairchild Family* (1818), described on its title-page as 'A child's manual, being a collection of stories calculated to show the importance and effects of religious education'. But despite this pious intention, the three Fairchild children Lucy, Emily and Henry all quarrel, get into mischief and disobey their parents in quite human (and sometimes unintentionally entertaining) ways. In the most famous passage, where Mr Fairchild shows them a rotting corpse hanging on a gibbet as a warning against family disputes, flesh-creeping suspense mingles with the solemn warning in a way that many young readers found not unagreeable. Later Victorian editions played down this section, and today Mrs Sherwood is unread.

**Sherwood, Robert E[mmet]** 1896–1955 American playwright. Sherwood was born in New Rochelle, New York, and educated at Harvard. Following his graduation he joined the Canadian army and was wounded in action in 1918. His war experiences led him to adopt an outspoken pacifist stance, which is evident in his first play, *The Road to Rome* (1927), a comedy about Hannibal's deferred march to Rome. His 1936 play, *Idiot's Delight*, was awarded a Pulitzer Prize, the first of four he was to receive. The advocacy of participation in a virtuous war in the late play, *There Shall Be No Night* (1940, Pulitzer Prize 1941), marked a celebrated change of heart in a man who was by then serving as Special Assistant to the Secretary of War as well as writing many of President Roosevelt's speeches. His other plays include *The Queen's Husband* (1928), *Reunion in Vienna* (1931), *The Petrified Forest* (1935), *Abe Lincoln in Illinois* (1938, Pulitzer Prize 1939), *The Rugged Path* (1945) and *Small War on Murray Hill* (1957). He also wrote screenplays and was awarded an Academy Award for his screenplay for *The Best Years of Our Lives* in 1946. His political memoir, *Roosevelt and Hopkins: An Intimate History* (1948), received the Pulitzer Prize in 1949.

**Shiel, M[atthew] P[hipps]** 1865–1947 Writer of fantasy, **detective fiction** and **science fiction**. Shiel was born in Montserrat in the West Indies; he came to London to study medicine but was absorbed instead into the literary world of the yellow 1890s. He wrote grotesque detective and horror stories in the collections *Prince Zaleski* (1895) and *Shapes in the Fire* (1896), before cashing in on the boom in future war stories with *The Yellow Danger* (1898). He was a fervent believer in social and evolutionary progress, combining a quasi-Nietzschean interest in 'overmen' with a fierce insistence on the necessity of altruism. His literary masterpiece is *The Purple Cloud* (1901), an allegorical fantasy which visits world-wide catastrophe upon the earth to test the faith of a modern Job. Other early futuristic works like *The Lord of the Sea* (1901) and *The Last Miracle* (1906) develop Shiel's philosophy further, as do non-fantasy novels like *The Weird o'It* (1902) and *The Evil That Men Do* (1904), but his ideas are more comprehensively and coherently displayed in later novels like *How the Old Woman Got Home* (1928) and *Dr Krasinski's Secret* (1929) and in his last scientific romance *The Young Men are Coming!* (1937). Shiel's luxuriant prose style and feverishly flamboyant plotting alienate some readers, but he is a fascinating and challenging writer who has been unjustly neglected.

**Shiels, George** 1881–1949 Irish playwright, born in Ballymoney, County Antrim. He emigrated to Canada and worked there for seven years before being permanently disabled in an accident whilst working for a railroad company. Back in Ballymoney, Shiels wrote articles and short stories for Ulster newspapers before turning to playwriting. After some success in Ulster theatres, he began writing for the **Abbey Theatre**, Dublin, in 1921 (*Bedmates* and *Insurance Money*), achieving his first major success with the characteristically sardonic comedy *Paul Twyning* (1922).

Shiels was the most consistently effective of the Abbey dramatists in the years that followed **O'Casey**'s departure to England. Among his best work, unrelentingly realistic in its presentation of acquisitive and unscrupulous 'decent' people, is *Cartney and Kevney* (1927), *Mountain Dew* (1929), the challenging comedy *The New Gossoon* (1930), *The Passing Day* (1936), *Give Him a House* (1939), *The Rugged Path* (1940) and its sequel *The Summit* (1941), *The Fort Field* (1942) and *The Caretakers* (1948).

***Shipman's Tale, The*** See *Canterbury Tales, The*.

***Shirley*** The second published novel by **Charlotte Brontë**, it appeared in 1849. The setting is Yorkshire at the time of the Luddite riots and the last stages of the Napoleonic war.

Robert Gérard Moore, a millowner, is determined to install new machinery and undeterred by the opposition of his workers, who attempt first to destroy the mill in protest and then to kill him. Robert's brother, Louis, is tutor to the wealthy Keeldar family and, even though he loves Caroline Helstone, the rector's niece, Robert sees that marriage to Shirley Keeldar would enable him to weather the financial difficulties caused by the troubled times. Shirley rejects him with contempt. The end of the war frees Robert from his difficulties and the devoted Caroline accepts him. Shirley, meanwhile, is more and more drawn to Louis.

The novelist's father, Patrick Brontë, had once been appointed to the parish of Hartshead-cum-Clifton, near Dewsbury, where a riot at Rawfold's Mill resulted in 14 men being hanged. Robert Moore was based on William Cartwright, who was decorated for his part in the defence of the mill. The character of Shirley is believed to have been modelled on **Emily Brontë**. (See also **The Condition of England novel**.)

**Shirley, James** 1596–1666 Dramatist. Born in London and educated at the Merchant Taylors' School and both Oxford and Cambridge, Shirley took holy orders after graduating and was headmaster of the grammar school in St Albans in 1623–5. After his conversion to Roman Catholicism in 1625 and the consequent loss of his post, he settled in London and began writing for the stage. The 36 plays he wrote between 1625 and the closing of the theatres in 1642 establish him as the leading dramatist of the Caroline theatre.

Shirley's avowed admiration for the work of **Beaumont** and **Fletcher** is evident in the cleverly contrived multiple plots of his comedies and tragicomedies. These include his first play, *The School of Compliment* (1625: later renamed *Love Tricks*), *Hyde Park* (1632), *The Gamester* (1633), *The Young Admiral* (1633), *The Lady of Pleasure* (1635), *The Imposture* (1640) and *The Sisters* (1642). His tragedies also reflect the influence of Beaumont and Fletcher in their vivid opposition of good and evil, uncomplicated by the moral shading of characterization associated with the best of Jacobean tragedy. They include *The Traitor* (1631), *Love's Cruelty* (1631), *The Politician* (c.1639) and *The Cardinal* (1641).

Various of Shirley's masques, including the spectacular *The Triumph of Peace* (1634) and *Cupid and Death* (1653), survive, as well as a modest volume of *Poems* (1646). His famous dirge, 'The glories of our blood and state', concludes a dramatization from Ovid of *The Contention of Ajax and Ulysses for the Armour of Achilles* (published 1658).

Having fought with the Royalists during the Civil War, Shirley was probably lucky to obtain employment as a schoolteacher during the Commonwealth. His death was caused by exposure and privation during the Great Fire of 1666.

*Shoemaker's Holiday, The*, or, *The Gentle Craft* A comedy by **Thomas Dekker**, first performed at the **Rose Theatre** in 1599. It is one of the finest of London city comedies, less remarkable for its various interrelated plots than for the gallery of characters it creates.

At the centre is Simon Eyre, a high-spirited shoemaker, whose bustling household of journeyman and apprentices is barely controlled by his comfortable and loving wife, Margery. One employee is a nobleman, Rowland Lacy, who has adopted the disguise of a Dutch shoemaker in order to pursue his love for Simon Eyre's daughter, Rose. Another is Ralph, loving husband of Jane, whose departure for the wars leaves Jane under threat from the attentions of the wealthy Hamond. Another is Firk, salt of the London earth and quite as good as his betters. The plot brings the true lovers together, and Simon Eyre is elevated to the office of Lord Mayor.

**Shorthouse, Joseph Henry** 1834–1903 Novelist. The son of a Quaker family of Birmingham, Shorthouse was a chemist in his father's business. He became an Anglican, and was preoccupied with the contemporary tensions between Anglicans and Roman Catholics in the aftermath of the **Oxford Movement**. This preoccupation is the matter of the one novel by which his name is remembered, *John Inglesant* (published in 1881 but privately printed the year before). His other works include further novels and *The Platonism of Wordsworth* (1882). Shorthouse edited **George Herbert**'s *The Temple* in 1882.

**Shute, Nevil** Pseudonym of Nevil Shute Norway (1899–1960), engineer and novelist. Educated at Shrewsbury and Oxford, he served in both world wars. He worked as an engineer at Howden Airship Works, and later became managing director of an aeroplane factory. His practical expertise was often skilfully worked into his novels: *No Highway* (1948) deals with the subject of metal fatigue in a manner which turns a technical subject into the stuff of mystery and suspense. He eventually settled at Langwarria in Victoria, Australia. Other novels include *Marazan* (1926), *So Disdained* (1928), *Lonely Road* (1932), *Ruined City* (1938), *What Happened to the Corbetts* (1939), *Pied Piper* (1942), *Pastoral* (1944), *The Far Country* (1952), *In the Wet* (1953), *The Breaking Wave* (1955), *On the Beach* (1957) and *The Trustee from the Toolroom* (1960). *Slide Rule* (1954) is an autobiography. *A Town Like Alice* (1949), by far his best-known novel, invests its bleak Australian setting with romance and adventure.

**Sidgwick, Henry** 1838–1900 Philosopher. Born at Skipton in Yorkshire, he was educated at Rugby and Trinity College, Cambridge, where he became a fellow. A leading advocate of reform in Cambridge (he opposed the religious test and supported women's education), he was appointed Knightbridge Professor of Moral Philosophy in 1883. A follower of **John Stuart Mill**, Sidgwick made ethics his special study, in *The Ethics of Conformity and Subscription* (1870), *The Methods of Ethics* (1874), *An Outline* *of the History of Ethics* (1886) and *The Scope and Limits of the Work of an Ethical Society* (1900). Other works include *The Principles of Political Economy* (1883) and *The Elements of Politics* (1891).

**Sidney, Sir Philip** 1554–86 Courtier, poet, critic and author of prose romance. Born at Penshurst in Kent, Philip Sidney was the eldest son of Sir Henry Sidney, Elizabeth's Lord Deputy in Ireland from 1559 onwards. Philip II of Spain, for whom he was named, was his godfather. After some private tutoring he went to school in Shrewsbury in 1564, entering it the same day as his life-long friend and future biographer, **Sir Fulke Greville**. In 1568 he entered Christ Church, Oxford, left without taking a degree and was licensed to travel abroad to learn foreign languages in 1572. He stayed at the embassy in Paris, leaving after the St Bartholomew's Day Massacre. At Frankfurt he met the scholar Languet with whom he was to exchange a long correspondence and who influenced him not a little. In Venice he studied music and astronomy. Before his return to England in 1575 he also visited Genoa, Padua, Vienna, Prague and Antwerp. In his journeys he greatly impressed those who met him ('wheresoever he went he was beloved and obeyed', according to Greville) and left behind a trail of books dedicated to him.

In 1577 he was given the formal mission of condoling with some German princes on the death of their fathers; in reality he was sounding out the possibilities of a Protestant league. This promising start to a public career was never fulfilled. His relations with the queen were chequered, his ardent Protestantism not finding favour with Elizabeth's more cautious religious policies. His suggestion that Elizabeth enter into an alliance to protect Holland received a cool reception, and his letter of 1579 advising the queen against marriage to the Duke of Anjou endeared him to Elizabeth even less. He seems to have chafed for lack of employment and his clandestine attempt to join Drake's expedition to the Spanish coast in 1585 resulted in Elizabeth's summoning him to court. He was finally given a minor appointment in the Low Countries as governor of Flushing and left England in 1585. In 1586 he was involved in an unimportant skirmish at Zutphen and wounded in the thigh. The wound did not heal and within 22 days he was dead, not having reached his 32nd birthday. The grief felt in England and in Europe was as profound as the long funeral progress from the Low Countries to St Paul's Cathedral was spectacular. The London crowds are said to have cried out 'Farewell, the worthiest knight that lived' as the funeral passed, and Sidney's death was generally mourned. His friend Fulke Greville was desolate

Sir Philip Sidney. Portrait by an unknown artist. National Portrait Gallery, London.

('The only question I now study is whether weeping sorrow or speaking sorrow may most honour his memory') and expressed the general sense of loss and Sidney's worth: 'What he was to God, his friends and country, fame hath told.' Lord Buckhurst noted that 'even Her Majesty and the whole realm besides do suffer no small loss'. England felt the loss of a man who had seemed to embody all the qualities and graces of the perfect courtier of Castiglione's *The Courtier*. **Arthur Golding** lamented the death of a Protestant knight in the field, **Thomas Nashe** the death of a 'Maecenas of learning' and the patron of virtue and wit. In *Astrophel* (1595) **Edmund Spenser** mourned the passing of 'a gentle shepherd' and poet.

Sidney's references to his literary works are the self-deprecating remarks of a Renaissance courtier. He speaks in the *Apology for Poetry* of 'having slipped into the title of a poet'. His massive prose romance, *Arcadia*, is this 'idle work of mine' and 'but a trifle'. Yet the debt of English literature to Sidney is enormous. *Astrophil and Stella* is the first English sonnet sequence, the *Apology* is the most important and best-written critical work of its period in English, and the *Arcadia*, as well as being the finest work of English prose fiction of the period, has also been seen as the ancestor of the English novel. His minor works include the playlet *The Lady of May*, composed in 1578 for the entertainment of Elizabeth, a translation of a work on the truth of the Christian religion by du Plessis Mornay, which was completed by Arthur Golding, and a metaphrase of the first 43 Psalms. Sidney was interested in metrical experimentation and his poems display an astonishing variety of stanzaic and metrical forms, some used for the first time in English. None of his works was published in his lifetime (the folio containing his major works appeared in 1598) but were circulated in manuscript. He asked for the *Arcadia* to be burned and repented of the 'vanity' that was Lady Rich, who is in some way masked as the Stella of his sonnets.

Soon after his death Sidney became the idealized representative of an idealized Elizabethan age. For **Samuel Daniel**, Sidney's eternal songs could show 'what great Eliza's reign hath bred'. The legend continued into the Romantic period and beyond. For **Shelley** in *Adonais*, Sidney fought and fell as he lived, 'Sublimely mild, a spirit without spot', and **W. B. Yeats**'s 'In Memory of Major Robert Gregory' paid Gregory the consummate compliment of comparison with Sidney: 'Our Sidney and our perfect man'.

**Sidney, Sir Robert** 1563–1626 Poet and courtier. Younger brother to **Sir Philip Sidney**, Robert accompanied him to Flushing in Holland in 1585; the following year he was knighted for his gallantry on the field of Zutphen 10 days before his brother's death from wounds sustained in the same battle. From 1589 until 1616, when the town was returned to the Dutch, he was governor of Flushing, and enjoyed a long and honourable career in public life. His poetry, which disappeared in the early 19th century, was never printed in his lifetime; it was recently rediscovered and edited by Peter Croft (1983). Consisting of a planned sequence of songs, sonnets and pastorals, it shows the influence of his elder brother's verse at every turn, and is chiefly remarkable for the form in which it survives: a manuscript notebook, in the poet's own hand, showing his alterations and corrections. It is the largest body of original verse to have descended to us from the Elizabethan period in a text entirely set down by the poet himself. A patron as well as a practitioner of poetry, Robert Sidney is paid noble tribute as the lord of the manor to whom **Ben Jonson**'s great poem *To Penshurst* is addressed.

**Siege of Jerusalem, The** A poem in **alliterative verse** written in the North-west Midlands between 1390 and 1400. Although the subject is mainly religious, it is given the courtly and chivalric setting of **verse romance**. The Roman Titus, hearing that belief in Christ and his miracles may cure his cancer, grieves over the Passion and is healed. He is baptized and travels to Rome where his leprous father Vespasian is cured by touching the veil of St Veronica. The remainder of the poem describes Vespasian and Titus's attack on Jerusalem. The Jews are eventually defeated and Vespasian becomes emperor of Rome. The greater part of the poem is concerned with describing the battles and chivalrous deeds of the siege. The principal sources are the *Legenda Aurea*, Higden's *Polychronicon* and the *Vindicta Salvatoris*. An inferior version in couplets written in or near London *c.*1400 is known as *Titus and Vespasian*.

**Siege of Rhodes, The** A spectacular entertainment by **William D'Avenant**, staged at Rutland House in 1656. It combined heroic drama with opera, both newcomers to the English stage. The music, which is lost, was by Henry Lawes and various collaborators. The text, in rhymed dialogue with frequent songs and choruses, is based on the account of the siege of Rhodes in **Richard Knolles**'s *General History of the Turks* (1603). The perspective scenes were designed for the first production by John Webb.

**Siege of Thebes, The** A poem by **John Lydgate** presented as an addition to **Chaucer**'s *The Canterbury Tales*, a tale told by the poet after meeting the pilgrims at Canterbury. At 9400 lines, however, it is longer than any of Chaucer's tales. It narrates the history of Thebes from the story of Oedipus to the war between Polyneices and Eteocles and the destruction of the city by Theseus. The poem acknowledges the influence of Boccaccio as well as Chaucer, and Lydgate also apparently used Martianus Capella, Seneca and a French version of the story of Thebes.

**Sign of Four, The** See **Sherlock Holmes stories**.

**Sigurd the Volsung and the Fall of the Niblungs, The Story of** An epic poem by **William Morris**, published in November 1876.

The poem is in four books, the first telling the story of Sigmund and the other three of his son Sigurd. Morris drew his material from the fuller Scandinavian rather than the German version of the Niblung legend. He eliminated Latin and Romance language words as far as possible and continued to use the long anapaestic line he had developed the year before for his *Aeneids of Virgil* (1875).

In August 1869 Eiríkr Magnússon sent a translation of the Icelandic *Volsunga Saga* to Morris in Germany. Morris initially thought it 'of the monstrous order' but by 1870, when he and Magnússon jointly published a prose translation, he had come to regard it as 'the Great Story of the North, which should be to all our race what the Tale of Troy was to the Greeks'. At the same time Richard Wagner was working to complete his opera epic *Der Ring des Nibe-*

*lungen* and in 1873 Morris complained: 'the idea of a sandy-haired German tenor tweedledeeing over the unspeakable woes of Sigurd, which even the simplest words are not typical enough to express! . . . I wish to see Wagner uprooted!' In October 1875 Morris began work on his own poetic version of the legend and the book appeared within three months of the first performances of the entire *Ring* at Bayreuth, news of which he took 'as a personal outrage'. Clearly Morris regarded the Icelandic saga as legitimate Teutonic material for a poem in the English language, and *Sigurd* is an important milestone in the 19th-century revival of northern European values. 'It is the central work of my father's life', wrote May Morris, which 'he held most highly and wished to be remembered by'.

**Silas Marner** A novel by **George Eliot**, first published in 1861.

Falsely judged guilty of theft, Silas Marner leaves his dissenting community and, as the novel opens, has been living for 15 years as a linen-weaver in the village of Raveloe where, an alien figure, he has worked hard to accumulate a goodly sum of gold. Squire Cass, 'the greatest man in Raveloe', has two sons: Godfrey, attracted to Nancy Lammeter but secretly and rashly married to the opium-ridden Molly Farren, and the good-for-nothing Dunstan (Dunsey) who, cognizant of his brother's clandestine marriage, blackmails him. Dunstan steals Marner's gold and promptly disappears. Molly dies in the snow-covered fields of Raveloe trying to reach the squire's residence to disclose her marriage, thus avenging Godfrey's refusal to acknowledge her. Their little girl, Eppie, toddles away from her dying mother to the threshold of Marner's cottage, where she is cared for by the lonely weaver. In his eyes she becomes more precious than his lost gold. The narrative moves forward 16 years to the discovery of the skeleton of Dunstan Cass and Silas's gold in the newly drained stone-pit. This revelation and his belief that 'everything comes to light' prompts Godfrey Cass to admit to Nancy, now his wife but childless, that Eppie is his daughter. Godfrey and Nancy try unsuccessfully to adopt the young girl, but neither Eppie nor Silas wish to be separated, and the novel concludes with her marriage to the worthy Aaron Winthrop who is more than willing to accept the weaver as part of the household.

*Silas Marner* is an impressive narrative, spiced with rustic humour and replete with forceful village characters.

**Silkin, Jon** 1930– Poet. Born into a Jewish family in London, Silkin was educated at Dulwich College. After national service and a series of manual jobs, he became Gregory Fellow in Poetry at Leeds University in 1958, staying on to read English. From 1952 to 1957 and from 1960 to the present day, he has edited the important literary magazine *Stand*. His first volume, *The Peaceable Kingdom* (1954), contained the excellent and much-anthologized 'Death of a Son'. After the over-grandiloquence of *The Two Freedoms* (1958), the three-beat line of *The Re-ordering of the Stones* (1961), and, especially, 'Flower Poems' in *Nature with Man* (1965), is more successful. A poet of commitment, Silkin writes of persecuted minorities, and his main theme is growth through the experience of pain, and the parallel existence of joy. Later poems, in *Amana Grass* (1971), *The Principle of Water* (1974), *The Psalms with their Spoils* (1980), *Selected Poems* (1980) and *Autobiographical Stanzas* (1984), are often obscure. Other publications include *Out of Battle: Poetry of the Great War* (1972), *The Penguin Anthology of First World War Poetry* (1979) and *Poetry of the Committed Individual: A Stand Anthology* (1973).

**Silko, Leslie Marmon** 1948– American poet, novelist and short-story writer. Born of mixed ancestry – Laguna Pueblo, Mexican, and Anglo-American – and raised in traditional Laguna ways but educated in white schools, she has written poetry and prose which incorporate material and techniques from the traditional sources of her Laguna people to explore contemporary issues and dilemmas. Since her first publication in 1969, a story entitled 'The Man To Send Rain Clouds', she has published three books: a collection of poems, *Laguna Woman* (1974), a novel, *Ceremony* (1977), and a collection of poetry and short fiction, *Storyteller* (1981).

Her best-known work, *Ceremony*, is the story of Tayo, a half-breed Laguna World War II veteran, shattered by his experience in the Pacific and his inability to save his half-brother, Rocky, a more Americanized, more successful soldier who was killed by the Japanese. Tayo is gradually able to heal himself and re-order his world by re-enacting a traditional ceremony with the help of a medicine man, Betonie, and a part-Mexican woman, T'seh, who embodies the female life-giving principle and wholeness of mother earth. The form of the novel is a mixture of modern, graphic realism with traditional Indian ways of seeing and telling, incorporating story, song and legend. In much the same way, Silko's poems have their roots in ritual but express themselves in the measures of contemporary free verse.

**Sillitoe, Alan** 1928– Novelist. Born and brought up in Nottingham, Sillitoe served in Malaya with the RAF. He began to write after demobilization when TB forced him to spend a year and a half convalescing. His first novel, *Saturday Night and Sunday Morning* (1958), remains his best known. Its anti-hero, Arthur Seaton, a young, anti-social, hedonistic Nottingham factory-worker, belonged to a fictional type found also in the work of other provincial realists of the late 1950s and early 1960s such as **John Braine** and **Stan Barstow**. Sillitoe's attachment to the anarchic outsider is further illustrated by the title story of his first collection of short stories, *The Loneliness of the Long-Distance Runner* (1959), which is narrated by a borstal boy who refuses to win the races he has been entered for.

Sillitoe has published several volumes of poetry, but his reputation rests on his fiction. Subsequent novels include two exceptions to his customary realistic narratives and Midlands settings: *The General* (1960), a political fable, and *Travels in Nihilon* (1971), a dystopian fantasy. A trilogy of novels, *The Death of William Posters* (1965), *A Tree on Fire* (1967) and *The Flame of Life* (1974), explores the notion of working-class revolution, but in the context of a modern industrialized provincial society. Sillitoe's most recent novels are *The Lost Flying Boat* (1983), an adventure narrative about flying, *Down from the Hill* (1984), a lyrical evocation of 1945, and *Life Goes On* (1985).

*Silver King, The* A melodrama by **Henry Arthur Jones**, first performed in London in 1882. Its success established Jones as a leading dramatist.

Wilfred Denver, dissipated but kindly, is persuaded that he has committed a murder. He is forced to abandon his family and flee to America. There he makes a fortune and is known as the Silver King. When he hears that his family is starving in England, he returns to save them. But he cannot reveal himself until he discovers not only that he is not guilty but also the identity of the murderer.

*Silver Tassie, The* A tragicomedy by **Sean O'Casey**, first staged in London in 1929 after its rejection by the directors of Dublin's **Abbey Theatre**.

The first act, set in the familiar O'Casey world of Dublin's tenements, shows Harry Heegan, on leave from World War I, leading his football team to victory and the trophy of the silver tassie. It was Act Two, originally performed in a startling stage-setting designed by Augustus John, that upset those who expected from O'Casey nothing but urban realism. It is a macabre theatrical poem, expressionist in technique and enacted in a battle-scarred landscape, which abandons the exploration of character in order to expose the futility of a foolish war. The remaining two acts return Harry Heegan to Ireland. Maimed and bitter, he cannot reconcile himself to his changed circumstances. The climactic final act, which takes place at the football club's dance, forces a recognition of how much has been lost and how little gained.

**Silver-fork School** A mocking name for early 19th-century novelists of fashionable life and manners, derived from the description by *Fraser's Magazine* of **Edward Bulwer Lytton** as a 'silver-fork polisher'. Although Lytton claimed his intent was satirical, the genre offered the reader a vicarious experience of high life. Among silver-fork writers were Lady Charlotte Bury (1775–1861), **Theodore Hook**, **Lady Blessington**, Lady Caroline Lamb (1785–1828), **Benjamin Disraeli**, **Frances Trollope**, Thomas Henry Lister (1800–42), Robert Plumer Ward (1765–1846), **Catherine Gore** and **Susan Ferrier**.

**simile** Where **metaphor** asserts the identity of unlike things, simile asserts their similarity: 'My love is like a red, red rose' (**Burns**). The concrete element of a simile, therefore, has to be taken figuratively not literally. Burns's love is not to be envisaged as suffering from some skin disease that renders her prickly and bright red, but as sweet, natural and voluptuous. Cognition, in fact, plays at least as large a part as visualization in the appreciation of simile.

Simile naturally lends itself to expansion – a process reaching its peak in the **epic simile** – while metaphor tends to condensation. The parallelism of simile has led some critics to see it as a paradigm of **allegory**, metaphor being more akin to a symbolic work, particularly one based on a central ramifying **symbol**.

Considering the deep-rooted involvement of metaphor in the development of language and its presence in almost every kind of expression, it is somewhat surprising to find how small a part it plays in literature before **Shakespeare**. In the earlier periods simile predominates.

**Simms, William Gilmore** 1806–70 American novelist, short-story writer and poet, born in Charleston, South Carolina. In 1825 he published his first book of verse and began contributing to *The Album*, a Charleston periodical. In 1827 he was admitted to the Bar. Between 1827 and 1830, in addition to practising law, he published four more volumes of poetry. From 1830 to 1832 he edited the Charleston *City Gazette*. His sixth book of verse, *Atalantis: A Story of the Sea*, appeared in 1832. In the following year he published his first novel, *Martin Faber*, a study of a murderer, and a collection of short stories entitled *The Book of My Lady: A Melange. Guy Rivers: A Tale of Georgia* (1834) is a romance of the Southern frontier. It was followed by his best-known novel, *The Yemassee: A Romance of Carolina* (1835), the fictional account of an actual uprising by the Yemassee Indians against British colonists. In the same year he published *The Partisan: A Tale* *of the Revolution.* A second Revolutionary War romance, *Mellichampe: A Legend of the Santee,* followed in 1836.

Simms continued to write historical romances – another 22 novels published in book form between 1838 and 1859, plus at least three more published serially (appearing in volume form only after his death). Perhaps the most notable of these later novels is *Woodcraft, or, Hawks about the Dovecote* (1854), which originally appeared in 1852 under the title of *The Sword and the Distaff, or, 'Fair, Fat, and Forty'.* During this period he also published three collections of short stories and 12 books of verse. His non-fiction works include the essay 'Slavery in America' (1837), *The History of South Carolina* (1840), *The Geography of South Carolina* (1843) and *The Life of Francis Marion* (1844). He was also connected with several periodicals, among them the *Southern Quarterly Review,* which he edited from 1849 to 1854. From 1844 to 1846 he served as a member of South Carolina's legislature. The Civil War broke him financially and spiritually. An extremely successful novelist in his own lifetime, Simms not only depicted the Old South in its essence but also helped to propagate the Southern myth of perfectibility – the myth that God had given the land to the Southern whites so that they could form an ideal society which would include benevolent enslavement of the blacks.

**Simon, (Marvin) Neil** 1927– American playwright, born in the Bronx, New York. Simon's prolific career in the American theatre began with revue sketches written with his brother Daniel. *Catch a Star!,* his first Broadway show, opened in 1955; *Come Blow Your Horn,* his first play, was written with his brother in 1961. A series of long-running successes followed in the 1960s: *Barefoot in the Park* (1963), *The Odd Couple* (1965), *The Star Spangled Girl* (1966), *Plaza Suite* (1968) and *The Last of the Red Hot Lovers* (1969). His later work includes *The Prisoner of Second Avenue* (1971), *The Sunshine Boys* (1972), *California Suite* (1976), the semi-autobiographical *Chapter Two* (1977) and *Brighton Beach Memoirs* (1983).

**Simple Cobler of Aggawam, The** A satire by **Nathaniel Ward,** written in America in 1645 and published in London in 1647. It is an appeal, in the midst of the English Civil War, for an end to hostilities and a return to national stability. Ward chides the king for having overreached his authority and supports the Parliamentary cause against the Royalists, but warns the radical Independents that their decentralizing, tolerationist policies will bring instability to England. He takes the side of the Presbyterians, urging the Parliamentarians to end the war and, in the interests of national unity, 'rather to compose than to tolerate differences in Religion'. Although orthodox, Ward's *Cobler* is unusual among Puritan texts for its ebullient style. Ward develops the 'simplicity' of his persona, the cobbler Theodore de la Guard, in terms of his living on the American frontier (Aggawam was the Indian name for Ipswich), quite removed from the London scene. Mixing a colloquial style with elaborate word play, puns and analogies and doggerel verses, *The Simple Cobler* is perhaps more reminiscent of Elizabethan than of Puritan literature.

**Simple Story, A** A novel by **Elizabeth Inchbald,** published in 1791. The story concerns Dorriforth, a priest, and his ward, the worldly and flirtatious Miss Milner, who falls in love with him. He loves her, but because of his calling they both conceal their feelings. Dorriforth inherits a peerage, is released from his vows, and, as Lord Elmwood, marries Miss Milner. However, her basic weakness of character leads to an affair with a former suitor, Sir Frederick Lawnley, and Elmwood banishes her from his house with their daughter, Matilda. Lady Elmwood dies of remorse and Matilda is left unprotected. Elmwood's feelings are brought back to life when Matilda is abducted by a reckless libertine and he restores her to her home and position. Another priest, Father Sandford, who succeeds Dorriforth as a spiritual guide, plays an important part in the course of the novel, which is frankly didactic, but notable for the author's attempt to portray emotions honestly.

**Simpson, Louis** 1923– American poet. Born in Jamaica, Simpson went to the USA in 1940; he attended Columbia University for three years before leaving to serve in the US Army. His poetry is characterized by its mythical and dream-like subject matter and its colloquial, often ironic tone. His first volume was *The Arrivistes: Poems 1940–49,* which was published in Paris in 1949. Subsequent publications include *The Father Out of the Machine: A Masque* (1951), *Good News of Death and Other Poems* (1955), *Andromeda* (1956), a play, *A Dream of Governors* (1959), *Riverside Drive* (1962), a novel, and *James Hogg: A Critical Study* (1962). He was awarded the Pulitzer Prize in 1963 for *At The End of The Open Road: Poems.* Recent volumes of poetry include *Adventures of the Letter I* (1971), *Searching for the Ox* (1976), *Caviare at the Funeral: Poems* (1980) and *The Best Hour of the Night* (1983). Simpson is also the author of *An Introduction to Poetry* (1967), *Three on the Tower* (1975), essays on **Ezra Pound, T. S. Eliot** and **William Carlos Williams,** *A Revolution in Taste: Studies of Dylan Thomas, Allen Ginsberg, Sylvia Plath and Robert Lowell* (1978) and *A Company of*

*Poets* (1981), published as part of a 'poets on poetry' series.

**Simpson, N[orman] F[rederick]** 1919– Dramatist. Born in London, he worked in a bank and served in the Intelligence Corps in World War II before becoming an adult education lecturer. The success of *A Resounding Tinkle* in a competition organized by *The Observer* in 1957 brought him to prominence. Like his other successful piece, *One-Way Pendulum* (1959), it is a zany disruption of middle-class normality. Written during the brief popularity of the **Theatre of the Absurd** in Britain, Simpson's work also belongs to a comic tradition that links Will Hay to the Goon Show and Monty Python.

**Sinclair, May (Mary Amelia St Clair)** 1863– 1946 Novelist. Born in Cheshire, she was educated at Cheltenham Ladies' College. Her first novel, *Audrey Craven* (1896), was followed by *Divine Fire* (1904). At this time she was involved in the suffragette movement. She later served with the Red Cross in Belgium during World War I. But before the outbreak of war she published *The Three Sisters* (1914), a study of middle-class women in the repressive society of Victorian and Edwardian Britain. The first of her 'psychological' novels, it showed the influence of Freud, Jung and **Havelock Ellis**. Sinclair was also an admirer of **Dorothy Richardson**'s *Pilgrimage*, the first volume of which appeared in 1915, and became one of the leading exponents of the technique of **stream of consciousness** used by Richardson. Her next psychological novel, *Mary Oliver* (1919), was an intense study of a mother–daughter relationship; it was followed by a third, *The Life and Death of Harriet Frean* (1922). In all, Sinclair wrote 24 novels as well as short stories and literary criticism.

**Sinclair, Upton** 1878–1968 American novelist, born in Baltimore, Maryland, and educated at the City College of New York and at Columbia. He had begun writing dime novels at the age of 15, and in 1906 he won international reputation with the publication of **The Jungle**. An exposé of the meat-packing industry in Chicago, and perhaps the most famous of all 'muckraking novels', it remains his best-known book. A prolific writer, he produced more than 100 works in all, among them a series of pamphlets on aspects of American life, including *The Profits of Religion* (1918), *The Brass Check* (1919), on journalism, *The Goslings* (1924), on education, *Money Writes!* (1927), on art and literature, and *The Flivver King* (1937), on the automobile industry.

By 1953 Sinclair had completed 11 volumes of his immense *roman fleuve*, *World's End*. Its hero, Lanny Budd, the illegitimate son of a munitions tycoon, travels the world and becomes involved in international political intrigues. The first novel in the series, also entitled *World's End*, was published in 1940 and narrates the events of Budd's life between 1913 and 1919; *Between Two Worlds* (1941) covers the period from the Treaty of Versailles to the 1929 stock-market crash; *Dragon's Teeth* (1942), which won the Pulitzer Prize, concerns Budd's encounters with anti-Nazi sentiment in Europe in the early 1930s; *Wide is the Gate* (1943) also deals with anti-Nazi sentiment, in Spain and France; *The Presidential Agent* (1944) recounts Budd's relationship with President Roosevelt; *Dragon Harvest* (1945) carries his history through to the fall of Paris; *A World to Win* (1946) and *A Presidential Mission* (1947) cover his experiences in Europe, North Africa, and the Orient during the early years of World War II; *One Clear Call* (1948) and *O Shepherd, Speak!* (1949) recount the last years of the war and the subsequent peace plans; the final novel in the series, *The Return of Lanny Budd* (1953) deals with hostile sentiment in the USA toward post-war Soviet Russia. Sinclair published his own selection from his correspondence, *My Lifetime in Letters*, in 1960, and his *Autobiography* in 1962.

**Singer, Burns (James Hyman)** 1928–64 Poet. Singer's birthplace was New York, but his Scottish parents brought him back to their native land when he was four. He was educated at Glasgow University, where he read English and biology. He worked as a marine biologist, before becoming a freelance writer. He died in Plymouth of a heart attack. One volume of poems, *Still and All* (1957), was published in his lifetime; an inadequate *Collected Poems* (1970) appeared posthumously. Much of his writing remains unpublished. Singer's poetry explores personal and public language and identity, and humanity's place in the complex and beautiful processes revealed by science; it is rhythmically subtle and intellectually complex, but never merely cerebral. He has been called highly original and praised for his attempt to combine science and poetry, but he remains largely unread. Singer was influenced by **W. S. Graham** and **Hugh MacDiarmid**, and by the philosopher Wittgenstein.

***Sinners in the Hands of an Angry God*** A sermon preached by **Jonathan Edwards** at Enfield, Connecticut, on 8 July 1741, at the height of the Great Awakening, and printed soon after its delivery. Developing the theme of the precariousness of the sinner's position and the imagery of the fire of damnation (invoking the famous image of the spider held over the fire by a slender thread), Edwards tried to move his hearers to feel the force of the Calvinist doctrine and to experience the first stirrings of a religious conversion.

**Sir Cleges** A **verse romance** in **tail-rhyme** stanzas written in the late 14th century in the North Midlands. Its source is unknown. Sir Cleges's generosity leads him into poverty. Praying in his garden at Christmas, he sees a cherry tree richly laden with fruit and determines to take the fruit to court for the king. Three officials demand a third each of his reward before they will admit him, so when he is asked to name his reward he requests 12 blows to be administered to the officials. The king is delighted to learn Cleges's identity, since he had supposed him dead. He is made a steward and given property.

**Sir Degare** A Middle English **verse romance** in couplets, written before 1325, probably in the South-west Midlands. Degare is conceived when his mother is raped in the forest by a fairy knight who leaves her a broken sword. He is abandoned at birth with his mother's glove and is brought up by a hermit. The adult Degare leaves to search for his parents, developing from an untrained and crude fighter into a proficient knight. He unwittingly marries his mother, who is revealed when the glove fits her. She gives him the sword and he goes to seek his father. He acquires a wife but puts off the wedding until after his quest. He eventually fights with his father who recognizes the sword and reveals himself. Degare's parents marry and he marries the lady he has won.

The romance sustains interest by its treatment of events rather than character, creating suspense and expectation through Degare's search. Its setting is Brittany, and it shows many of the features associated with the **Breton lay**.

**Sir Degrevant** An alliterative tail-rhyme romance of the late 14th century composed in the North or North-east Midlands. (See **tail-rhyme** and **verse romance**.)

Degrevant is recalled from a Crusade because his neighbour is persistently despoiling his forests. The earl will not make amends, and the two live in a state of hostility. Degrevant falls in love with the earl's daughter Melidor and defeats a suitor for her hand. She secretly entertains him every night but they remain chaste. When Degrevant is detected by the steward an ambush is prepared, but he escapes. Finally the earl relents and the couple are allowed to marry.

The poem contains various motifs common amongst the verse romances, but is distinguished by its vivid and realistic descriptions and its portrayal of feudal society.

**Sir Eglamour of Artois** A Middle English **verse romance** of the mid 14th century composed in the north of England. The poem is written in 12-line **tail-rhyme** stanzas. It contains motifs common to much romance and folk literature of the period, most notably the wife set adrift and the child stolen by animals.

Eglamour, in love with Christabelle, is set tasks by her father. These he accomplishes, killing a famous deer and boar and the giants who keep them. On his return he finds that Christabelle and her new-born son have been set adrift and leaves to seek them. The child, Degrebelle, is stolen by a griffin and later marries his own mother; she, however, recognizes him before the marriage is consummated. Eglamour recognizes his son when fighting in a tournament for Christabelle's hand and the family is reunited.

**Sir Firumbras** (or *Ferumbras*) A Middle English **verse romance** of the late 14th century, based on an Old French source. The story begins after the capture of Rome by the Saracens and the city is in the hands of the Sultan of Babylon. Charlemagne comes to Rome's aid and his champion, Oliver, fights and overcomes Firumbras, the Sultan's son. Firumbras is baptized. Roland and Oliver are captured and imprisoned by the Sultan but Floripas, his daughter, falls in love with another of the French prisoners, Guy, and arranges their escape and the Sultan's defeat. She marries Guy, and he and Firumbras are rewarded by Charlemagne. The story is substantially the same as the second half of *The Sowdon of Babylon*. The metre changes from septenary couplets to **tail-rhyme** stanzas (aabccb).

**Sir Gawain and the Carle of Carlisle** A **verse romance** composed c.1400 near Shropshire; it is in 12-line **tail-rhyme** stanzas.

After a hunting trip, Gawain, Kay and Bishop Baldwin seek shelter in the castle of the giant Carle of Carlisle. Baldwin and Kay behave rudely and disobediently, but Gawain is polite and obeys all his host's requests. He goes to bed with the Carle's wife at his bidding, but only kisses her and spends the night with the Carle's daughter instead. In the morning he reluctantly agrees to behead his host, who regains the shape of a normal knight, confesses and renounces his vow to kill any knight who disobeys him. The Carle becomes a knight of the Round Table and Gawain marries his daughter. The romance centres on the traditional courtesy of Gawain and rudeness of Kay.

**Sir Gawain and the Green Knight** An alliterative **verse romance** of the late 14th century written in the dialect of the West Midlands. The poem appears in the same manuscript as three others, *Pearl*, *Patience* and *Cleanness*. Although these are explicitly religious and *Sir Gawain and the Green Knight* is not, all four are usually taken to be the work of a single poet. In the debate over common authorship, the disparity of the poems' subject matter is set against verbal similarities and evidence of exceptional skill and artistry. The poem comprises 2500 lines of **alliterative verse** disposed into stanzas of unequal length and ending with a **bob and wheel**, a line of two syllables followed by four lines of seven syllables (three stresses) rhyming abab. The whole poem is divided into four fitts (or sections) of approximately equal length.

The story is set in the early days of Arthur's court. It is Christmas time and the court is about to dine when a huge, bright green knight rides into the hall and demands a game. He challenges any member of the court to borrow his axe and deal him a blow, to be returned the following year at his own home, the Green Chapel. Gawain accepts the challenge and beheads the knight, who promptly recovers his head, reminds Gawain of the bargain and rides out, leaving the dismayed court to resume its revelry.

The second fitt follows the course of the year and deals with Gawain's preparation for his departure in search of the Green Chapel, and his journey through the winter landscape from Camelot towards the north of England. The poet deals at length with the device of the pentangle on Gawain's shield and explains its significance in terms of the interlocking scheme of virtues by which Gawain endeavours to live. Gawain arrives at a castle where he is offered hospitality for Christmas. The castle, he is told, is very close to the Green Chapel and he is persuaded to stay until New Year's Day, the time appointed for his meeting.

The third fitt describes the last three days of Gawain's stay in the castle, during which time he and his host agree to exchange at dinner whatever they have gained during the day. While the host hunts (first deer, then a boar, and on the third day a fox), his beautiful wife attempts unsuccessfully to seduce Gawain. On the first two days Gawain exchanges successively one and two kisses for his host's game. On the third day the lady begs a gift of him and, when he refuses to give her one, offers him first a ring and then her green girdle. Gawain at first refuses, but is persuaded to accept it when told that the wearer cannot suffer violent death. However, he surrenders to his host only the three kisses he has received.

Gawain rides to the Green Chapel in the fourth fitt, accompanied at first by a guide who tries to persuade him to abandon his mission. The Green Knight swings at Gawain's exposed neck twice, and stops short each time. The third time he nicks the skin and Gawain leaps up, defiant and ready for battle. The Green Knight laughs and reveals that he is in fact Gawain's host, Sir Bertilak de Hautdesert. He knew of his wife's actions and gave Gawain the nick in the neck for his failure to keep the bargain of the

third day by concealing the green girdle. He explains that the whole episode was planned by Morgan le Fay with the purpose of frightening Guinevere to death. He invites Gawain to return to his castle, but Gawain refuses and returns to Arthur's court wearing his green girdle as a badge of shame. The court, however, are delighted at his return and all adopt the girdle as a badge of honour.

*Sir Gawain and the Green Knight* is the best of the surviving Middle English romances, characterized by passages of beautiful poetry, moments of gentle comedy and keenly observed psychology. The vigorous narrative includes sustained and detailed description conveying the poet's joy in the sensory world. The poem follows Gawain's psychological processes during the course of his testing and concentrates on the moral dilemmas he has to face in trying to live by the scheme of values he adopted at Arthur's court. The Green Knight's testing of Gawain and, by extension, of the Arthurian court, pits this idealistic scheme against man's natural urges, in particular his instinct to preserve his life. Critical controversy over a number of aspects of the poem remains unresolved; the 'identity' of the Green Knight and the adequacy of his explanation of the adventure's purpose are two such points.

The poem has no single known source, though it shares several episodes and motifs with earlier works and traditions of both French and Celtic origins. See also **Arthurian literature**.

**Sir Gowther** A **verse romance** in 12-line **tail-rhyme** stanzas composed *c.*1400 in the North-east Midlands; it is one of the Middle English **Breton lays**. The poem tells the popular story of **Robert the Devil**, and its source is a 12th-century French version, *Robert le Diable*.

Gowther, born after his mother was raped by a devil disguised as her husband, grows up to be very strong and violent. He leads an unremittingly evil life until he learns of his true parentage. At this he goes to Rome and confesses, then to Almayne where he eats food from the mouths of hounds as penance and is known as a fool. In disguise he defeats a Saracen suitor of the emperor's dumb daughter, with whom he has been having a chaste affair. After thinking him wounded and falling from a tower, she miraculously recovers her speech. The couple marry, and Gowther works miracles and is held as a saint. The poem has some features of the **saint's life**.

**Sir Harry Hotspur of Humblethwaite** A novel by **Anthony Trollope**, serialized in *Macmillan's Magazine* from May to December 1870, and published in a single volume in 1871.

Sir Harry Hotspur is a wealthy Cumberland squire whose only son and heir has died two years before the novel opens. He has a daughter, Emily, and the next male heir is a distant cousin, George Hotspur, charming but untrustworthy and a gambler. Rather than make George his heir, Sir Harry resolves that Emily shall have the property in the hope that when she marries her husband will take the family name. But the suitor favoured by her parents fails to win her heart, and her cousin George does, despite evidence which emerges of his lying, gambling debts, and liaison with an actress. Emily believes she can redeem him but promises not to marry without her father's consent, which Sir Harry refuses to give. It transpires that George has cheated at cards and, pressed by creditors and the threat of the law, he undertakes never to see Emily again in return for payment of his debts and an annuity. Emily is taken to Italy by her parents, where she learns of George's marriage to his mistress and dies broken-hearted.

A study in ancestral pride and the stubbornness born of high breeding and noble feelings, *Sir Harry Hotspur* has a tragic power and concentration unique in Trollope and rare in Victorian fiction.

## Sir John van Olden Barnavelt, The Tragedy of

A play about contemporary events in the Netherlands by **John Fletcher** and **Philip Massinger**. It was first produced in 1619 but not published until 1883, when the manuscript was discovered in the British Museum by A. H. Bullen.

Barnavelt (Johan van Oldenbarneveldt), permanent Advocate of the United Provinces, is disturbed by the increasing power of the Prince of Orange and the army. He organizes opposition under the guise of a religious movement and conspires to raise companies of burghers to counter the strength of the army. The prince's agents discover the conspiracy, the companies are disbanded, and Barnavelt's principal associates captured; one of them, Leidenberch, confesses. The prince is in favour of moderation towards Leidenberch. Barnavelt, because of his eminence, remains free – but he visits Leidenberch and convinces him that his honourable course, now, is suicide. Leidenberch does kill himself. The prince is convinced that Barnavelt is dangerous and orders his arrest; Barnavelt is tried for treason and executed.

The play is not faithful to history. Johan van Oldenbarneveldt was one of the architects of Dutch independence and prosperity; he was the loser in a struggle that involved both religious questions and the power of the princes. It culminated in the Synod of Dort and Oldenbarneveldt's principal antagonist was Prince Maurice of Nassau. The trial was highly irregular and the execution of the great advocate is regarded by most historians as judicial murder.

**Sir Launfal** (or *Launfalus Miles*) A late 14th-century **verse romance** written in South-east England. It is the only known work of **Thomas Chestre** (although he perhaps also wrote *Libeaus Desconus*), and is an adaptation of one of the 12th-century *Lais* of **Marie de France**, *Lanval*.

Launfal, a proud and generous knight, leaves Arthur's court because of his dislike of Guinevere and goes to Caerleon where his generosity leads him into poverty. When out riding he is summoned by two maidens to the pavilion of Tryamour, the daughter of a faery king. She becomes his mistress, gives him riches and comes at his command as long as their love remains secret. For a while Launfal prospers, then he returns to Arthur's court and annoys Guinevere by refusing her advances and telling her of Tryamour's beauty. He loses his mistress and his riches and is challenged to produce Tryamour within a year. She arrives at the last moment, blinds Guinevere, and takes Launfal to Olyroun where they still live.

Another translation of *Lanval*, in couplets, survives in three versions, *Sir Landeval*, *Sir Lambewell* and *Sir Lamwell*, which generally follow the Anglo-Norman source more closely than does *Sir Launfal*. See also **Arthurian literature** and **Breton lay**.

**Sir Orfeo** A Middle English **verse romance** probably written in the south of England early in the 14th century. The best of the English **Breton lays**, it has no known source, though Celtic and French features can be discerned; it is based loosely on the story of Orpheus and Eurydice told by Ovid and Virgil.

Orfeo loses his wife Herodis when she is abducted from beneath a tree by the king of faery. He entrusts his kingdom to his steward and wanders in the forest with his harp for years before eventually gaining access to the faery otherworld and winning back his wife as a reward for his harp-playing. The tragic ending of the legend is omitted, Orfeo and his queen regaining their own kingdom.

It is possible that the poet also wrote *Lai le Freine*, although the evidence – the appearance of the same prologue in *Le Freine* and two of the manuscripts of *Sir Orfeo* – is inconclusive.

**Sir Thomas More** A play that has been dated *c.* 1593–5, but for which there is no evidence of production. It was first printed in 1844. The incomplete manuscript is preserved in the British Museum, its great interest lying in the identification of **Shakespeare**'s handwriting and the proof of his contribution to a work by many hands. The other contributors are **Anthony Munday**, **Henry Chettle**, **Thomas Heywood** and **Thomas Dekker**.

The play is based on the main events of **More**'s life (already well chronicled by this date) from his rise to favour, through his friendship with **Erasmus** and opposition to the king, to his fall and death on the scaffold. Henry VIII does not appear.

*Sir Thopas, The Tale of* See *Canterbury Tales, The.*

*Sir Torrent of Portyngale* A **verse romance** in 12-line **tail-rhyme** stanzas, written in the late 14th or early 15th century in the East Midlands.

The cruel king of Portugal forces Torrent to undertake apparently impossible tasks before allowing him to marry his daughter, Desonell. Torrent is betrayed by the king who promises her to the prince of Aragon while he is absent on the appointed quests. Torrent defeats the prince and his champion and agrees to wait six months before marrying Desonell, then goes to Norway. Desonell meanwhile bears twins and is set adrift with them by her father. On his return Torrent sets the king adrift in a leaky boat and spends 15 years in battles before being reunited with his sons, each of whom he defeats unrecognized in tournaments. His armour is recognized by Desonell and they are married.

The work has no known source but is poorly constructed from a series of very familiar motifs (see *Sir Eglamour of Artois* and *Octavian*).

*Sir Triamour* A late 14th-century **verse romance** in 12-line **tail-rhyme** stanzas, written in the North or North-east Midlands.

King Ardus of Aragon leaves his wife, Margaret, to go on a pilgrimage to pray for an heir, unaware that she is already pregnant. The steward Marrok makes advances to her which she rejects. After Ardus's return Marrok tells him he had found Margaret with a lover; she is banished, accompanied by an old knight, Roger, and a dog. Marrock attacks them, killing Roger, but Margaret escapes and bears a son, Triamour. After guarding Roger's grave for 12 years (seven in one version), the dog returns to court, kills Marrok and leads the courtiers to the grave. Ardus seeks Margaret and is defeated by Triamour in a tournament for the hand of the daughter of the Hungarian king. He rescues Triamour from a rival whose father in turn besieges Ardus and is defeated by Triamour. The family is reunited and Triamour married.

The romance is notable for the number of conventional motifs incorporated in the plot: false steward, exiled wife, faithful hound, birth in the forest and combat between father and son.

*Sir Tristrem* A **verse romance** of the late 13th century, written in the north of England. Apart from **Sir Thomas Malory**'s prose treatment in *Le Morte Darthur*, it is the only rendering in Middle English of the story of Tristan and Iseult. The source is the Anglo-Norman poem *Le Roman de Tristan* by Thomas of Britain, of which only fragments survive.

Tristrem is born to the sister of King Mark of Cornwall after her husband has been killed; she dies in childbirth and he is brought up in Parmenie by a tutor. At the age of 15 he is abducted by pirates and abandoned on the Cornish shore where he educates Mark's hunters in proper hunting procedure and is taken into the court. He defeats the Irish champion who has come to collect a tribute, but is wounded. The wound does not heal and he eventually goes to Ireland where, known as Tramtris, he is healed by the queen, sister of the champion Moraunt. A year later he returns to claim the queen's daughter, Ysonde, as Mark's bride; he is recognized as Moraunt's killer but escapes death. He and Ysonde accidentally drink a love-potion intended for her and Mark and are compelled to conduct a secret affair after her marriage. Mark discovers their relationship and, despite trial by an ambiguous oath, Tristrem is eventually banished. He goes to Brittany where he marries Ysonde of the White Hands on account of her name, but the union is not consummated. On a return trip to England he is wounded again, but here the narrative breaks off. It is possible to supply the ending from other treatments of the same version: Tristrem sends for Ysonde to heal him in Brittany, demanding that the ship bear white sails if she is aboard and black if she is not. The ship returns but his jealous wife deceitfully tells him it has black sails and he dies of grief before Ysonde arrives; she dies beside him.

The story survives in many versions from most European countries, though in some it is greatly distorted. The most famous is that of Gottfried von Strassburg, based on the same source as *Sir Tristrem*. The English romance is a condensed and disappointing version, its uneven metre and uninspired rhyme rendering banal one of the greatest and most moving of European traditional tales.

**Sisson, C[harles] H[ubert]** 1914–   Poet, novelist, translator and essayist. Born in Bristol, he read English at Bristol University before pursuing his studies at the Universities of Berlin and Freiberg (1934–5) and at the Sorbonne (1935–6). Apart from active service in India (1942–5) – where his first novel, *An Asiatic Romance* (1953), is set – he worked from 1936 in the Civil Service, rising to Under-Secretary in the Ministry of Labour before his retirement in 1971. His dissatisfaction with the Civil Service is registered in *The Spirit of British Administration* (1959). Although he had published *Poems* (1959), *London Zoo* (1961), *Numbers* (1965) and *Metamorphoses* (1968), he achieved a wider recognition only with *In The Trojan Ditch: Collected Poems and Selected Translations* (1974). His themes are age, decline and death. His early work is a quest towards 'plain statement', but his belief in the unconsidered nature of poetic utterance has led to a 'softening' process, where dream states are reflected, meaning is unparaphrasable and syntax is ambiguous. He rejects whatever appears 'with the face of familiarity', and subtle, fluid rhythms are an outstanding feature of his work. An Anglican and a conservative, he is also a classicist – both in his pervading pessimism and rejection of Romantic possibilities, and in the influence of Roman literature. His range of translations is wide: they include Heine (1953), Catullus (1966), Horace's *Ars Poetica* (1975), Lucretius' *De Rerum Natura* (1976), La Fontaine (1979), Dante's *The Divine Comedy* (1979), *The Song of Roland* (1983), Du Bellay's *The Regrets* (1984) and Virgil's *The Aeneid* (1986). Later collections of verse include *Anchises* (1976), *Exactions* (1980), *Collected Poems 1943–1983* (1984) and *God Bless Karl Marx!* (1987). His critical works, *English Poetry 1900–1950: An Assessment* (1971) and *The Avoidance of Literature: Collected Essays* (1978), are characterized by a desire to debunk received opinion and a forceful independence of mind. His second novel, *Christopher Homm* (1965), told in reverse chronology, is a pessimistic masterpiece. His large *oeuvre* combines to make Sisson one of the handful of leading poets since the war.

**Sister Carrie** A novel by **Theodore Dreiser**, published in 1900. In 1901 it appeared in the Dollar Library series in England, Dreiser having condensed the first 200 pages into 80 to make it conform to the other volumes in the series. Its favourable reception by English reviewers was responsible for its reissue in the USA in 1907.

The novel tells the story of Carrie Meeber, a Midwestern country girl who moves to Chicago. She meets a salesman called Charles Drouet, and after a period of unemployment becomes his mistress. Soon, however, she becomes disillusioned with him and takes up with his friend George Hurstwood, a middle-aged, married restaurant manager. He embezzles money and elopes with Carrie to New York City, where he opens a saloon which proves a failure. Their liaison continues for some three years, until Carrie is forced by their impoverishment to work as a chorus girl to support them. Though she makes an impression in a small part and begins what is to become a successful career, she fails to find happiness. She deserts Hurstwood, who ends up a drunken beggar on Skid Row. Eventually, and unknown to Carrie, he commits suicide.

**Sister Helen** A poem by **Dante Gabriel Rossetti**, first published in 1870. Essentially in the **Pre-Raphaelite** tradition of the ballad revival, *Sister Helen* derives from the medieval superstition that revenge may be obtained by melting a waxen image of one's enemy. The narrative exchanges between Sister Helen and her younger brother reveal that Keith of Ewern has violated his troth and is to die in pain and fear, despite successive pleas from his relations. The poem is carefully wrought (Rossetti laboured on it over many years) and relies on irony, a subtly employed refrain, pointedly economical language and a pervading sense of doom for its striking effects.

**Sisters, The** A comedy by **James Shirley**, produced in 1642 and published in 1652.

The sisters are the presumptuous and haughty Paulina and the unassuming and modest Angellina. Frapolo, a bandit chief, comes to their house masquerading as a fortune teller and persuades Paulina that she is destined to marry a prince. He next appears as the Prince of Parma, and Paulina accepts him without hesitation. Then the real prince arrives on the scene and falls in love with Angellina. Frapolo is exposed and Paulina is discovered to be a changeling, the daughter of a peasant.

**Sitwell, Dame Edith (Louisa)** 1887–1964 Poet and critic. The older sister of **Osbert Sitwell** and **Sacheverell Sitwell**, she was born in Scarborough and brought up at Renishaw Hall, Derbyshire. Her first volume of verse, *The Mother and Other Poems* (1915), was a slim pamphlet of 10 pages published at her own expense. Between 1916 and 1921 she edited *Wheels*, an annual anthology intended as a radical alternative to **Edward Marsh**'s *Georgian Poetry*, which she and her brothers despised. The seven poems by **Wilfred Owen** it published in 1919 were among the first of his work to appear in print. Her poetic career continued prolifically throughout the 1920s, notably with *Façade* (1922), *Troy Park* (1925), which contained 'Colonel Fantock' and other poems about her family background, and *Gold Coast Customs* (1929). *Façade*, a suite of 'abstract poems' or 'patterns in sound' (as she later called them), typified her taste for experimentation, just as the controversy surrounding its performance to musical accompaniment by William Walton in 1923 typified her highly publicized role in literary life.

During the 1930s she turned to prose, publishing a study of **Pope** (1930), *English Eccentrics* (1933) and a biography of Queen Victoria (1936). *Aspects of Modern Poetry* (1934) examined the work of **Hopkins**, **Yeats**, **Eliot**, **Pound**, **Joyce** and **Gertrude Stein**; an ironic promise in the preface of a similar volume on the Georgian poets was never fulfilled. Her only novel, *I Live under a Black Sun* (1937), was based on the affairs of **Swift**, Vanessa and Stella.

A preoccupation with war and suffering marked her later poetry, notably *Street Songs*

Edith Sitwell, 1950.

(1942), which included the famous 'Still Falls the Rain', and *The Shadow of Cain* (1947), provoked by an eye-witness account of the first nuclear bomb on Hiroshima. *Collected Poems* appeared in the USA in 1954 and in an enlarged edition in Britain in 1957. Later prose work included two books on Elizabeth I, *Fanfare for Elizabeth* (1946) and *The Queens and the Hive* (1962); an appreciation of American poetry, *The American Genius* (1951); and a volume of autobiography, *Taken Care Of*, published posthumously in 1965. Her popularity was increased by lecture tours in America during the 1950s, and the eccentricities of her dress and appearance were made famous by Cecil Beaton's photographs. She was created a Dame of the British Empire in 1954, and entered the Roman Catholic Church in 1955.

**Sitwell, Sir (Francis) Osbert (Sacheverell)** 1892–1969 Novelist, critic and poet. He was born in London and educated at Eton, spending much of his youth at the family home, Renishaw Hall in Derbyshire. Like his sister **Edith Sitwell** and his brother **Sacheverell Sitwell**, he was an enemy of the Georgian poets, producing political and pacifist satires in *The Winstonburg Line* (1919). He wrote the text for William Walton's choral work, *Belshazzar's Feast*, first performed in 1931, and his *Collected Satires and Poems* (1931) was followed by *Demos*

*the Emperor* (1949), a 'Secular Oratorio'. Other work included several novels, the best known of which is *Before the Bombardment* (1926); travel writing in *Winters of Content* (1932), set in Italy, and *Escape with Me* (1939), about China and the Far East; and a collection of journalism, *Penny Foolish* (1935). His best-regarded work is his autobiography, which appeared in five volumes: *Left Hand, Right Hand* (1945), *The Scarlet Tree* (1946), *Great Morning!* (1948), *Laughter in the Next Room* (1949) and *Noble Essences* (1950). A later volume was *Tales My Father Taught Me* (1962).

**Sitwell, Sacheverell** 1897–1988 Poet, art historian and biographer. Brother of **Edith Sitwell** and **Osbert Sitwell**, he published over 40 books on a wide variety of subjects. His poetry, more traditional than his sister's, first appeared in *The People's Palace* (1918). He described *Dr Donne and Gargantua* (1930), a long poem which took 10 years to write, as 'a contest between Good and Evil'. His *Collected Poems* (1936), introduced by Edith, was followed by *The Dance of the Quick and the Dead* (1936). Sub-titled 'An Entertainment of the Imagination', it consisted of interrelated prose reflections and fantasias on art, literature, life and death. The similar but more despairing *Journey to the End of Time* (1959) was based on his belief that 'I have informed myself of nearly all works of art in the known world.' He published *Southern Baroque Art* (1924) and *German Baroque Art* (1927) at a time when these subjects had been little studied, and wrote biographies of Mozart (1932) and Liszt (1934). He also published *British Architects and Craftsmen* (1945) and a study of Japanese art, *The Bridge of the Brocade Sash* (1959). *A Retrospect of Poems* appeared in 1979.

*Sizwe Bansi Is Dead* A play written by **Athol Fugard** in collaboration with the two black South African actors who first performed it in 1972. A migratory worker is sent back to his homeland from Johannesburg because his passbook is not in order. Persuaded by a quick-witted friend to steal an identity card from a corpse, he 'becomes' Sizwe Bansi, but the loss of his own name threatens not only his sense of identity but also his dignity.

**Skeat, W[alter] W[illiam]** 1835–1912 Literary scholar and philologist. An architect's son, Skeat was born in London and educated at King's College School, Highgate School and Christ's College, Cambridge, where he became a fellow in 1860. He entered the ministry and practised as a curate for a time, but ill health obliged him to give up and return to Christ's College as a lecturer in mathematics.

His interest in early English texts, pursued privately, was the basis of his reputation. He edited texts for the Early English Text Society, the Chaucer Society, the Scottish Text Society and the English Dialect Society (which he founded in 1873). His editions of *Piers Plowman* (1867–85) and the works of **Chaucer** (1894–7) were standard authorities for a number of years. He was appointed Elrington and Bosworth Professor of Anglo-Saxon at Cambridge in 1878.

Skeat's study of the English language was scientific with a historical bias; his published works include *An Etymological Dictionary of the English Language* (1882), *A Concise Dictionary of Middle English* (1888), *A Primer of Classical and English Philology* (1905) and *The Science of Etymology* (1912). Skeat was also the author of numerous essays and editor of the poetry of **Thomas Chatterton** (1871).

**Skelton, John** ?1460–1529 Poet and satirist. Skelton may have been educated at Cambridge. Oxford conferred on him the title of laureate (a higher degree in rhetoric) in 1488, and Louvain and Cambridge also made him laureate in 1492 and 1493 respectively. In 1489 he was appointed court poet to Henry VII, by which time he had completed his translation of Diodorus Siculus (from a Latin version by Poggio) into English. From 1496 to 1501 he was tutor to the young prince Henry and was ordained priest in 1498. He obtained the rectorship of Diss in Norfolk *c.* 1503, a post he held until his death. In 1512 he received the title 'Orator Regius' from Henry VIII. He died in 1529, although the tradition that it was in sanctuary at Westminster, where he had taken refuge from Cardinal Wolsey, cannot be proved. Indeed, after the satirical attacks he made on Wolsey in the early 1520s in *Speak Parrot*, *Colin Clout* and *Why Came Ye Not To Court* he seems to have been reconciled with the Cardinal in the later 1520s, for Skelton's *How the Doughty Duke of Albany* was writtten at Wolsey's suggestion in 1523.

*The Bowge [i.e. rations] of Court* was written in the autumn of 1498 and printed by **Wynkyn de Worde** in the following year. It is a satirical dream-allegory about the court of Henry VII. *Philip Sparrow*, a lament by Jane Scroupe for her sparrow which was killed by Gib the cat, and which is also a requiem for the bird, was probably composed in 1505. *A Ballad of the Scottish King*, celebrating the English victory at Flodden, was printed in 1513. Skelton's huge secular morality play *Magnyficence* belongs to *c.* 1516. *The Tunning of Elinor Rumming*, probably written in 1517 and probably printed in 1521, portrays a drunken woman and the customers at her ale-house; it is largely responsible for **Pope**'s description of Skelton's subject matter as 'beastly'. 1521–2 saw the writing of his satirical attacks on Cardinal Wolsey. In *The Garland of Laurel* Skelton presents himself among the great poets, and if we are to believe the list of his works he gives there, many have been lost. A fairly complete collected edition of Skelton's poems was printed in 1568.

Skelton was highly regarded by most of his contemporaries: **Erasmus** called him 'the light and glory of English letters', **Caxton** praised him for his classical learning and his 'polished and ornate terms'. However, **Alexander Barclay** described him as 'devoid of wisdom' and attacked one of his poems for its 'wantonness' and William Lily described him as 'neither learned nor a poet'. Later readers have found his 'Skeltonics' – headlong, irregular lines with apparently no metre or rhyme scheme – difficult.

***Sketch Book, The*** A book of essays and tales by **Washington Irving**, published serially from 1819 to 1820 under the pseudonym of Geoffrey Crayon, Gent. Most of the pieces are descriptive and thoughtful essays on England, where Irving had been living for some years. Six sketches are set in America, among them Irving's most celebrated tales, 'The Legend of Sleepy Hollow' and 'Rip Van Winkle'. In its own day *The Sketch Book* brought great fame to Irving, both in England and America, making him the first American author to receive international recognition.

***Sketches by Boz*** A collection of essays, stories and sketches 'Illustrative of Every-Day Life and Every-Day People' by **Charles Dickens**, contributed mainly to periodicals between 1833 and 1836 and published in book form, with illustrations by **George Cruikshank**, in 1836–7.

The collection – Dickens's first published book – shows the variety of interest and the acuteness of observation fostered by his youthful training as a reporter. Whether driving home the moral lesson implicit in 'The Drunkard's Death', parodying middle-class pretensions in 'The Tuggses at Ramsgate' or simply visiting Astley's Circus, he shows a vivid eye for the pertinent detail. Casting his net widely, the author gives kindly accounts of the schoolmaster, the beadle, the curate and other timeless inhabitants of the local parish, and he records with sympathetic insight the events of a rural election or a dispossession. In comic vein, he writes of amateur theatricals in Clapham Rise. For grimmer subjects, he turns to the city life of Seven Dials, the gin shop, the criminal court and, above all, Newgate. Occasionally turgid and sometimes forced, *Sketches by Boz* nevertheless anticipates the literary achievement to come.

**Slessor, Kenneth** 1901–71 Australian poet. Born at Orange and educated in Sydney, he became a reporter on the Sydney *Sun*, and after serving in World War II was appointed literary editor. His earliest work, *The Thief of the Moon* (1924), was reprinted with illustrations by **Norman Lindsay** as *Earth-Visitors* (1926). Other works were 'Five Visions of Captain Cook' (in *Trio: A Book of Poems*, 1931), *Darlinghurst Nights and Morning Glories* (a volume also including verse by Virgil Gavan Reilly, 1933), *Five Bells: XX Poems* (1939) and *One Hundred Poems: 1919–1939* (1944). Slessor's verse, while controlled and formal, is elaborately decorative and displays an effective visual emphasis. His 'Five Bells' is a moving elegy for a drowned friend.

**Small House at Allington, The** A novel by **Anthony Trollope**, the fifth in the **Barsetshire** sequence, serialized in *The Cornhill Magazine* from September 1862 to April 1864, and published in two volumes in 1864.

The widowed Mrs Dale lives with her daughters Lily and Bell at the Small House at Allington, as family tenants of her brother-in-law Squire Dale, the unmarried proprietor of the adjacent Great House. Lily falls in love with a London civil servant, Adolphus Crosbie, but their engagement does not survive his visit to Courcy Castle and the attractions of rank in the person of Lady Alexandrina De Courcy. He jilts Lily and marries Lady Alexandrina, but the marriage is unhappy and they soon separate. Lily is deeply hurt and struggles to recover, but her continuing love for Crosbie prevents her marrying her honest and devoted local suitor Johnny Eames. Her more cautious sister resists a financially advantageous marriage with her cousin Bernard, the suitor favoured by her uncle the squire, and marries instead a local physician, Dr Crofts. A related plot deals with Johnny Eames and the romantic and financial entanglements brought on by his lonely life in London. He administers a public thrashing to Crosbie, which makes him a local hero at Allington.

The saddest of the Barsetshire novels, it is notable for the sympathetic power Trollope brings to the portrayal of Lily's loss and Crosbie's remorse. Lily Dale was his favourite heroine with the Victorian reading-public.

**Smart, Christopher** 1722–71 Religious poet. Born at Shipborne in Kent, Smart moved to Durham on the death of his father in 1733, and was educated at Pembroke College, Cambridge, where he was elected a fellow in 1745. A classical scholar of considerable standing, Smart also learned Hebrew, and was known as a writer of Latin verse. Around 1747, however, he began to display signs of erratic and obsessive behaviour – they were to intensify as he grew older – and he was arrested for debt. He returned to Pembroke in 1748, rescued by friends, but in the following year went to London where he worked as a journalist for the publisher **John Newbery**.

Between 1750 and 1755, Smart won the prestigious Seatonian Prize for sacred poetry on five occasions, with his verses on 'the Supreme Being'; his *Poems on Several Occasions* appeared in 1752, and *The Hilliad*, a somewhat weak satire on the quack doctor John Hill, was published in 1753. In 1756 there appeared a *Hymn to the Supreme Being* in thanks for his recovery from illness, but he was already teetering on the brink of what friends regarded as insanity. During the next seven years the poet was forcibly incarcerated in St Luke's Hospital for intermittent periods, during which time he busied himself with his writing, his gardening, and his cat Jeffrey.

His particular affliction was a religious mania which in his poetry manifests itself in convoluted patterns, puns, echoes and numerology, but which in his life gave rise to sudden and impassioned bouts of prayer and extravagant incantation. He was befriended by **Samuel Johnson**, a fellow contributor to *The Universal Visitor* (1756), who loyally declared: 'I'd as lief pray with Kit Smart as anyone else. Another charge was that he did not love clean linen; and I have no passion for it.' Legend has it that Smart, when not enthusiastically addressing the flowers or his cat, scratched certain of his verses with a key on the wainscot of his cell; whatever the means, he composed two quite exceptional poems during his confinement. The first, *A Song to David*, was published in 1763 and is now his best-known poem though it was largely disregarded by his contemporaries; it is a hymn of praise to the author of the Psalms, an alliterative ecstasy which combines the compression of lyric with the splendour of religious language. The second, more unconventional work was not published until 1939; *Jubilate Agno* demonstrates the poet's extraordinary linguistic range, and is unique in the history of 18th-century verse, an extended incantation on the divinely designed patterns in the natural world with catalogues of rousing, irregular stanzas in praise of the significative variety of Creation. A blend of biblical and Renaissance archaisms and exotic vocabulary, this remarkable poem also assumes a strangely prophetic note ('The English tongue shall be the language of the west') and appears to anticipate some of the verbal effects of more recent verse – 'the great flabber dabber flat clapping fish with hands' – though its obscurity seems at points to shade off into absurdity.

For a writer with such an idiosyncratic concept of the effects of language (he considered the bull and the mouse to be most important among the English fauna in view of the incidence of '-ble' and '-mus' suffixes), he was notably precise in his classical scholarship. He was much influenced by Horace's *Ars Poetica*, and translated the Latin poet's work into prose (1756) and verse (1767) imitating in the latter the complex variety of metrical schemes, including the notoriously difficult **Sapphics**. His other work included *A Translation of the Psalms of David* (1765), *The Parables . . . done into Familiar Verse* (1768) and *Hymns for the Amusement of Children*, which he wrote during his final imprisonment for debt (in 1770) before his death in prison. His more complicated work is only now attracting careful attention.

**Smart, Elizabeth** 1913–86 Canadian novelist and poet. Born of a wealthy Ottawa family, she was educated at private schools in Canada and finished her education by making 22 transatlantic trips during her teens. After working briefly as a journalist in Ottawa in 1938, she travelled to New York, Mexico and California. Her long liaison with the poet **George Barker** began in 1940. She returned to England in 1943 where she lived for the rest of her life, returning only once to Canada in 1982–3 as writer-in-residence at the University of Edmonton. Her best-known novel is *By Grand Central Station I Sat Down and Wept* (1945). A passionate love-poem in prose, infused with the language of the Song of Solomon and structured in a formal arrangement of movements like a symphony, it became popular in England and New York during the 1950s and 1960s but was not available in Canada till 1975. Smart published two collections of poems, *A Bonus* (1977) and *Eleven Poems* (1982), as well as a second short novel, *The Assumption of the Rogues and Rascals* (1978), and a collection of poetry and prose, *In the Mean Time* (1984). As an expatriate writer, Smart's closest affinities are with English poetry; she was closely involved with the activities of the London little poetry magazines during the late 1930s and 1940s.

**Smectymnuus** The name adopted by five Puritan writers – Stephen Marshall, Edward Calamy, Thomas Young, Matthew Newcomen and William Spurstow – for a pamphlet of 1641 against episcopacy. Their pamphlet was defended by **John Milton**.

**Smedley, Francis Edward** 1818–64 Novelist. Crippled from childhood, Smedley achieved some success as the author of novels blending romance with sport and adventure. The most popular was *Frank Fairleigh, or, Scenes from the life of a Private Pupil* (1850); others were *Lewis Arundel* (1852) and *Harry Coverdale's Courtship* (1855).

**Smiles, Samuel** 1812–1904 Biographer and essayist. Born in East Lothian, near Edinburgh, he was educated at Haddington High School and Edinburgh University. He became a doctor and later a journalist and company secretary in the expanding railway business. He held definite ideas on social and political reform, combined with a strong belief in work and self-improvement. These views emerge clearly in his biographies of successful men of the industrial age: *George Stephenson* (1857), *The Lives of the Engineers* (1867, expanded 1874) and *Josiah Wedgwood* (1894). He is best known for *Self-Help: With Illustrations of Character and Conduct* (1859), which sold in enormous numbers and was translated into several languages. Smiles continued his work as a popular moralist in *Character* (1871), *Thrift* (1875) and *Duty* (1880).

**Smith, Adam** 1723–90 Philosopher and political economist. The posthumous son of the local comptroller of customs, he was brought up in Kirkcaldy, Fife. He went to Glasgow University and as a Snell exhibitioner to Balliol College, Oxford, where his interest in **David Hume**'s *Treatise of Human Nature* brought him into conflict with the college authorities. In 1748 he was invited to Edinburgh under the auspices of **Henry Home, Lord Kames**, to give courses of lectures, which covered rhetoric and *belles-lettres*, jurisprudence and, probably, the history of philosophy. He also edited the poems of the Jacobite William Hamilton of Bangour (1748). Smith took up the Chair of Logic at Glasgow University in 1751 and the following year that of Moral Philosophy, a post he held until 1763. The foundations of his system of thought were laid down in this period. His lectures on ethics became *The Theory of Moral Sentiments* (1759). He published *On the First Formation of Languages* in *The Philological Miscellany* in 1761. His work on jurisprudence and government appeared posthumously as *Lectures on Jurisprudence* (1896).

Smith's international reputation was made by *The Theory of Moral Sentiments*. In 1766 he was elected a Fellow of the Royal Society and in 1764–6 he toured the Continent as tutor to the young Duke of Buccleuch, meeting Voltaire in Geneva and the Physiocrats in Paris. His major work, *The Wealth of Nations* (1776), was begun during the tour and continued in Kirkcaldy, Edinburgh and London. In London he spent time at the Club with **Gibbon, Burke, Joshua Reynolds, Johnson** (with whom he was not on good terms), **Boswell** and **Garrick**. He read a draft of parts of *The Wealth of Nations* to **Benjamin Franklin**. He was also intimate with the major figures of the Scottish Enlightenment, notably John Millar, **William Robertson, Adam Ferguson**, Joseph Black, James Hutton, Hugh Blair and **Dugald Stewart**. After Hume's death in 1776 Smith showed his independence of thought and loyalty in a spirited defence of his atheistic friend, which shocked many.

He moved to Edinburgh in 1778 as Commissioner of Customs for Scotland and of Salt Duties, taking an active part in the intellectual life of the city and becoming a founder-member of the Royal Society of Edinburgh in 1783. He was elected Lord Rector of Glasgow University in 1787, serving until 1789. His last major work was a revised, sixth edition of *The Theory of Moral Sentiments*. His literary executors were instructed to burn 16 folios of his unpublished writings, perhaps containing an unfinished version of a projected book on jurisprudence. Some essays, including the 'History of Astronomy', were spared and published in 1795 as *Essays on Philosophical Subjects*.

**Smith, Alexander** 1830–67 Poet. Born in Kilmarnock, Ayrshire, he earned his living as a lace-pattern designer in Glasgow. *Poems* (1853) contained 'A Life Drama', praised by the reviewers but ridiculed by **William Aytoun** as part of the **Spasmodic School of Poetry**. *Sonnets on the War*, with **Sydney Dobell**, appeared during the Crimean War in 1855. *City Poems* (1857) contained what is usually regarded as his best poem, 'Glasgow'. *Edwin of Deira* (1861) helped Smith live down his reputation as a Spasmodic but provoked the accusation that he had plagiarized from **Tennyson**'s *Idylls of the King*. Smith turned to prose. *Dreamthorpe* (1863) and *Last Leaves* (published posthumously, 1868) are collections of essays, *Alfred Hagart's Household* (1865) is a novel and *A Summer in Skye* (1865) is a description of the island and its people.

**Smith, A[rthur] J[ames] M[arshall]** 1902–80 Canadian poet. Born in Montreal and educated at McGill University and the University of Edinburgh, he taught at Michigan State University 1936–72. *News of the Phoenix and Other Poems* (1943), *A Sort of Ecstasy* (1954), *Collected Poems* (1962), *Poems: New and Collected* (1967) and *The Classic Shade* (1978) demonstrate his sharp and finely controlled style. He has published a number of anthologies of Canadian verse as well as works of criticism: *Towards a View of Canadian letters: Selected Essays 1928–72* (1973) and *On Poetry and Poets* (1977).

**Smith, Charlotte** 1749–1806 Novelist and poet. Born Charlotte Turner in London, she married a merchant in the West Indies trade in 1765. After the ruin of his business in 1782 he was imprisoned for debt and she turned industriously to writing. Her first published work was a translation of Prévost's *Manon Lescaut* (1785), though she became known as a poet and, chiefly, as a novelist. *Emmeline, or, The Orphan of the Castle* (1788) and *The Old Manor House* (1793) were widely admired by contemporaries.

**Smith, George (Murray)** 1824–1901 Publisher. Born of Scottish parents in London, he started work in his father's publishing firm, Smith & Elder, at the age of 14 and took charge of the business in 1843. An enormously energetic publisher, Smith was particularly good at recognizing authors. The **Brontë** sisters were his most famous discovery, but he added many great Victorians to his list: **Ruskin**, **Thackeray**, **Harriet Martineau**, **Elizabeth Gaskell**, **Rossetti**, **Wilkie Collins**, **Charles Reade**, **Robert Browning**, **Darwin**, **Meredith** and **Mrs Humphry Ward**. He founded *The Cornhill Magazine* in 1860, with Thackeray and later **Leslie Stephen** as editor, and, in collaboration with Frederick Greenwood, *The Pall Mall Gazette* in 1865. In 1882 he started to publish *The Dictionary of National Biography*, with Leslie Stephen as its first editor. His authors were his friends, and so were **Leigh Hunt**, John Everett Millais, Lord Leighton and **John Leech**.

**Smith, Goldwin** 1823–1910 Historian, literary critic and liberal reformer. Born in Reading, he was educated at Eton and Christ Church, Oxford, becoming Stowell Law Professor at University College in 1846 and Regius Professor of Modern History in 1859. Rejecting the **Oxford Movement**, Smith identified himself with the cause of liberal reform in Oxford and beyond, serving on the commission which led to the Oxford University Reform Act (1854), taking a sceptical position about religion in a disagreement with Bishop Wilberforce, attacking imperialism in *The Empire* (1863), supporting the North in the American Civil War, and joining **John Stuart Mill** on the committee urging the impeachment of Governor Eyre of Jamaica in 1867. An extended visit to America led to his appointment as the first Professor of English and Constitutional History at Cornell University in 1868. He settled in Toronto in 1871, at first advocating Canada's independence from Great Britain and then favouring its commercial union with the United States. His later works include political histories of the United States (1893) and the United Kingdom (1899), a volume on **Cowper** for the English Men of Letters series (1880) and a life of **Jane Austen** (1892).

**Smith, Iain Crichton** 1928– Scottish poet, translator, playwright, novelist and short-story writer. Born on the island of Lewis and educated at Aberdeen University, he worked as a schoolteacher in Clydebank from 1955 until 1977, when he became a full-time writer. He writes in English and Gaelic and is a notable translator of his own and other modern Scottish Gaelic poetry, such as that of **Sorley Maclean**. The Gaelic language and the landscape and people of the Scottish islands and highlands figure prominently in his work. His finest novel, *Consider the Lilies* (1968), is a moving account of the Highland Clearances, and a sequence of poems, 'Shall Gaelic Die?', expresses his intimate concern for the survival of the language. His work contains social criticism, particularly of contemporary urban life, but he writes best on the themes of language, exile, ageing and death in an essentially plain style which is exemplified by one of his most anthologized poems, 'Old Woman'. He has published two selections: *Selected Poems 1955–80* (1981) and *Selected Poems* (1985).

**Smith, John Thomas** 1766–1833 Artist, engraver and, after 1816, Keeper of Prints and Drawings at the British Museum. As well as the many antiquarian and topographical books which he wrote and illustrated, Smith published a maliciously candid biography of Joseph Nollekens (1828), the sculptor who had been his father's employer and his own teacher. *A Book for a Rainy Day, or, Recollections of the Events of the Years 1766–1833* (1845) is a mine of information on literary and artistic life.

**Smith, Ken[neth] (John)** 1938– Poet. Born in East Rudston, Yorkshire, he escaped the isolation of his childhood when he was called up for national service. After reading English at Leeds University, he taught at Dewsbury and Exeter Art Colleges. Despite the success of *The Pity* (1967) and his co-editorship, with **Jon Silkin**, of *Stand* magazine, he moved to America in 1967, where he learned from the poets **James Wright**, **Robert Bly** and William Stafford, and from oral poetry. Subsequent volumes – *Work, distances/poems* (1972), *Tristan Crazy* (1978) and *Fox Running* (1980) – are featured in *The Poet Reclining: Selected Poems 1962–1980* (1982), which marked Smith's re-establishment as a poet in Britain, where his work had been neglected. He writes a visionary poetry that is populist and humorous, anti-establishmentarian, and is concerned with the self, responses to nature, and politics. Other books include *Abel Baker* (1981), *Burned Books* (1981) and *Terra* (1985), and the prose *A Book of Chinese Whispers* (1987).

**Smith, Michael** 1954–83 Jamaican poet. Associated with the Rastafarian movement in Jamaica, Smith was also radically influenced by the writings of Marcus Garvey and by the teachings of the Guyanese political theorist Walter Rodney. As a result he had a large and youthful following from people in both the Caribbean and Britain who understood his anti-state and populist attitudes. He was stoned to death by unknown murderers; although he was not politically very active, his assassination may have been politically motivated. His success as a poet lay almost entirely in the performance of his work, since it relied a great deal on gesture, spoken emphases and at times musical accompaniment. As a result his poems are now best heard on records such as *Word* (1978), *Me Cyaan*

*Believe It* (1980) and *Roots* (1980). Although some of his poetry is available in anthologies Smith never brought out a printed collection, believing poetry to be an essentially oral art. Among the new generation of poets in the Caribbean and 'black' Britain he was, along with Bob Marley and **Linton Kwesi Johnson**, much the most influential.

**Smith, Pauline (Janet)** 1882–1959 South African short-story writer, born in Oudtshoorn. She was educated and lived mostly in Britain, yet the austere, rigorously crafted short stories in *The Little Karoo* (1925), and also the novel *The Beadle* (1926), about late 19th-century Boer peasant life, superbly demonstrate how a sensitive and sympathetic writer of one culture can penetrate the psychological hinterlands of another. To simulate Afrikaans speech in English sentences, she skilfully incorporates Afrikaans words and phrases into 'un-English' cadences with inverted word-order and unusual rhythms. *A.B.* (1933) is a modest, remarkably understanding tribute to **Arnold Bennett**, who first encouraged her.

**Smith, Stevie (Florence Margaret)** 1902–71 Poet and novelist. She was born in Hull but moved to an aunt's house in Palmers Green, London, when three years old and lived there for the rest of her life. She was educated at North London Collegiate School. Her lifelong employment was with the magazine publishers Newnes-Pearson, where she became private secretary to Sir George Newnes and Sir Neville Pearson. Her first book, *Novel on Yellow Paper* (1936), was followed by her first volume of poems, *A Good Time Was Had By All* (1937). These established her reputation and she published two more novels and eight collections of poetry, including *Not Waving But Drowning* (1957). Her wittily barbed poetry found a wide and enthusiastic audience, promoted by her distinctive public readings and recordings. Her work was often illustrated with naïve line drawings, rather in the manner of **Edward Lear**, with whom she shared an often sad but irrepressible love of life. *Collected Poems* appeared posthumously in 1975.

**Smith, Sydney** 1771–1845 Essayist, parson and wit. Sydney Smith, in the words of an admirer, 'the wisest of witty men, and the wittiest of wise men', was born at Woodford, Essex, educated at Winchester and New College, Oxford, and ordained in 1796. After a brief curacy in the West Country, Smith spent several years in Edinburgh where he was of the circle of **Walter Scott**, **Dugald Stewart** and **Francis Horner**. In company with **Francis Jeffrey**, **Henry Brougham**, John Allen and other intellectuals

Smith founded *The Edinburgh Review*, one of the most eminent journals of the century, in 1802.

Removing with his wife to London in 1804, Smith soon became a popular preacher, a lecturer in moral philosophy and, because of his brilliant wit, a familiar among the Whigs of Holland House. In 1808 he 'was suddenly caught up by the Archbishop of York and transported' to the living of Foston-le-Clay in Yorkshire where, 'not knowing a turnip from a carrot', he had to farm several hundred acres. Meanwhile, he had written for *The Edinburgh Review*, and in 1807 he began to publish *The Letters of Peter Plymley*, on Catholic Emancipation. After two decades in Yorkshire, Smith became a prebend in Bristol cathedral in 1828 and soon thereafter exchanged Foston for the living of Combe Florey in Somerset. A conscientious clergyman, Smith never achieved a bishopric, although in 1831 he was appointed Canon Residentiary at St Paul's. He died a wealthy man.

Charming, witty, and blessed with common sense, Sydney Smith is rare among divines of any age. He published some volumes of sermons as well as pamphlets on various subjects, and many reviews and discourses on matters as remote from each other as dissent and alehouse licensing, vice and female education.

**Smith, Sydney Goodsir** 1915–75 Scots poet. The son of Sir Sydney Smith, a celebrated Edinburgh professor of forensic medicine, he was born, despite the resolute Scottishness of his thinking and writing, in Wellington, New Zealand. He was educated at Edinburgh and Oxford Universities. Several minor books of verse appeared before *Under the Eildon Tree* (1948) showed his full power and established his reputation. These 24 elegies on the unhappy loves of poets have a wide range of literary reference to reinforce the autobiographical element. For all its background in earlier texts, his fluent and effective Scots has the suppleness of spoken language. His other major works are a play, *The Wallace* (Edinburgh Festival, 1960), patriotic but weak in structure, and a novel, *Carotid Cornucopius* (1947, revised 1964), an ambitious fantasy which owes something to **Joyce** but more to the Scottish Rabelaisian tradition of **Sir Thomas Urquhart**. Smith was in many ways the principal successor to **Hugh MacDiarmid**, with whom his linguistic affinities are strong.

**Smith, William Robertson** 1846–94 Biblical scholar. Born at Keig in Aberdeenshire, he studied at New College in Edinburgh and the universities of Bonn and Göttingen, and was appointed Professor of Oriental Languages and Old Testament Exegesis at Free College, Aberdeen, in 1870. His contributions to the ninth edition of the *Encyclopaedia Britannica*, which began publication in 1875, were influenced by the **Higher Criticism** and angered the General Assembly of the Free Church of Scotland by their failure to present the Bible as the authoritative word of God. He was dismissed from his post in 1881. After working as joint editor of the *Encyclopaedia Britannica*, he was appointed Professor of Arabic at Cambridge in 1883 and spent the rest of his career there.

**Smithyman, Kendrick** 1922– New Zealand poet. A schoolteacher, and university tutor in English, he was born and has always been based in Auckland. Where most modern New Zealand poets have been consistently preoccupied with what **Janet Frame** calls 'walking from paddock to field' ('paddock' being the New Zealand term for a field), he has rested securely and sanely in his New Zealand identity. His early poetry was tough, tortuous, and unashamedly 'difficult' in its wrestle with words and a sometimes too private context. The first major book of poems, *The Blind Mountain*, was published by the Caxton Press in 1950. His first journey to Europe in 1969 produced a series of 'travel' poems, which, being more conversational than the earlier work, seem to have clarified his New Zealand perspective, and seem also to have helped him to relax his contorting grip on language. Later books of poems, including *Earthquake Weather* (1972) and *Dwarf with a Billiard Cue* (1979), have won prizes, in part, perhaps, because of the way the new clarity has reinforced the cool, observant control of the earlier work. His book of criticism, *A Way of Saying* (1965), owes much to the influence and aesthetics of the poets of the American South, such as **John Crowe Ransom**. His other volumes include *The Gay Trapeze* (1955), *Flying to Palmerston* (1968), and *The Seal in the Dolphin Pool* (1974).

**Smollett, Tobias (George)** 1721–71 Novelist, travel-writer, critic, political controversialist, unsuccessful dramatist and poet. Smollett was the first of the Scots novelists, from the village of Leven, near Loch Lomond. While still at Dumbarton grammar school he wrote verses to the memory of the national hero, Wallace, and at 18 wrote a play, *The Regicide*, about James I of Scotland and his queen. Smollett wanted an army career, but was apprenticed to a surgeon in Glasgow, having at Glasgow University studied Greek, mathematics and natural philosophy. He studied medicine at Edinburgh University but left without taking a degree. Aged 19, he went to London, and became a surgeon's mate in the navy, under Admiral Vernon, at the siege of Carthagena in 1741.

In 1746 he published a satirical poem, 'Advice', and in 1747 one called 'Reproof' and another poem, 'The Tears of Scotland', which

Smollett. A detail from a portrait by an unknown artist, c.1770. National Portrait Gallery, London.

lamented the savage reprisals taken by the Duke of Cumberland after the 1745 rebellion. In *Roderick Random* (1748), he used his naval experience and theatrical disappointments. Most of the characters, in particular Crab, Potion and Squire Gawkey, were recognized as living portraits. The novel also contained an attack on Garrick (Marmozet). Smollett then wrote an opera, *Alceste*, to music by Handel, but when the piece was not staged, Handel adapted the music to **Dryden**'s 'Song for St Cecilia's Day'. Smollett worked tirelessly to get *The Regicide* performed, but without success. In 1749 it was published by subscription, with a preface attacking the duplicity of theatrical managers. In 1751 he published *Peregrine Pickle*. In 1752 he obtained the degree of Doctor of Physic and settled as a physician in Bath, publishing *An Essay on the External Use of Water, in a Letter to Dr—, with Particular Remarks upon the Present Method of Using the Mineral Waters at Bath in Somersetshire, and a Plan for Rendering Them More Safe, Agreeable and Efficacious*, his only professional publication.

He gave up medicine and moved to Chelsea, where he made a living writing for booksellers, who commissioned him for prefaces, translations and other hack work. He remained chronically short of money, and his wife, Anne Lascelles, was extravagant. In 1753 he published

*The Adventures of Ferdinand Count Fathom* and in 1755 a translation of *Don Quixote*, with explanatory notes. This was judged inadequate, as he lacked the requisite knowledge of Spanish language and culture. In 1756 appeared *A Compendium of Authentic Voyages, digested in a Chronological series* in seven volumes. Smollett was believed to be the editor, partly because the work included 'A Short Narrative of the Expedition to Carthagena, 1741' written 'with great spirit, but abounding with acrimony'. In 1757 his comedy, *The Reprisal, or, The Tars of Old England* was staged at **Drury Lane** by Garrick. From 1756 to 1763 he edited the *Critical Review or Annals of Literature*, in which he pursued quarrels with other authors. As a result of a libel on Admiral Knowles's conduct in the expedition to Rochford, 1758 ('an engineer without knowledge, an officer without resolution, and a man without veracity'), Smollett was fined £100 and served three months in prison. While there, he wrote *The Life and Adventures of Sir Launcelot Greaves*, later printed in *The British Magazine* (which he edited 1760–1) and in volume form in 1762. He published his *Complete History of England deduced from the defeat of Julius Caesar to the Treaty of Aix-la-Chapelle, 1748* in 1758. Written in 14 months, it made him £2000. In 1762 he began a weekly journal called *The Briton*, defending the Earl of Bute, then First Lord of the Treasury. **John Wilkes** replied with *The North Briton* and the controversy dissolved their friendship. Lord Bute resigned, but did not repay Smollett's loyal service.

Smollett, who complained most of his life of ill health (constant rheumatism and a neglected ulcer), went in June 1764 to France and Italy. *Travels through France and Italy* was published in 1766. Smollett, who considered himself 'traduced by malice, persecuted by fashion, and overwhelmed by . . . domestic calamity', was satirized by **Sterne** in *A Sentimental Journey* as 'the learned Smelfungus', who 'set out with the spleen and jaundice, and every object he passed by was discoloured and distorted'. In 1769 Smollett published *Adventures of an Atom*, a political satire supposed to be written in 1748 and showing, under Japanese names, the British political parties. In 1770 he went, again in search of health, to Edinburgh and Inverary. In 1771 appeared *The Expedition of Humphry Clinker*, in which, under the character of Matthew Bramble, he inserted the observations he made on revisiting his native country. He died at Leghorn on 21 October 1771.

**Snodgrass, W[illiam] D[eWitt]** 1926– American poet, born in Pennsylvania, and educated at the University of Iowa. His work is characterized by its autobiographical subject matter, its use of traditional verse forms, and its sensitive, often delicate tone. His first volume, *Heart's*

*Needle* (1959), centres on his divorce from his first wife and his subsequent separation from his daughter; it was awarded the Pulitzer Prize in 1960. His other volumes include *Gallows Songs of Christian Morgenstern* (1967), *After Experience: Poems and Translations* (1968), which includes his translations of Rilke, *The Führer Bunker: A Cycle of Poems in Progress* (1977), *Six Troubadour Songs* (1977), a book of translations and *Six Minnesinger Songs* (1983). His lectures and essays on poetry are collected in *In Radical Pursuit* (1975).

**Snow, C[harles] P[ercy], 1st Baron Snow of Leicester** 1905–80 Novelist. Born in Leicester, he was educated at Alderman Newton's School and Leicester University College, where he studied science. At Cambridge he took a PhD for research in physics, became a fellow of Christ's College in 1930 and taught science in 1935–45. He served as a scientific adviser during World War II and was a Civil Service Commissioner in 1945–60. He married the novelist **Pamela Hansford Johnson** in 1950 and was knighted in 1957. In 1964 he became Parliamentary Secretary to the Ministry of Science and Technology.

Snow's first novel, *Death Under Sail* (1932), was a conventional detective story; his second, *The Search* (1934), looked forward to his later work in its concern with power and the ethics of science. He is best known for the sequence *Strangers and Brothers*, which began in 1940 with a novel of that name (subsequently retitled *George Passant*) and continued with *The Light and the Dark* (1947), *Time of Hope* (1949), *The Masters* (winner of the James Tait Black Memorial Prize, 1951), *The New Men* (1954), *Homecomings* (1956), *The Conscience of the Rich* (1958), *The Affair* (1959), *Corridors of Power* (1963), *The Sleep of Reason* (1968) and *Last Things* (1970). The protagonist, Lewis Eliot, achieves fame and fortune after an inauspicious start; the various stages of his career permit Snow to offer a wide, leisurely survey of academic, scientific and political life. He also published critical studies, including a biography of **Trollope** (1975), but gained most impact with his Rede Lecture on *The Two Cultures and the Scientific Revolution* (1959). In this he contrasted the culture of 'literary intellectuals' and that of 'scientists', and argued that the two had ceased to communicate. His suggested remedy, involving a radical change in educational attitudes, was savagely attacked by **F. R. Leavis** for its utilitarian approach to the study of the humanities. *Science and Government* (1961, originally the Godkin Lectures at Harvard) examined the scientist's vocation and the factor of power involved in government-sponsored research. *Public Affairs* (1971) warned of the dangers and assessed the benefits of advanced technology, and *A Variety*

*of Men* (1967) was a group of biographical studies.

**Snyder, Gary** 1930– American poet, born in San Francisco, and educated at the University of California at Berkeley, where he met **Jack Kerouac**, **Allen Ginsberg** and other members of the **Beat** movement. He came to share many of the Beats' social and aesthetic views, including their rejection of mainstream American values and their use of experimental poetic forms.

Snyder's poetry reflects his interest in Buddhism as well as his experiences as a seaman, logger, and Forest Service trailman. His work often presents his views of nature, religion, and Western culture, and is meditative or philosophical in tone. His first book, *Riprap*, was published in 1959. Among his many other volumes are *Myths and Texts* (1960), *Six Sections from Mountains and Rivers Without End* (1965, revised 1970), *A Range of Poems* (1966), *The Back Country* (1968), *Regarding Wave* (1969) and *Axe Handles* (1983). *Turtle Island* (1974) includes both prose and poetry; *Earth House Hold* (1969) and *The Old Ways: Six Essays* (1977) are prose collections.

***Sohrab and Rustum****: An Episode* A poem by **Matthew Arnold**, published in *Poems: A New Edition* (1853). The story comes from Firdousi's *Shah Nameh*, a Persian epic, which Arnold encountered in an essay by the French critic Sainte-Beuve and Sir John Malcolm's *History of Persia* (1815).

Sohrab, son of the Persian hero Rustum, was born while his father was away at war. His mother, fearing that he would spend his life in fighting, gave out that she had borne a girl and returned to her own country with her son. Nevertheless, he grew up to be a warrior in the Tartar armies. When the Tartars attack Persia Sohrab challenges their bravest soldier to meet him in single combat. During the struggle the Persian champion calls out his own name, 'Rustum!', and Sohrab realizes that he is fighting his father. He recoils and his opponent strikes him down. Sohrab reveals his identity, by the seal pricked on his arm, but dies at his father's feet.

With its heroic subject and its frequent use of the **epic simile**, *Sohrab and Rustum* deliberately sets out to avoid that melancholy subjectivity which the preface to the volume where the poem first appeared had diagnosed as one of the ills of contemporary poetry. Arnold told his friend **Clough** in a letter: 'Homer *animates* – Shakespeare *animates* – in its poor way I think Sohrab and Rustum *animates*.'

***Soldiers Three*** A collection of 13 stories by **Rudyard Kipling**, first published separately in 1888 alongside the booklets entitled *Under the Deodars*, *The Phantom Rickshaw*, and *Wee Willie*

*Winkie*. They were included in a two-volume collection published in 1892.

Kipling depicts the soldierly virtues necessary to sustain the Empire. It is for his creation of the daily life of the British fighting man and of an army on the alert against potential invaders from Afghanistan that the stories are chiefly admired. Through the taxing ordeals of action and drilling, Mulvaney, one of the 'soldiers three', learns the stoical virtues. His rule-breaking individualism and imagination, qualities which are central to the later *Stalky & Co.*, finally reinforce the army system of values. The important elements of farce and melodrama are often seen most strongly in the short episodes of battle and skirmish; in these Kipling has been seen as a forerunner of cinematic vision. But the strongest ingredients are the atmosphere of the brooding landscape and the men's stoicism, companionship and ability to survive a tedious, emotionally cheerless routine.

**soliloquy** The convention that permitted an actor, alone on the stage, to address the audience directly was established in English drama from its earliest years, but the convention of soliloquy, which permitted an actor to talk revealingly to himself, was largely an invention of the Elizabethan dramatists. The opening speech of **Marlowe**'s *Doctor Faustus* is a flamboyant early example.

***Soliloquy of the Spanish Cloister*** A poem by **Robert Browning**, published in *Dramatic Lyrics* (1842). It takes the form of a dramatic monologue by a spiteful monk who envies the innocent happiness of his fellow, Brother Lawrence.

**Somerville, Edith** See **Somerville and Ross**.

**Somerville, William** 1675–1742 Sporting poetaster and gentleman. A resident of Edstone near Henley-in-Arden, Warwickshire, Somerville was educated at Winchester and at New College, Oxford, where he became a fellow. His pastime was to compose poetry, and in 1727 he published *Occasional Poems, Translations, Fables, Tales, etc*. His slender reputation depends on *The Chace* (1735), a poem in four books of Miltonic blank verse describing the pleasures of hunting and the variety of dogs, hounds, terrain and quarry. The work enjoyed a certain circulation and became the preferred poem of Mr Jorrocks in **Surtees**'s novel *Handley Cross*, though it prompted a scathing treatment of its author in **Johnson**'s *Lives of the Poets*. *Field Sports* (1742) is a less extended work, on hawking, and *Hobbinol* (1740) is a mock-heroic pastoral describing rustic May games in the Vale of Evesham.

**Somerville and Ross** The joint pseudonym of

Edith Anna Oenone Somerville (1858–1949) and Violet Florence Martin (1862–1915), cousins. Edith Somerville was born in County Cork and studied art in London and Paris; Violet Martin was born in County Galway and was educated in Dublin. Edith Somerville enjoyed some success as an artist, exhibiting from 1920 to 1938, but her literary career in collaboration with her cousin began as early as 1889, when the first book by Somerville and Ross, *An Irish Cousin*, was published. The two ladies are successful representatives – and at one time exceedingly popular ones – of the Anglo-Irish tradition of exploiting the humours of the true Irish in relation to the owners of the big houses and estates.

Other novels were *Naboth's Vineyard* (1891) and *The Real Charlotte* (1894); *In the Vine Country* (1893) related travels in France, and *Through Connemara in a Governess Cart* (1893) travels in the west of Ireland. *The Silver Fox* (1898) is a novel, and the enormously popular *Some Experiences of an Irish RM* (1899) contains stories about a resident magistrate in Ireland. *Beggars on Horseback* (1895) told of a riding tour of North Wales. *A Patrick's Day Hunt* (1902), *All on the Irish Shore* (1903), and *Further Experiences of an Irish RM* (1908) continued the short stories of Irish life; *Dan Russell the Fox* (1911) is a novel, the last collaboration before Violet Martin died.

Edith Somerville's later works were published under the familiar pseudonym and included *In Mr Knox's Country* (1915), *Mount Music* (1919), *The Big House of Inver* (1925), *The Sweet Cry of Hounds* (1936) and *Sarah's Youth* (1938).

***Song of Myself*** A poem by **Walt Whitman** which introduced the first edition of *Leaves of Grass* in 1855. Over 1300 lines long in its final version (1891–2), it set forth the major themes of Whitman's early work: the poet's celebration of the self and of its relation to the common men and women for whom 'leaves of grass' is a metaphor; the beauty and spiritual inheritance of the natural world; and the omnipresence and immortality of the cosmic 'I' who 'sings' the poem. The poem displays the influence of **Emerson**'s thought, and Emerson himself hailed it as 'the most extraordinary piece of wit and wisdom that America has yet contributed'. It is written in the long, free-verse lines that Whitman used for most of his poetry, and its endless catalogues – 'I will not have a single person slighted or left away, / The kept-woman, sponger, thief, are hereby invited' – attempt to take up into the poem the multiplicity of American life.

***Songs of Innocence and of Experience*** A collection of combined poems and etchings by **William Blake**. The 27 plates of *Songs of Innocence*

Blake's illustration for his *Songs of Innocence*, 1789. British Museum Print Room.

were published in 1789, the first of Blake's famous Illuminated Books. In the 'Introduction' a spirit child weeps with delight at the poet-piper's songs of 'happy chear' and commands him to 'sit thee down and write / In a book that all may read'. Some of the poems indeed appear to issue directly from the mouths of children (e.g. 'Little Lamb, who made thee?', 'The Little Black Boy', 'The Chimney Sweeper'); others view the state of infancy through the eyes of mothers and nurses ('Infant Joy', 'A Cradle Song', 'Nurse's Song'). Poems such as 'The Divine Image', 'Night' and 'On Another's Sorrow', on the other hand, quietly suggest an opposite world of sorrow and violence of which the child is necessarily unaware. In 1794 Blake issued *Songs of Innocence and of Experience Shewing the Two Contrary States of the Human Mind*, and since then the two cycles have always appeared together. The 'Songs of Experience' – containing 'The Tyger' and 'The Sick Rose', Blake's most frequently quoted and interpreted poems – include a number of poems bearing the same or similar titles to those in the earlier collection, but the poet now shows how the experiences of adult life corrupt and finally destroy innocence. The two Nurse's songs are a striking instance of Blake's antithetical procedure: where the children of the first song are encouraged to play on uninhibitedly, the soured and disillusioned nurse of the second undermines their play with thoughts of the transience of life and the fraudulence of adult sexual relations. Similarly, the paradisal anarchy of 'The Echoing Green' contrasts with the religious prohibitions of 'The Garden of Love'. Blake's angry attack on institutionalized coercion and enslavement embraces the ecclesiastical swindle of deferred gratification ('The Little Vagabond'), the creation of poverty in the midst of plenty ('Holy Thursday', 'Infant Sorrow'), and the moral and psychological devastations of early English capitalism ('London'). Only the Bard, who summons the Earth to awake from her materialist slumber and to return to the free life of the imagination, is able to envisage a healing of the grievous split between innocence and experience ('Introduction').

**sonnet Coleridge** defined the sonnet as 'a small poem, in which some lonely [i.e. single and coherent] feeling is developed'. Traditionally it is a short single-stanza lyric poem in iambic pentameters (see **metre**), usually consisting of 14 lines, rhyming in various patterns. The **Petrarchan** sonnet has an octave (8 lines) rhyming abba abba and a sestet (6 lines) rhyming cde cde (or some variation such as ccd ccd). **Sir Thomas Wyatt** was an early imitator of Petrarchan sonnets in England. There was also the so-called English or Shakespearean sonnet, developed by the **Earl of Surrey** and others in the 16th century, which consisted of three quatrains and a concluding couplet: Shakespeare's rhyme abab cdcd efef gg. The late 16th century saw a vogue for sonnet sequences, such as **Shakespeare's Sonnets**, **Sidney**'s *Astrophil and Stella* and **Spencer**'s *Amoretti*. The latter has a different rhyme scheme for its sonnet: three quatrains with interlinked rhymes abab bcbc cdcd ee. In the 17th century **John Donne** and **John Milton** expanded the sonnet's range from love poetry to include religious feelings and serious contemplation. Most of the Romantic poets wrote sonnets. The form was used by **W. H. Auden** and is still used by practising poets. **Wordsworth**'s sonnet beginning 'Scorn not the Sonnet' at once gives an example of his own use of the form and a brief history of the sonnet up to Milton.

**Sonnets of Shakespeare**   See **Shakespeare's Sonnets**.

**Sonnets from the Portuguese** Elizabeth Barrett Browning's sonnet sequence, published in *Poems* (1850). The deliberately misleading title – there are no Portuguese originals – was chosen to veil the intensely personal nature of these love poems, written before the poet's marriage to **Robert Browning** in 1846. The sequence was the object of a notorious bibliographical fraud, the so-called 'Reading edition' of 1847 fabricated by **T. J. Wise**.

**Sons and Lovers** A novel by **D. H. Lawrence**, published in 1913.

Gertrude Coppard becomes a schoolteacher to escape her harsh and overbearing father. She is fascinated by the miner, Walter Morel, whose earthy liveliness is in stark contrast to the Puritan atmosphere of her home.

She and Morel are married and live happily for a time; but he is a heavy drinker and a liar, sometimes brutal, and he resists her efforts to change him. Mrs Morel concentrates all her energies on her children, three sons and a daughter, and seeks some stimulus for her mind at the Co-operative Women's Guild. Her eldest son, William, goes to work and brings in a little more money for the family. Later he moves to London and dies there.

Mrs Morel is stunned by William's untimely death, but when Paul, her second son, also falls ill she nurses him back to health and transfers her emotions and aspirations to him. Walter Morel is scorned and excluded by his wife and children.

Paul starts work as a junior clerk in Nottingham. During his leisure he paints, achieving some success; he also falls in love with Miriam Leivers, an intense but reserved and rather 'spiritual' girl. Mrs Morel becomes possessive and jealous of Paul's relationship with Miriam. Eventually Paul meets and has an affair with Clara Dawes, a married woman, and is also powerfully drawn to her husband Baxter. Mrs Morel suffers a long and painful illness, which Paul relieves by administering morphia. After her death, at the end of the novel, he determines to set out and make his own life.

The novel is largely autobiographical and reflects Lawrence's life at Eastwood, Nottinghamshire, before he left home.

**Sontag, Susan** 1933– American critic, born in New York City, and educated at the University of Chicago and at Harvard. She has written two novels, *The Benefactor* (1963) and *Death Kit* (1967), and a collection of short fiction, *I, etcetera* (1978), all of which share an intense preoccupation with dreams and the unconscious. She is probably best known, however, for her essays on *avant-garde* film and for her literary criticism, much of which was first published in **The Partisan Review** and *New York Review of Books*, and later collected in *Against Interpretation* (1966). Another collection of essays, *Styles of Radical Will* (1969), also includes the autobiographical 'Trip to Hanoi'. She has written two film-scripts, *Duet for Cannibals* (1969) and *Brother Carl* (1971). When she contracted cancer she wrote *Illness as Metaphor* (1977), a study of the stereotypical thinking that surrounds disease in general, and cancer in particular. Another collection of essays, *Under the Sign of Saturn*, appeared in 1980.

**Sordello** A poem by **Robert Browning**, published in 1840. The action takes place in the early 13th century against the background of the struggles between Guelphs and Ghibellines, and concerns the troubadour Sordello, torn between his vocation as a poet and the duties of his birthright. Criticized by contemporary reviewers for its obscurity (a charge which dogged the poet throughout his career), *Sordello* remains the most challenging and impenetrable of Browning's works.

**Sorley, Charles (Hamilton)** 1895–1915 Poet. Born in Aberdeen, he grew up in Cambridge, where his father was Knightbridge Professor of Moral Philosophy, and Marlborough, where he gave remarkable talks to the school Literary Society on **John Masefield** and **A. E. Housman**. In 1913 he went to Germany and studied briefly at the University of Jena, before returning home in August 1914. He joined the Suffolk Regiment and was killed at the Battle of Loos in October 1915. 'What waste!' wrote **Robert Graves**, his exact contemporary and admirer.

*Marlborough and Other Poems* (1916) contained, as well as much juvenilia, several sonnets which anticipate the anti-romanticism of the later war poets, notably those beginning 'When you see millions of the mouthless dead' and 'Such, such is death; no triumph: no defeat.' *The Letters of Charles Sorley* (1919) contain some of his best writing, including his acute criticism of **Rupert Brooke**'s '1914' sequence: 'He has clothed his attitude in fine words; but he has taken the sentimental attitude.' His *Collected Poems* were edited by Jean Moorcroft Wilson (1985).

**Sound and the Fury, The** A novel by **William Faulkner**, published in 1929. A complex account of the history of the Compson family, the novel is divided into four sections, each under a different controlling perspective. The first section (April 7, 1928) is narrated by Benjy Compson, the youngest member of the family, and an 'idiot'. His section ('a tale told by an idiot, full of sound and fury') blends present and past events into a single present-day narrative. Like those of his brothers Quentin and Jason, Benjy's main focus is on his relationship with his sister Caddy. Indeed, much of the grief, anguish, guilt and anger expressed in the first three sections is prompted by Caddy's disappearance, which for Benjy amounts to the loss of the centre of his universe. The second section of the novel (June

2, 1910) is told by Quentin Compson, a freshman at Harvard. He is oppressed by his incestuous desire for Caddy and by the guilt this feeling evokes, and eventually he is driven to suicide. In the third section (April 6, 1928) Jason, the eldest of the Compson children, reveals his bitterness and anger at the opportunities he has lost because of the irresponsibility and selfishness which he feels predominate in his family. He is most enraged by the fact that Caddy, by leaving home, has evaded the family entrapment which he believes has ruined his life. The final section (April 8, 1928 – Easter Sunday) operates primarily as a commentary on the preceding three. In it the Compsons' black servant, Dilsey, and her grandson, Luster, expose the degeneration of the white family and the distortion of its values. In 1946 Faulkner added an appendix which reviews the history of the Compson family from 1699 to 1945. It concludes with Faulkner's assessment of the black people who have served the Compsons: 'They endured.'

**Souster, Raymond** 1921– Canadian poet. Born in Toronto, he has lived there all his life, apart from a period in World War II, when he served in the Canadian Air Force and spent time in Nova Scotia, Newfoundland and England. He has worked for the Canadian Imperial Bank of Commerce since leaving school at the age of 18. Souster is a prolific writer of short lyrics, and his work describes ordinary and often overlooked aspects of the urban experience in an economical, understated manner. The colloquialism of his style stands in marked contrast to the academicism of much modern Canadian verse. He is above all a poet of Toronto. His early verse is sometimes diffuse and over-explicit, but, after falling under the influence of **William Carlos Williams** in the early 1950s, he began to write in a spare, imagist style. At about the same time, along with **Louis Dudek** and Irving Layton, he founded Contact Press, the leading publisher of Canadian poetry in the 1950s, and throughout his career he has been active in editing, anthologizing and promoting the work of other poets. His many volumes of poetry include *When We Are Young* (1946), *Go To Sleep World* (1947), *Shake Hands with the Hangman* (1953), *Crêpe-Hanger's Carnival* (1958), *A Local Pride* (1962), *Place of Meeting* (1962), *The Colour of the Times* (1964), *As Is* (1967), *Change-Up* (1974) and *Hanging In* (1979). His *Collected Poems, 1940–80* (4 vols., 1980–3), is the definitive collection of his verse. He has also published two novels.

**Soutar, William** 1898–1943 Scottish poet. Born in Perth, he served in the Navy during World War I and contracted a spinal infection which made him an invalid. He graduated from Edinburgh University in 1923. He worked in the same vein as **Hugh MacDiarmid** to establish a distinctively contemporary Scots poetry (see **Scottish renaissance**). His first publication was *Gleanings by an Undergraduate* (1923), his last the posthumous *The Expectant Silence* (1944). Most of his work is brought together in *Collected Poems* (1948), edited with an introductory essay by Hugh MacDiarmid, and *Poems in Scots and English* (1961), edited by W. R. Aitken. An autobiographical volume, *Diaries of a Dying Man* (1954), was edited by A. Scott.

**South, Robert** 1634–1716 Preacher and theologian. Born in London, the son of a merchant, he attended Westminster School and Christ Church, Oxford. In 1660 he became chaplain to the **Earl of Clarendon**, who procured for him the degrees of BD and DD in 1663. Famous for his sermons, South was Public Orator to the University of Oxford from 1660 to 1667 and used his considerable wit to excellent effect. ('Piety', he declared, 'engages no Man to be dull.') After serving as chaplain to the English ambassador in Poland, he became rector of Islip in Oxfordshire in 1678. South opposed the Toleration Act of William and Mary (1689), which gave freedom of worship to Dissenters. He delivered a brilliant attack on **William Sherlock** in *Animadversions on Mr Sherlock's Book* (1693) and *Tritheism Charged* (1695). His sermons were collected and published in seven volumes in 1823.

*South English Legendary, The* A collection of narrative **exempla** incorporating biblical history and **saints' lives**, which developed by accretion through the 13th to 15th centuries. It survives in over 50 manuscripts, each in effect a different version as material was rearranged, omitted or expanded. The title reflects the belief, based on the dialect of the earliest versions, that the collection originated in the south. It was apparently written by friars for a secular audience, but no more precise details of the work's authorship or intention are known. A similar, earlier collection, the *Legenda Aurea* (translated as the **Golden Legend**), probably influenced the *South English Legendary* but the English collection is not directly dependent upon it.

*South Wind* A novel by **Norman Douglas**, published in 1917.
It is set on the island of Nepenthe in the Mediterranean (based upon the island of Capri where Douglas was living at the time). The Bishop of Bampopo, Thomas Heard, is visiting his cousin Mrs Meadows during the season of the *sirocco* (the south wind) which has a degenerative effect upon the populace's religious and moral standards. The bishop comes into contact with many of the island's exotic inhabitants,

including the Duchess of San Martino (an aspiring Catholic), Don Francesco ('a thoroughgoing pagan'), Mr Keith (a heretical eccentric) and Freddy Parker, the Commissioner. The plot revolves around a series of Rabelaisian conversation pieces in which various unorthodox moral and sexual opinions and practices are exposed. It is ironic in tone and contains many erudite passages about the legends and topography of the island. The bishop himself is caught under the pagan spell of the south wind and finds himself condoning much that he should not (including a murder).

Considered very *risqué* when it was first published, the novel caused considerable debate and became Douglas's most popular work.

**Southall, Ivan (Francis)** 1921– Australian children's novelist. Born and educated in Melbourne, Southall first trained as a journalist before serving with distinction in the Royal Australian Air Force. After the war he turned to children's fiction, producing orthodox adventure stories featuring Squadron Leader Simon Black, in many ways the Australian equivalent to **Captain W. E. Johns**'s flying hero Biggles. But Southall first found his true talents in *Hills End* (1962), a tough, realistic story about country children cut off by serious flooding. Something of the same formula also appears in subsequent novels such as *Ash Road* (1965), which has as its main disaster a ferocious bush fire, and *To the Wild Sky* (1967), which describes an air crash and its aftermath. *Finn's Folly* (1969) also deals in sudden danger, but, more controversially, with a central plot involving a road crash. Southall afterwards turned to novels concentrating more on inner conflict than external threat, a process already beginning with *Let the Balloon Go* (1968), which describes in meticulous detail a spastic boy's attempts to climb an 80-foot tree. Equally memorable is *Josh* (1971), a painful story of one child's social isolation. Subsequent books include *What About Tomorrow?* (1976) and *A City Out of Sight* (1985), which continues the earlier story of *To the Wild Sky*.

*Southern Literary Messenger* The longest-lived of American antebellum Southern literary magazines, founded in Richmond in 1834 by T. W. White, and intended to publish and promote Southern letters. Until it folded in 1864 it printed fiction, poetry, travel accounts, and sketches of Southern life and manners by such writers as **John Esten Cooke**, **William Gilmore Simms**, **Joseph G. Baldwin** and **Augustus Baldwin Longstreet**. One of its most prominent contributors was **Edgar Allan Poe**, many of whose tales and poems appeared for the first time in the *Messenger*'s pages; Poe also served as editor from December 1835 to January 1837, during which period his criticism and book reviews often sparked controversy. White wanted his magazine to promote Southern regional pride and achievement, and in the first few years of its existence he attempted to remain neutral on the question of slavery. But he and his successors were to adopt an increasingly defensive and sectional tone in their editorial statements as the Civil War approached, eventually identifying Southern literary regionalism with a defence of slavery.

**Southerne, Thomas** 1660–1746 Dramatist. Born near Dublin and educated at Trinity College, Dublin, Southerne went to London to study law in 1678. His first play, *The Loyal Brother* (1682), was a panegyric to the Duke of York. Of the remaining nine, the best are the comedies, *Sir Anthony Love* (1690) and the extraordinarily mixed *The Maid's Last Prayer* (1693), and the two sentimental tragedies adapted from stories by **Aphra Behn**, *The Fatal Marriage* (1694) and *Oroonoko* (1695). *The Wives' Excuse* (1691) is of interest as a transitional piece between the earlier comedy of **Etherege** and **Wycherley** and the more elegant comedy of **Congreve** and **Vanbrugh**. Southerne's last performed play was an unsuccessful comedy, *Money the Mistress* (1726).

**Southey, Robert** 1774–1843 Poet, historian and critic. The son of a Bristol linen draper, Southey spent a large part of his childhood in the care of an eccentric aunt, at whose home he acquired his insatiable appetite for books. He was educated at Westminster School, from which he was expelled for an attack on corporal punishment in his magazine, *The Flagellant*. A decidedly rebellious figure in his early years, he went on to Oxford, where he wrote the poem *Joan of Arc* (1792, published 1796) in support of the French Revolution, and the republican play *Wat Tyler* (first published 1817). In 1794 he became friendly with **Coleridge**, with whom he collaborated on another play, *The Fall of Robespierre*, and planned to set up a 'Pantisocratic' community in the United States. It was to have put into practice **Godwin**'s ideas of human perfectibility, but his enthusiasm soon waned, causing a break with Coleridge. Following his secret marriage to Elizabeth Fricker (he also played a significant role as matchmaker in Coleridge's marriage to her sister, Sara), he travelled to Portugal at the end of 1795, an experience which appears to have taught him to 'thank God for having made [him] an Englishman'. His poetry of this period includes many of the lyrics and ballads by which he is now chiefly remembered, and which in their own way contributed to the dismantling of the formal constrictions of late 18th-century verse: 'My days among the dead are past', 'The Inchcape Rock', 'The Battle of Blenheim', as well as 'The Holly

Tree', perhaps his best-known poem. The change from radical to Tory, which was to make him the *bête noire* of the Byronic generation of poets, was consolidated by a further visit to Portugal and Spain in 1800–1. Returned to England, he settled at Greta Hall, Keswick, in the Lake District, receiving the title of 'Lake poet', though his work has little in common with that of **Wordsworth** and Coleridge. His oriental verse epic, *Thalaba the Destroyer*, was indifferently received upon its appearance in 1801, though **Shelley** later borrowed its irregular verse form for **Queen Mab** (1813). It was followed by *Madoc* (1805), another exotic narrative, featuring the somewhat unlikely South American adventures of the son of the medieval Welsh king, Owen Gwyneth. Between 1804 and 1810 the Southeys had six children, and after Coleridge abandoned his family to go to Malta, Southey assumed for a while the additional responsibility of caring for his household. He was henceforth obliged to write virtually without pause: poetry, history, biography, translations and editions of earlier writers. His abridgement of *Amadis of Gaul* (1803) was followed in 1807 by a revised translation of *Palmerin of England*. In the same year he was awarded a government pension, and published *Letters from England by Don Manuel Alvarez Espriella*, a series of observations on English manners and society by a fictitious Spaniard. His translation of the *Chronicle of the Cid* appeared in 1808, and in 1809 he commenced his long association with the recently founded Tory **Quarterly Review**, which provided him with his first regular income, and for which he had, by 1838, written nearly a hundred political articles. His long poem, *The Curse of Kehama*, another tale in the fashionable oriental mode, appeared in 1810.

In 1813 Southey succeeded the abysmal **Henry James Pye** as Poet Laureate, a post which he did not particularly enjoy, but which inevitably set the seal on his reputation as a radical who had prostituted himself to the Establishment. His short and still very readable *Life of Nelson* appeared in the same year, and was followed in 1814 by his Christian romance *Roderick the Last of the Goths*. During the next three years he completed his three-volume *History of Brazil* (1810–19), and his *Life of Wesley* (1820). The poems of his laureateship include 'The Poet's Pilgrimage to Waterloo' (1816), 'Princess Charlotte's Epithalamium and her Elegy' (1817), and 10 odes on various public events. In 1817 he tried in vain to secure an injunction from chancery to stop the publication, by his liberal enemies, of *Wat Tyler*, the play of his Jacobinical youth. He was repeatedly attacked and lampooned during these politically tense years, notably by **Peacock**, who caricatures him as Mr Feathernest in the novel *Melincourt* (1817). In no way a shrinking violet, he typically responded with provocations of his own. *A Vision of Judgement* (1821), an apotheosis of the recently deceased King George III, is prefaced by a violent attack on **Byron**, whose rejoinder, *The Vision of Judgement*, is one of the great satirical parodies of English literature. Southey's prolific output continued with the publication of *The Book of the Church* (1824), his poem *A Tale of Paraguay* (1825), *Sir Thomas More* (1829), a conversation between the author and More's ghost, and the long ballads *All for Love* and *The Pilgrim to Compostella* (1829). *Essays Moral and Political* came out in 1832, and the same year saw the completion of his *History of the Peninsular War* (1823–32), which was followed in 1833 by the *Lives of the British Admirals*. A miscellany of anecdote, quotation and comment, *The Doctor*, appeared in 1834–7. In 1835 he was awarded a pension of £300 by Peel, but declined a baronetcy. His wife died in 1837, following a period of insanity, and in 1839 he married Caroline Bowles. His own mind was to become clouded during his last years.

**Southwell, Robert** ?1561–95 Poet and Catholic martyr. Southwell was sent abroad for his education, the usual practice in recusant families. He entered the Jesuit School at Douai in 1576 and was afterwards accepted for the Jesuit novitiate at Rome. He was ordained priest in 1585 and in 1586 came with Henry Garnett as part of the Jesuit mission to England. Southwell probably had to re-learn English in preparation, having forgotten his native tongue. Captured in 1592 while saying mass, he was tortured, imprisoned in the Tower, and finally executed in 1595. He was beatified along with other English martyrs by Pius XI in 1929. Some early Latin poems and meditations survive from the period of his novitiate, but the bulk of his poetry is in English and comes from 1586–92, the period of his mission. His longest poem, 'St Peter's Complaint' (printed 1616), is a narrative put into the mouth of the repentant saint. His best-known poem, *The Burning Babe*, first appeared with other short devotional poems in *Maeoniae*, a collection printed in 1595. A prose work, *An Epistle of Comfort*, was secretly printed in 1587 and his letters were circulated in manuscript. His *Fourfold Meditation on the Four Last Things* was printed in 1606.

*Sowdon of Babylon, The*   A **verse romance** written *c.* 1400 in the East Midlands.

The Sowdon attacks Rome and captures it before the arrival of Charlemagne's troops. He takes the holy relics back to his homeland; Charlemagne follows him and attacks his army there. The Sowdon's son, Ferumbras, is taken and submits to baptism (see **Sir Firumbras**), but the Saracens capture Roland and Oliver. The remainder of the 12 peers are sent to demand their release but they too are captured. The Sowdon's daughter, Floripas, is in love with one of them and succeeds in releasing them to expel the Sowdon from the city. He lays siege to it but is defeated by Charlemagne and eventually executed.

**Soyinka, Wole** 1934– Nigerian poet, novelist, playwright, born in Abeokuta. Gifted with verbal inventiveness and an ebullient imagination, Soyinka has an uncompromising sense of justice and humanity. His basic dramatic mode is comedy: genial in *The Trials of Brother Jero* (in *Three Plays*, 1963), *The Lion and the Jewel* (1963) and *Requiem for a Futorologist* (1985); politically satirical in *Kongi's Harvest* (1967); pungent in the anti-militarist *Madmen and Specialists* (1971) and *Jero's Metamorphosis* (1973); angrily farcical in *A Play of Giants* (1984). While trying to habilitate traditional African (in his case Yoruba) beliefs in modern life, as in his first novel *The Interpreters* (1965) and the long title-poem of *Idanre and Other Poems* (1968), Soyinka also satirizes precolonial African regimes, as in the complex but life-affirming play *A Dance of the Forests* (1963). In *Myth, Literature and the African World* (1976) he explicates Yoruba cosmography and culture, using them as dramatic themes, questioningly in *The Swamp Dwellers* and *The Strong Breed* (both in *Three Plays*, 1963), cryptically because semi-satirically in *The Road* (1965), and with tragic profundity in *Death and the King's Horseman*

Wole Soyinka.

The title-page illustration of an edition of Kyd's *The Spanish Tragedy* published in 1633. The play was first acted *c.*1589 and first published in 1592.

(1975). The powerful novel *Season of Anomy* (1973) tries to resolve issues of modern civil violence in terms of those Yoruba beliefs. In *The Bacchae* (1973) he successfully adapts Euripides, in *Opera Wanyosi* (1981) **Gay** and Brecht. He writes about his political imprisonment (1967–9) tumultuously in prose in *The Man Died* (1973), more meditatively in verse in *A Shuttle in the Crypt* (1972). *Ogun Abibiman* (1976), a poem, calls for black South Africa's liberation. *Aké* (1981) is an engaging autobiography.

**Spanish Curate, The** A comedy of intrigue by **John Fletcher** and, probably, **Philip Massinger**, produced in 1622 but not published until 1718.

**Spanish Gypsy, The** A poem by **George Eliot**, first published in 1868. Cast in pseudo-dramatic form and running to considerable length, it takes duty, happiness, love, race and loyalty as its themes. But these preoccupations overshadow the dramatic action, which is often unconvincing, and the characterization, which is weak. Although well received when it first appeared, *The Spanish Gypsy* is no longer ranked among George Eliot's distinguished writings.

**Spanish Tragedy, The**, or, *Hieronimo is Mad Again* A play by **Thomas Kyd**, produced *c.* 1589 and published in 1592. The first English **revenge tragedy**, it proved popular with Renaissance audiences, being revised for later productions. **Shakespeare**'s *Hamlet* is among its many successors.

Hieronimo is a marshal of Spain at the time of his country's victory over Portugal in 1580. His son Horatio and his nephew Lorenzo captured Balthazar, son of the Viceroy of Portugal, during the war and now Balthazar is courting Bel-imperia, Lorenzo's sister. Lorenzo favours the match and so does the King of Spain for political reasons but Bel-imperia loves Horatio. Lorenzo and Balthazar surprise the two lovers in Hieronimo's arbour at night: they murder Horatio and hang his body to a tree. Bel-imperia escapes but Hieronimo, hearing the disturbance, finds his son's body and is beside himself with grief. He ascertains the murderers' identity and plots their destruction with Bel-imperia. To accomplish this he engages them to take part in a play, with himself and Bel-imperia, to be acted before the court. Revenge on Lorenzo and Balthazar is carried out successfully in the play within the play; Hieronimo and Bel-imperia then take their own lives.

**Spark, Muriel (Sarah)** 1918– Novelist, poet and short-story writer. Born Muriel Sarah Camberg in Edinburgh, she was educated there at Gillespie's School for Girls. After some years in Africa (1936–44) she returned to Britain and worked in political intelligence at the Foreign Office. She had married S. O. Spark in 1938. From 1947 to 1949 she edited *Poetry Review*, publishing a volume of poems, *The Fanfarlo*, in 1952. After various works of literary criticism and biography, she published her well-received first novel, *The Comforters* (1957), which displayed her talent for irony and black humour. It was followed by *Memento Mori* (1959), about old age, and *The Ballad of Peckam Rye* (1960), about underworld life, which established her reputation as a satirical novelist with a sharp, oblique humour and a detached, elegant style. She is perhaps best known for **The Prime of Miss Jean Brodie** (1961), which was later successfully filmed, and for *Girls of Slender Means* (1963), a black comedy set in Kensington at the close of the war. Other novels include *The Mandelbaum Gate* (1965), *The Public Image* (1968), *The Driver's Seat* (1970) and *The Take-Over* (1976), set in Italy, where she eventually made her home. More recent novels include *Loitering With Intent* (1981), which explored her struggles with biography. *Collected Stories* and *Collected Poems* both appeared in 1967.

**Spasmodic School of Poetry** A term coined by **William Aytoun** to ridicule the extravagance of feeling and language in the work of **Philip James Bailey**, **Sydney Dobell** and **Alexander Smith**.

**Spectator, The** A periodical founded and jointly conducted by **Richard Steele** and **Joseph Addison**, appearing daily from 1 March 1711 to 6 December 1712 (a total of 555 issues). Addison revived it in 1714 for a further 80 issues. Among other contributors were **Alexander Pope**, **Ambrose Philips**, **Lady Mary Wortley Montagu**, **Thomas Tickell**, **Laurence Eusden**, and Eustace Budgell.

*The Spectator* was presented as the work of a small club of representative gentlemen from different walks of life: Sir Andrew Freeport (commerce), Captain Sentry (the army), Will Honeycombe (the townsman), and a lawyer and a clergyman, both anonymous. Sir Roger de Coverley, the periodical's most enduringly famous creation, was the country gentleman. Mr Spectator himself was the detached observer who took no 'practical part in life'. The papers addressed cultural, moral and topical concerns, and carried a series of entertaining character sketches.

**Speed, John** ?1552–1629 Historian and cartographer. By 1598 he had presented several maps to Queen Elizabeth, and from 1608 to 1611 he published a series of 44 maps of England and Wales, collected in 1611 as *The Theatre of the Empire of Great Britain*. He became a member of the Society of Antiquaries and was encouraged by **William Camden** and **Sir Robert Bruce Cotton** (who loaned him manuscripts) to begin the work published in 1611 as a continuation of the *Theatre of Great Britain* and entitled *The History of Great Britain*. The popularity of his biblical genealogies is attested by their numerous editions.

*Speed the Plough* A melodramatic comedy by **Thomas Morton**, first performed at **Covent Garden** in 1800. The play has a variety of plots. The 'main' one is a mawkish story of quarrelling brothers brought to reconciliation at the final curtain. Much better is a sub-plot in which the simple goodness of Farmer Ashfield is convincingly and humorously displayed. The play has been given a deserved place in cultural history by its author's invention of Mrs Grundy, a character who never appears but is constantly referred to by Farmer Ashfield's wife as an arbiter of acceptable behaviour.

**Speke, John Hanning** 1827–64 Explorer. Speke was **Richard Burton**'s companion on two expeditions to explore East Africa. They went to Somaliland (1854) and to the interior (1857–9), discovering Lake Tanganyika in 1858. Speke continued after Burton's physical condition obliged him to withdraw to Tabora, and discovered Lake Victoria. His belief that this was the source of the Nile had no supporting evidence, but was proved right. Speke's *Journal of the Discovery of the Source of the Nile* was published in 1863.

**Spencer, Elizabeth** 1921– American novelist, born in rural Mississippi. Her Southern experience is evident in many of her short stories, as well as in her first three novels – *Fire in The Morning* (1948), *This Crooked Way* (1952) and *The Voice At The Back Door* (1956) – in which she shows how the effort to preserve the ways of the antebellum South can sometimes overwhelm the sensitive members of the Mississippi upper-middle class. Her other novels include two set in Italy, *The Light in the Piazza* (1960) and *Knights and Dragons* (1965), and two set in New Orleans, *No Place For An Angel* (1968) and *The Snare* (1972). Her stories have been collected in two volumes: *Ship Island and Other Stories* (1968) and *The Stories of Elizabeth Spencer* (1981).

**Spencer, Herbert** 1820–1903 Philosopher and social scientist. Born to a Nonconformist family in Derby, he failed to thrive with the orthodox classical curriculum at the local day school, though his knowledge of science and other subjects was already advanced. He moved to the educational care of his radical uncle, Thomas Spencer, and left school at 16. He started a promising career as a railway engineer but then in 1848 became sub-editor of *The Economist*. His speculative and synthesizing bent of mind began to declare itself in powerful writing in the 1850s. His first book was the later much-admired *Social Statics, or, the Conditions Essential to Human Happiness Specified* (1851). His 1852 essay on the 'Development Hypothesis' sets forth a general theory of evolution before **Darwin**, though without Darwin's concept of natural selection and his compelling variety of evidence. Spencer's polymathism was uneven in depth. The determination to work from *First Principles* (1862) through to a 'synthetic philosophy' dominated his writing career. *Education* (1861) and *The Principles of Sociology* (1877–82) in particular caused great interest and controversy among his contemporaries. In *Education* he insisted on the importance of scientific study. Spencer's early writings seem to provide a model for the programme of upbringing invented by Sir Austin Feverel for his son in **George Meredith**'s *The Ordeal of Richard Feverel* (1859). Spencer insisted on individualism as the basis both of a free society and of ethics. This insistence created methodological problems for his classificatory systems within his syncretic philosophy. It also created difficulties in his personal life, since he was notoriously assertive about his intellectual property. Spencer was an intimate early friend of **George Eliot**, who loved him before she became a novelist. He maintained a difficult friendship with her and **G. H. Lewes** throughout their life together. He has been suggested as one model for Mr Casaubon in *Middlemarch* (1872).

Spencer's intellectual ordering power and his stamina and range of enquiry are remarkable, as can be seen from his works, *The Principles of Psychology* (1855–72), *The Principles of Biology* (1864–7) and *The Principles of Sociology* (1876–96). He was a productive influence on both **Thomas Hardy** and **H. G. Wells**.

**Spender, Sir Stephen (Harold)** 1909– Poet and man of letters. Born in London, he was educated at University College School, London, and at University College, Oxford, where he first met **W. H. Auden** and the other young writers of Auden's circle. Leaving Oxford without taking a degree, he went to Berlin in 1930, and was in Spain during the Civil War. He served as a fireman in London during World War II. Since 1948 he has split his time between England and the USA, holding many academic posts, including a professorship of English at University College, London, in 1970–5. He was co-editor of the magazine *Horizon* (1939–41), with **Cyril Connolly**, and of *Encounter* (1953–66). Many honours culminated in a knighthood in 1983.

His best work as a poet appeared in his first major collection, *Poems* (1933). 'I Think Continually of Those Who Are Truly Great' displays a natural lyric gift which was not fulfilled in later writing but, under Auden's influence, muted by a sense of obligation to include the detritus of contemporary life (as in the often-anthologized 'The Express' and 'The Pylons'). His work is dominated by an unsuccessful search for a faith and a quest to integrate the private and the political. *Vienna* (1934) is an unsuccessful long poem. *The Still Centre* (1939) contains effective poems about Spain but generally marks a movement towards more personal work. Although *Poems of Dedication* (1947), *The Edge of Being* (1949) and *The Generous Days* (1969) have appeared, Spender seems to have written little verse since the war. Instead, he has concentrated on critical works, which include *The Creative Element* (1953), *The Struggle of the Modern* (1963) and *Love–Hate Relations: A Study of Anglo-American Sensibilities* (1974). His brief flirtation with Communism, really an opposition to fascism, is analysed in his chapter in Richard H. Crossman's *The God That Failed* (1950). His candid autobiography, *World within World* (1951), is a revealing account of himself and his generation. 1987 saw the publication of *Journals 1939–1983*, and his poetic career can be surveyed in *Collected Poems 1928–1985* (1985).

**Spenser, Edmund** ?1552–99 Poet. Spenser was born in London, perhaps in Smithfield, although the family may have come from Lancashire. He entered Merchant Taylors' School in 1561, where the headmaster was the humanist **Richard Mulcaster** and fellow pupils included **Thomas Kyd**, **Lancelot Andrewes** and **Thomas Lodge**. In May 1569 he entered Pembroke Hall, Cambridge, as a sizar, graduating BA in 1573 and MA in 1576. At Cambridge he began his friendship with **Gabriel Harvey**. 1569 saw his first publication, anonymous translations, mainly of sonnets, of Petrarch and Du Bellay, in *A Theatre Wherein be Represented As Well the Miseries and*

Spenser. Engraving by J. Thomson from an original painting.

*Calamities That Follow the Voluptuous Worldlings*, an apocalyptic and anti-Catholic compilation by the Dutch Calvinist Jan van der Noodt. In 1578 he became secretary to John Young, Bishop of Rochester, and in 1579 entered Leicester's service where he became familiar with **Philip Sidney** and Edward Dyer. In the same year he married Maccabeus Chylde, by whom he had two children. In 1580 he became secretary to Lord Grey de Wilton, Lord Deputy of Ireland, arriving in Dublin in August of that year. Spenser lived in Ireland, apart from intermittent visits to England including an audience with the queen in 1589, until his return to London at the end of 1598. In Ireland Spenser held a succession of official posts such as commissioner for musters and deputy to the Clerk of the Council in Munster. He lived in a succession of houses, at Enniscorthy in Wexford, Dublin and the ruined castle of Kilcolman in Cork, which he leased in 1588. Kilcolman was sacked and burned during Tyrone's rebellion in October 1598, causing Spenser to take refuge in Cork and afterwards to return to England.

*The Shepheardes Calender*, dedicated to Sidney, was published anonymously in 1579, and Spenser's correspondence with Harvey a year later. In 1591 appeared a volume of nine of his poems entitled *Complaints*. This included revisions of his 1569 poems with other minor works such as *Virgil's Gnat* (a translation of the pseudo-Virgilian *Culex*) and *Muiopotmos* on the fate of a butterfly. In the same year *Daphnaida* was published, an elegy on the death of Lady Howard in imitation of **Chaucer**'s *Book of the Duchess*. In 1595 *Amoretti* and *Epithalamion* appeared together in one volume. The sonnet sequence and marriage hymn may in some way record respectively Spenser's courtship of and marriage to Elizabeth Boyle, whom he married in June 1594. They had one son, Peregrine. *Colin Clout's Come Home Again* (1595) is an autobiographical pastoral poem. *Four Hymns* (1596) are platonizing reflections on human and divine love, and *Prothalamion* (1596) celebrates the double betrothal of Katherine and Elizabeth, daughters of the Earl of Worcester. The prose dialogue, *A View of the Present State of Ireland*, was entered in the Stationers' Register in 1598 but not published until 1633. A translation of the pseudo-Platonic *Axiochus* is also attributed, very doubtfully, to him. The first three books of Spenser's great poem *The Faerie Queene* came out 1590 and these were published again in 1596 with the addition of Books IV–VI. The six completed books with the addition of the 'Mutability Cantos' appeared in folio in 1609, ten years after Spenser's death.

Spenser died at Westminster on 13 January 1599, 'for lack of bread' according to **Ben Jonson**. This assertion, although supported by the antiquary **William Camden**, is of doubtful authority. He was buried in Westminster Abbey and his hearse, according to Camden, was 'attended by poets, and mournful elegies and poems, with the pens that wrote them, thrown into the tomb'. The queen's order for a memorial to Spenser was never carried out, although a funeral memorial to 'the Prince of Poets in his time' was erected in Westminster Abbey in 1620 and restored in marble in 1778. His collected works were first published in 1611.

*The Shepheardes Calender* provided English literature with a series of pastorals that could stand comparison with European examples; *The Faerie Queene* with a great heroic romance that could justly claim to outshine the continental chivalric romances of Ariosto and Tasso. E. K.'s enthusiasm in *The Shepheardes Calender* for the emergence of an English Virgil was echoed by **William Webbe** in *Of English Poetry* (1586). Sidney's complaints about Spenser's archaisms were repeated by Ben Jonson, who claimed that he 'writ no language', and by Everard Guilpin, who objected to Spenser's 'grandam words'. But Jonson would still have him read for his 'matter', thus anticipating **Milton**'s commendation of the moral earnestness of the 'sage and serious' Spenser, whom he found a better teacher than either Thomas Aquinas or **Duns Scotus**. The 18th century was a great period of Spenser scholarship, with **Thomas Warton**'s *Observations on the Faerie Queene* (1754) and Upton's annotated edition of the poem. The Augustan age liked the pictorial quality of Spenser and saw *The Faerie Queene* as a poem of the imagination, although it found its allegory distasteful and its form disquieting. For the Romantics, Spenser was the poet's poet, a poet of dreams, beauty and sensuous appeal, but **Hazlitt** was not alone in not wishing to meddle with the allegory. **Wordsworth**'s *The White Doe of Rylstone* shows him to have liked the first book of *The Faerie Queene* and Book III of *The Prelude* describes Wordsworth at Cambridge reading 'Sweet Spenser, moving through his clouded heaven / With the moon's beauty and the moon's soft pace'. **W. B. Yeats** liked the 'charmed sleep' of Spenser's poetry but found his morality official and impersonal: he was for Yeats 'the first salaried moralist'. In 1932 **T. S. Eliot** doubted that any except scholars had read the whole of *The Faerie Queene* with delight. Fortunately in recent years, thanks partly to the championship of **C. S. Lewis**, readers and scholars on both sides of the Atlantic have found that Milton's didactic Spenser and the Romantics' recorder of charmed dreams are happily the same man, one whose speaking pictures both teach and delight.

**Spenserian stanza** **Edmund Spenser** invented this stanzaic form and used it in his *The Faerie Queene*. It varies **ottava rima**, and adds a final alexandrine to eight iambic pentameters to produce a nine-line stanza rhyming ababbcbcc. **Keats** used it in *The Eve of St Agnes* and **Shelley** in *Adonais*.

**Spirit of the Age, The** A volume of essays by **William Hazlitt**, published in 1825.

The collection is widely regarded as Hazlitt's critical masterpiece, and aspires to the status of a synthesis of the intellectual life of the Romantic age and the period preceding it. Written in an incisive and authoritative prose, the essays deal with the work and personalities of a number of Hazlitt's contemporaries, and contain some of his most mature and balanced criticism of **Godwin**, **Coleridge**, **Wordsworth**, **Byron**, **Lamb** and **Scott**.

**Spiritual Quixote, The, or, The Summer's Ramble of Mr Geoffry Wildgoose: A Comic Romance** A novel by **Richard Graves**, published in 1772.

Geoffry Wildgoose, a young man of property in the Cotswolds, is enthusiastic about Methodism. He sets forth with the village cobbler, Jerry Tugwell, on a summer tour to preach the Gospel and meet his hero, George Whitefield. With Tugwell as his Sancho Panza, Wildgoose encounters life on the road in 18th-century England. The Methodists generally, and Whitefield in particular, are satirized.

**Spoils of Poynton, The** A short novel by **Henry James**, serialized in *The Atlantic Monthly* from April to June 1896 under the title of *The Old Things*, and published in volume form as *The Spoils of Poynton* in the following year.

Poynton Park is the home of Owen Gereth, and the 'spoils' are the antiques and *objets d'art* with which his mother has filled it. When Mrs Gereth discovers that Owen has decided to marry the tasteless Mona Brigstock, she tries to interest him instead in Fleda Vetch, a kindred spirit who shares her own aesthetic taste. As Fleda secretly falls in love with Owen, he enlists her help in persuading his mother to vacate Poynton, which will now be the home of his bride. Mrs Gereth moves out, but takes the most prized possessions with her. Mona threatens to break off the engagement unless the spoils are returned. All the while Owen is becoming more and more attracted to Fleda; Mrs Gereth, certain that he has now transferred his affections to Fleda and will not marry Mona, returns the spoils to Poynton. Owen attempts to break his engagement with Mona, but, hearing of the replenishment of Poynton, she forces him to marry her. Fleda receives a letter from Owen, travelling abroad with Mona, asking her to choose from Poynton whatever object she would like to possess. She arrives at Poynton Park just as the house and its contents inexplicably go up in flames.

**spondee** See **metre**.

**Spoon River Anthology** A collection of 245 verse epitaphs by **Edgar Lee Masters**, published in 1915. The speakers of the epitaphs are the former residents of the fictional Spoon River, a small town in rural Illinois. Speaking from beyond the grave, they reveal the secret ambitions, transgressions, and misery – as well as the interconnectedness – of their lives. The volume was extremely popular and somewhat scandalous at the time, exploding as it did the myth of small-town respectability and morality. The epitaphs, often starkly realistic, are written in free verse.

**Spoonerism** The popular name for metathesis, the transposition of the initial letters of two or more words. The name derives from the Revd W. A. Spooner (1844–1930) of New College, Oxford.

**Sprigg, Christopher St John** See **Caudwell, Christopher**.

**sprung rhythm** See **Hopkins, Gerard Manley** and **metre**.

**Spy, The**: *A Tale of the Neutral Ground* A novel by **James Fenimore Cooper**, published in 1821, and his first successful book. It is set during the American Revolution and concerns Harvey Birch, a supposed loyalist who is actually a spy for George Washington. The complicated story involves Birch's activities in the 'neutral ground' of Westchester County, New York, and his friendship with the Whartons, a family whose loyalties in the conflict are divided: the father and son are loyalists (the son is in the British Army); the daughter, Frances, supports the rebel cause. General Washington appears several times disguised as 'Mr Harper'.

**Squire, Sir J[ohn] C[ollings]** 1884–1958 Critic and poet. The son of a veterinary surgeon, Squire was born in Plymouth, and attended Blundell's School, Tiverton, before studying history at St John's College, Cambridge. After a spell as a journalist, he began contributing to *The New Age*, and became literary editor of both *The New Statesman* (1913–19) and *Land and Water* (1914–20). As a regular reviewer for *The Observer* and as editor of *The London Mercury*, which he founded in 1919, Squire was a powerful influence in the literary world of the twenties, leading a clique of Georgian writers (known to its enemies as the 'Squirearchy') in a critical campaign against modernist writing. He published several volumes of parodies, and edited some successful anthologies of modern verse as well as *The Comic Muse* (1925). He was knighted in 1933. His *Collected Poems*, edited by **John Betjeman**, appeared in 1959.

***Squire of Low Degree, The*** A **verse romance** in couplets written *c*.1500 in the East Midlands. Apparently built up from a series of motifs familiar from other romances, it tells of a poor squire's love for a princess. She imposes a seven-year period of trial, but they are betrayed by the steward to the king, who nevertheless trusts the squire. The squire is ambushed by the steward on his way to take leave of the princess; he kills the steward and is himself captured. The disfigured body is dressed in the squire's clothing and the princess, finding it, embalms it and treasures it for seven years. The king meanwhile releases the squire to go abroad for seven years. He returns as the princess is about to become an anchoress and they are married. The poem is notable for its extravagant and picturesque descriptions of courtly life, though its use of the romance form is largely nostalgic and artificial.

***Squire's Tale, The*** See ***Canterbury Tales, The***.

**Stacpoole, Henry de Vere** 1863–1951 Novelist and short-story writer. Born in Kingstown, County Dublin, he was educated at an Irish public school, Portalington, and then at Malvern. He studied medicine at St George's and St Mary's Hospitals, qualifying in 1891. Stacpoole subsequently made several voyages as a ship's doctor which provided the background for much of his writing. His friends included **Oscar Wilde**, Lillie Langtry, **Warwick Deeping**, **A. J. Cronin** and **Aubrey Beardsley**. The influence of Beardsley and the other writers and artists associated with *The Yellow Book* is evident in his early novels, *The Intended* (1894) and *Pierrot!* (1896).

His first commercial successes were *The Crimson Azaleas* (1907) and *The Blue Lagoon* (1908). The latter is a romantic story of a boy and girl shipwrecked on a Pacific island and has been compared to **Barrie**'s *Peter Pan* and Maeterlinck's *The Blue Bird*. It was later filmed. Stacpoole wrote four more 'Blue Lagoon' novels: *The Beach of Dreams* (1919), *The Garden of God* (1923), *The Gates of Morning* (1925) and *The Girl of the Golden Reef* (1929). *The Street of the Flute Player* (1912) is set in Athens, *Monsieur de Rochefort* (1914) in 18th-century France and *Goblin Market* (1927) in the Isle of Wight. Stacpoole wrote well over 50 novels in lively descriptive prose, and deserves more recognition than he now enjoys. He was also a poet and the translator of Sappho and Villon.

**Stafford, Jean** 1915–79 American novelist and short-story writer, born in Covina, California. Her first novel, *Boston Adventure* (1944), deals with the social and economic barriers in Boston society in the early 20th century. Her second novel, *The Mountain Lion*, appeared in 1947, and her third, *The Catherine Wheel*, in 1952. She was associated with the literary circle which included **Robert Lowell** (her former husband), **Delmore Schwartz** and **Randall Jarrell**. She also published volumes of highly crafted short stories, including *Children Are Bored on Sunday* (1953) and *Bad Characters* (1964). *The Collected Stories of Jean Stafford* appeared in 1969 and received the 1970 Pulitzer Prize for literature.

***Stalky & Co.*** A collection of nine stories by **Rudyard Kipling**, first published in 1899. Five other Stalky tales appeared in separate collections; the 14 tales were brought together in *The Complete Stalky & Co.* (1929).

Kipling drew on his boyhood experiences at the United Services College at Westward Ho! in Devon, a school founded by retired army officers largely to fit its pupils for an army career. Stalky, M'Turk and Beetle (the last a loose self-portrait of Kipling) are the schoolboy trio who conduct a battle of wits with the masters and other boys. Stalky's cunning and self-reliance, his willingness to infringe the minor social rules of the school and to take his punishment when his transgressions are discovered come to represent a highly practical ethic. It is notable that the authority of the headmaster, 'Prooshian' Bates, is never seriously questioned, and that the laws of social responsibility and self-discipline are affirmed by the trio. Kipling's didactic intention in writing about the education of the young is clearly signalled in the final story, where the ex-schoolboys continue their exploits in India at the frontiers of the Empire they have implicitly been learning to defend.

**Standing Bear, Luther** 1868–1939 American Indian writer of Sioux extraction. Unhappy with reservation life, he joined Buffalo Bill's Wild West Show. After one tour, he returned to the reservation but decided to sell his allotment and become a US citizen. He then moved to California and became active in Indian affairs. In 1928 he published his autobiography, *My People, My Sioux*. His next book, *My Indian Boyhood* (1931), was written for children. This was followed by *The Land of the Spotted Eagle* (1933) and *Stories of the Sioux* (1934). His writings deal with Sioux customs and beliefs as well as the life of adjustment in white America, and are often critical of government Indian policy.

**Stanihurst, Richard** 1547–1604 Scholar and historian. Born in Dublin, he was educated at Oxford and later studied law at Furnival's and Lincoln's Inns. Stanihurst went to Leiden and took holy orders, becoming chaplain to the Governor of the Spanish Netherlands. Most of his writings are in Latin. He is best remembered for the *Description of Ireland* he contributed to the 1577 edition of **Holinshed**'s *Chronicles* and for his friendship with **Sir Philip Sidney**. He was one of the most important of the Roman Catholic 'Old English' writers in Ireland.

**Stanley, Arthur Penrhyn** 1815–81 Broad Churchman. The second son of a clergyman of aristocratic background, later created Bishop of Norwich in 1837, Stanley was born at Alderley, Cheshire, and educated at Rugby under **Dr Thomas Arnold**, whose favourite pupil and subsequent biographer he became. He entered Balliol College, Oxford, in 1833 and was elected a fellow of University College in 1838. Ecclesiastical preferment made him in turn a canon of Canterbury Cathedral and of Christ Church, Oxford, and finally, in 1864, Dean of Westminster.

Stanley's conciliatory, anti-dogmatic position won him admiration well beyond the bounds of the Anglican Church, but made him enemies within it, where those of an extreme High or Low Church persuasion believed his views to be tainted with German rationalism. He was the strong champion of those in danger of being pilloried for their theological views and defended the right of such men to express the most widely divergent views within the confines of the Anglican communion. *The Life of Dr Arnold* (1844) remained his most substantial work, whilst *Essays, chiefly on Questions of Church and State from 1850 to 1870* (1870) provides the best guide to his views on many topical controversies. His determination to celebrate uncontroversial absolutes such as Truth and Unity made the hymns he wrote blandly unremarkable.

**Stanley, Sir Henry Morton** 1841–1904 Journalist and explorer. He was born John Rowlands at Denbigh in Wales, and after the early death of his father spent most of his childhood in the workhouse. At the age of 15 he went as a cabin boy to New Orleans, where he was adopted by an English cotton merchant whose name, Henry Stanley, he took. (The 'Morton' was his own invention.) After an adventurous youth, he finally turned to journalism.

Stanley became world famous in 1871, when he successfully carried out his assignment for *The New York Daily Herald* to find the Scottish missionary and explorer, David Livingstone, in Africa. His own remarkable career as an explorer included the tracing of the Congo (Zaïre) river from its source to its mouth. His experiences are recorded in *How I Found Livingstone* (1872), *Through the Dark Continent* (1878), *In Darkest Africa* (1890) and the autobiography posthumously edited by his widow in 1909. Stanley eventually resumed British citizenship and was knighted in 1899.

**Stanley, Thomas** 1625–78 A descendant of the Stanley family who rose to prominence with the accession of Henry VII, Thomas Stanley wrote a *History of Philosophy* (1655–62), which was an early and commendable effort at popularization. He prepared an edition of Aeschylus (1663) and translated the work of Anacreon, Moschus, Bion, and other classical poets. Stanley was also the author of some little-known original poems, which were collected in 1650.

**stanza** A group of lines of verse, making up a unit which is repeated throughout the poem. It is often referred to as a 'verse', but strictly speaking a verse (from Latin, 'furrow' or 'turning') is a single line. Since that strict sense accords with such uses as 'rhymed verse', 'free verse' and 'blank verse' stanza is to be preferred for a repeated group of lines.

**Stapledon, W[illiam] Olaf** 1886–1950 Writer of **science fiction**. Although his early years were spent in the Middle East, Stapledon lived most of his life near Liverpool, supplementing a small private income mainly by teaching philosophy for the WEA. His novels are painstaking exemplary fictions displaying his ideas about ethics and evolution. The most famous are *Last and First Men* (1930), a history of man's descendants extending over billions of years, and *Star Maker* (1937), a spectacular vision of the whole universe and its creator. His more orthodox scientific romances – *Odd John* (1935), *Sirius* (1944), *The Flames* (1947) and *A Man Divided* (1950) – deal with exceptional individuals enabled by nature or artifice to catch glimpses of glorious possibility but doomed to frustrating personal failure. The combination of cosmic perspective and despairing anxiety gives Stapledon's work a poignant grandeur.

**Stark, Dame Freya** 1893– Travel-writer. She was born at Chagford, Devon, and educated at Bedford College, London University. A long lifetime of courageous solitary expeditions in Arabia, Turkey, etc., has provided material for her many travel books from *Bagdad Sketches* (1933) onwards. Vividly written, with a strong sense both of history and topography, they owe much to their author's indomitable personality, which also suffuses her six-volume collected *Letters* (1974–81). She was created a Dame of the British Empire in 1972.

**Stead, C[hristian] K[arlson]** 1932– New Zealand critic, novelist and poet. Karl Stead was born and educated in Auckland, where he was awarded his MA from the University in 1955. An outstanding scholar, he subsequently obtained his PhD from the University of Bristol in 1961. From 1959 he worked in the Department of English at the University of Auckland, rising to become a full professor before taking early retirement. Stead is best known as a critic and his book *The New Poetic: Yeats to Eliot* (1964) is a standard work on the poetry of **modernism**. *In the Glass Case: Essays on New Zealand Literature* (1981) is a collection of critical pieces on his native country's literature written between 1957 and 1981. His novels include *Smith's Dream* (1971), set in a future fascist New Zealand, and another political novel in which personal relationships are to the fore, *All Visitors Ashore* (1984). The latter novel describes events in Auckland in 1951, but is retrospectively narrated by the academic protagonist, who looks back on an early love-affair and his dreams of becoming a great writer, from the vantage-point of 30 years later. Written in a lucid expository style and frequently drawing on the arts for its inspiration, his poetry moves between the personal and the political. His volumes of verse include *Crossing the Bar* (1972), *Quesada* (1975), in which the title-sequence focuses on the Don Quixote figure, seen as a type of the journeying hero, *Geographies* (1982) and *Poems of a Decade* (1984).

**Stead, Christina (Ellen)** 1902–83 Novelist. Born in Rockdale, New South Wales, she was educated at Sydney University Teachers College, and travelled to London in 1928. She spent some time in Europe before settling in the United States. *The Salzburg Tales* (1934), a series of stories, was followed by *Seven Poor Men of Sydney* (1934), *The Beauties and Furies* (1936), *The Man Who Loved Children* (1940), *For Love Alone* (1944), *A Little Tea, A Little Chat* (1948), *The People with the Dogs* (1952), *Dark Places of the Heart* (1966 – published as *Cotter's England* in London), *The Little Hotel* (1975) and *Miss Herbert (The Suburban Wife)* (1976). *The Puzzleheaded Girl* (1968) is a collection of four novellas. Witty, satirical and highly wrought, Christina Stead's works, particularly *Seven Poor Men of Sydney* and *The Man Who Loved Children*, offer powerful psychological studies.

**Stead, W[illiam] T[homas]** 1849–1912 Journalist. Born at Embleton, Northumberland, he began his career on *The Northern Echo*, but by 1880 he had moved to London to work on *The Pall Mall Gazette*. His editorship of this vigorous London paper (1883–90) initiated the 'new journalism' of the 1880s – strident, courageous and itself influential in shaping political events. 'The Maiden Tribute of Modern Babylon', features on procuring a female child for sexual purposes, led to his imprisonment in 1889, but also to a change in the age of consent. He later edited *The Review of Reviews*, became a spiritualist, and died in the *Titanic* disaster.

**Steele, Sir Richard** 1672–1729 Dramatist and essayist. Born in Dublin, the son of an attorney, he was educated at Charterhouse and matriculated at Christ Church, Oxford, whence he migrated to Merton, leaving the latter without a degree in order to join the Life Guards. In 1700 he successfully fought a duel, seriously wounding his adversary, an experience which led to a lifelong campaign against duelling which first became clear in *The Christian Hero* (1701). The same year saw the first performance of *The Funeral*, which was followed by two unsuccessful dramatic pieces, derived from French originals by Corneille and Molière, in which Steele attempted to put into practice the advice of **Jeremy Collier** in his *Short View of the Immorality and Profaneness of the English Stage*. He was at this time attempting to discover the philosopher's stone, and these pseudo-scientific interests remained with him, as witness his 1718 patent for a 'Fish-pool', a fishing boat built like a water tank which transported its catch live. In 1707 he was appointed by **Robert Harley** to write the government-sponsored *Gazette*, which post he held till the change of government in October 1710. In 1709 under the pseudonym 'Isaac Bickerstaff' he started to produce the tri-weekly *Tatler*, a venture subsequently joined by **Addison**. The paper's sudden termination in January 1711 has not been satisfactorily explained. Two months later the partnership started to produce *The Spectator* to which Addison's contribution was the larger. *The Spectator* was followed by *The Guardian* (March–October 1713) and the more political *Englishman* (1713–14). During the run of *The Spectator*, Steele engaged in polemical pamphleteering, the most notable examples being *The Importance of Dunkirk Consider'd* (1713), which provoked a strong reply from **Swift**, and *The Crisis* (1714), a consideration of the Hanoverian succession so ill-timed as to result in Steele being charged with issuing a seditious libel and being deprived of his seat as MP for Stockbridge. With the accession of George I this expulsion was palliated by a number of official appointments, the most important being patentee of the Theatre Royal, **Drury Lane**. This patent was lost after a political difference with the Duke of Newcastle thus eliciting from Steele *The Theatre*, a periodical which ran from January to April 1720 full of details of the contemporary theatrical world. The following year Walpole arranged for the patent to be restored, and in November 1722 Steele produced *The Conscious Lovers*, derived from Terence's *Andria*. The instant success of this play was in part due to the publicity and acrimonious reactions provoked by *The Theatre*. It is Steele's only important dramatic work: its high moral tone, and frequent performance, made it influential on the later 18th-century pieces known as **sentimental comedy**.

**Steevens, George** 1736–1800 Shakespearean scholar. He was born in Poplar and educated at Eton and King's College, Cambridge, which he left without a degree. After a brief spell in the Temple he settled in Hampstead, where he built up a fine library and an impressive collection of **Hogarth**'s engravings. He did important bibliographical work on Hogarth, which was used in *The Genuine Works of Hogarth* (1803–17).

His greatest passion was **Shakespeare**. In 1766 he published reprints of the Shakespeare quartos which he had borrowed from **Garrick**'s library. **Johnson** agreed to Steevens's plan for a more fully annotated version of his own edition of 1765. The 10-volume Johnson–Steevens edition appeared in 1773; a revised edition (1778) included **Edmond Malone**'s account of the plays' chronology and a further revision (1785) was prepared by Isaac Reed. Three variorum editions appeared after Steevens's death, incorporating his unpublished notes, though the last, edited by James Boswell the younger in 1821, was based largely on Malone's work. In life Steevens had quarrelled with Malone and set out to displace his 1790 edition of Shakespeare with his own 15-volume edition (1793). Designed to differ from Malone as much as possible, it took emendation to ridiculous lengths; some notes bore witness to the spite for which Steevens was also known.

He knew most of literary London, was one of Johnson's circle – helping him with *The Lives of the Poets* – and became a member of the Club in 1774. Something of a journalist as well as a scholar, he revelled in epigrams and parodies. His interest in forgery was shown by his role in the controversies surrounding **Chatterton** and **William Henry Ireland**, as well as the tombstone of King Hardecanute which he fabricated in 1789 as a hoax against Richard Gough of the Society of Antiquaries.

See also **Shakespeare: performance and criticism**.

**Stein, Gertrude** 1874–1946 American woman of letters. Born in Allegheny, Pennsylvania, Stein spent her early childhood in Vienna and Paris and then moved with her family to Oakland, California. She was educated at Radcliffe College (1893–7), where she studied philosophy with **William James**, and then enrolled at The Johns Hopkins Medical School (1897–1901), but failed several courses in her fourth year and did not take a degree. From 1903 until her death she lived in France, remaining in Paris except for the period of Nazi occupation, when she moved to the south. A lesbian, she lived with another expatriate American, Alice B. Toklas, from 1907 onwards. Friends of painters such as Picasso, Braque, Matisse, and Juan Gris, Stein and Toklas found themselves at the centre of an art movement. During the 1920s Stein became a famous literary figure; her salon was a gathering place for both European artists and expatriate Americans such as **Ernest Hemingway**, **Sherwood Anderson**, and **F. Scott Fitzgerald**.

Her first books – *Fernhurst* and *Q.E.D.* (later retitled *Things as They Are: A Novel in Three Parts*) – were written during the period 1903–5 but were not published until much later. Her first published work, which she claimed to have written under the influence of Flaubert's *Trois Contes* and Cézanne's painting, was *Three Lives: Stories of the Good Anna, Melanctha, and the Gentle Lena* (1909). Its prose style is highly unconventional: she periodically repeats phrases, sentences, even whole paragraphs, and more or less dispenses with normal punctuation. Her subsequent works, which were even more experimental, were considered exciting by some and merely eccentric by others. In *Tender Buttons* (1914) she uses words so idiosyncratically that many of her sentences literally make no sense. *The Making of Americans, Being a History of a Family's Progress* (1925) is an extremely long novel in which she again employs her technique of repetition.

Altogether, Stein produced over 500 titles – novels, poems, plays, articles, portraits of famous people and memoirs. Among the most notable of them are *Composition as Explanation* (1926), a critical work, *Lucy Church Amiably* (1930), a novel, *Four Saints in Three Acts* (1929),

Gertrude Stein.

a lyric drama staged as an opera (with music by Virgil Thompson) in 1934, *Lectures in America* (1935), *Everybody's Autobiography* (1937), which is her own autobiography, *Wars I Have Seen* (1945), a memoir, and *Brewsie and Willie* (1946), a novel about the lives of American soldiers in France during and immediately after World War II. One of her best-known works from the later period is **The Autobiography of Alice B. Toklas** (1933), a fictionalized account of her own life from her companion's point of view.

**Steinbeck, John** 1902–68 American novelist. Born in Salinas, California, Steinbeck studied marine biology at Stanford. His literary career began in 1929 with a romantic novel, *Cup of Gold*, about the buccaneer Sir Henry Morgan. His next book was a collection of short stories portraying the people in a farm community, *The Pastures of Heaven* (1932). *To a God Unknown* (1933), his second novel, is about a California farmer whose religion is a pagan belief in fertility and who sacrifices himself on a primitive altar to bring an end to drought. It was *Tortilla Flat* (1935), however, with its vivid picture of life among the *paisanos* in Monterey, that brought Steinbeck to prominence. The tone of his work changed with *In Dubious Battle* (1936), a powerful novel about a strike among migratory workers in the California fruit orchards, and with *Of Mice and Men* (1937), the story of two itinerant farm workers who yearn for some sort of home.

*The Long Valley* (1938), which consists of 13 stories set in Salinas Valley, was followed by **The Grapes of Wrath** (1939), his best-known work and the high point of his career. This novel of a family fleeing from the dust bowl of Oklahoma to what they hope will be a better life in California was awarded the Pulitzer Prize in 1940 and became a classic American film in the same year. It was followed by *The Moon is Down* (1942), a short novel about Norwegian resistance to the Nazi occupation, *Cannery Row* (1945), in which he returned to the *paisanos* of Monterey, and *The Wayward Bus* (1947), in which the passengers on a stranded bus in California become a microcosm of contemporary American frustrations. His non-fiction includes *Bombs Away: The Story of a Bomber Team* (1942), *The Log of the Sea of Cortez* (1951), a selection of his dispatches as a war correspondent, *Once There Was a War* (1958) and his book about rediscovering his own country, *Travels with Charley* (1962). Among his other novels are *The Pearl* (1947), *East of Eden* (1952), *Sweet Thursday* (1954) and *The Winter of Our Discontent* (1961). He was awarded the Nobel Prize for literature in 1962.

**Steiner, (Francis) George** 1929– Critic. Born in Paris, to Austrian Jewish parents, Steiner fled with his family to the United States in 1940. Here he was educated at the Universities of Chicago and Harvard. In the 1950s he studied at Oxford as a Rhodes Scholar and worked on the staff of *The Economist*, then returned to the United States to research and teach at Princeton. He has been a fellow of Churchill College, Cambridge, since 1961, and Professor of English and Comparative Literature at Geneva since 1974.

Steiner's writings are those of a *Kulturkritik* in the humanist traditions of Central European Jewry, showing a truly international range of learning. Over all his work – especially *Language and Silence* (1967), *In Bluebeard's Castle* (1971), and the novel *The Portage to San Cristobal of A. H.* (1981) – falls the shadow of the Holocaust. His characteristic concern is with the status of language and the literary imagination in a century of barbarism and political terror. His other principal works are *Tolstoy or Dostoevsky* (1959), *The Death of Tragedy* (1961), *After Babel* (1975) and *Antigones* (1984). Steiner has also written on chess, and edited *The Penguin Book of Modern Verse in Translation* (1966). A varied selection of his writings has been published as *George Steiner: A Reader* (1984).

**Stephen, Sir Leslie** 1832–1904 Critic and scholar. Stephen came from a family involved in the Evangelical group known as the 'Clapham Sect', whose leading member was William Wilberforce. His father Sir James Stephen, Under-Secretary of State for the Colonies, played a role in the campaign to abolish slavery. His older brother was Sir James Fitzjames Stephen, a distinguished jurist. Stephen himself was educated at Eton, King's College in London and

Trinity Hall, Cambridge. He was ordained and became a college tutor at Trinity Hall. His reading, meanwhile, had embraced Kant, **John Stuart Mill** and **Herbert Spencer**; he resigned his orders in 1870, adopting the agnosticism he set forth in *Essays on Free Thinking and Plain Speaking* (1873) and the *Agnostic's Apology*, published in *The Fortnightly Review* for June 1876.

Stephen's literary career began in 1864, when he went to London and wrote for periodicals including *The Saturday Review* and *Fraser's Magazine*. These essays were published in the lively and enduring collections, *Hours in a Library* (1874, 1876 and 1879). Stephen continued his contribution to criticism with studies of **Johnson** (1878), **Pope** (1880), **Swift** (1882), **George Eliot** (1902) and **Thomas Hobbes** (1904) for the English Men of Letters series. *A History of English Thought in the Eighteenth Century* (1876) is generally regarded as his most important work.

From 1871 to 1882 Stephen was editor of *The Cornhill Magazine*, publishing (among many other works) the serial version of **Thomas Hardy**'s *Far from the Madding Crowd*. He left the post when he accepted the editorship, offered by **George Smith** of Smith & Elder, of *The Dictionary of National Biography*. He oversaw its first 26 volumes and wrote many entries himself, particularly for the 18th and 19th centuries. He continued to contribute to the dictionary after giving up the editorship in 1891. Also an enthusiastic mountaineer, he edited *The Alpine Journal* (1868–71) and published *The Playground of Europe* (1871), a collection of essays on mountaineering.

Stephen's first wife was Harriet Marian, the daughter of **Thackeray**, and he was the model for Vernon Whitford in **Meredith**'s *The Egoist*. Virginia Stephen, his youngest daughter, became famous as **Virginia Woolf**, and used him as the basis for the character of Mr Ramsay in *To the Lighthouse*.

**Stephen Hero** See *Portrait of the Artist as a Young Man, A*.

**Stephens, James** 1882–1950 Poet and novelist. Born in the Dublin slums, such education as he had he found for himself. He worked in an office and wrote in his spare time, working at stories and poems with no success until a meeting with **George Russell** (AE). Russell encouraged him and helped arrange the publication of his first collection of poems, *Insurrections* (1909). *The Lonely God and Other Poems* (1909) followed, and in 1911 his novel *The Charwoman's Daughter*, a humorous idyll of life in a Dublin tenement, was published in *The Irish Review*. In 1912 his prose fantasy, *The Crock of Gold*, made him famous. It was followed by *The Demi-Gods* (1914), in the same vein.

Stephens studied Irish literature and mythology and contributed to the revival of interest in the Gaelic language; he was also a busy journalist and an active Sinn Feiner, and edited the poems of his friend and colleague Thomas MacDonagh when the latter was executed after the Easter Rising. Two editions of *Collected Poems* by James Stephens were published in 1926 (enlarged 1954). Volumes of short stories were *Here are Ladies* (with poems, 1913), *In the Land of Youth* (1924), *Etched in Moonlight* (1928). His novel *Deirdre* (1923) takes Celtic legend for its subject. Among other works by James Stephens were *The Insurrection in Dublin* (1916), *Irish Fairy Tales* (1920) and several essays on poetry.

**Sterne, Laurence** 1713–68 Novelist. The son of an army subaltern, Sterne was born in Clonmel, Tipperary, spent his earliest years in various garrison towns, and was educated for eight years in Halifax until his father died in 1731 and left the family penniless. A cousin helped him to enter Jesus College, Cambridge, as a 'sizar' (poor scholar); he took his degree in 1737 and then took orders, becoming vicar of Sutton-on-the-Forrest, in Yorkshire, in 1738, and later prebendary of York Minster. The period until 1759, when he was working in the restricted social environment of Yorkshire, furnished his subsequent writings with a mass of minutely observed details.

In 1741 Sterne married Elizabeth Lumley, and they moved to Stillington and had a daughter, Lydia. In 1758 his wife suffered an emotional breakdown: Sterne was involved in a number of 'sentimental' dalliances with local ladies at this time. He also began work in 1759 on his monumental novel *Tristram Shandy*, excerpts from which he read to a circle of friends at Skelton Hall, the home of a Cambridge contemporary, John Hall-Stevenson. The first two volumes were published in 1760, and their author was at once catapulted to literary fame (further volumes appeared in 1761, 1762, 1765 and 1767). Sterne came to London in 1760, where he was lionized by fashionable society, an experience he relished after the parochial surroundings of Yorkshire. He had been granted the perpetual curacy of Coxwold as part of his new recognition, however, and established his residence there as Shandy Hall. Sterne was flamboyant and delighted in playing the parts of his own characters in real life; he became a cult figure in London, the subject of outlandish anecdotes and, to some, the object of disapproval.

He began to publish his sermons in 1760 as *The Sermons of Mr Yorick* (after the parson who features in *Tristram Shandy*), with subsequent volumes in 1766 and 1769. There was a prodigious level of subscription to these volumes, despite the singular lack of doctrinal content and the infrequency of attention to such devotional

Laurence Sterne. A detail from the portrait by Joshua Reynolds, 1760. National Portrait Gallery, London.

topics as faith. As with his fiction, Sterne was in his oratory a masterful user of shock tactics, while at the same time remaining capable of powerful emotion. Tolstoy is said to have been influenced by these sermons, which he read as a young man. From 1762–4 Sterne lived abroad in Toulouse, with his daughter and depressed spouse, and much of the rest of his time was spent in travelling the more clement regions of the Continent, in the interests of alleviating his consumptive condition. He spent seven months in France and Italy during 1765, and recorded some of his impressions in the fragmentary and fictionalized narrative of *A Sentimental Journey* (1768), which also takes an incidental swipe at **Smollett** (the learned Smelfungus) of whose more caustic travel writing Sterne disapproved.

During 1767 Sterne formed an attachment to Mrs Eliza Draper, the wife of an East India Company officer for whose eyes he kept a journal from April to August, published after his death, with Mrs Draper's consent, as *Letters from Yorick to Eliza* (1775). In 1768, Sterne died of pleurisy in his lodgings in Old Bond Street; despite his insolvency, the novelist's family was aided by John Hall-Stevenson and Mrs Draper, who raised subscriptions on his posthumous publications.

The full importance of *Tristram Shandy* has been acknowledged only since the author's death. **Johnson**, **Richardson** and **Goldsmith** were among contemporaries to denounce its whirling, anarchic method or to be offended by its playful indecency. Yet Sterne's oddity is neither an accident nor mere perversity; it is the strategy of an inventive, thoughtful comic talent. His novel dismantles previous conventions of narrative, substituting baffling changes of perspective and a subjective, fragmentary psychological presence for the clear storyline and the reliable story-teller. It thus points the way to later experiments (by **Joyce** and his successors, for example), though not all of these would be conducted with that vein of good humour, delicate yet often dark, which runs so riddlingly through Sterne's work.

**Steuart (or Steuart-Denham), Sir James** 1712–80 Political economist. Born in Edinburgh, Steuart was a Jacobite who returned from a long exile in 1763. In 1767 he published *An Inquiry into the Principles of Political Economy*, which in some respects anticipated the work of **Adam Smith** (who knew Steuart and his book), not least in its view of man as 'acting uniformly in all ages, in all countries, and in all climates, from the principles of self-interest, expediency, duty and passion'.

**Stevens, Wallace** 1879–1955 American poet, born in Reading, Pennsylvania, and educated at Harvard. In 1900 he got a job on the editorial staff of *The New York Tribune* and then on the periodical *The World's Work*. He was unhappy with journalism, though, and in 1901 he entered New York Law School. He was admitted to the Bar in New York in 1904.

His early verse was published in *Trend* and in **Harriet Monroe**'s magazine *Poetry*. In 1915 one of his most famous poems, 'Sunday Morning', appeared in *Poetry*. In 1916 he joined the legal staff of the Hartford Accident and Indemnity Company, and remained with the firm until his death. In the same year he published 'Three Travelers Watch a Sunrise', which won the *Poetry* magazine prize for a verse play. It was produced in the following year at New York's Provincetown Playhouse. His first collection of verse, *Harmonium*, appeared in 1923, and though it sold fewer than 100 copies it was well received by reviewers such as **Marianne Moore**. For the next few years he wrote very little, concentrating on his career in the business world (he became vice president of his company in 1934). His second volume of poetry, *Ideas of Order*, appeared in 1935 and was followed in 1936 by *Owl's Clover*. This latter collection included poems written in response to charges that he was unconcerned with social issues. Another of his most famous poems provided the title piece of his fourth collection, *The Man With The Blue Guitar and Other Poems* (1937). Two further collections, *Parts of a World* and *Notes Toward a Supreme Fiction*, appeared in 1942, *Esthétique du Mal* in 1945 and *Transport to Summer* in 1947. *The Auroras of Autumn* was published in 1950, the year after he was awarded the Bollingen Prize. *The Necessary Angel: Essays on Reality and* *the Imagination* (1951), a collection of essays and addresses on poetry and art, received the National Book Award. *Opus Posthumous* (1957) contains poems, essays and plays, many hitherto unpublished. *The Letters of Wallace Stevens* appeared in 1966.

Poetry for Stevens was 'a part of the structure of reality'. Throughout his poetic career he worked with the joint awareness of his Romantic heritage and his distinctively modern sensibility. His poetry reveals, on the one hand, an effort to reconcile the product of his imagination with fundamental reality, and on the other his disbelief in the possibility of any such reconciliation. His use of language is meticulous and frequently exotic; his habitual use of extended metaphors makes his poetry distinctly difficult at times.

**Stevenson, Anne (Katherine)** 1933– Poet. Born in Cambridge to American parents, she was educated at the University of Michigan, Ann Arbor. Subsequently she has worked in publishing, as a tutor at Glasgow University and as the proprietor of a poetry bookshop, and she has held many posts as writer-in-residence and writing fellow. The central theme of her work is an attempt to 'rationally' communicate 'the reality of the a-rational', to use finite language to express the infinite. This dilemma is often mirrored in a landscape, be it the Sierra Nevada in *Reversals* (1969), the flat, unassuming Fenlands, or the stark grandeur of the north-east coast of Scotland in *Enough of Green* (1977). Other collections have been *Living in America* (1965), *Correspondences: A Family History in Letters* (1974), *Minute by Glass Minute* (1982), *The Fiction Makers* (1985), and a *Selected Poems 1965–1986* (1987). Her admission of the limits of language – she speaks movingly of being unable to capture 'the mudness of mud' – makes her poems poignant and courageous. She has also written a study of **Elizabeth Bishop** (1966).

**Stevenson, Robert Louis** 1850–94 Romance writer, essayist and poet. He was born in Edinburgh, the son of Thomas Stevenson, joint-engineer to the Board of Northern Lighthouses. He entered Edinburgh University in 1867 to study engineering but, since he had no interest in his father's profession, changed to law and was admitted advocate in 1875. He showed his interest in a literary career by student contributions to *The Edinburgh University Magazine* in 1871 and *The Portfolio* in 1873. Even in his childhood his health was extremely poor; as an adult, there were times when he could not even wear a jacket for fear of bringing on a haemorrhage of the lungs. In spite of this, he was all his life an enthusiastic traveller: an account of his canoe tour of France and Belgium was published in 1878 as *An Inland Voyage*, and *Travels With a*

*Donkey in the Cevennes* followed in 1879. In this year he travelled to California by emigrant ship and train: his account of these experiences was published posthumously in 1895 as *The Amateur Emigrant*. In America he married Mrs Fanny Osbourne, whom he had previously met in France. It was for her young son, Lloyd, that **Treasure Island** (1883) was originally devised. After a brief stay at Calistoga – recorded in *The Silverado Squatters* (1883) – he returned to England, determined to stand or fall by his ability to earn a living by writing.

Stevenson contributed to various periodicals, including **The Cornhill Magazine** and *Longman's Magazine*, where his best-known article, 'A Humble Remonstrance', was published in 1884, in reply to **Henry James**'s 'The Art of Fiction'. This friendly controversy about the relationship between life and art led to a lifelong friendship. Stevenson's essays and short stories were collected in *Virginibus Puerisque* (1881), *Familiar Studies of Men and Books* (1882), *New Arabian Nights* (1882), *The Merry Men* (1887), *Memories and Portraits* (1887), *Across the Plains* (1892) and *Island Nights' Entertainments* (1893). In addition to *Treasure Island*, his novels include *Prince Otto* (1885), **The Strange Case of Dr Jekyll and Mr Hyde** (1886), **Kidnapped** (1886) and its sequel *Catriona* (1893), **The Black Arrow** (1888) and **The Master of Ballantrae** (1889). He left unfinished **Weir of Hermiston** (1896) and *St Ives* (1897 and 1898), which was completed by **Sir Arthur Quiller-Couch**. Minor works include his charming books of poems, *A Child's Garden of Verses* (1885) and *Underwords* (1887), and his fustian dramas, *Deacon Brodie* (1880), *Beau Austin* (1892) and *Admiral Guinea* (1897), written in collaboration with **W. E. Henley**.

Stevenson left England in search of health in 1888 and never returned. After sailing for a while among the Pacific islands, he settled in Samoa and bought the Vailima estate. Here he enjoyed a period of comparative good health and literary productivity. He died suddenly from a cerebral haemorrhage and was buried on the island where he had been known as 'Tusitala' or 'The Teller of Tales'. During his period of residence in Samoa, Stevenson had become fascinated by the Polynesian culture and incensed at the European exploitation of the islands, engaging in various letters to *The Times* in London on the islanders' behalf. *In The South Seas* (1896) and *A Footnote to History* (1892) document his indignation; even more important are his two South Sea novellas, *The Beach of Falesá* (1893) and *The Ebb-Tide* (1894). *The Ebb-Tide* is a condemnation of European colonial exploitation which prefigures **Conrad**'s **Heart of Darkness**, while *The Beach of Falesá* was so inimical to Stevenson's readers and publishers that its full text has only recently been published (1984). Both stories expose the myth of a romantic South Sea paradise, and indict a mercantile European culture which will sacrifice everything in its hope of financial gain.

Long categorized merely as a belletrist and writer for children, Stevenson is now being widely revalued. It is unlikely that his poems and plays will ever revive, but his novels are beginning to take their rightful place in the adult tradition of early **modernism**. His interest in the romance, which he explores in 'Victor Hugo's Romances' (1874), 'A Gossip on Romance' (1883) and 'A Humble Remonstrance' (1884), shows his search for a fiction which would avoid the trap of representationalism, his focus on 'incident' as a type of narrative epiphany, and his use of old forms for new purposes.

**Stewart, Douglas** 1913– Playwright and poet. Born in Eltham, New Zealand, and educated at university in Wellington, Stewart crossed to Australia in 1938 and has made Sydney his home. He was literary editor of the Sydney *Bulletin* in 1940–61; *The Flesh and the Spirit* (1948) and *The Broad Stream* (1975) are both selections from his critical writing. His consistent interest in the Australian bush ballad is evident in several of his poems, particularly in *Glencoe* (1947), and in his several editions, with Nancy Keesing, of bush ballads (1955, 1957, 1967 and 1968). His *Collected Poems, 1936–1967* were published in 1967.

Stewart's high reputation as a writer of verse plays rests on three written for radio, *The Fire on the Snow* (1941), which is about Captain Scott's doomed expedition, *The Golden Lover* (1943), a Maori love story, and *The Earthquake Shakes the Land* (1944), and three for the stage, *Ned Kelly* (1944), *Shipwreck* (1948) and *Fisher's Ghost* (1961).

**Stewart, Dugald** 1753–1828 Philosopher. Born in Edinburgh, he completed his education at Edinburgh and Glasgow Universities, becoming Professor of Moral Philosophy at Edinburgh in 1785 and remaining there until 1810. A disciple of **Thomas Reid**, he did much to encourage a distinguished generation of Scottish writers and philosophers. Among his pupils were **James Mill**, **Sir Walter Scott**, **Henry Brougham** and **Sydney Smith**. His philosophical works include *The Elements of the Philosophy of the Human Mind* (1792–1827), *Outlines of Moral Philosophy* (1794), and *The Philosophy of the Active and Moral Powers* (1828).

**Stewart, J[ohn] I[nnes] M[ackintosh]** 1906– Critic, novelist and, as Michael Innes, author of **detective fiction**. Born in Edinburgh, he studied at Oriel College, Oxford, and taught English at Leeds, Adelaide and Belfast before returning to Oxford in 1949 as Student (i.e. fellow) of Christ Church. Under his own name Stewart has written a number of novels and critical studies, notably *Eight Modern Writers* (1963). But he is better known for his long and prolific career as Michael Innes, beginning with *Death at the President's Lodging* (1936, as *Seven Suspects* in USA), *Hamlet, Revenge!* (1937), *Lament for a Maker* (1938) and *Stop Press* (1939). Ingenious, urbane and donnishly playful, packed with casual erudition and witty talk, these books remain classics of their form. Their policeman-hero, John (later Sir John) Appleby, has since featured in other, more heterogeneous types of adventure. *The Secret Vanguard* (1940), *From London Far* (1946), *The Journeying Boy* (1949) and *Operation Pax* (1951, as *The Paper Thunderbolt* in USA) are chase novels in the tradition of **John Buchan**. *Appleby on Ararat* (1941), *The Daffodil Affair* (1942) and *Appleby's End* (1945) are frankly fantastic. *A Private View* (1952), *Silence Observed* (1961) and *A Family Affair* (1969) deal with the world of art. A later attempt to replace Appleby by his son Bobby – in, for example, *An Awkward Lie* (1971) – was not successful. More promising has been the introduction of the painter and reluctant detective Honeybath, who first appears in *The Mysterious Commission* (1975).

**stichomythia** Dialogue in alternating lines of verse, usually signifying conflict or quarrel. It is a common device in classical drama; the exchange between Richard and Elizabeth in **Shakespeare**'s *Richard III* (Act Four, Scene Four) provides a famous example from the English theatre.

**Stoddard, Solomon** 1643–1729 American Puritan minister, born and educated at Harvard. In 1670 he became pastor of the church at Northampton, Massachusetts.

His appointment marked a major turning-point in colonial American history. At first a proponent of the Half-Way Covenant, which granted partial church membership to children of regenerate parents, in 1677 he ceased to distinguish between full and Half-Way church members because of his conviction that the sacraments were vehicles for God's grace and thus should be available to all seeking Christian salvation. This view, referred to as 'Stoddardeanism', secured for him not only the title of 'Pope' but also the wrath of the orthodox Ministry of Massachusetts Bay. At the synod held in 1679 he defended his theory and practice in 'Nine Arguments against Examinations Concerning a Work of Grace before Admission to the Lord's Supper', a paper attacked by **Increase Mather**. The exchange initiated a pamphlet war with the Mathers in which Stoddard defended himself with *The Doctrine of Instituted Churches* (1700), *The Inexcusableness of Neglecting the Worship of God, under the Pretence of Being in an*

*Unconverted Condition* (1708) and *An Appeal to the Learned* (1709). Most of the churches throughout western Massachusetts accepted Stoddard's admission policy, which laid the theological groundwork for the Great Awakening.

**Stoker, Bram** 1847–1912 Novelist. Abraham Stoker was born and educated in Dublin, entering Trinity College in 1866. He became a civil servant, as well as drama critic of *The Dublin Mail* and editor of *The Penny Press*, before settling in London and working as personal manager to Sir Henry Irving. His first publication, *The Duties of Clerks of Petty Sessions in Ireland* (1879), was followed by 15 works of fiction; *Dracula* (1897) is the most famous. Stoker also wrote the two-volume *Personal Reminiscences of Henry Irving* (1906).

**Stone, Louis** 1871–1935 Australian novelist. Born in Leicester, William Louis Stone was taken to Australia by his parents in 1884. After attending classes at the University of Sydney and training as a primary schoolteacher, he taught in country areas of New South Wales and the Sydney suburbs. His best-known novel, *Jonah* (1911), is a realistic account of the life of a working-class larrikin ('street rowdy' or 'Jack the lad') in Sydney. Today it is highly regarded, as the first classic novel of Sydney life and an important work in the naturalist tradition, which has suffered from neglect in Australia until comparatively recently, but at the time of its publication it failed to bring Stone the recognition he had hoped for. Lack of critical or financial success and a progressive nervous illness, which ultimately led to his early retirement from teaching, prevented him from realizing the promise suggested in *Jonah* and he produced only one further novel, *Betty Wayside* (1915), which describes the fortunes of a woman pianist in Sydney. Stone subsequently became interested in drama and in the 1920s travelled to London in the hope of getting his only play *The Last of the Gods* (1923) staged.

**Stones of Venice, The** A three-volume study of architecture, history and society by **John Ruskin**, published in 1851–3. The first volume (1851) is an architectural essay of authoritative dryness and stylistic restraint whose initial chapter, 'The Quarry', is a panoramic anticipation of the entire work. But it is with the publication in 1853 of the last two volumes that the work assumes epic scope with Ruskin's praise of Venetian Gothic architecture as an expression of the feelings and aspirations of those who laboured to form it. By contrast with earlier Greek, Egyptian or Ninevite workmen – slaves all – the Gothic workman, a child of Christianity, enjoyed freedom because his faith recog-nized the liberality of the individual soul. Then, bringing his argument up to his own time, Ruskin envisages the Victorian workman as dehumanized and enslaved. In a well-known passage he compares the Venetian glass-blower, whose work may be clumsily cut and imperfect in form, with his 19th-century counterpart who is compelled to be 'accurate' and 'perfect'. He concludes that the Gothic is superior and that the Victorian worker should be delivered from commercial slavery. The last part of *The Stones of Venice* – 'The Fall' – records the debasement and corruption of the state, a decline traced by Ruskin through Early, Roman, and Grotesque Renaissance architecture. Pride, Luxury, Self-adulation, Infidelity – these degradations resound in the pages of the last volume as the immense work reaches a 'Conclusion' recapitulating the controlling motifs and warning the reader of similar contemporary tendencies.

*The Stones of Venice* states a compelling (if debatable) thesis and – despite some digression, sweeping generalization and over-confident claims – the innate power of the work and the magisterial sweep of the prose bear the reader along. In its scope and magnanimity, its humanitarianism, and its belief in Imperfection under Divine Law, the book remains a central Victorian document.

**Stonor letters, The** The correspondence and papers of the Stonor family, from Stonor in Oxfordshire. The earliest piece in the collection is a Latin charter of *c.*1290 and the latest is from 1483. In between are personal letters, legal and official documents and household accounts written by or to various members of the family in English, Latin and Anglo-Norman. Some of the letters provide a valuable insight into everyday affairs and domestic details of the Middle Ages.

**Stoppard, Tom** 1937– Playwright. Born in Czechoslovakia, Stoppard was taken to Singapore in infancy and then, in 1946, to England, where he completed his education at Pocklington School. He was a journalist in Bristol and then London, 1954–63, working freelance for the last three years while writing plays. The modest success of some early radio and television pieces preceded the startling popularity of *Rosencrantz and Guildenstern Are Dead* (1966). Stoppard's highly intelligent and quizzical investigation of artistic conventions and cultural assumptions is characteristic, not only of this play, but also of subsequent work like *The Real Inspector Hound* (1968), the short farce *After Magritte* (1970), *Jumpers* (1972), in which a variety of philosophical perceptions occupy all the dialogue while the murder story that constitutes the plot is almost completely ignored, and *Travesties* (1974), in which ideas that mattered intensely to such of its characters as Tristan Tzara, **James Joyce** and Lenin are made to matter very little. The pervasive mockery of these plays, however good-humoured, leaves Stoppard with very little firm ground to stand on, and some of his later work suggests a greater engagement with social and political realities. *Every Good Boy Deserves Favour* (1977), written for performance by actors and a symphony orchestra, the short *Cahoot's Macbeth* (1979) and *Night and Day* (1979) raise issues about freeom and totalitarianism. A preoccupation with the farcical aspects of espionage enlivens the excellent television play *Professional Foul* (1977) as it does the earlier television thriller *Neutral Ground* (1968) and the reductively brilliant radio play *The Dog It Was That Died* (1982). That Stoppard remains interested in something like 'pure craftsmanship' is implied by his adaptation of a play by the Austrian master of farce, Nestroy, as *On the Razzle* (1981), but another adaptation for the **National Theatre**, of a play by Schnitzler as *Undiscovered Country* (1979), lies behind Stoppard's own exploration of adultery in *The Real Thing* (1982).

**Storey, David** 1933– Novelist and playwright. Born into a mining family in Wakefield, Storey went to the Queen Elizabeth Grammar School, Wakefield, and then to the Slade School of Art. He was subsequently a professional Rugby league footballer, a teacher, a farmer and a tent erector. His rugby-playing days gave him the subject for his first novel, *This Sporting Life* (1960), a grim, rawly realistic portrait of a Rugby League footballer. Though critics have often classed the novel with the work of **Angry Young Men** such as **Alan Sillitoe** and **John Braine**, *This Sporting Life* presents a particularly harsh and hapless vision which anticipates Storey's later, more extreme portraits of isolated male protagonists suffering mental and emotional crisis. *Radcliffe* (1963) and *Pasmore* (1973) are both striking examples of this preoccupation. In *Radcliffe* the hero's tense homosexual love-affair generates self-division and conflict which eventually build to a climax of horrifying breakdown and violence. Storey's subsequent novels, *Saville* (which won the 1976 Booker Prize), *A Prodigal Child* (1982) and *Present Times* (1985), continue his two major themes: the loss of working-class roots through upward social movement, and the crises of marriage and career arising out of mid-life stasis and the narrowing of future opportunity.

Storey is also a notable dramatist. His realistically set but tangentially plotted plays include *The Contractor* (1970), which draws on one of Storey's previous occupations for its enactment of the putting up of a marquee at a wedding; *Home* (1970), set in a mental home; and *The Changing Room* (1972), about football.

***Story of a Country Town, The*** A novel by **E. W. Howe**, published in 1883. The story is told by Ned Westlock, the son of a stern, Bible-quoting minister-farmer. John Westlock's religious gatherings each Sunday are the only social occasions for the neighbours in the Midwestern farming community, and their severity of doctrine is commonly accepted. The important people in young Ned's life are Jo Erring, his mother's younger brother, who works on the Westlock farm, the young schoolteacher Agnes Deming, and the miller Damon Barker, to whom Jo is later apprenticed. It is Damon who makes Ned aware that there is a rich and varied world outside.

Jo falls in love with Mateel Shepherd and develops an increasing dislike for Clinton Bragg, a friend of the Shepherd family. Then, to everyone's surprise, John Westlock leaves the land and moves his family to the country town of Twin Mounds. He trades in land and buys the local newspaper, which Ned helps him to edit. Jo builds a mill and a home of his own and is accepted by Mateel Shepherd. John Westlock runs off with Damon's sister; Ned's mother becomes ill with worry, and Ned keeps the paper going on his own. Damon himself turns out to be the father whom Agnes Deming never knew and she goes to live with him at the mill. Ned's mother dies just before his father comes back, alone. The return is brief; John Westlock is now a man without resolution or purpose and he soon disappears again. Jo has been prospering but now he discovers that Mateel and the hated Clinton Bragg were once lovers. His insane jealousy leads to Mateel's death, and he then murders Bragg. He surrenders to the police but commits suicide. Ned and Agnes marry and settle down happily. Thus the life of the country town continues.

**Stout, Rex** See **detective fiction**.

**Stow, John** 1525–1605 Stow is one of the best known and also one of the most accurate of Elizabethan historians and antiquaries. He was a tailor for many years, but from 1560 onwards he was collecting and transcribing manuscripts and writing histories. In 1561 his annotated edition of **Chaucer** was printed. A series of editions or summaries of chroniclers followed: his summary of English chronicles (1565), and then, with the encouragement of **Matthew Parker**, Matthew of Westminster's *Flores Historiarum* (1567), Matthew Paris's *Chronicle* (1571) and Thomas of Walsingham's *Chronicle* (1574). His *Chronicles of England* (1580) was known as *Annals* in its later editions. His most famous work is his *A Survey of London* (1598), an account of London arranged according to the city's wards which contains information about both the city and its customs. It was revised and enlarged in 1603.

**Stow, Randolph** 1935– Australian novelist and poet. Born in Geraldton, Western Australia, Stow was educated at the University of Western Australia. He graduated with an arts degree in 1956 and has subsequently held brief appointments as a lecturer at the Universities of Adelaide, Western Australia and Leeds. He has also studied anthropology and worked on a mission station for Aborigines in northwest Australia and as a patrol officer in Papua New Guinea. Since 1960 he has lived in England, mainly in East Anglia, but has travelled widely. He has won the Miles Franklin Award (1958) and the Patrick White Award (1979). Stow's reputation was established by five novels published between 1956 and 1965. The first two, *A Haunted Land* (1956) and *The Bystander* (1957), link a poetic feeling for landscape with an account of turbulent, emotional lives determined by family origins. Reminiscent of **Patrick White**'s *Voss*, *To the Islands* (1958; revised edition 1982) is a symbolic fable about an old missionary who experiences a spiritual crisis and journeys into a desolate inner landscape which takes him 'to the islands', an Aboriginal expression for death. *Tourmaline* (1963), Stow's densest symbolic novel, and the more realistic *The Merry-Go-Round in the Sea* (1965) are also concerned with self-exploration. After these novels he stopped writing fiction for some time, but continued to write poetry, a field in which he is best known for his technically assured lyrics. His verse is collected in *A Counterfeit Silence* (1969). During the years when he was not writing fiction, Stow wrote for musical theatre with the composer Peter Maxwell Davies. He returned to the novel with one of his finest books, *Visitants* (1979), an account of a confrontation between a developed and a primitive culture. His most recent novel, *The Suburbs of Hell* (1984), deals with a series of murders in a town on the East Anglian coast.

**Stowe, Harriet Beecher** 1811–96 American novelist, born in Litchfield, Connecticut, where her father, the influential and controversial Calvinist preacher Lyman Beecher, was rector of the First Church. In 1824 she went to Hartford, where her sister Catharine – later a prominent writer and ideologue of domesticity, feminine education, and woman's separate sphere – had founded the Hartford Female Seminary. Harriet was a student and then a teacher there until 1832, when the whole family accompanied Lyman to Cincinnati, where he became president of the new Lane Theological Seminary and took up the mission of converting the West. In 1834 Harriet began to write sketches and short fiction for the *Western Monthly* and other, mostly evangelical, periodicals. Her first book,

*The Mayflower: Sketches and Scenes and Characters Among the Descendants of the Puritans*, appeared in 1843. In 1836 she married Calvin E. Stowe, a professor at Lane, with whom she would eventually have seven children. The Cincinnati years were marked by poverty, isolation, and a cholera epidemic in which the Stowes lost a young son. In 1850 Calvin Stowe was offered a professorship at Bowdoin, and they moved to Brunswick, Maine.

There, amid household cares, Harriet wrote her first novel, **Uncle Tom's Cabin**, prompted by the passage of the Fugitive Slave Law. Like most of her subsequent novels, it was written as a serial, and began appearing in the *National Era* magazine in 1851. It was an immediate and scandalous best-seller, both in the USA and abroad. Stowe made three triumphal tours of Europe (1853, 1856 and 1859), where she formed important friendships with **George Eliot**, **Elizabeth Barrett Browning** and Lady Byron, among others, and gathered material for *Sunny Memories of Foreign Lands* (1854). Meanwhile, attacks on the veracity of her portrayal of the South led her to publish *The Key to Uncle Tom's Cabin* (1853), a book of source material. A second anti-slavery novel, *Dred: A Tale of the Great Dismal Swamp* (1856), told the story of a dramatic attempt at a slave rebellion, while attacking ministers who had failed to take a strong anti-slavery stand and demonstrating again the redemptive powers of Christian womanhood, white and black.

After this, however, Stowe turned away from the political sphere. *The Minister's Wooing* (1859), set in New England, is a novel of love and marriage in the context of Calvinist uncertainty about salvation and the dread of seeing a loved one die unconverted. (She drew on the experiences of her sister, whose fiancé had been lost at sea, and of her own grief at the drowning of her son Henry in 1837.) *Agnes of Sorrento* (1862) took up similar theological themes but was set in the Catholic Italy of Savonarola. *The Pearl of Orr's Island* (1862), another treatment of the redemption of wayward youth by female piety and example, drew heavily on the local colour of the New England shore; **Sarah Orne Jewett** credited this book with inspiring her own career. Stowe wrote three more works in a similar vein: **Oldtown Folks** (1869) and *Oldtown Fireside Stories* (1871) drew on her husband's childhood memories, and *Poganuc People* (1878), her last novel, on her own. She also wrote three novels of New York society: *Pink and White Tyranny* (1871), which attacks female frivolity, the French, and divorce, and *My Wife and I* (1871) and its sequel, *We And Our Neighbours* (1875), in which she shows how rural values can be brought to the city.

She was a remarkably prolific writer of both books and articles in many genres and styles.

She wrote children's books, travelogues, purely theological works, such as *In The Footsteps of the Master* (1877) and *Bible Heroines* (1878), temperance tracts and practical articles about housekeeping, decoration and the 'servant problem', including the highly influential *The American Woman's Home* (1869, co-written with her sister Catharine). Throughout her career she was both celebrated and financially successful.

**Strachey, (Giles) Lytton** 1880–1932 Biographer and essayist. The son of a distinguished soldier and Indian administrator, Sir Richard Strachey, he was born in London and educated at Leamington College and Liverpool University (1897–9). Then he went up to Trinity College, Cambridge, where his friends included **John Maynard Keynes, Leonard Woolf, E. M. Forster** and Saxon Sydney-Turner. He was elected to the **Apostles** in 1902. Later, in London, he became a prominent member of the **Bloomsbury Group**.

In 1904, Strachey became a reviewer for *The Spectator*; he was also to contribute to *The Edinburgh Review*, *The Nation*, *The Athenaeum* and *Life and Letters*. He published two collections of verse, *Prolusiones Academicae* (1902) and *Euphrosyne* (1905), and won the Chancellor's Medal for 'Ely: An Ode'. His first book, *Landmarks in French Literature*, was published in 1912 for the Home University Library series.

Strachey was a conscientious objector during World War I, and he gave up his attempt to make an academic career. *Eminent Victorians* (1918), containing controversial essays on Florence Nightingale, Cardinal Manning, **Dr Thomas Arnold**, and General Gordon, illustrated his contention that the biographer should 'attack his subject in unexpected places' and 'shoot a sudden, revealing searchlight into obscure recesses'. It was highly iconoclastic and, with *Queen Victoria* (1921), *Books and Characters, French and English* (1922), *Elizabeth and Essex: A Tragic History* (1928), *Portraits in Miniature* (1931) and *Characters and Commentaries* (1933), has been cited as originating the art of modern biography. Strachey was, perhaps, the first biographer to use Freudian insights, and these were accompanied by sharp but affectionate satire and fine narrative skill.

Throughout his life Strachey suffered from poor health. He died after losing the battle against cancer, and his close friend, the painter Dora Carrington (Mrs Ralph Partridge), who had nursed him throughout his last illness, committed suicide shortly afterwards.

*Spectatorial Essays*, a collection of reviews published in *The Spectator* (1904–14), appeared in 1964.

**Strand Magazine, The** A periodical founded by George Newnes in 1891, it survived until 1950.

Perhaps best known for publishing **Sir Arthur Conan Doyle**'s Sherlock Holmes stories, it also included fiction by **Rudyard Kipling, H. G. Wells, W. W. Jacobs, Somerset Maugham, Arthur Morrison, Stanley Weyman, Anthony Hope, Jerome K. Jerome** and **P. G. Wodehouse**, among others.

***Strange Case of Dr Jekyll and Mr Hyde, The*** A novel by **Robert Louis Stevenson**, published in 1886. Apart from *Treasure Island*, it is probably his best-known work.

The mystery of Jekyll and Hyde is gradually revealed to the reader through the disparate narratives of Mr Enfield, Mr Utterson, Dr Lanyon and Poole, the butler at Jekyll's house. The respectable Dr Jekyll wants to separate the good and evil aspects of his nature. By means of a transforming drug he has secretly developed in his laboratory, he succeeds in freeing his evil propensities into the repulsive form of Mr Hyde. Initially he finds it easy to return to the personality of Jekyll, but in time this becomes more difficult and he finds himself slipping involuntarily into being Hyde. Eventually his supplies of the drug run out and he cannot manage to reduplicate the chemical formula. Hyde is now wanted for murder, and Jekyll kills himself. The body discovered in his sanctum is that of Hyde, but the confession Jekyll leaves behind establishes that the two men were versions of the same person.

The story has attracted much commentary, being read as another version of the Scottish Arminianism of **James Hogg**'s *Private Memoirs and Confessions of a Justified Sinner*, as a variant of the *doppelgänger* myth, and as a pre-Freudian study of ego and libido. **G. K. Chesterton** noted, however, that Hyde is not a diabolic *alter ego* but a diminished part of Jekyll's whole personality, pure evil where Jekyll is a mixture of good and evil. Jekyll's deluded belief that, because man is dual rather than whole, the good in him can hence be separated from the evil, provides a study in degeneration and ultimate human responsibility.

***Strange Interlude*** A play in nine acts by **Eugene O'Neill**, first performed in New York in 1928. Its extreme length is largely the result of O'Neill's decision to have his characters articulate the sub-text of their speeches as well as the text, to say what they are thinking as well as what they actually voice. With this rather daring and unconventional use of dramatic 'asides', the play received a mixed critical reception, but won a Pulitzer Prize.

Nina Leeds, the daughter of a New England professor, has been prevented by her father from marrying the man she loves before he goes to war. His death in the war turns her against her father, and she leaves home to become a nurse. In homage to her dead lover, she offers herself as mistress to any war-wounded man who wants her, and is saved from this promiscuity by a fond but loveless marriage to Sam Evans, motivated by her wish for a child. When she discovers that there is madness in her husband's family she obtains a secret abortion and asks her husband's friend, Dr Edmund Darrell, to impregnate her. Darrell's life is destroyed by his love for her, and Nina's possessiveness for their son almost leads her to destroy that son's own hopes of marriage.

**stream of consciousness** A technique used by novelists to represent a character's thoughts and sense impressions without syntax or logical sequence. Four main types have been identified: soliloquy, omniscient narration of mental processes, and both direct and indirect interior monologue.

The phrase 'stream of consciousness' was first used by **William James** in his *Principles of Psychology* (1890) to describe the random flux of conscious and sub-conscious thoughts and impressions in the mind. A parallel description can be found in Bergson's account (1889) of the 'élan vital', popularized in England by **George Bernard Shaw**. Literature can show many examples before both James and Bergson of the attempt to capture inner consciousness, notably **Laurence Sterne**'s *Tristram Shandy* (1767). But stream of consciousness becomes important as a technique with the rise of **modernism** in the 20th century. It can be seen in the works of **Joyce** (who claimed to have inherited it from Edouard Dujardin's *Les Lauriers Sont Coupés*, 1888), **Dorothy Richardson**, **Virginia Woolf** and, among Americans, **William Faulkner**.

**Streatfeild, Noel** 1895–1986 Children's author. The daughter of a Sussex clergyman, she studied acting at RADA after a somewhat rebellious childhood. Her career on the stage was not greatly successful and by 1929 she gave it up in favour of writing. There followed some undistinguished novels for adults, beginning with *The Whicharts* (1931), and then her first and best book for children, *Ballet Shoes* (1936). Drawing freely on her own experience, it describes a family of orphans who eventually make good in the ballet and theatre world. Its success was instant, young readers relishing its blend of hard fact about auditions, drudgery and stage fright with the romance of final artistic triumph. Noel Streatfeild wrote a number of other 'career' novels, including *Tennis Shoes* (1937) and a novel about skating, *White Boots* (1951). *The Bell Family* (1954) chronicles the more domestic adventures of a gently idealized middle-class family that first featured in radio plays written for the BBC's programme *Children's Hour*.

*Street Scene* A three-act play by **Elmer Rice**, first presented in 1929. It was a critical and popular success, running for 601 performances and winning a Pulitzer Prize. In 1947 Rice worked with **Langston Hughes** and the composer Kurt Weill on a successful musical adaptation.

Despite many previous successes in the theatre, Rice had difficulty finding a producer for this ground-breaking drama, which required over 50 actors and an innovative and elaborate set to present a day in the life of a New York City tenement. In the course of one extremely hot day, the tenants, drawn from many ethnic groups, converse, complain, quarrel, and gossip, mostly about one of their number, Mrs Maurrant. A baby is born; a poor family is evicted after a visit from an unsympathetic social worker; the relative merits of socialism and capitalism are discussed; Mr Maurrant comes home to find his wife in bed with another man, shoots them both, and is captured by the police; and Rose Maurrant, the heroine, rejects the attentions both of her boss, the flashy Harry Easter, and of Sam Kaplan, the earnest young law student who lives in the building, and strikes out on her own.

*Streetcar Named Desire, A* A play by **Tennessee Williams**, first performed in New York in 1947. It ran for 855 performances and received both a New York Drama Critics Circle Award and a Pulitzer Prize.

The action revolves around the visit of Blanche Du Bois to her sister Stella, who lives in New Orleans, near the stop of the streetcar named Desire, with her brutish husband Stanley Kowalski. Blanche has an appearance of ladylike grace, and constantly refers to her early life at the family estate of Belle Rêve. Bewildered by her new environment and by the antagonism of her brother-in-law, she turns to his friend Mitch for consolation and company. Stanley, however, learns that Blanche is not the Southern belle she purports to be, and tells Mitch that she is in fact a lonely alcoholic who has been forced into bankruptcy and who has lost her job because of an affair with a young boy who reminded her of her dead husband. Blanche's antagonistic relationship with Stanley culminates in his raping her. She tells Stella but Stella does not believe her, and at the end of the play she is taken into psychiatric care.

**Strickland, Agnes** 1796–1874 Biographer. Born in London, the daughter of a landed family, she began her literary career as a poet. Later she turned to historical fiction for children and eventually to the short popular biographies for which she is remembered: *The Lives of the Queens of England from the Norman Conquest*

(1840–8) and *The Lives of the Queens of Scotland, and English Princesses* (1850–9).

**Strong, L[eonard] A[lfred] G[eorge]** 1896–1958 Author. Born in Plymouth, of mainly Irish stock, he was educated at Brighton College and at Wadham College, Oxford. He worked as a preparatory schoolmaster before becoming a full-time writer in 1930. The successful *Dewer Rides* (1929), a novel of Dartmoor, was followed by a great deal of fiction from his pen, some of it with Irish backgrounds. *Travellers* (1945) won the James Tait Black Prize. Extremely versatile and fluent, he wrote plays and radio scripts, compiled anthologies, and produced several biographies and autobiographies. His lyric verse, collected as *The Body's Imperfection* (1957), shows him pausing more reflectively than his vast output usually allowed.

**structuralism** Movement of thought affecting a number of intellectual disciplines, including anthropology, philosophy, history and literary criticism. The common element derives from linguistics and especially the writings of Ferdinand de Saussure (see **semiotics**). He argued that linguistics should study the 'synchronic' dimension of language (the system of relations within language operating at a given moment) rather than its 'diachrony' (temporal dimension). Speakers are able to use the system by registering the differences between possible elements within it. For example, at the level of the phoneme (minimum unit of sound) we distinguish between 'bus' and 'buzz' on the basis of a difference between a voiced (s) and an unvoiced (z) sibilant. Structuralists have applied the patterns of 'binary oppositions' derived from phonemics, syntax or grammar to human sign-systems of various kinds.

Claude Lévi-Strauss (1908– ) developed 'phonemic' analyses of kinship relations, myths, rites, and so on. Roland Barthes (1915–80) examined *haute cuisine*, narrative discourse, garments and all kinds of social artefacts. The underlying idea is that all human performances (*paroles*) presuppose a system (*langue*) of differential relations.

Structuralist narratology is especially well advanced. Tzvetan Todorov, Gérard Genette and A. J. Greimas are the key theorists. Propp developed the theories of the Russian Formalist Vladimir Propp, fitting them more closely to the linguistic model. The basic syntactical functions of subject and predicate have their equivalent functions in narrative: actor and action. In *The Morphology of the Folktale* (1968) Propp found 35 'functions' (basic narrative actions) and seven 'spheres of action' in the Russian folk-tale. Greimas's universal 'grammar' of narrative proposes three binary oppositions which include the six roles (*actants*) he requires: (1) subject/object; (2) sender/receiver; (3) helper/opponent. The pairs allow a description of all the fundamental patterns governing narrative: (1) aiming at something, (2) communicating, (3) helping or hindering. Lévi-Strauss developed a phonemic analysis of the Oedipus story; he aimed to establish the structural pattern which gives the myth its meaning. Todorov outlined a comprehensive application of the linguistic model, discovering the rules of agency, adjectival and verbal functions, mood, aspect and so on. Genette divided narrative into three levels: story, discourse and narration. These levels are related to one another through three aspects derived from three verbal qualities: tense, mood and voice.

The most influential theorist on modern criticism is probably Roman Jakobson (1896–1982) whose essays 'Linguistics and Poetics' and 'Two Aspects of Language' are especially important. The latter develops a theory of the binary structure of language which is typified in the opposition between metaphor and metonymy. **David Lodge** has applied the theory to develop a complete structural study of modern literature.

Jonathan Culler, using the mentalistic linguistics of Noam Chomsky (1928– ), argued for a reader-oriented structuralist poetics which sought the rules governing the reader's construction of a text's meaning. Culler has subsequently adopted and developed the deconstructive theories of Jacques Derrida (see **deconstructive criticism**).

**Strutt, Joseph** 1749–1802 Antiquary. Apprenticed as an engraver, Strutt was awarded both silver and gold medals at the Royal Academy. He devoted himself to antiquarian researches and published a number of important illustrated works which were often the first in their field, including: *The Regal and Ecclesiastical Antiquities of England* (1773), *Manners, Customs, Arms, Habits, &c. of the People of England* (3 vols., 1774–6), and his *Biographical Dictionary of Engravers* (2 vols., 1785–6), upon which all subsequent such dictionaries have been based. His best-known work is the curiously titled *Glig Gamena Angel Deod* (1801), a history of popular sports and pastimes. **Scott** acknowledged Strutt's unfinished romance 'Queenhoo Hall' as the original impetus for his Waverley novels.

**Strype, John** 1643–1737 Church historian. Born in London, he attended St Paul's School and went on to Jesus College, Cambridge, but transferred to St Catharine's Hall. After Cambridge he became curate and lecturer at Leyton in Essex (1669) and from 1689 to 1724 added a lectureship at Hackney to his activities. He was given the sinecure of West Tarring in Sussex in 1711.

Strype made a remarkable collection of Tudor

documents that are now in the British Library. The first of his documentary works was *Memorials of Thomas Cranmer* (1694). Works on the lives of Sir Thomas Smith (1698), John Aylmer (1701), and Sir John Cheke (1705) were followed by his magnum opus, *Annals of the Reformation and Establishment of Religion, and other Occurrences in the Church of England, during the First Twelve Years of Queen Elizabeth's Reign* (4 vols., 1709–31). Lives of Edmund Grindal (1710) and John Whitgift (1718) were also written while work proceeded on the *Annals*. Strype's *Ecclesiastical Memorials Relating Chiefly to Religion and the Reformation of It under Henry VIII, Edward VI and Mary* was published in 1721. He also edited and extended **John Stow**'s *Survey* as *A Survey of the Cities of London and Westminster*, adding a life of Stow (1720, with a much enlarged edition in 1754).

**Stuart, Francis** 1902– Irish novelist. Born in Australia of Irish parents, Stuart grew up in Ireland, and was educated in various English schools, including Rugby. In 1920 he married Iseult Gonne, daughter of Maud Gonne, the Irish nationalist loved by **Yeats**. He fought on the Republican side in the Irish Civil War and was imprisoned in 1922–3. Between 1931 and 1940, Stuart published 10 novels, but attracted little notice. In 1940 he went to the University of Berlin as a lecturer and stayed there throughout World War II. He was imprisoned for a year by French occupation forces after the war, probably because of the weekly broadcasts to Ireland he made in 1942–4, supporting Irish neutrality and sympathizing with IRA prisoners in the North and South. After some years in Germany he moved to London in 1951, and returned to Ireland in 1958, where he now lives. His wife Iseult died in 1954; his second wife, Gertrud Meissner, died in 1986.

The German experiences are reflected in *The Pillar of Cloud* (1948) and *Redemption* (1949). With *The Flowering Cross* (1950), these form a trilogy which is later balanced by three novels dealing variously with the Irish political crisis: *Memorial* (1973), *A Hole in the Head* (1977) and *The High Consistory* (1981). The fulcrum of these trilogies is *Black List, Section H* (1971), an autobiographical novel, first published in the USA, and the first of his novels to bring him wider acclaim and respect. Stuart's work is dominated by the artist's search for integrity, gained through disgrace and repudiation. This, in turn, becomes an analogue for the saintly life, lived fiercely and with a religious intensity which rebukes all official or institutionalized creeds and codes.

**Stubbes, Philip** ?1555–1610 Puritan pamphleteer. He is best known for *The Anatomy of Abuses* (1583), a denunciation of sinful customs

and fashions, which includes a section on stage plays. His earlier works had been broadside ballads, usually demonstrating God's vengeance on sin. *A Christal Glass for Christian Women* (1591), a biographical account of his wife Katherine, was extremely popular.

**Stubbs, William** 1825–1901 Historian. Born at Knaresborough in Yorkshire, he was educated at Ripon grammar school and Christ Church, Oxford, where he fell lastingly under the influence of the **Oxford Movement**. He became a fellow of Trinity College in 1848, rector of Navestock in Essex in 1850, and Regius Professor of Modern History at Oxford in 1866. In later years he was canon of St Paul's (1879), Bishop of Chester (1884) and Bishop of Oxford (1889). As a historian, he made major contributions to the medieval Rolls Series, beginning with *Registrum Sacrum Anglicanum* (1858). He is best remembered for *Select Charters and Other Illustrations of English Constitutional History from the Earliest Times to the Reign of Edward I* (1870) and *The Constitutional History of England* (1873–8), which takes his subject up to the accession of the Tudors.

**Studies in the History of the Renaissance** Essays by **Walter Pater** first published in book form in 1837, subsequently retitled *The Renaissance: Studies in Art and Poetry*.

This compendium of early writing in which Pater extends the chronology of the Renaissance from the Middle Ages to the 18th century is mainly concerned with Italy, although it includes his early essay on Winckelmann (that 'last fruit of the Renaissance'), one on Du Bellay and an initial essay titled 'Two early French stories'. Marked by grace and simplicity, elegance and disciplined fluency, the essays discuss the work of Pico della Mirandola, Botticelli, Leonardo, della Robbia and others, and explicate Pater's aesthetic theories. It is, however, the 'Conclusion' that is of signal importance. Excised from the second edition of *The Renaissance* for fear it might 'mislead' young men, its cry of 'Art for Art's sake' became the manifesto of the **Aesthetic Movement** even though Pater did not embrace it with the fervour of his disciples. He stresses that the intensity of the moment, the profundity of experience and the necessity of one's presence 'at the focus where the greatest number of vital forces unite in their purest energy' are central to self-realization and fullness of life: in Pater's memorable phrasing, 'To burn always with this hard, gemlike flame, to maintain this ecstasy, is success in life.'

**Study in Scarlet, A** See **Sherlock Holmes stories**.

**Stukeley, William** 1687–1765 Antiquary.

Born at Holbeach, Lincolnshire, Stukeley left the Free School there when he was 13 to join his father's legal business. Dissatisfied with the law, he persuaded his father to send him to Cambridge and he was admitted to Corpus Christi College in 1703. After Cambridge he practised medicine, first in Lincolnshire, then, from 1717, in London. At this time he was made a Fellow of the Royal Society and helped establish the Society of Antiquaries, whose first Secretary he became in 1718. He cultivated connections with painters, engravers and intellectual noblemen. He was interested in astronomy and was an early enthusiast of Gothic architecture.

His biographer Stuart Piggott demonstrates that Stukeley's work up until his ordination in 1729 was 'reliable and objective' but that from his ordination until his death it was 'speculative and fantastic'. His early work on Stonehenge and Avebury, though indebted to earlier scholars such as **John Aubrey**, was remarkable; and in his sense of nature Stukeley anticipates such figures as **Richard Jefferies** and **W. H. Hudson**. After 1729 an obsession with the Druids as builders of the stone circles took hold of him: he produced *Stonehenge: A Temple Restored to the British Druids* (1740) and *Abury: A Temple of the British Druids* (1743). Eccentric as this Druidism may now appear, poets such as **William Collins**, **William Mason, Thomas Gray** and the **William Blake** of the Prophetic Books stand clearly in his debt. Stukeley's particular kind of primitivism provides an interesting link between the early British antiquaries and the first Romantics.

**Sturt, George** 1863–1927 Essayist and historian of rural society. Sturt, whose early works were published under the name of 'George Bourne', was born at Farnham in Surrey and educated at Farnham grammar school, where he taught from 1878 to 1884. On the death of his father in 1884 Sturt inherited the family wheelwright business and, under **Ruskin**'s influence, advocated the traditions of local craftsmanship. He gave up business for writing in 1900. His books included *The Bettesworth Book* (1901) and its sequel, *Memoirs of a Surrey Labourer* (1907). *Change in the Village* (1912) was followed by *A Farmer's Life* (1922). In 1923 he published *The Wheelwright's Shop* under his own name, a chronicle of the family business which had begun at Farnham in 1706. It describes the stages in the construction of farm waggons before the advent of the tractor and notes that 'the provincial wheelwright could hardly help reading, from the waggon-lines, tales of haymaking and upland fields, of hilly roads and lonely woods and noble horses'.

**Styron, William** 1925– American novelist, born in Newport News, Virginia, and educated at Davidson College and Duke University. His first novel, *Lie Down in Darkness*, was published in 1951. Other novels include *The Long March* (1952), *Set This House on Fire* (1960), *The Confessions of Nat Turner* (1967), and *Sophie's Choice* (1979). His work generally concerns forms of oppression, ranging from that of the family to the wider social issues of racism and politics. His account of Nat Turner's rebellion met with considerable protest from the black community; *William Styron's Nat Turner: Ten Black Writers Respond* (1968) contains essays which reflect the animosity toward his 'white' approach to race relations. In *Sophie's Choice*, his most commercially successful novel to date, he deals with the horrors of the Holocaust as it affects the lives of those who survived the concentration camps and Nazi persecution. *This Quiet Dust* (1982) is a collection of essays.

*Subjection of Women, The* An essay by **John Stuart Mill**, published in 1869. 'The purpose of that book', Mill declared, 'was to maintain the claim of women, whether in marriage or out of it, to perfect equality in all rights with the male sex'.

In the last published work of his life Mill drew together the political, moral and social ideas diffused throughout the rest of his work in pungent rhetorical form. 20th-century feminism has drawn attention to the essay again. It remains an advanced piece of criticism, historically speaking, but is flawed by Mill undervaluing and therefore neglecting the sexual aspect of this political struggle.

**Suckling, Sir John** 1609–41 Poet and playwright. Born into a well-established Norfolk family (Suckling's father served as Comptroller of James I's household), the poet was educated at Trinity College, Cambridge, and at Gray's Inn. His early manhood was spent in military and ambassadorial adventures in Europe, and he was knighted in 1630. Suckling returned to England in 1632 and embarked on a career of less honourable if not less public activity: the prodigal dissipation of his patrimony. His reputation for both wit and extravagance led **John Aubrey** to characterize him as 'the greatest gallant of his time, and the greatest Gamester, both for Bowling and Cards . . . [he] invented the game of Cribbidge'. By the late 1630s, Suckling's literary reputation was fully fledged; his satire *The Wits* (or *Sessions of the Poets*), a mock-ballad in which contemporary writers contend for the laurel and are discomfited (Suckling himself refuses the summons, preferring bowls to the Muses), had been sung before the king in 1637, and his tragedy *Aglaura* was staged twice the next year, to great applause, the second time with a re-written fifth act, in which the catastrophe was averted. A bibliographically magnificent folio text, printed in 1638, was a popular subject for lampoon. In 1639, Suckling resumed soldiership, ingloriously participating in Charles I's defeat by the Scots; in 1641, he levied troops as part of the 'Army Plot' conspiracy to free the imprisoned Earl of Strafford by force. The plot was discovered, and Suckling fled to France to avoid arrest. There he committed suicide, according to Aubrey, by taking poison.

Apart from *Aglaura*, Suckling's plays comprise the unfinished *The Sad One* (a first draft of *Aglaura*), *The Goblins*, a musical comedy-romance indebted to **The Tempest**, and *Brennoralt*, a tragedy whose protagonist has often been considered a self-portrait (*The Discontented Colonel* is an alternative title). *The Goblins* and *Brennoralt*, both in the repertory of the **King's Men** by 1641, were printed in *Fragmenta Aurea* (1646), the collection which also includes Suckling's most famous poems, 'Ballade. Upon a Wedding' and 'Why So Pale and Wan, Fond Lover?' The influences of **Shakespeare**, **Jonson** and **Donne** can be variously felt throughout Suckling's work, and he shares many characteristics with his close friends **Carew** and **D'Avenant**; what **Rochester** aptly described as 'Suckling's easy pen' makes him one of the most attractive of the **Cavalier poets**.

**Summer of the Seventeenth Doll** A play by **Ray Lawler**, first performed in Melbourne, Australia, in 1955. It was the first Australian play to win an international audience. Its realistic appraisal of the Australian cult of 'mateship' and its reliance on female submissiveness administered a sharp shock to a theatre that had taken both for granted.

Roo and Barney are sugarcane cutters who work for half the year and return each summer to their waiting women, bringing always a kewpie doll among their gifts. Having failed to notice the needs of the women, they are unprepared for the discovery that the 17th summer can no longer be the same as the previous 16.

**Summoner's Tale, The** See *Canterbury Tales, The*.

**Sun Also Rises, The** A novel by **Ernest Hemingway**, published in 1926. The English edition which appeared the following year was entitled *Fiesta*. Set in the mid 1920s, it deals with the 'lost generation' of American and British expatriates who have settled in Paris, depicted here as a moral wasteland of drunkenness and promiscuity.

The story is narrated by Jake Barnes, an American journalist, who has been rendered sexually impotent by a wound suffered during World War I. Jake is in love with the queen of the pleasure-seekers, Lady Brett Ashley. Brett returns his love but, knowing that consum-mation is impossible, agrees to marry Mike Campbell. Jake lives according to a self-taught emotional pragmatism, which is contrasted with the self-pitying sentimentalism of his acquaintance Robert Cohn. Robert, under Brett's spell, joins her, Mike, and Jake on a jaunt to Spain to witness the fiesta and bullfights at Pamplona. At the bullring Jake finds meaning and hope in the ritual which pits man against beast, and life against death; he especially admires the young matador Pedro Romero, whose skill, bravery, and moral earnestness characterize him as a true Hemingway hero. The others in his group, however, remain true to form, and the fiesta degenerates into a series of brawls. Angered by Brett's seduction of the matador, Cohn beats up both Romero and Jake, and the party disintegrates. Brett runs off with Romero. Jake retreats to a seaside resort in an effort to regain moral stability, but his recovery is interrupted by a telegram from Brett pleading that he come to her aid in Madrid. There she tells him that she has sent Romero away because she does not want to corrupt him further. In a last taxi ride around the city, Brett and Jake face the hopelessness of their situation. Brett clings to the notion that they 'could have had such a damned good time together', but Jake responds ironically that it would be 'pretty' to think so – his word for his final rejection of a world of false hopes.

**Sunday Under Three Heads** A pamphlet by **Charles Dickens**, writing under the pseudonym of Timothy Sparks, addressed to the Bishop of London on the right of ordinary people to spend their Sundays in whatever way pleased them best. It was published in 1836.

**Surgeon's Daughter, The** See *Chronicles of the Canongate*.

**Surrey, Henry Howard, Earl of** ?1517–47 With **Thomas Wyatt**, Surrey is one of the early imitators of the Italian **sonnet** in English and his work represents one of the first flowerings of 16th-century poetry. Henry Howard received the courtesy title Earl of Surrey when his father became 3rd Duke of Norfolk in 1524. After some private tuition he became the companion of the Earl of Richmond, the bastard son of Henry VIII, at Windsor. At the same time came a suggestion from Anne Boleyn (who soon changed her mind) that Surrey should marry the Princess Mary. Norfolk affianced his son to the daughter of the Earl of Oxford and they were married in 1532. Surrey's fortunes declined in 1536, the year of the deaths of Anne Boleyn and of Richmond, and of Henry VIII's marriage to Jane Seymour. The Seymours schemed against the Howards and already in 1536 were accusing Surrey of secretly sympathizing with the Catho-

Earl of Surry

Henry Howard, Earl of Surrey. The portrait drawing by Holbein. The Royal Library, Windsor.

lic Pilgrimage of Grace rebellion. On this suspicion, Surrey was confined for a time at Windsor. In the 1540s Surrey campaigned successfully in Scotland and France. He was in favour again in the early 1540s, made Knight of the Garter in 1541, and became Commander of Boulogne in 1545–6. In 1546 Henry VIII's health was failing and Surrey made some ill-advised and public remarks about his father's obviously strong candidacy for the Protectorship of the young Prince Edward. He was arrested on the pretext of a heraldic nicety (he had been displaying royal quarterings in his shield), and after some damaging evidence from the Countess of Richmond (Surrey's sister) he was imprisoned in the Tower and executed on Tower Hill.

Even when Surrey was a child, his tutor had commended his translations from Latin and Italian. His translation of books II and IV of the *Aeneid* introduced blank verse for the first time in English poetry. His imitations of Italian sonnets, especially those of Petrarch, have a remarkable smoothness for their time. He was one of those instrumental in developing the English or Shakespearean sonnet. Much of his work was probably written during his confinement at Windsor and most of his work (some 40 poems) was published for the first time in *Tottel's Miscellany* (1557). **Sidney** found in Surrey's lyrics 'many things tasting of a noble birth, and worthy of a noble mind'.

**Surtees, R[obert] S[mith]** 1805–64 Sporting novelist and journalist. Surtees came of a long line of country gentlemen who had lived and owned land in County Durham for centuries; he spent his early life on his father's estate of Hamsterley Hall. After attending Durham School he studied law in Newcastle and London, qualifying in 1828. He does not seem to have practised very seriously, spending much time foxhunting with packs in the London area. He started writing for the *Sporting Magazine* and in 1831 founded in partnership with Rudolph Ackermann, the London publisher and printseller, the *New Sporting Magazine*, of which he became the first editor. In this capacity he made a number of hunting tours and paid summer visits to Brighton, indulging in various 'jaunts and jollities' which provided material for the doings of Mr Jorrocks, chronicled in the *NSM*. Surtees abandoned the law in 1835, continuing as editor of the *NSM* until the end of 1836. He returned to Hamsterley in 1837 and succeeded to the property on his father's death in 1838. He lived there for the rest of his life, hunting regularly and writing for pleasure rather than profit; he insisted that his books appeared anonymously. He married in 1841, became a JP and a Deputy Lieutenant for County Durham in 1842 and was created High Sheriff of Durham in 1856.

His major works were: *Jorrocks's Jaunts and Jollities* (1838; an enlarged, posthumous version appeared in 1869), *Handley Cross* (1843; enlarged version 1854), *Hillingdon Hall* (1845), *Mr Sponge's Sporting Tour* (1853), *Ask Mamma* (1858), *Plain or Ringlets?* (1860) and *Mr Facey Romford's Hounds*, which was being serialized when he died and appeared in book form in 1865. They are loosely, sometimes carelessly, constructed. What gives them life are the hard-bitten, talkative, closely observed characters taken from the whole spectrum of country life from dukes to 'chawbacons'. (One of **Kipling**'s characters describes his people as 'Dickens-and-horsedung', but changes his mind later when the books start to grip him.) There is much about foxhunting and the material rings true, being written by an expert. The notation of speech, especially North Country dialect, is masterly.

***Susanna, or, The Pistil of Swete Susan*** A poem in **alliterative verse** written between 1350 and 1380 in the North or North-west Midlands. It tells the story of Susanna and the Elders from an apocryphal addition to the Book of Daniel in the Vulgate Bible: Susanna, wife of a rich Babylonian, is accused of unchastity by two elders whose advances she had rebuffed but their dishonesty is discovered by Daniel and they are executed. The poem follows its source closely but has some additions and divergences including a description of a garden which draws on the

12th-century *Roman de la Rose* of Guillaume de Lorris and Jean de Meun. It has been suggested that it is the work of **Huchown of the Awle Ryale**, though there is little evidence to support this.

**Sutcliff, Rosemary** 1920– Children's historical novelist. Born in Surrey, the daughter of a naval officer, she started school only at the age of nine because of poor health. On leaving school at 14 she trained as an artist, specializing in miniatures, but soon gave this up in favour of writing. Her first book, *The Chronicles of Robin Hood* (1950), established her as a fine historical novelist: she has since gone on to write over 30 such books, including some that have become classics. Her favourite era is the Roman occupation of Britain, which also gives her the opportunity to write about the divided loyalties so often experienced by the characters in her books. Adding this type of psychological dilemma to stories of action was something new in the development of historical fiction for children, and is perhaps most memorably achieved in *The Eagle of the Ninth* (1954). The story of King Arthur offered another opportunity to explore character as well as events, the whole cycle beginning with *The Light Beyond the Forest* (1979). She has also reconstructed the story of Boadicea in *Songs for a Dark Queen* (1978), a savage novel which never falsifies the horrors of the time. *Blue Remembered Hills* (1983) tells the story of her own early life.

**Swan Theatre** Built in *c*.1595, the Swan's importance in the history of English theatre architecture is assured by the chance survival of a drawing by the Dutchman De Witt of its interior in 1596. It is the only reliable evidence we have of the auditoria of the open-air theatres of the Elizabethan period. The history of the Swan, which survived until *c*.1637, is unimpressive. It seems never to have recovered from the scandal surrounding the 1597 performance of *The Isle of Dogs*.

**Sweet, Henry** 1845–1912 Literary scholar. The son of a London solicitor, Sweet was educated at King's College School, London, and studied at Heidelberg before going on to Balliol College, Oxford. Here he invented his own system of phonetics and published an edition of **King Alfred**'s version of the *Cura Pastoralis*, but graduated with only a fourth-class degree in 1873. His *History of English Sounds* (1874) became a standard textbook, as did the *Anglo-Saxon Reader* (1876). These works were followed by his *Handbook of Phonetics* in 1877, the year in which Sweet persuaded the Oxford University Press to consider publishing the Philological Society's new dictionary (later to become the *Oxford English Dictionary*). Sweet's

leading position in the study of Old English and phonetics was not rewarded by the University until he was appointed to a Readership in 1901. His later works included *A New English Grammar* (1892), *The History of Language* (1900) and *The Sounds of English: An Introduction to Phonetics* (1908). It was on Sweet that **G. B. Shaw** based the character of the phonetician Professor Higgins in *Pygmalion*.

**Swift, Graham** 1949– Novelist. Swift's reputation rests on his most recent, third novel, *Waterland* (1983), an ambitious saga set in the Fenland region of East Anglia. Technically *Waterland* has much in common with **magic realism** and the early fiction of Günter Grass, while its themes of history and memory continue the preoccupations of Swift's first two works, *The Sweet-Shop Owner* (1980) and *Shuttlecock* (1981).

**Swift, Jonathan** 1667–1745 Satirist and poet. He was born in Dublin, the posthumous child of Jonathan Swift, an expatriate English lawyer, and Abigail Erick. His mother returned to her native Leicestershire when he was three, so from an early age Swift was looked after by his Uncle Godwin, who sent him to Kilkenny School in 1673, where **Congreve** was a fellow pupil. In April 1682 he entered Trinity College, Dublin, but his academic career there was not distinguished and he only managed to graduate *speciale gratia* in 1686. Swift seems in retrospect to have regarded the education he received as second-rate, though this is perhaps merely one of several instances of resentment on his part during the course of a long and disappointing life which he saw as characterized by the ingratitude of others.

Early in 1689 an outbreak of troubles in Ireland – the result of the arrival of James II – led Swift to visit his mother in England. He entered the household of **Sir William Temple** as his secretary, and settled at Moor Park, Surrey. From such a position the young Swift might reasonably have expected influential introductions that would lead to preferment, but neither a visit to William III nor an errand to Ireland on his patron's behalf advanced his ambitions for a public post. In July 1692, having already completed most of the required work, Swift took an MA from Hart Hall, Oxford, a qualification which would at least enable him to enter the Church.

Swift remained at Moor Park until May 1684, reading voraciously through Temple's library, and composing his largely unsuccessful Pindaric Odes, one of which was published in *The Athenian Mercury* in 1692, his first appearance in print. During this period he acted as tutor to the eight-year-old Esther Johnson (Stella), the daughter of the companion to Temple's sister.

Jonathan Swift. A detail from the portrait by Charles Jervas, c.1718. National Portrait Gallery, London.

Impatient for advancement, Swift was ordained in 1694 and returned to Ireland where he was granted the prebend of Kilroot, near Belfast, the following year.

Returning to Moor Park in 1696, he there edited Temple's correspondence and wrote *The Battle of the Books* in 1697, which further identified him with his patron's affairs. He was perhaps over-dependent on Temple's influence, for when the latter died in 1699 Swift found himself in effect 'unprovided both of friend and living', since he had resigned his prebend a year previously. He returned to Dublin as chaplain to Lord Berkeley, the new Lord Justice, managed to obtain the living of Laracor, and was granted a prebend in St Patrick's, Dublin, where Stella and her companion Rebecca Dingley were to join him.

He visited London with Lord Berkeley in 1701, and published his *Discourse of the Contests and Dissensions in Athens and Rome*, a political pamphlet concerning the impeachment of certain Whig lords. During his several trips to England during the period 1702–4 he made the acquaintance of **Addison** and **Steele**, and, with the anonymous publication in 1704 of his *Tale of a Tub*, a vehement and comprehensive satire on contemporary intellectual abuses, Swift began to gain notoriety and a certain popularity in Whig literary circles.

A period of writing on religious matters began in 1707, when he again visited England on a mission to obtain Queen Anne's Bounty for the Irish clergy. In 1708 he wrote his ironic

*Argument against Abolishing Christianity* (published 1711), followed by the *Letter Concerning the Sacramental Test*, an attack on the Presbyterians; a staunch Anglican, Swift was a strong supporter of the terms of the Revolutionary settlement and was intolerant of Dissent, especially those factions associated with 'enthusiasm', or a fanatical belief in inspiration. This attitude was one reason for his moving away from his former Whig associates and inclining towards the Tory circle of wits by 1710. In 1708 he invented the character of *Isaac Bickerstaff* for his *jeu d'esprit* at the expense of the astrologer John Partridge, and in 1709 he published two of his more celebrated short poems in *The Tatler*.

Allegiance to the Tory ministry of **Robert Harley, Earl of Oxford**, was sealed by Swift's acceptance in 1710 of the editorship of *The Examiner*, the Tory journal, a post he relinquished in June 1711 in order to concentrate on *The Conduct of the Allies*, his outstanding political pamphlet in support of the proposals for peace in the Continental campaign. He was by now on terms of close familiarity with Harley, and was enjoying an increasingly bright reputation in London where he befriended **Pope**, **Arbuthnot** and **Gay**; he began a series of intimate, playful letters addressed to Stella in Dublin, later collected as the *Journal to Stella*, which tell us much about his movements during these years. Meanwhile, he was also seeing Esther Vanhomrigh (whom he nicknamed Vanessa), a young London lady who fell in love with him, was encouraged and was then rebuffed; his poem *Cadenus and Vanessa* represents the equivocal nature of this affair. Indeed, his exact relationship with Stella has also been the cause of much speculation, one theory holding that they were secretly married in 1716, another that they were already related illegitimately by blood. The extent of his involvement with any of the women in his life remains unclear, but his reputation as a misogynist is patently unfounded, as the evidence of his charming 'Birthday poems' to Stella indicates.

Made Dean of St Patrick's Cathedral in 1713 (he had taken his DD in 1701), Swift's official appointments now reached a peak, but until the collapse of the Tory ministry with which he was socially and intellectually identified his literary stature in London continued to grow with the publication of various poems and pamphlets. But the death of Queen Anne in 1714 signalled for the Dean a period of self-imposed exile in Ireland, where he prudently retreated to avoid the recrimination of the new Whig administration. Swift realized that his hopes for preferment, both secular and ecclesiastical, were now to be thwarted for ever, and he based himself busily in Dublin where, despite persistent claims of loathing for the country, he proceeded to involve himself in championing the rights of

Ireland. He defended the cause of the Irish economy, in particular, with his *Proposal for the Universal Use of Irish Manufacture* (1720) and the famous *Drapier's Letters* of 1724, which effectively prevented the exploitation of Ireland through the issuing of debased coinage. He succeeded, ironically, in establishing himself as one of the leading Irish patriots of the century.

Despite his many protests to the contrary, Swift seemed fairly content with his new circle of friends in Dublin and its environs. He exchanged bantering correspondence with Delany and **Sheridan**, and maintained his contact with those friends in England whom he missed. As well as writing a good deal of satirical verse, it was probably around 1720 that he began work on his best-known book, *Gulliver's Travels*, which was published in 1726 to great acclaim and was the only piece of writing for which he was ever paid. He saw his old Scriblerian friends for the last time in the following year when, after a stay in England to remonstrate with Walpole, whom he detested, Swift had to return to Ireland, as Stella was desperately ill. She died in 1728, leaving him to an intermittently lonely existence, though there is certainly no evidence that his mental powers were fading until much later in his life. His writings prove the contrary case: as well as maintaining a vigorous correspondence with his many friends, he produced a diverse and talented body of work during these years, including his notoriously powerful *A Modest Proposal* in 1729, poems such as 'The Grand Question Debated' (1729), 'On Poetry: a Rhapsody' (1733) and the *Verses on the Death of Dr Swift* (published 1739), and the delightful dialogues of his *Polite and Ingenious Conversation* (1738).

Swift was both a prolific and a versatile writer, and, though his reputation has suffered many fluctuations, the originality of his imagination has never seriously been in question. A complicated man, the close and constant proximity of his personality and his writings has caused Swift to be misrepresented severely by many subsequent readers. There persists a misconception that his misanthropy was total, and that this eventually drove him insane, but in reality the senility of his later years was largely the result of physical causes such as the Ménière's syndrome from which he had suffered for years, a disease producing vertigo and nausea. The tenacity with which he held his views, his fierce dislike of injustice and his intolerance of folly which combine to make the satirist's *saeva indignatio* (fierce indignation) should be tempered with the popular esteem in which he was held by the ordinary people of Ireland (where he spent a third of his modest income on charity), his reputation as a prankster and lover of *la bagatelle*, and his devotion to the cause of common-sense. Although certain Victorian

readers such as **Thackeray** were appalled at the coarseness apparent in some of his work, he is generally admired as one of the finest authors of prose and satire in the English language.

**Swinburne, Algernon Charles** 1837–1909 Poet, playwright, novelist and critic. The son of an admiral, Swinburne was born in London but spent his childhood on the Isle of Wight. He was educated in France and at Eton and Balliol College, Oxford, which he left without a degree. As well as French and Italian, Swinburne mastered Greek and Latin and early showed interest in the intricacies of poetic form, especially the lyrical. Other influences impinged upon him to shape his future writings, among which the Bible, classical literature and the sea are pre-eminent. And such individualists as Mazzini, Hugo, and **Walter Savage Landor** cast their varied shadows upon him. Furthermore, Swinburne's attendance at university coincided with the ill-starred efforts of **Dante Gabriel Rossetti**, Edward Burne-Jones, **William Morris** and Holman Hunt to adorn the improperly prepared walls of the Oxford Union with frescoes; later Swinburne was briefly an inmate, with Rossetti and **George Meredith**, of their bizarre wombat-ridden household at Cheyne Walk, Chelsea. These influences – the literary, the rebellious, the classical, the medieval and the

Swinburne. A detail from the portrait by G. F. Watts, 1865. National Portrait Gallery, London.

nationalistic – severally make their presence felt upon Swinburne's vast output.

In 1860 Swinburne published two plays, *The Queen-Mother* and *Rosamund*, which were followed in 1865 by *Chastelard* (the first play of a trilogy about Mary Queen of Scots; *Bothwell* (1874) and *Mary Stuart* (1881) were the two others). Next came **Atalanta in Calydon**, whose lyrical 'When the hounds of spring are on winter's traces' and similar passages announced the young man's poetic presence.

But it was in 1866 with the publication of the notorious *Poems and Ballads* (including **Garden of Proserpine**, **Hymn to Proserpine** and **Laus Veneris**) that Swinburne's name truly reverberated through literary circles. The poems of this volume, with their themes of moral, spiritual and political rebellion, with their sadistic, blasphemous and sexually perverted subject matter, goaded the middle-class Victorian reading public to fury: **John Morley**'s review castigated Swinburne as the 'libidinous laureate of a pack of satyrs'. To a public attuned to the lyrical delicacy of **Tennyson**'s Amys and Mauds and Lilians the moral anarchy and explicitness of *Poems and Ballads* were quite horrifying. Yet these poems, in heralding a revolutionary form of poetical matter and expression, constitute a break with contemporary tastes and point to the *fin-de-siècle* and beyond.

From the mid 1860s to the late 1870s Swinburne's pen barely stopped. *Poems and Ballads* were followed in 1868 by **Ave Atque Vale** (an elegiac tribute to Baudelaire), the lyrically and politically charged *Song of Italy* and, in 1871, by *Songs Before Sunrise*. The poetic flow was temporarily diverted to prose, however, when he defended Dante Gabriel Rossetti against **Robert Buchanan**'s anonymous attack in 'The Fleshly School of Poetry' to which Swinburne retaliated with *Under the Microscope* (1872). Then, returning to his Greek models, he published *Erectheus* (1876) and, two years later, *Poems and Ballads: Second Series*, which despite their elegiac tone are touched by the old paganism. One novel, *Love's Cross-Currents: A Year's Letters* (1877), belongs to this period; a further novel, *Lesbia Brandon*, was not published until 1952.

Meanwhile, Swinburne had become seriously addicted to alcohol, so addicted as to engage the sympathy of Theodore Watts (later **Theodore Watts-Dunton**) who carried him off in 1879 to his home, The Pines, in Putney where, for the rest of his life, the *enfant terrible* of Victorian letters lived a passive, conventional suburban existence. But had Watts, yet to become the poet's legal and financial adviser and intimate, not rescued him Swinburne would surely have gone to an early and unpleasant death. Furthermore, if Watts's vigilance and supervision over the poet, his proprietary hold as well as his profit from that stewardship, are open to ques-

tion, it is only fitting to bear in mind that Swinburne, when Watts rescued him, was far from the perfect guest.

Under Watts-Dunton's care Swinburne experienced an abundant resurgence and in 1880 produced *The Heptalogia, or, The Seven against Sense* (anonymously published parodies) as well as *Songs of the Springtides* and *Studies in Song*. These were followed by *Tristram of Lyonnesse* (1882), *A Century of Roundels* (1883), *A Midsummer Holiday* (1884) and, in 1889, *Poems and Ballads: Third Series*. *Astrophel* appeared in 1894, followed by *The Tale of Balen* (1896) and *A Channel Passage* (1904).

Accompanying the foregoing came several verse plays, among them *Marino Faliero* (1885), *Locrine* (1887), *The Sisters* (1892), *Rosamund Queen of the Lombards* (1899) and *The Duke of Gandia* (1908). Swinburne was also a discerning if at times erratic and impetuous critic of literature and over the years cast his net widely by writing on Baudelaire, **Blake** (whose genius he was early to note), Hugo, **Webster**, **Shakespeare**, **Byron**, Rossetti, **Dickens** and others. Swinburne's criticism could reach the heights of enthusiasm and erudition, frequently displaying a mastery of technical analysis; on the other hand, his praise could be exaggerated and his ferocity of attack so uncontrollable, particularly with a pedant in his sights, as to preclude serious consideration of what he had written.

A child of both the romantic and classical traditions, Swinburne was an imaginative user of old forms and a bold experimenter with new ones. His poetry is chiefly notable for its verbal cascades, luxurious imagery and metrical pyrotechnics, for it would be difficult to make a case for its spiritual, philosophical or political profundity. Perhaps above all, Swinburne deserves to be remembered as one of the more courageous spirits to survive Victorian England, taking arms against the prudery of the age, reinvigorating its poetic language and fearlessly, if sometimes misguidedly, pronouncing on new currents of ideas that would be shaped and deepened by later literary men and women.

**Swinnerton, Frank (Arthur)** 1884–1982 Novelist and critic. Born in Wood Green, he left school at 14 to become an office-boy. He worked in 1902–7 as a confidential clerk at J. M. Dent, the publishers, and in 1907–26 as a reader at Chatto and Windus, reading manuscripts by **Aldous Huxley** and **Lytton Strachey** among others and 'discovering' **Daisy Ashford**'s *The Young Visiters*. He began his career as a novelist with *The Merry Heart* (1909) and *The Casement* (1911). *Nocturne* (1917) was a critical and commercial success which Swinnerton felt overshadowed his subsequent work. This consisted of nearly 40 more novels, including *Young Felix* (1923), *The Georgian*

*House* (1932) and *A Woman in Sunshine* (1944), and 20 books of criticism. Through his work as a publisher, and as a literary critic for *The Evening News* and *The Observer*, he knew and befriended the leading writers of his time, **Arnold Bennett** and **H. G. Wells** among them. A man of kindness and perception, he added the dimension of close personal contact to his criticism. Living to the age of 98 and continuing to write well into the second half of this century he thus provided an important link between the Georgian literary scene and later writing.

**Sword of Honour** A trilogy by **Evelyn Waugh**, comprising *Men at Arms* (1952), *Officers and Gentlemen* (1955) and *Unconditional Surrender* (1961). It was first published as a single work in 1965.

Guy Crouchback, an honourable man, has no place in the modern world. He receives no consolation from personal relationships or from his Catholicism, but World War II gives him the opportunity to establish his identity. He enlists in the Royal Corps of Halberdiers and much of the first volume, *Men at Arms*, is concerned with an eccentric fellow officer, Apthorpe, who eventually dies of a tropical disease in West Africa. Through the characters of Virginia Troy, Guy's beautiful but empty-headed ex-wife, her current husband, Tommy Blackhouse, and the extraordinary Brigadier Ritchie-Hook, Waugh blends nostalgia with a satirical portrait of upper-class English life.

By the end of the second volume, *Officers and Gentlemen*, Guy has been stripped of his illusions about the army. He has an affair with Virginia and departs for action in Alexandria. The novel ends with the withdrawal from Crete and Guy's capture by the enemy.

In the last volume, *Unconditional Surrender*, Guy volunteers for service in Italy with the military government, and he eventually goes to Yugoslavia as a liaison officer with the Partisans. Virginia gives birth to a son (not Guy's) and is killed in an air raid. At the end of the book Guy has again asserted himself, in the rescue of a group of Jewish refugees, and realizes what kind of man he used to be: one who believed that his private honour would be satisfied by war. In an Epilogue we learn that he has remarried and surrounded himself with a family.

**Sybil, or, The Two Nations** A novel by **Benjamin Disraeli**, published in 1845, about Chartist agitation. It was the earliest and in some ways the best **Condition of England novel**. Disraeli's description of the miserable living and working conditions of the poor is deservedly famous. With numerous historical disquisitions, the novel contrasts the lives of a spurious aristocracy, ennobled by monastic plunder and commercial greed, living in affluence and political selfishness, with the noble aspirations of the journalist, Stephen Morley, and his friend, Walter Gerard, thoughtful representatives of the working class. Walter's daughter, Sybil, is a Catholic who wishes to take the veil but eventually marries a member of the 'aristocracy'. Disraeli shows a keen, humane sympathy with the sufferings of England's oppressed working class but, like other novelists who tackled these themes, his view was paternalistic. With his deeply-entrenched prejudice in favour of 'ancient blood', he makes his 'daughter of the people' (who seems to be a lady of leisure, with no visible means of support), the heir to an ancient title and so fit to rule.

**Sydney Opera House** Designed by Jorn Utzon and opened in 1973, this remarkable building houses four separate auditoria, of which one is specifically for drama. Since 1979, it has been the home of the Sydney Theatre Company.

**syllabic metre** See **metre**.

**syllepsis** The application of one word to two semantically different parts of a sentence: 'Here, thou, great Anna! whom three realms obey,/ Dost sometimes counsel take – and sometimes tea' (**Pope**, *The Rape of the Lock*). Zeugma is the same thing, save that one of the applications is, strictly speaking, incorrect. Fluellen's 'Kill the boys and the luggage' in **Shakespeare**'s *Henry V* is the most famous example. Syllepsis, therefore, shares something with punning, zeugma with **metaphor**.

**Sylvester, Joshua** ?1562–1618 Poet and translator. Born in Kent of comfortable bourgeois stock, Sylvester was educated at Southampton grammar school, notable for the excellence of its instruction in French, until 1576, when he embarked on a career in the guild of Merchant Adventurers. His literary ambitions were realized in his once-renowned translation from Du Bartas, *The Divine Weeks and Works*, which, appearing piecemeal from 1592 to 1608, brought fame but little fortune. A member of Prince Henry's circle, he was friendly with the poet and cleric **Joseph Hall**; his translations from French and Latin are voluminous, and his original poems include the entertaining *Tobacco Battered; and the Pipes Shattered* (1617) and the allegorically autobiographical *The Wood-man's Bear*, written in 1587 but published posthumously in 1620. Folio editions of Sylvester's works appeared in 1621, 1633 and 1641.

**Sylvia's Lovers** A novel by **Elizabeth Gaskell**, first published in 1863.

Sylvia is the daughter of Daniel Robson, a former sailor and smuggler now a farmer near

Monkshaven (Whitby) on the north-east coast; he is also actively hostile to press gangs, whose grim activities are central to this novel of late 19th-century life. Sylvia is loved by her industrious Quaker cousin, Philip Hepburn, a shop assistant whose earnestness early secures him a partnership in the grocer-mercer-draper establishment of the Foster brothers. But Sylvia is more impressed by Charley Kinraid, a Lothario and 'spectioneer' (harpooner on a whaler), so an understanding, approved by her father, is established between them. Meanwhile, Philip is required to go to London on business at the same time that Kinraid is joining his ship. As their ways initially lie along the same coastal route Philip, from a hidden point of vantage, witnesses the illegal abduction of Kinraid by the press gang. Bound and put in a tender destined for a nearby frigate, Kinraid calls to Philip (now within hailing distance) and asks him to tell Sylvia he will return and that, because of a mutual oath, they are even now as married. Philip proceeds to London where work detains him for some weeks. Meanwhile Kinraid, whose hat is found at the water's edge, is presumed drowned, so that Philip returns from the city to find Sylvia in deep distress; instead of clarifying the situation he remains silent in his own interest. A resurgence of hatred toward the press gang's activities in Monkshaven causes a riot in which Daniel Robson plays a significant part and for which he is arrested and subsequently hanged. Soon afterwards Sylvia contracts a loveless marriage with Philip, but three years later Kinraid returns and tries unsuccessfully to get her to come away with him. True to her marriage vows, she refuses. Kinraid departs and Philip, whose concealment of Kinraid's position is now unmasked, is disdained by Sylvia and leaves Monkshaven in shame and disgrace. Almost immediately he encounters a marine sergeant who slips him the king's shilling and under the name of Stephen Freeman he serves at the siege of Acre where Kinraid, by now a naval officer, is also a participant and whose life Philip saves. Sick, shattered, and friendless, Philip finds his way to Monkshaven where Sylvia, her heart softened, is reconciled with him at his death. Kinraid, it is revealed, had upon leaving Sylvia for the final time married a Miss Jackson happily possessed 'with a fortune of £10,000'.

*Sylvia's Lovers* is notable for its dramatic evocations of press-gang cruelties and for such worthy characterizations as those of Kester (an honourable family servant), the Foster brothers (generous and decent Quaker shopkeepers) and Hester Rose, whose love for Philip remains unrequited throughout.

**symbol** A word that has been, and still is, used in very different ways. For literary purposes, as opposed to those of the mathematician, gram-marian, or computer programmer, it may profitably be distinguished from sign and **simile** to give an imprecise but usable meaning. Signs are purely conventional: green stands for Go, red for Stop, by agreement not by nature. In a simile some natural affinity between the two parts is presupposed but the difference is equally important, and the figurative part is not meant to be 'really' like its referent. The symbol, however, draws together different worlds, usually tangible and intangible, into a unity that purports to be more real than either. It tends to be less precise than a sign and more pretentious than a simile – and more powerful when the pretentions turn out to be justified. The symbol, therefore, may be thought of as a **metaphor** that purports to be more than 'merely metaphorical'. In practice, this means that metaphors apparently having a number of referents and an indefinite reverberation of suggestions tend to be distinguished as symbols. Thus **Blake**'s 'Sick Rose' seems to be a rose, a vulva, jealousy and corruption at least, but, rather than inviting translation into any or all of these, it offers itself as a complex unity of which they are all inseparable parts.

**Symbolism** A term specifically applied to the work of late-19th-century French writers who reacted against the descriptive precision and objectivity of **realism** and the scientific determinism of **naturalism**. It was first used in this sense by Jean Moréas in *Le Figaro* in 1886. Baudelaire's sonnet 'Correspondances' and the work of **Edgar Allan Poe** were important precursors of the movement, which emerged with Verlaine's *Romances Sans Paroles* (1874) and Mallarmé's *L'Après-midi d'un Faune* (1876). Other Symbolist writers included the poets Rimbaud and Laforgue, the novelists Joris-Karl Huysmans (*A Rebours*, 1884) and Edouard Dujardin, the dramatists Maurice Maeterlinck and Villiers de L'Isle Adam (*Axël*, 1890) and the critics Rémy de Gourmont and Marcel Schwob. Its influence on the other arts can be seen in the music of Debussy (who wrote many settings of Mallarmé's poems, notably 'Prélude à l'Après-midi d'un Faune') and the paintings of Odilon Redon, Gustave Moreau, Van Gogh and Gauguin.

Symbolism emphasized the primary importance of suggestion and evocation in the expression of a private mood or reverie. The symbol was held to evoke subtle relations and affinities, especially between sound, sense and colour, and between the material and spiritual worlds (although in the works themselves these were often antagonistic). The notion of affinities led to an interest in esoteric and occult writings (notably Swedenborg and the cabbala) and to ideas about the 'musicality' of poetry which, combined with the Wagner cult, stressed the possibility of orchestrating the theme of a poem through the evocative power of words.

Outside France **T. S. Eliot**, **Yeats**, **Pound**, **Joyce**, **Virginia Woolf** and **Wallace Stevens** were all variously interested in Symbolism. The most significant work was **Arthur Symons**'s *The Symbolist Movement in Literature* (1899), an introduction to the French literature which Eliot found 'a revelation'. It characterized Symbolism as a reaction against naturalism and realism, and as an 'attempt to spiritualise literature'. It was to be a reflection, not merely a sign, of spiritual reality: 'a kind of religion, with all the duties and responsibilities of the sacred ritual'. Yeats, the dedicatee of the book and himself a poet using symbols of the occult, agreed that Symbolism was 'the recoil from scientific materialism'. His essay, 'The Symbolism of Poetry', emphasized the importance of rhythm. In their poetry, however, both Yeats and Eliot returned to what the latter called the 'music latent in the common speech of its time'.

**Symonds, John Addington** 1840–93 Poet, translator and art historian. Born in Bristol, he was educated at Harrow and Balliol College, Oxford, where he studied under **Benjamin Jowett**. His poem 'The Escorial' won the Newdigate Prize, and he was made a fellow of Magdalen College in 1862, but following a nervous and physical breakdown he spent much of the following year in Italy and Switzerland. In an attempt to repress his homosexuality he married in 1864, and returned to Bristol where he studied law and began to publish criticism, reviews, studies in the Hellenism of the Renaissance and volumes of lyric verse. His circle of friends included **Edward Lear**, **Swinburne**, **Leslie Stephen** and **Robert Louis Stevenson**. Completion of the three-volume *The Renaissance in Italy* (1875–86) led to another breakdown, and he then settled at Davos Platz, Switzerland. He was buried near **Shelley**'s grave in the Protestant Cemetery in Rome.

His publications include studies of Dante (1872), the Greek poets (1873), **Whitman** (1893) and Michelangelo (1892); translations of Michelangelo and Campanella (1878), *Wine, Women and Song* (1884, translations of Goliardic songs) and the *Life of Cellini* (1888). His essays were collected in *Essays Speculative and Suggestive* (2 vols., 1890) and *In The Key of Blue* (1892). He published two privately printed pamphlets in a discreet campaign for legal reforms and recognition of 'inversion', *A Problem in Greek Ethics* (1883) and *A Problem in Modern Ethics* (1891), and he anonymously contributed his own case history to **Havelock Ellis**'s *Sexual Inversion* (1897). His volumes of poetry include the privately printed *Verses* (1871), followed by *Many Moods* (1878), *New and Old* (1880) and two sonnet sequences dealing obliquely with

'l'amour de l'impossible': *Anima Figura* (1882) and *Vagabundulis Libellus* (1884).

**Symons, Arthur (William)** 1865–1945 Critic and poet. Symons was born in Milford Haven of Cornish parents, his father being a Wesleyan minister. He was privately educated, became fluent in French and Italian, and, on taking up residence in London, frequented the **Rhymers' Club**, where he became the friend of **Ernest Dowson**, **Lionel Johnson** and **Oscar Wilde**. For a time he shared lodgings with **W. B. Yeats**.

A leading light of the Decadence in the 1890s, Symons contributed to *The Yellow Book* and in 1896 became editor of *The Savoy*. His own poetry, published in *Days and Nights* (1889), *Silhouettes* (1892), *London Nights* (1895) and *Images of Good and Evil* (1899), is forgotten now, but Symons is still remembered for *The Symbolist Movement in Literature* (1899), an influential study which introduced French **Symbolism** to English readers. He wrote several other critical studies, including *An Introduction to the Study of Robert Browning* (1886), *William Blake* (1907), *Charles Baudelaire* (1920), and *Studies in Elizabethan Drama* (1920), and translated Baudelaire's *Les Fleurs du Mal* and Zola's *L'Assommoir*.

**Symons, Julian** See **detective fiction**.

**synecdoche** A figure of speech which replaces the whole by the part, or vice versa. Thus a newly arrived person becomes a 'new face' and in the phrase 'Chelsea beat Liverpool' the proper nouns refer to football teams. See also **metonymy**.

**Synge, J[ohn] M[illington]** 1871–1909 Irish dramatist. Born into a moderately prosperous Protestant family in Rathfarnham, near Dublin, Synge was educated privately and at Trinity College, Dublin. His boyhood interest in music was allowed to flourish after his graduation, and he studied piano and violin at the Royal Irish Academy before travelling and studying music in Germany, Italy and France. It was while he was living in Paris that he met **W. B. Yeats** in 1896 and accepted his advice to develop his growing interest in the Irish language and traditions. Five summers in the Aran Islands between 1898 and 1902 excited his interest in the durability and humour of this isolated community. The notebooks he filled during these visits, and out of which he culled his commentary *The Aran Islands* (1907), show his developing ear for the music of speech. The posthumously published *In Wicklow, West Kerry and Connemara* (1911) is similarly observant, and the two books are the authentic background material of the group of plays, written in 1903–9, which made Synge the first great writer of the Irish Literary Theatre.

J. M. Synge, *c.*1896.

Involved with Yeats and **Lady Gregory** in the dramatic movement which would culminate in the opening of the **Abbey Theatre** in 1904 (he was one of its directors until his death), Synge wrote his first play, the one-act *In the Shadow of the Glen* (1903), as a conscious celebration of the independent spirit of the Irish. Set in a cottage in Wicklow, it shows Nora Burke choosing to forsake her ageing and suspicious husband in favour of the freedom of the open road. The prudish section of the Dublin audience declared its opposition to Synge's view of Ireland, as it would continue to declare it throughout Synge's brief dramatic career. The one-act tragedy *Riders to the Sea* (1904) is both a threnody and a song of praise to the indomitable spirit of the Aran islanders. *The Well of the Saints* (1905), set in the east of Ireland 'one or more centuries ago', is a bitter comedy, in which Synge's ironic pessimism finds expression in the decision of the blind beggars, Martin and Mary Doul, to reject the gift of sight because it has destroyed their illusions. *The Tinker's Wedding*, first performed in 1909, was written and revised between 1903 and 1907. It is a comedy which confronts Sarah Casey, a tinker, with the problem of reconciling her wandering life with the urge to be properly married by a priest. More inevitably even than Synge's masterpiece **The Playboy of the Western World** (1907), it offended the vocally pious of Dublin, who did not like to see a priest bundled into a sack. After the riots that had greeted *The Playboy of the Western World* at the Abbey, it was thought prudent to stage *The Tinker's Wedding* in London rather than Dublin.

Synge's last play, **Deirdre of the Sorrows** (1910), was his only dramatization of Irish mythology. Written during the late stages of Hodgkin's disease and never subjected to the rigorous revision that was Synge's habit, it was posthumously staged in 1910. The *Poems and Translations* (1909) give some indication of Synge's range, from the spiritual delicacy of Petrarch to the earthiness of Villon, from nature mysticism to the acute observation of Irish people in an Irish landscape.

**System of Logic, The**  This work by **John Stuart Mill** was first published in two volumes in 1843. It lays the groundwork for Mill's re-evaluation of **Utilitarianism**. His attack upon all forms in which an assumption of *a priori* knowledge of the external world manifested itself, led him first to an analysis of meaning and then to a discussion of inferential knowledge derived from the data of experience. He drew his proofs first from mathematics and then, by extension, from the world of the moral sciences of psychology and sociology. In this latter part Mill's tolerant liberalism is justified by asserting that human behaviour is both causally explicable and still free, and that society can never be greater than the sum of its constituent parts. The book's socio-political implications ensured a wide readership beyond the universities, but its adoption as a textbook by Oxford and Cambridge ensured that its discussion of the philosophy of logic created the agenda for much of the work in this field in the latter half of the 19th century.

# T

**tail-rhyme** A verse form which uses a short line followed by two or more long lines and then another short line rhyming with the first. The tail-rhyme stanza thus has various forms. It is common in medieval romance, but also features in the work of later poets, as in **Shelley**'s 'To Night'.

***Tale of a Tub, A*** A prose satire by **Jonathan Swift**, his first major work, written around 1696 but published in 1704. The principal narrative is the 'fable of the coats', an allegory following the fortunes of three brothers who are each left a coat by their father with strict instructions never to alter it. Peter (the Catholic Church), Martin (the Anglican) and Jack (the Calvinist) all exercise their utmost ingenuity in treating what they have inherited as they please, and the fable traces the squabbling that ensues.

The fable is of less interest, though, than the numerous formal digressions with which it is interspersed (on Critics, Madness and Digressions, for example) which, ironically, are designed to carry the main satiric force of the book. The title itself (as well as meaning 'flim-flam') refers to the nautical practice of throwing tubs off the back of ships to distract the attention of whales; the digressions act in similar fashion. The chief targets of this most complex and accomplished of Swift's early works include religious fanaticism (he was no advocate of Dissent), pedantry, scientific credulity, quackery and self-delusion. Swift frequently imitates the thought processes of those he is attacking, which gives rise to deliberate confusion in the reader. Although complicated, the book enjoys an intellectual symmetry in the 'tradition of learned wit', finding several precedents in the prose of **Browne**, **Burton** and **Marvell**. Its apparently chaotic nature, its paradoxes and contradictions, are similarly part of authorial design: with its clumsy paraphernalia of prefaces and notes, non-sequiturs and gaps, the *Tale* is, like *The Dunciad*, partly a parody of a bad book. The work made Swift notorious, and was widely misunderstood, especially by Queen Anne herself, who mistook its purpose for profanity. It effectively disbarred its author from proper preferment within the Church, but is often considered his most extraordinary work. Swift himself was certainly pleased with its imaginative flow; he is supposed to have remarked in later life 'Good God, what a genius I had when I wrote that book.'

***Tale of Gamelyn, The*** A **verse romance** in rhyming couplets, probably composed around 1350–70. It has been called *The Cook's Tale of Gamelyn*, and was at one time attributed to Chaucer (see **Chaucerian apocrypha**). It is one of the relatively few verse romances to have an English source. **Thomas Lodge** used some of the story in his *Rosalynde* (1590), which formed the basis of **Shakespeare**'s *As You Like It*.

Sir John de Boundys leaves his property in equal parts to his three sons, of whom Gamelyn is the youngest. The eldest brother seizes Gamelyn's share and the romance tells how Gamelyn grows up to be very strong, reclaims his inheritance and defeats the elder brother, who is ultimately hanged. It is a vigorous and violent tale, with none of the courtly elements usually associated with verse romance. Criticism of the clergy is a recurrent theme in the poem.

***Tale of Mystery, A*** The first English play to be advertised as a **melodrama**, *A Tale of Mystery* is a perfunctory adaptation by **Thomas Holcroft** of a French original by Pixérécourt. It was first performed as an afterpiece at **Covent Garden** in 1802.

***Tale of Two Cities, A*** A novel by **Charles Dickens**, published as a serial in *All the Year Round* from April to November 1859.

The novel is set in London and Paris at the time of the French Revolution, and was written in the shadow of **Carlyle**'s *The French Revolution*. Dr Manette is released after being imprisoned for 18 years in the Bastille for his innocent involvement in a discreditable secret of the aristocratic Evrémonde family. He comes to England, where his daughter Lucy has been brought up. She loves Charles Darnay, an honourable man cursed by his descent from the Evrémondes, and is hopelessly loved by the noble-minded wastrel, Sydney Carton. After his marriage to Lucy, Darnay finds that he must return to France to help a family servant imprisoned by the revolutionaries. Because of his heritage he is immediately arrested and imprisoned, but the intercession of Manette secures his release. Soon afterwards he is arrested again and this time, ironically, the evidence against him is a long denunciatory account of the Evrémonde family written by Manette during his imprisonment. Darnay is condemned to death but saved at the last moment by the heroic self-sacrifice of Sydney Carton, who exploits his strong physical resemblance to Darnay and takes his place on the scaffold.

The narrative includes several striking minor characters – among them the fanatical Madame Defarge, the upright Miss Pross and Jerry Cruncher, the odd-job man and part-time grave robber – but contemporaries were disappointed by the novel's lack of humour. Like *Barnaby Rudge*, Dickens's only other venture into historical fiction, it is most alive in its descriptions of mob violence.

**Tales from Shakespeare** A prose summary of 20 plays by **Shakespeare**, prepared by **Charles Lamb** and his sister Mary and published in 1807. Mary Lamb's name did not appear on the title-page until the edition of 1838, although she was responsible for 14 of the plays in the book. None of the history plays is included and the selection favours the comedies at the expense of the tragedies. The preface explained that the work was 'submitted to the young reader as an introduction to the study of Shakespeare'; it succeeded in becoming a classic for several generations.

**Talfourd, Sir Thomas Noon** 1785–1854 Judge, dramatist and literary critic. The son of a brewer, Talfourd was born at Reading and educated privately and then at Mill Hill Dissenting School and Reading Grammar School. After many years at the Bar he was elevated to the bench in the Court of Common Pleas in 1849, and was also thrice elected MP for Reading between 1835 and 1847. Comfortably dividing his time between law and literature, he was acquainted with most of the leading literary figures of the early 19th century, and his numerous contributions to *The New Monthly Magazine* included articles on **Scott**, **Godwin** and **Maturin** and a long and influential essay on **Wordsworth**. His vapid blank-verse tragedies, *Ion* (1836), *The Athenian Captive* (1838) and *Glencoe* (1840), have mercifully failed to withstand the passage of time, although they enjoyed brief fame as vehicles of the acting and directorial genius of Macready. Talfourd's most enduring work is his reverent edition of the letters of his friend **Charles Lamb**, with its accompanying 'Sketches' and 'Memorials' (1834 and 1848), and he is additionally remembered for his introduc-

tion of the Copyright Bill in 1837, which earned him the dedication of **Dickens's** *Pickwick Papers* and which was eventually passed in 1842.

**Talisman, The** A novel by **Sir Walter Scott**, the second of his *Tales of the Crusades*, published in 1825. The talisman of the title has a historical basis in the amulet, known as the Lee-penny, brought back from the Crusades by Sir Simon Lockhart and kept in the possession of his heirs, the Lockharts of the Lee. In Scott's novel the talisman is given to the hero, Sir Kenneth, the Knight of the Leopard, during his adventures in the Holy Land at the time of Richard I. The book was once enormously popular, rivalling Scott's more famous historical romance, *Ivanhoe*.

**Tam O'Shanter** A narrative poem by **Robert Burns**, first published in *The Edinburgh Magazine* in March 1791. Burns had asked the antiquary **Francis Grose** to include an engraving of Alloway Kirk, where the poet's father was buried, in his *Antiquities of Scotland*. Grose agreed, provided that Burns would supply an account of one of the witch legends surrounding the kirk to accompany the picture. Burns gave him three accounts, one of which told the story of Tam O'Shanter. After a satirical prologue, the drunken Tam is found in a tavern with his crony, Souter Johnnie. He lurches out, mounts his mare and starts for home. Passing Alloway Kirk, he sees a witches' celebration in progress and watches in fascination. The witches pour out of the kirk with Auld Nick himself, and Tam is pursued. He races away and is barely able to make it across the bridge over the Doon, one of the witches seizing his mare's tail at the last moment. Once on the other side he is safe, since witches will not cross water.

**Tamburlaine the Great** A tragedy by **Christopher Marlowe**, written in two parts and probably first performed in 1587. It was this play, more than any other, that determined the literary status of Elizabethan drama and drew into the public theatre the best writers of the age. Its towering central role, the first and most rhetorical of Marlowe's overreachers, was created by the actor **Edward Alleyn**.

Part I shows Tamburlaine's irresistible rise through military conquest from his Scythian origins as a shepherd-robber to unrivalled power. Having helped Cosroe to overthrow his brother, the Persian king Mycetes, Tamburlaine ousts Cosroe as King of Persia. He next conquers the forces of the Turkish Emperor Bajazet, whom he imprisons and humiliates until Bajazet and his Empress Zabina kill themselves by beating their heads against the bars of the cage in which Tamburlaine exhibits them. The only sign of tenderness in the cruel conqueror is his love for Zenocrate, at whose pleading he spares the life of the Soldan of Egypt, her father, when he captures Damascus. Part II continues the story of Tamburlaine's conquests, which reach their peak when he has his carriage drawn to Babylon by the captured kings of Trebizond and Soria, in relay with the kings of Anatolia and Jerusalem. But Zenocrate's death precipitates his raging against mortality whose victory over Tamburlaine himself is the concluding action of the play. It is *Tamburlaine the Great* that best exhibits the 'mighty line' of Marlowe.

**Taming of the Shrew, The** A comedy by **William Shakespeare**, first performed *c*.1594. The accepted text, published in the First Folio of 1623, has been presumed to have some relationship to a Quarto of *The Taming of a Shrew* (1594), but opinion is divided about the nature of that relationship. The source for the main plot is **George Gascoigne**'s *Supposes*, a translation from Ariosto. If *The Taming of a Shrew* is neither a pirated version of Shakespeare's play nor a source for it, it may be that both its anonymous author and Shakespeare relied on an earlier and now lost play, rather than on Gascoigne. The disappearance of Christopher Sly from the action of Shakespeare's comedy emphasizes the defectiveness of the copy from which the First Folio version was taken.

In the Induction, a lord plays a practical joke on the drunken tinker, Christopher Sly, treating him as a lord who has woken after 15 years of dreaming, and inviting him to witness the performance of a comedy, presented in his honour by a group of travelling players. This play is *The Taming of the Shrew*.

Baptista, a rich Paduan, has two daughters. He will not allow the marriage of the younger, Bianca, until a husband has been found for Katharina; but Katharina is notoriously illtempered, and nobody wants her. Petruchio, a visitor from Verona in search of a rich wife, decides to take her on. Oblivious of her rudeness and evidently delighting in what others find offensive, he succeeds in getting a marriage arranged. He arrives late at the wedding, wearing rags and riding an old nag, rushes Katharina off before the wedding feast and embarks on a programme of systematic humiliation. When he takes her back to Baptista's house, Petruchio can present her, in a not entirely jocular competition, as the most docile wife in the whole company. Even Bianca, who has married her Lucentio, cannot rival Katharina.

*The Taming of the Shrew* is an early comedy whose particular strength is the vigorous control of its central relationship. Modern audiences must accept an Elizabethan argument that Katharina is not the loser by her taming, though arguments about the possible ironies of her dutiful final speech will continue.

**Tancred, or, The New Crusade** A political novel by **Benjamin Disraeli**, published in 1847. The third in the trilogy begun by *Coningsby* and *Sybil*, it draws together characters from the earlier books and reintroduces the enigmatic Sidonia, who is revealed to be an international negotiator. Tancred, Lord Montacute, a thoughtful young man, retraces the journey made by his Crusader ancestors to Jerusalem, to find the roots of his Christian religion. There he becomes the unwitting pawn in political machinations, is kidnapped for ransom, discovers a community who worship the old Greek gods, and falls in love with Eva, daughter of the Jewish financier Besso. Eva is an acute theologian and lectures the willing Tancred on the history of Mediterranean civilization, which was ripe when 'flat-nosed Franks' were living as savages in the northern forests. In the final pages, Tancred declares his love for Eva, but she refuses him and swoons at the moment his parents come from England to claim him. The book is a piece of special pleading for Jewish culture, despite the disclaimer that Christianity is the 'perfection' of Judaism, but Tancred cannot fulfil the desire indicated by the drive of the narrative: like Disraeli, he is a 19th-century Christian, who cannot revert to Judaism, however deep his nostalgia.

**Tancred and Gismund** A tragedy by Robert Wilmot, Christopher Hatton, Henry Noel and others, based on a story by Boccaccio. It was presented before Elizabeth I at Greenwich, probably in 1568, as *Gismond of Salerne* and was in rhyming verse. The published version of 1591 changes the title and is in blank verse.

**Tannahill, Robert** 1774–1810 Poet and songwriter. Tannahill was a weaver of Paisley whose lyrics achieved a brief contemporary success. 'Jessie the Flower of Dunblane' was set to music by R. A. Smith, the editor of *The Scottish Minstrel. Poems and Songs* was published in 1807. Tannahill drowned himself after burning his manuscripts when Constable, the publisher, rejected a collection of his poems.

**Tarkington, (Newton) Booth** 1869–1946 American novelist and playwright, born in Indianapolis, Indiana, and educated at Purdue and Princeton. His first two novels, *The Gentleman From Indiana* (1899) and *Monsieur Beaucaire* (1900), were accepted for publication on the advice of **Hamlin Garland**; the former is an example of literary realism in the manner of **William Dean Howells**, the latter a historical romance.

In all, Tarkington went on to write over 40

volumes of fiction. Among his nostalgic novels of boyhood and adolescence for juvenile readers are *Penrod* (1914), *Seventeen* (1916), *Penrod and Sam* (1916) and *Penrod Jashber* (1929). His novels for adults include three – *The Turmoil* (1915), *The Magnificent Ambersons* (1918, Pulitzer Prize), and *The Midlander* (1924) – which in 1927 were published as a trilogy entitled *Growth*, and which treat the effects on society of the rise in social prominence of the *nouveau riche* businessman. *Alice Adams*, published in 1921 and awarded the Pulitzer Prize in the following year, is an ironic novel of manners about a middle-class American girl who seeks but fails to marry a rich man.

Tarkington's plays include an adaptation of his novel *Monsieur Beaucaire* (1901), *The Man From Home* (1908), *The Country Cousin* (1921), *The Intimate Strangers* (1921), *The Wren* (1922) and *Bimbo, the Pirate* (1926). In 1928 he published a volume of reminiscences, *The World Does Move*. He continued to write prolifically until his death at the age of 76; among his notable later works are the novels *The Heritage of Hatcher Ide* (1941), *Kate Fennigate* (1943), and *The Image of Josephine* (1945).

**Tarlton (or Tarleton), Richard** d. 1588 Clown. He is first heard of in 1570 as the supposed author of a ballad, and the Stationers' Register lists among his lost work *Tarlton's Toys* and *Tarlton's Tragical Treatises* (both 1576) and *Tarlton's Device upon this Unlooked for Great Snow* (1579). The manuscript of *Tarlton's Jig of a Horse Load of Fools* is now assumed to be a forgery by **John Payne Collier**, but Tarlton was almost certainly author of the popular play, *The Seven Deadly Sins* (1585), of whose second part an outline plot survives. It was performed by Queen Elizabeth's Men, which he joined on the company's formation in 1583; prior to that date he had probably been one of Leicester's Men. There is every indication that he was more suited to solo or extempore performance than to the faithful recitation of other men's lines. The spirit, though not the letter, of his comic routines is probably present in the posthumously published *Tarlton's Jests* (1611), an important source of biographical information. The well-known drawing by John Scottowe shows him as a rustic clown, with curly hair and broad nose, wearing a simple suit, buttoned cap and short boots, playing a pipe while beating a tabor. That Tarlton's fame outlived him is not surprising. He was the finest popular entertainer of his generation as well as a favourite at court. It is something more than sentiment that reinforces claims that **Shakespeare** had him in mind when he wrote Hamlet's reminiscence of Yorick.

***Task, The*** A poem in blank verse in six books by **William Cowper**, published in 1785. 'The Sofa' is the first part and the five books that follow are 'The Time-piece', 'The Garden', 'The Winter Evening', 'The Winter Morning Walk' and 'The Winter Walk at Noon'. The title comes from 'the task' that Lady Austen set him in writing a poem about his sofa. *The Task* is generally acknowledged as Cowper's masterpiece and earned the praise of **Robert Burns** and **Coleridge**. The poet, in a letter to William Unwin (10 October 1784), stated that his purpose was 'to recommend rural ease and leisure as friendly to the cause of piety and virtue'. His delight in the pleasures he found in country life is rendered with exactitude; there are also didactic passages concerned with abuses such as the failures of the clergy and the cruelty of blood sports.

**Tate, (John Orley) Allen** 1899–1979 American poet and critic, born in Winchester, Kentucky, and educated at Vanderbilt University. His first publication was the privately printed volume *The Golden Mean and Other Poems* (1923, with Ridley Wills). In 1928 he contributed several poems to *Fugitives: an Anthology of Verse*, among them 'Ode to the Confederate Dead', one of his most famous pieces. In the same year he published *Mr Pope and Other Poems* and a biography, *Stonewall Jackson: The Good Soldier*. Another Civil War biography, *Jefferson Davis: His Rise and Fall*, followed in 1929. He contributed to *I'll Take My Stand* (1930), a founding document of the Southern Agrarian movement. The volumes of poetry that followed include *Poems: 1928–1931* (1932), *The Mediterranean and Other Poems* (1936), *Selected Poems* (1937), *Poems: 1922–1947* (1948), *Poems* (1960) and *Collected Poems* (1977). He often took the history of the South as his subject and, especially in his later poetry, lamented the decline of Christianity in an increasingly mechanized and atheistic society. He received the Bollingen Prize for poetry in 1956.

His critical works include *Reactionary Essays on Poetry and Ideas* (1936), *Reason in Madness, Critical Essays* (1941), *On the Limits of Poetry, Selected Essays 1928–1948* (1948), *The Forlorn Demon: Didactic and Critical Essays* (1953), *Collected Essays* (1959) and *Essays of Four Decades* (1968). A leading proponent of the **New Criticism**, Tate also served as the editor of **The Kenyon Review** (1938) and **The Sewanee Review** (1944–6). His only novel, *The Fathers* (1938), is a first-person narrative in which the 65-year-old Lacy Buchan recalls his past – a past which spans the demise of the Old South and of the stability that it represented.

**Tate, Nahum** 1652–1715 Poet, translator and playwright. Born and educated in Dublin, Tate settled in London in 1672 and began a busy career in literature. He was appointed **Poet**

Laureate in 1692 and Historiographer Royal in 1702. His reputation as a poet is sustained by his collaboration with **Dryden** in the second part of *Absalom and Achitophel* and by the carol 'While shepherds watched their flocks by night', as a translator by his *New Version of the Psalms of David* (1696), undertaken with Nicholas Brady (see **Psalters**), and his version from Fracastoro of *Syphilus: A Poetical History of the French Disease* (1686). He is best remembered for his work in the theatre, particularly his libretto for Purcell's *Dido and Aeneas* (1689) and his scaled-down and immensely popular version of *King Lear* (1681), which spares Cordelia's life and betrothes her to Edgar in a happy ending.

*Tatler, The* A periodical founded by **Richard Steele**, appearing three times a week from April 1709 until January 1711. It presented its reports on various subjects as coming from different coffee and chocolate houses, the newly fashionable meeting places of the age: entertainment from White's, politics and foreign news from St James's, poetry from Will's. As it grew successful, *The Tatler* developed into an arbiter of conduct and taste, and the editor **Isaac Bickerstaff** (a pseudonym Steele borrowed from **Swift**) introduced the marriage of his sister Jenny Distaff to make it a family magazine. Of 271 numbers Steele wrote the entire contents of nearly 190, **Joseph Addison** wrote 42, and 36 were written in collaboration. *The Tatler* was succeeded by *The Spectator*.

**Taylor, Bayard** 1825–78 American travel-writer, poet and novelist, born to Quaker parents in Kennett Square, Pennsylvania. Taylor published his first collection of verse, *Ximena*, in 1844. That same year he travelled to Europe, and his experiences there furnished material for his second book, *Views A-Foot* (1846), and for a series of letters published in the *New York Tribune*. When he returned to America, the *Tribune*, impressed by these letters, appointed him manager of their literary section and sent him to California to cover the Gold Rush of 1849. He subsequently published an account of the Gold Rush, *Eldorado, or, Adventures in the Path of Empire* (2 vols., 1850). The following year he set off on an extensive journey which took him to Egypt, Abyssinia, Turkey, India and China, before he joined Commodore Perry in the Pacific. On his return to New York in 1853, Taylor began a series of lectures and wrote several accounts of travels and adventures, including *A Journey to Central Africa* (1854), *The Lands of the Saracen* (1855) and *A Visit to India, China and Japan in the Year 1853* (1855). In 1856 he travelled extensively in Europe and Russia and again published several accounts of the journey: *Northern Travel* (1857),

*Travels in Greece and Russia* (1859) and *At Home and Abroad* (1860).

He also wrote several novels, all of which are set in America and comment upon various aspects of Victorian American culture. They include: *Hannah Thurston* (1863), *John Godfrey's Fortunes* (1864), *Joseph and His Friend* (1870) and *Beauty and the Beast and Tales of Home* (1872). Throughout his life, he published numerous volumes of verse, a body of work which reflects his wide, international experience and varied tastes: *Rhymes of Travel, Ballads and Poems* (1849), *Lars, A Pastoral of Norway* (1873) and *The Echo Club and Other Literary Diversions* (1876).

**Taylor, Cecil P[hilip]** 1928–81 Dramatist. Throughout his life he kept faith with the socialism of his Glasgow Jewish childhood, but the revolutionary flavour of his early plays, such as his first, *Aa Went to Blaydon Races* (1962), gave way to the warm humour of such works as *The Black and White Minstrels* (1972). His most successful play, *Good* (1981), is about a liberal German professor whose moral cowardice leads to a military career and a job in Auschwitz. A prolific dramatist whose energy and charm were present in all his work, Taylor also adapted plays by Sternheim and Ibsen, as well as writing for television.

**Taylor, Edward** *c.*1645–1729 American poet. Born in Leicestershire, England, Taylor emigrated to Massachusetts in 1668. He graduated from Harvard in 1671 and served as minister to the church in the frontier town of Westfield, Massachusetts, for the rest of his life. A friend of the **Mathers** and of **Samuel Sewall**, he was a conservative in matters of church polity; he corresponded with **Solomon Stoddard**, his frontier neighbour, on the subject of the latter's open communion policy.

Today Taylor is considered the pre-eminent poet of early New England, but his poetry was not known in his own day; his manuscripts remained undiscovered in the Yale University library until 1937. Thomas H. Johnson edited the *Poetical Works* in 1939. In addition to a few occasional poems, he wrote the long series *Gods Determinations Touching His Elect; and the Elects Combat in Their Conversion, and coming Up to God in Christ: Together with the Comfortable Effects Thereof*, a poetic treatment of Puritan dogma; and the devotional *Meditations*, each exploring the imagery of a biblical text.

**Taylor, Elizabeth** 1912–75 Novelist and short-story writer. Born Elizabeth Coles in Reading, she was educated there and worked as a teacher and librarian until her marriage in 1936. Her first novel, *At Mrs Lippincote's* (1946), a gentle study of bourgeois life written with simplicity and precision, was followed by many others of similar quality: *Palladian* (1947), *A Wreath of Roses* (1950), about a middle-aged woman's emotional involvement with a younger man, *The Soul of Kindness* (1963), *Mrs Palfrey at the Claremont* (1972), about old age, and *Blaming* (1976), about a young woman whose life is thrown into emotional turmoil after her husband's death on their holiday in Istanbul. She is also the author of collections of short stories – *Hester Lilly* (1954), *The Blush* (1958), *A Dedicated Man* (1965) and *The Devastating Boys* (1962) – and a book for children, *Mossy Trotter* (1967).

**Taylor, Sir Henry** 1800–86 Playwright. Henry Taylor was born at Bishop-Middleham, Durham, and educated at home. He earned his knighthood for his long service in the Colonial Office. Taylor's verse dramas were never produced but one of them, *Philip van Artevelde* (1834), was much admired as a study of character. Others were *Isaac Comnenus* (1827), *Edwin the Fair* (1842), *The Virgin Widow* (1850) and *St Clement's Eve* (1862). Taylor was also the author of *The Statesman* (1836), a satirical essay on the art of succeeding as a civil servant, and *Autobiography (1800–75)* (1885). His *Collected Works* were published in 1877 and his *Correspondence* in 1888.

**Taylor, Jeremy** 1613–67 Religious writer. The son of a Cambridge barber, Taylor was educated at Gonville and Caius College and became a substitute preacher at St Paul's. He came to the notice of **Laud**, Archbishop of Canterbury, who gave him a fellowship at All Souls, Oxford. He became rector of Uppingham in 1638 and chaplain to both Charles I and the archbishop, leaving his rectorship in 1642 to join the king's personal attendants. He was at Cardigan Castle when it surrendered to the Parliamentary army, but found shelter as teacher and chaplain to the Earl of Carbery at Golden Grove in Carmarthenshire. Taylor spent ten years at Golden Grove and the best of his writing dates from this period. He moved next to London and Lord Conway, another friend, secured him a chaplaincy in Northern Ireland in 1658. He resumed his writing, and was given the see of Down and Connor at the Restoration, and later of Dromore, where he is buried in the cathedral. Taylor's place in English literature is as a devotional writer who did much to shape the Church of England. He wrote clear unadorned prose to set forth his plea for tolerance. men should be allowed to differ in opinion when they plainly agreed on Christian fundamentals. His principal works are *A Discourse on the Liberty of Prophesying* (1647), *The Golden Grove* (1655), *Discourse of the Nature, Offices and Measures of Friendship* (1657), *The Worthy Communicant* (1660) and, best known of all, *The Rule and Exercises of Holy Living* (1650) and *The Rule and Exercises of Holy Dying* (1651). The last was written in a period of deep personal grief following the deaths of his wife and of his patroness, Lady Carbery.

**Taylor, John** 1580–1653 The 'Water Poet'. Born in Gloucester and educated locally at the grammar school, he was apprenticed to a London waterman before being pressed into the navy. He was present at the siege of Cadiz in 1596, and, according to his own account, completed 16 voyages before retiring with a lame leg. He returned to working as a Thames waterman but found the trade damaged by excess of competition. He hit on the expedient of collecting sponsors for whimsical journeys, on foot or by water, and writing up his experiences in lively prose and doggerel. In this fashion he travelled to the Continent and Bohemia, and made water journeys from London to York, Salisbury and Queenborough, reaching the last destination in a brown-paper boat. *The Penniless Pilgrimage* (1618) describes a walk from London to Edinburgh and Braemar without money; when some of his sponsors complained that he had cheated, Taylor upbraided them in *A Kicksey Winsey* (1619). He eventually became an innkeeper, in Oxford from 1642 and in London from 1645.

**Taylor, Peter** 1917– American short-story writer. Born in Trenton, Tennessee, Taylor spent his youth in Nashville, St Louis, and Memphis. These cities, as well as the fictional town of Thornton, Tennessee, are the setting of many of his works, which frequently centre on the conflict between the values of small-town Southern life and those of an urban culture. He has published one novella, *A Woman of Means* (1950), and several collections of stories: *A Long Fourth and Other Stories* (1948), *The Widows of Thornton* (1954), *Happy Families Are All Alike* (1959), *Miss Leonora When Last Seen* (1963), *The Collected Stories of Peter Taylor* (1969), *In The Miro District and Other Stories* (1977), and *The Old Forest and Other Stories* (1985).

**Taylor, Tom** 1817–80 Dramatist, editor and critic. Born near Sunderland, Taylor attended the universities of Glasgow and Cambridge, where he taught in 1842–4. He was Professor of English in the University of London in 1845–7, during which time he qualified for the Bar. He practised law on the northern circuit in 1847–50, was Assistant Secretary and then Secretary to the London Board of Health in 1850–71 and editor of **Punch** from 1874 until his death. His phenomenal industry allowed him, during this time, to write 80 plays, leaders for *The Morning Chronicle* and *The Daily News*, art criticism for *The Times* and *The Graphic* and numerous contributions to *Punch*. He was house dramatist at the Olympic Theatre, 1853–60, and at the **Haymarket** 1857–70.

During his long theatrical career, Taylor wrote in almost all the current dramatic styles. His first play, *A Trip to Kissingen* (1844), was a farce. His pantomimes included such popular favourites as *Cinderella* (1845) and *Little Red Riding Hood* (1851). There was even a hippodrama, *Garibaldi* (1859), and a series of historical verse dramas, of which the best is *The Fool's Revenge* (1859), adapted from Hugo's *Le Roi s'Amuse*. Most of his work is derivative, as was typical of working Victorian playwrights, but there is merit in such melodramas as *Plot and Passion* (with John Lang, 1853) and particularly *The Ticket-of-Leave Man* (1863), and in the comedies, conventionally theatrical but not without social perception, *Masks and Faces* (with **Charles Reade**, 1852), *To Oblige Benson* (1854), *Still Waters Run Deep* (1855), *Victims* (1857), *The Contested Election* (1859), *The Overland Route* (1860) and *New Men and Old Acres* (with A. W. Dubourg, 1869). It is unjust that Taylor should be best remembered as the author of *Our American Cousin* (1858), whose success owed more to the actor E. A. Sothern's inventiveness as Lord Dundreary and whose notoriety was a result of Abraham Lincoln's being assassinated at a performance in Washington, DC.

**Tempest, The** A play by **William Shakespeare**, first performed *c*.1611 and published in the First Folio of 1623. No single main source has been established, and this very eclecticism has given strength to those who argue that, in writing what he felt might be his last work for the stage, Shakespeare was consciously summarizing his theatrical art.

Prospero, exiled Duke of Milan, has taken up a 12-year residence on a remote island, previously inhabited only by the airy spirit, Ariel, and the earthy Caliban, deformed son of the dead witch, Sycorax. With Prospero is his innocent daughter, Miranda, together with the books and the staff that enable him to practise magic. It is by magic that he brings about a storm and arranges for the arrival on the island of a group of shipwrecked figures from his past. From Milan come his usurping brother Antonio and the loyal counsellor Gonzalo, who gave Prospero what help he could when he was cast adrift 12 years before; and from Naples come King Alonso, his son Ferdinand and Sebastian, the king's scheming brother.

The play recounts the various adventures of these characters during their days on the island, all overseen by Prospero and organized by Ariel. The outcome is that Miranda, who could recall no man save Caliban and her father, falls in love with Ferdinand, that Sebastian's malice is exposed to Alonso, and that Antonio restores

'What have we here? A man or a fish?' Trinculo speaks thus of Caliban in *The Tempest* (Act II, scene 2). Scholars have long pondered on how Caliban was presented in Shakespeare's time and one possible solution may have been found in this creature, illustrated in Conrad Gessner's *Icones Anim Celium* (1560). Shakespeare shared the Elizabethan fascination with explorers' tales and descriptions of exotic and mythical animals.

the dukedom of Milan to Prospero. At the play's end, Prospero releases Ariel from his service, returns the island to a chastened Caliban, breaks his staff and buries his books. All will sail for home, guided by the gentle winds Ariel has conjured up.

Although formally a comedy, *The Tempest* is more aptly associated with the group of tragicomic romances with which Shakespeare greeted his company's move into the indoor theatre of the **Blackfriars**: *Pericles*, *Cymbeline* and *The Winter's Tale*. It is a complex poetic work, whose mechanical plotting serves to draw attention to wider aesthetic and philosophical themes.

**Temple, Sir William** 1628–99 Diplomat and essayist. The son of Sir John Temple, Master of the Rolls in Ireland, Temple was born in London and completed his education at Emmanuel College, Cambridge. In 1648 he met **Dorothy Osborne**, whom he married in 1655 despite the opposition of her father, a severe Royalist. Dorothy wrote regularly to William in the years 1652–4 and her letters were published in 1888. Temple became an envoy at Brussels in 1666, and in 1668 negotiated the Triple Alliance of England, Holland and Sweden to counterbalance the power of France and her ambitions in Spain. His work was negated, however, by Charles II's secret treaty with Louis XIV. Temple returned to Holland in 1674 and arranged the marriage of Princess Mary to William of Orange. He retired soon after and lived first at Sheen and then at Moor Park in Surrey, where **Jonathan Swift** worked as his secretary.

In literature Temple is remembered for his essays, his *Memoirs* (1692) and his letters, which were edited by Swift (1701). Apart from *Essay upon the Present State of Ireland* (1668), *Observations upon the United Provinces of the Netherlands* (1672) and *The Advancement of Trade in Ireland* (1673), the essays are brought together in three volumes of *Miscellanea* (1680, 1690 and 1701). Its second volume contains the *Essay upon the Ancient and Modern Learning*, in which he compared modern writers and philosophers un-

Sir William Temple. A detail from the portrait attributed to Lely, *c*.1660. National Portrait Gallery, London.

favourably with their classical counterparts and lavishly praised the epistles of Phalaris, the tyrant of Agrigentum in the 6th century BC. However, the scholar **Richard Bentley** showed the epistles to be forgeries and the result was a lively controversy which produced Swift's *The Battle of the Books*. **Macaulay** found Temple 'a man of the world among men of letters, a man of letters among men of the world'. He was an informed and opinionated amateur, whose best essays – on gardening or poetry, for example – still have at least historical interest.

*Temple of Glass, The*  A poem by **John Lydgate** in **rhyme royal** and couplets, written between 1400 and 1420. The form is an allegorical **dream-vision** and the poem draws extensively on the work of **Geoffrey Chaucer**, in particular *The House of Fame*, *The Parlement of Foules*, and *The Knight's Tale* (see *The Canterbury Tales*) as well as earlier poems in the tradition. The dreamer is transported to a temple of glass where he sees depicted famous lovers complaining to Venus. He then sees a woman complain that she is bound to a man she does not love and separated from her beloved. Venus promises her aid and a knight enters complaining of his unrequited love for the woman. They are united and blessed by Venus. The poem may refer to a historical event, but no specific references are found and it cannot be identified. The allegory is barely sustained and there is none of the philosophical and psychological complexity, or the humour, which characterize the poem's models.

*Tenant of Wildfell Hall, The*  **Anne Brontë**'s second novel, published in 1848, the year before she died. A much more ambitious work than *Agnes Grey*, it has a male narrator (Gilbert Markham).

Helen Graham, the tenant of Wildfell Hall, is young, beautiful and said to be a widow. Her reticence about herself provokes local gossip. Gilbert Markham, a neighbouring farmer who has fallen in love with her, defends Helen's reputation until he overhears her in affectionate conversation with her landlord, Frederick Lawrence. Markham and Lawrence quarrel violently.

Helen Graham is in fact in love with Markham, and writes of this in her diary, which also records the secret of her life. She was married young to Arthur Huntingdon and is the mother of his son. Huntingdon proved to be a drunkard and, despite her attempts to reclaim him, she led a life of misery and humiliation. Finally, afraid of the effect of his way of life on their son, she appealed to her brother, Lawrence, who provided her with the refuge of Wildfell Hall. She tells Markham the truth, and then has to go back to her husband, who is dangerously ill. Huntingdon dies of his excesses and Helen is free.

Markham is dismayed to learn that she is now a wealthy woman but is encouraged by Lawrence to win her hand.

Although the novel was a popular success, its frank portrait of Huntingdon's alcoholism and of Helen's struggle to free herself from such a husband struck some contemporaries as offensive and inappropriate subjects for a woman author. Even her sister **Charlotte Brontë** was disturbed, doubtless by the echoes of their brother Branwell's fate in the portrait of Huntingdon. Anne Brontë was unrepentant, defending herself in the preface to the second edition: 'I wished to tell the truth, for truth always conveys its own moral . . . To represent a bad thing in its least offensive light is doubtless the most agreeable course for a writer of fiction to pursue; but is it the most honest?'

**Tender is the Night** A novel by **F. Scott Fitzgerald**, published in 1934. Adverse criticism led Fitzgerald to believe that the story's time scheme was faulty, and a revised edition (based on his notes), which reorganized the action into chronological order, was published posthumously in 1948. However, most modern editions follow the original version.

*Tender is the Night* is a novel about the squandering of creative promise. It is the story of Dick Diver, a young American psychiatrist studying in Zurich in 1917. He becomes interested in the case of Nicole Warren, a beautiful and wealthy American suffering from schizophrenia. As she recovers, she comes to depend on Dick, and eventually they marry. The doctor–patient relationship, however, carries over to their marriage; caring for Nicole prevents Dick both from loving her and from pursuing his intellectual career. They have two children and lead a leisurely life on the Riviera. Their friends include Abe North, a composer who has become an alcoholic and who, like Dick, has failed to fulfil the creative promise of his youth. His failure is consummated when he is killed in a Paris bar. Dick's life as the impeccable host on the Riviera gradually deteriorates. He becomes infatuated with Rosemary Hoyt, an American actress much younger than himself; he begins to drink heavily; he is involved in a brawl in Rome; and his medical career is on the verge of ruin. Nicole falls in love with Tommy Barban, a French mercenary and member of their Riviera circle, and eventually divorces Dick, whose own failure is finalized when he returns to America to a small-town medical practice.

**Tennant, Emma** 1937– Novelist. Born in London and brought up in Scotland, she founded the literary newspaper *Bananas*, which during its short life in the early 1970s established a reputation for publishing quirky and adventur-

ous fiction. Of her 11 novels, the most original explore extreme psychological states and alternative notions of reality through striking fantasy and the extensive use of dream sequences and **stream of consciousness**. The most virtuoso performances are perhaps *The Bad Sister* (1978) and *Wild Nights* (1980). Recent novels such as *Queen of Stones* (1982) and *Woman Beware Woman* (1983) have tended towards a more conventionally realistic narrative and a strong element of mystery and suspense, while continuing Tennant's interest in the imprecise border of reality and its mythical implications.

**Tennant, Kylie** 1912–88 Australian novelist. Born in Manly and educated at the University of Sydney, she worked for the Australian Broadcasting Commission for a time. Her first novel, *Tiburon* (1935), was well received. It concerns the fate of an impoverished community in a small country town during the Depression years, a setting to which Tennant returned in later novels. *Foveaux* (1939) was followed by *The Battlers* (1941), *Ride on Stranger* (1943), *Time Enough Later* (1945), *Lost Haven* (1946), *The Joyful Condemned* (1953) and *The Honey Flow* (1956). Irony, humour and a vivid talent for the swift evocation of atmosphere, characterize her work.

**Tennant, William** 1784–1848 Poet. Born in Anstruther, Fifeshire, he completed his education at St Andrews University, where he later became Professor of Oriental Languages. His poem, *Anster Fair* (1812), is a mock-heroic description of a rural fair in the reign of James V of Scotland.

**Tenniel, Sir John** 1820–1914 Cartoonist and illustrator. Born in London, he studied art at the Royal Academy. After the success of his illustrations for *Aesop's Fables* (1848) he was invited to join **Punch** as leading cartoonist with **John Leech**. There followed over 50 years of political cartoons on all the great issues of the day, yet he is now remembered for his illustrations to **Lewis Carroll**'s *Alice's Adventures in Wonderland* (1865) and *Through the Looking-Glass* (1871). In all, he submitted over 90 drawings, of which only one was accepted without reservation by the author. The final result was extremely successful, with many of the details that Tenniel suggested in his pictures (such as the price label stuck in the Mad Hatter's top hat) now virtually a standard part of any new illustrator's reaction to Carroll's text. Tenniel agreed to illustrate the second Alice book only after much hesitation, and afterwards abandoned book illustration altogether.

**Tennyson, Alfred Lord** 1809–92 Poet. Alfred Tennyson was born, one of eight children, in Somersby, Lincolnshire, the son of the Revd George Clayton Tennyson and his wife, Elizabeth Fytche Tennyson. He was educated at Louth grammar school, privately by his father, and at Trinity College, Cambridge. As early as 1823–4 he had written *The Devil and the Lady*, a precocious fragment in the Elizabethan manner that remained unprinted until 1930. Matriculating at university in November 1827, Tennyson became a member of the **Apostles**, won the Chancellor's Gold Medal for poetry with 'Timbuctoo', and met **Arthur Henry Hallam** whose early death in 1833 prompted Tennyson's most enduring poem, *In Memoriam*, an elegy whose quatrains he started as early as 1834, jotting down his reflections until it became a vast compendium of 19th-century thought. In 1827 *Poems by Two Brothers*, unobtrusively published in Louth and including work by his brothers Frederick and Charles (see **Charles Tennyson Turner**), marked his début as a published poet and was followed in 1830 by *Poems, Chiefly Lyrical*. The next year his father, a past victim of severe physical and mental breakdown, died, and the young Tennyson left the university without a degree. In December 1832 he published *Poems* (title-page dated 1833), which received a savage mauling from **John Wilson Croker** in *The Quarterly Review*. There followed the 'Ten Years' Silence', a period of neurotic refusal to publish, when Tennyson's life lacked

Tennyson. A detail from the portrait by Samuel Laurence, c.1840. National Portrait Gallery, London.

direction and his emotional instability seemed unusually apparent. He suffered the shock of Hallam's death and the lesser shock of a family move to Epping, fell briefly in love with Rosa Baring, began his long and interrupted engagement to Emily Sellwood and made a disastrous investment in the woodcarving scheme of his friend Dr Allen. Had it not been for American pressures over copyright, the silence may well have continued, but Tennyson felt compelled to publish. The result was the masterly *Poems* of 1842, its first volume composed of earlier, revised work (*The Lady of Shalott*, *The Lotos-Eaters*) and the second containing new poems (*Locksley Hall*, *Ulysses*). This was followed in 1847 by *The Princess*, an amorous polemic on the rights of women and, three years later, by *In Memoriam*. In fact, 1850 was Tennyson's *annus mirabilis*, for in that year he succeeded **Wordsworth** as **Poet Laureate** and, finally, married Emily Sellwood.

Henceforth Tennyson trod the leonine, bardic path and, like many abnormally shy people, he trod it somewhat roughly. In 1853 he and Emily moved to Farringford on the Isle of Wight, where his privacy was constantly invaded. He became a member of the Athenaeum and was invited to join 'the Club', founded a century before by **Johnson** and **Reynolds**; but because of his obsessive shyness Tennyson invariably resigned or withdrew from such organizations. However, the poetry poured forth: in 1855 came *Maud and Other Poems*, in 1859 'Enid' (already privately printed in 1857), 'Vivien', 'Elaine' and 'Guinevere', the first four of the *Idylls of the King*. In 1862 the Laureate had his first of several audiences with Queen Victoria. In 1864 he published *Enoch Arden* in a volume which also included *Tithonus*, and in 1865 (as on several other occasions) he refused a baronetcy, though he did eventually agree to a title and took his seat in the Lords in 1883. Also in the 1860s the Tennysons built another home, in Aldworth near Haslemere, and he developed an interest in the Metaphysical Society. At the end of the decade he published *The Holy Grail and Other Poems* (1869, dated 1870). In 1872 came *Gareth and Lynette* followed in 1872–3 by the Imperial Library edition of the works which gathered up the *Idylls* (except *Balin and Balan* of 1885), added the Epilogue ('To the Queen') and rounded off that astonishing rendition of Arthurian legend. In 1875 Tennyson published his first play, *Queen Mary*, which was produced a year later; a clutch of dramatic works followed, among them *Harold* (1876), *Becket* (1884), and *The Cup* (1881), which latter even the combined talents of Henry Irving and Ellen Terry could not save from oblivion. His muse occasionally nodding, Tennyson nevertheless was poetically active during the 1880s, publishing *Ballads and Other Poems* (1880), *Tiresias and Other Poems* (1885), *Locksley*

'Mariana.' An illustration by John Everett Millais for the Moxon *Tennyson* (1857). Other illustrations were contributed by Holman Hunt and D. G. Rossetti.

*Hall Sixty Years After* (1886) and *Demeter and Other Poems* (1889), which contained **Crossing the Bar**. *The Death of Oenone, Akbar's Dream, and Other Poems* appeared posthumously in 1892. The output is substantial and, if not all of it measures up to his finest work, it is nevertheless impressive in quality and often revealing of his elusive genius.

Perhaps no poet's reputation has received – and withstood – so severe a buffeting since his death. Always highly neurotic, often roughly eccentric, a poet of twilight and half-shadows marked by his delicate poignancy and controlled sadness, yet also the trumpeter of Empire and exponent of a higher morality, Tennyson remained a supreme technician torn between the bardic voice and the solitary lyric.

**Tennyson Turner, Charles** 1808–79 Poet. Like his younger brother, **Alfred Tennyson**, he was born at Somersby in Lincolnshire and educated at Louth grammar school and Trinity College, Cambridge. He became vicar of Grasby, Lincolnshire, and changed his name to Turner on succeeding to his great-uncle's property in 1830. With Frederick and Alfred Tennyson he contributed to the misnamed *Poems by Two Brothers* (1827), and later produced four volumes of distinguished but restrained sonnets (1830, 1864, 1868, 1874).

***Terrible Temptation, A****: A Story of the Day* A novel by **Charles Reade**, published in 1871. The plot hinges on Richard Bassett's attempts to secure the inheritance of which he believes himself to have been defrauded, but the book is mainly notable for returning to the attack on asylums for the insane which Reade had begun in ***Hard Cash***.

**Terson, Peter** Pen-name of the dramatist Peter Patterson (1932– ). He was born and brought up on Tyneside, where he worked as a teacher for 10 years before his first play, *A Night to Make the Angels Weep*, was produced in 1964. Together with *The Mighty Reservoy* (1964), it showed him an amusing observer of life in the Midlands and the North, with the ability to seize on a symbolic idea which raised his naturalism toward myth. *Mooney and his Caravans* was seen on TV in 1966 before its stage production in 1968. Terson's association with the National Youth Theatre began with *Zigger Zagger* (1967), about football fans and hooligans, and continued with *The Apprentices* (1968), *Spring-Heeled Jack* (1970) and *Good Lads at Heart* (1971). *Strippers* (1984) describes the life of women in areas of high unemployment who take to stripping in pubs for pocket-money.

**terza rima** A series of three-line **stanzas** interlocked by rhyme, as follows: aba bcb cdc ded . . . The form was originally Italian, used by Dante in *The Divine Comedy*. The relative difficulty of rhyming in English makes it a less suitable form for English literature, but poets from **Chaucer** to **W. H. Auden** have used it successfully; **Shelley**'s 'Ode to the West Wind' is a famous example.

***Tess of the d'Urbervilles*** A novel by **Thomas Hardy**, first printed serially (in a bowdlerized form) in *The Graphic* from July to December 1891 and in book form the same year. Defiantly sub-titled 'A Pure Woman Faithfully Presented', the novel expresses Hardy's rejection of the conventional heroine of Victorian fiction. The controversy it provoked, renewed by the publication of ***Jude the Obscure***, contributed to Hardy's decision to abandon novels for poetry.

Unwisely, Parson Tringham tells John Durbeyfield, a haggler (local carrier) of Marlott, that he is descended from the ancient Norman family of d'Urbervilles. Fortified by this information, he and his wife Joan encourage their daughter Tess to seek the kinship of the parvenu Stoke-d'Urbervilles, themselves not entitled to the illustrious name. She is seduced by their son, the vulgar rake Alec, and bears a child that mercifully dies. To make a fresh start Tess goes to work in southern Wessex at the fertile Talbothays farm where she meets Angel Clare, younger son of a parson and, after a struggle within herself, accepts his offer of marriage. On their wedding night Tess confesses her unhappy past to Angel, who recoils in puritanical horror. He goes off to Brazil and Tess seeks employment at the grim upland farm, Flintcomb Ash, belonging to the tyrannical Farmer Groby. There she is again afflicted by the advances of Alec d'Urberville, now an itinerant preacher. He is insistent that Tess is more his wife than Angel's and relentless in his pursuit of her. Angel returns to England a wiser man and traces Tess to Sandbourne, where she is living as Alec's wife. She considers it too late for reconciliation and sends him away. In her despair and entrapment she kills Alec and, after a brief idyllic period with Angel, is arrested at Stonehenge, tried, and hanged in Wintoncester gaol.

*Testament of Cresseid, The*  A poem by **Robert Henryson**, continuing the story of **Chaucer**'s *Troilus and Criseyde*. The first printed version to survive is in Thynne's 1532 edition of Chaucer, and the poem regularly appeared in editions of Chaucer for some time after.

Abandoned by Diomede, Cresseid becomes promiscuous. She is taken in by her father, Calchas, and blasphemes against Cupid and Venus. The planetary gods in session depute Saturn and the Moon to punish her with leprosy (which, for Henryson's readers, would be identified with syphilis). Troilus, riding back to Troy, takes pity on the lepers and in a scene of exquisite pathos he and Cresseid meet, but 'not ane ane uther knew', although the meeting provokes in Troilus a faint memory of 'fair Cresseid sumtyme his awin darling'. Told by a leper that her benefactor was Troilus, Cresseid makes her 'testament' (will), bequeathing her wealth to the lepers and returning a ring given her by Troilus. The poem has many echoes of Chaucer's *Troilus*, but alters Chaucer's story in which Diomede killed Troilus. Henryson introduces elaborate astrological machinery and gives Cresseid a fine complaint on the familiar theme of the transitoriness of beauty and security in this world.

**tetrameter**  See **metre**.

**Tey, Josephine**  See **Mackintosh, Elizabeth**.

**Thackeray, William Makepeace** 1811–63 Novelist. Born in Calcutta of Anglo-Indian parents, Thackeray came to England in 1817, and was educated at private schools and, from 1822 to 1828, at Charterhouse, the 'Slaughterhouse' and 'Grey Friars' of his fiction. He spent two years at Trinity College, Cambridge, where he fell in with a fast set and lost heavily at cards, leaving in 1830 without taking a degree. A vacation visit to Paris in 1829 gave him a lifelong love of the city, and in 1830–1 he travelled to Germany and spent six months at

Weimar, where he met Goethe. This was followed by spells as a law student in London and as Paris correspondent of the *National Standard* newspaper, which failed in 1834. The prospect of a life of gentlemanly ease was shattered when Thackeray lost most of his patrimony in the Indian bank failures of 1833, and he decided to make his living as a painter, for which he had some aptitude, studying art in London and, from 1834 to 1837, in Paris. In 1836 he published his first book, lithograph caricatures of the ballet 'La Sylphide' entitled *Flore et Zéphyr*, and on the strength of his post as Paris correspondent of *The Constitutional*, a short-lived radical newspaper set up by his stepfather, he married Isabella Shawe, the young and mentally unstable daughter of an expatriate Anglo-Irish family.

Thackeray returned to London in 1837, where his daughter Anne (later to attain some literary fame as the novelist **Anne Thackeray Ritchie**) was born in June. A second daughter followed in 1838, but died eight months later, and in 1840 Harriet Marian ('Minny'), the future wife of **Leslie Stephen**, was born. By 1840 signs of his wife's incipient insanity were unmistakable, and she had to be confined. Forced to write for a living, Thackeray contributed a stream of reviews, comic sketches, burlesques, parodies and satires to a number of periodicals, most notably *Fraser's Magazine* and, from 1842, *Punch*. For *Fraser's* he wrote *The Yellowplush Papers* (1837–8), the comic memoirs of a footman, *Catherine* (1839–40), a pastiche of the then popular **Newgate fiction**, and *A Shabby Genteel Story* (1840). Many of his early works were published under such *noms de plume* as 'Charles James Yellowplush', a footman, 'Michael Angelo Titmarsh' (after Thackeray's sketching talent and broken nose), and 'George Savage Fitz-Boodle', the heavy, tobacco-addicted clubman who is the autobiographical subject of *The Fitz-Boodle Papers* (1842–3) and the editor of Thackeray's first real novel, *Barry Lyndon*, serialized in *Fraser's* in 1844. At this period Thackeray also published three travel books: *The Paris Sketch Book* (1840), *The Irish Sketch Book* (1843) and *Notes of a Journey from Cornhill to Grand Cairo* (1846).

Thackeray's growing reputation in the 1840s was consolidated by his writings for *Punch*, especially the highly successful *Book of Snobs* (1846–7), which anatomized the class-consciousness of the early Victorian age. This concern, and the discontent with contemporary fictional stereotypes evident in his masterly parodies, *Punch's Prize Novelists* (1847), are reflected in the satirical, anti-heroic vision of his first major novel, *Vanity Fair* (1847–8), published in the monthly-part form which **Dickens** had revived. An immediate popular and critical success, *Vanity Fair* was followed by *The History of*

William Makepeace Thackeray. Engraving from the portrait drawing by Samuel Laurence, c.1850.

In 1859 Thackeray became the founding editor of *The Cornhill Magazine*, a monthly literary journal set up by the publisher **George Smith** and launched with great success in January 1860. Now plagued by recurrent ill health, he found editorial duties irksome, and resigned in 1862. His last works were published in the *Cornhill*: the short novel *Lovel the Widower* (1860), the discursive essays gathered under the title of *The Roundabout Papers* (1860–3), and his last completed novel, *The Adventures of Philip* (1861–2). A reprise of many of the themes and situations from *Pendennis* and *The Newcomes*, *Philip* lends support to the view that by the end of his life Thackeray had little fresh to say. He died on Christmas Eve 1863, leaving *Denis Duval* (1864) unfinished.

Thackeray's reputation rests on *Vanity Fair*, *Henry Esmond*, and, less securely today, on *Pendennis* and *The Newcomes*. The authorial garrulity of his later fiction and essays, his sense of the novel as 'a sort of confidential talk between writer and reader' (preface, *Pendennis*), has not always been congenial to modern taste, but recently critics have rediscovered the keen satirical eye and comic irreverence of his early stories and travel books, which have the robust energy of the 18th-century writers he admired. Thackeray remains a central figure in the history of Victorian realism, and his sceptical, ironic but compassionate vision of human conduct in a society dominated by the power of money and class gives his best work the authority of major art.

*Pendennis* (1848–50), a semi-autobiographical **Bildungsroman** portraying one of 'the gentlemen of our age'. In 1848 Thackeray became attached to Jane Brookfield, the wife of a college friend, but their platonic relationship was brought to an end by her in 1851, and some of the melancholy of love unfulfilled enters *The History of Henry Esmond* (1852), the most carefully planned of his novels and the only one to be published originally in the three-volume format. A historical novel, set during the reign of Queen Anne, *Esmond* also reflects Thackeray's growing interest in that period. In 1851 he gave a series of lectures on *The English Humorists of the Eighteenth Century* (published 1853), and made them the basis of his first lecture tour of the United States in 1852–3. *The Newcomes* (1853–5), a panoramic novel of English social life during the first half of the 19th century, and *The Rose and the Ring* (1855), the last and best of his six Christmas Books, were followed by a second visit to the United States in 1855–6, during which he lectured on *The Four Georges* (1860). *The Virginians*, another historical novel continuing the Esmond family saga in 18th-century England and America, was published in monthly parts in 1857–9.

**Theatre, The** The first purpose-built public playhouse in England. Situated in Shoreditch, it was opened in 1576 as a commercial speculation by James Burbage, actor and master carpenter. It became the favourite home of the Lord Chamberlain's Men, to which **Shakespeare** belonged. When Burbage's lease ran out in 1597, his sons, together with other members of the acting company, dismantled it and carried its timbers over the Thames as building material for the **Globe**.

**Theatre of Cruelty** See **Cruelty, Theatre of**.

**Theatre of the Absurd** See **Absurd, Theatre of the**.

***Their Eyes Were Watching God*** A novel by **Zora Neale Hurston**, published in 1937. The story centres on Janie Crawford, a strong-willed seeker of beauty who is unwilling to lead an existence of drudgery and deprivation like that of the grandmother who raised her. She suffers through a marriage of convenience, finally leaving her husband for the smooth-talking and handsome visionary, Joe Starks. Janie and Joe establish Florida's first all-black town and Joe becomes its mayor. Following Joe's death Janie is left financially secure, fortyish, and sexually, romantically and spiritually oppressed. Rather than settle into comfortable widowhood, she falls passionately in love with Vergible Woods (known to everyone as Tea Cake), who is several years younger and penniless. Against friends' advice, she goes off with Tea Cake and marries him. Their marriage provides her with the idyllic love she had dreamed of but it ends tragically. Following a violent hurricane, Tea Cake is bitten by a rabid dog and contracts the disease. When, in his frenzy, he attacks Janie, she is forced to shoot him in self-defence. She is charged with murder, but quickly exonerated. She returns, saddened but victorious, to the town she and Joe Starks had founded. The novel openly confronts the issues of civil and social rights in both a racial and feminist context.

**Theobald, Lewis** 1688–1744 Scholar and dramatist. An exact contemporary of **Alexander Pope**, he was born at Sittingbourne, Kent, and became an attorney before turning to literature.

Theobald's earliest work was a Pindaric ode on the Union of England and Scotland in 1707. He then turned to translation as the readiest way to make money, producing versions of Plato's *Phaedo* (1713), plays by Sophocles and Aristophanes (1714–15) and the first Book of the *Odyssey* (1716). He wrote 'The Censor' for *Mist's Journal*, which brought him into conflict with **John Dennis**. Between 1715 and 1720 Theobald turned his hand to many forms: tragedy (*The Persian Princess* and *The Perfidious Brother*, 1715), prose romance (*The Loves of Antiochus and Stratonice*, 1717), opera (*Pan and Syrinx*, 1717; *The Lady's Triumph*, 1718), masque (*Decius and Paulina*, 1718), biography (*A Memoir of Sir Walter Raleigh*, 1719) and Shakespearean adaptation (of *Richard II*, 1720). He also played an important role in the history of the **pantomime**, writing several for John Rich, manager of **Drury Lane**: *The Rape of Proserpine*, *Harlequin a Sorcerer* (both 1725), *Perseus and Andromache* (1730) and *Merlin, or, the Devil at Stonehenge* (1734). Irritated by Pope's 1725 edition of **Shakespeare**, Theobald published *Shakespeare Restored, or A Specimen of the Many Errors as well Committed as Unamended by Mr Pope in his Late Edition of This Poet* (1726). This contains a number of fine emendations, which Pope incorporated in the second edition of 1728. Pope had not let this debt prevent him from satirizing Theobald as eel and swallow in *Peri Bathous* or from making him hero of the first *Dunciad* (1728). One of the works satirized in *Peri Bathous* was *The Double Falsehood* (acted 1727, published 1728), which Theobald claimed was by Shakespeare and derived from an old manuscript in his possession. Theobald never published his 'original', and the play may antici-

pate that tradition of Shakespearean forgery which became so strong later in the 18th century. (See also **Shakespeare apocrypha**.)

In 1728 Theobald published the first volume of the posthumous works of Pope's early friend **William Wycherley**; Pope pre-empted Theobald's second volume by publishing one himself. He failed to succeed **Eusden** as Poet Laureate in 1730. In 1731 he wrote *Orestes*, a tragedy, and contracted with **Tonson** to produce an edition of Shakespeare, which appeared in seven volumes in 1734. It went through three editions between 1734 and 1757 and was reprinted four times between 1757 and 1773. Lack of funds drove him back to writing for the stage: **George Steevens** suggested that Theobald is the subject of **Hogarth**'s *The Distressed Poet* (1737). He announced an edition of **Beaumont** and **Fletcher** in 1742 and was working on this when he died. His efforts formed the basis of the 10-volume Beaumont and Fletcher published in 1750.

***Theory of Moral Sentiments, The*** A treatise on ethics by **Adam Smith**, published in 1759 and derived from lectures at Glasgow University, where he was Professor of Moral Philosophy. It investigates the forms and objects of moral consciousness. Smith recognizes the social factor in morality and identifies sympathy as a source of moral sentiments. Sympathy can have real value only when it comes from an 'impartial and well-informed spectator' and such a spectator is an ideal, not an actual person. In ordinary life self-interest or imperfect understanding frequently affect our attitude to the situations of other men.

**Theroux, Paul** 1941– Novelist and travel-writer. Born in Massachusetts, Theroux wrote and set his first novel, *Waldo* (1967), in the United States before beginning an extended stay in East Africa as a university lecturer in English. He now lives in London. Theroux first found attention with his two original accounts of extended train journeys, *The Great Railway Bazaar* (1975), in which he crosses Europe and Russia to reach Japan, and *The Old Patagonian Express* (1978), about a railway odyssey down through the American continent. Theroux's fiction is stylish, witty, and essays many genres. *Girls at Play* (1969) and *Jungle Lovers* (1971) are tales of naïve, hapless westerners in Africa, reminiscent of **Somerset Maugham**; *Saint Jack* (1973) is a vigorous picaresque about a Singapore pimp; *The Family Arsenal* (1976) is an atmospheric London thriller after the manner of **Graham Greene**; *The Consul's File* (1977) and *The London Embassy* (1982) are collections of linked short stories about expatriate communities in Malaya and London whose method recalls **Kipling**'s *Plain Tales from the Hills*. Theroux's best novel is *The Mosquito Coast* (1981), set in Honduras, a powerful and resourceful parable of civilization courting barbarism. The futuristic fantasy *O-Zone* (1986) marks a fresh departure.

**Thersites** A comedy of unknown authorship, sometimes attributed to **Nicholas Udall**, first acted in 1537 and printed *c.*1562. It was adapted from the Latin of Ravisins Textor, a French scholar whose text was acted at Queens' College, Cambridge, in 1543. The setting is the siege of Troy.

The English version introduces a number of allusions to 'Robin John' and 'Little Hood' into the story of Thersites, who persuades Mulciber (Vulcan) to make him a suit of armour that will render him invulnerable. Thersites puts the armour on and immediately begins to defy young and old, heaven and hell – but runs to his mother for protection when threatened by another soldier and is completely demoralized by a snail. Eventually he abandons his splendid armour and deserts the field.

**Thirlwall, Connop** 1797–1875 Historian. Thirlwall, who became Bishop of St David's in 1840, was born in London and educated at Charterhouse School and Trinity College, Cambridge, where he became a fellow in 1818. He studied law at Lincoln's Inn, but eventually decided on the Church and was ordained in 1828. In the same year he published, with J. C. Hare, the first part of a translation of Barthold Niebuhr's *History of Rome* (1828–42). Thirlwall's principal work was *A History of Greece* (8 vols., 1835–44), published at the same time as the more highly regarded work by his former schoolfellow **George Grote**.

**Thomas, Audrey** 1935– Canadian novelist and short-story writer. Born in New York state and educated at Smith College, Massachusetts, she moved to England before emigrating to Canada in 1959. In 1964–6 she lived in Ghana, returning to British Columbia in 1967, where she has lived since. She has travelled extensively in Mexico and Europe, and was the first Canadian woman writer-in-residence at the University of Edinburgh in 1985–6. Her first short story was published in 1965 in *The Atlantic Monthly* and her first collection, *Ten Green Bottles*, in New York in 1967. She has since published four collections of short stories, including *Real Mothers* (1981) and *Goodbye Harold, Good Luck* (1986). Her novels include *Mrs Blood* (1970), *Songs My Mother Taught Me* (1973) and *Blown Figures* (1975), which form a trilogy centred on one female protagonist; *Latakia* (1979), set in Crete, Greece and Syria; and *Intertidal Life* (1985), set on Galiano Island, British Columbia. Her fiction is eclectic and post-modernist; it is also strongly feminist in its

exploration of women's ambitions and self-contradictions as they seek to redefine relationships between men and women.

**Thomas, Augustus** 1857–1934 American playwright, born in St Louis, Missouri. His early plays include *Alone* (1875) and *Alabama* (1891). The success of the latter allowed him to give up his job as an adapter of foreign works and to devote his time to his own plays, many of which depend on a specific American locality for their effect: *In Mizzoura* (1893), *Arizona* (1899), *Colorado* (1901) and *Rio Grande* (1916). He did, however, continue to adapt the work of others for the stage, notably F. H. Smith's *Colonel Carter of Cartersville* (1892), **Frances Hodgson Burnett**'s *Editha's Burglar* (first as a one-act play, then in a four-act adaptation entitled *The Burglar*, 1899) and **Richard Harding Davis**'s *Soldiers of Fortune*, dramatized in 1902 with the collaboration of the author. *The Witching Hour* (1907) and *The Harvest Moon* (1909) reflected Thomas's interest in mind-reading and hypnotism. His greatest success was *The Copperhead* (1918). His autobiography, *The Print of My Remembrance*, was published in 1922.

**Thomas, D[onald] M[ichael]** 1935– Poet, novelist and translator. Born in Redruth, Cornwall, he was educated at Redruth Grammar School, University High School, Melbourne, and, after national service, at New College, Oxford, where he read English. He has worked as a teacher and a lecturer. His early collections, *Personal and Possessive* (1964), *Two Voices* (1968) and *Logan Stone* (1971), feature erotic poems, science-fiction ballads, and the local colour of his Cornish lyrics. Later collections, such as the autobiographical *The Shaft* (1973), *Love and Other Deaths* (1975) and *The Honeymoon Voyage* (1978), develop greater depth and range, notably a strength in narrative and an ear for nuances of character in reported speech. His ability to enter another mind persuasively is shown in his translations from the Russian of Anna Akhmatova in *Requiem and Poem Without a Hero* (1974) and *Way of All the Earth* (1979); other Russian translations include Yevtushenko's *Invisible Threads* (1981) and Pushkin's *The Bronze Horseman* (1982). Thomas writes that his poetry is concerned with the twin poles of 'love and death', in the Freudian conception of 'Eros' and 'Thanatos'. It is with such themes that he has gained his widest public to date, in his novel *The White Hotel* (1981); other novels include *The Flute Player* (1979), *Birthstone* (1980) and the 'Russian Quartet', *Ararat* (1983), *Swallow* (1984), *Sphinx* (1986) and *Summit* (1987). They have been accused of self-indulgence, particularly in their almost pornographic erotic presentations. More recent books of poetry are *Dreaming in Bronze* (1981) and *Selected*

*Poems* (1983).

**Thomas, Dylan (Marlais)** 1914–53 Poet. Born in Swansea, South Wales, and educated at Swansea Grammar School, where his father taught English, Thomas began writing poetry during childhood. He left school in 1931 and worked as a reporter, writing prolifically in his spare time. He moved to London in 1934 and his first book, *18 Poems*, appeared the same year. *Twenty-five Poems* (1936) attracted the attention of **Edith Sitwell** and other poets and critics. Thomas married Caitlin Macnamara in 1937. Rejected as unfit for military service, he spent the war years in London, working as a script-writer and broadcaster for the BBC. He published two volumes of stories, *The Map of Love* (1939) and *Portrait of the Artist as a Young Dog* (1940), as well as *New Poems* (1943), which, together with his broadcast work, established his popular reputation. Two further volumes, *Deaths and Entrances* (1946) and *In Country Sleep* (1952), were followed by *Collected Poems* (1953), which was received rapturously by both critics and the public. Thomas undertook extensive reading-tours of the USA, mainly for financial reasons, in 1950, 1952 and 1953. His readings drew large audiences and the tours confirmed Thomas's reputation both as an extraordinarily charismatic reader of poetry and as a charming but disruptive and hard-drinking Bohemian. They also took a severe toll of his already fragile health. None the less, Thomas wrote his 'play for voices', *Under Milk Wood*, in 1952 and revised it for performance during his final tour in 1953. He also met Stravinsky, for whom he hoped to write a libretto. In October 1953 he returned, ill and exhausted, for a fourth visit to the USA, and died of alcoholic poisoning in New York the following month.

Overpraised during his lifetime, Thomas's work has since suffered critical disparagement. His elaborate and often highly obscure style, influenced centrally by **Hopkins** and more marginally by psychoanalysis and surrealism, deploys religious, archetypal and biological imagery in elaborate rhetorical patterns to evoke a sense of exuberant, pantheistic mysticism. The poems are romantic in their idiosyncratic individualism, their delight in emotion, and their idealization of natural energies. Many of them offer interesting verbal textures, and though some critics have found them sentimental or pretentious they retain a wide popular readership. A few at least of his poems – among them 'The Force that through the Green Fuse Drives the Flower', 'And Death Shall Have No Dominion', 'Do Not Go Gentle into that Good Night' and 'Fern Hill' – seem likely to remain popular, as does *Under Milk Wood*.

**Thomas, Edward (Philip)** 1878–1917 Poet, critic, biographer and writer on nature. Born in London soon after his parents had moved from Tredegar, Wales, he was educated at St Paul's School and Lincoln College, Oxford. Beginning with *The Woodland Life* (1897), he established himself as a full-time writer with a voluminous output, producing more than 40 books before his early death and regarding much of what he published as hackwork. His prose identified him as a nature writer in the tradition of **Richard Jefferies** and **George Borrow**, of whom he wrote critical biographies (1909 and 1912 respectively). He turned his walking tours into *The Heart of England* (1906), *The South Country* (1909), *The Icknield Way* (1913) and *In Pursuit of Spring* (1914). These travel narratives combine natural observation with passages of reflective description and an allegorical search for the spirit of England, which became one of the central themes of his poetry. He produced editions of **George Herbert** (1908), **Christopher Marlowe** (1909), *Celtic Stories* (1911) and *Norse Tales* (1912). His studies of Maurice Maeterlinck (1911) and **Lafcadio Hearn** (1912) included some acute criticism of **Symbolism**, while his books on **Swinburne** (1912) and **Walter Pater** (1913) argue against what he called these 'modern English half-martyrs, half-heroes of style'. He also wrote widely as a reviewer, and became part of a circle of friends which included **W. H. Davies**, **Walter de la Mare**, **Joseph Conrad**, **Arthur Ransome** and **Robert Frost**. After the outbreak of World War I he joined the Artists' Rifles in 1915 and was killed two years later.

All his poetry belongs to the last two and a half years of his life. Two prose experiments, *The Happy-Go-Lucky Morgans* (1913) and *The Childhood of Edward Thomas* (1938), preceded his discovery of a poetic form without 'the exaggerations of rhetoric'. Following a breakdown in 1911, the consequent elucidation of his own ideas about poetry in his criticism, and conversations with Robert Frost, he began in November 1914 to convert prose notes into the blank verse of 'Up in the Wind'. His characteristically subtle, quizzical poetry frequently used material from his nature writings, but with World War I providing a dark, metaphorical counterpart to the Kent and Wiltshire countryside. His landscapes become, like the past, something elusive and vulnerable to destruction. **Edward Garnett** thought the plain diction and irregular rhythm 'puzzling', and Thomas had much difficulty in finding a publisher. 27 poems appeared under the pseudonym of Edward Eastaway in *An Anthology of New Verse* in early 1917. *Poems* 'by E.E.' appeared posthumously in October 1917, followed by *Last Poems* (1918). The definitive *Collected Poems of Edward Thomas* (1978), edited by R. George Thomas, is the fullest of several collections which progressively established his reputation as a poet. His wife Helen Thomas wrote two memoirs, *As It Was* (1926) and *World without End* (1931).

**Thomas, R[onald] S[tuart]** 1913– Poet. Born in Cardiff, he was educated at the University College of North Wales, Bangor, where he read classics, and St Michael's College, Llandaff, where he studied theology. He was ordained a clergyman in the Church in Wales in 1937, and has subsequently worked in rural parishes. His first major book, *Song at the Year's Turning: Poems 1942–54* (1955), which collected earlier volumes, contains the first of his 'Iago Prytherch' poems. *Poetry for Supper* (1958), *Tares* (1961), *The Bread of Truth* (1963), *Pietà* (1966) and *Not That He Brought Flowers* (1968) display his rich early style, with its straightforward yet unexpected images. *H'm* (1972) is the major flowering of his later style, which has an increasing economy of language and is vulnerable because its fragility risks more. He has developed away from rootedness in a particular landscape towards allegory and prophecy. Subsequent volumes – *Young and Old* (1972), *Laboratories of the Spirit* (1975), *The Way of It* (1977), *Frequencies* (1978) and *Between Here and Now* (1981) – have disappointed many admirers of his early work. Honesty is Thomas's strength. His typically Welsh eschewal of the easy comforts of church polity gives much of his work a granitic vein. He attacks the hypocrisy with which people surround their lives, believing that the poet's task is to make them see a certain amount of reality. At the same time, he sets their pattern of life against a created world which, for all its grimness, is still 'stubborn with beauty'. The regular and traditional forms he prefers allow that beauty to emerge unromanticized and unmolested by showmanship. He remains the leading Anglo-Welsh poet since the death of **David Jones**. There are two selections: *Selected Poems 1946–1968* (1973, reissued 1986) and *Later Poems: A Selection* (1983).

**Thomas, (Walter) Brandon** 1856–1914 Actor and playwright. He made his stage début in 1879, supplementing his income by writing and singing coon-songs in London music halls. Of the many plays he wrote, mainly in collaboration, only the eighth is remembered. This was the immensely popular farce, **Charley's Aunt** (1892), which opened in Bury St Edmunds before running for four years at London's Royalty Theatre.

**Thomas, Lord Cromwell** (*The True Chronicle History of the Whole Life and Death of Thomas, Lord Cromwell*) A chronicle play published in 1602. Because its title-page gave the author as 'W.S.', it was for a time proposed as the work of **Shakespeare** but scholarship has rejected the attribution. See also **Shakespeare apocrypha**.

**Thompson, Edward** 1886–1946 Poet and critic. Thompson was born and educated at Bath and entered the Wesleyan Methodist ministry in 1909. He served in Bengal as a missionary teacher (1910–23) except for an interval as an army chaplain during World War I. Thompson became a lecturer in Bengali at Oxford (1923–33); he was later made Research Fellow in Indian history (1936–46). He had some reputation as a poet (his *Collected Poems* appeared in 1930) and as an interpreter of India. Among his books were *A History of India* and *An Indian Day* (both 1927), *A Farewell to India* (1930) and *Tagore: Poet and Dramatist* (1926).

**Thompson, Flora (Jane)** 1876–1947 Writer on rural life. Born Flora Timms at Juniper Hill, near Brackley, on the boundary between Oxfordshire and Northamptonshire, she went to school in nearby Cottisford and began work at the age of 14 as a Post Office clerk in Fringford. She later worked at Grayshott in Hampshire, and, after her marriage to another Post Office worker, John Thompson, in Bournemouth (1903–16), Liphook (1916–28) and Dartmouth. She began writing in Bournemouth, contributing essays and poems to magazines and later publishing a volume of verse, *Bog Myrtle and Peat* (1921). She is famous, though, for the subtle and unsentimentally precise evocation of the rural culture of her childhood in *Lark Rise to Candleford* (1945), a trilogy originally issued as *Lark Rise* (1939), *Over to Candleford* (1941) and *Candleford Green* (1943). *Still Glides the Stream*, posthumously published in 1948, weaves memories again drawn from childhood into a fictional story.

**Thompson, Francis** 1859–1907 Poet. Born in Preston, Lancashire, and educated at Ushaw College, he abandoned his first ambition of becoming a Roman Catholic priest and spent six years at Owens College (now the University of Manchester) in an unsuccessful attempt to become a doctor. In 1885 he went to London, rapidly sinking into opium addiction and destitution. He was rescued by **Alice Meynell** and her husband Wilfred, the editor of *Merry England*, to which Thompson first submitted his poems on ragged scraps of paper in 1887. After meeting him in 1888, they took charge of his life and work: finding him lodgings, introducing him to other writers, encouraging and publishing his poetry, and placing his literary criticism in *The Academy* and **The Athenaeum**. Despite their care and despite retreats at monasteries in Sussex and Wales, Thompson never fully recovered, dying from the combined effects of opium addiction and tuberculosis.

He published three volumes of poetry, *Poems* (1893), *Sister Songs* (1895) and *New Poems* (1897). The best-known example of his ornate, densely metaphorical style is 'The Hound of Heaven', which appeared in the first volume; it describes his flight from and recapture by God. Thompson's prose writings include 'Health and Holiness' (1905) and an essay on **Shelley** (1909). A three-volume *Works* (1913) was edited by Wilfred Meynell.

**Thomson, James** 1700–48 Poet and dramatist. He was born at Ednam, Roxburghshire, and educated at schools in Southdean and Jedburgh. In 1715 he entered Edinburgh University, where he joined a literary club, the Grotesques, and published pieces in *The Edinburgh Miscellany*. After his arrival in London in 1725 he acquired Lord Minto and Duncan Forbes of Culloden as patrons; the latter introduced him to **Arbuthnot, Pope** and **Gay**. He was also taken up by **David Mallet** and became tutor to Thomas Hamilton, the son of Charles, Lord Binning. Thomson established his reputation with *The Seasons*, still the poem for which he is best remembered. It was originally published in separate parts: *Winter* in 1726, *Summer* in 1727 and *Spring* in 1728. *Autumn* appeared in the first collective edition of *The Seasons* in 1730, for which Arbuthnot, **Bolingbroke**, Pope, Spence and **Young** subscribed. From 1738 onwards, aided perhaps by Pope and **George Lyttelton**, Thomson made extensive revisions to the poem. A corrected and much enlarged edition appeared in 1744.

In 1730 Thomson produced his tragedy *Sophonisba* (with its famous line, 'Oh! Sophonisba, Sophonisba, Oh!'). He then became tutor to Charles Talbot and escorted him around Europe. After Talbot's untimely death his father gave Thomson the first of his sinecures, the Secretaryship of Briefs. He retired to live at Richmond, where he is said to have grown so sybaritic that he ate 'the sunny side off the peaches in his garden with his hands in his pockets'. *Liberty*, a lengthy patriotic poem published in instalments between 1734 and 1736, was remarkable for its hyperbole and its failure to sell. After Talbot's death in 1737, Thomson turned again to the stage with a series of tragedies. Pope attended the first night of *Agamemnon* in 1738, but *Edward and Eleanora* was never acted. *Tancred and Sigismunda* enjoyed a vogue in 1745, and *Coriolanus* was performed posthumously in 1749 with his old friend James Quin in the leading role. Lyttelton, Thomson's new patron, secured him a pension of £100 a year from the Prince of Wales and he responded suitably with contributions to *The Masque of Alfred* (1740), including the words of the ode 'Rule Britannia'. In 1748 Thomson published the poem he had been working on for 15 years: *The Castle of Indolence*, an allegory written in Spenserian stanzas and admired by **Gray**. He died after catching a chill in a rowing-boat and

was buried in Richmond parish church. **William Collins** commemorated him in his ode 'In Yonder Grave a Druid Lies'.

**Thomson, James** 1834–82 Poet and essayist. Born in Port Glasgow, the son of an Irvingite mother and a merchant seaman, Thomson was educated at the Royal Caledonian Asylum, Hertfordshire, in 1842–50 and at the 'model school' of the Royal Military Asylum, Chelsea, in 1850–1, where he prepared to qualify as an army schoolmaster. Shortly afterwards he was sent to Ballincollig, Cork, as a student teacher in a garrison school. Here he fell deeply in love with Matilda Weller whose early death in 1853 accentuated his melancholia and influenced the writing of his poem *The Doom of a City* (1857). During his Irish period he also formed a friendship with the rationalist Charles Bradlaugh, whose atheistic ideas coloured Thomson's thought and work. A schoolmaster from 1854 to 1862, Thomson was dismissed the service for a trifling breach of discipline and subsequently served briefly as a solicitor's clerk. In 1872 secretaryship to a wildcat gold and silvermine company took him to the western United States and 1873 found him correspondent in Spain for *The New York World*. The rest of his life was spent in England. A victim of acute melancholia, insomnia and intemperance, Thomson died in London and was buried in the famous literary cemetery at Highgate.

Despite his psychological handicaps Thomson was surprisingly prolific both in poetry and prose. In the 1860s and early 1870s he wrote for Bradlaugh's *National Reformer*, often under the pseudonym B. V. (Bysshe Vanolis), and it was in that magazine that his masterpiece, *The City of Dreadful Night*, first appeared in 1874. After quarrelling with Bradlaugh, Thomson wrote for several years for that unique Liverpudlian magazine, *Cope's Tobacco Plant*, a publication that sought to peddle its wares by printing literature of quality. But it was through Thomson's friendship with the bookseller and publisher Bertram Dobell that his first volume of verse came out in 1880, entitled *The City of Dreadful Night and Other Poems*; later the same year a second volume, *Vane's Story, Weddah and Om-el-Bonain and Other Poems*, appeared. 1881 saw the publication of *Essays and Phantasies* and in 1884 came two posthumous volumes, *A Voice from the Nile and Other Poems* and *Satires and Profanities*. There were also many reviews, translations from Heine, and essays on divers subjects, for Thomson had written for *The Secularist, The London Investigator, The Liberal* and many other publications.

Although dubbed 'the laureate of pessimism' and influenced by the Continental figures of Heine, Novalis, and Leopardi, Thomson also had a vein of realistic humour apparent in

'Sunday at Hampstead' and 'Sunday up the River'; other verses show romantic yearnings after beauty, autobiographical glimpses, speculations on faith and atheism, and satirical barbs. But Thomson's major work is, above all, the poetry of despair, of life as futility, of man trapped and committed to loneliness and desolation. He is a fitting figure of late Victorian pessimism.

**Thoreau, Henry David** 1817–62 American man of letters. Born in Concord, Massachusetts, Thoreau spent most of his life in the area as a writer, teacher, essayist and orator, earning extra income by working as a gardener, pencil-maker and surveyor.

While attending Concord Academy and Harvard, he became known as an individualist who was often scornful of authority. Nevertheless, he was much influenced by many of the men he encountered during those years: **Edward Channing**, **Orestes Brownson**, and especially **Ralph Waldo Emerson**. Shortly after his graduation from Harvard in 1837, he and his brother John opened their own school in Concord, and operated it according to the **Transcendentalist** principles of Emerson, **Bronson Alcott** and Brownson. When John became fatally ill in 1841, Henry was unable to find another position, whereupon he lived in Emerson's home as a handyman. It was Emerson who encouraged him to keep the journals which form the basis of most of his major writings.

By this time Thoreau had already contributed several pieces to the Transcendentalist journal, **The Dial**; and he was also an occasional speaker at the Concord Lyceum, which he had started in 1838. His mature writing, however, dates from the two-year period (1845–7) when he lived at Walden Pond. There he put into final form **A Week on the Concord and Merrimack Rivers** (1849), based on a trip he took with his brother John in 1839. The experience at Walden itself, and the journal he kept there, became the source of his celebrated book **Walden** (1854), which takes the form of a lengthy autobiographical essay in which he sets forth many of his ideas on how the individual should live life to the best advantage of his nature and principles. Another of his best-known works, **On the Duty of Civil Disobedience** (1849), comes from the same period and reflects similar values: he was arrested in the summer of 1846 for refusing to pay his poll tax, and the night he spent in gaol prompted his reflections on a man's moral right passively to resist an unjust law.

The majority of Thoreau's work was published after his death. Aware that he was dying of tuberculosis, he cut short his therapeutic travels and returned to Concord, where he prepared some of his journals for publication. Selections from his manuscripts were edited and

Henry David Thoreau.

posthumously published as *The Maine Woods* (1864), *Cape Cod* (1865) and *A Yankee in Canada* (1866), all based on his various journeys. *Excursions* (1863) is a collection of pieces previously published in magazines. His letters were edited by his lifelong friend Emerson and published in 1865 (enlarged 1894). *Poems of Nature* appeared in 1895, *Collected Poems* in 1943. Finally, Thoreau's immense collection of journals was published in 1906 in 14 volumes.

**Three Clerks, The** A novel by **Anthony Trollope**, published in three volumes in 1858.

Harry Norman and Alaric Tudor, of the prestigious Weights and Measures office, and Alaric's cousin Charley Tudor, are regular visitors at the home of the widowed Mrs Woodward and her three daughters. Harry loves the eldest, Gertrude, but is supplanted by the ambitious Alaric, who is also promoted above him through success in the new system of competitive examination which has been introduced in the Civil Service. Alaric and Gertrude marry, but desire to succeed leads him to speculate in shares and then to embezzle a trust fund, for which he is tried and imprisoned. Alaric's rise and fall contrasts with the struggles of Charley, an honest scapegrace, to extricate himself from debt and an imprudent entanglement with an Irish barmaid, Norah Geraghty. Harry marries the second Woodward girl, Linda, and settles down as a country squire. Charley marries the third, Katie, and wins promotion to the Weights and Measures office. Alaric and his family emigrate to Australia.

*The Three Clerks* offers a lively picture of the Civil Service undergoing the Victorian reforms, and also in Charley Tudor a self-portrait of Trollope himself as a young man.

**Three Hours After Marriage** A comedy in three acts written collectively by **Gay**, **Pope** and **Arbuthnot** and performed with no great success in 1717. Partly a farce and partly a dramatized Varronian satire, the play takes as targets for its humour the characteristic concerns of the **Scriblerus Club** – pedantry, credulity and intellectual pretensions. It is densely written (the three playwrights observing the three unities of the three hours of action in three acts) and the plot turns on a number of elaborate metamorphoses and disguises. A jealous old man, Fossile, marries a younger wife, Townley, in secret at the start of the play; his moonstruck niece, Phoebe the poetess, reads her newest play to Sir Tremendous (the critic, **John Dennis**); Fossile intercepts amorous notes to his new wife from Plotwell (played by **Colley Cibber**) and decides to adopt various disguises to discover the fidelity of his spouse, posing as a footman, and then as Dr Lubomirski, a projector full of scientific gibberish. His suspicion and jealousy lead him to absurd contrivances that culminate in two amorous beaux hiding in his private museum, Plotwell in a mummy and Underplot in an alligator. The satire being no longer topical, the chief interest of the play is that it contains the only formal dramatic writing by Pope, and that its production prompted backstage fisticuffs between Gay and Cibber, the latter having discovered his part of Plotwell to be a lampoon on himself.

**Through the Looking-Glass and What Alice Found There** A fantasy (1871) by **Lewis Carroll**.

This sequel to *Alice's Adventures in Wonderland* was also immensely successful. In it, Alice passes through a mirror to the land behind, where everything happens back to front. Here she meets more memorable characters caught up like herself in a cosmic chess game; favourites among these include the Red Queen, the White Queen, Tweedledum and Tweedledee, the White Knight and the Walrus and the Carpenter. Humpty Dumpty also makes an appearance, with his oft-quoted remark 'When I use a word it means just what I choose it to mean – neither more nor less.' There is, too, Carroll's memorable and at times slightly sinister poem, 'Jabberwocky'. The book was vividly illustrated by **Sir John Tenniel**, despite his previous determination to have nothing further to do with so temperamental an author.

**Thurber, James (Grover)** 1894–1961 American short-story writer, born in Columbus, Ohio, and educated at Ohio State University. After working as a government clerk in Washington, he joined the embassy staff in Paris, and then became foreign correspondent for a Chicago newspaper. On his return to the USA he worked on the staff of *The New Yorker* (1927–33) and continued after that as a regular contributor. Both as a cartoonist and as a writer Thurber expressed the dilemma of the moral innocent in a complex modern world. A direct and disarming humorist, he frequently satirized such subjects as psychoanalysis, sexual awareness, the search for identity and the problem of communication.

Among his collections of stories and sketches are *The Owl in the Attic, and Other Perplexities* (1931), *The Seal in My Bedroom, and Other Predicaments* (1932), *Let Your Mind Alone* (1937), *My World – And Welcome To It!* (1942) and *The Beast in Me, and Other Animals* (1948). With **E. B. White**, his colleague on *The New Yorker*, he wrote *Is Sex Necessary?* (1929), and in collaboration with Elliot Nugent, he produced a successful dramatic comedy, *The Male Animal* (1940). *My Life and Hard Times* (1933) is autobiographical, and *The Years with Ross* (1959) a memoir of his years on the staff of *The New Yorker*. He also wrote several books for children, including *The Thirteen Clocks* (1950).

**Thwaite, Anthony (Simon)** 1930– Poet. Born in Chester, he was educated at Kingswood School, Bath, and, after national service, at Christ Church, Oxford. As well as having been the literary editor of *The New Statesman* and the co-editor of *Encounter*, he has taught in Japan and Libya and lectured abroad extensively for the British Council. His early work, in no. 17 of the Fantasy Poets series (1953), and in *Home*

One of James Thurber's celebrated dogs. A cartoon from *Fables for Our Time and Famous Poems Illustrated* (1940).

*Truths* (1957), is impersonal and aphoristic. His second collection, *The Owl in the Trees* (1963), captures items of everyday experience in tones of desolation and resignation. Like **Philip Larkin**, Thwaite adopts a man-in-the-street persona and uses intricate stanzas and rhyme schemes. Later volumes, including *The Stones of Emptiness* (1967), *Inscriptions* (1973) and *New Confessions* (1974), based on St Augustine, develop towards the dramatic monologue. *A Portion for Foxes* (1977) is mainly lyric but *Victorian Voices* (1980) contains 14 monologues by 19th-century literary and historical figures which also have a strong confessional, autobiographical element. *Poems 1953–1983* (1984) sums up his poetic career. Thwaite has edited *Larkin at 60* (1982), a collection of essays, and is currently editing Larkin's collected poems.

***Thyrsis*** A poem by **Matthew Arnold**, published in *New Poems* (1867). As the sub-title explains, it commemorates Arnold's friend, **Arthur Hugh Clough**, who had died at Florence in 1861. In the form of a pastoral lament, it recalls the Oxford countryside known to both men in their undergraduate days – a territory Arnold had earlier described in ***The Scholar-Gipsy***.

**Tickell, Thomas** 1686–1740 Poet. A protégé of **Joseph Addison**, Tickell was educated at The Queen's College, Oxford, where he became a fellow. His poem, *On the Prospect of Peace* (1712), was widely read in the period leading to the Treaty of Utrecht in 1713. Tickell contributed to ***The Guardian*** and ***The Spectator*** and published a translation of the first book of the *Iliad* at the same time as **Pope** published his. Pope believed that Addison had prompted Tickell and quarrelled with him. Tickell went to Ireland with Addison in 1709 and became Secretary to the Lords Justice in Ireland. He held this post for the rest of his life and edited Addison's works when his patron died. His work is largely forgotten, though his elegy on Addison's death (1721) is sometimes remembered.

***Ticket-of-Leave Man, The*** A melodrama by **Tom Taylor**, first performed at the Olympic Theatre, London, in 1863. It is notable for its introduction of a stage detective, Hawkshaw, adept at disguise and more than a match for the leaders of London's underworld. It is Hawkshaw's persistence that exonerates the hero, Bob Brierly, a convict released on ticket-of-leave.

**Till Eulenspiegel** Eulenspiegel (Owlglass) was the name of a German peasant prankster, supposedly born *c*.1300 in Brunswick. A collection of tales and jests grew up around his name, mainly of a farcical, broad and bawdy kind. In them Eulenspiegel is a cunning peasant who outwits the nobility, churchmen and townspeople. Stories connected with his name were probably first printed in German *c*.1500; the earliest extant text is 1515. An English translation of some stories was printed at Antwerp *c*.1510. The printer William Copland produced three editions, none of them dated: *Here Beginneth a Merry Jest of a Man that was Called Owlglass* was published *c*.1528.

**Tillotson, John** 1630–94 Archbishop of Canterbury. Born at Sowerby near Halifax, second son of a prosperous clothworker, he is believed to have attended first Colne Grammar School, then Heath Grammar School, Halifax. He entered Clare Hall, Cambridge, as a pensioner in 1647 and was elected a probationer fellow in 1651. There was a running dispute about this position and he was finally removed in 1661. Around this time he is believed to have been ordained. In 1664 he married Cromwell's niece, Elizabeth French. As a latitudinarian he was frequently in conflict with his superiors, but after a number of relatively lowly positions in the church he took the degree of DD in 1666 and was shortly afterwards made Charles II's chaplain. He was then successively Dean of Canterbury (1672), Dean of St Paul's (1689), and Archbishop of Canterbury (1691). His literary importance lies in his sermons, the copyright of which his widow sold for the immense sum of 2500 guineas. They were frequently reprinted during the 18th century and had considerable influence on both theological thought and English prose style not only in their own right but also because other sermon writers, such as **Sterne**, borrowed paragraphs with due acknowledgement. Evidence in ***The Spectator*** and in the diaries of **Woodforde** shows that some clergymen, rather than deliver their own work, would simply read one of Tillotson's sermons, which in 1742–4 were published weekly, presumably with this trade in mind.

**Tillyard, E[ustace] M[andeville] W[etenhall]** 1889–1962 Critic. A Cambridge man by birth and lifelong residence, Tillyard was educated at the Perse School and studied classics at Jesus College, where he returned to a fellowship in 1913 after studying archaeology in Athens. After serving in France and Greece in World War I, he helped to establish the new school of English at Cambridge University, devoting his work to **Milton** and **Shakespeare**. He published five books on Milton, of which the best known are *Milton* (1930) and *The Miltonic Setting* (1938), and three on Shakespeare: *Shakespeare's Last Plays* (1938), *Shakespeare's History Plays* (1944) and *Shakespeare's Problem Plays* (1950). His best-known work, *The Elizabethan World-Picture* (1943), is a brief explanation of the late medieval concept of a 'chain of being' as the harmonious design of the universe. Tillyard became Master of Jesus College in 1945, and later wrote *The Muse Unchained* (1958), an account of the early days of the Cambridge English school. His other works include *The Personal Heresy* (with **C. S. Lewis**, 1939) and *The English Epic and Its Tradition* (1954).

**Timber**, *or, Discoveries made upon Men and Matter* The commonplace book of **Ben Jonson**, published in the posthumous folio edition of 1640, a fascinating collection of notes, mordant observations on human behaviour and morality, aphorisms, short essays on a variety of subjects, and adaptations of Latin originals. It is a valuable repository of the learning and wisdom of England's first great neoclassical critic and poet, continually demonstrating the breadth of his reading.

**Time Machine, The** A short novel by **H. G. Wells**, developed by degrees from a series of speculative articles which he wrote in 1888 for *The Science Schools Journal*. The story appeared in two serial versions before book publication in 1895.

The central character, referred to throughout as the Time Traveller, tells a group of friends that he has invented a machine which can travel through time, enabling him to investigate the destiny of the human species. In the year 802,701, where he is temporarily stranded, he finds the meek and beautiful Eloi living in apparently idyllic circumstances, but discovers that they are the prey of the degenerate Morlocks, descendants of labourers who have lived underground for centuries. In later eras he sees the life-forms which survive the extinction of man, and thirty million years hence he is witness to the world's final decline as the sun cools. In his later writings Wells remained preoccupied with the need to save mankind from the kind of failure represented by the divided world of the Eloi and the Morlocks.

**Time's Laughingstocks and Other Verses** Poems by **Thomas Hardy**, first published in 1909. Divided into four parts – 'Time's Laughingstocks', 'More Love Lyrics', 'A Set of Country Songs' and 'Pieces Occasional and Various' – this third volume of Hardy's verse, some of which had already appeared in British and American publications, is stamped with many personal associations and recollections of rural and family life. There are short poems about his parents and grandparents set beside love lyrics written during his young manhood; there are country songs celebrating Casterbridge Fair as well as a small handful of Dorset dialect poems. Several are cast in ballad form, including Hardy's own favourite, the powerful 'Tramp-woman's Tragedy'. As in preceding volumes, the isolated incident, the minor key, the ironical flick, the robustly humorous and the poignancy of the unrealized in life inform one poem after another in these verses of bucolic memory and meditation.

**Times Literary Supplement, The** Originally, as its name suggests, a weekly section of *The Times* newspaper begun in 1902, the *TLS* became a separate paper in 1914. Its character and reputation were shaped by Bruce Richmond, the editor from 1903 to 1937, who commissioned reviews and articles from, among others, **T. S. Eliot**, **Herbert Read**, **Edgell Rickword** and **Virginia Woolf**. Reviews were anonymous until John Gross abolished this practice upon assuming the editorship in 1974. He was succeeded by Jeremy Treglown in 1981. The *TLS* publishes poems by established writers, but is devoted chiefly to reviewing books across a wide range from fiction to science, politics, music and the other arts.

**Timon of Athens** A tragedy by **William Shakespeare**, first performed *c.*1607 and published in the First Folio of 1623. Shakespeare probably found the story during his reading of Plutarch's life of Mark Antony, though he may also have known Lucian's satiric dialogue, *Timon Misanthropus*.

Timon is a rich and noble Athenian whose generosity leaves him penniless. When he asks his rich friends for help he is denied, and he finds that those who formerly sought his company now avoid him. He invites them all to a banquet, where he serves them with dishes of water, which he throws in their faces. He curses the city of Athens, and leaves it, followed only by his faithful servant Flavius.

Now a committed misanthrope, Timon lives in a cave, where, digging for roots, he uncovers a hoard of gold. He is visited by the exiled Athenian general, Alcibiades, who is on the way to Athens with an avenging army. Timon gives him gold to pay his soldiers. He also rewards the loyalty of Flavius, whom he swears to silence as he gives him all that remains of his treasure. It is the bitter philosopher Apemantus who spreads news of Timon's sudden riches, but the Athenian senators who come to seek his help against Alcibiades are spurned. The victorious Alcibiades promises to destroy only those who are his own or Timon's enemies, but a soldier brings him news that Timon is dead, and Alcibiades decides to offer peace with mercy.

*Timon of Athens* is the least loved of Shakespeare's great tragedies, perhaps because the bitter pride which Timon shares with Coriolanus is too readily justified by his experience. Recent criticism has sought to establish for the play a quality which it has still to prove in the theatre.

**Timrod, Henry** 1828–67 American poet, known as the 'Laureate of the Confederacy', born in Charleston, South Carolina, and educated at Franklin College (now the University of Georgia). With **William Gilmore Simms**, Basil Gildersleeve and his friend Paul Hamilton Hayne, he founded *Russell's Magazine* in Charleston in 1867, modelling it on the British journal *Blackwood's*. Some of his own poetry was published in the magazine. A volume entitled *Poems* had already appeared in 1860. He suffered from tuberculosis and was unable to serve in the Confederate Army in the Civil War, but he did manage to earn his living as an editor, and it was during these years that he wrote his best-known poems. They remained uncollected, however, until after his death, when Hayne published *The Poems of Henry Timrod* in 1827. *Katie*, a love poem addressed to his wife, was published in 1884 and *Complete Poems of Henry Timrod* in 1899.

**Tindal, Matthew** 1655–1733 Religious writer. Born in Devon and educated at Lincoln College and Exeter College, Oxford, he became a fellow of All Souls in 1678. After a brief period as a Catholic during the reign of James II, he returned to the Church of England in 1688 and thereafter became a leading proponent of **Deism**. His most influential work, *Christianity as Old as the Creation, or, The Gospel a Republication of the Religion of Nature* (1730), argued that the Gospels neither added to nor detracted from the perfect and unchanging law of reason, but freed man from superstition. His other writings include *The Rights of the Christian Church Asserted against the Romish and All Other Priests who Claim an Independent Power over It* (1706) and *A Defence of the Rights of the Christian Church* (1709).

**'Tis Pity She's a Whore** A tragedy by **John Ford**, the finest example of his psychological intensity. There is no certainty of the date of its first performance, though it probably took place between 1625 and the year of the play's first printing, 1633. The central theme is the incestuous love of Giovanni and Annabella, a pure thing in the enveloping context of corruption. Only when she discovers that she is pregnant does Annabella agree to marry, in the vain hope of shielding her brother. But Soranzo, whom she selects from a trio of unsatisfactory suitors, is the most tainted. He interrupts his adulterous affair with Hippolita to court Annabella and rejects Hippolita, despite earlier assurances, when the death of her husband is announced. But the husband, Richardetto, is not dead. Suspecting his wife's faithlessness, he has disguised himself as a physician, and he now plans the murder of Soranzo. He enlists the help of the second of Annabella's suitors, the jealous Grimaldi, but they bungle the attempt on Soranzo's life, killing the third suitor, the harmlessly idiotic Bergetto, instead. At the feast to celebrate the wedding of Annabella and Soranzo, Hippolita's plan to poison Soranzo is foiled by Soranzo's clever servant, Vasques, who contrives that Hippolita drink the poison herself. It is again Vasques who discovers the identity of Annabella's lover and reveals it to Soranzo. The play's climax is the banquet at which Soranzo intends to expose his wife and Giovanni. Forewarned of Soranzo's scheme, Giovanni kills Annabella and arrives at the banquet carrying her heart. Defiantly proclaiming their love, he kills Soranzo and is, in turn, killed by Vasques.

**Tithonus** A dramatic monologue in blank verse by **Alfred Tennyson**, published by **Thackeray** in *The Cornhill Magazine* in 1860. Its original form was the poem 'Tithon', which Tennyson wrote in 1833 as a companion piece to *Ulysses* but did not publish. In Greek myth Tithonus was loved by Aurora (Eos), goddess of the dawn, who begged her father Zeus to grant him eternal life. Zeus agreed, but Aurora had neglected to ask for eternal youth as well and so Tithonus grew ever older without dying.

**Titus Andronicus** A tragedy by **William Shakespeare**, perhaps written collaboratively. It was one of the earliest works with which his name was associated. Some critics have argued for a staging as early as 1590. It was published in Quarto (Q1) in 1594 and in the First Folio of 1623, where there is an additional scene. No certain source has been identified, although the influence of Seneca is manifest. The play is set in ancient Rome under the empire but is not related to any known emperor or historical event.

Titus Andronicus returns to Rome in triumph after defeating the Goths, whose queen Tamora and her three sons are among his prisoners. A chain of revenge is started when he sacrifices Tamora's eldest son to appease the spirits of his own dead sons. There follow, in relentless succession, acts of murder and violence which include the kidnapping of Titus's daughter Lavinia, the death of his son Mutius, the murder of the late emperor's son Bassianus, the death of Titus's son Martius, the rape and mutilation of Lavinia, the self-mutilation of Titus, the beheading of two more of his sons, the murder of Tamora's remaining sons and the use of their blood to make pies containing their severed heads, Titus's mercy-killing of Lavinia, his murder of Tamora after she has eaten the pies containing her son's heads, the killing of Titus by the Emperor Saturninus and of Saturninus by

The title-page illustration to the 1594 Quarto of *Titus Andronicus*. This is the only known copy and was found in Sweden in 1904, wrapped in an 18th-century lottery ticket. It is now in the Folger Shakespeare Library, Washington.

Titus's remaining son, Lucius. Lucius is elected emperor by the people of Rome, and he decrees honourable burial for Saturninus, Titus and Lavinia. He also orders that the body of Tamora be thrown to the birds and beasts of prey and that her black-skinned and black-hearted lover Aaron be buried up to his neck and left to starve to death.

*Titus Andronicus* gives notice of Shakespeare's later achievements only at rare moments and in the gathering bewilderment and madness of Titus himself.

**To Be Read at Dusk** A ghost story by **Charles Dickens**, published in 1852. It is narrated by a German courier in the Alps.

**To the Lighthouse** A novel by **Virginia Woolf**, published in 1927.

There is minimal action. The novel works through **stream of consciousness** and imagery to create an atmospheric and impressionistic record of the characters' moment-by-moment experiences, tracing the conflict between male and female principles (see *A Room of One's Own*) and making a statement about time, death and artistic transcendence.

Mr Ramsay is a tragic and self-pitying philosopher whose mind is rational but rather cold; Mrs Ramsay is a warm, creative and intuitive woman, the centre of the household. The first section, called 'The Window', describes a day during their summer holiday on the west coast of Scotland, where their guests include: a painter, Lily Briscoe; an ageing poet, Augustus Carmichael; a scientist, William Bankes; and a priggish young academic, Charles Tansley. The novel focuses on the conflict arising from young James Ramsay's desire to visit the lighthouse, and his father's quenching of this hope. The expedition takes on symbolic qualities and epitomizes the underlying tensions and differences

of perspective between Mrs Ramsay and her husband.

In the second section, 'Time Passes', Mrs Ramsay has died, her eldest son, Andrew, has been killed in the war, and the daughter, Prue, has died in childbirth. The Ramsays' seaside house lies deserted and desolate, but at the end of the section Lily Briscoe and Augustus Carmichael arrive to reawaken life.

Lily Briscoe assumes the 'visionary' mantle left by Mrs Ramsay, and during the final section ('The Lighthouse') Ramsay and his son, James, at last make the long-delayed voyage to the lighthouse. James, now 16 years old, is able to forgive his father and Lily Briscoe completes a painting which had been inspired by Mrs Ramsay. The mood at the end of the novel is one of muted optimism and triumph in which the two events, the visit to the lighthouse and the completion of the painting, are linked in Lily's mind: ' "He has landed," she said aloud. "It is finished." '

**Toccata of Galuppi's, A** A poem by **Robert Browning** in *Men and Women* (1855). The composer Baldassare Galuppi (1706–85) was organist of St Mark's Cathedral in Venice during the last years of his life; a toccata is a light piece of music displaying the musician's virtuosity. Browning's poem is designed to capture the rhythms of Galuppi's music, finding in them the decadent gaiety of Venice under Austrian rule in the 18th century.

**Tocqueville, Comte Alexis de** See *Democracy in America*.

**Todorov, Tzvetan** See **structuralism**.

**Toland, John** 1670–1722 Philosopher and religious controversialist. Born in Donegal, he abandoned Roman Catholicism at the age of 16 and studied successively at the universities of Glasgow, Leiden and Oxford. His *Christianity Not Mysterious* (1696) made a vital contribution to **Deism** by dismissing the 'mysteries' of Christianity as pagan intrusions maintained by the priesthood and arguing that God and his revelation were within the comprehension of all. Toland's subsequent writings showed the same gift for controversy and moved further away from orthodoxy. His biography of **Milton** (1698) contained a passage thought to question the authenticity of the New Testament; he replied with *Amyntor, or, A Defence of Milton's Life*, published the following year. *Nazarenus, or, Jewish, Gentile and Mahometan Christianity* (1718) displayed his remarkable knowledge of the apocryphal literature of the early Church. *Tetradymus* (1720) is a collection of essays on the natural explanation of biblical miracles. Toland coined the term 'pantheism', expressing the creed in *Pantheisticon* (1720).

**Tolkien, J[ohn] R[onald] R[euel]** 1892–1973 Scholar and fantasy writer. Born in South Africa, where his father was a bank manager, Tolkien came to England at the age of three. Educated first in Birmingham then at Oxford University, he went on to have a distinguished academic career at Leeds University and from 1925 at Oxford, where he was Merton Professor of English (1945–59). *The Hobbit* (1937), developed from the stories he told his children at bedtime, is about an amiable type of gnome called Bilbo Baggins, unwillingly required to destroy a menacing dragon who preys on the idealized, rural community in which the story is set. On his journeys he meets both friends and foes drawn from folklore, epic poetry and the author's own richly-stocked imagination. Best-known among these characters are the Orcs, a dangerous breed of goblins, and Gandalf, the benign wizard who helps Bilbo through his worst trials. The same characters also appear in *The Lord of the Rings* (1954–5), a much longer work in three parts, where once again an equally reluctant hobbit hero, Frodo, has to save the world from appalling evil. Opposed at every turn by supernatural obstacles and almost let down at the last moment by his own essentially human vulnerability to temptation, Frodo finally accomplishes his mission only to find that things also need to be put right back at home. This pessimism reflects Tolkien's own gloomy feelings about the development of England from rural village to industrial centre, chiming in well with new generations of readers and their own concern about conservation and the ever-present threat of nuclear extinction. For these and other reasons, Tolkien's novels became something of a cult in Europe and America and continue to be widely read today.

**Tom Brown's Schooldays** A novel by **Thomas Hughes**, published in 1857.

The first great school story, *Tom Brown's Schooldays* set a pattern for future writing in the genre. Written when its author was still young enough to remember his own days at Rugby, the novel describes the experiences of an upper middle-class boy going to boarding school for the first time. Shy at first, he learns how to put up with teasing from the older boys while carrying out various menial duties as their 'fag'. His two best friends represent opposite poles in behaviour and attitude, with Arthur gentle, law-abiding and idealistic and East mischievous and irreverent. But when some younger boys are picked on by the notorious school bully Flashman, it is East and Tom who bravely stand up to him, despite their still small size. The story ends with Tom as Head Boy under the kindly tutelage of **Thomas Arnold** himself. Hughes's affection for his own schooldays is never in doubt, and his story helped to found a long tradition of uncritical acceptance for public school values and practices in children's fiction.

**Tom Jones, A Foundling, The History of** A novel by **Henry Fielding**, published in 1749.

Mr Allworthy, a rich and benevolent country gentleman, finds a baby in his bed one night. He becomes the baby's guardian and gives him a home, later shared with Blifil, Mr Allworthy's nephew and heir. The mean-spirited Blifil is supported in his resentment of Tom by Thwackum the tutor and his friend Square, the philosopher. As he grows up, Tom enjoys the favours of Molly Seagrim, the gamekeeper's daughter, but falls in love with Sophia Western, the squire's daughter, who is intended for Blifil. Sophia detests Blifil and wants to marry Tom, who is confounded by Molly's declaration that she is pregnant. He is prepared to do the honourable thing in the face of Mr Allworthy's displeasure; fortunately, he learns that Molly has been very free with her favours and he is under no obligation. But Blifil's malice succeeds and Mr Allworthy closes his house to Tom. He sets out with the schoolmaster, Partridge, unsure where he is going but believing the army to be his best hope.

He encounters Sophia, who has run away from her father because he insists that she marry Blifil. With her maid, Mrs Honour, she is going to London to shelter with a relative. Tom finds a pocket book belonging to Sophia and follows her to London in order to return it. His adventures on the way are an opportunity for Fielding to portray a rich gallery of characters.

In London Tom drifts into an affair with Lady Bellaston, who keeps him. She tries to procure Sophia for her friend Lord Fellamar; the outraged girl also discovers Tom's relationship with Lady Bellaston and turns her back on him. Tom is forced into a duel and apparently kills his opponent. Lady Bellaston, furious at being left by Tom, and Lord Fellamar, furious at being rejected by Sophia, instigate Tom's arrest and imprisonment. Fortunately, Tom's opponent does not die, and it is revealed that Blifil knows the truth of Tom's birth and has concealed it. Tom is the son of Mr Allworthy's sister Bridget and as such is Mr Allworthy's proper heir. Sophia forgives him for his infidelities, and they are married.

The novel is Fielding's masterpiece. The introductory chapters that preface each of the novel's 18 books cultivate the reader in a way that was then unprecedented in English fiction; they establish a narrative voice satisfying the contemporary reader's fondness for moral commentary. The tangled comedies of coincidence are offset by the neat, architectonic structure of

The frontispiece to Vol. I of an edition of *Tom Jones* published in 1773. Left to right: Miss Bridget, Mr Allworthy, and Mrs Wilkins with the baby found in Mr Allworthy's bed. Fielding's novel was first published in 1749.

this most shapely novel. The portrait of the virtuous Sophia is triumphantly free from stereotypes (it is thought she was modelled on the author's wife, Charlotte) while Tom Jones himself is both a vital and a fallible hero, generous and imprudent, but ultimately happy in his pursuit of Sophia, or wisdom.

**Tom Sawyer, The Adventures of** See *Adventures of Tom Sawyer, The*.

**Tomlinson, (Alfred) Charles** 1927– Poet, translator and painter. Born in Stoke-on-Trent, he was educated at Longton High School, Queens' College, Cambridge – where his tutor was **Donald Davie** – and London University. He has taught at the University of Bristol since 1968, since 1982 as Professor of English. His first collection, *The Necklace* (1955), received wider recognition in the USA than in Britain, and his links with American literature are strong: his precursors are **Pound**, **Eliot**, **William Carlos Williams**, **Wallace Stevens** and **Louis Zukofsky**. His prose book, *Some Americans: A Personal Record* (1981), contains fascinating insights into these debts, and into Tomlinson's intellectual development. In attempting to accord 'objects their own existence', Tomlin-

son's poems are often imagistic, visual responses to landscapes, experiences and events. The title of his second collection, *Seeing is Believing* (1960), is apposite, and it should be remembered that Tomlinson is a visual artist of considerable originality and talent; *In Black and White* (1975) is a collection of his graphic work. His work has been criticized for being cold, humourless and without human interest – charges which led to the ironic title of his next book, *A Peopled Landscape* (1963). His best collection, *The Way of a World* (1969), contains the cinematic 'Swimming Chenango Lake' and the political poem 'Prometheus'. Later collections have been *Written on Water* (1972), *The Way In* (1974), *The Shaft* (1978), *The Flood* (1981), *Notes From New York and Other Poems* (1984) and *The Return* (1987), as well as *Selected Poems 1951–1974* (1978) and *Collected Poems* (1985). One source of originality in his work is the influence of Spanish-American writers. He has collaborated with Octavio Paz on a sonnet sequence, *Airborn/ Hijos del Aire* (1981), and produced many translations from the work of Paz and Antonio Machado, gathered in *Translations* (1983). He has also edited *The Oxford Book of Verse in Translation* (1980).

**Tomlinson, H[enry] M[ajor]** 1873–1958 Novelist and journalist. Born in the dockland area of East London, he entered a shipping office at the age of 12 but left to join the staff of *The Morning Leader* in 1904. In 1912 he went to South America, and *The Sea and the Jungle* (1912) was based on his experiences on the Amazon. During World War I he became a war correspondent in France for *The Daily News*, and he was literary editor of *The Nation* from 1917 to 1923.

His novels continued with *Old Junk* (1918), *London River* (1921) and *Waiting For Daylight* (1922), but he is chiefly remembered for *Gallions Reach* (1927) and the powerful anti-war novel *All Our Yesterdays* (1930), a quasi-historical account of British domestic and foreign affairs from 1900 to the Armistice in 1918. Its descriptions of the horrors of trench warfare were backed by Tomlinson's own experiences in Flanders and gave the novel considerable authority.

His other works include the novels *The Snows of Helicon* (1933), *All Hands* (1937) and *Morning Light* (1946), and the travel books *South to Cadiz* (1934) and *Malay Waters* (1950). *A Mingled Yarn* (1953) was a collection of autobiographical essays.

**Tono-Bungay** A novel by **H. G. Wells**, published in 1909.

Often regarded as a **Condition of England novel**, it follows George Ponderevo's quest for moral and intellectual certainties. As first-person narrator Ponderevo reviews his childhood at Bladesover, a country house where his mother worked as housekeeper. His admiration for the aristocratic order is overruled by his awareness of its obsolescence. After being sent as baker's apprentice to the narrow-minded Evangelist, Nicodemus Frapp, George is entered into the commercial world by his uncle Edward Ponderevo. He is required to be the salesman for 'Tono-Bungay', the quack medicine emanating from Teddy Ponderevo's chemist's shop. Tono-Bungay, the panacea of an irreligious age, brings prosperity to George's uncle and kindly Aunt Susan. George, less contented, can now marry Marion Ramboat.

Marriage is a failure for George, like his experiences of religion and commercialism. His real destiny is associated with the progress of scientific truth, and he becomes a student of aeronautics. Meanwhile Uncle Edward's fortunes decline, with his financial speculations and his ill-judged purchase of Lady Grove, a venerable estate. He appears less a country gentleman than a vulgar philanderer; his bankruptcy ensues. George undertakes an expedition to an island off Africa to collect 'quap', a radioactive material which will redeem the Ponderevo fortunes. The project fails, with 'quap' rotting the timbers of the ship. George's perpetual quest continues amid recurring disillusions. He flies his dying uncle to France to save him from imprisonment; a love affair with the Hon. Beatrice Normandy fails. Despite the presiding motif of decay in the nation, George is finally perceived as the producer of inexorable changes as he passes along the Thames on board a destroyer, his latest invention.

**Tonson, Jacob** (the elder) 1655–1736 Publisher. The second son of a shoemaker who was, nonetheless, a member of the Barber-Surgeons' Company, Tonson was apprenticed to Thomas Basset, a bookseller in Fleet Street, in 1670 and became a freeman of the Stationers' Company in December 1677. In 1679 he published **Dryden**'s version of *Troilus and Cressida*, and in 1684 started to publish the *Miscellany Poems*, which were edited and, in the earlier volumes, to a large extent written by Dryden, and are commonly referred to as *Tonson's Miscellany*. In two instalments, 1683 and 1690, he acquired the copyright of *Paradise Lost*, and in 1688, when still only owning half the copyright, published an edition of the poem by subscription. This was the first of a series of major publications issued in this fashion which Tonson, though not initiating, made popular. In 1705 he published **Addison**'s *Remarks on Several Parts of Italy*, and in 1713 the same author's *Cato*. The sixth volume of his *Miscellany* included **Pope**'s Pastorals. He also actively encouraged and published works by such figures as **Aphra Behn**, **Congreve**, **Lee**,

Otway, **Philips**, **Prior**, **Rowe**, **Steele**, **Swift** and **Tate**, and took over the publication of both *The Tatler* and *The Spectator*. Tonson was responsible for the founding of the **Kit-Cat Club**, the members of which were prominent among the leaders of the Whig party and in the literary field. As publisher of Dryden and Congreve alone Tonson would have a major claim to fame: bearing in mind his other activities, he may be regarded as the publisher of his age, and can be compared only with **Robert Dodsley**.

**Tooke, John Horne** 1736–1812 Radical politician and philologist. The son of a well-to-do poulterer named Horne, he was educated at Westminster School, Eton and St John's College, Cambridge. In 1782 he assumed the additional surname of Tooke, his wealthy friend William Tooke of Purley having apparently made him his heir. He was ordained and became vicar of New Brentford, Middlesex, in 1760, but resigned his living in 1773. Although he held a lifelong respect for things 'established', he had no religious calling and later bitterly regretted that he had not chosen the law. In 1765 he became friendly with **John Wilkes**, to whom he lent vigorous support in the Middlesex election of 1768. A skilled and witty speaker and pugnacious campaigner for constitutional reform, he was involved in numerous legal battles and skirmishes: his support for the American colonists against the King led to conviction and one year's imprisonment for blasphemous libel in 1777–8, but he was acquitted (with **Holcroft** and Thelwall) in the treason trials of 1794. Tooke represented an older type of British radicalism, appealing to Magna Carta and the revolution of 1688, and he treated the 'rights of man' generation of the 1790s with some scorn. In 1801 he was elected to the House of Commons, but immediately afterwards an Act (which is still in force) excluding the Anglican clergy from membership was passed, and he was disqualified. His literary reputation was established by *Epea Pteroenta, or, the Diversions of Purley* (1786–1805, two volumes of a projected three), which launched the science of comparative philology. He was among the first to see languages as historical developments rather than fixed structures, and stressed the importance of the study of Gothic and Anglo-Saxon. The work was extremely popular and greatly admired by **James Mill** and the Utilitarians. Tooke's friends and acquaintances included **Boswell**, **Bentham**, **Coleridge**, **Godwin** and **Thomas Paine**.

**Toole, John Kennedy** 1937–69 American novelist. Born in New Orleans, and educated at Tulane and Columbia universities. Toole wrote just one novel, *A Confederacy of Dunces*, which was not published until after his death; he committed suicide 11 years before his mother persuaded **Walker Percy** to read the manuscript. A satirical comedy on a depraved and depressed New Orleans society, *A Confederacy of Dunces* quickly won acclaim and was awarded a Pulitzer Prize in 1980, the year of its publication.

**Toomer, Jean (Nathan Eugene)** 1894–1967 Black American writer. A central figure of the **Harlem Renaissance**, Toomer was born in Washington, DC. He attended the University of Wisconsin and the City College of New York. In 1921 he worked as superintendent of a black rural school in Sparta, Georgia, an experience which provided the source for some of the material in his most widely read work, *Cane* (1923). During the 1920s he contributed poetry to the black journals *Opportunity* and *Crisis*, as well as to *avant-garde* magazines such as *Broom* and *The Little Review*. With the publication of *Cane*, a work composed of stories and poems, he attracted the attention of a number of prominent editors, critics, and authors, including **Waldo Frank** and **William Stanley Braithwaite**. In 1924 he studied in France under the mystic Georges Gurdjieff, whose influence is apparent in Toomer's later work. *Essentials*, a collection of aphorisms on philosophical subjects, appeared in 1931. He experimented with dramatic conventions in two unpublished plays, 'Natalie Mann' (1922) and 'The Sacred Factory' (1927). He also wrote numerous poems, stories, and autobiographical sketches which remained unpublished in his lifetime and were subsequently collected in *The Wayward and the Seeking* (1980), edited by Darwin T. Turner.

**Toplady, Augustus** 1740–78 Hymn writer and theologian. Born at Farnham in Surrey, he attended Westminster School and completed his education at Trinity College, Dublin. He was ordained in 1764 and became vicar of Broad Hembury in Devon in 1768. He is remembered for his hymns ('Rock of Ages' is the most famous) and for his violent reaction to the teaching of **John Wesley**, whom he had once admired. Toplady regressed into Calvinism and wrote *The Historic Proof of the Doctrinal Calvinism of the Church of England* (1774).

***Tottel's Miscellany*** The first of the poetic miscellanies popular in the later 16th century, brought out in 1557 by the printer Richard Tottel in collaboration with **Nicholas Grimald**. Its formal title was *Songs and Sonnets Written by the Right Honourable Lord Henry Howard Late Earl of Surrey and Other* (i.e. others). **Thomas Wyatt** is generously represented as well as **Surrey**, the first time that the work of either poet had appeared in print. Other writers include Grimald himself, Sir John Cheke and **Thomas Vaux**. There was a second edition in 1557 and many subsequent editions with additions and deletions in the 16th century.

***Tour of Dr Syntax in Search of the Picturesque, The*** A verse satire by **William Combe**, published in 1809. Between 1809 and 1811 Rudolph Ackermann produced his *Poetical Magazine*, for which Thomas Rowlandson offered him a series of plates depicting the comic adventures of a village schoolmaster. Combe was asked to write the letterpress for the illustrations, and thus began a collaboration between the writer and artist which lasted for over a decade. *The Schoolmaster's Tour*, as it was first called, was an enormous popular success, and was reissued in book form in 1812. Astride a shiftless old horse called Grizzle, the clergyman–schoolmaster sets out 'to make a *tour* and *write it*', in the course of which he suffers a series of absurd misfortunes. The book is perhaps in the first instance a satire of **William Gilpin**'s well-known expeditions to 'picturesque' Britain, but it also feeds off the host of 18th- and early-19th-century writers whose 'Tours', 'Travels' and 'Journeys' were vehicles of sententious moralizing, fake rapture and self-indulgent sentiment. It was followed by *The Second Tour of Dr Syntax in Search of Consolation* (1820), Mrs Syntax having expired at the end of the first Tour, and *The Third Tour of Dr Syntax in Search of a Wife* (1821). The three Tours were published together in 1826.

**Tourgée, Albion W[inegar]** 1838–1905 American novelist, born in Williamsfield, Ohio, and educated at the University of Rochester. He served with the Union forces during the Civil War and was seriously wounded. In 1864 he was admitted to the Bar and in the following year moved to North Carolina. A transplanted Northerner who disapproved of all the Old South stood for, he was labelled a carpetbagger. In 1868 he was elected a judge of North Carolina's Supreme Court, in which capacity he served for six years.

Tourgée's commitment to Reconstruction ideology and to the reform of the South is reflected in the novels he wrote there. *'Toinette: A Novel* (1874, republished as *A Royal Gentleman* 1881) is the story of a near-white slave girl who is freed but left in a tragic position when her lover, a white Southerner who has fathered her child, refuses to marry her. *A Fool's Errand* (1879) portrays the conflict between a former Confederate general and a former Union colonel who sides with the freed blacks and fights both the Ku Klux Klan and the carpetbaggers. The novel was republished in 1880 incorporating *The Invisible Empire*, a factual enquiry into the history of the Ku Klux Klan. *Bricks Without Straw* (1880) tells of a black's struggle to establish himself as a free and independent man; terrorized by the Klan, he is forced to move with his family to the North. After leaving the South in 1879, Tourgée continued to write fiction, producing a further 17 novels, among which are *Hot Plowshares* (1882), *Black Ice* (1888) and *Eighty-Nine, or, The Grand Master's Story* (1891), in which he returned to the theme of Republican reform of the South after the Civil War. From 1882 to 1884 he edited *Our Continent*, a weekly publication in which he continued to champion the rights of blacks and to expose the evil of the Ku Klux Klan. He served as US consul in Bordeaux from 1897 to his death in 1905.

**Tourneur, Cyril** *c.*1575–1626 Playwright. Virtually nothing is known of Tourneur's life before 1613, though he seems to have been at various times in the service of the Cecils, the Veres and the Earl of Essex, and probably combined military and diplomatic work both before and after 1613, when he was a government courier to Brussels. As Secretary to Sir Edward Cecil he was involved in the 1625 raid on Cadiz, and put ashore in Ireland after the raid's failure. He died there early in 1626, perhaps as a result of wounds suffered in the expedition.

Tourneur's first published work was an obscure poetic satire, *The Transformed Metamorphosis* (1600), but he is remembered as the author of two plays, the magnificent **The Revenger's Tragedy** (*c.*1607) and the greatly inferior **The Atheist's Tragedy** (published 1611). Tourneur is named as the author of the latter play on the title-page of the 1611 edition, but the disparity in quality between the two plays has led to doubts about the ascription of him of the former. **Thomas Middleton** is the most favoured of rival claimants, and the assignment to Tourneur has no stronger basis than the word of a certain Edward Archer in 1656. Tourneur is known, from a reference in the Stationers' Register, to have written a third play, called *The Nobleman* (1612–13), and was also asked to write one act of *The Arraignment of London* (1613). Neither play has survived. In effect, Tourneur's reputation rests on the splendours of a play he may not have written.

**Towneley cycle, the** See **miracle plays**.

**Townshend, Aurelian** ?1583–?1643 Poet. Little is known of Townshend's life. His family home was in Norfolk, and he entered Sir Robert Cecil's service at an early age, travelling to France and Italy. The linguistic proficiency he acquired is manifest in his letters (in both languages) to his patron. He made, however, undesirable connections, was recalled and was probably with Cecil when he died in 1612. Apart from registering his children, Townshend disappears until early in 1632, when he is found

supplanting **Ben Jonson** as literary collaborator with Inigo Jones on two court masques, *Albion's Triumph* and *Tempe Restored*. These, and a handful of lyrics and occasional poems, uncollected in his lifetime, constitute his literary work.

**Toynbee, Arnold (Joseph)** 1889–1975 Historian. Arnold Toynbee, nephew of Arnold Toynbee the social reformer, was born in London. He was educated at Winchester and Balliol College, Oxford, of which he became a fellow, and where he was a tutor (1912–15). After Oxford he served at the Foreign Office until 1919, when he was appointed Koraes Professor of Byzantine and Modern Greek Language, Literature and History at King's College, London. He was Director of Studies at the Royal Institute of International Affairs from 1925 to 1955. During World War II he directed the Foreign Office Research Department (1943–6) and at its conclusion was a member of the British delegation at the peace conference in Paris.

Toynbee's first work was a pamphlet, *Greek Policy Since 1882* (1914), and many of his subsequent works were concerned with European politics and ancient Greek culture. The first part of *A Study of History* appeared in 1934; it was completed in 12 volumes in 1961. A philosophy of world history from earliest to contemporary times, it views the history of mankind as a recurring cycle of growth, breakdown and eventual dissolution, and advances the proposition that a 'spiritual initiative' by a new universal church would provide the chrysalis from which a new civilization could emerge. The work proved highly controversial, but a two-volume condensation by D. C. Somervell (1946 and 1957) enjoyed a remarkable popular success.

Among other works by Toynbee were the texts of his notable Reith Lectures, *The World and the West* (1952), *Hellenism: The History of a Civilization* (1959) and *Hannibal's Legacy* (1965). An enthusiastic traveller, he was also the author of several travel books, *Between Oxus and Jumna* (1961), *Between Niger and Nile* (1965) and *Between Maule and Amazon* (1967). *Comparing Notes: A Dialogue Across a Generation* (1963) was written with his son, the critic and novelist Philip Toynbee (1916–81).

***Tracts for the Times*** An offshoot of the **Oxford Movement**, *Tracts for the Times* appeared from 1833 until 1841, providing another label for the ferment: the Tractarian Movement. **John Henry Newman** wrote the first tract; others were contributed by **John Keble**, **E. B. Pusey** and **Isaac Williams**. Originally brief leaflets, the tracts developed into learned theological treatises. In 1841 Newman's *Tract XC*, which argued that the 39 Articles of the Anglican Church were compatible with Catholic theology, caused an outcry which made it the last of the series. The Tractarians were officially banned, and in 1845 the group was further weakened by Newman's conversion to Catholicism.

***Traffics and Discoveries*** A collection of 11 stories and 11 poems by **Rudyard Kipling**, first published in 1904. The stories range in subject matter from the supernatural to the Boer War. Recent critical opinion has been divided on the best-known, 'They' and 'Mrs Bathurst'.

'They' hints at Kipling's feelings for his daughter Josephine, who died as a child in 1899. The narrator, driving across Sussex to the 'other side of the country', comes by chance upon an Elizabethan country house. He sees children at upper windows. The other-worldliness of the place, and especially of the children, is felt in the account of a blind lady; although childless, her life is devoted to the children. The narrator is drawn to the place a number of times; it is the children, who stay elusive, who have charmed him. At last, in the house, his hand is taken and kissed by an unseen child; contact has been established with a shadowy world of the departed, but the narrator knows that he must leave the house for good.

'Mrs Bathurst' has a strong element of unexplained mystery, but not of the supernatural. At the centre of a tale with widely spread geographical reference-points is the effect that Mrs Bathurst, a New Zealand hotel-keeper, has had on a naval warrant-officer, Vickery. One of the narrators, Pyecroft, has witnessed Vickery's obsession with the image of Mrs Bathurst seen on a news film on the local screen in Cape Town (one of the earliest uses of the cinematograph in fiction). Vickery's subsequent desertion and violent death in a thunderstorm are unexplained; tantalizingly, the story associates Mrs Bathurst with the terrible retribution of an otherwise random universe.

'Below the Mill Dam' and 'Wireless', stories in which mystery and the supernatural figure prominently, have also attracted favourable attention. However, the Boer War stories – notably 'A Sahibs' War' – have often been found muddled and disappointing, reflecting the more jingoistic Kipling.

**tragedy** There is no satisfactory explanation of the process by which a Greek word meaning 'goat song' came to be applied to the poetic dramas of ancient Greece, in which the kings and heroes of Greek mythology were displayed in the crisis of confrontation with their gods. The mature Greek tragedy of 5th-century BC Athens was analysed in Aristotle's influential *Poetics*, and the greater exactness of his neoclassical interpreters, particularly in Renaissance France, established the responsibility of tragedy to deal with the fall of great men (or, exceptionally, great women).

By an accident of scholarship, it was the Roman poet Seneca (c. 4 BC–AD 65), rather than the greater Greek writers Aeschylus, Sophocles and Euripides, who influenced the form of the earliest English tragedies. The Senecan atrocities of, for example, *Titus Andronicus*, were a readily acceptable part of Elizabethan tragedy, and the formal conventions of **revenge tragedy**, a distinctive sub-genre for 50 years after the first performance of **Kyd**'s *The Spanish Tragedy* (c. 1589), were originally adopted from Seneca. But English dramatists rejected the restrictions of their classical models. Their corpse-strewn stages owed much to Seneca, but their preparedness to use prose as well as verse, and to spread the action over comic as well as tragic characters and episodes gave a unique emotional breadth to English tragedy. Beside the colour of **Marlowe** and **Shakespeare**, the Senecan severity of **Ben Jonson**'s two Roman tragedies is unattractive. While Elizabethan and Jacobean tragedies were, with very few exceptions, obedient to the expectation that rulers or noblemen were the proper protagonists, their authors were more concerned to write popular plays than great literature.

English tragedy has suffered from the subsequent elevation of the genre. Whereas **comedy** thrived in the reopened post-Restoration theatres, the rhymed bombast of heroic tragedy led to dwindling popularity. Increasingly, through the 18th and 19th centuries, great tragic actors made their names in revivals, much altered, of Shakespeare. The most successful tragedies of **Lee**, **Otway**, **Dryden** and **Rowe** owed their attraction to their ability, however sporadically, to recall Shakespeare. It has been argued often that the increasing disunity of society, its loss of common spiritual values, was inimical to tragedy, which relies on the representative nature of individual disaster. A possible line of development was indicated by **George Lillo**, whose *The London Merchant* (1731) set a short-lived fashion for bourgeois tragedy. Lillo's moral directives, which push the audience towards thrift and industry, were absorbed into melodrama, and the further intrusion of tragedy into the lives of the middle classes had to await the emergence of Ibsen. Meanwhile, the conviction that tragedy was the proper preserve of poets continued to tempt most of the greatest from Dryden to **T. S. Eliot**. Some, like **Coleridge**, **Byron**, **Browning** and **Tennyson**, had fleeting success in the theatre, but few of their plays have lasted well. With the arguable exception of Byron, their model was Shakespeare, and the artistic outcome analogous to the reproduction of antique furniture.

Those who argue that the 20th-century English-speaking theatre has witnessed a revival of tragedy are more likely to base their claims on domestic and social dramas than on such historical works as the more conventionally tragic *Murder in the Cathedral*. **O'Neill** and **Arthur Miller** in the USA, **O'Casey** in Ireland and **Bond** in England have their adherents, but their determined emphasis on the world of everyman removes them from the Aristotelian world of high tragedy.

**Tragic Comedians, The**  A novel by **George Meredith**, published in 1880. It was based on Helene von Donniges's account of her love affair with the German socialist, Ferdinand Lassalle, who appears in the novel as Alvan. Helene von Donniges is represented as the character Clotilde, a nobleman's daughter who is prepared to marry Alvan in the face of her family's wrath. Quixotically honourable, Alvan insists that she gain their full consent. Clotilde returns to her family, who bully her mercilessly and in the end deceive her into accepting the suitor of their choice, Marko. When he learns what has happened, Alvan writes a furious and insulting letter to Clotilde's father. Marko challenges him, and in the ensuing fight Alvan is killed. Clotilde marries Marko after the tragedy.

**Traherne, Thomas** 1637–74 Religious poet and essayist. Born in Hereford, the son of a shoemaker, he studied at Brasenose College, Oxford, in 1653–6. Appointed by the Parliamentary Commissioners as rector of Credenhill near Hereford in 1657, he was ordained by the restored Church of England in 1660 and re-appointed to Credenhill. There he became part of a devotional circle around Mrs Susanna Hopton, for whom he is thought to have composed his *Centuries of Meditations*. He became chaplain to Sir Orlando Bridgeman, the Lord Keeper of the Great Seal, in 1667 and was buried in Teddington church, near Bridgeman's seat. In his lifetime, he published *Roman Forgeries* (1673), an account of the fabrication of false documents in the medieval church. *Christian Ethics* appeared in 1675, 'opening the way to blessedness by the rules of virtue and reason'. His *Thanksgivings* were published anonymously in 1699.

Traherne remained an unregarded writer until early this century when the discovery of his poems and the *Centuries of Meditations* revealed him as a man of outstanding religious sensibility. The *Centuries* transmit Traherne's childhood sense of living in an earthly paradise, surrounded by the beauty of the creation. He had no sense of property, division or limit; he felt, like Adam, that the world had been created entirely for his delight. His natural response was praise of the creator. Later, his spirit was clouded by a darkening sense of sin and of the sorrow of the world, but the experience of spiritual regeneration enabled him to recover the former intensity of delight in the world and its creator. This condition of spiritual elevation and joy he termed 'Felicity'. The *Centuries* are written in lucid metrical prose; they have a psalm-like quality of praise and thanksgiving, and they express a kind of luminous spirituality that is quite exceptional. Traherne sets himself apart from most of his contemporaries by his rejection of the doctrine of original sin; sin, he was inclined to believe, was a habit acquired by contact with society. His poems complement the experience of the *Centuries*, with much recall of the wonder of his childhood, and with a visionary sense of the divinity that permeates the creation.

**Traill, Catharine Parr** 1802–99  Canadian writer on emigrant life. The sister of **Agnes Strickland** and **Susanna Moodie**, she was born in London and moved to Canada in 1832, soon after her marriage. She published her first book, *The Blind Highland Piper and Other Tales*, at the age of sixteen and produced several popular books for children. In spite of a difficult life in Canada, marked by financial troubles, her most enduring works grew out of her pioneering days: *The Backwoods of Canada* (sub-titled 'Letters from the Wife of an Emigrant Officer, illustrative of the domestic economy of North America', 1836) and *The Female Emigrant's Guide* (1854). She was also an accomplished naturalist and published several books on Canadian wildlife.

**Traitor, The**  A tragedy by **James Shirley**, first produced in 1631 and published in 1635. The play has some basis in the history of the Medici family of Florence. The Duke of Florence is enamoured of Amidea, the sister of Sciarrha, one of his nobles. His kinsman, Lorenzo, plotting to seize power, does his best to further the duke's desires, while at the same time arousing Sciarrha's wrath at the threat to his sister's honour. Sciarrha kills Amidea to save her from dishonour and lays out her body where the duke will find her. When the duke comes upon the body he calls for Lorenzo, who seizes the opportunity to murder him. Lorenzo is killed by Sciarrha in the last moments of accusation and recrimination; Sciarrha dies of his wounds.

**Transcendentalism**  A literary and philosophical movement in New England in the early and middle part of the 19th century. Centred on Boston and Concord, some of its most notable voices were those of **Ralph Waldo Emerson**, **Henry David Thoreau**, **Margaret Fuller** and **Bronson Alcott**. Transcendentalism was opposed to the idea that man needs an intercessor through whom to reach the divine, and was critical of formalized religion. Like the physical universe itself, all constructive practical activity, all great literature, all forms of spiritual awareness were viewed as an expression of the divine spirit. The often-expressed ambition was to achieve vivid perception of the divine as it operates in common life, an awareness seen as leading at once to personal cultivation and to a sense of history as an at least potentially progressive movement.

*Traveller, The*, or, *A Prospect of Society* A poem by **Oliver Goldsmith**, published in 1764 and the first work to appear under his own name. It was dedicated to his brother Henry, to whom he had sent the rough draft from Switzerland during his own travels 10 years before. The traveller – or compulsive wanderer – is the poet himself. From a peak in the Alps he ponders the lessons of his travels and notes the faults and virtues of the countries he has visited. Happiness, he realizes, may be found in any place, as well as discontent. The poem is written in fluent rhyming couplets which encompass description and philosophy with apparent ease.

*Travels in France* (*Travels During the Years 1787, 1788, 1789 and 1790, Undertaken with a View of Ascertaining the Cultivation, Wealth, Resources and National Prosperity of the Kingdom of France*) A report by **Arthur Young** on his journeys in France, published in 1792. He observed conditions just before the Revolution and could see that the social order was ripe for change. His first journey took him through Berri, Poitou and Languedoc, the second through Brittany and Anjou, the third through Alsace–Lorraine, Franche-Comté, Burgundy and Provence. Young's examination of systems of land tenure has permanent value and his book has a considerable reputation in France. It was translated into a number of languages.

*Travels through France and Italy* A memoir of his travels from June 1764 to June 1765 by **Tobias Smollett**, published in 1766.

Smollett's health broke down in 1763, and in April of that year he was distressed by the death of his daughter Elizabeth at the age of 15. He set out for Europe with his wife in June of the following year and journeyed across France. After Nice, the Smolletts proceeded to Genoa and then through Italy, visiting Florence and continuing as far south as Rome. They returned to Nice in the winter and then made their way back to England. The book takes the form of letters to imaginary correspondents and gives a remarkable picture of mid 18th-century life on the Continent. Though his attitude may frequently be quarrelsome and resentful, Smollett remains a sharp and perceptive observer. **Laurence Sterne** met him during his wanderings and included him in *A Sentimental Journey* as Smelfungus: 'he set out with spleen and jaundice, and every object he passed by was discoloured or distorted'.

**Travers, Ben** 1886–1980 Dramatist. Born in Hendon and educated at Charterhouse, Travers worked for the family firm before joining the Royal Naval Air Service in 1914 and the Royal Air Force in 1918. Between 1922 and 1933, he wrote custom-made farces for the talented Aldwych company under the supervision of Tom Walls. The best include *A Cuckoo in the Nest* (1925), *Rookery Nook* (1926), *Thark* (1927) and *Plunder* (1928). Away from the Aldwych after 1933, Travers had less theatrical success, though his last play, *The Bed Before Yesterday* (1975), is a touching retrospect on the younger world of 1930.

**Travers, P[amela] L[yndon]** 1906– Children's writer. Born in Australia, she came to England in 1923 and worked as an actress-dancer until 1936. She based her first novel for children, *Mary Poppins* (1934), on stories she had originally told to children of her acquaintance. It was memorably illustrated by Mary Shepard (wife of **E. H. Shepard**). Its mixture of strong nursery discipline with exciting magic made it an immediate success and led to four sequels as well as a Walt Disney musical in 1964. Other novels for children include *The Fox at the Manger* (1963) and *Friend Monkey* (1971), a moving story about the adoption of an untamed animal. P. L. Travers is also a talented poet.

*Treasure Island* A novel of adventure and piracy in the 18th century by **Robert Louis Stevenson**. It was serialized as *The Sea Cook or Treasure Island*, by 'Captain George North', in *Young Folks* from October 1881 to January 1882 and published in book form in 1883. Stevenson himself regarded it as a digression from his serious work, but it was a popular success and has remained his most famous book.

The story is told by Jim Hawkins, whose mother keeps an inn, the 'Admiral Benbow', near the coast in the West Country. An old pirate, Billy Bones, comes to stay; he is dogged by his former confederates, for he has in his possession a map showing the location of Captain Flint's treasure. Jim outwits them and secures the map, which he and his mother take to Squire Trelawney. The squire and his old friend Dr Livesey charter a schooner, the *Hispaniola*, commanded by Captain Smollett, and set sail for Treasure Island with Jim as a member of the crew. Jim discovers that the crew includes pirates, led by the ship's one-legged cook, Long John Silver. The rest of the story tells how the pirates are defeated and the treasure found.

An illustration by Wal Paget for an edition of *Treasure Island* published in 1899. Jim Hawkins and Long John Silver walking along the quays. Stevenson's novel was first published as a serial in 1881.

**Treatise of Human Nature, A** A philosophical essay by **David Hume**, the first two volumes published in 1739 and the third in 1740.

Hume acknowledges his debt to **Locke** and earlier philosophers who had used experimental reasoning in the examination of moral subjects. Book I, on understanding, examines man's process of knowing, tracing the origin of ideas – of space, time, causality, etc. – in experience and the data of the senses. Book II, on the 'passions', provides an elaborate psychological machinery to explain the affective order in man, assigning a subordinate role to reason. Book III, on morals, describes 'moral goodness' in terms of 'feelings' of approval or disapproval generated by the agreeable or disagreeable consequences of human behaviour.

The *Treatise* is Hume's first and most comprehensive attempt to formulate his philosophical position. Its varying aspects are separately developed in *An Enquiry Concerning Human Understanding*, first published as *Philosophical Essays Concerning Human Understanding* in 1748, *An Enquiry Concerning the Principles of Morals* (1751) and the dissertation on the passions in *Four Dissertations* (1757).

**Treatise on the Astrolabe, A** A prose translation by **Geoffrey Chaucer** from Latin texts. Dedicated to his young son, Lewis, it offers a simplified account of the astrolabe, a mechanical device for making various astronomical and astrological measurements and calculations. Most of the work is translated from the 8th-century *Compositio et Operatio Astrolabii* of the Arabian Messahala, but some passages are apparently derived from John de Sacrobosco's *De Spaera* and others have not been traced to a source. The introduction is interesting as the only substantial piece of Chaucer's prose which is not a close translation from another author, but otherwise the work is of little literary interest. The *Treatise* is apparently the earliest complex scientific work to have been written in English. It is possible but not yet proven that Chaucer also wrote the more erudite astronomical treatise *The Equatorie of the Planets*.

**Treece, Henry** 1911–66 Poet and children's historical novelist. Born in Staffordshire and educated at Wednesbury Grammar School and Birmingham University, he became a schoolteacher before enlisting with the RAF during World War II. One of the founders of the **New Apocalypse** movement, he published several volumes of poetry, including *The Black Seasons* (1945) and *The Exiles* (1952). His critical works include *How I See Apocalypse* (1946) and the first book on **Dylan Thomas** (1949). His first children's book, *The Legion of the Eagle* (1954), describes battles between the Romans and the Celts. The many other novels which followed, dealing mostly with the Viking and Roman periods of British history, are distinguished by a feeling for the past that goes beyond mere accuracy of detail. He also produced a series of thrillers for children and a fine novel about one of the most baffling periods of medieval history, *The Children's Crusade* (1958), widely translated and probably his best book.

**Trelawny of the 'Wells'** A comedy by **Arthur Wing Pinero**, first performed at the **Royal Court Theatre**, London, in 1898.

The play is a nostalgic recollection of theatrical conditions in 1860, before the realism of **Tom Robertson** (alluded to in the character of Tom Wrench) had challenged the hold of melodrama. Rose Trelawny, star of Bagnigge Wells Theatre, is to quit the stage and marry. Her theatrical friends give her a farewell party, but she finds her fiancé's respectable family too unattractive, and returns to the theatre, determined to help stage the 'new' plays of Tom Wrench. All ends happily when her fiancé, having renounced his family, turns up as her leading man.

**Trelawny, Edward (John)** 1782–1881 Author and adventurer. The son of a senior army officer from an old Cornish family, Trelawny was born and brought up in London, and sent to a school in Bristol, from which he ran away. At the age of 13 he entered the Royal Navy, receiving his discharge in 1812. His experiences as a midshipman form the basis of the romantic account of his early years in his *Adventures of a Younger Son* (1831), in which he claims to have deserted the Navy in India and assumed command of a French privateer. In 1822 he surfaced in Pisa where he became a member of the circle round **Byron** and **Shelley**. He was acutely distressed by the news of Shelley's drowning in the Bay of Spezia, and it was he who supervised the recovery and cremation of the body, designed the tomb, and raised the money for **Mary Shelley** (to whom he some years later made a half-serious proposal of marriage) to return to England. In 1823 he accompanied Byron to Greece to take part in the struggle for national independence, where he got embroiled in the dissensions of the Greek leaders and survived an attempt on his life. He was married, for the second time, to a Greek girl in 1824. In 1833–5 he travelled in the United States, where, among other exploits, he swam the Niagara River just above the Falls and demonstrated his solidarity with the abolitionists by purchasing the freedom of a slave. His elopement in 1841 with the married Lady Augusta Goring caused a major social scandal and led to his third, and again unsuccessful, marriage. The second instalment of his autobiography appeared in 1858 under the title *Recollections of the Last Days of Byron and Shelley* (later altered to *Records of Byron, Shelley and the Author*, 1878), an extremely lively and readable account, though none too scrupulous on matters of fact. A truly larger-than-life figure of striking physical appearance and enormous social charm, Trelawny had become the ancient monument of the Byronic age by the end of his long life. His ashes were buried next to Shelley's in the Protestant Cemetery in Rome.

**Trench, Richard Chenevix** 1807–86 Philologist, theologian and poet. He made his name first as a poet with *The Story of Justin Martyr, and Other Poems* (1835), but, although he published other collections, few of his poems are read today. Fame came to him as a country clergyman with his *Notes on the Parables of Our Lord* (1841) written at Curdridge and *Notes on the Miracles of Our Lord* (1846) written at Itchenstoke. His most popular book *On the Study of Words* (1851) grew out of lectures given at the Winchester Diocesan Training School and was followed by *English Past and Present* (1855) from teaching at King's College, London. He played a part in launching **The Oxford English Dictionary** by reading two papers before the Philological Society, his *On Some Deficiencies in Our English Dictionaries*, in 1857 and proposing to the society in 1858 that a new dictionary be undertaken. Dean of Westminster from 1856, he returned to his birthplace to be consecrated Archbishop of Dublin (1864).

**Trespasser, The** A novel by **D. H. Lawrence**, first published in 1912.

The novel opens two years after Helena Verden, a young woman in her late twenties, has had an intense (though largely non-sexual) affair with her ex-violin teacher, Siegmund MacNair. Siegmund is dead and Helena continues to grieve, watched over by an adoring friend, Louisa, and her would-be suitor, Cecil Byrne, who wishes to 'bring her back from the dead'. Thereafter the burden of the novel retraces the tragic relationship between Helena and Siegmund, and 19 of the 31 chapters are occupied with their love experiences during a five days' stay on the Isle of Wight. Siegmund is a married man with children; Helena a member of 'that class of dreaming women with whom passion exhausts itself at the mouth'. She cannot give herself to him completely, and when they return to London Siegmund is tormented by his family's bitter reproaches. Unable to desert them for Helena, he feels trapped. Finally he commits suicide.

Beatrice, Siegmund's widow, begins a new and happier life as a boarding-house keeper in Highgate. Helena remains withdrawn and griefstricken. The novel ends with Cecil Byrne and Helena on an outing 'not yet a year after Siegmund's death'. Helena, though scarred by her experience, turns towards her new friend for 'rest and warmth'.

The novel was based on the experiences of Lawrence's friend Helen Corke, as revealed in her diaries.

**Trevelyan, G[eorge] M[acaulay]** 1876–1962 Historian. Trevelyan was the third son of the statesman and historian **Sir George Otto Trevelyan**. He was born at Stratford-upon-Avon and educated at Harrow and Trinity College, Cambridge. His dissertation, published as *England in the Age of Wycliffe* (1899), won him a fellowship at Trinity, where he taught until moving to London in 1903. During World War I he commanded an ambulance unit on the Italian front. He became Regius Professor of Modern History at Cambridge in 1927. An influential conservationist and keen walker, he was also a supporter of the National Trust and in 1931 became president of the newly founded Youth Hostels Association.

*England Under the Stuarts* (1904) confirmed

Trevelyan's reputation as a scholarly but popular writer, but his academic stature was established with the trilogy on Garibaldi: *Garibaldi's Defence of the Roman Republic* (1907), *Garibaldi and the Thousand* (1909) and *Garibaldi and the Making of Italy* (1911), published as a single work in 1933. *British History in the Nineteenth Century* (1922) and *History of England* (1926) were both popular successes, and his nostalgic *English Social History* (1944) became his most widely read book, though it was not considered his best.

Trevelyan's other publications include a three-volume history of *England Under Queen Anne* (1930–4) and *Grey of Falloden* (1937), a biography. His 1953 Clark lectures, *A Layman's Love of Letters* (published in 1954), acknowledged his love of English literature, notably **Browning**, **Scott**, **Meredith**, and **Housman**.

His *Autobiography and Other Essays* was published in 1949.

**Trevelyan, Sir George Otto** 1838–1928 Historian. The nephew of **Macaulay**, he was born in Leicestershire and educated at Harrow and Trinity College, Cambridge. He entered Parliament in 1865 and held a variety of public appointments.

Some of Trevelyan's early writings appeared in *The Dwak Bungalow* (1863), *The Competition Wallah* (1864) and *Cawnpore* (1865), all about India; other early humorous work was collected in *The Ladies of Parliament* (1869). A later, non-historical work, *Interludes in Prose and Verse*, appeared in 1905.

His first major historical writing was *The Life and Letters of Lord Macaulay* (1876). This was followed by *The Early History of Charles James Fox* (1880), intended as the first part of an exhaustive biography of the Whig politician; it is notable for its vivid presentation of social and political life in the late 18th century. However, his next work, *The American Revolution* (4 vols., 1899–1907), suggests that his intentions had changed, and *George III and Charles Fox* (1912–14) completed his study of the American Revolution.

**Trevisa, John de** 1326–1412 Born at Crocadon in St Mellion, Cornwall, he was a fellow of Exeter College, Oxford, in 1362–9. He became a fellow of The Queen's College in 1369 but was expelled in 1379 with others. Before 1387 he became chaplain to Lord Berkeley and vicar of Berkeley; he was also a canon of Westbury-on-Severn. He translated and augmented Higden's *Polychronicon* in 1387 and *De Proprietatibus Rerum* by Bartholomew de Glanville (or Bartholomaeus Anglicus) in 1398. The former is a **chronicle**, the latter an encyclopaedia. Several other works of lesser significance have been attributed to Trevisa, and **Caxton** credited him with a translation of the Bible. His work is notable as an example of early English prose treatment of secular topics.

**Trevor, William** 1928– Novelist and short-story writer. He was born William Trevor Cox in Mitcheldown, County Cork, and went to Trinity College, Dublin. Much of his fiction, which is divided equally into novels and short stories, is set in Ireland, where he has continued to live for extended periods. His work frequently deals with the corruption or destruction of innocence, for which childhood and old age are recurrent prototypes, and shows a penchant for settings of shabby, faded gentility. Novels include *The Old Boys* (1964); *Mrs Eckdorf in O'Neill's Hotel* (1969), which, like the more recent *Fools of Fortune* (1983), treats the civil struggle in Northern Ireland; *Elizabeth Alone* (1973); and *The Children of Dynmouth* (1976), about a psychopathic teenager menacing a quiet English retirement resort. Trevor's short stories were collected in a single volume in 1983.

***Trick to Catch the Old One, A*** A comedy by **Thomas Middleton**, performed by a **boys' company** *c*.1605 and published in 1608.

Theophilus Witgood, a young ne'er-do-well, wishes to get money from his miserly uncle, Pecunius Lucre. His former mistress, a courtesan known as the Widow Medler, agrees to pose as his wealthy 'intended'. In fact, Witgood is in love with Joyce, niece of the usurer Walkadine Hoard, Pecunius Lucre's sworn enemy. Scenting a good match for himself, Hoard courts and wins the Widow Medler. Thus disappointed of the money promised by his uncle on the prospect of a wealthy marriage, Witgood is arrested for debt, but persuades Hoard to pay off his debts by alluding to a breach of promise by the Widow. Witgood marries Joyce in secret. His uncle is delighted when Hoard learns, at the wedding feast, that he has married a courtesan, and, partly from malicious glee, agrees to forgive and finance his nephew. As for Hoard, he is consoled by the Widow's promise to be a good wife.

***Trilby*** A novel by **George Du Maurier**, published in 1894 and illustrated by himself. Originally, Du Maurier offered the outline to **Henry James**, suggesting that he should write it, but finally wrote it himself, to follow up the success of his first novel, *Peter Ibbetson*. Trilby is an artist's model who, manipulated by Svengali, becomes a famous singer. But at the moment of his death during a performance, her voice cracks and fails her. The novel was immediately and enduringly popular, because it combined the Victorian fascination with 'animal magnetism', hypnotism and occult powers with an archetypal story of demonic possession. Svengali, who has given his name to the language, was a German-Polish Jew, and the anti-semitism of the narrative jars on the modern reader. In 1895 the novel was adapted for the stage, Beerbohm Tree playing Svengali. A century later, Trilby's name survives as that of a man's felt hat, dented across the crown.

**Trilling, Lionel** 1905–75 American critic, born in New York City, and educated at Columbia, where he taught for most of his life. His publications include studies of *Matthew Arnold* (1939) and *E. M. Forster* (1943); and essays collected in *The Liberal Imagination* (1950), *The Opposing Self* (1955), *A Gathering of Fugitives* (1956), *Beyond Culture: Essays on Literature and Learning* (1965) and *Sincerity and Authenticity* (1972). Trilling addressed the broadest cultural questions: the relation of morality to politics, and the aesthetic as well as the political meaning of liberalism. His single novel, *The Middle of the Journey* (1947), also reflects these concerns. A volume of his short stories, *Of This Time, Of That Place and Other Stories*, was published posthumously in 1979.

**trimeter** See **metre**.

**triplet** A three-line **stanza**, usually on a single rhyme, or a variation of three rhyming lines in a poem of **heroic couplets**. As a stanza, it is also referred to as a tercet.

**Tristram and Iseult** A poem by **Matthew Arnold**, published in *Empedocles on Etna and Other Poems* (1852). In Brittany the dying Tristram remembers his happiness with Iseult of Ireland while her rival, Iseult of Brittany, watches over him. Iseult of Ireland arrives and there is one last passionate exchange between the lovers before he dies.

**Tristram Shandy, Gentleman, The Life and Opinions of** A novel by **Laurence Sterne**, published in instalments: Volumes I and II (1760), III and IV (1761), V and VI (1762), VII and VIII (1765) and Volume IX in 1767.

Despite its instant popularity and its ordinary-sounding title, *Tristram Shandy* is a novel with no clear beginning, middle and end: its narrative content is distributed across a bafflingly idiosyncratic time-scheme interrupted by numerous digressions, authorial comments and interferences with the printed fabric of the book. The comically fragmented storyline is a reaction against the linear narratives (of **Fielding**, for instance) or epistolary artifice (in particular, **Richardson**) in favour of a novelistic shape that depended on association of ideas, a realistic impressionism.

The story does start, however, *ab ovo* – with the narrator-hero describing his own conception. He is not actually born, though, for several volumes, and disappears from the book in Volume VI. In the meantime, the circumstances surrounding his birth are described in an apparently random fashion. Walter Shandy is Tristram's father, the science-smitten but benevolent head of Shandy Hall, where he lives in continuous exasperation with his wife. He has elaborate theoretical notions about society, the education of his son, and such projects as baptism by injection. His brother, 'my uncle Toby', is an old soldier wounded in the groin at the siege of Namur, whose obsessional hobby is the recreation of various military sieges, a pastime in which he is assisted by the devoted Corporal Trim (who received a wound in the knee, at Carden) and whose reflections on morality comprise Volume V. These are some of the characters whose behaviour can be understood in terms of their personal 'hobby-horses'. Dr Slop is the hilarious man-midwife so protractedly delayed in delivering the infant Tristram by a complex knot on his bag, Parson Yorick is the amiable local parson (Sterne adopted him as the persona for *A Sentimental Journey*) and the Widow Wadman casts a more than neighbourly eye over Uncle Toby.

After Tristram is born, Volume IV opens with the story of Slawkenbergius (a mock-

A detail from Hogarth's frontispiece to *Tristram Shandy*. Corporal Trim reads a sermon to Uncle Toby, Dr Slop, and Walter Shandy. British Museum Print Room.

encomium on noses) and an account of how the baby was christened 'Tristram' instead of the intended 'Trismegistus'. After Trim's discourse there is a fine dialogue between Tristram's parents, in Volume VI, about the 'breeching' (or dressing) of their child and the story of Le Fevre (a 'sentimental' set-piece of great popularity) after which the novel arbitrarily abandons the English village setting and follows the author's travels to France, reverting to an account of the amorous Widow Wadman's designs in Volume IX.

With its black pages, wiggly lines, chapters out of place and other intrusive devices, *Tristram Shandy* stands in part against the idea of literature as a finished product, its surfaces capable of reflecting with accuracy the conditions of life. Sterne's interest in the association of ideas (influenced by **John Locke**) involved the theory that time is only a convenient formula for the link between ideas, and the enormous personal importance of apparently trivial things is championed by the book's structure. Sterne teases the reader by mimicry and impersonation, and is virtually indivisible from Tristram himself, repeatedly drawing attention to his own presence in the fictional process, upbraiding and cajoling, indulging in a Swiftian war of nerves with his reader. The action of the book is intensely dramatic, with elaborate descriptions of physical posture, histrionic reactions, stage directions and scene-shifting. The setting of Shandy Hall, though never directly described, is nonetheless brilliantly evoked by impressions.

The novel has been extremely influential on the fictional writing of the 20th century, but Sterne's achievement was not the act of revolutionary isolation or iconoclasm that is sometimes suggested. **Stream of consciousness** and the anti-novel have few concerns in common with Sterne's, who was working in a long tradition of intellectual satire involving Montaigne, Rabelais, **Erasmus** and **Swift** as well as a mass of **picaresque** and travel literature. His dismantling of literary form is a matter of degree, but his system of distortion shows a genuinely comic perspective on the world, part of what has been called 'the religion of laughter'. Sterne's novel was also very much in keeping with the mood of his times, its interest in the growing 'cult of sensibility' (see **sentimental novel**) and also the fashion for ruins, for exciting fragments and the formally imprecise. As well as being extraordinarily popular in England, the novel was translated into German and French.

***Trivia, or, The Act of Walking the Streets of London*** A poem in three parts by **John Gay**, first published in 1716. An ambitious and very popular work, it subjects the topography of the capital to a Juvenalian treatment, surveying its dangers and delights in a splendid combination of the heroic classical style and the reality of contemporary conditions. The peripatetic narrator gives the reader a conducted tour that remains unrivalled for its atmospheric detail: there is advice on reading the weather signs, escaping the filth, taking one's bearings, recognizing the street cries, avoiding criminals and so forth. The poem incorporates several notable set-pieces and digressions.

**trochee** See **metre**.

***Troilus and Cressida*** A play by **William Shakespeare**, first performed *c.*1602 and published in Quarto (Q1) in 1609 as well as in the First Folio of 1623. Shakespeare's telling of the story owes something to oral tradition as well as to translations of Homer and, perhaps, to **Lydgate** and to **Chaucer**.

The story of the doomed love of Troilus and Cressida is interwoven with events in the Trojan war, in particular the death of Hector, the play's only consistently high-principled character. During a truce in the war, the weary Troilus confesses his love for Cressida to her uncle, Pandarus. True to his name, Pandarus contrives their meeting and oversees their love-making.

The Greek generals are quite as jaded with the war as most of their Trojan counterparts. In particular, the effeminate and indulgent behaviour of Achilles has damaged morale. It is at Achilles that Hector's challenge to single combat is directed, and the devious Greek generals attempt to manoeuvre him into confrontation with Hector.

Cressida's father Calchas, a seer, has deserted to the Greek camp. Wishing to be reunited with his daughter, he persuades the Greeks to offer a captured Trojan general in exchange for Cressida, and Diomedes arrives in Troy to collect her. Having promised eternal love to Troilus, Cressida finds herself admired and flattered by the Greeks. She becomes Diomedes' mistress.

Hector fights Ajax, but withdraws at the point of victory because he will not harm anyone related to his father's family. Achilles offers Hector hospitality on the eve of renewed hostility between Greeks and Trojans. The next day Troilus, embittered by Cressida's faithlessness, fights fiercely. Hector, having killed Achilles' friend Patroclus, is deceitfully murdered by Achilles. As the Trojans prepare to continue the war, Pandarus leaves Troy, rejected by Troilus, whose abuse of Pandarus is an attack also on the concupiscent Cressida.

*Troilus and Cressida* is neither a comedy nor a tragedy. Often grouped with the **problem plays**, *All's Well that Ends Well* and *Measure for Measure*, it is more accurately a tragicomedy than either of these associated pieces. It is not the least dispiriting feature of the play that the invective and cynicism of the scabrous Greek soldier

Thersites should be truer to our experience of it than the nobility of Hector.

*Troilus and Criseyde* A poem by **Geoffrey Chaucer**. Displaying a fully matured control of verse, narrative and characterization, it was probably a late work, perhaps written *c.*1385–90. Though the story has a Trojan setting it is not found in the Greek accounts of the war but first appears as an episode in the 12th-century *Roman de Troie* of Benoît de Sainte-Maure. This was translated into Latin prose by Guido delle Colonne as the *Historia Destructionis Troiae* from which Boccaccio developed the incident into a complete story in its own right as *Il Filostrato*. This latter was Chaucer's source, but he adapted, expanded and greatly improved it.

The poem relates the love of Troilus, a noble young warrior second only to Hector, and Criseyde, the widowed daughter of Calchas, an astronomer who had foreseen the fall of Troy and defected to the Greek camp. Troilus sees and falls in love with Criseyde and through the agency of her uncle and guardian, Pandarus, they begin a secret affair. They live very happily until Calchas and the Greeks demand Criseyde in exchange for a prisoner of war. Afraid of public scorn the lovers neither flee nor negotiate, and Criseyde goes to the Greeks promising to return as soon as possible. When she does not come Troilus becomes desolate, consumed with grief. Meanwhile, Criseyde has – reluctantly at first – taken the Greek Diomede as a lover. Troilus sees his betrayal in a dream, sees a brooch he had given Criseyde worn by Diomede and, on creeping into the enemy camp, hears the two together. In despair he devotes himself to the battle and dies in glory. He ascends to the seventh sphere whence he looks down on earth and recognizes the vanity of worldly concerns.

The poem is remarkable in particular for its characterization. Chaucer developed the rela-

Criseyde seeks Hector's compassion. An illustration for *Troilus and Criseyde* in R. Pynson's edition (1526) of Chaucer's *Works*.

tively simple lovers of Boccaccio's poem into complex individuals with a high degree of psychological realism in their behaviour and motivation. Troilus, perfectly noble and totally devoted to Criseyde, is at the same time incapable of decisive, assertive action and is prone to fatalism, passivity and self-pity. Criseyde, while genuinely loving Troilus, is fearful for her safety and her reputation, and lacks determination. Yet the characters are considerably more complex than any brief account can convey. Humour, coarseness, a sense of fun and boldness emerge in Criseyde's banter with her uncle, the character who is the main source of humour in the poem. The complexity and realism of the characterization has led some critics to argue that the poem approaches the form of a novel.

Characteristic of Chaucer is the subtle comedy maintained throughout, the articulate dialogue and the self-effacing narrator who is reluctant to speak ill of Criseyde. The poet's interest in Boethius' philosophy (which led to his translation **Boece**) is shown in Criseyde's discussion of false felicity and in Troilus's long monologue on free-will and predestination (in which he misunderstands the lesson of Boethius). Dante also contributes to the philosophical fabric of the poem, and the influence of Machaut, Petrarch, Ovid and Joseph of Exeter may be found in its content. The poem's concern with love is central and has been variously interpreted as in praise and in bitter criticism of the code of **courtly love**. More than a pair of courtly lovers, Troilus and Criseyde are fully developed individuals, and it is not with an artificial code but with the psychological realities of love that Chaucer is principally concerned.

**Trollope, Anthony** 1815–82 Novelist. Born in London, the fourth son of a Chancery barrister turned unsuccessful farmer, and of **Frances Trollope**, the future novelist, Trollope was educated at Harrow and Winchester. The humiliations of his schooldays, caused by the genteel poverty into which the family had sunk and by his parents' neglect, are poignantly described in his *Autobiography* (1883). He left school, 'a hobbledehoy of nineteen, without any idea of a career', and was found a position in the Post Office through the influence of his mother, who had started to retrieve the family fortunes with a successful literary career initiated, when she was over 50, by the best-selling *Domestic Manners of the Americans* (1832). His Civil Service career began inauspiciously, as an unpunctual and debt-ridden junior clerk – a period of his life portrayed in his novel *The Three Clerks* (1858) – but changed for the better when, at the age of 26, he volunteered to go to Ireland as a surveyor's clerk. There Trollope prospered: he organized the postal services in the district successfuly; he courted an English girl, Rose Heseltine, and married her in 1844; he acquired a lifelong passion for hunting, and he wrote his first novel, *The Macdermots of Ballycloran* (1847), a powerful study of a doomed Irish family. He spent 10 years in Ireland, from 1841 to 1851, and returned in 1853 for a further period before settling permanently in England in 1859.

A second novel of Irish life, *The Kellys and the O'Kellys* (1848), and a historical romance, were followed by his first real success, **The Warden** (1855), conceived, according to the *Autobiography*, while wandering round Salisbury cathedral on a summer evening, 'from whence came that series of novels of which Barchester, with its bishops, deans, and archdeacon, was the central site'. **Barchester Towers** followed in 1857, and then at intervals **Doctor Thorne** (1858), **Framley Parsonage** (1860), **The Small House at Allington** (1862–4), and **The Last Chronicle of Barset** (1866–7), which Trollope considered his finest novel. These 'Chronicles of Barsetshire', with their recurrent characters in a familiar, unfolding community, were a new departure for the English regional novel. Their realistic presentation of middle-class domestic relationships proved highly congenial to the mid-Victorian reading public, and when *Framley Parsonage* appeared as the lead serial in the new **Cornhill Magazine** in 1860, with illustrations by J. E. Millais, Trollope's reputation was established.

His other great novel-sequence, the political or **Palliser Novels**, grew out of Barsetshire, Plantagenet Palliser appearing as a dry, ambitious politician in *The Small House at Allington*. Political interests are peripheral in the first of the series, **Can You Forgive Her?** (1864–5), and in the third, **The Eustace Diamonds** (1871–3), but in **Phineas Finn** (1867–9), **Phineas Redux** (1873–4), **The Prime Minister** (1875–6) and **The Duke's Children** (1879–80) he painted an unrivalled portrait of Parliamentary political society in the high Victorian period. The strength of the series owes much to the steadily deepening presentation of Plantagenet Palliser and his wife Glencora, the two characters on whom, with Mr Crawley of *The Last Chronicle*, Trollope believed his reputation with posterity would rest. Trollope resigned from the Post Office in 1867, after a distinguished career – he introduced the pillar-box – which he felt had been unsufficiently recognized by his superiors. In 1868 he contested Beverley unsuccessfully as a Liberal, the constituency being subsequently disenfranchised because of bribery by the winning Conservative candidate. This experience is treated in *Ralph the Heir* (1870–1) and informs the pessimistic vision of political life in *Phineas Redux*. By now Trollope was an established figure in London literary society, the friend of **George Eliot** and **G. H. Lewes**, a member of the

Trollope. A detail from the portrait by Samuel Laurence, 1865. National Portrait Gallery, London.

Garrick and Athenaeum clubs, and the editor, from 1867 to 1870, of *St Paul's Magazine*. There are, however, signs of social pessimism in his later work, notably in **The Way We Live Now** (1874–5), a wide-ranging social satire which many consider Trollope's masterpiece, although in the *Autobiography* he declared that its 'accusations' were 'exaggerated'.

Trollope travelled widely during his Post Office career and after, producing travel books on *The West Indies and the Spanish Main* (1859), *North America* (1862), *Australia and New Zealand* (1873) and *South Africa* (1878). He wrote a *Life of Cicero* (1880) and a biography of Lord Palmerston (1882), a politician congenial to his own declared position as an 'advanced conservative liberal'; and he contributed the **Thackeray** volume (1879) to the English Men of Letters series, a study of the novelist he considered his master. The production of these works and of his 47 novels was made possible by a legendary work-routine, which involved Trollope getting to his desk by 5.30 a.m. and writing 250 words each quarter of an hour for three hours, a rate of 10 pages a day, before leaving for a day's work at the Post Office.

Few of Trollope's many novels are without interest. His prodigious productivity meant that he relied unduly on the conventional entanglements of romantic plot-making (for which he professed indifference), and it also involved an even professionalism of style which can lull the reader into ignoring the subtle and varied understanding of human nature on which his best work is based. He held, in his *Autobiography*, that the novelist's task was 'to make his readers so intimately acquainted with his characters that the creations of his brain should be to them speaking, moving, living, human creatures. This he can never do unless he know these fictitious personages himself, and he can never know them well unless he can live with them in the full reality of established intimacy.' To this 'intimacy' of portraiture should be added Trollope's understanding of the institutions of mid-Victorian England and the unobtrusive irony which informs his sympathetic vision of human fallibility. These qualities in his work are best displayed in the Barsetshire and Palliser sequences, but several other novels can claim to belong in the first rank of his achievement, among them *Orley Farm* (1861–2), *The Claverings* (1866–7), *He Knew He Was Right* (1868–9), *Sir Harry Hotspur of Humblethwaite* (1870), *The Way We Live Now* (1874–5), *Dr Wortle's School* (1880) and *Mr Scarborough's Family* (1882–3).

**Trollope, Mrs Frances** 1780–1863 Novelist and travel-writer. Born into a clergyman's family in Hampshire, Fanny Milton moved to London in 1803 and married Thomas Anthony Trollope in 1809. They had six children, of whom two – **Anthony Trollope** and **Thomas Adolphus Trollope** – were to become novelists. Her husband's failure as a barrister and farmer led him to conceive a scheme to repair the family fortunes by sending her to Cincinnati to set up a fancy goods emporium. The scheme failed but the travel book she wrote about her American experiences, *Domestic Manners of the Americans* (1832), made her a best-selling author at the age of 52. Driven on by the family debts, she was to publish a further 40 volumes in the next 25 years, mainly novels but also several travel books based on the many spells she spent abroad during the remainder of her life. Her career is remarkable more for her heroic productivity in the face of illness and debt than for the intrinsic quality of her writing, although two of her many novels have a place in the history of Victorian fiction: the anti-evangelical novel *The Vicar of Wrexhill* (1837), an early contribution to the novel of religious controversy in the period, and *The Life and Adventures of Michael Armstrong, the Factory Boy* (1840), one of the first of the Victorian 'industrial' novels.

**Trollope, Thomas Adolphus** 1810–92 Novelist and historian. Eldest son of **Frances Trollope** and older brother of **Anthony Trollope**, he was educated at Harrow and Winchester and, after some time in America, at Magdalen Hall, Oxford, where he took his degree in 1835. After a spell teaching at King Edward's School, Birmingham, he travelled abroad with his mother, settling in Florence in 1843. He married Theodosia Garrow in 1848 and their home in Florence became a centre of expatriate literary life. His first wife died in 1865 and he married the novelist Frances Eleanor Ternan, moving to Rome in 1873 as correspondent for the London *Standard*. Thomas Trollope wrote some 60 volumes of travel writing, history and fiction, all now forgotten, although his autobiography, *What I Remember* (1887–9), is valuable for its picture of expatriate life in Italy in mid-Victorian times, and for its reminiscences of famous writers, including **Dickens**, **Elizabeth Barrett Browning**, **Robert Browning**, **George Eliot** and **G. H. Lewes**.

*Troy Book, The* A poem by **John Lydgate**, written in 1412–20. It narrates the history of Troy, beginning with Jason's search for the Golden Fleece and ending with the death of Ulysses. Its principal source is Guido delle Colonne's *Historia Destructionis Troiae* (1287), a Latin prose translation of the *Roman de Troie* of Benoît de Sainte-Maure (*c.*1160), but it also draws on the works of Ovid, Isidore of Seville and of medieval authors, and the influence of **Chaucer** is evident throughout. The story is presented as historical fact (as it was believed to be) and Lydgate's expansion and elaboration of his source does not obscure that aim. Many of his additions are rhetorical or biographical, making the poem longer and more formal and complete than Guido's work. *The Troy Book* was very popular in the Middle Ages and influenced Renaissance writers such as **Christopher Marlowe**, **Thomas Kyd** and **Shakespeare**.

**Trumbull, John** 1750–1831 American poet, born in Connecticut, and educated at Yale. His valedictory poem, *An Essay on the Uses and Advantages of the Fine Arts* (1770), condemns neoclassical aesthetics, and in its closing verses, entitled 'Prospect of the Future Glory of America', celebrates the potential of American literature. While teaching at Yale (1770–3), Trumbull also wrote a satire on college education, *The Progress of Dulness, or, the Adventures of Tom Brainless* (1772). He left Yale to study law in Boston with John Adams, who inspired his patriotic poem *An Elegy on the Times* (1774). Practising law in New Haven and Hartford (1774–1825), he became associated with the **Connecticut Wits** and with them fought to broaden Yale's curriculum to include the study of contemporary American literature, and to defend Federalist politics. After publishing *M'Fingal* (1775, 1776 and 1782), a mock epic which satirizes British conduct during the American Revolution, he collaborated with others of the Connecticut Wits on *The Anarchiad* (1786–7) and *The Echo* (1791–1805).

**Trumpet-Major, The** A novel by **Thomas Hardy**, first published as a serial in *Good Words* from January to December 1880 and as a book the same year. It is set during the Napoleonic wars.

Anne Garland and her mother, the widow of a landscape painter, live in one part of Overcombe Mill, the other being occupied by Miller Loveday who has two sons – Robert, a sailor, and John, trumpet-major of a regiment of Dragoons sent to the West Country to ward off a possible Napoleonic invasion. An honourable, unselfish man, John loves Anne but she does not return his affection. She, however, is irked by the unwanted attentions of the buffoonish Festus Derriman, nephew of the local squire. The lively narrative follows the fortunes of these varied individuals. Robert falls prey to Matilda Johnson, a woman of questionable reputation, and is rescued by his brother; he also narrowly escapes the press-gang but ultimately goes off to fight at Trafalgar on the *Victory*. Mrs Garland succumbs to the charms of Miller Loveday. John thrashes Festus, and Robert returns a lieutenant to marry Anne. Sadly, John leaves his family and village and goes off 'to blow his trumpet till silenced for ever upon one of the bloody battle-fields of Spain'.

**Tucker, Abraham** 1705–74 Amateur philosopher and country gentleman. His first work, *Free Will, Foreknowledge and Fate* (1763), was published under the pseudonym Edward Search; his second, *Man in Quest of Himself* (also 1763), appeared under the pseudonym Cuthbert Comment. His principal work was the seven-volume *The Light of Nature Pursued* (1768–78), a book so long and diffuse that Tucker's ideas were not recognized until they were systematized by **William Paley** in *The Principles of Moral and Political Philosophy*. Tucker asserted that the principle of moral conduct was to be found in general happiness, while the motive of the individual could be found in his own content. The two do not always agree. Virtue may require self-sacrifice, despite considerations of prudence and self-interest. In disinterested goodness Tucker found a place for religion and the hope of a future life.

**Tuckerman, Frederick Goddard** 1821–73 American poet, born in Boston and educated at Harvard. He is best known for his sonnets, which are personal and often melancholy in tone. His only volume, *Poems*, appeared in 1860. **Nathaniel Hawthorne**, **Ralph Waldo Emerson** and **Henry Wadsworth Longfellow** all praised his work, but he was generally forgotten until the poet Witter Bynner published a selection from *Poems* in 1931 along with three previously unpublished sonnets. All of his work was later collected, edited and introduced by **N. Scott Momaday** in *The Complete Poems of Frederick Tuckerman* (1965).

**Tupper, Martin (Farquhar)** 1810–89 Poet. Born in London, he was educated at Charterhouse, where **Thackeray** was a contemporary, and Christ Church, Oxford, where Gladstone became a friend. His first volume, *Sacra Poesis* (1832), was religious; the second, *A Voice from the Cloister* (1835), warned undergraduates against vice. Tupper became famous with *Proverbial Philosophy: A Book of Thoughts and Arguments, Originally Treated* (1838), a collection of loosely versified commonplaces. It ran to over 50 editions in England, as well as being extremely popular in America. Tupper continued to write prolifically – publishing a continuation of **Coleridge's** *Christabel* (1838), three more series of *Proverbial Philosophy* (1842, 1867, 1869), three **Condition of England novels** (*The Crock of Gold*, *The Twins* and *Heart*, all 1844), a historical novel (*Stephan Langton*, 1858), several plays, an autobiography and many occasional verses – but his work, never well received by the critics, had lost popularity before his death.

**Turn of the Screw, The** A short novel by **Henry James**, first published in *Collier's Weekly*, and then with another story, 'Covering End', in a volume entitled *The Two Magics*, in 1898.

The story is about a governess who takes charge of two children at Bly, a lonely estate in England. Her employer, the children's uncle, has given her strict orders not to bother him with any of the details of their education or behaviour. The children, Flora and Miles, are attractive and intelligent, but also seem strained and secretive. Shortly after her arrival, the governess sees two former members of the household, the steward Peter Quint and the previous governess Miss Jessel; later she learns that both of them are dead. She is convinced that the children see the ghosts, too. But they display a remarkable talent for evading questions about them, and she becomes increasingly certain that they are under the maleficent influence of the pair. One day she challenges Flora directly; the little girl's reaction is explosive and hysterical and she falls ill. Miles is confronted next, and during this scene the governess sees Peter Quint at the window. She is determined to exorcize his influence, but despite her efforts to shield Miles from the apparition, the boy, frantic and terrified, dies in her arms. The story, told entirely from the point of view of the governess, raises doubts in the reader about her reliability as narrator, and about whether her visions are of real 'ghosts' or merely hallucinations.

**Turner, Ethel** 1872–1958 Australian children's writer. Born in Yorkshire, she emigrated to Australia with her family in 1880. Educated at the Sydney Girls' High School, she later contributed a children's column to *The Australian Town and Country Journal*. Her first novel, *Seven Little Australians* (1894), was an immediate success. It describes the unruly children of Captain Woolcott, an unsympathetic widower who has just remarried; far from mellowing, he becomes even more irritated by his family, finally sending his daughter Judy with her infant brother to a remote inland settlement. After learning about country ways, Judy dies saving her brother's life, and while this naturally sobers the other rebellious children they soon get back into trouble with authority in a sequel, *The Family at Misrule* (1895). The same theme reappears in many of the stories that followed, where good-hearted if mischievous children are constantly thwarted by parents who are either insensitive or negligent. Often very funny, Ethel Turner is comparable to **E. Nesbit** in her depictions of the ups and downs of family life and also looks forward to the novels of **Richmal Crompton** in her relish at the way children can discomfort adults.

**Turner, Frederick Jackson** 1861–1932 American historian, born in Portage, Wisconsin, and educated at the University of Wisconsin and Johns Hopkins University. He taught at the University of Wisconsin and at Harvard. Turner read his famous essay, 'The Significance of the Frontier in American History', to the American Historical Association in Chicago in 1893. In it he advanced the notion that the continual challenge presented by the frontier was the primary factor in American development, more important than the European influences of ancestry and culture. American life and values, he argued, were shaped above all by the waves of western movement. 'The Significance of the Frontier' was published with some of his other essays as *The Frontier in American History* (1920). His earlier publications include *The Character and Influence of the Indian Trade in Wisconsin* (1891) and *Rise of the New West, 1819–1829* (1906). For *The Significance of Sections in American History* (1932), Jackson was posthumously awarded the Pulitzer Prize for history. He won a second posthumous Pulitzer for *The United States, 1830–1850, The Nation and Its Sections* (1935), a continuation of *Rise of the New West*.

**Turner, Sharon** 1768–1847 Historian. Born and educated in London, he was intended for the law but abandoned it for the study of Old English manuscripts in the British Museum; he had long been interested in Norse antiquity and its connection with the history of England. Primarily an antiquarian, he nevertheless produced, after 16 years' work, *A History of England from the Earliest Period to the Norman Conquest* (1799–1805), which encouraged serious study of

England's ancient past. Other books by Turner were *The History of England from the Norman Conquest to 1500* (1814–23), *The History of the Reign of Henry VIII* (1826), and *The Reigns of Edward VI, Mary and Elizabeth* (1829). He also published *A Vindication of the Genuineness of the Ancient British Poems of Aneurin, Taliesin, Llynwarch Hen and Merdhin, with Specimens* (1803).

**Tusser, Thomas** ?1524–80 Agricultural writer and poet. Tusser was educated at Eton and Cambridge, and farmed in Suffolk, where he introduced the cultivation of barley. His verse *A Hundred Points of Good Husbandry* (1557) is a collection of instructions on farming and gardening, adorned with aphorisms on behaviour which make it a rich source of proverbs and maxims. The work was enlarged in later editions, by the addition of *A Hundred Good Points of Housewifery* in the 1570 edition; by 1573 the 100 good points had grown to 500.

**Tutuola, Amos** 1920– Nigerian writer, born in Abeokuta. Farmer, blacksmith, office messenger, he inaugurated West African Literature in English with *The Palm-Wine Drinkard* (1952), a sequence of 30 episodes of quest, endurance and the achievement of wisdom, mainly adapted from Yoruba folk-tales. Tutuola is in the living tradition of the village teller of tales, but instead of telling in Yoruba, he writes in the best English his scanty schooling permits. His linguistic idiosyncrasy proves a strangely suitable means of conducting his readers into the rich expanses of the Yoruba imagination – to which indeed he adds his own inventions, like the television-handed Goddess in *My Life in the Bush of Ghosts* (1954). His other books are: *Simbi and the Satyr of the Dark Jungle* (1955), *The Brave African Huntress* (1958), *Feather Woman of the Jungle* (1962), *Ajaiyi and His Inherited Poverty* (1967) and *The Witch-Herbalist of the Remote Town* (1981).

**Twain, Mark** Pseudonym of the American novelist, short-story writer and humorist Samuel Langhorne Clemens (1835–1910). Born in Florida, Missouri, he moved with his family to the Mississippi River town of Hannibal when he was 4. Later, he would make the scenes of his youth internationally famous in his most popular novels, *The Adventures of Tom Sawyer* and *Adventures of Huckleberry Finn*. Although always associated with the Mississippi River region, he travelled widely. He left school at the age of 12, and later travelled throughout the East and Midwest as a journeyman printer. He served briefly in the Confederate Army during the Civil War, but his division deserted and he spent the remainder of the war out West, some of it prospecting for silver in Nevada with his brother Orion, and then working with **Bret Harte**

Mark Twain carried to fame by *The Celebrated Jumping Frog of Calaveras County*. Contemporary cartoon.

as a journalist in San Francisco. In 1863 he began using the name Mark Twain, and in 1865 made it famous with his story **The Celebrated Jumping Frog of Calaveras County**.

Twain's rise to celebrity was impressive. His sparkling personality and his quotable phrases caught on fast and he soon began making lecture tours. His 1867 trip to Europe and the Holy Land produced his first major work, **The Innocents Abroad** (1869). He returned to America to settle in the East, and in 1870 married Olivia Langdon, the wealthy daughter of a New York coal magnate. His popularity continued to grow, through a series of works including **Roughing It** (1872), a humorous narrative of his early travels out West, **The Gilded Age** (1873), a satirical novel of the post-Civil War era which he co-wrote with **Charles Dudley Warner**, the ever popular *The Adventures of Tom Sawyer* (1876) and *A Tramp Abroad* (1880), another travel narrative. He travelled often in Europe, and especially in England, where he was received with even more enthusiasm than in the USA.

The last works of what might be called Twain's optimistic period were **The Prince and the Pauper** (1882) and **Life on the Mississippi** (1883). In 1884 his heavy investment in a badly

managed publishing firm and an inefficient typesetting invention drove him into bankruptcy. Ironically, the products of this harsh awakening are among his best works, most notably the renowned *Adventures of Huckleberry Finn* (1884), which has a moral dimension that is lacking in its predecessor *Tom Sawyer*. **A Connecticut Yankee in King Arthur's Court** (1889) and **The Tragedy of Pudd'nhead Wilson** (1894) are both characterized by a deep pessimism, though both were conceived simply as entertainments. In *The American Claimant* (1892), *Tom Sawyer Abroad* (1894), and *Tom Sawyer, Detective* (1896) he sought to recapture the innocent fun of his early works, but he was never quite able to write with his former casual ease.

He gradually overcame his debts, but after his daughter Susy died in 1896 Twain became increasingly alienated from the good-humoured wit on which his popularity was based. Books such as *The Man that Corrupted Hadleyburg* (1900) and *What Is Man?* (1906), as well as much of his posthumously published work, reflect a severe pessimism and dissatisfaction. However, when his personal life was devastated (his wife died in 1904 and his second daughter in 1909), his professional life carried him through. He continued to lecture widely, in the USA and abroad, though his opinions were often controversial, and he was supremely proud of the honorary doctorate of letters awarded to him by Oxford University in 1907. When he died in 1910 he left a wealth of unpublished material, including *The Mysterious Stranger* (1916) and *Letters From the Earth* (1962). His *Autobiography* was published in 1924.

**Twelfth Night, or, What You Will** A comedy by **William Shakespeare**, first performed *c.*1600 and published in the First Folio of 1623. The most direct source was probably **Barnabe Rich**'s *Apolonius and Silla*, a story derived from the Italian of Matteo Bandello.

A shipwreck brings to the sea coast of Illyria a mournful but still resourceful Viola, saddened by the loss in the same wreck of her 'identical' twin brother, Sebastian. Disguised as a boy, she seeks service in the court of Orsino, Duke of Illyria. Orsino is hopelessly in love with Olivia, a lady who rejects him ostensibly because she is mourning her dead brother. In her role as Cesario, Viola is sent to Olivia's house with messages of love from Orsino. Olivia is attracted to Viola, who is secretly falling in love with Orsino.

Unknown to Viola, Sebastian arrives in Illyria with his faithful friend Antonio. The two men are separated, and accidents of identical appearance and identical dress lead, through mistaken identity, to Antonio's belief that Sebastian has betrayed their friendship, to the astonished Sebastian's marriage to Olivia, and to a near-crisis when Orsino believes that Viola has stolen Olivia from him and threatens dire punishment. Only when, at the play's end, Sebastian and Viola are allowed on stage together do the confusions turn to clarity. Orsino is free to marry the loving Viola and Olivia to keep faith with her new husband, Sebastian.

In a busy sub-plot, Olivia's bibulous kinsman Sir Toby Belch takes advantage of the gullible Sir Andrew Aguecheek, plays an enthusiastic part in an inventive practical joke on Olivia's presumptuous steward Malvolio, and marries the plot's inventor, Olivia's lady-in-waiting Maria.

*Twelfth Night* is the most formally satisfying of Shakespeare's mature comedies. There is some evidence that the part of the worldly-wise clown, Feste, was rewritten to take account of the musical skills of **Robert Armin**, who had recently replaced **Will Kemp**. That is speculative, but Feste certainly has three of Shakespeare's finest songs, and the play is uncommonly confident in its use of music.

**Two Drovers, The** See **Chronicles of the Canongate**.

**Two Foscari, The** A tragedy by **Lord Byron**, first published in 1821, the same year as his other Venetian tragedy, **Marino Faliero**. The tragedy was produced at **Covent Garden** in 1837. Verdi's opera, based on Byron's tragedy, was first produced in Rome in 1844. It is set in the 15th century and Jacopo Foscari, son of the aged doge Francesco Foscari, is being interrogated on the rack. He was twice exiled, first for accepting bribes and then for complicity in the murder of Donato, one of the Council of Ten who had sentenced him to his first exile. He has been brought back from his second exile in Crete to answer charges of treason, and faces execution. But the council sentence him to perpetual exile and the aged Francesco has to sign the decree. The sentence is too much for Jacopo, who dies when he hears the news. The council then demand the abdication of his father, who dies as he leaves the palace, while the bells of St Mark's toll for the election of a new doge.

The historical Jacopo Foscari died in Crete six months after his perpetual banishment, too soon for the reprieve which followed the confession of the real murderer of Donato.

**Two Gentlemen of Verona, The** A comedy by **William Shakespeare**, first performed *c.*1593 and published in the First Folio of 1623. The source of the play is a story by Jorge de Montemayor, *Diana Enamorada*, but Shakespeare may have come upon it by way of a lost play, *The History of Felix and Philiomena*, known to have been acted at court in 1585.

Valentine leaves Verona and his friend Proteus and sets out for Milan. There he falls in love with the duke's daughter Silvia, whom the duke wishes to marry to the foolish Thurio. Proteus is sent by his father to Milan, and takes a solemn farewell of Julia, with whom he exchanges rings as a token of love. Welcomed by Valentine and Silvia, Proteus too becomes enamoured of Silvia and betrays to the duke the couple's intention of eloping. Valentine is banished.

Disguised as a boy, Julia has followed Proteus to Milan, where she enters his service. To her dismay, Proteus sends her – with the ring she had given him in Verona – to press his claims on Silvia. Heartily sick of both Thurio and Proteus, Silvia runs away to find Valentine and is captured by robbers. She does not know that Valentine has become the leader of a band of honourable outlaws. When Proteus rescues Silvia, Valentine is at hand to observe his former friend's treacherous attempts to force his love on her. The disguised Julia faints when Proteus asks Valentine's forgiveness, revealing the ring that Proteus had given her in Verona. The couples are reconciled, the duke willing to recognize the superior claims of Valentine as a match for his daughter and all return to Milan to celebrate a double wedding.

*The Two Gentlemen of Verona* is a charming romantic comedy, without the emotional or imaginative range of Shakespeare's mature work in the genre. Proteus's servant Launce, much troubled by his dog, has some of the best theatrical opportunities. The part was probably written for **Will Kemp**.

**Two Noble Kinsmen, The** A play first published in 1634, bearing on the title-page the inscription 'Written by the memorable Worthies of their Time; Mr **John Fletcher**, and Mr **William Shakespeare**. Gent.' Most critics agree that, whatever Shakespeare's contribution, it was not sufficient to make a good play of it. It is based on **Chaucer**'s *The Knight's Tale* (see **The Canterbury Tales**) with the addition of the character of the gaoler's daughter, who plays an active part in Palamon's escape and then goes mad with love for him.

**Two on a Tower** A novel by **Thomas Hardy**, first published serially in *The Atlantic Monthly*, an American journal, between May and December 1882 and in book form the same year.

Swithin St Cleeve, a young astronomer and son of a curate who married beneath himself, is found by Lady Viviette Constantine (some ten years his senior) using as his observatory a column known as Rings-Hill Speer, on the estate of her husband, Sir Blount Constantine, an unpleasant man given to big-game hunting. Upon being informed of the latter's death in Africa Viviette and Swithin marry in secret.

About the same time Swithin is left a generous inheritance, which he ignores because it is contingent upon his not marrying until the age of 25. Then he and Viviette learn that Sir Blount, although now dead, was alive when they were married, thus rendering void their clandestine union. Under pressure from Viviette, who has just discovered the conditions of the inheritance, Swithin claims it and goes to South Africa and elsewhere in the cause of astronomy. Very soon after his departure Viviette realizes she is pregnant and, to confer respectability on the child, accepts the hand of the Bishop of Melchester, who dies soon after their marriage. Swithin, after an absence of a few years, returns to England, meets her once more and proposes anew to her. But the shock is too much for Viviette and the 'sudden joy after despair' brings about her death.

**Two Treatises of Government** John Locke began his refutation of the doctrine of absolute power, and his proposals for reconciling individual liberty with collective order, during the last two years of his employment in the house of the Earl of Shaftesbury. By the time his work appeared in 1690 the idea of Divine Right had already died a natural death: Shaftesbury had fallen, Charles II had died, his successor James II had abdicated and a revolution had placed William and Mary on the throne. Nevertheless, Locke's *Treatises* had enormous influence on liberal thought, in France and America as well as England. The second treatise proposed Locke's theory of social contract: the people consent to be governed, resigning total freedom so that life, property and liberty can be maintained, while for their part those who govern remain accountable and lose their authority when they exceed their powers.

**Two Years Before the Mast** A personal narrative, by **Richard Henry Dana**, of life at sea in the 1830s, published in 1840. After leaving Harvard University, Dana sailed on the brig *Pilgrim* on a voyage of 150 days. In his clear-sighted, detailed, and unsparing account of the voyage from Boston around Cape Horn to California, he draws vivid portraits of his shipmates, telling how they were completely at the mercy of the captain, who ordered two of them to be flogged. His return trip, on the *Alert*, lasted 135 days, during which time he determined to quit the sea. Another chapter was added to the book 24 years later, telling of his return to California in 1859 and of the fortunes of some of the men described in the original narrative.

**Tyler, Royall** 1757–1826 American playwright, born in Boston and educated at Harvard. A distinguished legal career culminated in his appointments as chief justice of the Supreme

A scene from Royall Tyler's comedy *The Contrast*, first published in 1790. Jonathan goes to the defence of his master, Colonel Manly.

Court in Vermont (1807–13), and as Professor of Jurisprudence at the University of Vermont (1811–14).

His literary reputation is based largely on his first play, **The Contrast** (1787), said to have been written in the three weeks following his attendance at a performance of **The School for Scandal** in New York. *The Contrast* was the first comedy by a native American writer to be professionally produced. Tyler's second and less successful play was *Mad Day in Town, or, New York in an Uproar* (1787), a comic opera of which the manuscript has not survived. Two other plays of which no copy exists are *The Farm House, or, The Female Duellists* (1796), possibly an adaptation of J. P. Kemble's *The Farm House* (1789), and *The Georgia Spec, or, Land in the Moon* (1797), a satire of land speculation in Georgia. The texts of four other plays have survived, though none has been produced on stage: *The Island of Barrataria* is a three-act farce based on an episode from Cervantes's *Don Quixote*; *The Judgment of Solomon*, *The Origin of the Feast of Purim*, and *Joseph and his Brethren* are all sacred verse dramas. *The Yankey in London* (1809) is a collection of essays and sketches. **The Algerine Captive** (1797) was his only novel.

**Tynan, Katharine** 1861–1931 Irish poet, novelist and journalist. Born in County Dublin, she attended convent school at Drogheda. A literary hostess and close friend of **W. B. Yeats**, she married Henry A. Hinkson in 1893 and moved to England, where she became a regular contributor to a number of English, Irish and American journals and magazines. Her journalism won her a large public but did not help her career as a poet. She and her family returned to Ireland in 1911 and maintained a strong pro-British stance throughout the insurrectionary period. After her husband's death in 1919 she travelled through Europe, writing journalistic pieces on the chaotic conditions she found. A prolific writer, she produced 105 novels, 18 volumes of poetry and 38 other miscellaneous volumes as well as journalistic pieces that were not collected. Her *Collected Poems* appeared in 1930. Much of her work is strongly Roman Catholic in its preoccupations. She is widely regarded as one of the most promising but blighted poets of the Irish revival.

**Tynan, Kenneth (Peacock)** 1927–80 Drama critic. A short career as an actor and director preceded his appointment as a reviewer of plays for *The Observer* in 1954. Tynan's lifelong delight in controversy was the mercurial aspect of his passionate belief in the neglected importance of theatre in society. During his first spell at *The Observer* (1954–8), English drama experienced a revival, and Tynan undoubtedly contributed to it, not only by his trenchantly witty reviews, but also by his engagement in theoretical debates in the short-lived but influential journal, *Encore*. He became Brecht's most articulate English advocate. After two years as dramatic critic for *The New Yorker* (1958–60), Tynan returned to *The Observer* for a second spell (1960–3) and was then appointed Literary Manager of the **National Theatre** company (1963–9). It was he who spearheaded the assault on theatrical censorship in Britain and the erotic revue, *Oh! Calcutta!*, which he produced in 1968–9, was in part a celebration of the abolition of the Lord Chamberlain's powers. Tynan's theatrical criticism has been collected in several volumes, *He That Plays the King* (1950), *Curtains* (1961), *Tynan Right and Left* (1968) and *A View of the English Stage* (1975) among them. His enthusiasm for bullfighting is recorded in *Bull Fever* (1955). He spent his last years in the USA.

**Tyndale, William** ?1494–1536 Protestant martyr, humanist and translator of the Bible. He came from Gloucestershire, was educated at Oxford and later Cambridge. In 1522 he sought support for his project of an English translation of the Bible, but finding such figures as Tunstall, Bishop of London, opposed to the project left England for the Continent in 1524, never to return. The printing of his English New Testament (translated from the Greek text of **Erasmus**) was begun at Cologne in 1525 and completed at Worms in the same year, after the work at Cologne had been impeded by local magistrates. Such copies as found their way to England were ordered by the bishops to be burned. Tyndale spent most of the rest of his life in Antwerp where he revised his New Testament and completed English translations of the Pentateuch (1530) and Jonah (1531). Tyndale's translation was to become the basis for the King James Version (see also **The Bible in English**).

Doctrinally, he was close to Luther, whom he met at Wittenberg, on justification by faith, but Zwinglian in his view of the Eucharist. His view of the king as sole authority in the state was expressed in his *The Obedience of a Christian Man* (1528), which won him the approval of Henry VIII. Nonetheless Tyndale later opposed the king's divorce. Tyndale entered into controversy with **Thomas More**, notably in his *An Answer unto Sir Thomas More's Dialogue* (1530). A translation of Erasmus's *Enchiridion Militis Christianae* as *The Manual of the Christian Knight* is attributed to him.

Tyndale was arrested for heresy at Antwerp, imprisoned at Vilvorde near Brussels, and strangled and burned at the stake in 1536.

**Tyndall, John** 1820–93 Physical scientist and writer on the uses of imagination in science. Born to small landowners at Leighlin Bridge, County Carlow, Ireland, Tyndall was educated at the local national school and then worked on the Ordnance Survey of Ireland. Later, he attended the mechanics institute at Preston, Lancashire, and became a railway engineer and teacher. His career as a scientist began when he studied for a D. Phil. at Marburg University in 1848–50. His work on magnetic force and radiant heat made him famous among scientists, and his graphic and graceful expository style made him perhaps the greatest popularizer of 19th-century physical science. His essays in this field are published as *Fragments of Science for Unscientific People* (1871; 8 vols. by 1889). Tyndall is said to have had an extraordinarily developed mental awareness of relations in space, an intellectual talent trained, he suggested, by early study of the syntax of **Milton**'s *Paradise Lost*. The impact of his writing concerning wave-theory and the reasons for the blue colour of the sky can be traced in **George Eliot**'s *Middlemarch* and *Daniel Deronda*. He is fleetingly, but significantly, referrerd to in **Virginia Woolf**'s *Mrs Dalloway*. Her father, **Leslie Stephen**, was, with **Thomas Henry Huxley**, among Tyndall's closest friends, and, with them, he was a leader of agnostic opinion.

*Typee: A Peep at Polynesian Life. During a Four Months' Residence in a Valley of the Marquesas* **Herman Melville**'s first novel, published in 1846, and based on his own experiences in the South Seas.

Two seamen on a whaler, Tom and Toby, jump ship in the Marquesas Islands and make their way to an inland valley. They have heard that the Typee tribe is particularly savage, and hope instead to fall in with the peace-loving Happars. They meet the Typees first, however, and find them fairly friendly. Then the two become separated, and Tommo is left alone among the Typees. The natives are kind and generous, and he enjoys his island paradise in the company of Fayaway, a beautiful native girl. A sympathetic though not always comprehending observer of island culture, he criticizes white missionary efforts and their destructive effects on the islanders, as well as the facile dichotomy between 'civilization' and 'savagery' by which the whites justify their actions. However, some native customs are strange to him – he has heard uncomfortable rumours about cannibalism – and he becomes increasingly homesick for the Western world. He sees evidence of ritual cannibalism among the Typees and begins to fear that he will be their next victim. He decides to flee the valley, and though the tribe pursues him into the sea he is rescued by the boat of an Australian whaler.

*Tyrannick Love, or, The Royal Martyr* A heroic tragedy in rhymed couplets by **John Dryden**, produced in 1669 and published in 1670. The story concerns Princess Catharine of Alexan-dria, a Christian captive of the Roman Emperor Maximin. He falls in love with her but she does not respond. She succeeds in converting the Empress Berenice and the furious Maximin orders their death. Catharine is beheaded and becomes St Catharine, but Maximin is stabbed by Placidius, an officer who loves Berenice and is determined to save her.

**Tyrwhitt, Thomas** 1730–86 Scholar and editor. He was born at Westminster, educated at Eton College and The Queen's College, Oxford, and elected a fellow of Merton College in 1755. He was notable for the careful scholarship he brought to the study of **Chaucer**'s poetry. His edition of *The Canterbury Tales* (1775–8) helped establish the Chaucer canon but was most important for explaining the principles of Chaucer's heroic line, which had gone undiscerned for four centuries. Tyrwhitt also edited the Rowley poems of **Thomas Chatterton** in 1777, a time when they were still the object of great curiosity and dispute as to their authenticity. He himself became persuaded that they were forgeries and argued this view in an appendix added to his edition in the following year.

# U

*USA* A trilogy of novels by **John Dos Passos** consisting of *The 42nd Parallel* (1930), *1919* (1932) and *The Big Money* (1936). In all three novels Dos Passos interweaves the stories of fictional characters with biographies of real people and accounts of historical events. The trilogy begins roughly with the Spanish–American War (1898) and documents an era in America's history marked by rising tension between capitalists and labour unions, technological advances, involvement in World War I, and the Jazz Age; it ends in the early 1930s with the aftermath of the 1929 stock market crash.

Dos Passos's narrative technique is distinctly unconventional. His characters, types rather than fully developed individuals, lead lives that are interconnected in an almost random way. Although several of them appear in all three novels, their activities do not constitute a unified plot. But their lives have a common pattern: all are destroyed – either physically or spiritually – by a society that is becoming increasingly materialistic and inimical to individual freedom.

The characters come from all strata of society. J. Ward Moorehouse is from a fairly poor family; ambitious, he marries for money, sets aside his dream of being a song-writer, and becomes instead a successful public relations man. His success, however, does not bring him happiness. At the trilogy's end he is tired, ill and cynical. His young business associate, Richard Ellsworth Savage, repeats the pattern of his own life in several ways. A promising young poet from a relatively affluent family, Savage gives up writing poetry for the 'big money' in public relations. He leads a dissolute life, which puts him in debt. As his story comes to a close, he plans to court Myra Bingham, the homely daughter of one of his wealthy clients.

Joe Williams, a seaman, fights, drinks and womanizes whenever he is ashore. He never gets ahead, and eventually dies in a brawl in a bar in France where he had been celebrating the end of World War I. Charley Anderson, a likeable young aviator and inventor, becomes wealthy but is used by other people, most notably by Margo Dowling, an unscrupulous, greedy and ambitious actress. He dies from injuries sustained in an automobile accident.

Two female characters, Eleanor Stoddard and Eveline Hutchins, begin as friends. Stoddard is from a poor family, Hutchins from a wealthy one. They establish their own interior decorating firm in their native Chicago and later travel to New York to design the costumes and scenery for a friend's play. Though sexually frigid, Eleanor has an affair with J. Ward Moorehouse to advance herself socially. She becomes brittle and calculating and begins to snub her former friend Eveline, who now strikes her as unsophisticated. Eveline becomes pregnant, makes an unhappy marriage, becomes an alcoholic and eventually commits suicide.

Other characters attempt, not to advance themselves within America's capitalist society, but to change that society. Ben Compton, an organizer for the Communist Party, is eventually sentenced to a ten-year term in a federal prison for his radical activities. And because he refuses to be a 'yes man', he is abandoned by the Party he has served. Mary French, who for a while is Compton's lover, becomes a Party automaton. Initially a sensitive, bookish young woman who wants to help the downtrodden, she becomes so caught up in Party work – organizing marches, distributing leaflets, sheltering homeless Party members – that she no longer has a clear sense of what purpose, if any, it all serves.

Dos Passos does not rely only on his fictional characters to depict American life in the 20th century. In fact he makes use of four different kinds of narrative throughout the trilogy. He interrupts the stories of his fictional characters with brief biographies of politicians, inventors, intellectuals, labour leaders, businessmen and artists (people such as Eugene V. Debs, **Randolph Bourne**, **Thorstein Veblen**, Thomas Edison, Frank Lloyd Wright, Theodore Roosevelt, Woodrow Wilson, Henry Ford, Isadora Duncan and Rudolph Valentino). Impressionistic passages called 'Newsreels', in which he juxtaposes slogans, newspaper headlines, lyrics from popular songs, and parts of political speeches, give the reader a sense of the social and historical context in which the fictional characters move. The 'Camera Eye' sections, written in **stream-of-consciousness** form, present a subjective view of American life as experienced by a young boy who grows to manhood during the period covered by the trilogy.

**Udall (or Uvedale), Nicholas** 1505–56 Playwright. Udall was born in Southampton and educated at Winchester and Corpus Christi College, Oxford, where he became a fellow in 1524. At Oxford he was suspected of Lutheranism and investigated in 1528 but seems to have emerged unscathed. With his friend **John Leland** he contributed songs and verses for the coronation procession of Anne Boleyn in 1533, and in 1534 Udall published a book of selections from Terence with English translations, *Flowers for Latin Speaking*. In the same year he became headmaster of Eton and was soon notorious for the readiness with which he ordered floggings. He was dismissed in 1541, charged with theft and homosexual practices. He was imprisoned in the Marshalsea but apparently not for long, since he was settled in London in 1542 and in that year published his translation of the *Apophthegmata* of **Erasmus**. He was by now a declared supporter of the Reformation and in a lost play, *Ezechias*, celebrated the king's triumph over the Pope. Well on the way to rehabilitation with his translation of Erasmus's *Paraphrase upon Luke* (1545) under the patronage of Queen Catherine, he supervised the publication of the complete *Paraphrases* in 1549. He became canon of Windsor in 1551 and, in spite of his Reformist zeal, seems to have enjoyed the goodwill of Mary when she became queen. In 1555 he became headmaster of Westminster School.

At least four plays have been attributed to Udall and it is known that he was commissioned by Queen Mary to present masques and plays. But only one play can be called his with certainty, *Ralph Roister Doister*, which is probably the earliest English comedy.

**Ulster Literary Theatre** It was founded in 1902, with no encouragement from **Yeats**, by Bulmer Hobson and David Parkhill (Lewis Purcell), both of whom contributed plays. It proposed to enunciate a regional identity, a variant of the **Abbey Theatre**'s work, often in good-humoured satire. In 1915 its name changed to the Ulster Theatre. The company toured England and Ireland and gave the premières of some 50 Northern Irish plays. Apart from **Rutherford Mayne**, it cultivated no important dramatist and remained amateur to the end, though working to professional standards. Its demise in 1934 was due to the lack of either private or government financing.

**Ulysses** A **dramatic monologue** by **Alfred Tennyson**, published in 1842 but written in 1833. Its sources are Book IX of *The Odyssey* and Canto XXVI of Dante's *Inferno*. In old age Ulysses looks back on his past travels and forward to his last voyage, summoning the values of endurance, determination and hope to his aid. Tennyson said that there was more of himself in this poem than in *In Memoriam*: it was 'written under the sense of loss and that all had gone by, but that still life must be fought out to the end'.

**Ulysses** A novel by **James Joyce**, published in Paris in 1922. Chapters of the novel had appeared in *The Little Review* between April 1918 and December 1920, when the periodical was prosecuted for publishing obscene matter. Foreign copies were banned in America until 1933, and in England until 1936, when the first English edition appeared.

The novel encompasses events during a single calendar day in Dublin, 16 June 1904 (now known as 'Bloomsday'). Its main protagonists are: Leopold Bloom, a Jewish advertisement canvasser, his unfaithful wife Molly, a concert singer, and Stephen Dedalus, a young poet, the hero of Joyce's earlier autobiographical novel, *A Portrait of the Artist as a Young Man* (1916). The principal action follows Bloom and Stephen as they wander separately around Dublin, until they eventually meet, and each episode loosely corresponds with an episode in Homer's *Odyssey*. Bloom represents Odysseus, latinized as Ulysses, while Molly is Penelope, and Stephen Telemachus. Their largely mundane, and occasionally sordid lives are therefore ironically framed within an epic dimension. A highly allusive style, parodying numerous literary forms, interweaves great erudition with banal and scatological references.

Local landmarks visited during the course of the day include a public bath, a newspaper office, a cemetery, the National Library, a maternity hospital, a brothel, and various public houses. At the end of the novel Bloom and

St Stephen's Green, Dublin, in the first decade of the 20th century. James Joyce's vivid invocation of Dublin at this period provides the setting for *Ulysses*.

Stephen return to their starting-point, and neither has apparently found any answer to the bewildering sense of futility, frustration and loneliness within them. Molly Bloom alone achieves self-gratification, and much critical attention has been paid to her erotic monologue in the final chapter, a 20,000-word *tour de force* which employs the **stream of consciousness** technique.

*Uncle Remus: His Songs and His Sayings* The first collection of **Joel Chandler Harris**'s verse and tales based on black folklore, published in 1881. Uncle Remus, once a slave, is a valued family servant; the son of the house is a fascinated audience to whom he recounts the traditional stories of his people. Harris attempts to reproduce the speech of plantation blacks, and endows the animals in his fables with human qualities. Among the characters are Br'er Rabbit, Br'er Fox and Br'er Wolf.

*Uncle Silas: A Tale of Bartram-Haugh* A novel of suspense by **Sheridan Le Fanu**, published in 1864.

On her father's death Maud Ruthyn is made the ward of her uncle Silas, a sinister figure suspected of having murdered a gambling associate at his remote house, Bartram-Haugh, in Derbyshire. Silas, who will inherit if Maud should die, tries to force her into marriage to his own unpleasant son, Dudley. She escapes the marriage when it turns out that Dudley already has a wife, but Silas begins to plot her murder. The web of terror and intrigue tightens around the girl with the introduction of the grotesque and frightening French governess, Madame de la Rougierre. In the event, the plot against her fails, Dudley kills the governess by mistake and Maud makes her escape.

*Uncle Tom's Cabin, or, Life among the Lowly* An anti-slavery novel by **Harriet Beecher Stowe**, published serially in the *National Era* (1851–2) and in book form in 1852. It became the best-selling novel of the 19th century. Abraham Lincoln, in the midst of the Civil War, is reported to have remarked that Mrs Stowe was 'the little lady who wrote the book that made this great war'.

Uncle Tom is a saintly and faithful slave owned by the Shelby family. When the Shelbys find themselves in financial straits, Tom is separated from his wife and children and sold to a slave trader. Young George Shelby sympathizes with Tom and vows to redeem him some day. Tom is taken South, and on the voyage down the Mississippi he saves the life of Eva St Clare (known as little Eva) with the result that her father buys him out of gratitude. They go to the St Clare home in New Orleans, where Tom is happy and grows close to Eva and her black

'Uncle Tom saving Eva from a watery grave.' An illustration by George Cruikshank for the first English edition of *Uncle Tom's Cabin* (1852).

friend Topsy. After two years little Eva dies from a weakened constitution in a highly sentimental death scene. Her father is then killed in an accident and Tom is sold at auction to the villainous Simon Legree, a cruel and drunken Yankee. Legree is bewildered by Tom's ever-patient nature, and two of his female slaves capitalize on this by pretending to escape and going into hiding. Tom will not reveal their whereabouts, and Legree has him brutally whipped to death. As he is dying, George Shelby arrives to rescue him but it is too late. In despair, Shelby pledges to fight for the Abolitionist cause. 'God wrote the book', Mrs Stowe once said. 'I took His dictation.'

*Uncommercial Traveller, The* A collection of occasional pieces by **Charles Dickens**, published in 1860 and enlarged in 1865 and again in 1875. The articles originally appeared in *Household Words* and *All the Year Round*.

*Unconditional Surrender* See *Sword of Honour*.

**Under Milk Wood** A 'Play for voices' by **Dylan Thomas**, written in 1952, revised for its first public performance during his American tour in 1953, and first broadcast as a radio play in 1954. It describes, in liltingly poetic prose, a day in the life of some of the inhabitants of a small fishing town in South Wales. Called Llareggub (a jesting reversal of 'buggerall') in the play, the town is based on Laugharne, where Thomas lived.

**Under the Greenwood Tree**, *or, The Mellstock Quire* A novel by **Thomas Hardy**, first published in 1872.

Termed 'a rural painting of the Dutch school', this pastoral tale set in and about Mellstock (Stinsford) concerns the love of Dick Dewey, a tranter, for the flighty but charming Fancy Day. The narrative also traces the decline of the old church music to be supplanted at Mellstock by a 'cabinet-organ'. Fancy, the new teacher at the parish school and would-be organist, is sought not only by Dick (whom she really loves) but also by Farmer Shiner and Parson Maybold. In a weak moment she rashly agrees to marry the latter and then, recognizing her foolishness in time, breaks the engagement. The book ends with her cheery rustic marriage to Dick. *Under the Greenwood Tree* is a sunny, bucolic novel populated by simple, amusing countryfolk, but it is touched with regret at the changing of the old musical order and the duplicity of Fancy Day.

**Under the Volcano** A novel by **Malcolm Lowry**, published in 1947 and considered his masterpiece. It is the story of the final day in the life of Geoffrey Firmin, the British Consul in Cuernavaca, Mexico, in 1938, on the date of the festival of the Day of the Dead. On this day (the events of which are recalled in flashback exactly a year later by Firmin's former neighbour, Jacques Laruelle), Firmin's estranged wife Yvonne (who has had an affair with Laruelle) returns to visit her husband, who has become incorrigibly alcoholic. During the day they and Firmin's brother Hugh visit the festival, amid alarming premonitions of incipient local violence and symbolic intimations of doom. Finally, as the Consul is separated from Yvonne and Hugh during a torrential storm, Yvonne is killed by a runaway horse which the Consul has unleashed, and the Consul is murdered by a band of fascist thugs.

Dense with symbol and allusion to literature, religion and myth, the novel employs a complex, impacted time scheme and frequently achieves flights of remarkable prose reverie. It can be read as an unparalleled evocation of extreme alcoholism, as a virtuoso synthesis of arcane myth systems, or as an unforced allegory of a world in entropy as it stands on the brink of World War II.

**Under Western Eyes** A novel by **Joseph Conrad**, published in 1911. The narrator is an elderly English teacher of languages. He tells the story of Razumov, using the young Russian's diary for events in St Petersburg and his personal knowledge of Razumov once he has moved to Geneva and its community of Russian exiles.

Razumov's quiet student life in Russia is broken up by the arrival in his flat of Victor Haldin, a revolutionary idealist who has just assassinated a minister of state. Although Razumov agrees to shelter him, his loyalties swing towards the Tsarist state. He betrays Haldin to the police, only to find that the autocracy now regards him as a suspect. His isolation intensifies into moral solitude when he is dispatched to Geneva as a secret agent.

Razumov has the reputation of a hero among his fellow exiles: Haldin had written to his mother and young sister, Natalia, about his fellow student. Natalia's innocent devotion to the man she thinks tried to help her brother makes Razumov's guilt the harder to bear. He is repelled, further, by the cynical idealism of the revolutionaries, epitomized in the grotesque figure of Peter Ivanovitch. When he attempts to break free from his life of deceit, confessing both to Natalia (whom he loves) and to the revolutionaries, he brings ghastly retribution on himself. They burst his eardrums, and he is struck down and crippled by a tram he cannot hear.

**Underwoods** A collection by **Ben Jonson** of what he called 'lesser poems', published in 1640. It includes the poem on **Shakespeare** which had appeared in the First Folio of 1623; other notable pieces are 'An Ode: To Himself', 'A Celebration of Charis' and the 'Hymn on the Nativity'. **Robert Louis Stevenson** also adopted the title for a volume of his own poetry, published in 1887.

**Unfortunate Traveller, The** A pamphlet by **Thomas Nashe**, published in 1594. The dedicatory epistle (to the Earl of Southampton) promises 'some reasonable conveyance of history and variety of mirth' and the work has sometimes been claimed as the first **picaresque** novel in English. The story follows the adventures of Jack Wilton, a young English page, in France and Italy. It opens with Jack's tricks at the English camp at the siege of Tournai in the reign of Henry VIII and follows his travels as page to the Earl of Surrey. There is an account of the slaughter of the Anabaptists at Munster. In Italy Jack's adventures are hair-raising: he is involved with rapes, murders, revenges and schemings, and the sensational descriptions culminate in the horrific torture and execution of the Jew Zadoch. Another execution, that of Cutwolfe, causes Jack to flee Italy and reform his way of life. Nashe is nowhere more brutal or sensational in his writing, perhaps self-consciously so, in an attempt to burlesque the stock situations and tone of popular Elizabethan journalism.

**University Wits** The name popularly given to a group of playwrights, among whom **Marlowe, Greene, Nashe** and **Peele** are the most prominent, who received their education at Oxford or Cambridge, lived rashly in London and contributed significantly to the rapid development of a national repertoire of plays in the 1580s and 1590s. Most of the University Wits were hostile to the rising generation of playwrights, including **Jonson** and **Shakespeare**, who lacked their educational advantages.

*Unto this Last* Essays on political economy by **John Ruskin**, first published in *The Cornhill Magazine* in 1860 and in book form in 1862.

*Unto this Last* is Ruskin's most important and succinct social pronouncement, rejecting the *laissez-faire* doctrines of the 'Manchester School' of economic thought. So strongly were book and author reviled that publication in the *Cornhill*, then under **Thackeray**'s nervous editorship, was curtailed. The fundamental message of *Unto this Last* is that 'that country is the richest which nourishes the greatest number of noble and happy human beings'. Like his mentor, **Carlyle**, Ruskin calls for a benevolent paternalism in which enlightened 'Captains of Industry' work with their employees toward a way of life that will yield true wealth in an atmosphere of harmonious relationships and humane understanding. Honesty, justice, kindness, 'social affection', purity of commercial engagement – these are the values of *Unto this Last*, whose idealistic message was respected by both Tolstoy and Gandhi. The book is notable for its clear, eloquent style, touched by mordant humour.

**Updike, John (Hoyer)** 1932– American novelist, short-story writer and poet, born in Shillington, Pennsylvania, and educated at Harvard. He worked on the staff of *The New Yorker* for two years and his first work appeared in that magazine. In 1958 he published a volume of verse, *The Carpentered Hen* (called *Hoping for a Hoopoe* in England); his first novel, *The Poorhouse Fair*, came in the following year.

Updike established a reputation as a keen observer of modern American life with the short stories in *The Same Door* (1959), and enjoyed major success with the novel *Rabbit Run* (1960), whose central character, Harry Angstrom, appears also in the sequels, *Rabbit Redux* (1971) and *Rabbit is Rich* (1981). *Pigeon Feathers and Other Stories* (1962) and *The Magic Flute* (1962, a children's book) were followed by *The Centaur* (1963, National Book Award), in which the life

of a small-town teacher is linked to that of Chiron, the wise centaur of mythology. Updike's other works include the verse collections *Telephone Poles* (1963), *Seventy Poems* (1963), *Midpoint and Other Poems* (1969), *The Dance of the Solids* (1969) and *Tossing and Turning* (1977). Among his other novels are *Bech: A Book* (1970), *Bech is Back* (1982), *The Witches of Eastwick* (1984) and *Roger's Version* (1986). His collections of short stories include *The Ring* (1964, called *Olinger Stories* in England), *The Music School* (1966, O. Henry Award), *Museums and Women* (1972), *A Month of Sundays* (1975), *Marry Me* (1976), *Problems and Other Stories* (1979) and *Trust Me* (1987). *Hugging the Shore*, a collection of essays, was published in 1983.

**Upward, Edward (Falaise)** 1903– Novelist. Edward Upward was born at Romford in Essex and educated at Repton and Corpus Christi College, Cambridge. At school he met and became a lifelong friend of **Christopher Isherwood**, who was also a contemporary at Cambridge. He won the Chancellor's Medal for poetry and worked closely with Isherwood when both began to write.

During the 1930s Upward became a member of the Communist Party, and his *Journey to the Border* (1938) is a Kafkaesque political allegory about a private tutor's progress towards radicalism and the Workers' Movement. Like many radicals of his generation, Upward was caught in the trap of Party dogmatism during the Stalin era. His political 'soul-searching' was largely responsible for a period of silence which lasted for over two decades. He became a schoolteacher and, in 1962, published *In the Thirties*, the first part of a trilogy which gave an account of his personal struggles during the intervening years. *Rotten Elements* followed in 1969, then *No Home but the Struggle* (1977). The completed trilogy, *The Spiral Ascent*, was published the same year and traced Upward's career (through the person of Alan Sebrill, schoolteacher and Marxist poet) over several decades. The final volume presented Upward's artistic and political credo about the need for harmony between personal and social commitment.

*Urn Burial* See *Hydriotaphia*.

**Urquhart (or Urchard), Sir Thomas** *c*.1611–*c*.1660 Translator. A Scottish Royalist who fought against the Covenanters and was knighted in 1641, he took part in the Battle of Worcester and was imprisoned in the Tower for two years. On his return to Scotland he embarked on the spirited translation of Rabelais for which he is remembered; the first two books of *Gargantua and Pantagruel* appeared in 1653 and a third book was published posthumously (1693) by **Peter Anthony Motteux**, who completed the remainder in 1694. Urquhart was also the author of curious treatises on mathematics and language to which he gave elaborate Greek titles.

**Usk, Thomas** d.1388 Author of a religious prose work, *The Testament of Love*. Little is known of his life, but he was confidential clerk to John of Northampton, whom he betrayed in 1384; he was executed in 1388. His sole surviving work, written *c*.1387, is an **allegory** in three books describing how the imprisoned author was visited by Love (meaning divine love) after praying to Margaret, the Grace of God, for comfort. Love consoles him, condemns worldly fame and declares God's greatness and compassion. The second book contains complaints against the clergy, a discourse on women and a discussion on the route to salvation. The third book is concerned with predestination and free will; love finally shows how grace may be attained. The piece is obscure, poorly written and lacking in unity. It draws extensively on **Chaucer**'s *Boece* and on *The House of Fame* and was included in early editions of Chaucer's works (see **Chaucerian apocrypha**).

**Ussher, James** 1581–1656 Irish churchman and scholar. He was born in Dublin. His family was influential in legal and ecclesiastical affairs, and closely involved in the foundation of Trinity College, Dublin. Ussher was one of the first students in 1594 and became Professor of Divinity there in 1607. His frequent visits to England brought him in touch with **William Camden**, **Sir Robert Cotton** and **John Selden**, the leading scholars and antiquaries of the time. He contributed material on Irish antiquities to the 1607 edition of Camden's *Britannia*. Selden described him as 'learned to a miracle': he had an incomparable knowledge of patristic literature and of the history of the primitive church; he was famed too for his skill in languages, including Anglo-Saxon, Hebrew, Arabic and Persian. A tireless preacher, controversialist and antagonist of Rome, he was appointed Bishop of Meath in 1620, and Archbishop of Armagh, Primate of the Anglican church in Ireland, in 1625. In London during the 1630s he helped defend the episcopal system that was increasingly under attack, becoming a trusted associate of King Charles and moving with the court to Oxford in the 1640s. Ussher was admired by Cromwell, with whom he tried unsuccessfully to negotiate freedom of worship for Anglicans under the Protectorate. At his burial in Westminster Abbey, Cromwell permitted the proscribed Anglican funeral rites to be used as a mark of respect for Ussher's faith.

Most of his numerous scholarly works are in Latin. He explored in great detail early theological controversies and their bearing on contemporary religious positions, and he was especially interested in the history of the Pelagian heresy (which denied the doctrine of original sin) in Britain and Ireland. His outstanding works were *Britannicarum Ecclesiarum Antiquitates* (1639), a lengthy study of the early centuries of the church in the British Isles, and *Annales Veteris et Novi Testamenti* (1650), long accepted as providing a definitive chronology of the world up to the dispersion of the Jews. It was in this work that Ussher determined that the creation of the world had taken place on 23 October 4004 BC, and that the Flood had occurred in 1656 BC, dates of great use to contemporaries for working out the timetable of the Apocalypse.

**Utilitarianism** An ethical doctrine which judges an act to be right or wrong according to its tendency to promote the happiness of the majority affected by it. **Jeremy Bentham** is usually named as the founding father of Utilitarianism, although he acknowledged his debt to other 18th-century philosophers, including **David Hume** and the Frenchman Helvétius. For Bentham, Utilitarianism formed the ideological basis for a programme of moral and legal reforms that he and his followers, **James Mill**, **David Ricardo** and John Austin, a professor of jurisprudence, wished to introduce. In the next generation **J. S. Mill** was to widen the doctrine's scope, notably in the essay 'Utilitarianism' (1861), to include private as well as public moral sanctions and to refine the concept of 'pleasure'. Still working within the Utilitarian framework, later in the 19th century, **Henry Sidgwick** was to suggest that the method involved in determining the right course of action could frequently be more complex than early Utilitarian theory had allowed for, and, in the early 20th century, **G. E. Moore** argued for the recognition of non-hedonistic values, independent of the pain-pleasure principle.

Initially conceived as a doctrine of public morality, Utilitarianism had its widest effects in the fields of 19th-century law, politics and economics. In the popular mid-19th-century mind political economy was seen as a branch of Utilitarian theory, partly because of the close connection of many leading economists with the 'philosophical radicals'. The premise of the early political economists that the market had a self-regulating tendency towards the ultimate welfare of the greatest number was discountenanced by experience, and later Utilitarians were prepared to admit a greater degree of state intervention.

*Utopia* **Thomas More**'s work was originally written in Latin and printed at Louvain in 1516 as *Libellus Vere Aureus, nec Minus Salutaris quam Festivus, de Optimo Reipublicae Statu deque Nova*

'Utopia insulae figura.' A woodcut from the first edition of More's *Utopia*, Louvain 1516.

*Insula Utopia* (A truly golden little book, no less beneficial than entertaining, about the best state of a commonwealth and the new island of Utopia). It was begun in the Low Countries, completed in England, and opens with a historical event, a delegation to Bruges in 1515 of which More was part. More is then introduced to the traveller Raphael Hythlodaeus at Antwerp and enters into conversation with him. Raphael recalls conversations at the house of More's sometime patron Cardinal Morton which attempt criticism and analysis of contemporary European society, and offer solutions for its ills, in the course of which Raphael cites the example of the Utopians. Book I ends with More's request to hear further of Utopia and Book II (which was written first) contains Raphael's description of the happy island state where all things are held in common, gold is despised and the people live communally. The work ends with More's ambiguous reflections on the story: there are some things in Utopia he cannot agree with and others he would like to see implemented in Europe, although he doubts that they will be. Interpretations of *Utopia* (the name plays on two Greek words *eutopos*, 'a good place', and *outopos*, 'no place') are many and diverse. It has been seen as a programme for an ideal state, a vision of the ideal to be contemplated (like Plato's *Republic*), a satirical look at contemporary European society, and a humanist *jeu d'esprit*. It is part of a tradition of 'Utopian fiction' and begot others in the 16th century and later. In the 16th century *Utopia* was translated into Dutch, French, Italian, Spanish and into English, Ralph Robinson's version being printed in 1551.

Models for More's island state can be found in earlier literature. Plato's *Republic* is explicitly mentioned in the work itself, Plutarch had described an ideal Spartan commonwealth, and the most perfect island possible crops up in medievel theological debate. After the publication of *Utopia*, Italian humanists preoccupied themselves with works on ideal states, the most significant being Tommaso Campanella's *La Città del Sole* (The City of the Sun, written *c.* 1602). **Bacon**'s *New Atlantis* (1627) was one of many such works in the 17th century, when 'Utopian' became current as an adjective. The ambiguities of More's island, whether it is ideal, possible or even desirable, continue in subsequent Utopian literature, as does More's use of imagined strange lands for satirical purposes (**Swift**'s *Gulliver's Travels*, **Samuel Butler**'s *Erewhon*). 'Dystopian' was first used as an adjective in the late 19th century by **J. S. Mill**, to suggest an imagined state which was not desirable. But the desirability of Utopia is deliberately open to question even in More's own work. **Aldous Huxley**'s *Brave New World* and **George Orwell**'s *Nineteen Eighty-Four* describe apparent Utopias that reveal themselves to be dystopian.

**Uttley, Alison** 1884–1976 Children's author. A farmer's daughter born in Derbyshire, she went from the village school to study physics at Cambridge. After teaching science in a London girls' school she married and began writing. Her first children's book, *The Little Grey Rabbit* (1929), was followed by over 30 titles in the same series, all illustrated by Margaret Tempest and appearing in the same small format. Alison Uttley's imaginary world was gentle, reaching back into ancient legend and history at times and much taken up with the domestic details of the humanized squirrels, hares or moles about whom she wrote. A harsher side of rural life was brilliantly recorded in an autobiography, *The Country Child* (1931). In her finest story for older children, *A Traveller in Time* (1939), a modern child is transported back into dangerous 16th-century intrigues concerning the imprisoned Mary, Queen of Scots. *Tales of Four Pigs and Brock the Badger* (1939) saw the arrival of Sam Pig, a popular character with small readers eventually to feature in 35 separate adventures. Like all this author's characters, he helped provide town children with an idyllic but seldom sentimentalized vision of the countryside while also entertaining them with lively, well-crafted stories.

# V

*Valentinian* A tragedy by **John Fletcher**, performed about 1612 and published in 1647. The play has some basis in history – the last century of the Roman era – and includes some fine lyrics.

Valentinian III is guilty of dishonouring Lucina, wife of his general, Maximus. Lucina kills herself and Maximus plots his revenge. He poisons Valentinian's mind against his favourite general, Aecius, who commits suicide when he loses the emperor's favour. Two friends of Aecius kill Valentinian in revenge and Maximus is made emperor in his place. He takes Eudoxia, Valentinian's widow, as consort but makes the mistake of telling her how he reached the imperial throne. Eudoxia, revolted at hearing Maximus' false boast that he contrived in the dishonour of Lucina, poisons him before he can be crowned.

*Valley of Fear, The* See **Sherlock Holmes stories**.

**van der Post, Laurens** 1906– South African writer of rural Afrikaner origin, born near Philippolis. His openness to other cultures, and to the intuitive and the mythopoeic, derives from childhood exposure to San (Bushman) and other African myths and survival skills, reinforced by distinguished commando service in 1939–45 and friendship with Carl Jung. His first, most convincing novel, *In a Province* (1934), an early indictment of white South African racism, is realistic; *The Face Beside the Fire* (1953) is overburdened psychologically and symbolically, while *Flamingo Feather* (1955) is melodramatic. *The Hunter and the Whale* (1967), *A Story Like the Wind* (1972) and its sequel *A Far-off Place* (1974) are novels of vigorous action that emphasize individualism and intuition as correctives to Marxism and modern rationalism. *The Seed and the Sower* (1963) consists of three connected stories of Japanese prisoner-of-war camps.

He deploys his narrative skills most successfully, however, in non-fiction: *Venture to the Interior* (1952), about exploration in Malawi, and his recording of surviving San culture in *The Lost World of the Kalahari* (1958), *The Heart of the Hunter* (1961), *A Mantis Carol* (1975), and, with Jane Taylor, *Testament to the Bushman* (1984). His other books are: *The Dark Eye of Africa* (1955, essays), *Journey into Russia* (1964, as *A View of All the Russias*, USA), *A Portrait of Japan* (1968), *The Night of the New Moon* (1970, prisoner-of-war memoirs), *Jung and the Story of Our Time* (1976).

**Van Dine, S. S.** See **detective fiction**.

**Van Vechten, Carl** 1880–1966 American novelist, born in Cedar Rapids, Iowa, best known for a series of novels which deal with the cultural life of New York City in the 1920s. These include *Peter Whiffle* (1922), *The Blind Bow-Boy* (1923), *Firecrackers* (1925) and *Parties* (1930). His most highly acclaimed work is *Nigger Heaven* (1926), which takes place in the exotic world of Harlem's nightclubs and soirées, and which is often seen as epitomizing the renewed interest in black life shown by white writers during this period. His other novels include a satire of Hollywood entitled *Spider Boy* (1928) and *The Tattooed Countess* (1924), which is set in his home state of Iowa. He was also active as a music and drama critic and wrote several memoirs, the most notable of which are *Sacred and Profane Memoirs* (1932) and an account of his friendship with **Gertrude Stein**, published as an introduction to an edition of her *Three Lives* (1909).

**van Vogt, A[lfred] E[lton]** 1912– Canadian-born writer of **science fiction**, van Vogt became one of the most colourful pulp science fiction writers of the 1940s. His plots are convoluted, crowded with ideas, and often fail to make sense, but he compensates for these failings by the sheer verve of his inventiveness and the panache with which he delivers his imaginative flourishes. He has written many stories whose harassed heroes gradually achieve control of awesome superhuman powers, including *Slan* (1940; in book form 1948), *The World of Null-A* (1945; in book form 1948) and the two stories in *Masters of Time* (1950). His writing career was interrupted for some years when he tried to make these fantasies real by becoming a follower of L. Ron Hubbard's Scientology.

Although he is primarily an entertainer, his best work has intellectual substance, perhaps best displayed in his non-fantasy novel about brain-washing, *The Violent Man* (1962).

**Vanbrugh, Sir John** 1664–1726 Architect and playwright. Born in London, Vanbrugh was sent to school in Chester. He may have studied architecture in France, 1683–5. (His architectural genius is otherwise something of a mystery.) Commissioned ensign in the 13th Foot Regiment, Vanbrugh saw service in France and was arrested and imprisoned for espionage, 1688–92. He left the army in 1702 to become Comptroller to the Public Works, remaining in that office for 12 years. He was appointed Carlisle Herald in 1703 and Clarenceux King-at-Arms from 1704 until his death. He was knighted in 1723.

Public honours came Vanbrugh's way more because of his work as an architect than as a dramatist. Among his most famous designs were those for Castle Howard (1701), the Queen's Theatre in the Haymarket (1703), Blenheim Palace (1705) and Seaton Delavel (1720). He is said to have drafted a comedy during his French imprisonment, but his first performed play was provoked by his scepticism over the hero's reformation in **Colley Cibber**'s *Love's Last Shift*. **The Relapse**, *or, Virtue in Danger* (1696) shows the rakish Loveless reverting to

Sir John Vanbrugh. A detail from the portrait by Sir Godfrey Kneller, *c.*1704–10. National Portrait Gallery, London.

type. *The Provok'd Wife* (1697) is Vanbrugh's other major play. Both were singled out for attack by **Jeremy Collier** in his *Short View of the Immorality and Profaneness of the English Stage* (1698), and Vanbrugh was stung into writing *A Short Vindication of The Relapse and The Provok'd Wife from Immorality and Profaneness* (1698). His remaining plays are mostly adaptations, the two-part *Aesop* (1697) from Boursault, *The Country House* (1698) from Dancourt, *The Pilgrim* (1700) from **John Fletcher**, *The False Friend* (1702) from Le Sage, the best of them, *The Confederacy* (1705), from Dancourt and *The Mistake* (1705) from Molière. He collaborated with **Congreve** and William Walsh in *Squire Trelooby* (1704), another version of Molière, wrote the unsuccessful *The Cuckold in Conceit* (1707) and left unfinished a play called *A Journey to London*, which Colley Cibber completed and staged under the title *The Provok'd Husband* (1728).

**Vancouver, George** 1758–98 Explorer. Vancouver accompanied **Captain Cook** on his second voyage towards the South Pole (1772–5), and took part in Admiral Rodney's victory over the French at Les Saintes in the West Indies (1782). He was sent on a voyage of discovery (1791–5) during which he surveyed the south-west coast of Australia, the coast of New Zealand, and the Pacific coast of America. He returned by way of Vancouver Island (named after him) and Cape Horn. His *A Voyage of Discovery to the North Pacific* was published posthumously (1798).

**Vanderhaeghe, Guy** 1951– Canadian novelist and short-story writer. Born and raised in Esterhazy, Saskatchewan, he studied at the Universities of Saskatchewan and Regina. The twelve stories of his first collection of short fiction, *Man Descending* (1982), which won the Governor-General's Award for Fiction, chronicle the disillusionment and pain of daily life in the seemingly hostile environment of the contemporary world. Seven earlier stories were gathered together in *The Trouble with Heroes and Other Stories* (1983). His novel, *My Present Age* (1984), further explores the loneliness of modern man through the eyes of its 31-year-old narrator. In 1987 Vanderhaeghe won the Geoffrey Faber Memorial Prize.

*Vanity Fair* A novel by **W. M. Thackeray**, with illustrations by him, published in monthly parts from January 1847 to July 1848, and in volume form in 1848.

Sub-titled 'A Novel without a Hero', it traces the interweaving destinies of two contrasted heroines during the period of Waterloo and its aftermath. Becky Sharp, orphan daughter of a penniless artist, is resourceful and socially ambi-

'Mr Joseph entangled.' One of Thackeray's illustrations for his *Vanity Fair*, first published in monthly parts 1847–8. Joseph Sedley helping Becky Sharp wind a skein of green silk.

tious; her friend Amelia Sedley, at whose comfortable Bloomsbury home Becky goes to stay when the two leave school together, is affectionate, trusting and unworldly. Thwarted in her attempt to trap into marriage Amelia's brother, the fat Anglo-Indian Jos Sedley, Becky leaves to become governess at the Hampshire home of the Crawley family, where she soon makes herself indispensable to the dissolute old baronet, Sir Pitt, and charms his younger, soldier son, Rawdon. On the death of his second wife, Sir Pitt proposes to Becky, only to find that she is already married to Rawdon. This news alienates the wealthy aunt on whose fortune Rawdon depends, and the couple are forced to live by their wits.

The clouds of war gather and Amelia's fortunes decline. Her stockbroker father is ruined; her love affair with George Osborne, the handsome but vain and selfish son of a wealthy merchant, is opposed by his purse-proud father. George is persuaded to marry her by his best friend and fellow officer, William Dobbin, who secretly loves Amelia, and is disinherited. The principal characters move with the army to Brussels, where George flirts with Becky and is then killed in the battle of Waterloo. The grieving Amelia is brought back by Dobbin to her parents' home, where she gives birth to a son, Georgy, on whom and on the memory of George she dotes. Becky also has a son, Rawdon, whom she neglects.

As Amelia in genteel poverty struggles to bring up her son, supported in secret by the faithful Dobbin, now in India, Becky and Rawdon attempt 'to live well on nothing a year'. Through gambling, deceit, and the patronage of the wealthy Lord Steyne, Becky pursues a life of fashion until she is discovered by Rawdon in a compromising situation with Steyne. Rejected by both and ostracized by society, Becky escapes from her creditors to the Continent, where she is discovered leading a Bohemian life by Amelia, whose fortunes have revived with the return of Dobbin and Jos from India and Georgy's adoption by his wealthy grandfather. Amelia's kindness to Becky is disapproved by Dobbin, but leads to the revelation that George Osborne had proposed to elope with Becky on the eve of Waterloo, which destroys the sentimental memories of her husband Amelia has cherished. Older and disillusioned, Dobbin and Amelia can now marry. Becky meanwhile regains her hold over Jos, who gives her control of his finances and then dies in suspicious circumstances. Rawdon also dies abroad and his son inherits the Crawley estate. He pensions his mother but refuses to see her, and Becky ends the novel in the guise of a pious widow, busy with good works.

*Vanity Fair* is one of the greatest of English novels, a vast satirical panorama of a materialistic society and a landmark in the history of realistic fiction. Thackeray's sceptical, anti-heroic vision, and what **Bagehot** called his 'stern and humble realism', were important influences on the development of the Victorian domestic novel.

**Vanity Fair** An American magazine, published weekly in New York City from 1859 to 1863, offering humorous commentary on contemporary social and political issues. Edited by C. G. Leland and then by C. F. Brown, its contributors included **Thomas Aldrich**, **William Dean Howells**, **Fitz-James O'Brien** and **Richard Henry Stoddard**. It was revived in 1868. In 1913 it was purchased by Condé Nast and became a sophisticated review of literature, art and fashion. Frank Crowinshield was editor from 1914 to 1936, at which time it was absorbed by *Vogue*. It reappeared in 1983 under the editorship of Richard Locke, and is currently edited by Tina Brown. Though it remains a magazine of high fashion and living, it has also printed the work of such literary figures as Gabriel García Márquez, Joseph Brodsky, Italo Calvino and **Norman Mailer**.

**Vanity of Human Wishes, The** A poem by **Samuel Johnson**, in imitation of the tenth satire of Juvenal, published in 1749. With his customary generality of observation, the poet surveys the aspirations and delusions of mankind through the ages and across the busy geography of human ambition, selecting (as in the Latin original on which it is skilfully modelled) certain representative figures for examination. Wolsey, **Buckingham** and **Clarendon** are considered for their overreaching attitudes to power; the perils of intellectual eminence are adduced from the careers of Galileo and **Laud**; and Charles XII of Sweden (about whom the poet was thinking of writing a play) is the military leader in a world of power politics, brought low by a stray bullet. The section on the fearsomeness of old age is especially effective (it includes a terrifying vignette of the senile **Swift**) as is the treatment of physical beauty, though the poem ends with an affirmation of faith. The atmosphere of weary inevitability and the tragic irony of the human examples are enhanced by the poem's intensely regular movement.

**Vansittart, Peter** 1920– Novelist. Born in Bedford, he was educated at Marlborough House School, Haileybury College and Worcester College, Oxford, where he read modern history. His more than 20 novels include *I Am the World* (1942), *Broken Canes* (1950), *A Little Madness* (1953), *Carolina* (1961), *Quintet* (1976) and *Aspects of Feeling* (1986). An original and distinctive writer, he is preoccupied with language and has explored it at the expense of narrative. By doing so, he realizes that he is limiting his appeal and to some extent making himself a 'critics' novelist'. He is also concerned with time and how it can change or distort ideas and emotions. Although not all his novels have historical settings, Vansittart is recognized as a historical novelist who does not make the search for accuracy his main endeavour but prefers to speculate imaginatively on events.

*Varieties of Religious Experience, The* A book by **William James**, published in 1902, the compilation of two courses of lectures which he delivered at Edinburgh University in 1901–2. He focuses on a personal instead of an organized religion, which he found to be a matter of 'ritual acts' rather than of private importance. His argument, based on scientific analysis of a number of examples of the conversion process, asserts that the particulars of religious faith are true insofar as they provide the believer with emotional fulfilment. The book was especially influential in stimulating the study of the psychology of religion.

*Vathek: An Arabian Tale* A novel by **William Beckford**, written in French and first published in English in 1786. The translation, probably by Samuel Henley, may have been undertaken at Beckford's request and with his help, but was presented as Henley's own version from the Arabic. Beckford immediately issued the original in Paris and Lausanne (1786) and later revised the English text. *The Episodes of Vathek*, probably part of the original manuscript, were discovered and published with an English translation by F. T. Marzials in 1912.

The Caliph, Vathek, is the grandson of Haroun-al-Raschid; his mother, Catharis, is a Greek sorceress. Corrupted by power and a thirst for forbidden knowledge, Vathek becomes a servant of Eblis (the devil) in order to gain access to the treasures of the pre-Adamite sultans in the ruins of Istakar. He sacrifices 50 children and is given the power of death in the glance of one of his eyes, and sets off from his capital, Samarah. On his journey Vathek falls in love with Nouronihar, an emir's daughter, and she accompanies him. After exotic incidents in Istakar, Vathek gains admission to the halls of Eblis in the underworld, where he realizes the vanity of all the earthly treasures and wonders contained there. The story ends with Vathek and his companions awaiting their eternal torment: their bodies will remain intact but their hearts will burn for ever inside them.

Beckford's fantasy, finely sustained to its splendidly infernal conclusion, owes much to the contemporary fashion for **Gothic fiction**. Its setting, however, allies it with the tradition of Orientalism already apparent in **Samuel Johnson**'s *Rasselas* and later to reach its full flowering in the work of **Byron** and **Thomas Moore**.

**Vaughan, Henry** 1621 or 1622–95 Poet. The twin brother of **Thomas Vaughan**, he was born at Newton-upon-Usk in Wales. By 1638 he went up to Jesus College, Oxford, but did not take his degree, moving to London in 1640 to study law – 'which the sudden eruption of our late Civil Wars wholly frustrated'. He evidently fought on the Royalist side, then returned home to make his living as a physician.

In 1646 he published his *Poems, with the Tenth Satire of Juvenal Englished*, a slender offering of courtly Cavalier verse that he admitted was already out of fashion, although the translation of Juvenal remains a powerful and ominous work. *Olor Iscanus* ('The Swan of Usk') was ready for the press in 1647, but publication was delayed until 1651. Here Vaughan tried to create a poetry of rural retreat in a Welsh pastoral setting, but the violence of the age cannot be kept out. A complete change occurred in Vaughan's style and subject matter with *Silex Scintillans*, 1650, one of the outstanding volumes of meditative verse of the century. 'The Flashing Flint' of the title announces the theme of the hardened heart struck by affliction until it yields a holy fire. The experiences that lie behind the book are various: the sense of regeneration from sin, the death of a close friend, presumably the poet's younger brother William, moments of transcendence when the veil of mortality seems to lift, anticipations of the Day of Judgement. Stylistically the poems are deeply influenced by Vaughan's reading of **George Herbert**. The character of Vaughan's religious poems is, however, notably different from Herbert's: at their finest they transmit a visionary sense of the pervasive presence of the divine within the natural world. Frequently they are coloured by a mood of wistfulness induced by Vaughan's desire to reach some spiritual home.

An enlarged edition of *Silex Scintillans* appeared in 1655, and after a long silence came *Thalia Rediviva*, 1678, a dry miscellany of poems quite devoid of his earlier delicacy of spirit. His prose works include a meditative treatise *The Mount of Olives, or, Solitary Devotions*, 1652, and several translations of religious and medical writings. He liked to style himself Henry Vaughan, Silurist, a reference to his homeland in the border country of Wales once occupied by the ancient British tribe of the Silures.

**Vaughan, Thomas** 1621 or 1622–66 Hermetic philosopher. Twin brother of the poet **Henry Vaughan**, he was born at Newton-upon-Usk in Wales to a family belonging to the rural gentry. He went to Jesus College, Oxford, by 1638 and was ordained by 1645, although he did not exercise his calling. He probably fought on the Royalist side in the Civil War. He engaged in chemical research at Oxford and London, and died, according to **Anthony à Wood**, as a result of an experiment with mercury, 'which getting up into his nose, marched him off'. Under the name Eugenius Philalethes ('The well-born lover of Truth') he published in the 1650s a number of treatises of hermetic philosophy, and was regarded as one of the most notable alchemists of his time. His works explore the occult influences that operate throughout the creation, and he writes to justify the pursuit of alchemy as the supreme philosophic quest. His prose is learned, allusive and cryptic; it may however be admired for its aggressive ebullience. Vaughan was lampooned by **Samuel Butler** in *Hudibras*, and by **Swift** in *A Tale of a Tub*. His writings are: *Anthroposophia Theomagica, or, A Discourse of the Nature of Man and his State after Death* (1650), *Anima Magica Abscondita, or, A Discourse of the Universal Spirit of Nature* (1650), *Magia Adamica, or, The Antiquity of Magic, the Descent thereof from Adam Proved* (1650), *The Man-Mouse* (1650), a fulmination against **Henry More**, the **Cambridge Platonist**, *Lumen de Lumine, or, A New Magical Light Discovered* (1651), *The Second Wash, or, The Moore Scour'd* (1651), another attack on More for his scepticism about alchemy, *Aula Lucis, or, The House of Light* (1651), *The Fame and Confession of the Fraternity of the Rosie Cross* (1653), a translation of the Rosicrucian manifestos, and *Euphrates* (1655), on the elements of generation. Some of his poems were printed in Henry Vaughan's collection *Thalia Rediviva* (1678).

**Vaux, Thomas, 2nd Baron Vaux of Harrowden** 1510–56 Poet. Educated at Cambridge, he accompanied Wolsey on an embassy to France in 1527 and Henry VIII to Calais and Boulogne in 1532. He was made a Knight of the Bath in 1533. He contributed two poems to *Tottel's Miscellany*, one of them his best-known poem, 'The aged Lover Renounceth Love'; three of its stanzas were later garbled by the gravedigger in *Hamlet*. *The Paradise of Dainty Devices* (1576) contains 13 poems by Vaux.

**Veblen, Thorstein (Bunde)** 1857–1929 American economist and social critic. The son of Norwegian immigrant farmers, Veblen was born in Cato Township, Wisconsin, and educated at Carleton College, The Johns Hopkins University, and Yale.

His first and most famous book, *The Theory of the Leisure Class: An Economic Study in the Evolution of Institutions* (1899), was popular among radicals because it attacked the caste system that grew out of the pursuit of wealth. *The Instinct of Workmanship* (1914) considers two opposing tendencies within men – the disposition to workmanship which survives in the modern capitalist system and the predatory impulse which thrives in it. *The Place of Science in Modern Civilization* (1919) is a study of the two main sources of science – disorderly knowledge of a utilitarian character and disinterested interpretation of this knowledge. Veblen's abiding interest in the economic determinants of modern society – in particular his concern with the disjunction between those who actually produce goods and those who control the production process and the distribution of products – is evident in several of his other works: *The Theory of Business Enterprise* (1904), *The Vested Interests and the State of the Industrial Arts* (1919), *The Engineers and the Price System* (1921), and his last book, *Absentee Ownership* (1923).

*Vein of Iron* A novel by **Ellen Glasgow**, published in 1935, which tells the story of the Scottish-Irish Fincastle family, who have been ministers and leaders in Shut-In Valley in the Virginia mountains since Colonial times. The story focuses on a daughter of the family, Ada, and follows her from her childhood through the years of the Depression. John, Ada's father, has lost his position in the church because of his unorthodox ideas, and has started teaching. Ada is in love with her father's student, Ralph McBride, and is jealous when he marries the beautiful Janet Rowan. When Janet divorces Ralph to marry a richer man, he and Ada become lovers. He goes to fight in World War I, unknowingly leaving Ada pregnant. Rejected by the community after the death of her grandmother, whose good reputation has helped sustain the family, Ada moves to Queenborough to give birth to her son, Rannie. Ralph returns and they are married. Their happy reunion is upset, however, when Ralph is temporarily paralysed in a car accident. Ada, with her 'vein of iron', her undaunted pride and courage, goes back to work to support her husband, son and ailing father. After John Fincastle's death, the family uses the insurance money to buy back the family home in Shut-In Valley.

*Venetia* A novel by **Benjamin Disraeli**, published in 1837. The story is set in the 18th century but its two principal male characters, Marmion Herbert and Plantagenet Cadurcis, are loosely based on **Shelley** and **Byron**. It ends with both men drowning in a squall in the bay of Spezia. The heroine, Venetia Herbert, at length marries George Cadurcis, cousin and heir of Plantagenet.

*Venice Preserved* A tragedy in blank verse by **Thomas Otway**, first performed in 1682, with Betterton as Jaffeir and Elizabeth Barry as Belvidera.

Priuli, a Venetian senator, has repudiated his daughter Belvidera because of her marriage to the nobly born Jaffeir. He also repudiates Jaffeir's desperate request for help against poverty. The rejected Jaffeir is persuaded by his brave friend, Pierre, to join a conspiracy against the Venetian republic, and entrusts Belvidera to Renault, leader of the conspiracy, as proof of his loyalty. But Renault forces his attentions on Belvidera, and the disillusioned Jaffeir breaks his oath and reveals the conspiracy to her. She persuades him to warn her father, and Jaffeir does so on condition that the lives of the conspirators will be spared. But the Venetian senators break their promise, and Jaffeir kills Pierre to save him the agony of being broken on the wheel. He then kills himself, and Belvidera, her mind unbalanced by the tragedies she has witnessed, dies.

A sub-plot of surprising comic potential matches a courtesan called Aquilina with a masochistic senator called Antonio. It was known to some of the contemporary audience that Antonio and Renault formed a composite caricature of the Earl of Shaftesbury.

*Venus and Adonis* A narrative poem by **Shakespeare**, printed in 1593. The seven editions by 1602 and the 14 by 1640 testify to its enthusiastic readership. Like the slightly later *The Rape of Lucrece*, it was dedicated, as 'the first heir of my invention', to the Earl of Southampton. In both poems Shakespeare was laying claim to the status of a recognized professional poet. The poem is a sensuous and witty erotic **epyllion** like **Marlowe**'s *Hero and Leander* which Shakespeare took mainly from Ovid's *Metamorphoses*. Ovid's ver-

sion of the story is already a detached account of love and passion; Shakespeare's retelling increases the detachment and makes some changes. His coy, peevishly reluctant and epicene Adonis is unlike Ovid's willing lover, his Venus is aggressively sexual and the dominant partner. The poem tells of Venus' repeated, and simultaneously arousing and comic, attempts to woo Adonis. She warns him against hunting the boar but Adonis goes off to the hunt and Venus, hearing its sounds, runs distracted through the woods in search of her boy. She finds him dead, laments over the corpse, and finds the anemone sprung from his blood.

Like *The Rape of Lucrece*, the poem is full of rhetorical display, ornamented language, verbal display, elaborate conceits and witty play. In addition there are fine descriptions of the countryside and its animals. (An extended description of Adonis' horse drew from **Dowden** the query whether it was poetry or part of an advertisement for a horse sale.) The poem is like many of Shakespeare's comedies in its alternately sympathetic and ironic scrutiny of the pains, humour and pathos of wooing.

**Vercelli Book** A 10th-century manuscript of Old English verse and prose preserved in the cathedral library at Vercelli in northern Italy. It contains two poems by **Cynewulf** (*Elene* and *The Fates of the Apostles*), *The Address of the Soul to the Body*, *Andreas* and *The Dream of the Rood*, together with a prose life of St Guthlac and 22 prose homilies.

**verse romance** A poetic form originating in 12th-century France, where the greatest romances were the work of Chrétien de Troyes, and flourishing in England in the 13th and 14th centuries. Characteristically, the romance tells the story of a single knight, sometimes a character from **Arthurian literature**. He is separated from the court and exposed to various adventures, which often involve the supernatural, before making his triumphant return to court and prosperity; his rewards frequently include marriage to his beloved. Occasionally two central figures are involved, either a couple (as in *Floris and Blancheflour*) or close companions (as in *Amis and Amiloun*). The romance is courtly, concerned with the chivalric codes governing behaviour and manners in all aspects of social life, love and battle.

Most English romances are translations from the French, though they rarely match the quality of their originals. Early romances without French counterparts – such as *Athelston*, *King Horn* and *The Tale of Gamelyn* – tell old English stories. Those which are not translations, like *The Squire of Low Degree*, draw from a stock of common motifs. This type appeared more frequently towards the end of the 15th century when the form was in decline, and these late romances often have little to recommend them.

Although romances are not concerned with individual characterization, the better ones explore the psychological development of the hero through his various adventures and hardships. Criticism or examination of the courtly life and society also appear in the more distinguished examples – like *Sir Gawain and the Green Knight*, the best of the English romances. A love interest and some supernatural content are common but not necessarily central; some poems usually classified as verse romances (such as *The Sowdon of Babylon*) are more concerned with military campaigns and the opposition of Christianity to pagan religions. The verse forms most frequently used are **tail-rhyme**, **alliterative verse** and the octosyllabic couplet.

*Verses on the Death of Dr Swift* A poem by **Jonathan Swift** himself, published in 1739, in which he imagines the circumstances of his own death, the reaction of those who had known him and his subsequent misrepresentation for posterity. The poet's irony and raillery about contemporary values, and his good-natured gibes at the expense of his friends, do not conceal the genuinely felt impression of the ingratitude and fickleness of human nature. Swift's auto-elegy is distinguished – like so much of his verse – by the superb modulation of its rhythms, which frequently imitate conversation or speech, and allow the satirist to duck in and out of his own arguments. It is one of the outstanding examples of an 'apologia pro vita et satura sua', a writer's defence of his life and satire.

**Vertue, George** 1684–1756 Engraver and antiquary. Born in London, Vertue learned the art of engraving from van der Gucht and was a member of Kneller's academy. Throughout his life he was constantly employed on major projects, such as Tindal's translation of Rapin's *History of England* (1736) and the Oxford Almanacks. He became a member of the Society of Antiquaries in 1717 and was appointed its official engraver. He spent a good deal of time collecting materials for a history of the arts in England and published *A Description of the Works of Wenceslaus Hollar* (1745) and a catalogue of Simon's numismatical collection in 1753. After his death **Horace Walpole** bought all Vertue's working papers from his widow and incorporated much of the material in his *Andecdotes of Painting*. The notebooks have also been published separately (Walpole Society, 6 vols., 1929–52). Walpole also published Vertue's catalogue of the collection of Queen Caroline and his transcriptions of the catalogues of the collections of Charles I and James II.

**Very, Jones** 1813–80 American poet, born in Salem, Massachusetts, and educated at Harvard. His first book, *Essays and Poems* (1839), was edited and published by **Ralph Waldo Emerson**. A mystic who believed in the absolute surrender of the will to God, he wrote devotional verse in the vein of the 17th-century English metaphysical poets. His work was highly praised by **William Cullen Bryant** and **William Ellery Channing** as well as by Emerson. Two volumes were published posthumously: *Poems* (1883) and *Poems and Essays* (1886).

*Vicar of Bullhampton, The* A novel by **Anthony Trollope**, serialized in monthly numbers from July 1869 to May 1870, and published in a single volume in 1870.

The vicar is Frank Fenwick, a clergyman 'who talked more of life with its sorrows, and vices, and chances of happiness, and possibilities of goodness, than he did of the requirements of his religion'. His vigorous, practical Christianity shows in his concern for two erring children of the local miller Jacob Brattle. When Sam Brattle is accused of complicity in the murder of a local farmer, the vicar saves him by helping to bring the real murderers to trial. He also rescues Sam's sister Carry, a fallen woman, from a life of destitution, restoring her to the home and eventual forgiveness of her stern old father. Frank's support of the Brattle family leads him into conflict with the local landowner, who causes a Dissenting chapel to be built at the vicarage gates only to have it pulled down when the land is discovered to belong to the vicarage after all. Love-interest is provided by the hopeless passion of the local squire, Harry Gilmore, for Mary Lowther, and her eventual marriage to her cousin Walter Marrable.

*The Vicar of Bullhampton* is notable for its sympathetic, if conventional, handling of the fallen woman Carry Brattle, and for the portrayal of Gilmore's unhappiness and the flinty integrity of Jacob Brattle.

*Vicar of Wakefield, The* The only novel by **Oliver Goldsmith**, written in 1761 or 1762 but not published until 1766.

The story is told by the Vicar himself, Dr Primrose. He has a wife, Deborah, and six children; despite Deborah's social aspirations the family is both comfortable and contented. Their hardships begin when Dr Primrose loses his personal fortune in the bankruptcy of a merchant company. He finds a new living through the patronage of Squire Thornhill but the Squire proves a villain, persuading the eldest daughter, Olivia, into a false marriage ceremony and then deserting her. She is found by her father and brought back to his modest vicarage but further misfortune follows when the house is destroyed by fire. Thornhill calls in Dr Primrose's debts

An engraving by Thomas Bewick for an edition of *The Vicar of Wakefield* published in 1798. Goldsmith's novel was first published in 1766.

but the Vicar cannot pay and is thrown into prison. George Primrose, a captain, challenges Thornhill to a duel but the Squire has him overpowered by thugs and put in prison as well. The younger daughter, Sophia, is abducted by an unknown villain and the deserted Olivia, so the Vicar is told, has died of grief. Dr Primrose endures all these blows with stoicism.

A kind-hearted but apparently seedy gentleman, Mr Burchell, whose advice to Mrs Primrose about her daughters' marriage prospects has been rejected by that socially ambitious lady, effects the rescue of Sophia and she begins to feel affection for him. Burchell proves to be Sir William Thornhill, uncle of the evil Squire. The Squire was Sophia's abductor, and Sir William proves also that Olivia's marriage was after all a true one and that she is not dead. George is able to marry his love, Arabella Wilmot, and Dr Primrose's fortune is restored to him by the reformation of the swindler, Ephraim Jenkinson.

The most famous novel published in the period between **Sterne** and **Jane Austen**, *The Vicar of Wakefield* has the perennial charm of a fairy-tale: the rural setting is cosy, the characters are divided into stereotypes of good and evil, and all their sufferings can be magically relieved by a happy ending. **Sir Walter Scott** observed that 'we return to it again and again, and bless the memory of an author who contrives so well to reconcile us to human nature'.

Three of Goldsmith's most famous short poems appear in the course of the story: 'The Hermit: or Edwin and Angelina', 'When Lovely Woman Stoops to Folly' and 'Elegy on the Death of a Mad Dog'. The novel was adapted for the stage by **W. G. Wills** as *Olivia* (1878), the new title indicating the change of emphasis. Ellen Terry played the part with great success.

***Vices and Virtues*** The earliest dialogue in Middle English to survive, written *c.* 1200 in or near

Kent. The beginning is lost. A Soul confesses in detail its sins to Reason and the latter explains the nature and value of the Christian virtues. The Body complains that the Soul and Body are of different composition, and Reason answers that they should work in accord and continues to discuss various virtues. It is a dignified and carefully ordered series of expositions, held together by the loose dialogue form. It includes an interesting allegorical representation of the meeting between Mercy, Truth, Pity, Peace and Patience.

***Victory*** A novel by **Joseph Conrad**, published in 1915.

Axel Heyst has inherited a cynical and disillusioned attitude towards life from his father. His reluctance to involve himself with others, during a wandering existence, is ended at the Indonesian island of Timor, where he impulsively assists the captain of a trading brig, Morrison, by paying his fines. As a consequence, Heyst is offered a share in the Tropical Belt Coal Company and, when Morrison dies, he becomes its owner. The Company fails but Heyst remains on the island of Samburan, alone except for his servant Wang.

His involvement with Morrison has further unforeseen results. In Sourabaya, the hotel keeper Schomberg has circulated baseless rumours that Heyst murdered Morrison and has secreted a fortune on the island. Schomberg's malignancy increases when Heyst, on a rare visit to civilization, rescues a young English girl, Lela, from Schomberg's unwanted attentions, and takes her to his island. At his hotel, Schomberg invites a trio of desperadoes to raid Heyst's island: the woman-hating 'plain Mr Jones', his 'secretary' Ricardo, and the Caliban-like Pedro.

Lena, who has worked some changes upon the character of Heyst, is found by Ricardo; she feigns sympathy for his plan to steal the illusory fortune, and (conscious that Heyst is unarmed) manages to take Ricardo's knife from him. Jones, who has been unaware of Lena's existence, finds her with Ricardo and fires at him; he kills him, but his first shot has mortally wounded Lena. Jones is drowned while trying to escape from the island. Lena dies in Heyst's arms with the smile of private 'victory' on her lips. Heyst commits suicide in despair; the bungalow in which Lena dies becomes their joint pyre.

**Vidal, Gore** 1925– American novelist and essayist, born in West Point, New York, and educated at the University of New Hampshire. Vidal served on army transports in the Aleutian Islands in World War II and then made use of his war experiences in his early novels, *Williwaw* (1946) and *In a Yellow Wood* (1947). The novel *The City and the Pillar* (1948, revised 1965) dealt

Gore Vidal, 1986.

frankly with homosexual life in America and became a best-seller. He followed this with the novels *The Season of Comfort* (1949), *A Search for the King* (1950), *The Judgement of Paris* (1952), *Messiah* (1954, revised 1965) and the collection of short stories *The Thirsty Evil* (1956). He became a playwright, first for television, with *Visit to a Small Planet* (published with others in 1957), and then for the theatre with *The Best Man* (1960), about an election campaign – based on his own experience of running for Congress that same year. *Rocking the Boat* (1962) was his first book of essays, *Washington DC* (1964) his first satire on American politics. The novels *Myra Breckenridge* (1968), *Two Sisters* (1970), *Burr: A Novel* (1973), *Creation* (1982), *Duluth* (1983) and *Lincoln* (1984), and the essay collections *Reflections on a Sinking Ship* (1969), *An Evening with Richard Nixon* (1972), *Matters of Fact and Matters of Fiction: Essays, 1973–1976* (1977) and *The Second American Revolution* (1982), all, in their different ways, present his tart, penetrating view of American life. Vidal also writes detective stories under the name of Edgar Box.

*Village, The* A poem in two books by **George Crabbe**, published in 1783.

Conceived as a counter-pastoral, the poem opposes descriptions of pain, want and deprivation to the idyllic sentimentalism of conventional **pastoral**. The addressee is, in the first instance, the poet, and then, by extension, the complacent reader, who is implicitly challenged to recognize his indulgence in decorous dreams of 'rural ease' as a displaced form of the excessive consumerism of labour-exploiting landlords. Crabbe fails to sustain this kind of attack

in the second book, and the poem ends with a rather lame homily on misery and distress as the general human condition, though both are earlier seen as the special preserve of the rural poor. The work was warmly approved by **Johnson** and **Burke**, and established Crabbe's reputation.

*Villette* A novel by **Charlotte Brontë**, published in 1853. The story develops material that she had already used in her first novel, *The Professor*, rejected by publishers and never issued during her lifetime.

Lucy Snowe, an English girl, gains a post as teacher in a girls' school at Villette, a town in Belgium based on the author's experience of Brussels. Though lacking in friends, beauty or money, she proves her worth to Madame Beck, the headmistress. She is condescendingly befriended by one of the pupils, the beautiful and vain Ginevra Fanshawe, who counts among her admirers Dr John Bretton, the son of Lucy's godmother. Observing his infatuation with Ginevra, Lucy represses her own feelings for him and Bretton, realizing Ginevra's vanity, falls in love with Paulina Home. Lucy buries herself in her work but gradually awakens to the fascination of the professor, Paul Emmanuel, a sharp-tongued, waspish, unattractive man who finds in her a response that mellows and softens him. When he is obliged to depart for the West Indies he leaves Lucy in charge of his school, promising to return in three years.

*Virgin-Martyr, The* A tragedy by **Philip Massinger** and **Thomas Dekker**, first produced about 1620 and published in 1622. The martyr of the title, Dorothea, is recorded in Church history (*Hieronymian Martyrology*) and her feast day is 6 February. She is usually called St Dorothy.

The Princess Artemia, daughter of Emperor Diocletian, is exhorted by her father to marry. She chooses Antoninus, the son of the governor of Caesarea; but Antoninus is devoted to Dorothea and declines the princess's hand. Theophilus, a tireless persecutor, and his secretary Harpax (who personifies evil) inform Artemia that Dorothea is a Christian. The furious princess finds Antoninus and Dorothea together and orders their execution; but she is persuaded by Theophilus to let him attempt to detach Dorothea from the proscribed faith. He sends his daughters to convert Dorothea but, in fact, she converts them. The enraged Theophilus kills his own daughters, and Dorothea, attended by Angelo (who personifies good), suffers extremes of torture before being executed; Antoninus dies at her side. The last part of the play is concerned with the struggle between Harpax and Angelo for the soul of Theophilus. Angelo prevails and Theophilus himself suffers martyrdom as a Christian.

**Virginian, The**: *A Horseman of the Plains* A romantic novel of the old West by **Owen Wister**, published in 1902. Extremely popular in its day, it is the prototype for the whole genre of Western novels and the source of much Western lore. Perhaps the most celebrated episode is the first confrontation between the hero, known only as 'The Virginian', and his sworn enemy, Trampas. Trampas accuses him of cheating in a poker game, whereupon the bold but gentle hero lays his pistol on the table and replies, 'When you call me that, smile!'

Set mostly in the Wyoming cattle country of the 1870s, the novel portrays the unrefined manly life of the cowboys. Civilization is on the move, however, and appears in the form of the pretty Vermont schoolteacher, Miss Molly Wood. The plot builds toward the marriage day of Miss Wood and the Virginian, when the hero is forced to kill Trampas in a show-down duel (probably the first portrayed in literature). Molly, who detests violence, has sworn to break the engagement if such an event were to occur, but she decides to accept the Virginian anyway. Thus the bond between the civilized and pioneer America is closed, but not without some bitter-sweet undertones on a way of life that will be lost for ever.

**Virginians, The** A novel by **W. M. Thackeray**, with illustrations by him, published in monthly numbers from November 1857 to September 1859, and in two volumes in 1858–9.

The story concerns the twin grandsons of Henry Esmond, George and Harry Warrington, and follows their fortunes in America and England from the mid-18th century to the American War of Independence. George, the elder, is heir to the Castlewood estate in Virginia, a thoughtful and studious youth who joins General Braddock's expedition against the French and is reported killed in action. Harry is the favourite of his mother, Rachel Warrington, Henry Esmond's only child, and is active, spirited and pleasure-loving. Despite differences of temperament, the two brothers are devoted to each other. Harry comes to England after George's presumed death and visits his Castlewood relations, where he becomes a favourite of his aunt, the Baroness Bernstein – the Beatrix of *Esmond*, now an old woman – and falls in love with his middle-aged cousin, Lady Maria Esmond. Introduced to fashionable society by his aunt, he gets a reputation for fast living and comes to weary of his engagement to Lady Maria. After initial success at cards, he gambles away his patrimony and ends in a sponging-house, from which he is rescued by the return of his brother George, escaped from French imprisonment. Harry is released from his engagement by Maria, now that he is no longer the heir.

George settles in London, turns to writing plays, and marries Theo Lambert, daughter of the honest middle-class Lambert family. His mother disapproves and stops his allowance, and the couple are hard pressed until by the death of his English uncle, Sir Miles Warrington, George succeeds to the title and the Warrington estates in England. Meanwhile Harry, taunted for his idleness by Theo's witty younger sister Hetty, who secretly loves him, joins the army, and serves with General Wolfe at the capture of Quebec. Later he sells his commission and buys an estate in Virginia, aided by a legacy from the Baroness Bernstein; he marries the daughter of his mother's companion. The brothers find themselves on opposing sides during the Revolution and George, who has fought for the king, retires to England, resigning his Virginian estate to Harry.

This stately and rather static historical romance continues the story of the Esmond family from **The History of Henry Esmond**, but lacks the psychological inwardness that gives the earlier novel its power and classic status.

**Vision, A** An occult and historical study by **W. B. Yeats**, first published in Dublin in 1925, and revised, enlarged and published in London in 1937. It contains three sections: 'A Packet for Ezra Pound', 'Stories of Michael Robartes and His Friends' and 'The Phases of the Moon'. The text also includes four of Yeats's poems, 'The Phases of the Moon', 'Huddon, Duddon and Daniel O'Leary', 'Leda' and 'All Souls' Night', and there is a woodcarving of Yeats in the guise of Giraldus, fictional author of the fictional medieval source of the book, the *Speculum Angelorum et Hominum*. Based on the automatic writing of his wife, by whom the Instructors give him 'metaphors for poetry', and on the occult material of the Rosicrucian society, The Order of the Golden Dawn, it relates historical, occult and astrological material to three related symbols: the Phases of the Moon, the Great Wheel and the Gyres. These have in common that they are symbols of perpetual recurrence on many levels, and that Yeats never explicitly claims to believe in them other than as 'an impulse to create'. Their influence on his work can be seen in *The Tower*, *The Winding Stair*, *New Poems* and *Last Poems*, and in the play *The Resurrection*.

**Vision of Judgement, A** A poem by **Robert Southey**, published in 1821. George III died in 1820 and Southey, as Poet Laureate, produced the required elegy. In a trance the poet sees the king rise from his tomb. Before entering Heaven's gate he is informed about the condition of England by the prime minister. Apparently all is well, though fanatics pursue what they believe to be liberty. At Heaven's gate the good spirits assemble to stand by the king. Evil spirits led by Satan arrive, accompanied by **Wilkes** and **Junius**, to speak against him. The presence of the Deity overwhelms the king's enemies, who retire discomfited, and George Washington (of all people) speaks on the king's behalf. He is admitted to Paradise and greeted by all the monarchs and great men of English history.

This ill-judged performance infuriated **Byron**, who held different views on the condition of England and resented Southey's abandonment of the radical beliefs he had once held. Southey attacked Byron's work in his preface and Byron replied with his own satirical *The Vision of Judgement*, taunting Southey again in the preface to *Don Juan*.

**Vision of Judgement, The** A satirical poem by **Byron**, prompted by **Southey**'s eulogy of George III, *A Vision of Judgement*. It was published in 1822 by **Leigh Hunt** in *The Liberal* after Byron's usual publisher, **John Murray**, had refused it. Hunt incurred a £100 fine and would probably have suffered a heavier penalty if he had included Byron's preface, which charged Southey with attempting 'to canonize a monarch, who, whatever were his household virtues, was neither a successful nor a patriotic king'.

Byron imitated Southey's poem closely, transforming its solemn heroics into comedy. The parody opens with St Peter sitting at Heaven's gate, bored for lack of work. When he is told of the king's death, he has no idea who he is. There is a striking encounter between the archangel Michael and Satan, and a series of comments by the king's critics. These are cut short, and Washington and Franklin prevented from speaking, by the entry of a devil carrying Southey. St Peter implores him to speak in prose but Southey insists on reading his *A Vision of Judgement*. In the ensuing uproar St Peter fells Southey with his keys and George III slips unnoticed into Paradise, where Byron leaves him 'practising the hundredth psalm'.

**Vittoria** A novel by **George Meredith**, published in 1867. It continues the story begun in *Sandra Belloni*.

The setting is northern Italy in 1848, when the Italians, inspired by Mazzini, are moving towards revolt against their Austrian overlords. The singer, Sandra Belloni, places herself at the disposal of the independence movement and agrees to appear in the opera at Milan under the name 'Vittoria' to sing the song that will signal the revolt. Suspicion falls on her because her English friend, Wilfred Pole, is an officer in the Austrian army. She marries the gallant patriot Carlo Ammiani, but the climate of suspicion and the enmity of Violetta d'Isorella and Anna von Lenkenstein involve Vittoria, Carlo and

Wilfred in a series of dangerous situations and Carlo is killed. She is comforted by the arrival of her friend Merthyr Powys.

**Vivian Grey** The first novel by **Benjamin Disraeli**, written to pay off debts on a failed newspaper venture, and published in 1826. Although Disraeli had a good ear for society conversation, his sense of characterization was unreliable and he failed, in this instance, to construct a plot. Vivian, a clever, manipulative young man, rejects Oxford to embark on political intrigue and overreaches himself. His beloved suddenly dies in his arms. He kills his man in a duel and is forced to go to Germany, where he is soon embroiled in German political intrigue. The book's most interesting character is Essper George, a conjuror of mysterious origins who gives up showmanship to become Vivian's servant and entertain his employer with tall stories. The book may owe something to the tradition of *Tom Jones* and *Peregrine Pickle*, with their scapegrace heroes, accompanied by faithful servants.

**Vizenor, Gerald** 1934– American Indian poet, a member of the Minnesota Chippewa tribe, born in Minneapolis, and educated at the University of Minnesota. His first collection of poetry, *Born in the Wind*, was privately printed in 1960. He has since published several volumes of English haiku poetry, including *Raising the Moon* (1964), *Seventeen Chirps* (1964), *Two Wings the Butterfly* (1967) and *Matsushima: Haiku* (1984). He also has edited several collections of American Indian writings, including *Ojibwa Lyric Poems and Tribal Stories* (1981), *Earthdivers: Tribal Narratives on Mixed Descent* (1981) and *The People Named the Chippewa: Narrative Histories* (1984).

**Volpone, or, The Fox** A comedy by **Ben Jonson**, often regarded as his masterpiece. It was first performed by the **King's Men** in 1605–6 (published 1607) and is the most frequently revived of Jonson's plays. Although formally set in Venice, *Volpone* directs its merciless moral scrutiny on the customs and values of the rising merchant classes of Jacobean London. Volpone, a wealthy Venetian without heirs, lets it be known that he is near death in the confident belief that avaricious legacy-hunters will flock to his bedside, there to be duped by Volpone and his quick-witted servant, Mosca (fly). On the promise of inheriting the dying man's fortune, three of Venice's leading citizens reveal their true corruption. The lawyer Voltore (vulture) is prepared to infringe the laws he claims to sustain. The decrepit Corbaccio (crow) will disinherit his own son. The sanctimonious Corvino (raven) will send his virtuous wife, Celia, to Volpone's bed. The exuberance of the two plotters, Volpone and Mosca, together with the vileness of their victims, comes close to excusing the criminality of their schemes, but Volpone overreaches himself when, having willed his property to Mosca, he pretends to be dead. The infuriated Voltore takes the matter to court, where Mosca recognizes and exploits the personal advantage of his master's 'death'. To thwart Mosca, Volpone has to come alive and reveal the whole plot, on the strength of which revelation he, along with everyone else, is appropriately punished. Only the virtuous – Corvino's wife and Corbaccio's son – are rewarded.

**Vonnegut, Kurt, Jr** 1922–  American novelist, born in Indianapolis, Indiana, and educated at Cornell and the University of Chicago. While serving in the infantry during World War II he was captured by the Germans, and his subsequent experiences as a prisoner of war in Dresden were to influence much of his work. *Slaughterhouse Five* (1969), his most famous novel, is specifically concerned with the bombing of Dresden by the Allies, and offers ironic commentary on both our inhumanity and the appalling opportunity for destruction provided by 20th-century technology.

**vorticism** A movement in British art, part of **modernism**, which flourished in 1913–15 with the writer and painter **Wyndham Lewis** as its leading figure. In October 1913 he quarrelled with the art critic Roger Fry and broke away from the Omega Workshops, dominated by the **Bloomsbury Group.** His followers included the painters Frederick Etchells, Cuthbert Hamilton and Edward Wadsworth. In March 1914 they

Kurt Vonnegut.

created the Rebel Art Centre, which attracted more artists – the sculptor Jacob Epstein and several poets of **imagism** – who rejected the prevailing orthodoxy of post-impressionism. They preferred German aesthetics, expressionism, cubism and futurism to the decorative art of Matisse. The term 'vortex' had been first used by **Ezra Pound** to describe the *avant-garde* spirit of London's art world, and was adopted by Lewis to signify his version of the concentrated energy of the new arts of modernism. Vorticism, so its principal exponents claimed, was in favour of activity and significance in art, essential movement, and the energy of the individual human mind. Vorticist paintings and drawings tended towards sharp-lined and angular abstraction and non-representation, though they often celebrated modern machinery and industrial landscapes. The vorticist magazine *Blast* – of which only two issues appeared, in July 1914 and July 1915 – was largely produced by Wyndham Lewis.

**Voss** A novel by **Patrick White**, published in 1957, about an expedition into the interior of Australia in the 1840s. The first part, which can be read as a fairly straightforward novel of manners, is set in Sydney society and describes preparations for the expedition. The long central section, which employs a dense, metaphorical style, is the story of the journey itself and of how the megalomaniac explorer Voss, whose beliefs are based on Schopenhauer's theory of the Will, gradually comes to acknowledge humility. The final section returns to Sydney and deals ironically with the making of the myth of Voss, who has perished, along with all the members of the expedition except one. The novel incorporates aspects of Jungian theory, particularly the notions of the anima and the mandala. Voss's actual journey is complemented by the metaphorical journey of Laura Trevelyan, a woman he only meets briefly on a few occasions and who remains in Sydney, but who functions as his anima and 'spiritual wife'. *Voss* was inspired by White's reading of the journals of the Australian explorers Leichhardt and Eyre. These provided him with the starting-point for an epic novel about the creation of an Australian identity, which also explores psychological, spiritual and gender issues.

**Voyage Out, The** The first novel by **Virginia Woolf**. It was written in 1912–13 but publication was delayed until 1915.

Unlike Virginia Woolf's later works, the novel is realistic in form, though it contains passages of lyrical intensity for which she became well known in subsequent novels. The story concerns a young woman of 24, Rachel Vinrace, an innocent, 'unlicked' girl who voyages to South America on board her father's ship, the *Euphrosyne*. Accompanying her are her aunt, Helen Ambrose, and uncle Ridley, together with an assortment of English characters whose social interaction is delicately observed. During the voyage the ship puts in at Lisbon, and Rachel meets Richard and Clarissa Dalloway, who reappear more prominently in the later novel *Mrs Dalloway*.

In South America Rachel meets a young Englishman, Terence Hewet, an aspiring writer working on his first novel: ' "I want to write a novel about Silence," he said; "the things people don't say." ' Rachel attempts to broaden her education by reading but finds herself out of sympathy with the male perspective of standard classics. Terence, in contrast to other men, is interested in women's experiences and concerned about their position in society. 'Doesn't it make your blood boil? If I were a woman I'd blow some one's brains out.' He and Rachel fall in love and become engaged, determined to establish their future marriage on a new basis of equality. However, during an expedition Rachel contracts an unspecified disease and is confined to her bed with a fever. After a fortnight's illness she dies. The novel concludes with an image of the English party at the hotel retiring: 'a procession of objects, black and indistinct, the figures of people picking up their books, their cards, their balls of wool, their work-baskets, and passing . . . one after another on their way to bed'.

*Vulgar Errors* See *Pseudodoxia Epidemica*.

# W

**Wace** See **Arthurian literature**.

**Waddell, Helen (Jane)** 1889–1965 Scholar, translator and novelist. The daughter of an Ulster Presbyterian missionary, she was born in Tokyo and educated at Victoria College and Queen's University, Belfast. After an early career of miscellaneous writing, including *The Spoiled Buddha*, a play produced in 1915 by her brother **Rutherford Mayne**, and a volume of *Lyrics from the Chinese* (1915), she was able to go to Oxford in 1919 to study medieval literature. After further study in Paris and London she produced her masterpiece, *The Wandering Scholars* (1927), a pioneering study of European learning in the 12th century and the sometimes ribald Goliardic verse associated with it. Her distinguished book of verse translations, *Medieval Latin Lyrics*, and her learned but lively and moving novel *Peter Abelard* were both published in 1933. Her other writings include wartime journalism, translations of medieval saints' lives (*Beasts and Saints*, 1934) and the *Vitae Patrum* (*The Desert Fathers*, 1936) and a second play, *The Abbé Prévost* (1933), but her main achievement was to rekindle interest in the spirituality and the Latin literature of early medieval Europe.

**Waddell, Samuel J.** See **Mayne, Rutherford**.

**Waddington, Miriam (née Dworkin)** 1917– Canadian poet. Born in Winnipeg, the daughter of Russian Jewish immigrants, she was educated at the universities of Toronto and Pennsylvania. She has been a social worker in Montreal and Professor of English and Canadian Literature at York University in Toronto (1964–83). Her first poems were published in 1943 in the Montreal little magazine *First Statement* and her first collection of poetry, *Green World*, in 1945. Her other volumes include *The Second Silence* (1955), *The Glass Trumpet* (1966), *Say Yes* (1969), *Driving Home* (1972), *The Price of Gold* (1976) and *The Visitants* (1981). Her short stories are collected in *Summer at Lonely Beach* (1982). With their meticulous craft and their lyric celebration of the baffling richness within common things, her poems have appeared in many Canadian anthologies, and some have been set to music by Canadian and American composers. She is also a distinguished critic and translator of prose and poetry from the Yiddish.

**Wade, Thomas** 1805–75 Poet and playwright. Born at Woodbridge in Suffolk, Wade published a volume of poetry, *Tasso and the Sisters* (1825), before turning to a play in verse and prose, *Woman's Love, or The Trial of Patience* (1829), which his friend Charles Kemble produced successfully at **Drury Lane**. A farce, *The Phrenologists* (1830), was also successful but *The Jew of Arragon*, a tragedy produced in the same year, failed. Wade published some volumes of verse, wrote two other plays which were not produced, and was the editor of *Bell's Weekly Messenger* and *Wade's London Review*. His remarkable sonnets were published in a volume entitled *Mundi et Cordis: De Rebus Sempiternis et Temporariis: Carmina* (1835).

**Wain, John** 1925– Novelist, poet and critic. Born in Stoke-on-Trent, Wain was educated in Newcastle and at St John's College, Oxford, where he was subsequently a fellow from 1946–9. He lectured in English at Reading University in 1949–55, and was Professor of Poetry at Oxford in 1973–8. His own poetry, possessed of a dry, cerebral wit, is collected in *Poems 1949–79* (1981).

Wain's first novel, *Hurry On Down* (1953), remains his most famous; it narrates the picaresque career of the university graduate Charles Lumley, whose deliberate flight down the social scale away from all conventional expectations of self-advancement leads him to work as a window-cleaner and thence into other increasingly unpropitious occupations. It is regarded, along with **Kingsley Amis**'s *Lucky Jim* and **John Braine**'s *Room at the Top*, as one of the best **Angry Young Men** novels.

Wain's later novels, which have attracted less notice, include *The Contenders* (1958), *Strike the Father Dead* (1962), *The Smaller Sky* (1968) and *A Winter in the Hills* (1971), a rampageous comedy about a linguist's researches into local dialect among a suspicious and narrow North Wales community. His most recent novel, *Young Shoulders* (1982), a sensitive study of juvenile bereavement, won the Whitbread Prize for Fiction.

Wain has also published two volumes of short stories, *Nuncle* (1960) and *Death of the Hind Legs* (1966), a biography of **Samuel Johnson** (1974), several volumes of literary criticism, and is the author of many broadcast radio plays.

**Wainwright, Jeffrey** 1944– Poet and critic. He was born in Stoke-on-Trent and educated there and at the University of Leeds. He has taught at the University of Wales, Aberystwyth, Long Island University, Brooklyn, and Manchester Polytechnic. Early influences included **Geoffrey Hill**, **Jon Silkin** and **Ken Smith**. Wainwright's pamphlet *The Important Man* (1970) includes 'Three Poems on the Battle of Jutland 1916', '1815', 'Sentimental Education' and 'The Garden Master'. They are poems of political commitment although riven with irony and self-questioning, and his language is terse and humane. Poems from *The Important Man* were included in Wainwright's widely acclaimed first book, *Heart's Desire* (1978), which also added 'Thomas Muntzer', a major political poem about a 16th-century German radical and visionary executed during the Peasant War. Wainwright's adaptation of *Le Mystère de la charité de Jeanne d'Arc* by Péguy was performed by the **Royal Shakespeare Company** in 1984.

**Waiting for Godot** A play by **Samuel Beckett**, originally written in French and first performed in Paris in 1953. Beckett's own English translation was first presented at the Arts Theatre, London, in 1955, directed by Peter Hall.

In Act One, two tramps, Vladimir and Estragon, wait beside a leafless tree (the stage is otherwise bare) for the arrival of Godot, with whom they believe they have an appointment. In order to pass the time, or perhaps simply to accompany the passing of time, they play verbal games reminiscent of the cross-talk of music-hall comedians. When Pozzo arrives, holding his slave Lucky with a rope, the tramps wonder if he is Godot, but Pozzo denies all knowledge of Godot. To the discomfort and confusion of Vladimir, Estragon and the audience, he makes Lucky 'dance' and then 'think'. The long tirade of Lucky's thought is allusive and incoherent. Master and slave depart and a boy arrives to tell the tramps that Godot will not be coming that day 'but surely tomorrow'.

In Act Two the tree has leaves, but there is little other evidence of change as Vladimir and Estragon continue waiting. Pozzo enters again, but blind and dependent on the guiding rope that binds Lucky to him. Lucky is now dumb, but Pozzo is unaware of any difference. When they have gone, a boy, who may or may not be the same boy but who claims to be his brother,

The first production in English of *Waiting for Godot* took place at the Arts Theatre, London, on 3 August 1955. Peter Woodthorpe as Estragon (left), and Paul Daneman as Vladimir.

arrives with the same message. Still determining to go, the tramps do not move. As one critic observed, 'Nothing happens – twice.'

*Waiting for Godot* inspired a great variety of interpretative criticism, much of it centred on the character of the cryptic Godot. The play's allusiveness seemed mischievously to invite such speculation by its allusiveness. Its real subject, though, is not Godot but waiting.

**Waiting for Lefty** A play by **Clifford Odets**, first produced in New York in 1935, when its reference to the previous year's taxi strike gave it the urgency of political propaganda. It was published in England by the **Left Book Club** in 1937.

Within the framework of a corrupt union meeting – the theatre audience is addressed as if it were at the meeting – short naturalistic scenes involving characters and issues affected by the union's decision are acted out. The play ends when the union bosses are exposed and a rallying call for strike action is flung out at the actual theatre audience.

**Wake, William** 1657–1737 Divine. Born into a family of landowners at Blandford in Dorset, he completed his education at Christ Church, Oxford, and became chaplain to the English ambassador in Paris in 1682. His ambition to achieve a union between the Church of England and the Gallican Church came to nothing, but he is remembered in religious literature for his translation, *The Genuine Epistles of the Apostolic Fathers* (1693), and for *The State of the Church and Clergy of England* (1703). Wake became Archbishop of Canterbury in 1716.

**Wakefield cycle, the** See **miracle plays**.

**Wakoski, Diane** 1937– American poet, born in Whittier, California, and educated at the University of California at Berkeley. Her first volume of verse, *Coins and Coffins*, was published in 1962 and has been followed by over 30 more. With its frequent use of autobiographical material, much of her work resembles that of the **Confessional** poets. In particular, she focuses on her unhappy childhood and, in poems concerned with adult life, on her painful experiences with men. Her other volumes include *Discrepancies and Apparitions* (1966), *The George Washington Poems* (1967), *Greed Parts One and Two* (1968), *Thanking My Mother For Piano Lessons* (1969), *The Lament of the Lady Bank Dick* (1970), *The Pumpkin Pie, or, Reassurances Are Always False, Tho We Love Them, Only Physics Counts . . .* (1972), *Dancing on the Grave of a Son of a Bitch* (1973), *Looking For The King of Spain* (1974), *Waiting For The King of Spain* (1976), *The Lady Who Drove Me to the Airport* (1982) and *The Collected Greed, Parts 1–13* (1984). She has also published three volumes of prose: *Form Is an Extension of Content* (1972), *Creating a Personal Mythology* (1975) and *Towards a New Poetry* (1979).

**Walcott, Derek (Alton)** 1930– Theatre director, playwright, poet, born in Castries, St Lucia. His first three volumes of verse were published in Trinidad between 1948 and 1953 but his widespread recognition as a poet came with *In a Green Night* (1964), *The Castaway* (1965) and *The Gulf* (1969) – ironic, antithetical poetry of personal and artistic discovery, with delicate physical description as a means of taking psychological bearings and finding anchorage. Walcott has worked manfully for a Caribbean culture subsuming African, Indian and European origins in the region he describes as 'Our hammock swung between Americas' ('Elegy', *Gulf*). He tries to alchemize 'where nothing was/the language of a race' ('Crusoe's Journal', *Castaway*) out of various despised patois and metropolitan English, with which to confront Caribbean individual, historical and racial contradictions. With the impressive autobiographical poem, *Another Life* (1973), his poetry becomes both more supple in versification and even more linguistically disciplined. Poetry, detached and sceptical but simultaneously 'religious' in drift, has followed in *Sea Grapes* (1976), *The Star-Apple Kingdom* (1980) and *The Unfortunate Traveller* (1982). *Midsummer* (1984) disappointingly shows little further development. *Selected Poetry* appeared in 1981. Walcott's plays enact many of his interior explorations, combining much folk-activity, like singing, story-telling, and dancing, with colloquial, richly metaphorical speech: *Henri Christophe*

(1950), *Henri Dernier* (1951), *Ione* (1954), *Drums and Colours* (1961), *The Dream on Monkey Mountain* with *Ti-Jean and His Brothers, Malcochon, and The Sea at Dauphin* (1971), *The Joker of Seville* with *O Babylon* (1978), *Remembrance* with *Pantomime* (1980). 'What the Twilight Says', with which he introduces the *Monkey Mountain* volume, is an illuminating essay on the West Indian creative imagination.

***Walden, or, Life in the Woods*** An autobiographical narrative by **Henry David Thoreau**, published in 1854. It describes a two-year period from March 1845 to September 1847 during which the author retired from the town of Concord to live alone at nearby Walden Pond. This was Thoreau's own **Transcendentalist** experiment, equivalent in many ways to that of **Brook Farm**: he sought to put into action a programme of self-reliance, whereby the individual spirit might thrive in its detachment from the fractured world of mass society.

Much of the book was derived from the journals Thoreau kept during his stay. Comprising 18 essays, it effectively creates a sense of the multiple dimensions of the author's self. His prose can be complex and poetically evocative,

Walden Pond, *c*.1886. From an etching by W. B. Classon for *Homes and Haunts of the Poets*.

but also lucid, even scientifically direct; at times he engages in allegory and parable. Other passages catalogue the various animals and plants in the area. The narrative often digresses into lengthy discussions of philosophy and poetry; famous sections involve Thoreau's visits with a Canadian woodcutter and with an Irish family, a trip to Concord and a description of his bean field.

**Waldhere** An Old English poem of which only two brief fragments survive. It was apparently quite long and told a well-known story recorded in a Latin poem by Ekkehard of St Gall (d. 973). Hildegund, Walter and Hagen are prisoners of Attila of the Huns. Hagen escapes to join Gunther, king of the Franks. Walter and Hildegund, who are lovers, also escape with much treasure and Gunther persuades the reluctant Hagen to accompany him and 11 warriors going to rob them. In a narrow pass Walter kills all but Hagen and Gunther, and these three are maimed. The surviving fragments are from speeches, the first by Hildegund and the second from the end of Gunther's speech with Walter's reply.

**Waley, Arthur (David)** 1889–1966 Poet and Sinologist. He was born Arthur David Schloss in Tunbridge Wells, Kent, and educated at Rugby and King's College, Cambridge. Waley (he adopted his mother's surname in 1914) taught himself Chinese and Japanese while working in the Print Room of the British Museum. He is best known for his translations: *A Hundred and Seventy Chinese Poems* (1918); *The Tale of Genji* (6 vols., 1925–33), an 11th-century Japanese novel; *The Pillow-Book of Sei Shonagon* (1928); *The Analects of Confucius* (1938); and *Monkey* (1942), a 16th-century Chinese novel. His other work included *The No Plays of Japan* (1921), *The Poetry and Career of Li Po, AD 701–762* (1951) and the miscellany *The Secret History of the Moguls* (1964). Waley's work, which contributed greatly to the interest in the East during the 1920s, was related to **imagism**, especially to **Pound**'s *Cathay* (1915) and **Amy Lowell**'s *Fir Flower Tablets* (1921).

**Walker, Alice** 1944– American novelist and poet, born in Eatonton, Georgia, into a family of sharecroppers, and educated at Spelman College and Sarah Lawrence College.

Her first publications were two collections of poetry: *Once: Poems* (1968), which reflects her experience of the civil rights movement and her travels in Africa, *Revolutionary Petunias and Other Poems* (1973), which is a tribute to those who struggle against racism and oppression. Her first novel, *The Third Life of Grange Copeland* (1970), is the story of three generations of black tenant farmers from 1900 to the 1960s. A book of short stories, *In Love and Trouble: Stories of Black Women* (1973), explores the experience and heritage of black women, a theme to which Walker returns in a second collection, *You Can't Keep a Good Woman Down* (1981). The epistolary novel, *The Color Purple* (1982), which won a Pulitzer Prize, centres on the life of Celie, a black woman who has been raped by the man she believed to be her father. She bears his children, and then is forced to marry an older man whom she despises. The novel is made up of Celie's despairing letters to God and to her sister Nettie who has gone to Africa as a missionary, and of Nettie's letters to Celie. Walker's other publications include a biography for children, *Langston Hughes, American Poet* (1974), *Meridian* (1977), a novel about the lives of civil rights workers in the South during the 1960s, and two collections of poems, *Good Night, Willie Lee, I'll See You in the Morning* (1979) and *Horses Make a Landscape Look More Beautiful: Poems* (1984). A volume of essays appeared in 1983 entitled *In Search of My Mother's Garden: Womanist Prose*.

**Walker, George (Frederick)** 1947– Canadian playwright. He was born into a working-class family in Toronto's East End. Much of his work – including his first play, *The Prince of Naples* (1971), *Beyond Mozambique* (1974) and *Ramona and the White Slaves* (1976) – has resulted from his connection with the Factory Theatre Lab, where he has worked as playwright-in-residence and later as an associate director. *Gossip* (1977) and his gothic comedy *Zastrozzi* (1977) have enjoyed productions in the USA, Britain and Australia. An urban playwright, Walker is influenced by the **Theatre of the Absurd** as well as television and films. In his own words, his plays 'try to walk that fine line between the serious and the comic', their characters finding their obsessions 'a way of coping with life and surviving'.

**Walker, Kath[leen] (Jean Mary)** 1920– Australian Aboriginal poet, Kath Walker grew up on Stradbroke Island, Moreton Bay, Queensland, where many of the old Aboriginal customs survived. She did not begin writing until the 1950s, but swiftly gained popularity with a white Australian audience with her collection *We Are Going* (1964). The title poem is a moving elegy on the dispossession of the Aboriginal people. Other poems, including 'Municipal Gum', call attention to their plight. Later collections are *Dawn is at Hand* (1966) and *My People* (1970).

**Wallace** A poem written *c.*1477 by the Scottish poet **Blind Harry**, relating the life of Sir William Wallace and his struggle against the English. The work is divided into 12 books. The first two introduce the patriotic hero and Books III–VI give vivid descriptions of his battles and tell how he was made Guardian of Scotland. The poem continues to develop the figure of Wallace as a hero of mythic proportions. His final betrayal to the English and consequent execution by Edward I in 1305 (Book XII) are glossed over in favour of reinforcing the poem's image of Wallace as a saintly national hero. It enjoyed enduring popularity and influenced, amongst others, **Robert Burns** and **William Wordsworth**. Despite its exaggeration and the addition of some fictional incidents, the poem is a major source of information about the life of Wallace.

**Wallace, Lew[is]** 1827–1905 American novelist, born in Indiana. Wallace spent much of his life as a soldier. He served in the Mexican War and earned distinction in the Civil War, reaching the rank of major general. He lived for a time in Mexico, then returned to Indiana to practise law and to write. *The Fair God* (1873) tells of the Spanish conquest of Mexico. His next book, *Ben-Hur* (1880), was an enormous success, selling over two million copies. His third book was a work of non-fiction, *The Boyhood of Christ* (1888). He served as governor of New Mexico and in 1881 became the US minister to Turkey. He also wrote other works of fiction, a tragic poem, *The Wooing of Malkatoon* (1897), and an autobiography.

**Wallace, (Richard Horatio) Edgar** 1875–1932 Thriller writer. Born and brought up in the slums of south-east London, he worked in a printing firm, shoe shop and rubber factory and as a merchant seaman, plasterer, milk delivery boy and soldier before serving as correspondent for Reuters and *The Daily Mail* in the Boer War (1899–1902). For the rest of his life he combined newspaper work with a prodigious writing career which began with *The Four Just Men* (1906) and extended to nearly 100 more thrillers, over 50 volumes of short stories, nearly 30 plays and screenplays, four volumes of verse and many miscellaneous books, including three autobiographies and a ten-volume history of World War I. Critical success played no part in Wallace's ambition. He sought and gained the widest possible readership, becoming a wealthy and influential public figure. The 11 books featuring 'Sanders of the River' were among his most popular works. Of his **detective fiction**, the stories about J. G. Reeder were particularly successful: *Room 13* (1924), *The Mind of Mr J. G. Reeder* (1925), *Terror Keep* (1927), *Red Aces* (1929) and *The Guv'nor* (1932).

**Wallace-Crabbe, Chris** 1934– Australian poet and critic. Born in Melbourne, he was educated at Scotch College, Melbourne, and at Melbourne University. From 1965 to 1967 he was a Harkness Fellow at Yale University. He subsequently joined the Department of English at Melbourne University, where he is now a professor. Wallace-Crabbe's poetry is frequently concerned with the shaping of beliefs. An early absorption with rationalism quickly crystallized itself into an attempt to write poetry which moved beyond a purely personal lyrical vision to a more objective consideration of social and political issues. In his more recent poetry Australian themes loom larger. His *Selected Poems* (1973) reprints poems from his four earlier volumes, *The Music of Division* (1959), *In Light and Darkness* (1964), *The Rebel General* (1967) and *Where the Wind Came* (1971), as well as including a number of new poems. This volume also groups together a number of 'Meditations' inspired by his response to Turner's painting. Wallace-Crabbe has also published *The Emotions Are Not Skilled Workers* (1980). His critical writing includes *The Australian Nationalists* (1971) and *Three Absences in Australian Writing* (1983).

**Wallant, Edward (Lewis)** 1926–62 American novelist, born in New Haven, Connecticut. Wallant served in the US Navy during World War II, graduated from Pratt Institute in 1950, and worked in New York City advertising agencies until his death. His first story was published in 1955; *The Human Season*, his first novel, which appeared in 1960, is the story of a middle-aged immigrant Jew following the death of his wife. *The Pawnbroker* (1961), Wallant's most acclaimed work, is one of the first American novels to consider the atrocities that occurred during World War II. Sol Nazerman, a Polish Jew, is the sole member of his family to have survived a Nazi concentration camp; he is now living in Harlem, New York City, where he owns a pawnshop and relives the horrors he endured in his nightmares and in flashbacks. Wallant's early death cut short a brief yet accomplished career. Two works were published posthumously: *The Tenants of Moonbloom* (1963) and *The Children at the Gate* (1965).

**Waller, Edmund** 1606–87 Poet. The eldest son of a wealthy landowner, Waller was born at Coleshill, now in Buckinghamshire, and educated at Eton and King's College, Cambridge. Elected to Parliament when he was only 16, he gained a reputation as a brilliant orator, possessing (said **John Aubrey**) 'a great mastership of the English Language'. A member of **Lucius Falkland**'s philosophical circle at Great Tew, Waller sought, in the troubled 1640s, to steer a politically moderate course between the king and his opponents. In 1643, however, he plotted to oust the Parliamentary rebels and secure London for the royal cause. The plot was discovered and Waller confessed. Summoned before Parliament, he pleaded eloquently for clemency, was fined heavily and exiled. Settling in Paris, he also travelled in Italy and Switzerland with his friend, the diarist **John Evelyn**. In 1652 he was allowed to come home to England, and was returned to Parliament and into royal favour at the Restoration. He died in his bed, aged 82.

For most of his long lifetime, Waller was a famous wit and poet, renowned for both lyric and panegyric. To **Dryden**, he embodied both sweetness and correctness. **Pope** acknowledged him as a master and, as late as 1766, the *Biographia Britannica* proclaimed him 'the most celebrated Lyric Poet that ever England produced'. Waller's subsequent reputation fast declined: **Samuel Johnson** found evidence of moral vacuity in his willingness to pen panegyrics both on the death of Cromwell and the return of Charles. (When Charles trenchantly observed that the former was much the better poem, Waller is said to have replied: 'Sir, we poets never succeed so well in writing truth as in fiction.') Waller's eulogy of the Dutch Wars, *Instructions to a Painter* (1666), is unread, survived by its parody, **Andrew Marvell**'s *Last Instructions*. The lyrics addressed to Lady Dorothy Sidney, whom he courted in the 1630s, in the guise of Sacharissa were renowned in his own century, but today only two of his short pieces are well known: 'On a Girdle' and the exquisite song, 'Go, Lovely Rose'.

Waller deserves recognition for the refinement he brought to the **heroic couplet** and to standards of poetic eloquence and linguistic purity (he was a member of the Royal Society committee for 'improving the English tongue'): in this, he proved a significant model for 18th-century ideals of literature.

**Wallis, John** 1616–1703 Mathematician. Educated at Felsted School, near his birthplace, and at Emmanuel College, Cambridge, at a time when 'Mathematicks . . . were scarce looked upon as Academical Studies', Wallis became Savilian Professor of Geometry at Oxford (1649–1703) and was one of the founders of the Royal Society. His *Arithmetica Infinitorum* (1655) contains the first evaluation of $\pi$ as a method of measurement, the first use of the symbol for infinity, and the germ of the differential calculus. A moderate Puritan, Wallis used his mathematical skill to decipher Royalist code messages during the Civil War.

**Walmsley, Leo** 1892–1966 Novelist and playwright. Born in Shipley, West Yorkshire, Walmsley served with distinction in the Royal Flying Corps in Africa before settling first on the Yorkshire coast and later in Cornwall. He is best known for his regional novels, in which he portrayed the austere and often dangerous lives of the Yorkshire fishermen, with their loves, their hates, and their struggles with storm and tide. Of some dozen novels, charming for their simplicity and honesty rather than subtlety, *Three Fevers* (1932), *Foreigners* (1935) and *Sally Lunn* (1937, later dramatized) stand out. Walmsley also wrote an autobiography, *So Many Loves* (1944).

**Walpole, Horace, 4th Earl of Orford** 1717–97 Letter-writer and aesthetician. Born in London, the youngest son of Sir Robert Walpole, though malicious rumour of the time suggested that his true father was Lord Hervey, he was educated at Eton and King's College, Cambridge. In March 1739 he set off on a Grand Tour to Italy with **Gray** (during the course of which they disagreed and separated), returning in 1741 to England where Walpole in his absence had been elected MP for Callington, Cornwall. His *Aedes Walpolianae* (1747), an annotated catalogue of the extensive family collection of paintings, was his first contribution to art studies, and in the same year he moved to Twickenham and started to Gothicize Strawberry Hill, an activity which continued for nearly 25 years. The fame of this reconstruction, aided by the publication in 1774 of his *Description of the Villa of Horace Walpole*, was a major factor in the Gothic movement in both architecture and landscape gardening. The *Description* was printed on his own press installed at Strawberry Hill, the first important publication from which had been an edition of *Odes by Mr Gray* (1757). This was followed by Walpole's own *Catalogue of the Royal and Noble Authors of England* (1758), a combination of bibliography, antiquarianism and criticism which was a typical product of his interests and abilities. Other similar influential works were his reworking of the manuscripts of Vertue as *Anecdotes of Painting in England* (1762–71), his own *Catalogue of Engravers who Have Been Born or Resided in England* (1763), *Historic Doubts of the Life and Reign of Richard III* (1768), *Essay on Modern Gardening* (1785) and an edition of Lucan's *Pharsalia* with **Bentley**'s notes (1760). These works were distinguished both by their scholarship and the quality of the printing. In addition to contributing a number of minor pieces to journals, Walpole also wrote **The Castle of Otranto** (1764). This tale, which he initially attempted to pass off as a translation from an Italian original, set out 'to blend the wonderful of old stories with the natural of modern novels'. Its main interest resides in the fact that it was the first of a long line of far more successful **Gothic fiction** by writers such as **Reeve**, **Radcliffe** and **Lewis**. He followed *Otranto* with a blank-verse tragedy, *The Mysterious Mother* (1768), which, having as its central theme the protagonist's remorse for a previous act of

Horace Walpole's villa at Strawberry Hill. A detail from a watercolour by Paul Sandby, c.1775. Castle Museum, Nottingham.

incest, was not regarded as a suitable piece for presentation on stage, though later it was admired by **Byron**. In 1769 **Chatterton** sent Walpole a number of his forgeries, to which Walpole replied showing some interest. He was speedily disabused by Gray and **William Mason**, and wrote to Chatterton indicating that the pieces were not authentic. On hearing of the suicide of the forger Walpole appears to have been genuinely upset. Walpole's political connections and his own career as an MP for, successively, Callington, Castle Rising and Lynn, provided him with much inside information relating to government which he recorded and left sealed. His *Memoirs of the Last Ten Years of the Reign of George the Second* appeared in 1822; *Memoirs of the Reign of George the Third* in 1845; and *Journal of the Reign of King George the Third from the Year 1771 to 1783* in 1859. These editions are textually unreliable.

All his other works are insignificant in comparison with his letters. Throughout his life Walpole was an indefatigable letter-writer; over 4000 are extant, and he wrote with some *brio* covering a wide range of interests. Antiquarian topics were discussed with Cole; political matters with Mann; literature with Gray, Mason and Madame du Deffand (whose correspondence with Walpole is preserved only in letters from her, he having requested that his own be destroyed, presumably because of a feeling of inadequacy in his French); and social gossip with George Montagu and the Countess of Upper Ossory. He wrote his letters with an eye to publication, successfully requesting the return of about 1000, which he then annotated for the benefit of future editors. The first group to be treated in this way, a batch originally sent to Mann, were returned to Walpole as early as 1749. His reputation was impugned by **Wordsworth**, **Coleridge**, **Keats** and **Hazlitt** who

wrongly thought him responsible for the death of Chatterton; his literary works were praised by Byron and **Scott**; his political memoirs were considered poisonous by the Victorians.

**Walpole, Sir Hugh (Seymour)** 1884–1941 Novelist. Born in New Zealand, he was educated at King's School, Canterbury, and Emmanuel College, Cambridge. His first novels were *The Wooden Horse* (1910) and *Maradick at Forty* (1910), but it is for *Mr Perrin and Mr Traill* (1911) – which started the vogue for school stories and was based on his own brief experiences as a teacher – that he is chiefly remembered. *Fortitude* (1913) and *The Duchess of Wrexe* (1914) established his popular reputation.

During World War I he worked with the Russian Red Cross and was awarded the Order of St George. His experiences provided the background for *The Dark Forest* (1916) and *The Secret City* (1919), awarded the James Tait Black Memorial Prize. Other popular school stories followed with *Jeremy* (1919), *Jeremy and Hamlet* (1923), and *Jeremy at Crale* (1927). A family saga set in Cumberland, *The Herries Chronicle*, was enormously popular; it included *Rogue Herries* (1930), *Judith Paris* (1931), *The Fortress* (1932), and *Vanessa* (1933). *Farthing Hall* (1929) was written in collaboration with **J. B. Priestley**.

In total, Walpole produced over 40 popular novels, but he never achieved the literary status won by contemporaries like **Virginia Woolf**, whose **modernism** he envied. Among his nonfiction were *Joseph Conrad* (1916), *The Art of James Branch Cabell* (1920) and *Anthony Trollope* (1928). *The Crystal Box* (1924), *The Apple Trees* (1932) and *Roman Fountain* (1940) were autobiographical.

**Walsh, Jill [Gillian] Paton** 1937– Children's novelist. Born in London and educated at St

Michael's Convent and St Anne's College, Oxford, she began writing after she left the teaching profession in 1962 to raise a family. *Farewell the Great King* (1972) and several subsequent novels use a historical setting. *The Emperor's Winding-Sheet*, winner of the Whitbread Award in 1974, is about an English boy caught up in the final siege of Constantinople, while *A Parcel of Patterns* (1983) takes place in the village of Eyam during the plague. *A Chance Child* (1978) mixes historical elements with fantasy, linking the brutality of life in a modern slum to the horrors of child labour in Victorian England. She has also produced several powerful novels dealing with the problems of adolescence: *Goldengrove* (1972) and its sequel *Unleaving* (1976), tracing the growth of the heroine Madge, are her most ambitious works. *The Dolphin Crossing* (1967) and *Fireweed* (1969) are set during World War II.

**Walsh, William** 1663–1708 Critic and poet. His pastorals and amorous verses were fashionable at the end of the 17th century, but his more enduring claim to attention rests on his encouragement of the young **Alexander Pope**. Walsh praised Pope's *Pastorals* and suggested improvements to them. He advised Pope to work towards an ideal of 'correctness' in his poetry, and engaged in extensive critical correspondence with him. Pope published their letters in 1735. Walsh's *Works in Prose and Verse* were printed in 1736, and **Johnson** included a biography of Walsh in his *Lives of the English Poets*.

**Walton, Izaak** 1593–1683 Biographical and piscatorial writer. Born in Stafford, Walton went to London in 1618 and was apprenticed to a draper, and then an ironmonger, eventually making himself prosperous through his own drapery business. Until 1643 he lived in the parish of St Dunstan's, where **John Donne** was the vicar, and the two became friends. As a result of this, Walton made the acquaintance of **Herbert**, **King**, and **Wotton**, the distinguished Provost of Eton. From the latter, who died in 1639, Walton took over the writing of the 'Life' of Donne, which appeared in the 1640 edition of the poet's sermons. This was followed by a further series of 'Lives', each of which the author scrupulously updated, in his characteristic fashion; these were of Wotton himself (1651), **Richard Hooker** (1665), George Herbert (1670) and Bishop Sanderson (1678), all Anglican churchmen. Walton was a robust Royalist – but no Laudian – and his several ecclesiastical connections included the families of his two wives. After the Restoration of the monarchy he moved to Worcester as Steward to Bishop Morley, and then to Winchester, where he died in his ninetieth year, and was buried in the Cathedral. His unique place in English letters, and his international reputation, is really the result of *The Compleat Angler*, a classic book on fishes and fishing which was published in 1653 and has since been reprinted on many hundreds of occasions.

**Wanderer, The** An Old English poem preserved in **The Exeter Book**. The structure is somewhat ambiguous: the poem may represent a monologue containing two reported speeches or, alternatively, speeches by different characters. The first speech or quotation says that the solitary wanderer often experiences the grace of God despite the hardships he endures. There follows a long personal account of exile leading the speaker to wonder that his suffering and the general state of decay of the world do not make him miserable. Finally the voice of wisdom asserts that the world's wealth is transitory and faith in God is the only source of security. Although the dramatic form is obscure, the thought is clearly developed.

**Wanley, Nathaniel** 1634–80 Poet and cleric. He was born in Leicester, educated at Trinity College, Cambridge, and spent most of his adult life as vicar of Holy Trinity, Coventry. His religious verse, *Scintillulae Sacrae*, declares its debt to **Henry Vaughan** in its title; these meditations, and the narratives *The Witch of Endor* and *Lazarus* were first collected in 1928. His prose compilation, *The Wonders of the Little World* (1678), was one of the sources of **Robert Browning**'s *The Pied Piper of Hamelin*.

**War of the Worlds, The** A novel by **H. G. Wells**, published as a serial in *Pearson's Magazine* in 1897 and reprinted in book form in 1898.

The first part of the novel describes how missiles fired from Mars land in England, arousing only mild interest until they disgorge fearful war machines to devastate the country. Panic spreads as resistance fails and London is destroyed. In the second part survivors of the catastrophe live in hiding; a curate and an artilleryman offer opposed philosophies in reaction to the invasion, the latter dreaming hopelessly of revolution against the world's new masters. In the end, though, the loathsome Martians are unprotected by their armoured weapons against the ravages of earthly bacteria, which succeed where men's best efforts failed in destroying them. Wells takes a certain delight in contemplating the destruction of English society, but with characteristic ambivalence also displays a sympathetic appreciation of the magnitude of the tragedy.

This archetypal story of alien invasion provided a model for countless cruder imitations; a famous radio adaptation by Orson Welles was realistic enough to cause panic in the USA in 1938.

**Ward, Artemus** The pseudonym of the American humorist Charles Farrar Browne (1834–67). He was born in Waterford, Maine, and was for the most part self-educated. From 1857 to 1859 he wrote for *The Cleveland Plain Dealer*, and during this period created Artemus Ward – the writer of mock letters to the editor, full of colloquial language and misspellings that result in puns or malapropisms. Browne left Ohio in 1859 to join the staff of New York's *Vanity Fair*; later, as the journal's editor, he came to be known as the 'unofficial dean of American humor'.

He was a pioneer in the genre of the comic lecture – a form of entertainment **Mark Twain** would later capitalize on. His targets were Abolitionists, Mormons, Shakers, feminists, temperance movements, and anyone else he considered hypocritical or ineffectual. His publications include *Artemus Ward, His Book* (1862), *Artemus Ward, His Travels* (1865) and *Artemus Ward Among The Ferians* (1866). While on a lecture tour in England (1866–7, during which time he contributed to **Punch**), he died of tuberculosis. *Artemus Ward In London and Other Papers* was published posthumously in 1867.

**Ward, Edward** 1667–1731 A London tavern keeper with a gift for doggerel verse, Ned Ward was also a reporter of life in the capital. In *The London Spy*, begun in 1698, he uses the device of a countryman who meets a London friend while visiting the city and is taken everywhere to see almost everything. The 18 sketches were collected in 1703. Ward wrote quantities of verse in the manner of **Samuel Butler** and was notoriously indiscreet in his comments on the contemporary scene. He was sentenced to the pillory for passages in *Hudibras Redivivus* (1705).

**Ward, Mary Augusta** 1851–1920 Novelist. Mrs Humphry Ward, as she was better known, was born in Hobart, Tasmania, where her father, Thomas Arnold, younger brother of **Matthew Arnold**, had become inspector of schools, a post he relinquished on his conversion to Roman Catholicism in 1856. In 1858, two years after the family's return to England, Mary was sent to the first of a series of private boarding schools whilst her father worked in Roman Catholic educational institutions in Dublin and Birmingham. She rejoined her family in 1867 when her father's return to Anglicanism enabled him to teach in Oxford. In 1876 her father's reconversion to Roman Catholicism necessitated another move, but by this time Mary had been married for four years to Thomas Humphry Ward, an Oxford don and later the art critic for *The Times*.

Acquaintance with leading Oxford figures such as **J. R. Green**, **T. H. Green**, **Benjamin Jowett**, **Walter Pater** and **Mark Pattison** encour-

aged her academic interests. She contributed the lives of early Spanish ecclesiastics to the *Dictionary of Christian Biography* and became the first secretary of Somerville College in 1879. The Arnold family history, combined with her friendship with leading anti-dogmatic theologians, resulted in her defence, in pamphlet and novel form, of an unorthodox religious position close to that of her uncle Matthew Arnold's. She argued for a religious faith which, freed from the need to believe in the historical truth of the Gospel, could concentrate upon applying the spiritual truths of Christianity to practical humanitarian work. Her novel **Robert Elsmere** (1888) records the intellectual and emotional implications of such a spiritual pilgrimage, whilst the next phase of her own life showed its practical results. In 1881 the Wards moved to London where, in addition to literary reviewing, editing, and the writing of further novels, she involved herself in the work of the Passmore Edwards Settlement opened in Bloomsbury in 1897. Here she instituted recreational activities for children and developed an educational programme for the physically handicapped. Despite her support for higher education for women and her active political campaigning on behalf of her own son, she disapproved of female suffrage sufficiently to become President of the Women's Anti-Suffrage League (1908). During the war President Theodore Roosevelt persuaded her to write for the American public a series of letters and articles describing the Allied war effort, later published in England as *England's Effort* (1916), *Towards the Goal* (1917) and *Fields of Victory* (1919). In the year of her death she was appointed one of the first seven women magistrates. Apart from *Robert Elsmere*, the most notable of her 25 novels are, *The History of David Grieve* (1892) and *Helbeck of Bannisdale* (1898) for their treatment of religious issues, and *Marcella* (1894) and *Delia Blanchflower* (1915) for their debate of social and political issues. *A Writer's Recollections* (1918) provides interesting accounts of the many major literary figures she had met, including **George Eliot** and **Henry James**, and a record of the social and intellectual life of Oxford in her early years. Her translation of the *Journal Intime* of the Swiss mystic Henri Amiel (1885) long remained the standard English edition.

**Ward, Nathaniel** 1578–1652 American Puritan writer. Born in Essex, he emigrated to Massachusetts in 1634 and became influential in the colony's politics. His literary reputation rests on his **The Simple Cobler of Aggawam**, written in 1645 and published in London in 1647. He returned to England in 1646 and remained there for the rest of his life, but retained his ties with his American friends, and wrote a poem commending **Anne Bradstreet**'s collection, *The Tenth Muse*, which was included in the first edition (1650).

**Warden, The** A novel by **Anthony Trollope**, the first of the **Barsetshire** series, published in one volume in 1855.

The Revd Septimus Harding is an elderly clergyman who has been appointed by the Bishop of Barchester to be warden of Hiram's Hospital, an almshouse for 12 old men funded from a medieval charity. A gentle and unworldly man, Mr Harding never questions the discrepancy between his comfortable annual salary and the small weekly allowance given to the old men, until the issue is taken up by a local reformer, John Bold, and denounced as a flagrant Church abuse by the *Jupiter* newspaper (*The Times*). Bold is the suitor of Mr Harding's youngest daughter, Eleanor, and abandons the campaign at her request. But battle has been joined between the metropolitan reformers and the conservative clerical party led by Archdeacon Grantly, Mr Harding's son-in-law, and the warden resigns, 'not so anxious to prove himself right, as to be so'. Bold marries Eleanor, and Mr Harding leaves his pleasant home and garden for lodgings in Barchester.

A subtle study of the clash between public rhetoric and individual conscience, *The Warden* is one of the finest and most characteristic of Trollope's works. It contains an implicit defence of his own art and moral vision in the parodies of **Carlyle** as Dr Pessimist Anticant and **Dickens** as Mr Popular Sentiment.

**Ware, Sir James** 1594–1666 Irish antiquarian and historian. Born in Dublin, he was educated at Trinity College. His father was Attorney-General of Ireland, an office to which Ware succeeded in 1632, three years after he had been knighted. His great work, *Antiquities of Ireland*, began to appear in 1626; the final instalment did not appear until 1654. During this time Ware's political position exposed him to the hazards of the contemporary crises in England. He was imprisoned by the Parliamentarians for 10 months in the Tower of London in 1644 and exiled to France for two years in 1649 on the orders of the Puritan Deputy in Dublin. Before he died, in Ireland, Ware brought out a second edition of the *Antiquities* (1659), *Annals of Ireland* (1664), *Lives of the Irish Bishops* (1665) and *Works Ascribed to St Patrick* (1656). His most popular work for a time was *Writers of Ireland* (1639). Ware's reputation as a reliable scholar and historian suffered grievously because of the later interpolations and forgeries introduced into his writings by his son Robert. The full extent of these corruptions was not exposed until 1917.

**Warner, Charles Dudley** 1829–1900 American novelist and essayist. Born in Massachusetts, Warner received his BA in 1851 from Hamilton College and, following brief employment as a railroad surveyor in Missouri, studied law at the University of Pennsylvania. He practised law in Chicago until 1860, when he turned to writing professionally. He is best remembered for *The Gilded Age* (1873), his first published novel, which was written in collaboration with **Mark Twain**. He also produced several collections of essays, including *Summer in a Garden* (1870), *Being a Boy* (1878) and *The Relation of Literature to Life* (1896). He devoted his later years to writing a trilogy of novels: *A Little Journey in the World* (1889), *The Golden House* (1894) and *That Fortune* (1899).

**Warner, Rex** 1905–86 Poet, novelist and translator. Born in Gloucestershire, educated at St George's School, Harpenden, and Wadham College, Oxford, he became a schoolteacher in England and Egypt until the end of World War II. In 1945–7 he was director of the British Institute in Athens and became a respected translator. He was a professor at the University of Connecticut from 1964 to 1974.

Warner's first volume of poetry, *Poems* (1937), was inspired by anti-totalitarian fervour, a quality which he shared with many of his contemporaries during the 1930s, notably **W. H. Auden** and **Christopher Isherwood**. *The Wild Goose Chase*, a novel published in the same year, and *The Professor* (1938) were more bleak, showing the influence of Kafka in their use of mysterious allegory and an atmosphere of threat and guilt. *The Aerodrome* (1941) involved the conflict between an unnamed but quintessentially English village representing the fallen human condition, unregenerate but moderately happy, and the aerodrome, whose personnel believe in cleanliness, health and discipline.

Warner's many notable translations include: Euripides' *Medea* (1944), *Hippolytus* (1950) and *Helen* (1951); Aeschylus' *Prometheus Bound* (1947); Xenophon's *Anabasis* (1949); Thucydides (1954); and Plutarch (1958). In 1960 he produced a translation of the modern Greek poet George Seferis. His studies of classical subjects include *The Young Caesar* (1958) and *Pericles the Athenian* (1963).

**Warner, Susan B[ogert]** 1819–85 American novelist (pseudonym: Elizabeth Wetherell), born in New York City. At the age of 30 Warner began to write in order to assist her family's finances. Her first novel, *The Wide Wide World* (1850), describes the moral and religious development of a 13-year-old orphan. It was a best-seller, as was her second novel, *Queechy* (1852). She followed these with numerous other novels and children's books, some written with her sister, Anna B. Warner. Among her other novels are *Mrs Rutherford's Children* (1853–5), *The Old Helmet* (1863), *Melbourne House* (1864), *Daisy* (1868), *Wych Hazel* (1876), *My Desire* (1879), *Nobody* (1882) and *Stephan, MD* (1883).

**Warner, Sylvia Townsend** 1893–1978 Novelist, poet and short-story writer. The daughter of a master of Harrow School, she received no formal education but absorbed a wide range of knowledge from her parents and read voraciously. She joined the editorial board of the Church Music project in 1917 and spent the next 10 years working on the 10-volume *Tudor Church Music*. Her early poems were praised by **Housman** and **Yeats**, and Louis Untermeyer compared her to **Thomas Hardy**. Other writers who influenced Warner were **T. F. Powys**, whom she met in 1923, and **David Garnett**. She was a regular contributor to *The New Yorker* for many years. Her first novel, *Lolly Willowes*, was published in 1926. *Mr Fortune's Maggott* (1927) relates the story of a missionary, Mr Fortune, who goes to the island of Fanua to convert the natives, with little success. A month spent in the mysterious world of the Essex marshes inspired *The True Heart* (1929). A story of love, in its many forms, it shows Warner at her imaginative and lyrical best. Her volumes of poetry include *The Espalier* (1925), *Time Importuned* (1928), *Opus 7* (1931) and *Rainbow* (1932). Novels published after *The True Heart* were *Summer Will Show* (1936), *The Corner That Held Them* (1948), *The Flint Anchor* (1954). *A Garland of Straw* (1943) and *Museum of Cheats* (1947) were volumes of short stories. Warner lived with the writer Valentine Cunningham from the early 1930s until Cunningham's death in 1969.

**Warner, William** ?1558–1609 Poet and translator. Warner was educated at Oxford and became an attorney in London. His *Pan his Syrinx* (1584) is a collection of seven prose tales. He translated the *Menaechmi* of Plautus (1595), but it is unlikely that **Shakespeare** had seen the unpublished manuscript when he wrote his *The Comedy of Errors*, which also draws on *Menaechmi*. Warner's major work is *Albion's England*, a verse history of Britain in 14-syllable lines, which had a high reputation in its own time. The four-book first edition of 1586 tells the story from Noah to the Norman Conquest with many mythical episodes. Later editions carry the history on to the accession of Henry VII (1589) and that of Elizabeth (1592). It was further enlarged in the early 17th century and the 1612 version takes the history up to the reign of James I.

**Warren, Mercy Otis** 1728–1814 American playwright. The sister of James Otis, a Colonial political leader, and the wife of James Warren, the president of the Provincial Congress of Massachusetts, Mercy Warren was at the centre of Revolutionary politics and in frequent correspondence with Revolutionary leaders. She is best known for her anti-Loyalist political dramas *The Adulateur* (1773) and *The Group* (1775). Other plays have been attributed to her, most notably *The Blockheads* (1776) and *The Motley Assembly* (1779). She also published a collection of dramatic verse, *Poems Dramatic and Miscellaneous* (1790), which contains two verse tragedies, 'The Sack of Rome' and 'The Ladies of Castille', and a three-volume *History of the Rise, Progress and Termination of the American Revolution* (1805), which serves as an important contemporary record of the Revolutionary years.

**Warren, Robert Penn** 1905–89 American poet and novelist, born in Guthrie, Kentucky, and educated at Vanderbilt, the University of California at Berkeley, Yale, and Oxford. A member of the group of poets known as the 'Fugitives', he helped to found and edit the group's magazine, *The Fugitive* (1922–5). His first work, a biography entitled *John Brown, the Making of a Martyr*, was published in 1929. The following year he contributed to the Southern Agrarian manifesto, *I'll Take My Stand* (1930).

He published his first book of verse, *Thirty-Six Poems*, in 1935. It was followed by many others, including *Brother to Dragons: A Tale in Verse and Voices* (1953), *Promises: Poems 1954–1956* (1957), for which he was awarded a Pulitzer Prize, *Now and Then: Poems 1976–1978* (1978), for which he won a second Pulitzer, and most recently *Chief Joseph of the Nez Percé* (1983). In 1986 he was appointed the first US Poet Laureate. In addition to poetry, he wrote nine novels and two collections of short stories. His fiction often deals with Southern history and generally has Southern settings. *Night Rider* (1939), his first novel, is about the Kentucky tobacco wars; its protagonist, Percy Munn, helps to organize a group of 'night riders' to combat the tobacco buyers' ring and becomes a hunted outlaw. *All the King's Men* (1946), perhaps his most famous novel, is the story of Willie Stark, who enters the political arena, engages in corrupt politics, becomes governor of a Southern state, and then dies a tragic death. It was awarded the Pulitzer Prize for fiction in 1947 and was made into a movie in 1949. The story of *World Enough and Time* (1950) is based on an 1826 murder trial in Kentucky. *Band of Angels* (1955), a tragedy of miscegenation, was followed by *Wilderness: A Tale of the Civil War* (1961); *Flood: A Romance of Our Times* (1964), the story of a Tennessee Valley Authority dam project; and *A Place to Come To* (1977).

His numerous works of non-fictional prose include *Segregation: The Inner Conflict in the*

South (1956), *Remember the Alamo!* (1958), *Who Speaks for the Negro?* (1965), *Homage to Dreiser* (1971), *Democracy and Poetry* (1975) and *Jefferson Davis Gets His Citizenship Back* (1980). He also wrote or edited several volumes with **Cleanth Brooks**, including *Understanding Poetry: An Anthology for College Students* (1938, revised in 1950 and 1960), *Understanding Fiction* (1943, revised in 1958) and *Modern Rhetoric: With Readings* (1949, revised in 1958). Together, he and Brooks founded and edited *Southern Review* (1935–42).

**Warren, Samuel** 1807–77 Novelist. Born in Lancashire of a devoutly religious family, he studied medicine at the University of Edinburgh, changed to the law and was called to the English Bar in 1837. He became a bencher of the Inner Temple in 1851, Recorder for Hull in 1852–74 and Conservative MP for Midhurst in 1856–9. His first work of fiction, the melodramatic *Passages from the Diary of a Late Physician*, appeared in *Blackwood's Magazine* in 1830–7. *Ten Thousand a Year*, serialized in *Blackwood's* from 1839 and published complete in 1841, scored a great success and led some reviewers to compare Warren favourably with the young **Dickens**. Packed with sensational incident, as well as portraits of the legal profession and high society, the novel tells of the rise and fall of Mr Tittlebat Titmouse. *Now and Then* (1847) was less successful, and Warren turned to writing legal textbooks.

**Warton, Joseph** 1722–1800 Critic. The son of **Thomas Warton the elder** and brother of **Thomas Warton the younger**, he was born at Dunsfold in Surrey. He became headmaster of Winchester College, which he had attended before going to Oriel College, Oxford, and was prebendary of both Winchester and St Paul's cathedrals. He is remembered for his literary criticism, particularly his essays on **Pope** (1756, 1782), rather than for his own books of verse and his translations of the *Eclogues* and *Georgics* of Virgil. Warton also edited the works of Pope (1797) and **Sidney**'s *Apology for Poetry* (1787).

**Warton, Thomas, the elder** 1688–1745 Scholar, poet, and father of **Joseph Warton** and **Thomas Warton the younger**. He was educated at Hart Hall and Magdalen College, Oxford, where he was a fellow in 1717–24. He held the Professorship of Poetry from 1718 until 1728. In 1723 he also became vicar of Basingstoke and master of its grammar school, where **Gilbert White** was one of his pupils. Joseph Warton prepared his father's *Poems on Several Occasions* for posthumous publication in 1748. The two Runic Odes included in the volume influenced **Thomas Gray**.

**Warton, Thomas, the younger** 1728–90 Poet and literary historian. The younger son of **Thomas Warton the elder** and younger brother of **Joseph Warton**, he was educated at home in Basingstoke until he entered Trinity College, Oxford, in 1744. He became a fellow in 1751 and remained an academic all his life.

Warton encouraged Oxford literary life, writing occasional verse himself – 'The Pleasures of Melancholy' (1747), 'The Triumph of Isis' (1749), 'Newmarket, a Satire' (1751) – and editing anonymously *The Oxford Sausage, or, Select Poetical Pieces Written by the Most Celebrated Wits of the University of Oxford* (1764). He worked on the history of his college and produced lives of two distinguished Trinity men: Ralph Bathurst, a former President, and Sir Thomas Pope, the founder (1761 and 1772). He edited *The Union or Select Scots and English Poems* (Edinburgh, 1753).

Like his contemporary **Francis Grose**, Warton had a high regard for Gothic architecture. Some of his notes on the subject were used after his death in the volumes called *Essays on Gothic Architecture by the Rev. T. Warton, Rev. J. Bentham, Captain Grose, and the Rev. J. Milner* (1800). The records of his antiquarian tours of England and Wales are preserved in a manuscript now at Winchester College. He published *A Description of the City, College and Cathedral of Winchester* in 1750.

Along with this passion for the Gothic went a special love of early English literature. His *Observations on the Faerie Queene of Spenser* (1754; enlarged edition, 2 vols., 1762) earned the praise of **Samuel Johnson**. Thus began a long, if not always easy friendship. In 1755 Warton helped obtain for Johnson the MA degree which conferred academic respectability upon the title-page of the *Dictionary of the English Language*. *The Idler* papers 33, 93 and 96 were written by Warton; and he may have contributed pieces, as yet unidentified, to other periodicals. In 1782 he was admitted to the famous Club centred upon Johnson.

Warton was elected Professor of Poetry at Oxford in 1757 and, like his father, occupied the Chair for two successive five-year terms. He lectured in Latin on classical poetry. He produced editions of the Greek Anthology (1766) and Theocritus (1770).

Histories of English poetry had been projected by **Pope** and by **Gray**. Warton saw but did not use the latter's plans. His own *History of English Poetry from the Close of the Eleventh to the Commencement of the Eighteenth Century*, including discussions of 'the Origin of Romantic Fiction in Europe' and 'the Introduction of Learning into England', appeared in three volumes in 1774–81. 88 pages of a fourth volume were printed in Warton's lifetime but not published until Price's four-volume edition

Booker T. Washington.

for promoting vocational instruction at the expense of liberal education. Washington's publications include *The Future of the American Negro* (1899), *Sowing and Reaping* (1900), *Character Building* (1902), *Working with the Hands* (1904), *The Story of the Negro* (1909), *My Larger Education* (1911) and *The Man Farthest Down* (1912). His biography of **Frederick Douglass** (1906) is widely considered to be a pioneering work in the field. His autobiography, *Up From Slavery*, was published in 1901.

**Washington Square** A short novel by **Henry James** published serially in *The Cornhill Magazine* in 1880 and in volume form in 1881. The motherless daughter of a wealthy New York physician, Catherine Sloper is unappreciated and ignored by her father, and leads a lonely and bleak existence until she is courted by Morris Townsend. She accepts his proposal of marriage, but her father refuses to give his consent when he discovers Townsend to be a penniless fortune-hunter. Exasperated by Catherine's obstinate attachment, Dr Sloper takes her away to Europe for a year. This does not change her mind, but Morris, faced with the prospect of

An illustration by George Du Maurier for Henry James's *Washington Square* (1881).

of 1824. Warton's *History* is a mine of information about English literature down to the end of the reign of Elizabeth I. It ranks with **Thomas Percy**'s *Reliques* as a crucial document in the revival of interest in medieval and 16th-century poetry; and, in its shift away from exclusively classical tenets, it anticipates the spirit of Romanticism.

Warton's later years were in some ways his most illustrious. A collected edition of his poems was published in 1777 and went through four editions before his death. Much of his verse imitated **Spenser** and **Milton**, and he revived interest in the **sonnet**, a form so important to the next generation of poets. He contributed to the **Chatterton** controversy with *An Enquiry into the Authenticity of the Poems Attributed to Rowley* (1782). In 1785 he became Camden Professor of Ancient History at Oxford, published a first-rate edition of Milton's early poems and became Poet Laureate.

**Washington, Booker T[aliaferro]** 1856–1915 Black American leader, born in Hale's Ford, Virginia, the son of a slave mother and a white father. He urged a programme of gradual development for blacks, and emphasized training in the techniques of agricultural and industrial production. These policies soon brought him into conflict with **W. E. B. Du Bois** and other black leaders. Du Bois attacked him for not taking a sufficiently forceful stand on disenfranchisement in the South, and criticized him

Catherine having to forfeit her inheritance if she marries him, breaks off the engagement. Seventeen years later, after the death of her father has made Catherine a rich woman, Morris returns and proposes again. She rejects him absolutely and settles down to the life of a spinster in the family house in Washington Square.

**Waste Land, The** A poem by **T. S. Eliot**, published in 1922. At first attracting both praise and derision for its radically experimental technique, it became his most influential work and hence one of the most influential 20th-century poems.

The title, suggested by Jessie L. Weston's study of the Grail legend, *From Ritual to Romance* (1920), refers to a dry and desolate country which can be revived by a fertility ritual. Using this as his central symbol for European life after World War I, Eliot explores the various aspects of its sterility in five sections: 'The Burial of the Dead', 'A Game of Chess', 'The Fire Sermon', 'Death by Water' and 'What the Thunder Said'. The method throughout is deliberately fragmentary, abandoning traditional verse forms for **free verse** to juxtapose monologues or overheard snatches of conversation by the inhabitants of the waste land with allusions, not merely to the Grail legend, but to previous literature (**Shakespeare** and Dante in particular), religious teaching (the Bible, St Augustine, and the Upanishads) and myth. The resulting 'heap of broken images' both intensifies the portrait of spiritual decay and hints at the possibility of redemption. With its repeated chant of 'Shantih', which Eliot himself suggested can be translated as 'The Peace which passeth understanding', the ending is deliberately enigmatic. Much critical interpretation of *The Waste Land* has concentrated on gauging the extent of its pessimism.

The poem appeared in the first issue of *The Criterion*, which Eliot edited, in October 1922 and again a month later in *The Dial* (New York). When it appeared in book form, also in 1922, it included footnotes by Eliot, explaining his allusions but rarely resolving other complexities of the text. The original manuscript was published in facsimile, with an introduction by his widow, Valerie Eliot, in 1971. Considerably longer than the published version, it shows the cuts and revisions proposed by **Ezra Pound**, to whom the poem is dedicated.

**Water-Babies, The**: *A Fairy Tale for a Land Baby* A fantasy written by **Charles Kingsley** for his youngest son, as *The Heroes* was written for his older children. It was serialized by *Macmillan's Magazine* in 1862–3 and published in volume form in 1863. Tom, a young chimney-sweep, runs away from his brutal employer, Grimes. In his flight he falls into a river and is transformed into a water baby. Thereafter, in the river and in the seas, he meets all sorts of creatures and learns a series of moral lessons.

**Waterhouse, Keith (Spencer)** 1929– Novelist, dramatist and journalist. Born and educated in Leeds, he made his name as a novelist with *Billy Liar* (1959). Its superficial similarities with the provincial realism of contemporaries like **John Braine** and **Stan Barstow** are tempered by a whimsical streak: Billy is a compulsive dreamer who inhabits his own fantasy world of Ambrosia. A belated sequel, *Billy Liar on the Moon* (1976), takes up Billy's fortunes in London, with much satirical treatment of modern urban desolation – a theme Waterhouse returned to in his most recent novel, *Maggie Muggins* (1981). He has also pursued a successful career as a polemical, witty journalist and collaborated with **Willis Hall** in many works for stage, screen and television. Their plays together include an adaptation of *Billy Liar* (1960), *Celebration* (1961), *All Things Bright and Beautiful* (1963) and a comedy of adulteries, *Say Who You Are* (1965), as well as adaptations of Eduardo de Filippo's *Saturday, Sunday, Monday* (1973) and *Filumena* (1973).

**Waterman, Andrew (John)** 1940– Poet. He grew up in the South London suburbia which is the carefully evoked setting for many of his poems. After leaving home at the age of 17 he did various clerical and manual jobs before reading English at the University of Leicester. He teaches at the New University of Ulster, Coleraine. His first collection, *Living Room* (1974), announced his preoccupation with the journey from London childhood to present-day Ulster and his interest in conversational or demotic language. *From the Other Country* (1977) was followed by *Over the Wall* (1980), which showed a new assurance. The remarkable title sequence of *Out for the Elements* (1981) – 187 stanzas in a form borrowed from Pushkin but in spirit Wordsworthian – traces the growth of a poet's mind and, true to **Wordsworth**'s precepts, does so in determinedly ordinary language. *Selected Poems* appeared in 1986.

**Watership Down** A novel by **Richard Adams**, published in 1972. It found a large adult readership only after initial success as a children's book. *Watership Down* is a long and intricately plotted anthropomorphic fantasy about a community of rabbits in Berkshire who set out to found a new warren. While its allegory of human society extends to the semi-mystical overtones of an enigmatic God-rabbit, El-a-H'rairah, Adams's novel is also notable for its authentic account of rabbit behaviour and its sensitive evocation of the natural world of the Berkshire Downs.

**Watkins, Vernon (Phillips)** 1906–67 Poet. Born in Maesteg, Glamorganshire, to Welsh-speaking parents, Watkins was educated at Swansea Grammar School, Repton School, and Magdalene College, Cambridge. He worked as a clerk at Lloyds Bank in Swansea until 1965, apart from wartime service in the RAF. His collections include *The Ballad of the Mari Lwyd and Other Poems* (1941), *The Lady with the Unicorn: Poems* (1948), *The Death Bell: Poems and Ballads* (1954), and the posthumous volumes *Fidelities* (1968) and *The Collected Poems* (1986). Throughout his poetic career, Watkins pursued one theme: the time-annulling revelation of the transcendent. His poetry aims to create a controlled music through which we may enter into an experience that is both simple and overwhelming. He much admired **Yeats**, and this helped to offset the influence of the **New Apocalypse** poets and **Dylan Thomas**, his long-standing friend.

**Watson, Richard** 1737–1816 Polymath. Born at Heversham in Westmorland, he studied mathematics at Trinity College, Cambridge. With no training in the subject, Watson succeeded in becoming Professor of Chemistry at Cambridge in 1764. With no training in divinity, he became Regius Professor in that subject (1771) and held several church livings; he was appointed to the see of Llandaff in 1782 and went to live on Lake Windermere. His *Apology for Christianity, in a Series of Letters to E. Gibbon* (1776), prompted by Chapters XV and XVI of the first volume of **The Decline and Fall of the Roman Empire**, was courteously acknowledged by the historian. Watson was also the author of *Apology for the Bible, in Answer to Thomas Paine* (1796).

**Watson, Sheila** 1919– Canadian writer. Born in New Westminster, British Columbia, she was educated at the University of British Columbia and taught at various universities including the University of Alberta. Her first story, 'Brother Oedipus', was published in the *Queen's Quarterly* in 1954. Her novel, *The Double Hook* (1959), an attack upon the rural naturalism of much Canadian literature, received much critical and popular attention. *Four Stories* was published in 1980.

**Watson, Thomas** ?1557–92 A translator and minor Elizabethan poet, Watson was educated at Oxford and afterwards studied law in London. It was probably on a visit to Paris in 1581 that he first met Sir Thomas Walsingham, who was to become his patron. Watson had a reputation as a considerable classicist even at Oxford. His translation of Sophocles' *Antigone* with appendices of Latin allegorical poems and metrical exercises was printed in 1581. His Latin hexameter paraphrase of Tasso's *Aminta* (1585) was Englished by Abraham Fraunce without acknowledgement to Watson. *Raptus Helenae* (1586) is a Latin translation from the Greek of Coluthus. *The First Set of Italian Madrigals Englished* (1590) contains English versions of Italian madrigals, mainly those of Marenzio. Watson mourned his patron Walsingham's death in a Latin elegy (1590) which he translated into English and published in the same year. His Latin pastoral *Amintae Gaudia* was printed posthumously in 1592.

Watson is notable as an English poet largely for his sonnets. *The Hekatompathia, or Passionate Century of Love* (1582) is a collection of 18-line poems which Watson calls 'sonnets'. They are mainly imitations of classical, Italian and French models or contain paraphrases from classical and continental authors. It may well be that **Shakespeare** had one of these poems, an extended and highly wrought catalogue of a mistress's charms, in mind when he wrote sonnet 130, 'My mistress' eyes are nothing like the sun'. *The Tears of Fancy*, printed posthumously in 1593, contains 60 sonnets, largely inspired by Petrarch and Ronsard. The miscellanies also contain Watson's poems: **The Phoenix Nest** prints three previously unpublished poems, **England's Helicon** five (only one is new) and **A Poetical Rhapsody** prints ten poems from *Hekatompathia*.

**Watson, Sir William** 1858–1935 Poet. Born in Yorkshire, he published several volumes of poetry heavily indebted to **Tennyson**, among them *Wordsworth's Grave* (1890), *Lachrymae Musarum* (1892) which included poems on the death of Tennyson, *The Year of Shame* (1896) and *The Heralds of Dawn* (1912). His *Collected Poems* appeared in 1899 and 1906.

**Watts, Isaac** 1674–1748 Hymnwriter. The son of a Nonconformist minister and teacher, Watts was born in Southampton. His abilities marked him out at the local grammar school and a patron offered him a university education. However, Watts preferred to attend the Dissenters' Academy at Stoke Newington, where educational standards were exacting and where **Daniel Defoe** had also been taught. In 1700 Watts became assistant pastor, and then pastor, at the Independent Congregation in Mark Lane, but his health deteriorated after 1703 and he resigned in 1712. Thereafter he lived at Abney Hall, in Stoke Newington.

Watts promoted the practice of hymn singing in Nonconformist congregations where the Metrical Psalms had previously been the only music heard. His principal collections were *Hymns and Spiritual Songs* (1707) and *The Psalms of David* (1719); he also published *Divine Songs* (1715), the first hymn book composed for children, and a book of verse, *Horae Lyricae* (1706).

Among his lasting and popular hymns are 'Our God, our help in ages past', 'Jesus shall reign where'er the sun', and 'When I survey the Wondrous Cross'. **John Wesley** changed the opening of his most famous hymn to 'O God, our help in ages past' and **Lewis Carroll** parodied Watts in *Alice's Adventures in Wonderland* ('How doth the little busy bee').

**Watts–Dunton, (Walter) Theodore** 1832–1914 Novelist and critic. Born Theodore Watts (he changed his name by deed poll) at St Ives, now in Cambridgeshire, he went to school in Cambridge and practised as a solicitor in London. He published contributions to *The Athenaeum*, some Shakespearean criticism, a volume of poetry and *Aylwin* (1898), a novel which includes a thinly disguised portrait of **Dante Gabriel Rossetti**. Also a student of gypsy life, he edited **George Borrow**'s *Lavengro* in 1893 and *The Romany Rye* in 1900. His literary aspirations outpaced his abilities, and, if Watts–Dunton is remembered at all, it is for his care of the alcoholically ravaged **Swinburne** at The Pines, Putney, for the last 30 years of the poet's life.

**Waugh, Alec (Alexander Raban)** 1898–1981 Novelist. He was born in London, the son of Arthur Waugh, publisher and man of letters, and elder brother of **Evelyn Waugh**. He attended Sherborne School, Dorset, which provided the background for his precocious first novel *The Loom of Youth* (1917). This enjoyed some success (partly on account of its treatment of public-school homosexuality) and set Waugh on a long career as a middlebrow novelist. His greatest commercial success was *Island in the Sun* (1956). He lived latterly in Morocco and the United States, and produced several volumes of autobiography.

**Waugh, Evelyn (Arthur St John)** 1902–66 Novelist. Evelyn Waugh was born in Hampstead and educated at Lancing and Hertford College, Oxford, where he became a close friend of **Harold Acton**. After Oxford he became a teacher in various private schools, a frustrating experience, and then worked for *The Daily Express*.

A juvenile piece, *The World to Come: A Poem in Three Cantos* (1916), was followed by *PRB: An Essay on The Pre-Raphaelite Brotherhood 1847–1854* (1926), both of which were privately printed. *Decline and Fall*, his first great success, based on his teaching experience, was published in 1928. In the same year he published *Rossetti: His Life and Works*, married Evelyn Gardner (whom he divorced in 1930), and was received into the Roman Catholic Church.

Waugh's reputation as England's leading satirical novelist was established during the 1930s

Evelyn Waugh, 1964.

with *Vile Bodies* (1930), *Black Mischief* (1932), *A Handful of Dust* (1934) and *Scoop* (1938). These and *Put Out More Flags* (1942) caught the witty, cynical and irresponsible mood of upper-class life during the 1920s and 1930s.

He travelled extensively throughout the 1930s and produced several travel books. *Labels: A Mediterranean Journal* (1930) was followed by *Remote People* (1931; about Africa), *Ninety-Two Days* (1934; about South America), *Waugh in Abyssinia* (1936; covering Mussolini's invasion), and *Robbery Under Law: The Mexican Object-Lesson*, published in 1939. His last travel book, published towards the end of his life, was called *A Tourist in Africa* (1960).

In 1937 Waugh married Laura Herbert and settled in the West Country. Two chapters of an unfinished novel were published as *Work Suspended* (1942). He served in the Royal Marines during World War II, and was a member of the British Military Mission to Yugoslavia in 1944. *Brideshead Revisited*, one of his most popular novels, appeared in 1945. *Men at Arms* (1952), *Officers and Gentlemen* (1955) and *Unconditional Surrender* (1961) make up the trilogy *Sword of Honour*, published together in 1965.

*The Loved One* (1948), sub-titled 'An Anglo-American Tragedy', is a satire based on Waugh's experiences in Hollywood. *Helena* (1950), a historical novel set in the Rome of the Emperor Constantine, was Waugh's favourite work, but not his readers'. *The Ordeal of Gilbert*

*Pinfold* (1957), about a middle-aged writer who suffers a nervous breakdown but eventually finds salvation, is frankly autobiographical and held in high esteem by Waugh's admirers. *The Life of Ronald Knox* (1959) was a biography, and *A Little Learning* (1964) comprised a chapter of his autobiography, which Waugh did not live to complete. His *Diaries* were edited by M. Davie and published in 1976; his *Letters*, equally frank and revealing, appeared in 1980, edited by M. Amory.

**Waverley** A novel by **Sir Walter Scott**, published anonymously in 1814. Scott had worked on the book intermittently since 1805.

Edward Waverley, the hero, has been brought up partly by his uncle, Sir Edward Digby, who has Jacobite sympathies. When Edward receives his commission in the army and joins his regiment in Scotland, he visits Digby's friend Bradwardine, another Jacobite, and is attracted to Rose, Bradwardine's gentle daughter. Waverley's romantic disposition leads him to visit the Highlands and seek out a freebooting character, Donald Bean Lean, and there he meets Fergus Mac-Ivor and his beautiful sister Flora, both ardent Jacobites and active in the Stuart cause. His connection with the Jacobites gets Waverley into trouble with his colonel. An incipient mutiny is laid at his door and he is cashiered; the intervention of Rose, who is devoted to him, saves him from prison. But injustice leads him to join the other side; he is encouraged by Flora and well received by the Young Pretender. At the Battle of Prestonpans the Jacobite forces are routed; but Waverley saves the life of Colonel Talbot, a family friend, who secures a pardon for him. The other Jacobite prisoners are severely dealt with and Fergus Mac-Ivor is convicted of high treason. Waverley, meanwhile, is rejected by the beautiful Flora, who enters a convent when Fergus is executed; eventually he marries Rose.

*Waverley* was enormously popular: four editions were printed and sold in the first year of publication alone. Its success turned Scott's career decisively from poetry to fiction, and all his subsequent novels were described as being 'by the author of *Waverley*'.

**Waves, The** A novel by **Virginia Woolf**, published in 1931.

The most experimental of Virginia Woolf's novels, it traces the lives of six characters – Bernard, Susan, Rhoda, Neville, Jinny and Louis – from childhood to old age in a rotating series of interior monologues. These are interspersed with italicized passages which record the ascent and descent of the sun, the rise and fall of the waves, and the passing of the seasons. Each character's life story is revealed incidentally and, although there is no differentiation in their speech, their individual personalities are revealed by recurring phrases and images.

At the very beginning, as children, all six share a house by the seashore and are taught by a governess, Miss Hudson. Their lives soon diverge, but they gather later, first at a dinner in a French restaurant in London (to mark the departure to India of a friend, Percival, who dies soon afterwards), and secondly at Hampton Court. In a final monologue, Bernard as an elderly man reviews his life, those of his friends, and their influence on each other. He feels himself flowing into their consciousnesses like a wave into other waves.

The novel explores the continuity of memory and celebrates the potential for communion and love between individuals in the face of change and death. It is widely considered to be Virginia Woolf's masterpiece.

**Way of All Flesh, The** A novel by **Samuel Butler**, posthumously published in 1903.

The hero, Ernest Pontifex, endures an unhappy upbringing in the Evangelical parsonage at Battersby. His father, Theo, re-enacts the tyrannical ways of his own father, George, a religious publisher, but justifies them with the sanctimonious dictates of a spiritually bankrupt religious piety. At Cambridge Ernest is converted and then ordained, in accordance with his parents' wishes. As a curate, Ernest falls prey to the conflicting influences of a duplicitous Tractarian and a free-thinking tinker, before breaking out in an incident where his naïvety makes him mistake a respectable girl for a prostitute. The sudden shock of his subsequent imprisonment enables him to cast off his faith, his family and his class in an attempt to revert to the simple life of his artisan great-grandfather. Another false start leads him to marry a former maidservant at the Rectory, sacked when she was found to be pregnant. This time his freedom is achieved when his drunken wife is discovered to be already married. Anxious to avoid a repetition of the Pontifex paternal tyranny, Ernest farms out the children of his union. Having inherited an income from his aunt Alethea, Ernest embarks upon a solitary life, a literary vocation and eclectic interests much resembling Butler's own adult career.

The fortunes of the Pontifex family, as unfolded by the narrator, Overton, are designed to show that personal happiness is dependent upon the liberating effect of acting upon inherited and largely unconscious stores of vitality. The play between the conscious and unconscious also fuels the thrust of the novel's attack upon the conventions and hypocrisies of Victorian family life.

Butler started writing the novel in 1873, began revision in 1880, but abandoned it when his friend Miss Savage, model for Alethea, died in 1885. Although the realistic details, including actual letters from the Butler family, are taken from his own mid-century upbringing, for many of its first readers, such as **Arnold Bennett**, **E. M. Forster** and **G. B. Shaw**, Butler's debunking novel articulated their reaction against a whole range of orthodox Victorian pieties.

**Way of the World, The** A comedy by **William Congreve**, first performed in 1700, when its comparative failure contributed to Congreve's decision to turn away from the theatre. It is a complex play, whose elegant dialogue and wit cover with polish a plot that gradually reveals how far self-interest may go to make money and mar marriages.

Mirabell, in order to marry Millamant, whom he loves, must win the consent of her aunt, Lady Wishfort. His best hope lies in Lady Wishfort's eagerness for a lover of her own. But Lady Wishfort is only one of the obstacles. More threatening is the spite of Mrs Marwood, whose love Mirabell had not returned. Her liaison with Lady Wishfort's avaricious son-in-law Fainall takes them into a conspiracy which carries the play to the point of near-tragic confrontation. Nor is Millamant easily won.

The opening of Act IV, scene 10 of *The Way of the World*. At Lady Wishfort's, Sir Wilfull Witwoud is drunk and singing, to her annoyance. Also present are Millamant, young Witwoud, and Mrs Fainall. Frontispiece to Vol. III of Congreve's *Works*, published in 1753.

She is no milksop, as she makes clear in the famous 'proviso' scene in Act IV by laying down the conditions on which she would contemplate marriage to Mirabell. Lady Wishfort, gullible and constantly being gulled, is finally shaken into consenting to her niece's marriage when the villainies of Fainall and Mrs Marwood are exposed.

**Way We Live Now, The** A novel by **Anthony Trollope**, serialized in monthly numbers from February 1874 to September 1875, and published in two volumes in 1875.

At the centre of this huge satirical panorama of contemporary manners – Trollope's longest novel – is the fitfully heroic figure of Augustus Melmotte, a financier of obscure origins and seemingly fabulous wealth. Through the corrupt American Hamilton Fisker, Melmotte becomes involved in promoting a grandiose but fictitious American railway company, and quickly rises to social prominence in London as a consequence. Courted by impecunious aristocrats eager to get on the boards of his companies, he is chosen to entertain the Emperor of China in his Grosvenor Square house and is elected to Parliament as a Conservative MP. But the bubble bursts with the discovery of fraud, his titled friends desert him, and after getting drunk in the House of Commons, Melmotte goes home and commits suicide. A related plot involves the efforts of Lady Carbury to arrange a marriage between her dissolute son Sir Felix and Melmotte's only child, Marie, which collapses when Felix drunkenly gambles away the money Marie, who loves him, has obtained for their elopement. The only character to speak out against the widespread corruption is Lady Carbury's cousin Roger Carbury, a middle-aged country squire in love with her daughter Hetta. Another plot concerns Roger and his friend Paul Montague, a business partner of Hamilton Fisker and the erstwhile lover of Winifred Hurtle, a passionate American woman. Mrs Hurtle comes to England to win him back, but fails, Paul having fallen in love with Hetta. Although the marriage of Paul and Hetta provides the conventional happy ending, the loneliness and disappointment of Mrs Hurtle and Roger Carbury ensure that the mood of this most sombre of Trollope's novels is sustained to the end.

A study of what Trollope called 'the commercial profligacy of the age', *The Way We Live Now* portrays a society in which gambling – on the Stock Exchange and in the gentleman's club – has become a dominant activity. Undervalued in his own day, it is now seen as one of his finest works, a satire comparable in scope to **Vanity Fair** and **Little Dorrit**.

**Wealth of Nations, The** A treatise on political economy by **Adam Smith**, fully titled *An Inquiry*

into the *Nature and Causes of the Wealth of Nations*
and first published in 1776. During Smith's
lifetime it went through five editions, of which
the third (1784) was definitive.

It analyses the effects of the pursuit of self-
interest on different groups within an economic
system and recommends that market forces be
left to ensure the accumulation of wealth, albeit
within a framework of law and with some
government intervention. Book I analyses how
the division of labour lies behind increased
labour productivity and how the consequent
benefits are distributed as wages, rents and
profits to different groups in society. The pursuit of self-interest by one man will produce
unintended benefits for others. Book II analyses
the nature of capital (fixed and circulating), the
means and effects of individual accumulation of
it, and its different uses. He shows how the
expenditure of savings results in increased
income, thus making growth self-perpetuating.
Book III attempts to explain, partly historically,
different rates of growth in different countries,
beginning with an analysis of the economic
interdependence of country and town, and
showing how the growth of the town has been
beneficial to both. Book IV attacks mercantilism
for regarding wealth as money and not the
goods it can buy, and promotes the case for free
trade among nations. Book V turns to domestic
political economy and outlines the case for some
government intervention: market systems cannot produce armies, courts, roads and canals, all
of which increase welfare. The state has a duty
to ensure the education of the young where
private systems fail.

Eloquently argued, and showing Smith's
mastery of ethics, history, sociology, jurisprudence and economics, *The Wealth of Nations* has
exerted a profound influence over generations of
economists; indeed, it virtually defined the content of the subject for over 150 years. Marx was
influenced by its sociological underpinning, and
Smith's economics provided a manifesto for
British politicians seeking to reduce state intervention in economic life.

**Webb, (Martha) Beatrice (née Potter)** 1858–
1943 and **Webb, Sidney, 1st Baron Passfield**
1859–1947 Social historians. Beatrice and Sidney Webb constituted what has been called 'the
most prolific partnership in 20th-century British
history'. Both were committed Socialists before
they married in 1892, becoming leading figures
in the Fabian Society (founded 1884) and collaborating on numerous social and political
works. As Lord Passfield, Sidney Webb served
in the Labour governments of 1924 and 1929–
31.

With *The History of Trade Unionism* (1894) and
*Industrial Democracy* (1897) the Webbs established labour history as a separate study; and

their minority report of the Poor Law Commission (1905–9) laid the foundations for the Welfare State. Another major work was the seven-
volume *History of English Local Government* published between 1903 and 1930. In education and
publicity they wrote numerous pamphlets for
the Fabian Society, founded the London School
of Economics (1895), and established *The New
Statesman* in 1913.

Beatrice Webb also wrote two autobiographical works, *My Apprenticeship* (1926) and *Our
Partnership* (posthumously published, 1948).
Selections from her diaries appeared in 1952 and
1956, and the first full volume of the complete
*Diaries* (ed. N. and J. Mackenzie) appeared in
1982. These revealed an unsuspected gift of
psychological perception which, combined with
her acute social observation, have made them
classics of their kind.

Other titles written in collaboration included
*The State and the Doctor* (1910), *The Prevention of
Destitution* (1911), *The Decay of Capitalist Civilization* (1923), *Soviet Communism: A New Civilization?* (1935) and *The Truth about Soviet Russia*
(1942).

**Webb, Mary** 1881–1927 Novelist. Born
Gladys Mary Meredith in Shropshire, she was
educated at Southport. In 1912 she married
Henry Bertram Law Webb and they became
market gardeners before moving to London in
1921.

Mary Webb's early novels – *The Golden
Arrow* (1916), *Gone to Earth* (1917), *The House in
Dormer Forest* (1920) and *Seven for a Secret* (1922)
– met with little success, but *Precious Bane*
(1924), set in Shropshire, became an instant
best-seller after it had been praised by the Prime
Minister, Stanley Baldwin. He wrote an introduction to the 1928 edition of the novel, thereby
assuring her a large posthumous readership. Her
novels are infused with a romantic and often
naïve passion, unrelieved by any sense of humour – a style brilliantly parodied by Stella Gibbons in **Cold Comfort Farm** (1932) – but many
have found in her stark descriptions of the
countryside and rural life an original lyrical
intensity akin to that of **D. H. Lawrence**. *Armour
Wherein He Trusted*, an unfinished novel, and
*The Spring of Joy*, poems and essays, were both
published posthumously in 1929.

**Webbe, William** d.1591 Critic. After graduating from Cambridge, Webbe seems to have
supported himself by tutoring. He is the author
of *A Discourse of English Poetry* (1586).

**Webster, John** c.1580–c.1634 Playwright.
Almost nothing is known of the life of John
Webster. **Henslowe** records payments made to
him in 1602, but his first known work dates
from 1604. Then he wrote an Induction for the

revival of **Marston**'s *The Malcontent* by the **King's Men**, and collaborated with **Dekker** on *Westward Ho*. Another collaboration with Dekker, *The Famous History of Sir Thomas Wyatt*, may belong to the same year, and another, *Northward Ho*, to 1605. *Appius and Virginia* (*c.* 1608), a retelling from Roman history of a father's loving murder of his daughter, was probably written with **Thomas Heywood**. There followed three plays which are normally supposed to be Webster's alone. *The Devil's Law Case* (*c.*1610) is a sensational but uncharacteristically careless tragicomedy. *The White Devil* (*c.*1612 and *The Duchess of Malfi* (*c.*1613) are among the finest of all Jacobean tragedies. The new philosophy has put all in doubt, and Webster's characters strive unavailingly to fashion for themselves a meaningful life in a disintegrating world.

The last 20 years of Webster's life are as obscure as the first 20. A pageant survives (*Monuments of Honour*, 1624) and two collaborations, with **Middleton** on *Any Thing for a Quiet Life* (*c.*1621) and with **William Rowley** on *A Cure for a Cuckold* (*c.*1624). Other plays may have been lost. For so diligent a writer, the known output is improbably slight.

***Webster's Dictionary*** The American Noah Webster (1758–1843) was the author of two dictionaries (1806 and 1828). Although trained as a lawyer, he took up teaching and, from 1783 onwards, published elementary schoolbooks and monographs on the English language. *The American Spelling Book* (1806), a reissue of the first of his publications, sold over 80,000,000 copies within a hundred years and was to a great extent responsible for those spellings now considered markedly American. The real ancestor of the dictionaries that today bear Webster's name is his *An American Dictionary of the English Language* (1828). The word 'American' remained in subsequent editions of Webster until replaced by 'International'. The current *Webster's Third New International Dictionary*, much the size of the *Shorter Oxford English Dictionary*, was, when first published in 1961, greatly criticized for its relative lack of editorial prescriptivism.

See also **English dictionaries**.

***Wedding of Sir Gawen and Dame Ragnell, The*** A **verse romance** written *c.*1450 in the East Midlands. While hunting, King Arthur meets Sir Gromer Somer Joure, who threatens to kill him. He lets Arthur go on condition that he return in a year to tell him what women most desire. Arthur and Gawen seek the answer and after 11 months a hideous hag tells them in return for a promise of marriage to Gawen. Gromer Somer Joure curses his sister for revealing the answer, but has to allow Arthur to go.

Gawen marries Dame Ragnell and when he kisses her in bed she becomes young and beautiful. She asks him whether he would rather have her fair by day or night and when he allows her the choice she promises to be beautiful always. The same story is told by **Geoffrey Chaucer** as *The Wife of Bath's Tale* in *The Canterbury Tales*.

**Wedgwood, Dame C[icely] V[eronica]** 1910– Historian. Born in Northumberland, she was educated privately before going to Lady Margaret Hall, Oxford. *Strafford* (1935) and *The Thirty Years' War* (1938) were both well received and established her as a successful popular historian. *Oliver Cromwell* and her translation of Carl Brandi's *Charles V* (both 1939) were followed by *William the Silent* (1944) which won the James Tait Black Memorial Prize. Other works during this period included a translation of Canetti's novel *Auto da Fé* (1946), *Richelieu and the French Monarchy* (1949) and *Seventeenth-Century English Literature* (1950).

In 1955 Wedgwood published *The King's Peace*, the first part of her major history of the English Civil War. *The King's War* (1958) and *The Trial of King Charles* (1964; called *A Coffin for King Charles* in the USA) completed it. *Thomas Wentworth: A Revaluation* (1961) was a reconsideration of her first subject, Strafford. Other works included *Velvet Studies* (1946), a collection of essays, *Truth and Opinion* and *Poetry and Politics* (both 1960), *The World of Rubens* (1967), *Milton and His World* (1970) and *The Political Career of Peter Paul Rubens* (1975).

The author was created a Dame of the British Empire in 1968. She was a member of The Institute of Advanced Studies at Princeton from 1953 to 1968.

***Week on the Concord and Merrimack Rivers, A*** An account by **Henry David Thoreau**, published in 1849, of a boat trip to the White Mountains of New Hampshire, taken in 1839 with his brother John. Written during the period described in *Walden*, it resembles that better-known work in its thoughtful digressions on poetry, philosophy and religion. It was Thoreau's first major publication.

**Weever, John** 1576–1632 Poet and antiquary. Of Lancashire stock, Weever was educated at Queens' College, Cambridge. His early literary activity was in the field of contemporary satire; his *Epigrams* (1599) and *Faunus and Melliflora* (1600) are important sources of literary gossip. His later career as an antiquary culminated in the publication, in massive folio, of *Ancient Funeral Monuments within the United Monarchy of Great Britain* (1631).

***Weir of Hermiston*** An unfinished novel by **Robert Louis Stevenson**. The fragment published posthumously in 1896 does little more than set the scene and introduce the chief characters, but it is generally acknowledged as a potential masterpiece.

The Lord Justice-Clerk Adam Weir, Lord Hermiston, is a formidable hanging judge with a strength of character and will notably lacking in his son Archie. Archie's mother is dead, and he lives alone with his father, whom he loves and hates in equal proportions. Their relationship reaches a crisis when Archie, revolted by his father's brutal treatment of the defendant at a criminal trial, loses his temper and publicly insults him. He is banished to Hermiston, a remote and uncivilized village, where he lives as a recluse with his devoted housekeeper, Kirstie. Her four nephews, the 'Black Elliotts', are notorious for their ruthless hunting-down of the murderer of their father. Archie falls in love with their sister Christina. The couple's meetings become known to Kirstie and to Frank Innes, Archie's visitor and treacherous friend, and Archie tells Christina that their relationship must end.

The fragment ends here, but Stevenson's plans for the novel survive. Archie continues to avoid Christina and Frank Innes takes advantage of the situation by seducing her. The two men quarrel and Archie kills his rival. He is tried before his own father and condemned to death. Kirstie, meanwhile, has discovered the identity of Christina's seducer. She tells the 'Black Elliotts', who gather their followers and rescue Archie from prison. He escapes to America with Christina. Lord Hermiston is so much affected by the shock of having sentenced his own son that he collapses and dies.

**Welch, Denton (Maurice)** 1915–48 Novelist, short-story writer and artist. Born of British parents in Shanghai, he was educated at Repton School before going on to the Goldsmith School of Art in London. When he was 20 he suffered severe spinal injury in a cycling accident; he never recovered, and it greatly limited his life. This narrowing of capabilities caused him to concentrate almost exclusively on his writing and painting. Toward the end of his short life writing had become a painful and difficult exercise, performed only with great courage. Welch took pleasure in examining people and objects closely and in describing them in clear, vivid prose. He began by publishing an account of his meeting with the artist Walter Sickert (1942). It was followed by many poems, 60 short stories, three largely autobiographical novels – *Maiden Voyage* (1943), which was introduced by **Edith Sitwell**, *In Youth is Pleasure* (1945) and *A Voice through a Cloud* (1950) – and his *Journals* (1952).

**Welch, James** 1940– American novelist and poet. Born in Browning, Montana, Welch is Blackfoot Indian on his father's side and Gros Ventre on his mother's. He was educated at schools on the Blackfoot and Fort Belknap reservations, and then at the universities of Minnesota and Montana. His first publication, *Riding the Earthboy 40: Poems*, appeared in 1971. His first novel, *Winter in the Blood* (1974), is about a young Indian trying to make sense of his heritage in the modern world. A second novel, *The Death of Jim Loney* (1979), though set in contemporary Midwestern society, is concerned with the traditional codes of behaviour found in the mythic stories of the Gros Ventres. *Fool's Crew* appeared in 1986.

**Weldon, Fay** 1933– Novelist and television playwright. Born in Worcester, and later a student at the University of St Andrews, she worked as an advertising copywriter (coining the famous slogan, 'Go to work on an egg') before turning to full-time authorship. In addition to television plays and screenplays she has written several vigorous and resourceful novels articulating a contemporary feminist consciousness, prominent among which are *Female Friends* (1975) and *Praxis* (1978). A subsequent book, *Puffball* (1980), is unusual in essaying an extended evocation of the biological process of conception in the womb. *The President's Child* (1982) and *The Life and Loves of a She-Devil* (1983) are caustically satirical about the repressive and blinkered practices of male-dominated society. Weldon's latest books are a novella, *The Rules of Life* (1987), and a novel, *The Hearts and Lives of Men* (1987).

***Well at the World's End, The*** A late prose romance by **William Morris**, first published in 1896.

Ralph, youngest son of King Peter of Upmeads, sets out on a quest for the 'Well at the World's End', whose waters give the drinker long life and an ever-youthful 'lucky' appearance. He falls in love with the Lady of Abundance who has drunk from the Well, but she is killed before she can lead him to it. After a period of despair Ralph's quest for the Well finds a parallel in his search for Ursula, his first love. Together they reach the Well, drink from it and eventually return to rule Upmeads and 'to live in peace and patience without fear or hatred, and to succour the oppressed and love the lovely'.

Though largely unpalatable to a modern readership, the epic scale, pseudo-medieval setting and archaic language of Morris's late romances are an integral part of his attempt to recapture the spirit of bardic narrative literature. In 1895 Morris stated that he 'had not the least intention of thrusting an allegory' into a prose romance, which was rather 'meant for a tale pure and simple'. Political didacticism is abandoned in favour of a broad philanthropy, of which social concerns are only a part. The Well, from which only the 'Strong of Heart' may drink, is a source of human love and moral value. In reviewing the book **W. B. Yeats** wrote: 'there is scarcely a chapter in which there is not some moment for which one might almost give one's soul'.

***Well–Beloved, The*** A novel by **Thomas Hardy**, first published serially as *The Pursuit of the Well-Beloved* in *The Illustrated London News* from October to December 1892 and in book form, substantially revised, in 1897.

Jocelyn Pierston, sculptor and son of a prosperous stone merchant on the Isle of Slingers (Portland), seeks an ideal woman whose incarnation should take the form of the Well-Beloved. Jocelyn pursues this myth through the courtship of a mother, daughter, and granddaughter all named Avice. As the years and generations pass it becomes apparent that the ideal eludes Jocelyn, that 'all men are pursuing a shadow, the Unattainable'. With illness and encroaching age the ideal recedes and Jocelyn settles down on Portland, in due course marrying a woman he had known in earlier days, Marcia Bencomb.

**well–made play** Used strictly, this term applies to English imitations of the *pièce bien faite* whose formula was devised by the prolific French playwright Eugène Scribe (1791–1861). The aim is less to create a finely shaped overall structure than to space out effects and revelations in such a way as to keep the audience in suspense. Particularly suited to melodrama, the well-made-play formula has also been often applied in farce. Among its most successful English exponents are **Henry Arthur Jones** and **Pinero**.

**Wells, H[erbert] G[eorge]** 1866–1946 Novelist and author of works on politics, history and society. He was born at Bromley, where his father was an unsuccessful tradesman. His early life is reflected in the struggles of many of his novels' protagonists, and his father can be recognized in a number of fictional guises – most notably as Mr Polly. After two unhappy years as a draper's apprentice, Wells became a student assistant at Midhurst Grammar School. From here, in 1884, he won a scholarship to the Normal School of Science, now Imperial College, London. His year under **T. H. Huxley**, teacher of comparative anatomy, was seminal. Before taking a first-class honours degree in zoology in 1890, he had resumed the life of a schoolteacher. After an accident which damaged his kidneys, he determined that he would learn to write; his first full-length works were textbooks of biology and geography. In 1891 he

H. G. Wells, 1920.

made an unfortunate marriage to his cousin Isabel; his second marriage in 1895 to Amy Robbins (always 'Jane' to Wells) was to be lasting. From 1898 to 1909 they lived in Sandgate.

His literary career began with the publication of his first major novel, ***The Time Machine*** (1895). Other works of **science fiction** followed: *The Wonderful Visit* (1895), *The Island of Dr Moreau* (1896), a grim parable of the blind and bestial forces underlying civilization, *The Invisible Man* (1897), ***The War of the Worlds*** (1898), *When the Sleeper Wakes* (1899), *The First Men in the Moon* (1901) and *The War in the Air* (1908). By their satirical element and their implicit note of warning, these fables about the impact of alien races or advanced science on established society prefigure Wells's later concern with social and political realities. His interest in the changing social order again unites with a lesser element of fantasy in *A Modern Utopia* (1905). This, with other works like the later 'discussion' novel, *The New Macchiavelli* (1911), displays the didactic tendency in Wells. From 1903 he was a member of the Fabian Society, but his contact with its members was brief and mostly belligerent. His quarrel with **G. B. Shaw** was only one of his controversies with leading thinkers of the day.

Wells's major novels with a bias toward social

realism drew heavily on his own experiences as a youth from the lower middle classes. *Love and Mr Lewisham* (1900) and *Kipps: The Story of a Simple Soul* (1905) were followed by *Tono-Bungay* (1909), his most ambitious novel, and *The History of Mr Polly* (1910). *Ann Veronica* (1909) was considered scandalous for its portrayal of an emancipated woman.

Wells's public reputation survived the disgrace which attached to his views on sexual freedom. His liaison with **Rebecca West** between 1913 and 1923 attracted much attention. From 1912 until Jane's death in 1927, his home was in Essex. He wrote about his life there in *Mr Britling Sees It Through* (1916), one of his popular successes. Wells was not despairing about the major international crises of the modern world – the Great War and the rise of Fascism. He was an advocate of the League of Nations in 1919, and continued to see himself as an educator, writing *The Outline of History* (1920) for a large readership. His novel-writing continued, notably with *Mr Blettsworthy on Rampole Island* (1928) and *The Bulpington of Blup* (1932). At his last home in Regent's Park, which he refused to leave during the air raids of World War II, he wrote the lively and engaging self-portrait in *Experiment in Autobiography* (1934) as well as his pessimistic last work, *Mind at the End of Its Tether* (1945).

**Wells, Robert** 1947– Poet and translator. Wells was born in Oxford, where he received an intensively classical education before reading English and classics at King's College, Cambridge. He has taught in Italy and Iran, and translated Virgil's *Georgics* (1982) and Theocritus' *Idylls* (1988). Wells has worked for several years as a forester: it is the combination of classical precision with an intense physical awareness of the natural world which gives his work its unmistakable distinction. His poetry appeared in a Cambridge anthology, *Shade Mariners* (1970), which he shared with **Dick Davis** and Clive Wilmer, and in Michael Schmidt's *Ten English Poets* (1976) before the publication of *The Winter's Task* in 1977. The finest poems here mix rapturous sensuousness and muscular clarity: the reader may be reminded of **Thomas Traherne** and **Thom Gunn**. Other poems are epigrammatic in a style perhaps learned from **Ben Jonson** via **Yvor Winters** and **J. V. Cunningham**. *Selected Poems* appeared in 1986.

**Welty, Eudora** 1909– American short-story writer and novelist, born in Jackson, Mississippi, and educated at Mississippi State College for Women, the University of Wisconsin, and Columbia. Her first collection, *A Curtain of Green, and Other Stories*, appeared in 1941, with an introduction by **Katherine Anne Porter**, and established her as a major Southern writer with a powerful sense of place. Her second collection, *The Wide Net, and Other Stories* (1943), was less well received. *The Golden Apples* (1949) contains seven related stories about three generations of the MacLain, Morrison, Stark, Rainey and Carmichael families in the fictitious small town of Morgana, Mississippi. *The Bride of the Innisfallen, and Other Stories* (1955) includes stories set in London, Italy and Greece, as well as in the South.

Welty has also written a number of novels in the Southern Gothic tradition, among them *The Robber Bridegroom* (1942), *Delta Wedding* (1946), *The Ponder Heart* (1954), *Losing Battles* (1970) and *The Optimist's Daughter* (1972, Pulitzer Prize). She has published several volumes of critical essays, including *The Eye of the Story: Selected Essays and Reviews* (1979). Her literary autobiography, *One Writer's Beginnings*, was published in 1984.

**Wendt, Albert** 1939– Western Samoan novelist and poet. Born in what is now Western Samoa of mixed German and Polynesian ancestry, he won a government scholarship to study in New Zealand and attended high school in New Plymouth, teachers' college at Ardmore and the Victoria University of Wellington, where he gained an MA in History. He worked for a while as a schoolteacher in New Zealand before returning to Western Samoa in 1965. Shortly afterwards he became Principal of Samoa College and then in 1974 moved to Fiji, where he worked at the University of the South Pacific, playing an important role in the arts and encouraging young writers to develop their talents. He later became Director of the University's Centre in Western Samoa and has since moved back to Fiji to take up a Chair in South Pacific literature. The one writer from the South Pacific region with an international reputation, Wendt is best known for his novel, *Leaves of the Banyan Tree* (1979), a three-generation saga of Western Samoan life, which, in addition to providing a corrective to sentimentalized Western versions of the 'South Seas', provides a complex and powerfully written account of the psychological effects of colonialism and the possibility of achieving liberation from this situation through an existentialist individualism. While Wendt draws on traditional Polynesian culture, he takes the view that its fragmentation under the impact of Western civilization has given the artist a new freedom to develop a personal style. His other books include a volume of collected poetry, *Inside Us the Dead* (1976), and the novels *Sons for the Return Home* (1973), an autobiographical work telling the story of a young man from Samoa at university in New Zealand, and *Pouliuli* (1977), the tragedy of an old village chief forced to encounter Western ways.

**Wescott, Glenway** 1901–87 American novelist, born and raised in Wisconsin. His first publication was a book of **imagist**-influenced verse, *The Bitterns* (1920). His best-known works were published while he lived as an expatriate in France in the 1920s. These include *The Apple of the Eye* (1924) and his most successful novel, *The Grandmothers* (1926). Both are stories of frontier life in Wisconsin, and in both Wescott fashions a lyrical evocation of the past, a rich and deeply felt assessment of his heritage. *Good-Bye Wisconsin* (1928) is a collection of stories. He was friendly with **Gertrude Stein** and her literary circle; **Ernest Hemingway** based his character Robert Prentiss, in *The Sun Also Rises*, on him. After his return to the USA in 1933 his work grew more infrequent; his last publication of note, *The Pilgrim Hawk*, appeared in 1940. He also published several collections of essays, among them *Fear and Trembling* (1932) and *Images of Truth: Remembrances and Criticism* (1962).

**Wesker, Arnold** 1932– Dramatist. Born and educated in the East End of London, Wesker tells much about his early life in his first plays, the trilogy about Ronnie Kahn and his family and friends, made up of *Chicken Soup with Barley* (1958), *Roots* (1959) and *I'm Talking about Jerusalem* (1960). Less personal, *The Kitchen* (1959) nevertheless relies on Wesker's own experience as a kitchen porter and pastry cook in 1953–8. The intense social idealism that led him to found Centre 42 and to remain its director from 1961–70 was fed, like Ronnie Kahn's, by the atmosphere of his home. *Chips with Everything* perceives in military hierarchy the restraining outlines of the English class system. *Their Very Own and Golden City* (1965) is an expressionistic lament at the betrayal of a socialist vision. Wesker refused to settle into the working-class realism that had brought him to public attention, and *The Four Seasons* (1965) is an ambitiously poetic play about the changing patterns of a love affair. Its failure was the prelude to five years of theatrical silence, broken by the elegiac and almost despairing *The Friends* (1970). The essays in *Fears of Fragmentation* (1970) reveal Wesker's growing anger with his critics. Despite the quality and originality of such plays as *The Wedding Feast* (1974), the frankly satirical *The Journalists* (1975), *Love Letters on Blue Paper* (1978: televised in 1976), the provocative rewriting of **Shakespeare** in *The Merchant* (1977) and the questing *Caritas* (1981), Wesker has been nudged into the sidelines of the English theatre.

**Wesley, John** 1703–91 and **Wesley, Charles** 1707–88 Founders of Methodism. The two brothers were the 15th and 18th children of the rector of Epworth, Lincolnshire. A childhood rescue from their burning home in 1709 left John ever afterwards with a providential sense of mission, being 'a brand plucked out of the burning'. Both brothers were undergraduates at Christ Church, Oxford, though John had formerly attended Charterhouse and Charles had been at Westminster School. In 1726 John Wesley became a fellow of Lincoln College, Oxford, and spent two years acting as his father's curate. On his return to Oxford in 1729 he joined, and swiftly became leader of, a group, various nicknamed the 'Holy Club' or 'Methodists', of which Charles was already a member. Members, who were later to include **James Hervey** and George Whitefield, met for study and religious discussion, visited the poor, sick and imprisoned and practised strict self-discipline. Their self-examinations, frequently recorded in coded diaries, became the quarry for their *Journals*. John's was published periodically between 1739 and 1790 and Charles's posthumously in 1849.

In 1735 the brothers embarked on an abortive mission to the settlers and Indians in Georgia. On the voyage out they had been impressed by the piety of the Moravian passengers and, on their return to England (Charles in 1736 and John in 1737), they came under the influence of the Moravian pastor Peter Bohler and experienced conversions to 'saving faith' (Charles on 21 May and John on 24 May 1738).

In 1739 both brothers, having first tried to work through Church of England pulpits, resorted to open-air preaching. Using Bristol, London and Newcastle as their chief centres, they embarked on the life of itinerant preachers, establishing societies wherever they went, to provide discipline and mutual support for their converts. In 1743 John Wesley drew up *Rules* for these classes and in 1744 held the first conference for lay preachers whose help he had increasingly used since 1738. The implicit incompatibility of Methodism's evolving structure with the parochial discipline and apostolic claims of the Anglican Church was never admitted by John Wesley, but caused his brother to retire from itinerant work in 1756. John continued, covering some 250,000 miles of the British Isles by foot, horse and post-chaise and preaching three or four times a day.

John Wesley's *Journal*, a textbook of experiential religion, served to maintain contact between far-flung societies. Something of his authoritarian personality emerges from this grandly impersonal document of well over a million words, but his voluminous letters provide a more intimate picture of the detailed concern he expended on his devoted followers. John also engaged in polemical debate with the Moravians and Calvinists, wrote religious tracts and treatises, produced practical handbooks on medicine and translated, edited or abridged the work of others for more popular consumption.

John and Charles both recognized the value of hymns in worship as a method of instruction and a channel for spiritual fervour. Of the thousands of hymns composed by Charles, and often edited by John, many are still in use well beyond the confines of Methodism. Such favourites include 'Love divine, all loves excelling', 'Hark, the herald-angels sing' and 'Jesu, Lover of my soul'.

**Wessex Poems and Other Verses** The first collection of poetry published by **Thomas Hardy**, appearing in 1898. These 51 poems (some dating from the 1860s) are characteristically Hardyean in their diversity of subject matter, verse forms and instinct for the dramatic moment. They range from the speculative 'Hap' to the embittered 'Neutral Tones', from the mildly Chaucerian 'The Bride-Night Fire' to the poignant 'Thoughts of Phena' and from the gravity of 'Nature's Questioning' to the hearty 'Sergeant's Song'. *Wessex Poems* is the prelude to 30 years of sustained poetic writing.

**West, Nathanael** The pseudonym of Nathan Wallenstein Weinstein (1903–40), an American novelist born in New York City and educated at Brown University. His first novel, *The Dream Life of Balso Snell* (1931), is a garish and self-consciously *avant-garde* satire on the inner life of the intellectual introvert of the title. West's preoccupation with the barrenness of contemporary life was given further expression in *Miss Lonelyhearts* (1933), the story of a newspaperman who writes an advice-to-the-lovelorn column and who becomes obsessed with the need to be more than a phoney saviour. His initial professional detachment from his suffering correspondents turns into a tragic involvement which ends in his murder. The mockery of his sadistic editor accompanies his downfall. *A Cool Million: The Dismantling of Lemuel Pitkin* (1934) is a satire of the American Dream itself: Lemuel is naïve to the point of idiocy but this is no obstacle to his becoming a runner in the lethal race for riches and eminence. After he is murdered he is proclaimed a hero. West, who was earning his living as a journalist at the time, went to Hollywood in 1935 to write scripts for a minor studio. *The Day of the Locust* (1939) exposes the squalid hidden world of Hollywood – that apotheosis of the American Dream – of which the hypnotized public knows nothing. West was killed in a car crash at the age of 37.

**West, Dame Rebecca** 1892–1983 Born Cicily Isobel Fairfield in Kerry, Ireland, she was educated at George Watson's Ladies' College. After

Rebecca West, 1918. Photograph by E. O. Hoppé.

a brief career as an actress (her pseudonym originated from her role in Ibsen's *Rosmersholm*) she turned to journalism, reviewing books for *The Freewoman*, and then becoming a staff member of the *The Clarion* in 1912. She was deeply influenced by the Pankhursts and became an ardent and vocal supporter of women's suffrage. Her outspoken review of **H. G. Wells**'s *Marriage* (1912) started a relationship between the two which lasted for ten years and resulted in the birth of a son, Anthony West, in 1914.

Rebecca West's first book was a critical study of **Henry James** (1916). Her first novel, *The Return of the Soldier* (1918), about a shell-shock victim, was adapted for the stage in 1928 by John van Druten. Other novels were published at intervals: *The Judge* (1922), *The Strange Necessity* (1928), *Harriet Hume* (1929) and *The Thinking Reed* (1936). Three other novels appeared much later: *The Fountain Overflows* (1957), *The Birds Fall Down* (1966) and *This Real Night* (a sequel to *The Fountain Overflows*, published posthumously in 1984). An early novel, *Sunflower*, written during the 1920s, was published for the first time in 1986. Though her reputation as a novelist has never been of the first rank, recent studies have applauded the strong characterization of her heroines and stressed the radical qualities in her writing.

Her other works included a study of **D. H. Lawrence** (1930), a two-volume study of Yugoslavia, *Black Lamb and Grey Falcon* (1941–2) and *The Meaning of Treason* (1949, revised 1952 and 1965), an account of the cases of those convicted as traitors which originated from contributions to *The New Yorker* and *Harper's Magazine*. In *The Court and the Castle* (1958) she turned to the study of religion and politics in literature. This was followed by *McLuhan and the Future of Literature* (1969). *1900* (1982), her last work, was an evocation of the world of her childhood. Many of her earlier pieces were collected and reprinted as *The Young Rebecca* (1982, ed. Jane Marcus).

**Westminster Review, The** A quarterly periodical published between 1824 and 1914. It was conceived as the organ of 'philosophical radicalism' and intended to compete in its coverage of politics and literature with the Whig **Edinburgh Review** and the Tory **Quarterly Review**. Initially funded and inspired by **Jeremy Bentham**, it drew heavily on free contributions from **James Mill**, **John Stuart Mill** and their circles. Disenchanted with changes of proprietor and editor, the Mills began an alternative periodical, *The London Review*, in 1835. In 1836–40 these reviews were amalgamated under the effective but undeclared editorship of J. S. Mill. Under various changes of owner the review remained consistent in its radical campaign for social reform through legislation and education. When the publisher John Chapman bought it in 1851, he appointed **George Eliot** as assistant editor (1851–3) and gave the review a more free-thinking emphasis, accepting contributions from such progressive intellectuals as **J. A. Froude**, **T. H. Huxley**, **G. H. Lewes** and **John Tyndall**. The review at this period also offered extensive coverage of imperial politics and systematic reviewing of contemporary literature. With a further change of ownership and its conversion to a monthly in 1887, the review lost its former high seriousness and eventually dropped its literary coverage.

**Westward Ho** A comedy by **Thomas Dekker** and **John Webster**, produced about 1606 and published in 1607. The main plot concerns three wives who enjoy an escapade with three admirers, but are discovered by their husbands at an inn in Brentford. However, the innocence of the escapade is established and all is forgiven. The sub-plot concerns Justiniano, an Italian merchant in London, who believes his wife to be unfaithful and leaves her. Adopting a disguise, he does his best to enjoy the comedy of London life. Meanwhile, his wife nearly becomes involved with a dubious nobleman; but she loves her husband and they are reconciled at the end of the play.

**Westward Ho!** Historical novel by **Charles Kingsley**, published in 1855. Now remembered chiefly as a children's book, this was Kingsley's most ambitious novel, an epic of England's heroic victory over Spain and the fear of Catholic domination. Jesuits plot the ruin of England, the Inquisition tortures prisoners and roasts them alive; Englishmen fight fair, hang miscreants from the yard-arm, and win against the powers of darkness. The singeing of the Spanish king's beard is justified as liberation of the South American Indians and revenge for the cruelties practised upon them. The story is packed with incident and clotted with pedantry and preaching: Drake, **Raleigh**, **Spenser** and other real-life heroes crowd the pages, as do references to **Hakluyt** and Plato. Despite absurdities, the book has power. A heady mixture of patriotism, sentiment and romance, it set the attitudes of English children for several generations.

**Weyman, Stanley (John)** 1855–1928 Novelist. Born in Shropshire, he was educated at Shrewsbury and Christ Church, Oxford. He was a history teacher, then read for the Bar in 1877 – a profession he abandoned in 1891. His first ventures into literature were short stories for **The Cornhill Magazine** and *The English Illustrated Magazine*, but it was with *The House of the Wolf* (1890; previously serialized in the latter periodical in 1888–9) that he began his career as the author of highly successful historical romances. *A Gentleman of France* (1893), set in the period of Henry of Navarre, was praised by **R. L. Stevenson**; it was followed by *Under the Red Robe* (1894, successfully dramatized in 1896), *The Red Cockade* (1895), *The Castle Inn* (1898), *Count Hannibal* (1901, about the Massacre of St Bartholomew), *Chipping* (1906, set in England around the time of the Reform Bill) and many others.

A prolific author, Weyman continued to write popular novels until the year of his death; these were described by **Hugh Walpole** (in 1924) as 'the finest English historical romances since Scott'.

**Whale, The** An Old English poem preserved in **The Exeter Book**. The first section tells a common story about the whale from a version of the *Physiologus*. The whale's practice of lying with its back exposed encourages sailors to land on it thinking it an island, but when they are moored and light their fires it dives and drowns them. This is interpreted allegorically to illustrate the means by which the devil operates: fiends use deception to make the unwary complacent and then carry them off to hell.

**Wharton, Edith (Newbold)** 1862–1937 American novelist, born into a wealthy New York family. Her first book, written with Ogden Codman, Jr, was a work of non-fiction,

*The Decoration of Houses* (1897), in which she criticized the standards of taste exhibited by the wealthy of her parents' generation, and analysed old New York society and the effects of social snobbery based on economic status (concerns that were to dominate much of her fiction). A collection of short stories, *The Great Inclination*, appeared in 1899 and a short novel, *The Touchstone*, in 1900. Her first full-length novel, *The Valley of Decision*, set in 18th-century Italy, was published in 1902. This was followed by two collections of essays on Italy, and in 1905 by **The House of Mirth**, which was her first popular success.

The influence of her long-time friend **Henry James** is evident in *Madame de Treymes* (1907), the story of an American confronting the social customs of the French. Another novel, *The Fruit of the Tree*, appeared in the same year. In 1911 she published the popular novel **Ethan Frome**, which was uncharacteristically about the lower-middle class of New England. Prior to this she had moved to Paris and joined a group of expatriate friends that included Henry James. Two further novels appeared before the outbreak of World War I: *The Reef* (1912) and *The Custom of the Country* (1913). Both continued her attack on the hypocrisies of New York society. During the war she established American hostels and started an employment agency and day

Edith Wharton in 1905.

nursery for refugees. She was appointed a Chevalier of the Legion of Honour in 1916 for her wartime relief work. Experience of the war provided the material for two novels, *The Marne* (1918) and *A Son at the Front* (1923). Following a trip to North Africa in 1917, she produced a travel narrative, *In Morocco* (1920), and in the same year published **The Age of Innocence**, a novella, which earned her a Pulitzer Prize (making her the first woman to receive this honour). A series of four novelettes entitled *Old New York* appeared in 1924. Over the next few years she wrote three novels which deal with intergenerational differences in families: *The Mother's Recompense* (1925), *Twilight Sleep* (1927) and *The Children* (1928). Her next novels, *Hudson River Bracketed* (1929) and *The Gods Arrive* (1932), examine the artistic temperament through the character of Vance Western, a struggling novelist.

In addition to her many novels Wharton also produced eleven collections of short stories, of which the best known is probably *Xingu and Other Stories* (1916). In 1925 she published *The Writing of Fiction*, in which she discusses literary aesthetics and acknowledges her debt to Henry James. Her autobiography, *A Backward Glance*, appeared in 1934. At the time of her death she was working on another novel, *The Buccaneers* (1938), set in Saratoga in the 1860s.

**What Every Woman Knows** A comedy by **J. M. Barrie**, first performed at the Duke of York's Theatre, London, in 1908.

The father and brother of Maggie Wylie determine to get her a husband, despite her plainness. When the police report that an intruder has been seen climbing into their house, they keep watch and trap him. He is John Shand, a railwayman forced by poverty to discontinue his studies at Glasgow University. He explains that he has been breaking in to read the Wylies' books. The Wylies agree to finance his studies if, after five years, he gives Maggie the right to marry him. She does so after he has been elected to Parliament, where he quickly establishes a reputation as a brilliantly witty speaker. Shand falls for Lady Sybil Tenterden, and Maggie arranges for them to meet at a country cottage, secretly hopeful that they will bore each other. Her hope is fulfilled, and the humourless Shand realizes 'what every woman knows' – that he owes his success to Maggie who, as his typist, has added the brilliance to his dull speeches.

**What Maisie Knew** A novel by **Henry James**, first published in *The Chap Book* from January to August 1897. Later that same year it was serialized in revised form in the *New Review* and also published as a volume.

The story is set in England. Maisie's parents, Beale and Ida Farange, are divorced when she is six years old. She is to spend half of each year with her mother and half with her father. Both parents remarry. Beale marries Miss Overmore, who had been Maisie's governess until she and Maisie's mother quarrelled; Ida marries Sir Claude, but still has a succession of lovers. Maisie, now under the care of Mrs Wix, Miss Overmore's replacement, is shuttled back and forth between the two households. Her two new step-parents become attracted to one another and, when their marriages to her real parents dissolve, they marry. Abandoned to Mrs Wix's care by Ida and Beale, Maisie is invited by Sir Claude, who is fond of her, to make her home with him and the former Miss Overmore. Unfortunately, the former Miss Overmore cannot abide Mrs Wix, the one 'safe' adult whom Maisie absolutely refuses to give up. The final scene, which takes place in Boulogne, ends with Maisie's refusing to live with Sir Claude and his new wife: she departs for England with Mrs Wix, her means of subsistence guaranteed by Sir Claude.

It is ambiguous what sort of 'knowledge' Maisie has achieved at the novel's end, and debatable whether or not she has acquired a sense of morality (or an ability to recognize immorality), whether or not she has remained innocent in spite of the sordid worldliness that surrounds her. The entire story, though written in the third person, is told from the point of view of the perceptive but somewhat naïve Maisie.

**Wheatley, Phillis** 1753–84 A black American poet, born in Africa and sold as a slave in Boston at the age of eight to a tailor, John Wheatley, who educated her with his family. She studied English, Latin and Greek, and began to write poetry in her teens. She travelled to London when she was 18 and there published *Poems on Various Subjects, Religious and Moral* in 1773. When she returned to the USA she married John Peters, a free black, and died in poverty at a young age. Her poetry contains frequent allusions to classical mythology, and mixes topical or contemporary matter with religious and moral subjects. Her subjects include tributes to friends and famous people; discourses on Imagination, Recollection, Friendship and Morals; and occasionally references to incidents in her own life. *Memoirs and Poems of Phillis Wheatley* was published in 1834 and a volume of her letters in 1864.

**Wheelwright, John Brooks** 1897–1940 American poet, born in Boston, and educated at Harvard and the Massachusetts Institute of Technology. His poetry emphasizes his regional interests by focusing on Boston and its environs. It is frequently accompanied by prose 'arguments' which serve as interpretations

Phillis Wheatley. An engraving published in 1773.

rather than reiterations of the poems themselves. His first collection, *Rock and Shell*, was published in 1933. Like all the volumes published during his life, it was privately printed. The second, *Mirrors of Venus*, appeared in 1938, and a third, *Political Self-Portrait*, in 1940. While working on *Dusk to Dusk* Wheelwright was killed in an automobile accident. This fourth volume was published posthumously in *The Collected Poems of John Wheelwright* in 1972.

***Where Angels Fear to Tread*** A novel by **E. M. Forster**, published in 1905.

Lilia Herriton, a widow in her early thirties, is urged to spend a year in Italy by her brother-in-law, Philip, who believes that the experience will purify and ennoble her. Accompanying a younger but less impulsive neighbour, Caroline Abbott, Lilia departs. All goes well until news reaches the Herritons in Sawston that she intends to marry again. Mrs Herriton, a domineering social snob, dispatches Philip to prevent the catastrophe but he arrives too late. On reaching Monteriano he discovers that Lilia has already married Gino Carella, several years her junior and a dentist's son. Philip returns with Caroline to England.

The marriage fails and Lilia dies in childbirth. Mrs Herriton and her equally unsavoury daughter, Harriet, eventually decide to retrieve the baby from its father's dubious influence. Philip is again dispatched, this time with Harriet, and Caroline Abbott, guilt-ridden over her part in

Lilia's downfall, determines to adopt the child herself. All three meet in Monteriano (where Forster supplies a delightfully comic description surrounding a performance of the opera *Lucia di Lammermoor*) and Philip and Caroline begin to succumb to the charm of Italy.

Gino proves to be a devoted father and the mission is more or less abandoned. Harriet refuses to admit defeat, however, and attempts to steal the baby. The carriage in which she, Philip and the baby are travelling is involved in a collision. It overturns and the baby is killed. Gino assaults Philip and the three English characters retire. On the journey home, Philip discovers that he has fallen in love with Caroline, she with Gino; her future seems to hold spinsterhood and charitable works.

**Whetstone, George** ?1544–?1587 Writer of romances, dramatist, poet. Whetstone seems to have attempted to support his unstable fortunes by a military life and literary production. He fought in the Low Countries and was present at Zutphen when **Sir Philip Sidney** received his fatal wound. *The Rock of Regard* (1576) is mainly a collection of tales (largely drawn from Italian sources) in prose and verse. His play *Promos and Cassandra* (1578) was never acted. Its story is from Cinthio's *Hecatommithi*. The story of Promos and Cassandra is also one of the prose romances in Whetstone's 1582 collection *An Heptameron of Civil Discourses* where again many of the stories are from Cinthio. Whetstone's version of this story, either as play or romance or both, is probably the immediate main source for **Shakespeare**'s *Measure for Measure*. Among Whetstone's other works are a verse eulogy in commemoration of **George Gascoigne** (1577), and a series of biographical elegies of distinguished contemporaries, including a verse biography of Sir Philip Sidney.

**White, Antonia** 1899–1980 Novelist and short-story writer. Born Antonia Botting in London, she was educated at the Convent of the Sacred Heart, Roehampton, and at St Paul's Girls' School. She married H. T. Hopkinson, subsequently editor of *Picture Post*, in 1930. *Frost in May* (1933), her first book, was apparently written in six weeks and is mainly autobiographical. In it, Nanda Grey, the only daughter of a father recently converted to Roman Catholicism, is sent to be educated at the Convent of the Five Wounds, Lippington. The year is 1908 and she is nine. Her life there, with all its miseries and repressions, is cleverly evoked, and the same theme is picked up in Antonia White's subsequent novels, *The Lost Traveller* (1950), *The Sugar House* (1952) and *Beyond the Glass* (1954), whose heroine, Clara Batchelor, suffers in her relationships with men, is confined in an asylum, and eventually returns to the faith which she had rejected early in life.

Apart from the novels, Antonia White was the author of a play, *Three in a Room* (1947), and two books for children, *Minka and Curdy* (1957) and *Living with Minka and Curdy* (1970). She also translated many works from French, including novels by Christine Arnothy and Colette. Her *The Hound and the Falcon* (1965) recounts 'the story of a re-conversion to the Catholic faith'.

**White, Edmund** 1940– One of America's foremost homosexual authors. White's fiction includes *Forgetting Elena* (1973), *Nocturnes for the King of Naples* (1978) and *A Boy's Own Story* (1982), a novel which treats the coming of age of an adolescent who realizes his homosexuality and must find a place for himself in contemporary society. White has also published works of non-fiction dealing with issues of sociological and cultural interest. *States of Desire: Travels in Gay America* (1980) investigates the gay communities of several major American cities. With Dr Charles Silverstein he co-wrote *The Joy of Gay Sex* (1977).

**White, E[lwyn] B[rooks]** 1899–1985 American essayist, journalist and critic, born in Mount Vernon, New York, and educated at Cornell. After a period in Seattle as a reporter, he moved to New York City where he became a writer and contributing editor for *The New Yorker* in 1926. His long-term friendship with **James Thurber** included a collaboration, *Is Sex Necessary?*, in 1929. His other works include *Alice Through the Cellophane* (1933), *Quo Vadimus? Or the Case for the Bicycle* (1938), *One Man's Meat* (1942), *The Second Tree from the Corner* (1954) and *The Points of My Compass* (1962). He wrote several children's works, including *Stuart Little* (1945) and *Charlotte's Web* (1952).

**White, Gilbert** 1720–93 Naturalist. Born in Selborne, Hampshire, he was educated at Winchester College – where **Joseph Warton** and **Thomas Warton the younger** were his contemporaries – and at Oriel College, Oxford. He became a fellow of his college and later dean, but in 1758 returned to Selborne. He remained there for the rest of his life, holding several local curacies.

White recorded his observations of the local scene in letters to friends (chiefly the naturalists Thomas Pennant and Daines Barrington) and kept a journal, a sort of naturalist's calendar. Pennant and Barrington urged him to publish, returning his letters for that purpose. White added a description of Selborne and the surrounding country, also in the form of a letter, as an introduction and in 1789 published *The Natural History and Antiquities of Selborne. A Naturalists' Calendar*, edited by J. Aikin after

White's death, appeared in 1795. *The Natural History of Selborne*, as it is usually called, is a classic of natural history as well as a book of lasting charm. White was a keen observer of wildlife and the changing seasons, with a gift for painstaking fieldwork and an eye for luminous detail.

**White, Henry Kirke** 1785–1806 Poet. Born in Nottingham, where he received some elementary schooling, he educated himself further while serving as a solicitors' articled clerk. Increasingly evangelical in religion, he sought a university education to prepare for ordination, and published *Clifton Grove* (1803), a volume of verses in the style of **Goldsmith**'s *Deserted Village*, to raise funds. **Southey** encouraged his poetical bent, and others furthered his academic career. Already consumptive, he died at St John's College, Cambridge, where he was showing signs of promise as an undergraduate. Southey compiled *The Remains of Henry Kirke White* (1807) from his literary manuscripts; its evangelical tone ensured its brief popularity.

**White, Patrick** 1912–90 Australian novelist, short-story writer and dramatist. The son of a wealthy landowning family, he was born in London of Australian parents and taken to Australia at the age of six months. At the age of 13 he was sent to Cheltenham College, an experience which he has referred to as a 'four-year prison sentence'. He returned to Australia and worked for two years as a jackaroo on a sheep station before going to Cambridge to read Modern Languages. After graduating in 1935, he settled in London, hoping to make a career as a writer. He published an early volume of poetry and his first novel, *The Happy Valley* (1939). During World War II he served as an

Patrick White.

RAF Intelligence Officer in the Middle East and Greece. During these years he met Manoly Lascaris, a Greek officer who was to become his lifelong companion. After the war he settled with Lascaris at Castle Hill, near Sydney. The war years and his reading of the journals of the Australian explorers confirmed his sense of his Australianness and led ultimately to three of his finest novels, which discuss various aspects of Australian identity: *The Tree of Man* (1955), an epic novel covering a period from pioneer settlement to suburbanization, *Voss* (1957) and *Riders in the Chariot* (1961), which contains a powerful indictment of Australian suburban life, an aspect of White's work that has made him unpopular with some Australian readers. In 1964 he moved to an inner suburb of Sydney. The novels *The Solid Mandala* (1966), *The Vivisector* (1970) and *The Eye of the Storm* (1973) are all products of this milieu. In 1973 he won the Nobel Prize for Literature which confirmed his reputation as Australia's most important living writer. *A Fringe of Leaves* (1976), like *Voss*, takes a subject from 19th-century Australian history and uses it as a metaphor for self-exploration with national, psychological and gender implications. *The Twyborn Affair* (1979) is a wide-ranging work exploring various dualities in human nature, including that of male and female sexuality. White subsequently indicated that this was his last novel and that in future he would write only for radio and the stage, but in 1986 he published another novel, *Memoirs of Many in One* 'by Alex Xenophon Demirjian Gray, edited by Patrick White'. His autobiography, *Flaws in the Glass* (1981), openly acknowledges his homosexuality. He has also published the novels *The Living and the Dead* (1941) and *The Aunt's Story* (1948) and two volumes of short stories, *The Burnt Ones* (1964) and *The Cockatoos* (1974). White is also one of Australia's finest dramatists working in a non-naturalistic mode; his plays include *The Season at Sarsaparilla* (1961), *Night on Bald Mountain* (1962) and *Signal Driver* (1983).

**White, T[erence] H[anbury]** 1906–64 Children's writer. Born in Bombay, he was educated at Cheltenham College and Queens' College, Cambridge. For several years he was a schoolmaster at Stowe, then resigned his post to concentrate on his writing, living in a cottage at Stowe Ridings on the Stowe estate. Here he read and was profoundly affected by **Malory**'s *Le Morte Darthur*, which, as a pacifist, he considered to be about 'a quest for an antidote to war'. His own early works were hardly successful but *England Have My Bones* (1937), a paean of praise for the English countryside, its traditions and history, was admired by a number of contemporary readers. His major success began with *The Sword in the Stone* (1939), a quirky, humorous retelling of the Arthurian legend (see **Arthurian literature**), continued in *The Witch in the Wood* (1940), *The Ill-Made Knight* (1941) and *The Candle in the Wind* (1958). The series was revised and titled *The Once and Future King* (1958). A fifth title, *The Book of Merlyn*, posthumously discovered among the author's papers, was published in 1977.

Other works included *Mistress Masham's Repose* (1946), a fantasy about descendants of Gulliver's Lilliputians; *The Goshawk* (1951), an account of his training of a pet hawk; *The Book of Beasts* (1954), a translation from a medieval bestiary; and *The Master* (1957), part parable and part **science fiction**.

**White, William Hale** 1831–1913 Novelist and essayist under the pseudonym Mark Rutherford. White was born in the dissenting stronghold of Bedford, where his father, a printer and bookseller, played a prominent part in local dissenting politics. In a later capacity as doorman of the House of Commons his father, whom White continued to revere, wrote lively parliamentary sketches. White attended Bedford Modern School and, after the 'conversion' expected by his family's religious background, went to train as an Independent minister at the Countess of Huntingdon's college at Cheshunt and then to New College, St John's Wood, from which he and two other students were expelled in 1851 for raising issues of biblical criticism unacceptable to die-hard orthodoxy. During the 1850s he preached in Unitarian chapels and thereafter occasionally attended preachers whose life and teaching he respected. Having abandoned ministerial training White worked for John Chapman, publisher and editor of the *Westminster Review*, in whose offices he met **George Eliot** whom he much admired. In 1854 he entered the Civil Service, from which he was to retire in 1891 with the rank of Assistant Director of Contracts at the Admiralty. Meanwhile, he had turned to political and literary journalism, acting as London correspondent of *The Scotsman*. In his fifties White began to publish in two distinct – but for him related – fields: fiction and philosophy. In 1881 he published *The Autobiography of Mark Rutherford, Dissenting Minister*, allegedly edited by Reuben Shapcott, which, in thinly veiled form, retold White's own spiritual history. Rutherford finishes his ministerial training but becomes disillusioned with the morally and spiritually moribund nature of the congregations he attempts to serve. His subsequent journey, from Independent minister through Unitarianism to theism, agnosticism and finally a state of stoic resignation, not only resembles White's experience but charts the fluid nature of religious affiliation encountered by many a contemporary seceder from orthodoxy. What distinguishes White's account both here and in the sequel,

*Mark Rutherford's Deliverance* (1885), is the narrator's air of absolute fidelity to the truth as he sees it, however drab, sombre or inconvenient to the demands of fictional structure. These two novels together with *The Revolution in Tanner's Lane* (1887) provide a portrait of 19th-century dissent where nostalgia for the past glories of Puritanism informs the astringent analysis of its present decay. White never abandoned his Bedford religious heritage. An intimate knowledge of the Bible informed all his writings and gave rise to the essays on 'Gideon', 'Samuel', and 'Saul' and 'Notes on the Book of Job'; the Puritan daily habit of self-examination fed into the slow reflective commentaries on the inner lives of his characters; and the life and work of his early Puritan predecessor, **John Bunyan**, continued to fascinate him, as a study published under his own name in 1905 proved. White also published works under his own name on two philosophical writers who had deeply influenced his mature position, **Wordsworth** and Spinoza. His other writings, the novels *Catherine Furze* (1893), *Miriam's Schooling and other Papers* (1893) and *Clara Hopgood* (1896), and the essays and stories published in *Pages from a Journal* (1900), *More Pages from a Journal* (1910) and *Last Pages from a Journal* (1915), all serve to confirm the picture of a deeply self-critical moral earnestness schooling an innately depressive temperament for survival in an often uncongenial world, where it remains a duty to witness to the truth, however intermittently it may be glimpsed.

**White Book of Rhydderch** See *Mabinogion, The*.

**White Devil, The** A tragedy by **John Webster**, first produced c.1612 and published in 1612. The source of the play lies in historical events that took place in Italy in the 1580s.

The Duke of Brachiano is married to Isabella, sister of Francisco, the Duke of Florence. Brachiano is tired of Isabella and has fallen in love with Vittoria Corombona. Vittoria and Brachiano are encouraged and abetted in their adulterous relationship by Vittoria's brother, Flamineo, who helps Brachiano dispose of both Isabella and Vittoria's husband, Camillo. Flamineo also quarrels with his younger brother, Marcello, who is as honourable as Flamineo is evil; he kills him and their mother, Cornelia, is an involuntary witness of the murder. Vittoria is accused of murder and adultery; she is apprehended and sentenced to confinement in a house for fallen women. But Brachiano rescues her and they flee to Padua.

Francisco is determined to avenge Isabella's death. Flamineo, meanwhile, feels entitled to rich rewards for his services to Vittoria and Brachiano; but Francisco's men Gasparo and Lodovico, disguised as Capuchin friars, succeed in murdering Brachiano with the greatest possible cruelty. Vittoria and Flamineo now confront each other. Flamineo presses his claim to reward and Vittoria knows that destruction is only a hair's breadth from either of them. She would willingly kill him, but Gasparo and Lodovico return to complete Francisco's vengeance on both of them.

**White Goddess, The** A study by **Robert Graves**, published in 1948 and revised in 1952. Sub-titled 'A Historical Grammar of Poetic Myth', it is an eclectic and highly original exploration of poetic thinking in terms of Celtic and Mediterranean archaeology, anthropology and mythology. The central theme is that the Muse, or Moon-goddess, inspires poetry of a magical quality, in contrast to rational, classical verse. This is elaborated in terms of seasonal rituals of sacrifice and rebirth, in which the poet is identified with the God of the Waxing Year and his muse with the triple goddess who represents the 'ancient power of fright and lust'. The anthropological arguments for an ancient matriarchy and for the figure of the Muse have been attacked as historically implausible. On the other hand, the book has been admired for the creation of an extended metaphor of poetic inspiration, and as a scholastic extravaganza, erudite, inventive and riddling.

**White Hotel, The** A controversial best-selling novel by **D. M. Thomas**, published in 1981. *The White Hotel* attracted passionate support and notoriety in equal measures for its sensational sexual explicitness and direct treatment of Nazi war atrocities. Beginning with a virtuoso pastiche of a Freudian case history, the novel ultimately shows the neuroses of the patient and protagonist, Lisa Erdman, to have been premonitory of her eventual mutilation and murder in the Babi Yar massacre. Thomas's attempt to link what he regards as the 20th century's central body of 'myth' – Freud's collected case histories – with arguably its climactic experience – the Holocaust – in what Lisa sees as 'a universal struggle between the life instinct and the death instinct' has been charged inconclusively with pornography and plagiarism, but also acclaimed as a bold and powerful feat of modern myth-making.

**White Peacock, The** **D. H. Lawrence**'s first novel, published in 1911. Narrated in the first person by Cyril Beardsall, it describes the relationships of his sister, Lettie, with George Saxton, a tenant farmer's son, and Leslie Tempest, heir of a wealthy mineowner. Lettie flirts with both men, but eventually decides to marry Tempest to gain material security. Saxton is tormented by the knowledge that he could have won her had he been more strong-willed.

Instead he marries Meg, a commonplace girl – the beginning of a steady decline. Lettie makes the best of her prudent but unfulfilling marriage. Cyril himself shows a mild romantic interest in Saxton's sister, Emily, but nothing comes of it and she marries someone else. The most striking figure in the novel is the gamekeeper, Annable, the precursor of Oliver Mellors in *Lady Chatterley's Lover*. The characters are based loosely on friends and family members, and the countryside is recognizably the country around Eastwood.

**White Ship, The** A narrative poem by **Dante Gabriel Rossetti**, published in 1881 in *Ballads and Sonnets*. The tale of the loss of the White Ship and the death of Prince William, the heir to Henry I, is related by Berold of Rouen. The ship runs on a reef and the prince is placed in a boat so that he might be saved, but he insists on returning to the ship to save his sister. As a result, the boat is swamped. None of the courtiers can face the task of telling the king and a child is sent to carry the dreadful news.

**White-Jacket, or, The World in a Man-of-War** A novel by **Herman Melville**, published in 1850, and based on the author's experience of service on the man-of-war *United States* in 1844.

The narrative covers the homeward voyage of the frigate *Neversink* from Peru eastward round the Horn to Virginia. From scraps of cloth the narrator makes himself the white jacket that earns him his nickname and throughout the journey causes him grief, alienating him from his fellows, providing him with no protection against the elements, appalling and frightening him with its ghastly colour, and indeed nearly causing his death when the wind wraps it around his head so that he falls from the yard-arm into the sea. In this last incident, which occurs as they near home, he finally cuts himself free from the jacket, thus saving himself from drowning.

Most of the book, though, is devoted to describing life on board the man-of-war, emphasizing the degrading conditions the men live in, the tyrannies of the captain and officers over them, and especially the practice of flogging, which Melville criticizes on several occasions. The hierarchical organization of the navy, he argues, is dehumanizing to all involved and contradicts the spirit of American democracy. The issue of flogging was a timely one; copies of Melville's book were sent to Congress during its debate over the issue, and coincidentally the practice was abolished that year.

**Whitehead, Charles** 1804–62 Novelist, poet and dramatist. Whitehead was born in London, the son of a wine merchant. He was the author of several popular works: a poem, *The Solitary*

(1831), two romantic novels, *Jack Ketch* (1834) and *Richard Savage* (1842), and a verse drama, *The Cavalier* (1836). His career was blighted by drunkenness and he ceased writing about 1850. Whitehead died in Australia.

**Whitehead, William** 1715–85 Poet and dramatist. Born in Cambridge, he was educated at Winchester College and Clare College, Cambridge, where he was elected a fellow in 1742. Not wishing to be ordained, he resigned his fellowship in 1745 and became tutor to Viscount Villiers, son of the Earl of Jersey. The family remained his faithful patrons. Largely influenced by **Pope**, his early poems used the heroic couplet, but Whitehead explored blank verse too. **Garrick** produced his tragedy *The Roman Father* with some success in 1750. **Horace Walpole** and **William Mason** praised *Creusa, Queen of Athens* (1754). *Elegies, with an Ode to the Tiber, Written Abroad* (1757) was inspired by his experiences as tutor on the Grand Tour in 1754–6.

Whitehead became **Poet Laureate** on the death of **Cibber** in 1757, after **Gray** had declined the post, and attracted the disapproval of various contemporaries by the odes he wrote in performance of his duties. **Johnson** found his '*grand nonsense . . . insupportable*', but Whitehead's chief assailant was **Charles Churchill**, who wrote in *The Ghost* (1762): 'DULLNESS and METHOD still are one, / and WHITEHEAD is their darling Son.' Whitehead made a dignified reply in *A Charge to the Poets* (1762) and in *A Pathetic Apology for all Laureates, Past, Present, and to Come*. The latter was circulated among his friends and published posthumously in Mason's memoir.

Whitehead produced a successful comedy, *The School for Lovers*, in 1762 and a farce, *The Trip to Scotland*, in 1770. His later poems include *Variety: A Tale for Married People* (1776) and *The Goat's Beard* (1777), his last separate publication. His collected works appeared in two volumes in 1774. Mason added a third volume with a memoir for the collected edition of 1788.

**Whiteing, Richard** 1840–1928 Novelist and journalist. Born in London, he trained as an engraver before turning to fiction at the age of 48 with *The Island* (1888) and its sequel, *Number 5 John Street* (1889). The novels depict social unrest in late Victorian Britain and criticize accepted values. A series of satirical articles which date from Whiteing's time in Paris were published in *The Evening Star* from 1866.

**Whitfield, James M.** 1823–78 Black American Abolitionist poet born in Exeter, New Hampshire. He lived briefly in Boston, then settled in Buffalo, where he worked as a barber and began to write verse. His first volume, *Poems*, appeared in 1846, but it was not until the

publication of *America, and Other Poems* in 1853 that he stopped barbering and devoted his time to writing. In 1858 he founded the journal *African-American Repository*. His later poetry appeared primarily in journals such as the *Liberator* and *Frederick Douglass' Paper*. He died in California, en route to Central America to examine the possibilities of establishing a colony of free blacks in the region.

**Whiting, John** 1917–63 English playwright. He was born in Salisbury and educated at Taunton School and the Royal Academy of Dramatic Art. Whiting wrote against the stream of socially committed drama and acquired a following that was never quite large enough to constitute a paying audience. His best work includes a whimsical comedy, *A Penny for a Song* (1951), and several plays in which he dramatizes his own and his characters' spiritual struggles, *Saint's Day* (1951), *Marching Song* (1954), *The Gates of Summer* (1956) and *The Devils* (1961), derived from **Aldous Huxley**'s *The Devils of Loudun*. His perceptive criticism of the contemporary stage is collected in *Whiting on Theatre* (1966).

**Whitman, Walt[er]** 1819–92 American poet, born in West Hills on Long Island. In 1823 his family moved to Brooklyn. In 1830 he left school to become a printer's apprentice and then an itinerant teacher. He returned to Long Island in 1838 as a schoolteacher and printer, and in the same year started the newspaper *The Long Islander*, which he delivered personally to subscribers. In 1842 he went back to Brooklyn and became editor of the New York *Aurora*. Four years later he assumed editorship of the Brooklyn *Eagle*, but, because of the radical tone of his editorials, he did not keep the post for long. While working for these various newspapers he also began to write poetry and short stories. His early works include a temperance tract, *Franklin Evans* (1842), written in the form of a novel. His early stories are recollected in *The Half-Breed and Other Stories* (1927).

In 1848 he travelled south to work on the New Orleans *Crescent*. The experience of the vastness of the American landscape and the variety of its people made a deep impression on him. He returned to New York later that year and turned his attention increasingly toward poetry. In 1855 he borrowed a press from some friends and set up the 12 poems (including an early version of **Song of Myself**) which made up the first edition of *Leaves of Grass*. Although he himself published an anonymous laudatory review, the book received little attention. It did, however, elicit a letter of praise from **Ralph Waldo Emerson**, which Whitman printed in the second edition (1856). This edition also included 20 new poems, among them 'Crossing Brook-

Walt Whitman. The frontispiece portrait for the first edition of *Leaves of Grass* (1855).

lyn Ferry'. In 1857 he became editor of the Brooklyn *Times*, his contributions to which were subsequently published in *I Sit and Look Out* (1932). In 1860 he found a publisher (Thayer and Eldridge) for a new edition of *Leaves of Grass* which contained 124 new poems, including those of the 'Calamus' and 'Children of Adam' sections.

Whitman's verse, with its frequent use of colloquial language and everyday events, represents a turning-point in the history of American poetry – a poetic form fashioned out of specifically American experience in a distinctively American idiom. Some of his finest poems grew out of his personal experience of the horrors of the Civil War (during which he served as a volunteer nurse in army hospitals and as a correspondent for *The New York Times*), and out of his attempt to reconcile the destruction of the war with his visionary idea of America. *Drum Taps* was published in 1865, and with its companion volume, *Sequel*, appeared in the 1867 edition of *Leaves of Grass*. *Sequel* was written in the aftermath of Abraham Lincoln's assassination and includes Whitman's elegies for the dead president: 'When Lilacs Last in the Dooryard Bloom'd' and 'O Captain! My Captain!'.

After the war Whitman worked briefly as a clerk in the Department of the Interior, but was dismissed when the Secretary learned that he was the author of the sensual and shocking *Leaves of Grass*. He continued to hold minor posts in Washington, however, and his prose work *Democratic Vistas* (1871) is a passionate reaffirmation of democratic principles in the face of the widespread corruption of the Reconstruction era. In 1873 he suffered the first of a series of paralytic strokes. The 1871 edition of *Leaves of Grass* (which included the *Passage to India* group of poems) was reprinted in 1876 as the 'Author's' or 'Centennial' edition. In 1876 he also published a volume of prose pieces entitled *Two Rivulets*. In 1881 a newly augmented edition of *Leaves of Grass* appeared, then comprising 293 poems in all. The following year he published another volume of prose, *Specimen Days and Collect*. A collection of his newspaper pieces, *November Boughs*, appeared in 1888. His final volume was the 'Deathbed' edition of *Leaves of Grass*, which he prepared in 1891–2. It includes two annexes, the 'Sands at Seventy' and 'Good-bye My Fancy' groups of poems, and concludes with the prose piece 'A Backward Glance O'er Travel'd Roads', in which he attempts to explain his life and work.

**Whittier, John Greenleaf** *c.*1807–92 American poet, born into a Quaker family in East Haverhill, Massachusetts. His first poems were published by the Abolitionist **William Lloyd Garrison** in his paper *The Liberator*. Garrison became his friend and helped him obtain an editorial job on a Boston newspaper in 1829. His first book was *Legends of New-England in Prose and Verse* (1831). Early New England life also provided the subject for two long poems, *Moll Pitcher* (1832) and *Mogg Megone* (1836).

A career in journalism and letters seemed set, but Whittier's Quaker conscience and the influence of Garrison brought him into politics. He became involved in the anti-slavery cause and was elected to the Massachusetts legislature in 1835. He edited the *Pennsylvania Freeman* from 1838 to 1840, and published *Poems Written During the Progress of the Abolition Question* in 1838. He then became increasingly uncomfortable with Garrison's politics and founded the Liberty party, to which he contributed his skills as a journalist. *Lays of My Home and Other Poems* appeared in 1843, and further anti-slavery poems in *Voices of Freedom* in 1846. His first collected *Poems* (1849) testifies eloquently to his hatred of tyranny and his unshakeable concern for the suffering of others, as does *Songs of Labor* (1850).

He continued to write in support of Abolition throughout the Civil War, but also found time for creative efforts as a poet of the countryside with *The Chapel of the Hermits* (1853), *The Panorama and Other Poems* (1856) and *Home Ballads and Poems* (1860). The Civil War was the impulse for *In War Time and Other Poems* (1864). When the struggle was over, he turned back to New England and the countryside for his inspiration and produced what is probably his best work: *Snowbound* (1866), *The Tent on the Beach* (1867), *Among the Hills* (1869), *Miriam and Other Poems* (1871), *Hazel-Blossoms* (1875), *The Vision of Echard* (1878), *Saint Gregory's Guest* (1886) and *At Sundown* (1890).

**Who's Afraid of Virginia Woolf?** A play by **Edward Albee**, first performed in New York City in 1962. The first of his three-act dramas, it is also the most admired of Albee's plays.

George is a history professor at a small New England college. His wife Martha is the daughter of the college president. The play depicts the events of a single night, when George and Martha bring a young colleague and his nervous wife back from a party. The elder couple involve Nick and Honey in the verbal abuse that seems to be a nightly ritual with them. Honey drinks too much and becomes ill. Martha tries to seduce Nick. The sexuality of all four characters is impugned. Albee calls the second act a 'Walpurgisnacht', a night of conflict and purgation. The final purgative comes in Act Three, titled 'Exorcism', when George and Martha's imaginary son, created by them as some kind of sustenance, is declared dead by Martha, thereby acknowledging their illusions and allowing compassionate feelings to surface.

**Whyte-Melville, G[eorge] J[ohn]** 1821–78 Novelist. He was born of aristocratic parents and educated at Eton. He entered the Army and served in the Crimea; thereafter devoting himself to writing and foxhunting. He published some 23 novels and a volume of verse. His subjects were historical, romantic and sporting and his work in the latter area is generally felt to have survived best, being perceptive, vivid and curiously undated. A good example is *Market Harborough* (1861). He was killed, characteristically, in a hunting accident.

**Widow's Tears, The** A sour comedy by **George Chapman**, first performed by a **boys' company** in c.1605 and published in 1612.

The play is oddly broken-backed. The first three acts are largely concerned with what emerges as the sub-plot, in which the widowed Eudora, despite her vows of faithfulness to her dead husband, is wooed and won by Tharsalio, who, though well-born, was formerly her servant. Cynthia, one of the people most shocked by Eudora's fall, becomes the focus of the last two acts, which are based on the story of the widow of Ephesus in the *Satyricon* of Petronius. Chapman has given the story a twist by having Lysander feign his own death in order to test Cynthia's constancy. Disguised as a soldier, he woos his 'widow' in the tomb and succeeds in cuckolding himself. *The Widow's Tears* relies on conventional cynicism about the fickleness of women.

**Widowers' Houses** **George Bernard Shaw**'s first play, presented in London in 1892. The published sub-title insisted that it was both 'didactic' and 'realistic'. Its aim, certainly, was to instruct the Victorian age in the economic realities of capitalism.

Dr Henry Trench, a member of an aristocratic family, has fallen in love with Blanche Sartorius. Her father will consent to the match only if it can be guaranteed that Trench's family will accept Blanche. When Trench learns that Sartorius has gained his wealth, and continues to gain it, by extorting rent from impoverished tenants, he is horrified. But Sartorius turns the tables on him by pointing out that Trench's income, however little he may concern himself with it, is derived from the same sources. Trench capitulates, and agrees to marry Blanche, who is not much more admirable than her father and Trench.

**Widsith** An Old English poem preserved in **The Exeter Book**. Dating from the 7th century, it is one of the oldest surviving works in the vernacular. Purporting to be an account of the courts visited by the minstrel Widsith, the poem catalogues the heroes of the European tribes. The chronological span, from Eormanric (d.375) to Aelfwine's invasion of Italy in 568, makes it impossible that the work was based on the reminiscences of a real minstrel.

**Wiebe, Rudy (Henry)** 1934– Canadian novelist and writer of short stories. Born in Fairholme, Saskatchewan, of Russian parents, he grew up in Alberta and was educated at the University of Alberta where he now teaches. His first novel, *Peace Shall Destroy Many*, was published in 1962 to be followed by several novels, collections of short stories and anthologies, including *First and Vital Candle* (1966), *The Blue Mountains of China* (1970), *The Temptations of Big Bear* (1973), *Where is the Voice Coming From?* (1974), *The Scorched-Wood People* (1977) and *The Mad Trapper* (1980). Many of his short stories demonstrate an original and intelligent wit, 'The Naming of Albert Johnson' and 'The Angel of the Tar Sands' among them.

**Wieland, or, The Transformation** A Gothic romance by **Charles Brockden Brown**, published in 1798, and generally recognized as one of America's first major novels. Cast in the form of a letter from Clara, the only surviving member of the Wieland family, to an unnamed friend, the story begins with a brief biography of Wieland senior, a mystic who emigrated from

Germany to Pennsylvania and built a large estate there. While engaged one evening in an unidentified spiritual enterprise, he dies of spontaneous combustion. Following his wife's death, their children, Clara and Wieland Jr, are cared for by Catherine Pleyel, whom Wieland eventually marries. When Catherine's brother Henry arrives from Germany, Clara falls in love with him and the four enjoy each other's company insulated from the outside world.

The sense of spiritual and physical harmony is destroyed, however, following the intrusion of the mysterious Carwin. Shortly after his first appearance, disembodied voices issue various announcements and warnings. On one occasion they tell of the death of Henry Pleyel's fiancée, and this encourages him to fall in love with Clara. Later, when the voices suggest that Clara and Carwin are having an affair, Henry returns to Germany and, finding his fiancée alive, marries her. Back at the estate in Pennsylvania, the voices eventually drive Wieland insane; he murders his wife and children and is incarcerated in an asylum. He escapes, however, and returns on the very evening that Carwin confesses to Clara that he himself had created the voices by ventriloquism. Wieland's intention is to kill his sister, but when ordered not to by the concealed Carwin's voices, he commits suicide instead. Carwin disappears, and in time Clara marries Henry, when he returns to the estate after the death of his wife.

**Wife of Bath's Tale, The** See *Canterbury Tales, The*.

**Wife's Lament, The** An Old English poem preserved in **The Exeter Book**, recording the lament of a wife whose husband is in exile. She is apparently an alien in his homeland and friendless; he has committed a crime and been banished. Consequently she lives in an earth-barrow in the forest. The chronology of events is not completely clear and the circumstances of the husband's exile are not fully explained. Despite this obscurity the woman's lament poignantly expresses her solitude, isolation and longing for her husband.

**Wiggin, Kate Douglas (née Smith)** 1856–1923 American children's author. Born and educated in Philadelphia, she trained as a teacher and for a time ran a free nursery school in San Francisco. Her first novels were written to raise money for this enterprise, but her great bestseller, *Rebecca of Sunnybrook Farm* (1903), came many years later. Other works include the autobiographical *My Garden of Memory* (1923).

**Wigglesworth, Michael** 1631–1705 American Puritan minister and poet, born in Yorkshire. His family emigrated to New England in 1638

and settled in Quinnipiac (later named New Haven), Connecticut. He studied medicine at Harvard, and in 1656 he was ordained minister of the congregation at Malden, Massachusetts. Wigglesworth's writing not only states the most fundamental tenets of Puritan belief, but shows American Puritanism as it was lived by the individual and the community. His most widely read poems were written either to present the articles of faith in a form which allowed for easy memorization, or to prescribe behaviour fitting for a Christian: **The Day of Doom** (1662), *Meat Out of the Eater* (1670), a discourse on the uses the virtuous can find in the experience of ill health, and the posthumously-published verse jeremiad 'God's Controversy with New England', which interprets the drought of 1662 as a Providential warning to reform. His *Diary* articulates the psychological struggle inherent in spiritual growth.

**Wilbur, Richard (Purdy)** 1921– American poet, born in New York City and educated at Amherst College and at Harvard. He served in the US Army during World War II. His first volume of poetry, *The Beautiful Changes* (1947), was written in response to the personal and public dislocation he perceived in the war and its aftermath. He was awarded the Harriet Monroe Memorial Prize in 1948 and published his second collection, *Ceremony and Other Poems*, in 1950. Following the publication of *Things of This World* (1956), he received the Pulitzer Prize and the National Book Award in 1957. *Advice to a Prophet and Other Poems* appeared in 1961 and *The Poems of Richard Wilbur* in 1963. Subsequent volumes are *Complaint* (1968), *Walking to Sleep: New Poems and Translations* (1969), *Seed Leaves* (1974) and *The Mind-Reader* (1976). His verse is characterized by its formal strictness, its urbane wit, and its oblique quality: 'Poems', he argues, 'are not addressed to anybody in particular . . . they are conflicts with disorder, not messages from one person to another'. He has also published children's verse in *Loudmouse* (1963) and *Opposites* (1973), and a collection of essays, *Responses: Prose Pieces 1953–1976* (1976).

**Wild Wales** A travel book by **George Borrow**, published in 1862.

Based upon Borrow's holiday visits and solitary walking tours, *Wild Wales* retains its place as a document celebrating the Victorian rediscovery of rural Britain, not so much for its factual accuracy, but for the immediacy of its narrative, the high colouring given to simple episodes and the raciness of the dialogue. The writing is so direct that the book will serve as a guide even in the late 20th century, though Borrow's affectionate interpretation of the Welsh and their history draws its strength from a lifelong academic interest in the Welsh language and its literature, some of which he had translated.

**Wild-Goose Chase, The** A comedy by **John Fletcher**, first performed about 1621 and published in 1652, whose anticipation of the urbane manners comedy of Restoration England was recognized in **Farquhar**'s revision of it as *The Inconstant* (1702). The wild goose of the title is Mirabell, whose aversion to marriage leads Oriana, his betrothed, to desperate measures. She eventually wins him after disguising herself as a rich Italian.

**Wilde, Lady Jane Francesca** 1820–96 Irish poet and journalist, the wife of **Sir William Wilde** and mother of **Oscar Wilde**. Born in Wexford, she became a regular contributor to *The Nation*, the newspaper of the Young Ireland movement, using the pen-name 'Speranza' for her fiercely nationalistic poems and prose pieces. One of her articles, 'Jacta Alea Est' ('The Die is Cast'), led to the suppression of the issue of 29 July 1848. After her marriage to Sir William Wilde, she made their home at Merrion Square one of the best-known and most-frequented social centres in Dublin. After his death in 1876, she moved to London and resumed her career as the hostess of a salon at Chelsea. She died in London while Oscar Wilde was in prison. More famous as a personality than as a writer, she made something of a reputation as the author of *Ancient Legends, Mystic Charms, and Superstitions of Ireland* (1887).

**Wilde, Oscar (Fingal O'Flahertie Wills)** 1854–1900 Playwright, novelist, essayist, poet and epigrammatist. Wilde was born in Dublin, the son of **Sir William Wilde** and **Lady Jane Francesca Wilde**. He studied at Trinity College, Dublin, and later at Magdalen College, Oxford. A brilliant classicist, he won the Newdigate Prize in 1878 for his poem, 'Ravenna'. He made himself conspicuous by despising athleticism and espousing the **Aesthetic Movement**: he collected blue china and peacock's feathers, declared himself a disciple of **Walter Pater** and the cult of Art for Art's sake (which **Gilbert** and Sullivan mocked in *Patience*, 1881). That year his first volume of poems was published. Wilde affected velvet knee-breeches and advocated rational dress (which meant flowing robes and no corsets) for women. He also proclaimed himself a socialist, though his concern was less with egalitarianism than freedom for the artist. He went on a lecture tour of the United States in 1882, where he is said to have made the famous reply to the customs official who asked him whether he had anything to declare: 'Only my genius'. In 1883 he attended the first night of his play *Vera* in New York, but it was unsuccessful.

In 1884 he married and in 1888 published *The*

Oscar Wilde. A caricature by Max Beerbohm, 1894.

*Happy Prince and Other Tales*, fairy-stories written for his two sons. *The Picture of Dorian Gray* (1890) followed. In 1891 he brought out more fairy-stories, *A House of Pomegranates* and *Lord Arthur Savile's Crime and Other Stories*. His second play, *The Duchess of Padua*, came the same year; it is an uninspired tragedy in verse. But Wilde found his true theatrical voice with **Lady Windermere's Fan** (1892), **A Woman of No Importance** (1893), **An Ideal Husband** (1895) and his masterpiece, **The Importance of Being Earnest** (1895). *Salome*, written in French, was published in 1894 in an English translation by **Lord Alfred Douglas**.

Wilde's homosexuality was an open secret and the Marquess of Queensberry, Lord Alfred's father, publicly insulted Wilde in a note which accused him, curiously, of 'posing as a Somdomite' (*sic*). Wilde sued for libel but lost his case; he was prosecuted and imprisoned for homosexual acts in 1895. Prostitutes danced in the streets and ordinary decent people turned against art. Wilde's bitter letter of reproach to Lord Alfred was published (incomplete) in 1905 as *De Profundis*. Released in 1897, he went to France, calling himself 'Sebastian Melmoth', after the hero of **Charles Maturin**'s novel, *Melmoth the Wanderer*. *The Ballad of Reading Gaol* appeared in 1898. Wilde died in Paris after, it is said, becoming a Roman Catholic. He attracted many parodies, of which **Robert Hichens**'s *The Green Carnation* (1894) wears best.

**Wilde, Sir William** 1815–76 Irish antiquarian, the husband of **Lady Jane Francesca Wilde** and father of **Oscar Wilde**. Born in County Roscommon, he trained at the Royal College of Surgeons in Dublin and became a specialist in diseases of the eye and ear. He was also a gifted writer. Most of his early work was biographical and topographical, but it was in the field of antiquarian and archaeological history that he won his most enduring reputation. His *Irish Popular Superstitions* (1852), legendary tales and superstitions collected by him in the West of Ireland, helped to preserve a vanishing culture.

**Wilder, Laura Ingalls** 1867–1957 American children's writer. The daughter of a farmer, she was over 60 when her children suggested she write down the stories she remembered from her own pioneering childhood. The first of these, *Little House in the Big Woods* (1932), describes life in a log cabin with Laura herself, always appearing in the third person, observing the simple life going on around her, never minimizing its hardships but always remembering it with love. *Little House on the Prairie* (1935) tells how Laura's father takes his family out West, where they survive more difficulties before returning nearer home, this time to try wheat farming. Further adventures see the family on the move again, finally settling in a small town where they experience seven months of snow and ice in *The Long Winter* (1940). Once again, poverty and near-starvation are described with realism tempered by compassion and understanding. Subsequent novels take Laura to marriage and a teaching career.

**Wilder, Thornton (Niven)** 1897–1975 American playwright and novelist born in Madison, Wisconsin, the son of Calvinist parents. He attended missionary schools from 1905 to 1909, while his father served as consul general in Shanghai and Hong Kong. He completed high school in California, then attended Oberlin College, Yale, and Princeton.

His early writing included a series of 'three-minute' plays, 16 of which he later published in *The Angel That Troubled the Waters* (1928). His first publication, however, was the full-length play *The Trumpet Shall Sound*, which appeared serially in *The Yale Literary Magazine* in 1919.

His first novel, *The Cabala*, was published in 1926. Two years later he won a Pulitzer Prize for the novel *The Bridge of San Luis Rey* (1927), a complex study of the role of destiny, or providence, in the death of five travellers when the bridge near Lima, Peru, collapses in 1714. The story is supposedly taken from a manuscript written by a Franciscan monk, Brother Juniper. A third novel, *The Woman of Andros* (1930), set in ancient Greece, provoked an attack by critics who felt that Wilder was ignoring the bitter realities of contemporary American life. His other novels are *Heaven's My Destination* (1934), which concerns the fortunes of a good and simple man during the Depression; a historical novel of the last days of Julius Caesar, *The Ides of March* (1948), and two late works, *The Eighth Day* (1967) and *Theophilus North* (1973).

During the 1930s Wilder chose to concentrate most of his energies on the theatre. Stating that he wished to use the stage to capture 'not verisimilitude but reality', he spent some time studying the experimentalist drama which was flourishing in Europe at the time, and eventually resolved to 'shake up' the realistic theatre of the USA. *The Long Christmas Dinner and Other Plays* (1931) consists of six one-act sketches, three of which are written in the realistic mode he hoped to alter, and three in a radically experimental style. He received his second Pulitzer Prize for *Our Town* (1938), a drama set in the small town of Grover's Corners, New Hampshire, and played without scenery. *The Skin of Our Teeth* (1942) was also awarded the Pulitzer, and is an expressionistic play about mankind's precarious survival. *The Matchmaker* (1955) was a revision of an earlier play called *The Merchant of Yonkers* (1939), and in turn became another success as the musical comedy *Hello Dolly!* (1963). Several of Wilder's essays on the theatre are included in *American Characteristics and Other Essays* (1979).

**Wilding, Michael** 1942– Australian short-story writer, novelist, critic and editor. Born at Worcester in England, he attended Oxford University and, after graduating in 1963, lectured in English at the Universities of Sydney, 1963–6, and Birmingham, 1967–8. In 1969 he returned to the University of Sydney, where he is now Reader in English. Along with Frank Moorhouse, he founded *Tabloid Story*, a magazine for experimental imaginative prose, in 1972 and he has been an energetic champion of *avant-garde* fiction in Australia. Wilding's fiction is characterized by a strong sense of literary awareness and he frequently incorporates parodic and self-reflexive elements into his short stories, as in 'Emma: Memoirs of a Woman of Pleasure', which playfully juxtaposes extracts from **Jane Austen** and **John Cleland**. While much of his fiction takes its inspiration from the Sydney cultural scene, he is a believer in internationalism and his work has affinities with North American post-modernist writing. His short story collections are *Aspects of the Dying Process* (1972), *The West Midland Underground* (1975), *Scenic Drive* (1976), *The Phallic Forest* (1978) and *Reading the Signs* (1985). *A Man of Slow Feelings* (1985) is a selection which includes stories from each of these five volumes. Wilding has also published the novels *Living Together* (1974), *The Short Story Embassy* (1975), *Pacific Highway* (1982) and *The Paraguayan Experiment* (1985). His critical works include *Milton's Paradise Lost* (1969), *Marcus Clarke* (1977) and *Political Fictions* (1980). He has also been an influential editor, publishing *avant-garde* writing under the imprint of Wild and Woolley and acting as Australian editor for the English magazine *Stand*.

**Wilkes, John** 1727–97 Politician and journalist, the son of a maltster, Wilkes was born in Clerkenwell, London, and received his early schooling from a Presbyterian minister. He completed his education at the University of Leiden, and before he was 21 was married to an heiress some years his senior. Wilkes was hungry for something more exciting than the company of his wife and his mother-in-law and after a few years a separation was agreed. He became a lively young rake and a member of the Hellfire Club.

Wilkes was elected Member of Parliament for Aylesbury in Buckinghamshire in 1755. He supported the elder Pitt, but turned to journalism when Lord Bute came to power, finding a ready-made subject in the incompetence of the new Prime Minister. He contributed to *The Monitor*, wrote successful pamphlets, and in 1762 launched **The North Briton**, with the help of **Charles Churchill**, as a rival to *The Briton*, set up by Bute with another Scot, **Smollett**, as his editor. Lord Bute's growing unpopularity in the country gave *The North Briton*, with its ferocious attacks on the government, a wide public and popular success; but Wilkes grew too bold and in No. 45 of his weekly he libelled the crown by impugning the truth of the statements made, in the speech from the throne, regarding the Peace of Paris. He also published an 'obscene' essay on the female sex, and the paper was suppressed. Wilkes was expelled from the House of Commons and banished, though he escaped criminal prosecution by claiming parliamentary privilege.

He was able to return to England in 1768 when changes in the administration allowed his outlawry to be set aside. He became Member of Parliament for Middlesex but was expelled again in 1769 for a libel in *The St James's Chronicle*. He was elected for Middlesex again but the election was nullified; this happened three times but Wilkes's persistence in the face of an authority that the people were starting to question gave him the status of a popular hero. In 1774 he was made Sheriff of London and then Lord Mayor; he took his seat in the House of Commons without further opposition.

**Wilkinson, Anne (née Gibbons)** 1910–61 Born in Toronto and educated in Canada, England and the USA, she lived in Toronto for most of her life. She was a founding editor of *Tamarack Review* and published two volumes of poems, *Counterpoint to Sleep* (1951) and *The Hangman Ties the Holly* (1955). Her *Collected Poems*, edited by A. J. M. Smith, appeared in 1968. In their celebration of the elemental organic principles of life, her lyrics may be compared with the metaphysical poetry of **Marvell** and **Vaughan**, while her last poems about death stand with the best in Canadian literature.

*Will to Believe, The*, and Other Essays in Popular Psychology A book by **William James**, published in 1897, setting out his philosophy of 'radical empiricism'. James's career as a psychologist led him to emphasize the importance of instinct and to find a belief in absolute truth philosophically untenable. The essays in the volume all elucidate aspects of his objective position in regard to scientific and religious issues.

*William and Margaret* A poem by **David Mallet**, based on an old ballad and first published in 1724. The original, called 'Margaret's Ghost', is included in **Percy**'s *Reliques of Ancient English Poetry*. William has been faithless to Margaret, who goes to an early grave. Her ghost comes to William at dead of night, reproaches him, and tells him to come and see her grave. William goes to the grave, lies down on it, and joins her in death.

*William of Palerne* A **verse romance** in **alliterative verse** written *c.* 1350–61, probably in the South-west Midlands. It is a translation from the French romance *Guillaume de Palerne* (*c.* 1194–7) by an unknown 'William' whose patron was Humphrey de Bohun (d. 1361). The beginning of the English romance is missing, but the French poem opens with the infant prince William of Sicily being carried away by a werewolf to save him from the plots of his uncle. He is found and brought up by a cowherd and then by the emperor of Rome, who entrusts him to his daughter Melior. The couple fall in love and when the girl is promised to a Greek prince, they flee, dressed first in bearskins and later disguised as deer. With the help of the werewolf they reach Sicily and the plot is resolved. The werewolf, the bewitched heir of Spain, is released by his stepmother and marries William's sister. He identifies William who marries Melior. The tale is enchanting, unusual and well-told. It is not a close translation of the

French work, but is adapted to suit English tastes and the likely interests of its audience. It is also known as *William and the Werewolf*.

**William of Shoreham** 14th-century poet. Little is known of his life, but he lived in Kent, probably in Shoreham close to Sevenoaks. He is reported to have been vicar of Chart. Of his seven poems to survive, four are didactic, explaining points of Christian doctrine, discussing sin, the sacraments and the commandments. The remaining three poems are in praise of the Virgin, one a translation of the *Horae Canonicae Salvatoris* 'Patris sapientia, veritas divina', and another a translation from the work of **Robert Grosseteste**. Although difficult theological points are sometimes considered they are lucidly and simply expressed. The verse itself is unremarkable, and has frequent defects in metre and rhyme. The *Midland Prose Psalter* was at one time erroneously attributed to him.

**Williams, Charles (Walter Stansby)** 1886–1945 Poet, novelist and writer of theology. Born in London, Williams was educated at St Albans and University College, London. For many years he worked on the editorial staff of the Oxford University Press and lectured in London County Council evening institutes. During World War II he also lectured in Oxford and was made an honorary MA of Oxford University in 1944.

His first publication was *The Silver Stair* (1912), a volume of poetry influenced by **Yeats**. His later poetry reflected the contemporary vogue for verse drama initiated by **T. S. Eliot** and included his Canterbury Festival play *Thomas Cranmer* (1936) and *Seed of Adam* (posthumously published, 1948). He was also the author of several highly idiosyncratic and frequently obscure volumes on the Arthurian legend: *Taliessin Through Logres* (1938) and *The Region of the Summer Stars* (1944) which, with *The Arthur Torso*, was completed by his friend **C. S. Lewis** and published as one volume in 1948.

His novels, often described as 'supernatural thrillers' (Williams himself preferred 'metaphysical thrillers'), dealt with the conflict between good and evil in terms of sensational adventure, psychology, symbolism, black magic and fantastic miracles. They included *War in Heaven* (1930), *Many Dimensions* (1931), and *All Hallows Eve* (1944). Peter Stanhope, the hero of *Descent into Hell* (1937), is said to be a portrait of Eliot.

Williams's theological writings included: *He Came Down From Heaven* (1937), *Descent of the Dove* (1939), generally considered his most important, and *The Forgiveness of Sins* (1942). He also wrote *Witchcraft* (1941), and biographies of James I (1934) and Elizabeth (1936). His

literary criticism included a volume on Dante, *The Figure of Beatrice* (1943), and a critical introduction to the second edition of **Gerard Manley Hopkins**'s *Collected Poems* in 1930.

**Williams, Isaac** 1802–65 Poet and supporter of the **Oxford Movement**. Born in Aberystwyth, he was educated at Harrow and Trinity College, Oxford, where he won the Chancellor's Prize for Latin verse in 1823, an achievement which brought him into close association with **John Keble**. He was ordained in 1829, elected a fellow of Trinity in 1831 and appointed Dean in 1833, when he also acted as curate to **John Henry Newman** at St Mary's church. He contributed Tracts 80, 86 and 87 to *Tracts for the Times* and poems to *The British Magazine*, reprinted with verse by Newman and Keble in *Lyra Apostolica* (1836). After his support for the Oxford Movement stopped him succeeding Keble as Professor of Poetry in 1842, Williams left Oxford and eventually settled in Stinchcombe, Gloucestershire. His volumes of verse include *The Cathedral* (1838), *Thoughts in Past Years* (1838), *The Baptistery* (1842), *The Altar* (1847) and *The Christian Seasons* (1854).

**Williams, John (Alfred)** 1925– Black American novelist, born in Jackson, Mississippi. He served in the US Navy from 1943 to 1946, and graduated from Syracuse University in 1950. His first novel, *The Angry Ones* (1960), tells the story of Steve Hill, an artist who fights his own personal war against American racism. The protagonist of *Night Song* (1961) is a jazz musician who uses his art to combat discrimination. Williams's early work has often been compared to that of **Richard Wright**, but in his biography of Wright, *The Most Native of Sons* (1970), Williams himself criticized Wright's characterization of the black man as an individual who lacked racial and cultural consciousness. In *Sissie* (1963), *The Man Who Cried I Am* (1967), *Sons of Darkness, Sons of Light* (1969) and *Captain Blackman* (1972), Williams's voice is increasingly militant. *Mothersill and the Foxes* (1975), *The Junior Bachelor Society* (1976) and *!Click Song* (1982) are politically less radical, but remain firm in their emphasis on black unity. His non-fiction includes *Africa: Her History, Lands and People* (1962), *This Is My Country, Too* (1965) and *The King God Didn't Save* (1970).

**Williams, Raymond (Henry)** 1921–88 Critic. The son of a railway signalman, Williams was born in the Welsh border village of Pandy, and attended the grammar school at Abergavenny. His studies at Trinity College, Cambridge, were interrupted by wartime service as an anti-tank captain. He edited *Politics and Letters* (1947–8), and worked as an adult education tutor until his appointment as lecturer in English at Cambridge and fellow of Jesus College in 1961. He was Professor of Drama at Cambridge from 1974 to 1983, and wrote extensively on modern theatre in *Drama from Ibsen to Eliot* (1952, revised as *Drama from Ibsen to Brecht*, 1968), *Modern Tragedy* (1966) and other writings. His most influential work, especially in the celebrated *Culture and Society 1780–1950* (1958), and in *The Long Revolution* (1961) and *Keywords* (1976), was a sustained attempt to revise the concept of culture, away from the élitism of the Cambridge school and towards the socially responsible ideal of a 'common culture'. This has involved an extension of interests from literature to other media in *Communications* (1962) and *Television: Technology and Cultural Form* (1974). An active socialist, he showed a closer affiliation to Marxism in his later work, including *Orwell* (1971), *The Country and the City* (1973), *Marxism and Literature* (1977) and *Culture* (1981). His lectures on fiction were published in *The English Novel from Dickens to Lawrence* (1971), and his other lectures and essays were collected in *Problems in Materialism and Culture* (1980) and *Writings in Society* (1983).

**Williams, Roger** 1603–83 American Puritan minister, born in London, and educated at Charterhouse and Pembroke College, Cambridge. He emigrated to Massachusetts Bay in 1631, but did not easily find a home for his separatist views. He finally settled in Plymouth, a colony committed to a separatism which promised strict division between church and state. By 1633, however, he had found Plymouth disappointing, and he moved to Salem. Intent on moulding New England churches after the Apostolic model, he opposed the colony's attempt to establish synods at which representatives from each congregation would arrive at uniform answers to doctrinal and ecclesiastical questions. From 1633 to 1635 he repeatedly angered the General Court, and was finally banished from the colony in 1635 for refusing to correct doctrinal errors such as his conviction that an absolute division between church and state must be maintained.

During the next year Williams made his way to Rhode Island, where he founded its first settlement at Providence among the Narragansett Indians. By 1643 the Providence Plantations had expanded and Williams journeyed to England to secure a charter. En route, he wrote *A Key Into the Language of America* (London, 1643). Of interest today as a study of the habits, religion, and language of the Narragansett Indians, the treatise was used by Williams at the time to bolster his request for a charter, arguing that the Indians were in need of and prepared for conversion to Christianity. He remained in England for much of 1644 and during that time wrote some of his most frequently-read works.

*Mr Cotton's Letter Lately Printed, Examined, and Answered* contains his own version of the events which led to his banishment and severely criticizes the General Court's action. *The Bloudy Tenent of Persecution* presents his most fully developed defence of the freedom of conscience and the separation of church and state. *Christenings Make Not Christians*, published in 1645 after he had left England, examines the process of conversion and argues that the administration of the sacrament of baptism alone does not make one a Christian. In later years he assumed an unofficial but highly influential role in determining the policies of the Providence Plantations. For example, because of his conviction that citizenship should be granted irrespective of religious orientation, the colony admitted Jews and Quakers, two groups who could not otherwise find a home in the New World. In 1672, however, he wrote *George Fox Digg'd Out of his Burrows*, a critique of the Quaker reliance on the 'inner light'.

**Williams, Tennessee** 1911–83 American playwright, born Thomas Lanier Williams in Columbus, Mississippi, he graduated from the University of Iowa in 1938. His first plays were one-act pieces given in amateur and student performances between 1936 and 1940. They are partially collected in the volume *27 Wagons Full of Cotton and Other One-Act Plays* (1946, augmented 1953) and *Dragon Country: A Book of Plays* (1970).

His reputation was established by *The Glass Menagerie* (1944) and further enhanced by *A Streetcar Named Desire* (1947). Both plays show

Tennessee Williams, 1957.

Williams's sympathy for the lost and self-punishing individual, a characteristic of many of his subsequent dramas, such as *Summer and Smoke* (1947, revised as *The Eccentricities of a Nightingale* in 1964). His gift for comedy, often an undercurrent of his more serious dramas, is evident in *The Rose Tattoo* (1951). After the experimental *Camino Real* (1953), which was poorly received by the critics, he returned to the more familiar themes of the intricacies of Southern families and Southern culture with **Cat on a Hot Tin Roof** (1955), *Sweet Bird of Youth* (1956) and *The Night of the Iguana* (1959, revised 1961). Other plays include *Suddenly Last Summer* (1958), *The Milk Train Doesn't Stop Here Anymore* (1962), *In The Bar of A Tokyo Hotel* (1969), *Small Craft Warnings* (1974), *Vieux Carré* (1977) and *Clothes For a Summer Hotel* (1980).

Williams also published two volumes of poetry, *In the Winter of Cities* (1956) and *Androgyne, Mon Amour* (1977), several collections of prose and the novel *The Roman Spring of Mrs Stone* (1950). His *Memoirs*, published in 1975, present an account of a life consumed with guilt, anger, and a sense of failure, themes which are frequently associated with the major characters in his dramas. A volume of *Collected Stories* was issued in 1985.

**Williams, William Carlos** 1883–1963 American poet, born in Rutherford, New Jersey, the son of an English father and a Puerto Rican mother. He attended Swiss and French schools before studying medicine at the University of Pennsylvania, where he met **H. D.** and **Ezra Pound**. After further medical study in New York and Leipzig, and a visit to London where he met **William Butler Yeats**, Williams settled down to practise medicine in Rutherford in 1909.

Recognized as one of the most original and influential poets of the 20th century, his poetry is in fact deceptively simple. As critics have often noted, no object or occasion was 'unpoetic' to him. 'No ideas but in things', Williams declared, and he found his subjects in such homely items as refrigerated plums and wheelbarrows. His early work shows the influence of **imagism** in its objective, precise manner of description; his later poems, however, went beyond the interests of that movement, and became more personal. They also display his metrical invention, the 'variable foot', which he felt approximated colloquial American speech more closely than did traditional metres.

His first book, *Poems*, was privately printed in 1900. It was followed by *The Tempers* (1913), *Al Que Quiere!* (1917), *Kora in Hell: Improvisations* (1920), *Sour Grapes* (1921) and *Spring and All* (1923). Numerous other volumes followed. Among his last books were *The Desert Music and Other Poems* (1954), *Journey to Love* (1955) and

*Pictures from Brueghel and Other Poems* (1962), for which he received the Pulitzer Prize posthumously in 1963. Between 1946 and 1958 he published five books of the epic-length poem, **Paterson**, the work for which he is best known. Set in Paterson, New Jersey, the poem deals with the history and people of the town from its origins to modern times. Fragments of a sixth book were published posthumously in 1963. *The Collected Poems of William Carlos Williams: Volume One, 1909–1939* appeared in 1986.

Williams also published a number of prose works, both fiction and non-fiction, beginning with two collections of essays: *The Great American Novel* (1923) and *In the American Grain* (1925). *Selected Essays of William Carlos Williams* appeared in 1954. His short stories were collected in *The Farmer's Daughter: The Collected Stories* (1961); earlier volumes include *The Knife of the Times* (1932), *Life Along the Passaic River* (1938) and *Make Light of It: Collected Stories* (1950). His novels are *A Voyage to Pagany* (1928), *White Mule* (1937), *In the Money* (1940) and *The Build-Up* (1952). *The Autobiography of William Carlos Williams* was published in 1951; a collection of plays, *Many Lives and Other Plays*, appeared in 1961.

**Williamson, David** 1942– Australian dramatist. Born in Melbourne, he was educated in Bairnsdale, Victoria, and at Monash University, where he studied mechanical engineering. He subsequently lectured at the Swinburne College of Technology in Melbourne, an experience which appears to have provided material for his play, *The Department* (1974). His first full-length play, *The Coming of Stork*, was performed in 1970 at the La Mama Theatre in Melbourne, which had pioneered Alternative Theatre in Australia, and marked his emergence as one of the most important voices of the Australian 'New Wave'. It was followed by two plays, *The Removalists* and *Don's Party* (both 1971), which quickly established him as the nation's most popular contemporary dramatist. Both deal with personal confrontations which occur when repressed tensions find expression. *The Department* and *The Club* (1977) are about institutional power struggles. Williamson is a primarily naturalistic dramatist who anatomizes the Australian vernacular experience in a witty and satirical style. Despite his early association with the *avant-garde*, his work is formally far from radical. His more recent plays continue the anatomy of contemporary Australian society, but the satirical dimension is less prominent. His work is also notable for its portrayal of changing gender roles. His other plays include *Jugglers Three* (1972), *What If You Died Tomorrow* (1973), *A Handful of Friends* (1976), *Travelling North* (1979) and *The Perfectionist* (1982). He has also written screenplays for several major Australian films, including the screen versions of *Don's Party* and *The Club* and two immensely popular films about subjects of mythic significance in Australia, *Gallipoli* and *Phar Lap*.

**Williamson, Henry** 1895–1977 Novelist. Born in Bedfordshire, he was educated at Colfe's Grammar School, Lewisham. He joined the army at 17 and saw action on the Western Front during World War I, an experience which left him psychologically scarred. He later recorded the horrors of trench warfare in *The Wet Flanders Plain* (1929) and *A Patriot's Progress* (1930), a powerful account rendered from the point of view of the common soldier.

After the war Williamson spent a brief but unhappy period as a Fleet Street journalist, and it was during this time that he began *The Flax of Dreams*, a novel sequence comprising *The Beautiful Years* (1921), *Dandelion Days* (1922), *The Dream of Fair Women* (1924) and *The Pathway* (1928). Completed in Devon, to which he had retreated in 1921, it was much admired by **T. E. Lawrence**. The two men became close friends and Williamson later wrote a biography, *T. E. Lawrence: Genius of Friendship* (1941).

It was as a nature writer that Williamson achieved wider recognition and success. *The Peregrine's Saga* (1923) and *The Old Stag* (1926) were followed by *Tarka the Otter* (1927), a minutely observed and moving tale of animal life. It won the Hawthornden Prize and has become a popular classic. There followed other tales in the same genre, *Salar the Salmon* (1935), *The Phasian Bird* (1948) and *Tales of Moorland and Estuary* (1953), which reflect Williamson's debt to the 19th-century naturalist **Richard Jefferies**. He published a selection of Jefferies's work in 1937.

During the 1930s Williamson became a supporter of Oswald Mosley and an admirer of Hitler. This led to his internment at the end of World War II, and his political sympathies did much to mar his reputation. His most ambitious work, begun in his mid 50s, was a 15-novel sequence called *A Chronicle of Ancient Sunlight*: *The Dark Lantern* (1951), *Donkey Boy* (1952), *Young Phillip Maddison* (1953), *How Dear is Life* (1954), *A Fox Under My Cloak* (1955), *The Golden Virgin* (1957), *Love and Loveless* (1958), *A Test to Destruction* (1960), *The Innocent Moon* (1961), *It Was the Nightingale* (1962), *The Power of the Dead* (1963), *The Phoenix Generation* (1965), *A Solitary War* (1966), *Lucifer Before Sunrise* (1967) and *The Gale of the World* (1969). Largely autobiographical, *A Chronicle of Ancient Sunlight* recounts the career of Phillip Maddison, a writer whose life-story mirrors Williamson's own political and creative interests from the 1880s into the post-World War II years.

**Willobie, Henry** ?1574–?1596 Poet. Born in Wiltshire, he was educated at St John's College, Oxford. Willobie's reputation rests exclusively on a complex, riddling poem *Willobie His Avisa* (1594), the most comprehensive account of which explains it as a veiled history of the courtships of Queen Elizabeth. References within the poem to 'W. S.', characterized as 'the old player', have tantalized Shakespearean myth-makers.

**Wills, William Gorman** 1828–91 Anglo-Irish playwright and painter, born near Dublin. He provided the actor Henry Irving with many of his successes, including *Charles I* (1872), *Eugene Aram* (1873), *Vanderdecken* (1878) and *Faust* (1885). Wills believed poetry to be a higher form than drama, and his attempts to combine the two impressed contemporaries more than they have posterity. A noted clubman and an endearingly generous, if somewhat anachronistic, Bohemian, he made more money by painting fashionable portraits than by writing plays. His only enduring success was *Olivia* (1878), an adaptation of **Goldsmith**'s *The Vicar of Wakefield*, and even that endured only as long as Ellen Terry continued to perform in it.

**Wilson, A[ndrew] N[orman]** 1950– Novelist, born in Staffordshire and brought up in Wales. His prolific output of fiction began with baleful comedies in the manner of **Evelyn Waugh**, such as *The Sweets of Pimlico* (1977) and *Unguarded Hours* (1978), but his reputation rests mainly on *The Healing Art* (1980), *Who Was Oswald Fish?* (1981) and *Wise Virgin* (1982), intricately plotted tragicomedies which confront perplexing moral dilemmas. *The Healing Art* deals with the consequences of a mistaken diagnosis of cancer. He has also published a study of **Sir Walter Scott** (1980) and lives of **Milton** (1983) and **Belloc** (1984), and acquired (without great reluctance) a certain notoriety for stringent book reviewing while literary editor of *The Spectator* and for his uncompromising High-Church conservatism. *Lilibet* (1985), a pseudonymous verse eulogy addressed to the Queen, was not well received.

**Wilson, Sir Angus (Frank Johnstone)** 1913– 91 Novelist and short-story writer. Born of English and South African parents in Bexhill, Sussex, he was educated at Westminster School and Merton College, Oxford. He joined the staff of the British Museum Library in 1937 and, apart from service at the Foreign Office during World War II (1942–6), worked there until 1955. He retired as Deputy Superintendent of the Reading Room and subsequently became a university lecturer. In 1966 he held the Chair of English Literature at the University of East Anglia, and was appointed Chairman of the

National Book League in 1971. He was knighted in 1980.

Wilson's career as a writer began with two volumes of short stories, *The Wrong Set* (1949) and *Such Darling Dodos* (1950). *Hemlock and After* (1952), a novel about a middle-aged writer's attempt to establish a writers' colony, was in part intended to be 'a critique of the liberal humanism that is to be found in Forster's novels'. In fact, Wilson was often compared with **Forster** by critics who failed to observe his attempts to refute the tradition. *Anglo-Saxon Attitudes* (1956), another study of middle age, was followed by a further volume of short stories, *A Bit off the Map* (1957). *The Middle Age of Mrs Eliot* (1958) recounts the traumatic effect of widowhood and financial hardship on a previously wealthy and contented wife. *The Old Men at the Zoo* (1961), an uncharacteristic novel, is a bizarre and often violent fable about the 'near future' when England is at war with an alliance of European powers, and *Late Call* (1964), narrated from the perspective of Sylvia Calvert, a retired hotel manager, explores the spiritual desolation of life in a New Town in the English Midlands. In *No Laughing Matter* (1967), Wilson traces the fortunes of the Matthews family from 1912 to 1967. A long, ambitious work, its presentation of English social history and resourcefulness of language have been widely praised. Other works include *As if by Magic* (1973), about a world-ranging quest for meaning by Namo Langmuir and his god-daughter Alexandra, and *Setting the World on Fire* (1980), in which the lives and values of two brothers are contrasted.

Wilson's other writing includes studies of Zola (1950) and **Dickens** (1970). He is also the author of a play, *The Mulberry Bush* (1955). *Diversity and Depth in Fiction: Selected Critical Writings* was published in 1983.

**Wilson, Colin (Henry)** 1931– Critic, novelist and miscellaneous writer. Born in Leicester, he left school at the age of 16 to work in a variety of jobs – laboratory assistant, tax collector, labourer and hospital porter – before becoming a full-time writer in 1954. He shot to fame with his enthusiastic but disorganized study of alienation, *The Outsider* (1956). Its publication coincided with the first production of **John Osborne**'s *Look Back in Anger* and Wilson was hailed by some as a key thinker of the **Angry Young Men** generation. The critical euphoria quickly evaporated, and Wilson himself has complained that he has not been dealt with seriously ever since. But he has survived his abrupt rejection and has, by his prolific output, to some extent succeeded in removing himself from the influence exercised by critics. The first of his 'psychological thrillers' was *Ritual in the Dark* (published in 1960 but in fact completed

before *The Outsider*), based on the Jack the Ripper case. Other novels include *The Mind Parasites* (1967), *The Killer* (1970), *The Black Room* (1975) and *The Janus Murder Case* (1984). Numerous works of non-fiction deal with literature, philosophy (particularly existentialism), psychology, the occult and the paranormal, and crime. They include *The Strength to Dream: Literature and the Imagination* (1962), *Beyond the Outsider: The Philosophy of the Future* (1965) and *Mysteries: An Investigation into the Occult, the Paranormal and the Supernatural* (1980).

**Wilson, Edmund** 1895–1972 American man of letters, born in Red Bank, New Jersey, and educated at Princeton. During World War I he served in the US Army, first as a hospital aide, then with the Intelligence Corps. He became managing editor of *Vanity Fair* for one year in 1920. From 1926 to 1931 he was associate editor of *The New Republic*. He also reviewed books for *The New Yorker* – steadily from 1944 to 1948, occasionally thereafter. But Wilson was not simply a journalist; he was widely recognized as a learned and incisive critic, and in addition to critical and political essays, he wrote poetry, plays, novels and short stories. He was a close friend of several literary figures, among them **John Dos Passos**, **F. Scott Fitzgerald**, and **Edna St Vincent Millay**. The third of his four wives was **Mary McCarthy**, to whom he was married from 1938 to 1946.

Among his works of non-fiction are: *Axel's Castle: A Study in the Imaginative Literature of 1870–1930* (1931), a standard work on Symbolist literature; *Travels in Two Democracies* (1936), a Marxist critique of life in the USA and Russia; *To the Finland Station: A Study in the Writing and Acting of History* (1940), which describes the origins of the Russian Revolution; *The Boys in the Back Room: Notes on California Novelists* (1941); *The Wound and the Bow: Seven Studies in Literature* (1941); and *Patriotic Gore: Studies in the Literature of the American Civil War* (1962). He also edited several volumes, including an anthology of American literary criticism, *The Shock of Recognition: The Development of Literature in the United States Recorded by the Men Who Made It* (1943, enlarged in 1955), and a volume of his friend F. Scott Fitzgerald's uncollected pieces, *The Crack-Up: With Other Uncollected Pieces, Note-Books and Unpublished Letters* (1945). His own fiction consists of two novels, *I Thought of Daisy* (1929) and *Galahad* (1957), and a collection of short stories, *Memoirs of Hecate County* (1946, revised in 1958). He published two autobiographies, *A Piece of My Mind: Reflections at Sixty* (1956) and *A Prelude: Landscapes, Characters and Conversations From the Earlier Years of My Life* (1967). Since his death, three volumes of his memoirs have been published:

*The Twenties* (1975), *The Thirties* (1980) and *The Forties* (1983).

**Wilson, Ethel** 1890–1980 Novelist and writer of short stories. Born at Port Elizabeth in South Africa, Ethel Davis Bryant spent her early childhood in England, removing to Canada after the early deaths of her parents. She was educated in Vancouver and taught for some years. Her first short story, published in 1937, was followed by several novels and collections of stories including *Hetty Dorval* (1947), *The Innocent Traveller* (1949), *The Equations of Love* (1952), *Swamp Angel* (1954) and *Love and Salt Water* (1956).

**Wilson, John** 1626–*c*.1695 Playwright. Wilson was born in Plymouth and educated at Exeter College, Oxford. After Oxford he entered Lincoln's Inn, became a barrister and eventually Recorder of Londonderry. He wrote two comedies in the manner of **Ben Jonson**, *The Cheats* (1664) and *The Projectors* (1665). *Belphegor, or, The Marriage of the Devil* (1690) is a tragicomedy based on Machiavelli's story and *Andronicus Comnenius* (1664) a tragedy about the career of the Byzantine emperor. Wilson also wrote occasional verse.

**Wilson, John** 1785–1854 Critic and poet. He was born in Paisley, the son of a factory owner, and educated at Glasgow University and Magdalen College, Oxford, where he won the Newdigate Prize. His subsequent verse includes *The Isle of Palms* (1812) and *The City of the Plague* (1816). A novel, *The Trials of Margaret Lyndsay*, was published in 1823. In 1820 he was elected to the chair of moral philosophy at Edinburgh University on the strength of his firm Tory principles.

Wilson is remembered less for these achievements than for his connection with *Blackwood's Magazine*. Under the pseudonym of Christopher North he wrote the greatest number of the *Noctes Ambrosianae* papers and appeared as one of the characters in the dialogues. With **Hogg** and **Lockhart** he wrote the satirical *Chaldee MS* (October 1817) which gave *Blackwood's* its first considerable success.

**Wilson, J[ohn] Dover** 1881–1969 Literary scholar and critic. Born in Mortlake, Surrey, the son of an engraver, Wilson was educated at Lancing and at Gonville and Caius College, Cambridge, where he studied history. He spent three years teaching in Finland and another three years as lecturer at Goldsmiths' College, London (where he edited *Life in Shakespeare's England*, 1911), before becoming a school inspector in 1912 – thus following the example of **Matthew Arnold**, whose *Culture and Anarchy* he was to edit in 1932. His major contribution to literature began in 1919 when he was appointed co-editor of the New Cambridge Shakespeare series, which he saw through to completion in 1966 after publishing four books on **Shakespeare**: *The Essential Shakespeare* (1932), *What Happens in Hamlet* (1935) – which became something of an academic best-seller – *The Fortunes of Falstaff* (1943) and *Shakespeare's Happy Comedies* (1962). As a school inspector and later as Professor of Education at King's College, London (1924–35), Wilson was a keen advocate of literary education, contributing to the influential Newbolt Report on the teaching of English (1921) an impassioned appeal for literature to be taught to working-class children. From 1935 to 1945 he occupied the chair of English Literature at Edinburgh. His autobiography, *Milestones on the Dover Road*, appeared in 1969.

**Wilson, Robert** d. 1600 Actor and playwright. He was famous as an extemporizer but few details of his life have survived, except that he was a member of the Earl of Leicester's Men after 1572 and Queen Elizabeth's Men after 1583. Of several plays which he wrote or helped to write, the surviving three, *The Ladies of London* (*c*.1581), *The Three Lords and Three Ladies of London* (*c*.1589) and *The Cobbler's Prophecy* (*c*.1594), show his ability to adapt the **morality play** to the changing taste of the early public theatres.

**Wilson, Thomas** ?1528–81 Humanist and diplomat. Educated at Eton and Cambridge, he was engaged to tutor the two sons of the Duke of Suffolk; their death of the plague occasioned his first publication, a Latin eulogy, in 1551. Wilson spent most of Mary's reign abroad, and after his return to England in 1560 was successful over a period of years on embassies to Portugal and the Netherlands. He became a Privy Councillor *c*.1572 and Secretary of State in 1578. *The Rule of Reason* (1551) is an introduction to logic and the disposition and conduct of an argument. *The Art of Rhetoric* (1553) urges the use of English and discourages the affectation of foreign phrases and 'inkhorn terms'. His translation of some of Demosthenes' orations was printed in 1570 and his treatise on usury in 1572.

**Winchilsea, Anne Finch, Countess of** 1661–1721 Poet. Born Anne Kingsmill, the daughter of a Hampshire family, she became a maid-of-honour to the Duchess of York in 1683. She married Heneage Finch, who became 6th Earl of Winchilsea, in 1684. Her first poems appeared in 1701 and a collection, in a variety of metres, was published as *Miscellany Poems* in 1713. Her nature poetry, particularly the 'Nocturnal Reverie', was praised by **Wordsworth** in *Lyrical Ballads* (1801) and her small output is believed to have had some influence on the work of **Alexander Pope** (*Essay on Man*) and **Shelley** (*Epipsychidion*).

**Wind in the Willows, The** A novel by **Kenneth Grahame**, published in 1908.

Set in the country around the Thames, it chronicles the adventures of three bachelor animals living the easy lives of Edwardian landed gentry. The timid but friendly Mole moves in with his new acquaintance the Water Rat, a forceful character forever worrying about Toad, the owner of the local great house, Toad Hall. Given to sudden enthusiasms, Toad takes up motoring to such dangerous effect that he is finally sent to prison, at which point Toad Hall is invaded by the distinctly proletarian stoats and weasels who normally live in the Wild Wood beyond. Escaping from prison dressed as a washerwoman, Toad recaptures his ancestral home with his two friends and the curmudgeonly Badger. The book ends with Toad back in residence and promising to reform – a vain hope, according to a letter Grahame sent to a child admirer.

The strength of the book lies in its animal characterizations, but their adventures are interspersed with charming descriptions of the countryside and a meeting with the god Pan, here depicted as a friend to all dumb animals. Helped in its popularity by the illustrations of **E. H. Shepard** and then **Arthur Rackham**, *The Wind in the Willows* enjoyed a second and equally enduring life in the stage adaptation, *Toad of Toad Hall* (1929), by **A. A. Milne**.

**Winesburg, Ohio** A collection of 23 thematically related stories by **Sherwood Anderson**, published in 1919, which explores the nature of small-town life in the fictional town of the title. The stories gain further unity through the character of George Willard, a reporter for the local newspaper who has literary ambitions and to whom all the other characters gravitate in the course of the book. The stories can be related to Anderson's own life and to his experiences in his hometown in Ohio. Their style and thematic focus reflect his naturalistic approach to American life as well as his interest in the unusual or unfamiliar aspects of human existence. The various characters in the collection, referred to as 'grotesques', are portrayed in a manner which stresses both their alienation and their desperate attempts to communicate with others in their daily lives.

**Wings of the Dove, The** A novel by **Henry James**, published in 1902. Kate Croy, the daughter of a discredited social adventurer, is secretly engaged to Merton Densher, a journalist. While Merton is in America, Kate becomes friends with the wealthy Milly Theale, who confides to her that she is suffering from a mysterious illness, and that her doctor has told her that only happiness can postpone her death. When Merton returns to London, Kate encour-

ages him to take an interest in Milly, hoping that they will get married, thus soon making him a rich widower whom she herself can marry. The plot appears to be working until the fortune-hunting Lord Mark, rejected by Milly, reveals to her the true relationship between Kate and Merton. Milly's health deteriorates, and soon afterwards she dies in Venice. After her death Merton receives a letter from her: she has made him rich enough to marry Kate. In an agony of shame he confronts Kate and offers to marry her only if she agrees not to accept the wealth bestowed on him by Milly. Kate declines, and the novel closes as they separate for ever.

**Winnie-the-Pooh** See **Milne, A. A.**

**Winter Words in Various Moods and Metres** Poems by **Thomas Hardy**, posthumously published in October 1928. Written mostly after 1925, the poems of *Winter Words* stem from incidents and feelings of many decades before, some reaching back to the 1860s. In its unique diversity the volume is an astonishing compendium of Hardy the poet. Its pages reveal him in a variety of moods: philosophic, humorous, dramatic, observant of nature, narrative, lyric. Varied, too, are the technical devices employed by the poet to convey his feelings. The final poem of the volume is appropriately and movingly entitled 'He Resolves To Say No More'.

**Winter's Tale, The** A play by **William Shakespeare**, first performed *c.*1611 and published in the First Folio of 1623. The main source is **Robert Greene**'s romance, *Pandosto* (1588).

The first part of *The Winter's Tale* forms a rounded tragedy of jealousy. Leontes, King of Sicilia, has entertained his childhood friend, Polixenes, now King of Bohemia, for several months. Driven to a sudden and insane jealousy by the closeness of the friendship between his queen Hermione and Polixenes, he instructs his close adviser Camillo to poison Polixenes. Instead, Camillo warns Polixenes and escapes with him to Bohemia. Leontes claps his pregnant wife into prison and brings her to trial on a charge of adultery and a trumped-up accusation of conspiracy to poison him. When the Delphic oracle pronounces Hermione chaste and Leontes a 'jealous tyrant', he defies its message. His new-born daughter has already been carried off by Antigonus, unwillingly bound to expose the infant to the elements. Now comes news of the death of Leontes's son and the report from Antigonus's forceful and outraged wife Paulina that Hermione has also died. The shamed Leontes vows to spend the rest of his life in daily penance. Meanwhile Antigonus has brought the innocent daughter to the Bohemian shore, where he leaves her with a store of gold and a 'character', naming her Perdita. He is eaten by a bear while an old shepherd finds Perdita.

There follows a gap of 16 years, explained by Time as Chorus, and the second part, destined to be a comedy of rebirth and renewal, begins. Perdita, though brought up in the shepherd's humble home, has attracted the love of Polixenes's son, Prince Florizel. But Polixenes comes in disguise to attend the sheep-shearing feast and shatters the joy of the event by disclosing himself and demanding the end of the match. With Camillo's help, Perdita and Florizel escape and sail to Sicilia, where they are welcomed by Leontes. The vengeful Polixenes, who has followed them, learns, as they all do, the secret of Perdita's birth and welcomes the forthcoming marriage as a guarantee of his reconciliation with Leontes. Paulina gathers all the leading characters to see the statue of Hermione, newly completed. As Leontes looks at it with wonder, Paulina calls for music and the statue comes to life. Hermione is 'reborn' into her marriage with Leontes.

*The Winter's Tale* belongs with Shakespeare's other last plays *Pericles*, *Cymbeline* and *The Tempest*. It is a multi-faceted romance, written for indoor performance at the **Blackfriars**, where the stylish work of **John Fletcher** was much favoured. The second half focuses on the reconciliation that can be achieved through grace, a word which is allowed its full range from spiritual to physical reference.

**Winters, (Arthur) Yvor** 1900–68 American poet and critic, born in Chicago, and educated at the universities of Chicago, Colorado and Stanford. His verse, which is severely restrained and meticulously patterned, is among the first notable poetry of the American West. His first volume, *Poetry: The Immobile Wind*, was published in 1921. This was followed by *The Magpie's Shadow* (1922), *The Bare Hills* (1927) and *The Proof* (1930). During the 1930s and 1940s he published several more volumes, the last of which, *To the Holy Spirit*, appeared in 1947. His works of criticism include *In Defense of Reason* (1947), *The Function of Criticism* (1957) and *Forms of Discovery* (1967).

**Winthrop, John** 1588–1649 American Puritan leader, born in Suffolk, and educated at Trinity College, Cambridge. In appreciation for his aid in negotiating the colony's charter, the Massachusetts Bay Company elected him governor in 1629. He sailed aboard the *Arbella* in 1630 and during the voyage wrote and delivered 'A Modell of Christian Charity', a lay sermon which defined the social hierarchy he deemed necessary in order to preserve the commonwealth. He wrote a number of other pamphlets while serving, until his death, as governor or deputy governor. *A Defence of an Order of Court Made in the Yeare 1637* supports the legislation passed by the General Court after the trial of Anne Hutchinson, which denied citizenship to 'dissenters'. His account of the Hutchinson trial was incorporated into Thomas Welde's *A Short History of the Rise, Reign and Ruine of the Antinomians* (1644). His many comments on the political affairs of Puritan New England are collected in his journal, which was published in part in 1790 and complete in 1826, entitled *The History of New England 1630–1649*.

**Winthrop, Theodore** 1826–61 American novelist, born in Connecticut, and educated at Yale. None of his books was published until after he was killed while serving in the Union Army during the Civil War. His best-known work is *John Brent* (1862), a novel which exploits its Western setting to produce an exciting, melodramatic plot involving kidnappings and unscrupulous Mormons. His other works include two novels, *Cecil Dreeme* (1861) and *Edwin Brothertoft* (1862), and *Life in the Open Air* (1863) and *The Canoe and the Saddle* (1863), both travel books.

***Wisdom of the Ancients, The*** See *De Sapientia Veterum*.

**Wise, John** c.1652–1725 American Puritan minister, born in Roxbury, Massachusetts, and educated at Harvard. In 1682 he was ordained minister of the Second Church of Ipswich, Massachusetts. In 1687 he incited a vehement protest against paying taxes that violated the colony's charter rights, an act for which he was imprisoned briefly by Royal Governor Andros. Signing a petition to vindicate those accused of witchcraft in 1703, he helped the colony recover from the social damage done by the trials of 1692. He opposed the attempt to centralize church government, and his advocacy of autonomous congregations produced his two most important and popular publications: *The Churches Quarrel Espoused* (1710), a systematic refutation of the proposal for ecclesiastical centralization presented in *Questions and Proposals* by **Cotton Mather** and **Increase Mather**; and *A Vindication of the Government of New-England Churches* (1717), a definition and defence of Congregationalism. That both works advance egalitarian principles explains their subsequent appeal to American revolutionaries and Abolitionists in the 18th and 19th centuries, when they were reprinted in large quantities. *A Word of Comfort to a Melancholy Country* (1721), was a defence of paper money.

**Wise, T[homas] J[ames]** 1859–1937 Forger and bibliographer. Born at Gravesend and educated at home owing to lack of robustness, Wise joined the staff of an essential-oil merchants and rose eventually to be a partner. An early interest in the poetry of **Shelley** led him to start collecting editions of that poet and he became one of the greatest collectors of his age, at his death directing that his collection, known as the Ashley Library, be offered for sale to the British Museum. A catalogue of the library, now of debatable bibliographical value, was issued over a number of years. As a result of his prominence in the bibliographical world Wise was elected an honorary fellow of Worcester College, Oxford, was awarded an honorary MA by the University, and was elected President of the Bibliographical Society and a member of the Roxburghe Club.

For much of this period he was also engaged in the most reprehensible activities. In 1934 John Carter and Graham Pollard showed in *An Enquiry into the Nature of Certain Nineteenth Century Pamphlets* that Wise had been forging 'first editions' of major authors. Their work generated further investigation and at the present count it is known that Wise forged or pirated more than 50 works by, among others, **Arnold, Charlotte Brontë, Elizabeth Barrett Browning, Robert Browning, Dickens, George Eliot, William Morris, Dante Gabriel Rossetti**, Shelley, **Swinburne, Tennyson, Thackeray** and **Wordsworth**. The forgeries took a variety of forms: type facsimiles of genuine pamphlets; genuine works to which bogus title-pages with false dates were added; and works to which bogus cancels were added. The first two categories were surreptitiously disseminated through the antiquarian book trade with in the region of 25–30 copies being printed. When the Carter and Pollard study appeared Wise retreated behind his wife and doctor. In 1959 David Foxon demonstrated that Wise had also taken advantage of his standing in bibliographical circles to gain unsupervised access to Jacobean plays in the British Museum, many of them in the priceless Garrick Collection, and had torn out leaves from perfect copies in order to make up his own imperfect copies. These he then sold and are now to be found in the University of Texas at Austin. Carter aptly summed Wise up as 'vulgar, arrogant, and pretentious, a liar, a bully, and a thief'.

*Wise Blood* A novel by **Flannery O'Connor**, published in 1952. A highly disturbing book, it attempts to analyse the effects of religious belief and the nature of such belief in the 'fallen' world of the post-bellum South.

It concerns the spiritual quest of Hazel Motes, a Southerner recently returned from World War II. He is obsessed by the idea that redemption is impossible and that the whole notion of Jesus as saviour is suspect. As he sets himself up as a preacher of non-belief, he meets a variety of outcasts and social misfits. In particular, it is his encounter with the false preacher Asa Hawkes (who has supposedly blinded himself out of religious fervour) and his daughter Sabbath Lily that precipitates his downfall. Though apparently a non-believer, Hazel is devastated when he discovers that Asa is only pretending to be blind, having been too cowardly to carry out the act. Eventually, after Asa leaves town, Hazel murders another phoney preacher, who has been parodying Hazel's own 'Church of Christ Without Christ'. He then blinds himself and performs various acts of self-torture in atonement – although he cannot say for what. Finally, after being exposed to freezing wind and rain for two days, he is picked up by the police and clubbed into silence. He dies on the trip back to his landlady's house.

**Wiseman, Adele** 1928– Canadian novelist. Born in Winnipeg of Ukrainian Jewish parents, Wiseman attended the University of Manitoba and subsequently taught at McGill University and Sir George William University. She has also worked as a secretary and social worker. Her novels, *The Sacrifice* (1956) and *Crackpot* (1974), deal with the Jewish experience on the Canadian Prairies. *The Sacrifice* is a modern-day version of the Abraham and Isaac story, which can be read both as a realistic saga of immigrant family life, spanning three generations, and as a religious allegory. *Crackpot* is a more experimental novel which, like *The Sacrifice*, reflects the harshness of the immigrants' ghetto lives in their new country. It draws on traditional Jewish symbolism and humour. Wiseman has also written two plays and a number of shorter works which also deal with aspects of the Jewish diaspora.

**Wister, Owen** 1860–1938 American novelist and short-story writer, known primarily for Western fiction. Born in Pennsylvania and educated at Harvard, he first travelled west (to Wyoming) in order to improve his health, and this experience became the basis for his early writings. *Red Man and White* (1896), *Lin McLean* (1896) and *The Jimmyjohn Boss* (1900) are all collections of stories set in the Western cattle country. His best-known work, **The Virginian** (1902), was a popular novel of legendary proportions. Its heroic cowpuncher, unassumingly masterful, crude but innately gentle, became the standard for the Western hero in countless novels and movies. Having become famous for his Westerns, Wister decided to turn to the East for his subjects. *Philosophy Four* (1903) is a story about undergraduate life at Harvard. *Lady Baltimore* (1906) is a romantic novel set in Charleston. He also wrote a biography of Ulysses S. Grant (1900), and in 1930 published *Roosevelt, The Story of a Friendship, 1880–1919* from his own reminiscences of Theodore Roosevelt, the boyhood friend to whom he had dedicated *The Virginian*.

**wit** Like humour – so often, and usefully, compared with it – a concept that has varied not only from period to period but also within each period. Yet of both concepts it may be said that practically all the variations share the common property of being in some way in touch with, or derivable from, their etymological origins. Wit (Old English 'witan', to know) in all its manifestations remains within hailing distance of the idea of intelligence, cleverness or judgement. Humour (Latin 'humorem', moisture) can always be seen to have some relationship – eventually a rather distant one – with its early medical meaning: a bodily fluid. Wit, that is to say, is associated with qualities of mind and manners, humour with qualities of body and mood. The epigrammatic statement, then, that wit is the perception of resemblances, humour the perception of incongruities, is nearly true – if we bear in mind that while the wit himself always sees the resemblances, the incongruities are usually seen only by the audience.

In Elizabethan medical theory man was governed by four humours: black bile, yellow bile (or choler), phlegm, and blood. Properly mixed they rendered him a balanced, equable 'good-humoured' person. An excess of any one, however, rendered him melancholic, choleric, phlegmatic, or sanguine, respectively: unbalanced, obsessive and therefore absurd. **Ben Jonson** seizes on this medical theory and turns it into one for literary comedy (in the Prologue to *Every Man in His Humour*, 1598) by generalizing it to include any kind of obsession, whether for silence or sex or money, or any other such unbalancing folly. Straight away, then, physical imbalance becomes associated with temperamental oddity. Taken along with the gradual disappearance of humours from medical theory, this makes understandable the transition to the modern idea of humour as geniality about others or good-natured deprecation of oneself; it is in fact a modulation of what 'good-humoured' originally implied. So humorous comedy now implies something less moralistic than it used to; it is now amusement without judgement, attack without malice. However, it still tends to be associated with situation and type-characters – with clever plotting that manoeuvres people into situations that expose their one-sided unadaptability. The difference is that a method has become a mood. For Jonson's audience the humour lay in the action, the method of demonstrating absurdity and pointing a moral; for the modern audience it lies in the tone. Jonson's comedies can usually also be styled **satire**, whereas today a humorous satire is almost a contradiction in terms. Wit, on the other hand, has remained a method – which could in principle be used for any literary mode. Thus, a witty tragedy is not impossible, but a humorous tragedy is now inconceivable.

In Jonson and **Shakespeare**, wit is usually close to good sense, intelligence, inventiveness. In **Donne** and the **metaphysical poets** that shift towards ingenuity has begun which seems to be the source of the Restoration distinction between true wit and false wit – wit that illuminates and wit that merely dazzles. However, Shakespeare also sees wit as sharing some qualities of the imagination. Falstaff says of sherris-sack that:

It ascends me into the brain; dries me there all the foolish and dull and crudy vapours which environ it; makes it apprehensive, forgetive, full of nimble fiery and delectable shapes; which, delivered over to the voice, the tongue, which is the birth, becomes excellent wit.

This is not so far from **Hobbes**'s definition of wit as a combination of Fancy (imagination) and Judgement – an association that never quite drops out of sight, though for the Augustans wit was predominantly good sense, or propriety of idea and diction, or the natural civilized, or inventiveness, or perceptive cleverness. The Romantics tended to deprecate wit as frivolity; and indeed the idea of wit as witticism or joke, its modern meaning, was in being before the modern period.

Freud's *Jokes and their Relation to the Unconscious* (trs. James Strachey, 1960) brilliantly analyses and codifies the nature of this kind of wit – a kind of which Shakespeare and Hobbes were clearly not unaware, though neither linked it so specifically to jokes as we do today.

The essential perception is that such wit – as distinct from amusing cleverness of a fully conscious kind, like **irony** – has its roots in the subconscious, but only its roots. Such wit combines cognitive cleverness with emotional release or aggression; taken in the round, it is preconscious rather than subconscious. That is why the joker, though he cannot deliberately make up a good joke, is not quite so surprised as the hearer when he does so. However, such wit shares with dream the characteristics of latent significance, unexpectedness, disguise and compression.

But this does not exhaust the meaning of wit in the post-Romantic period. **Oscar Wilde**'s remark that 'the tragedy of age is not that one feels old; it is that one feels young' is so unexpected and unpredictable that one feels it has to be counted as wit, so profound that it might almost be a product of the unconscious; yet, unlike jokes, it touches on no taboo, and shows all those signs of acute perception and high intelligence that were earlier hallmarks of wit. Though there is a difference of emphasis today, it would appear that earlier meanings of wit have not come to seem foreign – as, indeed, is the case with humour. So too, in literature, witty comedy still tends to be characterized by dialogue rather than situation, verbal cleverness rather than type-characters, surprising congruities rather than incongruities, in contrast to humour.

**Witch of Edmonton, The** A tragicomedy performed in about 1621 but not published until 1658, when the title-page named the leading collaborators as **William Rowley**, **Thomas Dekker** and **John Ford**.

The play suffers from two plots that do not really fit together. The witch of the title is a poor and lonely old woman, Elizabeth Sawyer, persecuted by her neighbours until, in desperation, she makes a pact with the Devil and becomes a witch who can exact retribution for their thoughtless spite. The hand of Dekker is clearly discerned in these scenes, for they show his sympathy for the ill-used. The other part of the play, chiefly by Ford, is a domestic tragedy of crime and punishment. Frank Thorney secretly marries the servant Winifred against his father's wishes. Then his father orders him to marry a girl chosen for him, Susan Carter. Frank's inheritance depends on this, so he marries Susan and then murders her, having planned to throw the guilt on her two rejected suitors. But the truth is discovered and he is executed for the murder.

**With the Procession** A novel by **Henry Blake Fuller**, published in 1895. Set in Fuller's native Chicago, it tells the story of a family of social climbers, focusing on the bourgeois convention that a man should amass as much money as possible and then put it at the disposal of his wife and children, who squander it. This is the situation in which David Marshall finds himself: his eldest daughter, Jane, has social ambitions for the family which change all their lives; his son Truesdale spends four years abroad at his father's expense; the youngest daughter, Rosey, a social butterfly, continually demands money from her father. Exhausted by the demands made upon him – to build a new house, to be a philanthropist, to cut a public figure – David Marshall dies, sacrificed to his family's ambition to march 'with the procession'.

**Wither, George** 1588–1667 Poet. He was born at Bentworth in Hampshire and educated at Magdalen College, Oxford. His main claim to be remembered is as a pastoral poet. He contributed seven eclogues to **William Browne**'s *The Shepherd's Pipe* (1614) and continued in the same vein the next year with *The Shepherd's Hunting*. *Fidelia* (1617) is in the form of a letter from a faithful nymph to her inconstant lover. *Fair Virtue* (1622) is a hymn of love to his half-imagined mistress, Arete, and *Juvenilia* (1622) a collection of love and pastoral poetry. The merit

of these verses has been obscured by the notoriety of Wither's satire – *Abuses Stripped and Whipped, or, Satirical Essays* (1613) sent him to the Marshalsea, *Wither's Motto* (1621) to Newgate – and by the leaden didactic poetry of his later years: *The Hymns and Songs of the Church* (1624), *Britain's Remembrancer* (1628) and *Heleluiah, or, Britain's Second Remembrancer* (1641). A convinced Puritan, he attained the rank of major-general in the Civil War. **John Aubrey** records how, after Wither's arrest at the Restoration, '**Sir John Denham** went to the king and desired his majesty not to hang him, for that while George Wither lived, he should not be the worst poet in England.' Wither also worked with Marchamont Needham on the *Mercurius Britannicus*.

**Wives and Daughters** The last novel by **Elizabeth Gaskell**, almost complete at her untimely death in 1865. It ran serially in **The Cornhill Magazine** from August 1864 until January 1866 and was first published in book form in the latter year.

A series of skilfully interwoven plots, *Wives and Daughters* develops the story of Molly Gibson from girl to womanhood. She is the daughter of the local doctor of Hollingford who, after years as a widower, unwisely marries the flighty and vulgar widow, Clare Kirkpatrick, formerly governess and schoolmistress in the household of Lord and Lady Cumnor, the local Whig parvenu gentry. Molly is much beloved at Hamley Hall, home of Squire Hamley, a proud, unsophisticated, old-fashioned Tory landowner with two sons Roger (to become a respected scientist) and Osborne (to die young soon after a clandestine marriage to a French girl of lowly social status). Into this community comes Cynthia Kirkpatrick, daughter of Clare by her first husband, a beautiful young girl of Molly's age, flighty as her mother but far more intelligent and astute, and magnetically attractive to the opposite sex. A few years earlier Cynthia made an unwise commitment to Mr Preston, the tasteless, social-climbing land-agent of the Cumnors, but this is no deterrent to engaging herself to the temporarily bemused Roger Hamley. Their relationship, however, comes to an end and Cynthia ultimately marries a London barrister named Henderson. Molly, meanwhile, moves through the narrative, a participant in every major phase of its action: thus she extricates Cynthia from her difficulties with Preston (at the expense of her own passing embarrassment), is ministering angel at Hamley Hall, pacifies her tiresome stepmother, and secures Roger Hamley. The psychological development of Molly from a confused, insecure girl to a tranquil, poised young woman is one of Mrs Gaskell's major triumphs.

Socially, *Wives and Daughters* ranges in

descending order from the Cumnors, the Hamleys, and the Gibsons down to mob-capped spinsters, tenant farmers and ordinary labourers to register a lively, informative picture of early 19th-century England. And whilst the dominant figures in the novel (Molly, Cynthia and Roger in particular) are perceptively drawn, a host of lesser characters (Lady Harriet, Lord Cumnor, Mr Coxe and the Misses Browning) contribute a leavening humour, a dramatic moment, or a small turn to the narrative, to sustain the equilibrium and balance of the book. *Wives and Daughters* is an enduring work as narrative, social history and psychological study.

**Wodehouse, Sir P[elham] G[renville]** 1881–1975 Novelist. Born in Guildford, Surrey, and educated at Dulwich College, he worked as a bank clerk and gave this up for his writing in 1903. His school stories were serialized in *The Captain*, a magazine for boys, in which one of his famous later characters, Psmith, first appeared. After 1909 Wodehouse lived mainly abroad, in Paris and the United States. He wrote lyrics to a number of successful musical comedies with Cole Porter, Irving Berlin, and George Gershwin (*Oh, Kay!*, 1926, *Damsel in Distress*, 1928, etc.), but is most famous for his creation of Jeeves, who first appeared with Bertie Wooster in a collection of stories called *The Man with Two Left Feet* (1917). Numerous Jeeves volumes followed, beginning with *My Man Jeeves* (1919), and there were many adaptations for the stage in collaboration with **Ian Hay** and Guy Bolton.

During World War II Wodehouse was captured and interned in Germany. He was released but prevented from leaving the country, and subsequently made a number of broadcasts from Berlin for which he was later accused of pro-Nazi sympathies. After the war he settled in the United States and continued his prolific career (including work for Hollywood), eventually bringing his total number of novels and stories to something over 100. He received American citizenship in 1955. Among his later works were the autobiographical *Performing Flea* (1953) and *Over Seventy* (1957). He was knighted only weeks before his death.

**Wolcot, John** See **Pindar, Peter.**

**Wolfe, Thomas (Clayton)** 1900–38 American novelist and playwright, born in Asheville, North Carolina, and educated at the University of North Carolina and at Harvard. His first works were plays: *Welcome to Our City* (1923), which is set in his home town of Asheville, and *The Return of Buck Gavin* (1923). From 1924 to 1930 he taught English at New York University, where he wrote the play *Mannerhouse*, about the decay of a Southern family. Wolfe decided to become a full-time writer after the publication in 1929 of his first novel, *Look Homeward, Angel*. This strongly autobiographical work follows the life of Eugene Gant, the son of a stonecutter and a boarding-house matron, as he grows from a child in Altamont, Catawba, into the young adult who breaks with his family at the end of the novel. Wolfe's next book, a short novel entitled *A Portrait of Bascom Hawke* (1932), was later incorporated into *Of Time and the River* (1935), which continues the story of Eugene Gant, now at Harvard, and ends with his departure for Europe after a disappointing love affair. *From Death to Morning* (1935) is a collection of stories; *The Story of a Novel* (1936), Wolfe's last book to be published during his lifetime, is a critical examination of his own work. Wolfe died at the age of 38 after two operations for a brain infection following pneumonia. He left a considerable amount of material, from which Edward C. Aswell edited the semi-autobiographical novel *The Web and the Rock* (1939) and its sequel, *You Can't Go Home Again* (1940). A volume of short stories, *The Lost Boy*, was published in 1965.

**Wollstonecraft, Mary** 1759–97 Novelist, essayist and educational writer. She was born in Spitalfields, London. Her father dissipated his fortune in unsuccessful attempts to become a gentleman farmer, and she spent much of her childhood moving from farm to farm in England and Wales. Between the ages of 9 and 15, she received a certain amount of day-school instruction in Beverley, but like most of the educated women of her time she was largely self-taught. At 16 when living in Hoxton near London, she formed a close friendship with Fanny Blood, the accomplished daughter of a poor family, with whom she planned to live and work. At 19 she took a post as companion to a wealthy widow in Bath, a lonely and unhappy experience that quickened her distaste for the habits of the rich. In 1781 she returned to her family at Enfield to care for her sick mother, after whose death she assumed responsibility for the welfare of the younger children. With her sisters and Fanny Blood she opened a school at Newington Green, where she became acquainted with the famous polemicist **Richard Price** and other Dissenting ministers and intellectuals. Following the collapse of the school and the death of Fanny Blood, she began to write *Thoughts on the Education of Daughters*, published in 1787. In the same year she went to Ireland as governess to the daughters of Lord Kingsborough, another uncomfortable employment, during which she wrote *Mary: A Fiction* (1788), a self-pitying account of her childhood and friendship with Fanny Blood.

Upon her dismissal by Lady Kingsborough in 1787, Wollstonecraft resolved to try to make her living through writing and was soon working as translator and reader, and later as reviewer and editorial assistant, on Joseph Johnson's *Analytical Review*, a newly launched liberal journal. Through Johnson she met **Thomas Paine**, Henry Fuseli, **William Blake** and **William Godwin**. Between 1787 and 1790 she wrote two books for children, *Original Stories from Real Life; with Conversations Calculated to Regulate the Affections, and Form the Mind to Truth and Goodness*, and *The Female Reader*, a selection of texts for girls. She translated Jacques Necker's *Of the Importance of Religious Opinion* and Christian Gotthilf Salzmann's *Elements of Morality for the Use of Children*. Her *Vindication of the Rights of Men* (1790) replied to **Burke**'s attack on Price, among other radicals, in ***Reflections on the Revolution in France***. In it she defends the parliamentary reformers, identifies herself with the democratic programmes of the European Enlightenment and deplores both the complacency of British society and its trivialization of women. The latter theme is taken up at greater length in her most famous work, *A Vindication of the Rights of Woman* (1792), a sometimes chaotically written but rhetorically powerful plea for fundamental change in society's perception of the function, place and potential of women. It was dedicated to Tallyrand, in the vain hope of influencing the legislation on women's education before the French Assembly.

Following an obsessive, though unrewarding, relationship with Fuseli, she travelled alone to revolutionary France in 1792. Her *History and Moral View of the Origin and Progress of The French Revolution* (1794) condemns many of the events of the Revolution, while continuing to hold to its basic principles. In Paris she met Helen Maria Williams, leading members of the Girondist faction, and Gilbert Imlay, an American writer and businessman with whom she fell in love. Their daughter, Fanny, was born in Le Havre in 1794, though Imlay rapidly lost interest in the relationship. Learning of his infidelities on her return to England in 1795, she tried to commit suicide, agreeing afterwards to an unlikely solo journey to Scandinavia as his business representative which is fascinatingly described in *Letters Written during a Short Residence in Sweden, Norway and Denmark* (1796). Painful confirmation of Imlay's indifference awaited her in England, and she made another attempt on her own life. She slowly recovered from this affair and began to write and review again, meeting other writers such as Mary Hays, at whose home she again saw William Godwin. A mutual attachment developed, of which strong friendship was a welcome and stabilizing component after the near-fatality of passion. With Godwin's encouragement she began her last novel, *The Wrongs of Woman*, which expands many of her earlier ideas on the

institutionalized oppression and enfeeblement of middle- and lower-class women, and the legal expropriation of their labour, property and sexuality. She married Godwin after becoming pregnant, though they continued to maintain separate houses for a time. She died in 1797, eleven days after the birth of her daughter, the future **Mary Shelley**.

In 1798 Godwin published his *Memoirs* of his wife and edited her *Posthumous Works*, which included letters to Imlay, an autobiographical fictional fragment 'The Cave of Fancy' and the unfinished *Wrongs of Woman*. She is also portrayed in his novel *St Leon* (1799). By this time, conservative reaction had set in in England, and she was much attacked as an unsexed woman, 'a hyena in petticoats' and a 'philosophizing serpent'. *The Anti-Jacobin Review* represented her work as tending to the propagation of whores.

**Woman in White, The** A novel by **Wilkie Collins**, published in ***All the Year Round*** from November 1859 to August 1860 and in volume form in 1860.

The story is told through eyewitness accounts by the main characters. Walter Hartright goes to Limmeridge House in Cumberland as drawing master to Laura Fairlie and her half-sister Marian Halcombe. Laura is pretty and fair, while Marian is ugly and dark but also strong-minded and intelligent. Walter falls in love with Laura, even though she is to marry Sir Percival Glyde. Anne Catherick, a mysterious woman in white first encountered by Walter on his last night in London, reappears; she has escaped from the mental asylum to which she had been committed by Sir Percival because she and her mother know a discreditable secret about his past. Laura insists on going ahead with the marriage, and Walter leaves.

The investigation is continued by Marian. Determined to gain control of Laura's wealth, the baronet enlists the help of Count Fosco, a fat, suave and sinister Italian. Exploiting the resemblance between Laura and Anne Catherick, who has died, they bury Anne under Laura's name and commit Laura to an asylum as Anne. Marian helps her escape and is joined by Walter. They discover that Sir Percival's secret is his illegitimacy; he burns the parish registry containing the evidence and is killed in the resulting fire. Walter confronts Count Fosco, forcing him to admit his part in the conspiracy and so restore Laura to her true identity. The Count dies at the hand of the Italian secret societies he has betrayed, and Laura and Walter marry.

The novel shows Collins at the height of his powers. The careful plotting and manipulation of suspense are matched by his skill in creating atmosphere (notably in the scene where Walter first meets the woman in white) and his sharp

Title-page illustration for an edition of *The Woman in White* published in 1861. Marian and Laura, left; Count Fosco and Sir Percival Glyde, right. Collins's novel was first published as a serial in 1859–60.

eye for characterization. If he gives the reader a conventional heroine in Laura and a conventional villain in Sir Percival, he also offers, in Marian Halcombe and Count Fosco, the most interesting and evenly matched heroine and villain in Victorian **sensation fiction**.

**Woman Killed with Kindness, A** A tragicomedy by **Thomas Heywood**, first performed in 1603. It has claims to be considered, alongside *Arden of Feversham*, as an early masterpiece of domestic drama.

The main plot concerns the marriage of a country gentleman, John Frankford, to an exemplary wife, Anne Acton. Frankford's domestic peace is ruined for ever when he finds Anne in the arms of their guest Wendoll. He punishes her by sending her to live in comfort in a lonely house, barred from the sight of their children or himself. Living at ease but sick with remorse, Anne receives Frankford's forgiveness on her death-bed.

**Woman of No Importance, A** A play by **Oscar Wilde** (1893). The illegitimate Gerald is torn between his father, Lord Illingworth, and his long-suffering mother, Mrs Arbuthnot. Mrs Arbuthnot refuses Lord Illingworth's proposal of marriage, which has come 20 years too late. Lord Illingworth betrays his baseness by attempting to kiss a young American heiress, in love with Gerald. Gerald is able to secure his future by marrying her.

**Women Beware Women** A tragedy by **Thomas Middleton**, perhaps dating from as late as 1625. Like most of Middleton's plays, it has a complex plot and finely drawn characters, but it moves, in its climax of demented vengeance, towards a kind of black farce.

Bianca, daughter of a noble house, marries Leantio, a merchant's clerk, but soon tires of living in reduced circumstances and becomes the mistress of the Duke of Florence. Livia, who plays bawd to the adulterers, is a monster of cynical depravity, who is also instrumental in furthering the incestuous lust of her brother Hippolito for their niece Isabella. When the cardinal, brother to the Duke of Florence, upbraids the duke for his adultery, Leantio becomes an obstacle to their passion. The duke decides to have him killed, and the scheme is made easier when he discovers that Livia has become Leantio's lover. The outraged Hippolito kills Leantio and Livia takes her revenge initially by denouncing Hippolito's incestuous lust. But the climax of the various revenges is reached during a masque in the final act. Lethal incense, poisoned arrows, fatal trapdoors and tainted gold are used to kill off the victims of their own depravity.

**Women in Love** A novel by **D. H. Lawrence**, first published in 1920.

Ursula and Gudrun Brangwen (see *The Rainbow*) are teachers at a grammar school in the Midlands colliery town of Beldover. Both are bored by their limited horizon and searching for adventure and fulfilment. Ursula falls in love with Rupert Birkin, the school inspector, and Gudrun, an artist, is attracted to his friend, Gerald Crich, son of the local mineowner. Gerald replaces his father's benevolent management of the colliery with a more efficient but inhuman system. He has been haunted by feelings of guilt since the accidental death of his brother when they were children. These feelings are compounded when his sister, Diana, drowns during a water-party given by the Crich family.

Birkin and Gerald experience both attraction and repulsion in their respective relationships with the Brangwen sisters, and are also drawn towards each other. Gerald, however, rejects Birkin's attempt to establish a closer intimacy between them, complementing their relationships with women but based upon love between men. He pursues his passionate and ultimately destructive relationship with Gudrun.

Ursula and Birkin marry. Gerald and Gudrun have an affair. All four travel abroad, and at Innsbruck, after Birkin and Ursula have departed for Verona, Gudrun flirts with a German sculptor, Loerke. She and Loerke go tobogganing. Gerald follows, attacks the German and almost strangles Gudrun. Then he walks off into the mountains and is later found dead in the snow.

It is Birkin who feels Gerald's death most keenly. He attempts to explain to Ursula that he needed Gerald to complete his own idea of life and love, and is convinced that his love would have saved Gerald. Ursula cannot accept that two kinds of love are possible or necessary in the way that he asserts. The novel ends with this question left open.

**Wonder-Working Providence of Sion's Saviour in New-England, The** Sub-titled 'A History of New-England, from the English planting of the Yeere 1628 until the Yeere 1652', **Edward Johnson**'s *Wonder-Working Providence* was published anonymously in 1653. The work divides into three books and catalogues instances of divine intervention in New England's history which, Johnson argues, indicate God's approval of the New England Way. Book I (1628–37) considers the conditions in England which compelled removal to America, the journey across the Atlantic, and the settlement of towns and congregations. Book II (1637–45) and Book III (1645–51) portray the Puritans coping with those incidents – the Antinomian affair and the Pequot War, for example – which most seriously threatened the colony's existence.

**Wonderful Year, The** **Thomas Dekker**'s pamphlet (1603) begins with the death of Elizabeth and the accession of James. However, it soon reveals its nature as a typical 16th-century plague pamphlet, with descriptions of the dead and dying, coffins and charnel houses, and a cobbler's wife making her death-bed confession. Prosperous Londoners leave the city for the country (as Lovewit does in **Jonson**'s *The Alchemist*), only to carry the plague there.

**Wood, Anthony à** 1632–95 Antiquary and diarist. Anthony Wood (he archaized his name in later life) was born in Oxford, attending New College School (1641–4) and Lord Williams's School at Thame (1644–6) before entering Merton College in 1647. He lived in Oxford all his life, though he never became a fellow of his college, dying in the same house where he had been born.

*The Antiquities of Warwickshire* by **Sir William Dugdale** first aroused Wood's antiquarian interests, and he made collections for a similar book on Oxfordshire. Most of this work remained unpublished in his lifetime, but Dr John Fell saw that Wood's papers dealing with the University of Oxford went into print as *Historia et Antiquitates Universitatis Oxoniensis* (1674). Wood made an English version – *The History and Antiquities of the University of Oxford* – which John Gutch prepared for publication in 1791–6. In the biographical sections of his *History* and in the later *Athenae Oxonienses* (1691–2) – lives of illustrious Oxonians – Wood received

the invaluable help of **John Aubrey**, whom he later treated with ingratitude. In 1693 the *Athenae* were judged to contain a libel against Edward Hyde, first Earl of Clarendon (see **Clarendon**). The relevant pages were publicly burned and the guilty Wood was expelled from the University, blaming Aubrey for misinformation.

Besides his antiquarian collections, Wood left an autobiography and a remarkable diary for the years 1657–95, fully edited by Andrew Clark and published in five volumes as *The life and Times of Anthony Wood . . . as Described by Himself* (1891–1900).

**Wood, Charles (Gerald)** 1933– Dramatist. Born into a theatrical family, he served as a trooper in the Lancers from 1950 to 1955. His three short plays about the army, produced as *Cockade* in 1963, revealed his gift for terse, vivid dialogue and bitter satire. He has written attacks on militarism, British imperialism and the class system embodied in the army. *Dingo* (1967), set in North Africa during World War II, and *H: Being Monologues at Front of Burning Cities* (1969), about General Havelock and the Indian Mutiny, are epic tirades against the follies and hypocrisies of war. In lighter vein, he has written *Fill the Stage with Happy Hours* (1966), a comedy about a run-down repertory theatre, and *Veterans* (1972), based on his experiences collaborating with **John Osborne** on the screenplay for *The Charge of the Light Brigade*. *Has 'Washington' Legs?* (1978) is a farce about making a Hollywood flop.

**Wood, Mrs Henry** 1814–87 Novelist. She was born Ellen Price in Worcester, where her father was a wealthy glove-manufacturer, and after her marriage at the age of 22 spent 20 years living in France. Mrs Wood started publishing magazine short stories in 1855 and in 1860 won a prize offered for a temperance novel with *Danesbury House*, written in a month. Her second novel, *East Lynne* (1861), brought her world fame. Fifteen novels followed in the next seven years, among them *Mrs Halliburton's Troubles* (1862), which contained a portrait of her father as Mr Ashley, *The Channings* (1862), *Verner's Pride* (1862–3), *The Shadow of Ashlydat* (1863), which she considered her best novel, and *Lord Oakburn's Daughters* (1864). In 1867 she bought *The Argosy*, a journal whose reputation had been sullied by the scandal of **Charles Reade**'s *Griffith Gaunt*, and published many of her subsequent novels in it. They include *Anne Hereford* (1868), *Roland Yorke* (1869), *Bessy Rane* (1870), *Dene Hollow* (1871), *Within the Maze* (1872), *The Master of Greylands* (1873), *Parkwater* (1875), *Edina* (1876), *Pomeroy Abbey* (1878), *Court Netherleigh* (1881) and *Lady Grace* (1887). Her mixture of sentiment, melodrama and piety did not command universal admiration. A rival novelist, Mrs Riddel, said that Mrs Wood was 'simply a brute; she throws in bits of religion to slip her fodder down the public throat'. **Eliza Lynn Lynton** described her as a 'very, very shallow writer, a shallow observer of society, and a puerile and vulgar one'. But another woman writer, Sarah Tytler, reported that Mrs Wood 'considered hostile criticism, as mere envy or stupidity'. A memoir by her son appeared in 1894.

**Woodfall, Henry Sampson** See **Junius** and *Public Advertiser, The*.

**Woodforde, James** 1740–1803 Diarist. His father was rector of Ansford and vicar of Castle Cary, Somerset. Educated at Winchester and New College, Oxford, Woodforde held several curacies in Somerset, including those of his father's parishes. In 1776 he moved to Weston Longville, Norfolk, and remained there as rector until his death.

His diary begins in 1758, when he was an undergraduate, and continues for 45 years. Public events are mentioned briefly but Woodforde concentrates on the daily minutiae of domestic and parish life: meals, cricket matches, charities ('To a poor old Man that plays on the Dulcimer gave 0.0.6'), a glimpse of the Royal Family at Lord Digby's park in Sherborne, Dorset, hare-coursing, gains and losses at games of whist and quadrille, bastard children, household remedies, the payment of five shillings for black 'ribband' to prevent sore throats. The diaries reflect no intellectual interests, merely the surface of everyday life: 'I wore my largest gouty Shoes to Church today.' The eccentricities of grammar and spelling add piquancy to this trivial fond record of life in the second half of the 18th century, a rural life when news of the great world often took ten days to arrive.

**Woodlanders, The** A novel by **Thomas Hardy**, first published serially in *Macmillan's Magazine* from May 1886 to April 1887 and in book form in 1887.

Socially ambitious for his daughter Grace, whom he has educated above her class, the timber merchant George Melbury regrets comiting her to the rustic Giles Winterbourne and uses Winterbourne's financial and legal misfortunes as an excuse to end their relationship. Dr Edred Fitzpiers, scion of a once-prominent local family, expresses an interest in marrying Grace. She, knowing of Fitzpiers's dalliance with a local hoyden, Suke Damson, is not enthusiastic, but her father insists and the marriage takes place. Fitzpiers forms a liaison with Felice Charmond, who has returned from abroad to Hintock Manor House, and Melbury assaults him. Fitzpiers takes refuge with Mrs Charmond

and they go to the Continent where, after a foolish quarrel, their association comes to an end. It is on the Continent, too, that the shadowy figure of the 'gentleman from South Carolina' appears and kills Mrs Charmond in a jealous rage. Fitzpiers returns to England. Grace, meanwhile, supported by her father's vain hope that she can obtain a divorce, encourages Giles and is forced to seek shelter at his cottage in bad weather. Out of propriety he takes to a hopelessly inadequate outdoor retreat of hay and hurdles; already weakened by a previous illness, he dies of exposure. Grace is reunited with Fitzpiers, and the faithful Marty South, an outdoor worker deeply in love with Giles, is left to mourn him with the poignant elegy: 'But no, no, my love, I never can forget 'ee; for you was a good man, and did good things!'

**Woodstock**, *or, The Cavalier. A Tale of the Year 1651* A novel by **Sir Walter Scott**, published in 1826. It marks the beginning of Scott's unremitting labours to clear the huge debts which came as the result of improvident spending and his financial connection with James Ballantyne.

Sir Henry Lee, the old Cavalier, is ranger at Woodstock, the royal lodge. His daughter Alice loves her cousin Everard, but Lee disdains him because Everard serves Cromwell and has earned his favour. When Parliamentary commissioners come to seize Woodstock, however, Everard intervenes. They withdraw, but this is at Cromwell's orders. He knows Woodstock's royal connections and has it watched in the hope that Prince Charles, after his defeat at Worcester, will take refuge there.

Charles does arrive, as page to Albert, Alice's brother; he falls in love with Alice and this brings a clash with Everard, whereupon Charles reveals his identity. Everard gives his word not to betray Charles but Cromwell, informed of his presence, arrives with a force and surrounds the house. He orders the arrest of Everard. Albert Lee impersonates Charles, giving him a chance to escape. The furious Cromwell orders the execution of Everard and the Lees, but later relents and pardons them. Charles has left a parting message with his loyal friends at Woodstock, and this reconciles Sir Henry and Everard, who is now able to marry Alice.

**Woodworth, Samuel** 1785–1842 American poet and playwright, born in Massachusetts. Much of his poetry appeared in the collection *Melodies, Duets, Songs, and Ballads* (1826). He published one novel, *The Champions of Freedom* (2 vols., 1816), a romance set during the War of 1812. His plays include a melodrama, *Lafayette* (1824), a domestic tragedy of the Revolutionary period entitled *The Widow's Son* (1825) and a comedy, *The Forest Rose, or, American Farmers,* which is known for its presentation of the typical Yankee character, Jonathan Ploughboy.

**Woolf, (Adeline) Virginia** 1882–1941 Novelist. Virginia Woolf was born Virginia Stephen, daughter of **Sir Leslie Stephen** by his second wife, Julia Duckworth. The family lived at Hyde Park Gate, and Virginia was educated at home. After her father's death in 1904, Virginia moved to 46 Gordon Square, Bloomsbury, with her sister Vanessa (later the wife of **Clive Bell**) and her brothers Thoby and Adrian. The house was to be the original meeting-place of the **Bloomsbury Group**. When Thoby died of typhoid fever in 1906, she suffered a prolonged mental breakdown; throughout her life she was subject to nervous illness.

In 1912 she married **Leonard Woolf**, and completed her first novel, *The Voyage Out*, the following year – another breakdown delaying publication until 1915. She and Leonard founded the Hogarth Press, working on a hand press installed in their home at Hogarth House, Richmond; they began by publishing *Two Stories* in 1917 ('The Mark on the Wall' by Virginia, and 'Three Jews' by Leonard). **Katherine Mansfield**'s *Prelude* (1918) and **T. S. Eliot**'s *Poems* (1919) followed, and by the time they printed Eliot's *The Waste Land* in 1923 they were established publishers.

Virginia Woolf's career continued with *Night and Day* (1919), a realistic novel set in London, which contrasted the lives of two friends:

Virginia Woolf at the age of twenty. Photograph by G. C. Beresford.

Katherine, the daughter of a famous literary family, and Mary, who becomes involved with the suffragette movement. *Jacob's Room* (1922) was based upon the life and death of her brother, Thoby, and broke away from the realistic mode of her early writing. Like *Mrs Dalloway* (1925) it fulfilled the purposes of fiction laid down in her essay 'Modern Fiction' (1919): 'Life is not a series of gig-lamps symmetrically arranged; life is a luminous halo, a semitransparent envelope surrounding us from the beginning of consciousness to the end. Is it not the task of the novelist to convey this . . . with as little mixture of the alien and external as possible?' With *To the Lighthouse* (1927) and *The Waves* (1931) she fully established herself as a leading exponent of **modernism**.

*Orlando* (1928), a fantastic biography which traces the history of its androgynous protagonist through four centuries, is unlike any of her other novels and was her greatest commercial success. It was dedicated to **V. Sackville-West**, with whom the author had an intimate friendship. Another 'biography', *Flush* (1933), revolves around the life of **Elizabeth Barrett Browning**'s pet spaniel and gives a dog's-eye view of the love affair between his mistress and **Robert Browning**.

*The Years* (1937) was more conventional in form, but her last novel, *Between the Acts*, published posthumously in 1941, returned to the experimental and was completed just before the final attack of mental illness which drove her to suicide. In March 1941 she filled her pockets with stones and drowned herself in the River Ouse near her home at Rodmell in Sussex.

Virginia Woolf is now generally acknowledged as one of the major innovative novelists of the 20th century, best known, perhaps, for her use of **stream of consciousness**. Her contribution to feminist criticism has been widely recognized, and *A Room of One's Own* (1929), with its still more radical sequel, *Three Guineas* (1938), are now established feminist classics.

Her critical works, which began when she became a reviewer for *The Times Literary Supplement* in 1905 (a connection lasting until just before her death), included several collections of essays, notably *The Common Reader* (1925) and *The Second Common Reader* (1932). They were reprinted in *Collected Essays of Virginia Woolf* (4 vols., 1966–7).

Her letters, edited by Nigel Nicolson and J. Trautmann in six volumes (1975–80), include correspondence with nearly everyone associated with the Bloomsbury Group. Her diaries, edited in five volumes by Anne Olivier Bell and A. McNeillie (1977–84), give an invaluable picture of her creative method.

**Woolf, Leonard (Sidney)** 1880–1969 Author and social reformer. Born in London, he was educated at St Paul's and Trinity College, Cambridge, where he became a member of the **Apostles** and was profoundly influenced by the teachings of the philosopher **G. E. Moore**. He entered the Ceylon Civil Service in 1904 and served until 1911. On his return to England he wrote for various political journals and became an active member of the Fabian Society. He married Virginia Stephen (see **Virginia Woolf**) in 1912 and published his first novel, *The Village in the Jungle*, about life in Ceylon, in 1913. *The Wise Virgins* (1914), his only other novel and *Stories of the East* (1916) were also set in Ceylon.

Leonard and Virginia Woolf founded the Hogarth Press in 1917, and during the 1920s and 30s their Richmond house and later 52 Tavistock Square remained a focus for the **Bloomsbury Group**. His own publications continued with works on politics and international affairs, among them *Economic Imperialism* (1920), *Imperialism and Civilization* (1928), *After the Deluge* (2 vols., 1931 and 1939), and *Principia Politica* (1953). He was literary editor of *The Nation* from 1923 to 1930, and helped found *The Political Quarterly* (1931–59). His five volumes of autobiography are highly regarded for their literary qualities and for their portraits of notable figures: *Sowing* (1960), *Growing* (1961), *Beginning Again* (1964), *Downhill All the Way* (1967) and *The Journey not the Arrival Matters* (1969).

**Woolson, Constance (Fenimore)** 1840–94 American novelist, born in Claremont, New Hampshire. She lived in various parts of the USA and used her knowledge of the country as background material when she began to write. *Castle Nowhere: Lake-Country Sketches* (1875) tells of the French settlers in the Great Lakes region. *Rodman the Keeper: Southern Sketches* (1880) contrasts the life of the Old South with the South during Reconstruction. *Anna* (1882) tells of a Mackinac Island (Michigan) girl in New York City. *For the Major* (1883) is the story of a North Carolina woman helping to preserve her husband's illusions about the South. *East Angels* (1886) is set in Florida; *Jupiter Lights* (1889) portrays two sisters-in-law in conflict, one representing the North and the other the South. Her last novel, *Horace Chase* (1894), is a domestic drama about a woman who despises her self-made husband but discovers, almost too late, his sterling character. *Dorothy, and Other Italian Stories* (1896), her last book, concerns Americans in Europe. **Henry James** became a friend of Woolson, and portrayed her in his story *The Aspern Papers*.

**Worde, Wynkyn de** d.?1534 Printer. He was born Jan van Wynkyn in Worth, Alsace, hence the name by which he is usually known (i.e. Wynkyn from Worth). He arrived in London *c.* 1476 and became apprentice and assistant to **William Caxton**, inheriting Caxton's press and materials on the latter's death in 1491. Unlike Caxton, he contented himself with printing and did not make forays into translation and editing. Many important books came from his press in Westminster: editions of *The Golden Legend* of Jacobus de Voragine (1493), Caxton's translations of St Jerome's *Vitae Patrum* (1495), **Malory's** *Morte Darthur* (1498) and **Chaucer's** *The Canterbury Tales* (1498). In about 1500 he moved to Fleet Street and after that time printed some 600 books, mainly those likely to have a popular appeal, such as small service books (e.g. the Sarum *Hours*), grammar books and some popular romances. He was the first English printer to use italic type, in 1524.

**Wordsworth, Dorothy** 1771–1855 Sister of **William Wordsworth** and author of journals. Born a year and a half after William at Cockermouth, Cumberland, Dorothy spent her later childhood, after her parents' early death, with various relatives in Halifax, Penrith and Norfolk. The bond between her and William was exceptionally strong, and when he was left a legacy by his friend Raisley Calvert in 1795, they were able to realize a long-cherished plan of setting up house together, settling first at Racedown in Dorset, and then in the Quantocks at Alfoxden, Somerset, in order to be close to **Coleridge** at Nether Stowey. They were to remain inseparable through William's marriage until his death in 1850. Dorothy's *Alfoxden Journal*, of which only the entries for the months January–April 1798 have survived, is remarkable not only for the light it sheds on William and his friendship and collaboration with Coleridge in the *annus mirabilis* of the **Lyrical Ballads**, but also for its powerfully poetic quality as descriptive prose. Although she had no thought of professional authorship, and committed to paper her thoughts, impressions and responses to nature simply to 'give William pleasure by it', it is clear that the imaginative economy of her writing was an important source of stimulation to Wordsworth and Coleridge in the composition of individual poems. This is equally true of the *Grasmere Journals* for 1800–3, upon which William frequently drew for themes, motifs and images, most famously in the poem 'I wandered lonely as a cloud', whose daffodils are first observed by Dorothy as they 'tossed and reeled and danced and seemed as if they verily laughed with the wind that blew upon them over the lake, they looked so gay ever glancing ever changing'.

In the winter of 1798–9 she accompanied the friends to Germany, and in December 1799 she and William moved to Dove Cottage, Grasmere, where she continued to stay after his marriage (1802), participating as a matter of course in subsequent family moves to Allan Bank and Rydal Mount. She was with William on countless walking tours, excursions and foreign travels, on which she kept journals which remained unpublished until after her death. The German sojourn is briefly captured in her *Visit to Hamburgh and a Journey to . . . Goslar 1798–99*, and in 1805 she finished *Recollections of a Tour made in Scotland 1803*. Her strikingly lively accounts of *An Excursion on the Banks of Ullswater 1805* and *An Excursion to Scawfell Pike 1818* were used by Wordsworth in his *Guide to the Lakes* (1825). *The Journal of a Tour on the Continent 1820* is remarkable for its deeply emotional passages on the Swiss land-scape and its vivid portrait of Wordsworth in middle age. *A Journal of a Second Tour in Scotland* followed in 1822, and a *Journal of a Tour in the Isle of Man* in 1828. The unusual quality of Dorothy's personality left a deep impression on everyone who knew her. To Coleridge she was Wordsworth's 'exquisite sister . . . simple, ardent, innocent . . . her eye watchful in minu-test observation of nature'; **De Quincey** con-sidered her 'the most . . . natural person I have ever known . . . quickest in sympathy with joy and sorrow', and Wordsworth himself pays tribute to her beneficent influence upon his life and work in numerous poems. In 1829 she became seriously ill and was henceforth an invalid. From 1835 she developed arterioscler-osis, and apart from brief periods of remission her mind was clouded for the remaining 20 years of her life.

**Wordsworth, William** 1770–1850 Perhaps the most celebrated and lastingly influential of the English Romantic poets, Wordsworth was born at Cockermouth, Cumberland, the third of the five children of John Wordsworth, attorney to Sir James Lowther (later Earl of Lonsdale). He was educated at primary schools in Cocker-mouth and Penrith, and from 1779 to 1787 at the grammar school in Hawkshead, where he lived in lodgings. The children lost their mother when William was eight, and their father five years later, and were placed under the guard-ianship of uncles. Lowther's failure to pay large debts owing to his former employee left the orphans only modestly provided for, and new domestic arrangements caused William to be separated from his beloved sister, **Dorothy Wordsworth**. His first published poem, a sonnet 'On Seeing Miss Helen Maria Williams Weep at a Tale of Distress', and signed 'Axiologus', appeared in *The European Magazine* for March 1787. In October of that year he entered St John's College, Cambridge, where he was unsettled by the unfamiliar climate of world-liness and intellectual sophistication and read largely outside the curriculum, gradually shed-ding his awe of 'printed books and authorship'.

Rydal Water in the Lake District. Wordsworth's home was nearby. A 19th-century engraving.

The summer and autumn of 1790 were spent on a walking tour in France, Switzerland and Ger-many which is commemorated in *Descriptive Sketches* (composed 1792). At Cambridge he took an ordinary BA degree in January 1791, then spent some months in London and North Wales, before returning to France at the end of the year, where he stayed at Blois and Orleans, with occasional visits to Paris. This year in revolutionary France was one of the most important periods of his life. His friendship with Michel de Beaupuy, an aristocratic supporter of the Revolution, and later general in the Republi-can army, inspired a deep and passionate faith in the Revolution, and he fell in love with Annette Vallon, the daughter of a surgeon at Blois, by whom he had a daughter (Caroline, born in December 1792). Their affair is the basis of the poem *Vaudracour and Julia*, first published in 1820, when it was removed from its somewhat awkward position in Book IX of **The Prelude**. Wordsworth entertained ideas of offering his services to the Girondist faction of the Revolu-tion in Paris, and of marrying Annette, but he ran out of money and his uncles refused to fund further residence abroad. Bowing to 'harsh necessity' he returned to England in December 1792. In January 1793 he made his début as an author with 'An Evening Walk' and *Descriptive Sketches*, brought out by the radical publisher Joseph Johnson. He also wrote (but did not publish) a *Letter to the Bishop of Llandaff*, criticiz-ing his anti-revolutionary sermon on 'The Wisdom and Goodness of God in having made both Rich and Poor', and identifying himself with the ideas laid down by **Paine** in the recently published **Rights of Man**. The period 1793–5 was one of great personal unhappiness, uncertainty about his professional future, and moral and intellectual confusion, towards the end of which he seems to have been close to nervous break-down. Despite dismay at the drift of the Revo-lution into the political terror of the Jacobin dictatorship, he held fast to his belief in the French experiment as the future model for all European countries, but England's declaration of war against France in February 1793 left him grievously divided in his national loyalties, and was effectively to separate him for good from Annette and his child. He fell briefly under the spell of **Godwin**'s *Enquiry Concerning Political Justice*, but was soon repelled by its extreme rationalism. In the summer of 1793 he undertook a walking tour from Salisbury to North Wales, during which he first visited Tintern Abbey. Most of the first version of 'Salisbury Plain' (later 'Guilt and Sorrow'), published in part as 'The Female Vagrant' in the *Lyrical Ballads* of 1798, was written at this time. He probably visited Paris in late September and early October, where he witnessed the execution of Gorsas, the first Girondist to be guillotined. His revolutionary sympathies continued undaunted, however, and his joy at hearing the news of the death of Robespierre in August 1794 was accompanied by the expectation that the 'golden time' would now really come. He was not finally to become disenchanted with France until her occupation of Switzerland in 1798.

Wordsworth's precarious financial circumstances changed for the better in 1795, when his Penrith friend Raisley Calvert died, leaving him a legacy of £900. He was now in a position to follow his vocation as a poet, and to realize his long-cherished dream of setting up house with Dorothy, with whom he had been reunited in 1794. Taking charge of the small son of their widower friend, Basil Montagu, they settled first at Racedown in Dorset, where Wordsworth wrote the first version of 'The Ruined Cottage' and his only play, the blank-verse tragedy *The Borderers*, and then at the fine manor house at Alfoxden in Somerset, in order to be near to their exciting new friend, **Samuel Taylor Coleridge**, who was living at Nether Stowey. Wordsworth probably first met Coleridge, along with **Robert Southey** and the publisher Joseph Cottle, during a stay at Bristol in 1795. Encouraged and in many ways inspired by Dorothy, whose influence upon Coleridge was almost as strong as her influence upon her brother, both poets entered a period of intense creativity which produced the *Lyrical Ballads* (1798), a collection which inaugurated the Romantic epoch of English poetry. Largely in deference to Coleridge's desire to complete his philosophical education, the trio travelled to Germany in the autumn of 1798, splitting up to allow Coleridge to proceed to the University of Göttingen, while Dorothy and William entered winter quarters in the remote little town of Goslar. It was here that Wordsworth wrote the enigmatic 'Lucy' poems and began *The Prelude*, which was completed in its two-part version at the end of 1799.

Wordsworth. A detail from the portrait by Benjamin Robert Haydon, 1842. National Portrait Gallery, London.

On their return to England in May 1799, the Wordsworths stayed at Sockburn-on-Tees, before moving into Dove Cottage, Grasmere, in December. In the next year Wordsworth completed Book I of 'The Recluse' (later *The Excursion*) and wrote many of the poems included in the second edition of *Lyrical Ballads* (1800), which also contained a controversial new preface on poetic diction that became the aesthetic manifesto of conservative romanticism. On the death of Lord Lonsdale in 1802 his financial situation was substantially improved by the payment to the family of the money owed to John Wordsworth. During the short-lived Peace of Amiens he travelled with Dorothy to France to visit Annette Vallon and his daughter, and in the same year married Mary Hutchinson, with whom he had been friendly since childhood. It was agreed that Dorothy should retain her membership of the household. This was also the year in which he composed 'Resolution and Independence' and parts of his ode 'Intimations of Immortality from Recollections of Early Childhood', both of which appeared in *Poems in Two Volumes* (1807), along with other later work such as the 'Ode to Duty', 'Miscellaneous Sonnets' and 'Sonnets Dedicated to Liberty'. His son John, the first of five children by Mary, was born in 1803.

Wordsworth's life was now relatively uneventful. *The Prelude* was completed in its second, 13-book form in 1805. He was at the height of his creative powers and the head of a household unswervingly devoted to his fame, in which he maintained an unperturbed confidence despite sharp attacks in the literary press. New friends included **Sir Walter Scott**, Sir George Beaumont, and the young **De Quincey**, who wrote to him in tones bordering on hero-worship. His married life was contented, but the loss of his brother John at sea in February 1805 came as a cruel blow, and the Wordsworths' middle years were saddened by the deaths of two of their children in 1812. His estrangement from Coleridge in 1810 was a further disappointment for Wordsworth. A kind of reconciliation took place in 1812, but the old intimacy was never restored. In 1813 he was appointed to the sinecure of Distributor of Stamps for Westmorland, which carried the substantial salary of £400 a year, and moved from Allan Bank (where he had lived from 1808) to Rydal Mount, Ambleside, where he remained for the rest of his life. *The Excursion* was published in 1814, *The White Doe of Rylstone* in 1815, and *Poems, including Lyrical Ballads* in 1815 – the first of many collected editions of old and new poetical work, frequently revised and reclassified, to appear over the next 35 years. *Peter Bell: A Tale in Verse* (composed 1798) and *The Waggoner* (composed 1805) were both published in 1819. Arriving at Rydal Mount to pay his respects to the great poet in 1818, **Keats** was dismayed to discover that Wordsworth was busy campaigning for the Tory Lord Lonsdale in the general election. He was indeed now a long way from the cosmopolitan radicalism of his youth, and the openly reactionary politics and priestly patriotism of his middle age increasingly became a bone of contention between him and the second generation of Romantic poets, who were nonetheless lastingly indebted as practitioners to the great innovations of his poetry. Yet his poetic powers too began to decline as he neared 50, and the work of his later years is the inspiration of a less demanding muse. Much of the best of it commemorates his travels: *The River Duddon: A Series of Sonnets* was published in 1820, and a volume of poems entitled *Memorials of a Tour on the Continent* in 1822. In 1828 he toured the Rhineland with his daughter Dora, and Coleridge, and in 1831 stayed with Sir Walter Scott at Abbotsford, on the way to the Highlands. *Yarrow Revisited and Other Poems* was published in 1835. He was honoured by the Universities of Durham (1838) and Oxford (1839), and in 1842 received a Civil List pension of £300 a year. In 1843 he succeeded Southey as Poet Laureate. A monumental figure in English letters, he died at Rydal Mount, and *The Prelude*, now widely considered to be his most important work, was published posthumously in July 1850. His prose works include *The Convention of Cintra* (1809), an essay criticizing the agreement of Britain and Portugal to allow the beaten French army to return home during the Peninsular War; an 'Essay on Epitaphs', published in Coleridge's journal *The Friend* (1810); and *A Description of the Scenery of the Lakes in the North of England*, published in 1810 as an introduction to Joseph Wilkinson's *Select Views of Cumberland*.

**Work for Armourers** **Thomas Dekker**'s pamphlet (1609) is an allegory about the 'two nations'. The army of Poverty assaults the army of Money, entrenched in the City of London, and a final truce is reached. It denounces greed and corruption, is vehement about evictions and enclosures in the country and its motto is 'God help the poor, the rich can shift.'

**Workers in the Dawn** The first novel by **George Gissing**, published in 1880. Naturalist in method, it is about rich and poor, degradation, drink, destitution and the effects of heredity. Two solutions are proposed: revolution, which the author rejects as leading to incendiary madness, and education, which he endorses. But to educate the masses is seen as a hard struggle: the noble Helen, who has embraced the doctrines of 'Schopenhauer, Comte and **Shelley**', wears herself out giving free lessons in adult literacy and dies of inherited consumption. Arthur, in love with Helen, carelessly marries Carrie, a woman of low morals who resists his efforts to get her to speak correctly and learn to spell. Though gifted, Arthur suffers from inherited instability, which leads to his defeat by misfortune, despite his ability and heroic struggles. Although the minor characters are predictable (Whiffle the wastrel, Maud the heartless socialite), Helen and Arthur hold our interest. The descriptions of squalor are memorable.

**Wotton, Sir Henry** 1568–1639 Poet and diplomat. A Kentish man, Wotton was educated at Winchester and then at New College and The Queen's College, Oxford, before entering the Middle Temple. In 1595 he was engaged by the Earl of Essex as agent and secretary, collecting foreign intelligence. He was later appointed ambassador to Venice and worked as a diplomat until 1624, when he became Provost of Eton.

The only work published during his lifetime was *The Elements of Architecture* (1624). His poems and miscellaneous writings were collected as *Reliquiae Wottonianae* in 1651, and later enlarged. Among them were three poems that became favourite anthology pieces: 'Elizabeth of Bohemia', 'The Character of a Happy Life' and 'Upon the Sudden Restraint of the Earl of Somerset'. Wotton planned to write a life of his friend **John Donne** but the task devolved on their mutual friend **Izaak Walton**, who contributed a memoir of Wotton to the *Reliquiae*. Wotton's definition of an ambassador is famous: 'An Ambassador is an honest man, sent to lie abroad for the good of his country.'

**Wren, P[ercival] C[hristopher]** 1885–1941 Novelist. He was born in Devon and educated at Oxford. He then travelled the world, working as a schoolmaster, journalist, explorer and farmhand, serving in a British cavalry regiment and the French Foreign Legion, and living in India. During World War I he was an officer with the Indian forces in East Africa. From these varied experiences he drew inspiration for his many popular novels of romance and adventure, which reflect his belief in the values of the British Empire. His most famous book, *Beau Geste* (1924), dealt with the Foreign Legion; it was followed by more stories about the three Geste brothers, *Beau Sabreur* (1926), *Beau Ideal* (1928) and *Good Gestes* (1929). Other titles include *Dew and Mildew* (1912), *The Wages of Virtue* (1916), *Valiant Dust* (1932), *Sinbad the Sailor* (1935), *Rough Shooting* (1938) and *The Uniform of Glory* (1941).

**Wright, David (Murray)** 1920– Poet. Born in Johannesburg, he lost his hearing at the age of seven. In 1934 he came to England, where he attended the Northampton School for the Deaf and Keble College, Oxford. He was Gregory Poetry Fellow at the University of Leeds in 1965–7. With the painter Patrick Swift, he edited the brilliant but short-lived quarterly *X* magazine in 1959–62; it included contributions from **George Barker**, **Samuel Beckett**, **Hugh MacDiarmid**, **Patrick Kavanagh** and **Stevie Smith**. His anthologies include *The Faber Book of Twentieth-Century Verse* (with **John Heath-Stubbs**, 1953), *Mid-Century: English Poetry 1940–60* (1965) and the Penguin Books of *English Romantic Verse* (1968) and *Everyday Verse* (1976). In 1969 he published a remarkable autobiography, *Deafness*, and in 1985 a verse translation of **The Canterbury Tales**.

His volumes of poetry include *Moral Stories* (1954), *Monologue of a Deaf Man* (1958), *Adam at Evening* (1965), *Nerve Ends* (1969), *To the Gods the Shades: New and Selected Poems* (1976) and *Metrical Observations* (1980). His work is distinguished by a sense of the rhythm of ordinary speech which is more far-reaching than the merely aural and by a vivid rendering of appearances in language which is at once elegant and familiar. The poetry is above all celebratory, giving intimations of a deep-seated romanticism which, however, nowhere inflates the language.

**Wright, James** 1927–80 American poet, born in Martin's Ferry, Ohio, and educated at Kenyon College and the University of Washington. He taught at Hunter College in New York City from 1966 until his death. Whether writing about nature, politics, social outcasts, or his home town, Wright emphasizes the common human element in the subjects of his poems. His language is colloquial and unadorned, and his tone compassionate. He himself said that he wanted his poems to 'say something humanly important instead of just showing off with language'. His first volume, *The Green Wall*, was published in 1957; it was followed by *Saint Judas* (1959), *The Lion's Tail and Eyes* (1962), *This Branch Will Not Break* (1963), *Shall We Gather at the River?* (1968), *Collected Poems* (1971, Pulitzer Prize), *Two Citizens* (1973), *Moments of the Italian Summer* (1976) and *To a Blossoming Pear Tree* (1977).

**Wright, Judith (Arundell)** 1915– Australian poet. Educated at New England Girls School and Sydney University, she has written *The Moving Image* (1946), *Woman to Man* (1949), *The Gateway* (1953), *Five Senses* (1963), *The Other Half* (1966), *Collected Poems* (1971), *Alive* (1973), *Because I Was Invited* (1975), *The Double Tree* (1978) and *The Cry for the Dead* (1981). Her fresh and energetic poetry reveals her abiding concern for the environment which has led her to campaign for the protection of Australia's wildlife. She has also written a number of books on Australian literature, among them *Charles Harpur* (1963) and *Preoccupations in Australian Poetry* (1965).

**Wright, Richard** 1908–60 Black American novelist and social critic, born near Natchez, Mississippi. By the time he moved to New York City in 1937, after periods spent living in Memphis and Chicago, he had written most of the novel *Lawd Today*, which was published posthumously in 1963. His first published volume was a collection of short stories about Southern racism, ironically entitled *Uncle Tom's Children* (1938, enlarged edition 1940). The novel **Native Son** was published in 1940 and, with its memorable portrait of the rebellious Bigger Thomas, brought Wright widespread recognition.

In 1940 he left the USA to live in Mexico, and then in 1946 moved to Paris, where he remained for the rest of his life. His other novels are *The Outsider* (1953), which chronicles a black intellectual's search for identity, *Savage Holiday* (1954) and *The Long Dream* (1958). *Eight Men*, published posthumously in 1961, is a collection of short stories, radio plays, a novella, and an autobiography. Wright's non-fictional work includes *Twelve Million Black Voices* (1941), an illustrated folk history of American blacks, and the acclaimed autobiography *Black Boy* (1945). *American Hunger*, a continuation of *Black Boy*,

Richard Wright.

was published posthumously in 1977. He also published three books of social criticism inspired by his travels: *Black Power* (1954), about Africa, *The Color Curtain* (1956), about Asia, and *Pagan Spain* (1957). A collection of lectures on racial injustice, *White Man, Listen!*, appeared in 1957.

**Wright, Thomas** 1810–77 Antiquary. He was born at Tenbury, Shropshire, and educated at Ludlow and Trinity College, Cambridge. A founding member of the Camden Society (1838) and the Percy Society (1841), he edited many volumes of medieval texts for both societies. His most ambitious project was a biography of literary characters, *Biographia Britannica Literaria*, of which only the first two volumes were completed (1842 and 1846).

**Wrightson, (Alice) Patricia** 1921– Australian children's writer. Born in New South Wales and educated largely through correspondence school, she worked in hospital administration before taking up writing. Her best-known novel, *I Own the Racecourse!* (1968), deals sympathetically with the tragicomic delusions of a backward Australian adolescent loyally supported by an understanding group of friends. Since then she has linked her talent for realistic description to an exploration of Aboriginal folktales, most notably in *The Nargun and the Stars* (1973).

*Wulf and Eadwacer* An Old English poem preserved in **The Exeter Book**. It is short and enigmatic, yet poignantly expresses the sorrow of a woman separated from her lover by the enmity of their clans. Apparently she has or will soon have Wulf's child and expects it to be persecuted, but the nature of the events related by the poem is unclear.

**Wulfstan** d. 1023 Author of Old English **homilies**, tracts and law codes. He was Bishop of London (996–1002) and Worcester (1002–16) and Archbishop of York (1002–23), but nothing is known of his earlier life. His style is distinctive, enabling his homilies and legal texts to be identified, as well as his entries in a northern redaction of the **Anglo-Saxon Chronicle**. His main concerns were with problems of political and social organization and Church reform. His most famous work, written under the pseudonym Lupus, is *Sermo Lupi ad Anglos* (1014); it calls for repentance and reformation after the defeat of Aethelred. He also wrote *The Canons of Edgar* and the *Institutes of Polity* as well as many lesser-known pieces, and contributed to a vernacular version of the Benedictine office.

*Wuthering Heights* The only novel by **Emily Brontë**, first published in 1847.

The story is told from the viewpoint of Lockwood, a fashionable gentleman visiting the Yorkshire moors where the novel is set, and of Mrs Dean, servant to the Earnshaw family. Heathcliff, a foundling, is picked up on the streets of Liverpool by Mr Earnshaw and brought home by him to Wuthering Heights to be treated like his own children, Catherine and Hindley. But after Mr Earnshaw's death Heathcliff is bullied and degraded by Hindley, now married and head of the household. Heathcliff, of a passionate and ferocious nature, falls in love with Catherine, who returns his affection even though she feels it would be humiliating to marry him. Upon learning this Heathcliff slips quietly away. Meanwhile Hindley's wife has died leaving him a son, Hareton. Catherine, for all her affinity with Heathcliff, is attracted to the soft, luxurious life of the Lintons of Thrushcross Grange, and by the time he returns, after three years abroad, she has married Edgar Linton, master of the house.

Heathcliff remains at Wuthering Heights, and his vengeful nature begins to assert itself. His first victim is his beloved Catherine, whose death he hastens by incessant and vehement accusations of betrayal, of contempt for himself, and of cruelty; weakened by her pregnancy and unable to withstand such an emotional battering, she dies giving birth to a girl, another Catherine. A further victim is Isabella Linton, sister of Edgar, with whom Heathcliff, consumed with revenge and malevolence, contracts a loveless marriage that drives her to run away to the south. Their son, Linton Heathcliff, is claimed by his father and returned to the horrors of *Wuthering Heights*. Heathcliff also effects the destruction of Hindley, a heavy drinker and gambler, so that when the latter dies at the age of 27 he is deeply in debt and the mortgagee of Wuthering Heights is revealed as Heathcliff himself. As for Hindley's son, Hareton, he is not so much as taught to read or write, is allowed to develop brutishly and, despite glimmerings of kindness, is little more than a country lout.

Then, through trickery, Heathcliff engineers more havoc by forcing a marriage between young Catherine and his son, Linton, 'an ailing, peevish creature', and thus securing the Linton family property. But with the death of Linton Heathcliff the young widow develops an interest in Hareton; he reciprocates and she undertakes his education. By now Heathcliff, all passion spent, longs for death and union with Catherine. Increasingly alienated from daily life, he experiences visions and supernatural portents of reconciliation with his beloved Catherine. He dies having failed to extirpate the Earnshaws and the Lintons, and leaves to the younger generation, Catherine and Hareton, hopes of a richer life.

The novel's stern power, which disturbed and shocked contemporaries but has impressed later generations of readers, owes much to the deliberately enigmatic portrait of Heathcliff, who places instinct above moral or social obligation and seems the epitome of Romantic values. Hardly less remarkable is the way that the tortuous and violent plot, instead of seeming merely melodramatic, is given solidity by the precisely realized Yorkshire locations and subtlety by the shifting narrative viewpoints.

**Wyatt, Sir Thomas** ?1503–42 Poet. Wyatt was educated at St John's College, Cambridge, and became an important and popular member of the court of Henry VIII. In *c.* 1520 he married Elizabeth Brooke, from whom he separated *c.* 1525, charging her with adultery. He served Henry VIII on a number of missions (to the papal court and Venice in 1527), and in various offices (High Marshal of Calais in 1528–30), and was knighted in 1535. When Anne Boleyn lost the king's favour and was accused of adultery in 1536, Wyatt was arrested and imprisoned in the Tower, possibly on suspicion of being one of her lovers. He was released the same year and, in favour with the king again, was made ambassador to Charles V in 1537. In 1541 he was again arrested and confined to the Tower, this time on accusations of misconduct as ambassador first made against him in 1538 by Bonner, who was now Bishop of London. He wrote a spirited 'Defence' and was pardoned, perhaps at the request of Queen Catherine Howard. He died at Sherborne, Dorset, in 1542.

None of Wyatt's poems appeared in print in his lifetime and his first published work was *Certain Psalms . . . Drawn into English Metre* (1549), a version of the penitential psalms from a prose paraphrase by Aretino. More of his poetry, lyrics and satires, appeared in *Tottel's Miscellany* (1557). The rest remained in manuscript until the 19th and 20th centuries. With **Surrey**, Wyatt was the first to domesticate the **sonnet** into English, providing it with its characteristic final rhyming couplet. His versions of Petrarch show an extraordinary facility in the difficult task of imitation in another language: 'I find no peace' is a remarkably close rendering of Petrarch's 'Pace non trovo'. Wyatt's most famous sonnet, 'Whoso List to Hunt', imitates and transforms Petrarch's 'Una candida cerva' to produce a sonnet radically different in tone from its original. (The poem has sometimes been seen as containing covert allusions to Anne Boleyn, the hind with her diamond collar inscribed 'Noli me tangere [do not touch me], for Caesar's I am'.) Wyatt was also successful in his handling of such new forms in English as the **rondeau** and the **terza rima**. With their song-like refrains, his poems also continued native traditions of the English lyric. Some, especially those referring to the poet's lute (e.g. 'My Lute Awake' and 'Blame Not My Lute'), may have been sung by Wyatt himself to a courtly audience. One of Wyatt's best and most famous poems, 'They Flee From Me', shows his ability to combine native traditions and classical influence.

**Wycherley, William** 1640–1716 Playwright. Born at Clive, near Shrewsbury, Wycherley was sent to France by his prosperous family in 1655–60. There he became a Catholic, absorbed French literary culture and developed the social ambitions and financial greed that tarnished much of his later life. He was briefly at Oxford in 1660 and then at the Inner Temple, but he pursued fashion rather than the law, associating with such Restoration wits as the **Earl of Rochester**, **Etherege** and **Sir Charles Sedley**. His first publication, a verse burlesque of *Hero and Leander* (1669), was a bid for membership of the cleverly dismissive literary élite.

Wycherley may have had experience as an actor and a dabbler in theatrical management before he wrote his first play, *Love in a Wood, or, St James's Park* (1671). The mordant satire of a sexually and financially rapacious society that characterizes his best plays is already present in his first. *The Gentleman Dancing-Master* (1672), derived from a play by Calderón, is more generous to its characters than either of Wycherley's greatest comedies, *The Country Wife* (1675) and *The Plain Dealer* (1676). In these plays, Wycherley describes a world he knew. It is not a pleasant world, and although the comic contri-

William Wycherley. A detail from the painting after Lely, c.1668. National Portrait Gallery, London.

vance is masterly, there is no affection in the portraiture.

After 1676, Wycherley turned his back on the theatre and proceeded to live almost like a character in one of his plays. He forfeited the patronage of Charles II when he married the Countess of Drogheda, a wealthy widow, in 1679. She died in 1681, and Wycherley was imprisoned for debt on her estate in 1682–6. *Epistles to the King and Duke* (1683) is an expression, in lame verse, of pathetic need. James II arranged his release from prison in 1686, gave him a pension of £200 and paid his debts. From the seclusion of the family estate in Clive, Wycherley tried to guard his literary reputation, wrote unimpressive and sometimes obscene poems (published as *Miscellany Poems*, 1704), and became increasingly cantankerous. When he married a second time, shortly before his death, he seems to have been motivated by a wish to disinherit his nephew.

The strange friendship between the ageing Wycherley and the youthful **Alexander Pope** found expression in the edition by Pope and **Lewis Theobald** of Wycherley's *Posthumous Works* (2 vols., 1729), in which original Wycherley cannot be easily distinguished from sub-standard Pope.

**Wyclif (or Wycliffe), John** *c.*1320–84 Theologian and translator of the Bible. Born at Hipswell near Richmond into a wealthy family, he studied at Balliol College, Oxford, and later became Master of the college, resigning in 1361 to take up the living of Fillingham, Lincolnshire. In 1362 he accepted the prebend of Aust, Bristol, and in 1365 was appointed Warden of Canterbury Hall. The latter was contested and he lost it. In 1368 he moved from Fillingham to the curacy of Ludgershall and became a canon in Lincoln in 1371. In 1374 he was rector of Lutterworth and retained the post until his death.

He became a renowned lecturer in theology and philosophy. His writings took on a militant aspect after his engagement in negotiations with papal envoys in Bruges in 1374. He began to attack Rome's control of the English Church and his stance became increasingly anti-Papal resulting in condemnation of his teaching and threats of excommunication. He further antagonized the orthodox Church by disputing the doctrine of transubstantiation. He amassed a great following, particularly in Oxford, which developed into the **Lollard** movement and spread throughout England.

The majority of his writings are in Latin but his crucial contribution to the history of English literature was his project for vernacular translation of the Bible. His part in its execution was probably restricted to an unfinished version of the New Testament. (See also **The Bible in English**.) Many sermons, commentaries, glosses and tracts have been attributed to Wyclif, some of which are undoubtedly the work of his followers though most draw on his own material available in Latin. The large body of **Wyclifite writings** cannot be accurately attributed to individual authors but all share Lollard philosophy.

**Wyclifite writings** Religious works expressing **Lollard** sympathies, attributed to **John Wyclif** and his followers. They include sermons, tracts, commentaries and the satiric *Jack Upland* and *Upland's Rejoinder*. Some works may certainly be ascribed to Wyclif himself, others to John Purvey, his secretary, and others are of unknown authorship. They are concerned principally with attacking the worldliness and corruption of the friars and the orthodox Roman Church and with defending Lollard doctrine.

**Wyndham, John** Pseudonym of the novelist John Wyndham Parkes Lucas Beynon Harris (1903–69), who used various combinations of these names in different phases of his career. Before World War II he was active as John Beynon and as John Beynon Harris, but became known for his post-war **science fiction** novels, beginning with *The Day of the Triffids* (1951). His other novels include *The Kraken Wakes* (1953), *The Chrysalids* (1955), *The Midwich Cuckoos* (1957) and *The Trouble with Lichen* (1960). The best of his short fiction is in *Consider*

*Her Ways and Others* (1961). His stories focus on the reactions of ordinary people to terrible circumstances which plunge them into a struggle for survival. These anxious fantasies, preoccupied with the difficulty of preserving the values of English decency in hostile conditions, found favour with the British public while more colourful American science fiction still seemed alien, allowing Wyndham to carve out his own literary niche. His work provides a bridge between traditional British scientific romance and the more varied science fiction which has replaced it.

**Wynnere and Wastoure** A political **allegory** in **alliterative verse**, written in the west of England *c*.1352. The form is a **dream-vision**. The dreamer sees two armies arrayed for battle with all types of people under their two banners. The king forbids them to fight and calls upon their leaders to explain their respective causes. The first spokesman is Wynnere. He describes the practice and philosophy of those who produce and gain wealth through labour, and berates his opponent Wastoure, who spends freely and wastes resources. The ensuing debate sets Wynnere's selfish miserliness against Wastoure's laziness and profligacy, and reveals the disadvantages and scant benefits of each attitude. The king sends Wynnere to live with the Pope in Rome and Wastoure to Cheapside. The poem is satiric, with several contemporary political references, although its central issue is obviously relevant to all societies.

# Y

**Yates, Dornford** Pseudonym of the novelist Cecil William Mercer (1885–1960). Born in London and educated at Harrow and Oxford, Yates was called to the Bar before embarking on a career as a writer. His novels, almost invariably sustained by gently farcical plots and centred on an elegant leisured society, found a huge popular readership in the 1920s and 1930s. *Berry and Co.* (1921), *Jonah and Co.* (1922) and *Maiden Stakes* (1929) were among his many books about the activities of Berry Pleydell and his circle. *The Stolen March* (1926) was a fantasy of a hidden world; *Blind Corner* (1927) and *Perishable Goods* (1928) were two of his notable 'Chandos' thrillers. *As Berry and I Were Saying* (1952) and *Berry and I Look Back* (1958) were autobiographical.

**Years, The** A novel by **Virginia Woolf**, published in 1937.

Unlike Virginia Woolf's other later works, the novel is a conventional family saga with none of the experimental devices used elsewhere. It chronicles the lives of the Pargiters from 1880 to the 1930s. At the beginning, Colonel Pargiter's wife, Rose, is dying ('She was better today; would be worse tomorrow') and their seven children (ranging from early childhood to mid-20s) live under the oppressive weight of her illness. The first chapter ('1880') ends with her funeral.

Subsequent chapters trace the lives of each of the children in a series of separate but connected episodes which form a recurring cycle. Each chapter comprises a year; from '1907', through the years of World War I, to the present in 1936 when there is a large family reunion. There are many vivid descriptions of London life, and the novel sold well despite the author's reservations about her return to the 'novel of fact'.

**Yeast: A Problem** A novel by **Charles Kingsley**, serialized in *Fraser's Magazine* in 1848 and published in book form in 1850.

Its interest for posterity lies in its analysis of problems which the author admitted he could not solve. The main anxieties are what Kingsley saw as the insidious lure of the Roman Catholic church and the necessity for sanitary reform. The picture of rural degradation is vivid and the descriptions of the poor, sleeping 'like pilchards in a barrel', with no clean water and no sanitation, are memorable. Kingsley symbolically punishes the rich for their negligence by letting them catch fatal fevers, bred by filth. He deplores the waste of sewage, which fouls the rivers when it should be fertilizing the fields, and there are ironical attacks on the game laws and oppression. Heedless atheist Lancelot Smith, a gentleman, learns about life from Paul Tregarva, Lancelot's equal in intellect though not in education, one of the 'Dissenting poor'. This is a novel of ideas, ranging from the Early Church, Boehme and **Coleridge**, to symbolist theories of art. The book claims to avoid taking sides, but preaches that art is a mere self-indulgence when political action (reformist, not revolutionary) is needed, and that the 'true idea of Protestantism' is 'the universal symbolism and dignity of matter, whether in man or nature'.

**Yeats, William Butler** 1865–1939 Irish poet and dramatist. Born in Dublin, he spent two-thirds of his life out of Ireland. His father, John B. Yeats, was a lawyer turned painter, and in 1867 the family followed him to London, moving to the recently developed Bedford Park estate in Chiswick in 1879. Summer holidays, and two longer periods in 1869 and 1872, were spent with his mother's family, the Pollexfens, in Sligo. In 1881 the family returned to Dublin, and Yeats studied at the Metropolitan School of Art, where he met **George Russell**. Both were interested in mysticism, and in 1886 Yeats formed the Dublin Lodge of the Hermetic Society. At the Contemporary Club, a nationalist university debating group, he met **William Morris** and, most importantly, the old Fenian leader John O'Leary, who encouraged in him a cultural nationalism. He also began to publish in *The Dublin University Review*: an arcadian verse drama, *The Island of Statues* (1885), and a short verse-drama, *Mosada* (1886).

In 1887 the family returned to Bedford Park, and he began to build a reputation as an anthologist of Irish literature and as a poet of the **Rhymers' Club**, which he formed with Ernest

Rhys in 1890. He visited Mme Blavatsky (recalled in his autobiography, *The Trembling of the Veil*) and joined the Esoteric Section of the Theosophical Society, but was later asked to resign because his experiments were becoming too enthusiastic. He also joined MacGregor Mathers's Rosicrucian society, The Hermetic Order of the Golden Dawn, and quickly became a leading member. He met Maud Gonne in 1889, and she became the subject of his early love poetry. In 1892 he reformed an Irish Literary Society in London, and then the National Literary Society in Dublin, which aimed to promote the New Irish Library, as well as concerts and lectures on Irish themes. Through **Arthur Symons** he discovered French **Symbolism**, and in Paris in 1896 met Verlaine and **J. M. Synge**. In the following year he formed another important friendship with **Lady Gregory**; her estate, Coole Park, became the setting for several of his poems.

During the next decade he was preoccupied with 'theatre Business' (see 'The Fascination of What's Difficult'). With **George Moore** and Edward Martyn he formed the Irish Literary Theatre, inaugurated in 1899 with a production of *The Countess Kathleen* (1892), and collaborated with the Fay brothers and their Irish actors to produce his most successful play, *Cathleen Ni Houlihan* (1902), a propaganda piece with Maud Gonne in the title-role. A few members of this team became the Irish National Theatre, subsidized by Annie Horniman, which opened the

W. B. Yeats. A detail from the portrait by Augustus John, 1907. City Art Gallery, Manchester.

Abbey Theatre in December 1904. Yeats, Synge and Lady Gregory were joint directors. In 1912 he met **Pound**, who became his fencing master and secretary in the winters of 1913 and 1914, and who introduced him to Japanese Noh drama: this was a significant influence on his plays, starting with *At The Hawk's Well* (1916). Although he was out of Ireland at the time of the Easter Rising in 1916, he knew several of the executed rebels personally, as recorded in 'Easter, 1916'.

In early 1917 he bought Thoor Ballylee, a derelict Norman stone tower at Ballylee near Coole Park, and restored it as a summer home and a central symbol in his later poetry. In October 1917 he married Georgie Hyde-Lees, and on their honeymoon she began the automatic writing which led eventually to *A Vision* (1925, revised 1937). At the start of the guerrilla war in Ireland they settled in Oxford, but in 1922 returned to live in Dublin. The bridge at Thoor Ballylee was blown up, and shots were fired into their Dublin home. In the same year he became a Senator, and in 1923 was awarded the Nobel Prize for Literature. After a serious illness in 1929 he convalesced in Rapallo, Italy, where an emergency will had been witnessed by Pound and **Basil Bunting**. In 1932 he founded the Irish Academy of Letters, and in 1933 was briefly, but enthusiastically, involved with the fascist Blueshirts in Dublin. In 1936, while in Mallorca collaborating on a translation of the Upanishads, he again became seriously ill but survived to publish a controversial *Oxford Book of Modern Verse* (1936). He died at the Hôtel Idéal Séjour and was buried in Roquebrune, France. His coffin was disinterred and taken to Sligo in 1948; there is now some doubt as to the authenticity of the bones.

His work, which is now considered to be the most important in the revival of Irish literature, and which fruitfully engaged with Ireland's political independence, included poetry, drama, criticism, essays, journalism, novels and occult writings. A central theme is Ireland, its history, folklore and contemporary public life: 'Creative work must have a fatherland.' Beginning in the later years of the **Celtic revival**, the poetry developed from long allegorical nationalist poems, and Arcadian lyrics and verse dramas influenced by **Shelly** and **Spenser**, to a mature voice that was at once public and private in the work of the 1920s and a more deliberately passionate condemnation of Western civilization in the late poetry. A second important source was the occult, with which he was seriously involved throughout his life, because it provided a philosophy of poetry which emphasized the associative power of the imagination, and because it was a source of symbols, ideas and 'almost an infallible church of poetic tradition'. The obscure symbolism of *The Wind Among the*

*Reeds* (1899) was resolved in the later poetry into three symbols, themselves explained in *A Vision*: the Phases of the Moon, the Great Wheel and the Gyres.

His early work included *The Wanderings of Oisin and Other Poems* (1889), *The Countess Kathleen and Other Legends and Lyrics* (1892, the poetry from this volume subsequently organized into two sections, 'Crossways' and 'The Rose'), *The Wind Among the Reeds* (1899) and *In the Seven Woods* (1903). He wrote two short novels which deal with the opposition between the poet and the magician, *John Sherman and Dhoya* (1891) and *The Speckled Bird* (1897–1901), and published several anthologies of Irish writing and folklore, including *Fairy and Folk Tales of the Irish Peasantry* (1888), *Irish Fairy and Folk Tales* (1894), *The Celtic Twilight* (1893) and *The Secret Rose* (1897). *Ideas of Good and Evil* (1903) was a collection of essays, and 'Discoveries' (1906) was a long essay on art and drama. He also edited the poetry of **William Blake** (1893), in collaboration with Edwin Ellis, and of Spenser (1906).

*The Green Helmet and Other Poems* (1910) and *Responsibilities* (1914) showed him simplifying his poetry by turning to dramatic speech and public occasions, contrasting Greek mythology and Renaissance Italy with contemporary Dublin, the dispute over funding for the Municipal Gallery and the General Strike of 1913. *The Wild Swans at Coole* (1919) significantly extended his range, notably in the elegy 'In Memory of Major Robert Gregory', and introduced the symbols of *A Vision* and the magician-figure Michael Robartes, based on MacGregor Mathers, who appears in the occult stories *Rosa Alchemica* (1897) and the essays *Per Amica Silentia Lunae* (1917). *Michael Robartes and the Dancer* (1921) included 'Easter, 1916' and 'The Second Coming': the first had only been privately printed until its publication in 1920 in an issue of *The New Statesman* devoted to Irish politics and the British government's brutal 'Black and Tans' campaign. He also published two collections of plays, *Plays for an Irish Theatre* (1911) and *Four Plays for Dancers* (1920); a collection of essays, *The Cutting of an Agate* (1918); and two volumes of autobiography, *Reveries Over Childhood and Youth* (1914) and *The Trembling of the Veil* (1922).

*The Tower* (1928) included 'Sailing to Byzantium', 'Leda and the Swan', 'Among School Children' and two sequences on the Civil War. In these he achieved a rich lyricism that encompassed the apparent contradictions between art and politics. *The Winding Stair* (1933) was a powerfully pessimistic collection which included 'Byzantium', 'Coole Park, 1929' and 'Coole Park and Ballylee'. It also included the sequence 'Words for Music Perhaps', 25 songs written for the puppet-characters Crazy Jane,

Jack the Journeyman, the Bishop, Old Tom and God, set in a world of dreams, rhymes, madness songs and riddling refrains. *Parnell's Funeral and Other Poems* (1935) began the theme of 'lust and rage' which dominated *New Poems* (1938) and the posthumous *Last Poems and Two Plays* (1939); these included 'The Municipal Gallery Revisited' and 'The Circus Animals' Desertion', both retrospective judgements on the vision of Ireland in his work. 'Lapis Lazuli' drew on the ideas of Spengler, whose *The Decline of the West* had many similarities with his own *A Vision*. Other work included *Collected Poems* (1933), *Collected Plays* (1934), *Wheels and Butterflies* (1934), a further volume of autobiography in *Dramatis Personae* (1935), *Ten Principal Upanishads* (1937), *Essays 1931–36* (1937), *The Oxford Book of Modern Verse* (1936), and contributions to *Broadsides* and *On the Boiler*, intended as a bi-annual periodical, the only issue of which appeared in 1939.

Posthumous publications include *Collected Plays* (1953), *The Letters of W. B. Yeats* (1954), *Autobiographies* (1955), *Mythologies* (1959), *Essays and Introductions* (1961), *Explorations* (1962), *Uncollected Prose* (1970, 1975), *Memoirs* (1972) and *The Poems: A New Edition* (1984) edited by R. Finneran. Variorum editions of the *Poems* (1957) and *Plays* (1966) were edited by R. Alspach and P. Allt. Several volumes of his correspondence have been published, including that with Dorothy Wellesley (1940, 1964), Florence Farr and **G. B. Shaw** (1946), **T. Sturge Moore** (1953), **Katharine Tynan** (1953) and Margot Ruddock (1970). The first volume of *The Collected Letters*, edited by J. Kelly, appeared in 1986. The *Senate Speeches* (1960) were edited by D. Pearce.

**Yellow Book, The** A literary and art periodical which ran from 1894 to 1897, published by John Lane and edited by **Henry Harland**. Considered decadent and shocking by many readers, it had a distinctive yellow binding decorated by **Aubrey Beardsley**, the art editor. The first issue included **Max Beerbohm**'s controversial essay 'A Defence of Cosmetics'. Many of its contributors were to become major literary figures: **Henry James**, **Edmund Gosse**, **Arnold Bennett**, **H. G. Wells** and **W. B. Yeats** were all represented during its three years' existence, and Walter Sickert and Wilson Steer were among the many artists who also contributed.

**Yellowplush Papers, The** Comic sketches by **W. M. Thackeray**, serialized as *The Yellowplush Correspondence* in *Fraser's Magazine* from November 1837 to August 1838 and in January 1840, reprinted under its present title in his *Comic Tales and Sketches* (1841).

These comic memoirs of a footman, Charles James Yellowplush, are told in his aspiring cockney idiom, and deal with his life under two masters. The first is a respectable gentleman who turns out to be a crossing-sweeper; the second a card-sharping aristocrat, the Hon. Algernon Deuceace, who is outwitted in his pursuit of a wealthy marriage by his even more rascally father, the Earl of Crabs.

*Yemassee, The: A Romance of Carolina* A novel by **William Gilmore Simms**, published in 1835. Set in South Carolina, it is based on the 1715 uprising of the Yemassee Indians against the English colonists.

Sanutee, the Yemassee chief, perceives the threat the expanding colonies pose to his tribe. Urged on by the Spaniards, and aided by a renegade English officer named Chorley, he prepares to attack the white settlements. His son Occonestoga, who has been corrupted by white men's ways (and by alcohol in particular), sides with the whites against his tribe. Gabriel Harrison leads the defence of the settlement. Both he and Hugh Grayson, a young man who comes to emulate the naturally noble Harrison, are in love with Bess Matthews, who embodies the Southern ideal of womanhood. The Indians attack, led by Chorley, and kill many settlers. Harrison sends Occonestoga to spy on his tribe, but he is captured and formally expelled from the tribe. To be thus stripped of identity is a sentence more severe than death, and his mother kills him to save him from the disgrace. She also helps his friend Harrison to escape when he is captured by the Yemassee. Bess and her father are taken by Chorley, but Harrison saves them and kills Chorley. Matthews agrees to the union of Bess and Harrison, who then reveals his true identity: he is in fact Charles Craven, the governor of Carolina. He leaves Hugh Grayson in charge of the local forces and travels to Charleston to organize the force which finally destroys the Yemassee. The book ends with the death of Sanutee.

**Yerby, Frank** 1916– Black American novelist, born in Augusta, Georgia, and educated at Paine College in Augusta and Fisk University in Tennessee. Writing about racial injustice, he won early recognition (he received the O. Henry Award in 1944) for his stories 'Health Card' (1944) and 'The Homecoming' (1946). He then turned to historical novels, the first of which, *The Foxes of Harrow* (1947), won immediate success and sold over one million copies. He has since written some 30 melodramatic costume novels, most of them revolving around his favourite theme of the 'eternal warfare of the sexes'. The first six are set in the 19th century; he moves back in time to the 18th century in *The Devil's Laughter* (1953) and *Bride of Liberty* (1954), to the 17th century in *The Golden Hawk* (1948), and to biblical times in *Judas My Brother* (1968). *The Dahomean* (1971) is his only novel dealing primarily with blacks.

**Yezierska, Anzia** *c*. 1885–1970 A Russian-American novelist and short-story writer, Yezierska was born at Plinsk, in Russian Poland, and emigrated with her family to the USA in the 1890s. They settled in the ghetto of New York City's Lower East Side. She attended night school to improve her English, won a scholarship which enabled her to become a domestic science teacher, and taught cooking from 1905 to 1913. Her stories and novels deal realistically with the lives of struggling immigrants living in the ghetto. Her protagonists are usually women. *Hungry Hearts*, a collection of ten short stories, appeared in 1920; *Salome of the Tenements*, her first novel, in 1922. Subsequent works include another collection of short stories, *Children of Loneliness* (1923), *Bread Givers: A Novel: A Struggle Between a Father of the Old World and a Daughter of the New* (1925), *Arrogant Beggar* (1927), another novel, *All I Could Never Be* (1932), a semi-autobiographical novel, and her autobiography, *Red Ribbon on a White Horse* (1950). She died in poverty in Ontario, California.

**Yonge, Charlotte M[ary]** 1823–1901 Novelist. The daughter of a country gentleman who educated her himself, Charlotte M. Yonge was born at Otterbourne in Hampshire and spent the whole of her long life in the village. She was deeply influenced by **John Keble**, vicar of the neighbouring parish of Hursley, and expounded his religious views in her work. A prolific author of adult and children's fiction, she produced 160 books in all. The first was *Abbeychurch, or, Self-Control and Self-Conceit* (1844) but *The Heir of Redclyffe* (1854) began her popular success. It was followed by *The Daisy Chain* (1856) and several later volumes continuing the fortunes of the May family. The authenticity of her home and family backgrounds makes these works an excellent source of information about Victorian middle-class life. An admirer of **Sir Walter Scott**, she chose a historical setting for many of her novels, among them *The Little Duke* (1854), *The Lances of Lynwood* (1855), *The Prince and the Page* (1865) and *The Caged Lion* (1870). She also edited *The Monthly Packet* for nearly 50 years, and published biographies of Bishop Patterson (1874) and **Hannah More** (1888) and a *History of France* (1879).

**York cycle, the** See **miracle plays**.

**Yorke, Henry Vincent** See **Green, Henry**.

*Yorkshire Tragedy, A* A play, probably first performed in 1606, when it was part of the repertoire of the **King's Men** at the **Globe**

**Theatre**. The title-page of a 1608 edition claims it as Shakespeare's work (see **Shakespeare apocrypha**), but the most that could be supposed is that he had some hand in cutting the play down to the truncated form in which it has survived. **Thomas Middleton** has been suggested as a possible author.

The play is based on the story of Walter Calverley, executed for murder in 1605. It describes with grim haste the passage from gambling debts to the attempted murder of his family (wife and one son survive) to arrest and final repentance.

**Young, Andrew (John)** 1885–1971 Poet. Born at Elgin and educated in Edinburgh, he was ordained first as a Free Church minister and then as an Anglican clergyman. He was appointed canon of Chichester Cathedral in 1948. His long poetic career began with *Songs of Night* (1910). After the short nature lyrics of *The Green Man* (1947), he wrote two long meditative poems, *Into Hades* (1952) and *A Traveller in Time*, published together as *Out of the World and Back* (1958). In the preface to *Into Hades* he wrote that 'while my interest in nature was intense, it was not so deep as the underlying interest that prompted me to change my style'. Both poems attempt to reconcile philosophical and religious generalization with visionary narrative. Young also published prose pieces, including *A Prospect of Flowers* (1945), *A Retrospect of Flowers* (1950), *A Prospect of Britain* (1950) and *The Poet and the Landscape* (1962).

**Young, Arthur** 1741–1820 Writer on agriculture and travel. The son of a Suffolk clergyman, he was born in London and published a pamphlet, *The War in North America*, at the age of 17, but did not find his true subject as a writer until he had tried, and failed, to be a farmer and worked as an Irish land agent. He became known as an agricultural theorist with *A Farmer's Letters to the People of England* (1768), *A Six Weeks Tour Through the Southern Counties of England and Wales* (1768), *A Six Months Tour Through the North of England* (1771), and *The Farmer's Tour Through the East of England* (1771). Other works on farming followed, and he founded and edited *Annals of Agriculture* (1784–1809). *Political Arithmetic* (1774) and *A Tour in Ireland* (1780) showed that his shrewd observation was not confined to agriculture and in 1787 he set out on the first of his journeys in France. He made three tours of that country and published the results in 1792 in the book usually known as *Travels in France*, a damning indictment of the conditions which led to the Revolution. *The Example of France a Warning to England* (1793) appeared in the year he became Secretary to the Board of Agriculture. Young's family was connected to the Burneys and he is mentioned frequently by **Fanny Burney** in her diary and her letters.

**Young, Edward** 1683–1765 Poet and dramatist. Born at Upham, near Winchester, he was educated at Winchester College and at New College and Corpus Christi College, Oxford, becoming a fellow of All Souls in 1708. His early poems met with little success but his tragedy *Busiris, King of Egypt* (1719) was highly acclaimed. Another tragedy, *The Revenge* (1721), also became extremely popular after being coolly received at first. A series of seven satires, *The Universal Passion* (later called *The Love of Fame*, 1725–8), enjoyed a considerable vogue until eclipsed by **Pope**'s great satires of the 1730s.

The slow development of his career made Young look to the church. In 1730 he became rector of Welwyn, where he spent the rest of his life. His only published poem in the next decade was a patriotic ode, *The Foreign Address* (1735). The death of his stepdaughter in 1736 and his wife, Lady Elizabeth Lee, in 1740 prompted him to begin the work which made him famous. The first part of *The Complaint, or, Night-Thoughts on Life, Death and Immortality* appeared in 1742 and the last part (the ninth Night) in 1746. **Night Thoughts**, as it is usually known, allied him with both an older tradition of moral writing and the contemporary **graveyard poets**. Young's new

Edward Young. A detail from the portrait by Joseph Highmore, 1754. All Souls College, Oxford.

fame brought him into contact with **Mary Delany**, **Elizabeth Montagu** and the **bluestocking** circle, as well as **Cibber**, **Richardson** and **Johnson**, who rashly judged him 'a man of genius and a poet'. Latterly, he published *The Brothers* (1753), a play he had written earlier, and *The Centaur Not Fabulous* (1755). *Conjectures on Original Composition* (1759) seems to have been prompted by conversations with Richardson about the *Essay on the Genius and Writings of Pope* (1756), which **Joseph Warton** had dedicated to Young. His last published poem was the long *Resignation* (1762).

**Young, Francis Brett** 1884–1954 Novelist, short-story writer and poet. Born in Worcestershire, he was educated at Epsom School and at the University of Birmingham, where he studied medicine. He practised in Devon for several years, where he also began writing. His early novels, *Deep Sea* (1914), *The Dark Tower* (1914) and *The Iron Age* (1916), were all well received in critical circles.

During World War I he served in the Medical Corps in East Africa, and produced a valuable account of the campaign there, *Marching on Tanga* (1918). His post-war novels were situated in the West Midlands and included the titles for which he is best remembered, *Portrait of Clare* (1927) and *My Brother Jonathan* (1928). Towards the end of his life he returned to Africa, where he lived until his death. Novels with a South African setting included *Jim Redlake* (1930), *They Seek a Country* (1937), about the Great Trek, and *The City of Gold* (1939). *The Island* (1944) is a verse history of England, using verse forms appropriate to each period.

**Ywain and Gawain** A **verse romance** probably written in the first half of the 14th century in the north of England. A condensed version of *Yvain*, a late 12th-century French romance by Chrétien de Troyes, it omits much of the descriptive and reflective material in its source. Colloquial language replaces much of Chrétien's sophisticated literary diction and the irony of the source has been replaced by a straightforward and fluent account. It is the only Middle English translation of any of Chrétien's works.

Ywain defeats a knight who appears when water is cast over a stone. With the help of a go-between, Lunet, he marries the knight's widow. Gawain persuades him to leave his wife for a year to live as a knight, and when Ywain forgets to return she rejects him. After Ywain has spent a period of madness in the woods and undergone several adventures, Lunet eventually effects a reconciliation between the couple. Ywain is known as the Knight of the Lion because he is accompanied and helped by a lion he saved and befriended during his period of solitude. (See also **Arthurian literature**.)

# Z

**Zangwill, Israel** 1864–1926 Novelist, playwright and translator. Born in London of Russian-Jewish descent, he was educated there and at London University. For a number of years he edited the humorous periodical *Ariel* and worked as a teacher and journalist. After publishing several unsuccessful novels, he wrote *Children of the Ghetto* (1892), which brilliantly captured the stark reality of immigrant life in London. Other works in the same vein included *Ghetto Tragedies* (1893), *The Kings of Shnorrers* (1894) and *The Mantle of Elijah* (1900), which established him as a leading figure and powerful spokesman in the struggle for Jewish rights. *The Melting Pot* (1909), the best known of his plays, dealt with a similar theme – as did various non-fictional works, including *The War for the World* (1916) and *The Voice of Jerusalem* (1920). *The Big Bow Mystery* (1892) is Zangwill's one venture into **detective fiction**.

**Zanoni** A novel by **Edward Bulwer Lytton**, published in 1842, and set partly during the French Revolution. The hero is a mysterious sage and master of the occult arts possessed of the secret of eternal life, whose superhuman powers begin to fail him when he falls in love with a human being. Realizing that the affections of the heart, which he has hitherto shunned, can lead to a higher spiritual state than the abstractions of the intellect, he forsakes his immortality, marries the girl, and eventually dies in her place on the guillotine (prefiguring a similar, more famous sacrifice in **Dickens**'s *A Tale of Two Cities*).

**Zaturenska, Marya** 1902–82 Russian-American poet. Born in Kiev, Zaturenska emigrated to the USA in 1910 and attended Valparaiso University and the University of Wisconsin before marrying the poet **Horace Gregory** in 1925. With him she edited numerous anthologies and wrote *A History of American Poetry 1900–1940* (1946). *Threshold and Hearth* (1934) was her first volume of poetry. *Cold Morning Sky*, published in 1937, brought her critical acclaim and the Pulitzer Prize in 1938. Other collections of her poetry include *The Listening Landscape* (1941), *Golden Mirror* (1943),

*Terraces of Light* (1960) and *The Hidden Waterfalls* (1974).

**zeugma** See **syllepsis**.

**Zoo Story, The** A long one-act play by **Edward Albee**. The first of his plays to be performed professionally, it opened in Berlin in 1959 and in New York City in 1960. It concerns the confrontation in New York's Central Park between Jerry, an alienated and unhappy homosexual, and Peter, a middle-aged and distinctly ordinary man. Jerry frustrates all of Peter's attempts to leave with harangues about his alienated condition, and finally tricks Peter into helping him kill himself.

**Zukofsky, Louis** 1904–78 American poet, born in New York City and educated at Columbia. He was associated with the **Objectivist** school and his poetry was first published in *An 'Objectivists' Anthology* (1932), which he himself edited. His second publication, *First Half of 'A'*, appeared in 1940. Further sections of the long poem '*A*' were published over the next 38 years as Zukofsky kept expanding the work, which eventually comprised 24 separate sections. It was published in complete form in 1978. In it he explores the interrelationship of poetry and music, and treats questions of aesthetics, philosophy and history. His volumes of shorter poems include *55 Poems* (1941), *Anew* (1946), *Some Time* (1956), *Barely and Widely* (1958), *I's* (1963), *After I's* (1964) and *I Sent Thee Late* (1965). *All: The Collected Shorter Poems, 1923–1964* appeared in 1966. *A Test of Poetry* (1948) and *Prepositions* (1967) are collections of essays on modern poets and poetry. He also wrote a play, *Arise, Arise* (1965), and a novel, *Little: A Fragment for Careenagers* (1970).

**Zuleika Dobson**, *or, An Oxford Love Story* A novel by **Max Beerbohm**, published in 1911.
Zuleika, a stunningly beautiful girl, visits her grandfather, the Warden of Judas College, during Eights Week. With sustained irony, the novel recounts her devastating effect upon the undergraduates. Attracted only to men 'who would not bow down to her', Zuleika is disap-

pointed in her quest for one whom she herself could adore. To a man, the students fall madly in love with her, including the Duke of Dorset, a splendid young Apollo who had appeared the most promising candidate. He swears to lay down his life for her – and does so, by drowning himself. He is followed by the entire undergraduate population, who throw themselves into the Isis 'like lemmings'. Noaks, less agile than the others, is the only survivor. At the end of the novel Zuleika consults the train timetable to Cambridge.

# Photographic Acknowledgements

The illustrations on the following pages are reproduced by Gracious Permission of Her Majesty the Queen: 5, 685, 882, 961. The illustration on page 1106 is reproduced by permission of The Warden and Fellows of All Souls College, Oxford, that on page 637 by permission of the Master, Fellows and Scholars of Corpus Christi, Cambridge, and that on page 556 by permission of The National Trust and Macmillan London Limited.

The illustration on page 989 is © 1963 Hamish Hamilton.

Aldeburgh Museum Trust 235; Ashmolean Museum, Oxford 47, 1075; Australian Overseas Information Service, London 1066; B.B.C. Hulton Picture Library, London 158, 217, 243, 362, 450, 622, 982, 1012, 1058; Bassano & Vandyke, London 489; Bibliothèque Nationale, Paris 40; Birmingham Museums and Art Gallery 493, 648; Bodleian Library, Oxford 153, 780, 1106; British Library, London 7, 10, 13, 36, 39, 62, 68, 117, 160, 174, 180, 184, 194, 196, 211, 214, 253, 264, 267, 280, 282, 310 left, 332, 337, 338, 366, 372, 380, 386, 389, 418, 420, 423, 469, 470, 483, 503, 539, 556 top, 588, 609, 610, 631 top and bottom, 668, 677, 689, 690, 691, 695, 754, 757, 766, 770, 772, 774, 775, 781, 820, 840, 846, 848, 907, 995, 1002, 1007, 1023, 1026, 1031, 1054; Cambridge University Library 87; Camera Press, London 394, 947; Camera Press – Baron 923; Camera Press – Tom Blau 699; Camera Press – Bernard Charlon 58; Camera Press – Lionel Cherrault 576; Camera Press – Donald Cooper 626; Camera Press – Fay Godwin 80; Camera Press – Jacques Haillot 705; Camera Press – Tara Heinemann 861; Camera Press – Karsh of Ottawa 413, 869, 901, 1052; Camera Press – Sabine Weiss 345; Jonathan Cape Ltd – Frank Herman 1035; Courtauld Institute of Art, London 744; G.A. Duncan, Dublin 726, 784 right, 969; Faber and Faber Ltd – Rollie McKenna 784 left; Folger Shakespeare Library, Washington 662, 976, 993; Format Photographers, London – Val Wilmer 716, 938 left; John Fryer 120; Fay Godwin 25, 485, 832, 837 right; Hamlyn Group Picture Library 18, 101, 126, 179, 232, 237, 253, 311, 341, 390, 397, 414, 475, 476, 496, 504, 540, 546, 554, 556 right, 569, 604, 630, 651, 664, 717, 722, 735, 740, 777, 800, 806, 842, 853, 876, 933, 938 right, 980, 989, 1005, 1089; Hamlyn Group – Philip de Bay 73; Hodder & Stoughton Ltd – Jerry Bauer 536; Houston Rogers Collection, Theatre Museum, Victoria & Albert Museum, London 1038; The Huntington Library, San Marino, California 161, 162, 375; M. Knoedler & Co., New York 681; Library of Congress, Washington 64, 136, 236, 308, 315, 371, 441, 471, 502, 509, 514, 547, 570, 571, 599, 601, 616, 647, 654, 721, 739, 816, 988, 1014, 1018, 1039, 1049 left and right, 1063, 1064, 1072, 1098; Local Studies Library, Nottinghamshire County Council 564, 565; Manchester City Art Gallery 1103; Raymond Mander & Joe Mitchenson Theatre Collection, London 1, 173, 529; Mansell Collection, London 81, 133, 143, 310 right, 355, 379, 408, 432, 508, 593, 649, 736, 794, 865, 895, 941, 1061, 1094; John Murray Publishers Ltd 515; National Galleries of Scotland, Edinburgh 486, 549; National Library of Ireland, Dublin 1019; National Maritime Museum, London 673; National Portrait Gallery, London 48, 50, 55, 82, 98, 112, 127, 134, 141, 145, 146, 150, 193, 202, 233, 252, 260, 265, 274, 279, 283, 289, 295, 331, 350, 385, 391, 415, 443, 466, 519, 523, 544, 557, 580, 596, 642, 663, 749, 765, 769, 788, 837, 856, 862, 900, 904, 908, 912, 930, 949, 963, 964, 977, 979, 1008, 1025, 1092, 1095, 1100; New York Public Library 600, 745; City of Nottingham 1043; Popperfoto, London 550; Popperfoto – Douglas Glass 312, 1077; Roger-Viollet, Paris 545 bottom; Martin Secker and Warburg Ltd – Geraldine Farley 200; Society of Antiquaries of London 789; Larry B. Stevenson 1032; Tate Gallery, London 76, 753; Topham Picture Library, Edenbridge 14; United States Information Service 369; Victoria & Albert Museum, London 77, 351, 532, 902, 903; Virago Press 168; Martin Walters 582; Weidenfeld Publishers Ltd 704; Yale University Library, New Haven, Connecticut 526

U.S. research by Frances Rowsell, Washington.